HANDBOOK OF RESEARCH

ON EDUCATIONAL

COMMUNICATIONS AND

TECHNOLOGY

SECOND EDITION

HANDBOOK OF RESEARCH ON EDUCATIONAL COMMUNICATIONS AND TECHNOLOGY

SECOND EDITION

A Project of the Association for Educational
Communications and Technology

EDITED BY

DAVID H. JONASSEN

University of Missouri

LEA LAWRENCE ERLBAUM ASSOCIATES, PUBLISHERS
2004 Mahwah, New Jersey   London

Director, Editorial:	Lane Akers
Assistant Editor:	Lori Hawver
Cover Design:	Kathryn Houghtaling Lacey
Textbook Production Manager:	Paul Smolenski
Full-Service Compositor:	TechBooks
Text and Cover Printer:	Victor Graphics, Inc.

This book was typeset in 9/11 pt. ITC Garamond Roman, Bold, and Italic.
The heads were typeset in Novarese, Novarese Medium, and Novarese Bold Italic.

Lawrence Erlbaum Associates, Inc., Publishers
10 Industrial Avenue
Mahwah, New Jersey 07430
www.erlbaum.com

Library of Congress Cataloging-in-Publication Data

Handbook of research for educational communications and technology /
   edited by David H. Jonassen.—2nd ed.
      p. cm.
   "A project of the Association for Educational Communications and Technology."
   ISBN 0-8058-4145-8
    1. Educational technology—Research—Handbooks, manuals, etc.   2. Communication
in education—Research—Handbooks, manuals, etc.   3. Telecommunication
in education—Research—Handbooks, manuals, etc.   4. Instructional
systems—Design—Research—Handbooks, manuals, etc.   I. Jonassen, David H.,
1947-   II. Association for Educational Communications and Technology.

LB1028.3 .H355 2004
371.33'072—dc22

                                         2003015730

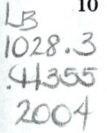

CONTENTS

Part I

THEORETICAL FOUNDATIONS FOR EDUCATIONAL COMMUNICATIONS AND TECHNOLOGY   1

v

Part II

HARD TECHNOLOGIES 247

Part III

SOFT TECHNOLOGIES 543

Part IV

INSTRUCTIONAL DESIGN APPROACHES   621

Part V

INSTRUCTIONAL STRATEGIES   717

Part VI

INSTRUCTIONAL MESSAGE DESIGN   863

Part
VII

RESEARCH METHODOLOGIES   1007

PREFACE

History

This second edition of the *Handbook of Research on Educational Communications and Technology* was begun some time in 2000 when Macmillan Reference, the publisher of the first edition, decided to discontinue publication of its handbook line. So the book went out of print and became unavailable, frustrating students and professors who wanted to use it in their courses. Lane Akers of Lawrence Erlbaum Associates, Inc. expressed interest in publishing a second edition. Erlbaum, AECT, and I agreed that we would work on a second edition, provided that Erlbaum would reprint the first edition until the second could be produced and that the second edition would also be available electronically. This is the fruit of our labors.

You will notice changes in the topics represented in this second edition of the *Handbook*. After agreeing to edit the second edition of the *Handbook,* I immediately invited every author from the first edition to revise and update their chapters for the second edition. Several authors declined. Because they would have been identical to the first edition, those chapters were not reprinted in the second edition. You can find them in the first edition (available in libraries and the AECT website), which is a companion document to this second edition. All of the chapters that were revised and updated are included in this second edition. Additionally, I conducted surveys and interviews with scholars in the field and content analyses of the journals in the field to identify new chapters that should be included and sought authors for those chapters. Some of those chapters were completed; others were not. Finally, I sought authors to write some of the chapters that were omitted from the first edition. Fortunately, some of those, such as programmed instruction, are now included in the second edition. While many scholars and practitioners may function a couple of paradigm shifts beyond programmed instruction, it was the first true technology of instruction that is *still* alive in computer-based instruction and reusable learning objects. So, the second edition represents the best compilation of research *in* the field that was possible in 2002.

Format of the Book

You may be reading this *Handbook* in its clumsy but comprehensive print version. You may also be downloading it from the AECT website via the World Wide Web. Each format has its distinct advantages and disadvantages. However, the only reason that I agreed to edit the second edition was so that students could have access to electronic versions of it. My convictions were egalitarian and intellectual. Affordable access to domain knowledge is an obligation of the field, I believe. Also, electronic versions afford multiple sense-making strategies for students. I hope that students will study this *Handbook,* not by coloring its pages with fluorescent markers, but by building hypertext front-ends for personally or collaboratively organizing the ideas in the book around multiple themes, issues, and practices. A variety of tools for building hypertext webs or semantic networks exist. They enable the embedding of hyperlinks in all forms of electronic files, including these *Handbook* files. Further, there are numerous theories and models for organizing the ideas conveyed in this *Handbook*. I would recommend that students and readers study cognitive flexibility theory, articulated by Rand Spiro and his colleagues, and apply it representing the multiple thematic integrations that run through the book. Rather than studying topics in isolation, I encourage readers to "criss-cross' our research landscape (a term introduced by Ludwig Wittgenstein in his *Philosophical Investigations,* which he wanted to be a hypertext before hypertexts were invented) of educational communications and technology.

You will notice that the headings in this *Handbook* are numbered in a hierarchical manner. Those numbers do not necessarily imply a hierarchical arrangement of content. Rather, the numbers exist to facilitate hyperlinking and cross-referencing so that you can build your hypertext front-end described in the previous paragraph. A Handbook should be a dynamic, working document that facilitates knowledge construction and problem solving for the readers. Hopefully, the numbers will facilitate those processes.

Limitations of the Book

Knowledge in any field is dynamic, especially one like educational communications and technology. Our field is assimilating and accommodating (to use Piagetian constructs) at an awesome pace. The focus on practice communities, computer-supported collaborative learning, and teachable agents, for a few examples, did not exist in our field when the first edition of the *Handbook* was published. But they are important concepts in the field today. The ideas that define our field represent a moving target that changes by the month, if not more frequently. Finding people to adequately represent all of those ideas in the *Handbook* has been a significant challenge. I had planned to include additional chapters on topics, such as problem-based learning, computer-supported collaborative learning, and design experiments, but they will have to wait for the next edition. By then, our field will have morphed some more, so representing even more contemporary ideas will constitute a significant challenge for the next editor.

The second challenge in comprehensively representing ideas in the field occurs within topics (chapters). For the chapter author, the process includes identifying research and articulating a structure for representing the issues implied by that research. The thousands of studies that have been conducted and reported in various forms require amazing analysis and synthesis skills on the part of the authors. Deciding which studies to report, which to summarize, and which to ignore has challenged all of the authors in this book. So, you will probably identify some omissions—important topics, technologies, or research studies that are not addressed in the book. I elicited all that I could from the authors.

Just as there may be gaps in coverage, you will notice that there is also some redundancy in coverage. Several chapters address the same topic. I believe that it represents a strength of the book, because it illustrates how technologies and designs are integrated, how researchers with different conceptual, theoretical, or methodological perspectives may address the same issue. Ours is an eclectic field. The breadth of the topics addressed in this *Handbook* attests to that. The redundancy, I believe, provides some of the conceptual glue that holds the field together.

My fervent hope is that you will find this *Handbook* to be an important conceptual tool for constructing your own understanding of research in our field, and that it will function as a catalyst for your own research efforts in educational communications and technology.

—David Jonassen, Editor

ABOUT THE EDITOR

David Jonassen is Distinguished Professor of Education at the University of Missouri where he teaches in the areas of Learning Technologies and Educational Psychology. Since earning his doctorate in educational media and experimental educational psychology from Temple University, Dr. Jonassen has taught at the Pennsylvania State University, University of Colorado, the University of Twente in the Netherlands, the University of North Carolina at Greensboro, and Syracuse University. He has published 23 books and numerous articles, papers, and reports on text design, task analysis, instructional design, computer-based learning, hypermedia, constructivist learning, cognitive tools, and technology in learning. He has consulted with businesses, universities, public schools, and other institutions around the world. His current research focuses on constructing design models and environments for problem solving and model building for conceptual change.

LIST OF CONTRIBUTORS

Gary Anglin, Department of Curriculum and Instruction, University of Kentucky, Lexington, Kentucky

Brock S. Allen, Department of Educational Technology, San Diego State University, San Diego, California

Eun-Ok Baek, Department of Instructional Technology, California State University, San Bernadino, California

Bela Banathy, Saybrook Graduate School and Research Center, San Francisco, California

Sasha A. Barab, School of Education, Indiana University, Bloomington, Indiana

Ann E. Barron, College of Education, University of South Florida, Tampa, Florida

Louis Berry, Department of Instruction and Learning, University of Pittsburgh, Pittsburgh, Pennsylvania

Gary Boyd, Department of Education, Concordia University, Montreal, Quebec, Canada

John K. Burton, Department of Teaching and Learning, Virginia Polytechnic Institute and State University, Blacksburg, Virginia

Alison Carr-Chellman, Department of Instructional Systems Program, Penn State University, University Park, Pennsylvania

Kathryn Cunningham, Distance Learning Technology Center, University of Kentucky, Lexington, Kentucky

Vanessa Paz Dennen, Department of Educational Psychology and Learning Systems, Florida State University, Tallahassee, Florida

Michael A. Evans, Indiana University, Bloomington, Indiana

Karen Fullerton, Celeron Consultant, Bothell. Washington

Evan M. Glazer, College of Education, University of Georgia, Athens, Georgia

Barbara Grabowski, Department of Instructional Systems Program, Penn State University, University Park, Pennsylvania

Margaret Gredler, Department of Educational Psychology, University of South Carolina, Columbia, South Carolina

Charlotte Nirmalani Gunawardena, College of Education, University of New Mexico, Albuquerque, New Mexico

Mark Guzdial, College of Computing, Georgia Institute of Technology, Atlanta, Georgia

Seungyeon Han, Department of Instructional Technology, University of Georgia, Athens, Georgia

Mike Hannafin, College of Education, University of Georgia, Athens, Georgia

James Hartley, Psychology Department, University of Keele, Keele, Staffordshire, United Kingdom

Philip H. Henning, School of Construction and Design, Pennsylvania College of Technology, Williamsport, Pennsylvania

Janette Hill, Department of Instructional Technology, University of Georgia, Athens, Georgia

Denis Hlynka, Centre for Ukrainian Canadian Studies, University of Manitoba, Winnipeg, Manitoba, Canada

Bob Hoffman, Department of Educational Technology, San Diego State University, San Diego, California

Laura J. Horn,

Patrick Jenlink, Department of Educational Leadership, Stephen Austin University, Nacogdoches, Texas

David W. Johnson, Department of Educational Psychology, University of Minnesota, Minneapolis, Minnesota

Roger T. Johnson, Department of Educational Psychology, University of Minnesota, Minneapolis, Minnesota

Steven Kerr, Department of Education, University of Washington, Seattle, Washington

James Klein, Department of Psychology in Education, Arizona State University, Tempe, Arizona

Randy Koetting, Department of Curriculum and Instruction, University of Nevada, Reno, Reno, Nevada

Janet L. Kolodner, College of Computing, Georgia Institute of Technology, Atlanta, Georgia

Kathy Krendl, College of Communications, Ohio University, Athens, Ohio

Jung Lee, Department of Instructional Technology, Richard Stockton College of New Jersey, Pomona, New Jersey

Barbara Lockee, Department of Teaching and Learning, Virginia Polytechnic Institute and State University, Blacksburg, Virginia

Susan G. Magliaro, Department of Teaching and Learning, Virginia Polytechnic Institute and State University, Blacksburg, Virginia

Mark Malisa, Department of Curriculum and Instruction, University of Nevada, Reno, Reno, Nevada

Robin Mason, Institute of Educational Technology, The Open University, Milton Keynes, United Kingdom

Joan M. Mazur, Department of Curriculum and Instruction, Kentucky University, Lexington, Kentucky

Marina Stock McIsaac, College of Education, Arizona State University, Tempe, Arizona

Hillary McLellan, McLellan Wyatt Digital, Saratoga Springs, New York

Robert Meyers, Department of Teaching and Learning, Virginia Polytechnic Institute and State University, Blacksburg, Virginia

David M. (Mike) Moore, Department of Teaching and Learning, Virginia Polytechnic Institute and State University, Blacksburg, Virginia

Edna Morey, Department of Specialty Studies, University of North Carolina at Wilmington, Wilmington, North Carolina

Gary Morrison, College of Education, Wayne State University, Detroit, Michigan

Laurie Miller Nelson, Department of Instructional Technology, Utah State University, Logan, Utah

Wayne Nelson, Department of Educational Leadership, Southern Illinois University-Edwardsville, Edwardsville, Illinois

Dehlia Neuman, College of Information Studies, University of Maryland, College Park, Maryland

Dale S. Niederhauser, Center for Technology in Learning and Teaching, Iowa State University, Ames, Iowa

Celestia Ohrazda, Department of Instructional Design, Development, and Evaluation, Syracuse University, Syracuse, New York

Chandra H. Orrill, College of Education, University of Georgia, Athens, Georgia

Richard G. Otto, National University, La Jolla, California

Jakita N. Owensby, College of Computing, Georgia Institute of Technology, Atlanta, Georgia

Ok-Choon Park, Institute of Education Sciences, U.S. Department of Education, Washington, D.C.

Tillman Ragan, Department of Educational Psychology, University of Oklahoma, Norman, Oklahoma

Rita Richey, College of Education, Wayne State University, Detroit, Michigan

Lloyd Rieber, Department of Instructional Technology, University of Georgia, Athens, Georgia

Rhonda Robinson, Department of Educational Technology, Research, and Assessment, Northern Illinois University, DeKalb, Illinois

Warren Roby, Department of Language Studies, John Brown University, Siloam Springs, Arizona

Alex Romiszowski, Department of Instructional Design, Development, and Evaluation, Syracuse University, Syracuse, New York

Steven M. Ross, Center for Research in Educational Policy, Memphis State University, Memphis, Tennessee

Wilhelmina C. Savenye, College of Education, Arizona State University, Tempe, Arizona

Mike Savoy, Department of Adult Education, Penn State University, University Park, Pennsylvania

Barbara Seels, Department of Instruction and Learning, University of Pittsburgh, Pittsburgh, Pennsylvania

Amy Shapiro, Department of Psychology, University of Massachusetts Dartmouth, N. Dartmouth, Massachusetts

Pat Smith, Department of Educational Psychology, University of Oklahoma, Norman, Oklahoma

Michael Spector, Department of Instructional Design, Development, and Evaluation, Syracuse University, Syracuse, New York

Hossein Vaez, Department of Physics and Astronomy, Eastern Kentucky University, Richmond, Kentucky

Ron Warren, Department of Communication, University of Arkansas, Fayetteville, Arkansas

David Wiley, Department of Instructional Technology, Utah State University, Logan, Utah

William Winn, College of Education, University of Washington, Seattle, Washington

Michael F. Young, Program in Educational Technology, University of Connecticut, Storrs, Connecticut

HANDBOOK OF RESEARCH

ON EDUCATIONAL

COMMUNICATIONS AND

TECHNOLOGY

SECOND EDITION ·

Part

• I •

THEORETICAL FOUNDATIONS FOR EDUCATIONAL COMMUNICATIONS AND TECHNOLOGY

BEHAVIORISM AND INSTRUCTIONAL TECHNOLOGY

John K. Burton
Virginia Tech

David M. (Mike) Moore
Virginia Tech

Susan G. Magliaro

Since the first publication of this chapter in the previous edition of the Handbook, some changes have occurred in the theoretical landscape. Cognitive psychology has moved further away from its roots in information processing toward a stance that emphasizes individual and group construction of knowledge. The notion of the mind as a computer has fallen into disfavor largely due to the mechanistic representation of a human endeavor and the emphasis on the mind–body separation. Actually, these events have made B. F. Skinner's (1974) comments prophetic. Much like Skinner's discussion of use of a machine as a metaphor for human behavior by the logical positivists who believed that "a robot, which behaved precisely like a person, responding in the same way to stimuli, changing its behavior as a result of the same operations, would be indistinguishable from a real person, even though," as Skinner goes on to say, "it would not have feelings, sensations, or ideas." If such a robot could be built, Skinner believed that "it would prove that none of the supposed manifestations of mental life demanded a mentalistic explanation" (p. 16). Indeed, unlike cognitive scientists who explicitly insisted on the centrality of the computer to the understanding of human thought (see, for example, Gardner, 1985), Skinner clearly rejected any characterizations of humans as machines.

In addition, we have seen more of what Skinner (1974) called "the current practice of avoiding" (the mind/body) "dualism by substituting 'brain' for 'mind.'" Thus, the brain is said to "use

data, make hypotheses, make choices, and so on as the mind was once said to have done" (p. 86). In other words, we have seen a retreat from the use of the term "mind" in cognitive psychology. It is no longer fashionable then to posit, as Gardner (1985) did, that "first of all, there is the belief that, in talking about human cognitive activities, it is necessary to speak about mental representations and to posit a level of analysis wholly separate from the biological or neurological on one hand, and the sociological or cultural on the other" (p. 6). This notion of mind, which is separate from nature or nurture, is critical to many aspects of cognitive explanation. By using "brain" instead of "mind," we get the appearance of avoiding the conflict. It is, in fact, an admission of the problem with mind as an explanatory construct, but in no way does it resolve the role that mind was meant to fill.

Yet another hopeful sign is the abandonment of generalities of learning and expertise in favor of an increased role for the stimuli available during learning as well as the feedback that follows (i.e., behavior and consequences). Thus we see more about "situated cognition," "situated learning," "situated knowledge," "cognitive apprenticeships," "authentic materials," etc. (see, for example, Brown, Collins, & Duguid, 1989; Lave, 1988; Lave & Wenger, 1991; Resnick, 1988; Rogoff & Lave, 1984; Suchman, 1987) that evidence an explicit acknowledgment that while behavior "is not 'stimulus bound'. . . nevertheless the environmental *history* is still in control; the genetic endowment of the species plus the contingencies to which the individual has been exposed still determine what he will perceive" (Skinner, 1974, p. 82).

Perhaps most importantly, and in a less theoretical vein, has been the rise of distance learning; particularly for those on the bleeding edge of "any time, any place," asynchronous learning. In this arena, issues of scalability, cost effectiveness, maximization of the learner's time, value added, etc. has brought to the forefront behavioral paradigms that had fallen from favor in many circles. A reemergence of technologies such as personalized system instruction (Keller & Sherman, 1974) is clear in the literature. In our last chapter we addressed these models and hinted at their possible use in distance situations. We expand those notions in this current version.

1.1   INTRODUCTION

In 1913, John Watson's *Psychology as the Behaviorist Views it* put forth the notion that psychology did not have to use terms such as consciousness, mind, or images. In a real sense, Watson's work became the opening "round" in a battle that the behaviorists dominated for nearly 60 years. During that period, behavioral psychology (and education) taught little about cognitive concerns, paradigms, etc. For a brief moment, as cognitive psychology eclipsed behavioral theory, the commonalties between the two orientations were evident (see, e.g., Neisser, 1967, 1976). To the victors, however, go the spoils and the rise of cognitive psychology has meant the omission, or in some cases misrepresentation, of behavioral precepts from current curricula. With that in mind, this chapter has three main goals. First, it is necessary to revisit some of the underlying assumptions of the two orientations and review some basic behavioral concepts. Second, we examine the research on instructional technology to illustrate the impact of behavioral psychology on the tools of our field. Finally, we conclude the chapter with an epilogue.

1.2   THE MIND/BODY PROBLEM

The western mind is European, the European mind is Greek; the Greek mind came to maturity in the city of Athens. (Needham, 1978, p. 98)

The intellectual separation between mind and nature is traceable back to 650 B.C. and the very origins of philosophy itself. It certainly was a centerpiece of Platonic thought by the fourth century B.C. Plato's student Aristotle, ultimately, separated mind from body (Needham, 1978). In modern times, it was René Descartes who reasserted the duality of mind and body and connected them at the pineal gland. The body was made of physical matter that occupied space; the mind was composed of "animal spirits" and its job was to think and control the body. The connection at the pineal gland made your body yours. While it would not be accurate to characterize current cognitivists as Cartesian dualists, it would be appropriate to characterize them as believers of what Churchland (1990) has called "popular

dualism" (p. 91); that the "person" or mind is a "ghost in the machine." Current notions often place the "ghost" in a social group. It is this "ghost" (in whatever manifestation) that Watson objected to so strenuously. He saw thinking and hoping as things we *do* (Malone, 1990). He believed that when stimuli, biology, and responses are removed, the residual is not mind, it is nothing. As William James (1904) wrote, "... but breath, which was ever the original 'spirit,' breath moving outwards, between the glottis and the nostrils, is, I am persuaded, the essence out of which philosophers have constructed the entity known to them as consciousness" (p. 478).

The view of mental activities as actions (e.g., "thinking is talking to ourself," Watson, 1919), as opposed to their being considered indications of the presence of a consciousness or mind as a separate entity, are central differences between the behavioral and cognitive orientations. According to Malone (1990), the goal of psychology from the behavioral perspective has been clear since Watson:

We want to predict with reasonable certainty what people will do in specific situations. Given a stimulus, defined as an object of inner or outer experience, what response may be expected? A stimulus could be a blow to the knee or an architect's education; a response could be a knee jerk or the building of a bridge. Similarly, we want to know, given a response, what situation produced it.... In all such situations the discovery of the stimuli that call out one or another behavior should allow us to influence the occurrence of behaviors; prediction, which comes from such discoveries, allows control. What does the analysis of conscious experience give us? (p. 97)

Such notions caused Bertrand Russell to claim that Watson made "the greatest contribution to scientific psychology since Aristotle" (as cited in Malone, 1990, p. 96) and others to call him the "... simpleton or archfiend ... who denied the very existence of mind and consciousness (and) reduced us to the status of robots" (p. 96). Related to the issue of mind/body dualism are the emphases on structure versus function and/or evolution and/or selection.

1.2.1   Structuralism, Functionalism, and Evolution

The battle cry of the cognitive revolution is "mind is back!" A great new science of mind is born. Behaviorism nearly destroyed our concern for it but behaviorism has been overthrown, and we can take up again where the philosophers and early psychologists left off (Skinner, 1989, p. 22)

Structuralism also can be traced through the development of philosophy at least to Democritus' "heated psychic atoms" (Needham, 1978). Plato divided the soul/mind into three distinct components in three different locations: the impulsive/instinctive component in the abdomen and loins, the emotional/spiritual component in the heart, and the intellectual/reasoning component in the brain. In modern times, Wundt at Leipzig and Titchener (his student) at Cornell espoused structuralism as a way of investigating consciousness. Wundt proposed ideas, affect, and impulse and Titchener proposed sensations, images, and affect as the primary elements of consciousness. Titchener eventually identified over 50,000 mental elements (Malone, 1990). Both relied heavily on the method of introspection (to be discussed later) for data. Cognitive notions such as schema, knowledge structures, duplex memory, etc. are structural explanations. There are no behavioral equivalents to structuralism because it is an aspect of mind/consciousness.

Functionalism, however, is a philosophy shared by both cognitive and behavioral theories. Functionalism is associated with John Dewey and William James who stressed the adaptive nature of activity (mental or behavioral) as opposed to structuralism's attempts to separate consciousness into elements. In fact, functionalism allows for an infinite number of physical and mind structures to serve the same functions. Functionalism has its roots in Darwin's *Origin of the Species* (1859), and Wittgenstein's *Philosophical Investigations* (Malcolm, 1954). The question of course is the focus of adaptation: mind or behavior. The behavioral view is that evolutionary forces and adaptations are no different for humans than for the first one-celled organisms; that organisms since the beginning of time have been vulnerable and, therefore, had to learn to discriminate and avoid those things which were harmful and discriminate and approach those things necessary to sustain themselves (Goodson, 1973). This, of course, is the heart of the selectionist position long advocated by B. F. Skinner (1969, 1978, 1981, 1987a, 1987b, 1990).

The selectionist (Chiesa, 1992; Pennypacker, 1994; Vargas, 1993) approach "emphasizes investigating changes in behavioral repertoires over time" (Johnson & Layng, 1992, p. 1475). Selectionism is related to evolutionary theory in that it views the complexity of behavior to be a function of selection contingencies found in nature (Donahoe, 1991; Donahoe & Palmer, 1989; Layng, 1991; Skinner, 1969, 1981, 1990). As Johnson and Layng (1992, p. 1475) point out, this "perspective is beginning to spread beyond the studies of behavior and evolution to the once structuralist-dominated field of computer science, as evidenced by the emergence of parallel distributed processing theory (McClelland & Rumelhart, 1986; Rumelhart & McClelland, 1986), and adaptive networks research (Donahoe, 1991; Donahoe & Palmer, 1989)".

The difficulty most people have in getting their heads around the selectionist position of behavior (or evolution) is that the cause of a behavior is the consequence of a behavior, not the stimulus, mental or otherwise, that precedes it. In evolution, giraffes did not grow longer necks in reaction to higher leaves; rather, a genetic variation produced an individual with a longer neck and *as a consequence* that individual found a niche (higher leaves) that few others could occupy. As a result, that individual survived (was "selected") to breed and the offspring produced survived to breed and in subsequent generations perhaps eventually produced an individual with a longer neck that also survived, and so forth. The radical behaviorist assumes that behavior is selected in exactly that way: by consequences. Of course we do not tend to see the world this way. "We tend to say, often rashly, that if one thing follows another that it was probably caused by it—following the ancient principle of *post hoc, ergo propter hoc* (after this, therefore because of it)" (Skinner, 1974, p. 10). This is the most critical distinction between methodological behaviorism and selectionist behaviorism. The former

attributes causality to the stimuli that are antecedent to the behavior, the latter to the consequences that follow the behavior. Methodological behaviorism is in this regard similar to cognitive orientations; the major difference being that the cognitive interpretation would place the stimulus (a thought or idea) inside the head.

1.2.2 Introspection and Constructivism

Constructivism, the notion that meaning (reality) is made, is currently touted as a new way of looking at the world. In fact, there is nothing in any form of behaviorism that requires realism, naive or otherwise. The constructive nature of perception has been accepted at least since von Helmholtz (1866) and his notion of "unconscious inference." Basically, von Helmholtz believed that much of our experience depends upon inferences drawn on the basis of a little stimulation and a lot of past experience. Most, if not all, current theories of perception rely on von Helmholtz's ideas as a base (Malone, 1990). The question is not whether perception is constructive, but what to make of these constructions and where do they come from? Cognitive psychology draws heavily on introspection to "see" the stuff of construction.

In modern times, introspection was a methodological cornerstone of Wundt, Titchener, and the Gestaltist, Kulpe (Malone, 1990). Introspection generally assumes a notion espoused by John Mill (1829) that thoughts are linear; that ideas follow each other one after another. Although it can (and has) been argued that ideas do not flow in straight lines, a much more serious problem confronts introspection on its face. Introspection relies on direct experience; that our "mind's eye" or inner observation reveals things as they are. We know, however, that our other senses do not operate that way.

The red surface of an apple does not *look* like a matrix of molecules reflecting photons at a certain critical wavelength, but that is what it is. The sound of a flute does not *sound* like a sinusoidal compression wave train in the atmosphere, but that is what it is. The warmth of the summer air does not feel like the mean kinetic energy of millions molecules, but that is what it is. If one's pains and hopes and beliefs do not *introspectively* seem like electrochemical states in a neural network, that may be only because our faculty of introspection, like our other senses, is not sufficiently penetrating to reveal such hidden details. Which is just what we would expect anyway ... unless we can somehow argue that the faculty of introspection is quite different from all other forms of observation. (Churchland, 1990, p. 15)

Obviously, the problems with introspection became more problematic in retrospective paradigms, that is, when the learner/performer is asked to work from a behavior to a thought. This poses a problem on two counts: accuracy and causality. In terms of accuracy, James Angell stated his belief in his 1907 APA presidential address:

No matter how much we may talk of the preservation of psychical dispositions, nor how many metaphors we may summon to characterize the storage of ideas in some hypothetical deposit chamber of memory, the obstinate fact remains that when we are not experiencing a sensation or an idea it is, strictly speaking, non-existent.... [W]e have no guarantee that our second edition is really a replica of the first, we have a good bit of presumptive evidence that from the content point of view the original never is and never can be literally duplicated. (Herrnstein & Boring, 1965, p. 502)

The causality problem is perhaps more difficult to grasp at first but, in general, behaviorists have less trouble with "heated" data (self reports of mental activities at the moment of behaving) that reflect "doing in the head" and "doing in the world" at the same time than with going from behavior to descriptions of mental thought, ideas, or structures and *then* saying that the mental activity *caused* the behavioral. In such cases, of course, it is arguably equally likely that the behavioral activities caused the mental activities.

A more current view of constructivism, social constructivism, focuses on the making of meaning through social interaction (e.g., John-Steiner & Mahn, 1996). In the words of Garrison (1994), meanings "are sociolinguistically constructed between two selves participating in a shared understanding" (p. 11). This, in fact, is perfectly consistent with the position of behaviorists (see, for example, Skinner, 1974) as long as this does not also imply the substitution of a group mind of rather than an individual "mind." Garrison, a Deweyan scholar, is, in fact, also a self-proclaimed behaviorist.

1.3 RADICAL BEHAVIORISM

Probably no psychologist in the modern era has been as misunderstood, misquoted, misjudged, and just plain maligned as B. F. Skinner and his Skinnerian, or radical, behaviorism. Much of this stems from the fact that many educational technology programs (or any educational programs, for that matter) do not teach, at least in any meaningful manner, behavioral theory and research. More recent notions such as cognitive psychology, constructivism, and social constructivism have become "featured" orientations. Potentially worse, recent students of educational technology have not been exposed to course work that emphasized history and systems, or theory building and theory analysis. In terms of the former problem, we will devote our conclusion to a brief synopsis of what radical behaviorism is and what it isn't. In terms of the latter, we will appeal to the simplest of the criteria for judging the adequacy and appropriateness of a theory: parsimony.

1.3.1 What Radical Behaviorism Does Not Believe

It is important to begin this discussion with what radical behaviorism rejects: structuralism (mind–body dualism), operationalism, and logical positivism.

That radical behaviorism rejects structuralism has been discussed earlier in the introduction of this article. Skinner (1938, 1945, 1953b, 1957, 1964, 1974) continually argued against the use of structures and mentalisms. His arguments are too numerous to deal with in this work, but let us consider what is arguably the most telling: copy theory. "The most important

consideration is that this view presupposes three things: (a) a stimulus object in the external world, (b) a sensory registering of that object via some modality, and (c) the internal representation of that object as a sensation, perception or image, different from (b) above. The first two are physical and the third, presumably something else" (Moore, 1980, p. 472-473).

In Skinner's (1964) words:

The need for something beyond, and quite different from, copying is not widely understood. Suppose someone were to coat the occipital lobes of the brain with a special photographic emulsion which, when developed, yielded a reasonable copy of a current visual stimulus. In many quarters, this would be regarded as a triumph in the physiology of vision. Yet nothing could be more disastrous, for we should have to start all over again and ask how the organism sees a picture in its occipital cortex, and we should now have much less of the brain available from which to seek an answer. It adds nothing to an explanation of how an organism reacts to a stimulus to trace the pattern of the stimulus into the body. It is most convenient, for both organism and psychophysiologist, if the external world is never copied—if the world we know is simply the world around us. The same may be said of theories according to which the brain interprets signals sent to it and in some sense reconstructs external stimuli. If the real world is, indeed, scrambled in transmission but later reconstructed in the brain, we must then start all over again and explain how the organism sees the reconstruction. (p. 87)

Quite simply, if we copy what we see, what do we "see" the copy with and what does this "mind's eye" do with its input? Create another copy? How do we, to borrow from our information processing colleagues, exit this recursive process?

The related problem of mentalisms generally, and their admission with the dialog of psychology on largely historical grounds was also discussed often by Skinner. For example:

Psychology, alone among the biological and social sciences, passed through a revolution comparable in many respects with that which was taking place at the same time in physics. This was, of course, behaviorism. The first step, like that in physics, was a reexamination of the observational bases of certain important concepts... Most of the early behaviorists, as well as those of us just coming along who claimed some systematic continuity, had begun to see that psychology did not require the redefinition of subjective concepts. The reinterpretation of an established set of explanatory fictions was not the way to secure the tools then needed for a scientific description of behavior. Historical prestige was beside the point. There was no more reason to make a permanent place for "consciousness," "will," "feeling," and so on, than for "phlogiston" or "vis anima." On the contrary, redefined concepts proved to be awkward and inappropriate, and Watsonianism was, in fact, practically wrecked in the attempt to make them work.

Thus it came about while the behaviorists might have applied Bridgman's principle to representative terms from a mentalistic psychology (and were most competent to do so), they had lost all interest in the matter. They might as well have spent their time in showing what an eighteenth century chemist was talking about when he said that the Metallic Substances consisted of a vitrifiable earth united with phlogiston. There was no doubt that such a statement could be analyzed operationally or translated into modern terms, or that subjective terms could be operationally defined. But such matters were of historical interest only. What was wanted was a fresh set of concepts derived from a direct analysis of newly emphasized data... (p. 292)

Operationalism is a term often associated with Skinnerian behaviorism and indeed in a sense this association is correct; not, however, in the historical sense of operationalism of Stevens (1939) or, in his attacks on behaviorism, by Spence (1948), or in the sense that it is assumed today: "how to deal scientifically with mental events" (Moore, 1980, p. 571). Stevens (1951) for example, states that "operationalism does not deny images, for example, but asks: What is the operational definition of the term "image?" (p. 231). As Moore (1981) explains, this "conventional approach entails virtually every aspect of the dualistic position" (p. 470). "In contrast, for the radical behaviorist, operationalism involves the functional analysis of the term in question, that is, an assessment of the discriminative stimuli that occasions the use of the term and the consequences that maintain it" (Moore, 1981, p. 59). In other words, radical behaviorism rejects the operationalism of methodology behaviorists, but embraces the operationalism implicit in the three-part contingency of antecedents, behaviors, and consequences and would, in fact, apply it to the social dialog of scientists themselves!

The final demon to deal with is the notion that radical behaviorism somehow relies on logical positivism. This rejection of this premise will be dealt with more thoroughly in the section to follow that deals with social influences, particularly social influences in science. Suffice it for now that Skinner (1974) felt that methodological behaviorism and logical positivism "ignore consciousness, feelings, and states of mind" but that radical behaviorism does not thus "behead the organism . . . it was not designed to 'permit consciousness to atrophy'" (p. 219). Day (1983) further describes the effect of Skinner's 1945 paper at the symposium on operationalism. "Skinner turns logical positivism upside down, while methodological behaviorism continues on its own, particular logical-positivist way" (p. 94).

1.3.2 What Radical Behaviorism Does Believe

Two issues which Skinnerian behaviorism is clear on, but not apparently well understood but by critics, are the roles of private events and social/cultural influences. The first problem, radical behaviorism's treatment of private events, relates to the confusion on the role of operationalism: "The position that psychology must be restricted to publicly observable, intersubjectively, verifiable data bases more appropriately characterizes what Skinner calls methodological behaviorism, an intellectual position regarding the admissibility of psychological data that is conspicuously linked to logical positivism and operationalism" (Moore, 1980, p. 459). Radical behaviorism holds as a central tenet that to rule out stimuli because they are not accessible to others not only represents inappropriate vestiges of operationalism and positivism, it compromises the explanatory integrity of behaviorism itself (Skinner, 1953a, 1974). In fact, radical behaviorism does not only value private events, it says they are the same as public events, and herein lies the problem, perhaps. Radical behaviorism does not believe it is necessary to suppose that private events have any special properties simply because they are private (Skinner, 1953b). They are distinguished only by their limited accessibility, but are assumed to be equally lawful as public events (Moore, 1980). In other words,

the same analyses should be applied to private events as public ones. Obviously, some private, or covert, behavior involves the same musculature as the public or overt behavior as in talking to oneself or "mental practice" of a motor event (Moore, 1980). Generally, we assume private behavior began as a public event and then, for several reasons, became covert. Moore gives three examples of such reasons. The first is convenience: We learn to read publicly, but private behavior is faster. Another case is that we can engage in a behavior privately and if the consequences are not suitable, reject it as a public behavior. A second reason is to avoid aversive consequences. We may sing a song over and over covertly but not sing it aloud because we fear social disapproval. Many of us, alone in our shower or in our car, with the negative consequences safely absent, however, may sing loudly indeed. A third reason is that the stimuli that ordinarily elicit an overt behavior are weak and deficient. Thus we become "unsure" of our response. We may think we see something, but be unclear enough to either not say anything or make a weak, low statement.

What the radical behaviorist does not believe is that private behaviors *cause* public behavior. Both are assumed to be attributable to common variables. The private event may have some discrimination stimulus control, but this is not the cause of the subsequent behavior. The cause is the contingencies of reinforcement that control both public and private behavior (Day, 1976). It is important, particularly in terms of current controversy, to point out that private events are in no way superior to public events and in at least one respect important to our last argument, very much inferior: the verbal (social) community has trouble responding to these (Moore, 1980). This is because the reinforcing consequence "in most cases is social attention" (Moore, 1980, p. 461).

The influence of the social group, of culture, runs through all of Skinner's work (see, e.g., Skinner, 1945, 1953b, 1957, 1964, 1974). For this reason, much of this work focuses on language. As a first step (and to segue from private events), consider an example from Moore (1980). The example deals with pain, but feel free to substitute any private perception. Pain is clearly a case where the stimulus is only available to the individual who perceives it (as opposed to most events which have some external correlate). How do we learn to use the verbal response to pain appropriately? One way is for the individual to report pain after some observable public event such as falling down, being struck, etc. The verbal community would support a statement of pain and perhaps suggest that sharp objects cause sharp pain, dull objects, dull pain. The second case would involve a collateral, public response such as holding the area in pain. The final case would involve using the word pain in connection with some overt state of affairs such as a bent back, or a stiff neck. It is important to note that if the individual reports pain too often *without* such overt signs, he or she runs the risk of being called a hypochondriac or malingerer (Moore, 1980). "Verbal behavior, is a social phenomenon, and so in a sense all verbal behavior, including scientific verbal behavior is a product of social–cultural influences" (Moore, 1984, p. 75). To examine the key role of social cultural influences it is useful to use an example we are familiar with, science. As Moore (1984) points out, "Scientists typically live the first 25 years of their lives, and 12 to 16 hours per day thereafter, in the lay community" (p. 61). Through the process of social and cultural reinforcers, they become acculturated and as a result are exposed to popular preconceptions. Once the individual becomes a scientist, operations and contact with data cue behaviors which lead to prediction and control. The two systems cannot operate separately. In fact, the behavior of the scientist may be understood as a product of the conjoint action of scientific and lay discriminative stimuli and scientific and lay reinforcer (Moore, 1984). Thus, from Moore:

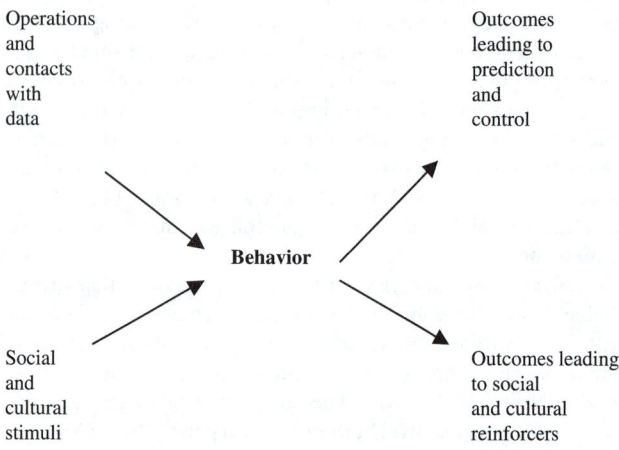

Operations and contacts with data

Outcomes leading to prediction and control

Behavior

Social and cultural stimuli

Outcomes leading to social and cultural reinforcers

Although it is dangerous to focus too hard on the "data" alone, Skinner (1974) also cautions against depending exclusively on the social/cultural stimuli and reinforcers for explanations, as is often the case with current approaches.

Until fairly late in the nineteenth century, very little was known about the bodily processes in health or disease from which good medical practice could be derived, yet a person who was ill should have found it worthwhile to call in a physician. Physicians saw many ill people and were in the best possible position to acquire useful, if unanalyzed, skills in treating them. Some of them no doubt did so, but the history of medicine reveals a very different picture. Medical practices have varied from epoch to epoch, but they have often consisted of barbaric measures—blood lettings, leechings, cuppings, poultices, emetics, and purgations—which more often than not must have been harmful. Such practices were not based on the skill and wisdom acquired from contact with illness; they were based on theories of what was going on inside the body of a person who was ill. . . .

Medicine suffered, and in part just because the physician who talked about theories seemed to have a more profound knowledge of illness than one who merely displayed the common sense acquired from personal experience. The practices derived form theories no doubt also obscured many symptoms which might have led to more effective skills. Theories flourished at the expense both of the patient and of progress toward the more scientific knowledge which was to emerge in modern medicine. (Skinner, 1974, pp. x–xi)

1.4 THE BASICS OF BEHAVIORISM

Behaviorism in the United States may be traced to the work of E. B. Twitmeyer (1902), a graduate student at the University of Pennsylvania, and E. L. Thorndike (1898). Twitmeyer's

doctoral dissertation research on the knee-jerk (patellar) reflex involved alerting his subjects with a bell that a hammer was about to strike their patellar tendon. As has been the case so many times in the history of the development of behavioral theory (see, for example, Skinner, 1956), something went wrong. Twitmeyer sounded the bell but the hammer did not trip. The subject, however, made a knee-jerk response in *anticipation* of the hammer drop. Twitmeyer redesigned his experiment to study this phenomenon and presented his findings at the annual meeting of the American Psychological Association in 1904. His paper, however, was greeted with runaway apathy and it fell to Ivan Pavlov (1849–1936) to become the "Father of Classical Conditioning." Interestingly enough, Pavlov also began his line of research based on a casual or accidental observation. A Nobel Prize winner for his work in digestion, Pavlov noted that his subjects (dogs) seemed to begin salivating to the sights and sounds of feeding. He, too, altered the thrust of his research to investigate his serendipitous observations more thoroughly.

Operant or instrumental conditioning is usually associated with B. F. Skinner. Yet, in 1898, E. L. Thorndike published a monograph on animal intelligence which made use of a "puzzle box" (a forerunner of what is often called a "Skinner Box") to investigate the effect of reward (e.g., food, escape) on the behavior of cats. Thorndike placed the cats in a box that could be opened by pressing a latch or pulling a string. Outside the box was a bowl of milk or fish. Not surprisingly, the cats tried anything and everything until they stumbled onto the correct response. Also, not surprisingly, the cats learned to get out of the box more and more rapidly. From these beginnings, the most thoroughly researched phenomenon in psychology evolves.

Behavioral theory is now celebrating nearly a century of contribution to theories of learning. The pioneering work of such investigators as Cason (1922a, 1922b), Liddell (1926), Mateer (1918), and Watson and Rayner (1920) in classical conditioning, and Blodgett (1929), Hebb (1949), Hull (1943), and Skinner (1938) in operant conditioning, has led to the development of the most powerful technology known to behavioral science. Behaviorism, however, is in a paradoxical place in American education today. In a very real sense, behavioral theory is the basis for innovations such as teaching machines, computer-assisted instruction, competency-based education (mastery learning), instructional design, minimal competency testing, performance-based assessment, "educational accountability," situated cognition, and even social constructivism, yet behaviorism is no longer a "popular" orientation in education or instructional design. An exploration of behaviorism, its contributions to research and current practice in educational technology (despite its recent unpopularity), and its usefulness in the future are the concerns of this chapter.

1.4.1 Basic Assumptions

Behavioral psychology has provided instructional technology with several basic assumptions, concepts, and principles. These components of behavioral theory are outlined in this section (albeit briefly) in order to ensure that the discussion of its applications can be clearly linked back to the relevant behavioral theoretical underpinnings. While some or much of the following discussion may be elementary for many, we believed it was crucial to lay the groundwork that illustrates the major role behavioral psychology has played and *continues* to play in the research and development of instructional technology applications.

Three major assumptions of selectionist behaviorism are directly relevant to instructional technology. These assumptions focus on the following: the role of the learner, the nature of learning, and the generality of the learning processes and instructional procedures.

1.4.1.1 The Role of the Learner. As mentioned earlier in this chapter, one of the most misinterpreted and misrepresented assumptions of behavioral learning theory concerns the role of the learner. Quite often, the learner is characterized as a passive entity that merely reacts to environmental stimuli (cf., Anderson's receptive–accrual model, 1986). However, according to B. F. Skinner, knowledge is action (Schnaitter, 1987). Skinner (1968) stated that a learner "does not passively absorb knowledge from the world around him but must play an active role" (p. 5). He goes on to explain how learners learn by doing, experiencing, and engaging in trial and error. All three of these components work together and must be studied together to formulate any given instance of learning. It is only when these three components are describable that we can identify what has been learned, under what conditions the learning has taken place, and the consequences that support and maintain the learned behavior. The emphasis is on the active responding of the learner—the learner must be engaged in the behavior in order to learn and to validate that learning has occurred.

1.4.1.2 The Nature of Learning. Learning is frequently defined as a change in behavior due to experience. It is a function of building associations between the occasion upon which the behavior occurs (stimulus events), the behavior itself (response events) and the result (consequences). These associations are centered in the experiences that produce learning, and differ to the extent to which they are contiguous and contingent (Chance, 1994). Contiguity refers to the close pairing of stimulus and response in time and/or space. Contingency refers to the dependency between the antecedent or behavioral event and either the response or consequence. Essential to the strengthening responses with these associations is the repeated continuous pairing of the stimulus with response and the pairing consequences (Skinner, 1968). It is the construction of functional relationships, based on the contingencies of reinforcement, under which the learning takes place. It is this functionality that is the essence of selection. Stimulus control develops as a result of continuous pairing with consequences (functions). In order to truly understand what has been learned, the entire relationship must be identified (Vargas, 1977). All components of this three-part contingency (i.e., functional relationship) must be observable and measurable to ensure the scientific verification that learning (i.e., a change of behavior) has occurred (Cooper, Heron, & Heward, 1987).

Of particular importance to instructional technology is the need to focus on the individual in this learning process. Contingencies vary from person to person based on each individual's genetic and reinforcement histories and events present at the time of learning (Gagné, 1985). This requires designers and developers to ensure that instruction is aimed at aiding the learning of the individual (e.g., Gagné, Briggs, & Wager, 1992). To accomplish this, a needs assessment (Burton & Merrill, 1991) or front-end analysis (Mager, 1984; Smith & Ragan, 1993) is conducted at the very beginning of the instructional design process. The focus of this activity is to articulate, among other things, learner characteristics; that is, the needs and capabilities of individual learners are assessed to ensure that the instruction being developed is appropriate and meaningful. The goals are then written in terms of what the learner will accomplish via this instructional event.

The material to be learned must be identified in order to clearly understand the requisite nature of learning. There is a natural order inherent in many content areas. Much of the information within these content areas is characterized in sequences; however, many others form a network or a tree of related information (Skinner, 1968). (Notice that in the behavioral views, such sequences or networks do not imply internal structures; rather, they suggest a line of attack for the designs). Complex learning involves becoming competent in a given field by learning incremental behaviors which are ordered in these sequences, traditionally with very small steps, ranging from the most simple to more complex to the final goal. Two major considerations occur in complex learning. The first, as just mentioned, is the gradual elaboration of extremely complex patterns of behavior. The second involves the maintenance of the behavior's strength through the use of reinforcement contingent upon successful achievement at each stage. Implicit in this entire endeavor is the observable nature of actual learning public performance which is crucial for the acknowledgment, verification (by self and/or others), and continued development of the present in similar behaviors.

1.4.1.3 The Generality of Learning Principles. According to behavioral theory, all animals—including humans—obey universal laws of behavior (a.k.a., equipotentiality) (Davey, 1981). In methodological behaviorism, all habits are formed from conditioned reflexes (Watson, 1924). In selectionist behaviorism, all learning is a result of the experienced consequences of the organisms' behavior (Skinner, 1971). While Skinner (1969) does acknowledge species-specific behavior (e.g., adaptive mechanisms, differences in sensory equipment, effector systems, reactions to different reinforcers), he stands by the fact that the basic processes that promote or inhibit learning are universal to all organisms. Specifically, he states that the research does show an

... extraordinary uniformity over a wide range of reinforcement, the processes of extinction, discrimination and generalization return remarkably similar and consistent results across species. For example, fixed-interval reinforcement schedules yield a predictable scalloped performance effect (low rates of responding at the beginning of the interval following reinforcement, high rates of responding at the end of the interval) whether the subjects are animals or humans. (Ferster & Skinner, 1957, p. 7)

Most people of all persuasions will accept behaviorism as an account for much, even most, learning (e.g., animal learning and perhaps learning up to the alphabet or shoe tying or learning to speak the language). For the behaviorist, the same principles that account for simple behaviors also account for complex ones.

1.4.2 Basic Concepts and Principles

Behavioral theory has contributed several important concepts and principles to the research and development of instructional technology. Three major types of behavior, respondent learning, operant learning, and observational learning, serve as the organizer for this section. Each of these models relies on the building associations—the simplest unit that is learned—under the conditions of contiguity and repetition (Gagné, 1985). Each model also utilizes the processes of discrimination and generalization to describe the mechanisms humans use to adapt to situational and environmental stimuli (Chance, 1994). Discrimination is the act of responding differently to different stimuli, such as stopping at a red traffic light while driving through a green traffic light. Generalization is the act of responding in the same way to similar stimuli, specifically, to those stimuli not present at time of training. For example, students generate classroom behavior rules based on previous experiences and expectations in classroom settings. Or, when one is using a new word processing program, the individual attempts to apply what is already known about a word processing environment to the new program. In essence, discrimination and generalization are inversely related, crucial processes that facilitate adaptation and enable transfer to new environments.

1.4.2.1 Respondent Learning (Methodological Behaviorism). Involuntary actions, called respondents, are entrained using the classical conditioning techniques of Ivan Pavlov. In classical conditioning, an organism learns to respond to a stimulus that once prompted no response. The process begins with identification and articulation of an unconditional stimulus (US) that automatically elicits an emotional or physiological unconditional response (UR). No prior learning or conditioning is required to establish this natural connection (e.g., US = food; UR = salivation). In classical conditioning, neutral stimulus is introduced, which initially prompts no response from the organism (e.g., a tone). The intent is to eventually have the tone (i.e., the conditioned stimulus or CS) elicit a response that very closely approximates the original UR (i.e., will become the conditional response or CR). The behavior is entrained using the principles of contiguity and repetition (i.e., practice). In repeated trials, the US and CS are introduced at the same time or in close temporal proximity. Gradually the US is presented less frequently with the CS, being sure to retain the performance of the UR/CR. Ultimately, the CS elicits the CR without the aid of the US.

Classical conditioning is a very powerful tool for entraining basic physiological responses (e.g., increases in blood pressure, taste aversions, psychosomatic illness), and emotive responses (e.g., arousal, fear, anxiety, pleasure) since the learning is paired with reflexive, inborn associations. Classical conditioning is a major theoretical notion underlying advertising, propaganda, and related learning. Its importance in the formations of biases, stereotypes, etc. is of particular importance in the design of instructional materials and should always be considered in the design process.

The incidental learning of these responses is clearly a concern in instructional settings. Behaviors such as test anxiety and "school phobia" are maladaptive behaviors that are often entrained without intent. From a proactive stance in instructional design, a context or environmental analysis is a key component of a needs assessment (Tessmer, 1990). Every feature of the physical (e.g., lighting, classroom arrangement) and support (e.g., administration) environment are examined to ascertain positive or problematic factors that might influence the learner's attitude and level of participation in the instructional events. Similarly, in designing software, video, audio, and so forth, careful attention is paid to the aesthetic features of the medium to ensure motivation and engagement. Respondent learning is a form of methodological behaviorism to be discussed later.

1.4.2.2 Operant Conditioning (Selectionist or Radical Behaviorism). Operant conditioning is based on a single, simple principle: There is a functional and interconnected relationship between the stimuli that preceded a response (antecedents), the stimuli that follow a response (consequences), and the response (operant) itself. Acquisition of behavior is viewed as resulting from these three-term or three-component contingent or functional relationships. While there are always contingencies in effect which are beyond the teacher's (or designer's) control, it is the role of the educator to control the environment so that the predominant contingent relationships are in line with the educational goal at hand.

Antecedent cues. Antecedents are those objects or events in the environment that serve as cues. Cues set the stage or serve as signals for specific behaviors to take place because such behaviors have been reinforced in the past in the presence of such cues. Antecedent cues may include temporal cues (time), interpersonal cues (people), and covert or internal cues (inside the skin). Verbal and written directions, nonverbal hand signals and facial gestures, highlighting with colors and boldfaced print are all examples of cues used by learners to discriminate the conditions for behaving in a way that returns a desired consequence. The behavior ultimately comes under stimulus "control" (i.e., made more probable by the discriminative stimulus or cue) though the contiguous pairing in repeated trials, hence serving in a key functional role in this contingent relationship. Often the behavioral technologist seeks to increase or decrease antecedent (stimulus) control to increase or decrease the probability of a response. In order to do this, he or she must be cognizant of those cues to which generalized responding is desired or present and be aware that antecedent control will increase with consequence pairing.

Behavior. Unlike the involuntary actions entrained via classical conditioning, most human behaviors are emitted or voluntarily enacted. People deliberately "operate" on their environment to produce desired consequences. Skinner termed these purposeful *responses operants.* Operants include both private (thoughts) and public (behavior) activities, but the basic measure in behavioral theory remains the observable, measurable response. Operants range from simple to complex, verbal to nonverbal, fine to gross motor actions—the whole realm of what we as humans choose to do based on the consequences the behavior elicits.

Consequences. While the first two components of operant conditioning (antecedents and operants) are relatively straightforward, the nature of *consequences* and interactions between consequences and behaviors is fairly complex. First, consequences may be classified as contingent and noncontingent. Contingent consequences are reliable and relatively consistent. A clear association between the operant and the consequences can be established. Noncontingent consequences, however, often produce accidental or superstitious conditioning. If, perchance, a computer program has scant or no documentation and the desired program features cannot be accessed via a predictable set of moves, the user would tend to press many keys, not really knowing what may finally cause a successful screen change. This reduces the rate of learning, if any learning occurs at all.

Another dimension focuses on whether or not the consequence is actually delivered. Consequences may be positive (something is presented following a response) or negative (something is taken away following a response). Note that positive and negative do not imply value (i.e., "good" or "bad"). Consequences can also be reinforcing, that is, tend to maintain or increase a behavior, or they may be punishing, that is, tend to decrease or suppress a behavior. Taken together, the possibilities then are positive reinforcement (presenting something to maintain or increase a behavior); positive punishment (presenting something to decrease a behavior); negative reinforcement (taking away something to increase a behavior); or negative punishment (taking away something to decrease a behavior). Another possibility obviously is that of no consequence following a behavior, which results in the disappearance or extinction of a previously reinforced behavior.

Examples of these types of consequences are readily found in the implementation of behavior modification. Behavior modification or applied behavior analysis is a widely used instructional technology that manipulates the use of these consequences to produce the desired behavior (Cooper et al., 1987). Positive reinforcers ranging from praise, to desirable activities, to tangible rewards are delivered upon performance of a desired behavior. Positive punishments such as extra work, physical exertion, demerits are imposed upon performance of an undesirable behavior. Negative reinforcement is used when aversive conditions such as a teacher's hard gaze or yelling are taken away when the appropriate behavior is enacted (e.g., assignment completion). Negative punishment or response cost is used when a desirable stimulus such as free time privileges are taken away when an inappropriate behavior is performed. When no consequence follows the behavior, such as ignoring an undesirable behavior, ensuring that no attention is given to the misdeed, the undesirable behavior often abates. But this typically is preceded by an upsurge in the frequency of responding until the learner realizes that the behavior will no longer receive the desired consequence. All in all, the use of each consequence requires consideration of whether one wants to increase or decrease a behavior, if it is to be done by taking away or giving some stimulus, and whether or not that stimulus is desirable or undesirable.

In addition to the type of consequence, the schedule for the delivery or timing of those consequences is a key dimension to operant learning. Often a distinction is made between simple and complex *schedules of reinforcement.* Simple schedules include continuous consequation and partial or intermittent consequation. When using a continuous schedule, reinforcement is delivered after each correct response. This procedure is important for the learning of new behaviors because the functional relationship between antecedent-response-consequence is clearly communicated to the learner through predictability of consequation.

When using intermittent schedules, the reinforcement is delivered after some, but not all, responses. There are two basic types of intermittent schedules: ratio and interval. A ratio schedule is based on the numbers of responses required for consequation (e.g., piece work, number of completed math problems). An interval schedule is based on the amount of time that passes between consequation (e.g., payday, weekly quizzes). Ratio and interval schedules may be either fixed (predictable) or variable (unpredictable). These procedures are used once the functional relationship is established and with the intent is to encourage persistence of responses. The schedule is gradually changed from continuous, to fixed, to variable (i.e., until it becomes very "lean"), in order for the learner to perform the behavior for an extended period of time without any reinforcement. A variation often imposed on these schedules is called limited hold, which refers to the consequence only being available for a certain period of time.

Complex schedules are composed of the various features of simple schedules. Shaping requires the learner to perform successive approximations of the target behavior by changing the criterion behavior for reinforcement to become more and more like the final performance. A good example of shaping is the writing process, wherein drafts are constantly revised toward the final product. Chaining requires that two or more learned behaviors must be performed in a specific sequence for consequation. Each behavior sets up cues for subsequent responses to be performed (e.g., long division). In multiple schedules, two or more simple schedules are in effect for the same behavior with each associated with a particular stimulus. Two or more schedules are available in a concurrent schedule procedure; however, there are no specific cues as to which schedule is in effect. Schedules may also be conjunctive (two or more behaviors that all must be performed for consequation to occur, but the behaviors may occur in any order), or tandem (two or more behaviors must be performed in a specific sequence without cues).

In all cases, the schedule or timing of the consequation is manipulated to fit the target response, using antecedents to signal the response, and appropriate consequences for the learner and the situation.

1.4.2.3 Observational Learning. By using the basic concepts and principles of operant learning, and the basic definition that learning is a change of behavior brought about by experience, organisms can be thought of as learning new behaviors by observing the behavior of others (Chance, 1994). This premise was originally tested by Thorndike (1898) with cats, chicks, and dogs, and later by Watson (1908) with monkeys, without success. In all cases, animals were situated in positions to observe and learn elementary problem-solving procedures (e.g., puzzle boxes) by watching successful same-species models perform the desired task. However, Warden and colleagues (Warden, Field, & Koch, 1940; Warden, Jackson, 1935) found that when animals were put in settings (e.g., cages) that were identical to the modeling animals and the observers watched the models perform the behavior and receive the reinforcement, the observers did learn the target behavior, often responding correctly on the first trial (Chance, 1994).

Attention focused seriously on observational learning research with the work of Bandura and colleagues in the 1960s. In a series of studies with children and adults (with children as the observers and children and adults as the models), these researchers demonstrated that the reinforcement of a model's behavior was positively correlated with the observer's judgments that the behavior was appropriate to imitate. These studies formed the empirical basis for Bandura's (1977) Social Learning Theory, which stated that people are not driven by either inner forces or environmental stimuli in isolation. His assertion was that behavior and complex learning must be "explained in terms of a continuous reciprocal interaction of personal and environmental determinants . . . virtually all learning phenomenon resulting from direct experience occur on a vicarious basis by observing other people's behavior and its consequences for them" (p. 11–12).

The basic observational or vicarious learning experience consists of watching a live or filmed performance or listening to a description of the performance (i.e., symbolic modeling) of a model and the positive and/or negative consequences of that model's behavior. Four component processes govern observational learning (Bandura, 1977). First, *attentional processes* determine what is selectively observed, and extracted valence, complexity, prevalence, and functional value influence the quality of the attention. Observer characteristics such as sensory capacities, arousal level, perceptual set, and past reinforcement history mediate the stimuli. Second, the attended stimuli must be remembered or retained (i.e., *retentional processes*). Response patterns must be represented in memory in some organized, symbolic form. Humans primarily use imaginal and verbal codes for observed performances. These patterns must be practiced through overt or covert rehearsal to ensure retention. Third, the learner must engage in *motor reproduction processes* which require the organization of responses through their

initiation, monitoring, and refinement on the basis of feedback. The behavior must be performed in order for cues to be learned and corrective adjustments made. The fourth component is *motivation*. Social learning theory recognizes that humans are more likely to adopt behavior that they value (functional) and reject behavior that they find punishing or unrewarding (not functional). Further, the evaluative judgments that humans make about the functionality of their own behavior mediate and regulate which observationally learned responses they will actually perform. Ultimately, people will enact self-satisfying behaviors and avoid distasteful or disdainful ones. Consequently, external reinforcement, vicarious reinforcement, and self-reinforcement are all processes that promote the learning and performance of observed behavior.

1.4.3 Complex Learning, Problem Solving, and Transfer

Behavioral theory addresses the key issues of complex learning, problem solving, and transfer using the same concepts and principles found in the everyday human experience. Complex learning is developed through the learning of chained behaviors (Gagné, 1985). Using the basic operant conditioning functional relationship, through practice and contiguity, the consequence takes on a dual role as the stimulus for the subsequent operant. Smaller chainlike skills become connected with other chains. Through discrimination, the individual learns to apply the correct chains based on the antecedent cues. Complex and lengthy chains, called procedures, continually incorporate smaller chains as the learner engages in more practice and receives feedback. Ultimately, the learner develops organized, and smooth performance characterized with precise timing and applications.

Problem solving represents the tactical readjustment to changes in the environment based on trial and error experiences (Rachlin, 1991). Through the discovery of a consistent pattern of cues and a history of reinforced actions, individuals develop strategies to deal with problems that assume a certain profile of characteristics (i.e., cues). Over time, responses occur more quickly, adjustments are made based on the consequences of the action, and rule-governed behavior develops (Malone, 1990).

Transfer involves the replication of identical behaviors from a task that one learns in an initial setting to a new task that has similar elements (Mayer & Wittrock, 1996). The notion of specific transfer or "theory of identical elements" was proposed by Thorndike and his colleagues (e.g., Thorndike, 1924; Thorndike & Woodworth, 1901). Of critical importance were the "gradients of similarity along stimulus dimensions" (Greeno, Collins, & Resnick, 1996). That is, the degree to which a response generalizes to stimuli other than the original association is dependent upon the similarity of other stimuli in terms of specific elements: The more similar the new stimulus, the higher probability of transfer. Critical to this potential for transfer were the strength of the specific associations, similarity of antecedent cues, and drill and practice on the specific skills with feedback.

1.4.4 Motivation

From a behavioral perspective, willingness to engage in a task is based on extrinsic motivation (Greeno et al., 1996). The tendency of an individual to respond to a particular situation is based on the reinforcers or punishers available in the context, and his or her needs and internal goals related to those consequences. That is, a reinforcer will only serve to increase a response if the individual wants the reinforcer; a punisher will only decrease a response if the individual wants to avoid being punished (Skinner, 1968). Essentially, an individual's decision to participate or engage in any activity is based on the anticipated outcomes of his/her performance (Skinner, 1987c).

At the core of the behavioral view of motivation are the biological needs of the individual. Primary reinforcers (e.g, food, water, sleep, and sex) and primary punishers (i.e., anything that induces pain) are fundamental motives for action. Secondary reinforcers and punishers develop over time based on associations made between antecedent cues, behaviors, and consequences. More sophisticated motivations such as group affiliation, preferences for career, hobbies, etc. are all developed based on associations made in earlier and simpler experiences and the degree to which the individual's biological needs were met. Skinner (1987c) characterizes the development of motivation for more complex activity as a kind of rule-governed behavior. Pleasant or aversive consequences are associated with specific behaviors. Skinner considers rules, advice, etc. to be critical elements of any culture because "they enable the individual to profit from the experience of those who have experienced common contingencies and described this in useful ways" (p. 181). This position is not unlike current principles identified in what is referred to as the "social constructivist" perspective (e.g., Tharp & Gallimore, 1988; Vygotsky, 1978).

1.5   THE BEHAVIORAL ROOTS OF INSTRUCTIONAL TECHNOLOGY

1.5.1   Methodological Behaviorism

Stimulus–response behaviorism, that is, behaviorism which emphasizes the antecedent as the *cause* of the behavior, is generally referred to as methodological behaviorism (see e.g., Day, 1983; Skinner, 1974). As such, it is in line with much of experimental psychology; antecedents are the independent variables and the behaviors are the dependent variables. This transformational paradigm (Vargas, 1993) differs dramatically from the radical behaviorism of Skinner (e.g., 1945, 1974) which emphasizes the role of reinforcement of behaviors in the presence of certain antecedents, in other words, the selectionist position. Most of the earlier work in instructional technology followed the methodological behaviorist tradition. In fact, as we have said earlier, from a radical behaviorist position cognitive psychology is an extension of methodological behaviorism (Skinner, 1974). Although we have recast and reinterpreted where possible, the differences, particularly in the film and television

research, are apparent. Nevertheless, the research is part of the research record in instructional technology and is therefore necessary, and moreover, useful from an S-R perspective.

One of the distinctive aspects of the methodological behavioral approach is the demand for "experimental" data (manipulation) to justify any interpretation of behavior as causal. Natural observation, personal experience and judgment fall short of the rules of evidence to support any psychological explanation (Kendler, 1971). This formula means that a learner must make the "correct response when the appropriate stimulus occurs" and when the necessary conditions are present.

Usually there is no great problem in providing the appropriate stimulus, for audiovisual techniques have tremendous advantages over other educational procedures in their ability to present to the learner the stimuli in the most effective manner possible. (Kendler, 1971, p. 36)

A problem arises as to when to develop techniques (in which appropriate responses to specific stimuli can be practiced and reinforced). The developer of an instructional medium must know exactly what response is desired from the students, otherwise it is impossible to design and evaluate instruction. Once the response is specified, the problem becomes getting the student to make this appropriate response. This response must be practiced and the learner must be reinforced to make the correct response to this stimulus (Skinner, 1953b). Under the S-R paradigm, much of the research on the instructional media was based upon the medium itself (i.e., the specific technology). The medium became the independent variable and media comparison studies became the norm until the middle 1970s (Smith & Smith, 1966). In terms of the methodological behavior model, much of the media (programmed instruction, film, television, etc.) functioned primarily upon the stimulus component. From this position, Carpenter (1962) reasoned that any medium (e.g., film, television) "imprints" some of its own characteristics on the message itself. Therefore, the content and medium have more impact than the medium itself. The "way" the stimulus material (again film, television, etc.) interacts with the learner instigates motivated responses. Carpenter (1962) developed several hypotheses based upon his interpretations of the research on media and learning and include the following possibilities:

1. The most effective learning will take place when there is similarity between the stimulus material (presented via a medium) and the criterion or learned performance.
2. Repetition of stimulus materials and the learning response is a major condition for most kinds of learning.
3. Stimulus materials which are accurate, correct, and subject to validation can increase the opportunity for learning to take place.
4. An important condition is the relationship between a behavior and its consequences. Learning will occur when the behavior is "reinforced" (Skinner, 1968). This reinforcement, by definition, should be immediately after the response.
5. Carefully sequenced combinations of knowledge and skills presented in logical and limited steps will be the most effective for most types of learning.

6. "...established principles of learning derived from studies where the learning situation involved from direct instruction by teachers are equally applicable in the use of instructional materials" (Carpenter, 1962, p. 305).

Practical aspects of these theoretical suggestions go back to the mid-1920s with the development by Pressey of a self-scoring testing device. Pressey (1926, 1932) discussed the extension of this testing device into a self-instruction machine. Versions of these devices later (after World War II) evolved into several, reasonably sophisticated, teaching machines for the U.S. Air Force which were variations of an automatic self-checking technique. They included a punched card, a chemically treated card, a punch board, and the Drum Tutor. The Drum Tutor used informational material with multiple choice questions, but could not advance to the next question until the correct answer was chosen. All devices essentially allowed students to get immediate information concerning accuracy of response.

1.6 EARLY RESEARCH

1.6.1 Teaching Machines

Peterson (1931) conducted early research on Pressey's self-scoring testing devices. His experimental groups were given the chemically treated scoring cards used for self checking while studying a reading assignment. The control group had no knowledge of their results. Peterson found the experimental groups had significantly higher scores than the group without knowledge of results. Little (1934), also using Pressey's automatic scoring device, had the experimental group as a test-machine group, the second group using his testing teaching machine as a drill-machine and the third group as a control group in a paired controlled experiment. Both experimental groups scored significantly higher mean scores than the control group. The drill- and practice-machine group scored higher than the test-machine group. After World War II additional experiments using Pressey's devices were conducted. Angell and Troyer (1948) and Jones and Sawyer (1949) found that giving immediate feedback significantly enhanced learning in both citizenship and chemistry courses. Briggs (1947) and Jensen (1949) found that self-instruction by "superior" students using Pressey's punch boards enabled them to accelerate their course work. Pressey (1950) also reported on the efficacy of immediate feedback in English, Russian vocabulary, and psychology courses. Students given feedback via the punch boards received higher scores than those students who were not given immediate feedback. Stephens (1960), using Pressey's Drum Tutor, found students using the device scored better than students who did not. This was true even though the students using the Drum Tutor lacked overall academic ability. Stephens "confirmed Pressey's findings that errors were eliminated more rapidly with meaningful material and found that students learned more efficiently when they could correct errors immediately" (Smith & Smith, 1966, p. 249). Severin (1960) compared the scores of students given the correct answers with no overt responses in a practice test with those of students using the punch board practice test and found

no significant differences. Apparently pointing out correct answers was enough and an overt response was not required. Pressey (1950) concluded that the use of his punch board created a single method of testing, scoring, informing students of their errors, and finding the correct solution all in one step (called telescoping). This telescoping procedure, in fact, allowed test taking to become a form of systematically directed self instruction. His investigations indicated that when self-instructional tests were used at the college level, gains were substantial and helped improve understanding. However, Pressey (1960) indicated his devices may not have been sufficient to stand by themselves, but were useful adjuncts to other teaching techniques.

Additional studies on similar self-instruction devices were conducted for military training research. Many of these studies used the automatic knowledge of accuracy devices such as The Tab Item and the Trainer-Tester (Smith & Smith, 1966). Cantor and Brown (1956) and Glaser, Damrin, and Gardner (1954) all found that scores for a troubleshooting task were higher for individuals using these devices than those using a mock-up for training. Dowell (1955) confirmed this, but also found that even higher scores were obtained when learners used the Trainer-Tester *and* the actual equipment. Briggs (1958) further developed a device called the Subject–Matter trainer which could be programmed into five teaching and testing modes. Briggs (1958) and Irion and Briggs (1957) found that prompting a student to give the correct response was more effective than just confirming correct responses.

Smith and Smith (1966) point out that while Pressey's devices were being developed and researched, they actually only attracted attention in somewhat limited circles. Popularity and attention were not generated until Skinner (1953a, 1953b, 1954) used these types of machines. "The fact that teaching machines were developed in more than one content would not be particularly significant were it not true that the two sources represent different approaches to educational design..." (Smith & Smith, 1966, p. 245). Skinner developed his machines to test and develop his operant conditioning principles developed from animal research. Skinner's ideas attracted attention, and as a result, the teaching machine and programmed instruction movement become a primary research emphasis during the 1960s. In fact, from 1960 to 1970, research on teaching machines and programming was the dominant type of media research in terms of numbers in the prestigious journal, *Audio-Visual Communication Review (AVCR)* (Torkelson, 1977). From 1960 to 1969, *AVCR* had a special section dedicated to teaching machines and programming concepts. Despite the fact of favorable research results from Pressey and his associates and the work done by the military, the technique was not popularized until Skinner (1954) recast self-instruction and self-testing. Skinner believed that any response could be reinforced. A desirable but seldom or never-elicited behavior could be taught by reinforcing a response which was easier to elicit but at some "distance" from the desired behavior. By reinforcing "successive" approximations, behavior will eventually approximate the desired pattern (Homme, 1957). Obviously, this paradigm, called shaping, required a great deal of supervision. Skinner believed that, in schools, reinforcement may happen hours, days, etc. after the desired behavior or behaviors and the effects would be greatly reduced. In addition, he felt that it was difficult to individually reinforce a response of an individual student in a large group. He also believed that school used negative reinforcers—to punish, not necessarily as reinforcement (Skinner, 1954). To solve these problems, Skinner also turned to the teaching machine concept. Skinner's (1958) machines in many respects were similar to Pressey's earlier teaching–testing devices. Both employed immediate knowledge of results immediately after the response. The students were kept active by their participation and both types of devices could be used in a self-instruction manner with students moving at their own rate. Differences in the types of responses in Pressey's and Skinner's machines should be noted. Skinner required students to "overtly" compose responses (e.g., writing words, terms, etc.). Pressey presented potential answers in a multiple choice format, requiring students to "select" the correct answer. In addition, Skinner (1958) believed that answers could not be easy, but that steps would need to be small in order for there to be no chance for "wrong" responses. Skinner was uncomfortable with multiple choice responses found in Pressey's devices because of the chance for mistakes (Homme, 1957; Porter, 1957; Skinner & Holland, 1960).

1.6.2 Films

The role and importance of military research during World War II and immediately afterward cannot be underestimated either in terms of amount or results. Research studies on learning, training materials, and instruments took on a vital role when it became necessary to train millions of individuals in skills useful for military purposes. People had to be selected and trained for complex and complicated machine systems (i.e., radio detection, submarine control, communication, etc.). As a result, most of the focus of the research by the military during and after the war was on the devices for training, assessment, and troubleshooting complex equipment and instruments. Much of the film research noted earlier stressed the stimulus, response, and reinforcement characteristics of the audiovisual device. "These [research studies] bear particularly on questions on the role of active response, size of demonstration and practice steps in procedural learning, and the use of prompts or response cues" (Lumsdaine & Glaser, 1960, p. 257). The major research programs during World War II were conducted on the use of films by the U.S. Army. These studies were conducted to study achievement of specific learning outcomes and the feasibility of utilizing film for psychological testings (Gibson, 1947; Hoban, 1946). After World War II, two major film research projects were sponsored by the United States Army and Navy at the Pennsylvania State University from 1947 to 1955 (Carpenter & Greenhill, 1955, 1958). A companion program on film research was sponsored by the United States Air Force from 1950 to 1957. The project at the Pennsylvania State University—the Instructional Film Research Program under the direction of C. R. Carpenter—was probably the "most extensive single program of experimentation dealing with instructional films ever conducted" (Saettler, 1968, p. 332). In 1954, this film research project was reorganized to include instructional films and instructional television because of the

similarities of the two media. The Air Force Film Research Program (1950–1957) was conducted under the leadership of A. A. Lumsdaine (1961). The Air Force study involved the manipulation of techniques for "eliciting and guiding overt responses during a course of instruction" (Saettler, 1968, p. 335). Both the Army and Air Force studies developed research that had major implications for the use and design of audiovisual materials (e.g., film). Although these studies developed a large body of knowledge, little use of the results was actually implemented in the production of instructional materials developed by the military. Kanner (1960) suggested that the reason for the lack of use of the results of these studies was because they created resentment among film makers, and much of the research was completed in isolation.

Much of the research on television was generated after 1950 and was conducted by the military because of television's potential for mass instruction. Some of the research replicated or tested concepts (variables) used in the earlier film research, but the bulk of the research compared television instruction to "conventional" instruction, and most results showed no significant differences between the two forms. Most of the studies were applied rather than using a theoretical framework (i.e., behavior principles) (Kumata, 1961).

However, Gropper (1965a, 1965b), Gropper and Lumsdaine (1961a), and others used the television medium to test behavioral principles developed from the studies on programmed instruction. Klaus (1965) states that programming techniques tended to be either stimulus centered on response centered. Stimulus-centered techniques stressed meaning, structure, and organization of stimulus materials, while response-centered techniques dealt with the design of materials that ensure adequate response practice. For example, Gropper (1965a, 1966) adopted and extended concepts developed in programmed instruction (particularly the response centered model) to televised presentations. These studies dealt primarily with "techniques for bringing specific responses under the control of specific visual stimuli and . . . the use of visual stimuli processing such control within the framework of an instructional design" (Gropper, 1966, p. 41). Gropper, Lumsdaine, and Shipman (1961) and Gropper and Lumsdaine (1961a, 1961b, 1961c, 1961d) reported the value of pretesting and revising televised instruction and requiring students to make active responses. Gropper (1967) suggested that in television presentations it is desirable to identify which behavioral principles and techniques underlying programmed instruction are appropriate to television. Gropper and Lumsdaine (1961a–d) reported that merely requiring students to actively respond to nonprogrammed stimulus materials (i.e., segments which are not well delineated or sequenced in systematic ways) did not lead to more effective learning (an early attempt at formative evaluation). However, Gropper (1967) reported that the success of using programmed instructional techniques with television depends upon the effective design of the stimulus materials as well as the design of the appropriate response practice.

Gropper (1963, 1965a, 1966, 1967) emphasized the importance of using visual materials to help students acquire, retain, and transfer responses based on the ability of such materials to cue and reinforce specified responses, and serve as examples.

He further suggests that students should make explicit (active) responses to visual materials (i.e., television) for effective learning. Later, Gropper (1968) concluded that, in programmed televised materials, actual practice is superior to recognition practice in most cases and that the longer the delay in measuring retention, the more the active response was beneficial. The behavioral features that were original with programmed instruction and later used with television and film were attempts to minimize and later correct the defects in the effectiveness of instruction on the basis of what was known about the learning process (Klaus, 1965). Student responses were used in many studies as the basis for revisions of instructional design and content (e.g., Gropper, 1963, 1966). In-depth reviews of the audiovisual research carried on by the military and civilian researchers are contained in the classic summaries of this primarily behaviorist approach of Carpenter and Greenhill (1955, 1958), Chu and Schramm (1968), Cook (1960), Hoban (1960), Hoban and Van Ormer (1950), May and Lumsdaine (1958), and Schramm (1962).

The following is a sample of some of the research results on the behavioral tenets of stimulus, response, and reinforcement gleaned from the World War II research and soon after based upon the study of audiovisual devices (particularly film).

1.6.2.1 Research on Stimuli. Attempts to improve learning by manipulating the stimulus condition can be divided into several categories. One category, that of the use of introductory materials to introduce content in film or audiovisual research, has shown mixed results (Cook, 1960). Film studies by Weiss and Fine (1955), Wittich and Folkes (1946), and Wulff, Sheffield, and Kraeling (1954) reported that introductory materials presented prior to the showing of a film increased learning. But, Jaspen (1948), Lathrop (1949), Norford (1949), and Peterman and Bouscaren (1954) found inconclusive or negative results by using introductory materials. Another category of stimuli, those that direct attention, uses the behavioral principle that learning is assisted by the association of the responses to stimuli (Cook, 1960). Film studies by Gibson (1947), Kimble and Wulff (1953), Lumsdaine and Sulzer (1951), McGuire (1953a), Roshal (1949), and Ryan and Hochberg (1954) found that a version of the film which incorporated cues to guide the audience into making the correct responses produced increased learning. As might be expected, extraneous stimuli not focusing on relevant cues were not effective (Jaspen, 1950; Neu, 1950; Weiss, 1954). However, Miller and Levine (1952) and Miller, Levine, and Steinberger (1952a) reported the use of subtitles to associate content to be ineffective. Cook (1960) reported that many studies were conducted on the use of color where it would provide an essential cue to understanding with mixed results and concluded it was impossible to say color facilitated learning results (i.e., Long, 1946; May & Lumsdaine, 1958). Note that the use of color in instruction is still a highly debated research issue.

1.6.2.2 Research on Response. Cook (1960) stated the general belief that, unless the learner makes some form of response that is relevant to the learning task, no learning will occur. Responses (practice) in audiovisual presentations may range from overt oral, written, or motor responses to an implicit response (not overt). Cook, in an extensive review of practice in audiovisual presentations, reported the effectiveness of students calling out answers to questions in an audiovisual presentation to be effective (i.e., Kanner & Sulzer, 1955; Kendler, Cook, & Kendler, 1953; Kendler, Kendler, & Cook, 1954; McGuire, 1954). Most studies that utilized overt written responses with training film and television were also found to be effective (i.e., Michael, 1951; Michael & Maccoby, 1954; Yale Motion Picture Research Project, 1947).

A variety of film studies on implicit practice found this type of practice to be effective (some as effective as overt practice) (i.e., Kanner & Sulzer, 1955; Kendler et al., 1954; McGuire, 1954; Michael, 1951; Miller & Klier, 1953a, 1953b). Cook (1960) notes that the above studies all reported that the effect of actual practice is "specific to the items practiced" (p. 98) and there appeared to be no carryover to other items. The role of feedback in film studies has also been positively supported (Gibson, 1947; Michael, 1951; Michael & Maccoby, 1954).

The use of practice, given the above results, appears to be an effective component of using audiovisual (film and television) materials. A series of studies were conducted to determine the amount of practice needed. Cook (1960) concludes that students will profit from a larger number of repetitions (practice). Film studies that used a larger number of examples or required viewing the film more than once found students faring better than those with fewer examples or viewing opportunities (Brenner, Walter, & Kurtz, 1949; Kendler et al., 1953; Kimble & Wulff, 1954; Sulzer & Lumsdaine, 1952). A number of studies were conducted which tested when practice should occur. Was it better to practice concepts as a whole (massed) at the end of a film presentation or practice it immediately after it was demonstrated (distributed) during the film? Most studies reported results that there was no difference in the time spacing of practice (e.g., McGuire, 1953b; Miller & Klier, 1953a, 1953b, 1954; Miller et al., 1952a, 1952b). Miller and Levine (1952), however, found results in favor of a massed practice at the end of the treatment period.

1.6.3 Programmed Instruction

Closely akin, and developed from, Skinner's (1958) teaching machine concepts were the teaching texts or programmed books. These programmed books essentially had the same characteristics as the teaching machines; logical presentations of content, requirement of overt responses, and presentation of immediate knowledge of correctness (a correct answer would equal positive reinforcement (Porter, 1958; Smith & Smith, 1966). These programmed books were immediately popular for obvious reasons, they were easier to produce, portable, and did not require a complex, burdensome, and costly device (i.e., a machine). As noted earlier, during the decade of the 60s, research on programmed instruction, as the use of these types of books and machines became known, was immense (Campeau, 1974). Literally thousands of research studies were conducted. (See, for example, Campeau, 1974; Glaser, 1965a; Lumsdaine & Glaser, 1960; Smith & Smith, 1966, among others, for extensive summaries of research in this area.) The term programming is taken here to mean what Skinner called "the construction of carefully arranged sequences of contingencies leading to the terminal performances which are the object of education" (Skinner, 1953a, p. 169).

1.6.3.1 Linear Programming.

Linear programming involves a series of learning frames presented in a set sequence. As in most of the educational research of the time, research on linear programmed instruction dealt with devices and/or machines and not on process nor the learner. Most of the studies, therefore, generally compared programmed instruction to "conventional" or "traditional" instructional methods (see e.g., *Teaching Machines and Programmed Instruction*, Glaser, 1965a). These types of studies were, of course, difficult to generalize from and often resulted in conflicting results (Holland, 1965). "The restrictions on interpretation of such a comparison arises from the lack of specificity of the instruction with which the instrument in questions is paired" (Lumsdaine, 1962, p. 251). Like other research of the time, many of the comparative studies had problems in design, poor criterion measures, scores prone to a ceiling effect, and ineffective and poor experimental procedures (Holland, 1965). Holland (1961), Lumsdaine (1965), and Rothkopf (1962) all suggested other ways of evaluating the success of programmed instruction. Glaser (1962a) indicated that most programmed instruction was difficult to construct, time consuming, and had few rules or procedures. Many comparative studies and reviews of comparative studies found no significance in the results of programmed instruction (e.g., Alexander, 1970; Barnes, 1970; Frase, 1970; Giese & Stockdale, 1966; McKeachie, 1967; Unwin, 1966; Wilds & Zachert, 1966). However, Daniel and Murdoch (1968), Hamilton and Heinkel (1967), and Marsh and Pierce-Jones (1968), all reported positive and statistically significant findings in favor of programmed instruction. The examples noted above were based upon gross comparisons. A large segment of the research on programmed instruction was devoted to "isolating or manipulating program or learner characteristics" (Campeau, 1974, p. 17). Specific areas of research on these characteristics included studies on repetition and dropout (for example, Rothkopf, 1960; Skinner & Holland, 1960). Skinner and Holland suggested that various kinds of cueing techniques could be employed which would reduce the possibility of error but generally will cause the presentation to become linear in nature (Skinner, 1961; Smith, 1959). Karis, Kent, and Gilbert (1970) found that overt responding such as writing a name in a (linear) programmed sequence was significantly better than for subjects who learned under covert response conditions. However, Valverde and Morgan (1970) concluded that eliminating redundancy in linear programs significantly increased achievement. Carr (1959) stated that merely confirming the correctness of a student's response as in a linear program is not enough. The learner must otherwise be motivated to perform (Smith & Smith, 1966). However, Coulson and Silberman (1960) and Evans, Glaser, and Homme (1962) found significant differences in favor of small (redundant) step programs over programs which had redundant and transitional materials removed. In the traditional linear program, after a learner has written his response (overt), the answer is confirmed by the presentation of the correct answer. Research on the confirmation (feedback)

of results has shown conflicting results. Studies, for example, by Holland (1960), Hough and Revsin (1963), McDonald and Allen (1962), and Moore and Smith (1961, 1962) found no difference in mean scores due the added feedback. However, Kaess and Zeaman (1960), Meyer (1960), and Suppes and Ginsburg (1962) reported in their research, positive advantages for feedback on posttest scores. Homme and Glaser (1960) reported that when correct answers were omitted from linear programs, the learner felt it made no difference. Resnick (1963) felt that linear programs failed to make allowance for individual differences of the learners, and she was concerned about the "voice of authority" and the "right or wrong" nature of the material to be taught. Smith and Smith (1966) believed that a "linear program is deliberately limiting the media of communication, the experiences of the student and thus the range of understanding that he achieves" (p. 293).

Holland (1965) summarized his extensive review of literature on general principles of programming and generally found that a contingent relationship between the answer and the content is important. A low error rate of responses received support, as did the idea that examples are necessary for comprehension. For long programs, overt responses are necessary. Results are equivocal concerning multiple choice versus overt responses; however, many erroneous alternatives (e.g., multiple choice foils) may interfere with later learning. Many of the studies, however, concerning the effects of the linear presentation of content introduced the "pall effect" (boredom) due to the many small steps and the fact that the learner was always correct (Beck, 1959; Galanter, 1959; Rigney & Fry, 1961).

1.6.3.2 Intrinsic (Branching) Programming.

Crowder (1961) used an approach similar to that developed by Pressey (1963) which suggested that a learner be exposed to a "substantial" and organized unit of instruction (e.g., a book chapter) and following this presentation a series of multiple choice questions would be asked "to enhance the clarity and stability of cognitive structure by correcting misconceptions and deferring the instruction of new matter until there had been such clarification and education" (Pressey, 1963, p. 3). Crowder (1959, 1960) and his associates were not as concerned about error rate or the limited step-by-step process of linear programs. Crowder tried to reproduce, in a self-instructional program, the function of a private tutor; to present new information to the learner and have the learner use this information (to answer questions); then taking "appropriate" action based upon learner's responses, such as going on to new information or going back and reviewing the older information if responses were incorrect. Crowder's intrinsic programming was designed to meet problems concerning complex problem solving but was not necessarily based upon a learning theory (Klaus, 1965). Crowder (1962) "assumes that the basic learning takes place during the exposure to the new material. The multiple choice question is asked to find out whether the student has learned; it is not necessarily regarded as playing an active part in the primary learning process" (p. 3). Crowder (1961), however, felt that the intrinsic (also known as branching) programs were essentially "naturalistic" and keep students working at the "maximum practical" rate.

Several studies have compared, and found no difference between, the type of constructed responses (overt vs. the multiple choice response in verbal programs) (Evans, Homme, & Glaser, 1962; Hough, 1962; Roe, Massey, Weltman, & Leeds, 1960; Williams, 1963). Holland (1965) felt that these studies showed, however, "the nature of the learning task determines the preferred response form. When the criterion performance includes a precise response . . . constructed responses seems to be the better form; whereas if mere recognition is desired the response form in the program is probably unimportant" (p. 104).

Although the advantages for the intrinsic (branching) program appear to be self-evident for learners with extreme individual differences, most studies, however, have found no advantages for the intrinsic programs over branching programs, but generally found time saving for students who used branching format (Beane, 1962; Campbell, 1961; Glaser, Reynolds, & Harakas, 1962; Roe, Massey, Weltman, & Leeds, 1962; Silberman, Melaragno, Coulson, & Estavan, 1961).

1.6.4 Instructional Design

Behaviorism is prominent in the roots of the systems approach to the design of instruction. Many of the tenets, terminology, and concepts can be traced to behavioral theories. Edward Thorndike in the early 1900s, for instance, had an interest in learning theory and testing. This interest greatly influenced the concept of instructional planning and the empirical approaches to the design of instruction. World War II researchers on training and training materials based much of their work on instructional principles derived from research on human behavior and theories of instruction and learning (Reiser, 1987). Heinich (1970) believed that concepts from the development of programmed learning influenced the development of the instructional design concept.

> By analyzing and breaking down content into specific behavioral objectives, devising the necessary steps to achieve the objectives, setting up procedures to try out and revise the steps, and by validating the program against attainment of the objectives, programmed instruction succeeded in creating a small but effective self-instructional system—a technology of instruction. (Heinich, 1970, p. 123)

Task analysis, behavioral objectives, and criterion-referenced testing were brought together by Gagné (1962) and Silvern (1964). These individuals were among the first to use terms such as systems development and instructional systems to describe a connected and systematic framework for the instructional design principles currently used (Reiser, 1987).

Instructional design is generally considered to be a systematic process that uses tenets of learning theories to plan and present instruction or instructional sequences. The obvious purpose of instructional design is to promote learning. As early as 1900, Dewey called for a "linking science" which connected learning theory and instruction (Dewey, 1900). As the adoption of analytic and systematic techniques influenced programmed instruction and other "programmed" presentation modes, early instructional design also used learning principles

from behavioral psychology. For example, discriminations, generalizations, associations, etc. were used to analyze content and job tasks. Teaching and training concepts such as shaping and fading were early attempts to match conditions and treatments, and all had behavioral roots (Gropper & Ross, 1987). Many of the current instructional design models use major components of methodological behaviorism such as specification of objectives (behavioral), concentration on behavioral changes in students, and the emphasis on the stimulus (environment) (Gilbert, 1962; Reigeluth, 1983). In fact, some believe that it is this association between the stimulus and the student response that characterizes the influence of behavioral theory on instructional design (Smith & Ragan, 1993). Many of the proponents of behavioral theory, as a base for instructional design, feel that there is an "inevitable conclusion that the quality of an educational system must be defined primarily in terms of change in student behaviors" (Tosti & Ball, 1969, p. 6). Instruction, thus, must be evaluated by its ability to change the behavior of the individual student. The influence of the behavioral theory on instructional design can be traced from writings by Dewey, Thorndike and, of course, B. F. Skinner.

In addition, during World War II, military trainers (and psychologists) stated learning outcomes in terms of "performance" and found the need to identify specific "tasks" for a specific job (Gropper, 1983). Based on training in the military during World War II, a commitment to achieve practice and reinforcement became major components to the behaviorist developed instructional design model (as well as other nonbehavioristic models). Gropper indicates that an instructional design model should identify a unit of behavior to be analyzed, the conditions that can produce a change, and the resulting nature of that change. Again, for Gropper the unit of analysis, unfortunately, is the stimulus–response association. When the *appropriate* response is made and referenced after a (repeated) presentation of the stimulus, the response comes under the control of that stimulus.

> Whatever the nature of the stimulus, the response or the reinforcement, establishing stable stimulus control depends on the same two learning conditions: practice of an appropriate response in the presence of a stimulus that is to control it and delivery of reinforcement following its practice. (Gropper, 1983, p. 106)

Gropper stated that this need for control over the response by the stimulus contained several components; practice (to develop stimulus construction) and suitability for teaching the skills.

Gagné, Briggs, and Wager (1988) have identified several learning concepts that apply centrally to the behaviorial instructional design process. Among these are contiguity, repetition, and reinforcement in one form or another. Likewise, Gustafson and Tillman (1991) identify several major principles that underline instructional design. One, goals and objectives of the instruction need to be identified and stated; two, all instructional outcomes need to be measurable and meet standards of reliability and validity. Thirdly, the instructional design concept centers on changes in behavior of the student (the learner).

Corey (1971) identified a model that would include the above components. These components include:

1. *Determination of objectives*—This includes a description of behaviors to be expected as a result of the instruction and a description of the stimulus to which these behaviors are considered to be appropriate responses.
2. *Analysis of instructional objectives*—This includes analyzing "behaviors under the learner's control" prior to the instruction sequence, behaviors that are to result from the instruction.
3. *Identifying the characteristics of the students*—This would be the behavior that is already under the control of the learner prior to the instructional sequence.
4. *Evidence of the achievement of instruction*—This would include tests or other measures which would demonstrate whether or not the behaviors which the instruction "was designed to bring under his control actually were brought under his control" (p. 13).
5. *Constructing the instructional environment*—This involves developing an environment that will assist the student to perform the desired behaviors as response to the designed stimuli or situation.
6. *Continuing instruction (feedback)*—This involves reviewing if additional or revised instruction is needed to maintain the stimulus control over the learner's behavior.

Glaser (1965b) also described similar behavioral tenets of an instructional design system. He has identified the following tasks to teach subject matter knowledge. First, the behavior desired must be analyzed and standards of performance specified. The stimulus and desired response will determine what and how it is to be taught. Secondly, the characteristics of the students are identified prior to instruction. Thirdly, the student must be guided from one state of development to another using predetermined procedures and materials. Lastly, a provision for assessing the competence of the learner in relation to the predetermined performance criteria (objectives) must be developed.

Cook (1994) recently addressed the area of instructional effectiveness as it pertains to behavioral approaches to instruction. He notes that a number of behavioral instructional packages incorporate common underlying principles that promote teaching and student learning and examined a number of these packages concerning their inclusion of 12 components he considers critical to instructional effectiveness.

1. Task analysis and the specification of the objectives of the instructional system
2. Identification of the entering skills of the target population, and a placement system that addresses the individual differences amongst members of the target population
3. An instructional strategy in which a sequence of instructional steps reflects principles of behavior in the formation of discriminations, the construction of chains, the elaboration of these two elements into concepts and procedures, and their integration and formalization by means of appropriate verbal behavior such as rule statements

4. Requests and opportunities for active student responding at intervals appropriate to the sequence of steps in #3
5. Supplementary prompts to support early responding
6. The transfer of the new skill to the full context of application (the facing of supporting prompts as the full context takes control; this may include the fading of verbal behavior which has acted as part of the supporting prompt system)
7. Provision of feedback on responses and cumulative progress reports, both at intervals appropriate to the learner and the stage in the program
8. The detection and correction of errors
9. A mastery requirement for each well-defined unit including the attainment of fluency in the unit skills as measured by the speed at which they can be performed
10. Internalization of behavior that no longer needs to be performed publicly; this may include verbal behavior that remains needed but not in overt form
11. Sufficient self-pacing to accommodate individual differences in rates of achieving mastery
12. Modification of instructional programs on the basis of objective data on effectiveness with samples of individuals from the target population

1.6.4.1 Task Analysis and Behavioral Objectives. As we have discussed, one of the major components derived from behavioral theory in instructional design is the use of behavioral objectives. The methods associated with task analysis and programmed instruction stress the importance of the "identification and specification of observable behaviors to be performed by the learner" (Reiser, 1987, p. 23). Objectives have been used by educators as far back as the early 1900s (e.g., Bobbitt, 1918). Although these objectives may have identified content that might be tested (Tyler, 1949), usually they did not specify exact behaviors learners were to demonstrate based upon exposure to the content (Reiser, 1987). Popularization and refinement of stating objectives in measurable or observable terms within an instructional design approach was credited by Kibler, Cegala, Miles, and Barker (1974), and Reiser (1987) to the efforts of Bloom, Engelhart, Furst, Hill, and Krathwohl (1956), Mager (1962), Gagné (1965), Glaser (1962b), Popham and Baker (1970), and Tyler (1934). Kibler and colleagues point out that there are many rational bases for using behavioral objectives, some of which are not learning-theory based, such as teacher accountability. They list, however, some of the tenets that are based upon behavioral learning theories. These include (1) assisting in evaluating learners' performance, (2) designing and arranging sequences of instruction, and (3) communicating requirements and expectations and providing and communicating levels of performance prior to instruction. In the Kibler et al. comprehensive review of the empirical bases for using objectives, only about 50 studies that dealt with the effectiveness of objectives were found. These researchers reported that results were inconsistent and provided little conclusive evidence of the effect of behavioral objectives on learning. They classified the research on objectives into four categories. These were:

1. *Effects of student knowledge of behavioral objectives on learning.* Of 33 studies, only 11 reported student possession

of objectives improved learning significantly (e.g., Doty, 1968; Lawrence, 1970; Olsen, 1972; Webb, 1971). The rest of the studies found no differences between student possession of objectives or not (e.g., Baker, 1969; Brown, 1970; Patton, 1972; Weinberg, 1970; Zimmerman, 1972).

2. *Effects of specific versus general objectives on learning.* Only two studies (Dalis, 1970; Janeczko, 1971) found that students receiving specific objectives performed higher than those receiving general objectives. Other studies (e.g., Lovett, 1971; Stedman, 1970; Weinberg, 1970) found no significant differences between the forms of objectives.

3. *Effects on student learning of teacher possession and use of objectives.* Five of eight studies reviewed found no significant differences of teacher possession of objectives and those without (e.g., Baker, 1969; Crooks, 1971; Kalish, 1972). Three studies reported significant positive effects of teacher possession (McNeil, 1967; Piatt, 1969; Wittrock, 1962).

4. *Effects of student possession of behavioral objectives on efficiency (time).* Two of seven studies (Allen & McDonald, 1963; Mager & McCann, 1961) found use of objectives reducing student time on learning. The rest found no differences concerning efficiency (e.g., Loh, 1972; Smith, 1970).

Kibler and colleagues (1974) found less than half of the research studies reviewed supported the use of objectives. However, they felt that many of the studies had methodological problems. These were: lack of standardization of operationalizing behavior objectives, unfamiliarity with the use of objectives by students, and few researchers provided teachers with training in the use of objectives. Although they reported no conclusive results in their reviews of behavioral objectives, Kibler and colleagues felt that there were still logical reasons (noted earlier) for their continued use.

1.7   CURRENT DESIGN AND DELIVERY MODELS

Five behavioral design/delivery models are worth examining in some detail: Personalized System of Instruction (PSI), Bloom's (1971) Learning for Mastery, Precision Teaching, Direct Instruction, and distance learning/tutoring systems. Each of the first four models has been in use for some 30 years and each share some distinctively behavioral methodologies such as incremental units of instruction, student-oriented objectives, active student responding, frequent testing, and rapid feedback. The fifth model, distance learning/tutoring systems, has grown rapidly in recent years due to the extensive development and availability of computers and computer technology. Increasingly, distance learning systems are recognizing the importance of and adopting these behavioral methodologies due to their history of success.

Additional class features of behavioral methodologies are inherent in these models. First and foremost, each model places the responsibility for success on the instruction/teacher as opposed to the learner. This places a high premium on validation and revision of materials. In fact, in all behavior models, instruction is always plastic; always, in a sense, in a formative

stage. Another major feature is a task or logical analysis which is used to establish behavioral objectives and serve as the basis for precise assessment of learner entry behavior. A third essential feature is emphasis on meeting the needs of the individual learner. In most of these models, instruction is self-paced and designed based on learner's mastery of the curriculum. When the instruction is not formally individualized (i.e., direct instruction), independent practice is an essential phase of the process to ensure individual mastery. Other common characteristics of these models include the use of small groups, carefully planned or even scripted lessons, high learner response requirements coupled with equally high feedback, and, of course, data collection related to accuracy and speed. Each of these programs is consistent with all, or nearly all, of the principles from Cook (1994) listed previously.

1.7.1   Personalized System of Instruction

Following a discussion of B. F. Skinner's Principles of the Analysis of Behavior (Holland & Skinner, 1961), Fred Keller and his associates concluded that "traditional teaching methods were sadly out of date" (Keller & Sherman, 1974, p. 7). Keller suggested that if education was to improve, instructional design systems would need to be developed to improve and update methods of providing instructional information. Keller searched for a way in which instruction could follow a methodical pattern. The pattern should use previous success to reinforce the student to progress in a systematic manner toward a specified outcome. Keller and his associates developed such a system, called Personalized System of Instruction (PSI) or the Keller Plan. PSI can be described as an interlocking system of instruction, consisting of sequential, progressive tasks designed as highly individualized learning activities. In this design, students determine their own rate and amount of learning, as they progress through a series of instructional tasks (Liu, 2001). In his seminal paper "Goodbye, Teacher . . ." (Keller, 1968), Keller describes the five components of PSI, which are:

1. The go-at-your-own pace feature (self-pacing)
2. The unit-perfection requirement for advancement (mastery)
3. The use of lectures and demonstrations as vehicles of motivation
4. The related stress upon the written word in teacher–student communication
5. The use of proctors for feedback

The first feature of PSI allows a student to move at his/her own pace through a course at a self-determined speed. The unit-perfection requirement means that before the student can move to the next unit of instruction, he/she must complete perfectly the assessment given on the previous unit. Motivation for a PSI course is provided by a positive reward structure. Students who have attained a certain level of mastery, as indicated by the number of completed units, are rewarded through special lectures and demonstrations. Communication, in classic PSI systems, relies primarily on written communication between student and teacher. However, the proctor–student relationship relies on both written and verbal communication, which provides valuable feedback for students (Keller, 1968).

A PSI class is highly structured. All information is packaged into small, individual units. The student is given a unit, reads the information, proceeds through the exercises, and then reports to a proctor for the unit assessment. After completing the quiz, the student returns the answers to the proctor for immediate grading and feedback. If the score is unsatisfactory (as designated by the instructor), the student is asked to reexamine the material and return for another assessment. After completion of a certain number of units, the student's reward is permission to attend a lecture, demonstration, or field trip, which is instructor-led. At the end of the course, a final exam is given. The student moves at his/her own pace, but is expected to complete all units by the end of the semester (Keller, 1968). PSI was widely used in the 1970s in higher education courses (Sherman, 1992). After the initial use of PSI became widespread, many studies focused on the effect that these individual features have on the success of a PSI course (Liu, 2001).

1.7.1.1 The Effect of Pacing.
The emphasis on self-pacing has led some PSI practitioners to cite procrastination as a problem in their classes (Gallup, 1971; Hess, 1971; Sherman, 1972). In the first semester of a PSI course on physics at the State University College, Plattsburgh, Szydlik (1974) reported that 20/28 students received incompletes for failure to complete the requisite number of units. In an effort to combat procrastination, researchers started including some instructor deadlines with penalties (pacing contingencies) if the students failed to meet the deadlines.

Semb, Conyers, Spencer, and Sanchez-Sosa (1975) conducted a study that examined the effects of four pacing contingencies on course withdrawals, the timing of student quiz-taking throughout the course, performance on exams, and student evaluations. They divided an introductory child development class into four groups and exposed each group to a different pacing contingency. Each group was shown a "minimal rate" line that was a suggested rate of progress. The first group received no benefit or punishment for staying at or above the minimum rate. The second group (penalty) was punished if they were found below the minimum rate line, losing 25 points for every day they were below the rate line. The third group (reward 1) benefited from staying above the minimum rate line by earning extra points. The fourth group (reward 2) also benefited from staying above the minimum rate line by potentially gaining an extra 20 points overall. All students were told that if they did not complete the course by the end of the semester, they would receive an Incomplete and could finish the course later with no penalty. Students could withdraw from the course at any point in the semester with a 'withdraw passing' grade (Semb et al., 1975).

The results of the course withdrawal and incomplete study showed that students with no contingency pacing had the highest percentage (23.8%) of withdrawals and incompletes. The second group (penalty) had the lowest percentage of withdrawals and incompletes (2.4%). With regard to procrastination, students in Groups 2–4 maintained a relatively steady rate of progress while Group 1 showed the traditional pattern of procrastination. No significant differences were found between any groups on performance on exams or quizzes. Nor were there any significant differences between groups regarding student evaluations (Semb et al., 1975).

In an almost exact replication of this study, Reiser (1984) again examined whether reward, penalty, or self-pacing was most effective in a PSI course. No difference between groups was found regarding performance on the final exam, and there was no difference in student attitude. However, students in the penalty group had significantly reduced procrastination. The reward group did not show a significant reduction in procrastination, which contradicts the findings by Semb et al. (1975).

1.7.1.2 The Effect of Unit Perfection for Advancement.
Another requirement for a PSI course is that the content be broken into small, discrete, units. These units are then mastered individually by the student. Several studies have examined the effect the number of units has on student performance in a PSI course. Born (1975) took an introductory psychology class taught using PSI and divided it into three sections. One section had to master 18 quizzes over the 18 units. The second section had to master one quiz every two units. The third section was required to master one quiz every three units. Therefore, each section had the same 18 units, but the number of quizzes differed. Surprisingly, there was no difference between the three groups of students in terms of performance on quizzes. However, Section one students spent a much shorter time on the quizzes than did Section three students (Born, 1975).

Another study examined the effect of breaking up course material into units of 30, 60, and 90 pages (O'Neill, Johnston, Walters, & Rashed, 1975). Students performed worst in the first attempt on each unit quiz when they had learned the material from the large course unit. Students exposed to a large unit also delayed starting the next unit. Also, more attempts at mastering the quizzes had to be made when students were exposed to a large unit. Despite these effects, the size of the unit did not affect the final attempt to meet the mastery criterion. They also observed student behavior and stated that the larger the unit the more time the student spent studying. Students with a large unit spent more time reading the unit, but less time summarizing, taking notes, and other interactive behaviors (O'Neill et al., 1975).

Student self-pacing has been cited as one aspect of PSI that students enjoy (Fernald, Chiseri, Lawson, Scroggs, & Riddell, 1975). Therefore, it could be motivational. A study conducted by Reiser (1984) found that students who proceeded through a class at their own pace, under a penalty system or under a reward system, did not differ significantly in their attitude toward the PSI course. The attitude of all three groups toward the course was generally favorable (at least 63% responded positively). These results agreed with his conclusions of a previous study (Reiser, 1980). Another motivating aspect of PSI is the removal of the external locus of control. Because of the demand for perfection on each smaller unit, the grade distribution of PSI courses is skewed toward the higher grades, taking away the external locus of control provided by an emphasis on grades (Born & Herbert, 1974; Keller, 1968; Ryan, 1974).

1.7.1.3 The Emphasis on Written and Verbal Communication.
Written communication is the primary means of communication for PSI instruction and feedback. Naturally, this would be an unacceptable teaching strategy for students whose writing skills are below average. If proctors are used, students may express their knowledge verbally, which may assist in improving the widespread application of PSI. The stress on the written word has not been widely examined as a research question. However, there have been studies conducted on the study guides in PSI courses (Liu, 2001).

1.7.1.4 The Role of the Proctor.
The proctor plays a pivotal role in a PSI course. Keller (1968) states that proctors provide reinforcement via immediate feedback and, by this, increase the chances of continued success in the future. The proctors explain the errors in the students' thought processes that led them to an incorrect answer and provide positive reinforcement when the students perform well. Farmer, Lachter, Blaustein, and Cole (1972) analyzed the role of proctoring by quantifying the amount of proctoring that different sections of the course received. They randomly assigned a class of 124 undergraduates into five groups (0, 25, 50, 75, and 100%) that received different amounts of proctoring on 20 units of instruction. One group received 0% proctoring, that is, no interaction with a proctor at all. The group that received 25% proctoring interacted with the proctor on five units, and so on. They concluded that the amount of proctoring did not affect performance significantly, as there was no significant difference between students who received the different amounts of proctoring. However, no proctoring led to significantly lower scores when compared with the different groups of students who had received proctoring (Farmer et al., 1972).

In a crossover experiment by Fernald and colleagues (1975), three instructional variables, student pacing, the perfection requirement, and proctoring, were manipulated to see their effects on performance and student preferences. Eight different combinations of the three instructional variables were formed. For example, one combination might have a student interact a lot with a proctor, a perfection requirement, and use student pacing. In this design, eight groups of students were exposed to two combinations of 'opposite' instruction variables sequentially over a semester: a student receiving much contact, perfection, and a teacher-paced section would next experience a little contact, no perfection, and student-paced section (Fernald et al., 1975).

The results of this experiment showed that students performed best when exposed to a high amount of contact with a proctor and when it was self-paced. These results were unexpected because traditional PSI classes require mastery. The variable that had the greatest effect was the pacing variable. Student pacing always enhanced performance on exams and quizzes. The mastery requirement was found to have no effect. However, the authors acknowledge that the perfection requirement might not have been challenging enough. They state that a mastery requirement may only have an effect on performance when the task is difficult enough to cause variation among students (Fernald et al., 1975).

1.7.1.5 Performance Results Using the PSI Method.
A meta-analysis by Kulik, Kulik, and Cohen (1979) examined 75 comparative studies about PSI usage. Their conclusion was that PSI produces superior student achievement, less variation in achievement, and higher student ratings in numerous college courses. Another meta-analysis on PSI conducted more recently by Kulik, Kulik, and Bangert-Downs (1990) found similar results. In this analysis, mastery learning programs (PSI and Bloom's Learning for Mastery) were shown to have positive effects on students' achievement and that low aptitude students benefited most from PSI. They also concluded that mastery learning programs had long-term effects even though the percentage of students that completed PSI college classes is smaller than the percentage that completed conventional classes (Kulik et al., 1990).

1.7.2 Bloom's Learning for Mastery

1.7.2.1 Theoretical Basis for Bloom's Learning for Mastery.
At about the same time that Keller was formulating and implementing his theories, Bloom was formulating his theory of Learning for Mastery (LFM). Bloom derived his model for mastery learning from John Carroll's work and grounded it in behavioral elements such as incremental units of instruction, frequent testing, active student responding, rapid feedback, and self-pacing. Carroll (as cited in Bloom, 1971) proposed that if learners is normally distributed with respect to aptitude and they receive the same instruction on a topic, then the achievement of the learners is normally distributed as well. However, if the aptitude is normally distributed, but each learner receives optimal instruction with ample time to learn, then achievement will not be normally distributed. Instead, the majority of learners will achieve mastery and the correlation between aptitude and achievement will approach zero (Bloom, 1971).

Five criteria for a mastery learning strategy come from Carroll's work (Bloom, 1971). These are:

1. Aptitude for particular kinds of learning
2. Quality of instruction
3. Ability to understand instruction
4. Perseverance
5. Time allowed for learning

The first criterion concerns aptitude. Prior to the concept of mastery learning, it was assumed that aptitude tests were good predictors of student achievement. Therefore, it was believed that only some students would be capable of high achievement. Mastery learning proposes that aptitude is the amount of time required by the learner to gain mastery (Bloom, 1971). Therefore, Bloom asserts that 95% of all learners can gain mastery of a subject if given enough time and appropriate instruction (Bloom, 1971).

Secondly, the quality of instruction should focus on the individual. Bloom (1971) states that not all learners will learn best from the same method of instruction and that the focus of instruction should be on each learner. Because understanding instruction is imperative to learning, Bloom advocates a variety of teaching techniques so that any learner can learn. These include the use of tutors, audiovisual methods, games, and small-group study sessions. Similarly, perseverance is required to master a task. Perseverance can be increased by increasing learning success, and the amount of perseverance required can be reduced by good instruction. Finally, the time allowed for learning should be flexible so that all learners can master the material. However, Bloom also acknowledges the constraints of school schedules and states that an effective mastery learning program will alter the amount of time needed to master instruction.

1.7.2.2 Components of Learning for Mastery.

Block built upon Bloom's theory and refined it into two sections: preconditions and operating procedures. In the precondition section, teachers defined instructional objectives, defined the level of mastery, and prepared a final exam over the objectives. The content was then divided into smaller teaching units with a formative evaluation to be conducted after instruction. Then the alternative instructional materials (correctives) were developed that were keyed to each item on the unit test. This provided alternative ways of learning for learners should they have failed to master the material after the first attempt (Block & Anderson, 1975). During the operating phase, the teacher taught the material to the learners and then administered the evaluation. The learners who failed to master the material were responsible for mastering it before the next unit of instruction was provided. After all instruction was given, the final exam was administered (Block & Anderson, 1975).

In the most recent meta-analysis of Bloom's LFM, Kulik et al., (1990) concluded that LFM raised examination scores by an average of 0.59 standard deviations. LFM was most effective when all five criteria were met. When the subject matter was social sciences, the positive effect that LFM had was larger. Secondly, LFM had a more marked effect on locally developed tests, rather than national standardized tests. However, LFM learners performed similarly to non-LFM learners on standardized tests. When the teacher controlled the pace, learners in an LFM class performed better. Fourthly, LFM had a greater effect when the level of mastery was set very high (i.e., 100% correct) on unit quizzes. Finally, when LFM learners and non-LFM learners receive similar amounts of feedback, the LFM effect decreases. That is, less feedback for non-LFM learners caused a greater effect of LFM (Kulik et al., 1990). Additional conclusions that Kulik et al. draw are: that low aptitude learners can gain more than high aptitude learners, the benefits of LFM are enduring, not short-term, and finally, learners are more satisfied with their instruction and have a more positive attitude (Liu, 2001).

Learning tasks are designed as highly individualized activities within the class. Students work at their own rate, largely independent from the teacher. The teacher usually provides motivation only through the use of cues and feedback on course content as students progress through the unit (Metzler, Eddleman, Treanor, & Cregger, 1989).

Research on PSI in the classroom setting has been extensive (e.g., Callahan & Smith, 1990; Cregger & Metzler, 1992;

Hymel, 1987; McLaughlin, 1991; Zencias, Davis, & Cuvo, 1990). Often it has been limited to comparisons with designs using conventional strategies. It has been demonstrated that PSI and similar mastery-based instruction can be extremely effective in producing significant gains in student achievement (e.g., Block, Efthim, & Burns, 1989; Guskey, 1985). Often PSI research focuses on comparisons to Bloom's Learning for Mastery (LFM) (Bloom, 1971). LFM and PSI share a few characteristics among these are the use of mastery learning, increased teacher freedom, and increased student skill practice time. In both systems, each task must be performed to a criterion determined prior to the beginning of the course (Metzler et al., 1989).

Reiser (1987) points to the similarity between LFM and PSI in the method of student progression through the separate systems. Upon completion of each task, the student is given the choice of advancing or continuing work within that unit. However, whereas PSI allows the student to continue working on the same task until mastery is reached, LFM recommends a "looping-back" to a previous lesson and proceeding forward from that point (Bloom, 1971).

This similarity between systems extends to PSI's use of providing information to the learners in small chunks, or tasks, with frequent assessment of these smaller learning units (Siedentop, Mand, & Taggert, 1986). These chunks are built on simple tasks, to allow the learner success before advancing to more complex tasks. As in PSI, success LFM is developed through many opportunities for practice trials with the instructor providing cues and feedback on the task being attempted. These cues and feedback are offered in the place of lectures and demonstrations. Though Bloom's LFM approach shares many similarities with Keller's design, PSI actually extends the concept of mastery to include attention to the individual student as he or she progresses through the sequence of learning tasks (Reiser, 1987).

Several studies have compared self-pacing approaches with reinforcement (positive or negative rewards) in a PSI setting. Keller (1968) has suggested that it was not necessary to provide any pacing contingencies. Others have used procedures that reward students for maintaining a pace (Cheney & Powers, 1971; Lloyd, 1971), or penalized students for failing to do so (Miller, Weaver, & Semb, 1954; Reiser & Sullivan, 1977). Calhoun (1976), Morris, Surber, and Bijou (1978), Reiser (1980), and Semb et al. (1975) report that learning was not affected by the type of pacing procedure. However, Allen, Giat, and Cheney (1974), Sheppard and MacDermot (1970), and Sutterer and Holloway (1975) reported that the "prompt completion of work is positively related to achievement in PSI courses" (Reiser, 1980, p. 200).

Reiser (1984), however, reported that student rates of progress is improved and learning is unhindered when pacing with penalties are used (e.g., Reiser & Sullivan, 1977; Robin & Graham, 1974). In most cases (except Fernald et al., 1975; Robin & Graham, 1974), student attitudes are as positive with a penalty approach as with a regular self-paced approach without penalty (e.g., Calhoun, 1976; Reiser, 1980; Reiser & Sullivan, 1977).

1.7.3 Precision Teaching

Precision teaching is the creation of O. R. Lindsley (Potts, Eshleman, & Cooper, 1993; Vargas, 1977). Building upon his own early research with humans (e.g., Lindsley, 1956, 1964, 1972, 1991a, 1991b; Lindsley & Skinner, 1954) proposed that rate, rather than percent correct, might prove more sensitive to monitoring classroom learning. Rather than creating programs based on laboratory findings, Lindsley proposed that the measurement framework that had become the hallmark of the laboratories of Skinner and his associates be moved into the classroom. His goal was to put science in the hands of teachers and students (Binder & Watkins, 1990). In Lindsley's (1990a) words, his associates and he (e.g., Caldwell, 1966; Fink, 1968; Holzschuh & Dobbs, 1966) "did not set out to discover basic laws of behavior. Rather, we merely intended to monitor standard self-recorded performance frequencies in the classroom" (p. 7). The most conspicuous result of these efforts was the Standard Behavior Chart or Standard Celeration Chart, a six–cycle, semi-logarithmic graph for charting behavior frequency against days.

By creating linear representations of learning (trends in performance) on the semi-logarithmic chart, and quantifying them as multiplicative factors per week (e.g., correct responses × 2.0 per week minus errors divided by 1.5 per week), Lindsley defined the first simple measure of learning in the literature: *Celeration* (either a multiplicative acceleration of behavior frequency or a dividing deceleration of behavior frequency per celeration period, e.g., per week). (Binder & Watkins, 1990, p. 78)

Evidence suggests that celeration, a direct measure of learning, is not racially biased (Koening & Kunzelmann, 1981).

In addition to the behavioral methodologies mentioned in the introduction to this section, precision teachers use behavioral techniques including applied behavior analysis, individualized programming and behavior change strategies, and student self-monitoring. They distinguish between operational or descriptive definitions of event, which require merely observation, versus functional definitions that require manipulative (and continued observation). Precision teachers apply the "dead man's test" to descriptions of behavior, that is, "If a dead man can do it, then don't try to teach it" (Binder & Watkins, 1990), to rule out objectives such as "sits quietly in chair" or "keeps eyes on paper." The emphasis of Precision Teaching has been on teaching teachers *and students* to count behaviors with an emphasis on counting and analyzing both correct and incorrect response (i.e., learning opportunities) (White, 1986). As Vargas (1977) points out, "This problem-solving approach to changing behavior is not only a method, it is also an outlook, a willingness to judge by what works, not by what we like to do or what we already believe" (p. 47).

The Precision Teaching movement has resulted in some practical findings of potential use to education technologists. For example, Precision Teachers have consistently found that placement of students in more difficult tasks (which produce higher error rates), results in faster learning rates (see e.g., Johnson, 1971; Johnson & Layng, 1994; Neufeld & Lindsley, 1980). Precision Teachers have also made fluency, accuracy plus speed of performance, a goal at each level of a student's progress. Fluency (or automaticity or "second nature" responding) has been shown to improve retention, transfer of training, and "endurance" or resistance to extinction (Binder, 1987, 1988, 1993; Binder, Haughton, & VanEyk, 1990). (It is important to note that fluency is not merely a new word for "overlearning," or continuing to practice past mastery. Fluency involves speed, and indeed speed may be more important than accuracy, at least initially). Consistent with the findings that more difficult placement produces bigger gains are the findings of Bower and Orgel (1981) and Lindsley (1990b) that encouraging students to respond at very high rates from the beginning, even when error rates are high, can significantly increase learning rates.

Large-scale implementations of Precision Teaching have found that improvements of two or more grade levels per year are common (e.g., West, Young, & Spooner, 1990). "The improvements themselves are dramatic; but when cost/benefit is considered, they are staggering, since the time allocated to precision teach was relatively small and the materials used were quite inexpensive" (Binder & Watkins, 1989, p. 82–83).

1.7.4 Direct Instruction

Direct Instruction (DI) is a design and implementation model based on the work of Siegfried Engelmann (Bereiter & Engelmann, 1966; Englemann, 1980), and refined through 30+ years of research and development. DI uses behavioral tenets such as scripted lessons, active student responding, rapid feedback, self-pacing, student-oriented objectives, and mastery learning as part of the methodology. According to Binder and Watkins (1990), over 50 commercially available programs are based on the DI model. The major premise of the DI is that learners are expected to derive learning that is consistent with the presentation offered by the teacher. Learners acquire information through choice–response discriminations, production–response discriminations, and sentence–relationship discriminations. The key activity for the teacher is to identify the type of discrimination required in a particular task, and design a specific sequence to teach the discrimination so that only the teacher's interpretation of the information is possible. Engelmann and Carnine (1982, 1991) state that this procedure requires three analyses: the analysis of behavior, the analysis of communications, and the analysis of knowledge systems.

The analysis of behavior is concerned with how the environment influences learner behavior (e.g., how to prompt and reinforce responses, how to correct errors, etc.). The analysis of communications seeks principles for the logical design of effective teaching sequences. These principles relate to the ordering of examples to maximize generalization (but minimize overgeneralization). The analysis of knowledge systems is concerned with the logical organization or classification of knowledge such that similar skills and concepts can be taught the same way and instruction can proceed from simple to complex. Direct instruction uses scripted presentations not only to support quality control, but because most teachers lack training in design and are, therefore, not likely to select and sequence examples effectively without such explicit instructions (Binder & Watkins, 1990). Englemann (1980) asserts that these scripted lessons release the teacher to focus on:

1. The presentation and communication of the information to children
2. Students' prerequisite skills and capabilities to have success with the target task
3. Potential problems identified in the task analysis
4. How children learn by pinpointing learner successes and strategies for success
5. Attainment
6. Learning how to construct well-designed tasks

Direct instruction also relies on small groups (10–15), unison responding (to get high response rates from *all* students) to fixed signals from the teacher, rapid pacing, and correction procedures for dealing with student errors (Carnine, Grossen, & Silbert, 1994). Generalization and transfer are the result of six "shifts" that Becker and Carnine (1981) say should occur in any well-designed program: overtized to covertized problem solving, simplified contexts to complex contexts, prompts to no prompts, massed to distributed practice, immediate to delayed feedback, and teacher's roles to learner's role as a source of information.

Watkins (1988), in the Project Follow Through evaluation, compared over 20 different instructional models and found Direct Instruction to be the most effective of all programs on measures of basic skills achievement, cognitive skills, and self concept. Direct Instruction has been shown to produce higher reading and math scores (Becker & Gersten, 1982), more high-school diplomas, less grade retention, and fewer dropouts than students who did not participate (Englemann, Becker, Carnine, & Gersten, 1988; Gersten, 1982; Gersten & Carnine, 1983; Gersten & Keating, 1983). Gersten, Keating, and Becker (1988) found modest differences in Direct Instruction students three, six, and nine years after the program with one notable exception: reading. Reading showed a strong long-term benefit consistently across all sites. Currently, the DI approach is a central pedagogy in Slavin's Success for All program, a very popular program that provides remedial support for early readers in danger of failure.

1.7.5 The Morningside Model

The Morningside Model of Generative Instruction and Fluency (Johnson & Layng, 1992) puts together aspects of Precision Teaching, Direct Instruction, Personalized System of Instruction with the Instructional Content Analysis of Markle and Tiemann (Markle & Droege, 1980; Tiemann & Markle, 1990), and the guidelines provided by Markle (1964, 1969, 1991). The Morningside Model has apparently been used, to date, exclusively by the Morningside Academy in Seattle (since 1980) and Malcolm X College, Chicago (since 1991). The program offers instruction for both children and adults in virtually all skill areas. Johnson and Layng report impressive comparative gains "across the board." From the perspective of the Instructional Technologist, probably the most impressive statistic was the average gain per hour of instruction; across all studies summarized,

Johnson and Layng found that 20 to 25 hours of instruction per skill using Morningside Model instruction resulted in nearly a two-grade level "payoff" as compared to the U.S. government standard of one grade level per 100 hours. Sixty hours of inservice was given to new teachers, and design time/costs were not estimated, but the potential cost benefit of the model seem obvious.

1.7.6 Distance Education and Tutoring Systems

The explosive rise in the use of distance education to meet the needs of individual learners has revitalized the infusion of behavioral principles into the design and implementation of computer-based instructional programs (McIssac & Gunawardena, 1996). Because integration with the academic environment and student support systems are important factors in student success (Cookson, 1989; Keegan, 1986), many distance education programs try to provide student tutors to their distance learners. Moore and Kearsley (1996) stated that the primary reason for having tutors in distance education is to individualize instruction. They also asserted that having tutors available in a distance education course generally improves student completion rates and achievement.

The functions of tutors in distance education are diverse and encompassing, including: discussing course material, providing feedback in terms of progress and grades, assisting students in planning their work, motivating the students, keeping student records, and supervising projects. However, providing feedback is critical for a good learning experience (Moore & Kearsley, 1996). Race (1989) stated that the most important functions of the tutors are to provide objective feedback and grades and use good model answers. Holmberg (1977) stated that students profit from comments from human tutors provided within 7–10 days of assignment submission.

The Open University has historically used human tutors in many different roles, including counselor, grader, and consultant (Keegan, 1986). The Open University's student support system has included regional face-to-face tutorial sessions and a personal (usually local) tutor for grading purposes. Teaching at the Open University has been primarily through these tutor marked assignments. Summative and formative evaluation by the tutor has occurred though the postal system, the telephone, or face-to-face sessions. Despite the success of this system (>70% retention rate), recently the Open University has begun moving to the Internet for its student support services (Thomas, Carswell, Price, & Petre, 1998).

The Open University is using the Internet for registration, assignment handling, student–tutor interactions, and exams. The new electronic system for handling assignments addresses many limitations of the previous postal system such as, turn-around time for feedback and reduced reliance upon postal systems. The tutor still grades the assignments, but now the corrections are made in a word processing tool that makes it easier to read (Thomas et al., 1998).

The Open University is also using the Internet for tutor–tutee contact. Previously, tutors held face-to-face sessions where students could interact with each other and the tutor. However, the cost of maintaining facilities where these sessions could take place was expensive and the organization of tutor groups and schedules was complex. Additionally, one of the reasons students choose distance learning is the freedom from traditional school hours. The face-to-face sessions were difficult for some students to attend. The Open University has moved to computer conferencing, which integrates with administrative components to reduce the complexity of managing tutors (Thomas et al., 1998).

Rowe and Gregor (1999) developed a computer-based learning system that uses the World Wide Web for delivery. Integral to the system are question–answer tutorials and programming tutorials. The question and answer tutorials were multiple choice and graded instantly after submission. The programming tutorials required the students to provide short answers to questions. These questions were checked by the computer and if necessary, sent to a human tutor for clarification. After using this format for two years at the University of Dundee, the computer-based learning system was evaluated by a small student focus group with representatives from all the levels of academic achievement in the class. Students were asked about the interface, motivation, and learning value.

Students enjoyed the use of the web browser for distance learning, especially when colors were used in the instruction (Rowe & Gregor, 1999). With regards to the tutorials, students wanted to see the question, their answer, and the correct answer on the screen at the same time, along with feedback as to why the answer was wrong or right. Some students wanted to e-mail answers to a human tutor because of the natural language barrier. Since the computer-based learning system was used as a supplement to lecture and lab sessions, students found it to be motivating. They found that the system fulfilled gaps in knowledge and could learn in their own time and at their own pace. They especially liked the interactivity of the web. Learners did not feel that they learned more with the computer-based system, but that their learning was reinforced.

An interesting and novel approach to distance learning in online groups has been proposed by Whatley, Staniford, Beer, and Scown (1999). They proposed using agent technology to develop individual "tutors" that monitor a student's participation in a group online project. An agent is self-contained, concurrently executing software that captures a particular state of knowledge and communicates with other agents. Each student would have an agent that would monitor that student's progress, measure it against a group plan, and intervene when necessary to insure that each student completes his/her part of the project. While this approach differs from a traditional tutor approach, it still retains some of the characteristics of a human tutor, those of monitoring progress and intervening when necessary (Whatley et al., 1999).

1.7.7 Computers as Tutors

Tutors have been used to improve learning since Socrates. However, there are limitations on the availability of tutors to distance learners. In 1977, Holmberg stated that some distance education programs use preproduced tutor comments and received favorable feedback from students on this method. However, advances in available technology have further developed the microcomputer as a possible tutor. Bennett (1999) asserts that using computers as tutors has multiple advantages, including self-pacing, the availability of help at any time in the instructional process, constant evaluation and assessment of the student, requisite mastery of fundamental material, and providing remediation. In addition, he states that computers as tutors will reduce prejudice, help the disadvantaged, support the more advanced students, and provide a higher level of interest with the use of multimedia components (Bennett, p.76–119). Consistent across this research on tutoring systems, the rapid feedback provided by computers is beneficial and enjoyable to the students (Holmberg, 1977).

Halff (1988, p. 79) identifies three roles of computers as tutors:

1. Exercising control over curriculum by selecting and sequencing the material
2. Responding to learners' questions about the subject
3. Determining when learners need help in developing a skill and what sort of help they need

Cohen, Kulik, and Kulik (1982) examined 65 school tutoring programs and showed that students receiving tutoring outperformed nontutored students on exams. Tutoring also affected student attitudes. Students who received tutoring developed a positive attitude toward the subject matter (Cohen et al., 1982). Since tutors have positive effects on learning, they are a desirable component to have in an instructional experience.

Thus, after over 25 years of research it is clear that behavioral design and delivery models "work." In fact, the large-scale implementations reviewed here were found to produce gains above two grade levels (e.g., Bloom, 1984; Guskey, 1985). Moreover, the models appear to be cost effective. Why then are they no longer fashionable? Perhaps because behaviorism has not been taught for several academic generations. Most people in design have never read original behavioral sources; nor had the professors who taught them. Behaviorism is often interpreted briefly and poorly. It has become a straw man to contrast more appealing, more current, learning notions.

1.8 CONCLUSION

This brings us to the final points of this piece. First, what do current notions such as situated cognition and social constructive add to radical behaviorism? How well does each account for the other? Behaviorism is rich enough to account for both, is historically older, and has the advantage of parsimony; it is the simplest explanation of the facts. We do not believe that advocates of either could come up with a study which discriminates between their position as opposed to behaviorism *except* through the use of mentalistic explanations. Skinner's work was criticized often for being too descriptive—for not offering explanation. Yet, it has been supplanted by a tradition that prides itself on qualitative, descriptive analysis. Do the structures and dualistic mentalisms add anything? We think not. Radical behaviorism provides a means to both describe events and ascribe causality.

Anderson (1985) once noted that the problem in cognitive theory (although we could substitute all current theories in psychology) was that of nonidentifiability; cognitive theories simply do not make different predictions that distinguish between them. Moreover, what passes as theory is a collection of mini-theories and hypotheses without a unifying system. Cognitive theory necessitates a view of evolution that includes a step beyond the rest of the natural world or perhaps even the purpose of evolution!

We seem, thus, to have arrived at a concept of how the physical universe about us—all the life that inhabits the speck we occupy in this universe—has evolved over the eons of time by simple material processes, the sort of processes we examine experimentally, which we describe by equations, and call the "laws of nature." Except for one thing! Man is conscious of his existence. Man also possesses, so most of us believe, what he calls his free will. Did consciousness and free will too arise merely out of "natural" processes? The question is central to the contention between those who see nothing beyond a new materialism and those who see—Something. (Vanevar Bush, 1965, as cited in Skinner, 1974)

Skinner (1974) makes the point in his introduction to *About Behaviorism* that behaviorism is not the science of behaviorism; it is the philosophy of that science. As such, it provides the best vehicle for Educational Technologists to describe and converse about human learning and behavior. Moreover, its assumptions that the responsibility for teaching/instruction resides in the teacher or designer "makes sense" if we are to "sell our wares." In a sense, cognitive psychology and its offshoots are collapsing from the weight of the structures it postulates. Behaviorism "worked" even when it was often misunderstood and misapplied. Behaviorism is simple, elegant, and consistent. Behaviorism *is* a relevant and viable philosophy to provide a foundation and guidance for instructional technology. It has enormous potential in distance learning settings. Scholars and practitioners need to revisit the original sources of this literature to truly know its promise for student learning.

ACKNOWLEDGMENTS

We are deeply indebted to Dr. George Gropper and Dr. John "Coop" Cooper for their reviews of early versions of this manuscript. George was particularly helpful in reviewing the sections on methodological behaviorism and Coop for his analysis of the sections on radical behaviorism and enormously useful suggestions. Thanks to Dr. David Jonassen for helping us in the first version of this chapter to reconcile their conflicting advise in the area that each did not prefer. We thank him again in this new chapter for his careful reading and suggestions to restructure. The authors also acknowledge and appreciate the research assistance of Hope Q. Liu.

References

Alexander, J. E. (1970). *Vocabulary improvement methods, college level*. Knoxville, TN: Tennessee University Press.

Allen, D. W., & McDonald, F. J. (1963). *The effects of self-instruction on learning in programmed instruction*. Paper presented at the meeting of the American Educational Research Association, Chicago, IL.

Allen, G. J., Giat, L., & Cherney, R. J. (1974). Locus of control, test anxiety, and student performance in a personalized instruction course. *Journal of Educational Psychology, 66*, 968–973.

Anderson, J. R. (1985). *Cognitive psychology and its implications* (2nd ed.). New York: Freeman.

Anderson, L. M. (1986). Learners and learning. In M. Reynolds (Ed.), *Knowledge base for the beginning teacher*. (pp. 85–99). New York: AACTE.

Angell, G. W., & Troyer, M. E. (1948). A new self-scoring test device for improving instruction. *School and Society, 67*(84–85), 66–68.

Baker, E. L. (1969). Effects on student achievement of behavioral and non-behavioral objectives. *The Journal of Experimental Education, 37*, 5–8.

Bandura, A. (1977). *Social learning theory*. Englewood Cliffs, NJ: Prentice Hall.

Barnes, M. R. (1970). *An experimental study of the use of programmed instruction in a university physical science laboratory*. Paper presented at the annual meeting of the National Association for Research in Science Teaching, Minneapolis, MN.

Beane, D. G. (1962). *A comparison of linear and branching techniques of programmed instruction in plane geometry* (Technical Report No. 1). Urbana: University of Illinois.

Beck, J. (1959). On some methods of programming. In E. Galanter (Ed.), *Automatic teaching: The state of the art* (pp. 55–62). New York: Wiley.

Becker, W. C., & Carnine, D. W. (1981). Direct Instruction: A behavior theory model for comprehensive educational intervention with the disadvantaged. In S. W. Bijou & R. Ruiz (Eds.), *Behavior modification: Contributions to education*. Hillsdale, NJ: Erlbaum.

Becker, W. C., & Gersten, R. (1982). A follow-up of Follow Through: Meta-analysis of the later effects of the Direction Instruction Model. *American Educational Research Journal, 19*, 75–93.

Bennett, F. (1999). *Computers as tutors solving the crisis in education*. Sarasota, FL: Faben.

Bereiter, C., & Engelmann, S. (1966). *Teaching disadvantaged children in the preschool*. Englewood Cliffs, NJ: Prentice-Hall.

Binder, C. (1987). *Fluency-building™ research background*. Nonantum, MA: Precision Teaching and Management Systems, Inc. (P.O. Box 169, Nonantum, MA 02195).

Binder, C. (1988). Precision teaching: Measuring and attaining academic achievement. *Youth Policy, 10*(7), 12–15.

Binder, C. (1993). Behavioral fluency: A new paradigm. *Educational Technology, 33*(10), 8–14.

Binder, C., Haughton, E., & VanEyk, D. (1990). Increasing endurance by building fluency: Precision Teaching attention span. *Teaching Exceptional Children, 22*(3), 24–27.

Binder, C., & Watkins, C. L. (1989). Promoting effective instructional methods: Solutions to America's educational crisis. *Future Choices, 1*(3), 33-39.

Binder, C., & Watkins, C. L. (1990). Precision teaching and direct instruction: Measurably superior instructional technology in schools. *Performance Improvement Quarterly, 3*(4), 75-95.

Block, J. H., & Anderson, L. W. (1975). *Mastery learning in classroom instruction.* New York: Macmillan.

Block, J. H., Efthim, H. E., & Burns, R. B. (1989). *Building effective mastery learning schools.* New York: Longman.

Blodgett, R. (1929). The effect of the introduction of reward upon the maze performance of rats. *University of California Publications in Psychology, 4,* 113-134.

Bloom, B. S. (1971). Mastery learning. In J. H. Block (Ed.), *Mastery learning: Theory and practice.* (pp. 47-63). New York: Holt, Rinehart & Winston.

Bloom, B. S. (1984). The 2-Sigma problem: The search for methods of group instruction as effective as one-to-one tutoring. *Educational Researcher, 13*(6), 4-16.

Bloom, B. S., Engelhart, N. D., Furst, E. J., Hill, W. H., & Krathwohl, D. R. (Eds.) (1956). *Taxonomy of educational objectives—The classification of education goals, Handbook I: Cognitive domain.* New York: McKay.

Bobbitt, F. (1918). *The curriculum.* Boston: Houghton Mifflin.

Born, D. G. (1975). Exam performance and study behavior as a function of study unit size. In J. M. Johnson (Ed.), *Behavior Research and Technology in Higher Education* (pp. 269-282). Springfield, IL: Charles Thomas.

Born, D. G., & Herbert, E. W. (1974). A further study of personalized instruction for students in large university classes. In J. G. Sherman (Ed.), *Personalized Systems of Instruction, 41 Germinal Papers* (pp. 30-35), Menlo Park, CA: W. A. Benjamin.

Bower, B., & Orgel, R. (1981). To err is divine. *Journal of Precision Teaching, 2*(1), 3-12.

Brenner, H. R., Walter, J. S., & Kurtz, A. K. (1949). The effects of inserted questions and statements on film learning. *Progress Report No. 10.* State College, PA: Pennsylvania State College Instructional Film Research Program.

Briggs, L. J. (1947). Intensive classes for superior students. *Journal of Educational Psychology, 38,* 207-215.

Briggs, L. J. (1958). Two self-instructional devices. *Psychological Reports, 4,* 671-676.

Brown, J. (1970). *The effects of revealing instructional objectives on the learning of political concepts and attitudes in two role-playing games.* Unpublished doctoral dissertation, University of California at Los Angeles.

Brown, J. S., Collins, A., & Duguid, P. (1989). Situated cognition and the culture of learning. *Educational Researcher, 18*(1), 32-42.

Burton, J. K. (1981). Behavioral technology: Foundation for the future. *Educational Technology, XXI*(7), 21-28.

Burton, J. K., & Merrill, P. F. (1991). Needs assessment: Goals, needs, and priorities. In L. J. Briggs, K. L. Gustafson, & M. Tillman (Eds.), *Instructional design: Principles and applications.* Englewood Cliffs, NJ: Educational Technology.

Caldwell, T. (1966). *Comparison of classroom measures: Percent, number, and rate* (Educational Research Technical Report). Kansas City: University of Kansas Medical Center.

Calhoun, J. F. (1976). The combination of elements in the personalized system of instruction. *Teaching Psychology, 3,* 73-76.

Callahan, C., & Smith, R. M. (1990). Keller's personalized system of instruction in a junior high gifted program. *Roeper Review, 13,* 39-44.

Campbell, V. N. (1961). *Adjusting self-instruction programs to individual differences: Studies of cueing, responding and bypassing.* San Mateo, CA: American Institute for Research.

Campeau, P. L. (1974). Selective review of the results of research on the use of audiovisual media to teach adults. *Audio-Visual Communication Review, 22*(1), 5-40.

Cantor, J. H., & Brown, J. S. (1956). *An evaluation of the trainer-tester and punchboard tutor as electronics troubleshooting training aids* (Technical Report NTDC-1257-2-1). (George Peabody College) Port Washington, NY: Special Devices Center, Office of Naval Research.

Carnine, D., Grossen, B., & Silbert, J. (1994). Direct instruction to accelerate cognitive growth. In J. Block, T. Gluskey, & S. Everson (Eds.), *Choosing research based school improvement innovations.* New York: Scholastic.

Carpenter, C. R. (1962). Boundaries of learning theories and mediators of learning. *Audio-Visual Communication Review, 10*(6), 295-306.

Carpenter, C. R., & Greenhill, L. P. (1955). *An investigation of closed-circuit television for teaching university courses, Report No. 1.* University Park, PA: Pennsylvania State University.

Carpenter, C. R., & Greenhill, L. P. (1956). *Instructional film research reports,* Vol. 2. (Technical Report 269-7-61, NAVEXOS P12543), Post Washington, NY: Special Devices Center.

Carpenter, C. R., & Greenhill, L. P. (1958). *An investigation of closed-circuit television for teaching university courses, Report No. 2.* University Park, PA: Pennsylvania State University.

Carr, W. J. (1959). *Self-instructional devices: A review of current concepts.* USAF Wright Air Dev. Cent. Tech. Report 59-503, [278, 286, 290].

Cason, H. (1922a). The conditioned pupillary reaction. *Journal of Experimental Psychology, 5,* 108-146.

Cason, H. (1922b). The conditioned eyelid reaction. *Journal of Experimental Psychology, 5,* 153-196.

Chance, P. (1994). *Learning and behavior.* Pacific Grove, CA: Brooks/Cole.

Cheney, C. D., & Powers, R. B. (1971). A programmed approach to teaching in the social sciences. *Improving College and University Teaching, 19,* 164-166.

Chiesa, M. (1992). Radical behaviorism and scientific frameworks. From mechanistic to relational accounts. *American Psychologist, 47,* 1287-1299.

Chu, G., & Schramm, W. (1968). *Learning from television.* Washington, DC: National Association of Educational Broadcasters.

Churchland, P. M. (1990). *Matter and consciousness.* Cambridge, MA: The MIT Press.

Cohen, P. A., Kulik, J. A., & Kulik, C. C. (1982). Educational outcomes of tutoring: A meta-analysis of findings. *American Educational Research Journal, 13*(2), 237-248.

Cook, D. A. (1994, May). *The campaign for educational territories.* Paper presented at the Annual meeting of the Association for Behavior Analysis, Atlanta, GA.

Cook, J. U. (1960). Research in audiovisual communication. In J. Ball & F. C. Byrnes (Eds.), *Research, principles, and practices in visual communication* (pp. 91-106). Washington, DC: Department of Audiovisual Instruction, National Education Association.

Cookson, P. S. (1989). Research on learners and learning in distance education: A review. *The American Journal of Distance Education, 3*(2), 22-34.

Cooper, J. O., Heron, T. E., & Heward, W. L. (1987). *Applied behavior analysis.* Columbus: Merrill.

Corey, S. M. (1971). Definition of instructional design. In M. D. Merrill (Ed.), *Instructional design: Readings.* Englewood Cliffs, NJ: Prentice-Hall.

Coulson, J. E., & Silberman, H. F. (1960). Effects of three variables in a teaching machine. *Journal of Educational Psychology, 51,* 135-143.

Cregger, R., & Metzler, M. (1992). PSI for a college physical education basic instructional program. *Educational Technology, 32,* 51-56.

Crooks, F. C. (1971). *The differential effects of pre-prepared and teacher-prepared instructional objectives on the learning of educable mentally retarded children.* Unpublished doctoral dissertation, University of Iowa.

Crowder, N. A. (1959). Automatic tutoring by means of intrinsic programming. In E. Galanter (Ed.), *Automatic teaching: The state of the art* (pp. 109-116). New York: Wiley.

Crowder, N. A. (1960). Automatic tutoring by intrinsic programming. In A. Lumsdaine & R. Glaser (Ed.), *Teaching machines and programmed learning: A source book* (pp. 286-298). Washington, DC: National Education Association.

Crowder, N. A. (1961). Characteristics of branching programs. In O. M. Haugh (Ed.), *The University of Kansas Conference on Programmed Learning: II* (pp. 22-27). Lawrence, KS: University of Kansas Publications.

Crowder, N. A. (1962, April). The rationale of intrinsic programming. *Programmed Instruction, 1,* 3-6.

Dalis, G. T. (1970). Effect of precise objectives upon student achievement in health education. *Journal of Experimental Education, 39,* 20-23.

Daniel, W. J., & Murdoch, P. (1968). Effectiveness of learning from a programmed text compared with a conventional text covering the same material. *Journal of Educational Psychology, 59,* 425-451.

Darwin, C. (1859). *On the origin of species by means of natural selection, or the preservation of the favored races in the struggle for life.* London: Murray.

Davey, G. (1981). *Animal learning and conditioning.* Baltimore: University Park.

Day, W. (1983). On the difference between radical and methodological behaviorism. *Behaviorism, 11*(11), 89-102.

Day, W. F. (1976). Contemporary behaviorism and the concept of intention. In W. J. Arnold (Ed.), *Nebraska Symposium on Motivation* (pp. 65-131) 1975. Lincoln, NE: University of Nebraska Press.

Dewey, J. (1900). Psychology and social practice. *The Psychological Review, 7,* 105-124.

Donahoe, J. W. (1991). Selectionist approach to verbal behavior. Potential contributions of neuropsychology and computer simulation. In L. J. Hayes & P. N. Chase (Eds.), *Dialogues on verbal behavior* (pp. 119-145). Reno, NV: Context Press.

Donahoe, J. W., & Palmer, D. C. (1989). The interpretation of complex human behavior: Some reactions to *Parallel Distributed Processing,* edited by J. L. McClelland, D. E. Rumelhart, & the PDP Research Group. *Journal of the Experimental Analysis of Behavior, 51,* 399-416.

Doty, C. R. (1968). *The effect of practice and prior knowledge of educational objectives on performance.* Unpublished doctoral dissertation, The Ohio State University.

Dowell, E. C. (1955). *An evaluation of trainer-testers.* (Report No. 54-28). Headquarters Technical Training Air Force, Keesler Air Force Base, MS.

Englemann, S. (1980). *Direct instruction.* Englewood Cliffs, NJ: Educational Technology.

Englemann, S., Becker, W. C., Carnine, D., & Gersten, R. (1988). The Direct Instruction Follow Through model: Design and outcomes. *Education and Treatment of Children, 11*(4), 303-317.

Englemann, S., & Carnine, D. (1982). *Theory of instruction.* New York: Irvington.

Engelmann, S., & Carnine, D. (1991). *Theory of instruction: Principles and applications* (rev. ed.). Eugene, OR: ADI Press.

Evans, J. L., Glaser, R., & Homme, L. E. (1962). An investigation of "teaching machine" variables using learning programs in symbolic logic. *Journal of Educational Research, 55,* 433-542.

Evans, J. L., Homme, L. E., & Glaser, R. (1962, June-July). The Ruleg System for the construction of programmed verbal learning sequences. *Journal of Educational Research, 55,* 513-518.

Farmer, J., Lachter, G. D., Blaustein, J. J., & Cole, B. K. (1972). The role of proctoring in personalized instruction. *Journal of Applied Behavior Analysis, 5,* 401-404.

Fernald, P. S., Chiseri, M. J., Lawson, D. W., Scroggs, G. F., & Riddell, J. C. (1975). Systematic manipulation of student pacing, the perfection requirement, and contact with a teaching assistant in an introductory psychology course. *Teaching of Psychology, 2,* 147-151.

Ferster, C. B., & Skinner, B. F. (1957). *Schedules of reinforcement.* New York: Appleton-Century-Crofts.

Fink, E. R. (1968). *Performance and selection rates of emotionally disturbed and mentally retarded preschoolers on Montessori materials.* Unpublished master's thesis, University of Kansas.

Frase, L. T. (1970). Boundary conditions for mathemagenic behaviors. *Review of Educational Research, 40,* 337-347.

Gagné, R. M. (1962). Introduction. In R. M. Gagné (Ed.), *Psychological principles in system development.* New York: Holt, Rinehart & Winston.

Gagné, R. M. (1965). The analysis of instructional objectives for the design of instruction. In R. Glaser (Ed.), *Teaching machines and programmed learning, II.* Washington, DC: National Education Association.

Gagné, R. M. (1985). *The condition of learning and theory of instruction* (4th ed.). New York: Holt, Rinehart & Winston.

Gagné, R. M., Briggs, L. J., & Wager, W. W. (1988). *Principles of instructional design* (3rd ed.). New York: Holt, Rinehart & Winston.

Gagné, R. M., Briggs, L. J., & Wager, W. W. (1992). *Principles of instructional design* (4th ed.). New York: Harcourt Brace Jovanovich.

Galanter, E. (1959). The ideal teacher. In E. Galanter (Ed.), *Automatic teaching: The state of the art* (pp. 1-11). New York: Wiley.

Gallup, H. F. (1974). Problems in the implementation of a course in personalized instruction. In J. G. Sherman (Ed.), *Personalized Systems of Instruction, 41 Germinal Papers* (pp. 128-135), Menlo Park, CA: W. A. Benjamin.

Gardner, H. (1985). *The mind's new science: A history of the cognitive revolution.* New York: Basic Books.

Garrison, J. W. (1994). Realism, Deweyan pragmatism, and educational research. *Educational Researcher, 23*(1), 5-14.

Gersten, R. M. (1982). High school follow-up of DI Follow Through. *Direct Instruction News, 2,* 3.

Gersten, R. M., & Carnine, D. W. (1983). *The later effects of Direction Instruction Follow through.* Paper presented at the annual meeting of the American Educational Research Association, Montreal, Canada.

Gersten, R. M., & Keating, T. (1983). DI Follow Through students show fewer dropouts, fewer retentions, and more high school graduates. *Direct Instruction News, 2,* 14-15.

Gersten, R., Keating, T., & Becker, W. C. (1988). The continued impact of the Direct Instruction Model: Longitudinal studies of follow through students. *Education and Treatment of Children, 11*(4), 318-327.

Gibson, J. J. (Ed.). (1947). *Motion picture testing and research* (Report No. 7). Army Air Forces Aviation Psychology Program Research Reports, Washington, DC: Government Printing Office.

Giese, D. L., & Stockdale, W. (1966). Comparing an experimental and a conventional method of teaching linguistic skills. *The General College Studies, 2*(3), 1-10.

Gilbert, T. F. (1962). Mathetics: The technology of education. *Journal of Mathetics,* 7–73.

Glaser, R. (1960). *Principles and problems in the preparation of programmed learning sequences.* Paper presented at the University of Texas Symposium on the Automation of Instruction, University of Texas, May 1960. [Also published as a report of a Cooperative Research Program Grant to the University of Pittsburgh under sponsorship of the U.S. Office of Education.

Glaser, R. (1962a). Psychology and instructional technology. In R. Glaser (Ed.), *Training research and education.* Pittsburgh: University of Pittsburgh Press.

Glaser, R. (Ed.). (1962b). *Training research and education.* Pittsburgh: University of Pittsburgh Press.

Glaser, R. (Ed.). (1965a). *Teaching machines and programmed learning II.* Washington, DC: Association for Educational Communications and Technology.

Glaser, R. (1965b). Toward a behavioral science base for instructional design. In R. Glaser (Ed.), *Teaching machines and programmed learning, II : Data and directions* (pp. 771–809). Washington, DC: National Education Association.

Glaser, R., Damrin, D. E., & Gardner, F. M. (1954). The tab time: A technique for the measurement of proficiency in diagnostic problem solving tasks. *Educational and Psychological Measurement, 14,* 283–93.

Glaser, R., Reynolds, J. H., & Harakas, T. (1962). *An experimental comparison of a small-step single track program with a large-step multi-track (Branching) program.* Pittsburgh: Programmed Learning Laboratory, University of Pittsburgh.

Goodson, F. E. (1973). *The evolutionary foundations of psychology: A unified theory.* New York: Holt, Rinehart & Winston.

Greeno, J. G., Collins, A. M., & Resnick, L. B. (1996). Cognition and learning. In D. C. Berliner & R. C. Calfee (Eds.), *Handbook of educational psychology* (pp. 15–46). New York: Simon & Schuster Macmillan.

Gropper, G. L. (1963). Why is a picture worth a thousand words? *Audio-Visual Communication Review, 11*(4), 75–95.

Gropper, G. L. (1965a, October). *Controlling student responses during visual presentations, Report No. 2. Studies in televised instruction: The role of visuals in verbal learning, Study No. 1—An investigation of response control during visual presentations. Study No. 2—Integrating visual and verbal presentations.* Pittsburgh, PA: American Institutes for Research.

Gropper, G. L. (1965b). *A description of the REP style program and its rationale.* Paper presented at NSPI Convention, Philadelphia, PA.

Gropper, G. L. (1966, Spring). Learning from visuals: Some behavioral considerations. *Audio-Visual Communication Review, 14:* 37–69.

Gropper, G. L. (1967). Does "programmed" television need active responding? *Audio-Visual Communication Review, 15*(1), 5–22.

Gropper, G. L. (1968). Programming visual presentations for procedural learning. *Audio-Visual Communication Review, 16*(1), 33–55.

Gropper, G. L. (1983). A behavioral approach to instructional prescription. In C. M. Reigeluth (Ed.), *Instructional design theories and models.* Hillsdale, NJ: Erlbaum.

Gropper, G. L., & Lumsdaine, A. A. (1961a, March). An experimental comparison of a conventional TV lesson with a programmed TV lesson requiring active student response. *Report No. 2. Studies in televised instruction: The use of student response to improve televised instruction.* Pittsburgh, PA: American Institutes for Research.

Gropper, G. L., & Lumsdaine, A. A. (1961b, March). An experimental evaluation of the contribution of sequencing, pre-testing, and active student response to the effectiveness of "programmed" TV instruction. *Report No. 3. Studies in televised instruction: The use of student response to improve televised instruction.* Pittsburgh, PA: American Institutes for Research.

Gropper, G. L., & Lumsdaine, A. A. (1961c, March). Issues in programming instructional materials for television presentation. *Report No. 5. Studies in televised instruction: The use of student response to improve televised instruction.* Pittsburgh, PA: American Institutes for Research.

Gropper, G. L., & Lumsdaine, A. A. (1961d, March). An overview. *Report No. 7. Studies in televised instruction: The use of student response to improve televised instruction.* Pittsburgh, PA: American Institutes for Research.

Gropper, G. L., Lumsdaine, A. A., & Shipman, V. (1961, March). *Improvement of televised instruction based on student responses to achievement tests, Report No. 1. Studies in televised instruction: The use of student response to improve televised instruction.* Pittsburgh, PA: American Institutes for Research.

Gropper, G. L., & Ross, P. A. (1987). Instructional design. In R. L. Craig (Ed.). *Training and development handbook* (3rd ed.). New York: McGraw-Hill.

Guskey, T. R. (1985). *Implementing mastery learning.* Belmont, CA: Wadsworth.

Gustafson, K. L., & Tillman, M. H. (1991). Introduction. In L. J. Briggs, K. L. Gustafson & M. H. Tillman (Eds.), *Instructional design.* Englewood Cliffs, NJ: Educational Technology.

Halff, H. M. (1988). Curriculum and instruction in automated tutors. In M. C. Polson & J. J. Richardson (Eds.), *The foundations of intelligent tutoring systems* (pp. 79–108). Hillsdale, NJ: Erlbaum.

Hamilton, R. S., & Heinkel, O. A. (1967). *English A: An evaluation of programmed instruction.* San Diego, CA: San Diego City College.

Hebb, D. O. (1949). *Organization of behavior.* New York: Wiley.

Heinich, R. (1970). *Technology and the management of instruction* (Association for Educational Communication and Technology Monograph No. 4). Washington, DC: Association for Educational Communications and Technology.

Herrnstein, R. J., & Boring, E. G. (1965). *A source book in the history of psychology.* Cambridge, MA: Harvard University Press.

Hess, J. H. (1971, October). *Keller Plan Instruction: Implementation problems.* Keller Plan conference, Massachusetts Institute of Technology, Cambridge, MA.

Hoban, C. F. (1946). *Movies that teach.* New York: Dryden.

Hoban, C. F. (1960). The usable residue of educational film research. *New teaching aids for the American classroom* (pp. 95–115). Palo Alto, CA: Stanford University. The Institute for Communication Research.

Hoban, C. F., & Van Ormer, E. B. (1950). *Instructional film research 1918–1950.* (Technical Report SDC 269-7-19). Port Washington, NY: Special Devices Center, Office of Naval Research.

Holland, J. G. (1960, September). *Design and use of a teaching-machine program.* Paper presented at the American Psychological Association, Chicago, IL.

Holland, J. G. (1961). New directions in teaching-machine research. In J. E. Coulson (Ed.), *Programmed learning and computer-based instruction.* New York: Wiley.

Holland, J. G. (1965). Research on programmed variables. In R. Glaser (Ed.), *Teaching machines and programmed learning, II* (pp. 66–117). Washington, DC: Association for Educational Communications and Technology.

Holland, J., & Skinner, B. V. (1961). *Analysis of behavior: A program of self-instruction.* New York: McGraw-Hill.

Holmberg, B. (1977). *Distance education: A survey and bibliography.* London: Kogan Page.

Holzschuh, R., & Dobbs, D. (1966). *Rate correct vs. percentage correct.*

Educational Research Technical Report. Kansas City, KS: University of Kansas Medical Center.

Homme, L. E. (1957). The rationale of teaching by Skinner's machines. In A. A. Lumsdaine & R. Glaser (Eds.), *Teaching machines and programmed learning: A source book* (pp. 133-136). Washington, DC: National Education Association.

Homme, L. E., & Glaser, R. (1960). Problems in programming verbal learning sequences. In A. A. Lumsdaine & R. Glaser (Ed.), *Teaching machines and programmed learning: A source book* (pp. 486-496). Washington, DC: National Education Association.

Hough, J. B. (1962, June-July). An analysis of the efficiency and effectiveness of selected aspects of machine instruction. *Journal of Educational Research, 55,* 467-71.

Hough, J. B., & Revsin, B. (1963). Programmed instruction at the college level: A study of several factors influencing learning. *Phi Delta Kappan, 44,* 286-291.

Hull, C. L. (1943). *Principles of behavior.* New York: Appleton-Century-Crofts.

Hymel, G. (1987, April). *A literature trend analysis in mastery learning.* Paper presented at the Annual Meeting of the American Educational Research Association, Washington, DC.

Irion, A. L., & Briggs, L. J. (1957). *Learning task and mode of operation variables in use of the Subject Matter Trainer,* (Tech. Rep. AFPTRC-TR-57-8). Lowry Air Force Base, Co.: Air Force Personnel and Training Center.

James, W. (1904). Does consciousness exist? *Journal of Philosophy, 1,* 477-491.

Janeczko, R. J. (1971). *The effect of instructional objectives and general objectives on student self-evaluation and psychomotor performance in power mechanics.* Unpublished doctoral dissertation, University of Missouri-Columbia.

Jaspen, N. (1948). Especially designed motion pictures: I. Assembly of the 40mm breechblock. *Progress Report No. 9.* State College, PA: Pennsylvania State College Instructional Film Research Program.

Jaspen, N. (1950). Effects on training of experimental film variables, Study II. Verbalization, "How it works, Nomenclature Audience Participation and Succinct Treatment." *Progress Report No., 14-15-16.* State College, PA: Pennsylvania State College Instructional Film Research Program.

Jensen, B. T. (1949). An independent-study laboratory using self-scoring tests. *Journal of Educational Research, 43,* 134-37.

Johnson, K. R., & Layng, T. V. J. (1992). Breaking the structuralist barrier; literacy and numeracy with fluency. *American Psychologist, 47*(11), 1475-1490.

Johnson, K. R., & Layng, T. V. J. (1994). The Morningside model of generative instruction. In R. Gardner, D. M. Sainato, J. O. Cooper, T. E. Heron, W. L. Heward, J. Eshleman, & T. A. Grossi (Eds.), *Behavior analysis in education: Focus on measurably superior instruction* (pp. 173-197). Pacific Grove, CA: Brooks/Cole.

Johnson, N. J. (1971). *Acceleration of inner-city elementary school pupils' reading performance.* Unpublished doctoral dissertation, University of Kansas, Lawrence.

John-Steiner, V., & Mahn, H. (1996). Sociocultural approaches to learning and development: A Vygotskian framework. *Educational Psychologist, 31*(3/4), 191-206.

Jones, H. L., & Sawyer, M. O. (1949). A new evaluation instrument. *Journal of Educational Research, 42,* 381-85.

Kaess, W., & Zeaman, D. (1960, July). Positive and negative knowledge of results on a Pressey-type punchboard. *Journal of Experimental Psychology, 60,* 12-17.

Kalish, D. M. (1972). *The effects on achievement of using behavioral objectives with fifth grade students.* Unpublished doctoral dissertation, The Ohio State University.

Kanner, J. H. (1960). The development and role of teaching aids in the armed forces. In *New teaching aids for the American classroom.* Stanford, CA: The Institute for Communication Research.

Kanner, J. H., & Sulzer, R. L. (1955). *Overt and covert rehearsal of 50% versus 100% of the material in filmed learning.* Chanute AFB, IL: TARL, AFPTRC.

Karis, C., Kent, A., & Gilbert, J. E. (1970). *The interactive effect of responses per frame, response mode, and response confirmation on intraframe S-4 association strength: Final report.* Boston, MA: Northeastern University.

Keegan, D. (1986). *The foundations of distance education.* London: Croom Helm.

Keller, F. S. (1968). Goodbye teacher… *Journal of Applied Behavior Analysis, 1,* 79-89.

Keller, F. S., & Sherman, J. G. (1974). *The Keller Plan handbook.* Menlo Park, CA: Benjamin.

Kendler, H. H. (1971). Stimulus-response psychology and audiovisual education. In W. E. Murheny (Ed.), *Audiovisual Process in Education.* Washington, DC: Department of Audiovisual Instruction.

Kendler, T. S., Cook, J. O., & Kendler, H. H. (1953). *An investigation of the interacting effects of repetition and audience participation on learning from films.* Paper presented at the annual meeting of the American Psychological Association, Cleveland, OH.

Kendler, T. S., Kendler, H. H., & Cook. J. O. (1954). Effect of opportunity and instructions to practice during a training film on initial recall and retention. *Staff Research Memorandum,* Chanute AFB, IL: USAF Training Aids Research Laboratory.

Kibler, R. J., Cegala, D. J., Miles, D. T., & Barker, L. L. (1974). *Objectives for instruction and evaluation.* Boston, MA: Allyn & Bacon.

Kimble, G. A., & Wulff, J. J. (1953). Response guidance as a factor in the value of audience participation in training film instruction. *Memo Report No. 36,* Human Factors Operations Research Laboratory.

Kimble, G. A., & Wulff, J. J. (1954). The teaching effectiveness of instruction in reading a scale as a function of the relative amounts of problem solving practice and demonstration examples used in training. *Staff Research Memorandum,* USAF Training Aids Research Laboratory.

Klaus, D. (1965). An analysis of programming techniques. In R. Glaser (Ed.), *Teaching machines and programmed learning, II.* Washington, DC: Association for Educational Communications and Technology.

Koenig, C. H., & Kunzelmann, H. P. (1981). *Classroom learning screening.* Columbus, OH: Merrill.

Kulik, C. C., Kulik, J. A., & Bangert-Downs, R. L. (1990). Effectiveness of mastery learning programs: A meta-analysis. *Review of Educational Research, 60*(2), 269-299.

Kulik, J. A., Kulik, C. C., & Cohen, P. A. (1979). A meta-analysis of outcome studies of Keller's personalized system of instruction. *American Psychologist, 34*(4), 307-318.

Kumata, H. (1961). *History and progress of instructional television research in the U.S.* Report presented at the International Seminar on Instructional Television, Lafayette, IN.

Lathrop, C. W., Jr. (1949). Contributions of film instructions to learning from instructional films. *Progress Report No. 13.* State College, PA: Pennsylvania State College Instructional Film Research Program.

Lave, J. (1988). *Cognition in practice.* Boston, MA: Cambridge.

Lave, J., & Wenger, E. (1991). *Situated learning: Legitimate peripheral participation.* Cambridge, UK: Cambridge University Press.

Lawrence, R. M. (1970). *The effects of three types of organizing devices on academic achievement.* Unpublished doctoral dissertation, University of Maryland.

Layng, T. V. J. (1991). A selectionist approach to verbal behavior: Sources of variation. In L. J. Hayes & P. N. Chase (Eds.), *Dialogues on verbal behavior* (pp. 146-150). Reno, NV: Context Press.

Liddell, H. S. (1926). A laboratory for the study of conditioned motor reflexes. *American Journal of Psychology, 37,* 418-419.

Lindsley, O. R. (1956). Operant conditioning methods applied to research in chronic schizophrenia. *Psychiatric Research Reports, 5,* 118-139.

Lindsley, O. R. (1964). Direct measurement and prosthesis of retarded behavior. *Journal of Education, 147,* 62-81.

Lindsley, O. R. (1972). From Skinner to Precision Teaching. In J. B. Jordan and L. S. Robbins (Eds.), *Let's try doing something else kind of thing* (pp. 1-12). Arlington, VA: Council on Exceptional Children.

Lindsley, O. R. (1990a). Our aims, discoveries, failures, and problems. *Journals of Precision Teaching, 7*(7), 7-17.

Lindsley, O. R. (1990b). Precision Teaching: By children for teachers. *Teaching Exceptional Children, 22*(3), 10-15.

Lindsley, O. R. (1991a). Precision teaching's unique legacy from B. F. Skinner. *The Journal of Behavioral Education, 2,* 253-266.

Lindsley, O. R. (1991b). From technical jargon to plain English for application. *The Journal of Applied Behavior Analysis, 24,* 449-458.

Lindsley, O. R., & Skinner, B. F. (1954). A method for the experimental analysis of the behavior of psychotic patients. *American Psychologist, 9,* 419-420.

Little, J. K. (1934). Results of use of machines for testing and for drill upon learning in educational psychology. *Journal of Experimental Education, 3,* 59-65.

Liu, H. Q. (2001). *Development of an authentic, web-delivered course using PSI.* Unpublished manuscript, Virginia Tech.

Lloyd, K. E. (1971). Contingency management in university courses. *Educational Technology, 11*(4), 18-23.

Loh, E. L. (1972). *The effect of behavioral objectives on measures of learning and forgetting on high school algebra.* Unpublished doctoral dissertation, University of Maryland.

Long, A. L. (1946). *The influence of color on acquisition and retention as evidenced by the use of sound films.* Unpublished doctoral dissertation, University of Colorado.

Lovett, H. T. (1971). *The effects of various degrees of knowledge of instructional objectives and two levels of feedback from formative evaluation on student achievement.* Unpublished doctoral dissertation, University of Georgia.

Lumsdaine, A. A. (Ed.). (1961). *Student responses in programmed instruction.* Washington, DC: National Academy of Sciences, National Research Council.

Lumsdaine, A. A. (1962). Instruction materials and devices. In R. Glaser (Ed.), *Training research and education* (p.251). Pittsburgh, PA: University of Pittsburgh Press (as cited in R. Glaser (Ed.), *Teaching machines and programmed learning, II* (Holland, J. G. (1965). Research on programmed variables (pp. 66-117)). Washington, DC: Association for Educational Communications and Technology.

Lumsdaine, A. A. (1965). Assessing the effectiveness of instructional programs. In R. Glaser (Ed.), *Teaching machines and programmed learning, II* (pp. 267-320). Washington, DC: Association for Educational Communications and Technology.

Lumsdaine, A. A., & Glaser, R. (Eds.). (1960). *Teaching machines and programmed learning.* Washington, DC. Department of Audiovisual Instruction, National Education Association.

Lumsdaine, A. A. & Sulzer, R. L. (1951). The influence of simple animation techniques on the value of a training film. *Memo Report No. 24,* Human Resources Research Laboratory.

Mager, R. F. (1962). *Preparing instructional objectives.* San Francisco: Fearon.

Mager, R. F. (1984). *Goal analysis* (2nd ed.). Belmont, CA: Lake.

Mager, R. F., & McCann, J. (1961). *Learner-controlled instruction.* Palo Alto, CA: Varian.

Malcolm, N. (1954). Wittgenstein's Philosophical Investigation. *Philosophical Review* LXIII.

Malone, J. C. (1990). *Theories of learning: A historical approach.* Belmont, CA: Wadsworth.

Markle, S. M. (1964). *Good frames and bad: A grammar of frame writing* (1st ed.). New York: Wiley.

Markle, S. M. (1969). *Good frames and bad: A grammar of frame writing* (2nd ed.). New York: Wiley.

Markle, S. M. (1991). *Designs for instructional designers.* Champaign, IL: Stipes.

Markle, S. M., & Droege, S. A. (1980). Solving the problem of problem solving domains. *National Society for Programmed Instruction Journal, 19,* 30-33.

Marsh, L. A., & Pierce-Jones, J. (1968). *Programmed instruction as an adjunct to a course in adolescent psychology.* Paper presented at the annual meeting of the American Educational Research Association, Chicago, IL.

Mateer, F. (1918). *Child behavior: A critical and experimental study of young children by the method of conditioned reflexes.* Boston: Badger.

May, M. A., & Lumsdaine, A. A. (1958). *Learning from films.* New Haven, CT: Yale University Press.

Mayer, R. E., & Wittrock, M. C. (1996). Problem solving and transfer. In D. C. Berliner & R. C. Calfee (Eds.), *Handbook of educational psychology* (pp. 47-62). New York: Simon & Schuster Macmillan.

McClelland, J. L., & Rumelhart, D. E. (1986). *Parallel distributed processing: Explorations into the microstructure of cognition: Vol. 2. Psychological and biological models.* Cambridge, MA: Bradford Books/MIT Press.

McDonald, F. J., & Allen, D. (1962, June–July). An investigation of presentation response and correction factors in programmed instruction. *Journal of Educational Research, 55,* 502-507.

McGuire, W. J. (1953a). *Length of film as a factor influencing training effectiveness.* Unpublished manuscript.

McGuire, W. J. (1953b). *Serial position and proximity to reward as factors influencing teaching effectiveness of a training film.* Unpublished manuscript.

McGuire, W. J. (1954). *The relative efficacy of overt and covert trainee participation with different speeds of instruction.* Unpublished manuscript.

McIssac, M. S., & Gunawardena, C. N. (1996). Distance education. In D. H. Jonassen (Ed.), *Handbook of research on educational communications and technology* (pp. 403-437). New York: Simon & Schuster Macmillan.

McKeachie, W. J. (1967). *New developments in teaching: New dimensions in higher education. No. 16.* Durham, NC: Duke University.

McLaughlin, T. F. (1991). Use of a personalized system of instruction with and without a same-day retake contingency of spelling performance of behaviorally disordered children. *Behavioral Disorders, 16,* 127-132.

McNeil, J. D. (1967). Concomitants of using behavioral objectives in the assessment of teacher effectiveness. *Journal of Experimental Education, 36,* 69-74.

Metzler, M., Eddleman, K., Treanor, L. & Cregger, R. (1989, February). *Teaching tennis with an instructional system design.* Paper presented at the annual meeting of the Eastern Educational Research Association, Savannah, GA.

Meyer, S. R. (1960). Report on the initial test of a junior high school vocabulary program. In A. A. Lumsdaine & R. Glaser (Eds.), *Teaching Machines and Programmed Learning* (pp. 229-46). Washington, DC: National Education Association.

Michael, D. N. (1951). Some factors influencing the effects of audience participation on learning form a factual film. *Memo Report 13 A* (revised). Human Resources Research Laboratory.

Michael, D. N., & Maccoby, N. (1954). A further study of the use of 'Audience Participating' procedures in film instruction. *Staff Research Memorandum*, Chanute AFB, IL: AFPTRC, Project 504-028-0003.

Mill, J. (1967). *Analysis of the phenomena of the human mind* (2nd ed.). New York: Augustus Kelly. (Original work published 1829).

Miller, J., & Klier, S. (1953a). *A further investigation of the effects of massed and spaced review techniques*. Unpublished manuscript.

Miller, J., & Klier, S. (1953b). *The effect on active rehearsal types of review of massed and spaced review techniques*. Unpublished manuscript.

Miller, J., & Klier, S. (1954). *The effect of interpolated quizzes on learning audio-visual material*. Unpublished manuscript.

Miller, J., & Levine, S. (1952). A study of the effects of different types of review and of 'structuring' subtitles on the amount learned from a training film. *Memo Report No. 17, Human Resources Research Laboratory*.

Miller, J., Levine, S., & Sternberger, J. (1952a). *The effects of different kinds of review and of subtitling on learning from a training film* (a replicative study). Unpublished manuscript.

Miller, J., Levine, S., & Sternberger, J. (1952b). *Extension to a new subject matter of the findings on the effects of different kinds of review on learning from a training film*. Unpublished manuscript.

Miller, L. K., Weaver, F. H., & Semb, G. (1954). A procedure for maintaining student progress in a personalized university course. *Journal of Applied Behavior Analysis, 7*, 87-91.

Moore, J. (1980). On behaviorism and private events. *The Psychological Record, 30*(4), 459-475.

Moore, J. (1984). On behaviorism, knowledge, and causal explanation. *The Psychological Record, 34*(1), 73-97.

Moore, M. G., & Kearsley, G. (1996). *Distance education: A systems view*. New York: Wadsworth.

Moore, J. W., & Smith, W. I. (1961, December). Knowledge of results of self-teaching spelling. *Psychological Reports, 9*, 717-26.

Moore, J. W., & Smith, W. I. (1962). A comparison of several types of "immediate reinforcement." In W. Smith & J. Moore (Eds.). *Programmed learning* (pp. 192-201). New York: D. VanNostrand.

Morris, E. K., Surber, C. F., & Bijou, S. W. (1978). Self-pacing versus instructor-pacing: Achievement, evaluations, and retention. *Journal of Educational Psychology, 70*, 224-230.

Needham, W. C. (1978). *Cerebral logic*. Springfield, IL: Thomas.

Neisser, U. (1967). *Cognitive psychology*. New York: Appleton-Century-Crofts.

Neisser, U. (1976). *Cognition and reality*. San Francisco: Freeman.

Neu, D. M. (1950). The effect of attention-gaining devices on film-mediated learning. *Progress Report No. 14-15, 16: Instructional Film Research Program*. State College, PA: Pennsylvania State College.

Neufeld, K. A., & Lindsley, O. R. (1980). Charting to compare children's learning at four different reading performance levels. *Journal of Precision Teaching, 1*(1), 9-17.

Norford, C. A. (1949). Contributions of film summaries to learning from instructional films. In *Progress Report No. 13*. State College, PA: Pennsylvania State College Instructional Film Research Program.

Olsen, C. R. (1972). *A comparative study of the effect of behavioral objectives on class performance and retention in physical science*. Unpublished doctoral dissertation, University of Maryland.

O'Neill, G. W., Johnston, J. M., Walters, W. M., & Rashed, J. A. (1975). The effects of quantity of assigned material on college student academic performance and study behavior. Springfield, IL: Thomas.

Patton, C. T. (1972). *The effect of student knowledge of behavioral objectives on achievement and attitudes in educational psychology*. Unpublished doctoral dissertation, University of Northern Colorado.

Pennypacker, H. S. (1994). A selectionist view of the future of behavior analysis in education. In R. Gardner, D. M. Sainato, J. O. Cooper, T. E. Heron, W. L. Heward, J. Eshleman, & T. A. Grossi (Eds.), *Behavior analysis in education: Focus on measurably superior instruction* (pp. 11-18). Pacific Grove, CA: Brooks/Cole.

Peterman, J. N., & Bouscaren, N. (1954). A study of introductory and summarizing sequences in training film instruction. *Staff Research Memorandum*, Chanute AFB, IL: Training Aids Research Laboratory.

Peterson, J. C. (1931). The value of guidance in reading for information. *Transactions of the Kansas Academy of Science, 34*, 291-96.

Piatt, G. R. (1969). *An investigation of the effect of the training of teachers in defining, writing, and implementing educational behavioral objectives has on learner outcomes for students enrolled in a seventh grade mathematics program in the public schools*. Unpublished doctoral dissertation, Lehigh University.

Popham, W. J., & Baker, E. L. (1970). *Establishing instructional goals*. Englewood Cliffs, NJ: Prentice-Hall.

Porter, D. (1957). A critical review of a portion of the literature on teaching devices. *Harvard Educational Review, 27*, 126-47.

Porter, D. (1958). Teaching machines. *Harvard Graduate School of Education Association Bulletin, 3*, 1-15, 206-214.

Potts, L., Eshleman, J. W., & Cooper, J. O. (1993). Ogden R. Lindsley and the historical development of Precision Teaching. *The Behavioral Analyst, 16*(2), 177-189.

Pressey, S. L. (1926). A simple apparatus which gives tests and scores—and teaches. *School and Society, 23*, 35-41.

Pressey, S. L. (1932). A third and fourth contribution toward the coming "industrial revolution" in education. *School and Society, 36*, 47-51.

Pressey, S. L. (1950). Development and appraisal of devices providing immediate automatic scoring of objective tests and concomitant self-instruction. *Journal of Psychology, 29* (417-447) 69-88.

Pressey, S. L. (1960). Some perspectives and major problems regarding teaching machines. In A. A. Lumsdaine & R. Glaser (Eds.), *Teaching machines and programmed learning: A source book* (pp. 497-505). Washington, DC: National Education Association.

Pressey, S. L. (1963). Teaching machine (and learning theory) crisis. *Journal of Applied Psychology, 47*, 1-6.

Race, P. (1989). *The open learning handbook: Selecting, designing, and supporting open learning materials*. New York: Nichols.

Rachlin, H. (1991). *Introduction to modern behaviorism* (3rd ed.). New York: Freeman.

Reigeluth, C. M. (1983). *Instructional-design theories and models*. Hillsdale, NJ: Erlbaum.

Reiser, R. A. (1980). The interaction between locus of control and three pacing procedures in a personalized system of instruction course. *Educational Communication and Technology Journal, 28*, 194-202.

Reiser, R. A. (1984). Interaction between locus of control and three pacing procedures in a personalized system of instruction course. *Educational Communication and Technology Journal, 28*(3), 194-202.

Reiser, R. A. (1987). Instructional technology: A history. In R. M. Gagné (Ed.), *Instructional technology: Foundations*. Hillsdale, NJ: Erlbaum.

Reiser, R. A., & Sullivan, H. J. (1977). Effects of self-pacing and instructor-pacing in a PSI course. *The Journal of Educational Research, 71*, 8-12.

Resnick, L. B. (1963). Programmed instruction and the teaching of complex intellectual skills; problems and prospects. *Harvard Education Review, 33*, 439-471.

Resnick, L. (1988). Learning in school and out. *Educational Researcher, 16(9),* 13-20.

Rigney, J. W., & Fry, E. B. (1961). Current teaching-machine programs and programming techniques. *Audio-Visual Communication Review, 9(3).*

Robin, A., & Graham, M. Q. (1974). Academic responses and attitudes engendered by teacher versus student pacing in a personalized instruction course. In R. S. Ruskin & S. F. Bono (Eds.), *Personalized instruction in higher education: Proceedings of the first national conference.* Washington, DC: Georgetown University, Center for Personalized Instruction.

Roe, A., Massey, M., Weltman, G., & Leeds, D. (1960). *Automated teaching methods using linear programs.* No. 60-105. Los Angeles: Automated Learning Research Project, University of California.

Roe, A., Massey, M., Weltman, G., & Leeds, D. (1962, June-July). A comparison of branching methods for programmed learning. *Journal of Educational Research, 55,* 407-16.

Rogoff, B., & Lave, J. (Eds.). (1984). *Everyday cognition: Its development in social context.* Cambridge, MA: Harvard University Press.

Roshal, S. M. (1949). Effects of learner representation in film-mediated perceptual-motor learning (*Technical Report SDC 269-7-5*). State College, PA: Pennsylvania State College Instructional Film Research Program.

Ross, S. M., Smith, L., & Slavin, R. E. (1997, April). Improving the academic success of disadvantaged children: An examination of Success for All. *Psychology in the Schools, 34,* 171-180.

Rothkopf, E. Z. (1960). Some research problems in the design of materials and devices for automated teaching. In A. A. Lumsdaine & R. Glaser (Eds.), *Teaching machines and programmed learning: A source book* (pp. 318-328). Washington, DC: National Education Association.

Rothkopf, E. Z. (1962). Criteria for the acceptance of self-instructional programs. *Improving the efficiency and quality of learning.* Washington, DC: American Council on Education.

Rowe, G.W., & Gregor, P. (1999). A computer-based learning system for teaching computing: Implementation and evaluation. *Computers and Education, 33,* 65-76.

Rumelhart, D. E., & McClelland, J. L. (1986). *Parallel distributed processing: Explorations into the microstructure of cognition: Vol. 1. Foundations.* Cambridge, MA: Bradford Books/MIT Press.

Ryan, B. A. (1974). *PSI: Keller's personalized system of instruction: An appraisal.* Paper presented at the American Psychological Association, Washington, DC.

Ryan, T. A., & Hochberg, C. B. (1954). *Speed of perception as a function of mode of presentation.* Unpublished manuscript, Cornell University.

Saettler, P. (1968). *A history of instructional technology.* New York: McGraw-Hill.

Schnaitter, R. (1987). Knowledge as action: The epistemology of radical behaviorism. In S. Modgil & C. Modgil (Eds.). *B. F. Skinner: Consensus and controversy.* New York: Falmer Press.

Schramm, W. (1962). What we know about learning from instructional television. In L. Asheim et al., (Eds.), *Educational television: The next ten years* (pp. 52-76). Stanford, CA: The Institute for Communication Research, Stanford University.

Semb, G., Conyers, D., Spencer, R., & Sanchez-Sosa, J. J. (1975). An experimental comparison of four pacing contingencies in a personalize instruction course. In J. M. Johnston (Ed.), *Behavior research and technology in higher education.* Springfield, IL: Thomas.

Severin, D. G. (1960). Appraisal of special tests and procedures used with self-scoring instructional testing devices. In A. A. Lumsdaine & R. Glaser (Eds.), *Teaching machines and programmed learning: A source book.* (pp. 678-680). Washington, DC: National Education Association.

Sheppard, W. C., & MacDermot, H. G. (1970). Design and evaluation of a programmed course in introductory psychology. *Journal of Applied Behavior Analysis, 3,* 5-11.

Sherman, J. G. (1972, March). *PSI: Some notable failures.* Paper presented at the Keller Method Workshop Conference, Rice University, Houston, TX.

Sherman, J. G. (1992). Reflections on PSI: Good news and bad. *Journal of Applied Behavior Analysis, 25(1),* 59-64.

Siedentop, D., Mand, C., & Taggart, A. (1986). *Physical education: Teaching and curriculum strategies for grades 5-12.* Palo Alto, CA: Mayfield.

Silberman, H. F., Melaragno, J. E., Coulson, J. E., & Estavan, D. (1961). Fixed sequence vs. branching auto-instructional methods. *Journal of Educational Psychology, 52,* 166-72.

Silvern, L. C. (1964). *Designing instructional systems.* Los Angeles: Education and Training Consultants.

Skinner, B. F. (1938). *The behavior of organisms.* New York: Appleton.

Skinner, B. F. (1945). The operational analysis of psychological terms. *Psychological Review, 52,* 270-277, 291-294.

Skinner, B. F. (1953a). *Science and human behavior.* New York: Macmillan.

Skinner, B. F. (1953b). Some contributions of an experimental analysis of behavior to psychology as a whole. *American Psychologist, 8,* 69-78.

Skinner, B. F. (1954). The science of learning and the art of teaching. *Harvard Educational Review, 24(86),* 99-113.

Skinner, B. F. (1956). A case history in the scientific method. *American Psychologist, 57,* 221-233.

Skinner, B. F. (1957). *Verbal behavior.* Englewood Cliffs, NJ: Prentice-Hall.

Skinner, B. F. (1958). Teaching machines. *Science, 128* (969-77), 137-58.

Skinner, B. F. (1961, November). Teaching machines. *Scientific American, 205,* 91-102.

Skinner, B. F. (1964). Behaviorism at fifty. In T. W. Wann (Ed.), *Behaviorism and phenomenology.* Chicago: University of Chicago Press.

Skinner, B. F. (1968). *The technology of teaching.* Englewood Cliffs, NJ: Prentice-Hall.

Skinner, B. F. (1969). *Contingencies of reinforcement: A theoretical analysis.* New York: Appleton-Century-Crofts.

Skinner, B. F. (1971). *Beyond freedom and dignity.* New York: Knopf.

Skinner, B. F. (1974). *About behaviorism.* New York: Knopf.

Skinner, B. F. (1978). Why I am not a cognitive psychologist. In B. F. Skinner (Ed.), *Reflections on behaviorism and society* (pp. 97-112). Englewood Cliffs, NJ: Prentice-Hall.

Skinner, B. F. (1981). Selection by consequences. *Science, 213,* 501-504.

Skinner, B. F. (1987a). The evolution of behavior. In B. F. Skinner (Ed.), *Upon further reflection* (pp. 65-74). Englewood Cliffs, NJ: Prentice-Hall.

Skinner, B. F. (1987b). The evolution of verbal behavior. In B. F. Skinner (Ed.), *Upon further reflection* (pp. 75-92), Englewood Cliffs, NJ: Prentice-Hall.

Skinner, B. F. (1987c). Cognitive science and behaviorism. In B. F. Skinner (Ed.), *Upon further reflection* (pp. 93-111), Englewood Cliffs, NJ: Prentice-Hall.

Skinner, B. F. (1989). *Recent issues in the analysis of behavior.* Columbus: OH. Merrill.

Skinner, B. F. (1990). Can psychology be a science of mind? *American Psychologist, 45,* 1206-1210.

Skinner, B. F., & Holland, J. G. (1960). The use of teaching machines in college instruction. In A. A. Lumsdaine & R. Glaser (Eds.), *Teaching machines and programmed learning: A source book* (159-172). Washington, DC: National Education Association.

Slavin, R. E., & Madden, N. A. (2000, April). Research on achievement outcomes of Success for All: A summary and response to critics. *Phi Delta Kappan, 82* (1), 38-40, 59-66.

Smith, D. E. P. (1959). Speculations: characteristics of successful programs and programmers. In E. Galanter (Ed.), *Automatic teaching: The state of the art* (pp. 91-102). New York: Wiley.

Smith, J. M. (1970). *Relations among behavioral objectives, time of acquisition, and retention*. Unpublished doctoral dissertation, University of Maryland.

Smith, K. U., & Smith, M. F. (1966). *Cybernetic principles of learning and educational design*. New York: Holt, Rinehart & Winston.

Smith, P. L., & Ragan, T. J. (1993). *Instructional design*. New York: Macmillan.

Spence, K. W. (1948). The postulates and methods of "Behaviorism." *Psychological Review, 55,* 67-78.

Stedman, C. H. (1970). *The effects of prior knowledge of behavioral objective son cognitive learning outcomes using programmed materials in genetics*. Unpublished doctoral dissertation, Indiana University.

Stephens, A. L. (1960). Certain special factors involved in the law of effect. In A. A. Lumsdaine & R. Glaser (Eds.), *Teaching machines and programmed learning: A source book* (pp. 89-93). Washington, DC: National Education Association.

Stevens, S. S. (1939). Psychology and the science of science. *Psychological Bulletin, 37,* 221-263.

Stevens, S. S. (1951). Methods, measurements, and psychophysics. In S. S. Stevens (Ed.), *Handbook of Experimental Psychology* (pp. 1-49). New York: Wiley.

Suchman, L. A. (1987). *Plans and Situated Actions: The Problem of Human-Machine Communication*. Cambridge, UK: Cambridge University Press.

Sulzer, R. L., & Lumsdaine, A. A. (1952). The value of using multiple examples in training film instruction. *Memo Report No. 25,* Human Resources Research Laboratory.

Suppes, P., & Ginsberg, R. (1962, April). Application of a stimulus sampling model to children's concept formation with and without overt correction response. *Journal of Experimental Psychology, 63,* 330-36.

Sutterer, J. E., & Holloway, R. E. (1975). An analysis of student behavior in a self-paced introductory psychology course. In J. M. Johnson (Ed.), *Behavior research and technology in higher education*. Springfield, IL: Thomas.

Szydlik, P. P. (1974). *Results of a one-semester, self-paced physics course at the State University College, Plattsburgh, New York*. Menlo Park, CA: W. A. Benjamin.

Tessmer, M. (1990). Environmental analysis: A neglected stage of instructional design. *Educational Technology Research and Development, 38*(1), 55-64.

Tharp, R. G., & Gallimore, R. (1988). *Rousing minds to life: Teaching, learning, and schooling in social context*. Cambridge, UK: Cambridge University Press.

Thomas, P., Carswell, L., Price, B., & Petre, M. (1998). A holistic approach to supporting distance learning using the Internet: Transformation, not translation. *British Journal of Educational Technology, 29*(2), 149-161.

Thorndike, E. L. (1898). Animal intelligence: An experimental study of the associative processes in animals. *Psychological Review Monograph, 2* (Suppl. 8).

Thorndike, E. L. (1913). The psychology of learning. *Educational psychology* (Vol. 2). New York: Teachers College Press.

Thorndike, E. L. (1924). Mental discipline in high school studies. *Journal of Educational Psychology, 15,* 1-22, 83-98.

Thorndike, E. L., & Woodworth, R. S. (1901). The influence of improvement in one mental function upon the efficiency of other functions. *Psychological Review, 8,* 247-261.

Tiemann, P. W., & Markle, S. M. (1990). *Analyzing instructional content: A guide to instruction and evaluation*. Champaign, IL: Stipes.

Torkelson, G. M. (1977). AVCR-One quarter century. Evolution of theory and research. *Audio-Visual Communication Review, 25*(4), 317-358.

Tosti, D. T., & Ball, J. R. (1969). A behavioral approach to instructional design and media selection. *Audio-Visual Communication Review, 17*(1), 5-23.

Twitmeyer, E. B. (1902). *A study of the knee-jerk*. Unpublished doctoral dissertation, University of Pennsylvania.

Tyler, R. W. (1934). *Constructing achievement tests*. Columbus: The Ohio State University.

Tyler, R. W. (1949). *Basic principles of curriculum and instruction*. Chicago: University of Chicago Press.

Unwin, D. (1966). An organizational explanation for certain retention and correlation factors in a comparison between two teaching methods. *Programmed Learning and Educational Technology, 3,* 35-39.

Valverde, H. & Morgan, R. L. (1970). Influence on student achievement of redundancy in self-instructional materials. *Programmed Learning and Educational Technology, 7,* 194-199.

Vargas, E. A. (1993). A science of our own making. *Behaviorology, 1*(1), 13-22.

Vargas, J. S. (1977). *Behavioral psychology for teachers*. New York: Harper & Row.

Von Helmholtz, H. (1866). *Handbook of physiological optics* (J. P. C. Southhall, Trans.). Rochester, NY: Optical Society of America.

Vygotsky, L. S. (1978). *Mind in society: The development of higher psychological processes*. Edited by M. Cole, V. John-Steiner, S. Scribner, & E. Souberman. Cambridge, MA: Harvard University Press.

Warden, C. J., Field, H. A., & Koch, A. M. (1940). Imitative behavior in cebus and rhesus monkeys. *Journal of Genetic Psychology, 56,* 311-322.

Warden, C. J., & Jackson, T. A. (1935). Imitative behavior in the rhesus monkey. *Journal of Genetic Psychology, 46,* 103-125.

Watkins, C. L. (1988). Project Follow Through: A story of the identification and neglect of effective instruction. *Youth Policy, 10*(7), 7-11.

Watson, J. B. (1908). Imitation in monkeys. *Psychological Bulletin, 5,* 169-178l

Watson, J. B. (1913). Psychology as the behaviorist views it. *Psychological Review, 20,* 158-177.

Watson, J. B. (1919). *Psychology from the standpoint of a behaviorist*. Philadelphia: Lippincott.

Watson, J. B. (1924). *Behaviorism*. New York: Norton.

Watson, J. B., & Rayner, R. (1920). Conditioned emotional reactions. *Journal of Experimental Psychology, 3,* 1-14.

Webb, A. B. (1971). *Effects of the use of behavioral objectives and criterion evaluation on classroom progress of adolescents*. Unpublished doctoral dissertation, University of Tennessee.

Weinberg, H. (1970). *Effects of presenting varying specificity of course objectives to students on learning motor skills and associated cognitive material*. Unpublished doctoral dissertation, Temple University.

Weiss, W. (1954). Effects on learning and performance of controlled environmental stimulation. *Staff Research Memorandum,* Chanute AFB, IL: Training Aids Research Laboratory.

Weiss, W., & Fine, B. J. (1955). *Stimulus familiarization as a factor in ideational learning*. Unpublished manuscript, Boston University.

West, R. P., Young, R., & Spooner, F. (1990). Precision Teaching: An introduction. *Teaching Exceptional Children, 22*(3), 4-9.

Whatley, J., Staniford, G., Beer, M., & Scown, P. (1999). Intelligent agents to support students working in groups online. *Journal of Interactive Learning Research, 10*(3/4), 361-373.

White, O. R. (1986). Precision Teaching—Precision learning. *Exceptional Children, 25,* 522-534.

Wilds, P. L., & Zachert, V. (1966). *Effectiveness of a programmed text in teaching gynecologic oncology to junior medical students, a source book on the development of programmed materials for use in a clinical discipline.* Augusta, GA: Medical College of Georgia.

Williams, J. P. (1963, October). A comparison of several response modes in a review program. *Journal of Educational Psychology, 54,* 253-60.

Wittich, W. A., & Folkes, J. G. (1946). *Audio-visual paths to learning.* New York: Harper.

Wittrock, M. C. (1962). Set applied to student teachings. *Journal of Educational Psychology, 53,* 175-180.

Wulff, J. J., Sheffield, F. W., & Kraeling, D. G. (1954). 'Familiarization' procedures used as adjuncts to assembly task training with a demonstration film. *Staff Research Memorandum,* Chanute AFB, IL: Training Aids Research Laboratory.

Yale Motion Picture Research Project. (1947). Do 'motivation' and 'participation' questions increase learning? *Educational Screen, 26,* 256-283.

Zencius, A. H., Davis, P. K., & Cuvo, A. J. (1990). A personalized system of instruction for teaching checking account skills to adults with mild disabilities. *Journal of Applied Behavior Analysis, 23,* 245-252.

Zimmerman, C.L. (1972). *An experimental study of the effects of learning and forgetting when students are informed of behavioral objectives before or after a unit of study.* Unpublished doctoral dissertation, University of Maryland.

·2·

SYSTEMS INQUIRY AND ITS APPLICATION

IN EDUCATION

Bela H. Banathy
Saybrook Graduate School and Research Center

Patrick M. Jenlink
Stephen Austin University

2.1   PART 1: SYSTEMS INQUIRY

The first part of this chapter is a review of the evolution of the systems movement and a discussion of human systems inquiry.

2.1.1   A Definition of Systems Inquiry

Systems inquiry incorporates three interrelated domains of disciplined inquiry: systems theory, systems philosophy, and systems methodology. Bertalanffy (1968) notes that in contrast with the analytical, reductionist, and linear–causal paradigm of classical science, *systems philosophy* brings forth a reorientation of thought and worldview, manifested by an expansionist, nonlinear dynamic, and synthetic mode of thinking. The scientific exploration of systems theories and the development of systems theories in the various sciences have brought forth a *general theory of systems,* a set of interrelated concepts and principles, applying to all systems. *Systems methodology* provides us with a set of models, strategies, methods, and tools that instrumentalize systems theory and philosophy in analysis, design, development, and management of complex systems.

2.1.1.1   Systems Theory. During the early 1950s, the basic concepts and principles of a general theory of systems were set forth by such pioneers of the systems movement as Ashby, Bertalanffy, Boulding, Fagen, Gerard, Rappoport, and Wiener. They came from a variety of disciplines and fields of study.

They shared and articulated a common conviction: the unified nature of reality. They recognized a compelling need for a unified disciplined inquiry in understanding and dealing with increasing complexities, complexities that are beyond the competence of any single discipline. As a result, they developed a transdisciplinary perspective that emphasized the intrinsic order and interdependence of the world in all its manifestations. From their work emerged systems theory, the science of complexity. In defining systems theory, we review the key ideas of Bertalanffy and Boulding, two of the founders of the Society for the Advancement of General Systems Theory. Later, the name of the society was changed to the Society for General Systems Research, then the International Society for Systems Research, and recently to the International Society for the Systems Sciences.

2.1.1.1.1   Bertalanffy (1956, pp. 1–10). Examining modern science, Bertalanffy suggested that it is "characterized by its ever-increasing specialization, necessitated by the enormous amount of data, the complexity of techniques, and structures within every field." This, however, led to a breakdown of science as an integrated realm. "Scientists, operating in the various disciplines, are encapsulated in their private universe, and it is difficult to get word from one cocoon to the other." Against this background, he observes a remarkable development, namely, that "similar general viewpoints and conceptions have appeared in very different fields." Reviewing this development in those fields, Bertalanffy suggests that there exist models, principles, and laws that can be generalized across various systems, their components, and the relationships among them. "It seems legitimate to ask for a theory, not of systems of a more or less special kind, but of universal principles applying to systems in general."

The first consequence of this approach is the recognition of the existence of systems properties that are general and structural similarities or isomorphies in different fields:

There are correspondences in the principles, which govern the behavior of entities that are intrinsically widely different. These correspondences are due to the fact that they all can be considered, in certain aspects, "systems," that is, complexes of elements standing in interaction. [It seems] that a general theory of systems would be a useful tool providing, on the one hand, models that can be used in, and transferred to, different fields, and safeguarding, on the other hand, from vague analogies which often have marred the progress in these fields.

The second consequence of the idea of a general theory is to deal with organized complexity, which is a main problem of modern science.

Concepts like those of organization, wholeness, directiveness, teleology, control, self-regulation, differentiation, and the likes are alien to conventional science. However, they pop up everywhere in the biological, behavioral, and social sciences and are, in fact, indispensable for dealing with living organisms or social groups. Thus, a basic problem posed to modem science is a general theory of organization. General Systems Theory (GST) is, in principle, capable of giving exact definitions for such concepts.

Thirdly, Bertalanffy (1956) suggested that it is important to say what a general theory of systems is not. It is not identical with the triviality of mathematics of some sort that can be applied to any sort of problems; instead "it poses special problems that are far from being trivial." It is not

a search for superficial analogies between physical, biological, and social systems. The isomorphy we have mentioned is a consequence of the fact that, in certain aspects, corresponding abstractions and conceptual models can be applied to different phenomena. It is only in view of these aspects that system laws apply.

Bertalanffy (1956) summarizes the aims of a general theory of systems as follows:

(a) There is a general tendency toward integration in the various sciences, natural and social.
(b) Such integration seems to be centered in a general theory of systems.
(c) Such a theory may be an important means of aiming at exact theory in the nonphysical fields of science.
(d) Developing unifying principles running "vertically" through the universe of the individual sciences, this theory brings us nearer to the goal of the unity of sciences.
(e) This can lead to a much needed integration in scientific education.

Commenting later on education, Bertalanffy noted that education treats the various scientific disciplines as separate domains, where increasingly smaller subdomains become separate sciences, unconnected with the rest. In contrast, the educational demands of scientific generalists and developing transdisciplinary basic principles are precisely those that GST tries to fill. In this sense, GST seems to make important headway toward transdisciplinary synthesis and integrated education.

2.1.1.1.2 Boulding (1956, pp. 11–17). Examining the state of systems science, Boulding underscored the need for a general theory of systems, because in recent years increasing need has been felt for a body of theoretical constructs that will discuss the general relationships of the empirical world. This is, as Boulding noted,

The quest of General Systems Theory (GST). It does not seek, of course, to establish a single, self-contained "general theory of practically everything," which will replace all the special theories of particular disciplines. Such a theory would be almost without content, and all we can say about practically everything is almost nothing.

Somewhere between the specific that has no meaning and the general that has no content there must be, for each purpose and at each level of abstraction, an optimum degree of generality.

The objectives of GST, then, can be set out with varying degrees of ambitions and confidence. At a low level of ambition, but with a high degree of confidence, it aims to point out similarities in the theoretical constructions of different disciplines, where these exist, and to develop theoretical models having applicability to different fields of study. At a higher level of ambition, but perhaps with a lower level of confidence, it hopes to develop something like a "spectrum" of theories—a system of systems that may perform a "gestalt" in theoretical constructions. It is the main objective of GST, says Boulding, to develop "generalized ears" that overcome the "specialized deafness" of the specific disciplines, meaning that someone who ought to know something that someone else knows isn't able to find it out for lack of generalized ears. Developing a framework of a general theory will enable the specialist to catch relevant communications from others.

In the subtitle, and later in the closing section of his paper, Boulding referred to GST as "the skeleton of science." It is a skeleton in the sense, he says, that:

It aims to provide a framework or structure of systems on which to hang the flesh and blood of particular disciplines and particular subject matters in an orderly and coherent corpus of knowledge. It is also, however, something of a skeleton in a cupboard-the cupboard in this case being the unwillingness of science to admit the tendency to shut the door on problems and subject matters which do not fit easily into simple mechanical schemes. Science, for all its success, still has a very long way to go. GST may at times be an embarrassment in pointing out how very far we still have to go, and in deflating excessive philosophical claims for overly simple systems. It also may be helpful, however, in pointing out to some extent where we have to go. The skeleton must come out of the cupboards before its dry bones can live.

The two papers introduced above set forth the "vision" of the systems movement. That vision still guides us today. At this point it seems to be appropriate to tell the story that marks the genesis of the systems movement. Kenneth Boulding told this story at the occasion when Bela Banathy was privileged to present to him the distinguished scholarship award of the Society of General Systems Research at our 1983 Annual Meeting.

The year was 1954. At the Center for Behavioral Sciences, at Stanford University, four Center Fellows—Bertalanffy (biology), Boulding (economics), Gerard (psychology), and Rappoport (mathematics)—had a discussion in a meeting room. Another Center Fellow walked in and asked: "What's going on here?" Ken answered: "We are angered about the state of the human condition and ask: 'What can we—what can science—do about improving the human condition?' ' "Oh!" their visitor said: "This is not my field. . . . " At that meeting the four scientists felt that in the statement of their visitor they heard the statement of the fragmented disciplines that have little concern for doing anything practical about the fate of humanity. So, they asked themselves, "What would happen if science would be redefined by crossing disciplinary boundaries and forge a general theory that would bring us together in the service of humanity." Later they went to Berkeley, to the annual meeting of the American Association for the Advancement of Science, and during that meeting established the Society for the Advancement of General Systems Theory.

Throughout the years, many of us in the systems movement have continued to ask the question: How can systems science serve humanity?

2.1.1.2 Systems Philosophy.

The next main branch of systems inquiry is systems philosophy. Systems philosophy is concerned with a systems view of the world and the elucidation of systems thinking as an approach to theoretical and real-world problems. Systems philosophy seeks to uncover the most general assumptions lying at the roots of any and all of systems inquiry. An articulation of these assumptions gives systems inquiry coherence and internal consistency. Systems philosophy (Laszlo, 1972) seeks to probe the basic texture and ultimate implications of systems inquiry. It "guides the imagination of the systems scientist and provides a general world view, the likes of which—in the history of science—has proven to be the most significant for asking the right question and perceiving the relevant state of affairs" (p. 10). The general scientific nature of systems inquiry implies its direct association with philosophy. This explains the philosophers' early and continuing interest in systems theory and the early and continuing interest of systems theorists and methodologists in the philosophical aspects of systems inquiry. In general, philosophical aspects are worked out in three directions. The first involves inquiry into the What: what things are, what a person or a society is, and what kind of world we live in. These questions pertain to what we call *ontology*. The second direction focuses on the question How: How do we know what we know; how do we know what kind of world we live in; how do we know what kind of persons we are? The exploration of these questions is the domain of epistemology. One might differentiate these two, but, as Bateson (1972) noted, ontology and epistemology cannot be separated. Our beliefs about what the world is will determine how we see it and act within it. And our ways of perceiving and acting will determine our beliefs about its nature. Whitehead (1978) explains the relationship between ontology and

epistemology such "That *how* an actual entity *becomes* constitutes *what* that actual entity is; so that the two descriptions of an actual entity are not independent. Its 'being' is constituted by its "becoming" (p. 23). Philosophically, systems are at once being and becoming. The third dimension of systems philosophy is concerned with the ethical/moral/aesthetic nature of a system. These questions reflect what we call axiology. Whereas ontology is concerned with what is, and epistemology is concerned with theoretical underpinnings, axiology is concerned with the moral and ethical grounding of the *What* and *How* of a system. Blauberg, Sadovsky, and Yudin (1977) noted that the philosophical aspects of systems inquiry would give us an "unequivocal solution to all or most problems arising from a study of systems" (p. 94).

2.1.1.2.1 Ontology.

The ontological task is the formation of a systems view of what is—in the broadest sense a systems view of the world. This can lead to a new orientation for scientific inquiry. As Blauberg et al. (1977) noted, this orientation emerged into a holistic view of the world. Waddington (1977) presents a historical review of two great philosophical alternatives of the intellectual picture we have of the world. One view is that the world essentially consists of things. The other view is that the world consists of processes, and the things are only "stills" out of the moving picture. Systems philosophy developed as the main rival of the "thing view." It recognizes the primacy of organizing relationship processes between entities (of systems), from which emerge the novel properties of systems.

2.1.1.2.2 Epistemology.

This philosophical aspect deals with general questions: How do we know whatever we know? How do we know what kind of world we live in and what kind of organisms we are? What sort of thing is the mind? Bateson (1972) notes that originating from systems theory, extraordinary advances have been made in answering these questions. The ancient question of whether the mind is immanent or transcendent can be answered in favor of immanence. Furthermore, any ongoing ensemble (system) that has the appropriate complexity of causal and energy relationships will (a) show mutual characteristics, (b) compare and respond to differences, (c) process information, (d) be self-corrective, and (e) no part of an internally interactive system can exercise unilateral control over other parts of the system. "The mental characteristics of a system are immanent not in some part, but in the system as a whole" (p. 316).

The epistemological aspects of systems philosophy address (a) the principles of how systems inquiry is conducted, (b) the specific categorical apparatus of the inquiry, and that connected with it, and (c) the theoretical language of systems science. The most significant guiding principle of systems inquiry is that of giving prominence to synthesis, not only as the culminating activity of the inquiry (following analysis) but also as a point of departure. This approach to the "how do we know" contrasts with the epistemology of traditional science that is almost exclusively analytical.

2.1.1.2.3 Axiology.

The axiological responsibility of systems philosophy is directed to the study of value, ethics, and aesthetics guided by the radical questions, What is good?, What is right?, What is moral?, What is elegant or beautiful? These questions directly fund the moral responsibility and practice of systems inquiry. Values, morals, ethics, aesthetics (elegance and beauty) are primary considerations in systems inquiry. Individuals and collectives engaged in systems inquiry must ask those questions that seek to examine, find, and understand a common ground from which the inquiry takes direction. Jantsch (1980) notes, in examining morality and ethics, that

The direct living experience of morality becomes expressed in the form of ethics—it becomes form in the same way in which biological experience becomes form in the genetic code. The stored ethical information is then selectively retrieved and applied in the moral process in actual life situations. (p. 264)

The axiological concern of systems philosophy is to ensure that systems inquiry is moral and ethical, and that those individuals/collectives who participate in systems inquiry are constantly questioning the implications of their actions. Human systems inquiry, as Churchman (1971, 1979, 1982) has stated, must be value oriented, and it must be guided by the social imperative, which dictates that technological efficiency must be subordinated to social efficiency. He speaks for a science of values and the development of methods by which to verify ethical judgments. Churchman (1982) explains that "ethics is an eternal conversation, its conversation retains its aesthetic quality if human values are regarded as neither relative or absolute" (p. 57). The methods and tools selected for the systems inquiry, as well as the epistemological and ontological processes that guide systems inquiry, work to determine what is valued, what is good and aesthetic, what is morally acceptable. Whereas traditional science is distanced from axiological considerations, systems philosophy in the context of social systems and systems inquiry embraces this moral/ethical dimension as a crucial and defining characteristic of the inquiry process.

2.1.1.3 Systems Methodology.

Systems methodology—a vital part of systems inquiry—has two domains of inquiry: (1) the study of methods in systems investigations by which we generate knowledge about systems in general and (2) the identification and description of strategies, models, methods, and tools for the application of systems theory and systems thinking for working with complex systems. In the context of this second domain, systems methodology is a set of coherent and related methods and tools applicable to (a) the analysis of systems and systems problems, problems concerned with the systemic/relational aspects of complex systems; (b) the design, development, implementation, and evaluation of complex systems; and (c) the management of systems and the management of change in systems.

The task of those using systems methodology in a given context is fourfold: (1) to identify, characterize, and classify the nature of the problem situation, i.e., (a), (b), or (c) above; (2) to identify and characterize the problem context and content in which the methodology is applied; (3) to identify and characterize the type of system in which the problem situation is embedded; and (4) to select specific strategies, methods, and tools that are appropriate to the nature of the problem situation, to the context/content, and to the type of systems in which the problem situation is located.

The brief discussion above highlights the difference between the methodology of systems inquiry and the methodology of scientific inquiry in the various disciplines. The methodology of a discipline is clearly defined and is to be adhered to rigorously. It is the methodology that is the hallmark of a discipline. In systems inquiry, on the other hand, one selects methods and methodological tools or approaches that best fit the nature of the identified problem situation, and the context, the content, and the type of system that is the domain of the investigation. The methodology is to be selected from a wide range of systems methods that are available to us.

2.1.1.4 The Interaction of the Domains of Systems Inquiry.

Systems philosophy, systems theory, and systems methodology come to life as they are used and applied in the functional context of systems. Systems philosophy presents us with the underlying assumptions that provide the perspectives that guide us in defining and organizing the concepts and principles that constitute systems theory. Systems theory and systems philosophy then guide us in developing, selecting, and organizing approaches, methods, and tools into the scheme of systems methodology. Systems methodology then is used in the functional context of systems. Methodology is confirmed or changed by testing its relevance to its theoretical/philosophical foundations and by its use. The functional context—the society in general and systems of all kinds in particular—is a primary source of placing demands on systems inquiry. It was, in fact, the emergence of complex systems that brought about the recognition of the need for new scientific thinking, new theory, and methodologies. It was this need that systems inquiry addressed and satisfied.

2.1.2 Evolution of the Systems Movement

Throughout the evolution of humanity there has been a constant yearning for understanding the wholeness of the human experience that manifests itself in the wholeness of the human being and the human society. Wholeness has been sought also in the disciplined inquiry of science as a way of searching for the unity of science and a unified theory of the universe. This search reaches back through the ages into the golden age of Greek philosophy and science in Plato's "kybemetics," the art of steermanship, which is the origin of modern cybernetics: a domain of contemporary systems thinking. The search intensified during the Age of Enlightenment and the Age of Reason and Certainty, and it was manifested in the clockwork mechanistic world view. The search has continued in the current age of uncertainty (Heisenberg, 1930) and the sciences of complexity (Nicolis & Prigogine, 1989; Prigogine, 1980), chaos (Gleick, 1987), relativity (general and special) (Einstein, 1955, 1959), quantum theory (Shrödinger, 1956, 1995), and the theory of wholeness and the implicate order (Bohm, 1995).

In recent years, the major player in this search has been the systems movement. The genesis of the movement can be timed as the mid-1950s (as discussed at the beginning of this chapter). But prior to that time, we can account for the emergence of the systems idea through the work of several philosophers and scientist.

2.1.2.1 The Pioneers. Some of the key notions of systems theory were articulated by the 18th-century German philosopher Hegel. He suggested that the whole is more than the sum of its parts, that the whole determines the nature of the parts, and the parts are dynamically interrelated and cannot be understood in isolation from the whole.

Most likely, the first person who used the term *general theory of systems* was the Hungarian philosopher and scientist Bela Zalai. Zalai, during the years 1913 to 1914, developed his theory in a collection of papers called *A Rendszerek Altalanos Elmelete*. The German translation was entitled *Allgemeine Theorie der Systeme* [General Theory of Systems]. The work was republished (Zalai, 1984) in Hungarian and was recently reviewed in English (Banathy & Banathy, 1989). In a three-volume treatise, *Tektologia*, Bogdanov (1921–1927), a Russian scientist, characterized *Tektologia* as a dynamic science of complex wholes, concerned with universal structural regularities, general types of systems, the general laws of their transformation, and the basic laws of organization. Bogdanov's work was published in English by Golerik (1980).

In the decades prior to and during World War II, the search intensified. The idea of a General Systems Theory was developed by Bertalanffy in the late 1930s and was presented in various lectures. But his material remained unpublished until 1945 (*Zu einer allgemeinen Systemlehre*) followed by "An Outline of General Systems Theory" (1951). Without using the term GST, the same frame of thinking was used in various articles by Ashby during the years 1945 and 1947, published in his book *Design for a Brain*, in 1952.

2.1.2.2 Organized Developments. In contrast with the work of individual scientists, outlined above, since the 1940s we can account for several major developments that reflect the evolution of the systems movement, including "hard systems science," cybernetics, and the continuing evolution of a general theory of systems.

2.1.3 Hard-Systems Science

Under hard-systems science, we can account for two organized developments: operations research and systems engineering.

2.1.3.1 Operations Research. During the Second World War, it was again the "functional context" that challenged scientists. The complex problems of logistics and resource management in waging a war became the genesis of developing the earliest organized form of systems science: the quantitative analysis of rather closed systems. It was this orientation from which operations research and management science emerged during the 1950s. This development directed systems science toward "hard" quantitative analysis. Operations research flourished during the 1960s, but in the 1970s, due to the changing nature of

sociotechnical systems contexts, it went through a major shift toward a less quantitative orientation.

2.1.3.2 Systems Engineering. This is concerned with the design of closed man–machine systems and larger scale sociotechnical systems. Systems engineering (SE) can be portrayed as a system of methods and tools, specific activities for problem solutions, and a set of relations between the tools and activities. The tools include language, mathematics, and graphics by which systems engineering communicates. The content of SE includes a variety of algorithms and concepts that enable various activities. The first major work in SE was published by A. D. Hall (1962). He presented a comprehensive, three-dimensional morphology for systems engineering. Over a decade later, Sage (1977) changed the directions of SE.

We use the word system to refer to the application of systems science and methodologies associated with the science of problem solving. We use the *word engineering* not only to mean the mastery and manipulation of physical data but also to imply social and behavioral consideration as inherent parts of the engineering design process. (p. xi)

During the 1960s and early 1970s, practitioners of operations research and systems engineering attempted to transfer their approaches into the context of social systems. It led to disasters. It was this period when "social engineering" emerged as an approach to address societal problems. A recognition of failed attempts have led to changes in direction, best manifested by the quotation of Sage in the paragraph above.

2.1.4 Cybernetics

Cybernetics is concerned with the understanding of self-organization of human, artificial, and natural systems; the understanding of understanding; and its relation and relevance to other transdisciplinary approaches. Cybernetics, as part of the systems movement, evolved through two phases: first-order cybernetics, the cybernetics of the observed system, and second-order cybernetics, the cybernetics of the observing system.

2.1.4.1 First-Order Cybernetics. This early formulation of cybernetics inquiry was concerned with communication and control *in* the animal and the machine (Wiener, 1948). The emphasis on the *in* allowed focus on the process of self-organization and self-regulation, on circular causal feedback mechanisms, together with the systemic principles that underlie them. These principles underlay the computer/cognitive sciences and are credited with being at the heart of neural network approaches in computing. The first-order view treated information as a quantity, as "bits" to be transmitted from one place to the other. It focused on "noise" that interfered with smooth transmission (Wheatley, 1992). The content, the meaning, and the purpose of information was ignored (Gleick, 1987).

2.1.4.2 Second-Order Cybernetics. As a concept, this expression was coined by Foerster (1984), who describes this shift as follows: "We are now in the possession of the truism that a description (of the universe) implies one who describes (observes it). What we need now is a description of the 'describer' or, in other words, we need a theory of the observer" (p. 258). The general notion of second-order cybernetics is that "observing systems" awaken the notion of language, culture, and communication (Brier, 1992); and the context, the content, the meaning, and purpose of information becomes central. Second-order cybernetics, through the concept of self-reference, wants to explore the meaning of cognition and communication within the natural and social sciences, the humanities, and information science; and in such social practices as design, education, organization, art, management, and politics, etc. (p. 2).

2.1.5 The Continuing Evolution of Systems Inquiry

The first part of this chapter describes the emergence of the systems idea and its manifestation in the three branches of systems inquiry: systems theory, systems philosophy, and systems methodology. This section traces the evolution of systems inquiry. This evolutionary discussion will be continued later in a separate section by focusing on "human systems inquiry."

2.1.5.1 *The Continuing Evolution of Systems Thinking.*
In a comprehensive report, commissioned by the Society of General Systems Research, Cavallo (1979) states that systems inquiry shattered the essential features of the traditional scientific paradigm characterized by analytic thinking, reductionism, and determinism. The systems paradigm articulates synthetic thinking, emergence, communication and control, expansionism, and teleology. The emergence of these core systems ideas was the consequence of a change of focus, away from entities that cannot be taken apart without loss of their essential characteristics, and hence can not be truly understood from analysis.

First, this change of focus gave rise to synthetic or systems thinking as complementary to analysis. In synthetic thinking an entity to be understood is conceptualized not as a whole to be taken apart but as a part of one or more larger wholes. The entity is explained in terms of its function, and its role in its larger context. Second, another major consequence of the new thinking is expansionism (an alternative to reductionism), which asserts that ultimate understanding is an ideal that can never be attained but can be continuously approached. Progress toward it depends on understanding ever larger and more inclusive wholes. Third, the idea of nondeterministic causality, advanced by Singer (1959), made it possible to develop the notion of objective teleology, a conceptual system in which such teleological concepts as fire will, choice, function, and purpose could be operationally defined and incorporated into the domain of science.

2.1.5.2 *Living Systems Theory (Miller, 1978).*
This theory was developed as a continuation and elaboration of the organismic orientation of Bertalanffy. The theory is a conceptual scheme for the description and analysis of concrete identifiable living systems. It describes seven levels of living systems, ranging from the lower levels of cell, organ, and organism, to higher levels of group, organizations, societies, and supranational systems.

The central thesis of living systems theory is that at each level a system is characterized by the same 20 critical subsystems whose processes are essential to life. A set of these subsystems processes information (input transducer, internal transducer, channel and net, decoder, associator, decider, memory, encoder, output transducer, and time). Another set of subsystems process matter and energy (ingestor, distributor, converter, producer, storage, extruder, motor, and supporter). Two subsystems (reproducer and boundary) process matter/energy and information.

Living system theory presents a common framework for analyzing structure and process and identifying the health and well-being of systems at various levels of complexity. A set of cross-level hypotheses was identified by Miller as a basis for conducting such analysis. During the 1980s, Living systems theory has been applied by a method—called living systems process analysis—to the study of complex problem situations embedded in a diversity of fields and activities. (Living systems process analysis has been applied in educational contexts by Banathy & Mills, 1988.)

2.1.5.3 *A General Theory of Dynamic Systems.*
The theory was developed by Jantsch (1980). He argues that an emphasis on structure and dynamic equilibrium (steady-state flow), which characterized the earlier development of general systems theory, led to a profound understanding of how primarily technological structures may be stabilized and maintained by complex mechanisms that respond to negative feedback. (Negative feedback indicates deviation from established norms and calls for a reduction of such deviation.) In biological and social systems, however, negative feedback is complemented by positive feedback, which increases deviation by the development of new systems processes and forms. The new understanding that has emerged recognizes such phenomena as self-organization, self-reference, self-regulation, coherent behavior over time with structural change, individuality, symbiosis and coevolution with the environment, and morphogenesis.

This new understanding of systems behavior, says Jantsch, emphasizes process in contrast to "solid" subsystems structures and components. The interplay of process in systems leads to evolution of structures. An emphasis is placed on "becoming," a decisive conceptual breakthrough brought about by Prigogine (1980). Prigogine's theoretical development and empirical conformation of the so-called *dissipative structures* and his discovery of a new ordering systems principle called *order through fluctuation* led to an explication of a "general theory of dynamic systems."

In the 1990s, important advancements in dynamical systems theory emerged in such fields as social psychology (Vallacher and Nowak, 1994), where complex social relationships integral to human activity systems are examined. The chaotic and complex nature of human systems, the implicit patterns of values and beliefs which guide the social actions of these systems, enfolded within the explicit patterns of key activities such as social judgement, decisioning, and valuing in social relations, may be made accessible through dynamic systems theory.

During the early 1980s and well into the 1990s, a whole range of systems thinking based methodologies emerged, based on what is called *soft systems thinking*. These are all relevant to human and social systems and will be discussed under the heading of human systems inquiry. In this section, four additional developments are discussed: systems thinking based on "unbounded systems thinking," "critical systems theory," "liberating systems theory" and "postmodern theory and systems theory."

2.1.5.4 Unbounded Systems Thinking (Mitroff & Linstone, 1993).
This development "is the basis for the 'new thinking' called for in the information age" (p. 91). In unbounded systems thinking (UST), "everything interacts with everything."

All branches of inquiry depend fundamentally on one another. The widest possible array of disciplines, professions, and branches of knowledge capturing distinctly different paradigms of thought—must be consciously brought to bear on our problems. In UST, the traditional hierarchical ordering of the sciences and the professions—as well as the pejorative bifurcation of the sciences into 'hard' vs. 'soft'—is replaced by a circular concept of relationship between them. The basis for choosing a particular way of modeling or representing a problem is not governed merely by considerations of conventional logic and rationality. It may also involve considerations of justice and fairness as perceived by various social groups and by consideration of personal ethics or morality as perceived by distinct persons. (p. 9)

2.1.5.5 Critical Systems Theory (CST).
Critical systems theory draws heavily on the philosophy of Habermas (1970, 1973). A CST approach to social systems is of particular import when considering systems wherein great disparities of power exist in relation to authority and control. Habermas (1973), focusing on the relationship between theory and practice, says:

The mediation of theory and praxis can only be clarified if to begin with we distinguish between three functions, which are measured in terms of different criteria; the formation and extension of critical theorems, which can stand up to scientific discourse; the organisation of processes of enlightenment, in which such theorems are applied and can be tested in a unique manner by initiation of processes of reflection carried on within certain groups towards which these processes have been directed; and the selection of appropriate strategies, the solution of tactical questions, and the conduct of political struggle. (p. 32)

Critical systems theory came to the foreground in the 1980s (Jackson, 1985; Ulrich, 1983), continuing to influence systems theory into the 1990s (Flood & Jackson, 1991; Jackson, 1991a, 1991b). As Jackson (1991b) explains, CST embraces five major commitments:

1. critical awareness—examining the commitments and values entering into actual systems design
2. social awareness—recognizing organizational and social pressures lead to the popularization of certain systems theories and methodologies

3. dedication to human emancipation—seeking for all the maximum development of human potential
4. complementary and informed use of systems methodologies
5. complementary and informed development of all varieties—alternative positions and different theoretical underpinnings—of systems approaches.

CST rejects a positivist epistemology of "hard" systems science, and offers a postpositivist epistemology for "soft" systems with a primary concern of emancipation or liberation through "communicative action" (Habermas, 1984).

2.1.5.6 Liberating Systems Theory (Flood, 1990).
This theory is situated, in part, within the CST. Flood, in his development of *liberating systems theory* (LST), acknowledged the value for bringing the work of both Habermas and Foucault together, a Marxist and poststructuralist, respectively. According to Flood, the effects of dominant ideologies or worldviews influence interpretations of some situations, thus privileging some views over others. LST provides a postpositivist epistemology that enables the liberation oppressed. Toward that purpose, LST is (1) in pursuit of freeing systems theory from certain tendencies and, in a more general sense, (2) tasking systems theory with liberation of the human condition. The first task is developed in three trends: (1) the liberation of systems theory generally from the natural tendency toward self-imposed insularity, (2) the liberation of systems concepts from objectivist and subjectivist delusions, and (3) the liberation of systems theory specifically in cases of internalized localized subjugations in discourse and by considering histories and progressions of systems thinking. The second task of the theory focuses on liberation and emancipation in response to domination and subjugation in work and social situations.

2.1.5.7 Postmodern Theory and Systems Theory.
In the 1990s, attention was turned to applying postmodern theories to systems theory. Postmodernism "denies that science has access to objective truth, and rejects the notion of history as the progressive realization and emancipation of the human subject or as an increase in the complexity and steering capacity of societies" (Jackson, 1991, p. 289). The work of Brocklesby and Cummings (1996) and Tsoukas (1992) suggests alternative philosophical perspectives, bringing the work of Foucault (1980) on power/knowledge to the fore of consideration in critical systems perspectives. Within postmodern theory, the rejection of objective truth and the argument that all perspectives, particularly those constructed across boundaries of time, culture, and difference (gender, race, ethnicity, etc.), are fundamentally incommensurate, renders reconciliation between worldviews impossible. Concern for social justice, equity, tolerance, and issues of difference give purpose and direction to the postmodern perspective. A postmodern approach to systems theory recognizes that the unknowability of reality, which renders it impossible to judge the truth, value, or worth of different perspectives, extant from the context of their origin, thus validating or invalidating all perspectives, equally, as the case may be.

2.1.6 Human Systems Inquiry

Human systems inquiry focuses systems theory, systems philosophy, and systems methodology and their applications on social or human systems. This section examines human systems inquiry by (1) presenting some of its basic characteristics, (2) describing the various types of human or social systems, (3) explicating the nature of problem situations and solutions in human systems inquiry, and (4) introducing the "soft-systems" approach and social systems design. The discussion of these issues will help us appreciate why human systems inquiry must be different from other modes of inquiry. Furthermore, inasmuch as education is a human activity system that gives to individuals the authority to act for the collectivity, and system, such understanding and a review of approaches to setting boundaries between the collectivity and the rest of the human systems inquiry will lead to our discussion on systems world.

2.1.6.1 The Characteristics of Human Systems. *Human Systems Are Different* is the title of the last book of the systems philosopher Geoffrey Vickers (1983). Discussing the characteristics of human systems as open systems, a summary of the open nature follows: (1) Open systems are nests of relations that are sustained through time. They are sustained by these relations and by the process of regulation. The limits within which they can be sustained are the conditions of their stability. (2) Open systems depend on and contribute to their environment. They are dependent on this interaction as well as on their internal interaction. These interactions/dependencies impose constraints on all their constituents. Human systems can mitigate but cannot remove these constraints, which tend to become more demanding and at times even contradictory as the scale of the organization increases. This might place a limit on the potential of the organization. (3) Open systems are wholes, but are also parts of larger systems, and their constituents may also be constituents of other systems. Change in human systems is inevitable. Systems adapt to environmental changes, and in a changing environment this becomes a continuous process. At times, however, adaptation does not suffice, so the whole system might change. Through coevolution and cocreation, change between the systems and its environment is a mutual recursive phenomenon (Buckley, 1968; Jantsch, 1976, 1980). Wheatley (1992), discussing stability, change, and renewal in self-organizing system, remarks that in the past, scientists focused on the overall structure of systems, leading them away from understanding the processes of change that makes a system viable over time. They were looking for stability. Regulatory (negative) feedback was a way to ensure the stability of systems, to preserve their current state. They overlooked the function of positive feedback that moves the system toward change and renewal.

Checkland (1981) presents a comprehensive characterization of what he calls human activity systems (HASs). HASs are very different from natural and engineered systems. Natural and engineered systems cannot be other than what they are. The concept of human activity systems, on the other hand, is crucially different for the concepts of natural and engineered systems. As Checkland explains,

human activity systems can be manifest only as perceptions by human actors who are free to attribute meaning to what they perceive. There will thus never be a single (testable) account of human activity systems, only a set of possible accounts all valid according to particular Weltanshaungen. (p. 14)

Checkland further suggests that HASs are structured sets of people who make up the system, coupled with a collection of such activities as processing information, making plans, performing, and monitoring performance. Relatedly, education as a human activity system is a complex set of activity systems such as curriculum design, instruction, assessment, learning, administrating, communicating, information processing, performing (student, teacher, administrator, etc.), and monitoring of performance (student, teacher, administrator, etc.).

Organizations, as human activity systems begin, as Argyris and Schön (1979) suggest, as a social group and become an organization when members

must devise procedures for: (1) making decisions in the name of the collectivity, (2) delegating to individuals the authority to act for the collectivity, and (3) setting boundaries between the collectivity and the rest of the world. As these conditions are met, members of the collectivity begin to be able to say 'we' about themselves; they can say, 'We have decided,' 'We have made our position clear,' 'We have limited our membership.' There is now an organizational 'we' that can decide and act. (p. 13)

Human systems form—self-organize—through collective activities and around a common purpose or goal. Ackoff and Emery (1972) characterize human systems as purposeful systems whose members are also purposeful individuals who intentionally and collectively formulate objectives. In human systems, "the state of the part can be determined only in reference to the state of the system. The effect of change in one part or another is mediated by changes in the state of the whole" (p. 218).

Ackoff (1981) suggests that human systems are purposeful systems that have purposeful parts and are parts of larger purposeful systems. This observation reveals three fundamental issues, namely, how to design and manage human systems so that they can effectively and efficiently serve (1) their own purposes, (2) the purposes of their purposeful parts and people in the system, and (3) the purposes of the larger system(s) of which they are part. These functions are called (1) self-directiveness, (2) humanization, and (3) environmentalization, respectively. Viewing human systems from an evolutionary perspective, Jantsch (1980) suggests that according to the dualistic paradigm, adaptation is a response to something that evolved outside of the systems. He notes, however, that with the emergence of the self-organizing paradigm, a scientifically founded nondualistic view became possible. This view is process oriented and establishes that evolution is an integral part of self-organization. True self-organization incorporates self-transcendence, the creative reaching out of a human system beyond its boundaries. Jantsch concludes that creation is the core of evolution, it is the joy of life, it is not just adaptation, not just securing survival. In the final analysis, says Laszlo (1987), social systems are value-guided systems, culturally embedded and interconnected. Insofar as they are independent of biological need fulfillment and reproductive needs, cultures satisfy not physical body needs, but individual and social values. All cultures respond to such supra-biological values. But in what form they do so depends on the specific kind of values people within the cultures happen to have.

2.1.6.2 Types of Human Systems.
Human activity systems, such as educational systems, are purposeful creations. People in these systems select, organize, and carry out activities in order to attain their purposes. Reviewing the research of Ackoff (1981), Jantsch (1976), Jackson and Keys (1984), and Southerland (1973), Banathy (1988a) developed a comprehensive classification of HASs premised on (1) the degree to which they are open or closed, (2) their mechanistic vs. systemic nature, (3) their unitary vs. pluralistic position on defining their purpose, and (4) the degree and nature of their complexity (simple, detailed, dynamic). Based on these dimensions, we can differentiate five types of HASs: rigidly controlled, deterministic, purposive, heuristic, and purpose seeking.

2.1.6.2.1 Rigidly Controlled Systems.
These systems are rather closed. Their structure is simple, consisting of few elements with limited interaction among them. They have a singleness of purpose and clearly defined goals, and act mechanically. Operational ways and means are prescribed. There is little room for self-direction. They have a rigid structure and stable relationship among system components. Examples are assembly-line systems and man–machine systems.

2.1.6.2.2 Deterministic Systems.
These are still more closed than open. They have clearly assigned goals; thus, they are unitary. People in the system have a limited degree of freedom in selecting methods. Their complexity ranges from simple to detailed. Examples are bureaucracies, instructional systems, and national educational.

2.1.6.2.3 Purposive Systems.
These are still unitary but are more open than closed, and react to their environment in order to maintain their viability. Their purpose is established at the top, but people in the system have freedom to select operational means and methods. They have detailed to dynamic complexity. Examples are corporations, social service agencies, and our public education systems.

2.1.6.2.4 Heuristic Systems.
Such systems as R&D agencies and innovative business ventures formulate their own goals under broad policy guidelines; thus, they are somewhat pluralistic. They are open to changes and often initiate changes. Their complexity is dynamic, and their internal arrangements and operations are systemic. Examples of heuristic systems include innovative business ventures, educational R&D agencies, and alternative educational systems.

2.1.6.2.5 Purpose-Seeking Systems.
These systems are ideal seeking and are guided by their vision of the future. They are open and coevolve with their environment. They exhibit dynamic complexity and systemic behavior. They are pluralistic,

as they constantly seek new purposes and search for new niches in their environments. Examples are (a) communities seeking to establish integration of their systems of learning and human development with social, human, and health service agencies, and their community and economic development programs, and (b) cutting-edge R&D agencies.

In working with human systems, the understanding of what type of system we are working with, or the determination of the type of systems we wish to design, is crucial in that it suggests the selection of the approach and the methods and tools that are appropriate to systems inquiry.

2.1.7 The Nature of Problem Situations and Solutions

Working with human systems, we are confronted with problem situations that comprise a system of problems rather than a collection of problems. Problems are embedded in uncertainty and require subjective interpretation. Churchman (1971) suggested that in working with human systems, subjectivity cannot be avoided. What really matters, he says, is that systems are unique, and the task is to account for their uniqueness; and this uniqueness has to be considered in their description and design. Our main tool in working with human systems is subjectivity: reflection on the sources of knowledge, social practice, community, and interest in and commitment to ideas, especially the moral idea, affectivity, and faith.

Relatedly, in working with human systems, we must recognize that they are unbounded. Factors assumed to be part of a problem are inseparably linked to many other factors. A technical problem in transportation, such as the building of a freeway, becomes a land-use problem, linked with economic, environmental, conservation, ethical, and political issues. Can we really draw a boundary? When we seek to improve a situation, particularly if it is a public one, we find ourselves facing not a problem but a cluster of problems, often called problematique. Peccei (1977), the founder of the Club of Rome, says that:

> Within the problematique, it is difficult to pinpoint individual problems and propose individual solutions. Each problem is related to every other problem; each apparent solution to a problem may aggravate or interfere with others; and none of these problems or their combination can be tackled using the linear or sequential methods of the past. (p. 61)

Ackoff (1981) suggests that a set of interdependent problems constitutes a system of problems, which he calls a mess. Like any system, the mess has properties that none of its parts has. These properties are lost when the system is taken apart. In addition, each part of a system has properties that are lost when it is considered separately. The solution to a mess depends on how its parts interact. In an earlier statement, Ackoff (1974) says that the era of "quest for certainty" has passed. We live an age of uncertainty in which systems are open, dynamic, in which problems live in a moving process. "Problems and solutions are in constant flux, hence problems do not stay solved. Solutions to problems become obsolete even if the problems to which they are addressed are not" (p. 31). Ulrich (1983) suggests that when working with human systems, we should reflect critically on problems. He asks: How can we produce solutions if the problems remain unquestioned? We should transcend problems as originally stated and should explore critically the problem itself with all of those who are affected by the problem. We must differentiate well-structured and well-defined problems in which the initial conditions, the goals, and the necessary operations can all be specified, from ill-defined or ill-structured problems, the kind in which initial conditions, the goals, and the allowable operations cannot be extrapolated from the problem. Discussing this issue, Rittel and Webber (1984) suggest that science and engineering are dealing with well-structured or tame problems. But this stance is not applicable to open social systems. Still, many social science professionals have mimicked the cognitive style of scientists and the operational style of engineers. But social problems are inherently wicked problems. Thus, every solution of a wicked problem is tentative and incomplete, and it changes as we move toward the solution. As the solution changes, as it is elaborated, so does our understanding of the problem. Considering this issue in the context of systems design, Rittel and Webber (1984) suggest that the "ill-behaved" nature of design problem situations frustrates all attempts to start out with an information and analysis phase, at the end of which a clear definition of the problem is rendered and objectives are defined that become the basis for synthesis, during which a "monastic" solution can be worked out. Systems design requires a continuous interaction between the initial phase that triggers design and the state when design is completed.

2.1.8 The Soft-Systems Approach and Systems Design

From the 1970s on, it was generally realized that the nature of issues in human/social systems is "soft" in contrast with "hard" issues and problems in systems engineering and other quantitative focused systems inquiry. Hard-systems thinking and approaches were not usable in the context of human activity systems. As Checkland (1981) notes, "It is impossible to start the studies by naming 'the system' and defining its objectives, and without this naming/definition, hard systems thinking collapses" (pp. 15–16).

Churchman in his various works (1968a, 1968b, 1971, 1979, 1981) has been the most articulate and most effective advocate of ethical systems theory and morality in human systems inquiry. Human systems inquiry, as valuing and value oriented, must be concerned with a social imperative for improving the human condition. Churchman situates systems inquiry in a context of ethical decision making, and calls for the design of human inquiry systems that are concerned with valuing of individuals and collectives, and which value humanity above technology. Human systems inquiry, should, Churchman argues, embody values and methods by which to constantly examine decisions. Relatedly, Churchman (1971) took issue with the design approach wherein the focus is on various segments of the system. Specifically, when the designer detects a problem

in a part, he moves to modify it. This approach is based on the separability principle of incrementalism. Churchman advocates "nonseparabilty" when the application of decision rules depends on the state of the whole system, and when a certain degree of instability of a part occurs, the designer can recognize this event and change the system so that the part becomes stable. "It can be seen that design, properly viewed, is an enormous liberation of the intellectual spirit, for it challenges this spirit to an unbounded speculation about possibilities" (p. 13). A liberated designer will look at present practice as a point of departure at best. Design is a thought process and a communication process. Successful design is one that enables someone to transfer thought into action or into another design.

Checkland (1981) and Checkland and Scholes (1990) developed a methodology based on soft-systems thinking for working with human activity systems. The methodology is considered a

a learning system which uses systems ideas to formulate basic mental acts of four kinds: *perceiving, predicating, comparing,* and *deciding* for action. The output of the methodology is very different from the output of systems engineering: It is learning which leads to decision to take certain actions, knowing that this will lead not to 'the problem' being now 'solved,' but to a changed situation and new learning. (Checkland, 1981, p. 17, italics in original)

The methodology defined here is a direct consequence of the concept, human activity system. We attribute meaning to all human activity. Our attributions are meaningful in terms of our particular image of the world, which, in general, we take for granted.

Systems design, in the context of social systems, is a future-creative disciplined inquiry. People engage in this inquiry to design a system that realizes their vision of the future, their own expectations, and the expectations of their environment. Systems design is a relatively new intellectual technology. It emerged only recently as a manifestation of open-system thinking and corresponding ethically based soft-systems approaches. This new intellectual technology emerged, just in time, as a disciplined inquiry that enables us to align our social systems with the new realities of the information/knowledge age (Banathy, 1991).

Early pioneers of social systems design include Simon (1969), Jones (1970), Churchman (1968a, 1968b, 1971, 1978), Jantsch (1976, 1980), Warfield (1976), and Sage (1977). The watershed year of comprehensive statements on systems design was 1981, marked by the works of Ackoff, Checkland, and Nadler. Then came the work of Argyris (1982), Ulrich (1983), Cross (1984), Morgan (1986), Senge (1990), Warfield (1990), Nadler and Hibino (1990), Checkland and Scholes (1990), Banathy (1991, 1996, 2000), Hammer and Champy (1993), and Mitroff and Linstone (1993).

Prior to the emergence of social systems design, the improvement approach to systems change manifested traditional social planning (Banathy, 1991). This approach, still practiced today, reduces the problem to manageable pieces and seeks solutions to each. Users of this approach believe that solving the problem piece by piece ultimately will correct the larger issue it aims to remedy. But systems designers know that "getting rid of what is not wanted does not give you what is desired." In sharp contrast with traditional social planning, systems design—represented by the authors above—seeks to understand the problem situation as a system of interdependent and interacting problems, and seeks to create a design as a system of interdependent and interacting solution ideas. Systems designers envision the entity to be designed as a whole, as one that is designed from the synthesis of the interaction of its parts. Systems design requires both coordination and integration. We need to design all parts of the system interactively and simultaneously. This requires coordination, and designing for interdependency across all systems levels invites integration.

2.1.9 Reflections

In the first part of this chapter, systems inquiry was defined, and the evolution of the systems movement was reviewed. Then we focused on human systems inquiry, which is the conceptual foundation of the development of a systems view and systems applications in education. As we reflect on the ideas presented in this part, we realize how little of what was discussed here has any serious manifestation or application in education. Therefore, the second part of this chapter is devoted to the exploration of a systems view of education and its practical applications in working with systems of learning and human development.

2.2 THE SYSTEMS VIEW AND ITS APPLICATION IN EDUCATION

In the first part of this section of the chapter we present a discussion of the systems view and its relevance to education. This is followed by a focus on the application of the intellectual technology of comprehensive systems design as an approach to the transformation of education.

2.2.1 A Systems View of Education

A systems view enables us to explore and characterize the system of our interest, its environment, and its components and parts. We can acquire a systems view by integrating systems concepts and principles in our thinking and learning to use them in representing our world and our experiences with their use. A systems view empowers us to think of ourselves, the environments that surround us, and the groups and organizations in which we live in a new way: the systems way. This new way of thinking and experiencing enables us to explore, understand, and describe the (Banathy, 1988a, 1991, 1996):

- Characteristics of the "embeddedness" of educational systems operating at several interconnected levels (e.g., institutional, administrational, instructional, learning experience levels).

- Relationships, interactions, and mutual interdependencies of systems operating at those levels within educational systems.

- Relationships, interactions, and information/matter/energy exchanges between educational systems and their environments.

- Purposes, the goals, and the boundaries of educational systems as those emerge from an examination of the relationship and mutual interdependence of education and the society.

- Nature of education as a purposeful and purpose-seeking complex of open system, operating at various interdependent and integrated system levels.

- Dynamics of interactions, relationships, and patterns of connectedness among the components of systems.

- Properties of wholeness and the characteristics that emerge at various systems levels as a result of systemic interaction and synthesis.

- Systems processes, i.e., the behavior of education as a living system, and changes that are manifested of systems and their environments over time.

The systems view generates insights into ways of knowing, thinking, and reasoning that enable us to apply systems inquiry in educational systems. Systemic educational change will become possible only if the educational community will develop a systems view of education, if it embraces the systems view, and if it applies the systems view in its approach to change.

Systems inquiry and systems applications have been applied in the worlds of business and industry, in information technology, in the health services, in architecture and engineering, and in environmental issues. However, in education—except for a narrow application in instructional technology (discussed later)—systems inquiry is highly underconceptualized and underutilized, and it is often manifested in misdirected applications.

With very few exceptions, systems philosophy, systems theory, and systems methodology as subjects of study and applications are only recently emerging as topics of consideration in educational professional development programs, and then only in limited scope. Generally, capability in systems inquiry is limited to specialized interests groups in the educational research community. It is our firm belief that unless our educational communities and our educational professional organizations embrace systems inquiry, and unless our research agencies learn to pursue systems inquiry, the notions of "systemic" reform and "systemic approaches" to educational renewal will remain hollow and meaningless rhetoric.

The notion of systems inquiry enfolds large sets of concepts that constitute principles, common to all kinds of systems. Acquiring a "systems view of education" means that we learn to think about education as a system, we can understand and describe it as a system, we can put the systems view into practice and apply it in educational inquiry, and we can design education so that it will manifest systemic behavior. Once we individually and collectively develop a systems view then—and only then—can we become "systemic" in our approach to educational change, only then can we apply the systems view to the reconceptualization and redefinition of education as a

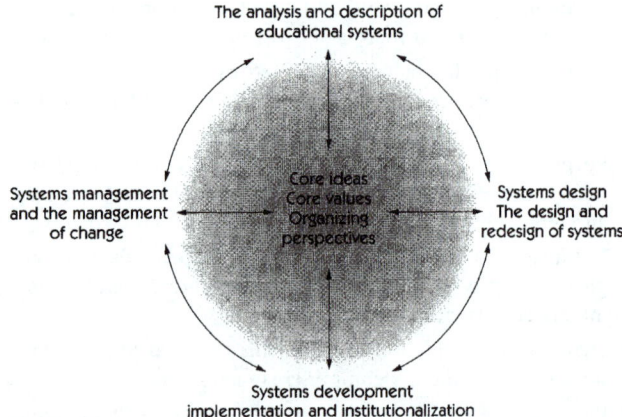

The analysis and description of
educational systems

Systems management
and the management
of change

Core ideas
Core values
Organizing
perspectives

Systems design
The design and
redesign of systems

Systems development
implementation and institutionalization

FIGURE 2.1. A comprehensive system of educational inquiry.

system, and only then can we engage in the design of systems that will nurture learning and enable the full development of human potential.

During the past decade, we have applied systems thinking and the systems view in human and social systems. As a result we now have a range of systems models and methods that enable us to work creatively and successfully with education as a complex social system. Banathy (1988b) organized these models and methods in four complementary domains of inquiry in educational organizations as follows:

- The systems analysis and description of educational systems by the application of three systems models: the systems environment, functions/structure, and process/behavioral models
- Systems design, conducting comprehensive design inquiry with the use of design models, methods, and tools appropriate to education
- Implementation of the design by systems development and institutionalization
- Systems management and the management of change

Figure 2.1 depicts the relational arrangement of the four domains of organizational inquiry. In the center of the figure is the integrating cluster.

In the center, the core values, core ideas, and organizing perspectives constitute bases for both the development of the inquiry approach and the decisions we make in the course of the inquiry.

Of special interest to us in this chapter is the description and analysis of educational systems and social systems design as a disciplined inquiry that offers potential for the development of truly systemic educational change. In the remainder of the chapter, we focus on these two aspects of systems inquiry.

2.2.2 Three Models That Portray Education as a System

Models are useful as a frame of reference to talk about the system the models represent. Because our purpose here is to understand and portray education as a system, it is important to create a common frame of reference for our discourse, to build systems models of education.

Models of social systems are built by the relational organization of the concepts and principles that represent the context, the content, and the process of social systems. Banathy (1992) constructed three models that represent (a) systems–environment relationships, (b) the functions/structure of social systems, and (c) the processes/behavior of systems through time. These models are "lenses" that can be used to look at educational systems and understand, describe, and analyze them as open, dynamic, and complex social systems. These models are briefly described next.

2.2.2.1 Systems–Environment Model. The use of the systems–environment model enables us to describe an educational system in the context of its community and the larger society. The concepts and principles that are pertinent to this model help us define systems–environment relationships, interactions, and mutual interdependencies. A set of inquiries, built into the model, guide the user to make an assessment of the environmental responsiveness of the system and, conversely, the adequacy of the responsiveness of the environment toward the system.

2.2.2.2 Functions/Structure Model. The use of the functions/structure model focuses our attention on what the educational system is at a given moment of time. It projects a "still-picture" image of the system. It enables us to (a) describe the goals of the system (that elaborate the purposes that emerged from the systems–environment model), (b) identify the functions that have to be carried out to attain the goals, (c) select the components (of the system) that have the capability to carry out the functions, and (d) formulate the relational arrangements of the components that constitute the structure of the system. A set of inquiries are built into the model that guide the user to probe into the function/structure adequacy of the system.

2.2.2.3 Process/Behavioral Model. The use of the process/behavioral model helps us to concentrate our inquiry on what the educational system *does* through time. It projects a "motion picture" image of the system and guides us in understanding how the system behaves as a changing and living social system; how it (a) receives, screens, assesses, and processes input; (b) transforms input for use in the system; (c) engages in transformation operations by which to produce the expected output; (d) guides the transformation operations; (e) processes the output and assesses its adequacy; and (f) makes adjustment in the system if needed or imitates the redesign of the system if indicated. The model incorporates a set of inquiries that guides the user to evaluate the systems from a process perspective.

What is important for us to understand is that no single model can provide us with a true representation of an educational system. Only if we consider the three models jointly can we capture a comprehensive image of education as a social system.

2.2.3 Systems Inquiry for Educational Systems

Systems inquiry is a disciplined inquiry by which systems knowledge and systems competencies are developed and applied in engaging in conscious self-guided educational change. In this section we focus on four domains of systems inquiry, explore their relationships, and define the modes of systems inquiry as discipline inquiry in relation to educational systems.

2.2.3.1 The Four Domains of Systems Inquiry in Educational Systems. Systems inquiry incorporates four interrelated domains: philosophy, theory, methodology, and application. Systems philosophy, as explicated earlier in this chapter, is composed of three dimensions: ontology, epistemology, and axiology. Of these, epistemology has two domains of inquiry. It studies the process of change or coevolution of the system within the systems inquiry space (systems design space) to generate knowledge and understanding about *how* systems change works, in our case, within educational systems. The ontological dimension, in relation to systems inquiry in education, is concerned with formation of a systems view of education, shifting from a view of education as inanimate ("thing view"), to a view of education as a living open system, recognizing the primacy of organizing—self-organizing—relationship processes. The axiological dimension of systems inquiry in social systems like education brings to the foreground concern for the moral, ethical, and aesthetic qualities of systems. In particular, social justice, equity, tolerance, issues of difference, caring, community, and democracy. Systems theory articulates interrelated concepts and principles that apply to systemic change process as a human activity system (Jenlink & Reigeluth, 2000). It seeks to offer plausible and reasoned general principles that explain systemic change process as a disciplined inquiry. Systems methodology has two domains of inquiry. The study of methods within the system by which knowledge is generated about systems and the identification and description of application-based strategies, tools, methods, and models used to design inquiry systems as well as used to animate the system inquiry processes in relation to the design of a solutions for complex system problems. Systems application takes place in functional contexts of intentional systems design and systemic change. Application refers to the dynamic interaction and translation of theory, philosophy, and methodology into social action through the systems inquiry process.

2.2.3.2 The Dynamic Interaction of the Four Domains. Systems philosophy, theory, methodology, and application come to life as they are used and applied in the functional context of designing systems inquiry and relatedly, as systems inquiry is used and applied in educational systems. It is in the practical context of application of systems inquiry in education that systems philosophy, theory, and methodology are confirmed, changed, modified, and reaffirmed. Systems philosophy provides the underlying values, beliefs, assumptions, and perspectives that guide us in "defining and organizing in relational arrangements the concepts and principles that constitute" (Banathy, 2000, p. 264) systems theory in relation to educational systems. Systems philosophy and theory dynamically work to

guide us in "developing, selecting, and organizing approaches, strategies, methods, and tools into the scheme of epistemology (p. 264) of educational systems design. Systems methodology and application interact to guide us in the confirmation and/or need for change/modification of systems theory and epistemology. The four domains, working dynamically, "continuously confirms and/or modifies the other" (p. 264). The four domains constitute the conceptual system of systems inquiry in educational systems. It is important to note that the relational influence of one domain on the others, recursive and multidimensional in nature, links one domain to the others.

2.2.3.3 Two Modes of Systems Inquiry. Systems inquiry, as disciplined inquiry, comes to life as the four domains of philosophy, theory, methodology, and application each interact recursively. In particular, when social systems design epistemology, in concert with methodological considerations for systems inquiry, work in relation to the philosophical and theoretical foundations, "faithfulness" of the systems design epistemology is tested. Simultaneously, the relevance of "its philosophical and theoretical foundations and its successes of application" (Banathy, 2000, p. 265) are examined in the functional context of systems inquiry and design—in the systems design space. In the course of this dynamic interaction, two modes of disciplined inquiry are operating: "decision-oriented disciplined inquiry and conclusion-oriented disciplined inquiry" (Banathy, 2000, p. 266). Banathy (2000) has integrated these two modes, first articulated by Cronbach and Suppes (1969) for educational systems, into systems inquiry for social systems design. Figure 2.2 provides a relational framework of these two modes of inquiry.

2.2.4 Designing Social Systems

Systems design in the context of human activity systems is a future-creating disciplined inquiry. People engage in design in

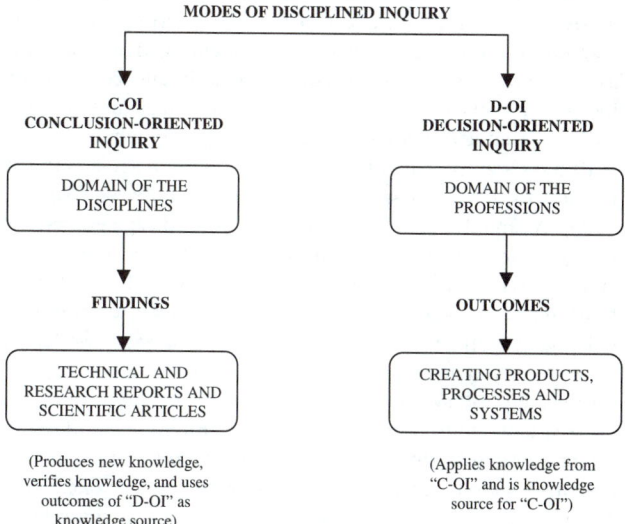

FIGURE 2.2. Relational framework of the two modes of inquiry.

order to devise and implement a new system, based on their vision of what that system should be.

There is a growing awareness that most of our systems are out of sync with the new realities, particularly since we crossed the threshold into a new millennium. Increasingly, the realization of postmodernity challenges past views and assumptions grounded in modernist and outdated modes of thinking. Those who understand this and are willing to face these changing realities call for the rethinking and redesign of our systems. Once we understand the significance of these new realities and their implications for us individually and collectively, we will reaffirm that systems design is the only viable approach to working with and creating and recreating our systems in a changing world of new realities. These new realties and the societal and organizational characteristics of the new millennium call for the development of new thinking, new perspectives, new insight, and—based on these—the design of social systems that will be in sync with those realities and emergent characteristics.

In times of accelerating and dynamic changes, when a new stage is unfolding in societal evolution, inquiry should not focus on the improvement of our existing systems. Such a focus limits perception to adjusting or modifying the old design in which our systems are still rooted. A design rooted in an outdated image is useless. We must transcend old ways of thinking and engage in new ways of thinking, at higher levels of sophistication. To paraphrase Albert Einstein, we can no longer solve the problems of education by engaging in the same level of thinking that created them, rather we must equip ourselves to think beyond the constraints of science, we must use our creative imagination. We should transcend the boundaries of our existing system, explore change and renewal from the larger vistas of our transforming society, envision a new image of our systems, create a new design based on the image, and transform our systems by implementing the new design.

2.2.4.1 Systems Design: A New Intellectual Technology.
Systems design in the context of social systems is "coming into its own as a serious intellectual technology in service of human intention" (Nelson, 1993, p. 145). It emerged only recently as a manifestation of open-systems thinking and corresponding soft-systems approaches. The epistemological and ontological importance of systems design is recognized when situated within the complex nature of social problems in society and in relation to the teleological issues of human purpose (Nelson, 1993). As an intellectual technology, systems design enables us to align our societal systems, most specifically our educational systems, with the "new realities" of the postmodern information/knowledge age. Individuals who see a need to transcend existing systems, in our case educational systems, and design new systems that enable the realization of a vision of the future society use systems design. This vision of the future society is situated within the societal and environmental context in which these individuals live and from which they envision new systems decidedly different from systems currently in existence. As a nascent method of disciplined inquiry and emergent intellectual technology, systems inquiry brings to the foreground a requirement of cognizance in systems philosophy, theory, and

methodology. As an intellectual technology and mode of inquiry, systems design

seeks to understand a problem situation as a system of interconnected, interdependent, and interacting issues and to create a design as a system of interconnected, interdependent, interacting, and internally consistent solution ideas. (Banathy, 1996, p. 46)

The need for systems knowledge and competencies in relation to accepting intellectual responsibility for designing the inquiry system as well as applying the inquiry system to resolve complex social problems, sets systems design apart from traditional social planning approaches. From a systems perspective, the individuals who comprise the social system, i.e., education, are the primary beneficiary or users of the system. Therefore, these same individuals are socially charged with the responsibility for constantly determining the "goodness of fit" of existing systems in the larger context of society and our environment, and engaging in designing new systems that meet the emerging needs of humanity.

2.2.5 When Should We Design?

Social systems are created for attaining purposes that are shared by those who are in the system. Activities in which people in the system are engaged are guided by those purposes. There are times when there is a discrepancy between what our system actually attains and what we designated as the desired outcome of the system. Once we sense such discrepancy, we realize that something has gone wrong, and we need to make some changes either in the activities or in the way we carry out activities. Changes within the system are accomplished by adjustment, modification, or improvement.

But there are times when we have evidence that changes within the system would not suffice. We might realize that our purposes are not viable anymore and we need to change them. We realize that we now need to change the whole system. We need a different system; we need to redesign our system; or we need to design a new system.

The changes described above are guided by self-regulation, accomplished, as noted earlier, by positive feedback that signals the need for changing the whole system. We are to formulate new purposes, introduce new functions, new components, and new arrangements of the components. It is by such self-organization that the system responds to positive feedback and learns to coevolve with its environment by transforming itself into a new state at higher levels of existence and complexity. The process by which this self-organization, coevolution, and transformation come about is systems design.

2.2.6 Models for Building Social Systems

Until the 1970s, design, as a disciplined inquiry, was primarily the domain of architecture and engineering. In social and sociotechnical systems, the nature of the inquiry was systems analysis, operation research, or social engineering. These approaches reflected the kind of systematic, closed systems, and hard-systems thinking discussed in the previous section. It was not until the 1970s that we realized that the use of these approaches was not applicable; in fact, they were counterproductive to working with social systems. We became aware that social systems are open systems; they have dynamic complexity; and they operate in turbulent and ever-changing environments. Premised on this understanding, a new orientation emerged, grounded in "soft-systems" thinking. The insights gained from this orientation became the basis for the emergence of a new generation of designers and the development of new design models applicable to social systems. Earlier we listed systems researchers who made significant contributions to the development of approaches to the design of open social systems. Among them, three scholars—Ackoff, Checkland, and Nadler— were the ones who developed comprehensive process models of systems design. Their work set the trend for continuing work in design research and social systems design.

2.2.6.1 Ackoff: A Model for the Design of Idealized Systems.

The underlying conceptual base of Ackoff's design model (1981) is a systems view of the world. He explores how our concept of the world has changed in recent time from the machine age to the systems age. He defines and interprets the implications of the systems age and the systems view to systems design. He sets forth design strategies, followed by implementation planning. At the very center of his approach is what he calls *idealized design.*

Design commences with an understanding and assessment of what is now. Ackoff (1981) calls this process *formulating the mess.* The mess is a set of interdependent problems that emerges and is identifiable only in their interaction. Thus, the design that responds to this mess "should be more than an aggregation of independently obtained solutions to the parts of the mess. It should deal with messes as wholes, systemically" (1981, p. 52). This process includes systems analysis, a detailed study of potential obstructions to development, and the creation of projections and scenarios that explore the question: What would happen if things would not change?

Having gained a systemic insight into the current state of affairs, Ackoff (1981) proceeds to the idealized design. The selection of ideals lies at the very core of the process. As he says: "it takes place through idealized design of a system that does not yet exist, or the idealized design of one that does" (p. 105). The three properties of an idealized design are: It should be (1) technologically feasible, (2) operationally viable, and (3) capable of rapid learning and development. This model is not a utopian system but "the most effective ideal-seeking system of which designers can conceive" (p. 107). The process of creating the ideal includes selecting a mission, specifying desired properties of the design, and designing the system. Ackoff emphasizes that the vision of the ideal must be a shared image. It should be created by all who are in the system and those affected by the design. Such participative design is attained by the organization of interlinked design boards that integrate representation across the various levels of the organization.

Having created the model of the idealized system, designers engage in the design of the management system that can guide the system and can learn how to learn as a system. Its three key functions are: (1) identifying threats and opportunities, (2) identifying what to do and having it done, and (3) maintaining and improving performance. The next major function is organizational design, the creation of the organization that is "ready, willing, and able to modify itself when necessary in order to make progress towards its ideals" (p. 149). The final stage is implementation planning. It is carried out by selecting or creating the means by which the specified ends can be pursued, determining what resources will be required, planning for the acquisition of resources, and defining who is doing what, when, how, and where.

2.2.6.2 Checkland's Soft-Systems Model.

Checkland in his work (1981) creates a solid base for his model for systems change by reviewing (a) science as human activity, (b) the emergence of systems science, and (c) the evolution of systems thinking. He differentiates between "hard-systems thinking," which is appropriate to work with, rather than closed, engineered type of systems and "soft-systems thinking," which is required in working with social systems. He says that he is "trying to make systems thinking a conscious, generally accessible way of looking at things, not the stock of trade of experts" (p. 162). Based on soft-systems thinking, he formulated a model for working with and changing social systems.

His seven-stage model generates a total system of change functions, leading to the creation of a future system. His conceptual model of the future system is similar in nature to Ackoff's idealized system. Using Checkland's approach, during the first stage we look at the problem situation of the system, which we find in its real-life setting as being "unstructured." At this stage, our focus is not on specific problems but the situation in which we perceive the problem. Given the perceived "unstructured situation," during Stage 2 we develop a richest possible structured picture of the problem situation. These first two stages operate in the context of the real world.

The next two stages are developed in the conceptual realm of systems thinking. Stage 3 involves speculating about some systems that may offer relevant solutions to the problem situation and preparing concise "root definitions" of what these systems are (not what they do). During Stage 4, the task is to develop abstract representations, models of the relevant systems, for which root definitions were formulated at Stage 3. These representations are conceptual models of the relevant systems, composed of verbs, denoting functions. This stage consists of two substages. First, we describe the conceptual model. Then, we check it against a theory-based, formal model of systems. Checkland adopted Churchman's model (1971) for this purpose.

During the last three stages, we move back to the realm of the real world. During Stage 5, we compare the conceptual model with the structured problem situation we formulated during Stage 2. This comparison enables us to identify, during Stage 6, feasible and desirable changes in the real world. Stage 7 is devoted to taking action and introducing changes in the system.

2.2.6.3 Nadler's Planning and Design Approach.

Nadler, an early proponent of designing for the ideal (1967), is the third systems scholar who developed a comprehensive model (Nadler, 1981) for the design of sociotechnical systems. During

Phase 1, his strategy calls for the development of a hierarchy of purpose statements, which are formulated so that each higher level describes the purpose of the next lower level. From this purpose hierarchy, the designers select the specific purpose level for which to create the, system. The formulation of purpose is coupled with the identification of measures of effectiveness that indicate the successful achievement of the defined purpose. During this phase, designers explore alternative reasons and expectations that the design might accomplish.

During Phase 2, "creativity is engaged as ideal solutions are generated for the selected purposes within the context of the purpose hierarchy," says Nadler (1981, p. 9). He introduced a large array of methods that remove conceptual blocks, nurture creativity, and widen the creation of alternative solutions ideas.

During Phase 3, designers develop solution ideas into systems of alternative solutions. During this phase, designers play the believing game as they focus on how to make ideal solutions work, rather than on the reasons why they won't work. They try ideas out to see how they fit.

During Phase 4, the solution is detailed. Designers build into the solution specific arrangements that might cope with potential exceptions and irregularities while protecting the desired qualities of solutions. As Nadler (1981) says: "Why discard the excellent solution that copes with 95% of the conditions because another 5% cannot directly fit into it?" (p. 11). As a result, design solutions are often flexible, multichanneled, and pluralistic.

During Phase 5, the implementation of the selected design solution occurs. In the context of the purpose hierarchy, the ideal solution is set forth as well as the plan for taking action necessary to install the solution. However, it is necessary to realize that the, "most successful implemented solution is incomplete if it does not incorporate the seeds of its own improvement. An implemented solution should be treated as provisional" (Nadler, 1981, p. 11). Therefore, each system should have its own arrangements for continuing design and change.

In a later book, coauthored by Nadler and Hibino (1990), a set of principles is discussed that guides the work of designers. These principles can serve as guidelines that keep designers focused on seeking solutions rather than on being preoccupied by problems. In summary form, the principles include:

- The "uniqueness principle" suggests that whatever the apparent similarities, each problem is unique, and the design approach should respond to the unique contextual situation.
- The "purposes principle" calls for focusing on purposes and expectations rather than on problems. This focus helps us strip away nonessential aspects and prevents us from working on the wrong problem.
- The "ideal design principle" stimulates us to work back from the ideal target solution.
- The "systems principle" explains that every design setting is part of a larger system. Understanding the systems matrix of embeddedness helps us to determine the multilevel complexities that we should incorporate into the solution model.
- The "limited information principle" points to the pitfall that too much knowing about the problem can prevent us from seeing some excellent alternative solutions.

- The "people design principle" underlines the necessity of involving in the design all those who are in the systems and who are affected by the design.
- The "betterment timeline principle" calls for the deliberate building into the design the capability and capacity for continuing betterment of the solution through time.

2.2.7   A Process Model of Social Systems Design

The three design models introduced above have been applied primarily in the corporate and business community. Their application in the public domain has been limited. Still, we can learn much from them as we seek to formulate an approach to the design of social and societal systems. In the concluding section of Part 2, we introduce a process model of social system design that has been inspired and informed by the work of Ackoff, Checkland, and Nadler, and is a generalized outline of Banathy's (1991) work of designing educational systems.

The process of design that leads us from an existing state to a desired future state is initiated by an expression of why we want to engage in design. We call this expression of want the *genesis of design*. Once we decide that we want to design a system other than what we now have, we must:

- Transcend the existing state or the existing system and leave it behind.
- Envision an image of the system that we wish to create.
- Design the system based on the image.
- Transform the system by developing and implementing the system based on the design.

Transcending, envisioning, designing, and transforming the system are the four major strategies of the design and development of social systems, which are briefly outlined below.

2.2.7.1   Transcending the Existing State. Whenever we have an indication that we should change the existing system or create a new system, we are confronted with the task of transcending the existing system or the existing state of affairs. We devised a framework that enables designers to accomplish this transcendence and create an option field, which they can use to draw alternative boundaries for their design inquiry and consider major solution alternatives. The framework is constructed of four dimensions: the focus of the inquiry, the scope of the inquiry, relationship with other systems, and the selection of system type. On each dimension, several options are identified that gradually extend the boundaries of the inquiry. The exploration of options leads designers to make a series of decisions that charts the design process toward the next strategy of systems design.

2.2.7.2   Envisioning: Creating the First Image. Systems design creates a description, a representation, a model of the future system. This creation is grounded in the designers' vision, ideas, and aspirations of what that future system should be. As the designers draw the boundaries of the design inquiry on the framework and make choices from among the options, they collectively form core ideas that they hold about the desired future. They articulate their shared vision and synthesize their core ideas into the first image of the system. This image becomes a magnet that pulls designers into designing the system that will bring the image to life.

2.2.7.3 Designing the New System Based on the Image.
The image expresses an intent. One of the key issues in working with social systems is: How to bring intention and design together and create a system that transforms the image into reality? The image becomes the basis that initiates the strategy of transformation by design. The design solution emerges as designers

1. Formulate the mission and purposes of the future system
2. Define its specifications
3. Select the functions that have to be carried out to attain the mission and purposes
4. Organize these functions into a system
5. Design the system that will guide the functions and the organization that will carry out the functions
6. Define the environment that will have the resources to support the system
7. Describe the new system by using the three models we described earlier—the systems–environment model, the functions/structure model, and the process/behavioral model (Banathy, 1992)
8. Prepare a development/implementation plan.

2.2.7.4 Transforming the System Based on the Design.
The outcome of design is a description, a conceptual representation, or modeling of the new system. Based on the models, we can bring the design to life by developing the system based on the models that represent the design and then implementing and institutionalizing it (Banathy, 1986, 1991, 1996).

We elaborated the four strategies in the context of education in our earlier work as we described the processes of (1) transcending the existing system of education, (2) envisioning and defining the image of the desired future system, (3) designing the new system based on the image, and (4) transforming the existing system by developing/ implementing/institutionalizing the new system based on the design.

In this section, a major step has been taken toward the understanding of systems design by exploring some research findings about design, examining a set of comprehensive design models, and proposing a process model for the design of educational and other social systems. In the closing section, we present the disciplined inquiry of systems design as the new imperative in education and briefly highlight distinctions between instructional design and systems design.

2.2.8 Systems Design: The New Imperative in Education

Many of us share a realization that today's schools are far from being able to do justice to the education of future generations. There is a growing awareness that our current design of education is out of sync with the new realities of the information/knowledge era. Those who are willing to face these new realities understand that:

- Rather than improving education, we should *transcend* it.
- Rather than revising it, we should revision it.
- Rather then reforming, we should transform it by design.

We now call for a metamorphosis of education. It has become clear to many of us that educational inquiry should not focus on the improvement of existing systems. Staying within the existing boundaries of education constrains and delimits perception and locks us into prevailing practices. At best, improvement or restructuring of the existing system can attain some marginal adjustment of an educational design that is still rooted in the perceptions and practices of the 19th century machine age.

Adjusting a design rooted in an outdated image, creates far more problems than it solves. At best, we resolve few if any of the issues we set out to address, and then only in superficial ways, while simultaneously risking the reification of many of the existing problems that problematize education and endanger the future for our children. We know this only too well. The escalating rhetoric of educational reform has created high expectations, but the realities of improvement efforts have not delivered on those expectations. Improving what we have now does not lead to any significant results, regardless of how much money and effort we invest in it.

Our educational communities—including our educational technology community—have reached an evolutionary juncture in our journey toward understanding and implementing educational renewal. We are now confronted with the reality that traditional philosophies, theories, methods, and applications are unable to attend to the complex nature of educational systems, in particular when we apply ways of thinking which further exacerbate fragmentation and incoherence in the system. There is a need for systems design that enables change *of* the system rather than limiting change to *within* the system (Jenlink, 1995). Improving what exists, when what exists isn't meeting the needs of an increasingly complex society, only refines the problem rather than providing solution. Change that focuses on design of an entire system, rather than change or improvement in parts of the system, moves to the forefront systems inquiry as a future-creating approach to educational renewal.

Systems philosophy, theory, methodology and relatedly systems thinking that emerges as we engage in a systems view of education guides the reenchantment of educational renewal. The purposeful and viable creation of new organizational capacities and individual and collective competencies and capabilities grounded in systems, enables us to empower our educational communities so that they can engage in the design and transformation of our educational systems by creating new systems of learning and human development. Systems inquiry and its application in education is liberating and renewing, which recognizes the import of valuing, nurturing, and sustaining the human capacity for applying a new intellectual technology in the design human activity systems like education.

2.2.9 Instructional Design Is Not Systems Design

A question, which frequents the educational technology community, reflects a longstanding discourse concerning systems design: Is there really a difference between the intellectual technology of instructional design and systems design? A review of this chapter should lead the reader to an understanding of the difference.

An understanding of the process of designing education as an open social system, reviewed here, and the comparison of this with the process of designing instructional or training systems, known well to the reader, will clearly show the difference between the two design inquiries. Banathy (1987) discussed this difference at some length earlier. Here we briefly highlight some of the differences:

- Education as social system is open to its environment, its community, and the larger society, and it constantly and dynamically interacts with its environment.
- An instructional system is a subsystem of an instructional program that delivers a segment of the curriculum. The curriculum is embedded in the educational system.
- An instructional system is three systems levels below education as a social system.
- We design an educational system in view of societal realities/expectations/aspirations and core ideas and values. It is from these that an image of the future system emerges, based on which we then formulate the core definition, the mission, and purposes of the system.
- We design an instructional system against clearly defined instructional objectives that are derived from the larger instructional program and—at the next higher level—from the curriculum.
- An instructional system is a closed system. The technology of its design is an engineering (hard-system) technology. An educational system is open and is constantly coevolving with its environment. Its design applies soft-systems methods.
- In designing an educational system we engage in the design activity those individuals/collectives who are serving the system, those who are served by it, and those who are affected by it.
- An instructional system is designed by the expert educational technologist who takes into account the characteristics of the user of the system.
- A designed instructional system is often delivered by computer software and other mediation. An educational system is a human/social activity system that relies primarily on human/social interaction. Some of the interactions, for example, planning or information storing, can be aided by the use of software.

2.2.10 The Challenge of the Educational Technology Community

As members of the educational technology community, we are faced with a four-pronged challenge: (1) We must transcend the constraints and limits of the means and methods of instructional technology. We should clearly understand the difference between the design of education as a social system and instructional design. (2) We must develop open-systems thinking, acquire a systems view, and develop competence in systems design. (3) We must create programs and resources that enable our larger educational community to develop systems thinking, a systems view, and competence in systems design. (4) We must assist our communities across the nation to engage in the design and development of their systems of learning and human development. Our societal challenge is to place our self in the service of transforming education by designing new systems of education, creating just, equitable, caring, and democratic systems of learning and development for future generations.

Accepting the responsibility for creating new systems of education means committing ourselves to systems inquiry and design and dedicating ourselves to the betterment of education, and therefore humankind. Through edcation we create the future, and there is no more important task and no nobler calling than participating in this creation. The decisions is ours today; the consequences of our actions are the inheritance of our children, and the generations to come.

References

Ackoff, R. L. (1981). *Creating the Corporate Future*. New York: Wiley.

Ackoff, R. L. & Emery, F. E. (1972). *On purposeful systems*. Chicago, IL: Aldine-Atherton.

Argyris, C. (1982). *Reasoning, learning and action*. San Francisco, CA: Jossey-Bass.

Argyris, C., & Schön, D. (1979). *Organizational learning*. Reading, MA: Addison Wesley.

Argyris, C., & Schön, D. (1982). *Reasoning, learning and action*. San Francisco, CA: Jossey-Bass.

Ashby, W. R. (1952). *Design for a brain*. New York: Wiley.

Argyris, C. (1982). Reasoning, Learning and action. San Francisco, CA: Jossey-Bass.

Banathy, B. A. (1989). A general theory of systems by Bela Zalai (book review). *Systems Practice 2*(4), 451–454.

Banathy, B. H. (1986). A systems view of institutionalizing change in education. In S. Majumdar, (Ed.), *1985–86 Yearbook of the National Association of Academies of Science*. Columbus, OH: Ohio Academy of Science.

Banathy, B. H. (1987). Instructional Systems Design, In R. Gagne, ed., *Instructional Technology Foundations*. Hillsdale, NJ: Erlbaum.

Banathy, B. H. (1988a). Systems inquiry in education. *Systems Practice, 1*(2), 193–211.

Banathy, B. H. (1988b). Matching design methods to system type. *Systems Research, 5*(1), 27–34.

Banathy, B. H. (1991). *Systems design of education.* Englewood Cliffs, NJ: Educational Technology.

Banathy, B. H. (1992). A *systems view of education.* Englewood Cliffs, NJ: Educational Technology.

Banathy, B. H. (1996). *Designing social systems in a changing world.* New York: Plenum Press.

Banathy, B. H. (2000). *Guided evolution of society: A systems view.* New York: Kluwer Academic/Plenum Press.

Banathy, B. H., & Mills, S. (1985). The application of living systems process analysis in education. San Francisco, CA: International Systems Institute.

Bateson, G. (1972). *Steps to an ecology of mind.* New York: Random House.

Bertalanffy, L., von (1945). *Zu EinerAllgemeinen System Lehre.* In F. Blaetter, *Deutsche Philosophie* 18 (3/4).

Bertalanffy, L., von (1951). General systems theory: A new approach to the unity of science. *Human Biology, 23.*

Bertalanffy, L., von (1956). General systems theory. In Vol. L, *Yearbook of Society for General Systems Research.*

Bertalanffy, L., von (1968). *General systems theory.* New York: Braziller.

Blauberg, J. X., Sadovsky, V. N., & Yudin, E. G. (1977). *Systems theory: Philosophical and methodological problems.* Moscow: Progress Publishers.

Bogdanov, A. (1921-27). Tektologia (a series of articles) *Proletarskaya Kultura.*

Bohm, D. (1995). *Wholeness and the implicate order.* New York: Routledge.

Boulding, K. (1956). General systems theory-the skeleton of science. In Vol I, *Yearbook of Society for General Systems Research.*

Brier, S. (1992). Information and Consciousness: A critique of the mechanistic foundation for the concept of Information. *Cybernetics and Human Knowing,* 1(2/3), 71-94.

Brocklesby, J., & Cummings, S. (1996). Foucault plays Habermas: An alternative philosophical underpinning for critical systems thinking. *Journal of Operational Research Society,* 47(6), 741-754.

Buckley, W. (1968). *Modem systems research for the behavioral scientist.* Chicago, IL: Aldine.

Cavallo, R. (1979). Systems research movement. *General Systems Bulletin IX, (3).*

Checkland, P. (1981). *Systems thinking, systems practice.* New York: Wiley.

Checkland, P., & Scholes, J. (1990). Soft *systems methodology.* New York: Wiley.

Churchman, C. W. (1968a). *Challenge to reason.* New York: McGraw-Hill.

Churchman, C. W. (1968b). *The systems approach.* New York: Delacorte.

Churchman, C. W. (1971). *The design of inquiring systems.* New York: Basic Books.

Churchman, C. W. (1979). *The systems approach and its enemies.* New York: Basic Books.

Churchman, C. W. (1982). *Thought and wisdom.* Salinas, CA: Intersystem.

Cronbach, L. J., & Suppes, P. (1969). *Research for tomorrow's schools: Disciplined inquiry in education.* New York: Macmillan.

Cross, N. (1974). *Redesigning the Future.* New York: Wiley.

Cross, N. (1981). *Creating the corporate future.* New York: Wiley.

Cross, N. (1984). *Developments in design methodology,* New York: Wiley.

Einstein, A. (1955). *The meaning of relativity.* Princeton, NJ: Princeton University Press.

Einstein, A. (1959). Relativity: The special and the general theory.

Flood, R. L. (1990). *Liberating systems theory.* New York: Plenum.

Foerster, H. von (1984). *Observing systems.* Salinas, CA: Intersystems.

Foucault, M. (1980). *Power/knowledge: Selected interviews and other writings 1972-1977* (C. Gordon, Ed.), Brighton, England: Harvester Press.

Gleick, J. (1987). *Chaos: Making a new science.* New York: Viking.

Golerik, G. (1980). *Essays in tektology.* Salinas, CA: Intersystems.

Habermas, J. (1970). Knowledge and interest. In D. Emmet and A. MacIntyre (Eds.), *Sociological theory and philosophical analysis* (pp. 36-54). London: Macmillan.

Habermas, J. (1973). *Theory and practice* (J. Viertel. Trans.). Boston, MA: Beacon.

Habermas, J. (1984). *The theory of communicative action* (T. McCarthy, Trans.). Boston, MA: Beacon.

Hall, A. (1962). *A methodology of systems engineering,* Princeton, NJ: Van Nostrand.

Hammer, M., & Champy, J. (1993). *Reengineering the corporation.* New York: HarperCollins.

Heisenberg, W. (1930). *The physical principles of the quantum theory* (C. Eckart & F. C. Hoyt, Trans). New York: Dover.

Hiller, W., Musgrove, J., & O'Sullivan, P. (1972). Knowledge and design. In W. J. Mitchell (Ed.), *Environmental design.* Berkeley, CA: University California Press.

Horn, R. A., Jr. (1999). The dissociative nature of educational change. In S. R. Steinberg, J. L. Kincheloe, & P.H. Hinchey (Eds.), *The post-formal reader: Cognition and education* (pp. 349-377). New York: Falmer Press.

Jackson, M. C. (1985). Social systems theory and practice: The need for a critical approach, *International Journal of General Systems, 10,* 135-151.

Jackson, M. C. (1991a). The origins and nature of critical systems thinking. *Systems Practice, 4,* 131-149.

Jackson, M. C. (1991b). Post-Modernism and contemporary systems thinking. In R. C. Flood & M. C. Jackson (Eds.), Critical Systems thinking (pp. 287-302). New York: John Wiley & Sons.

Jackson, M., & Keys, P. (1984). Towards a system of systems methodologies. *Journal of Operations Research, 3,* 473-486.

Jantsch, E. (1976). *Design for evolution.* New York: Braziller.

Jantsch, E. (1980). The self-organizing universe. Oxford: Pergamon.

Jenlink, P. M. (2001). Activity theory and the design of educational systems: Examining the mediational importance of conversation. *Systems Research and Behavioral Science,* 18(4), 345-359.

Jenlink, P. M. (1995). Educational change systems: A systems design process for systemic change. In P. M. Jenlink (Ed.), *Systemic change: Touchstones for the future school* (pp. 41-67). Palatine, IL: IRI/Skylight.

Jenlink, P. M. & Reigeluth, C. M. (2000). A guidance system for designing new k-12 educational systems. In J. K. Allen & J. Wilby (Eds.), *The proceedings of the 44th annual conference of the International Society for the Systems Sciences.*

Jenlink, P. M., Reigeluth, C. M., Carr, A. A., & Nelson, L. M. (1998). Guidelines for facilitating systemic change in school districts. *Systems Research and Behavioral Science,* 15(3), 217-233.

Jones, C. (1970). *Design methods.* New York: Wiley.

Laszlo, E. (1972). *The systems view of the world.* New York: Braziller.

Laszlo, E. (1987). *Evolution: A grand synthesis.* Boston, MA: New Science Library.

Lawson, B. R. (1984). Cognitive studies in architectural design. In N. Cross (Ed.), *Developments in design methodology.* New York: Wiley.

Miller, J. (1978). *Living systems.* New York: McGraw-Hill

Mitroff, I., & Linstone, H. (1993). *The unbounded mind.* New York: Oxford University Press.

Morgan, G. (1986). *Images of organization.* Beverly Hills, CA: Sage.

Nadler, G. (1976). *Work systems design: The ideals concept.* Homewood, IL: Irwin.

Nadler, G. (1981).*The planning and design approach.* New York: Wiley.

Nadler, G., & Hibino, S. (1990). *Breakthrough thinking.* Rocklin, CA: Prima.

Nelson, H. G. (1993). Design inquiry as an intellectual technology for the design of educational systems. In C. M. Reigeluth, B. H. Banathy, & J. R. Olson (Eds.), *Comprehensive systems design: A new educational technology* (pp. 145–153). Stuttgart: Springer-Verlag.

Nicolis, G., & Prigogine, I. (1989). *Exploring complexity: An introduction.* New York: W. H. Freeman.

Peccei, A. (1977). *The human quality.* Oxford, England: Pergamon.

Prigogine, I. (1980). *From being to becoming: Time and complexity in the physical sciences.* New York: W. H. Freeman.

Prigogine, I., & Stengers, I. (1980). *La Nouvelle Alliance.* Paris: Galfimard. Published in English: (1984). *Order out of chaos.* New York: Bantam.

Reigeluth, C. M. (1995). A conversation on guidelines for the process of facilitating systemic change in education. *Systems Practice, 8*(3), 315–328.

Rittel, H., & Webber, M. (1984). Planning problems are wicked problems. In N. Cross (Ed.), *Developments on design methodology.* New York: Wiley.

Sage, A. (1977). *Methodology for large-scale systems.* New York: McGraw-Hill.

Schrödinger, E. (1956). *Expanding universe.* Cambridge, England: Cambridge University Press.

Schrödinger, E. (1995). *The interpretation of quantum mechanics: Dublin seminars (1949–1955) and other unpublished essays.* Edited with introduction by Michel Bilbol. Woodbridge, CN: Ox Bow Press.

Senge, P. (1990). *The fifth discipline.* New York: Doubleday

Simon, H. (1969). *The science of the artificial.* Cambridge, MA: MIT.

Singer, E. A. (1959). *Experience and reflection.* Philadelphia, PA: University of Pennsylvania Press.

Southerland, J. (1973). *A general systems philosophy for the behavioral sciences.* New York: Braziller.

Thomas, John C., & Carroll, J. M. (1984). The psychological study of design. In N. Cross (Ed.), *Developments on design methodology.* New York: Wiley.

Tsoukas, H. (1992). Panoptic reason and the search for totality: A critical assessment of the critical systems perspectives. *Human Relations, 45*(7), 637–657.

Ulrich, W. (1983). *Critical heuristics of social planning: A new approach to practical philosophy.* Bern, Switzerland: Haupt.

Vallacher, R., & Nowak, A. (Eds.). (1994). *Dynamical systems in social psychology.* New York: Academic Press.

Vickers, G. (1983). *Human systems are different.* London, England: Harper & Row.

Warfield, J. (1976). Societal Systems. New York: Wiley

Waddington, C. (1977). *Evolution and consciousness.* Reading, MA: Addison-Wesley.

Warfield, J. (1990). *A science of general design.* Salinas, CA: Intersystems.

Wheatley, M. (1992). *Leadership and the new science.* San Francisco, CA: Barrett-Koehler.

Whitehead, A. N. (1978). *Process and reality* (Corrected Edition). (In D. R. Griffin, & D. W. Sherburne, Eds.). New York: The Free Press.

Wiener, N. (1948). *Cybernetics.* Cambridge, MA: MIT.

Zalai, B. (1984). *General theory of systems.* Budapest, Hungary: Gondolat.

I. BIBLIOGRAPHY OF SYSTEMS-RELATED WRITINGS

The Design of Educational Systems

Banathy, B. H. (1991). *Systems design of education.* Englewood Cliffs, NJ: Educational Technology.*

Banathy, B. H. (1992). *A systems view of education.* Englewood Cliffs, NJ: Educational Technology.*

Banathy, B. H., & Jenks, L. (1991). *The transformation of education by design.* Far West Laboratory.*

Reigeluth, C. M., Banathy, B. H., & Olson J. R. (Eds.). (1993). *Comprehensive systems design: A new educational technology.* Stuttgart: Springer-Verlag.*

Articles (Representative Samples)

From Systems Research and Behavioral Science.

Social Systems Design

Vol. 2, #3: A. N. Christakis, The national forum on non-industrial private forest lands.

Vol. 4, #1: A. Hatchel et al., Innovation as system intervention.

Vol. 4, #2: J. Warfield & A. Christakis, Dimensionality; W. Churchman, Discoveries in an exploration into systems thinking.

Vol. 4, #4: J. Warfield, Thinking about systems.

Vol. 5, #1: B. H. Banathy, Matching design methods to systems type.

Vol. 5, #2: A. N. Christakis et al., Synthesis in a new age: A role for systems scientists in the age of design.

Vol. 5, #3: M. C. Jackson, Systems methods for organizational analysis and design.

Vol. 5, #3: R. Ackoff, A theory of practice in the social sciences.

Vol. 6, #4: B. H. Banathy, The design of evolutionary guidance systems.

Vol. 7, #3: F. F. Robb, Morhostasi and morphogenesis: Context of design inquiry.

Vol. 7, #4: C. Smith, Self-organization in social systems: A paradigm of ethics.

Vol. 8, #2: T. F. Gougen, Family stories as mechanisms of evolutionary guidance.

Vol. 11, #4: G. Midgley, Ecology and the poverty of humanism: A critical systems perspective.

Vol. 13, #1: R. L. Ackoff & J. Gharajedaghi, Reflections on systems and their models; C. Tsouvalis & P. Checkland, Reflecting on SSM: The dividing line between "real world" and systems "thinking world."

Vol. 13, #2: E. Herrscher, An agenda for enhancing systemic thinking in society.

Vol. 13, #4: J. Mingers, The comparison of Maturana's autopoietic social theory and Gidden's theory of structuration.

Vol. 14, #1: E. Laszlo & A. Laszlo, The contribution of the systems sciences to the humanities.

---

*Primary and state of the art significance.

Vol. 14, #2: K. D. Bailey, The autopoiesis of social systems: assessing Luhmann's theory of selfreference.

Vol. 16, #2: A conversational framework for individual learning applied to the "learning organization" and the "learning society"; B. H. Banathy, Systems thinking in higher education: Learning comes to focus.

Vol. 16, #3: Redefining the role of the practitioner in critical systems methodologies.

Vol. 16, #4: A. Wollin, Punctuated-equilibrium: Reconciling theory of revolutionary and incremental change.

Vol. 18, #1: W. Ulrich, The quest for competence in systemic research and practice.

Vol. 18, #4: P. M. Jenlink, Special Issue

Vol. 18, #5: K. C. Laszlo, Learning, design, and action: Creating the conditions for evolutionary learning community.

From Systems Practice and Action Research:

Vol. 1, #1: J. Oliga: Methodological foundations of systems methodologies, p. 3.

Vol. 1, #4: R. Mason, Exploration of opportunity costs; P. Checkland, Churchman's Anatomy of systems teleology; W. Ulrich, Churchman's Process of unfolding.

Vol. 2, #1: R. Flood, Six scenarios for the future of systems problem solving.

Vol. 2, #4: J. Vlcek, The practical use of systems approach in large-scale designing.

Vol. 3, #1: R. Flood & W. Ulrich, Critical systems thinking.

Vol. 3, #2: S. Beer, On suicidal rabbits: A relativity of systems.

Vol. 3, #3: M. Schwaninger, The viable system model.

Vol. 3, #5: R. Ackoff, The management of change and the changes it requires in management; R Keys, Systems dynamics as a systems-based problem solving methodology.

Vol. 3, #6: 1 Tsivacou, An evolutionary design methodology.

Vol. 4, #2: M. Jackson, The origin and nature of critical systems thinking.

Vol. 4, #3: R. Flood & M. Jackson, Total systems intervention. 2. The systems design of education (very limited samples).

Vol. 8, #1, J. G. Miller & J. L. Miller, Applications of living systems theory.

Vol. 9, #2: B. H. Banathy, New horizons through systems design, Educational Horizons.

Vol. 9, #4, M. W. J. Spaul, Critical systems thinking and "new social movements": A perspective from the theory of communicative action.

Vol. 11, #3: S. Clarke, B. Lehaney, & S. Martin, A theoretical framework for facilitating methodological choice.

Vol. 12, #2: G. C. Alexander, Schools as communities: Purveyors of democratic values and the cornerstones of a public philosophy.

Vol. 12, #6: K. D. Squire, Opportunity initiated systems design.

Vol. 14, #5: G. Midgley & A. E. Ochoa-Arias, Unfolding a theory of systemic intervention.

II. ELABORATION

Books: Design Thinking–Design Action

Ackoff, R. L. (1974). *Redesigning the future: A systems approach to societal problems.* New York: John Wiley & Sons.

Ackoff, R. L. (1999). *Re-creating the corporation: A design of organizations for the 21st century.* New York: Oxford University Press.

Ackoff, R. L., Gharajedaghi, J., & Finnel, E. V. (1984). A *guide to controlling your corporation's future.* New York: John Wiley & Sons.

Alexander, C. (1964). *Notes on the synthesis of form.* Cambridge, MA: Harvard University Press.

Banathy B. et al., (1979). *Design models and methodologies.* San Francisco, CA: Far West Laboratory.

Banathy B., (1996). *Designing social systems in a changing world.* New York: Plenum Press.

Banathy B., (2000). *Guided evolution of society: A systems view.* New York: Kluwer Academic/Plenum Press.

Boulding, K. (1956). *The image.* Ann Arbor, MI: The University Michigan Press.

Checkland, P. (1981). *Systems thinking, systems practice.* New York: Wiley.

Checkland, P., & Scholes, J. (1990). Soft *systems methodology in action.* New York: Wiley.

Churchman, C. W. (1971). *The design of inquiring systems.* New York: Basic Books.

Emery, F., & Trist, E. (1973). *Towards a social ecology.* New York: Plenum.

Flood, R. L. (1993). *Dealing with complexity: An introduction to the theory and application of systems science.* New York: Plenum Press.

Flood, R. L. (1996). *Diversity management: Triple loop learning.* New York: John Wiley & Sons.

Flood, R. L., & Jackson, M. C. (1991). *Critical systems thinking.* New York: John Wiley & Sons.

Gasparski, W. (1984). *Understanding design.* Salinas, CA: Intersystems.

Gharajedaghi, J. (1999). *Systems thinking: Managing chaos and complexity: A platform for designing business architecture.* Boston, MA: Butterworth-Heinemann.

Harman, W. (1976). *An incomplete guide to the future.* San Francisco, CA: San Francisco Book Company.

Harman, W. (1988). *Global mind change.* Indianapolis, IN: Knowledge Systems.

Hausman, C. (1984). A *discourse on novelty and creation.* Albany, NY: SUNY Press.

Jantsch E. (1975). *Design for evolution.* New York: Braziller.

Jantsch E. (1980). *The self-organizing universe.* New York: Pergamon.

Jones C. (1980). *Design methods.* New York: Wiley.

Jones C. (1984). *Essays on design.* New York: Wiley.

Lawson, B. (1980). How *designers think.* Westfield, NJ: Eastview.

Lippit, G. (1973). *Visualizing change.* La Jolla, CA: University Associates.

Midgley, G. (2000). *Systemic intervention: Philosophy, methodology, and practice.* New York: Kluwer-Academic/Plenum.

Nadler, G. (1967). *Work systems design.* Ideals concept: Homewood, IL: Irwin.

Nadler, G (1981). *The planning and design approach.* New York: John Wiley & Sons.

Sage, A. (1977). *Methodology for large-scale systems.* New York: McGraw-Hill.

Scileppi, J. A. (1984). *A systems view of education: A model for change.* Lanham, MD: University Press of America.

Senge, P. (1990). *The fifth discipline.* New York: Doubleday/Currency.

Simon, H. (1969). *The sciences of the artificial.* Cambridge, MA: MIT Press.

Ulrich, W. (1983). *Critical heuristics of social planning.* Bern, Switzerland: Haupt.

van Gigch, J. (1974). *Applied systems theory.* New York: Harper & Row.

Whitehead, A. N. (1978). Process and reality (Corrected Edition). D. R. Griffin & D. W. Sherburne, Eds.). New York: The Free Press.

COMMUNICATION EFFECTS OF NONINTERACTIVE MEDIA: LEARNING IN OUT-OF-SCHOOL CONTEXTS

Kathy A. Krendl
Ohio University

Ron Warren
University of Arkansas

3.1 INTRODUCTION

Most of the chapters included in this collection focus specifically on the role of media in formal learning contexts, learning that occurs in the classroom in an institutional setting dedicated to learning. The emphasis is on specific media applications with specific content to assess learning outcomes linked to a formal curriculum. By contrast, the purpose of this chapter is to review research on the role of media, in particular, mass media, and learning outside the classroom, outside the formal learning environment. It focuses on the way in which media contribute to learning when no teacher is present and the media presentation is not linked to a formal, institutional curriculum with explicitly measurable goals.

Research on media and learning outside the classroom dates back to early studies of the introduction of mass media. As each new medium—film, radio, television, computer—was adopted into the home setting, a new generation of research investigations examined the role of the medium and its potential as a teacher. In addition to questions of how a new dominant mass medium would alter people's use of time and attention, one of the central research questions was how and to what extent audiences would learn from the new media system. Over time,

these questions broadened beyond media content to explore the manner in which audiences interpreted media messages and the social context in which that interpretation takes place. This chapter focuses on these unique perspectives in a review of communication and media research on learning.

Classic studies of the introduction of both film and television illustrate the broad-based questions regarding media and learning posed in relation to a new medium. In the case of film, the Payne Fund studies in the 1930s represented the first large-scale attempt to investigate the media's role in influencing people's beliefs and attitudes about society, other people, and themselves. Investigators (Cressey, 1934; Holaday & Stoddard, 1933; Peterson & Thurstone, 1933; Shuttleworth & May, 1933) examined three types of learning that have become dominant in studies of media and learning: (1) knowledge acquisition or the reception and retention of specific information; (2) behavioral performance, defined as the imitation or repetition of actions performed by others in media portrayals; and (3) socialization or general knowledge, referring to attitudes about the world fostered by repeated exposure to mass media content. Researchers found evidence in support of the medium's influence on learning on all three counts. In addition, the studies suggested that learning from film could go well beyond the specific content and the intended messages. According to Cressey (1934),

. . . when a child or youth goes to the movies, he acquires from the experience much more than entertainment. General information concerning realms of life of which the individual does not have other knowledge, specific information and suggestions concerning fields of immediate personal interest, techniques of crime, methods of avoiding detection, and of escape from the law, as well as countless techniques for gaining special favors and for interesting the opposite sex in oneself are among the educational contributions of entertainment films. (p. 506)

Compared to traditional classroom teaching, Cressey asserted, films offered an irresistible—and oppositional—new source of knowledge, especially for young people.

Early studies of the introduction of television adopted similar broad-based approaches and reached similar conclusions regarding the role of the new medium in shaping individuals' responses to, that is, helping them learn about, the world around them. The first rigorous exploration of television's effects on children (Himmelweit, Oppenheim, & Vince, 1959) set the stage for an examination of television's unintended effects on learning. Part of the study focused on the extent to which children's outlooks were colored by television: How were their attitudes affected? How were they socialized? Based on comparisons of viewers and nonviewers, the researchers found significant differences in attitudes, goals, and interests.

At about the same time Schramm, Lyle, and Parker (1961) initiated the first major examination of television's effects on children in North America in a series of 11 studies. This research emphasized how children learn from television. Based on their findings, the researchers proposed the concept of "incidental learning." "By this we mean that learning takes place when a viewer goes to television for entertainment and stores up certain items of information without seeking them" (Schramm et al., 1961, p. 75). They consistently found that learning in response to television programs took place whether or not the content was intended to be educational.

This concept of incidental learning has become a central issue in subsequent studies of media and learning. Some investigators have focused their studies on learning that resulted from programs or material designed as an *intentional* effort to teach about a particular subject matter or issue, while others were intrigued by the extent to which audience members absorbed aspects of the content or message that were *unintended* by the creators. As Schramm (1977) noted in his later work, "Students learn from *any* medium, in school or out, whether they intend to or not, whether it is intended or not that they should learn (as millions of parents will testify), providing that the content of the medium leads them to pay attention to it" (p. 267).

This notion of intended and unintended learning effects of media was anticipated in early discussions of education and learning in the writings of John Dewey. Dewey anticipated many of the issues that would later arise in communication research as investigators struggled to conceptualize, define, measure, and analyze learning that occurs in relation to media experiences. He devoted an early section of *Democracy and Education* (1916) to a discussion of "Education and Communication." In this discussion, he noted the significance of the role of communication in shaping individuals' understanding of the world around them as follows:

Society not only continues to exist *by* transmission, *by* communication, but it may fairly be said to exist *in* transmission, *in* communication.

There is more than a verbal tie between the words common, community, and communication. Men live in a community in virtue of the things which they have in common; and communication is the way in which they come to possess things in common. What they must have in common in order to form a community or society are aims, beliefs, aspirations, knowledge—a common understanding—like-mindedness as the sociologists say. (p. 4)

Later Dewey stated, "Not only is social life identical with communication, but all communication (and hence all genuine social life) is educative. To be a recipient of a communication is to have an enlarged and changed experience" (p. 5). That is, communication messages influence individuals' understanding of the world around them; they are changed or influenced by the messages.

Thus, for Dewey, one result of communication is to reflect *common understandings;* communication serves to educate individuals in this way, to help them understand the world around them, according to these shared views. The knowledge and understanding that they learn through this function of communication provide the foundation for the maintenance of society. Another function of communication in society, according to Dewey, is to *alter* individuals' understandings of the world; their perceptions of and knowledge about the world around them are influenced and shaped by the messages to which they are exposed.

Communication theorist James Carey (1989) expanded on Dewey's notions regarding both the social integration function of communication (communication as creating common understanding) and the change agent function of communication (communication as altering understandings) to propose two alternative conceptualizations of communication, the *transmission* view and the *ritual* view. The transmission view adopts the notion that "communication is a process whereby messages are transmitted and distributed in space for the control of distance and people" (Carey, 1989, p. 15). According to Carey, the transmission view of communication has long dominated U.S. scholarship on the role of media effects in general and learning from media in particular. However, the ritual view of communication "is directed not toward the extension of messages in space but toward the maintenance of society in time; not the act of imparting information but the representation of shared beliefs" (Carey, 1989, p. 18).

Because the ritual view of communication focuses on content that represents shared beliefs and common understandings, such content is not typically the focus of the message designer or producer. These messages are typically unintended because they are viewed by message designers as a reflection of shared attitudes, beliefs, and behaviors and not as a central purpose or goal of the communication.

By contrast, messages designed with the intention of altering responses are examples of the transmission view of communication. There is a specific intent and goal to the message: To change the audience member's view or understanding in a particular way. Research in this tradition focuses on the effects of messages intended to manipulate or alter audience attitudes, beliefs, and behaviors. Examples of such messages are conceived and designed by their creators as *intentional* efforts to influence audience responses.

These two contrasting conceptualizations of communication serve as a framework for organizing the first section of this chapter, which reports on research on media and learning as it relates to a focus on the *content* and intent of the message and its subsequent influence on learning. For the most part, these studies examine the effectiveness of media in delivering intentional messages with specific goals. However, we also discuss examples of research that propose some unintentional effects of media messages on audience members.

3.2 MEDIA AND LEARNING: CONTENT EFFECTS

The earliest models in the study of media and audiences were based on technical conceptions of message transmission. They developed in direct response to the advent of mass communication technologies that revolutionized the scale and speed of communication. The original intent was to assess the effects that the new and ubiquitous media systems had on their audience members and on society. From the beginning research was highly influenced by mass media's potential to distribute singular messages from a central point in space to millions of individuals in a one-way flow of information.

The components of the models stemmed from Lasswell's (1948) question of "Who says what to whom with what effect?" Some of the earliest theoretical work in mass communication was done in conjunction with the development of electronic mass media and was grounded in information theory. This approach examined both the process of how information is transmitted from the sender to the receiver and the factors that influence the extent to which communication between individuals proceeds in the intended fashion. As telephone, radio, and television technologies advanced, researchers looked for scientific means of efficiently delivering messages from one person to another. The goal was for the person receiving the message to receive only the verbal or electronic signals intentionally sent by another person. These theories were based on the 19th century ideas about the transfer of energy (Trenholm, 1986). Such scientific theories held that research phenomena could be broken into component parts governed by universal laws that permitted prediction of future events. In short, the technical perspective on communication held that objects (for example, messages,

their senders, and receivers) followed laws of cause and effect.

One of the most popular examples of the technical perspective was the mathematical model of Shannon and Weaver (1949), developed during their work for Bell Laboratories (see Fig. 3.1).

This linear, one-way transmission model adopted an engineering focus which treated information as a mathematical constant, a fixed element of communication. Once a message source converted an intended meaning into electronic signals, this signal was fed by a sender through a channel to a receiver that converted the signal into comprehensible content for the receiver of the message. Any interference in the literal transfer of the message (for example, from electronic static or uncertainty on the part of either party) constituted "noise" that worked against the predictability of communication. To the extent that noise could be kept to a minimum, the effect of a message on the destination could be predicted based on the source's intent.

This transmission paradigm viewed communication as a linear process composed of several components: source, message, channel, receiver, information, redundancy, entropy, and fidelity. Many of these concepts have remained fundamental concepts of communication theory since Shannon and Weaver's original work. Because of the emphasis on the transmission of the source's intended message, attention was focused on the design of the message and the extent to which the message's intent was reflected in outcomes or effects on the receiver. The greater the degree of similarity between the intention of the source and the outcome or effect at the receiver end, the more "successful" the communication was considered to be. If the intended effect did not occur, a breakdown in communication was assumed. The concept of feedback was added later to gauge the success of each message. This notion was derived from learning theory, which provided for the teacher's "checks" on students' comprehension and learning (Heath & Bryant, 1992).

The channel in this perspective was linked to several other terms, including the signal, the channel's information capacity, and its rate of transmission. The technical capabilities of media were fundamental questions of information theory. The ability of senders and receivers to encode and decode mental intentions into/from various kinds of signals (verbal, print, or electronic) were paramount to successful communication. Each of these concepts emphasized the technical capabilities of media and the message source.

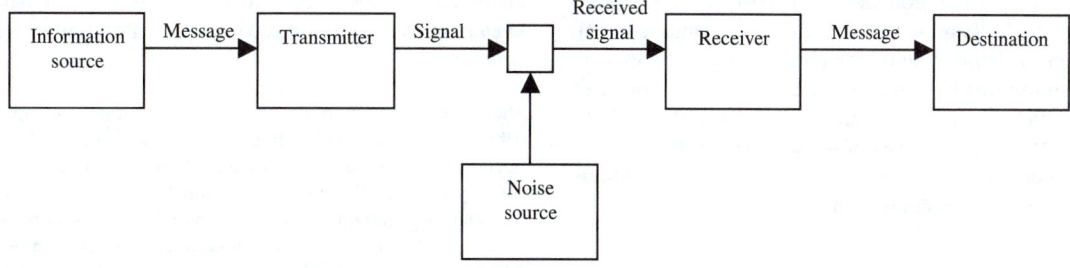

FIGURE 3.1. Shannon and Weaver's "mathematical model" of a one-way, linear transmission of messages. (From Shannon & Weaver, *The Mathematical Theory of Communication*, Urbana, IL, University of Illinois Press, 1949, p. 98. Copyright 1949 by the Board of Trustees of the University of Illinois. Used with permission of the University of Illinois Press.)

Two additional components critical within this perspective are *redundancy* and *entropy*. Redundancy refers to the amount of information that must be repeated to overcome noise in the process and achieve the desired effect. Entropy, on the other hand, is a measure of randomness. It refers to the degree of choice one has in constructing messages. If a communication system is highly organized, the message source has little freedom in choosing the symbols that successfully communicate with others. Hence, the systems would have low entropy and could require a great deal of redundancy to overcome noise. A careful balance between redundancy and entropy must be maintained in order to communicate successfully.

In the case of mass communication systems, the elements of the transmission paradigm have additional characteristics (McQuail, 1983). The sender, for example, is often a professional communicator or organization, and messages are often standardized products requiring a great deal of effort to produce, carrying with them an exchange value (for example, television air time that is sold as a product to advertisers). The relationship of sender to receiver is impersonal and non-interactive. A key feature here, of course, is that traditional notions of mass communication envision a single message source communicating to a vast audience with great immediacy. This audience is a heterogeneous, unorganized collection of individuals who share certain demographic or psychological characteristics with subgroups of their fellow audience members.

The technical perspective of communication, including information theory and the mathematical model of Shannon and Weaver (1949), focused attention on the channel of communication. Signal capacity of a given medium, the ability to reduce noise in message transmissions, and increased efficiency or fidelity of transmissions were important concepts for researchers of communication technologies. The use of multiple channels of communication (for example, verbal and visual) also received a great deal of attention. Three major assumptions characterize communication research in this tradition (Trenholm, 1986). First, it assumes that the components of communication execute their functions in a linear, sequential fashion. Second, consequently, events occur as a series of causes and effects, actions and reactions. The source's message is transmitted to a receiver, who either displays or deviates from the intended effect of the source's original intent. Third, the whole of the communication process, from this engineering perspective, can be viewed as a sum of the components and their function. By understanding how each element receives and/or transmits a signal, the researcher may understand how communication works.

These assumptions have important consequences for most research conducted using a transmission model (Fisher, 1978). A number of established bodies of research trace their origins to the transmission paradigm. Summaries of research traditions whose roots are grounded in this tradition follow.

3.2.1 Persuasion Studies

One of the most prolific and systematic research orientations examining the influence of message content on audience members is research on persuasion. Early programmatic research began with investigations of the *Why We Fight* films in the American Soldier studies, a series of studies designed to examine the effectiveness of film as a vehicle for indoctrination (Hovland, Lumsdaine, & Sheffield, 1949). Researchers were interested in the ability of media messages to provide factual information about the war, to change attitudes of new recruits towards war, and to motivate the recruits to fight. Learning was conceptualized as knowledge acquisition and attitude change.

The American Soldier studies adopted a learning theory approach and laid the foundation for future research on the role of mediated messages in shaping attitudes and behaviors. The body of work examining the persuasion process is extensive and spans more than five decades. Researchers initially adopted a single-variable approach to the study of the effectiveness of the message in changing attitudes including the design of the message (e.g., one-sided vs. two-sided arguments), the character of the message source (e.g., credible, sincere, trustworthy), and the use of emotional appeals (e.g., fear) in the message.

Over time, researchers have concluded that the single-variable approach, focused on the content of the message itself, has proven inadequate to explain the complexity of attitude change and persuasion. The number of relationships between mediating and intervening variables made traditional approaches theoretically unwieldy. They have turned, instead, to a process orientation. Current research focuses on the complex cognitive processes involved in attitude change (Eagly, 1992), and includes McGuire's (1973) information-processing approach, Petty and Cacioppo's (1986) elaboration likelihood model, as well as Chaiken, Liberman, and Eagly's (1989) heuristic–systematic model. The general approach to the study of persuasion and attitude change today examines multiple variables within a process orientation rather than focusing predominantly on the direct impact of message content on audience members. In addition, researchers seek to understand audience characteristics more thoroughly in creating intentional, targeted messages.

A subset of studies related to persuasion research is research on communication campaigns including product advertising, social marketing (e.g., health campaigns), and political campaigns. Research on the effectiveness of such campaigns has relied heavily on models and approaches from persuasion studies and reflects similar directions in terms of addressing process issues and a more detailed understanding of audience. This focus on audience is reflected in recent efforts in social marketing using a new approach referred to as the entertainment–education strategy.

The general purpose of entertainment–education programs is to contribute to social change, defined as the process in which an alteration occurs in the structure and function of a social system . . . Social change can happen at the level of the individual, community, an organization, or a society. Entertainment–education by itself sometimes brings about social change. And, under certain circumstances (in combination with other influences), entertainment–education creates a climate for social change. (Singhal & Rogers, 1999, p. xii)

This approach advocates embedding social action messages into traditional media formats (for example, soap operas) designed to change social attitudes and behaviors. For example, a series of studies in India examined the role of a popular radio soap opera, *Tinka Tinka Sukh,* to promote gender equality, women's empowerment, small family size, family harmony, environmental conservation and HIV prevention (Singhal & Rogers, 1999). The entertainment–education approach has become very popular in a variety of cultural settings in promoting social change in public attitudes and behaviors. The standard approach used in these studies relies on social modeling by using popular characters in a dramatic entertainment format to model the desired attitudes and behaviors associated with the intended goals of the program.

In discussing the future of entertainment–education initiatives, Singhal and Rogers (1999) concluded that the success of such efforts will depend, to a large extent, on the use of theory-based message design, and moving from a production-centered approach to an audience-centered approach (Singhal & Rogers, 1999), requiring that researchers understand more about audience perspectives and needs in creating appropriate and effective messages.

3.2.2 Curriculum-Based Content Studies

Other chapters in this volume provide detailed examinations of technology-based curriculum interventions. However, one television series deserves special mention in this chapter, with its focus on learning from media outside of the formal school setting. This series, *Sesame Street,* was designed with a formal curriculum for in-home delivery. It has generated more research over the past several decades and in many different cultures than any other single television series.

From the outset, the program was carefully designed and produced to result in specific learning outcomes related to the program content. Message designers included early childhood curriculum experts. The general goal was to provide preschoolers, especially underprivileged preschoolers (Ball & Bogatz, 1970; Bogatz & Ball, 1971), with a jump start on preparation for school. Reviews of research on the effectiveness of the program suggest that it did, indeed, influence children's learning with many of the intended results (Mielke, 1994). However, studies also concluded that situational and interpersonal factors influenced learning outcomes. For example, Reiser and colleagues (Reiser, Tessmer, & Phelps, 1984; Reiser, Williamson, & Suzuki, 1988) reported that the presence of adults who co-viewed the program with children, asked them questions, and provided feedback on the content increased learning outcomes. The most recent review of the Children's Television Workshop research (Fisch & Truglio, 2001) underscores the limitations of the program as a universal educator. Its producers see televised instruction as a beginning to adult–child interaction that results in the greatest learning gains. Again, the general conclusion from the research suggested that the emphasis on learning from message content provides only one part of the explanation for how learning from media takes place.

3.2.3 Agenda-Setting Research

Agenda-setting research is an example of a research orientation that focuses on learning outcomes directly related to message content but with unintentional outcomes, according to message designers. This established research tradition examines the relationship between the public's understanding of the relative importance of news issues and media coverage of those issues.

Agenda-setting research was inspired by the writings of Walter Lippmann (1922), who proposed that the news media created the "pictures in our heads," providing a view of the world beyond people's limited day-to-day experiences. The basic hypothesis in such research is that there is a positive relationship between media coverage of issues and what issues people regard as being important (McCombs & Shaw, 1972; Shaw & McCombs, 1977). Such research has routinely reported that individuals' rankings of the importance of daily news events reflect the level of importance (as measured by placement and amount of time or space allocated to it) attached to those news events by the news media. That is, when daily newspapers or broadcast news reports focus on specific news events, the message to the public is that those particular news events are the most significant events of the day and the ones on which their attention should be focused. The issue is, as one review concluded, that "There is evidence that the media are shaping people's views of the major problems facing society and that the problems emphasized in the media may not be the ones that are dominant in reality" (Severin & Tankard, 2001, p. 239).

Though this finding related to audience members' understanding of the significance of daily news events has been reported consistently, and researchers (McCombs & Shaw, 1977; Westley, 1978) have demonstrated that the direction of the influence is likely from the press to the audience, media practitioners argue that they perceive their role not as setting the public's news agenda but rather reflecting what they consider to be the most important issues of the day for their audience members.

Thus, the learning effect—identifying the most important issues of the day—reported by the public is unintentional on the part of the message producers. News reporters and editors are not intentionally attempting to alter the public's perception of what the important issues of the day are. Rather, they believe they are reflecting shared understandings of the significance of those events.

Agenda-setting studies over the past three decades have employed both short-term and longitudinal designs to assess public awareness and concern about specific news issues such as unemployment, energy, and inflation in relation to the amount and form of relevant news coverage (for example, Behr & Iyengar, 1985; Brosius & Kepplinger, 1990; Iyengar, Peters, & Kinder, 1982). Recent research has attempted to broaden understanding of agenda setting by investigating both attitudinal and behavioral outcomes (e.g., Ghorpade, 1986; Roberts, 1992; Shaw & Martin, 1992). Concern over possible mediating factors such as audience variations, issue abstractness, and interpersonal communication among audience members has fueled significant debate within the field concerning the strength of the agenda-setting effect on public learning. Some studies have suggested that agenda setting is strongly influenced by audience members' varying interests, the form of media employed, the tone of news stories toward issues, and the type of issue covered. Current directions in agenda-setting research suggest that though the agenda-setting function of media can be demonstrated, the relationship between media and learning is more complex than a simple relationship between message content and learning outcomes.

3.2.4 Violent Content Studies

Another learning outcome of media consumption in relation to television content, according to many critics (e.g., Bushman & Huesmann, 2001), is the notion that violent and aggressive behaviors are the most common strategies for resolving conflict in U.S. society. This line of research suggests that the lesson learned from television viewing is that violent and aggressive behavior is ubiquitous and effective. Investigators following this tradition (e.g., Gerbner, Gross, Morgan, & Signorielli, 1994; Potter, 1999) have argued that violent content represents the dominant message across television program genres—drama, cartoons, news, and so on. Program creators, on the other hand, argue that violence occurs in day-to-day experience, and the use of violence in television programming merely reflects real-life events (Baldwin & Lewis, 1972; Lowry, Hall, & Braxton, 1997). According to program producers, the learning effect examined in studies of television's violent content represents an unintentional effect.

The debate concerning violent content on television has focused, to a large extent, on the presence of such content in children's programming. The impetus for research on the topic emerged from public outcries that children were learning aggressive behaviors from television because the dominant message in televised content was that violence was a common, effective, and acceptable strategy for resolving conflicts.

The theoretical model applied in this research is grounded in social learning theory. The early work in social learning theory involved children and imitative aggressive play after exposure to filmed violence (Bandura, 1965). Studies were designed in the highly controlled methodology of experimental psychology. The social learning model, which attempts to explain how children develop personality and learn behaviors by observing models in society, was extended to the study of mediated models of aggression. The crux of the theory is that people learn how to behave from models viewed in society, live or mediated (Bandura, 1977). This approach examines learning as a broad-based variable that involves knowledge acquisition and behavioral performance. In a series of experiments (Bandura, 1965; Bandura, Ross, & Ross, 1961, 1963), Bandura and his colleagues demonstrated that exposure to filmed aggression resulted in high levels of imitative aggressive behavior.

For the past 4 decades research on the relationship between exposure to aggressive or violent content on television and resulting attitudes and behaviors has persisted in examining processes related to these basic questions: (1) To what extent does the presence of such content in children's programming influence children's understanding of the world around them? (2) How does such content influence children's perception of appropriate behaviors to adopt in response to that world? In general, this line of research has found a finite number of short-term learning effects of televised violence (see Potter, 1999). First, TV violence can lead to disinhibition—a removal of internal and social checks on aggressive behavior, though this effect is dependent on the viewer's personality, intelligence, and emotional state at the time of viewing, as well as on the nature of the portrayal of violent behavior (e.g., whether it is rewarded or punished, realistic, etc.). Second, televised violence can desensitize viewers to such content and, perhaps, to real-life aggression. In most cases, this effect is the result of repeated exposures, not the result on just one viewing (e.g., Averill, Malmstrom, Koriat, & Lazarus, 1972; Mullin & Linz, 1995; Wilson & Cantor, 1987). Here, too, the effect is dependent on both viewer and content characteristics (Cline, Croft, & Courrier, 1973; Gunter, 1985; Sander, 1995). In this way, children can acquire attitudes and behavioral scripts that tell them aggression is both an effective and appropriate response to a range of social situations (Bushman & Huesmann, 2001).

Recent questions have asked which children are most susceptible to such messages. Two comprehensive reviews of such literature (Potter, 1999; Singer & Singer, 2001) have charted the scope of this body of research. A wide range of viewer characteristics (e.g., intelligence, personality, age, hostility, arousal or emotional reactions, and affinity with TV characters) has been associated with children's varying displays of aggression subsequent to viewing televised violence. In addition, a separate line of studies has charted the environmental or contextual factors such as the role of parental mediation (e.g., Nathanson, 1999) that influence this process. Despite these findings, meta-analysts and critics alike maintain that the effects of violent content are universally significant across viewers, types of content, and methodological approaches (Bushman & Huesmann, 2001; Paik & Comstock, 1994). Most such studies cite a consistent concern with children's level of exposure to television content as a mediating factor in this process. This area of study culminated in a body of work referred to as cultivation research.

3.2.5 Cultivation Theory

Beginning in the late 1960s when initial research was underway to examine the links between level of exposure to violent content on television and subsequent behavior, research on the long-term socialization effects of television achieved prominence in the study of media and audiences. This approach, known as cultivation research, conceptualized learning as a generalized view of the world, the perception of social reality as conveyed by the mass media. Concerned primarily with television as the foremost "storyteller" in modern society, researchers argued that television's power to influence world views was the result of two factors. First, television viewing was seen as ritualistic and habitual rather than selective. Second, the stories on television were all related in their content.

Early cultivation research hypothesized that heavy television viewers would "learn" that the real world was more like that portrayed on television—particularly in regard to pervasive violence—than would light viewers (Gerbner, Gross, Eleey, Jackson-Beeck, Jeffries-Fox, & Signorielli, 1977, 1978; Gerbner, Gross, Morgan, & Signorielli, 1980, 1986). Heavy viewers were expected to estimate the existence of higher levels of danger in the world and feel more alienated and distrustful than would light viewers (i.e., the "mean world" effect—viewers come to believe that the real world is as mean and violent as the televised world). On one level, this effect is demonstrated with a "factual" check of viewer beliefs with real-world statistics. For example, heavy viewers in these studies have tended to overestimate crime rates in their communities. However, cultivation theorists argue that the effect is much more pervasive (Gerbner et al., 1994). For example, heavy viewers have tended to report more stereotypically sexist attitudes toward women and their roles at work and home (Signorielli, 2001). Heavy viewing adolescents were more likely to report unrealistic expectations of the workplace, desiring glamorous, high-paying jobs that afforded them long vacations and ample free time (Signorielli, 1990). Politically, heavy viewers were more likely to describe themselves as "moderates" or "balanced" in their political views (Gerbner et al., 1982). Though research following this model has been inconclusive in demonstrating direct content effects independent of other factors, the theoretical orientation associated with the possibility of direct effects continues to influence research on media and learning.

3.3 MEDIA AND LEARNING: BEYOND CONTENT

Research approaches based on understanding learning effects in response to specific media content have yielded mixed results. Researchers have concluded that further investigation of learning from media will require systematic investigation of other factors to understand learning processes associated with media experiences.

Because of the limitations of the traditional content-based models, a number of research orientations examining the relationship between media and learning have emerged that focus on factors that extend beyond message content. These orientations include the study of learning as it relates to the unique characteristics of individuals who process the messages, the expectations they bring to media situations, the way in which they process the messages, and the contextual and social factors that influence the communication process. Discussions of a series of such orientations follow.

3.3.1 Cognitive Processing of Media Messages

For several decades, communication research has attempted to apply the principles of cognitive psychology and information processing models to the reception of media content. The concerns of this research tradition are myriad, but can be grouped into three general categories: (1) examinations of the underlying processes of information acquisition (i.e., attention, comprehension, memory); (2) the relative activity or passivity with which viewers process content; and (3) media's capacity to encourage or discourage higher order cognition. While we do not attempt a comprehensive review of this literature (readers may find one in the edited work of Singer & Singer, 2001), a summary of its focal concerns and principle findings is in order.

Much research has been devoted to the study of what are called subprocesses of information processing. This model was introduced in cognitive and learning psychology (Anderson, 1990) and focuses on a sequence of mental operations that result

in learners committing information to memory. Studies of attention to television content, for example, have long attempted to resolve the relationship between visual and auditory attention (e.g., Anderson, Field, Collins, Lorch, & Nathan, 1985; Calvert, Huston, & Wright, 1987). At issue here is how children attend to or monitor TV messages, at times while engaged in other activities. Later research (Rolandelli, Wright, Huston, & Eakins, 1991) proposed that both types of attention contribute to children's comprehension of a program, but that a separate judgment of their interest in and ability to understand the content governed their attention to it. These judgments were often made by auditory attention. Children monitored verbal information for comprehensible content, then devoted concentrated attention to that content, resulting in comprehension and learning (Lorch, Anderson, & Levin, 1979; Verbeke, 1988).

3.3.1.1 Attention. If the goal is to encourage positive learning from television, a paramount concern becomes how to foster sustained attention to content. Berlyne (1960) was among the first researchers to identify the formal production features that encourage sustained visual attention (e.g., fast motion, colorful images). Comprehension was found to increase when attention was sustained for as little as 15 seconds (Anderson, Choi, & Lorch, 1987), though this kind of effect was more pronounced for older children (Hawkins, Kim, & Pingree, 1991) who are able to concentrate on complex, incomprehensible content for longer periods of time. According to one study (Welch, Huston-Stein, Wright, & Plehal, 1979), the use of these techniques explains boys' ability to sustain attention longer than girls, though this did not result in any greater comprehension of content. Indeed, gender has been linked to distinct patterns of attention to verbal information (Halpern, 1986). Attention to TV content also has been linked to other variables, including a child's ability to persist in viewing and learning activities, particularly in the face of distractions (Silverman & Gaines, 1996; Vaughn, Kopp, & Krakow, 1984).

3.3.1.2 Comprehension. A long line of research has examined the ways that media users make sense of content. In general, communication researchers examining cognitive processes agree that viewers employ heuristics (Chaiken, 1980) to minimize the effort required to comprehend content. One theory garnering extensive research attention is schema theory (Fiske & Taylor, 1991; Taylor & Crocker, 1981; Wicks, 2001). In the face of novel stimuli, viewers use schemata to monitor content for salient material. With entertainment programming, viewers are more likely to employ story related schemata—that is, their knowledge of story structure. This knowledge is acquired from prior experience with stories, elements of plot and character, and storytelling for others. Story grammar, as it is called, is usually acquired by age seven, though its signs show up as early as age two (Applebee, 1977; Mandler & Johnson, 1977). Story schemata are seen as most analogous to television programming, most easily employed by viewers, and (therefore) most easily used to achieve the intended outcomes of production. At least one study (Meadowcroft, 1985) indicated that use of story schemata results in higher recall of content and efficient use of cognitive resources to process incoming content.

Two other issues associated with content comprehension concern the nature of the televised portrayal. The first deals with the emphasis viewers place on either formal production features or storytelling devices when they interpret content. Formal production techniques like sound effects, peculiar voices, or graphics serve not only to attract attention, but also to reinforce key points or plot elements (Hayes & Kelly, 1984; Wright & Huston, 1981). Young viewers (ages three to five) have been found to rely on visual cues to interpret content more so than older children (Fisch, Brown, & Cohen, 1999). Storytelling devices such as sarcasm, figures of speech, and irony are more difficult to comprehend (Anderson & Smith, 1984; Christenson & Roberts, 1983; Rubin, 1986). Once child viewers reach 7 years of age, they are better able to identify storytelling devices that advance a program's plot rather than becoming distracted by production techniques designed to arrest their attention (Anderson & Collins, 1988; Jacobvitz, Wood, & Albin, 1991; Rice, Huston, & Wright, 1986).

The second issue concerns the realism of the content (Flavell, Flavell, & Green, 1987; Potter, 1988; Prawat, Anderson, & Hapkeiwicz, 1989). The relevant viewing distinction is between television as a "magic window" on reality (i.e., all content is realistic because it is on TV) and television as a fictional portrayal of events with varying bases in fact (i.e., the content is possible, but not probable in the real world). In both cases, a viewer's ability to isolate relevant information cues and make judgments about their realism are crucial to comprehension of content.

3.3.1.3 Retention.
Though there are differences between studies that test for viewers' recall or simple recognition of previously viewed content (Cullingsford, 1984; Hayes & Kelly, 1984), most research on recall shows that it is influenced by the same factors that govern attention and comprehension. Hence, there are several studies indicating that formal production features (e.g., fast pace, low continuity) result in lower content recall. Other studies (e.g., Hoffner, Cantor, & Thorson, 1988; van der Molen & van der Voort, 2000a, 2000b) have found higher recall of visual versus audio information, though the latter often supplements understanding and interpretation. Finally, two studies (Cullingsford, 1984; Kellermann, 1985) concluded children recalled more content when specifically motivated to do so. That is, viewers who were watching to derive specific information showed higher content recall than those who viewed simply to relax. Thus, motivation may enact a different set of processing skills.

3.3.1.4 Active vs. Passive Processing.
Communication research has long presented a passive model of media audiences. Some of the earliest work on mass media, the Payne Fund studies of movies, comic books, and other early 20th century media, for example (Cressey, 1934; Holaday & Stoddard, 1933; Peterson & Thurstone, 1933; Shuttleworth & May, 1933), examined the question of passive versus active message processing. Research on audience passivity typically examines viewing by young children and focuses on television production techniques. Researchers have suggested that rapid editing, motion, and whirls of color in children's programming, as well as the

frequency with which station breaks and commercials interrupt programs, are the prime detractors that inhibit elaborated cognition during viewing (Anderson & Levin, 1976; Greer, Potts, Wright, & Huston, 1982; Huston & Wright, 1997; Huston et al., 1981). The assumption, of course, is that these visual features sustain attention, thereby enhancing comprehension of the message. However, others (e.g., Lesser, 1977) have charged that these techniques produce "zombie viewers," rendering children incapable of meaningful learning from media. However, a series of experiments conducted by Miller (1985), concluded that television viewing produced brain wave patterns indicative of active processing rather than hypnotic viewing.

An active-processing model of television viewing also focuses on these production features. However, this model posits that such features are the basis of children's decisions about attending to content. Children do not always devote their attention to the television screen. One reason is that they often engage in other activities while viewing. A second theory is that they have a finite capacity of working memory available for processing narratives and educational content (Fisch, 1999). Hence, they must monitor the content to identify salient message elements. Some research has shown that children periodically sample the message to see if interesting material is being presented (Potter & Callison, 2000). This sampling may take the form of monitoring audio elements or periodically looking at the screen. When such samples are taken, children are looking for production features that "mark" or identify content directed specifically to them. For young children, these "markers" might include animation, music, and child or nonhuman voices. Older children and adolescents would conceivably rely on an age-specific set of similar markers (e.g., a pop music song or dialogue among adolescents) as a way of identifying content of interest to them. Content that includes complex dialogue, slow action, or only adult characters would consequently lose children's attention. Thus, some researchers (e.g., Rice, Huston, & Wright, 1982) have proposed a "traveling lens" model of attention and comprehension. This model holds that content must be neither too familiar nor novel to maintain attention. Similarly, content must strike a middle ground in its complexity, recognizability, and consistency to avoid boring or confusing viewers.

3.3.1.5 Higher Order Cognition.
Concerns about media's effects on cognition extend beyond the realm of attention and information processing to more complex mental skills. Television, in particular, has been singled out for its potentially negative impact on higher order thinking. Studies of children's imaginative thinking are a good case in point. Imagination refers to a number of skills in such work, from fantasy play to daydreaming. One group of scholars (Greenfield, 1984; Greenfield & Beagles-Roos, 1988; Greenfield, Farrar, & Beagles-Roos, 1986; Greenfield, Yut, Chung, Land, Kreider, Pantoja, & Horsley, 1990) has focused on "transcendent imagination," which refers to a child's use of ideas that cannot be traced to a stimulus that immediately precedes an experimental test. Creative children are said to transcend media content viewed immediately before testing, while imitative imagination is indicated when children use the content as the basis of their subsequent play. In general, this research argues that electronic media (as opposed to print media like

books) have negative effects on imaginative thought, though these effects are not uniform.

Research on television and creative imagination has included field investigations on the introduction of television to communities (Harrison & Williams, 1986), correlations of viewing with either teacher ratings of creativity or performance on standardized creative thinking tests (e.g., Singer, Singer, & Rapaczynski, 1984), and experimental studies on the effects of viewing alone (Greenfield, et al., 1990) and in comparison to other media (e.g., Greenfield & Beagles-Roos, 1988; Runco & Pezdek, 1984; Vibbert & Meringoff, 1981). While many studies reported that children drew ideas for stories, drawings, and problem solutions from televised stimuli (e.g., Greenfield & Beagles-Roos, 1988; Greenfield et al., 1990; Stern, 1973; Vibbert & Meringoff, 1981), virtually all of this literature reached one or both of two conclusions. First, TV fostered fewer original ideas than other media stimuli. Second, children who viewed more TV gave fewer unique ideas than those who viewed less TV. However, Rubenstein (2000) concluded that the content of TV and print messages had more to do with children's subsequent creativity than the delivery medium, per se.

Because of this, Valkenburg and van der Voort (1994) argued that these studies reveal a variation of the negative effects hypothesis—a visualization hypothesis. This argues that because television provides ready-made visual images for children, it is difficult to dissociate his/her thoughts from the visual images. As a result, creative imagination decreases. Anderson and Collins (1988) argue that in using an audio-only stimulus channel (e.g., radio), children are required to fill in added detail that visually oriented stimuli (e.g., television) would provide automatically. Most of the comparative studies of television, radio, and print media (e.g., Greenfield & Beagles-Roos, 1988; Greenfield et al., 1986) support the notion that television fosters fewer creative or novel ideas than other media that engage fewer sensory channels. When tested experimentally, then, such visual responses would be coded as novel and imaginative for those who listened to the radio, but not counted for those who just finished watching TV.

In this regard, research on media's impact on imagination is more concerned with the source of imaginative thought and play than the relative creativity or quantity of such behavior. Anderson and Collins (1988) called for a recategorization of television content, however, to better reflect the educational intent of some children's shows. The "animation" category, for example, is far too broad a distinction when several shows (e.g., *Sesame Street, Barney and Friends*) explicitly attempt to expand children's imagination.

3.3.2 Developmental Research on Media and Children

The collected work of cognitive processing research (e.g., Singer & Singer, 2001) demonstrates, if nothing else, the dominance of developmental psychology theories in work on learning from media. One foundation of the work on cognitive processing lies in the stage-based model of child development advanced by Piaget (1970, 1972). That model charts a child's intelligence as beginning in egocentric, nonreflective mental operations that respond to the surrounding environment. Children then progress through three subsequent stages of development (preoperational, concrete operational, formal operational) during which they acquire cognitive skills and behaviors that are less impulsive and deal more with abstract logic. Interaction with one's environment, principally other people, drives the construction of new cognitive structures (action schemes, concrete and formal operations). Three processes drive this development. Some novel events are assimilated within existing cognitive structures. When new information cannot be resolved in this way, existing structures must accommodate that information. Finally, the resolution of cognitive conflict experienced during learning events is referred to as equilibration.

When applied to media use, particularly audiovisual media, Piaget's model has revealed a series of increasingly abstract viewing skills that guide children's message processing. From infancy through the toddler years, the focus of processing skills is to distinguish objects on the screen by using perceptually salient visual (e.g., motion, color, shapes, graphics) and auditory (e.g., music, voices, sound effects) cues. This stage of childhood is devoted to perceiving and comprehending the complex code system of television and an evolving sense of story grammar. The task is to integrate novel stimuli with existing knowledge structures (assimilation) while familiarizing oneself with the dual processing demands of visual and verbal information. Children show greater visual attention to the TV screen during this developmental stage (Anderson et al., 1986; Ruff, Capozzoli, & Weissberg, 1998), partially because visual cues are more perceptually salient.

During their early school years (ages 6 to 12, or Piaget's concrete logical operations stage), children become much more adept at monitoring both video and audio information from the screen. It is during this stage that children spend less time looking at the screen and more time monitoring the audio content (Baer, 1994) for salient cues. However, salience is not determined by perceptual features (e.g., novel music, sound effects), but more by personally relevant features (e.g., the use of familiar voices or music). Thus, children develop more discriminating viewing patterns because of their increased familiarity with the medium. They are better able to sort out relevant from irrelevant information, concentrate on dialogue, and process video and audio information separately (Field & Anderson, 1985). Because so much of this developmental model is dependent upon the formal features and symbol systems of media, it has fostered a great deal of research on the link between production techniques and individual cognitive skills. Consequently, a discussion of these "media attributes" research is in order.

3.3.2.1 Media Attributes Studies. One research tradition that has been explored in an effort to explain why different individuals respond to media messages in different ways is research on media attributes. For the most part, studies following this line of research have focused on formal learning outcomes related to media experiences in formal settings. However, the approach has been examined in both in-school and out-of-school contexts, and, therefore is relevant here.

The media attributes approach to the study of media and learning explores unique media characteristics and their connections to the development or enhancement of students' cognitive skills. Researchers propose that each medium possesses inherent codes or symbol systems that engage specific cognitive abilities among users. In this research, the conceptualization of learning outcomes includes the learner's higher order interpretive processes. For example, according to the media attributes perspective, a researcher might ask how children interpret use of a fade between scenes in a television show and its connection to the viewer's ability to draw inferences about the passage of time in a story.

Early media attributes studies (Salomon, 1974, 1979; Salomon & Cohen, 1977) concluded that mastery of certain skills was a requisite for competent use of a medium. For instance, students had to be able to encode letters on a page as meaningful words in order to use a book. A series of laboratory and field experiments following this line of research reported that learning was mediated by the cognitive skills necessary for effective use of a particular medium.

In addition, scholars have analyzed the relationship between media attributes and the cultivation or development of certain cognitive skills. For television alone, studies have documented positive learning effects for the use of motion (Blake, 1977), screen placements (Hart, 1986; Zettl, 1973), split-screen displays (Salomon, 1979), and use of various camera angles and positions (Hoban & van Ormer, 1950). Researchers also explored cognitive skills linked to other media attributes, including the use of verbal previews, summaries, and repetition (Allen, 1973); amount of narration on audio/video recordings (Hoban & van Ormer, 1950; Travers, 1967); and the use of dramatization, background music, graphic aids, and special sound/visual effects (e.g., Beck, 1987; Dalton & Hannafin, 1986; Glynn & Britton, 1984; Morris, 1988; NIMH, 1982; Seidman, 1981). The list of cognitive skills linked to such attributes included increases in attention, comprehension and retention of information, as well as visualization of abstract ideas.

Critics have pointed out the potential weaknesses of this research, noting that assertions about media's cognitive-cultivation capacities remain unproven (Johnston, 1987). One detailed review of the research (Clark, 1983) argued that media attributes research rests on three questionable expectations: (1) that attributes are an integral part of media, (2) that attributes provide for the cultivation of cognitive skills for learners who need them, and (3) that identified attributes provide unique independent variables that specify causal relationships between media codes and the teaching of cognitive functions. A subsequent review found that no one attribute specific to any medium is necessary to learn any specific cognitive skill; other presentational forms may result in similar levels of skill development (Clark & Salomon, 1985). While some symbolic elements may permit audience members to cultivate cognitive abilities, these elements are characteristic of several media, not unique attributes of any one medium (Clark, 1987).

According to Salomon's original model, the relationships among these three constructs—perceived demand characteristics, perceived self-efficacy, and amount of invested mental effort—would explain the amount of learning that would result from media exposure. For example, he compared students'

learning from reading a book with learning from a televised presentation of the same content. Salomon found more learning from print media, which he attributed to the high perceived demand characteristics of book learning. Students confronted with high demands, he argued, would invest more effort in processing instructional content. Conversely, students would invest the least effort, he predicted, in media perceived to be the easiest to use, thus resulting in lower levels of learning.

In a test of this model, Salomon and Leigh (1984) concluded that students preferred the medium they found easiest to use; the easier it was to use, the more they felt they learned from it. However, measures of inference-making suggested that these perceptions of enhanced learning from the *easy* medium were misleading. In fact, students learned more from the *hard* medium, the one in which they invested more mental effort. A series of studies extended Salomon's work to examine the effect of media predispositions and expectations on learning outcomes. Several studies used the same medium, television, to deliver the content but manipulated instructions to viewers about the purpose of viewing. The treatment groups were designed to yield one group with high investments and one with low investments of mental effort.

Though this research began as an extension of traditional research on learning in planned, instructional settings, it quickly evolved to include consideration of context as an independent variable related to learning outcomes. Krendl and Watkins (1983) found significant differences between treatment groups following instructions to students to view a program and compare it to other programs they watched at home (entertainment context), as opposed to viewing in order to compare it to other videos they saw in school (educational context). This study reported that students instructed to view the program for educational purposes responded to the content with a deeper level of understanding. That is, they recalled more story elements and included more analytical statements about the show's meaning or significance when asked to reconstruct the content than did students in the entertainment context.

Two other studies (Beentjes, 1989; Beentjes & van der Voort, 1991) attempted to replicate Salomon's work in another cultural context, the Netherlands. In these studies, children were asked to indicate their levels of mental effort in relation to two media (television and books) and across content types within those media. The second study asked children either watching or reading a story to reproduce the content in writing. Beentjes concluded, "the invested mental effort and the perceived self-efficacy depend not only on the medium, but also on the type of television program or book involved" (1989, p. 55).

A longitudinal study emerging from the learner-centered studies (Krendl, 1986) asked students to compare media (print, computer and television) activities on Clark's (1982, 1983) dimensions of preference, difficulty, and learning. Students were asked to compare the activities on the basis of which activity they would prefer, which they would find more difficult, and which they thought would result in more learning. Results suggested that students' judgments about media activities were directly related to the particular dimension to which they were responding. Media activities have multidimensional, complex sets of expectations associated with them. The findings suggest that simplistic, stereotypical characterizations of media experiences (for example, books are hard) are not very helpful in understanding audiences' responses to media.

These studies begin to merge the traditions of mass communication research on learning and studies of the learning process in formal instructional contexts. The focus on individuals' attitudes toward, and perceptions of, various media has begun to introduce a multidimensional understanding of learning in relation to media experiences. Multiple factors influence the learning process—mode of delivery, content, context of reception, as well as individual characteristics such as perceived self-efficacy and cognitive abilities. Research on these factors is more prominent in other conceptual approaches to learning from media.

3.4 MEDIA AND LEARNING: WITHIN CONTEXT

Beginning in the 1970s, a reemergence of qualitative and interpretive research traditions signaled a marked skepticism toward content and cognitive approaches to media and learning. In communication research, these traditions are loosely referred to as cultural studies. This label refers to a wide range of work that derives from critical Marxism, structuralism, semiotics, hermeneutics, and postmodernism (among several others). Its fullest expression was made manifest by scholars of the Centre for Contemporary Cultural Studies at the University of Birmingham (Hall et al., 1978; Morley, 1980). The emphasis on media as cultural products is illustrative of these traditions' grounding in media messages as situated social acts inextricably connected with the goals and relationships of one's local environment. This section will briefly overview the theoretical tenets of this approach, illustrate its key theoretical concepts with exemplary studies, and discuss its implications for a definition of learning via media messages.

3.4.1 Theoretical Tenets of Cultural Analysis

Cultural studies as a research approach fits under Carey's ritual view of communication. It assumes that media messages are part of a much broader social, political, economic, and cultural context. Media messages are examined less in terms of content than in the relationship of the content and the social environment in which it is experienced. That is, media messages are not viewed in isolation, but rather as part of an integrated set of messages that confront audience members. One's definition of and experience with objects, events, other people, and even oneself, is determined through a network of interpersonal relationships. Basing his perspective on the work of Wilson and Pahl (1988), Bernardes (1986), and Reiss (1981), Silverstone (1994) argues that researchers must account for this social embeddedness of media users. Specifically, this means that any examination of media use must account for psychological motivations for viewing as well as the nature of the social relationships that give rise to such motivations. For example, office workers have strong motivations for viewing a TV sitcom if they know that their colleagues will be discussing the show at work the next day. Talk about the show might maintain social relationships that, in part, comprise the culture of a workplace. This talk can result in highlighting particularly salient aspects of a show

(e.g., a character's clothing or hair, a catch phrase from the dialogue). Together, viewers work out the meaning of the show through their social talk about content. That is, the meanings we form are products of social *negotiation* with other people. This negotiation determines both the symbols we use to communicate and the meanings of those symbols (Blumler, 1939, 1969; Mead, 1934).

3.4.1.1 Culture. On a micro level, then, participants arrive at shared meaning for successful communication. However, cultural analysts are concerned at least as much about macro-level phenomena. Individual action is influential when it becomes routine. Patterns of social action take on a normative, even constraining, force in interpersonal relationships. They become a set of social expectations that define life within specific settings (such as a home or workplace). Thus, social routines (such as office talk about favored TV shows) become the very fabric of cultural life. Hall (1980), in fact, defines culture as "the particular pattern of relations established through the social use of things and techniques." Whorf (1956) and his colleague Sapir hypothesized that the rules of one's language system contain the society's culture, worldview, and collective identity. This language, in turn, affects the way we perceive the world. In short, words define reality, reality does not give us objective meaning. When this notion is applied to media messages, the language and symbols systems of various media assume a very powerful influence over the structure and flow of individual action. They can determine not only the subject of conversation, but the tone and perspective with which individuals conduct that conversation. Hence, the role of media and other social institutions becomes a primary focus in the formation of culture.

3.4.1.2 Power. Because of its roots in the critical Marxism of theorists such as Adorno and Horkheimer (1972), cultural studies assigns a central role to the concept of power. Those theorists, and others in the Frankfurt School (Hardt, 1991; Real, 1989) believed that media institutions exerted very powerful ideological messages on mass audiences (particularly during the first half of the 20th century). Because the mass media of that time were controlled largely by social and financial elites, critical theorists examined media messages in reference to the economic and political forces that exercised power over individuals. Initially, this meant uncovering the size, organization, and influence of media monopolies in tangible historical/economic data. Consequently, an intense focus on the political economy of mass media became a hallmark of this approach. Media elites were seen as manufacturing a false consciousness about events, places, and people through their presentation of limited points of view. In news coverage, this meant exclusively Western perspectives on news events, largely dominated by issues of democracy, capital, and conquest. With entertainment programming, however, it usually meant privileging majority groups (e.g., Whites and males) at the expense of minority groups (e.g., African-Americans, Hispanics, females) in both the frequency and nature of their representation. The result, according to some analysts (e.g., Altheide, 1985; Altheide & Snow, 1979), was that TV viewers often received slanted views of cultural groups and social affairs.

3.4.1.3 Reaction to Transmission Paradigm. One ultimate goal of the Frankfurt School was audience liberation. Attention focused on the historical, social, and ideological contexts of media messages so that audiences might see through the message to its intended, sometimes hidden, purpose. Cultural studies scholars have taken these ideas and turned them on academia itself, communicating a deep mistrust of the research traditions discussed above. In her introduction to a collection of analyses of children's programs, Kinder expresses these sentiments specifically toward studies of TV violence. She explains,

> While none of these researchers endorse or condone violent representations, they caution against the kinds of simplistic, causal connections that are often derived from "effects studies." Instead, they advocate a research agenda that pays more attention to the broader social context of how these images are actually read. (Kinder, 1999, p. 4)

In contrasting the cultural studies approach and the transmission paradigm, Kinder (p. 12) characterizes the latter as "black box studies" that "address narrowly defined questions of inputs and outputs, while bracketing out more complex relations with school, family, and daily life, therefore yielding little information of interest." Instead, she calls for a move "... to a program of 'interactive research' which looks at how technology actually functions in specific social contexts, focuses on process rather than effects, and is explicitly oriented toward change."

This kind of skepticism is widespread among cultural studies scholars. Several (e.g., Morley, 1986: Silverstone, 1994) criticize scientific research as disaggregating, isolating relevant aspects of media use from their social context. To these scholars, merely measuring variables does not give us insight on the theoretical relationships between them. Media use must be studied in its entirety, as part of a naturalistic setting, to understand how and why audiences do what scientists and TV ratings companies measure them doing. To treat media use, specifically TV viewing, as a measurable phenomenon governed by a finite set of discrete variables is to suggest that the experience is equivalent for all viewers. Consistent with the emphasis on power and political economy, Morley (1986) reminds scholars that research is a matter of interpreting reality from a particular position or perspective, not from an objective, "correct" perspective. Audiences (i.e., learners) are social constructions of those institutions that study them. That is, an audience is only an audience when one constructs a program to which they will attend. Learners are only learners when teachers construct knowledge to impart. While they do have some existence outside our research construction, our empirical knowledge of them is generated only through that empirical discourse. Becker (1985) points to the perspectives offered by poststructural reader theories that define the learner as a creator of meaning. The student interacts with media content and actively constructs meaning from texts, previous experience, and outside influences (e.g., family and peers) rather than passively receiving and remembering content. According to this approach, cultural and social factors are seen as active forces in the construction of meaning. To understand viewers, then, is to approach them on their own terms—to illuminate and analyze their processes of constructing meaning whether or not that meaning is what academicians would consider appropriate. Thus, the purpose in talking to viewers is that we can open ourselves to the possibility of being wrong about them—and therefore legitimize their experience of media.

3.4.1.4 Viewing Pleasures. This celebration of the viewer raises an important tension within cultural studies. Seiter, Borchers, and Warth (1989) referred to this as "the politics of pleasure." Viewers' pleasure in television programming is an issue used to motivate many studies of pop culture and to justify the examination of popular TV programs. Innumerable college courses and academic studies of Madonna and *The Simpsons* are only the beginning of the examples we could provide on this score (e.g., Cantor, 1999; Miklitsch, 1998). However, Seiter et al. (1989) charge that some rather heady political claims have been made about the TV experience. Fiske (1989), for example, states that oppressed groups use media for pleasure, including the production of gender, subcultures, class, racial identities, and solidarity. One case in point would seem to be the appropriation of the Tinky Winky character on *Teletubbies* by gays and gay advocacy groups (Delingpole, 1997). The character's trademark purse gave him iconic status with adults that used the program as a means of expressing group identity (and creating a fair amount of political controversy about the show—see Hendershot, 2000; Musto, 1999). Questions of pleasure, therefore, cannot be separated from larger issues of politics, education, leisure, or even power. *Teletubbies* is clearly not produced for adults, and the publicity surrounding the show and its characters must have been as surprising to its producers as it was ludicrous. Still, the content became the site of a contest between dominant and subordinate groups over the power to culturally define media symbols.

According to Seiter et al. (1989), this focus on pleasure has drawbacks. There is nothing inherently progressive about pleasure. "Progressive" is defined according to its critical school roots in this statement. If the goal is to lift the veil of false consciousness, thereby raising viewers' awareness of the goals of media and political elites, then discussions of popular pleasures are mere wheel spinning. Talk about the polysemic nature and inherent whimsy of children's TV characters does little to expose the multinational media industries that encourage children to consume a show's toys, lunchboxes, games, action figures, and an endless array of other tie-in products. Thus, by placing our concern on audience pleasures, we run the risk of validating industry domination of global media. A discussion of audience pleasures, strictly on the audience's terms, negates the possibility of constructing a critical stance toward the media. The tension between the popular and the critical, between high versus low art, is inherent within the cultural studies perspective. Indeed, as we shall see below, it is an issue that analysts have studied as a social phenomenon all its own.

In summary, cultural studies analysts have proposed a very complex relationship where one's interpersonal relationships with others (e.g., as teacher, student, parent, offspring, friend) and one's social position (e.g., educated/uneducated, middle/working class) set parameters for one's acquisition and decoding of cultural symbols presented through the media. Any analysis of this relationship runs the risk of isolating some aspect (i.e., variable) of the phenomenon, cutting it off from its natural context and yielding an incomplete understanding of cultural life. Studying media's role in the production and maintenance of culture, then, is a matter of painstaking attention to the vast context of communication.

3.4.2 Applications of Cultural Studies

3.4.2.1 Studies of Everyday Life. One methodological demand of this approach, then, is to ground its analysis in data from naturalistic settings. Several cultural analysts (e.g., Morley, 1986; Rogge & Jensen, 1988; Silverstone, 1994) argue for the importance of studying viewing within its natural context and understanding the rules at work in those contexts. The effort to get at context partially justifies this argument, but these authors also point out that technological changes in media make received notions of viewing obsolete. Lindlof and Shatzer (1989, 1990, 1998) were among the first to argue this in response to the emergence of VCRs and remote control devices, both of which changed the nature of program selection and viewing. Media processes underwent significant change, meaning that the social routines of media use also changed. The central goal of cultural research, then, is to discover the "logic-in-us" for organizing daily life and how media are incorporated into daily routines.

The method most employed toward these ends is ethnographic observations of media use. Jordan (1992) used ethnographic and depth interview techniques for just such a purpose. The ostensible goal of her study was to examine media's role in the spatial and temporal organization of household routines. Ethnographers in her study lived with families for a period of 1 month, observing their interactions with media and one another at key points during the day (e.g., mornings before and evenings after work and school). She concluded that family routines, use and definition of time, and the social roles of family members all played a part in the use of media. Children learned at least as much, if not more, from these daily routines than any formal efforts to regulate media use. Parents, for example, controlled a great deal of their children's viewing in the patterned activities by which they accomplished household tasks like preparing dinner. In addition, she uncovered subtle, unacknowledged regulations of TV viewing during family viewing time (e.g., a parent shushing to quiet children during a program). Similarly, Krendl, Clark, Dawson, and Troiano (1993) used observational data to explore the nature of media use within the home. Their observations found that children were often quite skilled at media use, particularly the use of media hardware devices like a remote control. Their study also concluded that parents' and children's experience with media was often vastly different, particularly when parents exercised regulatory power over viewing. Many children in their study, for example, reported few explicit rules for media use, though parents reported going to extremes to control viewing (e.g., using the TV to view only videotapes).

3.4.2.2 Social Positioning. Studies of everyday social life revealed that media are important resources for social actors seeking to achieve very specific goals. The nature of these goals is dependent upon one's position in the local social setting. In the home, for example, children's goals are not always the same as, or even compatible with, parents' goals for TV viewing. Thus, one's position in relation to social others influences the goals and nature of media use. Cultural studies scholars foreground this purposeful activity as an entry point in our understanding of both local and global culture. In essence, this approach claims that individuals use media messages to stake out territory in their cultural environment. Media messages present images and symbols that become associated with specific social groups and subgroups (e.g., "yuppies," teens, the elderly). Media users, given enough experience, attain the ability to read and interpret the intended association of those symbols with those cultural identities (for example, a white hat as a symbol of the "good" cowboy). The display of such cultural competence is a means by which individuals identify themselves as part of certain social groups and distinguish themselves from others. In this way, social agents come to claim and occupy a social position that is the product of their cultural, social, educational, and familial background. This background instills in us our set of cultural competencies and regulates how we perceive, interpret, and act upon the social world. It creates mental structures upon which one bases individual action. Bourdieu (1977, p. 78) calls this the *habitus*, "the durably installed generative principle of regulated improvisation." It constitutes the deep-rooted dispositions that surface in daily social action.

3.4.2.3 Children "Reading" Television. The work of David Buckingham (1993, 2000) forcefully illustrates the roles of context, power, and social position in children's use of media. His extensive interviews with children about television programming reveal the dependence of their interpretation upon social setting and the presence of others. This principal surfaces in his analysis of children's recounts of film narratives. Buckingham's interviews revealed marked differences in the ways that boys and girls retold the story of various films. In several recounts, proclaiming any interest in romance, sex, or violence made a gender statement. Boys' social groups had strong norms against any interest in romantic content, resulting in several critical and negative statements about such content. Further, boys often referred to the fictional machinations of production when making such comments, further distancing themselves from any interest in love stories. Thus, boys claimed a social position by making a gendered statement about film content. They define their interests in terms similar to their same-sex friends, but they also deny any potential influence the content may have upon them. In short, they deny enjoying any romantic content and define themselves as separate from viewers who are affected by it. Such comments were also prevalent in boys' talk about soap operas and the American show *Baywatch*. Boys were more likely to indicate their disgust with the attractive male actors on the show, belittling their muscled physiques or attributing their attractiveness to Hollywood production tricks. Their talk was a matter of taking up a social position with their friends and peers, but it was also a statement on their own masculinity. Girls, on the other hand, had an easier time talking about the pleasures they derived from watching such programs (e.g., seeing attractive clothes, finding out about relationships), but only in same-sex groups. When placed in cross-sex discussion groups, girls were much more likely to suppress such remarks and talk more critically about TV shows. Particularly in same-sex peer groups, then, children's comments reveal the influence of gender and social position (i.e., peer groups) on their critical stance toward TV programs.

Gender was not the only factor of influence in these discussions, however. Buckingham also grouped children in terms of their social class standing (i.e., upper, middle, and working class children). Here Buckingham takes issue with social science findings that class and education are direct influences on children's ability to apply "critical viewing" skills. Through his interviews, Buckingham concluded that it might not be that social class makes some children more critical than others, but that critical discourse about television serves different social purposes for children of different social classes. This was especially true in his data from preadolescent, middle-class boys. During their discussions, these boys often competed to see who could think of the wittiest put-downs of popular TV shows. This had the consequence of making it problematic to admit liking certain television shows. If one's peer group, for example, criticizes *Baywatch* as "stupid," one's enjoyment of the show is likely to be suppressed. Indeed, children who admitted to watching shows their friends considered "dumb" or "babyish" often justified their viewing by saying they were just watching to find material for jokes with their friends. In other cases, children claimed they viewed only to accompany a younger sibling or to humor parents. This discussion pattern fits the theoretical notion of cultural capital and social distinction. Television provides children with images and symbols that they can exchange for social membership. Children seek to define their identities (e.g., as members of peer or gender groups) through their critical position toward TV.

This theoretical stance also works in children's higher order cognitions about the distinction between fantasy and reality on television, or its modality. Buckingham (1993) identifies the internal and external criteria by which children make modality judgments about TV content on two dimensions: (1) Magic Window (children's awareness of TV's constructed nature), and (2) social expectations (the degree to which children compare TV to their own social experiences). Internal criteria included children's discussion of genre-based forms and conventions (e.g., writing a script to make a character or situation seem scarier in a horror film) and specific production techniques (e.g., having a male *Baywatch* character lift weights right before filming to make him appear more muscular). External criteria referred to children's estimates of the likelihood that TV events could happen in real life. In general, children made such assertions based on their ideas about characters' psychological motivations or on the social likelihood that such events would actually happen. The latter could refer to direct personal experience with similar people or situations, or to a child's knowledge of the real-life setting for a show (e.g., their knowledge of New York when judging a fictional sitcom set in that real city).

As with comments about film narratives or characters, Buckingham found that children's assessment of TV's realism was a matter of social positioning and was dependent on their coconversants and the social setting. For example, all children (regardless of age) were likely to identify cartoon programming as unrealistic, a comment that was offered as a sign of their maturity to the interviewer. Cartoons were most frequently identified as "babyish" programming because of this distinction. When speaking with their peers, however, children were also likely to include humorous or appreciative comments about the jokes or violent content in cartoons. According to Buckingham, modality judgments are also social acts. Children make claims about the realism of a TV show as a means of affiliation or social distancing. They are claims of knowledge, mastery of content, and superiority over those who are easily influenced by such content. Such claims were far more prevalent when conversation was directed toward the adult interviewer, however, than they were with peers. When children perceive social capital (e.g., adult approval) in making critical comments about TV, such comments are easily offered and more frequent.

This conclusion reveals the extent to which power governs the relationship between children and media. As with most aspects of social life, adults have a great deal of power over what children can do with their time and with whom children share that time. This power stems chiefly from parents' formal role as decision maker, caregiver, and legal authority in most cultures. Much adult power is institutionalized, as Murray (1999) points out in her examination of "Lifers," a term used for fans of the 1994–1995 television drama *My So Called Life*. Murray's analysis of online chat group messages about the show tracks adolescent girls' struggle to maintain a personal relationship with the program even as network executives were considering its future. Several of the participants in this study saw the situation as another instance of adults taking away a good thing, or what Murray (1999, p. 233) calls a "struggle for control over representation." The chat rooms were often filled with negative comments about network executives' impending cancellation of the show in particular, and about adults' control over children's pleasures in general. Because the show's fans identified so strongly with the adolescent lead character (Angela), Murray's chapter documents the young viewers' struggle with their own identity and social relationships. Thus, media are resources with which viewers learn of and claim social positions in relation to the culture at large (Kinder, 1999)—a culture the media claim to represent and shape at the same time. However, because adults control media industries, children's entry into these cultures is at once defined and limited by adults. Only those needs recognized by adults are served; only those notions of childhood legitimized by adults are deemed "appropriate" for children. Children's voices in defining and serving their needs are lost in such a process (Buckingham, 2000).

3.5 IMPLICATIONS FOR RESEARCH ON LEARNING FROM MEDIA

The implications of these studies for learning from media are far reaching. First, the position of cultural studies scholars on scientific research is extended to developmental psychology.

Buckingham (2000) argues that one limitation of the Piagetian approach is its strict focus on individual differences, which isolates action from its social context. Audience activity is seen as an intervening variable between cause (TV programming) and effect (pro- or antisocial behavior). Viewing becomes a series of variables that are controlled and measured in isolation. Thus, developmental approaches have been criticized for oversimplifying children's social contexts and for neglecting the role of emotion (e.g., pleasures of viewing become guilty pleasures). Several cultural analysts (e.g., Buckingham, 1993; Hodge & Tripp, 1986) similarly critique Salomon's definition of TV attributes for its micro-level focus. They charge that Salomon ignores the levels of narrative structure, genre, and mode of address that go into TV messages. For example, a zoom can mean several things depending on its context. In one show, it might serve to highlight a fish so children can see its gills. In another show, however, it might serve to heighten the suspense of a horror movie by featuring a character's screaming mouth. The hierarchy of skills implied by developmental approaches, while having a legitimate basis in the biology of the brain, inevitably leads to mechanized teaching that subordinates children's own construction of meaning from television. The only legitimate meaning becomes the one teachers build for children.

Cultural studies takes a decidedly sociological view toward its research. Questions shift from the effects of media content to issues of meaning. Learning, consequently, is not an effort to impart approved instructional objectives upon children. To do so denies children's power to interpret media messages according to their own purposes and needs. Instead, cultural analysts favor an approach which recognizes children's social construction of meaning and uses that process to help children negotiate their social and cultural environments (Seiter, 1999). Hodge and Tripp (1986) offered a seminal effort to explicate the social, discursive, semiotic processes through which viewers construct meaning from television. Their work was seen as the first detailed explication of how children interpret a program (e.g., cartoon) and decode its symbol systems. To be sure, common meanings for television codes exist, much as Salomon's work (above) would indicate. The contribution of cultural studies research lies in the shifting nature of those codes as they operate within television's narrative structures and programming genres, as well as within local and global social systems.

A second implication is more obvious, that teachers and other adults assume very powerful positions when it comes to children's learning from media. Indeed, Buckingham argues, power is wrapped up in our notions of learning. Signs of "precocious" behavior both define and threaten the boundary between childhood and adulthood. To maintain this boundary, adults legitimize certain forms of learning from media, such as prosocial learning or the critical rejection of inappropriate programming (e.g., sex or violence). Thus, the fundamental issues are those of access and control. In the process, academic theorists ignore a great deal of children's media processing. However, this power belongs to peer groups as well. The power of a modality judgment can be inherent in the utterance, but it can also be challenged. The boys criticizing the male characters on *Baywatch* (above) were just as likely to criticize each other for not "measuring up" to the muscled men on the beach of that

show. Simultaneously, comments about the show's lack of quality suppressed any discussion of the viewing pleasures some children derived from such programming. Hence, this kind of discourse oppresses any expression of emotional involvement with a show. It is not cool to become engaged, so children do not discuss their engagement unless it is socially approved. Engaging in such critical discourse can also indicate a child's willingness to play the teacher or interviewer's "game." Therefore, we must regard children's critical comments about TV as a social act at least as much (if not more) as an indication of the child's cognitive understanding of TV. Rationalist discourses supplant the popular discourses through which children make meaning of media messages. We miss the opportunity to more deeply explore the meanings that children construct from their viewing, and consequently deeper insight into the way children learn from media content.

The cultural studies approach, adopting a research orientation focused on the role of media in learning within a broader social and cultural environment, is particularly appealing at this point in time given the changes in the nature of the media environment. Today the media environment is conceptualized not as individual, isolated experiences with one dominant media system. Rather, researchers consider the broad array of media choices and selections with the understanding that individuals live in a media-rich environment in which exposure to multiple messages shapes experiences and learning and creates complex interactions in the audience's understanding of the world around them.

3.6 CONCLUSION

Since the introduction of television into the home, broadcast television was the delivery system that commanded the most attention from researchers, characterized by its wide appeal to mass audiences, its one-way delivery of content, and its highly centralized distribution and production systems. Today the media environment offers an increasingly wide array of technologies and combinations of technologies. In addition, emerging technologies share characteristics that are in direct contrast to the broadcast television era and the transmission paradigm research that attempted to examine how people learned from it. Contemporary delivery systems are driven by their ability to serve small, specialized audiences, adopting a narrowcast orientation, as opposed to television's broadcast orientation. They are also designed to feature high levels of user control, selectivity, flexibility, and interactivity, as well as the potential for decentralized production and distribution systems.

As the media environment has expanded to offer many more delivery systems and capabilities, the audience's use of media has also changed. Audience members now select systems that are responsive to their unique needs and interests. Such changes in the evolution of the media environment will continue to have profound implications for research on media and learning.

In the same way that researchers have adopted different perspectives in studying the role and nature of the media system in understanding the relationship between media and learning, they have also adopted different theoretical orientations and assumptions about the nature and definition of learning in response to media experiences. This chapter has attempted to summarize those orientations and provide some perspective on their relative contributions to understanding media and learning in out-of-school contexts.

References

Adorno, T., & Horkheimer, M. (1972). *The Dialectic of Enlightenment.* New York: Herder and Herder.

Allen, W. H. (1973). *Research in educational media.* In J. Brown (Ed.), Educational media yearbook, 1973. New York: R. R. Bowker.

Altheide, D. L. (1985). *Media Power.* Beverly Hills, CA: Sage.

Altheide, D. L., & Snow, R. P. (1979). *Media Logic.* London: Sage.

Anderson, D. R., & Collins, P. A. (1988). The impact on children's education: Television's influence on cognitive development (Working paper No. 2). Washington, DC: U.S. Department of Education, Office of Educational Research and Improvement.

Anderson, D. R., Choi, H. P., & Lorch, E. P. (1987). Attentional inertia reduces distractibility during young children's TV viewing. *Child Development, 58,* 798-806.

Anderson, D. R., Field, D. E., Collins, P. A., Lorch, E. P., & Nathan, J. G. (1985). Estimates of young children's time with television: A methodological comparison of parent reports with time-lapse video home observation. *Child Development, 56,* 1345-1357.

Anderson, D. R., & Levin, S. R. (1976). *Young children's attention to "Sesame Street." Child Development, 47,* 806-811.

Anderson, D. R., Lorch, E. P., Field, D. E., Collins, P. A., & Nathan, J. G. (1986). Television viewing at home: Age trends in visual attention and time with TV. *Child Development, 52,* 151-157.

Anderson, D. R., & Smith, R. (1984). Young children's TV viewing: The problem of cognitive continuity. In F. J. Morrison, C. Lord, & D. P. Keating (Eds.), *Applied Developmental Psychology* (Vol. 1, pp. 116-163). Orlando, FL: Academic Press.

Anderson, J. R. (1990). *Cognitive psychology and its implications* (3rd ed.). New York: Freeman.

Applebee, A. N. (1977). A sense of story. *Theory Into Practice, 16,* 342-347.

Averill, J. R., Malmstrom, E. J., Koriat, A., & Lazarus, R. S. (1972). Habituation to complex emotional stimuli. *Journal of Abnormal Psychology, 1,* 20-28.

Baer, S. A. (1997). Strategies of children's attention to and comprehension of television (Doctoral dissertation, University of Kentucky, 1996). Dissertation Abstracts International, 57(11-B), 7243.

Baldwin, T. F., & Lewis, C. (1972). Violence in television: The industry looks at itself. In G. A. Comstock & E. A. Rubinstein (Eds.), Television and social behavior: Reports and papers: Vol. 1: Media content and control (pp. 290-373). Washington, DC: Government Printing Office.

Ball, S. & Bogatz, G. A. (1970). *The first year of Sesame Street: An evaluation.* Princeton, N.J.:Educational Testing Service.

Bandura, A. (1965). Influence of model's reinforcement contingencies on the acquisition of imitative responses. *Journal of Personality and Social Psychology, 1,* 589-595.

Bandura, A. (1977). *Social learning theory.* Englewood Cliffs, NJ: Prentice-Hall.

Bandura, A., Ross, D., & Ross, S. (1963). Imitation of film-mediated aggressive models. *Journal of Abnormal and Social Psychology, 66,* 3-11.

Bandura, A., Ross, D., & Ross, S. A. (1961). Transmission of aggression through imitation of aggressive models. *Journal of Abnormal and Social Psychology, 63,* 575-582.

Beck, C. R. (1987). Pictorial cueing strategies for encoding and retrieving information. *International Journal of Instructional Media, 14*(4), 332-345.

Becker, A. (1985). Reader theories, cognitive theories, and educational media research. Paper presented at the Annual Meeting of the Association for Educational Communications and Technology. (ERIC Document Reproduction Service No. ED 256 301).

Beentjes, J. W. J. (1989). Learning from television and books: A Dutch replication study based on Salomon's model. *Educational Technology Research and Development, 37*(2), 47-58.

Beentjes, J. W. J., & van der Voort, T. H. A. (1991). Children's written accounts of televised and printed stories. *Educational Technology, Research, and Development, 39*(3), 15-26.

Behr, R. L., & Iyengar, S. (1985). Television news, real world cues, and changes in the public agenda. *Public Opinion Quarterly, 49,* 38-57.

Berlyne, D. E. (1960). *Conflict, arousal, and curiosity.* New York: McGraw-Hill.

Bernardes, J. (1986). In search of "The Family"—Analysis of the 1981 United Kingdom Census: A research note. *Sociological Review, 34,* 828-836.

Blake, T. (1977). Motion in instructional media: Some subject-depth display mode interactions. *Perceptual and Motor Skills, 44,* 975-985.

Blumler, H. (1939). The mass, public & public opinion. In A. N. Lee (Ed.). *New outlines of the principles of sociology.* New York: Barnes & Noble.

Blumler, H. (1969). *Symbolic interactionism: Perspective and method.* Englewood Cliffs, NJ: Prentice Hall.

Bogatz, G. A., & Ball, S. (1971). The second year of Sesame Street: A continuing evaluation, Vols. I and II. Princeton, NJ: Education Testing Service. (ERIC Document Reproduction Service Nos. ED 122 800, ED 122 801).

Bourdieu, P. (1977). *Outline of a theory of practice.* New York: Cambridge University Press.

Brigham, J. C., & Giesbrecht, L. W. (1976). "All in the Family": Racial attitudes. *Journal of Communication, 26*(4), 69-74.

Brosius, H., & Kepplinger, H. M. (1990). The agenda setting function of television news. *Communication Research, 17,* 183-211.

Buckingham, D. (1993). *Children talking television: The making of television literacy.* London: The Falmer Press.

Buckingham, D. (2000). *After the death of childhood: Growing up in the age of electronic media.* London: Polity Press.

Bushman, B. J., & Huesmann, L. R. (2001). Effects of televised violence on aggression. In D. G. Singer & J. L. Singer (Eds.), *Handbook of children and the media* (pp. 223-254). Thousand Oaks, CA: Sage Publications.

Calvert, S. L., Huston, A. C., & Wright, J. C. (1987). Effects of television preplay formats on children's attention and story comprehension. *Journal of Applied Developmental Psychology, 8,* 329-342.

Cantor, P. A. (1999). The Simpsons. *Political Theory, 27,* 734-749.

Carey, J. (1989). *Communication as culture: Essays on media and society*. Boston: Unwin Hyman.

Chaiken, S. (1980). Heuristic versus systematic processing and the use of source versus message cues in persuasion. *Journal of Personality and Social Psychology, 39,* 752-766.

Chaiken, S., Liberman, A., & Eagly, A. H. (1989). Heuristic and systematic information processing within and beyond the persuasion context. In J. S. Uleman and J. A. Bargh, (Eds.), *Unintended thought* (pp. 212-252). New York: Guilford Press.

Christenson, P. G., & Roberts, D. F. (1983). The role of television in the formation of children's social attitudes. In M. J. A. Howe (Ed.), *Learning from television*. New York: Academic Press.

Clark, R. E. (1982). Individual behavior in different settings. *Viewpoints in Teaching and Learning, 58*(3), 33-39.

Clark, R. E. (1983). Reconsidering research on learning from media. *Review of Educational Research, 53*(4), 445-459.

Clark, R. E. (1987). Which technology for what purpose? The state of the argument about research on learning from media. Paper presented at the Annual Convention of the Association for Educational Communications and Technology. (ERIC Document Reproduction Service No. ED 285 520).

Clark, R. E., & Salomon, G. (1985). Media in teaching. In M. Wittrock (Ed.), *Handbook of research on teaching* (3rd ed.) (pp. 464-478). New York: MacMillan.

Cline, V. B., Croft, R. G., & Courrier, S. (1973). Desensitization of children to television violence. *Journal of Personality and Social Psychology, 27,* 260-265.

Cressey, P. (1934). The motion picture as informal education. *Journal of Educational Sociology, 7,* 504-515.

Cullingsford, C. (1984). *Children and television*. Aldershot, UK: Gower.

Dalton, D. W., & Hannafin, M. J. (1986). The effects of video-only, CAI only, and interactive video instructional systems on learner performance and attitude: An exploratory study. Paper presented at the Annual Convention of the Association for Educational Communications and Technology. (ERIC Document Reproduction Service No. ED 267 762)

Delingpole, J. (1997, Aug 30). Something for everyone. *The Spectator, 279*(8822), 10-11.

Dewey, J. (1916). *Democracy and education*. New York: The Free Press.

Eagly. A. H. (1992). Uneven progress: Social psychology and the study of attitudes. *Journal of Personality and Social Psychology, 63*(5), 693-710.

Field, D. E., & Anderson, D. R. (1985). Instruction and modality effects on children's television attention and comprehension. *Journal of Educational Psychology, 77,* 91-100.

Fisch, S. M. (1999, April). A capacity model of children's comprehension of educational content on television. Paper presented at the Biennial Meeting of the Society for Research in Child Development, Albuquerque, New Mexico.

Fisch, S. M., Brown, S. K., & Cohen, D. I. (1999, April). Young children's comprehension of television: The role of visual information and intonation. Poster presented at the Biennial Meeting of the Society for Research in Child Development, Albuquerque, New Mexico.

Fisch, S. M. & Truglio, R. T. (Eds.) (2001). *"G" is for growing: Thirty years or research on children and Sesame Street*. Hillsdale, NJ: Lawrence Erlbaum.

Fisher, B. A. (1978). *Perspectives on human communication*. New York: Macmillan.

Fiske, J. (1989). *Reading the Popular*. Boston, MA: Unwin and Hyman.

Fiske, S. T., & Taylor, S. E. (1991). *Social Cognition* (2nd ed.). New York: McGraw-Hill.

Flavell, J. H., Flavell, E. R., & Green, F. L. (1987). Young children's knowledge about the apparent-real and pretend-real distinctions. *Developmental Psychology, 23*(6), 816-822.

Gerbner, G., Gross, L., Eleey, M. F., Jackson-Beeck, M., Jeffries-Fox, S., & Signorielli, N. (1977). Violence profile no. 8: The highlights. *Journal of Communication, 27*(2), 171-180.

Gerbner, G., Gross, L., Eleey, M. F., Jackson-Beeck, M., Jeffries-Fox, S., & Signorielli, N. (1978). Cultural indicators: Violence profile no. 9. *Journal of Communication, 28*(3), 176-206.

Gerbner, G., Gross, L., Morgan, M., & Signorielli, N., (1980). The mainstreaming of America: Violence profile no. 11. *Journal of Communication, 30*(3), 10-28.

Gerbner, G., Gross, L., Morgan, M., & Signorielli, N. (1982). Charting the mainstream: Television's contributions to political orientations. *Journal of Communication, 32*(2), 100-127.

Gerbner, G., Gross, L., Morgan, M., & Signorielli, N., (1986). Living with television: The dynamics of the cultivation process. In J. Bryant & D. Zillman (Eds.), *Perspectives on media effects* (pp. 17-40). Hillsdale, NJ: Lawrence Erlbaum Associates.

Gerbner, G., Gross, L., Morgan, M., & Signorielli, N. (1994). Growing up with television: The Cultivation perspective. In J. Bryant & D. Zillmann (Eds.), *Media effects: Advances in theory and research* (pp. 17-42), Hillsdale, NJ: Lawrence Erlbaum Associates.

Ghorpade, S. (1986). Agenda setting: A test of advertising's neglected function. *Journal of Advertising Research, 25,* 23-27.

Glynn, S., & Britton, B. (1984). Supporting readers' comprehension through effective text design. *Educational Technology, 24,* 40-43.

Greenfield, P., & Beagles-Roos, J. (1988). Radio vs. television: Their cognitive impact on children of different socioeconomic and ethnic groups. *Journal of Communication, 38*(2), 71-92.

Greenfield, P., Farrar, D., & Beagles-Roos, J. (1986). Is the medium the message? An experimental comparison of the effects of radio and television on imagination. *Journal of Applied Developmental Psychology, 7,* 201-218.

Greenfield, P. M. (1984). *Mind and media: The effects of television, computers and video games*. Cambridge, MA: Harvard University Press.

Greenfield, P. M., Yut, E., Chung, M., Land, D., Kreider, H., Pantoja, M., & Horsley, K. (1990). The program-length commercial: A study of the effects of television/toy tie-ins on imaginative play . *Psychology and Marketing, 7,* 237-255.

Greer, D., Potts, R., Wright, J. C., & Huston, A. C. (1982). The effects of television commercial form and commercial placement on children's social behavior and attention. *Child Development, 53,* 611-619.

Gunter, B. (1985). *Dimensions of television violence*. Aldershot, UK: Gower.

Hall, S. (1980). Coding and encoding in the television discourse. In S. Hall et al. (Eds.), *Culture, media, and language* (pp. 197-208). London: Hutchinson.

Hall, S., Clarke, J., Critcher, C., Jefferson, T., & Roberts, B. (1978). *Policing the crisis*. London: MacMillan.

Halpern, D. F. (1986). *Sex differences in cognitive abilities*. Hillsdale, NJ: Lawrence Erlbaum Associates.

Hardt, H. (1991). *Critical communication studies*. London: Routledge.

Harrison, L. F., & Williams, T. M. (1986). Television and cognitive development. In T. M. Williams (Ed.), *The impact of television: A natural experiment in three communities* (pp. 87-142). San Diego, CA: Academic Press.

Hart, R. A. (1986). *The effects of fluid ability, visual ability, and visual placement within the screen on a simple concept task*. Paper presented at the Annual Convention of the Association for Educational Communications and Technology. (ERIC Document Reproduction Service No. ED 267 774)

Hawkins, R. P., Kim, J. H., & Pingree, S. (1991). The ups and downs of attention to television. *Communication Research, 18,* 53-76.

Hayes, D. S., & Kelly, S. B. (1984). Young children's processing of television: Modality differences in the retention of temporal relations. *Journal of Experimental Child Psychology, 38,* 505-514.

Heath, R. & Bryant, J. (1992). *Human communication theory and research.* Hillsdale, NJ: Erlbaum.

Hendershot, H. (2000). Teletubby trouble. *Television Quarterly, 31*(1), 19-25.

Himmelweit, H., Oppenheim, A. N., & Vince, P. (1959). *Television and the child: An empirical study of the effects of television on the young.* London: Oxford University Press.

Hoban, C. F., & van Ormer, E. B. (1950). Instructional film research, 1918-1950. Technical Report No. SDC 269-7-19, Port Washington, NY: U.S. Naval Special Devices Center.

Hodge, R., & Tripp, D. (1986). *Children and television: A semiotic approach.* Stanford, CA: Stanford University Press.

Hoffner, C., Cantor, J., & Thorson, E. (1988). Children's understanding of a televised narrative. *Communication Research, 15,* 227-245.

Holaday, P. W., & Stoddard, G. D. (1933). *Getting ideas from the movies.* New York: MacMillan.

Hovland, C. I., Lumsdaine, A. A., & Sheffield, F. D. (1949). *Experiments on mass communication* (vol. 3). Princeton, NJ: Princeton University Press.

Huston, A. C., & Wright, J. C. (1997). Mass media and children's development. In W. Damon (Series Ed.) & I. E. Siegel & K. A. Renninger (Vol. Eds.), *Handbook of child psychology: Vol. 4. Child psychology in practice* (4th ed., pp. 999-1058). New York: John Wiley.

Huston, A. C., Wright, J. C., Wartella, E., Rice, M. L., Watkins, B. A., Campbell, T., & Potts, R. (1981). Communicating more than content: Formal features of children's television programs. *Journal of Communication, 31*(3), 32-48.

Iyengar, E., Peters, M. D., & Kinder, D. R. (1982). Experimental demonstrations of the 'not-so-minimal' consequences of television news programs. *American Political Science Review, 76,* 848-858.

Jacobvitz, R. S., Wood, M. R., & Albin, K. (1991). Cognitive skills and young children's comprehension of television. *Journal of Applied Developmental Psychology, 12*(2), 219-235.

Johnston, J. (1987). *Electronic learning: From audiotape to videodisk.* Hillsdale, NJ: Lawrence Erlbaum Associates.

Jordan, A. B. (1992). Social class, temporal orientation, and mass media use within the family system. *Critical Studies in Mass Communication, 9,* 374-386.

Kellermann, K. (1985). Memory processes in media effects. *Communication Research, 12,* 83-131.

Kinder, M. (Ed.) (1999). *Kids' media culture.* Durham, NC: Duke University Press.

Krendl, K. A. (1986). Media influence on learning: Examining the role of preconceptions. *Educational Communication and Technology Journal, 34,* 223-234.

Krendl, K. A., Clark, G., Dawson, R., & Troiano, C. (1993). Preschoolers and VCRs in the home: A multiple methods approach. *Journal of Broadcasting and Electronic Media, 37,* 293-312.

Krendl, K. A., & Watkins, B. (1983). Understanding television: An exploratory inquiry into the reconstruction of narrative content. *Educational Communication and Technology Journal, 31,* 201-212.

Lasswell, H. D. (1948). The structure and function of communication in society. In L. Bryson (Ed.), *The communication of ideas.* New York: Harper & Brothers.

Lazarsfeld, P. F. (1940). *Radio and the printed page: An introduction to the study of radio and its role in the communication of ideas.* New York: Duell, Sloan, and Pearce.

Lesser, G. S. (1977). *Television and the preschool child.* New York: Academic Press.

Lindlof, T. R., & Shatzer, M. J. (1989). Subjective differences in spousal perceptions of family video. *Journal of Broadcasting and Electronic Media, 33,* 375-395.

Lindlof, T. R., & Shatzer, M. J. (1990). VCR usage in the American family. In J. Bryant (Ed.), *Television and the American family* (pp. 89-109). Hillsdale, NJ: Lawrence Erlbaum Associates, Inc.

Lindlof, T. R., & Shatzer, M. J. (1998). Media ethnography in virtual space: Strategies, limits, and possibilities. *Journal of Broadcasting & Electronic Media, 42,* 170-189.

Lippmann, W. (1922). *Public Opinion.* New York: Free Press.

Lorch, E. P., Anderson, D. R., & Levin, S. R. (1979). The relationship of visual attention to children's comprehension of television. *Child Development, 50,* 722-727.

Lowry, B., Hall, J., & Braxton, G. (1997, September 21). There's a moral to this. *Los Angeles Times Calendar,* pp. 8-9, 72-73.

Mandler, J., & Johnson, N. (1977). Remembrance of things parsed: Story structure and recall. *Cognitive Psychology, 9,* 111-151.

McCombs, M. E., & Shaw, D. L. (1972). The agenda setting function of mass media. *Public Opinion Quarterly, 36,* 176-187.

McGuire, W. J. (1973). Persuasion, resistance, and attitude change. In I. D. S. Pool, W. Schramm, F. W. Frey, N. Macoby, & E. B. Parker (Eds.), *Handbook of communication* (pp. 216-252). Chicago: Rand McNally.

McQuail, D. (1983). *Mass communication theory: An introduction.* Beverly Hills, CA: Sage.

Mead, G. H. (1934). *Mind, self, and society.* Chicago: University of Chicago Press.

Meadowcroft, J. M. (1985). *Children's attention to television: The influence of story schema development on allocation of cognitive capacity and memory.* Unpublished doctoral dissertation, University of Wisconsin-Madison.

Mielke, K. W. (1994). Sesame Street and children in proverty. *Media Studies Journal, 8*(4), 125-34.

Miklitsch, R. (1998). *From Hegel to Madonna: Toward a general economy of commodity fetishism.* New York: State University of New York Press.

Miller, W. (1985). A view from the inside: Brainwaves and television viewing. *Journalism Quarterly, 62,* 508-514.

Morley, D. (1980). *The "Nationwide" audience: Structure and decoding.* BFI TV Monographs No. 11. London: British Film Institute.

Morley, D. (1986). *Family television: Cultural power and domestic leisure.* London: Comedia Publishing Group.

Mullin, C. R., & Linz, D. (1995). Desensitization and resensitization to violence against women: Effects of exposure to sexually violent films on judgments of domestic violence victims. *Journal of Personality and Social Psychology, 69,* 449-459.

Murray, S. (1999). Saving our so-called lives: Girl fandom, adolescent subjectivity, and My So-Called Life. In M. Kinder (Ed.), *Kids' media culture* (pp. 221-236). Durham, NC: Duke University Press.

Musto, M. (1999, Feb 23). Purple passion. *The Village Voice, 44*(7), 55-57.

Nathanson, A. I. (1999). Identifying and explaining the relationship between parental mediation and children's aggression. *Communication Research, 26,* 124-143.

National Institute of Mental Health (NIMH) (1982). In D. Pearl, L. Bouthilet, & J. Lazar (Eds.), *Television and behavior: Ten years of scientific progress and implications for the eighties* (Vol. 2) (pp. 138-157). Washington, DC: U.S. Government Printing Office.

Paik, H., & Comstock, G. (1994). The effects of television violence on antisocial behavior: A meta-analysis. *Communication Research, 21,* 516-546.

Perse, E. M. (2001). *Media effects and society*. Mahwah: N.J.: Lawrence Erlbaum Associates.

Peterson, R. C., & Thurstone, L. L. (1933). *Motion pictures and the social attitudes of children*. New York: MacMillan.

Petty, R. E., & Cacioppo, J. T. (1986). *Communication and persuasion: Central and peripheral routes to attitude change*. New York: Springer-Verlag.

Piaget, J. (1970). Piaget's theory. In P. H. Mussen (Ed.), *Carmichael's manual of psychology* (chap. 9, pp. 703-732). New York: Wiley.

Piaget, J. (1972). *The principles of genetic epistemology*. (W. Mays, Trans.). New York: Basic.

Potter, R. F., & Callison, C. (2000). Sounds exciting!!: The effects of auditory complexity on listeners' attitudes and memory for radio promotional announcements. *Journal of Radio Studies, 1,* 59-79.

Potter, W. J. (1988). Perceived reality in television effects research. *Journal of Broadcasting & Electronic Media, 32,* 23-41.

Potter, W. J. (1999). *On media violence*. Thousand Oaks, CA: Sage.

Prawat, R. S., Anderson, A. H., & Hapkeiwicz, W. (1989). Are dolls real? Developmental changes in the child's definition of reality. *Journal of Genetic Psychology, 150,* 359-374.

Real, M. R. (1989). *Super media: A cultural studies approach*. Newbury Park, CA : Sage Publications.

Reiser, R. A., Tessmer, M. A. & Phelps, P. C. (1984). Adult-child interaction in children's learning from Sesame Street. *Educational Communications and Technology Journal, 32*(4), 217-33.

Reiser, R. A., Williamson, N. & Suzuki, K. (1988). Using Sesame Street to facilitate children's recognition of letters and numbers. *Educational Communications and Technology Journal, 36*(1), 15-21.

Reiss, D. (1981). *The family's construction of reality*. Cambridge, MA: Harvard Press.

Rice, M. L., Huston, A. C., & Wright, J. C. (1982). The forms and codes of television: Effects of children's attention, comprehension, and social behavior. In D. Pearl, L. Bouthilet, & J. Lazar (Eds.), *Television and behavior: Ten years of scientific progress and implications for the eighties*. Washington, DC: U.S. Government Printing Office.

Rice, M. L., Huston, A. C., & Wright, J. C. (1986). Replays as repetitions: Young children's interpretations of television forms. *Journal of Applied Developmental Psychology, 7*(1), 61-76.

Roberts, M. S. (1992). Predicting voting behavior via the agenda-setting tradition. *Journalism Quarterly, 69,* 878-892.

Rogge, J. U., & Jensen, K. (1988). Everyday life and television in West Germany: An empathic-interpretive perspective on the family as a system. In J. Lull (Ed.), *World families watch television* (pp. 80-115). Newbury Park, CA: Sage.

Rolandelli, D. R., Wright, J. C., Huston, A. C., & Eakins, D. (1991). Children's auditory and visual processing of narrated and nonnarrated television programming. *Journal of Experimental Child Psychology, 51,* 90-122.

Rubenstein, D. J. (2000). Stimulating children's creativity and curiosity: Does content and medium matter? *Journal of Creative Behavior, 34,* 1-17.

Rubin, A. M. (1986). Age and family control influences on children's television viewing. *The Southern Speech Communication Journal, 52*(1), 35-51.

Ruff, H. A., Cappozzoli, M., & Weissberg, R. (1998). Age, individuality, and context as factors in sustained visual attention during preschool years. *Developmental Psychology, 34,* 454-464.

Runco, M. A., & Pezdek, K. (1984). The effect of television and radio on children's creativity. *Human Communication Research, 11,* 109-120.

Salomon, G. (1974). Internalization of filmic schematic operations in interaction with learners' aptitudes. *Journal of Educational Psychology, 66,* 499-511.

Salomon, G. (1979). *Interaction of media, cognition, and learning*. San Francisco: Jossey-Bass.

Salomon, G., & Cohen, A. A. (1977). Television formats, mastery of mental skills, and the acquisition of knowledge. *Journal of Educational Psychology, 69,* 612-619.

Salomon, G., & Leigh T. (1984). Predispositions about learning from print and television. *Journal of Communication, 34*(2), 119-135.

Sander, I. (1995, May). How violent is TV-violence? An empirical investigation of factors Influencing viewers' perceptions of TV-violence. Paper presented at the annual conference of The International Communication Association, Albuquerque, NM.

Schramm, W. (1977). *Big media, little media*. Beverly Hills, CA: Sage.

Schramm, W., Lyle, J., & Parker, E. B. (1961). *Television in the lives of our children*. Stanford, CA: Stanford University Press.

Seidman, S. A. (1981). On the contributions of music to media productions. *Educational Communication and Technology Journal, 29,* 49-61.

Seiter, E. (1999). Power rangers at preschool: Negotiating media in child-care settings. In M. Kinder (Ed.), *Kids' media culture* (pp. 239-262). Durham, NC: Duke University Press.

Seiter, E., Borchers, H., & Warth, E. M. (Eds.) (1989). *Remote Control*. London: Routledge.

Severin, W. J., & Tankard, J. W., Jr., (2001). *Communication theories: Origins, methods, and uses in the mass media*. New York: Addison Wesley Longman.

Shannon, C. & Weaver, W. (1949). *The mathematical theory of communication*. Urbana, IL: University of Illinois Press.

Shaw, D. L., & Martin, S. E. (1992). The function of mass media agenda setting. *Journalism Quarterly, 69,* 902-920.

Shaw, D. L., & McCombs, M. E. (Eds.) (1977). *The emergence of American political issues: The agenda setting function of the press*. St. Paul, MN: West.

Shuttleworth, F. K., & May, M. A. (1933). *The social conduct and attitudes of movie fans*. New York: MacMillan.

Signorielli, N. (1990, November). *Television's contribution to adolescents' perceptions about work*. Paper presented at the annual conference of the Speech Communication Association, Chicago.

Signorielli, N. (2001). Television's gender role images and contribution to stereotyping: Past, present, and future. In D. G. Singer & J. L. Singer (Eds.), *Handbook of children and the media* (pp. 223-254). Thousand Oaks, CA: Sage Publications.

Silverman, I. W., & Gaines, M. (1996). Using standard situations to measure attention span and persistence in toddler-aged children: Some cautions. *Journal of Genetic Psychology, 16,* 569-591.

Silverstone, R. (1994). *Television and everyday life*. London: Routledge.

Singer, J. L., Singer, D. G., & Rapaczynski, W. S. (1984). Family patterns and television viewing as predictors of children's beliefs and aggression. *Journal of Communication, 34*(2), 73-89.

Singhal, A., & Rogers, E. M. (1999). *Entertainment-education: A communication strategy for social change*. Mahwah, NJ: Lawrence Erlbaum Associates.

Taylor, S. E., & Crocker, J. (1981). Schematic bases of social information processing. In E. T. Higgins, C. P. Herman, & M. P. Zanna (Eds.), *Social Cognition: The Ontario Symposium* (Vol. 1, pp. 89-134). Hillsdale, NJ: Lawrence Erlbaum Associates.

Travers, R. M. W. (1967). *Research and theory related to audiovisual information transmission*. Kalamazoo, MI: Western Michigan University Press.

Trenholm, S. (1986). *Human communication theory*. Englewood Cliffs, NJ: Prentice-Hall.

Valkenburg, P. A., & van der Voort, T. H. A. (1994). Influence of TV on daydreaming and creative imagination: A review of research. *Psychological Bulletin, 116,* 316-339.

van der Molen, J. H. W., & van der Voort, T. H. A. (2000a). The impact of television, print, and audio on children's recall of the news: A study of three alternative explanations for the dual-coding hypothesis. *Human Communication Research, 26,* 3–26.

van der Molen, J. H. W., & van der Voort, T. H. A. (2000b). Children's and adults' recall of television and print news in children's and adult news formats. *Communication Research, 27,* 132–160.

Vaughan, B. E., Kopp C. B., & Krakow, J. B. (1984). The emergence and consolidation of self-control from eighteen to thirty months of age: Normative trends and individual differences. *Child Development, 55,* 990–1004.

Verbeke, W. (1988). Preschool children's visual attention and understanding behavior towards a visual narrative. *Communication & Cognition, 21,* 67–94.

Vibbert, M. M., & Meringoff, L. K. (1981). *Children's production and application of story imagery: A cross-medium investigation (Tech. Rep. No. 23).* Cambridge, MA: Harvard University, Project Zero. (ERIC Document Reproduction Service No. ED 210 682)

Welch, R. L., Huston-Stein, A., Wright, J. C., & Plehal, R. (1979). Subtle sex-role cues in children's commercials. *Journal of Communication, 29*(3), 202–209.

Westley, B. (1978). Review of The emergence of American politicsl issues: The agenda-setting function of the press. *Journalism Quarterly, 55,* 172–173.

Whorf, B. (1956). In J. B. Carroll (Ed.), *Language, thought, and reality; selected writings.* Cambridge, MA: Technical Press of the Massachusetts Institute of Technology.

Wicks, R. H. (2001). *Understanding audiences: Learning to use the media constructively.* Mahwah, NJ: Lawrence Erlbaum.

Wilson, B. J., & Cantor, J. (1987). Reducing children's fear reactions to mass media: Effects of Visual exposure and verbal explanation. In M. McLaughlin (Ed.), *Communication yearbook 10.* Beverly Hills, CA: Sage.

Wilson, P., & Pahl, R. (1988). The changing sociological construct of the family. *The Sociological Review, 36,* 233–272.

Wright, J. C., & Huston, A. C. (1981). The forms of television: Nature and development of television literacy in children. In H. Gardner & H. Kelly (Eds.), *Viewing children through television* (pp. 73–88). San Francisco: Jossey-Bass.

Zettl, H. (1998). Contextual media aesthetics as the basis for media literacy. *Journal of Communication, 48*(1), 81–95.

Zettl, H. (2001). *Video Basics 3.* Belmont, CA: Wadsworth.

· 4 ·

COGNITIVE PERSPECTIVES IN PSYCHOLOGY

William Winn
University of Washington

4.1 INTRODUCTION

4.1.1 Caveat Lector

This is a revision of the chapter on the same topic that appeared in the first edition of the *Handbook,* published in 1996. In the intervening years, a great many changes have occurred in cognitive theory, and its perceived relevance to education has been challenged. As a participant in, and indeed as a promulgator of, some of those changes and challenges, my own ideas and opinions have changed significantly since writing the earlier chapter. They continue to change—the topics are rapidly moving targets. This has presented me with a dilemma: whether simply to update the earlier chapter by adding selectively from the last half dozen years' research in cognitive psychology and risk appearing to promote ideas that some now see as irrelevant to the study and practice of educational technology; or to throw out everything from the original chapter and start from scratch. I decided to compromise.

This chapter consists of the same content, updated and slightly abbreviated, that was in the first edition of the *Handbook,* focusing on research in cognitive theory up until the mid-1990s. I have added sections that present and discuss the reasons for current dissatisfaction, among some educators, with these traditional views of cognition. And I have added sections that describe recent views, particularly of mental representation and cognitive processing, which are different from the more traditional views. There are three reasons for my decision. First, the reader of a handbook like this needs to consider the historical context within which current theory has developed, even when that theory has emerged from the rejection, not the extension, of some earlier ideas. Second, recent collaborations with colleagues in cognitive psychology, computer science, and cognitive neuroscience have confirmed for me that these disciplines, which I remain convinced are centrally relevant to research in

educational technology, still operate largely within the more traditional view of cognition. Third, a great deal of the research and practice of educational technology continues to operate within the traditional framework, and continues to benefit from it. I also note that other chapters in the *Handbook* deal more thoroughly, and more ably, with the newer views. So, if readers find this chapter somewhat old fashioned in places, I am nonetheless confident that within the view of our discipline offered by the *Handbook* in its entirety, this chapter still has an important place.

4.1.2 Basic Issues

Over the last few years, education scholars have grown increasingly dissatisfied with the standard view of cognitive theory. The standard view is that people represent information in their minds as single or aggregated sets of symbols, and that cognitive activity consists of operating on these symbols by applying to them learned plans, or algorithms. This view reflects the analogy that the brain works in the same way as a computer (Boden, 1988; Johnson-Laird, 1988), a view that inspired, and was perpetuated by, several decades of research and development in artificial intelligence.

This computational view of cognition is based on several assumptions: (1) There is some direct relationship, or "mapping," between internal representations and the world outside, and this mapping includes representations that are analogous to objects and events in the real world, that is, mental images look to the mind's eye like the perceived phenomena from which they were first created (Kosslyn, 1985). (2) There is both a physical and phenomenological separation between the mental and the physical world, that is, perception of the world translates objects and events into representations that mental operations can work on, and the altered representations are in turn translated into behaviors and their outcomes that are observable in the external world. (3) This separation applies to the timing as well as to the location of cognitive action. Clark (1997, p. 105) calls the way that traditional cognitive theory conceives of the interaction between learner and environment "catch and toss." Information is "caught" from the environment, processed, and "tossed" back without coordination with or sensitivity to the real dynamics of the interaction. (4) Internal representations are idiosyncratic and only partially accurate. However, there is a standard and stable world out there toward which experience and education will slowly lead us, that is, there are correct answers to questions about the world and correct solutions to the problems that it presents.

Some scholars' dissatisfaction with the computational view of cognition arose from evidence that suggested these assumptions might be wrong. (1) Evidence from biology and the neurosciences, which we will examine in more detail later, shows that the central nervous system is informationally closed, and that cognitive activity is prompted by perturbations in the environment that are not represented in any analogous way in the mind (Maturana & Varela, 1980, 1987; Bickhard, 2000). (2) There is evidence that cognitive activity is not separate from the context in which it occurs (Lave, 1988; Suchman, 1987). Thinking, learning, and acting are embedded in an environment to which we are tightly and dynamically coupled and which has a profound influence on what we think and do. What is more, evidence from the study of how we use language (Lakoff & Johnson, 1980) and our bodies (Clark, 1997; Varela, Thompson & Rosch, 1991) suggests that cognitive activity extends beyond our brains to the rest of our bodies, not just to the environment. Many metaphorical expressions in our language make reference to our bodies. We "have a hand" in an activity. We "look up to" someone. Our gestures help us think (see the review by Roth, 2001) and the proprioceptive feedback we get from immediate interaction with the environment is an important part of thinking and learning. (3) Scholars have argued that cognitive activity results from the dynamic interaction between two complex systems— a person and the environment. Indeed, it is sometimes useful to think of the two (person and environment) acting as one tightly coupled system rather than as two interacting but separate entities (Beer, 1995; Roth, 1999). The dynamics of the activity are crucial to an understanding of cognitive processes, which can be described using the tools of Dynamical System Theory (Van Gelder & Port, 1995). (4) Finally, scholars have made persuasive arguments that the value of the knowledge we build lies not in its closeness to any ideal or correct understanding of the external world, but to how it suits our own individual needs and guides our own individual actions. This pragmatic view of what is called constructivism finds its clearest expression in accounts of individual (Winn & Windschitl, 2002) and situated (Lave & Wenger, 1991) problem solving. (The danger that this way of thinking leads inevitably to solipsism is effectively dispelled by Maturana & Varela, 1987, pp. 133–137.)

The constructivists were among the first to propose an alternative conceptual framework to the computational view of cognition. For educational technologists, the issues involved are clearly laid out by Duffy and Jonassen (1992) and Duffy, Lowyck, and Jonassen (1993). Applications of constructivist ideas to learning that is supported by technology are provided

by many authors, including Cognition and Technology Group at Vanderbilt (2000), Jonassen (2000), and White and Frederiksen (1998). Briefly, understanding is constructed by students, not received in messages from the outside simply to be encoded, remembered, and recalled. How knowledge is constructed and with what results depends far more on a student's history of adaptations to the environment (Maturana & Varela, 1987) than on particular environmental events. Therefore, learning is best explained in terms of the student's evolved understanding and valued on that criterion rather than on the basis of objective tests.

However, constructivism, in its most radical forms, has been challenged in its turn for being unscientific (Sokal & Bricmont, 1998; Wilson, 1998), even anti-intellectual (Cromer, 1997; Dawkins, 1997). There is indeed an attitude of "anything goes" in some postmodern educational research. If you start from the premise that anything that the student constructs must be valued, then conceptions of how the world works may be created that are so egregious as to do the student intellectual harm. It appears that, for some, the move away from the computational view of cognition has also been away from learning and cognition as the central focus of educational research, in *any* form. This is understandable. If the knowledge we construct depends almost entirely on our unique personal experiences with the environment, then it is natural to try to explain learning and to prescribe learning strategies by focusing on the environmental factors that influence learning, rather than on the mechanisms of learning themselves. Skimming the tables of contents of educational books and journals over the last 15 years will show a decline in the number of articles devoted to the mechanisms of learning and an increase in the number devoted to environmental factors, such as poverty, ethnicity, the quality of schools, and so on. This research has made an important contribution to our understanding and to the practice of education. However, the neglect of cognition has left a gap at the core that must be filled. This need has been recognized, to some extent, in a recent report from the National Research Council (Shavelson & Towne, 2002), which argues that education must be based on good science.

There are, of course, frameworks other than constructivism that are more centrally focused on cognition, within which to study and describe learning. These are becoming visible now in the literature. What is more, some provide persuasive new accounts of mental representation and cognitive processes. Our conceptual frameworks for research in educational technology must make room for these accounts. For convenience, I will place them into four categories: systems theoretical frameworks, biological frameworks, approaches based on cognitive neuroscience, and neural networks. Of course, the distinctions among these categories often blur. For example, neuroscientists sometimes use system theory to describe cognition.

4.1.2.1   System Theory.   System theory has served educational technology for a long time and in different guises (Heinich, 1970; Pask, 1975, 1984; Scott, 2001; Winn, 1975). It offers a way to describe learning that is more focused on cognition while avoiding some of the problems confronting those seeking biological or neurological accounts that, until recently, appeared largely intractable. A system-theoretic view of cognition is based on the assumption that both learners and learning environments are complex collections of interacting variables. The learner and the environment have mutual influences on each other. The interactions are dynamic, and do not stand still for scrutiny by researchers. And to complicate matters, the interactions are often nonlinear This means that effects cannot be described by simple addition of causes. What is cause and what is effect is not always clear. Changes in learners and their environments can be expressed by applying the mathematical techniques of dynamics (see relevant chapters in Port & Van Gelder, 1995). In practice, the systems of differential equations that describe these interactions are often unsolvable. However, graphical methods (Abraham & Shaw, 1992) provide techniques for side-stepping the calculus and allow researchers to gain considerable insight about these interacting systems. The accounts of cognition that arise from Dynamical System Theory are still abstractions from direct accounts, such as those from biology or cognitive neuroscience. However, they are closer to a description of systemic changes in understanding and in the processes that bring understanding about than accounts based on the computational or constructivist views.

4.1.2.2 *Biological Frameworks.*

Thinking about cognition from the standpoint of biology reminds us that we are, after all, living beings who obey biological laws and operate through biological processes. I know this position is offensive to some. However, I find the arguments on this point, put forward by Dawkins (1989), Dennett (1995), and Pinker (1997, 2002), among others, to be compelling and highly relevant. This approach to our topic raises three important points. First, what we call mind is an emergent property of our physical brains, not something that has divine or magical provenance and properties. This opens the way for making a strong case that neuroscience *is* relevant to education. Second, cognition is embodied in our physical forms (Clark, 1997; Kelso, 1999; Varela et al., 1991). This implies two further things. What we can perceive directly about the environment, without the assistance of devices that augment our perceptual capacities, and therefore the understanding we can construct directly from it, are very limited—to visible light, to a small range of audio frequencies, and so on (Nagel, 1974; Winn & Windschitl, 2001b). Also, we use our bodies as tools for thinking—from counting on our fingers to using bodily movement in virtual environments to help us solve problems (Dede, Salzman, Loftin, & Ash, 1996; Gabert, 2001). Third, and perhaps most important, the biological view helps us think of learning as adaptation to an environment (Holland, 1992, 1995). Technology has advanced to the point where we can construct complete environments within which students can learn. This important idea is developed later.

4.1.2.3 *Cognitive Neuroscience.*

The human brain has been called the most complex object in the universe. Only recently have we been able to announce, with any confidence, that some day we will understand how it works (although Pinker, 1997, holds a less optimistic view). In the meantime, we are getting closer to the point where we will be able to explain,

in general terms, how learning takes place. Such phenomena as memory (Baddeley, 2000; Tulving, 2000), imagery (Farah, 2001; Kosslyn & Thompson, 2000), vision (Hubel, 2000), implicit learning (Knowlton & Squire, 1996; Liu, 2002), and many aspects of language (Berninger & Richards, 2002) are now routinely discussed in terms of neurological processes. While much of the research in cognitive neuroscience is based on clinical work, meaning that data come from people with abnormal or damaged brains, recent developments in nonintrusive brain-monitoring technologies, such as fMRI, are beginning to produce data from normal brains. This recent work is relevant to cognitive theory in two ways. First, it lets us reject, once and for all, the unfounded and often rather odd views about the brain that have found their way into educational literature and practice. For example, there is no evidence from neuroscience that some people are right brained, and some left brained. Nor is there neurological evidence for the existence of learning styles (Berninger & Richards, 2002). These may be metaphors for observed human behaviors. But they are erroneously attributed to basic neural mechanisms. Second, research in cognitive neuroscience provides credible and empirically validated accounts of how cognition, and the behavior it engenders, change as a result of a person's interaction with the environment. Learning causes detectable physical changes to the central nervous system that result from adaptation to the environment, and that change the ways in which we adapt to it in the future (Markowitsch, 2000; see also Cisek, 1999, pp. 132-134, for an account of how the brain exerts control over a person's state in their environment).

4.1.2.4 *Neural Networks.*

This fourth framework within which to think about cognition crosses several of the previous categories. Neural networks are implemented as computer programs which, like people, can learn through iterative adaptation to input and can solve novel problems by recognizing their similarity to problems they already know how to solve. Neural network theory takes its primary metaphor from neuroscience— that even the most complex cognitive activity is an emergent property of the coordinated activation of networks of many atomic units (neurons) (Strogatz, 2003) that can exist in only two states, on or off. (See McClelland & Rumelhart, 1986, 1988; Rumelhart & McClelland, 1986, for conceptual and technical accounts.) The complexity and dynamics of networks reflect many of the characteristics of system theory, and research into networks borrows from systems analysis techniques. Neural networks also transcend the representation–computation distinction, which is fundamental to some views of cognition and to which we return later. Networks represent information through the way their units are connected. But the changes in these connections are themselves the processes by which learning takes place. What is known and the ways knowledge is changed are one and the same. Neural networks have been most successful at emulating low-level cognitive processes, such as letter and word recognition. Higher level operations require more abstract, more symbolic, modes of operation, and symbols are now thought to be compatible with network architectures (Holyoak & Hummel, 2000).

What has all this go to do with cognition and, particularly, with its relationship to educational technology? The rest of this chapter seeks answers to this question. It begins with a brief history of the precursors of cognitive theory and a short account of cognitive theory's ascendancy. It then presents examples of research and theory from the traditional cognitive perspective. This view is still quite pervasive, and the most recent research suggests that it might not be as far off the mark as suspected. The chapter therefore examines traditional research on mental representation and mental processes. In each of these two sections, it presents the major findings from research and the key objections to the traditional tenets of cognitive theory. It then discusses recent alternative views, based roughly on the four frameworks we have just examined. The chapter concludes by looking more closely at how traditional and more recent views of cognition can inform and guide educational technology research and practice.

4.2   HISTORICAL OVERVIEW

Most readers will already know that cognitive theory came into its own as an extension of (some would say a replacement of) behavioral theory. However, many of the tenets of cognitive theory are not new and date back to the very beginnings of psychology as an autonomous discipline in the late nineteenth century. This section therefore begins with a brief discussion of the new science of mind and of Gestalt theory before turning to the story of cognitive psychology's reaction to behaviorism.

4.2.1   The Beginnings: A Science of Mind

One of the major forces that helped Psychology emerge as a discipline distinct from Philosophy, at the end of the nineteenth century, was the work of the German psychologist, Wundt (Boring, 1950). Wundt made two significant contributions, one conceptual and the other methodological. First, he clarified the boundaries of the new discipline. Psychology was the study of the inner world, not the outer world, which was the domain of physics. And the study of the inner world was to be the study of thought, or mind, not of the physical body, which was the domain of physiology. Wundt's methodological contribution was the development of introspection as a means for studying the mind. Physics and physiology deal with phenomena that are objectively present and therefore directly observable and measurable. Thought is both highly subjective and intangible. Therefore, Wundt proposed, the only access to it was through the direct examination of one's own thoughts through introspection. Wundt developed a program of research that extended over many decades and attracted adherents from laboratories in many countries. Typically, his experimental tasks were simple—pressing buttons, watching displays, and the like. The data of greatest interest were the descriptions his subjects gave of what they were thinking as they performed the tasks.

On the face of it, Wundt's approach was very sensible. You learn best about things by studying them directly. The only direct route to thought is via a subject's description of his own thinking. There is a problem, however. Introspection lacks objectivity. Does the act of thinking about thinking interfere with and change the thinking that one is interested in studying? Perhaps. But the same general access route to cognitive processes is used today in developing think-aloud protocols (Ericsson & Simon, 1984), obtained while subjects perform natural or experimental tasks. The method is respected, judged to be valid if properly applied, and essential to the study of thought and behavior in the real world or in simulations of it.

4.2.2   Gestalt Psychology

The word Gestalt is a German noun, meaning both shape or form and entity or individual (Hartmann, 1935). Gestalt psychology is the study of how people see and understand the relation of the whole to the parts that make it up. Unlike much of science, which analyzes wholes to seek explanations about how they work in their parts, Gestalt psychology looks at the parts in terms of the wholes that contain them. Thus, wholes are greater than the sum of their parts, and the nature of parts is determined by the wholes to which they belong (Wertheimer, 1924). Gestalt psychologists therefore account for behavior in terms of complete phenomena, which they explain as arising from such mechanisms as insight. We see our world in large phenomenological units and act accordingly.

One of the best illustrations of the whole being different from the sum of the parts is provided in a musical example. If a melody is played on an instrument, it may be learned and later recognized. If the melody is played again, but this time in another key, it is still recognizable. However, if the same notes are played in a different sequence, the listener will not detect any similarity between the first and the second melody. Based on the ability of a person to recognize and even reproduce a melody (whole Gestalt) in a key different from the original one, and on their inability to recognize the individual notes (parts) in a different sequence, it is clear that, "The totals themselves, then, must be different entities than the sums of their parts. In other words, the Gestaltqualität (form quality) or whole has been reproduced: the elements or parts have not" (Hartmann, 1935).

The central tenet of Gestalt theory—that our perception and understanding of objects and events in the world depend upon the appearance and actions of whole objects not of their individual parts—has had some influence on research in educational technology. The key to that influence are the well-known Gestalt laws of perceptual organization, codified by Wertheimer (1938). These include the principles of "good figure," "figure–ground separation," and "continuity." These laws formed the basis for a considerable number of message design principles (Fleming & Levie, 1978, 1993), in which Gestalt theory about how we perceive and organize information that we see is used in prescriptive recommendations about how to present information on the page or screen. A similar approach to what we hear is taken by Hereford and Winn (1994).

More broadly, the influence of Gestalt theory is evident in much of what has been written about visual literacy. In this regard, Arnheim's book "Visual Thinking" (1969) is a key work. It was widely read and cited by scholars of visual literacy and proved influential in the development of that field.

Finally, it is important to note a renewal of interest in Gestalt theory in the 1980s (Epstein, 1988; Henle, 1987). The Gestalt psychologists provided little empirical evidence for their laws of perceptual organization beyond everyday experience of their effects. Using newer techniques that allow experimental study of perceptual organization, researchers (Pomerantz, 1986; Rock, 1986) have provided explanations for how Gestalt principles work. The effects of such stimulus features as symmetry on perceptual organization have been explained in terms of the "emergent properties" (Rock, 1986) of what we see in the world around us. We see a triangle as a triangle, not as three lines and three angles. This experience arises from the closeness (indeed the connection) of the ends of the three sides of the triangle. Emergent properties are the same as the Gestaltist's "whole" that has features all its own that are, indeed, greater than the sum of the parts.

4.2.3 The Rise of Cognitive Psychology

Behavioral theory is described in detail elsewhere in this handbook. Suffice it to say here that behaviorism embodies two of the key principles of positivism—that our knowledge of the world can only evolve from the observation of objective facts and phenomena, and that theory can only be built by applying this observation in experiments where the experimenter manipulates only one or two factors at a time. The first of these principles therefore banned from behavioral psychology unobservable mental states, images, insights, and Gestalts. The second principle banned research methods that involved the subjective techniques of introspection and phenomenology and the drawing of inferences from observation rather than from objective measurement. Ryle's (1949) relegation of the concept of mind to the status of "the ghost in the machine," both unbidden and unnecessary for a scientific account of human activity, captures the behaviorist ethos exceptionally well.

Behaviorism's reaction against the suspect subjectivity of introspection and the nonexperimental methods of Gestalt psychology was necessary at the time if psychology was to become a scientific discipline. However, the imposition of the rigid standards of objectivism and positivism excluded from accounts of human behavior many of those experiences with which we are extremely familiar. We all experience mental images, feelings, insight, and a whole host of other unobservable and unmeasurable phenomena. To deny their importance is to deny much of what it means to be human (Searle, 1992). Cognitive psychology has been somewhat cautious in acknowledging the ability or even the need to study such phenomena, often dismissing them as folk psychology (Bruner, 1990). Only recently, this time as a reaction against the inadequacies of cognitive rather than behavioral theory, do we find serious consideration of subjective experiences. (These are discussed in Bruner, 1990; Clancey, 1993; Dennett, 1991; Edelman, 1992; Pinker, 1997; Searle, 1992; Varela, et al., 1991, among others. They are also addressed elsewhere in this handbook.)

Cognitive psychology's reaction against the inability of behaviorism to account for much human activity arose mainly from a concern that the link between a stimulus and a response was not straightforward, that there were mechanisms that intervened to reduce the predictability of a response to a given stimulus, and that stimulus–response accounts of complex behavior unique to humans, like the acquisition and use of language, were extremely convoluted and contrived. (Chomsky's, 1964, review of Skinner's, 1957, S–R account of language acquisition is a classic example of this point of view and is still well worth reading.) Cognitive psychology therefore shifted focus to mental processes that operate on stimuli presented to the perceptual and cognitive systems, and which usually contribute significantly to whether or not a response is made, when it is made, and what it is. Whereas behaviorists claim that such processes cannot be studied because they are not directly observable and measurable, cognitive psychologists claim that they must be studied because they alone can explain how people think and act the way they do. Somewhat ironically, cognitive neuroscience reveals that the mechanisms that intervene between stimulus and response are, after all, chains of internal stimuli and responses, of neurons activating and changing other neurons, though in very complex sequences and networks. Markowitsh (2000) discusses some of these topics, mentioning that the successful acquisition of information is accompanied by changes in neuronal morphology and long-term potentiation of interneuron connections.

Here are two examples of the transition from behavioral to cognitive theory. The first concerns memory, the second mental imagery. Behavioral accounts of how we remember lists of items are usually associationist. Memory in such cases is accomplished by learning S–R associations among pairs of items in a set and is improved through practice (Gagné, 1965; Underwood, 1964). However, we now know that this is not the whole story and that mechanisms intervene between the stimulus and the response that affect how well we remember. The first of these is the collapsing of items to be remembered into a single "chunk." Chunking is imposed by the limits of short-term memory to roughly seven items (Miller, 1956). Without chunking, we would never be able to remember more than seven things at once. When we have to remember more than this limited number of items, we tend to learn them in groups that are manageable in short-term memory, and then to store each group as a single unit. At recall, we "unpack" (Anderson, 1983) each chunk and retrieve what is inside. Chunking is more effective if the items in each chunk have something in common, or form a spatial (McNamara 1986; McNamara, Hardy & Hirtle, 1989) or temporal (Winn, 1986) group.

A second mechanism that intervenes between a stimulus and response to promote memory for items is interactive mental imagery. When people are asked to remember pairs of items and recall is cued with one item of the pair, performance is improved if they form a mental image in which the two items appear to interact (Bower, 1970; Paivio, 1971, 1983). For example, it is easier for you to remember the pair "Whale–Cigar" if you imagine a whale smoking a cigar. The use of interactive imagery to facilitate memory has been developed into a sophisticated instructional technique by Levin and his colleagues (Morrison & Levin, 1987; Peters & Levin, 1986). The considerable literature on the role of imagery in paired-associate and other kinds of learning is summarized by Paivio and colleagues (Clark & Paivio, 1991; Paivio, 1971, 1983).

The importance of these memory mechanisms to the development of cognitive psychology is that, once understood, they make it very clear that a person's ability to remember items is improved if the items are meaningfully related to each other or to the person's existing knowledge. The key word here is "meaningful." For now, we shall simply assert that what is meaningful to a person is determined by what they can remember of what they have already learned. This implies a circular relationship among learning, meaning, and memory—that what we learn is affected by how meaningful it is, that meaning is determined by what we remember, and that memory is affected by what we learn. However, this circle is not a vicious one. The reciprocal relationship between learning and memory, between environment and knowledge, is the driving force behind established theories of cognitive development (Piaget, 1968) and of cognition generally (Neisser, 1976). It is also worth noting that Ausubel's (1963) important book on meaningful verbal learning proposed that learning is most effective when memory structures appropriate to what is about to be learned are created or activated through advance organizers. More generally, then, cognitive psychology is concerned with meaning, while behavioral psychology is not.

The most recent research suggests that the activities that connect memory and the environment are not circular but concurrent. Clark's (1997) "continuous reciprocal causation," and Rosch's (1999) idea that concepts are bridges between the mind and the world, only existing while a person interacts with the environment, underlie radically different views of cognition. We will return to these later.

Mental imagery provides a second example of the differences between behavioral and cognitive psychology. Imagery was so far beyond the behaviorist pale that one article that re-introduced the topic was subtitled, "The return of the ostracized." Images were, of course, central to Gestalt theory, as we have seen. But because they could not be observed, and because the only route to them was through introspection and self-report, they had no place in behavioral theory.

Yet we can all, to some degree, conjure up mental images. We can also deliberately manipulate them. Kosslyn, Ball, and Reiser (1978) trained their subjects to zoom in and out of images of familiar objects and found that the distance between the subject and the imagined object constrained the subject's ability to describe the object. To discover the number of claws on an imaged cat, for example, the subject had to move closer to it in the mind's eye.

This ability to manipulate images is useful in some kinds of learning. The method of "Loci" (Kosslyn, 1985; Yates, 1966), for example, requires a person to create a mental image of a familiar place in the mind's eye and to place in that location images of objects that are to be remembered. Recall consists of mentally walking through the place and describing the objects you find. The effectiveness of this technique, which was known to the orators of ancient Greece, has been demonstrated empirically (Cornoldi & De Beni, 1991; De Beni & Cornoldi, 1985).

Mental imagery will be discussed in more detail later. For now, we will draw attention to two methodological issues that are raised by its study. First, some studies of imagery are symptomatic of a conservative color to some cognitive research. As Anderson (1978) has commented, any conclusions about the existence and nature of images can only be inferred from observable behavior. You can only really tell if the Loci method has worked if a person can name items in the set to be remembered. On this view, the behaviorists were right. Objectively observable behavior is all the evidence even cognitive researchers have to go on. This means that, until recently, cognitive psychology has had to study mental representation and processes indirectly and draw conclusions about them by inference rather than from direct measurement. Now, we have direct evidence from neuroscience (Farah, 2000; Kosslyn & Thompson, 2000) that the parts of the brain that become active when subjects report the presence of a mental image are the same that are active during visual perception.

The second methodological issue is exemplified by Kosslyn's (1985) use of introspection and self-report by subjects to obtain his data on mental images. The scientific tradition that established the methodology of behavioral psychology considered subjective data to be biased, tainted and therefore unreliable. This precept has carried over into the mainstream of cognitive research. Yet, in his invited address to the 1976 AERA conference, the sociologist Uri Bronfenbrenner (1976) expressed surprise, indeed dismay, that educational researchers did not ask subjects their opinions about the experimental tasks they carry out, nor about whether they performed the tasks as instructed or in some other way. Certainly, this stricture has eased in much of the educational research that has been conducted since 1976, and nonexperimental methodology, ranging from ethnography to participant observation to a variety of phenomenologically based approaches to inquiry, are the norm for certain types of educational research (see, for example, the many articles that appeared in the mid-1980s, among them, Baker, 1984; Eisner, 1984; Howe, 1983; Phillips, 1983). Nonetheless, strict cognitive psychology has tended, even recently, to adhere to experimental methodology, based on positivism, which makes research such as Kosslyn's on imagery somewhat suspect to some.

4.2.4 Cognitive Science

Inevitably, cognitive psychology has come face to face with the computer. This is not merely a result of the times in which the discipline has developed, but emerges from the intractability of many of the problems cognitive psychologists seek to solve. The necessity for cognitive researchers to build theory by inference rather than from direct measurement has always been problematic.

One way around this problem is to build theoretical models of cognitive activity, to write computer simulations that predict what behaviors are likely to occur if the model is an accurate instantiation of cognitive activity, and to compare the behavior predicted by the model—the output from the program—to the behavior observed in subjects. Examples of this approach are found in the work of Marr (1982) on vision, and in connectionist models of language learning (Pinker, 1999, pp. 103–117). Marr's work is a good illustration of this approach.

Marr began with the assumption that the mechanisms of human vision are too complex to understand at the neurological level. Instead, he set out to describe the functions that these mechanisms need to perform as what is seen by the eye moves from the retina to the visual cortex and is interpreted by the viewer. The functions Marr developed were mathematical models of such processes as edge detection, the perception of shapes at different scales, and stereopsis (Marr & Nishihara, 1978). The electrical activity observed in certain types of cell in the visual system matched the activity predicted by the model almost exactly (Marr & Ullman, 1981).

Marr's work has had implications that go far beyond his important research on vision, and as such serves as a paradigmatic case of cognitive science. Cognitive science is not called that because of its close association with the computer but because it adopts the functional or computational approach to psychology that is so much in evidence in Marr's work. By "functional" (see Pylyshyn, 1984), we mean that it is concerned with the functions the cognitive system must perform not with the devices through which cognitive processes are implemented. A commonly used analogy is that cognitive science is concerned with cognitive software not hardware. By "computational" (Arbib & Hanson, 1987; Richards, 1988), we mean that the models of cognitive science take information that a learner encounters, perform logical or mathematical operations on it, and describe the outcomes of those operations. The computer is the tool that allows the functions to be tested, the computations to be performed. In a recent extensive exposition of a new theory of science, Wolfram (2002) goes so far as to claim that *every* action, whether natural or man-made, including all cognitive activity, is a "program" that can be recreated and run on a computer. Wolfram's theory is provocative, as yet unsubstantiated, but will doubtless be talked about in the literature for the next little while.

The tendency in cognitive science to create theory around computational rather than biological mechanisms points to another characteristic of the discipline. Cognitive scientists conceive of cognitive theory at different levels of description. The level that comes closest to the brain mechanisms that create cognitive activity is obviously biological. However, as Marr presumed, this level was at the time virtually inaccessible to cognitive researchers, consequently requiring the construction of more abstract functional models. The number, nature and names of the levels of cognitive theory vary from theory to theory and from researcher to researcher. Anderson (1990, chapter 1) provides a useful discussion of levels, including those of Chomsky (1965), Pylyshyn (1984), Rumelhart & McClelland (1986), and Newell (1982) in addition to Marr's and his own. In spite of their differences, each of these approaches to levels of cognitive theory implies that if we cannot explain cognition in terms of the mechanisms through which it is actually realized, we can explain it in terms of more abstract mechanisms that we can profitably explore. In other words, the different levels of cognitive theory are really different metaphors for the actual processes that take place in the brain.

The computer has assumed two additional roles in cognitive science beyond that of a tool for testing models. First, some have concluded that, because computer programs written to test cognitive theory accurately predict observable behavior that results from cognitive activity, cognitive activity must itself

be computer-like. Cognitive scientists have proposed numerous theories of cognition that embody the information processing principles and even the mechanisms of computer science (Boden, 1988; Johnson-Laird, 1988). Thus we find reference in the cognitive science literature to input and output, data structures, information processing, production systems, and so on. More significantly, we find descriptions of cognition in terms of the logical processing of symbols (Larkin & Simon, 1987; Salomon, 1979; Winn, 1982). Second, cognitive science has provided both the theory and the impetus to create computer programs that "think" just as we do. Research in artificial intelligence (AI) blossomed during the 1980s, and was particularly successful when it produced intelligent tutoring systems (Anderson, Boyle & Yost, 1985; Anderson & Lebiere, 1998; Anderson & Reiser, 1985; Wenger, 1987) and expert systems (Forsyth, 1984). The former are characterized by the ability to understand and react to the progress a student makes working through a computer-based tutorial program. The latter are smart "consultants," usually to professionals whose jobs require them to make complicated decisions from large amounts of data.

Its successes notwithstanding, AI has shown up the weaknesses of many of the assumptions that underlie cognitive science, especially the assumption that cognition consists in the logical mental manipulation of symbols. Scholars (Bickhard, 2000; Clancey, 1993; Clark, 1997; Dreyfus, 1979; Dreyfus & Dreyfus, 1986; Edelman, 1992; Freeman & Nuñez, 1999; Searle, 1992) have criticized this and other assumptions of cognitive science as well as of computational theory and, more basically, functionalism. The critics imply that cognitive scientists have lost sight of the metaphorical origins of the levels of cognitive theory and have assumed that the brain really does compute the answer to problems by symbol manipulation. Searle's comment sets the tone, "If you are tempted to functionalism, we believe you do not need refutation, you need help" (1992, p. 9).

4.2.5 Section Summary

This section has traced the development of cognitive theory up to the point where, in the 1980s, it emerged preeminent among psychological theories of learning and understanding. Although many of the ideas in this section will be developed in what follows, it is useful at this point to provide a short summary of the ideas presented so far. Cognitive psychology returned to center stage largely because stimulus-response theory did not adequately or efficiently account for many aspects of human behavior that we all observe from day to day. The research on memory and mental imagery, briefly described, indicated that psychological processes and prior knowledge intervene between the stimulus and the response making the latter less predictable. Also, nonexperimental and nonobjective methodology is now deemed appropriate for certain types of research. However, it is possible to detect a degree of conservatism in mainstream cognitive psychology that still insists on the objectivity and quantifiability of data.

Cognitive science, emerging from the confluence of cognitive psychology and computer science, has developed its own set of assumptions, not least among which are computer models of cognition. These have served well, at different levels of abstraction, to guide cognitive research, leading to such applications as intelligent tutors and expert systems. However, the computational theory and functionalism that underlie these assumptions have been the source of recent criticism, and their role in research in education needs to be reassessed.

The implications of all of this for research and practice in educational technology will be discussed later. It is nonetheless useful to anticipate three aspects of that discussion. First, educational technology research, and particularly mainstream instructional design practice, needs to catch up with developments in psychological theory. As I have suggested elsewhere (Winn, 1989), it is not sufficient simply to substitute cognitive objectives for behavioral objectives and to tweak our assessment techniques to gain access to knowledge schemata rather than just to observable behaviors. More fundamental changes are required including, now, those required by demonstrable limitations to cognitive theory itself.

Second, shifts in the technology itself away from rather prosaic and ponderous computer-assisted programmed instruction to highly interactive multimedia environments permit educational technologists to develop serious alternatives to didactic instruction (Winn, 2002). We can now use technology to do more than direct teaching. We can use it to help students construct meaning for themselves through experience in ways proposed by constructivist theory and practice described elsewhere in this handbook and by Duffy and Jonassen (1992), Duffy, Lowyck, and Jonassen, (1993), Winn and Windschitl (2001a), and others.

Third, the proposed alternatives to computer models of cognition, that explain first-person experience, nonsymbolic thinking and learning, and reflection-free cognition, lay the conceptual foundation for educational developments of virtual realities (Winn & Windschitl, 2001a). The full realization of these new concepts and technologies lies in the future. However, we need to get ahead of the game and prepare for when these eventualities become a reality.

4.3 MENTAL REPRESENTATION

The previous section showed the historical origins of the two major aspects of cognitive psychology that are addressed in this and the next section. These have been, and continue to be, mental representation and mental processes. The example of representation was the mental image, and passing reference was made to memory structures and hierarchical chunks of information. The section also talked generally about the input, processing, and output functions of the cognitive system, and paid particular attention to Marr's account of the processes of vision. In this section we look at traditional and emerging views of mental representation.

The nature of mental representation and how to study it lie at the heart of traditional approaches to cognitive psychology. Yet, as we have seen, the nature, indeed the very existence, of mental representation are not without controversy. It merits consideration here, however, because it is still pervasive in educational technology research and theory, because it has, in spite

of shortcomings, contributed to our understanding of learning, and because it is currently regaining some of its lost status as a result of research in several disciplines.

How we store information in memory, represent it in our mind's eye, or manipulate it through the processes of reasoning has always seemed relevant to researchers in educational technology. Our field has sometimes supposed that the way in which we represent information mentally is a direct mapping of what we see and hear about us in the world (see Cassidy & Knowlton, 1983; Knowlton, 1966; Sless, 1981). Educational technologists have paid a considerable amount of attention to how visual presentations of different levels of abstraction affect our ability to reason literally and analogically (Winn, 1982). Since the earliest days of our discipline (Dale, 1946), we have been intrigued by the idea that the degree of realism with which we present information to students determines how well they learn. More recently (Salomon, 1979), we have come to believe that our thinking uses various symbol systems as tools, enabling us both to learn and to develop skills in different symbolic modalities. How mental representation is affected by what a student encounters in the environment has become inextricably bound up with the part of our field we call "message design" (Fleming & Levie, 1993; Rieber, 1994, chapter 7).

4.3.1 Schema Theory

The concept of schema is central to early cognitive theories of representation. There are many descriptions of what schemata are. All descriptions concur that a schema has the following characteristics: (1) It is an organized structure that exists in memory and, in aggregate with all other schemata, contains the sum of our knowledge of the world (Paivio, 1974). (2) It exists at a higher level of generality, or abstraction, than our immediate experience with the world. (3) It is dynamic, amenable to change by general experience or through instruction. (4) It provides a context for interpreting new knowledge as well as a structure to hold it. Each of these features requires comment.

4.3.1.1 Schema as Memory Structure. The idea that memory is organized in structures goes back to the work of Bartlett (1932). In experiments designed to explore the nature of memory that required subjects to remember stories, Bartlett was struck by two things: First, recall, especially over time, was surprisingly inaccurate; second, the inaccuracies were systematic in that they betrayed the influence of certain common characteristics of stories and turns of event that might be predicted from everyday occurrences in the world. Unusual plots and story structures tended to be remembered as closer to normal than in fact they were. Bartlett concluded from this that human memory consisted of cognitive structures that were built over time as the result of our interaction with the world and that these structures colored our encoding and recall of subsequently encountered ideas. Since Bartlett's work, both the nature and function of schemata have been amplified and clarified experimentally.

4.3.1.2 Schema as Abstraction. A schema is a more abstract representation than a direct perceptual experience. When we look at a cat, we observe its color, the length of its fur, its size, its breed if that is discernible and any unique features it might have, such as a torn ear or unusual eye color. However, the schema that we have constructed from experience to represent "cat" in our memory, and by means of which we are able to identify any cat, does not contain these details. Instead, our "cat" schema will tell us that it has eyes, four legs, raised ears, a particular shape and habits. However, it leaves those features that vary among cats, like eye color and length of fur, unspecified. In the language of schema theory, these are "place-holders," "slots," or "variables" to be instantiated through recall or recognition (Norman & Rumelhart, 1975).

It is this abstraction, or generality, that makes schemata useful. If memory required that we encode every feature of every experience that we had, without stripping away variable details, recall would require us to match every experience against templates in order to identify objects and events, a suggestion that has long since been discredited for its unrealistic demands on memory capacity and cognitive processing resources (Pinker, 1985). On rare occasions, the generality of schemata may prevent us from identifying something. For example, we may misidentify a penguin because, superficially, it has few features of a bird. As we shall see below, learning requires the modification of schemata so that they can accurately accommodate unusual instances, like penguins, while still maintaining a level of specificity that makes them useful.

4.3.1.3 Schema as Dynamic Structure.

A schema is not immutable. As we learn new information, either from instruction or from day-to-day interaction with the environment, our memory and understanding of our world will change. Schema theory proposes that our knowledge of the world is constantly interpreting new experience and adapting to it. These processes, which Piaget (1968) has called "assimilation" and "accommodation," and which Thorndyke and Hayes-Roth (1979) have called "bottom up" and "top down" processing, interact dynamically in an attempt to achieve cognitive equilibrium without which the world would be a tangled blur of meaningless experiences. The process works like this: When we encounter a new object, experience, or piece of information, we attempt to match its features and structure to a schema in memory (bottom-up). Depending on the success of this first attempt at matching, we construct a hypothesis about the identity of the object, experience, or information, on the basis of which we look for further evidence to confirm our identification (top-down). If further evidence confirms our hypothesis we assimilate the experience to the schema. If it does not, we revise our hypothesis, thus accommodating to the experience.

Learning takes place as schemata change when they accommodate to new information in the environment and as new information is assimilated by them. Rumelhart and Norman (1981) discuss important differences in the extent to which these changes take place. Learning takes place by accretion, by schema tuning, or by schema creation. In the case of accretion, the match between new information and schemata is so good that the new information is simply added to an existing schema with almost no accommodation of the schema at all. A hiker might learn to recognize a golden eagle simply by matching it

to an already-familiar bald eagle schema noting only the absence of the former's white head and tail.

Schema tuning results in more radical changes in a schema. A child raised in the inner city might have formed a "bird" schema on the basis of seeing only sparrows and pigeons. The features of this schema might be: a size of between 3 and 10 inches; flying by flapping wings; found around and on buildings. This child's first sighting of an eagle would probably be confusing, and might lead to a misidentification as an airplane, which is bigger than 10 inches long and does not flap its wings. Learning, perhaps through instruction, that this creature was indeed bird would lead to changes in the "bird" schema, to include soaring as a means of getting around, large size, and mountain habitat. Rumelhart and Norman (1981) describe schema creation as occurring by analogy. Stretching the bird example to the limits of credibility, imagine someone from a country that has no birds but lots of bats for whom a "bird" schema does not exist. The creation of a bird schema could take place by temporarily substituting the features birds have in common with bats and then specifically teaching the differences. The danger, of course, is that a significant residue of bat features could persist in the bird schema, in spite of careful instruction. Analogies can therefore be misleading (Spiro, Feltovich, Coulson, & Anderson, 1989) if they are not used with extreme care.

More recently, research on conceptual change (Posner, Strike, Hewson, & Gertzog, 1982; Vosniadou, 1994; Windschitl, & André, 1998) has extended our understanding of schema change in important ways. Since this work concerns cognitive processes, we will deal with it in the next major section. Suffice it to note, for now, that it aims to explain more of the mechanisms of change, leading to practical applications in teaching and learning, particularly in science, and more often than not involves technology.

4.3.1.4 Schema as Context.

Not only does a schema serve as a repository of experiences; it provides a context that affects how we interpret new experiences and even directs our attention to particular sources of experience and information. From the time of Bartlett, schema theory has been developed largely from research in reading comprehension. And it is from this area of research that the strongest evidence comes for the decisive role of schemata in interpreting text.

The research design for these studies requires the activation of a well-developed schema to set a context, the presentation of a text, that is often deliberately ambiguous, and a comprehension posttest. For example, Bransford and Johnson (1972) had subjects study a text that was so ambiguous as to be meaningless without the presence of an accompanying picture. Anderson, Reynolds, Schallert, and Goetz (1977) presented ambiguous stories to different groups of people. A story that could have been about weight lifting or a prison break was interpreted to be about weight-lifting by students in a weight-lifting class, but in other ways by other students. Musicians interpreted a story that could have been about playing cards or playing music as if it were about music.

Finally, recent research on priming (Schachter & Buckner, 1998; Squire & Knowlton, 1995) is beginning to identify mechanisms that *might eventually* account for schema activation, whether conscious or implicit. After all, both perceptual and semantic priming predispose people to perform subsequent cognitive tasks in particular ways, and produce effects that are not unlike the contextualizing effects of schemata. However, given that the experimental tasks used in this priming research are far simpler and implicate more basic cognitive mechanisms than those used in the study of how schemata are activated to provide contexts for learning, linking these two bodies of research is currently risky, if not unwarranted. Yet, the possibility that research on priming could eventually explain some aspects of schema theory is too intriguing to ignore completely.

4.3.1.5 Schema Theory and Educational Technology.
Schema theory has influenced educational technology in a variety of ways. For instance, the notion of activating a schema in order to provide a relevant context for learning finds a close parallel in Gagné, Briggs, and Wager's (1988) third instructional "event," "stimulating recall of prerequisite learning." Reigeluth's (Reigeluth & Stein, 1983) "elaboration theory" of instruction consists of, among other things, prescriptions for the progressive refinement of schemata. The notion of a generality, that has persisted through the many stages of Merrill's instructional theory (Merrill, 1983, 1988; Merrill, Li, & Jones, 1991), is close to a schema.

There are, however, three particular ways in which educational technology research has used schema theory (or at least some of the ideas it embodies, in common with other cognitive theories of representation). The first concerns the assumption, and attempts to support it, that schemata can be more effectively built and activated if the material that students encounter is somehow isomorphic to the putative structure of the schema. This line of research extends into the realm of cognitive theory earlier attempts to propose and validate a theory of audiovisual (usually more visual than audio) education and concerns the role of pictorial and graphic illustration in instruction (Carpenter, 1953; Dale, 1946; Dwyer, 1972, 1978, 1987).

The second way in which educational technology has used schema theory has been to develop and apply techniques for students to use to impose structure on what they learn and thus make it more memorable. These techniques are referred to, collectively, by the term "information mapping."

The third line of research consists of attempts to use schemata to represent information in a computer and thereby to enable the machine to interact with information in ways analogous to human assimilation and accommodation. This brings us to a consideration of the role of schemata, or "scripts" (Schank & Abelson, 1977) or "plans" (Minsky, 1975) in AI and "intelligent" instructional systems. The next sections examine these lines of research.

4.3.1.5.1 Schema–Message Isomorphism: Imaginal Encoding.
There are two ways in which pictures and graphics can affect how information is encoded in schemata. Some research suggests that a picture is encoded directly as a mental image. This means that encoding leads to a schema that retains many of the properties of the message that the student saw, such as its spatial structure and the appearance of its features. Other research suggests that the picture or graphic imposes a structure on information first and that propositions about this structure rather than the structure itself are encoded. The schema therefore does not contain a mental image but information that allows an image to be created in the mind's eye when the schema becomes active. This and the next section examine these two possibilities.

Research into imaginal encoding is typically conducted within the framework of theories that propose two (at least) separate, though connected, memory systems. Paivio's (Clark & Paivio, 1992; Paivio, 1983) "dual coding" theory and Kulhavy's (Kulhavy, Lee, & Caterino, 1985; Kulhavy, Stock, & Caterino, 1994) "conjoint retention" theory are typical. Both theories assume that people can encode information as language-like propositions or as picture-like mental images. This research has provided evidence that (1) pictures and graphics contain information that is not contained in text and (2) that information shown in pictures and graphics is easier to recall because it is encoded in both memory systems, as propositions and as images, rather than just as propositions, which is the case when students read text. As an example, Schwartz and Kulhavy (1981) had subjects study a map while listening to a narrative describing the territory. Map subjects recalled more spatial information related to map features than nonmap subjects, while there was no difference between recall of the two groups on information not related to map features. In another study, Abel and Kulhavy (1989) found that subjects who saw maps of a territory recalled more details than subjects who read a corresponding text suggesting that the map provided "second stratum cues" that made it easier to recall information.

4.3.1.5.2 Schema–Message Isomorphism: Structural Encoding.
Evidence for the claim that graphics help students organize content by determining the structure of the schema in which it is encoded comes from studies that have examined the relationship between spatial presentations and cued or free recall. The assumption is that the spatial structure of the information on the page reflects the semantic structure of the information that gets encoded. For example, Winn (1980) used text with or without a block diagram to teach about a typical food web to high-school subjects. Estimates of subjects' semantic structures representing the content were obtained from their free associations to words naming key concepts in the food web (e.g., consumer, herbivore). It was found that the diagram significantly improved the closeness of the structure the students acquired to the structure of the content.

McNamara et al. (1989) had subjects learn spatial layouts of common objects. Ordered trees, constructed from free recall data, revealed hierarchical clusters of items that formed the basis for organizing the information in memory. A recognition test, in which targeted items were primed by items either within or outside the same cluster, produced response latencies that were faster for same-cluster items than for different-item clusters. The placement of an item in one cluster or another was determined, for the most part, by the spatial proximity of the items in the original layout. In another study, McNamara (1986) had subjects study the layout of real objects placed in an area on the floor. The area was divided by low barriers into four quadrants of equal size. Primed recall produced response latencies suggesting that the physical boundaries imposed categories on the objects when they were encoded that overrode the effect of absolute spatial proximity. For example, recall reponses were slower to items physically close but separated by a boundary than two items further apart but within the same boundary. The results of studies like these have been the basis for recommendations about when and how to use pictures and graphics in instructional materials (Levin, Anglin, & Carney, 1987; Winn, 1989b).

4.3.1.6 Schemata and Information Mapping. Strategies exploiting the structural isomorphism of graphics and knowledge schemata have also formed the basis for a variety of text- and information-mapping schemes aimed at improving comprehension (Armbruster & Anderson, 1982, 1984; Novak, 1998) and study skills (Dansereau et al., 1979; Holley & Dansereau, 1984). Research on the effectiveness of these strategies and its application is one of the best examples of how cognitive theory has come to be used by instructional designers.

The assumptions underlying all information-mapping strategies are that if information is well-organized in memory it will be better remembered and more easily associated with new information, and that students can be taught techniques exploiting the spatial organization of information on the page that make what they learn better organized in memory. We have already seen examples of research that bears out the first of these assumptions. We turn now to research on the effectiveness of information-mapping techniques.

All information-mapping strategies (reviewed and summarized by Hughes, 1989) require students to learn ways to represent information, usually text, in spatially constructed diagrams. With these techniques, they construct diagrams that represent the concepts they are to learn as verbal labels often in boxes and that show interconcept relations as lines or arrows. The most obvious characteristic of these techniques is that students construct the information maps for themselves rather than studying diagrams created by someone else. In this way, the maps require students to process the information they contain in an effortful manner while allowing a certain measure of idiosyncrasy in how the ideas are shown, both of which are attributes of effective learning strategies.

Some mapping techniques are radial, with the key concept in the center of the diagram and related concepts on arms reaching out from the center (Hughes, 1989). Other schemes are more hierarchical with concepts placed on branches of a tree (Johnson, Pittelman, & Heimlich, 1986). Still others maintain the roughly linear format of sentences but use special symbols to encode interconcept relations, like equals signs or different kinds of boxes (Armbruster & Anderson, 1984). Some computer-based systems provide more flexibility by allowing zooming in or out on concepts to reveal subconcepts within them and by allowing users to introduce pictures and graphics from other sources (Fisher, Faletti, Patterson, Thornton, Lipson, & Spring, 1990).

The burgeoning of the World Wide Web has given rise to a new way to look at information mapping. Like many of today's teachers, Malarney (2000) had her students construct web pages to display their knowledge of a subject, in this case ocean science. Malarney's insight was that the students' web pages were in fact concept maps, in which ideas were illustrated and connected to other ideas through layout and hyperlinks. Carefully used, the Web can serve both as a way to represent maps of content, and also as tools to assess what students know about something, using tools described, for example, by Novak (1998).

Regardless of format, information mapping has been shown to be effective. In some cases, information mapping techniques have formed part of study skills curricula (Holley & Dansereau, 1984; Schewel, 1989). In other cases, the technique has been used to improve reading comprehension (Ruddell & Boyle, 1989) or for review at the end of a course (Fisher et al., 1990). Information mapping has been shown to be useful for helping students write about what they have read (Sinatra, Stahl-Gemake, & Morgan, 1986) and works with disabled readers as well as with normal readers (Sinatra, Stahl-Gemake, & Borg, 1986). Information mapping has proved to be a successful technique in all of these tasks and contexts, showing it to be remarkably robust.

Information mapping can, of course, be used by instructional designers (Jonassen, 1990, 1991; Suzuki, 1987). In this case, the technique is used not so much to improve comprehension as to help designers understand the relations among concepts in the material they are working with. Often, understanding such relations makes strategy selection more effective. For example, a radial outline based on the concept "zebra" (Hughes, 1989) shows, among other things, that a zebra is a member of the horse family and also that it lives in Africa on the open grasslands. From the layout of the radial map, it is clear that membership of the horse family is a different kind of interconcept relation than the relation with Africa and grasslands. The designer will therefore be likely to organize the instruction so that a zebra's location and habitat are taught together and not at the same time as the zebra's place in the mammalian taxonomy is taught. We will return to instructional designers' use of information-mapping techniques in our discussion of cognitive objectives later.

All of this seems to suggest that imagery-based and information-structuring strategies based on graphics have been extremely useful in practice. Tversky (2001) provides a summary and analysis of research into graphical techniques that exploit both the analog (imagery-based) and metaphorical (information-organizing) properties of all manner of images. Her summary shows that they can be effective. Vekiri (2002) provides a broader summary of research into the effectiveness of graphics for learning that includes several studies concerned with mental representation. However, the whole idea of isomorphism between an information display outside the learner and the structure and content of a memory schema implies that information in the environment is mapped fairly directly into memory. As we have seen, this basic assumption of much of cognitive theory is currently being challenged. For example, Bickhard (2000) asks, "What's wrong with 'encodingism'?", his term for direct mapping to mental schemata. The extent to which this challenge threatens the usefulness of using pictures and graphics in instruction remains to be seen.

4.3.1.7 Schemata and AI. Another way in which theories of representation have been used in educational technology is to suggest ways in which computer programs, designed to "think" like people, might represent information. Clearly, this

application embodies the "computer models of mind" assumption that we mentioned above (Boden, 1988).

The structural nature of schemata make them particularly attractive to cognitive scientists working in the area of artificial intelligence. The reason for this is that they can be described using the same language that is used by computers and therefore provide a convenient link between human and artificial thought. The best early examples are to be found in the work of Minsky (1975) and of Schank and his associates (Schank & Abelson, 1977). Here, schemata provide constraints on the meaning of information that the computer and the user share that make the interaction between them more manageable and useful. The constraints arise from only allowing what typically happens in a given situation to be considered. For example, certain actions and verbal exchanges commonly take place in a restaurant. You enter. Someone shows you to your table. Someone brings you a menu. After a while, they come back and you order your meal. Your food is brought to you in a predictable sequence. You eat it in a predictable way. When you have finished, someone brings you the bill, which you pay. You leave. It is not likely (though not impossible, of course) that someone will bring you a basketball rather than the food you ordered. Usually, you will eat your food rather than sing to it. You use cash or a credit card to pay for your meal rather than offering a giraffe. In this way, the almost infinite number of things that can occur in the world are constrained to relatively few, which means that the machine has a better chance of figuring out what your words or actions mean.

Even so, schemata (or "scripts" as Schank, 1984, calls them) cannot contend with every eventuality. This is because the assumptions about the world that are implicit in our schemata, and therefore often escape our awareness, have to be made explicit in scripts that are used in AI. Schank (1984) provides examples as he describes the difficulties encountered by TALE-SPIN, a program designed to write stories in the style of Aesop's fables.

"One day Joe Bear was hungry. He asked his friend Irving Bird where some honey was. Irving told him there was a beehive in the oak tree. Joe walked to the oak tree. He ate the beehive." Here, the problem is that we know beehives contain honey, and while they are indeed a source of food, they are not themselves food, but contain it. The program did not know this, nor could it infer it. A second example, with Schank's own analysis, makes a similar point: "Henry Ant was thirsty. He walked over to the river bank where his good friend Bill Bird was sitting. Henry slipped and fell in the river. He was unable to call for help. He drowned."

This was not the story that TALE-SPIN set out to tell. [...] Had TALE-SPIN found a way for Henry to call to Bill for help, this would have caused Bill to try to save him. But the program had a rule that said that being in water prevents speech. Bill was not asked a direct question, and there was no way for any character to just happen to notice something. Henry drowned because the program knew that that's what happens when a character that can't swim is immersed in water. (Schank, 1984, p. 84)

The rules that the program followed, leading to the sad demise of Henry, are rules that normally apply. People do not usually talk when they're swimming. However, in this case, a second rule should have applied, as we who understand a calling-for-help-while-drowning schema are well aware of.

The more general issue that arises from these examples is that people have extensive knowledge of the world that goes beyond any single set of circumstances that might be defined in a script. And human intelligence rests on the judicious use of this general knowledge. Thus, on the rare occasion that we do encounter someone singing to their food in a restaurant, we have knowledge from beyond the immediate context that lets us conclude the person has had too much to drink, or is preparing to sing a role at the local opera and is therefore not really singing to her food at all, or belongs to a cult for whom praising the food about to be eaten in song is an accepted ritual. The problem for the AI designer is therefore how much of this general knowledge to allow the program to have. Too little, and the correct inferences cannot be made about what has happened when there are even small deviations from the norm. Too much, and the task of building a production system that embodies all the possible reasons for something to occur becomes impossibly complex.

It has been claimed that AI has failed (Dreyfus & Dreyfus, 1986) because "intelligent" machines do not have the breadth of knowledge that permits human reasoning. A project called "Cyc" (Guha & Lenat, 1991; Lenat, Guha, Pittman, Pratt, & Shepherd, 1990) has as its goal to imbue a machine with precisely the breadth of knowledge that humans have. Over a period of years, programmers will have worked away at encoding an impressive number of facts about the world. If this project is successful, it will be testimony to the usefulness of general knowledge of the world for problem solving and will confirm the severe limits of a schema or script approach to AI. It may also suggest that the schema metaphor is misleading. Maybe people do not organize their knowledge of the world in clearly delineated structures. A lot of thinking is "fuzzy," and the boundaries among schemata are permeable and indistinct.

4.3.2 Mental Models

Another way in which theories of representation have influenced research in educational technology is through psychological and human factors research on mental models. A mental model, like a schema, is a putative structure that contains knowledge of the world. For some, mental models and schemata are synonymous. However, there are two properties of mental models that make them somewhat different from schemata. Mayer (1992, p. 431) identifies these as (1) representations of objects in whatever the model describes and (2) descriptions of how changes in one object effect changes in another. Roughly speaking, a mental model is broader in conception than a schema because it specifies causal actions among objects that take place within it. However, you will find any number of people who disagree with this distinction.

The term envisionment is often applied to the representation of both the objects and the causal relations in a mental model (DeKleer & Brown, 1981; Strittmatter & Seel, 1989). This term draws attention to the visual metaphors that often accompany discussion of mental models. When we use a mental model, we see a representation of it in our mind's eye. This representation has spatial properties akin to those we notice with our biological eye. Some objects are closer to some than to others. And from seeing changes in our mind's eye in one object occurring simultaneously with changes in another, we infer causality between them. This is especially true when we consciously bring about a change in one object ourselves. For example, Sternberg and Weil (1980) gave subjects problems to solve of the kind "If A is bigger than B and C is bigger than A, who is the smallest?" Subjects who changed the representation of the problem by placing the objects A, B, and C in a line from tallest to shortest were most successful at solving the problem because envisioning it in this way allowed them simply to see the answer. Likewise, envisioning what happens in an electrical circuit that includes an electric bell (DeKleer & Brown, 1981) allows someone to come to understand how it works. In short, a mental model can be run like a film or computer program and watched in the mind's eye while it is running. You may have observed world-class skiers running their model of a slalom course, eyes closed, body leaning into each gate, before they make their run.

The greatest interest in mental models by educational technologists lies in ways of getting learners to create good ones. This implies, as in the case of schema creation, that instructional materials and events act with what learners already understand in order to construct a mental model that the student can use to develop understanding. Just how instruction affects mental models has been the subject of considerable research, summarized by Gentner and Stevens (1983), Mayer (1989a), and Rouse and Morris (1986), among others. At the end of his review, Mayer lists seven criteria that instructional materials should meet for them to induce mental models that are likely to improve understanding. (Mayer refers to the materials, typically illustrations and text, as "conceptual models" that describe in graphic form the objects and causal relations among them.) A good model is:

Complete—it contains all the objects, states and actions of the system
Concise—it contains just enough detail
Coherent—it makes "intuitive sense"
Concrete—it is presented at an appropriate level of familiarity
Conceptual—it is potentially meaningful
Correct—the objects and relations in it correspond to actual objects and events
Considerate—it uses appropriate vocabulary and organization.

If these criteria are met, then instruction can lead to the creation of models that help students understand systems and solve problems arising from the way the systems work. For example, Mayer (1989b) and Mayer and Gallini (1990) have demonstrated that materials, conforming to these criteria, in which graphics and text work together to illustrate both the objects and causal relations in systems (hydraulic drum brakes, bicycle pumps) were effective at promoting understanding. Subjects were able to answer questions requiring them to draw inferences from their mental models of the system using information they had not been explicitly taught. For instance, the answer (not explicitly taught) to the question "Why do brakes get hot?"

can only be found in an understanding of the causal relations among the pieces of a brake system. A correct answer implies that an accurate mental model has been constructed.

A second area of research on mental models in which educational technologists are now engaging arises from a belief that interactive multimedia systems are effective tools for model building (Hueyching & Reeves, 1992; Kozma, Russell, Jones, Marx, & Davis,1993; Seel & Dörr, 1994; Windschitl & André, 1998). For the first time, we are able, with reasonable ease, to build instructional materials that are both interactive and that, through animation, can represent the changes of state and causal actions of physical systems. Kozma et al. (1993) describe a computer system that allows students to carry out simulated chemistry experiments. The graphic component of the system (which certainly meets Mayer's criteria for building a good model) presents information about changes of state and causality within a molecular system. It "corresponds to the molecular-level mental models that chemists have of such systems" (Kozma et al., 1993, p. 16). Analysis of constructed student responses and of think-aloud protocols have demonstrated the effectiveness of this system for helping students construct good mental models of chemical reactions. Byrne, Furness, and Winn (1995) described a virtual environment in which students learn about atomic and molecular structure by building atoms from their subatomic components. The most successful treatment for building mental models was a highly interactive one. Winn and Windschitl (2002) examined videotapes of students working in an immersive virtual environment that simulated processes on physical oceanography. They found that students who constructed and then used causal models solved problems more effectively than those who did not. Winn, Windschitl, Fruland, and Lee (2002) give examples of students connecting concepts together to form causal principles as they constructed a mental model of ocean processes while working with the same simulation.

4.3.3 Mental Representation and the Development of Expertise

The knowledge we represent as schemata or mental models changes as we work with it over time. It becomes much more readily accessible and useable, requiring less conscious effort to use it effectively. At the same time, its own structure becomes more robust and it is increasingly internalized and automatized. The result is that its application becomes relatively straightforward and automatic, and frequently occurs without our conscious attention. When we drive home after work, we do not have to think hard about what to do or where we are going. It is important in the research that we shall examine below that this process of "knowledge compilation and translation" (Anderson, 1983) is a slow process. One of the biggest oversights in our field has occurred when instructional designers have assumed that task analysis should describe the behavior of experts rather than novices, completely ignoring the fact that expertise develops in stages and that novices cannot simply get there in one jump.

Out of the behavioral tradition that continues to dominate a great deal of thinking in educational technology comes the assumption that it is possible for mastery to result from instruction. In mastery learning, the only instructional variable is the time required to learn something. Therefore, given enough time, anyone can learn anything. The evidence that this is the case is compelling (Bloom, 1984, 1987; Kulik, 1990a, 1990b). However, enough time typically comes to mean the length of a unit, module or semester and mastery means mastery of performance not of high-level skills such as problem solving.

There is a considerable body of opinion that expertise arises from a much longer exposure to content in a learning environment than that implied in the case of mastery learning. Labouvie-Vief (1990) has suggested that wisdom arises during adulthood from processes that represent a fourth stage of human development, beyond Piaget's traditional three. Achieving a high level of expertise in chess (Chase & Simon, 1973) or in the professions (Schon, 1983, 1987) takes many years of learning and applying what one has learned. This implies that learners move through stages on their way from novicehood to expertise, and that, as in the case of cognitive development (Piaget & Inhelder, 1969), each stage is a necessary prerequisite for the next and cannot be skipped. In this case, expertise does not arise directly from instruction. It may start with some instruction, but only develops fully with maturity and experience on the job (Lave & Wenger, 1991).

An illustrative account of the stages a person goes through on the way to expertise is provided by Dreyfus and Dreyfus (1986). The stages are novice, advanced beginner, competence, proficiency, and expertise. Dreyfus and Dreyfus' examples are useful in clarifying the differences between stages. The following few paragraphs are therefore based on their narrative (1986, pp. 21–35).

Novices learn objective and unambiguous facts and rules about the area that they are beginning to study. These facts and rules are typically learned out of context. For example, beginning nurses learn how to take a patient's blood pressure and are taught rules about what to do if the reading is normal, high, or very high. However, they do not yet necessarily understand what blood pressure really indicates nor why the actions specified in the rules are necessary, nor how they affect the patient's recovery. In a sense, the knowledge they acquire is inert (Cognition and Technology Group at Vanderbilt, 1990) in that, though it can be applied, it is applied blindly and without a context or rationale.

Advanced beginners continue to learn more objective facts and rules. However, with their increased practical experience, they also begin to develop a sense of the larger context in which their developing knowledge and skill operate. Within that context, they begin to associate the objective rules and facts they have learned with particular situations they encounter on the job. Their knowledge becomes situational or contextualized. For example, student nurses, in a maternity ward, begin to recognize patients' symptoms by means that cannot be expressed in objective, context-free rules. The way a particular patient's breathing sounds may be sufficient to indicate that a particular action is necessary. However, the sound itself cannot be described objectively, nor can recognizing it be learned anywhere except on the job.

As the student moves into competence and develops further sensitivity to information in the working environment, the number of context-free and situational facts and rules begins to overwhelm the student. The situation can only be managed when the student learns effective decision-making strategies. Student nurses at this stage often appear to be unable to make decisions. They are still keenly aware of the things they have been taught to look out for and the procedures to follow in the maternity ward. However, they are also now sensitive to situations in the ward that require them to change the rules and procedures. They begin to realize that the baby screaming its head off requires immediate attention even if to give that attention is not something set down in the rules. They are torn between doing what they have been taught to do and doing what they sense is more important at that moment. And often they dither, as Dreyfus and Dreyfus put it, ". . . like a mule between two bales of hay" (1986, p. 24).

Proficiency is characterized by quick, effective, and often unconscious decision making. Unlike the merely competent student, who has to think hard about what to do when the situation is at variance with objective rules and prescribed procedures, the proficient student easily grasps what is going on in any situation and acts, as it were, automatically to deal with whatever arises. The proficient nurse simply notices that a patient is psychologically ready for surgery, without consciously weighing the evidence.

With expertise comes the complete fusion of decision-making and action. So completely is the expert immersed in the task, and so complete is the expert's mastery of the task and of the situations in which it is necessary to act, that ". . . When things are proceeding normally, experts don't solve problems and don't make decisions; they do what normally works" (Dreyfus & Dreyfus, 1986, 30–31). Clearly, such a state of affairs can only arise after extensive experience on the job. With such experience comes the expert's ability to act quickly and correctly from information without needing to analyze it into components. Expert radiologists can perform accurate diagnoses from x-rays by matching the pattern formed by light and dark areas on the film to patterns they have learned over the years to be symptomatic of particular conditions. They act on what they see as a whole and do not attend to each feature separately. Similarly, early research on expertise in chess (Chase & Simon, 1973) revealed that grand masters rely on the recognition of patterns of pieces on the chessboard to guide their play and engage in less in-depth analysis of situations than merely proficient players. Expert nurses sometimes sense that a patient's situation has become critical without there being any objective evidence and, although they cannot explain why, they are usually correct.

A number of things are immediately clear from his account of the development of expertise. The first is that any student must start by learning explicitly taught facts and rules even if the ultimate goal is to become an expert who apparently functions perfectly well without using them at all. Spiro et al. (1992) claim that learning by allowing students to construct knowledge for themselves only works for "advanced knowledge," which assumes the basics have already been mastered.

Second, though, is the observation that students begin to learn situational knowledge and skills as early as the "advanced beginner" stage. This means that the abilities that appear intuitive, even magical, in experts are already present in embryonic form at a relatively early stage in a student's development. The implication is that instruction should foster the development of situational, non-objective knowledge and skill as early as possible in a student's education. This conclusion is corroborated by the study of situated learning (Brown, Collins, and Duguid, 1989) and apprenticeships (Lave & Wenger, 1991) in which education is situated in real-world contexts from the start.

Third is the observation that as students becomes more expert, they are less able to rationalize and articulate the reasons for their understanding of a situation and for their solutions to problems. Instructional designers and knowledge engineers generally are acutely aware of the difficulty of deriving a systematic and objective description of knowledge and skills from an expert as they go about content or task analyses. Experts just do things that work and do not engage in specific or describable problem-solving. This also means that assessment of what students learn as they acquire expertise becomes increasingly difficult and eventually impossible by traditional means, such as tests. Tacit knowledge (Polanyi, 1962) is extremely difficult to measure.

Finally, we can observe that what educational technologists spend most of their time doing—developing explicit and measurable instruction—is only relevant to the earliest step in the process of acquiring expertise. There are two implications of this. First, we have, until recently, ignored the potential of technology to help people learn anything except objective facts and rules. And these, in the scheme of things we have just described, though necessary, are intended to be quickly superceded by other kinds of knowledge and skills that allow us to work effectively in the world. We might conclude that instructional design, as traditionally conceived, has concentrated on creating nothing more than training wheels for learning and acting that are to be jettisoned for more important knowledge and skills as quickly as possible. The second implication is that by basing instruction on the knowledge and skills of experts, we have completely ignored the protracted development that has led up to that state. The student must go through a number of qualitatively different stages that come between novicehood and expertise, and can no more jump directly from Stage 1 to Stage 5 than a child can go from Piaget's preoperational stage of development to formal operations without passing through the intervening developmental steps. If we try to teach the skills of the expert directly to novices, we shall surely fail.

The Dreyfus and Dreyfus (1986) account is by no means the only description of how people become experts. Nor is it to any great extent given in terms of the underlying psychological processes that enable it to develop. The next paragraphs look briefly at more specific accounts of how expertise is acquired, focusing on two cognitive processes: automaticity and knowledge organization.

4.3.3.1 Automaticity. From all accounts of expertise, it is clear that experts still do the things they learned to do as novices, but more often than not they do them without thinking about them. The automatization of cognitive and motor skills is a step along the way to expertise that occurs in just about every explanation of the process. By enabling experts to function without

deliberate attention to what they are doing, automaticity frees up cognitive resources that the expert can then bring to bear on problems that arise from unexpected and hitherto unexperienced events as well as allowing more attention to be paid to the more mundane though particular characteristics of the situation. This has been reported to be the case for such diverse skills as: learning psychomotor skills (Romiszowski, 1993), developing skill as a teacher (Leinhart, 1987), typing (Larochelle, 1982), and the interpretation of x-rays (Lesgold, Robinson, Feltovich, Glaser, Klopfer, & Wang, 1988).

Automaticity occurs as a result of overlearning (Shiffrin & Schneider, 1977). Under the mastery learning model (Bloom, 1984), a student keeps practicing and receiving feedback, iteratively, until some predetermined criterion has been achieved. At that point, the student is taught and practices the next task. In the case of overlearning, the student continues to practice after attaining mastery, even if the achieved criterion is 100 percent performance. The more students practice using knowledge and skill beyond just mastery, the more fluid and automatic their skill will become. This is because practice leads to discrete pieces of knowledge and discrete steps in a skill becoming fused into larger pieces, or chunks. Anderson (1983, 1986) speaks of this process as "knowledge compilation" in which declarative knowledge becomes procedural. Just as a computer compiles statements in a computer language into a code that will actually run, so, Anderson claims, the knowledge that we first acquire as explicit assertions of facts or rules is compiled by extended practice into knowledge and skill that will run on its own without our deliberately having to attend to them. Likewise, Landa (1983) describes the process whereby knowledge is transformed first into skill and then into ability through practice. At an early stage of learning something, we constantly have to refer to statements in order to be able to think and act. Fluency only comes when we no longer have to refer explicitly to what we know. Further practice will turn skills into abilities which are our natural, intuitive manner of doing things.

4.3.3.2 Knowledge Organization. Experts appear to solve problems by recognizing and interpreting the patterns in bodies of information, not by breaking down the information into its constituent parts. If automaticity corresponds to the cognitive process side of expertise, then knowledge organization is the equivalent of mental representation of knowledge by experts. There is considerable evidence that experts organize knowledge in qualitatively different ways from novices. It appears that the chunking of information that is characteristic of experts' knowledge leads them to consider patterns of information when they are required to solve problems rather than improving the way they search through what they know to find an answer. For example, chess masters are far less affected by time pressure than less accomplished players (Calderwood, Klein, & Crandall, 1988). Requiring players to increase the number of moves they make in a minute will obviously reduce the amount of time they have to search through what they know about the relative success of potential moves. However, pattern recognition is a much more instantaneous process and will therefore not be as affected by increasing the number of moves per minute. Since masters were less affected than less expert players by increasing the speed of a game of chess, it seems that they used pattern recognition rather than search as their main strategy.

Charness (1989) reported changes in a chess player's strategies over a period of 9 years. There was little change in the player's skill at searching through potential moves. However, there were noticeable changes in recall of board positions, evaluation of the state of the game, and chunking of information, all of which, Charness claims, are pattern-related rather than search-related skills. Moreover, Saariluoma (1990) reported, from protocol analysis, that strong chess players in fact engaged in less extensive search than intermediate players, concluding that what is searched is more important than how deeply the search is conducted.

It is important to note that some researchers (Patel & Groen, 1991) explicitly discount pattern recognition as the primary means by which some experts solve problems. Also, in a study of expert X-ray diagnosticians, Lesgold et al. (1988) propose that experts' knowledge schemata are developed through "deeper" generalization and discrimination than novices'. Goldstone, Steyvers, Spencer-Smith, and Kersten (2000) cite evidence for this kind of heightened perceptual discrimination in expert radiologists, beer tasters and chick sexers. There is also evidence that the exposure to environmental stimuli that leads to heightened sensory discrimination brings about measurable changes in the auditory (Weinberger, 1993) and visual (Logothetis, Pauls, & Poggio, 1995) cortex.

4.3.4 Internal and External Representation

Two assumptions underlie this traditional view of mental representation. First, we assume that schemata, mental models and so on change in response to experience with an environment. The mind is plastic, the environment fixed. Second, the changes make the internal representations somehow more like the environment. These assumptions are now seen to be problematic.

First, arguments from biological accounts of cognition, notably Maturana and Varela (1980, 1987), explain cognition and conceptual change in terms of adaptation to perturbations in an environment. The model is basically Darwinian. An organism adapts to environmental conditions where failure to do so will make it less likely that the organism will thrive, or even survive. At the longest time scale, this principle leads to evolution of new species. At the time scale of a single life, this principle describes cognitive (Piaget, 1968) and social (Vygotsky, 1978) development. At the time scale of a single course, or even single lesson, this principle can explain the acquisition of concepts and principles. Adaptation requires reorganization of some aspects of the organism's makeup. The structures involved are entirely internal and cannot in any way consist in a direct analogical mapping of features of the environment. This is what Maturana and Varela (1987) mean when the say that the central nervous system is "informationally closed." Thus, differences in the size and form of Galapagos finches' beaks resulting from environmental adaptations may be said to *represent* different environments, because they allow us to draw inferences about environmental characteristics. But they do not *resemble* the environment in any way. Similarly, changes in schemata or

assemblies of neurons, which may *represent* experiences and knowledge of the environment, because they are the means by which we remember things to avoid or things to pursue when we next encounter them, do not in any way *resemble* the environment. Mental representation is therefore not a one-to-one mapping of environment to brain, in fact not a mapping at all.

Second, since the bandwidth of our senses is very limited, we only experience a small number of the environment's properties (Nagel, 1974; Winn & Windschitl, 2001b). The environment we know directly is therefore a very incomplete and distorted version, and it is this impoverished view that we represent internally. The German word "Umwelt," which means environment, has come to refer to this limited, direct view of the environment (Roth, 1999). Umwelt was first used in this sense by the German biologist, Von Uexküll (1934), in a speculative and whimsical description of what the world might look like to creatures, such as bees and scallops. The drawings accompanying the account were reconstructions from what was known at the time about the organisms' sensory systems. The important point is that each creature's Umwelt is quite different from another's. Both our physical and cognitive interactions with external phenomena are, by nature, with our Umwelt, not the larger environment that science explores by extending the human senses through instrumentation. This means that the knowable environment (Umwelt) actually changes as we come to understand it. Inuit really do see many different types of snow. And as we saw above, advanced levels of expertise, built through extensive interaction with the environment, lead to heightened sensory discrimination ability (Goldstone et al., 2000).

This conclusion has profound consequences for theories of mental representation (and for theories of cognitive processes, as we shall see in the next section). Among them is the dependence of mental representation on concurrent interactions with the environment. One example is the reliance of our memories on objects present in the environment when we need to recall something. Often, we place them there deliberately, such as putting a post-it note on the mirror—Clark (1997) gives this example and several others. Another example is what Gordin and Pea (1995) call "inscriptions," which are external representations we place into our environment—drawings, diagrams, doodles—in order to help us think through problems. Scaife and Rogers (1996) suggest that one advantage of making internal representations external as inscriptions is that it allows us to rerepresent our ideas. Once our concepts become represented externally—become part of our Umwelt—we can interpret them like any other object we find there. They can clarify our thinking, as for example in the work reported by Tanimoto, Winn, and Akers (2002), where sketches made by students learning basic computer programming skills helped them solve problems. Roth and McGinn (1998) remind us that our environment also contains other people, and inscriptions therefore let us share our ideas, making cognition a social activity. Finally, some (e.g., Rosch, 1999) argue that mental representations cannot exist independently from environmental phenomena. On this view, the mind and the world are one, an idea to which we will return. Rosch writes, "Concepts and categories do not represent the world in the mind; they are a *participating part* [italics in the original] of the mind–world whole of which the sense of mind . . . is one pole, and the objects of mind. . . are the other pole" (1999, p. 72).

These newer views of the nature of mental representation do not necessarily mean we must throw out the old ones. But they do require us to consider two things. First, in the continuing absence of *complete* accounts of cognitive activity based on research in neuroscience, we must consider mental images and mental models as metaphorical rather than direct explanations of behavior. In other words, we can say that people act *as if* they represented phenomena as mental models, but not that they have models actually in their heads. This has implications for instructional practices that rely on the format of messages to induce certain cognitive actions and states. We shall return to this in the next section. Second, it requires that we give the nature of the Umwelt, and of how we are connected to it, a much higher priority when thinking about learning. Recent theories of conceptual change, of adaptation, and of embodied and embedded cognition, have responded to this requirement, as we shall see.

4.3.5 Summary

Theories of mental representation have influenced research in educational technology in a number of ways. Schema theory, or something very much like it, is basic to just about all cognitive research on representation. And schema theory is centrally implicated in what we call message design. Establishing predictability and control over how what appears in instructional materials and how the depicted information is represented has been high on the research agenda. So it has been of prime importance to discover (a) the nature of mental schemata and (b) how changing messages affects how schemata change or are created.

Mental representation is also the key to information mapping techniques that have proven to help students understand and remember what they read. Here, however, the emphasis is on how the relations among objects and events are encoded and stored in memory and less on how the objects and events are shown. Also, these interconcept relations are often metaphorical. Within the graphical conventions of information maps— hierarchies, radial outlines and so on—above, below, close to, and far from use the metaphor of space to convey semantic, not spatial, organization (see Winn & Solomon, 1993, for research on some of these metaphorical conventions). Nonetheless, the supposition persists that representing these relations in some kind of structure in memory improves comprehension and recall.

The construction of schemata as the basis for computer reasoning has not been entirely successful. This is largely because computers are literal minded and cannot draw on general knowledge of the world outside the scripts they are programmed to follow. The results of this, for story writing at least, are often whimsical and humorous. However, some would claim that the broader implication is that AI is impossible to attain.

Mental model theory has a lot in common with schema theory. However, studies of comprehension and transfer of changes of state and causality in physical systems suggest that well-developed mental models can be envisioned and run as students seek answers to questions. The ability of multimedia computer systems to show the dynamic interactions of components suggests that this technology has the potential for helping students develop models that represent the world in accurate and accessible ways.

The way in which mental representation changes with the development of expertise has perhaps received less attention from educational technologists than it should. This is partly because instructional prescriptions and instructional design procedures (particularly the techniques of task analysis) have not taken into account the stages a novice must go through on the way to expertise, each of which requires the development of qualitatively different forms of knowledge. This is an area to which educational technologists could profitably devote more of their attention.

Finally, we looked at more recent views of mental representation that require us to treat schemata, images, mental models and so on as metaphors, not literal accounts of representation. What is more, mental representations are of a limited and impoverished slice of the external world and vary enormously from person to person. The role of concurrent interaction with the environment was also seen to be a determining factor in the nature and function of mental representations. All of this requires us to modify, but not to reject entirely, cognitive views of mental representation.

4.4   MENTAL PROCESSES

The second major body of research in cognitive psychology has sought to explain the mental processes that operate on the representations we construct of our knowledge of the world. Of course, it is not possible to separate our understanding, nor our discussion, of representations and processes. Indeed, the sections on mental models and expertise made this abundantly clear. However, a body of research exists that has tended to focus more on process than representation. It is to this that we now turn.

4.4.1   Information Processing Accounts of Cognition

One of the basic tenets of cognitive theory is that information that is present in an instructional stimulus is acted upon by a variety of mediating processes before the student produces a response. Information processing accounts of cognition describe stages that information moves through in the cognitive system and suggests processes that operate at each step. This section therefore begins with a general account of human information processing. This account sets the stage for our consideration of cognition as symbol manipulation and as knowledge construction.

Although the rise of information processing accounts of cognition cannot be ascribed uniquely to the development of the computer, the early cognitive psychologists' descriptions of human thinking use distinctly computer-like terms. Like computers, people were supposed to take information from the environment into buffers, to process it before storing it in memory. Information processing models describe the nature and function of putative units within the human perceptual and cognitive systems, and how they interact. They trace their origins to Atkinson and Shiffrin's (1968) model of memory, which was the first to suggest that memory consisted of a sensory register, a long-term and a short-term store. According to Atkinson and Shiffrin's account, information is registered by the senses and then placed into a short-term storage area. Here, unless it is worked with in a "rehearsal buffer," it decays after about 15 seconds. If information in the short-term store is rehearsed to any significant extent, it stands a chance of being placed into the long-term store where it remains more or less permanently. With no more than minor changes, this model of human information processing has persisted in the instructional technology literature (R. Gagné, 1974; E. Gagné, 1985) and in ideas about long-term and short-term, or working memory (Gagné & Glaser, 1987). The importance that every instructional designer gives to practice stems from the belief that rehearsal improves the chance of information passing into long-term memory.

A major problem that this approach to explaining human cognition pointed to was the relative inefficiency of humans at information processing. This is to be a result of the limited capacity of working memory to roughly seven (Miller, 1956) or five (Simon, 1974) pieces of information at one time. (E. Gagné, 1985, p. 13, makes an interesting comparison between a computer's and a person's capacity to process information. The computer wins handily. However, humans' capacity to be creative, to imagine, and to solve complex problems do not enter into the equation.) It therefore became necessary to modify the basic model to account for these observations. One modification arose from studies like those of Shiffrin and Schneider (1977) and Schneider and Shiffrin (1977). In a series of memory experiments, these researchers demonstrated that with sufficient rehearsal people automatize what they have learned so that what was originally a number of discrete items become one single chunk of information. With what is referred to as overlearning, the limitations of working memory can be overcome. The notion of chunking information in order to make it possible for people to remember collections of more than five things has become quite prevalent in the information processing literature (see Anderson, 1983). And rehearsal strategies intended to induce chunking became part of the standard repertoire of tools used by instructional designers.

Another problem with the basic information processing account arose from research on memory for text in which it was demonstrated that people remembered the ideas of passages rather than the text itself (Bransford & Franks, 1971; Bransford & Johnson, 1972). This suggested that what was passed from working memory to long-term memory was not a direct representation of the information in short-term memory but a more abstract representation of its meaning. These abstract representations are, of course, schemata, which were discussed at some length earlier. Schema theory added a whole new dimension to ideas about information processing. So far, information processing theory assumed that the driving force of cognition was the information that was registered by the sensory buffers—that cognition was data driven, or bottom up. Schema theory proposed that information was, at least in part, top down. This meant, according to Neisser (1976), that cognition is driven as much as by what we know as by the information we take in at a given moment. In other words, the contents of long-term memory play a large part in the processing of information that passes through working memory. For instructional designers, it became apparent that strategies were required that guided top-down processing by activating relevant schemata and aided retrieval by providing the correct context for recall. The elaboration theory of instruction (Reigeluth & Curtis, 1987; Reigeluth & Stein, 1983) achieves both of these ends. Presenting an epitome of the content at the beginning of instruction activates relevant schemata. Providing synthesizers at strategic points during instruction helps students remember, and integrate, what they have learned up to that point.

Bottom up information processing approaches regained ground in cognitive theory as the result of the recognition of the importance of preattentive perceptual processes (Arbib & Hanson, 1987; Boden, 1988; Marr, 1982; Pomerantz, Pristach, & Carlson, 1989; Treisman, 1988). The overview of cognitive science, above, described computational approaches to cognition. In this return to a bottom up approach, however, we can see marked differences from the bottom-up information processing approaches of the 1960s and 1970s. Bottom-up processes are now clearly confined within the barrier of what Pylyshyn (1984) called "cognitive impenetrability." These are processes over which we can have no attentive, conscious, effortful control. Nonetheless, they impose a considerable amount of organization on the information we receive from the world. In vision, for example, it is likely that all information about the organization of a scene, except for some depth cues, is determined preattentively (Marr, 1982). What is more, preattentive perceptual structure predisposes us to make particular interpretations of information, top down (Duong, 1994; Owens, 1985a, 1985b). In other words, the way our perception processes information determines how our cognitive system will process it. Subliminal advertising works!

Related is research into implicit learning (Knowlton & Squire, 1996; Reber & Squire, 1994). Implicit learning occurs, not through the agency of preattentive processes, but in the absence of awareness that learning has occurred, at any level within the cognitive system. For example, after exposure to "sentences" consisting of letter sequences that do or do not conform to the rules of an artificial grammar, subjects are able to discriminate, significantly above chance, grammatical from nongrammatical sentences they have not seen before. They can do this even though they are not aware of the rules of the grammar, deny that they have learned anything and typically report that they are guessing (Reber, 1989). Liu (2002) has replicated this effect using artificial grammars that determine the structure of color patterns as well as letter sequences. The fact that learning can occur without people being aware of it is, in hindsight, not surprising. But while this finding has, to date, escaped the attention of mainstream cognitive psychology, its implications are wide-reaching for teaching and learning, with or without the support of technology.

Although we still talk rather glibly about short-term and long-term memory and use rather loosely other terms that come from information processing models of cognition, information processing theories have matured considerably since they first appeared in the late 1950s. The balance between bottom-up and top-down theories, achieved largely within the framework of computational theories of cognition, offers researchers a good conceptual framework within which to design and conduct studies. More important, these views have developed into full-blown theories of conceptual change and adaptation to learning environments that are currently providing far more complete accounts of learning than their predecessors.

4.4.2 Cognition as Symbol Manipulation

How is information that is processed by the cognitive system represented by it? One answer is, as symbols. This notion lies close to the heart of traditional cognitive science and, as we saw in the very first section of this chapter, it is also the source of some of the most virulent attacks on cognitive theory (Bickhard, 2000; Clancey, 1993). The idea is that we think by mentally manipulating symbols that are representations, in our mind's eye, of referents in the real world, and that there is a direct mapping between objects and actions in the external world and the symbols we use internally to represent them. Our manipulation of these symbols places them into new relationships with each other, allowing new insights into objects and phenomena. Our ability to reverse the process by means of which the world was originally encoded as symbols therefore allows us to act on the real world in new and potentially more effective ways.

We need to consider both how well people can manipulate symbols mentally and what happens as a result. The clearest evidence for people's ability to manipulate symbols in their mind's eye comes from Kosslyn's (1985) studies of mental imagery. Kosslyn's basic research paradigm was to have his subjects create a mental image and then to instruct them directly to change it in some way, usually by zooming in and out on it. Evidence for the success of his subjects at doing this was found in their ability to answer questions about properties of the imaged objects that could only be inspected as a result of such manipulation.

The work of Shepard and his colleagues (Shepard & Cooper, 1982) represents another classical case of our ability to manipulate images in our mind's eye. The best known of Shepard's experimental methods is as follows. Subjects are shown two three-dimensional solid figures seen from different angles. The subjects are asked to judge whether the figures are the same or different. In order to make the judgment, it is necessary to mentally rotate one of the figures in three dimensions in an attempt to orient it to the same position as the target so that a direct comparison may be made. Shepard consistently found that the time it took to make the judgment was almost perfectly correlated with the number of degrees through which the figure had to be rotated, suggesting that the subject was rotating it in real time in the mind's eye.

Finally, Salomon (1979) speaks more generally of "symbol systems" and of people's ability to internalize them and use them

as "tools for thought." In an early experiment (Salomon, 1974), he had subjects study paintings in one of the following three conditions: (a) A film showed the entire picture, zoomed in on a detail, and zoomed out again, for a total of 80 times; (b) The film cut from the whole picture directly to the detail without the transitional zooming, (c) The film showed just the whole picture. In a posttest of cue attendance, in which subjects were asked to write down as many details as they could from a slide of a new picture, low-ability subjects performed better if they were in the zooming group. High-ability subjects did better if they just saw the entire picture. Salomon concluded that zooming in and out on details, which is a symbolic element in the symbol system of film, television and any form of motion picture, modeled for the low-ability subjects a strategy for cue attendance that they could execute for themselves. This was not necessary for the high ability subjects. Indeed, there was evidence that modeling the zooming strategy reduced performance of high-ability subjects because it got in the way of mental processes that were activated without prompting. Bovy (1983) found results similar to Salomon's using "irising" rather than zooming. A similar interaction between ability and modeling was reported by Winn (1986) for serial and parallel pattern recall tasks.

Salomon continued to develop the notion of internalized symbol systems serving as cognitive tools. Educational technologists have been particularly interested in his research on how the symbolic systems of computers can "become cognitive," as he put it (Salomon, 1988). The internalization of the symbolic operations of computers led to the development of a word processor, called the "Writing Partner" (Salomon, Perkins, & Globerson, 1991), that helped students write. The results of a number of experiments showed that interacting with the computer led the users to internalize a number of its ways of processing, which led to improved metacognition relevant to the writing task. More recently (Salomon, 1993), this idea has evolved even further, to encompass the notion of distributing cognition among students and machines (and, of course, other students) to "offload" cognitive processing from one individual, to make it easier to do (Bell & Winn, 2000).

This research has had two main influences on educational technology. The first, derived from work in imagery of the kind reported by Kosslyn and Shepard, provided an attractive theoretical basis for the development of instructional systems that incorporate large amounts of visual material (Winn, 1980, 1982). The promotion and study of visual literacy (Dondis, 1973; Sless, 1981) is one manifestation of this activity. A number of studies have shown that the use of visual instructional materials can be beneficial for some students studying some kinds of content. For example, Dwyer (1972, 1978) has conducted an extensive research program on the differential benefits of different kinds of visual materials, and has generally reported that realistic pictures are good for identification tasks, line drawings for teaching structure and function, and so on. Explanations for these different effects rest on the assumption that different ways of encoding material facilitate some cognitive processes rather than others—that some materials are more effectively manipulated in the mind's eye for given tasks than others.

The second influence of this research on educational technology has been in the study of the interaction between technology and cognitive systems. Salomon's research, just described, is of course an example of this. The work of Papert and his colleagues at MIT's Media Lab. is another important example. Papert (1983) began by proposing that young children can learn the "powerful ideas" that underlie reasoning and problem solving by working (perhaps "playing" is the more appropriate term) in a micro-world over which they have control. The archetype of such a micro-world is the well-known LOGO environment in which the student solves problems by instructing a "turtle" to perform certain tasks. Learning occurs when the children develop problem definition and debugging skills as they write programs for the turtle to follow. Working with LOGO, children develop fluency in problem solving as well as specific skills, like problem decomposition and the ability to modularize problem solutions. Like Salomon's (1988) subjects, the children who work with LOGO (and in other technology-based environments [Harel & Papert, 1991]) internalize a lot of the computer's ways of using information and develop skills in symbol manipulation that they use to solve problems.

There is, of course, a great deal of research into problem solving through symbol manipulation that is not concerned particularly with technology. The work of Simon and his colleagues is central to this research. (See Klahr & Kotovsky's, 1989, edited volume that pays tribute to his work.) It is based largely on the notion that human reasoning operates by applying rules to encoded information that manipulate the information in such a way as to reveal solutions to problems. The information is encoded as a production system which operates by testing whether the conditions of rules are true or not, and following specific actions if they are. A simple example: "If the sum of an addition of a column of digits is greater than ten, then write down the right-hand integer and carry one to add to the next column". The "if . . . then . . . " structure is a simple production system in which a mental action is carried out (add one to the next column) if a condition is true (the number is greater than 10).

An excellent illustration is to be found in Larkin and Simon's (1987) account of the superiority of diagrams over text for solving certain classes of problems. Here, they develop a production system model of pulley systems to explain how the number of pulleys attached to a block, and the way in which they are connected, affects the amount of weight that can be raised by a given force. The model is quite complex. It is based on the idea that people need to search through the information presented to them in order to identify the conditions of a rule (e.g. "If a rope passes over two pulleys between its point of attachment and a load, its mechanical advantage is doubled") and then compute the results of applying the production rule in those given circumstances. The two steps, searching for the conditions of the production rule and computing the consequences of its application, draw upon cognitive resources (memory and processing) to different degrees. Larkin and Simon's argument is that diagrams require less effort to search for the conditions and to perform the computation, which is why they are so often more successful than text for problem-solving. Winn, Li, and Schill (1991) provided an empirical validation of Larkin and Simon's account. Many other examples of symbol manipulation

through production systems exist. In the area of mathematics education, the interested reader will wish to look at projects reported by Resnick (1976) and Greeno (1980) in which instruction makes it easier for students to encode and manipulate mathematical concepts and relations. Applications of Anderson's (1983, 1990, 1998) ACT* production system and its successors in intelligent computer-based tutors to teach geometry, algebra, and LISP are also illustrative (Anderson & Reiser, 1985; Anderson et al., 1985).

For the educational technologist, the question arises of how to make symbol manipulation easier so that problems may be solved more rapidly and accurately. Larkin and Simon (1987) show that one way to do this is to illustrate conceptual relationships by layout and links in a graphic. A related body of research concerns the relations between illustrations and text (see summaries in Houghton & Willows, 1987; Mandl & Levin, 1989; Schnotz & Kulhavy, 1994; Willows & Houghton, 1987). Central to this research is the idea that pictures and words can work together to help students understand information more effectively and efficiently. There is now considerable evidence that people encode information in one of two memory systems, a verbal system and an imaginal system. This "Dual coding" (Clark & Paivio, 1991; Paivio, 1983), or "Conjoint retention" (Kulhavy et al., 1985) has two major advantages. The first is redundancy. Information that is hard to recall from one source is still available from the other. Second is the uniqueness of each coding system. As Levin et al. (1987) have ably demonstrated, different types of illustration are particularly good at performing unique functions. Realistic pictures are good for identification, cutaways and line drawings for showing the structure or operation of things. Text is more appropriate for discursive and more abstract presentations.

Specific guidelines for instructional design have been drawn from this research, many presented in the summaries mentioned in the previous paragraph. Other useful sources are chapters by Mayer and by Winn in Fleming and Levie's (1993) volume on message design. The theoretical basis for these principles is by and large the facilitation of symbol manipulation in the mind's eye that comes from certain types of presentation.

However, as we saw at the beginning of this chapter, the basic assumption that we think by manipulating symbols that represent objects and events in the real world has been called into question (Bickhard, 2000; Clancey, 1993). There are a number of grounds for this criticism. The most compelling is that we do not carry around in our heads representations that are accurate maps of the world. Schemata, mental models, symbol systems, search and computation are all metaphors that give a superficial appearance of validity because they predict behavior. However, the essential processes that underlie the metaphors are more amenable to genetic and biological than to psychological analysis. We are, after all, living systems that have evolved like other living systems. And our minds are embodied in our brains, which are organs just like any other. The least that one can conclude from this is that students construct knowledge for themselves. The most that one can conclude is that new processes for conceptual change must be identified and described.

4.4.3 Knowledge Construction Through Conceptual Change

One result of the mental manipulation of symbols is that new concepts can be created. Our combining and recombining of mentally represented phenomena leads to the creation of new schemata that may or may not correspond to things in the real world. When this activity is accompanied by constant interaction with the environment in order to verify new hypotheses about the world, we can say that we are accommodating our knowledge to new experiences in the classic interactions described by Neisser (1976) and Piaget (1968), mentioned earlier. When we construct new knowledge without direct reference to the outside world, then we are perhaps at our most creative, conjuring from memories thoughts and expressions of it that are entirely novel. When we looked at schema theory, we saw how Neisser's (1976) "perceptual cycle" describes how what we know directs how we seek information, how we seek information determines what information we get and how the information we receive affects what we know. This description of knowledge acquisition provides a good account of how top-down processes, driven by knowledge we already have, interact with bottom-up processes, driven by information in the environment, to enable us to assimilate new knowledge and accommodate what we already know to make it compatible.

What arises from this description, which was not made explicit earlier, is that the perceptual cycle and thus the entire knowledge acquisition process is centered on the person not the environment. Some (Cunningham, 1992a; Duffy & Jonassen, 1992) extend this notion to mean that the schemata a person constructs do not correspond in any absolute or objective way to the environment. A person's understanding is therefore built from that person's adaptations to the environment entirely in terms of the experience and understanding that the person has already constructed. There is no process whereby representations of the world are directly mapped onto schemata. We do not carry representational images of the world in our mind's eye. Semiotic theory, which made an appearance on the Educational stage in the early 'nineties (Cunningham, 1992b; Driscoll, 1990; Driscoll & Lebow, 1992) goes one step further, claiming that we do not apprehend the world directly at all. Rather, we experience it through the signs we construct to represent it. Nonetheless, if students are given responsibility for constructing their own signs and knowledge of the world, semiotic theory can guide the development and implementation of learning activities as Winn, Hoffman, and Osberg (1999) have demonstrated.

These ideas have led to two relatively recent developments in cognitive theories of learning. The first is the emergence of research on how students' conceptions change as they interact with natural or artificial environments. The second is the emergence of new ways of conceptualizing the act of interacting itself.

Students' conceptions about something change when their interaction with an environment moves through a certain sequence of events. Windschitl & André (1998), extending earlier research by Posner et al. (1982) in science education, identified a number of these. First, something occurs that cannot be explained by conceptions the student currently has. It is a surprise. It pulls the student up short. It raises to conscious awareness processes that have been running in the background. Winograd & Flores (1986) say that knowledge is now "ready to hand." Reyes and Zarama (1998) talk about "declaring a break" from the flow of cognitive activity. For example, students working with a simulation of physical oceanography (Winn et al., 2002) often do not know when they start that the salinity of seawater increases with depth. Measuring salinity shows that it does, and this is a surprise. Next, the event must be understandable. If not, it will be remembered as a fact and not really understood, because conceptions will not change. In our example, the student must understand what both the depth and salinity readouts on the simulated instruments mean. Next, the event must fit with what the student already knows. It must be believable, otherwise conceptions cannot change. The increase of salinity with depth is easy to understand once you know that seawater is denser than fresh water and that dense fluids sink below less dense ones. Students can either figure this out for themselves, or can come to understand it through further, scaffolded (Linn, 1995), experiences. Other phenomena are less easily believed and assimilated. Many scientific laws are counterintuitive and students' developing conceptions represent explanations based on how things seem to act rather than on full scientific accounts. Bell (1995), for example, has studied students' explanations of what happens to light when, after traveling a distance, it grows dimmer and eventually disappears. Minstrell (2001) has collected a complete set of common misconceptions, which he calls "facets of understanding," for high school physics. In many cases, students' misconceptions are robust and hard to change (Chinn & Brewer, 1993; Thorley & Stofflet, 1996). Indeed, it is at this stage of the conceptual change process that failure is most likely to occur, because what students observe simply does not make sense, even if they understand what they see. Finally, the new conception must be fruitfully applied to solving a new problem. In our example, knowing that salinity increases with depth might help the student decide where to locate the discharge pipe for treated sewage so that it will be more quickly diffused in the ocean.

It is clear that conceptual change, thus conceived, takes place most effectively in a problem-based learning environment that requires students to explore the environment by constructing hypotheses, testing them, and reasoning about what they observe. Superficially, this account of learning closely resembles theories of schema change that we looked at earlier. However, there are important differences. First, the student is clearly much more in charge of the learning activity. This is consistent with teaching and learning strategies that reflect the constructivist point of view. Second, any teaching that goes on is in reaction to what the student says or does rather than a proactive attempt to get the student to think in a certain way. Finally, the kind of learning environment, in which conceptual change is easiest to attain, is a highly interactive and responsive one, often one that is quite complicated, and that more often than not requires the support of technology.

The view of learning proposed in theories of conceptual change still assumes that, though interacting, the student and the environment are separate. Earlier, we encountered Rosch's (1999) view of the one-ness of internal and external representations. The unity of the student and the environment has also influenced the way we consider mental processes. This requires us to examine more carefully what we mean when say a student interacts with the environment.

The key to this examination lies in two concepts, the embodiment and embeddedness of cognition. Embodiment (Varela et al., 1991) refers to the fact that we use our bodies to help us think. Pacing off distances and counting on our fingers are examples. More telling are using gestures to help us communicate ideas (Roth, 2001), or moving our bodies through virtual spaces so that they become data points on three-dimensional graphs (Gabert, 2001). Cognition is as much a physical activity as it is a cerebral one. Embeddedness (Clark, 1997) stresses the fact that the environment we interact with contains us as well as everything else. We are part of it. Therefore, interacting with the environment is, in a sense, interacting with ourselves as well. From research on robots and intelligent agents (Beer, 1995), and from studying children learning in classrooms (Roth, 1999), comes the suggestion that it is sometimes useful to consider the student and the environment as one single entity. Learning now becomes an emergent property of one tightly coupled, self-organizing (Kelso, 1999), student–environment system rather than being the result of iterative interactions between a student and environment, separated in time and space. Moreover, what is the cause of what effects is impossible to determine. Clark (1997, pp. 171–2) gives a good example. Imagine trying to catch a hamster with a pair of tongs. The animal's attempts to escape are immediate and continuous responses to our actions. At the same time, how we wield the tongs is determined by the animal's attempts at evasion. It is not possible to determine who is doing what to whom.

All of this leads to a view of learning as adaptation to an environment. Holland's (1992, 1995) explanations of how this occurs, in natural and artificial environments, are thought provoking if not fully viable accounts. Holland has developed "genetic algorithms" for adaptation that incorporate such ideas as mutation, crossover, even survival of the fittest. While applicable to robots as well as living organisms, they retain the biological flavor of much recent thinking about cognition that goes back to the work of Maturana and Varela (1980, 1987) mentioned earlier. They bear considering as extensions of conceptual frameworks for thinking about cognition.

4.4.4 Summary

Information processing models of cognition have had a great deal of influence on research and practice of educational technology. Instructional designers' day-to-day frames of reference for thinking about cognition, such as working memory and long-term memory, come directly from information processing theory. The emphasis on rehearsal in many instructional strategies arises from the small capacity of working memory. Attempts to overcome this problem have led designers to develop all manner of strategies to induce chunking. Information processing theories of cognition continue to serve our field well. Research into cognitive processes involved in symbol manipulation have been influential in the development of intelligent tutoring systems (Wenger, 1987) as well as in information processing accounts of learning and instruction. The result has been that the conceptual bases for some (though not all) instructional theory and instructional design models have embodied a production system approach to instruction and instructional design (see Landa, 1983; Merrill, 1992; Scandura, 1983). To the extent that symbol manipulation accounts of cognition are being challenged, these approaches to instruction and instructional design are also challenged by association.

If cognition is understood to involve the construction of knowledge by students, it is therefore essential that they be given the freedom to do so. This means that, within Spiro et al.'s (1992) constraints of "advanced knowledge acquisition in ill-structured domains," instruction is less concerned with content, and sometimes only marginally so. Instead, educational technologists need to become more concerned with how students interact with the environments within which technology places them and with how objects and phenomena in those environments appear and behave. This requires educational technologists to read carefully in the area of human factors (for example, Barfield & Furness, 1995; Ellis, 1993) where a great deal of research exists on the cognitive consequences human–machine interaction. It requires less emphasis on instructional design's traditional attention to task and content analysis. It requires alternative ways of thinking about (Winn, 1993b) and doing (Cunningham, 1992a) evaluation. In short, it is only through the cognitive activity that interaction with content engenders, not the content itself, that people can learn anything at all. Extending the notion of interaction to include embodiment, embeddedness, and adaptation requires further attention to the nature of interaction itself.

Accounts of learning through the construction of knowledge by students have been generally well accepted since the mid-1970s and have served as the basis for a number of the assumptions educational technologists have made about how to teach. Attempts to set instructional design firmly on cognitive foundations (Bonner, 1988; DiVesta & Rieber, 1987; Tennyson & Rasch, 1988) reflect this orientation. Some of these are described in the next section.

4.5 COGNITIVE THEORY AND EDUCATIONAL TECHNOLOGY

Educational technology has for some time been influenced by developments in cognitive psychology. Up until now, this chapter has focused mainly on research that has fallen outside the traditional bounds of our field, drawing on sources in philosophy, psychology, computer science, and more recently biology and cognitive neuroscience. This section reviews the work of those who bear the label "Educational Technologist" who have been primarily responsible for bringing cognitive theory to our field. The section is, again, of necessity selective, focusing on the applied side of our field, instructional design. It begins with some observations about what scholars consider design to be. It then examines the assumptions that underlay behavioral theory and practice at the time when instructional design became established as a discipline. It then argues that research in our field has helped the theory that designers use to make decisions about how to instruct keep up with developments in cognitive theory. However, design procedures have not evolved as they should have. The section concludes with some implications about where design should go.

4.5.1   Theory, Practice, and Instructional Design

The discipline of educational technology hit its stride during the heyday of behaviorism. This historical fact was entirely fortuitous. Indeed, our field could have started equally well under the influence of Gestalt or of cognitive theory. However, the consequences of this coincidence have been profound and to some extent troublesome for our field. To explain why, we need to examine the nature of the relationship between theory and practice in our field. (Our argument is equally applicable to any discipline.) The purpose of any applied field, such as educational technology, is to improve practice. The way in which theory guides that practice is through what Simon (1981) and Glaser (1976) call "design." The purpose of design, seen this way, is to select the alternative from among several courses of action that will lead to the best results. Since these results may not be optimal, but the best one can expect given the state of our knowledge at any particular time, design works through a process Simon (1981) calls "satisficing."

The degree of success of our activity as instructional designers relies on two things: first, the validity of our knowledge of effective instruction in a given subject domain and, second, the reliability of our procedures for applying that knowledge. Here is an example. We are given the task of writing a computer program that teaches the formation of regular English verbs in the past tense. To simplify matters, let us assume that we know the subject matter perfectly. As subject-matter specialists, we know a procedure for accomplishing the task—add "ed" to the infinitive and double the final consonant if it is immediately preceded by a vowel. Would our instructional strategy therefore be to do nothing more than show a sentence on the computer screen that says, "Add 'ed' to the infinitive and double the final consonant if it is immediately preceded by a vowel"? Probably not (though such a strategy might be all that is needed for students who already understand the meanings of infinitive, vowel, and consonant). If we know something about instruction, we will probably consider a number of other strategies as well. Maybe the students would need to see examples of correct and incorrect verb forms. Maybe they would need to practice forming the past tense of a number of verbs. Maybe they would need to know how well they were doing. Maybe they would need a mechanism that explained and corrected their errors. The act of designing our instructional computer program in fact requires us to choose from among these and other strategies the ones that are most likely to "satisfice" the requirement of constructing the past tense of regular verbs.

Knowing subject matter and something about instruction are therefore not enough. We need to know how to choose among alternative instructional strategies. Reigleuth (1983) has pointed the way. He observes that the instructional theory that guides instructional designers' choices is made up of statements about relations among the conditions, methods and outcomes of instruction. When we apply prescriptive theory, knowing instructional conditions and outcomes leads to the selection of an appropriate method. For example, an instructional prescription might consist of the statement, "To teach how to form the past tense of regular English verbs (outcome) to advanced students of English who are familiar with all relevant grammatical terms and concepts (conditions), present them with a written description of the procedure to follow (method)." All the designer needs to do is learn a large number of these prescriptions and all is well.

There are a number of difficulties with this example, however. First, instructional prescriptions rarely, if at all, consist of statements at the level of specificity as the previous one about English verbs. Any theory gains power by its generality. This means that instructional theory contains statements that have a more general applicability, such as "to teach a procedure to a student with a high level of entering knowledge, describe the procedure". Knowing only a prescription at this level of generality, the designer of the verb program needs to determine whether the outcome of instruction is indeed a procedure—it could be a concept, or a rule, or require problem solving—and whether or not the students have a high level of knowledge when they start the program.

A second difficulty arises if the designer is not a subject matter specialist, which is often the case. In our example, this means that the designer has to find out that "forming the past tense of English verbs" requires adding "ed" and doubling the consonant. Finally, the prescription itself might not be valid. Any instructional prescription that is derived empirically, from an experiment or from observation and experience, is always a generalization from a limited set of cases. It could be that the present case is an exception to the general rule. The designer needs to establish whether or not this is so.

These three difficulties point to the requirement that instructional designers know how to perform analyses that lead to the level of specificity required by the instructional task. We all know what these are. Task analysis permits the instructional designer to identify exactly what the student must achieve in order to attain the instructional outcome. Learner analysis allows the designer to determine the most critical of the conditions under which instruction is to take place. And the classification of tasks, described by task analysis, as facts, concepts, rules, procedures, problem solving, and so on links the designer's particular case to more general prescriptive theory. Finally, if the particular case the designer is working on is an exception to the general prescription, the designer will have to experiment with a variety of potentially effective strategies in order to find the best one, in effect inventing a new instructional prescription along the way. Even from this simple example, it is clear that, in order to be able to select the best instructional strategies, the instructional designer needs to know both instructional theory and how to do task and learner analysis, to classify learning outcomes into some theoretically sound taxonomy and to reason about instruction in the absence of prescriptive principles. Our field, then, like any applied field, provides to its practitioners both theory and procedures through which to apply the theory. These procedures are predominantly, though not exclusively, analytical.

Embedded in any theory are sets of assumptions that are amenable to empirical verification. If the assumptions are shown to be false, then the theory must be modified or abandoned as a paradigm shift takes place (Kuhn, 1970). The effects of these basic assumptions are clearest in the physical sciences. For example, the assumption in modern physics that it is impossible for the speed of objects to exceed that of light is so basic that, if it were to be disproved, the entire edifice of physics would come tumbling down. What is equally important is that the procedures for applying theory rest on the same set of assumptions. The design of everything from cyclotrons to radio telescopes relies on the inviolability of the light barrier.

It would seem reasonable, therefore, that both the theory and procedures of instruction should rest on the same set of assumptions and, further, that should the assumptions of instructional theory be shown to be invalid, the procedures of instructional design should be revised to accommodate the paradigm shift. The next section shows that this was the case when instructional design established itself within our field within the behavioral paradigm. However, this is not case today.

4.5.2   The Legacy of Behaviorism

The most fundamental principle of behavioral theory is that there is a predictable and reliable link between a stimulus and the response it produces in a student. Behavioral instructional theory therefore consists of prescriptions for what stimuli to employ if a particular response is intended. The instructional designer can be reasonably certain that with the right sets of instructional stimuli all manner of learning outcomes can be attained. Indeed, behavioral theories of instruction can be quite intricate (Gropper, 1983) and can account for the acquisition of quite complex behaviors. This means that a basic assumption of behavioral theories of instruction is that human behavior is predictable. The designer assumes that if an instructional strategy, made up of stimuli, has had a certain effect in the past, it will probably do so again.

The assumption that behavior is predictable also underlies the procedures that instructional designers originally developed to implement behavioral theories of instruction (Andrews & Goodson, 1981; Gagné et al., 1988; Gagné & Dick, 1983). If behavior is predictable, then all the designer needs to do is to identify the subskills the student must master that, in aggregate, permit the intended behavior to be learned, and select the stimulus and strategy for its presentation that builds each subskill. In other words, task analysis, strategy selection, try-out, and revision also rest on the assumption that behavior is predictable. The procedural counterpart of behavioral instructional theory is therefore analytical and empirical, that is reductionist. If behavior is predictable, then the designer can select the most effective instructional stimuli simply by following the procedures described in an instructional design model. Instructional failure is ascribed to the lack of sufficient information which can be corrected by doing more analysis and formative testing.

4.5.3   Cognitive Theory and the Predictability of Behavior

The main theme of this chapter has been cognitive theory. The argument has been that cognitive theory provides a much more complete account of human learning and behavior because it considers factors that mediate between the stimulus and the response, such as mental processes and the internal representations that they create. The chapter has documented the ascendancy of cognitive theory and its replacement of behavioral theory as the dominant paradigm in educational psychology and technology. However, the change from behavioral to cognitive theories of learning and instruction has not necessarily been accompanied by a parallel change in the procedures of instructional design through which the theory is implemented.

You might well ask why a change in theory should be accompanied by a change in procedures for its application. The reason is that cognitive theory has essentially invalidated the basic assumption of behavioral theory, that behavior is predictable. Since the same assumption underlies the analytical, empirical and reductionist technology of instructional design, the validity of instructional design procedures is inevitably called into question.

Cognitive theory's challenges to the predictability of behavior are numerous and have been described in detail elsewhere (Winn, 1987, 1990, 1993b). The main points may be summarized as follows:

1. Instructional theory is incomplete. This point is trivial at first glance. However, it reminds us that there is not a prescription for every possible combination of instructional conditions, methods and outcomes. In fact, instructional designers frequently have to select strategies without guidance from instructional theory. This means that there are often times when there are no prescriptions with which to predict student behavior.

2. Mediating cognitive variables differ in their nature and effect from individual to individual. There is a good chance that everyone's response to the same stimulus will be different because everyone's experiences, in relation to which the stimulus will be processed, are different. The role of individual differences in learning and their relevance to the selection of instructional strategies has been a prominent theme in cognitive theory for more than three decades (Cronbach & Snow, 1977; Snow, 1992). Individual differences make it extremely difficult to predict learning outcomes for two reasons. First, to choose effective strategies for students, it would be necessary to know far more about the student than is easily discovered. The designer would need to know the student's aptitude for learning the given knowledge or skills, the student's prior knowledge, motivation, beliefs about the likelihood of success, level of anxiety, and stage of intellectual development. Such a prospect would prove daunting even to the most committed determinist! Second, for prescriptive

theory, it would be necessary to construct an instructional prescription for every possible permutation of, say, high, low, and average levels on every factor that determines an individual difference. This obviously would render instructional theory too complex to be useful for the designer. In both the case of the individual student and of theory, the interactions among many factors make it impossible in practice to predict what the outcomes of instruction will be. One way around this problem has been to let students decide strategies for themselves. Learner control (Merrill, 1988; Tennyson & Park, 1987) is a feature of many effective computer-based instructional programs. However, this does not attenuate the damage to the assumption of predictability. If learners choose their course through a program, it is not possible to predict the outcome.

3. Some students know how they learn best and will not necessarily use the strategy the designer selected for them. Metacognition is another important theme in cognitive theory. It is generally considered to consist of two complementary processes (Brown, Campione, & Day, 1981). The first is students' ability to monitor their own progress as they learn. The second is to change strategies if they realize they are not doing well. If students do not use the strategies that instructional theory suggests are optimal for them, then it becomes impossible to predict what their behavior will be. Instructional designers are now proposing that we develop ways to take instructional metacognition into account as we do instructional design (Lowyck & Elen, 1994).

4. People do not think rationally as instructional designers would like them to. Many years ago, Collins (1978) observed that people reason "plausibly." By this he meant that they make decisions and take actions on the basis of incomplete information, of hunches and intuition. Hunt (1982) has gone so far as to claim that plausible reasoning is necessary for the evolution of thinking in our species. If we were creatures who made decisions only when all the information needed for a logical choice was available, we would never make any decisions at all and would not have developed the degree of intelligence that we have! Schon's (1983, 1987) study of decision making in the professions comes to a conclusion that is simliar to Collins'. Research in situated learning (Brown et al., 1989; Lave & Wenger, 1991; Suchman, 1987) has demonstrated that most everyday cognition is not "planful" and is most likely to depend on what is afforded by the particular situation in which it takes place. The situated nature of cognition has led Streibel (1991) to claim that standard cognitive theory can never act as the foundational theory for instructional design. Be that as it may, if people do not reason logically, and if the way they reason depends on specific and usually unknowable contexts, their behavior is certainly unpredictable.

These and other arguments (see Csiko, 1989) are successful in their challenge to the assumption that behavior is predictable. The bulk of this chapter has described the factors that come between a stimulus and a student's response that make the latter unpredictable. Scholars working in our field have for the most part shifted to a cognitive orientation when it comes to theory.

However, for the most part, they have not shifted to a new position on the procedures of instructional design. Since these procedures are based, like behavioral theory, on the assumption that behavior is predictable, and since the assumption is no longer valid, the procedures whereby educational technologists apply their theory to practical problems are without foundation.

4.5.4 Cognitive Theory and Educational Technology

The evidence that educational technologists have accepted cognitive theory is prominent in the literature of our field (Gagné & Glaser, 1987; Richey, 1986; Spencer, 1988; Winn, 1989a). Of particular relevance to this discussion are those who have directly addressed the implications of cognitive theory for instructional design (Bonner, 1988; Champagne, Klopfer & Gunstone, 1982; DiVesta & Rieber, 1987; Schott, 1992; Tennyson & Rasch, 1988). Collectively, scholars in our field have described cognitive equivalents for all stages in instructional design procedures. Here are some examples.

Twenty-five years ago, Resnick (1976) described "cognitive task analysis" for mathematics. Unlike behavioral task analysis which produces task hierarchies or sequences (Gagné et al., 1988), cognitive analysis produces either descriptions of knowledge schemata that students are expected to construct, or descriptions of the steps information must go through as the student processes it, or both. Greeno's (1976, 1980) analysis of mathematical tasks illustrates the knowledge representation approach and corresponds in large part to instructional designers' use of information mapping that we previously discussed. Resnick's (1976) analysis of the way children perform subtraction exemplifies the information processing approach. Cognitive task analysis gives rise to cognitive objectives, counterparts to behavioral objectives. In Greeno's (1976) case, these appear as diagrammatic representations of schemata, not written statements of what students are expected to be able to do, to what criterion and under what conditions (Mager, 1962).

The cognitive approach to learner analysis aims to provide descriptions of students' mental models (Bonner, 1988), not descriptions of their levels of performance prior to instruction. Indeed, the whole idea of "student model" that is so important in intelligent computer-based tutoring (Van Lehn, 1988), very often revolves around ways of capturing the ways students represent information in memory and how that information changes, not on their ability to perform tasks.

With an emphasis on knowledge schemata and the premise that learning takes place as schemata change, cognitively oriented instructional strategies are selected on the basis of their likely ability to modify schemata rather than to shape behavior. If schemata change, DiVesta and Rieber (1987) claim, students can come truly to understand what they are learning, not simply modify their behavior.

These examples show that educational technologists concerned with the application of theory to instruction have carefully thought through the implications of the shift to cognitive theory for instructional design. Yet in almost all instances, no one has questioned the procedures that we follow. We do cognitive task analysis, describe students' schemata and mental models, write cognitive objectives and prescribe cognitive instructional strategies. But the fact that we do task and learner analysis, write objectives and prescribe strategies has not changed. The performance of these procedures still assumes that behavior is predictable, a cognitive approach to instructional theory notwithstanding. Clearly something is amiss.

4.5.5 Can Instructional Design Remain an Independent Activity?

The field is at the point where our acceptance of the assumptions of cognitive theory forces us to rethink the procedures we use to apply it through instructional design. The key to what it is necessary to do lies in a second assumption that follows from the assumption of the predictability of behavior. That assumption is that the design of instruction is an activity that can proceed independently of the implementation of instruction. If behavior is predictable and if instructional theory contains valid prescriptions, then it should be possible to perform analysis, select strategies, try them out and revise them until a predetermined standard is reached, and then deliver the instructional package to those who will use it with the safe expectation that it will work as intended. If, as demonstrated, that assumption is not tenable, we must also question the independence of design from the implementation of instruction (Winn, 1990). There are a number of indications that educational technologists are thinking along these lines. All conform loosely with the idea that decision making about learning strategies must occur during instruction rather than ahead of time. In their details, these points of view range from the philosophical argument that thought and action cannot be separated and therefore the conceptualization and doing of instruction must occur simultaneously (Nunan, 1983; Schon, 1987) to more practical considerations of how to construct learning environments that are adaptive, in real time, to student actions (Merrill, 1992). Another way of looking at this is to argue that, if learning is indeed situated in a context (for arguments on this issue, see McLellan, 1996), then instructional design must be situated in that context too.

A key concept in this approach is the difference between learning environments and instructional programs. Other chapters in this volume address the matter of media research. Suffice it to say here that the most significant development in our field that occurred between Clark's (1983) argument that media do not make a difference to what and how students learn and Kozma's (1991) revision of this argument was the development of software that could create rich multimedia environments. Kozma (1994) makes the point that interactive and adaptive environments can be used by students to help them think, an idea that has a lot in common with Salomon's (1979) notion of media as "tools for thought." The kind of instructional program that drew much of Clark's (1985) disapproval was didactic—designed to do what teachers do when they teach toward a predefined goal. What interactive multimedia systems do is allow students a great deal of freedom to learn in their own way rather than in the way the designer prescribes. Zuccermaglio (1993) refers to them as "empty technologies" that, like shells, can be filled with anything the student or teacher wishes. By contrast, "full technologies" comprise programs whose content and strategy are predetermined, as is the case with computer-based instruction.

The implementation of cognitive principles in the procedures of educational technology requires a reintegration of the design and execution of instruction. This is best achieved when we develop stimulating learning environments whose function is not entirely prescribed but which can adapt in real time to student needs and proclivities. This does not necessarily require that the environments be "intelligent" (although at one time that seemed to be an attractive proposition [Winn, 1987]). It requires, rather, that the system be responsive to the student's intelligence in such a way that the best ways for the student to learn are determined, as it were, on the fly.

There are three ways in which educational technologists have approached this issue. The first is by developing highly interactive simulations of complex processes that require the student to used scaffolded strategies to solve problems. One of the best examples of this is the "World watcher" project (Edelson, 2001; Edelson, Salierno, Matese, Pitts, & Sherin, 2002), in which students use real scientific data about the weather to learn science. This project has the added advantage of connecting students with practicing scientists in an extended learning community. Other examples include Barab et al's (2000) use of such environments, in this case constructed by the students themselves, to learn astronomy and Hay, Marlino, and Holschuh's (2000) use of atmospheric simulations to teach science.

A second way educational technologists have sought to reintegrate design and learning is methodological. Brown (1992) describes "design experiments", in which designers build tools that they test in real classrooms and gather data that contribute both to the construction of theory and to the improvement of the tools. This process proceeds iteratively, over a period of time, until the tool is proven to be effective and our knowledge of why it is effective has been acquired and assimilated to theory. The design experiment is now the predominant research paradigm for educational technologists in many research programs, contributing equally to theory and practice.

Finally, the linear instructional design process has evolved into a nonlinear one, based on the notion of systemic, rather than simply systematic decision making (Tennyson, 1997). The objectives of instruction are just as open to change as the strategies offered to students to help them learn—revision might lead to a change in objectives as easily as it does to a change in strategy. In a sense, instructional design is now seen to be as sensitive to the environment in which it takes place as learning is, within the new view of embodiment and embeddedness described earlier.

4.5.6 Section Summary

This section reviewed a number of important issues concerning the importance of cognitive theory to what educational technologists actually do, namely design instruction. This has led to consideration of the relations between theory and the procedures employed to apply it in practical ways. When behaviorism was the dominant paradigm in our field both the theory and the procedures for its application adhered to the same basic assumption, namely that human behavior is predictable. However, our field was effective in subscribing to the tenets of cognitive theory, but the procedures for applying that theory remained unchanged and largely continued to build on the by now discredited assumption that behavior is predictable. The section concluded by suggesting that cognitive theory requires of our

design procedures that we create learning environments in which learning strategies are not entirely predetermined. This requires that the environments be highly adaptive to student actions. Recent technologies that permit the development of virtual environments offer the best possibility for realizing this kind of learning environment. Design experiments and the systems dynamics view of instructional design offer ways of implementing the same ideas.

References

Abel, R., & Kulhavy, R. W. (1989). Associating map features and related prose in memory. *Contemporary Educational Psychology, 14,* 33-48.

Abraham, R. H., & Shaw, C. D. (1992). *Dynamics: The geometry of behavior.* New York: Addison-Wesley.

Anderson, J. R. (1978). Arguments concerning representations for mental imagery. *Psychological Review, 85,* 249-277.

Anderson, J. R. (1983). *The architecture of cognition.* Cambridge, MA: Harvard University Press.

Anderson, J. R. (1986). Knowledge compilation: The general learning mechanism. In R. Michalski, J. Carbonell, & T. Mitchell (Eds.), *Machine Learning,* Volume 2. Los Altos, CA: Morgan Kaufmann.

Anderson, J. R. (1990). *Adaptive character of thought.* Hillsdale, NJ: Lawrence Erlbaum.

Anderson, J. R., Boyle, C. F., & Yost, G. (1985). *The geometry tutor.* Pittsburgh: Carnegie Mellon University, Advanced Computer Tutoring Project.

Anderson, J. R., & Labiere, C. (1998). *Atomic components of thought.* Mawah, NJ: Erlbaum.

Anderson, J. R., & Reiser, B. J. (1985). The LISP tutor. *Byte, 10*(4), 159-175.

Anderson, R. C., Reynolds, R. E., Schallert, D. L., & Goetz, E. T. (1977). Frameworks for comprehending discourse. *American Educational Research Journal, 14,* 367-381.

Andrews, D. H., & Goodson, L. A. (1980). A comparative analysis of models of instructional design. *Journal of Instructional Development, 3*(4), 2-16.

Arbib, M. A., & Hanson, A. R. (1987). Vision, brain and cooperative computation: An overview. In M. A. Arbib & A. R. Hanson (Eds.), *Vision, brain and cooperative computation.* Cambridge, MA: MIT Press.

Armbruster, B. B., & Anderson, T. H. (1982). *Idea mapping: The technique and its use in the classroom, or simulating the "ups" and "downs" of reading comprehension.* Urbana, IL: University of Illinois Center for the Study of Reading. Reading Education Report #36.

Armbruster, B. B., & Anderson, T. H. (1984). Mapping: Representing informative text graphically. In C. D. Holley & D. F. Dansereau (Eds.). *Spatial Learning Strategies.* New York: Academic Press.

Arnheim, R. (1969). *Visual thinking.* Berkeley, CA: University of California Press.

Atkinson, R. L., & Shiffrin. R. M. (1968). Human memory: A proposed system and its control processes. In K. W. Spence & J. T. Spence (Eds.), *The psychology of learning and motivation: Advances in research and theory, Volume 2.* New York: Academic Press.

Ausubel, D. P. (1968). *The psychology of meaningful verbal learning.* New York: Grune and Stratton.

Baddeley, A. (2000). Working memory: The interface between memory and cognition. In M. S. Gazzaniga (Ed.), *Cognitive Neuroscience: A reader.* Malden, MA: Blackwell.

Baker, E. L. (1984). Can educational research inform educational practice? Yes! *Phi Delta Kappan, 56,* 453-455.

Barab, S. A., Hay, K. E., Squire, K., Barnett, M., Schmidt, R., Karrigan, K., Yamagata-Lynch, L., & Johnson, C. (2000). The virtual solar system: Learning through a technology-rich, inquiry-based, participatory learning environment. *Journal of Science Education and Technology, 9*(1), 7-25.

Barfield, W., & Furness, T. (1995) (Eds.), *Virtual environments and advanced interface design.* Oxford: Oxford University Press.

Bartlett, F. C. (1932). *Remembering: A study in experimental and social psychology.* London: Cambridge University Press.

Beer, R. D. (1995). Computation and dynamical languages for autonomous agents. In R. F. Port & T. Van Gelder (Eds.), *Mind as motion: Explorations in the dynamics of cognition.* Cambridge, MA: MIT Press.

Bell, P. (1995, April). *How far does light go? Individual and collaborative sense-making of science-related evidence.* Annual meeting of the American Educational Research Association, San Francisco.

Bell, P., & Winn, W. D. (2000). Distributed cognition, by nature and by design. In D. Jonassen (Ed.), *Theoretical foundations of learning environments.* Mawah NJ: Erlbaum.

Berninger, V., & Richards, T. (2002). *Brain literacy for psychologists and educators.* New York: Academic Press.

Bickhard, M. M. (2000). Dynamic representing and representational dynamics. In E. Dietrich & A. B. Markman (Eds.), *Cognitive dynamics: Conceptual and representational change in humans and machines.* Mawah NJ: Erlbaum.

Bloom, B. S. (1984). The 2 sigma problem: The search for methods of group instruction as effective as one-to-one tutoring. *Educational Researcher, 13*(6), 4-16.

Bloom, B. S. (1987). A response to Slavin's Mastery Learning reconsidered. *Review of Educational Research, 57,* 507-508.

Boden, M. (1988). *Computer models of mind.* New York: Cambridge University Press.

Bonner, J. (1988). Implications of cognitive theory for instructional design: Revisited. *Educational Communication and Technology Journal, 36,* 3-14.

Boring, E. G. (1950). *A history of experimental psychology.* New York: Appleton-Century-Crofts.

Bovy, R. C. (1983, April). *Defining the psychologically active features of instructional treatments designed to facilitate cue attendance.* Presented at the meeting of the American Educational Research Association, Montreal.

Bower, G. H. (1970). Imagery as a relational organizer in associative learning. *Journal of Verbal Learning and Verbal Behavior, 9,* 529-533.

Bransford, J. D., & Franks, J. J. (1971). The abstraction of linguistic ideas. *Cognitive Psychology, 2,* 331-350.

Bransford, J. D., & Johnson, M. K. (1972). Contextual prerequisites for understanding: Some investigations of comprehension and recall. *Journal of Verbal Learning and Verbal Behavior, 11,* 717-726.

Bronfenbrenner, U. (1976). The experimental ecology of education. *Educational Researcher, 5*(9), 5-15.

Brown, A. L. (1992). Design experiments: Theoretical and methodological challenges in creating complex interventions in classroom settings. *Journal of the Learning Sciences, 2*(2), 141-178.

Brown, A. L., Campione, J. C., & Day, J. D. (1981). Learning to learn: On training students to learn from texts. *Educational Researcher, 10*(2), 14-21.

Brown, J. S., Collins, A., & Duguid, P. (1989). Situated cognition and the culture of learning. *Educational Researcher, 18*(1), 32-43.

Bruner, J. (1990). *Acts of meaning.* Cambridge, MA: Harvard University Press.

Byrne, C. M., Furness, T., & Winn, W. D. (1995, April). *The use of virtual reality for teaching atomic/molecular structure.* Paper presented at the annual meeting of the American Educational Research Association, San Francisco.

Calderwood, B., Klein, G. A., & Crandall, B. W. (1988). Time pressure, skill and move quality in chess. *American Journal of Psychology, 101,* 481-493.

Carpenter, C. R. (1953). A theoretical orientation for instructional film research. *AV Communication Review, 1,* 38-52.

Cassidy, M. F., & Knowlton, J. Q. (1983). Visual literacy: A failed metaphor? *Educational Communication and Technology Journal, 31,* 67-90.

Champagne, A. B., Klopfer, L. E., & Gunstone, R. F. (1982). Cognitive research and the design of science instruction. *Educational Psychologist, 17,* 31-51.

Charness, N. (1989). Expertise in chess and bridge. In D. Klahr & K. Kotovsky (Eds.), *Complex information processing: The impact of Herbert A. Simon.* Hillsdale, NJ: Lawrence Erlbaum.

Chase, W. G., & Simon, H. A. (1973). The mind's eye in chess. In W. G. Chase (Ed.), *Visual information processing.* New York: Academic Press.

Chinn, C. A., & Brewer, W. F. (1993). The role of anomalous data in knowledge acquisition: A theoretical framework and implications for science instruction. *Review of Educational Research, 63,* 1-49.

Chomsky, N. (1964). A review of Skinner's *Verbal Behavior.* In J. A. Fodor & J. J. Katz (Eds.), *The structure of language: Readings in the philosophy of language.* Englewood Cliffs, NJ: Prentice-Hall.

Chomsky, N. (1965). *Aspects of the theory of syntax.* Cambridge, MA: MIT Press.

Cisek, P. (1999). Beyond the computer metaphor: Behavior as interaction. *Journal of Consciousness Studies, 6*(12), 125-142.

Clancey, W. J. (1993). Situated action: A neuropsychological interpretation: Response to Vera and Simon. *Cognitive Science, 17,* 87-116.

Clark, A. (1997). *Being there: Putting brain, body and world together again.* Cambridge, MA: MIT Press.

Clark, J. M., & Paivio, A. (1991). Dual coding theory and education. *Educational Psychology Review, 3,* 149-210.

Clark, R. E. (1983). Reconsidering research on learning from media. *Review of Educational Research, 53,* 445-460.

Clark, R. E. (1985). Confounding in educational computing research. *Journal of Educational Computing Research, 1,* 137-148.

Cognition and Technology Group at Vanderbilt (1990). Anchored instruction and its relationship to situated learning. *Educational Researcher, 19*(3), 2-10.

Cognition and Technology Group at Vanderbilt (2000). Adventures in anchored instruction: Lessons from beyond the ivory tower. In

R. Glaser (Ed.), *Advances in instructional psychology, educational design and cognitive science, Volume 5.* Mawah, NJ: Erlbaum.

Collins, A. (1978). Studies in plausible reasoning: *Final report, October 1976 to February 1978. Vol. 1: Human plausible reasoning.* Cambridge MA: Bolt Beranek and Newman, BBN Report No. 3810.

Cornoldi, C., & De Beni, R. (1991). Memory for discourse: Loci mnemonics and the oral presentation effect. *Applied Cognitive Psychology, 5,* 511-518.

Cromer, A., (1997). *Connected knowledge.* Oxford: Oxford University Press.

Cronbach, L. J., & Snow, R. (1977). *Aptitudes and instructional methods.* New York: Irvington.

Csiko, G. A. (1989). Unpredictability and indeterminism in human behavior: Arguments and implications for educational research. *Educational Researcher, 18*(3), 17-25.

Cunningham, D. J. (1992a). Assessing constructions and constructing assessments: A dialogue. In T. Duffy & D. Jonassen (Eds.), *Constructivism and the technology of instruction: A conversation.* Hillsdale, NJ: Lawrence Erlbaum Associates.

Cunningham, D. J. (1992b). Beyond Educational Psychology: Steps towards an educational semiotic. *Educational Psychology Review, 4*(2), 165-194.

Dale, E. (1946). *Audio-visual methods in teaching.* New York: Dryden Press.

Dansereau, D. F., Collins, K. W., McDonald, B. A., Holley, C. D., Garland, J., Diekhoff, G., & Evans, S. H. (1979). Development and evaluation of a learning strategy program. *Journal of Educational Psychology, 71,* 64-73.

Dawkins, R. (1989). *The selfish gene.* New York: Oxford university Press.

Dawkins, R. (1997). *Unweaving the rainbow: Science, delusion and the appetite for wonder.* Boston: Houghton Mifflin.

De Beni, R., & Cornoldi, C. (1985). Effects of the mnemotechnique of loci in the memorization of concrete words. *Acta Psychologica, 60,* 11-24.

Dede, C., Salzman, M., Loftin, R. B., & Ash, K. (1997). Using virtual reality technology to convey abstract scientific concepts. In M. J. Jacobson & R. B. Kozma (Eds.), *Learning the sciences of the 21st century: Research, design and implementing advanced technology learning environments.* Mahwah, NJ: Erlbaum.

De Kleer, J., & Brown, J. S. (1981). Mental models of physical mechanisms and their acquisition. In J. R. Anderson (Ed.), *Cognitive skills and their acquisition.* Hillsdale, NJ: Lawrence Erlbaum.

Dennett, D. (1991). *Consciousness explained.* Boston, MA: Little Brown.

Dennett, D. (1995). *Darwin's dangerous idea: Evolution and the meanings of life.* New York: Simon & Schuster.

DiVesta, F. J., & Rieber, L. P. (1987). Characteristics of cognitive instructional design: The next generation. *Educational Communication and Technology Journal, 35,* 213-230.

Dondis, D. A. (1973). *A primer of visual literacy.* Cambridge, MA: MIT Press.

Dreyfus, H. L. (1972). *What computers can't do.* New York: Harper and Row.

Dreyfus, H. L., & Dreyfus, S. E. (1986). *Mind over machine.* New York: The Free Press.

Driscoll, M. (1990). Semiotics: An alternative model. *Educational Technology, 29*(7), 33-35.

Driscoll, M., & Lebow, D. (1992). Making it happen: Possibilities and pitfalls of Cunningham's semiotic. *Educational Psychology Review, 4,* 211-221.

Duffy, T. M., & Jonassen, D. H. (1992). Constructivism: New implications for instructional technology. In T. Duffy & D. Jonassen (Eds.), *Constructivism and the technology of instruction: A conversation.* Hillsdale, NJ: Lawrence Erlbaum Associates.

Duffy, T. M., Lowyck, J., & Jonassen, D. H. (1983). *Designing environments for constructive learning*. New York: Springer.

Duong, L-V. (1994). *An investigation of characteristics of pre-attentive vision in processing visual displays*. Ph.D. dissertation, College of Education, University of Washington, Seattle, WA.

Dwyer, F. M. (1972). *A guide for improving visualized instruction*. State College, PA: Learning Services.

Dwyer, F. M. (1978). *Strategies for improving visual learning*. State College, PA.: Learning Services.

Dwyer, F. M. (1987*). Enhancing visualized instruction: Recommendations for practitioners*. State College PA: Learning Services.

Edelman, G. M. (1992). *Bright air, brilliant fire*. New York: Basic Books.

Edelson, D. C. (2001). Learning-For-Use: A Framework for the design of technology-supported inquiry activities. *Journal of Research in Science Teaching, 38*(3), 355-385.

Edelson, D. C., Salierno, C., Matese, G., Pitts, V., & Sherin, B. (2002, April). *Learning-for-Use in Earth science: Kids as climate modelers*. Paper presented at the Annual Meeting of the National Association for Research in Science Teaching, New Orleans, LA.

Eisner, E. (1984). Can educational research inform educational practice? *Phi Delta Kappan, 65,* 447-452.

Ellis, S. R. (1993) (Ed.). *Pictorial communication in virtual and real environments*. London: Taylor and Francis.

Epstein, W. (1988). Has the time come to rehabilitate Gestalt Psychology? *Psychological Research, 50,* 2-6.

Ericsson, K. A., & Simon, H. A. (1984). *Protocol analysis: Verbal reports as data*. Cambridge, MA: MIT Press.

Farah, M. J. (1989). Knowledge of text and pictures: A neuropsychological perspective. In H. Mandl & J. R. Levin (Eds.), *Knowledge acquisition from text and pictures*. North Holland: Elsevier.

Farah, M. (2000). The neural bases of mental imagery. In M. Gazzaniga (Ed.), *The new cognitive neurosciences, second edition*. Cambridge, MA: MIT Press.

Fisher, K. M., Faletti, J., Patterson, H., Thornton, R., Lipson, J., & Spring, C. (1990). Computer-based concept mapping. *Journal of Science Teaching, 19,* 347-352.

Fleming, M. L., & , Levie, W. H. (1978). *Instructional message design: Principles from the behavioral sciences*. Englewood Cliffs, NJ: Educational Technology Publications.

Fleming, M. L., & Levie, W. H. (1993) (Eds.). *Instructional message design: Principles from the behavioral and cognitive sciences* (Second ed.). Englewood Cliffs, NJ: Educational Technology Publications.

Freeman, W. J., & Nuñez, R. (1999). Restoring to cognition the forgotten primacy of action, intention and emotion. In R. Nuñez & W. J. Freeman, (Eds.), *Reclaiming cognition: The primacy of action, intention and emotion*. Bowling Green, OH: Imprint Academic.

Gabert, S. L. (2001). *Phase world of water: A case study of a virtual reality world developed to investigate the relative efficiency and efficacy of a bird's eye view exploration and a head-up-display exploration*. Ph.D. dissertation, College of Education, University of Washington, Seattle, WA.

Gagné, E. D. (1985). *The cognitive psychology of school learning*. Boston: Little Brown.

Gagné, R. M. (1965). *The conditions of learning*. New York: Holt, Rinehart & Winston.

Gagné, R. M. (1974). *Essentials of learning for instruction*. New York: Holt, Rinehart & Winston.

Gagné, R. M., Briggs, L. J., & Wager, W. W. (1988). *Principles of instructional design: Third edition*. New York: Holt Rinehart & Winston.

Gagné, R. M., & Dick, W. (1983). Instructional psychology. *Annual Review of Psychology, 34,* 261-295.

Gagné, R. M., & Glaser, R. (1987). Foundations in learning research. In R. M. Gagné (Ed.), *Instructional Technology: Foundations*. Hillsdale, NJ: Lawrence Erlbaum Associates.

Gentner, D., & Stevens, A. L. (1983). *Mental models*. Hillsdale, NJ: Lawrence Erlbaum.

Glaser, R. (1976). Components of a psychology of instruction: Towards a science of design. *Review of Educational Research, 46,* 1-24.

Goldstone, R. L., Steyvers, M., Spencer-Smith, J., & Kersten, A. (2000). Interactions between perceptual and conceptual learning. In E. Dietrich & A. B. Markman (Eds.), *Cognitive dynamics: Conceptual and representational change in humans and machines*. Mawah NJ: Erlbaum.

Gordin, D. N., & Pea, R. (1995). Prospects for scientific visualization as an educational technology. *Journal of the Learning Sciences, 4*(3), 249-279.

Greeno, J. G. (1976). Cognitive objectives of instruction: Theory of knowledge for solving problems and answering questions. In D. Klahr (Ed.). *Cognition and instruction*. Hillsdale, NJ: Erlbaum.

Greeno, J. G. (1980). Some examples of cognitive task analysis with instructional implications. In R. E. Snow, P-A. Federico & W. E. Montague (Eds.), *Aptitude, learning and instruction, Volume 2*. Hillsdale, NJ: Erlbaum.

Gropper, G. L. (1983). A behavioral approach to instructional prescription. In C. M. Reigeluth (Ed.), *Instructional design theories and models*. Hillsdale, NJ: Erlbaum.

Guha, R. V., & Lenat, D. B. (1991). Cyc: A mid-term report. *Applied Artificial Intelligence, 5,* 45-86.

Harel, I., & Papert, S. (Eds.) (1991). *Constructionism*. Norwood, NJ: Ablex.

Hartman, G. W. (1935). *Gestalt psychology: A survey of facts and principles*. New York: The Ronald Press.

Hay, K., Marlino, M., & Holschuh, D. (2000). The virtual exploratorium: Foundational research and theory on the integration of 5-D modeling and visualization in undergraduate geoscience education. In B. Fishman & S. O'Connor-Divelbliss (Eds.), *Proceedings: Fourth International Conference of the Learning Sciences*. Mahwah, NJ: Erlbaum.

Heinich, R. (1970). *Technology and the management of instruction*. Washington DC: Association for Educational Communication and Technology.

Henle, M. (1987). Koffka's principles after fifty years. *Journal of the History of the Behavioral Sciences, 23,* 14-21.

Hereford, J., & Winn, W. D. (1994). Non-speech sound in the human-computer interaction: A review and design guidelines. *Journal of Educational Computing Research, 11,* 209-231.

Holley, C. D., & Dansereau, D. F. (Eds.) (1984). *Spatial learning strategies*. New York: Academic Press.

Holland, J. (1992). *Adaptation in natural and artificial environments*. Ann Arbor, MI: University of Michigan Press.

Holland, J. (1995). *Hidden order: How adaptation builds complexity*. Cambridge, MA: Perseus Books.

Holyoak, K. J., & Hummel, J. E. (2000). The proper treatment of symbols in a connectionist architecture. In E. Dietrich & A. B. Markman (Eds.), *Cognitive dynamics: Conceptual and representational change in humans and machines*. Mawah, NJ: Erlbaum.

Houghton, H. A., & Willows, D. H., (1987) (Eds.). *The psychology of illustration. Volume 2*. New York: Springer.

Howe, K. R. (1985). Two dogmas of educational research. *Educational Researcher, 14*(8), 10-18.

Hubel, D. H. (2000). Exploration of the primary visual cortex, 1955-1976. In M. S. Gazzaniga (Ed.), *Cognitive Neuroscience: A reader*. Malden, MA: Blackwell.

Hueyching, J. J., & Reeves, T. C. (1992). Mental models: A research focus for interactive learning systems. *Educational Technology Research and Development, 40,* 39-53.

Hughes, R. E. (1989). *Radial outlining: An instructional tool for teaching information processing.* Ph.D. dissertation. College of Education, University of Washington, Seattle, WA.

Hunt, M. (1982). *The universe within.* Brighton: Harvester Press.

Johnson, D. D., Pittelman, S. D., & Heimlich, J. E. (1986). Semantic mapping. *Reading Teacher, 39,* 778-783.

Johnson-Laird, P. N. (1988). *The computer and the mind.* Cambridge, MA: Harvard University Press.

Jonassen, D. H. (1990, January). *Conveying, assessing and learning (strategies for) structural knowledge.* Paper presented at the Annual Convention of the Association for Educational Communication and Technology, Anaheim, CA.

Jonassen, D. H. (1991). Hypertext as instructional design. *Educational Technology, Research and Development, 39,* 83-92.

Jonassen, D. H. (2000). *Computers as mindtools for schools: Engaging critical thinking.* Columbus, OH: Prentice Hall.

Kelso, J. A. S. (1999). *Dynamic patterns: The self-organization of brain and behavior.* Cambridge, MA: MIT Press.

Klahr, D., & Kotovsky, K. (Eds.) (1989). *Complex information processing: The impact of Herbert A. Simon.* Hillsdale, NJ: Erlbaum.

Knowlton, B., & Squire, L. R. (1996). Artificial grammar learning depends on implicit acquisition of both rule-based and exemplar-based information. *Journal of Experimental Psychology: Learning, Memory and Cognition, 22,* 169-181.

Knowlton, J. Q. (1966). On the definition of 'picture'. *AV Communication Review, 14,* 157-183.

Kosslyn, S. M. (1985). *Image and Mind.* Cambridge, MA: Harvard University Press.

Kosslyn, S. M., Ball, T. M., & Reiser, B. J. (1978). Visual images preserve metric spatial information: Evidence from studies of image scanning. *Journal of Experimental Psychology: Human Perception and Performance, 4,* 47-60.

Kosslyn, S. M., & Thompson, W. L. (2000). Shared mechanisms in visual imagery and visual perception: Insights from cognitive neuroscience. In M. Gazzaniga (Ed.), *The new Cognitive Neurosciences, Second edition.* Cambridge, MA: MIT Press.

Kozma, R. B. (1991). Learning with media. *Review of Educational Research, 61,* 179-211.

Kozma, R. B. (1994). Will media influence learning? Reframing the debate. *Educational Technology Research and Development, 42,* 7-19.

Kozma, R. B., Russell, J., Jones, T., Marz, N., & Davis, J. (1993, September). *The use of multiple, linked representations to facilitate science understanding.* Paper presented at the fifth conference of the European Association for Research in Learning and Instruction, Aix-en-Provence.

Kuhn, T.S. (1970). *The structure of scientific revolutions* (second ed.). Chicago: University of Chicago Press.

Kulhavy, R. W., Lee, J. B., & Caterino, L. C. (1985). Conjoint retention of maps and related discourse. *Contemporary Educational Psychology, 10,* 28-37.

Kulhavy, R. W., Stock, W. A., & Caterino, L. C. (1994). Reference maps as a framework for remembering text. In W. Schnotz & R. W. Kulhavy (Eds.), *Comprehension of graphics.* North-Holland: Elsevier.

Kulik, C. L. (1990). Effectiveness of mastery learning programs: A meta-analysis. *Review of Educational Research, 60,* 265-299.

Labouvie-Vief, G. (1990). Wisdom as integrated thought: Historical and development perspectives. In R. E. Sternberg (Ed.), *Wisdom: Its nature, origins and development.* Cambridge: Cambridge University Press.

Lakoff, G., & Johnson, M. (1980). *Metaphors we live by.* Chicago: University of Chicago Press.

Landa, L. (1983). The algo-heuristic theory of instruction. In C. M. Reigeluth (Ed.), *Instructional design theories and models.* Hillsdale, NJ: Erlbaum.

Larkin, J. H., & Simon, H. A. (1987). Why a diagram is (sometimes) worth ten thousand words. *Cognitive Science, 11,* 65-99.

Larochelle, S. (1982). *Temporal aspects of typing.* Dissertation Abstracts International, *43,* 3-B, 900.

Lave, J. (1988). *Cognition in practice.* New York: Cambridge University Press.

Lave, J., & Wenger, E. (1991). *Situated learning: Legitimate peripheral participation.* Cambridge: Cambridge University Press.

Lenat, D. B., Guha, R. V., Pittman, K., Pratt, D., & Shepherd, M. (1990). Cyc: Towards programs with common sense. *Communications of ACM, 33*(8), 30-49.

Leinhardt, G. (1987). Introduction and integration of classroom routines by expert teachers. *Curriculum Inquiry, 7,* 135-176.

Lesgold, A., Robinson, H., Feltovich, P., Glaser, R., Klopfer, D., & Wang, Y. (1988). Expertise in a complex skill: Diagnosing x-ray pictures. In M. Chi, R. Glaser, & M. J. Farr (Eds.), *The nature of expertise.* Hillsdale, NJ: Erlbaum.

Levin, J. R., Anglin, G. J., & Carney, R. N. (1987). On empirically validating functions of pictures in prose. In D. H. Willows & H. A. Houghton (Eds.). *The psychology of illustration.* New York: Springer.

Linn, M. (1995). Designing computer learning environments for engineering and computer science: The scaffolded knowledge integration framework. *Journal of Science Education and Technology, 4*(2), 103-126.

Liu, K. (2002). *Evidence for implicit learning of color patterns and letter strings from a study of artificial grammar learning.* Ph.D. dissertation, College of Education, University of Washington, Seattle, WA.

Logothetis, N. K., Pauls, J., & Poggio, T. (1995). Shape representation in the inferior temporal cortex of monkeys. *Current Biology, 5,* 552-563.

Lowyck, J., & Elen, J. (1994). *Students' instructional metacognition in learning environments (SIMILE).* Unpublished paper. Leuven, Belgium: Centre for Instructional Psychology and Technology, Catholic University of Leuven.

Mager, R. (1962). *Preparing instructional objectives,* Palo Alto, CA: Fearon.

Malarney, M. (2000). *Learning communities and on-line technologies: The Classroom at Sea experience.* Ph.D. dissertation, College of Education, University of Washington, Seattle, WA.

Mandl, H., & Levin, J. R. (Eds.) (1989). *Knowledge Acquisition from text and pictures.* North Holland: Elsevier.

Markowitsch, H. J. (2000). The anatomical bases of memory. In M. Gazzaniga (Ed.), *The new cognitive neurosciences* (second ed.). Cambridge, MA: MIT Press.

Marr, D. (1982). *Vision.* New York: Freeman.

Marr, D., & Nishihara, H. K. (1978). Representation and recognition of the spatial organization of three-dimensional shapes. *Proceedings of the Royal Society of London, 200,* 269-294.

Marr, D., & Ullman, S. (1981). Directional selectivity and its use in early visual processing. *Proceedings of the Royal Society of London, 211,* 151-180.

Maturana, H., & Varela, F. (1980). *Autopoiesis and cognition.* Boston, MA: Reidel.

Maturana, H., & Varela, F. (1987). *The tree of knowledge.* Boston, MA: New Science Library.

Mayer, R. E. (1989a). Models for understanding. *Review of Educational Research, 59,* 43-64.

Mayer, R. E. (1989b). Systematic thinking fostered by illustrations of scientific text. *Journal of Educational Psychology, 81,* 240–246.

Mayer, R. E. (1992). *Thinking, problem solving, cognition* (second ed.). New York: Freeman.

Mayer, R. E., & Gallini, J. K. (1990). When is an illustration worth ten thousand words? *Journal of Educational Psychology, 82,* 715–726.

McClelland, J. L., & Rumelhart, D. E. (1986). *Parallel distributed processing: Explorations in the microstructure of cognition. Volume 2: Psychological and biological models.* Cambridge, MA: MIT Press.

McClelland, J. L., & Rumelhart, D. E. (1988). *Explorations in parallel distributed processing.* Cambridge, MA: MIT Press.

McLellan, H. (1996) (Ed.) *Situated learning perspectives.* Englewood Cliffs, NJ: Educational Technology Publications.

McNamara, T. P. (1986). Mental representations of spatial relations. *Cognitive Psychology, 18,* 87–121.

McNamara, T. P., Hardy, J. K., & Hirtle, S. C. (1989). Subjective hierarchies in spatial memory. *Journal of Experimental Psychology: Learning, Memory and Cognition, 15,* 211–227.

Merrill, M. D. (1983). Component display theory. In C. M. Reigeluth (Ed.), *Instructional design theories and models.* Hillsdale, NJ: Erlbaum.

Merrill, M. D. (1988). Applying component display theory to the design of courseware. In D. Jonassen (Ed.), *Instructional designs for microcomputer courseware.* Hillsdale, NJ: Erlbaum.

Merrill, M. D. (1992). Constructivism and instructional design. In T. Duffy & D. Jonassen (Eds.), *Constructivism and the technology of instruction: A conversation.* Hillsdale, NJ: Erlbaum.

Merrill, M. D., Li, Z., & Jones, M. K. (1991). Instructional transaction theory: An introduction. *Educational Technology, 30*(3), 7–12.

Miller, G. A. (1956). The magical number seven, plus or minus two: Some limits on our capacity for processing information. *Psychological Review, 63,* 81–97.

Minsky, M. (1975). A framework for representing knowledge. In P. H. Winston (Ed.), *The psychology of computer vision,* New York: McGraw-Hill.

Minstrell, J. (2001). Facets of students' thinking: Designing to cross the gap from research to standards-based practice. In K. Crowley, C. D. Schunn, & T. Okada (Eds.), *Designing for science: Implications from everyday, classroom, and professional settings.* Pittsburgh PA: University of Pittsburgh, Learning Research and Development Center.

Morrison, C. R., & Levin, J. R. (1987). Degree of mnemonic support and students' acquisition of science facts. *Educational Communication and Technology Journal, 35,* 67–74.

Nagel, T., (1974). What it is like to be a bat. *Philosophical Review, 83,* 435–450.

Neisser, U. (1976). *Cognition and reality.* San Francisco: Freeman.

Newell, A. (1982). The knowledge level. *Artificial Intelligence, 18,* 87–127.

Norman, D. A., & Rumelhart, D. E. (1975). Memory and knowledge. In D. A. Norman & D. E. Rumelhart (Eds.), *Explorations in cognition.* San Francisco: Freeman.

Novak, J. D. (1998). *Learning, creating, and using knowledge: Concept maps as facilitative tools in schools and corporations.* Mawah NJ: Erlbaum.

Nunan, T. (1983). *Countering educational design.* New York: Nichols Publishing Company.

Owen, L. A. (1985a). Dichoptic priming effects on ambiguous picture processing. *British Journal of Psychology, 76,* 437–447.

Owen, L. A. (1985b). The effect of masked pictures on the interpretation of ambiguous pictures. *Current Psychological Research and Reviews, 4,* 108–118.

Paivio, A. (1971). *Imagery and verbal processes.* New York: Holt, Rinehart & Winston.

Paivio, A. (1974). Language and knowledge of the world. *Educational Researcher, 3*(9), 5–12.

Paivio, A. (1983). The empirical case for dual coding. In J. C. Yuille (Ed.). *Imagery, memory and cognition.* Hillsdale: Lawrence.

Papert, S. (1983). *Mindstorms: Children, computers and powerful ideas.* New York: Basic Books.

Pask, G. (1975). *Conversation, cognition and learning.* Amsterdam: Elsevier.

Pask, G. (1984). A review of conversation theory and a protologic (or protolanguage), Lp. *Educational Communication and Technology Journal, 32,* 3–40.

Patel, V. L., & Groen, G. J. (1991). The general and specific nature of medical expertise: A critical look. In K. A. Ericsson & J Smith (Eds.), *Toward a general theory of expertise.* Cambridge: Cambridge University Press.

Peters, E. E., & Levin, J. R. (1986). Effects of a mnemonic strategy on good and poor readers' prose recall. *Reading Research Quarterly, 21,* 179–192.

Phillips, D. C. (1983). After the wake: Postpositivism in educational thought. *Educational Researcher, 12*(5), 4–12.

Piaget, J. (1968). The role of the concept of equilibrium. In D. Elkind (Ed.), *Six psychological studies by Jean Piaget,* New York: Vintage Books.

Piaget, J., & Inhelder, B. (1969). *The psychology of the child.* New York: Basic Books.

Pinker, S. (1985). Visual cognition: An introduction. In S. Pinker (Ed.), *Visual cognition.* Cambridge, MA: MIT Press.

Pinker, S. (1997). *How the mind works.* New York: Norton.

Pinker, S. (1999). *Words and rules.* New York: Basic Books.

Pinker, S. (2002). *The blank slate: The modern denial of human nature.* New York: Viking.

Polanyi, M. (1962). *Personal knowledge: Towards a post-critical philosophy.* Chicago: University of Chicago Press.

Pomerantz, J. R. (1986). Visual form perception: An overview. In E. C. Schwab & H. C. Nussbaum (Eds.), *Pattern recognition by humans and machines. Volume 2: Visual perception.* New York: Academic Press.

Pomerantz, J. R., Pristach, E. A., & Carson, C. E. (1989). Attention and object perception. In B. E. Shepp & S. Ballesteros (Eds.) *Object perception: Structure and process.* Hillsdale, NJ: Erlbaum.

Port, R. F., & Van Gelder, T. (1995). *Mind as motion: Explorations in the dynamics of cognition.* Cambridge, MA: MIT Press.

Posner, G. J., Strike, K. A., Hewson, P. W., & Gertzog, W. A. (1982). Accommodation of scientific conception: Toward a theory of conceptual change. *Science Education, 66,* 211–227.

Pylyshyn Z. (1984). *Computation and cognition: Toward a foundation for cognitive science.* Cambridge, MA: MIT Press.

Reber, A. S. (1989). Implicit learning and tacit knowledge. *Journal of Experimental Psychology: General, 118,* 219–235.

Reber, A. S., & Squire, L. R. (1994). Parallel brain systems for learning with and without awareness. *Learning and Memory, 2,* 1–13.

Reigeluth, C. M. (1983). Instructional design: What is it and why is it? In C. M. Reigeluth (Ed.), *Instructional design theories and models.* Hillsdale, NJ: Erlbaum.

Reigeluth, C. M., & Curtis, R. V. (1987). Learning situations and instructional models. In R. M. Gagné (Ed.), *Instructional technology: Foundations.* Hillsdale NJ: Erlbaum.

Reigeluth, C. M., & Stein, F. S. (1983). The elaboration theory of instruction. In C. M. Reigeluth (Ed.), *Instructional design theories and models.* Hillsdale, NJ: Erlbaum.

Resnick, L. B. (1976). Task analysis in instructional design: Some cases from mathematics. In D. Klahr (Ed.), *Cognition and instruction*. Hillsdale, NJ: Erlbaum.

Reyes, A., & Zarama, R. (1998). The process of embodying distinctions: A reconstruction of the process of learning. *Cybernetics and Human Knowing, 5*(3), 19-33.

Richards, W. (Ed.), (1988). *Natural computation*. Cambridge, MA: MIT Press.

Richey, R. (1986). *The theoretical and conceptual bases of instructional design*. London: Kogan Page.

Rieber, L. P. (1994). *Computers, graphics and learning*. Madison, WI: Brown & Benchmark.

Rock, I. (1986). The description and analysis of object and event perception. In K. R. Boff, L. Kaufman & J. P. Thomas (Eds.), *The handbook of perception and human performance* (Volume 2, pp. 33-1-33-71). NY: Wiley.

Romiszowski, A. J. (1993). Psychomotor principles. In M. L. Fleming & W. H. Levie (Eds.) *Instructional message design: Principles from the behavioral and cognitive sciences* (second ed.) Hillsdale, NJ: Educational Technology Publications.

Rosch, E. (1999). Reclaiming concepts. *Journal of consciousness studies, 6*(11), 61-77.

Roth, W. M. (1999). The evolution of Umwelt and communication. *Cybernetics and Human Knowing, 6*(4), 5-23.

Roth, W. M. (2001). Gestures: Their role in teaching and learning. *Review of Educational Research, 71*, 365-392.

Roth, W. M., & McGinn, M. K. (1998). Inscriptions: Toward a theory of representing as social practice. *Review of Educational Research, 68*, 35-59.

Rouse, W. B., & Morris, N. M. (1986). On looking into the black box: Prospects and limits in the search for mental models. *Psychological Bulletin, 100*, 349-363.

Ruddell, R. B., & Boyle, O. F. (1989). A study of cognitive mapping as a means to improve summarization and comprehension of expository text. *Reading Research and Instruction, 29*, 12-22.

Rumelhart, D. E., & McClelland, J. L. (1986). *Parallel distributed processing: Explorations in the microstructure of cognition. Volume 1: Foundations*. Cambridge MA: MIT Press.

Rumelhart, D. E., & Norman, D. A. (1981). Analogical processes in learning. In J. R. Anderson (Ed.), *Cognitive Skills and their Acquisition*. Hillsdale, NJ.: Lawrence Erlbaum.

Ryle, G. (1949). *The concept of Mind*. London: Hutchinson.

Saariluoma, P. (1990). Chess players' search for task-relevant cues: Are chunks relevant? In D. Brogan (Ed.), *Visual search*. London: Taylor and Francis.

Salomon, G. (1974). Internalization of filmic schematic operations in interaction with learners' aptitudes. *Journal of Educational Psychology, 66*, 499-511.

Salomon, G. (1979). *Interaction of media, cognition and learning*. San Francisco: Jossey Bass.

Salomon, G. (1988). Artificial intelligence in reverse: Computer tools that turn cognitive. *Journal of Educational Computing Research, 4*, 123-140.

Salomon, G. (Ed.) (1993). *Distributed cognitions: Psychological and educational considerations*. Cambridge: Cambridge University Press.

Salomon, G., Perkins, D. N., & Globerson, T. (1991). Partners in cognition: Extending human intelligence with intelligent technologies. *Educational Researcher, 20*, 2-9.

Scaife, M., & Rogers, Y. (1996). External cognition: How do graphical representations work? *International Journal of Human Computer studies, 45*, 185-213.

Scandura, J. M. (1983). Instructional strategies based on the structural learning theory. . In C. M. Reigeluth (Ed.), *Instructional design theories and models*. Hillsdale, NJ: Erlbaum.

Schachter, D. L., & Buckner, R.L. (1998). Priming and the brain. *Neuron, 20*, 185-195.

Schank, R. C. (1984). *The cognitive computer*. Reading, MA: Addison-Wesley.

Schank, R. C., & Abelson, R. (1977). *Scripts, plans, goals and understanding*. Hillsdale, NJ: Erlbaum.

Schewel, R. (1989). Semantic mapping: A study skills strategy. *Academic Therapy, 24*, 439-447.

Schneider, W., & Shiffrin, R. M. (1977). Controlled and automatic human processing: I. Detection, search and attention. *Psychological Review, 84*, 1-66.

Schnotz, W., & Kulhavy, R. W. (Eds.) (1994). *Comprehension of graphics*. North-Holland: Elsevier.

Schon, D. A. (1983). *The reflective practitioner*. New York: Basic Books.

Schon, D. A. (1987). *Educating the reflective practitioner*. San Francisco, Jossey Bass.

Schott, F. (1992). The contributions of cognitive science and educational technology to the advancement of instructional design. *Educational Technology Research and Development, 40*, 55-57.

Schwartz, N. H., & Kulhavy, R. W. (1981). Map features and the recall of discourse. *Contemporary Educational Psychology, 6*, 151-158.

Scott, B. (2001). Conversation theory: A constructivist, dialogical approach to educational technology. *Cybernetics and Human Knowing, 8*(4), 25-46.

Searle, J. R. (1992). *The rediscovery of the mind*. Cambridge, MA: MIT Press.

Seel, N. M., & Dörr, G. (1994). The supplantation of mental images through graphics: Instructional effects on spatial visualization skills of adults. In W. Schnotz & R. W. Kulhavy (Eds.), *Comprehension of graphics*. North-Holland: Elsevier.

Seel, N. M., & Strittmatter, P. (1989). Presentation of information by media and its effect on mental models. In H. Mandl and J. R. Levin (Eds.), *Knowledge Acquisition from text and pictures*. North Holland: Elsevier.

Shavelson, R., & Towne, L. (2002). *Scientific research in Education*. Washington DC: National Academy Press.

Shepard, R. N., & Cooper, L. A. (1982). *Mental images and their transformation*. Cambridge, MA: MIT Press.

Shiffrin, R. M., & Schneider, W. (1977). Controlled and automatic information processing: II. Perceptual learning, automatic attending, and a general theory. *Psychological Review, 84*, 127-190.

Simon, H. A. (1974). How big is a chunk? *Science, 183*, 482-488.

Simon, H. A. (1981). *The sciences of the artificial*. Cambridge, MA: MIT Press.

Sinatra, R. C., Stahl-Gemake, J., & Borg, D. N. (1986). Improving reading comprehension of disabled readers through semantic mapping. *The Reading Teacher,* October, 22-29.

Sinatra, R. C., Stahl-Gemake, J., & Morgan, N. W. (1986). Using semantic mapping after reading to organize and write discourse. *Journal of Reading, 30*(1), 4-13.

Sless, D. (1981). *Learning and visual communication*. New York: John Wiley.

Skinner, B. F. (1957). *Verbal behavior*. New York: Appleton-Century-Crofts.

Snow, R. E. (1992). Aptitude theory: Yesterday, today and tomorrow. *Educational Psychologist, 27*, 5-32.

Sokal, A., & Bricmont, J. (1998). *Fashionable nonsense: Postmodern intellectuals' abuse of science*. New York: Picador.

Spencer, K. (1988). *The psychology of educational technology and instructional media*. London: Routledge.

Spiro, R. J., Feltovich, P. J., Coulson, R. L., & Anderson, D. K. (1989). Multiple analogies for complex concepts: Antidotes to analogy-induced misconception in advanced knowledge acquisition. In S. Vosniadou & A. Ortony (Eds.), *Similarity and analogical reasoning*. Cambridge: Cambridge University Press.

Spiro, R. J., Feltovich, P. J., Jacobson, M. J., & Coulson, R. L. (1992). Cognitive flexibility, constructivisim, and hypertext: Random access instruction for advanced knowledge acquisition in ill-structured domains. In T. M. Duffy & D. H. Jonassen (Eds.), *Constructivism and the technology of instruction*. Hillsdale, NJ: Lawrence Erlbaum.

Squire, L. R., & Knowlton, B. (1995). Learning about categories in the absence of memory. *Proceedings of the National Academy of Sciences, USA, 92*, 12,470-12,474.

Sternberg, R. J., & Weil, E. M. (1980). An aptitude X strategy interaction in linear syllogistic reasoning. *Journal of Educational Psychology, 72*, 226-239.

Streibel, M. J. (1991). Instructional plans and situated learning: The challenge of Suchman's theory of situated action for instructional designers and instructional systems. In G. J. Anglin (Ed.), *Instructional technology past, present and future*. Englewood, CO: Libraries Unlimited.

Strogatz, S. (2003). *Sync: The emerging science of spontaneous order*. New York: Hyperion.

Suchman, L. (1987). *Plans and situated actions: The problem of human/machine communication*. New York: Cambridge University Press.

Suzuki, K. (1987, February). *Schema theory: A basis for domain integration design*. Paper presented at the Annual Convention of the Association for Educational Communication and Technology, Atlanta, GA.

Tanimoto, S., Winn, W. D., & Akers, D. (2002). A system that supports using student-drawn diagrams to assess comprehension of mathematical formulas. *Proceedings: Diagrams 2002: International Conference on Theory and Application of Diagrams (Diagrams '02)*. Callaway Gardens, GA.

Tennyson, R. D. (1997). A systems dynamics approach to instructional systems design. In R. D. Tennyson, F. Schott, N. Seel, & S. Dijkstra (Eds.), *Instructional design, international perspectives. Volume 1: Theory, research and models*. Mahwah, NJ: Erlbaum.

Tennyson, R. D., & Park, O. C. (1987). Artificial intelligence and computer-based learning. In R. M. Gagné (Ed.), *Instructional Technology: Foundations*. Hillsdale, NJ: Lawrence Erlbaum Associates.

Tennyson, R. D., & Rasch, M. (1988). Linking cognitive learning theory to instructional prescriptions. *Instructional Science, 17*, 369-385.

Thorley, N., & Stofflet, R. (1996). Representation of the conceptual change model in science teacher education. *Science Education, 80*, 317-339.

Thorndyke, P. W., & Hayes-Roth, B. (1979). The use of schemata in the acquisition and transfer of knowledge. *Cognitive Psychology, 11*, 82-106.

Treisman, A. (1988). Features and objects: The fourteenth Bartlett Memorial Lecture. *Quarterly Journal of Experimental Psychology: Human Experimental Psychology, 40A*, 210-237.

Tulving, E. (2000). Memory: Introduction. In M. Gazzaniga (Ed.), *The new Cognitive Neurosciences, Second edition*. Cambridge, MA: MIT Press.

Tversky, B. (2001). Spatial schemas in depictions. In M. Gattis (Ed.), *Spatial schemas and abstract thought*. Cambridge MA: MIT Press.

Underwood, B. J. (1964). The representativeness of rote verbal learning. In A. W. Melton (Ed.), *Categories of human learning*. New York: Academic Press.

Van Gelder, T., & Port, R. F. (1995). It's about time. In R. F. Port & T. Van Gelder (Eds.) (1995). *Mind as motion: Explorations in the dynamics of cognition*. Cambridge, MA: MIT Press.

Van Lehn, K. (1988). Student modeling. In M. C. Polson & J. J. Richardson (Eds.), *Foundations of intelligent tutoring systems*. Hillsdale, NJ: Lawrence Erlbaum.

Varela, F. J., Thompson, E., & Rosch, E. (1991). *The embodied mind*. Cambridge, MA: MIT Press.

Vekiri, I. (2002). What is the value of graphical displays in learning? *Educational Psychology Review, 14*(3), 261-312.

Von Uexküll, J. (1934). A stroll through the worlds of animals and men. In K. Lashley (Ed.), *Instinctive behavior*. New York: International Universities Press.

Vosniadou, S. (1994). Conceptual change in the physical sciences. *Learning and Instruction, 4*(1), 45-69.

Weinberger, N. M. (1993). Learning-induced changes of auditory receptive fields. *Current opinion in neurobiology, 3*, 570-577.

Wenger, E. (1987). *Artificial intelligence and tutoring systems*. Los Altos, CA: Morgan Kaufman.

Wertheimer, M. (1924/1955). Gestalt theory. In W. D. Ellis (Ed.), *A source book of Gestalt psychology*. New York: The Humanities Press.

Wertheimer, M. (1938). *Laws of organization in perceptual forms in a source book for Gestalt psychology*. London: Routledge and Kegan Paul.

White, B. Y., & Frederiksen, J. R. (1998). Inquiry, modeling and metacognition: Making science accessible to all students. *Cognition and Instruction, 16*, 13-117.

Willows, D. H., & Houghton, H. A. (Eds.) (1987). *The psychology of illustration. Volume 1*. New York: Springer.

Wilson, E. O. (1998). *Consilience*. New York: Random House.

Windschitl, M., & André, T. (1998). Using computer simulations to enhance conceptual change: The roles of constructivist instruction and student epistemological beliefs. *Journal of Research in Science Teaching, 35*(2), 145-160.

Winn, W. D. (1975). An open system model of learning. *AV Communication Review, 23*, 5-33.

Winn, W. D. (1980). The effect of block-word diagrams on the structuring of science concepts as a function of general ability. *Journal of Research in Science Teaching, 17*, 201-211.

Winn, W. D. (1980). Visual Information Processing: A Pragmatic Approach to the "Imagery Question." *Educational Communication and Technology Journal, 28*, 120-133.

Winn, W. D. (1982). Visualization in learning and instruction: A cognitive approach. *Educational Communication and Technology Journal, 30*, 3-25.

Winn, W. D. (1986). Knowledge of task, ability and strategy in processing letter patterns. *Perceptual and Motor Skills, 63*, 726.

Winn, W. D. (1987). Instructional design and intelligent systems: Shifts in the designer's decision-making role. *Instructional Science, 16*, 59-77.

Winn, W. D. (1989a). Toward a rationale and theoretical basis for educational technology. *Educational Technology Research and Development, 37*, 35-46.

Winn, W. D. (1989b). The design and use of instructional graphics. In H. Mandl and J. R. Levin (Eds.). *Knowledge acquisition from text and pictures*. North Holland: Elsevier.

Winn, W. D. (1990). Some implications of cognitive theory for instructional design. *Instructional Science, 19*, 53-69.

Winn, W. D. (1993a). *A conceptual basis for educational applications of virtual reality*. Human Interface Technology Laboratory Technical Report. Seattle, WA: Human Interface Technology Laboratory.

Winn, W. D. (1993b). A constructivist critique of the assumptions of instructional design. In T. M. Duffy, J. Lowyck, & D. H. Jonassen

(Eds.), *Designing environments for constructive learning*. New York: Springer.

Winn, W. D. (2002). Current trends in educational technology research: The study of learning environments. *Educational Psychology Review, 14*(3), 331-351.

Winn, W. D., Hoffman, H., & Osberg, K. (1991). Semiotics, cognitive theory and the design of objects, actions and interactions in virtual environments. *Journal of Structural Learning and Intelligent Systems, 14*(1), 29-49.

Winn, W. D., Li, T-Z., & Schill, D. E. (1991). Diagrams as aids to problem solving: Their role in facilitating search and computation. *Educational Technology Research and Development, 39,* 17-29.

Winn, W. D., & Solomon, C. (1993). The effect of the spatial arrangement of simple diagrams on the interpretation of English and nonsense sentences. *Educational Technology Research and Development, 41,* 29-41.

Winn, W. D., & Windschitl, M. (2001a). Learning in artificial environments. *Cybernetics and Human Knowing, 8*(3), 5-23.

Winn, W. D., & Windschitl, M. (2001b). Learning science in virtual environments: The interplay of theory and experience. *Themes in Education, 1*(4), 373-389.

Winn, W. D., & Windschitl, M. (2002, April). *Strategies used by university students to learn aspects of physical oceanography in a virtual environment*. Paper presented at the annual meeting of the American Educational Research Association, New Orleans, LA.

Winn, W. D., Windschitl, M., Fruland, R., & Lee, Y-L (2002, April). *Features of virtual environments that contribute to students' understanding of earth science*. Paper presented at the Annual Meeting of the National Association for Research in Science Teaching, New Orleans, LA.

Yates, F. A. (1966). *The art of memory*. Chicago: University of Chicago Press.

Wolfram, S. (2002). *A new kind of science*. Champaign, IL: Wolfram Media Inc.

Zuchermaglio, C. (1993). Toward a cognitive ergonomics of educational technology. In T. M. Duffy, J. Lowyck, & D. H. Jonassen (Eds.), *Designing environments for constructive learning*. New York: Springer.

·5·

TOWARD A SOCIOLOGY OF EDUCATIONAL TECHNOLOGY

Stephen T. Kerr
University of Washington

5.1 PREFACE TO THE REVISED EDITION

By its nature, technology changes constantly. Technology in education is no different. At the time the original version of this chapter was prepared, the Internet was still the exclusive province of academic and a few educational enthusiasts; distance education was a clumsy congeries of TV broadcasts, correspondence, and the occasional e-mail discussion group; discussions of inequalities in how educational technology was used focused mostly on the mechanics of distribution of and access to hardware; perhaps most saliently, the developing wave of constructivist notions about education had not yet extended far into the examination of technology itself.

Internet connectivity and use in schools became a major issue in 1996 during the U.S. presidential campaign that year, and later became a central political initiative for the U.S. Government, with considerable success (PCAST, 1997; ISET, 2002). At about the same time, distance learning, as delivered via online environments, suddenly came to be seen as the wave of the future for higher education and corporate training, and was also the source for some of the inflated stock market hopes for "dot-com" companies in the late 1990s. As access to computers and networks became more affordable, those interested in the "digital divide" began to switch their attention from simple access to less tractable issues such as how technology might be involved in generating "cultural capital" among the disadvantaged. The intervening years have also witnessed emerging concerns about how technology seems to be calling into questions long-standing basic assumptions about educational technology: for example, might on-line learning in fact turn out to be less dehumanizing than sitting in a large lecture class? All the issues noted here are addressed in this revision.

5.2 INTRODUCTION

Common images of technology, including educational technology, highlight its rational, ordered, controlled aspects. These are the qualities that many observers see as its advantages, the qualities that encouraged the United States to construct ingenious railway systems in the last century, to develop a national network of telegraph and telephone communication, and later to blanket the nation with television signals. In the American mind, technology seems to be linked with notions of efficiency and progress; it is a distinguishing and pre-eminent value, a characteristic of the way Americans perceive the world in general, and the possible avenues for resolving social problems in particular (Boorstin, 1973; Segal, 1985).

Education is one of those arenas in which Americans have long assumed that technological solutions might bring increased efficiency, order, and productivity. Our current interest in computers and multi-media was preceded by a century of experimentation with precisely articulated techniques for organizing school practice, carefully specific approaches to the design of school buildings (down to the furniture they would contain), and an abiding enthusiasm for systematic methods of presenting textual and visual materials (Godfrey, 1965; Saettler, 1968).

There was a kind of mechanistic enthusiasm about many of these efforts. If we could just find the right approach, the thinking seemed to go, we could address the problems of schooling and improve education immensely. The world of the student, the classroom, the school was, in this interpretation, a machine (perhaps a computer), needing only the right program to run smoothly.

But technology frequently has effects in areas other than those intended by its creators. Railroads were not merely a better way to move goods across the country; they also brought standard time and a leveling of regional and cultural differences. Telephones allowed workers in different locations to speak with each other, but also changed the ways workplaces were organized and the image of what office work was. Television altered the political culture of the country in ways we still struggle to comprehend. Those who predicted the social effects that might flow from these new technologies typically either missed entirely, or foresaw inaccurately, what their impact might be.

Similarly with schools and education, the focus of researchers interested in educational technology has usually been on what is perceived to be the outcome of these approaches on what is thought of as their principal target—learning by pupils. Occasionally, other topics related to the way technology is perceived and used have been studied. Attitudes and opinions by teachers and principals about the use of computers are an example. Generally, however, there have been few attempts to limn a "sociology of educational technology" (exceptions: Hlynka & Belland, 1991; Kerr & Taylor, 1985. In their 1992 review, Scott, Cole, and Engel also went beyond traditional images to focus on what they called a "cultural constructivist perspective.") The task here, then, has these parts: to say what ought to be included under such a rubric; to review the relatively small number of works from within the field that touch upon these issues; and the larger number of works from related fields or on related topics that may be productive in helping us to think about a sociology of educational technology; and finally, to consider future directions for work in this field.

5.2.1 What to Include?

To decide what we should consider under the suggested heading of a "sociology of educational technology" we need to think about two sets of issues: those that are important to sociologists, and those that are important to educators and to educational technologists. Sociology is concerned with many things, but if there is a primary assertion, it is that we cannot adequately explain social phenomena if we look only at individuals. Rather, we must examine how people interact in group settings, and how those settings create, shape, and constrain individual action.

Defining what is central to educators (including educational technologists) is also difficult, but central is probably (to borrow a sociological term) cultural reproduction—the passing on to the next generation of values, skills, knowledge that are judged to be critical, and the improvement of the general condition of society. Three aspects of this vision of education are important here: first, interactions and relationships among educators, students, administrators, parents, community members, and others who define what education is to be ("what happens in schools and classrooms?"); second, attempts to deal with perceived social problems and inequities, and thus provide a better life for the next generation ("what happens after they finish school?"); and third, efforts to reshape the educational system itself, so that it carries out its work in new ways and thus contributes to social improvement ("how should we arrange the system to do its work?").

The questions about educational technology's social effects that will be considered here, then, are principally those relating (or potentially relating) to what sociologists call collectivities—groups of individuals (teachers, students, administrators, parents), organizations, and social movements.

5.2.1.1 Sociology of Organizations. If our primary interest is in how educational technology affects the ways that people work together in schools, then what key topics ought we to consider? Certainly a prime focus must be organizations, the ways that schools and other educating institutions are structured so as to carry out their work. It is important to note that we can use the term "organization" to refer to more than the administration of schools or universities. It can also refer to the organization of classrooms, of interactions among students or among teachers, of the ways individuals seek to shape their work environment to accomplish particular ends, and so forth.

Organizational sociology is a well-established field, and there have been some studies on educational organizations. Subparts of this field include the functioning of schools as bureaucracies; the ways in which new organizational forms are born, live, and die; the expectations of actors within the school setting of themselves and of each other (in sociological terms, the roles they play); and the sources of power and control that support various organizational forms.

5.2.1.2 Sociology of Groups and Classes. A second focus of our review here will regard the sociology of groups, including principally groups of ascription (that one is either born into or to which one is assumed to belong by virtue of one's position), but also those of affiliation (groups which one voluntarily joins, or comes to be connected with via one's efforts or work). Important here are the ways that education deals with such groups as those based on gender, class, and race, and how educational technology interacts with those groupings. While this topic has not been central in studies of educational technology, the review here will seek to suggest its importance and the value of further efforts to study it.

5.2.1.3 Sociology of Social Movements. Finally, we will need to consider the sociology of social movements and social change. Social institutions change under certain circumstances, and education is currently in a period where large changes are being suggested from a variety of quarters. Educational technology is often perceived as a harbinger or facilitator of educational change, and so it makes sense for us to examine the sociological literature on these questions and thus try to determine where and how such changes take place, what their relationships are to other shifts in the society, economy, or polity, etc.

Another aspect of education as a social movement, and of educational technology's place there, is what we might call the role of ideology. By ideology here is meant not an explicit, comprehensive and enforced code of beliefs and practices to which all members of a group are held, but rather a set of implicit, often vague, but widely shared set of expectations and assumptions about the social order. Essential here are such issues as the values that technology carries with it, its presumed contribution to the common good, and how it is perceived to interact with individuals' plans and goals.

5.2.1.4 *Questions of Sociological Method.* As a part of considering these questions, we will also examine briefly some questions of sociological method. Many sociological studies in education are conducted via surveys or questionnaires, instruments that were originally designed as sociological research tools. Inasmuch as sociologists have accumulated considerable experience in working with these methods, we need to note both the advantages and the problems of using such methods. Given especially the popularity of opinion surveys in education, it will be especially important to review the problem of attitudes versus actions ("what people say vs. what they do").

A further question of interest for educational technologists has to do with the "stance" or position of the researcher. Most of the studies of attitudes and opinions that have been done in educational technology assume that the researcher stands in a neutral position, "outside the fray." Some examples from sociological research using the ethnomethodological paradigm are introduced, and their possible significance for further work on educational technology are considered.

The conclusion seeks to bring the discussion back specifically to the field of educational technology by asking how the effects surveyed in the preceding sections might play out in real school situations. How might educational technology affect the organization of classes, schools, education as a social institution? How might the fates of particular groups (women, minorities) intersect with they ways educational technology is or is not used within schools? And finally, how might the prospects for long-term change in education as a social institution be altered by educational technology?

5.3 SOCIOLOGY AND ITS CONCERNS: A CONCERN FOR COLLECTIVE ACTION

In the United States, most writing about education has had a distinctly psychological tone. This is in contrast with what is the case in certain other developed countries, especially England and Western Europe, where there is a much stronger tradition of thinking about education not merely as a matter of concern for the individual, but also as a general *social* phenomenon, a matter of interest for the state and polity. Accordingly, it is appropriate that we review here briefly the principal focus of sociology as a field, and describe how it may be related to another field that in America has been studied almost exclusively through the disciplinary lenses of psychology.

Sociology as a discipline appeared during the nineteenth century in response to serious tensions within the existing social structure. The industrial revolution had wrought large shifts in relationships among individuals, and especially in the relationships among different social groups. Marx's interest in class antagonisms, Weber's focus on social and political structure under conditions of change, Durkheim's investigations of the sense of "anomie" (alienation; something seen as prevalent in the new social order)—all these concerns were born of the shifts that were felt especially strongly as Western social life changed under the impact of the industrial revolution.

The questions of how individuals define their lives together, and how those definitions, once set in place and commonly accepted, constrain individuals' actions and life courses, formed the basis of early sociological inquiry. In many ways, these are the same questions that continue to interest sociologists today. What determines how and why humans organize themselves and their actions in particular ways? What effects do those organizations have on thought and action? And what limitations might those organizations impose on human action?

If psychology focuses on the individual, the internal processes of cognition and motives for action that individuals experience, then sociology focuses most of all on the ways people interact as members of organizations or groups, how they form new groups, and how their status as members of one or another group affects how they live and work. The "strong claim" of sociologists might be put simply as "settings have plans for us." That is, the social and organizational contexts of actions may be more important to explaining what people do than their individual motivations and internal states. How this general concern for collective action plays out is explored below in relation to each of three topics of general concern here: organizations, groups, and social change.

5.3.1 Sociology of Organizations

Schools and other educational enterprises are easily thought of as organizations, groups of people intentionally brought together to accomplish some specific purpose. Education as a social institution has existed in various forms over historical time, but only in the last 150 years or so has it come to have a distinctive and nearly universal organizational form. Earlier societies had ways to ensure that young people were provided with appropriate cultural values (enculturation), with specific forms of behavior and outlooks that would allow them to function successfully in a given society (socialization), and with training needed to earn a living (observation and participation, formal apprenticeship, or formal schooling). But only recently have we come to think of education as necessarily a social institution characterized by specific organizational forms (schools, teachers, curricula, standards, laws, procedures for moving from one part of the system to another, etc.)

The emphasis here on education as a social organization leads us to three related sub-questions that we will consider in more detail later. These include: first, how does the fact that the specific organizational structure of schools is usually bureaucratic in form affect what goes on (and can go on) there, and how does educational technology enter into these relationships? Second, how are social roles defined for individuals and members of groups in schools, and how does educational technology affect the definition of those roles? And third, how does the organizational structure of schools change, and how does educational technology interact with those processes of organizational change? Each of these questions will be introduced briefly here, and treated in more depth in following sections.

5.3.1.1 *Organizations and Bureaucracy.* The particulars of school organizational structure are a matter of interest, for schools and universities have most frequently been organized as bureaucracies. That is, they develop well-defined sets of procedures for processing students, for dealing with teachers and other staff, and for addressing the public. These procedures deal with who is to be allowed to participate (rules for qualification, admission, assignment, and so forth), what will happen to them while they are part of the system (curricular standards, textbook selection policies, rules for teacher certification, student conduct, etc.), how the system will define that its work has been completed (requirements for receiving credit, graduation requirements, tests, etc.), as well as with how the system itself is to be run (administrator credentialing, governance structures, rules for financial transactions, relations among various parts of the system—accreditation, state vs. local vs. federal responsibility, etc.). Additional procedures may deal with such issues as how the public may participate in the life of the institution, how disputes are to be resolved, and how rewards and punishments are to be decided upon and distributed (Bidwell, 1965). Educational organizations are thus participating in the continuing transition from what German sociologists called "gemeinschaft" to "gesellschaft," from an earlier economic and social milieu defined by close familial bonds, personal relationships, and a small and caring community, to a milieu defined by ties to impersonal groups, centrally mandated standards and requirements, and large, bureaucratic organizations.

While bureaucratic forms of organization are not necessarily bad (and indeed were seen in the past century as a desirable antidote to personalized, arbitrary, corrupt, social forms), the current popular image of bureaucracy is exceedingly negative. The disciplined and impersonal qualities of the bureaucrat, admired in the last century, are now frequently seen as ossified, irrelevant, a barrier to needed change.

A significant question may therefore be, "What are the conditions that encourage bureaucratic systems, especially in education, to become more flexible, more responsive?" And since educational technology is often portrayed as a solution to the problems of bureaucracy, we need to ask about the evidence regarding technology and its impact on bureaucracies.

5.3.1.2 *Organizations and Social Roles.* To understand how organizations work, we need to understand not only the formal structure of the organization, the "organization chart." We also need to see the independent "life" of the organization as expressed and felt through such mechanisms as social and organizational roles. Roles have long been a staple of sociological study, but they are often misunderstood. A role is not merely a set of responsibilities that one person (say, a manager or administrator) in a social setting defines for another person (e.g., a worker, perhaps a teacher). Rather, it is better thought of as a set of interconnected expectations that participants in a given social setting have for their own and others' behaviors. Teachers expect students to act in certain ways, and students do the same for teachers, principals expect teachers to do thus and so, and teachers have similar expectations of principals. Roles, then, are best conceived of as "emergent properties" of social systems—they appear not in isolation, but rather when people interact and try to accomplish something together. Entire systems of social analysis (such as that proposed by George Herbert Mead (1934) under the rubric "symbolic interactionism") have been built on this basic set of ideas.

Educational institutions are the site for an extensive set of social roles, including those of teacher, student/pupil, administrator, staff professional, parent, future or present employer, and community member. Each of these roles is further ramified by the perceived positions and values held by the group with respect to which a member of a subject group is acting (for example, teachers' roles include not only expectations for their own activities, but also their perceptions of the values and positions of students, how they expect students to act, etc.). Especially significant are the ways in which the role of the teacher may be affected by the introduction of educational technology into a school, or the formal or informal redefinition of job responsibilities following such introduction. How educational roles emerge and are modified through interaction, how new roles come into existence, and how educational technology may affect those processes, then, are all legitimate subjects for our attention here.

5.3.1.3 *Organizations and Organizational Change.* A further question of interest to sociologists is how organizations change. New organizations are constantly coming into being, old ones disappear, and existing ones change their form and functions. How this happens, what models or metaphors best describe these processes, and how organizations seek to assure their success through time have all been studied extensively in sociology. There have been numerous investigations of innovation in organizations, as well as of innovation strategies, barriers to change, and so forth.

In education, these issues have been of special concern, for the persistent image of educational institutions has been one of unresponsive bureaucracies. Specific studies of educational innovation are therefore of interest to us here, with particular reference to how educational technology may interact with these processes.

5.3.2 Sociology of Groups

Our second major rubric involves groups, group membership, and the significance of group membership for an individual's life chances. Sociologists study all manner of groups—formal and informal, groups of affiliation (which one joins voluntarily) and ascription (which one is a member of by virtue of birth, position, class), and so on. The latter kinds of groups, in which one's membership is not a matter of one's own choosing, have been of special interest to sociologists in this century. This interest has been especially strong since social barriers of race, gender, and class are no longer seen as immutable but rather as legitimate topics for state concern. As the focus of sociologists on mechanisms of social change has grown over the past decades, so has their interest in defining how group membership affects the life chances of individuals, and in prescribing actions official institutions (government, schools, etc.) might take to lessen the negative impact of ascriptive membership on individuals' futures.

Current discussion of education has often focused on the success of the system in enabling individuals to transcend the boundaries imposed by race, gender, and class. The pioneering work by James Coleman in the 1960s (Coleman, 1966) on race and educational outcomes was critical to changing how Americans thought about integration of schools. Work by Carol Gilligan (Gilligan, Lyons, & Hanmer, 1990) and others starting in the 1980s on the fate of women in education has led to a new awareness of the gender nonneutrality of many schooling practices. The continuing importance of class is a topic of interest for a number of sociologists and social critics who frequently view the schooling system more as a mechanism for social reproduction than for social change (Apple, 1988; Giroux, 1981; Spring, 1989). These issues are of major importance for how we think about education in a changing democracy, and so we need to ask how educational technology may either contribute to the problems themselves, or to their solution.

5.3.3 Sociology of Social Change and Social Movements

A third large concern of sociologists has been the issue of social stability and social change. The question has been addressed variously since the days of Karl Marx, whose vision posited the inevitability of a radical reconstruction of society based on scientific "laws" of historical and economic development, class identification, and class conflict via newly mobilized social movements. Social change is of no less importance to those who seek not to change, but to preserve the social order. Talcott Parsons, an American sociologist of the middle of this century, is perhaps unjustly criticized of being a conservative, but he discussed in detail how particular social forms and institutions could be viewed as performing a function of "pattern maintenance" (Parsons, 1949, 1951).

Current concerns about social change are perhaps less apocalyptic today than they were for Marx, but in some quarters are viewed as no less critical. In particular, educational institutions are increasingly seen as one of the few places where society can exert leverage to bring about desired changes in the social and economic order. Present fears about "global economic competitiveness" are a good case in point; it is clear that for many policy makers, the primary task of schools in the current economic environment ought to be to produce an educated citizenry capable of competing with other nations. But other voices in education stress the importance of the educational system in conserving social values, passing on traditions. A variety of social movements have emerged in support of both these positions. Both positions contain a kernel that is essentially ideological—a set of assumptions, values, positions as regards the individual and society. These ideologies are typically implicit, and thus rarely are articulated openly. Nonetheless, identifying them is especially important to a deeper understanding of the questions involved.

It is reasonable for us to ask how sociologists have viewed social change, what indicators are seen as being most reliable in predicting how social change may take place, and what role social movements (organized groups in support of particular changes) may have in bringing change about. If education is to be viewed as a primary engine for such change, and if educational technology is seen by some as a principal part of that engine, then we need to understand how and why such changes may take place, and what role technology may rightly be expected to play. This raises in turn the issue of educational technology as a social and political movement itself, and of its place vis à vis other organizations in the general sphere of education. The ideological underpinnings of technology in education are also important to consider. The values and assumptions of both supporters and critics of technology's use in education bear careful inspection if we are to see clearly the possible place for educational technology.

The following section offers a detailed look at the sociology of organizations, the sociology of school organization and of organizational roles and the influences of educational technology on that organization. Historical studies of the impact of technology on organizational structures are also considered to provide a different perspective on how organizations change.

5.4 SOCIOLOGICAL STUDIES OF EDUCATION AND TECHNOLOGY: THE SOCIOLOGY OF ORGANIZATIONS

Schools are many things, but (at least since the end of the nineteenth century) they have been organizations—intentionally created groups of people pursuing common purposes, and standing in particular relation to other groups and social institutions; within the organization, there are consistent understandings of what the organization's purposes are, and participants stand in relatively well-defined positions vis à vis each other (e.g., the roles of teachers, student, parent, etc.) Additionally, the organization possesses a technical structure for carrying out its work (classes, textbooks, teacher certification), seeks to define job responsibilities so that tasks are accomplished, and has mechanisms for dealing with the outside world (PTSA meetings, committees on textbook adoption, legislative lobbyists, school board meetings).

Sociology has approached the study of organizations in a number of ways. Earlier studies stressed the formal features of organizations, and described their internal functioning and the relationships among participants within the bounds of the organization itself. Over the past twenty years or so, however, a new perspective has emerged, one that sees the organization in the context of its surrounding environment (Aldrich & Marsden, 1988). Major issues in the study of organizations using the environmental or organic approach include the factors that give rise of organizational diversity, and those connected with change in the organization.

Perhaps it is obvious that questions of organizational change and organizational diversity are pertinent to the study of how educational technology has come to be used, or may be used, in educational environments, but let us use the sociological lens to examine why this is so. Schools as organizations are increasingly under pressure from outside social groups and from political and economic structures. Among the criticisms constantly leveled at the schools are that they are too hierarchical, too bureaucratized, and that current organizational patterns make changing the system almost impossible. (Whether these perceptions are in fact warranted is entirely another issue, one that we will not address here; see Carson, Huelskamp, & Woodall, 1991). We might reasonably ask whether we should be focusing attention on the organizational structure of schools as they are, rather than discuss desirable alternatives. Suffice it to say that massive change in an existing social institution, such as the schools, is difficult to undertake in a controlled, conscious way.

Those who suggest (e.g., Perelman, 1992) that schools as institutions will soon "wither away" are unaware of the historical flexibility of schools as organizations (Cuban, 1984; Tyack, 1974), and of the strong social pressures that militate for preservation of the existing institutional structure. The perspective here, then, is much more on how the existing structure of the social organizations we call schools can be affected in desirable ways, and so the issue of organizational change (rather than that of organizational generation) will be a major focus in what follows.

To make this review cohere, we will start by surveying what sociologists know about organizations generally, including specifically bureaucratic forms of organization. We will then consider the evidence regarding technology's impact on organizational structure in general, and on bureaucratic organization in particular. We will then proceed to a consideration of schools as a specific type of organization, and concentrate on recent attempts to redefine patterns of school organization. Finally, we will consider how educational technology relates to school organization, and to attempts to change that organization and the roles of those who work in schools.

5.4.1 Organizations: Two Sociological Perspectives

Much recent sociological work on the nature of organizations starts from the assumption that organizations are best studied and understood as parts of an environment. If organizations exist within a distinctive environment, then what aspects of that environment should be most closely examined? Sociologists have answered this question in two different ways: for some, the key features are the resources and information that may be used rationally within the organization or exchanged with other organizations within the environment; for others, the essential focus is on the cultural surround that determines and moderates the organization's possible courses of action in ways that are more subtle, less deterministic than the resources-information perspective suggests. While there are many exceptions, it is probably fair to say that the resources-information approach has been more often used in analyses of commercial organizations, and the latter, cultural approach used in studies of public and nonprofit organizations.

The environmental view of organizations has been especially fruitful in studies of organizational change. The roles of outside normative groups such as professional associations or state legislatures, for example, were stressed by DiMaggio and Powell (1983; see also Meyer & Scott, 1983) who noted that the actions of such groups tend to reduce organizational heterogeneity in the environment and thus inhibit change. While visible alternative organizational patterns may provide models for organizational change, other organizations in the same general field exert a counterinfluence by supporting commonly accepted practices and demanding that alternative organizations adhere to those models, even when the alternative organization might not be required to do so. For example, an innovative school may be forced to modify its record-keeping practices so as to match more closely "how others do it" (Rothschild-Whitt, 1979).

How organizations react to outside pressure for change has also been studied. There is considerable disagreement as to whether such pressures result in dynamic transformation via the work of attentive leaders, or whether organizational inertia is more generally characteristic of organizations' reaction to outside pressures (Astley & Van de Ven, 1983; Hrebiniak & Joyce, 1985; Romanelli, 1991). Mintzberg (1979) suggested that there might be a trade-off here: large organizations have the potential to change rapidly to meet new pressures (but only is they use appropriately their large and differentiated staffs, better forecasting abilities, etc.; small organizations can respond to outside pressures if they capitalize on their more flexible structure and relative lack of established routines.

Organizations face a number of common problems, including how to assess their effectiveness. Traditional evaluation studies have assumed that organizational goals can be relatively precisely defined, outcomes can be measured, and standards for success agreed upon by the parties involved (McLaughlin, 1987). More recent approaches suggest that examination of the "street-level" evaluation methods used by those who work within an organization may provide an additional, useful perspective on organizational effectiveness (Anspach, 1991). For example, "dramatic incidents," even though they are singularities, may define effectiveness or its lack for some participants.

5.4.2 Bureaucracy as a Condition of Organizations

We need to pay special attention to the particular form of organization we call bureaucracy, since this is a central feature of school environments where educational technology is often used. The emergence of this pattern as a primary way for assuring that policies are implemented and that some degree of accountability is guaranteed lies in the nineteenth century (Peabody & Rourke, 1965; Waldo, 1952). Max Weber described the conditions under which social organizations would move away from direct, personalized, or "charismatic" control, and toward bureaucratic and administrative control (Weber, 1978).

The problem with bureaucracy, as anyone who has ever stood in line at a state office can attest, is that the organization's workers soon seem to focus exclusively on the rules and procedures established to provide accountability and control, rather than on the people or problems the bureaucratic system ostensibly exists to address (Herzfeld, 1992). The tension for the organization and those who work therein is between commitment to a particular leader, who may want to focus on people or problems, and commitment to a self-sustaining system with established mechanisms for assuring how decisions are made and how individuals work within the organization, and which will likely continue to exist after a particular leader is gone. In this sense, one might view many of the current problems in schools and concerns with organizational reform (especially from the viewpoint of teachers) as attempts to move toward a more collegial mode of control and governance (Waters, 1993). We will return to this theme of reform and change in the context of school bureaucratic structures below when we deal more explicitly with the concepts of social change and social movements.

5.4.3 Technology and Organizations

Our intent here is not merely to review what current thinking is regarding schools as organizations, but also to say something about how the use of educational technology within schools might affect or be affected by those patterns of organization. Before we can address those issues, however, we must first consider how technology has been seen as affecting organizational structure generally. In other words, schools aside, is there any consensus on how technology affects the life of organizations, or the course of their development? While the issue would appear to be a significant one, and while there have been a good many general discussions of the potential impact of technology on organizations and the individuals who work there (e.g., McKinlay & Starkey, 1998; Naisbitt & Aburdene, 1990; Toffler, 1990), there is remarkably little consensus about what precisely the nature of such impacts may be. Indeed, Americans seem to have a deep ambivalence about technology: some see it as villain and scapegoat, others stress its role in social progress (Florman, 1981; Pagels, 1988; Segal, 1985; Winner, 1986).

Some of these concerns stem from the difficulty of keeping technology under social control once it has been introduced (Glendenning, 1990; Steffen, 1993 especially chapters 3, 5). Perrow (1984) suggests that current technological systems are so complex and "interactive" (showing tight relationship among parts) that accidents and problems cannot be avoided—they are, in effect, no longer accidents but an inevitable consequence of our limited ability to predict what can go wrong. Even the systems approach, popularized after World War II as a generic approach to ferreting out interconnections in complex environments (including in education and educational technology), lost favor as complexity proved extraordinarily difficult to model effectively (Hughes & Hughes, 2000).

5.4.3.1   Historical Studies of Technology.   As a framework for considering how technology affects or may affect organizational life, it may be useful to consider specific examples of earlier technological advances now seen to have altered social and organizational life in particular ways. A problem here is that initial prognoses for a technology's effects—indeed, the very reason a technology is developed in the first place—are often radically different from the ways in which a technology actually comes to be used. Few of those who witnessed the development of assembly line manufacture, for example, had any idea of the import of the changes they were witnessing; although these shifts were perceived as miraculous and sometimes frightening, they were rarely seen as threatening the social status quo (Jennings, 1985; Marvin, 1988).

Several specific technologies illustrate the ways initial intentions for a technology often translate over time into unexpected organizational and social consequences. The development of printing, for example, not only lowered the cost, increased

the accuracy, and improved the efficiency of producing individual copies of written materials; it also had profound organizational impact on how governments were structured and did their work. Governments began to demand more types of information from local administrators, and to circulate and use that information in pursuit of national goals (Boorstin, 1983; Darnton, 1984; Eisenstein, 1979; Febvre & Martin, 1958; Kilgour, 1998; and Luke, 1989).

The telephone offers another example of a technology that significantly changed the organization of work in offices. Bell's original image of telephonic communication foresaw repetitive contacts among a few key points, rather than the multipoint networked system we see today, and when Bell offered the telephone patents to William Orton, President of Western Union, Orton remarked, "What use could this company make of an electrical toy?" (Aronson, 1977). But the telephone brought a rapid reconceptualization of the workplace; after its development, the "information workers" of the day—newspaper reporters, financial managers, and so forth—no longer needed to be clustered together so tightly. Talking on the telephone also established patterns of communication that were more personal, less dense and formal (de Sola Pool, 1977).

Chester Carlson, an engineer then working for a small company called Haloid, developed in 1938 a process for transferring images from one sheet of paper to another based on principles of electrical charge. Carlson's process, and the company that would become Xerox, also altered the organization of office life, perhaps in more local ways than the telephone. Initial estimates forecast only the "primary" market for Xerox copies, and ignored the large number of extra copies of reports that would be made and sent to a colleague in the next office, a friend, someone in a government agency or university. This "secondary market" for copies turned out to be many times larger than the "primary market" for original copies, and the resulting dissemination of information has brought workers into closer contact with colleagues, given them easier access to information, and provided for more rapid circulation of information (Mort, 1989; Owen, 1986).

The impact of television on our forms of organizational life is difficult to document, though many have tried. Marshall McLuhan and his followers have suggested that television brought a view of the world that breaks down traditional social constructs. Among the effects noted by some analysts are the new position occupied by political figures (more readily accessible, less able to hide failures and problems from the electorate), changing relationships among parents and children (lack of former separation between adult and children's worlds), and shifts in relationships among the sexes (disappearance of formerly exclusively "male" and "female" domains of social action; Meyrowitz, 1985).

Process technologies may also have unforeseen organizational consequences, as seen in mass production via the assembly line. Production on the assembly line rationalized production of manufactured goods, improved their quality, and lowered prices. It also led to anguish in the form of worker alienation, and thus contributed to the development of socialism and Marxism, and to the birth of militant labor unions in the United States and abroad, altering forms of organization within factories and the nature of worker-management relationships (Boorstin, 1973; Hounshell, 1984; Smith, 1981. See also Bartky, 1990, on the introduction of standard time; and Norberg, 1990, on the advent of punch card technology).

5.4.3.2 Information Technology and Organizations.

Many have argued that information technology will flatten organizational hierarchies and provide for more democratic forms of management; Shoshana Zuboff's study of how workers and managers in a number of corporate environments reacted to the introduction of computer-based manufacturing processes is one of the few empirically based studies to examine this issue (Zuboff, 1988). However, some have argued from the opposite stance that computerization in fact strengthens existing hierarchies and encourages top-down control (Evans, 1991). Still others (Winston, 1986) have argued that information technology has had minimal impact on the structure of work and organizations, or that information networks still necessarily rely at some level on human workers (Downey, 2001; Orr, 1996). Kling (1991) found remarkably little evidence of radical change in social patterns from empirical studies, noting that while computerization had led to increased worker responsibility and satisfaction in some settings, in others it had resulted in decreased interaction. He also indicated that computer systems are often merely "instruments in power games played by local governments" (p. 35; see also Danziger & Kraemer, 1986).

One significant reason for the difficulty in defining technology's effects is that the variety of work and work environments across organizations is so great (Palmquist, 1992). It is difficult to compare, for example, the record-keeping operation of a large hospital, the manufacturing division of a major automobile producer, and the diverse types of activities that teachers and school principals typically undertake. And even between similar environments in the same industry, the way in which jobs are structured and carried out may be significantly different. Some sociologists have concluded that it may therefore only make sense to study organizational impacts of technology on the micro level, i.e., within the subunits of a particular environment (Comstock & Scott, 1977; Scott, 1975, 1987).

Defining and predicting the organizational context of a new technology on such a local level has also proven difficult; it is extraordinarily complex to define the web of social intents, perceptions, decisions, reactions, group relations, and organizational settings into which a new technology will be cast. Those who work using this framework (e.g., Bijker, Hughes, & Pinch, 1987; Fulk, 1993; Joerges, 1990; Nartonis, 1993) often try to identify the relationships among the participants in a given setting, and then on that basis try to define the meaning that a technology has for them, rather than focus on the impact of a particular kind of hardware on individuals' work in isolation.

A further aspect of the social context of technology has to do with the relative power and position of the actors involved. Langdon Winner (1980) argues that technologies are in fact not merely tools, but have their political and social meanings "built in" by virtue of the ways we define, design, and use them. A classic example for Winner is the network of freeways designed by civil engineer Robert Moses for the New York City metropolitan region in the 1930s. The bridges that spanned the new arterials that led to public beaches were too low to allow passage by city buses, thus keeping *hoi polloi* away from the ocean front, while at the same time welcoming the more affluent, newly mobile (car-owning) middle class. The design itself, rather than the hardware of bridge decks, roads, and beach access points, defined what could later be done with the system once it had been built and put into use. Similar effects of predisposition-through-design, Winner argues, are to be found in nuclear power plants and nuclear fuel reprocessing facilities (Winner, 1977, 1993).

Many of these difficulties in determining how information technology interacts with organizations stem from the fact that our own stances as analysts contribute to the problem, as do our memberships in groups that promote or oppose particular (often technological) solutions to problems, as do the activities of those groups themselves in furtherance of their own positions. Technology creates artifacts which rarely stay in exactly the same form in which they were first created—their developers, and others interested, push these artifacts to evolve in new directions. These facets of information technology are reflections of a view of the field characterized as "the Social Construction of Technology" (SCOT), which has been hotly debated for the past 15 years (Bijker & Pinch, 2002; Clayton, 2002; Epperson, 2002).

5.4.3.3 Technology and Bureaucracy.

One persistent view of technology's role within organizations is as a catalyst for overcoming centralized bureaucratic inertia (Rice, 1992; Sproull & Kiesler, 1991a). Electronic mail is widely reputed to provide a democratizing and leveling influence in large bureaucracies; wide access to electronic databases within organizations may provide opportunities for whistle blowers to identify and expose problems; the rapid collection and dissemination of information on a variety of organizational activities may allow both workers and managers to see how productive they are, and where changes might lead to improvement (Sproull & Kiesler, 1991b). While the critics are equally vocal in pointing out technology's potential organizational downside in such domains as electronic monitoring of employee productivity and "deskilling"—the increasing polarization of the work force into a small cadre of highly skilled managers and technocrats, and a much larger group of lower-level workers whose room for individual initiative and creativity is radically constrained by technology (e.g., Garson, 1989)—the general consensus (especially following the intensified discussion of the advent of the "information superhighway" in the early 1990s) seemed positive.

But ultimately the role of technology in an increasingly bureaucratized society may depend more on the internal assumptions we ourselves bring to thinking about its use (Borgmann, 1999; Higgs, Light, & Strong, 2000). Rosenbrock (1990) suggests that we too easily confuse achievement of particular, economically desirable ends with the attainment of a more general personal, philosophical, or social good. This leads to the tension that we often feel when thinking about the possibility of replacement of humans by machines. Rosenbrock (1990) asserts that

Upon analysis it is easy to see that 'assistance' will always become 'replacement' if we accept [this] causal myth. The expert's skill is defined to be the application of a set of rules, which express the causal relations determining the expert's behavior. Assistance then can only mean the application of the same rules by a computer, in order to save the time and effort of the expert. When the rule set is made complete, the expert is no longer needed, because his skill contains nothing more than is embodied in the rules. (p. 167)

But when we do this, he notes, we lose sight of basic human needs and succumb to a "manipulative view of human relations in technological systems" (p. 159).

5.4.4 Schools as Organizations

One problem that educational sociologists have faced for many years is how to describe schools as organizations. Early analyses focused on the role of school administrator as part of an industrial production engine—the school. Teachers were workers, students—products, and teaching materials and techniques—the means of production. The vision was persuasive in the early part of this century when schools, as other social organizations, were just developing into their current forms.

But the typical methods of analysis used in organizational sociology were designed to provide a clear view of how large industrial firms operated, and it early became clear that these enterprises were not identical to public schools—their tasks were qualitatively different, their goals and outcomes were not equally definable or measurable, the techniques they used to pursue their aims were orders of magnitude apart in terms of specificity. Perhaps most importantly, schools operated in a messy, public environment where problems and demands came not from a single central location, but seemingly from all sides; they had to cater to the needs of teachers, students, parents, employers, and politicians, all of whom might have different visions of what the schools were for.

It was in answer to this perceived gap between the conceptual models offered by classical organizational sociology and the realities of the school that led to the rise among school organization theorists of the "loose-coupling" model. According to this approach, schools were viewed as systems that were only loosely linked together with any given portion of their surroundings. It was the diversity of schools' environment that was important, argued these theorists. Their view was consistent with the stronger emphasis given to environmental variables in the field of organizational sociology in general starting with the 1970s.

The older, more mechanistic vision of schools as mechanisms did not die, however. Instead, it lived on and gained new adherents under a number of new banners. Two of these—the "Effective Schools" movement and "outcome-based education"—are especially significant for those working in the field of educational technology because they are connected with essential aspects of our field. The effective schools approach was born of the school reform efforts that started with the publication of the report on the state of America's schools *A nation at risk* (National Commission on Excellence in Education, 1983).

That report highlighted a number of problems with the nation's schools, including a perceived drop in standards for academic achievement (but note Carson et al., 1991). A number of states and schools districts responded to this problem by attempting to define an "effective school"; the definitions varied, but there were common elements—high expectations, concerned leadership, committed teaching, involved parents, and so forth. In a number of cases these elements were put together into a "package" that was intended to define and offer a prescription for good schooling (Fredericks & Brown, 1993; Mortimer, 1993; Purkey & Smith, 1983; Rosenholtz, 1985; Scheerens, 1991.).

A further relative of the earlier mechanistic visions of school improvement was seen during the late 1980s in the trend toward definition of local, state and national standards in education (e.g., National Governors' Association, 1986, 1987), and in the new enthusiasm for "outcome-based" education. Aspects of this trend become closely linked with economic analyses of the schooling system such as those offered by Chubb and Moe (1990).

There were a number of criticisms and critiques of the effective schools approach. The most severe of these came from two quarters—those concerned about the fate of minority children in the schools, who felt that these children would be forgotten in the new drive to push for higher standards and "excellence" (e.g., Boysen, 1992; Dantley, 1990), and those concerned with the fate of teachers who worked directly in schools, who were seen to be "deskilled" and ignored by an increasingly top-down system of educational reform (e.g., Elmore, 1992). These factions, discontented by the focus on results and apparent lack of attention to individual needs and local control, have served as the focus for a "second wave" of school restructuring efforts that have generated such ideas as "building-based management," school site councils, teacher empowerment, and action research.

Some empirical evidence for the value of these approaches has begun to emerge recently, showing, for example, that teacher satisfaction and a sense of shared community among school staff are important predictors of efficacy (Lee, Dedrick, & Smith, 1991). Indications from some earlier research, however, suggest that the school effectiveness and school restructuring approaches may in fact simply be two alternative conceptions of how schools might best be organized and managed. The school effectiveness model of centrally managed change may be more productive in settings where local forces are not sufficiently powerful, well organized, or clear on what needs to be done, whereas the locally determined course of school restructuring may be more useful when local forces can in fact come to a decision about what needs to happen (Firestone & Herriott, 1982).

How to make sense of these conflicting claims for what the optimal mode of school organization might be? The school effectiveness research urges us to see human organizations as rational, manageable creations, able to be shaped and changed by careful, conscious action of a few well-intentioned administrators. The school restructuring approach, on the other hand, suggests that organizations, and schools, are best thought of as collectivities, groups of individuals who, to do their work better, need both freedom and the incentive that comes from joining with peers in search of new approaches. The first puts the emphasis on structure, central control, and rational action; the latter on individuals, community values, and the development of shared meaning.

A potential linkage between these differing conceptions is offered by James Coleman, the well-known sociologist who studied the issue of integration and school achievement in the 1960s. Coleman (1993) paints a broad picture of the rise of corporate forms of organization (including notably schools) and concomitant decline of traditional sources of values and social control (family, church). He sees a potential solution in reinvesting parents (and perhaps by extension other community agents) with a significant economic stake in their children's future productivity to the state via a kind of modified and extended voucher system. The implications are intriguing, and we will return to them later in this chapter as we discuss the possibility of a sociology of educational technology.

5.4.5 Educational Technology and School Organization

If we want to think about the sociological and organizational implications of educational technology as a field, we need something more than a "history of the creation of devices." Some histories of the field (e.g., Saettler, 1968) have provided just that; but while it is useful to know when certain devices first came on the scene, it would be more helpful in the larger scheme of things to know why school boards, principals, and teachers wanted to buy those devices, how educators thought about their use as they were introduced, what they were actually used for, and what real changes they brought about in how teachers and students worked in classrooms and how administrators and teachers worked together in schools and districts. It is through thousands of such decisions, reactions, perceptions, and intents that the field of educational technology has been defined.

As we consider schools as organizations, it is important to bear in mind that there are multiple levels of organization in any school—the organizational structure imposed by the state or district, that established for the particular school in question, and the varieties of organization present in both the classroom and among the teachers who work at the school. Certainly there are many ways of using technology that simply match (or even reinforce) existing bureaucratic patterns—districts that use e-mail only to send out directives from the central office, for example, or large-scale central computer labs equipped with integrated learning packages through which all children progress in defined fashion.

As we proceed to think about how technology may affect schools as organizations, there are three central questions we should consider. Two of these—the overall level of adoption and acceptance of technology into schools (i.e., the literature on educational innovation and change), and the impact of technology on specific patterns of organization and practice within individual classrooms and schools (i.e., the literature on roles and role change in education)—have been commonplaces in the research literature on educational technology for some years;

the third—organizational analysis of schools under conditions of technological change—is only now emerging.

5.4.5.1 The Problem of Innovation. We gain perspective on the slow spread of technology into schools from work on innovations as social and political processes. Early models of how new practices come to be accepted were based on the normal distribution; a few brave misfits would first try a new practice, followed by community opinion leaders, "the masses," and finally a few stubborn laggards. Later elaborations suggested additional factors at work—concerns about the effects of the new approach on established patterns of work, different levels of commitment to the innovation, lack of congruence between innovations and existing schemata, and so on (Greve & Taylor, 2000; Hall & Hord, 1984; Hall & Loucks, 1978; Rogers, 1962).

If we view technologies as innovations in teachers' ways of working, then there is evidence they will be accepted and used if they buttress a teacher's role and authority in the classroom (e.g., Godfrey, 1965, on overhead projectors), and disregarded if they are proposed as alternatives to the teacher's presence and worth (e.g., early televised instruction, programmed instruction in its original Skinnerian garb; Cuban, 1986). Computers and related devices seem to fall somewhere in the middle—they can be seen as threats to the teacher, but also as helpmates and liberators from drudgery (Kerr, 1991). Attitudes on the parts of teachers and principals toward the new technology have been well studied, both in the past and more recently regarding computers (e.g., Honey & Moeller, 1990; Pelgrum, 1993). But attitude studies, as noted earlier, rarely probe the significant issues of power, position, and changes in the organizational context of educators' work, and the discussion of acceptance of technology as a general stand-in for school change gradually has become less popular over the years. Scriven (1986) for example, suggested that it would be more productive to think of computers not simply as devices, but rather as new sources of energy within the school, energy that might be applied in a variety of ways to alter teachers' roles.

Less attention has been paid to the diffusion of the "process technology" of instructional development/instructional design. There have been some attempts to chart the spread of notions of systematic thinking among teachers, and a number of popular classroom teaching models of the 1970s (e.g., the "Instructional Theory into Practice," or ITIP, approach of Madeline Hunter) seemed closely related to the notions of ID. While some critics saw ID as simply another plot to move control of the classroom away from the teacher and into the hands of "technicians" (Nunan, 1983), others saw ID providing a stimulus for teachers to think in more logical, connected ways about their work, especially if technologists themselves recast ID approaches in a less formal way so as to allow teachers leeway to practice "high influence" teaching (Martin & Clemente, 1990; see also Shrock, 1985; Shrock & Higgins, 1990). More elaborated visions of this sort of application of both the hardware and software of educational technology to the micro- and macro-organization of schools include Reigeluth and Garfinkle's (1992) depiction of how the education system as a whole might change under the impact of new approaches (see also Kerr, 1989a, 1990a).

Recent years have seen increased interest among teachers in improving their own practice via professional development, advanced certification (for example, the National Board for Professional Teaching Standards), approaches such as "Lesson Study" and "Critical Friends," and so on. Internet- and computer-based approaches can clearly play a role here, as a number of studies demonstrate. Burge, Laroque, and Boak (2000) discovered significant difficulties in managing the dynamic tensions present in online discussions. Orrill (2001) found that computer-based materials served as a useful focus for a broader spectrum of professional development with teachers. A series of studies by Becker and his colleagues (e.g., Becker & Ravitz, 1999; Dexter, Anderson, & Becker, 1999) showed that an interest in working intensively with Internet-based materials is closely associated with teachers' holding more constructivist beliefs regarding instruction generally. A study by Davidson, McNamara, and Grant (2001) demonstrated that using networked resources effectively in pursuit of reform goals required "substantive reorganization across schools' practices, culture, and structure."

5.4.5.2 Studies of Technology and Educational Roles.
What has happened in some situations with the advent of contemporary educational technology is a quite radical restructuring of classroom experience. This has not been simply a substitution of one model of classroom life for another, but rather an extension and elaboration of what is possible in classroom practice. The specific elements involved are several: greater student involvement in project-oriented learning, and increased learning in groups; a shift in the teacher's role and attitude from being a source of knowledge to being a coach and mentor; and a greater willingness on the parts of students to take responsibility for their own learning. Such changes do not come without costs; dealing with a group of self-directed learners who have significant resources to control and satisfy their own learning is not an easy job. But the social relationships within classrooms can be significantly altered by the addition of computers and a well-developed support structure. (For further examples of changes in teachers' roles away from traditional direct instruction and toward more diverse arrangements, see Davies, 1988; Hardy, 1992; Hooper, 1992; Hooper & Hannafin, 1991; Kerr, 1977, 1978; Laridon, 1990a, 1990b; Lin, 2001; McIlhenny, 1991. For a discussion of changes in the principal's role, see Wolf, 1993.)

Indeed, the evolving discussion on the place of ID in classroom life seems to be drawing closer to more traditional sociological studies of classroom organization and the teacher's role. One such study suggests that a "more uncertain" technology (in the sense of general organization) of classroom control can lead to more delegation of authority, more "lateral communication" among students, and increased effectiveness (Cohen, Lotan, & Leechor, 1989). The value of intervening directly in administrators' and teachers' unexamined arrangements for classroom organization and classroom instruction was affirmed in a study by Dreeben and Barr (1988).

Technology may also exert and unanticipated impact on the existing structure of roles within a school or school district. Telem (1999), for example, found that school department heads' work was altered significantly with the introduction of computerization, with greater focus on "accountability, instructional evaluation, supervision, feedback, frequency of meetings, and shared decision making." And Robbins (2000) discovered potential problems and conflicts inherent in the style of collaboration (or lack thereof) between instructional technology and information services departments in school districts.

5.4.5.3 The Organizational Impact of Educational Technology.
If the general conclusion of some sociologists (as noted above) that the organizational effects of technology are best observed on the micro level of classrooms, offices, and interpersonal relations, rather than the macro level of district and state organization, then we would be well advised to focus our attention on what happens in specific spheres of school organizational life. It is not surprising that most studies of educational technology have focused on classroom applications, for that is the image that most educators have of its primary purpose. Discussions of the impact of technology on classroom organization, however, are rarer. Some empirical studies have found such effects, noting especially the change in the teacher's role and position from being the center of classroom attention to being more of a mentor and guide for pupils; this shift, however, is seen as taking significantly longer than many administrators might like, typically taking from 3 to 5 years (Hadley & Sheingold, 1993; Kerr, 1991).

Some models of application of technology to overall school organization do suggest that it can loosen bureaucratic structures (Hutchin, 1992; Kerr, 1989b; McDaniel, McInerney, & Armstrong, 1993). Examples include: the use of technology to allow teachers and administrators to communicate more directly, thus weakening existing patterns of one-way, top-down communication; networks linking teachers and students, either within a school or district, or across regional or national borders, thus breaking the old pattern of isolation and parochialism and leading to greater collegiality (Tobin & Dawson, 1992). Linkages between schools, parents, and the broader community have also been tried sporadically, and results so far appear promising (Solomon, 1992; Trachtman, Spirek, Sparks, & Stohl, 1991).

There have been some studies that have focused on administrators' changed patterns of work with the advent of computers. Kuralt (1987) for example, described a computerized system for gathering and analyzing information on teacher and student activity. Special educators have been eager to consider both instructional and administrative uses for technology, with some seeing the potential to facilitate the often-cumbersome processes of student identification and placement through better application of technology (Prater & Ferrara, 1990). Administrators concerned about facilitating contacts with parents have also found solutions using technology to describe assignments, provide supportive approaches, and allow parents to communicate with teachers using voice mail (Bauch, 1989). However, improved communication does not necessarily lead to greater involvement, knowledge, or feelings of "ownership" on the parts of educators. In a study of how schools used technology to implement a new budget planning process in school-based management schools, Brown (1994) found that many teachers simply did not have the time or the training needed to participate meaningfully in budget planning via computer.

The organizational structure of educational activities has been significantly affected in recent years by the advent of courses and experiences delivered via online distance learning. Researchers and policy makers have identified a number of issues in these environments that might become causes for concern: whether participants in such courses experience the same sense of community or "belonging" as those who work in traditional face-to-face settings, whether these environments provide adequate advising or support for learners, and whether such environments can appropriately support the sorts of collaborative learning now widely valued in education.

The presence (or absence) of community in online learning has been a concern for many investigators. A widely publicized book by Turkle (1995) suggested that the often-criticized anonymity of online settings is actually a positive social phenomenon, possibly associated with an improved self-image and a more flexible personality structure. In more traditional educational settings, studies of online learning have demonstrated that the experience of community during courses can grow, especially when supported and encouraged by instructors (Rovai, 2001). In another study, community among learners with disabilities was improved via both peer-to-peer and mentor-to-protégé interactions, with the former providing a more personally significant sense of community (Burgstahler & Cronheim, 2001).

Others who have examined online learning settings have considered how the environment may affect approaches to group tasks, especially problem solving. Jonassen and Kwon (2001) found that problem solving in an online environment was more task-focused, more structured, and led to more participant satisfaction with the work. Svensson (2000) found a similar pattern: learners were more oriented toward the specific tasks of problem solving, and so self-limited their collaboration to exclude interactions perceived as irrelevant to those goals.

One common rationale for the development and implementation of online courses is that they will permit easier access to educational experiences for those living in remote areas, and for those whose previous progress through the educational system has been hindered. An interesting study from Canada, however, calls these assumptions into question. Those most likely to participate in an online agricultural leadership development program lived in urban areas, and already possessed university degrees (McLean & Morrison, 2000).

Whether online environments themselves call forth new modes of interaction has been debated among researchers. At least some suggest that these settings themselves call forth new patterns. For example, Barab, Makinster, Moore, & Cunningham (2001) created an online project to support teachers in reflecting critically about their own pedagogical practice. As the project evolved, those studying it gradually shifted their focus from usability issues to sociability, and from a concern with the electronic structure to what they came to call a "sociotechnical interaction network." In another study, Järvelä, Bonk, Lentinen, & Lehti (1999) showed that carefully designed approaches to computer-based learning supported new ways for teachers and students to negotiate meanings in complex technological domains.

Several strands of current work show how preparing students to interact effectively in online environments may improve effectiveness of those environments for learning. Susman (1998) found that giving learners specific instruction on collaboration strategies improved results in CBI settings. But in a study in higher education, MacKnight (2001) found that current Web-based tools to encourage critical thinking (defined as finding, filtering, and assimilating new information) still do not generally meet faculty expectations.

But use of technology does not necessarily always translate into organizational change. Sometimes, existing organizational patterns may be extraordinarily strong. In higher education, for instance, some have suggested that the highly traditional nature of postbaccalaureate instruction and mentoring is ripe for restructuring via technology. Under the "Nintendo generation" hypothesis, new graduate students (familiar since childhood with the tools of digital technology) would revolutionize the realm of graduate study using new technologies to circumvent traditional patterns and experiment with new forms of collaboration, interaction, and authorship (Gardels, 1991). In a test of this argument, Covi (2000) examined work practices among younger doctoral students. She found that, while there were some differences in how these students used technology to communicate with others, elaborate their own specializations, and collect data, the changes were in fact evolutionary and cumulative, rather than revolutionary or transformative.

5.4.5.4 Educational Technology and Assumptions About Schools as Organizations.

There is clearly no final verdict on the impact educational technology may have on schools as organizations. In fact, we seem to be faced with competing models of both the overall situation in schools, and the image of what role educational technology might play there. On the one hand, the advocates of a rational-systems view of school organization and management—the effective school devotees—would stress technology's potential for improving the flow of information from administration to teachers, and from teachers to parents, for enabling management to collect more rapidly a wider variety of information about the successes and failures of parts of the system as they seek to achieve well-defined goals.

A very different image would come from those enticed by the vision of school restructuring; they would likely stress technology's role in allowing wide access to information, free exchange of ideas, and the democratizing potentials inherent in linking schools and communities more closely.

Is one of these images more accurate than the other? Hardly, for each depends on a different set of starting assumptions. The rational-systems adherents see society (and hence education) as a set of more or less mechanistic linkages, and efficiency as a general goal. Technology, in this vision, is a support for order, rationality, and enhanced control over processes that seem inordinately "messy." The proponents of the "teledemocracy" approach, on the other hand, are more taken by organic images, view schools as institutions where individuals can come together to create and recreate communities, and are more interested in technology's potential for making the organization of the educational system not necessarily more orderly, but perhaps more diverse.

At the moment, in the United States, the supporters of the rational-systems approach to the use of technology in education appear to have the upper hand at both federal and state levels. Budgetary reallocations, a deemphasis on exploratory experimentation, and an insistence on "scientifically proven" results on which to base educational policy decisions, combined with continued state and federal mandates for standards-based learning assessment, all have resulted in a focus on using technology to enforce accountability and to subject institutions to ever-more significant efforts at technologically enhanced data collection and analysis.

These images and assumptions, in turn, play out in the tasks each group sets for technology: monitoring, evaluation, assurance of uniformity (in outcomes if not methods), and provision of data for management decisions on the one hand; communication among individuals, access to information, diversification of the educational experience, and provision of a basis on which group decisions may be made, on the other. We shall discuss the implications of these differences further in the concluding section.

5.4.6 Social Aspects of Information Technology and Learning in Nonschool Environments

The discussion to this point has focused mostly on the use of educational technology in traditional school, settings, and the receptivity of those organizations to changed patterns of work that may result. But information technology does not merely foster change in traditional learning environments; it can also facilitate learning in multiple locations, at times convenient to the learner, and in ways that may not match traditional images of what constitutes "appropriate" learning. Two types of environments, both highly affected by developments in information technology and both loci for nonformal learning, call for attention here: digital online resources and museums.

5.4.6.1 *Informal Social Learning Using Online Digital Resources.* As use of the World Wide Web has become more widespread, increased numbers of young people regularly use it for informal learning projects of their own construction. There have been many studies of how children use the Web for school related projects and most of these have been highly critical of the strategies that young people employ (e.g., Fidel, 1999; Schacter, Chung, & Dorr, 1998).

A different approach, more attuned to what young people do on their own, in less constrained (i.e., adult-defined) environments, yields different sorts of results. For example, children may make more headway in searches if not required constantly to demonstrate and justify the relevance of results to adults, but rather turn to them for advice on an "as-needed" basis. Also, rather than see young peoples' differing standards for a successful search as a barrier, they might also be seen as a stimulus for deeper consideration of criteria for "success" and of how much to tolerate ambiguity (Dresang, 1999). Social aspects of informal online learning (collaboration, competition, types of informal learning projects undertaken, settings where explored, etc.) could also be profitably explored.

5.4.6.2 *Informal Social Learning via Information Technology in Museums.* Museums represent perhaps the quintessential informal learning environments. Museum visitors are not coerced to learn particular things, and museum visits are often social in nature, involving groups, families, or classes as a whole. Yet there are often expectations that one will learn something from the visit, or at least encounter significantly new perspectives on the world. Further, opportunities to explore museums for informal learning may constitute one form of educationally potent "cultural capital" (top be explored further below).

Information technology is increasingly being integrated into museums, and support for informal learning is a common rationale for these infusions. Individualized access to materials, to age-appropriate descriptions of them, and interaction around images of artifacts are examples of informal learning activities museums can foster using information technology (Marty, 1999). Other approaches suggest that information technology may be used productively to allow learners to bridge informal and formal educational environments, bringing images of objects back to classrooms from external locations, annotating and commenting on those objects in groups, and sharing and discussing findings with peers (Stevens & Hall, 1997).

All these new approaches to enhancing informal social learning bring with them significant and largely unstudied questions: How does informal social learning intersect with formal learning? How do learners behave in groups when working in these informal settings? How may the kinds of environments described here shape long-term preferences for ways of interacting around information generally, and for assumptions about the value of results from such work? Perhaps most saliently, how can such opportunities be provided to more young people in ways that ultimately support their further social and intellectual development?

5.5 THE SOCIOLOGY OF GROUPS

American sociologists have recently come to focus more and more on groups that are perceived to be in a position of social disadvantage. Racial minorities, women, and those from lower socioeconomic strata are the primary examples. The sociological questions raised in the study of disadvantaged groups include: How do such groups come to be identified as having special, unequal status? What forms of discrimination do they face? How are attitudes about their status formed, and how do these change, among the population at large? And what social or organizational policies may unwittingly contribute to their disadvantaged status? Because these groupings of race, gender, and class are so central to discussions of education in American society, and because there are ways that each intersects with educational technology, they will serve as the framework for the discussion that follows.

For each of these groups, there is a set of related questions of concern to us here. First, assuming that we wish to sustain a democratic society that values equity, equal opportunity, and equal treatment under law, *are we currently providing equal access to educational technology in schools?* Second, when we do provide access, are we providing access to the *same kinds of experiences*? In other words, are the experiences of males and females in using technology in schools of roughly comparable quality? Does one group or the other suffer from bias in content of the materials with which they are asked to work, or in the types of experiences to which they are exposed? Third, are there *differing perspectives on the use of the technology that are particular to one group or the other?* The genders, for example, may in fact experience the world differently, and therefore their experiences with educational technology may be quite different. And finally, so what? That is, *is it really important that we provide equality of access to educational technology,* bias-free content, etc., or are these aspects of education ultimately neutral in their actual impact on an individual's life chances?

5.5.1 Minority Groups

The significance of thinking about the issue of access to education in terms of racial groupings was underlined in studies beginning with the 1960s. Coleman's (1966) landmark study on the educational fate of American schoolchildren from minority backgrounds led to a continuing struggle to desegregate and integrate American schools, a struggle that continues. Coleman's findings—that African-American children were harmed academically by being taught in predominantly minority schools, and that Caucasian children were not harmed by being in integrated schools—provided the basic empirical justification for a whole series of federal, state, and local policies encouraging racial integration and seeking to abolish de facto segregation. This struggle continues, though in a different vein. As laws and local policies abolished de facto forms of segregated education, and access was guaranteed, the need to provide fully valuable educational experiences became more obvious.

5.5.1.1 Minorities and Access to Educational Technology. The issue of minority access to educational technology was not a central issue before the advent of computers in the early 1980s. While there were a few studies that explicitly sought to introduce minority kids to media production techniques (e.g., Culkin, 1965; Schwartz, 1987; Worth & Adair, 1972), the issue did not seem a critical one. The appearance of computers, however, brought a significant change. Not only did the machines represent a higher level of capitalization of the educational enterprise than had formerly been the case, they also carried a heavier symbolic load than had earlier technologies, being linked in the public mind with images of a better future, greater economic opportunity for children, and so forth. Each of these issues led to problems vis à vis minority access to computers.

Initial concerns about the access of minorities to new technologies in schools were raised in Becker's studies (1983), which seemed to show not only that children in poor schools (schools where a majority of the children were from low-socioeconomic-status family backgrounds) had fewer computers available to them, but also that the activities they were typically assigned by teachers featured rote memorization via use of simple drill-and-practice programs, whereas children in

schools with a wealthier student base were offered opportunities to learn programming and to work with more flexible software.

This pattern was found to be less strong in a follow-up set of studies conducted a few years later (Becker, 1986), but it has continued to be a topic of considerable concern. Perhaps school administrators and teachers became concerned and changed their practices, or perhaps there were simply more computers in the schools a few years later, allowing broader access. Nonetheless, other evidence of racial disparities in access to computing resources in schools was collected by Doctor (1991), and by Becker and Ravitz (1998), who noted continuing disparities. In 1992, the popular computer magazine *Macworld* (Borrell, 1992; Kondracke, 1992; Piller, 1992) devoted an issue (headlined "America's Shame") to these questions, noting critically that this topic seemed to have slipped out of the consciousness of many of those in the field of educational technology, and raising in a direct way the issue of the relationship (or lack of one) between government policy on school computer use and the continuing discrepancies in minority access. Access and use by minorities became a topic of interest for some researchers and activists from within the minority community itself (see Bowman, 2001 and related articles in a special issue of *Journal of Educational Computing Research*).

If the issue of minority access to computing resources was not a high priority in the scholarly journals, it did receive a good deal of attention at the level of federal agencies, foundations, state departments of education, and local school districts. States such as Kentucky (Pritchard, 1991), Minnesota (McInerney & Park, 1986), New York (Webb, 1986), and a group of southern states (David, 1987) all identified the question of minority access to computing resources as an important priority. Surveys of Advanced Telecommunications in U.S. education, conducted by NCES in the mid-1990s, showed gaps in access persisting along racial and SES lines (Leigh, 1999). Additionally, national reports and foundation conferences focused attention on the issue in the context of low minority representation in math and science fields generally (Cheek, 1991; Kober, 1991). Madaus (1991) made a particular plea regarding the increasing move toward high-stakes computerized testing and its possible negative consequences for minority students.

The issue for the longer term may well be how educational technology interacts with the fundamental problem of providing not merely access, but also a lasting and valuable education, something many minority children are clearly not receiving at present. The actual outcomes from use of educational technology in education may be less critical here than the symbolic functions of involvement of minorities with the hardware and software of a new era, and the value for life and career chances of their learning the language associated with powerful new forms of "social capital." We shall have occasion to return to this idea again below as part of the discussion of social class.

5.5.2 Gender

5.5.2.1 Gender and Technology. With the rise of the women's movement and in reaction to the perceived "male bias" of technology generally, technology's relationship to issues of gender is one that has been explored increasingly in recent years. One economic analysis describes the complex interrelationship among technology, gender, and social patterns in homes during this century. Technological changes coincided with a need to increase the productivity of household labor: as wages rose, it became more expensive for women to remain at home, out of the work force, and labor-saving technology, even though expensive, became more attractive, at first to upper-middle class women, then to all. The simple awareness of technology's effects was enough, in this case, to bring about significant social changes (Day, 1992). Changes in patterns of office work by women have also been intensively considered by sociologists (Kraft & Siegenthaler, 1989).

5.5.2.2 Gender and Education. Questions of how boys' and girls' experiences in school differ have come to be a topic of serious consideration. Earlier assertions that most differences were the result of social custom or lack of appropriate role models have been called into question by the work of Gilligan and her colleagues (Gilligan, 1982; Gilligan, Ward, & Taylor, 1988) which finds distinctive differences in how the sexes approach the task of learning in general, and faults a number of instructional approaches in particular.

5.5.2.3 Gender and Access to Technology in Schools. Several scholars have raised the question of how women are accommodated in a generally male-centric vision of how educational technology is to be used in schools (Becker, 1986; Damarin, 1991; Kerr, 1990b; Turkle, 1984). In particular, Becker's surveys (1983, 1986) found that girls tended to use computers differently, focusing more on such activities as word processing and collaborative work, while boys liked game playing and competitive work. Similar problems were noted by Durndell and Lightbody (1993), Kerr (1990b), Lage (1991), Nelson & Watson (1991), and Nye (1991). Specific strategies to reduce the effect of gender differences in classrooms have been proposed (*Neuter computer,* 1986). The issue has also been addressed through national and international surveys of computer education practices and policies (Kirk, 1992; Reinen & Plomp, 1993).

There is much good evidence that males and females differ both in terms of amount of computer exposure in school and in terms of the types of technology-based activities they typically choose to undertake. Some studies (Ogletree & Williams, 1990) suggest that prior experience with computers may determine interest and depth of involvement with computing by the time a student gets to higher grade levels. In fact, we are likely too close to the issues to have an accurate reading at present; the roles and expectations of girls in schools are changing, and different approaches are being tried to deal with the problems that exist. There have been some questions raised about the adequacy of the research methods used to unpack these key questions. Kay (1992), for example, found that scales and construct definitions were frequently poorly handled.

Ultimately, the more complex issue of innate differences in social experience and ways of perceiving and dealing with the world will be extraordinarily difficult to unknot empirically,

especially given the fundamental importance of initial definitions and the shifting social and political context in which these questions are being discussed. An example of the ways in which underlying assumptions may shape gender-specific experience with technology is seen in a study by Mitra, LaFrance, and McCullough (2001). They found that men and women perceived computerization efforts differently, with men seeing the changes that computers brought as more compatible with existing work patterns, and as more "trialable"—able to be experimented with readily on a limited basis.

The question of how males and females define their experiences with technology will continue to be an important one. Ultimately, the most definitive factor here may turn out to be changes in the surrounding society and economy. As women increasingly move into management positions in business and industry, and as formerly "feminine" approaches to the organization of economic life (team management styles, collaborative decision making) are gradually reflected in technological approaches and products (computer-supported collaborative work, "groupware"), these perspectives and new approaches will gradually make their way into schools as well.

5.5.3 Social Class

Surprisingly little attention has been paid to the issue of social class differences in American education. Perhaps this is because Americans tend to think of their society as "classless," or that all are "members of the middle class." But there is a new awareness today that social class may in fact play a very significant role in shaping and mediating the ways in which information resources are used educationally by both students and teachers

5.5.3.1 The Digital Divide Debated. Access to digital resources by members of typically disadvantaged groups became a more central social and political issues in the mid-1990s at the same time that Internet businesses boomed and the U.S. federal government moved to introduce computers and networks into all schools. Under the rubric of the "digital divide," a number of policy papers urged wider access to computer hardware and such digital services as e-mail and Web resources. Empirical evidence about the nature and extent of the divide, however, was slower to arrive. One major survey, after an extensive review of the current situation, suggested that further large-scale efforts to address the "divide" would be futile, due to rapid changes in the technology itself, and related changes in cost structures (Compaine, 2001).

Another important question is whether simple physical access to hardware or Internet connections lies at the root of problems that may hinder those in disadvantaged communities from fully participating in current educational, civic, or cultural life. Some have gone so far as to characterize two distinctly separate "digital divides." If the first divide is based on physical access to hardware and connectivity, then the second has more to do with how information itself is perceived, accessed, and used as a form of "cultural capital." The physical presence of a computer in a school, home, or library, in other words, may be less significant to overcoming long-standing educational or social inequalities than the sets of assumptions, practices, and expectations within which work with that computer is located. Imagine a child who comes from a family in which there is little value attached to finding correct information. In such a family, parents do not regularly encourage use of resources that support learning, and the family activity at mealtimes is more likely to involve watching television than engaging in challenging conversations based on information acquired or encountered during the day. In this setting, the child is much less likely to see use of a computer as centrally important, not only to educational success, but to success in life, success in becoming what one can become (Gamoran, 2001; Kingston, 2001; Persell & Cookson, 1987).

5.5.3.2 Information Technology, Cultural Capital, Class, and Education.

Some evidence for real interactions of cultural capital with educational outcomes has been provided by studies of the ways such resources are mediated in the "micropolitical" environment of classroom interaction and assessment. In one examination, such cultural capital goods as extracurricular trips and household educational resources were found to be less significant for minority children than for whites, a finding the researchers attributed to intervening evaluations by teachers and track placement of minority students (Roscigno & Ainsworth-Darnell, 1999). Similar findings emerged from a computer-specific study by Attewell and Battle (1999): The benefits of a home computer (and other cultural-capital resources) were not absolute, but rather accrued disproportionately to students from wealthier, more educated families. Clearly, cultural capital does not simply flow from access nor from increased incidental exposure to cultural resources; it is rather more deeply rooted in the structure of assumptions, expectations, and behavior of families and schools (Attewell, 2001).

With knowledge that the digital divide may exist at levels deeper than simple access to hardware and networks, sociologists of education may be able to assist in "designing the educational institutions of the digital age." A thoughtful analysis by Natriello (2001) suggests several specific directions in which this activity could go forward: advising on the structure of digital libraries of materials, to eliminate unintended barriers to access; helping to design online learning cooperatives so as to facilitate real participation by all who might wish to join; creating and operating distance learning projects so as to maximize interaction and availability; and assisting those who prepare corporate or other nonschool learning environments to "understand the alternatives and trade-offs" involved in design.

5.6 EDUCATIONAL TECHNOLOGY AS SOCIAL MOVEMENT

An outside observer reading the educational technology literature over the past half century (perhaps longer) would be struck by the messianic tone in much of the writing. Edison's enthusiastic pronouncement about the value of film in education in 1918 that "soon all children will learn through the eye, not the ear" was only the first in a series of visions of technology-as-panacea. And, although their potential is now seen in a very different light, such breakthroughs as instructional radio, dial-access

audio, and educational television once enjoyed enormous support as "solutions" to all manner of educational problem (Cuban, 1986; Kerr, 1982).

Why has this been, and how can we understand educational technology's role over time as catalyst for a "movement" toward educational change, for reform in the status quo? To develop a perspective on this question, it would be useful to think about how sociologists have studied social movements. What causes a social movement to emerge, coalesce, grow, and wither? What is the role of organized professionals versus lay persons in developing such a movement? What kinds of changes in social institutions do social movements bring about, and which have typically been beyond their power? How do the ideological positions of a movement's supporters (educational technologists, for example) influence the movement's fate? All these are areas in which the sociology of social movements may shed some light on educational technology's role as catalyst for changes in the structure of education and teaching.

5.6.1 The Sociology of Social Movements

Sociologists have viewed social movements using a number of different perspectives—movements as a response to social strains, as a reflection of trends and directions throughout the society more generally, as a reflection of individual dissatisfaction and feelings of deprivation, and as a natural step in the generation and modification of social institutions (McAdam, McCarthy, & Zald, 1988). Much traditional work on the sociology of mass movements concentrated on the processes by which such movements emerged, how they recruited new members, defined their goals, and gathered the initial resources that would allow them to survive.

More recent work has focused attention on the processes by which movements, once organized, contrive to assure the continued existence of their group and the long-term furtherance of its aims. Increasingly, social problems that in earlier eras were the occasion for short-lived expressions of protest by groups that may have measured their life-spans in months, are now the foci for long-lived organizations, for the activity of "social movement professionals," and for the creation of new institutions (McCarthy & Zald, 1973). This process is especially typical of those "professional" social movements where a primary intent is to create, extend, and preserve markets for particular professional services.

But while professionally oriented social movements enjoy some advantages in terms of expertise, organization, and the like, they also are often relatively easy for the state to control. In totalitarian governments, social movements have been controlled simply by repressing them; but in democratic systems, state and federal agencies, and their attached superstructure of laws and regulations, may in fact serve much the same function, directing and controlling the spheres of activity in which a movement is allowed to operate, offering penalties or rewards for compliance (e.g., tax-exempt status).

5.6.1.1 Educational Examples of Social Movements.

While we want to focus here on educational technology as a social movement, it is useful to consider other aspects of *education* that have recently been mobilized in one way or another as social movements. Several examples are connected with the recent (1983 to date) efforts to reform and restructure schools. As noted above, there are differing sets of assumptions held by different sets of actors in this trend, and it is useful to think of several of them as professional social movements: one such grouping might include the Governors' Conference, Education Council of the States, and similar government-level official policy and advisory groups with a political stake in the success of the educational system; another such movement might include the Holmes Group, NCREST (the National Center for the Reform of Education, Schools and Teaching), NCTAF (the National Council on Teaching and America's Future), the National Network for Educational Renewal, and a few similar centers focused on changing the structure of teacher education; a further grouping would include conservative or liberal "think tanks" such as the Southern Poverty Law Center, People for the American Way, or the Eagle Forum, having a specific interest in the curriculum, the content of textbooks, and the teaching of particularly controversial subject matter (sex education, evolutionism vs. creationism, values education, conflict resolution, racial tolerance, etc.) We shall return later to this issue of the design of curriculum materials and the roles technologists play therein.

5.6.1.1.1 Educational Technology as Social Movement. To conceive of educational technology itself as a social movement, we need to think about the professional interests and goals of those who work within the field, and those outside the field who have a stake in its success. There have been a few earlier attempts to engage in those sorts of analysis: Travers (1973) looked at the field in term of its political successes and failures, and concluded that most activities of educational technologists were characterized by an astonishing naiveté as regards the political and bureaucratic environments in which they had to try to exist. Hooper (1969) a BBC executive, also noted that the field had failed almost entirely to establish a continuing place for its own agenda. Of those working during the 1960s and 1970s, only Heinich (1971) seemed to take seriously the issue of how those in the field thought about their work vis a vis other professionals. Of the critics, Nunan (1983) was most assertive in identifying educational technologists as a professionally self-interested lobby.

The advent of microcomputers changed the equation considerably. Now, technology based programs moved from being perceived by parents, teachers, and communities as expensive toys of doubtful usefulness, to being seen increasingly as the keys to future academic, economic and social success. One consequence of this new interest was an increase in the number of professional groups interested in educational technology. Interestingly, the advantages of this new status for educational technology did not so much accrue to existing groups such as the Association for Educational Communication and Technology (AECT) or the Association for the Development of Computer-Based Instructional Systems (ADCIS), but rather to new groups such as the Institute for the Transfer of Technology to Education of the American School Board Association, the National Education Association, groups affiliated with such noneducational

organizations as the Association for Computing Machinery (ACM), groups based on the hardware or applications of particular computer and software manufacturers (particularly Apple and IBM), and numerous academics and researchers involved in the design, production, and evaluation of software programs. There is also a substantial set of cross connections between educational technology and the defense industry, as outlined in detail by Noble (1989, 1991). The interests of those helping to shape the new computer technology in the schools became clearer following publication of a number of federal and foundation sponsored reports in the 1980s and 1990s (e.g., *Power on!,* 1988).

Teachers themselves also had a role in defining educational technology as a social movement. A number of studies of the early development of educational computing in schools (Hadley & Scheingold, 1993; Olson, 1988; Sandholtz, Ringstaff, & Dwyer, 1991) noted that a small number of knowledgeable teachers in a given school typically assumed the role of "teacher-computer-buffs," willingly becoming the source of information and inspiration for other teachers. It may be that some school principals and superintendents played a similar role among their peers, describing not specific ways of introducing and using computers in the classroom, but general strategies for acquiring the technology, providing for teacher training, and securing funding from state and national sources. A further indication of the success of educational technology as a social movement is seen in the widespread acceptance of levies and special elections in support of technology based projects, and in the increasing incidence of participation by citizen and corporate leaders in projects and campaigns to introduce technology into schools.

5.6.1.1.2 Educational Technology and the Construction of Curriculum Materials. Probably in no other area involving educational technologists has there been such rancorous debate over the past 20 years as in the definition and design of curricular materials. Textbook controversies have exploded in fields such as social studies (Ravitch & Finn, 1987) and natural sciences (e.g., Nelkin, 1977); the content of children's television has been endlessly examined (Mielke, 1990); and textbook publishers have been excoriated for the uniformity and conceptual vacuousness of their products (Honig, 1989).

Perhaps the strongest set of criticisms of the production of educational materials comes from those who view that process as intensely social and political, and who worry that others, especially professional educators, are sadly unaware of those considerations (e.g., Apple, 1988; Apple & Smith, 1991). Some saw "technical," nonpolitical curriculum specification and design as quintessentially American. In a criticism that might have been aimed at the supposedly bias-free, technically neutral instructional design community, Wong (1991) noted:

Technical and pragmatic interests are also consistent with an instrumentalized curriculum that continues to influence how American education is defined and measured. Technical priorities are in keeping not only with professional interests and institutional objectives, but with historically rooted cultural expectations that emphasize utilitarian aims over intellectual pursuits. (p. 17)

Technologists have begun to enter this arena with a more critical stance. Ellsworth and Whatley (1990) considered how educational films historically have reflected particular social and cultural values. Spring (1992) examined the particular ways that such materials have been consciously constructed and manipulated by various interest groups to yield a particular image of American life. A study of Channel One by DeVaney and her colleagues (1994) indicates the ways in which the content selected for inclusion serves a number of different purposes and the interests of a number of groups, not always to educational ends.

All of these examples suggest that technologists may need to play a more active and more consciously committed role as regards the selection of content and design of materials. This process should not be regarded as merely a technical or instrumental part of the process of education, but rather as part of its essence, with intense political and social overtones. This could come to be seen as an integral part of the field of educational technology, but doing so would require changes in curriculum for the preparation of educational technologists at the graduate level.

5.6.1.1.3 The Ideology of Educational Technology as a Social Movement. The examples above suggest that educational technology has had some success as a social movement, and that some of the claims made by the field (improved student learning, more efficient organization of schools, more rational deployment of limited resources, etc.) are attractive not only to educators but to the public at large. Nonetheless, it is also worth considering the ideological underpinnings of the movement, the sets of fundamental assumptions and value positions that motivate and direct the work of educational technologists.

There is a common assumption among educational technologists that their view of the world is scientific, value-neutral, and therefore easily applicable to the full array of possible educational problems. The technical and analytic procedures of instructional design ought to be useful in any setting, if correctly interpreted and applied. The iterative and formative processes of instructional development should be similarly applicable with only incidental regard to the particulars of the situation. The principles of design of CAI, multimedia, and other materials are best thought of as having universal potential. Gagné (1987) wrote about educational technology generally, for example, that

fundamental systematic knowledge derives from the research of cognitive psychologists who apply the methods of science to the investigation of human learning and the conditions of instruction. (p. 7)

And Rita Richey (1986), in one of the few attempts to pull together the diverse conceptual strands that feed into the field of instructional design, noted that

Instructional design can be defined as the science of creating detailed specifications for the development, evaluation, and maintenance of both large and small units of subject matter. (p. 9)

The focus on science and scientific method is marked in other definitions of educational technology and instructional

design as well. The best known text in the field (Gagné, Briggs, & Wager, 1992) discusses the systems approach to instructional design as involving

carrying out of a number of steps beginning with an analysis of needs and goals and ending with an evaluated system of instruction that demonstrably succeeds in meeting accepted goals. Decisions in each of the individual steps are based on empirical evidence, to the extent that such evidence allows. Each step leads to decisions that become "inputs" to the next step so that the whole process is as solidly based as is possible within the limits of human reason. (p. 5)

Gilbert, a pioneer in the field of educational technology in the 1960s, supported his model for "behavioral engineering" with formulae:

We can therefore define behavior (B), in shorthand, as a product of both the repertory [of skills] *and* environment:

$$B = E \cdot P \qquad \text{(Gilbert, 1978, p. 81)}$$

The assumption undergirding these (and many other) definitions and models of educational technology and its component parts, instructional design and instructional development, is that the procedures the field uses are scientific, value neutral, and precise. There are likely several sources for these assumptions: the behaviorist heritage of the field and the seeming control provided by such approaches as programmed instruction and CAI; the newer turn to systems theory (an approach itself rooted in the development of military systems in World War II) to provide an overall rationale for the specification of instructional environments; and the use of the field's approaches in settings ranging from schools and universities to the military, corporate and industrial training, and organizational development for large public sector organizations.

In fact, there is considerable disagreement as to the extent to which these seemingly self-evident propositions of educational technology as movement are in fact value free and universally applicable (or even desirable). Some of the most critical analysis of these ways of thinking about problems and their solution are in fact quite old.

Lewis Mumford, writing in 1930 about the impact of technology on society and culture, praised the "matter of fact" and "reasonable" personality that he saw arising in the age of the machine. These qualities, he asserted, were necessary if human culture was not only to assimilate the machine but also to go beyond it:

Until we have absorbed the lessons of objectivity, impersonality, neutrality, the lessons of the mechanical realm, we cannot go further in our development toward the more richly organic, the more profoundly human. (Mumford, 1963, p. 363)

For Mumford, the qualities of scientific thought, rational solution to social problems, and objective decision making were important, but only preliminary to a deeper engagement with more distinctively human (moral, ethical, spiritual) questions.

Jacques Ellul, a French sociologist writing in 1954, also considered the relationship between technology and society. For

Ellul, the essence of "technical action" in any given field was "the search for greater efficiency" (1964, p. 20). In a description of how more efficient procedures might be identified and chosen, Ellul notes that the question is one

of finding the best means in the absolute sense, on the basis of numerical calculation. It is then the specialist who chooses the means; he is able to carry out the calculations that demonstrate the superiority of the means chosen over all the others. Thus a science of means comes into being—a science of techniques, progressively elaborated. (p. 21)

"Pedagogical techniques," Ellul suggests, make up one aspect of the larger category of "human techniques," and the uses by "psychotechnicians" of such technique on the formation of human beings will come more and more to focus on the attempt to

restore man's lost unity, and patch together that which technological advances have separated [in work, leisure, etc.]. But only one way to accomplish this ever occurs to [psychotechnicians], and that is to use technical means . . . There is no other way to regroup the elements of the human personality; the human being must be completely subjected to an omnicompetent technique, and all his acts and thoughts must be the objects of the human techniques. (p. 411)

For Ellul, writing in what was still largely a precomputer era, the techniques in question were self-standing procedures monitored principally by other human beings. The possibility that computers might come to play a role in that process was one that Ellul hinted at, but could not fully foresee. In more recent scholarship, observers from varied disciplinary backgrounds have noted the tendency of computers (and those who develop and use them) to influence social systems of administration and control in directions that are rarely predicted and are probably deleterious to feelings of human self-determination, trust, and mutual respect. The anthropologist Shoshana Zuboff (1988), for example, found that the installation of an electronic mail system may lead not only to more rapid sharing of information, but also to management reactions that generate on the part of workers the sense of working within a "panopticon of power," a work environment in which all decisions and discussion are monitored and controlled, a condition of transparent observability at all times.

Joseph Weizenbaum, computer scientist at MIT and pioneer in the field of artificial intelligence, wrote passionately about what he saw as the difficulty many of his colleagues had in separating the scientifically feasible from the ethically desirable. Weizenbaum (1976) was especially dubious of teaching university students to program computers as an end in itself:

When such students have completed their studies, they are rather like people who have somehow become eloquent in some foreign language, but who, when they attempt to write something in that language, find they have literally nothing to say. (p. 278)

Weizenbaum is especially skeptical of a technical attitude toward the preparation of new computer scientists. He worries

that if those who teach such students, and see their role as that of

a mere trainer, a mere applier of "methods" for achieving ends determined by others, then he does his students two disservices. First, he invites them to become less than fully autonomous persons. He invites them to become mere followers of other people's orders, and finally no better than the machines that might someday replace them in that function. Second, he robs them of the glimpse of the ideas that alone purchase for computer science a place in the university's curriculum at all. (p. 279)

Similar comments might be directed at those who would train educational technologists to work as "value-free" creators of purely efficient training.

Another critic of the "value-free" nature of technology is Neil Postman, who created a new term—Technopoly—to describe the dominance of technological thought in American society. This new world view, Postman (1992) observed,

consists of the deification of technology, which means that the culture seeks its authorization in technology and finds its satisfactions in technology, and takes its orders from technology. This requires the development of a new kind of social order. . . . Those who feel most comfortable in Technopoly are those who are convinced that technical progress is humanity's supreme achievement and the instrument by which our most profound dilemmas may be solved. They also believe that information is an unmixed blessing, which through its continued and uncontrolled production and dissemination offers increased freedom, creativity, and peace of mind. The fact that information does none of these things—but quite the opposite—seems to change few opinions, for such unwavering beliefs are an inevitable product of the structure of Technopoly. (p. 71)

Other critics also take educational technology to task for what they view as its simplistic claim to scientific neutrality. Richard Hooper (1990), a pioneer in the field and longtime gadfly, commented that

Much of the problem with educational technology lies in its attempt to ape science and scientific method. . . . An arts perspective may have some things to offer educational technology at the present time. An arts perspective focuses attention on values, where science's attention is on proof. (p. 11)

Michael Apple (1991), another critic who has considered how values, educational programs, and teaching practices interact, noted that

The more the new technology transforms the classroom into its own image, the more a technical logic will replace critical political and ethical understanding. (p. 75)

Similar points have been made by Sloan (1985) and by Preston (1992). Postman's (1992) assertion that we must

refuse to accept efficiency as the pre-eminent goal of human relations . . . not believe that science is the only system of thought capable of producing truth . . . [and] admire technological ingenuity but do not think it represents the highest possible form of human achievement. (p. 184) necessarily sounds unusual in the present content. Educational technologists are encouraged to see the processes they employ as beneficent, as value-free, as contributing to improved efficiency and effectiveness. The suggestions noted above that there may be different value positions, different stances toward the work of education, are a challenge, but one that the field needs to entertain seriously if it is to develop further as a social movement.

5.6.1.1.4 Success of Educational Technology as a Social Movement. If we look at the field of educational technology today, it has enjoyed remarkable success: legislation at both state and federal levels includes educational technology as a focus for funded research and development; the topics the field addresses are regularly featured in the public media in a generally positive light; teachers, principals, and administrators actively work to incorporate educational technology into their daily routines; citizens pass large bond issues to fund the acquisition of hardware and software for schools.

What explains the relative success of educational technology at this moment as compared with two decades ago? Several factors are likely involved. Certainly the greater capabilities of the hardware and software in providing for diverse, powerful instruction are not to be discounted, and the participation of technologists in defining the content of educational materials may be important for the future. But there are other features of the movement as well. Gamson (1975) discusses features of successful social movements, and notes two that are especially relevant here.

As educational technologists began to urge administrators to take their approaches seriously in the 1960s and 1970s, there was often at least an implied claim that educational technology could not merely supplement, but actually supplant classroom teachers. In the 1980s, this claim seems to have disappeared, and many key players (e.g., Apple Computer's Apple Classroom of Tomorrow (ACOT) project, GTE's Classroom of the Future, and others) sought to convince teachers that they were there not to replace them, but to enhance their work and support them. This is in accordance with Gamson's finding that groups willing to coexist with the status quo had greater success than those seeking to replace their antagonists.

A further factor contributing to the success of the current educational technology movement may be the restricted, yet comprehensible and promising, claims it has made. The claims of earlier decades had stressed either the miraculous power of particular pieces of hardware (that were in fact quite restricted in capabilities) or the value of a generalized approach (instructional development/design) that seemed both too vague and too like what good teachers did anyway to be trustworthy as an alternate vision. In contrast, the movement to introduce computers to schools in the 1980s, while long on general rhetoric, in fact did not start with large promises, but rather with an open commitment to experimentation and some limited claims (enhanced remediation for poor achievers, greater flexibility in classroom organization, and so on). This too is in keeping with Gamson's findings that social movements with single or limited issues have been more successful than those pushing for generalized goals or those with many sub-parts.

It is likely too early to say whether educational technology will ultimately be successful as a social movement, but the developments of the past dozen or so years are promising for the field. There are stronger indications of solidity and institutionalization now than previously, and the fact the technology is increasingly seen as part of the national educational, economic, and social discussion bodes well for the field. The increasing number of professionally related organizations, and their contacts with other parts of the educational, public policy, and legislative establishment are also encouraging signs. Whether institutionalization of the movement equates easily to success of its aims, however, is another question. Gamson notes that it has traditionally been easier for movements to gain acceptance from authorities and other sources of established power, than actually to achieve their stated goals. Educational technologists must be careful not to confuse recognition and achievement of status for their work and their field with fulfillment of the mission they have claimed. The concerns noted above about the underlying ideology that educational technology asserts—value neutrality, use of a scientific approach, pursuit of efficiency— are also problematic, for they suggest educational technologists may need to think still more deeply about fundamental aspects of their work than has been the case to date.

5.7 A NOTE ON SOCIOLOGICAL METHOD

The methods typically used in sociological research differ considerably from those usually employed in educational studies, and particularly from those used in the field of educational technology. Specifically, the use of two approaches in sociology— surveys and participant observation—differs sufficiently from common practice in educational research that it makes sense for us to consider them briefly here. In the first case, survey research, there are problems in making the inference from attitudes to probable actions that are infrequently recognized by practitioners in education. In the second case, participant observation and immersion in a cultural surround, the approach has particular relevance to the sorts of issues reviewed here, yet is not often employed by researchers in educational technology.

5.7.1 Surveys: From Attitudes to Actions

Survey research is hardly a novelty for educators; it is one of the most commonly taught methods in introductory research methods courses in education. Sociologists, who developed the method in the last century, have refined the approach considerably, and there exist good discussions of the process of survey construction that are likely more sophisticated than those encountered in introductory texts in educational research. These address nuances of such questions as sampling technique, eliciting high response rates, and so forth (e.g., Hyman, 1955, 1991). For our purposes here, we include all forms of surveys—mailed questionnaires, administered questionnaires, and in-person or telephone interviews.

An issue often left unaddressed in discussions of the use of survey research in education, however, is the difficulty of making the inference that if a person holds an attitude on a particular question, then the attitude translates into a likelihood of engaging in related kinds of action. For example, it frequently seems to be taken for granted that, if a teacher believes that all children have a right to an equal education, then that teacher will work to include children with disabilities in the class, will avoid discriminating against children from different ethnic backgrounds, and so forth.

Unfortunately, the evidence is not particularly hopeful that people do behave in accord with the beliefs that they articulate in response to surveys. This finding has been borne out in a number of different fields, from environmental protection (Scott & Willits, 1994), to smoking and health (van Assema, Pieterse, & Kok, 1993), to sexual behavior (Norris & Ford, 1994), to racial prejudice (Duckitt, 1992-93). In all these cases, there exists a generally accepted social stereotype of what "correct" or "acceptable" attitudes are—one is supposed to care for the environment, refrain from smoking, use condoms during casual sex, and respect persons of different racial and ethnic backgrounds. Many people are aware of these stereotypes and will frame their answers on surveys in terms of them even when their actions do not reflect those beliefs. There is, in other words, a powerful inclination on the part of many people to answer in terms that the respondent thinks the interviewer or survey designer wants to hear.

This issue has been one of constant concern to methodologists. Investigators have attempted to use the observed discrepancies between attitude and action as a basis for challenging people about their actions and urging them to reflect on the differences between what they have said and what they have done. But some studies have suggested that bringing these discrepancies to people's attention may have effects opposite to what is intended—that is, consistency between attitudes and behavior is reduced still further (Holt, 1993).

5.7.1.1 Educational Attitudes and Actions. The problem of discrepancies between attitudes and actions is especially pronounced for fields such as those noted above, where powerful agencies have made large efforts to shape public perceptions and, hopefully, behaviors. To what extent is it also true in education, and how might those tendencies shape research on educational technology? Differences between attitudes and actions among teachers have been especially problematic in such fields as special education (Bay & Bryan, 1991) and multicultural education (Abt-Perkins & Gomez, 1993), where changes in public values, combined with recent legal prescriptions, have generated powerful expectations among teachers, parents, and the public in general. Teachers frequently feel compelled to express beliefs in conformity to those new norms, whereas their actual behavior may still reflect unconscious biases or unacknowledged assumptions.

Is technology included among those fields where gaps exist between expressed attitudes and typical actions? There are occasions when teachers do express one thing and do another as regards the use of technology in their classrooms (McArthur & Malouf, 1991). Generally teachers have felt able to express ignorance and concerns about technology—numerous surveys have supported this (e.g., Dupagne & Krendl, 1992; Savenye, 1992). Most studies of teacher attitudes regarding technology, however, have asked about general attitudes toward computers,

their use in classrooms, and so on. And technology itself may be a useful methodological tool in gathering attitudinal data: A recent study (Hancock & Flowers, 2001) found that respondents were equally willing to respond to anonymous or nonanonymous questionnaires in a Web-based (as compared to traditional paper-and-pencil) environment.

As schools and districts spend large sums on hardware, software, and in-service training programs for teachers, the problem of attitudes and actions may become more serious. The amounts of money involved, combined with parental expectations, may lead to development of the kinds of strong social norms in support of educational technology that some other fields have already witnessed. If expectations grow for changes in patterns of classroom and school organization, such effects might be seen on several different levels. Monitoring these processes could be important for educational technologists.

5.7.2 Participant Observation

The research approach known as participant observation was pioneered not so much in sociology as in cultural anthropology, where its use became one of the principal tools for helping to understand diverse cultures. Many of the pioneering anthropological studies of the early years of this century by such anthropologists as Franz Boas, Clyde Kluckhohn, and Margaret Mead used this approach, and it allowed them to demonstrate that cultures until then viewed as "primitive" in fact had very sophisticated worldviews, but ones based on radically different assumptions about the world, causality, evidence, and so on (Berger & Luckmann, 1966). The approach, and the studies that it permitted anthropologists to conduct, led to more complex understandings about cultures that were until that time mysteries to those who came into contact with them.

The attempts of the participant observer both to join in the activities of the group being studied and to remain in some sense "neutral" at the same time were, of course, critical to the success of the method. The problem remains a difficult one for those espousing this method, but has not blocked its continued use in certain disciplines. In sociology, an interesting outgrowth of this approach in the 1960s was the development of ethnomethodology, a perspective that focused on understanding the practices and worldviews of a group under study with the intent to use these very methods in studying the group (Garfinkel, 1967; Boden, 1990). Ethnomethodology borrowed significant ideas from the symbolic interactionism of G. H. Mead and also from the phenomenological work of the Frankfurt School of sociologists and philosophers. Among its propositions were a rejection of the importance of theoretical frameworks imposed from the outside and an affirmation of the sense-making activities of actors in particular settings. The approach was always perceived as controversial, and its use resulted in a good many heated arguments in academic journals. Nonetheless, it was an important precursor to many of the ethnological approaches now being seriously used in the study of educational institutions and groups.

5.7.2.1 Participant Observation Studies and Educational Technology. The literature of educational technology is replete with studies that are based on surveys and questionnaires, and a smaller number of recent works that take a more anthropological approach. Olsen's (1988) and Cuban's (1986, 2001) work are among the few that really seek to study teachers, for example, from the teacher's own perspective. Shrock's (1985) study with faculty members in higher education around the use of instructional design offers a further example. A study by Crabtree et al. (2000) used an explicitly ethnomethodological approach in studying user behavior for the design of new library environments, and found that it generated useful results that diverged from what might have emerged in more traditional situations.

There could easily be more of this work, studies that might probe teachers' thought practices as they were actually working in classrooms, or as they were trying to interact with peers in resolving some educational or school decision involving technology. New video-based systems should allow exchange of much more detailed information, among more people, more rapidly. Similar work with principals and administrators could illuminate how their work is structured and how technology affects their activities. Also, studies from the inside of how schools and colleges cope with major educational technology-based restructuring efforts could be enormously valuable. What the field is missing, and could profit from, are studies that would point out for us how and where technology is and is not embedded into the daily routines of teachers, and into the patterns of social interaction that characterize the school and the community.

5.8 TOWARD A SOCIOLOGY OF EDUCATIONAL TECHNOLOGY

5.8.1 Organizations and Educational Technology

The foregoing analysis suggests that there is sociological dimension to the application of educational technology that may be as significant as its impacts in the psychological realm. But if this is true, as an increasing number of scholars seem to feel (see, e.g., Cuban, 1993), then we are perilously thin on knowledge of how technology and the existing organizational structure of schools interact. And this ignorance, in turn, makes it difficult for us either to devise adequate research strategies to test hypotheses or to predict in which domains the organizational impact of technology may be most pronounced. Nonetheless, there are enough pieces of the puzzle in place for us to hazard some guesses.

5.8.1.1 The Micro-Organization of School Practice. Can educational technology serve as a catalyst for the general improvement of students' experience in classrooms—improve student learning, assure teacher accountability, provide accurate assessments of how students are faring vis a vis their peers? For many in the movement to improve school efficiency, these are key aspects of educational technology, and a large part of the rationale for its extended use in schools. For example, Perelman (1987, 1992) makes the vision of improved efficiency through technology a major theme of his work. This also is a principal feature of the growing arguments for privatized, more efficient schools in the Edison Project and similar systems. On the other hand, enthusiasts for school restructuring through teacher empowerment and site-based management see technology as a tool for enhancing community and building new kinds of social relationships among students, between students and teachers, and among teachers, administrators, and parents. The increased pressures for assessment and for "high-stakes" graduation requirements may strengthen a demand for educational technology to be applied in service of these goals, as opposed to less structured, more creative instructional approaches.

5.8.1.1.1 Technologies and the Restructuring of Classroom Life. The possibilities here are several, and the approaches that might be taken are therefore likely orthogonal. We have evidence that technology can indeed improve efficiency in some cases, but we must not forget the problems that earlier educational technologists encountered when they sought to make technology, rather than teachers, the center of reform efforts (Kerr, 1989b). On the other hand, the enthusiasts for teacher-based reform strategies must recognize the complexities and time-consuming difficulties of these approaches, as well as the increasing political activism by the new technology lobbies of hardware and software producers, business interests, and parent groups concerned about perceived problems with the school system generally and teacher recalcitrance in particular.

Computers already have had a significant impact on the ways in which classroom life can be organized and conducted. Before the advent of computers, even the teacher most dedicated to trying to provide a variety of instructional approaches and materials was hard-pressed to make the reality match the desire. There were simply no easy solutions to the problem of how to organize and manage activities for 25 or 30 students. Trying to get teachers-in-training to think in more diverse and varied ways about their classroom work was a perennial problem for schools and colleges of education (see, e.g., Joyce & Weil, 1986).

Some applications of computers—use of large-scale Integrated Learning Systems (ILSs), for instance—support a changed classroom organization, but only within relatively narrow confines (and ones linked with the status quo). Other researchers have cast their studies in such a way that classroom management became an outcome variable. McLellan (1991), for example, discovered that dispersed groups of students working on computers could ease, rather than exacerbate, teachers' tasks of classroom management in relatively traditional settings.

Other studies have focused on the placement of computers in individual classrooms versus self-contained laboratories or networks of linked computers. The latter arrangements, noted Watson (1990), are "in danger of inhibiting rather than encouraging a diversity of use and confidence in the power of the resource" (p. 36). Others who have studied this issue seem to agree that dispersion is more desirable than concentration in fostering diverse use.

On a wider scale, it has become clear that using computers can free teachers' time in ways unimaginable only a few years ago. Several necessary conditions must be met: teachers must have considerable training in the use of educational technology;

they must have a view of their own professional development that extends several years into the future; there must be support from the school or district; there must be sufficient hardware and software; and, there should be a flexible district policy that gives teachers the chance to develop a personal style and a feeling of individual ownership and creativity in the crafting of personally significant individual models of what teaching with technology looks like (see Lewis, 1990; Newman, 1990a, 1990b, 1991; Olson, 1988; Ringstaff, Sandholz, & Dwyer, 1991; Sheingold & Hadley, 1990; Wiske et al., 1988 for examples).

5.8.1.1.2 Educational Organization at the Middle Range: Teachers Working with Teachers.

A further significant result of the wider application of technology in education is a shift in the way educators (teachers, administrators, specialists) collect and use data in support of their work. Education has long been criticized for being a "soft" discipline, and that has in many cases been true. But there have been reasons: statistical descriptions of academic achievement are not intrinsically easy to understand, and simply educating teachers in their use has never been easy; educational data have been seen as being more generalizable than they likely are, but incompatible formats and dissimilar measures have limited possibilities for sharing even those bits of information that might be useful across locations; and educators have not been well trained in how to generate useful data of their own and use it on a daily basis in their work.

In each of these areas, the wider availability of computers and their linkage through networks can make a significant difference in educational practice. Teachers learn about statistical and research procedures more rapidly with software tools that allow data to be presented and visualized more readily. Networks allow sharing of information among teachers in different schools, districts, states, or even countries; combined with the increased focus today on collaborative research projects that involve teachers in the definition and direction of the project, this move appears to allow educational information to be more readily shared. And the combination of easier training and easier sharing, together with a reemphasis on teacher education and the development of "reflective practitioners," indicates how teachers can become true "producers and consumers" of educational data. There is evidence that such changes do in fact occur, and that a more structured approach to information sharing among teachers can develop, but only over time and with much support (Sandholz, Ringstaff, & Dwyer, 1991). Budin (1991) notes that much of the problem in working with teachers is that computer enthusiasts have insisted on casting the issue as one of training, whereas it might more productively "emphasize *teaching* as much as computing" (p. 24).

What remains to be seen here is the extent to which the spread of such technologies as electronic mail and wide access to the Internet will change school organization. The evidence from fields outside of education has so far not been terribly persuasive that improved communication is necessarily equivalent to better management, improved efficiency, or flatter organizational structures. Rather, the technology in many cases merely seems to amplify processes and organizational cultures that already exist. It seems most likely that the strong organizational and cultural expectations that bind schools into certain forms will not be easily broken through the application of technology. Cuban (1993, 2001), Sheingold and Tucker (1990), and Cohen (1987) all suggest that these forms are immensely strong, and supported by tight webs of cultural and social norms that are not shifted easily or quickly. Thus, we may be somewhat skeptical about the claims by enthusiasts that technology will by itself bring about a revolution in structure or intra-school effectiveness overnight. As recent studies suggest (Becker & Reil, 2000; Ronnkvist, Dexter, & Anderson, 2000), its effects are likely to be slower, and to depend on a complex of other decisions regarding organization taken within schools and districts. Nonetheless, when appropriate support structures are present, teachers can change their ways of working, and students can collaborate in new ways through technology.

5.8.1.1.3 The Macro-Organization of Schools and Communities.

A particularly salient aspect of education in America and other developed nations is the linkage presumed to exist between schools and the surrounding community. Many forms of school organization and school life more generally are built around such linkages—relationships between parents and the school, between the schools and the workplaces of the community, between the school and various social organizations. These links are powerful determinants of what happens, and what may happen, in schools not so much because they influence specific curricular decisions, or because they determine administrative actions, but rather because they serve as conduits for a community's more basic expectations regarding the school, the students and their academic successes or failures, and the import of all of these for the future life of the community.

This is another domain in which technology may serve to alter traditional patterns of school organization. A particular example may be found in the relationships between schools and the businesses that employ their graduates. It is not surprising that businesses have for years seen schools in a negative light; the cultures and goals of the two types of institutions are significantly different. What is interesting is what technology does to the equation. Schools are, in industry's view, woefully undercapitalized. It is hard for businesses to see how schools can be so "wastefully" labor-intensive in dealing with their charges. Thus, much initial enthusiasm for joint ventures with schools and for educational reform efforts that involve technology appears, from the side of business, to be simply wise business practice: replace old technology (teachers) with new (computers). This is the initial response when business begins to work with schools.

As industry–school partnerships grow, businesses often develop a greater appreciation of the problems and limitations schools have to face. (The pressure for such collaboration comes from the need on the part of industry to survive in a society that is increasingly dominated by "majority minorities," and whose needs for trained personnel are not adequately met by the public schools.) Classrooms, equipped with technology and with teachers who know how to use it, appear more as "real" workplaces. Technology provides ways of providing better preparation for students from disadvantaged backgrounds, and thus is a powerful support for new ways for schools and businesses to work together.

The business community is not a unified force by any means, but the competitiveness of American students and American industry in world markets are an increasing concern. As technology improves the relationship between schools and the economy, the place of the schools in the community becomes correspondingly strengthened.

Relationships between schools and businesses are not the only sphere in which technology may affect school–community relations. There are obvious possibilities in allowing closer contacts between teachers and parents, and among the various social service agencies that work in support of schools. While such communication would, in an ideal world, result in improvements to student achievement and motivation, recent experience suggests many parents will not have the time or inclination to use these systems, even if they are available. Ultimately, again, the issues are social and political, rather than technical, in nature.

5.9 CONCLUSION: EDUCATIONAL TECHNOLOGY IS ABOUT WORK IN SCHOOLS

Contrary to the images and assumptions in most of the educational technology literature, educational technology's primary impact on schools may not be about improvements in learning or more efficient processing of students. What educational technology may be about is the work done in schools: how it is defined, who does it, to what purpose, and how that work connects with the surrounding community. Educational technology's direct effects on instruction, while important, are probably less significant in the long run than the ways in which teachers change their assumptions about what a classroom looks like, feels like, and how students in it interact when technology is added to the mix. Students' learning of thinking skills or of factual material through multimedia programs may ultimately be less significant than whether the new technologies encourage them to be active or passive participants in the civic life of a democratic society. If technology changes the ways in which information is shared within a school, it may thus change the distribution of power in that school, and thereby alter fundamentally how the school does its work. And finally, technology may change the relationships between schools and communities, bringing them closer together.

These processes have already started. Their outcome is not certain, and other developments may eventually come to be seen as more significant than some of those discussed here. Nonetheless, it seems clear that the social impacts of both device and process technologies are in many cases more important than the purely technical problems that technologies are ostensibly developed to solve. As many critics note, these developments are not always benign, and may have profound moral and ethical consequences that are rarely examined (Hlynka and Belland, 1991). What we need is a new, critical sociology of educational technology, one that considers how technology affects the organization of schools, classrooms, and districts, how it provides opportunities for social groups to change their status, and how it interacts with other social and political movements that also focus on the schools.

Much more is needed. Our view of how to use technologies is often too narrow. We tend to see the future, as Marshall McLuhan noted, through the rear-view mirror of familiar approaches and ideas from the past. In order to allow the potential inherent in educational technology to flourish, we need to shift our gaze, and try to discern what lies ahead, as well as behind. As we do so, however, we must not underestimate the strength of the social milieu within which educational technology exists, or the plans that it has for how we may bring it to bear on the problems of education. A better-developed sociology of educational technology may help us refine that vision.

References

Abt-Perkins, D., & Gomez, M. L. (1993). A good place to begin—Examining our personal perspectives. *Language Arts, 70*(3), 193–202.

Aldrich, H. E., & Marsden, P. V. (1988). Environments and organizations. In N. J. Smelser (Ed.), *Handbook of Sociology* (pp. 361–392). Newbury Park, CA: Sage.

Anspach, R. R. (1991). Everyday methods for assessing organizational effectiveness. *Social Problems, 38*(1), 1–19.

Apple, M. W. (1988). *Teachers and texts: A political economy of class and gender relations in education.* New York: Routledge.

Apple, M. W. (1991). The new technology: Is it part of the solution or part of the problem in education? *Computers in the Schools, 8*(1/2/3), 59–79.

Apple, M. W., & Christian-Smith, L. (Eds.) (1991). *The politics of the textbook.* New York: Routledge.

Aronson, Sidney H. (1977). Bell's electrical toy: What's the use? The sociology of early telephone usage. In I. de Sola Pool (Ed.), *The social impact of the telephone* (pp. 15–39). Cambridge, MA: MIT Press.

Astley, W. G., & Van de Ven, A. H. (1983). Central perspectives and debates in organization theory. *Administrative Science Quarterly, 28,* 245–273.

Attewell, P. (2001). The first and second digital divides. *Sociology of Education, 74*(3), 252–259.

Attewell, P., & Battle, J. (1999). Home computers and school performance. *The Information Society, 15*(1), 1–10.

Barab, S. A., MaKinster, J. G., Moore, J. A., & Cunningham, D. J. (2001). Designing and building an on-line community: The struggle to support sociability in the inquiry learning forum. *ETR&D—Educational Technology Research and Development, 49*(4), 71–96.

Bartky, I. R. (1989). The adoption of standard time. *Technology and Culture, 30*(1), 25–56.

Bauch, J. P. (1989). The TransPARENT model: New technology for parent involvement. *Educational Leadership, 47*(2), 32–34.

Bay, M., & Bryan, T. H. (1991). Teachers' reports of their thinking about at-risk learners and others. *Exceptionality, 2*(3), 127–139.

Becker, H. (1983). *School uses of microcomputers: Reports from a national survey*. Baltimore, MD: Johns Hopkins University, Center for the Social Organization of Schools.

Becker, H. (1986). *Instructional uses of school computers*. Reports from the 1985 national study. Baltimore, MD: Johns Hopkins University, Center for the Social Organization of Schools.

Becker, H. J., & Ravitz, J. L. (1998). The equity threat of promising innovations: Pioneering internet-connected schools. *Journal of Educational Computing Research, 19*(1), 1–26.

Becker, H. & Ravitz, J. (1999). The influence of computer and Internet use on teachers' pedagogical practices and perceptions. *Journal of Research on Computing in Education, 31*(4), 356–384.

Becker, H. J., & Riel, M. M. (December, 2000). *Teacher professional engagement and constructivist-compatible computer use*. Report #7. Irvine, CA: University of California, Irvine, Center for Research on Information Technology and Organizations.

Berger, P. L., & Luckmann, T. (1966). *The social construction of reality; a treatise in the sociology of knowledge*. Garden City, NY: Doubleday.

Bidwell, C. (1965). The school as a formal organization. In J. March (Ed.), *Handbook of organizations* (pp. 972–1022). Chicago: Rand-McNally.

Bijker W. E., Pinch, T. J. (2002). SCOT answers, other questions—A reply to Nick Clayton. *Technology and Culture, 43*(2), 361–369.

Bijker, W. E., Hughes, T. P., & Pinch, T. (Eds.). (1987). *The social construction of technology: New directions in the sociology and history of technology*. Cambridge: MIT Press.

Boden, D. (1990). The world as it happens. In G. Ritzer (Ed.), *Frontiers of social theory* (pp. 185–213). New York: Columbia University Press.

Boorstin, D. J. (1973). *The Americans: The democratic experience*. New York; Random House.

Boorstin, D. J. (1983). *The discoverers*. New York: Random House.

Borgmann, A. (1999). *Holding on to reality: The nature of information at the turn of the millennium*. Chicago: University of Chicago Press.

Borrell, J. (1992, September). America's shame: How we've abandoned our children's future. *Macworld, 9*(9), 25–30.

Bowman, J., Jr. (Ed.) (2001). Adoption and diffusion of educational technology in urban areas. *Journal of Educational Computing Research, 25*(1), 1–4.

Boysen, T. C. (1992). Irreconcilable differences: Effective urban schools versus restructuring. *Education and Urban Society, 25*(1), 85–95.

Brown, J. A. (1994). Implications of technology for the enhancement of decisions in school-based management schools. *International Journal of Educational Media, 21*(2), 87–95.

Budin, H. R. (1991). Technology and the teacher's role. *Computers in the Schools, 8*(1/2/3), 15–25.

Burge, E. J., Laroque, D., & Boak, C. (2000). Baring professional souls: Reflections on Web life. *Journal of Distance Education, 15*(1), 81–98.

Burgstahler, S., & Cronheim, D. (2001). Supporting peer-peer and mentor-protégé relationships on the internet. *Journal of Research on Technology in Education, 34*(1), 59–74.

Carson, C. C., Huelskamp, R. M., & Woodall, T. D. (1991, May 10). *Perspectives on education in America*. Annotated briefing—third draft. Albuquerque, NM: Sandia National Labs, Systems Analysis Division.

Cheek, D. W. (1991). *Broadening participation in science, technology, and medicine*. University Park, PA: National Association for Science, Technology, and Society. Available as ERIC ED No. 339671.

Chubb, J. E., & Moe, T. M. (1990). *Politics, markets, and America's schools*. Washington, DC: The Brookings Institution.

Clayton N. (2002) SCOT answers, other questions—Rejoinder by Nick Clayton. *Technology and Culture, 43*(2), 369–370.

Clayton N. (2002). SCOT: Does it answer? *Technology and Culture, 43*(2), 351–360.

Cohen, D. K. (1987). Educational technology, policy, and practice. *Educational Evaluation and Policy Analysis, 9*(2), 153–170.

Cohen, E. G., Lotan, R. A., & Leechor, C. (1989). Can classrooms learn? *Sociology of Education, 62*(1), 75–94.

Coleman, J. (1993). The rational reconstruction of society. *American Sociological Review, 58*, 1–15.

Coleman, J. S. (1966). *Equality of educational opportunity*. Washington, DC: US Department of Health, Education, and Welfare; Office of Education.

Compaine, B. M. (2001). *The digital divide: Facing a crisis or creating a myth?* Cambridge, MA: MIT Press.

Comstock, D. E., & Scott, W. R. (1977). Technology and the structure of subunits: Distinguishing individual and workgroup effects. *Administrative Science Quarterly, 22*, 177–202.

Covi, L. M. (2000). Debunking the myth of the Nintendo generation: How doctoral students introduce new electronic communication practices into university research. *Journal of the American Society for Information Science, 51*(14), 1284–1294.

Crabtree, A., Nichols, D. M., O'Brien, J., Rouncefield, M., & Twidale, M. B. (2000). Ethnomethodologically informed ethnography and information system design. *Journal of the American Society for Information Science, 51*(7), 666–682.

Cuban, L. (1984). *How teachers taught: Constancy and change in American classrooms, 1890–1980*. New York: Longman.

Cuban, L. (1986). *Teachers and machines: The classroom use of technology since 1920*. New York: Teachers College Press.

Cuban, L. (1993). Computers meet classroom: Classroom wins. *Teachers College Record, 95*(2), 185–210.

Cuban, L. (2001). *Oversold and underused: Computers in the classroom*. Cambridge, MA: Harvard.

Culkin, J. M. (1965, October). Film study in the high school. *Catholic High School Quarterly Bulletin*.

Damarin, S. K. (1991). Feminist unthinking and educational technology. *Educational and Training Technology International, 28*(2), 111–119.

Dantley, M. E. (1990). The ineffectiveness of effective schools leadership: An analysis of the effective schools movement from a critical perspective. *Journal of Negro Education, 59*(4), 585–98.

Danziger, J. N., & Kraemer, K. L. (1986). *People and computers: The impacts of computing on end users in organizations*. New York: Columbia University Press, 1986.

Darnton, R. (1984). *The great cat massacre and other episodes in French cultural history*. New York: Basic.

David, J. L. (1987). *Annual report, 1986*. Jackson, MS: Southern Coalition for Educational Equity. Available as ERIC ED No. 283924.

Davidson, J., McNamara, E., & Grant, C. M. (2001). Electronic networks and systemic school reform: Examining the diverse roles and functions of networked technology in changing school environments. *Journal of Educational Computing Research, 25*(4), 441–54.

Davies, D. (1988). Computer-supported cooperative learning systems: Interactive group technologies and open learning. *Programmed Learning and Educational Technology, 25*(3), 205–215.

Day, T. (1992). Capital-labor substitution in the home. *Technology and Culture, 33*(2), 302–327.

de Sola Pool, I. (Ed.) (1977). *The social impact of the telephone*. Cambridge: MIT Press.

DeVaney, A. (Ed.) (1994). *Watching Channel One: The convergence of students, technology, & private business*. Albany, NY: State University of NY Press.

Dexter, S., Anderson, R., & Becker, H. (1999). Teachers' views of computers as catalysts for changes in their teaching practice. *Journal of Computing in Education, 31*(3), 221–239.

DiMaggio, P. J., & Powell, W. W. (1983). The iron cage revisited: Institutional isomorphism and collective rationality in organizational fields. *American Sociological Review, 48,* 147-160.

Doctor, R. D. (1991). Information technologies and social equity: Confronting the revolution. *Journal of the American Society for Information Science, 42*(3), 216-228.

Doctor, R. D. (1992). Social equity and information technologies: Moving toward information democracy. *Annual Review of Information Science and Technology, 27,* 43-96.

Downey G. (2001). Virtual webs, physical technologies, and hidden workers—The spaces of labor in information internetworks. *Technology and Culture, 42*(2), 209-235.

Dreeben, R., & Barr, R. (1988). Classroom composition and the design of instruction. *Sociology of Education, 61*(3), 129-142.

Dresang, E. T. (1999). More research needed: Informal information-seeking behavior of youth on the Internet. *Journal of the American Society for Information Science, 50*(12), 1123-1124.

Duckitt, J. (1992-93). Prejudice and behavior: A review. *Current Psychology: Research and Reviews, 11*(4), 291-307.

Dupagne, M., & Krendl, K. A. (1992). Teachers' attitudes toward computers: A review of the literature. *Journal of Research on Computing in Education, 24*(3), 420-429.

Durndell, A., & Lightbody, P. (1993). Gender and computing: Change over time? *Computers in Education, 21*(4), 331-336.

Eisenstein, E. (1979). *The printing press as an agent of change.* Two vols. New York: Cambridge.

Ellsworth, E., & Whatley, M. H. (1990). *The ideology of images in educational media: Hidden curriculums in the classroom.* New York: Teachers College Press.

Ellul, J. (1964). *The technological society.* New York: Knopf.

Elmore, R. F. (1992). Why restructuring won't improve teaching. *Educational Leadership, 49*(7), 44-48.

Epperson B. (2002). Does SCOT answer? A comment. *Technology and Culture, 43*(2), 371-373.

Evans, F. (1991). To "informate" or "automate": The new information technologies and democratization of the workplace. *Social Theory and Practice, 17*(3), 409-439.

Febvre, L., & Martin, H.-J. (1958). *The coming of the book: The impact of printing, 1450-1800.* London: Verso.

Fidel, R. (1999). A visit to the information mall: Web searching behavior of high school students. *Journal of the American Society for Information Science, 50*(1), 24-37.

Firestone, W. A., & Herriott, R. E. (1982). *Rational bureaucracy or loosely coupled system? An empirical comparison of two images of organization.* Philadelphia, PA: Research for Better Schools, Inc. Available as ERIC Report ED 238096.

Florman, Samuel C. (1981). *Blaming technology: The irrational search for scapegoats.* New York: St. Martin's.

Fredericks, J., & Brown, S. (1993). School effectiveness and principal productivity. *NASSP Bulletin, 77*(556), 9-16.

Fulk, J. (1993). Social construction of communication technology. *Academy of Management Journal, 36*(5), 921-950.

Gagné, R. M. (1987). *Educational technology: Foundations.* Hillsdale, NJ: Erlbaum.

Gagné, R., Briggs, L., & Wager, W. (1992). *Principles of instructional design* (4th ed.). Fort Worth, TX: Harcourt Brace Jovanovich.

Gamoran, A. (2001). American schooling and educational inequality: A forecast for the 21st century. *Sociology of Education,* Special Issue - SI 2001, 135-153.

Gamson, W. (1975). *The strategy of social protest.* Homewood, IL: Dorsey.

Gardels, N. (1991). The Nintendo presence (interview with N. Negroponte). *New Perspectives Quarterly, 8,* 58-59.

Garfinkel, H. (1967). *Studies in ethnomethodology.* Englewood Cliffs, NJ: Prentice-Hall.

Garson, B. (1989). *The electronic sweatshop: How computers are transforming the office of the future into the factory of the past.* New York: Penguin.

Gilbert, T. (1978). *Human competence: Engineering worth performance.* New York: McGraw Hill.

Gilligan, C. (1982). *In a different voice: Psychological theory and women's development.* Cambridge: Harvard.

Gilligan, C., Lyons, N. P., & Hanmer, T. J. (1990). *Making connections: The relational worlds of adolescent girls at Emma Willard School.* Cambridge: Harvard University Press.

Gilligan, C., Ward, J. V., & Taylor, J. M. (Eds.). (1988). *Mapping the moral domain: A contribution of women's thinking to psychological theory and education.* Cambridge: Harvard.

Giroux, H. A. (1981). *Ideology, culture & the process of schooling.* Philadelphia: Temple University Press.

Glendenning, C. (1990). *When technology wounds: The human consequences of progress.* New York: Morrow.

Godfrey, E. (1965). *Audio-visual media in the public schools, 1961-64.* Washington, DC: Bureau of Social Science Research. Available as ERIC ED No. 003 761.

Greve, H. R., & Taylor A. (2000). Innovations as catalysts for organizational change: Shifts in organizational cognition and search. *Administrative Science Quarterly, 45*(1), 54-80.

Hadley, M., & Sheingold, K. (1993). Commonalties and distinctive patterns in teachers' integration of computers. *American Journal of Education, 101*(3), 261-315.

Hall, G., & Hord, S. (1984). Analyzing what change facilitators do: The intervention taxonomy. *Knowledge, 5*(3), 275-307.

Hall, G., & Loucks, S. (1978). Teacher concerns as a basis for facilitating and personalizing staff development. *Teachers College Record, 80*(1), 36-53.

Hancock, D. R., & Flowers, C. P. (2001). Comparing social desirability responding on World Wide Web and paper-administered surveys. *ETR&D—Educational Technology Research and Development, 49*(1), 5-13.

Hardy, V. (1992). Introducing computer-mediated communications into participative management education: The impact on the tutor's role. *Education and Training Technology International, 29*(4), 325-331.

Heinich, R. (1971). *Technology and the management of instruction.* Monograph No. 4. Washington, DC: Association for Educational Communications and Technology.

Herzfeld, M. (1992). *The social production of indifference: Exploring the symbolic roots of Western bureaucracy.* New York: Berg.

Higgs, E., Light, A., & Strong, D. (2000). *Technology and the good life?* Chicago, IL: University of Chicago Press.

Hlynka, D., & Belland, J. C. (Eds.) (1991). *Paradigms regained: The uses of illuminative, semiotic and post-modern criticism as modes of inquiry in educational technology.* Englewood Cliffs, NJ: Educational Technology Publications.

Holt, D. L. (1993). Rationality is hard work: An alternative interpretation of the disruptive effects of thinking about reasons. *Philosophical Psychology, 6*(3), 251-266.

Honey, M., & Moeller, B. (1990). *Teachers' beliefs and technology integration: Different values, different understandings.* Technical Report No. 6. New York: Bank Street College of Education, Center for Technology in Education.

Honig, B. (1989). The challenge of making history "come alive." *Social Studies Review, 28*(2), 3-6.

Hooper, R. (1969). A diagnosis of failure. *AV Communication Review, 17*(3), 245-264.

Hooper, R. (1990). Computers and sacred cows. *Journal of Computer Assisted Learning, 6*(1), 2-13.

Hooper, S. (1992). Cooperative learning and CBI. *Educational Technology: Research & Development, 40*(3), 21-38.

Hooper, S., & Hannafin, M. (1991). The effects of group composition on achievement, interaction, and learning efficiency during computer-based cooperative instruction. *Educational Technology: Research & Development, 39*(3), 27-40.

Hounshell, D. A. (1984). *From the American system to mass production, 1800-1932: The development of manufacturing technology in the United States.* Baltimore, MD: Johns Hopkins University Press.

Hrebiniak, L. G., & Joyce, W. F. (1985). Organizational adaptation: Strategic choice and environmental determinism. *Administrative Science Quarterly, 30,* 336-349.

Hughes, A. C., & Hughes, T. P. (Eds.). (2000). *Systems, experts, and computers: The systems approach in management and engineering, World War II and after.* Cambridge, MA: MIT Press.

Hutchin, T. (1992). Learning in the 'neural' organization. *Education and Training Technology International, 29*(2), 105-108.

Hyman, H. H. (1955). *Survey design and analysis: Principles, cases, and procedures.* Glencoe, IL: Free Press.

Hyman, H. H. (1991). *Taking society's measure: A personal history of survey research.* New York: Russell Sage Foundation.

ISET (Integrated Studies of Educational Technology). (May 2002). *Professional development and teachers' use of technology.* (Draft.) Menlo Park, CA: SRI International. Available at: http://www.sri.com/policy/cep/mst/

Järvelä, S., Bonk, C. J., Lehtinen, E., & Lehti, S. (1999). A theoretical analysis of social interactions in computer-based learning environments: Evidence for reciprocal understandings. *Journal of Educational Computing Research, 21*(3), 363-88.

Jennings, H. (1985). *Pandaemonium: The coming of the machine as seen by contemporary observers, 1660-1886.* New York: Free Press.

Joerges, B. (1990). Images of technology in sociology: Computer as butterfly and bat. *Technology and Culture, 31*(1), 203-227.

Jonassen, D. H., & Kwon H. I. (2001). Communication patterns in computer mediated versus face-to-face group problem solving. *ET&D—Educational Technology Research and Development, 49*(1), 35-51.

Joyce, B., & Weil, M. (1986). *Models of teaching.* (3rd ed.). Englewood Cliffs, NJ: Prentice Hall.

Kay, R. (1992). An analysis of methods used to examine gender differences in computer-related behavior. *Journal of Educational Computing Research, 8*(3), 277-290.

Kerr, S. T. (1977). Are there instructional developers in the school? A sociological look at the development of a profession. *AV Communication Review,*

Kerr, S. T. (1978) Consensus for change in the role of the learning resources specialist: Order and position differences. *Sociology of Education, 51,* 304-323.

Kerr, S. T. (1982). Assumptions futurists make: Technology and the approach of the millennium. *Futurics, 6*(3&4), 6-11.

Kerr, S. T. (1989a). Pale screens: Teachers and electronic texts. In P. Jackson and S. Haroutunian-Gordon (Eds.), *From Socrates to software: The teacher as text and the text as teacher* (pp. 202-223). 88th NSSE Yearbook, Part I. Chicago: University of Chicago Press.

Kerr, S. T. (1989b). Technology, teachers, and the search for school reform. *Educational Technology Research and Development, 37*(4), 5-17.

Kerr, S. T. (1990a). Alternative technologies as textbooks and the social imperatives of educational change. In D. L. Elliott & A. Woodward (Eds.), *Textbooks and schooling in the United States* (pp. 194-221). 89th NSSE Yearbook, Part I. Chicago: University of Chicago Press.

Kerr, S. T. (1990b). Technology : Education :: Justice : Care. *Educational Technology, 30*(11), 7-12.

Kerr, S. T. (1991). Lever and fulcrum: Educational technology in teachers' thinking. (1991). *Teachers College Record, 93*(1), 114-136.

Kerr, S. T. (2000). Technology and the quality of teachers' professional work: Redefining what it means to be an educator. In C. Dede (Ed.), *2000 State Educational Technology Conference Papers* (pp. 103-120). Washington, DC: State Leadership Center, Council of Chief State School Officers.

Kerr, S. T., & Taylor, W. (Eds.). (1985). Social aspects of educational communications and technology. *Educational Communication and Technology Journal, 33*(1).

Kilgour, F. G. (1998). *The evolution of the book.* New York: Oxford.

Kingston, P. W. (2001). The unfulfilled promise of cultural capital theory. *Sociology of Education,* Special Issue - SI 2001, 88-99.

Kirk, D. (1992). Gender issues in information technology as found in schools: Authentic/synthetic/fantastic? *Educational Technology, 32*(4), 28-35.

Kling, R. (1991). Computerization and social transformations. *Science, Technology, and Human Values, 16*(3), 342-267.

Kober, N. (1991). *What we know about mathematics teaching and learning.* Washington, DC: Council for Educational Development and Research. Available as ERIC ED No. 343793.

Kondracke, M. (1992, September). The official word: How our government views the use of computers in schools. *Macworld, 9*(9), 232-236.

Kraft, J. F., & Siegenthaler, J. K. (1989). Office automation, gender, and change: An analysis of the management literature. *Science, Technology, and Human Values, 14*(2), 195-212.

Kuralt, R. C. (1987). The computer as a supervisory tool. *Educational Leadership, 44*(7), 71-72.

Lage, E. (1991). Boys, girls, and microcomputing. *European Journal of Psychology of Education, 6*(1), 29-44.

Laridon, P. E. (1990a). The role of the instructor in a computer-based interactive videodisc educational environment. *Education and Training Technology International, 27*(4), 365-374.

Laridon, P. E. (1990b). The development of an instructional role model for a computer-based interactive videodisc environment for learning mathematics. *Education and Training Technology International, 27*(4), 375-385.

Lee, V. E., Dedrick, R. F., & Smith, J. B. (1991). The effect of the social organization of schools on teachers' efficacy and satisfaction. *Sociology of Education, 64,* 190-208.

Leigh, P. R. (1999). Electronic connections and equal opportunities: An analysis of telecommunications distribution in Public Schools. *Journal of Research on Computing in Education, 32*(1), 108-127.

Lewis, R. (1990). Selected research reviews: Classrooms. *Journal of Computer Assisted Learning, 6*(2), 113-118.

Lin, X. D. (2001). Reflective adaptation of a technology artifact: A case study of classroom change. *Cognition and Instruction, 19*(4), 395-440.

Luke, C. (1989). *Pedagogy, printing, and Protestantism: The discourse on childhood.* Albany, NY: SUNY Press.

MacKnight, C. B. (2001). Supporting critical thinking in interactive learning environments. *Computers in the Schools, 17*(3-4), 17-32.

Madaus, G. F. (1991). *A technological and historical consideration of equity issues associated with proposals to change our nation's testing policy.* Paper presented at the Ford Symposium on Equity and Educational Testing and Assessment (Washington, DC, March, 1992). Available as ERIC ED No. 363618.

Martin, B. L., & Clemente, R. (1990). Instructional systems design and public schools. *Educational Technology: Research & Development, 38*(2), 61-75.

Marty, P. F. (1999). Museum informatics and collaborative technologies: The emerging socio-technological dimension of information science in museum environments. *Journal of the American Society for Information Science, 50*(12), 1083-1091.

Marvin, C. (1988). *When old technologies were new: Thinking about electric communication in the late nineteenth century*. New York: Oxford.

McAdam, D., McCarthy, J. D., & Zald, M. N. (1988). Social movements. In N. J. Smelser (Ed.), *Handbook of sociology* (pp. 695-737). Newbury Park, CA: Sage.

McArthur, C. A., & Malouf, D. B. (1991). Teachers' beliefs, plans, and decisions about computer-based instruction. *Journal of Special Education, 25*(1), 44-72.

McCarthy, J. D., & Zald, M. N. (1973). *The trend of social movements in America: Professionalization and resource mobilization*. Morristown, NJ: General Learning Press.

McDaniel, E., McInerney, W., & Armstrong, P. (1993). Computers and school reform. *Educational Technology: Research & Development, 41*(1), 73-78.

McIlhenny, A. (1991). Tutor and student role change in supported self-study. *Education and Training Technology International, 28*(3), 223-228.

McInerney, C., & Park, R. (1986). *Educational equity in the third wave: Technology education for women and minorities*. White Bear Lake, MN: Minnesota Curriculum Services Center. Available as ERIC ED No. 339667.

McKinlay, A., & Starkey, K. (Eds.). (1998). *Foucault, management and organization theory: From panopticon to technologies of self*. Thousand Oaks, CA: Sage.

McLaughlin, M. W. (1987). Implementation realities and evaluation design. *Evaluation Studies Review Annual, 12*, 73-97.

McLean, S., & Morrison, D. (2000). Sociodemographic characteristics of learners and participation in computer conferencing. *Journal of Distance Education, 15*(2), 17-36.

McLellan, H. (1991). Teachers and classroom management in a computer learning environment. *International Journal of Instructional Media, 18*(1), 19-27.

Mead, G. H. (1934). *Mind, self & society from the standpoint of a social behaviorist*. Chicago: University of Chicago Press.

Meyer, J. W., & Scott, W. R. (1983). *Organizational environments: Ritual and rationality*. Beverley Hills, CA: Sage.

Meyrowitz, J. (1985). *No sense of place: The impact of electronic media on social behavior*. New York: Oxford.

Mielke, K. (1990). Research and development at the Children's Television Workshop. [Introduction to thematic issue on "Children's learning from television."] *Educational Technology: Research & Development, 38*(4), 7-16.

Mintzberg, H. (1979). *The structuring of organizations*. Englewood Cliffs, NJ: Prentice-Hall.

Mitra, A. , LaFrance, B., & McCullough, S. (2001). Differences in attitudes between women and men toward computerization. *Journal of Educational Computing Research, 25*(3), 227-44.

Mort, J. (1989). *The anatomy of xerography: Its invention and evolution*. Jefferson, NC: McFarland.

Mortimer, P. (1993). School effectiveness and the management of effective learning and teaching. *School Effectiveness and School Improvement, 4*(4), 290-310.

Mumford, L. (1963). *Technics and civilization*. New York: Harcourt Brace.

Naisbitt, J., & Aburdene, P. (1990). *Megatrends 2000: Ten new directions for the 1990s*. New York: Morrow.

Nartonis, D. K. (1993). Response to Postman's Technopoly. *Bulletin of Science, Technology, and Society, 13*(2), 67-70.

National Commission on Excellence in Education. (1983). *A nation at risk: The imperative for educational reform*. Washington, DC: US Government Printing Office.

National Governors' Association. (1986). *Time for results: The governors' 1991 report on education*. Washington, DC: Author.

National Governors' Association. (1987). *Results in education, 1987*. Washington, DC: Author.

Natriello, G. (2001). Bridging the second digital divide: What can sociologists of education contribute? *Sociology of Education, 74*(3), 260-265.

Nelkin, D. (1977). *Science textbook controversies and the politics of equal time*. Cambridge, MA: MIT Press.

Nelson, C. S., & Watson, J. A. (1991). The computer gender gap: Children's attitudes, performance, and socialization. *Journal of Educational Technology Systems, 19*(4), 345-353.

Neuter computer. (1986). New York: Women's Action Alliance, Computer Equity Training Project.

Newman, D. (1990a). *Opportunities for research on the organizational impact of school computers*. Technical Report No. 7. New York: Bank Street College of Education, Center for Technology in Education.

Newman, D. (1990b). *Technology's role in restructuring for collaborative learning*. Technical Report No. 8. New York: Bank Street College of Education, Center for Technology in Education.

Newman, D. (1991). *Technology as support for school structure and school restructuring*. Technical Report No. 14. New York: Bank Street College of Education, Center for Technology in Education.

Noble, D. (1989). Cockpit cognition: Education, the military and cognitive engineering. *AI and Society, 3*, 271-296.

Noble, D. (1991). *The classroom arsenal: Military research, information technology, and public education*. New York: Falmer.

Norberg, A. L. (1990). High-technology calculation in the early 20th century: Punched card machinery in business and government. *Technology and Culture, 31*(4), 753-779.

Norris, A. E., & Ford, K. (1994). Associations between condom experiences and beliefs, intentions, and use in a sample of urban, low-income, African-American and Hispanic youth. *AIDS Education and Prevention, 6*(1), 27-39.

Nunan, T. (1983). *Countering educational design*. New York: Nichols.

Nye, E. F. (1991). Computers and gender: Noticing what perpetuates inequality. *English Journal, 80*(3), 94-95.

Ogletree, S. M., & Williams, S. W. (1990). Sex and sex-typing effects on computer attitudes and aptitude. *Sex Roles, 23*(11-12), 703-713.

Olson, John. (1988). *Schoolworlds/Microworlds: Computers and the culture of the classroom*. New York: Pergamon.

Orr, J. E. (1996). *Talking about machines: An ethnography of a modern job*. Ithaca, NY: ILR Press.

Orrill, C. H. (2001). Building technology-based, learner-centered classrooms: The evolution of a professional development framework. *ETR&D—Educational Technology Research and Development, 49*(1), 15-34.

Owen, D. (1986, February). Copies in seconds. *The Atlantic*, 65-72.

Pagels, H. R. (1988). *The dreams of reason: The computer and the rise of the sciences of complexity*. New York: Simon & Schuster.

Palmquist, R. A. (1992). The impact of information technology on the individual. *Annual Review of Information Science and Technology, 27*, 3-42.

Parsons, T. (1949). *The structure of social action*. Glencoe, IL: Free Press.

Parsons, T. (1951). *The social system*. Glencoe, IL: Free Press.

PCAST (President's Committee of Advisors on Science and Technology). (March 1997). *Report to the President on the Use of Technology to*

Strengthen K-12 Education in the United States. Washington, DC: Author.

Peabody, R. L., & Rourke, F. E. (1965). The structure of bureaucratic organization. In J. March (Ed.), *Handbook of organizations* (pp. 802-837). Chicago: Rand McNally.

Pelgrum, W. J. (1993). Attitudes of school principals and teachers towards computers: Does it matter what they think? *Studies in Educational Evaluation, 19*(2), 199-212.

Perelman, L. (1992). *School's out: Hyperlearning, the new technology, and the end of education.* New York: Morrow.

Perelman, L. J. (1987). *Technology and transformation of schools.* Alexandria, VA: National School Boards Association, Institute for the Transfer of Technology to Education.

Perrow, C. (1984). *Normal accidents: Living with high-risk technologies.* New York: Basic.

Persell, C. H., & Cookson, P. W., Jr. (1987). Microcomputers and elite boarding schools: Educational innovation and social reproduction. *Sociology of Education, 60*(2), 123-134.

Piller, C. (1992, September). Separate realities: The creation of the technological underclass in America's schools. *Macworld, 9*(9), 218-231.

Postman, N. (1992). *Technopoly: The surrender of culture to technology.* New York: Knopf.

Power on! (1988). Washington, DC: Office of Technology Assessment, US Congress.

Prater, M. A., & Ferrara, J. M. (1990). Training educators to accurately classify learning disabled students using concept instruction and expert system technology. *Journal of Special Education Technology, 10*(3), 147-156.

Preston, N. (1992). Computing and teaching: A socially-critical review. *Journal of Computer Assisted Learning, 8,* 49-56.

Pritchard Committee for Academic Excellence. (1991). *KERA Update. What for....* Lexington, KY: Author. Available as ERIC ED No. 342058.

Purkey, S. C., & Smith, M. S. (1983). Effective schools: A review. *Elementary School Journal, 83,* 427-454.

Ravitch, D., & Finn, C. E. (1987). *What do our 17-year-olds know?* New York: Harper & Row.

Reigeluth, C. M., & Garfinkle, R. J. (1992). Envisioning a New System of Education. *Educational Technology, 32*(11), 17-23.

Reinen, I. J., & Plomp, T. (1993). Some gender issues in educational computer use: Results of an international comparative survey. *Computers and Education, 20*(4), 353-365.

Rice, R. E. (1992). Contexts of research on organizational computer-mediated communication. In M. Lea (Ed.), *Contexts of computer-mediated communication* (pp. 113-144). New York: Harvester Wheatsheaf.

Richey, R. (1986). *The theoretical and conceptual bases of instructional design.* New York: Kogan Page.

Ringstaff, C., Sandholtz, J. H., & Dwyer, D. C. (1991). *Trading places: When teachers utilize student expertise in technology-intensive classrooms.* ACOT Report 15. Cupertino, CA: Apple Computer, Inc.

Robbins, N. (2001). Technology subcultures and indicators associated with high technology performance in schools. *Journal of Research on Computing in Education, 33*(2), 111-24.

Rogers, E. (1962). *Diffusion of innovations* (3rd ed., 1983). New York: Free Press.

Romanelli, E. (1991). The evolution of new organizational forms. *Annual Review of Sociology, 17,* 79-103.

Ronnkvist, A. M., Dexter, S. L., & Anderson, R. E. (June, 2000). *Technology support: Its depth, breadth and impact in America's schools.* Report #5. Irvine, CA: University of California, Irvine, Center for Research on Information Technology and Organizations.

Roscigno, V. J., & Ainsworth-Darnell, J. W. (1999). Race, cultural capital, and educational resources: Persistent inequalities and achievement returns. *Sociology of Education, 72*(3), 158-178.

Rosenbrock, H. H. (1990). *Machines with a purpose.* New York: Oxford.

Rosenholtz, S. J. (1985). Effective schools: Interpreting the evidence. *American Journal of Education, 94,* 352-388.

Rothschild-Whitt, J. (1979). The collectivist organization: An alternative to rational bureaucracy. *American Sociological Review, 44,* 509-527.

Rovai, A. P. (2001). Building classroom community at a distance: A case study. *ETR&D—Educational Technology Research and Development, 49*(4), 33-48.

Saettler, P. (1968). *A history of instructional technology.* New York: McGraw Hill.

Sandholtz, J. H., Ringstaff, C., & Dwyer, D. C. (1991). *The relationship between technological innovation and collegial interaction.* ACOT Report 13. Cupertino, CA: Apple Computer, Inc.

Savenye, W. (1992). Effects of an educational computing course on pre-service teachers' attitudes and anxiety toward computers. *Journal of Computing in Childhood Education, 3*(1), 31-41.

Schacter, J., Chung, G. K. W. K., & Dorr, A. (1998). Children's internet searching on complex problems: Performance and process analysis. *Journal of the American Society for Information Science, 49,* 840-850.

Scheerens, J. (1991). Process indicators of school functioning: A selection based on the research literature on school effectiveness. *Studies in Educational Evaluation, 17*(2-3), 371-403.

Schwartz, Paula A. (1987). *Youth-produced video and television.* Unpublished doctoral dissertation, Teachers College, Columbia University, New York, NY.

Scott, D., & Willits, F. K. (1994). Environmental attitudes and behavior: A Pennsylvania survey. *Environment and Behavior, 26*(2), 239-260.

Scott, W. R. (1975). Organizational structure. *Annual Review of Sociology, 1,* 1-20.

Scott, W. R. (1987). *Organizations: Rational, natural, and open systems.* Englewood Cliffs, NJ: Prentice Hall.

Scott, T., Cole, M., & Engel, M. (1992). Computers and education: A cultural constructivist perspective. In G. Grant (Ed.), *Review of research in education* (pp. 191-251). Vol. 18. Washington, DC: American Educational Research Association.

Scriven, M. (1986 [1989]). Computers as energy: Rethinking their role in schools. *Peabody Journal of Education, 64*(1), 27-51.

Segal, Howard P. (1985). *Technological utopianism in American culture.* Chicago: University of Chicago Press.

Sheingold, K., & Hadley, M. (1990, September). *Accomplished teachers: Integrating computers into classroom practice.* New York: Bank Street College of Education, Center for Technology in Education.

Sheingold, K., & Tucker, M. S. (Eds.). (1990). *Restructuring for learning with technology.* New York: Center for Technology in Education; Rochester, NY: National Center on Education and the Economy.

Shrock, S. A. (1985). Faculty perceptions of instructional development and the success/failure of an instructional development program: A naturalistic study. *Educational Communication and Technology, 33*(1), 16-25.

Shrock, S., & Higgins, N. (1990). Instructional systems development in the schools. *Educational Technology: Research & Development, 38*(3), 77-80.

Sloan, D. (1985). *The computer in education: A critical perspective.* New York: Teachers College Press.

Smith, M. R. (1981). Eli Whitney and the American system of manufacturing. In C. W. Pursell, Jr. (Ed.), *Technology in America: A history of individuals and ideas* (pp. 45-61). Cambridge, MA: MIT Press.

Solomon, G. (1992). The computer as electronic doorway: Technology and the promise of empowerment. *Phi Delta Kappan, 74*(4), 327-329.

Spring, J. H. (1989). *The sorting machine revisited: National educational policy since 1945*. New York: Longman.

Spring, J. H. (1992). *Images of American life: A history of ideological management in schools, movies, radio, and television*. Albany, NY: State University of New York Press.

Sproull, L., & Kiesler, S. B. (1991a). *Connections: New ways of working in the networked organization*. Cambridge, MA: MIT Press.

Sproull, L., & Kiesler, S. B. (1991b). Computers, networks, and work. *Scientific American, 265*(3), 116-123.

Stafford-Levy, M., & Wiburg, K. M. (2000). Multicultural technology integration: The winds of change amid the sands of time. *Computers in the Schools, 16*(3-4), 121-34.

Steffen, J. O. (1993). *The tragedy of abundance*. Niwot, CO: University Press of Colorado.

Stevens, R., & Hall, R. (1997). Seeing tornado: How Video Traces mediate visitor understandings of (natural?) spectacles in a science museum, *Science Education, 18*(6), 735-748.

Susman, E. B. (1998). Cooperative learning: A review of factors that increase the effectiveness of cooperative computer-based instruction. *Journal of Educational Computing Research, 18*(4), 303-22.

Svensson, A. K. (2000). Computers in school: Socially isolating or a tool to promote collaboration? *Journal of Educational Computing Research, 22*(4), 437-53.

Telem, M. (1999). A case study of the impact of school administration computerization on the department head's role. *Journal of Research on Computing in Education, 31*(4), 385-401.

Tobin, K., & Dawson, G. (1992). Constraints to curriculum reform: Teachers and the myths of schooling. *Educational Technology: Research & Development, 40*(1), 81-92.

Toffler, A. (1990). *Powershift: Knowledge, wealth, and violence at the edge of the 21st century*. New York: Bantam Doubleday.

Trachtman, L. E., Spirek, M. M., Sparks, G. G., & Stohl, C. (1991). Factors affecting the adoption of a new technology. *Bulletin of Science, Technology, and Society, 11*(6), 338-345.

Travers, R. M. W. (1973). Educational technology and related research viewed as a political force. In R. M. W. Travers (Ed.), *Second handbook of research on teaching* (pp. 979-996). Chicago: Rand McNally.

Turkle, S. (1984). *The second self*. New York: Simon & Schuster.

Turkle, S. (1995). *Life on the screen: Identity in the age of the Internet,* New York, NY: Simon & Schuster.

Tyack, D. B. (1974). *The one best system: A history of American urban education*. Cambridge, MA: Harvard University Press.

van Assema, P., Pieterse, M., & Kok, G. (1993). The determinants of four cancer-related risk behaviors. *Health Education Research, 8*(4), 461-472.

Van de Ven, A. H., Polley, D. E., Garud, R., & Venkataraman, S. (1999). *The innovation journey.* New York: Oxford.

Waldo, D. (1952). The development of a theory of democratic administration. *American Political Science Review, 46,* 81-103.

Waters, M. (1993). Alternative organizational formations: A neo-Weberian typology of polycratic administrative systems. *The sociological review, 41*(1), 54-81.

Watson, D. M. (1990). The classroom vs. the computer room. *Computers in Education, 15*(1-3), 33-37.

Webb, M. B. (1986). *Technology in the schools: Serving all students*. Albany, NY: Governor's Advisory Committee for Black Affairs. Available as ERIC ED No. 280906.

Weber, M. (1978). *Economy and society*. In (Eds.). G. Roth & C. Wittich. Berkeley, CA: University of California Press.

Weizenbaum, J. (1976). *Computer power and human reason*. New York: W. H. Freeman.

Wilensky, R. (2000). Digital library resources as a basis for collaborative work. *Journal of the American Society for Information Science, 51*(3), 228-245.

Winner, L. (1977). *Autonomous technology*. Cambridge: MIT Press.

Winner, L. (1980). Do artifacts have politics? *Daedalus, 109*(1), 121-136.

Winner, L. (1986). *The whale and the reactor: A search for limits in an age of high technology*. Chicago: University of Chicago Press.

Winner, L. (1993). Upon opening the black box and finding it empty—Social constructivism and the philosophy of technology. *Science, Technology, and Human Values, 18*(3), 362-378.

Winston, B. (1986). *Misunderstanding media*. Cambridge, MA: Harvard University Press.

Wiske, M. S., Zodhiates, P., Wilson, B., Gordon, M., Harvey, W., Krensky, L., Lord, B., Watt, M., & Williams, K. (1988). *How technology affects teaching*. ETC Publication Number TR87-10. Cambridge, MA: Harvard University, Educational Technology Center.

Wolf, R. M. (1993). The role of the school principal in computer education. *Studies in Educational Evaluation, 19*(2), 167-183.

Wolfram, D., Spink, A., Jansen, B. J., & Saracevic, T. (2001). Vox populi: The public searching of the Web. *Journal of the American Society for Information Science and Technology, 52*(12), 1073-1074.

Wong, S. L. (1991). Evaluating the content of textbooks: Public interests and professional authority. *Sociology of Education, 64*(1), 11-18.

Worth, S., & Adair, J. (1972). *Through Navajo eyes: An exploration in film communication and anthropology*. Bloomington: Indiana University Press.

Zuboff, S. (1988). *In the age of the smart machine: The future of work and power*. New York: Basic.

EVERYDAY COGNITION AND SITUATED LEARNING

Philip H. Henning
Pennsylvania College of Technology

6.1 INTRODUCTION

Everyday cognition and situated learning investigates learning as an essentially social phenomena that takes place at the juncture of everyday interactions. These learning interactions are generated by the social relations, cultural history, and particular artifacts and physical dimensions of the learning environment. Brent Wilson and Karen Myers (2000) point out that there are distinct advantages in taking this approach. Taking a situated learning viewpoint promises a broader perspective for research and practice in instructional design. The diversity of disciplines that are interested in a social or practice learning point of view include linguistics, anthropology, political science, and critical theory among others allow researchers and practitioners to look beyond psychology-based learning theories.

In this chapter, I would like to take a broader look then is normally done some of the researchers that are engaged in exploring learning and local sense making from a situated perspective. The intent of this chapter is to provide a taste of some of the rich work being done in this field in the hopes that readers may explore ideas and authors in further detail in order to provide new avenues for investigation and to more critically examine learning, teaching, and instructional design from a practice-based approach. The term "practice" is defined as the routine, everyday activities of a group of people who share a common interpretive community.

6.2 THESIS: WAYS OF LEARNING

I would like to present an organizing argument to tie together the sections to follow. The argument runs as follows:

6.2.1 Ways of Knowing

There are particular ways of knowing, or ways of learning, that emerge from specific (situated) social and cultural contexts. These situated sites of learning and knowing are imbued with a particular set of artifacts, forms of talk, cultural history, and social relations that shape, in fundamental and generative ways, the conduct of learning. Learning is viewed, in this perspective, as the ongoing and evolving creation of identity and the production and reproduction of social practices both in school and out that permit social groups, and the individuals in these groups, to maintain commensal relations that promote the life of the group. It is sometimes helpful to think of this situated site of learning as a community of practice which may or may not be spatially contiguous.

6.2.2 Ethnomethods

Borrowing a term from ethnomethodology (Garfinkel, 1994), I am suggesting that these particular ways of learning are distinguishable by the operations or "ethnomethods" that are used to make sense of ongoing social interactions. These ethnomethods are used with talk (conversation, stories, slogans, everyday proverbs), inscriptions (informal and formal written and drawn documents) and artifacts to make specific situated sense of ongoing experiences including those related to learning and teaching.

The prefix "ethno" in ethnomethods indicates that these sense-making activities are peculiar to particular people in particular places who are dealing with artifacts and talk that are used in their immediate community of practice (Garfinkel, 1994a, p.11). These ethnomethods or, to put it in different words, these local methods of interpretation, that are used *in situ* to make sense of ongoing situations, are rendered visible to the investigator in the formal and informal representational practices people employ on a daily basis in everyday life (Henning, 1998a, p. 90).

6.2.3 Situated Nature of All Learning

The assumption is that learning in formal settings such as in schools and psychology labs is also situated (Butterworth, 1993; Clancey, 1993; Greeno & Group, M.S.M.T.A.P., 1998, see Lave, 1988. p. 25 ff. for her argument concerning learning in experimental laboratory situations and the problem of transfer). Formal and abstract learning is not privileged in any way and is not viewed as inherently better than or higher than any other type of learning.

6.2.4 Artifacts to Talk With

The gradual accumulation of practice-based descriptive accounts of learning in a diversity of everyday and nonschool situations within particular communities of practice holds the promise of a broader understanding of a type of learning that is unmanaged in the traditional school sense. Learning in nonschool settings has proven its success and robustness over many millennia. Multilingual language learning in children is one example of just this kind of powerful learning (Miller and Gildea, 1987, cited in Brown, Collins, & Duguid, 1989). How can we link these descriptive accounts of learning in a wide diversity of settings , as interesting as they are, so that some more general or "universal" characteristics of learning can be seen?

Attention paid to the representational practice of the participants in each of these diverse learning situations has some potential in establishing such a link. The representations that we are interested in here are not internal mental states that are produced by individual thinkers, but the physical, socially available "scratch pads" for the construction of meaning that are produced for public display. The representations of this type include speech, gesture, bodily posture, ephemeral written and graphical material such as diagrams on a whiteboard, artifacts, formal written material, tools, etc. What are the ways in which physical representations or inscriptions (Latour & Woolgar, 1986) are used to promote learning in these various communities of practice? These representations are not speculations by observers on the internal states produced by the learner that are assumed to mirror some outside, objective, reality with greater or lesser fidelity. The representations of interest are produced by the members of a community of practice in such a way that they are viewable by other members of the community of practice. Internal cognitive or affective states may be inferred from these practices, but the datum of interest at this stage in the analysis of learning is the physical display of these representations.

The representations that we are considering here are "inscribed" physically in space and time and may be "seen" with ear or eye or hand. They are not internal, individual, in the head symbolic representations that mirror the world, but are

physical and communal. A more descriptive word that may be used is "inscriptions" (Latour, 1986, p.7). Inscriptions must be capable of movement and transport in order to provide for the joint construction of making sense in everyday situations, but they also must retain a sense of consistency and immutability in order that they may be readable by the members of the community in other spaces and at other times. The act of inscribing implies a physical act of "writing," of intentionally producing a device to be used to communicate. Extending Latour's analysis, the immutability of inscriptions is a relative term- a gesture or bodily posture is transient yet immutable in the sense that its meaning is carried between members of a group.

These objects to "talk with" may consist of linguistic items such as conversation, stories, parables, proverbs or paralinguistic devices such as gestures and facial expressions. They may include formal written inscriptions such as textbooks and manuals and company policy, task analysis, tests and test scores which are usually a prime object of interest of educational researchers, but also may include a hand written note by a phone in the pharmacy that points to some locally expressed policy that is crucial for the operation of the store. Artifacts may also serve as representational devices. Commercial refrigeration technicians place spent parts and components in such a way to provide crucial information and instruction on a supermarket refrigeration system's local and recent history to technicians in an overlapping community of practice (Henning, 1998a).

The device produced may be of very brief duration such as a series of hand signals given from a roof to a crane operator who is positioning a climate control unit or an audio file of a message from the company founder on a web training page or the spatial arrangement of teacher's desk and the desks of students in a classroom or seminar room. The devices may be intentionally and consciously produced, but are more often done at the level of automaticity. Both individuals and collectivities produce these devices. The work of Foucault on prisons and hospitals (1994, 1995) describes some of these devices used for the instruction of prisoners and patients in the art of their new status.

Studies of the practice of language use (Duranti & Goodwin, 1992; Hanks, 1996), conversation (Goodwin, 1981, 1994), and studies of gestures and other "paralinguistic" events (Hall, 1959, 1966; Kendon, 1997; McNeill, 1992) are rich sources of new perspectives on how inscriptions are used in everyday life for coordination and instruction. Representational practice is an important topic in the field of science and technology studies. The representational practice in a science lab has been studied by Latour and Woolgar (1986) at the Salk Institute using ethnographic methods. An edited volume, *Representation in Scientific Practice* (Lynch & Woolgar, 1988a), is also a good introduction to work in this field.

Clancey (1995a) points out that a situated learning approach often fails to address internal, conceptual processes. The attention to communal and physical representational practices involved with teaching and learning and the production of inscriptions provides a way out of this dilemma. The study of the interpretive methods used by individuals to make sense of the representational practice, or what the American sociologist and ethnomethodologist Harold Garfinkel has termed the documentary method (Garfinkel, 1994a). The concept of the documentary method provides an analytical connection between the internal, conceptual processes that occur in individuals and the external practices of individuals in communities.

6.2.5 Constructing Identities and the Reconstruction of Communities of Practice

The ways in which individuals form identities as a member of a community of practice with full rights of participation is a central idea of the situated learning perspective. In all of these descriptions, some type of individual transformation reflected in a change in individual identity is involved. Examples of the production of identity in the literature include studies of the movement from apprentice to journeyman in the trades, trainee to technician, novice into an identity of an expert, the process of legitimate peripheral participation in Jean Lave and Etienne Wenger's work (1991), tribal initiation rites, among others. All of these transitions involve a progression into deeper participation into a specific community of practice. In most cases the new member will be associated with the community and its members over a period of time. However, for the majority of students graduating from high school in the industrialized world, the passage is out of and away from the brief time spent in the situated and local community of practice at school. Applying a community of practice metaphor for learning in school-based settings without questioning the particulars of identity formation in these settings can be problematic (Eckert, 1989).

A second important and symmetrical component of the formation of individual identity by the process of ever increasing participation, is the dialectical process of change that occurs in the community of practice as a whole as the new generation of members joins the community of practice. Implicit in this "changing of the guard" is the introduction of new ideas and practices that change the collective identity of the community of practice. The relation between increasing individual participation and changes in the community as a whole involves a dynamic interaction between individuals and community (Linehan & McCarthy, 2001). Conflict is to be expected and the evolution of the community of practice as a whole from this conflict to be assumed (Lave, 1993, p. 116 cited in Linehan & McCarthy, 2001).

The process of individual identity formation and the process of a community of practice experiencing evolutionary or revolutionary change in its collective identity are moments of disturbance and turbulence and offer opportunities for the researcher to see what otherwise might be hidden from view.

6.2.6 Elements of a Practice-Based Approach to Learning

A practice–based approach to learning is used here in this chapter to describe a perspective on learning that views learning as social at its base, that involves a dialectical production of individual and group identities, and is mediated in its particulars by semiotic resources that are diverse in their structure, are physical and not mental, and meant for display.

There are a number of advantages to be gained by treating learning from a practice-based approach. The basic outline of this approach as been used successfully in studying other areas of human interaction including scientific and technical work, linguistics, and work practice and learning (Chaiklin & Lave, 1993; Hanks, 1987, 1996, 2000; Harper & Hughes, 1993; Goodwin & Ueno, 2000; Pickering, 1992; Suchman, 1988).

The first advantage is that the artificial dichotomy between in-school learning and learning in all other locations is erased. Learning as seen from a practice based approach is always situated in a particular practice such as work, school, or the home. Organized efforts to create learning environments through control of content and delivery with formal assessment activities, such as those that take place in schools, are not privileged in any way. These organized, school based efforts stand as one instance of learning as an equal among others when seen from a practice based approach. By taking this approach to learning, our basic assumptions about learning are problematized in so far as we refuse to accept school learning as a natural order that cannot be questioned.

A second advantage of taking this approach is to stimulate comparative research activity that examines learning that is situated in locations that are both culturally and socially diverse. A matrix of research program goals is possible that allows for comparative work to be done on learning that is located socially within or across societies with diverse cultural bases. For instance, apprenticeship learning can be examined and contrasted with other forms of learning such as formal school learning or learning in religious schools within a culture or the comparative work can be carried out between cultures using the same or different social locations of learning.

A third significant advantage of taking a practice-based approach is that learning artifacts and the physical and cultural dimensions of the learning space are brought to the center of the analysis. Artifacts employed in learning are revealed in their dynamic, evolving and ad hoc nature rather than being seen as material "aids" that are secondary to mental processes. The social and physical space viewed from a practice based approach is a living theater set (Burke, 1945) that serves to promote the action of learning in dynamic terms rather than appearing in the analysis as a static "container" for learning. The construction of meaning becomes accessible by examining the traces made by material artifacts including talk as they are configured and reconfigured to produce the external representational devices that are central to all learning. The study of the creation of these external representational devices provides a strong empirical base for studies of learning. This approach holds the promise of making visible the "seen but unnoticed" (Garfinkel, 1994, p. 36; Schutz, 1962) background, implicit, understandings that arise out of the practical considerations of their particular learning circumstance. A brief description of some of the salient elements to be found in a practice-based approach to the study of learning follows below.

6.2.6.1 A Focus on the Creation of Publicly Available Representations. A practice-approach to learning asks: How do people build diverse representations that are available in a material form to be easily read by the community of practice in which learning is taking place? The representational practices of a community of learners produce an ever-changing array of artifacts that provide a common, external, in the world, map of meaning construction for both members and researchers alike. Attention to representational practices has proved fruitful for the study of how scientists carry out the work of discovery (Lynch & Woolgar, 1988a). David Perkins' (1993) concept of the person-plus is one example of this approach in studies of thinking and learning.

6.2.6.2 A Focus on the Specific Ways of Interpreting These Representations.
A practice-based approach asks what are the methods that are used by members of a particular community of practice to make sense of the artifacts that are produced. What are the features that are in the background of situations that provide the interpretive resources to make sense of everyday action and learning. Harold Garfinkel has termed this process of interpretation the "documentary method" (Garfinkel, 1994a)

6.2.6.3 A Focus on How New Members Build Identities.
A researcher who adopts a practice-based approach asks questions concerning the ways in which members are able to achieve full participation in a community of practice. Learning takes place as apprentice become journeyman, newcomer becomes an old-timer. This changing participation implies changes in the identities of the participants. How do these identity transformations occur and what is the relationship between identity and learning?

6.2.6.4 A Focus on the Changing Identities of Communities of Practice.
Learning involves a change in individual identity and an entry into wider participation in a community of practice. A practice-based approach to learning assumes that the situated identities of communities of practice are in evolution and change. These identities are situated (contingent) because of the particular mix of the members at a given time (old, young, new immigrants, etc.) and by virtue of changes taking place in the larger social and cultural arena. What can be said about the role of the individual members in the changes in identity of a community of practice? Do organizations themselves learn, and if so how? (Salomon & Perkins, 1998).

6.2.6.5 A Preference for Ethnographic Research Methods.
The methods used in ethnographic field studies are often employed in the study of the everyday practice of learning. Some studies include the use of "naturalistic" experiments in the field such as those carried out by Sylvia Scribner (1997) with industrial workers, or Jean Lave with West African apprentice tailors (1977, 1997).

6.2.6.6 Attention to the Simultaneous Use of Multiple Semiotic Resources.
A practice-based approach pays attention to the simultaneous use of a diversity of sign resources in learning. These resources for meaning construction are located in speech and writing in the traditional view of learning. However, multiple semiotic resources are also located in the body in activities such as pointing and gesturing (Goodwin, 1990), in

graphic displays in the environment, in the sequences within which signs are socially produced such as turn taking in conversation, and in the social structures and artifacts found in daily life (Goodwin, 2000).

6.3 TERMS AND TERRAIN

A number of overlapping but distinct terms are used to describe thinking and learning in everyday situations. It may be helpful to briefly review some of these terms as a means of scouting out the terrain before proceeding to the individual sections that describe some of the researcher's work in the field of situated learning broadly taken.

6.3.1 Everyday Cognition

Everyday cognition, the term used by Rogoff and Lave (1984), contrasts lab-based cognition with cognition as it occurs in the context of everyday activities. Lave (1998) uses the term just plain folk (jpf) to describe people who are learning in everyday activities. Brown et al. (1989) prefer the term apprentices and suggest that jfps (just plain folks) and apprentices learn in much the same way. Jfps are contrasted with students in formal school settings and with practitioners. When the student enters the school culture, Brown et al., maintain, everyday learning strategies are superceded by the precise, well-defined problems of school settings.

Everyday cognitive activity makes use of socially provided tools and schemas, is a practical activity which is adjusted to meet the demands of a situation, and is not necessarily illogical and sloppy, but sensible and effective in solving problems (Rogoff, 1984). The term "everyday cognition" is used by the psychologist Leonard Poon (1989) to distinguish between studies in the lab and real world studies or everyday cognition studies. Topics for these studies by psychologists include common daily memory activities by adults at various stages in their life span and studies of observed behavior of motivation and everyday world knowledge systems. In summary, the term refers to the everyday activities of learning and cognition as opposed to the formal learning that takes place in classrooms and in lab settings.

6.3.2 Situated Action

The term "situated action" was introduced by researchers working to develop machines that could interact in an effective way with people. The term points to the limitations of a purely cognitivist approach. The cognitive approach assumes that mentalistic formulations of the individual are translated into plans that are the driving force behind purposeful behavior (Suchman, 1987). The use of the term situated action

. . . underscores the view that every course of action depends in essential ways upon its material and social circumstances. Rather than attempting to abstract action away from its circumstances and represent it as

a rational plan, the approach is to study how people use their circumstances to achieve intelligent action. (Suchman, 1987, p. 50)

Plans, as the word is used in the title of Suchman's book, refers to a view of action that assumes that the actor has used past knowledge and a reading of the current situation to develop a plan from within the actor's individual cognitive process to intelligently meet the demands of the situation. The concept of situated purposeful action, in contrast, recognizes that plans are most often a retrospective construction produced after the fact to provide a rational explanation of action. A situated action approach sees that the unfolding of the activity of the actor is created by the social and material resources available moment to moment. Action is seen more as a developing, sense-making procedure than the execution of a preformulated plan or script that resides in the actor's mind.

6.3.3 Situated Cognition, Situated Learning

The term situated cognition implies a more active impact of context and culture on learning and cognition (Brown et al., 1989; McLellan, 1996) than is implied by the term everyday cognition. Many authors use these terms synonymously with a preference in the 1990s for the use of the term situated cognition. These views again challenge the idea that there is a cognitive core that is independent of context and intention (Resnick, Pontecorvo, & Säljö, 1997). The reliance of thinking on discourse and tools implies that it is a profoundly sociocultural activity. Reasoning is a social process of discovery that is produced by interactive discourse. William Clancey (1997) stresses the coordinating nature of human knowledge as we interact with the environment. Feedback is of paramount importance; knowledge in this view has a dynamic aspect in both the way it is formed and the occasion of its use. Clancey sees knowledge as "...a constructed capability-in-action" (Clancey, 1997, p. 4). Note the evolution of the term from everyday cognition as one type of cognition occurring in everyday activity, to the term, situated cognition, which implies a general and broader view of cognition and learning in any situation. Situated cognition occurs in any context, in school or out, and implies a view toward knowledge construction and use that is related to that of the constructivists (Duffy & Jonassen, 1992). Tools as resources, discourse, and interaction all play a role in producing the dynamic knowledge of situated cognition. Kirshner and Whitson (1997), in their introduction to an edited collection of chapters on situated cognition (p. 4), elevate the approach to a theory of situated cognition and define it in part as an opposition to the entrenched academic position that they term individualistic psychology. In this chapter I will not make any claims for a theory of situated learning. Rather, I am interested in providing a broad sketch of the terrain and some of the authors working in this field.

Perhaps the simplest and most direct definition of the term situated learning is given by the linguist William Hanks in his introduction to Lave and Wenger (1991). He writes that he first heard ideas of situated learning when Jean Lave spoke at a 1990 workshop on linguistic practice at the University of Chicago. The idea of situated learning was exciting because it located learning "at the middle of co-participation rather than in the heads of individuals." He writes of this approach that

...Lave and Wenger situate learning in certain forms of social co-participation. Rather than asking what kinds of cognitive processes and conceptual structures are involved, they ask what kinds of social engagements provide the proper contexts for learning to take place. (Lave & Wenger, 1991 p.14)

A focus on situated learning, as opposed to a focus on situated cognition, moves the study of learning away from individual cognitive activity that takes place against a backdrop of social constraints and affordances and locates learning squarely in co-participation. Hanks suggests that the challenge is to consider learning as a process that takes place in what linguists term participation frameworks and not in an individual mind. A participation framework includes the speakers "footing" or alignment toward the people and setting in a multiparty conversation. Goffman (1981) used this concept to extend the description of the traditional dyad of linguistic analysis to include a more nuanced treatment of the occasions of talk (Hanks, 1996, p. 207). The shift from situated cognition to situated learning is also a shift to a consideration of these participation frameworks as a starting point for analysis. One method of describing the substance of these frameworks is through the use of the concept of a community of practice which we will take up later in this chapter.

6.3.4 Distributed Cognition

Distributed cognition is concerned with how representations of knowledge are produced both inside and outside the heads of individuals. It asks how this knowledge is propagated between individuals and artifacts and how this propagation of knowledge representations effects knowledge at the systems level (Nardi, 1996, p. 77). Pea suggests that human intelligence is distributed beyond the human organism by involving other people, using symbolic media, and exploiting the environment and artifacts (Pea, 1993). David Perkins (1993) calls this approach to distributed cognition the person-plus approach, as contrasted with the person-solo approach to thinking and learning. Amplifications of a person's cognitive powers are produced by both high technology artifacts such as calculators and computers, but also by the physical distribution of cognition generally onto pencil and paper or simple reminders such as a folder left in front of a door. Access to knowledge, still conceived of in a static sense, is crucial. The resources are still considered from the perspective of the individual as external aids to thinking. The social and semiotic component of these resources is not generally considered in this approach.

6.3.5 Informal Learning

This term has been used in adult education and in studies of workplace learning. Marsick and Watkins (1990) define informal learning in contrast to formal learning. They include incidental learning in this category. Informal learning is not classroom based nor is it highly structured. Control of learning rests in the hands of the learner. The intellectual roots for this approach are in the work of John Dewey and in Kurt Lewin's work in group dynamics, and Argyris and Schön's work in organizational learning and the reflective practitioner. Oddly, there is not much if any reference to the work of everyday cognition or situated learning in these works.

6.3.6 Social Cognition

The last of these terms is social cognition. There is a large and new body of literature developing in social psychology on social cognition. Early studies in social cognition imported ideas from cognitive psychology and explored the role of cognitive structures and processes in social judgment. Until the late 1980s these "cold" cognitions involved representing social concepts and producing inferences. Recently there has been a renewed interest in the "hot" cognitions that are involved with motivation and affect and how goals, desires, and feelings influence what and how we remember and make sense of social situations (Kunda, 1999). In common with a constructivist and a situated action/participation approach, the emphasis is on the role individuals play in making sense of social events and producing meaning. Limitations of space preclude any further discussion of social cognition as seen from the social psychology tradition in this chapter. One recent introductory summary of work in this field may be found in Pennington (2000).

6.3.7 Sections to Follow

In the sections to follow, I discuss authors and ideas of situated cognition and practice loosely grouped around certain themes. It is not my intention to produce a complete review of the literature for each author or constellation of ideas, but will highlight certain unifying themes that support the ways of learning organizing thesis presented in the section above. One important area of interest for most authors writing on situated cognition, and for the somewhat smaller set of researchers carrying out empirical studies, is the ways in which representations are produced and propagated through the use of "artifacts" such as talk, tools, natural objects, inscriptions and the like. A second common theme is the development of identity. A third common theme is the co-evolution of social practice and individual situated action as it is expressed by the current state of a community of practice.

6.4 EVERYDAY COGNITION TO SITUATED LEARNING: TAKING PROBLEM SOLVING OUTDOORS

In 1973 Sylvia Scribner and Michael Cole wrote a now-classic chapter that challenged current conceptions of the effects of formal and informal education. This paper, and early work by Scribner and Cole on the use of math in everyday settings in a variety of cultures (Scribner, 1984; Carraher, Carraher, & Schliemann, 1985; Reed & Lave, 1979), asks: What are the relationships between the varied educational experiences of people and their problem solving skills in a variety of everyday settings in the United States, Brazil, and in Liberia?

Jean Lave extended this work to the United States in a study of the problem-solving activities of adults shopping in a supermarket (Lave, 1988). She concluded that adult shoppers used a gap closing procedure to solve problems, which turned out to yield a higher rate of correct answers than were achieved when the adults solved a similar problem in formal testing situations using the tools of school math. Lave developed an ethnographic critique of traditional theories of problem solving and learning transfer and elaborated a theory of cognition in practice (Lave, 1988). This work served as the basis for the development of situated learning by Lave (1991) and Lave and Wenger of legitimate peripheral participation (Lave & Wenger, 1991). Legitimate peripheral participation (LPP) is considered by Lave and Wenger to be a defining characteristic of situated learning. The process of LPP involves increasingly greater participation by learners as they move into a more central location in the activities and membership in a community of practice (Lave & Wenger, 1991, p. 29). Lave has continued her explorations of situated learning and recently has written extensively on the interaction of practice and identity (Lave, 2001).

6.4.1 Street Math and School Math

Studies on informal mathematics usage have been an early and a significant source for thinking about everyday cognition and the situated nature of learning. These studies have been carried out in Western and non-Western societies. The use of the distinction formal/informal is problematic. In this dichotomy, formal math is learned in school and informal math out of school. Using informal as a category for everything that is not formal requires us to find out beforehand where the math was learned. Nunes (1993, p. 5) proposes that informal mathematics be defined in terms of where it is practiced, thus mathematics practiced outside school is termed informal or street mathematics. The site, or as Nunes terms it, the scenario of the activities is the distinguishing mark. This has the advantage of not prejudging what is to be found within one category or the other and to a certain extent unseats the concept of a formal math from its position of preference that it holds as the most abstract of theoretical thinking. Formal math activity is redefined simply as math done at school. Another term that could be used instead of informal or everyday math is the term ethnomath, meaning mathematic activity done in the context of everyday life. The term is cognate with the term ethnobotany, for instance, indicating the types of local botanical understandings used by a group.

In order to investigate the relation between street math and school math, adults and children are observed using math, these people are interviewed, and certain "naturalistic experiments" are set up to lead people to use one or the other type of math. The aim is to see what various types of mathematic activities have in common.

If there are similarities in the processes of mathematical reasoning across everyday practices of vendors, foremen on construction sites, and fisherman, carpenters, and farmers, we can think of a more general description of street mathematics. Would a general description show that street mathematics is, after all, the same as school mathematics, or would there be a clear contrast? (Nunes, Schliemann, & Carraher, 1993, p.5)

Reed and Lave's work done in Liberia with tailors (1979) had shown there were differences in the use of mathematics between people who had been to school and who had not (see below). Carraher et al. (1985) asked in their study if the same person could show differences between the use of formal and informal methods. In other words, the same person might solve problems with formal methods in one situation and at other times solve them with informal methods. The research team found that context-embedded problems presented in the natural situation were much more easily solved and that the children failed to solve the same problem when it was taken out of context. The authors conclude that the children relied on different methods depending upon the situation. In the informal situation, a reliance on mental calculations closely linked to the quantities was used. In the formal test, the children tried to follow school-based routines. Field studies involving farmers, carpenters, fishermen, and school students have also been completed by the authors and have largely confirmed these findings.

Three themes stand out in this work. The first is the assumption that different situations or settings, occupational demands, and the availability of physical objects available for computation, influence the types of math activities that are used to solve problems. These settings and participants are diverse in terms of age (adults and children) and in terms of cultural location.

A second theme is that the practice of math is universal in all cultures and situations, both in school and out, and that a finer grained distinction than formal or informal needs to be made between math activities in various sites.

The third theme is the use of a "naturalistic" method that includes observational research combined with what Lave calls "naturally occurring experiments" (Lave, 1979, p. 438, 1997). This approach is preferred because of the recognition that the math practices are embedded in ongoing significant social activities. The change-making activities of the street vendors is linked to the intention of not shortchanging a customer or vendor rather than a high score on a school-based test. A fisherman estimating the number of crabs needed to make up a plate of crab fillet solves this math problem in a rich context that requires naturalistic or ethnographic methods as a research tool rather than statistical analysis of test results.

6.4.2 Sylvia Scribner: Studying Working Intelligence

Sylvia Scribner did her undergraduate work in economics at Smith and then found employment as an activities director of the electrical workers union in 1944. Later in the 1960s she worked in mental health for a labor group and became research director of mental health at a New York City health center. In her mid-forties she entered the Ph.D. program in psychology at the New School of Social Research in New York City doing her dissertation work on cross cultural perceptions of mental order. She had a strong commitment to promoting human welfare and justice through psychological research (Tobach, Falmagne, Parlee, Martin, & Kapelman, 1997, pp, 1–11). She died in 1991. Tributes to her work, biographical information, and a piece written by her daughter are found in *Mind and social practice: Selected writings of Sylvia Scribner* (Tobach et al., 1997), which is one of the volumes in the *Cambridge Learning in Doing* series. This volume collects together most of her important papers, some of which were printed in journals that are not easily obtainable.

At the end of the 1960s and into the 1970s the "cognitive revolution" in psychology had redirected the interests of many psychologists away from behavior and toward the higher mental functions including language, thinking, reasoning, and memory (Gardner, 1985). This change in psychology provided an open arena for Scribner's interests. In the 1970s, Scribner began a fruitful collaboration with Michael Cole at his laboratory at Rockefeller University. This lab later became the Laboratory of Comparative Human Cognition and has since relocated to the University of California, San Diego. Scribner spent several extended periods in Liberia, first working with the Kpelle people investigating how they think and reason (Cole & Scribner, 1974) and then with the Vai, also in Liberia, examining literacy (Scribner & Cole, 1981). During these years, Scribner studied the writings of Vygotsky and other psychologists associated with sociocultural-historical psychology and activity theory and incorporated many of their ideas into her own thinking (Scribner, 1990). During her entire research career, Scribner was interested in a research method that integrates observational research in the field with experiments conducted in the field on model cognitive tasks.

A central theme of Scribner and Cole's research is an investigation of the cognitive consequences of the social organization of education. In their 1973 paper that appeared in *Science* (Scribner & Cole, 1973) they wrote:

More particularly, we are interested in investigating whether differences in the social organization of education promote differences in the organization of learning and thinking. The thesis is that school practice is at odds with learning practices found in everyday activities. (p. 553)

Scribner and Cole state that cross-cultural psychological research confirms anthropological findings that certain basic cognitive capacities are found in all cultures. These include the ability to remember, generalize, form concepts and use abstractions. The authors found that, even though all informal social learning contexts nurture these same capacities, there are differences in how these capacities are used to solve problems in everyday activity. This suggests a division between formal and informal that is based not on location of the activities or where they were learned, but on the particular ways a given culture nurtures universal cognitive capacities.

Scribner and Cole's research on literacy practices among the Vai people in Liberia began with questions concerning the dependency of general abilities of abstract thinking and logical reasoning on mastery of a written language (Scribner & Cole, 1981; also a good summary in Scribner, 1984). The Vai are unusual in that they use three scripts: English learned in school, an indigenous Vai script learned from village tutors, and Arabic or Qur'anic literacy learned through group study with a teacher, but not in a school setting. Scribner and Cole found that general cognitive abilities did not depend on literacy in some general sense and that literacy without schooling (indigenous Vai and the Qur'anic script) was not associated with the same cognitive skills as literacy with schooling. The authors continued into a second phase of research and identified the particular linguistic and cognitive skills related to the two nonschooled literacies. The pattern of the skills found across literacies (English, Vai, Qur'anic) closely paralleled the uses and distinctive features of each literacy. Instead of conceiving of literacy as the use of written language which is the same everywhere and produces the same general set of cognitive consequences, the authors began to think of literacy as a term applying to a varied and open ended set of activities with written language (Scribner, 1984). At the conclusion of the research, Scribner and Cole called their analysis a practice account of literacy (Tobach et al., 1997, p. 202).

We used the term "practices" to highlight the culturally organized nature of significant literacy activities and their conceptual kinship to other culturally organized activities involving different technologies and symbol systems. Just as in the Vai research on literacy, other investigators have found particular mental representations and cognitive skills involved in culture-specific practice . . . (Scribner, 1984, p.13)

In the late 1970s, Scribner moved to Washington D.C. to work as an associate director at the National Institute of Education, and later, at the Center for Applied Linguistics. It was during this time that Scribner carried out observational studies on work in industrial settings. Scribner (1984) reported on this work and included a good summary of her research and ideas to date. In this paper, Scribner proposes the outline of a functional approach to cognition through the construct of practice. A consideration of practice offers the possibility ". . . of integrating the psychological and the social–cultural in such a way that makes possible explanatory accounts of the basic mental processes as they are expressed in experience " (Scribner, 1984, p. 13). Setting out with this approach to cognition, the practices themselves in their location of use become objects of cognitive analysis. A method is needed for studying thinking in context.

Scribner saw two difficulties with this approach. The first involves the problem of determining units of analysis. She proposes the construct of practice and the tasks that are associated with it to resolve this first difficulty. The second problem involves the supposed trade-off between the relevance of naturalistic settings and the rigor that is possible in laboratory settings (Scribner, 1984). The solution to this difficulty was found in the combination of observational, ethnographic, methods to provide information on the context and setting combined with experimental methods carried out at the site that were used to analyze the process of task accomplishment. Scribner saw the industry study which was done with workers in a dairy in Baltimore as a test of this method. The intention was to see if models of cognitive tasks can be derived empirically from a study of practices in a workplace setting.

Scribner and her fellow researchers chose the workplace as a setting to study cognitive activities because of the significance of these activities, the limited environment for practice that is offered by the tight constraints of the plant, and social concerns relating to the betterment of the conditions of workers. School experience is a dominant activity for children yet, for adults, work is the dominant activity. Due to the large percentage of time spent at work and the material and social consequences of work, work activity is highly significant for adults. In terms of research strategy, the choice of a single industrial plant meant that there is a constraint on activity and that in a certain sense the plant can be viewed as a semibounded cultural system. The social concern that motivated the choice of factory work as a site for study is the class related differences in educational attainment. Even though children from the lower rungs of the economic ladder don't do as well in school, they often go on to perform successfully complex skills in the workplace. A fine-grained analysis of how these successes in workplace learning take place could have implications for educational policy and practice in school and out. Scribner's varied background working with factory workers in unions probably played a part in the choice as well.

A note on the methods used is appropriate here as one of the main research objectives of the study was to try out a new practice based method of research. First, an ethnographic study was done of the dairy plant as a whole that included a general picture of the requirements in the various occupations for skills in literacy, math and other cognitive skills. Next, on the basis of the ethnographic case study, four common blue collar tasks were chosen for cognitive analysis. All the tasks, such as product assembly, involved operations with written symbols and numbers. Naturalistic observations were carried out under normal working conditions in and outside of the large refrigerated dairy storage areas for each of the tasks. Hypotheses, or as Scribner writes, ". . . more accurately 'hunches' " (Scribner, 1984, p. 17) were developed as a result of these observations. These "hunches" were generated about the factors in the task that might regulate how the task performance can vary. Modifications in the form of job simulations were made to test these hunches. A novice/expert contrast was also used. This contrast was performed between workers in different occupations within the plant. Workers in one occupation, such as product assemblers, were given tasks from another occupation, such as preloaders. A school and work comparison was also included. This group consisted of ninth graders chosen randomly from a nearby junior high school. These students received simulated dairy tasks with a paper and pencil math test. This paper and pencil math test was also given to dairy workers.

In addition to the methodological innovations of the study, some common features of the tasks studied offer a starting point for a theory of what Scribner in 1984 called practical intelligence. The outstanding characteristic is variability in the way in which the tasks were carried out. A top-down, rational approach to task analysis may not have revealed this diversity of practical operations. The variability in the way the dairy workers filled orders in the ice box for delivery or how the drivers calculated the cost of the order was not random or arbitrary, but served to reduce physical or mental effort. Skilled practical thinking was found to "... vary adaptively with the changing proprieties of problems and changing conditions of the task environment" (Scribner, 1984, p. 39).

Scribner terms her idea of practical thinking as "mind in action" (Scribner, 1997). For Scribner, the analysis of thought should take place within a system of activity and should be based on naturally occurring actions. A characteristic of all of Sylvia Scribner's work is this willingness to delve into the particular forms of experiences that form social practices as they are lived out in everyday situations. The ways in which the objects in the environment (artifacts) contribute to the execution of the skilled task are crucial in Scribner's view of practical intelligence. Reflecting on the dairy studies, Scribner says that "The characteristic that we claim for practical thinking goes beyond the contextualist position. It emphasizes the inextricability of task from environment, and the continual interplay between internal representations and operations and external reality..." (Scribner, 1997, p. 330).

This concern with the interaction between the individual and the environment and its objects stems directly from Scribner's reading of Vygotsky and other writers associated with sociocultural psychological theory and what has come to be termed activity theory. Activity theory is seen as making a central contribution to the mind and behavior debate in psychology. Scribner says that "... cognitive science in the United States, in spite of its youth, remains loyal to Descartes' division of the world into the mental and physical, the thought and the act" (Scribner, 1997, p. 367). In activity theory, the division is: outer objective reality, and the activity of the subject that includes both internal and external processes. Activity is both internal and concerned with motivation yet at the same time external and linked to the world through a mediated component, tools and more generally artifacts including language. Scribner suggests three features of human cognition: (1) human knowing is culturally mediated, (2) it is based on purposive activity, and (3) it is historically developing (Scribner, 1990). Cultural mediators, in this view, not only include language but "... all artifactual and ideational (knowledge, theories) systems through which and by means of which humans cognize the world" (Scribner, 1997, p. 269). The theory suggests a methodological direction. Changes in social practices (purposive activity), or changes in mediational means (such as the introduction of calculators) will be occasions for changes in cognitive activity (Scribner, 1990). Research efforts can be aimed at these interfaces of changing practices and changing uses of artifacts as mediators.

6.4.3 Jean Lave and the Development of a Situated, Social Practice View of Learning

It would be difficult to overstate the enormous contribution that Jean Lave has made to studies of everyday cognition and situated learning and to the formulation of a social practice theory of learning. I don't have space here to do justice to the richness and diversity of her work, but I will highlight some of her important articles and books and underscore some of her salient ideas in this section.

6.4.3.1 Tailor's Apprentices and Supermarket Shoppers.
Jean Lave, trained as an anthropologist, did research in West Africa on Vai and Gola tailors between 1973 and 1978. This research focused on the supposed common characteristics of informal education (Lave, 1977, 1996, p. 151). These assumed characteristics of informal education had been called into question by Scribner and Cole (1973). Does informal learning involve a context bound effort of imitation and mimesis that results in a literal, context bound understanding with limited potential for learning transfer? Is it true to assume that informal learning is a lower form of learning when contrasted with formal, abstract, school based learning? The results of Lave's research on apprentice tailors proved otherwise. The apprentice tailors started their learning fashioning simple articles of clothing such as hats and drawers and moved on to increasingly complex garment types culminating with the Higher Heights suit. These tailors were "... engaged in dressing the major social identities of Liberian society" (Lave, 1990, p. 312).

Far from simply reproducing existing social practices, they were involved in complex learning concerning the relations, identities and divisions in Liberian society. This learning was not limited to the reproduction of practices, but extended to the production of complex knowledge. (Lave, 1996, p. 152)

Reed & Lave (1979) examined arithmetic use in West Africa to investigate the consequences of formal (school) and informal (apprentice) learning. These studies compared traditional tribal apprenticeship with formal Western schooling among Vai and Gola tailors in Monrovia, Liberia. Arithmetic use was ideal for this study as it was taught and used in both traditional tailor activities and in formal school settings (Reed & Lave, 1979). In addition, arithmetic activity is found in all cultures and has been written about extensively. Reed and Lave also felt that arithmetic activity lends itself to a detailed description that makes comparisons possible. Traditional apprenticeship and formal schooling bear some similarities to each other: both involve long-term commitments, 5 years or more, and both involve the transmission of complex knowledge. They also differ in significant ways. Apprenticeship takes place at the site of tailoring practice in the shops, schooling takes place in a site removed from everyday activities although, of course it should be recognized that schooling itself is and important and dominant form of everyday activity. The juxtaposition of these two types of learning provide what Reed and Lave (1979) call:

... a naturally occurring experiment allowing the authors to compare the educational impacts of two types of educational systems of a single group within one culture. (p. 438)

In addition to the traditional ethnographic method of participant-observation and informal interviews, a series of experimental tasks with the tailors were carried out. Reed and Lave discovered that the tailors used four different types of arithmetic systems. The experimental tasks and the consequent error analysis and descriptions of task activities played a large role in discovering the use of these systems (Reed & Lave, 1979, p. 451). An iteration between observation and experimental tasks was used rather than using a linear succession of observation and then following up with experimental tasks. The conclusion was that a skill learned in everyday activities, such as in work in a tailor shop, led to as much general understanding as one learned in a formal school setting using a "top down approach" (Reed & Lave, 1979, p. 452).

In the late 1970s and early 1980s Lave and a group of researchers undertook studies in California of adult arithmetic practices in grocery shopping, dieting, and other everyday activities in what was called the Adult Math Project (Lave, 1988; Lave, Murtaugh, & de la Rocha, 1984). The term, dialectic, used in the title the chapter in the landmark 1984 edited volume by Rogoff and Lave points to the idea that problems are produced and resolved by the mutual creation that occurs as activity (the choice shoppers must make in the grocery store based on price) and the setting (the supermarket aisles visited) cocreate each other. Activity and setting are dialectically related to a larger and broader concept called arena. The construct of setting and arena is taken from the work of the ecological psychologist Barker (1968). Setting is the personal experience of the individual in the market. The arena is the more durable, and lasting components of the supermarket over time such as the plan of the market that is presented to all shoppers by the structure, aisles, etc. of the supermarket. The setting, as contrasted with the arena, is created by the shopper as specific aisles are chosen (Lave et al., 1984). The authors found that adults in this study did not use a linear formal school based process for solving problems, but rather a process of "gap closing."

The process of "gap closing" involves using a number of trials to bring the problem ever closer to a solution. The adults in this study demonstrated a high level of solution monitoring. This high level of monitoring, in the view of the authors, accounted for the very high level of successful problem solving that was observed (Lave et al., 1984). The supermarket setting itself stores and displays information in the form of the items that are under consideration for purchase. The supermarket setting interacts in a dynamic way with the activity of the actor to direct and support problem solving activities. Lave et al. make the very important point that this is true for all settings, not just supermarkets. All settings, they claim, provide a means of calculation, a place to store information, and a means for structuring activity (Lave et al., 1984, p. 94). These conclusions suggest that the study of cognition as problem solving in a socially and materially impoverished lab setting is unlikely to yield much information on the fundamental basis of cognition. The three components of activity: the individual, the setting (the phenomenological encounter with the supermarket), and the arena (the long term durability of the supermarket as it appears in many settings) are in constant interplay with each other. Dialectically, they cocreate each other as each impinges on the other. Learning as activity within a setting that is constrained by an arena is considered by Lave et al. as a particular form of social participation.

6.4.3.2 Missionaries and Cannibals: Learning Transfer and Cognition.

Learning transfer has always been a sticky subject in psychology. How can it be proven that transfer takes place if an individualistic view of psychological problem solving is rejected? What is the validity of experiments in the psychology lab that purport to prove or disprove that transfer had

taken place? In response to this difficulty, Lave sought to outline anew field that she termed "outdoors psychology" (Lave, 1988, p.1). This term had been coined by fellow anthropologist Clifford Geertz in his collection of essays *Local Knowledge* (Geertz, 1983). Lave's 1988 book, *Cognition in Practice,* is a concise refutation of the functionalist theory of education and cognition. The fact that Lave's 1998 book and Rogoff and Lave's 1984 edited book have been reprinted in paperback format and have found a new audience of readers attests to the pivotal importance of this research in everyday cognition and situated learning.

In the book's very tightly written eight chapters, Lave (1988) examines the culture of the experimental lab and its assumed, implicit ideas about learning and then moves the discussion toward a social practice theory of learning. The invention of this new "outdoors" psychology which Lave tentatively terms a social anthropology of cognition (Lave, 1988, p.1) would free the investigators of cognition and learning from the artificial confines of the psychology lab and from school settings. The very fact that all of us have experienced the school setting makes this setting appear as natural to learning and blinds researchers to investigating the everyday character and social situatedness of learning and thinking (Lave, 1990, pp. 325–326, note 1). Cognition seen in every day social practice is "... stretched over, not divided among- mind, body, activity, and culturally organized settings ..." (Lave, 1988, p.1). The solution to the problem of creating an outdoors psychology was to use the research tools of anthropology to carry out an ethnographic study of the lab practice of cognitive researchers who have studied problem solving. These laboratory problem solving experiments included a study of certain well known lab based problems such as the river crossing problem. In this problem, called missionaries and cannibals, missionaries and cannibals must be transported across a river on a ferry such that cannibals never outnumber the missionaries on shore or in the boat. The central topic for researchers studying problem solving in the lab is transfer of learning between problems of similar nature. Lave finds in her review of the work on problem solving that there is very little evidence that transfer takes place, especially when there were even small differences in problem presentation. Lave asks, if there appears to be little transfer between similar problems in tightly controlled lab experiments on problem solving, how is it possible to envision that learning transfer is an important structuring feature of everyday practice (Lave, 1988, p. 34)?

Lave concludes with the observation that learning transfer research is a part of the functionalist tradition of cognition. This tradition assumes that learning is a passive activity and that culture is a pool of information that is transmitted from one generation to another (Lave, 1988, p. 8). Functional theory presumes that there is a division of intellectual activity that places academic, rational thought in the preferred position. Theorists place schoolchildren's thought, female thought, and everyday thinking in a lower hierarchical position (Lave, 1988, p. 8). This view disassociates cognition from context. Knowledge exists, in this functionalist view, in knowledge domains independent of individuals. The studies reviewed show little support for using the learning transfer construct to study actual, everyday problem solving. In order to move the discussion of cognition out of the laboratory and off the verandah of the anthropologist, Lave proposes the development of a social practice theory of cognition. The argument is that activity, including cognition, is socially organized therefore the study of cognitive activity must pay attention to the way in which action is socially produced and to the cultural characteristics of that action (Lave, 1988, p. 177). Lave claims that "... the constitutive order of our social and cultural world is in a dialectical relation with the experienced, lived-in world of the actor" (Lave, 1988, p. 190).

6.4.3.3 Communities of Practice and the Development of a Social Practice Theory of Learning.

The community of practice construct is one of the most well-known ideas to emerge from the discussion of situated cognition and situated learning. Lave & Wenger (1991) use the term legitimate peripheral participation (LPP) as a way of characterizing the ways in which people in sites of learning participate in increasingly knowledgeable ways in the activities of what is termed a community of practice. The concept of changing participation in knowledgeable practice has its origins in Lave's work with apprentices in West Africa and in other anthropological studies of apprenticeship. The studies of apprenticeship indicate that apprenticeship learning occurs in a variety of phases of work production, teaching is not the central focus, evaluation of apprentices is intrinsic to the work practices with no external tests, and organization of space and the access of the apprentice to the practice being learned are important conditions of learning (Lave, 1991, p. 68). This view holds that situated learning is a process of transformation of identity and of increasing participation in a community of practice. Newcomers become old-timers by virtue of the fact that they are permitted by access to practice to participate in the actual practice of a group. One key feature of LPP is that the perspective of the learner, including the legitimate physical location of the learner from which action is viewed, changes as the learner becomes a complete participant. A second key feature is that a transformation of identity is implied. This transformation arises from the outward change of perspective and is one of the most interesting points being made by situated learning theorists.

The term community of practice is generally left as a somewhat vague statement in descriptions of situated learning. Lave and Wenger state that it is not meant as a primordial cultural identity, but that members participate in the community of practice in diverse ways and at multiple levels in order to claim membership. The term does not necessarily imply that the members are co-present or even are an easily identifiable group. What it does imply, for Lave and Wenger, is participation in a common activity system in which participants recognize shared understandings (Lave & Wenger, 1991, p. 98). The authors define community of practice as "... a set of relations among persons, activity, and world, over time and in relation with other tangential and overlapping communities of practice" (Lave & Wenger, 1991, p. 98). A community of practice, according to Lave and Wenger, provides the cultural, historical and linguistic support that makes it possible to "know" the particular heritage that defines knowledgeable practice. Lave and Wenger say that participation in practice is "... an epistemological principle of learning" (Lave & Wenger, 1991, p. 98).

Lave's research program in the 1980s moved from a consideration of traditional apprenticeship, such as those of weavers and midwives, to an investigation of the workplace and the school in contemporary culture. Lave finds that, when we look at formal, explicit educational sites such as contemporary school or formal educational programs in the workplace, it is difficult to find a community of practice, the concept of mastery, and methods of peripheral participation that lead to a change in identity. The reason for this apparent lack lies, in Lave's view, in the alienated condition of social life proposed by Marxist social theorists. The commodification of labor, knowledge, and participation limits the possibilities for developing identities (Lave, 1991).

Lave argues that this becomes true when human activity becomes a means to an end rather than an end in itself. The commodification of labor implies a detachment of labor from identity and seems, from Lave's view, to imply that the value of skill is removed from the construction of personal identity. Unfortunately, Lave does not cite any studies of contemporary apprenticeship learning in the United Sites to provide evidence for this claim. In a study of the situated work and learning of commercial refrigeration technicians, Henning (1998a) found that the formation of identity as knowledgeable participants was central to the increasing degree of participation in practice of apprentice refrigeration technicians. It appears, however, that in the school setting, the commodification of knowledge devalues knowledgeable skill as it is compared with a reified school knowledge used for display and evaluation within the context of school.

Lave and Wenger (1991) say that the problems in school do not lie mainly in the methods of instruction, but in the ways in which a community of practice of adults reproduces itself and the opportunities for newcomers to participate in this practice. A central issue is the acceptable location in space and in social practice that the newcomer can assume in a legitimate, recognized way that is supported by the members of the community of practice. Access to social practice is critical to the functioning of the community of practice. Wenger (1998) sees the term community of practice as being a conjunction of community and of practice. Practice gives coherence to a community through mutual engagement in a joint enterprise using shared resources such as stories, tools, words, and concepts (Wenger, 1998, p. 72).

The construct of a community of practice has provided a stimulus to thinking about the relations between activity in a culturally and socially situated setting and the process of learning by increasingly central participation in the practices of a community. The term, however, can be used to imply that there is a relatively unproblematic relationship between individual and community that tends to gloss over the actual process of the production of the varied and changing practices that make up the flesh and blood situatedness of people involved in joint engagement that changes over time. There is a certain disconcerting feeling in reading about the community of practice and its practitioners. At times, particularly in theoretical accounts, the practices and people referred to seem be disembodied, generic and faceless. The empirical work that is infrequently used in a general way to support the theoretical claims is mostly recycled and vintage work. Unlike Sylvia Scribner's work, which continued to be empirically based for the duration of her career and which conveys a sense of real people doing real tasks and learning important things, community of practice theorizing stays comfortably within the realm of theorizing. Lave relies exclusively on data from the early work with Liberian tailors and other early apprenticeship studies as well as work in the 1980s done with adults using math in everyday settings. Wenger's empirical data for his 1998 book appears to be largely derived from his research with insurance claims processing done in the 1980s. It should be noted, however, that Lave, as we will see in the next section, has recently been engaged in work with identity formation in Portugal (Lave, 2001) which has included extensive field work. Phil Agre (1997) commenting on Lave's (and also on Valerie Walkerdine's) sociological analysis of math activities as situated practice, points to the promise of this line of research and theoretical work. However, Agre makes the important point that the sophistication of the theoretical work and the unfamiliarity of Lave and Walkerdine's respective sociological methods to their intended audiences also makes for tough going for the reader. The contrast that Agre draws in this article between Lave's thinking on mathematical activity and that of Walkerdine's is helpful in gaining a broader view of the complexity of Lave's thinking. Jean Lave's introduction to the 1985 American Anthropological Association Symposium on the social organization of knowledge and practice (Lave, 1985) also provides a helpful summary of the role that the early work on apprenticeship and on adult math practices played in the development of situated learning and everyday problem solving.

6.4.3.4 Learning in Practice, Identity, and the History of the Person.
Lave asks in a 1996 chapter what the consequences are of pursuing a social theory of learning rather than an individual and psychological theory that has been the norm in educational and psychological research. Lave's answer is that theories that "...reduce learning to individual mental capacity/activity in the last instance blame marginalized people for being marginal" (Lave, 1996, p. 149). The choice to pursue a social theory of learning is more than an academic or theoretical choice but involves an exploration of learning that does not "...underwrite divisions of social inequality in our society" (Lave, 1996, p. 149). Just as Lave undertook an ethnographic project to understand the culture of theorizing about problem solving in *Cognition in Practice* (1988), here she asks a series of questions about theories of learning with the aim of understanding the social and cultural sources of theories of learning and of everyday life. Learning theories, as all psychological theories, are concerned with epistemology and involve a "third person singular" series of abstract questions to establish the *res* of the objects of the perceived world. The conclusion of Lave's inquiry was that it is the conception of the *relations* between the learner and the world that tends to differentiate one theory of learning from another. A social practice theory of learning stipulates that apprenticeship type learning involves a long-term project, the endpoint of which is the establishment of a newly crafted identity. Rather than looking at particular tools of learning, a social practice theory of learning is interested in the ways learners become full-fledged participants, the ways in which participants change and the ways in which communities of practice change.

The realization that social entities learn has been a topic for organizational studies for some time, but has not been a topic of educational theorists until recently (Salomon & Perkins, 1998). This dialectical relationship between participant (learner), setting, and arena first mentioned in 1984 (Lave, 1984) implies that both the setting, including the social practices of the community and the individual are changing rather than the individual alone. The trajectory of the learner is also a trajectory of changing practices within the community of practice.

This dialectical relationship is largely masked in school learning by the naturalization of learning as a process that starts and ends with changes within an individual. The consequence of this perspective taken from our own school experience and exposure to popular versions of academic psychology is that questions concerning learning are investigated from the point of view of making the teacher a more effective transmitter of knowledge. The solution, according to Lave, is to treat learners and teachers in terms of their relations with each other as they are located in a particular setting.

Ethnographic research on learning in nonschool settings has the potential of overcoming the natural, invisible, and taken for granted assumption that learning always involves a teacher and that the hierarchical divisions of students and teachers are normal and not to be questioned. The enormous differences in the ways learners in a variety of social situations shape their identities and are shaped in turn becomes the topic of interest. The process of learning and the experience of young adults in schools is much more than the effects of teaching and learning, but includes their own subjective understanding of the possible trajectories through and beyond the institution of the school (Lave, Duguid, Fernandez, & Axel, 1992).

The changing nature of this subjective understanding, and its impact on established practices in a variety of cultural and social situations, is not limited to schools and becomes the broader topic of research into learning. An investigation of learning includes an investigation of the artifacts and tools of the material world, the relations between people and the social world, and a reconsideration of the social world of activity in relational terms (Lave, 1993). In recent ethnographic work among British families living in the Port wine producing area of Portugal, Lave (2001) found that "getting to be British" involved both becoming British as a consequence of growing up British by virtue of school attendance in England, participation in daily practices of the British community in Porto, and also about the privilege of being British in Porto. Lave suggests that no clear line can be drawn between "being British" and between "learning to be British" (Lave, 2001, p. 313).

6.5 TALK, ACCOUNTS, AND ACCOUNTABILITY: ETHNOMETHODOLOGY, CONVERSATION ANALYSIS, AND STUDIES OF REFERENTIAL PRACTICE

A method of organizing the wealth of data obtained from empirical studies of various types of learning is needed to organize this material and to enable theoretical insights. Ethnomethodology, and work in conversation analysis and referential practice, can provide just such an organizing theoretical perspective for this wealth of detail. Microethnographic observations of practices that include learning, identity formation, and dialectical change become possible while preserving a theoretical scheme that permits the data obtained to be considered in general enough terms so as not to overwhelm the investigator with the infinite particulars of experience.

6.5.1 Garfinkel and Ethnomethodology

One core problem in any study of everyday cognition determining the nature of social action. A central issue for research in everyday cognition is to determine how the "actors" make sense of everyday events. Harold Garfinkel, a sociologist trained at Harvard under the social systems theory of Talcott Parsons, broke free of the constraints of grand theorizing and wrote a series of revolutionary papers derived from empirical studies that challenged the view that human actors were passive players in a social environment (Garfinkel, 1994a). A very valuable introduction to Garfinkel and the antecedents of ethnomethodology is given by John Heritage (1992). Garfinkel's emphasis on the moment by moment creation of action and meaning has informed and inspired the work of later researchers in the area of socially situated action such as Lucy Suchman and Charles Goodwin. Four tenets of ethnomethodology concern us here. These are (1) sense making as an on-going process in social interaction, (2) the morality of cognition, (3) the production of accounts and of account making concerning this action by actors, and (4) the repair of interactional troubles.

6.5.1.1 Ethnomethods and Sense Making. The term ethnomethodology is the study of the ways in which ordinary members of society make sense of their local, interactional situations. The members use what are termed "ethnomethods" or "members' methods" to perform this sense-making procedure. Making sense of the social and physical environment is a taken for granted and a largely invisible component of everyday life. The term ethnomethods is taken to be cognate with such other anthropological terms as ethnobotany or ethnomedicine. For the ethnomethodologists and their intellectual descendents, the application of these ethnomethods is not restricted to everyday, "non-scientific" thought and social action (Heritage, 1992). Ethnomethods applies equally well to sense making in the practice of the scientific lab (Latour and Woolgar, 1986) or of oceanographic research (Goodwin, C., 1995). In a paper coauthored by Harold Garfinkel with Harvey Sacks, the use of ethnomethods by members participating in social interaction is shown to be ". . . an ongoing attempt to remedy the natural ambiguity of the indexical nature of everyday talk and action"(Garfinkel & Sacks, 1986, p. 161).

Indexical is a term used in linguistics to describe an utterance or written message whose meaning can only be known in relation to the particulars of located, situated action. The meaning of an utterance such as "That is a good one" can only be known through an understanding of the context of the utterance. The utterance is indexed to a particular "that" in the immediate field of conversation and cannot be understood otherwise. Indexical expressions, and the problems these expressions present in ascertaining the truth or falsehood of propositions, have been a topic of intense discussion by linguists and philosophers (Hanks, 1996; Levinson, 1983; Pierce, 1932; Wittgenstein, 1953). These expressions can only be understood by "looking at" what is being pointed to as determined by the immediate situation. It does seem that the indexical quality of much of everyday interaction in conversation is centrally important to an understanding of cognition in everyday interaction.

Everyday interaction has an open ended and indeterminate quality to it. For this reason, constant misunderstandings normally arise in the course of conversation and social action. These misunderstandings or "troubles" must be resolved through the use of verbal and nonverbal ethnomethods. Ethnomethods are clearly shared procedures for interpretation as well as the shared methods of the production of interpretive resources (Garfinkel, 1994a). A key idea here is that these ethnomethods are used not in the sense of rules for understanding but as creative and continually unfolding resources for the joint creation of meaning. The use of ethnomethods produces a local, situated order (understanding) that flows with the unfolding course of situated action.

Sociologists such as Durkheim (1982) taught that the social facts of our interactional world consisted of an objective reality and should be the prime focus of sociological investigation. Garfinkel, however, claimed that our real interest should be in how this apparent objective reality is produced by the ongoing accomplishment of the activities of daily life. This accomplishment is an artful sense-making production done by members and is largely transparent to members and taken for granted by them (Garfinkel, 1994a). The accomplishment of making sense of the world applies to interactions using language, but also includes the artifacts that members encounter in their everyday life. This insight extended studies of situated and practical action to include the routine inclusion of nonlinguistic elements such as tools that play a role in the production of an ongoing sense of meaning and order.

6.5.1.2 The Morality of Cognition. Ethnomethods are used by members (actors) to produce an ongoing sense of what is taking place in every day action. A second question that arises in studies of everyday action is: How is the apparent orderliness produced in everyday action in such a way that renders everyday life recognizable in its wholeness on a day to day basis? The functionalist school of sociology represented by Talcott Parsons (1937) view the orderliness of action as a creation of the operation of external and internal rules that have a moral and thus a constraining force. On the other hand, Alfred Schultz (1967), a phenomenological sociologist who was a prime source of inspiration for Garfinkel's work, stressed that the everyday judgments of actors are a constituent in producing order in everyday life. Garfinkel is credited with drawing these two perspectives together. The apparent contradiction between a functionalist, rule regulated view and a view of the importance of everyday, situated judgments is reconciled by showing that cognition and action are products of an ongoing series of accountable, moral choices. These moral choices are produced in such a way as to

be seen by other members to be moral and rational given the immediate circumstances (Heritage, 1992, p. 76).

Garfinkel was not alone in his view of everyday action. Erving Goffman had presented similar ideas in *The Presentation of Self in Everyday Life* (1990). In a series of well-known experiments (sometimes called the breaching experiments), Garfinkel and his students demonstrated that people care deeply about maintaining a common framework in interaction. Garfinkel's simple and ingenious experiments showed that people have a sense of moral indignation when this common framework is breached in everyday conversation and action. In one experiment, the experimenter engaged a friend in a conversation and, without indicating that anything out of the ordinary was happening, the experimenter insisted that each commonsense remark be clarified. A transcription of one set of results given in Garfinkel (1963, pp. 221–222) and presented in Heritage (1992) runs as follows:

Case 1: The subject (S) was telling the experimenter (E), a member of the subject's car pool, about having had a flat tire while going to work the previous day.
S: I had a flat tire.
E: What do you mean, you had a flat tire?
She appeared momentarily stunned. Then she answered in a hostile way: "What do you mean? What do you mean? A flat tire is a flat tire. That is what I meant. Nothing special. What a crazy question!" (p. 80)

A good deal of what we talk about, and what we understand that we are currently talking about, is not actually mentioned in the conversation, but is produced from this implied moral agreement to accept these unstated particulars within a shared framework. This implied framework for understanding is sometimes termed "tacit" or hidden knowledge but, as we can see in the excerpt above and from our own daily experience, any attempt to make this knowledge visible is very disruptive of interaction. An examination of situated learning must take into account these implied agreements between people that are set up on an *ad hoc* basis or footing for each situation. These implied agreements somehow persist to produce orderliness and consistency in cognition and action.

The interpretation of these shared, unstated, agreements on the immediate order of things is an ongoing effort that relies on many linguistic and paralinguistic devices. Earlier, I used the term inscriptions to refer to these physical representations that are produced by members of a community of practice in such a way that they are visible to other members. These representations are not the mental states that are produced internally by individuals, but are physically present and may be of very long or very short duration. When the assumptions underlying the use of these representations are questioned or even directly stated, communication is in danger of breaking down as we have seen in the above example.

As a consequence of the dynamic nature of everyday cognition and action and the interpretation of these everyday representational devices, troubles occur naturally on a moment to moment basis in the production of sense making in everyday action. These troubles in communication do not mean that there is any kind of deficiency in the members of the community of practice and their ability to make sense of each other's actions, but is a normal state of affairs given the unstated, assumed nature of the frameworks for interpretation and the indexicality of the inscriptions used to help members make sense of what they are about.

6.5.1.3 Making Action Accountable and the Repair of Interactional Troubles.

Garfinkel says that in order to examine the nature of practical reasoning, including what he terms practical sociological reasoning (i.e., reasoning carried out by social scientists), it is necessary to examine the ways in which members (actors) not only produce and manage action in everyday settings, but also how they render accounts of that action in such a way that it is seen by others as being "reasonable" action (morally consistent in a practical sense). In fact, Garfinkel takes the somewhat radical view that members use identical procedures to both produce action and to render it "account-able" to others and to themselves (Garfinkel, 1994a). This process is carried on in the background and involves the ongoing activity of resolving the inherent ambiguity of indexical expressions. As mentioned above, indexical expressions depend for their meaning on the context of use and cannot be understood without that context. Garfinkel is saying that indexicality is a quality of all aspects of everyday expressions and action and that some means has to be used to produce an agreement among "cultural colleagues"(Garfinkel, 1994a, p. 11).

Garfinkel identifies the documentary method as the interpretive activity that is used to produce this agreement between members as action and talk unfolds (Garfinkel, 1994b, p. 40). The concept of the documentary method is taken from the work of the German sociologist, Karl Manheim (1952). The basic idea of the documentary method is that we have to have some method of finding patterns that underlie the variety of meanings that can be realized as an utterance or activity unfolds. A constructivist could easily reformat this statement and apply it to learning in the constructivist tradition. The documentary method is applied to the appearances that are visible in action and speech produced by members of the community of practice. These are the physical representations or inscriptions that I have referred to above. These inscriptions point to an underlying pattern by members to make sense of what is currently being said or done in terms of the presumed pattern that underlies what is being said or done.

This production of meaning, according to Garfinkel, involves a reciprocal relation between the pointers (the appearances) and the pattern. As the action or talk unfolds in time, latter instances of talk or action (the appearances in Garfinkel's terms) are used as interpretive resources by members to construct the underlying pattern of what is tacitly intended (Garfinkel, 1994b, p. 78). The documentary method is not normally visible to the members and operates in the background as everyday cognition and action take place. It is only recognized when troubles take place in interaction.

There are two crucial insights that Garfinkel makes here. The first relates to the sequential order of interaction. What is said later in a conversation has a profound impact on establishing the situated sense of what was said earlier. The possible meanings of earlier talk are narrowed down by later talk, most often, but not always, without the need for a question to provoke the later talk that situates the earlier talk. Take a moment and become aware of conversation in your everyday activities and of the unfurling of meaning as the conversation moves forward. An example of the importance of sequence in conversation is shown in this brief conversation taken from Sacks (Sacks 1995b, p. 102).

A: Hello
B: (no answer)
A: Don't you remember me?

The response of A to B's no answer provides a reason for the initial right that A had in saying hello. Consider the use of hello in an elementary classroom or on the playground in the neighborhood. What are the "rights" of saying hello for children and for adults? How does the "next turn" taken in the conversation further establish that right or deny it? A fundamental and often overlooked characteristic if the diachronic nature of all social action from the broad sweep of history to the fine grained resolution of turn taking and utterance placement in conversation. When it happens is as important as what happens.

The second crucial insight of the ethnomethodologists and researchers in conversation analysis is that troubles that occur in interaction are subjected to an ongoing process of repair. This repair process makes the instances of trouble accountable to some held in common agreement concerning just what it is that members are discussing. The empirical investigation of the process that members use to repair interactional troubles is a central topic for conversation analysis. This point of turbulence is an opportune moment for the researcher's ability to make visible what otherwise is hidden.

The specifics of meaning construction and the interpretive work and interpretive resources that members use to make sense of everyday action and settings for action are made visible in the investigation of these troubles and their repair. The *post hoc* examination of traditional educational research into the type and source of trouble in educational encounters in schools through the use of test instruments does not often provide access to the unfolding of meaning creation and the repair of interactional and cognitive troubles that occur as action unfolds in a school setting.

6.5.2 Conversation Analysis and Pragmatics

Everyday cognition studies can benefit from the insights of conversation analysis and the related field of pragmatics. The detailed transcriptions and microanalysis of everyday talk may be a barrier to an appreciation of the significant findings of conversation analysis, or CA as it is sometimes called, yet CA offers much that is useful for the study of everyday cognition.

John Searle (1992), writing on conversation, observes that traditional speech act theory deals with two great heroes, "S" and "H.' " S goes up to H and cuts loose with an acoustic blast; if all goes well, . . . if all kinds of rules come into play, then the speech act is successful and non-defective. After that there is silence; nothing else happens. The speech act is concluded and S and H go their separate ways" (Searle, 1992, p. 1). Searle asks if, as we know, real life speech acts do not resemble this

analytical sequence, could we develop an account of conversations and the rules that are followed as these conversations unfold in the same way that individual speech acts have been analyzed? Searle's response to this dilemma was to develop a more formal approach to the general use of utterances in actual conversation.

Conversation analysis, on the other hand, directs its attention to everyday talk in naturally occurring day-to-day interaction. In a review of literature on conversation analysis, Goodwin and Heritage (1990) suggest that there is a recognition that face-to-face interaction is a strategic area for understanding human action for researchers in psychological anthropology and learning theory. Conversation analysis grew out of sociology and the work of Harvey Sacks, Emanuel Schegloff, and Gail Jefferson in the 1960s and has its roots in the ethnomethodology of Harold Garfinkel. Studies of conversation involve an integrated analysis of action, shared knowledge, and social context (Goodwin & Heritage, 1990, p. 283). Education has often been described as an unfolding conversation between a learner and a teacher–coach. An understanding of the organization of talk in everyday life promises to elucidate the design conditions that make for good educational conversations. I will briefly mention one or two central ideas of conversation analysis but encourage the reader to explore the literature in this field.

6.5.2.1 Methodological Accounts of Action. Harvey Sacks, mentioned above in conjunction with his work with Harold Garfinkel and one of the founders of conversation analysis, was not looking for *a priori* rules in an idealized version of everyday talk that exist as independent entities beyond daily life. Sacks was looking for rules in practice that appear to produce an interactional effect in a real episode of talk. He asked: what are the situated methods that were used to produce this effect in actual conversation? These situated methods, then, are considered the "rules" under which talk proceeds (Sacks, 1995c).

As with most researchers in the area of situated learning the preference is for data from field experiences. Much of the material used for Sack's work in conversation analysis comes from recordings of telephone conversations made to an emergency psychiatric hospital (Sacks, 1995a). The methods used to produce the "rules" of conversational talk are situated because of their dependence on the immediate, on-going interactions of others in the conversation. A stable account of human behavior can be developed by producing an account of the methods that people use to produce it (Schegloff, 1991, 1995). Sacks says of the scientific descriptions of talk that are produced by this method that:

And we can see that these methods will be reproducible descriptions in the sense that any scientific description might be, such that the natural occurrences that we're describing can yield abstract or general phenomena which need not rely on statistical observability for their abstractness or generality. (Sacks, 1995c, pp. 10–11)

The focus of Sacks, and conversational analysis, is the interpretive methods individuals use to produce action and, at the same time as producing action to render it accountable. An account of action makes it visible to other members of the community of practice. These "background" methods of producing an account of action and making sense of everyday action seem to be prime methods in everyday learning. The "straight up," literal, this-is-what-I-am-about-to-say, approach taken for granted in formal and school education inevitably produces discomfort and confusion as to what is actually being said.

An example of an explanation of some of these background methods given by Sacks is found in the comparison of the two brief conversations reproduced below. At the time Sacks was working with a suicide prevention center in Los Angeles and was concerned with problems in getting the name of the person who is calling for help. Sacks wanted to see at what point in the course of a conversation could you tell that the person was not going to give their name. Obviously, without the person's name, the type of help that can be given is very limited.

First conversation:
A: This is Mr. Smith may I help you
B: Yes, this is Mr. Brown

Second conversation:
A: This is Mr. Smith may I help you
B: I can't hear you
A: This is Mr. Smith
B: Smith (Sacks, 1995c, p. 3).

The first conversation is an instance of an indirect method of posing the question "Who is this" and the normal response of the caller giving his name. The opening greeting "This is Mr. Smith may I help you" produces a conversational "slot" that appears in the next turn of conversation. The caller would normally fill in this slot by responding with his own name and in the first conversation does so. In the second conversation, however, the caller uses an indirect method of claiming not to hear properly as a method of not giving his name in response to the opening greeting and in fact in most conversations that started in this fashion the caller's name was never secured. The caller's method of avoiding giving the caller's name is reproducible in the sense that is recognizable in many calls to the suicide prevention center in which the person seeking help was not able to give his or her name. The caller provides a reasonable utterance ("I can't hear you") to fill the slot that would be normally used to identify himself and is thus able to continue the conversation. The rule or regularity of conversational action that emerges is a production used by the caller to produce a certain interactional effect, in this case an avoidance. The stable account of the callers behavior is made visible by the implied account of the avoidance: "I can't hear you." In Sack's terms, the reproducible nature of this conversational action is not attested by statistical frequency of occurrence but by the fact that we can recognize this situated and embodied "rule" in other instances of talk.

6.5.2.2 *The Importance of Sequence in Conversation.*
An important finding from the work of conversation analysis is that "conversational objects" such as a greeting, the offer of a caller's name are presented in particular conversational "slots" and that their significance varies with the placement. As mentioned above, everyday action has a diachronic quality. The diachronic location of an action in a time series of unfolding activity is crucial. Action is situated in time as well as place.

This diachronic quality of conversation and everyday action has significant implications for the type of research methods that are suitable for the investigation of everyday cognition. The research tools must be able to identify the time dependent creation of activity and action.

One example of many of the importance of sequencing in conversation is given by Sacks (1995a). The greeting term "Hello" is relevant for all conversations in the sense that the use of a greeting is normally a part of every conversation. Sacks points out that there is no set length for a conversation and, in fact the exchange "A: Hello, B: Hello" can constitute a conversation. In a two-party conversation, the format is normally carried out in turns such that A then B and then A, etc., repeated. These alternations are called conversational turns.

The content of an utterance and its sequential location in the course of the conversation are both found to be relevant for the type of meanings that are mutually constructed by the participants. As an example, if we answer the phone as we normally do with "Hello," this hello is taken as a greeting term. However, if we say "Hello" in the middle of the phone conversation, it is taken as a request to ascertain if someone is still on the other end of the line. A constructivist interpretation of learning must assume that there is some mechanism in a concrete sense that allows for the joint construction of knowledge in a learning situation. The exploration of the temporal, sequential quality of talk by conversation analysis provides the beginnings of the explication of the actual methods that people use to construct knowledge in these everyday situations.

6.5.3   A Baseline of a Practice Approach

The anthropological linguist William Hanks proposes a three-way division of language as (1) a semiformal system (the structure of language which is a traditional topic for formal linguistics), (2) the communicative activities of the participants, and (3) the way in which the participants create evaluations of the language structures and language use (Hanks, 1996, p. 230). The evaluations are ideological and take into account the broader range of values and beliefs. They may be misrecognitions or may be inaccurate, but are nevertheless social facts. These three analytical components of language use come together in what Hanks calls a moment of synthesis in "practice." He points out that participants have a sense of what is possible in language or what might fail through experimenting with various forms of utterances in conversational practice. The account of the success or failure of an utterance in conversation that is made by the speaker and hearer is a product of these experiments in practice rather than the result of a formal system known to the participants.

Hanks maintains that formalist systems that depend on rules for combining categories of utterance types make this same claim; however, for these formal systems, the generative capacity of the possible combinations is anonymous and does not take into consideration the indexical issues of time and place (Chomsky 1957; Hanks, 1996). In contrast to these general and formal analytical systems, Hanks proposes the concept of a person in practice who must estimate the potential effect of utterances based on the actual field of practice. The participants use the situated nature of language in use to make judgment calls in a particular situation. Notice the parallel with the creation of appropriate language slots in conversation described by Sacks. The slot created for the caller to respond with his name is produced in the use of language as the conversation unfolds. The idea here is that the judgment calls on what is possible in a conversation and in learning are produced by the local, situated unfolding of the conversation rather than a blind adherence to rules of interaction that lie outside of the situation. These possible language acts fall within a limited range and cannot be chosen from the total number of possible language acts. In other words, there are constraints on what is a possible utterance.

Finally, Hanks asserts that the participant in practice works within a diachronic situation. As mentioned above, this concern with temporal position is reflected in research work in conversation analysis and the concern with conversational sequence. Hanks links this diachronic quality to a sense of reflexivity. Donna Haraway terms the sense of reflexivity a partial perspective saying in reference to Hanks that:

We are accustomed to consider reflexive thought as a result of a conscious decision to think about our own approaches and actions, our own biases. The term that Hanks uses here refers to a situated sense of being in a particular place spatially. The term refers to the sense of the body that phenomenologists such as Merleau-Ponty use to describe active and situated knowing. We know things from a particular place. This place is both physical and bodily as well as social and intellectual. A partial perspective is what we have and in some sense this partial perspective in contestation holds the promise of objective vision (Haraway, 1991)

Hanks illustrates this practice approach to language use with examples from his work with the Maya and their language, also called Maya, which is spoken today in Mexico and parts of central America. For example, the terms used in the Maya language to indicate a front and back orientation for the body are not applied to a tree. Instead, the tree is given a front by the act of the woodsman's chopping it down. The word used is *taámbesik*, to cause the tree to have a front by the process of chopping, and involves the first cuts made on the tree on the side toward which it will fall (Hanks, 1996, p. 252). Once the chopping has begun, the term for bark is applied to designate the back of the tree. The final cut to the tree before it falls is referred to by a term that means "explode its back." Hanks is saying here that the shift in activity over the course of the tree cutting operation produces a semantic shift in frame of reference for potential use of terms for front and back in respect to a tree. The unfurling of the activity changes the meanings of the words used. It is reasonable to assume that a change in semantic framework as activity moves forward also takes place during learning. Exactly how these shifts take place and the creation of reproducible descriptions of these shifts in semantic frameworks in the course

of learning should be an interesting and fruitful topic of investigation.

6.6 PLANS, PRACTICES, AND SITUATED LEARNING

Lucy Suchman and many of her colleagues that have been associated with the Xerox Palo Alto Research Center during the creative years of the 1980s and 1990s focused their research interests on interactions that take place in ordinary practice, particularly those in the offices where the Xerox Corporation sold copy machines. These everyday interactions afford a view on the general scientific problem of how the situated structuring of action takes place (Suchman & Trigg, 1993, p. 144). In this section we will take a brief look at the empirical work and some of the theoretical conclusions of a number of researchers who are investigating everyday work practice.

6.6.1 Lucy Suchman: Centers of Coordination and the Study of the Structure of Action in Situated Practice

Suchman and her colleagues at Xerox were interested in learning how the practices at work sites, particularly those based on representational objects such as charts, whiteboards, schedules, etc., form the basis for the coordination of the activity at the sites (Suchman, 1993). How are activities articulated in such a way that an ongoing sense of social order is produced? Building on work in the sociology of science, Suchman is interested in the relation between practice and "devices for seeing" (Suchman, 1988, p. 305; Suchman & Trigg, 1993, p. 145). These devices for seeing include texts, diagrams, formulas, models and an infinite variety of other artifacts that are used to produce representations of the world at hand in everyday practice. A central focus of studies of work practice is the relationship between the physical underpinnings of work practice including artifacts of all types and the emerging structure of work activities (Suchman, 1997, p. 45). The artifacts in the work environment include not only tools but also architectural features, furnishings, video monitors, etc. This approach to work practices can be applied to any work site and may be very profitably used to analyze the coordination of practices in teaching and learning both in school and on the job with a detailed description of the ways in which inscriptions (physical representations) are produced and interpreted in everyday learning.

In her groundbreaking book, *Plans and Situated Actions*, Lucy Suchman (1987) challenged the cognitivist view that action is first generated solely by what takes place within the actor's head (Suchman, 1987, p. 9). Suchman states that when action is viewed from a cognitivist approach, people are thought to act on the basis of symbolic representations that are first internalized and processed solely at an individual level and then output as actions in the world. This approach assumes that people first use symbolic devices to prepare plans that are then carried out in action. According to the cognitivist view summarized by Suchman, "... intelligence is something independent of any 'human substrate' and can be implemented in any physical substrate, most specifically, the computer in the form of artificial intelligence" (Suchman, 1987, pp. 8–9). Suchman carried out an anthropological study to verify if this is actually the case in everyday action (Suchman, 1987). She undertook an ethnographic study of how people interacted with an early version of an expert help system built into a photocopier. As a result of this ethnographic study, she discovered that the apparent structure of people's actions is an emergent product of their actions that take place in a particular time and with particular people and is not the result of some sort of abstract computational process performed on symbolic representations that takes place apart from the lived world.

In one study, Suchman and Trigg (1993) examined the representational practices of researchers in artificial intelligence (AI). This ethnographic field study focused on the ways in which these researchers used graphical representations that are jointly produced in the course of their work on whiteboards. The representations produced on the whiteboard were a socially organized, public activity. These representations served as "artifacts to think with" and were used as a collaborative resource in small group meetings. Suchman and Trigg found that the actual production of the diagrams on the whiteboard left behind traces of its production and use and served to explicate the work practices of the AI researchers. These traces point to the situated and contingent nature of the production of representational forms as tools for coordination and articulation.

In another study of the ground operations at a large metropolitan airport on the west coast (Goodwin & Goodwin, 1995; Suchman, 1993, 1997), Suchman and her colleagues found that the work of servicing arriving and departing airplanes involved the reading of an extensive array of representational devices. A central finding of their research was that the work of ground operations required the assembly of knowledge about airplanes and schedules by the juxtaposition and relationship of a wide range of technologies and artifacts rather than with one form of technology. Using video records and observational studies, Suchman and her fellow researchers show that competent participation in the work of operations requires learning a way of seeing the environment. Video records can be useful in studies of work and situated learning. A video record of the setting of the work activity using a stationary camera, records of work from the perspective of a person doing the work, records of artifacts as they are used in the work setting, and records of tasks (Suchman & Trigg, 1991).

The making of these video recordings and the research work of Suchman and her colleagues at Xerox has been guided generally by ethnography and interaction analysis. These two related research methods have proved to be particularly fruitful for studies of work practice. Ethnography, used in cultural and social anthropology, involves the detailed study of activities and social relations as seen within the whole of a culture or social world. Interaction analysis takes a detailed look at the interactions between people and between people and artifacts (Jordan and Henderson, 1995). Interaction analysis is derived from work in anthropology, conversation analysis and ethnomethodology.

Goodwin (1994, p. 607)) has pointed out, however, that the placement of the camera and the type of shots that are chosen reflects the particular viewpoint of the person using the camera (p. 607).

6.6.2 Situated Learning and the Simultaneous Use of Multiple Semiotic Resources: Charles Goodwin, Marjorie Goodwin

Studies of the social and material basis of scientific practice have illustrated the interrelationship of situated social and cultural practices materials and tools in various fields of science and technology. The construction of knowledge in a scientific field can be described as an interaction between the practices surrounding the tools and materials of a particular scientific investigation and the cultural and historically established practices that define the scientific field (Suchman, 1998). Charles Goodwin shows these relations between artifacts and tools and the creation of scientific knowledge by looking at how scientists use tools in the day-to-day work of science.

Goodwin studied the work of oceanographers working at the mouth of the Amazon in one study. He examines how scientists on a research ship view a diversity of displays of the sea floor as representations on computer monitors in the ship's laboratory (Goodwin, C., 1995). The flow of images on the screens is accompanied by talk on a "squawk box" from a third person working in a different part of the ship. This person is positioning the scanning devices that are receiving the raw data from the sea floor that drives the computer monitors in the ship's lab. Goodwin points out that positioning in the social and physical space on and below the ship is central to the construction and interpretation of the scientific work that is focused on reading the representation created in the display of the sea floor.

Goodwin shows that the work of these scientists aboard the research ship depends upon the creation of new hybrid spaces that are constructed from multiple perceptual presentations. These hybrid spaces are constructed on the various computer screens by the scientists who respond to the positioning information that is a result of the interaction through talk with the third person, who is not a scientist and who is off stage. This third person is a crew member who raises and lowers the sensing device above the sea floor. The focus of Goodwin's analysis is not simply concerned with the abstract treatment of spatial organization as a mental entity produced in the individual minds of the scientists, but is extended to include an analysis of human cognition as "... a historically constituted, socially distributed process encompassing tools as well as multiple human beings situated in structurally different positions" (Goodwin, C., 1995. p. 268). The oceanographers aboard ship create a heterogeneous array of perceptual fields using a variety of tools (computer display screens, sonar probes etc) and a variety of social resources (verbal interaction with the crew member who is raising and lowering the probe).

The perceptual fields that are produced by the work of scientists with the particular tools and materials of their profession must be interpreted. These interpretations are used to produce what Latour and Woolgar (1986) term inscriptions. These objects in the form of various documents are circulated and commented on in the scientific community of practice. The inscriptions are not one-for-one representations of a slice of the natural order, but are a product of interpretive actions. This process of interpretation and the resultant inscription is, in Lynch and Woolgar's words, " . . . a rich repository of 'social' actions" (Lynch & Woolgar, 1988b, p. 103). The work of producing an inscription from these diverse perceptual fields is a form of what Charles Goodwin terms "professional vision."

In an article by that name, (Goodwin, 1994) Goodwin takes a look at the work of young archeologists in a field school and the work of a jury as it considers legal argumentation presented in the first Rodney King police brutality trial that took place in Los Angeles. Goodwin takes a look at three specific practices which are used to produce an account of what has been seen. These are (1) coding (the creation of objects of knowledge), (2) highlighting (making specific items salient in a perceptual field), and (3) producing and articulating material representations which support and contest socially organized ways of seeing.

The task of the young archaeologists at the field school is to learn to describe the characteristics of dirt from a current archaeological site. These characteristics which include color, consistency, and so forth, are used to classify the strata of the samples. Gradations in the color of earth also give clues to the location of wooden building posts and other cultural artifacts that have long since disappeared. The work of classifying soil samples includes the use of tools and documents such as the Munsell color chart and bureaucratic forms used to record the results. Goodwin shows that this work is intricately bound up with the discursive practices of the senior archaeologists at the field school. Goodwin concludes that ways of professional seeing are not developed in an individual's mind as an abstract mental process, but that these ways of professional seeing are " . . . perspectival and lodged within endogenous communities of practice" (Goodwin, 1994, p. 606).

In the second half of the article, jurors in the Rodney King trial develop a certain way of seeing by virtue of the presentation of a videotape of the police beating of King coupled with the testimony of expert witnesses. Although the graphical evidence in the tape seemed to insure a conviction, in the first trial the jury found the police officers innocent. The prosecution presented the tape as an objective report that was self-evident. However, the defense lawyers presented the events of the tape as situated in the professional work life of the police officers. King's actions and possible intent was made the focus of the presentation through a method of what Goodwin calls highlighting. As a consequence, the officers who are performing the beating in the tape are made to fade into the background.

In both the field school and the courtroom, the ways of seeing that arise from situated practices lodged within specific communities must be learned (Goodwin, 1994, p. 627). The process of learning in the two situations is quite different and, according to Goodwin referring to Drew and Heritage, the different ways of learning depend upon the alternative ways human interaction is organized (Drew & Heritage, 1992).

Although the settings of learning found in the work of the young archeologists in the field school and in the work of the jurors in establishing the "facts" of the Rodney King police

brutality case are very different, Goodwin (1994) concludes that there are common discursive practices used in each setting. First, he finds that the process of classification is central to human cognition. These classifications systems are social, and are organized as professional and bureaucratic knowledge structures. They carry within their structure the cognitive activity of the members of the community of practice that organize them. Second, the ability to modify the world to produce material representations for display to a relevant audience is as crucial to human cognition as are internal mental representations. Goodwin (1994) goes on to say on this second point:

. . . though most theorizing about human cognition in the 20th century has focused on mental events—for example, internal representations—a number of activity theorists, students of scientific and everyday practice, ethnomethodologists, and cognitive anthropologists have insisted that the ability of human beings to modify the world around them, to structure settings for the activities that habitually occur within them, and to build tools, maps, slide rules, and other representational artifacts is as central to human cognition as processes hidden inside the brain. The ability to build structures in the world that organize knowledge, shape perception, and structure future action is one way that human cognition is shaped through ongoing historical practices. (p. 628)

Goodwin and other researchers describe a process of producing and interpreting representational artifacts in various work and everyday settings. Marjorie Goodwin (1995), for instance, examined how workers at a midsized airport made use of multiple resources produce responses in routine work encounters. These work encounters occur in two types of social spaces that the sociologist Erving Goffman (1990) has described as back stage areas and front stage areas. In the operations room, a backstage area is hidden from public view, responses to pilots' requests to know the status of gates is constructed differently than in the front stage area of the gate agents dealing with passengers.

Marjorie Goodwin (1995) demonstrates that the construction of responses to coworkers at the airport is embedded in particular activity systems that are located in a specific social space. A key idea is that people interact within what are called participation frameworks. Marjorie Goodwin extends Goffman's (1961) concept of situated activity systems to include not only a single focus of interactional attention, but attention to coworkers who communicate at a distance. Goffman, using the activity surrounding a ride on a merry-go-round as an example says:

As is often the case with situated activity systems, mechanical operations and administrative purpose provide the basis for of the unit. Yet persons are placed on this floor and something organic emerges. There is a mutual orientation of the participants and—within limits, it is true—a meshing together of their activity. (Goffman 1961, p. 97)

Goffman's concept of mechanical operations and administrative purpose are loosely analogous to the concept of arena (Barker, 1968; Lave, 1988, p. 152) mentioned above. Goffman's early formulation of situated activity systems are an important precursor to the concept of participation frame works used in conversation analysis and pragmatics (Goodwin, 1997, p. 114–115).

Issues of uncertainty in finding an open gate for incoming planes can be resolved in the operations room by suspending radio contact with the pilot and working out the possibilities with other workers in the back stage space of the operations room. In the front stage area of the gate agents, communications between coworkers on the type of compensation to be offered to passengers for lost places on overbooked flights are handled in a short hand code between coworkers in the presence of the passenger. In this front stage area, the semiotic resources for producing action must be created and interpreted in a structurally different manner than the semiotic resources in the back stage area of the operations room. In both these situated activity systems, Goodwin shows that multiple representational artifacts and systems are used to construct responses to coworkers. Goodwin sees a connection between her research on the use of artifacts and collaboration as a way to understand the world with research in everyday cognition by Hutchins (1990), Lave (1988; Lave and Wenger, 1991; Rogoff and Lave 1984), and Scribner (1984). Hutchins (1996) found in a study of distributed cognition in an airline cockpit that a process of propagating representational states is carried out through the use of a variety of representational media types. The structure of these representational types have consequences for collaborative cognitive processes in the cockpit:

Every representational medium has physical properties that determine the availability of representations through space and time and constrain the sorts of cognitive processes required to propagate the representational state into and out of that medium. (Hutchins, 1996, p. 32)

Hutchins (1995) feels that the emphasis on internal, mental, structures results from a lack of attention to the ways in which internal representations are coordinated with what is outside (p. 369).

In Goodwin and Goodwin (2000), the production of powerful emotional statements within a situated activity system is examined. Field data on three girls playing hopscotch and data from another field study on the interaction in the family of a man with nonfluent aphasia are examined in this article. Intonation, gesture, body posture, and timing all provide a set of semiotic resources that are embodied in situated activity system of the girls playing hopscotch. These same semiotic resources are also found in the interaction of an aphasic man with his family allowing him to interact at an emotional level without the need for an explicit vocabulary of words that display emotion. Goodwin and Goodwin point out that the analysis of the actual talk of the participants as opposed to second hand reports of talk show how displays of emotion are produced within interaction. By making use of the participation framework produced by the words of the family members, the aphasic man was able to communicate emotion through an embodied performance of affect using intonation, gesture, body posture and timing without the need for an explicit vocabulary (Goodwin & Goodwin, 2000, p. 49).

Hutchins observes that the original proponents of a symbolic processing view of cognition such as Newell, Rosenbloom, & Laird (1989) were surprised that no one had been able to include emotion into their system of cognition (Hutchins, 1995). The problem, according to Hutchins, is that history, context and culture will always seem to be add-ons because they are by definition outside the boundaries of the cognitive system (p. 368). A learning theory that can't provide an account of emotion as it plays out in everyday interaction and cognition will be of limited value in understanding the breadth and diversity of learning experience in every life.

Anthropologically based field studies of the settings of talk provide a rich source of ideas about learning and everyday cognition that take place both in formal school and everyday settings. This perspective from studies in anthropological linguistics on situated action by the Goodwins described in brief above builds in part on the work of the Soviet sociohistorical tradition in psychology (Goodwin, 1994; Wertsch, 1981).

The Soviet sociohistorical tradition in psychology has produced much interesting work in activity theory and learning by Yrjö Engeström (1993, 1995, 1997, 1999) and others working in Scandinavia and the United States (Cole, 1997; Virkkunen, Engestrom, Helle, Pihlaja, & Poikela, 1997). The International Social and Cultural Activity Theory Research Association, ISCAR (*www.iscar.org*), holds a very lively conference every 5 years. The journal *Mind, Culture, and Activity* published by Lawrence Erlbaum and Associates (*www.erlbaum.com*) carries many good articles on situated cognition and activity theory. The special double issue on vision and inscription in practice (Goodwin & Ueno, 2000) is of particular interest for the discussion above.

Goodwin and others have advanced the idea that there is a continuity between the use of multiple semiotic fields in institutional settings such as in work based settings and in everyday settings that are not work related. The flexibility that is made possible by the various ways that these semiotic fields can be combined and used to construct meaning is thought to produce this continuity across settings. Following this view, an examination of the particulars of interpretive action in a work setting such as that of the dairy workers studied by Scribner (1984) should reveal the same basic semiotic resource production and interpretive practices as those found in, say, everyday math by Carraher and Schliemann (2000) or Nunes et al. (1993).

Cognition and, by implication, all learning following this view is a social process at its root and involves the public production and interpretation of a wide diversity of representations that are in the world in a variety of material forms. The sequential time dependent process of the construction of meaning becomes available to the lay person and to the researcher alike through the traces left by the production of these sometimes ephemeral semiotic resources. The locus of interest in the field of the study of cognition has shifted dramatically in recent years from internal structure and mental representations that must be inferred through protocols and tests to representational practice as a material activity that leave material traces in sound and artifact creation. We must still take a partial perspective (Harraway, 1991) on this activity because we carry out the act of interpretation from our own situated vantage point. Harraway (1991) says that:

Social constructionists make clear that official ideologies about objectivity and scientific method re particularly bad guides to how scientific knowledge is actually *made*. Just as for the rest of use, what scientists believe or say they do and what they really do have a very loose fit. (p. 184)

The "eyes" made available in modern technological sciences shatter any idea of passive vision; these prosthetic devices show us that all eyes, including our won organic ones, are active perceptual systems, building in translations and specific ways of seeing, that is, ways of life. (p. 190)

The viewpoint of privileged partial perspective is not to be confused with relativism which is in Harraway's words, " . . . a way of being nowhere while claiming to be everywhere equally" (Harraway, 1991, p. 191) and is a denial of responsibility and critical enquiry.

The inferences that can be made, however, are rooted in tangible and demonstrable evidence through records such as videotapes, screen grabs of graphic displays, actual artifacts, transcriptions of talk, and so forth. A focus on the production and use of these semiotic resources means that the investigation of cognition and of learning offers the promise of research firmly based in scientific practice which involves the production of both evidence rooted in experience and the production of theoretical formulations from that evidence.

6.6.3 Learning as a Process of Enculturation: Situated Cognition and the Culture of Learning

It is not surprising that the corporate world has in some cases been a leader in championing the development and application of situated learning. Given the amount of corporate spending on education, the bottom line requires corporations to be very aggressive in evaluating the results of formal and informal learning. The learning that companies tend to be interested in is very much situated in a particular industry and the cultural and technical practices of a particular firm. A series of articles by Brown, Collins and Duguid (1989, 1991) and by Brown and Duguid (1991, 1993) emerged from the fruitful collaboration of research scientists at the Xerox Palo Alto Research Center (PARC) and anthropologists, psychologists, and other academics at the University of California, Berkley and Stanford. The discussion centered on the role of practices and culture in learning. The work of Etienne Wenger on insurance claims processors (1990), Julian Orr (1990) with Xerox service technicians, and Jean Lave's work discussed above (Lave, 1988, 1991) with apprenticeship and adult math provided the solid empirical base that was needed to develop a convincing argument that the culture of school based learning is, in many ways, a deterrent to learning that is useful and robust and that other models of learning are worthy of consideration.

The argument put forward by Brown et al. (1989, 1991) follows the conclusions of Jean Lave that situations can be said to coproduce knowledge through activity (Brown et al., 1989, p. 32). Learning and cognition are viewed as being linked to arena and setting, to activity and situation in such a way that they can be said to coproduce each other. Concepts and knowledge are fully known in use, in actual communities of practice, and cannot be understood in any abstract way. Learning is a process of entering into full participation in a community of practice. This view of learning as a cultural process provides

a link to research in many other fields beyond educational and learning theory. Authentic activity, following Brown et al. (1989) are the ordinary activities of a culture (p. 34). School activity is seen as inauthentic because it is implicitly framed by one culture, that of the school, but is attributed to another culture, that of a community of practice of for example writers or historians (ibid, p. 34). Students are exposed to the tools of many academic cultures, but this is done within the all embracing presence of the school culture. The subtleties of what constitutes authentic and inauthentic activity probably are not as important as the fact that the situation within which activity occurs is a powerful cultural system which coproduces knowledge. High school chemistry students carry in their book bags a representation of chemistry knowledge in their 35-pound high school chemistry book. However, the knowledge representations that would be normally used by a person who works in a chemistry lab are typically diverse, multistructured, and are formulated in a variety of shapes and formats. The structure and format of the textbook is just the opposite in that it is homogeneous from front to back and is not a very handy representation to use for actual chemistry work. The school culture, or what Jean Lave calls the ideology of the school, including the specifics of the textbook selection process, drive the specific or situated manner in which chemistry knowledge is represented for the high school student.

A thorny problem in epistemology is the nature of the mediation between the world and idea. The approach in educational theory historically has been to focus on abstract conceptual representations which are assumed to be of a first order and prior to anything "in the world." The relation between these abstract, conceptual entities that exist in the mind and the practices, natural objects and artifacts of the world are left to conjecture and debate. Brown et al. (1989, p. 41) claim that an epistemology that is rooted in activity and perception is able to bypass the problem of conceptual mediation. This is thought possible by recognizing that knowledge or competent activity in a community of practice is an ongoing accomplishment that aligns publicly available, material representations with historically constituted practices that allow individuals to build valued identities. These changing identities and the movement into full participation are made possible by reciprocity in interaction and not by the accumulation of static bits of information. The problem of mediation between concept and world is no longer problematic because the construction of and use of interpretive practices provides the needed link between mind and activity to allow for the development of new views of knowledge production and the nature of knowledge.

Brown and Duguid (2000) have used the concept of reach and reciprocity to extend the idea of a community of practice. Communities of practice are, following Lave and Wenger (1991), relatively tight knit groups of people working together on a common or similar task. Brown and Duguid (2000) extend this idea to include what they term networks of practice. Networks of practice are made up of people who share certain practices and knowledge but do not necessarily know each other (Brown & Duguid, 2000, p. 141. Networks of practice have a greater reach than communities of practice and are linked by web sites, newsletters, bulletin boards, and listservs. The face-to-face interactions within a community of practice produce reciprocity. Reciprocity involves negotiation, communication, and coordination. A community of practice is limited in number by the fact that we can have reciprocal relations with a finite number of people. Following Weick (1973), Brown and Duguid go on to say that when reach exceeds reciprocity, the result is a loosely coupled system. Communities of practice allow for highly productive work and learning. These networks and communities have their own particular boundaries and definitions and result in a highly varied topography. The local configuration of these communities develop what has been termed an ecology of knowledge (Starr, 1995) such as those found in Silicon Valley in California or Route 128 in Massachusetts. This ecological diversity and heterogeneity across boundaries does not have a good fit with the normalizing concept of universal schooling. In fact, Brown (2002) says that a diversity of experience and practice is of paramount importance in becoming a part of a community of practice. Learning and innovation is a central activity in these ecologically diverse communities. Brown and Duguid describe this kind of learning as demand driven. The learner's position in the community of practice entails legitimate access to, among other things, the communication of the group (Brown & Duguid, 1991).

The unstated normative view of learning for most of us is derived from our school experience. The view of learning often is that it is somewhat like medicine—it is not supposed to taste good, but it will make you better, or in the case of learning in school, remedy an inherent defect that the student has when he or she enters the class. From this point of view, learning is supplied (delivered) to the learners rather than being demand driven by learners. Brown and Duguid make the point that when people see the need for learning and the resources are available, then people will go about devising ways to learn in whatever way suits the situation. It is not enough for schools to justify what is to be learned by claiming that it is relevant to some real world activity. Learning becomes demand driven when the need to learn arises from the desire to forge a new identity that is seen as valuable. This type of desirable knowledge that is productive of competent practice has been termed "stolen knowledge" by Brown and Duguid (1993) in reference to a story told by the Indian poet Tagore on his musical training. Tagore learned to play despite the explicit intentions of the musician employed to teach him.

The creation of a valued social identity shapes learning and provides the interpretive resources that are embedded in a particular community of practice. These interpretive resources are used to make sense of the representations that are constructed in language, bodily posture, and artifacts by members of the community for public display. The local appropriation of the meaning of these representational displays in turn contributes to the construction of competent knowledge in use which furthers the formation of desired identities.

The creation of an identity that serves as an outward reflection of the process of learning in its totality is produced by an encounter with both explicit and implicit knowledge. Implicit knowledge, Brown and Duguid (1992) claim, can only be developed in practice and does not exist as an abstract entity apart from practice. The term implicit is used instead of the more common term tacit knowledge. Tacit has the connotation of being hidden knowledge that could be revealed and made explicit. Brown and Duguid (1992) maintain that the act of explication of implicit knowledge changes the nature of the implicit codes that are used to interpret practice (p. 170).

As individuals move more centrally and confidently into participation in a community of practice, reciprocal processes of negotiation and feedback have an effect on the nature of the identity of the community of practice as a whole. Activity, setting, and knowledge coproduce each other in the dynamic arena of unfolding individual and community identity.

6.7 CONCLUSION: REPRESENTATIONS AND REPRESENTATIONAL PRACTICE

An examination of the representational practice of members of a community of practice promises a view of learning that is traceable to language and other artifacts that can be videotaped, transcribed and shared between researchers in ways that assumed mental states cannot. The success of this method is dependent on making a clear distinction between two senses in which the term "representation" can be used.

6.7.1 Two Senses of the Term Representation

It is important in discussing the construction of representations to discriminate between representations produced by an observer that are used to codify in words or in some other suitable form the actions of a group and the representations that are produced by the members of the group that make visible the "rational" and "logical" properties of action that is currently unfolding (Garfinkel, 1994a). Representations produced by an observer to construct, for instance, a knowledge base such as that used in a medical diagnostic program such as Mycin (Clancey, 1997) are of a different order and are not under discussion. Clancey warns that we must distinguish representations used by people such as maps and journal papers from representations that are produced by an observer and are assumed mental structures (Clancey, 1995b).

The representations that have been of interest in this chapter are produced in such a way that they are made visible to members of a community of practice (an interacting group) without the need for overt explication by the members of the group. Used in this second sense, the representations that are produced are physically present to the community although, as we have seen, the physical evidence is often not immediately recognizable by people who are the members of the community of practice. The nuanced changes in these representations appear to an outside observer as nonsensical or trivial to the task at hand, yet for the members these changes are an inscription in socially viewable objects. These semiotic resources in their diversity of form and structure are fundamental to the creation of an ongoing sense of what is actually happening from the participants current view. The description of these practical actions in and of themselves are not usually a topic of discussion.

The management of activities as an accountable practice (that is an activity that is defendable as a cultural reasonable activity) makes possible the organized and stable appearance of these activities. This management of activity is made possible by the ongoing production of representations in representational practice. In all of its aspects, this representational practice is social and dialectic.

Clancey illustrates clearly this sense of representations in his description of his own representational practice as a social accomplishment. He describes the process that shaped the diagrams reproduced in an article on knowledge and representations in the workplace (Clancey, 1995a). He clearly shows us how the diagram used to illustrate the divergent views of participants from multiple communities of practice who are working in a common design process has changed and evolved. The diagram is produced in a fundamental way by the process of social feedback that results from his use of the diagram in presentations. The diagram is made socially visible in a number of physical forms including a transparency and a whiteboard. The diagram is used to "hold in place" a variety of views. The varying conditions of use of the diagram and the affordances produced by the material method of inscription of the diagram (transparency, whiteboard) facilitated social feedback.

6.7.2 Why Study Representational Practice as a Means to Understand Learning?

The key point in studying the artifacts, including language and gesture, printed documents, and more ephemeral inscriptions such as notes and diagrams written on a plywood wall or on a post-it note stuck on the side of a keyboard produced in specific activity systems by a members of a community of practice, is to reveal the interpretive processes used by members to make everyday sense of what is going on. When learning is seen from a participation metaphor (Sfard, 1998), the movement into full participation depends fundamentally on being able to read the representations that are socially produced for common display. The situated interpretive practices that are used are learned practices. As Charles Goodwin (1994) has pointed out, these interpretive practices operate in similar ways across many settings for learning.

References

Agre, P. (1997). Living math: Lave and Walkerdine on the meaning of everyday arithmetic. In D. Kirshner & J. A. Whitson (Eds.), *Situated cognition: social, semiotic, and psychological perspectives* (pp. 71-82). Mahwah, NJ: Lawrence Erlbaum Associates.

Barker, R. (1968). *Ecological psychology: concepts and methods for studying the environment of human behavior.* Stanford: Stanford University Press.

Brown, J. S. (2002). Storytelling Passport to the 21st Century. http://www2.parc.com/ops/members/brown/storytelling/Intro4a-How-Larry & JSB.html.

Brown, J. S., Collins, A., & Duguid, P. (1989). Situated cognition and the culture of learning. *Educational Researcher, 18,* 32-42.

Brown, J. S., Collins, A., & Duguid, P. (1991). Situated cognition and culture of learning. In L. Yazdan & R. Lawler (Eds.), *Artificial Intelligence and Education.* Stamford, CT: Abex.

Brown, J. S., & Duguid, P. (1991). Organizational learning and communities of practice: toward a unified view of working, learning, and innovation. *Organization Science, 2*(1), 40-57.

Brown, J. S., & Duguid, P. (1992). Enacting design for the workplace. In P. Adler & T. Winograd (Eds.), *Design for usability.* Oxford: Oxford University Press.

Brown, J. S., & Duguid, P. (1993). Stolen knowledge. *Educational Technology, March 1993 (special issue on situated learning),* 10-14.

Brown, J. S., & Duguid, P. (2000). *The Social Life of Information.* Boston: The Harvard Business School Press.

Burke, K. (1945). *A Grammar of motives.* New York: Prentice-Hall.

Butterworth, G. (1993). Context and cognition in models of cognitive growth. In P. Light & G. Butterworth (Eds.), *Context and cognition: Ways of learning and knowing* (pp. 1-13). Hillsdale, NJ: Erlbaum.

Carraher, D. W., & Schliemann, A. D. (2000). Lesson from everyday reasoning in mathematics education: realism versus meaningfulness. In D. H. Jonassen & S. M. Land (Eds.), *Theoretical foundations of learning environments* (pp. 173-195). Mahwah, N.J.: L. Erlbaum Associates.

Carraher, T., Carraher, D., & Schliemann, A. (1985). Mathematics in the streets and in schools. *British Journal of Developmental Psychology, 3,* 21-29.

Chaiklin, S., & Lave, J. (Eds.). (1993). *Understanding practice: Perspectives on activity and context.* Cambridge, UK: Cambridge University Press.

Chomsky, N. (1957). *Syntactic Structures.* The Hague: Mouton.

Clancey, W. J. (1993). Situated action: a neuropsychological interpretation. *Cognitive Science 3, 17,* 87-116.

Clancey, W. J. (1995a,). *A tutorial on situated learning.* Paper presented at the Proceedings of the International Conference on Computers and Education (Taiwan).

Clancey, W. J. (1995b). Practice cannot be reduced to theory: Knowledge, representations, and change in the workplace. In S. Bagnara, C. Zuccermaglio, & S. Stuckey (Eds.), *Organizational learning and technological change* (pp. 16-46). Berlin: Springer Verlag.

Clancey, W. J. (1995c). A boy scout, Toto, and a bird: how situated cognition is different from situated robotics. In L. Steels & R. A. Brooks (Eds.), *The artificial life route to artificial intelligence: Building embodied, situated agents* (pp. ix, 288). Hillsdale, NJ: Lawrence Erlbaum Associates.

Clancey, W. J. (1997). *Situated cognition: On human knowledge and computer representations.* Cambridge, UK, New York: Cambridge University Press.

Cole, M., Engeström, Y., & Vasquez, O. A. (1997). *Mind, culture, and activity: Seminal papers from the Laboratory of Comparative Human Cognition.* Cambridge, New York: Cambridge University Press.

Cole, M., & Scribner, S. (1974). *Culture and thought: A psychological introduction.* New York: John Wiley and Sons.

Drew, P., & Heritage, J. (1992). *Talk at work: Interaction in institutional settings.* New York: Cambridge University Press.

Duffy, T. M., & Jonassen, D. H. (1992). *Constructivism and the technology of instruction: A conversation*. Hillsdale, NJ: Lawrence Erlbaum Associates Publishers.

Duranti, A., Goodwin, C., & (Eds.). (1992). *Rethinking context language as an interactive phenomenon*. New York: Cambridge University Press.

Durkheim, E. (1982). *The rules of sociological method (trans. W. D. Halls)*. London: Macmillan (original work published in 1895).

Eckert, P. (1989). *Jocks and burnouts: Social categories and identity in high school*. New York: Teachers College Press.

Engeström, Y. (1993). Developmental studies of work as a testbench of activity theory: The case of primary care medical practice. In S. Chaiklin & J. Lave (Eds.), *Understanding practice: Perspectives on activity and context*. Cambridge, UK: Cambridge.

Engeström, Y., & Cole, M. (1997). Situated cognition in search of an agenda. In D. Kirshner & J. A. Whitson (Eds.), *Situated cognition: Social, semiotic, and psychological perspectives* (pp. 301–309). Mahwah, NJ: Lawrence Erlbaum Associates.

Engeström, Y., Engeström, R., & Karkkainen, M. (1995). Polycontextuality and boundary crossing in expert cognition: Learning and problem solving in complex work activities. *Learning and Instruction, 5*, 319–336.

Engeström, Y., Miettinen, R., & Punamäki-Gitai, R.-L. (1999). *Perspectives on activity theory*. Cambridge, New York: Cambridge University Press.

Foucault, M. (1994). *The birth of the clinic: An archaeology of medical perception*. New York: Vintage Books.

Foucault, M. (1995). *Discipline and punish: The birth of the prison* (2nd Vintage Books ed.). New York: Vintage Books.

Gardner, H. (1985). *The mind's new science: A history of the cognitive revolution*. New York: Basic Books.

Garfinkel, H. (1963). A conception of, and experiments with, 'trust' as a condition of stable concerted actions. In O. J. Harvey (Ed.), *Motivation and social interaction* (pp. 187–238). New York: Ronald Press.

Garfinkel, H. (1978). On the origins of the term 'ethnomethodology.' In R. Turner (Ed.), *Ethnomethodology* (pp. 15–18). Hammondsworth: Penguin.

Garfinkel, H. (Ed.). (1986). *Ethnomethodological studies of work*. London; New York: Routledge & K. Paul.

Garfinkel, H. (1994a). *Studies in ethnomethodology*. Cambridge, UK: Polity Press (original work published 1967).

Garfinkel, H. (1994b). Studies of the routine grounds of everyday activities. In H. Garfinkel (Ed.), *Studies in ethnomethodology* (pp. 35–75). Cambridge, UK: Polity Press (original work published 1967).

Garfinkel, H., & Sacks, H. (1986). On formal structures of practical actions, *Ethnomethodological studies of work* (pp. 160–193). London: Routeledge (original work published 1967).

Geertz, G. (1983). *Local knowledge: Further essays in interpretive anthropology*. New York: Basic Books.

Goffman, E. (1961). *Encounters: Two studies in the sociology of interaction*. Indianapolis, IN: Bobbs-Merrill.

Goffman, E. (1981). *Forms of talk*. Oxford: Blackwell.

Goffman, E. (1990). *The presentation of self in everyday life*. New York NY: Anchor Books/Doubleday (original work published 1959).

Goodwin, C. (1981). *Conversational organization: Interaction between speakers and hearers*. New York: Academic Press.

Goodwin, C. (1994). Professional Vision. *American Anthropologist, 96*(2), 606–633.

Goodwin, C. (1995). Seeing in depth. *Social Studies of Science, 25*(2), 237–284.

Goodwin, C. (1997). Blackness of black: Color categories as situated practice. In L. Resnick, R. Säljö, C. Pontecorvo, & B. Burge (Eds.), *Discourse, tools, and reasoning: Essays on situated cognition*. Berlin, New York: Springer.

Goodwin, C. (2000). Action and embodiment within situated human interaction. *Journal of Pragmatics, 32*(2000), 1489–1522.

Goodwin, C., & Goodwin, M. (1995). Formulating planes: Seeing as situated activity. In D. Middleton & Y. Engeström (Eds.), *Cognition and communication at work*. Cambridge, UK: Cambridge University Press.

Goodwin, C., & Heritage, J. (1990). Conversation analysis. *Annual Review of Anthropology, 19*, 283–307.

Goodwin, C., & Ueno, N. (Eds.). (2000). *Vision and inscription in practice: A special double edition of Mind, Culture, and Activity*. Mahwah, N.J: Lawrence Erlbaum Associates.

Goodwin, M. (1995). Assembling a response: Setting and collaboratively constructed work talk. In P. ten Have & G. Psathas (Eds.), *Situated order: Studies in the social of talk and organization embodied activities* (pp. 171–186). Washington, DC: University Press of America.

Goodwin, M., & Goodwin, C. (2000). Emotion within situated activity. In N. Budwig, I. C. Uzgiris, & J. V. Wertsch (Eds.). *Communication: An arena of development* (pp. 33–53). Stamford, CT: Ablex Publishing Corporation.

Goodwin, M. H. (1990). *He-said-she-said: Talk as social organization among Black children*. Bloomington, IN: Indiana University Press.

Greeno, J. G., & Group, M. S. M. T. A. P. (1998). The situativity of knowing, learning, and research. *American Psychologist, 53*(1), 5–26.

Hall, E. T. (1959). *The Silent Language*. Garden City, NY: Doubleday.

Hall, E. T. (1966). *The Hidden Dimension*. Garden City, NY: Doubleday and Co.

Hanks, W. (1987). Discourse genres in a theory of practice. *American Ethnologist, 14*(4), 668–692.

Hanks, W. F. (1996). *Language & communicative practices*. Boulder, CO: Westview Press.

Hanks, W. F. (2000). *Intertexts: Writings on language, utterance, and context*. Lanham, MD: Rowman & Littlefield.

Haraway, D. (1991). Situated knowledges: the science question in feminism and the privilege of partial perspective. In D. Haraway (Ed.), *Simians, cyborgs, and women* (pp. 183–201). New York: Routledge.

Harper, R. H. R., & Hughes, J. A. (1993). 'What a F-ing system! Send 'em all to the same place and then expect us to stop 'em hitting' : Making technology work in air traffic control. In G. Button (Ed.), *Technology in working order* (pp. 127–144). London and New York: Routledge.

Henning, P. H. (1998a). Ways of learning: An ethnographic study of the work and situated learning of a group of refrigeration service technicians. *Journal of Contemporary Ethnography, 27*(1), 85–136.

Henning, P. H. (1998b). *'Artful integrations': Discarded artifacts and the work of articulation in overlapping communities of practice of commercial refrigeration technicians*. Paper given at The Fourth Congress of the International Society for Cultural Research and Activity Theory (ISCRAT). June, 1998: Aarhus, Denmark.

Heritage, J. (1992). *Garfinkel and ethnomethodology*. Cambridge, UK: Polity Press (original work published 1984).

Hutchins, E. (1995). *Cognition in the wild*. Cambridge, MA: MIT Press.

Hutchins, E., & Klausen, T. (1996). Distributed cognition in an airplane cockpit. In Y. Engeström & D. Middleton (Eds.), *Cognition & communication at work* (pp. 15–34). New York: Cambridge University Press.

Hutchins, E. L. (1990). The technology of team navigation. In J. Galegher, R. E. Kraut, & C. Egido (Eds.), *Intellectual teamwork: The social and technical foundations of cooperative work*. Hillsdale, NJ: Erlbaum.

Jordan, B., & Henderson, A. (1995). Interaction analysis: Foundations and practice. *Journal of the Learning Sciences, 4*(1), 39–103.

Kendon, A. (1997). Gesture. *Annual Review of Anthropology,* (26), 109-128.

Kirshner, D., & Whitson, J. A. (Eds.). (1997). *Situated cognition: Social, semiotic, and psychological perspectives.* Mahwah, NJ: Lawrence Erlbaum Associates.

Korzybski, A. (1941). *Science and sanity.* New York: Science Press.

Kunda, Z. (1999). *Social cognition: Making sense of people.* Cambridge, MA: The MIT Press.

Latour, B., & Woolgar, S. (1986). *Laboratory life: The construction of scientific facts.* Princeton, NJ: Princeton University Press.

Lave, J. (1977). Cognitive consequences of traditional apprenticeship training in Africa. *Anthropology and Education Quarterly, 7,* 177-180.

Lave, J. (1985). Introduction: Situationally specific practice. *Anthropology and Education Quarterly, 16,* 171-176.

Lave, J. (1988). *Cognition in practice: Mind, mathematics, and culture in everyday life.* Cambridge, New York: Cambridge University Press.

Lave, J. (1990). The culture of acquisition and the practice of understanding. In J. Stigler, R. A. Shweder, & G. Herdt (Eds.), *Cultural psychology: Essays on comparative human development.* Cambridge: Cambridge University Press.

Lave, J. (1991). Situating learning in communities of practice. In L. Resnick & S. Teasley (Eds.), *Perspectives on socially shared cognition* (pp. 63-82). Washington, DC: APA.

Lave, J. (1993). The practice of learning. In J. Lave & S. Chaiklin (Eds.), *Understanding practice: Perspectives on activity and context* (pp. 3-32). Cambridge, UK: Cambridge University Press.

Lave, J. (1996). Teaching, as learning, in practice. *Mind, Culture, and Activity, 3*(3), 149-164.

Lave, J. (1997). What's special about experiments as contexts for thinking. In M. Cole, Y. Engestrom, & O. A. Vasquez (Eds.), *Mind, culture, and activity: Seminal papers from the Laboratory of Comparative Human Cognition* (pp. 57-69). New York: Cambridge University Press.

Lave, J. (2001). Getting to be British. In D. H. Herring & J. Lave (Eds.), *History in person: Enduring struggles, contentious practice, intimate identities* (pp. 281-324). Santa Fe, NM: School of American Research Press.

Lave, J., Duguid, P., Fernandez, N., & Axel, E. (1992). Coming of age in Birmingham. *Annual Review of Anthropology (Palo Alto: Annual Reviews Inc.).*

Lave, J., Murtaugh, M., & de la Rocha, O. (1984). The dialectic of arithmetic in grocery shopping. In B. Rogoff & J. Lave (Eds.), *Everyday cognition: Its development in social context* (pp. 67-94). Cambridge, MA: Harvard University Press.

Lave, J., & Reed, H. J. (1979). Arithmetic as a tool for investigating relationships between culture and cognition. *American Ethnologist, 6*(3), 568-582.

Lave, J., & Wenger, E. (1991). *Situated learning: Legitimate peripheral participation.* New York: Cambridge University Press.

Levinson, S. C. (1983). *Pragmatics.* Cambridge, UK: Cambridge University Press.

Linehan, C., & McCarthy, J. (2001). Reviewing the "Community of Practice" metaphor: An analysis of control relations in a primary school classroom. *Mind, Culture, and Activity, 8*(2), 129-147.

Lynch, M., & Woolgar, S. (Eds.). (1988a). *Representation in scientific practice.* Cambridge: The MIT Press.

Lynch, M., & Woolgar, S. (1988b). Introduction: Sociological orientation to representational practice in science, *Representation in scientific practice* (pp. 99-116). Cambridge, MA: The MIT Press.

Mannheim, K. (1952). On the interpretation of 'weltanschauung.' In P. Kecskemeti (Ed.), *Essays in the Sociology of Knowledge* (pp. 33-83). New York: Oxford University Press.

Marsick, V. J., & Watkins, K. E. (1990). *Informal and incidental learning in the workplace.* London, New York: Routledge.

McLellan, H. (1996). Situated learning: Multiple perspectives. In H. McLellan (Ed.), *Situated learning perspectives* (pp. 5-17). Englewood Cliffs, NJ: Educational Technology Publications.

McNeill, D. (1992). *Hand and mind: What gestures reveal about thought.* Chicago, IL: University of Chicago Press.

Miller, G. A., & Gildea, P. M. (1987). How children learn words. *Scientific American, 257*(3), 94-99.

Nardi, B. (1996). Studying context: A comparison of activity theory, situated action models, and distributed cognition. In B. Nardi (Ed.), *Context and consciousness: Activity theory and human-computer interaction* (pp. 69-102). Cambridge, MA: The MIT Press.

Newell, A., Rosenbloom, P., & Laird, J. (1989). Symbolic architectures for cognition. In Posner, M. (Ed.), *Foundations of cognitive science.* Cambridge, MA: MIT Press.

Nunes, T., Schliemann, A., & Carraher, D. (1993). *Street mathematics and school mathematics.* Cambridge, New York: Cambridge University Press.

Orr, J. (1990). *Talking about machines: An ethnography of a modern job.* Cornell University, Department of Anthropology.

Parsons, T. (1937). *The structure of social action.* New York: McGraw-Hill.

Pea, R. (1997). Practices of distributed intelligence and designs for education. In G. Salomon (Ed.), *Distributed cognitions: Psychological and educational considerations (original work published 1993)* (pp. 47-87). New York: Cambridge University Press.

Peirce, C. (1932). *Collected papers, vol 2.* Cambridge, MA: Harvard University Press.

Peirce, C. S. (1955). Logic as semiotic: A theory of signs. In J. Buchler (Ed.), *Philosophical writings of Peirce* (pp. 98-119). New York: Dover Publications.

Pennington, D. C. (2000). *Social cognition.* London and Philadelphia: Routledge.

Perkins, D. (1997). Person-plus: A distributed view of thinking and learning. In G. Salomon (Ed.), *Distributed cognitions: Psychological and educational considerations (original work published 1993)* (pp. 88-109). New York: Cambridge University Press.

Pickering, A. (Ed.). (1992). *Science as practice and culture.* Chicago: Chicago University Press.

Poon, L. W., Rubin, D. C., & Wilson, B. A. (Eds.). (1989). *Everyday cognition in adulthood and late life.* Cambridge, UK: Cambridge University Press.

Reed, H. J., & Lave, J. (1979). Arithmetic as a tool for investigating relations between culture and cognition. *American Ethnologist,* (6), 568-582.

Resnick, L. B., Pontecorvo, C., & Säjö, R. (1997). Discourse, tools, and reasoning: Essays on situated cognition. In L. B. Resnick, C. Pontecorvo, R. Säjö, & B. Burge (Eds.), *Discourse, tools, and reasoning: Essays on situated cognition* (pp. 1-20). Berlin, New York: Springer.

Rogoff, B. (1984). Introduction: Thinking and learning in social context. In B. Rogoff & J. Lave (Eds.), *Everyday cognition: Its development in social context* (pp. 1-8). Cambridge, MA: Harvard University Press.

Rogoff, B., & Lave, J. (Eds.). (1984). *Everyday cognition: Its development in social context.* Cambridge, MA: Harvard University Press.

Sacks, H. (1995a). *Lectures on conversation: Volumes I and II. Edited by Gail Jefferson, with and Introduction by Emanuel Schegloff.* Oxford, UK: Basil Blackwell (original work published in 1992).

Sacks, H. (1995b). Lecture 12: Sequencing, utterances, jokes, and questions, *Lectures on conversation: Volumes I and II.*

Edited by Gail Jefferson, with and Introduction by Emanuel Schegloff (pp. 95-103). Oxford, UK: Basil Blackwell (original work published in 1992).

Sacks, H. (1995c). Lecture 1: Rules of conversational sequence, *Lectures on conversation: Volumes I and II.*

Edited by Gail Jefferson, with and Introduction by Emanuel Schegloff (pp. 3-11). Oxford, UK: Basil Blackwell (original work 1992).

Salomon, G. (Ed.). (1997). *Distributed cognitions: Psychological and educational considerations (original work published 1993).* Cambridge: Cambridge University Press.

Salomon, G., & Perkins, D. N. (1998). Individual and social aspects of learning. *Review of Research in Education, 23,* 1-24.

Schegloff, E. (1991). Conversation analysis and socially shared cognition. In L. B. L. Resnick, John M. et al. (Eds.), *Perspectives on socially shared cognition* (pp. 150-171). Washington, DC: American Psychological Association.

Schegloff, E. A. (1995). Introduction. In G. Jefferson (Ed.), *Lectures on conversation: Volumes I and II.*

Edited by Gail Jefferson, with and Introduction by Emanuel Schegloff. Oxford, UK: Basil Blackwell (original work published in 1992).

Schutz, A. (1962). *Collected papers.* (Vol. 1). The Hague: Martinus Nijhoff.

Schutz, A. (1967). *The phenomenology of the social world* (George Walsh Frederick Lehnert, Trans.) Northwestern University Press. (Originally published in 1936).

Scribner, S. (1984). Studying working intelligence. In B. Rogoff & J. Lave (Eds.), *Everyday cognition: Its development in social context* (pp. 9-40). Cambridge, MA: Harvard University Press.

Scribner, S. (1985). Thinking in action: Some characteristics of practical thought. In R. J. Sternberg & R. K. Wagner (Eds.), *Practical intelligence: Nature and origin of competence in the everyday world* (pp. 13-30). Cambridge, MA: Cambridge University Press.

Scribner, S. (1990). A sociocultural approach to the study of mind. In G. Greenberg (Ed.), *Theories of the evolution of knowing.* Hillsdale, NJ: Lawrence Erlbaum Associates.

Scribner, S. (1997). Mental and manual work: An activity theory orientation. In E. Tobach, R. Falmagne, M. Parlee, L. Martin, & A. Kapelman (Eds.), *Mind and social practice: Selected writings of Sylvia Scribner* (pp. 367-374). New York: Cambridge.

Scribner, S., & Cole, M. (1973). Cognitive consequences of formal and informal education. *Science, 182*(4112), 553-559.

Scribner, S., & Cole, M. (1981). *The psychology of literacy.* Cambridge: Harvard University Press.

Searle, J. R. (1992). *(On) Searle on conversation.* Philadelphia: Benjamins Publishing Company.

Sfard, A. (1998). On two metaphors for learning and the dangers of choosing just one. *Educational Researcher, 4-13.*

Star, S. L. (Ed.). (1995). *Ecologies of knowledge: Work and politics in science and technology.* Albany, NY: SUNY Press.

Suchman, L. (1987). *Plans and situated actions: The problem of human-machine communication.* New York: Cambridge University Press.

Suchman, L. (1988). Representing practice in cognitive science. *Human Studies, 11,* 305-325.

Suchman, L. (1993). Technologies of accountability: Of lizards and aeroplanes. In G. Button (Ed.), *Technology in working order.* London and New York: Routledge.

Suchman, L. (1997). Centres of coordination: A case and some themes. In L. Resnick, R. Saljo, & C. Pontecorvo (Eds.), *Discourse, tools, and reasoning* (pp. 41-62). New York: Springer-Verlag.

Suchman, L. (1998). Human/machine reconsidered. *Cognitive Studies, 5*(1), 5-13.

Suchman, L., & Trigg, R. (1993). Artificial intelligence as craftwork. In S. Chaiklin & J. Lave (Eds.), *Understanding practice: Perspectives on activity and context.* Cambridge, UK: Cambridge.

Suchman, L., & Trigg, R. H. (1991). Understanding practice: Video as a medium for reflection and design. In J. Greenbaum & M. Kyng (Eds.), *Design at work: Cooperative design of computer systems.* Hillsdale, NJ: Lawrence Erlbaum Associates.

Tobach, E., Falmagne, R., Parlee, M., Martin, L., & Kapelman, A. (Eds.). (1997). *Mind and social practice: Selected writings of Sylvia Scribner.* New York: Cambridge.

Virkkunen, J., Engestrom, Y., Helle, M., Pihlaja, J., & Poikela, R. (1997). The change laboratory: A tool for transforming work. In T. Alasoini, M. Kyllönen, & A. Kasvio (Eds.), *Workplace innovations: A way of promoting competitiveness, welfare and employment* (pp. 157-174). Helsinki, Finland.

Weick, K. E. (1976). Educational organizations as loosely coupled systems. *Administrative Science Quarterly, 21,* 1-19.

Wenger, E. (1998). *Communities of practice: Learning, meaning, and identity.* Cambridge, New York: Cambridge University Press.

Wenger, E. C. (1990). *Toward a theory of cultural transparency: Elements of a social discourse of the visible and the invisible.* Unpublished doctoral dissertation, University of California, Irvine.

Wertsch, J. V. (Ed.). (1981). *The concept of activity in soviet psychology.* Armonk, NY: Sharpe.

Wilson, B., G., & Myers, K. M. (2000). Situated Cognition in theoretical and practical context. In D. Jonassen & S. Land (Eds.), *Theoretical foundations of learning environments* (pp. 57-88). Mahwah, NJ: Erlbaum.

Wittgenstein, L., & Anscombe, G. E. M. (1953). *Philosophical investigations.* Oxford: B. Blackwell.

·7·

AN ECOLOGICAL PSYCHOLOGY OF INSTRUCTIONAL DESIGN: LEARNING AND THINKING BY PERCEIVING–ACTING SYSTEMS

Michael Young
University of Connecticut

7.1   INTRODUCTION

The word "ecological" in the title might bring to mind for the reader visions of plants and animals evolving to fill an environmental "niche," ecosystems changing too quickly creating endangered species or vanishing rainforests, or the complex climate systems for which advanced mathematical models have only limited success in predicting such things as hurricanes, ocean currents, global warming, climate changes, and daily weather. Perhaps surprisingly, these are the very issues that are relevant to instructional design. Much of what has been explored and defined for physico-chemo-biologic feedback systems has meaning when considering how people interact with learning environments, creating psycho-physico-chemo-biologic learning systems.

Ecological psychology finds its roots in the philosophy of rationalism (relying on reason rather than intuition, introspection, or gods) and empiricism (learning about the world through perception, not inborn understandings) and draws on models from physics and biology rather than information processing theory or traditional computer science. It presumes that learners have a basic "comportment" to explore their world and learn from their senses (Heidegger (1927a, 1927b), and prefers an integrated agent–environment view of learners as "embodied and embedded" in everyday cognition (Merleau-Ponty, 1962). Ecological psychology grew from Gibson's (1986) seminal description of how vision is the result of direct perception, rather than the reconstruction of meaning from lower-level detection of energy properties and complex geometrical processing. The ecological approach is often cited as the basis for a "situated cognition" approach to thinking and learning (e.g., Brown, Collins, & Duguid, 1989; CTGV, 1990, 1993; Greeno, 1994, 1998; Young, 1993) and relates to these and similar trends in contemporary educational psychology. There are current trends in computer science that have similar origins and address related issues, including the programming of autonomous agents and robots, autonomous living machines, and evolutionary computing, to name just a few. And there are also related issues across domains, particularly efforts that seek to integrate brain, body, and the lived-in world into a reciprocal codetermined system (e.g., Capra, 1996; Clark, 1997; Coulter, 1989; Sun, 2002; Vicente, 1999).

The emerging mathematics for an ecological description of cognition takes as its starting point the nonlinear dynamics of complex systems. For example, the "chaos" models used to predict the weather can be meaningfully applied as a metaphor to learners as autocatakinetic learning systems (Barab, Cherkes-Julkowski, Swenson, Garrett, Shaw & Young, 1999). Such theories of self-organizing systems rely on the presumption that higher degrees of complexity are more efficient at dissipating energy given an ongoing source of energy input (so-called open systems). Biological systems are such systems in that they take in energy from the environment (e.g., photosynthesis) or produce energy internally themselves (by eating and digesting). But a full analysis of the thinking and learning aspects of agent-environment interactions requires the modeling of an "information field" along with the energy fields and gradients that define the world (Shaw & Turvey, 1999). Such an information field is required to explain behavior in all forms of intentionally driven agents, slime molds, dragonflies, and humans alike.

With this as the contextual background, this chapter seeks to introduce the key ideas of ecological psychology that apply to instructional design. In addition to introducing these key concepts, a few examples of the reinterpretation of educational variables are given to illustrate how an ecological psychology approach leads to differences in conceptualizing learning environments, interactions among learners, and the related issues of instructional design.

7.2 THE BASICS

While much of the field of education in general, and the field of instructional design specifically, is controversial and not governed by absolute and generally accepted laws or even working principles, there are some things on which most educators would agree:

- Learners are self-directed by personal goals and intentions
- Learning improves with practice
- Learning improves with feedback

Considering these three time-honored educational principles for a moment, learners' goals and intentions are a part of nearly all learner-centered instructional designs. For example, the APA (1995) has endorsed 14 principles of optimal learning that take student-centered learning as fundamental. Similarly, whether from behavioral or information processing perspectives, practice is a powerful instructional variable. And likewise, one would be hard-pressed to find an instructional designer who did not acknowledge the essential role of feedback, from simple knowledge-of-result, to elaborated individualized or artificially intelligent tutoring systems' custom interactions. Perhaps reassuringly, these three are also basic principles that are fundamental to an ecological psychology perspective on learning and thinking.

Although, because of its emphasis on the role of the environment, at first blush one might want to equate an ecological approach to cognition with behaviorism, a fundamental distinction rests in ecological psychology's presumption of intentionality driving behavior on the part of the learner. While behaviorism in its purest form would have the environment selecting all the behaviors of the learner (operant conditioning), an ecological psychology description of behavior begins with the definition of a "goal space" or "Omega cell" (Shaw & Kinsella-Shaw, 1988) that consists of a theoretical set of paths that define a trajectory from the current state of the learner to some future goal state selected by the learner. In this way, the goals and intentions of the learner are given primacy over the interaction between environment and learner that subsequently arises. Perhaps the only additional constraint imposed by ecological psychology on this fundamental presumption is that goals and intentions are typically visible, attainable goals that have concrete meaning or

functional value to the individual. While this does not eliminate lofty abstract goals as potential sources for initiating behavior, it represents a sort of bias toward the realistic and the functional.

The second basic principle of learning, repeated trials, or practice, is an essential element of many of the basic perceptual-motor behaviors that serve as the basis for extending ecological psychology to instructional design. Things that people do in everyday life present many opportunities to "see" (perceive and act on) how the environment changes across repeated trials as they walk, crawl, step, catch, etc. Some fundamental studies include Lee's (1976) description of grasping, time-to-collision (tau), and optic flow as well as other midlevel intentional behaviors such as the perception of crawlable surfaces (Gibson, 1986), sittable heights (Mark, Balliett, Craver, Douglas, & Fox, 1990), steppable heights (Pufall & Dunbar, 1992; Warren, 1984), passable apertures (Warren & Wang, 1987), center of mass and center of percussion (Kugler & Turvey, 1987), and time to contact (Kim, Turvey, & Carello, 1993; Lee, Young, Reddish, Lough, & Clayton, 1983). In all these cases, it is experience with the environment across repeated trials (steps, tosses, grabs) than enable an agent to tune their attention to significant "invariants" across trials.

The third basic principle of learning, feedback, is one of the elements that has been mathematically modeled using principles of ecological psychology. Shaw, Kadar, Sim, & Repperger (1992) constructed a mathematical description for a hypothetical "intentional spring" situation showing how learning can occur through direct perception with feedback, without need for memory, storage, or retrieval processes. In a system that provides feedback by coupling the perceiving–acting of a trainer with the perceiving–acting of a learner (a dual of duals), the action and control parameters of the trainer can be passed to the learning (the coupled equations solved to identity) through repeated trials. These three principles, intentionality, practice, and feedback, are the basics on which a further description of an ecological psychology approach to instructional design can be described.

7.3 ECOLOGICAL TENETS

Perhaps the favorite metaphor for thinking about learners in traditional cognitive psychology is that they are like computers, taking in, storing, and retrieving information from temporary and long-term storage (memory)—the information processing model of learning. This model is presumed to explain all of human behavior including thinking and learning (e.g., Cognitive Science, 1993). While this model has produced a substantial body of research on rote memorization, semantic networks of spreading activation, and descriptions of expert–novice differences, attempts to take it further to create machines that learn, robots that move about autonomously, systems that can teach, and programs that can solve real-world problems have been difficult or impossible to achieve (e.g, Clancey, 1997; Clark, 1997). It seems that to some extent, computers work one way and people work another.

7.3.1 Ecological Psychology Posits an Alternative Metaphor Concerning How People Think and Learn: Learner as Detector of Information

This approach takes as fundamental the interaction of agent and environment. Rather than explain things as all inside the head of the learner, explanations emerge from learner–environment interactions that are whole-body embedded in the lived-in world experiences. Thermostats, rather than computers, might be the preferred metaphor. Thermostats represent a very simple form of detectors that can sense (perceive) only one type of information, heat, and can take only one simple action (turning the furnace on or off). But even such a simple detector provides a richer metaphor for learning than the computer storage/representation/processing/retrieval metaphor. The thermostat is a control device with a goal (the set point). It interacts continuously with the environment (ambient temperature), dynamically perceiving and acting (if you will) to detect changes in the temperature and to act accordingly. For our purposes, the most critical attributes of this metaphor are that interaction is dynamic and continuous, not static or linear, and the perceiving-acting cycle unfolds as a coupled feedback loop with control parameters and action parameters.

People, of course, are much more sophisticated and intentionally driven detectors, and they detect a wide range of information from their environment, not just temperature (which they can, of course, do through their skin). What this means is that rather than detect purely physically defined variables, people detect functionally defined informational-specified stable (invariant) properties of their world. Visual perception is the most studied and best understood perceptual system from the perspective of ecological psychology. Using vision as an example, rather than detecting the speed or velocity of an oncoming pie, people detect time-to-contact directly from the expansion rate of the image on their retinas (see Kim et al., 1993, for details). Thus the functional value here is not speed or velocity, it is time-to-pie-in-the-face, and once detected, this information enables avoidance action to be taken directly (ducking as needed).

In describing the functional value of things in the environment, Gibson (1986) coined the term "affordances," stating, "the *affordances* of the environment are what it *offers* the animal, what it *provides* or *furnishes,* either for good or ill" (p. 127). Affordances can be thought of as possibilities for action. Affordances are detected by a goal-driven agent as they move about in an "information field" that results from the working of their senses in concert with their body movements. As the agent moves, regularities within the information field emerge, invariants, that specify qualitative regions of functional significance to be detected. But affordances themselves cannot be thought of as simply stable properties of the environment that exist for all agents and for all times. Instead, the agent's skills and abilities to act, called "effectivities," codetermine the affordances. Such "duals," or terms that codefine each other are sometimes difficult to describe.

Consider that doorknobs have the affordance "turnable," lakes have the affordance "swimmable," onscreen buttons have the affordance "clickable," flower leaves have the affordance "landable," and open doorways have the affordance "passable." However, these affordances only exist for certain classes of agents and would only display high attensity (as defined in Shaw, McIntyre, & Mace, 1974) related to their functional value in situations where certain intentions arise. For example, doorknobs are turnable for human adults, but not for paraplegics (unaided by assistive technology) or young infants. Lakes are swimmable for ducks and for people who know how to swim, but not for bees or nonswimmers. Screen buttons are clickable if you know how to use a mouse or touchpad, but that affordance may not exist for immobilized users. For a dragonfly flying at 20 mph, a small flower leaf affords landing, but the small leaf does not have the same affordance for a human, who lacks the landing effectivity and can't even fly at 20 mph then land on any leaf. And doorways may have the affordance passable for walking adults, but that affordance may not exist for wheelchair users. Further, consider that until the related intention emerges, the functional value of these affordances can only be presumed; that is, affordances cannot be fully described until the moment of a particular occasion. Shaw and Turvey (1999) summarized this intentionally dynamic codeterminism of affordances and effectivities by stating that affordances propose while effectivities dispose. So to define an affordance, one must presume a related goal as a given, and must simultaneously codefine the related effectivities.

With the perceiving–acting cycle as a given, **action** (particularly moving one's body in space, but allowing for other more cognitive actions as well) **is an essential part of an ecological psychology description of thinking**. Thus an explanation of thinking is more a whole-body activity in context than simply an in-the-head process. Consider a classic example of thinking as "enacted" from Lave's (1988) description of a Weight Watchers member preparing cottage cheese as part of his lunch:

In this case [the Weight Watchers] were to fix a serving of cottage cheese, supposing that the amount allotted for the meal was three-quarters of the two-thirds cup the program allowed. The problem solver in this example began the task muttering that he had taken a calculus course in college (an acknowledgment of the discrepancy between school math prescriptions for practice and his present circumstances). . . . He filled a measuring cup two-thirds full of cottage cheese, dumped it out on a cutting board, patted it into a circle, marked a cross on it, scooped away one quadrant, and served the rest. Thus, "take three-quarters of two-thirds of a cup of cottage cheese" was not just the problem statement but also the solution to the problem and the procedure for solving it. The setting was part of the calculating process and the solution was simply the problem statement, enacted with the setting. (p. 165)

This exemplifies how perception is always *FOR* something, that activity drives perception which drives action, and from the ecological psychology perspective, activity is taken to be an inevitable part of thinking.

Lave's Weight Watcher is a beautiful example of how thinking, in this case problem solving, emerges from the interactions of the perceiving–acting cycle. But it also illustrates the dynamics of intentionality, as new goals and intentions emerge in situ.

The Weight Watcher did not begin his day with the goal to quarter and scoop cottage cheese. Rather, through interaction with the Weight Watchers instructors in the context of this exercise, he was induced to have the goal of apportioning the two-thirds cup daily allocation mostly for lunch and leaving a quarter for dinner. **The process of inducing students to adopt new goals is an essential element of instructional design from the ecological psychology perspective.** Further, as he proceeded to begin the task, the dumping and quartering procedure created the intention to scoop out a quarter. This new intention organized the perceiving–acting cycle for grasping a spoon and for the ballistic movements associated with scooping. In this way, the emergence of new intentions (dynamics of intentions) that drive the perceiving–acting cycle can be described.

The dynamics of intentions requires us to posit that intentions organize behaviors on multiple space–time scales (Kulikowich & Young, 2001). So a person can be pursuing multiple goals at once. Consider that as you read this paragraph, you may have several goals organizing your behavior. You may be enrolled in school to be a good provider in the role of wife, father, son, or daughter. You may be pursuing career goals. You may be in a class hoping for an A grade. But you may also be getting hungry or you may need to complete some personal errands. Some of these goals are organized in hierarchically nested space–time scales so they can be simultaneously pursued. Others, such as reducing hunger by getting up and making a snack, necessarily compete with the goal of reading this chapter. Given the premise that goals and intentions organize behavior, ecological psychology has proposed a cascading hierarchy of constraints that, at the bottom, end in the moment of a specific occasion on which a particular goal creates a goal path (Omega cell) that organizes behavior allowing the perceiving–acting cycle to unfold. But of course the dynamics of intentions must also allow for interruptions or new goals to emerge (like compactified fields), springing up in the middle of the pursuit of other goals. The cascade of hierarchically organized constraints has been described as "ontological descent" and is specified in more detail elsewhere (Kulikowich & Young, 2001; Young, DePalma, & Garrett, 2002). Understanding the nature of goals as organizers of behavior is a substantial part of guiding instructional design from an ecological psychology perspective.

7.3.2 The Bottom Line: Learning = Education of Intention and Attention

Any theory of instructional design must define what it means to learn. Behavioral theories define learning simply as the development of associations. Information processing theories also provide an in-the-head explanation of learning but prefer a memory-based storage and retrieval model in which things internally stored in short-term memory are encoded into long-term memory and rules are compiled through practice into automatic procedures. But ecological psychology raises questions about how such compiled procedures can be so elegantly and seemingly directly played out given the many changes in our contextual environment. For example, how can skilled drivers drive almost

mindlessly to work, talking and thinking about other things while engaged in such a skilled performance? Such questions suggest that something other than the simple playing out of compiled scripts may be at work. Ecological psychology looks for an answer in the direct perception of agent-environment interactions. Maybe such procedures are not stored in memory at all, but rather, the environment provides enough information so perception and action can proceed directly, without the need for retrieval and other representational cognitive processing.

With this thought in mind, consider the ecological psychology alternative:**learning is defined as the education of intention and attention**. The education of *intention* was described above, stating that new intentions can be induced through experiences with other people or they can emerge as compactified fields during the pursuit of existing goals. Consider that the many TV ads you encounter while pursuing the goal of watching your favorite show have as their primary mission to induce in you some new goals associated with the need to purchase the targeted product or service. The additional part of the definition, then, is the education of *attention*. Like the thermostats mentioned above, people can be "tuned" to detect information in the environment that they might not initially notice. Such "attunement" can take place through direct instruction, as a more knowledgeable person acts together with a more novice perceiver (scaffolding). A mathematical model of such a coupled two-person system has been described as the "intentional spring" model (see Shaw et al., 1992; Young, Barab, & Garrett, 2000).

Experience can also attune peoples' attention to aspects of their environment that have functional value for their purposes. As the perceiving–acting cycle unfolds, the environmental consequences of actions produce new experiences that can draw the attention of the perceiver to new affordances of the environment. This could also happen vicariously, as one student perceives another student operating within a shared environment. The actions of one student, then, can cause another to detect an affordance, enabling the perceiver to achieve a goal and "tuning" them to be able to detect similar functional values in the environment in the future. The resultant tuning of attention, along with the induction of new goals, represent the education of attention and intention that define learning.

Learning as the tuning of attention and intention is a differentiation process rather than a building up of associations as is classically the definition of learning from an information processing perception. This has implications for instructional design, in that the tools, activities, and instruction that are designed are not viewed as adding into the accumulating data in the heads of students. Such an information processing assertion is based on an assumption that perceptions are bare and meaningless until interpreted and analyzed by stored schemas. In contrast, an ecological presumption is that a sensitive exploring agent can pick up the affordance of an environment directly through exploration, discovery, and differentiation (Gibson & Spelk, 1983). So the learning environment and associated tool, activities, and instruction that are designed for instruction should serve to highlight important distinctions and focus the students' attention on previously unnoticed uses for things in the world.

7.4 REINTERPRETATIONS OF KEY LEARNING SYSTEM VARIABLES

7.4.1 Collaboration

Drawing from biology, as ecological psychology is prone to do, there is precedence for describing how isolated individuals can be drawn together to adopt a shared intentionality in the life cycle of *Dictyostelium discoideum* (Cardillo, 2001). *D. discoideum,* a type of slime mold, typically exists as a single-celled organism, called a myxamoeba. However, when food sources become scarce, the individual myxamoebae form a collective organism called a pseudoplasmodium, as seen in Fig. 7.1. This collective has the effectivity to move via protoplasmic streaming and, thus, is capable of responding to energy gradients in the environment in order to slither to better food sources—a capability well beyond that of any individual myxamoeba alone (Clark, 1997).

D. discoideum has a different set of effectivities as a myxamoebae than it does as a pseudoplasmodium. When the set of effectivities of the pseudoplasmodium, considering its current intentions (goals), becomes more appropriate to the environment at hand, individual myxameobae reconfigure to act collectively in order to more effectively cope with their environment. The collective behavior of learning groups may be similarly described.

By analogy, ecological psychology enables the description of groups of students using the same affordance/effectivity and perceiving/acting terms as applied to individuals (DePalma, 2001). The collaborative, intention-sharing group, becomes the unit of analysis. Analysis at the level of the collective forces the externalization, and subsequent observability, of aspects of intentionality that are not observable in an isolated agent and are thus a property of a higher order organization of behavior. Preliminary results from describing collaboration in these terms suggests that all definitions, metaphors, comparisons, and other instances of the ecological agent are applicable to the collective. Learning groups, termed "collectives" to highlight their shared

intentionality, are described as perceiving–acting wholes, with goals and intentions organizing their collective behavior.

7.4.2 Motivation

Ecological psychology has suggested that motivation may not be the all-explaining educational variable it is often proposed to be. Preliminary research into the motivation and interest of hypertext readers, using principles of ecological psychology, suggest that any stable description of "motivation" may be related to the stabilities of goals and intentions and affordances of environments (Young, Guan, Toman, DePalma, & Znamenskaia, 2000). Evidence suggests that both interest and motivation, as rated by the participant, change moment to moment, with the degree to which particular screens of information afford progress toward the reader's goal. This suggests the colloquial understanding of motivation may simply be an epiphenonmenon, the result of presuming such a variable exists and asking people to rate how much of it they have. Rather than being a relatively stable internal cognitive force that drives and sustains behavior (e.g., Ford, 1992), motivation is reinterpreted as an on-going momentary personal assessment of the match between the adopted goals for this occasion and the affordances of the environment. High motivation, then, would result from either adopting goals that are afforded by the present learning context or finding a learning context that affords progress toward one's adopted goals.

For instructional designers this means developing contexts that induce students to adopt goals that will be afforded by the learning contexts they design, especially one that enables students to detect the raison d'être of the material (Young & Barab, 1999). Likewise for students, the implications are that an honest assessment by the student of current goals will specify the level of motivation. Students whose goals are "to please the teacher," "to complete the course," or "to get an A" will be perceiving and acting to detect how the current context can further these goals. Consider two examples. A student who enrolls in a statistics course whose job is in qualitative market research. Such a student may not at first see the affordances of a quantitative approach to data reduction, but during the course may begin to see how the statistical analyses could move her forward to achive job-related goals. Similarly, consider a K-12 classroom teacher who comes back to school for ongoing

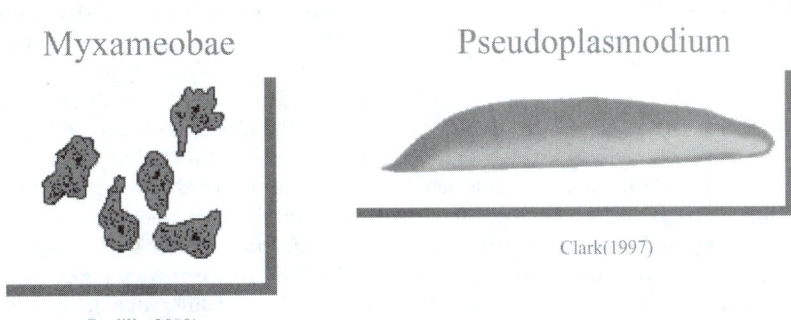

Myxameobae   Pseudoplasmodium

Cardillo(2000)   Clark(1997)

FIGURE 7.1. Organization of *D. discoideum* from individual myxameobae into a pseudoplasmodium for collective action.

inservice professional development in an educational technology course, thinking it will fulfill a school district requirement, but then detects how the technology he learns about can be applied to his existing lessons. Given learners with these goals rather than learning goals to master the content of instructional materials, instructional designers should not be surprised when the actions students take in a designed learning context appear unanticipated from the perspectives of the original designers.

7.4.3 Problem Solving

Ecological psychology principles have been used to describe the problem solving that takes place in the context of anchored instruction (CTGV, 1990, 1993). Young, Barab, and Garrett (2000) described a model of problem solving that presumes various phases of agent–environment interactions taking place as problem solvers view then work on the video-based problems. Viewers first detect information in the video presentation of the problem, then to a greater or lesser extent, adopt the goal of solving the problem (note some students may have the goal to get the right answer and display their mathematics prowess while others may have more genuine intentions to help the story protagonist solve a fictional dilemma). Perceiving and acting on the values using valid mathematical calculations then proceed until a solution is deemed to be reached (this must be seen as "enacted" activity in situ as described by Lave, 1988 above). All along the way, this model describes events as interactions between intention-driven learners and information-rich video environments.

This description of mathematical problem solving contrasts with that of information processing views. Rather than describing rules and procedures as stored inside the learner, this description focuses on activity in situ, describing it as behavior arising on a particular occasion the results from a cascade of environmental constraints imposed by contextual circumstances and personal goals. Understanding the goals that are actually organizing a student's behavior is a difficult task. Students cannot often just articulate their goals when asked. However, it seems no more difficult than speculating about the compiled rules and procedures that are stored in someone's memory. Both must be inferred from quantitative and qualitative assessment of what the problem solvers say and do, particularly the choices they make that may be evident when completing their problem solving with the aid of a computer.

7.4.4 "Flow," a Description of Optimal Performance

Csikszentmihalyi (1990) described how on some occasions people can be so fully engaged in achieving a goal that they lose track of time, concentrating so narrowly and consistently that they later report having had an optimal experience. He has titled this phenomenon "flow." Csikszentmihalyi (1990) described flow using a reprentation-based information processing perspective stating that "Everything we experience—joy or pain, interest or boredom—is represented in the mind as information." This description unfortunately leads inevitably to the questions that arise from mind–body or mind–matter dualism, such as "who or what is perceiving this mind-stored information and how does that perception and action occur?" This can quickly lead to infinite recursive descent and a less than satisfying account of how thinking and learning occur.

A more parsimonious description of flow can be provided using an ecological psychology perspective. From this perspective, flow emerges when the environment affords immediate and direct progress toward one's intended goals and affords opportunities for close coupling from which can arise immediate and continuous feedback. In short, flow is the result of an optimal match between the goals and intentions of a learner and the affordance of the environment on a specific occasion. This interactional account of flow does not place the controlling information inside the head of the learner, but leaves it out in the environment, with the learning bringing to it a goal, the path to which is clearly reachable under the environmental circumstances. Flow could be thought of as the ultimate level of motivation as ecologically defined, an ideal match of goals and affordances with clear and continuous opportunities for feedback. Flow is a good example of how variables and processes that have been discovered through research from the information processing perspective, can also and perhaps more parsimoniously be explained using ecological psychology.

7.4.5 Misconceptions

Young and Znamenskaia (2001) conducted a survey of preservice teachers in their junior year in college. The survey asked several online free-response questions about the student's understanding of what educational technology was, how it might be wisely integrated into the classroom, and the attributes one might look for in exceptionally good applications of technology to instruction. These novice preservice teachers gave responses that differed in quality and sometimes in quantity from those of experienced technology-using educators who had risen to the role of university scholars in the area of educational technology. The responses exhibited what might commonly be called "misconceptions" about educational technology. Ten such "misconceptions" were identified. They include the idea that educational technology only refers to computers and not other technologies such as video; the idea that the major cost of instructional computing is hardware, ignoring the costs of training, recurring costs of connections, and software; and the idea that the primary reason for using a program such as a word processor is for students to obtain pretty printout, ignoring the value of easy revisions, outlining, tracking changes or the multimedia capabilities of word processing programs.

But rather than label these observations "misconceptions," our preference was be to label them "naïve perceptions." This highlights our bias toward perception rather than memory, and clarifies that the differences may not lie solely in cognitive structures, but rather in the goals for perceiving and acting that future teachers have—goals that emerge from their environment (university classes) as compared to the environment of experts (applications development and K-12 classes) or even those of practicing teachers (have students learn content and/or perform well on standardized tests). We preferred naïve perceptions to "misperceptions" in that they were not "wrong," but rather were not seeing all the possibilities for action of educational technology. They needed to differentiate and pick up more of the affordances that were available to be detected.

Viewed this way, the "treatment" to remediate these naïve perceptions would not be simply informing students of the expert's responses, but instead, it would involve inducing future teachers to adopt new goals—goals that would enable them to see (detect) the many different ways in which educational technology (broadly defined) can be applied to lesson plans (i.e., enable teachers to detect the affordances of using educational technology). So rather than an instructional process, we advocated a "tuning" process of both intention and attention. Tuning *intention* in this case meant creating learning experiences in which future teachers could adopt realistic goals for integrating technology into instruction (Young & Barab, 1999). In this way they might experience the need to be driven by some sense of how students think and learn, rather than mindlessly applying the latest technology to every situation. Tuning *attention* in this case would be accomplished by providing rich contexts (hardware, software, and scaffolding for learning) that would afford students the broadest possible range of actions (e.g., integrating assistive technology, the Internet, simulations, productivity tools, video, construction kits, probeware, teleconferencing, manipulatives) through which to reach their newly adopted goals.

Further, Young and Barab (1999) proposed that such tuning of intention and attention, enhancing the naïve perceptions of preservice teachers so they can detect all the rich affordances for action that educational technology experts detect, would optimally take place within a community of practice (Lave & Wenger, 1991; Young, 1993). Such communities of practice (with goals to perform a profession competently) and communities of learners (with goals to engage in activities that optimize opportunities for tuning of intention and attention) are types of "collectives" with shared intentionality as discussed above. Future teachers with naïve perceptions of educational technology would be part of a community whose goals included the wise integration of technology into instruction, and whose members include a mix of relative novices and relative experts, working together toward a shared authentic purpose. This participation (action) in context might lead to the preservice teachers adopting the goals of the more-experienced peers.

7.4.6 Schemas

A schema is defined traditionally as an organized abstracted understanding, stored in memory, that is used to predict and make sense of events as they unfold. But from an ecological psychology perspective, schemata must be seen as the results of agent–environment interactions as they unfold on a specific occasion. The ecological psychology description of a schema

rests as much with regularities across events as it does with stored abstracted understandings in the head.

Evidence for schemas comes from the things people recall about sentences they read (Bransford & Franks, 1971) or add to their recollections of videos they watch (Loftus & Palmer, 1974) since they often recognize a holistic view rather than literal sentences and tend to incorporate and integrate information from subsequent events with recollections of initial events (e.g., postincident news reports biasing recall of video tapes of automobile accidents). Roger Schank provided a classic example of schemas in describing restaurant "scripts" (Schank & Abelson, 1977). He described the abstracted expectations that arise from the normal flow of events that typically happen in restaurants; namely, you arrive, are seated, you view the menu, order, wait, eat, pay, and leave. This "script" is then violated walking in to most fast-food restaurants in which you arrive, view the menu, order, pay, wait, find a seat, eat, and leave. Such violations of the script highlight the fundamental way in which scripts, as a particular type of schema, guide our understanding of the world.

However, the regularities of events that are believed to be abstracted and stored in scripts are a natural part of the environment as well. As we experience one restaurant after another, there is the possibility to directly pick up the invariance among the occasions. So after five traditional restaurant experiences, it may be possible to detect, and proactively perceive what is coming next, when entering the sixth traditional restaurant. The invariant pattern would also be violated on the occasion of a fast-food restaurant visit. That is, when defining events and perception that is meaningfully bounded rather than bounded in space and time, it is possible to say that the schema, at least the invariant information that defines the restaurant script pattern, is there to be directly perceived. It therefore does not require abstraction, representation or storage inside the head of the perceiver to be noticed and acted upon.

7.4.7 Assessment

Assessment is a theme running through nearly all instructional design models. Formative and summative assessments are integrated into the instructional design process, as well as individual and group assessment of learning outcomes that provide feedback to students. An ecological psychology approach to this focuses attention on the purpose or functional value of such assessments and leads to a recommendation that assessment should be seamless, continuous, and have functional value for the learners as well as the assessors (Kulikowich & Young, 2001). Young, Kulikowich, and Barab (1997) described such seamless assessments placing the target for assessment on the learner–environment interaction rather than using the individual or class as the unit of analysis. Kulikowich and Young have taken this further describing a methodology for an ecologically based assessment that provides direct assistance to learners throughout their engagement with the learning context, much like the flight instruments of a fighter jet enhance the pilot's abilities to detect distant threats and plan complex flight patterns.

From this perspective, a primary assessment goal for instructional designers is to assess a student's true goals and intentions, those organizing and guiding the student's behavior. Then, if they are reasonably educative goals, the instructional designer can use the problem space defined by such goals as criteria for determining whether the student is on course for success or whether some scaffolding must be implemented. However, if the student's current goals are not deemed to be educative, then the task is to induce in the student, new goals that will constrain and organize behavior in the learning context.

Young (1995) described how learners working on complex problems with the help of a computer could be assessed using time-stamped logs of their navigation patterns from screen to screen, indicating their goals and intentions as a trajectory of events and activities. Kulikowich and Young (2001) suggested as part of their methodology that such ecologically valid assessments must have demonstrable value in improving the performance of the learners, and further should be under the control of the learners so they could be tuned and optimized for individual intentions. In this sense an ecological psychology perspective on assessment suggests that primary attention be paid toward accurately assessing learner's true goals, and then using the state spaces that are known to be associated with those goals, in the context of well-documented properties (affordances) of learning environments, to anticipate, scaffold, guide, and structure the interactions of learners as they move toward achieving the goals. The "trick" for the instructional designer, then, is to induce students to adopt goals that closely match what the learning environments that they have designed afford.

7.5 THE FINAL WORD

So what is different in instructional design from the ecological psychology perspective? First, primary attention to goals. The first task for instructional designers is to induce learners to have goals related to the isntructional materials and learning environments they design. Videos, authentic real-world and online experiences, and stories have proven effective in inducing students to adopt new goals that they did not come to class with. Then, the events of instruction should be organized to enable the close coupling of the novice with someone (man or computer) more experienced, creating a shared intentionality and coordinated activity (collective). In this way the learner's attention can be tuned by jointly perceiving and acting or at least observing vicariously the environmental information that specifies previously unperceived affordances. Finally, assessments must be designed to have functional value for the learners, extending their perception and ability to act in ways that tune their intentions and attentions to critical affordances of the world. This, then, is how people learn, leverage that can be applied by the instructional designer.

References

American Psychological Association (APA) Board of Educational Affairs (1995, December). Learner-centered psychological principles: A framework for school redesign and reform [Online]. Available: *http://www.apa.org/ed/lcp.html*

Barab, S. A., Cherkes-Julkowski, M., Swenson, R., Garrett, S., Shaw, R. E., & Young, M. (1999). Principles of self-organization: Learning as participation in autocatakinetic systems. *Journal of the Learning Sciences, 8*(3 & 4), 349–390.

Bransford, J. D., & Franks, J. J. (1971). The abstraction of linguistic ideas. *Cognitive Psychology, 2*(4), 331–350.

Brown, J.S., Collins, A, & Duguid, P. (1989). Situated cognition and the culture of learning, *Educational Researcher,* Jan-Feb, 32–42.

Capra F. (1996). *The Web of Life.* New York: Anchor Books.

Cardillo, F. M. (2001). Dictyostelium. Classification of Plants. Available: *http://web1.manhattan.edu/fcardill/plants/protoc/dicty.html*

Clancey, W. J. (1997). *Situated cognition: On human knowledge and computer representations.* Cambridge: Cambridge University Press.

Clark, A. (1997). Being there: Putting brain, body, and world together again. Cambridge, MA: MIT Press.

Cognition and Technology Group at Vanderbilt (CTGV). (1990). Anchored instruction and its relationship to situated cognition. *Educational Research, 19*(6), 2–10.

Cognition and Technology Group at Vanderbilt (CTGV). (1993). Anchored instruction and situated cognition revisited. *Educational Technology,* March Issue, 52–70.

Cognitive Science (1993). *Special Issue: Situated Action, 17*(1), Jan-March. Norwood, NJ: Ablex.

Coulter, J. (1989). *Mind in action.* Atlantic Highlands, NJ: Humanities Press.

Csikszentmihalyi, M. (1990). *Flow: The psychology of optimal experience.* NY: Harper and Row.

DePalma, A. (2001). Collaborative programming in Perl: A case study of learning in groups described from an ecological psychology perspective. Dissertation, The University of Connecticut.

Ford, M. E. (1992). *Motivating humans: Goals, emotions, and personal agency beliefs.* Newbury Park, CA: Sage Publications, Inc.

Gibson, E. J., & Spelk, E. S. (1983). Development of perception. In P. H. Mussen (Ed.), *Handbook of Child Psychology.* New York: Wiley.

Gibson, J. J. (1986) *The ecological approach to visual perception.* Hillsdale, NJ: Erlbaum.

Greeno, J. G. (1994). Gibson's affordances. *Psychological Review, 101*(2), 236–342.

Greeno, J. G. (1998). The situativity of knowing, learning, and research. *American Psychologist, 53*(1), 5–26.

Heidegger, M. (1927a/ 1962). *Being and time.* New York: Harper and Row.

Heidegger, M. (1927b). *The basic problem of phenomenology.* New York: Harper and Row.

Kim, N-G, Turvey, M. T., & Carello, C. (1993). Optical information about the severity of upcoming contacts. *Journal of Experimental Psychology: Human Perception and Performance, 19,* 179-193.

Kugler, P. N., & Turvey, M. T. (1987). *Information, natural law, and the self-assembly of rhythmic movement.* Hillsdale, NJ: Erlbaum.

Kulikowich, J. M., & Young, M. F. (2001). Locating an ecological psychology methodology for situated action. *Journal of the Learning Sciences, 10*(1 & 2), 165–202.

Lave, J. (1988). *Cognition in practice: Mind, mathematics and culture in everyday life.* Cambridge, UK: Cambridge University Press.

Lave, J., & Wenger, E. (1991). *Situated learning: Legitimate peripheral participation.* New York: Cambridge University Press.

Lee, D. N. (1976). A theory of visual control of braking based on information about time to collision. *Perception, 5,* 437–459.

Lee, D. N., Young, D. S., Reddish, P. E., Lough, S., & Clayton, T. M. H. (1983). Visual timing in hitting an accelerating ball. *Quarterly Journal of Experimental Psychology, 35A,* 333–346.

Loftus, E. F., & Palmer, J. C. (1974). Reconstruction of automobile destruction: An example of the interaction between language and memory. *Journal of Verbal Learning and Verbal Behaviour, 13,* 585–589.

Mark, L. S., Bailliet, J. A., Craver, K. D., Douglas, S. D., & Fox, T. (1990). What an actor must do in order to perceive the affordance for sitting. *Ecological Psychology, 2,* 325–366.

Merleau-Ponty, M. (1962). *Phenomenology of perception.* London: Routledge and Kegan Paul.

Pufall, P., & Dunbar, C. (1992). Perceiving whether or not he world affords stepping onto or over: A developmental study. *Ecological Psychology, 4,* 17–38.

Schank, R. C., & Abelson, R. P. (1977). *Scripts, plans, goals and understanding: An inquiry into human knowledge structures.* Hillsdale, NJ: Erlbaum.

Shaw, R. E., Kadar, E, Sim, M., & Repperger, D. W. (1992). The intentional spring: A strategy for modeling systems that learn to perform intentional acts. *Journal of Motor Behavior, 24*(1), 3–28.

Shaw, R. E., & Kinsella-Shaw, J. M. (1988). Ecological mechanics: A physical geometry for intentioanl constraints. *Human Movement Science, 7,* 155–200.

Shaw, R. E., McIntyre, M., & Mace, W. (1974). The role of symmetry in event perception. In R. S. Macleod, & H. L. Pick, (Eds.), *Perception: Essays in honour of James Gibson.* Ithaca, NY: Cornell University Press.

Shaw, R. E., & Turvey, M. T. (1999). Ecological foundations of cognition: II. Degrees of freedom and conserved quantities in animal-environment system. *Journal of Consciousness Studies, 6*(11–12), 111–123.

Sun, R. (2002). *Duality of mind: A bottom-up approach toward cognition.* Mahwah, NJ: Erlbaum.

Vicente, K. J. (1999). *Cognitive work analysis: Toward safe, productive, and healthy computer-based work.* Mahwah, NJ: Erlbaum.

Warren, E. H. (1984). Perceiving affordances: Visual guidance of stair climbing. *Journal of Experimental Psychology: Human Perception and Performance, 10,* 683–703.

Warren, E. H., & Wang, S. (1987). Visual guidance of walking through apertures: Body-scaled information specifying affordances. *Journal of Experimental Psychology: Human Perception and Performance, 13,* 371–383.

Young, M. F. (1993). Instructional design for situated learning. *Educational Technology Research and Development, 41* (1), 43–58.

Young, M. (1995). Assessment of situated learning using computer environments. *Journal of Science Education and Technology, 4*(3), 89–96.

Young, M. F., & Barab, S. A. (1999). Perception of the raison d'être in anchored instruction: An ecological psychology perspective. *Journal of Educational Computing Research, 20*(2), 113–135.

Young, M. F., Barab, S., & Garrett, S. (2000). Agent as detector: An ecological psychology perspective on learning by perceiving-acting systems. In D. H. Jonassen & S. M. Land (Eds.), *Theoretical foundations of learning environments (pp. 147–172).* Mahwah, NJ: Erlbaum.

Young, M. F., DePalma, A., & Garrett, S. (2002). Situations, interaction, process and affordances: An ecological psychology perspective. *Instructional Science, 30,* 47–63.

Young, M., Guan, Y., Toman, J., DePalma, A., & Znamenskaia, E. (2000). Agent as detector: An ecological psychology perspective on learning by perceiving-acting systems. In B. J. Fishman & S. F. O'Connor-Divelbiss (Eds.), *Proceedings of International Conference of the Learning Sciences 2000.* Mahwah, NJ: Erlbaum.

Young, M. F., Kulikowich, J. M., & Barab, S. A. (1997). The unit of analysis for situated assessment. *Instructional Science, 25*(2), 133–150.

Young, M., & Znamenskaia, E. (2001). *Future teacher perceptions concerning educational technology.* Paper presented at the AERA Annual Meeting (#37.65), Seattle, WA, April 13.

· 8 ·

CONVERSATION THEORY

Gary McIntyre Boyd
Concordia University Canada

The object of the game is to go on playing it.
—John von Neumann (1958)

Is it, in some good sense, possible to design a character, and hence to generate some one kind of immortality? The fact of immortality is essential. Further, without this fact, our fine talk (as of societies and of civilizations and of existence) would be so much hogwash.
—Gordon Pask (1995)

8.1 OVERVIEW

Gordon Pask's Conversation Theory (CT) is based on his model of the underlying processes involved in complex human learning. As such it can be read as a radical cybernetic constructivist account of human cognitive emergence, a kind of ontology of human being. Conversational learning is taken to be a natural imperative, an "ought that is." So its elucidation in Pask's Conversation Theory can apply normatively to schemes for designing and evaluating technology-supported human learning. CT is relevant to the development of quasi-intelligent tutoring systems which enable learners to develop nontrivial understandings of the complex real underlying systemic processes of ecosystems and of themselves as multiactor systems. CT portrays and explains the emergence of knowledge by means of multilevel agreement-oriented conversations among participants, supported by modeling facilities and suitable communication and action interfaces; hence it is also very much an applied epistemology. When used for instructional system design, CT prescribes learning systems that involve at least two participants, a modeling facility and at least three levels of interaction: interaction with a shared modeling facility, conversational interaction about how to solve a problem, and conversation about why that method should be used. Higher metacognitively critical levels of learning

conversation, about the implications of carrying on robotically, are necessary to overcome the "cognitive fixity" arising when only two languaging levels are employed by a learner. In especially beneficial educational ventures, multiple participants and many levels of discourse are involved, and here CT is almost alone in providing a framework for developing multiactor multilevel networks of human–machine discourse.

Conversation Theory, when considered in depth, offers a critical transformative challenge to educational technology by deconstructing the conventionally understood psychology of the individual. The supposedly continuously present stable autonomous integrated individual learner is reunderstood rather as a collection of psychological individuals (P-individuals) whose presence is variable and hetrarchical. CT asserts that what it is we are mainly helping educate and self-construct is not simply one person but rather a wide variety of interwoven competitive P-individuals, some of whom execute in distributed fashion across many bodies and machines. Such a task is more complex and micropolitical than educational technologists usually assume to be their job.

This chapter provides a skeletal description of the theory, some practical explanations of how to use it, and a brief historical account of its evolution and future prospects. Pask's Conversation Theory has proven useful for designing, developing, evaluating and researching many sorts of partly computerized, more or less intelligent, performance support and learning support systems. The CT way of viewing human learning has very wide application and often has led to important new insights among those who have used it.

8.2 INTRODUCTION TO PASK'S CONVERSATION THEORY (CT)

8.2.1 Conversation for Responsible Human Becoming

The Conversation Theory (hereafter referred to as CT) conceived and developed by Gordon Pask (between 1966 and 1996) is primarily an explanatory ontology combined with an epistemology, which has wide implications for psychology and educational technology.

The object of THE game is not merely, as John von Neumann (1958) said, just "to go on playing it," but rather to go on playing it so as to have as many shared enjoyments and intimations of such Earthly immortality as are possible. Let us first look at an example of people attempting to teach and learn responsible and delightfully propitious habits of awareness and action. Subsequently we will look at ways to model and facilitate what are probably the real underlying processes that generate and propagate responsible human being and becoming.

In Mount Royal Park last week, Larry, aged eight and standing beside me, was watching his brother Eddy and Marie, a gentle young girl visiting them from Marseilles, crouched a little way down the hill trying to get near to a gray squirrel without frightening it. Suddenly, Larry clapped his hands as hard as he could; the squirrel scampered up a tree. I said, "Don't do that. You're spoiling their fun!" He said, "That's my fun!" I said gruffly, "Hey, wait a minute, Larry. They are really part of you, and you will go on suffering their dislike for a long time to come if that's how you get your fun." He just looked away. I strode off toward the lookout.

Possibly that event was both people-marring and an attempt at responsible peoplemaking through action-situated conversation. Was it a real learning conversation? Here we had two participants, both of whom had their attention fixed on an immediate concrete experience as well as on each other. On my part there was an intention to teach; Larry's obvious intent was to show how smart he was. Was there an intention to learn on both our parts? That is uncertain. The conversation was situated in an emotively meaningful way, and it was connected to direct actions and the cocausal interpretation of observations, and we will both remember it. However, we failed to come to an agreement as to how the acts should be named (just clever fun vs. gratuitous nastiness) and valued.

8.2.2 The Cycle of Conversational Coproduction of Learning

The essential activities of constructing knowledge through grounded conversation are pursued through cycles similar to A. N. Whitehead's (1949) description of learning through cycles of: Romance > Definition > Generalization > and so on again....

After the first touch of romance, a CT learning venture begins with the negotiation of an agreement between participants to learn about a given domain, and some particular topics and skills in that domain (see Fig. 8.1). One participant (A) who has some inkling of a topic starts by using the available resources to make a modeling move, to name it, and to explain why it is being made. Another participant (B) either agrees to try to do the same thing and compare it with what A did or disagrees

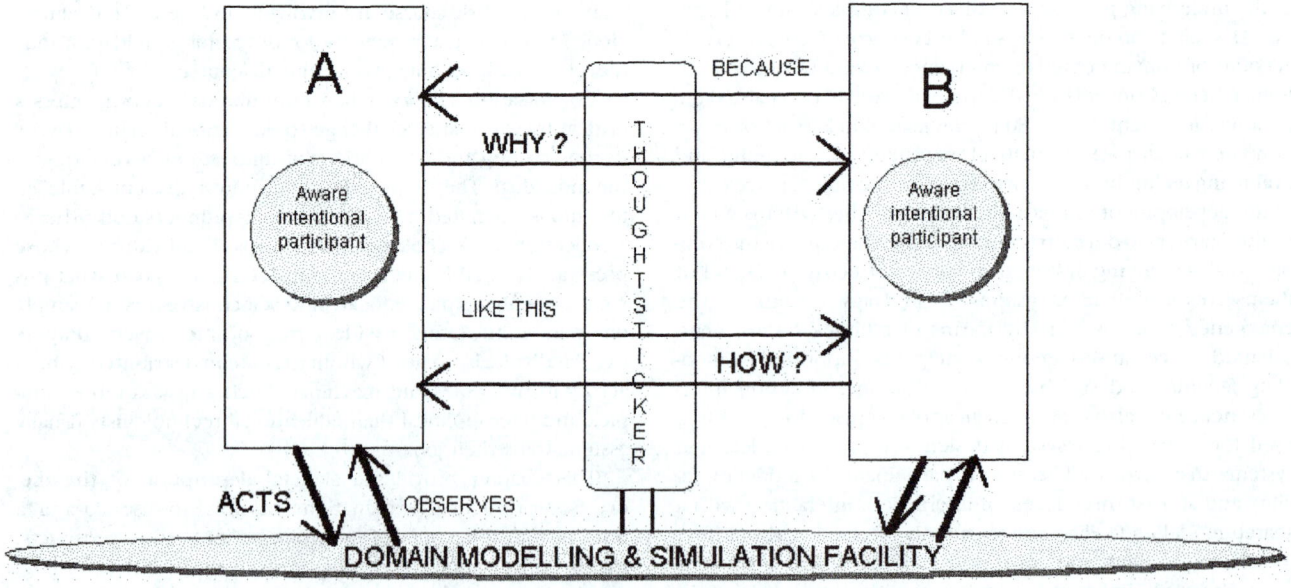

FIGURE 8.1. The simplest possible model of conversational learning.

with that foray and tries to make another start by acting on the model, naming the new act, and explaining why it is better. If there are other participants, they join in. If the modeling efforts are judged, on close investigation, to be different, they will be labeled differently and some relation will be constructed between them and will be appropriately labeled. If the two (or *n*) efforts are judged to be the same, they will be coalesced into one chunk of the domain model with one name.

Each chunk, or concept, of the model should consist of executable procedures that reconstruct relations among more elementary constituents, and possibly among other complex concepts. Various conjectures are made as to what a good extension, and/or predictive capability should be, and the participants attempt to extend and debug the model to achieve such. If they fail, then they reject the supposition as being incongruous with other parts of the domain knowledge and skill development endeavor. Each conversational learning cycle adds more agreed coherent well-labeled complexity and more autopoietic, predictive capability to the model.

8.2.3   Conversation Theory as an Explanatory, Also a Heuristic, Research and Development Framework

Pask's Conversation Theory is not yet a fully worked out conventional axiomatic-deductive scientific theory. What it offers is a framework for thought and a plausible model mechanism to account for the emergence of the domain of human conceptual knowledge, which Popper (1972) named "World 3." It is also a kind of Artificial-Life theory of human-becoming, which models the emergence of conscious cognizing human beings as essentially a matter of multilevel multiactor intercourse (CT conversations). This is carried forward among software-like actors called P-individuals, continually executing in biological processors or a combination of biological and hardware computer-communication systems, which are called, in general, M-individuals.

The physical world as we have learned to know it (including biological individuals) and the social world we have made together are both understood as being generated largely by contextually situated, multilevel conversations among our P-individuals who interpenetrate both. It is asserted that the reciprocal conversational construction, of active concepts and dynamic memories, is how psychological participants and perhaps indeed human beings arise as coconstructions.

Conversation Theory along with its child, Interaction of Actors Theory (IAT), amount to a sort of Artificial Life theory. They propose that, when employing the appropriate relational operators, a Strict Conversation, eventuating in appropriate agreements among its originating P-individual participants, can bifurcate and result in the emergence of a new Psychological individual (one able to engage in further broader and/or deeper conversations with others) and so on and on, constructing ever more complex extensive local and distributed P-individuals.

Pask's CT and IAT are, I believe, founded on a larger and deeper view of humanity than are many cognitive science theories. The underlying question is this: How do we together generate creatively complex psychological participant individuals that can interact to have plausible intimations of cultural immortality?

Conversation theory is a really radical psychological theory in that it places the understanding-constructing P-individuals and their world-reconstructing discourse in first place, ontologically. The biological individual persons are not the primary concern.

8.2.4   The Very General Ontological and Epistemological Nature of Conversation Theory

Gordon Pask's main premise is that reliable knowledge exists, is produced, and evolves in action-grounded conversations. Knowledge as an object distinct from learner–teachers does not exist. Learners always incorporate internalized teachers, and teachers always incorporate internalized learners who help construct their knowledge. We all incorporate all three, and our knowledge, as executable models of the world, in our physiological M-individual bodies and personal machines.

Conversation Theory, as well as being an ontology of human being, is also developed as a prescription for designing constructivist learning support systems. In going from "is" to "ought" there has always been the probability of committing the naturalistic fallacy, as David Hume (1740/1998) and G. E. Moore (1903) pointed out long ago. This has recently been an obvious problem when going from constructivist descriptions of how we (supposedly) actually learn, to prescriptions of how we ought to teach (Duffy & Jonassen, 1992). Where does this new "ought" come from? My own solution to this dilemma is to posit "The Ought That Is"—to assert that the ought has already been historically evolved right through the genetic and on into the neuronal systems of humanimals; so that as we learn and teach, what we are doing is uncovering and working with a biologically universally preexisting ought. The normative idea of constructivists is to design learning activities that facilitate a natural process rather than ones which hinder or frustrate it.

What is presented here is a much simplified composite of four decades of work, interpreted and somewhat elaborated by me (Boyd, 2001; Boyd & Pask, 1987), rather than a complete explanation of a finished theory. CT, like memetics theory, is not a mere finite game. Rather, they are parts of our infinite game as humankind. There are, therefore, inconsistencies and the theory remains incomplete. But many believe that CT/IAT is ahead of other current cognitivist and constructivist theories, at least as a heuristic for research progress.

8.2.5   Pask's Original Derivation of CT From the Basics of Problem Solving and Learning

Pask started with the definition that a *problem* is a discrepancy between a desired state and an actual state of any system, and then went to the question: What is the simplest problem solver possible? The simplest problem solver is a random trial and error operator that goes on trying changes in the model system until it hits upon the solution (if ever). The next simplest is a deviation-limiting feedback loop cybernetic solver which remembers how close the last change brought things and compares the result of the current action, to choose which direction to go next in the problem space in order to hill-climb to a good solution.

But hill-climbers are only "act pragmatists" (Rescher, 1977). Such problem solvers work, at least suboptimally, given enough time and in a restricted problem space But they don't learn anything. And they may end up on top of a foothill, rather than on the desired mountaintop.

That weakness can be partly fixed by adding some random decision dithering. The L_0 problem solvers of CT are of this type. If the L_0 level is augmented by a higher L_1 level adaptive feedback controller which remembers which sorts of L_0 solution paths were good for which classes of problems, then one has a rule-learning machine. These two level P-individuals are what Rescher (1977) calls rule pragmatists.

The minimal P-individual then has three components: a problem modeling and solution testing facility, together with a hill-climbing L_0 problem solver, and an L_1 rule learner, all executing on some M-individual (see Fig. 8.2.)

The problem with such a simple adaptive learning system is what Pask calls cognitive fixity; it develops one good way of learning and dumbly sticks to it, even when it repeatedly fails to generate a solution to some new type of problem. Harri-Augstein and Thomas (1991) refer to this as functioning as a "learning robot." The stability of selves depends on there being some cognitive fixity.

Pask also identified forms of metacognitive fixity as often occurring in two distinct learning styles: serialist and holist. However, many other sorts of limiting habits occur when only one P-individual is executing in one M-individual. The main ways beyond cognitive fixity are either to have several P-individuals executing and conversing in one M-individual, or to have P-individuals executing in a distributed way over many M-individuals.

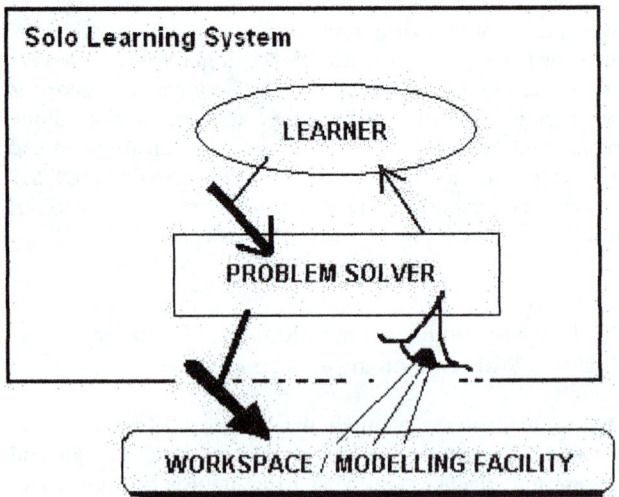

FIGURE 8.2. Simple solitary adaptive learning system.

If one particular way of rule learning doesn't help, what then? As Rescher (1977) showed, the next thing to do is see if you can invent a general method for creating good rules. Ideally higher levels of self conversation (L_1-L_n) would function as what he calls a methodological pragmatist. If you add some crossbreeding by conversation with another P-individual, such variation can yield an evolutionary system. Some genetic algorithm generators are of this nature: A-life crossbreeding.

8.3 HISTORICAL ROOTS AND EVOLUTION OF CONVERSATION THEORY

There are some similarities between CT and the ancient Socratic dialogue model as reported by Plato, also between the mediaeval dialectical antithesis debating strategy of Peter Abelard. And the first known educational technologist, Comenius, who (after Seneca) pointed out, "*Qui docet, discit,*" (He who teaches, learns)—although, admittedly, Seneca's Latin is not so broad as to imply reciprocal learning conversations. The Hegelian, Marxian, and Frankfurt-school forms of dialectic might also be seen as precursors of Conversation Theory, as might Martin Buber's profound *Ich und Du* conversations (1970).

Gordon Pask's Conversation Theory is a learning theory which initially arose from the perspectives of Wittgenstein and (Gordon's mentor) Heinz von Foerster. By putting reciprocal conversation-action in first place ontologically, Pask builds on Wittgenstein's (1958/1978) argument against private languages and on von Foerster's conception of second-order cybernetics (1981). And Pask can indeed be seen as putting forward a sort of posthuman (Hayles, 1999) critical social theory.

Conversation Theory seriously challenges both naive realists and folk psychology. However, CT is not irredeemably idealist, nor is it hyperrationalist, as some have accused Habermas of being. For those who care to think it through, CT can probably be accommodated within the new Critical Realist ontologies (Bhaskar & Norris, 1999). Gordon Pask usually assumed the perspective of conventional modern scientific realism.

Also the neurophysiological learning research of Pask's friend, Warren McCulloch (1969), was probably a related outgrowth of Pask's own experiments with dendritic physical–chemical learning systems. These latter were concretely embodied (unlike McCulloch's mathematical models) protoconnectionist systems. And now we see that CT is interestingly compatible with recent connectionist neurophysiological learning theories such as Edelman's Extended Theory of Neuronal Group Selection (Edelman, 1992).

At a more mundane level, the Personal Scientist and repertory-grids model (Kelly, 1955), each of us coconstruing our own scientific models of the world, can also be seen to correlate with CT, and has been used by Shaw (1985) and by Harri-Augstein and Thomas (1991) to extend CT.

Conversation Theory was developed interactively through a long series of experiments with new notations, adaptive teaching machines and computer aided learning environments. CASTE (Course Assembly and Tutorial Learning Environment) was the most notable of Pask's systems. CASTE served to interactively construct domain representations as entailment meshes and the associated topic tasks, but it also provided tutorial support to, and teachback acceptance from, the learners (Pask & Scott, 1973). The most striking features of CASTE were its large interactive display of the entailment mesh of the domain to be learned, and its smaller facility for actually carrying out learning conversations and teachbacks. The large domain display generally had an array of terminal competences at the top, and various supporting topics below. This was not a simple hierarchical tree graph of prerequisites but an hetrarchical net linked in the many valid ways. To start, the learner would mark the terminal competences he or she aimed for, and also some of supporting topics to be worked on. Then, after manipulation and conversation, when understanding of that topic had been demonstrated, the display indicated which other topics would be good choices to get on with. For more details, and photographs of various versions of CASTE, see Pask (1975), Mitchell and Dalkir (1986), and Pangaro (2002).

THOUGHTSTICKER, the next most noteworthy of Pask's machines, was originally produced in 1974, by Gordon Pask and Yitzhak Hayut-Man, as a system for filling and using a collection of pigeonholes for course-assembly topic files. The ultimate goal was to make THOUGHTSTICKER so simple to use that it could be, in Pask's words, "a children's toy." As Hayut-Man explained (2001), it was to be an "intelligent holographic Christmas tree" domain embodiment on which to hang topic knowledge as practical ornaments. Unfortunately, the hardware and software of the day was not adequate for this dream to be realized. Subsequently, in the 1980s, Paul Pangaro (2002) implemented a really usable and effective THOUGHTSTICKER on a LISP machine. (Functional, but far too expensive for a child's toy.)

Later many of these ideas were brought together and developed in various forms by, among others, Mildred Shaw (1985), Sheila Harri-Augstein and Laurie Thomas (1991) in their Learning Conversations methodology, and by Diana Laurillard (2002).

8.4 CYBERNETIC AND PSYCHOLOGICAL PREREQUISITES TO CONVERSATION THEORY

Do we need prerequisites here at all? Without some special prerequisite knowledge, Pask's Conversation Theory is very difficult to grasp. It is a transdisciplinary theory that draws on cybernetics, automata, and control theory in particular, and on formal linguistics and computer science concepts, theorems and notations, as well as on aspects of cognitive psychology and neurophysiology. Without certain ideas from those fields, CT is not really understandable. Throughout the chapter, I provide explicit references to sources that give detailed (and correct) accounts of these topics. However, for those unfamiliar with the literature and lacking the leisure to follow it up, here I will give very much simplified yet, I hope, plausible accounts of the few most needed key ideas.

8.4.1 Hypothetical Real Underlying Generative Entities

Important advances in science often require the postulation of new nonobservable entities and underlying generative mechanisms, which enable research to go forward to the point where either it turns out that these hypothetical entities are as real as Quarks or, like phlogiston, they are found to be expendable. Pask's once-novel use of an hierarchy of formal languages and meta-languages L_0, L_1, L_2-L_n has now become a normal approach in AI (artificial intelligence) and computational linguistics. Pask's various types of P-individuals (actors), his active-process definition of concepts, and his parturient (P-individual producing) bifurcations are more novel leveraging hypothetical constructs. Their reality has not yet been altogether validated nor, arguably, have they been replaced by any appreciably better learning process model components. They remain as working tools, which many have been finding to be helpful guiding heuristics for either learning systems research or for instructional systems design. So let us see how they can be used to carry our work forward.

8.4.2 Cybernetic Background Needed

8.4.2.1 Automata. The components of Conversation Theory are various kinds of automata functioning in parallel. Automata are abstract comprehensive generalizations of the idea of a machine. An automaton may be thought of as a box with an input, some stuff inside—part of which may amount to transformation rules, output rules—and an output. If you input a signal, it will cause changes in the internal state of the automaton. Sometimes an input will also prompt an automaton to produce an output. For example, if you type some data into a computer, it may simply store the data. Then if you type in a command to execute some program, the program can take the data and calculate and produce an output to the printer, say. The history of what programs and data have previously been fed into the computer determines what it will do with new inputs. This is true for all but trivial automata. Just about anything can be modeled by automata. However, as Searle (1969) pointed out, a model of digestion does not actually digest real food! Automata are not all that is. Automata may be deterministic—you get a definite output for a given series of inputs—or probabilistic—you get various possible outputs with different probabilities. Automata may also be fuzzy and/or rough, possibly as people are. But let's skip that, except to say that automata can be used to model very unmachinelike behavior such as the self-organizing criticality of mindstorms.

8.4.2.2 Self-Reproducing Automata. John von Neumann was, I believe, the first to demonstrate that for an automaton to be able to reproduce itself, it must possess a blueprint of itself. Consider a robot with arms and an eye. It can look at itself, choose parts, and pick them up, and put them together to copy itself... until the eye tries to look at the eye! Or until an arm has to disassemble part of the robot so the eye can look inside; then the whole procedure breaks down. However, if the robot has a "tail" with full plans for itself encoded on the tail, then all is well. The eye can read the tail and instruct the arms to do everything necessary. Well, that assumes there is a substrate or environment that provides the necessary parts and materials and energy. That von Neumann theorem is why self-reproducing, and indeed self-producing, automata must always have two main parts: the productive automaton itself, and a blueprint or a genetic or memetic code plan for producing itself. This also applies to living organisms. (Viruses, however, are just the blueprint and an injector to inject it into cells that have the producing machinery.) Since they are self-producing and reproducing, von Neumann's theorem is why the "bundles of executing procedures," which Pask calls P-individuals, always have at least the two main levels: L_0 problem-solving procedures and L_1 learning metaprocedures or plan-like programs, for guiding the choice of problem-solving procedures during execution—as well, of course, as some substrate to work on. Further levels will be discussed below.

8.4.2.3 Control Theory.
A large part of the problem solving which P-individuals do is to bring about and maintain desired relationships, despite disturbances over time. They do this by deviation-limiting (technically called negative) feedback controllers. (These are in principle just like the thermostat which controls a furnace and an air conditioner to keep room temperatures comfortable despite large variations in the outside weather.) They observe some condition, compare it with the desired condition and, if there is a difference, they set in motion some corrective action. When the difference gets small they stop and wait until it gets too large, then correct again. If anything at all stays more or less constant with small fluctuations it is because some natural, or person-made, negative feedback control loop is at work observing, comparing and correcting. (On diagrams such as Pask's, the comparison is usually indicated by a circle with a cross in it, and perhaps also a minus sign indicating that one signal is subtracted from the other, hence "negative" feedback.) We generally imagine what we would like to perceive, and then try to act on the world to bring *that* to be. If I am hungry I walk across the street to reduce the distance I perceive between myself and a restaurant. If I write something strange here (such as: negative feedback is far and away the most valuable sort), you probably try to reinterpret it to be the way you like to think of things (Powers, 1973), which may unfortunately emasculate the meaning.

8.4.2.4 Hetrarchical Control Theory.
What if a feedback controller cannot manage to iron out the disturbance well enough? One option is to use several controllers in series. Another is to change the requirement standard (or goal) being aimed at. (Too many kids failing? Lower the passing grade!). The standard changer (or goal changer) itself must have some higher level goal to enable it to choose the least bad alternative to the current unachievable standard. If this situation is repeated, a hierarchy of feedback controllers results. Bill Powers (1973) has shown how such feedback control hierarchies

are present and function in animals and especially in people, to enable us to behave precisely to control our perceptions to be what we need them to be in order to survive. The levels in a CT conversation are levels of negative feedback controllers for steering problem-solving activity.

Actual living systems and especially humanimals are of course very complicated. There are both parallel and series feedback controllers continually operating, not just in a single hierarchy capped by our conscious intentions, but rather in what Warren McCulloch defined as an hetrarchy: a complex multilevel network with redundancy of potential control. For example, redundancy and possible takeover occurs between conscious intentions and the nonconscious autonomous nervous system and the hormonal control systems (Pert, 1993). In Conversation Theory, a learning conversation among P-individuals is just such a complex hetrarchical learning system, with redundancy of potential control through different active memories taking over to lead the discourse as needed.

8.4.2.5 Evolving Automata and Genetic Algorithms.
Probabilistic self-reproducing automata, or sexually reproducing automata-like organisms, in an environment that imposes varying restrictions, will evolve by natural selection of the temporarily fittest. This is because those variant automata which best fit the environment will reproduce and those which don't fit cannot. The variation in P-individuals occurs through both probabilistic errors in their reproductive functioning (forgetting or confusing their procedures) and their conjugation with other P-individuals in the (mind-sex of) learning conversations that usually change both participants. The selection of P-individuals occurs through the initial (L* level) negotiations among persons, concerning which domains and which topics are to be studied when, and also through the limitations of available learning-support modeling facilities (L_0 level).

8.4.2.6 Second-Order Cybernetics.
Second-order cybernetics is the cybernetics of observing systems (von Foerster, 1981) and, most interestingly, of self-observing systems. We have already noted that a system cannot reproduce itself by observing itself unless it has a genetic or memetic blueprint on itself from which to build copies. There are other paradoxical effects occurring with self observing systems which can lead to pathological (recall Narcissus) and/or creative behavior. Rogerian psychotherapy is based partly on reflective technique, mirroring troubled persons' accounts of themselves back to them with unconditional positive regard. Martin Luther, on encountering a parishioner who repeatedly crowed like a cock, joined him in this incessant crowing for some days; then one day Luther simply said, "We have both crowed enough!" which cured the neurotic (though some might say Luther himself went on crowing).

In CT terminology when I hold a conversation with myself, two of my P-individuals are conversing with each other and also monitoring themselves in the internal conversation. For instance, one P-individual may be my poet persona throwing up poetic lines, while the other may be my critic pointing out which lines fail to scan or fail to rhyme. Each must monitor itself (at L_2 level) to be sure it is fulfilling its role, as well as carrying on the (L_0 and L_1 levels of) conversation. (Look ahead to Fig. 8.4.)

8.4.3 Psychological Background Needed

8.4.3.1 Awareness and Narrative Consciousness. Conversation Theory is about the mind-generating processes of which we are aware or can become aware. It is not about nonconscious neurophysiological and hormonal processes underlying the generation of minds at lower levels of emergence. The scope and nature of awareness and consciousness are therefore important considerations in CT.

The best current scientific theories of awareness and consciousness appear to be those expounded by Antonio D'Amasio (1994) and those of Edelman and Tononi (2000), which indeed are grounded in neurophysiological results. Peter Hobson's (2002) theory of emotional engagement and early attachment to others fits with Edelman's selectionist theory. One might also espouse Daniel Dennett's (1991) philosophical multiple-drafts theory of consciousness, as complementary to the multiple participants in conversations.

What are the points of contact with Conversation Theory? And is CT compatible with these newer models? There is not space here to give more than a bare indication of what is thought. All three deny the Cartesian theater idea that everything comes together on a single stage where "we" see, hear and feel it. Both D'Amasio (1994) and Edelman (1992) are convinced that there are two importantly different kinds of consciousness: the present-moment centered primary awareness of animals, and the linguistically mediated narrative consciousness of human beings which involves many more central nervous system components. If the drafts of multiple-draft narrative consciousness can be associated with the P-individuals of CT, then an interesting compatibility emerges.

8.4.3.2 Punctuated and Multiple Personae. The continuity of memory and being and the singleness of self, which most of us assume without question, are actually found to be partly illusory (Noë & O'Reagan, 2000). There seems to be a good deal of resistance to this knowledge, probably based on the widespread acceptance of the enlightenment ideology of the individual. Memories are not just recordings we can play back at will. When we recollect, we re-produce. When we reconstruct memories, we tend to interpolate to cover gaps, and frequently err in doing so. The more often we recall an old memory, the more it is overlaid by reconstructive errors. What we do remember for a long time is only what carried a fairly intense emotional loading at the time of experience (D'Amasio, 1994). If the emotional loading was too intense, the memory may be suppressed or assigned to an alternative persona, as in multiple personality syndrome. The very distinct and complexly differentiated personalities, which show up in pathological cases of multiple personality, are seemingly one extreme of a continuum, where

the other rare extreme is total single-mindedness (which is usually socially pathological, as with the "True Believer" of Hoffer (1951), if not also personally pathological).

According to CT, much of our really important learning is made possible because we *do* each embody different personae (P-individuals) with different intentions, and have to reconcile (or bracket) their conflicts within ourselves by internal dialog.

Less well recognized, until the recent emergence of social constructivism (Gergen, 1994), is that parts of each of us function as parts of larger actors who I like to call transviduals (such as families, teams, religious congregations, nations or 'linguigions,' etc.), which commandeer parts of many other people to produce and reproduce themselves. Conversation Theory, which takes generalized participants (P-individuals) as its central constituents, is one of the few theories of human being which seriously attempts to model both the multiple subviduals which execute within us, and the larger transvidual, actors of which we each execute parts in belonging to society.

8.5 BASIC ASSUMPTIONS AND HYPOTHESES OF CONVERSATION THEORY

1. The real generative processes of the emergence of mind and the production of knowledge can be usefully modeled as multilevel conversations between conversants (some called P-individuals, others merely "participants") interacting through a modeling and simulation facility.
2. Various emergent levels and meta-levels of command control and query (cybernetic) language (L_0 L_1—L_n L^*) need to be explicitly recognized, distinguished, and used in strategically and tactically optimal ways.
3. The concepts, the memories, the participants and their world-models all can be represented as bundles of procedures (programs) undergoing execution in some combination of biological (humanimals) and physical parallel-processing computers called M-individuals.
4. Useful first-cut models called "strict conversation models" can be made which bracket off the affective domain, but keep part of the psychomotor and perceptual domain. (I think this is a very unsatisfactory assumption, but one certainly needed by Pask at the time to enable work to go forward. GMB.)
5. New P-individuals can be brought into being when agreements in complex conversations result in a new coherent bundle of procedures capable of engaging in further conversations with other such P-individuals.
6. When such conversation occurs at high enough levels of complexity it is asserted that a new human actor, team, organization, or society emerges.

Insofar as I understand Conversation Theory, those six are the basic hypotheses. The overall basic scheme of CT is that of a ramifying mesh of concepts and participants in n-dimensional cultural space. The details concern just how multilevel interactive discourse must be carried out to be so productive, taking into account: precisely which formal languages are needed, and just what affordances the modeling facility should have, and what kinds of M-individual processors and networks are needed, to support all of these activities.

8.6 THE BUILDING BLOCKS OF CONVERSATION THEORY

There are 12 main building blocks of CT:

8.6.1 M-Individuals

M-individuals are the hosts, or supporting processors, for the bundles of procedures that in execution together learn. The abbreviation stands for mechanical individuals (term originated by Strawson, 1959), which are biological humanimals and/or computers with communication interfaces coupled to one another via communication channels of any suitable sort.

8.6.2 L-Languages

L, L_0 and $L_1 \ldots L_n$ are in general functionally stratified (hence the subscripts $[0,1,\ldots,n]$ and superscripts $[*]$ in Pask's texts). In the case of "strict" conversations, they are abstract formal or formalized languages and meta-languages that the M-individuals can interpret and process together. L_0 is the action naming and sequencing language, L_1 is for commands and questions about the building of models. The construction of models brings about relations and amounts to a practical explanation. L_2 is for verbal explanation and querying of actions. L_3 may be for debugging. L_4 is the operational meta-language for talking about experiments, describing the system, prescribing actions to pose and test hypotheses; and L^* is for negotiating the experimental contract. "Two Levels are not enough: you have not only to have the conversation and to be able to be critical of it (meta-level) but also to position it so that what is being talked about is known (meta-meta-level)" (Glanville, 2002).

8.6.3 P-Individuals

P-individuals is what Pask called "psychological" individuals, which are understood to be autopropagative discursive participant procedure-bundles, running (being executed) in one or among two or more M-individuals. A P-individual is a coherent self-aware cognitive organization consisting of a class of self-reproducing active memories. Simpler conversants lacking self-awareness are called merely 'participants.' The notion of P-individuals may become more plausible if you recall how you talk to yourself when trying to solve a difficult problem. What C. J. Jung called "personae" would be P-individuals, as would be the various personalities evident in cases of multiple personality syndrome (Rowan, 1990). P-individuals are taken to be the actual evolving conversational participants (i.e., learner–teachers), and thus the main self-building components of human persons, and on a larger scale of peoples and ultimately of the transvidual World–mind—insofar as such exists.

Note: all P-individuals are both learners and teachers at various levels of discourse. No P-individual is simply a learner, nor simply a teacher. (Note also that the emergence progression is from: procedures interacting in discourse, generating > concepts generating > memories generating > P-individuals.)

8.6.4 Procedures

Repertoires or collections of synchronizable procedure-bundles—usually nondeterministic programs or fuzzy algorithms—generate everything. Each P-individual is, and has as memory, a repertoire of executable procedures that may be executed in synchronism with one another and/or with those of other P-individuals. Information in the quotidian sense is not transferred; rather the procedures constituting concepts in participants become synchronized and thence similar. Incidentally, some of these procedures are probably of creative affective types that (so far) can be executed only in biological M-individuals.

(Note: As Baeker (2002) has pointed out, in second-order cybernetics such as CT, a system is recursively defined as a function of the system S and its environment E [i.e., $S' = f(S, E)$], not merely as $S = f$ (objects, relationships); and it is therefore a historical production whose history must be known to understand its current operation.)

8.6.5 Conversations

A "strict CT conversation" is constrained so that all topics belong to a fixed agreed domain and the level of language L_n of each action is specifically demarcated (a bit like Terry Winograd's Coordinator™, 1994). Understandings are recognized and used to mark occasions that are placed in order. A CT conversation is a parallel and synchronous evolving interaction between or among P-individuals, which if successful generates stable concepts agreed upon as being equivalent by the participants. Optionally, it also may generate new P-individuals at higher emergent levels. Participants may, and often do, hold conversations by simultaneously interacting through multiple parallel channels (e.g., neuronal, hormonal, verbal, visual, kinaesthetic). Most CT conversations involve reducing various kinds different of uncertainties, such as: Vagueness, Ambiguity, Strife, Nonspecificity (Klir & Weierman, 1999). This is done through questioning and through making choices, of which agreed concepts are to be included in a given domain of the participants' explanatory and predictive world construction. However, as learning proceeds, new kinds of uncertainties usually emerge.

8.6.6 Stable-Concepts

The confusingly broad and vague multifarious notions of concepts which currently prevail in cognitive science, are replaced by "Stable-Concepts" radically redefined by Pask to be a cluster of partly, or wholly, coherent L-processes undergoing execution in the processing medium M, which variously may: recognize, reproduce, or maintain a relation to/with other concepts and/or with P-individuals. CT stable-concepts are definitely not simple static rule-defined categories. A CT concept is a set of procedures for bringing about a relationship, not a set of things.

Such an understanding of concepts, as going beyond categories and prototypes to active processes, does also appear in the current USA literature; the version which appears to be closest to Pask's is that of Andrea diSessa (1998), whose "coordination processes" and "causal nets" roughly correspond to Pask's "concepts" and "entailment meshes."

8.6.7 The Meaning of a Concept

In my view, certain emergent levels of meaning should be carefully distinguished from each other, particularly Re-Enacted Affiliative Meaning [REAM]—such as that arising in historically rooted ritual performances—versus Rational-Instrumental Meaning [RIM] (Habermas, 1984, 1987; Weil, 1949).

It is worth noting here that Klaus Krippendorff (1994), who has specialized in discourse analysis, makes another important distinction: fully humanly embodied multimodal "conversations" which are unformalized, fluid, and emotionally loaded, versus "discourses," which he defines to be rule-governed, constrained, and formalized (and often dominative). Pask's "strict conversations" are "discourses" in Krippendorff's terminology, whereas Pask's own personal conversations with friends and students were dramatic examples of the former—inspiring, poetic, warmly human conversations.

Emotion is much more than just "feelings." The autistic author Donna Williams (1999) writes, "The emotions are the difference between 'to appear' and 'to be'; I would rather be." Pask himself said, "The meaning of a concept is the affect of the participants who are sharing it" (Barnes, 2001).

With shared emotion, meaning arises. This is compatible also with D'Amasio (1999) who has shown that emotional signals from the prefrontal cortex have to reach the hippocampus in order for short-term memories to be converted into long-term memories, really meaningful memories. Some emotional loading is essential for nontrivial cognition, although too much emotion paralyzes it.

There also appears to be an intrinsic motivation of all human participants to elaborate and improve the predictivity of their world models, in ways that can probably be delightfully and potently shared with others indefinitely into the future. This evolved-in imperative to clone chunks of ourselves (identity memeplexes) is what I call "The Ought That Is" (Boyd, 2000).

8.6.8 Topics

Many topics through a history of conversations compose a DOMAIN of study. Each topic is the focus of a particular conversation. A topic is a set of relations of the kind which, when brought about, solves a particular problem. Any problem, according to Pask, is a discrepancy between a desired state and an actual state.

Generally, P-individuals (learners) choose to work on and converse about only one topic at a time, if for no other reason than limited processing power and limited channel capacity. A topic is represented as a labeled node in an entailment structure.

8.6.9 Entailment and Entailment Structures

Chains, meshes, networks. . . . An "entailment" in CT is defined as any legal *derivation* of one topic-relation from another. Entailment meshes are computer-manipulable public descriptions of what may be known/learned of a domain. They show all the main topics and their various relationships in sufficient detail for the kinds of learners involved. They are generalized graphs (i.e., ones which include cycles, not simply graphs of strict logical entailments). They can be partitioned into topic structures. Their edges display various kinds of entailment relations between the nodes, which represent the "stable-concepts" in the given domain; the specific kinds can most unambiguously be exhibited through j-Map notation (Jaworski, 2002). Really useful representations of entailment structures are very complicated. (For a good example, see Plate 10, pp. 309–318 in Pask, 1975.) For a simplified (pruned) and annotated version of an entailment mesh, see Fig. 8.3.

Entailment structures are not simply hierarchies of prerequisites in the Gagne or Scandura (Pask, 1980) sense. They might be considered improved forms of Mind maps (Buzan, 1993) or of "concept maps" (Horn, Nicol, Kleinman, & Grace 1969; McAleese, 1986; Schmid, DeSimone, & McEwen, 2001; Xuan & Chassain, 1975, 1976). There is one similarity with Novak and Gowin's (1984) Vee diagrams, in that separate parallel portions of the graph (often the lefthand side vs. the righthand side) usually represent theoretical abstract relations versus concrete exemplifications of the domain (as in Plate 10 mentioned above).

Externalized, objectively embodied entailment meshes are principally tools for instructional designers and for learners. Although some analogues of them must exist inside human nervous systems, the entailment meshes are not intended to be direct models of our real internal M-individual neurohormonal physiological mind generating processes. (For what is known of those, see D'Amasio, 1994; Edelman & Tononi, 2000; Milner, 2001; Pert, 1993.)

8.6.10 Environments

Special conversation, modeling and simulation supporting machines and interfaces (which are [multimedia] facilities for externalizing multilevel conversations between/among P-individuals, in publicly observable and recordable form—e.g. CASTE, THOUGHTSTICKER [Glanville & Scott, 1973; Pask, 1975, 1984]) are required, for research and development. These environments, usually external hacked, or engineered, educational system components, provide necessary affordances. Most human learning is facilitated by the affordances of some external objects (blackboard and chalk, paper and pen, books, spreadsheets, DVDs, computers, etc.) which enable internal P-individuals to externalize large parts of their learning conversations.

(A)

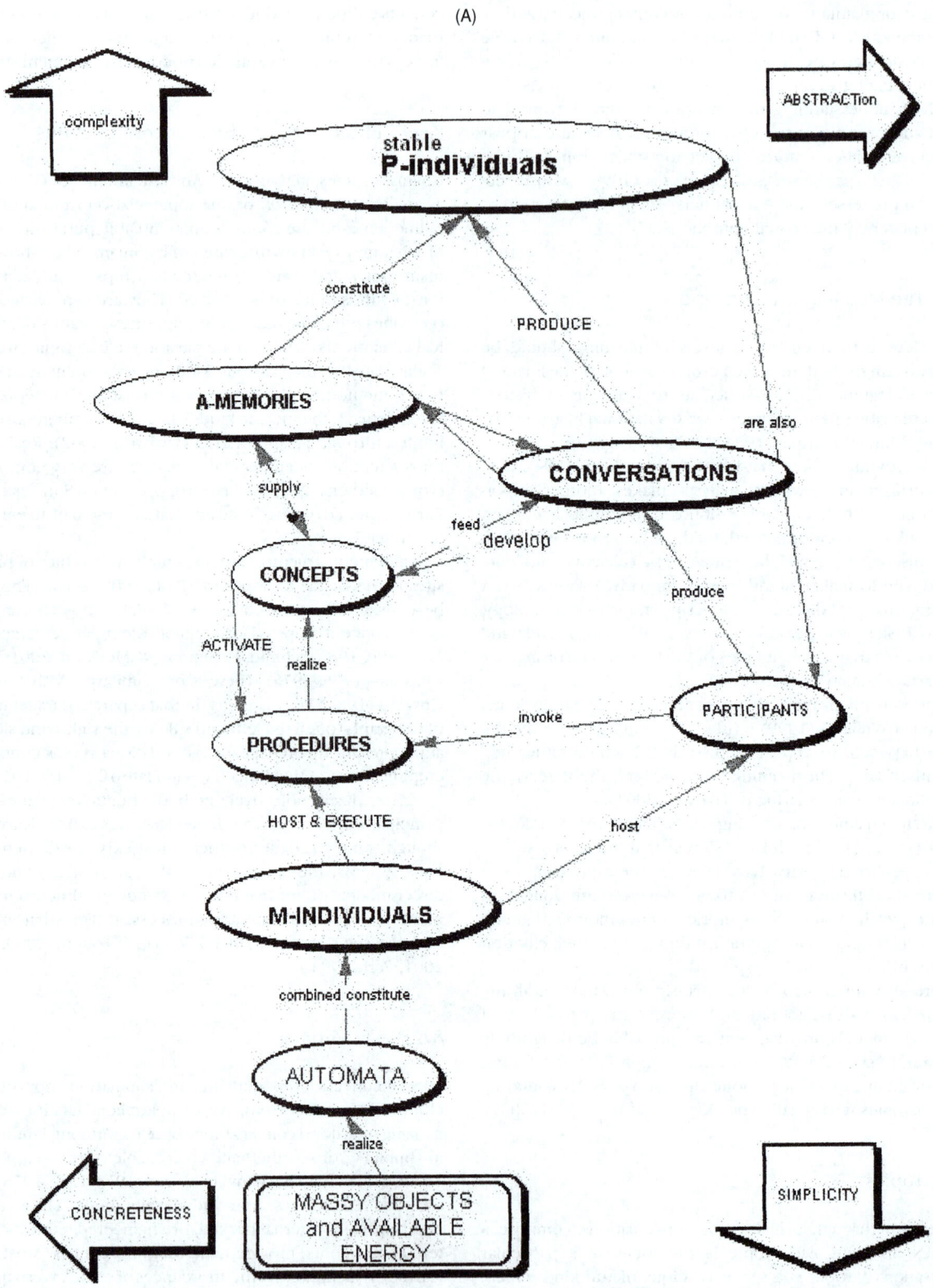

FIGURE 8.3.(A): An annotated entailment graph of the topic Conversational Learning.

(B)

ENTAILMENT MESH j-map derived from Fig.8.3a.

NOTATION = meaning of connector symbols used below
A::= set is 'cast' in *aggregations* role
v::= column (n-ary) is 'cast' in *part-of* role
E::= set is 'cast' in *edges* role
m::= edge descriptor is 'cast' in *middle* role
F::= set is 'cast' in *flow graph nodes* role
f::= node is 'cast' in *from* role
t::= node is 'cast' in *to* role
b::= node is 'cast' in both 'from' and *to* roles

N-ary RELATIONSHIPS / SETS AND ELEMENTS

1	2	3	4	5	6	7	8	9	10	11	12	13	14	15			
E	E	E	E	E	E	E	E	E	E	E	E	E	E	E	15	14	{Edge Descriptor}
m																1	constitute
	m															1	produce
		m														1	supply
	m															1	are aslo
			m													1	feed
				m												1	develop
					m											1	activate
						m										1	realize
				m												1	produce
							m									1	invoke
								m								1	host & execute
							m									1	host
									m							1	combine constitute
										m						1	realize
F	F	F	F	F	F	F	F	F	F	F	F	F	F	F	15	9	{Node names}
t	t	f														3	P-Individuals
f		b	b													3	A-Memories
	f		b	t	f	t										5	CONVERSATIONS
	t			f		f	t									4	Participants
		b		f	t		f	f								5	Concepts
					t	t	t		t							4	Procedures
								f	f	t						3	M-Individuals
										f	t					2	processors
											f					1	MASSY OBJECTS and AVAILABLE ENERGY
v	v	v	v	v	v	v	v	v	v	v	v	v	v	v	15		Syntax and Patterns © by W.M. Jaworski, 1988-2002

FIGURE 8.3.(continued)(B): A pruned version of the (A) entailment graph represented in j-Map type notation. The righthand side lists entities and symbol definitions; the lefthand side exhibits all the main connections among the entities by using the connector symbols.

8.6.11 Task Structures

For each topic structure in an entailment mesh there should be constructed an associated procedural (modeling and/or explaining) task structure giving operational meaning to the topic. In general, the tasks are uncertainty-reducing tasks. Uncertainties unfold about what should be constructed as our world, and how it should be constructed as our (subjectively) real worlds. We gradually reduce the uncertainties by carrying out these tasks and discussing them with each other.

(Note to critical realists, and monist humanists: Especially where human beings are concerned, there *is no implication* that all the procedures required to be executing in M-individual bodies, for our various P-individuals to function and to converse with one another, *can be directly accessed nor fully* modeled, let alone wholly separated from such biological bodies.)

8.6.12 Strategies and Protocols

For learning conversations to be effective two basic types of uncertainty, Fuzziness and Ambiguity (Klir & Weierman, 1999) have to be reduced. Distinct strategies are required for reducing each and each of their subtypes. The two different subtypes of ambiguity, strife and nonspecificity, call for characteristically distinct measures and strategies.

Cognitive "fixity" (Pask, 1975, p. 48) blocks further learning progress. When habits of action and old learning habits ("task-robots" and "learning robots" as Harri-Augstein and Thomas (1991) call them) block new learning, *uncertainty must actually temporarily be increased* by conflictual reframing conversational strategies, in order to allow for the construction of new habits.

It should be noted that every significant thing we learn, while reducing uncertainties we had in the past, opens vistas of new kinds of uncertainty opportunity if we allow it to do so.

8.7 CONVERSATION THEORY PER-SE

Now that we have reviewed the prerequisites, and exhibited the entities involved, we can go ahead and put a simple version of Conversation Theory together.

8.7.1 Putting the Building Blocks Together

For strict conversation learning to take place (as in Pask's CASTE, 1975), there are a number of requirements.

First, in order to start a learning conversation, there has to be an informal agreement in natural language (L*) between A and B, to embark on a learning venture concerned with some specific topics in a given domain. Second, there must be a modeling facility based interactive level of doing. Third, above that, there has to be a propositional assertive level using a formalized language (L_0) for commanding actions, and for naming and describing the demonstrations of concepts as sequences of actions, and for Teachback—for explaining actions, descriptions, and concepts. And again above that, there should be at least one illocutionary level of discourse using a meta-language (L_1), for questioning and for debugging explanations concluding how and why they are correct. Further meta-levels of linguistic interaction (languages $L_2 \ldots L_n$) are optional for (ecological, moral, political) pragmatic justifications, and for critically and creatively calling into being further P-individuals.

It is difficult to show the multiplicity of feedback loops in various modalities (verbal, visual, etc.) and of Deviation-Limiting, and sometimes Deviation-Amplifying feedback, which link all parts of this system. See Pask (1975, 1976, 1984, 1987) for a full unfolding of the complexities.

8.7.2 Elaboration of the Basic Learning Conversation

Here is a somewhat more formal example, in order to get across the characteristic features of a learning conversation as prescribed by Conversation Theory.

Consider two Participants A and B who both know something (mainly different things) about a domain, say cybernetics, and who have agreed to engage with each other, and who have agreed to use natural language conversation and a modeling and simulation facility, and a recording and playback facility, to learn a lot more (see Fig. 8.4).

A is a medical student and B is an engineering student. The modeling facility they have to work with might be Pask's CASTE (Course Assembly System and Tutorial Environment, Pask, 1975); equally possibly now one might prefer STELLA™ or prepared workspaces based on Maple™, MathCad™, or Jaworski's j-Maps™. The recording and playback system may conveniently be on the same computers as the modeling facility, and can keep track of everything done and said, very systematically. (If not those parts of a CASTE system, a version of Pask's tutorial recorder THOUGHTSTICKER (Pask, 1984) could well be used). See Fig. 8.4 for a schematic representation of somewhat complex, two participant, conversational learning.

Here are five separate, roughly synchronous, levels of interaction between A and B.

Level 0—Both participants are doing some actions in, say, CASTE (or, say, STELLA™), and observing results (with, say, THOUGHTSTICKER) all the while noting the actions and the results.

Level 1—The participants are naming and stating WHAT action is being done, and what is observed, to each other (and to THOUGHTSTICKER, possibly positioned as a computer mediated communication interface between them).

Level 2—They are asking and explaining WHY to each other, learning why it works.

Level 3—Methodological discussion about why particular explanatory/predictive models were and are chosen, why particular simulation parameters are changed, etc..

Level 4—When necessary the participants are trying to figure out WHY unexpected results actually occurred, by consulting (THOUGHTSTICKER and) each other to debug their own thinking.

The actual conversation might go as follows. In reply to some question by A such as, "HOW do engineers make closed loop control work without 'hunting'?" B acts on the modeling facility to choose a model and set it running as a simulation. At the same time B explains to A how B is doing this. They both observe what is going on and what the graph of the systems behavior over time looks like. A asks B, "WHY does it oscillate like that?" B explains to A, "BECAUSE of the negative feedback loop parameters we put in."

Then from the other perspective B asks A, "How do you model locomotor ataxia?" A sets up a model of that in STELLA and explains How A chose the variables used. After running simulations on that model, A and B discuss WHY it works that way, and HOW it is similar to the engineering example, and HOW and WHY they differ. And so on and on until they both agree about what generates the activity, and why, and what everything should be called.

This, at first glance, may now seem like a rather ordinary peer-tutoring episode using simulations. It is. But the careful metacognitive demarcation of levels of intercourse, according to their distinct cognitive functions, and the way in which multiple perspectives are brought together to construct a deep and transferable agreed understanding are the novel key aspects.

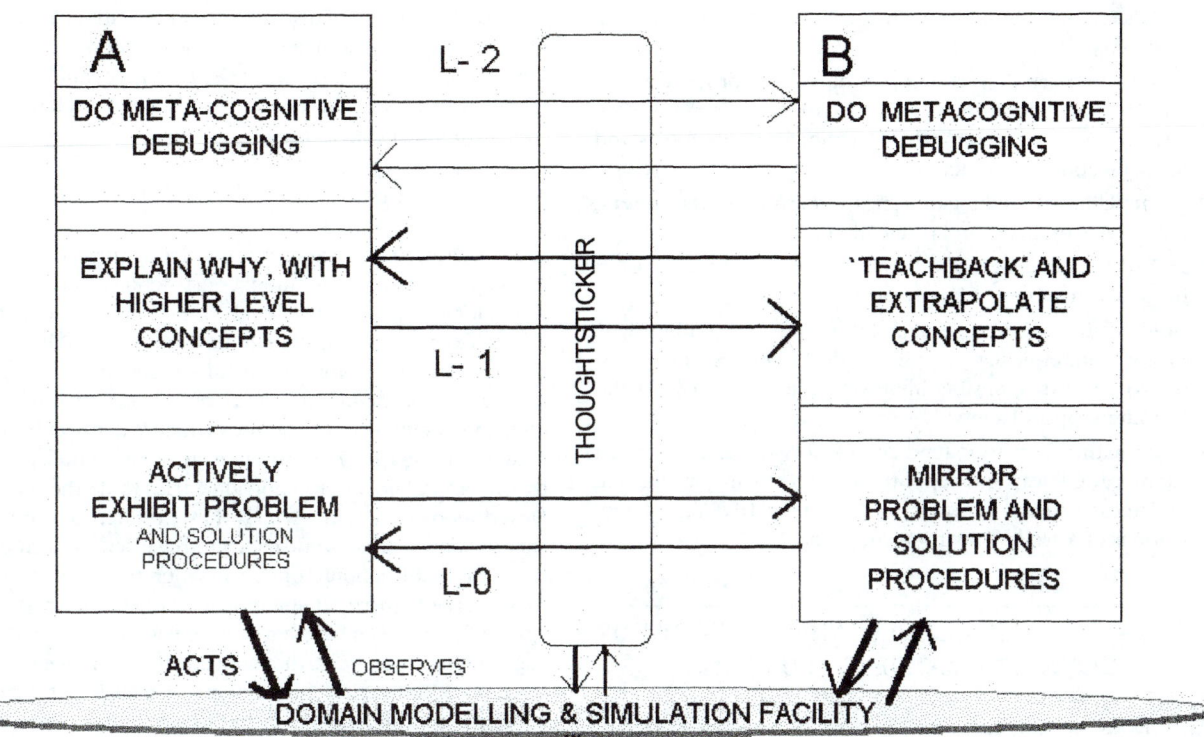

FIGURE 8.4. Conversational learning system—simplified to interaction at only three levels (after Pask, and somewhat after Bernard Scott, 2001).

8.8 HOW TO USE CONVERSATION THEORY AS A BASIS FOR LEARNING SYSTEM DESIGN

(The model for this is Course Assembly System and Tutorial Environment (CASTE), Pask, 1975; Mitchell & Dalkir, 1986.)

- Choose some domain, and some topic areas within it, of importance to you and to some population of other learners.

- Do a crude information mapping of the most important topics and their probable dependencies on each other—make a proto-entailment mesh, say, with stick-on notes on a whiteboard. Gather illustrations and exercises to exemplify the topics.

- Acquire or build a modeling and simulation running (and possibly gaming) facility which can be used to externalize and experientially exemplify those topics in the chosen domain. One could simply use an hypertext glossary system (Zimmer, 2001). One could use "Inspiration"™or AskSam™. One could use a generalized multidimensional matrix modeling facility such as Jaworski's j-Maps™. For more mathematical subjects one might use Maple™or MathCad™to construct modeling spaces. For stack-and-flow or predator–prey domains one might well use an existing dynamic systems modeling facility such as STELLA™. Fit the gathered domain material into the modeling facility using the sketched out mesh as a guide. The result is just a prototype domain model for improved conversational learning.

- Choose a small but diverse sample of learners from the target population.

- Set up multimodal recording arrangements with persons and machines in a pleasant tranquil environment.

- Discuss with the learners why understanding and ability to teachback topics in this domain can be lastingly valuable and timely for them and for you. Get their wholehearted agreement to participate and to commit enough time to the undertaking—if possible. (L* conversation)

- Pick a seemingly simple relation or operation and, using the facility, demonstrate it to the learners, name and explain what you are doing. (L_0)

- Answer their questions; explain why you are answering that way. (L_1)

- Ask the learners why they are asking those questions, in order to evoke metacognitive consciousness of how they are learning to learn. (L_2)

- Get each learner, and/or the group of learners, to use the facilities to teachback or to creatively demonstrate other versions of the relation/process back to you and the other learners. Note agreements; explain distinctions. Record the lot. Thus the domain representation is improved, and an understanding of it is cultivated in each participant. (L_3) Also look and listen for limiting habits: task robots and learning robots (Harri-Augstein & Thomas, 1991).

- Edit the transcriptions and dribble-files etc. to produce a master entailment mesh, and task structures, and appropriate tasks (exercises, tests) for that Domain, for Goals Topics and for Population of Learners.

- Prune! Eliminate redundant labels and links. Use the system, formatively evaluate, and prune more.

- Embed the entailment mesh and task structure protocols in the software of your support facility.

- Hold further learning (scientifically and philosophically—ecologically, ethically, morally—critical) conversations in order to go on responsibly improving the affordances of the learning support facility.

- Work with others to extend and clone what can become a canonical CT learning support facility for that domain, one which can generate working versions suited to different populations of learners, environments, etc.

8.9 HOW TO USE CONVERSATION THEORY FOR DOING FORMATIVE EVALUATIONS

Ask, "Does the support system provide the following desiderata?" And creatively suggest how they can be provided.

8.9.1 Shared Modeling/Simulation Tool-Space

Does it share a working space where all participants can carry out and observe actions made with appropriate tools, and various interactions of kinds appropriate to the particular field of study (e.g., C/CASTE—Mitchell & Dalkir, 1986; THOUGHTSTICKER—Pangaro, 2002)? If not readily available, then recommend an appropriate groupware modeling facility.

8.9.2 A Processable, Pluggable, Canonical Entailment Mesh and Task-Structure Representation-Model and Multiple Views Generator

Is a processable, canonical representation (model) of the relevant history of the domain language-field stored and readily accessible and rerunable—e.g., in j-Map^{TM}form (Jaworski, 2002)—together with variously versioned (e.g., graphical) views of its procedural entities and relationships (entailment meshes, task structures, etc.)? It is helpful if the important levels of a taxonomy of competencies, or of learning objectives such as Bloom and Krathwohl's (1956), or of human values such as Maslow's (1954), are incorporated.

8.9.3 Interaction Stratification

Is dialogue among participants stratified in terms of levels of languages and meta-languages? Are all participants aware of the need to converse at different levels roughly in parallel? Are clear distinctions made, and continually supported, between three or more levels of discourse: demonstration, L_0; and explanation (and teachback) agreement-negotiation, L_1; and debugging level, L_2; and situating levels, L_3. The commitment meta-negotiation level L^* may also have to be revisited if participants balk at so much engagement.

8.9.4 Scenarios

Are scenarios and/or exemplary model performances provided as rough guides to exploration, construction, evaluation and revision for all types of participants? If not, provide some models.

For example, about the simplest possible CT learning scenario would be like this: A pair of P-individuals having agreed to learn about a common topic, one P-individual originates a conceptual bundle of procedures which when applied (i.e., executed) produces a Description, image or an action, observable by the other. The other P-individual tries to do the same. If the Descriptions or actions, which they produce and display in a shared conversation workspace are regarded by each other after a reasonable amount of conversation to be about the same, then it is noted that an agreement has been reached, and the agreed Concept can be given one label which both participants can confidently use in further conversation. If, however, the productions differ, so that the participants realize that they are executing different concepts even though they both started from the same topic label, then the participants set about to externalize precisely these differences in the ways they are executing their concept-procedures, in order to establish a sharp distinction between the two. At this point they agree to assign two different labels (in which case each participant gains a new coherent distinctly labeled executable Concept).

8.9.5 Responsibility

Are reminders included, to philosophically and politically question who benefits and who is disadvantaged "malefits" by the kinds of productions of models of reality involved?

8.10 SOME IMPORTANT OMISSIONS FROM AND ADDITIONS TO CONVERSATION THEORY

8.10.1 Network of Actors

According to the extension of Conversation Theory and the Interactions of Actors Theory (IAT) each human biological being (humanimal) incorporates portions of many interbody P-individuals (transviduals). Thus, CT + IAT is a theory which potentially accommodates explanations of a wide variety of complex phenomena such as versatility of learning styles, autism, narrative-consciousness, multiple personality syndrome, the collective behavior of teams, families, churches, crowds, etc. Unlike other constructivist theories (e.g., Piaget, Gergen), Pask's CT and IAT nicely account for the emergence of coherent values (Scott, 2001) and also for what Habermas considers to be the universal essential human value—that of promoting rational understanding through nondominative discourse. Pablo Navarro (2001), an esteemed sociologist, accords CT praise for overcoming the false Hobbesian dichotomy between society and the individual.

8.10.2 Dominant Nonconversational Emergent Supra-Systems Ignored?

Pablo Navarro also notes that because of Pask's deliberate limitations of its scope to that of intra- and interpersonal intentional learning, CT ignores the nonintentional, nondiscursive, society-wide chaotic emergence of dominative systems such as global markets, and various wars and trade wars, which determine much of our lives—which indeed are very important parts of the E in the human system $S' = f(S, E)$.

8.10.3 Disembodiment Versus Integrity?

More concretely and viscerally, Klaus Krippendorff (1994) shows that serious limitations arise from Pask's expedient exclusion of the physiological and emotional conflictual dimensions of each human's being (Johnson,1987). And in the Kybernetes Festschrift (2001), Pablo Navarro also points out that CT (so far) does not contain a specification of whatever maintains the integrity of intentional P-individuals, despite their openness to conversational evolution. All this leads to the very important open research question: "How do the characteristics of the M-individuals impact the P-individuals executing and conversing through them?"

8.10.4 Motivation

Motivation is dealt with very little, in Pask's Conversation Theory writings, compared to its actual importance for human learning. Pask usually conducted L* negotiations with learners before the CT experiments, to get their agreement and commitment to participate wholeheartedly in the learning work. There is a formal description of the directional unfoldment of entailment meshes leading to possible action, but this is a very abstract and skeletal model of motivation; how it might relate to emotion is problematical.

Actually, it is now known that much cognition carries and generates affective loadings. In particular emotion, as distinguished from feelings, is essential to the formation of long-term memory (D'Amasio, 1994). Soon our improved models of teaching–learning conversations must specifically operationalize this. Also now it is clear that trans-M-individual P-individuals (transviduals) are deeply implicated in motivation for learning and (other) action, and this is not explicitly explored. It is, though, allowed for by Pask's theory, particularly by the L* level and more explicitly by the Interactions of Actors Theory (IAT) which he was working on at the time of his death (de Zeeuw, 2001).

Intellectual adolescents hold motivated learning conversations in their love relationships. Young professionals hold motivated learning conversations as part of the relevant credibility status games of scientific and professional societies. Elders' motivation for learning conversations is to distill the best of what they know and get it re-created in the young. How are such perspectives to be operationalized in CT systems?

8.11 EXAMPLES OF RESEARCH AND DEVELOPMENT WORK DONE WITH CONVERSATION THEORY

Second-order cybernetic (von Foerster, 1981) research on complex learning, where the researcher–experimenter–observers are acknowledged explicitly as part of the system which they are researching, can probably be better conducted by using versions of Conversation Theory and THOUGHTSTICKER-like or CASTE-like facilities; this was Pask's aim. However, to date, most CT research work (e.g., that of Pangaro, Harri-Augstein and Thomas, Scott, or Laurillard) has been done as a by-product of educative ventures, rather than with the study of complex learning as their primary aim.

Interesting possibilities beckon: study and overcoming of cognitive fixity (learning robots); study of various kinds and levels of conflict among personae and of their divergent motivations; study of multiple perspectives and cognitive switches, and so forth.

Pask's CT can be very helpful for improving the work of course development teams in Distance Education organizations, according to Zimmer (2001), of the UK Open University.

Also, as Diana Laurillard and Ray Ison (1999) have pointed out, there is a great opportunity for studying the learning of Learning Organizations and the learning of the Learning Society through the lens of Conversation Theory. Much of my own work (Boyd, 2002) has involved having graduate students collaboratively make cybersystemic models of teaching–learning systems that they have been (or are) in, and using CT and other cybernetic principles to diagnose and prescribe improvements to those systems.

Detailed examples of applications of CT are given in Pask's (1975) book *Conversation Cognition and Learning*. However, the text and notations there (and in the AECT journal paper) are rather difficult to work through. Some of the most practical and readable prescriptions for actually carrying out learning conversations have been provided by Diana Laurillard (2002) (Laurillard & Marnante, 1981), by Bernard Scott over the years up to the present (2001), and by Harri-Augstein and Thomas (1991). In at least one important respect, Harri-Augstein and Thomas and Mildard Shaw (1985), go beyond Pask, by combining his theory with that of George Kelly and by insisting upon two very important specific types of levels of discourse, one being a metacognitive level explicitly devoted to discussing and improving learning strategies (an L_n), and another a pragmatic level (an L*), explicitly dealing with why this particular learning is relevant and important to these participants in this context. Both these language levels exemplify aspects of $S' = f(S, E)$.

Jesus Vazquez-Abad and Real LaRose (1983) developed and researched an Operational Learning System based on Conversation Theory combined with Structural Learning Theory. It was implemented on the PLATO system to carry out research on instruction of rule-based procedures in science education.

Robert Barbour of the University of Waikato, New Zealand, used Pask's Conversation Theory to arrange for and study the learning of sixth and seventh form students using the UK Domesday Book interactive videodisks. Pask's and Husserl's views of cognition are both considered together (Barbour, 1992).

Steven Taylor (1999) developed a successful biology (photosynthesis) TEACHBACK/ computer aided learning system where the human learners try to teach the computer (playing the role of a simulated learner) the topic relations they have nominally already learned. Teachback has recently been rediscovered and rechristened as "Reciprocal Teaching" by Palthepu, Greer, and McCalla (1991) and Nichols (1993).

Conversation theory has also been found to be helpful in designing and understanding second-language learning (Miao and Boyd, 1992). Recently some quite good approaches have been cropping up for organizing conversational learning. Some have drawn on CT (Zeidner, Scholarios, & Johnson, 2001), but there are others which have not drawn on Conversation Theory but might gain from doing so (e.g., Keith Sawyer's Creating Conversations, 2001).

Another interesting informal and dramatic example of conversational learning using Pask's CT is in Yitzhak Hayut-Man's play (2002) "The Gospel of Judith Iscariot." In Act 2 Scene 3 Judith, at the Messiah Machine, conducts conversations with three cybernetic specters, to resolve her conflicts about Jesus. The solution is arrived at by conversing with all three conflicting parties until they agree on the betrayal of Jesus by Judith. The whole Academy of Jerusalem play is an exercise in transformative redemptive learning conversations, and indeed was directly inspired by Hayut-Man's years of work with Gordon Pask.

Gordon McCalla (2000), in his discussion of AI in education in 2010, asserts, "An explicit focus on learning and teaching, using computational models, can bring together a wide range of issues that considered separately or in other contexts would be intractable or incoherent." Conversation Theory provides a framework for creating better forms of such computational models.

Conversational learning is not limited to P-individuals within biological persons but may be carried out with P-individuals who execute in a distributed fashion across many persons and machines. Two important cases of transvidual P-individuals are Learning Organizations and Learning Societies. Laurillard (1999) explains just how Conversation Theory can be applied to realize better learning organizations such as e-universities and truly learning societies. *One might well dream of creating organizations which use communicating AI agent supported CT to learn to be wiser than even their wisest members.*

8.12 CONCLUSION: THERE ARE GOOD OPPORTUNITIES TO DO MORE WITH CONVERSATION THEORY

Conversation Theory begins to constitute a new kind of comprehensive ontology of subindividual, individual, and collective human being, which gets beyond the sterile individual—society dichotomy. To my mind, this understanding of human being implies a profound criticism of simplistic individualism. Competitive possessive individualism and freemarket ideology are evidently self-defeating ideologies if one understands that every person is inextricably woven into the fabric of other human beings.

CT now seems an even more plausible theory of participant beings than it did in 1975, since it fits well with so much other more recent work. Proto-conversations probably start right down at Edelman & Tononies (2000) second level of consciousness, where the selection of neuronal groups occurs through mimetic and linguistic interaction (although NOT much below that), and functions as a good explanatory and heuristic model (with the caveats listed above), on up to the level of competing global cultural memeplexes (such as the English language, Arabic-Islam, capitalism, socialism, etc.).

8.12.1 Conversation Theory as Open-Ended

Conversation Theory has not at any time been a fixed finished theory. De Zeeuw (private communication, 2002) sees it as a set of procedures itself (L_0 and L_1) that helps learners to create "languages"(L's) to talk "to" what is observed, such that actions may be performed with "limited" (pre-state-able) effects. Many versions of CT exist because it evolved steadily, through conversations and experiments from early proto theory in the 1950s, to the IAT—Interactions of Actors Theory (de Zeeuw, 2001; Pask, 1992)—which itself continued to evolve in his various ongoing conversations until Pask's death in March of 1996.

Conversation Theory has proven to be a very inspiring and practically useful theory for many other educational cyberneticists and technologists, because it indicates how realistically complex n-personae learning, for actors(P-individuals) with different learning styles (e.g., holist; serialist; versatile), should be supported by second-order cybernetic technology.

Cognitive fixity—learners being trapped by their habitual ontologies and their habitual ways of learning, remains a central problem especially for any science education which aspires to the cultivation of a deep understanding of the complex systems in which we live (Jacobson, 2000). The multiple P-individual, and distributed processing across multiple M-individuals, reconceptualization which CT offers may be the most promising way to liberate persons from inadequate ontologies and epistemologies.

Conversation Theory and Interaction of Actor Theories initially generated by Pask and his collaborators, continue to evolve their own sort of immortality as educational development heuristics—particularly among those of us who knew Gordon Pask and studied with him and who have incorporated those systems into our own thinking (e.g., de Zeeuw, 2001; Laurillard, 1999; Scott, 2001).

Pask's P-individuals forever seek to engage in new conversational learning ventures, which change them, enlarge domains of knowledge, and change other participants, and sometimes replace both. When one considers real persons *and communities,* rather than quasi-algorithmic A-life models, there are clearly aesthetic, ethical, moral, and biophysical dimensions which must be democratically taken into account Wenger (1999). This is especially so when we apply our theory in our educational and human performance system interventions. How to fit these into a coherent universally ethically acceptable cybersystemic theory of selves-researching, selves-changing human community systems?

Interactive intermittently, positively reinforcing aesthetically engaging systems, without scientifically and philosophically critical levels of learning conversation, are pathological addiction machines (e.g., Video Lottery Terminals and Massive Multiplay Games like Doom). Can our simulation systems and conversational learning tools be augmented with appropriate artificial intelligence to bring harmony among vast numbers of competing communities, as Gordon McCalla (2000) envisions? And how do such augmented learning conversations fit into our understanding of, and obligations toward, the closely coupled system of all Life on this delicate little planet Earth?

ACKNOWLEDGMENTS

First of all, I must acknowledge the benefit of many learning conversations with Prof. Gordon Pask, who was resident codirector, with Prof. P. David Mitchell, of the Centre for System Research and Knowledge Engineering of Concordia University from 1982 to 1987. Much helpful criticism and many good suggestions have been received from the AECT editor, David Jonassen, and from Ms. Shelly Bloomer. Especially important points came from persons closely associated with Pask's work, notably: Bernard Scott, Ranulph Glanville, Gerard deZeeuw, Paul Pangaro, David Mitchell, and Vladimir Zeman. However, the author takes full responsibilty for any weaknesses, errors, or omissions which remain.

References

Baeker, D. (2002). The joker in the box, or the theory form of the system. *Cybernetics and Human Knowing, 9*(1), 51–74.

Barbour, R. H. (1992). Representing worlds and world views. Available from Dr. Bob Barbour: R.Barbour@cs.waikato.ac.nz.

Barnes, G. (2001). Voices of sanity in the conversation of psychotherapy. *Kybernetes: The International Journal of Systems and Cybernetics, 30*(5), 537.

Bhaskar, R. (1978). *A realist theory of science.* Hemel Hempstead: Harvester Wheatsheaf.

Bhaskar, R., & Norris, C. (1999, Autumn). Roy Bhaskar interviewed. *The Philosophers' Magazine 8.* Retrieved October 1, 2002, from *The Critical Realist Website.* http://www.raggedclaws.com/criticalrealism

Bloom, B. S., & Krathwohl, D. R. (1956). *Taxonomy of educational objectives: The classification of educational goals, by a committee of college and university examiners. Handbook I: Cognitive domain.* New York: Longman, Green.

Boyd, G. M. (1993). Educating symbiotic P-individuals through multilevel conversations. In R. Glanville (Ed.), Gordon Pask, a Festschrift. *Systems Research 10*(3), 113–128.

Boyd, G. M. (2000, July). The educational challenge of the third millenium: eco-co-cultural SYMVIABILITY. *Patterns V,* 1–6. Soquel, CA: ASCD Systems Network.

Boyd, G. M. (2001). Reflections on the conversation theory of Gordon Pask. In R. Glanville & B. Scott (Eds.), Festschrift in celebration of Gordon Pask. *Kybernetes: The International Journal of Systems and Cybernetics 30*(5–6), 560–570.

Boyd, G.M. (2002). Retrieved October 1, 2002 from http://alcor.concordi.ca/~boydg/drboyd.html

Boyd, G. M., & Pask, G. (1987). Why do instructional designers need conversation theory? In D. Laurillard (Ed.), *Interactive media: Working methods and practical applications* (pp. 91–96). Chichester: Ellis Horwood.

Buber, M. (1970). *I and Thou* (W. Kaufman, Trans.). New York: Charles Scribner's Sons.

Buzan, T. (1993). *The mind map book. How to use radiant thinking to maximize your brain's untapped potential.* London: Penguin Group.

D'Amasio, A. (1994). *Descartes's error. Emotion, reason and the human brain.* New York: Putnam.

D'Amasio, A. (1999). *The feeling of what happens: Body and emotion in the making of consciousness.* New York: Harcourt Brace.

Dennett, D. (1991). *Consciousness explained.* New York: Little Brown.

de Zeeuw, G. (2001). Interaction of actors theory. *Kybernetes: The International Journal of Systems and Cybernetics, 30*(7–8), 971–983.

de Zeeuw, G. (2002). "What I like about conversation theory. . . ." Private communication, on reading a draft of this chapter.

diSessa, A. A. (1998). What changes in conceptual change. *International Journal of Science Education, 20*(10), 1155–1191.

Duffy, T. M., & Jonassen, D. H. (Eds.). (1992). *Constructivism and the technology of instruction.* Mahwah, New Jersey: Lawrence Erlbaum Associates.

Edelman, G. M. (1992). *Bright air brilliant fire: On the matter of the mind.* New York: Harper Collins.

Edelman, G. M., & Tononi, G. (2000). *Consciousness: How matter becomes imagination.* London: Allen Lane.

Gaines, B., & Shaw M. (2000). Conversation theory in context. *Kybernetes: The International Journal of Systems and Cybernetics.* Unpublished manuscript.

Gergen, K. J. (1994). *Realities and relationships.* Cambridge, MA: Harvard University Press.

Glanville, R. (1993). Pask: A slight primer. In R. Glanville (Ed.), Gordon Pask, a Festschrift. *Systems Research, 10*(3), 213–218.

Glanville, R. (2002). "Two levels are not enough. . .". Private communication with the author upon reviewing a draft of this chapter.

Glanville, R. & Scott, B. (1973). CASTE : A system for exhibiting learning strategies and regulating uncertainty. *International Journal of Man Machine Studies, 5.*

Habermas, J. (1984). *The theory of communicative action, volume 1, Reason and the rationalization of society.* Boston, MA: Beacon Press.

Habermas, J. (1987). *The theory of communicative action, volume 2, System and lifeworld: a critique of functionalist reason.* Boston, MA: Beacon Press.

Harri-Augstein, S., & Thomas, L. (1991). *Learning conversations.* London: Routledge.

Hayles, K. (1999). *How we became posthuman.* Chicago: University of Chicago Press.

Hayut-Man, Y.I. (2001). My Paskalia and the genesis of the Christmas intelligent tree. *Kybernetes: The International Journal of Systems and Cybernetics, 30*(5-6), 723-725.

Hayut-Man, Y.I. (2002). The gospel of Judith Iscariot. Retrieved October 1, 2002, from http://www.thehope.org/gosplink.htm

Hobson, P. (2002). *The cradle of thought.* London: MacMillan.

Hoffer, E. (1951). *The true believer.* New York: Harper and Row.

Horn, R. E. (1975). Information mapping for design and development. *Datamation, 21*(1), 85-88.

Horn, R. E. (1993, February). Structured writing at twenty-five. *Performance and Instruction, 32*, 11-17.

Horn, R. E., Nicol, E., Kleinman, J., & Grace, M. (1969). *Information mapping for learning and reference.* A. F.Systems Command Report ESD-TR-69-296. Cambridge, MA: I.R.I.

Hume, D. (1998). *The works of David Hume.* Oxford: Clarendon-Press. (Original work published 1740.)

Ison, R. (1999). Applying systems thinking to higher education. *Systems Research and Behavioral Science, 16(2),* 107-12.

Jackendoff, R. (2002), Foundations *of language: Brain, meaning, grammar, evolution.* Oxford, Oxford University Press.

Jacobson, M. J. (2000). *Butterflies, traffic jams, and cheetahs; problem solving and complex systems.* Paper presented at the American Educational Research Association annual meeting. Atlanta, Georgia.

Jaworski, W. (2002). General strategies j-maps. Retrieved October 1, 2002, from http://www.gen-strategies.com/papers/w_paper/white.htm

Johnson, M. (1987). *The body in the mind.* Chicago, IL: University of Chicago Press.

Kelly, G. A. (1955). *The psychology of personal constructs.* New York: W. W. Norton.

Klir, J. & Weierman, M. (1999). *Uncertainty-based information.* New York: Springer-Physica Verlag.

Krippendorff, K. (1994). A recursive theory of communication. In D. Crowley & D. Mitchell (Eds.), *Communication theory today* (pp. 78-104). Palo Alto, CA: Stanford University Press.

Laurillard, D. M. (1999). A conversational framework for individual learning applied to the 'learning organization' and the 'learning society.' *Systems Research and Behavioral Science, 16*(2), 113-122.

Laurillard, D. M. (2002). *Rethinking university teaching: A conversational framework.* London: Routledge.

Laurillard, D. M., & Marnante, D. J. (1981). *A view of computer assisted learning in the light of conversation theory.* Milton Keynes: Open University Institute of Educational Technology.

Loefgren, L. (1993). The wholeness of a cybernetician. *Systems Research, 10*(3), 99-112.

MacLennan, B. (1992). Synthetic ethology: An approach to the study of communication. In C. Langton, C. Taylor, J. Farmer, & S. Rasmussen (Eds.), *Artificial life II* (pp. 631-655). Redwood City, CA: Addison Wesley.

Maslow, A. (1954). *Motivation and personality.* New York: Harper.

McAleese, R. (1986). The knowledge arena, an extension to the concept map. *Interactive Learning Environments, 6*(10), 1-22. Retrieved October 1, 2002, from http://www.cst.hw.ac.uk/~ray/McAleese

McCalla, G. (2000). The fragmentation of culture, learning, teaching and technology: Implications for the Artificial Intelligence in Education research agenda in 2010. *International Journal of Artificial Intelligence in Education, 11,* 177-196.

McCulloch, W. (1969). A hetrarchy of values determined by the topology of nervous nets. In H. von Foerster (Ed.), *Cybernetics of cybernetics* (pp. 65-78). Champaign-Urbana: University of Illinois, Biological Computer Laboratory.

Miao, Y., & Boyd, G. (1992). Conversation theory as educational technology in second language lexical acquisition. *Canadian Journal of Educational Communications, 21*(3), 177-194.

Milner, P. (2001). *The autonomous brain.* Mahwah, NJ: Lawrence Erlbaum.

Mitchell, P. D. (1990). Problems in developing and using an intelligent hypermedia tutoring system: A test of conversation theory. In N. Estes, J. Heene, & D. LeClercq (Eds.), *Proceedings of the Seventh World Conference on Technology and Education.* Edinburgh: C.E.P.

Mitchell, P. D., & Dalkir, K. (1986). C/CASTE: An artificial intelligence based computer aided learning system. *Proceedings of the Fifth Canadian Symposium on Instructional Technology.* (On 3.5" diskettes.) Ottawa: National Research Council.

Moore, G. E. (1903). *Principia ethica.* Cambridge: Cambridge University Press.

Navarro, P. (2001). The limits of social conversation: A sociological approach to Gordan Pask conversation theory. *Kybernetes, 30,* 5-16, 771-788.

Nichols, D. (1993). Intelligent student systems: learning by teaching. In P. Brna, S. Ohlson, & H. Pain (Eds.), *Artificial intelligence and education: Proceedings of the Conference on Artificial Intelligence in Education '93* (p. 576). Charlottesville, VA: AACE.

Noë, A., & O'Reagan, J. K. (2000, October). Perception, attention and the grand illusion. *Psyche, 6*(15), 123-125.

Novak, J., & Gowin, D. (1984). *Learning how to learn.* Cambridge: Cambridge University Press.

Palthepu, S., Greer, J. E., & McCalla, G. I. (1991). Learning by teaching. In L. Birnbaum (Ed.), *Proceedings of the International Conference on the Learning Sciences* (pp. 357-363). Retrieved October 1, 2002, from http://www.cs.usask.ca/homepages/faculty/greer/greercv.html

Pangaro, P. (2002). Gordon Pask archive. Retrieved October 1, 2002, from http://www.pangaro.com/Pask-Archive/Pask-Archive.html

Pask, G. (1961). *An approach to cybernetics.* London: Methuen.

Pask, G. (1975). *Conversation cognition and learning: A cybernetic theory and methodology.* Amsterdam: Elsevier.

Pask, G. (1976). *Conversation theory: Applications in education and epistemology.* Amsterdam: Elsevier.

Pask, G. (1980). In contrast to Scandura: An essay upon concepts, individuals and interactionism. *Journal of Structural Learning, 6,* 335-346.

Pask, G. (1984). Review of conversation theory and a protologic or protolanguage. *Educational Communication and Technology Journal, 32*(1), 3-40.

Pask, G. (1987). *Developments in conversation theory Part II: Conversation theory and its protologic.* Unpublished manuscript held by G. Boyd.

Pask, G. (1988). Learning strategies, teaching strategies and conceptual or learning styles. In R. R. Schmeck (Ed.), *Learning strategies and learning styles.* London: Plenum Press.

Pask, G. (1995). One kind of immortality. *Systemica, 9*(1-6), 225-233.

Pask, G., & Scott, B. (1973). "CASTE: A system for exhibiting learning strategies and regulating uncertainty." *Intl. Journal of Man Machine Systems, 5,* 17-52.

Pask, G., & de Zeeuw, G. (1992). A succinct summary of novel theories. In R. Trappl (Ed.), *Cybernetics and systems research* (pp. 263-265). Washington: Hemisphere.

Pert, C. (1993). *Molecules of emotion*. New York: Simon and Schuster.

Popper, K. R. (1972). *Objective knowledge. An evolutionary approach*. Oxford: Clarendon.

Powers, W. T. (1973). *Behavior: The control of perception*. Chicago: Aldine.

Rescher, N. (1977). *Methodological pragmatism*. New York: New York University Press.

Rowan, J. (1990). *Sub-personalities: The people inside us*. London: Routledge.

Sawyer, R. K. (2001). *Creating conversations: Improvisation in everyday discourse*. Cresskill, NJ: Hampton Press. Retrieved October 1, 2002, from http://www.artsci.wustl.edu/~ksawyer/cc.htm

Schmid, R., DeSimone, C., & McEwen, L. (2001). Supporting the learning process with collaborative concept mapping using computer-based communication tools and processes. *Educational Research and Evaluation, 7*(2-3), 263-283.

Scott, B. (2000). The cybernetics of systems of belief. *Kybernetes: The International Journal of Systems and Cybernetics, 29*(7-8), 995-998.

Scott, B. (2001). Conversation theory: A constructivist, dialogical approach to educational technology. *Cybernetics and Human Knowing, 8*(4), 25-46.

Searle, J. R. (1969). *Speech acts: An essay on the philosophy of language*. Cambridge: Cambridge University Press.

Searle, J. R. (1984). *Minds, brains and science*. Cambridge, MA: Harvard University Press.

Shaw, M. L. G. (1985). Communities of knowledge. In F. Epting & A. Landfield (Eds.), *Anticipating personal construct psychology* (pp. 25-35). Lincoln, NE: University of Nebraska Press.

STELLA (2002). *Systems thinking software*. Retrieved October 10, 2002, from http://www.hps-inc.com

Strawson, P. F. (1959). *Individuals: An essay in descriptive metaphysics*. London: Methuen. (1963). Garden City, New York: Doubleday Anchor. ("P-predicates apply to states of consciousness. M-predicates apply to bodily characteristics".... p.100 Anchor edition).

Taylor, S. (1999). *Exploring knowledge models with simulated conversation*. Doctoral dissertation. Montreal, QC: Concordia University.

Varela, F., Maturana, H., & Uribe, R. (1974). Autopoiesis: The organisation of living systems, *Biological Systems, 5,* 187.

Vazquez-Abad, J., & LaRose, R. (1983). Computers adaptive teaching and operational learning systems. In P. R. Smith (Ed.), *CAL 83: Selected Proceedings from the computer assisted learning 83 symposium, University of Bristol, UK, April 13-15, 1983* (pp. 27-30). Amsterdam: Elsevier Science.

von Foerster, H. (1981). *Observing systems*. Seaside, CA: Intersystems.

von Glasersfeld, E. (1995). *Radical constructivism. A way of knowing and learning*. London: The Falmer Press.

von Neumann, J. (1958). *The computer and the brain*. New Haven, CT: Yale University Press.

Watanabe, S. (1969*). Knowing and guessing: A quantitative study of inference and information*. New York: John Wiley.

Weil, S. (1949). *L'enracinement*. Paris: Gallimard. (1952) trans. A. F. Wills, as *The need for roots*. London: Ark.

Wenger E. (1997). *Communities of practice, learning memory and identity*. Cambridges: Cambridge Univ. Press.

Whitehead, A. N. (1949). *The aims of education and other essays*. New York: New American Library.

Williams, D. (1994). *Somebody somewhere breaking free from the world autistic*. New York: Doubleday.

Winograd, T. (1994). Categories, disciplines, and social co-ordination. *Computer Supported Cooperative Work, 2,* 191-197.

Wittgenstein, L., (1978). *Philosophical Investigations* (G.E.M. Anscombe, Trans). Oxford: Basil Blackwell. (Original work published 1958)

Xuan, L., & Chassain, J-C. (1975). *Comment élaborer systèmiquement une séquence pédagogique*. Paris: Bruand Fontaine.

Xuan, L., & Chassain, J-C. (1976). *Analyse comportementale et analyse de contenu*. Paris: Nathan.

Zeidner, J., Scholarios, D., & Johnson, C. (2001). Classification techniques for person-job matching, an illustration using the U.S. Army procedures. *Kybernetes: The International Journal of Systems and Cybernetics, 30*(7-8), 984-1005.

Zimmer, R. S. (2001). Variations on a string bag: Using Pask's principles for practical course design. *Kybernetes: The International Journal of Systems and Cybernetics, 30*(7-8), 1006-1023.

·9·

ACTIVITY THEORY AS A LENS FOR CHARACTERIZING THE PARTICIPATORY UNIT

Sasha A. Barab
Indiana University

Michael A. Evans
Indiana University

Eun-Ok Baek
California State University

9.1   INTRODUCTION

Since the cognitive revolution of the sixties, representation has served as the central concept of cognitive theory and representational theories of mind have provided the establishment view in cognitive science (Fodor, 1980; Gardner, 1985; Vera & Simon, 1993). Central to this line of thinking is the belief that knowledge exists solely in the head, and instruction involves finding the most efficient means for facilitating the "acquisition" of this knowledge (Gagne, Briggs, & Wager, 1993). Over the last two decades, however, numerous educational psychologists and instructional designers have begun abandoning cognitive theories that emphasize individual thinkers and their isolated minds. Instead, these researchers have adopted theories that emphasize the social and contextualized nature of cognition and meaning (Brown, Collins, & Duguid, 1989; Greeno, 1989, 1997; Hollan, Hutchins, & Kirsch, 2000; Lave & Wenger, 1991; Resnick, 1987; Salomon, 1993). Central to these reconceptualizations is an emphasis on contextualized activity and ongoing participation as the core units of analysis (Barab & Kirshner, 2001; Barab & Plucker, 2002; Brown & Duguid, 1991; Cook & Yanow, 1993;

Gherardi, Nicolini, & Odella, 1998; Henricksson, 2000; Yanow, 2000). Sfard (1998) characterized the current shift in cognitive science and educational theory as a move away from the "acquisition" metaphor towards a "participation" metaphor in which knowledge, reconceived as "knowing about," is considered a fundamentally situated activity.

In spite of the wealth of theoretical contributions in terms of conceptualizing learning as participation, there have been less empirical and methodological contributions to aid researchers attempting to characterize a participatory unit of activity. This reconceptualization of knowledge as a contextualized act, while attractive in theory, becomes problematic when attempting to describe one's functioning in a particular context. Of core consequence is the question: What is the ontological unit of analysis for characterizing activity?[1] Defining the participatory unit is a core challenge facing educators who wish to translate these theoretical conjectures into applied models. In this chapter we describe Activity Theory (Engeström, 1987, 1993, 1999a; Leont'ev, 1974, 1981, 1989) and demonstrate its usefulness as a theoretical and methodological lens for characterizing, analyzing, and designing for the participatory unit. Activity Theory is a psychological and multidisciplinary theory with a naturalistic emphasis

---

[1] See Barab & Kirshner, 2001, or Barab, Cherkes-Julkowski, Swenson, Garret, Shaw, & Young, 1998, for further discussion on this topic.

that offers a framework for describing activity and provides a set of perspectives on practice that interlink individual and social levels (Engeström, 1987, 1993; Leont'ev, 1974; Nardi, 1996). Although relatively new to Western researchers, Activity Theory has a long tradition as a theoretical perspective in the former Soviet Union (Leont'ev, 1974, 1981, 1989; Vygotsky, 1978, 1987; Wertsch, 1985) and over the last decade has become more accepted in the United States.

When accounting for activity, activity theorists are not simply concerned with "doing" as a disembodied action, but are interested in "doing in order to transform something," with the focus on the contextualized activity of the system as a whole (Engeström, 1987, 1993; Holt, & Morris, 1993; Kuutti, 1996; Rochelle, 1998). From an activity theory perspective, "the 'minimal meaningful context' for understanding human actions is the activity system, which includes the actor (subject) or actors (subgroups) whose agency is chosen as the point of view in the analysis and the acted upon (object) as well as the dynamic relations among both" (Barab, 2002, p. 533). It is this system that becomes the unit of analysis and that serves to bind the participatory unit. As such, Activity Theory has much potential as a theoretical and methodological tool for capturing and informing the design of activity. It is in making clear the theoretical assumptions and the applied value of activity theory for research and design that this chapter is targeted. In terms of instructional design, assumptions underlying activity highlight the need for a more participatory unit of analysis, thereby, complicating design in that the design process is recognized as involving much more than simply producing an artifact.

It is much simpler to conceive the design process as the development of an artifact than as supporting the emergence of a mediated activity system. The latter fundamentally situates and complicates our work as designers. In our own work, we have found that conceiving design work as producing a series of participant structures and supports that will facilitate the emergence of activity to be a productive and useful characterization. Further, as if designing participation structures (opposed to objects) was not complex enough, many of the designs that our work has been focused on are in the service of social interaction (Barab, Kling, & Gray, in press). This is evident in the building of virtual communities in which designers move beyond *usability* strategies to employ what might be referred to as *sociability* strategies—that is, strategies to support people's social interactions, focusing on issues of trust, time, value, collaboration, and gatekeeping (Barab, MaKinster, Moore, Cunningham, & the ILF Design Team, 2001; Preece, 2000; Trentin, 2001). In these cases, it is not that we design artifacts but rather that we design *for* social participation—the latter characterization highlighting that designs are actualized in practice and not in the design laboratory. In these cases, especially when designing for something like community, the focus is not simply to support human–computer interactions but human–human interactions that transact with technology.

A key concept underlying this perspective is the notion of transaction, which has as its base assumption the interdependency and interconnection of components—components that only remain separate in name or in researchers' minds, for in their materiality they change continuously in relation to other components (Dewey & Bentley, 1949/1989). Through transactions the tools we design for, the subjects who use the tools, the objects they transform, and the context in which they function are all changed—we can never treat our designs as a static thing. Instead, our designs must be understood in situ, as part of a larger activity system. It is here, in providing a characterization of the larger activity through which our tools transact, that Activity Theory can serve as a useful tool for designers. Toward that end, we begin with a discussion of activity more generally, overviewing the work of Vygotsky, Leont'ev and others who focused on the mediated nature of activity. This discussion is then followed by Engeström's (1987, 1993) and Cole's (1996) treatment of mediated activity as part of a larger context, extending Leont'ev's (1974, 1981) commitment to situate action as part of larger activity systems. Implications for instructional design are then summarized. Armed with this appreciation of Activity Theory we highlight the application of activity theory to three different contexts. From here, we then offer some cautionary notes for those applying activity theory to their respective designs.

9.2 LITERATURE REVIEW

In the following sections, we sketch the genealogy of a version of Activity Theory that is commonly invoked by researchers and practitioners in instructional and performance technology, along with cognate fields including educational psychology (Bonk & Cunningham, 1998; Koschmann, 1996), human-computer interaction (Kuutti, 1999; Nardi, 1996) and organizational learning (Blackler, 1995; Holt & Morris, 1993). Our intent is not only to provide the reader with a sufficient background of the origins of the theory, but also to gradually make apparent its usefulness for understanding learning and design from a truly systemic perspective that emphasizes the participatory unit.

9.2.1 Conceptualizing Learning as Mediated Activity

Beginning around 1920, Russian revolutionary psychologists Lev Vygotsky (1978, 1987), A. R. Luria (1961, 1966, 1979, 1982) and A. N. Leont'ev (1978, 1981) initiated a movement that is now referred to as Cultural-Historical Activity Theory (Cole & Engeström, 1993; Engeström & Miettinen, 1999). Recognizably the most central character in this movement, Vygotsky laid bare what he argued as the then problem in psychological investigation that limited experimental research to reductionist laboratory studies separated from the contexts of human lives (Luria, 1979; Scribner, 1997; Vygotsky, 1978). From his perspective, this research tradition led to the erroneous principle that to understand human cognition and behavior the individual (or organism) and environment had to be treated as separate entities. Consequently, to transcend this Cartesian dichotomy, Vygotsky formulated on a Marxist basis a new unified perspective concerning humanity and its environment (Cole, 1985).

The central notion of this revolutionary standpoint revolved about the triadic relationship between the object of cognition, the active subject, and the tool or instrument that mediated the interaction. As he notes,

The use of artificial means [tool and symbolic artifact], the transition to mediated activity, fundamentally changes all psychological operations just as the use of tools limitlessly broadens the range of activities within which the new psychological functions may operate. In this context, we can use the term higher psychological function, or higher [truly human] behavior as referring to the combination of tool and sign in psychological activity. (Vygotsky, 1978, p.55)

Thus, in contrast to his intellectual peers (e.g., Thorndike, Wundt, and Hull) who accepted the behaviorally rooted proposal of a direct link between the object (stimulus) and subject (respondent), Vygotsky maintained that all psychological activity is *mediated* by a third element. This third element he labeled *tool* or *instrument*. Generally speaking, tools fall into two broad categories—*material tools,* such as hammers or pencils, and *psychological tools,* such as signs and symbols. Eventually, to Vygotsky, these *semiotic* tools (i.e., signs and symbols), would take on enormous importance in his work. To some (e.g., Engeström, 1987), this imbalance in the emphasis of the cognitive over the material limited Vygotsky's work, a point we will take up later. Vygotsky's triangular schema of mediated activity, composed of the subject, object, and mediating tool, is represented in Fig. 9.1. In the schematic, the subject refers to the individual or individuals whose agency is selected as the analytical point of view (Hasu & Engeström, 2000). The object refers to the goals to which the activity is directed. Mediating tools include artifacts, signs, language, symbols, and social others. Language, including nonword items like signs, is the most critical psychological tool through which people can communicate, interact, experience, and construct reality.

What Vygotsky contended, and this is an important point regarding the inseparability of the elements of mediated activity, is that individuals engaging in activities with tools and others in the environment have undertaken the development of humanity (Cole, 1996). Throughout history, humans have constructed and transformed tools that influence their transformation and likewise tools embedded in social interactions have triggered human development. In essence, humans and their environment mutually transform each other in a dialectical relationship. Culturally, these tools and the knowledge pertinent to their continued use are passed from generation to generation. As such, learning is not solely an individual activity but a collectively shared process with significant cultural and historical dimensions (Stetsenko, 1999). It is important to note that although tools are present whenever we are engaged in a certain activity, they are also constructed through our activity (Bannon & Bødker, 1991). In this way, mediating action involves subject, object, and tools that are constantly transformed through the activity.

To explain this cultural–historical interrelationship between human and environment, Vygotsky (1978, 1987) proposed the concept of a zone of proximal development (ZPD). Put simply, the ZPD is conceptualized as the distance between what an individual can achieve on her own (the actual level of cognitive development) and what she can accomplish when guided by more capable peers or adults (the potential level of development). The primary idea of the ZPD is that humans learn through social interaction, this interaction taking place in a historical context and imbued with cultural artifacts. Thus, social interaction emerges through "the genetic law of cultural development" that incorporates intermental and intramental planes:

Every function in the child's cultural development appears twice: first, on the social level, and later on the individual level; first, between people (intermental), and then inside the child (intramental). (Vygotsky, 1978, p. 57)

The intermental plane is a place where shared cognition emerges through interaction between and among individuals and the intramental plane is a place where this shared cognition is internalized or appropriated. This is in contrast to the view of learning as a mere response to outside stimuli. Very definitely, it posits that learning is inevitably a collaboration with others in a cultural and social environment. In this sense, learning is a collaborative mediated action between individuals and objects of environment mediated by cultural tools and others (Rogoff, 1990; Vygotsky, 1978; Wertsch, 1985).

The concept of mediated activity within ZPD lead us to a perspective of learning that sees the learner as actively constructing meaning within a cultural–historical context. Although the learner is conceived of as active, it is the responsibility of the culturally more advanced facilitator (e.g., teacher), to provide opportunities for acceptable constructions. As Vygotsky indicates, "instruction is good only *when it proceeds ahead of development,* when it awakens and rouses to life those functions that are in the process of maturing or in the zone of proximal development" (1987, p. 222, emphasis in original). The ultimate burden then, is placed on the facilitator. With increasing breadth of impact, Vygotsky's perspective has influenced both educational psychology and instructional design over the past 20 years.

While Vygotsky made tremendous strides in breaking free of the Cartesian dichotomy, by framing learning as mediated activity within a cultural–historical milieu, he was criticized for two critical shortcomings. First, his articulation of what was meant by activity was never fully developed. It took his colleague, Leont'ev, to formulate more elaborate schemes of activity and the relationship between external and internal activity. Moreover, as was hinted at earlier, Vygotsky overemphasized the cognizing individual or individuals as the unit of analysis. As we will see shortly, Engeström has come a long way to bring back into

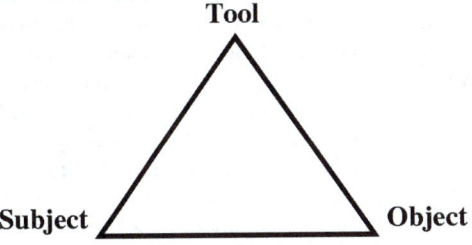

FIGURE 9.1. The basic schematic of mediated activity as developed by Vygotsky (1978, 1987).

current formulations of Activity Theory the importance of cultural–historical elements.

9.2.2 Characterizing Activity

In his search for an answer to the riddle of the origin and development of the mind, A. N. Leont'ev formulated the concept of *activity* as the fundamental unit of analysis to understand the objective and subjective worlds of complex organic life (Leont'ev, 1974, 1978, 1981, 1989). Like his mentor and colleague Vygotsky, his driving intention was to break away from the conventional Cartesian-inspired theories and methodologies of psychology to develop a conceptualization that could wed both the objective, material world and subjective, psychic world. While his radical approach had similar beginnings to those of Vygotsky, Leont'ev was able to articulate a conceptualization of activity that more clearly emphasized the inherently collective nature of learning and, the inspiration for the entire lineage of this line of thought, work (or labor). The stride that was made was that instead of focusing on the psychologically developing individual within a cultural-historical milieu, Leont'ev emphasized the *object's* place in the concept of activity. His agenda to locate the focus of the conceptualization and study of activity on the object is unmistakably stated in the following excerpt:

Thus, the principal "unit" of a vital process is an organism's activity; the different activities that realise its diverse vital relations with the surrounding reality are essentially determined by their object; we shall therefore differentiate between separate types of activity according to the difference in their objects [emphasis in original]. (Leont'ev, 1981, p. 37)

A key move in Leont'ev's work was to emphasize the importance of the object (as opposed to the subject) of activity and to distinguish between the immediate action and the larger overall activity system. It was in this way that he began the process of situating activity within a larger system, a point that Engeström (1987) would take up and extend in his subsequent work.

Within Leont'ev's framework, the most fundamental principle of analysis is, therefore, the hierarchical structuring of activity. Thus, to understand the development of the human psyche, Leont'ev (1978, 1981) proposed three hierarchical levels—operation, action, and activity. At the risk of sacrificing the subtleties of the conceptualization, an activity system can be thought of as having three hierarchical levels corresponding roughly to automatic, conscious, and cultural levels of behavior (Kuutti, 1996; Leont'ev, 1978). Starting at the automatic level, he referred to these as *operations*. Operations are habitual routines associated with an action and, moreover, are influenced by current conditions of the overall activity. This construct in many ways parallels the view Simon takes of human behavior as he presents the parable of the ant making his "laborious way across a wind- and wave-molded beach" (1981, p. 63). In Simon's words:

A man (sic), viewed as a behaving system, is quite simple. The apparent complexity of his behavior over time is largely a reflection of the complexity of the environment in which he finds himself [emphasis in original]. (1981, p. 65)

For Leont'ev, nevertheless, *operations* are the most basic level of activity. *Actions* occur at the next higher level and are often associated with individual knowledge and skills. Thus, within the activity of project management, there are possibly several associated actions, including, for example, consulting, accounting, and writing (Kuutti, 1996). These actions, either separately or in various combinations, are subordinated to individual needs. At the highest, or cultural, level is *activity,* which is essentially defined at the level of motives and goals (Gilbert, 1999). The motivation of an activity is to transform the object into an outcome. It should be noted that within this hierarchy individuals are usually aware only of action at the conscious level, on immediate goals with local resources. This "action" level is conditioned by a larger cultural scope, and supported by automatic behaviors previously learned. Again, the focus here is on attempting to characterize the nature of the activity and not the processes of the individual mind.

In a now famous passage from *Problems of the Development of Mind,* Leont'ev describes the case of hunters on the savannah to illustrate more definitely the relationship of the concepts of activity and action and how they contribute to a unique understanding of human production:

Let us now examine the fundamental structure of the individual's activity in the conditions of a collective labour process from this standpoint. When a member of a group performs his labour activity he also does it to satisfy one of his needs. A beater, for example, taking part in a primaeval collective hunt, was stimulated by a need for food or, perhaps, a need for clothing, which the skin of the dead animal would meet for him. At what, however, was his activity directly aimed? It may have been directed, for example, at frightening a herd of animals and sending them toward other hunters, hiding in ambush. That, properly speaking, is what should be the result of the activity of this man. And the activity of this individual member of the hunt ends with that. The rest is completed by the other members. This result, i.e., the frightening of the game, etc. understandably does not in itself, and may not, lead to satisfaction of the beater's need for food, or the skin of the animal. What the processes of his activity were directed to did not, consequently, coincide with what stimulated them, i.e., did not coincide with the motive of his activity; the two were divided from one another in this instance. Processes, the object and motive of which do not coincide with one another, we shall call "actions". We can say, for example, that the beater's activity is the hunt, and the frightening of the game his action. (1981, p. 210)

Here then, we have the distinction between activity and action and how collective labor, with its inherent division of labor, necessitates such a conceptualization. That is, in collective work, activity occurs at the group level while action occurs at the individual level. Thus, what may be of particular interest to researchers and practitioners is the concept of the action level of activity. Here the task would be to analytically represent and further understand (Engeström, 2000) the processes involved in using tools (either conceptual or artifactual), the meditative effects (either enabling or constraining) these tools have on object-oriented activity, and the outcomes (e.g., knowledge) that result. Necessarily attractive to instructional and performance technologists, then, is that this hierarchy of activity

TABLE 9.1. The Hierarchical Distribution of Components in an Activity System: Three Examples

Hierarchy of Activity Components	Activity Systems		
	Hunters[a]	Flute Makers[b]	Preservice Teachers[c]
Activity	Hunting	Flute making	Preservice Training
Motive(s)	Survival	Production of world-class quality flutes	Professional qualification
Action(s)	Drum beating; spear throwing	Carving flute body; tuning mechanisms	Participating in lectures, writing field notes
Need(s)	Clothing; sustenance	Professional reputation; flute making skill maintenance; compensation	Professional teaching position; course credit; intellectual development
Operation(s)	Striking drum; gripping spear	Gripping and manipulating instruments; striking or carving materials	Gripping writing and manipulating instruments; expressing preconceived beliefs and attitudes
Conditions	Material of drum skin, drumstick, and spear; savanna landscape and climate	Materials for crafting flutes; working conditions; organizational standards	Classroom and online environment and tools; learning materials and resources; faculties' teaching styles

[a]Adapted from Leont'ev (1981).
[b]Adapted from Crook & Yanow (1996) and Yanow (2000).
[c]Adapted from Blanton et al. (2001).

provides a comprehensive view of mediation. Moreover, development, or learning, might be defined as the process of activity passing from the highest (i.e., social) to the lowest (i.e., automatic) level of activity, or vice versa (Engeström, 1987). More poignantly, an activity theory perspective prompts the designer to look beyond the immediate operation or action level and to understand the use of the designed tool in terms of the more comprehensive, distributed, and contextualized activity. This shift places emphasis on understanding not simply the subject but the entire context. The implications of this radical idea should be obvious to instructional and performance technologists, particularly those occupied with the assessment of needs and the analysis of tasks. An illustration of this hierarchy using both the hunting example and one from the organizational learning literature is provided in Table 9.1.

9.2.3 Contextualizing Mediated Activity

Whereas Vygotsky began the process of moving the locus of cognition and knowing more generally outside of the individual mind, and Leont'ev refined the emphasis of the role of contexts and actions as part of larger activities, Engeström further contextualized the unit of activity. More specifically, Engeström (1987) provided a triangular schematic (see Fig. 9.2) for the structure of activity that can be described as follows. Similar to Vygotsky (1978), the most basic relations entail a *subject* (individual or group) oriented to transform some *object* (outward goal, concrete purpose, or objectified motive) using a cultural–historically constructed *tool* (material or psychological). For example, an employee (the subject) in an organization may use an electronic library and reference (the tool) to compose new accounting procedures (the concrete purpose) for her colleagues in an effort to improve customer satisfaction. What this example has introduced, which emphasizes Engeström's contribution and thus completes the schematic, are

the components of *community* (the organization) and *outcome* (the intended or not implications of activity). Moreover, the subject relates to the community via *rules* (norms and conventions of behavior) while the community relates to the object via *division of labor* (organization of processes related to the goal) and to the subject via rules (Rochelle, 1998). It is the bottom part of the triangle (rule, community, division of labor) that acknowledges the contextualized nature of activity.

One dimension of this reconceptualized activity system that is potentially critical for design is the concept of *contradiction*. According to Engeström (1987), any activity system has four levels of contradictions that must be attended to in analysis of a learning and work situation. These contradictions are as follows:

- Level 1: Primary contradiction arise *within* each node of the central activity under investigation; this contradiction emerges from the tension between use value and exchange value

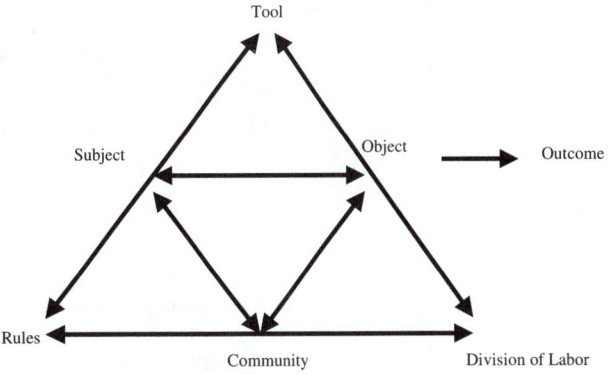

FIGURE 9.2. The basic schematic of an activity system as developed by Engeström (1987).

- Level 2: Secondary contradiction arises *between* the constituent nodes (e.g., between the Subject and the Tool) of the central activity system
- Level 3: Tertiary contradiction arises *between* the object/motive of the central activity and the object/motive of a culturally more advanced form of the central activity
- Level 4: Quaternary contradictions arise *between* the central activity and adjacent activities, for example, instrument-producing, subject-producing, and rule-producing activities.

As an empirical example of this notion, Barab, Barnett, Yamagata-Lynch, Squire, and Keating (2002) used Activity Theory as an analytical lens for understanding the transactions and pervasive tensions that characterized course activities. Reflecting on their analyses, they interpreted course tensions and contradictions in the framework of the overall course activity system, modeled in general form using Engeström's (1987) triangular inscription for modeling the basic structure of human activity (see Fig. 9.3). Each of the components Engeström hypothesized as constituting *activity* is depicted in bold at the corners of the triangle.

The figure illuminates the multiple and interacting components that from an activity theory perspective constitute activity. In this figure, Barab et al. (2002) illustrate the pervasive

tensions of the course, characterizing them in the form of dilemmas within each component of the triangle (e.g., subject: passive recipient vs. engaged learner). Contradictions within a component are listed under each component, and dotted arrows (see a, b, c in Fig. 9.3) illustrate cross-component tensions. Viewing the class as an activity system allowed for an appreciation of pervasive tensions and how these fueled changes in the course. Below, we further discuss this case example and further illustrate the use of contradictions for understanding medical surgical teams.

In summary, Activity Theory (Cole & Engeström, 1993; Engeström, 1987, 1999a) can be conceptualized as an organizing structure for analyzing the mediational roles of tools and artifacts within a cultural–historical context. According to the principles of activity theory, an *activity* is a coherent, stable, relatively long-term endeavor directed to an articulated or identifiable goal or *object* (Rochelle, 1998). Moreover, activity can only be adequately understood within its culturally and historically situated context. Examples of activity might include the collaborative authoring of a book, the management of investments in mutual funds, the raising of a child or even the hunting of game on the savannah. Importantly, the unit of analysis is an activity directed at an object that motivates activity, giving it a specific direction. Activities are composed of goal-directed actions that must be undertaken to fulfill the object. Actions

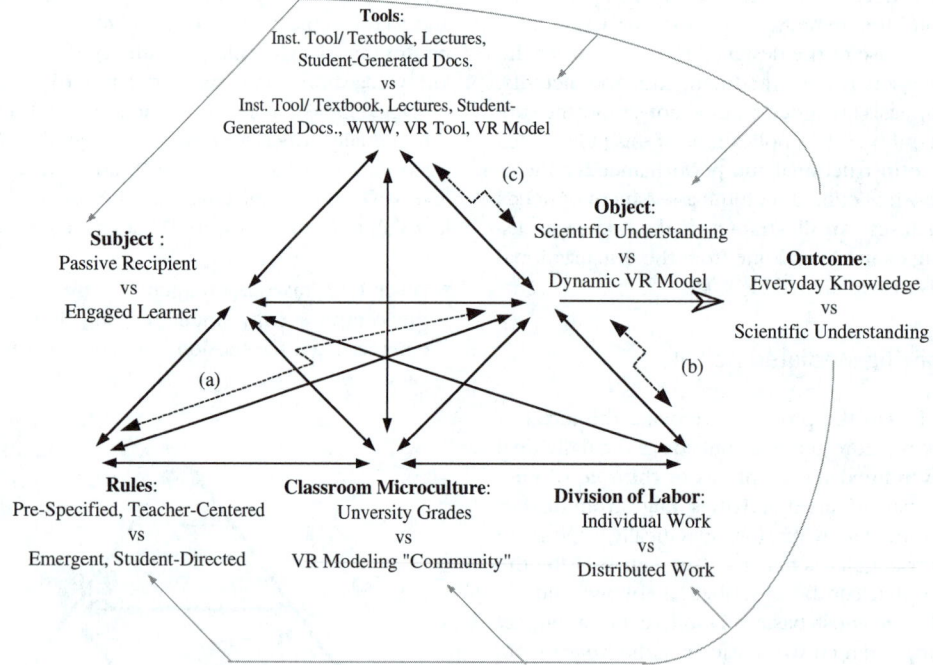

FIGURE 9.3. The mediated relationship between subject and object, and the interrelations among the various components of the system in the VSS course. The figure illustrates the mediated relationship between subject and object, and the interrelations among the various components of the system. Specifically, it illuminates the systemic dynamics and pervasive tensions of the course activity of students participating in the VSS course (see Barab, Barnett et al., 2002).

are conscious, and different actions may be undertaken to meet the same goal. Actions are implemented through automatic operations. Operations do not have their own goals; rather they provide an adjustment of actions to current situations. Activity Theory holds that the constituents of activity are not fixed, but can dynamically change as conditions change.

9.3 DESIGN IMPLICATIONS

In the design of instructional materials or constructivist learning environments, the following design guidelines have been drawn from Vygotsky's (1978) notions more generally:

(1) instructor's role as a facilitator to support students in becoming active participants in the learning process;
(2) instructional materials structured to promote student collaboration;
(3) instruction designed to reach a developmental level that is just above the students' current developmental level;
(4) use of a wide variety of tools, such as raw materials and interactive technology (e.g., computers) in order to provide a meaningful learning context; and
(5) student evaluations focusing on the students' understanding, based upon application and performance (Brooks & Brooks, 1993; Brown, et al., 1989; Hausfather,1996; Jonassen, 1991).

Examples of these learning environments include (1) anchored instruction (Cognition and Technology Group at Vanderbilt, 1991, 1992, 1993); (2) apprenticeship modeling (Collins, Brown, & Newman, 1989); (3) problem-based learning (Barrows, 1985, 1992; Savery & Duffy, 1995; Dabbagh, Jonassen, Yueh, & Samouilova, 2000); and (4) case-based learning (Jarz, Kainz, & Walpoth, 1997; Jonassen & Hernandez-Serrano, 2002).

From our perspective, taking into account the hierarchical layers of activity described by Leont'ev (1974, 1981) may provide instructional designers or performance technologists with a broad picture of the entire collective activity systems, not just isolated actions or automated operations. We believe that understanding participation at these broader levels is necessary to truly facilitate development/changes in activity systems. For instance, Hyppönen (1998) used the hierarchy to link user activity with product functions and features, by associating the process of the activity with results of usability evaluations of the technology, in the entire stages of a product's development. Furthermore, Activity Theory might provide an ideal position—one with sufficient scope and depth—for observing individuals at work, alone or in collaboration with others, using electronic tools. As an example, the designers of an electronic performance support system (EPSS) might be able to use Activity Theory to determine the effectiveness of the specific functions of the tool, depending on where the behavior is located in the hierarchy and whether and how the tool is enabling or constraining a particular goal-oriented behavior.

The schematic advanced by Engeström (1987) provides a framework for viewing and designing tool-mediated activity as it occurs in a naturally organized setting. As Jonassen (2000) has pointed out, "Activity theory provides an alternative lens for analyzing learning [and work] processes and outcomes that capture more of the complexity and integratedness with the context and community that surround and support it" (p. 11). Given our goal in instructional and performance technology to understand collective practice, Activity Theory provides a potentially rich and useful description of how practice is culturally and historically situated. Acknowledging design work as targeted toward supporting contextualized activity while a useful move also brings with it a host of challenges that designers must engage. This is because when designers shift from focusing on the production of artifacts to the development of tools in the service of larger activity many complications arise.

It is an appreciation for the complexities of supporting activity in situ that we have shifted from our understanding of design as the application of a series of principles to a balancing of tensions (Barab, MaKinster, & Scheckler, in press; Wenger, 1998, 2000). In our work, this has meant identifying relevant tensions in the use of our work and supporting the coemergence of participant structures that best balance the potentially conflicting and frequently complementary struggles. Engeström (1993) has argued that it is in the balancing of these tensions that systems are energized and continue to evolve and grow. It is important to note that these tensions cannot be designed and controlled from the outside or in some design document, but must be managed in situ as part of contextualized activity. It is for this reason that many of the complex design projects in which we are engaged are not simply about designing an artifact, or even designing learning, but are about designing for change. Such a process does not involve the simplistic application of those principles advanced by other researchers. Instead it involves reading other rich descriptions, relating these accounts and local struggles to that confronting one's own work and determining how to best balance local tensions that emerge through design.

For an ingenious interpretation of activity theory in applied settings, the reader is referred to Mwanza's (2001) case study on the requirements for a computer system to facilitate customer support (operated by a firm in the industrial computing sector); Hasan's (1998) longitudinal case study that analyzes the progress of university management support systems and highlights benefits of the use of activity theory in the field of information systems (IS) and HCI; Petersen, Madsen, and Kjær's (2002) usability study—a long-term empirical study conducted in the homes of two families, that illustrates how the development of television use is supported or hampered by users' backgrounds, needs, experiences, and specific contexts; and the collection of studies in Nardi's (1996) book on *Context and Consciousness*. In the next section we briefly illustrate three examples in which activity theory was applied to understand and enrich contexts of participation. However, we encourage the interested reader to also refer to the case examples above.

9.4 APPLICATION OF ACTIVITY THEORY

Below, we briefly highlight three research and design projects that have usefully integrated activity theory to understand and evolve activity. We begin with a technology-rich astronomy course in which Activity Theory was applied to understand particular course actions and resulting in a more general characterization of course activity and systemic tensions that fueled more useful iterations of the course. From here, our unit of analysis expands to focus on applying Activity Theory to make sense and evolve the design and participation of an online community consisting of over 1600 members. Finally, our unit expands even farther as we relate a case in which Activity Theory was useful for exposing and intervening on the practices of the medical profession more generally. While each case is useful in its own right, taken as a collection they highlight the ever expanding unit of analysis and different time and space scales that can be examined from an Activity Theory perspective. In this way, operations, actions, and even activities are always nested in more complex contexts all of which might be considered when designing and researching activity systems.

9.4.1 Case I: Tensions Characterizing a Technology-Rich Introductory Astronomy Course

In the design project discussed above, Barab, Barnett et al. (2002) used Activity Theory to understand the systemic tensions characterizing a technology-rich, introductory astronomy course. More specifically, in this work they designed and examined a computer-based three-dimensional (3–D) modeling course for learning astronomy, using the central tenets of Activity Theory to analyze participation by undergraduate students and instructors, illuminating the instances of activity that characterized course dynamics. They focused on the relations of subject (student) and object (3-D models and astronomy understandings) and how, in their course, object transformations leading to scientific understandings were mediated by tools (both technological and human), the overall classroom microculture (emergent norms), division of labor (group dynamics and student/instructor roles), and rules (informal, formal, and technical). In addition to characterizing course activity in terms of Engeström's (1987) system components, through analysis of the data they interpreted and then focused on two systemic tensions as illuminative of classroom activity (see Fig. 9.3).

With respect to the first systemic tension, they examined the dialectic between learning astronomy and building 3-D models, with findings suggesting that frequently participation in the development of model building (using the 3-D modeling tool) coevolved with the outcome of astronomy learning. This is not to say that there were not times when the using of 3-D modeling tools did not frustrate the students or detract time from actually learning astronomy content. However, there were many times when grappling with the limitations of the tool actually highlighted inconsistencies that were supportive of developing a rich appreciation for astronomy content. With respect to the second tension, an examination of the interplay between prespecified, teacher-directed instruction versus emergent, student-directed learning indicated that it was rarely teacher-imposed or student-initiated constraints that directed learning; rather, rules, norms, and divisions of labor arose from the requirements of building and sharing 3-D models.

The authors found that viewing the class as an activity system allowed them to understand how "dualities, analyzed as systemic tensions, led to outcomes that were inconsistent with students developing astronomical understandings" (p. 25). By understanding the tensions in the context of the larger activity system they made appropriate changes in the course participant structures (see Barab, Hay, Barnett, & Keating, 2001) that leveraged emergent tensions in ways that would best support learning. As part of a larger design experiment work, they found the characterization of course actions and activity in terms of Engeström's (1987) schematic, with its focus on understanding how tools and community mediate object transformation, to be useful for identifying particular tensions and making necessary changes in future iterations of the course.

9.4.2 Case II: Conceptualizing Online Community

In one instructional design project, Barab, Schatz, and Scheckler (in press) applied Activity Theory as an analytical lens for characterizing the process of designing and supporting the implementation of the Inquiry Learning Forum (ILF), an online environment designed to support a web-based community of in-service and preservice mathematics and science teachers sharing, improving, and creating inquiry based pedagogical practices. In this research they found Activity Theory to be a useful analytical tool for characterizing design activity. For example, when they attempted to characterize the design and implementation struggles, they realized that when applying Engeström's (1987) triangle it was necessary to develop two separate triangles—one from the perspective of designers and the other from that of users. As they attempted to determine how to relate these two systems, they realized the schism in their design work. While the team was already becoming uncomfortable with the divide, characterizing activity in terms of two distinct systems made this even more apparent. It is in understanding their lack of a participatory design framework that Activity Theory proved particularly useful. Additionally, it helped them account for the more complex dynamics and influences that come into play when thinking about online community. In their work, they began to develop an appreciation that design activity when targeted towards designing for online community does not simply involve the development of a tool or object but establishing a system of activity.

As one moves toward trying to design community, especially one in which the members are expected to engage in new practices that challenge their current culture, many contradictions emerge. Since Lave and Wenger's (1991) seminal book on communities of practice, it has become generally accepted to look at community in which action is situated as an essential mediating artifact of action. This is particularly true when viewing communities of practice designed to support learning (Barab, Kling, & Gray, in press), where the community itself is a tool that mediates the interaction between the subject and object. In terms of Engeström's triangle, this treatment elevates the notion of community from simply occupying the bottom of the triangle to an entity whose reach is distributed across multiple components as it functions as tool, object, outcome, and, at one unit of analysis, even subject. Barab, Schatz, and Scheckler (in press) show how their online environment for learning functioned in multiple roles and, thereby, occupied multiple components of Engeström's triangle. They stated, "when the community itself is considered a tool as well as an outcome it comes to occupy multiple components with its compartmentalization being an acknowledgment of function—not form."(p. 28). As such, they concluded that while an activity theory framework as advanced by Engeström (1987, 1993) was useful for understanding the design and use process and some of their faulty design decisions, isolating components to particular components of the triangle did not appear to be ontologically consistent with the activities through which the community of practice emerged and functioned.

9.4.3 Case III: Analyzing Discoordinations in Medical Consultations/Care

Engeström (1999b, 2000) presents an elegant example of how the concept of secondary contradictions between the principle nodes of a central activity system can provide powerful insights for analysis and redesign of work environments. In the case of a medical team working in an outpatient clinic at Children's Hospital in Helsinki, primary contradictions were detected that resulted in costly gaps, overlaps and discoordinations of care.

As chronic patients passed through the system of encounters with physicians, specialists, and practitioners, the first contradictions detected were between the object (patients moving smoothly from hospital to primary care) and the instruments, or tools. In the Children's Hospital, so-called critical pathways were the officially accepted instruments for dealing with complex cases. The critical pathways are normative guidelines providing step-by-step procedures for moving a child with a given diagnosis through the health care system. The contradiction arises when a physician must use the critical pathway for a patient with multiple diagnoses. On the contrary, the critical pathways were designed to handle only one diagnosis at a time. When the conventional critical pathways were applied to patients with multiple diagnoses, the inadequacy, and possible contribution to additional disturbances, was revealed in the analysis. Multiproblem patients who move between different care providers and thus require interinstitutional coordination instigated two additional contradictions within the overall system. As for the contradiction between the traditional rules of the hospital (which emphasize solo responsibility on the part of the physician) and the object, multiproblem patients forced physicians to request assistance from other institutions. Likewise, the contradiction between the division of labor (where physicians are socialized and trained to act as solo performers) and the object created a disturbance among physicians, specialists, and practitioners. Against tradition, the needs of multiproblem patients demanded that cooperation and collaboration be enacted to ensure the object was achieved.

Consequently, given the case presented here, the concept of contradictions becomes most useful, for researchers and practitioners in our field because it permits for the formulation of hypotheses about contradictions in the central activity system.

Thus, in the case of the medical team study, Engeström (1999b, 2000) constructed hypotheses to be used in the redesign of work practices that could lead to innovations and, ideally, expansive learning opportunities. One of these innovations was a *care agreement* formulated by physicians, nurses, and parents that permitted for continued attention to conventions, but also required the coordination and collaboration among individuals and institutions to meet emerging and unforeseen needs. In a way, contradictions became a source for the design of innovative work practices.

9.5 UTILIZING ACTIVITY THEORY FOR ANALYSIS AND DESIGN

Undoubtedly, Activity Theory can at times be an overwhelmingly complex framework, making it difficult for the novice and expert alike to utilize the concepts and principles efficiently and effectively for analysis and design. Nonetheless, from our own experience and through reviewing the extant literature, we have found that a general heuristic for taking advantage of Activity Theory can be derived to aid both researcher and practitioner. One thing we wish to make certain, though, is that the order of tactics presented here should not be taken as a prescription or as generally accepted practice. Although certain researchers may consistently apply a preferred strategy, there currently is no accepted methodology for using Activity Theory, particularly in the fields of instructional and performance technology.

9.5.1 Characterize Components of Activity

One of the most powerful and frequently invoked uses of Activity Theory is as a *lens, map,* or *orienting device* to structure the analysis of complex sociocultural learning and performance contexts (Barab, Schatz, & Scheckler, in press; Blanton, Simmons, & Warner, 2001; Cole & Engeström, 1993; Engeström, 1999a; Engeström & Miettinen, 1999; Rochelle, 1998). That is, by attending to the primary components of Engeström's (1987) activity system triangle—Subject(s), Tools, Object(s), Outcome(s) Rules, Community, and Division of Labor—an investigator can begin to structure her analysis without the burden of too overt a prescription. However, before activity more generally can be segmented into components the researcher must select a unit of analysis for investigation (micro or macro). In the case descriptions described above, the first case has a more fine-grained unit of analysis, focusing on particular learning episodes in the course, than does Case II, focusing on community participation in the ILF, which is still finer than Case III in which Engeström (1999b) is characterizing medical practice more generally. Once the unit or grain size is selected, the researcher than mines collected data to determine the content that they view as constituting a particular component of the triangle with the goal of developing a triangular characterizing of activity. These components may be used as "buckets" for arranging data collected from needs and task analyses, evaluations, and research.

As an example, Blanton, Simmons, and Warner (2001, p. 443) utilized the components of the activity system triangle to contextualize a computer technology and telecommunications mediated learning system designed to promote conceptual change in prospective teachers' perceptions of teaching, learning, and pupils. As a precursor to analysis, the researchers filled each node with empirical data collected from their site. For example, under Subjects the investigators placed the college faculty developing and implementing the course curriculum; under Tools they placed items such as "discourse," "distance learning," "field notes," and "telecommunications"; under Objects they placed "undergraduates," "meaning-making," and "reflection." In essence, the authors were using the activity system triangle as an aid to account for the meaningful participants, processes, and elements of the learning intervention so as to ensure a more thorough analysis.

9.5.2 Structuring Levels of Activity

A second increasingly used tactic generated from the Activity Theory perspective is the attention to the *hierarchical structure of activity*. Here, the analyst is interested in discovering and constructing the motives of the overall activity system, the needs associated with the actions of individual participants and users, and the conditions that enable or inhibit accompanying operations (Gilbert, 1999; Hyppönen, 1998; Kuutti, 1996; Leont'ev, 1978, 1981). Metaphorically speaking, attention to the hierarchical structure of activity provides "depth" to the initial "breadth" gained from the activity triangle orientation. Whereas we have already offered an abbreviated exercise using this hierarchical notion to analyze the motives, needs, and conditions of three activity systems from the literature (see Table 9.1), a more detailed example may provide further aid and insight. In an elegant attempt to bridge user needs with product specifications (in this case, an alarm system for disabled users incorporated into an existing mobile telephone technology), Hyppönen (1998) drew upon the hierarchical notions of activity (Leont'ev, 1978, 1981) to capture requirements for design and development. At the activity level, the researcher inferred that the principle motive was the gaining of easy access to alarm services. This motive implied cooperation among relevant actors and organizations in regard to, for example, locating reliable network services to carry the technology, distributing and maintaining the technology, and educating users on its use. At the action level, it was revealed that several need-driven tasks had to be addressed, including the making of ordinary calls, recalling previous calls from memory, and using a remote alarm key. Finally, the operational level of analysis oriented the researcher to the conditions under which reliable, easy access could be promoted. These included locating the phone, remembering the sequence of operations, and requirements for layout of keys and functions. As seasoned needs analysts and researchers, we find that the riches gained from this perspective provide insights not possible with more conventional views or practices.

9.5.3 Locating Points of Contradiction

A final, equally insightful, tactic taken from an activity theoretical posture is to identify *contradictions* within and between

nodes in the central activity system as well as across entire activity systems (Barab, Barnett et al., 2002; Engeström, 1999b, 2000; Holt & Morris, 1993; Nardi, 1996). If you will recall from an earlier section, Engeström (1987) has indicated four levels of contradiction that need particular attention during analysis: primary contradictions within each node of the central activity system, secondary contradictions between constituent nodes (e.g., Subject(s) and Community), tertiary contradictions between object/motive of central activity and culturally advanced form of central activity, and quaternary contradictions between central activity system and adjacent activities. The importance of contradictions to Activity Theory is that they serve as indications of both discordance and, more positively, potential opportunities for intervention and improvement. Paradoxically, contradictions should not be mistaken as *dysfunctions,* but as *functions* of a growing and expanding activity system. Another way to think of the process of contradiction identification is "gap analysis." To illustrate, whereas in the third case from the previous section (concerning discoordinations of medical consultation and care), we presented an example of how secondary contradictions between nodes disrupted care in a children's hospital, Holt and Morris (1993) provide a concise tutorial in detecting primary contradictions. In their retrospective analysis of the space shuttle Challenger disaster, the authors used the notion of primary contradictions to hypothesize possible causes of failure of NASA's Flight Readiness System (the system installed to ensure unqualified safety for each launch). By indicating contradictions within each node (p.105), for example, in the Rules node ("safety first" vs. timely flight) in the Community node (defense-dependent vs. self-sustaining shuttle program), and in the Division of Labor node (priority given to Flight Readiness Review vs. timely flight by Flight Readiness Team), it was concluded that fundamental differences in priority (i.e., safety vs. timeliness) between contracted engineers and NASA officials may have contributed substantially to the decision to launch, ending in disaster. Thus, a substantial "gap" was detected between the mindsets or cultures of officials and engineers involved in the space shuttle program, a significant discovery that could inform a number of possible performance interventions.

Before ending this section, we want to make certain the reader is clear on three important points. First, as mentioned in the opening paragraph, there currently is no generally accepted methodology for utilizing concepts and principles from Activity Theory. Through a review of the literature and from our own experience applying Activity Theory, we have offered at best a loose heuristic for use. Our recommendation is that the reader access the works cited above (particularly Barab, Barnett et al., 2002; Blanton et al., 2001; Hyppönen, 1998; and Holt & Morris, 1993) to gain a deeper understanding of how Activity Theory is used for analysis. Second, speaking of methodology, it can be confidently stated that researchers and designers adopting an Activity Theory perspective are often committed, although not explicitly obligated, to the use of strategies and tactics from methodologies such as case study (Stake, 1995; Yin, 1994), ethnography (Hollan et al., 2000; Metz, 2000; Spindler & Hammond, 2000), and design experiment (Brown, 1992; Collins, 1990). The commitment is to take an extended, holistic view that allows for the contribution of multiple perspectives. Third, and arguably most importantly, Activity Theory as promoted by Vygotsky, Leont'ev, and Engeström is to be used *descriptively*. That is, the framework in its original intention aids in the *understanding* and *description* of learning and work in socioculturally rich contexts; it does not claim to advocate a prescription for *change*. Nevertheless, in the domains of instructional and performance technology, our efforts are often focused on bringing about positive change. Consequently, although we encourage the exploration of using Activity Theory in more prescriptive endeavors, researchers and designers must take heed of the origins and original intentions of the theory and respect inherent limitations. For ideas on how to adapt Activity Theory to more practical uses, the reader is referred to the work of Kaptelinin, Nardi, and Macaulay (1999), Mwanza (2001), and Turner, Turner, and Horton (1999).

9.6 CAUTIONARY NOTES

Despite the obvious opportunities Activity Theory provides to understand and redesign for learning and work (Engeström, 1987, 1999b, 2000), there are unresolved issues that still must be addressed. Life tends not to compartmentalize itself or act in ways that are always wholly consistent with our theoretical assumptions. As such, just as we identify the strengths of any theory we must also understand its limitations so that we can most usefully apply it to impact practice. Below, we briefly highlight three issues that seem particularly problematic as cautionary notes for those using Activity Theory to make sense and evolve their particular contexts.

9.6.1 Issue 1: Move from Interactive to Transactive Framework

Engeström's (1987) triangle provides an analytical focus and allows researchers to identify components of activity and to gain insight into the interaction among the components of the triangle. However, Garrison (2001) has argued that while activity theory has much usefulness as an analytical lens, it can frequently be used in ways that suggest system dynamics are less transactive those they are trying to represent. Instead of treating each component as independent and simply interactional with other components, transactional thinking "allows us to see things as belonging together functionally . . . [and] allows us to recognize them as subfunctions of a larger function [the ILF]" (Garrison, 2001, p. 23). Transactional thinking assumes that components of the world transact through a dialectic in which both sides continually are transformed. Dewey and Bentley (1949/1989, p. 101–102) distinguished among three forms of action:

(1) Self-action: where things are treated as functioning independently and viewed as acting under their own powers; (2) Inter-action: where one thing is balanced against another thing in casual interconnection; and (3) Trans-action: where systems of description and naming are used to deal with aspects and phases of action, without attribution to "elements" or other presumptively detachable or independent "entities," "essences," or "realities," and without isolation of presumptively detachable "relations" from such detachable "elements."

Central to the notion of transaction is the interdependency and interconnection of components that only remain separate in name or in researchers' minds, for in their materiality they are transformed continuously in relation to other components.

Garrison (2001) argued that applications of Activity Theory must be careful to ensure that all components, when examined in the context of activity, are treated as subfunctions (not separate entities) of a larger transactive function—the activity. Without such an appreciation, researchers will strip the overall activity and its nested components of their ecological functioning as part of larger system. As long as we treat the components as interacting we run the risk of thinking that tools (or subjects) are somewhat isolated and that they can be understood in isolation from their contextualized transactions. Instead, we argue, that they must be considered fundamentally situated and transactive and reinterpreted as they come to transact as part of new systems. Said succinctly, they are always situated. This does not entail that subjects, tools, and communities have no invariant properties that persist across contexts, but rather that these are re-situated as part of each context through which they function (Barab et al., 1999).

9.6.2 Issue 2: Move from Static to Dynamic Characterization

The temptation is to look at any activity system as a black box, static in both time and structure. This temptation is exacerbated when the researcher characterizes the system using a static representation such as occurs when using Engeström's (1987) triangle on paper. Any generalized and static account of an activity system obfuscates the numerous nested levels of activity that occur throughout the making of the system. As such, while Activity Theory offers an excellent characterization of the dynamics of a system and as such does useful work, the compartmentalization also runs the risk of leading to the ontological compartmentalization and static portrayal of reciprocally defining and transacting components. This is because most segmentation is based on a compartmentalization that frequently treats the components it compartmentalizes as independent ontological entities, essences, or realities. Barab, Schatz, and Scheckler (in press) argued that in their analysis of their online community, they found that components treated as, for example, tools were at other times objects or even the community. As such, they suggested that researchers should view Engeström's (1987) triangle as illuminating a functional and not ontological distinction.

By functionally relating each component (subject, tools, community, and objects) as subfunctions of the larger system, one comes to appreciate how activity systems function as a unit that is transformed over time through transactions inside and outside the system. For example, reflecting on the Inquiry Learning Forum, Barab, MaKinster, and Scheckler (in press) suggest that at times the Inquiry Learning Forum was the tool, at other times the object to be transformed, and still others it is the community. Further, as subjects transact with tools both the subject and the tool are transformed in ways. They stated that:

... while an activity theory framework as conceptualized by Engeström (1987, 1993) was useful for understanding this process and some of our faulty design decisions, isolating components to particular locations along the triangle did not appear to be ontologically consistent with the activities through which this community of practice was made and functioned. (p. 23)

We argue that any description of an activity should be treated as continually in the making with the segmented characterization simply being a static snapshot that informs at the same time it reifies. Every system, however, has a history and nested actions, which when viewed from different vantage points and from different points in time may be construed and represented differently and constitute their own activity systems. It is for this reason that some researchers have used Activity Theory in conjunction with other theoretical perspectives.

9.6.3 Issue 3: Move from Isolated to Complementary Theoretical Perspectives

Several researchers have noted the similarities between Activity Theory and other theories that address collective knowledge and practice (Davydov, 1999; Engeström, 1987; Schwen, 2001; Wenger, 1998). The particular theories that we find to have a great deal of potential include Communities of Practice Theory (Lave & Wenger, 1991; Wenger, 1998, 2000), Actor Network Theory (Latour, 1987), and Institutional Theory (Berger & Luckmann, 1966). Although space does not permit us to go more in-depth into the comparison, a cursory survey should pique the reader's interest enough to explore the issue further.

To begin, Wenger (1998) has noted that Activity Theory and Communities of Practice Theory both are concerned with the tensions and contradictions that exist between the collective (or community) and the individual. For Wenger (1998, pp. 230), the notions of identification (to indicate the individual) and negotiability (to indicate the community) exist in a duality that stimulates both harmony and tension. Interestingly, both Wenger and Engeström see this tension as an opportunity for learning and development for both the individual/subject and community. Researchers in instructional technology are also picking up on this notion of integrating these perspectives when describing collective activity. For example, Hung and Chen (2001) attempted to derive certain heuristics to describe the sufficient conditions for online participation. Using situated cognition, Communities of Practice Theory and Activity Theory, they concluded that community-oriented web-based design should take note of at least four dimensions as follows: situatedness, commonality, interdependency, and infrastructure.

Next, Engeström (1999b) himself admits that Actor Network Theory and Activity Theory are simultaneously attempting to attend to multiple activity systems as the cross-cultural (be it professional, organizational, national, or multinational) dimension of learning and work has come to the forefront of research and practice in the latter part of the last century. Thus, it would be beneficial both conceptually and practically to make an attempt to integrate these overlapping approaches. Ideally, this work would provide us the means to analyze collective practice and (re)design the technology that supports and facilitates the involved actors. In the work of Barab, Schatz, and Scheckler (in press) as one example, they combined activity theory with a network theoretical approach, resulting in a richer characterization in which the network approach was used to illuminate the transactional nature of the system and Activity Theory helped to characterize the various functioning of the system and further illuminated pervasive tensions. In other words, while actor-network theory is particularly useful for characterizing the system and understanding its functioning, network approaches can prove useful for observing the dynamic transactions of a system as a simultaneously functioning unit.

Finally, as for Activity Theory and Institutional Theory, we have not found a piece that explicitly attempts to wed these two perspectives. Nonetheless, there is a remarkable congruence to the way the two positions articulate the construction of objective and subjective reality involving processes of internalization and externalization. Like Berger and Luckmann (1966) emphasize a triadic process of externalization–objectivation–internalization. Critical here is the notion of an "obdurate" reality that shapes and is shaped by human production. Of note is that both draw heavily from dialectical materialism.

9.7 CONCLUSIONS AND IMPLICATIONS

Our intentions have been to provide the reader a brief sketch of a theory that we feel can have tremendous impact upon the fields of instructional and performance technology. First, Activity Theory provides us the means to overcome the limiting heritage of the Cartesian dichotomy that has misled us into believing that individuals and their environments can be separated for analytical and synthetic activities. Next, in its development Activity Theory has given us powerful conceptualizations for thinking about learning and work as an activity. Leont'ev's distinctions between activity and action have clear consequences for needs assessment and task analysis and for conceptualizing the targets of our designs. Finally, Engeström has provided a lens for better coordinating the evidently complex task of taking account of activity at a systemic level. Although other approaches have made claims of accomplishing this feat (e.g., Heinich's instructional systems [see Heinich, 1984; Schwen, 2001]), none have been developed from psychological perspectives that conceptualize *collective* production. Another way to put this is that conventional so-called "systemic" approaches have mistakenly taken individual aggregation as being equal to "collective." Additionally, it is one thing to design to support existing systems and another design with the goal of changing the system.

Designing for change is a complex activity that involves balancing many tensions. It is one thing to design tools that support users in doing what they already do but in a more efficient manner. It is another thing to support tools that focus on bringing about change. Barab, Thomas, Dodge, Carteaux, Tuzun, and Goodrich (in press) stated that:

The goal of improving the world is a messy business, with numerous struggles, opposing agendas, multiple interpretations, and even unintended and controversial consequences. Instead of simply building an artifact to help someone accomplish a specific task, the goal is to develop a design that can actually support the user (and the culture) in his or her own transformation. (p. 3)

Design work targeted towards transformation, or what Barab et al. (in press) refer to as empowerment design work, requires establishing buy in and commitment, honoring people wherever they are at the same time supporting them in envisioning and accomplishing what they can be, and balancing multiple agendas and tensions. Understanding the context of the activity through which the design work transacts is a necessary part of any design work (Norman, 1990). We view Activity Theory in general and Engeström's (1987) schematic framework with its acknowledgment of the larger community (including norms and division of labor) of activity as providing useful starting points for understanding the tensions that emerge in this type of work.

Despite its clear advantages in helping instructional and performance technology make strides in accounting and designing for learning and work in the 21st century, there are still many obstacles ahead, a few of which we have mentioned here. As a closing remark, we want to emphasize that a perspective inspired by Activity Theory can be well supplemented with a desire to make meaningful and lasting contributions to society (Coleman, Perry, & Schwen, 1997; Driscoll & Dick, 1999; Reeves, 2000; Reigeluth, 1997). That is, our choice of taking Activity Theory with us on design projects is grounded in a belief that it will permit us to recognize and respect the culture of the collective we are engaged with and support them longitudinally in their aspirations for better lives (Eisenhart, 2001; Metz, 2000; Spindler & Hammond, 2000). It is in this way that we view Activity Theory as a transactional tool that can help us improve local practice and, hopefully, the world through which these practices occur.

References

Bannon, L. J., & Bodker, S. (1991). Beyond the interface: Encountering artifacts in use. In J. Carroll (Ed.), *Designing interaction: Psychology at the human–computer interface* (pp. 227–253). New York: Cambridge University Press.

Barab, S. A. (2002). Commentary: Human-field interaction as mediated by mobile computers. In T. Koschmann, R. Hall, & N. Miyake (Eds.), *Computer supported collaborative learning* (pp. 533–538). Mahwah, NJ: Erlbaum.

Barab, S., A., Barnett, M., Yamagata-Lynch, L., Squire, K., & Keating, T. (2002). Using activity theory to understand the contradictions characterizing a technology-rich introductory astronomy course. *Mind, Culture, and Activity, 9*(2),76–107.

Barab, S. A., Cherkes-Julkowski, M., Swenson, R., Garrett. S., Shaw, R. E., & Young, M. (1999).Principles of self-organization: Ecologizing the learner-facilitator system. *The Journal of The Learning Sciences, 8*(3&4), 349–390.

Barab, S. A., & Duffy, T. (2000). From practice fields to communities of practice. In D. Jonassen & S. M. Land (Eds.), *Theoretical foundations of learning environments* (pp. 26–56). Mahwah, NJ: Lawrence Erlbaum Associates.

Barab, S. A., Hay, K. E., Barnett, M. G., & Keating, T. (2000). Virtual solar system project: Building understanding through model building. *Journal of Research in Science Teaching, 37*(7), 719–756.

Barab, S. A., & Kirshner, D. (2001). Guest editors' introduction: Rethinking methodology in the learning sciences. *The Journal of the Learning Sciences, 10*(1&2), 5–15.

Barab, S. A., Kling, R., & Gray, J. (in press). (Eds.). To appear as *Designing for Virtual Communities in the Service of Learning*. Cambridge, MA: Cambridge University Press.

Barab, S. A., MaKinster, J., Moore, J., Cunningham, D., & the ILF Design Team (2001). The Inquiry Learning Forum: A new model for online professional development. *Educational Technology Research and Development, 49*(4), 71–96.

Barab, S. A., MaKinster, J., & Scheckler, R. (in press). Designing system dualities: Characterizing a websupported teacher professional development community. In S. A. Barab, R. Kling, R., & J. Gray (Eds.), *Designing for virtual communities in the service of learning.* Cambridge, MA: Cambridge University Press.

Barab, S. A., & Plucker, J. A. (2002). Smart people or smart contexts? Cognition, ability, and talent development in an age of situated approaches to knowing and learning. *Educational Psychologist, 37*(3), 165–182.

Barab, S. A., Schatz, S., & Scheckler, R. (in press). Using Activity Theory to conceptualize online community and using online community to conceptualize Activity Theory. To appear in *Mind, Culture, and Activity.*

Barab, S. A., Thomas, M., Dodge, T., Carteaux, R., Tuzun, H., & Goodrich, T. (in press). Empowerment design work: Building participant structures that transform. In *The Conference Proceedings of the Computer Supported Collaborative Learning Conference*, Seattle, WA.

Barrows, H. S. (1985). *How to design a problem based curriculum for the preclinical years.* New York: Springer Publishing Co.

Barrows, H. S. (1992). *The tutorial process.* Springfield, IL: Southern Illinois University School of Medicine.

Bednar, A. K., Cunningham, D., Duffy, T. M., & Perry, J. D. (1992). Theory into practice: How do we link? In T. M. Duffy & D. H. Jonassen (Eds.), *Constructivism and the technology of instruction: A conversation* (pp. 17–35). Hillsdale, NJ: Lawrence Erlbaum Associates.

Berger, P., & Luckmann, T. (1966). *The social construction of reality: A treatise in the sociology of knowledge.* New York: Anchor Books.

Blackler, F. (1995). Knowledge, knowledge work and organizations: An overview and interpretation. *Organization Studies, 16*(6), 1021–1046.

Blanton, W. E., Simmons, E., & Warner, M. (2001). The fifth dimension: Application of Cultural-Historical Activity Theory, inquiry-based learning, computers, and telecommunications to change prospective teachers' preconceptions. *Journal of Educational Computing Research, 24*(4), 435–63.

Bonk, C. J., & Cunningham, D. J. (1998). Searching for learner-centered, constructivist, and sociocultural components of collaborative educational learning tools. In C. J. Bonk & K. S. King (Eds.), *Electronic collaborators: Learner-centered technologies for literacy, apprenticeship, and discourse* (pp. 25-50). Mahwah, NJ: Lawrence Erlbaum Associates.

Brooks, J. G., & Brooks, M. G. (1993). *In search of understanding: The case for constructivist classrooms,* Alexandria, VA: American Society for Curriculum Development.

Brown, A. L. (1992). Design experiments: Theoretical and methodological challenges in creating complex interventions in classroom settings. *The Journal of The Learning Sciences, 2,* 141-178.

Brown, J. S., Collins, A., & Duguid, P. (1989). Situated cognition and the culture of learning. *Educational Researcher, 18,* 32-42.

Brown, J.S., & Duguid, P. (1991). Organizational learning and communities-of-practice: Toward a unified view of working, learning, and innovation. *Organization Science, 2*(1), 40-57.

Cognition and Technology Group at Vanderbilt (1991). Some thoughts about constructivism and instructional design. In T. M. Duffy & D. H. Jonassen (Eds.), *Constructivism and the technology of instruction: A conversation.* (pp. 115-119). Hillsdale, NJ: Lawrence Erlbaum Associates.

Cognition and Technology Group at Vanderbilt (1992). Emerging technologies, ISD, and learning environments: Critical perspectives. *Educational Technology Research and Development, 40*(1), 65-80.

Cognition and Technology Group at Vanderbilt (1993). Designing learning environments that support thinking: The Jasper series as a case study. In T. M. Duffy, J. Lowyeh, & D. H. Jonassen (Eds.), *Designing environments for constructive learning* (pp. 9-36). Berlin: Springer-Verlag.

Cole, M. (1985). The zone of proximal development: Where cultural and cognition create each other. In J. Wertsch (Ed.), *Culture, communication, and cognition* (pp. 146-161). New York: Cambridge University Press.

Cole, M. (1996). *Cultural psychology: A once and future discipline.* Cambridge, MA: Harvard University Press.

Cole, M., & Engeström, Y. (1993). A cultural-historical approach to distributed cognition. In G. Salomon (Ed.), *Distributed cognitions: Psychological and educational considerations* (pp. 1-46). New York: Cambridge University Press.

Coleman, S. D., Perry, J. D., & Schwen, T. M. (1997). Constructivist instructional development: Reflecting on practice from an alternative paradigm. In C. R. Dills & A. J. Romiszowski (Eds.), *Instructional development paradigms* (pp. 269-282). Englewood Cliffs, NJ: Educational Technology Publications.

Collins, A. (1990): *Toward a design science of education [Technical Report #1].* Cambridge, MA: Bolt Beranek and Newman.

Collins, A., Brown, J. S., & Newman, S. (1989). Cognitive apprenticeship: Teaching the crafts of reading, writing, and mathematics. In L. Resnick (Ed.) *Knowledge, learning, and instruction,* (pp. 453-494). Englewood Cliffs, NJ: Erlbaum.

Cook, S. D. N., & Yanow, D. (1993). Culture and organizational learning. *Journal of Management Inquiry, 2*(4), 373-390.

Dabbagh, N., Jonassen, D. H., Yueh H. P., & Samouilova, M. (2000). Assessing a problem-based learning approach in an introductory instructional design course: A case study. *Performance Improvement Quarterly, 13*(3), 60-83.

Davydov, V. V. (1999). The content and unsolved problems of activity theory. Perspectives on activity theory. In Y. Engeström, R. Miettinen, & R. Punamaki (Eds.), *Perspectives on activity theory* (pp. 39-53). Cambridge, MA: Cambridge University Press.

Dewey, J., & Bentley, A. (1949/1989). Knowing and the known. In Jo Ann Boydston (Ed.), *John Dewey: The later works, volume 16* (pp. 1-279). Carbondale, IL: Southern Illinois University Press.

Driscoll, M. P., & Dick, W. (1999). New research paradigms in instructional technology: An inquiry. *Educational Technology Research & Development, 47*(2), 7-18.

Duffy, T. M., & Cunningham, D. J. (1996). Constructivism: Implications for the design and delivery of instruction. In D. J. Jonassen (Ed.), *Handbook of research for educational communication and technology* (pp. 170-198). New York: McMillan Library Reference USA.

Duffy, T. M., & Jonassen, D. H. (1991). New implications for instructional technology? *Educational Technology, 31*(3), 7-12.

Eisenhart, M. (2001). Educational ethnography past, present, and future: Ideas to think with. *Educational Researcher, 30*(8), 16-27.

Engeström, Y. (1987). *Learning by expanding: An activity-theoretical approach to developmental research.* Helsinki, Finland: Orienta-Konultit.

Engeström, Y. (1993). Developmental studies of work as a test bench of activity theory: The case of primary care medical practice. In S. Chaiklin & J. Lave (Eds.) *Understanding practice: Perspectives on activity and context* (pp. 64-103). Cambridge, MA: Cambridge University Press.

Engeström, Y. (1999a). Activity theory and individual and social transformation. In Y. Engeström, R. Miettinen, & R. Punamaki (Eds.), *Perspectives on activity theory* (pp. 19-38). Cambridge, MA: Cambridge University Press.

Engeström, Y. (1999b). Innovative learning in work teams: Analyzing cycles of knowledge creation in practice. In Y. Engeström, R. Miettinen, & R. Punamaki (Eds.), *Perspectives on activity theory* (pp. 377-404). Cambridge, MA: Cambridge University Press.

Engeström, Y. (2000). Activity Theory as a framework for analyzing and redesigning work. *Ergonomics, 43*(7), 960-974.

Engeström, Y., & Miettinen, R. (1999). Introduction. In Y. Engeström, R. Miettinen, & R. Punamaki (Eds.), *Perspectives on activity theory* (pp. 1-16). Cambridge, MA: Cambridge University Press.

Fodor, J. A. (1980). Methodological solipsism considered as a research strategy in cognitive psychology. *Behavioral and Brain Science, 3,* 63-109.

Gagne, R. M., Briggs, L. J., & Wager, W. W. (1993). *Principles of instructional design* (4th *ed*). Fort Worth, TX: Harcourt Brace.

Gardner, H. (1985). *The mind's new science.* New York: Basic Books.

Garrison, J. (2001). An introduction to Dewey's theory of functional "trans-action": An alternative paradigm for activity theory. *Mind, Culture, and Activity, 8*(4), 275-296.

Gherardi, S., Nicolini, D., & Odella, F. (1998). Toward a social understanding of how people learn in organizations: The notion of situated curriculum. *Management Learning, 29*(3), 273-297.

Gifford, B., & Enyedy, N., (1999). Activity centered design: Towards a theoretical framework for CSCL. *Proceedings of the Third International Conference on Computer Support for Collaborative Learning.*

Gilbert, L. S. (1999). Where is my brain? Distributed cognition, activity theory, and cognitive tools. In K. Sparks & M. Simonson (Eds.), *Proceedings of Selected Research and Development Papers Presented at the National Convention of the Association for Educational Communications and Technology [AECT]* (pp. 249-258). Washington, DC: Association for Educational Communications and Technology.

Greeno, J. G. (1989). A perspective on thinking. *American Psychologist, 44,* 134-141.

Greeno, J. G. (1997). On claims that answer the wrong question. *Educational Researcher, 26*(1), 5-17.

Hasan, H. (1998). Integrating IS and HCI using activity theory as a philosophical and theoretical basis. [Electronic version]. Retrieved July 6, 2002, from *http://www.cba.uh.edu/~parks/fis/hasan.htm#s5*

Hasu, M., & Engeström, Y. (2000). Measurement in action: An activity-theoretical perspective on producer-user interaction. *International Journal Human-Computer Studies. 53,* 61-89.

Hausfather, S. J. (1996, Summer). Vygotsky and schooling: Creating a social context for learning. *Action in Teacher Education 18*(2), 1-10.

Heinich, R. (1984). ERIC/ECTJ annual review paper: The proper study of instructional technology. *Educational Communication and Technology: A Journal of Theory, Research, and Development, 32*(2), 67-87.

Henricksson, K. (2000). *When communities of practice came to town: On culture and contradiction in emerging theories of organizational learning* (Working Paper Series No. 2000/3). Lund, Sweden: Lund University, Institute of Economic Research.

Hollan, J., Hutchins, E., & Kirsh, D. (2000). Distributed cognition: Toward a new foundation for human-computer interaction research. *ACM Transactions on Computer-Human Interaction, 7*(2), 174-196.

Holt, G. R., & Morris, A. W. (1993). Activity theory and the analysis of organizations. *Human Organization, 52*(1), 97-109.

Honebein, P. C., Duffy, T. M. and Fishman, B. J. (1993). Constructivism and the design of learning environments: context and authentic activities for learning. In T. M. Duffy, J. Lowyck, and D. H. Jonassen (Eds.) *Designing environments for constructive learning* (pp. 87-108). Berlin: Springer-Verlag.

Hung, D. W. L., & Chen, D. T. (2001). Situated cognition, Vygotskian thought and learning from the communities of practice perspective: Implications for the design of web-based e-learning. *Educational Media International, 38*(1), 3-12.

Hyppönen, H. (1998). Activity theory as a basis for design for all. *In Proceedings of the Technology for Inclusive Design and Equality [TIDE] Conference.* 23-25 June, Marina Congress Center Helsinki, Finland. [Electronic version]. Retrieved July 10, 2002, from http://www.stakes.fi/tidecong/213hyppo.htm

Jarz, E. M., Kainz, G. A., & Walpoth, G. (1997). Multimedia-based case studies in education: Design, development, and evaluation of multimedia-based case studies, *Journal of Educational Multimedia and Hypermedia, 6*(1), 23-46.

Jonassen, D. H. (1991). Objectivism versus constructivism: Do we need a new philosophical paradigm? *Journal of Educational Research, 39*(3), 5-14.

Jonassen, D. H. (1999). Designing constructivist learning environments. In C. M. Reigeluth (Ed.), *Instructional design theories and models: Their current state of the art. 2nd ed.* Mahwah, NJ: Lawrence Erlbaum Associates.

Jonassen, D. (2000, October). *Learning as activity.* Paper presented at the international meeting of the Association for Educational Communication and Technology, Denver, CO.

Jonassen, D., Davidson, M., Collins, M., Campbell, J. and Haag, B. B. (1995). Constructivism and computer-mediated communication in distance education. *The American Journal of Distance Education, 9*(2), 17-25.

Jonassen, D., & Hernandez-Serrano, J. (2002). Case-based reasoning and instructional design: Using stories to support problem solving, *Educational Technology Research & Development, 50*(2), 65-77.

Kaptelinin, V., Nardi, B., & Macaulay, C. (1999). Methods & tools: The activity checklist: A tool for representing the "space" of context. *Interactions, 6*(4), 27-39.

Koschmann, T. (1996). Paradigm shifts and instructional technology: An introduction. In T. Koschmann (Ed.), *CSCL: Theory and Practice of an Emerging Paradigm* (pp. 1-23). Mahwah, New Jersey: Lawrence Erlbaum Associates.

Kuutti, K. (1996). Activity theory as a potential framework for human-computer interaction research. In B. Nardi (Ed.), *Context and consciousness: Activity theory and human-computer interaction.* Cambridge, MA: The MIT Press.

Kuutti, K. (1999). Activity theory, transformation of work, and information systems design. In Y. Engeström, R. Miettinen, & R. Punamaki (Eds.), *Perspectives on activity theory* (pp. 360-376). Cambridge, MA: Cambridge University Press.

Lave, J., & Wenger, E. (1991). *Situated learning: Legitimate peripheral participation.* New York: Cambridge University Press.

Leont'ev, A. N. (1974). The problem of activity in psychology. *Soviet Psychology, 13*(2), 4-33.

Leont'ev, A. N. (1978). *Activity, consciousness, and personality.* Englewood Cliffs: Prentice-Hall.

Leont'ev, A. N. (1981). *Problems of the development of mind.* Moscow: Progress.

Leont'ev, A. N. (1989). The problem of activity in the history of Soviet psychology. *Soviet Psychology, 27*(1), 22-39.

Luria, A. R. (1961). *The role of speech in the regulation of normal and abnormal behavior.* New York: Liveright.

Luria, A. R. (1966). *Higher cortical functions in man.* New York: Basic Books.

Luria, A. R. (1979). *The making of mind: A personal account of Soviet psychology.* Cambridge, MA: Harvard University Press.

Luria, A. R. (1982). *Language and cognition.* New York: Interscience.

Metz, M. H. (2000). Sociology and qualitative methodologies in educational research. *Harvard Educational Review, 70*(1), 60-74.

Mwanza, D. (2001). *Where theory meets practice: A case for an Activity Theory based methodology to guide computer system design.* (Tech. Rep. No. 104). United Kingdom: The Open University, Knowledge Media Institute.

Nardi, B. (Ed.). (1996). *Context and consciousness: Activity theory and human-computer interaction.* Cambridge, MA: The MIT Press.

Norman, D. (1990). *The design of everyday things.* New York: Currency Doubleday.

Petersen, M. G., Madsen, K. H., & Kjær, A. (2002, June). The usability of everyday technology: Emerging and fading opportunities. *ACM Transactions on Computer-Human Interaction, 9*(2), 74-105.

Preece, J. (2000). *Online communities: Designing usability, supporting sociability.* Chichester, UK: John Wiley & Sons.

Reeves, T. C. (2000). Socially responsible educational technology research. *Educational Technology, 31*(6), 19-28.

Reigeluth, C. M. (1997). Instructional theory, practitioner needs, and new directions: Some reflections. *Educational Technology, 37*(1), 42-47.

Resnick, L. B. (1987). Introduction. In L. B. Resnick (Ed.), *Knowing, learning and instruction: Essays in honor of Robert Glaser* (p. 1-24). Hillsdale, NJ: Lawrence Erlbaum Associates, Inc.

Rochelle, J. (1998). Activity theory: A foundation for designing learning technology? *The Journal of the Learning Sciences, 7*(2), 241-255.

Rogoff, B. (1990). *Apprenticeship in thinking: Cognitive development in social context.* NY: Oxford University Press.

Salomon, G. (Ed.). (1993). *Distributed cognitions: Psychological and educational considerations.* New York: Cambridge University Press.

Savery, J. R., & Duffy, T. M. (1995). Problem based learning: an instructional model and its constructivist framework. *Educational Technology, 35*(5), 31-38.

Schwen, T. M. (2001, December). *The digital age: A need for additional theory in instructional technology.* Paper presented at the meeting of The Instructional Supervision Committee of Educational Technology in Higher Education Conference, Guangzhou, China.

Scribner, S. (1997). A sociocultural approach to the study of mind. In E. Toback, R. J. Flamagne, M. B. Parlee, L. M. W. Martin, & A. S. Kapelman (Eds.), *Mind and social practice: Selected writings of Sylvia Scribner* (pp. 266-280). New York: Cambridge University Press.

Sfard, A. (1998). On two metaphors for learning and the dangers of choosing just one. *Educational Researcher, 27,* 4-13.

Simon, H. A. (1981). *The science of the artificial, 2 ed.* Cambridge, MA: MIT Press.

Spindler, G., & Hammond, L. (2000). The use of anthropological methods in educational research: Two perspectives. *Harvard Educational Review, 70*(1), 39-48.

Stake, R. E. (1995). *The art of case study research.* Thousand Oaks: Sage.

Stetsenko, A. P. (1999). Social interaction, cultural tools and the zone of proximal development: In search of a synthesis. In S. Chaiklin, M. Hedegaard, & U. J. Jensen (Eds.), *Activity theory and social practice: Cultural-historical approach* (pp. 225-234). Aarhus, DK: Aarhus University Press.

Trentin, G. (2001). From formal training to communities of practice via network-based learning. *Educational Technology,* 5-14.

Turner, P., Turner, S., & Horton, J. (1999). From description to requirements: An activity theoretic perspective. In S. C. Hayne (Ed.), *Proceedings of the International ACM SIGGROUP Conference on Supporting Group Work* (pp. 286-295). New York: ACM Press.

Vera, A. H., & Simon, H. A. (1993). Situated action: A symbolic interpretation. *Cognitive Science, 17,* 7-49.

Verenikina, I. & Gould. E. (1997) Activity Theory as a framework for interface design. ASCIlITE. Retrieved July 1, 2002. *http://www.curtin.edu.au/conference/ascilite97/papers/Verenikina/Verenikina.html*

Vygotsky, L. S. (1978). *Mind in society: The development of higher psychological processes.* Cambridge: Harvard University Press.

Vygotsky, L. S. (1987). *Thinking and speech.* In R. W. Rieber & A. S. Carton (Eds.), *The collected works of L. S. Vygotsky, Volume 1: Problems of general psychology.* New York: Plenum.

Wasson, B. (1999). Design and evaluation of a collaborative telelearning activity aimed at teacher training. In *Proceedings of the Computer Support for Collaborative Learning (CSCL) 1999 Conference,* C. Hoadley & J. Roschelle (Eds.) Dec. 12-15, Stanford University, Palo Alto, California. Mahwah, NJ: Lawrence Erlbaum Associates.

Wells, G. (1999). *Dialogic inquiry: Towards a sociocultural practice and theory of education.* New York: Cambridge University Press.

Wenger, E. (1998). *Communities of practice: Learning, meaning, and identity.* New York: Cambridge University Press.

Wenger, E. (2000). Communities of practice and social learning systems. *Organization, 7*(2), 225-246.

Wertsch, J. V. (1985). *Vygotsky and the social construction of mind.* Cambridge, MA: Harvard University Press.

Yanow, (2000). Seeing organizational learning: A "cultural" view. *Organization, 7*(2), 247-268.

Yin, R. K. (1994). *Case study research: design and methods* (2nd ed.). Thousand Oaks, CA: Sage.

· 10 ·

MEDIA AS LIVED ENVIRONMENTS:
THE ECOLOGICAL PSYCHOLOGY
OF EDUCATIONAL TECHNOLOGY

Brock S. Allen
San Diego State University

Richard G. Otto
National University

Bob Hoffman
San Diego State University

We live in an era when everyday activities are shaped by environments that are not only *artificial*—almost half of humanity lives in cities—but also *mediated*. Emotional and cognitive activities in all levels and segments of society are increasingly vested in information-rich venues supported by television, radio, telephone, and computer networks. Even in very remote areas, hunters and farmers watch satellite broadcasts and play battery-operated video games. And in the depths of the Amazon River basin, tribes use tiny video cameras to document territorial encroachments and destruction of rain forest habitat.

10.1   OVERVIEW

This chapter explores the metaphor of media as lived environments. A *medium* can be considered an environment to the extent that it supports both the perception of opportunities for acting and some *means* for acting. This environmental metaphor can help us understand how media users exercise their powers of perception, mobility, and agency within the constraints imposed by particular media technologies and within the conventions established by various media cultures.

The ergonomic utility of many media environments is based on metaphors and mechanics that invite users to participate in worlds populated by semiautonomous objects and agents—ranging from buttons and windows to sprites and computer personas. Attempts to model user engagement with these worlds as the processing of symbols, messages, and discourse are limited because the channel-communications metaphor fails to specify many of the modalities by which humans interact with situations. These modalities include locating, tracking, identifying, grasping, moving, and modifying objects. There is a profound, but not always obvious, difference between receiving communication and acquiring information through these interactive modalities.

Much of the philosophy and neuropsychology of the last century concerned explanations of the mechanisms by which organisms create and store information about their external environment and their relationship to that environment. These explanations have generated a superabundance of terminology for describing internal representations including *memory, stimulus-response mechanisms, neural networks, productions, associations, propositions, scripts, schemata, mental images and models,* and *engrams.*

For simplicity's sake, we will often use a single acronym, *MIROS,* to stand for all such *Mental-Internal Representations of Situations.*[1] Much of the discussion in this chapter assumes that MIROS are incomplete—functioning as complements to rather than substitutes for the external representation of situations provided by media and by realia,[2] that is, real things. The metaphor of media as environments helps us reconsider trade-offs between the "cost" of (a) *external* storing and processing of information via realia and media and the "cost" of (b) *internal-mental* storing and processing of information.

Investment of organic resources in improved perceptual capacities, whether acquired through learning or by natural selection, offers an important alternative to construction of more complete MIROS. Improved perception allows organisms to more effectively use information reflected in the structure of the environment, information maintained at no biological "cost" to the organism. The tradeoff between internal and external storage and processing provides a basis for coordinating media with MIROS so that they "share the work" of representing situations.

This chapter also seeks to link paradigms of ecological psychologists with the concerns of researchers, designers, and developers who are responsible for understanding and improving the person–environment fit. It examines ways ecological psychology might inform the design of products and systems that are efficient in promoting wise use of human cognitive resources yet humane in enabling authentic modes of being.

Theories that treat media as mere conveyances of symbols and messages often neglect the differences in actions enabled by media, MIROS, and realia. The pages of a book on human anatomy, for example, afford examination of structures of the human body as does a film of an autopsy. However, each of these media offers different possibilities for exploratory action. The anatomy book affords systematic surveys of body structure through layouts and cross sections, while the film affords observation of the mechanics of the dissection process.

The advantages of storage and transmission provided by media technologies should be weighed against possible loss in representational fidelity. Older technologies such as print and film employ well-established conventions that help users to reconstitute missing circumstances and perspectives. Prominent among these conventions are the captions and narratives that accompany two-dimensional (2-D) pictures that guide viewers in constructing the MIROS required for interpretation and understanding. These conventions help us understand how perception in mediated environments can substitute for actions that might have been available to hypothetical observers of or participants in the represented situation.

The actions afforded by media are rarely the same as those afforded by imaginary or real environments represented by these media. Media technologies can partially overcome dislocations in time and space by storing and transferring information. Opportunities for perceiving and acting on media, however, are rarely identical to the opportunities for perceiving and acting on corresponding realia or MIROS.

Emerging technologies challenge us to rethink conventional ideas about learning from and with media by reminding us that we humans are embodied beings with a long heritage of interactions in complex spatiotemporal and quasi-social environments—a heritage much older than our use of symbols and language. Like other organisms whose capabilities are shaped by niche or occupation, our modes of perception are adapted to opportunities for action in the environment. The conclusion of this chapter examines problems that can result when media technologies so degrade opportunities for integrating action with perception that users face a restricted range of options for moral thought and behavior.

10.2 BACKGROUND

Many important issues in ecological psychology were first identified by J. J. Gibson, a perceptual psychologist whose powerful, incomplete, and often misunderstood ideas have played a seminal role in technologies for simulating navigable environments. Although we do not entirely agree with Gibson's theories, which were still evolving when he died in 1979, his work serves as a useful organizing framework for examining the implications of ecological psychology for media design and research.

We provide here a list of phenomena that Gibson identified in personal notes as critical to the future of ecological psychology (J. J. Gibson, 1971/1982, p. 394).

1. Perceiving environmental layout (inseparable from the problem of the ego and its locomotion)
2. Perceiving objects of the environment including their texture, color, shape, and their affordances
3. Perceiving events and their affordances
4. Perceiving other animals and persons ("together with what they persistently afford and what they momentarily do")
5. Perceiving expressive responses of other persons
6. Perceiving communication or speech
   Also,
7. Knowledge mediated by artificial displays, images, pictures, and writing
8. Thought as mediated by symbols
9. Attending to sensations
10. Attending to structure of experience (aesthetics)
11. Cultivating cognitive maps by traveling and sightseeing

According to Gibson (1971/1982), everyday living depends on *direct perception,* perception that is independent of internal propositional or associational representations—perception that guides actions intuitively and automatically. Direct perception,

---

[1] A situation can be defined as a structured relation between one or more objects. A MIROS is a mental representation of such a structured relationship. If perception is understood to be *acquisition of information* about the environment, percepts are not considered to be MIROS.

[2] *Realia* (Latin, *ralis,* relating to real things): (a) objects that may be used as teaching aids but were not made for the purpose; and (b) real things, actual facts, especially as distinct from theories about them (1987 *Compact Edition of the Oxford English Dictionary, Volume III Supplement*). Oxford: Oxford University Press.

for example, guides drivers as they respond to subtle changes in their relationship to roadway centerlines. Direct perception adjusts the movements required to bring cup to lip, and guides the manipulation of tools such as pencils, toothbrushes, and scalpels. Direct perception is often tightly linked in real time with ongoing action. "The child who sees directly whether or not he can jump a ditch is aware of something more basic than is the child who has learned to say how wide it is in feet or meters" (J. J. Gibson, 1977/1982, p. 251).

Perhaps the most widely adopted of Gibson's (1979) contributions to the descriptive language of ecological psychology are his concepts of *affordances* (roughly, opportunities for action) and *effectivities* (roughly, capabilities for action). Natural selection gradually tunes a species' effectivities to the affordances associated with its niche or "occupation." Thus are teeth and jaws the effectivities that permit killer whales to exploit the "grab-ability" of seals. Thus are wings the effectivities that allow birds to exploit the flow of air.

In contrast to direct perception, *indirect perception* operates on intermediaries, such as signs, symbols, words, and propositions, that inform an organism about its environment via indexical bonds (Nichols, 1991). Following verbal directions to locate a hidden object is a good example of indirect perception. Indirect perception permits, even promotes, reflection and deliberation.

Gibson acknowledged the importance of intermediaries such as symbols and language-based propositions to human thought. However, he was skeptical about claims that general cognitive processes could be modeled in terms of such intermediaries. He argued that models relying excessively on internal manipulation of symbols and propositions would inevitably neglect critical relationships between perceiving and acting.

Every media technology from book, to video, to computer simulation, imposes profound constraints on representation or description of real or imaginary world and requires tradeoffs as to which aspects of a world will be represented. Even museums, as repositories of "unmediated" authentic artifacts and specimens, must work within the technical limitations of display technologies that favor some modalities of perception over others—looking in lieu of touching, for instance.

Although Gibson (1977/1982) did not develop a complete theory of *mediated* perceiving—that is, perceiving through intermediaries such as pictures and text—he posited that such intermediaries are effective because they are "tools for perceiving by analogy with tools for performing" (p. 290). Careful appraisal of this idea reminds us that in the Gibsonian worldview, everyday perceiving cannot be separated from acting. Therefore, there is no contradiction in the assertion that "tools for perceiving" might serve as analogs for action. Static media such as text, diagrams, pictures, and photos have traditionally achieved many of their most important informative effects by substituting acts of perception for acts of exploration.

THE MISSION MUSEUM: NAVIGATIONAL SHORT CUTS AND ANALOGS FOR ACTION

Almost every fourth grader in California's public schools learns about the chain of late 18th century Franciscan missions that inaugurated the Spanish colonial era in California.

A CD-ROM product now makes the mission at La Purísima, Lompoc, more accessible. *The Mystery of the Mission Museum* (Hoffman, et al., 2002) offer a through-the-screen virtual reality model coordinated with curriculum materials that challenge students to become "museum guides" by researching, developing, and giving presentations using the virtual mission environment.

The virtual mission encompasses 176 photographically generated 360-degree "panoramas"—scrollable views of interior and exterior spaces. Users move from one panorama to another by clicking on doors and passageways. Like their colleagues at other museums, curators at the La Purísima mission populated their museum with realia—authentic artifacts of mission life. To represent these artifacts virtually, Mission Museum designers embedded within the various panoramas over 50 virtual objects ranging from kitchen utensils to weapons.

FIGURE 10.1. Sample screens from the Mystery of the Mission Museum software. Interactive maps (lower left corner insets, and top screen) afford faster movement across longer distances. Users click in panoramas to view 60 short videos, featuring costumed docents demonstrating mission crafts or telling life stories. Users can also manipulate virtual objects. In the Cuartel (bottom), for example, they can open and close the stocks (second from bottom) by dragging the computer mouse along a top-to-bottom axis. For more information, see http://mystery.sdsu.edu

In many virtual environments, designers provide some degree of manipulability of virtual objects by creating computer-generated 3-D graphic objects that can be rotated for inspection. However, capturing La Purísima objects from every viewpoint would have been complex and costly.

Making the virtual objects "rotate-able" would have wasted production resources on representation of spatial features with dubious educational relevance, such as the back of a storage chest, the bottom of an ox cart, or the entire circumference of a bell. More importantly, such a strategy would have focused user attention on spatial and physical properties of artifacts at the expense of anthropologically significant affordance properties related to the way real people might have used the artifacts to accomplish their goals.

The designers therefore decided to simulate affordance properties that were especially characteristic of each object as mission inhabitants might use it. The limited affordance properties of the through-the-screen system, which assumed users would employ a standard computer mouse, led designers to a solution in which users employ mouse actions roughly analogous to actions real people at the real museum would use to manipulate "real things." Thus, in the finished version of the virtual museum, students can "operate" a spinning wheel by clicking on ("grasping") the wheel and moving the mouse in a circular fashion. (Some objects, such as bells, also respond with sounds when manipulated.) By means of similar analogs for action, olive-mill and wheat-mill donkeys are lead-able; the mission's cannon is point-able and shoot-able; and the mission bell rope is pull-able. In small-scale usability testing, McKean, Allen, and Hoffman (1999) found that fourth-grade boys manipulated these virtual artifacts more frequently than did their female counterparts. However, videotapes of the students suggested that girls were more likely to discuss the social significance of the artifacts.

Another kind of trade-off confronted *Mission Museum* designers as they created affordances for macro- and micronavigation. Traversing the real La Purísima requires more than a few minutes, even at a brisk walk, and reaching some locations requires diligent wayfinding through hallways, corridors, and rooms. Initially the designers had planned to require node-by-node navigation as a means of representing the scale and complexity of the real mission. However, early usability testing revealed that users found this requirement tedious and frustrating. Moving in the most direct line from one end to the other of the main building complex alone takes 26 mouse clicks.

On reflection it became clear to the designers that the initial approach sacrificed educational utility to a more literal notion of spatial authenticity. As a result, they provided a high-level map to afford "jumps" among a dozen major areas, each represented by a local map. This approach essentially collapsed the space–time affordance structures of the real museum while preserving the potential value associated with direct navigation of specific environs such as rooms, shops, and courtyards.

10.3 NATURAL AND CULTURAL DYNAMICS OF INFORMATION AND MEDIA TECHNOLOGIES

What distinguishes contemporary humans from our pre-ice age ancestors is that our adaptations are primarily cultural. The human evolutionary clock may have slowed for the moment in some respects because we accommodate some "natural selection pressure" technically and socially rather than biologically.

Donald's (1991) reconstruction of the origins of the modern mind claims that the unfolding drama of our distinctly human cognitive capacity has been characterized primarily by increasing externalization of information—first as gestures and "rudimentary songs," later as high-speed articulate speech, and eventually as visual markings that enabled storage of information in stable nonbiological systems.

Norman (1993) succinctly captures this theme of information externalization in the title of his trade book, *Things that Make Us Smart*. He argues that the hallmark of human cognition lies not so much in our ability to reason or remember, but rather in our ability to construct external cognitive artifacts and to use these artifacts to compensate for the limitations of our working and long-term memories. Norman defines cognitive artifacts as artificial devices designed to maintain, display, or operate upon information in order to serve representational functions.

As Greeno (1991) claims, "a significant part of what we call 'memory' involves information that is in situations . . . rather than just in the minds of the behaving individual" (p. 265). Indeed, a sizable body of literature describes some profound limitations of internal representations (or in our terms, MIROS) and suggests that without the support of external devices or representations, MIROS are typically simplistic, incomplete, fragmentary, unstable, difficult to run or manipulate, lacking firm boundaries, easily confused with one another, and generally unscientific. See, for example, Carroll and Olson, 1988; Craik, 1943; di Sessa, 1983, 1988; D. Gentner and D. R. Gentner, 1983; D. Gentner and Stevens, 1983; Greeno, 1989; Johnson-Laird, 1983; Larkin and Simon, 1987; Lave, 1988; Payne, 1992; Rouse and Morris, 1986; Wood, Bruner, and Ross, 1976; and Young, 1983.

10.3.1 Thermodynamic Efficiency of Externalization

The scope and complexity of MIROS are constrained by the thermodynamics of information storage and processing in biological systems. Seemingly lost in three decades of discussion on the problems of internal representation is Hawkins' (1964) insight that *external* representations can confer gains in thermodynamic efficiency.

Hawkins suggested that the capacity to learn evolved when nervous systems made it possible for organisms to store information outside the structure of the cell nucleus proper. Resulting increases in capacity and flexibility meant that a species' genome was no longer the only repository for survival-enhancing information.

Hawkins argued that the first law of thermodynamics, conservation of energy, established conditions that favor development of higher levels of cognition in animal species. He based this line of argument partly on the work of Shannon and Weaver (1949), the mathematicians who applied thermodynamic analysis to technical problems such as the coding and transmission of messages over channels, maximum rate of signal transmission over given channels, and effects of noise.

Hawkins (1964) reasoned further from Shannon and Weaver's (1949) theoretical treatment of information that learning, whether the system that learns be machine or human, confers its benefits through increased thermodynamic efficiency. He considers two simple learning mechanisms: conditioned reflexes and network switches. In both of these mechanisms, the essential thermodynamic condition is the availability of free energy to reduce entropy and increase order. A network of switches can transmit flows of energy much larger than incoming signals that direct switching operations. "Through reinforcement and inhibition, relatively simple stimuli come to release complex responses adapted to the character and behavior of the environment" (p. 273). In both these cases, the patterning found in the operation of the switches and complex responses represents, vis-à-vis the environment, lowered entropy of arrangement.

Externalization of information beyond the limits of cell nuclei and the appearance of simple learning mechanisms referred to by Hawkins (1964) are only the first of many strategies life has evolved for increasing thermodynamic efficiency. Even greater gains accrue if an organism can off-load the work of information storage and processing to the external environment itself and thus reduce biological costs associated with maintaining and processing that information in neural networks. "Investment" of organic resources in improved perception, whether acquired by learning or by natural selection, is an important alternative to construction of more complete MIROS.

Improved perception allows organisms to more effectively use information reflected in the structure of the environment, information maintained at no biological "cost" to the organism. Environments rich in information related to the needs, goals, or intentions of an organism favor development of enhanced perception. Environments lacking such information favor development of enhanced MIROS.

This tradeoff between internal and external storage and processing provides a basis for coordinating media with MIROS so that they "share the work" of representing situations. All things being equal, we might expect investment of organic resources in improved capabilities of perception to be a more effective strategy for organisms than construction of elaborate MIROS. Regardless of whether such capabilities are acquired through learning or natural selection, improved perception allows organisms to more effectively exploit information reflected in the structure of the environment—information that is maintained with no direct biological "cost" to the organism.

Yet all things are not equal: A number of factors determine how biological resources are divided between perceptual capabilities and MIROS. These factors include the niche or occupation of the organism; the availability in the environment of information related to the niche; the biological "costs" of action requisite to information acquisition; the costs of developing and maintaining perceptual organs; and the costs of developing and maintaining the MIROS. Also, when the organism's acquisition of information involves exploring or investigating, there is a "cost" of opportunities forgone: Moving or adjusting sensory organs to favor selection of information from one sector of the environment may preclude, for some time, selection of information from other sectors.

Consider in the following scenario how these factors operate at the extremes to favor development of, respectively, perception and MIROS in two hypothetical groups of people concerned with navigation in a high-security office building.

The first group are ordinary workers who move into a building and after a short time are able to navigate effectively using an environment rich in information such as signage, landmarks, changes in color schemes, and the like. If the building is well designed, it is unlikely the workers will invest much mental effort in remembering the actual details of the spatial layout. "Why bother," they might say. "It's obvious: You just keep going until you find a familiar landmark or sign and then you make your next move. We don't need a mental model because we can see where to go." Norman and Rumelhart (1975) have demonstrated that living in buildings for many months is no guarantee that inhabitants will be able to draw realistic floor plans. In fact, such residents often make gross errors in their representation of environmental layouts—incorrectly locating the position of doors, furniture, and balconies.

Now, suppose a second group, more nefarious and transient, is hired to steal company secrets in the same building during the dead of night when visual information about the environment is not so easily obtained. Each use of flashlights by these commandos would entail risk of discovery (a kind of cost) and each act of exploration or orientation would increase the possibility of being caught. In preparing for their raid, therefore, the commandos might be willing to spend a great deal of time developing a mental model of the layout of a building they may only raid once. "Sure," they might say, "we have to invest a lot of mental resources to memorize floor plans, but it's an investment that pays off in saved time and reduced risk."

Unfortunately, explanatory models in the cognitive sciences still tend to favor notions of mental models as complete representations of the external environment rather than as elements in a distributed information system in which the brain is only one component with representational capacities. As Zhang and Norman (1994) suggest, traditional approaches assume that cognitive processes are exclusively internal and that external representations of information are merely peripheral to internal processing (e.g., numerals are memory aids for calculation and letters represent utterances). They argue that these explanatory models fail to acknowledge external representations in their own right and therefore rely on postulations of complicated internal representations to account for complexity of behavior when much of this behavior merely reflects the complexity of the environment itself.

10.3.2 Coupling and Information Transfer

According to ecological psychologists, perception cannot be separated from action; perceiving involves selecting and attending to some sources of information at the expense of others. Human eyes, for instance, constantly flick across the visual field in rapid eye movements called saccades. Natural interaction with environments cannot be easily modeled in terms of communications channels because such environments typically contain numerous independent sources of information.

Organisms attend to these sources selectively depending on the relevance of the information to their needs and intentions. To stretch a communications metaphor that already seems inadequate, organisms constantly "switch channels." Moreover, most organisms employ networks of sensors in multiple sense modalities and actively manipulate their sensor arrays. It is unclear how we should think of such networks in a way that would be consistent with Shannon and Weaver's (1949) rigorous technical meaning for *channel* in which they model information flow as a single stream of serial bits.

According to Gibson's paradigm (1979), information contained in situations is actively selected or "picked up" rather than passively "filtered" as suggested by some metaphors associated with popular models of memory and perception. In a thermodynamic context, selective perception of the environment confers benefits similar to the switching mechanisms of learning described by Hawkins (1964): Organisms often expend small amounts of energy attending to aspects of the environment that might yield large returns.

Hawkins (1964) extends another Shannon and Weaver (1949) insight by noting that some kind of coupling is a necessary condition for duplication or transmission of patterns. He notes that the idea of coupling—widely misinterpreted by communications and media theorists to mean mechanical, deterministic coupling—was used by Shannon and Weaver to refer to thermodynamic (probabilistic, stochastic) coupling. Thermodynamic coupling is a many-to-many form of linkage. It is a concept of coupling that accounts for possible gains in efficiency and preserves the ancient Greek sense of information as transference of form (*in + formatio*).

Hawkins (1964) argues that human influence on the environment is primarily thermodynamic. Humans exert this influence through subtle changes in the structure of the environment that cause natural processes to flow in new ways. Competent use of this influence requires detecting invariant patterns in the environment so that attention and intention can be directed toward those aspects of the environment that *do* vary or that can be influenced. As Maturana (1978) notes, conceptualizing information as a continuous interactive transformation of pattern or form implies that learning is not merely the collection of photograph-like representations but involves continuous change in the nervous system's capacity to synthesize patterns of interaction with the environment when certain previously encountered situations reoccur. In other words, learning is more usefully described as the development of representations about how to interact with the environment than the retention of models of the environment itself.

Such learning represents a lowered state of entropy—that is, a greater orderliness of arrangement. Chaotic or arbitrary aspects of an organism's activity are ameliorated by attention and intention directed toward aspects of the environment related to survival in the organism's ecological niche. The orderliness and organization of behavior that results from niche-related attention and intention can be characterized as *intelligence,* which is thermodynamically efficient because it "leverages" the expenditure of small amounts of biological energy (Gibbs Free Energy) to guide much larger flows of energy in the external environment. Media users, for example, benefit from this thermodynamic leverage when they expend modest attentional resources to acquire information about how to control large amounts of energy. A speculator who makes a quick killing on Wall Street after reading a stock quote is making thermodynamically efficient use of media technology.

The use of media to extend human cognitive capacities reflects long-term biological and cultural trends toward increasing externalization of information storage and processing. Externalization increases the individual's thermodynamic efficiency. It reduces organic "costs" of cognitive processing by distributing the "work" of representing situations between individuals and their cognitive artifacts. Indeed, one way to define higher order learning is by the degree to which it permits individuals to benefit from externalization of information storage and processing. This can be conceptualized as *literacy* or more generally, we propose, as *mediacy*. Both literacy and mediacy are qualities of intelligence manifested by the facility with which an individual is capable of perceiving and acting on mediated information. Bruner and Olson (1977–78) invoke this concept of mediacy succinctly when they define intelligence as "skill in a medium."

10.3.3 Simplicity and Complexity

Ecology in general attempts to explain how matter and energy are transferred and organized within biological communities. Since transfer and organization of matter and energy are ultimately governed by thermodynamics rather than by processes that are solely mechanical, ecological sciences eschew purely deterministic explanation (one-to-one, reversible couplings) in favor of stochastic, probabilistic explanation (many-to-many, nonreversible couplings). Stochastic description and analysis is based on information transfer and formalized by measures of *entropy* or, organized complexity. Information is thought of essentially as a measure of *level of organization* or relatedness. Entropy can also be thought of as a measure of *degrees of freedom* (Gatlin, 1972; von Bertalanffy, 1967) or *opportunities for action*. From this perspective, complex systems offer more freedom of action than simple systems because complex systems are more highly organized, with more and higher level relations.

Complex biosystems encompass more species and support longer food chains than simple biosystems. For example, a rain forest affords more freedom of action, more opportunities to hunt and gather than does arctic tundra. Cities offer more opportunities for human action—different types of work, recreation, and socializing—than, say, a large cattle ranch. Extremely simple systems may offer no opportunities for action because (a) there is no organization—all is chance and chaos, or (b) organization is rigid—all relations are already absolutely determined. For instance, a square mile of ocean surface is simple and chaotic, whereas a square mile of sheer granite cliff is simple and rigid.

10.3.4 A Multiplicity of Media

Amidst dramatic changes enabled by convergent computing and telecommunications technologies, concepts associated with the word *media* have shifted fundamentally. Many connotations of this term originated in the late 19th century when leaders of publishing and advertising industries became concerned with large scale dissemination of commercial information. In the latter half of the 20th century, the term *medium* was applied variously to:

- storage surfaces such as tapes, discs, and papers;
- technologies for receiving, recording, copying, or playing messages;
- human communication modalities such as text, diagrams, photos, speech, or music;
- physical and electronic infrastructures such as broadcast networks or cyberspace; and
- cultures of creation and use such as sports media, edutainment, the paparazzi, and "cyburbia" (Allen, 1991, p. 53).

These forms of usage are broadly consistent with a more general concept of a medium as "a substance through which something is carried or transmitted" (*MSN Encarta*, 2002). This notion of transmission underlies technical use and popular imagination of media as channels for sending and receiving messages.

Transmission was also implicit in the metaphors of cognitivists in the 1970s and 1980s that characterized human cognition as information processing in which symbols flow through registers and processing modules in a progression of transformations akin to serial computation. Common extensions of this metaphor led many to believe that the way humans (should) work with computers is to "communicate" with them through symbols and language-based discourse including verbal commands.

We have grounded this chapter in a different paradigm that conceptualizes a medium as "a substance or the environment in which an organism naturally lives or grows" (*MSN Encarta*, 2002). Applying this metaphor to human affairs seems particularly relevant in an era when electronic information pervades virtually every aspect of everyday life. Our perceptions of the planet earth are influenced by world-wide "supermedia" events (Real, 1989) even as we are surrounded by "info-cocoons" patched together from components such as facsimile machines, computers, copiers, cellular phones, radios, TVs, and video games. Public awareness of virtual realities and other immersive environments grew steadily in the 1990s as these technologies were popularized in films and amusement parks, and as they were more widely used in architecture, medicine, aviation, and other disciplines.

However, the notion of media as channels for transmitting information is limited because it tends to ignore many of the modalities of perception and action that people use when interacting with contemporary computer-based media. Attempts to model as "communication" user interactions with graphical user interfaces such as those associated with Macintosh or Windows operating systems seem particularly dubious to us. When a user drags a folder to a trashcan icon, does the user intend to "communicate" with the computer? Possibly. When the trash can icon puffs up after receiving the file, does the user interpret this as evidence of the trashcan's intention to communicate? Possibly.

Yet, under normal circumstances, one does not interpret the act of tossing an actual file into a *real* trashcan as an act of communication but rather as an act of disposition. Similarly, a file in a real trashcan is not normally interpreted by the tosser as an effort on the part of the trashcan to communicate its status as "containing something." What is the difference between virtual file tossing and real file tossing? To computer users, both virtual and real trashcans share certain analogous functional properties: From the user's point of view, trashcans are not receivers of messages, but receivers of unwanted objects.

GUIs and similar environments also challenge conventional notions of symbols. In conventional usage, the meaning of a symbol is determined by its referents—that is, a symbol refers to a set of objects or events, but is not in and of itself the means for initiating events. For example, letters refer to sounds and numerals refer to quantities. In arranging letters to spell a word, however, one is not voicing actual sounds; in arranging numerals to represent a mathematical operation, one is not manipulating actual quantities of objects.

The dispositional properties of computer icons and tools set them apart from conventional symbols because icons and tools afford opportunities for direct action. Double-clicking on a selected file icon does not merely *symbolize* the action of opening the selected file. Rather, it *is* the action of opening the file. The double-click action causes the operating system to execute the code associated with the selected icon. Clicking on a selected file does not symbolize file opening anymore than toggling a light switch symbolizes light bulb activation.

However useful engineers may find the communications metaphor in rationalizing the logic of information flows in hardware and software subsystems, questions about the research and design of contemporary user interfaces center on object perception and manipulation partly because perception and manipulation of objects invoke powerful cognitive abilities that are also used in many everyday activities: locating, tracking, and identifying objects; grasping and moving them; altering the properties of the objects; or "switching" them from one modality to another.

The means by which users carry out such activities in a GUI are often partially or completely removed from language-based communication: Pointing, dragging, and pushing allow users to perceive and to continuously adjust virtual tools or other devices without using propositions or commands such as "Erase selected file." Ecological psychologists recognize that, in spite of their apparent modernity, such activities represent very ancient modes of unified action–perception employed by many organisms: Every predator worthy of the name must be able to locate, track, identify, grasp, move, and modify objects. The cognitive faculties used by an artist who cuts objects from a complex computer-based drawing and saves them in her electronic library have much in common with the faculties employed by a wolf who snatches white rabbits from a snow field and buries them until spring.

Developers of computer-based environments of all types, especially interactive multimedia, increasingly rely on object-oriented design and programming (Martin, 1993). Object technologies challenge the media-as-channels and "media-as-conveyors" (R. E. Clark, 1983) metaphors because the objects—files and segments of code—contain instruction sets that enable the objects to assume varying degrees of behavioral autonomy.

Contemporary, object-oriented regimes for interface design result in complex communities of semi-autonomous entities—windows, buttons, "hot spots," and other objects—that exchange messages with each other, usually by means that are invisible to the user. Thus, the user is in a very real sense only one of many agents who populate and codetermine events in cyberspace. Increasingly, human computer users are not the only senders and receivers of messages; they are participants in arenas that have been likened to theaters (Laurel, 1986), and living communities ("vivaria"; Kay, cited in Rheingold, 1991, p. 316).

10.3.5 Integrated Perception and Action

Perceiving is an achievement of the individual, not an appearance in the theater of his consciousness. It is a keeping-in-touch with the world, an experiencing of things, rather than a having of experiences. It involves awareness-of instead of just awareness. It may be awareness of something in the environment or something in the observer or both at once, but there is no content of awareness independent of that of which one is aware. This is close to the act psychology of the nineteenth century except that perception is not a mental act. Neither is it a bodily act. Perceiving is a psychosomatic act, not of the mind or of the body, but of a living observer. (J. J. Gibson, 1979, p. 239)

Dominated by information processing theories, perceptual psychology in the mid and late 20th century emphasized research paradigms that constrained action and isolated sensation from attention and intention. This predilection for ignoring codeterminant relations between perception and action resulted in a relatively weak foundation for design of media products and a limited basis for understanding many traditional media forms.

Ulric Neisser's (1976) perceptual cycle—which acknowledges the influence of both J. J. Gibson and his spouse, developmental psychologist Eleanor Gibson—served as an early framework for examining the relationship between action and perception. Neisser (1976) was concerned with the inability of information processing models to explain phenomena associated with attention, unit formation, meaning, coherence, veridicality, and perceptual development.

Information processing models of the 1970s typically represented sensory organs as fixed and passive arrays of receptors. Neisser asked how then would such models explain why different people attend to different aspects of the same situation? How would information processing models help explain why even infants attend to objects in ways that suggest the brain can easily assign to *things* stimuli obtained through distinct sensory modalities? How would information processing models explain the remarkable ability of the brain to respond to scenes as if they were stable and coherent even though the act of inspecting such scenes exposes the retina to rapidly shifting and wildly juxtaposed cascades of images?

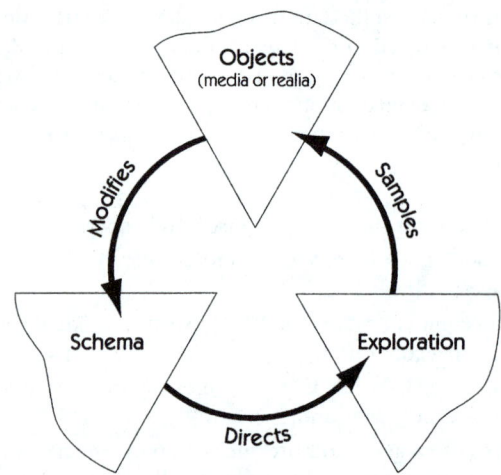

FIGURE 10.2. **Neisser's Perceptual Cycle.** In the language of ecological psychologists, an organism selectively samples available information in accord with the requirements of its niche. An organism's perceptions are tuned to the means that the environment offers for fulfilling the organism's intentions (after Neisser, 1976, p. 21).

The Neisser–Gibson alternative to the information processing models added the crucial function of exploration. This addition, illustrated in Neisser's Perceptual Cycle (Fig. 10.2), reflects the fact that organisms *selectively sample* available information in accord with the demands of their niches. An organism's perceptual capabilities are tuned to the means that its accustomed environment offers for realizing that organism's intentions.

Neisser's emphasis on exploratory perception reminds us that schemata can never be entirely complete as representations of realia. In his opinion, schemata are not templates for conceptualizing experiences. They are more like plans for interacting with situations. "The schema [is] not only the plan but also the executor of the plan. It is a pattern of action as well as a pattern for action" (Neisser, 1991, pp. 20–21).

The idea of the action-perception cycle, which is similar in some respects to early cybernetic models, can be reframed as a dialectic in which action and perception are codeterminant. In visual tracking, for example, retinal perception is codeterminant with eye movement. (See Clancey, 1993, and Churchland, 1986, on tensors as neural models of action-perception dialectics.)

Cyclic models such as Neisser's represent perception and action as separate phases or steps: "See the button, position the cursor, click the mouse." Dialectic models represent perception and action as covariates, in which action and perception are constantly adjusting to each other: "Use the mouse to drag the object to a new location, carefully positioning it at just the right spot." This kind of operation requires continuous integration and reciprocal calibration of perception and action that cannot be easily modeled as discrete steps; the eyes track the cursor *while* the hand moves the mouse.

Detection and analysis of covariation is a critical neural function which, according to psychologists such as MacKay (1991) often obviates the need for more complex models of cognition involving representations of the environment. "...the system has all it needs by way of an internal representation of the tactile world-as-perceived for the organization of relevant action.... readiness for action using other dimensions of the effector system, such as walking, can be derived directly from this representation, without any need for an explicit 'map'" (MacKay, 1991, p. 84).

Neisser's use of *schemata* and *plans* echoes a multiplicity of meanings from Kant (1781/1966) to Bartlett (1932) to Piaget (1971) to Suchman (1987). His meaning is close to what we will define as *actionable mental models*. An actionable mental model integrates perception of the environment with evolving plans for action including provisions for additional sampling of the environment. Actionable mental models draw not so much on memories of how the *environment* was structured in the past as they do on memories of how past actions were related to past perceptions. Rather than mirroring the workings of external reality, actionable models help organisms to attend to their perceptions of the environment and to formulate intentions, plans, and/or action sequences.

Our use of actionable mental models assumes first that mental models are rarely self-sufficient (see D. Gentner & Stevens, 1983). That is, mental models cannot function effectively (are not "runnable") without access to data. Actionable mental models must be "situated" (Collins, Brown, & Newman, 1989; Greeno, 1994) in order to operate.

Ecological psychology assumes that much if not most of the information required to guide effective action in everyday situations is directly perceivable by individuals adapted to those situations. It seems reasonable to assume that natural selection in favor of cognitive efficiency (Gatlin, 1972; Minsky, 1985; von Foerster, 1986) will work against the development and maintenance of complex MIROS if simple MIROS contribute to survival equally well. That is, the evolution of cognitive capacities will not favor unnecessary repleteness in mental models, or the neurological structures that support them, even when such models might be more truthful or veridical according to some "objective" standard of representation.

In many cases, MIROS cannot serve (or do not serve efficiently) as equivalents for direct perception of situations in which the environment does the "work" of "manipulating itself" in response to the actions of the perceiver. It is usually much easier, for instance, to observe how surroundings change in response to one's movement than it is to construct or use MIROS to predict such changes.

Even when humans *might* employ more complete MIROS, it appears they are often willing to expend energy manipulating things physically to avoid the effort of manipulating such things internally. Lave (1988) is on point in her discussion of a homemaker responsible for implementing a systematic dieting regime. After considering the effort involved in fairly complex calculations for using fractional measures to compute serving sizes, the homemaker, who had some background in higher mathematics, simply formed patties of cottage cheese and manipulated them physically to yield correct and edible solutions.

There are tradeoffs between elaborate and simple MIROS. Impoverished environments are likely to select *against* improvement of elaborate sensory and perceptual faculties and may even favor degradation of some of these faculties: We can assume that the blindness of today's cave fish evolved because eyes contributed little to the survival of their sighted ancestors. It seems reasonable to assume that, in the long run, the calculus of natural selection balances resources "invested" in perception against resources "invested" in other means of representing the environment.

In any case, for reasons of parsimony in scientific explanation (in the tradition of Occam's razor), descriptions of MIROS—which are of necessity often hypothetical—should not be any more complex than is necessary to explain observed facts. Accounting for observed behavior, then, with the simplest possible MIROS will assume that natural selection frequently favors organisms that attend to the environment directly because this is often more economical and more reliable than maintaining internal models of the environment or reasoning about it.

10.3.6 Perception

Gibson's seminal works (1966 and 1979, for example) established many of the theories, principles, concepts, and methods employed by contemporary ecological psychologists. Developed over a 35-year span of research on the problems of visuospatial perception, his "ecological optics" now serves as a framework for extending the ecological approach to other areas of psychology. The implications of Gibson's research go beyond the purely theoretical. He was instrumental in producing the first cinematic simulations of flying to use small cameras and miniature airfields to represent landings from a pilot's point of view. Gibson's novel conception of the retinal image[3] substituted dynamic, flowing imagery of the mobile observer for the static, picture-like image of classical optics. This inspired techniques of ground plane simulation and texture gradients that are the basis for many contemporary video games.

10.3.7 Invariants

In developing his radical ecological optics, Gibson (1979) focused on the practical successes of an organism's everyday behavior as it lives in and adapts to its environment. He was particularly concerned with characteristics and properties of the environment that supported such success.

Generalizing this interest, ecological psychologists investigate "information transactions between living systems and their environments, especially as they pertain to perceiving situations of significance to planning and execution of purposes activated in an environment" (Shaw, Mace, & Turvey, 1986, p. iii).

---

[3] "...the natural retinal image consists of a binocular pair of ordinal structures of adjacencies and of successive transpositions and transformations of regions of texture delimited by steps or margins, which are characterized by gradients and changes in gradients" (Reed on Gibson, 1988, p. 136).

Ecological psychologists focus on ordinary everyday perceiving as a product of active and immediate engagement with the environment. An organism selectively "picks up" information in its habitat when such information is related to its ecological niche. In this context, it is useful to think of *habitat* as roughly equivalent to address, and *niche* as roughly equivalent to occupation.

While ecologists describe habitats in generally spatial terms, *niche* is essentially a thermodynamic concept. Selection pressure tends to drive "niche differentiation," in which two species competing for identical resources gradually come to exploit different resources. Since the perceptual capabilities of organisms are tuned to opportunities for action required to obtain enough energy and nutrients to reproduce, such perceptual capabilities also are shaped differentially by niche demands.

"Attunement to constraints" (attributed to Lashley, 1951, by Gibson, 1966) reflects the most fundamental type of information that an organism can obtain about its environment. With this in mind, ecologists such as von Foerster (1986) contend that "one of the most important strategies for efficient adjustment to an environment is the detection of invariance or unchanging aspects of that environment" (p. 82).

The detection of invariants—constrained and predictable relations in the environment—simplifies perception and action for any organism. Detection of invariants is also critical to successful adaptation by humans to any mediated environment. Perhaps the most ubiquitous invariants in media environments are the rectangular frames that contain moving and still images, bodies of text, and computer displays—pages, borders, windows, and the like.

The concept of invariance should not be taken so literally as to imply a complete lack of change in the environment. It is more useful to think of invariance as reliable *patterns of change* that organisms use as a background for detection of less predictable variation. Tide pool animals, for instance, are superb at detecting underlying patterns in the apparent chaos of the surf and adjusting their activity patterns to these fluctuations.

A beginning computer user who at first struggles to understand how movement of a mouse is linked to movement of a cursor will eventually come to understand "directly" and "intuitively" the higher order patterns that link movement of a handheld object across a horizontal surface with the changing position of a cursor on the vertical computer screen.

10.3.7.1 A Simple Experiment in Detecting Invariants. As an example of the importance of detecting invariants, consider the human visual system as it is often presented in simple diagrammatic models. Millions of rods and cones in the retina serve as a receptor array that transmits nerve impulses along bundled axons to an extensive array of neurons in the primary visual cortex. Neurons in this part of the brain are *spatiotopically mapped*—laid out in fields that preserve the spatial organization of the information captured by the retina. These fields of neurons then transmit information to specialized centers that process color, form, and motion.

There is much more to seeing than the processing of such retinal imagery. Seeing also integrates complex systems that focus lenses, dilate irises, control vergence and saccades, and enable rotation of the head and craning of the neck. Perception by the visual system of invariants in the environment can be thrown into complete confusion by interfering with the brain's detection of head and eye movement.

Try this simple experiment. Close your left eye and cock your head repeatedly to the side by two or three inches. Proprioceptors in your neck muscles allow the brain to assign this jerkiness to movements of your head rather than to changes in the environment. Without this natural ability to assign movement of retinal images to self-induced changes in head position, simply turning to watch an attractive person would "set one's world spinning."

Now close your left eye again and, keeping the right eye open, gently press on the right eyeball several times from the side. Your visual system now assigns roughly the same amount of eyeball jerkiness to radical movement of the environment itself. Your brain is temporarily unable to recognize the invariant structure of the environment and the walls of the room, furniture, or other spatial markers appear to be in motion.

Under normal circumstances, the brain does not attribute variation in retinal images resulting from head or eye movement to change in the environment. Rather, an elaborate system of proprioceptive and locomotor sensors operates automatically in concert with retinal data to generate a framework of perceptual invariants against which true environmental change can be detected.

10.3.8 Perception of Invariants: Some Implications for Media Design

Invariants remind us that the perceived quality or realism of mediated environments is not necessarily determined by the degree to which they approach arbitrary standards of "photographic" realism. Perceptual invariants play a key role in determining the degree of realism experienced by viewers.

Omissions of minor detail from a simulated road race—lug nuts on wheels, for example—are likely to remain unnoticed if they aren't connected to important tasks or goals. However, omitting key invariants that affect user actions are very likely to adversely affect perceived fidelity.

Gibson, for example, discovered that most people are very sensitive to texture gradients as cues to depth and distance. When a driver looks down a real asphalt road, the rough surface immediately in front of the car gradually transitions into an apparently smooth surface a few hundred feet away. The driver's perceptual system assumes that the "grain size" of the road texture is invariant, so the gradient suggests distance.

Texture gradients are also critical to realistic representations of depth in smaller spaces such as rooms. Thus, even when painters and computer artists follow rules of linear perspective and carefully render light reflection, pictures will look "flat" without such gradients.

While Gibson's work in the 1970s met with skepticism from his contemporary psychologists, he did generate a considerable following among human-factors engineers and ergonomicists and his work is now appreciated by virtual-world and interface designers. The central concern for these designers is how to engineer the relationship between perceptual variants and perceptual invariants so as to optimize the user's ability to perceive and act in complex, information-rich environments. The strongest invariants in such environments are ratios, gradients, calibration references, and optical flows tied to motion parallax, the ground plane, and ego perception (Gardner, 1987). By simulating the perceptual invariants that people use to navigate the real world, creators of virtual worlds invite exploration and action.

10.3.9   Perceptual Learning

Gibson did not believe that sensory inputs are "filtered" or processed by propositional or symbolic schemes. He favored a bottom-up paradigm in which exploratory action, rather than propositions, drives processes of selective perception. Yet none of Gibson's ideas preclude *learning* to perceive directly—as when children learn that they must automatically respond to icy sidewalks with flat-footed caution. Nor did Gibson deny the importance of "top-down" reasoning about perceptions—as when a mountaineer carefully analyzes the complex textures of an ice-covered cliff in planning an ascent.

Gibson believed that perceptual learning entails the tuning of attention and perception, not merely the conforming of percepts to concepts, as argued by many cognitive psychologists, or the linking of stimulus to response as posited by behaviorists. Perceptual learning is, in the words of Gibson's spouse, Eleanor, "an increase in the ability of an organism to get information from its environment as a result of practice with the array of stimulation provided by the environment" (E. J. Gibson, 1969, p. 77). In perceptual learning, the organism responds to variables of stimulation not attended to previously rather than merely emitting new responses to previously encountered stimulus. "The criterion of perceptual learning is thus an increase in specificity. What is learned can be described as detection of properties, patterns, and distinctive features" (Ibid).

10.3.10   Propositional Versus Nonpropositional Learning

Gibson's (1979) research on visual perception in everyday rather than laboratory situations led him to think of perceiving as a process in which organisms acquire information directly, without the mediation of propositional reasoning. Gibson thought our perception of objects and events is an immediate response to higher order variables of stimulation, not merely the end-product of associative processes that enrich otherwise meaningless sensations (Hochberg, 1974).

Gibson sometimes used the term "associative thought" in ways that implied that he meant propositional reasoning. Therefore, we have substituted the term "propositional reasoning" in this chapter when we discuss his ideas in order to avoid confusion with current usage of the term "associative," which is broadly inclusive of a variety of neurological processes. In any case, a brief review of the controversy regarding propositional and nonpropositional reasoning seems in order here (for more, see Vera & Simon, 1993, and Clancy's 1993 reply).

Cognitive psychologists and computer scientists have long used symbols and propositions to model human thought processes. Anderson's influential ACT* model (1983) was typical of rigorous efforts in the 1980s to use propositional logic to model learning. The ACT* model converted declarative knowledge—that is, knowledge that can be stated or described—into production rules through a process of *proceduralization*. The resulting *procedural knowledge* (roughly, skills) is highly automatic and not easily verbalized by learners.

Gordon (1994) offers this simplified example of how Anderson's (1983) notion of proceduralization might be used to model the way an agent learns to classify an object:

IF the figure has four sides
    and sides are equal
    and sides are touching on both ends
    and four inner angles are 90°
    and figure is black
THEN classify as [black] square.
(p. 139; content in brackets added)

Such instructions might have some value as a script for teaching students about logic, or perhaps even as a strategy for teaching them to recognize squares. Yet even the most sophisticated computer models fail almost entirely to recognize more complex patterns and contexts when programmed to use this kind of reasoning even when such patterns are easily recognized by animals and humans.

There are other reasons to doubt assertions that the brain represents perceptual skills as propositions or production rules. While declarative knowledge expressed through language and propositions is obviously useful for teaching perceptual skills, the ultimate mechanisms of internal representation need not be propositional. The observation that propositions help people to learn to recognize patterns could be explained, for example, by a model in which propositional frameworks are maintained by the brain merely as temporary scaffolding ("private speech"; see Berk, 1994) that supports repeated rehearsal required for perceptual development. Once the perceptual skills have been automated, the brain gradually abandons the propositional representations and their encumbrance on processing speed. It then becomes difficult for learners to verbalize "how" they perceive.

Having decided that perceptual learning is not directly dependent on internalized propositions or production rules, many cognitive scientists have turned to models of non-symbolic representation. We suspect that Gibson would have found considerable support for many of his ideas in these models.

Kosslyn and Konig (1992), for instance, offers an excellent treatment of the ways in which connectionist models can explain the details of perceptual processing. Connectionist models (see also A. Clark, 1989) employ networks of processing units that learn at a *subsymbolic* level. These networks (also called *neural networks*) can be trained, without using formal rules or propositions, to produce required outputs from given inputs. The processing units mathematically adjust the weighting of connections through repeated trials. Neural nets are typically superior to proposition-based programs in learning tasks such as picture recognition.

A trained subsymbolic network cannot be analyzed or dissected to yield classical rules or propositions because the learned information is represented as weighted connections. The network represents learned information not stored as symbols or bits of code located at specific sites but in the fabric of connections. However, subsymbolic processing networks can serve as *substrates* for conventional symbolic processing and have shown some promise for modeling forms of human thought that *do* rely on symbols and language.

10.3.11   Affordances

In Gibson's (1974/1982) view, sensory information alone is insufficient for guiding and controlling the activities of living organisms. He believed that sensory discrimination was distinct from perceptual discrimination. Sensory discrimination accounts for properties that belong to objects—qualities that are measurable in concrete terms such as intensity, volume, duration, temperature, or timbre. Perceptual discrimination on the other hand, accounts for properties that belong to the environment—qualities that indicate opportunities for action. Therefore, perception involves meaning while sensation does not.

Selective perception generates much more information about an experienced event than can be obtained by sensation alone because during the selection process, the organism is informed by traces of its activities relating to location, orientation, and other conditions. In all but extreme laboratory settings, organisms employ the natural means available to them for locomotion in and manipulation of their environment—both to obtain additional information and to act on that information. For Gibson (1979), perception and action were inextricably and seamlessly coupled. To describe this coupling, he introduced the concepts of *affordances* (roughly, opportunities for action) and *effectivities* (roughly, capabilities for action).

Affordances are functional, meaningful, and persistent properties of the environment (J. J. Gibson, 1979)—"nested sets of possibilities" (Turvey & Shaw, 1979, p. 261) for activity. In active perceiving, "the affordances of things is what gets attended to, not the modalities, qualities, or intensities of the accompanying sensations . . ." (J.J. Gibson, 1977/1982, p. 289). In other words, organisms attend to functional properties and the opportunities implied by these properties rather than sensations and physical properties per se.

Thus, an affordance is a pathway for action that enhances the survivability of an organism in its niche: having a firm surface for support, a tree limb to grasp, or a mate. Gibson claimed that affordances such as these are specified by the structure of light reflected from objects, and are directly detectable. "There is, therefore, no need to invoke representations of the environment

intervening between detection of affordances and action; one automatically leads to the other" (Bruce & Green, 1990, p. 382).

In the Gibsonian (1979) paradigm, affordances are opportunities for action rather than physical artifacts or objects. Nevertheless, it is useful to think of sets of affordances as bundled in association with tools or devices. The affordance of "browse-ability" is itself composed of clusters of affordances; one exploits the turnability of a book's pages in order to exploit the readability of their text. We can characterize a telephone by its "handle-ability," "dial-ability," "listen-to-ability," or "talking-into-ability"—affordances that in some cases serve multiple ends. The complete action pathway for realizing the opportunity afforded by a phone for talking to someone at a distance must be perceived, though not necessarily all at once, and "unpacked" through the effectivities of a human agent. Interface designers refer to this unpacking as *entrainment*.

It may seem peculiar or contrived to use *climb-ability* as an alternative to the familiar forms of the verb *to climb*. The grammar of most human languages is, after all, centered on action in the form "agent-action-object" or "agent-object-action." Organizing propositions in terms of action, however, is a serious limitation if one wants to describe mediated environments as complex fields of potentialities. The language of affordances and effectivities refocuses attention on *how* the environment structures activity rather than on descriptions of activities per se.

Affordances simultaneously enable some possibilities and constrain others. Hence, they make some actions more predictable and replicable, more closely coupled to, and defined by, the structure and order of the environment. This in no sense reduces the statistical variety of environmental features; rather, it is the affordance properties associated with these features that reduce the statistical variety in a population's perceptions and actions (Hawkins, 1964).

As a general rule, we can assume that organisms will not squander sensory or cognitive resources on aspects of the environment that have no value as affordances. Natural selection (or learning) will have effectively blinded organisms to objects and phenomena which they cannot exploit. "We see the world not as *it is* but as *we are*," in the words of the Jewish epigram. To paraphrase this from the perspective of ecological psychology, organisms perceive the world not as it is, but as they can exploit it.

10.3.12   Automaticity

One of the reasons Gibson argued that direct perception is independent of deliberate reasoning is because, by definition, the properties of an affordance are persistent, even invariant. They are the knowns of the problem—the "climb-ability" of a branch for the squirrel, the "alight-ability" of a rock for the seagull, or the "grab-ability" of a deer for the wolf. Such affordances are perceived automatically as the result of repeated engagement with consistent circumstances—"hard wired" in the form of dendrites and synaptic connections.

Although Gibson almost certainly would have disagreed with the lexicon of Shiffrin and Schneider (1977), their seminal theories of automaticity, broadly conceptualized, overlap Gibson's concept of direct perception. Shiffrin and Schneider contrasted *automatic* and *controlled* cognitive processing. Automatic processing relies on long-term memory (LTM), requiring relatively little in the way of attentional effort or cognitive resources. Controlled processing, which is typically invoked when an individual is challenged by less familiar circumstances or some degree of novelty, relies much less on processing routines previously stored in LTM and therefore demands deliberate, effortful attention. Controlled and automatic processes can be viewed as ends of a continuum.

Mature human beings have typically developed tens of thousands of "automaticities." While the number of these automaticities may be less in other mammals, they are critical to success in complex environments. All mammals, humans included, are fundamentally limited in their ability to accommodate novelty. Moreover, the evidence is overwhelming that the development of human expertise proceeds primarily through a reinvestment of mental resources that become available as a result of automating interactions with environmental regularities.

Unfortunately, many laypersons associate the term "automaticity" with development of "automatons," people who resemble machines "by obeying instructions automatically, performing repetitive actions, or showing no emotion" (MSN Encarta, 2002). In any case, we use automaticity in this chapter to refer to capabilities that are so well developed as to minimize demands on working memory and other cognitive functions associated with conscious, controlled, deliberate processing.

Much of an organism's capacity to detect and respond to affordances results from encounters, that, over time—in the life of the individual or the species—are consistent enough to induce automaticity in perception and action. Affordances influence the interaction of the organism with its environment by enabling and constraining action and by entraining the organism's perceiving and acting in predictable, repeatable sequences.

In the natural calculus of planning and action, detection of the invariant properties of affordances allows some aspects of a situation to be stipulated or assumed, freeing cognitive resources to attend to unknowns—those aspects of the environment that vary in less predictable ways: Is this branch too thin? Are the waves too frequent? Is the bison too big?

10.3.13 Effectivities

Effectivities (roughly, capabilities), are intentional, meaningful properties of a perceiving organism that trigger, guide, and control ongoing activities directed toward exploiting inherent possibilities of affordances (Turvey, Shaw, Reed, & Mace, 1981). An effectivity encompasses the structures, functions, and actions that might enable the organism to realize an intention. Using its "climber-things," the squirrel exploits the climb-ability of branches to escape predators. Using its "alighter-things," the seagull exploits the alight-ability of rocks for rest. Using its "grabber-things," the wolf exploits the grab-ability of deer to obtain nutrients.

Effectivities are geometrical, kinetic, and task constrained. The geometric and kinetic constraints are measurable by external reference frames such as one's height or weight. Task constraints are more functional and "psychological," encompassing such factors as intentions, goals, or disposition (Mark, Dainoff, Moritz, & Vogele, 1991).

Affordances and effectivities are mutually grounded in and supported by both regularities of the physical structure of the environment and by psychosomatic structures of the perceiver. Affordances and effectivities are neither specific organs of perception nor specific tools of execution but rather emergent properties produced by interactions between the perceiver and his/her environment. It is meaningless to consider whether an object provides an affordance without also considering the nature of corresponding effectivities that some organism might employ to exploit that affordance to achieve the organism's intentions: A flat, two-foot-tall rock affords convenient sitting for a human, but not for a bull elephant.

A well-tuned relationship between affordances (opportunities) and effectivities (abilities) generates a dialectic, which Csikszentmihalyi (1990) argues, is experienced by humans as a highly satisfying "flow experience" (p. 67). Fundamental meaning is extant in the relationship of organisms to their environments. Here is our working definition of *ecological meaning: Those clusters of perceptions associated with the potential means—that is, affordances and effectivities—by which an organism pursues opportunities related to its ecological niche.* Our definition does not assume that organisms are conscious or that they use semantics or syntax. It does not necessarily assume that organisms are purposeful. However, our definition does assume that many organisms engage in activities that can be characterized as intentional or goal oriented.

Many biologists and psychologists would criticize these notions of intentionality or goal orientation, especially when applied to simpler forms of life. Intentionality implies teleological thinking and such critics typically hold teleology in disrepute because it has been associated with doctrines that seek evidence of deliberate design or purpose in natural systems—vitalism and creationism, for example.

A narrower conception of intentionality is convenient in studying self-organizing and cybernetic systems that involve feedback mechanisms. When input is controlled by output, resulting system stability tends to resist disturbing external influences. Thus, stability of output may be considered the "goal" of such a system (Gregory, 1987, p. 176). When ecological psychologists attribute intentions and goals to nonhumans, they typically do so in this more limited sense associated with functional maintenance of homeostasis (or in Maturana's (1980) terms *autopoesis*) rather than as a result of deliberate design or purpose.

10.3.14 Unification of Effectivities and Affordances

A curious phenomenon emerges in humans when effectivities engage with affordances. The affordances often seem to disappear from awareness. Winograd and Flores (1986) cite Heidegger's example of hammering a nail. The hammer user is unaware of the hammer because it is part of the background ("readiness-to-hand" in translations of Heidegger) that is taken for granted. The hammer is part of the user's world, but is not present to awareness any more than the muscles and tendons of the user's arm.

Likewise, a computer user is no more aware of a mouse than she or he is aware of his or her fingers. As observers, we may talk about the mouse and reflect on its properties, but for the user, the mouse does not exist as an entity although the user may be very aware of certain objects he or she is manipulating with the mouse.

Such skilled but unaware tool use is the hallmark of automaticity. It can also be seen in people who, having lost both arms, adapt their feet to function as secondary "hands." With time, such individuals often learn to write, type, even sew or play the guitar. Presumably the same neural plasticity that engenders such prehensile adaptation also allows amputees to become skilled users of prosthetic devices. Norman (1993) asks the next question in this progression: Is the neural "rewiring" that underlies prehensile and prosthetic adaptation essentially the same as the rewiring that supports highly skilled use of *discrete* tools such as hammers, pencils, keyboards, and computer mice? Are the underlying mechanisms of neural adaptation essentially the same whether we are using a body part or a tool?

While a foot is clearly an effectivity in Gibson's terms, should we think of a prosthetic foot as an effectivity or an affordance? And why should a computer mouse be considered an affordance when it's clearly a means for effecting action? These apparent inconsistencies can be resolved by thinking of the linked effectivities and affordances as a kind of pathway of opportunity. As the user becomes increasingly familiar with the interaction between his/her effectivities and the affordance properties of the tool, the effectivities merge psychologically with the tool.[4]

One can think of this union as an extension of the effectivity by the affordance or as establishment of a *way,* or *route* for action-perception. In everyday activity, the *routinization* of such effectivity-affordance pathways renders them "transparent" to the individual's conscious awareness.

Factors that influence the transparency and learnability of these pathways include:

(a) Availability of opportunities that users will perceive as relevant to his or her needs, wants, or interests;
(b) Tightness of coupling in real time ("feedback")—basically the immediacy and resolution with which users can perceive the results of his or her own actions;
(c) Invariants or regularities in the relationship between the users' actions and perceptions; and
(d) Opportunities for sustained and repeated engagement.

As a child uses a mouse to manipulate objects on a computer screen, the effectivity-affordance pathway for such manipulation becomes increasingly transparent and "intuitive." In less metaphorical terms, we can say that the child's consistent engagement with invariant structures associated with mouse movement (e.g., moving the mouse forward on a horizontal surface moves the cursor toward the top of the computer screen) automates patterns of action and perception associated with these invariants.[5] This in turn frees up cognitive resources for engaging more complex patterns which at first appear novel and then also reveal underlying invariant patterns. For example, most mouse control systems incorporate an "acceleration" feature which moves the mouse proportionately greater distances with a quick stroke than with a slow stroke.

As effectivity-affordance links become transparent, new affordances become apparent: an icon leads to a web page which leads to a password field which leads to a simple control system for a camera at the bottom of a kelp bed off the Southern California coast. With repetitive engagement, this entrainment of affordances progressively extends the user's effectivities, creating a reliable and robust pathway to new opportunities. And if the transparency is sufficient, the affordances seem to fall away as the user perceives directly and intuitively new possibilities in a distant world.

10.3.15 Extension of Effectivities and Breakdown

Eventually, the action-perception pathways formed through coupling of effectivities and affordances rupture and corresponding opportunities for immediate action diminish or terminate. Heidegger's hammer reemerges in awareness when it breaks or slips from the user's hand or if the user wants to drive a nail and the hammer cannot be found (Winograd & Flores, 1986). Dirt accumulates on the mouse ball and the mouse no longer provides an accurate reading of x-y coordinates. Thus, as most readers know, the mouse loses its transparency and becomes annoyingly obvious.

In terms of ecological psychology, we can think of the reemergence of the mouse to awareness as a kind of decoupling of an effectivity from its corresponding affordances. Such decoupling ("breakdown" in most translations of Heidegger) advances awareness and understanding by "revealing to us the nature of our practices and equipment, making them 'present-to-hand' to us, perhaps for the first time. In this sense they function in a positive rather than a negative way" (Winograd & Flores, 1986, p. 78).

This reminds us that while automaticities play a critical role in constructing human competencies, broader aims of education almost always involve challenging and reshaping automaticity of perception and action. Efforts to help students to surface and confront highly automatic stereotypes, prejudices, and misconceptions often involve arranging circumstances that force

---

[4]The psychological and cultural reality of this unification has become an enduring literary theme, from Thoreau, who warned that "Men have become the tools of their tools" to Antoine de Saint Exupéry (1939) who waxed rhapsodically about unification with his airplane. Exploration of the relationship of effectivities and affordances also underlies postmodern literary exploration of the prospects and pitfalls of cyborgian culture.

[5]Readers wishing to simulate early childhood mouse learning may want to try turning their mouse around so the cord or "tail" points opposite the normal direction (towards the computer screen). This effectively inverts the mouse's x-y coordinate system, removing some of the interface transparency available to skilled mouse users. In Heidegger's framework, this "breakdown" of normal "readiness-to-hand" reveals properties of the mouse that are rarely "visible" to skilled users.

students to experience "breakdowns" in automatic cognitive processes.

Thus, metaphorically, educators search for ways to "add dirt to the mouse ball," so as to help students see the nature of their dispositions and practices—making automated, transparent processes visible, making nonproblems problematic. Reasoning and propositional logic can play a role in structuring such challenges. "Only critical vision," in the words of Marshall McLuhan (1965), can "mitigate the unimpeded operation of the automatic."

The Constructing Physics Understanding (CPU) curriculum discussed later in this chapter develops this critical vision by asking students to develop theories and models that explain familiar phenomena. The students then examine the adequacy of these theories and models by interacting with real and simulated laboratory apparatus. CPU pedagogy assumes that challenging students to make explanatory ideas explicit and testable forces the students to confront the inadequacy of their ideas and fosters a search for ideas with greater predictive validity and explanatory power.

10.3.16 Everyday Learning and Media Environments

For Gibson, the world of everyday learning and perception was not necessarily the world as described by conventional physics textbooks, not the world of atoms and galaxies, but the "geological environment:" earth, water, sky, animate and inanimate objects, flora and fauna. Gibson insisted that these sources of information must be analyzed in ecological, rather than physical, terms. "Psychology must begin with ecology, not with physics and physiology, for the entities of which we are aware and the means by which we apprehend them are ecological" (cited in Reed, 1988, p. 230).

The popularity of Donald Norman's (1990) book, *The Design of Everyday Things,* which shares key ideas with Gibson's work, testifies to an increased awareness by the general public that media engineers and scientists must look beyond the merely physical properties and attributes of systems. In an age of post-industrial knowledge workers, human habitats and artifacts must accommodate mentality as well as physicality, and support creativity as well as consumption. Cognitive ergonomics (Zucchermaglia, 1991) is becoming just as important as corporal ergonomics. Both depend on understanding fundamental human capabilities that were tuned by ecological circumstances long ago.

If new media are to support the development and use of our uniquely human capabilities, we must acknowledge that the most widely distributed human asset is the ability to learn in everyday situations through a tight coupling of action and perception.

10.3.17 Direct Perception, Context Sensitivity, and Mechanicalism

The modern theory of automata based on computers . . . has the virtue of rejecting mentalism but it is still preoccupied with the brain instead of the whole observer in his environment. Its approach is not ecological.

The metaphor of inputs, storage, and consulting of memory still lingers on. No computer has yet been designed which could learn about the affordances of its surroundings. (J. J. Gibson, 1974/1982, p. 373)

In the process of reinventing the concept of retinal imagery that underlay his radical theoretical postulates concerning perception, Gibson (1966) implicitly relied on the context and situatedness of ambulatory vision. In his empirical research, he paid particular attention to the boundary conditions that affect and constrain visual perception in everyday living. This investigatory focus led Gibson to findings that he could not explain within the paradigms of the positivist tradition. Thus, Gibson was forced to rethink much of what psychologists had previously supposed about perception and to propose a new approach as well as new theoretical concepts and definitions.

Positivisim, in addressing questions of perception and knowledge, relies almost exclusively on the conventional physicist's characterization of reality as matter in motion in a space–time continuum. This "mechanicalism" of Newtonian physics and engineering is allied with sensationalism—a set of assumptions permeating philosophy, psychology, and physiology since the beginning of the modern era.

Roughly speaking, sensationalism maintains that only that which comes through the senses can serve as the basis for objective scientific knowledge. Sensations, however, as Gibson consistently argued, are not specific to the environment: "They are specific to sensory receptors. Thus, sensations are *internal states* that cannot be used to ensure the objectivity of mechanistic descriptions. Gibson argued that what has been left out of the picture in most twentieth-century psychology is the active self observing its surroundings" (Reed, 1988, p. 201).

Conventional psychology, with its roots in positivism, relies on sensationalism and mechanicalism to treat perception as a mental process applied to sensory inputs from the real world. This treatment of perception, however, fails to bridge the gap between (a) incomplete data about limited physical properties such as location, color, texture, and form, and (b) the wider, more meaningful "ecological awareness" characterized by perception of opportunities for action.

Such actions are not always easy to describe within the confines of traditional Cartesian metrics. Ecological psychologists employ "geodesics" (Kugler, Shaw, Vincente, & Kinsella-Shaw, 1991, p. 414) to complement mechanistic systems of description. Examples of geodesics are least work, least time, least distance, least action, and least resistance. Ecological psychology conceives of these pathways as "streamlines" through the organism's niche structure.

Ecological psychologists often think of habitats as environmental layouts rather than as simple traversals of Cartesian space. Geodesics are constrained by factors such as gravity, vectors associated with the arc of an organism's appendages or sensory organs, and energy available for exertion. For a simple example of geodesics, consider how cow paths are created by animals avoiding unnecessary ascents and descents on an undulating landscape. In addition to serving as records of travel through Cartesian space, the paths reflect cow energy expenditure and the ability of the cows to detect constraints imposed by gravity.

Geodesics are essentially a thermodynamic construct and as such can be applied to human activity in media environments. Optimal perceiving and acting in mediated environments does not necessarily follow boxes, frames, or other contrivances based on arbitrary grids imposed in the Cartesian tradition such as pages, tables, rules, keyboards, or screens. True optimums for action and perception must be measured in terms of cognitive and corporal ergonomics rather than the metrical efficacy assumed by a one-grid-fits-all-organisms approach. Designing keyboards to conform to a grid may simplify circuitry and manufacture, but such keyboards may strain the human wrist.

Media designers and researchers can use geodesic analysis to study how users interact with print and computer-based media by, for example, tracking the extent to which users recognize opportunities for action afforded by features such as headers, indexes, icons, "hot buttons," and modal dialog boxes. In terms of thermodynamic efficiency, skilled use of short cuts and navigational aids to wend one's way through a media environment is similar to the challenge faced by the cows: What pathway of action yields the desired result with the least expenditure of energy?

10.4 ECOLOGICAL VERSUS EMPIRICAL APPROACHES

The act of perceiving is one of becoming aware of the environment, or picking up of information about the environment, but...nothing like a *representation* of the environment exists in the brain or the mind which could be in greater or lesser correspondence with it—no "phenomenal" world which reflects or parallels the "physical" world. (J. J. Gibson, 1974/1982, pp. 371–372)

Gibson (1979) found himself at odds with both the fading metaphors of behaviorists who often likened the brain to a mechanical device and the emergent metaphors of the cognitivists who frequently spoke of the brain as an information processing computer. One of his important insights was that *actions* involved in detecting and selecting information are just as important to subsequent understanding of what is perceived as the processing of sensory stimuli. As in the sport of orienteering—the use of a map and compass to navigate between checkpoints along an unfamiliar course—locomotion informs perception by providing critical data regarding origin, path, and orientation.

Gibson's ideas about the importance of orientation led him to question the mind–body dualism of behaviorists and cognitivists who treated the brain metaphorically as a mechanical device or computer and therefore made it seem reasonable to separate mind from body. Essentially, Gibson converted this ontological dualism into a useful tool to distinguish differences in observational conditions regarding stimulus variables (J. J. Gibson, 1979).

According to Reed (1988), this methodological innovation led Gibson to a novel distinction between *literal* and *schematic* perceptions. Gibson realized that laboratory psychophysical experiments are often arranged so that subjects will make the best observations of which they are capable, resulting in perception that is veridical and accurate—the "literal visual world." Experiments that employ impoverished or ambiguous stimulation or

that constrain observation time typically result in schematic perception. While such "quick and dirty" perception usually grasps the gist of situations, it is notoriously prone to inaccuracies and errors.

Perhaps Gibson's (1979) greatest doubt about information processing models was the emphasis they placed on analytical processing of stimulus information at the expense of processes involved in *detection* and *selection*. Thus, information processing models of the last three decades have tended to minimize the *context* of stimuli—their locality, temporality, and relatedness to other factors in the environment and in the organism.

10.4.1 Situation and Selectivity

In place of a sensation-based theory of perception, Gibson (1974/1982) proposed a theory based on situations and selectivity: Perception entails detecting information, not the experiencing of sensations. Rather than building his theories around an idealized perceiver, or an objective "God's Eye View" (Putnam, 1981), Gibson opted for a real, everyday perceiver, with all the possibilities and limitations implied by ordinary contexts. He situated this perceiver in an environment populated by ordinary, everyday people, living organisms, and natural as well as artificial affordances, rather than imagining the perceiver in an objectively accessible world defined and measured by conventional, mechanistic physics.

Gibson also appropriated familiar terms to create a new ecological vocabulary designed to complement the lexicon of physics (Reed, 1988):

1. Substances, surfaces, and media as complements for matter;
2. Persistence and change as complements for space and time;
3. Locomotion as a complement for motion; and
4. Situatedness in a niche as a complement for location in space and time.

Gibson's (1979) development of ecological theory began with studies of the properties of surfaces. He identified several issues that have become important to designers of virtual realities and simulations. He noted that surfaces are not discrete, detached objects but are nested within superordinate surfaces. According to Gibson, a surface does not have a location—a locus—as does an object, but is better thought of as situated relative to other surfaces in an "environmental layout" (1979, p. 351).

The concept of environmental layouts reflects a persistent concern expressed in the writings of ecological psychologists that successful systems of formal description and analysis employed by classical physics have been misapplied in describing fields of action and perception available to organisms.

There is little doubt that descriptions derived from classical physics are well suited to disciplines such as mechanical engineering and even biomechanics. Nevertheless, if we infer from thermodynamic principles that opportunities for action are ultimately determined by complexity of organization rather than space and time per se, then the usefulness of space–time grid maps for analyzing and explaining organic behavior is only partial. Such Cartesian representations can be complemented by environmental layout maps that indicate opportunities and pathways for action and perception.

Critics such as Fodor and Pylyshyn (1981) have questioned the empirical foundations of ecological psychology, demanding that its new lexicon be verified within the conventions of laboratory-bound experimentalism. On the other hand many ecological psychologists (e.g., Johansson, 1950; Koffka 1935; Lashly, 1951; McCabe, 1986; and Turvey, Shaw, Reed, & Mace,1981) share concerns with field biologists and anthropologists that excessive reliance on laboratory experiments often results in factual but misleading findings based on unrealistic contexts. Indeed, some of the most serious conceptual errors in the history of psychology—errors that misled researchers for decades—began with naive attempts to remove phenomena from their natural contexts. We would argue that context effects are impossible to eliminate, and that we should not try to eliminate them totally, but study them. There is no zero point in the flow of contexts. They are not merely incidental phenomena that confound experiments: They are quintessential in psychology. "There is no experience without context" (Baars, 1988, p. 176).

Like many other life scientists, Gibson (1979) had to defend his ideas against some fairly vociferous opponents. Many of his defenses were polemical. In our reading of his work, we have learned to tolerate an imprecision in terminology and syntax that unfortunately left his ideas and arguments open to misunderstanding and marginal criticism. Nevertheless, we believe Gibson's views on empiricism reflect the philosophical dispositions of many ecological psychologists and offer a basis for reconciling current conflicts between constructivist thinking and traditional scientific paradigms.

First, empiricism can be distinguished from objectivism. Eschewing objectivist theories of description need not imply abandonment of the scientific method, only rejection of unwarranted extensions that impute to human descriptions of reality a God-like objective status. Second, the risks of misunderstanding inherent in cultural relativism, objectivism, and scientism can be ameliorated if reports of empirical observations are taken as instructions to others about how to share, replicate, and verify findings and experiences rather than as veridical descriptions of reality.

10.4.2 Indirect Perception, Mediated Perception, and Distributed Cognition

Our species has invented various aids to perception, ways of improving, enhancing, or extending the pickup of information. The natural techniques of observation are supplemented by artificial techniques, *using tools for perceiving by analogy with tools for performing*. (J. J. Gibson, 1977/1982, p. 290; emphasis added)

Although he never developed a clear definition or theory of indirect perception, Gibson clearly considered it an important topic and recognized degrees of directness and indirectness. His writing on this issue, which consists mostly of unpublished notes, is inconsistent—as if he were still vacillating or cogitating about the idea. While we have found the concept of *direct perception* useful as an approximate synonym for perception that

is mostly automatic, we will only briefly summarize Gibson's views on indirect perception here.

According to Gibson, indirect perception is assisted perception: "the pick-up of the invariant in stimulation after continued observation" (1979, p. 250). Reed suggests that Gibson's preliminary efforts to distinguish direct and indirect forms of perception assumed that (a) ambient energy arrays within the environment (e.g., air pressure, light, gravity) provide the information that specifies affordance properties and (b) the availability of these arrays has shaped the evolution of perceptual systems. Gibson thought the exploratory actions of an organism engaged in perceiving energy arrays evidenced the organism's "awareness" that stimulus information specifies affordance properties relevant to the requirements of its niche. On the other hand, Gibson recognized that "simpler pictures" can also support direct perception.

Gibson referred to knowledge gained through language and numbers as *explicit* rather than direct and noted that "not all information about the world can be captured by them" (J. J. Gibson, 1977/1982, p. 293). Gibson also argued that symbols (i.e., *notational symbols* in Goodman's 1976 sense) are quite different from pictures and other visual arrays. He believed that symbols constitute perhaps the most extreme form of indirect perception because symbolic meanings are derived via association:

The meaning of an alphanumeric character or a combination of them fades away with prolonged visual fixation, unlike the meaning of a substance, surface, place, etc. . . . They make items that are unconnected with the rest of the world. Letters can stand for nonsense syllables (but there is no such thing as a nonsense place or a nonsense event). (1977/1982, p. 293)

Like other ecological psychologists, Gibson recognized the constructive nature of indirect perception, especially the important role that it plays in the creation and use of language. He argued that language helped fix perceptual understandings. However, since the range of possible discriminations in most situations is unlimited, selection is inevitable, "the observer can always observe more properties than he can describe" (J. J. Gibson, 1966, p. 282).

10.5 DISTRIBUTED COGNITION

We argued earlier that humans and other organisms may benefit from a thermodynamic "leverage" when they can off-load information storage and processing to nonbiological systems such as mediated representations and cognitive artifacts.

Such off-loading may require improved perception—more reliable access to external information. It is not always easy to compare the "costs" associated with internal and external representation because the information is often allocated dynamically between internal and external storage-processing systems. For example, after repeatedly forgetting some information item, one might decide to write it down (external, mediated representation), or alternatively, to make a deliberate effort to memorize it (internal representation). Computer designers and users similarly attempt to optimize dynamics of storage and processing between *internal* mechanisms (fast, but energy-consuming and volatile CPUs and RAMs) and *external* media (slow but energy-efficient and stable DVDs and CDs).

Where humans are concerned, such dynamic allocation of storage and processing can be modeled as *distributed cognitive tasks*—defined by Zhang and Norman (1994) as "tasks that require the processing of information across the internal mind and the external environment" (p. 88). Zhang and Norman conceive of a *distributed representation* as a set of representations with (a) *internal* members, such as schemas, mental images, or propositions, and (b) *external* members such as physical symbols and external rules or constraints embedded in physical configurations. *Representations* are abstract structures with referents to the represented world.

Zhang and Norman (1994) propose a theoretical framework in which internal and external representations form a "distributed representational space." Task structures and properties are represented in "abstract task space" (p. 90). Zhang and Norman developed this framework to support rigorous and formal analysis of distributed cognitive tasks and to assist their investigations of "representational effects [in which] different isomorphic representations of a common formal structure can cause dramatically different cognitive behaviors" (p. 88). Figure 10.3 freely adapts elements of the Zhang–Norman framework (1994, p. 90) by substituting MIROS for "internal representational space" and by further dividing external representational space into media (media space) and realia (real space).

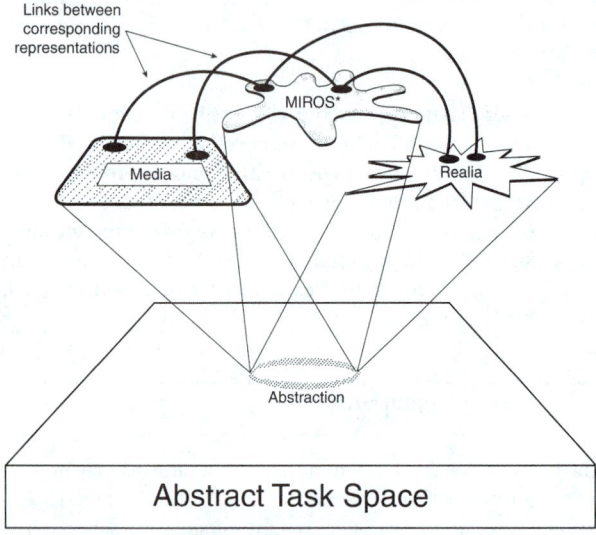

FIGURE 10.3. **A tripartite framework for distributing cognition among media, realia, and mental–internal representations of situations (MIROS).** Freely elaborated from Zhang and Norman (1994, p. 90), this framework subdivides external representational space into media space (media) and real space (realia). The framework does not assume that corresponding elements in three spaces will necessarily be isomorphic in function or structure. On the contrary, there are usually profound differences.

We do not propose in this chapter to rigorously define mutually exclusive categories for media and realia. There are many types of hybrids. Museums, for example, often integrate realia with explanatory diagrams and audio. Recursion is also a problem: A portrait of George Washington is of interest as a physical artifact and also as a mediated representation of a real person; a spreadsheet program may include representations of itself in online multimedia tutorials. Our modification of the Zhang–Norman framework distinguishes real space from media space nevertheless because there are often considerable differences between the affordance properties of realia and the affordance properties of media.

Our adaptation of the Zhang–Norman model does not assume that corresponding elements in the media space, real space, and internal representational space will necessarily be isomorphic in function or structure. On the contrary, there are often profound differences between the way information is structured in each space. Furthermore, as we noted earlier, MIROS vary in completeness and complexity. As Zhang and Norman (1994) demonstrated in their study of subjects attempting to solve the Tower of Hanoi problem, incongruent internal and external representations can interfere with task performance if critical aspects of the task structure are dependent on such congruence.

Whatever the degree of correspondences between the structures of media, MIROS, and realia, external representations allow individuals to distribute some of the burden of storing and processing information to nonbiological systems, presumably improving their individual thermodynamic efficiency. A key to intelligent interaction with a medium is to know how to optimize this distribution—to know when to manipulate a device, when to look something up (or write something down), and when to keep something in mind.

Of course media and realia can also support construction of MIROS that function more or less independently of interactions with external representational space. Salomon (1979, p. 234) used the term *supplantation* to refer to internalization of mediated representations as when viewers perform a task after watching a videotaped demonstration. Salomon thought of such learning by observation, not as a simple act of imitation, but as a process of elaboration that involves recoding of previously mastered constituent acts.

Distributed cognition informs the design of more efficient systems for supporting learning and performance. Yet new representational systems afforded by emergent computer and telecommunications technologies will challenge media researchers and designers to develop better models for determining which aspects of a given situation are best allocated to media or realia, and which are best allocated to MIROS.

10.6   MEDIA AND MIROS

To describe the evolutions or the dances of these gods, their juxtapositions and their advances, to tell which came into line and which in opposition, to describe all this without visual models would be labor spent in vain. (Plato, *The Timaeus*)

Gibson's (1977/1982) insights about visual displays remind us that, like other primates, humans have well-developed faculties for managing information about objects and spaces when that information is derived through locomotor and stereoscopic functions.

As mediated perception extends and substitutes for direct perception, so do the affordance properties of mediated environments extend and substitute for the affordance properties of real environments. Effective use of media requires that users understand implicit conventions and explicit instructions that guide them in constructing the MIROS required to compensate for missing affordance properties of mediated representations—the properties that are lost when such things are represented by text descriptions, pictures, functional simulations, and the like.

Media technologies impose profound constraints on representation of real or imaginary worlds and require tradeoffs as to which aspects of a world will be represented. A topographical map, for instance, represents 3-D landforms on a 2-D surface. For much of the 20th century such maps were constructed through electromechanical processes in which numerous aerial photos taken from different angles were reconciled to yield a single image. Aided by human interpreters, this process encoded some of the visual indications of affordance properties available to actual aerial observers—shadings, textures, angles, occlusions, for instance—as well as ways the values for these properties change in response to the observer's movement. The original affordance information—the climb-ability and walk-ability of the terrain, for example—was represented on the map as a flat image that indicated elevation through contour intervals and ground cover or other features through color coding. Much of the information detected by the aerial observer was thus available vicariously to map viewers, *provided* that the viewers could use the affordances of the map—contours, color coding, legends, grids—in concert with their mental models of map viewing to imagine the affordances of the actual terrain. Thus,

$$Media + MIROS \approx Realia.$$

Mediated habitats encompass a range of affordances and effectivities related to cognitive artifacts such as a book, a calculator, or a television. These artifacts do some of the work of storing and transforming information and thus lessen the user's need to construct or maintain more complex MIROS. But such artifacts also afford opportunities to engage in reasoning. "Reasoning is an activity that transforms a representation, and the representation affords that transformational activity" (Greeno, Moore, & Smith, 1993, p. 109).

10.6.1 Depiction

Pictorial representations of complex environments often pose problems for writers of captions and narratives. Picture captions also impose task-irrelevant cognitive processing burdens when readers must hunt through large bodies of text to find and correlate descriptions with depictions. A typical illustration (see

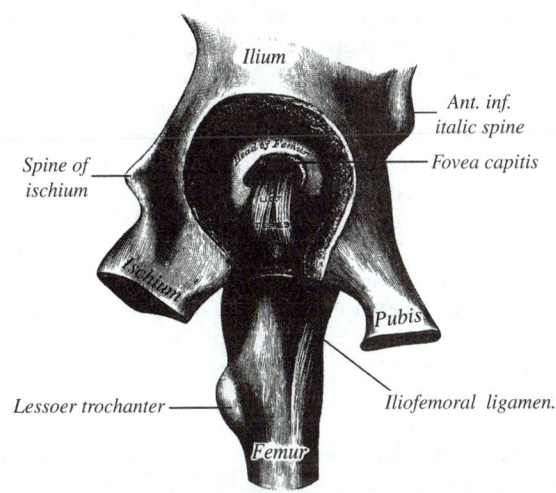

FIGURE 10.4. A drawing from *Gray's Anatomy* (1930, p. 334).

Fig. 10.4) and its caption from *Gray's Anatomy* (Gray, 1930, p. 334) makes it clear that, lacking information about the viewpoint of the artist, and lacking information about more subtle relationships between the components depicted in the drawing, viewers will be unable to construct a suitable MIROS to complement mediated representations.

Fortunately, anatomists have developed a rich lexicon for describing relationships between viewers and depictions. For example, the text description matched to the preceding figure from *Gray's* reads:

The ligament teres femoris is a triangular, somewhat flattened band implanted by its apex into [a small pit on the head of the femur]; its base is attached by two bands, one into either side of the ace tabular notch . . . (p. 334).

Using only propositions to tell people about how to construct a MIROS for a 3-D structure may be a misappropriation of cognitive resources if better means are feasible—a physical or pictorial model, for instance. The issue is partly a matter of instructional intent. Designers of an anatomy course might decide to use animated 3-D renderings of a situation—with orienting zooms and pans—to teach gross structure. If the goal is to teach spatial nomenclature as preparation for dissection through a particular structure, however, the designers might select a strategy with less emphasis on explicit visual representation of operations and more emphasis on narration. The two approaches are not mutually exclusive.

10.6.1.1 Photography. Consider the camera as a tool for capturing photographic images. A photograph excludes large quantities of information that would have been available to bystanders at the scene who could have exercised their powers of exploratory action, ranging from gross motor movements to tiny adjustments in eye lenses. To create a photographic image, the photographer selects a single viewpoint in space and time, one of many possible viewpoints.

A subsequent user of the photograph might be able to manipulate the position and orientation of the photo itself, take measurements of objects as they are depicted, and engage in selective visual exploration. However, such exploration will be an imperfect substitute for ambulatory perception at the original scene. Both the user's perception of the depictions in photographs and the user's interpretation of these depictions require prior knowledge of conventions of photographic culture as well as knowledge of ways in which photography distorts situational factors such as orientation, distance, texture, hue, contrast, and shadows. The user's ability to perceive and interpret the photo may be enhanced if he or she can integrate information in the photo with adjunct–verbal information such as captions, scales, and dates that, however inadequately, support development of MIROS complementary to depiction of the actual situation.

Scanning a photo is not the same as scanning a scene, although ecological psychologists will argue that much is similar about the two acts. Viewing a scene vicariously through a photo frees one of the need to monitor or respond immediately to events depicted in it—permitting, even promoting, reflection not possible at the scene.

10.6.1.2 Cinematography.

Cinematographs record the transformation of imagery as a camera moves through multiple viewpoints. Like photographs, cinematographs evoke mediated perceptions in the end user which are fundamentally decoupled from the exploratory ambulation that would have been possible in the actual situation. In other words, attention is partially decoupled from action and from intention: Viewers can attend to changes in imagery, but are unable to affect these changes or engage in exploratory actions.

Conventional cinematography substitutes camera dynamics for dimensionality by recording the way the appearance of objects transforms in response to motion parallax associated with camera movement. Reed (1988) suggests that more importantly cinematographs establish invariant structure by presenting the environment from many viewpoints. Filming multiple views of a scene helps viewers to construct MIROS representing the unchanging physical layout of objects and events.

However, film directors and editors must work carefully to orchestrate camera movement and shot sequences so they help viewers build a consistent understanding. Beginning film students fail to do this when they "cross the director's line" by splicing two shots of a scene taken from opposite positions on a set. By omitting a "traveling shot" showing the camera's movement from one side of the scene to the other, the spliced sequence will depict a strange violation of assumptions about the invariant structure: the whole environment will suddenly appear to flip horizontally so that actors and props on the left suddenly appear on the right and visa versa.

Reduced possibilities for ambulation when viewing conventional film and video remind us of the importance of exploration in mammalian perceptual development. Numerous studies demonstrate that interfering with proprioception and ambulation retards adaptation by mammalian visual systems. For example, when experimenters require human subjects to view their surroundings through an inverting prism apparatus, the subjects adapt to the upside-down imagery after several weeks, achieving a high degree of functionality and reporting that their vision seems "normal" again (Rock, 1984). This adaptation does not occur, however, if the experimenters restrict the subjects' kinesthetic and proprioceptive experience or subjects' ability to engage in self-controlled locomotion.

In a study more directly related to use of media in education and training, Baggett (1983) found that subjects who were denied an opportunity to explore the parts of a model helicopter were less effective at a parts-assembly task than subjects who explored the parts in advance—even though both types of subjects saw a videotape depicting the assembly process before performing the task.

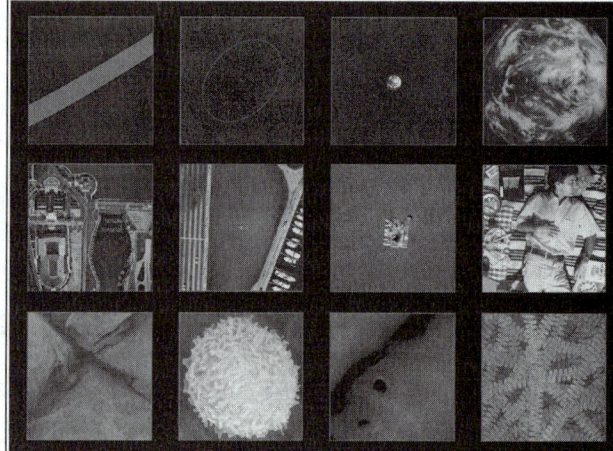

POWERS OF TEN:
LANGUAGE AND INDIRECT PERCEPTION

FIGURE 10.5. **Images from *Powers of Ten*** (courtesy of The Office of Charles and Ray Eames, http://www. powersof10.com)

The short film *Powers of Ten* (C. Eames & R. Eames, 1977/1986) offers a neatly constrained example of language as an aid to interpreting mediated representations. Created by the Office of Charles and Ray Eames to help viewers grasp "the relative size of things in the universe," *Powers of Ten* opens on a picnic blanket in Chicago, initiating a trip that takes the viewer to the farthest reaches of universe and back. The trip ends nine and one-half minutes later, in the nucleus of a carbon atom embedded in the hand of a man lying on the blanket. The film version of *Powers of Ten* is now available in CD-ROM and DVD versions with extensive collateral material.

Such a visual experience would be meaningless for many viewers without a verbal narrative guiding interpretations of the film's rapidly changing imagery which includes diverse depictions ranging from galaxies, to the solar system, to Lake Superior, to a cell nucleus, to the DNA double helix. The book version of *Powers of Ten* (Philip Morrison & Phylis Morrison, 1982) displays 42 frames from the film, supplemented by elaborative text and supplementary photos. The authors use a set of "rules" (pp. 108–110) to describe the film's representation of situations including propositions such as . . .

Rule 1. The traveler moves along a straight line, never leaving it.

Rule 2. One end of that line lies in the darkness of outermost space while the other is on the earth in Chicago, within a carbon atom beneath the skin of a man asleep in the sun.

Rule 3. Each square picture along the journey shows the view one would see looking toward the carbon atom's core, views that would encompass wider and wider scenes as the traveler moves further away. Because the journey is along a straight line, every picture contains all the pictures that are between it and the nucleus of the carbon atom . . .

Rule 4. Although the scenes are all viewed from one direction, the traveler may move in either direction, going inward toward the carbon atom or outward toward the galaxies . . .

Rule 5. The rule for the distance between viewpoints [is that] . . . each step is multiplied by a fixed number to produce the size of the next step: The traveler can take small, atom-sized steps near the atom, giant steps across Chicago, and planet-, star-, and galaxy-sized steps within their own realms.

The Morrison rules can be taken as an invitation to propositional reasoning. Yet the rules can also be construed as instructions for constructing a MIROS that complements and partially overlaps the work of representation carried out by the film. Rule 2, for example, provides a framework for the reader to imagine moving back and forth on the straight line connecting the starting point (outermost space) and ending point (carbon nucleus), thus substituting for the action of the imaginary camera "dollying" (moving forward) across outer and finally inner space. Rule 3 describes the way in which each square picture encompasses a wider or narrower scene.

Rules 2 and 3 can also be directly perceived in the film itself by attending to the symmetricalness of image flow as various objects and structures stream from a fixed center point and move at equal rates toward the edge of the visual field. The film also depicts movement via changes in the texture gradients of star fields and other structures. Such cues to both movement and direction epitomize the appropriation by filmmakers and other media producers of visual processing capabilities that are widespread among vertebrates, and as common among humans as a jog on a forest trail or a drive down a two-lane highway.

What viewers cannot obtain by direct perception of either the film or the photos, however, is information indicating deceleration of the hypothetical camera as it dollies toward earth. Rule 5, which concerns the logarithm governing the speed of camera motion, cannot be perceived directly because (a) the camera motion simulates a second-order derivative (deceleration rather than speed) that humans cannot distinguish from gravity and (b) because the objects flowing past the camera are largely unfamiliar in everyday life and therefore have little value as scalars.

10.6.2 Collapsing Multivariate Data

The limitations of photography and cinematography reflect the central challenge for authors and designers of other media products: how to collapse multivariate data into flat, 2-D displays while optimizing the ability of the end user to exploit the affordances of the displays.

As Tufte explains in *Envisioning Information* (1992), techniques for collapsing multivariate data to paper-based representations involve opportunities as well as constraints. Yet Tufte believes most of our methods for representing multidimensional data on 2-D surfaces are a hodgepodge of conventions and "particularistic" solutions. "Even our language, like our paper, often lacks immediate capacity to communicate a sense of dimensional complexity" (p. 15). Tufte quotes Paul Klee on this issue: "It is not easy to arrive at a conception of a whole which is constructed from parts belonging to different dimensions . . . For with such a medium of expression, we lack the means of discussing in its constituent parts, an image which possesses simultaneously a number of dimensions" (cited in Tufte, 1992, p. 15). On the other hand, as Tufte so richly illustrates, tradeoffs so necessary to successful compression of a data set with four or five variables into a 2-D representation may serve the end user very well if the sacrificed data would have been confusing or superfluous.

Regardless of medium, designers and producers must always sacrifice options for exploratory action that would have been available to unimpeded observers or actors in the represented situation. Media cannot represent realia in all their repleteness. What is critical is that enough information be provided so that users can construct useful, actionable mental models appropriate to their needs and goals.

10.6.3 Distributed Cognition and the Construction of Physics Understanding

How might educational product designers apply the tripartite framework of distributed cognition reflected in Fig. 10.3? Constructing Physics Understanding (CPU) represents a rethinking of the relationship between media, mental models, and realia as well as a rethinking of the roles of students and teachers (CPU, 2002). Led by San Diego State University professor Fred Goldberg, the CPU development team designed a physics curriculum based on student investigations of the interplay between experiments involving real and simulated laboratory apparatus.

These apparatus simulators include special part and layout editors that allow students considerable flexibility in varying the organizations and components of any particular apparatus. Students can use the simulator to view a particular layout in different modalities, each with its own representational conventions.

A current electricity simulator, for example, allows students to connect various types of virtual batteries, bulbs, and switches in different combinations and thereby test theories of current flow. One view of the simulator represents the components and interconnections fairly concretely as "pictorial" representations seen from a high angle and rendered with simplified color, shading, and depth cues. The students can also switch to a formal circuit diagram representing the same setup. When students make changes in one view, these changes are immediately updated in the other view. However, only the pictorial view represents events such as the illumination of a light bulb.

This approach provides opportunities to correlate different representations of similar setups and to reconcile differences in representational conventions. The students come to learn, for example, that while illuminating a "real" or "pictorial" bulb requires that it be connected to a battery with two wires, the corresponding circuit diagram represents these wires with a single line.

CPU designers also struggle to reconcile differences in representational capabilities. Illumination of bulbs in the real apparatus for studying electrical currents ranges from a dull red glow to white hot. But computer monitors used to display the pictorial representations typically have fairly limited contrast ratios and are thus unable to fully simulate this range of luminosity.

The primary purpose of the CPU curriculum is to support science learning through experimentation and discourse. Students are responsible for the development and critical evaluation of ideas, models, and explanations through interactions with each other in small groups.

Teachers act as guides and mentors. During the "elicitation phase" of a particular unit, CPU challenges students to predict the results of other hands-on experiments with other phenomena such as waves and sound, force and motion, and light and color.

Students articulate their models (MIROS)—including prior knowledge, ideas, assumptions, and preconceptions—related to the featured phenomena. They then use real apparatus (realia) to conduct traditional experiments, often revealing their misconceptions when their predictions fail. Then they pursue new ideas using simulated apparatus (media) that emulate, with an appropriate degree of functional fidelity, properties and behaviors associated with the featured phenomena.

The students abandon ideas that don't work and construct new theories and models to explain what they observe in the simulated experiments. During the "application" phase of the curriculum, students further explore the featured phenomena by conducting experiments of their own design using the lab apparatus, computer simulations, and other resources to further refine their mental models and clarify their understanding.

10.6.4 Media as Arenas for Unified Perception and Action

Emerging media systems and technologies appear headed toward a technical renaissance that could free media products from constraints that now limit end users: the static symbols and limited dimensionality of paper and ink; the shadows captured and cast from a single point of view in photographs and films; and the fixed sequences and pacing of analog broadcast technology.

Paradoxically, trends toward ever more rapid and extensive externalization of cognitive functions in nonbiological media leaves us as creatures with an ancient, largely fixed core of perception–action modalities surrounded by rapidly fluctuating and increasingly powerful technological augmentation frameworks. Thus, whether emergent media technologies serve human beings well depends on the extent to which they honor ancient human capabilities for perceiving and acting—capabilities that are grounded in the fundamental ecological necessities of long ago.

10.6.4.1 *Alienation and Transformation.* While glib marketers of computer-based media tantalize us with vast fields of electronic action and apparently unlimited degrees of freedom, skeptics (W. Gibson, 1984; Mander, 1978; McKibbin, 1989) have served up warnings of isolation, manipulation, and diminished authenticity that can be traced back through McLuhan (1965) to Rousseau's (1764/1911) classic treatise on alienation from nature.

Much public discussion of the limitations and negative effects of so-called "passive" media such as television implicitly acknowledges both the epistemological and moral dimensions of mediated experience. During the 1990s some advocates of multimedia technology argued that interactivity might help address the putative problems of an obese couch potato nation that mindlessly surfs television channels in search of sex and violence. Such advocacy was partly based on the assumption that somehow interactivity would empower viewers with more choices and promote a greater awareness and understanding of nature and culture.

The hope of human history has often been that technological augmentation would make us gods or angels or at least make us superior to enemies and aliens. Media technologies and the cognitive artifacts associated with them have played a special role in this regard by offering seductive possibilities of transformation: more than mere augmentation, a permanent acquisition of special knowledge and experience through recorded sounds and images. Yet receiving the word or beholding a revelation, whether real or artifactual, without active and appropriate participation risks distorted understanding and resultant alienation. Recognition of such risks underlay the prohibition of graven images that has figured strongly in Judaic, Islamic, and Buddhist religious traditions. And in Christianity, doubts about religious imagery peaked in the eighth century with the radical proscriptions of the iconoclasts, who wanted to eliminate all religious depictions as demonic; such doubts dampened Western artistic exploration until the Renaissance.

For humans and all organisms, integration of action with perception is a necessary but not sufficient condition for living well. "Perception is the mechanism that functions to inform the actor of the means the environment affords for realizing the actor's goals" (Turvey, Shaw, Reed, & Mace, 1982, p. 378). Perceptual faculties languish and degrade when they are decoupled from opportunities for action. Separated from action, perception cannot serve as a basis for formulating hypotheses and principles,

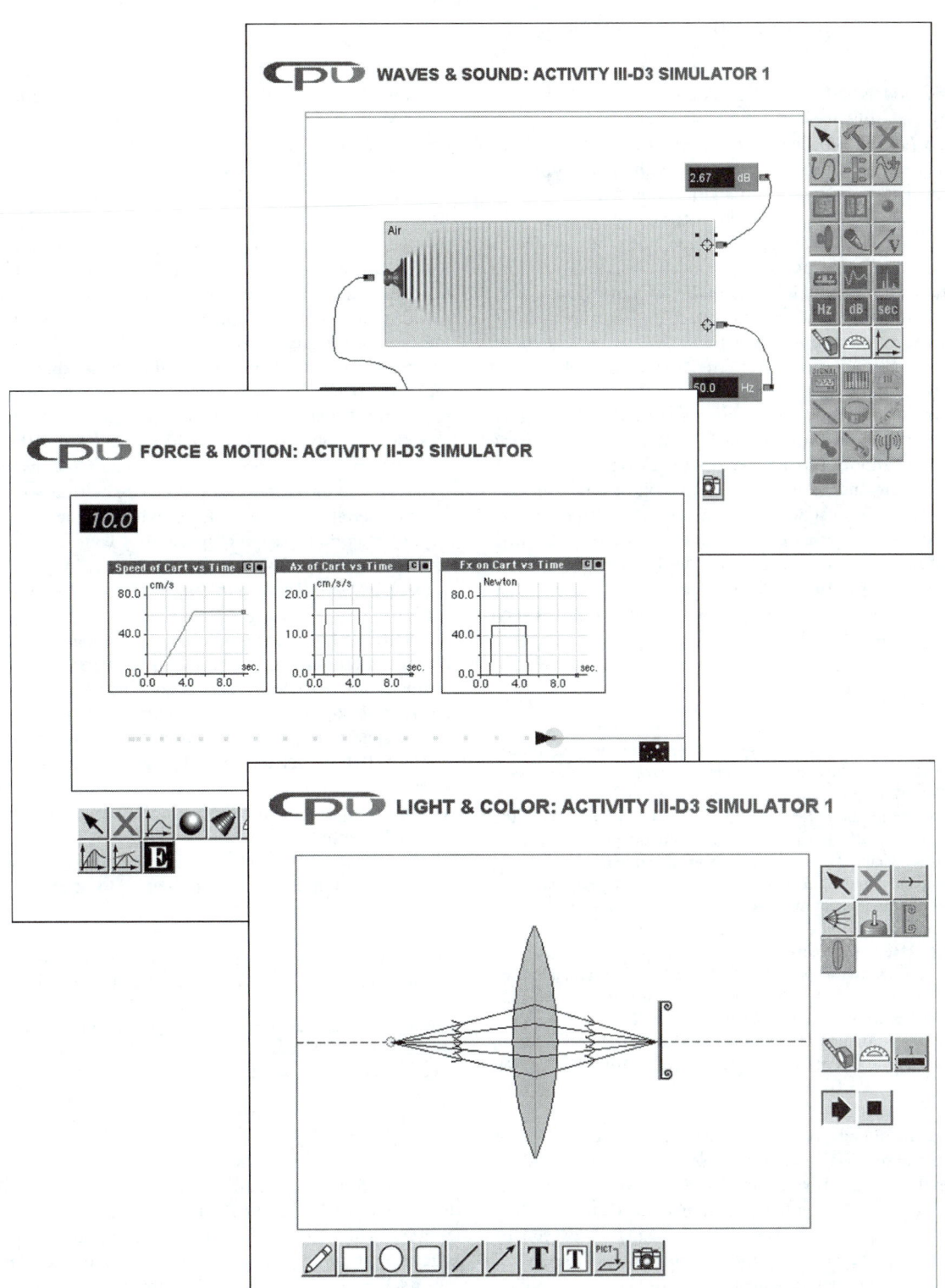

FIGURE 10.6. **Sample simulator screens from** *Constructing Physics Understanding.* These Java applets complement hands-on laboratory activities in a wide variety of contexts, providing students with both phenomenological and conceptual (model-based) evidence that helps them develop mental models with greater robustness and predictive validity. *For more information, see http://cpuproject.sdsu.edu/CPU*

for testing models and theories, for choosing alternatives, or for exploring consequences.

Indeed, Eleanor Gibson (1994) has reviewed a growing body of evidence which strongly suggests that without opportunities for action, or appropriate substitutes for action, perception does not develop at all or takes on wildly distorted forms. Behavioral capabilities likewise languish and degrade when they are decoupled from perception. "Action is the mechanism that functions to select the means by which goals of the actor may be effected" (Turvey, Shaw, Reed, & Mace, 1982, p. 378). Deprived of information concerning opportunities for action, perception alone results in ritualistic performance unrelated to any real task and hence any realizable goal.

It is worth noting in this context that *sin* in the original Christian sense of the word meant *to miss the mark,* implying a failure that cannot be assigned to either action or perception alone. A similar understanding of the incompleteness of perception isolated from action can be found in other traditions—notably Zen (see, for example, Herrigel's 1953 classic *Zen and the Art of Archery*). Many meditative disciplines teach integration of perception and action by training students to unify attention (perception) and intention (action), using exercises such as "following one's breathing."

Caves and Consciousness

We need to move from our exclusive concern with the logic of processing, or reason, to the logic of perception. Perception is the basis of wisdom. For twenty-four centuries we have put all our intellectual effort into the logic of reason rather than the logic of perception. Yet in the conduct of human affairs perception is far more important. Why have we made this mistake? We might have believed that perception did not really matter and could in the end be controlled by logic and reason. We did not like the vagueness, subjectivity and variability of perception and sought refuge in the solid absolutes of truth and logic. To some extent the Greeks created logic to make sense of perception. We were content to leave perception to the world of art (drama, poetry, painting, music, dance) while reason got on with its own business in science, mathematics, economics and government. We have never understood perception. Perceptual truth is different from constructed truth. (Edward de Bono, *I Am Right—You are Wrong: From Rock Logic to Water Logic,* 1991, p. 42)

Among the ancient perplexities associated with the human condition, the relationship between perception, action, and environment has endured even as technical context and consciousness have continued to evolve. In the annals of Western Civilization, Plato's Allegory of The Cave (Plato, *The Republic*) remains one of the most elegant and compelling treatments of the central issues. Chained and therefore unable to move, his cave-dwelling prisoners came to perceive shadows cast on the walls by firelight as real beings rather than phantasms. Why? Plato argues that this profound misperception resulted from external as well as internal conditions.

First consider the external conditions: We will take some license in imagining that if the prisoners were rigidly bound and deprived of ambulatory vision, then they were probably (a) denied the cues of motion parallax that might have indicated the two-dimensionality of the shadows; (b) suffering from degraded stereopsis and texture recognition due to lighting conditions; and (c) incapacitated in their ability to investigate the source of illumination or its relationship to the props that were casting the shadows that captured their imagination.

Many readers of Plato's allegory have been tempted to assume that they would not personally be fooled in such a situation, leading us to consider the internal conditions: With a rudimentary knowledge of optics and commonsense understanding of caves, it might have been possible for the prisoners to entertain plausible alternatives to their belief that the shadows were real beings. For the prisoners to entertain such an alternative would have required that they be able to construct a model of the situation that would be "runnable," that is, serve as an internal analog for the physical actions of inspecting the layout of the cave, the pathways of light, and so on. In our (re)interpretation of Plato's Cave, what doomed the prisoners to misperception was not only that they were constrained from exploratory action by external conditions, but also that they were unable to integrate working mental models with what they saw.

Plato's allegory involves both epistemological and moral dimensions. Epistemology considers problems involved in representing knowledge and reality (knowing–perceiving), whereas moral philosophy considers problems involved in determining possible and appropriate action (knowing–acting). Plato reminds us that perceiving and acting are complementary and inseparable: The prisoners cannot perceive appropriately without acting appropriately, and they cannot act appropriately without perceiving appropriately.

Alan Kay (1991) summarized our thoughts about this dilemma as it applies to contemporary education over a decade ago:

Up to now, the contexts that give meaning and limitation to our various knowledges have been all but invisible. To make contexts visible, make them objects of discourse and make them explicitly reshapable and inventable are strong aspirations very much in harmony with the pressing needs and on-rushing changes of our own time. It is therefore the duty of a well-conceived environment for learning to be contentious and even disturbing, seek contrasts rather than absolutes, aim for quality over quantity and acknowledge the need for will and effort. (p. 140)

Who knows what Plato would say about the darkened cave-like structures we call movie theaters and home entertainment centers, where viewers watch projections cast upon a wall or screen, only dimly aware of the original or true mechanics of the events they perceive? Our ability to interpret the shadowy phantasms of modern cinema and television is constrained not only by collapsed affordances of cinematography—two-dimensional, fixed-pace sequencing of images—but also by the lack of affordances for exercising action and observing consequences. We also often lack the mental models that might allow us to work through in our minds alternatives that are not explored on the screen. Yet even when we possess such mental models, it is often impossible to "run" or test them due to interference from the relentless parade of new stimuli. And as McLuhan (1965) noted in the middle of the last century, we frequently succumb to the unconscious inhibition that attends most television and movie watching: Reflect too much on what you observe and you will be left behind as the medium unfolds its plans at a predetermined pace.

ACKNOWLEDGMENTS

The authors wish to thank Sarah N. Peelle and Barbara E. Allen for their assistance in editing this chapter. Kris Rodenberg was particularly helpful in revising the text of this second edition of the chapter to make it more readable. Thanks are also due to David Kirsh, William Montague, Dan Cristianez, George W. Cox, David W. Allen, and Kathleen M. Fisher for offering advice on the first edition of this chapter (without holding them responsible for the final results).

Research for this chapter was partially supported by a fellowship from the American Society for Engineering Education and the Naval Personnel Research and Development Center, San Diego. Opinions expressed by the authors do not necessarily reflect the policies or views of these funding organizations.

References

Allen, B. S. (1991). Virtualities. In B. Branyan-Broadbent & R. K. Wood (Eds.), *Educational Media and Technology Yearbook, 17*(pp. 47–53). Englewood, CO: Libraries Unlimited.

Anderson, J. R. (1983). *The architecture of cognition*. Cambridge, MA: Harvard University.

Baars, B. J. (1988). *A cognitive theory of consciousness*. Cambridge, England: Cambridge University Press.

Baggett, P. (1983). *Learning a procedure for multimedia instructions: The effects of films and practice* (Eric No. ED239598). Boulder, CO: Colorado University Institute of Cognitive Science.

Balzano, G. J., & McCabe, V. (1986). An ecological perspective on concepts and cognition. In V. McCabe & G. J. Balzano (Eds.), *Event cognition* (pp. 133–158). Hillsdale, NJ: Lawrence Erlbaum Associates.

Bartlett, F. C. (1932). *Remembering*. Cambridge, England: Cambridge University Press.

Berk, L. E. (1994). Why children talk to themselves. *Scientific American, 271*(5), 78–83.

Bruce, V., & Green, P. (1990). *Visual perception: Physiology, psychology, and ecology* (2nd ed.). Hillsdale, NJ: Lawrence Erlbaum Associates.

Bruner, J. S., & Olson, D. R. (1977–78). Symbols and texts as tools for the intellect. *Interchange, 8*, 1–15.

Carroll, J. M., & Olson, D. R. (1988). Mental models in human–computer interaction. In M. Helander (Ed.), *Handbook of human–computer interaction*. Amsterdam: Elsevier.

Churchland, P. S. (1986). *Neurophilosophy: Towards a unified theory of the mind-brain*. Cambridge, MA: MIT Press.

Clancey, W. J. (1993). Situated action: A neuropsychological interpretation. *Cognitive Science,* 17, 87–116.

Clark, A. (1991). *Microcognition: Philosophy, cognitive science, and parallel distributed processing*. Cambridge, MA: MIT Press.

Clark, R. E. (1983). Reconsidering research on learning from media. *Review of Educational Research, 53*, 445–459.

Collins, A., Brown, J. S., & Newman, S. E. (1989). Cognitive apprenticeship: Teaching the crafts of reading, writing, and mathematics. In L. B. Resnick (Ed.), *Knowing, learning, and instruction: Essays in honor of Robert Glaser* (pp. 453–494). Hillsdale, NJ: Lawrence Erlbaum Associates.

CPU. (2002). *CPU Project: Constructing Physics Understanding*. San Diego State University. Retrieved April 16, 2002 from http://cpuproject.sdsu.edu/CPU

Craik, K. (1943). *The nature of explanation*. Cambridge, England: Cambridge University Press.

Crutcher, K. A. (1986). Anatomical correlates of neuronal plasticity. In J. L. Martinez & R. P. Kesner (Eds.), *Learning and memory: A biological view*. New York: Academic Press.

Csikszentmihalyi, M. (1990). *Flow: The psychology of optimal experience*. New York: Harper Perennial.

De Bono, E. (1991). *I am right—You are wrong: From rock logic to water logic*. New York: Viking/Penguin.

de Saint Exupéry, A. (1939/1967). *Wind, sand, and stars*. Fort Washington, PA: Harvest Books.

di Sessa, A. (1983). Phenomenology and the evolution of intuition. In D. Gentner & A. L. Stevens (Eds.), *Mental models*. Hillsdale, NJ: Lawrence Erlbaum Associates.

di Sessa, A. (1988). Knowledge in pieces. In G. Froman & P. Pufrall (Eds.), *Constructivism in the computer age*. Hillsdale, NJ: Lawrence Erlbaum Associates.

Donald, M. (1991). *Origins of the modern mind: Three stages in the evolution of culture and cognition*. Cambridge, MA: Harvard University Press.

Eames, C., & Eames, R. (Producers). (1986). Powers of ten: A film dealing with the relative size of things in the universe and the effect of adding another zero. In M. Hagino (Executive Producer) & Y. Kawahara (Producer/Director), *The world of Charles and Ray Eames* [videodisc], Chapter 3. Tokyo, Japan: Pioneer Electronic Corporation. (Original work published 1977.)

Fodor, J. A., & Pylyshyn, S. W. (1981). How direct is visual perception? Some reflections on Gibson's ecological approach. *Cognition, 9*, 139–196.

Gardner, H. (1987). *The mind's new science: A history of the cognitive revolution*. New York: Basic Books, Inc.

Gatlin, L. L. (1972). *Information theory and the living system*. New York: Columbia University Press.

Gentner, D., & Gentner, D. R. (1983). Flowing waters or teeming crowds: Mental models of electricity. In D. Gentner & A. L. Stevens (Eds.), *Mental models*. Hillsdale, NJ: Lawrence Erlbaum Associates.

Gentner, D., & Stevens, A. L. (Eds.). (1983). *Mental models*. Hillsdale, NJ: Lawrence Erlbaum Associates.

Gibson, E. J. (1969). *Principles of perceptual learning and development*. New York: Appleton Century-Crofts.

Gibson, E. J. (1994). Has psychology a future? *Psychological Science, 5*, 69–76.

Gibson, J. J. (1950). *The perception of the visual world*. Boston: Houghton-Mifflin.

Gibson, J. J. (1960). The concept of stimulus in psychology. *American Psychologist, 17*, 23–30.

Gibson, J. J. (1966). *The senses considered as perceptual systems*. Boston: Houghton-Mifflin.

Gibson, J. J. (1971/1982). A note on problems of vision to be resolved. In E. Reed & R. Jones (Eds.), *Reasons for realism: Selected essays of James J. Gibson* (pp. 391–396). Hillsdale, NJ: Lawrence Erlbaum Associates. (Unpublished manuscript, Spring, 1971.)

Gibson, J. J. (1974/1982). A note on current theories of perception. In E. Reed & R. Jones (Eds.), *Reasons for realism: Selected essays of James J. Gibson* (pp. 370–373). Hillsdale, NJ: Lawrence Erlbaum Associates.(Unpublished manuscript, July, 1974.)

Gibson, J. J. (1977/1982). Notes on direct perception and indirect apprehension. In E. Reed & R. Jones (Eds.), *Reasons for realism: Selected essays of James J. Gibson* (pp. 289–293). Hillsdale, NJ: Lawrence Erlbaum Associates. (Unpublished manuscript, May, 1977.)

Gibson, J. J. (1979). *The ecological approach to visual perception*. Boston: Houghton-Mifflin.

Gibson, W. (1984). *Neuromancer*. New York: Berkeley Publications Group.

Goodman, N. (1976). *Languages of art*. Indianapolis, IN: Bobbs-Merrill.

Gordon, S. E. (1994). *Systematic training program design: maximizing effectiveness and minimizing liability*. Englewood Cliffs, NJ: Prentice Hall.

Gray, H. (1930). *Anatomy of the human body* (22nd edition). New York: Lea & Febiger.

Greeno, J. G. (1989). Situations, mental models, and generative knowledge. In D. Klahr & K. Kotovsky (Eds.), *Complex information processing*. Hillsdale, NJ: Lawrence Erlbaum Associates.

Greeno, J. G. (1991). Mathematical cognition: Accomplishments and challenges in research. In R. R. Hoffman & D. S. Palermo (Eds.), *Cognition and the symbolic processes: Applied and ecological perspectives* (pp. 255–281). Hillsdale, NJ: Lawrence Erlbaum Associates.

Greeno, J. G. (1994). Gibson's affordances. *Psychological Review, 101,* 336–342.

Greeno, J. G., Moore, J. L., & Smith, D. R. (1993). Transfer of situated learning, In: D. K. Detterman & R. J. Sternberg (Eds). *Transfer on trial: intelligence, cognition and instruction*. Norwood, N. J.: Ablex, pp. 99–167.

Gregory, R. L. (1987). *The Oxford companion to the mind*. Oxford: Oxford University Press.

Hawkins, D. (1964). *The language of nature: An essay in the philosophy of science*. San Francisco: W.H. Freeman & Company.

Herrigel, E. (1953). *Zen in the art of archery* (R. F. C. Hull, trans.). New York: Pantheon Books.

Hochberg, J. (1974). Higher-order stimuli and inter-response coupling in the perception of the visual world. In R. B. MacLeod & H. L. Pick, Jr. (Eds.), *Perception: Essays in honor of James J. Gibson* (pp. 17–39). Ithaca, NY: Cornell University Press.

Hoffman, B. et al. (2002). *The mystery of the mission museum*. San Diego State University. Retrieved April 16, 2002, from http://mystery.sdsu.edu

Johansson, G. (1950). *Configurations in event perception*. Uppsala, Sweden: Almqvist & Wiksell.

Johnson, M. (1987). *The body in the mind: The bodily basis of meaning, imagination, and reason*. Chicago: The University of Chicago Press.

Johnson-Laird, P. N. (1983). *Mental models*. Cambridge, England: Cambridge University Press.

Kant, I. (1781/1966). *The critique of pure reason* (2nd ed., F. Max Muller, Trans.). New York: Anchor Books.

Kay, A. (1991). Computer networks and education. *Scientific American, 265*(3), 138–148.

Koffka, K. (1935). *Principles of gestalt psychology*. New York: Harcourt-Brace.

Kosslyn, S. M., & Koenig, O. (1992). *Wet mind: The new cognitive neuroscience*. New York: Free Press.

Kugler, P. N., Shaw, R. E., Vicente, K. J., & Kinsella-Shaw, J. (1991). The role of attractors in the self-organization of intentional systems. In R. R. Hoffman & D. S. Palermo (Eds.), *Cognition and the symbolic processes: Applied and ecological perspectives* (pp. 371–387). Hillsdale, NJ: Lawrence Erlbaum Associates.

Kupfermann, I. (1991). Learning and memory. In E. R. Kandel, J. H. Schwartz, & T. S. Jessell (Eds.), *Principles of neural science* (3rd ed.). Norwalk, CT: Appleton & Lange.

Larkin J., & Simon, H. (1987). Why a diagram is (sometimes) worth ten thousand words. *Cognitive Science, 11,* 65–100.

Lashly, K. S. (1951). The problem of serial order in behavior. In L. A. Jeffress (Ed.), *Cerebral mechanism in behavior*. New York: Hafner.

Laurel, B. K. (1986). *The art of human–computer interface design*. Reading, MA: Addison-Wesley.

Lave, J. (1988). *Cognition in practice*. Cambridge, England: Cambridge University Press.

MacKay, D. M. (1991). *Behind the eye*. Cambridge, MA: Basil Blackwell, Inc.

Mander, J. (1978). *Four arguments for the elimination of television*. New York: Quill.

Mark, L. S., Dainoff, M. J., Moritz, & Vogele, D. (1991). An ecological framework for ergonomic research and design. In R. R. Hoffman & D. S. Palermo (Eds.), *Cognition and the symbolic processes: Applied and ecological perspectives* (pp. 477–507). Hillsdale, NJ: Lawrence Erlbaum Associates.

Martin, J. (1993). *Principles of object-oriented analysis and design*. Englewood Cliffs, NJ: Prentice Hall.

Maturana, H. R. (1978). Biology of language: The epistemology of reality. In G. A. Miller & E. Lenneberg (Eds.), *Psychology and biology of language and thought: Essays in honor of Eric Lenneberg*. New York: Academic Press.

Maturana, H. R., & Varela, F. J. (1980). *Autopoesis and cognition: The realization of the living*. Dordrecht, The Netherlands: Reidel.

McCabe, V. (1986). The direct perception of universals: A theory of knowledge acquisition. In V. McCabe & G. J. Balzano (Eds.), *Event cognition* (pp. 29–44). Hillsdale, NJ: Lawrence Erlbaum Associates.

McCabe, V., & Balzano, G. J. (Eds.). (1986). *Event cognition*. Hillsdale, NJ: Lawrence Erlbaum Associates.

McKean, M., Allen, B. S., & Hoffman, B. (2000, April 27). Sequential data analysis: Implications for assessment of usability in virtual museums. In Janette Hill (Chair), *Learning in Virtual and Informal Learning Environments*. Symposium Conducted at the Annual Meeting of the American Educational Research Association, New Orleans.

McKibbin, B. (1989). *The end of nature*. New York: Random House.

McLuhan, M. (1965). *Understanding media: The extensions of man*. New York: Bantam Books.

Minsky, M. (1985). *Society of mind*. New York: Simon & Schuster.

Morrison, Philip, & Morrison, Phylis. (1982). *Powers of ten*. New York: W. H. Freeman and Company.

MSN Encarta (2002). *Encarta world dictionary* (North American Edition) Retrieved from *http://dictionary.msn.com*

Neisser, U. (1976). *Cognition and reality*. San Fransico: W. H. Freeman.

Neisser, U. (1991). Direct perception and other forms of knowing. In R. R. Hoffman & D. S. Palermo (Eds.), *Cognition and the symbolic processes: Applied and ecological perspectives* (pp. 17–33). Hillsdale, NJ: Lawrence Erlbaum Associates.

Nichols, B. (1991). *Representing reality: Issues and concepts in documentary*. Bloomington, IN: Indiana University Press.

Norman, D. A. (1990). *The design of everyday things*. New York: Currency/Doubleday.

Norman, D. A. (1993). *Things that make us smart*. Reading, MA: Addison-Wesley.

Norman, D. A., & Rumelhart, D. E. (1975). *Explorations in cognition*. San Fransico: W. H. Freeman.

Payne, S. J. (1992). On mental models and cognitive artifacts. In Y. Rogers, A. Rutherford & P. Bibby (Eds.), *Models in the mind: Theory, perspective, and application*. New York: Academic Press.

Piaget, J. (1971). *Biology and knowledge: An essay on the relations between organic regulations and cognitive processes*. Chicago: University of Chicago Press.

Putnam, H. (1981). *Reason, truth and history*. Cambridge, England: Cambridge University Press.

Real, M. R. (1989). *Super media: A culutral studies approach*. Newbury Park, CA: Sage Publications.

Reed, E. S. (1988). *James J. Gibson and the psychology of perception*. New Haven, CT: Yale University Press.

Reed, E. S., & Jones, R. (Eds.). (1982). *Reasons for realism: Selected essays of James J. Gibson*. Hillsdale, NJ: Lawrence Erlbaum Associates.

Reference Software [Computer software]. (1993). *Random House Webster's electronic dictionary & thesaurus*. New York: Random House.

Rheingold, H. (1991). *Virtual reality*. New York: Simon & Schuster.

Rock, I. (1984). *Perception*. New York: Scientific American Library.

Rosch, E. (1978). Principles of categorization. In E. Rosch & B. B. Lloyd (Eds.), *Cognition and categorization*. Hillsdale, NJ: Lawrence Erlbaum Associates.

Rouse, W. B., & Morris, N. M. (1986). On looking into the black box: Prospects and limits in the search for mental models. *Psychological Bulletin, 100*, 349-363.

Rousseau, J. J. (1764/1911). *Emile*. (B. Foxley, Trans.). New York: Dutton.

Salomon, G. (1979). *Interaction of media, cognition, and learning*. San Francisco: Jossey-Bass.

Shannon, C., & Weaver, W. (1949). *The mathematical theory of communication*. Urbana, IL: University of Illinois Press.

Shaw, R. E., & Hazelett, W. M. (1986). Schemas in cognition. In V. McCabe & G. J. Balzano (Eds.), *Event cognition*. Hillsdale, NJ: Lawrence Erlbaum Associates.

Shaw, R. E., Mace, W. M., & Turvey, M. T. (1986). Resources for ecological psychology. In V. McCabe & G. J. Balzano (Eds.), *Event cognition*. Hillsdale, NJ: Lawrence Erlbaum Associates.

Shaw, R. E., Turvey, M. T., & Mace, W. M. (1982). Ecological psychology: The consequences of a commitment to realism. In W. Wiemer & D. Palermo

(Eds.), *Cognition and the symbolic processes* II. Hillsdale, NJ: Lawrence Erlbaum Associates.

Shiffrin, R. & Schneider, W. (1977). Controlled and automatic human information processing II. *Psychological Review, 84.* 127-190.

Sternberg, R. J. (1977). *Intelligence, information processing and analogical reasoning*. Hillsdale, NJ: Lawrence Erlbaum Associates.

Suchman, L. A. (1987). *Plans and situated actions: The problem of human-machine communications*. Cambridge, England: Cambridge University Press.

Tufte, E. R. (1992). *Envisioning information*. Cheshire, CN: Graphic Press.

Turvey, M. T., & Shaw, R. E. (1979). The primacy of perceiving: An ecological reformulation of perception for understanding memory. In L. Nilsson (Ed.), *Perspectives on memory research: Essays in honor of Uppsala University's 500th anniversary*. Hillsdale, NJ: Lawrence Erlbaum Associates.

Turvey, M. T., Shaw, R. E., Reed, E. S., & Mace, W. M. (1981). Ecological laws of perceiving and acting: In reply to Fodor and Pylyshyn. *Cognition, 9*, 237-304.

Varela, F. J., Thompson, E., & Rosch, E. (1991). *The embodied mind: Cognitive science and human experience*. Cambridge, MA: MIT Press.

Vera, A. H., & Simon, H. A. (1993). Situated action: A symbolic interpretation. *Cognitive Science, 17*, 7-48.

von Bertalanffy, L. (1967). *Robots, men, and minds*. New York: George Braziller.

von Foerster, H. (1986). From stimulus to symbol. In V. McCabe & G. J. Balzano (Eds.), *Event cognition: An ecological perspective* (pp. 79-91). Hillsdale, NJ: Lawrence Erlbaum Associates.

Winograd, T., & Flores, F. (1986). *Understanding computers and cognition: A new foundation for design*. Norwood, NJ: Ablex.

Wood, D. J., Bruner, J. S., & Ross, G. (1976). The role of tutoring in problem solving. *Journal of Child Psychology and Psychiatry, 17*, 89-100.

Young, R. M. (1983). Surrogates and mappings: Two kinds of conceptual models for interactive devices. In D. Gentner & A. L. Stevens (Eds.), *Mental models*. Hillsdale, NJ: Lawrence Erlbaum Associates.

Zhang, J., & Norman, D. A. (1994). Representations in distributed cognitive tasks. *Cognitive Science, 18*, 87-122.

Zuchermaglia, C. (1991). Towards a cognitive ergonomics of educational technology. In T. M. Duffy, J. Lowyck, & D. H. Jonassen (Eds.), *Designing environments for constructive learning*. New York: Springer-Verlag.

POSTMODERNISM IN EDUCATIONAL TECHNOLOGY: UPDATE: 1996–PRESENT

Denis Hlynka
University of Manitoba

Since the first edition of the *Handbook of Research in Educational Technology,* postmodernism as a philosophy, a concept, and a methodology has integrated itself firmly and solidly within nearly all scholarly domains. In the area of curriculum theory, one need not search too far into contemporary developments of curriculum without coming upon postmodernist foci. Yet in the field of educational technology, this is not so. Scholarship in educational technology is surprisingly resistant to postmodern activity in any systematic way. While there are many sporadic and isolated examples, the field of educational technology is weak in postmodern analyses.

This entry will bring the postmodern up-to-date. The first edition of this handbook was published in 1996. Therefore this entry will backtrack to 1995 and include work until 2001, focusing on (1) postmodernism as philosophy, (2) postmodernism in curriculum theory, (3) doing postmodern research, (4) postmodernism in educational technology, and (5) borderline postmodern educational technology. This latter section focuses mainly upon the literature within the "information technology" domain. Finally, this review is not intended to be comprehensive, but rather to highlight directions and examples of the kind of work that is being done and can be done.

11.1 POSTMODERNISM AS PHILOSOPHY

At the most generic level, postmodernism has now entered the literature as the philosophy of our times. Of a myriad of popular and scholarly texts available, only two will be noted here, given for their conscious placement of postmodernism within the broad perspective of philosophy. Cooper (1996) provides a panoramic picture of world philosophies, beginning in the ancient worlds of India, China, and Greece, and ending with twentieth century philosophies, the last of which he identifies as postmodernism. Cooper concentrates his postmodern analysis on Derrida, Lyotard, and Rorty, with their "enthusiasm [in varying degrees] for irony and play, parody and pastiche, pluralism and eclecticism" (p. 465). A similar broad treatment is given in an earlier work by Tarnas (1991) who argues that the postmodern search for truth "is constrained to be tolerant of ambiguity and pluralism, and its outcome will necessarily be knowledge that is relative and fallible rather than absolute and certain" (p. 396).

11.2 POSTMODERNISM IN CURRICULUM THEORY

Of all the contemporary studies of curriculum theory, the most comprehensive overview is arguably that provided by Pinar, Reynolds, Slattery, and Taubman (2000). Their outline of contemporary curriculum discourses provides a useful template, which one might adapt for educational technology scholarship. Their nine categories of curriculum research identify curriculum as

1. Political text
2. Racial text
3. Gender text
4. Phenomenological text
5. Poststructuralist, deconstructed, and postmodern text
6. Autobiographical/biographical text
7. Aesthetic text

8. Theological text
9. Institutionalized text

Category 5 specifically lumps poststructuralism, deconstruction, and postmodernism into one. Nevertheless, postmodern scholars might find it difficult to pigeonhole themselves that narrowly. Many would include several items of the longer Pinar et al list as in fact falling *within* the postmodern domain, including gender text, phenomenological text and political text. Contrarily, the authors choose to discuss the feminist writings of Patti Lather under the category of postmodern, but not under the equally appropriate heading "gender text."

Slattery (1995) working on his own (before his teaming with Pinar et al.) had suggested a rather all-inclusive analysis of postmodern curriculum development paradigms, including hermeneutics, race, gender, ethnicity, and "qualitative aesthetics"(p. 207), to name only a few. Indeed, Slattery (1997) provides

a vision of the postmodern curriculum that is radically eclectic, determined in the context of relatedness, recursive in its complexity, autobiographically intuitive, aesthetically intersubjective, phenomenological, experiential, simultaneously quantum and cosmic, hopeful in its constructive dimension, radical in its deconstructive movement, liberating in its poststructural intents, empowering in its spirituality, ironic in its kaleidoscopic sensibilities, and ultimately, a hermeneutic search for greater understanding that motivates and satisfies us on the journey. (p. 267)

Ellsworth (1997) writes about curriculum theory from the vantage point of film theory, thus providing a totally different, and very useful, entry into educational technology. Ellsworth focuses on the importance of the cinematic construct of "mode of address." Film theory, she says, defines "mode of address" by the question: "Who does this film think you are ? " (p. 22). The answer points out the necessary and inevitable gap between sender–receiver, filmmaker–audience, or teacher–learner. The question (Who does this film think you are?), seemingly straightforward, immediately becomes entangled and complex. This is because a focus on mode of address "makes assumptions about who the audiences are—in terms of their aesthetic sensibilities, attention spans, interpretive strategies, goals and desires, previous reading and viewing experiences, biases and preferences. These assumptions are predicated on further assumptions about audience members locations within dynamics of race, gender, social status, age, ideology, sexuality, educational achievement and geography" (p. 45). Instructional designers need to keep in mind this postmodern concept of "mode of address" by asking critical questions about an instructional product or design:

- What actually exists?
- What is supposed to exist?
- What is wanted?
- What is needed?
- How do alternative communities perceive its function?
- Who does this *instructional product* think you are?

The significance given to the postmodern within curriculum theory is perhaps best illustrated by the acceptance to be found in the work of the *American Educational Research Association* and its journal *Educational Researcher*. Most noteworthy are the debates stimulated by Constas (1998), Pillow (2000), and St. Pierre (2000).

11.3   DOING POSTMODERN RESEARCH

It is problematic to find methodological texts that guide the novice researcher into the difficult realm of the postmodern. Two such texts may prove useful, although they are ostensibly both outside the domain of education, let alone educational technology. Cheek (2000) focuses on research in the field of nursing, but her chapters provide a useful walk-through "situating postmodern thought," "researching poststructurally," and "doing research informed by postmodern and poststructuralist approaches" (p. v–vi). Scheurich (1997) provides another, albeit more generic, approach for examining postmodern research methodology.

11.4   POSTMODERNISM IN EDUCATIONAL TECHNOLOGY

As was stated earlier, postmodern scholarship in educational technology is not mainstream. Yet, on the other hand, there would seem to be a plethora of individual scholars working in the field. And clearly, they do work together. Having said that, there seems to be no strongly unified body of work that presents a clear postmodern strand of scholarship. This *Handbook of Research in Educational Technology* would appear to be the exception rather than the rule. In the first edition of the *Handbook,* postmodern issues were very clearly identified within the broad topic of "Foundations." Major work was summarized there by Yeaman, Damarrin, Hlynka, Anderson, and Mufoletto. Today one must add scholarship by Bromley, Wilson, and Solomon as major contributors to that list, even though some of those listed might not consider themselves postmodernists.

Bromley (1998) is one who may not claim to be a postmodernist, but who nevertheless has questioned the prevailing discourse of computers in schools. His focus is on the social practices of technology utilization, broadly in schools and more narrowly in classrooms.

Wilson (1997) has been consistently intrigued by the postmodern paradigm within a series of important writings. He too, claims not to be a postmodernist, but rather an "instructional designer," and more specifically a *constructivist* instructional designer. Nevertheless, in several papers he explores postmodern implications for instructional design. For example, he provides an interesting comparison of postmodernism and constructivism, and notes the irony that while constructivism seems to have gained acceptance in educational technology, postmodernism has not, even though "the roots of many constructivist beliefs about cognition are traceable to postmodern philosophies" (Wilson, 1997). Elsewhere (Wilson, Osman-Jouchoux, & Teslow, 1995), he provides a similar comparison. Reeves and Hedberg (1997) explore evaluation decisions within different paradigms, one of which is identified as "critical theory-neomarxist-postmodern-praxis".

Mason and Hlynka (1998) present a scenario on the use of PowerPoint in the classroom, then in a follow-up tandem paper (Hlynka & Mason, 1998) they examine PowerPoint from six postmodern frames: multiple voicing, breakup of the canon, supplementarity, slippery signifies, nonlinearity, and ironic juxtaposition.

Solomon (2000) in a paper designated the AECT "Young Scholar" award winner for 1999, has provided a tentative postmodern agenda for instructional technology, and has stressed the importance of a postmodern component to the field.

Yeaman (1994, 1997, 2000) has written extensively on postmodern instructional technology focusing most recently on cyberspace, technology discourse, and the cyborg.

Several authors have noted the correspondence of hypertext to postmodern philosophy. Within educational technology, the most interesting approach has been that of Rose (2000).

In addition, a variety of doctoral dissertations have explored a variety of dimensions of postmodern educational technology. Elshof (2001) looks at cultural discourses on technology teachers' worldviews and curriculum. Waltz (2001) provides a fascinating critical and close reading of a learning space, specifically a distance-learning classroom. Hartzell (2000) provides a postmodern framework from which to examine technology integration. Maratta (2001) focuses on the "unification of distance learning foundations and critical thought paradigms, especially postmodernism, through the creation of an educational prototype and an actual web-based course syllabus template" (p. 1). Finally, following the lead of Yeaman (1994), several studies have focused on the cyborg within technology and what it means to be human (Lucek 1999; Stein,1997).

11.5 BORDERLINE POSTMODERN EDUCATIONAL TECHNOLOGY

In addition to the research noted in the previous sections, a huge body of literature exists in closely related fields, especially information technology, but also media theory and sociology.

Marshall McLuhan has been reinterpreted by a variety of scholars as a postmodernist before his time. For example, Levinson (1999) makes it clear that Mcluhan's aphorisms and phrases, once thought as quaint and throw-away lines, now seem to be a description of nothing less than the postmodern condition: "discarnate man," "centers everywhere; margins nowhere," "hot and cool," "surf-boarding electronic waves," and of course, "the medium is the message." Genosko (1999) begins his study linking Baudrillard with McLuhan by pointing out that a McLuhan revolution is "in full swing" (p. 1), and that his focus is "what every reader of Baudrillard already in some respect knows: Baudrillard's debts to McLuhan are substantial (p. 3)." Finally he acknowledges that, "McLuhan and Baudrillard are the key thinkers to whom postmodernists turn to situate their deviations from them (ibid.)." Stamps (1995) moves in different directions by coupling McLuhan with another noted Canadian communications theorist Harold Innis, and explores their work from the perspective of the Frankfurt School.

The relation of information technology to contemporary postmodern literary theory has been explored by Coyne (1997), and Landow (1997).

In an only slightly different but parallel vein, Manovich (2001), combining film theory and art history on the one hand with computer science on the other, attempts to develop and explicate a language of new media. He argues: "In the 1980s many critics described one of the key effects of postmodernism as that of spatialization—privileging space over time, flattening historical time, refusing grand narratives. Computer media, which evolved during the same decade accomplished this spatialization quite literally" (p. 78). Manovich goes on to explore those relationships and to propose that new media is grounded in five principles: numerical representation, modularity, automation, variability, and cultural transcoding.

11.6 CONCLUSION

The intersection of postmodernist thinking and educational technology has developed haphazardly since the first edition of this *Handbook of Research on Educational Technology*. While independent scholarship thrives, nevertheless, postmodern educational technology, at this writing remains on the margins. It may be that this field is simply too close to a technical model which continually needs to know *how* more often than *why*. Progress in instructional design seems to be measured by the success of instructional design models, which promise accurate, efficient and "just-in-time" learning, often grounded today in new developments within artificial intelligence research. Interest shifts from how to teach people to think, to how to teach machines to think like people. Postmodern instructional designers and postmodern instructional technologists are more curious about *why* rather than *how*. Postmodernists are aware and have always been aware that multiple discourses need to be recognized, understood, and explicated. There are unquestionably those individuals, including instructional designers, who are more comfortable with searching for the one best solution to a given learning problem. It is clearly comforting to believe that there is still one best solution that can always be found, if one only tries hard enough, and has time enough to cycle and recycle. There are still those who fear the postmodern as bringing uncertainty and chaos into the world. Yet alternative worldviews do exist and will always exist, even within our own boundaries and borders. It is paradoxical that as we move inexorably toward a global village, in which we are united instantly with the entire world, primarily due to technology, at the same time we discover that village in our own backyard. The world today *is* postmodern. Educational technology must also be.

References

Bromley, H., & Apple, M. (Eds.). (1998). *Education/Technology/Power: Educational computing as a social practice.* Buffalo: SUNY Press.

Bromley, H. (1998). Data-driven democracy: Social assessment of educational computing. In H. Bromley, & M. Apple, (Eds.), *Education/Technology/Power: Educational computing as a social practice.* Buffalo: SUNY Press.

Cheek, J. (2000). *Postmodern and poststructural approaches to nursing education.* Thousand Oaks, CA: Sage Publications.

Constas, M. (1998). Deciphering postmodern educational research. *Educational Researcher, 27*(9), 36–42.

Cooper, D. (1996). *World philosophies: An historical introduction.* Oxford, UK: Blackwell.

Coyne, R. (1997). *Designing information technology in the postmodern age: From method to metaphor.* Cambridge, MA: MIT Press.

Ellsworth, E. (1997). *Teaching positions: Difference, pedagogy and the power of address.* New York: Teachers College Press.

Elshof, L. (2001). *Worldview research with technology teachers.* Unpublished doctoral dissertation, University of Toronto.

Genosko, G. (1999). *McLuhan and Baudrillard: The masters of implosion.* London: Routledge.

Hartzell, F. (2000). *Contradictions in technology use: Stories from a model school.* Unpublished doctoral dissertation, Oklahoma State University.

Hlynka, D., & Mason, R. (1998). PowerPoint in the Classroom: What is the Point?. *Educational Technology, 38*(5), 45–48.

Landow, G. (1997). *Hypertext 2.0: The convergence of contemporary critical theory and technology.* Baltimore, MD: Johns Hopkins University Press.

Levinson, P. (1999). *Digital Mcluhan: A guide to the information millennium.* London: Routledge.

Lucek, L. (1999). *A modest intervention: Reframing cyborg discourse for educational technologists.* Unpublished doctoral dissertation, Northern Illinois.

Manovich, L. (2001). *The language of new media.* Cambridge, MA: MIT Press.

Maratta, W. H. (2001). *The nexus of postmodernism and distance education: Creating empowerment with educational technology and critical paradigms.* Unpublished doctoral dissertation, Florida State University.

Mason, R., & Hlynka, D. (1998). PowerPoint in the Classroom: Who has the power? *Educational Technology, 38*(5), 42–45.

Pillow, W. (2000). Deciphering attempts to decipher postmodern educaitonal research. *Educational Researcher, 29*(5), 21–24.

Pinar, W., Reynolds, W., Slattery, P., & Taubman, P. (2000). *Understanding curriculum: An introduction to the study of historical and contemporary curriculum discourses.* New York: Peter Lang.

Reeves, T., & Hedberg, J. (1997). Decisions, decisions, decisions. Available http://nt.media.hku.hk/webcourse/references/eval_decisions.htm

Rose, E. (2000). *Hypertexts: The language and culture of educational computing.* Toronto: Althouse Press.

Scheurich, J. (1997). *Research method in the postmodern.* New York: RoutledgeFalmer.

Slattery, P. (1995). *Curriculum development in the postmodern era.* New York: Garland Publishing, Inc..

Solomon, D. (2000). Towards a post-modern agenda in instructional technology. *Educational Technology: Research and Development, 48*(4), 5–20.

St. Pierre, E. (2000). The call for intelligibility in postmodern educational research. *Educational Researcher, 29*(5), 25–28.

Stamps, J. (1995). *Unthinking modernity: Innis, McLuhan and the Frankfurt school.* Montreal: McGill-Queens University Press.

Stein, S. (1997). *Redefining the human in the age of the computer: Popular discourses, 1984 to the present.* Unpublished doctoral dissertation, University of Iowa.

Tarnas, R. (1991). *The passion of the western mind: Understanding the ideas that have shaped our world view.* New York: Ballantine Books.

Waltz, S. (2001). *Pedagogy of artifacts in a distance learning classroom.* Unpublished doctoral dissertation, State University of New York at Buffalo.

Wilson, B. (1997). The postmodern paradigm. In C. R. Dill & A. J. Romiszowski (Ed.), *Instructional develoment paradigms* (pp. 105–110). Englewood Cliffs, NJ: Educational Technology. (Available http://carbon.cudenver.edu/~bwilson/postmodern.html)

Wilson, B., & Osman-Jouchoux, R., & Teslow, J. (1995). The impact of constructivism (and postmodernism) on ID fundamentals. In B. Seels (Ed.), *Instructional design fundamentals.* Englewood Cliffs, NJ: Educational Technology.

Yeaman, A. (1994). Cyborgs are us *Arachnet Electronic Journal on Virtual Culture* [On-Line serial], *2*(1). (Available *http://www.infomotions.com/serials/aejvc/aejvc-v2n01-yeaman-cyborgs.txt*)

Yeaman, A. (1997). The discourse on technology. In R. Branch & B. Minor (Eds.), *Educational media and technology yearbook* (pp. 46–60). Englewood, CO: Libraries Unlimited.

Yeaman, A. (2000). Coming of age in cyberspace. *Educational technology: Research and development, 48*(4), 102–106.

HARD TECHNOLOGIES

·12·

RESEARCH ON LEARNING FROM TELEVISION

Barbara Seels
University of Pittsburgh

Karen Fullerton
Celeron Consultants

Louis Berry
University of Pittsburgh

Laura J. Horn

This chapter summarizes a body of literature about instructional technology that is unique not only in its depth but also in its breadth and importance. A recent search of articles about television yielded 20,747 citations in the Educational Resources Information Center (ERIC) database while a similar search in the PsycINFO database produced 6,662 citations. It is fitting, therefore, that there be a chapter in this handbook which reviews how instructional technology has used research on television as well as how the field has contributed to this body of research.

After the first edition of this handbook appeared, several excellent review books were published including *Children, Adolescents and the Media* by Strasburger and Wilson (2002), *Handbook of Children and the Media* by Singer and Singer (2001), and *Television and Child Development* by Van Evra (1998). These books do such a thorough job of updating the literature that the authors decided to refer you to these books rather than adding major sections to this chapter.

We feel these books address literature in areas such as sexuality, drugs, new media, and violence that is germane to learning from television because parents and teachers need to mediate the viewing experience. It is clear from our recent review that the literature on mass media dominates although there are also many studies on distance education and educational television. This stress on societal issues reflects concern for pressures on children that influence learning and behavior.

There is some evidence that the essential relationships among variables are beginning to be understood. Thus, television viewing affects obesity, which can impact school achievement. Programming affects beliefs, such as stereotypes about mental illness, which create a need for mediation. Therefore, the concept of the television viewing system (programming, viewing environment, and behavior) gains importance.

There are areas that seem important but are not well researched. The most important of these areas is controversial programming, such as MTV, World Wrestling Federation programs, reality shows, and talk shows. There have been minor changes. For example, ITV now means interactive or two-way television as well as instructional television (Robb, 2000), and the Center for Research on the Influences of Television on Children (CRITC) at the University of Kansas is now at the University of Texas, Austin. However, the most important service we can provide is not to detail minor changes. Rather, it is to give you an overview of the major evolutionary trends in this body of literature. We do this under the heading "Current Issues" near the end of each major section.

12.1 NATURE OF THE CHAPTER

In order to address research on learning from television,[1] it is necessary to define this phrase. For the purposes of this chapter, learning is defined as changes in knowledge, understanding, attitudes, and behavior due to the intentional* or incidental effects* of television programming. Thus, learning can occur intentionally as a result of programming that is planned to achieve specific instructional outcomes or incidentally through programming for entertainment or information purposes.

Three elements of the television viewing system* are covered: the independent variable or stimulus, mediating variables, and the resulting behavior or beliefs. The television viewing experience* is based on the interaction of these three components of the viewing system, which are usually described as programming, environment, and behavior. Each of these elements encompasses many variables; for example, message design* and content are programming variables. Viewer preferences and habits are environmental variables that mediate. Individual differences are also mediating variables in that they affect behavior. Learning and aggressive or cooperative behaviors are dependent variables.

For this review to serve an integrative function, it was necessary to be selective in order to comprehensively cover many areas. Several parameters were established to aid in selectivity. The first decision was that film and television research would be integrated. Although they are different mediums, their cognitive effects are the same. The technologies underlying each medium are quite different; however, for instructional purposes, the overall appearance and functions are essentially the same, with television being somewhat more versatile in terms of storage and distribution capabilities. Furthermore, films are frequently converted to television formats, a fact that blurs the distinction even more. Research on learning from television evolved from research on learning from motion pictures. Film research dominated until about 1959 when the Pennsylvania State University studies turned to research on learning from television. Investigations related to one medium will be identified as such; however, effects and other findings will be considered together. Classic research on both film and television is reviewed.

Nevertheless, relatively little space is devoted to film research because an assumption was made that there were other reviews of this early research, and its importance has diminished. It seemed more important to emphasize contributions from the last 20 years, especially since they are overwhelming the consumer of this literature by sheer volume.

Another decision was that although some important international studies would be reported, the majority of studies covered would be national. This was essential because the international body of literature was gargantuan. Those who wish to pursue international literature are advised to start with a topic that has existing cross-cultural bibliographies, such as the *Sesame Street Research Bibliography* (1989) available from Children's Television Workshop (CTW).

In addition, it was necessary to determine what to include and exclude in relation to the other chapters in the handbook. All distance learning and interactive multimedia studies were excluded because other chapters cover these technologies. Some media literacy* will be covered because it is a very important variable in learning from television. Nevertheless, it is assumed that aspects of visual literacy (i.e., visual learning and communication) will be covered throughout the handbook, not just in this chapter.

It was further decided that a variety of methodological approaches would be introduced, but that discussion should be limited because the final section of this handbook covers methodologies. Methodological issues, though, will be addressed throughout this chapter.

Our final decision was that this chapter would make a comprehensive effort to integrate research from both mass media* and instructional television*. Although other publications have done this, generally one area dominates, and consequently the other is given inadequate attention. It was our intent to start the process of integrating more fully the literature from mass media and instructional television.

12.1.1 Relevance to Instructional Technology

Research on learning from television encompasses more than formal instruction. This body of research addresses learning in home as well as school environments. Many of the findings are relevant to the instructional technologist; for example, research on formal features* yields guidelines for message design. Instructional technologists can both promote students' learning to regulate and reinforce their own viewing* and educate parents and teachers about media utilization.

In addition, instructional technologists are also responsible for recommending and supporting policy that affects television utilization. The literature provides support for policy positions related to (a) control of advertising and violence, (b) parent and teacher training, (c) provision of special programming, and (d) media literacy education.

Researchers in instructional technology can determine gaps in the theoretical base by using reviews such as this. In the future, more research that relates variables studied by psychologists to variables studied by educators will be required in order to identify guidelines for interventions and programming.

12.1.2 Organization of the Chapter

The chapter is organized chronologically and categorically in order to cover both research on the utilization of television in education and mass media research on television effects. The beginning of the chapter chronologically traces the evolution

---

[1]A glossary of terms related to learning from television is given at the end of the chapter. The first time a term defined in the glossary appears, it will be marked with an asterisk.

of research in this area. Other sections, which are organized by subject, review theoretical and methodological issues and synthesize the findings. A glossary of terminology related to television research is given at the end of this chapter.

The chapter starts with a historical overview. After this introductory background, the chapter turns to sections organized categorically around major issues, some of which are independent or mediating variables, and others of which are effects. The first section synthesizes research on message design and mental processing. It reviews how formal features affect comprehension* and attention.* The next issue section deals with the effects of television on school achievement. Turning to what is known about the effects of the family, viewing context, viewing environments,* and coviewing* are reviewed next. The effects of television on socialization* are explored through attitudes, beliefs, and behaviors. The next section covers programming and its utilization in the classroom and home. The final section covers theory on media literacy and mediation* through critical-viewing skills.* The organization of the chapter follows this outline:

1. Historical overview
2. Message design and cognitive processing*
3. School achievement
4. Family-viewing context
5. Attitudes, beliefs, and behaviors
6. Programming and utilization
7. Critical-viewing skills
8. Glossary of terms

It was necessary to approach the literature broadly in order to synthesize effectively. Despite the disparity in types of research and areas of focus, most of the studies provided information about interactions that affect learning from television.

12.2 HISTORICAL OVERVIEW

Much research on the effects of television is contradictory or inconclusive, but that doesn't make the research useless, wasteful, or futile. We need to know as much as we can about how children learn, and conscientious research of any kind can teach us, if nothing else, how to do *better* research (Rogers & Head, 1983, p. 170).

As Fred Rogers and Barry Head suggest, to use research on television, one needs a historical perspective. The purpose of this section is to provide that perspective. It will briefly explain the evolution of the technologies, important historical milestones, the evolution of the research, and the variety of methodological approaches used. After reading this section, you should be able to place the research in historical context and understand its significance.

12.2.1 Contributors to the Literature

This large body of research is the result of individuals, organizations, and fields with constituencies naturally interested in the

effects of television. The disciplines that are most dedicated to reflecting on learning from television are education, communications, psychology, and sociology. Within education, the fields of educational psychology, cognitive science, and instructional technology have a continuing interest. Educational psychology and cognitive science have focused on mental processing. Instructional technology has made its greatest contributions to television research through the areas of message design, formative evaluation,* and critical-viewing skills.

12.2.1.1 Organizations. Groups associated with research on television operate in diverse arenas. Government institutions, such as the National Institute of Mental Health (NIMH), the Educational Resources Clearinghouse on Information Resources (ERIC), and the Office of Research in the Department of Education have been the catalyst for many studies. Government has influenced research on television through hearings and legislation on violent programming and commercials for children. Government legislation also created the Public Broadcasting System (PBS).

Many universities have established centers or projects that pursue questions about the effects of television. These include the Family Television Research and Consultation Center at Yale University, the Center for Research on the Influence of Television on Children at the University of Kansas, the National Center for Children and Television at Princeton, and Project Zero at Harvard University. Foundations have supported research in the areas of media effects and instructional television, including the Spencer, Ford, and Carnegie Foundations. Public service organizations such as Action for Children's Television and church television awareness groups have spurred policy and research.

Research and development (R&D) organizations, such as the Southwest Educational Development Laboratory, have generated curricula on critical-viewing skills. Children's Television Workshop (CTW), the producer of *Sesame Street*, is an R&D organization that not only develops programming but also does research on the effects of television.

12.2.1.2 Review Articles and Books. Despite such long-term efforts, much of the literature on television lacks connection to other findings (Clark, 1983, 1994; Richey, 1986). The conceptual theory necessary to explain the relationship among variables is still evolving. Because of this, consumers of the literature are sometimes overwhelmed and unable to make decisions related to interactions in the television viewing system of programming, environment, and behavior.

Comprehensive and specialized reviews of the literature are helpful for synthesizing findings. Individual studies contribute a point of view and define variables, but it takes a review to examine each study in light of others. Fortunately, there have been many outstanding reviews of the literature. For example, Reid and MacLennan (1967) and Chu and Schramm (1968) did comprehensive reviews of learning from television that included studies on utilization. Aletha Huston-Stein (1972) wrote a chapter for the National Society for the Study of Education (NSSE) yearbook on Early Childhood Education entitled *Mass Media and Young Children's Development* which presented a conceptual framework for studying television's effects. In 1975, the Rand Corporation published three books by George Comstock that reviewed pertinent scientific literature, key studies, and the state of research. Jerome and Dorothy Singer reviewed the implications of research for children's cognition, imagination, and emotion (Singer & Singer, 1983). In that article, they described the trend toward studying cognitive processes and formal features. By 1989, the American Psychological Association had produced a synthesis of the literature titled *Big World, Small Screen.*

Other reviews have concentrated on special areas like reading skills (Williams, 1986); cognitive development (Anderson & Collins, 1988); instructional television (Cambre, 1987); and violence (Liebert & Sprafkin, 1988). Lawrence Erlbaum Publishers offers a series of volumes edited by Dolf Zillmann and Jennings Bryant on research and theory about television effects.

Light and Pillemer (1984) argue against the single decisive-study approach and propose reviews around a specific research question that starts by reporting the main effects, then reports special circumstances that affect outcomes, and finishes by reporting special effects on particular types of people. This integrated research strategy is especially appropriate for reviews of research on television effects.

12.2.2 Evolution and Characteristics of the Technologies

The evolution of the technologies of motion pictures and television during the latter part of the 19th century and early 20th century can be described in terms of media characteristics, delivery systems, and communication functions. It is also important to know the terminology essential to understanding research descriptions and comparisons. This terminology is given in the glossary at the end of this chapter.

12.2.2.1 *Functional Characteristics.* These media characteristics of film and television are primarily realism or fidelity, mass access, referability, and, in some cases, immediacy. Producers for both of these technologies wanted to make persons, places, objects, or events more realistic to the viewer or listener. The intent was to ensure that the realistic representation of the thing or event was as accurate as possible (i.e., fidelity). The ability to transmit sounds or images to general audiences, or even to present such information to large groups in theaters, greatly expanded access to realistic presentations. In the case of television, the characteristic of immediacy allowed the audience to experience the representation of the thing or event almost simultaneously with its occurrence. The notion of "being there" was a further addition to the concept of realism. As these various forms of media developed, the ability to record the representations for later reference became an important characteristic. Viewers could not only replay events previously recorded but could also refer to specific aspects or segments of the recording time and time again for study and analysis. Each of these characteristics has driven or directed the use of film or television for instructional purposes.

12.2.2.2 *Delivery Systems.* The State University of Iowa began the first educational television broadcasts in 1933. Educational broadcasting quickly grew, with several universities producing regular programming and commercial stations broadcasting educational materials for the general population. During the 1950s and 60s, other technical innovations emerged that expanded the flexibility and delivery of educational television. These included the development in 1956 of magnetic videotape and videotape recorders, the advent of communications satellites in 1962, and the widespread growth of cable television in the 1960s and 70s. Delivery systems encompass both transmission and storage capabilities. The various means whereby the message is sent to the intended audience differ in terms of the breadth of the population who can access the message. These means of transmission include broadcast television, communications satellite, closed-circuit television (CCTV), cable access television (CATV), and microwave relay links.

Broadcast television programming is generally produced for large-scale audiences by major networks and, with the exception of cable or microwave relay agreements, can be received free of charge by any viewer with a receiver capable of receiving the signal. Satellite communication has the capability of distributing the television signal over most of the populated globe. Closed-circuit television is produced for limited audiences and for specified educational purposes. Cable television often presents programming produced by public television organizations, public service agencies, or educational institutions for educational purposes. Today, many of the microwave relay functions have been replaced by satellite relays; however, this transmission medium is still used to distribute closed circuit programming within prescribed areas such as school districts.

12.2.2.3 *Storage Media.* In the beginning, television productions were often stored in the form of kinescopes, which are rarely, if ever, used today, although some early television recording may still exist in kinescope form. Today, most video programs are stored on videotape cassette format, which is convenient and is produced in a variety of tape widths. Videotape permits a large number of replays; however, it can deteriorate after excessive use.

12.2.2.4 *Communications Functions.* From an instructional point of view, the most important factor in the development of any of these technologies is not the technical aspect of their development but rather the impact of the medium on the audience. Terms that relate to communications functions include instructional television (ITV), educational television (ETV), mass media, incidental learning, and intentional learning. Today, ITV programming is often transmitted by satellite to a school where it is either recorded for use when convenient or used immediately and interactively through a combination of computers and telecommunications. Educational television programming is typically not part of a specific course of study and may be directed to large and diverse groups of individuals desiring general information or informal instruction.

The distinction between mass media and educational television is frequently difficult to make since most educational television programming is distributed via broadcast television, the primary mass-media mode. What differentiates mass media from educational television is the notion of intended purpose. With educational television, intentional effects are achieved through purposeful intervention to achieve educational objectives. Incidental effects, on the other hand, typically result from mass media or entertainment oriented programming.

12.2.3   Legislative Milestones

The history of research on television effects has been tied to important government policy actions (Wood & Wylie, 1977). In the 1930s the government declared air channels to be public property and created the Federal Communications Commission (FCC) to regulate systems such as radio. After lengthy hearings, in 1952 the Federal Communications Commission reserved 242 television channels for noncommercial, educational broadcasting.

12.2.3.1   *The 1950s and 60s.* The first congressional hearings on violence and television occurred in 1952. In 1954, hearings were held to investigate the link between television and juvenile crime. When he was doing his Bobo doll social-psychology experiments in the early 1960s, Albert Bandura published an article in *Look* magazine entitled "What Television Violence Can Do to Your Child." This article popularized the term "TV violence."

In 1964, Newton Minow assumed the chair of the FCC. He would prove to be a strong commissioner, remembered for his statement that television was "a vast wasteland." By 1965, advertisers had discovered that they could reach young children with advertisements for toys, candy, and cereal more cheaply and effectively on Saturday mornings than in prime time. Also in the 1960s, Congress created the Public Broadcasting System (PBS) and the Corporation for Public Broadcasting (CPB). By the end of the 1960s, the National Commission on the Causes and Prevention of Violence had issued a report stating that exposure to violence on television had increased rates of physical aggression. This led to the Surgeon General's appointing a committee to study the effects television programs have on children. The decade concluded by the Supreme Court's upholding the fairness doctrine, which required stations to give equal time to political candidates.

12.2.3.2   *The 1970s.* The decade of the 1970s started with a ban on cigarette advertising on television, which had been initiated after the Surgeon General's report that there was a relationship between cancer and smoking. In 1972, the Surgeon General issued a report on violence that alleged that there was also a causal link between violent behavior and violence on television and in motion pictures. This first major government report on television and violence (NIMH, 1972) consisted of five volumes of reports and papers gathered through an inquiry process directed by the National Institute of Mental Health (NIMH). To prepare for this report, NIMH was empowered to solicit and fund a million dollars worth of research on the effects of television violence (Liebert & Sprafkin, 1988). By 1975,

the FCC had received 25,000 complaints about violent or sexually oriented programs on television. As a consequence, in 1975 the Ford Foundation, the National Science Foundation, and the Markle Foundation cosponsored a major conference on television and human behavior. The Supreme Court ruled that the FCC could regulate hours in which "indecent" programming could be aired.

12.2.3.3   *The 1980s.* In 1982, the National Institute of Mental Health confirmed the link between television and aggression and stated that, "violence on television does lead to aggressive behavior by children and teenagers who watch the programs" (NIMH, 1980, p. 6); thus television was labeled a cause of aggressive behavior. In 1985, the American Psychological Association (APA) publicly concluded that violence can cause aggressive behavior and urged broadcasters to reduce violence. As the decade ended, the FCC decided that the Fairness Doctrine was no longer necessary because there was no longer a scarcity of stations and that it was perhaps unconstitutional. Congress passed a bill to reinstitute the doctrine, but the President vetoed it. The President also vetoed legislation that would place limits on advertising during children's programs. In 1989, Congress passed the Television Violence Act granting television executives the authority to hold discussions on the issues of television violence without violating antitrust laws.

12.2.3.4   *The 1990s.* This brings us to the current decade, which started with Congress's passing the Children's Television Act that requires limits on advertising and evidence that stations provide programming to meet children's needs. This is the first legislation to establish the principle that broadcasters have a social responsibility to their child audiences. The advantage of this approach is that it avoids the thorny issue of censorship. The bill became a law without presidential signature. Congress established the National Endowment for Children's Television to provide resources for production of quality children's programming as well as the Television Decoder Circuitry Act, which requires all new sets to have closed-caption capability. Over presidential veto, Congress approved the Cable Television Consumer Protection and Competition Act to regulate the cable industry. In 1993, the National Research Council of the National Academy of Sciences published a comprehensive report on the causes of violence in American society, entitled "Understanding and Preventing Violence," which addressed the role of television. The Senate Commerce Committee held hearings on television violence during which Senator Hollings complained that Congress has been holding hearings on television violence for 40 years. The idea of "V-chip" legislation to require the technology in all sets to block showing of programs rated violent was introduced at these hearings. The Telecommunications Act of 1996 required that this V-chip be installed on all new television sets. This landmark legislation had other important provisions, including one for discounted service rates for telecommunication lines into schools, especially for lines for compressed video and the Internet (Telecommunications Act of 1996). This overview of societal concerns about television documents the impetus for much research.

12.2.4 Historical Evolution of the Research

The first major research initiatives in both film and television began in the 1950s and 1960s. Research foci and variables of interest, as well as the social orientation of research, have changed considerably over the years.

Bowie (1986) reviewed research on learning from films and grouped the research into three phases:

1. Research on whether films can teach (1910–1950)
2. Research on how films teach (1940–1959)
3. Research on who learns from films (1960–1985)

Research from the last phase includes a great many experimental studies. The results of these experimental studies can be grouped in these areas: (a) use of films to teach higher-level cognitive skills, (b) effects of film viewing on individual learning, and (c) effects of film viewing on self-concept. Bowie concluded that the literature reviewed in these three areas suggests that:

- Films are effective in teaching inquiry learning and problem solving.
- Unstructured films are more effective for teaching problem solving.
- Films are effective in teaching observation skills and attention to detail.
- Low-aptitude students tend to benefit more from films.
- Films tend to be more effective for field-independent students.
- Films can positively influence self-concept.

Research on learning from films also served as a basis for research on instructional television.

Television research began with attention being devoted almost solely to its instructional effectiveness in formal instructional environments. The types and foci of research evolved into more varied agendas that considered not only the formal instructional implications of television but also the social, psychological, and instructional effects of broadcast television in less formal environments.

Sprafkin, Gadow, and Abelman (1992) describe the research on television as falling into three distinct chronological phases. The first of these they refer to as the "medium-orientation phase" in which television was seen as a powerful instructional tool that required research to describe its effectiveness. At this point, little attention was devoted to assessing the interaction of the media with developmental or individual differences in the viewers. The second phase that Sprafkin et al. describe is the "child orientation phase" in which research focused more closely on the relationship of television to young viewers' individual characteristics and aptitudes. Media effects were thought to be due to a child's mental processing characteristics, not to programming. They termed the third phase the "interaction phase" in which television effects were seen as complex three-way interactions between characteristics of the medium (such as type of content), the child or viewer variables (such as age), and factors in the viewing environment (such as parents and teachers).

These three phases correspond approximately to the three eras of film and television research: the period of comparative media research during the 1950s and early 1960s (Greenhill, 1967); the media effects and individual differences research of the late 1960s through the 1970s (Anderson & Levin, 1976; Wright & Huston, 1983); and die interaction research characterized by the work of Salomon (1979, 1983) during the later 1970s through the present time.

The purpose of this section is to chronicle the evolution of these research trends and describe the nature of the research associated with each phase. In doing so, we will attempt to relate the trends to methodologies and variables.

12.2.4.1 Research Prior to 1965. Before the mid-1950s, the vast majority of research was focused on the effects of instructional films*, usually in controlled educational or training environments, both in formal education and in military and industrial training. This period was marked primarily by the widely quoted Instructional Film Research Program conducted at the Pennsylvania State University. This program was initiated under the auspices of the U.S. Naval Training Devices Center to study a variety of variables related to the use of instructional films for personnel training purposes. One report issued through this research project summarized and evaluated over 200 film research studies from 1918 until 1950 (Hoban & VanOrmer, 1950). The major focus of the Instructional Film Research Program, however, was the conduct of an extensive series of experiments that compared instruction delivered via film with "conventional" or "face-to-face instruction." Within these comparisons, researchers also investigated the effects of various production techniques, the effect of film-based instruction on learner attitudes, and the effectiveness of various applications of instructional films (Carpenter & Greenhill, 1956; Greenhill, 1967). This series of studies represents one of the first, and certainly most extensive, attempts to evaluate thoroughly the effectiveness of the medium. The findings of these studies, however, indicated no significant differences in most cases and have been criticized for a number of methodological procedures (Greenhill, 1967).

Typical among the studies conducted in this program were those that sought to compare the relative effectiveness of motion-picture-based instruction with conventional classroom instruction. A study by VanderMeer (1949) compared ninth-grade biology students taught by: (1) sound films, (2) sound films plus study guides, and (3) standard lecture–demonstration classroom instruction. No significant differences were found across all groups on either immediate or 3-month-delayed achievement testing, although the film-only group showed a shorter completion time. This study is quite characteristic of most of these film studies in that no significant differences were found across both the experimental and control groups. Other studies focused on the relative effectiveness of instructional films for teaching performance skills and generally found no significant difference or only slight benefit from the film treatment (Greenhill, 1967). The effects of production variables were also of interest to researchers, and the relative effects of such variables as inserted questions, variants in the sound track, color versus monochrome, animation versus still pictures, and the use of attention gaining and directing devices were all studied, albeit with few, if any, significant differences across groups.

The period between the mid-1950s and the mid-1960s was characterized by a great deal of instructional television research by a group of researchers at the Pennsylvania State University, reconstituted as the Instructional Television Research Project (Carpenter & Greenhill, 1955), as well as by other individuals (Hagerstown Board of Education, 1959; Holmes, 1959; Kumata, 1956; Niven, 1958; Schramm, 1962). These projects and summaries of research included literally hundreds of studies covering many content areas and many different age groups. In most cases, the summary reports issued by these researchers or projects provided fairly comprehensive descriptions of the general findings and conclusions. As with the film research initiatives, the television research projects focused strongly on comparative research designs and similarly resulted in "no significant differences." Few studies reported findings entirely supportive of television, and conversely few found television instruction to be less effective than conventional classroom instruction. The finding of no significant difference was seen by Greenhill (1967) as a positive result because it implied that television could be a reasonable alternative to classroom instruction and consequently, for reasons of administrative, fiscal, and logistical benefit, could be a more desirable choice of instructional method.

The comparative studies of television conducted during this time were later criticized on methodological grounds by Stickell (1963) and Greenhill (1967). Stickell analyzed 250 comparisons and determined that only 10 were "interpretable" methodologically. Those 10 had employed random assignment of subjects, control of extraneous variables, and application of appropriate tests of significance in which the underlying assumptions of the test were met. Of the studies Stickell found to be "interpretable," none revealed significant differences.

The majority of these early comparative studies were designed to compare various forms of televised instruction to a vaguely specified standard known as "face-to-face instruction," "conventional," or "traditional classroom instruction" (Carpenter & Greenhill, 1956; Lumsdaine, 1963). Instructional techniques and formats included (a) a single instructor teaching the same content, (b) a "live instructor" teaching a class while the same class was being televised to a remote class, (c) a number of different instructors teaching the same general lesson as the televised lesson, and (d) kinescope recordings of a lesson augmented by various, instructor-led activities. In most cases, there was little or no means of equating the instructional formats being used in terms of instructor equivalence, content congruence, or environmental similarity (Greenhill, 1967; Wilkinson, 1980; Williams, Paul, & Ogilvie, 1957). Among the large number of comparative studies, there are many that simply compared the medium with some standard of live classroom instruction, while a smaller proportion made comparisons with the audio message only, comparisons of film versus kinescope, and television versus an in-studio classroom (Kumata, 1956).

As mentioned, this matter was further complicated by the fact that the vast majority of the studies, in both film and television, produced results of "no significant difference" (Greenhill, 1967; Stickell, 1963). This finding, when considered in conjunction with the general comparative nature of the research, makes it difficult to draw specific conclusions or recommendations from most of these comparative studies. Other methodological problems also plagued this early research, including: lack of equivalence of experimental groups, confounding of variables, and statistical analysis procedures that were not powerful enough to detect differences that may have been present (Greenhill, 1967).

In terms of group equivalence, two problems were apparent. First, groups were rarely pretested to determine if prerequisite knowledge was approximately equivalent. Second, little attention was given to ensuring equivalence of assignment to experimental groups. In some cases, correlative data such as IQ scores or grade point averages were used as matching variables, but because of the use of intact classes, randomization was rarely employed to assign subjects (Chu & Schramm, 1968; Stickell, 1963). Because the variables of televised instruction and conventional instruction were not clearly defined, it was almost impossible to separate other mediating variables related to production methods, technologies, viewing and teaching environments, viewer characteristics, and content organization. The result was often a serious confounding of many variables, only some of which were of interest. In terms of statistical analysis, t and F tests were used only occasionally, and analysis of covariance procedures were employed rarely because adjusting variables were infrequently assessed (Stickell, 1963). Additionally, content-related factors and objectives as well as types of learning were often not addressed or confounded (Miller, 1968).

Other more carefully defined variables continued to be investigated during this time, including: technical or production variables such as color, camera techniques, and attention-gaining and directing devices (Ellery, 1959; Harris, 1962; Kanner & Rosenstein, 1960; Schwarzwalder, 1960); pedagogical variables, such as inserted questions and presentation modes (Gropper & Lumsdaine, 1961; Rock, Duva, & Murray, 1951); and variables in the viewing environment, such as viewing angle, group size, and distractions (Carpenter & Greenhill, 1958; Hayman, 1963; McGrane & Baron, 1959). In addition, attitudes toward televised instruction and the use of television to teach procedural skills were studied (Hardaway, Beymer, & Engbretson, 1963; Pasewark, 1956).

Later studies, conducted during the 1960s and early 1970s, focused more specifically on individual variables, media characteristics, and die interaction between viewer characteristics and television effects. These studies typically employed the aptitude–treatment–interaction paradigm described by Cronbach and Snow (1976) and were intended to explore specific effects of television on particular individuals. These designs were inherently more precise and more powerful and consequently enabled researchers to identify the effects of individual variables as well as the interaction of variables and other factors (Levie & Dickie, 1973).

During this time period, studies employed quantitative experimental methods almost, exclusively to evaluate the relative effectiveness of film and televised instruction in generally controlled environments such as laboratories, studios, classrooms, and schools. Researchers did not have the resources or research interest to investigate or describe specific effects on larger or noncontrolled populations, such as the effect of incidental learning resulting from noneducational broadcast television.

12.2.4.2 Research after 1965.
After 1965, research focus was increasingly directed toward mass media and social effects. The formation of Children's Television Workshop (CTW) in the late 1960s directed research interest to formal features and formative evaluation (Polsky, 1974). The 1970s were also devoted to research on the relationship between televised violence and aggression. With the 1980s, a change from the behavioral to cognitive paradigm in psychology stimulated further research on mental processing and formal features. Some research questions have persisted from the 1960s until the present, such as effect on school achievement and aggression. Research evolved from a focus on specifying variables to describing the relationships and interactions among variables. More varied research agendas have considered not only the formal instructional implications of television but also the social, psychological, and instructional effects of broadcast television in various, less-formal environments (Comstock & Paik, 1987; Huston et al., 1992).

12.2.5 Methodological Approaches

Historically, research on television has employed four methodologies: experimental, qualitative, descriptive, and developmental. There has been a general chronological correspondence between certain methodologies and research foci, for example, between comparative studies and instructional effectiveness and between correlational studies and school achievement. For this reason, it is important to understand that research related to television has, over the years, come to address more than simply the effects of televised instruction on learning. Evolving societal demands brought about the need for different methodological approaches to study the disparate effects of television on types of viewers, on variations in viewing environments, on socialization effects, and on interaction with programming variables (Cambre, 1987). Such a broad base of research agendas has necessitated reliance on research methodologies other than those of a traditional empirical nature.

The vast majority of current television research reflects these four methodological approaches: experimental, qualitative, descriptive, and developmental. This section deals with these various research methodologies with regard to their purposes, strengths, and weaknesses as they apply to film and television research.

12.2.5.1 Experimental Methodology.
Early research in television effects utilized traditional experimental designs, albeit with different levels of robustness and precision. The era of film and television research conducted during the 1940s through the mid-1960s, which has been referred to as the period of comparative research studies generally used traditional experimental designs, such as those described by Campbell and Stanley (1963). Although many of these studies were methodologically weak in that they did not employ randomization of groups, pretests, or control groups, and have been subsequently criticized for these reasons (Greenhill, 1967; Stickell, 1963), it is important to note that there were many methodologically rigorous studies conducted during this period which continue to provide useful insights, not only into the comparative effects of television and traditional classroom instruction but also into the effects of specific variables, such as color, inserted questions, and presentation techniques (Greenhill, 1967; Reid & MacLennan, 1967). During the period of time from the mid-1960s through the 1970s, other empirical studies were prompted by (a) better design conceptualization such as the aptitude treatment interaction paradigm, (b) more robust statistical analysis techniques, and (c) greater attention to the individual characteristics of the medium, the child, and the viewing environment. Increasingly, research moved from the laboratory or classroom to the home and social environment. Two types of experimental studies that compare variables are common in research on television: laboratory and field experiments. The former has advantages when comparing theories, testing hypotheses, and measuring effects; the latter is suited to checking the results of laboratory experiments in real-life settings (Comstock, 1980). An example of a laboratory experiment would be three treatments (i.e., violent first segment, violent last segment, and nonviolent segment) given to three randomly assigned groups who are given written instruments assessing recall.* An example of a field experiment would be randomly assigning children to watch specific television shows at home and then administering attitude surveys and comprehension measures.

The major advantage of the laboratory experiment is that random assignment of subjects to specific treatment conditions can control for the effect of other variables. The disadvantage is that there is no certainty that the setting is realistic. The major disadvantage of the field experiment is that it produces little consistent evidence because control of variables is less rigorous. Nevertheless, one can be more confident in how realistic the findings are with a field experiment; however, realism and validity are gained at the expense of control of variables and the possibility of drawing causal conclusions. Laboratory research, on the other hand, generally allows one to draw cause–effect conclusions about interactions.

12.2.5.2 Qualitative Methodology.
Qualitative research methodology includes approaches that typically use nonexperimental methods, such as ethnography or case studies, to investigate important variables that are not easily manipulated or controlled and which emphasize the use of multiple methods for collecting, recording, and analyzing data (Seels & Richey, 1994). Although case histories have been used frequently in television research, ethnographic studies are becoming more common. The trend toward qualitative research emerged after new research questions began to be asked about the mediating effect of the home context for television viewing (Leichter et al., 1985). Often with qualitative research, the purpose is hypothesis generating rather than hypothesis testing. Unlike survey methodology, qualitative research cannot present a broad picture because it concentrates on single subjects or groups, although longitudinal studies can describe how groups, or individuals change over time. There is no attempt at representative sampling as in survey research. Examples of case studies abound in literature on early ITV and ETV projects. Ethnographic studies have been

conducted by photographing or videotaping the home environment, which mediates television viewing (Allen, 1965; Lewis, 1993). An example of a recent ethnographic study on learning from television is the *Ghostwriter* study conducted by CTW (Children's Television Workshop' October 1994). *Ghostwriter* is an after school literacy* program that encompasses a mix of media including television and utilizes outreach programs with community organizations. Ethnographic techniques were used to gather data on wide variations in observed phenomena in disparate settings. For example, case studies were done at Boys' and Girls' Clubs in Los Angeles and Indianapolis and at Bethune Family Learning Circle in Baltimore.

12.2.5.3 Descriptive Methodology.
Studies in this category include survey research such as demographic, cross-cultural, and longitudinal, in addition to content and meta-analyses.* The common denominator among such studies is the use of survey techniques for the purpose of reporting characteristics of populations or samples.

Survey research uses samples of group populations to study sociological and psychological variables. To do this, data can be collected by personal or telephone interview, questionnaires, panels, and structured observation. Demographic research uses facts and figures collected by others, such as the census bureau or television information offices. Cross-cultural studies based on surveys use factual data about groups to draw generalizations.

There are many longitudinal* and cross-sectional* studies in the body of literature on learning from television Sometimes these are based on qualitative research, sometimes on quantitative research, and sometimes on both. The longitudinal method can reveal links between earlier and later behavior and changes in individuals over time, but the changes may be the result of many factors not just developmental maturation. Cross-sectional studies can demonstrate age differences in behavior by observing people of different ages at one point in time. They provide information about change over time in cohort groups but not change in individuals. A sequential* method combines the cross-sectional and longitudinal approaches by observing different groups on multiple occasions. Obviously, the more variables are controlled in each of these methods, the more reliably results can be interpreted. If there is not sufficient control of variables, the results from a cross-sectional study can conflict with the results of a longitudinal study. The longitudinal method is more extensively used, perhaps because it is easier and less expensive.

Parallel longitudinal studies in Australia, Finland, Israel, Poland, and the United States (Heusman & Eron, 1986, cited in Huston et al., 1992) revealed a pattern of involvement with violence related to amount of television viewing. The amount of violence viewed at age 8 predicted aggression at age 18 and serious criminal behavior at age 30. Because this was a relational study, however, it could not be determined whether more violence was viewed because of the viewer's personality or whether violent programming affected the viewer through desensitization* or some other mechanism (Eron, 1982; Huesmann, Eron, Lefkowitz, & Walder, 1984, cited in Huston et al., 1992). Milavsky, Kessler, Stripp, and Rubens (1982) conducted a similar study and concluded that other research did not support

the hypothesis. On the other hand, methodology experts who examined other studies supported the hypothesis on violence and aggression (Cook, Kendzencky, & Thomas, 1983, cited in Huston et al., 1992).

Content analyses are used to determine variables such as (1) the number of violent, antisocial, or prosocial incidents in a program; (2) characteristics of roles* given ethnic groups, gender, age, or occupations portrayed; and (3) values presented on television, such as in commercials. Meta-analyses, which use statistical techniques for synthesis of the literature, and integrated research studies, which use comprehensive surveys and graphic comparison of the literature, are used to draw conclusions from multiple studies on a research question.

12.2.5.4 Developmental Methodology.
Formative evaluation as a research methodology developed in response to a need for procedures to systematically try out and revise materials during a product development process (Cambre, 1987). It is one of the major contributions of television research. According to Flagg (1990), "The goal of formative evaluation is to inform the decision making process during the design, production, and implementation stages of an educational program with the purpose of improving the program" (p. 241). The techniques used in formative evaluation of television programs are important areas of competency for instructional technologists. Formative evaluation studies pose research questions rather than hypotheses, and techniques employed range from oral reports and videotaping reactions to short questionnaires. Evaluation models incorporate phases, such as pre- and postproduction, in the research process.

An example of formative evaluation studies on television is the AIT report on the development of a lesson in the form of a program entitled "Taxes Influence Behavior" (Agency for Instructional Television, 1984). Students were questioned about attention to the program, interest, story believability, character perceptions, storyline comprehension, and program objectives. Teachers were asked about the program's appeal, curriculum fit, objectives, and utilization. Revisions and recommendations for teachers were based on the data collected.

It was Children's Television Workshop (CTW) that pioneered techniques for formative and summative evaluation* (Flagg, 1990). After specifying message design variables and then investigating the effect of these variables on psychological phenomena such as attention, CTW developed techniques for investigating relationships formatively, so that designs could be changed, and summatively, so that effects on behavior could be reported. In doing so, CTW forever put to rest the assumption that one style of television is best for all young children (Lesser, 1974) and the assumption that television was not an interactive enough medium to teach intellectual skills to young children.

Periodic bibliographies issued by CTW document not only the research done there but also research related to CTW productions. Sammur (1990) developed a *Selected Bibliography of Research on Programming at the Children's Television Workshop* that annotated 36 formative, summative, and theoretical research studies on the four educational children's television series produced by CTW. The CTW research program reflects the systematic application of design, development, and evaluation procedures that is necessitated by the expense of producing for sophisticated educational technologies.

12.2.6 Current Issues

The current issues of importance are how television should be regulated and how the technology will evolve. Therefore, legislation in the 1990s and the consequences of new technological innovation are discussed.

12.2.6.1 Legislation. The Children's Television Act was passed in 1990 and revised in 1992. The revision was prompted by the difficulty of enforcing a law that did not clearly define children's programming (Strasburger & Donnerstein, 1999). The Federal Communications Commission (FCC) concluded that it was not within their role to determine the value of specific programs because there are constitutional limits to the public interest standard in relation to the first amendment to the Constitution. The FCC decided to require licensees to justify how they serve the needs of a community within the construction of the law (Corn-Revere, 1997). The Telecommunications Act of 1996 fostered implementation of the Children's Television Act by requiring ratings and V-chips. Those concerned about television's affect on children stressed that there should be increased regulation of television by the FCC and of the Internet by the Federal Trade Commission. The most active research area related to legislation has been the affect of the ratings system. Unfortunately, research has shown few effects from the ratings. Another active area is the effect of captions. The Television Decoder Circuitry Act of 1993 mandated all new television sets in the United States have the capability for closed captions that are used for deaf children and those learning English as a second language (ESL) (Parks, 1995).

12.2.6.2 The Changing Television Environment. The television landscape has been restructured with the advent of new technologies. This shift began with the diffusion of television hardware into every home, and continued to the everyday adoption of associated television technologies such as cable and satellite delivery systems and the ubiquity of the videotape recorder. During the past decade, the number of television receivers per home has skyrocketed, with many children each having a TV set in their bedroom. Through cable and satellite access, families have a choice of a hundred or more channels, most broadcasting twenty-four hours a day. The videotape recorder has enabled viewers to delay watching or to rewatch television programs at any time and thereby shift the traditional viewing hours to virtually any time of the day. The research studies directed at these phenomena have confirmed, however, that little effect has been seen in children's viewing habits. There was simply more of the same programming fare and it was available through a broader time frame. The distribution of television sets into various areas of the home and the less traditional hours of availability have, if anything, reduced the opportunities for parental coviewing and control. The V-chip was predicted to enhance the ability of parents to exercise such control, but appears to have been a failure with many parents not even aware of the existence of such a device.

The second factor contributing to this changing environment was the advent of all the digital technologies, but dominated by the Internet. World Wide Web based materials have become a parallel media which often interact with existing television programming to produce a unique "hybrid" technology that incorporates some of the characteristics of the parent technologies as well as some unique new applications. Internet based educational sites have become a stock-in-trade in most schools and have recently merged with the television industry through the creation of web sites for many of the educational channels or programs. It is not unusual today to see news or science programs that have their own web sites and that display a web site-like screen display during their programming. These complementary technologies can enhance the attention gaining power of the programming as well as the ability of children to better comprehend what is presented enabling them to interact with the program content in a more meaningful way.

The further developments and diffusion of purely digital forms of television media such as digital television, digital video disks (DVD), broadband delivery, and the ability of individuals to produce and incorporate sophisticated video material will be additional steps in the restructuring of television.

What does this mean in terms of the way children interact with and learn from television? First, the greater flexibility, versatility, and accessibility will increase the options children are faced with and the need for structure and guidance from parents and teachers. Children will also clearly need to develop more sophisticated literacy and interpretation skills. Whether or not these can or will be provided by schools and families is hard to predict at this point, given the poor success of critical viewing skills and the looser family structure.

Second, the highly interactive nature of the Internet and Internet–television hybrid types of media will provide children with more activities to interact with the technology and the information provided by it, rather than functioning as lower-level receptors of the broadcast medium. In this way, the full effect of the active theory will become apparent.

A third future lies in the increasingly enhanced realism of computer-television technology. Researchers are predicting that the innovations of virtual reality technology, which are now evolving commercially in video game formats, will enhance the realism of the computer-television medium particularly for educational purposes.

12.2.7 Summary

Film research during the 1950s contributed an identification of variables, especially variables related to message design. However, much of this research was methodologically flawed. Therefore, today it is useful primarily for the model it set for television research and the variables it identified. During the 1960s television research emphasized comparative studies and frequently focused on message design variables.

The 1970s were a period of transition in that there was a move from ITV to ETV research and a move from comparative studies to the study of specific variables and effects via the aptitude treatment interaction paradigm. There was also a methodological shift to qualitative, descriptive, and developmental studies in addition to traditional empirical studies.

During the 1980s and 1990s, variables began to be categorized into a viewing system consisting of programming, environment, and behavior, all of which interrelated. We turn now from a chronological consideration of the historical context of film and television research to findings in the major areas of interest to researchers.

12.3 MESSAGE DESIGN AND COGNITIVE PROCESSING

The vast majority of early instructional films and television programs were essentially documentary works that were developed by commercial, noneducational producers. At this early point in the evolution of instructional technology, little attention was given to the use of instructional techniques or design principles. Similarly, the technology of film or television was still in its infancy, and few, if any, editing or special visual effects were available to the producers of such materials. In light of this, it is not surprising that most of the earlier research focused on simple comparisons between the technology and some form of standard instruction. Since the two technologies did not incorporate many of the production elements that have become part of their unique symbol systems as we understand them today, little attention was given to assessing the effects of specific media characteristics on student learning.

12.3.1 The Evolution of Message Design

During the period of the Pennsylvania State University film studies, however, some research was directed at determining how the intentional incorporation of instructional techniques and media characteristics interacted with learner achievement from the materials. The variables studied included: the use of inserted questions, color, subjective camera angle, sound track modifications, and the use of visual cueing devices (Greenhill, 1956; Hoban & van Ormer, 1951). Similar studies were further conducted on instructional television in the late 1950s and early 1960s, generally on adult audiences in controlled environments (Chu & Schramm, 1967; Greenhill, 1967). From this time on, a growing number of researchers have investigated, in increasingly greater levels of detail, the instructional effectiveness of television productions incorporating specialized features that are intended to facilitate learning. The process of specifying and organizing these components has come to be called *message design*.

Fleming and Levie (1993) define an instructional message as "a pattern of signs (words, pictures, gestures) produced for the purpose of modifying the psychomotor, cognitive, or affective behavior of one or more persons" (p. x). Grabowski (1991) describes message design as "planning for the manipulation of the physical form of the message" (p. 206). The concept of message design was not used in the literature until the 1970s, although the general principles of message design were being synthesized from research on perception, psychology, and instruction. Early researchers focused primarily on visual perception (Fleming, 1967; Knowlton, 1966; Norberg, 1962, 1966); however, later researchers addressed auditory and print media as well. Fleming and Levie (1978, 1993) first defined the term *message design* and comprehensively articulated its general principles for instructional designers. Today, the concept of message design in television includes all of the scripting, production, and editing decisions that are made separate from the actual content of the program.

The design of the instructional television message has become increasingly important as a greater understanding of instructional and cognitive principles has emerged from the study of learning and psychology, and with the growing sophistication of television production technology, particularly in broadcast television. The intentional use of various video effects such as zooms, cuts, dissolves, and the designer's manipulation of program pacing and use of various audio and graphic effects became a standard procedure among instructional designers wishing to maximize the effectiveness of television programming. For the most part, however, these production effects* were not systematically investigated, and, consequently, the television producer had few reliable research guidelines on which to base production decisions.

During the mid-1970s, Aletha Huston and John Wright used the term *formal features* to collectively describe the various production techniques employed in designing and producing the television message (Huston & Wright, 1983). They describe television as being distinguished by its unique forms, rather than simply by the content of the programming. These researchers and their associates at the University of Kansas began a systematic investigation of the formal attributes or features* of television, particularly with respect to how these techniques interact with cognitive processes, such as attention and comprehension (Rice, Huston, & Wright, 1982).

By the late 1970s, much of the television research focused on how children view television and those processes that relate to attention and comprehension of the televised information. This era of research can be best characterized as the conjunction of interest in both the developmental aspects of learning and in cognitive processing of information. Two events in the area of children's television prompted this research: the initial success of *Sesame Street* and associated programming by the Children's Television Workshop (Mielke, 1990), and the increased criticism of television and its alleged negative effects by a number of popular writers (Mander, 1978; Postman, 1982; Winn, 1977).

With the advent of The Children's Television Workshop and *Sesame Street,* a number of researchers began to explore the value of using many of these production techniques. These studies were typically formative in nature, intended for in-house use to assess the adequacy of particular techniques, and consequently did not appear regularly in the research literature (Sammur, 1990). Thus, researchers began to focus on those unique features that promote children's attention and comprehension during television viewing. In this research, the cognitive effects of formal features such as pacing, audio cues, camera effects, animation, and editing techniques were also explored with regard to the role that they played in attention and comprehension (Meyer, 1983).

During this time, public interest was also drawn to the possible negative effects of television programming on children in addition to the continuing public concern for the effects of television violence on children, interest increased into the possibly debilitating effects on children's cognitive processing abilities. In her book, *The Plug-in Drug,* Winn (1977) charged that television and the formal features inherent in the programming were causing excessive cognitive passivity* and depressed processing capabilities.*

Organized research, which was prompted by these events and criticisms, investigated the general effects on both attention and comprehension, as well as on the specific effects of television's formal production features in a fairly comprehensive manner. Such research has given us a remarkably thorough understanding of how television promotes cognitive activities (Anderson & Collins, 1988).

As interest in the cognitive aspects of children's television grew, hypotheses were developed to account for these effects in a broad manner, irrespective of particular types of programming. While a number of these theoretical perspectives are unconfirmed, they have provided the impetus and base for substantial, systematic research.

12.3.2 The Effects of Television on Cognitive-Processing Abilities

Television has been both lauded and criticized for the ways in which it presents information to the viewer, irrespective of the information itself (Anderson & Collins, 1988). It is this area, that of the relationship between the ways in which information is presented on television and the effect of that presentation on the cognitive-processing abilities of the viewer, which has continued to attract a great deal of theoretical as well as supporting research interest (Huston et al., 1992).

12.3.2.1 Theoretical Orientations. One critical view that has persisted over the years, despite contrary research findings, is that the television image and associated presentation effects are cognitively debilitating (Mander, 1978; Winn, 1977). The central assertion of this viewpoint is that the rapidly changing television image-enhanced by production features such as cuts, zooms, animation, and special effects-is cognitively mesmerizing. This is hypothesized to result in cognitive passivity, shortened attention spans, and, paradoxically enough, hyperactive behavior (Dumont, 1976, cited in Winn, 1977, Winn, 1977). Such a view is more conjecture than substantiated fact or articulated theory and has been drawn substantially from subjective observation rather than from extensive empirical research. The notion, however, has appealed to many who associate these behavioral manifestations with general, adult entertainment forms of television and who are more critical of the content of television programming rather than the presentation formats. It should be noted that most researchers in the area of cognitive

science and educational technology have not supported these assertions, which remain, to a large degree, open to definitive and methodologically rigorous research (Anderson & Collins, 1988).

12.3.2.2 Empirical Research. For the most part, research related to this aspect of television effects has been drawn from studies done in the area of advertising and marketing or in electroencephalography (EEG). Krugman (1970, 1971) compared the EEGs of subjects viewing rear projected visual images and those of subjects reading, and concluded that television viewing resulted in different brain wave patterns than did reading. It is important to note that these studies were conducted on a single subject and only used the subject's EEG obtained while browsing a magazine as a baseline index. The length of time the EEG was recorded was also only 15 minutes, and readings were taken at only one location on the head. The two brain wave patterns of interest were the alpha rhythm, which is associated with an inactive or resting brain state, and the beta rhythm, which is usually indicative of cognitive activity. These experiments were repeated by Krugman, using actual television images with similar results (Krugman, 1979). Similar findings were produced by several other researchers who indicated that television viewing produced more alpha activity than reading, which resulted in greater beta activity (Appel, Weinstein, & Weinstein, 1979; Featherman, Frieser, Greenspun, Harris, Schulman, & Crown, 1979; Walker, 1980; Weinstein, Appel, & Weinstein, 1980). In these cases, alpha activity was associated with periods of low cognitive activity, which was interpreted to be the mesmerizing effect described by critics.

Drawing from the work of Krugman (1979), Emery and Emery (1975, 1980) criticized television images as "habituating" because the continuously scanned image emitted an overload of light-based information, potentially resulting in an overload of the processing system. This claim was substantially refuted, however, in studies by Silberstein, Agardy, Ong, and Heath (1983), who, in methodologically rigorous experiments with 12-year-old children, found no differences in brain wave activity between projected text and text presented on the television screen. Furthermore, differences were found between text presented on the television screen and documentary or interview programming whereas no differences were found between the two types of programming. A third interesting finding was that both the text and interview program produced right and left hemisphere effects, while the documentary alone resulted in greater right hemisphere activity. A comprehensive and critical review of most of the EEG research was published by Fite (1994). In this report, Fite found virtually no substantiation of the detrimental effects of television evidenced by EEG-based studies.

Focusing specifically on viewer attention, Rothshild, Thorson, Reeves, Hirsch, and Goldstein (1986) found that alpha activity dropped immediately following the introduction of a scene change or formal feature in the program material, which in these studies were commercial advertisements. Winn (1977) has further criticized children's television and Sesame Street, in particular, for contributing to shortened attention spans and hyperactive behavior. A study by Halpern (1975) has been frequently cited as providing evidence that programming such as Sesame Street contributed to hyperactive and compulsive behavior. This study has been seriously criticized on methodological grounds by Anderson and Collins (1988), and the findings have not been successfully replicated by Halpern. Other studies related to children's concentration and tolerance for delay reported moderate decreases in tolerance for delay associated with action programs (Friedrich & Stein, 1973) and actually increased concentration resulting from television viewing among children rated as low in imagination (Tower, Singer, Singer, & Biggs, 1979). Anderson, Levin, and Lorch (1977) investigated the effect of program pacing on attention, activity, and impulsivity levels and found no differences in 5-year-old children's degree of activity, impulsivity, or perseverance levels. Salomon (1979), however, found that Sesame Street viewing, when compared to other general types of children's programming, produced a decrease in perseverance in a laboratory task. This effect may have been related to differences in the audience's age and the intended target age of the Sesame Street programming and the relative ease of the task.

12.3.3 The Television Symbol System or Code

For the most part, research into the cognitive effects of television has focused more specifically on how televised information is processed rather than on how television affects cognitive processing abilities (Anderson & Collins, 1988). This research is based on theory related to both the symbol system or formal features used in television and the ways that information is attended to and comprehended.

12.3.3.1 *The Role of Filmic Codes* in Processing.* One of the most universal views of television as a medium was described by McLuhan (1964) when he suggested that the formal attributes of a medium, such as television, influence how we think and process information. Furthermore, McLuhan put forth the idea that different media present information in unique ways that are idiosyncratic to the individual medium. Goodman (1968) and Gardner, Howard, and Perkins (1974) further elaborated on the function of such symbol systems,* implying that similarities between the symbol system and mental representations of the content will facilitate comprehension of the instructional message. More recently, Kozma (1991) suggests that different media are defined by three characteristics: the technology,* the symbol systems employed, and the methods of processing information. Of these, the symbol system is crucial to the mental processing of the person interacting with the medium. The individual symbol systems may be idiosyncratic to the particular medium and consequently may need to be learned by the user. This thesis has been elaborated on by Gavriel Salomon, who has attempted to test it empirically with regard to television (Salomon, 1972, 1974, 1979; Salomon & Cohen, 1977). He suggested that different symbol systems or codes can represent information in different ways during encoding in memory, making it necessary to process the information in unique ways. Salomon contended that children learn to interpret these "filmic codes," which can be incorporated into

cognitive activities in two ways (Salomon, 1979). The first function of symbolic or filmic codes is that they can call on or activate cognitive skills within the learner and can become internalized into the learner's repertoire of processing skills (Salomon & Cohen, 1977). In this way, such production features as montage* or cuts can activate respective cognitive processes such as inferencing and sequencing. The second role of filmic codes lies in the assumption that these codes, which model cognitive processes, can actually "stand in" for or "supplant" the cognitive skills themselves, thereby facilitating learning (Salomon, 1974). In this manner, features such as zooms and dissolves can be used to model the cognitive skills they represent and consequently enhance the processing skills of the viewer.

Rice, Huston, and Wright (1983) further differentiated the types of representation within the television code into three levels. These include at the most basic level, literal visual or auditory portrayal of real-world information. At the second level are media forms and conventions that have no real-world counterpart, such as production effects and formal features. The third level consists of symbolic code that is not distinctive to the television medium. These third level codes consist of linguistic, nonlinguistic, and auditory code such as language, which may be used to "double encode" or describe the visual codes presented on the screen. Of the three, the media forms and conventions are of most interest to the researcher because they are idiosyncratic to the media of television and film and relate most specifically to the child's processing of the television message (Rice, Huston, & Wright, 1983).

12.3.3.2 *Research on Filmic Codes.* There is not a great deal of empirical work related to the cognitive effects of television code. However, the work of Gavriel Salomon constitutes the most comprehensive series of empirical studies focused on the symbol system and code of television. Drawing on his theoretical position, he devised a series of experiments that explored the use of filmic codes to model or supplant cognitive skills and to call on or activate specific cognitive skills. He conducted the first group of studies with Israeli eighth-graders to determine if the camera effect of zooming could indeed model the relation of the part to the whole (Salomon, 1974). The results indicated that the children exposed to the experimental treatment performed significantly better than did those students either shown the individual close-up and overall pictures or those receiving no treatment. In this case, the use of explicit modeling of the cognitive skill improved the student's ability to focus attention on the detailed parts of the overall display. A second experiment, using fewer visual transformations, was not as effective as the first possibly indicating that extensive modeling of these skills is necessary for this effect to occur. In a third experiment, Salomon confirmed that the internalization of the filmic codes could enhance the cognitive skills of the viewer by presenting scenes where the three-dimensional unfolding of an object was compared with the same representation in two dimensions. In this case, the three-dimensional animation effect modeled the cognitive analog of mentally unfolding the object from three dimensions to two dimensions more effectively than did simple presentation of the two-dimensional object. A study conducted by Rovet (1983) using a spatial rotation task with third-grade

children further confirmed Salomon's findings, although conclusive confirmation of this theory has not been provided through research.

The second assertion made by Salomon suggested that filmic, codes could also activate or "call upon" specific cognitive skills. In a series of studies, Salomon (1979) tested this hypothesis on groups of preschool, second-grade, and third-grade Israeli students using *Sesame Street* programming as the content. After 6 months, the groups of school-aged children demonstrated significantly higher comprehension scores. This was interpreted by Salomon to indicate that students were able to learn the meanings of the filmic codes, and in so doing activated the respective cognitive skills. However, the effects were limited to the older children and have been qualified by Salomon to suggest that these mental skills can be activated by the appropriate filmic codes, but are not necessarily always activated in this manner.

12.3.4 Children's Attention to Television

The effect of the television symbol system on learning has been addressed through two areas of cognitive processing: attention and comprehension. For each of these areas, we discuss theoretical approaches and empirical research.

12.3.4.1 Reactive/Active Theory.
Two approaches to understanding the way in which children attend to television have emerged. These positions include the reactive theory* which generally views the child as passive and simply a receptor of information or stimuli delivered by the television, and the active theory* which suggests that children cognitively interact with the information being presented as well as with the viewing environment (Anderson & Lorch, 1983). These two viewpoints generally parallel theoretical orientations to human information processing in that early concepts of the human information processing system were reasonably linear and viewed attention as a relatively receptive process where the learner merely reacted to stimuli that were perceived (Atkinson & Shiffrin, 1968). Later conceptions of how we process information took the position that we are active participants in selecting and processing incoming stimuli (Anderson, 1980).

The first theoretical orientation, the reactive theory, is derived from Bandura's Social Learning Theory* (Bandura, 1977). In this conceptualization, the salient formal features of the television programming gain and maintain the viewer's attention. Continued attention and comprehension occur more or less automatically as the child's information processing system functions reactively. Singer (1980) describes this process as one where the continually changing screen and auditory patterns create an ongoing series of orienting reflexes in the viewer. Key to this orientation is the role of the viewer as a passive, involuntary processor of information that is absorbed from the screen. The reactive theory of attention to television is supported by little direct research, with most of the foundation for the theory being based on the early human information processing theories such as those described by Atkinson and Shiffrin (1968, 1971), Broadbent (1959), and Neisser (1967). The work of Singer (1980) included little direct research relative

to this perspective, but rather drew on what was, at that time, a popular theory of memory that described the human information processing system as one in which information was processed in the sensory store, received further processing in short-term memory, and was then transferred to long-term memory, all without a great deal of active or purposeful selection, processing, or coding by the learner.

It is generally accepted today that the reactive theory requires much revision, particularly with regard to the learner's role in initiating and actively processing new information in relation to prior knowledge. For these reasons, little substantiation of the theory can be put forth, especially in light of the support that current research provides to the opposing theory, the active theory.

The alternative theory, the active theory, defines the child as an active processor who is guided by previous knowledge, expectations, and schemata* (Anderson & Lorch, 1983). In this way, the child does not merely respond to the changing stimuli presented, but rather actively applies strategies based on previous experience with the content and formal features, personal knowledge structures, and available cognitive skills. Key to this view is the assumption that the child will apply existing schemas to the perception and processing of the televised information. Anderson and Lorch (1983) suggest that a number of premises underlie the functioning of the active theory. These include consideration of competing stimuli, the need to maintain a reasonable level of stimulus unfamiliarity, the role of auditory cues to refocus attention, and the effect of attentional inertia* to maintain cognitive involvement (Anderson, Alwitt, Lorch, & Levin, 1979). Additionally, a key component of the active theory is the role of viewing schemata, which Anderson and Lorch suggest develop through increased interaction with television forms, as well as with general cognitive growth.

The notion of representational codes or formal features and their role and effects in the processing of television information has become an area of particular interest and the central focus of much research regarding how children attend to and process the television message. Formal features are defined by Anderson and Collins (1988) as characteristic attributes of the medium, which can be described without reference to specific content. In reality these include, but are not limited to, the visual features of zooms, camera movements, cuts and dissolves, montage techniques, animation, ellipses, program pace, and special visual effects, as well as the auditory features of music, sound effects, and unusual voices. A fairly comprehensive taxonomy of formal features has been developed by the research group at the Center for Research on the Influence of Television on Children (CRITC) (Huston & Wright, 1983; Rice, Huston, & Wright, 1983).

Two constructs related to the visual message and the forms of television have emerged and become important to an understanding of how these forms function in the processing of the television message. These constructs, which include visual complexity or the amount and degree of change of information (Watt & Welch, 1983; Welch & Watt, 1982) and perceptual salience* or those attributes of the stimulus that increase its intensity, contrast, change, or novelty (Berlyne, 1960; Rice, Huston, & Wright, 1983), relate to both quantitative and qualitative characteristics of the message. Researchers associated with each of these positions have developed or adapted models that can be used to conceptualize the effects of these attributes on the message and how it is processed by the viewer. Watt and Welch employed an information theory model for entropy to explain the relationship between static and dynamic complexity and learning from television content (Watt & Welch, 1983; Welch & Watt, 1982). Rice, Huston, and Wright (1982) presented a model that described the relationship between attention and stimulus complexity. For the most part, however, the effects of the formal features of television have been considered with regard to the particular cognitive processes or skills with which they are associated, attention and comprehension, and consequently, they are best examined from that perspective.

12.3.4.2 Research on Attention.

The variable of attention to the television program has received extensive research interest, of which the most comprehensive group of studies has been conducted by Daniel Anderson and his associates at the University of Massachusetts. This group of researchers was the first to propose that the process of attending to television programming was active rather than simply a reaction to the stimuli presented.

One of the first questions relative to attention to television is a qualification of exactly what attention is and how it can appropriately be measured. Anderson and Field (1983) describe five methodologies that may constitute an effective measure of this attention. These include (a) visual orientation, the physical orientation of the viewer toward the television screen; (b) eye movements and fixations; (c) comprehension and recognition testing, which measures attention through inferences drawn from objective recognition and comprehension tests; (d) interference methods, which pinpoint attention as that time when a viewer responds to and removes some form of interfering information from the message; and (e) physiological measures that include cardiac, galvanic skin response, and electroencephalographic records of arousal. Of these, the most frequently employed have been visual orientation and the use of recognition and comprehension tests.

Anderson and Field (1983) identify a number of settings and contexts for viewing that impinge on the attentional process. They differentiate between the home viewing environment and laboratory settings in terms of the accuracy of data obtained. Home viewing generally results in overly inflated estimates of attentional time (Bechtel, Achepohl, & Akers, 1972). The use of monitoring cameras revealed that attention does not continue for long periods of time but rather consists of frequent interruptions, conversations, distractions* and the viewer's exits and returns to the room (Allen, 1965; Anderson, 1983). Allen used time-lapse movie cameras, and Bechtel, Achepohl, and Akers videotaped in the home. The results of these studies appear consistent, indicating that children up to age 10 averaged about 52 percent of the time in the viewing room actually attending to the program, while children aged 11 to 19 years showed an average attention of about 69 percent (Bechtel et al., 1972). In all cases, attention to children's programs was substantially higher than to adult-level programming, although this may not

remain true today because of changes in programming and the increased viewing sophistication of children. In laboratory settings, where more control over outside distractions could be maintained, it was found that children still were frequently distracted and demonstrated only sporadic attention to the program (Becker & Wolfe, 1960). In several studies, preschool children were observed to look at and away from the television 150 to 200 times per hour (Alwitt, Anderson, Lorch, & Levin, 1980; Anderson & Levin, 1976; Field, 1983). The lengths of "looks" were also seen as important characteristics of attention. Anderson, Lorch, Smith, Bradford, and Levin (1981) found that looks of more than 30 seconds were infrequent and that the majority of look lengths were less than 5 seconds.

The viewing context was also identified as an influential factor in attention. Sproull (1973) suggested that toys and other activities were strong attention-diverting stimuli, in the absence of which attention rose to 80 percent. Studies by Lorch, Anderson, and Levin (1979) concluded that attention is strategic in children, because audio cues were used heavily to monitor program content and indicate instances when attention should be redirected to the television. The presence of other children with whom they could discuss the program and use as models of attention was also shown to be a strong factor contributing to attentional control (Anderson et al., 1981).

The factor of viewer age has frequently emerged as a variable of significance, particularly with regard to determining at what age children begin to attend to and comprehend the content of the television program. Very young children (6 to 12 months of age) appear to direct attention to the television screen about half the time in controlled situations (Hollenbeck & Slaby, 1979; Lemish & Rice, 1986), with a dramatic increase between 12 and 48 months (Anderson & Levin, 1976). In their study, Anderson and Levin observed an increase in look lengths by a factor of 4 at approximately 30 months of age. Other researchers have reported similar findings (Carew, 1980; Schramm, Lyle, & Parker, 1961).

Attention appears to increase continuously beyond this age to about 12 years, at which point it plateaus (Alwitt et al., 1980; Anderson, 1983; Anderson, Lorch, Field, Collins, & Nathan, 1986; Anderson, Lorch, Field, & Sanders, 1981; Calvert, Huston, Watkins, & Wright, 1982).

The unique role of the formal features of television has been the focus of much research on children's attention. Such features include both visual and auditory production effects that are integral to the television program composition and presentation. Formal features have significant implications for attention, comprehension, and, as has been discussed previously, modeling and activating cognitive skills. In terms of attention, the research has indicated that only some formal features, specifically special visual effects, changes in scene, character change, and high levels of action, are reasonably effective at eliciting attention, while conventional camera effects such as cuts, zooms, and pans have substantially less power to gain attention (Rice, Huston, & Wright, 1983). The visual feature that most inhibited attention was the long zoom effect. Other program components, such as animation, puppets, and frequent changes of speaker, while not actually production features, were also found to promote attention. Those components that decreased attention were live animals, song and dance, and long speeches (Alwitt et al., 1980; Anderson & Levin, 1976; Calvert, Huston, Watkins, & Wright, 1982).

Several researchers have observed that the sound track of the television program plays a major role in attention, particularly in gaining the attention of the nonviewing child (Anderson & Field, 1983). With respect to the generalized use or effect of the audio track to direct attention, Lorch et al. (1979) found that auditory attention parallels visual attention* and increases with age at a rate similar to that of visual attention. When the audio message was experimentally degraded so as to be unintelligible, either through technical reversal or substitution, children at ages 2, 3, 3½, and 5 years evidenced significant drops in attention to *Sesame Street* programs, with the most significant drop being observed with the older children (Anderson, Lorch, Field, & Sanders, 1981). It has also been reported that children employ the audio message to monitor the program for critical or comprehensible content, which they can then attend to visually (Anderson & Lorch, 1983). Auditory attention to television is, to a large degree, mediated by the formal attributes of the auditory message, including type, age, and gender of voice, and the novelty of particular sound, sound effects, or music. Research conducted by Alwitt et al. (1980) revealed that certain audio effects were effective in gaining attention from nonviewing children. These included auditory changes, sound effects, laughter, instrumental music, and children's, women's, and "peculiar" voices; alternatively men's voices, individual singing, and slow music inhibited attention (Anderson & Lorch, 1983). The researchers concluded that auditory devices such as those described cued the children that an important change was taking place in the program which might be of interest, thereby prompting attention. They also reported that audio effects do not appear to have any significant effect before the age of 24 to 30 months, which parallels approximately the beginning of general attending behavior noted previously.

When all types of formal features, both visual and auditory, are considered in terms of their ability to facilitate attention, it becomes apparent that those, which are most obvious, are generally most effective (Wright, Huston, Ross, Calvert, Rolandelli, Weeks, Raeissi, & Potts, 1984). These researchers contend that the more perceptually salient a feature is, such as fast action or pace, the more effectively it will gain attention. This was partially confirmed in research they described in which those programs identified as high in feature saliency also had larger viewing audiences. Interestingly, *Sesame Street,* which has a high viewership and attention gaining power, has been found to be slower paced (in terms of shot length) than other entertainment programs (Bryant, 1992). Evidence was also found which suggests that violence per se is not necessarily attention gaining, but rather the high saliency of formal features in violent programs may be responsible for the higher viewer numbers (Huston & Wright, 1983; Wright et al., 1984; Wright & Huston, 1982).

The differential effects of both visual and auditory formal features have been cited by several researchers as significant evidence supporting the active theory of attention to television (Anderson & Field, 1983; Rice, Huston & Wright, 1983). They contend that for the reactive theory to be an apt descriptor

of children's attentional behavior, all formal features should be effective at virtually all ages, because they should all automatically elicit an orienting reaction due to their movement, stimulus change, or salient visual patterns. Since the research consistently identifies only certain features at particular ages as attention gaining and conversely finds that other features are inhibiting to attention, this hypothesis is strongly rejected (Anderson & Field, 1983). With regard to the active theory, they describe the viewing child as actively and selectively in command of his or her own attentional strategies. For this reason, the child could be expected to respond differentially to the various stimuli and features, which is the case made by current research findings (Hawkins, Kin & Pingree, 1991). Alwitt et al. (1980) conclude:

An attribute (feature) comes to have a positive or negative relationship to attention, we hypothesize, based on the degree to which it predicts relevant and comprehensible content. A child can thus use an attribute to divide attention between TV viewing and other activities: Full attention is given when an attribute is predictive of understandable content and terminated when an attribute predicts irrelevant, boring, and incomprehensible content. (p. 65)

12.3.5 Children's Comprehension of Television

Anderson and Field (1983) explain that formal features perform two significant functions: First, they mark the beginning of important content segments, and second, they communicate producer-intended concepts of time, space, action, and character (Anderson & Field, 1983). The notion that the formal features, which comprise such television effects as montage, are able to convey changes in time, place, or movement is integral to a viewer's ability to comprehend story content and plot as well as simply to gain or hold attention. It is in the area of comprehension that formal features appear to play the most important role.

12.3.5.1 Relationship of Comprehension to Attention. The basic theory related to children's comprehension of television relates to and derives from theoretical bases for attention (Anderson & Lorch, 1983). They cite the reactive theory for suggesting that once attention has been gained, comprehension will automatically follow as a natural consequence. Interestingly, Singer (1980) and Singer and Singer (1982), proponents of the reactive theory, suggest that the rapid pace or delivery of most television messages that gain or hold attention, may not permit the viewer to process adequately the information at a deep enough level to ensure high levels of comprehension. The active theory, on the other hand, maintains that attention itself is directed by children's monitoring* of the program for comprehensible content, which serves as a signal to focus more direct attention to the message (Anderson & Lorch, 1983). To represent the relationship, Rice, Huston, and Wright (1982) offered the attentional model presented in Fig. 12.1. In this model, both high and low levels of comprehensibility inhibit attention. At the high end (incomprehensibility), the content is complex and not understood by the child and consequently elicits little interest or attention. At the low end (boredom), the content is familiar

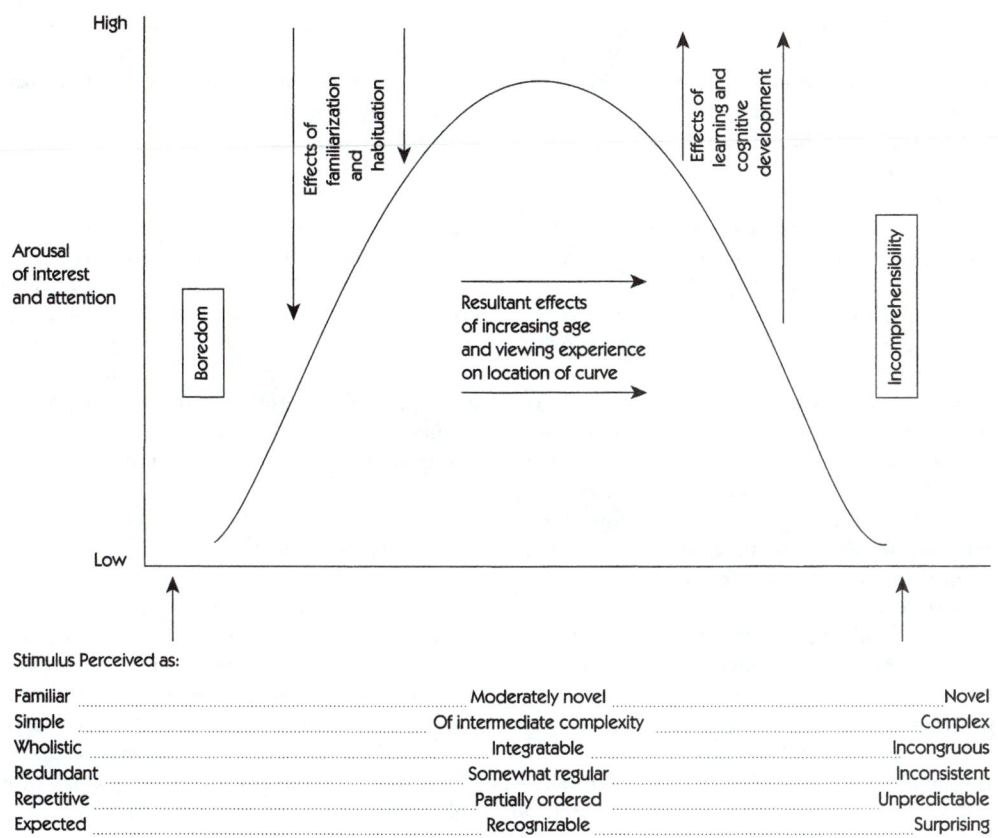

FIGURE 12.1. A model of developmental changes in interest and attention. (From Rice, Huston & Wright, 1982.)

and lacking in information, making it less attention gaining. In this way, comprehension is interpreted to drive attention (Rice, Huston, & Wright, 1983).

A good deal of the theory related to the formal features of television has relevance for the area of comprehension as well as attention. Of particular interest is the concept of montage, one of the formal features previously described. A montage is a series of scenes interrupted by special effects such as cuts, dissolves, changes in point of view, and overlays, the purpose of which is to show various shifts in time, place, or personal point of view. Such actions call on the viewer to maintain a sequence of events, infer changes of scene or time, and to relate or integrate individual scenes to one another (Anderson & Field, 1983). In this way, any two scenes can be joined together to generate a new idea or suggest a relationship that has not been explicitly shown.

Piaget (1926) suggested that younger children (under 7 years) were limited in story comprehension because of weak seriation abilities and the inability to infer and comprehend transformations between events in a story that differ temporally. These limitations reduce the ability to develop complete schemas and consequently impair comprehension. Inconsistencies across theories such as these, however, have produced a dilemma among researchers concerning the ability of children to comprehend fully information presented in this manner via television (Wartella, 1979).

12.3.5.2 Research on Comprehension. Substantial research has addressed the interrelationship between comprehension and attention and the resultant support of the active theory suggested by Anderson and Lorch (1983). Lorch et al. (1979) compared different experimental attention situations in terms of recall of *Sesame Street* content by 5-year-olds. Their findings revealed that variations in the amount of attention a child demonstrated did not differentially affect comprehension scores. However, a significant positive correlation was found between the comprehension scores and the amount of attention exhibited during the specific program content that was related to the comprehension test items. These findings were further supported in research reported by Krull and Husson (1979) and Pezdek and Hartman (1981) who also identified the significance of audio cues in promoting comprehension as well as directing visual attention. A later study, however, by Anderson, Lorch, Field, and Sanders (1981, Study 2), which controlled for extraneous confounding effects of formal features inserted in the programs, produced data that fully supported the earlier findings of Lorch et al. (1979). All in all, these studies provided strong support for the active theory over the reactive theory, in that attention appeared to be significantly directed by the comprehensibility of the program content.

Understandably, the role of formal features in comprehension is directly related to the active theory of television viewing. Anderson and Field (1983) suggest that the employment of formal features in a montage serve the purposes of the producers of the program to convey or infer changes in time, space, action, or point of view. They further contend that the active comprehension hypothesis is consequently supported, in that if children did not actively make the inferences, they would perceive the program as meaningless segments of video and would, therefore, not attend to it.

The earliest research on comprehension of film montage suggested that young children were incapable of comprehending the elements of montage (Piaget, 1926). Empirical research supported these contentions (Baron, 1980; Noble, 1975; Tada, 1969). In these cases, assessment of children's comprehension was made via verbal explanations of what had occurred, a process that has been criticized as being extremely difficult for younger children (Smith, Anderson, & Fisher, 1985). In research that employed nonverbal testing methods such as reconstructing the story using dolls and the original television sets, these researchers found that children aged 3 and 5 years showed substantial comprehension of program content. It is interesting to note that no differences were found between treatments that employed the formal features of pans, zooms, fades, and dissolves and those treatments that relied solely on still photographic representation. Montage that incorporated formal features was apparently not necessary for comprehension of the story. Rather, children were able to comprehend the message presented via either montage or still pictures with equal ability. In a second experiment, Smith et al. (1985) examined the effects of specific montage elements in terms of the outcomes (ellipsis, spatial relationships, character point of view, and simultaneity of action) intended by the producer. In this case, both 4- and 7-year-olds demonstrated good comprehension via the nonverbal evaluation technique, with 7-year-old children showing greater comprehension. The researchers attribute this result to a greater amount of life experience on the part of the older children. A later study conducted by Huston and Wright (1989) indicated that formal features used in montage, such as those used to depict distorted perceptions, memory flashbacks, and instant replays were not comprehended well by school age children. Anderson and Collins (1988) have generally concluded that the features incorporated in montage are well comprehended by children, particularly those who are older and have greater prior experience and knowledge. Anderson and Field (1983) contend that the results of these studies indicate that young children make frequent, active inferences as they interpret montage effects in television programming. Furthermore, they suggest that this fact provides strong support for the active-comprehension hypothesis.

The comprehension of longer segments of programming that necessitated integration and inferencing skills was investigated by Lorch, Bellack, and Augsbach (1987). In two experiments, they determined that both 5-year-olds and 4- and 6-year-olds were capable of selectively recalling 92 percent of ideas that were central to the television stories. Much lower recall rates were found for incidental or noncentral information. In an earlier study, however, Calvert, Huston, Watkins, and Wright (1982) found that children recalled central content that was presented by means of highly salient formal features better than that which used low-salience features. In studies in which the programming content was of much longer duration, such as in commercially broadcast programs, older viewers were generally able to discriminate central content better than younger viewers (Collins, 1983). Collins further suggested that an inability to make inferences contributed to comprehension difficulties, although this research was conducted using entertainment programming that was intended primarily for adult audiences. Anderson and Collins (1988) concluded, however, that the poor comprehension of both central and implied content should be attributed primarily to less developed knowledge bases rather than to any cognitive disability. More recent research (Sell, Ray, & Lovelace, 1995) suggests, however, that repeated viewing of the program results in improved comprehension by 4-year-old children. They attribute this effect to more complete processing of the formal features that enabled children to focus on essential information critical to understanding the plot.

12.3.6 Current Issues

Contemporary research in the cognitive effects of the television medium has generally continued along the same agendas as in previous decades. Additional research into the nature of the television viewing act has further confirmed the active theoretical approach. Recent researchers have explored the role of the auditory message and reported findings that demonstrate the power of audio cues in helping children identify critical information in the visual track which direct their attention to comprehensible program content. Research has shown that the relationship between attention and comprehension, previously identified, is a complex and interactive process which relies on both visual and auditory information as well as prior knowledge of content (Bickham, Wright, & Huston, 2000).

Researchers have also addressed the variable of comprehension in recent research. Studies by Clifford, Gunter, and McAleer (1995) found that children demonstrate different information processing and conceptualizing abilities than do older individuals, and they caution that much of this area has received little research attention. Further work by Kelly and Spear (1991) indicated that comprehension could be improved by the addition of viewing aids such as synopses, which are placed at strategic points in the program.

Research involving the use of closed captioning for deaf students demonstrated the critical nature of the audio track in facilitating comprehension of television program content as well as the beneficial effects of such captioning for all students (Jelinek-Lewis & Jackson, 2001).

12.3.7 Summary and Recommendations

Two theoretical orientations have emerged with regard to the cognitive processing of television program content and the effect of the formal production features on that processing. The earlier, reactive theory suggested that the child was a passive entity that could only react to the stimuli being presented. A number of writers accepted this theory and employed it to further describe the viewer as not only passive but also mesmerized by the flickering stimuli presented on the screen. Only modest data, however, reflect a negative effect of certain types of television programming on attention and cognitive processing, and virtually no reliable research confirms the strong, deleterious effects claimed by a number of popular writers and critics of television.

A second opposing position, the active theory (or the active comprehension theory), drew on more contemporary cognitive views of the learner and described the child as actively exploring and analyzing the program content being presented. This theory suggests that attention to the television program is not a reaction to stimuli but rather a monitoring and comprehension process to identify meaningful content requiring more directed attention.

Research has generally supported the active hypothesis, describing the attentional and comprehension processes as highly interrelated, with comprehension being a precondition to attention. Comprehension is further facilitated through the effects of formal features that function as elements of montage to infer meaningful changes in space, time, and point of view.

The television image has been shown to incorporate a unique symbol system that has certain specifiable capabilities it shares with no other medium. The modes of symbolic representation in television exist as a singular language that must be learned by the child. The specific effects of formal features have received substantial research attention with regard to both attention and comprehension processes, as well as to their ability to model and activate cognitive skills. The importance of formal features as they interact with content has also been underscored by many findings; however, their interaction with other variables has not been pursued sufficiently by researchers. Any research agenda should include continuing investigation of formal features, especially their complex interactions with other variables.

The simple act of a child viewing television has been demonstrated not as a response to stimuli but as a complex, purposeful cognitive activity that becomes progressively sophisticated as the child matures to adulthood. The cognitive effects of such activity have far-reaching consequences for both formal and informal educational activities.

12.4 SCHOLASTIC ACHIEVEMENT

Television viewing has gained the widespread reputation of being detrimental to scholastic achievement. This perception of many teachers, parents, and researchers stems primarily from the negative statistical relationship sometimes found between amount of time spent watching television and scholastic performance (Anderson & Collins, 1988). The relationship between television and scholastic achievement is much more complicated and complex than such a simple inverse relationship suggests (Beentjes & Van der Voort, 1988; Comstock & Paik, 1987, 1991; Neuman, 1991). A review of the research on scholastic achievement, focusing particularly on that produced since the early 1980s, reveals the likelihood of many interacting variables influencing the impact of television.

This section of the chapter will first discuss some theoretical assumptions and major theories about television's impact on scholastic achievement, including a brief review of the body of research and methodological issues. A summary of the intervening variables that have been studied with regard to the television/achievement association and the current conclusions about that relationship will follow.

12.4.1 Theoretical Assumptions

Research on television's impact on scholastic achievement hinges on two assumptions. The first is the belief that an objective measurement of television viewing can be obtained. The second concerns the assessment and measurement of achievement. The methods used to gather data on both are similar.

Television viewing is often defined by hours of viewing per day or week. This information is primarily gathered through self-reporting instruments or parental diaries. Rarely is a distinction made about how the student is relating to the television set, whether or not others are in the room, or if there are concurrent activities being performed. A few studies record the type of programming watched, but again, these data are usually gathered from the subjects within a self-reporting context instead of by direct observation.

Scholastic achievement is overwhelmingly defined in the literature as reading. Reading assessments in the form of achievement tests on vocabulary and comprehension are the primary source of comparison. Some studies measure other school-related achievement such as mathematics but commonly discuss their study results mainly in terms of the reading scores. While this may be limiting in terms of our understanding of scholastic achievement, it has allowed for more comprehensive meta-analyses and comparisons between studies than otherwise would have been possible.

12.4.2 Major Theories

Research in this arena of television's effects has had two major thrusts. Researchers first sought to discover if there was an association between television and scholastic achievement. Many, having concluded that there was such an association, expanded their studies to search for the nature of the relationship. A number of theories attempt to explain and account for the often conflicting and confusing results of studies.

12.4.2.1 Frameworks for Theory. Homik (1981) suggested a number of hypotheses for the relationship between television viewing and achievement. Television may (a) replace study time, (b) create expectation for fast paced activities, (c) stimulate interest in school-related topics, (d) teach the same content as schools, (e) develop cognitive skills that may reinforce or conflict with reading skills, and (f) provide information concerning behaviors. Except for the first hypothesis, Reinking and Wu (1990), in their meta-analysis of studies examining television and reading achievement, found little research systematically investigating Homik's theories.

Beentjes and Van der Voort (1988) grouped potential theories by impact. The facilitation hypothesis asserts a positive association, while the inhibition hypothesis asserts a negative association, and the no-effect hypothesis asserts no association. They found the most support for the inhibition hypothesis but noted that heavy viewers, socially advantaged children, and intelligent children are most vulnerable to the negative impact of television.

In her book *Literacy in the Television Age*, Neuman (1991) examined four prevailing perspectives of the television/achievement relationship: the displacement theory,* the information processing theory, the short-term gratifications theory, and the interest stimulation theory. Her analysis of the evidence supporting and refuting each of these hypotheses is one of the most accessible and comprehensive to date. She also includes practical suggestions to help parents and teachers delineate situations where television can be beneficial for scholastic achievement and literacy development. Through Neuman's framework, we can examine the body of literature on the association between television viewing and scholastic achievement.

12.4.2.2 Displacement Theory.

The displacement theory emerged in the late 1950s out of studies demonstrating that children watch many hours of television weekly. The displacement hypothesis* has been proposed by many theorists and critics to explain the effect of television viewing on other activities. This hypothesis states that, "television influences both learning and social behavior by displacing such activities as reading, family interaction, and social play with peers" (Huston et al., 1992, p. 82). Since children are not spending those hours doing something else, television is displacing other activities. Theorists suggested that the negative relationship sometimes found between television and achievement occurs because the activities being replaced are those that would enhance school performance (Williams, 1986). This theory is the most consistently present construct in achievement research.

Research supports the displacement hypothesis to some extent. The functional displacement hypothesis* holds that one medium will displace another when it performs some of the functions of the displaced medium (Himmelweit, Oppenheim, & Vince, 1958, cited in Comstock & Paik, 1991). Therefore, television does displace other activities, but mostly similar activities such as use of other media (Huston et al., 1992). "Moreover, when children watch television together, their play is less active—that is, they are less talkative, less physically active, and less aggressive than during play without television" (Gadberry, 1974, cited in Huston et al., 1992, p. 86).

Trend studies, which analyze the change in scholastic (reading) achievement over the decades of television's diffusion into everyday life (Stedman & Kaestle, 1987; M. Winn, 1985), have generally supported the displacement theory. Their results provided weak evidence of the existence of a negative television/achievement relationship, since societal changes during the time periods studied include much more than the advent of television.

Another type of longitudinal research design uses surveys to measure a link between television viewing and achievement using measures of the same subjects' media use and achievement (Gaddy, 1986; Gortmaker, Salter, Walker, & Dietz, 1990; Ritchie, Price, & Roberts, 1987). Gaddy's analysis of 5,074 high

school students during their sophomore and their senior years attempted to ascertain whether television viewing was impacting achievement by replacing more enriching activities. He found no significant correlations when other variables were controlled, nor did he find that television viewing rates predict 2-year reading-skill changes. Gaddy hypothesized that other researchers have found significant results due to their failure to consider important intervening variables.

The displacement theory received more rigorous support from quasi-experimental studies typified by the analysis of the impact of television's introduction into a community or the comparison of children in households with and without a television set (Greenstein, 1954; Hornik, 1978). Corteen and Williams's 1986 study of three British Columbia communities, one without television (Notel), one with a single television channel (Unitel), and one with multiple channels (Multitel), is a classic example of this design. In the first phase, the 217 children in all three communities attending grades 2, 3, and 8 were tested for reading fluency before the Notel community received television transmissions. Two years later when the children were in grades 4, 5, and 10, they were retested. In the second phase, 206 new second-, third-, and eighth-graders were tested. In a connected data-gathering activity, a reading assessment of vocabulary and comprehension was administered to students in grades 1 through 7 in all three communities 6 months after television came to Notel.

The cross-sectional and longitudinal analyses of these data sets produced very complex findings: (a) Over the 2 years, those Notel children who started the study in second and third grades showed gains in reading fluency that were not significantly different from their Unitel and Multitel counterparts; (b) the eighth-graders showed less progress if they lived in Notel; (c) Phase 1 second- and third-graders had higher fluency scores than Phase 2 second- and third-graders; and (d) Notel's second- and third-grade scores were higher than those in Unitel and Multitel on the assessment of reading comprehension and vocabulary.

Corteen and Williams's somewhat conflicting results also epitomize the difficulty and complexity of studies of television effects. Although not unequivocal, as a whole their data suggested that television might hinder the development in reading skills for children at certain ages (Beentjes & Van der Voort, 1988).

A number of correlational studies, which focused on the same two variables—amount of time spent watching television and cognitive development as measured by reading achievement test scores—have also found support for the displacement theory. However, the data, on the whole, from such simple correlational studies have been shown to be conflicting, finding negative, positive, or no significant relationship between television viewing and reading achievement (Bossing & Burgess, 1984; Quisenberry & Klasek, 1976; Zuckerman et al., 1980). Further analysis of more recent studies with larger sample sizes suggests that the relationship is likely to be curvilinear rather than linear, with achievement rising with light television watching (1 to 2 hours per day), but falling progressively with heavier viewing (Anderson et al., 1986; Feder, 1984; Searls et al., 1985).

This curvilinear view of the negative association between television and achievement has been addressed by researchers using meta-analysis, a technique that attempts to discover trends through arithmetic aggregation of a number of studies. A key study of this type is Williams, Haertel, Haertel, and Walberg's 1982 analysis of 23 studies that examined the relationship between scholastic achievement and television viewing. The results of these meta-analyses were the basis for Comstock and Paik's discussion of scholastic achievement (1991). The five large-scale studies that became their major sources include:

1. The 1980 California Assessment Program (including Feder & Carlson, 1982) that measured 282,000 sixth-graders and 227,000 twelfth-graders for mathematics, reading, and writing achievement, and for television viewing
2. The 1980 High School and Beyond study (Keith, Reimers, Fehrman, Pottebaum, & Aubey, 1986) that compared 28,000 high school seniors' television viewing in terms of achievement scores in mathematics and reading
3. The 1983–1984 National Assessment of Educational Progress data (Anderson, Mead, & Sullivan, 1988) that described the relationship between viewing and reading for 100,000 fourth-, eighth- and eleventh-graders across 30 states
4. Neuman's synthesis of eight state reading assessments that included measures of attitudes toward television representing nearly 1 million students from fourth through twelfth grades (1988)
5. Gaddy's data from several thousand students who were studied during their sophomore and senior years (1986). A small average negative effect was obtained for the relationship between television and scholastic achievement by Williams and his associates. Interestingly, effects were slightly positive for lighter viewers (up to 10 hours weekly) and grew increasingly negative as students' viewed more television.

Comstock and Paik (1991) noted that for students who are not fluent in English, the opposite is true, with some important qualifications: (a) Family socioeconomic status has a stronger negative correlation with achievement than the negative correlation between television viewing and achievement; (b) as socioeconomic status rises, the inverse association between amount of television viewed and achievement increases; (c) this relationship is stronger for older students; and (d) for low socioeconomic status families there is only a slight rise in achievement associated with television viewing, especially for younger students.

A number of researchers augmented our understanding of the characteristics of television's impact on scholastic achievement by controlling for variables suspected of intervening (Anderson, Mead, & Sullivan, 1988; Feder & Carlson, 1982; Keith, Reimers, Fehrmann, Pottebaum, & Aubey, 1986; Morgan, 1982; Morgan & Gross, 1980; Neuman, 1988; Potter, 1987; Ridley-Johnson, Cooper, & Chance, 1982). In these studies, one or more third variables, often intelligence and socioeconomic status, are controlled. As a result, the relationship measured between achievement and television is not confounded by the third variable. For instance, controlling for intelligence tends to reduce the degree of negative association. However, the relationship remains intact for certain viewers and some content, such as adventure or entertainment programs (Beentjes & Van

der Voort, 1988). Data from this form of research permit more precise analysis of variables that are involved in the complex interaction of television watching and scholastic achievement.

Neuman argued that the two pieces of evidence needed to validate the displacement theory, proof that other activities are being replaced and a demonstration that those activities are more beneficial to scholastic achievement than television, have not been adequately established in the literature (Neuman, 1991). Neither leisure reading at home nor homework activities were found to have been displaced consistently by television. Instead, functionally equivalent media activities such as movies or radio seem to have been affected by television viewing (Neuman, 1991). Since other activities have not been proved to be more beneficial than television, Neuman found the displacement theory unsubstantiated. The body of literature on achievement supports the need for a much more complex and sophisticated model than the simplistic one represented by pure displacement theory. Another trend in achievement research identified by Neuman is information processing theory that examines the ways television's symbol system impacts mental processing. This theory was discussed in the section on message design and cognitive processing.

12.4.2.3 Short-Term Gratification Theory. Short-term gratification theory deals primarily with affective and motivational components of the learner: enthusiasm, perseverance, and concentration. Proponents of this theory, many of whom are teachers, believe that television's ability to entertain a passive viewer has "fundamentally changed children's expectations toward learning, creating a generation of apathetic spectators who are unable to pursue long-term goals" (Neuman, 1991, p. 105). They argue that students have come to believe that all activities should be as effortless as watching television and that students' attention spans are shorter due to such fast-paced programming as *Sesame Street* (Singer & Singer, 1983). This issue was presented in the section on mental processing and will be discussed in the section on "Programming and Utilization."

Writers in the 1970s claimed that the children's program *Sesame Street* had a number of undesirable unintended effects, namely, increased hyperactivity (Halpern, 1975) and reinforced passivity (Winn, 1977), especially when compared to its slower-paced competition *Mister Rogers' Neighborhood* (Tower, Singer, Singer, & Biggs, 1979, cited in Neuman, 1991). These unintended effects gave credence to the short-term gratification theory and the general bias against the television medium. However, further investigations shed doubt on the accuracy of these conclusions (Anderson, Levin, & Lorch, 1977; Neuman, 1991) by discovering that individual differences, family-viewing context, and other intervening variables were interacting within the association between television and achievement.

Salomon's theory of amount of invested mental effort (AIME*) suggested that children approach television as an "easy" source of information and, therefore, tend not to expend much mental effort to understand, process, and remember the information in television programs (Salomon, 1983, 1984). He explained that this caused most to perform below their capabilities unless they were specifically directed or encouraged to learn from the source. He further speculated that this "effort-free" experience became the expectation for other sources of information as well.

Gaddy's (1986) theory of diminishing challenge concurred with the concept that as children grow older they find television less cognitively challenging; thus, they need less effort to understand the information. Typical teenagers will spend less time watching television. Gaddy concluded that those who continue to watch at high levels are therefore spending an inordinate amount of time in cognitive "laziness."

12.4.2.4 Interest Stimulation Theory.

The fourth trend in achievement research discussed by Neuman is the interest stimulation theory. This hypothesis suggests that television can potentially spark a student's interest in or imagination about a topic, fostering learning and creativity.

Examples of television's initiating interest, as demonstrated by increased reading and study around a topic, can be taken from most of our lives. For instance, after the broadcast of the miniseries *Roots,* Fairchild, Stockard, and Bowman (1986) reported that 37 percent of those sampled indicated increased interest and knowledge about issues of slavery. Similarly, Hornik (1981) has shown that adult book sales will boom after a special program airs on television. Morgan (1980) found that children who watch more television when they are younger are likely to read more when they are older. While this phenomenon has been measured, the arousal of interest and generation of incidental knowledge about subjects broadcast on television has been described as fleeting (Comstock & Paik, 1991; Leibert & Sprafkin, 1988; Neuman, 1991).

Neuman (1991) summarized three reasons to account for the ephemeral nature of incidental learning from ordinary entertainment viewing. First, most people who casually view television lack the intention to learn. Therefore, they do not engage in active cognitive processing of the material. Second, the redundancy of plot and character and the low intellectual level in most television programming increases the likelihood that any information intended for learning was previously mastered. Finally, unless the material has direct relevance to the viewer, any incidental information learned is quickly forgotten due to lack of reinforcement and practice. She suggests a series of concomitant strategies of parental and teacher mediation that can activate, broaden, and focus television's potential to stimulate interest in school-related topics under natural home-viewing conditions (Neuman, 1991).

12.4.2.5 Theories Related to Imagination.

The idea of television as a stimulator of imagination and creativity has been an area of debate among scholars and researchers. Admittedly, studying the imagination is a difficult prospect at best. Techniques to do so have ranged from observations and self-reports to imagination tests using inkblots or inventories to teacher and parental descriptions. In his work *Art, Mind and Brain: A Cognitive Approach to Creativity* (1982), Howard Gardner recounts observations and research that support the idea that television is a rich medium for imaginative activity. "The child's imagination scoops up these figures from the television screen and then, in its mysterious ways, fashions the drawings and stories of his own fantasy world" (p. 254). He purports that

television stimulates the sensory imagination of the young much more successfully than it generates the abstract, conceptual lines of thought important to older viewers' creativity.

Other researchers have found evidence of television's stimulation of imaginative play. Alexander, Ryan, and Munoz (1984) found brothers who used television-generated conversation to initiate fantasy play. James and McCain (1982) recorded children's play at a daycare center and observed that many games created by those children were taken from television characters and plots. They noted that the themes occurring in such television-activated play were similar to those in play not stimulated by television. Commercials in particular have been demonstrated in certain circumstances to contribute to imaginative activity (Greer, Potts, Wright, & Huston, 1982; Reid & Frazer, 1980.)

A considerable amount of research in the area of television's impact on the imagination of the viewer, particularly that of children, has been conducted by Jerome and Dorothy Singer and various associates. They have concluded that television can present general information, models for behavior, themes, stories, and real and make-believe characters who are incorporated into creative play (Singer & Singer, 1981, 1986). This process is not guaranteed, nor is it always positive. Rather, a pattern emerges of a conditional association between television and developing imagination.

The first condition is the type of programming viewed. A number of studies have linked high-violence action adventure programs to decreased imagination, and low-violence situation comedies or informative programs with increased imagination (Huston-Stein, Fox, Greer, Watkins, & Whitaker, 1981; J. Singer & Singer, 1981; Singer, Singer, & Rapaczynski, 1984; Zuckerman, Singer, & Singer, 1980). Singer and Singer have also argued that the pacing of television can impact the amount of imaginative play, with slower, carefully designed programs, such as *Mister Rogers' Neighborhood,* generating conditions for optimal creative thought and play (Singer & Singer, 1983). Dorothy Singer reported two studies on the effect of *Sesame Street* and *Mister Rogers' Neighborhood* on children's imagination (Friedrich & Stein, 1975, cited in Singer, 1978; Tower, Singer, Singer, & Biggs, 1978). *Mister Rogers' Neighborhood* produced a significant increase in imagination. *Sesame Street* did not.

The type of programming watched may also affect the nature of fantasy activities. Rosenfeld, Heusmann, Eron, and Torney-Purta (1982) used Singer and Antrobus's (1972) Imaginal Processes Inventory to categorize types of fantasy. They found three types: (a) fanciful play around fairy tales and implausible events, (b) active play around heroes and achievement, and (c) aggressive negative play around fighting, killing, and being hurt. Children, chiefly boys, who demonstrated aggressive negative fantasy were those who tended to watch violent action adventure programs regularly (Singer & Singer, 1983). McIlwraith and Schallow (1982, 1983) and Schallow and McIlwraith (1986, 1987) investigated various media effects on imaginativeness in children and undergraduates and found connections between programming genre and type of imaginative thinking. For instance, pleasant, constructive daydreams came from watching drama, situation comedies, or general entertainment programs.

The second condition of television's association with imagination is the amount of time spent viewing television. Heavy viewers have been shown to be less imaginative (Peterson, Peterson, & Carroll, 1987; Singer & Singer, 1986; Singer, Singer, & Rapaczynski, 1984). Children who watch television many hours weekly tend to also exhibit traits within their fantasies similar to those who watch action adventure programs. This is evidenced by the fact that they tend to be aggressive and violent in their play (Singer & Singer, 1983).

The final condition within the television and imagination association is that of mediation or family viewing context. Singer, Singer, and Rapaczynski's (1984) study found parental attitudes* and values about imagination to be a stronger indicator of child imaginativeness than type or amount of television viewing. D. Singer and Singer's (1981) year-long examination of 200 preschoolers within three treatment groups found that the greatest gains in imaginativeness were associated with adult mediation. The first group had television exposure and teacher-directed lesson plans designed around 2- to 3-minute televised segments intended to improve the child's cognitive, social, and imaginative skills. The second group received the specialized lesson plans without television exposure. The final group received the ordinary school curriculum. The results from the first group showed gains in imagination and other social skills such as leadership and cooperation.

Though the results of these studies examining television's effects on imagination are not universal, they reveal a pattern of conditional benefit. Children who are exposed to a limited amount of television, who watch carefully selected programs in terms of content and pacing, and who engage in conversations with adults who mediate that exposure are likely to use their television experience as a springboard to positive, creative, and imaginative activities.

12.4.2.6 Future Directions for Theory. Neuman (1991) concluded that we need a conceptual model to account for (a) the many uses for television, (b) the "spirited interplay" between various media including television, and (c) the impact of television on scholastic achievement. The writings of Comstock and Paik (1991), Beentjes and Van der Voort (1988), and Reinking and Wu (1990) support the need for a conceptual model that links research variables. The difficulty researchers have encountered in finding consistent, definitive evidence about the magnitude and shape of an association and a functional description of such an association between television viewing and scholastic achievement may be due to the presence of negative bias toward television. Additionally, there is the aforementioned difficulty of the lack of a conceptual model that adequately explains the complex interactions of variables such as age, socioeconomic status, family viewing context, and intelligence.

12.4.3 Methodological Concerns

While many early studies found significant negative correlations between television viewing and achievement, reviewers (Beentjes & Van der Voort, 1988; Homik, 1981; Neuman, 1991; Reinking & Wu, 1990) note that severe flaws in design shed

doubt on the veracity of those early findings. These include (a) small sample size, (b) lack of control for intervening variables, (c) less powerful analysis techniques, (d) relative inattention to the content of programming, and (e) unreliable self-reporting instruments, whereas subsequent studies with larger sample sizes, better controls, and more rigorous analysis have continued to discover consistently significant relationships between television viewing and scholastic achievement (Anderson et al., 1986; Feder & Carlson, 1982; Gaddy, 1986; Keith et al., 1986; Neuman, 1988).

Ritchie, Price, and Roberts (1987) postulated that television might have the most profound impact during the preschool years. Another concern they raise is the question of long-term exposure to the effects of television. This is a dilemma for researchers that can be addressed by more rigorous longitudinal studies.

Neuman (1991) itemized additional concerns about the television and achievement literature: (a) The majority of the research lacks a driving theory; (b) many studies purport to be qualitative but are actually anecdotal; (c) scholastic achievement has been narrowly defined and measured, focusing on reading achievement scores; and (d) due to an assumption that print is the intellectually superior medium, a negative bias pervades the literature.

12.4.4 Intervening Variables

A brief look at the variables that have been studied for their potential differential effects throughout the research will help illustrate the complexity of the interaction between the individual and television in terms of subsequent scholastic achievement.

12.4.4.1 Age. As with many other variables, there is conflicting evidence regarding how the variable of age affects scholastic achievement. The literature suggests that the negative correlation between television viewing and achievement is stronger for older students, which implies that older students may replace study time with television viewing, while younger children are monitored more closely by parents with regard to studying (Anderson et al., 1986; Neuman, 1988; Roberts, Bachen, Hornby, & Hernandez-Ramos, 1984; Searls, Mead, & Ward, 1985).

12.4.4.2 Gender. Studies comparing the effects of television viewing on the scholastic achievement of boys and girls have produced conflicting findings. Morgan and Gross (1980) found a negative relationship for boys between television viewing and scholastic achievement. In contrast, Williams, Haertel, Haertel, and Walberg's (1982) meta-analysis identified a negative relationship for girls.

12.4.4.3 Intelligence. Morgan (1982) and Morgan and Gross (1980) found that the negative association between television and achievement was strongest for children of higher abilities. They found no significant effect for low and medium levels of intelligence. As with older children, television may have a greater impact on highly intelligent students because it displaces more cognitively stimulating activities (Beentjes & Van der Voort, 1988).

12.4.4.4 Home-Viewing Environment.
Researchers have found that television-watching and leisure-reading patterns of children often reflect those of their parents (Morgan, 1982; Neuman, 1986). Many factors of the home environment are statistically significant indicators of television watching, especially for younger children (Roberts et al., 1984). Behavioral patterns of leisure reading and television watching seem to persist into adulthood (Reinking & Wu, 1990; Ritchie et al., 1987).

12.4.4.5 Reading Skills.
Research on various levels of reading skill is inconclusive, due mainly to the habit of measuring reading skill with one overall score (Beentjes & Van der Voort, 1988). Corteen and Williams (1986) found a connection to comprehension, but not vocabulary, in their study of three Canadian towns.

12.4.4.6 Socioeconomic Status.
Although heavy viewers universally have lower scholastic achievement, for light and moderate viewers socioeconomic status seems to have a place in the interaction. Contrary to high socioeconomic status children who demonstrate a negative correlation, low socioeconomic status children can improve achievement with television viewing (Anderson et al., 1986; Feder, 1984; Searls et al., 1985). Combined with findings on the effect of intelligence, many scholars have reached a conclusion that supports the displacement theory in specific situations. "The pattern invites a proposition: television viewing is inversely related to achievement when it displaces an intellectually and experientially richer environment, and it is positively related when it supplies such an environment" (Comstock & Paik, 1987, p. 27).

12.4.4.7 Type of Programming Watched.
Purely entertaining television programming such as cartoons, situation comedies, and adventure programs have a negative correlation with school achievement (Neuman, 1981; Zuckerman, Singer, & Singer, 1980). News programs and other highly informative shows, on the other hand, have a positive relationship to achievement (Potter, 1987).

12.4.4.8 Various Levels of Viewing Time.
Many studies have found different levels of viewing time to be an important element in television's relationship to achievement (Anderson et al., 1986; Feder, 1984; Neuman, 1988; Potter, 1987; Searls et al., 1985). In their discussion of Williams et al. (1982), Comstock and Paik (1987, 1991) concluded that there was a good possibility of curvilinearity at the intermediate and primary grades, especially for households of lower socioeconomic status or using English as a second language. For these groups, television can have a beneficial effect at moderate levels of viewing.

One of the problems of interpreting studies of the effect of viewing time on achievement is that the content or context of that viewing time is often ignored, yet may have an effect. For example, in the early evaluations of *Sesame Street*, viewing time was positively correlated with learning outcomes when it was measured as an approximation of "time on task." If a more undifferentiated measure of viewing time—one unconnected with the content of sequences or programs—had been used, the findings may have been different. What is the relationship of intentional and incidental learning conditions to the interaction of viewing time and achievement? Is it important to distinguish between viewing as a primary activity and viewing as a secondary activity? Questions such as these need to be raised when researchers study the interaction of viewing time and achievement.

12.4.5 Current Issues

Researchers continue to investigate how television watching affects children's use of time, the affect of viewing on ability to read, and the extent to which television stimulates imagination. In addition, there is burgeoning interest in the effect of television on obesity and body image and whether there is a related effect on school achievement.

12.4.5.1 Time.
Within the last five years, two major studies related to children's use of time have been reported: *Kids and Media @ the New Millennium* (Kaiser Family Foundation, 1999) and *Healthy Environments, Healthy Children* (Hofferth, 1999). The University of Michigan's Institute for Social Research conducted the latter. The Kaiser Foundation study reported that the typical American child spends an average of more than 38 hours a week and nearly five and a half hours a day consuming media outside of school. For children age eight and older, the amount of watching rises to six and three fourths hours a day. The study investigated children's use of television, computers, video games, movies, music and print media. Drew Altman, President of the Kaiser Foundation, concluded that, "watching television, playing video games, listening to music and surfing the Internet have become a full-time job for the typical American child" (Kaiser Family Foundation, 1999).

The University of Michigan Institute for Social Research gathered information on a group of families from 1981 to 1997. This data allowed a comparison of the way children 12 and under occupied themselves in 1981 and what activities dominate now. While television still consumes more time than any other activity than sleep, total watching time was decreased about two hours for 9–12 year olds. The study did not determine whether these two hours are now devoted to using computers. Children have less leisure time and the time they have is more structured. These findings are attributed to some extent to society placing more value on early childhood education and the working family crunch because everyone is busier. Time away from home has limited the hours some children spend watching television (Study Finds Kids . . . , 1998; Hofferth, 1999a, 1999b; Research Uncovers How . . . , 1998).

12.4.5.2 Reading.
Another continuing issue is: To what extent is television viewing related to the increasing gap in reading ability between the best and worse readers? Over the years research has indicated small positive or negative correlations to watching television depending on the amount of viewing. It is clear that when there is an effect, television is not a major

variable. The amount of time parents spend reading to children is a more significant variable (Zemike, 2001).

12.4.5.3 Imagination.
Two important articles extend the debate about the effect of television on imagination. Rubenstein (1999) investigated the effect of content and the medium on creativity. The results suggest that content has more effect on creativity and attitude than the medium. The study compared high and low content television and print. Valkenberg and Beentjes (1997) tried to find evidence to support the visualization hypothesis. This hypothesis states that viewers have more difficulty disassociating themselves from ready-made television images; therefore, imagination may be adversely affected. If this hypothesis is supported, radio is likely to stimulate imagination more. The results support the visualization hypothesis. In the older age group, radio stories elicited more novel responses than television stories.

12.4.5.4 Obesity.
Another new direction is the study of how the television viewing environment is related to childhood obesity (Horgen, Choate, & Brownell, 2001). Studies on obesity may relate to learning from television because they address children's use of time and the effect of this on physical fitness. Physical fitness, in turn, affects achievement in sports and physical education (Baranowski, 1999; Armstrong et al., 1998; Durant, Anderson, et al., 1998).

12.4.6 Summary and Recommendations

Few researchers today doubt that there is a relationship between television viewing and scholastic achievement. The debate centers instead around the nature of that association. Regardless of the seeming disparity of results, some patterns are emerging:

1. Heavy television viewers of all intellectual abilities and home environments tend to have lower scholastic achievement and demonstrate less imaginativeness when compared to their lighter-viewing peers. This effect is especially severe among students with high IQs and otherwise stimulating home environments.
2. For light-to-moderate viewers, a number of intervening variables come into play: age, ability, socioeconomic status, home-viewing environment, and type of programming watched. It has been shown that light television viewing may increase scholastic performance for children of lower abilities and lower socioeconomic status.
3. Within certain stages of intellectual and emotional development, television viewing can have a greater impact on achievement.
4. Parental attitudes and viewing patterns* are strong indicators of the child's current and future television viewing and its effect on scholastic achievement.
5. Home-viewing environment and adult mediation of viewed material are significantly related to the incidental and intentional learning and imaginative play that come from television viewing.

There has been a call by many for television to cease being seen as intrinsically bad or good (Gomez, 1986; Hatt, 1982; Neuman, 1991; Reinking & Wu, 1990). The perception of television as detrimental has colored the attitudes of researchers and educators alike. Jankowski said:

It is a source of constant amazement to me that the television set, an inert, immobile appliance that does not eat, drink, or smoke, buy or sell anything, can't vote, doesn't have a job, can't think, can't turn itself on or off, and is used only at our option, can be seen as the cause of so much of society's ills by so many people in education. (cited in Neuman, 1991, p. 195)

The last decade of research has shown that the relationship of television viewing to scholastic achievement is a complex proposition with many interacting variables, not just a simple, negative relationship. The impact of this medium on achievement remains far from clear. However, research continues to improve our understanding of how each individual may be influenced by television.

Future research should seek to avoid these obvious problems while building on the body of literature available. Emphasis on mulitvariate relationships through correlation and on meta-analyses seems the most direct route to increasing our understanding of the nature of the television/ achievement relationship.

12.5 FAMILY-VIEWING CONTEXT

By the late 1970s, two reviews of research on child development had concluded that television was more than a communicator of content because it organized and modified the home environment (Atman & Wohlwill, 1978; Majoriebanks, 1979). Conversely, it was known that the home environment organized and modified television viewing. For example, Frazer (1976) found that the family routine established the viewing habits* of preschoolers, not vice versa. Today we know that demographic differences, such as ethnicity (Tangney & Feshbach, 1988) and individual differences, such as genetics (Plomin, Corley, DeFries, & Fulker, 1990), also influence the family-viewing context. This section deals with variables that mediate the effects of television in the home setting, including the home environment, coviewing, and viewing habits. For "television viewing occurs in an environmental context that influences what and when viewing occurs, as well as the ways in which viewers interpret what they see" (Huston et al., 1992, p. 98).

12.5.1 Variables That Mediate

The variables in the family context for television viewing can be grouped into three categories: (a) the environment, which encompasses the number and placement of sets, the toys and other media available, options for other activities, rules for viewing, and parental attitudes and style; (b) coviewing, which includes the nature and frequency of interactions, the effect of attitudes, and the effect of age and roles; and (c) viewing habits, which are based on variables such as amount of viewing, viewing patterns or preferences, and audience involvement.* These variables interact to create a social environment that mediates the effects of viewing.

Mediating variables can be separated into two types of variables: direct and indirect. Direct mediating variables are those that can be controlled, such as the situation or habits. Indirect mediating variables are those that are fixed, such as educational or socioeconomic level.

The research on television as a socializing agent is extensive and will be discussed later in this chapter. Although research on family context abounds, many findings are contradictory or inconclusive. Nevertheless, there is enough research to suggest some important interactions.

One approach to visualizing the relationship between program variables (e.g., formal features, content), context variables (e.g., environment, habits, coviewing), and outcome variables (e.g., attention, comprehension, attitudes) was presented by Seels in 1982 (see Fig. 12.2).

Another approach to conceptualizing visually the relationship of some of these mediating variables to exposure and outcomes was presented by Carolyn A. Stroman (1991) in Fig. 12.3, which appeared in the Journal of Negro Education.

12.5.2 Theoretical Assumptions

At the level of operational investigation of these variables, assumptions are made that affect the questions researched, methodologies used, and interpretation of findings. One such issue is how television viewing should be defined. As discussed in the message design and cognitive-processing section, classic studies by Allen (1965) and Bechtel, Achelpohl, and Akers (1972) found there was a great deal of inattention while the television set was turned on. If viewing is defined as a low level of involvement, i.e., nothing more then being in the room when the television set is on, the result is estimates of the big role of television in children's lives. When estimates of viewing by 5-year-olds made from parent-kept viewing diaries and time-lapse video recordings are compared, diaries yield estimates of 40 hours a week and time-lapse video recordings analyzed for attentive viewing yield $3\frac{1}{2}$ hours per week (Anderson, Field, Collins, Lorch, & Nathan, 1985, cited in Comstock & Paik, 1987). Viewing is often defined as "including entering and leaving the room while intermittently monitoring what is unfolding on the screen" (Comstock & Paik, 1991, p. 19).

On the other hand, current research on mental activities that occur during the television experience suggests that a great deal of mental activity can occur while viewing. Comstock and Paik (1991) suggest that a distinction be made between monitoring (paying attention to audio, visual, and social cues that indicate the desirability of attention to the screen) and viewing (paying attention to what is taking place on the screen).

The issue of whether the viewer is active or passive arises from differing conceptions of viewing and from the fact that research has established that the viewer can be either, depending on programming and the mediating variables. Comstock and Paik (1991) cite several classic and recent studies that established a high level of mental activity despite an often

low level of involvement (Bryant, Zillmann, & Brown, 1983; Huston & Wright, 1989; Krendl & Watkins, 1983; Krull, 1983; Lorch, Anderson, & Levin, 1979; Meadowcroft & Reeves, 1989; Thorson, Reeves, & Schleuder, 1985). As previously noted in the section on message design and cognitive processing, the notion of hypnotic watching of television has been largely discredited (Anderson & Lorch, 1983; Bryant & Anderson, 1983).

Three studies by Argenta, Stoneman, and Brody (1986), Wolf (1987), and Palmer (1986) reinforce this conclusion. Wolf and Palmer interviewed children about their viewing to determine interest, thoughtfulness, and insight. Their study, therefore, is susceptible to the biases of self-reporting. Argenta et al. (1986) analyzed the visual attention of preschoolers to cartoons, Sesame Street, and situation comedies. They observed social interaction, viewing, and use of toys. With Sesame Street and situation comedies, attention was divided among social interaction, viewing, and toys. Only with cartoons did social interaction decrease. "The image of children mesmerized in front of the television set, forsaking social interaction and active involvement with their object environment, held true for only one type of programming, namely, cartoons" (Argenta et al., 1986 p. 370). Thus, findings will differ depending on how viewing is defined.

Another assumption is that incidental learning and intentional learning are separate during the television experience. Yet, if an adult reinforces or intervenes while coviewing a program for children, intentional learning will increase. Additionally, if a child learns indirectly through informative programming, incidental learning will increase. The nature of the television experience today, especially with cable and video-cassette recorder (VCR) technology, may be that incidental and intentional learning happen concurrently and may even interact or reinforce each other. Coviewing with discussion may be a way to join incidental and intentional learning. In an article on *Family Contexts of Television*, Leichter et al. (1985) point out that ways of representing and thinking about time may be learned from the television experience. Children can incidentally learn to recognize the hour of the day from the programming schedule. They can intentionally learn time concepts by watching *Mister Rogers' Neighborhood* and *Sesame Street*

A methodological assumption underlying much research on the television viewing environment is the acceptability of self-reporting instruments and diaries. Although these techniques are valid, often they need to be compared with research results from other methodologies. This may be especially true in television research, because self-reporting techniques are used so extensively, particularly in studies on the family-viewing context.

12.5.3 The Television Viewing Environment

The television viewing environment is part of the television viewing system, which results in a television viewing experience. This section will next address several categories and subcategories of mediating variables starting with the viewing environment.

12.5.3.1 Number and Placement of Sets. Leichter and her colleagues (1985) discuss the temporal and spatial organization of the television viewing environment. According to Leichter

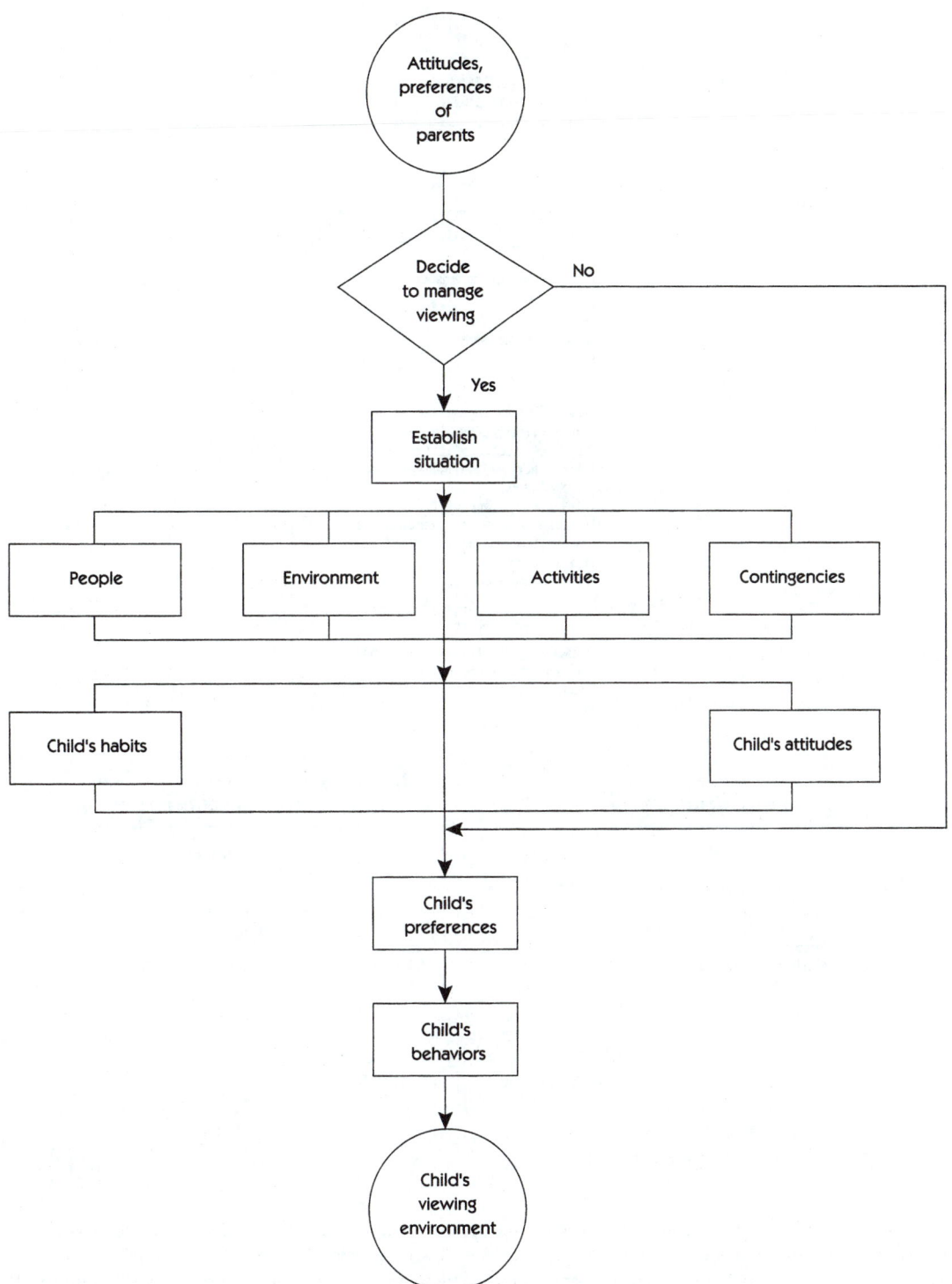

FIGURE 12.2. Relationship among variable in the family-viewing context. (From Seels, 1982.)

et al., there are symbolic meanings associated with the placement of television sets in the home. In their discussion of the methodological approaches to the study of family environments, they stress the need "to obtain a detailed picture of the ways in which television is interwoven with the underlying organization of the family" (p. 31). They decided that ethnographic or naturalistic data gathering through a variety of observation techniques was best. Therefore, they used participant observation, interviewing, recording of specific behaviors, and video and audio recording of interactions. To gather data over a sufficient time span, one observer moved in with the family. Leichter and her colleagues generated research questions through a study

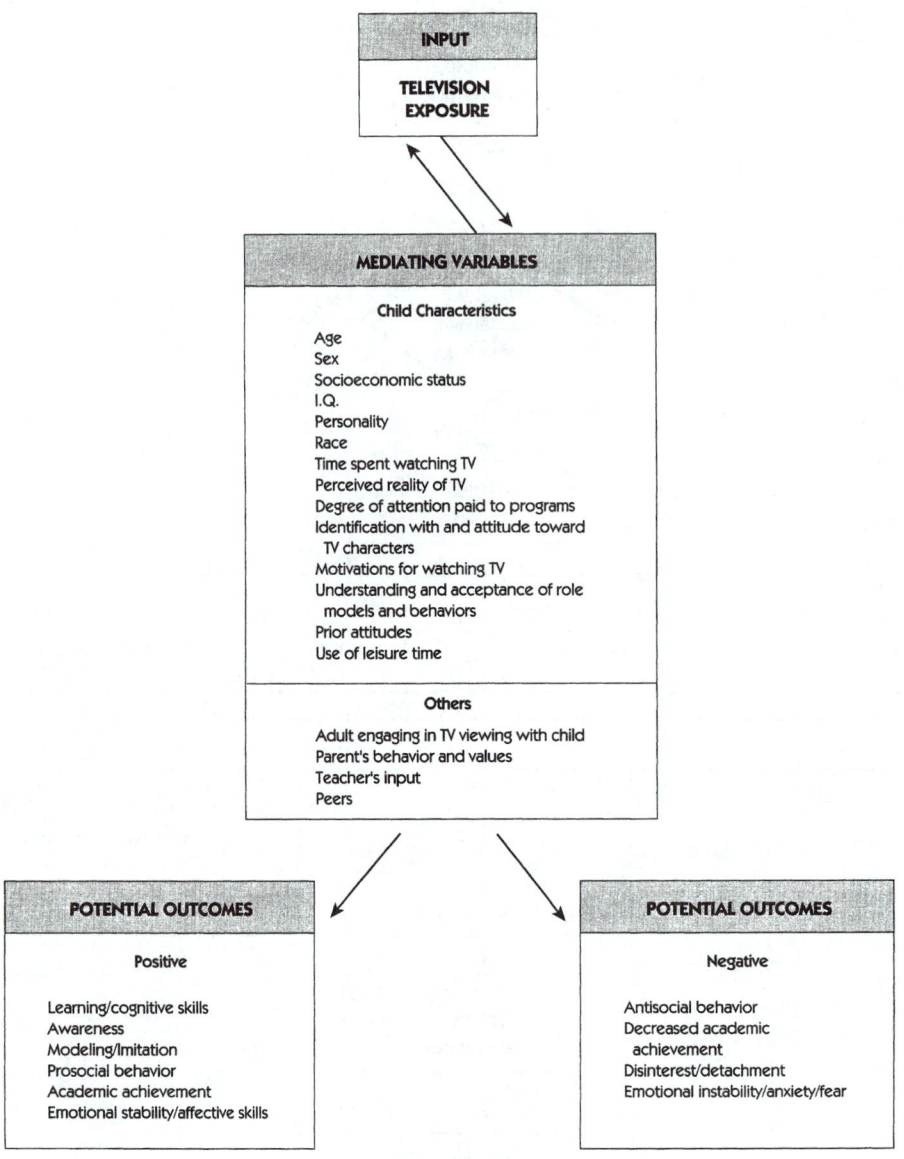

FIGURE 12.3. Hypothesized model for understanding television's socializing impact. (From Stroman, C. A., (1991). Television's role in the socialization of African American children and adolescents. *Journal of Negro Education, 60*(3), 314–327. Copyright ©1991 by Howard University. All rights reserved.)

of three families followed by a study of ten families. They compared the data generated with a similar cross-cultural study done in Pakistan (Ahmed, 1983) and concluded that placement varies with the architecture of the home and with family perceptions. As a result, a set can be "fixed" or "static" in terms of its placement, just as individual position for viewing can be fixed or static. The area of placement can be close to traffic patterns or places of activity, or it can be set in out-of-the-way places reserved just for viewing. Where the set is placed may lead to conflict because of other activities.

Even though television is a "magnet," especially for young viewers, the physical design of the area where the set is

placed can inhibit the amount of time someone spends viewing. This conclusion is supported by research on use of dormitory viewing areas in college (Preiser, 1970, cited in Ross, 1979), Young children engage in many other activities in the television area even if the television isn't in a desirable location for other activities (Rivlin, Wolfe, & Beyda, 1973, cited in Ross, 1979).

Winn (1977) argues that the television should be put in an out-of-the-way area such as the basement in order to minimize its dominance. Others argue that the more centrally located the set, the more likely viewers will be influenced by other powerful variables such as coviewing.

One concept that could be used in research on placement is "household centrality."* Medrich et al. (1982, cited in Comstock & Paik, 1991) proposed that families can be classified on a dimension reflecting behavior and norms* that favor viewing. If there is high use by parents and children and there are few rules governing viewing, the household can be said to have "centrality" of television. Research is needed on the effect of placement of set(s) on centrality. Generally, if there is only one set, it is in a living or group recreational area. If there is a second set, it is usually placed in a bedroom (Leichter et al., 1985). The more central the location, the greater is the likelihood that social interaction or coviewing will mediate the effects of television.

The majority of households in the United States have two or more sets, subscribe to cable, and own a VCR (Huston et al., 1992). Children in multiple-set homes tend to watch more television than those in single-set homes (Webster, Pearson, & Webster, 1986). Christopher, Fabes, and Wilson (1989) found that parents who owned one television set tended to exert more control over their children's viewing than did parents owning multiple sets. They also found that parents who owned three or more sets were more positive about their children's watching television and spent twice as much time watching as those with fewer sets. Webster et al. (1986) cautioned that multiple sets could lead to decreased parent–child interactions.

Since additional sets are used to resolve conflicts over program choices, children may view more since they have more control over their own viewing. In sum, one obvious guideline is that young children should not have access to more sets than parents can monitor. The experience of resolving conflicts over who watches what can provide valuable lessons in sharing.

12.5.3.2 Availability of Toys.
Children develop strategies for viewing, including strategies that allow for competing activities, such as playing with dolls (Levin & Anderson, 1976). Rapid television pacing has no effect on the number of toys used during a play period (Anderson, Levin, & Lorch, 1977). Family rules govern the placement and use of toys during viewing. Some families forbid toys in the television room; others permit toys to be available during viewing (Leichter et al., 1985). Where the set is placed may affect the use of toys during viewing. If the set is in the living room where no toys are permitted, the use of toys as distracters or reinforcers during viewing will be less than if the set is in the playroom or recreation room where toys and games are available.

The availability of toys may distract young children from the television set. In a study by Lorch, Anderson, and Levin (1979), when attractive toys were available to 5-year-olds, attention to *Sesame Street* dropped from 87 to 44 percent. One of the methods employed in the earliest research on *Sesame Street* was to conduct formative evaluation by having children watch a sequence while seated at a table filled with toys. If the children played with the toys rather than watching, the sequence was deemed ineffective in holding attention. Among these now classic studies were studies by Lesser in 1972 and 1974, and by Lorch and his colleagues in the late 1970s. When Lorch, Anderson, and Levin (1979) showed a version of *Sesame Street* to two groups, one group of children surrounded by toys and one group with no toys in the environment, the children in the group without toys attended twice as much. However, there

was no difference between the groups in comprehension of television content. Thus, toys may be seen as positive elements of the viewing environment in that they can reinforce viewing and provide a basis for interaction with others about television and other topics. On the other hand, toys can decrease attention, but this phenomenon does not seem to affect cognitive learning.

It is commonly believed that children learn about life through forms of play and social interaction (D. Winn, 1985). Although television can model prosocial forms of interaction, the time spent watching television results in less time for play, practice, and real interactions with other children or family members.

Television has no sign on it: 'Trespassers will be prosecuted.' Television is living made easy for our children. It is the shortest cut yet devised, the most accessible back door to the grown-up world. Television is never too busy to talk to our children. Television plays with them, shares its work with them. Television wants their attention, needs it, and goes to any length to get it. (Shayon, 1950, p. 9)

It is likely that children watching television in an environment rich with toys and the opportunity for other activities will not be as mesmerized by television programming. Opportunities for elaboration, interaction, and creativity that extend the effect of the television stimulus should be richer in such an environment. However, research is not available at this time to support such suppositions.

12.5.3.3 Relationship to Other Activities.
Television impacts other activities, and other activities impact television. A study on television's impact conducted by Johnson in 1967 (cited in Liebert & Sprafkin, 1988) showed that of those surveyed, 60 percent changed their sleep patterns, 55 percent altered meal times, and 78 percent used television as an electronic babysitter. Liebert and Sprafkin also cite a study by Robinson in 1972 that showed reductions in sleep, social gatherings away from home, leisure activities, conversation, household care, and newspaper reading.

Television is frequently secondary to other activities, or there is frequently another activity even when viewing is primary (Comstock, Chaffee, Katzman, McCombs, & Roberts, 1978). Krugman and Johnson (1991) report that compared to traditional programming, VCR movie rental is associated with less time spent on other activities.

Parental mediation and the incorporation of other activities as adjuncts to the viewing process may be beneficial for children. Friedrich and Stein (1975) concluded that when adults provide discussion after viewing or read storybooks that summarize important concepts conveyed in programming, children increase their understanding of concepts and are able to generalize them to new situations better than children not provided with summaries. Singer, Singer, and Zuckerman (1981) reached the same conclusion when they had teachers lead discussions following viewing of prosocial programs.

Some families engage in orienting activities prior to viewing that lead to awareness of program options. According to Perse (1990), heavy viewers tend to use television guides and newspaper listings to select programs. They reevaluate during exposure by grazing* (quickly sampling a variety of programs using zapping* techniques with remote controls) while they are viewing.

Some studies have shown that television viewing reduces time devoted to other activities (Murray & Kippax, 1978; Williams, 1986). Murray and Kippax collected data from three towns in Australia: a no-television town, a low-television town, and a high-television town. The low-television town was defined as one receiving television for only 1 year, and the high as one receiving television for 5 years. Comparisons between the no-television town and the low-television town showed a marked decrease in other activities for all age levels when television was available. Television led to a restructuring of children's time use (Himmelweit, Oppenheim, & Vince, 1958, cited in Comstock & Paik, 1994; Murray & Kippax, 1978). The displacement theory discussed in the section on school achievement attempts to explain the relationship of other activities to television viewing in the family context.

12.5.3.4 Rules for Viewing. The National Center for Educational Statistics conducted the National Education Longitudinal Study (NELS) of 1988. The study surveyed 25,000 eighth-graders, their parents, principals, and teachers.

A follow-up study was undertaken in 1990 when the same students were tenth-graders. Results of these surveys are given in two reports (National Center for Education Statistics, 1991; Office of Educational Research and Improvement, 1991). According to these reports, "69% of parents reported monitoring their eighth-grader's television viewing, 62% limited television viewing on school nights, and 84% restricted early or late viewing" (National Center for Educational Statistics, 1992, p. 1). These statistics are not as reassuring as one would hope:

Two-thirds of the parents reported they *did* enforce rules limiting television viewing, while the same number of students reported their parents *did not* limit their television viewing. In fact, these eighth-graders spent almost 4 times as much time watching television each week as they did doing their homework. (Office of Educational Research and Improvement, Fall 1991, p. 5)

Generally, research does not support the myth that children watch more television because their parents are absent. Even parents who are present rarely restrict children's viewing. The older the child, the less influence the parents have (Pearl, 1982). This pattern is disturbing in light of evidence that heavy viewers (4 hours a day or more) do less well in school and have fewer hobbies and friends (Huston et al., 1992). Gadberry (1980) did an experimental study in which parents restricted 6-year-olds to about half their normal viewing amount. When compared with a control group whose viewing was not restricted, the treatment group improved in cognitive performance and time spent on reading.

Parents who are selective viewers are more likely to encourage or restrict viewing and to watch with their children. Parents who believe television is a positive influence watch more television with children (Dorr et al., 1989). The least-effective position for parents to take is a laissez-faire one, because children whose parents neither regulate or encourage viewing watch more adult entertainment television, usually without an adult

present. This puts children more at risk from the negative effects of television (Wright, St. Peters, & Huston, 1990).

Lull (1990) describes the many roles television can play in family interaction. The roles are structural (time and activity cues) or relational (facilitation of either shared communication or avoidance of communication and demonstration of competence or authority). Thus, television is an important variable in how family members relate to each other. Using surveys, Bower (1988) has compared parents' use of rules for viewing in 1960, 1970, and 1980. The results indicated a trend toward an increase in the restrictions and prescriptions parents impose on viewing. This increase in rules about amount of viewing and hours for viewing was indicated for 4- to 6-year-olds and 7- to 9-year-olds. For younger children, this also included an increase in rules about changing the channel or "grazing." Bower found that the higher the educational level of parents, the more likely they had rules about viewing. This confirms the findings of Medrich et al. who also found that the likelihood of rules increased with parental education for all households, but African-American households at every socioeconomic level were less restrictive about television viewing (Bower, 1985; Medrich, Roizen, Rubin, & Buckley, 1982, cited in Comstock & Paik, 1991).

Several studies discuss the effects of new technology, such as cable and VCRs, on parental restrictions. Comstock and Paik (1991) reviewed these studies. Lin and Atkin (1989) found that several variables interact with rulemaking* for adolescent use of television and VCRs, including school grades, child media ownership, child age, and gender. They point out the difficulty in separating the research on rulemaking, parental mediation, and coviewing:

Within this realm of parental guidance, the relationship between mediation and rulemaking is, itself, worthy of separate consideration. Few researchers have considered mediation (e.g., encouraging, discouraging, discussing viewing) apart from the notion of rulemaking (established guidelines about acceptable and/or prohibited behaviors). Those making mediation–rulemaking distinctions (Brown & Linne, 1976; Reid, 1979; Bryce & Leichter, 1983) found a fair degree of correspondence between the two. Although these two concepts may appear as indicators of the same general process, we maintain that they should be theoretically distinguished. Actual mediation isn't necessarily contingent upon established rules. Clearly, one can have mediation without making explicit rules (and vice versa). (Lin & Atkin, 1989, p. 57)

Even so, Lin and Atkin found that mediation and rule making were predicted by each other.

There is also the question of whether information or training can increase parental involvement. Greenberg, Abelman, and Cohen (1990) provided television guides that reviewed programs to parents who did not use them. However, the children used them to find programs with the warning "parental discretion is advised" so that they could watch them (Greenberg et al., 1990, cited in Comstock & Paik, 1991). The jury is out, however, on whether training can help parents guide children in using television wisely. There are many books available for parents, including the Corporation for Public Broadcasting's *Tips for Parents: Using Television to Help Your Child Learn* (1988); the more recent American Psychological Association's (APA) *Suggestions for Parents* (Huston et al., 1992); Chen's

The Smart Parent's Guide to KIDS' TV (1994a); and the USOE Office of Educational Research and Improvement publication *TV Viewing and Parental Guidance* (1994).

There has been little training of parents and almost no research on the effectiveness of such training. There have been many materials for television awareness training, such as critical-viewing teaching materials, which have been evaluated formatively. These will be discussed later in this chapter.

12.5.3.5 Parental Attitude and Style. Several studies found that parents did not mediate or enforce rules about television viewing because they did not believe television was either a harmful or beneficial force (Messaris, 1983; Messaris & Kert, 1983, cited in Sprafkin, Gadow, & Abelman, 1992; Mills & Watkins, 1982). There is some research that reports that a parent's positive attitude towards television is an important mediator (Brown & Linne, 1976; Bybee, Robinson, & Turow, 1982; Doff, Kovaric, & Doubleday, 1989). In 1991, St. Peters, Fitch, Huston, Wright, and Eakins concluded that attitudes about television were correlated with parents' regulation and encouragement of viewing. The next year, they reported that parents' negative attitudes about television were not sufficient to modify the effects of television viewing. To reach their conclusions, the researchers collected data from 326 children and their families through diaries, questionnaires, standardized instruments, and one-way mirror experiments. This research led to a finer delineation of the variable "parental attitude" toward television:

Positive attitudes were positively associated with parents' encouragement of viewing certain types of programs. Negative attitudes were positively related to regulating children's television viewing. Those parents who both regulated and encouraged discriminating viewing had children who viewed less television than parents who were high on encouragement of viewing. However, the present analysis shows that while parents appear to criticize and regulate television's content because of its negative influence and coview violent programming (news and cartoons) with their children, parents may not be taking advantage of the opportunity to discuss the programs they watch with their children and moderate the effects of content either directly or indirectly. Parents' education and attitudes about television were not associated with children's social behavior towards others (St. Peters, Huston, & Wright, 1989, p. 12).

Abelman found that parents who were more concerned with cognitive effects were more likely to discuss and criticize television content, whereas parents who were more concerned about behavioral effects were more likely to mediate by restricting viewing (Abelman, 1990, cited in Sprafkin, Gadow & Abelman, 1992). Earlier, Abelman and Rogers (1987) presented findings that compared the television mediation of parents of exceptional children. Parents of nonlabeled (no disability* identified) children were restrictive in style; parents of gifted children were evaluative in style; and parents of emotionally disturbed, learning disabled, or mentally retarded children were unfocused in style. The actions of parents with restrictive styles included forbidding certain programs, restricting viewing, specifying viewing time, specifying programs to watch, and switching channels on objectionable programs. Parents with an evaluative style explained programs and advertising, evaluated character roles, and

discussed character motivations and plot/story lines. Parents with an unfocused style were characterized by one or two of these actions: (a) coviewed with the child, (b) encouraged the use of a television guide, (c) used television as reward or punishment, and (d) talked about characters (Abelman & Rogers, 1987).

Singer and Singer and their colleagues have studied parental communication style as it interacts with television viewing and affects comprehension of television (Desmond et al., 1985, 1990; Singer, Singer, & Rapaczynski, 1985, cited in Sprafkin et al., 1992). In a summary of these research findings, Desmond et al. (1990) suggest that, "general family communication style may have been more critical than specific television rules and discipline for enhancing a range of cognitive skills, including television comprehension" (p. 302). Children are helped by an atmosphere that promotes explanation about issues instead of just comments on people and events. Similarly, Korzenny et al. conducted a study at Michigan State University to determine under what conditions children's modeling of antisocial portrayals on television was strongest. They found that parents who disciplined by reasoning and explanation had children who were less affected by antisocial content than children whose parents disciplined through power (Korzenny et al., 1979, cited in Sprafkin et al., 1992).

12.5.4 Coviewing as a Variable

Coviewing refers to viewing in a group of two or more, such as a child and parent or three adolescent peers. Since discussion has been shown in many studies to be an important variable in learning from television (Buerkel-Rothfuss, Greenberg, Atkin, & Neuendorf, 1982, cited in Comstock & Paik, 1991; Desmond, Singer, & Singer, 1990), one would expect coviewing to be a significant variable in the home viewing context. Unfortunately, studies suggest that although coviewing is an important variable, there are few effects due to coviewing. The reasons for this conclusion will be explained in this section. Three categories will be discussed: the nature and frequency of interaction, the effect of attitudes, and the effects of age and roles.

12.5.4.1 Nature and Frequency of Interaction. Based on a review of several articles, Comstock and Paik (1991) speculate that the time adolescents and adults spend coviewing is declining. The greatest concern in the literature is that most parents don't spend time coviewing, and when parents do coview, their level of involvement is usually low. It is not just the amount of time spent coviewing; the type of interaction during coviewing is critical. Most conversation during coviewing is about the television medium itself, the plots, characters, and quality of programs (Neuman, 1982, cited in Comstock & Paik, 1991). These conversations help educate young viewers and make them more critical. According to Comstock and Paik, however, they are not as crucial as conversations that deal with the reality of the program or the rightness or wrongness of the behavior portrayed.

The evidence suggests that parental mediation—when it employs critical discussions and interpretations of what is depicted and sets some guidelines on television use—can increase the understanding of television, improve judgments about reality and fantasy, and reduce total viewing (Comstock & Paik, 1991, p. 45).

Nevertheless, parental coviewing is not always a positive influence. Parents can give implicit approval to violence, prejudice, or dangerous behavior (Desmond, Singer, & Singer, 1990, cited in Comstock & Paik, 1991). After surveying 400 second-, sixth-, and tenth-graders, Dorr, Kovaric, and Doubleday (1989, cited in Comstock & Paik, 1991) found that coviewing basically reflected habits and preferences, rather than parental mediation or conversational involvement. In 1989, Dorr et al. reported only weak evidence for positive consequences from coviewing. They concluded that coviewing is an imperfect indicator of parental mediation of children's viewing. In their review, they identify several methodological problems that make it difficult to use the literature, including differing definitions of coviewing, overestimates by parents, and the assumption that coviewing is motivated by parents' desire to be responsible mediators of children's' interactions with television. They report that coviewing with young children is infrequent (Hopkins & Mullins, 1985, cited in Dorr et al., 1989). Moreover, several studies have found that parent–child coviewing decreases as the number of sets in the house increase (Lull, 1982; McDonald, 1986, cited in Dorr et al., 1989). Dorr and her colleagues investigated several hypotheses about coviewing using data from seven paper-and-pencil instruments given to both parents and children. Their subjects included 460 middle-class second-, sixth-, and tenth-grade children and one parent for each of 372 of these children. The results indicated that coviewing by itself had little relationship to children's judgment of reality. It did predict satisfaction with family viewing.

Thus, research shows that most coviewing takes place because parents and children have similar viewing interests and tastes. Little of the coviewing has been planned by the parent to aid with the child's understanding and comprehension of the show (MacDonald, 1985, 1986, cited in Dorr et al., 1989; Wand, 1968). Nevertheless, it is possible that coviewing may help parents deal with difficult issues. Through viewing scenarios on television, the child may discuss the television character's dilemma with a parent, or the child may simply accept the television portrayal as the appropriate solution.

12.5.4.2 *Effect of Attitudes.*

Dorr and her colleagues also found that parental attitudes toward television were predictors of coviewing. Parents who were more positive coviewed with children more frequently. Coviewing also correlated moderately with parents' belief that children can learn from television and with parents' encouragement of viewing. They concluded that it has a greater effect when motivated by parents' determination to mediate television experiences. This is an important finding, because coviewing occurs least with those who need it most, young children. Children are willing to discuss television content with their parents. Gantz and Weaver (1984) found that children initiate discussions of what they view with their parents; however, children did not initiate discussions about programs unless the programs were coviewed.

12.5.4.3 *Effect of Age and Roles.*

Coviewing is usually described in terms of whether the viewers are children, adolescents, or adults, and whether the social group is of mixed age or not. The usual roles referred to are siblings, peers, and parents.

Haefner and Wartella (1987) used an experimental design to test hypotheses about coviewing with siblings. By analyzing verbal interactions in coviewing situations, they determined that relatively little of the interaction helped younger children interpret the content. Some teaching by older siblings did occur but was limited to identifying characters, objects, words, and filmic conventions. The result was that older siblings influenced evaluation of characters and programs in general, rather than interpretation of content. Haefner and Wartella (1987) noted that other variables needed to be accounted for, such as gender, birth order, viewing style, and attitude, because they could affect differences in learning from siblings. Pinon, Huston, and Wright (1989) conducted a longitudinal study of family viewing of *Sesame Street* using interviews, testing sessions, and diaries with 326 children from ages 3 to 5 and 5 to 7. The presence of older children was found to reduce viewing, the presence of younger children to increase it. Alexander, Ryan, and Munoz (1984, cited in Pinon et al., 1989) found that younger children imitated the preferences of older children and that coviewing with older siblings promoted elaboration of program elements.

Salomon (1977) conducted an experimental study on mothers who coviewed *Sesame Street* with their 5-year-olds. He found:

Mothers' co-observation significantly affected the amount of time that lower-SES children watched the show, as well as their enjoyment of the program, producing in turn an effect on learning and significantly attenuating initial SES differences. Co-observation effects were not found in the middle-class group, except for field dependency performance where encouragement of mothers accentuated SES differences. (p. 1146)

Salomon speculated that the performance of lower-class children is more affected, because the mother as coviewer acts as a needed energizer of learning.

On the other hand, television viewing activity may restrict parent–child interaction. Gantz and Weaver (1984) reviewed the research on parent–child communication about television. They used a questionnaire to examine parent–child television viewing experiences. They report conflicting research, some of which revealed a decrease in family communication, and some of which revealed facilitation of communication. Generally, they found that when parents and children watched together, conversations were infrequent. Moreover, there seems to be a socioeconomic variable interacting with coviewing, because more effective mediation of the viewing experience occurs with higher socioeconomic and educational levels. When viewing occurs with the father present, he tends to dominate program selection (Lull, 1982, cited in Gantz & Weaver, 1984).

Hill and Stafford (1980) investigated the effect of working on the time mothers devote to activities such as childcare, leisure television viewing, and housework. The addition of one child increased the time devoted to housework by 6 to 7 hours a week. Mothers who worked took this time from personal care time, including sleep and television watching. Because early childhood may be an important time for the establishment of long-term patterns of television use, it becomes essential that parental patterns of viewing continue to include coviewing with children, even when family routine mandates changes.

Collett (1986) used a recording device to study coviewing. The device, a C-Box,* consisted of a television set and video camera that recorded the viewing area in front of the television. In addition, subjects were asked to complete a diary. He pointed out that:

It is a sad fact that almost everything we know about television has come from asking people questions about their viewing habits and opinions, or from running them through experiments. The problem with asking people questions is that they may not be able to describe their actions reliably, or they may choose to offer accounts which they deem to be acceptable to the investigator. (p. 9)

In 1988, Anderson and Collins examined the research literature on the relationship between coviewing by parents and critical-viewing skills programs, school achievement, and learning outcomes. The review concluded that there was little support for most of the beliefs about the negative influence of television on children. This opinion contrasts to some extent with conclusions of Haefner and Wartella (1987) and Winn (1977). Anderson and Collins concluded that adults can be helpful to children's comprehension through coviewing, but that it is not clear that interactions are common.

12.5.5 Viewing Habits

Another factor in the family viewing context is the viewing habits or patterns of the household. Because television viewing is often a social as well as a personal act, viewing habits both effect and are affected by other family variables. The factors that seem to emerge from research on viewing habits are the amount of viewing, viewing patterns, and audience involvement.

12.5.5.1 The Amount of Viewing. So far research related to this variable centers around the effects of heavy viewing. Estimates for the typical number of hours television is watched in the American home each day vary from 7 hours (Who are the biggest couch potatoes?, 1993) to 21 hours (Would you give up TV for a million bucks?, 1992). Those over age 55 watched the most; teenage girls, who averaged 3 hours a day, watched the least (Who are the biggest couch potatoes?, 1993). If heavy viewing is defined as more than 3 to 4 hours a day, many Americans are heavy viewers, which makes it difficult to research and draw conclusions about heavy viewing. Research does indicate that heavy viewing is associated with more negative feelings about life. Adults who watch television 3 or more hours daily are twice as likely to have high cholesterol levels as those who watch less than an hour daily according to Larry Tucker, director of health promotion at Brigham Young University, who examined the viewing habits of 12,000 adults.

Children who are heavy viewers often have parents who are heavy viewers. Such parents are usually less educated and enforce fewer family rules about appropriate programs (Roderick & Jackson, 1985). The amount of viewing changes over a life span. Teenagers are relatively light viewers when compared with children and adults (Comstock & Paik, 1987). Some studies reported that children of mothers who work outside the home watch no more or less television than children of mothers at home (Brown, Childers, Bauman, & Koch, 1990; Webster, Pearson, & Webster, 1986); yet Atkin, Greenberg, and Baldwin (1991) summarized research that concluded that children view more in homes where the father is absent (Brown, Bauman, Lenz, & Koch, 1987, cited in Atkin, Greenberg & Baldwin, 1991) and where the mother works (Medrich, Rozien, Rubin, & Buckley, 1982, cited in Atkin, Greenberg, & Baldwin, 1991).

Using a questionnaire, Roderick and Jackson (1985) identified differences in television viewing habits between gifted and nongifted viewers. More nongifted students were found to have their own television sets, which may account for the heavier viewing habits of nongifted students. Gifted students preferred different programs (educational, documentaries) from nongifted students (sitcoms, soaps, game shows). Gifted students were more likely to have VCRs in their home. They did not engage in the wishful thinking or fantasizing about television characters that was common with nongifted students. Roderick and Jackson had nongifted students respond in their classrooms and gifted students respond at home, which may have introduced bias.

The CPB participated in the 1993 Yankelovich Youth Monitor in order to answer some questions about viewing patterns in the 1990s (Corporation for Public Broadcasting, 1993). The Youth Monitor survey studied 1,200 children ages 6 to 17 with an in-home interview in randomly selected households. Today 50 percent of children have a television set in their bedroom. They watch 3 hours per weekday and 4 hours per weekend day. Less than 20 percent watch an hour or less per day. Viewing decreases as income increases. African-American and Hispanic children view the most. Television viewing is the number one activity in the hours between school and dinner time. Nearly half the children reported viewing television with their family each evening. This is especially true for children who watch public television.

12.5.5.2 Viewing Patterns. "Viewing patterns" refers to content preferences, but content does not dictate viewing, because, with few exceptions, other variables have more effect on preferences. This concept can be misleading, because, although there are few discernable patterns of preferences by program types, viewers would be unlikely to watch test patterns or the scrolling of stock market reports. Research supports the conclusion that viewers are relatively content indifferent.* Huston, Wright, Rice, Kerkman, and St. Peters (1990) conducted a longitudinal investigation of the development of television viewing patterns in early childhood, focusing on types and amounts of viewing from ages three to seven. They were interested in developmental changes resulting from maturation or cognitive development, individual and environmental variables affecting viewing patterns, and the stability of individual differences in viewing patterns over time. Viewing was measured from diaries kept by parents who were instructed to record as a viewer anyone who was present for more than one-half of a 15-minute interval when the television was on. While there were many individual differences, these differences tended to be stable over time. As they grew older, children watched programs that required more cognition, such as programs with less redundancy and increasing complexity. Nevertheless, the researchers concluded that family patterns and external variables are more important determinants of viewing than individual or developmental differences. They also found that boys watched more cartoons, action-adventure, and sports programs than did girls. Boys watched more television overall. Viewers of humorous children's programs evolve into viewers of comedy at a later age. Viewers of adventure stories become viewers of action-adventure by age seven. In comparison to this study, Lyle and Hoffman (1972, cited in Comstock & Paik, 1991) documented through questionnaires that preferences change with age.

Plomin, Corley, DeFries, and Fulker (1990) conducted a longitudinal study of 220 adopted children from age three to five. Evidence for both significant genetic and environmental influences on television viewing patterns was found. Neither intelligence nor temperament was responsible for this genetic influence.

McDonald and Glynn (1986) examined adult opinion about how appropriate it is for children to view certain kinds of content. Telephone interviews were conducted with 285 respondents. Adults did not approve of crime detective and adult-oriented programming for children.

Over 4 years, Frank and Greenberg (1979) conducted personal interviews with 2,476 people aged 13 years or older. They found support for their thesis that viewing audiences are more diverse than usually assumed. From the information collected, they constructed profiles of 14 segments of the television audience. Their study is an example of research that clusters variables. More of such research is needed, because so many variables interact in the television environment.

12.5.5.3 Audience Involvement.
Research shows that selectivity and viewing motives can affect viewing involvement (Perse, 1990). Using factor analysis techniques with data generated from questionnaires, Perse investigated viewing motives classified as ritualistic* (watching for gratification) or instrumental* (watching for information). The study included four indications of audience involvement: (a) intentionality, or anticipating television viewing; (b) attention, or focused cognitive effort; (c) elaboration, or thinking about program content; and (d) engaging in distractions while viewing. Ritualistic television use, which indicates watching a broad variety of programs, is marked by higher selectivity before watching but lower levels of involvement while viewing. The study confirms the value of the Levy-Windahl Audience-Activity Typology (Levy & Windahl, 1985, cited in Perse, 1990).

The Experience-Sampling Method* was used to study media habits and experiences of 483 subjects aged 9 to 15 years (Kubey & Larson, 1990). Respondents carried electronic paging devices, and whenever contacted, they reported on their activities and subjective experiences. The utilization of three new forms of video entertainment (music videos, video games, and videocassettes) and traditional television was subsequently analyzed. Traditional television viewing remains the dominant video media form for preadolescents and adolescents. New video media are a relatively small part of their lives. However, the percentage of time spent alone with the new media is growing, perhaps because they offer chances for adolescents to be more independent of the family. Boys had more positive attitudes towards the new media. There could be many reasons for this, including gender differences or the content of the new media.

12.5.6 Current Issues

12.5.6.1 Ratings.
A new component of the viewing environment is use of ratings as guides. Originally, age-based ratings were established (e.g., TV-M for mature audiences). These ratings were criticized for being vague and confusing. To revamp the ratings, content ratings were introduced using symbols such as V for violence and L for coarse language. Researchers have investigated whether parents use the ratings guide (Greenberg & Rampoldi-Hnilo, 2001). A study by Elkoff (1999) reported the strength of the relationship between parental socioeconomic status and children's television viewing. Contrary to expectations based on previous research, parental attitudes seemed to be a stronger variable in parental regulation of viewing than parental style. The parenting style most associated with using the ratings was a communication-oriented, discussion-based style. Discussions helped children to understand parental regulations and created a positive viewing environment. The success of the V-chip technology will affect the success of the ratings system (Ableman, 1999). Strasburger and Wilson (2002) suggested that one way to increase the power of parental mediation was to have the same rating system across media. Krcmar and Cantor (1997) compared the effect of the ratings on parents and children. Parent-child dyads avoided choosing programs with restrictive ratings, but the ratings increased stress in the decision making process. Parents gave more commands when discussing programs with restricted ratings. Children spoke more positively of programs with restrictive ratings.

12.5.6.2 Coviewing.
There seems to be a consensus that models of coviewing need refinement. Current studies distinguish between coviewing and mediation. Coviewing is now described as a condition where an adult does not give comments and shows a neutral attitude towards the program watched. Alternatively, mediation occurs when an adult provides children with additional comments and shows a positive attitude towards the program (Valkenburg, Kremar & deRoos, 1998). Previous studies tended to lump coviewing with varying types and levels of mediation. For children to benefit from viewing with an adult, the adult must discuss the program to clear up any misconceptions (Austin, Bolls, Fujioka, & Engelbertson, 1999). The current trend reflects a need to be more specific about coviewing and mediation. Parental mediation seems to make children less vulnerable to the negative effects of television, for example, to aggressive behavior (Nathanson, 1999).

12.5.6.3 Viewing Habits.
A decade ago not much research was done on the viewing habits of adolescents and college

students. Today, there is evidence of increasing interest in how television influences adolescents and college students and their needs for self-monitoring (Granello & Pauley, 2000; Haferkamp, 1999; Kunkel, Cope, & Biely, 1999). To some extent this interest arises from a concern about programming and how it influences behavior that may negatively affect school achievement. A student who is a heavy viewer because of fascination with formal features or content is likely to achieve less.

12.5.7 Summary and Recommendations

In 1978, Wright, Atkins, and Huston-Stein listed some characteristics of the setting in which a child views television:

- Presence of others who are better informed or who can answer questions raised by a child
- Behavior of others, who through well-timed comments and questions model elaboration of content
- Preparation of the child through previous reading, viewing, or discussion
- Opportunity to enact or rehearse, role play plots, characters, and situations viewed
- Distractions in the environment.

Much is known today about each of these aspects of the family viewing context. In addition, new variables and interactions have been identified such as rulemaking, parental communication style, socioeconomic level, and ethnicity.

Nevertheless, many gaps exist in the research literature, especially about interactions. The well-supported conclusion that learning from television increases when an adult intervenes to guide and support learning, even if the program is an entertainment one (Johnston, 1987), suggests that much more needs to be done to relate the findings of mass media research to research from instructional television and message design. Therefore, it is essential to relate findings about learning from television with findings about the family context for viewing* in order to design interventions that will ensure the positive benefits of television. Findings need to be related theoretically in order to develop recommendations for interventions.

St. Peters et al. (1991) summarized the situation:

Whatever the effects of parental coviewing, encouragement, and regulation, it is clear that the family context is central to the socialization of young children's television use. Families determine not only the amount of television available to children, but also the types of programs, and the quality of the viewing experience. (p. 1422)

12.6 ATTITUDES, BELIEFS, AND BEHAVIORS

Since the early days of broadcast television, educators, parents, and legislators have been concerned about the effects of televised messages on the socialization of children. In 1987, a Louis Harris poll indicated that more than two-thirds of the adults surveyed were concerned about the effects of television on the

values and behaviors of their children (Huston et al., 1992). Attention has also been directed to television's potential for cultivating prosocial behavior.* The cause–effect relationship between televised violence and violent behavior has not been conclusively supported by the research literature. Although there have been significant correlations in certain groups, such as those predisposed to aggressive behavior, the effects cannot be easily generalized to all children. As reported in the section on family viewing context, there are many mediating variables that influence the effects of television on attitudes and behaviors.

As in other areas of television research, methods vary between laboratory experiments, field studies, and surveys. Variables studied can include subject characteristics such as age, sex, ethnicity, socioeconomic status, aggressive tendencies or predispositions, parental style, or amount of viewing. Other studies focus on the type of content that is presented, such as aggression that is realistic, rewarded, or justified. Still other studies focus on the influence of the physical and social context by manipulating variables such as parental approval (Hearold, 1986). More complex interactions may exist among these variables as well. Outcomes can be measured through observing spontaneous play, through teacher and peer ratings, or through monitoring the intensity of responses that presumably produce pain. Treatments and behaviors can be delineated as antisocial,* prosocial,* or neutral.* As defined, each of these categories encompasses many variables.

During the seven hours per day that the television set is typically turned on, it plays a subtle role as a teacher of rules, norms, and standards of behavior (Huston et al., 1992). This section will examine how television can impact beliefs and attitudes. It will also look at issues of desensitization,* oversensitization,* and disinhibition.* Finally, it will review what has been learned about the effects of television on both antisocial and prosocial behavior.

12.6.1 Major Theories

Socialization is the process of learning over time how to function in a group or society. It is a set of paradigms, rules, procedures, and principles that govern perception, attention, choices, learning, and development (Dorr, 1982). Although there have been hundreds of studies conducted that examined the socialization effects of television, a consistent theoretical basis is lacking. Social learning theory,* catharsis theory,* arousal or instigation theory,* and cultivation theory* are commonly cited when researchers examine the effects of television on attitudes, beliefs, and behaviors.

12.6.1.1 Social Learning Theory. Many studies of television effects are based on Bandura's social learning theory, which "assumes that modeling influences operate principally through their informative function, and that observers acquire mainly symbolic representations of modeled events rather than specific stimulus-response associations" (Bandura, 1971, p. 16). According to Bandura and Walters (1963), the best and most effective way to teach children novel ways of acting is to show them the behavior you want them to display. Children can imitate modeled behaviors almost identically (Bandura, Ross, & Ross, 1961). Bandura (1971) states that although much social learning is fostered through observation of real life models, television provides symbolic, pictorially presented models. Because of the amount of time that people are exposed to models on television, "such models play a major part in shaping behavior and in modifying social norms and thus exert a strong influence on the behavior of children and adolescents" (Bandura & Walters, 1963, p. 49).

Bandura and others conducted a series of studies known popularly as the "Bobo doll studies." In each of them, a child saw someone assaulting a Bobo doll, a five-foot tall inflated plastic clown designed to be a punching bag. In some experiments, the model was in the room; in others, a film of either the model or a cartoon figure was projected onto a simulated television (Bandura, Ross, & Ross, 1961, 1963; Liebert & Sprafkin, 1988). Different treatment groups saw the model receiving different consequences. A model who acted aggressively was either rewarded, punished, or received no consequences. Some groups saw a nonaggressive model. After exposure, trained observers counted the children's spontaneous, imitative aggressive acts during play with toys.

The results showed that (a) children spontaneously imitated a model who was rewarded or received no consequences; (b) children showed far more aggression than children in other groups when they observed an aggressive model who was rewarded; (c) children showed little tendency towards aggression when they saw either the aggressive model who was punished or a nonaggressive model who was inhibited; and (d) boys showed more imitative aggression than girls (Bandura, Ross, & Ross, 1961, 1963; Bandura & Walters, 1963; Liebert & Sprafkin, 1988).

Bandura also found that children could learn an aggressive behavior but not demonstrate it until motivated to do so. After children were told they would receive treats if they could demonstrate what they had seen, children in all treatment conditions, even those who saw the model punished, were able to produce a high rate of imitation (Liebert & Sprafkin, 1988; Sprafkin, Gadow, & Abelman, 1992; Wolf, 1975).

Although these studies provided evidence that modeled or mediated images can influence subsequent behavior, they are criticized for being conducted in laboratory conditions and for measuring play behavior toward a toy that was designed to be hit (Liebert & Sprafkin, 1988). Consequently, the results may not transfer to real life situations. Environmental variables, such as parental approval or disapproval, also played an important role in eliciting or inhibiting aggressive behavior in naturalistic settings (Bandura, Ross, & Ross, 1963).

12.6.1.2 Catharsis Theory.
In contrast to social learning theory, catharsis theory suggests that viewing televised violence reduces the likelihood of aggressive behavior (Murray, 1980). The basic assumption is that frustration* produces an increase in aggressive drive, and because this state is unpleasant, the person seeks to reduce it by engaging in aggressive acts or by viewing fantasy aggressions such as those seen in action-adventure

television (Sprafkin, Gadow, & Abelman, 1992). Children who view violence experience it vicariously and identify with the aggressive action, thereby discharging their pent-up aggression (Murray, 1980).

Scheff and Scheele (1980) delineated two conditions needed for catharsis*: stimuli that give rise to distressful emotion and adequate distancing from the stimuli. They suggested that characters in violent cartoons may provide enough distancing and detachment for catharsis to occur, but that realistic violence may be too overwhelming to feel and subsequently discharge.

Since catharsis involves a particular type of emotional response, viewing television may or may not elicit that response depending on characteristics of the stimuli, viewers, and other conditions (Scheff & Scheele, 1980). Feshbach and Singer (1971) took a slightly different theoretical approach to their investigations of the relationship between fantasy aggression and overt behavior. They stated that specific types of fantasies could cause either arousal, which leads to an increase in activity, or inhibition, which in turn leads to drive reduction. In looking at the effects of televised violence over a 6-week period, they studied approximately 400 boys who were divided into two treatment groups based on whether they watched aggressive or nonaggressive television. Feshbach and Singer found no significant differences between these groups. However, when they analyzed the data by type of residential school (private vs. boys' home), they found that in the boys' home the nonaggressive television group became more aggressive, while the aggressive television group became less aggressive. When they analyzed private schools, they found the opposite to be true. Thus, the catharsis theory was supported in the boys' home setting only. Other factors, such as the boys' resentment of not being allowed to watch preferred programming, may have been more influential than the nonaggressive television treatment. The researchers also suggested that, "violence presented in the form of fiction is less likely to reinforce, stimulate, or elicit aggressive responses in children than is violence in the form of a news event" (p. 158).

In general, catharsis theory has failed to receive support in studies on children (Liebert & Sprafkin, 1988) but has found some support in studies on adolescents (Sprafkin, Gadow, & Abelman, 1992). More research is needed on the effects on different populations. Scheff and Scheele (1980) cautioned that catharsis theory has never been adequately tested due to the lack of a careful definition and of systematic data collection. They recommended that studies be conducted that identify and separate viewers of violent programming who experience a cathartic emotional response from those who do not.

12.6.1.3 Instigation or Arousal Theory.
Arousal theory* is related to catharsis theory only in its emphasis on an increase in a physiological state. This theory suggests that generalized emotional arousal influences subsequent behaviors rather than just resulting in drive reduction. Televised messages about emotion, sexuality, or violence can lead to "nonspecific physiological and cognitive arousal that will in turn energize a wide range of potential behaviors" (Huston et al., 1992, p. 36). For example, increased aggression following televised violence would be interpreted as the result of the level of arousal elicited by

the program, not as a result of modeling (Liebert & Sprafkin, 1988). In over a dozen studies, Tannenbaum (1980) varied the content in film clips to include aggressive, sexual, humor, music, and content-free abstract symbols and movement. He compared subjects who viewed more arousing (using physiological measures) though less aggressive (in content) film clips to those who viewed less arousing, more aggressive clips. Subjects were required to make some form of aggressive or punitive response, usually the administration of alleged electric shocks. The subjects could only vary the intensity, frequency, or duration of the shocks. Tannenbaum found more aggression after subjects had seen the more arousing though less aggressive films. He cautioned, however, that a necessary feature of these studies was a target, the researcher's accomplice, who had earlier angered the subjects and, therefore, may have been considered as deserving an aggressive response.

This theory suggests that when aroused, people will behave with more intensity no matter what type of response they are called upon to make (Tannenbaum, 1980). An important implication of this theory is that behavior may be activated that is quite different from what was presented (Huston et al., 1992). Thus, arousal may stimulate a predisposition towards aggression.

Arousal levels can be measured by pulse amplitudes, a type of heart response measured by a physiograph (Comstock & Paik, 1991). With this method the measurement of effects is not influenced by extraneous factors such as observer bias or counting errors.

12.6.1.4 Cultivation Hypothesis and Drip Versus Drench Models.

Cultivation theory "predicts that the more a person is exposed to television, the more likely the person's perceptions of social realities will match those represented on television ..." (Liebert & Sprafkin, 1988, p. 148). In other words, a person's view of the world will be more reflective of the common and repetitive images seen on television than of those actually experienced (Signorielli, 1991; Signorielli & Lears, 1992).

Television may influence viewers by the "drip model," the subtle accumulation of images and beliefs through a process of gradual incorporation of frequent and repeated messages (Huston et al., 1992). George Gerbner conducted a number of studies that demonstrated a cultivation effect. He found that individuals who watch greater amounts of television, and therefore see more crime-related content, develop beliefs about levels of crime and personal safety that reflect those risks as portrayed on television (Gunter, 1987).

Greenberg (1988, cited in Williams & Condry, 1989) asserted that critical images that stand out or are intense may contribute more to the formation of impressions than does the frequency of images over time. Huston et al. also found support for the "drench model" where single programs or series may have a strong effect when they contain particularly salient portrayals. For example, programs designed to counteract stereotypes,* such as *The Golden Girls,* can change children's attitudes and beliefs about older women.

The "drip versus drench models" illustrate a common problem in theory building. Even though the drip model is associated with cultivation theory, neither model explains the cognitive mechanisms that operate.

12.6.2 Attitudes and Beliefs

Television is just one of many sociological factors that influence the formation of beliefs and attitudes. Many of the poorest and most vulnerable groups in our society such as children, the elderly, ethnic minorities, and women are the heaviest users of television in part because it is used when other activities are not available or affordable (Huston et al., 1992; Stroman, 1991). In general, people with low incomes and with less formal education watch more television than people with high incomes and with higher education (Huston et al., 1992).

Liebert and Sprafkin (1988) reported that heavy viewers (those who watched more than 3 to 4 hours per day) are more likely than light viewers to have outlooks and perceptions congruent with television portrayals, even after controlling for income and education. They cautioned that some groups, such as adolescents with low parental involvement, were more susceptible than others. Huston et al. (1992) concluded that children and adults who watched a large number of aggressive programs also tended to hold attitudes and values that favored the use of aggression to resolve conflicts, even when factors such as social class, sex-role identity, education level, or parental behavior were controlled.

The beliefs and attitudes learned from television can also be positive. Bandura and Walters (1963) stated that exemplary models often reflect social norms and the appropriate conduct for given situations. Children can acquire a large number of scripts and schemes for a variety of social situations based on television prototypes (Wright & Huston, 1983). Television can also impact children's understanding of occupations with which they have no experience (Comstock & Paik, 1991). Viewing positive interactions of different ethnic groups on *Sesame Street* led to an increase in positive intergroup attitudes among preschool children (Gom, Goldberg, & Kamungo, 1976, cited in Huston et al., 1992) Unfortunately, many television producers continue to rely on stereotypes due to the desire to communicate images and drama quickly and effectively.

12.6.2.1 Stereotypes.

A group is described as stereotyped "whenever it is depicted or portrayed in such a way that all its members appear to have the same set of characteristics, attitudes, or life conditions" (Liebert & Sprafkin, 1988, p. 189). Durkin (1985) described stereotypes as being based on extreme characteristics attributed to the group, with usually negative values attached to that group. The less real-world information people have about social groups, the more inclined they are to accept the television image of that group. According to Gross (1991), nonrepresentation in the media maintains the powerless status of groups that possess insignificant material or power bases. He stated that mass media are especially powerful in cultivating images of groups for which there are few first-hand opportunities for learning.

Many studies assess stereotypes both quantitatively, with counts of how many and how often subgroups are portrayed, and qualitatively, with analyses of the nature and intent of the portrayals. "Recognition* refers to the frequency with which a group receives TV roles at all. Respect* refers to how characters behave and are treated once they have roles" (Liebert & Sprafkin, 1988, p. 187). Television can reflect and affect the position of groups in society, since the number and types of portrayals of a group symbolize their importance, power, and social value (Huston et al., 1992). For example, when Davis (1990) studied network programming in the spring of 1987, he concluded that television women are more ornamental than functional.

Huston et al. (1992) cautioned, "despite extensive documentation of television content, there is relatively little solid evidence about the effects of television portrayals on self-images, or on the perceptions, attitudes, and behaviors of other groups" (p. 33). As with other areas of television research, it may be too difficult to isolate the effects of television from other social effects. On the other hand, programs that are designed specifically to produce positive images of subgroups appear to be successful.

12.6.2.1.1 Gender Stereotypes. The effects of television in sex role* socialization is another area of concern (Signorielli & Lears, 1992). According to Durkin (1985), "The term sex role refers to the collection of behaviours or activities that a given society deems more appropriate to members of one sex than to members of the other sex" (p. 9). Television viewing has been linked with sex-stereotyped attitudes and behaviors. Correlational studies show a positive relationship between amount of viewing and sex-stereotyped attitudes, and experimental studies demonstrate that even brief exposure to television can increase or decrease sex-stereotyped behaviors, depending on the type of program viewed (Lipinski & Calvert, 1985). Several studies showed that in the United States, women were portrayed on television as passive, dominated by men, deferential, governed by emotion or overly emotional, dependent, younger or less intelligent than men, and generally weak (Davis, 1990; Higgs & Weiller, 1987; Liebert & Sprafkin, 1988; Pryor & Knupfer, 1997; Signorielli & Lears, 1992). During prime time, dramas feature two to three men for every woman (Pryor & Knupfer, 1997). Additionally, women comprised only 30 percent of starring characters (Kimball, 1986).

The formal features of television could contribute to stereotyping by gender. Commercials aimed at women used soft background music and dissolves, and employed female narrators primarily for products dealing with female body care (Craig, 1991; Durkin, 1985; Signorielli & Lears, 1992; Zemach & Cohen, 1986). In the meantime, male narrators were used in 90 percent of all commercials (Zemach & Cohen, 1986). Commercials aimed at men more often incorporated variation in scenes, away-from-home action, high levels of activity, fast-paced cuts, loud and dramatic music and sound effects, and fantasy and excitement (Bryant & Anderson, 1983; Craig, 1991; Durkin, 1985). Additionally, men were shown as authority figures or experts even while at leisure (Pryor & Knupfer, 1997).

Presenting a group in a way that connotes low status deprives that group of respect (Liebert & Sprafkin, 1988). Women were typically assigned marital, romantic, or family roles (Liebert & Sprafkin, 1988) and were depicted in subservient roles allocated

to them by a patriarchal society (Craig, 1991). Davis (1990) also found that the television woman's existence was a function of youth and beauty. Women were younger than men by 10 years, and those aged 35 to 50 were not apparent. They were also five times more likely to have blond hair and four times more likely to be dressed provocatively. They were also frequently defined by their marital or parental status.

A higher proportion of working women were portrayed in professional and entrepreneurial roles than actually existed. They were rarely shown to combine marriage and employment successfully (Signorielli, 1991). Furthermore, television women rarely experienced problems with childcare, sex discrimination, harassment, or poverty (Huston et al., 1992).

Although many studies identified female role stereotypes, fewer examined male stereotypes and their characteristics (Craig, 1991; Langmeyer, 1989). In general, men on television tended to be active, dominant, governed by reason, and generally powerful (Liebert & Sprafkin, 1988). Meyers (1980) examined how men were portrayed in 269 television commercials. Her analysis found four main characteristics: authoritative-dominant, competitive/success hungry, breadwinner, or emotionless male. Commercials aimed at men are more likely to "stress the importance of being capable, ambitious, responsible, and independent and physically powerful, and of seeking accomplishment, physical comfort, and an exciting and prosperous life" (Scheibe & Condry, 1984, cited in Craig, 1991, p. 11).

Craig (1991) found that portrayals differed according to the time of day. For example, daytime television commercials that were aimed at women portrayed men from the perspective of home and family. Men appeared in the home, were hungry, were potential partners for romance, were rarely responsible for childcare, and were portrayed as husbands or celebrities (Craig, 1991). During the weekends, ads were "replete with masculine escapist fantasy" (Craig, p. 53). Men were primary characters 80 percent of the time and appeared in settings outside the home. In contrast, women were completely absent in 37 percent of the ads, and when they did appear, they were sex objects or models 23 percent of the time.

In examining effects, heavy television viewing was associated with stronger traditional sex role development in boys and girls (Comstock & Paik, 1991; Gunter, 1986; Liebert & Sprafkin, 1988; Murray, 1980). Signorielli and Lears (1992) found a significant relationship between heavy television viewing and sex-stereotyped ideas about chores for preadolescent children. They found that children who watched more television were more likely to say that only girls should do the chores traditionally associated with women, and only boys should do those associated with men. Jeffery and Durkin (1989) found that children were more likely to accept a sex role transgression (i.e., a man doing domestic chores) when the character was presented as a powerful executive than when he was shown as a cleaner/custodian. When Kimball (1986) studied three Canadian communities, she found that 2 years after the introduction of television, children's perceptions relating to sex roles were more sex typed than before television was available. Although she recognized the influence of peers, parents, school, and other media, she concluded that the introduction of television to the Notel town added enough of an effect to produce an increase in sex stereotyping.

Additionally, Bryant and Anderson (1983) reported that viewing public television (which contained less stereotyping than commercial television) was characteristic of children who made less stereotypical toy choices.

According to Dambrot, Reep, and Bell (1988), the role played by an actor or actress was more critical to viewers' perceptions than their sex. In their study examining crime action shows, they found that "viewers ascribe masculine traits to both female and male characters" (p. 399). When women were portrayed in nontraditional roles and situations, viewers did not attribute traditional stereotyped traits to them.

Hansen and Hansen (1988) studied the effect of viewing rock music videos on perception. Subjects who viewed stereotypic music videos were more likely to have a distorted impression of an interpersonal interaction than were subjects who viewed neutral videos. Although research studies on the effects of sex role portrayals suggested a link to beliefs about gender roles, Gunter (1986) cautioned that many studies do not account for other variables, such as the effect of parental role modeling, nor do they measure precisely what viewers actually watch.

Even in sports programming, television reinforced stereotypes (Higgs & Weiller, 1987; Weiller & Higgs, 1992). Commentators described men as strong, aggressive, and unstoppable. They used surnames and provided technical information about male athletes. On the other hand, in the limited coverage of women's sports, women were described by their pain and the difficulty of the competition, by their first names, and with derisive adjectives, such as "the best *little* center" in basketball (Higgs & Weiller, 1992, p. 11).

On a positive note, television altered expectations when it purposely deviated from stereotypic portrayals in order to change beliefs (Comstock & Paik, 1987; Gunter, 1986). Johnston and Ettema (1982) conducted summative evaluations of *Freestyle,* the 13-part public television program designed to change attitudes about sex roles among children aged 9 to 12. Their study included four experimental conditions spread among seven research sites. Although limited positive effects were seen with unstructured viewing, positive short-term and long-term effects were seen when the program was viewed in the classroom and discussion took place (Comstock & Paik, 1987; Durkin, 1985). Effects with home viewers were small and were found only for the heaviest viewers. Among female children who viewed the programs in school, however, there were significant changes in beliefs, attitudes, and interests. While there were few changes in boys' beliefs, attitudes, or interests, there were no cases of negative effect on males or females (Johnston & Ettema, 1982, cited in Johnson, 1987). The program was particularly successful in promoting greater acceptance of (a) girls who displayed independence and abilities in athletics, mechanical activities, and leadership; (b) boys who were nurturing; and (c) men and women who chose nontraditional roles (Gunter, 1986; Johnston & Ettema, 1982). Overall, Johnston and Ettema concluded that the programs could impact children's beliefs and attitudes more than their interests in nontraditional pursuits.

12.6.2.1.2 Minority Stereotypes. The effects of television on beliefs and perceptions related to ethnicity have not received as much attention as those related to sex roles (Comstock & Paik, 1991). Because children are less likely to have contact with people of different racial or ethnic backgrounds, television may be the primary source of information about minorities (Takanishi, 1982; Williams & Condry, 1989). By 2080, Caucasians in the United States will no longer be the majority (Fitzgerald, 1992). In response to the United States being more racially integrated than at any other time in history, television is becoming more racially diverse.

According to Huston et al. (1992), television is particularly important for African-Americans because they watch more than many other groups, have more favorable attitudes toward it, rely more on it for news and information, and perceive it as reflecting reality, Additionally, young, well-educated African-American adults are heavy viewers. Furthermore, television may provide minority children with important information about the world that is not available to them in their immediate environment (Stroman, 1991). Therefore, the effects may be greater.

Minority children on average spent more time watching television regardless of socioeconomic status (Comstock & Cobbey, 1982; Dorr, 1982) and ascribed more reality or credibility to television portrayals (Dorr, 1982). Stroman cited a study by Lee and Browne (1981) that reported that 26 percent of third- and fourth-graders and 15 percent of adolescents watched more than 8 hours of television per day. Since their families were less able to afford alternative forms of entertainment, African-American children relied more on television for entertainment and guidance and to learn about occupations (Stroman, 1991). The images of successful African-Americans on television were as far removed from reality as negative portrayals were (Wilson & Gutierrez, 1985, cited in Fitzgerald, 1992).

In the early days of television, African-Americans appeared in minor roles, frequently as servants or as comedians (Liebert & Sprafkin, 1988). According to Williams and Condry (1989), in the 1970s, however, racism became subtle. Black characters were younger, poorer, and less likely to be cast in professional occupations, dramatic, or romantic roles. They often appeared in segregated environments. From their study of 1,987 network programs and commercials, Williams and Condry concluded that minorities were portrayed with blue-collar or public-service jobs, appeared as children, or appeared as perpetrators or victims of criminal and delinquent acts.

Ethnic identity* is the "attachment to an ethnic group and a positive orientation toward being a member of that group" (Takanishi, 1982, p. 83). Children are particularly vulnerable to negative portrayals of African-Americans. "Black children are ambivalent about their racial identity, and studies still show that many prefer whites, prefer to be white, and prefer white characters on television to characters like themselves" (Comer, 1982, p. 21). Graves (1982) cited several studies that demonstrated that preschoolers imitated televised Caucasian models more than African-American models, even when imitating toy selection. Other variables could be contributing to these studies, however. The results could be interpreted as relating more to the perceived status of the models than to their ethnicity (Comstock & Cobbey, 1982).

Although he criticized situation comedies for their portrayals of African-Americans as frivolous and stupid, Comer

(1982) commented that these programs helped Caucasian third-through fifth-graders gain positive images of minorities, and many African-American children gained positive images about themselves. Graves (1982) found positive effects, including the acceptance and imitation of minority role models. Additionally, Mays and colleagues (1975) found that after viewing 16 episodes of *Vegetable Soup*, a program that featured the interactions of children of different ethnic backgrounds, children aged 6 to 10 years expressed greater friendliness toward those differing in ethnicity (cited in Comstock & Paik, 1991). Mays and colleagues also found that those who were African-American expressed enhanced acceptance of their own ethnicity. Takanishi (1982) and Greenberg and Atkin (1982) cautioned that the effects of minority character portrayals were complicated by the different values, attitudes, and characteristics that children bring to viewing in addition to the effects of social influences and the attributes of content.

According to Davis (1990) and Berry (1982), minority group portrayals have improved in terms of frequency. In 1987, African-Americans comprised 12.4 percent of television characters and 12.9 percent of the population (Davis, 1990). Although African-Americans were appearing more on television, segregation and isolation continued to be a problem (Berry, 1982). In 1980, cross-racial interactions appeared in only 2 percent of dramas and 4 percent of comedies (Weigel, Loomis & Soja, 1980, cited in Liebert & Sprafkin, 1988). In their study of 1987 network programming, Williams and Condry found that 40 percent of minorities were in segregated environments with no contact with whites. They did find an interesting trend in that cross-racial friendships among youth were commonplace. In contrast, they found that cross-racial relationships among adults were limited to job-related situations.

Audience viewing patterns have the potential to counteract the negative effects of televised stereotypes. Greenberg and Atkin (1982) stated that African-American parents were more likely than Caucasian parents to sit down and watch television programs with their children, especially minority programs. Grayson (1979) and Stroman (1991) advised direct intervention by parents to reduce the impact of negative portrayals, including (a) selectively viewing programs and excluding those that portray minorities in distorted or stereotyped roles; (b) looking for and coviewing programs that portray minorities in a positive, realistic, and sensitive manner; (c) viewing and discussing the program's applicability and relevance to real-life people and events; (d) providing exposure to content beyond television and to activities that will promote physical and intellectual growth, such as trips to zoos and museums; and (e) providing opportunities for children to be in real situations with minorities, elderly persons, and others.

Other minority groups were rarely portrayed. By the mid-1970s, however, other subgroups were complaining to the networks about their portrayals. Common stereotypes at the time included Arabs as terrorists or oil sheiks, Italians as Mafia hoodlums, Asians as invaders, docile launderers, or karate experts, Chicanos/Hispanics as comics, banditos, or gang members, homosexuals as effeminate, and Native Americans as savages, victims, cowards, or medicine men (Davis, 1990; Williams

& Condry, 1989; Willis, 1990). Relatively little is known about how television is used by other minority groups.

12.6.2.1.3 Elderly Stereotypes. As a group, the elderly have been under-represented on television, occupying no more than 3 percent of all roles (Bell, 1991; Huston et al., 1992; Liebert & Sprafkin, 1988). Of that number, men outnumbered women two to one and were likely to be more powerful, active, and productive. In a study of children's Saturday morning programs, Bishop and Krause (1984) found that over 90 percent of the comments made about the elderly were negative (cited in Liebert & Sprafkin, 1988). The elderly were also portrayed as unhappy and having problems they could not solve themselves. According to Davis and Davis (1986), they were shown as "more comical, stubborn, eccentric, and foolish than other characters. They are more likely to be treated with disrespect" (cited in Bell, 1991, p. 3).

This image of the elderly may be changing as the media recognize that one out of every six Americans is over 60 years of age, and marketing decisions begin to incorporate the elderly into television's prime time (Bell, 1991). According to Nielsen ratings, in 1989 the five most popular dramas for the over-age-55 audience featured older characters: *Murder She Wrote, The Golden Girls, Matlock, Jake and the Fatman,* and *In the Heat of the Night* (Bell, 1991). Bell found that they portrayed elderly who were at the center of the show as powerful characters, affluent, healthy, physically and socially active, quick witted, and admired. He concluded that while the elderly were portrayed better than they had been in the past, there were still problems. "When men appear with women, the old stereotypes of male prominence and power still operate" (Bell, 1991, p. 11). In his observation, these shows depicted two worlds: one where there were older women but no men, and one where there were older men with young women but no older women.

Some evidence exists for the potential of television to promote positive outcomes regarding the elderly. Keegan (1983) found that a planned program, *Over Easy,* which was designed to reach viewers over 55 years, was effective in fostering positive attitudes about aging (cited in Huston et al., 1992). The effects of images of the elderly need to be researched further and with different populations.

12.6.2.1.4 Disability Stereotypes. According to the World Health Organization, disability is defined as "any restriction or lack (resulting from an impairment) of ability to perform an activity in the manner or within the range considered normal for a human being" (cited in Cumberbatch & Negrine, 1992, p. 5). Television tends to concentrate on the disability rather than on the individual aspects of the character portrayed. People with disabilities wish to be treated as ordinary people on television, not as superheroes or villains or with sentimentality. Cumberbatch and Negrine (1992) studied televised images of disability on programs produced in Great Britain from 1988 to 1989 and compared them to shows produced in the United States. By recording and coding 1,286 programs, they found that characters with disabilities were shown to have locomotor, behavioral, or disfigurement disabilities since these are visible.

"The wheelchair has apparently become a ready symbol of the experience of disability, a shorthand for a variety of difficulties that someone suffering from disabilities may encounter" (Cumberbatch & Negrine, p. 136). They concluded that in feature films, characters with disabilities were stereotyped most commonly as criminals, as being barely human, or as powerless and pathetic. In British programs, they were portrayed as villains, moody, introverted, unsociable, or sad. In the United States, however, characters with disabilities were shown more positively and were more likely to be sociable, extroverted, moral, and nonaggressive. Research on the effects of portraying characters with disabilities is needed.

12.6.2.2 Sensitization and Inhibition Issues.

In addition to effects on stereotyping, some modeled behaviors can desensitize viewers, oversensitize viewers, or temporarily remove inhibitions (disinhibition*). Variables include the type of behavior exhibited on screen as well as how victims' responses are portrayed.

Repeated exposure to specific types of violent programming, especially sexual violence and sports, may result in some viewers becoming desensitized or disinhibited. For example, Stein (1972, cited in Friedrich & Stein, 1973) found that emotional arousal declined with repeated exposure to violence, but it was unclear if behavioral responses also declined.

Although exposure to erotic content does not appear to induce antisocial behavior,* research on sexual violence suggests that it can reinforce certain attitudes, perceptions, and beliefs about violence toward women (Huston et al., 1992). After seeing sexual assault modeled, men behaved toward women differently than those shown sexual intimacy without aggression (Donnerstein, 1980, cited in Bandura, 1986). Bandura (1986) found:

Showing women experiencing orgasmic pleasure while being raped stimulates greater punitiveness than if they are depicted expressing pain and abhorrence. Depictions of traumatic rape foster less aggression even though they are as arousing and more unpleasant than depictions of rape as pleasurable. (p. 295)

Bandura also suggested that since sexual modeling served as a source of arousal and disinhibition, it could also heighten aggressiveness. Both male and female viewers who were massively exposed to pornography:

... regard hard-core fare as less offensive and more enjoyable, they perceive uncommon sexual practices as more prevalent than they really are, they show greater sexual callousness toward women, they devaluate issues of importance to women, and they are more lenient toward rape offenses. (Zillmann & Bryant, 1984, cited in Bandura, 1986, p. 294)

Although broadcast television is usually sexually suggestive rather than explicit, cable channels and videotape rentals can make violent and explicit sexual images readily available to children. Huston et al. (1992) called for more research to be done regarding the impact of these materials on children. Bandura (1986) expressed concern that while society exercises control over injurious actions, it presents discontinuities in the socialization of and boundaries for sexual behavior.

Although some viewers may become desensitized by what they watch on television, other viewers may become oversensitive. Television may cultivate or intensify distorted perceptions of the incidence of crime in the real-world, especially for heavy viewers (Gunter, 1987; Gunter & Wakshlag, 1988; Murray, 1980; NIMH, 1982). Heavy viewers may think the world is more dangerous than it really is and perceive that the world is a mean and scary place (Liebert & Sprafkin, 1988). This may be the result of a circular effect where "greater fear of potential danger in the social environment may encourage people to stay indoors, where they watch more television, and are exposed to programmes which tell them things which in turn reinforce their anxieties" (Gunter & Wakshlag, 1988, pp. 208–209).

On the other hand, programs such as crime dramas in which the antagonists end up being punished can have the countereffect of providing comfort and reassurance in a just world (Gunter & Wakshlag, 1988). Gunter and Wober (1983) found a positive relationship between beliefs in a just world and exposure to crime drama programming (cited in Gunter, 1987).

The amount of viewing may be less important than the types of programs watched, the perception of and interpretation of content, and the actual level of crime where people live (Gunter, 1987). More detailed analyses are needed before causal conclusions can be drawn,

In addition to sensitization effects, another area of concern is disinhibition. For example, disinhibition effects* that lead to increased aggressive behavior have also been observed. In a study conducted by Bandura and Walters (1963), experimental subjects were instructed to administer electrical shocks (simulated) to individuals who gave incorrect responses. In this study, subjects who were exposed to aggressive content (a scene of a knife fight) administered stronger electrical shocks than did their counterparts who were shown constructive or neutral films (Liebert & Sprafkin, 1988). They cautioned that many of the laboratory studies that supported disinhibition occurred in contrived circumstances with television segments that were taken out of context. They also found a trend for disinhibition effects among those who are initially more aggressive.

Some evidence exists that disinhibition also occurs when violence is viewed in real-life settings. For adults, disinhibition may be a factor in the increase in violence against women that occurs after football games. White, Katz, and Scarborough (1992) studied the incidence of trauma after National Football League games. Although Walker found that calls to women's shelters increased on the day that a team lost (cited in Nelson, 1994), White et al. found that women were more likely to be hospitalized for trauma from assaults on the day after a team won. They concluded that violence against women could be stimulated by some aspect of identification with an organization that dominates through violent behavior. "In a domestic context, the example of being successful through violent behavior may provide the male viewer with a heightened sense of power and may increase domination over his spouse or partner. This feeling of power can act to disinhibit constraints against violence" (White et al., p. 167). Additionally, calls to women's shelters increased in the first four to five hours after a Super Bowl game, with more calls being reported in some cities than on any other day of the year (Nelson, 1994). The director of a domestic abuse center stated that when men describe battering incidents that involve sports, "the men talk about being pumped up from the game" (p. 135). Other variables, such as intoxication, may confound these data.

12.6.3 Behaviors

A substantial body of research has been conducted relative to the positive and negative effects of television on behavior. Behavior patterns that are established in childhood and adolescence may affect the foundations for lifelong patterns that are manifested in adulthood (Huston et al., 1992). According to Wright and Huston (1983), "producers, advertisers, and broadcasters use violence in children's programming largely because they believe that dramatic content involving anger, aggression, threat, and conquest is essential to maintain the loyalty and attention of child audiences" (p. 838), even though the research on formal features has suggested alternative ways of maintaining attention, such as with high rates of child dialogue, high pace, auditory and visual special effects, salient music, and nonhuman speech. According to Hearold (1986), whether or not what is learned is ever put to use depends on a variety of factors:

There must be the capability to perform the act, sufficient motivation, and some remembrance of what is viewed; performance also depends on the restraints present, including the perceived probability of punishment and the values held in regard to violence (p. 68).

It is difficult to make definitive statements about the cause of behaviors or about correlations between causes and effects because of inconsistencies in the labels for gross treatment effects. Antisocial and prosocial are broad terms that can represent diverse treatments or outcomes. There is also ambiguity in more specific terms such as frustration or aggression (Bandura & Walters, 1963).

In her meta-analysis of 230 studies that were conducted through 1977, however, Hearold (1986) made 1,043 treatment comparisons. Overall, she found a positive effect for antisocial treatments on antisocial behaviors and a positive effect for prosocial treatments on prosocial behaviors. When she looked at the most ecologically valid studies, Hearold found that effect sizes* continued to be positive, although they were lower. She cautioned, however, that some of the differences might be understood by the intention of the treatments. For example, antisocial programs are generally created to entertain audiences. Alternatively, many prosocial programs have prosocial instruction as their goal. Other moderating variables can be the degree of acceptance of antisocial and prosocial behaviors.

12.6.3.1 Antisocial Outcomes. For decades, people have been concerned about the effect of television on antisocial behavior*, particularly violence and aggression. Violence* can be defined as "the overt expression of physical force against others or self, or the compelling of action against one's will on pain of being hurt or killed" (NIMH, 1972, p. 3). Aggression* can be defined as an action intended to injure another person or object (Friedrich & Stein, 1973), but its designation as antisocial depends on the act as well as the circumstances and participants (NIMH, 1972). In observational studies, these antisocial acts include physical assault, nonverbal teasing, verbal aggression, commanding vigorously, tattling, injury to objects, and playful or fantasy aggression (Friedrich & Stein, 1973). Some laboratory studies use a "help–hurt" game in which the intensity, quantity, or length of pain-producing responses are measured when the subjects believe they are affecting another child or a researcher's accomplice.

Two decades of content analysis show that violence remains at approximately 5 violent acts per hour in primetime television and at 20 to 25 acts per hour in children's Saturday morning programming. This translates into an average of 8,000 murders and over 100,000 acts of violence viewed by the time a child graduates from elementary school (Huston et al., 1992).

Initiated in 1994, the National Cable Television Association funded the National Television Violence Study, a 3-year effort that went beyond counting the number of violent incidents portrayed on television. The study also assessed the contexts of violence in entertainment and reality-based shows, examined the effect of ratings and content advisories, and explored the effectiveness of antiviolence television messages and public service announcements (Federman, 1998; Mediascope, 1996). Important conclusions included:

- During the study, 60 percent of entertainment programs contained violence compared to 39.2 percent of reality programs; in these, on average six violent incidents per hour were shown.
- Most perpetrators of violence were presented as attractive role models and they rarely showed remorse or experienced negative consequences.
- About half of the violent incidents showed no harm or pain to the victim; less than 20 percent showed long-term damage to victim's family or friends.
- Overall, 40 percent of violent scenes included humor.
- For children under age seven, portrayals of violence were found most often in cartoons where perpetrators were attractive role models, violence was justified or unpunished, and victims suffered few consequences.
- Less than 5 percent of violent programs employed an antiviolence theme (Federman, 1998).

Early results showed that "viewer discretion" advisories and "PG-13" or "R" ratings made programs more attractive for boys, particularly those aged 10 to 14, while the opposite was true for girls, especially those aged 5 to 9 (Mediascope). Public service announcements and antiviolence programming were not effective in changing adolescents' attitudes about using violence to resolve conflict unless they showed negative consequences (Federman).

Antisocial outcomes have been shown to occur after exposure to antisocial programming. Although Huston et al.'s review of the literature stated that "there is clear evidence that television violence can cause aggressive behavior and can cultivate values favoring the use of aggression to resolve conflicts" (1992, p. 136), this statement should be treated with caution because definitions of antisocial behavior, violence, and aggression can vary from study to study. Results can also vary depending on other variables such as age, sex, parenting style, or environmental cues. For example, Bandura and Walters' (1959) study of childrearing practices found that parents of aggressive boys were more likely to encourage and condone aggression than the parents of nonaggressive boys (cited in Bandura & Walters, 1963). A predisposition for aggressiveness may also be a catalyst that produces increases in mediated behavior (Murray, 1980). Comstock and Paik (1987) list others factors that have been identified as heightening television's influence or contributing to viewers' antisocial behavior. These include the portrayal of violence as: (a) justified, rewarded, not criticized, unpunished, or seemingly legal; (b) violence resulting in numerous victims or mass killings; (c) violence among friends or gang members; (d) viewers who are angered or provoked prior to viewing; and (e) viewers who are in a state of frustration or unresolved excitement after viewing (Comstock & Paik, 1987).

The accumulated research shows a positive correlation between viewing and aggression, i.e., "heavy viewers behave more aggressively than light viewers" (Huston et al., 1992, p. 54). But when a correlation is made between viewing televised violence and aggressive behavior, it does not mean that there is a causal relationship. Alternate explanations are possible such as those who are predisposed to being aggressive tend to watch more violent television. Multiple factors including biological predispositions, family or peer characteristics, and situational variables can influence tendencies toward aggression (Bushman & Huesmann, 2001).

Although experimental studies such as the Bandura Bobo doll studies have shown that aggression can increase after exposure to televised violence, the research has not proved that aggression demonstrated in laboratory settings transfers to real-life settings. Field studies show conflicting results, and naturalistic studies are frequently confounded by uncontrollable environmental factors.

In an effort to find more precise answers, a major endeavor was sponsored by the Surgeon General of the United States to study the effects of television on social behavior with a focus on the effects of televised violence on children and youth (NIMH, 1972). From 1969 to 1971, 23 independent projects were conducted, a number of which were field studies that showed correlations ranging from .0 to .30 (Atkin, Murray, & Nayman, 1971). The end result was a very cautious report that stated, "On the basis of these findings . . . we can tentatively conclude that there is a modest relationship between exposure to television and aggressive behavior or tendencies . . . " (NIMH, 1972, p. 8). Only two of the studies showed +.30 correlations between earlier viewing and later aggression.

Finding positive correlations did not lead to statements of causality. The advisory committee cautioned that "a correlation coefficient of .30 would lead to the statement that 9% of the variance in each variable is accounted for by the variation in the other" (NIMH, 1972, p. 167). They also wrote, "The majority of the values are trivially small, but the central tendency for the values is clearly positive. En masse, they indicate a small positive relationship between amount of violence viewing and aggressive behavior . . ." (NIMH, 1972, p. 168). They also speculated that the correlations could be the result of any of three causal sequences: (a) viewing violence led to aggression, (b) aggression led to violence viewing, or that (c) both viewing and aggression were the products of some unidentified conditions. Such conditions could have included preexisting levels of aggression, underlying personality factors, or parental attitudes and behavior.

The committee found the experimental evidence to be weak and inconsistent. However, they felt there was a convergence of evidence for short-term causation of aggression among some children, but less evidence for long-term manifestations. They pointed out that the viewing-to-aggression sequence most likely applied to some children predisposed to aggressive behavior and that the manner in which children responded depended on the environmental context in which violence was presented and received (Atkin, Murray & Nayman, 1971–1972).

Overall, the Surgeon General's Advisory Committee concluded that there was a tentative indication of a causal relationship between viewing violence on television and aggressive behavior. Any relationship operated only on some children, those who were predisposed to be aggressive, and it operated only in some environmental contexts (NIMH, 1972).

In 1982, the National Institute of Mental Health (NIMH) published another report that reviewed research conducted during the ten years that followed the original report. In their summary, they concluded that the convergence of evidence supported the conclusion that there was a causal relationship between viewing televised violence and later aggressive behavior (NIMH, 1982). They cautioned that all the studies demonstrated group differences, not individual differences, and that no study unequivocally confirmed or refuted the conclusion that televised violence leads to aggressive behavior.

As stated earlier in this section, Hearold (1986) found similar results when she conducted a meta-analysis of studies conducted through 1977 that measured antisocial and prosocial behaviors or attitudes of subjects assigned to film or video treatment conditions. She included only those studies with valid comparison groups such as pre/post comparison studies or those with control groups. Hearold found that the most frequently measured antisocial behavior was physical aggression, and concluded that positive findings have not been confined to a method, measure, or age group. While responses to television violence were undifferentiated by sex among young children under the age of nine, they became more differentiated with age as sex role norms were learned. Male–female differences were greatest for physical aggression in the later teen years when effect sizes for boys markedly increased, while those for girls decreased. When looking at outcome characteristics, Hearold found that physical aggression was a variable in 229 comparisons with a mean effect size of .31. She also found that when subjects were frustrated or provoked, the effect size increased (Hearold, 1986).

Paik and Comstock (1994, cited in Bushman and Huesmann, 2001) conducted a meta-analysis that looked at the results of

217 studies of media violence and aggression. They also found a .31 overall correlation between television violence and antisocial behaviors. They included both laboratory (.40 correlation) and field (.30 correlation) experiments.

Other studies support the importance of individual predispositions and environmental contexts in predicting the negative effects of television. Because studying the effects of television in naturalistic settings is so complex, researchers called for a move away from determining if there are effects to seeking the explanations and processes responsible for causing effects (Joy, Kimball, & Zabrack, 1986; NIMH, 1982). For example, Friedrich and Stein's (1973) study of 93 preschoolers found that children who were initially above average in aggression showed greater interpersonal aggression after exposure to aggressive cartoons than when exposed to neutral or prosocial programs. They also showed sharp declines in self-regulation such as delay tolerance and rule obedience. Children who were initially below average in aggression did not respond differently to the various treatment conditions.

In their longitudinal study, Joy, Kimball, and Zabrack (1986) found that after 2 years of exposure to television, children in the formerly Notel town were verbally and physically more aggressive than children in the Unitel and Multitel towns. They also found that boys were more aggressive than girls, and children who watched more television tended to be more physically aggressive. They speculated that this might have been due to a novelty effect rather than a cultivation effect.

Special populations of children can react to and use television differently from their nondisabled peers. When Sprafkin, Gadow and Abelman (1992) reviewed field studies conducted with emotionally disturbed and learning disabled children, they found that these children demonstrated more physical aggression after viewing control material or cartoons with low levels of aggression than did nonlabeled children. In laboratory studies of exceptional children, however, they found that children who were naturally more aggressive were more likely to be reactive to televised violence. Other variables may have impacted the results, including the use of nonaggressive but highly stimulating or suspenseful treatment materials.

There also seems to be a relationship between heavy viewing and restlessness. Studies conducted by Singer and colleagues and Desmond and colleagues (1990) found positive associations between heavy television viewing and greater restlessness for children whose parents were not involved in coviewing (cited in Comstock & Paik, 1991).

Furthermore, most young children do not know the difference between reality and fantasy (NIMH, 1982). Some of the negative effects of violence and stereotypes may be attenuated if children can separate fiction from reality (Wright & Huston, 1983). Sprafkin, Gadow, and Dussault developed a test called the Perceptions of Reality on Television (PORT) to assess children's knowledge of the realism of people and situations shown on television (Sprafkin, Gadow & Abelman, 1992). It consisted of showing a series of video excerpts about which children answered questions. The PORT questions were based on judging the realism of aggressive content, nonaggressive content, and superhuman feats, on differentiating between the actor and the role played, and on differentiating between cartoons and nonan-

imated programs. PORT has been found to be a reliable and valid measure of children's perceptions of reality on television (Sprafkin, Gadow, & Abelman, 1992). Research on the applicability of PORT to developing interventions in critical viewing skills is needed.

At least three areas of concern arise from the literature about violence on television. The obvious ones are the relationship between television violence and aggression, even if the aggression is not directed against society, and the desensitization of children to pain and suffering (Smith, 1994). The less obvious one is the potential for children who are sensitive and vulnerable to become more fearful and insecure upon exposure to violence on television (Signorielli, 1991).

In response to these concerns, the United States Congress included in the Telecommunications Act of 1996 a requirement for television manufacturers to install an electronic device in every set produced after 1998. This device, popularly referred to as the V-chip, enables parents to identify and block programming they determine is undesirable for their children (Murray, 1995; Telecommunications Act of 1996). In order for this technology to work, the Telecommunications Act called for programs to be rated and encoded according to their level of sex and violence.

Alfred Hitchcock was reputed to have said, "Television has brought murder into the home, where it belongs" (Elkind, 1984, p. 103). Murders and crime occur about ten times more frequently on television than in the real world. A third of all characters in television shows are committing crime or fighting it, most with guns. It becomes, therefore, a chicken-and-egg question. Does television programming include more violence because society is more violent, or does society become more violent because people are desensitized to violence through television? The answer is probably both. Too many factors interact for the extent of each influence to be determined.

When one examines violence in films the trend towards increased gore and explicit horror is easily documented. Rather than reflecting the content and meaning associated with myths and fairy tales, horror films today are pure sensation with little serious content (Stein, 1982, cited in Elkind, 1984). If violence on television is controlled, children and adults will still be able to experience violence vicariously through other media such as films, books, and recordings. Research on television suggests that the messages sent about violence do have an effect, but many other factors can mediate these effects.

Recognizing this, members of the television industry decided to play an active role. In 1994, the Corporation for Public Broadcasting (CPB) partially funded *The National Campaign to Reduce Youth Violence* The purpose of the campaign was to identify and support interventions to counter the effects of violence on television. Its goals were (a) to focus on successful, community-based solutions, (b) to collaborate with multiple community resources and organizations, and (c) to involve youth in the problem-solving process (Head, 1994). Over an initial 2-year period, it was to have provided technical assistance with telecommunications services, two program series, and accompanying outreach programs. This campaign was designed to involve television, print, radio, government agencies, and community, educational, and industrial organizations.

12.6.3.2 *Prosocial Outcomes.*

Although concerns about the negative effects of television are certainly valid, television also can be used to teach positive attitudes and behaviors. Prosocial behaviors include generosity, helping, cooperation, nurturing, sympathy, resisting temptation, verbalizing feelings, and delaying gratification (Friedrich & Stein, 1973; Rushton, 1982; Sprafkin, Gadow, & Abelman, 1992). Liebert and Sprafkin (1988) divided prosocial behavior into two categories: (a) altruism* which includes generosity, helping, cooperation, and (b) self-control* which includes delaying gratification and resisting the temptation to cheat, lie, or steal. Children must be able to comprehend television content, however, if prosocial messages are to be effectively conveyed.

Content analyses revealed an average of 11 to 13 altruistic acts per hour, 5 to 6 sympathetic behaviors, and less than 1 act of control of aggressive impulses or resistance to temptation (Liebert & Sprafkin, 1988). Although viewers were exposed to prosocial interpersonal behaviors, there were infrequent displays of self-control behaviors on television (Liebert & Sprafkin, 1988). Most of these prosocial behaviors appeared in situation comedies and dramas. Additionally, many prosocial acts appeared in an aggressive context (Mares & Woodard, 2001).

In her meta-analysis, Hearold (1986) found 190 tests for effects of prosocial behavior. The average effect size for prosocial television on prosocial behavior (.63) was far higher than that for the effects of antisocial television on antisocial behavior (.30) (cited in Liebert & Sprafkin, 1988). "The most frequently measured prosocial behavior, altruism (helping or giving), had one of the strongest associations, with a mean effect size of .83" (Hearold, 1986, p. 105). Other noteworthy average effect sizes included .98 for self-control, .81 for buying books, .57 for a positive attitude toward work, and .57 for acceptance of others (Hearold, 1986). Due to these large effect sizes, Hearold called for more attention to and funding for the production of prosocial programs for children.

One such prosocial program was *Mister Rogers' Neighborhood,* which has been lauded for its ability to promote prosocial behavior in preschool children. Field experiments showed that children increased self-control (Liebert & Sprafkin, 1988) and learned nurturance, sympathy, task persistence, empathy, and imaginativeness from viewing it (Huston et al., 1992). Positive interpersonal behavior was enhanced when viewing was supplemented with reinforcement activities such as role-playing and play materials, especially for lower socioeconomic status children (Huston et al., 1992; Sprafkin, Gadow & Abelman, 1992). After exposing children to 12 episodes of *Mister Rogers' Neighborhood* over a 4-week period, Stein and Friedrich (1972, cited in Murray, 1980) found that preschool children became more cooperative and willing to share toys and to delay gratification than children who watched antisocial cartoons. Friedrich and Stein (1973) also found that preschoolers showed higher levels of task persistence, rule obedience, and delay tolerance than subjects who viewed aggressive cartoons. These effects of increased self-regulatory behavior were particularly evident for children with above-average intelligence. Paulson (1974) reported that children who viewed *Sesame Street* programs designed to portray cooperation behaved more cooperatively in test situations than did nonviewers.

Sprafkin (1979) compiled the following results of research on other prosocial programs: *Sesame Street* improved children's racial attitudes toward African-Americans and Hispanics; *Big Blue Marble* caused fourth- through sixth-graders to perceive people around the world as being similar and "children in other countries as healthier, happier, and better off than before they had viewed the program" (p. 36); *Vegetable Soup* helped 6- to 10-year-olds become more accepting of children of different races; and finally, *Freestyle* helped 9- to 12-year-olds combat sex role and ethnic stereotyping in career attitudes.

Commercial television programs that reach larger audiences can also promote prosocial behavior. First-graders who viewed a prosocial *Lassie* episode were more willing to sacrifice good prizes to help animals seemingly in distress than a control group was (Sprafkin, Liebert, & Poulos, 1975, cited in Sprafkin, Gadow, & Abelman, 1992). Children who viewed the cartoon *Fat Albert and the Cosby Kids* understood its prosocial messages and were able to apply them (Huston et al., 1992; Liebert & Sprafkin, 1988). Anderson and Williams (1983, cited in Stroman, 1991) found that after African-American children viewed an episode of *Good Times,* the children reported that they learned that street gangs were bad and that family members should help each other. Television can also explain to children how to handle fearful events such as going to the dentist or demonstrate that frightening situations are not so bad (Stroman, 1991).

Forge and Phemister (1982) sought to determine whether a prosocial cartoon would be as effective as a live-model prosocial program. Forty preschoolers were shown one of four different 15-minute videotapes. Subjects were then observed during 30 minutes of free play. The prosocial cartoon was as effective as the live-model program in eliciting prosocial behavior.

Unfortunately, some commercial superhero cartoons and crime/adventure programs may deliver prosocial or moral messages via characters who behave aggressively. Lisa, Reinhardt, and Fredriksen (1983, cited in Liebert & Sprafkin, 1988) used episodes of the cartoon *Superfriends* to compare a prosocial/aggressive condition to a purely prosocial condition. In their study of kindergarten, second-, and fourth-grade children, subjects were put in a situation where they could hurt or help another child within the context of a help–hurt game. They found that children exposed to a purely prosocial condition helped more than they hurt, tended to hurt less, and understood the plot and moral lesson significantly better than those in the prosocial/aggressive condition. Liebert and Sprafkin concluded that prosocial behavior should not be presented in an aggressive context.

Prosocial television has its critics, too. There are "legitimate moral objections to using a public medium to indoctrinate socially a whole nation of children" (Liebert & Sprafkin, 1988, p. 240). When Liebert and Sprafkin assisted with the production of an internationally broadcast public-service announcement that modeled cooperation by showing children sharing a swing, they were accused of trying to manipulate children's behavior and moral values and were told that their efforts could potentially be seen as "a highly objectionable form of psychological behavior control" (p. 243).

Although television can influence children and does so in an indiscriminate manner, an important question is whether anyone should purposely try to harness its power for specific socialization goals. Even so, Hearold (1986) makes a good point:

Although fewer studies exist on prosocial effects, the effect size is so much larger, holds up better under more stringent experimental conditions, and is consistently higher for boys and girls, that the potential for prosocial effects overrides the smaller but persistent negative effects of antisocial programs. (p. 116)

12.6.4 Current Issues

Since the first edition of this handbook was published, the research on attitudes, beliefs, and behaviors has not seen major changes. In general, more recent analyses of program content and effects have served to reinforce the results of past investigations. The factors under investigation, however, are being more carefully defined and described. In the future, the displacement of television viewing by the Internet and the increased integration of the two technologies will likely impact research and findings in this field.

12.6.4.1 Stereotypes. In terms of respect and recognition, concerns continue to be raised about both the quality and quantity of portrayals of specific groups on television. Among the large number of cable channels now available are those devoted to specific audiences such as women or ethnic minorities. Although this has lead to increased numbers of portrayals overall, little growth has been seen on the major networks. For example, although Ryan (2001) found an increase in the number of Hispanic programs on cable, Soriano (2001) found a decrease in the number of Hispanics represented during prime-time programs on the six major networks. Furthermore, in the 26 network programs that premiered in autumn of 1999, no minority characters held a leading role (Berry & Asamen, 2001). Because of the lack of minority representation among news reporters and in prime-time programs, the networks came under attack by minority advocacy groups. The National Association for the Advancement of Colored People (NAACP) even threatened to boycott the four major networks unless more minorities were employed as actors, as news reporters, and in production management.

By 2001, some of the networks had slightly increased the number of minority actors (African-American, Hispanic, and Asian-American) and African-American shows (Allen, 2002). The diversity and quality of those portrayals remained problematic, however. According to Allen, many of the minority actors appeared in secondary roles and not as lead characters. Additionally, in 2000 the National Hispanic Foundation for the Arts found that Hispanic actors were still being cast as criminals or blue-collar workers and, of the only 48 Hispanic actors seen during prime time, 40 percent played token characters with no relevance to the plot (Soriano, 2001).

In terms of gender representation, even though positive portrayals have become more frequent, negative stereotypes continue to be used widely. For example, Signorielli (1997, 2001) continued to find that girls were being exposed to stereotyped messages about their appearance, relationships, and careers even though there were positive adult role models on television. By numbers, women continued to be underrepresented in prime time, children's programming, and music videos. When portrayed, they were usually younger than men, rarely overweight, and when thin, received numerous positive comments about their appearances (Signorielli, 2001). Especially for adolescents, media usage has been associated with unrealistic expectations about body image and eating disorders (Botta, 1999, 2000; Harrison, 2000; Van Den Bulck, 2000). During the 1990s, some improvements were made in the occupational portrayals of women and minorities, but these were inconsistent (Signorielli, 2001). Furthermore, women continued to rarely be seen combining marriage and work successfully.

Men on television also continue to be stereotyped, typically shown as working in traditional roles and portrayed as the breadwinners (Signorielli, 2001). Heintz-Knowles et al. (1999) polled 1,200 youths aged 10 to 17. The children reported that the males they see on television are different from those they encounter in real life. Among other findings, the researchers' content analyses revealed that male characters rarely cried or performed domestic chores, and that one in five used aggression to solve problems.

12.6.4.2 Sensitization and Disinhibition. Instead of focusing on dramatized or fantasy violence, some researchers have directed more attention to the effects of viewing real crime and violence on television. In the past, researchers found that news broadcasts could frighten people and lead to their becoming oversensitized. More recently, developmental differences were found to play a role in the reactions of children. For example, Cantor and Nathanson (1996) and Smith and Wilson (2000) found that all age groups of children could be frightened by news stories. This was especially true for older children, however, who better understood the reality of events and who were more frightened by local stories about crime.

Over the past decade, researchers have also begun to pay more attention to the impact of specific types of news stories, such as televised disasters and war coverage. When events like these are visually explicit and pervasive on television, their impact can be long lasting. Many parents are not aware of how much or how frequently their children are frightened by the news (Cantor, 2001). In particular, natural disasters frighten young children more than older ones (Cantor & Nathanson, 1996). More recently, the live broadcasts and replays of the September 11, 2001 acts of terrorism appeared to have affected adults and children alike. Silver et al. (2002) found that 17 percent of the population outside New York City reported symptoms of posttraumatic stress 2 months after the attacks and that 5.8 percent continued to report these symptoms at 6 months. The media attempted to address these issues with suggestions to viewers to stop watching news coverage and by reporting techniques for coping with depression and connecting with family and friends.

12.6.4.3 Prosocial and Antisocial Behavior. The impact of television on behavior remains an important issue for parents, teachers, and policy makers. Although many studies on prosocial behavior were published in the 1970s and 1980s, few studies have been conducted recently even though many questions remain about how to best design content to achieve prosocial outcomes (Mares & Woodard, 2001). The majority of attention continues to be directed toward the selection and effects of antisocial programming, especially programs that show violence and aggression. Policy efforts to control viewing and, hopefully, impact behavior have not been widely accepted even though parents continue to complain about the amount of violence and sexual content on television. For example, the V-chip technology required in new television sets by the U.S. Telecommunications Act of 1996 has not gained wide spread use among families. According to a 2001 survey conducted by the Kaiser Family Foundation, although 40 percent of all parents had a V-chip equipped television in their homes, 53 percent of those with the chip didn't know about it. Of those who were aware of owning one, 30 percent chose not to use it while only 17 percent have used it. The report found greater use of the ratings systems: 56 percent of all parents said they used television ratings to decide what programs their children could watch (Kaiser Family Foundation, 2001). Unfortunately, during the previous year Woodard and Gridina (2000) found that parental awareness of the ratings system had dropped from 70 percent in 1997 to 50 percent in 2000. They also found that parents were confused about the labels, especially regarding what was educational for children. Although age ratings seem to be used and understood, both studies found that many parents don't understand the content ratings. Training efforts are clearly needed for parents to make better use of the *TV Parental Rating Guidelines* and V-chip technology.

The effects of specific types of programming on different populations continue to be of interest, especially when a new genre becomes very popular. For example, O'Sullivan (1999) looked at the effects of professional wrestling programs and found a correlation between viewing and subsequent aggressive behaviors among first-grade boys. The popularity of televised contact sports programs and their appeal to boys and adolescent males is a concern, especially because preschoolers (Silva, 1996; Simmons, Stalsworth & Wentzel, 1999) and elementary school boys (O'Sullivan, 1999; Reglin, 1996; Singer & Miller, 1998) frequently imitate violent and aggressive behavior they see on television. In addition to concerns about behavior, some of the formal features of sports programs and their commercials can be problematic. Messner et al. (1999) studied sports programming and found that aggression and violence among men were depicted as exciting and rewarding, women were absent or portrayed as stereotypes, and commercials often used images of speed, danger and aggression. The commentary aired during sports programming may also be contributing to the problem. Aicinena (1999) analyzed 355 comments about behavior in 102 editions of a sports news program. He found few comments about good sportsmanship but 352 comments about poor sportsmanship, violence, or immoral behavior.

In contrast, viewing educational programs during the preschool years has been associated with positive outcomes,

both short term and long term. For example, in their recontact study of 570 adolescents, Anderson et al. (2001) found higher grades, more book reading, more value on achievement, greater creativity, and less aggressive behavior among boys who viewed educational programming during preschool.

Although children continue to be the focus of most studies, fewer studies have been conducted with adults. This leaves a gap in the literature. Because adults' viewing choices can influence their children, research is needed on adult viewing habits, their relationship to resultant attitudes and behaviors, and their impact on children.

Additionally, more longitudinal studies that range from childhood to adulthood are needed. One such study conducted by Johnson et al. (2002) on 707 individuals assessed television viewing and aggressive behavior from 1975 to 2000. They concluded that the amount of television viewing by adolescents and young adults was significantly associated with subsequent acts of aggression even after controlling for factors such as family income, neighborhood violence, and psychiatric disorders. Viewing 3 or more hours per day of television at mean age 14 was significantly associated with aggression (according to self-reports and law enforcement records) at mean ages 16 and 22. Of the total sample, 28.8 percent of those who watched 3 or more hours per day at age 14 committed aggressive acts against others at ages 16 or 22. Compared to this, only 5.7 percent of those who watched less than 1 hour per day reported aggression. Youths who were considered aggressive at mean age 16 also watched significantly more television at age 22. Additionally, the researchers found that more than 3 hours of viewing per day at age 22 was associated with aggression at age 30.

More attention is being directed to the search for personality factors that lead to the amount of viewing choices. For example, Krcmar and Greene (1999) examined the relationships among sensation seeking, risk-taking, and exposure to violent television. They found that for adolescents, especially males, higher disinhibition lead to greater exposure to contact sport and real crime shows while higher levels of sensation seeking lead to less exposure. They concluded that televised violence did not compensate for exposure to real risk-taking. Therefore, for these viewers television did not provide appropriate levels of stimulation to satisfy their social and psychological needs.

Although most of the studies mentioned in this section have been based in the United States, the international community is also concerned about the effects of television viewing and violent programming. A major study sponsored by the United Nations Educational, Scientific, and Cultural Organization (USESCO) questioned 5,000 12-year-olds from 23 countries and analyzed the relationships between their media preferences, aggression, and environment (Groebel, 2001). The study found that, on average, the children watched 3 hours of television per day. Groebel reported that among the one third who lived in high-aggression (war or crime) or problematic environments, one third believed that "most people in the world are evil" (p. 264). She also reported that a preliminary analysis showed a link between a preference for media violence and the need to be involved in aggression. For a compilation of additional studies based in other cultures, also see *Media, Sex, Violence, and Drugs in the Global Village* edited by Kamalipour and Rampal (2001).

12.6.4.4 Media Convergence. At the turn of the century, about 98 percent of Americans had a television in their homes (Nielsen Media Research, cited in Woodard & Gridina, 2000). As of 2001, 72.3 percent of Americans also had access to the Internet and were spending about 9.8 hours per week online (Lebo, 2001). Of note, *The UCLA Internet Report 2001* found that Internet users watched 4.5 hours per week less television than did nonusers, and that the top reason for using the Internet was to obtain information quickly (Lebo, 2001).

Initially, it appears that television, considered to be primarily a passive entertainment medium, is being partially displaced by the Internet, considered to be an interactive information and communication medium. Some television programs, however, are beginning to use these differences to their advantage and are attempting to foster simultaneous use. Many programs, especially news programs, now direct viewers to their web sites for more information. During live broadcasts, some encourage viewers to log-on to their website and participate in surveys so they can report the results during the show. Many educational programs offer websites that provide enrichment activities and expanded information. This convergence of television and the Internet offers rich opportunities for further investigation into media and selection effects. On the one hand, there is tremendous potential for the users of blended technologies to benefit from more active engagement and exploration of content. Users can become exposed to a much wider range of information than by either medium alone and can receive this information via preferred delivery formats and at their preferred pace. The flexible natures of the Internet and delayed-delivery options for television allow viewers to explore topics either broadly or in depth, as they desire and when they choose.

On the other hand, users may only expose themselves to content with which they are familiar or with which they agree. Due to the increase in the number of cable channels available, television audiences have already become more fragmented along lines of social, economic and personal interest (Putnam, 2000). Due to self-selection, the vast array of information on the Internet might not be utilized and alternative viewpoints might remain unknown. In turn, this selectivity may support a viewer's superficial or prejudicial worldview and could potentially reinforce sensitization or disinhibition effects. Once selection and usage habits for both media are better understood and tracked, their effects may be studied and, as necessary, mediated or reinforced. Literacy programs that address multiple types of media may be key to these efforts.

12.6.5 Summary and Recommendations

After decades of research, we know that television can teach and change attitudes, beliefs, and behaviors. The nature and longevity of these effects, however, as well as their interactions with other variables need to be identified and explored further. In particular, the beneficial impacts of prosocial programming need to be studied more extensively, especially on populations of adolescents and adults, and the results communicated to media producers and advertisers.

The question remains: How do we best design effective interventions and training for children and adults and, in particular, counteract the effects of antisocial programming? First of all, more research is needed on identifying the variables, psychological as well as contextual, that influence viewing choices. Additionally, we need to know more about what elicits or suppresses recall and imitation of the attitudes, beliefs and behaviors that are portrayed and why. In the end, the results may help persuade the producers of programming and advertising to alter their use of violence and stereotypes. Currently, producers believe they are providing what their audiences want and, more importantly for them, what their advertisers need. To persuade them to change, more evidence is needed such as Bushman's (1998) study that found television violence increased viewers' anger, which in turn, impaired memory of commercials. This suggested, therefore, that sponsorship might not be profitable for the advertisers who currently value violent programs because they attract younger viewers.

In general, the research on antisocial programming needs to be considered carefully. For example, many inferences of causation tend to be based on correlational data. An additional problem with many studies is that they examine behavior immediately following exposure to a short program. As research continues in this area, it is important to examine the long-term and cumulative effects of exposure, especially since television appears to negatively affect heavy users.

The viewing environment and parental influence also need to be considered when results are examined. For example, child-rearing practices are a factor that can interact with antisocial programming. Korzenny, Greenberg, and Atkin (1979, cited in Sprafkin, Gadow, & Abelman, 1992) found that the children of parents who disciplined with power were most affected by antisocial content while the children of parents who disciplined with reasoning and explanation were less affected. Although Rushton (1982) speculated that television has become one of the most important agencies of socialization for our society, it is important to identify the other variables in the home, school, and society that are more important than television to the socialization of children.

The type of experiment that is conducted is also a consideration. Although some laboratory experiments have shown a positive correlation between television violence and antisocial behavior, naturalistic studies are not as clear. In terms of causation, it appears that some populations in specific settings are sometimes affected. Researchers need to continue to move away from determining if there is a relationship to determining the causes, nature, and direction of that relationship. The identification of the most influential variables will help inform the design of policy, programming, and interventions.

Another area that should yield fruitful research is the interaction between formal features and the effects of television on aggression. If, as some research indicates, aggression increases in the presence of specific formal features such as fast-paced action regardless of the violence of the content, then researchers need to explore such interactions.

As early as 1961, Schramm, Lyle, and Parker stated:

For some children, under some conditions, some television is harmful. For some children under the same conditions, or for the same children under other conditions, it may be beneficial. For most children, under most conditions, most television is probably neither particularly harmful nor particularly beneficial. (cited in Hearold, p. 68)

Decades later, it remains important to conduct research that identifies the variables and conditions that do matter, and thus, be able to apply the results to appropriate action.

12.7 PROGRAMMING AND UTILIZATION

We now turn to programming and its effects and to utilization studies. This section will critically review:

- Programming for preschoolers
- Programming for classrooms
- Programming for subject-matter teachers
- News programs
- Advertising on television
- Utilization studies

12.7.1 Programming for Preschoolers

12.7.1.1 Mister Rogers' Neighborhood. Fred Rogers has stated that television can either facilitate or sabotage the development of learning readiness. According to Rogers, for a child to be ready to learn, the child must have at least six fundamentals: (a) a sense of self-worth, (b) a sense of trust, (c) curiosity, (d) the capacity to look and listen carefully, (e) the capacity to play, and (f) times of solitude. Television can help children develop the sense of uniqueness essential to their self-worth, or it can undermine this sense of uniqueness by teaching children to value things rather than people and by presenting stereotyped characters (Rogers & Head, 1963).

Rogers' program to develop learning readiness is the longest-running series on public television. Its goals are affective in that the programs are designed to increase self-esteem and valuing of self and others. Research shows that the program is successful in achieving these goals (Coates, Pusser, & Goodman, 1976). Research has also shown that the program uses almost exclusively positive reinforcement to accomplish this goal (Coates & Pusser, 1975).

In 1992, McFarland found that the program helped childcare teachers and providers enhance the emotional development of preschool children. Parents had positive attitudes toward the use of quality children's programming in childcare. She found that while the behavior of adult childcare providers could be positively affected by watching *Mister Rogers' Neighborhood*, there were ambiguous effects for children's behavior. She concluded that Fred Rogers provided positive modeling that helped childcare providers to develop attitudes and behaviors that enhance the emotional development of preschool children. McFarland used a three-part study that included surveys,

observations, and written feedback. Part 2 of the study used the programs plus accompanying materials for 5 months. To some extent, the success of the program is due to the use of supplementary materials, such as books, puppets, and tapes of songs on the show. Research has not determined the role of such materials in the instructional effectiveness of the program.

One issue that has been pursued in the research is the comparative effect of *Sesame Street* and *Mister Rogers' Neighborhood* on attention span. Studies on the effects of pacing on attention span are equivocal. Children who watched an hour of fast-paced programming were compared with children who watched an hour of slow-paced programming. No significant differences were found in effects on attention or perseverance. Two other studies showed that children who watched typical children's programming had increased impulsiveness and reduced perseverance. In another study, children who watched the slow-paced *Mister Rogers' Neighborhood* were found to be increasingly persistent in preschool activities (Anderson & Collins, 1988; Friedrich & Stein, 1973, cited in Huston et al., 1992). Anderson, Levin, and Lorch (1977) found no evidence that rapid television pacing had a negative impact on preschool children's behavior. Nor did they find a reduction in persistence or an increase in aggression or hyperactivity. Their research was an experiment using slow-paced and rapid paced versions of *Sesame Street,* followed by a free-play period in a room full of toys.

12.7.1.2 Sesame Street. In a series of classic studies of cognitive learning, Bogatz and Ball (1970, 1971) found that children who watched the most learned the most, regardless of age, viewing or geographic location, socioeconomic status, or gender. Not only did children who watched gain basic skills in reading and arithmetic, they also entered school better prepared than their nonviewing or low-viewing peers. Encouragement to view was found to be an important factor in viewer gains. Paulson (1974) did an experiment to determine whether children learned social skills from watching. When tested in situations similar to those presented on the program, children who watched learned to cooperate more than children who did not. Reiser and his colleagues conducted two studies (1988, 1984) and concluded that cognitive learning increased when adults who watched *Sesame Street* with children asked them questions about letters and numbers and gave feedback.

More recent research on the relationship of viewing by preschool children to school readiness has been reported (Zill, Davies, & Daly, 1994). Zill et al. used data from the 1993 National Household Education Survey to determine who viewed the program and how regularly. Data from the survey were also examined to determine the relationship between viewing and (a) literacy and numeracy in preschool children, and (b) school readiness and achievement for early elementary students. The study found that the program reached the majority of children in all demographic groups including the "at risk" children. The findings revealed:

- Children of highly educated parents stopped watching the program earlier than children of less-educated parents.

- Children from disrupted families were more likely to watch the program.

- Children whose parents did not read to them regularly were less likely to watch the program.

- Children from low-income families who watched television showed more signs of emerging literacy than children from similar families who did not watch.

- Children who watched the program showed greater ability to read and had fewer reading problems in first and second grade.

- First- and second-graders who watched the program did not show less grade repetition or better academic standing.

The established value of *Sesame Street* for children in poverty is reviewed by Mielke (1994). In an article for a special issue of *Media Studies Journal* on "Children and the Media," he argued that the program is reaching and helping low-income children who have a narrower range of educational opportunities in the critical preschool years and, therefore, it should be an important element in a national strategy for reaching our educational goals by the year 2000.

Recent research on CTW's educational programming is summarized in several documents that can be obtained from their research division, including:

- *"Sesame Street" Research Bibliography 1989–1994* (Petty, 1994a)

- *A review of "Sesame Street" Research 1989–1994* (Petty, 1994b)

- *"Sesame Street" Research Bibliography: Selected Citations to "Sesame Street" 1969–1989* (Research Division, CTW, June 1990)

The first of these documents provides an annotated bibliography. The second is a report of research in the areas of (a) educational, cognitive, and prosocial implications; (b) effects of nonbroadcast materials; (c) formal features and content analyses; and (d) *Sesame Street* as stimulus material for other investigations. The third is also an annotated bibliography, but it covers research done both nationally and internationally.

12.7.1.3 Cartoons.

Much of the discussion about the effects of cartoon programming has centered around the extent to which children of different ages assume that the fantasy presented in such shows is real. Fictional characters vary from realistic portrayals to superheroes and heroines.

The photographic and dynamic qualities of television can make characters seem real. Children were shown photographs of television cartoon characters intermixed with photographs of familiar real people. Then, children were given tasks and asked questions designed to reveal their beliefs about these characters. There were 70 boys aged 5 to 12 participating. All the boys attributed unique physical characteristics to the characters, but the younger children generalized this uniqueness to other characteristics. For example, they believed a superhero could live forever because he was strong, or that he was happy because he

could fly. Older children described the characters more realistically and were aware that physical ability doesn't ensure happiness. The study concluded that young children might miss important traits and consequences because visual effects heighten the physical dimension (Fernie, 1981, cited in Meringoff et al., 1983).

One of the problems with research on cartoons is that it is commonly done and reported within the Saturday morning children's programming context. A cartoon is typically a fantasy program with humor, mayhem, action, and drama. However, today realism is often mixed with animation, and *there are* many types of content represented in cartoons for children. Furthermore, religious training or calculus lessons can be put within an animated format that will influence children differently than will a Saturday morning entertainment cartoon. There has been much debate about whether cartoons are violent. All of these questions suggest that it is difficult to generalize from the research, because content becomes as important as format, and often these two variables are not separated, nor is their interaction studied.

12.7.2 Programming for Classrooms

After 40 years, the collective evidence that film and television can facilitate learning is overwhelming. This evidence is available for all forms of delivery, film, ITV, ETV, and mass media. It is reinforced by evaluation of programming prepared for these formats and delivered by newer delivery systems such as cable and satellite. The next section will review recent representative examples of this body of research. The section will be organized by these topics: general findings; video production*; educational series programming, including Children's Television Workshop productions; programming for subject-matter areas; satellite programming; and utilization studies.

12.7.2.1 General Findings.

The findings reported here are the ones that are most important for further research. In 1993, Katherine Cennamo critiqued the line of investigation initiated by Gavriel Salomon in the 1980s with his construct of amount of invested mental effort, or AIME. Cennamo posed the question: Do learner's preconceptions of the amount of effort required by a medium influence the amount of effort they invest in processing such a lesson and consequently the quantity and quality of information they gain? Factors influencing preconceptions of effort required and actual effort expended were found to include characteristics of the task, media, and learners. In her summary, she noted that, in general, learners perceive television as a medium requiring little mental effort and believe they learn little from television. However, learners reported attending more closely to educational television programs than to commercial programs. The topic of the program also influenced preconceptions. She stated that in actuality, learning from television may be more difficult than learning from a single-channel medium because of its complexity. Learners achieved more from a lesson they were told to view for instructional reasons than from a lesson they were told to view for fun. This is consistent with many other findings about the importance of intentional use of the medium to help children learn, such as those reported in the Reiser et al. (1988, 1984) *Sesame Street* studies, which concluded that children learn more when an adult is present to guide and reinforce learning.

It is important to identify the types of learning that programs are designed to facilitate and the types of learning for which television can be used most effectively. Cennamo (1993) points out that the types of achievement tests used may not reveal mental effort or achievement in intended areas. For example, tests of factual recall cannot document increased mental effort or inferential thinking. Beentjes (1989) replicated Salomon's study on AIME and found that Dutch children perceived television to be a more difficult medium to learn from than did the American children in Salomon's study.

In 1967, Reid and MacLennan reviewed 350 instructional media comparisons and found a trend of no significant differences when televised instruction was compared to face-to-face instruction. However, their analysis of other uses of video instruction yielded different conclusions:

When videotapes were used in observation of demonstration teaching, teacher trainees gained as much from video observations as from actual classroom visits. In addition, when used in teaching performance skills–such as typing, sewing, and athletic skills–films often produced a significant increase in learning and an improvement in student attitudes. (Cohen, Ebeling, & Kulik, 1981, p. 27)

Another general finding is that the potential for television's effectiveness is increased when teachers are involved in its selection and utilization, and when teachers are given specialized training in the use of television for instruction (Graves, 1987). Teachers can integrate television in the curriculum, prepare students, extend and elaborate on content, encourage viewing, and provide feedback. They do this best if they themselves are prepared. If a distinction is made between television as a stand-alone teacher and television's capacity to teach when used by a teacher, the evidence indicates that although television can teach in a stand-alone format, it can teach more effectively when utilized by a competent teacher (Johnson, 1987). We turn now to the effects of specific programming used in classroom settings.

12.7.2.2 Film/Video Production. Interest in the effects of production experience on students started many years ago. In the early 1970s students learned how to produce Super 8-mm films. With easy access to half-inch videotape and portable equipment, they ventured into producing video. Since cable television has made more equipment, facilities, and training available, there has been an increase in video production by schools for educational purposes. Nevertheless, students have been producing programs for class assignments and school use since the 1960s. It is surprising, therefore, that there is very little research on the effects of video production by students on learning and attitudes. This may be due to the fact that most researchers are in university settings, and most video production is in school buildings, or to the difficulty of controlling variables in a field setting. Nevertheless, the effects of video production and the variables that mediate these effects are not

being investigated. It may be that the strongest effects related to learning from television come from student productions, because the strongest commitment and identification is possible in these cases.

The Ford Foundation funded studies related to learning from film and television production. One such study reported on the effects of filmmaking on children (Sutton-Smith, 1976). Subjects attended a workshop on filmmaking. The researchers used the workshop to determine (a) the processes through which children of the same or different ages proceeded in the acquisition of filmmaking mastery, and (b) the perceptual, cognitive, and affective changes that resulted in the children. Observation, videotaping, and interviews were used for documentation. One interesting finding was that there were striking differences between younger and older children in filmmaking, despite repeated instruction in the same areas. Young children tended not to make:

- Establishing shots
- Films about a major character
- Films about a group of characters
- Multiple scenes
- Markers in films (titles, ends, etc.)
- Story themes
- Story transitions
- Causal linkages
- Use of long shots, close-ups, pans, zooms, or changes in camera position
- Long films (18 seconds vs. 65 seconds for older children)

Children 5 to 8 years old were considered young, and children 9 to 11 constituted the older group. It would be interesting to replicate this study today, because sophistication with the television code could generate different results.

Tidhar (1984, cited in Shutkin, 1990) researched the relationships between communication through filmmaking and the development of cognitive skills in children. She compared classes of students who studied scenario design, photography, and editing in different combinations and concluded that necessary mental skills for decoding film texts are developed during film production.

Those who encourage students to produce video assert that the process teaches them goal setting, creative problem solving, cooperative learning, interpersonal skills, and critical analysis skills. In addition, they claim the experience improves a student's self-esteem and self-concept. Furthermore, they contend that students who have trouble verbalizing or are "at risk" can succeed with this approach to learning when they can't in traditional classroom activities. There is little evidence to support such claims, because little research has been reported other than testimonials from teachers and students. Generally, the studies reported are subjective case histories that are likely to be both perceptive and biased. Another frequent problem is that intact classes are compared over long periods of time. Thus, lack of control of variables limits interpretation and confidence.

Barron (1985, cited in Shutkin, 1990) found that a comprehensive course for fifth-graders, involving both video production and media studies, led to the development of mental skills necessary for understanding television programming. Torrence (1985) reviewed research findings about the features that should be incorporated in school video production experiences. These features are offered through guidelines on message design and utilization factors. Laybourne (1981, cited in Valmont, 1995) states that children who make their own television productions become more critical viewers.

This assertion of an association between video production experience and media literacy is common in the literature, although few report studies that investigated the phenomena. Messaris (1994) addresses "production literacy," meaning competency in the production of images. He conducted a study in 1981 (cited in Messaris, 1994) that compared subjects with various levels of competency in filmmaking, from expert to apprentice to novice. They were shown a film containing both traditional naturalistic style (narrative) editing and experimental editing. All three groups ignored visual conventions in their interpretations of the traditional editing sequences and instead discussed the events in the film as if they actually occurred. With the experimental sequences, however, there were differences among the groups. The novices became confused and struggled to interpret. The apprentices and especially the experts discussed explicit intentions of the filmmaker and the visual conventions used. In a follow-up study (Messaris & Nielsen, 1989), the significance of production experience was confirmed. The researchers interpreted the findings as indications that production experience heightened awareness of manipulative conventions and intent and thus improved media literacy.

Shutkin (1990) has urged the development of a critical media pedagogy, because the adoption of video equipment in the schools is not politically neutral and, therefore, is potentially problematic. In support of his theoretical position, Shutkin offers a review of the research and theory around video production education and filmmaking. He points out that video production involves interpersonal and group process skills that can be researched, as well as other aspects of the communication process that suggest variables for researchers to pursue. Shutkin argues that video production is being used to lower the dropout rate, raise self-esteem, and develop technological skill; yet no one is determining whether or how these results occur and what mediates such learnings.

12.7.2.3 Educational Series Programming.

The most important research on educational programs designed for home and classroom use comes from Children's Television Workshop (CTW). The contribution of this organization to television research is of such overwhelming importance that this section will devote much of its discussion to CTW. In 1990, Keith Mielke, senior research fellow at CTW, edited a special issue of *Educational Technology Research and Theory* devoted to CTW. In a case study of CTW, Polsky (1974) concluded that historical research supports the conclusion that systematic planning was the key to CTW's success.

CTW produced several series that were used in the classroom as well as broadcast to the home. Among these series were *Sesame Street,* which was used in some elementary schools, *Electric Company, 3-2-1 Contact,* and *Square One* Research on *Sesame Street* has already been discussed. The research on each of the other series will be discussed separately in this section.

12.7.2.4 Electric Company.

Electric Company was aimed at children in early elementary grades who were deficient in reading skills. It focused on blending consonants, chunking of letter groups, and scanning for patterns. Learning outcomes were supposed to be discrimination of vowels from consonants, scanning text for typical word structures, and reading for meaning by using context. The series was an experiment in using a video medium to teach decoding skills for a print medium.

Stroman (1991) stated that summative evaluations of *Sesame Street* and the *Electric Company* indicated that African-American children improve their cognitive skills after exposure to these programs. Graves (1982) pointed out the importance of adult coviewing. Learning increased and reading performance improved after children viewed these programs with an adult present. When teachers made sure children viewed, used additional learning materials, and provided practice, children learned these skills, with the greatest gains being made by the youngest children and children in the bottom half of the class. A comparison made with home viewing indicated that it was important to attract the viewers for a sufficient number of shows to have a measurable impact on reading skills. Research on the series suggested the difficulty of depending on the home as the context for learning (Johnson, 1987).

12.7.2.5 3-2-1 Contact.

3-2-1 Contact was designed to harness the power of television to convey to children the excitement and fascination of science. Its objective was to create a climate for learning about science, in other words to provide science readiness. It was aimed at 8- to 12-year old children. After two years of research, CTW offered some surprising insights about 8- to 12-year-olds and television:

- They attended to stories where a problem was posed and resolved through relations between recurring characters, particularly those dealing with life and death themes.
- They attended primarily to the visual channel. A dense or abstract audio track overwhelmed them.
- They thought in terms of their personal experiences rather than abstractly.
- Boys favored action and adventure programs while girls favored programs about warm, human relationships.
- They identified with and preferred cast members like themselves in terms of gender or ethnicity.
- They preferred role model's who were somewhat older. They preferred the characters on the show who were competent or striving to be competent.
- They liked humor in sequences only when it was age and subject appropriate.
- They had a traditional image of scientists as middle-aged white males working in laboratories to invent or discover. However,

younger scientists were often more impressive to these children than Nobel Prize winners.

- They needed a wrap-up at the end of the program to make connections and to reinforce learning.

All of these findings were taken into account when the format and content of the program were determined (Iker, 1983). Research on the program indicated that significant gains occurred in comprehension and in interest and participation in science activities. However, there were no significant effects on career attitudes (Revelle, 1985; Research Communications, 1987, cited in Sammur, 1990). Gotthelf and Peel (1990) reported the steps CTW took to make the program, which was originally designed for home viewing, a more effective science teaching tool when used in school classrooms. Instructional technologists who read their article will be interested in the barriers that needed to be removed and the resources that needed to be provided. An annotated research bibliography on *3-2-1 Contact* is available from CTW (Research Division, CTW, n.d.).

12.7.2.6 Square One.
This series was introduced in 1987 with the objective of addressing the national need for early positive exposure to mathematics. Its primary audience was intended to be 8- to 12-year-olds viewing at home. The content was to go beyond arithmetic into areas such as geometry, probability, and problem solving. However, the program was designed to be motivational rather than to teach cognitive skills. The program was used in classrooms. Chen, Ellis, and Hoelscher (1988) investigated the effectiveness of reformatted cassettes of the program. Chen et al. mentioned that previous studies of educational television identified two classes of barriers to school use: technological (i.e., obtaining equipment), and instructional (i.e., finding supplementary materials, designing lessons, and finding time). Teachers found the cassettes especially helpful in demonstrating connections between mathematical ideas and real-world situations. The most researched variable related to this program is problem-solving outcomes. In studies done in the Corpus Christi, Texas, public elementary schools, viewers demonstrated more skill in problem solving than nonviewers. This was generally true in the research done on the effects of *Square One* (Debold, 1990; Hall, Esty, & Fisch, 1990; Peel, Rockwell, Esty, & Gonzer, 1987; Research Communications, 1989, cited in Sammur, 1990). In addition, viewers recalled aspects of mathematics presented on the show and displayed more positive attitudes and motivation towards science (Schauble, Peel, Sauerhaft, & Kreutzer, 1987, as reported in Sammur, 1990; Debold, 1990). A five-volume report on a National Science Foundation study of the effects of the series reported an interesting finding:

Across all of these themes, there were no substantive differences among the viewers' reactions as a function of their gender or socioeconomic status. The reactions described above came from both boys and girls and from children of different economic backgrounds. (Fisch, Hall, Esty, Debold, Miller, Bennett, & Solan, 1991, p. 13)

A research history and bibliography on *Square One* is available from CTW (Fisch, Cohen, McCann, & Hoffman, 1993).

12.7.2.7 ThinkAbout.
ThinkAbout was a series created by the Agency for Instructional Television in the early 1980s. It consisted of sixty 15-minute episodes designed to strengthen reasoning skills and reinforce study skills. There were 13 program clusters on topics such as estimating, finding alternatives, and collecting information. The series was aimed at upper elementary students. Research on *ThinkAbout* is reported in a series of ERIC documents from the late 1970s and early 1980s (Carrozza & Jochums, 1979; Sanders & Sonnad, 1982).

Students who spent two hours a week watching the program improved their thinking skills to a very limited extent. Although the program added a new element to the classroom, research did not support its effectiveness (Sanders, 1983, cited in Johnson, 1987). Johnson also reported that the research itself was flawed in two ways. First, the criterion of effectiveness was performance on the California Test of Basic Skills, which was too general a test to provide a realistic measure of success. Secondly, the research was done after one year of uncontrolled use. There was no assurance that teachers had been trained to use the series as intended or that they did. This is documented by a series of case studies on how *ThinkAbout* was used in classrooms, which reported that the series was both used effectively and misused (Johnson, 1987). Over 80 percent of the teachers reported that the series presented complex ideas better than they could and that the programs stimulated discussion (Sanders, 1983, cited in Johnson, 1987).

Television series for classroom use as well as home use have come from other sources. The British government funded the Open University, which has a library of over 3,000 instructional video programs keyed to courses. The British have also produced many series, such as *The Ascent of Man,* which are suitable for instructional purposes. Several series for secondary and postsecondary education in the United States have been funded by the Annenberg Foundation. Unfortunately, most of these fine series have neither been researched nor used in classroom settings.

12.7.2.8 Subject-Matter Instruction.
Secondary teachers in subject-matter areas have used film and video to enhance their teaching. The areas in which they have been used most extensively are social studies and science.

Because television is the main source of news for most Americans, the area of social studies has a mandate to teach critical-viewing skills. In addition, television has become the primary medium for political campaigning in the United States. Thus, educating voters requires attention to television and its effects. Fortunately, there is plentiful research on learning from television news, some of which will be discussed later in this section (Hepburn, 1990). The other area in which research is available to help the social-studies teacher use television is economics. Huskey, Jackstadt, and Goldsmith (1991) conducted a replication study to determine the importance of economics knowledge to understanding the national news. Of the total news program, 13 percent (or 3 minutes) was devoted to economic stories, but knowledge of economic terms was essential to understand the stories (Huskey, Jackstadt, & Goldsmith, 1991).

There are many studies on the effectiveness of using television and film to teach science and mathematics. Two recent interesting approaches need to be researched. One suggests that science fiction films and programming be used to teach science (Dubeck, Moshier, & Boss, 1988); another uses teacher-training institutes for science, television, and technology to impact classroom teaching. This project is called the National Teacher Training Institutes for Science, Television and Technology. Managed by Thirteen/WNET, the New York City public television station, it was an alliance between education, business, and public television (Thirteen/WNET, 1992). The research was supported by Texaco Corporation. By the end of 1993, the Teacher Training Institutes planned to have reached 17,000 teachers and 2 million students. So far, findings indicated that students in classes exposed to ITV outperformed peers in non-ITV classes, they scored higher on creative imagery and writing, they were more confident in problem solving, and they learned more in proportion to the time spent on ITV.

12.7.2.9 Satellite Programming. Programming delivered to the classroom via satellite can be divided into two categories: news programs and subject-matter courses. The most famous of the news programs was *Channel One,* but there are others, such as *CNN Newsroom,* which was broadcast by Ted Turner's news network (Wood, 1989). The courses were distributed from many sources, the most commonly known of which was the Satellite Educational Resource Consortium (SERC). Very little research has been done on courses distributed by satellite to schools because this is a relatively recent phenomenon.

Zvacek (1992) compared three classroom news programs: *Channel One, CNN Newsroom,* and the front-end news segment of *Today.* Although each show followed a pattern of different segments, there was variability between the programs. Zvacek found differences in the proportion of time devoted to news and features, in the content of news stories, in the length of the news stories, in a national or international orientation, and in format. *Channel One* devoted slightly more time to features than did the other programs. *Today* spent more time on news than did the other programs. *CNN Newsroom* had more stories on world events and *Channel One* had more on national events. Late-breaking news often did not make it onto the pretaped school news programs. *Channel One* included advertisements, while *CNN Newsroom* did not.

Some research has been done specifically on *Channel One* Generally, the findings from different studies were consistent about these points:

- Viewers liked the features more than the news.
- Viewers ignored the advertisements.
- Knowledge of current events did not improve significantly.
- The program was not integrated in the school curriculum; teachers had not prepared students for watching nor discussed what was watched.
- Knowledge of geography and map reading increased (Knupfer, 1994; Knupfer & Hayes, 1994; Thompson, Carl, & Hill, 1992; Tiene, 1993, 1994).

There are many ethical and social issues associated with the use of *Channel One* in the schools. These issues arose because Whittle Communications offered free equipment to each school that would agree to require students to watch the news program for 10 minutes a day for 3 years. In exchange, a school received a satellite dish, two videocassette recorders, a color television set for every classroom, and all necessary internal wiring, installation, and servicing. By the mid-1990s, over 8 million teenagers in more than 12,000 schools were viewing the program and its advertisements. The issues provoked by the acceptance of the program are explored in *Watching Channel One,* a book of research edited by Ann De Vaney (1994). In many ways, the book is an example of a postmodernist approach to research on television effects. As such it is interesting both for the methodologies incorporated and the ideas presented. In the book, John Belland raises questions such as whether it is ethical for educators to deliver a mass audience for advertisers, and whether the time invested is defensible even if used for a discussion of popular culture.

12.7.3   News Programs

Television news programs are essential sources of information for citizens of all countries. Because learning from television news programs is important, especially in a democracy, extensive research on learning from television news programs has been done nationally and internationally. Unfortunately, methodological problems have hampered researchers and limited the usefulness of this body of literature. For example, Robinson and Levy (1986) discredited the methodology of studies, which determined that television is the primary purveyor of news. Their criticism centered on poorly designed survey questions.

This section will address four variables after methodological issues are explained. Two of the variables will be independent variables: news item or story (content) characteristics and presentation variables.* One will be a mediating variable, viewer characteristics, and one will be a dependent variable, learning outcomes.

12.7.3.1 Methodological Issues. The major methodological issue is the confounding of variables. For example, it is difficult to determine to what extent differences in knowledge are affected by exposure to other media or by talking with family and friends. Without controls for other important variables, the independent effects of television news viewing on learning cannot be determined (Gunter, 1987). Another example is the confounding of two independent variables, content and presentation. It is difficult to determine whether effects are due to design or content factors or to an interaction of the two, because a message must incorporate both factors. This confounding is further complicated by additional mediating factors outside of television (Berry, 1983). Research that examines the relationship between dependence on newspapers or television for news and mediating factors, such as viewer characteristics or exposure to a variety of media, provides another example of the difficulty of controlling for confounding variables (Gunter, 1987).

A second major methodological issue is consistent with definitional issues reported in other sections, such as scholastic achievement and family context. It is difficult to make comparisons across studies, because variables are defined or interpreted differently. This is especially true with the variables of attention, recall, and comprehension. There are at least three distinct levels at which attention to news can be measured: (a) regularity of watching, (b) deliberateness of watching, and (c) degree of attentiveness to the screen (Berry, 1983). Recall can be free,* cued,* or aided*, and can vary within each of these categories. Recall is sometimes incorrectly interpreted as comprehension of news stories.

An additional weakness in television news research is the generally narrow interpretation of the data without reference to a theoretical base. Consequently, it is difficult to relate the findings of different studies, and it's especially hard to relate them to what is known about learning in general. One reason for this is that research on television news is often done by those in mass-media areas who do not focus on theories of learning. This issue has been addressed from an information-processing perspective by Woodall, Davis, and Sahin (1983) in an article on news comprehension.

12.7.3.2 Viewer Characteristics.
Educational level, gender, intelligence, frequency of watching, interest, motivation, and knowledge of current events have all been found to be significantly related to learning from television news. Of these factors, the most significant seems to be knowledge of current events, because the other factors are only slightly related, or there are conflicting studies. Berry (1983) speculated on whether the importance of knowledge of current events is due to its correlation with education or its role as an indicator of ability to assimilate knowledge and thus retain it.

While there has been considerable interest in the effect of motivation on learning from television news, the evidence is not clear. Several studies claim to show motivational effects; however, there are not many studies that can be compared (Berry, 1983; Gunter, 1987). For example, differences in mean news recall from television bulletins were found to be greater in those with higher motivation than with higher educational level (Neuman, 1976). However, statistical controls for the effects of knowledge might change these results. Nevertheless, the finding that those who watch for information learn more than those who watch for purely entertainment is consistent with other research in education on learning from intentional set (Gantz, 1979, cited in Gunter, 1987).

Research on the effect of frequency of viewing is characterized by the same methodological problems as other research on learning from television news (Gunter, 1987). Cairns has studied comprehension of television news since 1980, using children from the North and South of Ireland and has found an interaction with age. Children aged 11 years who reported greater viewing frequency knew more about current events (Cairns, 1984, cited in Gunter, 1987). In 1990, Cairns reported research on how quantity of television news viewing influenced Northern Irish children's perceptions of local political violence. Based on a correlation between viewing frequency and perceptions that matched social reality, Cairns (1990) concluded that children's

frequency of viewing affected comprehension. The findings on gender as they interact with learning from violent segments on television news will be discussed under the next topic, news item characteristics.

12.7.3.3 News Item Characteristics.
This variable describes the content of news stories. Much of the research has centered on the effects of violent segments and the interaction of violent content with presentation and viewer variables. An important finding in the literature is that there is an interaction between gender and violence in television news. Visual presentation of violence affected how well females recalled the news. Violence negatively affected females' recall of other contiguous, nonviolent news stories, but male subject recall was not affected similarly (Gunter, Furnharn, & Gietson, 1984; Furnham & Gunter, 1985, cited in Gunter, 1987a).

This finding highlights an important aspect of the content of television news, its visuals. The visuals are important because they are selected by the producers and thus influence story interpretation, just as the words and announcer's tone do. Cognitive scientists have argued that imagery has an important role in memory. It is generally concluded that memory for pictures is better than memory for words (Fleming & Levie, 1993). The selection of dramatic visuals, therefore, can enhance or impair memory and comprehension.

Violence in a news story can increase interest. However, violent events can distract from attention and learning even though they heighten impact (Gunter, 1987a). This finding is in contrast to findings that violent visuals are often remembered better. Gunter (1980) reported on Neuman's study of recall associated with economic news as compared with news of the war in Vietnam. Recall of the war news was much greater, probably due to the visuals used.

The organization of the message is also an important aspect of a news story. Cognitive frames of reference, known variously as schemata or scripts, which individuals utilize during learning, facilitate memory and comprehension. Thus, the absence of an organization compatible with the learner's schemata can contribute to poor comprehension and recall (Graber, 1984; Collins, 1979, cited in Gunter, 1987). Krendl and Watkins (1983) examined the components of a television narrative schema and the effect of set on learning. They concluded that the process of learning from television becomes a function of both the messages sent and the perceptual set with which the messages are received and interpreted. The groups with an educational set scored consistently higher than groups given an entertainment set. There were no significant differences between groups in understanding the plot; however, groups with an educational set had better recall and higher-level processing. Thus, the organization of die message seems to interact with motivation for watching.

Lang (1989) has studied the effects of chronological sequencing of news items on information processing. She hypothesized that a chronological organization would facilitate episodical processing and reduce the load on semantic memory, thereby reducing effort and increasing amount of information processed. This hypothesis was supported, in that chronological presentation of events was easier to remember than broadcast structure, which presented what is new followed by causes and consequences of the change.

12.7.3.4 Presentation Variables. Another term for these aspects of television news is formal features. With television news, research has centered on factors such as humor, recapping* and titles, narrator versus voice-over, and still and dynamic visuals. Kozma (1986) wrote a review article that examined the implications of the cognitive model of instruction for the design of educational broadcast television. In the article he reviews research related to pacing, cueing, modeling, and transformation that has implications for design of presentation features. By transformation he meant having the learner change knowledge in one form to another form, such as from verbal to visual form. He suggested that designers cue cognitive strategies for older learners and increase salience for younger learners.

Perloff, Wartella, and Becker (1982) and Son, Reese and Davie (1987) investigated the use of recaps in television news. Both articles reported an increase in retention when the news was recapped. Son et al. (1987) speculated that this was due to time for rehearsal. Snyder (1994) analyzed scripts and stories used in television news and concluded that comprehension can be increased by captioning.

Edwardson, Grooms, and Pringle (1976) compared the effect of a filmed news story with the same story related by an anchorperson without visualization. They found that the filmed news story was remembered no better than the story told by the anchor. Slattery (1990) conducted an experiment to determine whether viewer evaluation of a news story would be influenced by visuals when the verbal information was held constant. Treatment number 1 used visuals both related and relevant to the information presented by the audio channel, i.e., visuals of a landfill when a landfill issue was presented. Treatment number 2 used only related visuals, i.e., a shot of a council meeting where an issue was discussed instead of a visual of the home or people involved. Treatment number 3 consisted of audio information only; no visuals were used. The hypothesis was supported because the visuals influenced the interpretation of the news. Those in treatment number 1 found the story more interesting, important, informative, unforgettable, clear, and exciting than those in treatments number 2 or 3.

12.7.3.5 Learning Outcomes. The learning outcomes related to television news that have been investigated are attention, recall and retention, comprehension, and attitude change. Of these, the most researched areas are recall and comprehension. One important finding related to recall is that there are dramatic increases when cued or aided recall* is used (Neuman, 1976, cited in Gunter, 1987). Educational level is related to amount of recall. Stauffer, Frost and Rybolt (1978, 1980, cited in Gunter, 1987) found that spontaneous recall was highest among educated subjects and lowest among illiterate subjects. It is not surprising that education and social class/occupational status were correlated with comprehension of television news (Trenaman, 1967, cited in Gunter, 1987). One must be careful when findings on recall and comprehension are reported, because sometimes measures of comprehension are actually measures of recall.

12.7.4 The Effects of Advertising

Ellen Notar (1989) argued that television is a curriculum, and as such it is the ultimate example of individualized instruction. She questioned why we have left it almost entirely in the hands of the profit makers and why children are not being taught to question the assumptions presented by advertising. She summarizes the situation:

Recently, I did an analysis of both programming and commercials aimed at children. Unbelievable results! The data were worse than an analysis I did in the late 1970s. Commercials were at least 12 to 14 minutes of each hour, repeated over and over again. The sound levels were higher than the regular programs. The messages were *violence solves problems, advertisers' products will make you happy, and popular, sugar products are selected by the best and the brightest.* The graphics, photography, and audio were invariably superior to the programs they surrounded, guaranteed to capture children's attention if program interest waned. Television advertisers spend over $800 million a year on commercials directed at children under age 12! The average child watching television 4 hours a day sees more than 50 of these spots daily and about 18,000 per year! (p. 66)

12.7.4.1 Evolution of the Research Base. Concern for the effects of advertising on television has a 30-year history. In 1977, the National Science Foundation (NSF) published a review of the literature on the effects of television advertising. The issues addressed are still controversial today:

1. Children's ability to distinguish television commercials from program material
2. The influence of format and audiovisual techniques on children's perceptions of commercial messages
3. Source effects and self-concept appeals in children's advertising
4. The effects of advertising containing premium offers
5. The effects of violence and unsafe acts in television commercials
6. The impact on children of proprietary medicine advertising
7. The effects on children of television food advertising
8. The effects of volume and repetition of television commercials
9. The impact of television advertising on consumer socialization
10. Television advertising and parent-child relations. (National Science Foundation, 1977, p. ii)

The report considered both fantasy violence in commercials and commercials adjacent to violent programs. They concluded that there was relatively little violence in commercials, that the types of violence in commercials were rarely imitable, and that the duration of the violence was too short to suggest instigational effects on viewers. The question of definition arose again in regard to research on television; what should be interpreted as violence in commercials and in programming for children is still being debated.

The principal investigator for this report and some of his coinvestigators (Adler, Lesser, Meringoff, Robertson, Rossiter, & Ward, 1980) subsequently published another review of the literature on the effects of television advertising. In 1987,

Comstock and Paik recognized the importance of the issue for public policy formation by reviewing its evolution, the points of contention, and the empirical evidence in a report commissioned by the Educational Clearinghouse on Information Resources (ERIC). In 1988, Liebert and Sprafkin reviewed the studies on effects of television violence and advertising on children. The areas they synthesized reflect the continuing issues: children's understanding of commercials, effects of common advertising tactics, concerns about products advertised, and training young consumers. A British review of advertising effects of television (Young, 1990) brought attention to many variables that need to be investigated: for example, the effects of formal features used in advertising. In 1991, Comstock and Paik expanded their ERIC review into a book on *Television and the American Child* that reviewed empirical evidence in five areas related to television advertising: recognition and comprehension, harmfulness, parenting, programming, and program content.

The report of the American Psychological Association task force on television effects included a review of research on advertising around topics such as nutrition and health, advertising content and effects, and cognitive abilities necessary to process advertising (Huston et al., 1992). The members of the task force concluded that although the number of commercials increased due to federal deregulation in the early 1980s, many issues related to advertising were not addressed by the research. Some of these issues are the effects of (a) heavy viewing on materialistic values, (b) interruptions for commercials on attention span, (c) health-related commercials, and (d) individual differences in persuadability. Today, new issues have arisen that need to be investigated, because information is important for shaping public-policy positions. The effects of home shopping channels, infomercials, and *Channel One* are among these issues.

12.7.4.2 Consistent Findings.
Some findings have been consistent over these 30 years of research. The strongest is that the effects of television advertising diminish and change as the child ages. Attention to commercials decreases as children get older (Ward, Levinson, & Wackman, 1972). Young children have difficulty distinguishing commercials from programming (Zuckerman, Ziegler, & Stevenson, 1978), although this ability increases throughout the preschool years. Eventually by age 8, most viewers can make this distinction (Levin, Petros, & Petrella, 1982). Kunkel (1988) found that children ages 4 to 8 were less likely to discriminate commercials from regular programming when a host-selling format was used, and that older children were more favorably influenced by commercials in this format. Television commercials influence children's food selections (Gorn & Goldberg, 1982), but the degree of influence is disputed (Bolton, 1983). The combined information seems to indicate that television commercials do have an effect on product selection that is limited when all aspects of a child's environment are taken into account. Nevertheless, young children may be affected greatly by television advertising and need help dealing with it.

Another finding of consistent importance over the years is the interrelationship of formal features and the effects of advertising. As early as the 1977 NSF report, there was speculation on this relationship. The report stated that the type of violence

in children's commercials and programming almost always fell in the fantasy category. Thus, the impact of violence might vary according to the number of fantasy cues. Cartoons have at least three cues to indicate violence (animation, humor, and a remote setting); make-believe violence generally has two cues (humor and a remote setting); and realistically acted violence generally has only one cue (the viewer's knowledge that the portrayal is fictional). Real-life violence (i.e., news footage) has no cues to suggest fantasy. It easy to imagine a young child without media literacy becoming confused and misunderstanding such messages.

12.7.4.3 Important Findings.
An important study, *A Longitudinal Analysis of Television Advertising Effects on Adolescents*, was conducted by Moore and Moschis and reported in 1982. This study is mentioned because the effects of television advertising on a society of widely differing economic groups is another area that needs researching. Moore and Moschis (1982) reported that television advertising affects the development of materialism* and the perception of sex roles. The greatest effects occur in families where consumption matters are not discussed.

Jalongo did an important study in 1983. She investigated *The Preschool Child's Comprehension of Television Commercial Disclaimers*. She used a questionnaire to assess general knowledge about television. Results indicated that linguistic ability was a poor predictor of paraphrase and standard/modified disclaimer scores. Scores reflecting general knowledge about television were the most effective predictors of disclaimer comprehension.

12.7.5 Utilization Studies

Research that investigates the use of instructional television, including factors such as (a) availability of equipment, programming, support personnel, and training; (b) attitudes towards television in the classroom and informally; and (c) the impact of instructional television, is grouped in a category called "utilization studies." There is a long tradition of utilization studies that dates back to the early 1950s when the FCC reserved channels for education and to film studies done earlier. Nevertheless, there are many gaps in this area of the literature. In a comprehensive review of ETV as a tool for science education, Chen (1994b) outlines the lack of research, especially developmental research, on the many science series broadcast nationally. Compared to the investment in production, minimal resources have been devoted to research on learning from most of these series.

The category "utilization studies" encompasses research on using television processes and resources for learning (Seels & Richey, 1994). This discussion of utilization research will cover several topics:

1. Variables investigated
2. Projects of historical interest
3. Studies from the Agency for Instructional Technology (AIT), formerly the Agency for Instructional Television
4. Studies from the Corporation for Public Broadcasting (CPB)
5. Other utilization studies.

12.7.5.1 *Variables Investigated.* Chu and Schramm (1968) reviewed research on television before the ERIC Clearinghouse began to compile and organize the literature on learning from television. They summarized the variables that interacted with learning from instructional television. Today, many of these variables are being investigated under questions related to message design. The remaining variables are still pursued in the area of utilization studies. As identified by Chu and Schramm, these variables are:

• Viewing conditions, e.g., angle, context, grouping, interaction
• Attitudes towards ITV, e.g., students, teachers
• Learning in developing regions, e.g., visual literacy, resistance
• Educational level, e.g., elementary, adult
• Subject matter, e.g., health education, current events
• Relationship to other media, e.g., effectiveness, cost, integration.

Over the years, two of Chu and Schramm's variables have assumed increasing importance: the variable of effectiveness of instruction as measured by formative and summative evaluation, and the variable of impact on the individual, organization, and society.

12.7.5.2 *Projects of Historical Interest.* A good overview of the television utilization studies done in the 1950s, 60s, and 70s is obtained when projects in the Midwest, Hagerstown (Maryland), Samoa, and El Salvador are examined. Most of these projects received funding through Ford Foundation grants, local funds, and corporate equipment. Three district-wide patterns emerged. Studies revolved around investigation of the effectiveness of these patterns, which were (a) total instructional program presented by television teacher, (b) supplemented television instruction, and (c) television as a teaching aid. Total instruction meant that all curriculum was presented through television and the teacher acted as supervisor. With supplemented instruction, the teacher prepared the class and followed up after the program. Only part of the curriculum was presented through television. When television was used as a teaching aid, the classroom teacher just incorporated television into lessons, and use of television was more infrequent (Cuban, 1986).

The Hagerstown, Maryland, project was an early demonstration of supplemented television. Up to one-third of the school day was devoted to televised lessons, with teacher preparation and follow-up. From 1956 to 1961, the Fund for the Advancement of Education and corporations invested about $1.5 million in improving education in the Hagerstown schools through closed-circuit broadcasting. The initial experiment was a success, because costs were reduced while standardized test scores improved.

By the end of the experiment, over 70 production staff, including 25 studio teachers, telecast lessons in 8 different subjects at the elementary level and 15 subjects at the secondary level. All teachers were involved in the planning, because a team approach was used. Assessment of programs was continuous.

Elementary students spent about 12 percent of their time with televised programs, the junior high students about 30 percent of their time, and high school students about 10 percent of their time. Fewer teachers were hired; however, master teachers were hired to teach televised classes. Student improvement was most dramatic when students who learned by television were compared with those in rural schools who did not receive televised lessons. Although standardized test scores were used to compare groups, there was no control for socioeconomic background. Still, when surveyed, parents, teachers, and administrators favored use of televised instruction.

Unfortunately, when funding was withdrawn after 5 years, problems began to arise because local resources were insufficient, especially for capital expenditures. This is a common pattern in utilization of instructional television. By 1983, the project had been reduced to a service department for the district, using a variety of technologies. The annual budget of $334,000 was justified, because all art and music lessons were offered through television, thus saving the cost of 12 itinerant teachers, a practice that would certainly be debated by aesthetic educators. Despite this and other exemplary supplemental television instruction projects, most schools used television simply as a teaching aid during this period (Cuban, 1986).

The Midwest Program of Airborne Instructional Television Instruction (MPATI) began in 1959 and continued in conjunction with the Purdue Research Foundation at Purdue University. Thirty-four courses were televised to 2,000 schools and 40,000 students through 15 educational television stations in six states. In addition, to reach schools not served by these stations, MPATI transmitted programs from an airplane circling at 23,000 feet over North-Central Indiana. Broadcasting began in 1961 with a cost of about $8 to 10 million annually (Seattler, 1968).

In contrast, television provided the total instructional program in American Samoa between 1964 and 1970. This approach was justified because the existing teaching staff and facilities were totally inadequate in 1961 when Governor H. Rex Lee was appointed. When Lee made restructuring the school system his top priority, Congress approved over $1 million in aid for the project. Soon four of every five students were spending one-quarter to one-third of their time watching televised lessons, especially in the elementary schools. The rest of the day was built around preparing for the televised lessons. The packets of material that accompanied the programs became the textbooks.

Researchers examined test scores before and after the introduction of television and found little difference in language scores, although slight advantages in reading and arithmetic were documented. There was little control for mediating variables. The English-speaking ability of the classroom teachers was generally poor, while English was the native language of television teachers. It is interesting, therefore, that the greatest advantage was found in the area of mathematics, not English language (Wells, 1976).

The project was initially reported a success, but by the early 1970s, objections to orienting the whole curriculum to televised lessons increased among students, teachers, and administrators, especially at grades 5 and above. By the eighth year of the project, students wanted less television, and teachers wanted more control over lessons. In 1973, policymakers shifted authority from the television studio to the classroom teacher and cut back the amount of television. In 1979, a utilization study conducted by Wilbur Schramm and his colleagues concluded that television's role had been reduced to supplemental or enrichment instruction, or at the high school level to little more than a teaching aid (Cuban, 1986).

In El Salvador, a major restructuring of education included the use of television to increase enrollment without a loss of quality. Overall educational reforms included (a) reorganization of the Ministry of Education, (b) teacher retraining, (c) curriculum revision, (d) development of new study materials, (d) development of more diverse technical program, (e) construction of new classrooms, (f) elimination of tuition, (g) use of double sessions and reduced hours to teach more students, (h) development of a new evaluation system, and (i) installation of a national television systems for grades 7 through 9. An evaluation project showed no advantage for the instructional television system. The only advantage was in the seventh grade. However, in the eighth and ninth grades, the nontelevision classrooms often obtained better scores. Positive scores during the first year of the reform were dismissed as due to the "halo effect," because scores diminished as novelty of the delivery method diminished (Wells, 1976). As with the Hagerstown project, however, an advantage was found for rural students (Hornik, Ingle, Mayo, McAnany, & Schramm, 1973). Thus, "the consistent advantage of television seems to be in improving the test scores of rural students. One of the reasons for this improvement is that the technology provides for the distribution of the scarce resource of high-quality teaching ability" (Wells, 1976, p. 93).

Each of these projects generated related research and guidelines for practice. As television personnel learned about utilization, they shared their experience through handbooks for teachers on how to use television for instruction (Hillard & Head, 1976). Studies of process and impact were done. For example, Nugent (1977) reported a Nebraska State Department of Education field experiment that addressed whether teacher activities increased learning from television. She concluded that telelessons impacted learning, achievement in television classes was higher, and the nature of activities used had an affect on achievement but not the number of activities.

Tiffin (1978) used a multiple case study approach to analyze "Problems in Instructional Television in Latin America." After doing case studies on 8 of the 14 ITV systems in Latin America, critical subsystems were analyzed, especially in regard to conditions that were symptomatic of problems. Thus, problems and causes were traced until root causes were revealed. In many instances, these turned out to originate outside the ITV system. A hierarchy of casually interrelated problems, called a *problem structure,* was generated. Problems of utilization subsystems were analyzed. "In four cases the visual component of television was not being used and did not appear to be needed. If the television receiver were replaced by radio it appears unlikely that the measured learning outcomes would be appreciably affected" (Tiffin, 1978, p. 202).

Another project of historical significance is the research done by Educational Facilities Laboratories around the best use of space for the utilization of television. A nonprofit corporation

established by the Ford Foundation, Educational Facilities Laboratories (EFL), encouraged research, experimentation, and dissemination about educational facilities. In their 1960 publication on "Design for ETV Planning for Schools with Television," EFL recommended effective designs for seeing, hearing, and learning, and for group spaces. The issues of cost, equipment, and support were also discussed (Chapman, 1960).

12.7.5.3 Agency for Instructional Technology Studies.
AIT is a nonprofit United States–Canadian organization established in 1962 to strengthen education. AIT, which is located in Bloomington, Indiana, provides leadership and services through development, acquisition, and distribution of technology-based instructional materials. Although AIT's research program currently centers primarily on formative evaluation of materials, the organization has sponsored utilization studies. A few representative ones will be mentioned here. Dignam (1977) researched problems associated with the use of television in secondary schools, including equipment, scheduling, availability of programs, and teacher resistance. She reported a continuing debate about the extent to which teacher training should be emphasized in relation to systematic evaluation of utilization. Her report, which is based on a review of the literature, concluded that the relaxation of off-air taping regulations granted by some distributors eased scheduling and equipment difficulty, as did videocassette and videodiscs.

It Figures is a series of twenty-eight 15-minute video programs in mathematics designed for grade 4, in use since 1982. AIT (1984) did a survey of 117 teacher-users of this series. This survey gathered information on (a) teacher's backgrounds, (b) how teachers discovered and used the series, (c) perceived cognitive and attitudinal effects of the series, (d) teachers' reactions to the teacher's guide, and (e) overall reactions to the series. Seventy-six teachers responded that they perceived the series positively and used it in diverse ways. This is an example of an impact study.

AIT used a series of mini-case studies to report on "Video at Work in American Schools" (Carlisle, 1987). This report takes the form of a compilation of experiences the author, Robert Carlisle, had during his travels through 12 states, visiting applications of ITV. He talked to almost 160 people about television utilization and documented them and their projects through photographs. Carlisle concluded that access to equipment is no longer a sizable problem, nor is availability of programming, and the VCR has proved to be a very flexible tool for instruction. Nevertheless, the strength of the human support network behind the teacher was questionable.

12.7.5.4 Corporation for Public Broadcasting Studies.
Peter Dirr, director of the Catholic Telecommunications Network, did the first school use television studies for the Corporation for Public Broadcasting. Dirr and Petrone (1978) conducted a study in 1976–1977 that documented the pattern of greatest use of ITV in lower grades and diminishing use in higher grades. They used a stratified sample of 3,700 classroom teachers. This was the first in-depth and rigorously conducted study of public school use since the introduction of television in schools (Cuban, 1986). Estimating based on data collected,

they speculated that over 15 million students watched televised lessons daily. As is typical with most subsequent utilization studies, they investigated teacher attitudes, accessibility of equipment, and patterns of use in schools.

CPB sponsored two subsequent school utilization studies, one covering 1982–83 and another covering 1990–91. The research was conducted by CPB and the National Center for Education Statistics (NCES). The final report of the 1982–83 study compared the use of instructional television in 1977 and 1983 (Riccobono, 1985). This 1982–83 study surveyed the availability, use, and support (financial, personnel, and staff development) of instructional media in public and private elementary and secondary schools.

While the 1977 survey focused on television, this study was expanded by adding audio/radio and computers. Queries about instructional applications and equipment were directed to 619 superintendents, 1,350 principals, and 2,700 teachers. Responses were grouped by district size, wealth, and school level. The results indicated that although media use varied across districts and levels, almost all teachers had access to audio, video, and digital media. Over 90 percent of the districts offered in-service teacher training in media. The status of television for instruction remained relatively stable since 1977, except that fewer elementary teachers and more secondary teachers reported using television (CBP & NCES, 1984).

CPB sponsored the "1991 Study of School Uses of Television and Video," which surveyed almost 6,000 educators (CPB, n.d.). The results can be generalized to virtually all of the nation's public education system: 11,218 school districts, 72,291 public elementary and secondary schools, and 2,282,773 schoolteachers. The survey measured the use of instructional television and video, the availability of equipment and programming, and the support and resources devoted to instructional television. It replaced the audio/radio and computer component of the 1982–83 report with questions related to several new television-based technologies. The results of the survey show that instructional television is a firmly established teaching tool that is positively regarded by classroom teachers and increasingly well supported with equipment and programming. Programming availability was reported to be one source of frustration for teachers.

12.7.5.5 Other Utilization Studies. The major methodologies used for utilization studies have been experimentation and questionnaire survey. An example of an experimental design would be a study designed to investigate the relative effectiveness of three methods of instruction: conventional classroom instruction, televised instruction only, and a combination of classroom and televised instruction for teaching science content and vocabulary. A 1971 study done in the Santa Ana Unified School District reported no significant difference obtained by either classroom or televised instruction alone. The combination of televised and classroom instruction resulted in the greatest achievement (Santa Ana Unified School District, 1971). Such comparative studies have fallen into disfavor because they cannot be related to individual differences or mediating variables.

An example of a questionnaire approach is Turner and Simpson's (1982) study of the factors affecting the utilization of educational television in schools in Alabama. The researchers gathered information pertaining to five variables:

1. The percentage of students using ITV
2. The ratio of students to videotape recorders
3. The ratio of students to television receivers
4. The ratio of students to color television receivers
5. Students within districts using television

Scheduling was found to be the most important variable. This finding holds true in some cases today. Many districts that contracted for satellite telecourses when they were first offered were surprised to learn that some of the programs required one and a half of their regular periods and that students scheduled for such classes were therefore unable to take some regular classes.

Utilization studies in the United States have focused on the availability of resources, attitudes towards ITV and ETV, and impact of programming. In comparison, utilization studies of television in developing countries have looked at resource issues from the perspective of the design and support of both educational and television systems.

12.7.6 Current Issues

Many issues have been generated by changes in programming. Major trends in programming include:

- An expansion of advertising into infomercials and shopping channels
- The replacement of cigarette advertising with advertisements for drugs
- An increasing emphasis on sexuality through innuendo, dress, dance and topics as exemplified on the Fox Network and MTV
- The popularity of controversial programming such as wrestling, reality, and talk shows
- The evolution of news programming into news/entertainment including tabloid style video magazines
- More centralized responsibility for programming as mergers and monopolies lead to cross-media collaboration
- The use of public service announcements as vehicles for affecting attitudes
- The of ratings as required by national legislation
- An increased emphasis on children's programming without a concurrent increase in the quality of children's experiences with television.

Some of these trends have led to research; others have not generated enough studies to report findings. The areas that have drawn the most attention from researchers are: sexuality, public service announcements and the use of ratings.

12.7.6.1 Sexuality. The Henry J. Kaiser Family Foundation studies provide a basis for comparison of sexual content in 1996–97, 1997–98, and 1999–2000. Using content analysis, researchers found about a 10 percent increase in sexual content in dramas and situation comedies, but not in soap operas or talk shows. Two in every three programs addresses sexuality.

Depiction of intercourse has increased from 3 to 9 percent. Risks and responsibilities associated with sex were discussed in about 10 percent of the programs. Using focus groups, researchers also investigated whether sexual jokes, innuendos, and behavior on television goes over children's heads. The findings were:

- Children understood the sexual content.
- They preferred shows with prosocial messages about sexual issues.
- Shows with mixed messages left children confused.
- Most children, especially younger ones, were made uncomfortable.
- Some parents say television helps them to broach the subject of sex (Kaiser Foundation, 1996a, 1996b).

While the Kaiser Foundation found no increase in sexuality on soap operas from 1996–2000, another study (Greenberg & Buselle, 1996) compared soap opera content from 1984 to 1994 and found increased incidence in visual as well as verbal content. Kunkel et al. (1996) reported that a Kaiser Foundation study documented a 118 percent increase in sexual behaviors on television over the last 20 years. Although risks and responsibilities were addressed about 10 percent of the time, shows involving teens presented consideration of issues of sexual responsibility 29 percent of the time.

12.7.6.2 Controversial Programming.
There have been a few studies on talk shows and MTV. Davis and Mares (1998) found that high school viewers of talk shows were not desensitized to the suffering of other, although viewers overemphasized the frequency of deviant behaviors. Among some age groups, talk show viewing was positively related to the perceived importance of social issues. Many parents are concerned about sexuality on MTV. Pardun and McKee (1995) found that religious imagery was twice as likely to be paired with sexual imagery than without. However, the religious symbolism was rarely connected to the content of the lyrics or story of the video. Seidman (1999) replicated a 1987 study examining sex roles in music videos. Both the original and the recent study showed that music videos tend to stereotype the sexes behaviorally and occupationally and that women were portrayed primarily as sex objects.

12.7.6.3 Children's Programming.
A major change in children's programming is the decreasing importance of network programming and the increasing importance of cable and Public Broadcasting System (PBS) offerings (Adgate, 1999). Networks devote about 10 percent of total programming time to educational or prosocial programming for children. This is about 30 minutes each Saturday morning as required by the Children's Television Act (Calvert et al., 1997). The Corporation for Public Broadcasting (CPB) has made a concerted effort to become the premier provider of children's programming. The CPB's Public Television Programming Survey documents this (CPB, 1996). Children's programming on the networks has little educational value, while programming on cable and PBS is increasing in educational value including literacy education and prosocial learning (Wan, 2000).

Researchers continue to investigate the effects of both prosocial programming and the lack of prosocial messages. Swan (1995) examined the effects of Saturday morning cartoons on children's perceptions of social reality using content analysis techniques. The study found that the cartoons reviewed presented many negative portrayals based on age, gender, and ethnicity. Weiss and Wilson (1996) investigated television's role as a socializing agent in emotional development. The results revealed that family sitcoms focus on common emotions and emotional situations. Emotions were strongly related to two contextual factors: type of plot (main plot, subplot) and type of character (featured, nonfeatured).

12.7.6.4 News.
Research has continued on children's reactions to news of violent situations, such as the Oklahoma City bombing. Sixty-eight percent of children regularly watch television news programs (Tuned in or tuned out, 1995). Smith and Wilson (2000) studied two variables in children's reactions to news: video footage and the proximity of the crime. The reported proximity of the crime affected 10- to 12-year-olds, but not 6- to 7-year-olds. Video footage decreased fear among children in both age groups. Children from kindergarten through elementary school years continue to be frightened by news programs. On the other hand, fantasy programs became less and less frightening to children as they aged (Cantor & Nathanson, 1996).

12.7.6.5 Advertising.
The most important issue related to advertising is the increasing emphasis on advertising for children. This is true for other media as well as for television (Center for New American Dream, 2001; Lambert, Plunkett et al., 1998). Children as young as 3 years of age are influenced by pressure from advertising. Brand loyalty can begin to be established as early as age two (National Institute on Media and the Family, 2002). Singh, Balasubramanian, and Chakraborty (2000) found that the 15-minute long infomercial was more effective than the 1-minute advertisement or the 30-minute infomercial.

12.7.6.6 School Utilization.
One major change in school utilization is the availability of new resources for the teacher, such as databases and web pages that support learning from television. In some instances multiple resources are provided by one source. The cable industry funds KidsNet, which provides a database for teachers and lesson plans through a "Cable in the Classroom" component. The cable industry foundation encourages communities to build a collection of educational series on videotape for the local library, so that teachers have access to extended resources. The Corporation for Public Broadcasting offers virtual tours through the Internet. The trend towards expansion of resources will continue. As broadband becomes available, schools are likely to use video streaming (Butler, 2001; Holmes & Branch, 2000).

12.7.7 Summary and Recommendations

Although a great deal of research has been done on programming for preschoolers and classrooms, there are major gaps in the literature. One such gap is in the effects of video production by students. Another area in which the research is confusing is that of newer programming genres for which it is difficult to compare findings. Contemporary varieties of advertising on television also present a very complex topic that warrants more research. Greater attention should be paid to the effects of genre differences and program formats, as well. It is important for researchers to investigate the interaction of the content and form of programming with other variables.

Many areas identified by research have not been adequately pursued, such as the effect of programs and utilization practices on rural children. Barriers to greater utilization are teachers' lack of knowledge about sources of programming for their subject-matter area and research on utilization. Utilization may be facilitated through "Cable in the Classroom," a nonprofit service of the cable television industry, which will offer educational programming for the classroom, curriculum-based support materials, and a clearinghouse for information on cable use in schools. Over 500 hours of high-quality programs will be delivered to schools each month, without commercial interruption (Kamil, 1992). Opportunities for research will arise as a result. KIDSNETT, a computerized clearinghouse concerned with programs for children preschool through high school, will be another source of information for researchers. Its "Active Database" has detailed information on 5,000 children's programs and public-service announcements and on 20,000 programs available for use in classrooms (Mielke, 1988).

12.8 CRITICAL-VIEWING SKILLS

To some extent, the critical-viewing skills movement was motivated by the gradual deregulation of the broadcasting industry. During the mid-1980s, as research turned more to the study of the interaction of variables, it became apparent that parents and teachers could have an important mediating role to play (Palmer, 1987; Sprafkin, Gadow & Abelman, 1992). This discussion of the critical-viewing skills movement will address (a) its relationship to the media literacy movement, (b) the assumptions underlying critical-viewing skills, (c) the goals adopted by the movement, (d) the curriculum projects developed to attain these goals, (e) the research findings on these projects, and (f) the impact of these projects. In an article on developmentally appropriate television, Levin and Carlsson-Paige (1994) suggested, "Now, the children who first fell prey to deregulated children's TV in 1984 are entering middle and high school; among them we see an alarming increase in violence" (p. 42). This inference is not easily supported in the literature, however, because there are other factors interacting with the effects of television. Nevertheless, violence has increased in society and on television. The authors point out that a content analysis of television programming reveals:

- A dangerous, rather than secure world
- A world where autonomy means fighting, and connectedness means helplessness, rather than a world of independent people helping each other

- A world where physical strength and violence equal power, rather than a world where people have a positive effect without violence
- A world with rigid gender divisions, rather than complex characters
- A world where diversity is dangerous and dehumanizing and stereotyping abounds, rather than a world of respect where people enrich each others lives
- A world where people are irresponsible and immoral, rather than a world where empathy and kindness pervade
- And a world full of imitative play, rather than creative, meaningful play.

Based on this review and what is on television, it could be argued that this perception is biased towards negative effects. Nevertheless, there are plenty of instances of negative content to support this framework. Arguments about content on television and the role of mediation have stimulated efforts to emphasize media literacy.

12.8.1 Media Literacy

The media literacy debate encompasses issues around the role of content in relation to format and media literacy. It can be argued that today the medium dominates "symbol production and myth/reality dissemination in contemporary society" (Brown, 1991, p. 18). Others argue that to divorce content from examination of variables is illogical and self-defeating (K. W. Mielke, personal communication, Nov. 15, 1994). Another point of view is that television is decoded by a viewer drawing on a unique social and cognitive background, and thus the effects of television depend more on the receiver than on content or media literacy. The argument as to whether content should be controlled or taken into account in research is set in opposition to the development of media literacy, when probably both perspectives are important (Brown, 1991).

Worth raises another concern that reinforces the argument for attention to both content and media literacy:

Throughout the world, the air is being filled with reruns of "Bonanza" and ads for toothpaste, mouthwash, and vaginal deodorants.... If left unchecked, Bantuy, Dani, and Vietnamese children, as well as our own, will be taught to consume culture and learning through thousands of "Sesame Streets," taught not that learning is a creative process in which they Participate, but rather that learning is a consumer product like commercials.

If left unchecked, we, and perhaps other nations like us, will continue to sell the technology which produces visual symbolic forms, while at the same time teaching other peoples our uses only, our conceptions, our codes, our mythic and narrative forms. We will, with technology, enforce our notions of what is, what is important, and what is right. (Worth, 1981, p. 99, cited in Brown, 1991, p. 21)

A concern for receivership skills* developed from the perception that television was being used as a consumer product. Receivership skills "involve comprehending overt and hidden meanings of messages by analyzing language and visual and aural images, to understand the intended audiences and the intent of the message" (Brown, 1991, p. 70). Thus, an attempt is made to extend the tradition of teaching critical reading and critical thinking to include critical viewing.

Concern for media literacy is not new. When films were a prevalent audiovisual medium, there were many publications about the need for film literacy (Peters, 1961). A 1970 article by Joan and Louis Foresdale proposed film education to help students develop levels of comprehension and learn filmic code. As mentioned earlier under the topic filmic code, Salomon (1982) redirected attention to television literacy.* He theorized that comprehension occurred in two stages, both employing cognitive strategies for decoding and recoding. The first stage was specific television literacy dependent on knowing the symbol system associated with television viewing. The second stage required using general literacy skills to move to higher levels of learning. He also theorized that, except for small children, the general literacy skills were more important. He based his theory of a television symbol system on research others and he conducted (Salomon, 1982).

By the 1990s, books were available on television literacy (Neuman, 1991). Some of these came from the visual literacy movement, such as Messaris's *Visual Literacy: Image, Mind, and Reality* (1994). In this book, he synthesized research and practice in order to identify four aspects:

• Visual literacy is a prerequisite for comprehension of visual media.

• There are general cognitive consequences of visual literacy.

• Viewers must be made more aware of visual manipulation.

• Visual literacy is essential for aesthetic appreciation.

In responding to Clark's argument (1983, 1994) that media research tells us little, Kozma (1994) brought attention to the centrality of media literacy for instructional technology research. Kozma argued that we needed to consider the capabilities of media and their delivery methods as they interact with the cognitive and social processes by which knowledge is constructed. "From an interactionist perspective, learning with media can be thought of as a complementary process within which representations are constructed and procedures performed, sometimes by the learner and sometimes by the medium"(Kozma, 1994, p. 11). Thus, Kozma extended the attention directed to the interaction of media and mediating variables that began in the 1980s.

12.8.2 Critical-Viewing Education

During the 1980s, critical-viewing curricula were developed based on a number of underlying assumptions. These assumptions will be discussed next.

12.8.2.1 Assumptions About Critical Viewing. A significant assumption used in developing curricula on critical viewing was drawn from the analogy between positive television-viewing patterns and a balanced menu or diet. In fact, the

terms "good TV diets" (O'Bryant & Corder-Bolz, 1978), "media diets" (Williams, 1986), "television diets" (Murray, 1980), and "balanced diet" (Searching for Alternatives, 1980) appeared frequently in the literature on television viewing. The assumption was that if television was watched in moderation and a variety of age-appropriate program genres were selected, the television experience would be positive. The only evidence we have found to support this assumption is the finding that moderate amounts of watching can increase school achievement. Other than indications that young children can become fearful or confused from watching adult programming, little evidence exists to support the need to view diverse and appropriate types of programs. Such research has not been done. It may be that individual or family differences can balance and thereby justify an "unbalanced TV diet."

A second unstated assumption was that a critical viewer,* like a critical reader, would have the critical-thinking skills of an adult. But "the efficacy of children imitating adult reasoning remains untested" (Anderson, 1983, p. 320). Children, especially young children, process information concretely and creatively. Therefore, they may not benefit from more logical analyses. The critical viewer may be less like a critical reader and more like an art critic.

Another assumption was that the critical-viewing process had to have as its primary purpose education rather than entertainment. Consequently, viewers had to become more knowledgeable, and the best way to do this was through classroom curricula (Anderson, 1983). Critical-viewing curriculum projects had to meet the criteria of systematic instruction and the provision of a variety of audiovisual materials. For years, some anthropologists have argued that much visual literacy is learned naturally from the environment. Presumably, critical viewing could be learned in the home environment without instructional materials.

Primarily, the tests of these three assumptions were formative evaluations of the success of the educational interventions conducted in the name of critical-viewing skills curricula. While these efforts were found to improve learning, there was little other evidence to use. Nevertheless, positive reports from parents, teachers, experts, and students were given credence. On the other hand, the positive effects could be the result of maturation (Watkins, Sprafkin, Gadow, & Sadetsky, 1988). Anderson (1980) has traced the theoretical lineage of critical-viewing curricula.

12.8.2.2 Goals for Critical-Viewing Curricula. Amy Doff Leifer (1976) conducted a comparative study to identify critical evaluative skills associated with television viewing. Five skills were tentatively proposed:

1. Explicit and spontaneous reasoning
2. Readiness to compare television content to outside sources of information
3. Readiness to refer to industry knowledge in reasoning about television content
4. Tendency to find television content more fabricated or inaccurate
5. Less positive evaluation of television content (Doff, 1976, p. 14)

At the end of the 1970s, the U.S. Office of Education (USOE) sponsored a national project, *Development of Critical Television Viewing Skills in Students,* which was intended to help students become more active and discriminating viewers. Separate curricula were developed for elementary, middle school, secondary, and postsecondary students. Four critical television skills emphasized in the secondary curriculum were the ability to:

- Evaluate and manage one's own television-viewing behavior
- Question the reality of television programs
- Recognize the arguments employed on television and to counter-argue
- Recognize the effects of television on one's own life (Lieberman, 1980; Wheeler, 1979)

In 1983, Anderson identified 11 objectives in 8 curriculum projects. He interpreted these as reflecting four goals common to all the projects. The goals were: (a) ability to grasp the meaning of the message; (b) ability to observe details, their sequence and relationships, and understand themes, values, motivating elements, plot lines, characters, and characterization; (c) ability to evaluate fact, opinion, logical and affective appeals, and separate fantasy and reality; and (d) the ability to apply receivership skills to understand inherent sources of bias (cited in Brown, 1991). The goals and objectives of the major critical-viewing skills projects were summarized by Brown (1991).

A common approach to attaining these goals was to include content on the various programming genre. Participants would be taught to distinguish types of programming and to use different analysis approaches with each. Brown (1991) reviewed the various approaches to defining genre, such as types, classifications, and typology. Bryant and Zillmann (1991) dedicated Part II of their book of readings on *Responding to the Screen* to an in-depth analysis of research and theory on each genre and associated literacy issues including news and public affairs, comedy, suspense and mystery, horror, erotica, sports, and music television.

12.8.2.3 Critical-Viewing Skills Curricula.

Over the years, there have been many curricula to develop television literacy in addition to the USOE project curricula described above. In the United States, these curricula were developed by local television stations, national networks underwriting social research, school districts, research centers, and national coalitions. Most of these have been summarized by Brown in his book on major media literacy projects (1991). Some have been developed by companies (i.e., J. C. Penny's), some by researchers [i.e., the Critical Viewing Curriculum (KIDVID) and the Curriculum for Enhancing Social Skills Through Media Awareness (CESSMA)], some by practitioners (i.e., O'Reilly & Splaine, 1987), and some by nonprofit associations (i.e., Carnegie Corporation) or coalitions, such as Action for Children's Television. A few will be described here, especially those that have been summatively researched or that address unique populations or content.

The recommendations of Action for Children's Television (ACT) are summarized in *Changing Channels: Living (Sensi-*

bly) with Television (Charren & Sandler, 1983). This is an example of an educational plan intended for general use rather than specifically for the classroom. A more current example of general recommendations is Chen's (1994a) *The Smart Parent's Guide to KIDS' TV.*

The Curriculum for Enhancing Social Skills through Media Awareness (CESSMA) was designed to be used with educationally disabled and learning-disabled children to improve their prosocial learning from television. CESSMA was field tested in an elementary school for educationally disabled children on Long Island. The curriculum group significantly outperformed the control group on television knowledge. Children in the intervention group identified less with aggressive television characters than those in the control group. Nevertheless, there was no evidence that CESSMA significantly altered attitudes or behavior.

KIDVID has been used with gifted and learning disabled children. It was designed to facilitate children's ability to recognize the prosocial content from a television program. The three-week curriculum, originally developed for intellectually average and gifted children, was tested in intact fourth-grade classrooms using indices to measure the children's ability to identify and label the types of prosocial behaviors portrayed in commercial television programs. The curriculum was effective because all who participated were better able to recognize and label prosocial behaviors (Sprafkin, Gadow, & Abelman, 1992).

Previously, in 1983, Abelman and Courtright had conducted a study on television literacy in the area of prosocial learning. In that study they found evidence that curriculum can be effective in amplifying the cognitive effects of commercial television's prosocial fare. They concluded:

For children who rely on television information as an accurate source of social information, who spend the majority of their free time with the medium, and who are unable to separate television fantasy from reality, some form of mediation is imperative. (p. 56)

A practitioner's approach to a curriculum on television literacy for gifted learners was reported by Hunter (1992). This approach used video production to teach fifth- through eighth-graders. Students were divided into three treatment groups. One of the two critical-viewing treatment groups showed significant gains, while the control/no treatment group did not.

Another practitioner approach was reported by Luker and Johnston (1989). Teachers were advised to help adolescent social development by using television shows in the classroom with a four-step process:

There are four steps to take after viewing a show: (1) Establish the facts of the conflict, (2) establish the perspectives of the central characters, (3) classify the coping style used by the main character, and (4) explore alternatives that the main character could take and the consequences of each alternative both for the main character and the foil. (p. 51)

They found that teachers were effective in completing the first two steps, but had greater difficulty with steps 3 and 4.

The effect of learning about television commercials was studied in an experiment by Donohue, Henke, and Meyer (1983). Two instructional units, one role-playing unit and one traditional, were designed to examine if young children can be taught general and specific intent of television commercials. Both treatment groups of 6- to 7-year-olds experienced significant increases in comprehension of commercials. The researchers concluded that:

Through mediation via an instructional unit at the seven-year mark, the process of building defense mechanisms against the manipulative intent of countless television commercials can be considerably accelerated to the point where children are able to effectively and correctly assimilate commercial messages into their developing cognitive structures. (p. 260)

Rapaczynski, Singer, and Singer (1980) looked at children in kindergarten through second grade. They introduced a curriculum designed to teach how television works, which was produced by simplifying the content of a curriculum intended for older children. Although a control group was not used, this curriculum intervention did appear to produce substantial knowledge gains. Another curriculum developed for kindergarteners and second-graders also was found to produce significant knowledge gains (Watkins, Sprafkin, & Gadow, 1988). In this case, the study used another class at each grade level as nontreatment controls.

Currently, the Academy of Television Arts and Sciences is mounting a critical-viewing skills campaign. Its members offer free workshops that use a videotape and exercises developed by Dorothy and Jerome Singer under the auspices of the Pacific Mountain Network in Denver.

12.8.2.4 Evaluation of the Curricula.

The major thrust in critical-viewing skills came with the four curriculum development projects sponsored by the U.S. Office of Education at the end of the 1970s. Each project addressed a different age group. A final report on the development of the curriculum for teenagers was prepared by Lieberman (1980). The formative evaluation of the curriculum, which is reported in a series of Educational Resource Information Center (ERIC) documents, was done by the Educational Testing Service.

To evaluate the curriculum for teenagers, Educational Testing Service identified 35 reviewers representing various constituencies (Wheeler, 1979). Generally, the review revealed effective use of an instructional systems design and development process.

Based on his review of the literature, Brown (1991) presented 20 descriptive criteria for assessing critical-viewing skills curricula or projects. The criteria fall into these categories:

- Breadth: meaning social, political, aesthetic, and ethical perspectives
- Scope: meaning adaptability and wide utilization
- Individuality and values: meaning reflecting diverse heritages and sensitization of viewers to their role
- Validity and reliability (accuracy): meaning based on research
- Cognition (developmental): meaning age-appropriate education
- Cognition (reasoning skills): meaning training in analysis and synthesis

- Pragmatics of media education: meaning incorporating the content and form of media literacy projects.

12.8.2.5 Impact of Critical-Viewing Projects.

How effective have these curricula been across the country and over the years? Berger (1982) suggested that it would take 30 years before the results would be known. Bell (1984), however, concluded that several indicators pointed to the rapid demise of curricula on critical television viewing. Although he found little evidence that the curriculum materials produced under the aegis of the USOE had been assimilated into school curricula, he noted that the skills promoted have not been completely forgotten by instructional technologists. The impact of content and strategy was greater than the influence of the movement or subsequent use of the materials, many of which are no longer available. Bell also reported another troublesome indicator. The Boston University Critical Television Viewing Skills Project for adults, directed by the highly regarded Donis Dondis, dean of the School of Communication, was given the Golden Fleece award by Senator William Proxmire. This was his monthly prize for ridiculous and wasteful government spending. The lack of clear understanding of the need for such projects and their potential was clear in the statement he read in 1978:

If education has failed to endow college students with critical facilities that can be applied to the spectrum of their lives, a series of new courses on how to watch television critically will not provide it. (cited in Bell, 1984. p. 12)

12.8.3 Current Issues

12.8.3.1 Use of Sources.

There has never been a greater need for media literacy education. As mergers and monopolies in the communication industry increase, control of programming is more and more centralized. What is frightening is that fewer and fewer companies control all forms of media: books, films, television, and magazines. A company such as Viacom or Disney can be the gatekeeper to many media formats. Hearings on monopolies in communications industries are common (Moyers, 2002). The popularity of alternatives to mainstream media (e.g., National Public Radio, Frontline, The Nation, Adbusters.org, Bill Moyer's NOW) documents interest in analyzing media. One issue that arises is whether the media literacy goal of using a variety of media sources to elaborate and triangulate learning is still relevant today since different forms of media often present the same content, for example: television news magazines, television news, and magazines. It may be that sources other than mainstream media need to be included and emphasized in media literacy.

12.8.3.2 Resources.

New resources for media literacy are available including curriculum units and web sites. There are many web sites that support media literacy including commercial sites (e.g., Apple Corporation), software sites (e.g., ImageForge, www.simtel.net/pub/dl/57671.shtml), and organizational sites (e.g., Media Literacy Clearinghouse, *http://www.med.sc.edu:1081/default.htm*). Television literacy is supported by many sites, such as those sponsored by the Public Broadcasting System, the Cable Industry (e.g., Cable in the Classroom), and the Pediatrics Association. Hugh Rank's Persuasion Analysis Homepage (*http://www.govst.edu/users/gbrank*) is another valuable site.

At the least, we must note three outstanding curricula in television literacy that have been disseminated over the past decade. The first was developed in 1990 and has proven to be an excellent resource for elementary teachers. This is the *Behind the Scenes: Resource Kit for Television Literacy* (TV Ontario, 1990). These resources are available for less than $50. The Academy of Television Arts and Sciences (1994) developed the second curricula during the 1990's. This curriculum was called *Creating Critical Viewers: A Partnership Between Schools and Television Professionals* and was developed under the auspices of the Pacific Mountain Network in Denver, Colorado. The academy makes workshop leaders from the profession available for secondary schools and provides teaching materials developed in cooperation with Dorothy and Jerome Singer. The curriculum provides a videotape of six 10-minute sequences that can be used to stimulate study about such topics as editing, commercials, the industry, and the creative process.

The third curriculum reflects one trend in media education, that is, media literacy that enables health education. The New Mexico Visual Literacy Project, *Understanding Media,* was developed to help children and adolescents deal with alcohol advertising on television. The curriculum was implemented at six New Mexico Schools. The materials include a CD-ROM on *Media Literacy: Reversing Addiction in our Compulsive Culture*. The state Department of Education related the curriculum to standards and benchmarks and provided another CD-ROM on *Understanding Media* and a video called *Just Do Media*. This curriculum contributed another list of critical viewing goals or objectives (McCannon, 2002).

12.8.3.3 International Efforts. The United States has been outpaced by Australia, the United Kingdom, Canada, Germany, and Latin America where media literacy programs have been incorporated as part of school curricula. Researchers in Italy investigated whether media literacy education enhanced comprehension of television news reporting. They found that even brief critical viewing instruction had an impact of the comprehension and attitudes of seventh- and eleventh-graders (Siniscalo, 1996).

Nevertheless, media literacy education has not addressed many areas of concern, such as reality programming, MTV, sexuality on television, infomercials. shopping channels and the World Wrestling Federation. Duncum (1999) argues that art education should incorporate everyday experiences like shopping and watching television because aesthetic experiences from pop culture can significantly impact life.

12.8.4   Summary and Recommendations

From formative and summative evaluation and a few experimental studies, there is evidence that intervening with instruction on critical viewing increases knowledge of and sophistication about television. Abelman and Courtright (1983) summarize the situation well: "... television literacy curricula can be as much a social force as the medium itself" (p. 56).

The need for field research on the effects of interventions is documented by the paucity of literature on applying the findings of research through interventions. We know that children learn more from any form of television if adults intervene. The various ways of intervening need to be researched using methods other than formative evaluation. Systematic programs of intervention need to be developed and their impact measured.

12.9   CONCLUDING REMARKS

This chapter has dealt only with research on traditional forms of television and instructional film. The research on newer technologies, such as interactive multimedia, has been left for others to review. We have endeavored to identify the important variables that have surfaced from the enormous mass of research that has been published about learning from television. It was not possible to narrow this list of variables to any great extent, because most were relevant either to the design, development, or utilization functions of this field. Nor could we narrow the list by concentrating on research about film and television solely in the classroom, because instructional technology as a field has a responsibility to media literacy and learning in many environments. The review was not limited to research done within the field because, in this case, many disciplines contribute information useful to the practitioners and researchers in our field. Therefore, the chapter has traced the progress of research in many fields over decades and summarized the important variables related to areas of interest to our field. These areas are message design, mental processing, school achievement, family context for viewing, socialization, programming, utilization, and critical-viewing skills. Research in these areas has investigated independent variables, mediating variables, and effects. This chapter concludes with consideration of myths about learning from television in the light of this review.

Milton Chen (1994c), director for the Center for Education and Lifelong Learning at KQED in San Francisco, summarized many myths about the effects of television. He argued that to conclude that television is primarily responsible for "turning kids into couch potatoes, frying their brains, shortening their attention spans, and lowering their academic abilities" is too simplistic. Indeed, there are several suppositions about the effects of television that seem mystifying in light of the research reviewed in this chapter.

The first myth is that television encourages mental and physical passivity. Research reveals that a great deal of mental activity takes place while viewing, some in reaction to programming and the rest in reaction to elements in the environment. In his essay on whether television stimulates or stultifies children, psychologist Howard Gardner (1982) argued that there is little if any support for the view that the child is a passive victim of television. Gardner said that, on the other hand, there is a great deal of evidence that children are active transformers of what they see on television. He concluded that during the early childhood years, television is a great stimulator.

Similarly, it is often assumed that television has a negative effect on school achievement and reading. In reality, it has little effect if the home environment establishes rules that control the negative influences of television. In fact, for some students with difficulty in reading, it can provide another source of vocabulary and language development. Television can assist with reading and school readiness. A 1988 study by Anderson and Collins investigated the premise that television viewing has a detrimental effect on the cognitive development of children. They found that children comprehend programs produced for them, that they are cognitively active during learning, and that effect on reading achievement is small relative to other factors (Anderson & Collins, 1988). Generally, the evidence shows that moderate amounts of television viewing are positively related to academic achievement, while heavy viewing is negatively associated.

Another myth is that television is a great leveler because rich and poor alike watch the same programming. It is obviously an oversimplification to assume that all variables including socioeconomic ones are thus equalized by watching the same television programs. It would be more accurate to say that television can help provide a common conceptual framework for a community. Socioeconomic groups use television differently, and television has different effects on these groups. Lower-income children watching *Sesame Street* gained more in every area except knowledge of the alphabet (Zill, Davies, & Daly, 1994). On the other hand, the more educated the family, the more likely there will be supervised use of television. Children who experience rules related to television viewing are likely to gain the most from the television experience. Television may be helpful to individuals from a lower socioeconomic class because it provides stimulation rather than displacing more valuable activities. Television has the potential both to positively and negatively affect minorities' self-concept (Stroman, 1991).

Another common belief is that television causes violent behavior. The research shows that while there is a relationship between television and aggression, the effects of this relationship vary depending on individual and environmental variables:

In sum, the empirical and theoretical evidence suggests that in general the effects of television's content depend in part on the extent to which contradictory messages are available, understood, and consistent. In the case of sex role attitudes, messages from television are consistent and either absent or reinforced in real life, whereas in the case of aggressive behavior, most viewers receive contradictory messages from both sources. All viewers may learn aggression from television, but whether they will perform it will depend on a variety of factors. If we wish to predict behavior, that is, performance, we need to know something of the viewers' social milieu. (Williams, 1986, p. 411).

It is true that research has shown that television has the potential to incite aggressive or antisocial behavior, to create problems resulting from advertising, and to portray characters in ways that foster stereotypes. Despite these potentially negative effects, television has the capability to educate, stimulate, persuade, and inform. Enough is known about how to use television positively to make a difference; however, the research has not led to successful interventions. There are several reasons for this: the lack of conceptual theory relating findings, poor dissemination of findings, and little support for interventions.

What is most remarkable about the literature on learning from television is that the concerns haven't changed greatly in 40 years. Although the research questions have become more sophisticated as the medium evolved, the same issues—i.e., violence, commercialism, effect on school achievement—have continued. Yet, while interest in the negative aspects of television remains steady, efforts to increase positive effects seem to be more sporadic. Interventions are tried and discarded even if successful. The research on prosocial effects is reported and largely ignored. In fact, there is the danger that applying some of these findings could fuel a debate about "political correctness" that could lead to loss of funding. Perhaps the reason there seems to be less progress than warranted after 40 years is that the emphasis on negative effects has been more salient than efforts to ensure positive effects through interventions. Far more attention needs to be paid to the positive effects of television on learning and the potential for overcoming negative effects with these positive effects.

We would like to conclude by stressing the importance of emphasizing the positive through research on interventions, rather than through perpetuation of myths that emphasize negative effects. If this review has revealed anything, it is that the findings on learning from television are complex and so interrelated that there is a great danger of oversimplification before research can provide adequate answers to sophisticated questions. Other reviews, such as Signorielli's *A Sourcebook on Children and Television* (1991), have reached similar conclusions. It seems important, therefore, to urge action in areas where research or intervention are both needed and supported, but to caution about sweeping generalizations that create distortions that affect policy. Finally, we hope that by extending this review beyond the usual consideration of either mass media literature or literature from instruction to a review combining both, we have established support for increased attention to design factors and to interventions that affect utilization.

A conscious effort by teachers and parents to use television positively makes a difference. Discussion of programming, for example, enhances learning through elaboration and clarification. Most parents who think they discuss television with their children, however, do so only in a minimal way. Therefore, the belief that parents and teachers guide the use of television is a myth. Generally, they don't. Neither teachers nor parents are given assistance in developing the skills to intervene successfully in the television-viewing experience.

From the research, one can surmise that different variables are important at different points in the life span of viewers. Thus, research on preschool viewers concentrates on mental processing, imagination, and attention span, while research on school age viewers asks questions about television's effect on school achievement and language development. Research on adolescents turns to questions of violence and the learning of roles and prosocial behavior. Adult learners are questioned about attitude change and viewing habits. These foci cause discontinuities in the literature because the same research questions are not asked across all life span periods. Thus, we know very little about the mental processing of adults viewing television or the effect of television on adult achievement. One recommendation for a research agenda would be to ask the same questions about all life span periods.

In pursuing the same questions across different life span periods, researchers need to ensure that self-reporting instruments measure the same phenomena for each age studied. When data are collected through self-reporting measures such as interviews, questionnaires, and psychological tests, there are limitations to take into account. Self-reporting instruments are used less effectively with young children and those with language disabilities. Moreover, subjects of different ages may interpret questions differently due to comprehension or interest. In addition, respondents may try to present themselves in a positive or socially desirable manner, thus misleading the researcher (Sigelman & Shaffer, 1995).

Which brings us to final conclusions. The need to study research questions through a variety of methodologies appropriate to respective variables and through investigations of interactions among variables is apparent from this review. One can only hope that enough researchers become interested enough, especially those open to interdisciplinary research, to provide some of the answers society, teachers, and parents need.

12.10 GLOSSARY OF TERMS

Active Theory Describes the child as an active processor of information, guided by previous knowledge, expectations, and schemata (Anderson & Lorch, 1983).

Aggression An antisocial "behavior, the intent of which is injury to a person or destruction of an object" (Bandura, Ross, & Ross, 1963, p. 10).

Aided Recall When interviewers probe for further detail by cuing (Gunter, 1987, p. 93).

AIME The amount of invested mental effort in nonautomatic elaboration of material (Salomon, 1981a, 1981b). Theory that the amount of invested mental effort that children apply to the television-viewing experience influences their program recall and comprehension (Sprafkin, Gadow, & Abelman, 1992, p. 55).

Altruism The prosocial "unselfish concern for the welfare of others" (Neufeldt & Sparks, 1990, p. 18). Evidenced by generosity, helping, cooperation, self-control, delaying gratification, or resisting the temptation to cheat, lie, or steal.

Antisocial Behavior Behavior that goes against the norms of society including "physical aggression, verbal aggression, passivity, stereotyping, theft, rule breaking, materialism, unlawful behaviors, or pathological behavior" (Hearold, 1986, p. 81).

Arousal Theory Contends that communication messages can evoke varying degrees of generalized emotional arousal and that this can influence any behavior an individual is engaged in while the state of arousal persists (Sprafkin, Gadow, & Abelman, 1992, p. 79).

Attention The cognitive process of orienting to and perceiving stimuli. With regard to television research, this may be measured by visual orientation to the television or "looking" by eye movements, by electrophysiological activity, and by inference through secondary recall and recognition tests (Anderson & Collins, 1988). See Visual Attention.

Attentional Inertia "The maintenance of cognitive involvement across breaks or pauses in comprehension and changes of content" (Anderson & Lorch, 1983, p. 9).

Attribute A characteristic of programming, e.g., when advertising uses a hard-sell tone. See Formal Features.

Audience Involvement The degree to which people personally relate to media content; one dimension of the construct audience activity (Perse, 1990, p. 676). Indications of audience involvement include anticipating viewing (intentionality), attention (focused cognitive effort), elaboration (thinking about content), and engaging in distractions while viewing.

Broadcast Television Refers to any television signal that is transmitted over FCC-regulated and licensed frequencies within the bandwidth of 54 to 890 megahertz. Broadcast television messages may be received by home antenna, or they may be relayed via cable, satellite, or microwave to individual subscribers.

Cable Access Television (CATV) Used to describe the distribution of broadcast, locally originated, or subscription television programming over a coaxial cable or fiber optic network. Such distribution frequently includes locally produced or syndicated programming intended for specialized audiences; also known as narrowcasting.

Catharsis Drive reduction (Feshbach & Singer, 1971, p. 39); "The notion that aggressive impulses can be drained off by exposure to fantasy aggression ..." (Liebert & Sprafkin, 1988, p. 75).

Catharsis Theory Suggests that antisocial behaviors can be reduced by viewing those behaviors on television, e.g., watching fantasy aggression may provide viewers with a means to discharge their pent-up emotions vicariously.

C-Box A recording device consisting of a television set and a video camera that records the viewing area in front of the television set.

Closed-Circuit Television (CCTV) Refers to the transmission of the television signal over a wire or fiber optic medium. The most important aspect of closed-circuit television for education is the ability to distribute a television signal within a school building or district. Also called wire transmission (which includes fiber optic transmission).

Cognitive Processing Refers collectively to the various mental processes involved in perception, attention, semantic encoding, and retrieval of information from memory. Typically used to describe activities associated with learning.

Cohort "A group of people born at the same time, either in the same year or within a specified, limited span of years" (Sigelman & Shaffer, 1995, p. 18).

Commercial Broadcast Stations Stations that are privately owned and supported primarily by commercial advertising revenues.

Communications Satellite Refers to the transmission and reception of a television signal via a geocentric communications satellite. This form of communication link involves the transmission of a television signal to a satellite (uplink) that is placed in a geocentric orbit (one that is synchronized with the rotation of the Earth so as to appear motionless over approximately one-third of the populated planet). The satellite then rebroadcasts the signal to dish-type receiver antennas at other geographic locations (downlink).

Comprehension The extraction of meaning; the first step in critically analyzing any presentation regardless of medium (Anderson, 1983, p. 318). Comprehension may include the ability to recall or recognize content information and to infer story sequence or plot.

Content Indifference The theory that content does not dictate viewing; that, with a few exceptions, other variables have more effect on preferences (Comstock & Paik, 1991, p. 5).

Coviewing Viewing television in the presence of others; viewing in a group of two or more such as with a parent, child, or peers.

Critical Viewer "One who can first grasp the central meaning of a statement, recognize its ambiguities, establish its relationship with other statements, and the like; one who plans television viewing in advance and who evaluates programs while watching" (Anderson, 1983, pp. 313–318).

Critical-Viewing Skills The competencies specified as objectives for television literacy curricula.

Cross-Sectional Method A research method that involves the observation of different groups (or cohorts) at one point in time.

Cued Recall Recall based on questions about specific program details (Berry, 1993, p. 359).

Cultivation Theory Suggests that heavy television viewing over time or viewing images that are critical or intense can lead to perceptions of reality that match those images seen on television instead of those experienced in real life.

Desensitization A decline in emotional arousal or the decreased likelihood of helping victims of violence due to repeated exposure to violent programming.

Disability "Any restriction or lack (resulting from an impairment) of ability to perform an activity in the manner or within the range considered normal for a human being" (Cumberbatch & Negrine, 1992, p. 5).

Disclaimer Aural and/or visual displays designed to delineate an advertised item's actual performance and to dispel misconceptions that might be created by demonstration of a product (Jalongo, 1983, p. 6).

Disinhibition Temporary removal of an inhibition through the action of an unrelated stimulus.

Disinhibitory Effects "The observation of a response of a particular class (for example, an aggressive response) that leads to an increased likelihood of displaying other different responses that belong to the same class" (Liebert & Sprafkin, 1988, p. 71).

Displacement Hypothesis The notion that television influences both learning and social behavior by displacing such activities as reading, family interaction, and social play with peers (Huston et al., 1992, p. 82).

Displacement Theory Other activities are replaced by watching television.

Distractions Alternatives to television viewing such as toys, other children, music, or some combination of these.

Educational Television (ETV) Consists of commercial or public broadcast programming targeted at large audiences over wide geographic areas with the express purpose of providing instruction in a content or developmental area.

Effect Size In meta-analysis studies, "the mean difference between treated and control subjects divided by the standard deviation of the control group" (Hearold, 1986, pp. 75–76). See Meta-analysis.

Ethnic Identity The "attachment to an ethnic group and a positive orientation toward being a member of that group" (Takanishi, 1982, p. 83).

Experience-Sampling Method The use of paging devices to gather data on television activities and experiences.

Exposure Measures Measures of hours of television watched per day or of watching specific content, e.g., frequency of watching news (Gunter, 1987, p. 125).

Family Context for Viewing An environmental context that influences what and when viewing occurs as well as the ways in which viewers interpret what they see (Huston et al., 1992, p. 99); created through the interaction of variables in the home setting that mediate the effects of television, including environment, coviewing, and viewing habits.

Filmic/Cinematic Code Describes the collective formal features of television as a symbol system unique to both film and television (Salomon, 1979).

Formal Features Program attributes that can be defined independently from the content of a program, such as action, pace, and visual techniques (Huston & Wright, 1983). Synonymous with Production Effects or Presentation Variables.

Formative Evaluation Gathering information on the adequacy of an instructional product or program and using this information as a basis for further development (Seels & Richey, 1994).

Free Recall Recall where viewers must recall all they can from a specified program [without cues] (Berry, 1983, p. 359).

Frustration An unpleasant state caused by "delay in reinforcement" (Bandura & Walters, 1963, p. 116).

Functional Displacement Hypothesis One medium will displace another when it performs the function of the displaced medium in a superior manner (Comstock & Paik, 1991, p. 78).

Genre A category of programming having a particular form, content, and purpose as in comedy, news, drama, or music television.

Grazing Quickly sampling a variety of programs using remote controls while viewing.

Household Centrality Dimension reflecting behavior and norms that favor viewing (Comstock & Paik, 1991, p. 69).

Incidental Effects Those behavioral or cognitive outcomes that result as a by-product of the programming. These are usually not planned and may be negative or positive in nature. They may result from observational learning, role modeling, prosocial or antisocial messages, or attitude formation.

Instructional Films/Motion Pictures Motion pictures that have been designed to produce specific learning outcomes through the direct manipulation of the presentation format and sequence.

Instructional Television (ITV) Programming that has as its primary purpose the achievement of specified instructional objectives by students in school settings. In practice, it has usually referred to programming that is formally incorporated into a particular course of study and presented to intact classes or groups of students or trainees.

Instrumental Viewing Watching for information.

Intentional Effects Those mental processes or behaviors that occur as a direct result of organized instructional events or practices and that are generally expected to occur through the viewer's interaction with the television programming.

Interactive Television (ITV) Conferencing technology that allows two-way communication with both video and audio components. Also known as two-way video. Used for distance education and videoconferencing.

Kinescope Medium consisting of a motion picture recording of a live television program, in which the television frame rate was synchronized with the film frame rate.

Learning from Television Changes in knowledge, understanding, attitudes, and behaviors due to the intentional or incidental effects of television programming.

Literacy "One's ability to extract information from coded messages and to express ideas, feelings, and thoughts through them in accepted ways; the mastery of specific mental skills that become cultivated as a response to the specific functional demands of a symbol system" (Salomon, 1982, p. 7).

Longitudinal Method A research method that involves the observation of people or groups repeatedly over time.

Mass Communication "The process of using a mass medium to send messages to large audiences for the purpose of informing, entertaining, persuading" (Vivian, 1991, p. 15).

Mass Media Delivery systems (i.e., television, newspapers, radio) that channel the flow of information to large and diverse audiences and that are characterized by unlimited access and by the vast amount of noncontent-related (incidental) learning that occurs as a byproduct. Generally intended to provide entertainment-oriented programming. See Mass Communication.

Materialism "An orientation emphasizing possession and money for personal happiness and social progress" (Ward & Wackman, 1981, cited in Moore & Moschis, 1982, p. 9).

Media Dependency Relying on the media for information and guidance (Comstock & Paik, 1991, p. 143).

Media Literacy The ability to learn from media; capable of comprehending filmic code. See Literacy and Visual Literacy.

Mediation "Parents or teachers intervening in the television viewing experience by encouraging, discouraging, or discussing viewing" (Lin & Atkin, 1989, p. 54).

Mesmerizing Effect Describes a passive, hypnotic state in the viewer, presumably associated with reduced cognitive processing and high alpha activity (Mander, 1978).

Message "A pattern of signs (words, pictures, gestures) produced for the purpose of modifying the psychomotor, cognitive, or affective behavior of one or more persons" (Fleming & Levie, 1994, p. x).

Message Design "Planning for the manipulation of the physical form of the message" (Grabowski, 1991, p. 206).

Meta-analysis "A statistical approach to summarizing the results of many studies that have investigated basically the same problem" (Gay, 1992, p. 590). See Effect Size.

Microwave Relay Links Technology that employs a series of microwave transmission towers to transmit and relay the television signal. Such transmission is generally used in areas where cable distribution systems are not practical or where television network signals must be transmitted over long distances. Microwave relays are also used to transmit location broadcast signals from remote locations to the television studio for news or public-events coverage.

Monitoring Attention to audio, visual, and social cues as to the desirability of paying attention to the screen (Comstock & Paik, 1991, p. 23).

Montage Television sequence that incorporates formal features to imply changes in space, time, action, mental state, or character point of view (Anderson & Field, 1983, p. 76).

Neutral Behavior Behavior that observers would not describe as being antisocial or prosocial (Hearold, 1986, p. 81).

Norm Belief held by a number of members of a group that the members ought to behave in a certain way under certain circumstances (Holmans, 1961, p. 6).

Oversensitization As a result of overexposure to televised violence, the belief that the world is mean and scary or that the incidence of crime and risk of personal injury are greater than they really are.

Parental Attitude "Parents' perceptions of television's impact on their children" (Sprafkin et al., 1992, p. 103).

Passivity Acted upon rather than acting or causing action.

Presentation Variables See Formal Features.

Processing Capabilities "The ability of a medium to operate on available symbol systems in specified ways; in general, information can be displayed, received, stored, retrieved organized, translated, transformed, and evaluated" (Kozma, 1994, p. 11).

Production Effects See Formal Features.

Prosocial Behavior Behaviors that are socially desirable and that in some way benefit another person or society at large (Rushton, 1979, cited in Liebert & Sprafkin, 1988, p. 228). Includes behaviors such as generosity, helping, nurturing, or delaying gratification.

Public Stations Stations that derive funding from government, public, and philanthropic sources. On such stations, commercial messages are either not aired or are used only for the recognition of the contributor.

Reactive Theory Describes the child as a passive, involuntary processor of information who simply reacts to stimuli (Singer, 1980).

Recall Memory for content and features from television viewing; can be cued or uncued.

Recapping Refers to repeating the most important facts; it is a source redundancy (Son, Reese, & Davie, 1987, p. 208).

Receivership Skills "The comprehension of overt and hidden meanings of messages by analyzing language and visual and aural images, to understand the intended audiences and the intent of the message" (Brown, 1991, p. 70).

Recognition "Refers to the frequency with which a group receives TV roles at all" (Liebert & Sprafkin, 1988, p. 187).

Respect "Refers to how characters behave and are treated once they have roles" (Liebert & Sprafkin, 1988, p. 187).

Ritualistic Viewing Watching for gratification.

Roles "Refers to expectations about activities that are performed and to beliefs and values attributed to performers" (Birenbaum, 1978, pp. 128–129).

Rulemaking Establishing guidelines about acceptable and/or prohibited behavior (Lin & Atkin, 1989, p. 54); "also called restrictive mediation" (Atkin, Greenberg, & Baldwin, 1991, p. 43).

Salience Highlighting certain components of the program for viewers through formal or production features; perceptual salience may elicit and maintain attention and influence comprehension by aiding in selection of content (Huston & Wright, 1983, p. 44).

Schemata "Conceptual frames of reference that provide organizational guidelines for newly encoded information about people and social or behavioral roles and events; they can be important mediators of learning" (Taylor & Crocker, 1981, cited in Gunter, 1987, p. 65).

Self-Control "Specific kinds of prosocial action, including a willingness to work and wait for long-term goals, as well as the ability to resist the temptation to cheat, steal, or lie" (Liebert & Sprafkin, 1988, p. 229).

Sequential Method A research method that combines cross-sectional and longitudinal approaches by observing different groups at multiple points in time.

Sex Role "Refers to the collection of behaviors or activities that a given society deems more appropriate to members of one sex than to members of the other sex" (Durkin, 1985, p. 9).

Socialization Learning the values, norms, language, and behaviors needed to function in a group or society; socialization agents often include mass media, parents, peers, and the school (Moore & Moschis, 1982, p. 4). Learning over time how to function in a group or society by assimilating a set of paradigms, rules, procedures, and principles that govern perception, attention, choices, learning, and development (Doff, 1982).

Social Learning Theory (1) Acquiring symbolic representations through observation. (2) Learning through imitation of observed behavior (Bandura & Walters, 1963).

Stereotype "A generalization based on inadequate or incomplete information" (Stern & Robinson, 1994), "A group is said to be stereotyped whenever it is depicted or portrayed in such a way that all its members appear to have the same set of characteristics, attitudes, or life conditions" (Liebert & Sprafkin, p. 189).

Summative Evaluation "Involves gathering information on adequacy and using this information to make decisions about utilization" (Seels & Richey, 1994, p. 134).

Symbol Systems Sets of symbolic expressions by which information is communicated about a field of reference, e.g., spoken language, printed text, pictures, numerals and formulae, musical scores, performed, music, maps, or graphs (Goodman, 1976, cited in Kozma, 1994, p. 11).

Technology "The physical, mechanical, or electronic capabilities of a medium that determine its function and, to some extent, its shape and other features" (Kozma, 1994, p. 11).

Television Literacy Understanding television programming, including how it is produced and broadcast, familiarity with the formats used, ability to recognize overt and covert themes of programs and commercial messages, and appreciation of television as an art form (Corder-Bolz, 1982, cited in Williams, 1986, p. 418). Also see Critical-Viewing Skills.

Video Production Producing television programming in the community or schools.

Videotape Format generally used today to record and play back video programming. It consists of an oxide-coated roll of acetate, polyester, or Mylar tape on which a magnetized signal is placed.

Viewing Visual attention to what is taking place on the screen (Comstock & Paik, 1991, p. 22).

Viewing Environment A social context created by the interaction of variables, such as the number and placement of sets, toys, and other media, other activities, rules, and parental communication.

Viewing Experience Result of interaction of programming, mediating variables, and outcomes; variously described as active or passive and positive or negative. See Viewing System.

Viewing Habits When and what children watch and for how long as determined by the amount of time a child spends in front of a television set, program preferences, and identification with characters (Sprafkin et al., 1992, p. 23).

Viewing Patterns Content preferences of viewers.

Viewing System Components of the viewing process, including programming, environment, and behavior and their interaction. See Viewing Experience.

Violence "The overt expression of physical force against others or self, or the compelling of action against one's will on pain of being hurt or killed" (NIMH, 1972, p. 3).

Visual Attention "Visual orientation (eyes directed towards the screen) and visual fixation (precise location on the screen toward which eyes are directed given visual orientation)" (Anderson & Lorch, 1983, p. 2).

Visual Literacy The ability to understand and use images, including the ability to think, learn, and express oneself in terms of images (Braden & Hortin, 1982, p. 41). See Media Literacy.

Zapping Changing channels quickly using a remote control.

ACKNOWLEDGMENTS

The authors would like to acknowledge the significant contribution that our reviewers have made to this article: Keith Mielke, senior research fellow, Children's Television Workshop; Marge Cambre, associate professor, Ohio State University; and Dave Jonassen, professor, Pennsylvania State University. In addition, Mary Sceiford of the Corporation for Public Broadcasting and Ray McKelvey of the Agency for Instructional Technology gave valuable advice. Barbara Minor assisted with searching through the resources of the Educational Clearinghouse on Information Resources (ERIC). Many students at the University of Pittsburgh also helped with the research.

References

Ableman, R. (1999). Preaching to the choir: Profiling TV advisory ratings users. *Journal of Broadcasting and Electronic Media, 43*(4), 529-550.

Ableman, R., & Rogers, A. (1987). From "plug-in drug" to "magic window": The role of television in special education. Paper presented at the Seventh Annual World Conference on Gifted Education, Salt Lake City, UT.

Ableman, R., & Courtright, J. (1983). Television literacy: Amplifying the cognitive level effects of television's prosocial fare through curriculum intervention. *Journal of Research and Development in Education, 17*(1), 46-57.

Academy of Television Arts and Sciences in cooperation with D. G. and J. L. Singer (1994). *Creating critical viewers: A partnership between schools and television professionals.* Denver, CO: Pacific Mountain Network.

Adgate, B. (1999 July 21). Market research kids and TV, past, present and future, part 3. *Reports/Selling to Kids.* Retrieved from www.mediachannel.org

Adler, R. P., Lesser, G. S., Meringoff, L. K., Robertson, T. S., Rossiter, J. R. & Ward, S. (1980). *The effects of television advertising on children: review and recommendations.* Lexington, MA: Lexington.

Agency for Instructional Television (1984). *Formative evaluation of "taxes influence behavior" (lesson #2) from "Tax whys: understanding taxes," Research Report 91.* Bloomington, IN: Agency for Instructional Television. (ERIC Document Reproduction Service No. ED 249 974.)

Agency for Instructional Television (1984, Jun.) *"It figures": A survey of users. Research report* 91. Bloomington, IN: Agency for Instructional Television. (ERIC Document Reproduction Service No. ED 249 975.)

Ahmed, D. (1983). *Television in Pakistan.* Unpublished doctoral dissertation. New York: Columbia University Teacher's College.

Aicinena, S. (1999). *One hundred and two days of "Sportscenter": Messages of poor sportsmanship, violence and immorality.* (ERIC Document Reproduction Service No. ED 426 998.)

Alexander, A., Ryan, M., & Munoz, P. (1984). Creating a learning context: investigations on the interactions of siblings during television viewing. *Critical Studies in Mass Communication, 1,* 345-364.

Allen, C. L. (1965). Photographing the TV audience. *Journal of Advertising Research, 28*(1), 2-8.

Allen, T. (2002, June 21). Out of focus. Numbers indicate little has changed for African Americans in broadcasting journalism. *The Call Internet Edition.* Retrieved October 10, 2002, from httl://www.kccall.com/News/2002/0621/Front_Page/006.html

Alwitt, L., Anderson, D., Lorch, E., & Levin, S. (1980). Preschool children's visual attention to television. *Human Communication Research, 7,* 52-67.

Anderson, B., Mead, M., & Sullivan, S. (1988). *Television: What do national assessment results tell us?* Princeton, NJ: National Assessment of Educational Progress, Educational Testing Service. (ERIC Document Reproduction Service No. ED 277 072.)

Anderson, D., & Field, D. (1983). Children's attention to television: Implications for production. In M. Meyer (Ed.), *Children and the formal features of television* (pp. 56-96). Munich: Saur.

Anderson, D., Alwitt, L., Lorch, E., & Levin, S. (1979). Watching children watch television. In G. Hale & M. Lewis (Eds.), *Attention and cognitive development* (pp. 331-361). New York: Plenum.

Anderson, D., Levin, S., & Lorch, E. (1977). The effects of TV program pacing on the behavior of preschool children. *AV Communication Review, 25,* 159-166.

Anderson, D., Lorch, E., Field, D. & Sanders, J. (1981). The effects of TV program comprehensibility on preschool children's visual attention to television. *Child Development, 52,* 151-157.

Anderson, D., Lorch, E., Field, D., Collins, P., & Nathan, J. (1986). Television viewing at home: age trends in visual attention and time with television. *Child Development, 57,* 1024-1033.

Anderson, D., Lorch, E., Smith, R., Bradford, R., & Levin, S. (1981). Effects of peer presence on preschool children's visual attention to television. *Developmental Psychology, 17,* 446-453.

Anderson, D. R., & Collins, P. A. (1988). *The impact on children's education: Television's influence on cognitive development.* Washington, DC: U.S. Department of Education, Office of Educational Research and Improvement. (ERIC Document Reproduction Service No. ED 295 271.)

Anderson, D. R., Huston, A. C., Schmitt, K. L., Linebarger, D. L., & Wright, J. C. (2001). Early childhood television viewing and adolescent behavior: The recontact study. *Monographs of the Society for Research in Child Development, 66*(1), 1–147.

Anderson, D. R., & Levin, S. R. (1976). Young children's attention to "Sesame Street." *Child Development, 47,* 806–811.

Anderson, D. R., Levin, S. R., & Lorch, E. P. (1977). The effects of TV program pacing on the behavior of preschool children. *AV Communication Review, 25,* 159–166.

Anderson, D. R., & Lorch, E. P. (1983). Looking at television: action or reaction. *In* J. Bryant & D. R. Anderson, eds. *Children's understanding of television: Research on attention and comprehension* (pp. 1–34). San Diego, CA: Academic.

Anderson, J. A. (1980). The theoretical lineage of critical viewing curricula. *Journal of Communication, 30*(3), 64–70.

Anderson, J. A. (1981). Receivership skills: an educational response. In M. Ploghoft & J. A. Anderson (Eds.), *Education for the television age* (pp. 19–27). Springfield, IL: Thomas.

Anderson, J. A. (1983). Television literacy and the critical viewer. In J. Bryant & D. R. Anderson (Eds.), *Children's understanding of television: research on attention and comprehension* (pp. 297–330). San Diego, CA: Academic.

Anderson, J. R. (1980). *Cognitive psychology and its implications.* San Francisco, CA: Freeman.

Anderson, R. E., Crespo, C. J., Bartlett, S. J., et. al. (1998 August). Relationship of television watching with body weight and level of fatness among children. *Southern Medical Journal, 91*(8), 789–793. Retrieved from http://jama.ama-assn.org/issues/v79n12/rfull/joc71873.html

Appel, V., Weinstein, S., & Weinstein, C. (1979). Brain activity and recall of TV advertising. *Journal of Advertising Research, 19*(4), 7–15.

Argenta, D. M., Stoneman, Z., & Brody, G. H. (1986). The effects of three different television programs on young children's peer interactions and toy play. *Journal of Applied Developmental Psychology, 7,* 355–371.

Armstrong, C. A., et al. (1998 July–August). Children's television viewing, body fat, and physical fitness. *Journal of Health Promotion, 12*(6), 363–368.

Atkin, C. K., Murray, J. P., & Nayman, O. B. (1971–72). The surgeon general's research program on television and social behavior: a review of empirical findings. *Journal of Broadcasting, 16*(1), 21–35.

Atkin, D. J., Greenberg, B. S., & Baldwin, T. F. (1991). The home ecology of children's television viewing: parental mediation and the new video environment. *Journal of Communication, 41*(3), 40–52.

Atkinson, R. C., & Shiffrin, R. M. (1968). Human memory: a proposed system and its control processes. In K. W. Spence & J. T. Spence (Eds.), *The psychology of learning and motivation: advances in research and theory, Vol. 2* (pp. 89–193). San Diego, CA: Academic.

Atman, I., & Wohlwill, J. F. (Eds.) (1978). *Children and environment* New York: Plenum.

Austin, E. W., Bolls, P. Fujioka, Y., & Engelbertson, J. (1999). How and why parents take on the tube. *Journal of Broadcasting and Electronic Media, 43*(2), 175–192.

Ball, S., & Bogatz, G. A. (1970). *The first year of Sesame Street: An evaluation.* Princeton, NJ: Educational Testing Service.

Bandura, A. (1965). Influence of models' reinforcement contingencies on the acquisition of imitative responses. *Journal of Personality and Social Psychology, 1,* 585–595.

Bandura, A. (1971). Analysis of modeling processes. In Bandura, A., ed. *Psychological modeling: conflicting theories* (pp. 1–62). Chicago, IL: Aldine Atherton.

Bandura, A. (1977). *Social learning theory.* Englewood Cliffs, NJ: Prentice Hall.

Bandura, A. (1986). *Social foundations of thought and action: a social cognitive theory.* Englewood Cliffs, NJ: Prentice Hall.

Bandura, A., & Walters, R. H. (1963). *Social learning and personality development.* New York: Holt, Rinehart & Winston.

Bandura, A., Ross, D. & Ross, S. A. (1961). Transmission of aggression through imitation of aggressive models. *Journal of Abnormal and Social Psychology, 63*(3), 575–82.

Bandura, A., Ross, D., & Ross, S. A. (1963). Imitation of film-mediated aggressive models. *Journal of Abnormal and Social Psychology, 66*(1), 3–11.

Baron, L. (1980). *What do children really see on television?* Paper presented at the annual meeting of the American Educational Research Association, Boston, MA.

Baughman, J. L. (1985). *Television's guardians: the FCC and the politics of programming* 1958–1967. Knoxville, TN: University of Tennessee Press.

Bechtel, R. P., Achepohl, C., & Akers, R. (1972). Correlates between observed behavior and questionnaire responses on television viewing. In E. A. Rubinstein, G. A. Comstock & J. P. Murray (Eds.), *Television and social behavior: Vol. 4. Television in day-to-day life: Patterns of use* (pp. 274–344). Washington, DC: Government Printing Office.

Becker, S., & Wolfe, G. (1960). Can adults predict children's interest in a television program? In W. Schramm (Ed.), *The impact of educational television* (pp. 195–213). Urbana, IL: University of Illinois Press.

Beentjes, J. W. J. (1989). Learning from television and books: A Dutch replication study based on Salomon's model. *Educational Technology Research and Development, 37,* 47–58.

Beentjes, J. W. J., & Van der Voort, T. H. A. (1988). Television's impact on children's reading skills: a review of research. *Reading Research Quarterly 23(4),* 389–413.

Bell, J. (1984). *"TV's sort of . . . just there": Critical television viewing skills* (ERIC Document Reproduction Service No. ED 249 945.)

Bell, J. (1991, Jun.) *The elderly on television: Changing stereotypes.* Paper presented at the Annual Visual Communication Conference, Brackenridge, CO. (ERIC Document Reproduction Service No. ED 337 836.)

Belland, J. (1994). Is this the news? In A. De Vaney (Ed.), *Watching channel one: The convergence of students, technology, and private business.* Albany, NY SUNY Press.

Berger, A. A. (1982). Televaccinations. [Review of: *Television: a family focus; critical television viewing; inside television: a guide to critical viewing;* and *critical television viewing skills*]. *Journal of Communication 32*(1), 213–215.

Berlyne, D. E. (1960). *Conflict, arousal, and curiosity.* New York: McGraw-Hill.

Berry, C. (1982). Research perspectives on the portrayals of Afro-American families on television. In A. Jackson (Ed.), *Black families and the medium of television* (pp. 147–159). Ann Arbor, MI: Bush Program in Child Development & Social Policy, University of Michigan.

Berry, C. (1983). Learning from television news: A critique of the research. *Journal of Broadcasting, 27,* 359–370.

Berry, G. L., & Asamen, J. K. (2001) Television, children, and multicultural awareness: Comprehending the medium in a complex multimedia society. In D. G. & J. L. Singer (Eds.), *Handbook of Children and the Media* (pp. 359–373). Thousand Oaks, CA: Sage Publications.

Bickham, D. S., Wright, J. C., & Huston, A. C. (2000). Attention, comprehension, and the educational influences of television. In D. G. & J. L. Singer (Eds.), *Handbook of Children and the Media* (pp. 101–120). Thousand Oaks, CA: Sage Publications.

Birenbaum, A. (1978). Status and role. In E. Sagan, ed. *Sociology: The basic concepts* (pp. 128–139). New York: Holt, Rinehart & Winston.

Bogatz, G. A., & Ball, S. (1971). *The second year of Sesame Street: a continuing evaluation, Vols. 1,2.* Princeton, NJ: Educational Testing Service. (ERIC Document Reproduction Service Nos. ED 122 800, ED 122 801.)

Bolton, R. N. (1983). Modeling the impact of television food advertising on children's diets. In J. H. Leigh & C. R. Martin, Jr. (Eds.), *Current issues and research in advertising.* Ann Arbor, MI: Graduate School of Business Administration, University of Michigan.

Bossing, L., & Burgess, L. B. (1984). *Television viewing: Its relationship to reading achievement of third-grade students* (ERIC Document Reproduction Services No. ED 252 816.)

Botta, R. A. (1999, Spring). Television images and adolescent girls' body image disturbance. *Journal of Communication, 49*(2), 22–41.

Botta, R. A. (2000, Summer). The mirror of television: A comparison of black and white adolescents' body image. *Journal of Communication, 50*(3), 144–159.

Bower, R. T. (1985). *The changing television audience in America.* New York: Columbia University Press.

Bowie, M. M. (1986, Jan.). *Instructional film research and the learner.* Paper presented at the Annual Convention of the Association for Educational Communications and Technology, Las Vegas, NV. (ERIC Document Reproduction Service No. ED 267 757.)

Braden, R. A., & Hortin, J. L. (1982). Identifying the theoretical foundations of visual literacy. *Journal of Visual/Verbal Languaging, 2,* 37–42.

Bred, D. J., & Cantor, J. (1988). The portrayal of men and women in U.S. television commercials: a recent content analysis and trends over 15 years. *Sex Roles, 18*(9/10), 595–609.

Broadbent, D. (1958). *Perception and communication.* London: Pergamon.

Brown, J. A. (1991). *Television "critical viewing skills" education: Major media literacy projects in the United States and selected countries.* Hillsdale, NJ: Erlbaum.

Brown, J. D., Childers, K. E., & Koch, C. C. (1990). The influence of new media and family structure on young adolescents' television and radio use. *Communication Research, 17*(1), 65–82.

Brown, J. R., & Linne, 0. (1976). The family as a mediator of television's effects. In R. Brown (Ed.), *Children and television* (pp. 184–198). Beverly Hills, CA: Sage.

Bryant, J. (1992).*Examining the effects of television program pacing on children's cognitive development.* Paper presented at the U.S. Department of Health and Human Service, Administration for Children and Families' Conference on "Television and the preparation of the mind for learning: critical questions on the effects of television on the developing brains of young children," Washington, DC.

Bryant, J., & Anderson, D. R. (Eds.) (1983). *Children's understanding of television: Research on attention and comprehension* San Diego, CA: Academic.

Bryant, J., & Zillmann, D., eds. (1991). *Responding to the screen: Reception and reaction processes.* Hillsdale, NJ: Erlbaum.

Bryant, J., Zillmann, D. & Brown, D. (1983). Entertainment features in children's educational television: effects on attention and information acquisition. In J. Bryant & D. R. Anderson (Eds.), *Children's understanding of television: research on attention and comprehension* (pp. 221–240). San Diego, CA: Academic.

Bryce, JW., & Leichter, H. J. (1983). The family and television. *Journal of Family Issues, 4,* 309–328.

Bushman, B. J. (1998, December). Effects of television violence on memory for commercial messages. *Journal of Experimental Psychology Applied, 4*(4), 291–307.

Bushman, B. J., & Huesmann, L. R. (2001). Effects of televised violence on aggression. In D. G. & J. L. Singer (Eds.), *Handbook of Children and the Media* (pp. 223–254). Thousand Oaks, CA: Sage Publications.

Butler, T. P. (2001). Cable in the classroom: A versatile resources. *Book Report, 19*(5), 50–53. (ERIC Document Reproduction No. ED 413 4212.)

Bybee, C., Robinson, D., & Turow, J. (1982). Determinants of parental guidance of children's television viewing for a special subgroup: mass media scholars. *Journal of Broadcasting, 16,* 697–710.

Cairns, E. (1990). Impact of television news exposure on children's perceptions of violence in Northern Ireland. *Journal of Social Psychology, 130*(4), 447–452.

Calvert, S., Huston, A., Watkins, B., & Wright, J. (1982), The effects of selective attention to television forms on children's comprehension of content. *Child Development, 53,* 601–610.

Calvert, S. L., et al. (1997). *Educational and prosocial programming on Saturday morning television.* Paper presented at the Biennial Meeting of the Society for Research in Child Development (62cd) in Washington, DC. April 3–6, 1997. (ERIC Document Reproduction Service No. ED 406 062.)

Cambre, M. A. (1987). *A reappraisal of instructional television* ERIC Clearinghouse on Information Resources. Syracuse, NY. Syracuse University.

Campbell, D. T., & Stanley, J. C. (1963). *Experimental and quasi-experimental designs for research* Chicago, IL: Rand McNally.

Cantor, J. (2001). The media and children's fears, anxieties, and perceptions of danger. In D. G. & J. L. Singer (Eds.), *Handbook of Children and the Media,* (pp. 207–221). Thousand Oaks, CA: Sage Publications.

Cantor, J., & Nathanson, A. I. (1996). Children's fright reactions to television news. *Journal of Communication, 46*(4), 139–152.

Carew, J. (1980). Experience and the development of intelligence in young children at home and in day care. *Monographs of the Society for Research in Child Development, 45*(187), 1–89.

Carlisle, R. D. B. (1987). *Video at work in American schools.* Bloomington, IN: Agency for Instructional Technology.

Carpenter, C. R., & Greenhill, L. P. (1955). *Instructional television research project number one: An investigation of closed circuit television for reaching university courses.* University Park, PA: Pennsylvania State University.

Carpenter, C. R., & Greenhill, L. P. (1956). *Instructional film reports, Vol. 2* (Technical Report No. 269-7-61). Port Washington, NY. Special Devices Center, U.S. Navy.

Carpenter, C. R., & Greenhill, L. P. (1958). *Instructional television research. Report No. 2.* University Park, PA: Pennsylvania State University.

Carrozza, F., & Jochums, B. (1979, Apr.). A *summary of the "Think-About" cluster evaluation: collection information.* Bloomington, IN: Agency for Instructional Television. (ERIC Document Reproduction Service No. ED 249 947.)

Cennarno, K. S. (1993). Learning from video: Factors influencing learner's preconceptions and invested mental effort. *Educational Technology Research and Development, 41*(3), 33–45.

Center for the New American Dream. (2001). Just the facts about advertising and marketing to children. *Kids and Commercialism* [On-line]. Retrieved from http://www.newdream.org/campaign/kids/facts.html

Chapman, D. (1960). *Design for ETV: planning for schools with television.* (rev. by F. Carioti, 1968). New York: Educational Facilities.

Charren, P., & Sandler, M. (1983). *Changing channels: Living (sensibly) with television.* Reading, MA: Addison-Wesley.

Chen, M. (1994a). *The smart parent's guide to KIDS' TV* San Francisco, CA: KQED.

Chen, M. (1994b). Television and informal science education: Assessing the past, present, and future of research. In V. Crane, H. Nicholson, M. Chen, & S. Bitgood (Eds.), *Informal science learning: What the research says about television, science museums, and community-based projects* (pp. 15-60). Dedham, MA: Research Communications.

Chen, M. (1994c). Six myths about television and children. *Media Studies Journal, 8*(4), 105-114.

Chen, M., Ellis, J., & Hoelscher, K. (1988). Repurposing children's television for the classroom: teachers' use of "square one" TV videocassettes. *Educational Communications and Technology Journal, 36*(3), 161-178.

Children's Television Workshop. (1994, Oct.). *Ghostwriter and youth-serving organizations: Report to Carnegie Corporation of New York.* New York: Children's Television Workshop.

Children's Television Workshop. (1989). Sesame Street research bibliography: selected citations relating to Sesame Street 1969-1989. New York: Author.

Christopher, F. S., Fabes, R. A., & Wilson, P. M. (1989). Family television viewing: Implications for family life education. *Family Relations, 38*(2), 210-214.

Chu, G., & Schramm, W. (1967). *Learning from television: What the research says.* Stanford, CA: Institute for Communications Research.

Clark, R. E. (1983). Reconsidering research on learning from media. *Review of Educational Research, 53*(4), 445-459.

Clark, R. E. (1994). Media will never influence learning. *Educational Technology Research and Development, 42*(2), 21-29.

Clifford, B. R., Gunter, B., & McAleer, J. (1995). *Television and children: Program evaluation, comprehension, and impact.* Hillsdale, NJ: Lawrence Erlbaum Associates.

Coates, B., & Pusser, H. E. (1975). Positive reinforcement and punishment in "Sesame Street' and "Mister Rogers." *Journal of Broadcasting, 19*(2), 143-151.

Coates, B., & Pusser, H. E., & Goodman, I. (1976). The influence of "Sesame Street" and "Mister Rogers' Neighborhood" on children's social behavior in preschool. *Child Development, 47,* 138-144.

Cohen, P. A., Ebeling, B., & Kulik, J. (1981). A meta-analysis of outcome studies of visual-based instruction. *Educational Communications and Technology Journal, 29*(1), 26-36.

Collett, P. (1986). Watching the TV audience. Paper presented at the International Television Studies Conference, London. (ERIC Document Reproduction Service No. ED 293 498.)

Collins, W. A. (1983). Interpretation and inference in children's television viewing. In J. Bryant & D. R. Anderson (Eds.), *Children's understanding of television: Research on attention and comprehension.* San Diego, CA: Academic.

Comstock, G. (1980). New emphases in research on the effects of television and film violence. In E. L. Palmer & A. Dorr (Eds.), *Children and the faces of television.* New York: Academic.

Comstock, G., Chaffee, S., Katzman, N., McCombs, M., & Roberts, D. (1978). *Television and human behavior.* New York: Columbia University Press.

Comstock, G., & Cobbey, R.E. (1982). Television and the children of ethnic minorities: Perspectives from research. In G. L. Berry & C. Mitchell-Kernan (Eds.), *Television and the socialization of the minority child* (pp. 245-259). San Diego, CA: Academic.

Comstock, G., & Paik, H. (1987). *Television and children: a review of recent research.* JR-71). Syracuse, NY. ERIC Clearinghouse on Information Resources.

Comstock, G., & Paik, H. (1991). *Television and the American child.* San Diego, CA: Academic.

Comer, J. (1982). The importance of television images of black families. In A. Jackson (Ed.), *Black families and the medium of television* (pp. 19-25). Ann Arbor, MI: Bush Program in Child Development & Social Policy, University of Michigan.

Corn-Revere, R. (1997). Policy analysis: Regulation in newspeak: The FCC's children's television rules [On-line]. Retrieved from http://www.cato.org/pubs/pas/pa-268.html

Corporation for Public Broadcasting & National Center for Educational Statistics. (1984, May). *School utilization study, 1982-83: Executive summary.* Washington, DC: Author. (ERIC Document Reproduction Service No. ED 248 832.)

Corporation for Public Broadcasting & National Center for Educational Statistics (1988). *TV tips for parents: Using television to help your child learn.* Washington, DC: Corporation for Public Broadcasting. (ERIC Document Reproduction Service No. 299 946.)

Corporation for Public Broadcasting & National Center for Educational Statistics. (1993, Nov.). Kids and television in the nineties: Responses from the Youth Monitor. *CPB Research Notes No. 64.*

Corporation for Public Broadcasting & National Center for Educational Statistics. (1996). Highlights of the public television programming survey: Fiscal year 1996 (CPB Research Notes, No. 106). Washington, DC: Corporation for Public Broadcasting. (ERIC Document Reproduction No. ED 421 958.)

Corporation for Public Broadcasting & National Center for Educational Statistics. (n.d.). *Summary report: Study of school uses of television and video* 1990-1991 *School Year* Washington, DC: Author.

Corporation for Public Broadcasting & National Center for Educational Statistics. (n.d.). *Technical report of the 1991 study of school uses of television and video.* Washington, DC: Author.

Corteen, R. S., & Williams, T. M. (1986). Television and reading skills. In T. M. Williams (Ed.), *The impact of television: A natural experiment in three communities* (pp. 39-86). San Diego, CA: Academic.

Craig, R. S. (1991). *A content analysis comparing gender images in network television commercials aired in daytime, evening, and weekend telecasts.* (ERIC Document Reproduction Service No. ED 329 217.)

Cronbach, L. J., & Snow, R. E. (1977). *Aptitudes and instructional methods.* New York: Irvington.

Cuban, L. (1986). *Teachers and machines: the classroom use of technology since 1920.* New York: Teachers College Press, Columbia University.

Cumberbatch, C., & Negrine, R. (1992). *Images of disability on television.* London: Routledge.

Dambrot, F. H., Reep, D. C., & Bell, D. (1988). Television and sex roles in the 1980's: Do viewers' sex and sex role orientation change the picture? *Sex Roles, 19*(5-6), 387-401.

Davis, D. M. (1990). Portrayals of women in prime-time network television: Some demographic characteristics. *Sex Roles, 23*(5-6), 325-331.

Davis, S., & Mares, M-L. (1998 Summer). Effects of talk show viewing on adolescents. *Journal of Communication, 48*(3).

Debold, E. (1990). *Children's attitudes towards mathematics and the effects of square one: Vol. 111. Children's problem solving behavior and their attitudes towards mathematics: A study of the effects of square one TV.* New York: Children's Television Workshop.

Dee, J. (1985). *Myths and mirrors: A qualitative analysis of images of violence against women in mainstream advertising.* (ERIC Document Reproduction Service No. Ed 292 139.)

Desmond, R. J., Singer, J. L., & Singer, D. G. (1990). Family mediation: Parental communication patterns and the influence of television on children. In J. Bryant, (Ed.), *Television and the American Family* (pp. 293-310). Hillsdale, NJ: Erlbaum.

De Vaney, A. (Ed.) (1594). *Watching channel one: The convergence of students, technology and private business.* New York: SUNY Press.

Dignam, M. (1977, Jun.). *Research on the use of television in secondary schools. Research report 48*. Bloomington, IN: Agency for Instructional Television. (ERIC Document Reproduction Service No. ED 156 166.)

Dirr, P., & Pedone, R. (1978, Jan.). A national report on the use of instructional television. *AV Instruction,* 11–13.

Donohue, T.R., Henke, L. L., & Meyer, T. P. (1983). Learning about television commercials: The impact of instructional units on children's perceptions of motive and intent. *Journal of Broadcasting, 27*(3), 251–261.

Dorr, A. (1982). Television and its socialization influences on minority children. In G. L. Berry & C. Mitchell-Kernan (Eds.), *Television and the socialization of the minority child* (pp. 15–35). San Diego, CA: Academic.

Dorr, A., Kovaric, P., & Doubleday, C. (1989). Parent-child coviewing of television. *Journal of Broadcasting & Electronic Media, 33*(1), 15–51.

Dubeck, L. W., Moshier, S. E., & Boss, J. E. (1988). *Science in cinema.* New York: Teachers College Press, Columbia University.

Dumont, M. (1976). [Letter to the editor]. *American Journal of Psychiatry, 133.*

Duncum, P. (1999). A case for an art education of everyday aesthetic experiences. *A Journal of Issues and Research, 40*(4), 295–311.

DuRant, R. H., & Baranowski, T. (October 1999). The relationship among television watching, physical activity, and body composition of young children. *Pediatrics, 94*(4), 449–456.

Durkin, K. (1985). *Television, sex roles, and children.* Philadelphia: Open University Press.

Edwardson, M., Grooms, D., & Pringle, R (1976). Visualization and TV news information gain. *Journal of Broadcasting, 20*(3), 373–380.

Elkind, D. (1984). *All grown up and no place to go: Teenagers in crisis.* Reading, MA: Addison-Wesley.

Elkoff, J. (1999 March). Predictors of the regulation of children's television and video viewing as reported by highly educated mothers. *Dissertation Abstracts International, 59*(9-B), 5165. (University Microfilms No. AAM99-08268.)

Ellery, J. B. (1959). *A pilot study of the nature of aesthetic experiences associated with television and its place in education.* Detroit, MI: Wayne State University.

Emery, M., & Emery, F. (1975). *A choice of futures: To enlighten and inform.* Canberra, Australia: Center for Continuing Education, Australian National University.

Emery, M., & Emery, F. (1980). The vacuous vision: The TV medium. *Journal of the University Film Association, 32,* 27–32.

Engelhardt, T. (1995). *The end of victory culture: Cold war America and the disillusioning of a generation.* NY: Basic Books/HarperCollins.

Eron, L. D. (1982). Parent child interaction: Television violence and aggression of children. *American Psychologist, 37,* 197–211.

Fairchild, H. H., Stockard, R., & Bowman, R (1986). Impact of roots: Evidence of the national survey of black Americans. *Journal of Black Studies, 16,* 307–318.

Featherman, G., Frieser, D., Greenspun, D., Harris, B., Schulman, D., & Crown, R (1979). *Electroencephalographic and electrooculographic correlates of television watching.* Final Technical Report. Hampshire College, Amherst, MA.

Feshbach, S., & Singer, R. D. (1971). *Television and aggression.* San Francisco, CA: Jossey-Bass.

Feder, M. (1984). Television viewing and school achievement. *Journal of Communication, 34*(2), 104–118.

Feder, M., & Carlson, D. (1982). *California assessment program surveys of television and achievement.* New York: Annual Meeting of the American Educational Research Association, March. (ERIC Document Reproduction Services No. ED 217 876.)

Federman, J. (Ed.). (1998). *National television violence study, volume 3, executive summary.* Santa Barbara, CA: University of California Center for Communication and Social Policy.

Field, D. (1983). *Children's television viewing strategies.* Paper presented at the Society for Research in Child Development, biennial meeting, Detroit, MI.

Fisch, S., Cohen, D., McCann, S. & Hoffman, L. (1993, Jan.). *"Square one" TV—Research history and bibliography.* New York: Children's Television Workshop.

Fisch, S. M., Hall, E. R., Esty, E. T., Debold, E., Miller, B. A., Bennett, D. T., & Solan, S. V. (1991). *Children's problem solving behavior and their attitudes towards mathematics: A study of the effects of square one TV Vol. V Executive summary.* New York: Children's Television Workshop.

Fite, K. V. (1994). *Television and the brain: A review.* New York: Children's Television Workshop.

Fitzgerald, T. K. (1992). Media, ethnicity and identity. In R Scannell, P. Schlesinger & C. Sparks (Eds.), *Culture and power: A media, culture & society reader* (pp. 112–133). Beverly Hills, CA: Sage.

Flagg, B. N. (1990). *Formative evaluation for educational technologies.* Hillsdale, NJ: Erlbaum.

Fleming, M., & Levie, W. H. (Eds.). (1978). *Instructional message design: Principles from the behavioral sciences.* Englewood Cliffs, NJ: Educational Technology.

Fleming, M., & Levie, W. H. (Eds.). (1993). *Instructional message design: Principles from the behavioral sciences* (2d ed.). Englewood Cliffs, NJ: Educational Technology.

Fleming, M. (1967). Classification and analysis of instructional illustrations. *Audio-visual Communication Review, 15*(3), 246–258.

Forge, K. L. S., & Phemister, S. (1982). Effect of prosocial cartoons on preschool children (unpublished report). (ERIC Document Reproduction Service No. ED 262 905.)

Forsdale, J. R., & Forsdale, L. (1970). Film literacy. *AV Communication Review, 18*(3), 263–276.

Frank, R. E., & Greenberg, M.G. (1979). Zooming in on TV audiences. *Psychology Today, 13*(4), 92–103, 114.

Frazer, C. F. (1976). *A symbolic interactionist approach to child television viewing.* Unpublished doctoral dissertation. University of Illinois at Urbana, Champaign, IL.

Friedrich, L. K., & Stein, A. H., (1973). Aggressive and prosocial television programs and the natural behavior of preschool children. *Monographs of the Society for Research in Child Development, 38*(4, serial no. 151).

Gadbeny, S. (1980). Effects of restricting first-graders' TV viewing on leisure time use, IQ change, and cognitive style. *Journal of Applied Developmental Psychology, 1,* 45–58.

Gaddy, G. D. (1986). Television's impact on high school achievement. *Public Opinion Quarterly, 50,* 340–359.

Gantz, W., & Weaver, J. P. (1984). *Parent-child communication about television: a view from the parent's perspective.* Paper presented at the annual convention of the Association for Education in Journalism and Mass Communication, Gainesville, FL. (ERIC Document Reproduction Service No. ED 265 840.)

Gardner, H. (1982). *Art, mind and brain: A cognitive approach to creativity.* New York: Basic Books.

Gardner, H., Howard, V. A., & Perkins, D. (1974). Symbol systems: A philosophical, psychological and educational investigation. In D. Olson (Ed.), *Media and symbols: The forms of expression, communication and education* (73d annual yearbook of the National Society for the Study of Education). Chicago, IL: University of Chicago Press.

Gay, L. R. (1992). *Educational research: Competencies for analysis and application.* (4th ed.). New York: Merrill.

Gomez, G. O. (1986, Jul.). *Research on cognitive effects of non-educational TV—an epistemological discussion.* London. International Television Studies Conference. (ERIC Document Reproduction Service No. ED 294 534.)

Goodman, N. (1968). *Languages of art.* Indianapolis, IN: Hackett.

Gom, G. J., & Goldberg, M.E. (1982). Behavioral evidence of the effects of televised food messages on children. *Journal of Consumer Research, 9,* 200-205.

Gortmaker, S. L., Salter, C. A., Walker, D. K., & Dietz, W. H. Jr. (1990). The impact of television viewing on mental aptitude and achievement: a longitudinal study. *Public Opinion Quarterly, 54,* 594-604.

Gotthelf, C., & Peel, T. (1990). The Children's Television Workshop goes to school. *Educational Technology Research and Development, 38(4),* 25-33.

Grabowski, B. L. (1991). Message Design: issues and trends. In G. J. Anglin (Ed.), *Instructional technology: Past, present and future* (pp. 202-212). Englewood, CO: Libraries Unlimited.

Granello, D. H., & Pauley, P. S. (2000) Television viewing habits and their relationship to tolerance of people with mental illness. *Journal of Mental Health Counseling, 22(2),* 162-175.

Graves, S. B. (1982). The impact of television on the cognitive and affective development of minority children. In G.L. Berry & C. Mitchell-Keman (Eds.), *Television and the socialization of the minority child* (pp. 37-69). San Diego, CA: Academic.

Graves, S. B. (1987). *Final report on Newburgh, New York, sample.* New York: Children's Television Workshop.

Grayson, B. (1979). Television and minorities. In B. Logan & K. Moody (Eds.), *Television awareness training: The viewer's guide for family and community* (pp. 139-144). New York: Media Action Research Center.

Gredler, M. E. (1992). *Learning and instruction: Theory into practice* (2nd ed.). New York: Macmillan.

Greenberg, B. S., & Atkin, C. K. (1982). Television, minority children, and perspectives from research and practice. In G.L. Berry & C. Mitchell-Kernan (Eds.), *Television and the socialization of the minority child* (pp. 215-243). San Diego, CA: Academic.

Greenberg, B. S., & Busselle, R. W. (1996). Soap operas and sexual activity: A decade later. *Journal of Communication, 46(4),* 153-160.

Greenberg, B. S., & Rampoldi-Hnilo, L. (2001). Child and parent responses to the age-based and content-based television ratings. In D. G. & J. L. Singer (Eds.), *Handbook of Children and the Media,* (pp. 621-634). Thousand Oaks, CA: Sage Publications.

Greenhill, L. P. (1956). *Instructional film research program: Final report.* University Park, PA: Pennsylvania State University.

Greenhill, L. P. (1967). Review of trends in research on instructional television and film. In J. C. Reid & D. W. MacLennan (Eds.), *Research in instructional television and film.* U.S Office of Education.

Greenstein, J. (1954). Effects of television on elementary school grades. *Journal of Educational Research, 48,* 161-176.

Greer, D., Potts, R., Wright, J., & Huston, A.C. (1982). The effects of television commercial from and commercial placement on children's social behavior and attention. *Child Development, 53,* 611-619.

Groebel, J. (2001). Media violence in cross-cultural perspective: A global study on children's media behavior and some educational implications. In D. G. & J. L. Singer (Eds.), *Handbook of Children and the Media* (pp. 255-268). Thousand Oaks, CA: Sage Publications.

Gropper, G. L., & Lumsdaine, A. A. (1961). *The use of student response to improve televised instruction: An overview.* Pittsburgh, PA: American Institutes for Research.

Gross, L. (1991). Out of the mainstream: sexual minorities and the mass media. In M. A. Wolf & A. P. Kielwasser (Eds.), *Gay people, sex and the media* (pp. 19-46). New York: Haworth.

Gunter, B. (1980). Remembering television news: Effects of picture content. *Journal of General Psychology, 102,* 127-133.

Gunter, B. (1986). *Television and sex role stereotyping.* London: Libbey.

Gunter, B. (1987a). *Poor reception: Misunderstanding and forgetting broadcast news.* Hillsdale, NJ: Erlbaum.

Gunter, B. (1987b). *Television and the fear of crime.* London: Libbey.

Gunter, B., & Wakshlag, J. (1988). Television viewing and perceptions of crime among London residents. In P. Drummond & R. Paterson (Eds.), *Television and its audience: International research perspectives* (pp. 191-209). London: BFI Books.

Haefner, M. J., & Wartella, E. A. (1987). Effects of sibling coviewing on children's interpretations of television programs. *Journal of Broadcasting & Electronic Media, 31(2),* 153-168.

Haferkamp, C. J. (1999). Beliefs about television in relation to television viewing, soap opera viewing, and self-monitoring. *Current Psychology, 18(2),* 193-204.

Hagerstown: The Board of Education (1959). *Closed circuit television: Teaching in Washington County 1958-68*

Halpern, W. (1975). Turned-on toddlers. *Journal of Communication, 25,* 66-70.

Hansen, C. H., & Hansen, R. D. (1988). How rock music videos can change what is seen when boy meets girl: Priming stereotypic appraisal of social interactions. *Sex Roles, 19(5-6),* 287-316.

Hardaway, C. W., Beymer, W. C. L., & Engbretson, W. E. (1963). *A study of attitudinal changes of teachers and pupils of various groups toward educational television.* USOE Project No. 988. Terre Haute, IN: Indiana State College.

Harris, C. O. (1962). *Development of problem-solving ability and learning of relevant-irrelevant information through film and TV versions of a strength of materials testing laboratory.* USOE Grant NO. 7-20-040-00. East Lansing, MI: College of Engineering, Michigan State University.

Harrison, K. (2000, Summer). The body electric: Thin-ideal media and eating disorders in adolescents. *Journal of Communication, 50(3),* 119-143.

Hatt, P. (1982). *A review of research on the effects of television viewing on the reading achievement of elementary school children.* (ERIC Document Reproduction Service No ED 233297.)

Hawkins, R., Kin, Y., & Pingree, S. (1991). The ups and downs of attention to television. *Communication Research, IS* (1), 53-76.

Hayman, J. L., Jr. (1963). Viewer location and learning in instructional television. *AV Communication Review, 11,* 96-103.

Head, C. (1994, Nov.-Dec.). Partners against youth violence. *Focus,* 3-4.

Hearold, S. (1986). A synthesis of 1043 effects of television on social behavior. In *G.* Comstock (Ed.), *Public communication and behavior Vol. 1* (pp. 65-133). San Diego, CA: Academic.

Heintz-Knowles, K., Li-Vollmer, M., Chen, P., Harris, T., Haufler, A., Lapp, J., & Miller, P. (1999). Boys to men: Entertainment media. Messages about masculinity: A national poll of children, focus groups, and content analysis of entertainment media. (ERIC Document Reproduction Service No. ED 440 774.)

Hepburn, M. A. (1990). Americans glued to the tube: mass media, information and social studies. *Social Studies Education, 54(4),* 233-236.

Higgs, C. T., & Weiller, K. H. (1987, Apr.). *The aggressive male versus the passive female: An analysis of differentials in role portrayals.* Paper presented at the National Convention of the American Alliance for Health, Physical Education, Recreation, and Dance, Las Vegas, NV. (ERIC Document Reproduction Service No. ED 283 796.)

Hill, C. R., & Stafford, F. P. (1980). Parental care of children: Time diary estimates of quantity, predictability, and variety. *The Journal of Human Resources, 15*(2), 219–39.

Hilliard, R. L., & Field, H. H. (1976). *Television and the teacher.* New York: Hastings House.

Hoban, C. F., & VanOrmer, E. B. (1950, Dec.). *Instructional film research 1918–1959.* Technical Report No. 269-7-19. Port Washington, NY U.S. Naval Training Devices Center.

Hofferth, S. L. (1999a May). Changes in American children's time, 1981–1997. *Tri State Area School Study Council, The Forum, 2*(9), 1–2.

Hofferth, S. L. (1999b March). Changes in American children's time, 1981–1997. *The Brown University Child and Adolescent Behavior Letter,* pp. 1, 5–6.

Hollenbeck, A. & Slaby, R. (1979). Infant visual responses to television. *Child Development, 50,* 41–45.

Holmes, G. & Branch, R. C. (2000). Cable television in the classroom. *ERIC Digest.* (ERIC Document Reproduction No. ED 371 727 1994-06-00.)

Holmes, P. D. (1959). *Television research in the teaching learning process.* Detroit, MI: Wayne State University Division of Broadcasting.

Homans, G. C. (1961). *Social behavior: Its elementary forms.* New York: Harcourt, Brace & World.

Horgen, K. B., Choate, M., & Brownell, K. D. (2000). Television food advertising: Targeting children in a toxic environment. In D. G. & J. L. Singer (Eds.), *Handbook of Children and the Media* (pp. 447–462). Thousand Oaks, CA: Sage Publications.

Hornik, R. (1978). Television access and the slowing of cognitive growth. *American Educational Research Journal, 15,* 1–15.

Hornik, R. (1981). Out-of-school television and schooling: Hypotheses and methods. *Review of Educational Research, 51,* 193–214.

Hornik, R., Ingle, H. T., Mayo, J. K., McAnany, E. G., & Schramm, W. (1973). *Television and educational reform in El Salvador: Final Report.* Palo Alto, CA: Institute for Communication Research, Stanford University.

Huesman, L. R., Eron, L. D., Lefkowitz, M. M., & Walder, L. O. (1984). Stability of aggression over time and generations. *Developmental Psychology, 20,* 1120–1134.

Hunter, P. (1992). Teaching critical television viewing: an approach for gifted learners. *Roeper Review, 15*(2), 84–89.

Huskey, L., Jackstadt, S. L., & Goldsmith, S. (1991). Economic literacy and the content of television network news. *Social Education, 55*(3), 182–185.

Huston, A. C., & Wright, J. C. (1983). Children's processing of television: the informative functions of formal features. In J. Bryant & DR. Anderson (Eds.), *Children's understanding of television: Research on attention and comprehension* (pp. 35–68). San Diego, CA: Academic.

Huston, A. C., Donnerstein, E., Fairchild, H., Feshbach, N. D., Katz, P. A., Murray, J. P., Rubinstein, E. A., Wilcox, B. L., & Zuckerman, D. (1992). *Big world, small screen: The role of television in American society.* Lincoln, NE: University of Nebraska Press.

Huston, A. C., & Watkins, B. A. (1989). The forms of television and the child viewer. In G. Comstock (Ed.), *Public communication and behavior Vol. 21* (pp. 103–159). San Diego, CA: Academic.

Huston, A. C., Watkins, B. A., & Kunkel, D. (1989). Public policy and children's television. *American Psychologist, 44*(2), 424–433.

Huston, A. C., Watkins, B. A., Rice, M. L., Kerkman, D., & St. Peters, M. (1990). Development of television viewing patterns in early childhood: a longitudinal investigation. *Developmental Psychology, 26*(3), 409–420.

Huston-Stein, A. (1972). Mass media and young children's development. In I. Gordon (Ed.), *Early childhood education.* The 71st yearbook of the National Society for the Study of Education (pp. 180–202). Chicago, IL: University of Chicago Press.

Huston-Stein, A., Fox, S., Greer, D., Watkins, B. A., & Whitaker, J. (1981). The effects of TV action and violence on children's social behavior. *The Journal of Genetic Psychology, 138,* 183–191.

Iker, S. (1983, Nov./Dec.). Science, children and television. *MOSAIC,* 8–13.

Jalongo, M. R. (1983). *The preschool child's comprehension of television commercial disclaimers.* Paper presented at the Research Forum of the Annual Study Conference of the Association for Childhood Education International, Cleveland, OH. (ERIC Document Reproduction Service No. ED 229 122.)

James, N. C., & McCain, T. A. (1982). Television games preschool children play: Patterns, themes, and uses. *Journal of Broadcasting, 26*(4), 783–800.

Jeffery, L., & Durkin, K. (1989). Children's reactions to televised counter-stereotyped male sex role behaviour as a function of age, sex, and perceived power. *Social Behaviour, 4,* 285–310.

Jelinek-Lewis, M. S., & Jackson, D. W. (2001 Winter). Television literacy: Comprehension of program content using closed captions for the deaf. *Journal of Deaf Studies and Deaf Education, 6*(13), 43–53.

Johnson, J. (1987). *Electronic learning: From audiotape to videodisc.* Hillsdale, NJ: Erlbaum.

Johnson, J. G., Cohen, P., Smailes, E. M., Kasen, S., & Brook, J. S. (2002, March 29). Television viewing and aggressive behavior during adolescence and adulthood. *Science, 295,* 2468–2471.

Johnston, J., & Ettema, J. S. (1982). *Positive images: Breaking stereotypes with children's television.* Beverly Hills, CA: Sage.

Jones, G. (2002). *Killing monsters: Why children need fantasy, super heroes, and make-believe violence.* New York: Basic/Perseus Books.

Joy, L. A., Kimball, M. M., & Zabrack, M. L. (1986). Television and children's aggressive behavior. In T. M. Williams (Ed.), *The impact of television: A natural experiment in three communities* (pp. 303–360). San Diego, CA: Academic.

Kaiser Family Foundation. (1996a).*The family hour focus groups: Children's responses to sexual content on TV and their parent's reactions.* Oakland, CA: Kaiser Foundation and Children Now.

Kaiser Family Foundation (1996b). *A Kaiser Family Foundation and Children Now national survey: Parents speak up about television today: A summary of findings.* Oakland, CA: Kaiser Foundation and Children Now.

Kaiser Family Foundation (1999 November 17). *Kids & media @ the new millennium.* NY. Retrieved from www.kff.org (Contact: Amy Weitz 650-854-9400)

Kaiser Family Foundation (2001, July). *Parents and the V-Chip 2001: A Kaiser Family Foundation Survey. How parents feel about TV, the TV ratings system, and the V-Chip.* Retrieved June 3, 2002, from *http://www.kff.org/content/2001/3158/*

Kamalipour, Y. R., & Rampal, K. R., eds. (2001). *Media, sex, violence, and drugs in the global village.* Lanham, MD: Rowman & Littlefield Publishers.

Kamil, B.L. (1992). Cable in the classroom. In D. Ely & B. Minor (Eds.), *Educational Media Yearbook, Vol. 18.* Englewood, CO: Libraries Unlimited in cooperation with the Association for Educational Communications & Technology.

Kanner, J. H., & Rosenstein, A. J. (1960). Television in army training: Color vs. black and white. *AV Communication Review, 8,* 243–252.

Keith, T. Z., Reimers, T. M., Fehrmann, P. G., Pottebaum, S. M., & Aubey, L. W. (1986). Parental involvement, homework, and TV time: Direct and indirect effects on high school achievement. *Journal of Educational Psychology, 78*(5), 373–380.

Kelly, A. E., & Spear, P. S. (1991). Intraprogram synopses for children's comprehension of television content. *Journal of Experimental Child Psychology, 52*(1), 87-98.

Kimball, M. M. (1986). Television and sex-role attitudes. In T. M. Williams (Ed.), *The impact of television: A natural experiment in three communities* (pp. 265-301). San Diego, CA: Academic.

Knowlton, J. Q. (1966). On the definition of "picture." *Audiovisual Communication Review, 14*(2), 157-183.

Knupfer, N. N. (1994). Channel one: Reactions of students, teachers and parents. In A. De Vaney (Ed.), *Watching channel one: The convergence of students, technology, and private business* (pp. 61-86). Albany, NY: SUNY Press.

Knupfer, N. N. & Hayes, P. (1994). The effects of the channel one broadcast on students' knowledge of current events. In A. De Vaney (Ed.), *Watching channel one: The convergence of students, technology, and private business* (pp. 42-60). Albany, NY: SUNY Press.

Kozma, R. B. (1986). Implications of instructional psychology for the design of educational television. *Educational Communications and Technology Journal, 34*(1), 11-19.

Kozma, R. B. (1991). Learning with media. *Review of Educational Research, 61*(2), 179-211.

Kozma, R. B. (1994). Will media influence learning? Reframing the debate. *Educational Technology Research and Development, 42*(2), 7-19.

Krcmar, M., & Cantor, J. (1997). The role of television advisories and ratings in parent-child discussion of television viewing choices. *Journal of Broadcasting and Electronic Media, 41*(3), 393-411.

Krcmar, M., & Greene, K. (1999, Summer). Predicting exposure to and uses of television violence. *Journal of Communication, 49*(3), 24-44.

Krendl, K. A., & Watkins, B. (1983). Understanding television: an exploratory inquiry into the reconstruction of narrative content. *Educational Communications and Technology Journal, 31*(4), 201-212.

Krugman, D. M., & Johnson, K. F. (1991). Differences in the consumption of traditional broadcast and VCR movie rentals. *Journal of Broadcasting, 35*(2), 213-232.

Krugman, H. (1970). *Electroencephalographic aspects of low involvement: Implications for the McLuhan hypothesis.* Cambridge, MA: Marketing & Science Institute.

Krugman, H. (1979, January 29). The two brains: New evidence on TV impact. *Broadcasting*, 14.

Krugman, H. (1971). Brain wave measures of media involvement. *Journal of Advertising Research, 11*, 3-9.

Krull, R. (1983). Children learning to watch television. In J. Bryant & D. R. Anderson (Eds.), *Children's understanding of television: Research on attention and comprehension*, (pp. 103-123). San Diego, CA: Academic.

Kubey, R., & Larson, R. (1990). The use and experience of the new video media among children and young adolescents. *Communication Research, 17*(1), 107-130.

Kumata, H. (1956). *An inventory of instructional television research.* Ann Arbor, MI: Educational Television and Radio Center.

Kunkel, D. (1988). Children and host-selling television commercials. *Communication Research, 15*(1), 71-92.

Kunkel, D., et al. (1996). *Sexual messages on family hour television: Content and context.* Oakland, CA: Kaiser Foundation and Children Now. (ERIC Document Reproduction Service No. ED 409 080.)

Kunkel, D., Cope, K. M., & Biely, E. (1999 August). Sexual messages on television: Comparing findings from three studies. *Journal of Sex Research, 36*(3), 230-236.

Lambert, E., Plunkett, L., et al. (1998). Just the facts about advertising and marketing to children. *Kids and Commercialism.* Retrieved from *http://www.newdreams.org.campaign/kids/facts/html*

Lang, A. (1989). Effects of chronological presentation of information on processing and memory for broadcast news. *Journal of Broadcasting and Electronic Media, 33*(4), 441-452.

Langmeyer, L. (1989, Mar.). *Gender stereotypes in advertising: A critical review.* Paper presented at the annual meeting of the Southeastern Psychological Association, Washington, DC. (ERIC Document Reproduction Service No. ED 309 484.)

Lashly, K. S., & Watson, J. B (1922). *A psychological study of motion pictures in relation to venereal disease campaigns.* Washington, DC: U.S. Interdepartmental Social Hygiene Board.

Lebo, H. (2001). *The UCLA Internet Report 2001. Surveying the Digital Future Year Two.* Los Angeles. UCLA Center for Communication Policy.

Leichter, H. J., Ahmed, D., Barrios, J. B., Larsen, E., & Moe, L. (1985). Family contexts of television. *Educational Communication and Technology Journal, 33*(1), 26-40.

Leifer, A. D. (1976). *Factors which predict the credibility ascribed to television.* Paper presented at the annual convention of the American Psychological Association, Washington, DC. (ERIC Document Reproduction Service No. ED 135 332.)

Lernish, D., & Rice, M. (1986). Television as a talking picture book: A prop for language acquisition. *Journal of Child Language, 13*, 251-274.

Lesser, G. S. (1972). Language, teaching and television production for children: The experience from "Sesame Street." *Harvard Educational Review, 42*, 232-272.

Lesser, G. S. (1974). *Children and television: lessons from "Sesame Street* " New York: Random House.

Levie, H. W., & Dickie, K. E. (1973). The analysis and application of media. In R. M. W. Travers (Ed.), *Second handbook of research on teaching* (pp. 858-882). Chicago, IL: Rand McNally.

Levin, D. E., & Carlsson-Paige, N. (1994, Jul.). Developmentally appropriate television: Putting children first. *Young Children, 49*(5), 38-44.

Levin, S. R., & Anderson, D. R. (1976). "Sesame Street" around the world: The development of attention. *Journal of Communication, 26*(2), 126-135.

Levin, S. R., Petros, T. V., & Petrella, F. W. (1982). Preschoolers' awareness of television advertising. *Child Development, 53*, 933-937.

Lewis, C. (1993). The interactive dimension of television: Negotiation and socialization in the family room. *Journal of Visual Literacy, 13*(2), 9-50.

Lieberman, D. (1980). *Critical TV viewing workshops for high school teachers, parents, and community leaders [trainer's manual], Vol. II: workshop handouts.* San Francisco, CA: Far West Laboratory for Educational Research and Development. (ERIC Document Reproduction Service No. ED 244 585.)

Lieberman, D. (1980). *Critical television viewing skills curriculum.* Final Report (Oct. 1, 1979-Nov. 30, 1980.) San Francisco, CA: Far West Laboratory for Educational Research & Development. (ERIC Document Reproduction Service No. ED 215 668.)

Liebert, R. M., & Sprafkin, J. (1988). *The early window: Effects of television on children and youth* (3d ed.). New York: Pergamon.

Light, R. J. & Pillemer, D. B. (1984). *Summing up: The science of reviewing research.* Cambridge, MA: Harvard University Press.

Lin, C. A., & Atkin, D. J. (1989). Parental mediation and rulemaking for adolescent use of television and VCRs. *Journal of Broadcasting & Electronic Media, 33*(1), 53-67.

Lipinski, J. W., & Calvert, S. L. (1985). *The influence of television on children's sex typing.* (ERIC Document Reproduction Service No. ED 280 586.)

Lloyd-Kolkin, D., Wheeler, P., & Strand, T. (1980). Developing a curriculum for teenagers. *Journal of Communication, 30*(3), 119-125.

Lorch, E. P., Anderson, D. R., & Levin, S. R. (1979). The relationship of visual attention to children's comprehension of television. *Child Development, 50,* 722-727.

Lorch, E. P., Bellack, D., & Augsbach, L. (1987). Young children's memory for televised stories: Effects of importance. *Child Development, 58,* 453-63.

Luker, R., & Johnston, J. (1989). Television in adolescent social development. *Education Digest, 54*(6), 50-51.

Lull, J. (1990). Families' social uses of television as extensions of the household. In J. Bryant (Ed.), *Television and the American family* (pp. 59-72). Hillsdale, NJ: Erlbaum.

Lumsdaine, A. A. (1963). Instruments and media of instruction. In N. L. Gage (Ed.), *Handbook of Research on Teaching* (pp. 583-682). Chicago, IL: Rand McNally.

Mander, J. (1978). *Four arguments for the elimination of television.* New York: Morrow.

Mares, M-L., & Woodard, E. H. (2001). Prosocial effects on children's social interactions. In D. G. & J. L. Singer (Eds.), *Handbook of children and the media* (pp. 183-205). Thousand Oaks, CA: Sage Publications.

Marjoriebanks, K. (1979). *Families and their learning environments.* Boston, MA: Routledge & Kegan Paul.

McCannon, B. (2002). Media literacy: What? Why? How? In V. C. Strasburger and B. J. Wilson (Eds.), *Children, Adolescents, & the Media* (pp. 322-367). Thousand Oaks, CA: Sage Publications.

McDonald, D. G. & Glynn, C. J. (1986). *Television content viewing patterns: Some clues from societal norms.* Paper presented to the Mass Communication Division of the International Communication Association Annual Convention, Chicago, IL. (ERIC Document Reproduction Service No. ED 278 063.)

McFarland, S. L. (1992). *Extending "the neighborhood" to child care. Research report.* Toledo, OH: Public Broadcasting Foundation of Northwest Ohio. (ERIC Document Reproduction Service No. ED 351 136.)

McGrane, J. E., & Baron, M. L. (1959). A comparison of learning resulting from motion picture projector and closed circuit television presentations. *Society of Motion Picture and Television Engineers Journal, 68,* 824-827.

McIlwraith, R. D., & Schallow, J. (1983). Adult fantasy life and patterns of media use. *Journal of Communication, 33*(1), 78-91.

McIlwraith, R. D., & Schallow, J. (1982-83). Television viewing and styles of children's fantasy. *Imagination, Cognition and Personality, 2*(4), 323-331.

McLuhan, M. (1964). *Understanding media: The extensions of man.* New York: McGraw-Hill.

Meadowcroft, J. M., & Reeves, B. (1989). Influence of story schema development on children's attention to television. *Communication Research, 16*(3), 352-374.

Mediascope, Inc. (1996). *National television violence study: Executive summary.* Studio City, CA: Author.

Meringoff, L. K., Vibbert, M. M., Char, C. A., Fernie, D. E., Banker, G. S., & Gardner, H. (1983). How is children's learning from television distinctive? Exploiting the medium methodologically. In J. Bryant & D. R. Anderson (Eds.), *Children's understanding of television* (pp. 151-177). San Diego, CA: Academic.

Messaris, R. (1994). *Visual literacy: Image, mind, & reality.* Boulder, CO: Westview.

Messaris, R., & Nielsen, K. (1989, Aug.). *Viewers' interpretations of associational montage: The influence of visual literacy and educational background.* Paper presented to the Association for Education in Journalism and Mass Communication, Washington, DC.

Messner, M., Hunt, D., Dungar, M., Chen, P., Lapp, J., & Miller, P. (1999). *Boys to men: Sports media messages about masculinity: A national poll of children, focus groups, and content analyses of sports programs and commercials.* (ERIC Document Reproduction Service No. ED 440 775).

Meyer M. (1983). *Children and the formal features of television.* Munich: Saur.

Meyers, R. (1980, Nov.). *An examination of the male sex role model in prime-time television commercials.* Paper presented at the annual meeting of the Speech Communication Association, New York. (ERIC Document Reproduction Service No. ED 208 347.)

Mielke, K. (Ed.). (1990). Children's learning from television: research and development at the Children's Television Workshop [special issue]. *Educational Technology Research and Development, 38*(4).

Mielke, K. (Ed.). (1988, Sep.). Television in the social studies classroom. *Social Education,* 362-364.

Mielke, K. (Ed.). (1994). "Sesame Street" and children in poverty. *Media Studies Journal, 8*(4), 125-134.

Milavsky, J. R., Kessler, R. C., Stipp, H. H., & Rubens, W. S. (1982). *Television and aggression: A panel study.* San Diego, CA: Academic.

Miller, W. C. (1968, Dec.). Standards for ETV research. *Educational Broadcasting Review,* 48-53.

Moore, R. L., & Moschis, G. P. (1982). *A longitudinal analysis of television advertising effects on adolescents.* Paper presented at the annual meeting of the Association for Education in Journalism, Athens, OH. (ERIC Document Reproduction Service No. ED 219 753.)

Morgan, M., (1980). Television viewing and reading: does more equal better? *Journal of Communication, 32,* 159-165.

Morgan, M. (1982, Mar.). *More than a simple association: Conditional patterns of television and achievement.* Paper presented at the annual meeting of the American Educational Research Association, New York. (ERIC Document Reproduction Services No. ED 217 864.)

Morgan, M., & Gross, L. (1980). Television and academic achievement. *Journal of Broadcasting, 24,* 117-232.

Moyers, B. (2002, April 26). Mergers and monopolies. In *Now with Bill Moyers.* New York: WNET.

Murray, J. P. (1995, Spring). Children and television violence. *The Kansas Journal of Law & Public Policy,* 7-15.

Murray, J. P. (1980). *Television and youth: 25 years of research and controversy.* Boys Town, NE: Boys Town Center for the Study of Youth Development. (ERIC Document Reproduction Service No. ED 201302.)

Murray, J. P., & Kippax, S. (1978). Children's social behavior in three towns with differing television experience. *Journal of Communication, 28*(1), 19-29.

Nathanson, A. (1999 April). Identifying and explaining the relationship between parental mediation and children's aggression. *Communication Research, 26*(2), 124-143.

National Center for Education Statistics. (1991). *NELS—A profile of the American eighth grader* (Stock No. 065-000-00404-6). Washington, DC: U.S. Government Printing Office.

National Center for Education Statistics. (1992, Sep.). *New reports focus on eighth graders and their parents* (Announcement NCES 92-488A). Washington, DC: Office of Educational Research & Improvement.

National Institute of Mental Health (NIMH). (1972). *Television and growing up: The impact of televised violence.* Report to the Surgeon General, U.S. Public Health Service, from the Surgeon General's Scientific Advisory Committee on Television and Social Behavior, U.S. Department of Health, Education, & Welfare; Health Services & Mental Health Administration. Rockville, MD: National Institute of Mental Health. [DHEW Publication No. 72-9090.]

National Institute of Mental Health (NIMH). (1982). *Television and behavior: Ten years of scientific progress and implications for the eighties (Vol. 1: summary report)* Rockville, MD: National Institute of Mental Health. [DHHS Publication no. 82-1195.]

National Institute on Media and the Family. (2001). *Factsheets: Children and advertising*. Retrieved from http://www.mediaandthefamily.org/childadv.html

National Science Foundation. (1977). *Research on the effects of television advertising on children: A review of the literature and recommendations for future research* (NSFIRA 770115). Washington, DC: U.S. Government Printing Office No. 0-246-412.

Neisser, U. (1967). *Cognitive psychology.* New York: Appleton Century-Crofts.

Nelson, M. B. (1994). *The stronger women get, the more men love football: Sexism and the American culture of sports.* New York: Harcourt, Brace.

Neufeldt, V., & Sparks, A.X., eds. (1990). *Webster's new world dictionary.* New York: Warner Books.

Neuman, S. B. (1986). Television reading and the home environment. *Reading Research and Instruction, 25,* 173–183.

Neuman, S. B. (1988). The displacement effect: Assessing the relation between television viewing and reading performance. *Reading Research Quarterly, 23,* 414–440.

Neuman, S. B. (1991). *Literacy in the television age: The myth of the TV effect.* Norwood, NJ: Ablex.

Niven, H.F. (1958). *Instructional television as a medium of teaching in higher education.* Unpublished doctoral dissertation, Ohio State University.

Noble, G. (1975). *Children in front of the small screen.* Beverly Hills, CA: Sage.

Norberg, K. (1966). Visual perception theory and instructional communication. *Audio-visual Communication Review, 3*(14), 301–317.

Norberg, K. (Ed.). (1962). Perception theory and AV education [supplement 5]. *Audio-visual Communication Review, 10*(5).

Notar, E, (1989). Children and TV commercials "wave after wave of exploitation." *Childhood Education, 66*(2), 66–67.

Nugent, G. (1977). *Television and utilization training: How do they influence learning?* Lincoln, NE: Nebraska University. (ERIC Document Reproduction Service No. ED 191433.)

O'Bryant, S. L., & Corder-Bolz, C. R. (1978). Children and television. *Children Today.* DHEW Publication No. (OHDS) 79-30169. Washington, DC: U.S. Government Printing Office.

Office of Educational Research and Improvement (1991). *The executive summary of "NAEP—The state of mathematics achievement"* (NCES Publication No. 91-1050). Washington, DC: Office of Educational Research & Improvement, U.S. Office of Education.

Office of Educational Research and Improvement (1991, Fall). Data indicate lack of parent involvement (No. ED/OERI 91-1). *OERI Bulletin, 5.*

Office of Educational Research and Improvement (1994, Oct.). *TV viewing and parental guidance.* Washington, DC: Office of Educational Research & Improvement, U.S. Office of Education.

O'Reilly, K., & Splaine, J. (1987, May/Jun.). *Critical viewing: Stimulant to critical thinking.* South Hamilton, MA: Critical Thinking. (ERIC Document Reproduction Service No. ED 289796.)

O'Sullivan, C. (1999). *Professional wrestling: Can watching it bring out aggressive and violent behaviors in children?* (ERIC Document Reproduction Service No. ED 431 526.)

Palmer, E. L. (1987). *Children in the cradle of television* Lexington, MA: Lexington Books, Heath.

Palmer, P. (1986). *The lively audience* Boston, MA: Allen & Unwin.

Pardun, C., & McKee, K. (1995). Strange bedfellows. Symbols of religion and sexuality on MTV. *Youth and Society, 26*(4), 438–449.

Parks, C. (1995). *Closed caption TV: A resource for ESL literacy.* Washington, DC: Corporation for Public Broadcasting.

Pasewark, W. R. (1956). *Teaching typing through television.* Research Report No. 17. East Lansing, MI: Michigan State University.

Paulson, R. L. (1974). Teaching cooperation on television: An evaluation of Sesame Street social goals program. AV *Communication Review, 22*(3), 229–246.

Pearl, D., Bouthilet, L., & Lazar, J. (Eds.). (1982). *Television and behavior: Ten years of scientific progress and implications for the eighties, Vol. 1, summary report.* Washington, DC: U.S. Government Printing Office.

Pearl, D., Bouthilet, L., & Lazar, J. (Eds.). (1982). *Television and behavior: Ten years of scientific progress and implications for the eighties, Vol. 2, technical reviews.* Rockville, MD: National Institute of Mental Health. [DHHS Publication no. 82-1195.]

Perloff, R. M., Wartella, E. A., & Becker, L. B. (1982). Increasing learning from TV news. *Journalism Quarterly, 59,* 83–86.

Perse, E. M. (1990). Audience selectivity and involvement in the newer media environment. *Communication Research, 17*(5), 675–697.

Peters, J. M. L. (1961). *Teaching about the film.* New York: International Document Service, Columbia University Press.

Peterson, C. C., Peterson, J. L., & Carroll, J. (1987) Television viewing and imaginative problem solving during preadolescence. *The Journal of Genetic Psychology, 20*(1), 61–67.

Petty, L. I. (1994a, Sep.). *"Sesame Street" research bibliography* 1989–1994. New York: Children's Television Workshop.

Petty, L. I. (1994b, Sep.). *A review of "Sesame Street" research 1989–1994.* New York: Children's Television Workshop.

Piaget, J. (1926). *The language and thought of the child.* New York: Harcourt, Brace.

Pinon, M. F, Huston, A. C., & Wright, J. C. (1989). Family ecology and child characteristics that predict young children's educational television viewing. *Child Development, 60,* 846–56.

Plomin, R., Corley, R., DeFries, J. C., & Fulker, D. W. (1990). Individual differences in television viewing in early childhood: nature as well as nurture. *Psychological Science, 1*(6), 371–377.

Pryor, D., & Knupfer, N. N. (1997, February 14-18). Gender stereotypes and selling techniques in television advertising: Effects on society. *Proceedings of Selected Research and Development Presentations at the 1997 National Convention of the Association for Educational Communication and Technology.* (ERIC Document Reproduction Service No. ED 409 861.)

Polsky, R. M. (1974). *Getting to Sesame Street: Origins of the Children's Television Workshop.* New York: Praeger.

Postman, N. (1982). *The disappearance of childhood.* New York: Delacorte.

Potter, W. J. (1987). Does television viewing hinder academic achievement among adolescents? *Human Communication Research, 14,* 27–46.

Potter, W. J. (1990). Adolescents' perceptions of the primary values of television programming. *Journalism Quarterly, 67*(4), 843–851.

Putnam, R. D. (2000). *Bowling alone: The collapse and revival of American community.* New York: Simon & Schuster.

Quisenberry, N., & Klasek, C. (1976). *The relationship of children's television viewing to achievement at the intermediate level.* Carbondale, IL: Southern Illinois University. (ERIC Document Reproduction Service No. ED 143 336.)

Rapaczynski, W., Singer, D. G., & Singer, J. L. (1982). Teaching television: A curriculum for young children. *Journal of Communication, 32*(2), 46–55.

Reglin, G. (1996). *Television and violent classroom behaviors: Implications for the training of elementary school teachers.* (ERIC Document Reproduction Service No. ED 394 687.)

Reid, J. C., & MacLennan, D. W., eds. (1967). *Research in instructional television and film.* Washington, DC: U.S. Department of Health, Education, & Welfare.

Reid, L. N. (1979). Viewing rules as mediating factors of children's responses to commercials. *Journal of Broadcasting, 23*(1), 15–26.

Reid, L. N., & Frazer, C. F. (1980). Children's use of television commercials to initiate social interaction in family viewing situations. *Journal of Broadcasting, 24*(2), 149–158.

Reinking, D., & Wu, J. (1990). Reexamining the research on television and reading. *Reading Research and Instruction, 29*(2), 30–43.

Reiser, R. A., Tessmer, M. A., & Phelps, P. C. (1984). Adult–child interaction in children's learning from "Sesame Street." *Educational Communications and Technology Journal, 32*(4), 217–233.

Reiser, R. A., Williamson, N., & Suzuki, K. (1988). Using "Sesame Street" to facilitate children's recognition of letters and numbers. *Educational Communications and Technology Journal, 36*(1), 15–21.

Research Division, Children's Television Workshop (n.d.). *"3-2-1 Contact" research bibliography.* New York: Children's Television Workshop.

Research Uncovers How Kids Spend Their Time. (1998 December 30). Information Legislative Service published by the Pennsylvania School Boards Association, p. A4.

Riccobono, J. A. (1985). *School utilization study: Availability, use, and support of instructional media, 1982-83, final report.* Washington, DC: Corporation for Public Broadcasting. (ERIC Document Reproduction Service No. ED 256 292.)

Rice, M., Huston, A., & Wright, J. (1982). The forms of television: effects on children's attention, comprehension, and social behavior. In D. Pearl, L. Bouthilet & J. Lazar (Eds.), *Television and behavior: Ten years of scientific inquiry and implications for the eighties: Vol. 2. Technical review* (pp. 24–38). Washington, DC: U.S. Government Printing Office.

Rice, M., Huston, A., & Wright, J. (1983). The forms of television: effects on children's attention, comprehension, and social behavior. In M. Meyer (Ed.), *Children and the formal features of television* (pp. 21–55). Munich: Saur.

Richey, R. (1986). *The theoretical and conceptual bases of instructional design.* London: Kogan Page.

Ridley-Johnson, R., Cooper, H., & Chance, J. (1982). The relation of children's television viewing to school achievement and I.Q. *Journal of Educational Research, 76*(5), 294–297.

Ritchie, D., Price, V., & Roberts, D.E. (1987). Television, reading and reading achievement: A reappraisal. *Communication Research, 14,* 292–315.

Robb, D. (2000). *The changing classroom role of instructional television.* Retrieved from http://horizon.unc.edu/ts/editor/218.html

Roberts, D. F., Bachen, C. M., Homby, M. C., & Hernandez-Ramos, R. (1984). Reading and television predictors of reading achievement at different age levels. *Communication Research, 11,* 9–49.

Robinson, J. R & Levy, M. R. (1986). *The main source: Learning from television news.* Beverly Hills, CA: Sage.

Rock, R. T., Duva, J. S., & Murray, J. E. (1951). *The effectiveness of television instruction in training naval air reservists, instructional TV research reports* (Technical Report SDC 476-02-S2). Port Washington, NY: U.S. Naval Special Devices Center.

Roderick, J., & Jackson, P. (1985, Mar.). *TV viewing habits, family rules, and reading grades of gifted and nongifted middle school students.* Paper presented at the Conference of the Ohio Association for Gifted Children. (ERIC Document Reproduction Service No. ED 264 050.)

Rogers, F., & Head, B. (1963). *Mister Rogers talks to parents.* New York: Berkley Publishing Group and Family Communications.

Rosenfeld, E., Heusmann, L. R., Eron, L. D., & Torney-Purta, J. V. (1982). Measuring patterns of fantasy behavior in children. *Journal of Personality and Social Psychology, 42,* 347–366.

Ross, R. P. (1979, Jun.). *A part of our environment left unexplored by environmental designers: Television.* Paper presented at the annual meeting of the Environmental Design Research Association, Buffalo, NY. (ERIC Document Reproduction Service No. ED 184 526.)

Rothschild, M., Thorson, E., Reeves, B., Hirsch, J., & Goldstein, R. (1986). EEG activity and the processing of television commercials. *Communication Research, 13,* 182–220.

Rovet, J. (1983). The education of spatial transformations. In D. R. Olson & E. Bialystok (Eds.), *Spatial cognition: The structures and development of mental representations of spatial relations* (pp. 164–181). Hillsdale, NJ: Erlbaum.

Rubenstein, D. J. (2000). Stimulating children's creativity and curiosity: Does content and medium matter? *Journal of Creative Behavior, 34*(1), 1–17.

Rushton, J. P. (1982). Television and prosocial behavior. In D. Pearl, L. Bouthilet & J. Lazar (Eds.), *Television and behavior: Ten years of scientific progress and implications for the eighties, Vol 2: Technical reviews* (pp. 248–257). Rockville, MD: National Institute of Mental Health. [DHHS Publication no. 82-1195.]

Ryan, S. C. (2001, March 25). Latinos finally beginning to see themselves on television. *The Boston Globe,* p. L8.

Salomon, G. (1972). Can we affect cognitive skills through visual media? A hypothesis and initial findings. *AV Communication Review, 20*(4), 401–422.

Salomon, G. (1974). Internalization of filmic schematic operations in interaction with learner's aptitudes. *Journal of Educational Psychology 66,* 499–511.

Salomon, G. (1977). Effects of encouraging Israeli mothers to co-observe "Sesame Street" with their five-year-olds. *Child Development, 48,* 1146–1151.

Salomon, G. (1979). *Interaction of media, cognition, and learning: An exploration of how symbolic forms cultivate mental skills and affect knowledge acquisition.* San Francisco, CA: Jossey-Bass.

Salomon, G. (1981a). Introducing AIME: The assessment of children's mental involvement with television. In H. Gardner & H. Kelly (Eds.), *Children and the worlds of television.* San Francisco, CA: Jossey-Bass.

Salomon, G. (1981b). *Communication and education: Social and psychological interactions.* Beverly Hills, CA: Sage.

Salomon, G. (1982), Television literacy vs. literacy. *Journal of Visual Verbal Languaging, 2*(2), 7–16.

Salomon, G. (1983). Television watching and mental effort: a social psychological view. In J. Bryant & D. R Anderson (Eds.), *Children's understanding of television: Research on attention and comprehension* (pp. 181–198). San Diego, CA: Academic.

Salomon, G. (1984). Television is "easy" and print is "tough": The differential investment of mental effort in learning as a function of perceptions and attributions. *Journal of Educational Psychology, 76,* 647–658.

Salomon, G., & Cohen, A. A. (1977). Television formats, mastery of mental skills, and the acquisition of knowledge. *Journal of Educational Psychology, 69*(5), 612–619.

Sammur, G. B. (1990). Selected bibliography of research on programming at the Children's Television Workshop. *Educational Technology Research and Development, 38*(4), 81–92.

Sanders, J. R., & Sonnad, S. R. (1982, Jan.). *Research on the introduction, use, and impact of the "ThinkAbout" instructional television series: Executive summary.* Bloomington, IN: Agency for Instructional Television. (ERIC Document Reproduction Service No. ED 249 948.)

Santa Ana Unified School District (1971, Apr.). *The effect of instructional television utilization techniques on science achievement in the sixth grade.* Santa Ana, CA: Author. (ERIC Document Reproduction Service No. ED 048 751.)

Schallow, J. R., & McIlwraith, R. D. (1986-87). Is television viewing really bad for your imagination? Content and process of TV viewing and imaginal styles. *Imagination, Cognition and Personality, 6*(1), 25-42.

Scheff, T. J., & Scheele, S. C. (1980). Humor and catharsis: The effect of comedy on audiences. In P. H. Tannenbaum (Ed.), *The entertainment functions of television* (pp. 165-182). Hillsdale, NJ: Erlbaum.

Schramm, W. (1962). *What we know about learning from instructional television, educational television: The next ten years.* Stanford, CA: Institute for Communication Research.

Schramm, W., Lyle, J., & Parker, E. (1961). *Television in the lives of our children.* Stanford, CA: Stanford University Press.

Schwarzwalder, J. C. (1960). *An investigation of the relative effectiveness of certain specific TV techniques on learning* (USOE Project No. 985). St. Paul, MN: KTCA-TV.

Searching for alternatives: Critical TV viewing and public broadcasting. (1980, Summer) [special issue]. *Journal of Communication, 30*(3).

Searls, D. T., Mead, N. A., & Ward, B. (1985). The relationship of students' reading skills to TV watching, leisure time reading and homework. *Journal of Reading, 29,* 158-162.

Seattler, P. (1968). *A history of instructional technology.* New York: McGraw-Hill.

Seels, B. (1982). Variables in the environment for pre-school television viewing. In R. A. Braden & A. D. Walker (Eds.), *Television and visual literacy* (pp. 53-67). Bloomington, IN: International Visual Literacy Association.

Seels, B. B., & Richey, R. C. (1994). *Instructional technology: The definition and domains of the field.* Washington, DC: Association for Educational Communications & Technology.

Seidmen, S. (1999). Revisiting sex-role stereotyping in MTV videos. *International Journal of Educational Media, 26*(1), 11-22.

Sell, M. A., Ray, G. E., & Lovelace, L. (1995). Preschool children's comprehension of a "Sesame Street" video tape: The effects of repeated viewing and previewing instructions. *Educational Technology Research and Development, 43*(3), 49-60.

Shayon, R. L. (1950, Nov. 25). The pied piper of video. *Saturday Review of Literature, 33.*

Shutkin, D. S. (1990). Video production education: Towards a critical media pedagogy. *Journal of Visual Literacy, 10*(2), 42-59.

Sigelman, C. K., & Shaffer, D. R. (1995). *Understanding lifespan human development.* Pacific Grove, CA: Brooks/Cole.

Signorielli, N. (1989). Television and conceptions about sex roles: Maintaining conventionality and the status quo. *Sex Roles, 21*(5-6), 341-360.

Signorielli, N. (1991a). *A sourcebook on children and television.* New York: Greenwood.

Signorielli, N. (1991b, Sep.). Adolescents and ambivalence toward marriage: A cultivation analysis. *Youth & Society, 23,* 121-149.

Signorielli, N. (1997). *Reflections of girls in the media: A content analysis. A study of television shows and commercials, movies, music videos, and teen magazine articles and ads.* (ERIC Document Reproduction Service No. ED 444 214).

Signorielli, N. (2001). Television's gender role images and contribution to stereotyping. In D. G. & J. L. Singer (Eds.), *Handbook of children and the media* (pp. 341-358). Thousand Oaks, CA: Sage Publications.

Signorielli, N., & Lears, M. (1992). Children, television, and conceptions about chores: Attitudes and behaviors. *Sex Roles, 27*(3-4), 157-169.

Silberstein, R., Agardy, S., Ong, B., & Heath, D. (1983). *Electroencephalographic responses of children to television.* Melbourne: Australian Broadcasting Tribunal.

Silva, D. (1996). *Moving young children's play away from TV violence. A how-to guide for early childhood educators: Child care providers, head start instructors, preschool and kindergarten teachers.* (ERIC Document Reproduction Service No. ED 400 052.)

Silver, R. C., Holman, E. A., McIntosh, D. N., Poulin, M., & Gil-Rivas, V. (2002, September 11). Nationwide longitudinal study of psychological responses to September 11. *JAMA, 288*(10), 1235-1244.

Simmons, B. J., Stalsworth, K., & Wentzel, H. (1999, Spring). Television violence and its effect on young children. *Early Childhood Education Journal, 26*(3), 149-153.

Singer, D. G. (1978). Television and imaginative play. *Journal of Mental Imagery, 2,* 145-164.

Singer, D. G., & Singer, J. L. (1981). Television and the developing imagination of the child. *Journal of Broadcasting, 25,* 373-387.

Singer, D. G., & Singer, J. L. (Eds.). (2001). *Handbook of children and the media.* Thousand Oaks, CA: Sage Publications.

Singer, D. G., Singer, J. L., & Zuckerman, D. M. (1981). *Teaching television: How to use TV to your child's advantage.* New York: Dial.

Singer, D. G., Zuckerman, D. M., & Singer, J. L. (1980). Helping elementary school children learn about TV. *Journal of Communication, 30*(3), 84-93.

Singer, D. G., Zuckerman, D. M., & Singer, J. L. (1981). Teaching elementary school children critical television viewing skills: An evaluation. In M. E. Ploghoft & J. A. Anderson (Eds.), *Education for the television age* (pp. 71-81). Athens, OH: Ohio University.

Singer, J. (1980). The power and limitations of television: A cognitive affective analysis. In P. H. Tannenbaum (Ed.), *The entertainment functions of television* (pp. 31-65). Hillsdale, NJ: Erlbaum.

Singer, J. L., & Antrobus, L. S. (1972). Dimensions of daydreaming and the stream of thought. In K. S. Pope & J. L. Singer (Eds.), *The stream of consciousness.* New York: Plenum.

Singer, J. L., & Singer, D. G. (1981). *Television, imagination, and aggression: A study of preschoolers.* Hillsdale, NJ: Erlbaum.

Singer, J. L., & Singer, D. G. (1983). Implications of childhood television viewing for cognition, imagination and emotion. In J. Bryant & D. R. Anderson (Eds.), *Children's understanding of television: Research on attention and comprehension* (pp. 265-295). San Diego, CA: Academic.

Singer, J. L., & Singer, D. G. (1986). Family experiences and television viewing as predictors of children's imagination, restlessness, and aggression. *Journal of Social Issues, 42,* 107-124.

Singer, J. L., Singer, D. G., & Rapaczynski, W. S. (1984). Family patterns and television viewing as predictors of children's beliefs and aggression. *Journal of Communication, 34*(2), 73-89.

Singer, M. I., & Miller, D. (1998). *Mental health and behavioral sequelae of children's exposure to violence.* (ERIC Document Reproduction Service No. ED 433644.)

Singh, M., Balasubramanian, S. K., & Chakraborty, G. (2000). A comparative analysis of three communication formats; Advertising, infomercial, and direct experience. *Journal of Advertising, 29*(4), 59-76.

Siniscalco, M. T. (1996). Television literacy: Development and evaluation of a program aimed at enhancing TV news comprehension. *Studies in Educational Evaluation, 22*(3), 207-221.

Slattery, K. F. (1990). Visual information in viewer interpretation and evaluation of television news stories. *Journal of visual Literacy, 10*(1), 26-44.

Smith, M. E. (1994). Television violence and behavior: a research summary. In D. P. Ely & B. Minor (Eds.), *Educational media and technology yearbook,* Vol. 20 (pp. 164-168). Englewood, CO: Libraries Unlimited.

Smith, R., Anderson, D., & Fischer, C. (1985). Young children's comprehension of montage. *Child Development, 56,* 962-71.

Smith, S. L., & Wilson, B. J. (2000). Children's reactions to a television news story. *Communication Research, 27*(5), 641-673.

Snyder, R. (1994). Information processing: A visual theory for television news. *Journal of Visual Literacy, 14*(1), 69-76.

Son, J., Reese, S. D., & Davie, W. R. (1987). Effects of visual-verbal redundancy and recaps on television news learning. *Journal of Broadcasting and Electronic Media, 31*(2), 207-216.

Soriano, D. G. (2001, September 26). Latino TV roles shrank in 2000, report finds. *USA Today.* Retrieved September 26, 2001, from *http://www.usatoday.com/usatonline/20010926/3482996s.htm*

Sprafkin, J. N. (1979). Stereotypes on television. In B. Logan & K. Moody (Eds.), *Television awareness training: The viewer's guide for family and community* (pp. 33-37). New York: Media Action Research Center.

Sprafkin, J., Gadow, K. D., & Abelman, R. (1992). *Television and the exceptional child: The forgotten audience.* Hillsdale, NJ: Erlbaum.

Sproull, N. (1973). Visual attention, modeling behaviors, and other verbal and nonverbal metacommunication of prekindergarten children viewing Sesame Street. *American Educational Research Journal, 10,* 101-114.

Stedman, L. C., & Kaestle, C. F. (1987). Literacy and reading performance in the United States from 1880 to the present. *Reading Research Quarterly, 22,* 8-46.

Stern, R. C., & Robinson, R. S. (1994). Perception and its role in communication and learning. In D. M. Moore & F. M. Dwyer (Eds.), *Visual literacy.* Englewood Cliffs, NJ: Educational Technology.

Stickell, D. W. (1963). *A critical review of the methodology and results of research comparing televised and face-to-face instruction.* Unpublished doctoral dissertation, The Pennsylvania State University.

St. Peters, M., Fitch, M., Huston, A. C., Wright, J. C., & Eakins, D. J. (1991). Television and families: What do young children watch with their parents? *Child Development, 62,* 1409-1423.

St. Peters, M., Huston, A. C., & Wright, J. C. (1989, Apr.). *Television and families: Parental coviewing and young children's language development, social behavior, and television processing.* Paper presented at the conference of the Society for Research in Child Development, Kansas City, KS.

Strasburger, V. C., & Wilson, B. J. (2002). *Children, adolescents, and the media.* Thousand Oaks, CA: Sage Publications.

Strasburger, V. C., & Donnerstein, E. (1999 January). Children, adolescents, and the media. *Pediatrics, 103*(1), 129-139. Retrieved from *http://136.142.56.160/ovid/web/ovidweb.cgi*

Strasburger, V. C., & Wilson, B. J. (2002). *Children, adolescents, & the media.* Thousand Oaks, CA: Sage Publications.

Stroman, C. A. (1991). Television's role in the socialization of African-American children and adolescents. *The Journal of Negro Education, 60*(3), 314-327.

Study finds kids spend less time watching television and playing; Spend more time working and studying. (1998 November 30). *Jet.* Johnson Publishing Co. in association with The Gale Group and LookSmart.

Sutton-Smith, B. (1976). *A developmental psychology of children's film making: Annual report No. 1, 1974-75 and annual report No. 2, 1975-76.* New York: Ford Foundation. (ERIC Document Reproduction Service No. ED 148 330.)

Swan, K. (1995). *Saturday morning cartoons and children's perceptions of social reality.* Paper presented at the Annual Meeting of the American Educational Research Association in San Francisco, CA, April 18-22, 1995. (ERIC Document Reproduction No. ED 390 579.)

Tada, T. (1969). Image-cognition: A developmental approach. In S. Takashima & H. Ichinohe (Eds.), *Studies of broadcasting.* Tokyo: Nippon Hoso Kyokai.

Takanishi, R. (1982). The influence of television on the ethnic identity of minority children: A conceptual framework. In G. L. Berry & C. Mitchell-Kernan (Eds.), *Television and the socialization of the minority child* (pp. 81-103). San Diego, CA: Academic.

Talking with TV: A guide to starting dialogue with youth (1994). Washington, DC: The Center for Population Options.

Tangney, J. P., & Feshbach, S. (1988). Children's television viewing frequency: Individual differences and demographic correlates. *Personality and Social Psychology Bulletin, 14*(1), 145-158.

Tannenbaum, P. H. (1980). Entertainment as vicarious emotional experience. In P. H. Tannenbaum (Ed.), *The entertainment functions of television* (pp. 107-31). Hillsdale, NJ: Erlbaum.

Telecommunications Act of 1996, Pub. L., No. 104-S.652, Title V, Subtitle B, Sec. 551. *Parental choice in television programming.* Retrieved October 2002, from Federal Communications website: http://www.fcc.gov/Reports/tcom1996.txt

Thirteen/WNET (1992). *Evaluation of thirteen/Texaco teacher train* New York: Author.

Thompson, M. E., Carl, D., & Hill, F. (1992). Channel One news in the classroom: Does it make a difference? In M. Simonson (Ed.), *Proceedings of selected research & development presentations at the convention of the Association for Educational Communications & Technology.* Washington, DC: AECT, Research and Theory Division. (ERIC Document Reproduction Service No. ED 348 032.)

Thorson, E., Reeves, B., & Schleuder, J. (1985). Message complexity and attention to television. *Communication Research, 12,* 427-454.

Tiene, D. (1993). Exploring the effectiveness of the Channel One school telecasts. *Educational Technology, 33*(5), 36-20.

Tiene, D. (1994). Teens react to Channel One: a survey of high school students. *Tech Trends, 39*(3), 17-38.

Tiffin, J. W. (1978). Problems in instructional television in Latin America. *Revista de Tenologia Educativa, 4*(2), 163-234.

Torrence, D. R. (1985). How video can help: video can be an integral part of your training effort. *Training and Development Journal, 39*(12), 50.

Tower, R., Singer, D., Singer, J., & Biggs, A. (1979). Differential effects of television programming on preschooler's cognition, imagination and social play. *American Journal of Orthopsychiatry, 49,* 265-281.

Tuned in or tuned out? America's children speak out on the news media. (1995). A Children Now poll conducted by Fairbank, Maslin, Maulin, & Associates [On-line]. Retrieved from http://www.mediascope.org/pubs/ibriefs/aynm.htm

Turner, P. M., & Simpson, W. (1982, Mar.). *Factors affecting instructional television utilization in Alabama.* (ERIC Document Reproduction Service No. ED 216 698.)

TV Ontario. (1990). *Behind the scenes: Resource guide for television literacy.* (1990). Toronto, Ontario, Canada: The Ontario Educational Communications Authority.

Valkenburg, P. M., & Beentjes, J. W. J. (1997 Spring). Children's creative imagination in response to radio and television stories. *Journal of Communication, 47*(2), 21-37.

Valkenburg, P. M., Kremar, M., & deRoss, S. (1998 Summer). The impact of a cultural children's program and adult mediation on children's knowledge of and attitudes towards opera. *Journal of Broadcasting and Electronic Media, 42*(3), 315-326.

Valmont, W. J. (1995). *Creating videos for school use.* Boston, MA: Allyn & Bacon.

Van den Bulck, J. (2000). Is television bad for your health? Behavior and body image of the adolescent "couch potato." *Journal of Youth and Adolescence, 29*(3), 273-288.

VanderMeer, A. W. (1950, Jul.). *Relative effectiveness of instruction by films exclusively, films plus study guides, and standard lecture methods* (Technical Report No. SDC 269-7-13). Port Washington, NY: U.S. Naval Training Devices Center.

Van Evra, J. (1998). *Television and child development.* Mahwah, NJ: Lawrence Erlbaum Associates.

Vivian, J. (1991). *The media of mass communication.* Boston, MA: Allyn & Bacon.

Walker, J. (1980). Changes in EEG rhythms during television viewing: Preliminary comparisons with reading and other tasks. *Perceptual and Motor Skills, 51,* 255-261.

Wan, G. (2000). *"Barney and Friends": An evaluation of the literacy learning environment created by the TV series for children.* (ERIC Document Reproduction No. ED 438 900.)

Ward, S., Levinson, D., & Wackman, D. (1972). Children's attention to television advertising. In E. A. Rubinstein, G. A. Comstock, & J. P. Murray (Eds.), *Television and social behavior. (Vol. 4), Television in day-to-day life: Patterns of use* (pp. 491-515). US Government Printing Office, 1972.

Ward, S., Wackman, D. B., & Wartella, E. (1975). *Children learning to buy: The development of consumer information processing skills* Cambridge, MA: Marketing Science Institute.

Wartella, E. (1979). The developmental perspective. In E. Wartella (Ed.), *Children communicating: Media and development of thought, speech, understanding* (pp. 7-20). Beverly Hills, CA: Sage.

Watkins, L. T., Sprafkin, J., Gadow, K. D., & Sadetsky, I. (1988). Effects of a critical viewing skills curriculum on elementary school children's knowledge and attitudes about television. *Journal of Educational Research, 81*(3), 165-170.

Watt, J., & Welch, A. (1983). Effects of static and dynamic complexity on children's attention and recall of televised instruction. In J. Bryant & D. R. Anderson (Eds.), *Children's understanding of television: Research on attention and comprehension* (pp. 69-102). San Diego, CA: Academic.

Webster, J. G., Pearson, J. C., & Webster, D. B. (1986). Children's television viewing as affected by contextual variables in the home. *Communication Research Reports, 3,* 1-7.

Weiller, K. H., & Higgs, C. T. (1992, Apr.). *Images of illusion, images of reality: Gender differences in televised sport—the 1980's and beyond.* Paper presented at the National Convention of the American Alliance for Health, Physical Education, Recreation, & Dance, Indianapolis, IN. (ERIC Document Reproduction Service No. ED 346 037.)

Weinstein, S., Appel, V., & Weinstein, C. (1980). Brain activity responses to magazine and television advertising. *Journal of Advertising Research, 20*(3), 57-63.

Weiss, A. J., & Wilson, B. J. (1996). Emotional portrayals in family television series that are popular among children. *Journal of Broadcasting and Electronic Media, 40,* 1-29.

Welch, A., & Watt, J. (1982). Visual complexity and young children's learning from television. *Human Communication Research, 8*(2), 13-45.

Wells, S. (1976). *Instructional technology in developing countries: Decision making processes in education.* New York: Praeger.

Wheeler, R. (1979). *Formative review of the critical television viewing skills curriculum for secondary schools, Vol. I: Final report. Vol. 11: Teacher's guide: Reviewers' suggested revisions* (OE Contract No. 300-78-0495). San Francisco, CA: Far West Laboratory for Educational Research & Development. (ERIC Document Reproduction Service No. ED 215 669.)

White, G. F., Katz, J., & Scarborough, K. (1992). The impact of professional football games upon violent assaults on women. *Violence and Victims, 7*(2), 157-171.

Who are the biggest couch potatoes? (1993, May 23). *Parade Magazine,* p. 17.

Wilkinson, G. L. (1980). *Media in instruction: 60 years of research.* Washington, DC: Association for Educational Communications & Technology.

Williams, D. C., Paul, J., & Ogilvie, J. C. (1957). Mass media, learning, and retention. *Canadian Journal of Psychology, 11,* 157-163.

Williams, M. E., & Condry, J. C. (1989, Apr.). *Living color: Minority portrayals and cross-racial interactions on television.* Paper presented at the Biennial Meeting of the Society for Research in Child Development, Kansas City, MO. (ERIC Document Reproduction Service No. ED 307 025.)

Williams, P., Haertle, E., Haertel, G., & Walberg, H. (1982). The impact of leisure time television on school learning. *American Educational Research Journal, 19,* 19-50.

Williams, T. M. (Ed.). (1986). *The impact of television: A natural experiment in three communities.* San Diego, CA: Academic.

Willis, G. (1990). *Stereotyping in TV programming: Assessing the need for multicultural education in teaching scriptwriting.* Doctoral dissertation, University of Pittsburgh.

Winn, D. (1985a). *TV and its affect on the family.* Paper presented at the annual Weber State College "Families Alive" Conference, Ogden, UT. (ERIC Document Reproduction Service No. ED 272 314.)

Winn, M. (1977). *The plug-in drug.* New York: Viking.

Winn, M. (1985b). *The plug-in drug: Television, children and the family.* New York: Viking.

Wolf, M. A. (1987). How children negotiate television. In T. R. Lindlof (Ed.), *Natural audiences: Qualitative research of media uses and effects* (pp. 58-94). Norwood, NJ: Ablex.

Wolf, T. M. (1975). Response consequences to televised modeled sex-inappropriate play behavior. *Journal of Genetic Psychology, 127,* 35-44.

Wood, D. B. (1989, Sep. 29). Schoolroom newscasts-minus ads. *Christian Science Monitor,* pp. 10-11.

Wood, D. N., & Wylie, D. G. (1977). *Educational telecommunications.* Belmont, CA: Wadsworth.

Woodall, W. G., Davis, D. K., & Sahin, H. (1983). From the boob tube to the black box: Television news comprehension from an information processing perspective. *Journal of Broadcasting, 27*(1), 1-23.

Woodard, E. H., & Gridina, N. (2000). *Media in the home 2000. The fifth annual survey of parents and children.* Retrieved on October 7, 2002, from *http://www.appcpenn.org/mediainhome/survey/survey7.pdf*

Would you give up TV for a million bucks? (1992, Oct. 10). *TV Guide,* pp. 10-17.

Wright, J. C., & Huston, A. C. (1983). A matter of form: Potentials of television for young viewers. *American Psychologist, 38,* 835-843.

Wright, J. C., & Huston, A. (1989). Potentials of television for young viewers. In G. A. Comstock (Ed.), *Public communication and behavior, Vol. 1.* San Diego, CA: Academic.

Wright, J. C., Atkins, B., & Huston-Stein, A. C. (1978, Aug.). *Active vs. passive television viewing: A model of the development of information processing by children.* Paper presented at the annual meeting of the American Psychological Association, Toronto. (ERIC Document Reproduction Service No. ED 184 521.)

Wright, J. C., St. Peters, M., & Huston, A. C. (1990). Family television use and its relation to children's cognitive skills and social behavior. In J. Bryant (Ed.), *Television and the American family* (pp. 227-252). Hillsdale, NJ: Erlbaum.

Young, B. M. (1990). *Television advertising and children.* Oxford, England: Clarendon.

Zemach, T., & Cohen, A. A. (1986). Perception of gender equality on television and in social reality. *Journal of Broadcasting & Electronic Media, 30*(4), 427–444.

Zemike, K. (2001, April 7). Reading gap widens between top, bottom. *Pittsburgh Post-Gazette*, p. A-6. Reprinted from the *New York Times*.

Zill, N., Davies, E., & Daly, M. (1994, Jun.). *Viewing of "Sesame Street" by preschool children in the United States and its relationship to school readiness.* New York: Children's Television Workshop.

Zuckerman, D. M., Singer, D. G., & Singer, J. L. (1980). Television viewing, children's reading, and related classroom behavior. *Journal of Communication, 30*(1), 166–174.

Zuckerman, P., Ziegler, M., & Stevenson, H. W. (1978). Children's viewing of television and recognition memory of commercials. *Child Development, 49,* 96–104.

Zvacek, S. M. (1992, Feb.). *All the news that's fit to watch in school.* Paper presented at the annual meeting of the Association for Educational Communications & Technology, Washington, DC.

·13·

DISCIPLINED INQUIRY AND THE STUDY
OF EMERGING TECHNOLOGY

Chandra H. Orrill
University of Georgia

Michael J. Hannafin
University of Georgia

Evan M. Glazer
University of Georgia

Few developments have piqued researchers' interest as has the growth of computers in their various hybrid forms as educational tools. A seemingly infinite range of methods and strategies has evolved to exploit the potential of technology. The problem has not been a scarcity of research. Literally thousands of studies related to computers and learning have been published during the past three decades. The problem has been one of making sense of the enormous, and growing, body of available research.

This dilemma is compounded by the continuous metamorphosis of technologies—hardware, software and design—and the relatively short shelf-life of what is considered "state of the art." Present-day technologies often bear little resemblance to the computers of even a decade ago; new hardware and design technologies continue to emerge. During the past 40 years alone, computers have evolved from cumbersome, expensive room-size machines with typewriter displays to inexpensive hand-held devices of substantially greater power, flexibility, and ease of use. Applications have shifted from primitive tutorials to tools for individual inquiry, from typed text to high-fidelity visual images and immersive three-dimension CAVEs (computer-aided virtual environments), and from systems that present information to systems in which individuals construct knowledge. Indeed, the construct of "emerging" technology seems apropos in a field of such rapid and continuous change. The purpose of this chapter is to present one way of making sense of the vast body of educational technology research by organizing and categorizing research related to technology in education along a number of facets. As part of this organization, we examine how differences in the values and assumptions underlying teaching and learning research, theory, and practice have influenced disciplined inquiry related to emerging technologies.

13.1 PERSPECTIVES ACROSS RESEARCH COMMUNITIES

Different communities emphasize different perspectives—at times modest, at times profound. The problems and issues related to teaching, learning and emerging technologies, as well as the methods of study, develop along different paths. Much "educational technology" research focused on the effectiveness of technology in improving test scores, using past achievement as evidence of a problem or need (e.g., Wenglinksy, 1998). "Learning science research," in contrast, might address misconceptions by allowing students to hypothesize, test and reconcile naïve individual beliefs. Each adopts a different epistemological perspective, which influences the questions studied, the literature

Considerations of Use?

		No	Yes
Quest for fundamental understanding?	Yes	Basic and foundational research (Foundation Research)	Use-inspired basic research (Theory-building Research)
	No	X	Pure applied research (Application Research)

FIGURE 13.1. Quadrant model applied to educational technology research

base used to frame and interpret the problem, and the methods of study (Hannafin, Hannafin, Land, & Oliver, 1997).

While it is important to understand goals and distinctions unique to different perspectives, it is beyond the scope of this chapter to do so comprehensively. Rather, we have chosen to highlight particular research processes that characterize particular approaches, then look across the work of researchers from different "schools," to identify patterns and implications not apparent within any single approach. As illustrated in Fig. 13.1, Stokes' (1997) model contrasts research on understanding and use as the key dimensions, each of which is considered as being either central or not central to the aims of the researcher. The extent to which research manifests each dimension (i.e., the pursuit of fundament understanding and use) determines the quadrant (or focal point for impact) of the research.

Basic (or foundation) research, in this context, is concerned with developing principles and standards that may be drawn upon in other settings. In contrast, application research focuses on technology use in a given setting and/or meeting a particular need. Application researchers focus on how the tools work in a particular setting. Rather than attempting to derive principles, application researchers often try to answer practical questions about the use or implementation of an innovation. Theory builders conduct what Stokes terms "use-inspired basic research." They are interested in both practical questions and the development of fundamental understanding. However, their research typically focuses not on the technology (though the technology is important), but on understanding theories about learning as well as ideas for supporting learning. Theory builders are concerned with how well theories embodied in innovations work in practice. (Note. Stokes does not attempt to legitimize research perceived as advancing neither fundamental understanding nor use implications to warrant detailed attention in his presentation of Pasteur's Quadrant. For our purposes, we adopt similar distinctions in our application of Pasteur's quadrant to instructional technology research.)

13.2 PASTEUR'S QUADRANT AND EMERGING TECHNOLOGY RESEARCH

In education—and particularly in educational technology—the dimensions of Fig. 13.1 relate questions about *using* innovations with *developing principles* for designing and developing the innovations. The distinctions are important to establishing

important conceptual distinctions among the growing universe of research, and researchers, related to teaching, learning and emerging technology. The matrix shown in Table 13.1 provides a common set of perspectives across three key research communities represented in Pasteur's Quadrant: foundation, application, and theory building, or use-inspired, research. Throughout this chapter, each column of Table 13.1 will be elaborated into its own matrix focused on a wide range of sample projects within the research perspective. Each matrix provides a means for exploring the kinds of questions posed, the evolution of research threads, differences among the focus and methods of contrasting communities, and distinctions as to the goals and audience of different research communities, classifying seemingly disparate educational technology research. It should be noted that the matrices, as well as the text accompanying them, attempt to broadly define the research field rather than offer a comprehensive review of the literature for that research perspective.

13.2.1 Foundation Research

Analogous to Stokes' pure basic research quadrant, *foundation research* identifies underlying principles and processes that provide core principles to guide, influence, or direct other researchers' efforts. The research appropriate to this quadrant focuses on basic information about an innovation independent of setting. Foundation research focuses on developing fundamental knowledge about technology and its use that is necessary before an innovation or instructional approach can be considered for use in educational settings, while concurrently defining underlying principles and processes for use-inspired research. For the educational technology field, foundation researchers include psychologists, engineers, programmers, and others interested in issues related to how technology can work and what happens when people use it.

13.2.1.1 Goals of the Research. As implied by their placement in the quadrant model, foundation researchers are interested in fundamental knowledge independent from real-world application. For example, Abnett, Stanton, Neale, and O'Malley (2001) examined the consequences of young children working in pairs using more than one mouse. They found that students sharing mice while engaged in a collaborative writing activity exhibited greater levels of shared input and produced higher

TABLE 13.1. Framework for Considering Research on and with Learning Technologies

Community	Foundation (Psychology, Computer Science, Information Management, Engineering)	Application (Educational Technology, Instructional Design)	Theory Building (Learning Sciences)
Nature of the Research	Basic and foundation research—focused on developing fundamental understanding about the technology itself or about affective aspects of technology use (e.g., motivation or efficacy).	Application research—focused on how people interact with and learn from an innovation. Often concerned with innovation in use in a particular setting.	Theory Application & Development (use-inspired basic research)—focused on learning with technology acting as a vehicle. Combination of other two as focus is on developing understanding about learning while focusing on questions about learning in context.
Problem Definition	Concerned with whether the technology is achieving a desired effect. Foundation research provides principles and processes that can be adopted and adapted in other settings.	Concerned with the user's experience. Typically concerned with supporting decision-making regarding adoption and adaptation.	Concerned with implementation and refinement of theory embodied in or captured by technology tools. Often leads to further refinement and retesting of theories and tools.
Research Question Categories	Can people learn from this technology? How does this technology work best? What happens when people use this technology? How do we overcome problems inherent to this technology?	How do users benefit from this innovation? Is the innovation practical? What is the innovation's return on investment? Is the innovation usable? Is the innovation worth using?	How do certain theories enacted in the innovation work? Is the theory underlying my innovation/implementation appropriate? What happens when I test this theory/innovation in context?
Target Audience(s) for the Research	Developers Engineers Programmers Instructional designers	Policy makers Evaluators Decision makers Practitioners	Researchers Instructional designers Practitioners

quality stories. While this research could be considered application research, the intent of the research was to build a body of baseline evidence of a need that might warrant further inquiry, not a solution to a defined problem. Foundation research can also serve as initial steps in the development of educational applications of technology. The work undertaken by Dede's (e.g., Dede, Salzman, & Loftin, 2000) and Winn's (e.g., Winn et al., 1997) virtual reality groups provided insight into whether students could learn from virtual reality as well as how they interacted with the virtual environments but without the expectation of addressing a manifest need or a common classroom problem. Their work served as foundation for subsequent researchers interested in educational virtual reality environments.

The goals of the foundation research are typically twofold: (1) The researchers are interested in particular technology innovation, and (2) more importantly, they are interested in testing a hypothesis related to some facet of that innovation. Often, hypothesis testing drives the research. Investigators may be interested in increased motivation related to the use of technology, information search processes on the Internet, or patterns of reading in a hypermedia environment (see Table 13.2 for a snapshot of the variety of questions and issues addressed in foundation research). Researchers set out to test or reveal focused, but potentially generalizable, principles. Once conclusions are drawn, the foundation researcher or other researchers may embody the findings in later work that is more explicitly

contextualized. For example, Antonietti, Imperio, Rasi, and Sacco's (2001) work with hypermedia and virtual reality was focused on a single learning task—learning about lathes. However, their research questions were focused on the hypothesis that seeing the virtual reality version of the lathe before interacting with related hypermedia information would yield different results than interacting first with the information, then with the virtual tool. In the end, their research yielded a principle about using virtual reality and hypermedia that is largely context-independent—that is, users with no previous mental model seem to benefit from interacting with the virtual environment before reading about it, whereas the users with previous experience benefit more from interacting with the hypermedia materials followed by the virtual experiences.

Various foundation researchers' work reflects different assumptions about learning or interaction. For example, many questions are concerned with information processing issues such as how young students navigate using CD-ROMs (e.g., Large, Beheshti, & Breleux, 1998). However, some are interested in sociocultural theories as evidences by their work focused on the role of an instructor in a learning environment (e.g., Hmelo, Nagarajan, & Day, 2000). Often, foundation researchers concentrate on sets of closely linked questions of a highly interdependent nature, such as the research on information processing and human memory. Foundation researchers often develop more inclusive, generalizable theories and principles through

TABLE 13.2. Sample Questions and Findings from Foundation Research

Selected Research Questions	Studies	Findings
Scaffolding		
How is a joint problem space constructed? How is the process influenced by incoming knowledge levels?	Hmelo, Nagarajan, & Day, 2000	Low incoming knowledge students and high incoming knowledge students used different processes to solve a problem. However, both relied on computer tools to structure their activity and to prompt them to consider certain factors.
Do different versions of a concept-mapping system affect performance?	Chang, Sung, & Chen, 2001	Students using a scaffold that was a partially completed expert concept map scored better on performance outcomes than those who created their own maps.
Do students who take notes have better achievement than those who do not?	Trafton & Trickett, 2001	Found that students using note taking answered more questions correctly than those who did not. Found different levels of scaffolding in note taking affected both use of learning strategy and task performance.
Hypermedia/Multimedia		
Can students learn using a virtual lathe? Given a virtual and hypermedia environment, which is better for students to encounter first?	Antonietti, Imperio, Rasi, & Sacco, 2001	Students can learn from virtual lathe. Trend emerged that it was beneficial to experience VR condition before hypermedia if students do not know about lathes. The opposite is true if they do have a prior mental model for a lathe.
Do users react better to more or less information in a hypertext system?	Dimitroff, Wolfram, & Volz, 1995	Found complex relationships between maneuverability and usability in the systems. In the system with more information, users felt it was usable, but rated it low for accessing the information they wanted.
Does a hypertext system better support information location than a print-based system?	Egan, Remde, Landauer, Lochbaum, & Gomez, 1995	Found hypertext users had better search accuracy, fewer erroneous responses, and produced superior essays than those using print-based system.
Is there evidence that the brain processes various media types differently?	Gerlic & Jausovec, 1999	Used EEG readings to determine that the brain reacts differently to images and movies than to text.
Information Organization/Seeking		
What strategies do young novices use when seeking information?	Marchionini, 1989	Older searchers were able to find information faster and with more success. Younger searchers generally used whole sentence searches indicating a lack of understanding of information organization.
What kinds of strategies do adults use in searching for information?	Van Der Linden, Sonnentag, Frese, & Van Dyck, 2001	Systematic efforts led to better task performance. Trial and error can be effective, but also leads to a number of negative errors. Noneffective strategies lead to lower self-evaluation. Repeating unsuccessful searches or excessive searches led to low performance.
Usability of Innovations/Human Factors		
Does using two mice influence student collaboration?	Abnett, Stanton, Neale, & O'Malley, 2001	Presence of second mouse did not impact communication amount. Gender of students in pair influenced kind of communication, but second mouse seemed to promote equity. Quality of student work was improved.
How do users react to and use a "programming by example" system?	Cypher, 1995	Subjects were uncomfortable giving up control to automated system. There were important interface flaws that kept users from understanding what was happening.
What kinds of virtual reality cues lead to the most learning in an immersive VR environment?	Dede et al., 2000; Dede, Salzman, & Loftin, 1996	Found that three-dimensional representations were more effective than two-dimensional representations. Found that users preferred multimodal cues (haptic, sound, & sight).
Motivation		
How do student motivation, inquiry quality, and the interactions between these develop?	Hakkarainen, Lipponen, Jarvela, & Niemivirta (1999)	Student motivation was no different in computer environment than on self-report. Significant differences emerged between motivation orientation and knowledge production.
How are student and teacher motivation related in a design and technology project?	Atkinson, 2000	Found a positive correlation between teacher motivation and student motivation for project.

TABLE 13.2. Continued

Selected Research Questions	Studies	Findings
What is virtual reality's potential as a motivating learning tool?	Bricken & Byrne, 1992; Byrne, Holland, Moffit, Hodas, & Furness, 1994	Found that students were motivated in virtual environments—particularly those they created themselves.
Learning from Technology		
Can students learn content in an immersive virtual reality environment?	Winn et al., 1997; HITL, 1995; Winn, 1995	Yes, students can learn content. Lower achieving students may particularly benefit.
Can VR aid in eliminating student science misconceptions?	Dede et al., 2000	Found that students learn correct content and that they seem to have their incoming misconceptions challenged by participation in immersive environment.

multiple studies related to a single topic. These studies, however, are not inherently related except by topic strand—a researcher may choose to focus on motivation, for instance, and conduct a number of separate motivation studies over a period of years. Further, this research tends not to be iterative in nature or self-correcting. After all, making revisions in the conditions during a study removes the controlled environment that basic research requires to develop understandings about the phenomenon of interest.

13.2.1.2 Questions Asked.
Research questions asked in foundation research tend to be tightly focused, discrete, and largely unconcerned with specific contextual factors except those variables that impact the theory. To-be-learned content, for example, is often described more in terms of characteristics and complexity (e.g., problem solving, inquiry) than as specific to a domain (e.g., determining how far light waves travel, use of specific pedagogical approaches in scientific inquiry). Whereas an application researcher may study the practical value of tool use in a particular domain or setting, and theory builders may attempt to study how (or if) an innovation supports learning in particular ways, foundation researchers study whether and how an idea works—under particular circumstances and with a particular subject pool.

Foundation researchers study questions such as whether or an innovation works, under what conditions it works, and how people work with the innovation, but not questions about the users' experience with the innovation or whether the innovation was worth using. Often, the research questions require the innovation be compared against a control group so that researchers can determine the statistical reliability of the observed differences. In some cases, foundation questions focus on a specific prototype. For example, Chang, Sung, and Chen (2001) created a concept-map scaffolding system to support their inquiry. In other cases, questions rely on a specific innovation only as a vehicle for understanding a phenomenon, such as Marchionini's (1989) early hypertext research on student search strategies. While some structure was provided for the search activity, there was no overt attempt to test a particular product; rather, Marchionini attempted to understand how children of different ages conducted an information search. Table 13.2 presents a representative selection of foundation research studies

related to emerging technologies, many of which are elaborated throughout this section.

13.2.1.3 Methodologies.
Research conducted by foundation researchers is often experimental or quasi-experimental in nature. This is largely related to the historical roots of the instructional technology field, where experimental designs dominated most of the foundation research dome prior to the 1990s, and questions typically asked: *whether* the innovation works and *to what extent* it works. From the perspective of the emerging technology research community, it provides a baseline from which to chart growth or measure change. Foundation researchers often do not know the extent to which an innovation or idea is effective without also knowing what performance would be elicited from similar subjects who have not interacted with the innovation.

How questions examine the ways in which people interact with an innovation. In these studies, quasi-experimental studies are often employed (or in many cases should be employed), often featuring pre/postmeasures or other within-group or within-subject measures rather than the between-groups measures often appropriate for other questions. Typically, though not exclusively, data collected during these studies tend to be objective in nature. Participant surveys, pre/postmeasures, and observational checklists are commonly employed in these studies, and hypotheses are tested using data are analyzed statistically to establish objective baseline indicators and threshold data. Interestingly, however, recent efforts have adapted approaches from usability testing and observational qualitative approaches, broadening both the methodological toolkit of the researcher and the question and method options for inquiry.

13.2.1.4 Audience.
Foundation researchers provide information about people and innovations for a wide spectrum of technology-related research. Instructional developers use foundation research for decision making; educational technologists use it for selecting appropriate classroom materials; while learning scientists use this research to formulate and test their contextualized hypotheses. Foundation researchers also inform one another. Programmers, engineers, and psychologists deepen their understanding of relevant principles from their own or other disciplines to design future studies or implement future

innovations. Research agendas emerge by linking together separate foundation studies that center on a hypothesis and refine it over time through progressive refinements in underlying principles.

13.2.1.5 Examples of Foundation Research.

13.2.1.5.1 Virtual Reality Usability Research. Early VR researchers were interested in whether learning could occur in virtual environments and to what extent it occurred as well as on the usability issues of such systems. Dede's (e.g., Dede et al., 2000; Dede, Salzman, & Loftin, 1996) research, for example, centered on ScienceSpace, a series of immersive microworlds designed to promote the learning of physical science principles, but considered questions that were not specific to that tool. In addition to student satisfaction and learning, the researchers studied what happens as learners attempt to use an immersive VR program. These and related studies helped to provide principles about VR learning that can be used in a wide array of settings. For example, these early studies found that users prefer multimodal (haptic, sight, and sound) systems and that there is a tendency for disorientation sickness. These studies, and the findings from them were not related to the mastery of particular content or the use of the tools in a particular setting, rather they focused on foundational questions about the potential of VR.

Further VR research focused on understanding frames of reference—an issue unique to immersive technologies. One study indicated the importance of using the egocentric view to see details and the exocentric view to understand the big picture (Salzman, Dede, Loftin, & Ash, 1998). Another study found that students in the 3D environment could construct two-dimensional representations of the concept, however those in the two-dimensional space were unable to create a 3D representation (Dede et al., 2000)—important principles related to learning in immersive environments developed through foundation research.

13.2.1.5.2 Hypermedia Research. As alluded to thus far in the discussion of foundation research, much hypermedia research can be considered foundation research. From the early hypermedia studies that attempted to determine differences in the use of hypertext versus linear text (see McKnight, Dillon, & Richardson, 1996, or Thompson, Simonson, & Hargrave, 1996, for overviews of early hypermedia research) to the current research focused on understanding factors that impact learning with hypertext, there has been a consistent focus on foundation questions related to what makes hypertext work best and what happens when people use it.

Shapiro (1999), for example, has studied the relevance of hierarchies and other organizational structures on the way people learn information. In her study, Shapiro offered adults information on a made-up topic (life forms on another planet) organized in different ways. The same body of information was available to each participant, however, some saw it hierarchichally organized, some saw it clustered, others saw it in a linear form, and the final group saw the information unstructured. Her findings

indicated that there was no difference in the amount of factual knowledge learned across the three groups, but that there was a bias for structured groups, particularly the hierarchical group, in cued association tests and information mapping. In fact, she found that those who were given the hierarchy used it readily while those who were not given the hierarchy tended to try to develop their own hierarchical organization as they moved through the tasks.

Dimitroff, Wolfram, and Volz (1995) studied the effects of different factors on participant information retrieval using a hypertext system. While their methods varied considerably from Shapiro's, they had at least one finding in common—that participants' mental model, or lack thereof, impacted their interactions with a hypertext system. In their study, Dimitroff and colleagues looked at a basic and enhanced version of their hypertext information retrieval system. The enhanced system varied from the basic system only in that it included additional hyperlinked information. The abstract and titles of materials were included in a keyword link. The researchers assigned their 83 adult participants to either a basic system group or an enhanced system group and asked them to complete five searches (known item, keyword, descriptor, and two different subject searches) then complete a user survey. In their factor analysis of the survey results, the researchers found that for both conditions maneuverability was rated quite low. This included factors such as the fun and frustration levels the participants reported, whether the system was easier than other systems they had used, and whether the system was confusing. In fact, 74 percent of the negative comments reported in both groups were related to system maneuverability. Conversely, the participants found the system to be quite useful. They reported it was easier to use than they expected and felt the navigation was not overwhelming. While these are only two of a host of hypermedia research efforts, they demonstrate how foundation research has moved our understanding forward.

13.2.2 Application Research

Application research focuses on in-context technology innovations and issues of practice. Application researchers include instructional developers, educational technologies, and educational evaluators, as well as teachers conducting action research in their own classrooms. In terms of Stokes' model, the research is applied in nature; questions are mainly concerned with the application of principles in the real-world rather than the development of underlying design or learning theories to guide future use or development. Further, questions often focus on the user's experience with the innovation rather than the innovation itself. Often, the work of the application researchers supports decision making ranging from the actual cost of instructional technology for a school district (Keltner & Ross, 1995) to whether an EPSS system is effective for supporting teachers in conducting their day-to-day activities (Moore & Orey, 2001).

13.2.2.1 Goals of the Research. Often, application research focuses primarily on whether innovations are effective and worthwhile in a given context. Application research

questions vary widely, tending to focus on whether technology should be used in a given setting or by a particular audience. This research transcends experimental settings, focusing on technology as used in classrooms such as WebQuests or computer aided instruction systems, and performance technologies, such as electronic performance support systems and training simulations. For example, the Moore & Orey (2001) research included in Table 13.3 focused on whether EPSS systems were effective in supporting teachers as they conducted everyday activities. The researchers found that only elements of the EPSS were used and, consistent with the applied nature of the research, the investigators identified some key attributes that impacted the innovation's effectiveness in practice.

Another common goal of application research is to improve the implementation of an innovation rather than focusing on improving the innovation itself. For example, the research will address whether the innovation is worthwhile, as well as factors that impaired or facilitated the innovation's utility or value, speculations on elements that might make it more effective, and principles of broader implications. Stuhlmann and Taylor (1999), for example, in their examination of factors influencing student-teacher technology use, identified both factors that impacted the student-teachers and hypothesized about effective ways of supporting student-teacher technology integration during classroom experiences.

13.2.2.1.1 Questions Asked. Application research is most concerned with understanding the practical issues related to the use of technology by learners—whether in classrooms, informal settings, or just-in-time training situations. In simplest terms, this area of research is concerned with the kinds of questions summarized in Table 13.3: "Did it work?" "How will it work best?" and "What matters to the users as they use it?" To this end, researchers are concerned with questions of effectiveness as measured through defined criteria, such as return on investment, cost effectiveness, and usability. Often, the questions answered by research out of this group have straightforward "yes," "no," or "it depends" answers. While the researcher generally provides clear rationales and foundations for the questions asked the way they are considered, the answer is a clear one. For example, Wenglinsky's (1998) review of NAEP data asked questions about how technology could be used to support achievement in mathematics. His study yielded simple guidance on the effectiveness of computers for supporting mathematics achievement. Findings included suggestions that drill and practice do not increase student achievement and, in some cases, may actually lower achievement. Further, Wenglinsky found a correlation between teacher professional development and reported effectiveness of technology used in the classroom.

13.2.2.2 Methodologies. Unlike foundation research, application research tends to be concerned with users and their experiences with technologies—particularly as their experience relates to specified goal attainment. Because of this, much of the research takes the form of case studies or of evaluations of particular innovations in use. Another common approach to application research is analysis of standardized test results to determine whether set goals were achieved through the use of the innovation.

Research focused on practical use, however, may also use approaches such as teacher (or action) research, evaluation, think-alouds, cost modeling, or usability studies. Given the goal of determining whether an innovation is efficient or effective, almost any approach to research that allows measurable growth to be witnessed or allows the researcher to interact with the learners as they are experiencing an innovation becomes a viable method for conducting the research.

13.2.2.3 Audience. The audience for application research includes any of a variety of decision makers. These may include administrators or financial agents in education or business, teachers, curriculum specialists, or other people placed in the position of selecting or implementing instructional materials in any school district, university, corporate, or military setting.

13.2.2.4 Examples of Application Research. Cost effectiveness research. One form the "did it work?" question has taken focuses on the return-on-investment versus cost of developing technology innovations. This has been considered as the measure for defining effectiveness (see Niemiec, 1989, for a review of several early cost effectiveness studies related to computer-based instruction). As an historical example of application research, cost effectiveness as a research area evolved to meet a series of locally bound needs. Early in the evolution of computer-assisted instruction, it became clear that developing courseware and acquiring needed hardware would be an expensive proposition. To achieve useful results to research considering costs, researchers have taken different approaches. For example, some researchers applied "value-added" models, where the gains associated with such systems were evaluated relative to the additional costs incurred in obtaining them (see, for example, the methods described by Levin & Meister, 1986, and Niemeier, Blackwell, & Walberg, 1986, in Kappan's issue on the effects of computer-assisted instruction). This approach rarely yielded favorable results. Another perspective considered cost-replacement approaches to evaluate the relative costs associated with learning via "traditional" approaches—usually teacher-led, textbook-based methods—versus computer-aided methods. The underlying question shifted from assessing the marginal gains of "add-on" technologies, to one in which the costs of replacing existing methods were assessed (e.g., Bork, 1986). Judgments as to the true value of computers versus traditional classroom-based teaching on learning could then be assessed, appropriate designs and models could be implemented, true costs (immediate, recurring, long-term) associated with each could be identified, and the relative effectiveness of each method could be benchmarked without undue confounding.

There are countless ways researchers can consider effectiveness of innovations. They range from reasonable to questionable (e.g., media comparison studies) and provide a variety of information to the audience for which they are intended.

TABLE 13.3. Sample Questions and Findings from Application Research

Selected Research Question	Studies	Findings
Tool Use & Design		
Are first graders able to make productive use of a synchronous collaborative workspace?	Tewissen, Lingnau, Hoppe, Mannhaupt, & Nischk, 2001	Synchronous workspace can be effective in literacy development if the students are properly prepared to use it.
What are the critical success factors for implementing MOOSE (a virtual reality MUD) into classrooms?	Bruckman & DeBonte, 1997	Case study showed that the 4 critical success factors were student access to computers, presence of peer experts, student freedom to choose to use versus being told to use, and teacher tolerance for productive chaos.
What kinds of interface elements are best suited to multimedia for primary school children and do multimedia tools have a role to play in the classroom?	Large, 1998	Students showed confidence in navigation in each product, but were hesitant to use searching. Children are not naïve users and can discern between attractive interfaces and useful tools. Multimedia should only be used when there is a clear need for it.
How can a problem-based learning tool be best used in a classroom?	Laffey, Tupper, Musser, & Wedman, 1998	Found that for successful use, teacher must be philosophically aligned with pedagogical approach and the tool must fit with the authentic activity of the classroom.
How did participants use an asynchronous conferencing tool to support learning in an online problem-based environment?	Orrill, 2002	Found that students tended to use tool for logistics and often did not provide rationales for comments. Students were persistent in getting their point across. Recommendations about ways to promote meaningful interactions are provided.
Performance		
Can a custom-designed EPSS support teachers in carrying out day-to-day activities?	Moore & Orey, 2001	The teachers were able to use it to facilitate certain record keeping. There was a strong relationship between usage of the system, performance on teacher tasks, and attitudes toward the system and technology.
Does EPSS use by instructional designers lead to high learning and/or better performance on an analysis task?	Bastiaens, 1999	EPSS users had lower levels of learning, but exhibited higher levels of performance. There was no difference in time on task or satisfaction with training in two groups.
How can we best structure student experiences with information seeking?	Bowler, Large, & Rejskind, 2001	Provides findings about how students seek information as well as a list of issues that determine student success with information finding, interpretation, and use.
Usefulness/Utility Research		
What factors influence student teachers' experience with technology integration?	Stuhlmann & Taylor, 1999	Identified 3 factors that influence student teachers' experience (computer availability, technological attitude and competency of cooperating teacher, and attitude of principal toward use). Also made recommendations about supporting student teachers.
Do navigational assistants improve search experiences?	Mazlita & Levene, 2001	Novice users were able to navigate with this system more easily than traditional search engines. Expert searchers who were about the same on both. Users found the interface too complex.
How do student frustrations with an online learning environment inhibit their learning experience?	Hara & Kling, 1999	Three main areas caused frustration: technological problems; minimal and untimely feedback from instructor; ambiguous instructions. Impacted course because students gave up on learning content.
Return on Investment		
What is the Return on Investment (ROI) for a set of EPSSs?	Hawkins, Gustafson, & Nielson, 1998	Provides a rationale and model for determining ROI.

TABLE 13.3. Continued

Selected Research Question	Studies	Findings
What does it cost to have a K-12 technology program?	Keltner & Ross, 1995	Considered all related costs as well as effectiveness. Provided figures between $142 per student to over $400 per student.
Meta-analyses of Implementation/Application Studies		
What does research say about the impact of technology on student achievement?	Schacter, 1999	According to the research reviewed, students with access to various kinds of learning technologies see gains on a variety of outcome measures.
Does small group learning enhance student achievement? What features moderate small-group success? Are there optimal conditions for using small groups with computer technology?	Lou, Abrami, & d'Apollonia, 2001	Small group learning had positive effects on individual performance and small group performance. The best outcomes occurred when tasks were difficult, groups had 3–5 members, and no or minimal feedback was available from the computer.
What is the observed effectiveness and efficiency of computer simulations for supporting scientific discovery learning?	De Jong & van Joolingen, 1998	Findings indicate that students do not perform better on outcome tests, but do exhibit indicators of deeper understanding and implicit application than those who did not use simulations. Also included outcomes of particular designs.

13.2.2.4.1 Computer-Supported Collaborative Learning.
Computer-supported collaborative learning (CSCL) research, like many other research strains reported here, spans across the three major research groups of interest in this chapter. Numerous studies of CSCL consider when, how, and under what conditions students use CSCL tools (e.g., Kynigos, Evangelia, & Trouki, 2001; Laffey, Tupper, Musser, & Wedman, 1998). Consistent with application research, these questions focus on whether "it" worked—whether "it" was an instructional approach or a tool. For example, as shown in Table 13.3, Laffey et al.'s (1988) work on the PBLSS examined issues of use with online tools for supporting problem-based learning. Their research indicated that, for technology to scaffold authentic inquiry in school, the tool must align with the teacher's assessment needs work as well as the students' needs in their inquiry process. Kynigos and colleagues (2001) explored how elementary-aged Greek students used CSCL. In their study, students in two classrooms were to work together via email to plan a trip to each other's location. Their findings indicated that collaborating this way promoted greater student attention to written communication; students learned that they could not make basic assumptions in their communications. They also found that the students, perhaps because of the teacher, often focused on school questions rather than personal questions. As a result the students learned about each other's locations, little was learned about the other students and their cultures. Finally, the authors described a "question and answer game" that emerged. This was a pattern of communication where students answered incoming questions and asked new questions. Typically, students did not offer alternatives to the questions asked. For example, one of the classes asked the other about routes to travel to visit their city. The queried students immediately identified that there was another possible route, but chose not to share that information because they had not been asked about it. In another example of the question and answer game, the students were encouraged by their teacher

to generate new questions if they received a response that did not include questions. This indicated that the teachers' roles in the communication impacted the students' experiences. Clearly, these studies offered advice about what it means for CSCL to work and under what conditions it may work.

Another group of CSCL application questions focus on the ways in which participants use the tools to communicate. In one study of collocated CSCL learning, Lipponen, Rahikainen, Lallimo, and Hakkarainen (2001), analyzed the patterns and quality of participation among 12- to 13-year-old Finnish students as they worked individually or in a dyad or triad to complete a unit on human senses. Lipponen et al. found that 39 percent of the class participated in the online tool and posted between 7 and 39 notes (mean = 16, s.d. 8.02). They found that the thread size—that is, the number of messages posted in a continuous thread—ranged from 2 to 11 notes (mean = 3.4, s.d. 2.13). They differentiated among central participants and isolated participants by analyzing the number of responses to postings. Of the on-topic postings (63 percent overall), they found that 75 percent provided information and 25 percent asked for clarification. Overall, even younger students could benefit from online communications. Overall, these findings suggested that students can and will use CSCL to share relevant information—particularly to share information with one another.

In a study of the ways students use CSCL tools, education graduate students used an online tool to support distributed problem-based learning (Orrill, 2002). The research showed that students used rationales only 34 and 41 percent of the time even though rationales should provide the basis for agreeing on a problem definition and a plan of action. Perhaps related, the same students were often reluctant to take a stance most of the time, preferring to label messages in neutral ways almost 52 percent of the time. While the students were able to apply labels to their messages, more than one-third of the time, the label was not used in an anticipated way (e.g., "Summary" was used to label a question), but that socially negotiated meanings for the labels emerged. This was complicated by the presence of multiple ideas in each message. Orrill also detected two ways that students used the collaborative space. Some groups used it to engage in problem definition discussions focused on the issues, while others used the space to coordinate effort and tasks. The findings from this research indicate that students can use distributed, online tools to identify problems and plan for their solution, but that the depth and meaningful nature of the conversation is tentative.

Interestingly, Jonassen and Kwon (2001) considered some similar aspects of adult student problem solving using four conditions: online or face-to-face as well as ill-structured or well-structured. In their analyses, the instance of off-task messages was lower for online groups than face-to-face. This suggests that perhaps Lipponen et al.'s (2001) students would have been more off-task if they had worked face-to-face rather than online. Like Orrill, Jonassen and Kwon (2001) found a high degree of "simple agreement" postings in their computer-based groups, that is, postings that simple state a position ("I agree") with no further elaboration or moving forward of the conversation. Here, findings indicated that adult learners may be more focused using CSCL than in a face-to-face group, though the interaction dynamics are quite different.

In a study of how and whether CSCL supports a particular goal, problem solving, Hurme and Järvelä (2001) considered emergent metacognitive processes in the CSCL environment as students construct solutions for math problems. Finnish students, ages 12 and 13 years varied in their use of the CSCL space to work based on the task they were given but very little metacognition was present in their work regardless of the situation. Only the highest-level group in the class was able to use the discussion features for this project; the remaining students posted only their final plan. Consistent with the findings presented above, factors not yet identified seem to impact student success in the use of these tools for higher-level thinking. This collection of application research studies provides insight into the body of CSCL literature examining how students actually use CSCL software in a variety of classroom settings.

Another branch of CSCL research focuses on effectiveness studies. In application research, effectiveness refers to the degree to which an approach meets the needs of the local learners. In short, this research considers whether an innovation is practical and worthwhile. Goldman (1992) considered whether online learning was practical and worthwhile. She found that, as a result of CSCL tool use, student discourse was often rich, involving a variety of materials, resources, and methods. The findings indicated that the environment supported student exploration, investigation, and communication, where the "social glue" served as a mechanism for promoting deeper understanding. This study indicated that the social element appeared to be an important factor in student performance.

Similarly, in a study concerned with implementation of a CSCL software package to support writing skills, Neuwirth and Wojahn (1996) described the importance of instructor–student discourse when using a CSCL writing software to improve writing and reduce frustration. The inquiry centered on the effectiveness of the system for supporting student writing skills. Then

software not only allowed many iterations of feedback, but also supported instructor coaching of peer reviews and supported students' articulation of knowledge about revisions. Students and teacher were able to track editorial changes and use their comments on the screen as a basis for communicating and reflecting on their ideas. Findings indicated that students liked using the tools, were able to see the editing process as one of two-way communication rather than one-way feedback, and were able to make meaningful improvements to their work. In short, the tools proved to be practical and effective for meeting a set of needs.

In a separate effectiveness study, Muukkonen, Lakkala, and Hakkarainen (2001) compared a computer-supported, shared journaling effort with maintaining a written journal. Effectiveness was determined by the extent to which students were engaged in the inquiry process. Students in the CSCL group were asked to post a message where it became public as part of a shared module. The journal group was asked to keep a journal in which they recorded working theories and had peers comment regularly on entries. The results indicated very different entries between the two groups. While both had more working theories than other kinds of note (Control 65.2%, online 40.4%) and similar numbers of scientific explanation notes (11.5% in online group, 10.7% in control), the online group had far more quotes from others (10.3 vs. 3.8% in the control group), more meta-comments (16.8 vs. 9.0% in the control group), and more problem presentations (20.9 vs. 11.3% in the control group). The findings indicated that the journal group was more focused on explaining their own understanding whereas the online group had many interlinked ideas. In short, the online journal fostered a socially shared understanding of the content. In their results, the authors recommended the use of either tool, noting that both bring valuable benefits. These three studies offer insight into application research aimed at answering questions of effectiveness. That is, they all define what it means for the CSCL environment to be considered effective and how their environment did or did not meet those criteria in implementation.

13.2.3 Theory-Building Research

Theory-building research converges where application and foundation knowledge overlap—what Stokes labels as "use-inspired research." Like application researchers, theory builders attempt to address real-world issues; like foundation researchers, they develop fundamental understanding about learners and learning. Theory builders, such as researchers in the learning sciences, are primarily concerned with enacting theories so that hypotheses about learning and learning environments may be tested. However, this group is highly concerned with contexts and the interaction between tools and learning in complex settings such as real classrooms. In theory-building research, technology is viewed as a tool that can support, scaffold, capture, and promote student and teacher thinking, communication, and archival of ideas. The work of the theory builders has fostered long-term, iterative development efforts to better understand learning, teaching, and design.

TABLE 13.4. Common Characteristics of Theory-Building Research

Theory-Building research efforts:

- Feature a research and design process that is intertwined and iterative
- Embody one or more explicit theories about learning and aim to evolve those theories
- Aim to inform design, learning, and instructional theories
- Use a variety of research approaches including case studies and quasi-experimental designs
- Span considerable lengths of time
- Stay within their design group—the tools may be used by others, but the research agenda remains with the developers

As exemplified in significant R& D undertakings such as *The Adventures of Jasper Woodbury* (Jasper) and CSILE, theory builders have created a host of tools and complex systems to support learners in developing conjectures, testing hypotheses, critiquing ideas, and articulating understandings (Stahl, 1999) as they engage in learning activities. Collectively, these systems have become known as "knowledge building environments" (KBEs) and are typically technologically enhanced environments concerned with a specific facet of learning. KBEs are grounded in a particular theory or theories about learning and knowledge; research refines that theory and leads to other theories, such as theories about instruction and school change (See Table 13.4). [In addition to the examples discussed in this chapter, see research from the CoVis (Edelson, Gordin, & Pea, 1999; Edelson, Pea, & Gomez, 1995; O'Neill & Gomez, 1994) and Inquiry Learning Forum (Barab, MaKinster, & Sheckler, in press; Barab, MaKinster, Moore, Cunningham, & ILF Team, 2001) projects for other detailed examples of the theory-based development and research-centered evolution of KBEs.]

13.2.3.1 Goals of the Research.

Theory-building research has a variety of goals subsumed within a single research agenda. Whereas foundation and application research often focus on individual studies and attends to technology and/or human–technology interaction, theory-building efforts focus on extended, in-depth exploration centering on a single theory or hypothesis. Theory-building research focuses on innovations and design that embodies central theories about teaching and learning in authentic situations. Such theories may be broad, such as the theories underlying CSILE: (1) Learning should be intentional; (2) Expertise is a process, not just a performance; and (3) Intentional learning, necessary for building expertise, requires a reframing of schools into knowledge-building communities (Scardamalia & Bereiter, 1996). Similarly, the theories may be well-defined and easier to enact, such as those embodied in the KIE/WISE project: (1) choose topics and models that are accessible to students; (2) use visual representations and help make students' thinking visible; (3) students need opportunities to learn from each other; and (4) science instruction should promote the development of autonomous lifelong learning skills

(Linn, 2000; Linn & Hsi, 2000). Regardless of the set of theories the researchers are interested in, the very existence of rich, interconnected ideas underlying a single intervention requires a different approach to research—one that simultaneously considers interrelationships among the parts of the underlying theory set, yet takes the necessary steps to understand the impact of the various facets of that set by themselves and in context.

Research goals, guided by the underlying theoretical biases, often focus on developing understandings of the learning, teaching, and designing processes. Consistent with application research, the goals of theory-building research center not only on the viability of the theories and processes in controlled settings, but extend to consider the viability and nuances of the theories and processes as they are enacted in the context for which they were intended. The fundamental difference between application research and theory building is the intent. Theory building is concerned with the enactment and refinement of generalizable theories while application research is concerned with considering effectiveness of single implementations of an innovation. Further, theory builders are concerned with the processes involved with the design and implementation of the innovation as well as the outcomes of that implementation. For example, in one report of Jasper, the authors cautioned, "It is emphasized that the research has not been done to 'prove that Jasper works.' Rather, it has been undertaken to understand the kinds of thinking and problem solving that students engage in when they tackle the Jasper challenges ..." (CTGV, 1992b, p. 118).

13.2.3.2 Questions Asked.

Theory-building research looks both inward and outward simultaneously. That is, the research typically informs the design of interest, typically a KBE, itself while simultaneously evolving the community's understanding of generalizable issues related to theories of teaching and learning. For example, KIE research led to the development of several new tools as specific student needs have emerged from classroom-based experiments and case studies (Bell & Linn, 2000; Bell & Davis, 2000). *Sensemaker* was developed to help students organize arguments about science-related controversies, and to sort links to Web sites into categories of "Evidence" in support of their arguments. Simultaneously, these studies led to a fuller understanding about supporting students as they develop the processes and skills necessary to become lifelong science learners.

Findings from theory-building research efforts often spark new questions about the innovations as well as about the theories upon which innovations are built. In the case of Jasper Woodbury, for example, there were many evolving and new themes that emerged. In the assessment research effort, early implementation studies focused on classrooms already invested in the reform ideas championed by national mathematics organizations (e.g., Pellegrino, Hickey, Heath, Rewey, & Vye, 1992); however, later studies focused on schools that were not complying with recommended standards (Hickey, Moore, & Pellegrino, 2001). The research shifted to examine the implementation requirements in environments that were not philosophically or epistemologically aligned with problem-based approaches. Similarly, findings from the nine-state implementation effort for Jasper led to the development of new assessment tools and approaches including the evolutionary development of a "Challenge Series" which allowed students in one classroom to "compete" against students in other classrooms on extension questions related to the Jasper series (CTGV, in press). The evolution of the Challenge series led to simultaneous development of new research questions and development of new design ideas.

Because of the nature of design research, theory-building research efforts tend to evolve over time, and involve multiple collaborators including instructional designers, psychologists, teachers, and programmers. Research questions evolve to make them more responsive to the emerging realities of classroom use as they arise during iterations of research. The Jasper Project, for example, initially focused on several related issues: (1) changes in the students' abilities to solve complex problems over time; (2) effects of different approaches to using Jasper in classroom settings; (3) assessment of problem-solving ability and attitudes about mathematics; and (4) ways of supporting teachers as they implemented these new materials (Cognition and Technology Group at Vanderbilt, 1992a). Over time, however, the research shifted to examine the implementation requirements in environments that were not philosophically or epistemologically aligned with problem-based approaches. Similarly, research was broadened to develop an understanding not only of how learning and instruction principles influence learning in classrooms, but also to compare that to informal learning settings.

13.2.3.3 Methodologies.

Because theory-building research and design efforts are intertwined, research efforts are typically iterative, with successive efforts focusing on different aspects of learning, design, and educational change as they are embodied in the KBE of interest. Design experiments (Brown, 1992; Collins, 1992), formative research (Reigeluth & Frick, 1999), and development research (Reeves, 2000) are commonly employed in the theory-building research efforts. Design-based approaches utilize both traditional quantitative and qualitative research methodologies, often creating and testing new ways to analyze and collect data. The iterative nature allows questions of various scope and complexity to be studied; the findings of successive implementations form a rich base of information to refine theories about learning, design, and teacher change (Edelson, 2002). For example, in a theory-building research effort, an early implementation of a KBE may focus on its use in an after-school club to learn how students interact with a single facet of the KBE environment. Later studies in the research effort may include larger groups (such as whole classes or schools), more specific questions (e.g., "How does this tool support the development of problem-solving strategies?") or more general questions (e.g., "What kinds of changes occur in classrooms using this innovation?"). Hoadley (2002) outlines an evolution of research on one facet of WISE. He provides a roadmap of design decisions, iterations of research and design, research

questions that emerged, and participant groups—starting from a pilot study that included graduate students and focused on proof-of-concept issues, through final iterations that considered how to support middle school students in reveling their identity in their postings. This was relevant because research efforts had uncovered a tendency for students to post anonymously in cases where others had done so.

13.2.3.4 Audience.

Because of the nature of theory-building research, the audiences for the work varies. The attention given to design processes and theory development in theory-building research informs communities of developers (e.g., software designers, programmers, instructional writers) as well as theorists (e.g., psychologists and sociologists). The focus on innovations in use, on the other hand, appeals to decision makers, teachers, and other practitioners who are concerned with whether they should adopt a given innovation for their classroom.

13.2.3.5 Examples of Theory-Building Research.

CSILE/Knowledge Forums The Computer-Supported Intentional Learning Environment (CSILE) is an online information organization and evolution system that supports student learning by capturing information, allowing users to organize it, and sharing the information among participants. CSILE, now known as Knowledge Forums (available at http://www.learn.motion.com/lim/kf/KF0.html), uses an interface that allows users to communicate about their own learning as well as to support others in learning-by-doing activities such as attaching notes to images, displaying notes in a threaded format, and creating "rise-above" notes that allow users to group ideas together (Hewitt, 2000).

Consistent with theory-building research, CSILE was initially developed to research and support students as they learned how to learn, set cognitive goals, and applied comprehension, self-monitoring, and knowledge organization strategies (Scardamalia et al., 1989). The design group held strong beliefs about learning as process rather than product which, in turn, influenced CSILE's affordances. (e.g., Bereiter, 1994; Bereiter, Scardamalia, Cassells, & Hewitt, 1997).

Consistent with design-based research, CSILE's creators employed iterative research cycles to stimulate the refinement of existing tools and the development of tools as student needs were clarified (Scardamalia & Bereiter, 1991). The initial research agenda centered on three main issues: supporting students engaged in intentional learning; transitioning from novice toward expertise; and fundamentally changing schools. The problems were contextualized in actual classrooms, but the researchers aimed to build a more generalizable theory as well: "Nobody wants to use technology to recreate education as it is, yet there is not much to distinguish what goes on in most computer-supported classrooms versus traditional classrooms" (Scardamalia & Bereiter, 1996, p. 249).

CSILE research has focused on learning, pedagogy, and design as well as refining the original theory upon which it was based. A series of case studies and experimental studies were undertaken in a variety of classrooms, from fifth grade through graduate school, and included students who were new to the environment as well as those who had used it for multiple projects. CSILE researchers have explored student goal-setting behaviors (Ng & Bereiter, 1991) as well as conversational interaction among students using CSILE (Cohen & Scardamalia, 1998).

Pedagogically, research has explored whether and how students learn using CSILE (e.g., Bereiter & Scardamalia, 1992; Hewitt & Scardamalia, 1998; Scardamalia & Bereiter, 1993). Research has yielded both generalizable strategies for supporting knowledge building and a range of use-inspired questions about CSILE in the classroom, such as providing multiple entry points to a conversation (e.g., allowing notes to be text-based, graphical, etc.), emphasizing the work of the community over the work of the individual, and encouraging students to participate by both adding notes and exploring the information already present.

CSILE's evolution has been tightly linked to ongoing research on learning and pedagogy, that is, design requirements evolved by watching students use the CSILE system. Design changes were examined to determine not only whether they improved learning, but also how they influenced the students' abilities to engage in intentional knowledge building. Hewitt's research (e.g., Hewitt, 1997, 2000; Hewitt & Scardamalia, 1998; Hewitt, Webb, & Rowley, 1994) has been particularly relevant to the design and development of communal knowledge systems. Hewitt examined the interaction between students and CSILE's affordances to better understand how information is organized, inter-connected, and reused in the service of learning. These efforts resulted in the development of new CSILE functionalities (e.g., an annotation tool) and guided the transition of CSILE to WebCSILE and ultimately Knowledge Forums.

13.2.3.5.1 The Adventures of Jasper Woodbury. Jasper is a videodisc-based mathematics curriculum that serves as an enactment of anchored instruction. Consistent with the design experiment approach, Jasper arose from an identified need in the schools, was based on a series of design principles, enacted and tested a learning theory, relied on and evolved because of partnerships with practitioners, and was studied through a series of experiments and case studies that, combined, offer a holistic image of the effectiveness of the tool, but separated represent a variety of grain sizes, questions, and approaches (e.g., CTGV, 1994, in press).

13.2.3.5.2 The Adventures of Jasper Woodbury, in its final form, includes 12 episodes that fall into four categories of mathematical activities: trip-planning, statistics and business plans, geometry, and algebra. Consistent with the Jasper design principles, the episodes are divided evenly among these categories (see Table 13.5 for a list of the Jasper Design Principles). Each episode is designed to present a problem to the students grounded in a real-world context. For example, in the "Journey to Cedar Creek" episode, the students watch as Jasper Woodbury purchases a boat, buys gas for the boat, gets it repaired, and spends time with a friend. They are provided with a variety of relevant and irrelevant data that would be common to some-

one actually in a boat on a lake or river. The students are asked at the end of the scenario what time Jasper must leave to get home before dark and whether he has enough fuel to make the trip. Each problem, as shown in this example, includes a number of subproblems that the students must complete in order to answer the episode problem.

Jasper was originally developed to address shortcomings in student problem-solving ability identified in previous research by members of the Jasper team. In work leading to Jasper, Bransford's group identified a need for meaningful contexts for mathematical problem solving (e.g., Bransford et al., 1988). Through a series of experiments using commercial videos (e.g., *Raiders of the Lost Ark*), then low-fidelity prototypes, the research team was able to develop and refine a set of design principles as well as develop an understanding about the benefits of anchored instruction (CTGV, 1992b, in press).

In the first round of studies on Jasper, the goals of the research were focused on understanding whether Jasper was, indeed, addressing an actual need. To this end, the researchers presented the Cedar Creek episode to high-achieving sixth graders and college students, then asked a series of increasingly-prompting questions about the main problem and the subproblems ranging from Level 1 (What problems did he have to solve?) to Level 3 (What is the distance from the Marina to get home?) (Van Haneghan et al., 1992; CTGV, 1992b, in press). Findings showed that as the researchers asked more explicit questions, both college and middle schools students were more able to provide reasonable answers to the questions. However, at both college and middle school level, the students showed a very low ability to identify subproblems and solve them. Once this baseline data had been set, the researchers attempted to determine whether short-term instruction with Jasper would impact learning. To this end, both a field-test and a controlled study were undertaken to determine the effects of Jasper on student learning and attitude. Results from the field tests indicated that Jasper was liked by the teachers and students and that students were able to engage in the Jasper activities in a sustained way. Further, students reported that the problems were challenging, but not too hard and students, parents, and teachers reported instances of students thinking about the problems outside of math class. The controlled study posed questions about whether anchored instruction with Jasper would produce learning and transfer that was not experienced by students instructed in word-problem solving activities as instructed in a traditional curriculum. This study of fifth grade students found that, on posttests, both the Jasper and the control group were equally able to solve unrelated context problems. This was surprising given that the control group students had received more instruction related to this skill. Further, Jasper students showed significant gains in the ability to match pertinent information to problems that needed to be solved while the control group did not. Finally, Jasper students we more able than the control students to identify the main problem and subproblems in a similar Jasper activity both in prompted and unprompted cases. From this work, the researchers were able to determine a set of research issues that drove the next phases of development and research on Jasper. These included a need to work with a larger variety of students,

TABLE 13.5. Seven Design Principles Underlying *The Adventures of Jasper Woodbury*

Design Principle	Hypothesized Benefits
Video-based	a) more motivating; b) easy to search; c) support complex cognition; d) good for poor readers, yet can support reading.
Narrative with realistic problem (rather than a lecture on video)	a) makes situation easier to remember; b) more engaging for students; c) promotes student realization of relevance of mathematics and reasoning.
Generative (the story ends and students generate problems to be solved)	a) motivates students to determine ending; b) teaches students to find and define problems to be solved; c) provides enhanced opportunity for reasoning.
Embedded data design (all necessary data is included in the story)	a) permits reasoned decision making; b) motivating to students to find the information in the episode; c) all students have the same knowledge to work from; d) clarifies that relevant data depends on specific goals.
Problem complexity (each problem is at least 14 steps)	a) promote persistence—overcome student tendency to try for a few minutes, then quit; b) introduce students to levels of complexity seen in real, everyday problems; c) help student learn to deal with complexity; d) develop student confidence in abilities.
Pairs of related adventures (the Jasper adventures were originally all paired by key activities)	a) extra practice with core mathematical ideas; b) helps students clarify what is or is not transferable; c) illustrates analogical thinking.
Links across the curriculum	a) helps extend mathematical thinking to other areas; b) encourages knowledge integration; c) support information finding and publishing.

Note. This table adapted from CTGV, 1992a.

to provide professional development to teachers, and to develop assessment tools.

The next generation of Jasper work focused on a nine-state implementation that involved over 1300 students, included a 2-week professional development component for teachers, and collected large amounts of Jasper and control data from a subset of the implementation sites (e.g., CTGV, 1992c,1994, in press). The research goals at this phase were to better understand student abilities to represent and solve complex problems; to determine the effects of different teaching approaches on the experiences with Jasper; to assess instructional outcomes on problem solving and student attitudes toward math; and to better understand how to support teachers as they learned the new materials (CTGV, 1992a). Research on these questions included qualitative, quasi-experimental, and anecdotal evidence. The findings indicated that in the development of complex problem solving skills Jasper students made significant gains in their abilities to generate subproblems and subgoals as well as to determine which subproblem a calculation belonged with while control group students did not. Jasper students also outperformed control group students on one-step, two-step, and multistep word problems. Changes in student attitudes toward mathematics and their perceived abilities during the implementation year were significantly higher in Jasper groups except on questions of the students' abilities. It should be noted that while Jasper students saw mathematics as being more relevant and felt more self-confidence, their overall ratings of these items were still not

particularly high. Further measures of mathematical skills indicated that Jasper had a positive impact on basic concepts and skills in most classrooms. Further, findings indicated that Jasper had a small, but not significant, positive impact on student scores on standardized tests.

Jasper research on teacher professional development focused on the same nine-state implementation. Teachers attended a summer workshop as members of triads that included two teachers from each participating school and a corporate partner who would help support the teacher in the implementation of the series. The professional development focused on solving Jasper adventures, providing teachers with the opportunity to develop some basic computer skills, and the opportunity for teachers to learn some multimedia skills. The teachers rated the workshop very highly and felt confident in their abilities to implement Jasper. As the implementation occurred, the researchers determined, based on artifacts they were receiving, that the implementation was very different based on implementation site. Further, they found that teachers did little more than focus on the adventures—they did not use the multimedia materials. In the follow-up workshop, researchers learned that the teachers felt strongly that they needed more support in the initial implementation and that they saw the use of the multimedia elements as a new idea to implement in Year 2. Based on the findings from this effort, the Jasper team developed plans for ongoing professional development (CTGV, 1994, in press).

Finally, the assessment strand of the implementation research was concerned with not only finding ways to determine what kinds of learning was occurring, but to do so in ways that the students and teachers approved of. In the initial implementation, teachers reported significant negative reaction to the paper-and-pencil assessments developed by the Jasper team (CTGV, 1994, in press). In response to this negative attitude, the team developed a new approach to assessment called the "Jasper Challenge Series" which was like a call-in game show in which classrooms of students competed against each other. A succession of design experiments were undertaken to develop and refine the challenges beyond the initial implementation (e.g., CTGV, 1994).

Like all of the major research projects discussed in this theory-building research section, Jasper has proven a fertile ground for experimenting with new ideas, refining them, and understanding their impact on student thinking and mathematical ability. The research that has grown out of the Jasper effort has shown not only that Jasper might be construed as "effective" but also attempts to add to the dialogue about what "success" means, what it looks like when students learn, and how we can promote meaningful experiences. Even now, more than a decade after the initial premier of the Jasper series, we are seeing worthwhile studies of learning being published ranging from those considering the interplay of a number of variables on trying to understand Jasper's success (Hickey, Moore, & Pellegrin, 2001) and those concerned with what elements of cooperation impact the success of group problem solving (Barron, 2000). Also, consistent with good design research, Jasper simultaneously developed solutions and looked for problems, partnered with teachers, and focused on the theories and beliefs that the solutions were built on.

13.2.3.5.2 Web-Based Inquiry Science Environment (WISE). WISE (http://wise.berkeley.edu) is a 3rd generation technology built upon enabling projects: Computers as Learning Partners (CLP) (Linn & Hsi, 2000), which focused on knowledge integration and teaching as design, and the Knowledge Integration Environment (KIE) (Linn, Bell, & Hsi, 1998; Slotta & Linn, 2000), which focused on scaffolding knowledge integration with technology. WISE was designed to embody the principles of "scaffolded knowledge integration" (Linn & Hsi, 2000) by "engag(ing) students in sustained investigation, providing them with cognitive and procedural supports as they make use of the Internet in their science classroom" (Slotta & Linn, 2000, p. 193).

WISE research has focused simultaneously on questions of use and the development of fundamental understanding about learning. WISE researchers have studied and developed tools and supports to help students learn science, support online collaborative learning, make thinking visible, and search for information (Bell, 1996; Slotta & Linn, 2000). Recent work has focused on supporting teachers as they develop modules—from developing a partnership program to developing discipline-specific support tools within the system (Linn & Slotta, 2000; Linn, Clark, & Slotta, in press). As shown in Table 13.6, the research questions asked in a theory-building line of research require a variety of research methods be employed. In the case of WISE, these include methods commonly associated with the fundamental research group such as quasi-experimental, comparison designs (e.g., Clark & Slotta, 2000; Hoadley, 2000), as well as methods more common to application research such as analysis of longitudinal data collected through authentic use of the system (e.g., Bell & Davis, 2000).

Characteristic of theory-building research, the WISE effort has informed design, learning, and pedagogy. WISE technology and curriculum have evolved continuously through research resulting in easy-to-use software. WISE scientists, teachers, and educational researchers projects have developed a library of teaching and learning activities. As WISE matured from its earlier versions in KIE and CLP, researchers confronted new questions focusing on professional development, teacher practice, and curriculum and assessment. Over the past several years, thousands of teachers and tens of thousands of students have participated in WISE activities (Slotta, 2002). WISE research demonstrates the value of intertwining iterative tool development, curriculum design, and theory building and the importance of longitudinal approaches to theory-building research.

13.3 THE FUTURE OF RESEARCH AND EMERGING TECHNOLOGIES

This chapter has attempted to provide a representative rather than exhaustive review of contrasting, and in some cases complementary, community perspectives advanced by emerging technology researchers. It seems to us naïve and perhaps impossible to examine research in terms of hardware per se—computers, video, CD-ROM, and the like. By design, we have avoided attempts to organize these trends in terms of technological "things." Rather, we focus our perspectives and analysis on the kinds of questions researchers from diverse epistemological backgrounds pose and address related to technology. Our matrix attempts to overlay a framework on emerging technology research to better understand the kinds of questions asked, the communities who ask them, and the underlying beliefs on which they are based. We build on the distinctions made by Stokes and others who describe research in terms of the underlying intent of the research community—whether concerned with solving real-world problems of use or developing fundamental building-block knowledge across settings.

Are there really "new" research questions, or are they variations of existing themes? To be certain, the questions posed and the methods employed vary as a function of the epistemological biases, contextual factors, social and community values and mores of the researchers. So, perhaps conventional wisdom—the problem and question drive the method—is oversimplified: The very same "things" are often examined in dramatically different ways—different questions, different theoretical frameworks, different methods and measures. It is the unique lens through which innovation is viewed that influences what is studied and how it is studied. To refine and understand one's lens is to define the researchers frame; to communicate this frame effectively is to reveal the basic foundations, assumptions and biases underlying a research study or program of research.

TABLE 13.6. Sample Questions and Findings from WISE Research

Selected Research Questions	Design or Pedagogical Strategy from Research Findings	Selected Studies	Findings
Make Science Accessible			
How can we use Internet resources to make learning accessible?	Setting appropriate scope and goals	Slotta & Linn, 2000; Linn, 2000	Advance guidance helps students use Internet materials effectively
How do we help students connect a variety of ideas	Build from current ideas, provide richer models	Linn, Bell, & Hsi, 1998; Clark & Linn, in press	Depth of coverage leads to more coherent understandings
Make Thinking Visible			
How do we support students in engaging in scientific learning process?	Development of activity checklist—leads to integrated learning rather than memorizing	Linn, Shear, Bell & Slotta, 1999	Controversy-based curriculum can introduce ideas about the nature of science
How do we support students in modeling expert thinking?	Ways to use advance organizers with student arguments	Bell & Linn, 2000	Technology scaffolds can enable richer arguments
How can we support students in engaging in knowledge integration through debate?	Development and refinement of SenseMaker argumentation tool	Bell & Linn, 2000; Bell & Davis, 2000	Design of debate activities includes use of evidence, critique of peers, revision of arguments
Help Students Learn from Each Other			
How do we engage all students in meaningful conversation	Development and refinement of SpeakEasy online discussion tool	Hoadley, 2000; Hsi & Hoadley, 1997	Student participation increases dramatically in online forums
How can students learn from debate?	Research use of online discussions in inquiry projects	Hsi, 1997; Hoadley & Linn, 2000	Social representations add value to discussions Careful design is required to integrate online discussions with curriculum
Promote Lifelong Science Learning/Promoting Autonomy			
How do we help students become lifelong science learners?	Development of principles for supporting student knowledge integration	Linn & Hsi, 2000; Clark & Slotta (2000)	Articulated a set of design principles for knowledge integration activities
How do we support students in conducting their own knowledge integration?		Linn & Clancy, 1992; Linn and Hsi, 2000; Slotta and Linn, 2000	A case study approach benefits students. Explored the use of personally relevant topics
How do we support students in integrating knowledge through reflection?	Development of Mildred—an online scaffolding & reflection system	Davis & Linn, 2000; Bell, & Davis, 2000; Davis, 2000	Explored the nature of effective prompts
How does perceived credibility impact student use of evidence?	Development of principles for selecting media to support all learners	Clark & Slotta, 2000; Slotta & Linn, 2000	Manipulated evidence credibility in studies of student argumentation Showed that critiquing skills can be promoted by advance guidance

References

Abnett, C., Stanton, D., Neale, H., & O'Malley, C. (2001). *The effect of multiple input devices on collaboration and gender issues*. Paper presented at EuroCSCL 2001: Maastricht, Netherlands. Available online http://www.mmi.unimaas.nl/euro-cscl/presentations.htm [2002, November 4].

Antonietti, A., Imperio, E., Rasi, C., & Sacco, M. (2001). Virtual reality and hypermedia in learning to use a turning lathe. *Journal of Computer Assisted Learning, 17*, 142–155.

Atkinson, S. (2000). An investigation into the relationship between teacher motivation and pupil motivation. *Educational Psychology, 20*(1), 45–57.

Barab, S., MaKinster, J., & Sheckler, R. (in press). Designing system dualities: Building online community. In S. A. Barab, R. Kling, & J. Gray (Eds.), *Designing for virtual communities in the service of learning*. Cambridge, MA: Cambridge University Press.

Barab, S. A., MaKinster, J. G., Moore, J. A., Cunningham, D. J., & The ILF Design Team (2001). Designing and building an on-line community: The struggle to support sociability in the Inquiry Learning

Forum. *Educational Technology Research & Development, 49*(4), 71-96.

Barron, B. (2000). Achieving coordination in collaborative problem solving groups. *The Journal of the Learning Sciences, 9*(4), 403-436.

Bastiaens, T. J. (1999). Assessing an electronic performance support system for the analysis of jobs and tasks. *International Journal of Training and Development, 3*(1), 54-61.

Bell, P., (1996). *Designing an activity in the Knowledge Integration Environment.* Paper presented at the Annual Meeting of the American Educational Research Association: New York.

Bell, P., & Davis, E. A. (2000). Designing Mildred: Scaffolding students' reflection and argumentation using a cognitive software guide. In B. Fishman & S. O'Connor-Divelbliss (Eds.), *Fourth International Conference of the Learning Sciences* (pp. 142-149). Mahwah, NJ: Erlbaum.

Bell, P. & Linn, M. C. (2000). Scientific arguments as learning artifacts: Designing for learning from the web with KIE. *International Journal of Science Education, 22*(8), 797-817.

Bereiter, C. (1994). Implications of postmodernism for science, or, science as progressive discourse. *Educational Psychologist, 29*(1), 3-12.

Bereiter, C., & Scardamalia, M. (1992). Two models of classroom learning using a communal database. In S. Dijkstra (Ed.), *Instructional models in computer-based learning environments.* Berlin: Springer-Verlag.

Bereiter, C., Scardamalia, M., Cassells, C., & Hewitt, J. (1997). Postmodernism, knowledge building, and elementary science. *The Elementary School Journal, 97*(4), 329-340.

Bork, A. (1986). Let's test the power of interactive technology. *Educational Leadership, 43*(6), 36-37.

Bowler, L., Large, A., & Rejskind, G. (2001). Primary school students, information literacy, and the web. *Education for Information, 19,* 201-223.

Bransford, J., Hasselbring, T., Barron, B., Kulewicz, S., Littlefield, J., & Goin, L. (1988). Uses of macro-contexts to facilitate mathematical thinking. In R. I. Charles & E. A. Silver (Eds.), *The teaching and assessing of mathematical problem solving* (pp. 125-147). Hillsdale, NJ: Erlbaum & National Council of Teachers of Mathematics.

Bricken, M., & Byrne, C. (1992). Summer students in virtual reality: A pilot study on educational applications of virtual reality technology. In A. Wexelblat (Ed.), *Virtual reality applications and explorations.* Cambridge, MA: Academic Press Professional.

Brown, A. L. (1992). Design experiments: Theoretical and methodological challenges in creating complex interventions in classroom settings. *Journal of the Learning Sciences, 2*(2), 141-178.

Bruckman, A., & De Bonte, A. (1997). *MOOSE goes to school: A comparison of three classrooms using a CSCL environment.* Paper presented at Computer Support for Collaborative Learning: Toronto. Available online: http://www.oise.utoronto.ca/cscl/papers/bruckman.pdf [2002, November 4].

Byrne, C., Holland, C., Moffit, D., Hodas, S., & Furness, T. A. (1994). *Virtual reality and "at risk" students* (R-94-5). Seattle: University of Washington.

Chang, K. E., Sung, Y. T., & Chen, S. F. (2001). Learning through computer-based concept mapping with scaffolding aid. *Journal of Computer Assisted Learning, 17,* 21-33.

Clark, D., & Linn, M. C. (in press). Scaffolding knowledge integration through curricular depth. *The Journal of Learning Sciences.*

Clark, D. B., & Slotta, J. D. (2000). Evaluating media-enhancement and source authority on the internet: The Knowledge Integration Environment. *International Journal of Science Education, 22*(8), 859-871.

Cognition and Technology Group at Vanderbilt (CTVG) (1992a). The Jasper experiment: An exploration of issues in learning and instructional design. *Educational Technology Research & Development, 40*(1), 65-80.

Cognition and Technology Group at Vanderbilt (CTVG) (1992b). The Jasper Series. A generative approach to improving mathematical thinking. In K. Sheingold, L. G. Roberts, & S. M. Malcolm (Eds.), *This year in school science1991: Technology for learning and teaching.* Washington, DC: American Association for the Advancement of Science.

Cognition and Technology Group at Vanderbilt (CTVG) (1992c). The Jasper Series as an example of anchored instruction: Theory, program description, and assessment data. *Educational Psychologist, 27*(3), 291-315.

Cognition and Technology Group at Vanderbilt (CTVG) (1994). From visual word problems to learning communities: Changing conceptions of cognitive research. In K. McGilly (Ed.), *Classroom lessons: Integrating cognitive theory and classroom practice.* Cambridge, MA: MIT Press/Bradford Books.

Cognition and Technology Group at Vanderbilt (CTVG) (in press). The Jasper series: A design experiment in complex mathematical problem solving. In J. Hawkins & A. Collins (Eds.), *Design experiments: Integrating technologies into schools.* New York: Cambridge University Press.

Cohen, A., & Scardamalia, M. (1998). Discourse about ideas: Monitoring and regulation in face-to-face and computer-mediated environments. *Interactive Learning Environments, 6*(1-2), 93-113.

Collins, A. (1992). Toward a Design Science of Education. In E. Scanlon & T. O'Shea (Eds.), *New Directions in Educational Technology.* Berlin/New York: Springer-Verlag.

Cypher, A. (1995). Eager: Programming repetitive tasks by example. In R. M. Baecker, J. Grudin, W. A. S. Buxton, & S. Greenberg (Eds.), *Readings in human-computer interaction: Toward the year 2000,* 2nd ed. (pp. 804-810). San Francisco: Morgan Kaufman Publishers, Inc.

Davis, E. A., & Linn, M. C. (2000). Scaffolding students' knowledge integration: Prompts for reflection in KIE. *International Journal of Science Education, 22*(8), 819-837.

De Jong, T., & van Jooligen, W. R. (1998). Scientific discovery learning with computer simulations of conceptual domains. *Review of Educational Research, 68* (2), 179-201.

Dede, C., Salzman, M., Loftin, R. B., & Ash, K. (2000). The design of immersive virtual learning environments: Fostering deep understandings of complex scientific knowledge. In M. J. Jacobson & R. B. Kozma (Eds.), *Innovations in science and mathematics education: Advanced designs for technologies of learning* (pp. 361-414). Mahwah, NJ: Lawrence Erlbaum Associates.

Dede, C., Salzman, M. C., & Loftin, R. B. (1996). *ScienceSpace: Virtual realities for learning complex and abstract scientific concepts.* Paper presented at the IEEE Virtual Reality Annual International Symposium, New York.

Dimitrof, A., Wolfram, D., & Volz (1995). Affective response and retrieval performance: Analysis of contributing factors. *Library and Information Science Research, 18,* 121-132.

Edelson, D. C. (2002). Design research: What we learn when we engage in design. *The Journal of the Learning Sciences, 11*(1), 105-121.

Edelson, D. C., Gordin, D. N., & Pea, R. D. (1999). Addressing the challenges of inquiry-based learning through technology and curriculum design. *The Journal of the Learning Sciences, 8*(3 & 4), 391-450.

Edelson, D. C., Pea, R. D., & Gomez, L. M. (1995). Constructivism in the collaboratory. In B. G. Wilson (Ed.), *Constructivist Learning Environments: Case Studies in Instructional Design* (pp. 151-164). Englewood Cliffs, NJ: Educational Technology Publications.

Egan, D. E., Remde, J. R., Landauer, T. K., Lochbaum, C. C., & Gomez, L. M. (1995). Behavioral evaluation and analysis of a hypertext browser. In R. M. Baecker, J. Grudin, W. A. S. Buxton, & S. Greenberg (Eds.), *Readings in human–computer interaction: Toward the year 2000*, 2nd ed. (pp. 843-848). San Francisco: Morgan Kaufman Publishers, Inc.

Gerlic, I., & Jausovec, N. (1999). Multimedia: Differences in cognitive processes observed with EEG. *Educational Technology Research & Development, 47*(3), 5-14.

Goldman, S. V. (1992). Mediating microworlds: Collaboration on high school science activities. In T. Koschmann (Ed.), *CSCL: Theory and practice of an emerging paradigm* (pp. 45-82). Mahwah, NJ: Lawrence Erlbaum Associates.

Goldman, S. V. (1996). Mediating microworlds: Collaboration on high school science activities. In T. Koschmann (Ed.), *CSCL: Theory and Practice* (pp. 45-82). Mahwah, NJ: Lawrence Erlbaum Associates, Inc.

Hakkarainen, K., Lipponen, L., Jarvela, S., & Niemivirta, M. (1999). The interaction of motivational orientation and knowledge-seeking inquiry in computer-supported collaborative learning. *Journal of Educational Computing Research, 21*(3), 263-281.

Hannafin, M. J., Hannafin, K. M., Land, S., & Oliver, K. (1997). Grounded practice and the design of constructivist learning environments. *Educational Technology Research and Development, 45*(3), 101-117.

Hara, N., & Kling, R. (1999). Students' frustrations with a web-based distance education course. *First Monday, 4*(12). Available online: http://firstmonday.org/issues/issue4_12/hara/index.html [2002, November 4].

Hawkins, C. H., Gustafson, K. L., & Neilsen, T. (1998). Return on investment (ROI) for electronic performance support systems: A Web-based system. *Educational Technology, 38*(4), 15-21.

Hewitt, J. (1997). *Beyond threaded discourse.* Paper presented at the WebNet '97, Toronto.

Hewitt, J. (2000, April). *Sustaining interaction in a Knowledge Forum classroom.* Paper presented at the American Educational Research Association, New Orleans.

Hewitt, J., & Scardamalia, M. (1998). Design principles for distributed knowledge building processes. *Educational Psychology Review, 10*(1), 75-96.

Hewitt, J., Webb, J., & Rowley, P. (1994, April). *Student use of branching in a computer-supported discussion environment.* Paper presented at the American Educational Research Association, New Orleans.

Hickey, D. T., Moore, A. L., & Pellegrino, J. W. (2001). The motivational and academic consequences of elementary mathematics environments: Do constructivist innovations and reforms make a difference? *American Educational Research Journal, 38*(3), 611-652.

HITL (1995). *The US West Virtual Reality Roving Vehicle program.* HITL. Available: http://www.hitl.washington.edu/projects/education/vrrv/vrrv-3.95.html [2002, June 1].

Hmelo, C. E., Nagarajan, A., & Day, R. S. (2000). Effects of high and low prior knowledge on construction of a joint problem space. *Journal of Experimental Education, 69*(1), 36-56.

Hoadley, C. M. (2000). Teaching science through online, peer discussions: SpeakEasy in the Knowledge Integration Environment. *International Journal of Science Education, 22*(8), 839-857.

Hoadley, C. M. (2002). Creating context: Design-based research in creating and understanding CSCL. In *Proceedings of CSCL 2002.* Boulder, CO. January, 2002.

Hoadley, C. M., & Linn, M. C. (2000). Teaching science through online peer discussions: SpeakEasy in the Knowledge Integration Environment. *International Journal of Science Education*, Special Issue(22), 839-857.

Hsi, S. (1997). *Facilitating knowledge integration in science through electronic discussion: The Multimedia Forum Kiosk.* Unpublished doctoral dissertation, University of California, Berkeley, CA.

Hsi, S., & Hoadley, C. M. (1997). Productive discussions in science: Gender equity through electronic discourse. *Journal of Science Education and Technology, 6*, 23-36.

Hurme, T., & Järvelä, S. (2001). *Metacognitive processes in problem solving with CSCL in math.* Paper presented at Euro CSCL 2001. Maastricht, Netherlands. Available: http://www.mmi.unimaas.nl/euro-cscl/presentations.htm.

Jonassen, D. H., & Kwon, H. I. (2001). Communication patterns in computer-mediated versus face-to-face group problem solving. *Educational Technology Research and Development, 49*(1), 35-51.

Keltner, B., & Ross, R. L. (1995). *The cost of school-based educational technology programs.* RAND Corporation. Arlington, VA. Available: http://www.rand.org/publications/MR/MR634/. [2002, November 5].

Kynigos, C., Evangelia, V., & Trouki, E. (2001). *Communication norms challenged in a joint project between two classrooms.* Paper presented at Euro CSCL 2001. Maastricht, Netherlands. Available: http://www.mmi.unimaas.nl/euro-cscl/presentations.htm.

Laffey, J., Tupper, T., Musser, D., & Wedman, J. (1998). A computer-mediated support system for project-based learning. *Educational Technology Research & Development, 46*(1), 73-86.

Large, A., Beheshti, J., & Breuleux, A. (1998). Information seeking in a multimedia environment by primary school students. *Library & Information Science Research, 20*(4), 343-376.

Levin, H., & Meister, G. (1986). Is CAI cost-effective? *Phi Delta Kappan, 67*, 745-749.

Linn, M. C. (2000). Designing the Knowledge Integration Environment. *International Journal of Science Education, 22*(8), 781-796.

Linn, M. C., Bell, P., & Hsi, S. (1998). Using the Internet to enhance student understanding of science: The Knowledge Integration Environment. *Interactive Learning Environments, 6*(1-2), 4-38.

Linn, M. C., & Clancy, M. J. (1992). The case for case studies of programming problems. *Communications of the ACM, 35*(3), 121-132.

Linn, M. C., Clark, D., & Slotta, J. D. (in press). WISE design for knowledge integration. In S. Barab & A. Luehmann (Eds.), *Building sustainable science curriculum: Acknowledging and accommodating local adaptation, Science Education.*

Linn, M. C., & Hsi, S. (2000). *Computers, teachers, peers: Science learning partners.* Mahwah, NJ: Lawrence Erlbaum Associates.

Linn, M. C., Shear, L., Bell, P., & Slotta, J. D. (1999). Organizing principles for science education partnerships: Case studies of students' learning about 'rats in space' and 'deformed frogs'. *Educational Technology Research and Development, 47*(2), 61-85.

Linn, M. C., & Slotta, J. D. (2000). WISE science. *Educational Leadership, 58*(2), 29-32.

Lipponen, L., Rahikainen, M., Lallima, J., & Hakkarainen, K. (2001). *Analyzing patterns of participation and discourse in elementary students' online science discussion.* Paper presented at Euro CSCL 2001. Maastricht, Netherlands. Available: http://www.mmi.unimaas.nl/euro-cscl/presentations.htm.

Lou, Y., Abrami, P. C., & d'Apollonia, S. (2001). Small group and individual learning with technology: A meta-analysis. *Review of Educational Research, 71*(3), 449-521.

Marchionini, G. (1989). Information-seeking strategies of novices using a full-text electronic encyclopedia. *Journal of the American Society for Information Science, 40*(1), 54-66.

Mazlita, M. H., & Levene, M. (2001). Can navigational assistance improve search experience? *First Monday, 6*(9), online: http://firstmonday.org/issues/issue6_9/mat/index.html

McKnight, C., Dillon, A., & Richardson, J. (1996). User-centered design of hypertext/hypermedia for education. In D. H. Jonassen (Ed.), *Handbook of research for educational communications and technology* (pp. 622-633). New York: Simon & Schuster Macmillan.

Moore, J. L., & Orey, M. (2001). The implementation of an electronic performance support system for teachers: An examination of usage, performance, and attitudes. *Performance Improvement Quarterly, 14*(1), 26-56.

Muukkonen, H., Lakkala, M., & Hakkarainen, K. (2001). *Characteristics of university students' inquiry in individual and computer-supported collaborative study process.* Paper presented at Euro CSCL 2001. Maastricht, Netherlands. Available: http://www.mmi.unimaas.nl/euro-cscl/presentations.htm.

Neuwirth, C. M., & Wojahn. P. G. (1996). Learning to write: Computer support for a cooperative process. In T. Koschmann (Ed.), *CSCL: Theory and Practice* (pp. 45-82). Mahwah, NJ: Lawrence Erlbaum Associates, Inc.

Ng, E., & Bereiter, C. (1991). Three levels of goal orientation in learning. *The Journal of the Learning Sciences, 1*(3), 243-271.

Niemeier, R., Blackwell, M., & Walberg, H. (1986). CAI can be doubly effective. *Phi Delta Kappan, 67,* 750-751.

Niemiec, R. (1989). Comparing the cost-effectiveness of tutoring and computer-based instruction. *Journal of Educational Computing Research, 5,* 395-407.

O'Neill, D. K., & Gomez, L. M. (1994). *The collaboratory notebook: A networked knowledge-building environment for project learning.* Paper presented at the Ed-Media, Vancouver, B. C.

Orrill, C. H. (2002). Supporting online PBL: Design considerations for supporting distributed problem solving. *Distance Education, 23*(1), 41-57.

Pellegrino, J. W., Hickey, D., Heath, A., Rewey, K., & Vye, N. (1992). *Assessing the outcomes of an innovative instructional program: The 1990-1991 implementation of "The Adventures of Jasper Woodbury Program"* (Tech. Rep. No 91-1). Nashville: Vanderbilt University, Learning & Technology Center.

Reeves, T. C. (2000). Socially responsible educational technology research. *Educational Technology, 40*(6), 19-28.

Reigeluth, C. M., & Frick, T. W. (1999). Formative research: A methodology for creating and improving design theories. In C. M. Reigeluth (Ed.), *Instructional-design theories and models: A new paradigm of instructional theory* (Vol. II, pp. 633-651). Mahwah, NJ: Lawrence Erlbaum Associates, Publishers.

Salzman, M., Dede, C., Loftin, R. B., & Ash, K. (1998). *Using VR's frames of reference in mastering abstract information.* Paper presented at the Third International Conference of the Learning Sciences, Atlanta.

Saye, J. W., & Brush, T. (2002). Scaffolding critical reasoning about history and social issues in multimedia supported environments. *Educational Technology Research and Development, 60*(3), 77-96.

Scardamalia, M., & Bereiter, C. (1991). Higher levels of agency for children in knowledge building: A challenge for the design of new knowledge media. *The Journal of the Learning Sciences, 1*(1), 37-68.

Scardamalia, M., & Bereiter, C. (1993). Technologies for knowledge-building discourse. *Communications of the ACM, 36*(5), 37-41.

Scardamalia, M., & Bereiter, C. (1996). Computer support for knowledge-building communities. In T. Koschmann (Ed.), *CSCL: Theory and practice of an emerging paradigm* (pp. 249-268). Mahwah, NJ: Lawrence Erlbaum Associates.

Scardamalia, M., Bereiter, C., McLean, R. S., Swallow, J., & Woodruff, E. (1989). Computer-supported intentional learning environments. *Journal of Educational Computing Research, 5*(1), 51-68.

Schacter, J. (1999). *The impact of education technology on student achievement: What the most current research has to say.* Santa Monica, CA: Milken Exchange on Education Technology: Available: http://www.mff.org/publications/publications.taf?page=161 [2002, Novermber 5]

Selman, R. L. (1980). *The growth of interpersonal understanding.* New York: Academic Press.

Shapiro, A. M. (1999). The relevance of hierarchies to learning biology from hypertext. *The Journal of the Learning Sciences, 8*(2), 215-243.

Slotta, J. D. (2002). Designing the Web-based Inquiry Science Environment. In S. Hooper (Ed). *Educational technology, 42*(5), 5-28.

Slotta, J. D., & Linn, M. C. (2000). The Knowledge Integration Environment: Helping students use the internet effectively. In M. J. Jacobson & R. B. Kozma (Eds.), *Innovations in science and mathematics education: Advanced designs for technologies of learning* (pp. 193-226). Mahwah, NJ: Lawrence Erlbaum Associates.

Stahl, G. (1999). *Reflections on WebGuide: Seven issues for the next generation of collaborative knowledge-building environments.* Paper presented at the CSCL, Stanford.

Stokes, D. E. (1997). *Pasteur's Quadrant: Basic science and technological innovation.* Washington DC: Brookings Institution Press.

Stuhlmann, J. M., & Taylor, H. G. (1999). Preparing technologically competent student teachers: A three-year study of interventions and experiences. *Journal of Technology and Teacher Education, 7*(4), 333-350.

Tewissen, F., Lingnau, A., Hoppe, U., Mannhaupt, G., & Nischk, D. (2001). *Collaborative writing in a computer-integrated classroom for early learning.* Paper presented at EuroCSCL 2001: Maastricht, Netherlands. Available online: http://www.mmi.unimaas.nl/euro-cscl/Papers/161.pdf [2002, November 4].

Thompson, A. D., Simonson, M. R., & Hargrave, C. P. (1996). *Educational technology: A review of the research* (2nd ed.). Washington, DC: Association for Educational Communications and Technology.

Trafton, J. G., & Trickett, S. B. (2001). Note-taking for self-explanation and problem solving. *Human-Computer Interaction, 16*(1), 1-38.

Van Der Linden, D., Sonnentag, S., Frese, M., & Van Dyck, C. (2001). Exploration strategies, performance, and error consequences when learning a complex computer task. *Behavior & Information Technology, 20*(3), 189-198.

Van Haneghan, J. P., Barron, L., Young, M., Williams, S., Vye, N., & Bransford, J. (1992). The Jasper series: An experiment with new ways to enhance mathematical thinking. In D. F. Halpern (Ed.), *Enhancing thinking skills in the sciences and mathematics* (pp. 15-38). Hillsdale, NJ: Lawrence Erlabum Associates, Inc.

Wenglinsky, H. (1998). *Does it computer: The relationship between educational technology and student achievement in mathematics* . Princeton, NJ: Educational Testing Service.

Winn, W. D. (1995). The Virtual Reality Roving Vehicle project. *Technological Horizons in Education, 23*(5), 70-74.

Winn, W., Hoffman, H., Hollander, A., Osberg, K., Rose, H., & Char, P. (1997). *The effect of student construction of virtual environments on the performance of high- and low-ability students.* Paper presented at the Annual meeting of the American Educational Research Association, Chicago.

DISTANCE EDUCATION

Charlotte Nirmalani Gunawardena
University of New Mexico

Marina Stock McIsaac
Arizona State University

14.1 INTRODUCTION

The field of distance education has changed dramatically in the past ten years. Distance education, structured learning in which the student and instructor are separated by place, and sometimes by time is currently the fastest growing form of domestic and international education. What was once considered a special form of education using nontraditional delivery systems, is now becoming an important concept in mainstream education. Concepts such as networked learning, connected learning spaces, flexible learning and hybrid learning systems have enlarged the scope and changed the nature of earlier distance education models. Web-based and web-enhanced courses are appearing in traditional programs that are now racing to join the "anytime, anyplace" educational feeding frenzy. In a 2002 survey of 75 randomly chosen college distance learning programs, results revealed an astounding rate of growth in the higher education distance learning market (Primary Research Group, 2002). In a time of shrinking budgets, distance learning programs are reporting 41 percent average annual enrollment growth. Thirty percent of the programs are being developed to meet the needs of professional continuing education for adults. Twenty-four percent of distance students have high speed bandwidth at home. These developments signal a drastic redirection of traditional distance education.

With the rise and proliferation of distance learning systems has come the need to critically examine the strengths and weaknesses of various programs. A majority of new programs have been developed to meet the growing needs of higher education in responding to demands for flexible learning environments, continuing education and lifelong learning. David Noble, the Ralph Nader of Distance Education, has written a series of papers examining what he calls the private, commercial hijacking of higher education. He makes the case that the banner touting cheap online education waved in front of administrators has resulted in much higher costs than expected. The promotion of online courses, according to Noble, has resulted in a huge, expensive infrastructure that he describes as a technological tapeworm in the guts of higher education (Noble 1999, November). In a later piece, Noble describes the controversy in 1998 that developed at UCLA over its partnership with a private company, the Home Education Network (THEN). The controversy, over public and private partnerships and great expectation of financial returns, he says, is fueled by extravagant technological fantasies which underly much of today's enthusiasm for distance education. Noble describes this expectation as a pursuit of what appears increasingly to be little more than fool's gold (Noble 2001, March).

Noble is one of a growing group of scholars becoming increasingly disillusioned with the commercialization of distance learning, particularly in the United States. They call for educators to pause and examine the enthusiastic claims of distance educators from a critical perspective. With the recent developments in hybrid combinations of distance learning, flexible learning, distributed learning, web-based and web-enhanced instruction, the questions facing educators are how to examine new learning technologies from a wider perspective than we have in the past, and to examine how distance education fits into the changing educational environment. Scholars are exploring information technologies from the critical perspectives of politics, hidden curriculum, pedagogy, cost effectiveness, and the global impact of information technologies on collective intelligence (Vrasidas, & Glass, 2002).

Due to the rapid development of technology, courses using a variety of media are being delivered to students in various locations in an effort to serve the educational needs of growing populations. In many cases, developments in technology allow distance education programs to provide specialized courses to students in remote geographic areas with increasing interactivity between student and teacher. Although the ways in which distance education is implemented differ markedly from country to country, most distance learning programs rely on technologies which are either already in place or are being considered for their cost effectiveness. Such programs are particularly beneficial for the many people who are not financially, physically or geographically able to obtain traditional education. Although there is an increase in the number of distance services to elementary and secondary students, the main audience for distance courses continues to be the adult and higher education market. Most recently, Kaplan College launched the nation's first online certificate program for security manager and crime scene technicians under their certificate program for homeland security (Terry, 2002, August 27).

Distance education has experienced dramatic growth both nationally and internationally since the early 1980s. It has evolved from early correspondence education using primarily print based materials into a worldwide movement using various technologies. The goals of distance education, as an alternative to traditional education, have been to offer degree granting programs, to battle illiteracy in developing countries, to provide training opportunities for economic growth, and to offer curriculum enrichment in non traditional educational settings. A variety of technologies have been used as delivery systems to facilitate this learning at a distance.

In order to understand how research and research issues have developed in distance education, it is necessary to understand the context of the field. Distance education relies heavily on communications technologies as delivery media. Print materials, broadcast radio, broadcast television, computer conferencing, electronic mail, interactive video, satellite telecommunications and multimedia computer technology are all used to promote student-teacher interaction and provide necessary feedback to the learner at a distance. Because technologies as delivery systems have been so crucial to the growth of distance education, research has reflected rather than driven practice. Early distance education research focused on media comparison studies, descriptive studies, and evaluation reports. Researchers have examined those issues that have been of particular interest to administrators of distance education programs such as; student attrition rates, the design of instructional materials for large scale distribution, the appropriateness of certain technologies for delivery of instruction, and the cost effectiveness of programs.

However, the growth of flexible learning, networked learning and distributed learning models, is blurring the distinctions between distance and traditional education. These models and their related network technologies also have the capability of creating new environments for learning such as "virtual communities." For more than 8 years students in traditional settings have been given entire courses on CD-ROM multimedia disks through which they have progressed at their own pace, interacting with the instructor and other students on electronic mail or face to face according to their needs (Technology Based Learning, 1994). These materials are now available using web-based multimedia technologies. In earlier collaborative projects, students around the world participated in cooperative learning activities sharing information using computer networks (Riel, 1993). In these cases, global classrooms often have participants from various countries interacting with each other at a distance. Many mediated educational activities have allowed students to participate in collaborative, authentic, situated learning activities (Brown, Collins, & Duguid, 1989; Brown & Palincsar, 1989). In fact, the explosion of information technologies has brought learners together by erasing the boundaries of time and place for both site based and distance learners.

Research in distance education reflects the rapid technological changes in this field. Although early research was centered around media comparison studies, recent distance education research has examined four main underlying research issues: learner needs, media and the instructional process, issues of access, and the changing roles of teachers and students (Sherry, 1996). Educators have become more interested in examining pedagogical themes and strategies for learning in mediated environments (Berge & Mrozowski, 2001; Collis, deBoer, Vander-Jeen, 2001; Salomon, Perkins, & Gloperson, 1991; Vrasidas & McIsaac, 1999) Knowledge construction and mediated learning offer some of the most promising research in distance education (Barrett, 1992; Glaser, 1992; Harasim, 2001; Salomon, 1993).

This chapter traces the history of the distance education movement, discusses the definitions and theoretical principles which have marked the development of the field and explores the research in this field which is inextricably tied to the technology of course delivery. A critical analysis of research in distance education was conducted for this chapter. Material for the analysis came from four primary data sources. The first source was an ERIC search, which resulted in over 900 entries. This largely North American review was supplemented with international studies located in the International Centre for Distance Learning (ICDL) database. The entries were then categorized according to content and source. Second, conference papers were reviewed which represented current, completed work in the field of distance education. Third, dissertations were obtained from universities that produced the majority of doctoral dissertations in Educational Technology doctoral programs. Finally, five journals were chosen for further examination because of their recurrent frequency in the ERIC listing. Those journals were *Open Learning, American Journal of Distance Education, International Review of Research in Open and Distance Learning, Distance Education,* and *Journal of Distance Education.*

14.2 HISTORY OF DISTANCE EDUCATION

Distance Education is not a new concept. In the late 1800s, at the University of Chicago, the first major correspondence program in the United States was established in which the teacher and learner were at different locations. Before that time, particularly in preindustrial Europe, education had been available primarily to males in higher levels of society. The most effective form of instruction in those days was to bring students together in one place and one time to learn from one of the masters. That form of traditional education remains the model today. The early efforts of educators like William Rainey Harper in 1890 to establish alternatives were laughed at. Correspondence study, which was designed to provide educational opportunities for those who were not among the elite and who could not afford full time residence at an educational institution, was looked down on as inferior education. Many educators regarded correspondence courses as simply business operations. Correspondence education offended the elitist, and extremely undemocratic educational system that characterized the early years in this country (Pittman, 1991). Indeed, many correspondence courses were viewed as simply poor excuses for the real thing. However, the need to provide equal access to educational opportunities has always been part of our democratic ideals, so correspondence study took a new turn.

As radio developed during the First World War and television in the 1950s, instruction outside of the traditional classroom had suddenly found new delivery systems. There are many examples of how early radio and television were used in schools to deliver instruction at a distance. Wisconsin's School of the Air was an early effort, in the 1920s, to affirm that the boundaries of the school were the boundaries of the state. More recently, audio and computer teleconferencing have influenced the delivery of instruction in public schools, higher education, the military, business and industry. Following the establishment of the Open University in Britain in 1970, and Charles Wedemeyer's innovative uses of media in 1986 at the University of Wisconsin, correspondence study began to use developing technologies to provide more effective distance education. The United States was slow to enter the distance education marketplace, and when it did, a form of distance education unique to its needs evolved. Not having the economic problems of some countries nor the massive illiteracy problems of developing nations, the United States nevertheless had problems of economy of delivery. Teacher shortages in areas of science, math, and foreign language combined with state mandates to rural schools produced a climate, in the late 1980s, conducive to the rapid growth of commercial courses such as those offered via satellite by the TI-IN network in Texas, and Oklahoma State University. In the United States, fewer than 10 states were promoting distance education in 1987. A year later that number had grown to two-thirds of the states and by 1989 virtually all states were involved in distance learning programs. Perhaps the most important political document describing the state of distance education in the 1980s was the report done for Congress by the Office of Technology Assessment in 1989 called *Linking for Learning* (Office of Technology Assessment, 1989). The report gives an overview of distance learning, the role of teachers, and reports of local, state and federal projects. It describes the state of distance education programs throughout the United States in 1989, and highlights how technology was being used in the schools. Model state networks and telecommunication delivery systems are outlined with recommendations given for setting up local and wide area networks to link schools. Some projects, such as the Panhandle Shared Video Network and the Iowa Educational Telecommunications Network, have served as examples of operating video networks which are both efficient and cost effective. The 1990s saw a rapid rise in the number of institutions wanting to offer network- based flexible learning through traditional programs. As they looked at the potential market and at the growth of online degree programs using a commercial portal, a conceptual battle began between the for-profit and non-profit providers. The success of joint business ventures capitalizing on the information needs of the educational community in the digital age will depend on how these partnerships are viewed by educational institutions, commercial courseware providers and the students themselves.

In the United States, national interest and federal involvement in virtual learning is reflected in the creation of The Bipartisan Web-based Education Commission by Congress in 1998, as part of the reauthorization of the Higher Education Act under Title VIII. Chaired by former Nebraska Senator J. Robert Kerrey and co-chaired by Georgia Congressman Johnny Isakson, the 16-member commission was charged with studying how the Internet can be used in education—from pre-kindergarten to job retraining—and what barriers may be slowing its spread." The Commission's report, titled "*The Power of the Internet for Learning*" (2000) urges the new administration and 107th Congress to make E-learning a center-piece of the nation's education policy. "The Internet is perhaps the most transformative technology in history, reshaping business, media, entertainment, and society in astonishing ways. But for all its power, it is just now being tapped to transform education. . . . There is no going back. The traditional classroom has been transformed" (Web-Based Education Commission, 2000, p. 1).

The House Education and Workforce Committee and the Subcommittee on 21st Century Competitiveness approved H.R. 1992, a bill to expand Internet learning opportunities in higher education. The "Internet Equity and Education Act of 2001" (2001) would repeal the rule that requires schools to provide at least 50 percent of their instruction in person, as well as the "12-hour" rule that requires students enrolled in classes that do not span a typical quarter or semester to spend at least 12 hours per week in class. The bill would allow students to use federal loans to pay for a college education delivered entirely over the Internet. This bill is the first step toward making the Web-based Education Commission's recommendations a reality. By allowing students to use federal loans to pay for on-line courses, H.R. 1992 will make the on-line option available to more students.

14.2.1 Defining Distance Education

In 1982, the International Council for Correspondence Education changed its name to the International Council for Distance Education to reflect the developments in the field. With the rapid growth of new technologies and the evolution of systems for delivering information, distance education with its ideals of providing equality of access to education, became a reality. Today there are distance education courses offered by dozens of public and private organizations and institutions to school districts, universities, the military and large corporations. Direct satellite broadcasts are produced by more than 20 of the country's major universities to provide over 500 courses in engineering delivered live by satellite as part of the National Technological University (NTU). In the corporate sector, more than 40 billion dollars a year are spent by IBM, Kodak, and the Fortune 500 companies on distance education programs. Distance education is the broad term that includes distance learning, open learning, networked learning, flexible learning, distributed learning and learning in connected space. Definitions vary with the distance education culture of each country, but there is some agreement on the fundamentals. Distance learning is generally recognized as a structured learning experience that can be done away from an academic institution, at home or at a workplace. Distance education often offers programs leading, to degrees or credentials. Colleges and universities in the United States offer existing courses through distance learning programs as an alternative to traditional attendance. Educators in the United Kingdom describe their distance strategies as flexible or open learning. They were the first to develop an Open University on a large scale. Open learning is flexible, negotiated and suited to each person's needs. It is characterized by open entry–open exit courses, and the courses begin and end when the student is ready.

The rapid growth of networks, particularly the Internet and the World Wide Web, have spawned an interest in networked learning, sometimes referred to as learning in connected space or learning in the virtual classroom. This type of instruction may take place in traditional classrooms with web-enhanced features such as online syllabus, readings and assignments but with major portions of discussion and assessment done in the traditional classroom. Or the network may facilitate web-based instruction in which the entire course is online. Networked learning is particularly useful in providing information resources to remote geographic areas. It has vast implications for educating large populations of people who have an adequate technology infrastructure.

These distance education strategies may form hybrid combinations of distance and traditional education in the form of distributed learning, networked learning or flexible learning in which multiple intelligences are addressed through various modes of information retrieval. What, then, are the definitions of distance education? Desmond Keegan (1980) identified six key elements of distance education:

- Separation of teacher and learner
- Influence of an educational organization
- Use of media to link teacher and learner
- Two-way exchange of communication
- Learners as individuals rather than grouped
- Education as an industrialized form

Distance education has traditionally been defined as instruction through print or electronic communications media to persons engaged in planned learning in a place or time different from that of the instructor or instructors.

The traditional definition of distance education is slowly being changed as new technological developments challenge

educators to reconceptualize the idea of schooling and lifelong learning. At the same time, interest in the unlimited possibilities of individualized distance learning is growing with the development of each new communication technology. Although educational technologists agree that it is the systematic design of instruction which should drive the development of distance learning, the rapid development of computer related technologies has captured the interest of the public and has been responsible for much of the limelight in which distance educators currently find themselves. Asynchronous or time-delayed computer conferencing has shown the capability to network groups of learners over a period of time thereby challenging Keegan's 1980 definition that learners need to be taught as individuals rather than in groups.

Holmberg refined the definition by stating that

Distance education is a concept that covers the learning-teaching activities in the cognitive and/or psycho-motor and affective domains of an individual learner and a supporting organization. It is characterized by non-contiguous communication and can be carried out anywhere and at any time, which makes it attractive to adults with professional and social commitments. (Holmberg, 1989 p. 168)

We have taken the position that the most inclusive and currently workable definition of distance education comes from Garrison and Shale (1987) who include in their essential criteria for formulation of a distance education theory, the elements of *noncontiguous communication, two-way interactive communication,* and the *use of technology to mediate the necessary two-way communication.*

14.2.2 Distance Education as a Global Movement

Distance education has developed very differently in the United States from the way it has in the rest of the world. Current international issues regarding the development of distance learning will be discussed at greater length later in this chapter, but it is important to recognize here the importance that many countries have played in the history of distance education and its corollaries, distance and open learning.

The establishment of the British Open University in the United Kingdom in 1969 marked the beginning of the use of technology to supplement print based instruction through well designed courses. Learning materials were delivered on a large scale to students in three programs; undergraduates, postgraduates and associate students. Although course materials were primarily print based, they were supported by a variety of technologies. No formal educational qualifications have been required to be admitted to the British Open University. Courses are closely monitored and have been successfully delivered to over 100,000 students. As a direct result of its success, the Open University model has been adopted by many countries in both the developed and developing world (Keegan, 1986). Researchers in the United Kingdom continue to be leaders in identifying problems and proposing solutions for practitioners in the field (Harry, Keegan, & Magnus, 1993). The International Centre for Distance Learning, at the British Open University, maintains the most complete holdings of literature in both research and practice of international distance learning. Research studies, evaluation reports, course modules, books, journal articles and ephemeral material concerning distance education around the world are all available through quarterly accessions lists or online.

In Europe and other Western countries, a global concern was beginning to emerge. In a 1992 report, the 12 members of the European Association of Distance Teaching Universities proposed a European Open University to begin that year. This was in direct response to the European Parliament, the Council of Europe, and the European Community (Bates, 1990). In this report, articles from authors in nine European countries describe the use of media and technology in higher education in Europe and reflect upon the need for providing unified educational access in the form of a European Open University to a culturally diverse population.

Since that time, telecommunication networks have grown to circle the globe, linking people from many nations together in novel and exciting ways. As the borders of our global community continue to shrink, we search for new ways to improve communication by providing greater access to information on an international scale. Emerging communication technologies, and telecommunications in particular, are providing highly cost effective solutions to the problems of sharing information and promoting global understanding between people. In today's electronic age, it is predicted that the amount of information produced will increase exponentially every year. Since economic and political power is directly related to access to information, many educators like Takeshi Utsumi, President of GLOSAS (Global Systems Analysis and Simulation) have worked to develop models of the "Global University" and the "Global Lecture Hall" which provide resources allowing less affluent countries to keep up with advances in global research and education (Utsumi, Rossman, & Rosen, 1990). International issues will be discussed in more detail later in this chapter, so let us turn our attention now to the issue of theory in distance education.

There have been a variety of efforts to identify theoretical foundations for the study of distance education. Thus far, there has been little agreement about which theoretical principles are common to the field and even less agreement on how to proceed in conducting programmatic research.

14.3 THEORY OF DISTANCE EDUCATION

Theories serve to satisfy a very human "need" to order the experienced world (Dubin, 1978). This order will reflect the principles, standards and ideals that will influence and shape practice. Theories can be derived from efforts to explain or make sense of observed phenomena, or by reasoning through the implications of existing theories. Theories are necessary because they help us to understand, communicate and predict the nature of a discipline or a field of practice, its purpose, goals, and methods. Theories help to shape practice, and practice in turn contributes to the development of theory.

One of the critical challenges the field of distance education has faced is the need for the continuous development of theory necessitated by the rapid changes brought about by the development of new communications technologies used as delivery media. Theorists are challenged to adapt theories to understand the learning environments created by new technological developments or to develop new theories to explain or make sense of these new and emerging technologies. Another challenge that has faced theory development is whether theorists should borrow theories from other disciplines to explain distance education or develop unique theories that describe the nature of the field.

Distance education has come of age and matured as a field of education developing theoretical constructs that describe its unique nature. It has moved beyond debates about defining the field to focus on the systematic development of theoretical constructs and models. In a seminal article addressing the theoretical challenges for distance education in the 21st century, Garrison (Garrison, 2000) observes that in "surveying the core theoretical contributions of the last three decades, we see evidence of a sound theoretical foundation." (p. 11). He notes however, that it is less obvious as to whether the current state of knowledge development is adequate to explain and shape new practices for a broad range of emerging educational purposes and experiences. Garrison argues that the 21st century represents the postindustrial era where transactional issues (i.e., teaching and learning) will predominate over structural constraints (i.e., geographical distance). He observes that distance education in the 20th century was primarily focused on distance constraints and approaches that bridged geographical distance by way of organizational strategies such as the mass production and delivery of learning packages. This period has been identified as the industrial era of distance education consistent with Otto Peter's (1971, 1983) description of the field as an industrial form of education.

Garrison notes that more recently the focus in the study of distance education has shifted to educational issues associated with the teaching–learning process, specifically concerns regarding real, sustained communication, as well as emerging communications technology to support sustained communication anytime, anywhere. Therefore, issues that involve the learner, the instructor, the technology, and the process of teaching and learning are becoming increasingly important. Because distance education has moved away from the industrialization of teaching to learner-centered instruction, distance educators must move ahead to investigate how the learner, the instructor and the technology collaborate to generate knowledge.

In order to understand the theoretical issues that face the field today, it is important to reflect on the development of theoretical constructs in the last century. Traditionally, both theoretical constructs and research studies in distance education have been considered in the context of an educational enterprise which was entirely separate from the standard, classroom-based, classical instructional model. In part to justify, and in part to explain the phenomenon, theoreticians like Holmberg, Keegan, and Rumble explored the underlying assumptions of what it is that makes distance education different from traditional education. With an early vision of what it meant to be a nontraditional learner, these pioneers in distance education defined the distance learner as one who is physically separated from the teacher (Rumble, 1986) has a planned and guided learning experience (Holmberg, 1986), and participates in a two-way structured form of distance education which is distinct from the traditional form of classroom instruction (Keegan, 1988). In order to justify the importance of this nontraditional form of education, early theoretical approaches attempted to define the important and unique attributes of distance education.

Keegan (1986) identifies three historical approaches to the development of a theory of distance education. Theories of autonomy and independence from the 1960s and 1970s, argued by Wedemeyer (1977) and Moore (1973), reflect the essential component of the independence of the learner. Otto Peters' (1971) work on a theory of industrialization in the 1960s reflects the attempt to view the field of distance education as an industrialized form of teaching and learning. The third approach integrates theories of interaction and communication formulated by Bääth (1982), Sewart (1987), and Daniel & Marquis (1979). Keegan presents these three approaches to the study and development of the academic discipline of distance education. The focus at this time was on the concept of industrialized, open, and nontraditional learning.

14.3.1 Theoretical Developments

In this section we discuss the major theoretical developments and contributions that have influenced the field of distance education.

14.3.1.1 The Industrial Model of Distance Education.
One of the most influential theoretical developments of the 20th century was the industrial production model of distance education described by Otto Peters (1971, 1983). Otto Peters characterized distance education as a method of imparting knowledge, skills and attitudes which is rationalized by the application of division of labor and organizational principles as well as by the extensive use of technical media, especially for the purpose of reproducing high quality teaching material which makes it possible to instruct great numbers of students at the same time wherever they live. Distance education was therefore described as an industrialized form of teaching and learning. This model emphasizes instructional units as products which can be mass-produced and distributed like cars or washing machines. This view and definition emerged during the time when behaviorism was at its height of popularity, together with the related approaches of programmed instruction and instructional systems design (ISD). The use of highly specific performance objectives, characteristic of the ISD approach, is probably essential to the true mass production and administration of instructional packages.

This industrial approach had a major impact on distance education specifically in the development of Open Universities such as the British Open University. As Moore and Kearsley (1996) and Garrison (2000) have pointed out, Peters' theory was an organizational theory and not a theory of teaching, nor of learning. It was an organizational model that talked about organizing the educational process to realize economies of scale. Garrison (2000) observes that this industrial model placed in clear contrast the need to choose between independence and inter-

action, which generated a debate about the worth of each approach in implementing distance education. Daniel and Marquis (1979) in their discussion of the pros and cons of interaction versus independence, point out the impact of these two approaches on the costing of distance education systems, as interactive activities were much more expensive to fund because of the personnel required, than independent activities. Garrison (2000) declares that with the advent of computer-mediated communication (CMC) this debate was rendered useless as this medium made both independent and interactive activities possible.

In his more recent writing on the possibilities and opportunities afforded by digital environments for distance education, Peters (2000) remains a proponent of independent self-study even within a networked learning environment. He observes that the "digital environment will probably be the most efficacious 'enabler' of independent and self-determined learning" (p. 16). He believes that this approach is promising because it does not modify the traditional methods of presentational teaching and receptive learning, but provides a completely different fundamental challenge for learning.

14.3.1.2 Guided Didactic Conversation.
Börje Holmberg has been recognized as a prominent theorist in distance education for the substantial contributions he has made to the field. Central to Holmberg's (1989) theory of distance education is the concept of "guided didactic conversation" (p. 43), which refers to both real and simulated conversation. Holmberg (1991) emphasized simulated conversation, which is the interaction of individual students with texts and the conversational style in which preproduced correspondence texts are written. According to his theory of didactic conversation, which he developed while seeking an empathy approach to distance education (Homberg, 1991), course developers are responsible for creating simulated conversation in self-instructional materials. The role of the teacher is largely simulated by written dialogue and comments. Garrison (2000) questions whether an inert learning package, regardless of how well it is written, is a sufficient substitute for real communication with the teacher. Homberg's theory of guided didactic conversation while closely associated with the correspondence movement and the industrial organization of distance education, introduces an empathy approach focusing on the importance of discourse both real and simulated.

14.3.1.3 Independence and Autonomy.
Charles Wedemeyer, considered by many to be the father of American distance education, moved away from the concept of correspondence study and emphasized independent study or independent learning. Wedemeyer (1977, 1981) identifies essential elements of independent learning as greater student responsibility, widely available instruction, effective mix of media and methods, adaptation to individual differences, and a wide variety of start, stop and learn times. He focused on freedom and choice for the learner, on equity and access. His vision of independent study was consistent with self-directed learning and self-regulation, and his thinking was in line with principles of Humanism and Andragogy. Garrison (2000) observes that Wedemeyer's focus

on the peadagogoical assumptions of independent study was a shift from the world of correspondence study dominated by organizational and administrative concerns to an emphasis on educational issues concerning learning at a distance. He notes that Wedemeyer's work is surprisingly relevant to a new era of theory development.

14.3.1.4 Transactional Distance.

Moore's theory of "transactional distance" which became known since 1986 combines both Peter's perspective of distance education as a highly structured mechanical system and Wedemeyer's perspective of a more learner-centered, interactive relationship with a tutor (Moore & Kearsley, 1996). As Garrison (2000) has noted, it incorporates the structure of the industrial approach with the interaction of the transactional approach. The major contribution of the theory of transactional distance is that it defined distance not as a geographical phenomenon but as a pedagogical phenomenon. Moore's (1990) concept of "transactional distance" encompasses the distance, which, he says, exists in all educational relationships. This distance is determined by the amount of dialog which occurs between the learner and the instructor, and the amount of structure which exists in the design of the course. Greater transactional distance occurs when an educational program has more structure and less student-teacher dialogue, as might be found in some traditional distance education courses. Moore acknowledges that even face-to-face teaching environments have high transactional distance such as a class of 100 students offered in a large, auditorium-style classroom where there is little or no opportunity for the individual student to interact directly with the instructor. Education offers a continuum of transactions from less distant, where there is greater interaction and less structure, to more distant where there may be less interaction and more structure.

Moore's theory of transactional distance takes into account learner autonomy which is a personal characteristic, in varying degrees. The learner's capacity and desire to determine the course of his or her own learning, which may be called learner "autonomy" implies a corresponding decrease in the degree of instructor control over the process. Moore classifies programs according to the degree of autonomy they offer the learner in three areas: planning, implementation and evaluation of instruction. The highest degree of autonomy is found in programs that allow the learner to participate in all three aspects of instruction; the lowest degree of autonomy is offered by those programs in which instruction is planned, implemented, and evaluated entirely according to the dictates of the course designer(s) and/or instructor(s).

The theory of transactional distance blurs the distinctions between conventional and distance programs because of the variety of transactions which occur between teachers and learners in both settings. Thus distance is not determined by geography but by the relationship between dialog and structure with learner autonomy taken into account in varying degrees. It is also worthwhile to explore other types of distance that exist in an educational transaction that contributes to the distance of understandings and perceptions. These distances can be described as intellectual distance (i.e., the level of knowledge,

prerequisite learning) social distance (affinity, closeness, support), and cultural distance (language, class, ethnicity, age, gender and religion).

Saba and Shearer (1994) carry the concept of transactional distance a step farther by proposing a system dynamics model to examine the relationship between dialog and structure in transactional distance. In their study, they used a system modeling program called STELLA, to model the relationship between dialogue and structure using distance students' exchanges with instructors. Saba and Shearer conclude that as learner control and dialog increase, transactional distance decreases. The more control the teacher has, the higher the level of structure and the greater the transactional distance in the learning experience. Saba and Shearer claim that their results support the validity of Moore's theory of transactional distance. This concept has implications for traditional classrooms as well as distant ones. The use of integrated telecommunication systems may permit a greater variety of transactions to occur, thus improving dialogue to minimize transactional distance.

14.3.1.5 Control.

Focusing their attention on the teaching and learning process in education at a distance, Garrison and Baynton (1987), Garrison (1989), and Baynton (1992) developed a model to explain the concept of "control" in an educational transaction. Control was defined as the opportunity and ability to influence the educational transaction, and was intended to develop a more comprehensive view of independence, a core element of distance education. Garrison and Baynton (1987) argued that the concept of independence, alone, does not account for, nor address adequately, the complexity of interacting variables present in the communication process that occurs in distance education. They proposed moving beyond the concept of independence to the concept of control to encompass more fully the interactive aspects of distance education, particularly the interaction between the teacher, learner, and other resources in the distance education context. Their model proposed that control of the learning process results from the combination of three essential dimensions: a learner's independence (the opportunity to make choices), a learner's proficiency or competence (ability, skill, and motivation), and support (both human and nonhuman resources). They argued that independence must be examined in relation to competence and support and that it is the dynamic balance among these three components that enables the student to develop and maintain control over the learning process. Therefore, it is pointless to give the learner independence in selecting learning objectives, activities and evaluation procedures if the learner does not have the competence or the necessary support to make use of that independence.

14.3.1.6 Interaction.

A theoretical construct of recent interest to distance educators, and one that has received much attention in the literature, is that of interaction. Garrison (1989), and Garrison and Shale (1990) in their definition of distance education explicitly place sustained real two-way communication at the core of the educational experience, regardless of the separation of teacher and student. This was a clear attempt to place the teaching and learning transaction at the core of distance education practice and to break loose from the organizational assumptions of the industrial model. The concept of interaction is fundamental to the effectiveness of distance education programs as well as traditional ones.

Examining instructional interaction in distance education, Moore (1989) makes a distinction between three types of interaction: learner-content interaction, learner-instructor interaction, and learner-learner interaction. Learner-content interaction is the process of intellectually interacting with lesson content that results in changes in the learner's understanding, and perspective. This is similar to Holmberg's (1989) didactic conversation where learners interact with printed text. In multimedia web-based learning formats, learner-content interaction can be associated with "system interactivity." This is when the technical system may interact with learner inputs or interactions. Web pages that interact with students by changing their form and displaying new information in response to the position of the cursor or mouse clicks are one form of learner-content interaction.

Learner-instructor interaction is that component of Moore's (1989) model that provides motivation, feedback, and dialog between the teacher and student. This type of interaction is regarded as essential by many educators and highly desired by many learners. Moore states that the instructor is especially valuable in responding to the learners' application of new knowledge.

Learner-learner interaction is the exchange of information, ideas and dialog that occur between students about the course whether this happens in a structured or nonstructured manner. It is this type of interaction that will challenge our thinking and practice in the 21st century as we move to designing networked learning communities. Facilitating this type of interaction would contribute immensely to a learner-centered view of learning, and provide the opportunity for the social negotiation of meaning and construction of knowledge between learners connected to each other. Dinucci, Giudice, and Stiles (1998), and Dede (1992) have shown that newer three-dimensional (3D) virtual reality environments can carry learner-learner interaction into another level of reality. These systems offer graphic stand-ins called "avatars" which students can use to represent themselves online. An avatar can actually walk up to other students (or to their avatars) and exchange conversation, usually as text strings displayed in the window.

Hillman, Willis, and Gunawardena (1994) have taken Moore's (1989) concept of interaction a step farther and added a fourth component to the model, learner-interface interaction, necessitated by the addition of high technology communications systems to mediate the communication process. They note that the interaction between the learner and the technology that delivers instruction is a critical component of the model that has been missing thus far in the literature. They propose a new paradigm that includes understanding the use of the interface in all transactions. Learners who do not have the basic skills required to use the interface of a communication medium spend inordinate amounts of time learning to interact with the technology in order to be able to communicate with others or learn the lesson. Hillman et al. (1994) state that it is important to make a distinction between the perception of interface as an independent, fourth mode of interaction, and the use of an interface as a mediating element in all interaction. With the increasing use of the Web for distance education and training user-friendly interface design is becoming extremely important. Instructional designers must include learner-interface interactions which enable the learner to have successful interactions with the mediating technology.

Fulford and Zhang (1993) have shown us that the perception of interaction is as important as actual interaction. They examined learner perceptions of interaction in a course delivered via instructional television and found that the critical predictor of student satisfaction was not the extent of personal interaction but the perception of overall or vicarious interaction. If students perceived that there had been a high level of student interaction in the course, they were satisfied regardless of how much personal interaction they had. Based on these results they conclude that instructors teaching through interactive TV probably should be concerned with overall group dynamics than with engaging every individual equally, or with soliciting overt individual responses.

In discussing the nature and value of interaction in distance education, Kearsley (1995) argues that a distinction needs to be made between immediate (real time) and delayed (asynchronous) interaction. The distinction is significant because it determines the logistic and "feel" of the distance learning experience. Delayed interaction provides more student control and flexibility, while immediate interaction may have a sense of excitement and spontaneity that is not present with delayed interaction. Another factor that needs to be considered is that individual learners differ in their propensity for interaction depending upon their personality, age, or cognitive/learning styles. For example, students who are more self-directed or autonomous may want /need less interaction than others. Therefore, Kearsley argues that the concept of interaction as it applies to distance education is more complicated than traditional face to face contexts, as it needs to be differentiated according to content versus teacher versus student, immediate versus delayed, and types of learners.

14.3.1.7 Sociocultural Context.
The sociocultural context in which distance learning takes place is emerging as a significant area for theory building and research. Theorists are examining how the sociocultural environment affects motivation, attitudes, teaching and learning. Evans and Nation (1992) contribute some of the most thoughtful and insightful comments on theory building when they suggest that we examine broader social and historic contexts in our efforts to extend previously narrow views of theories in open and distance education. They urge us to move toward deconstruction of the instructional industrialism of distance education, and toward the construction of a critical approach which, combined with an integration of theories from the humanities and social sciences, can enrich the theory building in the field.

It is particularly important to examine the sociocultural context in distance learning environments where the communication process is mediated and where social climates are created that are very different from traditional settings. Spears and Lea (1992) stress the importance of studying the social environment to understand computer-mediated communication. Feenberg and Bellman (1990) propose a social factor model to examine computer networking environments that create specialized electronic social environments for students and collaborators working in groups. Computer-mediated communication attempts to reduce patterns of discrimination by providing equality of social interaction among participants who may be anonymous in terms of gender, race and physical features. However, there is evidence that the social equality factor may not extend, for example, to participants who are not good writers but who must communicate primarily in a text-based format (Gunawardena, 1993).

There is a widespread notion that technology is culturally neutral, and can be easily used in a variety of settings. However media, materials and services are often inappropriately transferred without attention being paid to the social setting or to the local recipient culture (McIsaac, 1993). Technology-based learning activities are frequently used without attention to the impact on the local social environment.

14.3.1.8 Social Presence. One social factor that is particularly significant to distance education that has been studied previously by communication researchers, is social presence. Social presence is the degree to which a person feels "socially present" in a mediated situation or the degree to which a person is perceived as a "real person" in mediated communication. (Short, Williams, & Christie, 1976). Social presence is described as a construct that comprises a number of dimensions relating to the degree of interpersonal contact. Two concepts associated with social presence are Argyle and Dean's 1965 concept of "intimacy," and Wiener and Mehrabian's 1968 concept of "immediacy" (cited in Short et al., 1976). Short et al. suggest that the social presence of the communications medium contributes to the level of intimacy that depends on factors such as physical distance, eye contact, and smiling. Therefore, television rather than audio-only communication makes for greater intimacy, other things being equal, because of its ability to convey nonverbal cues such as eye contact and smiling. Text-based CMC, devoid of nonverbal codes that are generally rich in relational information occupies a relatively low position as a medium that is capable of generating intimacy. On the other hand, immediacy is a measure of the psychological distance, which a communicator puts between himself or herself and the object of his/her communication. A person can convey immediacy or non-immediacy nonverbally (physical proximity, formality of dress, and facial expression) as well as verbally. Immediacy enhances social presence. Therefore, according to Short et al.'s argument, social presence is both a factor of the medium, as well as that of the communicators and their presence in a sequence of interaction.

In the distance education context, several studies (Gunawardena & Zittle, 1997; Hackman & Walker, 1990; Jelfs & Whitelock, 2000; Rourke, Anderson, Garrison, & Archer, 1999; Tu & McIsaac, 2002) have examined social presence and its relationship to learner satisfaction and learner perception of learning.

These studies are discussed in more detail in the research section of this chapter. Discussing the role of social presence in online learning, McIsaac and Gunawardena (1996) and Tammelin (1998) observe that it can be linked to the larger social context including motivation, interaction, group cohesion, verbal and nonverbal communication, and social equality. Constructs such as social presence, immediacy and intimacy are social factors which deserve further inquiry as we move toward theoretical formulations related to community building in networked learning environments.

14.3.2 Theoretical Challenges

As Garrison (2000) has observed, the challenge facing distance education theorists in the 21st century is to provide an understanding of the opportunities and limitations of facilitating teaching and learning at a distance with a variety of methods and technologies. This will demand theories that reflect a collaborative approach to distance education (i.e., as opposed to independent learning) and have at their core an adaptive teaching and learning transaction. "This adaptability in designing the educational transaction based upon sustained communication and collaborative experiences reflects the essence of the postindustrial era of distance education" (p. 13). He adds that asynchronous text-based collaborative learning may well be the defining technology of this era that will challenge theorists to recognize that this form of communication may impact the facilitation of learning outcomes in different ways.

Many distance educators are beginning to call for a theoretical model based on constructivist epistemology (Jegede, 1991). Technological advances have already begun to blur the distinction between traditional and distance education settings. Time and place qualifiers are no longer unique. The need to test assumptions and hypotheses about how and under what conditions individuals learn best, leads to research questions about learning, teaching, course design and the role of technology in the educational process. As traditional education integrates the use of interactive, multimedia technologies to enhance individual learning, the role of the teacher changes from knowledge source to knowledge facilitator. As networks become available in schools and homes to encourage individuals to become their own knowledge navigators, the structure of education will change and the need for separate theories for distance education will blend into the theoretical foundations for the mainstream of education.

In an effort to theoretically define the field of distance education, Deshler and Hagen (1989) advocate a multidisciplinary and interdisciplinary approach resulting in a diversity of perspectives. They caution that anything short of this approach may "Produce theory that suffers from a view that is narrow, incomplete, discipline-based and restricted . . . to a predominant view of reality"(p. 163). Gibson (1993) calls for a broader conceptualization of distance education using an ecological systems perspective. She argues that "as distance educators we are not only interested in learning, but also in the interaction of those properties of the person and their multiple environments which produce constancy and change in the characteristics of that person over time" (p. 86).

A strategy for theory development from an international perspective has been proposed by Sophason and Prescott (1988). They caution that certain lines of questioning are more appropriate in some countries than in others, thus the emanating theory "may have a particular slant" (p. 17). A comparative analysis strategy would undoubtedly be influenced by cultural bias and language barriers (Pratt, 1989). Pratt further indicates that understanding different culturally related beliefs about the nature of the individual and society may be critical in defining appropriate distance education theories. Pratt clarifies his belief through a description of how differences in societies' historical traditions and philosophies can contribute to differing orientations toward self-expression and social interactions within educational settings.

We believe that the theoretical challenges for distance education will center on issues related to learning and pedagogy in technology mediated learning environments. One such issue is understanding and evaluating knowledge construction in online collaborative learning communities. Increasingly we are subscribing to a knowledge construction view of learning as opposed to an information acquisition view, as we design web-based distance learning environments. The knowledge construction perspective views computer networks not as a channel for information distribution, but primarily as a new medium for construction of meaning, providing new ways for students to learn through negotiation and collaboration with a group of peers. The challenge however, is to develop theory to explain how new construction of knowledge occurs through the process of social negotiation in such a knowledge-building community.

A related area of theoretical challenge is to determine how the social dimension of an online learning environment influences learning. The online learning environment has been described as a sociotechnical system incorporating both technical and social aspects. Unique aspects such as the time-independent nature of an asynchronous environment can create communication anxiety, or the lack of visual cues in a text-based medium can give rise to the development of emoticons (icons that express emotion, such as ☺) to express feelings. This environment forces us to reformulate the way in which we view the social dimension and how learners actively influence each other's knowledge and reasoning processes through social networks.

With the expansion and acceptance of the Internet and the World Wide Web across the globe for education and training, the significance of culture and its impact on communication, and the teaching and learning process at a distance will provide an impetus for further research and theory building. If we design learner-centered learning environments, how do we build on the conceptual and cultural knowledge that learners bring with them? How does culture influence perception, cognition, communication, and the teaching–learning process in an online course? How do we as instructors engage in culturally responsive online teaching? These types of questions need to be addressed in research and in theoretical frameworks as we move toward making distance education a more equitable learning experience.

14.4 EVOLUTION OF DISTANCE EDUCATION MEDIA

As stated in Keegan's (1980), and more recent definitions of distance education, media plays a critical role in linking the teacher and learner and providing for the two-way exchange of communication that is so necessary for the teaching and learning process. Until the advent of telecommunications technologies, distance educators were hard pressed to provide for two-way real time interaction, or time-delayed interaction between students and the instructor or among peers. In the correspondence model of distance education, which emphasized learner independence, the main instructional medium was print and it was usually delivered using the postal service. Interaction between the student and the instructor usually took the form of correspondence of self-assessment exercises that the student completed and sent to the instructor for feedback. Formal group work or collaborative learning was very rare in distance education even though attempts have been made to facilitate group activities at local study centers. Also, traditionally, distance education courses were designed with a heavy emphasis on learner independence and were usually self-contained. With the development of synchronous (two-way, real time interactive technologies) such as audio teleconferencing, audiographics conferencing and videoconferencing it became possible to link learners and instructors who are geographically separated for real time interaction.

These technologies facilitated interaction between an instructor and a group of learners, or among learners. They are not very suitable for promoting collaborative learning among a group of learners over an extended period of time. Also, the synchronous nature of these technologies may not be suitable or convenient for many distance learners as it requires instantaneous responses when questions are asked, and often learners had to travel to a site to participate in an audio or video teleconference. The asynchronous (time-delayed) feature of computer-mediated communications (CMC), on the other hand, offers an advantage in that the CMC class is open 24 hours a day, 7 days a week to accommodate the time schedules of distance learners. Although CMC systems may be either synchronous (real-time), or asynchronous (time-delayed), it is asynchronous CMC, because of it's time independent feature that is an important medium for facilitating collaborative group work among distance learners.

Current developments in digital communications and the convergence of telecommunications technologies exemplified by international standards such as ISDN (Integrated Services Digital Network), make available audio, video, graphic and data communication through an ordinary telephone line on a desktop workstation. Therefore, as we look at distance learning technologies today and look to the future, it is important to think in terms of integrated telecommunication systems rather than simply video versus audio, versus data systems. More and more institutions that teach at a distance are moving toward multimedia systems integrating a combination of technologies both synchronous and asynchronous that meets learner needs. Therefore, while in the 1970s and 1980s many distance education institutions throughout the world used print as a major delivery medium, by the year 2002 many institutions in the United States have adopted telecommunications-based systems for the delivery of distance education. This does not necessarily mean that print will no longer be used in distance education. It is still a very important medium as books, reading packets, study guides and even computer files are downloaded and used in printed format. However, in the future it is more likely that print will be used as a supplementary medium in most telecommunications-based systems, and better ways of communicating information through print will be investigated and incorporated into the design of study guides and other print-based media.

We have seen distance education evolve from highly individualized forms of instruction as in correspondence education, to formats that encourage teaching students as a group, to formats that facilitate extended dialogue and collaborative learning among peers. In this section we describe the advantages and limitations of various media that have been used in distance education. What is important to remember is that each medium whether it is low cost or high cost has advantages and limitations. It is critical to select media that is most appropriate for the task and compensate for a medium's weakness by using another medium. As we evolve to more multimedia and hybrid formats for distance education, we must also remember the importance of providing access to the learner using the medium or media that they can readily access.

14.4.1 Print

Until the beginning of the 1970s and the advent of two-way telecommunications technologies, print and the mail system were the predominant delivery medium for distance education. Correspondence study relied primarily on print to mediate the communication between the instructor and the learner. Currently many distance education institutions in developing countries use print based correspondence study as the main distance education medium as the use of communications technologies is often cost prohibitive. Garrison (1990) refers to print based correspondence study as the first generation of distance education technology. It is characterized by the mass production of educational materials that Peters (1983) describes as an industrial form of education. The difficulty with correspondence education has been the infrequent and inefficient form of communication between the instructor and the students. Further, it was difficult to arrange for peer interaction in correspondence based distance education. The development of broadcast technologies and two-way interactive media has mitigated the limitations of correspondence study, specially in relation to facilitating two-way communication. However, print remains a very important support medium for electronically delivered distance education. Printed study guides have become a very important component of electronic distance education.

In a survey of distance teaching institutions in the United States that use television as a main delivery medium, Gunawardena (1988) found that a majority of institutions cited the study guide which provides printed lesson materials and guidelines for studying, the most important form of support for distance learners. A study guide can steer and facilitate the study of correspondence texts, television programs, and other components in a distance education course. A study guide, if well designed, can provide the integration between various media components and activate students to read and or listen to presentations of various kinds, to compare and criticize them, and to try to come to conclusions of their own. In a study guide or correspondence text, simulated conversation can be brought about by the use of a conversational tone which Holmberg (1989) refers to as "guided didactic conversation." In addition, cognitive strategies such as advance organizers, mathemagenic devices such as directions and underlining, and self-assessment and self remediation exercises can be used to help students learn how to learn from printed material.

14.4.2 Broadcast Television and Radio

Broadcast television and radio can be used to instruct a vast number of students at the same time even though the students may not have the ability to call back and clarify a statement or ask a question in real time. Many distance education institutions in developing countries as well as institutions in developed countries such as the British Open University, use broadcast television and radio extensively to deliver programming to a large number of distant learners.

In the past two decades, television, both open-broadcast and cable and interactive instructional television (ITV) have been the most popular media for delivering distance education in the United States. Radio has remained an underutilized medium for distance education (Gunawardena, 1988). It is in the developing countries that radio programming has been used innovatively to either support and supplement print based materials or to carry the majority of the course content.

Bates (1984) observes that broadcasts are ephemeral, cannot be reviewed, are uninterruptible, and are presented at the same pace for all students. A student cannot reflect upon an idea or pursue a line of thought during a fast paced program, without losing the thread of the program itself. A student cannot go over the same material several times until it is understood. Access to a videotape of the broadcast, however, will alleviate these problems by giving the learner control over the medium with the ability to stop and rewind sections that were not clear.

Despite its ability to reach a large section of the student population, open-broadcast television has remained a one-way communication medium. To make the system interactive, open-broadcast distribution requires an added system to provide either an audio or audio-video return circuit. While many talk shows have utilized open-broadcast television and radio interactively with participants calling in from their home phones to interact with the talk show host, this application has hardly been utilized for distance education partly because of the difficulty of arranging for appropriate broadcast times.

14.4.3 Cable Television

In the United States, cable television began in remote rural areas, expanded into the suburbs, and has now penetrated into large urban areas. Cable has evolved from a way of improving reception in rural areas to a technology that is capable of providing many television channels and even two-way video communication and high speed Internet access. Today, cable technology is readily available and reaches a large number of homes and apartment units in the United States.

Cable can be used to replay programming offered over open-broadcast television, usually at more convenient times for the students than open-broadcast schedules, or used as a means of delivering nationally distributed television programs, where terrestrial broadcasting facilities are not available.

14.4.4 Interactive Instructional Television

When State governments began to establish statewide distance education networks, interactive television became a popular medium. Interactive Instructional Television (ITV) systems usually use a combination of Instructional Television Fixed Service (ITFS) and point-to-point microwave. They can transmit either two-way video and two-way audio, or one-way video and two-way audio to several distant locations. The advantage of combining ITFS and microwave is that microwave is a point-to-point system while ITFS is a point-to-multipoint system. Therefore, large geographical areas can be covered by the combination of the two technologies. Microwave connects one location to another electronically with its point-to-point signals, while ITFS distributes that signal to several receiving stations around a 20-mile radius. In the United States, several states such as Iowa and Oklahoma support statewide networks that use a combination of ITFS, microwave, satellite, fiber optics, and coaxial cable.

14.4.5 Recorded Audio and Video Media

Both audiocassettes and videocassettes afford the learner control over the learning material because learners can stop, rewind, and fast forward the tape. Audiocassettes offer great flexibility in the way they can be used, either at home or while driving a car. Audiocassettes can be used to tape lectures or can be specially designed with clear stopping points in order to supplement print or video material. For example, audiocassettes can be used to describe diagrams and abstract concepts that students encounter in texts in order to facilitate student learning.

An audiocassette can be used to record the sound portion of a television program if a videocassette recorder is not available, and an audiocassette can provide a review of a television program in order to assist students to analyze the video material. They can also be used to provide feedback on student assignments and is a very useful medium to check student pronunciation when teaching languages at a distance. Audiocassettes can be an excellent supplementary medium to enrich print or other media and can provide resource material to distance learners. Since they can be produced and distributed without much cost, audiocassettes are also a very cost-effective medium for use in distance education.

Videocassettes are like broadcast television in that they combine moving pictures and sound but unlike broadcast television are distributed differently and viewed in different ways. An institution using videocassettes for distribution of video material to distant learners can use them as (a) a copy technology for open-broadcast, satellite, or cablecast programming; (b) a supplementary medium—for instance, providing the visual component for educational material carried over audio teleconferencing networks; (c) a specially designed video program that takes advantage of the cassette medium such as its stop/review functions, so that students can be directed at the end of sequences to stop and take notes on, or discuss, what they have seen and heard.

An important advantage in using videocassettes is that students can exercise "control" over the programming by using the stop, rewind, replay, and fast forward features to proceed at their own pace. Videocassettes are also a very flexible medium allowing students to use the cassettes at a time that is suitable to them. Bates (1987), observes that the "videocassette is to the broadcast what the book is to the lecture" (p. 13).

If videocassettes are designed to take advantage of their "control" characteristics and students are encouraged to use the "control" characteristics, then there is opportunity for students to interact with the lesson material. Students can repeat the material until they gain mastery of it by reflecting on and analyzing it. The control features that videocassettes afford the learner give course designers the ability to integrate video material more closely with other learning materials, so that learners can move between lesson material supplied by different media.

The ability to create "chunks" of learning material, or to edit and reconstruct video material, can help develop a more questioning approach to the presentation of video material. Recorded television therefore considerably increases the control of the learner (and the teacher) over the way video material can be used for learning purposes. (Bates, 1983, pp. 61–62)

Bates (1987) discusses the implications of the "control" characteristics for program design on videocassettes: (a) use of segments, (b) clear stopping points, (c) use of activities, (d) indexing, (e) close integration with other media (e.g., text, discussion), and (f) concentration on audiovisual aspects.

When videocassettes are used in a Tutored Video Instruction (TVI) program, where tutors attend video-playback sessions at work places or study centers to answer questions and to encourage student discussion, students can take advantage of the features of a lecture (on videocassette) and a small group discussion, which gives them the opportunity for personal interaction available in on-campus instruction.

14.4.6 Teleconferencing

Teleconferencing is a meeting through a telecommunications medium where participants who are separated by geographic distance can interact with each other simultaneously.

Teleconferencing can be classified into four separate categories depending on the technologies that they use: audio teleconferencing, audiographics teleconferencing, video tele-conferencing and computer conferencing. There are two types of computer conferencing systems: synchronous computer con-ferencing when two or more computers are linked at the same time so that participants can interact with each other, and asynchronous computer conferencing when participants interact with each other at a time and place convenient to them.

The four major types of teleconferencing vary in the types of technologies, complexity of use and cost. However, they have several features in common. All of them use a telecommunica-tion channel to mediate the communication process, link in-dividuals or groups of participants at multiple locations, and provide for live, two-way communication or interaction. One advantage of teleconferencing systems is that they can link a large number of people who are geographically separated. If satellite technology is used for the teleconference, then, there is no limit to the number of sites that can be linked through the combination of several communications satellites. In order to participate in a teleconference, participants usually have to assemble at a specific site in order to use the special equipment that is necessary for a group to participate in the conference. The only exceptions are audio teleconferences which can link up any individual who has access to a telephone, computer conferences that can link up individuals, their computers and modems at home, or direct broadcast satellites that can deliver information directly to participant's homes. However, if more than two people are present at a participating site then it is necessary for the participants to gather at a location which is equipped with teleconferencing equipment in order to partici-pate in a teleconference. This may restrict access for some learn-ers. In terms of control, participants will have control over the interaction that takes place in a teleconference only to the ex-tent that the instructional design allows for it. However, if the teleconference is taped for later review, students will have more control in viewing the conference.

The unique advantage of teleconferences is that they pro-vide for two-way interaction between the originators and the participants. Teleconferences need to be designed to optimize the interaction that takes place during the conference. Interac-tion needs to be thought of not only as interaction that occurs during the teleconference but pre- and post conference activi-ties that allow groups to interact. Monson (1978) describes four design components for teleconferences: humanizing, participa-tion, message style and feedback. Humanizing is the process of creating an atmosphere which focuses on the importance of the individual and overcomes distance by generating group rapport. Participation is the process of getting beyond the technology by providing opportunities for the spontaneous interaction be-tween participants. Message style is presenting what is to be said in such a way that it will be received, understood and remem-bered. Feedback is the process of getting information about the message which helps the instructor and the participants com-plete the communications loop. Monson (1978) offers excellent guidelines for incorporating these four elements into teleconfer-encing design. The symbolic characteristics and the interfaces that are unique to each medium are discussed with the descrip-tion of each technology.

14.4.6.1 Audio Teleconferencing.
Audio teleconferencing or audio conferencing is voice-only communication. Even though it lacks a visual dimension, audio teleconferencing has some major strengths: it uses the regular telephone system which is readily available and a familiar technology, it can con-nect a large number of locations for a conference using an au-diobridge, the conferences can be set up at short notice, and it is relatively inexpensive to use when compared with other technologies.

Olgren and Parker (1983) observe that one should keep in mind that voice communication is the backbone of any telecon-ferencing system with the exception of computer conferencing. Sophisticated video or graphics equipment can be added to any audio system. But, it is the audio channel that is the primary mode of communication. If the audio is of poor quality it will have a negative impact on users of even the most sophisticated graphics and video technologies. Audio teleconferences can be enhanced by adding a visual component to the conference by mailing or e-mailing ahead of time printed graphics, transparen-cies or a video cassette to be used during the conference. Each site must be equipped with a projection device and a VCR if such graphical or video support is used.

14.4.6.2 Audiographics Conferencing.
While popular a decade ago, audiographics systems have been gradually replaced by compressed video systems. Audiographics used ordinary tele-phone lines for two-way voice communication and the trans-mission of graphics and written material. Audiographics add a visual element to audio teleconferencing while maintaining the flexibility and economy of using telephone lines. Audio telecon-ferencing is now combined with written, print, graphics and still or full motion video information. Most audiographics sys-tems use two telephone lines, one for audio and one for the transmission of written, graphic and video information.

The simplest audiographics system was the addition of a fax machine using a second telephone line to an audio telecon-ference. As a result of developments in computer, digital and video compression technology, fairly sophisticated computer-based audiographics systems were available in the market. These systems combine voice, data, graphics, and digitized still video to create a powerful communications medium. The PC-based systems have specially designed communications software that control a scanner; graphics tablet, pen, keyboard, video camera, printer, and a modem.

One of the key advantages of an audiographics system is the ability to use the screen-sharing feature of the system. Partici-pants at different sites can use different colored pens to create a graphic on the same screen at the same time. This feature enables the use of collaborative learning methods that involve learners at the remote locations.

14.4.6.3 Video Teleconferencing.
Video teleconferencing systems transmit voice, graphics and images of people. They have the advantage of being able to show an image of the speaker, three dimensional objects, motion, and preproduced video footage. The teleconference can be designed to take ad-vantage of the three symbolic characteristics of the medium: iconic, digital and analog, where the iconic or the visual

properties of the medium which is television's foremost strength can be manipulated to convey a very convincing message. Because of its ability to show the images of people, video teleconferences can create a "social presence" that closely approximates face-to-face interaction. Video teleconferencing systems are fully interactive systems that either allow for two-way video and audio, where the presenters and the audience can see and hear each other, or one-way video and two-way audio, where the audience sees and hears the presenter, and the presenter only hears the audience. During a video teleconference, audio, video and data signals are transmitted to distant sites using a single combined channel as in the use of a fiber optic line. Audio only feedback is most often transmitted over a dial-up telephone line. The transmission channel can be analog or digital; signals can be sent via satellite, microwave, fiber optics or coaxial cable or a combination of these delivery systems.

The term video teleconferencing has become popular as an ad hoc one-time, special event conference that usually connects a vast number of sites in order to make the conference cost effective. A video teleconference is usually distinguished from interactive Instructional Television (ITV) that is generally used to extend the campus classroom and carries programming for a significant length of time such as a semester. ITV may use the same transmission channels as a video teleconference, but is distinguished from video teleconferencing because of its different applications; video teleconferencing, an ad hoc conference, and ITV extending the classroom over a longer period of time.

Video teleconferences can be classified into two broad areas according to the technology used for transmission: full-motion video teleconferencing or compressed (or near-motion) video teleconferencing. Full-motion video teleconferencing uses the normal TV broadcast method or an analog video channel which requires a wideband channel to transmit pictures. The range of frequencies needed to reproduce a high quality motion TV signal is at least 4.2 million Hz (4.2 MHZ). The cost of a full-motion video teleconference is therefore extremely high. In the 1970s, conversion of the analog video signal to a digital bit stream enabled the first significant reductions in video signal bandwidth, making compressed video conferencing less cost prohibitive. Therefore, in compressed video, full video information is compressed by a piece of technology known as a Codec in order to send it down the narrower bandwidth of a special telephone line. The compressed video method is cheaper and more flexible than the TV broadcast method.

14.4.6.3.1 Full-Motion Video Teleconferencing. This became popular with the advent of satellite technology. For the past decade educational developers have provided credit courses via satellite television. Video compression standards and the introduction of fiber optic cable infrastructure by many telephone and cable companies has made terrestrial line transmission of video much cheaper. There are, however, at least two reasons that satellite television will probably remain available and, in fact, increase in the foreseeable future. First, there are still many remote areas of the world, even in North America, where telephone service, if it exists at all, is supported by antiquated technology barely able to provide a usable audio or data

signal, let alone carry video. These remote areas simply need to point a relatively inexpensive satellite dish, powered by solar panels, batteries, or generators, at the appropriate satellite to receive its signal. The new generation of Ku-band satellite is already offering direct broadcast service (DBS) to households. The proliferation of smaller, less expensive satellite television reception technology, along with the continued launching of new, higher powered satellites will insure a continuing niche for this technology to deliver instructional video and data to even the remotest areas of the world that lack other information infrastructure.

Fiber optics is gaining in popularity as a transmission medium for video teleconferencing. Fiber optics offers several advantages: it can carry a tremendous amount of data at high transmission speeds; it does not experience signal degradation over distance as does coaxial cable, and it is a multipurpose system which can transmit video, audio, data, and graphics into a school through a single cable. A single fiber optic cable can carry over a billion bits per second, enabling several video teleconferences to run simultaneously. Many companies, universities and States in the United States are building fiber optic transmission networks to carry voice, data and video.

Video teleconferencing can also use digital or analog microwave systems, or dial-up digital transmission lines. Current developments center on converging the different transmission channels and using a combination of telecommunications channels, satellite, fiber optic, microwave, coaxial cable to deliver full-motion video teleconferencing.

14.4.6.3.2 Compressed Video Teleconferencing. Video compression techniques have greatly reduced the amount of data needed to describe a video picture and have enabled the video signal to be transmitted at a lower, and less expensive data rate. The device used to digitize and compress an analog video signal is called a video codec, short for COder/DEcoder which is the opposite of a modem (MOdulator/DEModulator). Reduction of transmission rate means trade-offs in picture quality. As the transmission rate is reduced, less data can be sent to describe picture changes. Lower data rates yield less resolution and less ability to handle motion. Therefore, if an image moves quickly, the motion will "streak" or "jerk" on the screen.

Currently most compressed video systems use either T-1 or half a T-1 channel. In a T-1 channel, video is compressed at 1.536 Mbps which is the digital equivalent of 24 voice-grade lines. Digital video compression technology has allowed video teleconferencing to become less cost-prohibitive. However, it is not as cost effective as audio teleconferencing.

14.4.6.3.3 Desktop Video Teleconferencing. Integrated desktop video teleconferencing combining audio, video and data is becoming increasingly popular. This technology allows users to see each other, speak to each other, transfer application files and work together on such files at a distance. Most systems do not require advanced digital communications technologies such as ISDN to operate. For those wanting to utilize ISDN, it is possible to purchase an ISDN card while most systems are now being designed to work with telecommunications standards such as ISDN.

Education can use this technology as a method of presenting class material and forming work groups even though students may be at a considerable distance from each other. An instructor could conceivably present material to the entire class either "live" or through delivery of an audio file to each students electronic mail account. Students could then work together in real time if they wished to share information over telephone lines.

As more technologies begin to dovetail desktop videoconferencing becomes laptop videoconferencing. The use of cellular telephone technology combined with high speed laptop modems will make it possible for people to hold meetings and work group sessions whether they are at home, in an office or on the beach.

14.4.6.3.4 Integrated Services Digital Network (ISDN). ISDN is an international telecommunications standard that offers a future worldwide network capable of transmitting voice, data, video, and graphics in digital form over standard telephone lines or fiber optic cable. ISDN transmits media using digital rather than analog signals. In order to move toward a global network, ISDN promises end-to-end digital connectivity, multiple services over the same transmission path and standard interfaces or conversion facilities for ubiquitous or transparent user access. ISDN's applications for distance education include convergence, multitasking and shared communications.

14.5 CURRENT TECHNOLOGY FOR DISTANCE EDUCATION

The technologies discussed in the previous section; print, broadcast television and radio continue to deliver instruction for much of the distance education that is delivered around the world. All of the mega universities, those distance teaching institutions with over 100,000 students, rely heavily on print, television, radio and videocassettes. However, in many countries newer technologies have been integrated into distance delivery systems.

The field of distance education is in the midst of dynamic growth and change. The directions that distance education takes depend on each country's technology infrastructure, pedagogy, and goals for education. In many countries, the development of new media and computing technologies, the different methods of group learning and information gathering, and the development of government telecommunications policies have promoted the use of new technologies, particularly computer based media. Computer-supported learning has been the fastest growing component of distance education.

14.5.1 Computers and Learning

The development of cheaper and faster computers and the proliferation of computer applications to education have encouraged a growing interest in exploring ways that pedagogy, flexible learning, and knowledge building can be integrated using computer and network based technology. Computers are not new as technology, but they are rapidly evolving into new areas. Personal computers have long been used in education to run tutorials and teach students to use word processing, database management, and spreadsheets. Now, new interest in learner-centered pedagogies has led educators to discover ways that learners can be given strategies and tools to help them construct their own knowledge bases using networked computers. Not only learning, but teaching is affected by the use of computers. Teaching in technology based environments is shifting away from the acquisition model to the participation model (Collis, deBoer, van der Veen 2001). Teacher training models are directing teachers to become facilitators of learning rather than simply expert authorities. A number of tools have made this possible.

14.5.1.1 Laptop Computers. Personal computers have been the mainstay of electronic information appliances. They have been used to control incoming video over cable and fiber optic lines, handle both incoming and outgoing electronic mail over the Internet and even search globally for text, audio, graphic, and video files needed by the user. Children in many schools have discovered such computer-based uses by navigating the Internet to find files, downloading information from the networks and electronically copying and pasting reference material from network resources to their papers. They have discovered the ease of communicating with their peers around the world using their computers. Conexiones is one of many projects that provide laptops to children of migrant workers. This project models innovative approaches to using network communications and educational computer applications by leveraging technology to actively engage educators, students, and the community to educate traditionally under served minority students (http://conexiones.asu.edu/).

Laptops provide the portability to carry all files, papers, financial records, and any other text based materials on a small machine. New software is making communication, writing, publishing and learning easier and more portable. Laptops are being used in classrooms at all levels of education to access the Web, to communicate with others around the world, and to stay in touch with teachers and fellow students. Increasing numbers of schools and colleges are finding them useful.

14.5.1.2 Personal Digital Assistants (PDAs). Further miniaturization and the increased power of microprocessors have resulted in the widespread growth and use of personal digital assistants (PDAs). Each year these handheld microprocessors are produced with more memory and smaller physical size. The smallest versions of personal computers, personal digital assistants are used in many schools just as the early laptops were used, to communicate with others, to retrieve information, and to keep databases. As protocols are standardized so that PDAs can work with various computers, one's personal network becomes seamless and processors can control fax, copying, and telecommunications functions as well as environment and power utilization from a very small machine. As PDAs become more powerful, incorporating data storage devices that store the same amount of information as CD-ROMs in a smaller space, it becomes possible to create even more useful personal computing tools. Forsyth County Day School in North Carolina is one of a number of schools mandating that all of its high school students purchase a Palm IIIc and portable keyboard. According to school officials, the PDA, at around $300. is more affordable than a computer and will allow students to organize homework assignments, take notes, make vocabulary cards, and take quizzes through the integrated use of technology. Effective summer 2001, UCLA School of Medicine required PDAs for two reasons: to "enable point of contact access to information resources; and to prepare students for practicing medicine in the 21st century" (UCLA, 2001).

Through wireless connectivity PDA manufacturers already offer Web and telephone access. With the profusion of microprocessor technology in offices, homes, cars and all forms of electronics, PDAs can become the ultimate remote control allowing people to access records on home or office computers and control functions of electronics in these locations using cellular phone technology.

14.5.1.3 CD-ROM.
Computer-based instruction (CBI), developed in the 1980s, has expanded to include multimedia available on CD-ROM, allowing students greater access to large digital audio and video files on individual computers. CD-ROMs have replaced videocassettes in many settings where computers are used, and the proliferation of integrated multimedia systems with electronic networks allows the greater individualization of instruction envisioned by early CBI developers. An ever-increasing amount of text, graphic and even full motion video data is being recorded and distributed on CD-ROM. There is also a constantly expanding hardware base for CD-ROM drives built into computers. As digital video compression improves, CD-ROM and similar optical storage formats such as DVD are replacing videocasettes as the most popular media for distributing full motion video programming, films, and telecourses.

Current versions of CD-ROMs hold over 600 mb of digitized information. Most multimedia applications are CD-ROM-based since video, audio, and graphic files require enormous amounts of storage space. An example of a popular CD-ROM title is the Compton's Multimedia Encyclopedia that provides both the traditional text and still images along with animation and video. Essentially a hypermedia database, the encyclopedia allows random access to any of its material guided by the interests of the user.

An early example of how CD-ROMs have affected education was the creation of a graduate media design course developed by the College of Education at Arizona State University. With the help of a grant from the Intel Corporation, this course was redesigned and transferred to CD-ROM (Technology Based Learning, 1994).

There are currently nearly 10,000 CD-ROM titles listed in media directories. Although heralded as the wave of the future for years, CD-ROM was slow in developing as a technology while suffering a "chicken-or-the-egg" problem. CD-ROM titles grew slowly because there was only a small installed hardware base. Meanwhile many people were hesitant to buy CD-ROM drives until more titles were offered. Recently, however, the market has

begun to snowball as faster, less expensive drives are available in virtually all computers.

14.5.1.4 Course Management Tools.
The earlier computer-managed instruction (CMI) has evolved into course management tools used on the Web. These tools have begun to shift the focus away from the presentation of content to the integration of student contributions, building communities of learners and constructing a community of knowledge using Web-based templates.

WebCT and Blackboard, are examples of course management tools. They offer a well developed structure for teachers who are unfamiliar with Web-based teaching, and they make putting courses online fairly easy.

But there are other course management tools such as Tele-TOP that are built around the central concept of a new, Web-based pedagogy (Collis et al. 2001). Course management tools such as these shift the focus from teacher presented to learner constructed materials and are leading the way toward truly collaborative communities of learning.

14.5.2 Computer-Mediated Communication (CMC)

CMC supports three types of online services: electronic mail (e-mail), computer conferencing, and online databases. These services are useful to educators in building learning communities around course content. E-mail among students and between student and instructor form the fundamental online form of communication. Online databases enhance students' abilities to retrieve information, construct their own knowledge bases, and contribute to the community. The computer conference, based on the use of networks, is the collaborative working environment in which learning takes place through discussion and exchange of ideas.

14.5.2.1 Electronic Networks.
The past few years have produced an explosion of electronic information resources available to students, teachers, library patrons, and anyone with a computer. Millions of pages of graphics and text-based information can be accessed directly online through hundreds of public, private and commercial networks, including the biggest network of all: the Internet. The Internet is, in fact, a collection of independent academic, scientific, government and commercial networks providing electronic mail, and access to file servers with free software and millions of pages of text and graphic data that even thousands of elementary and secondary students are now using.

Students in developing countries with limited assets may have very little access to these technologies and thus fall further behind in terms of information infrastructure. On the other hand, new telecommunications avenues such as satellite telephone service are opening channels at reasonable cost to even the remotest areas of the world. One very encouraging sign from the Internet's rapidly developing history is not only the willingness, but the eagerness with which networkers share information and areas of expertise. Networks have the potential of providing a broad knowledge base to citizens around the world, and will offer opportunities for expanded applications of distance education. Research is just beginning to indicate how these newer technologies can benefit learners. The most widespread use of electronic networks is the World Wide Web.

The World Wide Web project is a distributed hypermedia environment that originated at CERN with the collaboration of a large international design and development team. World Wide Web applications are Internet-based global hypermedia browsers that allow one to discover, retrieve, and display documents and data from all over the Internet. For example, using these interfaces, learners can search the databases in museums all over the world that are connected to the Internet by navigating in a hypermedia format. Browsing tools such as these help learners explore a huge and rapidly expanding universe of information and gives them the powerful new capabilities for interacting with information.

The Clinton–Gore administration developed the first comprehensive U.S. high-speed electronic network that extended the capabilities of Internet services to learners through an information superhighway. The plan, *The National Information Infrastructure: Agenda for Action* (U.S. Department of Commerce, 1993) had far-reaching effects on education by expanding access to information. Since that time, electronic networks have continued to expand. Today there are more than 105 million Internet users, and an increasing number each year comes from minority groups (Cyberatlas, 2002). Partially responsible for this growth in access are recent efforts to help schools acquire the hardware necessary to access the Internet.

The fiber optic infrastructure in the United States that provides the backbone of the NII has expanded through both public and commercial efforts. Fiber optics are capable of carrying much greater bandwidth technologies such as full motion video. These lines can provide two-way videoconferencing, on-line multimedia, and video programming on demand. Iowa was one of the early adopters and installed nearly 3000 miles of fiber optic cable linking 15 community colleges and three public universities with a 48-channel interactive video capability (Suwinski, 1993). The next wave of developments in electronic networks will center on applications designed for Internet II, a research-based high-speed network that will link higher education institutions in the United States and Overseas.

14.5.2.2 Wireless Networks.

Laptops with Airport connections and PDAs with wireless connectivity are the forerunners of greater satellite-based wireless tools. Although PDAs are used mainly for writing notes and keeping track of schedules, their growing value may be more in the order of complete wireless telecommunications devices.

Combined with the rapid proliferation of cellular telephone service in the United States, wireless technologies can free learners from the need to be tied to a particular hard-wired location to access information. Additionally, a consortium of major telecommunications, electronics, and aerospace companies has worked on global satellites to offer direct telephone service without the need for satellite dishes to literally any location on Earth. This could provide not only voice but direct data and fax access to anyone anywhere utilizing PDA technology. How viable this is for remote populations depends on the cost for this service, but the technology is in place. What we see in all of these technologies is that once separate devices are now merging to form information appliances that eventually will allow users to seamlessly communicate with each other, control home and office environments, and, most importantly of all, access most of the world's information whether in text, audio, or visual forms, at any place and any time.

14.5.2.3 Computer Conferencing.

Computer conferencing systems use computer-mediated communication (CMC) to support group and many-to-many communication. In these systems, messages are linked to form chains of communication and these messages are stored on the host computer until an individual logs on to read and reply to messages. Most conferencing systems offer a range of facilities for enhancing group communication and information retrieval. These include directories of users and conferences, conference management tools, search facilities, polling options, cooperative authoring, the ability to customize the system with special commands for particular groups, and access to databases. Recent developments in groupware, the design of software that facilitates group processes especially in the CMC environment will have a tremendous impact on facilitating group work between participants who are separated in time and place. Webcourse authoring tools such as WebCT and Blackboard provide a computer conferencing feature to enhance group dialogue. Computer conferencing is also available on stand alone systems such as WebBoard.

The key features of computer conferencing systems that have an impact on distance education are the ability to support many-to-many interactive communication, the asynchronous (time-independent), and place-independent features. It offers the flexibility of assembling groups at times and places convenient to participants. The disadvantage, however, is that since online groups depend on text-based communication, they lack the benefit of nonverbal cues that facilitates interaction in a face-to-face meeting. Levinson (1990) notes that research into education via computer conferencing must be sensitive to the ways in which subtle differences in the technology can impact the social educational environment. Harasim (1989, 2001) emphasizes the necessity to approach on-line education as a distinct and unique domain. "The group nature of computer conferencing may be the most fundamental or critical component underpinning theory-building and the design and implementation of on-line educational activities" (1989, p. 51). Gunawardena (1991, 1993) reviews research related to the essentially group or socially interactive nature of computer conferences focusing on factors that impact collaborative learning and group dynamics.

Computer conferencing provides an environment for collaborative learning and the social construction of knowledge. Researchers are using conferencing platforms to examine social presence, cognitive presence and interaction. Using the model of learning as socially situated, scholars are examining collaboration, knowledge construction and learner satisfaction in computer conferences (Gunawardena & Duphorne 2000). Research indicates that student satisfaction is strongly related to the learner's perception of social presence (Gunawardena & Zittle, 1997). Garrison and colleagues (2001) suggest that cognitive presence, (critical, practical inquiry) is an essential part of a critical community of inquiry, and can be supported in a computer conference environment that models effective teaching and contains activities for encouraging social presence. Communities of practice are developing in computer-mediated environments using strategies based on distributed models of learning (Lea & Nicoll, 2002).

14.5.3 Virtual Reality

Virtual reality offers the promise of training future students in ways that currently are far too dangerous or expensive. Virtual reality combines the power of computer generated graphics with the computer's ability to monitor massive data inflows in real time to create an enclosed man/machine interactive feedback loop. VR participants wearing visors projecting the computer images react to what they see while sensors in the visor and body suit send information on position and the head and eye movement of the wearer. The computer changes the scene to follow the wearer and give the impression of actually moving within an artificial environment.

Medical students wearing a virtual reality visor and data suit can perform any operation on a computer generated patient and actually see the results of what they are doing. Pilots can practice maneuvers, as they do now in trainers but with far more realism. The U.S. Defense Department has already used primitive networked versions in their SIMNET training. This network was one of the first to connect and control training simulators in the U.S. and Europe so that hundreds of soldiers could practice armored maneuvers while the computer reacted to their judgments and allowed them to see each other's moves as if they were all together (Alluisi, 1991).

Beyond practical training needs, virtual reality can put students on a street in ancient Rome, floating inside of a molecule, or flying the length of our galaxy. Many scientists are now beginning to understand the power of visualization in understanding the raw data they receive. Virtual reality can be used by students and professionals alike to interpret and understand the universe.

Individuals interacting in a virtual world will undoubtedly create unanticipated communities and possibly even new and unique cultures. There are concerns, however. Dede (1992) warns that "the cultural consequences of technology-mediated physical social environments are mixed." While providing a wider range of human experience and knowledge bases, these environments can also be used for manipulation and to create misleading depictions of the world.

Recent investigations into student learning in virtual environments is examining whether students can use immersive Virtual Reality and other advanced technologies for learning complex tasks, and retain that learning longer than in traditional classrooms (Winn, 1997). Research has shown that learning in artificial environments allows students to learn in ways that are different from those that occur in the regular classroom, and virtual reality offers an alternative or supplemental tool for learning.

14.6 COURSE DESIGN AND COMMUNICATION

A number of research studies have been conducted around the issues of designing course material for distance education. A brief review of the literature reveals that the most frequently expressed concern in courses designed for distance learners has to do with providing the learner with adequate feedback (Howard, 1987; McCleary & Eagan, 1989). Learner feedback is listed as one of the five most important considerations in course design and instruction, and it is identified by Howard (1987) as the most significant component in his model for effective course design.

Other major issues that relate to course design are effective instructional design, selection of appropriate media based on instructional needs, basic evaluation, and programmatic research. There appears to be little reported systematic research in this area because of the time and costs involved in conducting such large scale projects. McCleary and Egan (1989) examined course design and found that their second and third courses received higher ratings as a result of improving three elements of course design, one of which was feedback. In a review of the research, Dwyer (1991) proposes the use of instructional consistency/congruency paradigms when designing distance education materials in order to pair content of material with level of learners' ability. Others suggest models combining cognitive complexity, intellectual activity and forms of instruction for integrating the use of technology in course delivery.

Although consideration is given in the literature to elements of course design such as interactivity, student support, media selection, instructional design issues and feedback, little research has been reported other than evaluative studies. Few are generalizable to global situations. Although course design is a primary component of large scale international distance education programs, little attention has been paid to the underlying social and cultural assumptions within which such instruction is designed. Critical theorists have examined how teaching materials and classroom practices reflect social assumptions of validity, authority and empowerment. Although the thread of critical theory has woven its way through the fabric of the literature in education, nowhere is it more important to examine educational assumptions underlying course design than in distance education.

Courses designed for distance delivery often cost thousands of dollars to produce and reach hundreds of thousands of students. Not only are hidden curricula in the classroom well documented, there is a growing body of evidence in the literature which critically analyzes the impact of social norms on the production of educational media. In their book, Ellsworth and Whatley (1990) examine the ways in which particular historical and social perspectives combine to produce images in educational media that serve the interests of a particular social and historical interpretation of values. Distance learning materials are designed to rely heavily on visual materials to maintain student interest. Film, video and still photography should no longer be viewed as neutral carriers of information. In a seminal book of readings Hlynka and Belland (1991) explore critical inquiry in the field of Educational Technology as a third paradigm, equally as important as the qualitative and quantitative perspectives. This collection of essays encourages instructional designers to examine issues in educational media and technology using paradigms drawn from the humanities and social sciences, sociology and anthropology.

The examination of issues concerning the use of technology is especially important when designing courses for distance education. There are many factors that are particularly critical and need to be considered. In order to distinguish the characteristics of the communications technologies currently being used in distance education it is necessary to adopt a classification system, although any classification system may not remain current for very long with the constant development of new technologies.

14.6.1 Media and Course Design

Several classification models have been developed to describe the technologies used in distance education (Barker, Frisbie, & Patrick, 1989; Bates, 1991; Johansen, Martin, Mittman, & Saffo, 1991). In an early attempt to classify the media used in distance education, Bates (1993) noted that there should be two distinctions. The first is that it is important to make a distinction between "media" and "technology." Media are the forms of communication associated with particular ways of representing knowledge. Therefore, each medium has its own unique way of presenting knowledge, and organizing it that is reflected in particular formats or styles of presentation. Bates (1993) notes that in distance education, the most important four media are: text, audio, television, and computing. Each medium, however, can usually be carried by more than one technology. For example, the audio medium can be carried by audiocassettes, radio, and telephone, while the television medium can be carried by broadcasting, videocassettes, DVD, cable, satellite, fiber optics, ITFS and microwave. Therefore, a variety of different technologies may be used to deliver one medium. The second distinction is the one between primarily one-way and primarily two-way technologies. One way technologies such as radio and broadcast television, do not provide opportunities for interaction, while two-way technologies such as videoconferencing or interactive television, allow for interaction between learners and instructors and among learners themselves.

For the purpose of this chapter, we would like to expand on a definition adopted by Willen (1988) who noted that where distance teaching and learning is concerned, three characteristics have proved critical to the optimization of the study situation: (a) the ability of the medium to reach all learners, or provide access, (b) the flexibility of the medium; and (c) the two-way communication capability of the medium. We feel that it is necessary to expand these three characteristics to include three others: the symbolic characteristics of the medium, the social presence conveyed by the medium, and the human–machine interface for a particular technology. Whatever classification system is used to describe the technologies, we feel that six important characteristics need to be kept in mind in the adoption and use of these technologies for distance education:

1. Delivery and access—the way in which the technology distributes the learning material to distance learners and the location to which it is distributed: homes, places of work, or local study centers. Student access to technologies in order to participate in the learning process is an important consideration.

2. Control—the extent to which the learner has control over the medium (the extent to which the medium provides flexibility in allowing the students to use it at a time and place and in a manner which suits them best). For example, the advantage of using videocassettes over broadcast television is that students can exercise "control" over the programming by using the stop, rewind, replay, and fast forward features to proceed at their own pace. Videocassettes are also a very flexible medium allowing students to use the cassettes at a time that is suitable to them.

3. Interaction—the degree to which the technology permits interaction (two-way communication) between the teacher and the student, and among students. Technologies utilized for distance education can be classified as one-way transmission, or two-way interactive technologies. One-way transmission media include printed texts and materials, radio programs, open broadcast or cablecast television programs, audiocassettes and videocassettes. Technologies that permit two-way interaction can be classified as either synchronous (real time communication) or asynchronous (time-delayed communication) systems. Audio teleconferencing, audiographics teleconferencing, video teleconferencing, interactive television, and real-time computer chatting when two or more computers are linked so that participants can talk to each other at the same time, are synchronous technologies that permit real time two-way communication. Computer-Mediated Communications (CMC) including electronic mail (e-mail), bulletin boards, and computer conferencing when used in a time-delayed fashion are asynchronous technologies that permit two-way communication.

4. Symbolic (or audiovisual) characteristics of the medium. Salomon (1979) distinguishes between three kinds of symbol systems: iconic, digital, and analog. Iconic systems use pictorial representation; digital systems convey meaning by written language, musical notation, and mathematical symbols; and analog systems are made up of continuous elements which nevertheless have reorganized meaning and forms, such as voice quality, performed music, and dance. Television, or multimedia, for example, use all three coding systems to convey a message. Salomon (1979) observes that it is the symbol system that a medium embodies rather than its other characteristics that may relate more directly to cognition and learning. "A code can activate a skill, it can short-circuit it, or it can overtly supplant it" (Salomon, 1979 p.134).

5. The social presence created by the medium. Telecommunication systems, even two-way video and audio systems that permit the transmission of facial expressions and gestures, create social climates which are very different from the traditional classroom. Short et.al. (1976) define social presence as the "degree of salience of the other person in the interaction and the consequent salience of the interpersonal

relationships . . . " (p. 65). This means the degree to which a person is perceived as a "real person" in mediated communication. Social presence can be conveyed both by the medium (video can convey a higher degree of social presence than audio) and by the people who are involved in using the medium for interaction (instructors who humanize the classroom climate may convey a higher degree of social presence than those who do not). Gunawardena and Zittle (1997) showed that social presence is an important predictor of learner satisfaction.

6. Human–machine interface for a particular technology that takes into consideration how the equipment interfaces with the end users. The learner must interact with the interface or the technological medium in order to interact with the content, instructor, and other learners. This may include an activity such as using a keyboard to interact with a web interface. With the rapid growth of new telecommunications technologies, ergonomics or the design of human–machine interfaces has become an important area of research and development within the broader area of research related to human factors. The kinds of interfaces the technology employs has implications for the kind of training or orientation that both teachers and students must receive in order to be competent users of the medium.

When selecting technologies for a distance learning program, or when designing instruction for distance learning, these six factors need to be kept in mind (see Fig. 14.1). They are not entities in and of themselves but interact with each other to make up the total environment in which a specific medium operates. The diagram below indicates this interaction.

The evolution of geographic space into cyberspace has profound implications for communication, instruction and the design of the instructional message. One recent trend in course design is the shift from a teacher-centered to a learner-centered paradigm based on constructivist and social constructivist learning principles. Using the features of networked learning technologies, designers are exploring how to build communities of inquiry to facilitate collaborative learning and knowledge construction in online learning designs. Current research on course design issues such as learner control, interaction and

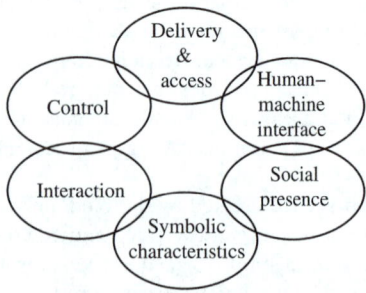

FIGURE 14.1. Factors impacting selection and use of distance education technologies.

social presence are discussed under the section (14.10) on Research in Distance Education.

14.6.2 Course Design and the International Market

Issues that examine course design in distance education cross geographic boundaries. Courses that are produced in North America are exported across the world. There is a widespread belief that Western technologies, particularly the computer, are culturally neutral and can be used to modernize traditional societies. When distance education programs are delivered to developing countries, cultural differences are often dealt with by simply translating the existing software, or by writing new software in the local language. What remains is still instruction based on a set of cultural assumptions emphasizing the view that Western technology and science represent the most advanced stage in cultural evolution. This rationalist, secularist and individualist philosophy remains at the tacit level and suggests that, for any country, true modernization relies on the scientific method and the adoption of culture-free technology. The imported technology boasts capabilities based on assumptions that are frequently in direct opposition to traditions and social practices in the local culture.

Critical theorists, and others, have engaged in the debate over obvious discrepancies between the ideal Western view of life and the reality of deteriorating social fabric, loss of traditional values, high crime and drug rates and other visible social ills. The Western view of modernization and progress has not been universally accepted as ideal. However by embracing new communication technologies, non-Western countries are buying into a new set of cultural assumptions. The danger is that this may occur at the cost of their own indigenous traditions.

UNESCO has argued that when urban, individualistic, images of life are part of the cultural agendas of Western media, people in developing countries will aspire to these to be modern. The long-term effects of technological innovations on cultural traditions have not yet been well documented. It may be, that in racing to embrace modernism and technological innovations, social and traditional patterns of life will be altered to the extent that local traditions may be irrevocably changed. The cultural values of individualism, secularism, and feminism are not all recognized as desirable in other cultures that place higher values on religion, group efforts and well defined gender roles (McIsaac, 1993). Course materials designed with a particular cultural bias embedded in the instruction may have a negative effect on learning.

Moral issues surrounding loss of local culture can result from wholesale importation of foreign values. At the minimum, educators engaged in technology transfer should analyze local social customs and consider those customs, whenever possible. Such social conventions as extended hospitality, differing perceptions of time and the perceived importance of the technology project can all affect the credibility of the program and, ultimately, its success (McIsaac & Koymen, 1988).

Course designers should first determine the underlying assumptions conveyed by the educational message being designed. Designers should consider the social and political setting in which the lessons will be used. They should determine whether the instructional design model has implicit cultural and social bias. And finally tacit messages and hidden agendas should be examined and eliminated wherever possible so that course materials do not reflect particular ideological points of view. Distance education research in course design should include programs of social research that explore the effects of technological innovations on cultural traditions.

14.7 INSTRUCTION AND LEARNER SUPPORT

The issue of learner support has received wide attention in distance education. The research, however, has been varied and inconclusive. After examining one hundred seven articles to determine whether there were predictors of successful student support, Dillon and Blanchard (1991) conclude that the reported research was mixed. They propose a model to examine the support needs of the distance student, related to institutional characteristics, course content and the technology. In a study analyzing learner support services in a state-wide distance education system, Dillon, Gunawardena and Parker (1992) outline the function and effectiveness of one learner support system and make recommendations for examining student–program interactions. Feasley (1991) comments that although research on student support falls largely into the evaluation category, there are some very useful case studies and institutional surveys such as reports issued by FernUniversitat, National Home Study Council which summarize statistics about student services for a number of institutions. Wright (1991) comments that the largest number of studies related to student support have been conducted outside the United States with large distance education programs. The student support activities reported are preenrollment activities, tutorial services, and counseling and advising services.

In addition to student support, several ethical and administrative issues related to students are repeated in the literature as well. The mediation of technology coupled with the distance between instructor and student poses questions related to admission, counseling and retention. Reed and Sork (1990) provide evidence that admission criteria and intake systems should take into account the unique demands of the adult learner (i.e., motivation, anxiety, interactions and learning style). Nelson (1988) states that admission requirements should consider the effects of the individual's cognitive styles as these often affect student achievement in programs characterized by mediated communications and limited personal contact.

Combined with the institutions' responsibilities related to admissions procedures is the responsibility of counseling students into and out of programs where the learner and advisor are physically separated (Reed & Sork, 1990). Herein two issues arise. First, the nearly impossible task of understanding the life situation of the learner when distance and time interfere with communication, makes counseling a difficult task at best. Second, the monetary requirements of the distance education institution and the well-being of the student who may or may not be advised into a distance education environment must be

considered. Reed and Sork (1990) observe that students counseled out of distance education represent a loss of revenue. Counseling in a traditional setting requires expertise in a number of psychological and academic areas. However, counseling from a distance is a highly complex process which calls for a variety of methods, materials, and a knowledge of adult learner characteristics (Verduin & Clark, 1991). The literature has offered various profiles of the distance education student. Counseling professionals should review the research on student needs and develop new methodologies for assisting students at a distance. Additional research is called for in all areas of student interaction with the learning environment.

14.7.1 Learning and Characteristics of Learners

The study of learning and characteristics of learners engages the largest number of researchers and includes studies of learning styles, attitudes, personality, locus of control, motivation, and attrition. Included are general studies about cognition and metacognition as well as specific studies related to the particular needs of the distance learner. Many studies have been single group evaluations, few with randomization of subjects or programmatic investigations. Some exploratory research has involved a small number of participants in short interventions. Although these efforts yield interesting insights, they have not helped solve the problem of isolating and testing variables which might predict academic success. Often, experimental studies use thin descriptions and do not provide deep contextual information. Similarly, descriptive studies often lack generalizability and are not qualitatively rich.

Research reports that do appear in the literature are often inconclusive. Reports in the literature suggest that some combination of cognitive style, personality characteristics, and self-expectations can be predictors of success in distance education programs. It appears that those students who are most successful in distance learning situations tend to be independent, autonomous learners who prefer to control their own learning situations.

Characteristics besides independence which appears to be predictors of success are high self-expectations and self-confidence (Laube, 1992), academic accomplishment (Coggins, 1988; Dille & Mezack, 1991) and external locus of control (Baynton, 1992). Another motivation which reportedly influences academic persistence is the desire to improve employment possibilities (von Prummer, 1990). Research findings suggest that it is the combination of personal (such as learning style), environmental and social factors which must be taken into account when predicting academic success in distance learning programs.

Verduin and Clark (1991) examined learning styles within the distance education setting and reviewed the research done on learning styles by Canfield in 1983. Canfield developed a learning style inventory that conceptualized learning styles as composed of preferred conditions, content, mode and expectancy scores. Verduin and Clark (1991) believe this information can be helpful to educators in planning courses for students who will receive the instruction from a distance. They indicate that an understanding of how individual learners approach learning may make it possible for the distance educator to see a pattern of learning styles and plan or adjust course presentations accordingly. They conclude by saying that adults may or may not learn more easily when the style of presentation matches the students learning style, but when the two do match, the students report being more satisfied with the course.

Perhaps the most interesting work in cognition appears outside the traditional confines of the distance education literature. Research that examines the interaction of learners and delivery media is currently being conducted with multimedia. These studies examine learning and problem solving in asynchronous, virtual environments in which the learner is encouraged to progress and interact with learning materials in a very individual way. In the Jasper experiment, for example, math problems are anchored in authentic real world situations portrayed on videodisc (Van Haneghan et.al., 1992). It was hypothesized that the attributes of videodisc, which allow the portrayal of rich audio and visual images of a problem situation, would enhance the problem solving abilities of learners. Research results showed significant gains for the video-based group over the text based group, not only in solving the original Jasper problems, but in identifying and solving similar and related problems. The rich video-based format context was found to simulate a real world context for problem solving (Van Haneghan et al., 1992). In a similar vein, the Young Children's literacy project uses a Vygotsky scaffolding approach to support the construction of mental model building skills for listening and storytelling (Cognition and Technology Group at Vanderbilt, 1991). Programs like Jasper and the Young Children's literacy project provide robust sensory environments for developing metacognitive strategies and participating in critical thinking. These cognitive approaches to teaching abstract thinking skills have found fertile ground in the design and development of multimedia programs.

Individualized instruction delivered in multimedia settings has begun to blur the distinction between distance education and traditional education. The use of computer technologies to enhance thinking has generated interest in all areas of the curriculum. Researchers are examining ways to decontextualize classroom learning by anchoring and situating problems to be solved as real life events (Brown, Collins, & Duguid, 1989). Collaborative interactions between learner and technology have caused cognitive psychologists to reexamine the effects of computer technology on intellectual performance. Salomon, Perkins, and Globerson (1991) call on educators to investigate the learning activities which new technologies promote. They argue that it is this collaborative cognitive processing between intelligent technology and learner that may have the potential for affecting human intellectual performance.

The authors make the distinction between effects *with* technology in which the learner enters into a partnership where the technology assumes part of the intellectual burden of processing information (calculator), and effects *of* technology and related transfer of skills. The former role of technology is what has been referred to by Pea (1993) as distributed cognition. The distributed model of cognition has its roots in the cultural-historical tradition and is reflected in the work of Luria (1979) and Vygotsky (1978). This view of the distribution of cognition from a cultural-historical perspective maintains that learning is not an individual process but is part of a larger activity which involves the teacher, pupil and cultural artifacts of the classroom. Knowledge does not reside with an individual alone but is distributed among the tools and artifacts of the culture. The technologies of today have created graphic interfaces which offer symbiotic and virtual environments distributed between human and machine.

One example of such a symbiotic environment is a computer conference network called The WELL. It is a "virtual community" where people meet, converse and socialize. This "digital watering hole for information-age hunters and gatherers" has developed into a unique social and communication phenomenon (Rheingold, 1993). It functions as cafe, beauty shop, town square, pub, lecture hall, library. In short it is network of communications in cyberspace; a true virtual community. The social and cultural ramifications of this type of community which functions in cognitive and social space rather than geographic space has vast implications for research in distance education.

These new learning environments are distance learning settings and they prompt researchers to ask further questions. How do these environments enhance cognitive activities? Which personal learning style factors are important to consider in designing interactive materials for effective instruction? Can we predict which program elements are likely to enhance student learning? Current research on the distance learner is discussed under the section (14.10.3.1) on Research in Distance Education.

14.8 ISSUES RELATED TO TEACHING

Studies that examine teaching in distance education address the developing role of the instructor, the need for decreasing resistance as traditional educators begin to use distance delivery systems and finally, faculty attitude toward the use of technology. Altered roles for faculty who teach in distance education settings is a common thread found throughout the literature. Sammons (1989) saw a need for definition of the role of teacher. He stresses that without this definition, prepackaged, mass distribution of education will result. Holmberg's (1989) theory of guided didactic conversation suggests that a relationship exists between the faculty's role in the conversation and student performance. Smith's (1991) qualitative study places students' involvement at the center of the foundation for distance education teaching activities. The extent to which faculty roles are modified by the distance education environment is related to how the technology is used (Dillon & Walsh, 1992). Some educators express concern that the use of packaged television courses creates negative consequences for mediated instruction. Sammons (1989) notes that the teaching role is an interactive, social process and questions whether presenting a telecourse or mass producing learning material for presentation at a distance is teaching. Peters (1983) lends an organizational perspective in his comparison of distance teaching to an industrial enterprise. He reports on the mass production of learning materials, mechanization, automation, quality control and other operational activities. According to Peters, the teacher need not teach in a personal, face-to-face mode, but rather should provide cost-effective instruction which can reach large numbers of students.

The emergence of increasingly student-centered learning activities of the 1970s, facilitated by technology in the 1980s, contributed to an evolution of the role of faculty in the 1990s (Beaudoin, 1990). In particular, the increase in distance education enrollment will profoundly impact faculty members' instructional roles. Rather than transmit information in person, many faculty have to make the adjustment to monitoring and facilitating the work of geographically distant learners (Bates, 1991). Faculty accustomed to the more conventional teaching roles are required to accommodate new skills and assume expanding roles (Kember & Murphy, 1990).

This role shift from the European model of teacher as the exclusive source of information to one of facilitator is a difficult and threatening situation for most teachers. The role of teacher is not becoming obsolete but instead is being transformed (Beaudoin, 1990). Educators, and in particular those in distance educational environments, must be proficient at both delivery of content and the operation of the technology. Beaudoin goes on to point out that the teacher's role in the 1990s is becoming one of facilitator and bridge between student and the learning source (i.e., computer, television).

With new technologies being capable of delivering instruction, teachers are entering into a partnership with the technology. Garrison (1989) notes that while the teacher must be aware of the external aspects of learning, those related to the technology, it is the internal cognitive aspects of the learning experience that remain in the hands of the teacher. Ramsden (1988) sees the role of the distance education instructor as including the challenge of dialogue and interaction. "Machines," Ramsden says, "transmit information as if it were an unquestionable truth" (1988, p. 52). The teacher's role, which must include dialogue, is to challenge the seemingly unquestionable truths and to elicit meaning for the student.

Dillon and Walsh (1992) see a lack of research focus on the role adaptations of faculty, and they recommend future research on this topic. In their review of literature, Dillon and Walsh (1992) found only 24 of 225 articles on faculty roles. Research by Garrison (1990) indicated that educators are resistant to adaptation and to introduction of technology into previously designed classes. The literature suggests that faculty attitudes improve as experience with distance education increases, and as faculty become more familiar with the technology. Taylor and White (1991) support this idea in their findings of positive attitudes from faculty who have completed the first distance education class, but their study also indicates a faculty preference for face-to-face traditional teaching. The reason most often cited in their qualitative study is lack of student interaction. Additionally Taylor and White (1991) found through interviews and surveys that faculty agree that distance teaching is not appropriate for all content areas or for all students. In a recent study of faculty participation in distance education, Wolcott (2003) points out that although faculty participation has been an issue of interest among distance education administrators, research has been sparse over the past two decades. Studies have focused on mostly obstacles to participation and incentives to participate. She points out that from a research perspective, there has been less interest in faculty motivation.

There is a lack of training opportunity in distance education, which could help faculty to overcome anxieties about technology and might improve teacher attitudes. Most teacher inservice programs that deal with technology teach how to operate equipment, with little attention paid to the more important aspects of how to incorporate technology into instruction. Virtually none address the concept and practice of distance education as a unique enterprise with different techniques of instruction from the traditional classroom.

In addition to conducting research on the emerging roles of faculty involved in distance education activities, studies are needed to examine faculty attitudes. Many teachers have a natural concern that technology will replace them in the classroom. It is important, says Hawkridge (1991), for teachers in training to be stimulated to a positive attitude toward technology as a means of enhancing the quality of the human interaction, and not to see technology as a dehumanizing influence. Hawkridge is joined by current researchers who call for future study in the area of instructor role development. As technology becomes a means for future educational delivery, a new view of the profession of teaching may need to be developed.

14.9   POLICY AND MANAGEMENT

State and national policies on the use of telecommunication technologies for distance education have been slow to develop in the United States. Many other countries have had well-developed national plans for the implementation of distance education delivery systems over large geographic areas. Countries in which education is centralized at the national level are often those with the largest distance education enterprises. Countries in Asia, the Middle East, Latin America, and Europe that have national policies for the development of distance education often use communication infrastructures which are already in place to deliver massive programs over broadcast media (McIsaac, Murphy, & Demiray, 1988).

In the United States, the most significant early study to be done on a large scale was Linking for Learning (Office of Technology Assessment, 1989). This report was the first to examine national and state telecommunication initiatives, and make recommendations for a plan of action, based on needs of state and local schools. Because distance education in the United States is not supported by a central educational authority as in other countries, development of national and state policy has been slow. Key policy issues that have received attention include: funding, equal access to high quality education, effectiveness of educational systems, licensing of distance education programs, and equal access to delivery systems (Dirr, 1991). Donaldson (1991) called for application of organization theory to issues of management and administration in distance education. Simonson & Bauck (2003) and Dirr (2003) discuss recent trends in distance education policy and management.

Most recently, distance educators have been concerned about quality assurance and setting policies that assure quality both from the standpoint of students and faculty. The Pew Symposium in Learning and Technology produced a seminal report on issues surrounding policy formulation and quality assurance from the perspectives of institutions and agencies (Twigg, 2001). Another report, prepared for the Canadian Association for Community Education, established quality guidelines for online training and education in Canada (Barker, 2001). In 2000, the Web-based Education Commission focused their attention on policy issues that would help educators use the Web to transform learning. Policies were drafted for technology trends, pedagogy, access and equity, technology costs, teacher training and support, regulatory barriers, standards and assessment, accreditation and certification, intellectual property protection, online privacy and research and development (*http://www.hpcnet.org/wbec/issues*). The commission continues to collect data and examine research to better understand how the Web can best be used for learning.

It seems evident that research has been conducted from many perspectives and in many disciplines. As the body of research studies grows, methods such as meta-analysis can help us analyze the growing body of information. Meta-analysis, the application of qualitative and quantitative procedures for the purpose of integrating, synthesizing and analyzing various studies, would be particularly useful (McIsaac, 1990). Sophason and Prescott, (1988), believe that single studies cannot expect to provide definitive answers to theoretical questions. Instead a method such as meta-analysis is needed to identify underlying trends and principles emerging from the research.

14.10 RESEARCH IN DISTANCE EDUCATION

This section provides an overview of early research studies in distance education, explores issues related to the development of research in the field, and discusses current trends in distance education research.

14.10.1 Early Research Studies

Much of the early research in distance education since the 1960s has focused on comparisons between delivery media such as television, video, or computer and traditional face-to-face teaching. Other research compared the effectiveness of one distance delivery medium over another. Most of these media comparison studies found no significant differences (NSD) in learning (Boswell, Mocker, & Hamlin, 1968; Chu & Schramm, 1967; Chute, Bruning, & Hulick, 1984; Hoyt & Frye, 1972; Kruh, 1983; Whittington, 1987). Critiquing these early media comparison studies, Spenser (1991) points out that they tended to report comparative statistics which gave no indication of the size of differences, if any, between the types of instruction. Conclusions tended to be based on the presence or absence of a statistically significant result. "When groups of research were reviewed there was a tendency to use a 'box score' tally approach,

frequently resulting in a small number of studies favoring the innovation, a similar number favoring the traditional approach, and the vast majority showing NSD" (p. 13). Problems associated with research design and methods in these early comparison studies are discussed at length by Lockee, Burton, and Cross (1999), Smith and Dillon (1999), and Saba (2000).

Whatever methods have been used to report the results of media comparison studies and their instructional impact, these studies have yielded very little useful guidance for distance education practice. This prompted Clark (1984) to make the following observation: "Learning gains come from adequate instructional design theory and practice, not from the medium used to deliver instruction" (p. 3). Although Clark's statement has been debated (Kozma, 1994), educational technologists agree that the quality of the instructional design has a significant impact on learning. Winn (1990) suggests that the technology chosen for instruction may not affect the eventual achievement outcome but "it greatly affects the efficiency with which instruction can be delivered" (p. 53). Distance education developers, worldwide, face the challenge of selecting the most efficient medium for delivery of instruction. Wagner (1990) believes that as technologies become more complex (i.e., interactive television, computer-based instruction, and teleconferencing), the need to be more accountable and effective when selecting and utilizing instructional delivery systems becomes increasingly more important.

It is time, therefore, to move away from media comparison studies that often yield no significant differences, and begin to examine factors such as instructional design, learning and instructional theory, and theoretical frameworks in distance education, which when applied to learning, might account for significant differences in levels of performance. The questions that need to be asked are not which medium works best, but rather how best to incorporate media attributes into the design of effective instruction for learning. Studies which compare two different instructional designs using the same medium may yield more useful results for practice than simple media comparisons. Little research has been done to examine what happens in the learning process when students interact with various technologies.

Early research literature in distance education was brief and inconclusive. Both quantitative and qualitative studies have generally lacked rigor. Suen and Stevens (1993) identified several common problems associated with the analysis of data in quantitative distance education research. Driven by practice, much research has taken the form of program evaluation, descriptions of individual distance education programs, brief case studies, institutional surveys, and speculative reports. Although well reported case studies offer valuable insights for further investigation, the early literature in distance education lacked rich qualitative information or programmatic experimental research which would lead to testing of research hypotheses. Many studies were reported in journals that were not peer reviewed. A number of research reports were generated by governmental agencies and institutions responsible for large scale distance delivery programs. These were often proprietary and not readily available.

14.10.2 Issues in Research

One significant issue in early research studies in distance education is the lack of a sound theoretical foundation. This reflected an emerging field where theoreticians spent their energy trying to define the field and advance constructs that described its unique nature. Shale (1990) commented that research within the field is not productive because the field has limited itself to studies of past and present practice that look at "distance" as the significant concept. He calls for an examination of broader issues in education which look at the educational transaction mediated by communication technologies. Coldeway (1990) notes that researchers in the field have not tested the various theories which have been advanced, and hypotheses have not been identified for experimental research. Saba (2000) points out that most comparative research in distance education lacks a discussion of theoretical foundations of the field. He observes:

Research questions are rarely posed within a theoretical framework or based on its fundamental concepts and constructs. Although research within a theoretical framework is not a requirement for inductive inquiry, a post facto theoretical discussion of research results would be helpful in making studies relevant to the work of other researchers, and possibly even to the practitioners in the field. Comparative researchers, however, have shown little or no interest in the theoretical literature of the field either before or after conducting their studies. (pp. 2-3)

This view is echoed by Perraton (2000), who declares that "an examination of existing research literature confirms that much of it suffers from an apparently atheoretical approach" (p. 4). He emphasizes that research in open and distance learning needs to be grounded in theory, and that there are often benefits in drawing theory from outside narrow educational confines, and that research will suffer unless this is done. Dillon and Aagaard (1990) supported this stance of borrowing from other fields in their response to Gibson's (1990) argument on the perils of borrowing. While they agree that distance education could use further definition as a field, they also believe that the process is an evolutionary one that proceeds as we try out theories from other disciplines and then either accept them as applicable or discard them as unusable in the context of distance education. They argue that it is only after research indicates that we must discard existing theories that we truly will be able to define distance education as a unique applied field of endeavor. Dillon and Aagaard (1990) point out that the very nature of an applied field such as distance education demands reliance upon an interdisciplinary approach to research. With the rapid spread of online learning into many disciplines, we will increasingly observe an interdisciplinary approach to research in distance education. Model studies, often exploratory, are appearing across disciplines where researchers are examining the interaction of learners with the new online media.

Berge and Mrozowski (2001) in their review of distance education research in four major journals in the United States, Australia, Canada, and the United Kingdom and Dissertation Abstracts International covering the period between 1990 and 1999 observe that pedagogical themes such as design issues, learner characteristics, and strategies for active learning and increased interactivity, dominate the research and appear to be increasing. Research in the areas of equity and accessibility, operational issues, and policy and management issues is less common. In reviewing the research methodologies used in the articles and dissertations, they note that 75 percent used descriptive methods, 12 percent used case studies, 7 percent used correlational methods, and 6 percent used experimental methods. However, they point out several limitations in the methodology used for this review. One of the drawbacks was the categorization of articles and dissertations only by what seemed to be the main research methodology used. This may have resulted in placing publications in inappropriate categories. From their review, Berge and Mrozowski (2001) identify the following gaps in what is being researched:

- Research has tended to emphasize student outcomes for courses rather than for an entire academic program.
- Research does not adequately explain dropout rates.
- Research focuses mostly on the impact of individual technologies rather than on the interaction of multiple technologies.
- Research does not adequately address the effectiveness of digital libraries.

In Perraton's (2000) discussion of issues in research in open and distance learning from a European perspective, he observes that in a review of literature conducted before launching of the International Research Foundation for Open Learning, they found that most research fell under five headings: (1) description, (2) audience studies, (3) cost-effectiveness studies, (4) methodology (methodologies used to teach and support distance students), and (5) social context. He critiques many of these studies for their lack of a theoretical base and for their lack of understanding about the distance education "context." He states that research on the context of open and distance learning, considering its purposes, outcomes, and relevance to major educational problems, has been relatively neglected as contrasted with research on its application. It is findings about the context of distance education that are particularly significant for policy makers.

14.10.3 Current Trends in Distance Education Research

Saba (2000) observes that in the past ten years, a few researchers have conducted rigorous studies that are based on theoretical foundations of the field, or theories of fields closely related to distance education. Among them he cites Fulford and Zhang's (1993), and Sherry, Fulford, and Zhang's (1998) studies on learner perception of interaction, Gunawardena's (1995), and Gunawardena and Zittle's (1997) studies on the implications of social presence theory for community building in computer conferencing, Tsui and Ki's (1996) study on social factors affecting computer mediated communication at the University of Hong Kong, McDonald and Gibson's (1998) study on group development in asynchronous computer conferencing, and Chen and Willits' (1999) study of interaction in a synchronous video-conferencing environment. Saba (2000) observes that a common theme in these and other distance education research in the past 10 years is the concept of "interaction," which indicates its centrality in conceptualizing the process of teaching and learning. Further, he states that these studies are paradigmatic because their discussion of interaction transcends the idea of distance in its physical sense, and embraces the discussion of teaching and learning in general.

Recent trends in distance education research indicate a preponderance of studies focused on understanding pedagogical issues in the CMC environment. Some of these studies are being conducted outside the field of distance education such as in communication and management and bring an interdisciplinary perspective to the research questions addressed. What is of significance is that new methods are being explored for understanding interaction and the learning process, specifically collaborative learning in CMC using interaction analysis, content analysis, conversational analysis, and discourse analysis; research techniques made possible by the availability of computer transcripts of online discussions. Rourke et al. (2001) in a comprehensive analysis of several studies discuss the potential and the methodological challenges of analyzing computer conference transcripts using quantitative content analysis. (See Chapter by Joan Mazur for a detailed discussion of conversation analysis.)

Another emerging trend is the attempt made by distance education researchers to understand the social and cultural contexts of distance learning. Recent psychological theories are challenging the view that the social and the cognitive can be studied independently, arguing that the social context in which cognitive activity takes place is an integral part of that activity, not just the surrounding connect for it (Resnick, 1991.) These views are exemplified in discussions on the relationship of affect and cognition from a neurobiological perspective in which emotion is seen as an integral attribute of cognition (Adolphs & Damasio 2001; Davidson 2002), socially shared cognition (Resnick, 1991), socioconstructivism, which emphasizes the importance of social processes in individual knowledge building (Vygotsky 1978; Teasley, S., & Roschelle, J.,1993), and sociocultural perspectives which describe learning from a cultural point of view. By stressing the interdependence of social and individual processes in the coconstruction of knowledge, sociocultural approaches view semiotic tools or cultural amplifiers as personal and social resources, and hence, mediating the link between the social and the individual construction of meaning (Vygotsky, 1978).

Lave (1991) extends the interdependence of social and individual processes in the coconstruction of knowledge further by stating that we need to rethink the notion of learning, treating it as an emerging property of whole persons' legitimate peripheral participation in communities of practice. Such a view sees mind, culture, history, and the social world as interrelated processes that constitute each other, and intentionally blurs social scientists' divisions among component parts of persons, their activities, and the world. As the Internet spreads rapidly to many parts of the world we will increasingly see learners from diverse social and cultural contexts in online courses. Therefore,

understanding the sociocultural context of learning will be an important challenge for future research.

In the following section we discuss some of the major trends we have observed in distance education research during the past 10 years and point out avenues for future research. Research has focused on the distance learner, and pedagogical and design issues associated with learning and satisfaction such as interaction, the social dynamic, and social presence. It is also evident that research is beginning to examine the sociocultural context of distance learning and address factors that influence interaction, group dynamics and community building in the online environment. Research has begun to address the complexity of distance education through systems modeling techniques and there is a recent trend toward rethinking and redesigning experimental and quasi-experimental comparative studies to yield more useful results.

14.10.3.1 The Distance Learner.
Perhaps one of the earliest theory based research studies on the distance learner was the study conducted by Baynton (1992) to test the theoretical model developed by Garrison and Baynton (1987), and refined by Garrison (1989), to explain the learner's sense of "control" in an educational transaction. The model proposed that control of the learning process results from the combination of three essential dimensions: a learner's independence (the opportunity to make choices), a learner's proficiency or competence (ability, skill, and motivation), and support (both human and nonhuman resources). Baynton's factor analysis (1992) confirms the significance of these three factors and suggests other factors which may affect the concept of control and which should be examined to accurately portray the complex interaction between teacher and learner in the distance learning setting.

A comprehensive collection of research and thinking on distance learners in higher education was published in a book edited by Chere Campbell Gibson in 1998. Research addressed by the chapter authors included improving learning outcomes, academic self-concept, gender and culture, roles and responsibilities in learning in a networked world, learner support, and understanding the distance learner in context. Based on her dissertation research, Olgren (1998) discusses three factors that have a major impact on learning: (1) cognitive learning strategies for processing information, (2) metacognitive activities for planning and self-regulation, and (3) the learner's goals and motivations. Research suggests that academic self-concept plays an important role in persistence in distance education and that this aspect of general self-concept is a dynamic and situational attribute of the distance learner, and one that is amenable to intervention (Gibson 1998). Sanchez and Gunawardena (1998) in their development of a profile of learning style preferences for the Hispanic adult learner in their study population based on nine instruments, show learner preferences for motivational maintenance level, task engagement level, and cognitive processing level. Burge (1998) discusses gender-related differences in distance education. Recent research and issues related to the distance learner are discussed by Gibson (2003) and Dillon and Greene (2003).

A review of research related to learner characteristics and CMC variables published in refereed distance education journals revealed the emergence of studies analyzing learner experiences with computer conferencing: learner perspectives (Burge, 1994; Eastmond, 1994); critical thinking (Bullen, 1998); group dynamics (McDonald & Gibson, 1998); equity of access (Ross, Crane, & Robertson 1995); computer self-efficacy (Lim, 2001), and practice-based reflection (Naidu, 1997). Of these, three studies (Bullen, 1998; Burge, 1994; Eastmond, 1994) investigated the relationship between learner characteristics and the unique aspects of the online environment. Burge (1994) explored the salient features of the CMC environment and the effects of these features on learning from the learners' perspective. Bullen (1998) noted that the factors most frequently identified by students as either facilitating or inhibiting their participation and critical thinking in online discussions were those related to the attributes of computer conferencing technology, described by Harasim (1990) as time-independence, text-based communication, computer-mediated communication, and many-to-many communication.

Employing grounded theory, and the constant comparative model for qualitative research (Glaser & Strauss, 1967), Eastmond (1994) examined adult students' experience of learning in an online course. Then, using data from various dimensions of the study, Eastmond (1994) developed the Adult Distance Study Through Computer Conferencing (ADSCC) model as a framework from which to understand the dynamics of successful learning by computer conferencing. Surrounding the model is the context within which the computer conference is held and the larger institutional and societal milieu that influences the distance learning experience. Within this context there are three major aspects which sequentially influence the student's study experience:

1. Readiness—the personal and environmental factors that prepare the student for study in this instructional situation
2. Online features—the unique elements that make up the computer conferencing environment
3. Learning approaches—the general and specific learning strategies a student uses to make the conference an effective learning experience.

Eastmond notes that the educational institution can positively impact readiness, online features, and learning approaches. The individual also can improve each dimension iteratively as the person uses new knowledge about learning approaches or online features to enhance readiness or elements of the online environment. Gunawardena and Duphorne (2000) tested the ADSCC model which Eastmond developed using grounded theory principles by employing a quantitative approach to data analysis.

The purpose of the Gunawardena and Duphorne (2000) study was to determine if the three variables in the Eastmond (1994) ADSCC model, learner readiness, online features, and CMC-related learning approaches, are (i) related to learner satisfaction, (ii) intercorrelated, and (iii) able to predict learner satisfaction with an academic computer conference. The study was based on the inter-university "GlobalEd" computer conference that provided a forum for graduate students in distance education to share and discuss research, and experience distance education by using CMC. All three variables showed a positive relationship to learner satisfaction. The strongest positive correlation was found between online features and learner satisfaction. The variable, online features, was also the best predictor of learner satisfaction. This has implications for designing computer conferences where attention must be paid to orienting adult learners to the unique elements that make up the computer conferencing environment. This includes the design of both the technical aspects and the social environment of an academic computer conference.

14.10.3.2 *Interaction and Learning.*

The issue of "interaction" has been an area of much debate in the practice of distance education. Often debated questions are: What type and level of interaction is essential for effective learning? Does interaction facilitate learning and transfer? How does synchronous (real-time) and asynchronous (time-delayed) interaction contribute to learning? Is interaction more important for certain types of learners? Should patterns of interaction change over time when designing a distance education course? Is it worth the cost? Computer-mediated communication (CMC) has led to the emergence of networked learning communities, or "cybercommunities" bound by areas of interest, transcending time and space (Jones, 1995, 1997). It is the ability to facilitate communities of inquiry to engage in higher order thinking in many disciplines that is one of the most important contributions of this medium for online learning. Many of the studies on interaction have tried to examine the "interaction" that occurs in such collaborative learning environments using methods such as content analysis and interaction analysis of computer transcripts.

Henri (1992) makes a significant contribution to understanding the relationship between interaction and learning by proposing an analytical framework for assessing the learning process through the facilitation of interaction in a collaborative computer conferencing environment. She proposes a system of content analysis which involves breaking messages down into units of meaning and classifying these units according to their content. The model consists of five dimensions of the learning process: participation, interaction, social, cognitive and the metacognitive. This framework has informed studies of collaborative learning (Hara, Bonk, & Angeli, 2000; McDonald & Gibson, 1998; Newman, Webb, & Cochrane, 1995). Garrison (2000) has noted that Henri's real contribution is that it is a collaborative view of teaching and learning that provides a potential structure for coding CMC messages to study the nature and quality of the discourse.

Utilizing Henri's (1992) model as a starting point, Gunawardena, Lowe, and Anderson (1997) began to address questions related to the process and type of learning that occurred in an online professional development conference conducted as a debate across international time lines They used interaction analysis (Jordan & Henderson, 1995) of the computer transcript as their method. They were interested in examining the relationship of interaction to learning evident in the following two questions:

1. Was knowledge constructed within the group by means of the exchanges among participants? And

2. Did individual participants change their understanding or create new personal constructions of knowledge as a result of interactions within the group?

In using Henri's (1992) model as a framework of analysis to address these two questions, Gunawardena et al. (1997) found that Henri's definition of the concept of interaction was unsuited for the interactions that occur in a computer conferencing environment. They, therefore, proceeded to define interaction within the CMC environment and develop a framework of interaction analysis that would be more appropriate for analyzing the debate transcript. Gunawardena et al. (1997) believed that the metaphor of a patchwork quilt better describes the process of shared construction of knowledge that occurs in a constructivist learning environment. The process by which the contributions are fitted together is interaction, broadly understood, and the pattern that emerges at the end, when the entire gestalt of accumulated interaction is viewed, is the newly-created knowledge or meaning. They defined interaction as the essential process of putting together the pieces in the cocreation of knowledge.

Based on this new definition of interaction, the debate was analyzed for the (1) type of cognitive activity performed by participants (questioning, clarifying, negotiating, synthesizing, etc.), (2) types of arguments advanced throughout the debate, (3) resources brought in by participants for use in exploring their differences and negotiating new meanings, and (4) evidence of changes in understanding or the creation of new personal constructions of knowledge as a result of interactions within the group.

Their development of an interaction analysis model (Gunawardena et al., 1997) is based on social constructivist theory to examine the negotiation of meaning that occurred in the online conference. They described the model in phases, as they saw the group move from sharing and comparing of information (Phase I), through cognitive dissonance (Phase II), to negotiation of meaning (Phase III), the testing and modification of the proposed coconstruction (Phase IV), and to the application of the newly constructed meaning (Phase V). In applying the model to the analysis of the debate they note that the debate format influenced the process of coconstruction by sometimes supporting and sometimes hindering the efforts made by participants to reach a synthesis.

The efficacy of the Gunawardena et al. (1997) interaction analysis model was tested in other studies. Kanuka and Anderson (1998) analyzed a professional development forum with this model and found that the majority of learning occurred at the lower phases of the interaction analysis model (Phase I and II). The model was applied to a study at the MonterreyTechnology Institute's Virtual University in Mexico by Lopez-Islas and his research team (2001). An interesting observation they made is that the phases of cognitive dissonance, and the testing and modification of the proposed coconstruction were almost absent in the conferences as the Latin culture does not favor the open expression of disagreements, and therefore, there is no need to extensively test and modify group proposals. Jeong (2001) applied the Gunawardena et al. (1997) model and developed a model of 12 critical thinking event categories, while Reschke (2001) applied the model and developed the Degree of Synthesis Model.

Another interaction analysis model that has been developed for understanding learning in computer-mediated environments is Garrison, Anderson, and Archer's (2001) model that describes the nature and quality of critical discourse in a computer conference. Utilizing content analysis techniques, they suggest that cognitive presence (i.e., critical, practical inquiry) can be created and supported in a computer conference environment with appropriate teaching and social presence. Cognitive presence is defined as the extent to which learners are able to construct and validate meaning through sustained reflection and discourse in a critical community of inquiry. Cognitive presence reflects higher-order knowledge acquisition and application and is associated with critical thinking. Garrison et al. (2001) note that this practical inquiry model is consistent with the one developed by Gunawardena et al. (1997).

These interaction analysis models, an emerging area of research in distance education, present a means to evaluate the process of learning through the analysis of computer discussions. However, there are issues that need to be addressed in relation to interaction analysis or content analysis methods. Issues related to validity and reliability of the findings were addressed by Rourke et al. (2001). The need to triangulate findings with other data gathering methods such as interviews, surveys and journals is evident. As Hara et al. (2000) point out each computer conference will have its own unique attributes and researchers may have to design electronic discussion group analysis criteria on a case by case basis. For instance, a problem solving activity online will require different types of skills from a debate, or using the medium for sharing of information. While detailed analyses of computer transcripts fall within the realm of research and are very time consuming, a practitioner with relevant skills should be able to analyze small segments of computer discussions (for example, a two-week discussion) to determine the process of learning.

14.10.3.3 Social Dynamic.
With the growing interest in facilitating collaborative learning in the online environment, distance education research is beginning to address the social dynamic that underlies learning and satisfaction. Recent studies have tried to examine the relationship of cognitive and social processes (Cecez-Kecmanovic & Webb, 2000; Kanuka & Anderson, 1998; Kumpulainen & Mutanen, 2000; Nolla, 2001; Wegerif, 1998). Kanuka and Anderson (1998) in their study showed that social discord served as a catalyst to the knowledge construction process observed. Kumpulainen and Mutanen (2000) introduce an analytical framework of peer group interaction that can be modified to apply to different studies of peer group interaction and learning. On the one hand, it can be used to highlight the dynamics between social and individual learning, and on the other hand to investigate how cognitive and social aspects of learning interrelate and interact in synergistic ways. Based on the results of their study, Vrasidas and McIsaac (1999) reconceptualize interaction as a theoretical construct and emphasize the importance of socially constructed meanings from the participants' perspectives.

Nolla (2001) in her dissertation research used content analysis techniques to investigate the social nature of online learning and its relationship to cognitive learning, and found that: (1) Equilibrium can exist between socioemotional-affective areas such as encouraging, supporting, and praising, and task areas; (2) in a positive, encouraging environment, participants are willing to give opinions more than they are requested to; (3) moderators had a prevalent role in maintaining the social environment of the conferences, thus, facilitating information exchange and providing the shared space essential for collaborative group work; and that (4) social interaction is linked to academic discussions and therefore, to separate them for analysis is artificial. She concludes that instructors should consider providing the opportunities and the environment for the identified social interaction categories to occur within a flexible course framework and that future research should focus on the impact different moderating styles have on student participation.

Wegerif (1998) used ethnographic research methods to investigate an online course offered by the British Open University and concluded that collaborative learning was central to feelings of success or failure on the course and that social factors were critical to collaborative learning. Those who felt that they had gained most from the course moved from feeling like outsiders to feeling like insiders. Those who dropped out or felt that they had failed to learn as much as they might were those who felt that they had remained outsiders unable to cross the threshold to insider status. The findings of the study point to several factors which can move students from being outsiders to becoming insiders, including features of the course design, the role of moderators, the interaction styles of course participants and features of the technological medium used. McDonald and Gibson's (1998) study of interpersonal dynamics and group development in computer conferencing found that there is a definite pattern to interpersonal issues in group development. Their results indicate that people meeting, discussing, and collaborating as a group via computer conferencing have similar interpersonal issues, at comparable stages and proportions, as reported in the literature for face-to-face groups. Carabajal, La Pointe and Gunawardena (2003) in their analysis of research on group development in online learning communities point out that there is empirical evidence that online groups can form, interact, and accomplish tasks through the online technology, yet the addition of a technological dimension distinguishes the online groups from the face-to-face groups in several ways. For example, online groups take longer to complete their tasks than face-to-face groups. However, there are many things that we still do not know about CMC's impact on group structure, process and development. Ravitz (1997) notes that the assessment of social interactions that occur online must use ethnographic approaches such as discourse analysis of messages that tell more about the interactions that occurred. He focuses attention on the importance of assessing questions such as "How did the interactions change the participants?" and proposes one methodology described as the Interactive Project Vita.

14.10.3.4 Social Presence.
Social presence (defined in the theory section of this chapter) is one factor that relates to the social dynamic of mediated communication, as well as to other factors such as interaction, motivation, group cohesion, social equality, and in general to the socioemotional climate of a learning experience. The importance of studying CMC from a social psychological perspective has been emphasized by

international communication research (Jones, 1995; Spears & Lea, 1992; Walther, 1992). Lombard and Ditton (1997) in an extensive review of literature on the concept of presence in telecommunications environments identify six interrelated but distinct conceptualizations of presence, and equates "presence as social richness" with social presence.

A detailed discussion of the literature on social presence is found in Gunawardena (1995). A common theme in the conclusions of social presence studies conducted in traditional face-to-face classrooms is that teacher "immediacy" is a good predictor of student affective learning across varied course content (Christophel, 1990; Gorham, 1988; Kearney, Plax, & Wendt-Wasco 1985). In CMC research, social presence theory has been used to account for interpersonal effects. CMC with its lack of nonverbal communication cues is said to be extremely low in social presence in comparison to face-to-face communication. However, field research in CMC often reports more positive relational behavior and has indicated the development of "online communities" and warm friendships (Baym 1995; Walther 1992).

Walther (1992) notes that a significant number of research studies that have explored the effects of CMC have failed to account for the different social processes, settings, and purposes within CMC use as well. Research has reported that experienced computer users rated e-mail and computer conferencing "as rich" or "richer" than television, telephone and face-to-face conversations. Therefore, he notes that the conclusion that CMC is less socioemotional or personal than face-to-face communication is based on incomplete measurement of the latter form. Walther's (1992) "social information-processing perspective" (P. 67) considers how relational communication changes from initial impersonal levels to more developed forms in CMC. This perspective recognizes that extended interactions should provide sufficient information exchange to enable communicators to develop interpersonal knowledge and stable relations.

The relationship of social presence to learner satisfaction and learner perception of learning have been studied by distance education researchers using a variety of research designs. Hackman and Walker (1990), studying learners in an interactive television class, found that cues given to students such as encouraging gestures, smiles and praise were factors that enhanced both students' satisfaction and their perceptions of learning. Utilizing two stepwise regression models, Gunawardena and Zittle (1997) have shown that social presence is a strong predictor of learner satisfaction in an academic computer conference. This finding, supports the conclusions of Hackman and Walker's (1990) study, and the view that the relational or social aspect of CMC is an important element that contributes to the overall satisfaction of task-oriented or academic computer conferences (Baym 1995; Walther 1992).

An additional finding in the Gunawardena and Zittle (1997) study was that participants who felt a higher sense of social presence within the conference, enhanced their socio-emotional experience by using emoticons (icons that express emotion, such as ☺, ;-), ☹), to express missing nonverbal cues in written form. At low levels of social presence the use of emoticons had no effect on satisfaction, while at higher levels of social presence, there was an improvement on satisfaction as emoticon use increased. This raises the question of individual differences along personality or social-psychological lines, and begs the need for future research to investigate individual differences (other than learning styles) as mediating factors in developing the social environment for online learning. These findings have implications for designing online learning where equal attention must be paid to designing techniques that enhance social presence and the social environment. Instructors who are used to relying on nonverbal cues to provide feedback and who have a lesser-developed ability to project their personality will need to learn to adapt to the CMC medium by developing skills that create a sense of social presence.

Rourke et al. (1999) examine the relationship of social presence and interaction in an online community of inquiry. They define social presence as the ability of learners to project themselves socially and affectively into a community of inquiry. They present a template for assessing social presence in computer conferencing through content analysis of conferencing transcripts and conclude with a discussion of the implications and benefits of assessing social presence for instructors, conference moderators, and researchers.

In other research, Jelfs and Whitelock (2000) explored the notion of presence in virtual reality environments and found that audio feedback and ease of navigation engendered a sense of presence. Tu and McIsaac (2002) examined dimensions of social presence and privacy. The dimensions that emerged as important elements in establishing a sense of community among online learners were social context, online communication and interactivity. The privacy factor was important in maintaining a comfort level for students working online.

The relationship between social presence and interactivity need to be examined more fully in future research. Examining these two concepts, Rafaeli (1988, 1990) observes that social presence is a subjective measure of the presence of others as Short et al. (1976) defined it, while "interactivity" is the actual quality of a communication sequence or context. Interactivity is a quality (potential) that may be realized by some, or remain and unfulfilled option. When it is realized, and when participants notice it, there is "social presence." There is a need for future research to examine the relationship between social presence and interaction to further understand how each affects the other. Research on social presence and CMC has indicated that despite the low social bandwidth of the medium, users of computer networks are able to project their identities whether "real" or "pseudo," feel the presence of others online, and create communities with commonly agreed on conventions and norms that bind them together to explore issues of common interest.

14.10.3.5 Cultural Context.
Reflecting the globalization and internationalization of distance education and the importance of cultural factors that influence the teaching learning process in distance education, two recognized journals in the field devoted special issues to addressing cultural factors that influence the use of technology (The *British Journal of Educational Technology*, Volume 30, number 3, published in 1999), and cultural considerations in online learning (*Distance Education*, Volume 22, number 1, published in 2001). With the rapid expansion of international online course delivery, some of the questions that have emerged as discussed by Mason and Gunawardena (2001) include:

- What does it mean to design course content for a multicultural student context?
- What kind of environment and tutor/instructor support most encourages nonnative students to participate actively in online discussions?
- What are the organizational issues involved in supporting a global student intake?

One factor related to online learning that has sometimes been a barrier is the issue of language, even language differences within the same country. Non-native students, using a second language to communicate, find the asynchronous interactions of online courses easier to understand than the faster pace of verbal interaction in face-to-face classes. However, the jargon, in-jokes, culture-specific references and acronyms of typical online native speaker communication can become a barrier (Mason & Gunawardena, 2001.) There are clear disadvantages of working in another language in online courses, when students have to contribute toward collaborative assignments or participate in discussion forums with those for whom English is the first language (Bates, 2001). Global universities are faced with the choice between continuing to expect all students to adjust to traditional English-Western academic values and uses of language, or changing their processes to accommodate others (Pincas, 2001).

McLoughlin (2001) who has been actively researching cross-cultural issues in the online learning environment offers a theoretically grounded framework that links culturally inclusive learning with authentic curriculum and assessment design using the principle of constructive alignment. She points out that a goal of culturally inclusive online learning is to ensure that pedagogy and curriculum are flexible, adaptable and relevant to students from a diverse range of cultural and language backgrounds. Pincas (2001) alerts us to literature, findings and research that impact on the cultural, linguistic and pedagogical issues of global online learning.

Researching cross-cultural issues pose many challenges. We see the emergence of research studies beginning to address cultural issues based on established theoretical frameworks or by progressing to develop grounded theory frameworks. Goodfellow, Lea, Gonzalez, and Mason (2001) investigate some of the ways that cultural and linguistic differences manifest themselves in global online learning environments. They present outcomes of a qualitative study of student talk from a global Masters Program taught largely online, and identify the areas of "cultural otherness," "perceptions of globality," "linguistic difference," and "academic convention," as focal constructs around which student experiences could be recounted.

Two teams of researchers from the University of New Mexico in the United States and Universidad Virtual del Tec de Monterrey in Mexico (Gunawardena, Nolla, Wilson, López-Islas, Ramírez-Angel, & Megchun-Alpízar, 2001) examine differences in perception of online group process and development between participants in the two countries. Their mixed method design using survey and focus group data, based on Hofstede's (1980) and Hall's (1976, 1984) theoretical frameworks for determining cultural differences, identified several factors that could be described as cultural factors that influence online group process and development. Survey data indicated significant differences in perception for the Norming and Performing stages of group development, with the Mexican group showing greater agreement with collectivist group values. The groups also differed in their perception of collectivism, low power distance, femininity, and high context communication. Country differences rather than age and gender differences, accounted for the differences observed. For the Mexican participants the medium of CMC equalized status differences, while USA participants were concerned that the lack of non-verbal cues led to misunderstanding. Both groups felt that the amount of time it takes to make group decisions in asynchronous CMC, and the lack of commitment to a fair share of the group work, were problems. Focus group participants in Mexico and the United States identified several factors that influence online group process and development:

1. Language, or forms of language used
2. Power distance in communication between teachers and students
3. Gender differences
4. Collectivist versus individualist tendencies
5. Perception of "conflict" and how to manage it
6. Social presence
7. The time frame in which the group functions
8. The varying level of technological skills.

Focus group data indicated both similarities and differences in perception of these factors between the two groups.

In a subsequent exploratory study, which extended the Gunawardena et al. (2001) study, the researchers examined the negotiation of "face" in an online learning environment (Gunawardena, Walsh, Reddinger, Gregory, Lake, & Davies, 2002). Utilizing a qualitative research design, the study addressed the question: How do individuals of different cultures negotiate "face" in a non face-to-face learning environment? Results of interviews conducted with sixteen participants representing six cultural groups indicated that cultural differences do exist in presentation and negotiation of "face" in the online environment. In evaluating responses to the three scenarios presented in this study, they found that regardless of cultural heritage, the majority of participants expressed the importance of establishing positive face in an online course environment. They wanted to project a positive, knowledgeable image with association to dominating facework behavior. With regard to conflict behavior, responses were mixed and indicated cultural as well as individual differences.

These research studies expose the problem inherent in categorizing comparison groups in cross-cultural studies, since groups that are defined as nationally or culturally different can differ in many other background characteristics. Therefore, it is usually difficult to determine if differences observed are related to culture or other factors. Other problems in cross-cultural research relate to translation of instruments and construct equivalence. Future researchers need to conceptualize identity issues in cross-cultural studies to go beyond simplistic stereotyping, and use qualitative methods to understand how people define themselves.

The other types of studies that address cultural issues in distance education, examine design issues for the online environment based on reviews of literature or on experience designing for diverse audiences. Incorporating cultural differences and individual preferences in online course design, means that instructors and designers must understand the cultural contexts of the learners, be willing to be flexible, and provide choices in activities and methods to achieve the goals of the course. Based on a review of literature and research studies on cultural factors influencing the online environment, Gunawardena, Wilson, and Nolla (2003) developed a framework, AMOEBA (Adaptive, Meaningful, Organic, Environmental-Based Architecture) for online course design that helps to visualize these options in a flexible, open-ended learning environment that can be molded to the needs identified. In this framework, an instructor becomes a facilitator and a colearner with the students by involving them in curricular decisions and providing choices in language, format, activities, methods, and channels for communication.

Chen, Mashhadi, Ang, and Harkrider (1999) propose that social and cultural understanding need to be explicit and up front, before participants are able to build the on-line networks of trust upon which effective communication and learning is based. Feenberg (1993) argues that most online groups need a familiar framework adapted to their culture and tasks, otherwise "they are repelled by what might be called contextual deprivation." (p. 194). Social rules and conventions of communication are vital to understanding the norms according to which we carry out conversations and judge others. For instance, cultural variations in the use of silence might well lie behind some lack of participation in online discussions.

Discussing cultural issues in the design of Web-based course-support sites, Collis (1999) notes that cultures differ on willingness to accommodate new technologies, acceptance of trial-and-error in terms of computer use, differences in expectations for technical support, preferences for precision versus browsing, preferences for internal versus system/instructor control, and differences for tolerance of communication overlaps and interruptions. Chen et al. (1999), drawing from Stoney and Wild's 1998 study, point out that in designing culturally appropriate Web-based instruction,

... the interface designer must be aware how different cultures will respond to issues of the layout of the graphical interface, images, symbols, colour and sound, inferring that culture itself cannot be objectified unproblematically as just another factor to be programmed into a learning course. (p. 220)

Such apparently simple issues of layout and format become increasing complex as the plurality of learners increase. Malbran and Villar (2001) discuss how to incorporate cultural relevance into a Web-based course design by showing how they adapted a university level course on cognitive processing to the local context in Argentina using familiar images and metaphors.

Another area of research that is increasingly gaining prominence is studies examining gender differences in online communication. One of the early studies examining gender differences and learner support in distance education was conducted by Kirkup and von Prummer (1990). Results of Blum's (1999) study examining gender differences in asynchronous learning employing content analysis of student messages, suggests there are differences between male and female distance education students, which contribute toward inequitable gender differences. These differences are both similar and different from the traditional learning environment. Herring (2000) provides a detailed review of literature while addressing gender differences in CMC, and also examines issues related to gender and ethics in CMC (Herring, 1996). Burge (1998) argues that gender-related differences in how adults learn "require sustained attention, knowing that 'distance' raises psychological barriers to programs and course completions as well as geographical and fiscal barriers" (p. 40).

These studies indicate a growing awareness of issues related to culture and gender in distance education. As the Internet spreads, researching these issues in the online environment will become increasingly important. Current research on the relationship between the social and the cognitive processes of learning will provide impetus for examining culture and gender issues further. While designing sound and rigorous studies to examine cultural factors is a challenging task, it is a challenge that must be taken up if we are to clearly understand the sociocultural context of online learning. Future research using qualitative and ethnographic methodology may provide useful answers to many of the questions in this area.

14.10.3.6 Distance Education as a Complex System.

Distance education is a complex system consisting of many subsystems that interact with each other over time. Moore and Kearsley (1996) believe that a systems approach is helpful to an understanding of distance education as a field of study and is essential to its successful practice. They note that a distance education system consists of all the component processes such as learning, teaching, communication, learner support, design, management, and several other factors that form subsystems and interact to make the whole system work. Further, there are other factors such as social, political, economic, and global issues that influence distance education. Therefore, the ability to visualize interactions and see patterns becomes increasingly important in order to gain a better understanding of how distance education works within different contexts. Recently, research has begun to emerge that examines distance education from a systems perspective, and promises to be a direction that future research will adopt.

Saba (1999) argues that a systems approach is necessary to describe distance education and define a set of principles and rules for its effective use, as well as a set of criteria to determine its effectiveness. This holistic view of the process reveals the behavior of each individual learner. Saba (2000) advocates using methods related to systems dynamics as well as hierarchy and complexity theories to provide a more comprehensive understanding of the field. Saba and Shearer (1994) demonstrated how to understand the concept of transactional distance through their research using systems modeling techniques. Transactional distance is seen as representative of the interaction of many variables affecting and being affected by each other over time. The data points representing several variables that interact over time are numerous. What is of interest, however, is not each data point, but the pattern that emerges from observing each individual learner (Saba, 1999).

14.10.3.7 Rethinking Comparative Studies.

While comparative studies have been widely criticized for problems related to research design and lack of theoretical and practical value to the field, Smith and Dillon (1999) note the renewed interest in comparative studies that examine the effectiveness of online learning. This interest has been fueled by the U.S. Department of Education's Strategic Plan for 2002–2007 <http://www.ed.gov/pubs/stratplan2002-07/index.html> which calls to transform education into an evidence-based field. This plan encourages the use of scientifically based methods (often described as randomized trials with control groups) to evaluate federally funded distance education programs.

Smith and Dillon (1999) argue that the problem with comparative studies is not in the "comparison," but in the media/method confound. They believe that comparison studies designed with clearly defined constructs of both media and delivery systems can serve to advance our understanding of the phenomenon of distance education. They propose a framework based on media attribute theory that can be used to categorize both media and delivery systems based on research related to learning and motivation. Their framework is based on identifying and defining categories of attributes embedded within each delivery system and the media used by the delivery system that may support learning in different ways. Their categories or attributes include (1) realism/bandwidth, (2) feedback/interactivity, and (3) branching/interface. They note: "It is important that comparative studies explain more than just which technologies were used; they must also explain why and how the media and delivery systems were used to support learning and motivation" (p. 6). As Saba (2000) notes, Smith and Dillon have shown that a new set of categories and clearly defined constructs of both media and delivery systems could improve comparative studies and cure the "no significant difference" phenomenon.

Lockee, Burton, and Cross (1999) advocate longitudinal studies as a more beneficial approach to conducting future research in distance education. They argue that the collection of data over time can provide a more accurate perspective, whether through qualitative case studies or more quantitative time-series analyses which might demonstrate patterns in certain variables.

Another type of research that is gaining increasing prominence with funded Web-based projects, is developmental research which provides opportunities to study processes while implementing the distance education programs. Not unlike the process of formative evaluation, developmental research enables the testing of prototypes by methods such as interface evaluation studies. In complex Web-based learning environments, developmental research can provide timely feedback for the improvement of the learning design to facilitate learning.

This discussion on research in distance education has shown the development of research from early media comparison studies that yielded "no significant differences" which were clearly conducted to justify distance education as a worthwhile endeavor, to research that is focusing on critical pedagogical, design, and sociocultural context issues based on theoretical constructs in the field and related fields such as communication. The newer studies have focused on the distance learner, issues associated with the teaching learning process such as interaction, transactional distance, and control, and the sociocultural context of learning including factors such as social presence, group dynamics, community building, culture, and gender. It is evident from recent research studies that these lines of questioning would continue in future research. Research has also begun to address the complexity of distance education systems through a systems perspective, and it is likely that this would be an avenue for future research with the development of system modeling computer programs such as STELLA and Star Logo that are capable of modeling entire systems. An area of research that has received scant attention in the literature so far is related to policy, management, organization and administration of distance education. Future research will need to address these issues as distance education moves on to become an international and global movement.

14.11 INTERNATIONAL ISSUES

The United States is a relative newcomer to the distance education scene. The British Open University led the way in the early 1970s and was soon providing leadership to developing countries, each with a unique need to educate, train, and provide job opportunities for growing populations.

Drawing upon the well-known model of the British Open University, countries such as Pakistan, India, and China have combined modern methods of teaching with emerging technologies in order to provide low-cost instruction for basic literacy and job training. Turkey has recently joined those nations involved in large-scale distance learning efforts. Sir John Daniel, UNESCO's Assistant Director-General for Education, and former Vice-Chancellor of the British Open University, has called these largest distance learning institutions mega-universities, those having more than 100,000 students enrolled in learning at a distance (Daniel, 1996). One example of a rapidly growing mega-university is Anadolu University in Turkey. Now 20 years old, Anadolu's distance education program currently enrolls over 600,000 students and is one of the three largest distance education program in the world (Demiray, 1998; Demiray & McIsaac, 1993; McIsaac, Askar & Akkoyunla, 2000; McIsaac, 2002). These mega-universities are huge enterprises that require organization, resources and effective delivery systems. Traditionally these media delivery systems have relied heavily on print, supported by film, video, and most recently computers. However mega-universities are now looking toward other information and communication technologies.

Distance learning delivery systems, particularly those that rely on ICTs (information and communication technologies) have benefited from the economic growth of the telecommunications industry. As early as 1990, telecommunication equipment and services accounted for $350 billion and employed 2.8 million workers. The communication industry in OECD countries has continued as an extremely profitable and competitive business with public telecommunication operators developing new ISDN and satellite services. The increased development of mobile communications is being matched with increased deregulation and privatization of networks, increasing competition and lowering costs.

In many countries, although the existing communication infrastructure is old and may be dysfunctional, newer technologies have been used to provide for the flow of information to the majority of the population through distance education delivery systems (McIsaac, 1992). Today, the newer cellular radio technologies, which can handle a greater number of users than previous fixed link networks, are providing leapfrog technologies. Such mobile technologies can be put in place with less cost than wired networks and, in addition, occupy a very small spectrum of the radio frequencies.

According to an NUA Internet Survey in August 2002, more than 553 million people worldwide have Internet access. That is ten percent of the world's population, with the percentage of use growing rapidly (*http://www.nua.ie/survey/index.cgi*). Other relevant facts illustrate the current growth of Internet access, and, in some countries, broadband use.

Africa—has between 1.5 and 2.5 million Internet users in the 49 sub-Saharan African countries

Asia—will have more Internet users than either Europe or North America by the end of 2002. South Korea has the highest broadband penetration in the world, 60 percent, and more DSL lines than any other country.

Australia/New Zealand—number of broadband connections doubled from July 2001 to March 2002 to 251,000

Europe—UK lags behind rest of Europe with only 9 percent using broadband. Germany 39 percent broadband, Sweden has 33 percent.

Middle East—the highest use led by United Arab Emirates, Kuwait, and Israel.

North America—25 percent in Canada have broadband, 12 percent in the USA

Latin America—most have narrowband Internet access. Use expected to increase from 25 million in 2002 to 65 million by 2007.

What does this rapid increase in the use of ICTs mean for international distance education? Although the future of new technological developments promises increased accessibility to information at low cost, this access is not without its own pitfalls. Economic power remains largely within the hands of developed countries. From an economic point of view, some disadvantages include the selection of a costly technological solution when a simpler and existing technology might suffice. Technology used over long physical distances with primitive and unreliable electricity and telephone services is not the most appropriate solution.

The most important consideration for the majority of developing countries is economic independence. It is in many of the economically developing countries that the largest distance learning projects are undertaken. A top educational priority for many such countries is to improve the cost effectiveness of education and to provide training and jobs for the general population. Researchers across the globe have called for the establishment of national priorities for research in areas such as distance education (Jegede, 1993). One particularly important collection of research articles on Open and Distance Learning (ODL) provides valuable information from 20 countries about the status of open and distance education in Asia and the Pacific Rim. Organized by the Centre for Research in Distance and Adult Learning (CRIDAL) at the Open University of Hong Kong, these articles provide comprehensive information on distance learning and much needed empirical data from which to examine the future prospects of ODL development in the region (Jegede & Shive, 2001)

Two additional groups that are leading international developments in distance education are the Commonwealth of Learning (COL), and UNESCO. COL is an intergovernmental organization made up of leaders of more than 50 commonwealth governments including Australia, Britain, Canada, India, New Zealand, and Nigeria. Created in 1989 to encourage the development and sharing of knowledge and resources in distance learning, the COL is the only intergovernmental organization solely concerned with the promotion and development of distance education and open learning.

Highlighting the human dimension of globalization and its impact on education, COL's 3-year plan (2000–2003) focuses on providing new opportunities using communication technologies for transfer of knowledge and development of skills-based industries. COL, believing that education offers the best way to overcome the cycles of poverty, ignorance, and violence, is committed to using open and distance learning with appropriate technologies to deliver education to people in all parts of the world. A recent study carried out by COL and funded by Britain found that the state of virtual education depended on where it was carried out. Surging interest in virtual education is emphasizing technology to deliver traditional educational programs by making them more accessible, flexible, and revenue-generating (Farrell, 2001). Most of the growth, COL found, was in countries with mature economies. Developing countries have not yet succeeded in using these new ICTs to bring mass educational opportunities to their people. However, the report continues by identifying new trends that are likely to have an impact on the evolution of distance education systems in developing countries.

One of COL's recent innovations is the creation of a Knowledge Finder portal using Convera's RetrievalWare as a search and categorization engine (http://www.convera.com). This tool provides online sources in the public domain, filtered to select only educational materials and helps developing nations access quality education inexpensively and effectively by providing resources and information in 45 languages.

The second organization that is a leader in the international arena is the United Nations Educational, Scientific and Cultural Organization (UNESCO). In a recent report prepared by UNESCO and the Academy for Educational Development, scholars addressed the effective use of Information and Communication Technologies (ICTs) for the 21st century (Haddad & Draxler 2002). Emphasizing ways that ICTs can be integrated into the educational programs of various countries, the study examines objectives and strategies using case studies. UNESCO has emphasized that there can be no sustainable development without education, and the organization is charged with using the power of education to being about the holistic and interdisciplinary strategies needed to create a sustainable future for the next generation. The new vision of education needed for a sustainable future involves changes in values, behavior and lifestyles. (http://www.unesco.org)

Cultural issues become important in many aspects of distance education delivery. In programs that are developed outside the native environment where it will be used, there are often conflicts in goals, perspectives and implementation. A danger is that the cultural values of program providers become dominant, desirable, and used as the standard. There have been many examples of programs from North America, Australia, Great Britain, and Europe that were purchased but never used in Africa and Asia because the material was not relevant in those countries. Because the appropriate design of instructional material is a critical element in its effectiveness, the issue of "who designs what and for whom" is central to any discussion of the economic, political, and cultural dangers that face distance educators using information technologies (McIsaac, 1993).

Research on distance education programs face a number of obstacles around the world. The lack of financial resources available for conducting adequate needs assessment in many countries, particularly prior to embarking on a massive distance education plan, is a common problem (McIsaac, 1990). In many cases investing money in research is perceived to be unnecessary and a drain from areas in which the money is needed. Time is an additional problem, since programs are often mandated with very little start-up time. In the interest of expedience, an existing distance learning program from another country may be used and revised but many times this does not adequately answer the needs of the specific population.

One solution to the lack of adequate resources available locally has traditionally been the donation of time and expertise by international organizations to help in developing project goals and objectives. The criticism of this approach is that visiting experts seldom have adequate time to become completely familiar with the economic, social and political factors influencing the success of the project. A second, and more appropriate solution, has been to train local experts to research, design and implement sound distance learning programs based on the needs of the particular economy.

Distance education and its related delivery systems are often called upon to support national educational priorities and the current political system. One goal of education, particularly in developing countries, is to support the political organization of the country and to develop good citizens. Distance education programs that endorse this priority will have greater chance for success. National political philosophies and priorities are found reflected in the diversity of distance education programs around the world. These programs conform to prevailing political, social and economic values. Research, particularly of the applied variety, is essential to avoid the trial and error approach that costs international distance education projects millions of dollars.

14.12 SUMMARY

Distance education programs will continue to grow both in the United States and abroad. One of the reasons for this growth is related to the ever growing global need for an educated workforce combined with financial constraints of established educational systems. Distance education offers life-long learning potential to working adults and will play a significant part in educating societies around the world. Distance education will become of far greater importance in the United States in the years ahead because it is cost efficient and because it allows for independent learning by working adults. If society is to cope with this growing need for an educated workforce, distance education must continue to make its place in the educational community.

A major development in the changing environment of distance education in the United States is the rise of corporate universities and commercial institutions selling academic programs. Commercial companies are increasingly supporting the online infrastructure of universities, and universities are becoming more corporate. The globalized economy will be an increasing factor in the growth of the alternative education market in the United States, and of major educational development in many countries of the world. The growth of an information society will continue to put pressure on those countries without adequate technology infrastructure, and there will be increasing demands for access to higher education to upgrade skills for employment. Information as a commodity and the distributed nature of new knowledge will offer educators opportunities to explore alternative pedagogies and student centered learning. These developments should be questioned and examined critically through a scholarly lens.

Future research should focus on establishing theoretical frameworks as a basis for research, and should examine the interactions of technology with teaching and learning. Researchers should address issues of achievement, motivation, attrition, and control.

Distance education is no longer viewed as a marginal educational activity. Instead, it is regarded internationally as a viable and cost effective way of providing individualized and interactive instruction. Recent developments in technology are erasing the lines between traditional and distance learners as more students have the opportunity to work with multimedia designed for individual and interactive learning. Print, once the primary method of instructional delivery, is now taking a backseat to modern interactive technologies.

The content of future research should:

- Move beyond media comparison studies and reconceptualize media and instructional design variables in the distance learning environment.
- Examine the characteristics of the distance learner and investigate the collaborative effects of media attributes and cognition
- Explore the relationship between media and the socio-cultural construction of knowledge
- Identify course design elements effective in interactive learning systems
- Contribute to a shared international research database
- Examine the cultural effects of technology and courseware transfer in distance education programs

Research methodologies should:

- Avoid microanalyses
- Progress beyond early descriptive studies
- Generate a substantive research base by conducting longitudinal and collaborative studies
- Identify and develop appropriate conceptual frameworks from related disciplines such as cognitive psychology, social learning theory, critical theory, communication theory and social science theories
- Explore thorough qualitative studies that identify the combination of personal, social and educational elements that create a successful environment for the independent learner
- Combine qualitative and experimental methodologies, where appropriate, to enrich research findings

Technology may be driving the rapid rise in popularity of distance education, but it is the well designed instructional situation which allows the learner to interact with the technology in the construction of knowledge. It is the effective interaction of instructor, student and delivery system that affords distance education its prominence within the educational community. Distance education can offer the opportunity for a research-based, practical, integration of technology, instruction and instructor creating a successful educational environment.

References

Adolphs, R., & Damasio, A. R. (2001). The interaction of affect and cognition: A neurobiological perspective. In J. P. Forgas (Eds.), *Handbook of affect and social cognition* (pp. 27–49). Mahwah, NJ: Lawrence Erlbaum Associates.

Alluisi, E. A. (1991). The development of technology for collective training: SIMNET, a case history. *Human Factors, 33*(3), 343–362.

Bääth, J. (1982). Distance students' learning—empirical findings and theoretical deliberations. *Distance Education, 3*(1), 6–27.

Barker, B. O., Frisbie, A. G., & Patrick, K. R. (1989). Broadening the definition of distance education in light of the new telecommunications technologies. *The American Journal of Distance Education, 3*(1), 20–29.

Barker, K. (2001). *Creating quality guidelines for online education and training*. Vancouver, BC, Canadian Association for Community Education.

Barrett, E. (Ed.). (1992). *Sociomedia: Multimedia, hypermedia and the social construction of knowledge*. Cambridge, MA: The MIT Press.

Bates, A. W. (1983). Adult learning from educational television: The open university experience. In M. J. A. Howe (Eds.), *Learning from television: Psychological and educational research* (pp. 57-77). London: Academic Press.

Bates, A. W. (1984). Broadcast television in distance education: A worldwide perspective. In A. W. Bates (Ed.), *The role of technology in distance education* (pp. 29-41). London: Croom Helm.

Bates, A. W. (1987). *Television, learning and distance education*. Milton Keynes, UK: The Open University, Institute of Educational Technology.

Bates, A. W. (1990). *Media and technology in European distance educaton*. Milton Keynes, UK: Open University.

Bates, A. W. (1991). Third generation distance education: The challenge of new technology. *Research in Distance Education, 3*(2), 10-15.

Bates, T. (1993). Theory and practice in the use of technology in distance education. In D. Keegan (Ed.), *Theoretical principles of distance education* (pp. 213-233). London: Routledge.

Bates, T. (2001). International distance education: Cultural and ethical issues. *Distance Education, 22*(1), 122-136.

Baym, N. K. (1995). The emergence of community in computer-mediated communication. In S. G. Jones (Ed.), *Cybersociety,* (pp. 138-163). Thousand Oaks, CA: Sage.

Baynton, M. (1992). Dimensions of control in distance education: A factor analysis. *The American Journal of Distance Education, 6*(2), 17-31.

Beaudoin, M. (1990). The instructor's changing role in distance education. *The American Journal of Distance Education, 4*(2), 21-29.

Berge, Z. L., & Mrozowski, S. (2001). Review of research in distance education: 1990 to 1999. *American Journal of Distance Education, 15*(3), 5-19.

Blum, K. D. (1999). Gender differences in asynchronous learning in higher education: Learning styles, participation barriers and communication patterns. *Journal of Asynchronous Learning Networks (JALN), 3*(1), 46-66.

Boswell, J. J., Mocker, D. W., & Hamlin, W. C. (1968). Telelecture: An experiment in remote teaching. *Adult Leadership, 16*(9), 321-322, 338.

Brown, A. L., & Palincsar, A. S. (1989). Guided, cooperative learning and individual knowledge acquisition. In L. B. Resnick (Ed.), *Knowing, Learning and Instruction: Essays in Honor of Robert Glaser* (pp. 393-452). Hillsdale, NJ: Lawrence Erlbaum Associates.

Brown, J. S., Collins, A., & Duguid, P. (1989). Situated cognition and the culture of learning. *Educational Researcher, 18*(1), 32-42.

Bullen, M. (1998). Participation and critical thinking in online university distance education, *Journal of Distance Education, 13*(2), 1-32.

Burge, E. (1998). Gender in distance education. In C. Campbell Gibson (Ed.), *Distance learners in higher education: Institutional responses for quality outcomes* (pp. 25-45). Madison, WI: Atwood Publishing.

Burge, E.J. (1994). Learning in computer conferenced contexts: The learners perspective' *Journal of Distance Education, 9*(1), 19-43.

Canfield, A. A. (1983) *Canfield learning styles inventory form S-A: manual* (3rd edition). Birmingham, Michigan: Humanics Media.

Carabajal, K., La Pointe, D., Gunawardena, C. N. (2003). Group development in online learning communities. In M. G. Moore & W. G. Anderson (eds.) *Handbook of distance education* (pp. 217-234). Mahwah, NJ: Lawrence Erlbaum Associates Inc.

Cecez-Kecmanovic, D., & Webb, C. (2000). A critical inquiry into web-mediated collaborative learning. In A. Aggarwal (Ed.), *Web-based learning and teaching technologies* (pp. 307-326). Hershey, PA: Idea Group Publishing.

Chen, A-Y., Mashhadi, A., Ang, D., & Harkrider, N. (1999). Cultural issues in the design of technology-enhanced learning systems. *British Journal of Educational Technology, 30,* 217-230.

Chen, Y-J., & Willits, F. K. (1999). Dimensions of educational transactions in a videoconferencing learning environment. *The American Journal of Distance Education, 13*(1), 45-59.

Christophel, D. (1990). The relationship among teacher immediacy behaviors, student motivation, and learning. *Communication Education, 39,* 323-340.

Chu, G. C., & Schramm, W. (1967). *Learning from television: What the research says*. Washington, DC: National Association of Educational Broadcasters.

Chute, A. G., Bruning, K. K., & Hulick, M. K. (1984). *The AT&T Communications national teletraining network: Applications, benefits and costs*. Cincinnati, OH: AT&T Communication Sales and Marketing Education.

Clark, R. E. (1984). Research on student thought processes during computer-based instruction. *Journal of Instructional Development, 7*(3), 2-5.

Coggins, C. C. (1988). Preferred learning styles and their impact on completion of external degree programs. *The American Journal of Distance Education, 2*(1), 25-37.

Cognition and Technology Group at Vanderbilt (1991). Integrated media: Toward a theoretical framework for utilizing their potential. In *Multimedida Technology Seminar* (pp. 1-21). Washington, DC.

Coldeway, D. (1990). Methodological issues in distance education research. In M. G. Moore (Ed.), *Contemporary issues in American distance education* (pp. 386-396). Oxford: Pergamon Press.

Collis, B. (1999). Designing for differences: Cultural issues in the design of the WWW-based course-support sites. *British Journal of Educational Technology, 30,* (3) 201-215.

Collis, B., de Boer, W. & van der Veen, J. (2001). Building on learner contributions: A web-supported pedagogic strategy. *Educational Media International, 38*(4), 229-240.

Cyberatlas (2002). Latinos Outpace Other Groups' Online Growth. 2002. Accessed at http://search.internet.com/cyberatlas.internet.com

Daniel, J. (1996). *Mega-universities and knowledge media: Technology strategies for higher education*. London: Kogan Page.

Daniel, J., & Marquis, C. (1979). Interaction and independence: getting the mixture right. *Teaching at a Distance, 15,* 25-44.

Davidson, R. (2002, April). *Emotion, plasticity and the human brain: An overview of modern brain research and its implications for education*. The Decade of Behavior Distinguished Lecture presented at the American Educational Research Association Annual Conference, New Orleans, LA.

Dede, C. J. (1992). The future of multimedia: Bridging to virtual worlds. *Educational Technology*(32), 54-60.

Demiray, U., Ed. (1998). *A review of the literature on the open education faculty in Turkey (1982-1997)*. Open Education Faculty Publicatins No. 558. Eskisehir, Turkey, Anadolu University Publications.

Demiray, U., & McIsaac, M. S. (1993). Ten years of distance education in Turkey. In B. Scriven, R. Lundin, & Y. Ryan (Eds.), *Distance education for the twenty-first century* (pp. 403-406). Oslo, Norway: International Council for Distance Education.

Deshler, D., & Hagan, N. (1989). Adult education research: Issues and directions. In S. Merriam & P. Cunningham (Eds.), *The handbook of adult and continuing education* (pp. 147-167). San Francisco: Jossey-Bass.

Dille, B., & Mezack, M. (1991). Identifying predictors of high risk among community college telecourse students. *The American Journal of Distance Education, 5*(1), 24-35.

Dillon, C., & Aagaard, L. (1990). Questions and research strategies: Another perspective. *The American Journal of Distance Education, 4*(3), 57-65.

Dillon, C., & Blanchard, D. (1991). Education for each: Learner driven distance education. In *Second American Symposium on Research in Distance Education*. University Park, PA. Pennsylvania State University.

Dillon, C., & Greene, B. (2003). Learner differences in distance learning: Finding differences that matter. In M. G. Moore & W. G. Anderson (eds.) *Handbook of distance education* (pp. 235-244). Mahwah, NJ: Lawrence Erlbaum Associates Inc.

Dillon, C. L., Gunawardena, C. N., & Parker, R. (1992). Learner support: The critical link in distance education. *Distance Education, 13*(1), 29-45.

Dillon, C. L., & Walsh, S. M. (1992). Faculty: The neglected resource in distance education. *The American Journal of Distance Education, 6*(3), 5-21.

Dinucci, D., Giudice, M., & Stiles, L. (1998). *Elements of Web Design.* Berkeley, CA: Peachpit Press.

Dirr, P. (1991). Research issues: State and national policies in distance education. In *Second American Symposium on Research in Distance Education*. University Park, PA: Pennsylvania State University.

Dirr, P. J. (2003). Distance education policy issues: Towards 2010. In M. G. Moore & W. G. Anderson (eds.) *Handbook of distance education* (pp. 461-479). Mahwah, NJ: Lawrence Erlbaum Associates Inc.

Donaldson, J. (1991). Boundary articulation, domain determination, and organizational learning in distance education: Practice opportunities and research needs. In *Second American Symposium on Research in Distance Education,* University Park, PA. Pennsylvania State University.

Dubin, R. (1978). *Theory building.* New York: The Free Press (A Division of Macmillan Publishing Co.).

Dwyer, F. (1991). A paradigm for generating curriculum design oriented research questions in distance education. In *Second American Symposium on Research in Distance Education,* University Park, PA: Pennsylvania State University.

Eastmond, D. V. (1994). Adult distance study through computer conferencing. *Distance Education, 15*(1), pp. 128-152.

Ellsworth, E., & Whatley, M. (1990). *The ideology of images in educational media:Hidden curriculums in the classroom.* New York: Teachers College Press.

Evans, T., & Nation, D. (1992). Theorising open and distance education. *Open Learning*(June), 3-13.

Farrell, G. (Team Leader) (2001). The changing faces of virtual education. London: Commonwealth of Learning.

Feasley, C. (1991). Does evaluation = research lite? In *Second American Symposium on Research in Distance Education*. University Park, PA: Pennsylvania State University.

Feenberg, A. (1993). Building a global network: The WBSI Experience. In L. M. Harasim (Ed.), *Global networks: Computers and international communication* (pp. 185-197). Cambridge, MA: The MIT Press.

Feenberg, A., & Bellman, B. (1990). Social factor research in computer-mediated communictions. In L. M. Harasim (Ed.), *Online education: Perspectives on a new environment* (pp. 67-97). New York: Praeger.

Fulford, C. P., & Zhang, S. (1993). Perceptions of interaction: The critical predictor in distance education. *The American Journal of Distance Education* **7**(3), 8-21.

Garrison, D. R. (1989). *Understanding distance education: A framework for the future.* London: Routledge.

Garrison, D. R. (1990). An analysis and evaluation of audio teleconferencing to facilitate education at a distance. *The American Journal of Distance Education, 4*(3), 13-24.

Garrison, D. R., Anderson, T., & Archer W. (2001). Critical thinking, cognitive presence, and computer conferencing in distance education. *American Journal of Distance Education, 15*(1), 7-15.

Garrison, D. R., & Baynton, M. (1987). Beyond independence in distance education: The concept of control. *The American Journal of Distance Education, 1*(1), 3-15.

Garrison, D. R., & Shale, D. (1987). Mapping the boundaries of distance education: Problems in defining the field. *The American Journal of Distance Education, 1*(1), 7-13.

Garrison, D. R., & Shale, D., Ed. (1990). *Education at a distance: from issues to practice.* Melbourne, FL: Krieger.

Garrison, R. (2000). Theoretical challenges for distance education in the 21st century: A shift from structural to transactional issues. *International Review of Research in Open and Distance Learning, 1*(1), 1-17 http://www.irrodl.org/content/v1.1/randy.pdf.

Gibson, C. C. (2003). Learners and learning: The need for theory. In M. G. Moore & W. G. Anderson (eds.) *Handbook of distance education* (pp. 147-160). Mahwah, NJ: Lawrence Erlbaum Associates Inc.

Gibson, C. C. (1993). Towards a broader conceptualization of distance education. In D. Keegan (Ed.), *Theoretical principles of distance education* (pp. 80-92). London: Routledge.

Gibson, C. C. (1990). Questions and research strategies: One researcher's perspectives. *The American Journal of Distance Education, 4*(1), 69-81.

Gibson, C. C. (1998a). The distance learner's academic self-concept. In C. C. Gibson (Ed.), *Distance learners in higher education: Institutional responses for quality outcomes* (pp. 65-76). Madison, WI: Atwood.

Gibson, C. C. (Ed.). (1998b). *Distance learners in higher education: Institutional responses for quality outcomes.* Madison, WI: Atwood.

Glaser, B. G., & Strauss, A. L. (1967). *The discovery of grounded theory: strategies for qualitative research.* Chicago: Aldine.

Glaser, R. (1992). Expert knowledge and processes of thinking. In D. F. Halpern (Ed.), *Enhancing thinking skills in the sciences and mathematics* (pp. 63-76). Hillsdale, NJ: Lawrence Erlbaum Associates.

Goodfellow, R., Lea, M., Gonzalez, F., & Mason, R. (2001). Opportunity and e-quality: Intercultural and linguistic issues in global online learning. *Distance Education, 22*(1), 65-84.

Gorham, J. (1988). The relationship between verbal teacher immediacy behaviors and student learning. *Communication Education 37*(1), 40-53.

Gunawardena, C. N. (1991). Collaborative learning and group dynamics in computer-mediated communication networks. In *The Second American Symposium on Research in Distance Education*. University Park: PA: Pennsylvania State University.

Gunawardena, C. N. (1993). The Social Context of Online Education. In *Proceedings of the Distance Education Conference*, Portland, Oregon.

Gunawardena, C. N., Campbell Gibson, C., Cochenour, J., et al. (1994). Multiple perspectives on implementing inter-university computer conferencing. In *Proceedings of the Distance Learning Research Conference* (pp. 101-117). San Antonio, TX: Texas A&M University, Dept. of Educational Human Resources.

Gunawardena, C. N. (1995). Social presence theory and implications for interaction and collaborative learning in computer conferences.

International Journal of Educational Telecommunications, 1(2/3), 147–166.

Gunawardena, C. N., Lowe, C. A., & Anderson, T. (1997). Analysis of a global online debate and the development of an interaction analysis model for examining social construction of knowledge in computer conferencing, *Journal of Educational Computing Research, 17*(14), 395–429.

Gunawardena, C. N., & Zittle, F. (1997). Social presence as a predictor of satisfaction within a computer-mediated conferencing environment. *The American Journal of Distance Education, 11*(3), 8–25.

Gunawardena, C. N., & Duphorne, P. L. (2000). "Predictors of learner satisfaction in an academic computer conference." *Distance Education, 21*(1), 101–117.

Gunawardena, C. N., Nolla, A. C., Wilson, P. L., López-Islas, J. R., Ramírez-Angel, N., Megchun-Alpízar, R. M. (2001). A cross-cultural study of group process and development in online conferences. *Distance Education: An International Journal, 22*(1).

Gunawardena, C. N., Walsh, S. L., Reddinger, L., Gregory, E., Lake, Y., Davies, A. (2002). Negotiating "Face" in a non-face-to-face learning environment (pp. 89–106). In F. Sudweeks and C. Ess (Eds.), *Proceedings Cultural Attitudes Towards Communication and Technology, 2002,* University of Montreal, Canada.

Gunawardena, C. N., Wilson, P. L., & Nolla, A. C. (2003). Culture and online education. In M. G. Moore and W. G. Anderson (Eds.), *Handbook of distance learning* Mahwah, NJ: Lawrence Erlbaum Associates, Inc. (pp. 753–775).

Hackman, M. Z., & Walker, K. B. (1990). Instructional communication in the televised classroom: The effects of system design and teacher immediacy on student learning and satisfaction. *Communication Education, 39*(3), 196–209.

Haddad, W., & Draxler, A., Ed. (2002). *Technologies for Education: Potential, Parameters and Prospects,* UNESCO and Academy for Educational Development.

Hall, E. T. (1976). *Beyond culture.* Garden City, NY: Anchor Books.

Hall, E. T. (1984). *The dance of life: The other dimension of time.* Garden City, NY: Anchor Press.

Hara, N., Bonk, C. J., Angeli, C. (2000). Content analysis of online discussion in an applied educational psychology course. *Instructional Science, 28,* 115–152.

Harasim, L. (2001). Shift happens: Online education as a new paradigm in learning. *The Internet and Higher Education (3)1.* Accessed online at: *http://virtual-u.cs.sfu.ca/vuweb.new/papers.html* July 10, 2002.

Harasim, L. (1989). Online education: A new domain. In R. Mason & A. Kaye (Eds.), *Mindweave* (pp. 50–62). Oxford: Pergamon.

Harasim, L. M. (1990). Online education: An environment for collaboration and intellectual amplification. In L. M. Harasim (Ed.), *Online education: Perspectives on a new environment* (pp. 39–64). New York: Praeger.

Harry, K., Keegan, D., & Magnus, J. (Eds.). (1993). *Distance education: New perspectives.* London: Routledge.

Hawkridge, D. (1991). Challenging educational technologies. *Educational and Training Technology International, 28*(2), 102–110.

Henri, F. (1992). Computer conferencing and content analysis. In A. R. Kaye (Ed), *Collaborative learning through computer conferencing: The Najaden papers* (pp. 117–136). Berlin: Springer-Verlag.

Herring, S. C. (1996). Posting in a different voice: Gender and ethics in computer-mediated communication. In Charles Ess (Ed.), *Philosophical perspectives on computer-mediated communication* (pp. 115–145). Albany: SUNY Press.

Herring, S. C. (2000). Gender differences in CMC: Findings and implications. In *The Computer Professionals for Social Responsibility (CPSR) Newsletter,* Winter 2000. http://www.cpsr. org/publications/newsletters/issues/2000/Winter2000/index.html (accessed 9-15-02).

Hillman, D. C., Willis, D. J., & Gunawardena, C. N. (1994). Learner-interface interaction in distance education: An extension of contemporary models and strategies for practitioners. *The American Journal of Distance Education, 8*(2), 30–42.

Hlynka, D., & Belland, J. (Ed.). (1991). *Paradigms regained: The uses of illuminative, semiotic and post-modern criticism as modes of inquiry in educational technology.* Englewood Cliffs, NJ: Educational Technology Publications.

Hofstede, G. (1980). *Culture's consequences: International differences in work-related values.* Beverly Hills, CA: Sage.

Holmberg, B. (1986). *Growth and structure of distance education.* London: Croom Helm.

Holmberg, B. (1989). *Theory and practice of distance education.* London: Routledge.

Holmberg, B. (1991). Testable theory based on discourse and empathy. *Open Learning, 6*(2), 44–46.

Howard, D. C. (1987). Designing learner feedback in distance education. *The American Journal of Distance Education, 1*(3), 24–40.

Hoyt, D. P., & Frye, D. (1972). *The effectiveness of telecommunications as an educational delivery system.* Manhattan, KS: Kansas State University.

Jegede, O. (1991). Constructivist epistemology and its implications for contemporary research in distance learning. In T. Evans & P. Juler (Eds.), *Second research in distance education seminar.* Victoria: Deakin University.

Jegede, O. (1993). *Distance education research priorities for Australia: A study of the opinions of distance educators and practitioners.* Adelaide: University of South Australia.

Jegede, O., & Shive, G., Ed. (2001). *Open and distance education in the Asia Pacific region.* Hong Kong: Open University of Hong Kong Press.

Jelfs, A., & Whitelock, D. (2000). The notion of presence in virtual learning environments: what makes the environment real. *British Journal of Educational Technology, 31*(2), 145–152.

Jeong, A. (2001). *Supporting critical thinking with group discussion on threaded bulletin boards: An analysis of group interaction.* Unpublished doctoral dissertation, University of Wisconsin, Madison.

Johansen, R., Martin, A., Mittman, R., & Saffo, P. (1991). *Leading business teams: How teams can use technology and group process tools to enhance performance.* Reading, MA: Addison-Wesley Publishing Company.

Jones, S. G. (1995). *Cybersociety: Computer-mediated communication and community.* Thousand Oaks, CA: Sage.

Jones, S. G. (Ed.). (1997). *Virtual culture: Identity and communication in cybersociety.* London: Sage.

Jordan, B. & Henderson, A. (1995). Interaction analysis: Foundations and practice. *The Journal of the Learning Sciences, 4*(1), 39–103.

Kanuka, H., & Anderson, T. (1998). Online social interchange, discord, and knowledge construction. *Journal of Distance Education, 13*(1), 57–74.

Kearney, P., Plax, T., & Wendt-Wasco, N. (1985). Teacher immediacy for affective learning in divergent college classes. *Communication Quarterly 3*(1), 61–74.

Kearsley, G. (1995). *The nature and value of interaction in distance learning.* Paper presented at the Third Distance Education Research Symposium., May 18–21. The American Center for the Study of Distance Education, Pennsylvania State University.

Keegan, D. (1980). On defining distance education. *Distance Education, 1*(1), 13–36.

Keegan, D. (1986). *The foundations of distance education* (second ed.). London: Routledge.

Keegan, D. (1988). Problems in defining the field of distance education. *The American Journal of Distance Education, 2*(2), 4–11.

Kember, D., & Murphy, D. (1990). A synthesis of open, distance and student contered learning. *Open Learning, 5*(2), 3–8.

Kirkup, G., & von Prummer, C. (1990). Support and connectedness: The needs of women distance education students. *Journal of Distance Education, V*(2), 9–31.

Kozma, R. B. (1994). Will media influence learning? Reframing the debate. *Educational Technology Research and Development, 42*(2), 7–19.

Kruh, J. (1983). Student evaluation of instructional teleconferencing. In L. Parker & C. Olgren (Eds.), *Teleconferencing and electronic communications 11* Madison, WI: University of Wisconsin-Extension, Center for Interactive Programs.

Kumpulainen, K., & Mutanen, M. (2000). Mapping the dynamics of peer group interaction: A method of analysis of socially shared learning processes. In H. Cowie & van der Aalsvoort (Eds.), *Social interaction in learning and instruction: The meaning of discourse for the construction of knowledge* (pp. 144–160). Advances in Learning and Instruction Series. Amsterdam: Pergamon.

Laube, M. R. (1992). Academic and social integration variables and secondary student persistence in distance education. *Research in Distance Education, 4*(1), 2–5.

Lave, J. (1991). Situating learning in communities of practice. In L. B. Resnick, J. M. Levine, & S. D. Teasley (Eds.), (1991). *Perspectives on socially shared cognition* (pp. 63–82) Washington, DC: American Psychological Association.

Lea, M. R., & Nicoll, K., Ed. (2002). *Distributed learning: Social and cultural approaches to practice*. London: Routledge, Falmer

Levinson, P. (1990). Computer conferencing in the context of the evolution of media. In L. Harasim (Ed.), *Online education: Perspectives on a new environment* (pp. 3–14). New York: Praeger.

Lim, C. K. (2001). Computer self-efficacy, academic self-concept, and other predictors of satisfaction and future participation of adult distance learners, *The American Journal of distance Education, 15*(2), 41–51.

Lockee, B. B., Burton, J. K., & Cross, L. H. (1999). No comparison: Distance education finds a new use for 'no significant difference.' *Educational Technology Research and Development, 47*(3), 33–42.

Lombard, M., & Ditton, T. (1997 September). At the heart of it all: The concept of presence, *JCMC, 3*(2).

Lopez-Islas, J. R. (2001). *Collaborative learning at Monterrey Tech-Virtual University*. Paper presented at the invited Symposium on Web-based Learning Environments to Support Learning at a Distance: Design and Evaluation, December 7–9, Asilomar, Pacific Grove, California.

Luria, A. R. (1979). *The making of mind: A personal account of Soviet psychology*. Cambridge, MA: Harvard University Press.

Malbran, M. D. C. & Villar, C. M. (2001). Incorporating cultural relevance into online courses: The case of VirtualMente. *Distance Education, 22*(1), 168–174.

Mason, R., and Gunawardena, C. (2001). Editorial. *Distance Education, 22*(1), 4–6.

McCleary, I. D., & Eagan, M. W. (1989). Program design and evaluation: Two-way interactive television. *The American Journal of Distance Education, 3*(1), 50–60.

McDonald, J., & Gibson, C. C. (1998). Interpersonal dynamics and group development in computer conferencing. *The American Journal of Distance Education, 12*(1), 7–25.

McIsaac, M. S. (1990). Problems affecting evaluation of distance education in developing countries. *Research in Distance Education, 2*(3), 12–16.

McIsaac, M. S. (1992). Networks for Knowledge: The Turkish electronic classroom in the twenty-first century. *Educational Media International, 29*(3), 165–170.

McIsaac, M. S. (1993). Economic, political and social considerations in the use of global computer-based distance education. In R. Muffoletto & N. Knupfer (Eds.), *Computers in education: Social, political, and historical perspectives* (pp. 219–232). Cresskill, NJ: Hampton Press, Inc.

McIsaac, M. S.(2002) Online learning from an international perspective. *Educational Media International, 39*(1), 17–22.

McIsaac, M. S., Askar, P. & Akkoyunlu, B. (2000) Computer links to the West: Experiences from Turkey. In A. DeVaney, S. Gance & Y. Ma (Eds.) *Technology and resistance: Digital communications and new coalitions around the world.* Counterpoints: Studies in the Postmodern Theory of Education Series. Vol. 59. (pp. 153–165). New York: Peter Lang.

McIsaac, M. S., & Gunawardena, C. L. (1996). Distance Education. In D. Jonassen (Ed.), *Handbook of research for educational communications and technology* (pp. 403–437). New York: Simon & Schuster Macmillan.

McIsaac, M. S., & Koymen, U. (1988). Distance education opportunities for women in Turkey. *International Council for Distance Education Bulletin,* 17(May), 22–27.

McIsaac, M. S., Murphy, K. L., & Demiray, U. (1988). Examining distance education in Turkey. *Distance Education, 9*(1), 106–113.

McLoughlin, C. (2001). Inclusivity and alignment: Principles of pedagogy, task and assessment design for effective cross-cultural online learning. *Distance Education, 22*(1), 7–29.

Monson, M. (1978). *Bridging the distance: An instructional guide to teleconferencing*. Madison, WI: Instructional Communications Systems, University of Wisconsin-Extension.

Moore, M. G. (1973). Toward a theory of independent learning and teaching. *Journal of Higher Education,* 44, 66–69.

Moore, M. G. (1989). Three types of interaction. *The American Journal of Distance Education, 3*(2), 1–6.

Moore, M. G. (Ed.). (1990a). *Contemporary issues in American distance education*. Oxford: Pergamon Press.

Moore, M. G. (1990b). Recent contributions to the theory of distance education. *Open Learning, 5*(3), 10–15.

Moore, M. G., & Kearsley, G. (1996). *Distance education: A systems view*. Belmont, CA: Wadsworth Publishing Company.

Naidu, S. (1997). Collaborative reflective practice: An instructional design Architecture for the Internet. *Distance Education, 18,* (2) 257–283.

Nelson, A. (1988). Making distance education more efficient. *ICDE Bulletin, 18,* 18–20.

Newman, D. R., Webb, B. & Cochrane. C. (1995). A content analysis method to measure critical thinking in face-to-face and computer supported group learning, *Interpersonal Computing and Technology: An Electronic Journal for the 21st Century,* 3(2), 56–77. *http://jan.ucc.nau.edu/~ipct-j/1995/n2/newman.txt* accessed 9-14-02.

Noble, D. (1999, November). Rehearsal for the revolution: Digital diploma mills, Part IV. Accessed online at:http://communication.ucsd.edu/dl/ddm4.html June 4, 2002.

Noble, D. (2001, March). *Fool's gold: Digital diploma mills,* Part V. Accessed online at: http://communication.ucsd.edu/dl/ddm5.html June 6, 2002.

Nolla, A. C. (2001). Analysis of social interaction patterns in asynchronous collaborative academic computer conferences. Unpublished dissertation. University of New Mexico: Albuquerque, NM.

Office of Technology Assessment (1989). *Linking for learning*. Washington, DC: United States Government Printing Office.

Olgren, C. H. (1998). Improving learning outcomes: The effects of learning strategies and motivation. In C. C. Gibson (Ed.), *Distance learners in higher education: Institutional responses for quality outcomes* (pp. 77-95). Madison, WI: Atwood.

Olgren, C. H., & Parker, L. A. (1983). *Teleconferencing technology and applications.* Artech House Inc.

Pea, R. (1993). Practices of distributed intelligence and designs for education. In G. Salomon (Ed.), *Distributed cognitions: Psychological and educational considerations* (pp. 47-87). Cambridge: Cambridge University Press.

Perraton (2000). Rethinking the research agenda. In *International Review of Research in Open and Distance Learning,* vol 1(1). *http://www.irrodl.org/content/v1.1/hilary.pdf*

Peters, O. (1971). Theoretical aspects of correspondence instruction. In O. Mackenzie & E. L. Christensen (Eds.), *The changing world of correspondence study.* University Park, PA: Pennsylvania State University.

Peters, O. (1983). Distance teaching and industrial production: A comparative interpretation in outline. In D. Sewart, D. Keegan, & B. Holmberg (Eds.), *Distance education: International perspectives* (pp. 95-113). London: Croom-Helm.

Peters, O. (2000). Digital learning environments: New possibilities and opportunities. *International Review of Research in Open and Distance Learning, 1*(1), 1-19. *http://www.irrodl.org/content/v1.1/otto.pdf.*

Pincas, A. (2001). Culture, cognition and communication in global education. *Distance Education, 22*(1), 30-51.

Pittman, V. (1991). Rivalry for respectability: Collegiate and proprietary correspondence programs. In *Second American Symposium on Research in Distance Education.* University Park, PA: Pennsylvania State University.

Pratt, D. D. (1989). Culture and learning: A comparison of western and Chinese conceptions of self and individualized instruction. In *30th Annual Adult Educational Research Conference.* Madison, WI.

Primary Research Group (2002). *The survey of distance and cyber-learning programs in higher education, 2002 edition.* New York: Primary Research Group.

Rafaeli, S. (1988). Interactivity: From new media to communication. In R. P. Hawkins, S. Pingree, & J. Weimann (Eds.), *Advancing Communication Science: Sage Annual Review of Communication Research, 16,*110-134. Newbury Park, CA: Sage.

Rafaeli, S. (1990). Interaction with media: Parasocial interaction and real interaction. In B. D. Ruben & L. A. Lievrouw (Eds.), *Information and Behavior, 3,* 125-181. New Brunswick, NJ: Transaction Books.

Ramsden, P. (1988). *Studying learning: Improved teaching.* London: Kogan Page.

Ravitz, J. (1997). Evaluating learning networks: A special challenge for web-based instruction. In B. H. Khan (Ed.), *Web-based instruction* (pp. 361-368). Englewood Cliffs, NJ: Educational Technology Publications.

Reed, D., & Sork, T. J. (1990). Ethical considerations in distance education. *The American Journal of Distance Education, 4*(2), 30-43.

Reschke, K. (2001). *The family child care forum: An innovative model for effective online training for family child care providers.* Unpublished doctoral dissertation, Indiana State University.

Resnick, L. B. (1991). Shared cognition: Thinking as social practice. In L. B. Resnick, J. M. Levine, & S. D. Teasley (Eds.), (1991). *Perspectives on socially shared cognition* (pp. 1-20) Washington, DC: American Psychological Association

Rheingold, H. (1993). *The virtual community: Homesteading on the electronic frontier.* New York: Addison-Wesley Publishing Company.

Riel, M. (1993). Global education through learning circles. In L. M. Harasim (Ed.), *Global networks* (pp. 221-236). Cambridge, MA: The MIT Press.

Ross, J. A., Crane, C. A. & Robertson, D. (1995). Computer-mediated distance education. *Journal of Distance Education, 10,*(2), 17-32.

Rourke, L., Anderson, T., Garrison, D. R., & Archer, W. (1999). Assessing social presence in asynchronous text-based computer conferencing. *Journal of Distance Education, 14*(2).

Rourke, L., Anderson, T., Garrison, D. R., & Archer, W. (2001). Methodological issues in the content analysis of computer conference transcripts. *International Journal of Artificial Intelligence in Education, 12,* 8-22.

Rumble, G. (1986). *The planning and management of distance education.* London: Croom Helm.

Saba, F. (2000). Research in distance education: A status report. *The International Review of Research in Open and Distance Learning 1*(1). Accesses at *http://www.icaap.org/iuicode?149.1.1.3*

Saba, F. (1999). Toward a systems theory of distance education. *The American Journal of Distance Education, 13*(2).

Saba, F., & Shearer, R. (1994). Verifying key theoretical concepts in a dynamic model of distance education. *American Journal of Distance Education, 8*(1), 36-59.

Salomon, G. (1979). *Interaction of media, cognition and learning: An exploration of how symbolic forms cultivate mental skills and affect knowledge acquisition.* San Francisco: Jossey-Bass.

Salomon, G. (Ed.). (1993). *Distributed cognitions: Psychological and educational considerations.* Cambridge: Cambridge University Press.

Salomon, G., Perkins, D. N., & Globerson, T. (1991). Partners in cognition: Extending human intelligence with intelligent technologies. *Educational Researcher, 20*(3), 2-9.

Sammons, M. (1989). An epistemological justification for the role of teaching in distance education. *The American Journal of Distance Education, 2*(3), 5-16.

Sanchez, I., & Gunawardena, C. N. (1998). Understanding and supporting the culturally diverse distance learner. In C. C. Gibson (Ed.), *Distance learners in higher education: Institutional responses for quality outcomes* (pp. 47-64). Madison, WI: Atwood.

Sewart, D. (Ed.). (1987). *Staff development needs in distance education and campus-based education: Are they so different?* London: Croom Helm.

Shale, D. (1990). Toward a reconceptualization of distance education. In M. G. Moore (Eds.), *Contemporary issues in American distance education* (pp. 333-343). Oxford: Pergamon Press.

Sherry, A. C., Fulford, C. P., & Zhang, S. (1998). Assessing distance learners' satisfaction with interaction: A quantitative and a qualitative measure. *The American Journal of Distance Education, 12*(3), 4-8.

Sherry, L. (1996). Issues in distance learning. *International Journal of Educational Telecommunications 1*(4), 337-365.

Short, J., Williams, E., & Christie, B. (1976). *The social psychology of telecommunications.* London: John Wiley & Sons.

Simonson, M., & Bauck, T. (2003). Distance education policy issues: Statewide perspectives. In M. G. Moore & W. G. Anderson (eds.) *Handbook of distance education* (pp. 417-424). Mahwah, NJ: Lawrence Erlbaum Associates Inc.

Smith, P. L., & Dillon, C. L. (1999). Comparing distance learning and classroom learning: Conceptual considerations, *The American Journal of Distance Education, 13*(2), 6-23.

Sophason, K., & Prescott, C. (1988). *The VITAL/THAI system: A joint development of computer assisted instruction systems for distance education*. Nonthaburi, Thailand: Sukothai Thammathirat University.

Spears, R. & Lea, M. (1992). Social influence and the influence of the 'social' in computer-mediated communication. In M. Lea (Ed.), *Contexts of computer-mediated communication* (pp. 30–65). New York: Harvester Wheatsheaf.

Spenser, K. (1991). Modes, media and methods: The search for educational effectiveness. *British Journal of Educational Technology*, *22*(1), 12–22.

Stoney, S., & Wild, M. (1998). Motivation and Interface Design: Maximising Learning Opportunities. *Journal of Computer-Assisted Learning, 14,* 40–50.

Suen, H. K., & Stevens, R. J. (1993). Analytic considerations in distance education research. *The American Journal of Distance Education,* *7*(3), 61–69.

Suwinski, J. H. (1993). Fiber optics: Deregulate and deploy. *Technos,* *2*(3), 8–11.

Tammelin, M. (1998). The role of presence in a network-based learning environment. *Aspects of Media Education: Strategic Imperatives in the Information Age*. Tella. Helsinki, Finland, Media Education Center, Department of Teacher Education, University of Helsinki, Media Education Publications 8 available online at: http://www.hkkk.fi/~tammelin/MEP8.tammelin.html.

Taylor, J. C., & White, V. J. (1991). Faculty attitudes towards teaching in the distance education mode: An exploraory investigation. *Research in Distance Education, 3*(3), 7–11.

Teasley, S., & Roschelle, J. (1993). Constructing a joint problem space: The computer as a tool for sharing knowledge. In S. P. Lajoie & S. J. Derry (Eds.), *Computers as cognitive tools* (pp. 229–257). Hillsdale, NJ: Lawrence Erlbaum Associates.

Technology Based Learning (1994). *Instructional Media Design on CD ROM.* Tempe, AZ: Arizona State University.

Terry, R. (2002, August 27). Online Education's New Offerings. *Washington Post.* Washington, DC.

Tsui, A. B. M., & Ki, W. W. (1996). An analysis of conference interactions on TeleNex—A computer network for ESL teachers. *Educational Technology Research and Development, 44*(4), 23–44.

Tu, C., & McIsaac, M.S. (2002). "The relationship of social presence and interaction in online classes." *American Journal of Distance Education 16*(3), 131–150.

Twigg, C. (2001). Quality Assurance for Whom? Providers and Consumers in Today's Distributed Learning Environment: The Pew Learning and Technology Program, 2001. Troy, NY, Center for Academic Transformation: Rensselaer Polytechnic Institute.

UCLA (2001). PDA Requirement. Accessed online at http://www.medstudent.ucla.edu/pdareq/print.cfm on July 15, 2002

U.S. Department of Commerce (1993). *The national information infrastructure: Agenda for action.* Available online: FTP:ntia.doc.gov/pub/niiagenda.asc.

Utsumi, T., Rossman, P., & Rosen, S. (1990). The global electronic university. In M. G. Moore (Ed.), *Contemporary issues in American distance education* (pp. 96–110). New York: Pergamon Press.

Van Haneghan, J., Barron, L., Young, M., Williams, S., Vye, N., & Bransford, J. (1992). The Jasper series: An experiment With new ways to enhance mathematical thinking. In D. F. Halpern (Eds.), *Enhancing thinking skills in the sciences and mathematics* Hillsdale, NJ: Lawrence Erlbaum Associates.

Verduin, J. R., & Clark, T. A. (1991). *Distance education: The foundations of effective practice*. San Francisco: Jossey-Bass.

von Prummer, C. (1990). Study motivation of distance students: A report on some results from a survey done at the FernUniverität in 1987/88. *Distance Education, 2*(2), 2–6.

Vrasidas, C. & Glass, G. V. (2002). Distance education and distributed learning. Greenwich, Connecticut: Information Age Publishing.

Vrasidas, C., & McIsaac, M. S. (1999). "Factors influencing interaction in an online course." *The American Journal of Distance Education, 13*(3), 22–36.

Vygotsky, L. S. (1978). *Mind in society: The development of the higher psychological processes*. Cambridge, MA: Harvard University Press.

Wagner, E. (1990). Looking at distance education through an educational technologist's eyes. *The American Journal of Distance Education, 4*(1), 53–67.

Walther, J. B. 1992, Interpersonal effects in computer-mediated interaction: A relational perspective. *Communication Research, 19*(1), 52–90.

Web-based Education Commission (2000, December 19). *The power of the Internet for learning: Final report of the Web-Based Education Commission*. Washington, D. C. Available: *http://www.ed.gov/offices/AC/WBEC/FinalReport/* (Accessed April 27, 2003).

Wedemeyer, C. (1981). *Learning at the back door: Reflections on non-traditional learning in the lifespan.* Madison, WI: University of Wisconsin.

Wedemeyer, C. A. (1977). Independent study. In A. S. Knowles (Ed.), *The International Encyclopedia of Higher Education* Boston: Northeastern University.

Wegerif, R. (1998). The Social Dimension of Asynchronous Learning Networks, *Journal of Asynchronous Learning Networks, 2*(1). <*http://www.aln.org/alnweb/journal/jaln_vol2issue1. htm#Wegerif*> Accessed 9-14-02.

Whittington, N. (1987). Is instructional television educationally effective?: A research review. *The American Journal of Distance Education, 1*(1), 47–57.

Willen, B. (1988). What happened to the Open University?: Briefly. *Distance Education, 9,* 71–83.

Winn, B. (1990). Media and instructional methods. In D. R. Garrison & D. Shale (Eds.), *Education at a distance: From issues to practice* (pp. 53–66). Malabar, FL: Krieger Publishing Co.

Winn, W. (1997). The impact of three-dimensional immersive virtual environments on modern pedagogy. Seattle, WA: University of Washington, Human Interface Technology Laboratory.

Wolcott, L. L. (2003). Dynamics of faculty participation in distance education: Motivations, incentives, and rewards. In M. G. Moore & W. G. Anderson (eds.) *Handbook of distance education* (pp. 549–565). Mahwah, NJ: Lawrence Erlbaum Associates Inc.

Wright, S. (1991). Critique of recent research on instruction and learner support in distance education with suggestions for needed research. In *Second American Symposium on Research in Distance Education*. University Park, PA:Pennsylvania State University.

·15·

COMPUTER-MEDIATED COMMUNICATION

Alexander Romiszowski
Syracuse University

Robin Mason
The Open University

15.1 INTRODUCTION AND OVERVIEW

15.1.1 Scope of the Chapter

15.1.1.1 Principal Focus. This chapter will focus essentially on asynchronous text-based computer-mediated communication (CMC). By this, we mean email, whether one-to-one or one-to-many, e-mail-based discussion lists, bulletin boards, computer conferencing environments, and the growing number of Web-mediated manifestations of these types of communication.

As technologies change, the forms of CMC evolve. Sometimes there is divergence, for example, the newer audiovisual possibilities to contrast with the purely text-based, while in other aspects there is convergence, as in the amalgamation of many forms within a single Web-browser environment. Some forms of CMC are purely synchronous, some purely asynchronous, while others (e.g., NetMeeting™, ICQ™) are now allowing the two to occur in the same environment.

Technological issues, such as system and interface design, and speed of message transmission, have been known for many years to influence CMC use (Collins & Bostock, 1993; Perrolle, 1991; Porter, 1993). With this in mind, the technology should "be transparent, so that the learner is most conscious of the content of the communication, not the equipment" (Mason, 1994).

15.1.1.2 Partly in Scope. Many other forms of CMC exist, and especially many more synchronous (real-time) forms. All of these have been proposed and tested for educational purposes, in the same way that synchronous one-to-one telephone conversations have been used to provide learner support and telephone conference calls have been used for discussions among groups of students and their teachers.

However, as the advantages of distance and online education, and the various models of e-learning, are posited around the idea of overcoming the need for students to meet together in real time, the use of real-time interactions of this type are open to question. Chat forums, mediated through IRC chat and other software, such as the many proprietary forms of instant messaging now available, have been used for educational purposes, but usually as an adjunct to other modes of delivery. Thus, for example, they might be used to provide an additional communication channel to accompany a web broadcast of a lecture, and to provide the facility for students to pose questions to the lecturer and to other students. One of the major advantages of such synchronous CMC is to bring together geographically dispersed students, and in doing so, add immediacy and increase motivation, although it also reduces flexibility. This whole area merits further study, as we may be on the verge of seeing some really significant changes with real time electronic communications in developing social presence and hence community.

Some have advocated the use of MOOs (multiuser object-oriented environments) for learning, especially because they see the real-time role-playing aspects fitting with aspects of professional continuing education, or less formal forms of education (Collis, 1996; Horton, 2000). Fanderclai (1995), Looi (2002) suggests that MOOs and MUDs (Multiuser Dungeon, Dimension, or Domain) can provide learning environments that support constructivist approaches to learning, due in large part to the students controlling the timing of learning, and through the construction of knowledge within the online environments. Collis (2002) views them as still peripheral forms of online education, due to the technical support that is often needed, and the difficulties of scheduling the synchronous interactions needed for them to function effectively.

15.1.1.3   Out of Scope. Many other forms of computer, Internet and web-based technologies exist and can be used for educational purposes. One can stretch definitions of communication to possibly include them. However, we will exclude from our definitions and discussions the use of computer networks for accessing remote databases, or library systems, or for the transmission of large amounts of text. Online journals are another area that we will exclude, although evolving models of journals, which encourage interaction of readers with the authors through feedback, are starting to blur the distinctions (Murray & Anthony, 1999). One example of this latter area is the *Journal of Interactive Media in Education* (JIME – http://www-jime.open.ac.uk), which promotes an interactive online review process, while many health journals, for example, the *British Medical Journal,* regularly publish responses to the articles, appended to the articles themselves.

15.1.2   Basic Concepts

15.1.2.1   What is CMC? A working definition of CMC that, pragmatically and in light of the rapidly changing nature of communication technologies, does not specify forms, describes it as "the process by which people create, exchange, and perceive information using networked telecommunications systems that facilitate encoding, transmitting, and decoding messages" (December, 1996). This seems to encompass both the delivery mechanisms, derived from communication theory, and the importance of the interaction of people that the technologies and processes mediate (Naughton, 2000). It also provides for great flexibility in approaches to researching CMC, as "studies of cmc can view this process from a variety of interdisciplinary theoretical perspectives by focusing on some combination of people, technology, processes, or effects" (December, 1996).

The social aspects of the communication, rather than the hardware or software, form the basis of the more recent definitions. Jonassen et al. (1995) focus on the facilitation of sophisticated interactions, both synchronous and asynchronous, by computer networks in their definition of CMC. One of the most overt examples of the move away from a technological focus in definitions describes it thus: "CMC, of course, is not just a tool; it is at once technology, medium, and engine of social relations. It not only structures social relations, it is the space within which the relations occur and the tool that individuals use to enter that space" (Jones, 1995). In our selection of research studies for the present review, we have been guided more by the social and organizational aspects of specific projects than by their use of specific varieties of CMC and the associated technologies.

15.1.2.2   Synchronous and Asynchronous Communication. One of the main distinctions that has been made in CMC has been between synchronous (real-time) and asynchronous (delayed time) communications. Synchronous, real-time communications, as between two people in a face-to-face discussion, or talking on the telephone, or as in a one-to-many form, such as

a lecture, has its equivalent within CMC in chat rooms and similar environments. Much software exists to mediate this form of communication (e.g., IRC and various forms of instant messaging). These forms have had some use within educational contexts, but, in general, asynchronous forms seem to predominate, wherein there is a, potentially significant, time delay between sending a message and it being read. In offline communication, this latter form is similar to letter writing, or sending faxes, and online has its usual manifestations in email, discussion lists, and most forms of bulletin board and computer conference. For reasons that will become obvious as the reader proceeds, we do not plan to review synchronous and asynchronous applications of CMC in separate sections. Instead, we will refer to both of these categories as relevant in any or all of the sections of our review.

15.1.2.3   Highly Interactive Communication. CMC provides for complex processes of interaction between participants. It combines the permanent nature of written communication (which in itself has implications for research processes) with the speed, and often the dynamism of spoken communications, for example via telephone. The possibilities for interaction and feedback are almost limitless, and are not constrained as they are in some of the "electronic page turning" forms of computer-aided instruction, wherein the interaction is limited to a selection among a small number of choices. It is only the creativity, imagination, and personal involvement of participants, that constrains the potential of online discussions. The potential for interaction in a CMC environment is both more flexible and potentially richer than in other forms of computer-based education. The textual aspects of CMC, and in particular of asynchronous CMC, support the possibility of greater reflection in the composition of CMC than is seen in many forms of oral discourse, with implications for levels of learning. We reflect these aspects of CMC in specific sections dealing with the dynamics of CMC processes in educational contexts.

15.1.2.4   Oral or Textual. There is a substantial body of work within the discussion of CMC practice and research on the nature of CMC, in particular whether it is akin to oral discourse or to written texts, or whether it is a different form (Kaye, 1991; Yates, 1994). CMC has been likened to speech, and to writing, and considered to be both and neither simultaneously. Some have criticized this oral/literate dichotomy, believing that it "obscures the uniqueness of electronic language by subsuming it under the category of writing." (Poster, 1990).

Discussion list archives, and the saving of interesting messages by individuals, which they may then reuse within later discussions, provide for new forms of group interaction, and suggest features unlike those seen in communities based on face-to-face interaction and the spoken word. Such a group can exist and "through an exchange of written texts has the peculiar ability to recall and inspect its entire past." (Feenberg, 1989).

This ability to recall and examine the exact form of a communication has profound significance for research conducted on or using CMC (McConnell, 1988). From a poststructuralist theoretical perspective, "the computer promises to redefine the relationship between author, reader and writing space." Bolter (1989).

For the reasons implied by the above, our review will place special emphasis on discourse analysis studies. Many of these have been performed by researchers especially interested in questions of language acquisition and use and are reported in journals and websites that are not part of the "mainstream" literature of educational technology.

15.1.2.5 Active or Passive Participation (Lurking).

In most discussion forums, a majority of subscribers do not contribute to the discussion list in any given time period. Of those who do contribute, most tend to make only a small number of contributions, while a small number of active subscribers provide a larger proportion of message contributions.

One of the criticisms of many forms of CMC discussion is this tendency for a few members to dominate the discussions, or for the majority to lurk and not actively participate or contribute messages to the discussion forum. However, face-to-face discussions in educational contexts are often designed to be, or can become, monologues, with "silence filled by the teacher, or an exchange of unjustified opinions" (Newman et al., 1996). The fact that it is technologically possible for everyone to speak leads initially to the assumption that it is a good thing if they do, and to the measurement of a successful conference being related to the number of students who input messages.

Most members of discussion forums are, most of the time, passive recipients of the messages, rather than active contributors to discussions; they are, de facto, lurkers. Lurking, that is, passive consumption of such electronic discussions, has been the subject of much discussion in CMC research. However, despite all that has been written, it remains under-theorized and under-researched. In most face-to-face group discussion environments, most participants lurk most of the time, and make occasional contributions. Indeed, most discussion forums, whether online or offline, would be impossible if all participants tried to actively contribute more frequently than they do. In addition, there is an assumption, one that has been insufficiently challenged in the research, of lurkers as passive recipients, rather than actively engaged in reading. Reading cannot be assumed to be passive. Much reading, whether online or offline, can encompass active engagement, thought, even reflection on what has been read. The fact that it does not elicit an overt contribution to the discussion forum should not, as has generally been the case in CMC research, be taken to assume lack of such engagement, or of learning.

15.2   RESEARCH ON CMC SYSTEMS IN GENERAL

The above mentioned comments on active/passive participation and the comparison drawn between how this issue is interpreted and handled in CMC and face-to-face (F2F) contexts, is one major justification for inclusion of just a few studies that compare learning in these two contexts. However, the majority of comparative research studies have been omitted for reasons now well understood and accepted in the general educational

technology community. This point will be addressed from a research methodology perspective later in out review in the section on research methodologies. The present "general research studies" section is subdivided into studies that focus pedagogical and instructional design issues and those that raise general issues regarding the technologies employed.

15.2.1   Pedagogical/Instructional Aspects

Do online learning environments (Web courses) work? Do people learn in these environments? The literature on the topic is large and growing, but most of it is anecdotal rather than empirical. The many outstanding research questions will not be resolved quickly, since many variables need to be accounted for and control groups established for comparisons, which is a difficult task in real-life "intact" educational environments (Mayadas, F., 1997).

Early studies of online education focused on the viability of online instruction when compared to the traditional classroom. Recently, researchers have begun to examine instructional variables in courses taught online. Berge (1997) conducted a study of 42 postsecondary online instructors to discover strategies that educators might use to improve their online teaching. The instructors indicated that they believed learner-centered strategies to be more effective than instructor-centered strategies. They also indicated that they preferred the following methods: discussion, collaborative learning activities, and authentic learning activities. However, what was not discussed in the study was the effect the strategies had on the students.

Carswell et al. (2000) go a bit further than most previous studies when they describe the use of the Internet on a distance-taught undergraduate computer science course. This paper examines students' experience of a large-scale trial in which students were taught using electronic communication exclusively. The paper compares the experiences of a group of Internet students to those of conventional distance learning students on the same course. Learning styles, background questionnaires, and learning outcomes were used in the comparison of the two groups. The study reveals comparable learning outcomes with no difference in grade as the result of using different communication media. The student experience is reported, highlighting the main gains and issues of using the Internet as a communication medium in distance education. This paper also shows that using the Internet in this context can provide students with a worthwhile experience.

The students elected to enroll for either the conventional course or the Internet version. In a typical year, the conventional course attracts about 3500 students; of this, about 300 students elected to study the Internet version. The target groups were as follows:

- Internet: all students who enrolled on the Internet presentation (300);
- Conventional: students enrolled on the conventional course, including students whose tutors also had Internet students (150) and students of selected tutors with only conventional students.

The composition of the conventional target group allowed the researchers to consider tutor differences as well as to make conventional-Internet comparisons for given tutors.

The data sources for this analysis included:

- *Background questionnaires:* used to establish students' previous computing experience and prior knowledge, helping to assess group constitution;
- *Learning style questionnaires:* used to assess whether any student who displayed a preferred learning style fared better in one medium or the other, and to compare the learning style profiles of the groups overall;
- *Final grades* including both continuous assessment and final examination; used to compare the two groups' learning outcomes.

The student's final grade was used as an indicator of learning outcomes; the final grade is the average of the overall continuous assessment score and the final exam grade. Eight continuous assessment assignments were spread over the course. Each assignment typically had four parts which related to the previous units of study. The background questionnaire and the learning style questionnaire were sent to students in the target populations at the beginning of the course. Conventional students received these materials by post and Internet students received them by electronic mail.

The research results suggest that the Internet offers students a rapid and convenient communication medium that can enable increased interaction with fellow students (both within and beyond their tutor groups) and tutors. Possibly the biggest gain for Internet students was the improved turnaround time of assignments, so that students received timely feedback. A summary of gains includes:

- Faster assignment return; more immediate feedback;
- Robust model for queries, with greater perceived reliability;
- Increased interaction with tutor and other students;
- Extending learning experiences beyond the tutorial;
- Internet experience.

Learning outcomes (as indicated by continuous assessment and final examination) were comparable, and the Internet students' experience was favorable and was one they would wish to repeat—a major factor in maintaining the enthusiasm and motivation of distance education students throughout a complete degree program.

The biggest obstacle to Internet presentation was inexperience—and cultural inexperience presented tougher obstacles than technical inexperience:

Internet presentation requires a culture shift by students and tutors. Both must learn how to cultivate communication in a largely asynchronous environment, and both must develop a sensitivity to the emerging etiquette and conventions of Internet culture. Using the Internet does imply higher expectations: students (both Internet and conventional) expect electronic communication to be faster. One of the keys to successful Internet presentation is to instill appropriate expectations among all participants (Carswell et al., 2000)

A comparison, by Collins (2000), of correspondence and Web versions of the same course indicated that, although the students were very satisfied with the Web version, the correspondence section achieved the higher mean final scores in three of the four semesters while the Web course achieved the higher mean final scores in only one semester. Each module ends with a multiple-choice quiz (with text and diagrams) which students can complete and submit for immediate online scoring and feedback. The feedback informs the student as to whether each response was correct or incorrect, and in the case of the latter gives the correct response as well as a hot-link to the subunit containing the information related to that particular question. The Web version of the course is, therefore, much more interactive than the correspondence version in which students receive, by mail, a course manual, containing the text and diagrams, in addition to the course objectives and glossary of terms, and multiple-choice quizzes with the answers provided. Students taking the correspondence version of the course do not have access to the class Web forum, and their only access to the instructor is by the phone during weekly office hours, or by email.

While most other studies, with the notable exception of Zhang (1998), have reported that there was seemingly no significant difference between the performances of students in the Web and traditional versions of courses, Collins found that the students in the Web course achieved lower mean final marks than those in the correspondence and lecture sections, although the differences were not statistically significant. As with other studies the students were very satisfied with the Web course, and gave a number of reasons they liked this approach, including the ability to study at one's own convenience, being able to communicate easily with both the instructor and classmates, and the opportunity of gaining experience with email and the Internet. But, the learning effects, as measured through the instruments used, was inferior for the Web-based students. This important aspect will be addressed further—and in depth—in the remainder of this section of our review.

In recent years, partially as a result of the so-called "technology revolution" and partially due to paradigmatic shifts in educational philosophy, both the theories and the practice of instruction have undergone significant change. In the area of learning theories, there has been a shift from a behaviorist to a constructivist view of learning as a process involving the construction of knowledge. This, in turn, has led to an increasing emphasis on collaborative learning strategies, in which people work together in small groups. The physical environment of learning is also shifting ever more from face-to-face classroom instruction, to distance-learning on the Internet.

Constructivist theory states that students should be encouraged to construct their own knowledge. Computer-mediated communication, it is argued, effectively supports constructivism because of the emphasis on access to resources and the extent of collaboration between students promoted through the use of discussion boards. Therefore, many constructivists argue, students in an online environment can construct their knowledge through active learning and collaboration and, therefore, would presumably learn more effectively. Another theoretical perspective—engagement theory—suggests that learners must be actively engaged in meaningful tasks for effective learning to take place (Kearsley & Schneiderman, 1998) and one means of providing such meaningful tasks is to engage the students in discussions. Researchers also argue that collaborative learning and social interaction play a major role in cognitive development. Collaborative learning is the "acquisition of knowledge, skills or attitudes that take place as a result of people working together to create meaning, explore a topic or improve skills" (Graham & Scarborough, 1999). Hiltz (1997) states that collaborative learning is crucial to the effectiveness of online learning environments.

Both engagement theory and collaborative learning theory would suggest that the use of discussion forums brings the students directly into contact with the content material of the course instead of leaving them on the outside as passive learners. Through this interaction, it is postulated, students are building their knowledge instead of relying on simple memorization skills. If these theoretical positions are valid, one could expect the use of discussion forums to be more effective than, for example, quizzes or objective testing as a means of promoting learning. However, both these theoretical positions seem to espouse online learning mainly because it offers tools for collaboration and so is in tune with the latest philosophical views on education in general and the learning process in particular. We see a certain circularity in the arguments presented in the literature. This lack of clarity in the arguments makes it particularly important to investigate the relative effectiveness of the two levels of interaction represented by the two most-used forms of online learning exercises: individual quizzes and group discussion forums.

The substitution of interactive "CAI" tutorial sequences, or individually completed quizzes, by online group discussions is observed to be an increasingly common practice among teachers who modify previously existing courses for online delivery. This trend is often justified from the standpoint of Collaborative Group Learning principles drawn from theories of Active Learning based on modern educational philosophies such as Constructivism. However, the available research data that would confirm these claims is scarce and inconclusive. Furthermore, given that the popularity of this trend seems to have grown with the increasing availability of efficient technology for the organization and management of threaded discussions, one may question whether theoretical principles or technological fashion are the real driving forces. It also seems that some of the specific new strategies that are being implemented in the name of new theoretical positions do not always exhibit the characteristics that these strategies should (theoretically speaking) embody. In some cases it seems that the changes are driven more by the appearance and availability of the new technologies than by any coherent set of theoretical principles.

Lewis (2002) addressed exactly these concerns when she investigated the learning effectiveness in online course contexts of two alternative forms of practice activities: asynchronous online discussion forums and individually completed quizzes. The study was conducted in existing regular courses, where learning effectiveness is formally assessed by means of objective tests derived from the subject matter content of the course. The goal of this study was to investigate the extent to which one specific change in methods and media, namely the use of asynchronous discussion environments as a component of online courses can be seen to be theory driven or technology driven. Another motivation for the study arose from the desire to understand the effectiveness of such discussion forums on students' achievement scores. Among the many as yet unanswered questions regarding Web-based courses is whether the use of asynchronous online discussion activities, as a means for providing opportunities for practice and learning, is necessarily an improvement over previously used strategies, such as quizzes.

The theory and practice of the discipline of instructional design suggests that in order to implement a new instructional approach, based on a different theory of learning, it is usually necessary to modify not one, but maybe all or most of the components of a lesson (Dills & Romiszowski, 1997; Romiszowski & Chang, 2001). However, it is currently quite common to utilize the newly available online discussion environments as the practice component of lessons that are otherwise unaltered in their basic instructional design. Existing content-presentation materials, previously used in conventional courses, are posted to the Web without any modification. The same final evaluation tests and procedures are employed, regardless of the implied modifications to the underlying course philosophy and shift in key objectives from the content to the process of learning.

The Lewis (2002) study intentionally selected just such a context for its investigation. An existing course that has for some time been offered as a conventional face-to-face course is now also being offered as an online course. This course is based on a well-established basic textbook that not only is a major source for the course content, but also includes a large questions bank from which instructors may create a variety of learning assessment instruments and practice quizzes. In the process of transforming the conventional course to an online version, little instructional design change was introduced as regards the presentation phase, in that the same textbook was made available online and similar instructor advice and support was offered. Also, little change occurred with respect to the final test or assessment phase, in that the same questions bank was used to generate final examinations. However, some of the instructors involved chose to modify the practice phase by introducing online discussion activities in place of the previously used quizzes.

This particular course that Lewis analyzed is a 15 week online course in a major university setting. The course and the instructional materials it uses (i.e., the content of 12 chapters of the set book, the test bank and any tests and unit quizzes derived from the bank) is a standard online course that is offered by three different instructors each semester at the university. The enrollment is 50 students per course. Therefore, on an average, 150 students per semester take the online version of the course, using the same course materials. The entire course syllabus, quizzes, and discussion activities are available online in a WebCT course shell.

An intact cohort of 50 students, registered to take the above-mentioned course was randomly subdivided into two experimental groups who were subjected to different treatments as regards the practice phases of the online lessons that compose the course. All students participated in quizzes for some of the lessons and in online discussions for other lessons, according to the experimental design explained below. This procedure allowed the investigator to compare the learning effectiveness of the two alternative practice procedures and also to investigate some other secondary questions. The following procedures were applied to the assignment of the participants to the treatment sequences and measurement of the results. Each participant:

- Completed an online pretest which was based upon the information contained in 12 chapters of the required textbook;
- Read the book and the lecture notes, one chapter per course unit;
- Completed six online quizzes for six of the course units (based on randomized assignment to one of two groups: Group 1 in odd and Group 2 in even units);
- Completed six threaded discussion forums for the other six course units, which were based on questions posted by the instructor on issues in the unit.
- Completed an online posttest based upon information in the textbook (exactly the same assessment procedure that has been used for years for grading both on-line and face-to-face versions of the course);
- Completed an end of course evaluation questionnaire.

The tests were taken from the test bank prepared by the publisher of the book used in the course. This book and test bank have been used for the past 3 years at the university. As stated above, the course is offered three times a semester as an online course for a total of nine times a year. Besides the online version of the course, this course is also offered three times a semester as a traditional course using the same test bank. Therefore, even though there is no available statistical analysis of the reliability of the test items, it could be inferred that the test questions do have general acceptance by expert teachers of the subject as a valid instrument by which to measure learning of the course material. Different versions of the assessment instrument (i.e., test) have been used at least six times a semester (including traditional and online courses), three times a year, over a period of 3 years, for a total of 54 times.

Fifty students began the class; however, only 37 students finished the course. Thirteen students either dropped out of the course or took an incomplete grade. The concluding 37 students remained in the same random groups and subgroups as assigned in the beginning of the course. The first step of the experiment involved the administering of a pretest. The main reason for administering a pretest was to verify that the randomly selected groups were indeed equivalent as regards entry level. Once this was established, all comparisons between the groups were made on the basis of posttest scores. Each posttest score was divided into the 12 chapter units scores. The investigator found some interesting differences among the subunit scores.

Several one-way ANOVAs were performed to test the null hypothesis: "there is no difference in the learning outcome for those who engage in discussion activities versus those who complete the quizzes." This analysis revealed that the null hypothesis is accepted for subunits 1, 3, 5, 6, 7, and 9. However, the null hypothesis was rejected for subunits 2, 4, 6, 8, 10, 11, and 12. This finding is interesting in that the Chapters 2, 4, 8, 10, and 12 are the chapters for which Group 2 did the discussion forums and Group 1 did the quizzes. These results, taken on their own, seem to suggest quite strongly that the quiz-taking activity generally leads to superior posttest performance than the discussion activity.

However, the other half of the results did not tally with this finding. The only time when there was significance when Group 2 did the quizzes and Group 1 did the discussion forums was in subunit 11. In all the other 5 such cases, the differences were not significant. The question that arises out of the data, therefore, is why is there generally no significance when Group 2 takes the quizzes and Group 1 engages in online discussion.

Let us examine these findings from yet another theoretical position—the objectivist theory of instructional design. This position has a long history of practical use and acceptance. It is arguably rather incorrect and unfair to label the position as behaviorist, because it really represents the established practice of the teaching profession from times way before the development of behaviorism. However, this position did tend to get formalized as a result of the growing popularity of the use of behavioral objectives as a basis for the design of learning activities. The practical influence of programmed instruction models reinforced the widespread acceptance, almost as an axiom, of the principle of designing the learning activities as a mirror image of the final evaluation activities. In the case of this particular study, the objectivist position would argue that we should expect the quizzes to be more effective learning activities than the discussions, because they better reflect the final test conditions used to evaluate the learning. Once more, however, one must observe that, in the present study, one part of the results supports this position, but the other part does not.

Further light is, however, shed on the results of this study if one examines the objectivist position a bit more critically. The partial result that students who participated in the discussion activities scored just as well as those who took the quizzes is in line with Mouton's (1988) findings that success on lower level testing can be achieved by the review of "higher-order learning" problem-solving questions during the practice assignments. In his study, Mouton looked at what types or combination of types of practice activities should be provided to students, studying through mediated self-instruction. The finding of the study showed that a "more stable and durable memory trace results if deeper cognitive processing occurs during encoding" (p. 97) and "students when engaged in higher level thinking questions will do as well on lower level thinking test items as students just doing lower level thinking questions."

Also predating the constructivist movements of today, Bloom (1981) suggested that, in order to be independent and active learners, the learners should engage in so-called "higher-level thinking." They should also " possess the ability to learn and solve problems, be intrinsically motivated, and possess a degree of social responsibility to interact with others in the acquisition of learning." Using the logic of Mouton and Bloom, the use of online discussion forums can be postulated to serve as an avenue for learners to obtain higher levels of achievement, even on lower-level rote-memory test instruments, than by means of participation in lower-level forms of learning activities, such as quizzes. From this theoretical position, the use of higher level thinking questions and discussions does not hinder but enhances a student's learning, even if tested by lower level thinking tests. This theoretical analysis helps to explain the partial finding in the present study that Group 1 students studying in the higher-order-thinking mode of the discussion forum did just as well as Group 2 students who studied these same subunits in the lower-order-thinking mode that was a mirror image of the final test conditions.

However, we still have the other partial result that seems to support the conventional objectivist position of designing the learning activities as a mirror-image of the testing procedures. It is difficult to escape the conclusion that, despite the apparent equivalence of the two groups, as demonstrated by means of analysis of overall pretest scores, something differentiated them during the course of the study. One factor that may have played a part is the intensity and frequency of participation in the group discussions.

To explore this question, Lewis looked at the content of the online discussions. She reviewed the number of messages read and number of messages posted to see if any differences may have had an effect on the posttest scores. A one-way ANOVA was conducted on both the messages read and messages posted by the students. There was a significant difference on messages read by students between groups. However, there was no significant difference on messages posted within the groups.

Palloff and Pratt (1999) claimed that interaction and collaboration become critical in Web-based training. They also suggested that the successful online learner is a "noisy learner" who is active and creative in the instructional environment. Students in Group 1 were more active than students in Group 2. This is apparent from the number of messages read by the students. Students who participated frequently and intensively in the online discussions could be expected to have benefited from the higher level thinking activity more than those students who engaged less thoroughly and less frequently in the discussions. Thus, a possible, though by no means proven, interpretation of the results of this study is that the difference between Group 1 and Group 2 scores is due to the varying amount of effort and frequency of participation in group discussion activities. The higher level of engagement of Group 1, as compared to Group 2, led that group to get more value out of the discussion activities and thus compensate for the "handicap" imposed by the lack of a practice exercise that directly mirrored the final evaluation.

Further research would be required in order to establish whether this hypothesis is consistently supported in practice. If it proves to be supported, one may gain some important insights into the factors that must be designed into online learning activities in order to ensure that they are effective learning experiences as measured and evaluated by the conventional, content-based, criteria that are commonly utilized by most educational systems. Finally, we may add that the study

here analyzed illustrates the importance of adopting a theory and research-based instructional design approach to Web-based education and training. One outcome of such a design approach would be to reexamine right from the start whether the maintenance of the same conventional testing procedures for the online course was theoretically justified, or was just the result of overlooking an opportunity for the improvement of that aspect of the course as well.

15.2.2 Technological Aspects

In this section, we shall address just a few of the technology-related design and use aspects of modern Web-based CMC systems. Space precludes the analysis of all the many technological solutions that have been launched on the CMC market in recent years. The approach of this section is to critique some general aspects of the current trends, rather than to focus on specific technologies and products.

The variety of Internet-based synchronous and asynchronous communication systems keeps growing. In addition to the already well-known forms of asynchronous computer-mediated communication systems, such as email, listserv and threaded discussion lists, we now use a variety of new synchronous communication alternatives, such as electronic whiteboards, Internet relay chat, Web-based audio and video conferencing, and a growing variety of "groupware" packages. As the power of the Internet grows, so does the complexity of the material posted. Ever more ambitious examples of interactive multimedia are launched on the Web every day.

A number of novel research questions and issues arise in relation to the design and use of these new systems. Much existing research is related to earlier forms of text-based CBT. Some of these results may be equally valid within the context of multimedia distance education/training systems. However, we may expect many new issues and questions to emerge as these broad band multimedia, multimodal communication systems link both people and remote databases into one seamless information and communication environment. One recurrent problem is that we tend to hop from one recently emerged technology to another currently emerging technology that promises some new potential, without ever learning to fully exploit the potential of the old. It is a sobering thought that in all the centuries since the Gutenberg print technology facilitated the mass dissemination of text, we are still struggling with the issues of mediocre textbooks, instructional manuals that fail to instruct, and communications (including online texts and hypertexts) that just do not communicate (Romiszowski & Villalba, 2000).

In addition to the communication technology and instructional design variables, another aspect to consider for improvement of existing online learning environments is the promotion of effective conversational interaction between groups of students (and instructors) engaged on a joint project. There is a growing need for the implementation of learning exercises that prepare students for the new profession of "knowledge work." These exercises should allow students to work creatively, collaboratively and at a distance on complex, leading-edge problems that impact their life and work. Teaching methods such as seminars or case studies are traditionally employed for developing creative thinking skills through collaborative effort. They are typically implemented in small or medium sized groups, led by skilled and experienced facilitators. The success of these methods depends much on the facilitators and the skill with which they perform their roles: focus the discussion; guide the approaches adopted by the participants; use the natural group dynamics to stimulate interest; promote and support participation and deep involvement by all; and pull together what has been learned in the final debriefing discussion. Can such participatory discussion methods be effectively orchestrated at a distance? How might this be done? And, most importantly, how might we do it so as to create practical and sustainable WBT systems that will survive the test of time as the initial enthusiastic "early adopters" move on to other projects and their place is taken by the rank and file of the teaching/training profession?

In a recent study, Villalba and Romiszowski (1999) performed a comparative analysis of typical online learning environments currently used in higher education and the typical ways in which these environments are used to implement collaborative group learning activities. The findings indicated that few currently implemented online courses actually include a strong emphasis on collaborative small-group learning and, when such activities are implemented, this is generally as a relatively unstructured online group discussion, using either synchronous chat sessions or, more frequently, asynchronous email driven discussion lists. There is little if any research, however, indicating that such environments are conducive to in-depth reflective discussions of the type required to develop critical and creative thinking skills. And there are some studies (e.g., Romiszowski & DeHaas, 1989; Romiszowski & Chang, 1992) that suggest they are singularly ineffective in this respect. As a means of verifying these suggestions, the authors selected one of the previously evaluated online learning environments, Aulanet, for further in-depth study.

Aulanet is a Web-based instruction environment, developed in Brazil (Lucena et al., 1998), which is also available in an English language version. It was selected as it offered a wider variety of online discussion environments than most other currently available systems. In addition to the regular e-mail, both threaded and unthreaded asynchronous discussion environments and text-based synchronous chat rooms, options are available for audio audiographic and full video-conference sessions in small or large groups. In addition, the creators of Aulanet claim the system is based on or influenced by contemporary theories of cognition and constructivism. Villalba and Romiszowski (1999) analyzed the use of Aulanet as a delivery system for four courses running through several semesters. The study involved both the observation of student use of different collaborative learning environments provided within Aulanet and the analysis of student questionnaire responses and user-evaluations administered during the course of the academic year.

In that study the students made some quite significant suggestions for enhancement of the learning environment. A major observation is concerned with the structure of facilities for constructive educational "conversations." The many and various components of Aulanet that permit both synchronous and asynchronous student/teacher and student/student interaction

are seen to be no different from the facilities that exist in many other online learning packages currently on the market. Both faculty and students have come across limitations in the available group communication facilities that limit what they can implement in the way of "creative group work at a distance."

In a similar vein, Chen and Hung (2002) highlight a technology-related concern with using online discussion for learning. They argue that there is a lack of technological support for the development of personalized knowledge representation in most online discussion forums. Analyses of existing discussion forums suggest that there is a range of collective knowledge representation mechanisms which support a group or a community of learners. However, such mechanisms "may not necessarily lead to learners' internalization of collective knowledge into personalized knowledge." They discuss how internalization can be facilitated through the notion of "knowledge objects," while externalization can be mediated by "idea artefacts." These notions are translated into technological supports and suggestions of how online discussions can be designed differently from the common threaded discussion.

> The recent proliferation of student online discussions calls for a re-examination of the meaning of knowledge. Though not explicitly or intentionally so designed, most discussion forums seem to focus more on supporting the construction of collective knowledge rather than on the construction of personalized understanding. There seems to be an assumption that during the processes of social dialogue, students' personal understanding is automatically guaranteed. The situation could well be that individual students have developed personalized understanding differently and perhaps with misconceptions. In essence, how can we better facilitate the process of constructing personalized understanding in relation to collective understanding? (Chen & Hung, 2002)

The distinction between personalized and collective knowledge representations questions the assumption that participants in the social dialogue will automatically acquire "the intersubjectivity reached within a particular community of learners." By *only* supporting the construction of the collective knowledge representation the authors argue that:

> . . . we may unknowingly discourage or even impede students' personal understanding because (a) such support does not foster/facilitate personalized understanding; (b) it provides limited opportunity for multiple foci in discussion and thus does not cater for the varying needs of individuals; and (c) the mass of contributions remains overwhelming. We argue for the necessity of technological supports for this transformation. In addition, we also challenge the adequacy of the traditional threaded discussion representations, which, we believe, are problematic in at least four areas: (a) difficulty in summarizing the current state of the discussion, (b) difficulty in referring (or linking) to a message posted earlier (thus, the need for an easy way to index and refer to messages), (c) difficulty in determining which thread to go to because a message could be related to more than one message, and (d) difficulty in tracking all messages and filtering only the relevant ones. (Chen & Hung, 2002)

Chen and Hung (2002) propose that knowledge representations, though not the knowledge itself, can be transitional aids and supports to the dialectic internalization and externalization processes. For example, the threads of a discussion are visual representations that bring together all externalizations from participants. In other words, these visualizations facilitate and coordinate the organization of the collective knowledge representation. In a similar manner, the personalized knowledge representation would assist individuals to internalize the current state of the discussion, translate it into personalized knowledge objects, and later integrate it into their own existing schema. It is then logical to think of two types of technological support, one for collective knowledge representation (for externalization and negotiation) and the other for personalized representation (for internalization).

In an ideal online discussion environment, students would have access to both collective and personalized representations. They could even superimpose the two to perform further compare and contrast. It is also possible to design the system in such a way that if a learner wishes, he/she could publish annotated remarks on why certain messages are included or excluded and why certain links are made the way they are. Most current online discussion systems only support collective knowledge representation, which primarily facilitates the externalization and negotiation of intuitive inspirations or ideas. Chen and Hung (2002) argue for the need to support personalized knowledge representations in order to cater for individual differences:

Personalized knowledge representations are the transitional states of knowledge and understanding in the process of internalization from objective knowledge to subjective knowledge. When translated to technological supports, the objective knowledge could be represented by the collective knowledge representation of an online discussion forum; the knowledge objects could be illustrated by personalized knowledge representations; and idea artifacts could be messages, which every individual learner contributes. Without these supporting mechanisms, students may soon be overwhelmed by the massive number of messages or de-motivated to participate due to inflexibility in choosing the more relevant topics to pursue. (Chen & Hung, 2002)

It is clear that more research studies are needed to test the arguments and approaches proposed in this paper, in particular of the internalization process. But, we believe that the authors have suggested an attractive alternative to current states of online discussions. As CMC systems are used ever more frequently in contexts of continuing adult education in the workplace, the issues related to knowledge capture, knowledge management and its storage in forms that serve the purposes of other users of the newly created knowledge base will take on ever greater importance. So will the development of online tools that may help the users of this knowledge to use it productively in the process of knowledge work. An underlying process of importance in this context is productive learning which, according to Collis and Winnips (2002), is defined as:

...learning that can be reused, in application to new problem situations in an organization or for assimilation and reflection in structured learning situations such as courses. An important but under-exploited form of productive learning relates to the capture and reuse of the tacit knowledge of members of an organization. (Collis & Winnips, 2002)

Collis and Winnips describe two approaches for this reuse of tacit knowledge, along with instructional strategies and technologies to support the knowledge capture and reuse process

within each of the approaches. In one of the approaches the emphasis is on how those in mentor or supervisor positions can more systematically support the diffusion of their own tacit knowledge to those of their mentees and in the process create new knowledge for reuse in other situations. In the second illustration, a change in orientation from knowledge transfer to knowledge creation and sharing in the formal training programs of the organization is the focus. An underlying database as well as easy-to-use tools for resource entry and indexing are key elements in facilitating the reuse of experience-based resources within and across both informal and formal learning.

15.3 THE CMC PROCESS

15.3.1 Student Participation

15.3.1.1 Dynamics of the CMC Process. In one of several early studies, Warschauer (1996, 1997) examined the nature of computer-mediated communication (CMC) and its potential in promoting collaborative language learning. He examined various features of CMC in terms of their relationship to theories of collaboration and interaction in education and in language teaching. The most significant of these theories in this study is the "*text-mediational*" interpretation of Vygotsky. Warschauer (1997) states that by bringing together the concepts of expression, interaction, reflection, problem solving, critical thinking, and literacy, and seeing how these concepts are tied together through various uses of talk, text, inquiry, and collaboration in the classroom, the text-mediational view of Vygotsky provides an extremely useful framework for understanding collaborative learning in the language classroom and for evaluating the potential of online education to assist that process. The author then explores several aspects of text-based and computer-mediated interaction and how these aspects relate to the text-mediational interpretation of Vygotsky. Among the apects of CMC examined by Warschauer (1987) are "many-to-many communication," "synchronous discussion in the composition classroom," "synchronous discussion in the foreign language classroom," "time- and place-independent communication," "long-distance exchanges" (both one-to-one and many-to many), and "hypermedia information and student publishing." Warschauer (1997) that all of the long-distance activities described above have several important elements in common. First, the activities are experiential and goal-oriented, with collaborative projects carried out and shared with classmates and foreign partners via the Internet and other means. Second, issues of linguistic form are not dropped out but rather are subsumed within a meaningful context. Finally, international collaboration is combined with in-class collaboration; students work in groups to decide their research questions, evaluate responses from afar, and report and discuss their findings.

These words would seem to summarize many of the dynamic process factors of CMC that are of relevance to much more than the context of language learning. However, much of the early in-depth research into the dynamics of the online learning process seems to have been performed in this context. For example,

Leppänen and Kalaja (1995) discuss an "experiment where computer conferencing (CC) was used in English for Academic Purposes (EAP) in the context of a content-area course." They tested the possibilities offered by CC in the Department with a group of first-year students taking a two-term course in British and American Institutions consisting of a series of lectures, discussions in small groups and reading and writing assignments on relevant topics. Of interest are the class discussions in which the students participated electronically. In these discussions, the

... tutor's role turned out to be a fairly passive one. In CC it was the students, and not the teacher, who dominated. In the ESL classroom, in contrast, the teacher normally dominates and does most of the talking. The students, in turn, when they talk, tend to respond only to the teachers question. In the experiment, the students also started off by responding to the tutor's questions, but soon they did other things as well—asked questions, argued, initiated new topic, expressed opinions, commented on each other's messages, etc. (Leppänen & Kalaja, 1995)

Toyoda and Harrison (2002) examined the negotiation of meaning that took place between students and native speakers of Japanese over a series of chat conversations and attempted to categorize the difficulties encountered. The data showed that the difficulties in understanding each other did indeed trigger negotiation of meaning between students even when no specific communication tasks were given. Using discourse analysis methods, the negotiations were sorted into nine categories according to the causes of the difficulties: recognition of new word, misuse of word, pronunciation error, grammatical error, inappropriate segmentation, abbreviated sentence, sudden topic change, slow response, and intercultural communication gap. Through the examination of these categories of negotiation, it was found that there were some language aspects that are crucial for communication but that had been neglected in teaching, and that students would not have noticed if they had not had the opportunity to chat with native speakers. In light of these findings, the authors make pedagogical recommendations for improving chat conversations.

In another language-learning-related study, Sotillo (2000) investigated discourse functions and syntactic complexity in English-as-a-second-language (ESL) learner output obtained via two different modes of computer-mediated communication (CMC): asynchronous and synchronous discussions. Two instructors and 25 students from two advanced ESL writing classes participated in this study. Answers were sought to the following questions:

(a) Are the discourse functions present in ESL learners' synchronous discussions of reading assignments quantitatively and qualitatively different from those found in asynchronous discussions?

(b) Which mode of CMC shows more syntactically complex learner output?

The results showed that the quantity and types of discourse functions present in synchronous discussions were similar to the types of interactional modifications found in face-to-face conversations that are deemed necessary for second language acquisition. Discourse functions in asynchronous discussions were more constrained than those found in synchronous discussions and similar to the question–response–evaluation sequence of the traditional language classroom. Concerning syntactic complexity, the delayed nature of asynchronous discussions gives learners more opportunities to produce syntactically complex language. Sotillo concludes that "asynchronous and synchronous CMC have different discourse features which may be exploited for different pedagogical purposes."

We now proceed from the language-learning context to consider some general aspects of thinking and learning. Writers such as Schon (1983) have alerted the educational community to the importance on reflection-in-action as a learning strategy. Salmon (2000) suggests that, through the provision of opportunities for reflection-in-action at critical learning stages and with the support of a trained e-moderator, the participants in computer mediated conferencing (CMC) can be encouraged to engage in reflecting about their online experiences. Such reflection aids the building of a productive online community of practice. In addition, by encouraging participants to reflect on later stages of their online training experiences, a reflection-on-action record can be built up. Participants' reflective processes can be captured through analysis of their onscreen text messages and so be available for research purposes. Examples of conference text message reflections are given throughout the paper, drawn from the onscreen reflections of Open University Business School (OUBS) associate lecturers who were working online through the medium of computer mediated conferencing for the first time. The conclusion is that reflection-on-practice in the online environment is beneficial for helping the participants to learn from online conferencing and can provide an excellent tool for qualitative research. Opportunities for reflection, says Salmon, need to be built into the design of online conferences and facilitated by a trained e-moderator.

Curtis and Lawson (2001) investigated the extent to which evidence of collaborative learning could be identified in students' textual interactions in an online learning environment. The literature on collaborative learning has identified a range of behaviors that characterize successful collaborative learning in face-to-face situations. Evidence of these behaviors was sought in the messages that were posted by students as they interacted in online work groups.

Analysis of students' contributions revealed that there is substantial evidence of collaboration, but that there are differences between conventional face-to-face instances of collaborative learning and what occurs in an asynchronous, networked environment. There is some commonality between the collaborative behaviors in face-to-face situations and those observed in this study, although there are some important differences. Those differences include the lack of 'challenge and explain' cycles of interaction that are thought to characterize good interchanges in face-to-face tutorials. The significant presence of planning activities within groups interactions, the extent of which seems to be related to communication limitations imposed by the lack of good real-time interaction support tools, was another notable difference between face-to-face and asynchronous online interactions.

In a similar vein of inquiry, Jonassen and Kwon (2001) compared the perceptions of participants, the nature of the comments made, and the patterns of communication in face-to-face and computer-mediated groups in terms of problem-solving activities while solving well-structured and ill-structured problems. Findings indicated that students in the computer-conferencing groups perceived that communicating asynchronously through the conference was a higher quality and more satisfying experience than did F2F students; that students in the computer-conferencing environment used more task-directed and focused communications while solving both well-structured and ill-structured problems; and that students' patterns of communications in the computer-conferencing groups better reflected the problem-solving nature of the task when compared with the F2F environment. Although most participants indicated in their comments that the major advantage of computer conferencing was its flexibility and convenience, the more important implication is that participants perceived the flexibility to be conducive to deep and reflective thinking, as indicated in participants' comments.

Participants believed that even though they had to make a greater effort to communicate with other group members in the computer conferencing environment, they were satisfied with the group process because the greater levels of personal reflection and critical thinking facilitated better decisions.

That computer conferencing groups required four to six days to complete a group assignment, while most face-to-face groups finished their group assignments within one hour, confirms the greater opportunity for reflection and supports the beliefs of Kaye, Mason, and Harasim (1991) that the computer conferencing environment leads to more reflection and debate. (Jonassen and Kwon, 2001, p. 46)

The authors comment that these results are not consistent with the findings of Olaniran et al. (1996) who found that F2F groups were perceived as more effective, easier, and more satisfying than CMC groups. However, this study confirmed other research that found that group interactions in computer conferences are more task-oriented compared to face-to-face discussions (Olaniran, Friedrich, & VanGrundy, 1992). Both the total number of messages and the number of nontask messages in computer conferencing were smaller than those in face-to-face group negotiations. The study also supports previous research which showed that virtual groups tend to be more task oriented and exchange less social-emotional information (Chidambaram, 1996).

In addition to differences in participants' perceptions and the content of their messages, the patterns of reasoning, as reflected in their communications, also differed. The group interaction patterns in the computer conference were more complex and more similar to problem-solving processes than those in the F2F meetings.

Results of the cluster analysis indicated that the group interaction patterns were influenced by communication mode and to a lesser degree influenced by task variables. Activities were grouped into four different clusters that generally reflected the communication mode as well as the nature of the task (well-structured vs. ill-structured problem solving). Therefore, interaction between communication mode and task variable was a primary predictor of group activities into four patterns. (Jonassen and Kwon, 2001, p. 48)

15.3.1.2 Online Community Development. As Internet-based education applications began to proliferate, educators and researchers turned their attention to issues related to building community among the online learners (Bruffee, 1993; Dede, 1990, 1996; Harasim, Hiltz, Teles & Turoff, 1995; Kaye, 1995). As online programs replace the on-campus experience, there is increasing interest in understanding how interactions among learners are being addressed in the online world. There is, among other issues, a need to understand what community means in these environments. The emphasis on creating community is fueled by research that reveals a number of positive outcomes for individuals and the learning communities to which they belong. The strong interpersonal ties shared by community members increase the flow of information among all members, the availability of support, commitment to group goals, cooperation among members, and satisfaction with group efforts (Argyle, 1991; Bruffee, 1993; Dede, 1996; Harasim et al., 1995; Wellman, 1999). Individuals tend to benefit from community membership by experiencing a greater sense of well being and happiness, and having a larger set of colleagues to call on for support in times of need (Haines & Hurlbert, 1992; Haines, Hurlbert & Beggs, 1996; Walker, Wasserman, & Wellman, 1994; Wellman & Gulia, 1999b).

However, the situation in many learning communities is different from what many of these authors describe. First, the classic community model is bound to the notion of people living close to each other, interacting face-to-face to share companionship and support of all kinds (Wellman, 1999). So, too, our concept of learning communities is typically bound up with the notions of university campuses and physical colleges. How can we build community without a physical place, and through computer media that are unable to transmit the full range of verbal and nonverbal cues necessary to support strong interpersonal ties?

Second, there are different classes of communities described in the literature. Some authors focus on learning communities, as a general category (Baker & Moss, 1996; Bauman, 1997; Cross, 1998; Haythornthwaite, 1998; Hill & Raven, 2000; Kowch & Schwier, 1997; Palloff & Pratt, 1999; Rasmussen & Skinner, 1997; Raymond, 1999; Riel, 1998; Schwier, 1999; Wilson & Ryder, 1996). Others distinguish between learning communities and communities of practice (Lave, 1993; Lave & Wenger, 1991; Wenger, 1998). Yet others single out the special characteristics of virtual or online communities (Kim, 2000; Preece, 2000; Wellman, 1999; Wellman, Carrington, & Hall, 1988; Wellman & Guila, 1999a, 1999b).

Some studies of online environments have found that one can indeed create community and sustain strong ties through electronic media (e.g., Baym 1995, 1997; McLaughlin, Osborne, & Smith, 1995; Reid, 1995; Rheingold, 1993; Smith, McLaughlin, & Osborne, 1996). These studies show that when we view community as what people do together, rather than where or through what means they do them, we can see that community can exist separate from physical boundaries such as campuses (Wellman, 1999). Yet other studies suggest that online participants in email networks, newsgroups, chat rooms and MUD environments support common goals and a strong commitment to the purpose and tone of their community (Baym,

1995; Curtis, 1997; Donath 1999; King, Grinter, & Pickering, 1997; Reid, 1995; Rheingold, 1993). They recognize boundaries that define who belongs and who does not, establishing their own hierarchies of expertise, their own vocabularies and modes of discourse (Marvin, 1995; Sproull & Kiesler, 1991). They may develop special rules and behaviors, even community rituals (Bruckman, 1997; Fernback, 1999; Jones, 1995, 1998; Kollock & Smith, 1999; McLaughlin, Osborne, & Smith, 1996).

In one study, singled out from this plethora for its unusual and unique contribution to the literature, Bruckman (1997) asserts that too much attention is paid to the Internet's ability to provide access to information and not enough to its use as a "context for learning through community-supported collaborative construction."

A constructionist approach to use of the Internet makes particularly good use of its educational potential. The Internet provides opportunities to move beyond the creation of constructionist tools and activities to the creation of constructionist cultures.

These issues are explored through a specific example: MOOSE Crossing, a text-based virtual world (or MUD) designed to be a constructionist learning environment for children ages 8 to 13. On MOOSE Crossing, children construct a virtual world together, making new places, objects, and creatures. Bruckman's thesis discusses the design principles underlying a new programming language (MOOSE) and client interface (MacMOOSE) designed to make it easier for children to learn to program. It presents a detailed analysis, using an ethnographic methodology, of children's activities and learning experiences on MOOSE Crossing, with special focus on seven children who participated in a weekly after-school program. In its analysis of children's activities, this thesis explores the relationship between construction and community. It describes how the MOOSE Crossing children motivated and supported one another's learning experiences: community provided support for learning through design and construction. Conversely, construction activities helped to create a particularly special, intellectually engaging sort of community. Finally, it argues that the design of all virtual communities, not just those with an explicitly educational focus, can be enhanced by a constructionist approach.

However, the special characteristics of groups (cohorts) in formal educational contexts are rather specific and in many ways different from the types of communities described in much of the literature quoted above (including Bruckman's thesis). For example, the virtual community literature puts much emphasis on attracting members and defining the community based on common interests. But in many educational contexts the students are "forced" to form a community by the structure of the course they are taking. Outsiders, who are not registered on the given course, are not allowed to participate. And the course participants are not a special-interest group of people who share common goals and can share relevant experience and knowledge. Unlike an informal learning community, which is based on a self-selected group of people coming together for informal learning purposes, the formal learning community is largely defined and structured by others than the actual community members. Obviously, students may be encouraged to bring their experience and knowledge to bear on their coursework, but nevertheless, the learning in question will be much more restricted and externally defined than an informal learning community.

Misanchuk and Anderson (2002) discuss the above mentioned argument in a paper that proposes specific strategies for moving an online class "from cohort to community." The authors give suggestions for instructional and noninstructional strategies that have students interacting at the levels of communication, cooperation and collaboration. Strategies that fall into the instructional category include: ways of presenting material; assignment design; team management; content covered; strategies for discussing material. Noninstructional strategies include: creating a computer support system so that students look beyond the technology; making reserve readings and other library resources readily available to distance students; designing an onsite orientation that encourages students to quickly bond with each other at the beginning of the program; creating an online café for off-topic discussions; dealing with team/class disputes. The authors also identify a range of questions requiring further research. These include:

- What are valid measures of community development?
- How can learners be motivated to take part in community activities?
- What are the special features of the "forced community"?
- What is the expected/observed life cycle of the typical learning community?
- How does this community develop and maintain its history?
- Should the distance community be integrated with the residential graduate community? If so, how can this be accomplished?
- How can the community best be mentored?
- What are the different roles for instructors, graduate assistants, volunteers, etc?
- What communication/collaboration tools foster the development of a learning community?
- What are the best practices for using existing communication tools in distance education?
- What tool features lend themselves to different aspects of collaboration and community building?

Some recent research studies have addressed at least a few of this list of questions. Rovai (2002a, 2002b) investigated how the sense of community differs between students enrolled in traditional face-to-face and those enrolled in asynchronous learning network (ALN) courses. Subjects consist of 326 adult learners who were enrolled in a mix of 14 undergraduate and graduate courses at two urban universities. As operationalized by the Sense of Classroom Community Index (SCCI), there appears no significant difference in classroom community between the two groups of subjects. However, a discriminant analysis shows a significant overall difference in community structure between the two groups. Variations between groups on feelings of similarity of needs, recognition, importance of learning, connectedness, friendship, thinking critically, safety, acceptance, group identity, and absence of confusion are the characteristics contributing mostly to this difference in learning effectiveness.

Brown (2001) discusses the process of community building in CMC, very much from the perspective of the students participating in the learning community. Based on interviews with 21 adult learners participating in online courses, she outlines a three-stage process of community development. The first stage was making friends online with whom students felt comfortable communicating. The second stage was community conferment (acceptance) which occurred when students were part of a long, thoughtful, threaded discussion on a subject of importance after which participants felt both personal satisfaction and kinship. The third stage was camaraderie which was achieved after long-term or intense association with others involving personal communication. Each of these stages involved a greater degree of engagement in both the class and the dialogue. She lists several helpful strategies to get the students to participate more fully in the social aspects of the forming community:

- Early discussion of community and its potential benefits may create a perceived need that students will then want to fill. Certainly the discussion will convey that community is a course expectation so students will work to meet it.
- Building opportunities for the students to learn more about each other to facilitate early discovery of commonalities. Asking the students to provide e-mail addresses, phone numbers (suggested but not required) and FAX numbers to encourage communication beyond the required responses.
- Asking them to note in the cafeteria when they are planning to go to what conferences or to be on-site because others from class may be there, and they could meet face-to-face.
- Using a "community reflection piece," perhaps three times a semester, in which students note what they have done to contribute to community, what others have done to help them feel more a part of a community, what this has accomplished, and what still needs to be attained.

Another perspective on community building is offered by Oren, Mioduser, and Nachmias (2002), reporting on five studies at Tel Aviv University, that explored social climate issues in both synchronous and asynchronous online activities in academic courses. These studies focused on the following questions: Does a social atmosphere develop in online learning discussion groups? What are the different modes of social interaction are manifest in online learning discussion groups? What is the role of the virtual teacher with regard to the social climate in online learning discussion groups?

Their research shows that teachers find it difficult to change their dominant role to that of moderators and facilitators of learning. As a result, students neither have enough opportunities to interact with each other, nor are they directed to develop self-initiative and make active contributions to the collaborative learning process. Social behavior is a natural human need and is acknowledged as an important factor in the development of learning processes. In their tutoring and moderating of virtual learning groups, teachers should explicitly support creation of a social climate with learning groups. With respect to the teachers' role in promoting community, the authors suggest that online teachers should:

- Moderate the group's work in a way that enables students to interact;
- Encourage participants to create a relaxed and calm atmosphere;
- Be attentive to participants' social needs;
- Offer a legitimate platform for messages that have social significance;
- Enhance the social atmosphere by using supportive feedback, discussing with the group ways to facilitate the creation of social interactions, emphasizing the importance of peer feedback, and by encouraging students to relate to each other during the learning activities and beyond.

Further observations at the level of the *pedagogical rationale* of online courses are related to aspects such as the character of the assignments included in the course, the focus of the discussion forums, or the identities assumed by the students. Examples of these are:

- Group work should be encouraged and course developers should aim to define learning assignments that demand varied forms of interaction and collaboration.
- Teachers should implement learning strategies that support communication such as appointing students to moderate discussion groups or encouraging students to help each other and to refer to each other.
- Course developers should create a varied range of virtual spaces in order to respond to different social needs evolving during the group's work.
- A distance learning course should include a social forum as a place for social integration of the learning group.
- It should also include a forum in which students can find contextual (e.g., technical, content-related) help.
- In order to achieve the degree of intimacy required for significant exchanges within online interactions, the number of participants be limited to 20.

This list of suggestions quite clearly places to responsibility for the building of a social climate and community on the course developers and teaching staff involved. It is not surprising, therefore, that in the remainder of their paper, the authors stress appropriate teacher training as a key factor in the "design of successful models of socially sound technology based learning."

15.3.2 Teacher Participation

15.3.2.1 Teaching Strategies in CMC. Online teachers have at their disposal a variety of novel strategies that they may incorporate in their lesson plans. Some of these, such as online threaded discussion lists, have already been discussed earlier. Others will be mentioned in this section. They also face some novel problems, for example the relatively greater difficulty of keeping a virtual group working in an asynchronous mode "on task" or "on topic" (Romiszowski & DeHaas, 1989). Recent studies have begun to offer solutions to some of these problems.

Beaudin (1999) identifies various techniques recommended and used by online instructors for keeping online learners on topic during asynchronous discussion and researches what factors affected their selection. A 37-item online questionnaire was developed and completed by 135 online instructors. Thirteen techniques for keeping online asynchronous learners on topic were rated using a six-point Likert scale. The online instructors rated the following as the top four techniques for keeping asynchronous online discussion on topic:

1. Carefully design questions that specifically elicit on-topic discussion.
2. Provide guidelines to help online learners prepare on-topic responses.
3. Reword the original question when responses are going in the wrong direction.
4. Provide discussion summary on a regular basis.

A common element for learning in a typical classroom environment is the social and communicative interactions between student and teacher, and student and student. In examinations of interaction, the concept of presence or a sense of being in a place and belonging to a group also has received attention. However, as this concept is studied, the definition is expanding and being refined to include telepresence, cognitive presence, social presence, teaching presence, and other forms of presence. The term community is related to presence and refers to a group of individuals who belong to a social unit such as students in a class. In an online course, terms such as communities of inquiry, communities of learners, and knowledge-building communities have evolved. As the definition of presence has expanded and evolved, a distinction is being made between interaction and presence, emphasizing that they are not the same. Interaction may indicate presence but it is also possible for a student to interact by posting a message on an electronic bulletin board while not necessarily feeling that she or he is a part of a group or a class. If they are different, then it is also possible that interaction and presence can affect student performance independently.

Anderson et al. (2001) developed a tool for the purpose of assessing *teaching presence* in online courses that make use of computer conferencing. The concept of *teaching presence* is defined as having three categories—design and organization, facilitating discourse, and direct instruction. Indicators that we search for in the computer conference transcripts identify each category. Pilot testing of the instrument reveals differences in the extent and type of teaching presence found in different graduate level online courses. Results show the pattern of teaching presence varying considerably between two courses (in education and health) facilitated by two experienced online teachers.

Liu and Ginther (2002) review the knowledge base for verbal and nonverbal factors affecting impression formation in both FtF and CMC environments. Based on this review, instructional strategies for achieving effective communication and a positive impression in CMC distance education courses are proposed.

These recommendations cover both verbal and nonverbal strategies. The verbal strategies discussed include:following language norms for greetings, information sequencing, reciprocity, and appropriate compliment giving; using standard discourse schemas—interpersonal, rhetorical, and narrative—selectively, in accordance with the nature of the topic being communicated; using pragmatic and syntactic codes selectively; using intense language, such as strongly worded messages, to express their attitudes toward the topic being communicated; using immediate language; using a wide range of vocabulary; using powerful language style; selecting appropriate verbal influence strategies when being involved in disagreements and/or persuasive learning tasks; using appropriate ironic remarks.

The nonverbal strategies discussed include: using paralinguistic cues such as emoticons appropriately; taking into account chronemics; maintaining a high frequency of messaging; maintaining longer duration messages; maintaining a fast reply of messaging; manipulating primacy effect; manipulating recency effect; ensuring no typing errors. Rossman (1999) performed a document analysis of more than 3000 course evaluations from 154 courses conducted during 11 consecutive quarters. The narrative responses were grouped into the following categories: faculty feedback, learner discussions, and course requirements. General observations related to these categories are presented followed by several tips for successful teaching in an online environment using an asynchronous learner discussion forum. The tips were initially generated by the document analysis. Additional tips were then added and the list was revised each quarter following the end-of-quarter teleconference with the instructors. The tips discussed include the following.

A. Faculty Feedback: Weekly notes on class business; encourage learners to send private e-mail messages or to phone the instructor as appropriate; send personal notes throughout the online course to simulate the informal chat that often occurs at the beginning of a traditional class; keep track of those who respond and those who do not; encourage learners to complete course evaluations; encourage learners to engage each other in debate; post relevant citations or URLs; encourage learners to be on the lookout for URLs that interface with the course content units and to post them to the discussion forum for all to see; keep track of these to enhance the next offering of the course.

B. Facilitating Discussion: Present a personal introduction the first week. Send a picture of yourself to all learners at all sites. Encourage learners to pass on to one another any helpful hints they may have or hear about regarding success at the home institution. Let learners know if you are comfortable with a first name basis for those who wish to address you by your first name. Use synchronous postings to the discussion forum and allow learners to post at their convenience. Post a weekly summary of the class discussion for the prior week. Make every effort to keep learners up to speed with the discussion's progress. Monitor the quality and regularity of learner postings. Keep all comments positive in the forum— discuss negative feedback privately. Learners frequently have expertise related to the subject matter of the course and should be encouraged to share their knowledge with their classmates. Keep notes about each learner so that you are reminded about learner interests and experience.

C. Course Requirements Be sure to let the class know what your expectations are for the course. Be sure to negotiate the final project requirements, if required, with the learner well in advance of the time it is due. Be sure to find the time at the end to go through all the final papers or projects.

Campos, Laferrière, and Harasim (2001) analyse the teaching practices of postsecondary educators who integrated asynchronous electronic conferencing in over 100 mixed-mode courses at eight North American institutions between 1996 and 1999. Quantitative and qualitative research methods were applied to assess their practices and to further understand the correlation between the use of electronic conferencing and the degree of collaboration achieved. Based on the findings, pedagogical approaches for the use of electronic conferencing are provided, and are grouped according to the level of collaboration. As a result of this study, the authors present a suggested model for the networked classroom to foster and guide the transformation of pedagogical practice.

The study suggests that educators are integrating conferencing technology into their teaching in creative and dynamic ways. Results point to a re-discovery of the art of teaching with the support of new technologies. The authors suggest that even the most individualized activity presents a minimal level of collaboration. The findings highlight the pedagogical opportunities that technology offers to education and the profound changes that networked classrooms may bring to the very nature of the teaching and learning experience. This study also demonstrates the more online experience educators possess, the less they focus on individual processes and the more they benefit from the advantages and collaborative possibilities that new learning technologies bring. Finally, the authors claim that educators are learning how to integrate networked activities through applying and transferring their face-to-face expertise into the online environment. The findings and model identified present a first step for considering the dynamics of online course design.

15.3.2.2 Teacher Training and Development.

One question raised by the previous paragraphs might be: So where do the online teachers gain their initial experience and expertise in online teaching? The answer most commonly offered is "On the Internet." This response may imply "learning by doing," but it also implies "learning from others, through knowledge-sharing in virtual communities of like-minded teachers." The literature on the use of such communities of practice is, as we have seen, quite extensive. However, in the case of the use of such communities for in service teacher development (whether for online or conventional teaching duties), the literature is not very conclusive.

Zhao and Rop (2000) present a critical review of the literature on networks as reflective discourse communities for teachers, that merits more detailed analysis. The study was guided by five questions.

First, why were electronic networks developed for teacher professional development? Second, what beliefs about the benefits of electronic teacher networks for professional development are evidenced by the goals of the networks? Third, to what extent were these claims evaluated in the literature? Fourth, to what extent were the claimed benefits realized? And last, what factors (e.g., technological and social arrangements, and participants' cognitive and affective characteristics) seem to be related to the degree of success or failure?

Twenty-eight papers, describing 14 networks that "ranged from small local efforts to huge national projects, and from early, pioneering ventures to very recent and current undertakings," were analyzed according to criteria established for the five research questions. It may be interesting to summarize the findings related to each of these questions, as they shed much light on the current state of the research on many topics associated with CMC.

Why Electronic Teacher Networks? The characteristics of CMC technologies that have been most frequently promoted in the literature as having the potential to counter the difficulties in teacher professional development are their power to transcend time and space. Furthermore, CMC technologies are believed to have the potential to individualize professional development. In addition, telecommunications technology may encourage the reflection needed for long-term teacher growth in several ways. Written interaction allows time to carefully shape discourse. This may encourage reflection and enable participation for some teachers. Network interactions also offer various degrees of anonymity. For some individuals this may encourage a freedom of expression and comfort level that allows them to address issues that they may not feel free to share with school colleagues (Hawkes, 1997; Zhao, 1998).

What Claims Were Made for the Effects of the Network? It is often claimed that networks had a number of positive effects on their participants: they supposedly reduced teacher isolation, enabled cooperative curriculum development, facilitated the dissemination of information, and provided easy access to curricular materials. The network also connected teachers to "local, national, and global communities of peers and experts," providing links to subject matter Internet resources, providing support for teachers and students in using community-based projects for math and science learning, and providing collaborative research opportunities. The network also supported conversations and "philosophical" discussions in addition to information and practical suggestions, and increased teachers' understanding of the national standards. Finally, it was claimed that networks provided emotional support for their participants and encouraged the feeling of belonging to a group. The general tendency is to assume that a group of people connected and periodically interacting via some kind of CMC technology constitutes an online community. Both in the larger body of literature that we initially explored and in the set of papers on the 14 networks examined, community is a term that generally is used as casually as it is pervasively. Although these networks were identified as communities, they were not necessarily identified as reflective discourse communities. The number of networks identified as "reflective discourse communities" is much smaller (about 34%). The concept of reflection and discourse as terms for substantive, thoughtful conversations, although not as commonly occurring as ideas of community, do appear repeatedly in the literature.

To What Extent Were the Claims Evaluated? It is evident that beliefs about benefits shaped the network goals, but it is not common that the subsequent claims were carefully examined in the literature. Very few of these networks were subjected to a research process to determine if community did indeed exist; further, there were very limited indications of what community might be, and no concerted effort to define the concept. In most cases the only evidence that could be garnered for the existence of a community was that a number of people were communicating with each other.

Were the Claimed Benefits Realized? Most of the literature does not provide enough evidence to answer this question in any scientific fashion. In some cases authors made effective cases for specific claims. The more limited and specific the claims, the more likely that they were supported. However, in many cases, broad claims were made without supporting evidence. It is also safe to suggest that not many reflective discourse communities, in the true sense of the words reflective, discourse, and community, were realized in these efforts.

What Factors Are Related to the Success of Networks? Although a lot of time, money, energy, and commitment are being spent in trying to use telecommunications to link teachers, it seems apparent that the majority of these efforts are only mildly successful, even on their own terms. Some common factors surface which are necessary but not sufficient conditions for simply getting teachers talking to each other. We highlight some of these in the following paragraphs.

Technology. Teachers' technological proficiency, access to equipment, and the stability of the technology have been reported to influence the success of networks. Several of the networks in this study found that their greater goals were limited or prevented by the teachers' technical difficulties.

Motivation. Teachers must have some reason to talk to each other in the first place. We found that most of the networks were developed by university researchers with support from government agencies or private foundations. Very often the reasons for using the networks were determined by these researchers or project leaders, and not by teachers.

Project Time Frames. Most of the networks had a relatively short life span. Consequently, few networks reached a point where a clear assessment of the project was viable. Many reports focused on suggestions for the future, rather than evidence of success.

Time to Participate. Teachers cite a lack of available time as a primary reason for foregoing online communication. This problem must be addressed before it is reasonable to expect that reflective discourse communities can be effectively supported.

Project Goals. The development of teacher reflective discourse communities in electronic contexts demands significant amounts of funding, with little to show for it in traditional terms. It also requires the development of a research base that supports the effects of this type of teacher development.

To summarize, it seems that the interest in development of computer networks for teachers results from two considerations: (1) CMC technologies can transcend time and space to bring together teachers who may not be able to communicate with each other in face-to-face situations, and (2) the nature of CMC technologies may enhance reflections and community-building among teachers. Many networks have pursued the goal of building learning and reflective communities of teachers. However, the authors found a general lack of rigorous research on these networks. Little is known about their effectiveness for teacher learning. Few researchers seriously examined the degree to which the networks indeed were communities that promoted reflective discourse.

We now turn to some important issues highlighted by the study findings. First, although it seems that claims about the power of CMC technology to create reflective communities for teachers have not been well supported by systematic empirical evidence, on a theoretical level these claims seem logical and reasonable. Secondly, the study shows that although much has been written about the teacher networks, most of the studies have been descriptions of the design and implementation of networks, or a priori arguments for CMC's potential benefits for teacher professional development. Furthermore, the evaluative studies relied mostly on surface features, such as number of participants, number of messages/turns, or simple topic/thread counts, and anecdotal evidence, such as selected comments by participants.

Collaboration is generally described as a process of willing cooperation with peers and colleagues to reach educational objectives. In schools, however, teachers often work more in isolation from—than in collaboration with—each other. In a study of teachers' collegial relations, Rosenholtz (1988), using case study methods and repeated measures, arrived at some conclusions about the effects on teachers working in isolation. In interviews with 55 teachers from schools classified as having isolating characteristics, Rosenholtz found that collaboration included little if any sharing of existing materials and ideas; that planning and problem solving with colleagues rarely happened at all; and that teachers preferred to keep discipline problems to themselves.

Newer visions of professional development emphasize critical reflection on teaching practice through collaboration and collegial dialogue. Research on approaches bearing these qualities indicate that by using them, teachers are better able to make and sustain unproved instructional practices with greater consistency than when attempting to make these improvements alone or when supported by traditional professional development approaches (Corcoran, 1995; Darling-Hammond, 1996; Lichtenstein, McLaughlin, & Knudsen, 1992; Lieberman & McLaughlin, 1993). Unfortunately, the research also indicates that due to time, cost, and lack of will and vision, opportunities to engage in professional development experiences that are collaborative, collegial, and reflective are limited (Lichtenstein, McLaughlin, & Knudsen, 1992; Little, 1993, Lieberman, 1995).

In its role of bringing together diverse voices, CMC is thought to be especially suited to the task of linking teachers together in experiences that may be both professionally and personally rewarding (Honey, 1995; Kimball, 1995; Ringstaff, Sandholtz, & Dwyer, 1994).

Despite CMC's ability to connect teachers, little is known about the technology's ability to facilitate teacher collaborative reflective processes. Studies that do address reflection are usually done in the highly controlled context of pre-service teachers development (Colton & Sparks-Langer, 1993; Kenny, Andrews, Vignola, Schilz, & Covert, 1999; Mickelson & Paulin, 1997; Ropp, 1998). Only a few studies address the reflective quality of computer-mediated discourse for practicing teachers. Of those studies, little description of the reflective processes or outcomes of collaborative teacher discourse is offered.

One of the earliest efforts offering an insight into the application of network-based communications is the LabNet project. In 1989 the Technical Education Research Center (TERC) launched the LabNet project as a technology-supported teacher-enhancement program aimed at high school physics teachers. LabNet organized 99 physical science teachers from across the county into clusters of 6 to 10 teachers in a summer workshop experience. Teachers used the asynchronous network to communicate with peers both in and out of their clusters. An analysis of the conversation of these teachers showed discourse outcomes of growing teacher confidence for teaching physics, increased enthusiasm for teaching, and a sense of belonging to the physics teaching community (Spitzer, Wedding, & DiMauro, 1995). These outcomes are attributed in part to the reflective nature of the teacher discourse. Unfortunately, the study does not treat reflection as a systematic variable, and no discussion on the nature of the reflection or the process used to examine the reflective content is made.

Another informative study of reflective outcomes of CMC is McMahon's (1996) research on the PBS Mathline project. This project brought together middle school teachers using a wide range of technologies—video, computers, satellite, and closed circuit broadcast television—to deliver and discuss material aligned with National Council of Teachers of Mathematics (NCTM) standards in curriculum, teaching, and assessment. The online electronic support system linked 25 to 30 teachers at a time. McMahon studied the flow, frequency, and volume of the 393 messages posted to the listserv over the 8 weeks of the course. Using a four-point reflection rubric to determine the reflective nature of electronic messages in the listserv, McMahon discovered that 29 percent of the participants posted at least one critically reflective message. A message was critically reflective when it "raised issues exploring underlying beliefs, motivations, and implications related to teaching and learning" (p. 91).

In a similar vein, Hawkes & Romiszowski (2001) describe a study that explored the professional development experiences of 28 practicing teachers in 10 Chicago suburban schools involved in a 2-year technology supported problem-based learning (PBL) curriculum development effort. Asynchronous computer-mediated communications were used as the communication tools of the project. The computer-mediated discourse produced by the teachers was compared with the discourse produced by teachers in face-to-face meetings. Research methods including discourse analysis and archival data analysis were applied to determine the nature of the teacher discourse and its reflective content.

The primary goal at the outset of the program involved building teacher capacity for developing PBL curricula. Teacher teams completed and delivered their first PBL unit in the spring of the first project year. Teachers provided written critiques on their units shortly after, and planned for refinements to the first PBL units and the development of a second unit through the summer. The focus of the second year of the initiative was to use new technology tools to expand teacher instructional practices and skills in PBL curricular development.

To determine what levels of collaborative reflection are present when teachers interact under normal circumstances, researchers recorded face-to-face work meetings of school teams consisting of two to five teachers. The collection of computer-mediated communication commenced through the same four month period that face-to-face data were gathered. Collection and storage of CMC discourse between members of the group was ongoing. Researchers categorized messages posted to the common project forums as they were produced. Reading the posts as they appeared provided an indication of the pace of online activity and the topics that were addressed.

All computer-mediated and face-to-face communications between project participants were scored on a seven-point reflection rubric. The rubric is based on Simmons, Sparks, Starko, Pasc, Colton, & Grinberg's (1989) taxonomy for assessing reflective thinking. This framework for analyzing the reflective discourse embraces a model of teacher development in which teachers acquire new information that helps them reach "new and creative solutions" to decision making through collaborative dialogue-leading to reflection (Colton & Sparks-Langer, 1993; p. 49). Independent rater assessments show that computer-mediated discourse achieves a higher overall reflective level than reflections generated by teachers in face-to-face discourse. Although more reflective, CMC proved not to be as interactive as face-to-face discourse.

Teachers found that the convenience, quality, breadth, and volume of peer-provided information facilitated by network technology improved their knowledge of educational theory, policy, and the educational community. Still some teachers in this study remained hesitant about the use of technology for an intimate level of discussion. Follow-up interviews revealed that nearly half the teachers participating in this study firmly believe that CMC cannot a replace face-to-face conversation; that the disjointed presentation of information on the medium is difficult to understand; and that disclosure on a public forum brings professional risks. These and other reservations remind us that network technology is not an answer to every teacher's professional development needs.

15.4 THE INDIVIDUALS INVOLVED IN THE PROCESS

15.4.1 Student-Related Questions

15.4.1.1 Gender Issues. Issues of gender have been studied ever since the first computer networks and email systems were invented. Recently, the intensity of this particular strand of research seems to have become less popular. It is not clear whether this is due to the "answers being known" or to other reasons. The few selected research studies on gender influences in the context of educational CMC, reported below, would seem to indicate that there is still much to learn regarding this question.

Tella's (1992) study focused on "students' attitudes and preferences to teaching practices and teaching tools." The study examined the "gender sensitivity" of e-mail and "the question of equality" in education. Tella addressed the following issues: "computer equity/inequity," "equality education," "opinions and preferences between boys and girls concerning the use of communications NetWorks and e-mail," "achievability of aims and goals," "student-generated disturbances," and "students' initiative."

In the course of the study, Tella found that girls' comments were "more analytical" than those of boys. "When expressing a critical opinion, many girls motivated their views while the boys often contented themselves with blunt statements. More girls than boys appeared to be ready to commit themselves to a new kind of learning environment." Tella concludes that computer-mediated instruction should take into account the differences which tend to surface regarding boys' and girls' preferences and aptitudes in computing. Boys tend to have an interest in the hardware and technology used in itself, while girls tend to focus on "manipulat[ing] the word-processors" and "exchang[ing] ideas in writing." In the end,

both boys and girls could enjoy working in a learning environment focused on computer-mediated communication", becoming "deeply committed to working in an e-mail-equipped co-operative environment". In such an environment they would "learn not only from each other but also learn from and interact productively with the computer.

Hardy et al. (1994) open their article with a review of important studies dealing with "Gender and CMC," "Gender and education," and "Gender and language." The article principally deals with three small-scale studies which Hardy and her colleagues performed on three computer-mediated graduate courses in management learning. The first study looks at the number and length of turns taken by men and women in online conferences. The results of this study showed that women take more turns, but that the length of turns is approximately the same for men and women. Many previous studies had claimed that men generally took more turns.

The second study treats "the nature of men's talk and of women's talk and their impact as experienced by women." This study's results showed that women spent more time "being themselves or using their own language" and finding "the ease of feeling connected to and responding to other women." On the other hand, women commented on the men's contributions, referring to the length, "the language used and something about the style, 'heavy and cerebral' and their [own] reactions such as to be 'intimidated', or to 'shy away'".

The third study deals with comments on how "some people behaved online and how easy or not it was to read and respond to their inputs." Women tended to engage in "rapport" talk, while men engaged in "report" talk. While women would speak of feelings or relationships between participants, men tended to distance themselves emotionally and intellectualize all responses. Sometimes, when "feelings" were at issue male participants would address other males about something a female had written, rather than respond to the female directly.

The authors conclude that while CMC does have certain egalitarian potential (in the realm of turn taking) there is still a "subtle potential for gender imbalance in online conversations."

In contrast, Ory, Bullock, and Burnaska (1997) present the results of an investigation of male and female student use of and attitudes about CMC after 1 year of implementation in a university setting. Results of this study revealed no significant gender differences.

Blum's (1999) research project was an interpretative qualitative case study of higher education students learning through asynchronous, CMC-based distance education. Subjects consisted of adult professionals studying for bachelor and master's degrees. Male and female preferred learning styles, communication patterns, and participation barriers were compared for differences in gender. Differences were then contrasted with traditional gender differences in face-to-face (FTF) higher education learning environments. Results of content analysis from one month of online student messages suggests there are gender differences between male and female distance education students which contribute toward inequitable gender differences which are both similar and different from the traditional learning environment. There are higher dispositional, situational, and institutional barriers for female distance education students. This helps to create an inequitable learning environment for distance education students because the nature of the medium requires at least some technical skills and a degree of confidence about distance education. Furthermore, the CMC-based environment supported a tolerance of male domination in online communication patterns, which effectively silenced female students. Implications for practice are discussed.

15.4.1.2 Discourse Analysis.
Kilian (1994) treats what he refers to as the "passive–aggressive paradox" in online discussions as it applies to the classroom. While many claim that electronic media help to eliminate the domination of discussion by a small minority, this may not in fact be the case. Kilian holds that in electronic bulletin board systems, for example, a few contributors dominate while everyone else "lurks." This is what he calls the passive–aggressive syndrome. The same phenomenon, he contends, occurs in the classroom: "Most teachers and students who go on line are passive readers of other people's postings; they rarely, if ever, respond to what they read. That leaves the aggressives in charge—teachers and students who post often and, of course, have only one another to respond to." This is due to the fact that people who are not computer specialists do not know the "rituals" of cyberspace—which is to say that there is no easily identifiable linguistic register on line. As a short-term solution, Kilian (1994) suggests that: "Cyberspace democracy, like the classroom itself, will need to rely for a time on teacher domination of the medium to ensure that a disinterested moderator is there to look after the interests of the less aggressive." For the long term, he writes that "we need to get beyond mere netiquette to find the real registers of on-line communication."

Uhlíøová (1994) examined the "textual properties of a corpus of computer-mediated messages" to "show the effects of the computer as a new technological medium upon the message." The corpus of messages studied was composed of over 100 messages written by two correspondents in Prague to various recipients, and approximately 50 messages which these same two correspondents received. Uhlíøová outlines the "*contexts of situations*" in which e-mail is used. These include the following: common *subject matters;* more or less private issues; secondary messages (e.g., a proposal for an official wording of an agreement or of a project, a curriculum vitae, a list of e-mail names); and messages about the technology of e-mailing. Also included in the article are descriptions of the mix of spoken and written language features in e-mail. Uhlíøová concludes that e-mail ". . . contributes significantly to the development of language use offering new writing strategies in the frame of new constraints and requirements of the medium." This is because "although *written* in its substance, e-mail messages are in some respects no less interactive than speech," and this "blurs" the categories of writing and speaking. Not only does the "capability of e-mail to widen the possibilities of language use" affect the content of messages sent, but may eventually lead to the creation of new registers."

Warschauer, Turbee, and Roberts (1996) analyze the potential of computer learning networks to empower second language learners in three ways: (1) by enhancing student's opportunities for autonomous control and initiative in language learning, (2) by providing opportunities for more equal participation by those students who may be otherwise excluded or discriminated against, and (3) by developing students' independent and critical learning skills. The article reviews the literature as it relates to these three points and also includes a discussion of potential problems. The final section, "Suggestions for the Practitioner," discusses some general principles for effective use of computer learning networks.

In a related paper, Warschauer (1996a) compared ESL students' discourse and participation in two modes: (1) face-to face discussion and (2) electronic discussion. A repeated measures, counterbalanced experiment was set up to compare student participation and language complexity in four-person groups in the two modes. Using a formula which measured relative balance based on words per student, the study found that the electronic discussion featured participation which was twice as balanced (i.e., more equal among participants) than the face-to-face discussion. This was due in part to the fact that the Japanese students in this multiethnic class were largely silent in the face-to-face discussion, but participated much more regularly in the electronic discussion. The study found that students' increased participation in the electronic mode correlated highly with their relative feelings of discomfort in face-to-face discussion.

Finally, the study looked at the lexical complexity of the discourse in the two modes as well as the comparative syntactic complexity. The electronic discussion was found to be significantly more complex both lexically and syntactically. This finding was highlighted by the use of examples which illustrated some of the lexical and syntactic differences between the discourse of the two environments.

15.4.1.3 Individual Student Styles, Perceptions, and Attitudes.

The research literature regarding the importance of interaction in education especially in Web-based distance learning is extensive. Both students and faculty typically report increased satisfaction in online courses depending on the quality and quantity of interactions. For example, Shea, Fredericksen, Pickett, Pelz, and Swan (2001) in a survey of 3,800 students enrolled in 264 courses through the SUNY Learning Network (SLN), conclude that the "greater the percentage of the course grade that was based on discussion, the more satisfied the students were, the more they thought they learned from the course, and the more interaction they thought they had with the instructor and with their peers." Dziuban and Moskal (2001), likewise report very high correlations and relationships between interaction in online courses and student satisfaction.

Related to the research on interaction is the concept of presence. Students who feel that they are part of a group or present in a community will, it is argued, wish to participate actively in group and community activities. Lombard and Ditton (1997) define presence as the perceptual "illusion of nonmediation." An illusion of nonmediation occurs when a person fails to perceive or acknowledge the existence of a medium in his/her communication environment and responds as he/she would if the medium were not there. Furthermore, because it is a perception, presence can and does vary from individual to individual. It can also be situational and vary across time for the same individual, making it a complex subject for research. Researchers studying applications related to virtual reality software, CMC and online learning increasingly are redefining our understanding of presence in light of the ability of individuals to communicate extensively in a group via digital communications networks. The term "telepresence" has evolved and has become popular as an area of study.

Biocca (1995) classifies presence into three types: spatial presence, self-reflective presence and social presence. Rourke, Anderson, Garrison, and Archer (2001a; 2001b) have proposed a community of inquiry model with three presence components: cognitive, social, and teaching. Their model supports the design of online courses as active learning environments or communities dependent on instructors and students sharing ideas, information, and opinions. What is critical here is that presence in an online course is fundamentally a social phenomenon and manifests itself through interactions among students and instructors.

Interaction and presence in a an online course can be studied for many reasons. Ultimately, however, student performance outcomes need to be evaluated to determine the overall success of a course. An extensive amount of literature exists on performance outcomes as related to distance learning. Course completion and attrition rates are considered to be important student performance measures especially as related to adult and distance learning. The literature on quality issues in distance learning suggests that multiple measures related to individual academic program and course objectives should be used in studying student performance (Dziuban & Moskal, 2001; Shea et al., 2001). Performance data can be in the form of tests, written assignments, projects, and satisfaction surveys. The above discussion sets the scene for an extensive study (Picciano, 2002) that utilizes this multiple measure approach. The major research questions that guided this study are as follows:

1. What is the relationship between actual student interaction/participation and performance?
2. What is the relationship between student perception of social presence and performance?
3. What is the relationship between student perceptions of social presence and actual participation?
4. Are there differences in student perceptions of their learning experiences and actual performance?
5. Are there differences in student perceptions of their interaction and actual participation?

Data on student participation in online discussions were collected throughout the semester. Students also completed a satisfaction survey at the end of the course, which asked a series of questions addressing their overall experiences, especially as related to their learning and interaction with others and the technology used. A series of questions that relate to social presence was included as part of this survey.

In addition to student perceptions of their learning as collected on the student satisfaction survey, two further student performance measures were collected: scores on an examination and scores on a written assignment. The latter measures relate to the course's two main objectives: to develop and add to the student's knowledge base regarding contemporary issues in education, as well as to provide future administrators with an appreciation of differences in points of view and an ability to approach issues that can be divisive in a school or community. The results are summarized below.

Student Perceptions of Interaction and Learning. These results indicated that there is a strong, positive relationship between student perceptions of their interaction in the course and their perceptions of the quality and quantity of their learning.

Actual Student Interaction and Performance. The overall conclusion was that actual student interaction as measured by the number of postings on the discussion board had no relationship to performance on the examination. Actual student interaction as measured by the number of postings on the discussion board did have a relationship to the written assignment for students in the high interactive grouping.

Social Presence and Performance. In comparing student perceptions of social presence with actual performance measures, the results are somewhat different. The overall conclusion is that student perception of social presence did not have a statistically significant relationship to performance on the examination, while student perception of social presence had a positive, statistically significant relationship to performance on the written assignment.

Student Perceptions of Interaction and Actual Participation. The last area for analysis in this study was the relationship between the perceived interaction of students and actual interaction. While the perceptions of the number of postings of

the moderate interaction group of students are consistent with their actual postings, the low interaction group perceived themselves to have made a higher number of postings than they actually did and the high interaction group perceived themselves to have made fewer postings than they actually did. The results indicate that student perceptions of their interaction in a course need to be viewed with a bit of caution.

Daughenbaugh et al. (2002) sought to determine if different personality types express more or less satisfaction with courses delivered online versus those delivered in the classroom. The methodology employed two online surveys—the Keirsey Temperament Sorter (KTS) and a course satisfaction instrument. The four hypotheses are that Introvert, Intuition, Thinking, and Perceiving personalities express greater satisfaction with online courses than Extrovert, Sensing, Feeling, and Judging personalities. Both descriptive and inferential statistics were used in the study.

This study resulted in a statistically significant difference between the preference for online courses between Introvert personalities and Extrovert personalities. However, the findings of this study were exactly opposite of what had been hypothesized. Extroverts expressed stronger preference for online courses than did Introverts. No statistically significant difference was found in the preference for online courses between students with predominately Intuition personalities and those with predominately Sensing personalities, between students with predominately Thinking personalities and those with predominately Feeling personalities, and between students with predominately Perceiving personalities and those with predominately Judging personalities.

There were, however, six other interesting findings of this study.

1. There were statistically significant differences in the responses to certain course satisfaction variables among those in the Extrovert/Introvert temperament group.
2. There were statistically significant differences in the responses to certain course satisfaction variables among those in the Intuition/Sensing temperament group.
3. There were no statistically significant differences in the responses to any course satisfaction variables among those in the Thinking/Feeling temperament group.
4. There were statistically significant differences in the responses to certain course satisfaction variables among those in the Perceiving/Judging temperament group.
5. There was a statistically significant difference in satisfaction with student interaction between students taking online courses and those taking in-class courses. Students taking in-class courses had greater satisfaction with their level of student interaction than students in online courses.
6. There was no statistically significant difference related to gender in the preference for online or in-class courses. Females and males in this study expressed nearly identical levels of preference for online or in-class course.

Based on the findings of this study, the authors recommend that instructors teaching online (a) should consider the personality types of students in their courses and (b) should provide a variety of ways for students to interact with each other.

15.4.2 Teacher Related Questions

15.4.2.1 Faculty Participation Issues. Most of the literature on Asynchronous Learning Networks (ALNs) has focused on the pedagogical and technological advantages of this educational delivery mode and the way ALNs can respond to the changing demands and pressures placed on institutions of higher education. However, there are considerable obstacles preventing the widespread implementation of ALNs. These obstacles, and the associated forms of opposition and resistance, were analyzed by Jaffee (1998) in an organizational context that examines the prevailing academic culture and the widely institutionalized value placed on classroom-based teaching and learning. The writer argues that the recognition of the classroom as a "sacred institution in higher education, and a major source of professorial identity," is a necessary first step toward developing strategies for organizational change and pedagogical transformation.

Various strategies for change are discussed, with the objective to convert what may be outright hostility and a perception that ALNs are totally illegitimate into a greater acceptance of ALNs on the basis of their ability to address some of the pedagogical problems faced by all faculty. While faculty members may be unwilling to relinquish their attachment and devotion to the conventional classroom institution, they can better appreciate the reasons why other faculty might want to experiment with ALNs and they may even be interested in developing some kind of on-line web conference for their classroom course as a way to extend the classroom beyond the spatial and temporal confines of four walls and seventy-five minute time limits. This is an important intermediate application of instructional technology between the pure classroom and the exclusively online delivery modes. As human organizations, institutions of higher education are constrained by habit, tradition, and culture. These represent the most significant obstacles to organizational change and they therefore must be recognized and addressed in order to realize genuine pedagogical and institutional transformation.

Schifter (2000) compares the top five motivating and inhibiting factors for faculty participation in Asynchronous Learning Networks or CMC as reported by faculty participators and non-participators, and administrators. While faculty and administrators agreed strongly on what inhibits faculty from participating in such programs, there were significantly different perceptions on what motivates faculty to participate. "Personal motivation to use technology" was a strong motive for participating in ALN/DE at this institution, as noted by all parties involved. The faculty, participators and non-participators, rated issues that could be considered intrinsic factors as motivating for participation in DE, while administrators indicated a perception that faculty would be more motivated by factors that could be considered extrinsic.

The top inhibiting factors were rated very similarly across groups and all five top inhibiting factors appear to be more extrinsic in nature than intrinsic. Determining what factors would deter faculty from participating in ALN/DE appears easier than what would motivate. The results of this study suggest that faculty are more likely to participate in CMC programs due to interest in using computers in teaching, interest in exploring new opportunities for programs and students and interest in the intellectual challenge, rather than monetary or personal rewards.

Hislop and Atwood (2000) surveyed teacher attitudes and behaviors in CMC courses in the College of Information Science and Technology (IST) at Drexel University that began a long-term initiative in early 1994 to develop online teaching capabilities. The survey consisted primarily of a series of statements to which respondents were asked to indicate their agreement or disagreement using a seven-point scale. In addition to the quantitative response, the survey allowed for comments on each statement and included several open-ended questions inviting comment about concerns and potential of ALN. The researchers received 19 responses out of a possible 26.

Overall the survey seems to show broad support for online education among the faculty, tempered by some sources of concern. There is strong agreement that the College should continue work in this area, although there are clearly differences in the types of degrees the faculty feel are most appropriate for online delivery. There is some concern about the effectiveness of online education compared to traditional education. There is also some personal preference for teaching face-to-face. However, many of the faculty are willing to have a substantial portion of their teaching assignment be online.

Full-time faculty members have been involved with all phases of the project from course conversion to teaching, development, administration, and evaluation. A variety of factors were found to affect faculty motivation for the online program.

- The faculty who started the project formed a natural group of early adopters.
- All of the faculty members teaching in the program have substantial technical ability and generally enjoy working with new technologies.
- Courses taught online count as a part of regular faculty teaching load, with online and traditional courses counting the same. To provide some additional incentive, faculty members teaching online also receive extra compensation.
- New faculty members are hired with the understanding that they are likely to teach in the online program. On the other hand, all faculty members who teach online also teach traditional classes.
- Participation by faculty members in the online program is recognized as a desirable activity in the university performance appraisal process for faculty.

Berg (2000) investigated the compensation practices for faculty developing and teaching distance learning courses. The research divides itself into two basic lines of inquiry: direct and indirect compensation (including royalties, training, and professional recognition). Also, economic models for distance learning are examined with a view towards understanding faculty compensation within attempts to reduce labor costs. The primary questions this research attempts to answer are:

- What are the current policies and practices in higher education for compensating faculty who develop and teach distance learning format courses?
- Will the increased use of distance learning format courses alter overall labor conditions for American faculty? If so, how?

Although information is limited, it is found that faculty work in both developing and teaching CMC courses tends thus far to be seen as work-for-hire under regular load with little additional indirect compensation or royalty arrangements.

15.4.2.2 Teacher Opinions—Some Case Studies.

The State University of New York (SUNY) Learning Network (SLN) is the on-line instructional program created for the 64 colleges and nearly 400,000 students of SUNY. The foundation of the program is "freedom from schedule and location constraints for faculty and students." The primary goals of the SLN are to bring SUNY's diverse and high-quality instructional programs within the reach of learners everywhere, and to be the best provider of asynchronous instruction for learners in New York State and beyond.

Fredericksen et al. (2000) examine the factors that have contributed to the high level of faculty satisfaction we have achieved in the SLN. A faculty satisfaction survey revealed a number of indicators that address the issue of teaching satisfaction. Eighty-three percent responded that they found their online teaching experiences very satisfying and 17 percent found them somewhat satisfying. One-hundred percent of the faculty responded that they plan to continue teaching online courses. Asked to evaluate the effectiveness of the online teaching strategies they used, 83 percent responded that they were very satisfied. Sixty-seven percent of the faculty characterized the quantity of student-to-student interaction, and student-to-professor interaction as "more than in the classroom." In response to a question about the quality of interaction, 67 percent said that the quality of student-to student interaction was higher than in the classroom, and 50 percent responded that the quality of student-to-professor interaction was higher than in the classroom.

When asked why some mainstream faculty might resist online teaching, they gave the following responses:

- Afraid of the technology. Unsure of the pedagogy. Questions the authenticity.
- Afraid of the unknown and the potential work involved in trying something new.
- It threatens the territory they have become comfortable in.
- Technophobia and not having thorough knowledge or exposure to the methodology.
- Online teaching is too impersonal and does not allow for meaningful interaction.

Asked what could be done to break down this resistance, they replied:

- Demonstrate effective pedagogy. Testimonials from respected colleagues.
- Roundtable discussions with experienced onliners.
- Set a good example and outline the positive features of teaching via the Internet.
- Convince them it's not a threat, just an enhancement.
- Professional development seminars where faculty are interactive within a course.
- One-on-one demonstrations with faculty who are cautious but interested.
- Show them a course and answer their questions.
- Suggest they take a course online themselves before teaching one.

Hartman, Dziuban, and Moskal (2000) describe relationships among infrastructure, student outcomes, and faculty satisfaction at the University of Central Florida (UCF). The model focuses on a developmental process that progresses from courses with some Web presence to those that are driven by CMC. Faculty receive support for online teaching in the form of release time for training and development, upgraded hardware, and complete course development services. The results of the impact evaluation at UCF indicate that faculty feel that their teaching is more flexible and that interaction increases in the ALN environment. On the other hand, they are concerned that online teaching may not fit into the academy culture. Uniformly, faculty using the CMC environments indicate that their workload increases along with the amount and quality of the interaction with and between students.

Kashy et al. (2000) present a case study that describes the implementation and continued operation of a large on-campus CMC system for a 500-student course in introductory physics. A highly positive impact on student success rates was achieved. Factors that increased faculty satisfaction and instances of dissatisfaction are presented. The potential increase in the latter with technology is of some concern. To put the faculty satisfaction issues in perspective, the researchers interviewed faculty, including some who have not used CMC in their disciplines and looked at previous studies of issues that affect faculty satisfaction. The principal factors, which emerge include collegiality, workload, and autonomy. An interesting observation concerns the role conflict that occurs at the intersection between faculty and administrative domains of responsibility. While it does not appear to affect general faculty satisfaction, it can be a source of disaffection and dissatisfaction. The authors describe several specific cases of such critical factors.

Arvan and Musumeci (2000) present the results of interviews with the principal investigators of the current Sloan Center for Asynchronous Learning Environments (SCALE) Efficiency Projects. There are six such projects: Spanish, microbiology, economics, math, chemistry, and physics. The paper reviews each project individually, summarizes the results, and then discusses some common lessons learned as well as some still open issues. The paper considers satisfaction both from the perspective of the course director/designer and from the perspective of other instructors and graduate teaching assistants. The evidence appears to show that all of these groups are satisfied with ALN, relative to the prior situation. Nonetheless, it is not clear whether these results would translate to other high enrollment courses.

Almeda and Rose (2000) investigated instructor satisfaction in 14 online courses in freshman-level composition and literature, business writing, and ESL offered in the University of California (UC) Extension's online program. The results of an informal instructor survey also are discussed. Obstacles to adoption, effective and problematic practices, and critical programmatic and individual course factors gleaned from this analysis are outlined. The obstacles identified include: lack of face-to-face interaction; the workload is greater than in other teaching experiences; compensation is seen as inadequate.

The paper by Turgeon, Di Biase, and Miller (2000) describes two of the distance education programs offered through the Penn State World Campus during its first year of operation in 1998. Detailed information is provided on how these programs were selected and supported, the nature of the students who enrolled and the faculty who developed and taught the courses, and the technology and infrastructure employed for delivering content and engaging students in collaborative learning. The organization of the World Campus, the evolution of these programs, and the results obtained from them during the first 18 months of operation are presented. Several contemporary issues are addressed from a faculty perspective, including: teaching effectiveness, relationship with students, satisfaction with product, compatibility with other responsibilities, ethical concerns, incentives and rewards, team efforts, support services, perceptions by colleagues, scholarly value, opportunity cost for faculty, intellectual property concerns, and compensation.

15.5 RESEARCH METHODOLOGIES

The methods used to research the theory and practice of CMC applications in education have evolved over the 15 years or so that the medium has been available. As the technologies have matured and become more widespread, a greater range of researchers have become interested in investigating all aspects of their educational use. In the 1980s and early 1990s, much research seems to have been grounded in positivistic paradigms, while from the mid-1990s onwards, there has been a shift to much more use of qualitative methods. In addition, there has been a move away from experimental environments, so that much more use is made of data from real-life interactions between CMC students, rather than quasi-scientific laboratory studies of user reactions. CMC researchers now, on the whole, are taking a naturalistic approach to the collection and interpretation of data. Early researchers shied away from analyzing the content of messages, partly because there were no precedents or methods for carrying out the task, and partly because it was highly time consuming. However these barriers have been overcome and the field has, finally, moved away from the situation wherein real data from CMC interactions is "paradoxically the least used" (Mason, 1991).

15.5.1 Evolving Approaches to CMC Research

Much of the early research on CMC focused on quantitative measures such as numbers of messages per participant, message length and frequency, and particularly message maps showing patterns of response to key inputs. Furthermore, early adopters seemed to feel it necessary to prove that studying online produced the same results—measured by examination results—as campus based education. The massive amount of research of this kind has now been collected together on the "No significant difference" web site at http://teleeducation.nb.ca/nosignificantdifference/.

Many early researchers drew on the automatic computer-based recording of communications transactions, and examined usage and interaction. Harasim (1987) used mainframe computer records to analyze student access times and dispersion of participation in a graduate computer conference. There was, up to the early 1990s, relatively little use of qualitative approaches based in observation and interviewing of CMC users—survey questionnaires were the preferred method. Some studies did begin to use these methods in the early 1990s (e.g., Burge, 1993; Eastmond, 1993).

The variety of methods and approaches to CMC research that began to develop in the mid-1990s is reflected in two volumes in particular. Ess' (1996a) book examines a range of issues in the analysis, application and development of CMC. In particular, the volume addresses philosophical issues and the effect of gender on CMC use. It presents a range of philosophical approaches and frameworks for the analysis, including poststructuralist perspectives (e.g., Yoon, 1996), semiotics (Shank & Cunningham, 1996), critical theory (Ess, 1996b), and ethnography (Herring, 1996b).

Herring's (1996c) collection of essays on linguistic, social and other issues in CMC presents more analyses based in mixed methods and philosophical approaches and frameworks. These include conversation and discourse analyses and ethnographic studies of online communities. While there does seem to be a general convergence of methods for researching CMC, some researchers note that "CMC is not homogeneous, but like any communication modality, manifests itself in different styles and genres" (Herring, 1996c).

15.5.1.1 Content Analysis. Various forms of content analysis, some grounded in specific theoretical frameworks and others not, have been used over at least the past 10 years in CMC studies. The need to move away from gathering quantitative data and to analyze the interactive exchanges of CMC and to demonstrate the effects and advantages of interactive exchange in learning is now well established in the research community.

An early solution (Henri, 1991) was a model and analytic framework that analysed the text of the messages from a number of dimensions, including levels of participation, social aspects of the interactions, types and levels of interaction and intertextuality, and evidence of cognitive and metacognitive aspects of the messages. While a step towards some of the more integrated, qualitative methods developed, this analysis seems to have taken the text in isolation, rather than including consideration of the social and other contexts within which the messages were being exchanged.

Bowers (1997), the listowner of a psychiatric nursing discussion list, presents a content analysis of discussions on the list during the first 16 months of its existence. His findings are congruent with other studies from that era (e.g., Murray, 1996), noting the use of discussions to explore and challenge current practice.

Some attempts have also been made to use postmodern and poststructuralist approaches or frameworks in the analysis of CMC. Aycock (1995) explored synchronous CMC (Usenet) discussions within Foucault's (1988) concept of the technologies of self. Other researchers (e.g., Baym, 1995) have moved away from focusing on building predictive models of CMC, and favor more naturalistic, ethnographic, and microanalytic research to refine our understanding of both influences and outcomes.

A review of the issues and methodologies related to CMC content analysis has been carried out by Rourke, Anderson, Garrison, and Archer (2001a). Their paper explores six fundamental issues of content analysis: criteria of objectivity, reliability, replicability, and systematic consistency in quantitative content analysis; descriptive and experimental research designs; manifest content and latent content; the unit of analysis in content analysis of transcripts; software packages to facilitate the process and ethical issues. They note:

The analysis of computer conference transcripts is beset with a number of significant difficulties, which is why this technique is more often praised than practiced. First, it is impossible to avoid some degree of subjectivity in the coding of segments of transcripts into categories; however, the degree of subjectivity must be kept to a minimum, or the value of the study will be seriously compromised. Second, the value of quantitative studies that do not report the reliability of their coding (and many do not) is also questionable . . .

When the content being analysed is manifest in the transcript—e.g., when the researcher is counting the number of times participants address each other by name—then reliability is a much less significant problem and the analysis can in at least some cases be automated. However, in most cases the researcher is interested in variables that are latent—i.e., have to be inferred from the words that appear in the transcript. Various techniques have been developed for dealing with such variables. The most popular has been to define the latent variables and then deduce manifest indicators of those variables. This is the technique that has been used by our own research group, as well as a number of the other researchers whose work we examined. (Archer, Garrison, Anderson, & Rourke, 2001, p. 6)

Content analysis is one of the key areas of research in the CMC field. It is beginning to develop theoretical foundations and a variety of frameworks within which analysis can be situated.

15.5.1.2 Case Study Methodologies.
However, by far the majority of research papers on CMC are case studies and are usually based on survey research, through electronic or conventionally distributed questionnaires (e.g., Phillips, 1990; Phillips & Pease, 1987; Ryan, 1992). While this kind of research is appropriate and necessary in a newly developing field such as CMC was in the early 1990s, there is now an urgent need for methodologies that provide generalizable evidence and meta-analyses that build upon the results of the extensive case study literature.

An example of a case study that makes good use of the methodology is a paper by Creanor (2002), in which she compares her experience of tutoring on two contrasting courses. While much of the paper is inevitably descriptive, the author does use the five-stage model of online interactivity as defined by Salmon (2000), to understand the differences between the two courses. Her conclusion is indicative of the kind of results that case study methodologies produce:

Measures of success are relative to the learning context. As online education reaches out to homes, communities and workplaces on a global scale, factors such as those described are more likely to impact on success or failure than the technology itself. Issues such as the preparation of tutors through specialist training and the links between tutor and student engagement certainly merit further research, perhaps through wider comparative studies. There can be no doubt, however, that the experienced tutor with well-developed moderating skills, organisation abilities, and above all an awareness of the external influences will become highly prized as the keystone of the e-learning experience. (Creanor, 2002, p 67)

Despite this weakness in CMC research, there are outstanding examples of appropriate methodologies being applied and adapted to the CMC environment. Three such methods are: ethnography, surveys and focus groups.

15.5.1.3 Ethnographic Methodologies.
Ethnographic perspectives, through using interviews and participant observation (Murray, 2002; Schrum, 1995) in the study of asynchronous CMC are becoming increasingly popular. Similar approaches have been adopted in the study of synchronous interactions (e.g., Waskul & Douglass, 1997).

A classic example of the application of ethnographic methodologies to the CMC field is the paper by McConnell (2002). Using over 1000 messages running to 240 pages of text, McConnell adapted a grounded theory approach of reading and rereading the data from a postgraduate problem-based online MEd. He sought to answer the questions, "How does a group of distributed learners negotiate its way through the problem that it is working on? How does it come to define its problem, produce a method for investigating it, and produce a final 'product'?" He describes his method of working thus:

As a category emerged from the analysis, I would make a note of it and proceed with the analysis of the transcript, trying to find evidence that might support or refute each category being included in the final set of categories. I would then look in depth at these emerging categories, re-read the margin annotations and notes to myself, moving back and forward from the text of the transcripts to my notes. A new set of notes was made on the particular category, clarifying, for example, who said what or who did what, how others reacted to that, and how the group worked with members' ideas and suggestions. (McConnell, 2002, p. 65)

In this way, categories were re-worked and reconceptualized on the basis of analysis of the transcripts, and the final categories and emergent theories were grounded in rigorous analysis of the data. In addition, he developed a flow chart indicating the work of the online students, detailing significant events, agreements reached and steps in understanding. This acted as an aide-memoire for him as he read through the transcripts and refined his categories. For triangulation of results, he carried out face-to-face interviews with students, which he recorded and transcribed. These also were subjected to grounded theory analysis.

McConnell then goes on to use the categories and phases his research has produced to discuss the implications of his analysis for practice—both his own and that of other CMC tutors and instructors. The depth and groundedness of his research method lends weight to his conclusions and substance to his generalizations.

Research of this kind—open ended, exploratory, descriptive, grounded in real learning situations and contexts, addressing both broad themes and micro issues—helps us understand the complexity of learning and teaching in distributed Problem Based Learning environments and offers insights which can be useful in developing our practice. (McConnell, 2002, p. 80)

Ethnographic research is inevitably labor intensive and time consuming, but is ideally suited to providing a rich understanding of the nature of learning in the CMC environment.

15.5.1.3.1 Survey Methodologies. Survey research is very commonly used in studying educational computer conferencing, but is most effective when used with large numbers of students. The shortcomings of surveys—superficiality of the data, reliability of individual answers—are less problematic, and the scale of the responses provide a broad overview of the issues addressed. Where it is used with 20–50 students, as it too often is in CMC research, it tends to raise far more questions than it ever answers. Two good examples of effective use of survey questionnaires are an Australian study of online education across all universities, sponsored by the Australian Department of Education, Science and Training (Bell, Bush, Nicholson, O'Brien, & Tran, 2002), and a paper by an American academic interested in measuring the development of community in online courses (Rovai, 2002b).

The Australian study had a simple aim: to ascertain the current extent of online education in Australian universities. All universities were sent a questionnaire and 40 out of 43 responded. This high response rate is one of the factors which contributes to the effectiveness of the study. Many other research reports using survey questionnaires base results on return rates of 60 percent and some make do with return rates below 50 percent! One of the problems is that with the proliferation of surveys, people are less and less willing to fill them out and return them. Another problem is the reliability of the responses. A statement of the limitations perceived by the survey are common in most research papers. The Australian report notes:

The quality of responses was not always as high as expected. For instance, data was not divided into undergraduate and postgraduate figures; data was missing; errors in calculating percentages were common; information was not always returned in the form required. In one case, the university's system of recording units made it difficult to extract the number of units without double-counting. (Bell et al., 2002, p. 8)

Because the report sought factual information, the aim was well matched with the methodology. Questionnaires asking students to reflect on their use of CMC or worse still, to categorize their feelings based on Likert scale responses, are usually less satisfactory. The fact that the Australian survey went to 100 percent of universities adds to the validity of the findings. The report provides comprehensive figures on the numbers and types of online courses, the systems used to manage online interaction and other support services such as library, administration, and fee payment.

The article by Rovai (2002b) aimed to develop and field-test an instrument to measure classroom community with university students taking courses online. The survey questions did ask students to rate their feelings about community on 1–5 Likert scales. However, the strength of the research lies in the development of a Classroom Community Scale measuring sense of community in a learning environment. It aims to help educators identify ways of promoting the development of community. Data were collected from 375 students enrolled in 28 different courses, offered to postgraduates learning online.

The 40-item questionnaire was developed by several means: a review of the literature on the characteristics of sense of community, use of both face-to-face and virtual classroom indicators of community and finally ratings from a panel of experts in educational psychology on the validity of each item in the scale. Half of the items related to feelings of connectedness and half related to feelings regarding the use of interaction within the community to construct understanding, and to the extent to which learning goals were being satisfied in the online learning environment. The findings lack the depth and richness of those resulting from the McConnell ethnographic study, but they provide breadth from the relatively large sample studied and a sort of dip stick methodology for educators to easily assess the growth of community. The researcher provides further suggestions for strengthening the research:

In the future, other target populations, such as traditional students and high school students, as well as other university populations, could be used for the purpose of norming the Classroom Community Scale. Other forms of distance education, such as broadcast television, video and audio teleconferencing could also be examined. Resultant scores could then be standardized for ease of interpretation. (Rovai, 2002b, p. 208)

Survey questionnaires are likely to be used increasingly in CMC research, if only because the numbers of students studying via CMC is increasing. It is interesting to compare the findings of the Rovai research with those of a study on the same topic—the process of community building in online courses—which used ethnographic methodologies (extensive interviews, analysis of conference interactions, coding of the data into categories based on rereading and refining the emergent issues (Brown, 2001). The paper presents rich and reliable outputs:

Nine themes or categories emerged through open coding that characterized community-building in asynchronous text-based distance education graduate classes . . . Relationships between categories were explored through axial coding. A paradigm model was developed that portrayed the interrelationships of the axial coding categories by using the following headings: causal conditions, phenomenon, context, intervening conditions, strategies and consequences. From this, selective coding generated a theory which is shown as a visual model with accompanying explanation. (Brown, 2001, p. 4)

The researcher was able to generate theoretical propositions grounded in the data, to identify a variety of levels of community engagement in the online environment, and to develop a community building paradigm.

15.5.1.4 Focus Groups.

As a methodology, the focus group is a form of structured group discussion that offers the potential of richer and broader feedback than individual interviews. Whether face-to-face or online, focus groups use a facilitator to manage a structured protocol in facilitating group discussion. The aim is usually to obtain qualitative, affective information from the group. In many ways, the method is ideally suited to the online medium because it supports distributed, reflective, asynchronous interaction. Not surprisingly, online focus groups are being used in a wide range of contexts: for universities to gather feedback from students, and for organizations of all kinds to collect the views of their clients or stakeholders. In many cases, the onus is on users to join a focus group. In formal research studies, it is more usual for the researchers to select the participants according to a set of appropriate criteria.

A study by Killingsworth, Schellenberger and Kleckley (2000) reports on the experiences and associated benefits of using face-to-face focus groups, in this case to design and develop a U.S. labor exchange system to be used on the Internet. The researchers note:

If focus groups are to provide useful information it is necessary to use valid and effective methods. Selection of facilitators and selection of the focus group members are critical to ultimate success. If possible, an experienced and properly trained contractor should be selected to conduct the focus groups. Adequate planning time must be provided . . . It is also important to identify all stakeholder groups so that all can be represented. Finally it is necessary to conduct sessions with multiple focus groups. (Killingsworth et al., pp. 2–3)

Greenbaum (2000), an experienced focus group leader, makes a case against online focus groups as a tool for gathering marketing information:

The authority role of the moderator is one of the most important reasons why traditional focus groups are so important. An experienced moderator is in complete charge of the group activities and is able to ensure that everyone participates and that the focus of the discussion remains on target.

It is virtually impossible to establish authority from behind a computer screen.

One of the major benefits of traditional focus groups is the interaction among the various participants. A well conducted focus group utilizes this interaction to explore topics in more detail and to draw out the feelings of each of the participants based on their reactions to what others in the room have said.

This is not viable in an Internet environment.

A competent focus group moderator will use non-verbal cues from participants to direct the discussion in the room. Often the non-verbal inputs can be as important as the verbal in determining the reactions to various ideas.

It is impossible to address non-verbal reactions in an online focus group. (Greenbaum, 2000, p. 1)

Nevertheless, for educational research online focus groups are increasingly the source of innovative studies. For example, a paper by Rezabek (2000) used online focus groups to formulate the key issues and questions to be explored in a large scale questionnaire survey and in small scale in-depth interviews.

The members of the focus group were first asked to consider a question, respond with their thoughts, feelings, experiences and suggestions, and then react to the responses given by the various members of the group. In this way, a discussion was generated, resulting in a rich environment of thought and idea formation.

The focus group discussion commenced with an invitation to present some biographical information as an introduction of each person. Then, an initial question from this researcher was presented. The discussion and concept threads then evolved as the members of the focus group considered the question and responded with their thoughts, feelings, and experiences. They were then asked to also react to the responses given by the various members of the group. Subsequent questions were then posed to the group after everyone had had a chance to comment and react to the others' comments. (Rezabek, 2000, paragraphs 30–31)

15.5.2 Ethical Issues and Intellectual Property in CMC Research

In an area as relatively new (compared with the history of methods for face-to-face research techniques) as CMC research, one would expect methods and conventions around ethical issues, especially those of accessing sources of data, quoting communications, etc., to be in an early stage of development. This is certainly the case. There are still ongoing debates on the ethics of CMC research, especially in terms of the rights of the researcher and the researched, and of who owns or should give permission for the use of materials from online discussions, be they from closed educational conferences or open access discussion lists. Little seems to have changed or been resolved in the years since Mason (1988) said that "quoting from a conference raises the vexed question of privacy and ownership of messages . . . issues that have yet to be settled formally by the conferencing community." Different researchers have adopted positions depending, often, on their own research traditions and methods, and the particular studies they have undertaken. The thorny issue of precisely whose permission might be needed to use a particular contribution to a list discussion, or other form of CMC, still lies generally unresolved. This may be no bad thing, and a plurality of approaches may be needed, depending on the nature and context of any particular study. This plurality is, however, situated within the context of general ethical principles of research, of doing no harm to participants, (e.g., Herring 1996a), and the time and virtual space within which the research is conducted.

This seems akin to the ethical principle of beneficence (i.e., maximizing possible benefit and minimizing possible harm from one's actions; Engelhardt & Wildes, 1994), a principle that seems to underpin implicitly, if not explicitly, the views of many CMC researchers. Coupled with this it seems to be common practice to consider anything posted to any list or newsgroup as public information. One early view (Howard, 1993) was that completing the study and then going back to seek permission to quote was both labor-intensive and inefficient. To overcome the problems, Howard (1993) decided not to seek authors' specific permission, but always to anonymize any quoted materials, while providing sufficient material to establish context.

The issues of ownership and permission are compounded by the fact that much of the communication is across national boundaries, each of which may have their own peculiarities of copyright, and more recently of data protection legislation. Whose permission is needed, for example, for a researcher based in the United Kingdom to use a message posted by a participant in Australia to a list that is distributed via a computer in Canada? And what if the researcher happens to be in the United States or France when they access the message? Is it that of the original author, the contributor who has included part of that message in their own response, the list owner, or the general consent of all who have been party to the discussions through their reading, or by virtue of being a member of the list, whether they have been active participant or lurker? This is reflected in the fact that, at the beginning of the 21st century we are seeing attempts by national and international legislation to catch up with developments as the reality of e-commerce, technological change and CMC continue to evolve faster than laws.

In relation to the ownership of messages in discussion lists and other forms of CMC, a distinction between publicly accessible and publicly distributed messages is suggested (Waskul & Douglass, 1996). The same researchers also question the nature and possibility of informed consent in a CMC group that is in a constant state of flux in terms of its membership. They acknowledge that, in reality, online interactions often render attempting to obtain informed consent a practical impossibility.

Not all CMC researchers would advocate a cautious approach. In one of the pivotal publications addressing the area (a special edition of the journal *The Information Society*), Thomas (1996) summarized key points of the issues raised in a variety of articles and views. These included the statements that:

- Research in cyberspace provides no special dispensation to ignore ethical precepts;
- There may not be exact analogues in the offline world to ethical issues in cyberspace;
- While certain research activities may be possible, or not precluded, this doesn't mean they are necessarily allowable or ethical; and
- The ultimate responsibility lies with the individual researcher for honesty and ethical integrity.

Some recommendations on the approach to be taken reveal opposing views, with each seeming to assume only one particular type of CMC and seeking to generalize recommendations based on that type to other forms of CMC (Herring, 1996d). One view, from a legal perspective, sees all CMC as published work, protected by copyright law, and thus necessitating full referencing if used, including authors' names and other identifying details (Cavazos & Morin, 1994).

Few CMC researchers would adopt this viewpoint, which is in direct contradiction of the usual anonymization of sources in much research. King's (1996) standpoint is that all messages in online discussion groups are potentially private, and so if used in research should be totally anonymized, even to the extent of not identifying the discussion group itself and paraphrasing, in preference to directly quoting, the contributions. Obviously, such paraphrasing would make many of the forms of textual, linguistic and discourse analysis that have been employed impossible to use on CMC interactions. Herring (1996a) criticizes both extremes of absolutist position as untenable in the reality of CMC research, as they assume only one form of CMC exists, or one approach to CMC research. They also imply that generalizations from one form can be applied to all other variants and forms. She also criticizes both sets as not allowing for critical research, excluding the complex reality of both cyberspace and research, and excluding legitimate forms of research on CMC.

Schrum (1995) proposes a set of guidelines (Fig. 15.1) for the conduct of ethical electronic research, using an amalgam of techniques, including an ethnographic perspective, use of interviews and participant observation, and the need to maintain a delicate balance between protecting the subjects and the freedoms of the researcher.

15.6 A RESEARCH AGENDA

15.6.1 Mobile Learning

We are beginning to move from e-learning environments, where despite the flexibility offered, learners are still tied to a place-based mode of educational delivery, to the possibility of more mobile access to education. With the rise in use of mobile telephones, and their convergence with PDAs (personal digital assistants) and similar devices, new vista are opened for the intersection of communication and education.

Few would have predicted, for example, the extent to which text messaging via mobile phones is now a common part of the everyday life of many young people, people who are, or soon will be, our students. It is a form of CMC, and while some universities have used text alerts to students as reminders of submission dates, for example, there has yet been little study of the potential of this form of interaction. The European Commission, through its Information Society initiatives, has funded some research and development projects that are exploring the use of mobile devices for providing distance education.

In addition to the range of technological issues to be explored in enabling truly mobile education, there are many interesting social issues that probably present more opportunities for research and the development of new ways of education. If students can provide instant text responses, are they likely to do so, and perhaps not engage in reflection on issues before providing such a response?

Mobile and wireless networks might have additional effects on personalisation and/or intimacy of the learning experience if the student is truly able to study anywhere, anytime, and both receive information and provide information and interaction wherever they may be.

Researchers:

1. Must begin with an understanding of the basic tenets of conducting ethical qualitative research;

2. Should consider the respondents and participants as owners of the materials; the respondents should have the ability to modify or correct statements for spelling, substance, or language;

3. Need to describe in detail the goals of the research, the purposes to which the results will be put, plans of the researcher to protect participants, and recourse open to those who feel mistreated;

4. Should strive to create a climate of trust, collaboration, and equality with electronic community members, within an environment that is non-evaluative and safe;

5. Should negotiate their entry into an electronic community, beginning with the owner of the discussion, if one exists. After gaining entry, they should make their presence known in any electronic community (e.g., a listserv, specialized discussion group, or electronic class format) as frequently as necessary to inform all participants of their presence and engagement in electronic research;

6. Should treat electronic mail as private correspondence that is not to be forwarded, shared, or used as research data unless express permission is given;

7. Have an obligation to begin by informing participants as much as possible about the purposes, activities, benefits, and burdens that may result from their being studied;

8. Must inform participants as to any risks that might result from their agreeing to be part of the study—especially psychological or social risks;

9. Researchers must respect the identity of the members of the community, with special efforts to mask the origins of the communication, unless express permission to use identifying information is given;

10. Must be aware of the steep learning curve for electronic communications. Information about the research should be placed in a variety of accessible formats; and

11. Have an obligation to the electronic community in which they work and participate to communicate back the results of their work.

FIGURE 15.1. Schrum's ethical electronic research guidelines (from Schrum, 1995).

15.6.2 Vicarious Learning and Informal Discussion Environments

Communities of practice may be formally constituted, but there is increasing scope, with the widespread adoption of flexible approaches to continuing professional education and the recording of supporting evidence, for more informal approaches, generated from the needs of practitioners. McKendree et al. (1998) discuss vicarious learning and the fact that much real learning occurs through observation of other learners engaged in active dialogues. Murray's (2002) research identified a number of the issues arising, including the potential benefits of lurking. Boyle and Cook (2001) have used assessed online discussion groups to attempt to foster a community of enquiry (Lipman, 1991) and to foster vicarious learning. Many issues around the nature and extent of such vicarious learning would seem to be ripe for research over the coming years.

15.6.3 Structured Learning Activities

Asynchronous discussions and individual messaging are an important component of most models of online courses (Mason, 1998). In order to encourage discussion, in practical implementation of discussion within taught courses, it has been found to be important for course designers to structure the online environment. This involves devising stimulating individual and group activities, providing small group discussion areas and supporting students through facilitative rather than instructive moderating (Salmon, 2000).

Coomey and Stephenson (2001) stress the importance of dialogue, involvement and support in learning online, identifying four major features essential for good practice. They also state that dialogue must be carefully structured into a course to be successful, with the role of the moderator being, in part, to facilitate active participation through dialogue, in-depth reflection and thoughtful responses. Involvement through structured tasks, support, including periodic face to face contact, online tutor supervision, peer support, and advice from experts are seen to be important components, while the extent to which learners have control of key learning activities, and the extent to which students are encouraged to exercise that control have been shown, from the existing research, to facilitate online learning through CMC (Coomey & Stephenson 2001).

However, this evidence of a need for structure may seem to be at odds with the opportunities introduced above for informal learning opportunities, with potentially much less structured development. The possible tension between these two approaches is an important area of future research, as it may be that quite different processes are at work in the different environments.

15.6.4 Assessment Based on CMC

Much of the assessment of e-learning, as with many of the teaching and learning methods, used essentially offline methods, usually with little variation. Many current forms of online assessment are based on what we have used in the classroom for decades, including quizzes and submission of essays. The benefits of online assessment are measured in terms of automation and time and cost savings (McCormack & Jones, 1998). There has been relatively little attempt to explore new forms of assessment that might be made possible by online interaction, especially among groups of learners. Online assessment is a vital area for research over the next few years, in terms of investigating not only the appropriateness of transferring offline methods to e-learning, but also the development of new assessment methods grounded in the opportunities offered by the online world. Joint assessment and group web work are only two of the possibilities that have had some exploration so far, but which merit much more. Some collaborative CMC projects, which might form the basis of assessments, are suggested by Collis (1996), such as discussion of news items from the viewpoints of different cultural contexts, or exploring issues of cultural sensitivity through exploration of customs and lifestyles among students in a culturally diverse, international group.

As Mason (1998) notes, in group work integrated with assessment and examination, most students overcome their inhibitions and play their part in joint activities. The assessment procedures currently used in tertiary education are particularly ill suited to the digital age in which the ways people use information are more important than simply rote learning and regurgitation. She adds a further challenge that reusing material should be viewed as a skill to be encouraged, not as academic plagiarism to be despised. Through taking this approach, novel assessment methods might be developed, for example, through devising assignments and assessment procedures that reflect team working ability and knowledge management skills. These might also include the assessment of new knowledge jointly generated by students through online discussions.

15.6.5 Different Learners

For learners who come to e-learning from a cultural tradition that is based around a teacher-centered approach, rote learning or individual as opposed to group achievement, collaboration and discussion may not work well, and research will be needed into how best to use CMC within multicultural and unicultural groups.

Similarly, gender differences between and among online learners has received some attention within the CMC research (e.g., Spender, 1995), but there are still many areas to be examined. Different approaches to the use of CMC and collaborative learning between different professional groups, or within professions, merit much further work.

It is suggested that e-learning facilitates different learning styles, but research is needed into the practical application of different learning styles in the development of e-learning. Related questions include whether, or to what extent, different types of learner need to belong to a community in order to maximize the chances of success in both the development of the learning community and the meeting of individuals' learning needs.

15.6.6 Beyond Replicating Face-to-Face Teaching

Much CMC use has been grounded in replication of what can be done offline, in face-to-face encounters or by those mediated by other technologies, such as the telephone. However, just as the ways in which telephone use changed after it became widespread within the population, and in some unexpected ways, so we should expect that the use of CMC will change. Dillenbourg & Schneider (2002) state that, currently, most e-learning is in a stage of design-by-imitation, often reproducing classroom activities and with virtual campuses mimicking physical campuses. Practically-oriented texts on the development of online education (e.g., Collis, 1996; McCormack & Jones, 1998) tend to base their approaches in modeling classroom-based methods and interactions in the online environment.

What Mason (1998) terms "pedagogical evolution" refers not to a notion of teaching getting better, or the invention of new and different methods, but working with the technology (itself a moving target) and with course participants to arrive at new perspectives on how learning is best encouraged and supported in the online environment. Whether such new perspectives can be achieved is, to some degree, an assumption, and itself needs testing in the crucible of practice-based research. Two concepts that may emerge from research-based examination of the potential of the technologies, and new learning environments are a break down of the distinction between teacher and taught, and the collective construction of the educational course and, more broadly, of new knowledge. The online environment, with its resources, places to interact and people to contact, can form the backdrop against which a learning community comes together briefly to collaborate in a shared course.

Dillenbourg and Schneider (2002) view the most promising work in e-learning as investigating functionalities that do not exist in face-to-face interactions, for instance the possibility for learners to analyze their own interactions, or to see a display of their group dynamics. A group of learners and their e-learning tools might constitute a distributed system which self-organizes in a different way than a group of learners face to face. To investigate, and perhaps realize, some of this vision, is the greatest challenge facing the research and policy agendas for educators. This is especially so when we seem to be in a climate where funders of education provision are seeking materials and courses linked to specific occupational skills, rather than education for its own sake.

References

Almeda, M. B., and Rose, R. (2000). Instructor satisfaction in University of California Extension's on-line writing curriculum. *Journal of Asynchronous Learning Networks, 4*(3).

Anderson, T., Rourke, L., Garrison, D. R., & Archer, W. (2001). Assessing teaching presence in a computer conferencing context. *Journal of Asynchronous Learning Networks, 5*(2). From http://www.aln.org/alnweb.journal/

Archer, W., Garrison, D. R., Anderson, T., & Rourke, L. (2001). *A framework for analyzing critical thinking in computer conferences.* Paper presented at EURO-CSCL, Maastricht.

Argyle, M. (1991). Cooperation in working groups. In *Cooperation: The basis of sociability* (pp. 115-131). London: Routledge.

Arvan, L. and Musumeci, D. (2000). Instructor attitudes within the SCALE efficiency projects. *Journal of Asynchronous Learning Networks, 4*(3).

Aycock, A. (1995). Technologies of the self: Michael Foucault online. *Journal of Computer-Mediated Communication, 1*(2). From http://www.ascusc.org/jcmc/vol1/issue2/aycock.html

Baker, P., & Moss, K. (1996). Building learning communities through guided participation. *Primary Voices K-6, 4*(2), 2-6.

Bauman, M. (1997). *Online learning communities.* Paper presented at the Teaching in the Community Colleges Online Conference.

Baym, N. K. (1995). The emergence of community in computer-mediated communication. In S. Jones (Ed.) *CyberSociety: Computer-mediated communication and community* (pp. 138-63). Thousand Oaks, CA: Sage.

Baym, N. K. (1997). Interpreting soap operas and creating community: Inside an electronic fan culture. In S. Kiesler (Ed.) *Culture of the Internet* (pp. 103-20). Mahwah, NJ: Lawrence Erlbaum.

Beaudin, B. P. (1999). Keeping online asynchronous discussions on topic. *Journal of Asynchronous Learning Networks, 3*(2). From http://www.aln.org/alnweb.journal/

Becker, D., & Dwyer, M. (1998). The impact of student verbal/visual learning style preference on implementing groupware in the classroom. *Journal of Asynchronous Learning Networks, 2*(2). From http://www.aln.org/alnweb.journal/

Bell, M., Bush, D., Nicholson, P., O'Brien, D., & Tran, T. (2002). *Universities online. A survey of online education and services in Australia, Commonwealth Department of Education Science & Training.* From http://www.dest.gov.au/highered/occpaper/02a/default.htm

Berg, G (2000). "Early Patterns of Faculty Compensation for Developing and Teaching Distance Learning Courses." *Journal of Asynchronous Learning Networks, 4*(1).

Berge, Z. (1997). Characteristics of online teaching in post-secondary formal education. *Educational Technology, 37*(3), 35-47.

Biocca, F. (1995). *Presence.* Presentation at a workshop on Cognitive Issues in Virtual Reality, VR '95 Conference and Expo, San Jose, CA.

Bloom, B. (1981). *A Primer for parents, instructors and other educators: All our children learning.* New York: McGraw-Hill.

Blum, K. D. (1999). Gender differences in asynchronous learning in higher education: Learning styles, participation barriers and communication patterns. *Journal of Asynchronous Learning Networks, 3*(1). From http://www.aln.org/alnweb.journal/

Bolter J. D. (1989). Beyond word processing: The computer as a new writing space. *Language and Communication, 9*(2/3), 129-142.

Bowers, L. (1997). Constructing international professional identity: What psychiatric nurses talk about on the Internet. *International Journal of Nursing Studies, 34*(3), 208-212.

Boyle, T., & Cook, J. (2001) Online interactivity: Best practice based on two case studies. *ALT-J, Association of Learning Technology Journal, 9*(1), 94-102.

Brown, R. E. (2001). The process of community-building in distance learning classes. *Journal of Asynchronous Learning Networks, 5*(2). From http://www.aln.org/alnweb/journal/

Bruckman, A. (1998). Community support for constructionist learning. *CSCW: The Journal of Collaborative Computing, 7,* 47-86.

Bruckman, A. S. (1997). *MOOSE crossing: Construction, community, and learning in a Networked virtual world for kids.* Dissertation, School Of Architecture And Planning, Massachusetts Institute of Technology. From http://asb.www.media.mit.edu/people/asb/thesis/0-front-matter.html#abstract

Bruffee, K. A. (1993). *Collaborative learning: Higher education, interdependence, and the authority of knowledge.* Baltimore: John Hopkins University Press.

Burge, E. J. (1993). *Students' perceptions of learning in computer conferencing: A qualitative analysis.* EdD thesis (unpublished), Graduate Department of Education, University of Toronto, Canada.

Campos, M., Laferrière, T., & Harasim, L. (2001). The post-secondary networked classroom: Renewal of teaching practices and social interaction. *Journal of Asynchronous Learning Networks, 5*(2). From http://www.aln.org/alnweb/journal/

Carswell, L., Thomas, P., Petre, M., Price, B., & Richards, M. (2000). Distance education via the Internet: the student experience. *British Journal of Educational Technology, 31*(1), 29-46.

Cavazos, E. A., & Morin, G. (1994). *Cyberspace and the law: your rights and duties in the on-line world.* Cambridge, MA: The MIT Press.

Chen, D. T., & Hung, D. (2002). Personalized knowledge representations: The missing half of online discussions. *British Journal of Educational Technology, 33*(3), 279-290.

Chidambaram, L. (1996). Relational development in computer supported groups. *MIS Quarterly, 20*(2), 443-470.

Collins, D., & Bostock, S. J. (1993) Educational effectiveness and the computer conferencing interface. *ETTI, 30*(4), 334-342.

Collins, M. (2000). Comparing Web, correspondence and lecture versions of a second-year non-major biology course. *British Journal of Educational Technology, 31*(1).

Collis, B. (1996). *Tele-learning in a digital world: The future of distance learning.* London: International Thomson Computer Press.

Collis, B., & Winnips, K. (2002). Two scenarios for productive learning environments in the workplace. *British Journal of Educational Technology, 33*(2), 133-148.

Collis. B. (2002). Information technologies for education and training. In Adelsberger, H. H., Collis, B., & Pawlowski, J. M. (Eds.), *Handbook on information technologies for education and training.* Berlin: Springer-Verlag.

Colton, A. B., & Sparks-Langer, G. M. (1993). A conceptual framework to guide the development of teacher reflection and decision making. *Journal of Teacher Education, 44*(1), 45-54.

Coomey, M. & Stephenson, J. (2001). Online learning: it is all about dialogue, involvement, support and control - according to the research. In J. Stephenson (Ed.) *Teaching and learning online: Pedagogies for new technologies.* London: Kogan Page.

Corcoran, T. C. (1995). *Transforming professional development for teachers: A guide for state policymakers.* Washington, DC: National Governors Association.

Creanor, L. (2002). A tale of two courses: A comparative study of tutoring online. *Open Learning, 17*(1), 57-68.

Cross, P. K. (1998). Why learning communities? Why now? *About Campus, 3*(3), 4-11.

Curtis, D. D., & Lawson, M. J. (2001). Exploring collaborative online learning. *Journal of Asynchronous Learning Networks, 5*(1). From http://www.aln.org/alnweb/journal/

Curtis, P. (1997). MUDDING: Social phenomena in text-based virtual realities. In S. Kiesler (Ed.), *Culture of the Internet* (pp. 121-142). Mahwah, NJ: Lawrence Erlbaum.

Darling-Hammond, L. (1996). The right to learn and the advancement of teaching: Research, policy, and practice for democratic education. *Educational Researcher, 25*(6), 5-17.

Daughenbaugh, R., Ensminger, D., Frederick, L., & Surry, D. (2002). *Does personality type effect online versus in-class course satisfaction?* Paper presented at the Seventh Annual Mid-South Instructional Technology Conference on Teaching, Learning, & Technology.

December, J. (1996). What is Computer-mediated Communication? From http://www.december.com/john/study/cmc/what.html

Dede, C. J. (1990). The evolution of distance learning: Technology-mediated interactive learning. *Journal of Research on Computers in Education, 22*, 247-264.

Dede, C. (1996). The evolution of distance education: Emerging technologies and distributed learning. *American Journal of Distance Education, 10*(2), 4-36.

Dillenbourg, P., & Schneider, D. K. (2002). *A call to break away from imitating schooling.* From http://musgrave.cqu.edu.au/clp/clpsite/guest_editorial.htm (Accessed 31/10/02)

Dills, C. & Romiszowski, A. J. (Eds.). (1997). *Instructional development paradigms.* Englewood Cliffs, NJ: Educational Technology Publications.

Donath, J. S. (1999). Identity and deception in the virtual community. In M. A. Smith & P. Kollock (Eds.), *Communities in cyberspace* (pp. 29-59). New York: Routledge.

Dziuban, C. & Moskal, P. (2001). *Emerging research issues in distributed learning.* Paper delivered at the 7th Sloan-C International Conference on Asynchronous Learning Networks.

Eastmond, D. V. (1993). *Adult learning of distance students through computer conferencing.* PhD dissertation. Syracuse, NY: Syracuse University.

Engelhardt, H. T., & Wildes, K. W. (1994). The four principles of health care ethics and post-modernity: why a libertarian interpretation is unavoidable. In R. Gillon (Ed.), *Principles of health care ethics.* Chichester, UK: John Wiley & Sons.

Ess, C. (Ed.) (1996a). *Philosophical perspectives on computer-mediated communication.* Albany, NY: State University of New York Press.

Ess, C. (1996b). Introduction: Thoughts along the I-way: philosophy and the emergence of computer-mediated communication. In C. Ess (Ed.), *Philosophical perspectives on computer-mediated communication.* Albany, NY: State University of New York Press.

Fanderclai, T. L. (1995). MUDs in Education: New Environments, New Pedagogies. Computer-Mediated Communication Magazine, From http://www.ibiblio.org/cmc/mag/1995/jan/fanderclai.html

Feenberg, A. (1989). The written world: On the theory and practice of computer conferencing. In R. Mason & A. Kaye (Eds.), Mindweave: Communication, computers and distance education, Pergammon Press, Oxford, pp. 22-39.

Fernback, J. (1999). There is a there there: Notes toward a definition of cyberspace. In S. G. Jones (Ed.), *Doing Internet research.* Thousand Oaks, CA: Sage.

Foucault, M. (1988). *Technologies of the self: A seminar with Michel Foucault.* In L. H. Martin et al. (Eds.). Amherst, MA: University of Massachusetts Press.

Fredricksen, E., Pickett, A., Shea, P., Pelz, W., & Swan, K. (2000). Student satisfaction and perceived learning with online courses: Principles and examples from the SUNY Learning Network. Journal of Asynchronous Learning Networks, 4. Retrieved october 30, 2002, from http://www.aln.org/alnweb/journal/Vol4_issue2/le/Fredericksen/LE-fredericksen.htm

Graham, M., & Scarborough, H. (1999). Computer mediated communication and collaborative learning in an undergraduate distance education environment. *Australian Journal of Educational Technology, 15*(1), 20-46. From http://wwwasu.murdoch.edu.au/ajet/

Greenbaum, T. (2000). Focus Groups vs Online. *Advertising Age* (Feb, 2000). From http://www.isixsigma.com/offsite.asp?A=Fr&Url=http://www.groupsplus.com/pages/

Haines, V. A., & Hurlbert, J. S. (1992). Network range and health. *Journal of Health and Social Behavior, 33*, 254-266.

Haines, V. A., Hurlbert, J. S. & Beggs, J. J. (1996). Exploring the determinants of support provision: Provider characteristics, personal networks, community contexts, and support following life events, *Journal of Health & Social Behavior, 37*(3), 252-64.

Harasim, L., Hiltz, S. R., Teles, L., & Turoff, M. (1995). *Learning networks: A field guide to teaching and learning online.* Cambridge, MA: MIT Press.

Harasim, L. M. (1987). Teaching and learning on-line; issues in computer-mediated graduate courses. *Canadian Journal of Educational Communication, 16*(2), 117-135.

Hardy, V., Hodgson, V., & McConnell, D. (1994). Computer conferencing: A new medium for investigating issues in gender and learning. *Higher Education, 28*, 403-418.

Hartman, J., Dziuban, C., & Moskal, P. (2000). Faculty Satisfaction in ALNs: A dependent or independent variable? *Journal of Asynchronous Learning Networks, 4*(3).

Haythornthwaite, C. (1998). A social network study of the growth of community among distance learners. *Information Research, 4*(1).

Hill, J., R., & Raven, A. (2000). *Creating and implementing Web-based instruction environments for community building.* Paper presented at the AECT International Conference, Denver, CO.

Hiltz, S. R. (1994). *The virtual classroom.* Norwood, NJ: Ablex Publishing Corporation.

Hawkes, M. (1997). *Employing educational telecommunications technologies as a professional development structure for facilitating sustained teacher reflection.* Paper presented at the Annual Meeting of the American Educational Research Association, Chicago, IL.

Hawkes, M., & Romiszowski, A. J. (2001). Examining the reflective outcomes of asynchronous computer-mediated communication on in-service teacher development. *Journal of Technology and Teacher Education, 9*(2), 285–308.

Henri, F. (1991). Computer conferencing and content analysis. In A. R. Kaye (Ed.), *Collaborative learning through computer conferencing: The Najaden papers.* pp. 117–135. Berlin: Springer-Verlag/NATO Scientific Affairs Division.

Herring, S. (1996a). Linguistic and critical analysis of computer-mediated communication: Some ethical and scholarly considerations. *The Information Society, 12,* 153–168.

Herring, S. (1996b). Posting in a different voice: Gender and ethics in computer-mediated communication. In C. Ess (ed.), *Philosophical perspectives on computer-mediated communication.* Albany, NY: State University of New York Press.

Herring, S. (Ed.) (1996c). *Computer-mediated communication: Linguistic, social and cross-cultural perspectives.* Amsterdam: John Benjamins Publishing Company.

Herring, S. (1996d). Two variants of an electronic messaging schema. In S. Herring (Ed.), *Computer-mediated communication: Linguistic, social and cross-cultural perspectives.* Amsterdam: John Benjamins Publishing Company.

Hightower, R., & Sayeed, L. (1995). The impact of computer-mediated communication systems on biased group discussion. *Computers in Human Behavior, 11,* 33–44.

Hiltz, S. R. (1997). *Impacts of college-level courses via asynchronous learning networks: Some preliminary results.* From http://eies.njit.edu/~hiltz/workingpapers/philly/philly.htm

Hislop, G. (2000). ALN teaching as a routine faculty workload. *Journal of Asynchronous Learning Networks, 4*(3).

Hislop, G., and Atwood, M., (2000). ALN Teaching as Routine Faculty Workload. *Journal of Asynchronous Learning Networks, 4*(3). From http://www.aln.org/alnweb/journal/Vol4_issue3/fs/hislop/fs-hislop.htm

Hollingsworth, S. (1994). *Teacher research and urban literacy education: Lessons and conversations in a feminist key.* New York: Teachers College.

Honey, M. (1995). Online communities: They can't happen without thought and hard work. *Electronic Learning 14*(4), 12–13.

Horton, S. (2000). Web teaching guide: A practical approach to creating course web sites. New Haven, CT: Yale University Press.

Howard, T. (1993). The property issue in e-mail research. *Bulletin of the Association of Business Communications, 56*(2), 40–41.

Jaffee, D. (1998). Institutionalized resistance to asynchronous learning networks. *Journal of Asynchronous Learning Networks, 2*(2).

Jonassen, D. H. & Kwon, H. II. (2001). Communication patterns in computer mediated versus face-to-face group problem solving. *Educational Technology Research and Development, 49*(1), 35–51.

Jonassen, D., Davidson, M., Collins, M., Campbell, J. & Haag, B. B. (1995). Constructivism and computer-mediated communication in distance education. *The American Journal of Distance Education, 9*(2), 7–26.

Jones, S. G. (1995). Understanding community in the information age. In S. G. Jones (Ed.) Cybersociety - computer-mediated communication and community. Thousand Oaks, CA: Sage Publications Inc.

Jones, S. G. (Ed.) (1995). *CyberSociety: Computer-mediated communication and community.* Thousand Oaks, CA: Sage.

Jones, S. G. (Ed.) (1998). *CyberSociety 2.0: Revisiting computer-mediated communication and community.* Thousand Oaks, CA: Sage.

Kashy, E., Thoennessen, M., Albertelli, G. & Tsai, Y. (2000). Implementing a large on-campus ALN: Faculty perspective. *Journal of Asynchronous Learning Networks, 4*(3).

Kaye, A. (1991). Learning together apart. In A. R. Kaye (ed.), *Collaborative learning through computer conferencing: The Najaden papers.* Berlin: Springer-Verlag/NATO Scientific Affairs Division.

Kaye, A., Mason, R., & Harasim, L. (1991). Computer conferencing in the academic environment. ERIC Document Reproduction Service, No. 320 540.

Kaye, A. (1995). Computer supported collaborative learning. In N. Heap et al. (Eds.), *Information technology and society* (pp. 192–210). London: Sage.

Kearsley, G., & Shneiderman, B. (1998). Engagement theory. *Educational Technology, 38*(3).

Kenny, R. F., Andrews, B. W., Vignola, M., Schilz, A., & Covert, J. (1999). Toward guidelines for the design of interactive multimedia instruction: Fostering the reflective decision-making of preservice teachers. *Journal of Technology and Teacher Education, 71,* 13–31.

Kilian, C. (1994). The passive-aggressive paradox of on-line discourse. *The Education Digest, 60,* 33–36.

Killingsworth, B., Schellenberger, R., & Kleckley, J. (2000). The use of focus groups in the design and development of a national labor exchange system. *First Monday, 5*(7), 1–18. From http://firstmonday.org/issues/issue5_7/killingsworth/index.html

Kim, A. J. (2000). *Community building on the Web.* Berkeley, CA: Peachpit Press.

Kimball, L. (1995). Ten ways to make online learning groups work. *Educational Leadership, 53*(2), 54–56.

King, J. L., Grinter, R. E., & Pickering, J. M. (1997). The rise and fall of Netville: The saga of a cyberspace construction boomtown in the great divide. In S. Kiesler (Ed.), *Culture of the Internet* (pp. 3–33). Mahwah, NJ: Lawrence Erlbaum.

King, S. A. (1996). Researching Internet communities: Proposed ethical guidelines for the reporting of results. *The Information Society, 12,* 119–127.

Kollock, P., & Smith, M. A. (1999). Communities in cyberspace. In M. A. Smith & P. Kollock (Eds.), *Communities in cyberspace* (pp. 3–25). New York: Routledge.

Kowch, E., & Schwier, R. (1997). Considerations in the construction of technology-based virtual learning communities. *Canadian Journal of Educational Communication, 26*(1).

Lave, J. (1993). *Understanding practice : Perspectives on activity and context.* Cambridge, UK/New York: Cambridge University Press.

Lave, J., & Wenger, E. (1991). *Situated learning : Legitimate peripheral participation.* Cambridge, UK/New York: Cambridge University Press.

Leppänen, S., & Kalaja, P. (1995). Experimenting with computer conferencing in English for academic purposes. *ELT Journal, 49,* 26–36.

Lewis, B. A. (2001). *Learning effectiveness: Efficacy of quizzes vs. discussions in on-line learning.* Doctoral Dissertation. IDD&E, Syracuse University School of Education.

Lewis, B. A. (2002). The effectiveness of discussion forums in on-line learning. *Brazilian Review of Education at a Distance, 1*(1). From http://www.abed.org.br

Lichtenstein, G., McLaughlin, M., & Knudsen, J. (1992). Teacher empowerment and professional knowledge. In A. Lieberman (Ed.), *The National Society for Studies in Education 91st yearbook* (Part II). Chicago, IL: University of Chicago.

Lieberman, A. (1995). Practices that support teacher development: Transforming conceptions of professional learning. *Phi Delta Kappan, 76*(8), 591–596.

Lieberman, A., & McLaughlin, M. W. (1993). Networks for educational change: Powerful and problematic. *Phi Delta Kappan, 75*(9), 673–677.

Lipman, M. (1991). *Thinking in education*. New York: Cambridge University Press.

Little, J. W. (1993). Teachers' professional development in a climate of educational reform. *Educational Evaluation and Policy Analysis, 15*(2), 129–152.

Liu, Y., & Ginther, D. W. (2002). *Instructional strategies for achieving a positive impression in computer mediated communication (CMC) distance education courses*. Proceedings of Teaching, Learning, & Technology Conference, Middle Tennessee State University.

Lombard, M., & Ditton, T. (1997). At the heart of it all: The concept of presence. *Journal of Computer Mediated Communications, 3*(2). From http://www.ascusc.org/jcmc/

Looi, C.-K. (2002). Communication techniques. In Adelsberger, H. H., Collis, B., & Pawlowski, J. M. (Eds.), *Handbook on information technologies for education and training*. Berlin: Springer-Verlag

Lucena, C. P. J., Fuks, H., Milidiu, R., Laufer, C., Blois, M., Choren, R., Torres, V., and Daflon, L. (1998). AulaNet: helping teachers to do their homework. Proceedings of the Multimedia Computer Techniques in Engineering Seminar/Workshop, Technische Universitat Graz, Graz, Austria (pp. 16–30).

Marvin, L. (1995). Spoof, spam, lurk and lag: The aesthetics of text-based virtual realities. *Journal of Computer-Mediated Communication, 1*(2). From http://www.ascusc.org/jcmc/

Mason, R.. (1991). Evaluation methodologies for computer conferencing applications. In A. R. Kaye (Ed.), *Collaborative learning through computer conferencing: The Najaden papers*. Berlin: Springer-Verlag/NATO Scientific Affairs Division.

Mason, R. (1992). Computer conferencing for managers. *Interactive Learning International, 8*, 15–28.

Mason, R. (1998). Models of online courses. *ALN Magazine 2*(2). From http://www.aln.org/alnweb/magazine/vol2_issue2/Masonfinal.htm

Mayadas, F. (1997). Asynchronous learning networks: A Sloane Foundation perspective. *Journal of Asynchronous Learning Networks, 1*(1). From http://www.aln.org/alnweb.journal/issue1/mayadas.htm)

McConnell, D. (2002). Action research and distributed problem-based learning in continuing professional education. *Distance Education, 23*(1), 59–83.

McCormack, C., & Jones, D. (1998). *Building a web-based education system*. New York: Wiley Computer Publishing.

McKendree, J., Stenning, K., Mayes, T., Lee, J., & Cox, R. (1998). Why observing a dialogue may benefit learning. *Journal of Computer Assisted Learning, 14*(2), 110–119.

McMahon, T. A. (1996). *From isolation to interaction? Computer-mediated communications and teacher professional development*. Doctoral dissertation. Bloomington, IN: Indiana University.

McLaughlin, M. L., Osborne, K. K., & Smith, C. B. (1995). Standards of conduct on Usenet. In S. G. Jones (Ed.), *CyberSociety: Computer-mediated communication and community* (pp. 90–111). Thousand Oaks, CA: Sage.

Mickelson, K. M., & Paulin, R. S. (1997). *Beyond technical reflection: The possibilities of classroom drama in early preservice teacher education*. Paper presented at the annual meeting of the American Educational Research Association. Chicago, IL.

Misanchuk, M., & Anderson, T. (2002). Building community in an online learning environment: Communication, cooperation and collaboration. *Proceedings of the Teaching Learning and Technology Conference*, Middle Tennessee State University, April 7–9.

Moore, G. (1997). Sharing faces, places, and spaces: The Ontario Telepresence Project Field Studies. In K. E. Finn et. al (Eds.), *Video-mediated communication* (pp. 301–321). Mahwah, NJ: Lawrence Erlbaum.

Moore, M. G., & Kearsley, G. (1996). *Distance education: A systems view*. Boston, MA: Wadsworth Publishing.

Mouton, H. (1988). *Adjunct questions in mediated self-instruction: Contrasting the predictions of the "levels of processing" perspective, the "transfer-appropriate processing" perspective, and the "transfer across levels of processing" perspective*. Doctoral dissertation. IDD&E, Syracuse University, School of Education.

Murray, P. J. (1996). Nurses' computer-mediated communications on NURSENET: A case study. *Computers in Nursing, 14*(4), 227–234.

Murray, P. J., & Anthony, D. M. (1999). Current and future models for nursing e-journals: Making the most of the web's potential. International *Journal of Medical Informatics, 53*, 151–161.

Murray, P. J. (2002). *Subject:talk.to/reflect—reflection and practice in nurses' computer-mediated communications*. PhD Thesis. Institute of Educational Technology, The Open University, UK.

Naughton, J. (2000). *A brief history of the future: The origins of the internet*. London: Phoenix

Newman, D. R., Johnson, C., Cochrane, C. & Webb, B. (1996) An experiment in group learning technology: Evaluating critical thinking in face-to-face and computer-supported seminars. Interpersonal Computing and Technology: An Electronic Journal for the 21st century, *4*(1), 57–74. From http://jan.ucc.nau.edu/~ipctj/1996/n1/newman.txt

Olaniran, B. A. (1994). Group performance in computer-mediated and face-to-face communication media. *Management Communication Quarterly, 7*(3), 256–281.

Olaniran, B. A., Savage, G. T., & Sorenson, R. L. (1996). Experimental and experiential approaches to teaching the advantages of face-to-face and computer-mediated group discussion. *Communication Education, 45*, 244–259.

Oren, A., Mioduser, D. & Nachmias, R. (2002). The development of social climate in virtual learning discussion groups. *International Review of Research in Open and Distance Learning (IRRODL)*, April 2002. http://www.irrodl.org/content/v3.1/mioduser.html

Ory, J. C., Bullock, C., & Burnaska, K. (1997). Gender similarity in the use of and attitudes about ALN in a university setting. *Journal of Asynchronous Learning Networks, 1*(1). From http://www.aln.org/alnweb.journal/

Palloff, R. M., & Pratt, K. (1999). *Building learning communities in cyberspace: Effective strategies for the online classroom*. San Francisco, CA: Jossey-Bass.

Perrolle, J. A. (1991). Conversations and trust in computer interfaces. In C. Dunlop & R. Kling (Eds.), *Computerization and controversy: Value conflicts and social choices*, Academic Press Inc., Boston.

Phillips, A. F., & Pease, P. S. (1987). Computer conferencing and education: Complementary or contradictory concepts? *The American Journal of Distance Education, 1*(2), 38–51.

Phillips, C. (1990) Making friends in the electronic student lounge. *Distance Education, 11*(2), 320–333.

Phipps, R. A., & Merisotis, J. P. (1999). *What's the difference: A review of contemporary research on the effectiveness of distance learning in higher education*. Washington, DC: The Institute for Higher Education Policy. From http://www.chea.org/Events/QualityAssurance/98May.html

Picciano, A. G. (2002). Beyond student perceptions: Issues of interaction, presence, and performance in an online course. *Journal of Asynchronous Learning Networks, 6*(1). From http://www.aln.org/alnweb.journal/

Poster, M. (1990) *The mode of information: Poststructuralism and social context.* Cambridge: Polity Press.

Porter, J. E. (1993). E-mail and variables of rhetorical form. *Bulletin of the Association of Business Communications, 56*(2), 41–42

Preece, J. (2000). *Online communities.* Chichester, UK: John Wiley & Sons.

Rasmussen, G., & Skinner, E. (1997). *Learning communities: Getting started.* ERIC Clearinghouse (ED433048).

Raymond, R. C. (1999). Building learning communities on nonresidential campuses. *Teaching English in the Two-Year College, 26*(4), 393–405.

Reid, E. (1995). Virtual worlds: Culture and imagination. In S. G. Jones (Ed.), *CyberSociety: Computer-mediated communication and community* (pp. 164–183). Thousand Oaks, CA: Sage.

Rezabek, R. (2000). Online focus groups: Electronic discussions for research. *Forum Qualitative Sozialforschung/Forum: Qualitative Social Research, 1*(1). Online at: http://qualitative-research.net/fqs

Rheingold, H. (1993). *The virtual community: Homesteading on the electronic frontier.* Reading, MA: Addison Wesley.

Riel, M. (1998). *Education in the 21st century: Just-in-time learning or learning communities.* Paper presented at the Fourth Annual Conference of the Emirates Center for Strategic Studies and Research, Abu Dhabi.

Ringstaff, C., Sandholtz, J. H., & Dwyer, D. (1994). Trading places: When teachers use student expertise in technology intensive classrooms. *People and Education, 2*(4), 479–505.

Romiszowski, A. J. and DeHaas, J. (1989). Computer-mediated communication for instruction: Using E-mail as a seminar. *Educational Technology, 24*(10).

Romiszowski, A. J., Jost, K. & Chang, E. (1990). Computer-mediated communication: A hypertext approach to structuring distance seminars. In proceedings of the 32nd Annual ADCIS International Conference. Association for the Development of Computer-based Instructional Systems (ADCIS).

Romiszowski, A. J. and Chang, E. (1992). Hypertext's contribution to computer-mediated communication: In search of an instructional model. In M. Giardina (Ed.), *Interactive Multimedia Environments* (pp. 111–130).

Romiszowski, A. J., & Mason, R. (1996). Computer-mediated communication. In D. Jonassen (Ed.), *Handbook of research for educational communications and technology* (pp. 438–456). New York: Simon & Schuster Macmillan.

Romiszowski, A. J., and Villalba, C. (2000). Structural Communication and Web-based Instruction. Proceedings of the ED-MEDIA2000 International Conference, Montreal.

Romiszowski A. J. & Chang E. (2001). A practical model for conversational Web-based training. In B. H. Khan (Ed.), *Web-based training.* Educational Technology Publications.

Ropp, M. M. (1998). *Exploring individual characteristics associated with learning to use computers in preservice teacher preparation.* Paper presented at the annual meeting of the American Educational Research Association, San Diego, CA.

Rossman, M. H. (1999). Successful online teaching using an asynchronous learner discussion forum. *Journal of Asynchronous Learning Networks, 3*(2). From http://www.aln.org/alnweb.journal/

Rourke, L., Anderson, T., Garrison, D. R., & Archer, W. (2001a). Methodological issues in analyzing text-based computer conferencing transcripts. *International Journal of Artificial Intelligence in Education, 12*, 8–22.

Rourke, L., Anderson, T., Garrison, D. R., & Archer, W. (2001b). Assessing social presence in asynchronous text-based computer conferencing. *Journal of Distance Education/Revue de l'enseignement*

à distance, 14(2). From http://cade.athabascau.ca/vol14.2/rourke_et_al.html

Rovai, A. A. P. (2002a). A preliminary look at the structural differences of higher education classroom communities in traditional and ALN courses. *Journal of Asynchronous Learning Networks, 6*(1). Online at: http://www.aln.org/alnweb.journal/

Rovai, A. (2002b). Development of an instrument to measure classroom community. *The Internet and Higher Education, 5*, 197–211.

Rutter, J., & Smith, G. (1999): *Presenting the offline self in an everyday, online environment.* Paper presented at the Identities in Action Conference, Gregynog.

Russell, D. and Daugherty, M. (2001). Web Crossing: a context for mentoring. *Journal of Technology and Teacher Education, 9*(3), 433–446.

Ryan, R. (1992). International connectivity: A survey of attitudes about cultural and national differences encountered in computer-mediated communication. *The Online Chronicle of Distance Education and Communication, 6*(1).

Tella, S. (1992). *Boys, girls, and e-mail: A case study in Finnish senior secondary schools.* Helsinki: University of Helsinki, Department of Teacher Education.

Tella, S. 1992. Boys, Girls, and E-Mail: A Case Study in Finnish Senior Secondary Schools. Department of Teacher Education. University of Helsinki. Research Report 110. (In English) [http://www.helsinki.fi/~tella/110.pdf]

Turgeon, A., Di Biase, D. and Miller, G. (2000). Introducing the Penn State World Campus through certificate programmes in turf grass management and geographic information systems. From http://www.aln.org/alnweb/journal/Vol4_issue3/fs/turgeon/fs-turgeon.htm

Salmon, G. (2000). *E-moderating: The key to teaching and learning online.* London: Kogan Page.

Salmon, G. (2002). Mirror, mirror, on my screen: Exploring online reflections. *British Journal of Educational Technology, 33*(4), 379–391.

Schifter, C. C. (2000). Faculty participation in Asynchronous Learning Networks: A case study of motivating and inhibiting factors. *Journal of Asynchronous Learning Networks, 4*(1), 15–22.

Schon, D. A. 1983. *The Reflective Practitioner: How professionals think in action.* New York: Basic Books.

Schrum, L. (1995). Framing the debate: Ethical research in the information age. *Qualitative Inquiry, 1*(3), 311–326.

Schwier, R. A. (1999). *Turning learning environments into learning communities: Expanding the notion of interaction in multimedia.* Paper presented at the World Conference on Educational Multimedia, Hypermedia and Telecommunications, Seattle, WA, Association for the Advancement of Computers in Education.

Shank, G., & Cunningham, D. (1996). Mediated phosphor dots: Toward a post-cartesian model of CMC via the semiotic superhighway. In C. Ess (Ed.), *Philosophical perspectives on computer-mediated communication.* Albany, NY: State University of New York Press.

Shea, P., Fredericksen, E., Pickett, A., Pelz, W., & Swan, K. (2001). Measures of learning effectiveness in the SUNY Learning Network. In J. Bourne & J. Moore (Eds.), *Online education: Proceedings of the 2000 Sloan summer workshop on asynchronous learning networks.* Volume 2 in the Sloan-C series. Needham, MA: Sloan-C Press.

Simmons, J. M., Sparks, G. M., Starko, A., Pasch, M., Colton, A., & Grinberg, J. (1989). *Exploring the structure of reflective pedagogical thinking in novice and expert teachers: The birth of a developmental taxonomy.* Paper presented at the annual conference of the American Educational Research Association, San Francisco, CA.

Smith, C. B., McLaughlin, M. L., & Osborne, K. K. (1996). Conduct control on Usenet. *Journal of Computer-Mediated Communication, 2*(4). From http://www.ascusc.org/jcmc/vol2/issue4/smith.html.

Smith, M. A., & Kollock, P. (Eds.) (1999). *Communities in cyberspace*. London: Routledge.

Sotillo, S. M. (2000). Discourse functions and syntactic complexity in synchronous and asynchronous communication. *Language Learning & Technology, 4*(1), 82-119.

Spender, D. (1995). *Nattering on the net: Women, power and cyberspace*. North Melbourne, Australia: Spinifex Press.

Spitzer, W., Wedding, K., & DiMauro, V. (1995). *Strategies/or the purposeful uses of the network for professional development*. Cambridge, MA: Technical Education Research Centers. From http://hub.terc.edu/terc/LabNet/Guide/00-Pubinfor.htm

Sproull, L., & Kiesler, S. (1986). Reducing social context cues: Electronic mail in organizational computing. *Management Science, 32*(11), 1492-1512.

Sproull, L., & Kiesler, S. (1991). *Connections: New ways of working in the networked organization*. Cambridge, MA: The MIT Press.

Swan, K. (2002). Building learning communities in online courses: The importance of interaction. *Education, Communication & Information, 2*(1), 23 -49.

Thomas, J. (1996). A debate about the ethics of fair practices for collecting social science data in cyberspace. *Information Society, 12*(2), 7-12.

Toyoda, E., & Harrison, R. (2002). Categorization of text chat communication between learners and native speakers of Japanese. *Language Learning & Technology, 6*(1), 82-99.

Turkle, S. (1995). *Life on the screen: Identity in the age of the Internet*. Phoenix.

Uhlíøová, L. (1994). E-mail as a new subvariety of medium and its effects upon the message. In S. Mejrková & P. Franti_ek (Eds.), *The Syntax of Sentence and Text: A Festschrift for Franti_ek Dane_*. (pp. 273-282). Philadelphia, PA: John Benjamins.

Villalba, C. and Romiszowski, A. J. (1999). AulaNet and other Web-based learning environments: A comparative study in an International context. Proceedings of the 1999 ABED International conference, Rio de Janeiro, Brazil. http://www.abed.org.br

Villalba, C. and Romiszowski, A. J. (2001). Current and ideal practices in designing, developing, and delivering web-based training. In B. H. Khan (Ed.) *Web-based training*. Englewood Cliffs, NJ: Educational Technology Publications.

Walker, J., Wasserman, S., & Wellman, B. (1994). Statistical models for social support networks. In S. Wasserman & J. Galaskiewicz (Eds.), *Advances in social network analysis*. (pp. 53-78). Thousand Oaks, CA: Sage.

Walther, J., & Burgoon, J. (1992). Relational communication in computer-mediated interaction. *Human Communication Research, 19*, 50-88.

Warschauer, M. (1996). Comparing face-to-face and electronic discussion in the second language classroom. *CALICO Journal, 13*(2/3), 7-26.

Warschauer, M. (1997). Computer-mediated collaborative learning: Theory and practice. *Modern Language Journal, 81*(3), P470-481.

Warschauer, M., Turbee, L., & Roberts, B. (1996). Computer learning NetWorks and student empowerment. *SYSTEM, 24*(1), 1-14.

Waskul, D., & Douglass, M. (1996). Considering the electronic participant: Some polemical observations on the ethics of on-line research. *The Information Society, 12*, 129-139.

Waskul, D. & Douglass, M.. (1997). Cyberself: The emergence of self in on-line chat. *The Information Society, 13*, 375-397.

Wellman, B. (1979). The community question. *American Journal of Sociology, 84*, 1201-1231.

Wellman, B. (1999).The network community: An introduction to networks in the global village. In B. Wellman (Ed.), *Networks in the global village* (pp. 1-48). Boulder, CO: Westview Press.

Wellman, B., & Gulia M. (1999a). Net surfers don't ride alone: Virtual communities as communities. In M. Smith & P. Kollock (Eds.) *Communities in cyberspace* (pp. 167-194). London: Routledge.

Wellman, B., & Gulia, M. (1999b). The network basis of social support: A network is more than the sum of its ties. In B. Wellman (Ed.). *Networks in the global village* (pp. 83-118). Boulder, CO: Westview Press.

Wellman, B., Carrington, P., & Hall, A. (1988). Networks as personal communities. In B. Wellman & S. D. Berkowitz (Eds.), *Social structures: A network approach* (pp. 130-184). Cambridge, UK: Cambridge University Press.

Wenger, E. (1998). *Communities of practice: Learning, meaning, and identity*. Cambridge, UK: Cambridge University Press.

Wilson, B., & Ryder, M. (1996). *Dynamic learning communities: An alternative to designed instructional systems*. ERIC Clearinghouse (ED397847).

Yates, S. J. (1994). The textuality of computer-mediated communication: Speech, writing and genre in CMC discourse. PhD thesis (unpublished), The Open University, Milton Keynes, UK.

Yoon, S. H. (1996). Power online: A poststructuralist perspective on computer-mediated communication. In C. Ess (ed.), *Philosophical perspectives on computer-mediated communication*. Albany, NY: State University of New York Press.

Zhang, P. (1998). A case study of technology use in distance learning *Journal of Research on Computers in Education, 30*(4), 398-419.

Zhao, Y. (1998). The effects of anonymity on peer review. *International Journal of Educational Telecommunication, 4*(4), 311-346.

Zhao, Y., & Rop, S. (2000). *A critical review of the literature on electronic networks as reflective discourse communities for inservice teachers*. Paper presented at the Annual Meeting of American Education Research Association, New Orleans, LA. Available as CIERA Report #3-014, University of Michigan School of Education.

EXPLORING RESEARCH ON INTERNET-BASED LEARNING: FROM INFRASTRUCTURE TO INTERACTIONS

Janette R. Hill
University of Georgia

David Wiley
Utah State University

Laurie Miller Nelson
Utah State University

Seungyeon Han
University of Georgia

16.1 INTRODUCTION

Internet-based technologies are expanding and changing at an exponential rate. Few technologies have had such a global impact; further, few technologies have impacted such a wide range of sectors in our society across and within various socioeconomic groups. This is particularly true of the World Wide Web (Web). Business to education, youth to elders, world powers to third world countries—all have felt the impact of the web.

The Internet and Web have not only received the greatest attention, they have also experienced the greatest distribution. According to the U.S. Department of Commerce (2002), Internet access and use in the United States has expanded exponentially. As of September 2001, approximately 54 percent of the population were using the Internet. This increase was seen across demographic groups and geographic regions, representing one of the most significant shifts in terms of technology infusion.

Education has certainly been impacted by the Web. As stated by Owston (1997), "nothing before has captured the imagination and interests of educators simultaneously around the globe more than the World Wide Web" (p. 27). From the individual classroom to the media center, it is difficult to imagine not having some form of access to the Internet in schools, both K–12 and higher education, to support the learning and work that needs to be done.

Surprisingly, despite the seemingly widespread infusion and use of the Internet, we have yet to develop a clear understanding of the impact these technologies have had and are having on the processes of learning. Theoretical and research foundations have not kept pace with technological growth and use. Several questions have been posed and answered; yet many more remain. We are developing a good idea of "what" the technology can do, while "how's" (e.g., *How can the Internet assist us with teaching and learning processes?*) and "why's" (e.g., *Why this technology now?*) remain relatively unclear. It is important that we examine the how's and why's in our research to understand the value (current and potential) the Internet can bring to the learning process. The purpose of this chapter will be to explore the research that has been completed to date, and to identify unresolved issues and problems that might help guide future research.

16.1.1 Organization of the Chapter

The chapter is organized categorically to cover research related to the Internet. Theoretical foundations underlying research related to the Internet-based learning are described in the first section, including instructional approaches and learning styles. The subsequent four sections of the chapter represent major topical areas revealed in our review of the literature:

1. Designing Internet-based learning environments,
2. Teaching and the Internet: uncovering challenges and opportunities,
3. Learning from and with the Internet: learner perspectives, and
4. Learning through the Internet: interactions and connections in online environments.

We close the chapter with emerging issues and considerations for future research.

We recognize there are other areas that could be included in the review; indeed, we found it challenging to make decisions regarding major topical areas to cover for our review. Furthermore, we recognize that the "prime" areas will continue to shift and change over time. Rather than being all-inclusive and definitive review, we feel the topics included in our chapter reflect current trends in Internet-based research, indicating areas where future research may be leveraged.

16.2 THEORETICAL FOUNDATIONS UNDERLYING INTERNET-BASED RESEARCH

Internet-based learning has been occurring since the start of ARPANET (the precursor of the current Internet) in the 1960s. More formal uses of the Internet for learning were established in the 1980s with the formation of moderated newsgroups (Schrum & Berenfeld, 1997). The Internet technology of the Web is also a newcomer to the distance learning movement, with one of the first educational applications documented by ERIC in 1994 with Blumberg's report on the use of MendelWeb.

Despite the relative newness of these technologies, researchers have sought to establish a theoretical foundation to guide research and practice. In the following section, we discuss theoretical constructs related to learning and the Internet that have been empirically investigated.

16.2.1 Theoretical Constructs for Internet-Based Learning

In 1973, Michael Moore issued a call for examination of and research related to more "macro-factors" in distance learning in general. As reported by Moore & Kearsley (1995), Moore's list included: defining the field of distance learning, identifying the critical components of teaching and learning at a distance, and building a theoretical framework for distance learning. While not directly related to Internet-based learning, there are connections between the two areas. Almost 30 years later, a common definition is still not agreed upon, the critical components continue to be examined, and a unified theory of distance or Internet-based learning has not been established. There has, however, been significant progress made with research examining each of the macro-factors described by Moore: transactional distance, interaction, control, and social context.

16.2.1.1 Transactional Distance. Michael Moore first introduced his theory of transactional distance at a conference in 1972 (Moore & Kearsley, 1995). In his explanation, Moore emphasized that his theory was a pedagogical theory. As explained by Moore and Kearsley, what is of interest is the effect that distance has on instruction and learning. Moore's theory focuses on the shifts in understanding and perception that are created by the separation of teachers and learners.

There are two primary variables in the theory: structure and dialogue. The structure is determined during the design of the course, whereas the dialogue is a function of the communication between the instructor and learner during implementation. In Moore's theory, *distance* is not a geographical concept but rather a concept defined in the relationship between structure and dialogue. According to McIsaac and Gunawardena (1996), "education offers a continuum of transactions from less distant, where there is greater interaction and less structure, to more distant, where there may be less interaction and more structure" (p. 407).

Moore's theory has received recent attention in the research literature. Jung (2001) analyzed previous research related to teaching and learning processes of Web-based instruction (WBI) in order to develop a theoretical framework of WBI using Moore's Transactional Distance Theory as a foundation. The purpose of Jung's research was to provide a better understanding of the essential pedagogical components of WBI. Jung's proposed model extends Moore's theory and includes the following elements: infrastructure (content expandability, content adaptability, visual layout), dialogue (academic interaction, collaborative interaction, interpersonal interaction), and learner collaborativity (learner collaboration) and learner autonomy. One conclusion from Jung's work is that previous work has not been widely explored—thus creating an opportunity for more theory-based research as well as theory development.

16.2.1.2 Interaction. The concept of interaction has received considerable attention in the literature related to distance Internet-based learning. Four types of interaction have been described in the literature: learner–instructor, learner–learner, learner–content, and learner–interface (Hillman, Willis, & Gunawardena, 1994; Moore, 1989). Each is briefly described below.

Learner–instructor interaction is a key element that provides dialogue between the learner and the instructor. This form of interaction enables feedback as well as opportunities to motivate and support the learner. Learner–learner interaction encompasses the dialogue among and between students in the online course. This dialogue may include the exchange of information or ideas.

Learner–content interaction is critical to the learning process, particularly at a distance. Articles, textbook chapters, and Web sites are all examples of the kinds of materials a learner may need to interact with to extend their understanding in an online course. Finally, learner–interface interaction relates to the learners' ability to use the communication medium facilitating the online course.

In a recent study, the concepts of learner–instructor, learner–learner, and learner–interface interactions were described as having an impact in online courses (Hill, Raven, & Han, 2002). Learners reported that reminder messages [things you **C**ould be doing, **S**hould be doing and **M**ust be doing (**CSMs**)] sent by the instructor were particularly helpful with time management. Participants also mentioned that motivational statements of support and encouragement from their peers were valuable. Finally, the study indicated that the learners' inability to successfully interact with the mediating technology had the potential of being a significant source of frustration, leading to dissatisfaction with the online course.

16.2.1.3 Control. The issues associated with control have been a part of the theoretical foundations of education for many years. Alessi and Trollip (2001) have conducted considerable research in this area, particularly as it relates to multimedia systems. As one of the most robust multimedia systems currently available, the Internet, and particularly the Web, provides much more user control than in most educational software. Alessi and Trollip's research indicates that control—in the forms of learner and system—are critical in to the development of effective learning environments. Further, they suggest that the proper availability and use of controls is particularly important for learners when working on the Web.

In distance or Internet-based learning, the two concepts that have been linked with control are independence and learner control. Independence relates to the learners impressions of how well they can function on their own. Independence was one factor that Bayton (1992) found relevant in her research. According to Bayton, a balance needs to be obtained between independence, competence and support to have a successful online experience.

The notion of independence is directly tied to internal and external locus of control (see Hayes, 2000, for an extensive overview of the research). When a student has an internal locus of control, she or he perceives that success is a result of personal accomplishments and effort. An external locus of control, in contrast, leads the student to feel that she or he is dependent on factors outside of her/his control for success

(e.g., fate, luck). Each of these has implications for learning in Internet-based learning contexts. Students with internal locus of control have been found to have a higher completion rate than students with external locus of control (Rotter, 1989). Assisting learners with adjusting their perceptions of control, especially from external to internal, can greatly facilitate increases in completion of Internet-based learning experiences.

16.2.1.4 Social Context. The social context in which a learning experience takes place is an important consideration whether the interaction is face-to-face or at a distance. However, recent research has emphasized the import role that social and cultural attributes play in learning from and with the Internet. As pointed out by McIssac and Gunawardena (1996), technology may not be culturally neutral; therefore, it is important to attend to the context in which the interactions will take place so that learning experiences can be planned appropriately.

Other researchers have focused on the concept of presence as it relates to social context. In her work on community building, Hill (2002) discusses the importance of knowing there is a **there,** there—meaning it is important for learners and facilitators to have a sense that others are a part of the interactions and that although the space is virtual, that it does share some of the same properties as a physical space.

Moller (1998) also talks about the role of presence and being there in his work in asynchronous Web-based environments. According to Moller, social presence is the degree to which an individual feels or is seen as *real* by colleagues working in the online context. When a learner has a higher degree of social presence, they are more likely to feel connected to the group, which in turn typically leads to greater satisfaction and reduces the likelihood that the learner will leave the environment.

Jelfs and Whitelock (2000) also found that a sense of presence was important in their work in virtual environments. Based on interviews with experts in the area of computer-based learning, Jelfs and Whitelock concluded that audio feedback is one of the most important features that can help engender a sense of presence. They also found that ease of navigation within a virtual environment can impact perceptions of presence. While the research conducted by Jelfs and Whitelock were not restricted to virtual environments enabled by the Internet, there are clear implications for what we can do in Internet-enabled contexts. Looking to incorporate audio into the interactions may have a positive impact, as would making the interface easy to navigate. The use of systems like PlaceWare® and HorizonLive®, which incorporate sound and video into Internet-based learning experiences, may prove particularly useful for future design and development work.

16.2.1.5 Other Areas to Consider. While the four constructs described above have received the most attention by researchers, there are other areas that have been explored. Saba and his colleagues (Saba, 1988; Saba & Shearer, 1994) extended the theoretical work to a systems level. Employing a systems dynamics modeling technique, Saba and his colleagues sought to gain a better understanding of learner autonomy and transactional distance. Kember (1995) created a model to explain the relationships among a variety of factors (e.g., social integration,

external attribution, GPA) and their impact on student success within the learning context.

While the work described in the paragraph above focused on extending Moore's work from the 1980s, others have looked to analyze guidelines and/or recommendations from individual design and development efforts to create theory. Levin (1995) did an analysis of individual Internet-based learning activities to suggest a theory of networked learning environments. In his theory, Levin suggests five main factors as important for Internet-based activities: structure, process, mediation, community building, and institutional support. According to Levin, each plays a critical role in successful online interactions.

Still others have looked to other theories to help inform theory for developing Internet-based interactions. For example, Leflore (2000) presents an overview of how gestalt theory and cognitive theory can be used to create guidelines for Web-based instruction. Miller and Miller (2000) describe how one's epistemological perspective (beliefs about knowledge, reality and truth) and theoretical orientation (e.g., information processing, constructivism) influence the design of Web-based instruction.

As we move forward and use of the Internet for learning continues to expand, development of a theory—or theories—to support the work remains important. Fortunately, there are techniques and methods that can strengthen and extend theory development. Grounded theory methodologies offer particular promise for this work. The grounded theory method, first made popular by Glaser and Strauss (1967) and later extended by Strauss and Corbin (1998), enables researchers to analyze and interpret their data with a goal toward building theory from it. We certainly have a growing data set from which this can occur.

16.3 DESIGNING INTERNET-BASED LEARNING ENVIRONMENTS

All goal-oriented creation is prefaced by design. In the case of moving to Internet-based learning environments, significant design and redesign work must be done to prepare face-to-face courses to survive and thrive in a networked environment. This section reviews literature related to the design and redesign of courses, assignments, and assessments, and discusses studies of online course evaluation, scalability, development, and management. It is important to note that there is a close relationship between these topics, and many studies actually shed light on more than one of the areas. Deciding which category to list each study under was troublesome and we recognize that they may overlap. Indeed, we hope that the overlap will help further illustrate the complexity of learning, particularly when it is Internet based.

16.3.1 Design and Redesign: Courses, Assignments, and Assessments

16.3.1.1 Course Redesign. Initial attempts to move courses onto the Internet were solidly grounded current practice, and generally attempted to perfectly duplicate the face-to-face class

experience online. However, instructional designers and educational researchers have begun exploring new ways of exploiting the capabilities of the Internet in their online courses, and Internet-specific course designs are beginning to emerge. This section reviews literature regarding several redesigned courses.

Arvan, Ory, Bullock, Burnaska, and Hanson (1998) redesigned and studied nine courses at University of Illinois at Urbana–Champagne using networked technology in an attempt to achieve higher student/faculty ratios without sacrificing instructional quality, the goal being to actually effect more learning per unit cost. The courses were in chemistry, circuit analysis, differential equations, economics, microbiology, Spanish, and statistics. Increases in the number of students an instructional team (faculty and teaching assistants) could serve were viewed as positive outcomes, as were decreases in the size of a team serving the same number of students. Three key strategies were employed in the redesigns: automating the grading of assignments as appropriate, using less expensive undergraduate peer tutors as graders when human grading was more appropriate, and relying on peer support. No summary information was presented regarding the difference in size between the traditional sections and the online sections taught with larger groups, though the data presented suggest that the online sections were approximately twice the size of the traditional sections. While somewhat reserved in their conclusions, the researchers report that student academic performance in the redesigned online environment is not negatively impacted when compared to parallel traditional sections, and may be improved in some cases.

Arvan et al. (1998) also presented detailed financial information for one of the nine courses. Cost savings were estimated to range between $55 and $209 per student in the redesigned course, depending on how faculty were compensated and how many students enrolled in the course. These cost savings were used to estimate the time required to recoup the costs of developing the new online course. In best case scenarios, the courses would be turning a profit by the end of their initial offering. In the most pessimistic scenario, approximately a year would be required before the development cost was completely recouped.

Jewett (1998) implemented the redesign of a philosophy course in an online environment using CMC technology to include more frequent personal interaction, writing, and challenging of opinion regarding philosophical works. The group of students in the restructured version of the course significantly outperformed traditional course counterparts in 8 of 16 criteria critical to philosophical discourse, no differences were found for 7 criteria, and the traditional group significantly outperformed the redesigned group on one criteria: succinctness.

Wegner, Holloway and Crader (1997) studied a redesigned traditional upper level course in curriculum design, implementation, and evaluation. According to the authors, the movement of the course to the Internet allowed Southwest Missouri State faculty to revisit the pedagogy of the course, resulting in a new online version using a problem-based approach coupled with technology-mediated Socratic questioning. Analysis of student learning outcomes for those enrolled in the new course with outcomes from students in a traditional section showed no significant differences. Student comments about the new course design show that, while far from perfect, students appreciated the focus on real-world (non-busy-work) assignments, the sense of group they developed, gaining practical skills, and the guiding questions provided by the instructor.

16.3.1.2 Assignments.
In addition to redesigning entire courses, some educators have changed individual assignments to better fit the networked nature of the Internet. And teachers aren't the only ones changing, as researchers begin to suggest that students may complete online assignments differently from in class assignments.

Schutte (2000) reports a study in which students in a social statistics course were randomly assigned to two sections, one face-to-face course and one course taught on the Web. With text, lectures, and exams held constant between the two classes, only the weekly assignments differed significantly. The face-to-face class completed and submitted a weekly problem assignment, while the virtual class had this assignment plus mandatory weekly e-mail with others in their randomly assigned work group, newsgroup discussion of a weekly topic, and IRC interactions.

The original hypothesis was that without weekly face-to-face contact with the instructor, students in the virtual sections would suffer negative consequences. Contrary to the hypothesis, results showed that the virtual class outperformed the traditional class an average of 20 percent on both the midterm and final. Virtual students also exited with significantly higher perceptions of peer contact, time spent on task, flexibility, understanding of the material, and positive affect toward mathematics. Shutte attributes the findings to virtual students bonding together to "pick up the slack of not having a real classroom," and taking advantage of the collaborative opportunities afforded by the networked medium.

Blum (1999) found evidence of differences between gender interaction and participation in discussion assignments in online environments. The results from this study were similar to previous research in face-to-face environments in some areas (e.g., males tend to dominate discussion). However, Blum also found evidence that barriers to female participation in online discussion are even higher than barriers to participation in traditional classroom settings. According to Blum, the additional barriers are a result of worries regarding technology use and the rate at which the online course and discussions progressed.

16.3.1.3 Assessment.
Much of the research in online assessment has focused on automating the scoring process. Automated scoring of selected response formats such as multiple choice items has been practiced in classrooms for decades using bubble sheets. Features of the online environment afford variations on the automated scoring theme. For example, Campbell (2001) describes a "Speedback" system used to score and provide feedback for selected response items in online environments. When instructors initially create items they also create detailed feedback for each distracter to be presented to the learner should the learner choose the distracter. Campbell describes Speedback as an important factor in the cost

effectiveness of distance education in that it enables quick responses to the learner without instructor interaction.

More advanced efforts have also been made in the automated scoring of constructed response items like essays. Page's (1994) Project Essay Grade (PEG) used multiple regression with 20 variables to score 1194 senior essays. Results indicate that PEG was able achieve correlation coefficients of .87, which was close to the reliability of the group of human judges.

Burstein et al. (1998) describe an automated essay scoring system developed by Educational Testing Service (ETS) called Electronic Essay Rater (e-rater). In this study, e-rater predicts human scores for essays written for the Graduate Management Admission Test (GMAT) and Test of Written English (TWE) using a hybrid model including syntactic structural analysis, rhetorical structure analysis, and topical analysis. The system gave the same or an adjacent score to the questions between 87 percent and 94 percent of the time.

Finally, Rudner and Liang (2002) report a study using Bayesian Essay Test Scoring sYstem (BETSY), in which Bayesian networks were used to grade essays. Bayesian networks model cause-and-effect relationships between variables by weighting each relation according the probability of one variable affecting another. Several models were run and compared; however, the best approach combined a Bernoulli model versus a multinomial model, matching against arguments versus words or phrases, and refraining from stemming and the elimination of stopwords such as *the*, *of*, and *or*. With a training set of only 462 essays, the scoring algorithm was able to assign the same score as two human raters to over 80 percent of the set of 80 essays that were machine scored.

In addition to automating the scoring process, several issues in online assessment remain open. For example, the Internet can make transgressions from small acts of plagiarism to wholesale duplication of papers easy for students. Automated, Internet-based systems that detect plagiarism are becoming popular, but research needs to be conducted into their effectiveness. Learner authentication issues also continue to plague designers and accreditors of online programs.

16.3.2 Online Courses and Issues of Evaluation, Scalability, Development, and Management

For reasons both ethical and institutional teachers are obligated to evaluate their online course offerings. This section reviews studies regarding student satisfaction with online courses and students' perceptions of learning in online courses. Faculty satisfaction is dealt with in a later section on faculty issues.

16.3.2.1 Student Satisfaction.
Rossman (1999) performed a document analysis of more than 3,000 course evaluations from 154 online courses at Capella University over 11 consecutive quarters. The design of the online courses, which are tailored specifically to adults, contained "small lectures, assigned readings," and a significant online discussion component. Three broad categories of feedback emerged from the analysis of the

online course evaluations, with specific issues in each theme including:

A. Faculty Responsibility
   1) Learners want prompt feedback from faculty and seem to appreciate it when these comments were posted in the discussion forum in a timely manner.
   2) Learners want specific feedback and view comments such as "nice job" or "good response" as being indicative of a disinterested or lazy faculty member.
   3) Learners do not object to opinions being challenged as long as the individual was not belittled or humiliated for offering the response.
   4) Learners prefer that negative comments be given privately, preferably through a phone call.
B. Facilitating Discussions
   1) Learners appreciate and seemed to learn much from the responses of other learners.
   2) Learner responses seem to be a valuable aspect of the course.
   3) There is perceived guilt among some learners about not posting when postings of other learners have captured the essence of what they wanted to say.
   4) Learners do not like it when fellow classmates did not keep current with the weekly online posting requirements.
   5) Learners prefer discussion forums that encourage open and honest dialog; are not dominated by one or two "dominant voices"; and are not used to express non-course-related concerns or complaints.
C. Course Requirements
   1) Learners want guidelines from faculty regarding course requirements.
   2) Learners were dissatisfied when URLs were inoperative or incorrect.
   3) Learners want to immediately apply information gleaned in class to life or work situations.
   4) Learners did not like being required to purchase books, articles, various programs or other required material that were not fully utilized by the course instructor.

Rossman suggests that these evaluation results demonstrate the need for a significant shift in faculties' understanding of their role; specifically, online teachers must focus more on facilitating learning than instructing.

Hiltz (1997) conducted a study comparing face-to-face courses with online courses offered using "Virtual Classroom" software at the New Jersey Institute of Technology. Courses taught in this mode also had significant online collaboration requirements. In a postcourse questionnaire including responses from 390 students, 71 percent of students reported that the online environment provided them with better access to their instructor and 69 percent felt that the virtual course was more convenient. Further, 58 percent indicated that they would take another virtual course and 40 percent felt that they had learned more than in their traditional classes (and 21% felt they had not). Finally, 47 percent felt that the online environment increased the efficiency of education (23% disagreed) and 58 percent said

the online environment increased the quality of education (20% disagreed).

Satisfaction with online courses is not limited to higher education. Students in secondary education are also reporting positive feedback in relation to their Internet-based learning experiences. In a similar study including four surveys across 2 years, Shapely (1999) also reports high levels of student satisfaction with an online upper-level organic chemistry course. Students compared the course favorably to other chemistry courses they had taken, and 70 percent of students said they would like to take another online course.

Not all students are satisfied with their online experiences, however. For example, Picciano (1998) reports that working adults evaluating an online class on principalship in the public schools actually reported that they would rather have been in class, citing family and workplace distractions by children and coworkers as disruptive to their studies.

Fredericksen, Pickett, Shea, Pelz, and Swan (2000) report the factors that contribute to students' perceptions of levels of learning through the results of a survey of over 1400 students in online courses in the SUNY Learning Network (SLN). Their findings state that interaction with the teacher is the most significant contributor to perceived learning in students. Further, the study indicated that students with the highest levels of perceived learning:

- Had high levels of interaction with their online classmates,
- Participated in their online classes at higher levels than in their traditional classroom experiences,
- Had positive experiences with the supporting Help Desk,
- Chose to take the course online (as opposed to those situations where the online course was the only option),
- Were female, and
- Were in the 36–45 year age range.

The gender finding is particularly interesting in that it conflicts with the Blum (1999) study reported above, which found that women experienced significant barriers to success in online courses. Obviously the issue of gender interactions with networked learning environments warrants further study.

Wegner, Holloway, and Garten (1999) report an experimental study in which students self-selected into either an online or traditional course in curriculum design and evaluation. While evaluation results did not support the hypothesis that students in the online section would experience better academic achievement or have a more positive perception of their learning, the results did support the more conservative claim that Internet-based delivery appears to not negatively impact achievement or perception of learning.

16.3.2.2 Scalability. Scalability, the facility to go from serving a few students with online learning programs to serving very many students with such programs, is of critical concern to those involved in the design and delivery of online education. Many people generally associate scalability with the technological facility to serve large numbers of students; for example, having sufficient bandwidth to deliver large video files or having sufficient computing power respond to large numbers of requests for web pages. Through the development of very large e-commerce sites and massive research computing clusters many of the problems with this technology side of scalability have been worked out satisfactorily. However, many of our pedagogical approaches were developed for use in a face-to-face classroom environment with 30 to 40 students. Most of the difficult scalability problems encountered in online learning relate not to the technology of networked computers, but to the pedagogy of large numbers of students. The costs associated with scaling to serve large numbers of students are also a concern. Specifics related to scalability challenges are discussed in the following paragraphs.

The cost of scaling online offerings to large numbers of students is a significant challenge. When "tried and true" face-to-face instructional models are moved online, the assumptions about appropriate faculty-to-student ratios move online as well. When this assumption is held constant, scaling to a larger number of students often means hiring additional teachers, which costs more. When faculty are paid to teach online courses on a per student basis, as Johnston, Alexander, Conrad, and Feiser (2000) found to be the case, this presents the "worst-case scenario of the future." If the cost of educating more individuals will forever scale linearly with the number of students, one of the main promises of online education will surely fail to be fulfilled.

While automation of certain portions of the online learning experience seems to be the clear path toward scaling to larger numbers of learners online, automation is not necessarily the answer. Thaiupathump, Bourne, and Campbell (1999) studied the effects of replacing the repetitive actions carried out by human instructors (e.g., reminding students when homework is due, providing rudimentary feedback on student assignments, and notifying the instructor when students take certain actions (like submitting homework)) with similar actions performed by intelligent agents or "knowbots." The study suggested that employing the intelligent agents significantly raised the number of assignments students completed in an online course. In two versions of the same course, with populations similar in size and characteristics, the number of assignments completed rose from 64 before the introduction of the agents to 220 afterward ($t = 5.96$, $p < 0.001$, DF = 83).

However, analyses of messages posted in the conferencing system suggested that the introduction of the intelligent agents actually *increased* the average facilitation time spent by the instructor per student, causing the research team to reject their hypothesis that the use of knowbots would be associated with a decrease in facilitation time. No information was reported about other time savings (e.g., time spent in grading assignments), so it is not possible to tell if there was a net loss or gain of instructor time attributable to the introduction of the intelligent agents. However, the result that automating portions of instructors' online course responsibilities can actually increase instructor responsibilities elsewhere is worthy of further attention. While there are many researchers continuing to pursue automation of various portions of the online learning experience in order to scale it to greater numbers of learners, the path forward is not

entirely clear, and the area of scalability remains wide open for additional research and understanding.

16.3.2.3 Development and Management Tools.

Development and management tools are the technical foundation of online instruction. Without facilities for uploading and storing syllabi, lecture notes, and other materials, creating quizzes, communicating announcements, and answering student questions, online instruction grinds to a halt for all but those who write their own HTML and maintain their own Unix accounts. Landon (2002) maintains a very thorough online comparison of development and management tools, including detailed descriptions of their characteristics and features. There are a multitude of smaller comparisons and published narratives regarding individual institutions' stories of selecting official platforms for their online programs (see, for example, Bershears, 1998, or Hazari, 1998). In this section we review two broader studies describing the functions of development and management tools which students and faculty believe to be most critical to success in online teaching and learning.

The Digital Learning Environment (DLE) Group at Brigham Young University carried out an extensive evaluation of online course development and management tools as part of a campus effort to select an official, supported platform for e-learning (Seawright et al., 2000). The study began with a campus-wide survey whose findings would be used to prioritize criteria for the selection process. Findings from the 370 faculty survey respondents included ranked reports of current and intended future use of the internet for instruction. Highlights from these findings include reports that faculty were currently using the Internet mainly for communication and announcements, and posting syllabi, 47 percent intended to use "interactive learning activities" in online courses in the future, and 20 percent or more of the faculty members surveyed indicated no intention of ever putting syllabi online or communicating with students via the Internet. The DLE survey also included questions about faculty barriers to using development and management tools. The largest barrier perceived by respondents was the lack of time necessary to utilize such tools, followed by lack of funds, lack of training, and lack of technical support.

An extended usability study was performed with the three systems (WebCT, Blackboard's CourseInfo, and WBT Systems' TopClass) including faculty from all the University colleges representing a range of self-reported computer experience. The tests centered on faculty performing four real world tasks (upload a syllabi, create a one item quiz, e-mail a student, and post a course announcement) in a 20-minute period. All participants attempted all three systems, with the order of systems randomized to account for learning effects. The mean number of tasks completed in CourseInfo was 4.0, while the mean number of tasks completed in both WebCT and TopClass was 1.0. An ANOVA showed strong significance in the difference between the number of tasks participants were able to complete ($F = 45$, $p < .001$). A follow-up attitudinal survey regarding perceived ease of use confirmed these results, with CourseInfo receiving a mean rating of 3.8, and WebCT and TopClass receiving ratings of 2.3. Again, strong statistical significance was observed ($F = 49.8$, $p < .001$).

Halloran (2000) carried out a similar study for the U.S. Air Force Academy. Her study employed both faculty and students, all of whom self-reported as being familiar with Web-based curriculum materials. In addition to prioritizing faculty needs for development and management tools, the Halloran study included a survey of student needs. Students completed a survey rating system functions on a 6-point scale according to their perceptions of the functions' importance. The tool functions of most importance to students were access to information about their progress, an online student manual, and a tool for searching for content. As in previous studies, faculty survey responses in this study suggest that CourseInfo was again significantly easier to use than either WebCT or Intralearn, empirical investigations of the average time taken by faculty to complete a series of representative tasks in each of the three tools showed no significant differences whatsoever.

16.3.3 Continuing the Dialogue

As can be clearly seen from the studies reviewed in this section, there remains much to be done in researching the design and deployment of Internet-based courses. One study finds significant gender differences, another does not. One study finds that students prefer the flexibility of working remotely and asynchronously, another finds that students prefer to be in class. One study finds that relieving teachers of responsibility for repetitive tasks increases efficiency and even saves dollars, another finds that such relief is actually associated with faculty needing to spend even more time in their online courses. These and other contradictory results seem to indicate an inherent complexity of the educational domain as a research area, and a lack of clarity regarding the nature and purpose of educational research. It is an exciting time to be an instructional designer.

16.4 TEACHING AND THE INTERNET: UNCOVERING CHALLENGES AND OPPORTUNITIES

Designing meaningful, effective learning environments, whether on the Internet or elsewhere, is a challenging task. The hours of development work associated with the creation of the context (web pages, graphics, video/audio files, interactions, etc.) is also demanding. Indeed, many professionals are working full-time in the area of Internet-based learning and many researchers, as we have indicated in previous sections, are spending many hours exploring how to improve practices related to these endeavors.

What we would like to devote this section to is an area often overlooked in the literature: implementation. More specifically, we want to focus on one of the primary players in the implementation of many Internet-based learning events: the instructor. In the following section we will explore three topics that have been represented in the literature regarding opportunities instructors have taken advantage of as well as challenges they continue to face: professional development and shifting from face-to-face to Internet-based learning.

16.4.1 Professional Development

Professional development has traditionally received considerable attention in the technology-related literature. Entire journals have focused on professional development, with issues filled cover to cover with stories from the trenches (i.e., this is what happened to me) and a multitude of stories relaying tips and hints for how to. Many other articles and books have been published in an effort to assist instructors in their move to Internet-based learning (see, for example, Boaz et al., 1999; deVerneil & Berge, 2000; Simonson, Smaldino, Albright, & Zvacek, 2000). While this literature is important, particularly for the practitioner looking to do something tomorrow, it is not sufficient to sustain continued growth in professional development related to Internet-based learning. For growth to occur, we need insight from the research literature to guide our discussions related to professional development.

Several researchers have started the exploration of professional development in Internet-based learning. The research to date appears to be related to uncovering guidelines for professional development as well as how to support professional development via Internet-based environments. We will discuss trends in each area in the following subsections.

16.4.1.1 Guidelines for Professional Development. The research related to this area of professional development in Internet-based learning has focused on generic skills or competencies needed by faculty seeking to teach in Internet-based contexts. In the mid-1990s, Cyrs (1997) conducted a meta-analysis of the literature related to professional development and the Internet. His analysis identified four areas of general competence needed by instructors teaching via the Internet or Web: course planning and organization, verbal and nonverbal presentation skills, collaborative teamwork, and questioning strategies. While focused primarily on *courses* taught at a distance, Cyrs work remains viable for a variety of interactions via the Internet, whether short lessons/interactions or more in-depth courses.

Schoenfeld-Tacher and Persichitte (2000) explored the distinct skills and competencies required in Internet-based courses. To guide their research, Schoenfeld-Tacher and Persichitte interviewed six faculty members with experience in teaching courses via the Web. The results of their research resulted in a list of 13 skills and competencies needed by instructors when teaching via the Internet. These are summarized in the following list: familiarity with learner characteristics and needs, and how those differ from learners in a face-to-face context; application of basic instructional design; thorough knowledge of subject matter; understanding of learner-centered environments; ability to design constructivist environments; practical applications of adult learning theories, self-paced learning and computer-mediated communication; appropriate selection of Internet-based strategies for reflection and interaction; fostering a sense of community; adaptability and flexibility with media; familiarity with delivery medium; ability to multi-task; time management; and overall professional characteristics (e.g., motivated to teach, self-confident). While Schoenfeld-Tacher and Persichitte point out that more research is needed, they have presented a good starting point for beginning a professional development effort.

Lan (2001) has also explored the general needs of instructors working in Internet-based learning contexts. Lan focused her research on interviews with 31 instructors representing 26 universities and colleges throughout the United States. Four variables were explored in the study: environment, incentives, motivation, and skills/knowledge needed to perform the task. In terms of environment, Lan found that a priori technological infrastructure was one of the highest predictors of use by instructors. Incentives were also key components for instructors; specifically, they are carrots and encourage the faculty to get involved. Motivation of instructors was also a key finding in Lan's work. As stated by Lan, "there must be convincing evidence of the value and benefits of technology" before the faculty will adopt it. In relation to skills/knowledge, Lan's found that prior technology experience was a key predictor of instructor participation in Internet-based environments. Further, she concluded that perceptions of pedagogical value were a key variable in instructor decisions to integrate technology.

16.4.1.2 Using the Internet for Professional Development.
Professional development guidelines are important in our continued work to improve Internet-based learning. Exploring how to use the Internet to facilitate professional development is also important. Efforts related to this initiative are described in the following paragraphs.

Researchers have spent considerable time exploring how to build Internet-based professional development communities. One sustained effort is occurring at Indiana University. Barab and his colleagues have been working in the last few years to develop a system called the *Inquiry Learning Forum* (ILF) (Barab, MaKinster, Moore, Cunningham, & The ILF Design Team, 2001). ILF is a Web-based professional development system based on learning and community models. ILF provides teachers with a virtual space where they can observe, discuss and reflect on classroom practices [for more information see http://ilf.crlt.indiana.edu/]. Research is on-going, but the studies completed to date indicate that the ILF has been effective for assisting with professional development and community building.

Moore (2002) is also conducting research in the area of Internet-based professional development. Moore completed research exploring the Learning Study Group (LSG), a professional development effort focused on connecting in-service and preservice teachers with subject-matter experts to improve educational practices. In choosing to become part of the LSG Project the participants also utilized the Inquiry Learning Forum (ILF). Moore focused her efforts on in-depth interviews and document analysis of five participants in the LSG project over a 2-year period.

In terms of their experiences with the LSG and ILF projects, Moore found that overall the participants thought the LSG project to be most profitable and engaging (in comparison with ILF), highlighting the collaborative aspects of the project and the time to focus on teaching as important aspects. Moore

reports that the participants saw "potential" in the ILF, particularly in terms of specific features (e.g., video), but reported that their participation in the online environment was not all that meaningful or useful. In general, they found their face-to-face interactions via LSG to be more useful for their day-to-day work.

Gold (2001) focused his research on the training that an online instructor needs to become an effective Internet-based teacher. A 2-week Internet-based faculty development course was examined. Participants included 44 experienced college teachers with little online teaching or studying experience. Online data collection and surveys were used to gather data to explore effects of the pedagogical training on the participants.

Gold reported two major findings. First, the research indicated that instructors exposed to the professional development course significantly changed their attitudes toward online instruction. After completing the course, instructors viewed Internet-based learning as more participatory and interactive than traditional face-to-face instruction. Second, the research indicated that after completing the course, instructors were more willing to use the online instruction.

16.4.2 Shifting from Face-to-Face to Online Contexts

Another area that has received considerable attention in the literature is related to moving from face-to-face environments to online contexts. In these studies, several factors have been explored. We will discuss four of the most prevalent factors in the following section: workload, communication, satisfaction, and cultural considerations.

16.4.2.1 Workload.
Workload has received considerable attention in the literature, specifically examining how the move from a face-to-face context impacts workload in a variety of ways. Ryan, Carlton, and Ali (1999) conducted a study focusing on viewpoints related to classroom versus World Wide Web modules. A questionnaire was distributed to 96 graduate students to evaluate perceptions of their experiences in the classroom and on the Web. Several issues were raised from the results of the study, one of which related to workload. According to the researchers, the Internet-based modules required more time on the part of the faculty to respond to the students, as each student was required to respond to each topic. As a result, a group approach in the face-to-face classroom became a one-on-one approach in the Internet-based environment. The researchers indicated a need to rethink how many students might be included in an Internet-based learning context as well as how we engage dialogue in learning environments.

Kearsley (2000) has also reported on workload implications for Internet-based learning. Citing Brown, Kearsley indicates that designing a course that is highly interactive creates the high workload. Providing good feedback to students also creates high workload. While Kearsley also offers suggests for how to reduce the workload for instructors (e.g., peer evaluation, use of teaching assistants, multiple choice tests vs. discussion), more research is needed to fully understand the ways in which we might help reduce the amount of work associated with Internet-based learning.

16.4.2.2 Communication.

One of the key characteristics of Internet-based learning is communication—asynchronous and synchronous. Researchers have explored a variety of factors impacting Internet-based communication.

Berger (1999) describes communication lessons she learned from teaching a human resource management course via the Web. The course consisted of 54 students located around the world. The course was the first online experience for Berger, although she had 10 years of teaching experience. Suggestions for management of communication were one result of Berger's experience. Recommendations include: create a single Web page for personal and professional information for all course participants; place all operational procedures for the course in one location; have students submit assignments within the body of e-mail messages instead of attachments; have students use the e-mail address to which they want responses sent, enabling easy replying; create separate folders for each course requirement to enable easy filing; and be very specific with expectations (e.g., turnaround time with messages and postings) and requirements regarding assignments so as not to confuse students.

Tiene (2000) looked specifically at the advantages and disadvantages of Internet-based discussions. Tiene surveyed 66 students involved in five graduate-level online courses over a 2-year period to find out their perceptions of online discussions. Results indicated positive reactions to most aspects of the online discussions, particularly the asynchronous aspects and use of written communication. However, when given a choice, most students indicated a preference for face-to-face discussions, noting that online discussions are useful additions to face-to-face discussions. One conclusion that Tiene draws is that instructors use online discussions to enrich face-to-face interactions when such an arrangement is feasible.

Smith, Ferguson, and Caris (2002) also focused on communication in their research. In their study, Smith et al. (2002) interviewed 21 college instructors who had taught online and face-to-face courses. Results from the analysis of the interviews indicated that instructors perceived a difference in communication style in online versus face-to-face classes. Instructors attributed the differences to bandwidth limitations, the asynchronous nature of how the courses were designed, and an emphasis on the written word. Smith et al. indicate that the differences provide opportunities and challenges. Opportunities include greater student/instructor equality, deeper class discussions and anonymity. Challenges include a need for greater explicitness in instructions for class activities, increased workload for instructors and emerging online identities for all participants.

16.4.2.3 Instructor Satisfaction.

Several studies have explored learner satisfaction with Internet-based learning. We were interested in uncovering research related to instructor perceptions of their Internet-based experiences. Several studies have sought to provide insight into the positive and negative reactions that instructors have to working in Internet-based contexts (see the *Journal of Asynchronous Learning Networks* for a comprehensive review of faculty satisfaction, http://www.aln.org/alnweb/journal/jaln-vol4issue2-3.htm).

A recent issue of *Distance Education Report* (2001) presented pros and cons related to instructor satisfaction in Internet-based learning. Fifty faculty members at a major university in the northeast were involved in the 2001 research study focused on uncovering factors leading to satisfaction and dissatisfaction with Internet-based learning. Results of the research indicate three key factors contributed to faculty satisfaction: reaching new audiences, highly motivated students, and high levels of interaction. Three key factors were also identified as creating discontent: heavier workload, loss of some degree of control over the course, and lack of recognition of the work associated with Internet-based work in the higher education reward system.

Lee (2001) also explored the factors contributing to instructor satisfaction. The overall purpose of Lee's research was to examine faculty perceptions of instructional support in relation to a faculty member's satisfaction in distance teaching. A survey was used to gather data from 237 faculty members from 25 institutions affiliated with the Western Cooperative for Educational Telecommunication. Lee found that the perception of support from the institution has an impact on instructor satisfaction. Further, Lee reported that in the context of insufficient support faculty tended to be less satisfied with their teaching. A clear implication is that institutional support is not only needed for logistical reasons, it is important for instructor satisfaction with the online experience.

16.4.2.4 Cultural Considerations.

Internet-based learning has the clear potential for international impact unlike any other instructional medium to date. Clearly teaching and learning on a global scale is quite a different experience from one that is more situated in a local context. An area that is receiving increased attention in the research literature is the impact of cultural issues on teaching via the Internet. Research to date offers insights regarding the promise of Internet-based learning on an international scale.

McLoughlin (1999) examined the impact of culturally responsive design in the creations of an online unit for indigenous Australian learners. The model used was adapted from Lave's (1991) community of practice model. McLoughlin reported that the experience indicated that designers of Internet-based environments need to be aware of the sociocultural background and learning styles of their learners. Further, educators and designers need to respect cultural identity, participation styles and expectations of learners from various cultures. As stated by McLoughlin, it is possible to support local communities as well as to support virtual communities that include a multitude of local entities.

Cifuentes and Murphy (2000) conducted a case study exploring the effectiveness of distance learning and multimedia technologies in facilitating an expanded learning community in two K–12 contexts in Texas and Mexico. Data sources used in the research included portfolios, written reflections, and interviews. Four themes emerged from the data analysis: growth, empowerment, comfort with technology, and mentoring. Overall, the researchers concluded that powerful teacher relationships were formed as a result of the Internet-based connections, students' multicultural understandings were enhanced, and students developed a more positive self-concept as a result of their online interactions. The project offers encouraging insights into the potential of Internet-based learning for breaking down cultural stereotypes.

16.4.3 Continuing the Dialogue

The research conducted to date related to instructors and Internet-based learning provides many insights into the challenges and opportunities associated with teaching in online contexts. We are beginning to gain insights into what is needed for professional development, both in terms of content and in relation to providing professional development via the Internet. We are also gaining a deeper understanding of the challenges and opportunities associated with shifting from a face-to-face to an Internet-based learning environment. As we continue our movement toward more Internet-based interactions for learning, we also need to continue to strengthen the research base upon which the decisions are made.

16.5 LEARNING FROM AND WITH THE INTERNET: LEARNER PERSPECTIVES

Much attention has been given to how to use various technologies to facilitate learning. The Internet is no exception. While not specifically focused on these information technologies, the arguments raised by Clark (1994) and Kozma (1994) in the early 1990s certainly offer important insights for how we think about the use of any technology for learning. Related arguments have been built around the concepts of *tutor–tool–tutee* (Taylor, 1980) and *cognitive tools* (Jonassen & Reeves, 1996; Lajoie, 1993). Jonassen and Reeves discuss the specific concepts of *learning from* and *learning with* in their work on cognitive tools. These concepts are described in more detail in the following paragraphs.

The *learning from* perspective is grounded in a behaviorist view of learning that proposes that information is transmitted from the medium and absorbed by the learner (Hayes, 2000). The learner's role in the *learning from* model is passive with occasional and limited interaction. The teacher's role in the *learning from* model is that of manager—managing the use of the preestablished, often "teacher-proof" content. When *learning from,* the Internet is a vehicle for the delivery of information (Kozma, 1994).

Learning with the Internet is a perspective founded in constructivist (Piaget, 1954; von Glasersfeld, 1993, 1989) and constructionist (Harel & Papert, 1991; Kafai & Resnick, 1996) principles of teaching and learning. *Learning with* moves the orientation from passive learning to one of active creation. The effectiveness of *learning with* technology is a function of the skills and experience learners have with it and the degree to which curriculum has been designed to support desirable pedagogical dimensions (Reeves, 2002, personal communication).

The learner is no longer solely taking the information; s/he is also contributing to the knowledge base, designing and creating artifacts that enable the learning process to occur (Perkins, 1986).

In the following section we will explore two primary threads of arguments that have been presented by researchers regarding strategies for how the Internet can/should be used for *learning from* and *learning with* in educational settings. To facilitate the discussion, we will look at three subtopics closely tied to *learning from* and *learning with:* learner characteristics, activities, and achievement with the Internet. We will focus our review on research related to learners and how they are engaged in *learning from* and *learning with* the tool (see section four in this chapter for research related to the instructor).

16.5.1 Learner Characteristics

Learner characteristics have received considerable attention in the literature related to the use of the Internet for learning. We will focus on three specific constructs: learners as receivers of information, learners as information users and creators, and demographic traits.

16.5.1.1 Learners as Receivers. The primary role played by learners when *learning from* the Internet is that of receiver. The learner is reading and viewing information provided by others. This may sound a simple task; indeed, it is a modality that continues to predominate our educational infrastructure. However, there are many underlying variables that need to be taken into consideration in facilitating learners as receivers. These variables are explored in the following paragraphs.

One variable that has received considerable attention in relation to learners as receivers is that of evaluation of information. Although the learner may not be actively creating the resource, they do need to be actively engaged in evaluating the viability and reliability of the resource. Fitzgerald (2000) did an extensive study of university-level students' evaluation of information and found that there are many factors that influence information evaluation, including: prior knowledge, format of information, and epistemology. Fitzgerald also found that emotions, beliefs, and metacognition were influential factors in evaluation. While work like Fitzgerald's assists us in developing a greater understanding of the information evaluation process and where we need to focus when helping learners evaluate information, we still have more work to do. As stated by Fitzgerald: "Evaluation [of information] is messy and complex" (p. 184). Working to make the evaluation activity less complex will be an important area of research in the coming decade.

Interpretation of the information is another important variable when the learner is the receiver of information. Research conducted by Hill and Hannafin (1997) with a group of university-level graduate students indicated that there are several factors that impact how information is interpreted once it is found during a search. In the Hill and Hannafin study, students selected the topic and searched for information using a search engine on the Web. Results concluded that even when the information presented would appear to address the students' self-stated need, they would often not see it as relevant. Hill and Hannafin concluded that this disparity in interpretation could be attributed to several factors, including prior knowledge and metacognitive knowledge. In related work, Yang (2001) found that students' attitudes and perceptions also played a role in the interpretation of information during information seeking. How the students approached the task influenced their perceptions of the activity.

Use of the information is also a variable that has been considered in research related to *learning from* the Internet. For example, Doring (1999) emphasized that the use of information in the production of knowledge was a key component in the retrieval process. As users seek information, they have in mind how that information will be used. This, in turn, influences what they view as relevant and useful in the overall effort.

16.5.1.2 Learners as Information Users and Creators.
In learning with the Internet, learners become users of the information as they actively construct their understanding and create artifacts to represent the understanding. Many types of products have been used to help facilitate the representation of understanding.

Perhaps one of the most widely known tools is the Webquest. Webquests (Dodge, 2001, 2002; Yoder, 1999) are another formal learning tool that has been used in a variety of contexts to meet the information needs of students and teachers. Webquests have been used in social studies to assist learners with understanding Latin American contexts (Milson, 2001), in math to teach probability (Arbaugh, Scholten, & Essex, 2001), and in language arts to teach literature, library and computer skills (Truett, 2001). Webquests have also been implemented across grade levels, with children and adults.

To date, the majority of Webquests have been constructed by teachers and then used by students. Research related to teacher-directed implementations indicates that Webquests are a success (see, for example, Dutt-Doner, Wilmer, Stevens, & Hartman, 2000; Kelly, 2000). However, recent research indicates that a more constructionist approach can be used to place students in the position of designer of the Webquest. Peterson and Koeck (2001) found it very effective to have students construct Webquests in a chemistry course to explore nuclear energy in the 21st century. Results from Peterson's and Koeck's research indicate that students engaged in intellectual struggles to solve problems, created interdisciplinary connections as they constructed their Webquests, and used the technology as a tool to communicate meaning. While more research is needed in this area, the prospect of students as developers of Webquests is encouraging.

16.5.1.3 Demographic Traits.
Specific learner traits have also been explored in the research. Gender is one trait that has received considerable attention. Stewart, Shields, Monolescu, and Taylor (1999) looked at the impact of gender on participation within a synchronous learning environment employing Internet Relay Chat (IRC) as the delivery technology. Seventeen undergraduates enrolled in a course in a university in an urban area in the United States. Stewart et al. (1999) examined gender differences in the following areas: online participation, language

styles, computer skills, socialization, attitudes, and prior experience. Results indicated that participants were similar in background and experience levels as well as attitudes toward technology. However, the researchers found significant differences in the amount and type of communication by gender. Men sent more and longer messages than women. They also found that men tended to look at the task as more of a game, with the women taking the task more seriously. Further, the men tended to take control of the discussion, while women tended to work toward agreement in the discussions.

Two other specific characteristics have been explored in the literature: culture and disabilities. Although neither characteristic has received as much considerations as other characteristics, we feel the need for further exploration of these constructs will continue to increase. A study was conducted by Wilson (2001) to explore the potential impact of text created by Westerners for West African students. Wilson specifically sought to develop understanding of the impact of cultural discontinuities on learning. In this qualitative study, Wilson discovered that several cultural discontinuities existed, including: differences in worldviews, culturally specific knowledge and conceptualizations, first-language linguistic challenges, and reading cognition profiles. Further, Wilson discovered that the discontinuities had an impact on learning for the native language speakers. Wilson's research helps provide an insight into the importance of culture, providing insights into the viability of globally based Internet learning.

Fichten et al. (2000) explored issues related to disabilities and Internet-based learning. Fichten et al. specifically explored access issues in relation to physical, sensory, and learning disabilities. Using focus groups, interviews and questionnaires, the researchers gathered data in three empirical studies. Results from the studies indicated that learners made use of the Internet for learning, however physical adaptation of the technology was needed to enable effective use.

Many studies examining use of the Internet for learning have explored multiple learner characteristics within the same study. For example, Hargis (2001) examined a variety of learner characteristics in her study of the use of the Internet to learn science. An objectivist and constructivist instructional format was created online. Both contained the same content. Specific characteristics studied in the research included: age, gender, racial identity, attitude, aptitude, self-regulated learning and self-efficacy. No significant differences were found with specific variables, with the exception of older participants performing better using an objectivist approach. Hargis concluded that individual learner characteristics should not be barriers to Internet-based learning.

16.5.2 Supporting Learner Activities in Online Environments

Learners are often engaged in several activities when learning from or with the Internet. Further, these activities often occur simultaneously. In this subsection, we explore four specific activities: information gathering, knowledge construction, use of distributed resources and distributed processing.

16.5.2.1 Information Gathering. While this topic is covered more in-depth in another chapter in the book, it would be remiss not to mention it here within the context of learners and *learning from*. Information gathering is a critical activity in the *learning from* model of using the Internet and Web for learning. In fact, research indicates that information gathering is perhaps the most widely used application of the Internet (Hill, Reeves, Grant, & Wang, 2000). And with the continued exponential growth in available resources, it is likely to continue to be one of the most widely used applications of networked technologies.

What are we doing when we are gathering information on the Internet? According to Hill (1999), learners are engaged in a variety of activities, including purposeful thinking, acting, evaluation, transformation and integration, and resolution. Fitzgerald (2000) points out other processes that are occurring as we seek information. According to her research with adult learners at the university level, learners evaluate, analyze, choose, critique, construct, argue and synthesize. Clearly, the gathering of information is a complex cognitive task that has many rewards, but as a complex activity, it also has the potential to create significant challenges.

One significant challenge indicated by the research is the potential of getting lost in hyperspace. Marchionini's work in the late 1980s through the mid-1990s documented the information seeking process, including the impacts of getting lost, as users worked in various information systems. This work culminated in his book, *Information Seeking in Electronic Environments* (Marchionini, 1995). Marchionini concludes that we need to work to create "... positive and natural [systems] rather than sophisticated workarounds" (p. 196) so that learners can have an easier time with locating and using the information they find.

This appears to be a proposition that is easier said than done. More recent research indicates that the potential of "getting lost" continues to be a challenge for information gathering. In a study with learners in a technology-based course, Hill and Hannafin (1997) found that learners struggled to keep track of where they were and what they were looking for within a Web-based information context. Indeed, results indicated that learners often got "lost" and then struggled to figure out where they were and what they were looking for to begin with. Hill (1999) also discusses the struggles faced by learners as they seek information in open-ended information systems like the Internet. This challenge continues today. How to make systems more "positive and natural" remains an area in need of further research.

Another challenge relates to support. As pointed out by Hill (1999), information gathering needs to be well supported if learners are to be successful in the task of information retrieval. Several researchers have posed potential solutions to the challenges associated with information seeking. Some researchers have focused on strategies related to the learners themselves. Fornaciari and Roca (1999) pose that there are several strategies that learners can use to help facilitate the information seeking process, including: "... defining problems effectively, determining information needs, identifying and evaluating information, and questioning source credibility and quality" (p. 732). Pirolli and Card (1999) likened information seeking behavior

to foraging for food with an "information foraging theory," in which they proposed that people "modify their strategies or the structure of their environment to maximize their rate of gaining valuable information" (p. 643).

Other researchers have focused on how to use technology to assist with the process. For example, Baylor (1999) has conducted research using intelligent agents to assist with information retrieval and overload. Baylor concluded that intelligent agents can indeed be useful for assistance. Other researchers have examined specific characteristics related to the interface to help the learner with the information seeking process. Cole, Mandelblatt, and Stevenson (2002) as well as Heo and Hirtle (2001) indicate that visual schemes appear to be promising for assisting learners with information seeking and not getting lost in the overwhelming amount of information.

16.5.2.2 Knowledge Construction. While *learning from* entails the somewhat passive use of resources found on the Internet, *learning with* extends the effort to one of construction. The learner is actively involved in constructing something unique based on what is uncovered as they use the Internet for information gathering. The learner is not only engaged in retrieving the information; s/he uses it to solve problems (Simon, 1987).

When the Internet is used to facilitate knowledge construction it becomes what Jonassen and Reeves (1996) refer to as a "cognitive tool." Cognitive tools are technologies (tangible or intangible) that "... enhance the cognitive powers of human beings during thinking, problem solving, and learning" (p. 693). When used as a cognitive tool, the Internet becomes a tool for creation that enables the learner to express what they know; that is, it becomes a technology of the mind (Salomon, 1994).

Kafai and Resnick (1996) also describe the power of knowledge construction in their work. According to Kafai and Resnick, when learners are engaged in developing representations of what they know, it can lead to a greater level of understanding. Learners become creators of rather than consumers of; communicators versus receivers. When learners are full participants in the learning process, from planning to evaluation of the process, personally meaningful learning is viable in ways not possible prior to now.

One well-researched environment for knowledge construction is Slotta and Linn's (2000) Web-based Knowledge Integration Environment (KIE). In one research project related to KIE, eighth graders were asked to evaluate Web sites related to passive solar energy. As the students evaluated the sites, they were also asked to address questions that would assist them in creating knowledge, relating the Web site content to a specific project. Results indicated that with the use of scaffolding tools, students were able to generate knowledge and ask critical questions of the content.

In another study related to Web-based contexts, Linn and her colleagues (1999) explored the use of the Web-based Integrated Science Environment (WISE), seeking to find out how student analyze information and create knowledge within the system. Researchers found that students were able to successfully analyze scientific content related to why frog mutations occur. Further, they also found that students with low academic performance demonstrated gains in cognitive engagement.

16.5.2.3 Use of Distributed Resources.
The Internet has enabled access to millions of resources, distributed on a global scale heretofore impossible. These resources are like "knowledge bubbles" that learners and teachers encounter as they are moving through virtual space. A resource-based structure is not a new pedagogical innovation (see Haycock, 1991), however interest has grown over the last few years in terms of how to take advantage of the rich amount of information now available (see, for example, Hill & Hannafin, 2001; MacDonald & Mason, 1998).

Research related to the use of resources in Web-based environments have provided some insight into how resources can be used for learning. Research conducted by Slotta and Linn (2000) explored how eighth grader's used Web resources during a learning task. Their findings indicate that when students are provided orientation and ongoing scaffolding on the use of the resources and tools, they perform quite effectively on the task. These findings were similar to what Oliver (1999) found in his research related to Web-based learning environments. Oliver concluded that students need orientation and guidance for effective use of the available resources.

While the prospects are exciting, the implications in our current context can be somewhat daunting. As stated by Hill and Hannafin (2001), "... current [educational] practices may prove insufficient in optimizing available resources..." (p. 37). Defining strategies that will enable the efficient and effective use of the multitude of electronic resources is an area in need of further exploration.

Distributed resources also create challenges from a standardization perspective. Standards and tools for sharing resources are emerging (e.g., SCORM, IMS), yet they are not adhered to nor systematically applied in all areas (Hill & Hannafin, 2001; Robson, 2002). We need to find ways to enable the creation of mechanisms that allow for flexible retrieval and use of resources within a structured context. Research to date has been limited. However, investigations underway by Wiley (2000) promise to provide insight into how resource distribution might be accomplished.

16.5.2.4 Distributed Processing.
One of the benefits often associated in the *learning with* literature relates to the notion of distributed cognition. According to Pea (1985), media can become cognitive technologies if they assist learners to overcome limitations (e.g., limits on memory, problem solving). With the vast number of resources and relative ease associated with resource creation, the Internet has the potential to assist learners with cognitive challenges associated with memory, knowledge creation, and problem solving.

In addition to assisting with cognitive challenges, distributed processing also enables the establishment of intellectual partnerships through the sharing of cognitive artifacts. The sharing of artifacts can happen in real-time (e.g., in synchronous chat rooms, virtual conferencing) or asynchronously (e.g., posted Web pages, bulletin board interactions). By sharing artifacts— either created individually or collaboratively—learners are adding to the knowledge base, thereby further extending the capabilities of the system and the individuals using the system (Perkins, 1993).

This area has received considerable attention in the literature, particularly at the university level. Brush and Uden (2000) found that distributed processing worked well in two university instructional design courses. Students worked with each other in two different countries to create products and provide feedback. Students reported that when the collaboration occurred they worked well, although the researchers indicated that participation could have been much higher.

Distributed processing has also been explored in the area of assessment. Kwok and Ma (1999) researched the use of a Group Support System (GSS) for collaborative assessment of student projects in an undergraduate Distributed Information Systems course. To explore the use of the GSS, Kwok and Ma set up two groups: one group that used the tool online and one group that met face-to-face. Results indicated that the students that used the GSS had a higher level of "deep approach" strategies to learning and better project grades. While not conclusive, the use of tools like the GSS appears to be promising.

Distributed processing does not come without challenges. For example, the very nature of the activity creates a dependence on others for the information needed. If others in the environment have not shared their information and/or encouraged others to do so, it may well be that the information will not be accessible when needed. This can lead to frustration on the part of the learner.

Another challenge associated with distributed processing is the time it can take to get others to respond. While one user may be a frequent and thorough responder to e-mail, bulletin board postings, etc., another may have a completely different work style. Providing guidelines for response times can go a long way in reducing potential frustration (Hill, 2002). Other research suggests that this problem diminishes in proportion to the size of the community (Wiley & Edwards, 2002), although more research is needed to gain a more complete picture of why this occurs.

16.5.3 Achievement in Internet-Based Learning Environments

Achievement is another variable often explored in Internet-based learning. This construct has been explored in formal and informal environments, looking at both intentional and incidental learning. We will explore the research in this area within two subsections: required learning and meaningful learning.

16.5.3.1 Required Learning.
There is a reality in our educational practice that some things are just required in terms of learning. Basic facts related to English, history, math and science continue to be taught by teachers and memorized by students in schools, and are valued in the larger social context. The resurgence of interest in standardized curriculum and testing is placing considerable emphasis on required learning, and does not look to be diminishing in the foreseeable future.

The *learning from* model of using the Internet offers considerable promise in assisting teachers and learners with required learning activities. Researchers and developers have been working on creating Web sites to assist teachers in finding the resources they need that will assist with matching instruction to standards and other requirements. For example, Peck and his colleagues at Penn State have created a Web portal that links national standards, resources and tools together for teachers to use in their classrooms (for more information, see http://ide.ed.psu.edu/aectweb). This system is grounded in some of Peck's (1998) earlier work in which he sought to show connections between standards and the use of technology in schools. Initial review of the system has been positive, although formal research has not yet been published.

Studies have also explored how students have performed in online environments versus other types of learning environments (e.g., face-to-face, television). The vast majority of the studies report no significant difference in terms of achievement (see Russell, 1999, for a comprehensive review). However, many of the studies are reporting differences in other areas. These are described in the following paragraphs.

Ostiguy and Haffer (2001) conducted a study in a general education science course exploring academic achievement in a face-to-face course versus other delivery modes. While they did not find differences in achievement, they did find differences in interaction levels. Students enrolled in the television and Web-based versions of the course reported greater levels of interaction with the instructor. Further, they were also more likely to report dissatisfaction with the interaction when it was less than they wanted.

Sinyor (1998) also found that the Internet did not greatly facilitate achievement. Sinyor studied 74 students involved in three intermediate and advanced Italian second language classes. Results from her study indicated that while the Internet was useful as a source of information, specific resources for learning Italian were inadequate and limited. In this instance, the Internet did not meet the needs for required learning.

Despite the majority of studies reporting no significant differences in achievement, there are some studies indicating an impact on performance. For example, in a study of a middle school atmospheric science program, Lee and Songer (2001) reported an improvement in performance. Students involved in the study were involved in an Internet-enhanced version of the program. Using discourse analysis of electronic messages between students and scientists as well as interviews and a teacher survey, Lee and Songer reported that students had an enhanced understanding of atmospheric science following their involvement in the program.

Research by Gilliver, Randall, and Pok (1998) indicated an impact on performance in a college in Singapore. Gilliver and his colleagues examined the use of the Internet as an adjunct to learning in an undergraduate financial accounting course. Results indicated that the examination scores of those using the Internet as a learning supplement were superior to those who did not use the electronic version.

Follansbee et al. (1997) also found an increase in performance. Follansbee et al. (1997) explored the use of the Internet, with an emphasis on the use of the Scholastic Network, on student learning. Using a quasi-experimental design, results indicated that students in experimental classes produced better results on a civil rights unit than those in the control classes.

There are also studies reporting both positive and negative impacts of the Internet on learning. Ali and Franklin (2001) conducted a study of 22 undergraduates enrolled in a technological applications in education course. The study focused on one-on-one interviews, participant observation and a survey. Results from the Ali and Franklin (2001) study indicated several positive and negative influences on learning. Positively, participants reported the Internet enabled access to vast resources, provided opportunities for independent and individualized learning via online tutorials, created opportunities for in-depth learning, and increased motivation. On the negative side, participants reported the Internet created interference with concentration in class; was time consuming, both in terms of finding information and assessing it; and created a dependency on the network for information, even when it may have been inappropriate to use the Internet to find information.

16.5.3.2 *Meaningful Learning.*

A construct that is central to the *learning with* model is that of meaningful learning. When learning is meaningful, it is student-centered, focusing on the needs and intents of the individual learner (Hannafin, Hill, & Land, 1997). According to Jonassen and Reeves (1996), meaningful learning is critical to the cognitive partnership inherent in the *learning with* approach.

Meaningful learning occurs within authentic contexts (Kafai & Resnick, 1996). Unlike more traditional approaches in which learning occurs in an isolated classroom, meaningful learning is grounded in the "real world" context in which it occurs. The authenticity of the activity is also critical to meaningful learning. According to several researchers (Brown, Collins, & Duguid, 1989; Greeno, Smith, & Moore, 1992), knowledge created while involved in authentic activities is more readily transferred to different contexts that when the activities are abstract. Cognitive apprenticeship (Collins, Brown, & Newman, 1989), anchored instruction (Cognition and Technology Group at Vanderbilt, 1992), and problem-based learning (Barrows, 1986) are often associated with meaningful learning.

When learners are engaged in meaningful learning, they are defining the goals and/or context in which the learning will occur. Because they are creating it, they own it. The creation/ownership link enables a different level of thinking and understanding—one that is likely to enable a more fulfilling learning experience (Kafai & Resnick, 1996).

One example of research related to meaningful learning is found in the Teaching as Intentional Learning program. Moss (1999, 2000) has been actively involved in the creation of and research related to the Teaching as Intentional Learning (TIL) program at Duquesne University in Pennsylvania. TIL is a part of a larger research effort investigating "... professional learning, reflective practice, teacher beliefs, teacher inquiry and the role of technology in learning environments" (Moss, 2000, p. 46). As stated by Moss (2000), teachers involved in the network (over 400 worldwide) come with the goal of revealing, examining and challenging the assumptions that underlie their teaching practice—with the intent to improve that practice as "scholarly practitioners." Moss' ongoing research in this area is an important step in bringing the examination of intentional learning into online contexts.

Incidental learning has also received some attention in *learning with* contexts. Baylor (2001) conducted a study in which she examined the incidental learning of adult learners during a search task in a Web environment. Initial results indicated incidental learning did occur, particularly in the absence of distracting links. Oliver and McLoughlin (2001) also explored incidental learning within a Web-based context, focusing their attention on the acquisition of generic skills (e.g., self-management, task, information). Like Baylor, Oliver and McLoughlin's (2001) results indicate that the generic skills were acquired as a result of working within the learning environment, although this was not the focus of the environment. While more research is needed, these initial studies are an important contribution to the examination of incidental learning, an area of study that has proved challenging, particularly in terms of measuring "real world" incidental learning that occurs within a meaningful context (Kelly, Burton, Kato, & Akamatsu, 2001).

16.5.4 Continuing the Dialogue

Use of the Internet for learning—from or with, intentionally or incidentally—has grown exponentially in the last 5 years. We have also greatly enhanced how we are using the tool. However, issues and questions remain that continue to impact the long-term viability of Internet use for learning. Gibson and Oberg (1997) conducted a case study research project in Alberta, Canada exploring how schools were using the Internet, how teachers were learning to use it, and perceptions of its value as an educational tool. While the study is somewhat dated, and while use and access have certainly changed in the years since the data was gathered, many of the issues uncovered in the study remain relevant. For example, quality of information found on the Internet remains a concern as does the control of access to information. Other areas that call to question the viability of the Internet for learning include: impact of standardized teaching on resource use in the classroom, robustness and reliability of the network, and shifts in expectations (for the teacher and learner) associated with Internet-based learning. Examination of these issues, along with many others, will provide a foundation for research well into the future.

16.6 LEARNING THROUGH THE INTERNET: INTERACTIONS AND CONNECTIONS IN ONLINE ENVIRONMENTS

Perhaps the most pervasive research area related to the use of the Internet for learning in the last 5 years has come in the area of interaction, particularly in the form of interpersonal exchanges. According to Schrum (1995), high levels of interactivity helped drive the popularity of the Internet as an instructional medium when it first started—and this has continued today. The tool has

been used in a variety of ways to facilitate learning. Harris (1995) discussed six types of interpersonal exchanges transpiring on the Internet:

- *Keypals:* individual students in two or more locations matched with each other for discussion via electronic mail,
- *Global classrooms:* two or more classrooms in two or more locations studying a common topic together,
- *Electronic "appearances:"* newsgroups or bulletin boards sponsor special guests with whom students correspond,
- *Electronic mentoring:* one-to-one link between an apprentice and an expert for purposes of providing guidance and answering questions,
- *Question and answer services:* questions are submitted and then answered by a subject-matter expert, and
- *Impersonation activity structures:* any—or all—participants communicate with each other "in character" fitting the topic under discussion.

Researchers continue to talk about the uses described by Harris, as well as other applications, including the use of e-mail with students to assist with motivation and greater academic achievement (Miller, 2001), e-mail mentors to connect girls with professional women for career advice (Duff, 2000), facilitating learning via e-mail games (Jasinski & Thiagarajan, 2000), using listservs to facilitate brainstorming and creativity (Siau, 1999), using e-mail for collaborative projects (Buchanan, 1998), and extending deaf students' access to knowledge through the use of listservs (Monikowski, 1997). These activities are well aligned with the review of research reported by Berge and Mrozowski (2001). In their review, Berge and Mrozowski indicated the emphasis placed on the use of a variety of technologies to support interaction. Research as also focused on the type of interactions occurring as well as how best to use the tools to facilitate these interactions. We explore this research in the following sections.

16.6.1 Instructor–Learner and Learner–Learner Interactions

Traditionally, three types of interaction are described in distance or Internet-based learning: instructor–learner, learner–learner, and learner–content (Moore & Kearsley, 1995). While research has examined all three areas, the majority of the current research has focused on human interactions involving instructors and learners. In the following paragraphs, we will examine three specific areas of research related to human interactions: identity, communication challenges, and factors influencing interactions.

16.6.1.1 Identity. When individuals prepare to interact with others online, whether for learning or other social reasons, they must project an identity into the interaction space. Online conversations frequently entail identity-probing questions such as "a/s/l everyone?" in which individuals are asked to self-disclose their age, sex, and location (Barzeski, 2002). Yet research is confirming what many have already experienced: self-disclosures online regarding identity are sometimes purposely deceptive (Donath, 2002). When being someone else is so simple, individuals may attempt to manipulate this ease of deception toward their own academically dishonest ends (e.g., portraying him/herself as a professor).

Aside from purposive deception with regards to identity, Gergen (1991) has argued that the Internet has led to the "social saturation" of individuals. E-mail, chat, the web, and other technologies expose each of us to more people of greater variety more frequently than humans have ever interacted with before. This broad and frequent exposure to individuals and viewpoints can make appropriate attribution (i.e., citation of ownership of ideas) difficult. Indeed, the notion of what type of attribution is appropriate online appears to be changing. Questions of identity as they relate to assessment strategies and citation must be dealt with before the Internet can be deployed more broadly within formal educational environments.

16.6.1.2 Communication Challenges.
Internet-based interactions are primarily text based, relying on many of the conventions associated with written communication. However, because of the ability to rapidly exchange the text-based information in chat rooms or with instant messaging, the interactions can also resemble verbal communication. This hybrid form of communication creates several exciting opportunities as well as several challenges.

One challenge relates to the temporal gap associated with sharing information in Internet-based learning contexts. Researchers have started exploring the impact of this gap on the learning and interaction processes. Garcia and Jacobs (1999) concluded that chat systems, a popular Internet-based tool used to facilitate communication, are "quasi-synchronous" communication tools. According to Garcia and Jacobs (1999), chat messages primarily serve the composer of the message in terms of the communication process. While only a slight delay in providing a reply in many instances, the delay creates a shift in the dialogue structure.

The expository nature of communication is another challenge associated with Internet-based learning. Fahy, Crawford, and Aely (2001) explored the communication patterns of thirteen students enrolled in a 15-week online graduate course. Communication was facilitated by several Internet-based tools: e-mail, file sharing, and a conferencing application. Fahy et al. explored the interactional and structural elements of the interactions using the Transactional Analysis Tool (TAT).

Results from the TAT analysis revealed that the size of the network has an impact on the level of involvement. That is, as the network grew, the number of links to other messages also grew. Overall, the researchers found that levels of participation and connectedness of participants varied considerably, and intensity and persistence of participation among individuals were unequal. The majority of the students' contributions were direct statements, with the next largest category being reflections. Thus the focus of the "conversation" was on transfer of information rather than a dynamic dialogue. The challenge of assisting students with learning how to communicate

in dynamic ways using Internet-based technologies remains largely unexplored and an area in need of further investigation.

Facilitating dialogue in any learning context is certainly important, and many researchers have explored ways to support and facilitate dialogue. Gay, Boehner, and Panella (1997) explored how to support online learning through conversations. ArtView, developed by the Interactive Multimedia Group at Cornell University, was designed to enable learners to converse in a shared space while viewing art-related images selected by the instructor. Gay et al. (1997) examined the effectiveness of this tool in a college art course. Learners enrolled in the course were asked to compare and contrast their experience with ArtView to a face-to-face guided visit and discussion in an art museum.

Participants reported limitations as well as positive aspects to the application. Limitations of ArtView included a lack of personal choice of what to view as well as a lack of an outstanding physical viewing environment. They also mentioned the limitations of the 2-D display of the images. Despite the limitations, Gay et al (1997) reported that most participants reported that the limitations were outweighed by the quality and convenience of the online tools.

16.6.1.3 Factors Influencing Communication.
Interaction and communication are impacted by several factors. Researchers have been exploring specific interactions in an attempt to define exactly what the factors are so that we might better understand how to accommodate needs and enable enhanced communication in Internet-based learning environments.

Vrasidas and McIsaac (1999) examined interactions in a blended delivery graduate course that involved face-to-face and Internet-based communication. Eight learners and one instructor participated in the course. The researchers used several sources of data to inform their results: observations, interviews, course work, and online messages. Results indicated that course structure, class size, level of feedback and prior experience of the learners influenced communication in the course. Participants also indicated that their understanding was influenced by group interactions; yet the researchers indicated a lack of interaction in asynchronous discussions. Finding ways to assist learners in becoming comfortable in communicating in multiple venues may facilitate increased understanding.

Wolfe (2000) focused her work on communication patterns of college students in a blended environment as well. In this study, the researcher focused on two specific characteristics: ethnicity and gender. Wolfe (2000) found that white male students participated more in the face-to-face class interactions, while the white female students benefited from the Internet-based communication tools. Wolfe also found that Hispanic female students participated frequently in face-to-face interactions, speaking more than their male counterparts, and, in general, disliked the Internet-based interactions.

16.6.2 Facilitating Interactions: Strategies and Tools

In addition to uncovering specific factors that impact communication, researchers have also attempted to discover strategies and tools that assist and facilitate interaction in Internet-based learning. We discuss these techniques in three main areas: collaboration strategies, discourse strategies, and tools.

16.6.2.1 Collaboration Strategies.

Collaboration is a strategy frequently used to facilitate interactions in Internet-based learning. In a collaborative model, learners are not working in isolation. Rather, they are working with others to extend their own learning, as well as to help facilitate the learning of others. As a result, the orientation changes from what *I* know to what *we* know.

According to Slavin (1990), the social construction of knowledge enables a deeper level of processing and understanding than could occur on an individual level. With its extensive communication capabilities, the Internet readily facilitates collaboration. Internet-based technologies such as e-mail, listservs, and chat rooms enable content to be pushed to learners on a local or global scale. Web-based tools such as web boards virtual classrooms, and blogs extend and enhance communication capabilities, extending the opportunities for collaboration amongst and between learners (Sugrue, 2000).

Oliver, Omari, and Herrington (1998) explored the collaborative learning activities of university level students engaged in an Internet-based learning environment. The researchers found that the environment, based on constructivist principles, encouraged cooperation and reflection amongst and between participants. Oliver et al. (1998) found that specific elements influenced collaboration within the course: group composition and specific collaborative components. Results also indicated that having suggested roles for group members influenced collaboration.

By collaborating using the Internet, learners have the capabilities to engage in dynamic meaning-making (Hooper-Greenhill, 1999). According to hermeneutic theory, meaning is created through the hermeneutic circle involving continuous activity and movement. Hooper-Greenhill (1999) explains this process as follows: ". . . understanding develops through the continuous movement between the whole and the parts . . . and . . . meaning is constantly modified as further relationships are encountered. . . . The process of constructing meaning is like holding a conversation . . . [and] is never static" (p. 49).

The use of a strong theory to guide research was also found in research by Cecez-Kecmanovic and Webb (2000a, 2000b). Habermas' theory of communicative action was used to create a model of collaborative learning that was used to analyze the data gathered during the study. Based on their analysis, Cecez-Kecmanovic and Webb found that the model assisted them in uncovering what was said and how it contributed to the conversation. This is an important finding in that more robust models are needed to assist with the analysis of online discourse in terms of learning.

Many researchers have explored the challenges associated with collaboration and group work within Internet-based contexts. Bruckman and Resnick (1996) describe one of the first online professional communities, MediaMOO, established using an Internet technology known as a MUD—a multiuser dungeon. According to Bruckman and Resnick, MediaMOO was a text-based, networked, virtual reality environment designed to facilitate member-created and organized projects and events. Within this context, users decided what to build and when to build it, encouraging self-expression, diversity, and meaningful engagement.

More recently, attention has turned to the development of computer-supported collaborative learning (CSCL). In CSCL environments, online groups are used for instructional purposes. Brandon and Hollingshead (1999) provide a nice overview of some of the research on CSCL environments, including associated benefits and challenges. Benefits include: increased student responsibility, greater opportunities for communication, potential for increased learning, and preparation for work in virtual teams. Challenges include: reconciling technological, pedagogical, and learning issues; and becoming adept at creating activities that involve CSCL environments. Brandon and Hollingshead (1999) conclude with the presentation of a model for the creation of effective CSCL groups, which includes the interaction of collaboration, communication, and social context.

16.6.2.2 Discourse Strategies.

Expert intervention and group formation seem to impact discourse in Internet-based learning. Daley (2002) analyzed over 450 contributions to an Internet-based discussion by 52 adult learners. Results indicated that interactions progressed to a high analytical level, which Daley attributes to group process development. She also indicates that communication was supported by faculty synthesizing and linking contributions for learners. This intervention by the faculty might indicate to learners that the faculty member values Internet-based communication, thus adding to motivation levels and contributions to the discussion. The significance of the faculty's framing of the importance of the Internet-based interactions was also corroborated in another study. Yagelski and Grabill (1998) found that the ways in which the instructor framed and managed the uses of Internet-based technologies impacted rates of student participation. It also had an impact on students' perceptions of the importance of the technologies within the learning context.

The importance on the value of assisting participants in learning how to communicate in Internet-based dialogue has been discussed by several researchers. Werry (1996) and Hutchby (2001) discuss the value of speaking directly to or addressing individuals in Internet-based discourse. Addressing involves putting the name of the person being addressed at the front of a message or post. This enables everyone engaged in the dialogue to understand the order of communication.

Edens (2000) evaluated the use of an Internet-based discussion group with preservice teachers. Edens specifically sought to explore how the use of such a group might strengthen communication, inquiry, and reflection. While the group did benefit the students in that they communicated observations and concerns across grade-level placements, Edens pointed out that there were pitfalls encountered, one of which was the importance of fostering communication and reflective inquiry in Internet-based discussion groups.

Hill (2002) also described the importance of monitoring activities to facilitate discourse based on her research in community building. Hill (2002) found that facilitation of Internet-based dialogue, either by the instructor or peer participants, had an impact on the perceived value of the interaction by participants.

16.6.2.3 Tools.
The exploration of specific tools to use to help facilitate interactions has also received considerable attention in the literature. Miller and Corley (2001) explored the effect of e-mail messages on student participation in an asynchronous online course. The 8-week course had 62 participants, most of whom identified that they had limited prior computer experience. Participation was measured by the number of minutes a student spent in an individual module in the course. An activity report was generated every 5 days to indicate the amount of time each student spent engaged in course activities. Depending on the amount of time (none to significant), a coded e-mail message was sent to each student following the generation of the activity report. If there was no activity, a negatively worded message was sent to the student. If there was significant activity, a positively worded message was sent to the student.

Results indicated that the negative messages resulted in increased activity by the student. The positive messages resulted in no change, or in some instances, a decrease in effort. As indicated by Miller and Corley (2001), e-mail messages seemed to increase the motivation of the students who were not progressing at a satisfactory level. While the positive messages did not have a positive impact, the researchers were careful to point out this did not indicate that positive messages should not be sent. Rather, Miller and Corley suggested that the students appear to be sufficiently self-regulated and may not require as much feedback.

16.6.3 Opportunities and Challenges Associated with Intentional Community Building

Community building has received considerable attention in the literature at the turn of the new century. Rheingold (1993) provided the seminal work on online communities in *The Virtual Community*. Rheingold discusses the Internet's first large, thriving community (*The Well*), grassroots organization and activism online, MUDs, and individual identity online. More recently, Palloff and Pratt (1999) discuss building communities in online environments. The authors describe both the opportunities and challenges associated with the creation of community in Web-based learning contexts.

Earlier research in the area of community building focused on Internet-based technologies. Parson (1997) documented the use of electronic mail for the creation of community in an online learning context. According to Parson, the use of e-mail served to draw students together, enabling the formation of a community where information could be shared and everyone could learn from one another.

Many other researchers followed in the path of such early pioneers as Rheingold, Parson, and Palloff, and Pratt, examining a variety of issues associated with community building. For example, Weedman (1999) explored the capabilities of electronic conferences for facilitating peer interactions. Weedman's research indicates that the conference environment was effective for the extension of the educational community and that posters to the conference noticed the impact significantly more than lurkers on the forum. Wiley and Edwards (2002) have also conducted research in this area, exploring self-organizing behavior in very large web boards. Wiley and Edwards concluded that very valuable informal learning occurred even in these informal, ill-structured environments.

Moller, Harvey, Downs, and Godshalk (2000) explored the impact of the strength of the community on learning achievement, studying 12 graduate students in an asynchronous course. The primary means of interaction and community building for the students occurred through an Internet-based conferencing tool. Results from the study indicated a relationship between learning achievement and strength of the community. While not conclusive, this study would seem to indicate that spending time on community-building activities would be valuable in an Internet-based interaction.

The study of the impact of community on learning is not a new construct. Wegerif (1998) studied the impact of community in an asynchronous context. He specifically conducted an ethnographic study of how social factors impact learning. Results indicated that participants felt their learning was a part of the process of becoming a part of a community of practice. More specifically, the participants reported that a supportive learning environment greatly facilitated their learning.

Murphy and Collins (1997) also found that a supportive learning environment is important for learning in their research. Participants in their study indicated that it was important to know other learners in the course. Participants stated this enabled them to establish trust, and provide support to each other. Knowing each other, trust, and support (among other things) enabled the creation of a safe and secure learning environment, a factor other researchers have indicated as important for interactions in online enviornments (Hill, 2002).

Hill along with her colleagues Raven and Han (2002) have proposed a research-based model for community building in higher education contexts. This work is an extension of Hill's (2001) earlier work in community building in online contexts. In the model, Hill et al. (in press) propose that attention must be given to a variety of issues if community is to be enabled within a Web-based learning environment. While the model has not yet been tested, it holds considerable promise for the creation of presence within a virtual context.

16.6.3.1 Building Community in Informal Learning Environments.
Wiley and Edwards (2002) reviewed informal learning in large-scale web board environments and found strong similarities between the group processes employed there and those described in Nelson's Collaborative Problem Solving process (Nelson, 1999). Wiley and Edwards explained the communities' ability to engage in these activities without central leadership in terms of biological self-organization. Stigmergy, "the influence on behavior of the persisting environmental effects of previous behavior," allows social insects to communicate with each other indirectly by operating on their

environment (Holland & Melhuish, 2002, p. 173). Web boards provide individuals the same opportunity to operate on the environment, leaving traces that will spur others onto further action.

Kasper (2002) explored open source software communities from a communities of practice perspective. An open source software community consists of a group of geographically disbursed individuals working together to create a piece of software. Each community is distinct, and the cultural expectations in terms of interaction patterns, programming style, and other conventions can take a significant investment to master. Kasper found that the significant learning necessary for individuals to become productive members of the group frequently occurs without formal instruction, conforming to Lave and Wenger's model of legitimate peripheral participation (Lave & Wenger, 1990). Netscape's open source browser project Mozilla (*http://www.mozilla.org/*) provides an excellent example of the type of support necessary for movement from the periphery into the core of an open source community.

While the social component of informal learning is significant, there is also considerable informal learning that occurs on an individual basis. To date, this area has not been widely explored via research outside of museum settings (Falk & Dierkins, 2000; Hein, 1998). More research is needed in other contexts to extend our understanding of how and why the Internet is used for learning outside of formal contexts.

16.6.3.2 Continuing the Dialogue. A need for interactivity and making connections continue to be two appealing aspects of Internet-based learning. The increased proliferation of Web-based courses along with the growth in use of technologies like chat rooms, bulletin boards, and virtual classrooms that enable two-way audio and video, are indicators that the interest in Internet-based learning has grown beyond enabling the retrieval of content online. Indeed, the focus has increasingly shifted to exploring ways to assist learners in communicating with other learners and teachers and other experts, and for teachers to communicate with teachers, administrators and, in some instances, parents.

While the opportunities are considerable and the appeal continues to grow, much work remains in the area of *learning through* the Internet. The infrastructure—both in terms of hardware and software—is a challenge. The physical network of the Internet can only support so much activity. Limited bandwidth is a significant barrier to robust, sustained use of the Internet for learning. The software currently available is also problematic. Exploration of how to increase throughput, along with how to make the interface into this promising world of learning, is greatly needed.

We are also faced with much more daunting question: what is the value-add from Internet-based learning? As we have reported in section three of this chapter, the research is mixed and inconclusive. In a recent broadcast on National Public Radio exploring the benefits of an online law degree program, a primary benefit cited was convenience. In our own informal research with our students, convenience was often mentioned as a key benefit to Internet-based learning. But is convenience enough? Does it justify the costs—tangible and intangible—associated with Internet-based learning? Until we have completed more research related to the value that Internet-based learning affords, this may be the best answer we have.

16.7 EMERGING ISSUES AND CONSIDERATIONS FOR FUTURE RESEARCH

The Internet is wide open for research and investigation. Research is needed at micro and macro levels, and across learning contexts. Continuing research related to Internet technologies will enable the continued expansion and growth of online environments for learning.

The Internet has demonstrated its capability as an information technology. Its success in this realm is abundantly clear across all sectors of our culture. Internet technologies also offer significant promise as tools for learning. As the Internet continues to grow in popularity as a means for delivering instruction at a distance—formally and informally—the need for research also expands. In the late 1980s, Kaye (1987) suggested a need for research examining how best to use the Internet to facilitate cooperative learning, discovery learning, and development of problem-solving skills and critical thinking skills. In the early 1990s, Schrum (1992) also put forth several questions for research consideration, including:

- In what ways do educators who learn in this manner [using the Internet] integrate the technology into their professional work?
- What is the nature of communication and interaction online and in what ways is it similar or different from other communications? (p. 50)

These are areas that continue to be, and need to be, investigated today. In addition to the broader issues associated with Internet-based learning, there are more specific areas that are in need of further investigation. We have divided these into three main areas—theoretical frameworks, issues related to practice, and ethical considerations. Each of the areas is explored in the following sections.

16.7.1 Theoretical Frameworks

Each of the areas described in the chapter could be built upon and extended as we continue to refine our theoretical understanding of learning and the Internet. However, as stated by Merisotis (1999), "...there is a vital need to develop a more integrated, coherent, and systematic program of research based on theory" (p. 50). Clearly there are researchers and theorists seeking to describe a theory related to distance learning, including the use of the Internet for learning. What is needed is a more comprehensive perspective to guide future work: what is needed to move the field toward a more comprehensive framework related to the Internet and learning? Until that question is answered, individual efforts will continue but fail to bring about a constructive progression in understanding.

16.7.2 Issues Related to Practice

16.7.2.1 Exploration of Best Practices. Best practices remain an area in need of systematic investigation. We would like to suggest a variation on a question posed in the report *What's the Difference?* in which Phipps and Merisotis (1999) asked: what is **the best way** to teach students? Like other researchers before us (see, for example, Reigeluth, 1999), we propose that there is not **one** best way, but rather several best ways. A primary challenge for researchers examining learning from and learning with the Internet is to uncover those best practices relative to specific conditions, learning goals, contexts, and learners. Perhaps that leaves us with one fundamental question: What are **the best ways** to teach students within specific contexts and under certain conditions?

16.7.2.2 Expansion of Use and Research Practices. Instructional uses of the Web have ranged from enhancement to full-engagement in Web-based learning environments. Loegering and Edge (2001) described their efforts to enhance their science courses by enabling students access to Web-based exercises. Web-based portfolios have also been used to enhance courses (see, for example, Chen, Liu, Ou, & Lin, 2001). Researchers have explored immersive Web environments, describing experiences within specific courses (Hill et al., 2002; Lawson, 2000) as well as experiences with providing entire degree programs online (see Boettcher, 2002, for a review). Research related to the Web has focused primarily on pedagogical issues (Berge & Mrozowski, 2001). While these efforts hold much promise for the future of the technology, particularly for learning, some researchers contend that, the majority of the educational uses of these tools simply replicate classroom practice (Jonassen, 2002). The use of the tool, as well as the research practices surrounding it, are in need of expansion if it is to reach its potential as a platform for educational innovation (Berge & Mrozowski, 2001; Jonassen, 2002).

16.7.2.3 Formal and Informal Learning Environments. The call for formal instructional environments on the Internet is clear, and a variety of organizations are rushing to design and provide this training. However, a need exists for structured environments supporting the important informal learning described by Brown and Duguid (2000). The success of the design of these environments will be highly dependent on our understanding of the processes underlying informal learning on the Internet. Hence a great deal more research on this topic is needed.

16.7.2.4 Intentional and Incidental Learning. Interest in and exploration of intentional and incidental learning is documented in the research literature; however, the majority of the studies completed to date have been situated in

face-to-face contexts or in electronic environments outside the realm of Internet-based learning (e.g., information seeking). Both of these type of learning—intentional and incidental—need more study if we are to realize their role in and relationship to Internet-based learning.

16.7.3 Ethical Considerations

16.7.3.1 Using the Internet to Support Learning. Research grounded in ethical considerations is needed. Clark and Salomon (1996) encouraged researchers of media use in education to move beyond the how and why a particular medium operates in instruction and learning. Clark and Salomon (1996) point out that there is an historical precedence related to the adoption of technology for learning: "... there has been a pattern of adoption by schools in response to external pressures from commercial and community special interests rather than as a result of identified and expressed need" (p. 475). We call for an ethical consideration of promoting the adoption of technology, pointing out that we have not addressed several basic questions: How can media support instructional objectives? What other roles do media play? What role will teachers play with students using computers to guide learning? How can schools, already overburdened by multiple demands, meet the demands created by the new technologies?

16.7.3.2 Research From, With, and Through the Internet. The 1999 formation of the Association of Internet Researchers (AoIR; http://aoir.org/) provides evidence of the interdisciplinary recognition that research on the Internet is not the same animal as research in the "real world." Many of the differences between these two research loci relate to ethical concerns for the protection of research participants. An AoIR ethics committee preliminary report recounts some of the challenges faced by Internet researchers:

- *Greater risk to individual privacy and confidentiality* because of greater accessibility of information about individuals, groups, and their communications—and in ways that would prevent subjects from knowing that their behaviors and communications are being observed and recorded (e.g., in a large-scale analysis of postings and exchanges in a USENET newsgroup archive, in a chatroom, etc.);
- *Greater challenges to researchers* because of greater difficulty in obtaining informed consent;
- *Greater difficulty of ascertaining subjects' identity* because of use of pseudonyms, multiple online identities, etc.
- *Greater difficulty in discerning ethically correct approaches* because of a greater diversity of research venues (private e-mail, chatroom, webpages, etc.)
- *Greater difficulty of discerning ethically correction approaches* because of the global reach of the media involved – i.e., as CMC (and legal) settings. (AoIR, 2002)

In addition to AoIR, a number of organizations and researchers are rethinking the ethics of research, and even the techniques of research, when the Internet is involved (AAAS,

1998; Hine, 2000; Dicks & Mason, 1998; Schrum, 1995; Waern, 2002).

How must our research methods change to reflect the different affordances and opportunities presented by the Internet? How does our obligation to gain informed consent change when people make statements in "public" settings like an open Web board? Are these environments public like a street corner, or do posters to a web board enjoy an expectation of privacy and protection regarding the comments they make there? These and many other questions are open and must be answered before we can fully engage the Internet as a research site.

16.7.4 Continuing the Dialogue

We have taken a rather broad look at research related to various aspects of Internet-based learning. While there are many other issues that can be explored, perhaps the most pressing issue relates to the broader use of technology for learning. Saettler (in press) has done an excellent job of reminding us where we have come from and the relatively little progress we have made with integrating technology into teaching and learning.

Clark and Salomon (1996) offer assistance in recalling why we may not have seen indicators of significant progress with technology in education in our research. The lessons they recall for us in their work apply to thinking about learning from and with the Internet. These lessons include: (1) no medium enhances learning more than any other media, (2) instructional materials and learner motivation are usually enhanced with new technologies, (3) a need to link technology-based research with cognitive science research, and (4) a need to move beyond the how and why a technology operates in teaching and learning. We would add a fifth "lesson": while traditional notions of "control" may be difficult (if not impossible) to achieve in educational research, research reports must include more information describing the research setting in order to facilitate meaningful comparisons across studies. If we can learn these lessons, we may be able to extend our research efforts with the Internet and Web 10-fold.

16.8 CONCLUSIONS

In a presentation to the National School Board Association's Technology and Learning Conference (Dallas, 1992), Alan Kay of Apple Computers drew the analogy between the invention and use of the movie camera to the exploration and use of computer technologies in education. In the comparison Kay related that the movie camera was, at first, only used as a stationary recording device.... It was not, according to Kay, until D. W. Griffith realized that by moving the camera and using different shots... to focus the attention of the audience and to shape the mood and perceptions of the audience that the movie became it own art form... (from Riedel, 1994, p. 26)

As of the publication of this chapter a decade later, the Internet remains in the same position as the movie camera once was—it is primarily a delivery mechanism. However, Internet-based technologies have most certainly reached the phase where Griffith-type interventions are possible. Research related to the Internet has been represented in the literature for over a decade (see, for example, Baym, 1995; Bechar-Israeli, 1995; Schrum, 1992); reports on Internet-based implementations for learning also date back over a decade (see, for example, Cheng, Lehman, & Armstrong, 1991; Davie, 1988; Hill & Hannafin, 1997; Phelps, Wells, Ashworth, & Hahn, 1991; Whitaker, 1995). While some of the research has been critiques in terms of its quality and rigor (Berge & Mrozowski, 2001; Phipps & Meriotis, 1999; Saba, 2000), we do have a foundation and can continue to expand our efforts based on studies from the last 5 to 10 years.

Use of the Internet for learning is an area growing at an exponential rate. K–12 educators to higher education faculty to business and industry trainers are exploring and/or have moved into this arena to reach learners. As educators are exploring and implementing Internet-based learning environments, they are also exploring how to reach their learners. Indeed, the Internet is a technology that has the potential for enabling the creation of learning-centered distance education environments—ones in which students, teachers, and experts are working together in the learning process.

While the exploration of how to reach learners on a psychological level is underway, there is also a movement toward a blended approach to the use of the Internet for teaching and learning. As stated by Mason and Kaye (1990), "... the distinctions currently drawn between distance and classroom-based education may become less clear as applications of new technologies become more widespread" (p. 16). Blended approaches will enable a use of a variety of technologies to meet the needs of learners.

In 1995, Dede presented the idea that Internet-based learning has potential for significant expansion, moving from a "traditional" distance learning to a "distributed learning" paradigm. According to Dede, it is the emerging technologies such as the Internet that make this possible:

The innovative kinds of pedagogy empowered by these emerging media, messages, and experiences make possible a transformation of conventional distance education—which replicates traditional classroom teaching across barriers of distance and time—into an alternative instructional paradigm: distributed learning.... (p. 4)

We have yet to realize the promise that Dede described in the mid-1990s. The Internet remains on the threshold as learning tools. The promise of the technology is vast; yet, the potential can be lost if steps are not taken to realize the true potential of these information technologies for learning. What remains to be crystallized are the applications in a learning environment. As we continue to implement and examine the use of the Internet in our learning environments, the factors contributing to their successful implementation will become clearer. Taking the next steps toward the creation of active learning environments using the Internet is just a matter of choice; choosing not to take these next steps will leave the technologies like many other educational technologies before them: great ideas whose true potential was never realized.

Perhaps it is time to reexamine the questions we are posing related to learning from, learning with, and learning through the Internet. Clark and Salomon (1996) close their chapter in the *Handbook on Teaching Research* with the following statement: "This, then, suggests a new class of questions to be asked: not only what technology, for whom, and so forth, but **why this technology now**?" (p. 475). We have an opportunity to take a critical perspective on the technologies that have captured the attention of all sectors in our society. In taking this step we

seize another opportunity: making a difference in teaching and learning

ACKNOWLEDGMENTS

The authors would like to extend thanks to the students at the University of Georgia and Utah State University. This chapter would not have been possible without the hours of conversations and resources we have shared.

References

AAAS (1998). *Ethical and legal aspects of human subjects research in cyberspace*. Available online: *http://www.aaas.org/spp/dspp/sfrl/projects/intres/main.htm*

Alessi, S. M., & Trollip, S. R. (2001). *Multimedia for learning: Methods and development* (3rd ed.). Boston, MA: Allyn and Bacon.

Ali, A., & Franklin, T. (2001). Internet use in the classroom: Potential and pitfalls for student learning and teacher-student relationships. *Educational Technology, 41*(4), 57-59.

Anonymous (2001). Identifying faculty satisfaction in distance education. *Distance Education Report, 5*(22), 1-2.

AoIR (2002). *Association of Internet Researchers ethics report*. Available online: http://aoir.org

Arbaugh, F., Scholten, C. M., & Essex, N. K. (2001). Data in the middle grades: A probability WebQuest. *Mathematics Teaching in the Middle School, 7*(2), 90-95.

Arvan, L., Ory, J. C., Bullock, C. D., Burnaska, K. K., & Hanson, M. (1998). The SCALE efficiency projects. *Journal of Asynchronous Learning Network, 2*(2). Retrieved November 27, 2002, from *http://www.aln.org/alnweb/journal/vol2_issue2/arvan2.htm*

Barab, S. A., MaKinster, J. G., Moore, J. A., Cunningham, D. J., & The ILF Design Team (2001). Designing and building an on-line community: The struggle to support sociability in the Inquiry Learning Forum. *Educational Technology, Research & Development, 49*(4), 71-96.

Barrows, H. S. (1986). A taxonomy of problem-based learning methods. *Medical education, 20,* 481-486.

Barzeski, E. (1999). A/S/L to death. *Le Mega Byte*. Retrieved from *http://www.macopinion.com/columns/megabyte/99/10/28/*

Baylor, A. (1999). *Multiple intelligent mentors instructing collaboratively (MIMIC): Developing a theoretical framework*. (ERIC Document: ED 438790).

Baylor, A. (2001). Perceived disorientation and incidental learning in a web-based environment: Internal and external factors. *Journal of Educational Multimedia & Hypermedia, 10*(3), 227-251.

Baym, N. (1995). The performance of humor in computer-mediated communication. *Journal of Computer-Mediated Communication, 1*(2).

Bayton, M. (1992). Dimensions of control in distance education: A factor analysis. *The American Journal of Distance Education, 6*(2), 17-31.

Bechar-Israeli, H. (1995). From to: Nicknames, play and identify on Internet relay chat. *Journal of Computer-Mediated Communication, 1*(2).

Berge, Z. L., & Mrozowski, S. (2001). Review of research in distance education, 1990 to 1999. *The American Journal of Distance Education, 15*(3), 5-19.

Berger, N. S. (1999). Pioneering experiences in distance learning: Lessons learned. *Journal of Management Education, 23*(6), 684-690.

Bershears, F. M. (2002). *Demystifying learning management systems*. Retrieved November 27, 2002, from *http://socrates.berkeley.edu/~fmb/articles/demystifyinglms/*

Blum, K. D. (1999). Gender differences in asynchronous learning in higher education: Learning styles, participation barriers and communication patterns. *Journal of Asynchronous Learning Networks, 3*(1). Retrieved November 27, 2002, from *http://www.aln.org/alnweb/journal/vol3_issue1/blum.htm*

Blumberg, R. B. (1994). *MendelWeb: An electronic science/math/history resource for the WWW.* Paper presented at the 2nd World Wide Web Conference: Mosaic and the Web in Urbana-Champaign, Illinois (ERIC Document ED 446896) Available online: *http://archive.ncsa.uiuc.edu/SDG/IT94/Proceedings/Educ/blumberg.mendelweb/MendelWeb94.blumberg.html*

Boaz, M., Elliott, B., Foshee, D., Hardy, D., Jarmon, C., & Olcott, D. (1999). *Teaching at a distance: A handbook for instructors*. Fort Worth, TX: League for Innovation in the Community College & Archipelago (Harcourt).

Boettcher, J. V. (2002). The changing landscape of distance education. *Syllabus, 15*(12), 22-24, 26-27.

Brandon, D. P., & Hollingshead, A. B. (1999). Collaborative learning and computer-supported groups. *Communication Education, 48*(2), 109-126.

Brown, J. S., Collins, A., & Duguid, P. (1989). Situated cognition and the culture of learning. *Educational Researcher, 18*(1), 32-42.

Brown, J. S., & Duguid, P. (2000). *The social life of information*. Boston, MA: Harvard Business School.

Bruckman, A., & Resnick, M. (1996). The MediaMOO project: Constructionism and professional community. In Y. Kafai & M. Resnick (Eds.), *Constructionism in practice: Designing, thinking, and learning in a digital world* (pp. 207-221). Hillsdale, NJ: Lawrence Erlbaum.

Brush, T. A., & Uden. L. (2000). Using computer-mediated communications to enhance instructional design classes: A case study. *International Journal of Instructional Media, 27*(2), 157-164.

Buchanan, L. (1998). O how wonderous is e-mail! *MultiMedia Schools, 5*(3), 42-44.

Burstein, J., Kukich, K., Wolff, S., Lu, C., Chodorow, M., Braden-Harder, L., & Harris, M. D. (1998). Automated scoring using a hybrid feature identification technique. In the *Proceedings of the Annual Meeting of the Association of Computational Linguistics,* August, 1998. Montreal, Canada. Retrieved November 27, 2002, from *http://www.ets.org/reasearch/aclfinal.pdf*

Campbell, O. J. (2001). *Factors in ALN Cost Effectiveness at BYU.* Retrieved November 27, 2002, from *http://sln.suny.edu/sln/public/original.nsf/dd93a8da0b7ccce0852567b00054e2b6/2daa5ea4eb5205f185256a3e0067197f/$FILE/Brigham%20Young%20Cost%20Effectiveness.doc*

Cecez-Kecmanovic, D., & Webb, C. (2000a). A critical inquiry into Web-mediated collaborative learning. In A. Aggarwal (Ed.), *Web-based learning and teaching technologies: Opportunities and challenges* (pp. 307-326). Hershey, PA: Idea Group Publishing.

Cecez-Kecmanovic, D., & Webb, C. (2000b). Towards a communicative model of collaborative Web-mediated learning. *Australian Journal of Educational Technology, 16*(1), 73-85.

Chen, G., Lin, C. C., Ou, K. L., & Lin, M. S. (2001). Web learning portfolios: A tool for supporting performance awareness. *Innovations in Education and Training International, 38*(1), 19-30.

Cheng, H., Lehman, & Armstrong (1991). Comparison of performance and attitude in traditional and computer conferencing classes. *American Journal of Distance Education, 5*(3), 51-64.

Cifuentes, L., & Murphy, K. (2000). Promoting multicultural understanding and positive self-concept through a distance learning community: Cultural Connections. *Educational Technology, Research & Development, 48*(1), 69-83.

Clark, R. E. (1994). Media will never influence learning. *ETR&D, 42*(2), 21-29.

Clark, R. E., & Salomon, G. (1996). Media in teaching. In M. C. Wittrock, (Ed.), *Handbook of research on teaching* (3rd ed.) (pp. 464-478). New York: Macmillan.

Cole, C., Mandelblatt, B., & Stevenson, J. (2002). Visualizing a high recall search strategy output for undergraduate in an exploration stage of researching a term paper. *Information Processing and Management, 38*(1), 37-54.

Cognition and Technology Group at Vanderbilt (CTGV) (1992). Technology and the design of generative learning environments. In T. M. Duffy & D. H. Jonassen (Eds.), *Constructivism and the technology of instruction: A conversation* (pp. 77-89). Hillsdale, NJ: Lawrence Erlbaum Associates.

Collins, A., Brown, J. S., & Newman, S. E. (1989). Cognitive apprenticeship: Teaching the crafts of reading, writing, and mathematics. In L. B. Resnick (Ed.), *Knowing, learning, and instruction: Essays in honor of Robert Glaser* (pp. 453-494). Hillsdale, NJ: Lawrence Erlbaum Associates.

Cyrs, T. E. (1997). Competence in teaching at a distance. *New Directions for Teaching and Learning, 71,* 15-18.

Daley, B. (2002). An exploration of electronic discussion as an adult learning strategy. *PAACE Journal of Lifelong Learning, 11,* 53-66.

Davie, L. E. (1988). Facilitating adult learning through computer-mediated distance education. *Journal of Distance Education, 3*(2), 55-69.

Dede, C. J. (1995). The evolution of constructivist learning environments: Immersion in distributed, virtual worlds. *ETR&D, 35*(5), 4-36.

deVerneil, M., & Berge, Z. L. (2000, Spring/Summer). Going online: Guidelines for faculty in higher education. *Educational Technology Review, 13,* 13-18.

Dicks, B. & Mason, B. (1998). Hypermedia and ethnography: Reflections on the construction of a research approach. *Sociological Research Online, 3*(3). Retrieved November 27, 2002, from http://www.socresonline.org.uk/socresonline/3/3/3.html

Dodge, B. (2001). FOCUS: Five rules for writing a great WebQuest. *Learning & Leading with Technology, 28*(8), 6-9, 58.

Dodge, B. (2002). *The WebQuest Page.* Available online: http://webquest.sdsu.edu/webquest.html

Donath, J. (2002). A semantic approach to visualizing online conversations. *Communications of the ACM 45*(4), 45-49.

Donath, J. S. (1998). *Identity and deception in the virtual community.* Retrieved November 27, 2002, from http://smg.media.mit.edu/people/Judith/Identity/IdentityDeception.html

Doring, A. (1999). Information overload? *Adult Learning, 10*(10), 8-9.

Duff, C. (2000). Online mentoring. *Educational Leadership, 58*(2), 49-52.

Dutt-Doner, K., Wilmer, M., Stevens, C., & Hartmann, L. (2000). Actively engaging learners in interdisciplinary curriculum through the integration of technology. *Computers in the Schools, 16*(3-4), 151-66.

Edens, K. M. (2000). Promoting communication, inquiry and reflection in an early practicum experience via an online discussion group. *Action in Teacher Education, 22*(2), 14-23.

Fahy, P. J., Crawford, G., & Ally, M. (2001, July). Patterns of interaction in a computer conference transcript. *International Review of Research in Open and Distance Learning.* Available online: http://www.irrodl.org/content/v2.1/fahy.html

Falk, J. H., & Dierkins, L. D. (2000). *Learning from museums: Visitor experiences and the making of meaning.* Lanham, MD: Altamira.

Fichten, C. S., Asuncion, J. V., Barile, M., Fossey, M., & DeSimone, C. (2000). Access to educational and instructional computer technologies for post-secondary students with disabilities: Lessons form three empirical studies. *Journal of Educational Media, 25*(3), 179-201.

Fitzgerald, M. A. (2000). The cognitive process of information evaluation in doctoral students. *Journal of Education for Library and Information Science, 41*(3), 170-186.

Follansbee, S., Hughes, R., Pisha, B., & Stahl, S. (1997). The role of online communications in schools: A national study. *ERS Spectrum, 15*(1), 15-26.

Fornaciari, C. J., & Roca, M. F. L. (1999). The age of clutter: Conducting effective research using the Internet. *Journal of Management Education, 23*(6), 732-42.

Fredrickson, E., Pickett, A., Shea, P., Pelz, W., & Swan, K. (2000). Student satisfaction and perceived learning with on-line courses: Principles and examples for the SUNY Learning Network. *Journal of Asynchronous Learning Networks, 4*(2). Retrieved November 27, 2002, from *http://www.aln.org/alnweb/journal/Vol4_issue2/le/Fredericksen/LE-fredericksen.htm*

Garcia, A. C., & Jacobs, J. B. (1999). The eyes of the beholder: Understanding the turn-taking system in quasi-synchronous computer-mediated communication. *Research on language and social interaction, 32*(4), 337-368.

Gay, G., Boehner, K., & Panella, T. (1997). ArtView: Transforming image databases into collaborative learning spaces. *Journal of Educational Computing Research, 16*(4), 317-332.

Gergen, K. J. (1991). *The saturated self: Dilemmas of identity in contemporary life.* New York: Basic Books.

Gibson, S., & Oberg, D. (1997). Case studies of Internet use in Alberta Schools: Emerging issues. *Canadian Journal of Educational Communication, 26*(3), 145-164.

Gilliver, R. S., Randall, B., & Pok, Y. M. (1998). Learning in cyberspace: Shaping the future. *Journal of Computer Assisted Learning, 14*(3), 212-222.

Glaser, B. G., & Strauss, A. L. (1967). *Discovery of grounded theory: Strategies for qualitative research.* Hawthorne, NY: Aldine de Gruyter.

Gold, S. (2001). A constructivist approach to online training for online teachers. *Journal of Asynchronous Learning Networks, 5*(1). Available online: http://www.aln.org/alnweb/journal/jaln-vol5issue1.htm

Greeno, J. G., Smith, D. R., & Moore, J. L. (1992). Transfer of situated learning. In D. Detterman & R. J. Sternberg (Eds.), *Transfer on trial: Intelligence, cognition, and instruction* (pp. 99-167). Norwood, NJ: Ablex.

Halloran, M. E. (2002). *Evaluation of web-based course management software from faculty and student user-centered perspectives.* Retrieved November 27, 2002, from *http://www.usafa.af.mil/iita/Publications/CourseManagementSoftware/cmseval.htm*

Hannafin, M. J., Hill, J. R., & Land, S. M. (1997). Student-centered learning and interactive multimedia: Status, issues and implication. *Contemporary Education, 68*(2), 94-99.

Harel, I., & Papert, S. (1991). *Constructionism.* Norwood, NJ: Ablex.

Hargis, J. (2001). Can students learn science using the Internet? *Journal of Research on Technology in Education, 33*(4).

Harris, J. (1995). Educational telecomputing projects: Interpersonal exchanges. *The Computing Teacher, 22*(6), 60-64.

Haycock, C. A. (1991). Resource based learning: A shift in the roles of teacher, learner. *NASSP Bulletin, 75*(535), 15-22.

Hayes, N. (2000). *Foundations of psychology* (3rd ed.). London, England: Thomson Learning.

Hazari, S. (2002). *Evaluation and selection of web course management tools.* Retrieved November 27, 2002, from *http://sunil.umd.edu/webct/*

Heo, M., & Hirtle, S. C. (2001). An empirical comparison of visualization tools to assist information retrieval on the Web. *Journal of the American Society for Information Science and Technology, 52*(8), 666-675.

Hein, G. E. (1998). *Learning in the museum.* New York: Routledge.

Hill, J. R. (1999). A conceptual framework for understanding information seeking in open-ended information systems. *Educational Technology Research & Development, 47*(1), 5-28.

Hill, J. R. (2001). *Building community in Web-based learning environments: Strategies and techniques.* Paper presented at the Southern Cross University AUSWEB annual conference. Coffs Harbour, Australia.

Hill, J. R. (2002). Strategies and techniques for community building in Web-based learning environments. *Journal of Computing in Higher Education, 14*(1), 67-86.

Hill, J. R., & Hannafin, M. J. (1997). Cognitive strategies and learning from the World Wide Web. *Educational Technology Research & Development, 45*(4), 37-64.

Hill, J. R., & Hannafin, M. J. (2001). Teaching and learning in digital environments: The resurgence of resource-based learning. *Educational Technology Research & Development, 49*(3), 37-52.

Hill, J. R., Raven, A., & Han, S. (2002). Connections in Web-based learning environments: A research-based model for community-building. *Quarterly Review of Distance Education, 3*(4), 383-393.

Hill, J. R., Reeves, T. C., Grant, M. M., & Wang, S. K. (2000). *Year one report: Athens Academy laptop evaluation.* Athens, GA: University of Georgia. Available online: http://lpsl.coe.uga.edu/~projects/AAlaptop

Hillman, D., C., A., Willis B., & Gunawardena, C. N. (1994). Learner-interface interaction in distance education: An extension of contemporary models and strategies for practitioners. *American Journal of Distance Education, 8*(2), 30-42.

Hiltz, S. R. (1997). Impacts of college-level courses via asynchronous learning networks: some preliminary results. *Journal of Asynchronous Learning Networks, 1*(2). Retrieved November 27, 2002, from *http://www.aln.org/alnweb/journal/issue2/hiltz.htm*

Hine, C. (2000). *Virtual Ethnography.* Thousand Oaks, CA: Sage.

Holland, O. E. & Melhuish, C. (2000). Stigmergy, self-organization, and sorting in collective robotics. *Artificial Life, 5*(2), 173-202.

Hooper-Greenhill, E. (1999). Learning in art museums: Strategies of interpretation. In E. Hooper-Greenhill (Ed.), *The educational role of the museum* (2nd ed.) (pp. 44-52). New York: Routledge.

Hutchby, I. (2001). *Conversation and technology: From the telephone to the Internet.* Cambridge, UK: Polity.

Jasinski, M., & Thiagarajan, S. (2000). Virtual games for real learning: Learning online with serious fun. *Educational Technology, 40*(4), 61-63.

Jelfs, A., & Whitelock, D. (2000). The notion of presence in virtual learning environments: What makes the environment "real." *British Journal of Educational Technology, 31*(2), 145-152.

Jewett, F. (1998). *Course restructuring and the instructional development initiative at Virginia Polytechnic Institute and State University: A benefit cost study.* Blacksburg, VA: Report from a project entitled Case Studies in Evaluating the Benefits and Costs of Mediated Instruction and Distributed Learning. Virginia Polytechnic Institute and State University. (ERIC Document: ED 423 802)

Johnston, T. C., Alexander, L., Conrad, C., & Fieser, J. (2000). Faculty compensation models for online/distance education. *Mid-South Instructional Technology Conference,* April 2000. Murfreesboro, Tennessee. Retrieved November 27, 2002, from *http://www.mtsu.edu/~itconf/proceed00/johnston.html*

Jonassen, D. H. (2002). Engaging and supporting problem solving in online learning. *Quarterly Review of Distance Education, 3*(1), 1-13.

Jonassen, D. H., & Reeves, T. C. (1996). Learning *with* technology: Using computers as cognitive tools. In D. H. Jonassen (Ed.), *Handbook of research for educational communications and technology* (pp. 693-719). New York: Simon & Schuster.

Jung, I. (2001). Building a theoretical framework of web-based instruction in the context of distance education. *British Journal of Educational Technology, 32*(5), 525-534.

Kafai, Y., & Resnick, M. (1996). *Constructionism in practice: Designing, thinking, and learning in a digital world.* Mahwah, NJ: Erlbaum.

Kasper, E. (2001). *Epistemic communities, situated learning and open source software.* Retrieved November 27, 2002, from *http://opensource.mit.edu/papers/kasperedwards-ec.pdf*

Kaye, T. (1987). Introducing computer-mediated communication into a distance education system. *Canadian Journal of Educational Communication, 16*(2), 153-166.

Kearsley, G. (2000). *Online education: Learning and teaching in cyberspace.* Belmont, CA: Wadsworth.

Kelly, R. (2000). Working with Webquests: Making the Web accessible to students with disabilities. *TEACHING Exceptional Children, 32*(6), 4-13.

Kelly, S. W., Burton, A. M., Kato, T., & Akamatsu, S. (2001). Incidental learning of real-world regularities. *Psychological Science, 12*(1), 86-89.

Kember, D. (1995). Learning approaches, study time and academic performance. *Higher Education, 29*(3), 329-343.

Kozma, R. (1994). Will media influence learning? Reframing the debate. *ETR&D, 42*(2), 7-19.

Kwok, R. C. W., & Ma, J. (1999). Use of a group support system for collaborative assessment. *Computers and Education, 32,* 109-125.

Lajoie, S. P. (1993). Computer environments as cognitive tools for enhancing learning. In S. Lajoie & S. Derry (Eds.), *Computers as cognitive tools* (pp. 261–88). Hillsdale, NJ: Erlbaum.

Lan, J. (2001). Web-based instruction for education faculty: A needs assessment. *Journal of Research in Computing in Education, 33*(4), 385–399.

Landon, B. (2002). *Course management systems: Compare products.* Retrieved November 27, 2002, from *http://www.edutools.info/course/compare/index.jsp*

Lawson, T. J. (2000). Teaching a social psychology course on the Web. *Teaching of Psychology, 27*(4), 285–289.

Lave, E. (1991). *Communities of practice: Learning, meaning, and identity.* New York: Cambridge.

Lave, J., & Wenger, E. (1990). *Situated learning: Legitimate peripheral participation.* Cambridge, UK: Cambridge University.

Lee, J. (2001). Instructional support for distance education and faculty motivation, commitment, satisfaction. *British Journal of Educational Technology, 32*(2), 153–160.

Lee, S. Y., & Songer, N. B. (2001). Promoting scientific understanding through electronic discourse. *Asia Pacific Education Review, 2*(1), 32–43.

Leflore, D. (2000). Theory supporting design guidelines for Web-based instruction. In B. Abbey (Ed.), *Instructional and cognitive impacts of Web-based instruction* (pp. 102–117). Hershey, PA: Idea.

Levin, J. (1995). *Organizing educational network interactions: Steps toward a theory of network-based learning environments.* Paper presented at the American Educational Research Association Annual Meeting, San Francisco CA, April 1995. Available online: *http://lrs.ed.uiuc.edu/guidelines/Levin-AERA-18Ap95.html*

Linn, M., Shear, L., Bell, P., & Slotta, J. (1999). Organizing principles for science education partnerships: Case studies of students learning about rats in space and deformed frogs. *Educational Technology Research and Development, 47*(2), 61–84.

Loegering, J. P., & Edge, W. D. (2001). Reinforcing science with Web-based exercises. *Journal of College Science Teaching, 31*(4), 252–257.

MacDonald, J., & Mason, R. (1998). Information handling skills and resource-based learning in an open university course. *Open Learning, 13*(1), 38–42.

Marchionini, G. (1995). *Information seeking in electronic environments.* Cambridge, MA: Cambridge University.

Mason, R., & Kaye, A. (1990). Toward a new paradigm for distance education. In L. M. Harasim (Ed.), *Online education: Perspectives on a new environment* (pp. 15–38). New York: Praeger.

McIsaac, M. S., & Gunawardena, C. N. (1996). Distance education. In D. H. Jonassen (Ed.), *Handbook of research for educational communications and technology* (pp. 403–437). New York: Simon & Schuster.

McLoughlin, C. (1999). Culturally responsive technology use: Developing an on-line community of learners. *British Journal of Educational Technology, 30*(3), 231–143.

Merisotis, J. P. (1999, Sept-Oct). The "What's-the-Difference?" debate. *Academe,* 47–51.

Miller, M. D. (2001). The effect of e-mail messages on student participation in the asynchronous on-line course: a research. *Online Journal of Distance Learning Education, 4*(3).

Miller, M. D., & Corley, K. (2001). The effect of e-mail messages on student participation in the asynchronous online-course: A research note. *Online Journal of Distance Learning Education, 4*(3). Available online: http://www.westga.edu/~distance/ojdla/fall43/miller43.html

Miller, S. M., & Miller, K. L. (2000). Theoretical and practical considerations in the design of Web-based instruction. In B. Abbey (Ed.), *Instructional and cognitive impacts of Web-based instruction* (pp. 156–177). Hershey, PA: Idea.

Milson, A. J. (2001). Fostering civic virtue in a high-tech world. *International Journal of Social Education, 16*(1), 87–93.

Moller, L. (1998). Designing communities of learners for asynchronous distance education. *Educational Technology Research and Development, 46*(4), 115–122.

Moller, L. A., Harvey, D., Downs, M., & Godshalk, V. (2000). Identifying factors that effect learning community development and performance in asynchronous distance education. *Quarterly Review of Distance Education, 1*(4), 293–305.

Monikowski, C. (1997). Electronic media: Broadening deaf students' access to knowledge. *American Annals of the Deaf, 142*(2), 101–104.

Moore, J. A. (2002). *The design of and desire for professional development: A community of practice in the making?* Unpublished doctoral dissertation, Indiana University, Bloomington, IL.

Moore, M. G. (1989). Distance education: A learner's system. *Lifelong Learning, 12*(8), 11–14.

Moore, M. G., & Kearsley, G. (1995). *Distance education: A systems view.* New York: Wadsworth.

Moss, C. M. (1999). *Teaching as intentional learning…in service of the scholarship of practice.* Available online: *http://castl.duq.edu*

Moss, C. M. (2000). Professional learning on the cyber sea: What is the point of contact? *CyberPsychology and Behavior, 3*(1), 41–50.

Murphy, K. L., & Collins, M. P. (1997). Communication conventions in instructional electronic chats. *Journal of Distance Education, 2*(11), 177–200. Available online: http://www.firstmonday.dk/issues/issue2_11/murphy/index.html

Nelson, L. M. (1999). Collaborative problem solving. In C. M. Reigeluth (Ed.), *Instructional-design theories and models.* Volume ii. *A new paradigm of instructional theory* (pp. 241–268). Mahwah, NJ: Lawrence Erlbaum Associates.

Oliver, K. (1999). *Student use of computer tools designed to scaffold scientific problem solving with hypermedia resources: A case study.* Unpublished doctoral dissertation, University of Georgia, Athens GA.

Oliver, R., & McLoughlin, C. (2001). Exploring the practice and development of generic skills through web-based learning. *Journal of Educational Multimedia & Hypermedia, 10*(3), 207–225.

Oliver, R., Omari, A., & Herrington, J. (1998). Exploring student interactions in collaborative World Wide Web computer-based learning environments. *Journal of Educational Multimedia and Hypermedia, 7*(2/3), 263–287.

Ostiguy, N., & Haffer, A. (2001). Assessing differences in instructional methods: Uncovering how students learn best. *Journal of College Science Teaching, 30*(6), 370–374.

Owston, R. D. (1997). The World Wide Web: A technology to enhance teaching and learning? *Educational Researcher, 26*(2), 27–33.

Page, E. B. (1994). Computer grading of student prose, using modern concepts and software. *Journal of Experimental Education, 62*(2), 127–42.

Palloff, R. M., & Pratt, K. (1999). *Building learning communities in cyberspace: Effective strategies for the online classroom.* San Francisco, CA: Jossey-Bass.

Parson, P. T. (1997). Electronic mail: Creating a community of learners. *Journal of Adolescent and Adult Literacy, 40*(7), 560–565.

Pea, R. D. (1985). Beyond amplification: Using the computer to reorganize mental functioning. *Educational Psychologist, 20*(4), 167–182.

Peck, K. L. (1998). Ready…fire…aim! Toward meaningful technology standards for educators and students. *TechTrends, 43*(2), 47–53.

Perkins, D. N. (1986). *Knowledge as design*. Hillsdale, NJ: Erlbaum.

Perkins, D. N. (1993). Person-plus: A distributed view of thinking and learning. In G. Salomon (Ed.), *Distributed cognitions: Psychological and educational considerations* (pp. 88-110). Cambridge, UK: Cambridge University.

Peterson, C. L., & Koeck, D. C. (2001). When students create their own WebQuests. *Learning and Leading with Technology, 29*(1), 10-15.

Phelps, R. H., Wells, Ashworth, & Hahn (1991). Effectiveness and costs of distance education using computer-mediated communication. *American Journal of Distance Education, 5*(3), 7-19.

Phipps, R., & Merisotis, J. P. (1999). *What's the difference?* Washington, D.C.: Institute of Higher Education Policy. Available online: *http://www.nea.org/he/abouthe/diseddif.pdf*

Piaget, J. (1954). *The construction of reality in the child*. New York: Ballantine.

Picciano, A. (1998). Developing an asynchronous course model at a large, urban university. *Journal of Asynchronous Learning Networks, 2*(1). Retrieved November 27, 2002, from http://www.aln.org/alnweb/journal/vol2_issue1/picciano.htm.

Pirolli, P., & Card, S. K. (1999). Information foraging. *Psychological Review, 106*(4), 643-675.

Reigeluth, C. M. (1999). What is instructional design theory and how is it changing? In C. M. Reigeluth (Ed.), *Instructional design theories and models: A new paradigm of instructional theory* (pp. 5-29). Mahwah, NJ: Lawrence Erlbaum Associates.

Rheingold, H. (1993). *The Virtual Community*. Reading, MA: Addison-Wesley.

Riedel, D. (1994). Bandwidth and creativity: An inverse relationship? *TIE News, 5*(3), 25-26.

Robson, R. (2002, September 1). Standards connections: SCORM steps up. *E-learning*. Available online: http://www.elearningmag.com

Rossman, M. H. (1999). Successful online teaching using an asynchronous learner discussion forum. *Journal of Asynchronous Learning Networks, 3*(2). Retrieved November 27, 2002, from *http://www.aln.org/alnweb/journal/vol3_issue2/Rossman.htm*

Rotter, J. (1989). Internal versus external control of reinforcement. *American Psychologist, 45*(4), 489-93.

Rudner, L. M. & Liang, T. (2002). Automated essay scoring using Bayes theorem. *Journal of Technology, Learning, and Assessment, 1*(2). Retrieved November 27, 2002, from *http://www.bc.edu/research/intasc/jtla/journal/pdf/v1n2_jtla.pdf*

Russell, T. (1999). *The no significant difference phenomenon*. Raleigh, NC: North Carolina State University.

Ryan, M., Carlton, K. H., & Ali, N. S. (1999). Evaluation of traditional classroom teaching methods versus course delivery via the World Wide Web. *Journal of Nursing Education, 38*(6), 272-277.

Saba, F. (1988). Integrated telecommunications systems and instructional transaction. *American Journal of Distance Education, 2*(3), 17-24.

Saba, F. (2000). Research in distance education. A status report. *International Review of Research in Open and Distance Learning, 1*. Available online.

Saba, F., & Shearer, R. L. (1994). Verifying key theoretical concepts in a dynamic model of distance education. *American Journal of Distance Education, 8*(1), 36-59.

Saettler, P. (in press). *The evolution of American educational technology* (2nd ed.). Englewood, CO: Libraries Unlimited.

Salomon, G. (1994). *Interaction of media, cognition, and learning: An exploration of how symbolic forms cultivate mental skills and affect knowledge acquisition*. Hillsdale, NJ: Lawrence Erlbaum Associates.

Schoenfeld-Tacher, R., & Persichitte, K. A. (2000). Differential skills and competencies required of faculty teaching distance education courses. *International Journal of Educational Technology, 2*(1). Available online: http://www.outreach.uiuc.edu/ijet/v2n1/schoenfeld-tacher/index.html

Schrum, L. (1992). Professional development in the information age: An online experience. *Educational Technology, 32*(12), 49-53.

Schrum, L. (1995). *On-line education: A study of pedagogical, organizational, and institutional issues*. Paper presented at ICEM.

Schrum, L., & Berenfeld, B. (1997). *Teaching and learning in the information age: A guide to educational telecommunications*. Boston, MA: Allyn & Bacon.

Schutte, J. (2000). *Virtual teaching in higher education*. Retrieved November 27, 2002, from *http://www.csun.edu/sociology/virexp.htm*

Seawright, L., Wiley, D. A., Bassett, J., Peterson, T. F., Nelson, L. M., South, J. B., & Howell, S. L. (2000). *Online course management tools research and evaluation report*. Retrieved November 27, 2002, from *http://wiley.ed.usu.edu/dle/research/final_report.pdf*

Shapely, P. (1999). On-line education to develop complex reasoning skills in organic chemistry. *Journal of Asynchronous Learning Networks, 4*(3). Retrieved November 27, 2002, from http://www.aln.org/alnweb/journal/Vol4_issue2/le/shapley/LE-shapley.htm

Siau, K. (1999). Internet, World Wide Web, and creativity. *Journal of Creative Behavior, 33*(3), 191-201.

Simon, H. A. (1987). Computers and society. In S. B. Kiesler & L. S. Sproul (Eds.), *Computing and change on campus* (pp. 4-15). New York: Cambridge University.

Simonson, M., Smaldino, S., Albright, M., & Zvacek, S. (2000). *Teaching and learning at a distance: Foundations of distance education*. Upper Saddle River, NJ: Merrill.

Sinyor, R. (1998). Integration and research aspects of Internet technology in Italian language acquisition. *Italica, 75*(4), 532-40.

Slavin, R. E. (1990). Research on cooperative learning: Consensus and controversy. *Educational Leadership, 47*(4).

Slotta, J. D., & Linn, M. C. (2000). The knowledge integration environment: Helping students use the Internet effectively. In M. J. Jacobson & R. B. Kozma (Eds.), *Innovations in science and mathematics education: Advanced designs for technologies of learning* (pp. 193-226). Mahwah, NJ: Lawrence Erlbaum Associates.

Smith, G. G., Ferguson, D., & Caris, M. (2002). Teaching over the Web versus in the classroom: Differences in the instructor experience. *International Journal of Instructional Media, 29*(1), 61-67.

Stewart, C., M., Shields, S. F., Monolescu, D., & Taylor, J. C. (1999). Gender and participation in synchronous CMC: An IRC case study. *Interpersonal Computing and Technology*. Available online: http://www.emoderators.com/ipct-j/1999/n1-2/stewart.html

Strauss, A. L., & Corbin, J. M. (1998). *Basics of qualitative research: Techniques and procedures for developing grounded theory*. Thousand Oaks, CA: Sage.

Sugrue, B. (2000). Cognitive approaches to Web-based instruction. In S. P. Lajoie (Ed.), *Computers as cognitive tools, volume two: No more walls. Theory change, paradigm shifts, and their influence on the use of computers for instructional purposes* (pp. 133-162). Mahwah, NJ: Lawrence Erlbaum Associates.

Taylor, R., ed. (1980). *The computer in the school: Tutor, tool, tutee*. New York: Teachers College.

Thaiupathump, C., Bourne, J., & Campbell, O. J. (1999). Intelligent agents for online learning. *Journal of Asynchronous Learning Networks, 3*(2). Retrieved November 27, 2002, from *http://www.aln.org/alnweb/journal/Vol3_issue2/Choon2.htm*

Tiene, D. (2000). Online discussions: A survey of advantages and disadvantages compared to face-to-face discussions. *Journal of Educational Multimedia and Hypermedia, 9*(4), 371–384.

Truett, C. (2001). Sherlock Holmes on the Internet: Language Arts teams up with the computing librarian. *Learning and Leading with Technology, 29*(2), 36–41.

U. S. Department of Commerce (2002). *A nation online: How Americans are expanding their use of the Internet.* Washington, DC: U.S. Department of Commerce.

von Glasersfeld, E. (1989). An exposition of constructivism: Why some like it radical. In R. B. Davis, C. A. Maher, & N. Noddings (Eds.), *Constructivist views on the teaching and learning of mathematics.* Athens, GA: JRME Monographs.

von Glasersfeld, E. (1993). Questions and answers about radical constructivism. In K. Tobin (Ed.), *The practice of constructivism in science education* (pp. 23–38). Hillsdale, NJ: Erlbaum.

Vrasidas, C., & McIsaac, M. S. (1999). Factors influencing interaction in an online course. *The American Journal of Distance Education, 13*(3), 22–36.

Waern, Y. (2002). *Ethics in global internet research.* Report from the Department of Communication Studies, Linköping University.

Weedman, J. (1999). Conversation and community: The potential of electronic conferences for creating intellectual proximity in distributed learning environments. *Journal of the American Society for Information Science, 50*(10), 907–928.

Wegerif, R. (1998). The social dimension of asynchronous learning networks. *JALN, 2*(1). Available online: http://www.aln.org/alnweb/journal/vol2_issue1/wegerif.htm

Wegner, S., Holloway, K. C., & Garton, E. M. (1999). The effects of Internet-based instruction on student learning. *The Journal of Asynchronous*

Learning Network, 3(2), 98–106. Retrieved November 27, 2002, from *http://www.aln.org/alnweb/journal/Vol3_issue2/Wegner.htm*

Wegner, S. B., K. C. Holloway, K. C., & Crader, A. B. (1997). *Utilizing a problem-based approach on the World Wide Web.* (Report No. SP 037 665). Southwest Missouri State University. (ERIC Document: ED 414 262)

Werry, C. C. (1996). Linguistic and interactional features of Internet Relay Chat. In S. C. Herring (Ed.), *Computer-mediated communication: Linguistic, social and cross-cultural perspectives* (pp. 47–64). Philadelphia, PA: John Benjamins.

Whitaker, G. W. (1995). First-hand observations of tele-course teaching. *T.H.E. Journal, 23*(1), 65–68.

Wiley, D. A. (2000). *Learning object design and sequencing theory.* Unpublished doctoral dissertation, Brigham Young University. Available: *http://davidwiley.com/papers/dissertation/dissertation.pdf*

Wiley, D. A. & Edwards, E. K. (2002). Online self-organizing social systems: The decentralized future of online learning. *Quarterly Review of Distance Education, 3*(1), 33–46.

Wilson, M. S. (2001). Cultural considerations in online instruction and learning. *Distance Education, 22*(1), 52–64.

Wolfe, J. (2000). Gender, ethnicity, and classroom discourse: Communication patterns of Hispanic and white students in networked classrooms. *Written Communication, 17*(4), 491–519.

Yagelski, R. P., & Grabill, J. T. (1998). Computer-mediated communication in the undergraduate writing classroom: A study of the relationship of online discourse and classroom discourse in two writing classes. *Computers and Composition, 15*(1), 11–40.

Yang, S. C. (2001). Language learning on the World Wide Web: An investigation of EFL learners' attitudes and perceptions. *Journal of Educational Computing Research, 24*(2), 155–181.

Yoder, M. B. (1999). The student WebQuest. *Learning & Leading with Technology, 26*(7), 6–9, 52–53.

·17·

VIRTUAL REALITIES

Hilary McLellan
McLellan Wyatt Digital

17.1 INTRODUCTION

Virtual realities are a set of emerging electronic technologies, with applications in a wide range of fields. This includes education, training, athletics, industrial design, architecture and landscape architecture, urban planning, space exploration, medicine and rehabilitation, entertainment, and model building and research in many fields of science (Aukstalnis, & Blatner, 1992; Earnshaw, Vince, Guedj, & Van Dam, 2001; Hamit, 1993; Helsel, 1992a, 1992b, 1992c; Helsel & Roth, 1991; Hillis, 1999; Mayr, 2001; Middleton, 1992; Pimentel & Teixiera, 1992; Rheingold, 1991; Vince, 1998). Virtual reality (VR) can be defined as a class of computer-controlled multisensory communication technologies that allow more intuitive interactions with data and involve human senses in new ways. Virtual reality can also be defined as an environment created by the computer in which the user feels present (Jacobson, 1993a). This technology was devised to enable people to deal with information more easily. VR provides a different way to see and experience information, one that is dynamic and immediate. It is also a tool for model-building and problem solving. VR is potentially a tool for experiential learning. The virtual world is interactive; it responds to the user's actions. Virtual reality evokes a feeling of immersion, a perceptual and psychological sense of being in the digital environment presented to the senses. The sense of presence or immersion is a critical feature distinguishing virtual reality from other types of computer applications. An excellent extensive set of web links for companies involved with the production of virtual reality technologies, applications, and consulting services is available at http://www.cyberedge.com/4f.html.

Virtual reality is a new type of computer tool that adds vast power to scientific visualization. Buxton (1992) explains that "Scientific visualization involves the graphic rendering of complex data in a way that helps make pertinent aspects and relationships within the data more salient to the viewer. The idea is to tailor the visual presentation to take better advantage of the human ability to recognize patterns and see structures" (p. 27). However, as Erickson (1993) explains, the word "visualization" is really too narrow when considering virtual reality. "Perceptualization" is probably more appropriate. With virtual reality, sound and touch, as well as visual appearance, may be used effectively to represent data. Perceptualization involving the sense of touch may include both tactile feedback (passive touch, feeling surfaces and textures) and haptic feedback (active touch, where there is a sense of force feedback, pressure, or resistance) (Brooks, 1988; Delaney, 2000; Dowding, 1991; Hon, 1991, 1992; Marcus, 1994; McLaughlin, Hespanha, & Sukhatme, 2001; Minsky, 1991; Sorid, 2000). The key to visualization is in representing information in ways that can engage any of our sensory systems and thus draw on our extensive experience in organizing and interpreting sensory input (Erickson, 1993).

The term Virtual Reality was coined by Jaron Lanier one of the developers of the first immersive interface devices (Hall, 1990). Virtual often denotes the computer-generated counterpart of a physical object: a "virtual room," a "virtual glove," a "virtual chair." Other terms such as "virtual worlds," "virtual environments," and "cyberspace" are used as global terms to identify this technology. For example, David Zelter of the MIT Media Lab suggests that the term "virtual environments" is more appropriate than virtual reality since virtual reality, like artificial intelligence, is ultimately unattainable (Wheeler, 1991). But virtual reality remains the most commonly used generic term (although many researchers in the field vehemently dislike this term).

Virtual reality provides a degree of interactivity that goes beyond what can be found in traditional multimedia programs. Even a sophisticated multimedia program, such as the Palenque DVI program, which features simulated spatial exploration of an ancient Mayan pyramid, is limited to predetermined paths. With a virtual world you can go anywhere and explore any point of view.

461

Virtual reality emerged as a distinctive area of computer interfaces and applications only during the 1980s. Any assessment of this technology must keep in mind that it is at an early stage of development and the technology is evolving rapidly. Many exciting applications have been developed. Furthermore, researchers are beginning to collect valuable information about the usefulness of virtual reality for particular applications, including education and training. And a great deal of theory building has been initiated concerning this emerging technology and its potentials in education and training.

17.2 HISTORICAL BACKGROUND

Woolley (1992) explains that, "Trying to trace the origins of the idea of virtual reality is like trying to trace the source of a river. It is produced by the accumulated flow of many streams of ideas, fed by many springs of inspiration." One forum where the potentials of virtual reality have been explored is science fiction (Bradbury, 1951; W. Gibson, 1986; Harrison, 1972; Stephenson, 1992; Sterling, 1994), together with the related area of scenario building (Kellogg, Carroll, & Richards, 1991).

The technology that has led up to virtual reality technology—computer graphics, simulation, human–computer interfaces, etc.—has been developing and coalescing for over three decades. In the 1960s, Ivan Sutherland created one of the pioneering virtual reality systems which incorporated a head-mounted display (Sutherland, 1965, 1968). Sutherland's head-mounted display was nicknamed 'The Sword of Damocles' because of its strange appearance. Sutherland did not continue with this work because the computer graphics systems available to him at that time were very primitive. Instead, he shifted his attention to inventing many of the fundamental algorithms, hardware, and software of computer graphics (McGreevy, 1993). Sutherland's work provided a foundation for the emergence of virtual reality in the 1980s. His early work inspired others, such as Frederick P. Brooks, Jr., of the University of North Carolina, who began experimenting with ways to accurately simulate and display the structure of molecules. Brooks' work developed into a major virtual reality research initiative at the University of North Carolina (Hamit, 1993; Rheingold, 1991; Robinett, 1991).

In 1961, Morton Heilig, a filmmaker, patented Sensorama, a totally mechanical virtual reality device (a one-person theater) that included three-dimensional, full color film together with sounds, smells, and the feeling of motion, as well as the sensation of wind on the viewer's face. In the Sensorama, the user could experience several scenarios, including a motorcycle ride through New York, a bicycle ride, or a helicopter ride over Century City. The Sensorama was not a commercial success but it reflected tremendous vision, which has now returned with computer-based rather than mechanical virtual reality systems (Hamit, 1993; Rheingold, 1991).

During the 1960s and 1970s, the Air Force established a laboratory at Wright–Patterson Air Force Base in Ohio to develop flight simulators and head-mounted displays that could facilitate learning and performance in sophisticated, high-workload, high-speed military aircraft. This initiative resulted in the Super-Cockpit that allows pilots to fly ultra-high-speed aircraft using only head, eye, and hand movements. The director of the Super-Cockpit project, Tom Furness, went on to become the director of the Human Interface Technology Lab at the University of Washington, a leading VR R&D center with a strong focus on education. And VR research continues at Wright–Patterson Air Force Base (Amburn, 1993; Stytz, 1993, 1994). Flight simulators have been used extensively and effectively for pilot training since the 1920s (Bricken & Byrne, 1993; Lauber & Fouchee, 1981; Woolley, 1992).

In the 1960s, GE developed a simulator that was adapted for lunar mission simulations. It was primarily useful for practicing rendezvous and especially docking between the lunar excursion module (LEM) and the command module (CM). This simulator was also adapted as a city planning tool in a project at UCLA—the first time a simulator had been used to explore a digital model of a city (McGreevy, 1993).

In the 1970s, researchers at MIT developed a spatial data management system using videodisc technology. This work resulted in the *Aspen Movie Map* (MIT, 1981; Mohl, 1982), a recreation of part of the town of Aspen, Colorado. This "map" was stored on an optical disk that gave users the simulated experience of driving through the town of Aspen, interactively choosing to turn left or right to pursue any destination (within the confines of the model). Twenty miles of Aspen streets were photographed from all directions at 10-foot intervals, as was every possible turn. Aerial views were also included. This photo-based experiment proved to be too complicated (i.e., it was not user friendly) so this approach was not used to replicate larger cities, which entail a higher degree of complexity (Hamit, 1993).

Also in the 1970s, Myron Krueger began experimenting with human–computer interaction as a graduate student at the University of Wisconsin-Madison. Krueger designed responsive but nonimmersive environments that combined video and computer. He referred to this as Artificial Reality. As Krueger (1993) explains,

...you are perceived by a video camera and the image of your body is displayed in a graphic world. The juxtaposition of your image with graphic objects on the screen suggests that perhaps you could affect the graphic objects. This expectation is innate. It does not need to be explained. To take advantage of it, the computer continually analyzes your image with respect to the graphic world. When your image touches a graphic object, the computer can respond in many ways. For example, the object can move as if pushed. It can explode, stick to your finger, or cause your image to disappear. You can play music with your finger or cause your image to disappear. The graphic world need not be realistic. Your image can be moved, scaled, and rotated like a graphic object in response to your actions or simulated forces. You can even fly your image around the screen. (p. 149)

The technologies underlying virtual reality came together at the NASA Ames Lab in California during the mid-1980s with the development of a system that utilized a stereoscopic head-mounted display (using the screens scavenged from two miniature televisions) and the fiber-optic wired glove interface device. This breakthrough project at NASA was based on a long tradition of developing ways to simulate the environments and the procedures that astronauts would be engaged in during space flights such as the GE simulator developed in the 1960s (McGreevy, 1993).

During the late 1980s and early 1990s, there was widespread popular excitement about virtual reality. But the great expense of the technology and its inability to meet people's high expectations at this early stage of development, led to a diminution of excitement and visibility that coincided with the emergence of the World Wide Web. Although the hype for this technology receded, eclipsed by enthusiasm for the World Wide Web, serious research and development has continued. Rosenblum, Burdea and Tachi (1998) describe this transition to a new phase:

Unfortunately, the excitement about virtual reality turned into unrealizable "hype". The movie *Lawnmower Man* portrayed a head-mounted display raising a person's IQ beyond the genius level. Every press report on the subject included the topic of cybersex (which still pervades TV commercials). Fox TV even aired a series called "VR5". Inevitably, the public (and, worse, research sponsors) developed entirely unrealistic expectations of the possibilities and the time scale for progress.

Many advances occurred on different fronts, but they rarely synthesized into full-scale systems. Instead, they demonstrated focused topics such as multiresolution techniques for displaying millions of polygons, the use of robotics hardware as force-feedback interfaces, the development of 3D audio, or novel interaction methods and devices. So, as time passed with few systems delivered to real customers for real applications, attention shifted elsewhere. Much of the funding for VR began to involve network issues for telepresence (or telexistence) that would enable remote users, each with their own VR system, to interact and collaborate. Medical, military, and engineering needs drove these advances.

As Rosenblum et al (1998) point out, the field of virtual reality faces difficult research problems involving many disciplines. Thus, it realistically, major progress will require decades rather than months. The area of systems, in particular, will require the synthesis of numerous advances. According to Rosenblum et al., "the next advance depends on progress by non-VR researchers. Thus, we may have to wait for the next robotics device, advanced flat-panel display, or new natural language technique before we can take the next step in VR."

As Rosenblum et al. (1998) explain, there have been important developments in the areas of multiresolution rendering algorithms, texture mapping, and image rendering. Both texture mapping and image rendering benefited from the dramatic improvements in computer processing speeds that took place over the past decade. Advances have also taken place in advances have taken place in lighting, shadowing, and other computer graphics algorithms for realistic rendering (Rosenblum et al., 1998). There have also been improvements in commercial software platforms for building VR computer application software. This includes SGI Performer, DIVE, Bamboo, Cavern, and Spline. In terms of VR display technologies, Rosenblum et al. report,

The 1990s saw a paradigm shift to projective displays that keep viewers in their natural environment. The two most prominent of these, the Responsive Workbench and the CAVE, use see-though stereoscopic shutter glasses to generate 3D images. Current advances in generating lighter, sharper HMDs let low-budget VR researchers use them. (p. 22)

Rosenblum et al. point out that R&D concerning other interfaces and nonvisual modalities (acoustics, haptics, and olfactory) has lagged behind (Delaney, 2000; Sorid, 2000). Improved navigational techniques are needed. Overall, Rosenblum et al. recommend,

We know how to use wands, gestures, speech recognition, and even natural language. However, 3D interaction is still fighting an old war. We need multimodal systems that integrate the best interaction methods so that, someday, 3D VR systems can meet that Holy Grail of the human–computer-interface community—having the computer successfully respond to "Put that there."

17.3 DIFFERENT KINDS OF VIRTUAL REALITY

There is more than one type of virtual reality. Furthermore, there are different schema for classifying various types of virtual reality. Jacobson (1993a) suggests that there are four types of virtual reality: (1) immersive virtual reality, (2) desktop virtual reality (i.e., low-cost homebrew virtual reality), (3) projection virtual reality, and (4) simulation virtual reality.

Thurman and Mattoon (1994) present a model for differentiating between different types of VR, based on several "dimensions." They identify a "verity dimension" that helps to differentiate between different types of virtual reality, based on how closely the application corresponds to physical reality. They propose a scale showing the verity dimension of virtual realities (see Fig. 17.1). According to Thurman and Mattoon (1994),

The two end points of this dimension—physical and abstract—describe the degree that a VR and entities within the virtual environment have the characteristics of reality. On the left end of the scale, VRs simulate or mimic real-world counterparts that correspond to natural laws. On the right side of the scale, VRs represent abstract ideas which are completely novel and may not even resemble the real world. (p. 57).

Thurman and Mattoon (1994) also identify an "integration dimension" that focuses on how humans are integrated into the computer system. This dimension includes a scale featuring three categories: batch processing, shared control, and total inclusion. These categories are based on three broad eras of human–computer integration, culminating with VR—total inclusion. A third dimension of this model is interface, on a scale ranging between natural and artificial. These three dimensions

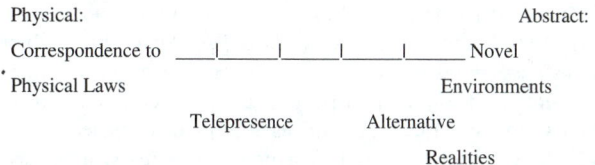

FIGURE 17.1. Thurston and Mattoon's verity scale for virtual reality (adapted from Thurston and Mattoon, 1994).

are combined to form a three-dimensional classification scheme for virtual realities. This model provides a valuable tool for understanding and comparing different virtual realities.

Another classification scheme has been delineated by Brill (1993, 1994b). This model will be discussed in detail here together with some new types of virtual reality that have emerged. Brill's model features seven different types of virtual reality: (1) Immersive first-person, (2) Through the window, (3) Mirror world, (4) Waldo World, (5) Chamber world, (6) Cab simulator environment, and (7) Cyberspace. Some of Brill's categories of virtual reality are physically immersive and some are not. The key feature of all virtual reality systems is that they provide an environment created by the computer or other media where the user feels present, that is, immersed physically, perceptually, and psychologically. Virtual reality systems enable users to become participants in artificial spaces created by the computer. It is important to note that not all virtual worlds are three-dimensional. This is not necessary to provide an enriching experience. And to explore a virtual world, the user doesn't have to be completely immersed in it: first-person (direct) interaction, as well as second-person and third-person interaction with the virtual world are all possible (Laurel, 1991; Norman, 1993), as the following discussion indicates.

The new types of virtual reality that will be discussed are: (1) the VisionDome, and (2) the Experience Learning System under development at the Institute For Creative Technologies (ICT) at the University of Southern California. Not everyone would agree that these technologies constitute virtual reality, but they all appear to be part of the initiative to implement computer-controlled, multisensory, immersive experiences. And these technologies all have important implications for education and training.

To summarize, we will be examining 10 types of virtual reality: (1) Immersive first-person, (2) Augmented reality (a variation of immersive reality), (3) Through the window, (4) Mirror world, (5) Waldo World (Virtual characters), (6) Chamber world, (7) Cab simulator environment, (8) Cyberspace, (9) the VisionDome, and (10) the Experience Learning System.

17.3.1 Immersive First-Person

Usually when we think of virtual reality, we think of immersive systems involving computer interface devices such as a head-mounted display (HMD), fiber-optic wired gloves, position tracking devices, and audio systems providing 3-D (binaural) sound. Immersive virtual reality provides an immediate, first-person experience. With some applications, there is a treadmill interface to simulate the experience of walking through virtual space. And in place of the head-mounted display, there is the BOOM viewer from Fake Space Labs which hangs suspended in front of the viewer's face, not on it, so it is not as heavy and tiring to wear as the head-mounted display. In immersive VR, the user is placed inside the image; the generated image is assigned properties which make it look and act real in terms of visual perception and in some cases aural and tactile perception (Begault, 1991; Brooks, 1988; Gehring, 1992; Isdale, 2000b; Markoff, 1991; McLaughlin,

Hespanha, & Sukhatme, 2001; Minsky, 1991; Trubitt, 1990). There is even research on creating virtual smells; an application to patent such a product has been submitted by researchers at the Southwest Research Institute (Varner, 1993).

Children are already familiar with some of this technology from video games. Mattel's Power Glove™, used as an interface with Nintendo Games, is a low-cost design based on the DataGlove™ from VPL Research, Inc. The Power Glove™ failed as a toy, but it achieved some success as an interface device in some low-cost virtual reality systems in the early 1990s, particularly in what are known as "homebrew" or "garage" virtual reality systems (Jacobson, 1994). Inexpensive software and computer cards are available that make it possible to use the Power Glove™ as an input device with Amiga, Macintosh or IBM computers (Eberhart, 1993; Hollands, 1995; Jacobson, 1994; Stampe, Roehl, & Eagan, 1993). Robin Hollands (1996) published *The Virtual Reality Homebrewer's Handbook*. In addition, there are many homebrew resources on the World Wide Web, including the web sites:

- http://www.cms.dmu.ac.uk/~cph/hbvr.html.
- http://www.geocities.com/mellott124/
- http://www.phoenixgarage.org/homevr/

Homebrew VR has expanded to include web-based resources such as VRML. The low cost of homebrew virtual reality makes it accessible to educators.

17.3.2 Augmented Reality

A variation of immersive virtual reality is **Augmented Reality** where a see-through layer of computer graphics is superimposed over the real world to highlight certain features and enhance understanding (Isdale, 2001). Azuma (1999) explains, "Augmented Reality is about augmentation of human perception: supplying information not ordinarily detectable by human senses." And Behringer, Mizell, and Klinker (2001) explain that "AR technology provides means of intuitive information presentation for enhancing the situational awareness and perception of the real world. This is achieved by placing virtual objects or information cues into the real world as the user perceives it."

According to Isdale (2001), there are four types of augmented reality (AR) that can be distinguished by their display type, including:

1. Optical See-Through AR uses a transparent Head Mounted Display (HMD) to display the virtual environment (VE) directly over the real wold.
2. Projector Based AR uses real world objects as the projection surface for the VE.
3. Video See-Through AR uses an opaque HMD to display merged video of the VE with and view from cameras on the HMD.
4. Monitor-Based AR also uses merged video streams but the display is a more conventional desktop monitor or a hand held display. Monitor-Based AR is perhaps the least difficult to set up since it eliminates HMD issues.

Augmented reality has important potential in athletic training. Govil, You, and Neumann (2000) describe a video-based augmented reality golf simulator. The "Mixed Reality Lab" in Yokohama has developed an augmented reality hockey game (Satoh, Ohshima, Yamamoto, & Tamura, 1998). Players can share a physical game field, mallets, and a virtual puck to play an air-hockey game.

One important application of augmented reality is spatial information systems for exploring urban environments as well as planetary environments in space. In particular, a research initiative concerning "mobile augmented reality"—using mobile and wearable computing systems—is underway at Columbia University (Feiner, MacIntyre, Höllerer, & Webster, 1997; Höllerer, Feiner, & Pavlik, 1999; Höllerer, Feiner, Terauchi, Rashid, & Hallaway, 1999).

Another important application of augmented reality is in industrial manufacturing, where certain controls can be highlighted, for example the controls needed to land an airplane. Groups at Boeing are exploring these types of applications. Behringer, Mizell, and Klinker (2001) report that David Mizell has conducted a pilot experiment of an application of AR in the actual industrial airplane construction (specifically, the construction of wirebundle connections). This research found that with the aid of the AR system, a nontrained worker could assemble a wirebundle—faster than a trained worker who was not using this system. Behringer et al. (2001) report that Dirk Reiners developed an AR system that can be used for the car manufacturing process. Based on visual marker tracking, this system guides the user through an assembly sequence of a door-lock assembly process. Reiners' system requires an HMD and is running on a SGI O2 (180 MHz) for tracking and an SGI Onyx RE2 for rendering.

Many medical applications of augmented reality are under development (Isdale, 2001; Taubes, 1994b). Recently, for the first time, a surgeon conducted surgery to remove a brain tumor using an augmented reality system; a video image superimposed with 3-D graphics helped the doctor to see the site of the operation more effectively (Satava, 1993).

Similar to this, Azuma (1999) explains that

...applications of this technology use the virtual objects to aid the user's understanding of his environment. For example, a group at UNC scanned a fetus inside a womb with an ultrasonic sensor, then overlayed a three-dimensional model of the fetus on top of the mother's womb. The goal is to give the doctor "X-ray vision," enabling him to "see inside" the womb. Instructions for building or repairing complex equipment might be easier to understand if they were available not in the form of manuals with text and 2D pictures, but as 3D drawings superimposed upon the machinery itself, telling the mechanic what to do and where to do it.

An excellent resource is the Augmented Reality web page at http://www.cs.rit.edu/~jrv/research/ar/.

Azuma (1999) reports,

Unfortunately, registration is a difficult problem, for a number of reasons. First, the human visual system is very good at detecting even small misregistrations, because of the resolution of the fovea and the sensitivity of the human visual system to differences. Errors of just a few pixels are noticeable. Second, errors that can be tolerated in Virtual Environments are not acceptable in Augmented Reality. Incorrect viewing parameters, misalignments in the Head-Mounted Display, errors in the head-tracking system, and other problems that often occur in HMD-based systems may not cause detectable problems in Virtual Environments, but they are big problems in Augmented Reality. Finally, there's system delay: the time interval between measuring the head location to superimposing the corresponding graphic images on the real world. The total system delay makes the virtual objects appear to "lag behind" their real counterparts as the user moves around. The result is that in most Augmented Reality systems, the virtual objects appear to "swim around" the real objects, instead of staying registered with them. Until the registration problem is solved, Augmented Reality may never be accepted in serious applications. (p. 2)

Azuma's research is focused upon improving registration in augmented reality. He has developed calibration techniques, used inertial sensors to predict head motion, and built a real system that implements these improved techniques. According to Azuma, "I believe this work puts us within striking distance of truly accurate and robust registration." (p. 3).

For information about Azuma's research at the University of North Carolina, and copies of his publications (Azuma, 1993, 1997; Azuma & Bishop, 1994, 1995), go to http://www.cs.unc.edu/~azuma/azuma-AR.html. Milgram and Kishino (1994) present an excellent taxonomy of mixed reality. And Isdale's (2001) article, available on the web at http://www.vrnews.com/issuearchive/vrn0905/vrn0905 tech.html, presents a comprehensive overview of developments in artificial reality/mixed reality.

17.3.3 Through the Window

With this kind of system, also known as "desktop VR," the user sees the 3-D world through the window of the computer screen and navigates through the space with a control device such as a mouse (Fisher & Unwin, 2002). Like immersive virtual reality, this provides a first-person experience. One low-cost example of a Through the window virtual reality system is the 3-D architectural design planning tool *Virtus WalkThrough* that makes it possible to explore virtual reality on a Macintosh or IBM computer. Developed as a computer visualization tool to help plan complex high-tech filmmaking for the movie *The Abyss, Virtus WalkThrough* is now used as a set design and planning tool for many Hollywood movies and advertisements as well as architectural planning and educational applications. A similar, less expensive and less sophisticated program that is starting to find use in elementary and secondary schools is *Virtus VR* (Law, 1994; Pantelidis, nd).

The Virtus programs are still available, but now a number of other low-cost virtual reality programs are available for educational applications. This includes web-based applications based upon the Virtual Reality Modeling Language (VRML) and other tools, including Java-based applications. It helps that computers have improved dramatically in power and speed since the early 1990s.

Another example of Through the window virtual reality comes from the field of dance, where a computer program called *LifeForms* lets choreographers create sophisticated human motion animations. *LifeForms* permits the user to access "shape" libraries of figures in sitting, standing, jumping, sports poses, dance poses, and other positions. *LifeForms* supports the compositional process of dance and animation so that choreographers can create, fine-tune, and plan dances "virtually" on the computer. The great modern dancer and choreographer Merce Cunningham has begun using *LifeForms* to choreograph new dances (Calvert, Bruderlin, Dill, Schiphorst, & Welman, 1993; Schiphorst, 1992). Using *LifeForms,* it is possible to learn a great deal about the design process without actually rehearsing and mounting a performance. The program LifeForms is now available commercially through Credo-Interactive (http://www.credo-interactive.com/products/index.html), which offers several different low-end VR software tools.

The field of forensic animation is merging with Through the window VR (Baird, 1992; Hamilton, 1993). Here, dynamic computer animations are used to recreate the scene of a crime and the sequence of events, as reconstructed through analysis of the evidence (for example, bullet speed and trajectory can be modeled). These dynamic visualizations are used in crime investigations and as evidence in trials. The London Metropolitan Police has used VR to document witnesses' descriptions of crime scenes. Similarly, the FBI has used *Virtus WalkThrough* as a training tool at the FBI Academy and as a site visualization tool in hostage crisis situations.

17.3.4 Mirror World

In contrast to the first-person systems described above, Mirror Worlds (Projected Realities) provide a second-person experience in which the viewer stands outside the imaginary world, but communicates with characters or objects inside it. Mirror world systems use a video camera as an input device. Users see their images superimposed on or merged with a virtual world presented on a large video monitor or video projected image. Using a digitizer, the computer processes the users' images to extract features such as their positions, movements, or the number of fingers raised. These systems are usually less expensive than total immersion systems, and the users are unencumbered by head gear, wired gloves, or other interfaces (Lantz, 1992). Four examples of a Mirror World virtual reality system are: (1) Myron Krueger's artificial reality systems such as VIDEOPLACE, (2) the Mandala system from the Vivid Group (http://www.vividgroup.com/), created by a group of performance artists in Toronto, (3) the InView system which has provided the basis for developing entertainment applications for children, including a TV game show, and (4) Meta Media's wall-sized screen applications such as shooting basketball hoops and experiencing what happens when you try to throw a ball under zero gravity conditions (Brill, 1995; O'Donnell, 1994; Wagner, 1994).

In Krueger's system, users see colorful silhouettes of their hands or their entire bodies. As users move, their silhouette mirror images move correspondingly, interacting with other silhouette objects generated by computer. Scale can be adjusted so that one person's mirror silhouette appears very small by comparison with other people and objects present in the VIDEOPLACE artificial world. Krueger suggests that, "In artificial realities, the body can be employed as a teaching aid, rather than suppressed by the need to keep order. The theme is not learning by doing in the Dewey sense, but instead doing is learning, a completely different emphasis" (Krueger, 1993, p. 152)."

The Mandala and InView systems feature a video camera above the computer screen that captures an image of the user and places this image within the scene portrayed on the screen using computer graphics. There are actually three components: (1) the scene portrayed (usually stored on videodisc), (2) the digitized image of the user, and (3) computer graphics-generated objects that appear to fit within the scene that are programmed to be interactive, responding to the "touch" of the user's image. The user interacts with the objects on the screen; for example, to play a drum or to hit a ball. (Tactile feedback is not possible with this technique.) This type of system is becoming popular as an interactive museum exhibit. For example, at the National Hockey Museum, a Mandala system shows you on the screen in front of the goalie net, trying to keep the "virtual" puck out of the net. Recently, a Mandala installation was completed for Paramount Pictures and the Oregon Museum of Science and Industry that is a simulation of Star Trek: The Next Generation's holodeck.

Users step into an actual set of the transporter room in the real world and view themselves in the "Star Trek virtual world" on a large screen in front of them. They control where they wish to be transported and can interact with the scene when they arrive. For example, users could transport themselves to the surface of a planet, move around the location, and manipulate the objects there. Actual video footage from the television show is used for backgrounds and is controlled via videodisc. (Wyshynski & Vincent, 1993, p. 130)

Another application is an experimental teleconferencing project—"Virtual Cities"—for children developed by the Vivid Group in collaboration with the Marshal McLuhan Foundation (Mandala VR News, 1993). In this application, students in different cities around the world are brought into a networked common virtual environment using videophones.

The Meta Media VR system is similar to the Mandala and InView systems, but the image is presented on a really large wall-sized screen, appropriate for a large audience. Applications of this system, such as Virtual Hoops, are finding widespread use in entertainment and in museums (Brill, 1995). One fascinating aspect of this type of VR mirror world is that it promotes a powerful social dimension: people waiting in the bleachers for a turn at Virtual Hoops cheer the player who makes a hoop—it's very interactive in this way. And preliminary evidence suggests that learners get more caught up in physics lessons presented with this technology, even when they are only sitting in the audience (Wisne, 1994).

17.3.5 Waldo World (Virtual Characters)

This type of virtual reality application is a form of digital puppetry involving real-time computer animation. The name

"Waldo" is drawn from a science fiction story by Robert Heinlein (1965). Wearing an electronic mask or body armor equipped with sensors that detect motion, a puppeteer controls, in real-time, a computer animation figure on a screen or a robot. This type of technology has come to be known more commonly as "virtual characters" as well as "virtual animation" rather than Waldo World VR.

An early example of this type of VR application is the Virtual Actors™ developed by SimGraphics Engineering (Tice & Jacobson, 1992). These are computer-generated animated characters controlled by human actors, in real-time. To perform a Virtual Actor (VA), an actor wears a "Waldo" which tracks the actor's eye brows, cheek, head, chin, and lip movements, allowing them to control the corresponding features of the computer generated character with their own movements. For example, when the actor smiles, the animated character smiles correspondingly. A hidden video camera aimed at the audience is fed into a video monitor backstage so that the actor can see the audience and "speak" to individual members of the audience through the lip-synced computer animation image of the character on the display screen. This digital puppetry application is like the Wizard of Oz interacting with Dorothy and her companions: "Pay no attention to that man behind the curtain!"

The Virtual Actor characters include Mario in Real Time (MIRT), based on the hero of the Super Mario Nintendo games, as well as a Virtual Mark Twain. MIRT and the Virtual Mark Twain are used as an interactive entertainment and promotional medium at trade shows (Tice & Jacobson, 1992). Another Virtual Actor is Eggwardo, an animation character developed for use with children at the Loma Linda Medical Center (Warner, 1993; Warner & Jacobson, 1992). Neuroscientist Dave Warner (1993) explains:

We brought Eggwardo into the hospital where he interacted with children who were terminally ill. Some kids couldn't even leave their beds so Eggwardo's image was sent to the TV monitors above their beds, while they talked to the actor over the phone and watched and listened as as Eggwardo joked with them and asked how they were feeling and if they'd taken their medicine. The idea is to use Eggwardo, and others like him, to help communicate with therapy patients and mitigate the fears of children who face surgery and other daunting medical procedures.

Another type of Waldo World has been developed by Ascension, using its Flock of Birds™ positioning system (Scully, 1994). This is a full-body waldo system that is not used in real time but as a foundation for creating animated films and advertisements.

Manners (2002) describes how this type of technology is used to create virtual characters for TechTV cable television (http://www.techtv.com). TechTV features two virtual characters, Tilde and Dash, that are driven by software developed by the French company MediaLab (http://www.medialabtechno.com). Manners explains that the performances constitute an impressive piece of choreographed collaboration between the body performers and the voice artists who read the scripts since the two must perform in coordination.

17.3.6 Chamber World

A Chamber World is a small virtual reality projection theater controlled by several computers that gives users the sense of freer movement within a virtual world than the immersive VR systems and thus a feeling of greater immersion. Images are projected on all of the walls that can be viewed in 3-D with a head-mounted display showing a seamless virtual environment. The first of these systems was the CAVE, developed at the Electronic Visualization Laboratory at the University of Illinois (Cruz-Nierna, 1993; DeFanti, Sandin, & Cruz-Neira, 1993; Sandin, DeFanti, & Cruz-Nierna, 2001; Wilson, 1994). Another Chamber World system—EVE: Extended Virtual Environment—was developed at the Kernforschungszntrum (Nuclear Research Center) Karlsruhe in collaboration with the Institut fur Angewandte Informatik (Institute of Applied Informatics) in Germany (Shaw, 1994; Shaw & May, 1994). The recently opened Sony Omnimax 3-D theaters where all members of the audience wear a head-mounted display in order to see 3-D graphics and hear 3-D audio is another—albeit much larger—example of this type of virtual reality (Grimes, 1994).

The CAVE is a 3-D real-projection theater made up of three walls and a floor, projected in stereo and viewed with "stereo glasses" that are less heavy and cumbersome than many other head-mounted displays used for immersive VR (Cruz-Nierna, 1993; Rosenblum et al., 1998; Wilson, 1994). The CAVE provides a first-person experience. As a CAVE viewer moves within the display boundaries (wearing a location sensor and 3-D glasses), the correct perspective and stereo projections of the environment are updated and the image moves with and surrounds the viewer. Four Silicon Graphics computers control the operation of the CAVE, which has been used for scientific visualization applications such as astronomy.

17.3.7 Cab Simulator Environment

This is another type of first-person virtual reality technology that is essentially an extension of the traditional simulator. Hamit (1993) defines the cab simulator environment as:

Usually an entertainment or experience simulation form of virtual reality, which can be used by a small group or by a single individual. The illusion of presence in the virtual environment is created by the use of visual elements greater than the field of view, three-dimensional sound inputs, computer-controlled motion bases and more than a bit of theatre. (p. 428).

Cab simulators are finding many applications in training and entertainment. For example, AGC Simulation Products has developed a cab simulator training system for police officers to practice driving under high-speed and dangerous conditions (Flack, 1993). SIMNET is a networked system of cab simulators that is used in military training (Hamit, 1993; Sterling, 1993). Virtual Worlds Entertainment has developed BattleTech, a location-based entertainment system where players in six cabs are linked together to play simulation games (Jacobson, 1993b). An entertainment center in Irvine, California called Fighter Town features actual flight simulators as "virtual environments." Patrons pay for a training session where they learn how to operate the simulator and then they get to go through a flight scenario.

17.3.8 Cyberspace

The term cyberspace was coined by William Gibson in the science fiction novel *Neuromancer* (1986), which describes a future dominated by vast computer networks and databases. Cyberspace is a global artificial reality that can be visited simultaneously by many people via networked computers. Cyberspace is where you are when you're hooked up to a computer network or electronic database—or talking on the telephone. However, there are more specialized applications of cyberspace where users hook up to a virtual world that exists only electronically; these applications include text-based MUDs (Multi-User Dungeons or Multi-User Domains) and MUSEs (Multi-User Simulated Environments). One MUSE, Cyberion City, has been established specifically to support education within a constructivist learning context (Rheingold, 1993). Groupware, also known as computer-supported cooperative work (CSCW), is another type of cyberspace technology (Baecker, 1993; Bruckman & Resnick, 1993; Coleman, 1993; Miley, 1992; Schrage, 1991; Wexelblat, 1993).

The past decade has seen the introduction of a number of innovations that are changing the face of cyberspace. The introduction of the World Wide Web during the early 1990s has extended the realms of cyberspace to include a vast area where, in addition to text, graphics, audio, multimedia, video and streaming media are all readily available throughout much of the world. And the increasing availability of wireless technologies and cable-based Internet access are extending access to cyberspace. For example, in Africa, where land-based telephone networks are not well developed, wireless cell phones offer an alternative. They have become very widespread in some parts of Africa. Wireless Internet access will not be far behind.

Habitat, designed by Chip Morningstar and F. Randall Farmer (1991, 1993) at Lucasfilm, was one of the first attempts to create a large-scale, commercial, many-user, graphical virtual environment. Habitat is built on top of an ordinary commercial on-line service and uses low-cost Commodore 64 home computers to support user interaction in a virtual world. The system can support thousands of users in a single shared cyberspace. Habitat presents its users with a real-time animated view into an online graphic virtual world. Users can communicate, play games, and go on adventures in Habitat. There are two versions of Habitat in operation, one in the United States and another in Japan.

Similar to this, researchers at the University of Central Florida have developed ExploreNet, a low-cost 2-D networked virtual environment intended for public education (Moshell & Dunn-Roberts, 1993, 1994a, 1994b). This system is built upon a network of 386 and 486 IBM PCs. ExploreNet is a role-playing game. Students must use teamwork to solve various mathematical problems that arise while pursuing a quest. Each participant has an animated figure on the screen, located in a shared world. When one student moves her animated figure or takes an action, all the players see the results on the networked computers, located in different rooms, schools, or even cities. ExploreNet is the basis for a major research initiative.

Habitat and ExploreNet are merely early examples of graphical user environments. With the emergence of the World Wide Web, a wealth of applications have been developed, including a number of educational applications.

Online video games such as Ultima Online (http://www. uo.com/), are as well as other types of online communities designed with graphical user interfaces are now a big part of the Internet. Ultima Online provides a fascinating case study in how people respond to cyberspace—and how much cyberspace can be just like the real world—especially within the framework of virtual reality. Dell Computer Corporation (1999) explains that players buy the game software and set up an account at the Ultima Online Web site for a monthly fee. Players choose a home "shard," or city and create up to six characters, selecting the occupations, skills and physical appearance for each. Characters start off in relative poverty, having 100 gold pieces in their pockets. From there on, the characters are free to roam—to barter for goods, talk to other players (via text bubbles) or make goods to sell to get more gold—all the while building up their powers and strength to the point where they can, among other chivalrous duties, slay mystical beings. It takes time to develop a truly memorable character and to establish a virtual home and a thriving virtual business. To bypass the effort of establishing wealth and real estate online, players can make deals with other players in the real world, via the Ebay auction site, to buy virtual real estate for real money.

As Dell Computer Corporation (1999) explains:

It started with a Texan firefighter named Dave Turner, who went by the online moniker Turbohawk. Turner decided he'd been spending too much time playing the game. So he put his account—his veteran character—up for sale on Ebay, asking for $39. It sold for $521. This was in early 1999. Within days, hundreds of other Ultima characters and property and, eventually, gold caches and other accessories were being bought and sold. One account went for $4,000.

Daren Sutter, for one, put a large tower on the auction block last August. He made 600 bucks on the sale. He's been prospecting ever since. On any given day, he will have a couple of dozen items up for auction. These are mostly lump sums of gold in parcels of 500,000 or 1 million units. At present the market value is about $20 to $30 per half-million units. A "one million uo gold!" check sold recently for $71. (Buyers send Sutter hard currency, and Sutter leaves gold checks for them at virtual banks in Britannia.) This puts the exchange rate at around 15,000 to 25,000 Ultima Online gold units to the U.S. dollar, making a unit of Ultima gold nearly equal in value to the Vietnamese dong.

It raises the question: who are these people who figure that a unit of currency in a fictional online world is worth about the same as actual Vietnamese money? Sutter says there are two kinds: impatient newcomers and upwardly mobile longtime players. The former, Sutter reckons, "just want to jump into the game with good weapons and armor and have a good-sized home for their character." The latter group is closer in mindset to that of overambitious parents. "A lot of people," says Sutter, "want to give their characters big homes and unique items that other characters don't have. Just like real life, people just want to get ahead."

And if you're starting to think that the operative phrase here is "just like real life" (if you're wondering, that is, if maybe some of these 60-hours-a-week Ultima junkies no longer even notice the distinction), then check out the Sunday-real-estate-supplement jargon used in pitches for Ultima property. (Britannia, fantasy world or not, has a finite amount of land, so real estate is in particularly high demand.) "We all know real estate is hard to find," begins the description of one tower, "and a great house in a great location even harder to find." Another reads, "a hop skip from the city of Trinsic-perfect for all you miners out there." Elsewhere, a suit of "Rare Phoenix Armor" is described as a "status-symbol piece." It sold for $445. It was no aberration: there are literally hundreds of Ultima-related trades made every day, and the winning bids are in the hundreds of dollars as often as not. To be sure, this is not some ready-for-Letterman, stupid-human trick. Rather, it is a high-end niche market.

Another example of cyberspace is the Army's SIMNET system. Tank simulators (a type of cab simulator) are networked together electronically, often at different sites, and wargames are played using the battlefield modeled in cyberspace. Participants may be at different locations, but they are "fighting" each other at the same location in cyberspace via SIMNET (Hamit, 1993; Sterling, 1993). Not only is the virtual battlefield portrayed electronically, but participants' actions in the virtual tanks are monitored, revised, coordinated. There is virtual radio traffic. And the radio traffic is recorded for later analysis by trainers. Several battlefield training sites such as the Mojave Desert in California and 73 Easting in Iraq (the site of a major battle in the 1991 war) are digitally replicated within the computer so that all the soldiers will see the same terrain, the same simulated enemy and friendly tanks. Battle conditions can be change for different wargame scenarios (Hamit, 1993; Sterling, 1993). The Experience Learning System, to be described, shows the latest development in virtual military training. And there are many examples of how digital networks can be used to enhance military training and performance. The American soldiers in Afganistan in 2001–2002 relied heavily upon digital technologies to enhance their performance in the field in coordination with others.

17.3.9 Telepresence/Teleoperation

The concept of cyberspace is linked to the notion of **telepresence,** the feeling of being in a location other than where you actually are. Related to this, **teleoperation** means that you can control a robot or another device at a distance. In the Jason Project (http://www.jason.org), children at different sites across the United States have the opportunity to teleoperate the unmanned submarine Jason, the namesake for this innovative science education project directed by Robert Ballard, a scientist as the Woods Hole Oceanographic Institute (EDS, 1991; McLellan, 1995; Ulman, 1993). An extensive set of curriculum materials is developed by the National Science Teachers Association to support each Jason expedition. A new site is chosen each year. In past voyages, the Jason Project has gone to the Mediterranean Sea, the Great Lakes, the Gulf of Mexico, the Galapagos Islands, and Belize. The 1995 expedition went to Hawaii.

Similar to this, NASA has implemented an educational program in conjuction with the Telepresence-controlled Remotely Operated underwater Vehicle (TROV) that has been deployed to Antarctica (Stoker, 1994). By means of a distributed computer control architecture developed at NASA, school children in classrooms across the United States can take turns driving the TROV in Antarctica. NASA Ames researchers have focused on using telepresence-controlled scientific exploration vehicles to perform field studies of space-analog environments on the Earth including the Mars Pathfinder project.

Telepresence offers great potential for medicine (Coleman, 1999; SRI, 2002; Green, Hill, Jensen, & Shan, 1995; Satava, 1997; Shimoga & Khosla, 1994; Wong, 1996). A variety of telepresence medical devices are in use. Surgeon Richard Satava is pioneering telepresence surgery for gall bladder removal without any direct contact from the surgeon after an initial small incision is made—a robot does the rest, following the movements of the surgeon's hands at another location (Satava, 1992; Taubes, 1994b). Satava believes that telepresence surgery can someday be carried out in space, on the battlefield, or in the Third World, without actually sending the doctor. In conjunction with its series on *Twenty First Century Medicine*, PBS offers a teacher's guide to "cybersurgery," including learning activities, at http://www.pbs.org/safarchive/4_class/45_pguides/pguide-605/4565_cyber.html.

17.3.10   The VisionDome

The VisionDome from the Elumens Corporation (formerly ARC) is an immersive, multiuser, single projection Virtual Reality environment featuring a full-color, raster based, interactive display (Alternate Realities Corporation (ARC), 1998; Design Research Laboratory, 2001; Elumens Corporation, 2001). This differs from the chamber world type of virtual reality in that it does not require goggles, glasses, helmets, or other restrictive interface devices. Upon entering the VisionDome, the user views are into its hemispherical structure, which forms a fully immersive 180–degree hemispheric screen. The user sees vivid images that take on depth and reality inside the VisionDome. Combining computer generated 3-D models with advanced projection equipment, the VisionDome immerses users in a 360 degree by 180 degree virtual environment. As ARC (1998) explains,

The tilted hemispherical screen is positioned so as to fill the field-of-view of the participants, creating a sense of immersion in the same way that large-screen cinemas draw the audience into the scene. The observer loses the normal depth cues, such as edges, and perceives 3D objects beyond the surface of the screen. The dome itself allows freedom of head motion, so that the observer can change their direction of view, and yet still have their vision fully encompassed by the image. (web publication, p. 3)

Three-dimensional immersive environments (3-D Models) are developed for the VisionDome in modeling applications such as AutoCad, 3D Studio Max, or Alias Wavefront. Models are exported in VRML or Inventor format. These interactive files types can be displayed over the Web by using a VRML plug-in with a Web browser.

Since this system does not require interface devices such as head-mounted displays for individual users, it is less expensive than immersive VR systems and it can accommodate a much larger audience. The VisionDome is available in several different models. For example, the V-4 model can accommodate from 1 to 10 people while the V-5 model can accommodate up to

45 people. The larger model is finding use in museums and trade shows. Both models are relevant to education. In addition, there is the smaller VisionStation that offers great potential ofr training and related applications. The projection system and 3-D images are scalable across the different VisionDome models so that content can be developed once and used on different models.

The VisionDome is highly interactive. For example, it allows designers and clients to interact in real-time with a proposed design. The spaces of a building or landscape plan can be visualized in a photo-realistic way.

The VisionDome can be used wherever an effective wide field-of-view immersive display is needed. Potential application areas include:

- Simulation and Training
- Research, commercial, military and academic
- Oil and gas exploration
- Product design, research and prototyping
- Marketing, presentation of products and services
- Medical, diagnosis, surgical planning and teaching hospitals
- Urban planning, geophysical research and planning
- Architectural presentation and walk-throughs
- Entertainment, arcades, museums, and theme parks

North Carolina State University was the first university to obtain a VisionDome in 1998. The Design Research Laboratory (DRL) at NCSU reports that it has plans to use the VisionDome for educational applications, research initiatives and projects in the fields of architecture, landscape architecture, industrial design, urban planning, engineering, chemistry, and biology. Projects are already underway concerning architectural planning and terrain visualization.

The Colorado School of Mines is installing a VisionDome at its new Center for Multidimensional Engineered Earth Systems which has an educational component to its mission. The Center will design software to project 4-D images of the earth's subsurface on a VisionDome. This facility is similar to a planetarium, with the viewer sitting inside the earth looking up at tectonic plate movements, migration of oil, environmental impact of natural seeps, or human exploitation of natural resources, etc. It will be used to educate people about energy literacy.

17.3.11 The Experience Learning System

The Institute for Creative Technologies (http://www.ict.usc.edu/) has recently been established at the University of Southern California to provide the Army with highly realistic training simulations that rely on advances in virtual reality, artificial intelligence and other cutting-edge technologies (Hafner, 2001; Kaplan, 1999). This research center at USC will develop core technologies that are critical to both the military and to the entertainment industry. Kaplan (1999) explains, "The entertainment industry is expected to use the technology to improve its motion picture special effects, make video games more realistic and create new simulation attractions for virtual reality arcades (p. 7)." According to Kaplan,

The Army will spend $45 million on the institute during its first five years, making it the largest research project at USC. Entertainment companies are expected to contribute not only money but also their know-how in everything from computer special effects to storytelling. Altogether, the center could raise enough funds from entertainment companies and government sources to nearly double its budget. (p. 7)

According to the Institute for Creative Technologies (ICT) Web site,

The ICT's work with the entertainment industry brings expertise in story, character, visual effects and production to the Experience Learning System. In addition, game developers, who bring computer graphics and modeling resources; and the computer science community bring innovation in networking, artificial intelligence, and virtual reality technology. The four basic research vectors of the ICT are: entertainment industry assets, photoreal computer graphics, immersive audio, and artificial intelligence for virtual humans.

The Web site also explains that the ICT is working closely with several of USC's schools, including the School of Cinema-TV, the School of Engineering and its Information Sciences Institute (ISI) and Integrated Media Systems Center (IMSC), and the Annenberg School of Communication.

The Institute for Creative Technologies, established in 1999, will develop a convergence of core technologies into "the experience learning system." This system will include:

- Artificial intelligence to create digital characters for military simulations that respond to situations like real people.
- Computer networks that can run simulations with hundreds—or even thousands—of participants who are spread around the globe.
- Technologies to create immersive environments for simulations, ranging from better head-mounted displays to force-feedback devices to surround-sound audio systems (Kaplan, 1999, p. 7).

Hafner (2001) explains that when these virtual learning simulations are ready, they will be used at bases around the country to train soldiers and officers alike to make decisions under stress. The ICT initiative highlights that the critical R&D challenge in developing virtual learning systems extends beyond the technology. Today's challenge is "to focus on the more unpredictable side of the human psyche, simulating emotions and the unexpected effects that panic, stress, anxiety and fear can have on actions and decisions when an officer or a soldier is deep in the fog of war" (Hafner, 2001). Hafner explains that the growing interest among researchers in these kinds of simulations comes with the rise in computer processing power and the growing sophistication of psychological theories.

To enhance the realism, the Institute for Creative Technologies has built a theater with a screen that wraps around roughly half the room. Three projectors and a sound system make the theater so realistic and directional that it can trick the listener into believing that a sound's source is coming from anywhere in the room. Several virtual learning exercises have been developed, including this one described by Hafner:

On a quiet street in a village in the Balkans, an accident suddenly puts an American peacekeeping force to the test. A Humvee has hit a car, and a child who has been injured in the collision lies unmoving on the ground. A medic leans over him. The child's mother cries out. A crowd of local residents gathers in the background. How they will react is anyone's guess.

A lieutenant arrives at the scene and is confronted by a number of variables. In addition to the chaos unfolding in the village, a nearby unit is radioing for help. Emotions—not only the lieutenant's own and those of his sergeant, but also those of the panicked mother and the restive townspeople—will clearly play a role in any decision he makes.

This seven-minute situation is a simulation, generated on a large computer screen with sophisticated animation, voice synthesis and voice recognition technology. It is the product of about six months of work here by three research groups at the University of Southern California: the Institute for Creative Technologies, largely financed by the Army to promote collaboration among the military, Hollywood and computer researchers; the Information Sciences Institute; and the Integrated Media Systems Center.

The only human player is the lieutenant. The rest of the characters, including the sergeant who has been conferring with the lieutenant, have been generated by the computer. (p. 34)

Hafner explains that as the simulation becomes more sophisticated, there will be more choices for the lieutenant, and software will put the story together on the fly.

17.4 INTRODUCTION TO VIRTUAL REALITY APPLICATIONS IN EDUCATION AND TRAINING

Virtual reality appears to offer educational potentials in the following areas: (1) data gathering and visualization, (2) project planning and design, (3) the design of interactive training systems, (4) virtual field trips, and (5) the design of experiential learning environments. Virtual reality also offers many possibilities as a tool for nontraditional learners, including the physically disabled and those undergoing rehabilitation who must learn (or relearn) communication and psychomotor skills (Delaney, 1993; Knapp, & Lusted, 1992; Loge, Cram, & Inman, 1995; Murphy, 1994; Pausch, Vogtle, & Conway, 1991; Pausch, & Williams, 1991; Powers & Darrow, 1996; Sklaroff, 1994; Trimble, 1993; Warner & Jacobson, 1992). Virtual reality has been applied to teaching foreign languages (Osberg, Winn, Rose, Hollander, Hoffman, & Char, 1997; Rose, 1995a, 1995b, 1996; Rose & Billinghurst, 1995; Schwienhorst, 1998). Virtual reality offers professional applications in many disciplines—robotics, medicine, scientific visualization, aviation, business, architectural and interior design, city planning, product design, law enforcement, entertainment, the visual arts, music, and dance. Concomitantly, virtual reality offers potentials as a training tool linked to these professional applications (Donelson, 1994; Dunkley, 1994; Earnshaw et al., 2001; Goodlett, 1990; Hughes, 1993; Hyde & Loftin, 1993; Jacobson, 1992).

Virtual reality offers tremendous potential in medicine, both as a tool for medical practice (Carson, 1999) and for training medical students, especially those training to become surgeons. There is an annual Medicine Meets Virtual Reality Conference (MMVR) where research concerning VR in medicine,

including training applications, is presented. The Web site is http://www.nextmed.com/mmvr_virtual_reality.html. The U.S. Army has a Telemedicine & Advanced Technology Research Center (http://www.tatrc.org/). The VRepar Project (Virtual Reality Environments in Psychoneuro-physiological Assessment and Rehabilitation) has a useful Web site at http://www.psicologia.net/.

In terms of medical training, several companies have introduced surgical simulators that feature virtual reality, including both visual and tactile feedback (Brennan, 1994; Burrow, 1994; Hon, 1993, 1994; Marcus, 1994; McGovern, 1994; Merril, 1993, 1994, 1995; Merril, Roy, Merril, & Raju, 1994; Rosen, 1994; Satava, 1992, 1993; Spritzer, 1994; Stix, 1992; Taubes; 1994b; Weghorst, 1994). Merril (1993) explains:

Anatomy is 3-dimensional and processes in the body are dynamic; these aspects do not lend themselves to capture with two dimensional imaging. Now computer technology has finally caught up with our needs to examine and capture and explain the complex goings-on in the body. The simulator must also have knowledge of how each instrument interacts with the tissues. A scalpel will cut tissue when a certain amount of pressure is applied; however, a blunt instrument may not—this fact must be simulated. In addition the tissues must know where their boundaries are when they are intersecting each other. (p. 35)

Virtual reality simulators are beginning to offer a powerful dynamic virtual model of the human body that can be used to improve medical education (Taubes, 1994b). In his autobiography, *The Big Picture*, Ben Carson (1999), the head of pediatric neurosurgery at the Johns Hopkins University Medical Center describes how a virtual reality system helped him prepare for an operation that successfully separated two Siamese twins joined at the head. The visualization was developed on the basis of CAT scans and other types of data that were integrated to create a three-dimensional, interactive model:

However it worked, I can say it was the next best thing to brain surgery—at least in terms of my preparation and planning for the scheduled operation on the Banda twins. In a Johns Hopkins research lab in Baltimore, Maryland, I could don a special set of 3-D glasses and stare into a small, reflective screen which then projected an image into space so that I could virtually "see" inside the heads of two little Siamese twins who were actually lying in a hospital on another continent. Using simple hand controls I manipulated a series of virtual tools. A turning fork or spoke could actually move the image in space—rotating the interwoven brains of these two boys to observe them from any and all angles. I could magnify the image in order to examine the smallest details, erase outer segments of the brain to see what lay hidden underneath, and even slice through the brains to see what different cross-sections would reveal about the inner structure of the brains. This allowed me to isolate even the smallest of blood vessels and follow them along their interior or exterior surface without difficulty or danger of damaging the surrounding tissue. All of which, of course, would be impossible in an actual operating room.

The chief benefit of all this was knowledge. I could observe and study the inner structure of the twins' brains before we opened them up and began the actual procedure on the operating table. I could note abnormalities ahead of time and spot potential danger areas—which promised to reduce the number of surprises we would encounter in the real operation. (p. 31)

Carson's account illustrates what a powerful tool virtual reality offers for medical practice—and for medical training.

Virtual reality is under exploration as a therapeutic tool for patients. For example, Lamson (1994) and Carmichael, Kovach, Mandel, and Wehunt (2001) report that psychologists and other professionals are using virtual reality as tool with patients that are afraid of heights. Carmichael et al. (2001) also report that the Virtual Vietnam program is being used with combat veterans to help them overcome post-traumatic stress syndrome. Carmichael et al. also report that virtual reality techniques are proving useful with panicky public speakers and nervous golfers. The company Virtually Better, Inc. (http://www.virtuallybetter.com/) creates virtual reality tools for the treatment of various anxiety disorders.

Oliver and Rothman (1993) have explored the use of virtual reality with emotionally disturbed children. Knox, Schacht, and Turner (1993) report on a proposed VR application for treating test anxiety in college students.

A virtual reality application in dentistry has been developed for similar purposes: virtual reality serves as a "dental distraction," distracting and entertaining the patient while the dentist is working on the patient's teeth (Weissman, 1995). Frere, Crout, Yorty, and McNeil (2001) report that this device is "beneficial in the reduction of fear, pain and procedure time." The "Dental Distraction" headset is available for sale at http://www.dentallabs.co.uk/distraction.htm as well as other Web sites.

Originally designed as a visualization tool to help scientists, virtual reality has been taken up by artists as well. VR offers great potential as a creative tool and a medium of expression in the arts (Moser & MacLeod, 1997). Creative virtual reality applications have been developed for the audio and visual arts. An exhibit of virtual reality art was held at the Soho Guggenheim Museum in 1993 and artistic applications of VR are regularly shown at the Banff Center for the Arts in Canada (Frankel, 1994; Laurel, 1994; Stenger, 1991; Teixeira, 1994a, 1994b). This trend is expanding (Brill, 1995; Cooper, 1995; Krueger, 1991; Treviranus, 1993). Virtual reality has been applied to the theater, including a venerable puppet theater in France (Coats, 1994). And virtual reality has a role to play in filmmaking, including project planning and special effects (Manners, 2002; Smith, 1993). This has important implications for education.

One of VR's most powerful capabilities in relation to education is as a data gathering and feedback tool on human performance (Greenleaf, 1994; Hamilton, 1992; Lampton, Knerr, Goldberg, Bliss, Moshell, & Blau, 1994; McLellan, 1994b). Greenleaf Medical has developed a modified version of the VPL DataGlove™ that can be used for performance data gathering for sports, medicine, and rehabilitation. For example, Greenleaf Medical developed an application for the Boston Red Sox that records, analyzes, and visually models hand and arm movements when a fast ball is thrown by one of the team pitchers, such as Roger Clemens. Musician Yo Yo Ma uses a virtual reality application called a "hyperinstrument," developed by MIT Media Lab researcher Tod Machover, that records the movement of his bow and bow hand (Markoff, 1991; Machover, n.d.). In addition to listening to the audio recordings, Yo Yo Ma can examine data concerning differences in his bowing during several performances of the same piece of music to determine what works best and thus how to improve his performance. Other researchers at the MIT Media Lab have conducted research on similar interfaces. For a list of publications, go to http://www.media.mit.edu/hyperins/publications.html.

NEC has created a prototype of a virtual reality ski training system that monitors and responds to the stress/relaxation rate indicated by the skier's blood flow to adjust the difficulty of the virtual terrain within the training system (Lerman, 1993; VR Monitor, 1993). Flight simulators can "replay" a flight or battletank wargame so that there can be no disagreement about what actually happened during a simulation exercise.

In considering the educational potentials of virtual reality, it is interesting to note that the legendary virtual reality pioneer, Jaron Lanier, one of the developers of the DataGlove™, originally set out to explore educational applications of virtual reality. Unfortunately this initiative was ahead of its time; it could not be developed into a cost-effective and commercially viable product. Lanier explains, "I had in mind an ambitious scheme to make a really low-cost system for schools, immediately. We tried to put together something that might be described as a Commodore 64 with a cheap glove on it and a sort of cylindrical software environment" (quoted in Ditlea, 1993, p. 10). Subsequently, during the mid-1980s, Lanier teamed up with scientists at the NASA Ames Lab on the research and development project where immersive virtual reality first came together.

Another virtual reality pioneer, Warren Robinett, designed the educational software program *Rocky's Boots* (Learning Company, 1983) during the early 1980s. This highly regarded program, which provides learners with a 2-D "virtual world" where they can explore the basic concepts of electronics, was developed before virtual reality came into focus; it serves as a model for experiential virtual reality learning environments.

Newby (1993) pointed out that, "Education is perhaps the area of VR which has some of the greatest potential for improvement through the application of advanced technology" (p. 11). The Human Interface Technology Lab (the HIT Lab) at the University of Washington has been a pioneer in exploring educational applications of virtual reality for K–12 education. The HIT Lab publications (Bricken, 1990; Bricken & Byrne, 1992; Byrne, 1993, 1996; Emerson, 1994; Jackson, Taylor, & Winn, 1999; Osberg, 1993, 1994; Osberg, Winn, Rose, Hollander, Hoffman, & Char, 1997; Rose, 1995a, 1995b; Rose & Billinghurst, 1995; Taylor, 1998; Winn, 1993; Winn, Hoffman, Hollander, Osberg, Rose, & Char, 1997; Winn, Hoffman, & Osberg, 1995) are all available on the Web site. HIT Lab educational projects have included:

- **Chemistry World:** Chemistry world is a VR world in which participants form atoms and molecules from the basic building blocks of electrons, protons and neutrons. The world is a balance of theoretically real objects following the laws of chemistry along with symbolism to help participants interpret the information.
- **HIV/AIDS Project:** The HIT Lab collaborated with Seattle Public Schools for "Virtual Reality and At-Risk Youth—The HIV/AIDS Project." The goals were to motivate the students and to learn more about VR as an educational tool within a curriculum.

- **Learning Through Experiencing Virtual Worlds:** The Learning Center provided the Teacher/Pathfinder project an advanced technology component for their Internet resources for teachers. The Learning Center has developed a web site that that introduces teachers to virtual reality and world building, using the Global Change World as a model. Through this site teachers have the ability to review the world building process, experience a 3-D environment by "flying through" it, and provide feedback on the potential usefulness of building virtual worlds.
- **Puzzle World:** Puzzle World examines the use of VR to help students in developing spatial concepts and relationships through experience in multiperceptual alternative learning environments.
- **Pacific Science Center:** The Pacific Science Center sponsored projects that taught children to build and experience their own virtual worlds.
- **US West Virtual Reality Roving Vehicle Program (VRRV):** The VRRV program enables students in grades 4–12 to experience and use VR technology and provide and instructional unit for children to build their own VR worlds.
- **Zengo Sayu:** Zengo Sayu is the first functioning virtual environment ever created specifically to teach foreign language. The environment is a world of building blocks endowed with the power to speak. Students absorb and practice the target language—Zengo Sayu was originally designed to teach Japanese—as they move through the environment and interact with virtual objects (Rose, 1995).

For more information about these applications, go to Imprintit, on the Web at http://www.imprintit.com/CreationsBody.html.

The Virtual Reality and Education Lab (VREL) East Carolina University, in Greenville, North Carolina is one organization that provides leadership in promoting education in the schools (Auld & Pantelidis, 1994; Pantelidis, 1993, 1994). The Web site for VREL is http://www.soe.ecu.edu/vr/vrel.htm. VREL has as its goals, "to identify suitable applications of virtual reality in education, evaluate virtual reality software and hardware, examine the impact of virtual reality on education, and disseminate this information as broadly as possible" (Auld & Pantelidis, 1994, p. 29). Researchers at VREL have focused intensively on assembling and sharing information. For example, VREL regularly releases an updated bibliography concerning VR and education via the internet. Veronica Pantelidis, Co-Director of VREL, has prepared several reports, including: *North Carolina Competency-Based Curriculum Objectives and Virtual Reality* (1993), *Virtus VR and Virtus WalkThrough Uses in the Classroom,* and *Virtual Reality: 10 Questions and Answers*.

VR Learning from the Virtual Reality Education Company (http://www.vrlearning.com/index.html), provides software and curriculum modules for using virtual reality in the K–12 classroom. As the company Web site explains:

VR Learning's mission is to provide software that promotes student achievement through virtual worlds, and meets the highest standards of classroom teachers and technology coordinators for K–12 software. Our products incorporate the following core principles:

- use of virtual reality helps with visualization and spatial memory, both proven keys to learning.
- the process of manipulating objects in virtual space engages students and promotes active learning.

- classroom software should be teacher-created and teacher and student tested to improve learner outcomes.—classroom software should be available for all computing platforms.
- classroom software should be cross-platform. That is, software and user-created files should function exactly the same on any platform.
- classroom software that is Intranet and Internet accessible (works in standard web browsers) is more cost-effective for many schools to acquire and maintain than stand—alone software.
- students should build on knowledge they discover by manipulating objects in virtual worlds, by reflecting on concepts and building their own virtual worlds.

This initiative started as a result of a project funded through the U.S. West Foundation, in partnership with the HIT Lab) designed to introduce virtual reality to the schools in and around Omaha Nebraska. Specifically, this was part of the HIT Lab's VRRV project described above.

As the VR Learning Web site explains, the staff from Educational Service Unit #3 took a fully immersive VR computer on loan from the HIT Lab on 1-day visits to over 60 schools and 4000 students experience immersive VR. The purpose of these visits was to expose the educational system to the VR concept, and start educators as well as students thinking about how virtual reality could be integrated into the curriculum. In addition, teachers were able to use the system to teach using one of five "Educational Worlds," including the Atom Building World and Hydrogen Cycle World. Teachers can see not only the technology, but also how to use the VR worlds to effectively teach content. For example, the Atom Building World teaches the structure of an atom by assembling a Neon atom one particle at a time. This application can be used in science classes, as well as computer-aided design (CAD) classes: a CAD teacher has used this system to show 3-D design in an immersive environment. The project featured low-end as well as high-end VR applications. The excitement generated by this funded project led to the formation of VR Learning in partnership with Educational Service Unit #3 to continue the momentum. VR Learning is focused on its home school district in Omaha, Nebraska, but its resources are available to all K–12 educators.

There have been other initiatives to explore the potential of virtual reality in the schools. For example, the Academy for the Advancement of Science and Technology in Hackensack, New Jersey, the West Denton High School in Newcastle-on-Tyne in Great Britain, and the Kelly Walsh High School in Natrona County, Wyoming have explored virtual reality in the K–12 classroom. Gay (1994a) describes how immersive virtual reality was implemented in Natrona County "on a school budget" using public domain software and other resources.

Museums are adopting virtual reality for displays as well as educational programs (Brill, 1994a, 1994b, 1994c, 1995; Britton, 1994; Gay, 1994b; Greschler, 1994; Holden, 1992; Jacobson, 1994b; Lantz, 1992; Loeffler, 1993; O'Donnell, 1994; Wagner, 1994; Wisne, 1994). In particular, the recently introduced VisionDome offers great potential in museums since it can accommodate up to 45 people without requiring individual head-mounted displays or other interfaces for each member of the audience.

Newby (1993) points out

... that VR for education, even if developed and proven successful, must await further commitment of funds before it can see widespread use. This situation is common to all countries where VR research is being undertaken with the possible exception of Japan, which has followed through on an initiative to provide technological infrastructure to students. (p. 11)

So far most educational applications of virtual reality have been developed for professional training in highly technical fields such as medical education, astronaut and cosmonaut training (Stone, 2000), military training (Earnshaw et al., 2001; Eckhouse, 1993; Merril, 1993, 1995). In particular, military training has been an important focus for the development of virtual reality training systems since VR-based training is safer and more cost-effective than other approaches to military training (Amburn, 1992; Dovey, 1994; Fritz, 1991; Gambicki & Rousseau, 1993; Hamit, 1993; Sterling, 1993; Stytz, 1993, 1994). It is important to note that the cost of VR technologies, while still expensive, has substantially gone down in price over the last few years. And options at the lower end of the cost scale such as garage VR and desktop VR are expanding, especially via the World Wide Web.

NASA (http://www.vetl.uh.edu) has developed a number of virtual environment R&D projects. This includes the Hubble Telescope Rescue Mission training project, the Space Station Coupola training project, the shared virtual environment where astronauts can practice reconnoitering outside the space shuttle for joint training, human factors, engineering design (Dede, Loftin, & Salzman, 1994; Loftin, Engleberg & Benedetti (1993a) 1993). And NASA researcher Bowen Loftin has developed the Virtual Physics Lab where learners can explore conditions such as changes in gravity (Loftin, Engleberg, & Beneditti 1993a, 1993b, 1993c). Loftin et al. (1993a) report that at NASA there is a serious lag time between the hardware delivery and training since it takes time to come to terms with the complex new technological systems that characterize the space program. Virtual reality can make it possible to reduce the time lag between receiving equipment and implementing training by making possible virtual prototypes or models of the equipment for training purposes. Bowen Loftin and his colleagues have conducted extensive research exploring virtual reality and education (Bell, Hawkins, Loftin, Carey, & Kass, 1998; Chen, Kakadiaris, Miller, Loftin, & Patrick, 2000; Dede, 1990, 1992, 1993; Dede, Loftin, & Salzman, 1994; Harding, Kakadiaris, & Loftin, 2000; Redfield, Bell, Hsieh, Lamos, Loftin & Palumbo, 1998; Salzman, Dede, & Loftin, 1999; Salzman, Loftin, Dede, & McGlynn, 1996).

17.5 ESTABLISHING A RESEARCH AGENDA FOR VIRTUAL REALITIES IN EDUCATION AND TRAINING

Since virtual reality is a fairly new technology, establishing a research agenda—identifying the important issues for research—is an important first step in exploring its potential. So far, work in virtual reality has focused primarily on refining and improving the technology and developing applications. Many

analysts suggest that VR research needs to deal with far more than just technical issues. Laurel (1992) comments, "In the last three years, VR researchers have achieved a quantum leap in the ability to provide sensory immersion. Now it is time to turn our attention to the emotional, cognitive, and aesthetic dimensions of human experience in virtual worlds." Related to this, Thurman (1993) recommends that VR researchers need to focus on instructional strategies, because "device dependency is an immature perspective that almost always gives way to an examination of the effects of training on learners, and thereby finetune how the medium is applied." To date, not much research has been conducted to rigorously test the benefits—and limitations—of learning and training in virtual reality. This is especially true of immersive applications. And assessing the research that has been carried out must take into consideration the rapid changes and improvements in the technology: improved graphics resolution, lighter head-mounted displays, improved processing speed, improved position tracking devices, and increased computer power. So any research concerning the educational benefits of virtual reality must be assessed in the context of rapid technological improvement.

Any research agenda for virtual realities must also take into consideration existing research in related areas that may be relevant. The Learning Environment systems project at the University of Southern California illustrates the importance of interdisciplinary expertise in developing virtual reality training systems. Many analysts (Biocca, 1992a, 1992b; Heeter, 1992; Henderson, 1991; Laurel, 1991; Pausch, Crea, & Conway, 1992; Piantanida, 1993, 1994; Thurman & Mattoon, 1994) have pointed out that there is a strong foundation of research and theory-building in related areas—human perception, simulation, communications, computer graphics, game design, multimedia, ethology, etc.—that can be drawn upon in designing and studying VR applications in education and training. Increasingly, research and development in virtual reality is showing an overlap with the field of artificial intelligence (Badler, Barsky, & Zeltzer, 1991; Taubes, 1994a; Waldern, 1994). And Fontaine (1992) has suggested that research concerning the experience of presence in international and intercultural encounters may be valuable for understanding the sense of presence in virtual realities. This example in particular gives a good indication of just how broad the scope of research relevant to virtual realities may be.

Furthermore, research in these foundation areas can be extended as part of a research agenda designed to extend our understanding of the potentials of virtual reality. For example, in terms of research related to perception that is needed to support the development of VR, Moshell and Dunn-Roberts (1993) recommend that theoretical and experimental psychology must provide: (1) systematic measurement of basic properties; (2) better theories of perception, to guide the formation of hypotheses—including visual perception, auditory perception, movement and motion sickness, and haptic perception (the sense of force, pressure, etc.); (3) careful tests of hypotheses, which result in increasingly valid theories; (4) constructing and testing of input and output devices based on empirical and theoretical guidelines, and ultimately (5) evaluation metrics and calibration procedures.

Human factors considerations will need careful attention (Pausch et al., 1992; Piantanida, 1993; Piantanida, 1994).

Waldern (1991) suggests that the following issues are vital considerations in virtual reality research and development: (1) optical configuration; (2) engineering construction; (3) form; (4) user considerations; (5) wire management; and (6) safety standards. According to Waldern, the single most difficult aspect is user considerations, which includes anthropometric, ergonomic and health and safety factors. Waldern explains: "If these are wrong, even by a small degree, the design will be a failure because people will choose not to use it." One issue that has come under scrutiny is the safety of head-mounted displays (HMDs), especially with long-term use. This issue will need further study as the technology improves. Wann, Rushton, Mon-Williams, Hawkes, and Smyth (1993) report, "Everyone accepts that increased screen resolution is a requirement for future HMDs, but equally we would suggest that a minimum requirement for the reduction of serious visual stress in stereoscopic presentations is variable focal depth."

Thurman and Mattoon (1994) comment,

It is our view that VR research and development will provide a foundation for a new and effective form of simulation-based training. However, this can be achieved only if the education and training communities are able to conceptualize the substantial differences (and subsequent improvements) between VR and other simulation strategies. For example, there are indications that VR is already misinterpreted as a single technological innovation associated with head-mounted displays, or sometimes with input devices such as sensor gloves or 3-D trackballs. This is analogous to the mistaken notion that crept into the artificial intelligence (AI) and subsequently the intelligence tutoring system (ITS) community in the not too distant past. That is, in its infant stages, the AI and ITS community mistakenly assumed that certain computer processors (e.g., lisp machines) and languages (e.g., Prolog) constituted artificial intelligence technology. It was not until early implementers were able to get past the "surface features" of the technology and began to look at the "deep structure" of the concept that real inroads and conceptual leaps were made. (p. 56)

This is a very important point for VR researchers to keep in mind.

It will be important to articulate a research agenda specifically relating to virtual reality and education. Fennington and Loge (1992) identify the following issues: (1) How is learning in virtual reality different from that of a traditional educational environment? (2) What do we know about multisensory learning that will be of value in determining the effectiveness of this technology? (3) How are learning styles enhanced or changed by VR? and (4) What kinds of research will be needed to assist instructional designers in developing effective VR learning environments? Related to this, McLellan (1994b) argues that virtual reality can support all seven of the multiple intelligences postulated by Howard Gardner—linguistic, spatial, logical, musical, kinesthetic, interpersonal and intrapersonal intelligences. VR researchers may want to test this notion.

A detailed research agenda concerning virtual reality as applied to a particular type of training application is provided by a front-end analysis that was conducted by researchers at SRI International (Boman, Piantanida, & Schlager, 1993) to determine the feasibility of using virtual environment technology in Air Force maintenance training. This study was based on interviews with maintenance training and testing experts at Air Force and

NASA training sites and at Air Force contractors' sites. Boman et al. (1993) surveyed existing maintenance training and testing practices and technologies, including classroom training, hands-on laboratory training, on-the-job training, software simulations, interactive video, and hardware simulators. This study also examined the training-development process and future maintenance training and testing trends. Boman et al. (1993) determined that virtual environments might offer solutions to several problems that exist in previous training systems. For example, with training in the actual equipment or in some hardware trainers, instructors often cannot see what the student is doing and cannot affect the session in ways that would enhance learning.

The most cited requirements were the need to allow the instructor to view the ongoing training session (from several perspectives) and to interrupt or modify the simulation on the fly (e.g., introducing faults). Other capabilites included instructional guidance and feedback to the student and capture the playback of a session. Such capabilities should be integral features of a VE system. (V. II, pp. 26–27)

Boman et al. (1993) report that the technicians, developers, and instructors interviewed for this study were all in general agreement that if the capabilities outlined above were incorporated in a virtual environment training system, it would have several advantages over current training delivery methods. The most commonly cited advantages were availability, increased safety, and reduced damage to equipment associated with a simulated practice environment. Virtual reality was seen as a way to alleviate the current problem of gaining access to actual equipment and hardware trainers. Self-pacing was also identified as an advantage. For example, instructors could "walk through" a simulated system with all students, allow faster learners to work ahead on their own, and provide remediation to slower students. Boman et al. (1993) report that another potential benefit would be if the system enforced uniformity, helping to solve the problem of maintaining standardization of the maintenance procedures being taught.

Boman et al. (1993) report that some possible impacts of virtual environment simulations include: (1) portraying specific aircraft systems; (2) evaluating performance; (3) quick upgrading; (4) many hardware fabrication costs are avoided; (5) the computer-generated VR model can be disassembled in seconds; (6) the VR model can be configured for infrequent or hazardous tasks; and (7) the VR model can incorporate modifications in electronic form. Their findings indicate that (1) a need exists for the kind of training virtual reality offers and (2) virtual environment technology has the potential to fill that need. To provide effective VR maintenance training systems, Boman et al. (1993) report that research will be needed in three broad areas: (1) Technology development to produce equipment with the fidelity needed for VR training; (2) Engineering studies to evaluate functional fidelity requirements and develop new methodologies; (3) Training/testing studies to develop an understanding of how best to train using virtual reality training applications. For example, Boman et al. (1993) recommend the development of new methods to use virtual environment devices with simulations, including: (1) evaluating methods for navigating within a simulated environment, in particular, comparing the use of speech, gestures, and 3-D/6-D input devices for navigation commands; (2) evaluating methods for manipulating virtual objects including the use of auditory or tactile cues to detect object colision; (3) evaluating virtual menu screens, voice, and hand gesture command modes for steering simulations; (4) evaluating methods for interaction within multiple-participant simulations, including methods to give instructors views from multiple perspectives (e.g., student viewpoint, God's-eye-view, panorama); and (5) having the staff from facilities involved in virtual environment software and courseware development perform the studies on new methodologies.

In sum, virtual environments appear to hold great promise for filling maintenance and other technical training needs, particularly for tasks for which training could not otherwise be adequate because of risks to personnel, prohibitive costs, environmental constraints, or other factors. The utility of virtual environments as more general-purpose maintenance training tools, however, remains unsubstantiated. Boman et al. (1993) make a number of recommendations:

- Develop road maps for virtual environment training and testing research;
- Identify and/or set up facilities to conduct virtual environment training/testing research;
- Conduct experimental studies to establish the effectiveness of VE simulations in facilitating learning at the cognitive process level;
- Develop effective principles and methods for training in a virtual environment;
- Assess the suitability of VE simulation for both evaluative and aptitude testing purposes;
- Develop criteria for specifying the characteristics of tasks that would benefit from virtual environment training for media selection;
- Conduct studies to identify virtual environment training system requirements;
- Develop demonstration systems and conduct formative evaluations;
- Conduct studies to identify guidelines specifying when and where virtual environment or other technologies are more appropriate in the total curriculum, and how they can be used in concert to maximize training efficiency and optimize the benefits of both;
- Develop integrated virtual environment maintenance training system and curriculum prototypes; and
- Conduct summative evaluation of system performance, usablity, and utility, and of training outcomes. (V IV, pp. 12-16)

This study gives a good indication of the scope of the research still needed to assess the educational potentials of virtual realities. As this study indicates, a wide gamut of issues will need to be included in any research agenda concerning the educational potentials of VR. Virtual realities appear to hold great promise for education and training, but extensive research and development is still needed to refine and assess the potentials of this emerging technology.

Imprintit (n.d.) presents a valuable report on its approach to developing education virtual reality applications. This report is available at *http://www.imprintit.com/Publications/VEApp.doc*.

17.6 THEORETICAL PERSPECTIVES ON VIRTUAL REALITIES

Already there has been a great deal of theory building as well as theory adapting vis-à-vis virtual reality. Theorists have looked to a broad array of sources—theater, psychology, ethology, perception, communication, computer science, and learning theories—to try to understand this emerging technology and how it can be applied in education and other fields.

17.6.1 Ecological Psychology Perspective— J. J. Gibson

The model of ecological psychology proposed by J. J. Gibson (1986) has been particularly influential in laying a theoretical foundation for virtual reality. Ecological psychology is the psychology of the awareness and activities of indivduals in an environment (Gibson, 1986; Mace, 1977). This is a theory of perceptual systems based on direct perception of the environment. In Gibson's theory, "affordances" are the distinctive features of a thing which help to distinguish it from other things that it is not. Affordances help us to perceive and understand how to interact with an object. For example, a handle helps us to understand that a cup affords being picked up. A handle tells us where to grab a tool such as a saw. And door knobs tell us how to proceed in opening a door. Affordances provide strong clues to the operations of things.

Affordance perceptions allow learners to identify information through the recognition of relationships among objects or contextual conditions. Affordance recognition must be understood as a contextually sensitive activity for determining what will (most likely) be paid attention to and whether an affordance will be perceived. J. J. Gibson (1986) explains that the ability to recognize affordances is a selective process related to the individual's ability to attend to and learn from contextual information.

Significantly, Gibson's model of ecological perception emphasizes that perception is an active process. Gibson does not view the different senses as mere producers of visual, auditory, tactile, or other sensations. Instead he regards them as active seeking mechanisms for looking, listening, touching, etc. Furthermore, Gibson emphasizes the importance of regarding the different perceptual systems as strongly inter-related, operating in tandem. Gibson argues that visual perception evolved in the context of the perceptual and motor systems, which constantly work to keep us upright, orient us in space, enable us to navigate and handle the world. Thus visual perception, involving head and eye movements, is frequently used to seek information for coordinating hand and body movements and maintaining balance. Similar active adjustments take place as one secures audio information with the ear and head system.

J. J. Gibson (1986) hypothesized that by observing one's own capacity for visual, manipulative, and locomotor interaction with environments and objects, one perceives the meanings and the utility of environments and objects, i.e., their affordances. McGreevy (1993) emphasizes that Gibson's ideas highlight the importance of understanding the kinds of interactions offered by real environments and the real objects in those environments. Some virtual reality researchers (Ellis, 1991, 1992; McGreevy, 1993; Sheridan & Zeltner, 1993; Zeltner, 1992) suggest that this knowledge from the real world can inform the design of interactions in the virtual environment so that they appear natural and realistic, or at least meaningful.

Michael McGreevy, a researcher at the NASA Ames Lab, is studying the potential of virtual reality as a scientific visualization tool for planetary exploration, including virtual geological exploration. He has developed a theoretical model of the scientist in the virtual world as an explorer, based on J.J. Gibson's theory of ecological psychology. In particular, McGreevy links the Gibsonian idea that the environment must "afford" exploration in order for people to make sense of it to the idea that we can begin to learn something important from the data retrieved from planetary exploration by flying through the images themselves via immersive VR, from all different points of view. McGreevy (1993) explains:

Environments afford exploration. Environments are composed of openings, paths, steps, and shallow slopes, which afford locomotion. Environments also consist of obstacles, which afford collision and possible injury; water, fire, and wind, which afford life and danger; and shelters, which afford protection from hostile elements. Most importantly, environments afford a context for interaction with a collection of objects. (p. 87).

As for objects, they afford "grasping, throwing, portability, containment, and sitting on. Objects afford shaping, molding, manufacture, stacking, piling, and building. Some objects afford eating. Some very special objects afford use as tools, or spontaneous action and interaction (that is, some objects are other animals)" (McGreevy, 1993, p. 87).

McGreevy (1993) points out that natural objects and environments offer far more opportunity for use, interaction, manipulation, and exploration than the ones typically generated on computer systems. Furthermore, a user's natural capacity for visual, manipulative, and locomotor interaction with real environments and objects is far more informative than the typically restricted interactions with computer-generated scenes. Perhaps virtual reality can bridge this gap. Although a virtual world may differ from the real world, virtual objects and environments must provide some measure of the affordances of the objects and environments depicted (standing in for the real-world) in order to support natural vision (perceptualization) more fully.

Related to this, Rheingold (1991) explains that a wired glove paired with its representation in the virtual world that is used to control a virtual object offers an affordance—a means of literally grabbing on to a virtual world and making it a part of our experience. Rheingold explains: "By sticking your hand out into space and seeing the hand's representation move in virtual space, then moving the virtual hand close to a virtual object, you are mapping the dimensions of the virtual world into your internal perception-structuring system" (p. 144).

And virtual reality pioneer Jaron Lanier (1992) has commented that the principle of head-tracking in virtual reality suggests that when we think about perception—in this case, sight—we shouldn't consider eyes as "cameras" that passively take in a scene. We should think of the eye as a kind of spy submarine moving around in space, gathering information. This creates a picture of perception as an *active* activity, not a *passive* one, in keeping with J. J. Gibson's theory. And it demonstrates a fundamental advantage of virtual reality: VR facilitates active perception and exploration of the environment portrayed.

17.6.2 Computers-as-Theater Perspective— Brenda Laurel

Brenda Laurel (1990a, 1990b, 1991) suggests that the principles of effective drama can be adapted to the design of interactive computer programs, and in particular, virtual reality. Laurel (1990) comments, "millennia of dramatic theory and practice have been devoted to an end that is remarkably similar to that of human–computer interaction design; namely, creating artificial realities in which the potential for action is cognitively, emotionally and aesthetically enhanced" (p. 6). Laurel has articulated a theory of how principles of drama dating back to Aristotle can be adapted to understanding human-computer interaction and the design of virtual reality.

Laurel's (1991) ideas began with an examination of two activities that are extremely successful in capturing people's attention: games and theater. She distinguishes between two modes of participation: (1) first-person—direct participation; and (2) third-person—watching as a spectator with the subjective experience is that of an outsider looking in, detached from the events.

The basic components of Laurel's (1991) model are:

1. Dramatic storytelling (storytelling designed to enable significant and arresting kinds of actions)
2. Enactment (for example, playing a VR game or learning scenario as performance)
3. Intensification (selecting, arranging, and representing events to intensify emotion)
4. Compression (eliminating irrelevant factors, economical design)
5. Unity of action (strong central action with separate incidents that are linked to that action; clear causal connections between events)
6. Closure (providing an end point that is satisfying both cognitively and emotionally so that some catharsis occurs)
7. Magnitude (limiting the duration of an action to promote aesthetic and cognitive satisfaction)
8. Willing suspension of disbelief (cognitive and emotional engagement)

A dramatic approach to structuring a virtual reality experience has significant benefits in terms of engagement and emotion. It emphasizes the need to delineate and represent human–computer activities as organic wholes with dramatic structural characteristics. And it provides a means whereby people experience agency and involvement naturally and effortlessly. Laurel (1991) theorizes that engagement is similar in many ways to the theatrical notion of the "willing suspension of disbelief." She explains: "Engagement involves a kind of complicity. We agree to think and feel in terms of both the content and conventions of a mimetic context. In return, we gain a plethora of new possibilities for action and a kind of emotional guarantee" (p. 115). Furthermore, "Engagement is only possible when we can rely on the system to maintain the representational context" (p. 115).

Magnitude and closure are two design elements associated with enactment. Magnitude suggests that limiting the *duration* of an action has aesthetic and cognitive aspects as well as physical ones. Closure suggests that there should be an end point that is satisfying both cognitively and emotionally, providing catharsis.

> In simulation-based activities, the need for catharsis strongly implies that what goes on be structured as a whole action with a dramatic "shape." If I am flying a simulated jet fighter, then either I will land successfully or be blown out of the sky, hopefully after some action of a duration that is sufficient to provide pleasure has had a chance to unfold. Flight simulators shouldn't stop in the middle, even if the training goal is simply to help a pilot learn to accomplish some midflight task. Catharsis can be accomplished, as we have seen, through a proper understanding of the nature of the whole action and the deployment of dramatic probability. If the end of an activity is the result of a causally related and well-crafted series of events, then the experience of catharsis is the natural result of the moment at which probability becomes neccesity. (Laurel, 1991, p.122)

Instructional designers and the designers of virtual worlds and experiences within them should keep in mind the importance of defining the "whole" activity as something that can provide satisfaction and closure when it is achieved.

Related to this theory of design based upon principles of drama, Laurel has recently introduced the concept of "smart costumes" to describe characters or agents in a virtual world. She has developed an art project, PLACEHOLDER, that features smart costumes—a set of four animal characters—crow, snake, spider, and fish (Frenkel, 1994; Laurel, 1994). A person visiting the PLACEHOLDER world may assume the character of one of these animals and thereby experience aspects of its unique visual perception, its way of moving about, and its voice. For example, snakes can see the infrared portion of the spectrum and so the system tries to model this: the space appears brighter to someone wearing this "smart costume." The "smart costumes" change more than the appearance of the person within. Laurel (1991) explains that characters (or "agents") need not be complex models of human personality; indeed, dramatic characters are effective precisely because the they are less complex and therefore more discursive and predictable than human beings.

Virtual agents are becoming an increasingly important area of design in virtual reality, bridging VR with artificial intelligence. For example, Waldern (1994) has described how virtual agents based on artificial intelligence techniques such as neural nets and fuzzy logic form a basis of virtual reality games such as *Legend Quest*. Bates (1992) is conducting research concerning dramatic virtual characters. And researchers at the Center for Human Modeling and Simulation at the University of Pennsylvania are studying virtual agents in "synthetic-conversation group" research (Badler et al., 1991; Goodwin Marcus Systems,

Creative artists		Performing artists
	writer	storyteller
	speech writer	orator
	joke writer	comedian
	poet	bard
novelist	choreographer	dancer, mime
architect	composer	instrumentalist
sculptor	coach	athlete
painter	songwriter	singer
	playwright	stage actor
	filmmaker	film actor
user interface designer	dungeon master	D & D role player
	spacemaker	cyberspace player

FIGURE 17.2. Walser's media spectrum, including spacemaker and cyberspace player categories. Adapted from Walser (1991).

Ltd., n.d. Taubes, 1994a). The virtual agent Jack™, developed at the Center for Human Modeling and Simulation, has been trade marked and is used as a 3-D graphics software environment for conducting ergonomic studies of people with products (such as cars and helicopters), buildings, and interaction situations (for example, a bank teller interacting with a customer) (Goodwin Marcus Systems, n.d.). Researchers at the MIT Media Lab are studying ethology—the science of animal behavior—as a basis for representing virtual characters (Zeltner, 1992).

17.6.3 Spacemaker Design Perspective— Randal Walser

Randall Walser (1991, 1992) draws upon ideas from filmmaking, performance art, and role-playing games such as Dungeons and Dragons to articulate his model of "spacemaking."

> The goal of spacemaking is to augment human performance. Compare a spacemaker (or world builder) with a film maker. Film makers work with frozen virtual worlds. Virtual reality cannot be fully scripted. There's a similarity to performance art. Spacemakers are especially skilled at using the new medium so they can guide others in using virtual reality. (Walser, 1992)

Walser (1991) places the VR roles of spacemaker (designer) and cyberspace player (user) in the context of creative and performing artists, as shown in Fig. 17.2.

Walser (1992) places virtual reality (or cyberspace, as he refers to VR) in the context of a full spectrum of media, including film as well as print, radio, telephony, television, and desktop computing. In particular, Walser compares cyberspace with desktop computing. Just as desktop computing, based on the graphic user interface and the desktop metaphor, created a new paradigm in computing, Walser proposes that cyberspace is based on still another new paradigm, which is shown in Fig. 17.3.

Walser (1992) is particularly concerned with immersive virtual reality. He explains that in the desktop paradigm, computers

Desktop paradigm	Cyberspace paradigm
mind	body
ideas	actions
creative arts	performing arts
products	performances

FIGURE 17.3. Walser's (1992) comparison of the desktop and cyberspace paradigms of media design.

are viewed as tools for the mind — mind as dissembodied intellect. In the new cyberspace paradigm, computers are viewed as engines for worlds of experience where mind and body are inseparable. Embodiment is central to cyberspace, as Walser (1992) explains:

Cyberspace is a medium that gives people the feeling they have been bodily transported from the ordinary physical world to worlds of pure imagination. Although artists can use any medium to evoke imaginary worlds, cyberspace carries the various worlds itself. It has a lot in common with film and stage, but is unique in the amount of power it yields to its audience. Film yields little power, as it provides no way for its audience to alter screen images. The stage grants more power than film does, as stage actors can "play off" audience reactions, but the course of the action is still basically determined by a script. Cyberspace grants seemingly ultimate power, as it not only enables its audience to observe a reality, but also to enter it and experience it as reality. No one can know what will happen from one moment to the next in a cyberspace, not even the spacemaker (designer). Every moment gives each participant an opportunity to create the next event. Whereas film depicts a reality to the audience, cyberspace grants a virtual body and a role, to everyone in the audience.

Similar to Brenda Laurel, Walser (1992) theorizes that cyberspace is fundamentally a theatrical medium, in the broad sense that it, like traditional theater, enables people to invent, communicate, and comprehend realities by "acting them out." Walser explains that acting out roles or points of view is not just a form of expression, but a fundamental way of knowing.

17.6.4 Constructivist Learning Perspective—Meredith and William Bricken

Focusing primarily on immersive applications of VR, Meredith Bricken theorizes that virtual reality is a very powerful educational tool for constructivist learning, the theory introduced by Jean Piaget (Bricken, 1991; Bricken & Byrne, 1993). According to Bricken, the virtual reality learning environment is experiential and intuitive; it provides a shared information context that offers unique interactivity and can be configured for individual learning and performance styles. Virtual reality can support hands-on learning, group projects and discussions, field trips, simulations, and concept visualization; all successful instructional strategies. Bricken envisions that within the limits of system functionality, it is possible to create anything imaginable and then become part of it.

Bricken speculates that in virtual reality, learners can actively inhabit a spatial multi-sensory environment. In VR, learners are both physically and perceptually involved in the experience; they perceive a sense of presence within a virtual world. Bricken suggests that virtual reality allows natural interaction with information. In a virtual world, learners are empowered to move, talk, gesture, and manipulate objects and systems intuitively. And according to Bricken, virtual reality is highly motivational: it has a magical quality. "You can fly, you can make objects appear, disappear, and transform. You can have these experiences without learning an operating system or programming language, without any reading or calculation at all. But the magic trick of creating new experiences requires basic academic skills, thinking skills, and a clear mental model of what computers do" (Bricken, 1991, p. 3).

Meredith Bricken points out that virtual reality is a powerful context, in which learners can control time, scale, and physics. Participants have entirely new capabilities, such as the ability to fly through the virtual world, to occupy any object as a virtual body, to observe the environment from many perspectives. Understanding multiple perspectives is both a conceptual and a social skill; virtual reality enables learners to practice this skill in ways that cannot be achieved in the physical world.

Meredith Bricken theorizes that virtual reality provides a developmentally flexible, interdisciplinary learning environment. A single interface provides teachers and trainers with an enormous variety and supply of virtual learning "materials" that do not break or wear out. And as Bricken (1991) envisions it, virtual reality is a shared experience for multiple participants.

William Bricken (1990) has also theorized about virtual reality as a tool for experiential learning, based on the ideas of John Dewey and Jean Piaget. According to him, "VR teaches active construction of the environment. Data is not an abstract list of numerals, data is what we perceive in our environment. Learning is not an abstract list of textbook words, it is what we do in our environment. The hidden curriculum of VR is: make your world and take care of it. Try experiments, safely. Experience consequences, then choose from knowledge" (Bricken, 1990, p. 2).

Like his wife Meredith Bricken, William Bricken's attention is focused primarily on immersive virtual reality. William Bricken (1990) suggests that virtual reality represents a new paradigm in the design of human–computer interfaces. Bricken's model of the new virtual reality paradigm, contrasted with the "old" desktop computing paradigm, is presented in Fig. 17.4. This new VR paradigm is based on the transition from multiple points of view external to the human, to multiple points of view that the human enters, like moving from one room to another. Related to this, William Bricken and William Winn (Winn & Bricken, 1992a, 1992b) report on how VR can used to teach mathematics experientially.

17.6.5 Situated Learning Perspective— Hilary McLellan

McLellan (1991) has theorized that virtual reality-based learning environments can be designed to support situated learning, the model of learning proposed by Brown, Collins, and Duguid

Desktop paradigm (Old)	Virtual reality paradigm (New)
symbol processing	reality generation
viewing a monitor	wearing a computer
symbolic	experiential
observer	participant
interface	inclusion
physical	programmable
visual	multimodal
metaphor	virtuality

FIGURE 17.4. William Bricken's (1990) comparison of the desktop and virtual reality paradigms of media design.

(1989). According to this model, knowledge is situated; it is a product of the activity, context, and culture in which it is developed and used. Activity and situations are integral to cognition and learning. Therefore, this knowledge must be learned in context—in the actual work setting or a highly realistic or "virtual" surrogate of the actual work environment. The situated learning model features apprenticeship, collaboration, reflection, coaching, multiple practice, and articulation. It also emphasizes technology and stories.

McLellan (1991) analyzes a training program for pilots called Line-Oriented Flight Training (LOFT), featuring simulators (virtual environments), that exemplifies situated learning. LOFT was introduced in the early 1980s in response to data showing that most airplane accidents and incidents, including fatal crashes, resulted from pilot error (Lauber & Foushee, 1981). Concommitently, this data showed that pilot error is linked to poor communication and coordination in the cockpit under crisis situations. So the LOFT training program was instituted to provide practice in team building and crisis management. LOFT teaches pilots and co-pilots to work together so that an unexpected cascade of small problems on a flight doesn't escalate into a catastrophe (Lauber & Foushee, 1981).

All six of the critical situated learning components—Apprenticeship; Collaboration; Reflection; Coaching; Multiple practice; Articulation of learning skills—are present in the LOFT training program (McLellan, 1991). Within the simulated flight, the environmental conditions are controlled, modified, and *articulated* by the instructor to simulate increasingly difficult conditions. The learning environment is contextually rich and highly realistic. *Apprenticeship* is present since the instructor decides on what array of interlocking problems to present on each simulated flight. The pilots must gain experience with different sets of problems in order to build the skills neccesary for *collaborative teamwork and coordination*. And they must learn to solve problems for themselves: there is no instructor intervention during the simulated flights. *Reflection* is scheduled into the training after the simulated flight is over, when an instructor sits down with the crew to critique the pilots' performance. This involves *coaching* from the instructor as well.

The simulation provides the opportunity for *multiple practice*, including practice where different factors are *articulated*. Related to this, it is noteworthy that many virtual reality game players are very eager to obtain feedback about their performance, which is monitored electronically.

The LOFT training program emphasizes stories: stories of real disasters and simulated stories (scenarios) of crisis situations that represent all the possible kinds of technical and human problems that a crew might encounter in the real world. According to Fouchee (1992), the pilots who landed a severely crippled United Airlines airplane in Sioux City, Iowa several years ago, saving many lives under near-miraculous conditions, later reported in debriefing that they kept referring back to their LOFT training scenarios as they struggled to maintain control of the plane, which had lost its hydraulic system. The training scenarios were as "real" as any other experience they could draw upon.

Another example of situated learning in a virtual environment is a program for corporate training in team building that utilizes the Virtual Worlds Entertainment games (BattleTech, Red Planet, etc.), featuring networked simulator pods (Lakeland Group, 1994; McLellan, 1994a). This is a fascinating example of how an entertainment system has been adapted to create a training application. One of the advantages of using the VWE games is that it creates a level playing field. These virtual environments eliminate contextual factors that create inequalities between learners, thereby interfering with the actual learning skills featured in the training program, that is, interpersonal skills, collaboration, and team-building. Thus, McGrath (1994) reports that this approach is better than other training programs for team building. The Lakeland team training program suggests that virtual reality can be used to support learning that involves a strong social component, involving effective coordination and collaboration with other participants. Since both LOFT and the Lakeland Group training program are based upon virtual environments (cab simulators), it remains to be seen how other types of virtual reality can be used to support situated learning. Mirror world applications in particular seem to offer potential for situated learning.

The new Experience Learning System at the University of Southern California (Hafner, 2001) appears to be informed by the situated learning perspective. The central role of stories is noteworthy. Of course stories are also central to the experience design perspective discussed below and to Brenda Laurel's "Computers-as-theater" perspective discussed above.

17.6.6 Experience Design Perspective

Experience design is an important emerging paradigm for the design of all interactive media, including virtual reality. Experience design draws upon the theory building in virtual reality concerning the concept of presence. It also builds on theory building in a range of other fields, including psychology (Csikszentmihalyi, 1990), economics (Pine & Gilmore, 1999) and advertising (Schmitt, 1999) as well as media design (Carbone & Haecke, 1998; Ford and Forlizzi, 1999; Shedroff, 2001).

According to Ford & Forlizzi (1999), experience is built upon our perceptions, our feelings, our thoughts. Experiences are usually induced not self-generated; they are born of something external to the subject. Experience is:

- A private event that occurs in response to some kind of stimulus, be it emotional, tactile, aesthetic, or intellectual.
- Made up of an infinite amount of smaller experiences, relating to other people, surroundings, and the objects encountered.
- The constant stream of thoughts and sensations that happens during conscious moments (Ford & Forlizzi, 1999).

Ford and Forlizzi (1999) suggest that "As designers thinking about experience, we can only design situations—levers that people can interact with—rather than outcomes that can be absolutely predicted."

Shedroff (2002) explains,

One of the most important ways to define an experience is to search its boundaries. While many experiences are ongoing, sometimes even indefinitely, most have edges that define their start, middle, and end. Much like a story (a special and important type of experience), these boundaries help us differentiate meaning, pacing, and completion. Whether it is due to attention span, energy, or emotion, most people cannot continue an experience indefinitely; they will grow tired, confused, or distracted if an experience, however consistent, doesn't conclude.

At the very least, think of an experience as requiring an *attraction*, an *engagement*, and a *conclusion*.

Shedroff explains that the attraction is necessary to initiate the experience. This attraction should not be synonymous with distraction. An attraction can be cognitive, visual, auditory, or it can signal any of our senses. Shedroff recommends that there need to be cues as to where and how to begin the experience.

Shedroff further explains that engagement is the experience itself. The engagement needs to be sufficiently different from the surrounding environment of the experience to hold the attention of the experiences. The engagement also needs to be cognitively important or relevant enough for someone to continue the experience.

According to Shedroff, the conclusion can come in many ways, but it must provide some sort of resolution, whether through meaning or story or context or activity to make an otherwise enjoyable experience satisfactory—and memorable. Shedroff refers to this factor that endures in memory as the *takeaway*. As Shedroff (2001) explains that takeaways help us derive meaning from what we experience. Narrative is becoming recognized as an increasingly important design element (Packer & Jordan, 2001). For example, Murray (1997) reports that increasingly, people want a story in their entertainment. Entertainment rides such as those at Universal Studios (a form of virtual reality) are designed with a story element. The traditional amusement ride with small surprises, hints of danger, and sensory experiences—they want a story to frame the experience.

Shedroff (2002) reports, "Most technological experiences—including digital and, especially, online experiences—have paled in comparison to real-world experiences and they have been relatively unsuccessful as a result. What these solutions require is developers that understand what makes a good experience first, and then to translate these principles, as well

as possible, into the desired medium without the technology dictating the form of the experience." This is a very important design goal.

Psychologist Mihalyi Csikszentmihalyi has conducted extensive research exploring what makes different experiences optimally engaging, enjoyable, and productive. This research is a foundation for any understanding of experience design. Csikszentmihalyi (1991) explains, "The autotelic experience, or flow, lifts the course of life to a different level. Alienation gives way to involvement, enjoyment replaces boredom, helplessness turns into a feeling of control, and psychic energy works to reinforce the sense of self, instead of being lost in the service of external goals" (p. 69). Csikszentmihalyi has found that an optimum state of flow or "autotelic experience" is engaged when there is a clear set of goals requiring an appropriate response; when feedback is immediate; and when a person's skills are fully involved in overcoming a challenge that's high but manageable. When these three conditions are met, attention to task becomes ordered and fully engaged. A key element of an optimal experience is that it is an end in itself; even if undertaken for other reasons, the activity that engages us becomes intrinsically rewarding. This type of experience is fundamentally enjoyable.

Ackerman (1999) refers to this type of optimal experience as "deep play." As she explains, "play feels satisfying, absorbing, and has rules and a life of its own, while offering rare challenges. It gives us the opportunity to perfect ourselves. It's organic to who and what we are, a process as instinctive as breathing. Much of human life unfolds as play." Optimal experiences are the ultimate goal of experience design.

Economists Pine and Gilmore (1999) put this into a broader perspective (see Fig. 17.5). They hypothesize that we are moving from a service economy to an experience economy. "When a person buys a service, he purchases a set of intangible activities carried out on his behalf. But when he buys an experience, he pays to spend time enjoying a series of memorable events that a company stages—as in a theatrical play—to engage him in a personal way" (p. 2). In this context, experience type transactions occur whenever a company intentionally uses services as the stage and goods as props to engage an individual. "Buyers of experiences—we'll follow Disney's lead and call them guests—value being engaged by what the company reveals over a duration of time. Just as people have cut back on goods to spend more money on services, now they also scrutinize the time and money they spend on services to make way

Economic Offering	Services	Experiences
Economic Function	Deliver	Stage
Nature of Offering	Intangible	Memorable
Key Attribute	Customized	Personal
Method of Supply	Delivered on demand	Revealed over a duration
Seller	Provider	Stager
Buyer	Client	Guest
Factors of Demand	Benefits	Sensations

FIGURE 17.5. Economic distinctions between service and experience-based economic activities. Adapted from Pine and Gilmore (1999).

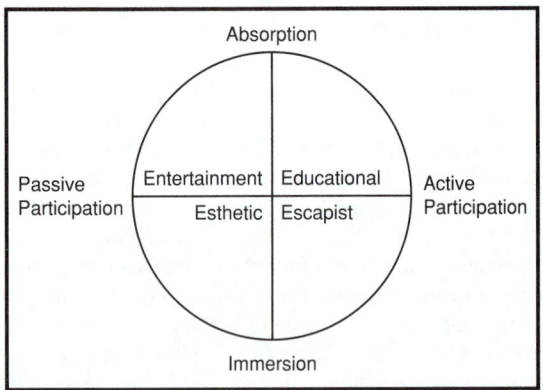

FIGURE 17.6. Realms of experience. Source: Pine and Gilmore (1999).

for more memorable—and more highly valued—experiences" (Pine & Gilmore, p. 12). While the work of the experience stager perishes, the value of the experience lingers, in contrast to service transactions.

Pine and Gilmore have proposed a model of different types of experience (Fig. 17.6). They recommend using this model as a framework for conceptualizing the aspects of each realm that might enhance the particular experience you wish to stage.

The coupling of these dimensions defines the four "realms" of an experience—entertainment, education, escape, and estheticism—mutually compatible domains that often commingle to form uniquely personal encounters. The kind of experiences most people think of as entertainment occur when they passively absorb the experiences through their senses, as generally occurs when viewing a performance, listening to music, or reading for pleasure.

Pine and Gilmore emphasize that in setting out to design a rich, compelling, and engaging experience, it is not necessary to stay in just one realm or quadrant. While many experiences engage the audience primarily through one of the four realms, most experiences in fact cross boundaries, combining elements from all four realms: the key is to find the best balance for each type of experience. The designer's goal is to find "the sweet spot"—the ideal combination—for any compelling experience to create the optimum experience, one that is memorable and that people want to return to again and again.

17.7 DESIGN MODELS AND METAPHORS

Developing design models and design metaphors will be an important aspect of theory-building, research, and development in the emerging virtual reality medium. A few models and design metaphors have emerged that are specifically for education and training.

Wickens (1993) and Wickens and Baker (1994) have proposed a model of virtual reality parameters that must be considered for instructional design. These analysts suggest that virtual reality can be conceptualized in terms of a set of five features,

	Less Real	More Real
1. Dimensionality	2D	3D
2. Motion	Static	Dynamic
3. Interaction	Open Loop	Closed Loop
4. Frame of reference	Outside-In	Inside-Out
	(God's eye)	(User's Eye)
	World-Referenced	Ego-Referenced
5. Multimodal Interaction	Limited	Multimodal
(Enhanced sensory experience)		

FIGURE 17.7. Five components of virtual reality. Adapted from Wickens and Baker (1994). (1) Three-dimensional (perspective and/or stereoscopic) viewing vs. two-dimensional planar viewing. Three-dimensional viewing potentially offers a more realistic view of the geography of an environment than a 2-D contour map. (2) Dynamic vs. static display. A dynamic display appears more real than a series of static images of the same material. (3) Closed-loop (interactive or learner-centered) vs. open-loop interaction. A more realistic closed-loop mode is one in which the learner has control over what aspect of the learning "world" is viewed or visited. That is, the learner is an active navigator as well as an observer. (4) Inside-out (ego-referenced) vs. outside-in (world-referenced) frame-of-reference. The more realistic inside-out frame of reference is one in which the image of the world on the display is viewed from the perspective of the point of ego-reference of the user (that point which is being manipulated by the control). (5) Multimodal interaction (enhanced sensory experience). Virtual environments employ a variety of techniques for user input, including speech recognition and gestures, either sensed through a "data glove" or captured by camera.

which are shown in Fig. 17.7. Any one of these five features can be present or absent to create a greater sense of reality. These analysts suggest that, based on these five elements, several justifications can be cited for using virtual reality as an educational tool. These justifications include: (1) Motivational value; (2) Transfer of learning environment; (3) Different perspective; and (4) Natural interface. According to Wickens and Baker (1994),

We may conceptualize the features of VR in terms of two overlapping goals: that of increasing the naturalness of the interface to reduce the cognitive effort required in navigation and interpretation, and that of creating dynamic interaction and novel perspective. It is important to keep the distinctions between these goals clear as we consider the conditions in which VR can facilitate or possibly inhibit learning. Specifically, we argue that those features of an interface that may reduce effort and increase performance, may actually reduce retention. (p. 4)

Based on this model, these analysts discuss the cognitive issues involved in using virtual reality for task performance and for learning applications. They suggest that virtual reality may prove useful for four types of educational tasks: (1) online performance; (2) off-line training and rehearsal; (3) online comprehension; and (4) off-line learning and knowledge acquisition. These four categories, and the examples of each category that the authors present, clearly reflect emerging training needs linked to high technology, as well as more traditional training needs.

Online performance refers to systems where the virtual environment is providing the operator with direct manipulation capabilities in a remote, or nonviewable environment. One example of this is the operation of a remote manipulator, such as an undersea robot, space shuttle arm, or hazardous waste handler, the control of a remotely piloted vehicle, or the task of navigating through a virtual data base to obtain a particular item. Wickens and Baker (1994) suggest that three general human performance concerns are relevant in these environments. These include: (a) closed-loop perceptual motor performance should be good (that is, errors should be small, reactions should be fast, and tracking of moving targets should be stable); (b) situation awareness should be high; and (c) workload or cognitive efforts should be low.

Concerning off-line training and rehearsal, Wickens and Baker (1994) suggest that virtual environments may serve as a tool for rehearsing critical actions in a safe environment, in preparation for target performance in a less forgiving one. According to Wickens and Baker (1994), "This may involve practicing lumbar injection for a spinal or epidural anesthesia, maneuvering a space craft, carrying out rehearsal flights prior to a dangerous mission, or practicing emergency procedures in an aircraft or nuclear power facility. The primary criterion here is the effective transfer of training from practice in the virtual environment to the true reality target environment" (p. 5). In terms of online comprehension, Wickens and Baker (1994) explain that the goal of interacting with a virtual environment may be to reach insight or understanding regarding the structure of an environment. This type of application is particularly valuable for scientists and others dealing with highly abstract data. Finally, off-line learning and knowledge acquisition concerns the transfer of knowledge, acquired in a virtual environment, to be employed, later in a different more abstract form (Wickens & Baker, 1994).

Wickens (1994) cautions that the goals of good interface design for the user and good design for the learner, while overlapping in many respects, are not identical. He points out that

a key feature in this overlap is the concern for the reduction in effort; many of the features of virtual reality may accomplish this reduction. Some of these features, like the naturalness of an interface which can replace arbitrary symbolic command and display strings, clearly serve the goals of both. But when effort-reduction features of virtual reality serve to circumvent cognitive transformations that are necessary to understanding and learning the relationships between different facets of data, or of a body of knowledge, then a disservice may be done. (p. 17)

Wickens also recommends that these design considerations should be kept in mind as virtual reality concepts are introduced into education. Also care should be taken to ensure redundancy of presentation formats, exploit the utility of visual momentum, exploit the benefits of closed-loop interaction, and use other principles of human factors design.

Wickens (1994) recommends that related human factors research concerning the characteristics of cognitive processes and tasks that may be used in a virtual environment should be taken into account. These factors include task analysis,

including search, navigation, perceptual biases, visual-motor coupling, manipulation, perception and inspection, and learning (including procedural learning, perceptual motor skill learning, spatial learning and navigational rehearsal, and conceptual learning). And Wickens suggests that there are three human factors principles relevant to the design of virtual environments—consistency, redundancy, and visual momentum—which have been shown to help performance and, also, if carefully applied, facilitate learning in such an environment.

A design metaphor for representing the actions of the VR instructional developer has been proposed by researchers at Lockheed (Grant, McCarthy, Pontecorvo, & Stiles, 1991). These researchers found that the most appropriate metaphor is that of a television studio, with a studio control booth, stage, and audience section. The control booth serves as the developer's information workspace, providing all the tools required for courseware development. The visual simulation and interactions with the system are carried out on the studio stage, where the trainee may participate and affect the outcome of a given instructional simulation. The audience metaphor allows passive observation, and if the instructional developer allows it, provides the trainee the freedom of movement within the virtual environment without affecting the simulation. For both the instructional developer and the student, the important spatial criteria are perspective, orientation, scale, level of visual detail, and granularity of simulation (Grant et al., 1991).

17.8 VIRTUAL REALITIES RESEARCH AND DEVELOPMENT

17.8.1 Research on VR and Training Effectiveness

Regian, Shebilske, and Monk (1992) report on empirical research that explored the instructional potential of immersive virtual reality as an interface for simulation-based training. According to these researchers, virtual reality may hold promise for simulation-based training because the interface preserves (a) visual-spatial characteristics of the simulated world, and (b) the linkage between motor actions of the student and resulting effects in the simulated world. This research featured two studies. In one study, learners learned how to use a virtual control console. In the other study, learners learned to navigate a virtual maze. In studying spatial cognition, it is useful to distinguish between small-scale and large-scale space (Siegal, 1981). Small-scale space can be viewed from a single vantage point at a single point in time. Large-scale space extends beyond the immediate vantage point of the viewer, and must be experienced across time. Subjects can construct functional representations of large-scale space from sequential, isolated views of small-scale space presented in two-dimensional media such as film (Hochberg, 1986) or computer graphics (Regian, 1986). Virtual reality, however, offers the possibility of presenting both small-scale and large-scale spatial information in a three-dimensional format that eliminates the need for students to translate the representation from 2-D to 3-D. The resulting reduction in cognitive load may benefit training. Regian et al. (1992) investigated the use of immersive virtual reality to teach procedural tasks requiring performance of motor sequences within small-scale space (the virtual console) and to teach navigational tasks requiring configurational knowledge of large-scale space (the virtual maze). In these studies, 31 subjects learned spatial-procedural skills and spatial-navigational skills in immersive virtual worlds accessed with head-mounted display and Dataglove™. Two VR worlds were created for this research: a virtual console and a virtual maze. Both were designed to support analogs of distinctly different tasks. The first was a procedural console-operations task and the second was a three-dimensional maze-navigation task. Each task involved a training phase and a testing phase. The console data show that subjects not only learned the procedure, but continued to acquire skill while being tested on the procedure, as the tests provided continued practice in executing the procedure. The maze data show that subjects learned three-dimensional, configurational knowledge of the virtual maze and were able to use the knowledge to navigate accurately within the virtual reality.

17.8.2 Research on Learners' Cognitive Visualization in 2-D and 3-D Environments

Merickel (1990, 1991) carried out a study designed to determine whether a relationship exists between the perceived realism of computer graphic images and the ability of children to solve spatially related problems. This project was designed to give children an opportunity to develop and amplify certain cognitive abilities: imagery, spatial relations, displacement and transformation, creativity, and spatially related problem solving. One way to enhance these cognitive abilities is to have students develop, displace, transform and interact with 2-D and 3-D computer-graphics models. The goal of this study was to determine if specially designed 2-D and 3-D computer graphic training would enhance any, or all, of these cognitive abilities. Merickel reports that experiments were performed using 23 subjects between the ages of 8 and 11 who were enrolled in an elementary summer school program in Novato, California. Two different computer apparatuses were used: computer workstations and an immersive virtual reality system developed by Autodesk, Inc. The students were divided into two groups. The first used microcomputers (workstations) equipped with AutoSketch and AutoCAD software. The other group worked with virtual reality. The workstation treatment incorporated three booklets to instruct the subjects on how to solve five different spatial relationship problems. The virtual reality system provided by Autodesk that was used in the virtual reality treatment included an 80386-based MS-DOS microcomputer, a head-mounted display and a VPL DataGlove™, a Polhemus 6D Isotrak positioning and head-tracking device; Matrox SM 1281 real-time graphics boards; and software developed at Autodesk. The cyberspace part of the project began with classroom training in the various techniques and physical gestures required for moving within and interacting with cyperspace modes. Each child was shown how the DataGlove™ and the head-mounted display would feel by first trying them on without being connected to the computer.

Merickel reports that after the practice runs, 14 children were given the opportunity to don the cyberspace apparatus and interact with two different computer-generated, 3D virtual realities. The DataGlove™ had to be calibrated. Students looked around the virtual world of an office, and using hand gesture commands, practiced moving toward objects and "picked up" objects in the virtual world. Students also practiced "flying" which was activated by pointing the index finger of the hand in the DataGlove™.

The second cyberspace voyage was designed to have students travel in a large "outdoor" space and find various objects including a sphere, a book, a chair, a racquet, and two cube models—not unlike a treasure hunt. But this treasure hunt had a few variations. One was that the two cube models were designed to see if the students could differentiate between a target model and its transformed (mirrored) image. The students' task was to identify which of the two models matched the untransformed target model. Students were instructed to fly to the models and study them; they were also instructed to fly around the models to see them from different viewpoints before making a choice. Most students were able to correctly identify the target model. Merickel reports that during this second time in cyberspace, most students were flying with little or no difficulty. Their gestures were more fluid and, therefore, so was their traveling in cyberspace. They began to relax and walk around more even though walking movement is restricted by the cables that attach the DataGlove™ and head-mounted display to the tracking devices. Students began to turn or walk around in order to track and find various items. They appeared to have no preconceived notions or reservations about "traveling inside a computer." In sum, these children had become quite proficient with this cutting-edge technology in a very short time.

Merickel reports that four cognitive ability tests were administered to the subjects from both treatment groups. The dependent variable (i.e., spatially related problem solving) was was measured with the Differential Aptitude Test. The three other measures (Minnesota Pager Form Board Test, Mental Rotation Test, and the Torrance Test of Creative Thinking) were used to partial out any effects which visualization abilities and the ability to mentally manipulate two-dimensional figures, displacement and transformation of mental images abilities, and creative thinking might have had on spatially related problem solving.

Merickel concluded that the relationships between perceived realism and spatially related problem solving were inconclusive based on the results of this study, but worthy of further study. Furthermore, Merickel points out that the ability to visualize and mentally manipulate two-dimensional objects are predictors of spatially related problem solving abilities. In sum, Merickel concluded that virtual reality is highly promising and deserves extensive development as an instructional tool.

17.8.3 Research on Children Designing and Exploring Virtual Worlds

Winn (1993) presented an overview of the educational initiatives that are either underway or planned at the Human Interface Technology Lab at the University of Washington: One goal is to establish a learning center to serve as a point of focus for research projects and instructional development initiatives, as well as a resource for researchers in kinesthesiology who are looking for experimental collaborator. A second goal is to conduct outreach, including plans to bring virtual reality to schools as well as pre- and in-service teacher training. Research objectives include the development of a theoretical framework, knowledge construction, and data-gathering about effectiveness of virtual reality for learning in different content areas and for different learners. Specific research questions include: (1) Can children build Virtual Reality worlds?, (2) Can children learn content by building worlds? and (3) Can children learn content by being in worlds built for them? Byrne (1992) and Bricken and Byrne (1993) report on a study that examined this first research issue—whether children can build VR worlds. This study featured an experimental program of week-long summer workshops at the Pacific Science Center where groups of children designed and then explored their own immersive virtual worlds. The primary focus was to evaluate VR's usefulness and appeal to students ages 10 to 15 years, documenting their behavior and soliciting their opinions as they used VR to construct and explore their own virtual worlds. Concurrently, the researchers used this opportunity to collect usability data that might point out system design issues particular to tailoring VR technology for learning applications.

Bricken and Byrne (1993) report that the student groups were limited to approximately 10 new students each week for 7 weeks. Participants were ages 10 years and older. A total of 59 students from ages 10 to 15 self-selected to participate over the 7-week period. The average age of students was 13 years, and the gender distribution was predominantly male (72%). The students were of relatively homogeneous ethnic origin; the majority were Caucasians, along with a few Asian Americans and African Americans. The group demonstrated familiarity with Macintosh computers, but none of the students had worked with 3-D graphics, or had heard of VR before coming to the VR workshops. The Macintosh modeling software package Swivel 3-D™ was used for creating the virtual worlds. Each student research group had access to five computers for 8 hours per day. They worked in groups of two or three to a computer. They used a codiscovery strategy in learning to use the modeling tools. Teachers answered the questions they could, however, the software was new to them as well so they could not readily answer all student questions. On the last day of each session, students were able to get inside their worlds using VR interface technology at the HIT Lab (the desktop Macintosh programs designed by the children with Swivel 3-D™ were converted over for use on more powerful computer workstations). Bricken and Byrne (1993) report that they wanted to see what what these students were motivated to do with VR when given access to the technology in an open-ended context. The researchers predicted that the participants would gain a basic understanding of VR technology. In addition, the researchers expected that in using the modeling software, this group might learn to color, cluster, scale, and link graphic primatives (cubes, spheres), to assemble simple geometric 3-D environments, and to specify basic interactions such as "grab a ball, fly it to the box, drop it in."

The participants' experience was designed to be a hands-on student-driven collaborative process in which they could learn about VR technology by using it and learn about virtual worlds by designing and constructing them. Their only constraints in this task were time and the inherent limitations of the technology. At the end of the week, students explored their worlds one at a time, while other group members watched what the participant was seeing on a large TV monitor. Although this was not a networked VR, it was a shared experience in that the kids "outside" the virtual world conversed with participants, often acting as guides. Bricken and Byrne (1993) report that the virtual worlds constructed by the students are the most visible demonstrations of the success of the world-building activity. In collecting information on both student response and system usability, Bricken and Byrne (1993) reported that they used three different information-gathering techniques. Their goal was to attain both cross-verification across techniques and technique-specific insights. They videotaped student activities, elicited student opinions with surveys, and collected informal observations from teachers and researchers. Each data source revealed different facets of the whole process. Bricken and Byrne (1993) reported that the students who participated in these workshops

were fascinated by the experience of creating and entering virtual worlds. Across the seven sessions, they consistently made the effort to submit a thoughtfully planned, carefully modeled, well-documented virtual world. All of these students were motivated to achieve functional competence in the skills required to design and model objects, demonstrated a willingness to focus significant effort toward a finished product, and expressed strong satisfaction with their accomplishment. Their virtual worlds are distinctive and imaginative in both conceptualization and implementation. Collaboration between students was highly cooperative, and every student contributed elements to their group's virtual world. The degree to which student-centered methodology influenced the results of the study may be another fruitful area for further research. (p. 204)

Bricken and Byrne (1993) report that students demonstrated rapid comprehension of complex concepts and skills.

They learned computer graphics concepts (real-time versus batch rendering, Cartesian coordinate space, object attributes), 3-D modeling techniques, and world design approaches. They learned about VR concepts ("what you do is what you get," presence) and enabling technology (head-mounted display, position and orientation sensing, 6-D interface devices). They also learned about data organization: Students were required by the modeling software to link graphical elements hierarchically, with explicit constraints; students printed out this data tree each week as part of the documentation process. (p. 205)

According to these researchers, this project revealed which of the present virtual reality system components were usable, which were distracting, and which were dysfunctional for this age group. The researchers' conclusion is that improvement in the display device is mandatory; the resolution was inadequate for object and location recognition, and hopeless for perception of detail. Another concern is with interactivity tools. This study showed that manipulating objects with the DataGlove™ is awkward and unnatural. Bricken and Byrne (1993) also report that the head-mounted display has since been replaced with a boom-mounted display for lighter weight and a less intrusive cable arrangement. In sum, students, teachers, and researchers agreed that this exploration of VR tools and technology was a successful experience for everyone involved (Bricken & Byrne, 1993; Byrne, 1992). Most important was the demonstration of students' desires and abilities to use virtual reality *constructively* to build expressions of their knowledge and imagination. They suggest that virtual reality is a significantly compelling environment in which to teach and learn. Students could learn by creating virtual worlds that reflected the evolution of their skills and the pattern of their conceptual growth. For teachers, evaluating comprehension and competence would become experiential as well as analytical, as they explored the worlds of thought constructed by their students.

17.8.4 Research on Learners in Experiential Learning Environments

An experiential learning environment was developed and studied at the Boston Computer Museum, using immersive virtual reality technology (Gay, 1993, 1994b; Greschler, 1994). The Cell Biology Project was funded by the National Science Foundation. David Greschler, of the Boston Computer Museum, explains that in this case, the NSF was interested in testing how VR can impact informal education (that is, self-directed, unstructured learning experiences). So an application was developed in two formats (immersive VR and flat panel screen desktop VR) to study virtual reality as an informal learning tool. A key issue was: what do learners do once they're in the virtual world? In this application, participants had the opportunity to build virtual human cells and learn about cell biology. As Greschler explains, they looked at

the basics of the cell. First of all the cell is made up of things called organelles. Now these organelles, they perform different functions. Human cells: if you open most textbooks on human cells they show you one picture of one human cell and they show you organelles. But what we found out very quickly, in fact, is that there are different kinds of human cells. Like there's a neuron, and there's an intestinal cell, and there's a muscle cell. And all those cells are not the same at the basic level. They're different. They have different proportions of organelles, based on the kinds of needs that they have. For instance, a muscle cell needs more power, because it needs to be doing more work. And so as a result, it needs more mitochondrias, which is really the powerhouse. So we wanted to try to get across these basic principles.

In the Cell Biology Virtual World, the user would start by coming up to this girl within the virtual world who would say, "Please help me, I need neuron cells to think with, muscle cells to move with, and stomach cells to eat with." So you would either touch the stomach or the leg or the head and "you'd end up into the world where there was the neuron cell or the muscle cell or the intestinal cell and you would have all the pieces of that cell around you and marked and you would actually go around and build." You would go over, pick up the mitochondria, and move it into the cell. As Greschler (1994) explains, "there's a real sense of accomplishment, a real sense of building. And then, in addition to that, you would build this person." Greschler reports that before trying to compare the different media versions of the cell biology world, "[the designers] sort of said, we have to make sure our virtual world is good and people like it. It's one thing to just go for the educational point of

view but you've got to get a good experience or else big deal. So the first thing we did, we decided to build a really good world. And be less concerned about the educational components so much as a great experience." That way, people would want to experience the virtual world, so that learning would occur. A pilot virtual world was built and tested and improvements were made. Greschler reports,

...we found that it needed more information. There needs to be some sort of introduction to how to navigate in the virtual world. A lot of people didn't know how to move their hand tracker and so on. So what we did is we felt like, having revised the world, we'd come up with a world that was...I suppose you could say "Good." It was compelling to people and that people liked it. To us that was very important.

They defined virtual reality in terms of immersion, natural interaction (via hand trackers), and interactivity—the user could control the world and move through it at will by walking around in the head mount (within a perimeter of 10 × 10 feet).

Testing with visitors at the Boston Computer Museum indicated that the nonimmersive desktop group consistently was able to retain more information about the cells and the organelles (at least for the short term). This group retained more cognitive information. However, in terms of level of engagement, the immersive VR group was much stronger with that. They underestimated the amount of time they were in the virtual world by, on average, more than 5 minutes, far more than the other group. In terms of conclusions, Greschler (1994) suggests that immersive virtual reality "probably isn't good for getting across factual information. What it might be good for is more general experiences; getting a sense for how one might do things like travel. I mean the whole idea [of the Cell Biology Project] is traveling into a cell. It's more getting a sense of what a cell is, rather than the facts behind it. So it's more perhaps like a visualization tool or something just to get a feel for certain ideas rather than getting across fact a, b, or c."

Furthermore, "I think the whole point of this is it's all new...We're still trying to figure out the right grammar for it, the right uses for it. I mean video is great to get across a lot of stuff. Sometimes it just isn't the right thing to use. Books are great for a lot of things, but sometimes they're just not quite right. I think what we're still trying to figure out is what is that 'quite right' thing for VR. There's clearly something there—there's an incredible level of engagement. And concentration. That's I think probably the most important thing." Greschler (1994) thinks that virtual reality will be a good tool for informal learning. "And my hope in fact, is that it will bring more informal learning into formal learning environments because I think that there needs to be more of that. More open-endedness, more exploration, more exploratory versus explanatory" (Greschler, 1994).

17.8.5 Research on Attitudes Toward Virtual Reality

Heeter (1992, 1994) has studied people's attitudinal responses to virtual reality. In one study, she studied how players responded to BattleTech, one of the earliest virtual reality location-based entertainment systems. Related to this, Heeter has examined differences in responses based on gender, since a much higher proportion of BattleTech players are males (just as with videogames). Heeter conducted a study of BattleTech players at the Virtual Worlds Entertainment Center in Chicago.

In the BattleTech study, players were given questionnaires when they purchased playing times, to be turned in after the game (Heeter, 1992). A total of 312 completed questionnaires were collected, for a completion rate of 34 percent. (One questionnaire was collected per person; at least 45 percent of the 1,644 games sold during the sample days represented repeat plays within the sample period.) Different questionnaires were administered for each of three classes of players: novices, who had played 1 to 10 BattleTech games ($n = 223$; veterans, who had played 11 to 50 games ($n = 42$); and masters, who had played more than 50 games ($n = 47$).

According to Heeter (1992), the results of this study indicate that BattleTech fits the criteria of Czikszentmihalyi's (1990) model of "flow" or optimal experience: (1) require learning of skills; (2) have concrete goals; (3) provide feedback; (4) let person feel in control; (5) facilitate concentration and involvement; and (6) are distinct from the everyday world ("paramount reality"). Heeter (1992) explains:

BattleTech fits these criteria very well. Playing BattleTech is hard. It's confusing and intimidating at first. Feedback is extensive and varied. There are sensors; six selectable viewscreens with different information which show the location of other players (nearby and broader viewpoint), condition of your 'Mech, heat sensors, feedback on which 'Mechs are in weapon range (if any), and more. After the game, there is additional feedback in the form of individual scores on a video display and also a complete printout summarizing every shot fired by any of the six concurrent players and what happened as a result of the shot. In fact, there is far more feedback than new players can attend to. (p. 67).

According to Heeter (1992), "BattleTech may be a little too challenging for novices, scaring away potential players. There is a tension between designing for novices and designing for long term play. One-third of novices feel there are too many buttons and controls" (p. 67). Novices who pay to play BattleTech may feel intimidated by the complexity of BattleTech controls and some potential novices may even be so intimidated by that complexity that they are scared away completely, that complexity is most likely scaring other potential novices away. But among veterans and masters, only 14 percent feel there are too many buttons and controls, while almost 40 percent say it's just right.).

Heeter (1992) reports that if participants have their way, virtual reality will be a very social technology. The BattleTech data identify consistently strong desires for interacting with real humans in addition to virtual beings and environments in virtual reality. Just 2 percent of respondents would prefer to play against computers only. Fifty-eight percent wanted to play against humans only, and 40 percent wanted to play against a combination of computers and humans. Respondents preferred playing on teams (71 percent) rather than everyone against everyone (29 percent). Learning to cooperate with others in team play was considered the most challenging BattleTech skill by masters, who estimated on average that it takes 56 games to learn how

to cooperate effectively. Six players at a time was not considered enough. Veterans rated "more players at once" 7.1 on a 10-point scale of importance of factors to improve the game; more players was even more important to masters (8.1). In sum, Heeter concludes that "Both the commercial success of BattleTech and the findings of the survey say that BattleTech is definitely doing some things right and offers some lessons to designers of future virtual worlds" (p. 67).

Heeter (1992) reports that BattleTech players are mostly male. Masters are 98 percent male, veterans are 95 percent male, and novices are 91 percent male. BattleTech is not a child's game. Significant gender differences were found in reactions to BattleTech. Because such a small percentage of veterans and masters were female, gender comparisons for BattleTech were conducted only among novices. (Significant differences using one-way ANOVA for continuous data and Crosstabs for categorical data are identified in the text by a single asterisk for cases of $p < .05$ and double asterisk for stronger probability levels of $p < .01$.) Specifically, 2 percent of masters, 5 percent of veterans, and 9 percent of novices were female. This small group of females who chose to play BattleTech might be expected to be more similar to the males who play BattleTech than would females in general. Even so, gender differences in BattleTech responses were numerous and followed a distinct, predictable stereotypical pattern. For example, on a scale from 0 to 10, female novices found BattleTech to be LESS RELAXING (1.1 vs. 2.9) and MORE EMBARRASSING (4.1 vs. 2.0) than did male novices. Males were more aware of where their opponents were than females were (63 vs. 33 percent) and of when they hit an opponent (66 vs. 39 percent). Female BattleTech players enjoyed blowing people up less than males did, although both sexes enjoyed blowing people up a great deal (2.4 vs. 1.5 out of 7, where 1 is VERY MUCH). Females reported that they did not understand how to drive the robot as well (4.6 compared to 3.1 for males where 7 is NOT AT ALL). Fifty-seven percent of female novices said they would prefer that BattleTech cockpits have fewer than its 100+ buttons and controls, compared to 28 percent of male novices who wanted fewer controls.

Heeter (1994) concludes, "Today's consumer VR experiences appear to hold little appeal for the female half of the population. Demographics collected at the BattleTech Center in Chicago in 1991 indicated that 93 percent of the players were male." At FighterTown the proportion was 97 percent. Women also do not play today's video games. Although it is clear that women are not attracted to the current battle-oriented VR experiences, what women DO want from VR has received little attention. Whether from a moral imperative to enable VR to enrich the lives of both sexes, or from a financial incentive of capturing another 50 percent of the potential marketplace, or from a personal curiosity about the differences between females and males, insights into this question should be of considerable interest.

In another study, Heeter (1993) explored what types of virtual reality applications might appeal to people, both men and women. Heeter conducted a survey of students in a large-enrollment "Information Society" Telecommunications course at Michigan State University, where the students were willing to answer a 20-minute questionnaire, followed by a guest lecture about consumer VR games. The full study was conducted with 203 students. Sixty-one percent of the 203 respondents were male. Average age was 20, ranging from 17 to 32. To summarize findings from this exploratory study, here is what women DO want from VR experiences. They are strongly attracted to the idea of virtual travel. They would also be very interested in some form of virtual comedy, adventure, MTV, or drama. Virtual presence at live events is consistently rated positively, although not top on the list. The females in this study want very much to interact with other live humans in virtual environments, be it virtual travel, virtual fitness, or other experiences. If they play a game, they want it to be based most on exploration and creativity. Physical sensations and emotional experiences are important. They want the virtual reality experience to have meaningful parallels to real life.

Heeter (1993) reported that another line of virtual reality research in the Michigan State University Comm Tech Lab involves the development of virtual reality prototype experiences demonstrating different design concepts. Data is collected from attendees at various conferences who try using the prototype.

17.8.6 Research on Special Education Applications of VR

Virtual reality appears to offer many potentials as a tool that can enhance capabilities for the disabled in the areas of communication, perception, mobility, and access to tools (Marcus, 1993; Murphy, 1994; Middleton, 1993; Pausch, Vogtle, & Conway, 1991; Pausch & Williams, 1991; Treviranus, 1993; Warner and Jacobson, 1992). Virtual reality can extend, enhance, and supplement the remaining capabilities of people who must contend with a disability such as deafness or blindness. And virtual reality offers potential as a rehabilitation tool. Delaney (1993) predicts that virtual reality will be instrumental in providing physical capabilities for persons with disabilities in the following areas:

1. Individuals with movement restricting disabilities could be in one location while their "virtual being" is in a totally different location—this opens up possibilities for participating in work, study, or leisure activities anywhere in the world, from home, or even a hospital bed
2. Individuals with physical disabilities could interact with the real world through robotic devices they control from within a virtual world
3. Blind persons could navigate through or among buildings represented in a virtual world made up of 3-D sound images—this will be helpful to rehearse travel to unfamiliar places such as hotels or conference centers
4. Learning disabled, cognitively impaired, and brain injured individuals could control work processes that would otherwise be too complicated by transforming the tasks into a simpler form in a VR environment
5. Designers and others involved in the design of prosthetic and assistive devices may be able to experience the reality of a person with a disability—they could take on the disability in

virtual reality, and thus experience problems firsthand, and their potential solutions.

At a conference on "Virtual Reality and Persons with Disabilities" that has been held annually in San Francisco since 1992 (sponsored by the Center on Disabilities at California State University Northridge) researchers and developers report on their work. This conference was established partly in response to the national policy, embedded in two separate pieces of legislation: Section 504 of the Rehabilitation Act of 1973, and the Americans with Disabilities Act (ADA). Within these laws is the overriding mandate for persons with disabilities to have equal access to electronic equipment and information. The recently-enacted American Disabilities Act offers potential as a catalyst for the development of virtual reality technologies. Harry Murphy (1994), the Director of the Center on Disabilities at California State University Northridge, explains that "Virtual reality is not a cure for disability. It is a helpful tool, and like all other helpful tools, television and computers, for example, we need to consider access" (p. 59). Murphy (1994) argues that, "Virtuality and virtual reality hold benefits for everyone. The same benefits that anyone might realize have some special implications for people with disabilities, to be sure. However, our thinking should be for the general good of society, as well as the special benefits that might come to people with disabilities" (p. 57). Many virtual reality applications for persons with disabilities are under development, showing great promise, but few have been rigorously tested. One award-winning application is the Wheelchair VR application from Prairie Virtual Systems of Chicago (Trimble, 1993). With this application, wheelchair-bound individuals "roll through" a virtual model of a building such as a hospital that is under design by an architect and tests whether the design supports wheelchair access. Related to this, Dean Inman, an orthopedic research scientist at the Oregon Research Institute is using virtual reality to teach kids the skills of driving wheelchairs (Buckert-Donelson, 1995).

Virtual Technologies of Palo Alto, California has developed a "talking glove" application that makes it possible for deaf individuals to "speak" sign language while wearing a wired glove and have their hand gestures translated into English and printed on a computer screen, so that they can communicate more easily with those who do not speak sign language. Similar to this, Eberhart (1993) has developed a much less powerful noncommercial system that utilizes the Power Glove™ toy as an interface, together with an Echo Speech Synthesizer. Eberhart (1993) is exploring neural networks in conjunction with the design of VR applications for the disabled. Eberhart trained the computer to recognize the glove movements by training a neural network.

Newby (1993) described another much more sophisticated gesture-recognition system than the one demonstrated by Eberhart. In this application, a DataGlove™ and Polhemus tracker are employed to measure hand location and finger position to train for a number of different hand gestures. Native users of American Sign Language (ASL) helped in the development of this application by providing templates of the letters of the manual alphabet, then giving feedback on how accurately the program was able to recognize gestures within various tolerance calibrations. A least-squares algorithm was used to measure the difference between a given gesture and the set of known gestures that the system had been trained to recognize.

Greenleaf (1993) described the GloveTalker, a computer-based gesture-to-speech communication device for the vocally impaired that uses a modified DataGlove™. The wearer of the GloveTalker speaks by signaling the computer with his or her personalized set of gestures. The DataGlove™ transmits the gesture signals through its fiber optic sensors to the Voice Synthesis System, which speaks for the DataGlove™ wearer. This system allows individuals who are temporarily or permanently impaired vocally to communicate verbally with the hearing world through hand gestures. Unlike the use of sign language, the GloveTalker does not require either the speaker or the listener to know American Sign Language (ASL). The GloveTalker itself functions as a gesture interpreter: the computer automatically translates hand movements and gestures into spoken output. The wearer of the GloveTalker creates a library of personalized gestures on the computer that can be accessed to rapidly communicate spoken phrases. The voice output can be sent over a computer network or over a telephone system, thus enabling vocally impaired individuals to communicate verbally over a distance. The GloveTalker system can also be used for a wide array of other applications involving data gathering and data visualization. For example, an instrumented glove is used to measure the progress of arm and hand tremors in patients with Parkinson's disease.

The Shepherd School, the largest special school in the United Kingdom, is working with a virtual reality research team at Nottingham University (Lowe, 1994). The Shephard School is exploring the benefits of virtual reality as a way of teaching children with complex problems to communicate and gain control over their environment.

Researchers at the Hugh Macmillan Center in Toronto, Canada are exploring virtual reality applications involving Mandala and the Very Nervous System, a responsive musical environment developed by artist David Rokeby that is activated by movement so that it "plays" interactive musical compositions based on the position and quality of the movement in front of the sensor; the faster the motions, the higher the tones (Treviranus, 1993). Rokeby has developed several interactive compositions for this system (Cooper, 1995).

Salcedo and Salcedo (1993) of the Blind Children Learning Center in Santa Ana, California report that they are using the Amiga computer, Mandala software, and a videocamera to increase the quantity and quality of movement in young children with visual impairments. With this system, children receive increased feedback from their movements through the musical sounds their movements generate. Related to this is the VIDI MICE, a low-cost program available from Tensor Productions which interfaces with the Amiga computer (Jacobs, 1991).

Massof (1993) reports that a project is underway (involving collaboration by Johns Hopkins University, NASA, and the Veterans Administration) where the goal is to develop a head-mounted video display system for the visually impaired that incorporates custom-prescribed, real-time image processing

designed to enhance the vision of the user. A prototype of this technology has been developed and is being tested.

Nemire, Burke, and Jacoby (1993) of Interface Technologies in Capitola, California report that they have developed a virtual learning environment for physics instruction for disabled students. This application has been developed to provide an immersive, interactive, and intuitive virtual learning environment for these students.

Important efforts at theory building concerning virtual reality and persons with disabilities have been initiated. For example, Mendenhall and Vanderheiden (1993) have conceptualized two classification schemes (virtual reality versus virtual altered reality) for better understanding the opportunities and barriers presented by virtual reality systems to persons with disabilites. And Marsh, Meisel, and Meisel (1993) have examined virtual reality in relation to human evolution. These researchers suggested that virtual reality can be considered a conscious reentering of the process of evolution. Within this reconceptualization of the context of survival of the fittest, disability becomes far less arbitrary. In practical terms, virtual reality can bring new meaning to the emerging concepts of universal design, rehabilitation engineering, and adaptive technology.

Related to this, Lasko-Harvill (1993) commented,

In Virtual Reality the distinction between people with and without disabilities disappears. The difference between Virtual Reality and other forms of computer simulation lies in the ability of the participant to interact with the computer generated environment as though he or she was actually inside of it, and no one can do that without what are called in one context "assistive" devices and another "user interface" devices.

This is an important comparison to make, pointing out that user interfaces can be conceived as assistive technologies for the fully abled as well as the disabled. Lasko-Harvill explains that virtual reality can have a leveling effect between abled and differently abled individuals. This is similar to what the Lakeland Group found in their training program for team-building at Virtual Worlds Entertainment Centers (McGrath, 1994; McLellan, 1994a).

17.9 IMPLICATIONS

This emerging panoply of technologies—virtual realities—offers many potentials and implications. This chapter has outlined these potentials and implications, although they are subject to change and expansion as this very new set of educational technologies, virtual realities, develops. It is important to reiterate that since virtual realities as a distinct category of educational technology are little more than a decade old, research and development are at an early stage. And rapid technological improvements mean that existing research concerning virtual realities must be assessed carefully since it may be rapidly outdated with the advent of improved technological capabilities such as graphics resolution for visual displays, increased processing speed, ergonomically enhanced, lighter-weight interface design, and greater mobility. The improvements in technology over the past decade give testament to the speed of technological improvements that researchers must keep in mind. Research and development programs are underway throughout the world to study the potentials of virtual reality technologies and applications, including education and training. There is a wealth of possibilities for research. As discussed in this chapter, the agenda for needed research is quite broad in scope.

And as many analysts have pointed out, there is a broad base of research in related fields such as simulation and human perception that can and must be considered in establishing a research agenda for virtual reality overall, and concerning educational potentials of virtual reality in particular. Research can be expected to expand as the technology improves and becomes less expensive.

References

Ackerman, D. (1999). *Deep Play.* New York: Random House.

Alternate Realities Corporation (ARC) (1998). *How does the VisionDome work?* Durham, NC: Alternate Realities Corporation. http://www.acadia.org/competition-98/sites/integrus.com/html/library/tech/www.virtual-reality.com/technology.html (pp. 1–6).

Amburn, P. (1992, June 1). *Mission planning and debriefing using head-mounted display systems.* 1992 EFDPMA Conference on Virtual Reality. Education Foundation of the Data Processing Management Association. Washington, D.C.

Aukstalnis, S., & Blatner, D. (1992). *Silicon mirage: The art and science of virtual reality.* Berkeley, CA: Peachpit Press.

Auld, L., & Pantelidis, V. S. (1999, November). The Virtual Reality and Education Laboratory at East Carolina University. *THE Journal, 27*(4), 48–55.

Auld, L. W. S., & Pantelidis, V. S. (1994, January/February). Exploring virtual reality for classroom use: The Virtual Reality and Education Lab at East Carolina University. *TechTrends, 39*(2), 29–31.

Azuma, R. (1993, July). Tracking requirements for augmented reality. *Communications of the ACM, 36*(7) 50–51.

Azuma, R. (August 1997). A survey of augmented reality. *Presence: Teleoperators and Virtual Environments, 6*(4), 355–385.

Azuma, R. (1999). *Augmented reality.* http://www.cs.unc.edu/~azuma/azuma_AR.html (pp. 1–4).

Azuma, R., & Bishop, G. (1994). Improving static and dynamic registration in an optical see-through HMD *Proceedings of SIGGRAPH '94,* 197–204.

Azuma, R., & Bishop, G. (1995, August). A frequency-domain analysis of head-motion prediction. *Proceedings of SIGGRAPH '95,* 401–408.

Badler, N. I., Barsky, B., & Zeltzer, D. (Eds.). (1991). *Making them move: Mechanics, control and animation of articulated figures.* San Mateo, CA: Morgan Kaufman.

Baecker, R. M. (Ed.). (1993). *Readings in groupware and computer-supported cooperative work.* San Mateo, CA: Morgan Kaufman.

Baird, J. B. (1992, September 6). New from the computer: 'Cartoons' for the courtroom. *New York Times.*

Barfield, W., & Furness, T. A., III. (Eds). (June 1997). *Virtual environments and advanced interface design.* Oxford University Press.

Bates, J. (1992). Virtual reality, art, and entertainment. *Presence, 1*(1), 133–138.

Begault, D. R. (1991, September 23). *3-D sound for virtual reality: The possible and the probable.* Paper presented at the Virtual Reality '91 Conference, San Francisco, CA.

Behringer, R., Mizell, D., & Klinker, G. (2001, August). International Workshop on Augmented Reality. *VR News, 8*(1). http://www.vrnews.com/issuearchive/vrn0801/vrn0801augr.html

Bell, B., Hawkins, J., Loftin, R. B., Carey, T., & Kass, A. (1998). The Use of 'War Stories' in Intelligent Learning Environments. *Intelligent Tutoring Systems,* 619.

Bevin, M. (2001, January). Head-mounted displays. *VR News, 10*(1).

Biocca, F. (1992a). Communication within virtual reality: Creating a space for research. *Journal of Communication, 42*(4), 5–22.

Biocca, F. (1992b). *Communication design for virtual environments.* Paper presented at the Meckler Virtual Reality '92 Conference, San Jose, California.

Boman, D., Piantanida, T., & Schlager, M. (1993, February). *Virtual environment systems for maintenance training.* Final Report, Volumes 1–4. Menlo Park, CA: SRI International.

Bradbury, Ray (1951). The Veldt. In *Illustrated man.* New York: Doubleday.

Brennan, J. (1994, November 30). *Delivery room of the future.* Paper presented at the Virtual Reality Expo '94. New York City.

Bricken, W. (1990). *Learning in virtual reality.* Memorandum HITL-M-90-5. Seattle, WA: University of Washington, Human Interface Technology Laboratory.

Bricken, M. (1991). *Virtual reality learning environments: Potentials and challenges.* Human Interface Technology Laboratory Technical Publication No. HITL-P-91-5. Seattle, WA: Human Interface Technology Laboratory.

Bricken, M., & Byrne, C. (1992). *Summer students in virtual reality: A pilot study on educational applications of VR technology.* Report R-92-1. Seattle, WA: University of Washington, Human Interface Technology Laboratory.

Bricken, M., & Byrne, C. M., (1993). Summer students in virtual reality: A pilot study on educational applications of virtual reality technology. In Alan Wexelblat (Ed.), *Virtual reality: Applications and explorations.* (pp. 199–218). Boston: Academic Press Professional.

Brill, L. (1993). Metaphors for the traveling cybernaut. *Virtual Reality World, 1*(1), q-s.

Brill, L. (1994a, January/February). The networked VR museum. *Virtual Reality World, 2*(1), 12–17.

Brill, L. (1994b, May/June). Metaphors for the traveling cybernaut—Part II. *Virtual Reality World, 2*(3), 30–33.

Brill, L. (1994c, November/December). Museum VR: Part I. *Virtual Reality World, 1*(6), 33–40.

Brill, L. (1995, January/February). Museum VR: Part II. *Virtual Reality World, 3*(1), 36–43.

Britton, D. (1994, December 1). *VR tour of the LASCAUX Cave.* Paper presented at the Virtual Reality Expo '94. New York City.

Brooks, F. P., Jr. (1988). Grasping reality through illusion: Interactive graphics serving science. In E., Soloway, D., Frye, & S. Sheppard, (Eds.), *CHI'88 Proceedings,* (pp. 1–13).

Brown, J. S., Collins, A., & Duguid, P. (1989). Situated cognition and the culture of learning. *Educational Researcher, 18*(1), 32–42.

Bruckman, A., & Resnick, M. (1993, May). *Virtual professional community, results from the Media MOO Project.* Paper presented at the Third International Conference on Cyberspace (3Cybercon). Austin, TX.

Buckert-Donelson, A. (1995, January/February). Dean Inman. *Virtual Reality World, 3*(10), 23–26.

Burrow, M. (1994, November 30). *Telemedicine.* Paper presented at the Virtual Reality Expo '94, New York.

Buxton, B. (1992). Snow's two cultures revisited: Perspectives on human-computer interface design. In Linda Jacobson (Ed.). *Cyber-Arts: Exploring art and technology* (pp. 24–38).

Byrne, C. (1992, Winter). Students explore VR technology. *HIT Lab Review,* 6–7.

Byrne, C. (1993). Virtual reality and education. *Proceedings of IFIP WG3.5 International Workshop Conference,* pp. 181–189.

Byrne, C. (1996). *Water on tap: The use of virtual reality as an educational tool.* Doctoral Dissertation, University of Washington, Human Interface Technology Lab.

Calvert, T. W., Bruderlin, A., Dill, J., Schiphorst, T., & Welman, C. (1993, May). Desktop animation of multiple human figures. *IEEE Computer Graphics and Applications, 13*(3), 18–26.

Carande, R. J. (1993). *Information sources for virtual reality: A research guide.* Westport, CT: Greenwood Press.

Carmichael, M., Kovach, G., Mandel, A., & Wehunt, J. (2001, June 25). Virtual-reality therapy. *Newsweek,* 53.

Carson, B. (1999). *The big picture.* Grand Rapids, MI: Zondervan Publishing House.

Chen, D. T., Kakadiaris, I. K., Miller, M. J., Loftin, R. B., & Patrick, C. (2000). Modeling for plastic and reconstructive breast surgery. *Medical Image Computing and Computer-Assisted Intervention (MICCAI) Conference Proceedings,* pp. 1040–1050.

Coats, G. (1994, May 13). *VR in the theater.* Paper presented at the Meckler Virtual Reality '94 Conference, San Jose, CA.

Coleman, D. D. (Ed.). (1993). *Groupware '93 Proceedings.* San Mateo, CA: Morgan Kaufman.

Coleman, M. M. (Nov. 15, 1999). The cyber waiting room: A glimpse at the new practice of telemedicine. *The Internet Law Journal.* http://www.tilj.com/content/healtharticle11159902.htm.

Connell, A. (1992, September 18). *VR in Europe.* Preconference Tutorial. Meckler Virtual Reality '92 Conference, San Jose, California.

Cooper, D. (1995, March). Very nervous system. *Wired, 3*(3), 134+.

Cruz-Nierna, C. (1993, May 19). *The cave.* Paper presented at the Meckler Virtual Reality '93 Conference, San Jose, CA.

Czikszentmihalyi, M. (1990). *Flow: The psychology of optimum experience.* New York: Harper & Row.

Dede, C. (1990, May). Visualizing cognition: Depicting mental models in cyberspace (Abstract). In M. Benedikt, (Ed.), *Collected abstracts from the first conference on cyberspace.* (pp. 20–21). Austin, TX: School of Architecture, University of Texas.

Dede, C. (1992, May). The future of multimedia: Bridging to virtual worlds. *Educational Technology, 32*(5), 54–60.

Dede, C. (1993, May 7). *ICAT-VET conference highlights.* Paper presented at the 1993 Conference on Intelligent Computer-Aided Training and Virtual Environment Technology, Houston, TX.

Dede, C., Loftin, R. B., & Salzman, M. (1994, September 15). *The potential of virtual reality technology to improve science education.* Paper presented at the Conference on New Media for Global Communication from an East West Perspective. Moscow, Russia.

Dede, C. J., Salzman, M. C., & Loftin, R. B. (1994). The development of a virtual world for learning Newtonian mechanics. *MHVR 1994,* 87–106.

DeFanti, T. A., Sandin, D. J., & Cruz-Neira, C. (1993, October). A 'room' with a view. *IEEE Spectrum, 30*(10), 30–33.

Delaney, B. (1993, Fall). VR and persons with disabilities. *Medicine and Biotechnology: Cyberedge Journal Special Edition,* 3.

Delaney, B. (2000, April/May). Thoughts on the state of virtual reality. *Real Time Graphics, 8*(9), 1–2.

Dell Computer Corporation (1999). *Ultima online.* http://www.dell.com/us/en/dhs/browser/article_0103_ultima_2.htm.

Design Research Laboratory. (2001). *The VisionDome.* Durham, NC: Design Research Laboratory of North Carolina State University. http://www.design.ncsu.edu/research/Design-Lab/dome/

Ditlea, S. (1993, June). Virtual reality: How Jaron Lanier created an industry but lost his company. *Upside, 5*(6), 8–21.

Donelson, A. (1994, November/December). Fighting fires in virtual worlds. *Virtual Reality World, 2*(6), 6–7.

Dovey, M. E. (1994, July). Virtual reality: Training in the 21st century. *Marine Corps Gazette, 78*(7), 23–26.

Dowding, T. J. (1991, September 23). *Kinesthetic training devices.* Paper presented at the Virtual Reality '91 Conference, San Francisco, CA.

Dowding, T. J. (1992, A self-contained interactive motorskill trainer. In: S. K. Helsel (Ed.). *Beyond the vision: The technology, research, and business of virtual reality: Proceedings of Virtual Reality '91, the Second Annual Conference on Virtual Reality, Artificial Reality, and Cyberspace.* Westport, CT: Meckler.

Dunkley, P. (1994, May 14). Virtual reality in medical training. *Lancet,* 343(8907), 1218.

Earnshaw, R. A., Vince, J. A., Guedj, R. A., & Van Dam, A. (Ed.). (2001). *Frontiers in human-centred computing, online communities and virtual environments.* New York: Springer-Verlag.

Eberhart, R. (1993, June 17) *Glove Talk for $100.* Paper presented at the 1993 Conference on Virtual Reality and Persons with Disabilities, San Francisco, CA.

Eckhouse, J. (1993, May 20). Technology offers new view of world. *San Francisco Chronicle,* A1, A15.

EDS (1991). *EDS: Bringing JASON's vision home.* Dallas, TX: Author. [Brochure].

Ellis, S. (1991). Nature and origins of virtual environments: A bibliographical essay. *Computing Systems in Engineering, 2*(4), 321–347.

Ellis, S. (Ed.). (1992). *Pictorial communication in virtual and real environments.* New York: Taylor and Francis.

Elumens Corporation, Inc. (2001). VisionDome Models. http://www.elumens.com/products/visiondome.html

Emerson, T. (1994). Virtual interface technology: Selected citations on education and training applicatons (EdVR). Bibliography B-94-3. Seattle, WA: University of Washington, Human Interface Technology Laboratory.

Erickson, T. (1993). Artificial realities as data visualization environments. In Alan Wexelblat (Ed.), *Virtual reality: Applications and explorations* (pp. 1–22). Boston: Academic Press Professional.

Feiner, S., MacIntyre, B. Höllerer, T., & Webster, T. (1997, October). A touring machine: Prototyping 3D mobile augmented reality systems for exploring the urban environment. In *Proceedings of the ISWC '97 (First International Symposium on Wearable Computers),* 208–217.

Fennington, G., & Loge, K. (1992, April). Virtual reality: A new learning environment. *The Computing Teacher, 20*(7), 16–19.

Fisher, P. and Unwin, D. (2002). *Virtual reality in geography.* London: Taylor & Francis.

Flack, J. F. (1993, May 19). *First person cab simulator.* Paper presented at the Meckler Virtual Reality '93 Conference, San Jose, California.

Fontaine, G. (1992, Fall). The experience of a sense of presence in intercultural and international encounters. *Presence, 1*(4), 482–490.

Frenkel, K. A. (1994). A conversation with Brenda Laurel. *Interactions, 1*(1), 44–53.

Frere, C. L., Crout, R., Yorty, J., & McNeil, D. W. (2001, July). Effects of audiovisual distraction during dental prophylaxis. *The Journal of the American Dental Association (JADA), 132*(7), 1031–1038.

Fritz, M. (1991, February). The world of virtual reality. *Training, 28*(2), 45-50.

Galloway, I., & Rabinowitz, S. (1992). Welcome to "Electronic Cafe International": A nice place for hot coffee, iced tea, and virtual space. In L. Jacobson (Ed.), *CyberArts: Exploring art and technology* (pp. 255-263). San Fransisco: Miller Freeman.

Gambicki, M., & Rousseau, D. (1993). Naval applications of virtual reality. *AI Expert Virtual Reality 93 Special Report*, 67-72.

Gay, E. (1993). VR sparks education. *Pix-Elation,* (10), 14-17.

Gay, E. (1994a, November/December). Virtual reality at the Natrona County school system: Building virtual worlds on a shoestring budget. *Virtual Reality World, 2*(6), 44-47.

Gay, E. (1994b, Winter). Is virtual reality a good teaching tool? *Virtual Reality Special Report, 1*(4), 51-59.

Gibson, J. J. (1986). *The ecological approach to visual perception.* Hillsdale, NJ: Lawrence Erlbaum Associates.

Gibson, W. (1986). *Neuromancer.* New York: Bantam Books.

Gold, S. (nd). *Forensic animation—its origins, creation, limitations and future.* http://www.shadowandlight.com/4NsicArticle.html.

Goodlett, J. Jr. (1990, May). Cyberspace in architectural education (Abstract). In M. Benedikt, (Ed.), *Collected abstrats from the first conference on cyberspace* (pp. 36-37). Austin, TX: School of Architecture, University of Texas.

Goodwin Marcus Systems, Ltd. (nd). *Jack™: The human factors Modeling System.* Middlewich, England: Goodwin Marcus Systems, Ltd. [Brochure].

Govil, A., You, S., & Neumann, U. (2000, October). A video-based augmented reality golf simulator. *Proceedings of the 8th ACM International Conference on Multimedia,* pp. 489-490.

Grant, F. L., McCarthy, L. S., Pontecorvo, M. S., & Stiles, R. J. (1991). Training in virtual environments. *Proceedings of the 1991 Conference on Intelligent Computer-Aided Training,* Houston, TX. November 20-22, 1991, pp. 320-333.

Green, P. S., Hill J. W, Jensen J. F., & Shan A. (1995). Telepresence surgery. *IEEE Engineering In Medicine and Biology,* 324-329.

Greenleaf, W. (1993). Greenleaf DataGlove: The future of functional assessment. *Greenleaf News, 2*(1), 6.

Greenleaf, W. (1994, November 30). *Virtual reality for ergonomic rehabilitation and physical medicine.* Paper presented at the Virtual Reality Expo '94, New York City.

Grimes, W. (1994, November 13). Is 3-D Imax the future or another Cinerama? *New York Times.*

Hafner, K. (2001, June 21). Game simulations for the military try to make an ally of emotion. *New York Times,* p. 34.

Hale, J. (1993). *Marshall Space Flight Center's virtual reality applications program.* Paper presented at the Intelligent Computer-aided Training and Virtual Environments (ICAT-VE) Conference. NASA Johnson Space Center, Houston, TX.

Hall, T. (1990, July 8). 'Virtual reality' takes its place in the real world. *New York Times,* p. 1.

Hamilton, J. (1992, October 5). Virtual reality: How a computer-generated world could change the world. *Businessweek,* (3286), 96-105.

Hamit, F. (1993). *Virtual reality and the exploration of cyberspace.* Carmel, IN: Sams.

Harding, C., Kakadiaris, I. A., & Loftin, R. B. (2000). A multimodal user interface for geoscientific data investigation. *ICMI 2000,* 615-623.

Harrison, H. (1972). Ever branching tree. In A. Cheetham (Ed.), *Science against man.* New York: Avon.

Heeter, C. (1992). BattleTech masters: Emergence of the first U.S. virtual reality subculture. *Multimedia Review, 3*(4), 65-70.

Heeter, C. (1994a, March/April). Gender differences and VR: A non-user survey of what women want. *Virtual Reality World, 2*(2), 75-85.

Heeter, C. (1994b, May 13). *Comparing child and adult reactions to educational VR.* Paper presented at the Meckler Virtual Reality '94 Conference, San Jose, California.

Heinlein, Robert (1965). *Three by Heinlein: The Puppet Master; Waldo; Magic, Inc.* Garden City, NY: Doubleday.

Helsel, S. K. (1992a). Virtual reality as a learning medium. *Instructional Delivery Systems, 6*(4), 4-5.

Helsel, S. K. (1992b). CAD Institute. *Virtual Reality Report, 2*(10), 1-4.

Helsel, S. K. (1992c, May). Virtual reality and education. *Educational Technology, 32*(5), 38-42.

Helsel, S. K., & Roth, J. (Eds.). (1991). *Virtual reality: Theory, practice, and promise.* Westport, CT: Meckler.

Henderson, J. (1990). Designing realities: Interactive media, virtual realities, and cyberspace. In S. Helsel (Ed.), *Virtual reality: Theory, practice, and promise* (pp. 65-73). Westport, CT: Meckler Publishing.

Henderson, J. (1991, March). Designing realities: Interactive media, virtual realities, and cyberspace. *Multimedia Review, 2*(3), 47-51.

Hillis, K. (1999). *Digital sensations: Space, identity, and embodiment in virtual reality.* Minneapolis: University of Minnesota Press.

Hochberg, J. (1986). Representation of motion and space in video and cinematic displays. In K. Boff, L. Kaufman, & J. Thomas (Eds.), *Handbook of perception and human performance.* New York: Wiley.

Holden, L. (1992, October/November). Carnegie Mellon's STUDIO for creative enquiry and the Interdisciplinary Teaching Network (ITeN) and Interactive Fiction and the Networked Virtual Art Museum. *Bulletin of the American Society for Information Science, 19*(1), 9-14.

Hollands, R. (1995, January/February). Essential garage peripherals. *Virtual Reality World, 2*(1), 56-57.

Hollands, R. (1996). *The virtual reality homebrewer's handbook.* New York: John Wiley and Sons.

Höllerer, T., Feiner, S., & Pavlik, J. (1999, October). Situated documentaries: Embedding multimedia presentations in the real world In *Proceedings of the ISWC '99 (Third International Symposium on Wearable Computers),* pp. 79-86.

Höllerer, T., Feiner, S., Terauchi, P., Rashid, G., & Hallaway, D. (1999, December). Exploring MARS: Developing indoor and outdoor user interfaces to a mobile augmented reality system. *Computers and Graphics, 23*(6), 779-785

Hon, D. (1991, September 23). *An evolution of synthetic reality and tactile interfaces.* Paper presented at the Virtual Reality '91 Conference, San Francisco, CA.

Hon, D. (1993, November 30). *Telepresence surgery.* Paper presented at the New York Virtual Reality Expo '93, New York.

Hon, D. (1994, November 30). *Questions enroute to realism: The medical simulation experience.* Paper presented at the Virtual Reality Expo '94, New York.

Hughes, F. (1993, May 6). *Training technology challenges for the next decade and beyond.* Paper presented at the Intelligent Computer-aided Training and Virtual Environments (ICAT-VE) Conference. NASA Johnson Space Center, Houston, TX.

Hyde, P. R., & R. B. Loftin, (Eds.). (1993). *Proceedings of the Contributed Sessions: 1993 Conference on Intelligent Computer-Aided Training and Virtual Environment Technology.* Houston, TX: NASA/Johnson Space Center.

Imprintit (nd). *Virtual environment development.* http://www.imprintit.com/Publications/VEApp.doc.

Isdale, J. (1999a, January/February). Information visualization. *VR News, 8*(1).

Isdale, J. (1999b, April). Motion platforms. *VR News, 8*(3).

Isdale, J. (2000a, January/February). 3D Workstations. *VR News, 9*(1).

Isdale, J. (2000b, March). Alternative I/O technologies. *VR News, 9*(2).

Isdale, J. (2000c, April). Motion platforms. *VR News, 9*(3).

Isdale, J. (2000d, May). Usability engineering. *VR News, 9*(4).

Isdale, J. (2000e, November/December). Augmented reality. *VR News, 9*(5).

Isdale, J. (2001, January). Augmented reality. *VR News, 10*(1).

Jackson, R., Taylor, W., Winn, W. (1999). Peer collaboration and virtual environments: A preliminary investigation of multi-participant virtual reality applied in science education. *Proceedings of the 1999 ACM Symposium on Applied Computing*, pp. 121-125.

Jacobs, S. (1991, August/September). Modern day storyteller. *info*, 24–25.

Jacobson, L. (Ed.). (1992). *CyberArts: Exploring art and technology*. San Francisco, CA: Miller Freeman.

Jacobson, L. (1993a). Welcome to the virtual world. In: Richard Swadley (Ed.). *On the cutting edge of technology* (69-79). Carmel, IN: Sams.

Jacobson, L. (1993b, August). BattleTech's new beachheads. *Wired, 1*(3), 36-39.

Jacobson, L. (1994a). *Garage virtual reality*. Carmel, IN: Sams.

Jacobson, L. (1994b, September/October). The virtual art world of Carl Loeffler. *Virtual Reality World, 2*(5), 32-39.

Johnson, A. D., & Cutt, P. S. (1991). Tactile feedback and virtual environments for training. *Proceedings of the 1991 Conference on Intelligent Computer-Aided Training*, Houston, TX. November 20-22, 1991, p. 334.

Kaplen, K. (1999, august 19). Army signs contract for institute at USC. *Los angeles times*, p. 7.

Karnow, C. (1993, December 1). *Liability and emergent virtual reality systems*. Paper presented at the New York Virtual Reality Expo '93, New York.

Kellogg, W. A., Carroll, J. M., & Richards, J. T. (1991). Making reality a cyberspace. In M. Benedikt (Ed.), *Cyberspace: First steps*. (pp. 411-431). Cambridge, MA: MIT Press.

Knapp, R. B., & Lusted, H. S. (1992). *Biocontrollers for the physically disabled: A direct link from the nervous system to computer*. Paper presented at the Conference on Virtual Reality and Persons with Disabilities, San Francisco, CA. June 15, 1992.

Knox, D., Schacht, C., & Turner, J. (1993, September). Virtual reality: A proposal for treating test anxiety in college students. *College Student Journal, (3)*, 294-296.

Kreuger, M. (1991). *Artificial reality II*. Reading, MA: Addison Wesley.

Krueger, M. W. (1993). An easy entry artificial reality. In A. Wexelblat (Ed.), *Virtual reality: Applications and explorations* (pp. 147-162). Boston: Academic Press Professional.

Lakeland Group (1994). *Tomorrow's team today . . . Team development in a virtual world*™. [brochure]. San Francisco, CA: The Lakeland Group, Inc.

Lampton, D. R., Knerr, B. W., Goldberg, S. L., Bliss, J. P., Moshell, J. M., & Blau, B. S. (1994, Spring). The virtual environment performance assessment battery (VEPAB): Development and evaluation. *Presence, 3*(2), 145-157.

Lamson, R. (1994, November 30). *Virtual therapy: Using VR to treat fear of heights*. Paper presented at the Virtual Reality Expo '94, New York.

Lanier, J. (1992, July). The state of virtual reality practice and what's coming next. *Virtual Reality Special Report/AI Expert* (pp. 11-18). San Francisco, CA: Miller Freeman.

Lantz, E. (1992). Virtual reality in science museums. *Instructional Delivery Systems, 6*(4), 10-12.

Lasko-Harvill, A. (1993). *User interface devices for virtual reality as technology for people with disabilities*. Paper presented at the Conference on Virtual Reality and Persons with Disabilities, San Francisco, CA.

Lauber, J. K., & Foushee, H. C. (January 13-15, 1981). *Guidelines for line-oriented flight training: Proceedings of a NASA/Industry workshop held at NASA Ames Research Center, Moffett Field, California*. United States. National Aeronautics and Space Administration. Scientific and Technical Information Branch.

Laurel, B. (1990a). On dramatic interaction. *Verbum, 3*(3), 6-7.

Laurel, B. (1990b, Summer). Virtual reality design: A personal view. *Multimedia Review, 1*(2), 14-17.

Laurel, B. (1991). *Computers as theater*. Reading, MA: Addison Wesley.

Laurel, B. (1992). Finger flying and other faulty notions. In L. Jacobson (Ed.), *CyberArts: Exploring art and technology* (pp. 286-291). San Fransico: Miller Freeman.

Laurel, B. (1994, May 13). *Art issues in VR*. Paper presented at the Virtual Reality '94 Conference, San Jose, CA.

Learning Company (1983). *Rocky's Boots*. Freemont, CA: Author. [Computer software].

Lerman, J. (1993, February). Virtue not to ski? *Skiing, 45*(6), 12-17.

Lin, C. R., Loftin, R. B., Nelson, H. R., Jr. (2000). Interaction with geoscience data in an immersive environment. *IEEE Virtual Reality 2000 Conference Proceedings*, pp. 55-62.

Loeffler, C. E. (1993, Summer). Networked virtual reality: Applications for industry, education, and entertainment. *Virtual reality World, 1*(2), g-i.

Loftin, R. B. (1992). *Hubble space telescope repair and maintenance: Virtual environment training*. Houston, TX: NASA Johnson Space Center.

Loftin, R. B., Engelberg, M., & Benedetti, R. (1993a). Virtual environments for science education: A virtual physics laboratory. In P. R. Hyde & R. Bowen Loftin (Eds.), *Proceedings of the Contributed Sessions: 1993 Conference on Intelligent Computer-Aided Training and Virtual Environment Technology*, Volume I, 190.

Loftin, R. B., Engelberg, M., & Benedetti, R. (1993b). Virtual controls for interactive environments: A virtual physics laboratory. *Proceedings of the Society for Information Display, 1993 International Symposium, Digest of Technical Papers, 24*, 823-826.

Loftin, R. B., Engelberg, M., & Benedetti, R. (1993c). Applying virtual reality in education: A prototypical virtual physics laboratory. *Proceedings of the IEEE 1993 Symposium on Research Frontiers in Virtual Reality*, pp. 67-74.

Loge, K., Cram, A., & Inman, D. (1995). *Virtual mobility trainer operator's guide*. Virtual Reality Labs, Oregon Research Institute. http://www.orclish.org/5_disability_res/Guide.html.

Lowe, R. (1994, March/April). Three UK case studies in virtual reality. *Virtual Reality World, 2*(2), 51-54.

Mace, W. M. (1977). James J. Gibson's Strategy for perceiving: Ask not what's inside your head, but what your head's inside of. In R. Shaw and J. Bransford (Eds.), *Perceiving, acting, and knowing: Toward an ecological psychology*. Hillsdale, NJ: LEA.

Machover, T. (n.d.). *Hyperinstruments*. MIT Media Lab. http://www.media.mit.edu/hyperins/.

Mandala VR News (1993, Fall/winter). Future watch: Interactive teleconferencing. *Mandala VR News*. Toronto, Canada: The Vivid Group. p. 3.

Manners, C. (2002, March). Virtually live broadcasting. *Digital Video, 10*(3), 50-56.

Marcus, B. (1994, May 12). *Haptic feedback for surgical simulations*. Paper presented at the Virtual Reality '94 Conference, San Jose, CA.

Marcus, S. (1993, June 17). *Virtual realities: From the concrete to the barely imaginable*. Paper presented at the 1993 Conference on Virtual Reality and Persons with Disabilities, San Francisco, CA.

Markoff, J. 1991, February 17). Using computer engineering to mimic the movement of the bow, *New York Times*, p. 8F.

Marsh, C. H., Meisel, A., & Meisel, H. (1993, June 17). *Virtual reality, human evolution, and the world of disability*. Paper presented at the 1993 Conference on Virtual Reality and Persons with Disabilities, San Francisco, CA.

Massachusetts Institute of Technology (MIT) (1981). *Aspen movie map*. Cambridge, MA: Author. [videodisc].

Massof, R. (1993, June 17). *Low vision enhancements: Basic principles and enabling technologies*. Paper presented at the 1993 Conference on Virtual Reality and Persons with Disabilities, San Francisco, CA.

Mayr, H. (2001). *Virtual automation environments*. New York: Marcel Dekker, Inc.

McCarthy, L., Pontecorvo, M., Grant, F., & Stiles, R. (1993). Spatial considerations for instructional development in a virtual environment. In P. R. Hyde & R. Bowen Loftin (Eds.), *Proceedings of the Contributed Sessions: 1993 Conference on Intelligent Computer-Aided Training and Virtual Environment Technology,* Volume I, 180–189.

McLaughlin, M., Hespanha, J. P., & Sukhatme, G. S. (2001). *Touch in virtual environments: Haptics and the design of interactive systems*. Saddle River, NJ: Prentice Hall.

McGovern, K. (1994, November 30). *Surgical training*. Paper presented at the Virtual Reality Expo '94, New York.

McGrath, E. (1994, May 13). *Team training at virtual worlds center*. Paper presented at the Meckler Virtual Reality '94 Conference, San Jose, CA.

McGreevy, M. W. (1993). Virtual reality and planetary exploration. In A. Wexelblat (Ed.), *Virtual reality: Applications and explorations* (pp. 163–198). Boston: Academic Press Professional.

McKenna, Atherton, & Sabiston (1990). *Grinning evil death*. Cambridge, MA: MIT Media Lab. [computer animation].

McLellan, H. (1991, Winter). Virtual environments and situated learning. *Multimedia Review, 2*(3), 25–37.

McLellan, H. (1992). *Virtual reality: A selected bibliography*. Englewood Cliffs, NJ: Educational Technology Publications.

McLellan, H. (1994a). The Lakeland Group: Tomorrow's team today . . . Team development in a virtual world. *Virtual Reality Report, 4*(5), 7–11.

McLellan, H. (1994b). Virtual reality and multiple intelligences: Potentials for higher education. *Journal of Computing in Higher Education, 5*(2), 33–66.

McLellan, H. (1995, January/February). Virtual field trips: The Jason Project. *Virtual Reality World, 3*(1), 49–50.

Mendenhall, J., & Vanderheiden, G. (1993, June 17). *Two classification schemes for better understanding the opportunities and barriers presented by virtual reality systems to persons with disablities*. Paper presented at the 1993 Conference on Virtual Reality and Persons with Disabilities, San Francisco, CA.

Merickel M. L. (1990, December). The creative technologies project: Will training in 2D/3D graphics enhance kids' cognitive skills? *T.H.E. Journal*, 55–58.

Merickel M. L. (1991). *A study of the relationship between perceived realism and the ability of children to create, manipulate and utilize mental images in solving problems*. Oregon State University. Unpublished doctoral dissertation.

Merril, J. R. (1993, November/December). Window to the soul: Teaching physiology of the eye. *Virtual Reality World, 3*(1), 51–57.

Merril, J. R. (1994, May 12). *VR in medical education: Use for trade shows and individual physician education*. Paper presented at the Virtual Reality '94 Conference, San Jose, California.

Merril, J. R. (1995, January/February). Surgery on the cutting-edge. *Virtual Reality World, 1*(3&4), 51–56.

Merril, J. R., Roy, R., Merril, G., & Raju, R. (1994, Winter). Revealing the mysteries of the brain with VR. *Virtual Reality Special Report, 1*(4), 61–66.

Middleton, T. (1992). Applications of virtual reality to learning. *Interactive Learning International, 8*(4), 253–257.

Middleton, T. (1993, June 18). *Matching virtual reality solutions to special needs*. Paper presented at the 1993 Conference on Virtual Reality and Persons with Disabilities. San Francisco, CA.

Miley, M. (1992). Groupware meets multimedia. *NewMedia, 2*(11), 39–40.

Milgram, P., & Kishino, F. (1994, December). A Taxonomy of Mixed Reality Visual Displays. *IEICE Transactions on Information Systems,* E77-D(12). http://gypsy.rose.utoronto.ca/people/paul_dir/IEICE94/ieice.html.

Minsky, M. (1991, September 23). *Force feedback: The sense of touch at the interface*. Paper presented at the Virtual Reality '91 Conference, San Francisco, CA.

Mohl, R. F. (1982). *Cognitive space in the interactive movie map: An investigation of spatial learning in virtual environments*. Massachusetts Institute of Technology. Unpublished doctoral dissertation.

Morningstar, C., & Farmer, F. R. (1991). The lessons of Lucasfilm's habitat. In M. Benedikt (Ed.), *Cyberspace: First steps* (pp. 273–302). Cambridge, MA: MIT Press.

Morningstar, C., & Farmer, F. R. (1993). The lessons of Lucasfilm's Habitat. *Virtual Reality Special Report/AI Expert* (pp. 23–32). San Francisco, CA: Miller Freeman.

Moser, M. A. & MacLeod, D. (Eds). (September 1997). *Immersed in technology art & visual environments*. Cambridge, MA: MIT Press.

Moshell, J. M., & Dunn-Roberts, R. (1993). Virtual environments: Research in North America. In J. Thompson, (Ed.), *Virtual reality: An international directory of research projects* (pp. 3–26). Westport, CT: Meckler.

Moshell, J. M., & Hughes, C. E. (1994a, January). *The virtual school*. Orlando, FL: Institute for Simulation and Training. Document JMM94.2.

Moshell, J. M., & Hughes, C. E. (1994b, January/February). Shared virtual worlds for education. *Virtual Reality World, 2*(1), 63–74.

Moshell, J. M., & Hughes, C. E. (1994c, February). *The virtual academy: Networked simulation and the future of education*. Proceedings of the IMAGINA Conference, Monte Carlo, Monaco. 6–18.

Murphy, H. (1994). The promise of VR applications for persons with disabilities. In S. Helsel, (Ed.), *London Virtual Reality Expo '94: Proceedings of the fourth annual conference on Virtual Reality*. London: Mecklermedia, pp. 55–65.

Murray, J. H. (1997). *Hamlet on the holodeck: The future of narrative in cyberspace*. Cambridge, MA: MIT Press.

Nemire, K., Burke, A., & Jacoby, R. (1993, June 15). *Virtual learning environment for disabled students: Modular assistive technology for physics instruction*. Paper presented at the 1993 Conference on Virtual Reality and Persons with Disabilities, San Francisco, CA.

Newby, G. B. (1993). Virtual reality: Tomorrow's information system or just another pretty interface? *Proceedings of one american society for information science annual meeting, 30*. 199–203. Medford, NJ: Learned Information.

Norman, D. (1993). *Things that make us smart*. Reading, MA: Addison-Wesley.

O'Donnell, T. (1994, December 1). *The virtual demonstration stage: A breakthrough teaching tool arrives for museums*. Paper presented at the Virtual Reality Expo '94, New York.

Oliver, D., & Rothman, P. (1993, June 17). *Virtual reality games for teaching conflict management with seriously emotionally disturbed (SED) and learning disabled (LD) children*. Paper presented at the First Conference on Virtual Reality and Persons with Disabilities, San Francisco, CA. (http://www.csun.edu/cod/93virt/Vrgame~1.html)

Orange, G., & Hobbs, D. (Eds). (2000). *International perspectives on tele-education and virtual learning environments*. Burlington, VT: Ashgate Publishing Company.

Osberg, K. (1993). *Virtual reality and education: A look at both sides of the sword*. Technical Report R-93-7. Seattle: University of Washington, Human Interface Technology Laboratory.

Osberg, K. (1994). *Rethinking educational technology: A postmodern view*. Technical Report R-94-4. Seattle: University of Washington, Human Interface Technology Laboratory.

Osberg, K. M., Winn, W., Rose, H., Hollander, A., Hoffman, H., & Char, P. (1997). The effect of having grade seven students construct virtual environments on their comprehension of science. In *Proceedings of Annual Meeting of the American Educational Research Association*.

Packer, R., & Jordan, K. (Eds). (2001). *Multimedia: From Wagner to virtual reality*. New York: Norton & Company.

Pantelidis, V. S. (n.d.). *Virtus VR and Virtus WalkThrough uses in the classroom*. Unpublished document. Greenville, NC: Department of Library Studies and Educational Technology, East Carolina University.

Pantelidis, V. S. (1993). *North Carolina competency-based curriculum objectives and virtual reality*. Unpublished document. Greenville, NC: Virtual Reality and Education Laboratory, School of Education, East Carolina University.

Pantelidis, V. S. (1994). *Virtual reality and education: Information sources*. Unpublished document. Greenville, NC: Virtual Reality and Education Laboratory, College of Education, East Carolina University. (Note: This document is regularly updated.)

Pausch, R., Crea, T., & Conway, M. (1992). A literature survey for virtual environments: military flight simulator visual systems and simulator sickness. *Presence, 1,* 344-363.

Pausch, R., Vogtle, L., & Conway, M. (1991, October 7). *One dimensional motion tailoring for the disabled: A user study*. Computer Science Report No. TR-91-21. Computer Science Department, University of Virginia, Charlottesville, VA.

Pausch, R., & Williams, R. D. (1991). *Giving CANDY to children: User-tailored gesture input driving an articulator-based speech synthesizer*. Computer Science Report No. TR-91-23. Computer Science Department, University of Virginia. Charlottesville, VA.

Piantanida, T. (1993). Another look at HMD safety. *CyberEdge Journal, 3*(6), 9-12.

Piantanida, T. (1994a, November 29). *Low-cost virtual-reality head-mounted displays and vision*. Paper presented at the Virtual Reality Expo '94, New York.

Piantanida, T. (1994b, December 2). *Health and safety issues in home virtual-reality systems*. Paper presented at the Virtual Reality Expo '94, New York.

Pimentel, K., & Teixeira, K. (1992). *Virtual reality: Through the new looking glass*. New York: McGraw Hill.

Powers, D. A., & Darrow, M. (1996, Winter). Special education and virtual reality: Challenges and possibilities. *Journal of Research on Computing in Education, 27*(1).

Redfield, C. L., Bell, B., Hsieh, P. Y., Lamos, J., Loftin, R. B., Palumbo, & D. (1998). Methodologies for Tutoring in Procedural Domains. *Intelligent Tutoring Systems,* 616.

Regian, J. W. (1986). *An assessment procedure for configurational knowledge of large-scale space*. Unpublished doctoral dissertation. University of California, Santa Barbara.

Regian, J. W., Shebilske, W. L., & Monk, J. M. (1992). Virtual reality: An instructional medium for visual-spatial tasks. *Journal of Communication, 42*(4), 136-149.

Regian, W. (1993, May 6). *Virtual reality—Basic research for the effectiveness of training transfer*. Paper presented at the 1993 Conference on Intelligent Computer-Aided Training and Virtual Environment Technology 9ICAT-VET).

Rheingold, H. (1991). *Virtual reality*. Reading, MA: Addison Wesley.

Rheingold, H. (1993). *The virtual community: Homesteading on the electronic frontier*. Reading, MA: Addison Wesley.

Robinette, W. (1991, Fall). Electronic expansion of human perception. *Whole Earth Review,* pp. 16-21.

Rose, H. (1995a). *Assessing learning in VR: Towards developing a paradigm virtual reality in roving vehicles (VRRV) Project*. HIT Lab Report R-95-1 (pp. 1-46). Seattle, WA: Human Interface Technology Laboratory, University of Washington.

Rose, H. (1995b). *Zengo Sayu: An immersive educational environment for learning japanese*. Technical Report P-95-16 (pp. 1-9). Seattle, WA: Human Interface Technology Laboratory, University of Washington.

Rose, H. (1996). *Zengo Sayu: An immersive educational environment for learning japanese*. Technical Report R-96-6. Seattle: University of Washington, Human Interface Technology Laboratory. pp. 1-9.

Rose, H., & Billinghurst, M. (1995). *Zengo Sayu: An immersive educational environment for learning japanese*. Technical Report R-95-4 (pp. 1-14). Seattle, WA: Human Interface Technology Laboratory, University of Washington.

Rosen, J. (1994, November 30). *Telemedicine*. Paper presented at the Virtual Reality Expo '94, New York.

Rosenblum, L., Burdea, G. and Tachi, S. (1998, November/December). VR Reborn. *VR News* (pp. 21-23). Based on an article that appeared in *IEEE Computer Graphics and Applications*.

Salcedo, M., & Salcedo, P. (1993, June 17). *Movement development in preschool children with visual impairments*. 1993 Conference on Virtual Reality and Persons with Disabilities, San Francisco, CA.

Salzman, M. C., Dede, C. J., & Loftin, R. B. (1999). VR's frames of reference: A visualization technique for mastering abstract multidimensional information. *Computer-Human Interaction (CHI) Conference Proceedings,* 489-495.

Salzman, M. C., Loftin, R. B., Dede, C. J., & McGlynn, D. (1996). ScienceSpace: Lessons for designing immersive virtual realities. *CHI Conference Companion,* 89-90.

Sandin, D., Defanti, T., and Cruz-Nierna, C. (2001). Room with a view. In R. Packer & K. Jordan (Eds.), *Multimedia: From Wagner to virtual reality*. New York: W. W. Norton & Company.

Satava, R. (1992, June 9). *Telepresence surgery*. Paper presented at the 1992 EFDPMA Conference on Virtual Reality. Education Foundation of the Data Processing Management Association, Washington, D.C.

Satava, R. M. (Editor). (1997). *Cybersurgery: Advanced technologies for surgical practice*. New York: Wiley & Sons.

Satava, R. V. (1993, May 6). *Virtual reality for anatomical and surgical simulation*. Paper presented at the Intelligent Computer-aided Training and Virtual Environments (ICAT-VE) Conference. NASA Johnson Space Center, Houston, TX.

Satoh, K., Ohshima, T., Yamamoto, H., & Tamura, H. (1998). Case studies of see-through augmentation: Mixed reality projects. *IWAR 98: First IEEE International Workshop on Augmented Reality.* http://www.mr-system.co.jp/public/abst/iwar98satoh.html.

Schiphorst, T. (1992). The choreography machine: A design tool for character and human movement. In Linda Jacobson (Ed.), *CyberArts: Exploring art and technology* (pp. 147-156). San Francisco, CA: Miller Freeman.

Schlager, M., & Boman, D. (1994, May 13). *VR in education and training*. Paper presented at the Meckler Virtual Reality '94 Conference, San Jose, CA.

Schmitt, B. H. (1999). *Experiential marketing*. New York: Free Press.

Schrage, Michael (1991). *Shared minds: The new technologies of collaboration*. New York: Random House.

Schwienhorst, K. (1998). The "third place"—virtual reality applications for second language learning. *ReCALL, 10*(1), 118-126.

Scully, J. (1994, December 2). *Tracking technologies and virtual characters*. Paper presented at Virtual Reality Expo '94, New York.

Shaw, J. (1994). EVE: Extended virtual environment. *Virtual Reality World, 2*(3), 59–62.

Shaw, J., & May, G. (1994). EVE: Extended virtual environment. In S. Helsel, (Ed.), *London virtual reality expo '94: Proceedings of the fourth annual conference on Virtual Reality*. London: Mecklermedia, pp. 107–109.

Shedroff, N. (2001). *Experience design*. Indianapolis, IN: New Riders.

Shedroff, N. (2002). Experience design. *Web Reference*. http://www.webreference.com/authoring/design/expdesign/2.html

Sheridan, T. B., & Zeltzer, D. (1993, October). Virtual reality check. *Technology Review, 96*(7), 20–28.

Shimoga, K., & Khosla, P. (1994, November). Touch and force reflection for telepresence surgery. *Proceedings of the 16th Annual International Conference of the IEEE Engineering in Medicine and Biology, 2*, 1049–1050.

Siegal, A. W. (1981). The externalization of cognitive maps by children and adults: In search of ways to ask better questions. In L. Liben, A. Patterson, & N. Newcombe (Eds.), *Spatial representation and behavior across the life span* (pp. 163–189). New York: Academic Press.

Singhal, S., & Zyda, M. (1999). *Networked virtual environments: Design and implementation*. Reading, MA: Addison-Wesley.

Sklaroff, S. (1994, June 1). Virtual reality puts disabled students in touch. *Education Week, 13*(36), 8.

Smith, D. (1993, May 19). *Through the window*. Paper presented at the Virtual Reality '93 Conference, San Jose, CA.

Sorid, D. (2000, March 23). What's next: Giving computers a sense of touch. *New York Times*.

Spritzer, V. (1994, November 30). *Medical modeling: The visible human project*. Paper presented at the Virtual Reality Expo '94, New York.

SRI (2002). *Telepresence surgery*. http://www.sri.com/ipet/ts.html.

Stampe, D. Roehl, B., & Eagan, J. (1993). *Virtual reality creations*. Corta Madiera, CA: The Waite Group.

Stenger, N. (1991, September 23). *"Angels," or "Les Recontres Angeliques."* Paper presented at the Virtual Reality '91 Conference, San Francisco, CA.

Stephenson, N. (1992). *Snow crash*. New York: Bantam Books.

Sterling, B. (1994). *Heavy weather*. New York: Bantam Books.

Sterling, B. (1993). War is virtual hell. *Wired, 1*(1), 46–51+.

Stix, G. (1992, September). See-through view: Virtual reality may guide physicians hands. *Scientific American*, 166.

Stoker, C. (1994, July). Telepresence, remote vision and VR at NASA: From Antarctica to Mars. *Advanced Imaging, 9*(7), 24–26.

Stone, R. (2000, April). VR at the Gagarin Cosmonaut Training Centre. *VR News, 9*(3).

Stuart, R. (2001). *Design of virtual environments*. Fort Lee, NJ: Barricade Books.

Stytz, M. (1993, May 20). *The view from the synthetic battlebridge*. Virtual Reality '93 Conference, San Jose, CA.

Stytz, M. (1994, December 1). *An overview of US military developments in VR*. New York Virtual Reality Expo '94 Conference, New York.

Sutherland, I. E. (1965). The ultimate display. *Proceedings of the IFIPS, 2*, 506–508.

Sutherland, I. E. (1968). A head-mounted three dimensional display. *Proceedings of the Fall Joint Computer Conference, 33*, 757–764.

Taubes, G. (1994a, June). Virtual Jack. *Discover, 15*(6), 66–74.

Taubes, G. (1994b, December). Surgery in cyberspace. *Discover, 15*(12), 84–94.

Taylor, W. (1997). Student responses to their immersion in a virtual environment. *Proceedings of Annual Meeting of the American Educational Research Association*, pp. 12.

Taylor, W. (1998). *E6–A aviation maintenance training curriculum evaluation: A case study*. Doctoral Dissertation, University of Washington.

Teixeira, K. (1994a, May/June). Behind the scenes at the Guggenheim. *Virtual Reality World, 2*(3), 66–70.

Teixeira, K. (1994b, May 13). *Intel's IDEA Project and the VR art exhibit at the Guggenheim*. Paper presented at the Virtual Reality '94 Conference, San Jose, CA.

Thompson, J. (Ed.). (1993). *Virtual reality: An international directory of research projects*. Westport, CT: Meckler.

Thurman, R. (1992, June 1). *Simulation and training based technology*. Paper presented at the EFDPMA (Educational Foundation of the Data Processing Management Association) Conference on Virtual Reality.

Thurman, R. A., & Mattoon, J. S. (1994, October). Virtual reality: Toward fundamental improvements in simulation-based training. *Educational Technology, 34*(8), 56–64.

Tice, S., & Jacobson, L. (1992). VR in visualization, animation, and entertainment. In: Jacobson, L. (Ed.), *CyberArts: Exploring art and technology*. San Francisco, CA: Miller Freeman.

Treviranus, J. (1993, June 17). *Artists who develop virtual reality technologies and persons with disabilities*. Paper presented at the 1993 Conference on Virtual Reality and Persons with Disabilities, San Francisco, CA.

Trimble, J. (1993, May 20). *Virtual barrier-free design ("Wheelchair VR")*. Paper presented at the 1993 Conference on on Virtual Reality and Persons with Disabilities, San Francisco, California.

Trubitt, D. (1990, July). Into new worlds: Virtual reality and the electronic musician. *Electronic Musician, 6*(7), 30–40.

Ulman, N. (1993, March 17). High-tech connection between schools and science expeditions enlivens classes. *Wall Street Journal*, B1, B10.

Van Nedervelde, P. (1994, December 1). *Cyberspace for the rest of us*. Paper presented at the Virtual Reality Expo '94, New York.

Varner, D. (1993). *Contribution of audition and olfaction to immersion in a virtual environment*. Paper presented at the 1993 Conference on Intelligent Computer-Aided Training and Virtual Environment Technology.

Vince, J. (1998) *Essential virtual reality fast: How to understand the techniques and potential of virtual reality*. New York: Springer Verlag.

VR Monitor (1993, January/February). VR si training system by NEC. *VR Monitor, 2*(1), 9.

Wagner, E. (1994, December 1). *Virtual reality at "The Cutting Edge."* Paper presented at the Virtual Reality Expo '94, New York.

Waldern, J. D. (1991). Virtuality: The world's first production virtual reality workstation. In T. Feldman (Ed.), *Virtual reality '91: Impacts and applications (pp. 26–30). Proceedings of the First Annual Conference on Virtual Reality 91*. London: Meckler.

Waldern, J. (1992, June 1). *Virtual reality: The serious side*. Paper presented at the EFDPMA (Educational Foundation of the Data Processing Management Association) Conference on Virtual Reality.

Waldern, J. (1994). Software design of virtual teammates and virtual opponents. In S. Helsel (Ed.), *London Virtual Reality Expo '94: Proceedings of the fourth annual conference on Virtual Reality*. London: Mecklermedia, pp. 120–125.

Walser, R. (1991). *Cyberspace trix: Toward an infrastructure for a new industry*. Internal paper. Advanced Technology Department. Autodesk, Inc.

Walser, R. (1992, June 1). *Construction in cyberspace*. Paper presented at the EFDPMA (Education Foundation of the Data Processing

Management Association) Conference on Virtual Reality, Washington, DC.

Wann, J., Rushton, S., Mon-Williams, M., Hawkes, R., & Smyth, M. (1993, September/October). *What's wrong with our head mounted display?* CyberEdge Journal Monograph. Sausalito, CA: CyberEdge, pp. 1–2.

Warner, D. (1993, May 20). *More than garage nerds and isolated physicians who make VR medical technology.* Paper presented at the Meckler Virtual Reality '93 Conference, San Jose, California.

Warner, D., & Jacobson, L. (1992, July). Medical rehabilitation, cyberstyle. *Virtual Reality Special Report/AI Expert.* San Francisco, CA: Miller Freeman. 19–22.

Weghorst, S. (1994, November 30). *A VR project: Parkinson disease.* Paper presented at the Virtual Reality Expo '94, New York.

Weishar, P. (1998). *Digital space: Designing virtual environments.* New York: McGraw-Hill.

Weissman, D. (1995, February 6). Dental distraction not 'just a gimmick': Dentists enlist new technology to soothe fears among patients. *The Journal of the American Dental Association (JADA), 126*(2), 14.

Wexelblat, A. (1993). The reality of cooperation: Virtual reality and CSCW. In A. Wexelblat (Ed.), *Virtual reality: Applications and explorations* (pp. 23–44). Boston: Academic Press Professional.

Wheeler, D. L. (1991, March 31). Computer-created world of 'virtual reality' opening new vistas to scientists. *The Chronicle of Higher Education, 37*(26), A6+.

Wickens, C. D. (1993, April). *Virtual reality and education.* Technical Report ARL-93-2/NSF-93-1 prepared for the National Science Foundation. Aviation Research Laboratory Institute of Aviation. University of Illinois at Urbana-Champaign, Savoy, IL.

Wickens, C. D., & Baker, P. (1994, February). *Cognitive issues in virtual reality.* Human Perception and Performance Technical Report UIUC-BI-HPP-94-02. The Beckman Institute, University of Illinois at Urbana-Champaign, Urbana, IL. also appeared in W. Barfield and T. Furness (Eds.) (1995). *Virtual environments and advanced interface design.* Oxford: Oxford University Press.

Wilson, D. L. (1994, November 16). A key for entering virtual worlds. *Chronicle of Higher Education,* A19.

Winn, W. (1993). *A conceptual basis for educational applications of virtual reality.* Report R-93-9. Seattle: University of Washington, Human Interface Technology Laboratory.

Winn, W. (1993, December 1). *A discussion of the human interface laboratory (HIT) and its educational projects.* Paper presented at the Virtual Reality Expo '93, New York.

Winn, W., and Bricken, W. (1992a, April). *Designing virtual worlds for use in mathematics education.* Paper presented at the Annual Meeting of the American Educational Research Association, San Francisco, CA.

Winn, W., and Bricken, W. (1992b, December). Designing virtual worlds for use in mathematics education: The example of experiential algebra. *Educational Technology, 32*(12), 12–19.

Winn, W., Hoffman, H., Hollander, A., Osberg, K., Rose, H., & Char, P. (1997, March). *The effect of student construction of virtual environments on the performance of high- and low-ability students.* Paper presented at Annual Meeting of the American Educational Research Association, Chicago, IL.

Winn, W., Hoffman, H., & Osberg, K. (1995). Semiotics and the design of objects, actions and interactions in virtual environments. In *Proceedings of Annual Meeting of American Educational Research Association,* April 18–22, 1995, San Francisco, CA (pp. 21). (ERIC Document Reproduction Service No. ED385236)

Wisne, J. (1994, December 1). *VR at the Ohio's Center of Science & Industry.* Paper presented at the Virtual Reality Expo '94, New York.

Wong, V. (1996). *Telepresence in medicine: An application of virtual reality.* http://www.doc.ic.ac.uk/~nd/surprise_96/journal/vol2/kwc2/article2.html

Woolley, B. (1992). *Virtual worlds: A journey in hype and hyperreality.* Oxford, England: Blackwell.

Wyshynski, & Vincent, V. J. (1993). Full-body unencumbered immersion in virtual worlds. In A. Wexelblat (Ed.), *Virtual reality: Applications and explorations* (pp. 123–146). Boston: Academic Press Professional.

Zeltner, D. (1992, June 1). *Virtual environment technology.* Paper presented at the EFDPMA (Education Foundation of the Data Processing Management Association) Conference on Virtual Reality, Washington, DC.

·18·

THE LIBRARY MEDIA CENTER: TOUCHSTONE FOR INSTRUCTIONAL DESIGN AND TECHNOLOGY IN THE SCHOOLS

Delia Neuman
University of Maryland

> Perhaps...the school media specialist will become an instrumental player in this transformation [of teachers' roles], an instructional designer from within.
>
> (Gustafson, Tillman, & Childs, 1991, p. 460)

Echoing a goal that has long been held by the school library media field, these authors capture both the promise and the uncertainty that characterize any fond hope. In fact, many scholars and other leaders in the field have been vocal champions of a strong relationship linking the library media specialist, various learning technologies, and instructional design; however, the realities of life in the public schools have presented serious obstacles to the full flowering of this relationship. Today, as at other periods in the evolution of the library media field, internal and external changes affecting the school environment suggest that the library media specialist is poised to assume a much more active role as an instructional designer/instructional technologist than has been possible in the past. Understanding the nature and history of the field will enable school library media professionals and others to make a realistic assessment of the opportunities that lie ahead and to devise strategies to take advantage of them.

This chapter discusses the history of the role of the library media specialist since the field began to emphasize a design-and-technology focus in the 1960s; the various instructional design models created specifically for library media specialists to use in the schools; the nature of the library media specialist's role today, particularly as it relates to instructional design and technology; the accumulated research on the impact of library media programs on student learning and achievement; and the issues related to instructional design and technology that are likely to engage school library media researchers in the near future. The chapter is intended to provide a wide-ranging context for a consideration of the issues the library media field faces in the early twenty-first century and to lay a realistic yet sanguine foundation for its future progress in the areas of instructional design and technology.

18.1 SOME "EARLY" HISTORY: 1960–1989

The nature of the long and often challenging evolution of the school librarian from a provider of services and materials into a central member of a school's instructional team has had a profound effect on the roles, responsibilities, and image of the library media specialist today. The history of that evolution is tied inextricably to the official standards and guidelines for the field, a set of documents dating to the 1920s that over the years have served a dual purpose: to describe the library media specialist's roles and responsibilities in the periods in which they were written and to urge the field forward toward an ever-increasing degree of professionalism in the periods to follow. A brief review of the modern editions of those documents (i.e., those published since 1960) provides an overview of this evolutionary process as it has played out during the post-Sputnik decades that have seen both technology and the library media specialist's instructional role grow more and more important in the schools.

The field's first three sets of standards were published in 1920, 1925, and 1945. Since at least the publication of the fourth set—*Standards for School Library Programs,* released by the American Association of School Librarians (AASL) in 1960—library media specialists have been expected to serve as instructors as well as librarians. The professional role has included not only helping teachers select appropriate learning materials (including the "audiovisual materials" newly mentioned in the 1960 standards) but also working collaboratively with teachers to integrate library skills into ongoing classroom instruction. There is no question that the "information specialist" aspect of the role reigned supreme at that time and remains prominent to this day. However, it is important to note that school librarians—now library media specialists—have spent decades taking on increasing responsibility for providing instruction and for integrating technology into the curriculum as well as for providing library services.

The publication of *Standards for School Media Programs* (AASL & DAVI, 1969) ushered in the widespread use of the terms "media" and "media specialist" and gave increasing emphasis to the library media specialist's instructional role. This fifth set of standards—the first set jointly prepared by AASL and what would one day become AECT—signaled an important confluence of the two major foci of the field, librarianship and educational technology. Now, the "library girls" and the "AV boys" officially joined forces and became "library media specialists"; the issues, cultures, and expertise of the two areas have remained intertwined ever since. The 1969 *Standards* formally established for school library media practitioners and theorists alike the view that the library media program is the center of instructional design and technology activity within the school. For the most part, however, this recognition has been at the theoretical level, as professional practice has struggled to keep pace with professional aspirations.

The sixth set of national standards, *Media Programs: District and School* (AASL & AECT, 1975), provided a further step in the evolution of the library media specialist as an instructional technologist and designer. These guidelines "elevated the curricular and instructional role of the school library media specialist and began to specify the requirements of such a role" (Cleaver & Taylor, 1989, p. 5), charging library media specialists with such tasks as:

Initiating and participating in curriculum development and implementation

Designing in-service education

Developing materials for self-instructional use by learners for specified objectives ...

Determining the effectiveness or validity of instructional materials and sequences.

—(*Media Programs* ..., p. 7, cited in Cleaver & Taylor, 1989, p. 5)

The years following the release of *Media Programs* ... saw an explosion of publications related to the instructional design role of the library media specialist. In what has become known as the primer on the topic, Margaret Chisholm and Don Ely published *Instructional Design and the Library Media Specialist* in 1979. This slim volume both provided a rationale for the new role and described how it should be practiced by the library media specialist. The book also set the tone for much of the writing that followed:

The process of instruction will continue into the future, and those who are active in its design are those who will survive. ... It is possible that many of the functions which are now performed by traditional librarians and audiovisual specialists can be handled by clerks and technicians. ... Therefore, in order to justify a professional position, it is incumbent upon library media professionals to use the talents which they have to become active members of the instructional team. (p. 6).

Although Chisholm and Ely's predictions seem unremarkable—even quaint—in hindsight, they were visionary at the time. For many current library media specialists, achieving these authors' vision is still a struggle.

18.2 INSTRUCTIONAL DESIGN MODELS FOR LIBRARY MEDIA SPECIALISTS

After 1975, the question became, how would library media specialists rise to the new opportunities and mandates presented to them? While the field's leaders and professional organizations touted the importance of instructional design, there was little guidance for practicing library media specialists who wished to take on the designer's role. In 1982, for example, Turner surveyed all library-education programs in the United States that were accredited by the American Library Association and found that a substantial number had no instructional design requirements for their school library media students.

In the early 1980s, several authors tackled the details of helping practitioners use the methods and techniques of instructional design in the schools—notably Kerry Johnson (1981), Philip Turner and Janet Naumer (1983), and Betty Cleaver and William Taylor (1983). The first two sets of authors looked to traditional instructional design models and developed variations that were tailored to the needs of the library media specialist; the third developed a contextual model that offered guidance about implementing the overall design process. All three of these earliest models assumed that the library media specialist had a basic role in providing access to, and assisting teachers and students with, the technology of the day. Perhaps even more importantly, all three assumed that the library media specialist would work in collaboration with teachers—not as an individual designer who presented teachers with finished products. Today, over 20 years later, these central assumptions persist: the library media specialist is to use the concepts and skills of instructional design to integrate technology into instruction and to serve as a member of instructional teams that form and dissolve according to the needs of teachers and the curriculum.

18.2.1 The SID Model

Johnson (1981) noted that "The library media specialist as instructional developer has not been specifically considered in [instructional design] model development" (p. 257) in any of the dozens of models that were then in the instructional design literature. His solution was SID (the School Instructional Development model), which he created to "describe instructional development in terms appropriate to the role of school library media specialist" (p. 271). Johnson identified three general stages—define, design, and evaluate—and provided details related to each in both graphic and narrative forms (Fig. 18.1). The boxes and lines of the graphic make it look like a typical instructional design model, and both the illustration and its accompanying narrative include specific guidance for the library media specialist. The graphic notes the "sources of curriculum" that underlie the development of an "ideal component outline," for example, while the narrative explains that "It is the major role of the library media specialist during this [project selection] stage of the project to elicit from the teacher all possible approaches to the instructional problem at hand and to encourage creative thinking" (p. 259).

Johnson intended his sophisticated model to be "a framework within which the library media specialist can operate" (p. 271). He noted, however, that its successful use assumes several key factors: the willingness of library media specialists to become designers and the adequacy of their educational preparation for the role. He further "posits the condition that principals and teachers are equally aware and supportive of the library media specialist's proactive role" as an instructional designer (p. 271). Over the years, all three of Johnson's assumptions have proven problematic, as other school personnel's understanding of the library media specialist's once-new role has continued to lag.

18.2.2 The Turner Model

Two years after Johnson's model appeared, Turner and Naumer noted that the library media specialist "who has accomplished the transition to this role [of instructional design consultation with teachers] is in a distinct minority. Most school library media specialists seem either never to have chosen to pursue this expanded role or to have soon become frustrated in the attempt" (p. 29). To remedy this situation, Turner and Naumer offered their own eight-step instructional design model (Fig. 18.2) and expanded upon its basic elements to suggest the appropriate level of involvement for the library media specialist at each step. Identifying four levels—involvement, passive participation, reaction, and action/education—the authors provided an ingenious and pragmatic guide for library media specialists to follow in using instructional design in a staged and gradual

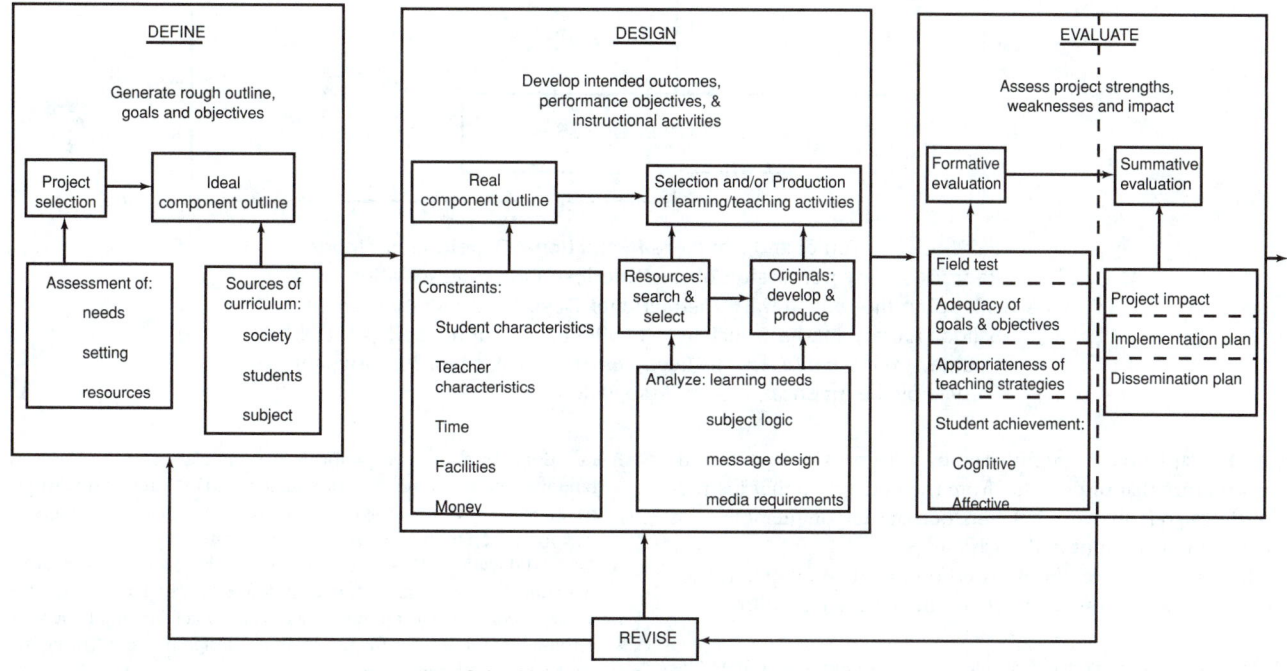

FIGURE 18.1. Johnson's School Instructional Development Model (SID). Reproduced by permission of the American Library Association from "Instructional Development in Schools: A Proposed Model," by Kerry A. Johnson, from *School Library Media Quarterly*, vol. 9, p. 270; copyright © 1981 by the American Library Association.

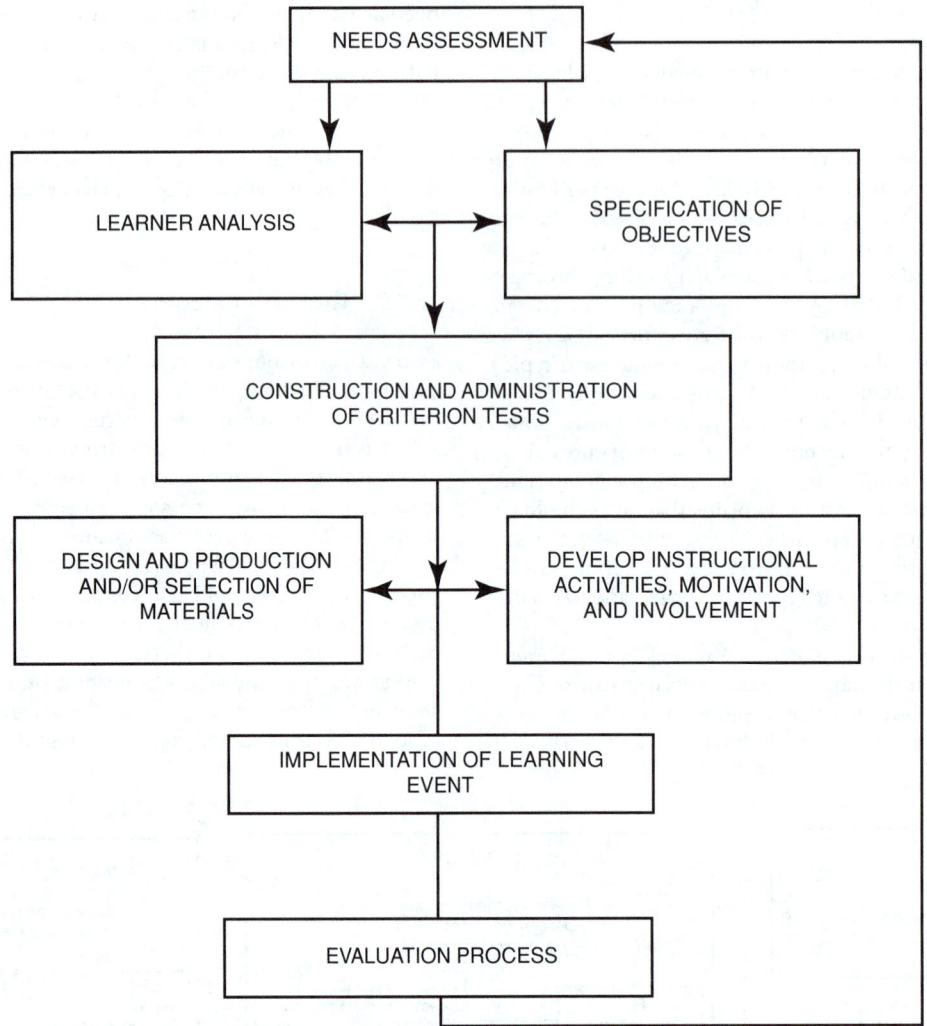

FIGURE 18.2. Turner and Naumer's Instructional Development Model. Reproduced by permission of the American Library Association from "Mapping the Way Toward Instructional Design Consultation by the School Library Media Specialist," by Philip M. Turner and Janet N. Naumer, from *School Library Media Quarterly*, vol. 10, p. 30; copyright © 1983 by the American Library Association.

way. Perhaps even more importantly, they provided a theoretical structure that offers relief from the perception that instructional design is an overwhelming, perhaps unconquerable, task for anyone to attempt in the schools.

In 1985, in his textbook based on the 1983 article, Turner described each of the four levels of involvement as follows:

1. No Involvement. Perhaps no intervention is required. Perhaps the teacher has not requested involvement by the center. Perhaps the library media specialist is unwilling or unable to intervene.
2. Passive Participation. This level . . . involves little or no interaction between the library media specialist and the faculty member. The library media specialist selects and maintains materials, equipment, and facilities which assist the faculty member in implementing a particular step.

3. Reaction. As a teacher performs a particular step, he/she may randomly request some sort of assistance. . . . This intervention would be informal and not designed to increase the teacher's ability to perform a step more effectively at a later date.
4. Action/Education. This level . . . most closely resembles formal instructional design consultation as described in the literature. . . . the library media specialist often works as part of a team, implementing a number of the steps in the instructional design process. The library media specialist might present an inservice on one or more of the steps. Often the purpose of involvement at this level is to increase the teacher's ability to perform one or more of the steps subsequent to the intervention. (Turner, 1985, p. 15)

Not surprisingly, in the original article Turner and Naumer discouraged library media specialists from adopting the

"No Involvement" level at any step. They argued that *"all levels, except the very lowest, be considered involvement in the instructional design consultation process"* [italics in original] (p. 30). For each step of their design model, they provided a brief definition of the step, succinct descriptions of the levels as they apply to that step, and a series of sample activities that illustrate how each level might be attained. Step 2, Specification of Objectives, for example, is defined as "Derives terminal and enabling objectives from goal statements, identifies as to type of learning and arranges in a learning hierarchy." The Reaction level for this step involves "Upon request, assists in any aspect of creating and using objectives," while the sample activity states that "After being informed by the Principal that her objective, 'The students will *really* understand the value of good citizenship,' was not adequate, the new social studies teacher asked for help. The [library media specialist] helped her re-write the objective" (p. 31).

Testimony to the value of Turner and Naumer's contribution to the library media specialist's evolving design role is provided by its uniqueness and longevity: Turner's book, based on the 1983 model, has remained for many years the sole text on instructional design developed specifically for the library media field. Originally published in 1985, it was revised and reissued in 1993. While the "levels" idea remained, several of the levels were renamed and slightly reconceptualized: in-depth, moderate, initial, and no involvement. The essential structure and content of the model, however, remained unchanged. Turner continues to write on the topic (Turner, 1991; Turner & Zsiray, 1990) and plans a new edition of *Helping Teachers Teach* for 2003.

18.2.3 The TIE Model

Like the Johnson and the Turner and Naumer works, the Cleaver and Taylor (1983) model "attempts to bridge the gap between theory and practice" (Cleaver & Taylor, 1989, p. ix) for the library media specialist attempting to adapt to the designer's role. In contrast to the models described above, however, Cleaver and Taylor focus primarily on how the library media specialist can fold instructional design into his or her many other responsibilities within a school. Thus, their TIE model (Fig. 18.3) does not address the specific concepts and principles of instructional systems design but "gives the school library media specialist a structure for the process of initiating cooperative planning with a teacher." The focus of the model is on "helping the library media specialist to examine, step-by-step, the processes of his or her interactions" (p. ix) as he or she establishes a cooperative relationship with a teacher, works through the process of instructional planning with that teacher, and implements and evaluates the results of the effort. The TIE model—Talking, Involving, Evaluating—complements and enriches Johnson's and Turner and Naumer's work.

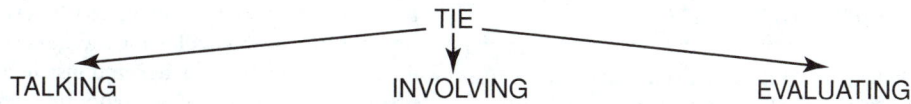

TALKING	INVOLVING	EVALUATING
MEETING WITH THE TEACHER IN THE CLASSROOM	WORKING WITH THE TEACHER IN THE LIBRARY MEDIA CENTER	PROVIDING OPPORTUNITIES FOR FEEDBACK

TALKING — MEETING WITH THE TEACHER IN THE CLASSROOM

A. Select teacher for cooperative effort.
B. Discuss reasons for seeking a meeting.
C. Set time and place.
D. Select a trial unit.
E. Determine teacher's resources and strategies for this unit and identify the areas for cooperation.
F. Describe what you expect to do before your next meeting.

INVOLVING — WORKING WITH THE TEACHER IN THE LIBRARY MEDIA CENTER

A. Identify and locate information resources for the unit in preparation for your meeting.
  1. Examine library media center collection.
  2. Use the Information Resources Checklist.
B. Review and analyze information resources.
  1. Presort and organize resources.
  2. Analyze resources.
C. Meet with teacher in the library media center.
  1. Discuss resources available.
  2. Examine and preview resources with the teacher.
  3. Develop a plan matching resources and strategies to student characteristics.

EVALUATING — PROVIDING OPPORTUNITIES FOR FEEDBACK

A. Evaluate the effectiveness of the information resources and instructional strategies.
  1. Discuss criteria for observation and evaluation.
  2. Observe strategies and resources being used in the classroom and library media center.
B. Evaluate cooperative efforts.
  1. Discuss mutual classroom and library media center.
  2. Plan for future cooperation.

FIGURE 18.3. Cleaver and Taylor's Talking-Involving-Evaluating Model (TIE). Reproduced by permission from *The Instructional Consultant Role of the Library Media Specialist* by Betty P. Cleaver and William D. Taylor; copyright © 1989 by the American Library Association.

Out of print for several years, the book explaining the TIE model was reissued in 1989. Honed by the authors' experiences conducting staff development workshops with library media specialists in Ohio, the revised edition provides extensive guidance for each of its steps and includes a number of ancillary documents designed to meet the needs the workshop participants had identified. For example, a Curriculum Awareness Checklist is provided to help library media specialists be proactive rather than reactive in initiating the instructional design process; an Information Resources Checklist is included to help remind them of sources for the materials they might need to support the materials selection part of that process. Advice includes tips for choosing a teacher—one "who has a reputation for being an effective classroom teacher, a teacher regarded highly by students and other teachers" (p. 32) who will be skilled and secure enough to enhance the chances of a successful cooperative effort. Advice for selecting a trial unit includes descriptions of the Ho-Hum Unit, the Undernourished Unit, the Student Involvement Unit, the Mandated Unit, the Expanded Unit, and the New Unit—any one of which is likely to be improved by an infusion of cooperative instructional design. Clearly, the authors were determined to provide direct and specific help for the library media specialist who was willing to attempt what Turner and Naumer (1983) had identified as a potentially frustrating experience.

18.3 THE FIRST INFORMATION POWER: THE 1988 GUIDELINES

It is no accident that the revised and expanded TIE model was issued in the wake of the publication of the seventh national standards for the school library media field: *Information Power: Guidelines for School Library Media Programs* (AASL & AECT, 1988). A landmark document for the field, these standards—now known as *Information Power 1*—broke new ground in many ways that are beyond the scope of this chapter. However, the reappearance of the TIE model a year after the guidelines' publication is a clear example of the excitement the new document spawned about the library media specialist's instructional design role. In fact, it is difficult today to overestimate the influence of *Information Power 1* on the emergence and solidification of that role.

18.3.1 Mission and Goals

According to these guidelines, the mission of the library media program was "to ensure that students and staff are effective users of ideas and information" (AASL & AECT, 1988, p. 1). Library media specialists were to accomplish that mission not only by helping teachers select and use appropriate resources but by providing intellectual and physical access to information. Library media specialists were to offer instruction related to the use of information and to work with other educators "to design learning strategies to meet the needs of individual students" (p. 1). Two goals related to the overall mission further delineated the key relationship between the library media program and the

field of instructional design and technology. These goals called upon the library media specialist

> To provide learning experiences that encourage students and others to become discriminating consumers and skilled creators of information through introduction to the full range of communications media and use of the new and emerging information technologies [and]
> To provide leadership, instruction, and consulting assistance in the use of instructional and information technology and the use of sound instructional design principles. (AASL & AECT, 1988, p. 2)

The position of these statements within the overall context of *Information Power 1* is in itself significant: they are the third and fourth of seven goals listed in the document—appearing immediately after the goals dealing with the provision of intellectual and physical access to information, the most obvious of the library media specialist's functions. Their prominence within the document underlines the unquestioned importance of instructional design and technology to the leaders in the library media field by this point in its history. After years of moving toward a full instructional role in the school, the field was now staking a claim to what would become the central focus of education in the 1990s and beyond—helping students and others learn how to use informational/instructional technology for learning.

18.3.2 Roles of the Library Media Specialist

Information Power 1 highlighted its claim by formally identifying three distinct roles for the library media specialist: information specialist, teacher, and instructional consultant. The first two roles, of course, were nothing new: library media specialists had always been their schools' information specialists and had long been expected to teach library skills. Although the document noted that "the importance and complexity of this [information specialist] function have increased dramatically in recent years" (AASL & AECT, 1988, p. 27) and that the teaching of "information skills" now involved helping students to develop skills in critical thinking and "to become effective producers and users of media" (p. 33), little in the updated descriptions of these roles was totally unfamiliar to the document's audience. The formal specification of the role of instructional consultant, however, was another matter: a stunning innovation in the field's national guidelines and a direct and purposeful call to library media specialists to adopt a new and greatly enlarged role within their schools. *Information Power 1*'s anointing of library media specialists as instructional consultants is arguably the most significant contribution of this set of standards to the progress of the field.

18.3.3 Instructional Consulting

As an information consultant, the library media specialist was now expected to use "a systematic process" to

> contribute to the development of instructional activities in the school by participating in the design, production, implementation, and

evaluation of complete instructional units. Throughout the instructional development process, library media specialists [are expected to] assist classroom teachers with the following tasks:

- developing unit objectives that build viewing, listening, reading, and critical thinking skills and that respond to student needs, as determined by a formal assessment process;
- analyzing learner characteristics that will influence design and use of media in an instructional unit;
- evaluating present learning activities and advising appropriate changes;
- organizing the instructional plan, indicating when, where, how, and by whom activities will be presented;
- examining and identifying resources that may be helpful in teaching the unit;
- identifying materials that must be produced locally and or adapted from other materials, within copyright guidelines, and determining how they will be developed;
- identifying logistical problems that must be addressed in order to implement the instructional plan;
- securing equipment, materials, and services required to implement the learning unit;
- assisting in the delivery of unit content and activities;
- determining types of assessment, especially when learning alternatives include various types of media; [and]
- evaluating and modifying learning activities, based on feedback gained from observation and interaction with students. (AASL & AECT, 1988, p. 36)

Wittingly or unwittingly, the writers of *Information Power 1* had developed their own instructional design model for the field.

18.3.4 Theory and Rationale

Information Power 1 did not appear in a vacuum, of course, and its focus on the two instructional roles of the library media specialist—teacher and instructional consultant—reflected the writings of a number of leaders who were intent on moving the field to a more integral place within the schools' instructional programs. In a 1982 special issue of the *Wilson Library Bulletin* devoted to the library media center, David Loertscher had touted instructional development as a "second revolution" in the emergence of the library media field, one which was a "natural extension of the role of the library media specialist" (p. 417). This special issue also introduced Loertscher's 11-level scheme describing successive levels of the library media specialist's involvement in the school's instructional program. At each of its levels, the taxonomy assumes that the library media specialist will be involved in providing, selecting, and/or promoting the use of audiovisual materials—the instructional technologies of the time; levels nine and ten, however, speak specifically to the library media specialist's involvement in instructional design:

Level Nine—Instructional design, level I: the library media specialist participates in every step of the development, execution, and evaluation of an instructional unit, but there is still some detachment from the unit.

Level Ten—Instructional design, level II: the library media center staff participates in grading students and feels an equal responsibility with the teacher for their achievement. (Loertscher, 1982, p. 420)

Acknowledging that the differences between the two levels are subtle, Loertscher (1982) explained that in both levels the library media specialist "works with teachers to create the objectives of the unit, assembles materials, understands unit content, and participates in the instructional process." The latter level also involves the library media specialist as "a coequal teacher not only as a resource person but also as an evaluator of student progress" (p. 420). A conceptual framework rather than a specific instructional design model like Johnson's (1981) and Turner's (1983), Loertscher's taxonomy rapidly became influential and joined with these others in helping to create an environment in which the library media specialist's instructional consultant role could be successfully promoted. Loertscher's 1988 book—*Taxonomies of the School Library Media Program,* which grew out of his 1982 article—remained an important resource for the field throughout the 1990s.

One especially significant piece from this era—written, in fact, while *Information Power 1* was under development—was Mancall, Aaron, and Walker's (1986) "Educating Students to Think: The Role of the School Library Media Program." In this concept paper resulting from a 1985 meeting sponsored by the National Commission on Libraries and Information Science, the authors reviewed then-current learning theory and tied it to the library media specialist's instructional role, advancing a compelling argument for the library media program's centrality in this arena. They wrote that "Library media specialists . . . realize that a major part of their time must be spent helping students develop the thinking skills that will equip them to not only locate but also evaluate and use information effectively and thereby become information literate." The article also noted that among the "primary functions performed by the library media staff that contribute directly to the development of these skills" are "materials production, student instruction, and instructional development activities" (p. 19). Overall, the piece had a major influence not only because it articulated the theoretical grounding for the library media specialist's instructional consultant role but also because it introduced the idea of "information literacy" to the field. It is considered a classic today.

18.4 BARRIERS TO INSTRUCTIONAL CONSULTING

Cautionary notes had been sounded even before *Information Power 1* appeared. In a 1987 special issue of the *Journal of Instructional Development* devoted to the question of instructional design and the public schools, Schiffman hypothesized that "School library media centers represent a viable means of gradually infusing [instructional design] theory and practice into public education" (p. 42) but posed a number of questions about the library media specialist's assumption of the instructional consultant role:

Anyone familiar with the demands placed on school library media specialists... knows that their role as instructional consultants is vastly overshadowed by the management and clerical responsibilities required to keep a resource center operating smoothly. The tendency to schedule school library media centers with classes most of the day... bites into most of the remaining time that might allow for instructional design activities. Furthermore, school library media specialists have generally not been trained in instructional design skills... beyond those required for media production. (Schiffman, 1987, p. 2)

Schiffman's caveats—other responsibilities, inflexible scheduling, and inadequate training—are recurring themes in the library media specialist's evolution into a fuller instructional role (see, for example, Baumbaugh, 1991; Craver, 1986, 1990; Small, 1998b).

In the years following the publication of *Information Power 1,* numerous writers chronicled the stumbling blocks in that evolution. Craver—whose series of important publications (1986, 1990, 1994) have both traced the evolution of the library media specialist's instructional role and envisioned its potential at various stages in this evolution—noted in 1990 "a clear pattern of disagreement between the contemporary literature, standards, and actual practice" that persisted throughout the 1980s and suggested that "the instructional consultant role visualized by practitioners and researchers [that had] preceded the 1988 standards" had by that point "evolved into... a reaction to educational changes brought about by technological advances" rather than solidifying into a distinct role in its own right. Indeed, she concluded that "there is little evidence to suggest that this new role has been accepted and is being practiced by the majority of librarians–despite the numerous books and articles that have discussed it" (pp. 11-12). Eisenberg and Brown (1992), reviewing studies of library skills instruction in K-12 settings, reinforced Craver's view: they found considerable interest in the library media specialist's instructional role but little research in support of the assumptions and acclamations of its value that fill the literature of the field.

Pickard (1993), in a small survey that was limited to library media specialists in a single county ($N = 83$) but that echoes Schiffman's insights, found that a large majority of her respondents agreed with the importance of the instructional consultant role but that "The library media specialists were not practicing [that] role to any great extent. In fact, fewer than half reported that they were practicing to a great or very great extent the actual instructional design levels of Loertscher's taxonomy" (p. 119). In one of the most widely published studies from this period, Putnam (1996) echoed Pickard's design and methodology in a national survey of library media specialists in elementary schools ($N = 197$) and found similar results. Using an 18-item questionnaire designed to capture respondents' perceptions of various aspects of the library media specialist's overall role, she asked them to use a Likert-like scale to rate each item (1) for its importance to the profession and (2) for the degree to which they implemented it in their daily practice. Overall, "with only one exception, all statements rating actual work practice had means lower than the means for perceived importance to professional role, and the mean differences were significant... at the .05 level" (p. 46). For the purposes of this paper, it is interesting to note that two of the four statements relating to the library media specialist's role in instructional design garnered top-half ratings for their importance to the profession but none was ranked higher than eleventh in the responses related to actual practice.

Perhaps the most telling insight into the effectiveness of the library media specialist's instructional consulting role in the 1980s and early 1990s came from outside the library media field. Martin and Clemente (1990), in an article that purported to explain "why ISD has not been accepted by public schools" (p. 61), never discuss the role—actual or potential—of the library media specialist in infusing the concepts and processes of instructional design into public education. Never mentioning the library media specialist at all, the article suggests that the authors—and by extension, many others—were unaware that such a role existed or was mandated by the library media field.

18.4.1 Flexible Scheduling and Instructional Collaboration

Library media researchers, of course, began to look for reasons that the key new role promoted by *Information Power 1* had failed to materialize. Putnam (1996) and others have suggested that the culprit behind the lack of the full implementation of that role is the way in which library media center offerings are often scheduled. Under "fixed scheduling," which is still widely practiced throughout the country, library media specialists teach "library" classes or supervise groups of students' use of resources regularly throughout the school week and have little (if any) opportunity to collaborate with teachers—who often use the students' time in the library as the planning period to which they are entitled by contract. Under "flexible scheduling," the scheduling pattern endorsed by the profession as a whole, students still use the library regularly—however, "The library media specialist and the teacher plan together for instruction or use of resources based on student learning needs in each curriculum unit and schedule on that basis. The schedule is arranged on an *ad hoc* basis and varies constantly" (van Deusen & Tallman, 1994, p. 18).

The issue of fixed vs. flexible scheduling has been a staple of professional discussions for well over a decade. Van Deusen's (1993) survey of 61 Iowa library media specialists nominated by their supervisors as "effective [professionals] whom... they would rehire based on performance" (p. 174) provided some of the earliest research on the issue. Her *t*-tests comparing the independent variable "schedule" to a series of specific instructional design tasks (gather, design, collaborate, deliver, evaluate) revealed that library media specialists who were flexibly scheduled were statistically more likely to participate in the evaluation of students' work and that, moreover, "scheduling and teachers' planning styles interacted significantly to produce more curriculum involvement when flexible scheduling and team planning were implemented together" (p. 173). Van Deusen concluded that successful instructional consulting occurred in elementary schools in which flexible scheduling joined with a "culture of planning" to create an environment in which meaningful collaboration between teachers and the library media specialist could occur.

Reporting on a national survey of elementary school library media specialists ($N = 362$) that echoed her earlier methodology and was funded by the 1993/94 AASL/Highsmith Research Award Study—a well-respected research grant available through the American Association of School Librarians—van Deusen and Tallman confirmed and expanded these earlier findings. After participants had identified instances of five types of curriculum consulting in which they had participated over a 6-week period—gather, identify, plan, teach, and evaluate—the researchers used a variety of descriptive statistical techniques as well as a series of ANOVAs to determine the relationships among scheduling, consulting, information skills instruction performed by library media specialists, specific aspects of the planning process, and a variety of other variables (e.g., full- and part-time status of the program, requirements to provide planning time for teachers, etc.). In an issue of *School Library Media Quarterly* devoted primarily to the three parts of this study the authors wrote that

Library media specialists in schools that used fixed scheduling defined slightly more than one-fifth of their units as collaboratively planned. In contrast, those library media specialists in schools that used flexible scheduling defined slightly more than three-fifths of their units as collaboratively planned. Perhaps the best scenario for implementation of the consultation and teaching roles defined in *Information Power* includes flexible scheduling, with a full-time certified library media specialist who meets with teams of teachers to plan for instruction. (van Deusen & Tallman, 1994, pp. 36-37)

McCarthy (1997) confirmed these and Putnam's (1996) findings through a survey of library media programs in 48 schools in the New England region. She found that the second-ranked barrier to the full realization of the vision of *Information Power 1*—after the predictable "lack of support for budget, resources, technology, and staff"—was the "lack of a flexible schedule to allow for collaborations" (p. 209). Whatever the reasons, it was clear that, almost a decade after the publication of the 1988 guidelines that had formalized the instructional consultant role, library media specialists supported the role but were not practicing it to the extent to which it could make a difference in their contribution to student learning.

18.4.2 The Library Power Project

One exception to this general pattern was uncovered during the Library Power Project, a 3-year effort funded by the DeWitt Wallace–Reader's Digest Fund launched in 1988. With almost $50 million in support from the Fund, Library Power involved 19 communities across the country in the largest school library media project ever funded. "Designed to promote the full use of the school library program in instruction" (Hopkins & Zweizig, 1999, p. i), the project sought to surmount the barriers to the full implementation of the vision of *Information Power 1* by (1) stocking newly refurbished facilities with up-to-date resources, (2) ensuring adequate staffing by full-time library media specialists, (3) requiring flexible scheduling, (4) supporting collaboration among teachers and library media specialists, and (5) offering professional development. Using a mixture of

survey and case-study approaches, project evaluators addressed a wide range of questions. What Webb and Doll (1999) found from their content analyses of data from over 400 schools (i.e., "collaboration log forms" completed by library media specialists and questionnaires completed by a variety of school personnel) was that

participation in Library Power increased the percentage of schools where teachers and librarians collaborated to plan instruction and to develop the library collection. Library Power also apparently increased the percentage of teachers who collaborated with the librarian in schools where collaboration already existed. (Webb & Doll, 1999, p. 29)

While such a finding is hardly surprising—participants simply did what the grant money funded them to do—it is notable that the barriers to instructional consulting that have been cited by other researchers can, in fact, be removed. Van Deusen's most recent study on the topic (1996) suggests that vast sums of money are not the only mechanism for engineering such a removal. Using traditional qualitative methods—interviews with teachers, the principal, and the library media specialist; observations of planning sessions and of instruction; analysis of various documents, including email messages related to planning; and analysis of a checklist on which teachers identified the roles the library media specialist tended to play in their teams—van Deusen investigated the library media specialist's contributions to teaching teams in a new elementary school "designed and staffed to feature collaboration" (p. 232). She identified three categories of assistance the library media specialist provided: gathering and presenting resources, planning and focusing teaching and learning experiences, and serving as a communication link among the teams and the other instructional specialists in the school.

Ultimately, van Deusen concluded that the library media specialist worked effectively with all four of the school's teaching teams, functioning as an "insider/outsider" who was able to participate fully as a member of each team while at the same time using her status as someone with neither teaching responsibilities nor authority over the teachers to serve as "a catalyst for reflective thought" (p. 245). Many of the conditions in the school seemed ideal for fostering the collaboration she found: a resource-based curriculum, a commitment "to create for itself an identity as a community" (p. 232), "a high priority for the use of instructional technology" (p. 235), and a library media specialist who had been a successful classroom teacher. Once again, her findings suggest that the culture of the school—which is analogous to the environment enabled by the Library Power funding—is the most important variable in determining the library media specialist's effectiveness in the instructional consultant role.

18.5 RESEARCH ON THE LIBRARY MEDIA PROGRAM'S IMPACT ON LEARNING

One can argue that the library media specialist's instructional design role has been largely overlooked because library media programs have been largely unconnected with learning—that, despite the field's protestations, library media centers are largely "circulation depots" that are generally removed from the classroom and that library media specialists focus only on delivering "containers" of information rather than on designing instruction that helps students learn from the information in those containers. While it is undoubtedly true that many well-documented barriers have prevented library media programs from fully meeting the field's current expectation that "The library media program is essential to learning and teaching and must be fully integrated into the curriculum to promote students' achievement of learning goals" (AASL & AECT, 1998, p. 58), it is also true that the widespread perception that library media programs are removed from the schools' instructional mission is an inaccurate stereotype. In fact, research suggests that library media programs have had a steady, if small and little-documented, impact on student learning over the years.

18.5.1   Early Studies

As early as 1984, Elaine Didier's analysis of 38 studies of library media programs' impact on student achievement revealed a number of positive findings. Although the review is plagued by the problems endemic to any such "meta-analysis"—variations in definitions of achievement (GPA, test scores, problem-solving ability); in samples (elementary through postsecondary students); and in areas studied (primarily those like language arts that are usually associated with library media services but with scattered findings in such other areas as mathematics and the natural sciences)—the patterns that emerged allowed Didier to conclude in a later article that "Overall, the findings show much evidence that school library media programs can be positively related to student achievement" (Didier, 1985, p. 33). The studies indicated that the presence of library media programs, knowledge of library skills, and levels of library media service in a school were all associated with both general and specific improvements in achievement. Interestingly, while some of the studies in Didier's review addressed the curricular and instructional roles of the library media specialist, these were more descriptions of the barriers to implementing those roles than examinations of their effectiveness. Nevertheless, Didier's review makes it clear that for decades researchers in the field have held the assumption that the instructional role is an important component of library media programs that relates them directly to student learning.

Despite the positive trends in Didier's findings, she was able to muster only minimal evidence for library media programs' effectiveness in fostering learning. This is not surprising: Lance (1994) noted that fewer than forty studies had focused on the topic by the mid-1990s and that the majority of these had been conducted between 1959 and 1979. Many in the field "know" that library media programs are valuable in fostering learning and can point to individual studies and experiences to buttress that view, but little widespread and rigorous research has been conducted to support such claims. The fact that the calls for the library media specialist's instructional consulting role didn't appear in the field's official guidelines until the late1980s both offers a reason for the dearth of studies before that period and

suggests that it is now time to conduct more extensive research into the relationship of the library media specialist's instructional and instructional consultant roles to student learning.

One of the first current library media researchers to investigate that relationship was Ross Todd, who conducted a series of studies in Australia over a period of several years and found that "integrated information-skills [instruction] can add a positive dimension to learning" (Todd, 1995, p. 133). Reporting specifically on the culminating study in this series, Todd described one of the few experimental attempts to investigate the connection between the library media specialist's instructional role and student achievement: a posttest-only comparison group study that took place over three terms and involved 40 high school students who'd received traditional science instruction and 40 who'd received instruction in information seeking as part of the science curriculum. Analyses of variance of students' mean annual science scores (based on marks from their midyear and final exams) and of mean scores on an information-skills test devised by the research team led Todd to conclude that "integrated skills instruction appears to have had a significant positive impact on students' mastery of prescribed science content and on their ability to use a range of information skills" (p. 137). This finding that the library media specialist's instruction in information literacy improved students' achievement not only in the information skills but also in content knowledge was an important and tantalizing step in the field's quest to state with confidence that its programs and services have a direct and positive effect on learning.

18.5.2   Learning with Information

In the past decade, various other library media researchers have also worked mightily to capture the elusive relationships among the library media program, the library media specialist's instructional and instructional consultant roles, and student learning. Although much of this work has simply *assumed* the importance of information use to learning rather than actually testing the relationship, the stream of writing in this area deserves attention in any discussion of research on library media programs' role in student achievement. In fact, it is obvious today that the theories and arguments underlying the literature on information use and learning must be a key component undergirding any future research on the impact of library media programs on learning.

18.5.2.1   Resource-Based   Learning. Throughout the 1990s, researchers and theorists associated with the resource-based learning movement (also known as the information-based learning movement) sought to demonstrate the benefits of a kind of learning that was grounded in students' direct use of information—that is, in their use of original sources and reference materials to answer self-generated questions (see, for example, Eisenberg & Small,1995; Meyer & Newton, 1992; Ray, 1994). Their ideas (1) that students' personal questions are more important than teachers' packaged assignments and (2) that information is a more valuable tool for learning than textbooks and other traditional learning tools are obviously consistent with constructivist learning theory. Moreover, the emergence of this stance within the library media field marked an important stage in the field's movement toward a specific focus on learning and in its understanding that library media programs have an essential role in fostering authentic, meaningful learning.

18.5.2.2 Learning as Process.

Other library media researchers also began to use ideas from contemporary learning theory and to focus less on information retrieval and more on the cognitive dimensions of using information as the basis for learning. Moore and St. George (1991), for example, used think-alouds and retrospective interviews with 23 sixth graders in New Zealand to explore the cognitive demands that libraries place on children. McGregor (1994a, 1994b) used participant observation, interviews, think-aloud protocols, and document analysis to investigate the higher-order thinking skills that gifted Canadian twelfth graders in two classes (English and social studies) brought to bear during the process of finding information for three research papers. She found that students thought intuitively rather than in any planned way, that they thought at all levels of Bloom's taxonomy during the process, that they were product-oriented as they sought to complete their projects, and that the nature of the question they were asked (i.e., factual or analytical) had an effect on their levels of thinking about the information they encountered.

Pitts (1994) also used qualitative methods—observation, interviews, and the examination of documents—in a study funded by the 1993–94 AASL/Highsmith Research Award to investigate how and why 26 eleventh- and twelfth-grade science students in a Florida high school made decisions about seeking and using information for a video documentary on a topic related to marine biology. Pitts concluded that the students' learning experience consisted of four intertwined "learning strands"—life skills, information seeking and use, subject matter, and video production—and that they employed these strands differentially according to the immediate task at hand as the research project progressed. Unfortunately, the students' "limited mental models" related to all four strands and the lack of systematic support for any of them from the teachers and library staff involved in the project conspired to limit the students' success.

More recently, McGregor and Streitenberger (1998) used qualitative methods to look at students' understanding of the relationship between learning and the everyday details of the research process. Todd (1999) used a quasi-experimental, repeated-phases design to examine the way information use changed the cognitive models of four above-average Australian girls in their last year of secondary education. In this study, Todd elicited and mapped the girls' initial knowledge structures about heroin and then repeated this process after each of three exposures to different information about the drug. He found that the students used three different strategies—appending new information to an existing node, inserting new information between two existing nodes, and deleting nodes—as they integrated the new information into their original structures: "Overall, the predominant change to the girls' knowledge structures was through elaborating a more inclusive, general idea

through set membership, providing more specific layers in the hierarchy of ideas" (p. 21).

All these studies presume a focus that is grounded in the core ideas that spawned information-based learning—that is, they assume that the learning that is important to investigate involves the processes students use to identify questions, interact with a wide range of resources and information, and generate their own answers. This focus on the processes of learning with information rather than only on the outcomes of those processes marked a significant advance in library media researchers' contributions to the understanding of library media specialists' instructional role.

18.5.2.3 Learning and Electronic Information Sources.

For years, a smattering of information science researchers investigating students' use of electronic resources for information retrieval have drawn implications for learning from their findings (e.g., Kafai & Bates, 1997; Liebscher & Marchionini, 1988; Marchionini, 1989; Marchionini & Teague, 1987; Solomon, 1993, 1994). Others have gone beyond looking at electronic information resources only as venues for information retrieval or for fostering skills directly related to that retrieval to investigate them specifically as learning resources (e.g., Crane & Markowitz, 1994; Kuhlthau, 1997; Neuman, 1993, 1995, 1997). While this research thread remains minor within the information science field, questions about the relationship of information seeking and learning with the products and services available today—particularly those on the World Wide Web—seem to be entering the field almost by osmosis. Recently, for example, Bilal (2000, 2001) used response-capturing software and exit interviews to examine seventh graders' cognitive behaviors as they searched for information to answer a specific question—How long do alligators live in the wild and how long in captivity—on Yahooligans! Among other things, she found that students' search processes "showed an interaction between the concrete cognitive operational stage and the formal cognitive operational stage" (p. 660) and that their navigational prowess had a greater impact on their success as searchers than "factors such as reading ability, topic knowledge, or domain knowledge" (p. 661).

Fidel involved seven of her graduate students in a class project to use observations, think-alouds, and interviews to study eight high school students' Web-searching behaviors in connection with their homework assignments (Fidel et al., 1999). The group was unavoidably drawn into questions about learning when they encountered the students' many problems in completing their searches and tried to determine how to make the students' experiences more successful: "the team's first and strongest recommendation is to provide teachers and students with formal training in Web searching. . . . without such training, the introduction of the Internet into schools will not help to improve learning and may even help some students to develop unproductive learning habits" (p. 34).

To date, the work of Large and his colleagues offers the most intensive and extensive look at information use and learning in electronic environments from an information science perspective. For approximately a decade, this group has studied sixth graders in primary schools in the Montreal area as they have used various electronic information technologies—first a CD-ROM encyclopedia and, later, the Web. Their two series of studies have been multiphased and comprehensive, using experimental and qualitative methods to look at a variety of aspects of interface and information design, students' searching, and the kinds of learning associated with working in this environment. The first series, funded by the Social Sciences and Humanities Research Council of Canada, comprised three phases:

- Phase 1 involved 120 students and compared their abilities to recall information and draw inferences from it after using either the print or the CD-ROM version of *Compton's Multimedia Encyclopedia* (Large et al., 1994b).
- Phase 2 involved 71 students and examined their abilities to recall and enact a procedure presented under various conditions, including several involving animation and captioning, in the same encyclopedia (Large et al., 1995).
- Phase 3 involved 122 students and further investigated the effects of animation and captioning and added a focus on spatial skills in an overall attempt to determine the specific factors that enhance students' abilities to recall text and to comprehend it (Large et al., 1996).

A related study that was not actually a part of the three-phase work (Large et al., 1994a) compared 48 students' retrieval steps and times when looking at questions of varying complexity in the print and CD-ROM versions of the encyclopedia.

All these investigations used experimental designs and a variety of analytic techniques. The first-published study (Large et al., 1994a) randomly assigned the students to two equal groups and had each student retrieve text to answer four questions in either the print or the CD-ROM version of the encyclopedia in a randomized sequence over two searching sessions. The questions ranged from simple (involving one key term) through various stages of complexity (involving two, three, or four key terms). Most students (75%) were able to retrieve the appropriate text from whichever source they searched, and analysis of variance revealed that both groups took seven times longer to retrieve the text containing the answer for the most complex question than the text related to the simplest one. Students in the CD-ROM group used one or more of the three search paths offered by the interface and exhibited a wide range of retrieval times to find their answers.

The studies that comprised the three phases of the larger investigation changed in both complexity and focus as the work progressed. All the studies, however, were interested in the contributions of animation to students' recall and comprehension and were heavily influenced by work found in the instructional design literature (e.g., Hannafin & Rieber, 1989; Reiber, 1990; Rieber & Hannafin, 1988). Each involved the establishment of various numbers of randomly assigned groups (five in Large et al., 1994b, and four in each of the other two studies) that viewed the same semantic content under different presentation conditions—each involving text alone and then a variation of additional conditions depending upon the particular focus of the study. Data analysis involved a variety of techniques, including multivariate repeated measures analysis of variance for all the studies and additional measures as appropriate—for example, Large et al. (1996) also involved the analysis of taped interviews.

As might be expected, the findings for the collection of studies are wide-ranging and various. The following highlights review the findings that seem most germane to the focus of this chapter:

- Students shown the text-only version of the CD-ROM version of the encyclopedia did better on the measure of literal recall of content than either (1) students who saw printed text and illustrations or (2) those who saw multimedia (text, still images, and animation). However, the "multimedia subjects did significantly better than their print or text-on-screen counterparts at this deeper level [drawing inferences]. The animations, then, appeared to help subjects better understand the topics" (Large et al., 1994b).
- While recall and inference levels were similar for the four groups in this study, recall of procedural information—that is, of a sequence of executable steps—was highest in the group that saw the richest presentation: text plus animations plus captions (Large et al., 1995).
- While animation did not have any effect on students' recall and understanding of descriptive text—that is, of text that describes persons, events, and processes related to a common theme—it had a significant effect on students' ability to perform a problem-solving task, the task in the study that "involved the highest level of cognitive effort." Moreover, "Students with high spatial ability in general performed better than students with low spatial ability regardless of presentation condition" (Large et al., 1996, p. 437).

For their next series of studies—another 3-year effort supported by the Social Sciences and Humanities Research Council of Canada—Large and his associates used qualitative methods to explore in depth some of the issues related to children's searches of multimedia CD-ROMs and the World Wide Web. Again using sixth graders from the Montreal area, the researchers investigated students' search strategies, information extraction, and use of information for assignments in both environments and elicited their suggestions for Web design. While this series of studies is less targeted to learning than the earlier series, it nevertheless adds to the growing amount of data available to the designers of these resources that could help them create products that are more suitable for younger users (Large & Beheshti, 2000; Large, Beheshti, & Breuleux, 1998; Large, Beheshti, & Rahman, 2002).

Large and his collaborators are unique in the breadth and depth of their studies of the relationship of information seeking and learning, and they stand almost alone in presenting such findings in the information science literature. Others in the field who are working on similar problems include Chung (2003)—who has used qualitative techniques and concept mapping to identify connections between information seeking in various library media center resources, including electronic ones, and learning at each of the six levels in Anderson and Krathwohl's (2001) revision of Bloom's taxonomy—and Neuman (2001), who argues that synthesizing—the process of creating a personal conceptual structure from information elements found in discrete electronic resources—is the key to learning with the World Wide Web.

18.5.2.4 *Kuhlthau's Information Search Process (ISP).*
One indication of the importance of emerging ideas about the relationship of information to learning was the appearance of the inaugural issue of *School Libraries Worldwide* (Oberg, 1995), which was devoted entirely to the topic. Carol Kuhlthau was invited to write the lead article in that journal both because her work in the area is considered seminal and because her Information Search Process (ISP) has found wide acceptance not only within school library media but within the larger field of library and information science.

Kuhlthau (1983) initially identified the ISP in a library media setting through a qualitative study in which she identified the cognitive, affective, and physical dimensions of 25 advanced high school seniors' information seeking as they worked on research papers. Over the years, she has verified the model through a series of related studies: with "process surveys" of a broader population of 147 high school seniors in six sites (Kuhlthau, 1989); with similar surveys of 385 academic, public, and school library users in 21 sites (Kuhlthau et al., 1990); and with two longitudinal studies of her original participants after their college graduations (Kuhlthau, 1988a, 1988b). In *Seeking Meaning: A Process Approach to Library and Information Services* (Kuhlthau, 1993), she argued that both learning and information seeking are constructivist processes and that "information seeking in libraries [should be] placed in a larger context of learning" if library and information science theorists are to overcome "a lack of theory within library and information science to explain fully the user's perspective of information seeking" (pp. 14-15).

Although Kuhlthau's original intent was to illuminate information seeking rather than learning—indeed, the ISP doesn't include the word "learning" at all—her interweaving of information seeking and learning has been deeply influential throughout the library media field. She captured what the field believes to be its core contribution in schools, and she has expanded and explained her ideas in a variety of forums. In 1993, for example, she identified "zones of intervention" during which library media specialists could apply practices related to Vygotsky's theory to help their students in various stages of the ISP; in 1997, she presented an adaptation of the model for use in electronic environments; in 1999, she was invited to participate in the Library Power Project to analyze the effects of that effort on student learning.

18.5.3 Learning and Library Power

One of a cadre of researchers involved in evaluating the Library Power Project, Kuhlthau (1999) was asked to address the question of "learning in the library," only one of many questions of interest to the project as a whole. Designed to assess the extent to which the project achieved its primary goal—that is, to improve "opportunities for learning" rather than to assess learning itself—the overall Library Power evaluation component

reflected the traditional library science approach to assessing the value of library services by focusing on the nature and extent of the opportunities provided rather than on the actual results achieved. Despite this limitation, Kuhlthau was able to tease out several findings that are relevant to learning in school library media centers.

Working with responses to a single open-ended question about learning on each of three years of annual surveys of all Library Power librarians ($N = 405$) and with data from case studies of learning in three Library Power schools, Kuhlthau identified five levels of learning:

Level 1: Input—emphasis on what librarian did, not on students, i.e., adding to collection, adding new technology, describing lesson or unit plan.
Level 2: Output—emphasis on quantitative measure of student use, i.e., more visits, more use of materials and technology.
Level 3: Attitude—emphasis on change in student attitude, i.e., increased interest and enthusiasm.
Level 4: Skills—emphasis on location of resource and use of technology, i.e., locating books, using CDROM encyclopedia.
Level 5: Utilization—emphasis on content learning, i.e., using resources to learn through inquiry in content areas of the curriculum. (Kuhlthau, 1999, p. 83)

Focusing on the fifth level—"the most pertinent level of evaluation for addressing the question of impact on student learning" (p. 92)—Kuhlthau cataloged a number of indicators of learning identified by the librarians on the survey. The most frequent of these—"independence in applying skills"—accounts for about 20% of the 251 of these responses (62% of the 405) that included any descriptive statement related to learning; indicators related to documented evidence like final products, "recalls content at a later time," and test results accounted for only 15% (39 responses). Case-study data—analyzed according to the same levels noted above—revealed that the three schools had various levels of success in fostering learning and that the most successful was School 1, where "the librarian was a full partner with teachers in learning through research" (p. 94). Able to answer only "a qualified 'yes' that Library Power has influenced student learning opportunities" (p. 94), Kuhlthau pointed out that many of the library media specialists had been "grappling with the task of identifying and assessing learning related to use of library resources.... This study suggests further expertise was needed for assessing, evaluating, and documenting the learning related to libraries" (pp. 87-88). The fact that this expertise was lacking suggests, once again, that the concepts and techniques of instructional systems design had not yet permeated library media specialists' understanding of their instructional role.

18.5.4 The "Colorado" Research

Against the background of this limited research into the effectiveness of library media programs, the task of demonstrating any robust or widespread relationship between such programs and learning fell to Keith Curry Lance and his colleagues. Lance's group and others who adopted their methodology conducted a

series of studies that "have confirmed a positive relationship between library media programs and student achievement virtually
across the United States: the two 'Colorado' studies (Lance et al.,
1993; Lance, Rodney, & Hamilton-Pennell, 2000b) and the studies in Alaska (Lance, Hamilton-Pennell, & Rodney, 2000), Oregon (Lance, Rodney, & Hamilton-Pennell, 2001), Pennsylvania
(Lance, Rodney, & Hamilton-Pennell, 2000a), and Texas (Smith,
2001) that are based on the 'Colorado' methodology" (Neuman,
2003, p. 505).

For the first of these studies, Lance drew a nonrandom sample of 221 Colorado public elementary and secondary schools
that (1) had library media centers that had responded to a 1989
survey of library media centers in Colorado and (2) used either the Iowa Tests of Basic Skills or Tests of Achievement and
Proficiency to assess student achievement. He applied a combination of statistical techniques to data from (1) the 1980 U.S.
Census about each district that had a school in the sample and
(2) building-level files from the Colorado Department of Education (where he is the Director of the Library Research Service)
in order to identify the relationships of 23 independent variables to students' academic achievement as measured by the
Iowa tests. Following an approach that might best be characterized as "peeling the onion," he used first correlational analysis, then factor analysis, then path analysis conducted through
multiple-regression techniques to determine the relationship of
specific variables to student achievement. The first two methods provided a way to combine and reduce the original set of
variables to nine: a "community" variable (the "at-risk" factor);
three "school" variables (teacher-pupil ratio, per-pupil expenditures, and a combination of salary and other teacher data he
labeled the "career teacher" factor); and five "library media center" variables (a "library media specialist role" factor and factors
related to the library media center's size, use, computing facilities, and per-pupil expenditures). The third method—path
analysis—resulted in the ranking of the variables as predictors
of student achievement.

Not surprisingly, the "at-risk" factor emerged as the strongest
direct predictor of that achievement. Among all the other variables, however, the library media center ones were found to be
the most powerful—even more powerful than other "school"
predictors:

- The size of a library media program, as indicated by the size of its
  staff and collection, is the best school predictor of academic achievement.
- Library media center expenditures predict the size of the library media center's staff and collection and, in turn, academic achievement.
- The instructional role of the library media specialist shapes the collection and, in turn, academic achievement.
- Library media center expenditures and staffing vary with total school
  expenditures and staffing.
- The degree of collaboration between library media specialist
  and classroom teacher is affected by the ratio of teachers to
  pupils.
- The other potential predictors analyzed during the study—the career
  teacher, library media center use, and library media center computing
  factors—were not found to have significant relationships to student
  achievement. (Lance, 1994, p. 172)

These were extraordinary findings, and so the "Colorado
study" swept the school library media field. Most significantly for
the purposes of this paper, it is important to note that many of
the findings—particularly the third and the fifth—relate specifically to the library media specialist's roles as teacher and/or
instructional partner; we must also note that the final finding
suggests that library media specialists' use of instructional technology, at least computer technology, was either lagging or had
not yet borne fruit. (Lance has since postulated that his initial work failed to take into account networked computers that
tapped into library media center resources but were not physically housed in the library media facility.) In any case, drawing
from across his data, Lance ultimately concluded that "Students
whose library media specialists played [an instructional] role
tended to achieve higher average test scores" (p. 172).

Criticized for its small sample size, its reliance on existing (rather than original) data related to both demographics
and achievement, and its nonexperimental design, the first
"Colorado study" nevertheless provided new insights into the relationships of library media programs and learning. Lance specifically called for replications of his work in other states, and later,
in the 1990s and into the current century, he and others have
drawn on his methodology to conduct such replications across
the country. These later studies have generally included greater
numbers of schools, original data as well as available data, and
variations on Lance's original study design. While they have continued to reinforce the importance of the instructional role of
the library media specialist, they have found additional predictors of academic achievement as well: not surprisingly, for example, the library media center's provision and use of technology,
especially the Internet, has emerged as a major predictor.

Invited to the White House Conference on School Libraries
on June 4, 2002, to present an overview of his work—including
several studies that are currently underway—Lance identified
three sets of findings about library media center factors that
predict academic achievement that figure prominently across
the studies he's conducted in recent years:

- the *level of development* of the school library,
- the extent to which school librarians engage in *leadership* and *collaboration* activities that foster information literacy, and
- the extent to which instructional *technology* is utilized to extend the
  reach of the library program beyond the walls of the school library.
  (Lance, 2002, p. 2; italics in original)

The first of these factors relates primarily to physical issues:
"the ratios of professional and total staff to students, a variety of
per student collection ratios, and per student spending on the
school library." The second two, however, relate directly to the
library media specialist's role in instruction and in the use of
technology for learning. According to Lance, library media specialists who exercise leadership in creating a collaborative environment in which they perform such functions as "planning instruction cooperatively with teachers . . . and teaching students
both with classroom teachers and independently" (p. 4) have
a direct effect on students' higher reading scores. Additionally,
"Perhaps the most dramatic changes since the original Colorado
study have been in the realm of instructional technology. . . . In

our recent studies, we have found that in schools where computer networks provide remote access to library resources, particularly the Web and licensed databases, test scores tend to be higher" (p. 5).

The importance of this series of studies is that it establishes—for the first time—a clear and widespread connection between library media programs and learning. Moreover, since all the studies have included a mechanism to control for such "school differences" as teachers' characteristics and total per pupil expenditures and such "community differences" as poverty and minority demographics, the connection is difficult to dismiss. Overall, the pattern that has emerged, while still based on correlational data rather than experimental findings, is strong enough to allow Lance to claim that "School libraries are a powerful force in the lives of America's children. The school library is one of the few factors whose contribution to academic achievement has been documented empirically, and it is a contribution that cannot be explained away by other powerful influences on student performance" (pp. 6–7).

18.6 THE CURRENT NATIONAL STANDARDS AND THE LIBRARY MEDIA SPECIALIST'S ROLE TODAY

It is no accident that Lance couches his most recent findings in language taken directly from the latest national guidelines for school library media programs, *Information Power: Building Partnerships for Learning* (AASL & AECT, 1998). That document identifies "collaboration, leadership, and technology" as the three "integrating issues" that "underlie the vision of library media programs presented" there (p. 47). Lance's (2002) focus on these subtle but significant elements reflects the field's belief that a focus on these issues is imperative:

Collaboration, leadership, and **technology** [bold in original] are integral to every aspect of the library media program and every component of the library media specialist's role. They furnish theoretical and practical grounding both for the program and for all the activities of the library media specialist.... They suggest a framework that surrounds and supports the authentic student learning that is the goal of a successful, student-centered library media program. (AASL & AECT, 1998, p. 49)

All three of these themes relate to the library media specialist's role in instructional design and technology, and both the theoretical and the practical thrusts of *Information Power 2* leave no doubt about the current understanding of that role. For example, the document retained the same mission statement as *Information Power 1* and modified the goals only insofar as necessary to update them to reflect current language and emphases. Thus, the third and fourth goals now argue that the role of the library media specialist is

To provide learning experiences that encourage students and others to become discriminating consumers and skilled creators of information through comprehensive instruction related to the full range of communications media and technology [and]

To provide leadership, collaboration, and assistance to teachers and others in applying principles of instructional design to the use of instructional and information technology for learning. (AASL & AECT, 1998, p. 7)

Concepts and suggested practices related to these goals as well as to collaboration, leadership, and technology are embedded throughout the guidelines.

18.6.1 Today's Library Media Specialist

While the general thrust of *Information Power 2* remains the same as that of its predecessor, the document reflects some significant changes in the field's understanding of the library media specialist's overall role for the new century and its "information age." Acknowledging the library media specialist's substantial responsibilities in the areas of program management, budgeting, staff supervision, and resource acquisition and maintenance, the new guidelines elevate "program administrator" to the library media specialist's fourth official role. And bowing to the field's continuing dislike of the term "instructional consultant" because of its negative connotations, the guidelines substitute the phrase "instructional partner" for this function. No longer having to explain away their own reservations about the separateness inherent in the word "consultant" and the concerns of teacher colleagues who bridled at the notion of superiority implied by the term, library media specialists can more easily assume a collaborative stance—joining "with teachers and others to identify links across student information needs, curricular content, learning outcomes, and a wide variety of print, nonprint, and electronic information resources" (AASL & AECT, 1998, p. 4).

Two other changes in role descriptions from earlier standards documents are also important to note. First, in *Information Power 2*'s listing of the four roles now prescribed for the field, "teacher" is listed first; "instructional partner," second; "information specialist," third; and "program administrator," fourth. The committee that prepared the guidelines have been adamant that their intent was not to diminish the traditional "information specialist" role but to highlight the importance of the two instructional roles in an age in which "Core elements in both learning and information theory . . . converge to suggest that developing expertise in accessing, evaluating, and using information is in fact the authentic learning that modern education seeks to promote" (AASL, AECT, 1998, p. 2). Nevertheless, the order of presentation underlines the full evolution of the library media specialist from a provider of supplementary resources and services to an essential part of the school's instructional team with a mandate to use both instructional design and instructional technology to enhance students' learning.

18.6.2 The Information Literacy Standards for Student Learning

The second important innovation in the document is the inclusion of a mechanism intended specifically to help the library media specialist implement the "teacher" and "instructional partner" roles. The Information Literacy Skills for Student Learning (ILSSL) are the core of *Information Power 2* and the first learning outcomes related to information use ever endorsed by the two national organizations that represent the library media field. The nine standards and 29 indicators presented in the ILSSL are intended to provide a conceptual framework for the library media specialist's teaching of "information literacy"—the greatly expanded notion of "library skills"—and for integrating this key element of information-age learning throughout the curriculum. The schema begins with three standards related to basic information literacy, develops through three standards that foster independent learning with information, and culminates in three standards that relate to using information and information technology in socially responsible ways. The ILSSL are undoubtedly the most important contribution that *Information Power 2* makes to the school library media field.

Several features were designed specifically to make the ILSSL useful as tools to support the library media specialist's instructional design role: the format in which they appear, the provision of suggestions for assessing their achievement, and the inclusion of direct links to standards from a variety of content areas to show their relevance to learning across the curriculum. First, the ILSSL reflect the typical instructional design approach of creating goals and objectives to structure and direct student learning. The first Standard, for example, is "The student who is information literate accesses information effectively"—a statement that describes an outcome at a broad, general level. This Standard encompasses five "indicators," statements that detail specific outcome behaviors that lend themselves to assessment: for example, "Identifies a variety of potential sources of information" (Standard 1, Indicator 4; AASL & AECT, 1998, p. 11).

For each indicator, three levels of proficiency are suggested "to assist in gauging the extent to which individual students have mastered the components of information literacy." Examples rather than specific assessment items, these statements "allow local teachers and library media specialists full flexibility in determining the amount and kind of detail that should structure student evaluations" (AASL & AECT, 1998, p. x). For Standard 1, Indicator 4, the levels are as follows:

Basic Lists several sources of information and explains the kind of information found in each.
Proficient Brainstorms a range of sources of information that will meet an information need.
Exemplary Uses a full range of information sources to meet differing information needs. (AASL & AECT, 1998, p. 11)

The format of the statements and the inclusion of suggestions for assessing students' learning clearly give library media specialists a useful tool for designing information literacy instruction according to the concepts and principles of instructional systems design. Moreover, providing specific guidance but assuming more latitude than traditional objectives and assessment strategies often allow, the ILSSL are broad enough to encompass a variety of learning and evaluation activities that are both consistent with current learning theory and that call for the use of "the full range of communications media and technology" (AASL & AECT, 1998, p. 7).

Thus, the theory underlying the development of the ILSSL supports the library media specialist's role in designing and implementing learning experiences that involve authentic tasks and that use a variety of technologies as "information vehicles for exploring knowledge to support learning-by-constructing" (Jonassen, Peck, & Wilson, 1999, p. 13). For example, comparing and contrasting commercial and public service ads to determine the kinds of information featured in each addresses an information issue of interest to many students and can involve the use of a comprehensive range of information technology—newspapers, magazines, radio, television, and the World Wide Web—as venues for learning. The ILSSL provide theoretical and practical guidance for melding the library media specialist's instructional design and instructional/informational technology responsibilities.

18.6.3 Links to the Content Areas

The third aspect of the ILSSL that supports their use as an instructional-partnering tool is the provision of links between these statements of information literacy outcomes and the content area standards developed by various national educational groups in science, mathematics, geography, civics, English language arts, etc. Each of the ILSSL is accompanied by a series of outcome statements developed by these groups, over 80 of which—related to 14 content areas—were selected to highlight the connections between information literacy and learning in the content areas. Extracted from Kendall and Marzano's *Content Knowledge: A Compendium of Standards and Benchmarks for K-12 Education* (2nd ed., 1997), the statements are linked with specific ILSSL to provide "a tool for library media specialists and teachers to use as they collaboratively design learning experiences that will help students master both disciplinary content and information literacy" (AASL & AECT, 1998, pp. x–xi). By offering guidance for linking information access, evaluation, and use specifically to the subject matter areas, this feature gives the library media specialist a clear and specific mechanism to use in approaching teachers, showing them the relevance of information literacy to achievement in their own content areas, and initiating the collaborative instructional design process envisioned by *Information Power 1* and *2*.

One of the 11 content area standards provided for our example (ILSSL Standard 1) illustrates the utility of these statements for supporting the collaborative design of learning experiences that address both information literacy and content area expertise and that incorporate the meaningful use of technology as well:

Geography Knows the characteristics and purposes of geographic databases (e.g., databases containing census data, land-use data, topographic information). Standard 1, Grades 6-8 Indicator. (Kendall and Marzano, pp. 511, quoted in AASL & AECT, 1998, p. 13)

Armed with this standard and an ILSSL indicator that focuses on the importance of identifying the most appropriate sources for finding specific information on a topic, the library media specialist can readily collaborate with the middle school geography teacher to design, implement, evaluate, and revise interesting and authentic learning experiences that provide students an opportunity to build their knowledge of geographic sources and their uses.

It may be that *Information Power 2*'s multiple supports for the library media specialist's instructional design function—its newly stated goals, its emphasis on the "instructional partner" role, and its inclusion of the Information Literacy Standards for Student Learning—will be the catalysts that finally enable library media specialists to become full partners on schools' instructional design teams. The potential is certainly in place: over 56,000 copies of the guidelines have been sold in over 24 countries (Robert Hershman, personal communication, March 11, 2002).

18.7 RESEARCH ISSUES FOR THE FUTURE

Now that *Information Power 2* has been available for 5 years, research should begin in earnest on its impact on the teaching-and-learning mission of library media programs and on the contributions those programs bring to student achievement (Neuman, 2003). Such research is clearly necessary. Despite the promising developments of the past decade, there are at present no data to suggest that library media specialists have stepped fully into the role of "an instructional designer from within" as envisioned over a decade ago (Gustafson, Tillman, & Childs, 1991). In fact, in their chapter on instructional design and technology in the schools published in 2002, Carr-Chellman and Reigeluth fail even to mention library media programs or library media specialists in their survey of various types of instructional design and technology initiatives in the schools. Even their recommendations—"building sincere coalitions with teacher groups, moving toward proactive relationships with teachers, and working to understand what teachers need from our field and what will be both useful and sustainable" (p. 251)—suggest a lack of awareness that such activities have been occurring through library media programs for over 20 years.

18.7.1 Understanding the Status of the Field: Too Little Done, Too Little Studied, Too Narrowly Communicated

There are many reasons for the lack of awareness of library media specialists' forays into instructional design and their contributions to learning in schools. One, surely, is the limited amount of integrated instruction and instructional consulting that is actually accomplished. Scholars in the field have lamented this situation for close to two decades (see, for example, Baumbach, 1991; Craver, 1986, 1990; Pickard, 1993; Putnam, 1996; Schiffman, 1987; Small, 1998b; Turner & Zsiray, 1990; van Deusen & Tallman, 1994). To this day, library media specialists with fixed schedules and fixed expectations on the part of principals and teachers often have little opportunity to engage in any instruction beyond teaching isolated classes in what are still too widely called "library skills." Even a library media specialist fortunate enough to have a flexible schedule is often the only professional working in a school's library media center—with an astonishing

array of "librarian" responsibilities and little time for the kind of collaboration envisioned by the field. Those "consulting moments" that do occur are often silently folded into a larger context rather than trumpeted as a distinct and distinctly valuable role. Publicizing successful efforts is rarely a high priority in a hectic schedule.

Another reason for the lack of awareness of the library media program's role in student learning is undoubtedly the limited amount of research that has been conducted on the learning outcomes associated with library media programs and with the instructional efforts of library media specialists. Lance's (1994) observation that fewer than 40 studies had addressed these issues by the mid-1990s and that most of these had been conducted before 1979 is indeed sobering to anyone looking for solid evidence of library media programs' effectiveness in fostering learning. Some of this lack of research on outcomes reflects the limited amount of instructional consulting done in the past, some reflects the comparatively small size of the library media research community, and some seems to reflect the culture of librarianship—a commitment to providing free and unfettered access to information and a firm belief in guarding the privacy of all who use that information.

Growing out of this culture, library and information science (LIS) research has traditionally focused on improving access to information rather than on assessing any outcomes based on its use. Most LIS research on user needs—the closest analog to "learning" issues in the field—has traditionally been survey research (Wang, 1999). Only in 1999, for example, did the Association of Research Libraries begin its "Higher Education Outcomes Research Review" to "investigate strategies for assessing the library's value to the community and to explore the library's impact on learning, teaching, and research" (ARL, 2002). School library media research often follows this long-standing LIS research pattern—using survey and other descriptive methodologies to address the nature and extent of library media programs in schools, the adequacy of funding and collections of resources, the installation and use of networked resources, instances of censorship, the education of library media specialists, factors related to the implementation of the instructional consultant role, and other issues more closely related to providing "opportunities for learning" than to assessing any outcomes related to those opportunities.

A third reason for the lack of awareness of library media programs' value seems to be the library media field's own history and the compartmentalization of education in general and of educational research in particular: while the library media field has moved steadily toward a more complex and valuable instructional presence for decades, few outside the field are aware of the changes. Still seen as "only librarians" by many of their colleagues and generally ignored by researchers outside the library media community, library media specialists have not yet had substantial success in breaking out of their isolation from their fellow practitioners or into the attention of the larger body of educational researchers—all busy professionals who are themselves absorbed in the issues and concerns of their own immediate disciplines.

Moreover, library media researchers themselves have not addressed the issue successfully: talking about Didier's (1984) "benchmark" review of research studies "intended to identify an association between school library media programs and student achievement," Callison (2002) noted that

Tracing these studies 20 years later . . . reveals a problematic trend . . . in that none is published in respected educational research journals, few investigators published their findings beyond the initial dissertation, and an awareness of these collective findings seldom extended beyond the narrow school library research arena. (p. 351)

While this situation has improved somewhat, it is still true that library media research rarely finds its way into journals beyond the limited number devoted specifically to the field: "Until research strands reported here move into a broader educational research framework, it is likely that findings, no matter how dramatic or significant, will remain dormant without causing change" (Callison, 2002, p. 362).

The chief problems, then, in linking the library media program to student achievement are that too little has been done, too little has been studied, and what has been found has been too narrowly communicated. Can this situation be overcome? Can library media programs and the library media specialists responsible for them emerge as recognized contributors to student learning over the next decade? And can research, theory, and practice in instructional design and technology contribute to that emergence? Several promising elements are in place both to support such emergence and to chronicle its nature and effects. Perhaps never before in the history of the field has there been a better environment in which library media specialists can engage more fully in their instructional and instructional design roles and in which library media researchers can study the impact of those efforts and report their results to an interested educational research community.

18.7.2 A Partial Answer to "Too Little Done"

Underlying the factors that suggest a more prominent and visible instructional contribution for library media specialists are the societal and cultural changes that have affected schooling in general and library media programs in particular. Foremost among these, of course, is the World Wide Web. The Web epitomizes the merger of information, communication, and instructional technologies—a merger that has placed the library media program at the heart of one of modern education's most important challenges: to determine how to use information and information technology for effective, meaningful teaching and learning. With teachers eager to find the "best" Web sites to enrich their teaching and students intent on importing Web-based text and visuals into their final products, today's library media specialists often find themselves at the center of the instructional questions that are most pressing in the everyday life of their schools.

It is library media specialists' responsibility to select, maintain, and provide instruction on how to use their schools' electronic information resources—a responsibility that gives them greater opportunities than ever before to promote their instructional design and technology skills to affect learning, teaching,

and student achievement. Sought out for their expertise rather than seeking chances to provide it, today's library media specialists are poised to collaborate in designing information-based instruction as a matter of course rather than as an add-on or an unwarranted distraction. Both conceptually and practically, it is a short step from helping students and teachers locate specific information to helping them use information and information resources in meaningful ways. Library media specialists—trained in both information skills and instructional design—have the knowledge and skills and now an unprecedented opportunity to take that step.

Another cultural and societal engine that is driving library media specialists to a greater focus on learning outcomes is the increasing national emphasis on student achievement, which grew as part of the movement toward developing national standards throughout the 1990s and culminated in the No Child Left Behind Act of 2001. Like all other educators, library media specialists are reexamining their programs and approaches to align them with state and national requirements to foster and demonstrate improved student performance. While the idea of assessing student learning is relatively new to library media specialists (see, for example, Kuhlthau, 1994; Neuman 2000; Thomas, 1999), the current national focus on accountability is encouraging library media specialists to be assessment partners with their teachers and thus—as a by-product—to set the stage for more research opportunities to delineate the relationship of library media programs to learning.

Opportunities, of course, cannot be confused with outcomes. There is certainly a possibility that the tsunami of the Web will overwhelm library media specialists with technical demands rather than spurring them to new heights of instructional and instructional design activity. Even with an increased emphasis on assessment, the field's commitment to integrating information literacy into content instruction rather than treating it as a stand-alone curriculum makes it difficult to trace a straight line between the library media program and learning. Nevertheless, the Web has sparked unprecedented popular and educational interest in "educational technology," and the national focus on accountability is finding its way into library media centers (see, for example, Grover, 1994; Grover, Lakin, & Dickerson, 1997). It seems likely at this juncture that researchers will soon find a much greater number of instances of library media specialists' teaching, instructional partnering, and participation in stipulating and assessing student learning outcomes to use as the basis for studying library media programs' contributions to student learning.

18.7.3 A More Extensive Answer to "Too Little Studied"

To take advantage of the research possibilities afforded by the increasing instructional and instructional design activities now available for library media specialists, library media researchers will need new conceptual frameworks to guide their investigations. Neuman (1997) has argued that the notion of "information literacy," particularly as defined by the American Library Association, provides a compelling framework for such research because of its close interweaving of learning and information studies:

To be information literate, a person must be able to recognize when information is needed and have the ability to locate, evaluate, and use effectively the needed information. . . . Ultimately, information literate people are those who have learned how to learn. They know how to learn because they know how knowledge is organized, how to find information, and how to use information in such a way that others can learn from them. They are people prepared for lifelong learning because they can always find the information needed for any task or decision at hand. (*ALA Presidential Committee Report,* p. 1, quoted in Behrens, 1994, p. 315)

This definition, which "makes explicit the link between information use and learning" and integrates "concepts inherent to learning with those essential to information use, suggests a theoretical structure that . . . anchors [the two fields] within [the] larger framework" of information literacy that provides a compelling rationale for studying the links between information use and learning and for determining the relationship of learning with information to student achievement (Neuman, 1997, pp. 703–704).

Within this framework, several approaches—outgrowths of long-standing views as well as approaches that have emerged in recent years—hold promise for guiding studies of library media programs' contributions to student learning. For example, the field's instructional models for teaching information-seeking skills—such as Eisenberg and Berkowitz's Big Six Skills (1990), Joyce and Tallman's I-Search Process (1997), Stripling and Pitts REACTS model (1988), and Pappas' Pathways to Knowledge (1997)—lend themselves to research that will build on their implied focus on the learning that can occur as part of information seeking. Research designs that make that focus explicit and use it to undergird studies of how library media specialists use the models to foster learning through information seeking can test the models' value as tools for learning. Since many library media practitioners and researchers are already familiar with one or more of the models, using them as the basis for such studies could be a reasonably straightforward way to address the issue.

In addition to the "traditional" information-seeking models that could be expanded to ground research on information seeking and learning, research related to several new instructional design models created specifically for library media specialists can extend knowledge and understanding of the relationship between learning and the instructional design role of the library media specialist. Turner's new textbook, based on his original model, is slated for publication in 2003. A book based on Small's IM-PACT model (Information Motivation—Purpose, Audience, Content, Technique) is also about to appear (Small, 2000a). Turner's model has been a potent force in discussions of library media specialists' instructional design role for some 20 years, and Small's approach builds on her research agenda on motivation (see, for example, Small, 1998a, 1999, 2000b) to create a model in which "motivation theories and concepts inform and are integrated into" each of four design phases. "Based on principles of instructional design, industrial psychology, information science, and communications theory," Small's model focuses on generating "information motivation"—that is, "interest and excitement for using information resources, services, and technologies to solve information problems, satisfy intellectual curiosity, and stimulate a desire to seek and gain knowledge" (Ruth Small, personal communication, September 11, 2002). Research conducted both to verify Turner's and Small's models and to determine their effectiveness in promoting the library media specialist's use of the concepts and skills of instructional design could augment our understanding of library media specialists as instructional partners.

Chief among the tools that can focus studies of library media programs' relationship to student learning, however, are the Information Literacy Standards for Student Learning (ILSSL) presented in *Information Power 2.* Designed both to "describe the content and processes related to information that students must master to be considered information literate" (AASL & AECT, 1998, p. x) and to "provide the basis for the library media specialist's role in collaborative planning and curriculum development" (p. 63), these statements tie the field directly to learning and instruction as nothing has done before. Using them as a framework for structuring studies of their effectiveness—both as tools for planning and as measures for assessing the nature and extent of student learning—is an obvious research approach for the coming decade.

Case studies of how the ILSSL function as tools for collaborative planning and teaching—the processes and outcomes of using them to structure the library media specialist's instructional-partnering role—could provide insights into the specific ways in which library media specialists contribute to sound instructional design and therefore to student achievement. Perhaps even more importantly, studies designed to measure students' achievement related to each of the 29 indicators could provide specific evidence of the contributions of library media programs not only to students' information literacy but to their mastery of content knowledge. These central components of *Information Power*—with their outcomes-based format, built-in guidelines for assessment, and links to a range of subject-matter areas—could prove central components in the field's efforts to establish library media programs as essential to learning in the twenty-first century.

18.7.4 A Partial Answer to "Too Narrowly Communicated"

Changes in the way theorists and practitioners have come to view teaching and learning suggest that library media research that focuses on learning—and particularly on learning with the information that surrounds us in this "information age"—has a focus that could be of wide interest to the educational research community as a whole. Constructivist theory in particular has renewed and strengthened all educators' understanding that learning is in fact a process and that this process is interwoven with a variety of the individual and contextual elements, including information in its various forms. Carey's (1998) argument for designing information literacy instruction according to constructivist ideas makes explicit the connection between constructivism and information literacy.

The constructivist conception of learning is a comfortable fit for the library media field, which has long been associated with learning as a process rather than only an outcome: "Our content *is* process" is a frequent refrain among library media theorists and practitioners who see the field's essential role as helping students master the processes of finding, evaluating, and using information. The long-standing and widespread popularity of Eisenberg and Berkowitz's "Big Six Skills"—designated as skills "for information problem solving" (Eisenberg & Berkowitz, 1990)—provides evidence of the commitment of library media specialists to the view that their work goes well beyond attention to the specific content of a particular information-gathering effort.

Ironically, in some respects it seems almost as if education at large and instructional design in particular are catching up with the library media field's views about learning with information. For example, Mayer (1999) defines learning in terms of information processing and uses this definition as the basis for his SOI Model for designing constructivist learning: "Constructivist learning depends on the activation of several cognitive processes in the learner during learning, including selecting relevant information, organizing incoming information, and integrating incoming information with existing knowledge. I refer to this analysis as the SOI model to highlight three crucial cognitive processes in constructivist learning: S for selecting, O for organizing, and I for integrating" (p. 148). While it is true that Mayer's theoretical stance as well as his suggestions for encouraging students in each process reflect a focus that is somewhat different from the kind of learning with information that concerns library media specialists, his design of a model based on information use suggests a strong conceptual commonality between instructional design and library media. Indeed, Chung (2003) used it as part of the theoretical framework for her study of high school students' use of library media resources for meaningful learning.

Similarly, Duffy and Cunningham's (1996) six-step model for an undergraduate minor in "Corporate and Community Education" is based on the processes of information seeking and use and employs terms similar to the skills advocated by Eisenberg and Berkowitz (1990), including a central step in which students are instructed in the

Use of information resources. Given a learning issue, how efficiently can you use the variety of information repositories to identify and obtain potentially relevant information? This includes your ability to:
- Locate and acquire information or expertise from the library, experts, and using electronic resources like e-mail, World Wide Web, and Newsreaders.
- Reformulate your learning issue in a way appropriate to searching, using the particular information resource, i.e., ability to develop key words, restrict searches, identify related topics, etc. (Duffy & Cunningham, 1996, p. 192)

Although a model for university undergraduates rather than for the P-12 audience that library media specialists serve, Duffy and Cunningham's steps clearly reflect the library media field's orientation.

Mayer's (1999) and Duffy and Cunningham's (1996) models both suggest a commonality of research interests across age groups and even specific fields. The need to explore questions about "how students represent knowledge in their own minds at various stages of the information-seeking process, how they extract information from both textual and visual presentations and construct personal meaning from it, how they integrate various kinds of information into their own understandings, how they move from one level of understanding to another, and how information use supports the growth and development of students' changing conceptual structures as they move forward along the novice-to-expert continuum" (Neuman, 2003, pp. 513–514) suggests parallel agendas for instructional design research in general, for library media research that focuses on learning with information, and for content area research addressed to understanding how the process of extracting information from content area databases and other resources can foster content learning. Although the caveat against mistaking opportunities for outcomes remains in force, it does seem that mutual interests in the many facets of learning with information suggest that researchers across a variety of fields might publish in one another's journals to the benefit of all.

18.8 SUMMARY AND CONCLUSION

For over 40 years, library media specialists have been moving closer and closer to a full instructional role in the schools. Each new version of the field's national standards and guidelines published during that period has advanced that movement, and instructional design models created especially for library media specialists have provided specific strategies and techniques to further its momentum. The linking of AASL and what would become AECT to prepare the 1969 standards and the resultant conceptual merger of the "library" and "audiovisual" aspects of the field in that document situated library media directly within the field of educational communications and technology. With the growing awareness of the library media specialist's role as an instructional technologist and designer throughout the 1970s, leaders in library media began to call for formal training in instructional systems design as part of the preparation of library media specialists—a focus that culminated with the appearance of the "instructional consultant" role in *Information Power 1* in 1988.

Research tying the field directly to student learning is limited but suggests that library media programs have made a small but important contribution to student achievement over the years. While much of the field's early research focused on "opportunities for learning"—sizes of collections, presence of certified staff, etc.—contemporary researchers are becoming more sensitive to the need to demonstrate library media programs' effects on student learning. Since the early 1990s, research has been discovering and documenting this effect, and research into the concepts and strategies related to information seeking and learning from information has augmented our understanding of the ways in which students' encounters with information and information resources affect their performance in schools.

The emergence of the library media specialist's instructional consulting/instructional partnering role over the last 15 years holds the key to forging and documenting the library media program's contribution to student learning and achievement. While a variety of factors have prevented individual library media specialists and the field as a whole from moving fully into an instructional design role, today's library media specialist—generally the one professional in the school with formal training in instructional systems design—is in an ideal position to adopt it. With the convergence of instructional, informational, and communications technology into the electronic resources that are the library media specialist's purview and teachers' newest instructional tool, library media programs have an unprecedented opportunity to contribute to student learning. As an information specialist, as a program administrator, and as a teacher and instructional partner charged with "ensur[ing] that students and staff are effective users of ideas and information" (AASL & AECT, 1998, p. 6), the library media specialist is in a unique position to engage students and teachers in authentic, information-based learning. The Information Literacy Standards for Student Learning provide an innovative and powerful tool for fostering that engagement.

Over 30 years ago, Joyce and Joyce (1970) became the first researchers in the library and information science field to explore children's use of information systems. Then, the focus was primarily on retrieval; today, it is on learning. Just as the library media specialist has an unprecedented opportunity to contribute to student learning, the library media researcher has an unprecedented opportunity to chronicle and report that contribution to a wide audience of educators who are interested in similar questions and issues. As Neuman (2003) notes,

Student learning is at the heart of the school library media field, and the question of how students learn with electronic information sources is one of the field's key research questions for the coming decade.... it is [these] interactive resources that hold the greatest promise for enabling students to engage meaningfully with information and to use it as the basis for developing sophisticated understandings of the world in which they live. Learning with information is the authentic learning that is sought by all educators today, and fostering learning with information is the library media program's central contribution to student learning and achievement. Research that explores students' learning with the emerging... electronic resources that will provide the richest venue for their learning throughout their lives should be a central focus of the field. (Neuman, 2003, p. 510)

Such a research focus would fuse the cultures of librarianship, instructional design and technology, and school library media in an important and unprecedented way. If the research and practice opportunities before the school library media field today do, in fact, become outcomes, Gustafson, Tillman, and Childs' (1991) goal could be met and library media programs could actually become the touchstone for instructional design and technology in the schools. Like that "black...stone used to test the purity of gold and silver," the library media program could become "a test or criterion for the qualities of [the] thing" (Urdang, 1968, p. 1389).

ACKNOWLEDGMENT

The author gratefully acknowledges Ruth V. Small, Professor and Director, School Media Program, School of Information Studies, Syracuse University, for the information and encouragement she provided throughout the development of this chapter.

References

American Association of School Librarians (1960). *Standards for school library programs.* Chicago: American Library Association.

American Association of School Librarians and Department of Audiovisual Instruction, National Education Association (1969). *Standards for school media programs.* Chicago: American Library Association.

American Association of School Librarians and Association for Educational Communications and Technology (1975). *Media programs: District and school.* Chicago and Washington, DC: Authors.

American Association of School Librarians and Association for Educational Communications and Technology (1988). *Information power: Guidelines for school library media programs.* Chicago and Washington, DC: Authors.

American Association of School Librarians and Association for Educational Communications and Technology (1998). *Information power: Building partnerships for learning.* Chicago and Washington, DC: Authors.

Anderson, L. W., & Krathwohl, D. R. (2001). *A taxonomy for learning, teaching, and assessing: A revision of Bloom's Taxonomy of Educational Objectives.* New York: Addison Wesley Longman.

Association of Research Libraries (ARL) (2002). *Higher education outcomes research review.* Retrieved October 13, 2002, from the World Wide Web: *http://www.arl.org*

Baumbach, D. J. (1991). The school library media specialist's role in instructional design: Past, present, and future. In Gary J. Anglin (Ed.), *Instructional systems design: Past, present, and future* (pp. 221-226). Englewood, CO: Libraries Unlimited.

Behrens, S. J. (1994). A conceptual analysis and historical overview of information literacy. *College & Research Libraries, 55*(4), 309-322.

Bilal, D. (2000). Children's use of Yahooligans! Web Search Engine: I. Cognitive, physical, and affective behaviors on fact-based search tasks. *Journal of the American Society for Information Science, 51*(7), 646-665.

Bilal, D. (2001). Children's use of Yahooligans! Web Search Engine: II. Cognitive and physical behaviors on research tasks. *Journal of the American Society for Information Science, 52*(2), 118-136

Callison, D. (2002). The twentieth-century school library media research record. In A. Kent & C. M. Hall (Eds.), *Encyclopedia of library and information science, 71*(Suppl. 34), pp. 339-369. New York: Marcel Dekker.

Carey, J. O. (1998). Library skills, information skills, and information literacy: Implications for teaching and learning. *School Library Media Quarterly Online.* Retrieved November 16, 2001, from the World Wide Web: *http://ala.org/aasl/SLMQ/skills.html*

Carr-Chellman, A. A., & Reigeluth (2002). Whistling in the dark? Instructional design and technology in the schools. In R. A. Reiser & J. V. Dempsey (Eds.), *Trends and issues in instructional design and technology* (pp. 239–255). Upper Saddle River, N.J.: Merrill/Prentice Hall.

Chisholm, M. & Ely, D. (1979). *Instructional design and the library media specialist*. Chicago: American Library Association.

Chung, J. (2003). *Information use and meaningful learning*. Unpublished doctoral dissertation. University of Maryland.

Cleaver, B. P., & Taylor, W. D. (1983). *Involving the school library media specialist in curriculum development*. Chicago: American Library Association.

Cleaver, B. P., & Taylor, W. D. (1989). *The instructional consultant role of the school library media specialist*. Chicago: American Library Association.

Crane, B., & Markowitz, N. L. (1994). A model for teaching critical thinking through online searching. *Reference Librarian, 44,* 41–52.

Craver, K. W. (1986). The changing instructional role of the high school library media specialist: 1950–1984. *School Library Media Quarterly, 14*(4), 183–191.

Craver, K. W. (1990). The instructional consultant role of the school library media specialist: 1980–1989. In J. B. Smith (Ed.), *School library media annual 1990* (pp. 8–14). Englewood, CO: Libraries Unlimited.

Craver, K. W. (1994). *School library media centers in the 21st century: Changes and challenges*. Westport, CN: Greenwood Press.

Didier, E. K. (1984). Research on the impact of school library media programs on student achievement–Implications for school media professionals. In S. L. Aaron and P. R. Scales (Eds.), *School library media annual 1984* (pp. 343–361). Littleton, CO: Libraries Unlimited.

Didier, E. K. (1985). An overview of research on the impact of school library media programs on student achievement, *School Library Media Quarterly, 14*(1), 33–36.

Duffy, T. M., & Cunningham, D. J. (1996). Constructivism: Implications for the design and delivery of instruction. In D. H. Jonassen (Ed.), *Handbook of research for educational communications and technology*. Mahwah, NJ: Erlbaum.

Eisenberg, M. B., & Berkowitz, R. E. (1990). *Information problem solving: The Big Six Skills approach to library and information skills instruction*. Norwood, NJ: Ablex.

Eisenberg, M. B., & Brown, M. K. (1992). Current themes regarding library and information skills instruction: Research supporting and research lacking. *School Library Media Quarterly, 20*(2), 103–110.

Eisenberg, M. B., & Small, R. V. (1995). Information-based education: An investigation of the nature and role of information attributes in education. *Information Processing and Management, 29*(2), 263–275.

Fidel, R., Davies, R. K., Douglass, M. H., Holder, J. K., Hopkins, C. J., Kushner, E. J., Miyagishima, B. K., & Toney, C. D. (1999). A visit to the information mall: Web searching behaviors of high school students. *Journal of the American Society for Information Science, 51*(7), 646–665.

Grover, R. (1994). Assessing information skills instruction. *Reference Librarian, 44,* 173–189.

Grover, R., Lakin, J. McM., & Dickerson, J. (1997). An interdisciplinary model for assessing learning. In L. Lighthall & K. Haycock, (Eds.), *Information rich but knowledge poor? Emerging issues for schools and libraries worldwide*. Paper presented at the 26th annual conference of the International Association of School Librarianship, 6–11 July 1997, pp. 85–94. Vancouver, BC.

Gustafson, K., L., Tillman, M. H., & Childs, J. W. (1991). The future of instructional design. In L. J. Briggs, K. L. Gustafson, & M. H. Tillman (Eds.). *Instructional design: Principles and applications* (2nd ed) (pp. 451–467). Englewood Cliffs, NJ: Educational Technology Publications.

Hannafin, M. J., & Reiber, L. P. (1989). Psychological foundations of instructional design for emerging computer-based instructional technologies. Part II. *Educational Technology Research & Development, 37*(2) 102–114.

Hopkins, D. McA., & Zweizig, D. L. (1999). Introduction to the theme issue: Library Power Program evaluation. *School Libraries Worldwide, 5*(2), i–vi.

Johnson, K. (1981). Instructional development in schools: A proposed model. *School Library Media Quarterly, 9*(4), 256–271.

Jonassen, D. H., Peck, K. L., & Wilson, B. G. (1999). *Learning with technology: A constructivist approach*. Upper Saddle River, NJ: Prentice Hall/Merrill.

Joyce, B. R., & Joyce, E. A. (1970). The creation of information systems for children. *Interchange, 1*(70), 1–12.

Joyce, M. Z., & Tallman, J. I. (1997). *Making the writing and research connection with the I-Search Process*. New York: Neal-Schuman.

Kafai, Y., & Bates, M. (1997). Internet Web-searching instruction in the elementary classroom: Building a foundation for information literacy. *School Library Media Quarterly, 25*(2), 103–111.

Kendall, J. S., & Marzano, R. J. (1997). *Content knowledge: A compendium of standards and benchmarks for K-12 education* (2nd ed.). Denver, CO: Midcontent Research and Evaluation Laboratory.

Kuhlthau, C. C. (1983). *The research process: Case studies and interventions with high school seniors in advanced placement English classes using Kelly's Theory of Constructs*. Unpublished doctoral dissertation, Rutgers University.

Kuhlthau, C. C. (1988a). Longitudinal case studies of the Information Search Process of users in libraries. *Library and Information Science Research, 10*(3), 257–304.

Kuhlthau, C. C. (1988b). Perceptions of the Information Search Process in libraries: A study of changes from high school through college. *Information Processing and Management, 24*(4), 419–427.

Kuhlthau, C. C. (1989). The information search process of high-middle-low achieving high school seniors. *School Library Media Quarterly, 17*(4), 224–228.

Kuhlthau, C. C. (1993). *Seeking meaning: A process approach to library and information services*. Norwood, NJ: Ablex.

Kuhlthau, C. C. (1994). *Assessment and the school library media center*. Englewood, CO: Libraries Unlimited.

Kuhlthau, C. C. (1997). Learning in digital libraries: An Information Search Process approach. *Library Trends, 45*(4), 708–724.

Kuhlthau, C. C. (1999). Student learning in the library: What Library Power librarians say. *School Libraries Worldwide, 5*(2), 80–96.

Kuhlthau, C. C., Turock, B. J., George, M. W., & Belvin, R. J. (1990). Validating a model of the search process: A comparison of academic, public, and school library users. *Library and Information Science Research, 12*(1), 5–32.

Lance, K. C. (1994). The impact of school library media centers on academic achievement. *School Library Media Quarterly, 22*(3), 167–170.

Lance, K. C. (2002). *What research tells us about the importance of school libraries*. Paper presented at the White House Conference on School Libraries, June 4, 2002. Retrieved September 15, 2002, from the World Wide Web: *http://www.imls.fed.us/pubs/whitehouse0602/keithlance.htm*

Lance, K. C., Hamilton-Pennell, C., & Rodney, M. (2000). *Information empowered: The school librarian as an agent of academic achievement in Alaska schools* (rev. ed.). Juneau: Alaska State Library.

Lance, K. C., Rodney, M., & Hamilton-Pennell, C. (2001). *Good schools have school librarians: Oregon school librarians collaborate to improve academic achievement*. Terrebonne, OR: Oregon Educational Media Association.

Lance, K. C., Rodney, M., & Hamilton-Pennell, C. (2000a). *Measuring up to standards: The impact of school library programs and information literacy in Pennsylvania schools*. Greensburg, PA: Pennsylvania Citizens for Better Libraries.

Lance, K. C., Rodney, M., & Hamilton-Pennell, C. (2000b). *How school librarians help kids achieve standards: The second Colorado study*. Castle Rock, CO: Hi Willow.

Lance, K. C., Welborn, L., Hamilton-Pennell, C., & Rodney, M. (1993). *The impact of school library media centers on academic achievement*. Castle Rock, CO: Hi Willow.

Large, A., & Beheshti, J. (2000). The web as classroom resource: Reactions from users. *Journal of the American Society for Information Science, 51*(12), 1069-1080.

Large, A., Beheshti, J., & Breuleux, A. (1998). Information seeking in a multimedia environment by primary school students. *Library & Information Science Research, 20*(4), 343-376.

Large, A., Beheshti, J., Breuleux, A., & Renaud, A. (1994a). A comparison of information retrieval from print and CD-ROM versions of an encyclopedia by elementary school students. *Information Processing & Management, 30*(4), 499-513.

Large, A., Beheshti, J., Breuleux, A., & Renaud, A. (1994b). Multimedia and comprehension: A cognitive study. *Journal of the American Society for Information Science, 45*(7), 515-528.

Large, A., Beheshti, J., Breuleux, A., & Renaud, A. (1995). Multimedia and comprehension: The relationship between text, animation, and captions. *Journal of the American Society for Information Science, 46*(5), 340-347.

Large, A., Beheshti, J., Breuleux, A., & Renaud, A. (1996).The effect of animation in enhancing descriptive and procedural texts in a multimedia learning environment. *Journal of the American Society for Information Science, 47*(6), 437-448.

Large, A., Beheshti, J., & Rahman, T. (2002). Design criteria for children's Web portals: The users speak out. *Journal of the American Society for Information Science and Technology, 53*(2), 79-94.

Liebscher, P., & Marchionini, G. (1988). Browse and analytical search strategies in a full-text CD-ROM encyclopedia. *School Library Media Quarterly, 16*(4), 223-233.

Loertscher, D. V. (1982). The second revolution: A taxonomy for the 1980s. *Wilson Library Bulletin, 56*(6), 417-21.

Loertscher, D. V. (1988). *Taxonomies of the school library media program*. Englewood, CO: Libraries Unlimited.

Mancall, J. C., Aaron, W. L., & Walker, S. A. (1986). Educating students to think: The role of the school library media program. *School Library Media Quarterly, 15*(1), 18-27.

Marchionini, G. (1989). Information-seeking strategies of novices using a full-text electronic encyclopedia. *Journal of the American Society for Information Science, 40*(1), 54-66.

Marchionini, G., & Teague, J. (1987). Elementary students' use of electronic information services: An exploratory study. *Journal of Research on Computing in Education, 20*, 139-155.

Martin, B. L., & Clemente, R. (1990). Instructional systems design and public schools. *Educational Technology Research & Development, 38*(2), 61-75.

Mayer, R. E. (1999). Designing instruction for constructivist learning. In C. M. Reigeluth (Ed.), *Instructional-design theories and models: A new paradigm of instructional theory*. Volume II. Mahwah, NJ: Erlbaum.

McCarthy, C. A. (1997). A reality check: The challenges of implementing *Information Power* in school library media programs. *School Library Media Quarterly, 25*(4), 205-214.

McGregor, J. H. (1994a). Cognitive processes and the use of information: A qualitative study of higher-order thinking skills used in the research process by students in a gifted program. In C. C. Kuhlthau (Ed.), *School library media annual 1994* (pp. 124-133). Englewood, CO: Libraries Unlimited.

McGregor, J. H. (1994b). Information seeking and use: Students' thinking and their mental models. *Journal of Youth Services in Libraries, 8*(1), 69-76.

McGregor, J. H., & Streitenberger, D. C. (1998). Do scribes learn? Copying and information use. *School Library Media Quarterly Online*. Retrieved February 20, 2002, from the World Wide Web: *http://www.ala.org/aasl/SLMQ/scribes.html*.

Meyer, J., & Newton, E. (1992). Teachers' views of the implementation of resource-based learning. *Emergency Librarian, 20*(2), 13-18.

Moore, P. A., & St. George, A. (1991). Children as information seekers: The cognitive demands of books and library systems. *School Library Media Quarterly, 19*(3), 161-168.

Neuman, D. (1993). Designing databases as tools for higher-level learning: Insights from instructional systems design. *Educational Technology Research & Development, 41*(4), 25-46.

Neuman, D. (1995). High school students' use of databases: Results of a national Delphi study. *Journal of the American Society for Information Science, 46*(4), 284-298.

Neuman, D. (1997). Learning and the digital library. *Library Trends, 45*(4), 6687-6707.

Neuman, D. (2000). *Information Power... and assessment: the other side of the standards coin*. In R. Branch & M. A. Fitzgerald (Eds.), *Educational media and technology yearbook 2000* (pp. 110-119). Englewood, CO: Libraries Unlimited.

Neuman, D. (2001, November). *Students' strategies for making meaning from information on the Web*. Paper presented at the annual conference of the American Society for Information Science and Technology, Washington, DC.

Neuman, D. (2003). Research in school library media for the next decade: Polishing the diamond. *Library Trends, 51*(4), 508-524.

Oberg, D. (Ed.). (1995). Learning from information [Special issue]. *School Libraries Worldwide, 1*(1).

Pappas, M. (1997). *Introduction to the Pathways to Knowledge*. McHenry, IL: Follett.

Pickard, P. W. (1993). The instructional consultant role of the school library media specialist. *School Library Media Quarterly, 21*(2),115-121.

Pitts, J. M. (1994). *Personal understandings and mental models of information: A qualitative study of factors associated with the information seeking and use of adolescents*. Unpublished doctoral dissertation.

Putnam, E. (1996). The instructional consultant role of the elementary-school library media specialist and the effects of program scheduling on its practice. *School Library Media Quarterly, 25*(1), 43-49.

Ray, J. T. (1994). Resource-based teaching: Media specialists and teachers as partners in curriculum development and the teaching of library and information skills. *Reference Librarian, 44*, 19-27.

Rieber, L. P. (1990). Using computer animated graphics in science instruction with children. *Journal of Educational Psychology, 82*, 135-140.

Rieber, L. P., & Hannafin, M. J. (1988). Effects of textual and animated orienting activities and practice on learning from computer-based instruction. *Computers in the Schools, 5*(1-2), 77-89.

Schiffman, S. (1987). Influencing public education: A "window of opportunity" through school library media centers. *Journal of Instructional Development, 10*(4), 41-44.

Small, R. V. (1998a). Designing motivation into library and information skills instruction. *School Library Media Quarterly Online*.

Retrieved March 18, 2002, from the World Wide Web: *http://ala. org/aasl/SLMQ/skills.html*

Small, R. V. (1998b). School librarianship and instructional design: A history intertwined. In K. H. Latrobe (Ed.), *The emerging school library media center: Historical issues and perspectives* (pp. 227-237). Englewood, CO: Libraries Unlimited.

Small, R. V. (1999). An exploration of motivational strategies used by library media specialists during library and information skills instruction. *School Library Media Research*. Retrieved March 18, 2002, from the World Wide Web: *http://ala.org/aasl/SLMR/vol2/motive/html*

Small, R. V. (2000a). Having an IM-PACT on information literacy. *Teacher-Librarian, 28*(1), 30-35.

Small, R. V. (2000b). Motivation in instructional design. *Teacher Librarian, 27*(5), 29-31.

Smith, E. G. (2001). *Texas school libraries: Standards, resources, services and students' performance*. Retrieved March 1, 2002, from the World Wide Web: *http://castor/tsl.state.tx.us/ld/pubs/schlibsurvey/index.html*.

Solomon, P. (1993). Children's information retrieval behavior: A case analysis of an OPAC. *Journal of the American Society for Information Science, 44*(5), 2245-2263.

Solomon, P. (1994). Children, technology, and instruction: A case study of elementary school children using an online public access catalog (OPAC). *School Library Media Quarterly, 23*(1), 43-53.

Stripling, B. K., & Pitts, J. M. (1988). *Brainstorms and blueprints: Library research as a thinking process*. Englewood, CO: Libraries Unlimited.

Thomas, N. P. (1999). *Information literacy and information skills instruction: Applying research to practice in the school library media center*. Englewood, CO: Libraries Unlimited.

Todd, R. J. (1995). Integrated information skills instruction: Does it make a difference? *School Library Media Quarterly, 23*(2), 133-138.

Todd, R. J. (1999). Utilization of heroin information by adolescent girls in Australia: A cognitive analysis. *Journal of the American Society for Information Science, 50*(1), 10-23.

Turner, P. (1982). Instructional design competencies taught at library schools. *Journal of Education for Librarianship, 22*(4), 276-282.

Turner, P. (1985, 1993). *Helping teachers teach*. Littleton, CO: Libraries Unlimited.

Turner, P. (1991). Information skills and instructional consulting: A synergy? *School Library Media Quarterly, 20*(1), 13-18.

Turner, P., & Naumer, J. (1983). Mapping the way toward instructional design consultation by the school library media specialist. *School Library Media Quarterly, 10*(1), 29-37.

Turner, P., & Zsiray, S. (1990). The consulting role of the library media specialist: A review of the literature. In *Papers for the Treasure Mountain Research Retreat*. Englewood, CO: Hi Willow.

Urdang, L. (Ed.). (1968). The Random House dictionary of the English language (college ed.). New York: Random House.

van Deusen, J. D. (1993). The effects of fixed versus flexible scheduling on curriculum involvement and skills integration in elementary school library media centers. *School Library Media Quarterly, 21*(3), 173-182.

van Deusen, J. D. (1996). The school library media specialist as a member of the teaching team: "Insider" and "outsider." *Journal of Curriculum and Supervision, 11*(3), 249-258.

van Deusen, J. D., & Tallman, J. I. (1994). The impact of scheduling on curriculum consultation and information skills instruction, Parts I-III. *School Library Media Quarterly, 23*(1), 17-37.

Wang, P. (1999). Methodologies and methods for user behavioral research. In M. E. Williams (Ed.), *Annual review of information science and technology* (pp. 53-99). Medford, NJ: Information Today.

Webb, N. L., & Doll, C. A. (1999). Contributions of Library Power to collaborations between librarians and teachers. *School Libraries Worldwide, 5*(2), 29-44.

TECHNOLOGY IN THE SERVICE OF FOREIGN LANGUAGE LEARNING: THE CASE OF THE LANGUAGE LABORATORY

Warren B. Roby
John Brown University

19.1 HISTORY

Foreign language learning lends itself naturally to the use of media. Linguists stress the primacy of speech over writing in language: children can listen and speak before they learn to read and write and all languages of the world are spoken, but not all have a writing system. Accordingly, foreign-language educators have been heavily involved in the use of audio equipment. They welcomed the first audio device, the phonograph, and have immediately adopted other advances in audio technology such as magnetic tape and digital media. (Delcoque, Annan, & Bramoullé, 2000). Unfortunately, the history of the use of technology to teach languages has not been duly noted by historians of educational technology. Paul Saettler, in his definitive *The Evolution of American Educational Technology*, only makes passing references to foreign-language teaching, and language laboratories are granted merely one paragraph (p. 187). It will be demonstrated that this disregard is startling in view of the extensive use and massive investment in instructional equipment by foreign-language educators. Moreover, it will be shown that the research that accompanied these commitments has not been appreciated by the larger educational technology community.

This chapter belongs in this handbook because the language laboratory represents a unique use of educational technology. It will be shown that language laboratories are discipline-specific equipment configurations. The focus is on specialized audio installations. The use of equipment in foreign language classroom teaching and the use of computers in language teaching are touched upon briefly. The discussion is largely confined to the language laboratory in the United States.

19.1.1 Forerunners to the Language Laboratory: 1877 to 1945

Léon (1962) and Peterson (1974) have documented the early use of audio recordings by foreign-language educators since the invention of the phonograph by Thomas Edison in 1877. By 1893 there were commercial record sets available for Spanish and English as a foreign language. The phonograph was used in regular classes and for self-study at home, but to what extent is difficult to ascertain. In their 340-page annotated bibliography of "modern" language methodology (the references commence in 1880s), Buchanan and MacPhee (1928) include only nine entries concerning the phonograph. Three of these are listings of recorded courses; none of the six articles is a controlled study of the merit of the phonograph. The 491-page Bagster-Collins et al. volume (1930) contains no mention of the phonograph. This paucity of references is surprising when one considers that in the 1880s the field of phonetics was born out of the effort to teach proper foreign-language pronunciation. The literature of the period is full of articles on phonetics, and many pronunciation textbooks and teaching materials were published. One would have expected greater enthusiasm in the language-teaching community for the equipment that could provide native speaker models.

According to a contemporary (Keating, 1936), initial use of the phonograph and other devices such as the stereopticon (an early slide projector) was haphazard, and interest waned because there was "no real absorption of modern inventions into the teaching program" (p. 678). The Depression may have prohibited a wider use of the phonograph in the 1930s. A definite discouragement to its use was the Carnegie-funded Coleman report of 1929, which stated that the reading skill should be emphasized (Parker, 1961). Nevertheless, it should be noted that the decade saw much interest in the use of radio for foreign-language instruction. From October 1935 (volume 20) through December 1946 (volume 30), the *Modern Language Journal* had a radio "department."

It is not until 1908 that there is any evidence of a laboratory arrangement of phonographic equipment (Léon, 1962). By this is meant a dedicated facility for foreign-language study. This lab was at the University of Grenoble in France. An American, Frank C. Chalfant, who studied there in the summer of 1909, appears to have been the one who brought the idea back to this country. He installed a "phonetics laboratory" at Washington State College in Pullman during the 1911–1912 academic year. Pictures of this installation in use show students listening via networked earphones. This lab also had a phonograph-recording machine so that students could compare their pronunciation with the native-speaker models.

Near the time that Chalfant established his phonetics laboratory, the U.S. Military and Naval Academy set aside rooms for listening to foreign-language records (Clarke, 1918). Another early facility was set up at the University of Utah in 1919 by Ralph Waltz (1930). He moved to Ohio State and built another lab about which he published several articles (Waltz, 1930, 1931, 1932). Waltz is usually credited with coining the term *language laboratory* in 1930 (Hocking, 1967). In fact, Chalfant had used it synonymously with phonetics laboratory as early as 1916 in the Washington State College yearbook, the *Chinook,* and probably in the regional foreign-language education circles of which he was a leader. In any event, it appears that the preferred term until after WWII was "phonetics laboratory." That is what Middlebury College called the lab it installed in 1928 (Marty, 1956). Also in use was "language studio" (Eddy, 1944) and "conversation laboratory" (Bottke, 1944). Whitehouse (1945) used the terms "workshop" and "language laboratory" together for the lab at Birmingham-Southern college. Bontempo (1946) also used "workshop" to describe the elaborate foreign language training program he created at the College of the City of New York in 1940. The use of audio-visual equipment was part of the "implementation (p. 325) phase. The "language discothèque" described by Gaudin (1946) was a carefully selected set of records used in class and presumably in some kind of lab because she went on to publish several articles about labs in the next few years.

In the 1930s and during the second world war many other institutions established labs (Gullette, 1932; Hocking, 1967), but, as in the case of the phonograph, discussions of their use did not loom large in the methodological literature. For example, the *Modern Language Journal's* annual annotated bibliography of monographs and articles only had four entries prior to 1945 besides the three articles by Waltz. The 105-item bibliography

of the language laboratory for the years 1938–1958 compiled by Sanchez (1959) brought the total for the prewar period up to eight.

19.1.2 The First Language Laboratory Proper: 1946 to 1958

The year 1946 is considered to mark the beginning of the modern language laboratory movement (Hocking, 1967; Koekkoek, 1959). The labs at Louisiana State University (Hocking, 1967) and the University of Laval in Quebec City, Canada (Kelly, 1969), were built that year. By 1949 Cornell University had a lab thanks to a grant of $125,000 from the Rockefeller Foundation (Harvigurst, 1959). Whether these postwar labs owed anything to the previous phonetics labs is unclear, but probable. Claudel's (1968) use of "predecessor" (p. 221) expresses linkage. However, according to Koekkoek, "the beginning of the language laboratory movement was a new start, albeit with similar means and ends, rather than a direct expansion of the limited phonetics laboratory tradition" (1959, p. 4). Sanchez (1959) is ambiguous on the question. The earliest entry in his annotated bibliography of the "modern" language laboratory is a reference to a phonetics laboratory (Peebles, 1938), but he included the note "not related to the Modern Language lab, as such' (p. 231). The record at the universities of Iowa (Funke, 1949) and Tennessee (Stiefel, 1952) indicate continuity with phonetics labs. It thus appears that Koekkoek's statement must be tempered. Most institutions that built language labs after the war did so for the first time, whereas a few others updated their prewar phonetics labs. Clearly, "language laboratory" became the common term for labs after 1946, but the old terms were still in circulation (Funke, 1949) and new ones were introduced, such as "sound rooms" (Mazzara, 1954).

A point of difference between phonetics labs and language labs were individual booths or carrels. Although the lab at Ohio State had long tables divided into "compartments" (Waltz, 1930, p. 28) by 18-inch-tall boards, these did not provide sufficient acoustic isolation (Schenk, 1930). Levin (1931) suggested that the facility he described would be improved by the installation of soundproof booths. These became standard equipment in the postwar labs (MLA, 1956). Middlebury College had a more elaborate arrangement with seven feet by seven feet "roomlets" or "cabins" in which students worked individually (Marty, 1956, p. 53). Labs of the period were principally audio installations, but movie, slide, and filmstrip projectors were sometimes present as well (Hirsch, 1954; Marty, 1956; Newmark, 1948). A quaint description of the use of the Middlebury College lab is provided by a (then) 18-year-old coed who interviewed several students (Reed, 1958).

Also at issue is the impulse for the modern lab movement. It is certain that the military's success in language training during the war caught the attention of the foreign-language teaching profession at large. The technique was actually a wartime civilian creation: the Intensive Language Program of the American Council of Learned Societies, with Rockeller Foundation funding (Science comes to languages, 1944), was responsible for it (Lado, 1964). Nevertheless, the army got the credit in the public's eyes and in 1945 the *Modern Language Journal's* annual bibliography began a separate category for the "Army" (Army Specialized Training Program, ASTP) method. It contained far more entries than any of the other 21 categories. Regarding labs specifically, Koekkoek maintained that 'The language laboratory and its spread is a postwar development, fostered by a climate of experimentation which was stimulated by the Army language teaching program during the war" (1959, p. 4). Pictures of labs in the 1950s certainly have a military air to them. Rows of students with eyes straight ahead suggest columns of soldiers at attention. The individual student in a booth wearing a headset is like unto a navigator or radar technician at his or her post on a ship or airplane.

Hocking, however, adamantly denied that the ASTP method drove the establishing of labs. He was echoed by Barrutia:

... we have Elton Hocking to thank for almost single-handedly trying to keep the record straight about the fiction of the supposed extended use of recording equipment and aural-oral techniques in the A.S.T.P... the Army Specialized Training Program did not, as is so widely believed, pioneer language laboratories... (1967, p. 890).

In fact, much nearer the war effort Gaudin claimed that the so-called Army method was "far from revolutionary" and that language teachers had been using phonograph records "for the past fifteen or twenty years" (1946, p. 27).

To what, then, did Hocking and Barrutia and others attribute the postwar interest in labs? They cite the availability of magnetic tape and tape-recording machines from 1946. Hitherto, labs were outfitted with phonographs or wire recorders. These had several problems: their sound fidelity was low, they were fragile, and they were difficult to edit. Plastic disc player/recorders such as the SoundScriber (first advertised in the *Modern Language Journal* in October 1946) were in use at Yale University (Harvigurst, 1949) and other schools. This was an improvement over wire mechanisms, but as Hocking could note in retrospect: "the superiority of the tape recorder-reproducer was immediately apparent" (1967, p. 18).

This major technological improvement does not fully account for the language laboratory movement. Roughly concurrent with the invention of magnetic tape was the development of the audiolingual method. It is here that the ASTP can be given some deserved credit. It stressed the listening and speaking skills more than reading and writing—the priorities of prewar methods. The Army method relied much on small-group practice to develop the learners' aural and oral abilities. Another important feature of the ASTP was the preponderate use of native-speaker instructors. It was also known as the "mim–mem" method because of its emphasis on mimicry of target language models (whether live or recorded) and the memorization of dialogues. Stack connects these developments in equipment and methodology:

The language laboratory owes its existence to the recognition that the spoken form of language is central to effective communication, and that it should have as large a share in instruction as do written forms. In order to implement this new orientation of language teaching, the textbook (which is essentially graphic) was supplemented by sound recordings

of native speakers. The coincidental advent of the tape recorder created a fortuitous juncture of technology and pedagogy. (1971, p. 3)

By 1958, in the United States there were 64 labs in secondary schools and 240 in colleges and universities (Johnston & Seerley, 1960). Forty-nine universities responded to Mustard and Tudisco's (1959) survey of lab usage. They found that the lab was used mainly in first-year classes. A majority of the respondents judged that courses which involved lab work resulted in better listening and speaking skills on the part of students compared with classes that made no use of the lab. The Sanchez (1959) bibliography contains descriptions of at least 35 labs. The passage of the National Defense Education Act the previous year ushered in a new phase in language laboratory history.

19.1.3 The Language Laboratory Boom: 1959 to 1969

The Soviet Union's launching of Sputnik on October 4, 1957 represented a challenge to the preeminence of Yankee know-how and American ingenuity. In response Congress passed the National Defense Education Act (NDEA), which President Eisenhower signed into law on September 2, 1958. The act sought to strengthen the teaching of mathematics, science, and foreign languages in America's schools. The intent of the foreign-language provisions of this important legislation has been described by Derthick (1959). The history of the language laboratory in the first years following the NDEA has been written by Parker (1961), Diekhoff (1965), and Hocking (1967).

Unquestionably, the 1960s were the golden years of the language laboratory. There was an explosion in the number of facilities, thanks to generous federal support: $76 million in matching funds by 1963 (Diekhoff, 1965). It is difficult to quantify how many labs there were. According to Hocking (1967) by 1962 there were approximately 5,000 installations in secondary schools. Another 1,000 secondary schools had labs by 1964 (Diekhoff, 1965). If the figure of 6,000 is accurate, this represents a thousand-fold increase in the number of labs at the secondary level from 1958! Most of these were in medium-to-large school districts (Godfrey, 1967). Although colleges and universities were not eligible for equipment funds under the NDEA, they were caught up in the national enthusiasm for language study, and thus committed their own monies to labs. By 1962 there were 900 labs in higher education (Hocking, 1967). More postsecondary labs were built from 1965 when matching funds became available under Title VI-A of the Higher Education Act (Ek, 1974). Although they did not cite a source for their information, Keck and Smith claimed: "By mid-decade an estimated 10,000 language laboratories had been installed in secondary schools; 4,000 more could be found in institutions of higher learning" (1972, p. 5).

Those involved in these facilities felt an urgent need to gather and compare experiences. William Riley Parker wrote this about the motivation for the first of the Indiana and Purdue universities-sponsored language laboratory conferences in 1960 (the others were in 1961, 1962, and 1965):

... foreign language teachers feel themselves suddenly involved in a technological revolution, suddenly chin-deep in a tide of new demands upon their competencies, and they seek, some almost frantically, enlightenment and practical help. (1960, p. v)

In addition to the Indiana conferences, there were many lab-related presentations at meetings of the various professional associations to which language educators belonged: the Modern Language Association (MLA), the American Association of Teachers of French (AATF), the American Association of Teachers of German (AATG), and the American Association of Teachers of Spanish and Portuguese (AATSP). The sessions at these gatherings were principally for professors. Language laboratory directors held caucuses at the conventions of the MLA and the Department of Audiovisual Instruction of the National Education Association (NEA), but they soon felt the need for their own organization. The National Association of Language Laboratory Directors (NALLD) was founded in 1965. The NALLD began publishing a newsletter the following year. The inaugural issue reported that at the first NALLD meeting in Chicago in December 1965, there had been much discussion of the lab director's job description and the problem schools face in recruiting qualified applicants. Job openings were featured regularly from the start of this publication.

A spate of publications also accompanied the flow of money and the installation of many labs. Most of the entries in Davison's (1973) 780-item bibliography of the language laboratory from 1950 through 1972 are from the 1960s, and thus post-NDEA. The first edition of Edward Stack's textbook, *The Language Laboratory and Modern Language Teaching,* appeared in 1960. It should be consulted by those interested in the literature of the period, because it explains the terminology of installations and operations current at the time. Foreign language teacher-training textbooks of the decade included a chapter on the language laboratory (e.g., Brooks, 1960; Lado, 1964). Also appearing in the early 1960s were Hutchinson's monograph concerning labs in high schools (1961), and the technical guide to facilities by Hayes (1963). Leon's book *Laboratoire des Langues et Correction Phonétique* (1962), although written in French and published in France, circulated widely in this country, as evidenced by the numerous citations of it. The Scherer and Wertheimer (1964) book-length report of an experiment involving language labs will be discussed in the section on research.

As for articles, hundreds appeared in all ranges of periodicals from school district newsletters to long-established refereed journals such as *The Modern Language Journal, Language Learning, Hispania, The French Review,* and *The German Quarterly.* A publication that focused on language laboratories, *The Audio-Visual Language Journal,* was founded in Great Britain in 1962. Both *The International Review of Applied Linguistics* and *Foreign Language Annals* carried articles about the language laboratory from their inceptions in 1963 and 1967, respectively. The bibliographies compiled by Keck and Smith (1972), Davison (1973), and Charoenkul (n.d.) list many of these articles. The major research articles of the period will be noted in a later section.

B. F. Skinner spoke at the first of the Indiana/Purdue language laboratory meetings on January 22, 1960. His subject was the use of teaching machines for foreign language instruction. One of the respondents to Skinner's paper was Robert Glaser. Neither of these men were foreign-language educators by training, but both were already well-known in the educational technology community. Their presence at this conference is testimony to the willingness of foreign-language professionals to accept insights from other disciplines, notably psychology. In reciprocal fashion, the larger educational community of the day showed interest in foreign language education. The October, 1966 issue of *Audiovisual Instruction* (published by the forerunner of the AECT, the Department of Audiovisual Instruction of the NEA) was devoted entirely to foreign language learning, and two articles focused specifically on the language laboratory.

No discussion of instructional technology in the 1960s would be complete without a mention of programmed instruction. Both Skinner and Glaser were involved in this movement. A pioneer was Ralph Tyler, who was working at Ohio State University in the 1930s. The reader will recall that a pioneer of the phonetics lab movement was Ralph Waltz, who also was at Ohio State in the 1930s. One wonders whether the two may have shared ideas. Edgar Dale, also of Ohio State, provides an overt link between the educational technology field, the programmed instruction movement, and the foreign language profession. The author of a language teaching methodology book of the period under discussion, Ruth R. Cornfield, acknowledged in her preface "all the inspiration, philosophy, and ideas given me" (1966, p. vi) by Dale. The books by Carroll (1962), Marty (1962), and the pedagogy textbook of Grittner (1969) provide further evidence of the embrace of programmed instruction by foreign language educators who were also interested in the language laboratory.

The major technical development of note during the decade was the audiocassette (Dodge, 1968). The advantages of cassette were a lower price and that smaller, lighter machines could play it. However, it did have the drawbacks of lower fidelity and greater difficulty of editing by cutting and splicing. The quality of sound was eventually ameliorated, and the editing problem was not sufficient to prevent the cassette from replacing reel tape in language labs in the 1970s. Machines with a repeat or skip-back function came on the scene at this time as well. This feature permitted students to easily replay a tape segment, and thus was well suited to dictations and audio-lingual listen-and-repeat drills. The cassette *Canon Repeat-Corder L* was first advertised in the *NALLD Journal* in the October 1970 issue. Aikens and Ross (1977) wrote an article in the same journal describing a reel-to-reel machine they fabricated. By the end of the decade, the major manufacturers, such as Sony and Tandberg, were producing machines with skip-back capability.

Another technical advance was the speech compressor-expander. This device allowed a recording to be sped up (compressed) or slowed down (expanded). Articles on this technology were numerous in the general educational literature from the start of the decade. Sanford Couch (1973), a professor of Russian, advocated its use. Paradoxically, it was not until 1978 that anything on speech compression appeared in the NALLD Journal (Harvey, 1978). One would have expected a greater enthusiasm for this feature among language laboratory professionals. The ability to slow down a tape would seem to be a boon to students struggling with a difficult passage. Moreover, variable-speed technology was not unknown in foreign-language teaching, for Hirsch (1954) had commended the use of the *sound stretcher (p.* 22) in the early 1950s.

Huebener, in his mid-decade (1965), *How to teach foreign languages effectively,* provides a helpful synthesis of all the above factors. By design a methodology textbook should present the state-of-the art so that the next generation of teachers can be inducted into the profession. In his section on "Recent Trends," he noted that "the entire philosophy . . . was completely changed." To what did he attribute this change? He said the ASTP was "influential in introducing the intensive method in the colleges and universities and in stressing the spoken aim." The result was the "'new key' or audio-lingual" method. The new method "received powerful support from three sides." He cited the federal government for financial and moral support and pointed to NDEA. He noted the technical support of tape recorders, teaching machines, language laboratories, films, and programmed courses. "There is a veritable *embarrass de richesses* in the field of audio-visual aids." The third source of support was theoretical: "the new method was based on the findings of the structural linguists, who developed a psychology and a philosophy of language learning quite different from the traditional" (p. 11). With so much undergirding it, audiolingualism became the orthodoxy in the field:

The audio-lingual approach, enjoying Federal sanction and financial support, was announced with the aura of authority of Moses delivering the Decalogue on Mt. Sinai. Anathema to anyone who dared oppose the new dispensation! (Huebener, 1963, p. 376)

The language laboratory was an integral, but not the only, article of the prevailing creed.

Language laboratories ended the 1960s on a sour note. Federal funding was diminished:

. . . the amount of equipment funding in Title III-A of the National Defense Education Act (NDEA) and Title VI-A of the Higher Education Act (HEA), two large sources for equipment funds, dropped from an allotment in fiscal year 1968–69 of $91.24 million to nothing in fiscal year 1969–70. The portent of this budgetary reduction is not as black as it might seem: any program for which the federal government is still offering subsidy, e.g., bilingualism, poverty, etc., still has access to equipment funds, but the inflated years of the mid-sixties have come to a close. (Dodge, 1968, p. 331)

Based on his observations in several schools and with discussions he had at five NDEA summer institutes, Turner noted that labs were

"electronic graveyards," sitting empty and unused, or perhaps somewhat glorified study halls to which students grudgingly repair to don headphones, turn down the volume, and prepare the next period's history or English lesson, unmolested by any member of the foreign language faculty. (1969, p. 1)

Smith (1970) did not view this decline in federal support as entirely negative, because he candidly acknowledged that "the recent years have seen much professional neglect and misuse of the language laboratory (p. 191). On the matter of misuse, earlier in the decade Charest had complained that students were being treated as "guinea pigs on whom pet ideas are tried out in the lab" and asked whether "experimentation has gotten a bit out of hand" (1962, p. 268). On the other hand, Smith sensed a positive development in the unanimous agreement that the laboratories should be used to "individualize instruction," in the university community and provide the corresponding "increase in expenditures for equipment and materials for tutorial and individualized instruction" (p. 192). Heinich (1968) also commented on the problems associated with labs and the insights that were gained by both language educators and instructional technologists:

The *language laboratory* movement threw content and media specialists together in an intimate working relationship that produced very strange and startling experiences. For the first time, language teachers discovered that the mode and materials of instruction interact with instructional behavioral objectives and methods. Many language teachers did not understand that a language laboratory requires a different method of instruction: that print stimulus methods are not audio stimulus methods. On the other hand, the audiovisual specialist was shaken out of a comfortable bookkeeping-procurement function and introduced, often for the first time, to the rigors of developing curriculum materials to meet specific curricular objectives. The novelty of the roles played by both has caused so many difficulties that the language laboratory has not yet reached its potential value. One of the lessons learned by audiovisual directors in this encounter is the incredible quantity of materials required by technology when media are used for direct instruction. The classroom teacher, at the same time, was experiencing another instance of shared responsibility with media. (pp. 50–51)

19.1.4 The Evolution of the Language Laboratory: 1969 to Present

The 1970s and early 1980s were a period of malaise for the language laboratory. Coinciding with the drying up of funds was a sharp drop off in the number of articles published. An index of this change can be seen in the ACTFL yearbooks. The first two volumes contained the articles by Dodge (1968) and Smith (1970), with 84 and 95 citations, respectively. The 1971 volume had one paragraph about labs and two references! From then on until 1983, many volumes contained no mention of labs, and those that did accorded a page at most. Holmes (1980) was the last article on the language laboratory ever to be published by the leading organ of the field, the Modern Language Journal. Labs had their vocal defenders to be sure (Jarlett, 1971), and those who offered constructive suggestions (Couch, 1973), but frank avowals of their problems (Altamura, 1970; Racle, 1976) and their need for revitalization (Strei, 1977) were prominent. Stack's book on language laboratories did not go through any more editions after the third in 1971, but Dakin's *The Language Laboratory and Language Teaching* appeared in 1973. It was a very different kind of book in that it had almost no mention of lab equipment or lab management issues. It was focused on the pedagogical use of the lab and anticipated Ely's (1984) and Stone's (1988) books which will be discussed below.

A turnaround in the decline of the language lab could be seen from the early 1980s. A 3-day colloquium with the theme "A Renaissance for the Language Lab" was held at Concordia University in July of 1981 (Kenner, 1981). The next month the Language Laboratory Association of Japan and the NALLD teamed up to sponsor the first Foreign Language Education And Technology (FLEAT) conference in Tokyo. McCoy and Weible maintained that the recent "revival of interest in language laboratories" was "directly attributable to the 'domestication' of the tape recorder, made possible through the invention of the audiocassette" (1983, p. 110). What this indicates is that it took nearly 2 decades for the audiocassette, from its invention in the mid 1960s, to fully work its way into the instructional mores of teachers.

The lab of the 1980s was not to be limited to audio technology. Nineteen eighty-three, the year after *Time* magazine named the computer the "machine of the year," saw the founding of the Computer Assisted Learning and Instruction Consortium (CALICO). This group was (and still is) dominated by language educators. It should not be thought that the invention of the personal computer in the late 1970s was solely responsible for the interest in computer-assisted language instruction. Mainframes had already been much used for this purpose, most notably in the PLATO system at the University of Illinois. Computers were welcomed for their potential, but cautions were issued about the need to avoid the unrealistic expectations associated with early language labs and the need to learn other lessons from language lab history (LeMon, 1986; Marty, 1981; McCoy & Weibel, 1983; Otto, 1989; Pederson, 1987).

Ely's *Bring the Lab Back to Life* was published in 1984. In 1985 the president of the International Association of Learning Laboratories (IALL, the new name for the NALLD as of November 1982), Glyn Holmes, could affirm that the professional group was showing new signs of vitality (Holmes, 1985). This rebirth was also indicated by volumes 18 and 19 of the ACTFL Foreign Language Education Series, which were devoted entirely to technology (Smith, 1987, 1989). With new life came a new look. In 1988 the reinvigorated IALL published the first of several monographs dealing with learning-center design and pedagogical use (Stone, 1988) and in 1989 started producing several "video tours" of facilities around the country. By 1989, Otto could write that "language laboratories have been redefined as multimedia learning centers that deliver computer and video services to faculty and students in addition to familiar audio resources" (1989, p. 38). A new name for facilities often went with the expanded media offerings: some variation containing the words *language, learning, media, resource,* and *center* became widespread (Lawrason, 1990).

A further sign of the broadening of focus of language laboratories in the 1980s was the new attention given to reading and writing. The reader will recall that the early labs were devoted solely to the "sound" skills of listening and speaking. Personal computers, which became popular in the 1980s, first made their entrance into the language laboratory because they could handle the "paper" skills of reading and writing. A prime example of reading software was the popular *Language Now!* series produced by the *Transparent Language* Company. The *Système-D* writing assistant program, winner of the 1988 EDUCOM/NCRIPTAL Higher Education Software Award (Garrett, 1991), of *Heinle & Heinle* Publishers came into extensive use and major research was done on its effectiveness (Bland et al., 1990).

Although there had been numerous foreign language film series produced from the 1950s, these were intended for classroom, not laboratory use. With the domestication of the VCR in the 1980s, the use of video became firmly established in language laboratory sessions. A prominent instance was the innovative first- and second-year French course that appeared in 1987, *French in Action*. Interestingly, an early leader in the post-NDEA labs, Pierre Capretz, was the driving force behind it. It received major funding from the Annenberg Foundation and was broadcast on many Public Broadcasting System stations. Video episodes form the core of *French in Action*. That is, the textbook was one of the ancillaries (along with audiocassettes and lab workbook). It was widely adopted in universities and high schools. Many language laboratory carrels that once housed audio equipment now had small TV/VCR combinations instead so that students could watch these excellent videos.

The momentum of the 1980s carried over into the early part of the next decade. This can be seen among lab professionals. The IALL gathered sponsorship from three educational technology companies to produce a monograph on "Designing the Learning Center of the Future" (Kennedy, 1990). The IALL produced more video tours of labs in 1990, 1991, and 1993. Lab directors and other language professionals interested in technology were able to share questions and keep in touch through the *Language Learning Technology International* (LLTI) listserv that began in 1991. This was cosponsored by the IALL and Dartmouth College. As an aid to those who were planning new labs, the IALL put together guidelines on language laboratory design in 1991. This organization teamed up again with the Language Laboratory Association of Japan to put on the FLEAT II conference in August, 1992. To help instructors make effective use of the lab, LeeAnn Stone edited a second volume on communicative activities (Stone, 1993). A valuable resource for lab directors appeared in 1995: *Administering the Learning Center: The IALL Management Manual* (Lawrason, 1995).

The use of technology in language learning and teaching appeared ready to increase because of several developments. New monies for the use of technology in foreign language instruction appeared. In 1990 the U.S. Department of Education funded the first National Foreign Language Resource Centers. Two centers, the University of Hawaii and San Diego State University, began offering workshops on the use of technology. With initial funding from IBM, the FLAME (Foreign Language Applications in Multimedia Environment) project was began at the University of Michigan in 1990. The success of *French in Action* in the late 1980s led to a similar video program for Spanish, *Destinos,* (1992). It benefited from Annenberg/CPB funding as did its predecessor and *Fokus Deutsch,* for German (1999). The amount of computer courseware grew steadily. Publishers began packaging textbook-specific software as standard components along with audio and video materials. With the explosive rise of the World Wide Web from 1993, companion web sites also became commonplace and many "third party" web sites concerning language learning started springing up.

Did language laboratory traffic increase because of all these developments? It would appear that many teachers and learners were hesitant to use the lab and technology. Richards and Nunan (1992) judged that "technology at present is underexploited in language learning and teaching" (p. 1203). Nina Garrett, herself a veteran of the language laboratory, wrote an article (1991) "for teachers making little or no use of technology" (p. 74). She gave a detailed list of all the resources available at the start of the decade. Interestingly, she paid almost no attention to the language laboratory: "'Conventional' audio technology, that of the tape and the language lab, needs no explanation here." (p. 75). Yet she did cite the expertise of some lab personnel in the use of computers—the main subject of her article: "some major language laboratories have enough experience with computers in language teaching so that their staff members can field inquiries" (p. 78).

As regards learners Mullen (1992) noted that "Since their heyday in the 1960s, language laboratories have fallen under something of a cloud" (p. 54). It would appear that the language laboratory had "an image problem" that needed to be addressed before teachers and learners were ready to use it. Wiley (1990) depicts the image vividly:

Many second language students shudder at the thought of entering into the bowels of the "language laboratory" to practice and perfect the acoustical aerobics of proper pronunciation skills. Visions of sterile white-walled, windowless rooms, filled with endless bolted-down rows of claustrophobic metal carrels, and overseen by a humorless, lab director, evoke fear in the hearts of even the most stout-hearted prospective second-language learners. (p. 44)

Despite a mixed start, as the decade progressed, the use of technology in language teaching and learning increased. It was clear, from articles such as Garrett's (1991) and other indications, that the movement of computers into the language laboratory, which as noted above, began in earnest in the 1980s, was bound to increase in the 1990s. Schwartz (1995) helped make the bridge between the history of the language laboratory and computer-assisted language learning:

Without proper teacher-training, evaluation of CALL materials, and research on student use of computers, CALL is likely to meet the same fate as the language laboratory of the 50s and 60s. (p. 534)

It would appear that the foreign language teaching profession had indeed learned a lesson from the experience of the language laboratory. Research was promoted via a new refereed journal, *Language Learning & Technology, http://llt.msu.edu/* that was founded in 1997. The same year saw the publication of the Bush and Terry (1997) volume and a CALICO monograph (Murphy-Judy & Sanders, 1997), both of which sought to equip teachers and prompt research.

That computers were to occupy center stage in the language laboratory is not surprising. Afterall, computers are omnibus machines that can provide audio, video, text, and interactive written exercises. Moreover, the Internet now provides equivalents to the shortwave radio that language educators made some use of from the 1920s, and an approximation of the satellite television programming that became popular in the 1980s. There is a universal standard emerging: "there is one certainty: we know that all current technologies are converging into one digital environment" (Scinicariello, 1997, p. 186). There was speculation

on LLTI and in professional gatherings that because so many students were buying computers and networking was installed on all university campuses, that perhaps the language laboratory should go "virtual" (Pankratz, 1993). Quinn (1990) describes the transition of the language laboratory brought about by the computer:

Rather than say that audio laboratories have been abandoned, it might be more accurate to say these are no longer used in schools where they did not live up to the promise made for them, but have evolved beyond just being "audio labs" in others. Actually, schools still use "language labs," and technologically-advanced learning centers have recently been installed in numerous universities." (p. 303)

In the first two years of the 21st century, the LLTI listserv has carried announcements of language laboratory closings and offers of entire audio labs for sale. So it is certain that some schools have indeed decided to dispense with a dedicated facility for foreign language study. This could be because the problem of the language laboratory's image has not been resolved:

Despite of (sic) their undoubted contribution to the development of language teaching and learning, the term "lab" nowadays also triggers memories about a place where students disappear behind technology, separated from each other, delving head first into the electronic environment and fighting a lone battle with linguistic requests from mysterious authorities. (Bräuer, 2001, p. 185)

What is the future of the language laboratory? Will it cease to exist? At least its name seems destined to change: "the term *language lab* is obsolescent, a form of shorthand that represents a variety of entities responsible for delivering technology-based language instruction. New names like 'language media center' or 'learning resource center' attempt to reflect new goals and new technologies" (Scinicariello, 1997, p. 186). Whatever they be called, it is probable that no two places will look alike: "There is no ideal language lab for the twenty-first century" (Scinicariello, 1997, p. 186).

19.1.5 Conclusion of Language Laboratory History

Surely language laboratories represent the single largest investment and installment of audio resources in education. It is no accident that the foreign-language teaching community has been heavily involved in using audio. Audio has face validity in foreign language instruction simply because much of language use is oral/aural. Granted, there has been concern that the reading and writing skills might be neglected in methodologies that make much use of recordings such as audio-lingualism. Nevertheless, for foreign-language educators it has never been an issue of whether to use audio technology; it has been a question of how.

19.2 RESEARCH ON THE EFFECTIVENESS OF THE LANGUAGE LABORATORY

The preceding historical account detailed the growth and extent of a particular application of audio technology, the language laboratory. What has not yet been assessed is the effectiveness of this massive expenditure of effort and money. This is the task of research. This section will give the main currents of research for each period in the language laboratory's history. Details of each study will not be mentioned except insofar as they are crucial to interpreting the chief findings. The bibliography will permit the interested reader to locate and directly consult the reports cited for further information about the design and conditions of each study.

19.2.1 Research on the Forerunners to the Language Laboratory: 1877 to 1946

There appears to have been very little attempt to provide an empirical justification for the use of the phonograph and phonetics laboratories before World War II. This is not entirely surprising, given that before the 1960s very few foreign-language scholars had training in quantitative experimental techniques: They were humanists schooled in literary and philological research methods. There are, however, accounts of problems with the use of phonographs and phonetics labs which can perhaps be classified as observational research. These observations will be noted, for they raise issues that were to be examined more rigorously later. Moreover, these records demonstrate that there was some notion of accountability among those who used early audio resources. That is, the phonograph and phonetics labs were not accepted and used uncritically.

Based on his "long experimentation," C. C. Clarke (1918, p. 120) provided the first guidelines to appear in the scholarly literature on the proper use of the phonograph in teaching foreign languages. He granted that some teachers found the "mechanism" (p. 122) troublesome, time-consuming, and distracting. To this he countered that it afforded learners the opportunity to hear consistent native-speaker models that never suffered fatigue. He concluded that "the true success of the speech record is in teaching pronunciation and that nothing else should be expected of it" (p. 120). The emphasis on pronunciation training certainly became the hallmark of the phonetics laboratories. Waltz, the founder of the lab at Ohio State University, also cited the benefit of having tireless native-speaker models to imitate. By having the "constant control sounding in his ears" (p. 29), the student could exclude the imperfect approximations of his peers and gain confidence in his own speaking ability. However, a colleague of Waltz, Emma Schenk, complained that the earphones did not adequately keep out others' voices (1930). In addition, she deplored the poor audio quality and the lack of supervision in the Ohio State lab. She worried that students would "cultivate errors" (p. 30). She also noted much cheating on time slips and many students who were not on task while in the lab. Levin (1931) was sympathetic to labs and sought to offer constructive criticism of their use. He stressed the need for immediate feedback so as to avoid the problem Schenk had feared, namely, the development of bad speech habits. Gullette (1932) showed that this fear was justified. He noted with consternation that many students working alone in the lab reverted back to the poor pronunciation practices that earlier had been eradicated in class drill sessions. He stressed that imitation was

not sufficient; what was needed was ear training such as was done in music classes. This would allow for self-diagnosis and correction.

Waltz's report (1932) of two studies he consulted on, but did not conduct himself, is the first record of an attempt to establish empirically the phonetic/language laboratory's effectiveness. It is ironic, in view of the identification of the language laboratory with foreign languages, that neither investigation involved their teaching! The first experiment had to do with the teaching of the Irish accent; the second was concerned with correct English diction. Both studies can be faulted for the low number of subjects (20 and 24), the apparent nonrandom assignment of subjects to treatments, and the lack of statistical analysis beyond a comparison of group means. Nevertheless, Waltz did note that the groups were equivalent by using scores on standardized tests of intelligence, hearing, and pitch discrimination. In the first study, the lab group's mean was 10. 1 (out of a possible 20 points). The control group's mean was 8.04. In the second study, both the lab and nonlab groups showed similar gains. Waltz argued that the comparable improvement was actually evidence in favor of the efficiency of the lab: Class and instructor time was saved by having students work independently in the lab.

For the sake of comprehensiveness, Peebles' master's thesis (1938) must be mentioned. It was included in the annotated bibliography compiled by Sanchez (1959). Students who volunteered to use the Phonetics Laboratory at the University of Colorado and who received one or two French pronunciation tutorial sessions were compared with students who did not avail themselves of these opportunities. Amazingly, she did not specify how much the volunteers used the lab. Neither were the total number of subjects, nor the number of subjects per group, specified. These omissions bespeak a blatant lack of control that invalidates any conclusions that might be drawn from her data, which in fact consisted only of mean numbers of pronunciation mistakes on a posttest.

19.2.1.1 Summary. Obviously, no firm conclusions can be drawn about the effectiveness of the phonograph and the prewar phonetics laboratory from these few observations and two cursory investigations. There appears to have been a consensus among practitioners that the best use of this equipment was for pronunciation training. All saw a potential benefit in untiring, consistent, native speaker models for students to imitate. However, complaints were raised about the sound quality of recordings, and it was observed that many learners lacked the self-monitoring ability to profit fully from them. Just as the next period of language laboratory history saw an increase in the number and sophistication of facilities, so there was similar growth in the inquiries concerning their value.

19.2.2 Research: 1946 to 1958

Language laboratory research of the postwar and pre-NDEA period may be described as nascent. Certain features of empirical research are seen; some are only partially present, and others are completely absent. For example, one sees the first use of standardized tests as criterion measures, and this use is universal. On the other hand, only one study (Allen, 1960) randomly assigned subjects to treatments; intact classes were used otherwise. Only two-group designs and t tests were used. The number of subjects, when reported, was uniformly low. There certainly was not an agreed-upon research agenda. In fact, researchers of the day were either unaware of what their peers were doing (there is little citation of others' work) or they simply ignored it. With these limitations in view, the following discussion will list five studies of the period in chronological order and present their conclusions. According to Kelly (1969), more experiments were conducted than this number would suggest, "but we only know of those whose authors had the time and energy to write articles about them" (p. 245). This is corroborated by Johnson and Seerley (1960), who refer to studies done at a high school and two universities (all unnamed) and of research that was planned at the University of Massachusetts.

Stiefel's description (1952) of the language laboratory at the University of Tennessee and its usage is barely beyond the anecdotal level. Yet its mention of the University of Chicago language investigation tests and the cooperative tests (created by the forerunner of Educational Testing Services) does represent the first, inchoate desire of those involved in language labs to have an objective benchmark with which to compare groups of learners who used the lab with those who did not. In this case, Stiefel compared the scores of lab classes on these measures and on an in-house test with classes from previous years. Thus, this is an ex post facto study. He, noted higher scores for lab groups on the in-house tests, but he was hesitant to draw any strong conclusions from these. He found that both groups were comparable on the standardized tests. This he took as heartening evidence that the reading ability (as measured by the cooperative test) of the lab groups did not suffer because of their emphasis on the listening and speaking skills. This last point was of great concern to the scholarly community of the day, as further evidenced by the following study.

Supported by a grant from the Carnegie Foundation for the Advancement of Teaching, Brushwood and Polmantier (1953) at the University of Missouri sought to determine whether dialogue repetition and memorization in the language lab increased learners' aural skills. Although for administrative reasons they were unable to randomly assign subjects to treatments, these researchers did take the trouble to administer the Iowa Foreign Language Aptitude Test to the intact classes that constituted the treatment groups. Moreover, the researchers obtained access to the scores on two English proficiency tests that all the subjects had taken previously. All these tests revealed that the control and experimental groups were matched on these measures, as they were in age.

Four groups were formed: two groups of 19 subjects each who were enrolled in elementary Spanish, and two groups of 23 who were enrolled in elementary French. The control groups simply attended the standard 5-hour per week (1 hour daily) course as taught at the University of Missouri. The experimental groups covered the same material (grammar, reading, and composition) as the control groups, but did so in 4 hours instead of 5. The experimental groups also attended two 1-hour laboratory sessions during the first 4 days of the week. In these sessions, they worked with a dialogue written for the experiment

that incorporated the grammar and vocabulary that had been studied that week. The work consisted of listening to the dialogue via earphones and chorally repeating until it was memorized. A graduate student or upperclassman lab attendant controlled the tape player and thus directed the sessions. His or her only other task was to correct gross pronunciation errors. The experimental group then had a fifth class session in which the regular instructor had the students review and act out the dialogues. The dialogue was then manipulated by changing number, person, tense, object, etc., as a transition to free conversation. This fifth hour was deemed "the crucial point in the achievement of the oral-aural objective" (p. 8).

At the end of the semester the groups were given the cooperative tests on reading, vocabulary, and grammar, and an aural comprehension test created for the experiment. For whatever reason, both t tests and F tests were calculated for the two Spanish and two French groups, but no tests were run on a combination of control and experimental groups across languages. The results showed that there were no significant differences on the cooperative measures. There were significant ts, but not Fs, in favor of the experimental groups on the aural comprehension test.

This study can be faulted on several grounds, but perhaps the most serious flaw may be the lack of control for amount of instruction. Although the authors claimed that the 2 hours of lab practice for the experimental groups were in lieu of homework required of the students in the control groups, it must be noted that the lab sessions were scheduled and monitored. Whether students in the control sections did their work or not is unknown. Moreover, the significant difference between the groups on aural comprehension was measured by a nonstandardized test, the validity and reliability of which is open to question. All of these criticisms aside, Brushwood and Polmentier's study was certainly more rigorous than previous investigations of the use of audio resources in foreign-language teaching.

Next in chronological order are two ex post facto studies that are included here for the sake of completeness. The first is the description by Fotos (1955) of the use of the language laboratory at Purdue University. In direct opposition to the Brushwood and Polmentier study, the lab at Purdue was used for "*predrilling* [emphasis added] the student on the French text of the basic grammar or reading lesson" (p. 142) that was to be covered in class. Fotos reported that students in first-year French scored 60.1 on the cooperative tests; second-year students scored 71.3. The national averages were 56.7 and 68.8, respectively. Whether this was a significant difference cannot be ascertained.

Mueller and Borglum (1956) looked at correlations between lab attendance and course grade, final exam score, and cooperative test score at Wayne University. They noted that students who voluntarily attended the lab more than the minimum requirement of 30 minutes per week generally did better on these measures. They drew special attention to the heavy lab users' 10% increase on the cooperative reading test: "an unprecedented jump in 8 years of recorded scores" (p. 325). Moreover, they observed that even students who only attended the lab 30 minutes per week scored better than students from previous years who had no lab experience. They also noted a lower drop rate for heavy lab users. One can surmise that greater time-on-task naturally produced greater learning. In their discussion, Mueller and Borglum also acknowledged a significant teacher effect: The lab's director "succeeded in getting the students of his sections to attend the laboratory 2 or 3 times more frequently than other instructors" (p. 322).

Allen (1960) conducted a study during the 1957-58 academic year which represents the last investigation of Language laboratories in the 1946-58 period. The 54 subjects were 15- and 16-year-old students in a high school operated by Ohio State University. Allen created eight groups based on level (elementary or intermediate), language (French or Spanish), and use of the lab (55 minutes per week or none). These divisions made for groups as small as five. He administered three standardized tests in order to have a basis for pairing subjects. Once the pairs were established, he used a random-choice technique to assign students to the lab or nonlab treatments.

The lab groups spent one classroom hour listening to instructor-made tapes of "humorous or suspenseful tales" (p. 355) and answering questions about them in the target language. They recorded their answers and then spent the rest of the period listening to commercially prepared recordings. There was absolutely no written material presented during the lab hour. The nonlab group read the same stories and answered the questions in writing. If any time remained, they did free reading from a collection of books at their level.

At the end of the school year, all groups were given three standardized tests (including the cooperative) that measured reading, vocabulary, grammar, speaking, and listening. Allen only reports means and standard deviations. In all cases except one, the laboratory groups scored identical to or higher than the nonlab groups. The exception was the Intermediate Spanish lab group ($n = 5$), which scored lower on the speaking test. In several cases, the differences between the means were large, but Allen did not compute any test of significance. In his brief conclusion, however, he claimed that the laboratory groups "achieved significantly higher scores in reading, vocabulary, and grammar" (p. 357), but that there were no differences in speaking or listening. The author of this chapter calculated a t test on the cooperative French test means for the largest groups, those in Elementary French ($n = 10$ each). The lab group had a mean of 57 (s.d. = 23); the nonlab group mean was 39.4 (s.d. = 20). This turned out to be significant at the 0.001 level.

It is fitting that the last of the studies of the 1946-58 period should be the one with the highest methodological standards. Yet the number of subjects was quite low for the design chosen, and it is baffling that Allen claimed to have found a significant difference in favor of the lab groups, but did not bother to report any data beyond means and standard deviations. Moreover, it is ironic that reading, grammar, and vocabulary scores were enhanced by listening in the language laboratory, whereas listening scores proper did not reveal any difference between the lab and nonlab groups. Thus, Allen's study gives weak but curious evidence of the language laboratory's contribution to foreign language learning.

19.2.2.1 Summary. Writing in the early 1960s, Carroll (1963) stated that virtually all previous foreign-language research "has only rarely been adequate with respect to research

methodology" (p. 1094). For him, language laboratory research was not an exception to this rule. He briefly reviewed three studies concerning labs; these were not included in this section because they did not contain important results, were not widely circulated at the time (two were institutional reports), and were not cited by subsequent researchers. Therefore, what one can conclude from Carroll's review and this summary is that while the research during the 1946-1958 period did not firmly establish the positive value of language laboratories, it did provide circumstantial, and in one case (Allen, 1960) empirical, evidence in favor of this conclusion.

Writing at the close of the period under consideration, Koekkoek (1959) stated that labs were so "firmly established" in language teaching that "no teacher can remain today unaffected and disengaged" (p. 5). He went on to describe the ambivalence about them within the profession and closed his article with the hope that subsequent experience would resolve "basic questions to be expected from the use of laboratory machines and the best methods of obtaining the results" (p. 5). If the nascent body of research could only offer a cautious "thumbs-up" assessment, it also showed that those promoting labs were willing to be held responsible for their use. This was fortunate, for during the next phase of the lab's existence, a period of great growth because of major expenditures, the public would eventually demand an accounting.

19.2.3 Research on Language Laboratories: 1959 to present

The massive increase in the number of language laboratories, thanks to the NDEA, prompted a comparable increase in the amount of research concerning their effectiveness. In fact, some of the studies were funded by the NDEA under its Title VI provisions. The extent of this research is such that this section cannot detail every investigation that was undertaken. The several dissertations listed by Davison (1973) will not be treated. This discussion will focus on four large-scale studies of labs: three in high schools and one in a university. These all received much attention at the time. Moreover, those studies that have been thoroughly reviewed elsewhere will be only briefly described.

19.2.3.1 Major Studies. During the 1961-62 school year, Keating (1963) conducted a study of the use of the language laboratory in French classes in New York City high schools. He cited Allen's study (1960) as the "only exception" (he was evidently unaware of the Brushwood & Polmantier study) to the rule that "the literature abounds with articles that describe the benefits of using language laboratories" but " contains virtually no reports upon the empirical validation" (p. 8) of them. He called Allen's results "quite interesting" but noted a possible Hawthorne effect, which he felt "severely compromised" (p. 8) them. Keating knew of the research being simultaneously conducted in New York City by Lorge (to be described later).

Keating's was a large-scale study involving approximately 5,000 subjects in 21 school districts. Schools were divided between laboratory and nonlaboratory users based on a questionnaire filled out by each district's foreign-language coordinator.

Besides this factor, groups were formed according to year of study (first through fourth years) and IQ scores (five levels). The dependent measures were reading comprehension, listening comprehension, and speech production. The cooperative test was used to test the first two skills; however, first-year students were not given the listening portion because it was designed for intermediate and advanced students. The French speech production test was used to evaluate speaking. This instrument was constructed specifically for the study. Of note is that it was not administered to all subjects: only 519 students from 12 of the participating school districts were given it. The results showed a sole significant finding in favor of the lab groups, on speaking among first-year students. Otherwise, there were several cases of the nonlab groups scoring significantly higher.

Keating's findings were promptly and vehemently disputed. The April 1964 issue of the *Modern Language Journal* included four rebuttals (by Anderson, Grittner, Porter & Porter, and Stack). The criticisms showed much overlap. Keating was taken to task for numerous methodological flaws: failure to define what was meant by language laboratory and the activities that went on there, failure to control for amount of time spent in the lab, failure to control for the socioeconomic level of the schools and the quality of their lab installations, use of *t* tests when ANOVAs were called for, and sloppy reporting of results (the number of subjects per group was not consistent). Keating was also criticized for using several different IQ tests, rather than one, to group subjects. The validity of his speaking test was challenged for being in fact only a pronunciation measure. Keating was shown no mercy: Despite the disclaimers he gave about the generalizibility of his results, he was accused of spreading anti-lab propaganda by Grittner.

Because the literature of the period contains no defense of Keating's study, it can be concluded that it was dismissed by the scholarly community of the day. Unfortunately, the public was of another mind. It seized on the notion that if language laboratories are not useful, then the massive investment of tax dollars in facilities was a waste. An example of this attitude was a newspaper editorial about the Keating study entitled "Backwards Via 'Aid" that was reprinted in the *Modern Language Journal* issue containing the four rebuttals. Such a response gives credence to the propaganda charge made by Grittner. He and Stack and Anderson pointed out, with great dismay, that the Institute of Administrative Research of Columbia Teacher's College, which had sponsored Keating's study, mailed out a five-page preliminary report to school administrators across the country. They viewed such an action as unprofessional; it was clearly inflammatory in its impact.

Lorge (1964) conducted two experiments in New York City high schools. The first took place during the 1961–62 school year, and the second was done the following year. Thus, the first study coincided with Keating's investigation. Whether there was any overlap of subjects between the two studies is unknown, but could hardly be problematic given that only two schools were involved in Lorge's first inquiry; Keating's entailed 21 districts. Lorge described the purpose of her study thus:

The object of the study was not to compare what a student learns from a teacher alone as opposed to what he learns from laboratory work alone.

The question was whether the teacher improves the teaching-learning situation by using the laboratory as a teaching aid. The research was intended not to give the laboratory a passing or failing mark-if it passes, use it; if it fails, rip it out—but rather to determine in which areas it had proved to be successful, and how its use could be made more effective. (p. 409)

The first study compared first-, second-, and third-year French classes. Unfortunately, the number of classes and subjects is not specified in the article, and the full report of the study is not available for consultation; by 1965 it was already out of print (Lorge, 1965). All that is known is that the classes were determined to be comparable based on the Stanford reading test and the Gallup–Thorndike vocabulary test. Half of the classes had 60 minutes a week of supervised lab practice in lieu of a fifth class period. The other half had five class meetings. The course content was the same for both groups. At the end of the school year, all classes were given the cooperative French test to gauge reading, vocabulary, and grammar skills. A speaking test and a listening test, both written by the experimenters, were also administered. All the tests contained subtests for which separate statistics were calculated. There were no differences between the groups on the cooperative test. The first and second-year laboratory groups tested significantly higher than the control groups on the fluency component of the speaking test. The second-year laboratory group also scored significantly higher on the intonation component. The third-year laboratory group was significantly superior in listening.

The second experiment compared two types of laboratory equipment: audio-active and recording-playback. The first was a headset with earphones and a microphone; the second was an identical headset plus a tape recorder for each student. The other factor was time. Daily usage of 20 minutes was compared to a once-a-week 60-minute session. Five groups of second-year French students were formed. It should be stressed that none of the subjects had previous laboratory experience. Moreover, during the study, the control group did not use any equipment. The other four groups were formed by crossing equipment type and usage time. The dependent measures were the same as in the first study, with the addition of a mimicry test.

The t test results from the 14 components are difficult to interpret. Some differences are reported at a .01 level of significance, others at a .05 level, but it is impossible to determine whether one group was significantly higher than all the other groups or only some of them. The rankings that were also reported are more helpful, for they allow trends to be detected. On measures of enunciation, the order was thus: (1) daily record-playback, (2) daily audio-active, (3) weekly record-playback, (4) weekly audio-active, and (5) control. Thus greater time, frequency, and more elaborate equipment favor one aspect of the speaking skill. However, as regards lexical and syntactic features of speech, the control group was ranked first, with the daily record-playback group coming in second. This finding should be considered along with the result from the composite score on the cooperative test. Here, the daily record-playback group ranked first and the control group was second. The difference between the two groups was not significant, but both groups were significantly higher than the other three groups. What emerges is this: The daily record-playback group and the control group scored similarly, and significantly better than the other groups, on both oral and written measures of vocabulary and grammar.

From the above findings, one is tempted to draw an "all or nothing" conclusion: Either use a fully equipped lab daily or dispense with it altogether. It seems that certain outcomes will be the same in either case. The corollary is that infrequent usage of a modest lab actually appears to be detrimental to the lexical and syntactic aspects of language learning! However, Lorge does not make such a counterintuitive deduction. She noted that in the first study, there were no differences between the lab and nonlab groups on the vocabulary and grammar tests. In the second study, she maintained that any measure showing statistically significant differences showed at least one laboratory group that equaled or exceeded the gains made by the control group. This appears to indicate that time spent in the laboratory contributes to conventional learnings as well as to listening and speaking skills (p. 419).

The last sentence is crucial. Taken together, these studies indicated an overall advantage for the language lab. Lorge also noted that a higher percentage of students in lab sections continued studying French beyond the 3 years required for high school graduation and college admission.

Lorge's study appears to have been well received by the scholarly community. Stack (1964) praised Lorge's work in his critique of the Keating study. Only Green (1965) ventured criticisms. Some of his complaints had to do with the manner in which the results were reported. He was more concerned with the apparent addition of another group after the study was underway. Lorge (1965) answered these objections easily in her rebuttal, which was included in the same issue of the *Modern Language Journal* as Green's piece.

In 1966, Philip D. Smith began an investigation of beginning high school French and German teaching and learning, which lasted through 1969. It was sponsored by the Federal Office of Education under Titles VI and VII of the NDEA and is commonly referred to in the literature as the Pennsylvania project because all the participating schools were in that state. Smith summarized his findings in 1969 articles in *Foreign Language Annals* (Smith, 1969a) and the *French Review* (Smith, 1969b), which are more accessible than the technical reports he submitted as part of the grant's requirements. The October 1969 issue (volume 53, number 6) of the *Modern Language Journal* contained six articles critiquing the Pennsylvania studies. The December 1969 issue (volume 3, number 2) of *Foreign Language Annals* contained the summary article by Smith and two review articles. Contemporary synopses of the project and its reviews by D. L. Lange (1968) and W. F. Smith (1970) will be relied on for this discussion.

In the first year of the study, 2,171 students participated. Three teaching strategies and three language laboratory systems were compared. The strategies were: traditional, functional skills, and functional skills with grammar. By *traditional* was meant that an emphasis was placed on vocabulary acquisition, reading and writing skills, translation, and grammatical analysis. *Functional skills* was a synonym for the audio lingual method; the command of a core vocabulary and key syntactic patterns was emphasized, as were the speaking and listening skills. *Functional skills with grammar* was, as the name indicates, the addition of grammatical explanations to the audio lingual method. The three language laboratory systems were: audio-active, audio-active record, and tape recorder in the classroom. The first consisted of two, 25-minute practice sessions each week in which a 10-minute drill tape was played twice. The second arrangement differed from the first in that the students recorded their first practice with the tape and then listened to their own responses. Both of the audio-active groups also practiced in the classroom with a tape recorder each day under the supervision of the instructor for one-fifth of the period. The tape recorder in the classroom group did no lab practice. What they did was at least 10 minutes of guided practice with the tape each day in class.

The results from the first year indicated no significant differences between the teaching strategies, except for reading, where the traditional group outperformed the two audio-active groups. There were no significant differences detected between laboratory systems. During the second year of the project, 639 first-year students participated in a replication study, and 1,090 of the original 2,171 subjects were observed in their second year of language study. The results from this second year of the investigation were in line with those of the first. In the third year the number of subjects (third-year students) dropped to 277, and by the fourth year it was down to 144 fourth-year students. The findings from these last 2 years showed the traditional students faring significantly better than the audio-active students in both reading and listening. In none of the 4 years of the study was a significant difference in outcomes found according to the laboratory system.

Although the Pennsylvania project generally received higher marks for its methodology than did the Keating report with which it was often compared, there were nevertheless several critiques leveled and questions raised. Some of these involved control issues, such as the degree of teacher adherence to experimental guideline, the consistency of laboratory installations and maintenance between schools, and the lack of data as to the amount of time the labs where actually used. Carroll (1969b) detected stowaway variables and practice effects. Perhaps the most serious criticism was the claim (Valette, 1969) that the cooperative test was an inappropriate measure of listening achievement. It was maintained that the vocabulary in this test was closer to what was in the textbook used by traditional groups than the one used by the lab groups. Moreover, evidence from other sources was cited which indicated that the cooperative test was simply too difficult for students in their first 3 years of foreign-language study. This second criticism had broad implications: It cast doubt on the instrument that had been used in all previous language laboratory studies and in many other studies of foreign-language teaching.

Carroll (1969b) and Smith (1970) assessed the implications of the Pennsylvania project. For them, the supposed findings in favor of the traditional groups did not warrant a return to former means of teaching. Rather, they viewed the report, despite its faults, as a credible demonstration that the enthusiastic adoption of new approaches and accompanying materiel does not guarantee success. "The Pennsylvania studies have removed us from our tower of false security" (Smith, 1970, p. 208). For Carroll, the specific lessons to be learned were that audio lingual textbooks needed more linguistic content and that less emphasis should be placed on drills and other "habit formation" activities (1969; p. 235). Smith ended his review on an upbeat note: "It is time to meet the challenge of a new decade" (1970, p. 208). But such a positive attitude did not prevail. As was noted in the historical section above, language laboratories were in the doldrums in the 1970s and early 1980s. Davies (1982) singled out the Pennsylvania project for making complete the growing disillusionment of the period with labs. Moreover, it appears that the study discouraged other research, for it was the last of the large scale inquiries into the language laboratory's effectiveness.

The only major inquiry of the language laboratory involving postsecondary students will now be discussed. Scherer and Wertheimer (1964) described in a 246-page book, *A psycholinguistic experiment in foreign-language teaching,* the 2-year NDEA-sponsored investigation they conducted from September 1960. Their goal was to compare the audio-lingual approach to the traditional grammar-reading method. Thus, this was not an examination of the language laboratory per se; rather, it was an inquiry similar to the Pennsylvania project (not yet conducted), which was interested in the language lab because of its intimate connection to the audio-lingual method. The subjects were beginning German students at the University of Colorado. Intact classes were used, and these were determined to be similar on measures of general academic ability, language learning aptitude, and motivation, as well as sex, age, and year in school. It should be noted that Wertheimer was a psychologist and this study was published in a psychology series. This reinforces what was noted in the previous *History* section, namely, that the general educational community in the 1960s was very interested in the language laboratory and that the foreign language community looked outside of itself for guidance in implementing and evaluating the language laboratory.

All of the teaching staff received a week of training in the respective methods prior to the start of the experiment. In addition, there were weekly meetings and frequent observations by the principal investigators and outside consultants to ensure that the instructors adhered to the experiment's guidelines. The traditional approach is only scantily described, but the audio-lingual procedures are elaborately detailed in Scherer and Wertheimer's book. The essence of the latter was dialogue memorization and related drill and practice in class. The frequency and duration of the lab sessions were unfortunately not specified; they were for "overlearning" (p. 83) the material presented in class. It is stated that the lab sessions were unmonitored and were of the "library-type" (p. 83), which presumably means the students attended at their convenience. Of note is the postponement of reading for the audio-lingual group until the 12th week of the semester. To be specific, the audio-lingual group saw absolutely no written German until that point. When reading began, it consisted of the dialogues that had been previously memorized and recombinations of the vocabulary contained in them.

The investigators claimed that they conducted a "persistent and continuous search" (p. 108) for standardized tests to use to measure the outcomes of the two teaching approaches. They

were not satisfied with what they found, because "nothing that the major test distributors had to offer seemed to meet the requirements of our situation" (p. 108). They therefore constructed tests of the four language skills and two for translation: German-to-English and vice versa. The *t* test statistic was used for comparisons. At the end of the first year, the audio-lingual students were significantly superior to the traditional students in speaking and listening. The superiority in speaking was maintained in the second year, but the advantage for listening was not. On the other hand, the traditional students significantly outperformed the audio-lingual students on reading and writing during the first year, and maintained their edge on the latter skill during the second year. The traditional students also were higher in German-to-English translation during both years, and better in English-to-German translation in the first year.

In addition to these measures of linguistic proficiency, Scherer and Wertheimer also used standardized scales and questionnaires they constructed to evaluate the subjects' motivation to study German and their attitude to it and its speakers. They were also concerned with "habituated direct association." By this was meant the ability of the students to think in German, their inclination to translate or not, and their sensitivity to semantic nuances between the two languages. Numerous intercorrelations between these and measures of affective constructs such as anomie, social inhibition, and desire for further German study were calculated. The researchers summarized their work thus:

The experiment has demonstrated that the two methods, while yielding occasionally strong and persisting differences in various aspects of proficiency in German, result in comparable overall proficiency. But the audio-lingual method, whether its results are measured objectively or estimated by the students themselves, appears to produce more desirable attitudes and better habituated direct association. (p. 245)

John B. Carroll (1969a) characterized the Scherer and Wertheimer study as "ambitious" (p. 869) and more rigorously designed than any previous examination of the audio-lingual approach. He accepted the investigators' conclusions as valid, but offered the following:

The conclusion that emerges from this experiment is that the differences between the audio-lingual and traditional methods are primarily differences of objectives; not surprisingly, students learn whatever skills are emphasized in the instruction. (pp. 869–870)

19.2.3.2 Minor Studies. Besides the large-scale and well-publicized studies of Keating, Lorge, Smith, and Scherer and Wertheimer, there have been many smaller investigations since 1959. Eight studies that appeared in major journals have been selected for inclusion here according to chronological order. Only their main findings will be given, since these studies in general did not generate the interest of the larger studies that were described above.

Bauer (1964) found that university students who used the language laboratory in a supervised group-practice condition performed significantly better on oral and dictation measures, but not on a writing measure, than students who studied individually and were not supervised. Two drawbacks to the study were the low number of subjects ($N = 24$) and the use of nonstandardized tests. Moreover, a close examination of the data reveals that the supervised subjects as a group used the lab 125 minutes more over a 3.5-week period than the unsupervised subjects, so the observed differences could possibly be attributed to greater time-on-task.

Young and Choquette's NDEA-sponsored study (1965) was a series of seven experiments that sought to determine whether any of four language laboratory equipment configurations made a difference in the subjects' abilities to self-monitor their pronunciation. The systems were characterized by the feedback options they presented: (1) passive, (2) active, (3) long-delayed comparison, and (4) short-delayed comparison. The first three systems were standard options for language laboratory installations at the time. An apparatus for the fourth condition was specially fashioned for the study by the investigators. In the passive arrangement, the subjects repeated after taped prompts, but they could not clearly hear their responses because the headsets muffled their voices. In the active arrangement, subjects could hear their responses amplified through their headsets as they spoke. In the third option, subjects could record their answers for later comparison. In the fourth setup, the students could hear their recorded response within 1.5 seconds of making them. Subjects in the active feedback configuration were found to have slightly superior pronunciation than subjects in the other arrangements. However, the authors qualified this finding on several grounds. Of note was the lower sound quality of the fabricated equipment used in the short-delay condition. The authors admitted that this hampered a true comparison with the other three conditions.

Buka, Freeman, and Locke (1962) and Freeman and Buka (1965) conducted experiments that sought to establish psychoacoustic parameters for language laboratory equipment. The first study determined that a high-frequency cutoff of less than 7,300 cps hindered subjects (high school students) from perceiving certain phonemic contrasts in German and French. The second study found that a low-frequency cutoff of 500 cps caused subjects (again high school students) to make significantly more errors in German phoneme discrimination than a 50-cps cutoff. However, no significant differences were found between these two levels for French phoneme discrimination. It was also found that consonant distinctions were more affected than vowel distinctions by the degradation of sound quality brought on by filtering.

Benathy and Jordan (1969) reported on a post hoc comparison of achievement scores in Bulgarian courses at the Defense Language Institute. The scores of 13 classes (87 students) that completed the course between August 1959 and September 1963 were compared to the scores of 15 classes (103 students) that finished between November 1963 and July 1967. The difference between these classes was the introduction in the fall of 1963 of the Classroom Laboratory Instructional System (CLIS): CLIS is a designed interaction of live instruction and a set of different kinds of learning experiences that make use of prepared and recorded instructional materials, delivered through the electronic media (p. 473).

The authors stressed that the CLIS system kept the learners on task much more than in a typical classroom. This was because the earphones both isolated each learner from the erroneous responses and pronunciations of others and provided quality native-speaker models. Moreover, the learner did not wait to be called on as in a regular class; it was always his or her "turn." The equipment used appeared to be that of a typical audioactive language laboratory, although the authors do not use the term in their article. Curiously, they do not cite any language laboratory literature in their discussion, yet their description and justification for CLIS are identical to those commonly found in language laboratory writings.

The two groups were found to be very similar in ages and scores on the Army Language Aptitude Test. Class sizes were nearly identical, and the same textbooks and proficiency test were used throughout the 8-year period. It was found that the CLIS classes scored significantly higher than the pre-CLIS classes on the two skills measured by the test, namely, reading and listening. The differences were especially pronounced in the case of the latter skill.

Despite the many experimental controls and the marked differences between the groups, there are three questions that may be raised about this study. First of all, as no mention of instructors is made, one wonders whether teacher effects were held constant. Secondly, the generalizability of the results to high school and university students is doubtful, given that the subjects were all adults studying for specific career purposes at the Defense Language Institute. A third consideration is a question: Why did Benathy and Jordan not more fully report on the synchronous study that Preceded the longitudinal one? They claimed similar significant results from it in favor of the CLIS. More information (i.e., number of subjects, a showing t values) about it would give greater credibility to their overall conclusion.

The Chomei and Houlihan (1970) study compared three language laboratory systems: instant playback, long-delay playback, and audio-active. The instant playback option allowed the subjects to have their recorded response to the program stimulus echoed back within half a second. The long-delay group had to rewind the tape to hear their recordings. The audio-active group did not record their responses. It can thus be seen that this study closely resembled what had been done by Young and Choquette (1965), but, surprisingly, this earlier work was not cited. The subjects in the Chomei and Houlihan investigation were 140 Japanese 10th-graders, who were all taught by the same instructor. It was found that the instant-playback group performed significantly better than the other groups on one out of five translation tests and on four out of five speaking tests that had been specially created for the experiment.

Sisson (1970) did a study that was sponsored by the U.S. Office of Education. Its aim was to settle the controversy among language educators as to the benefit (or lack thereof) of delayed comparison on students' ability to perceive and produce the phonemes of another language. Thus, this study shared the same goal as the work of Young and Choquette (1965) and Chomei and Houlihan (1970). That Sisson did not cite the latter is understandable, since it was contemporary to his own. What is surprising is that he ignored the former, yet did cite 39 other articles. In this oversight he followed Chomei and Houlihan, as pointed out before. Why a major study published in a leading journal was so ignored is an unanswered question in the record.

Sisson claimed that "the variables of learning environment were controlled as closely as possible with respect to identity of instructors, scheduling of laboratory lessons, and use of class-room and laboratory materials" (p. 82). The special equipment used in the study, the Plurilingua language laboratory, was thoroughly described. The subjects were 24 students of English as a second language at the University of Michigan. They were in three intact classes of eight students each. The classes were matched on the basis of a modified version of the test of Aural Perception for Latin American Students. This instrument had a phoneme discrimination section and two phoneme production portions.

Two conditions were compared. Half of the students (four from each of the three classes) listened to a taped stimulus and recorded their answer. On completion of an exercise, these subjects rewound the tape and repeated the exercise in the same manner. These subjects formed the "active group." The other group of subjects recorded their responses, as did the active group. However, at the completion of the exercise, these subjects rewound their tape and listened to their first responses rather than record them a second time. This was the "delayed-comparison group." Both groups spent 1 hour per week in the language laboratory during the 8-week term. The modified version of the test of Aural Perception for Latin American Students, which had been used as the pretest was also used as the posttest. Sisson found no significant difference between the two groups on either discrimination or production.

Morin (1971) compared three types of laboratory equipment: (1) an instructor-supervised lab with listening and recording functions, (2) a cassette recorder with "minimal supervision" (p. 65), and (3) an audio-active lab with no recording capability. At the outset 80 students were given the Modern Language Aptitude Test (MLAT) and the LA form of the MLA Cooperative speaking test as pretests. The students were then assigned at random to 8 classes which contained 10 students each. This resulted in two classes per treatment condition (there was also a control group). The *Voix et Images de France* textbook and tapes were used. After three days of instruction, the classes were further divided into "fast" and "slow" groups. What was meant by these terms and the basis for assignment to groups is not explained. Nor is there mention of teacher assignment. A total of 16 groups/cells of 5 students each resulted. After a total of 120 hours of instruction over a three-week period, Form LB of the MLA Cooperative test was administered. The results were analyzed by ANCOVA, although which of the pretests was used for the covariant was not given. No significant differences were found. Morin concluded that "inexpensive equipment produces results comparable to more sophisticated ones" and then suggested that "further study should bear mainly on improving ways and means of utilizing present equipment rather than on equipment proper" (p. 67). The conclusions of this study are suspect because of the low N and the apparent lack of control for teacher effect.

Smith (1980) conducted a study to determine whether the slowing down of recorded material had a beneficial effect on listening comprehension. The reader will recall from the *History* section that during the 1960s equipment became available which was capable of slowing down (expanding) or speeding up (compressing) recordings without distortion. Smith claimed that his search of the literature turned up no reference to studies addressing the specific application of this technology to foreign-language instruction. This claim was incorrect: Driscoll (1981) listed two such studies which predated Smith's by several years and three that were done at about the same time as Smith's (i.e., the late 1970s). However, in fairness, it should be pointed out that Driscoll was also guilty of oversight; he omitted Smith's study even though it was in the same outlet, the *NALLD Journal,* as his own article.

Smith's subjects were second-semester students of French at West Chester State College in Pennsylvania. The control group had 11 members, and the experimental, 12. The cooperative test was administered as a pretest, and the control group was found to be significantly better in reading ability than the experimental group, but both groups were equal in listening comprehension, the skill at issue in the investigation. The study stretched over the fall 1978 semester. The control group covered 12 audio lessons that were recorded at normal speed. The experimental group listened to four lessons that were slowed by 20 percent, four that were slowed by 10 percent, and four that were at normal speed. At the end of semester, the students were again given the cooperative tests. Contrary to expectations, the ANCOVA and Finney t test procedures showed that the control group scored significantly higher on listening comprehension than the experimental group who listened to expanded material.

Despite such a clear-cut albeit counterintuitive finding, Smith cautioned that the study needed to be replicated with a larger number of subjects and for other languages before it could be reasonably concluded that expanded speech was not beneficial, or perhaps even harmful, for the acquiring of listening proficiency in a foreign language. Unfortunately, there is no record of replications by Smith or others. Whether the magnitude of Smith's findings squelched any other initiatives can only be conjectured. Driscoll (1980) concluded from his review of the studies that the results "do not add up to much more than implication" (p. 49) that either expanded or compressed speech is a boon to foreign language study. Nevertheless, language laboratory manufacturers continued to include expansion and compression capabilities in the "deluxe" models of their equipment. It can only be concluded that many practitioners appreciated these features and purchased them, although they had no independent, empirical confirmation of their effectiveness.

19.2.3.3 Summary of Research. Twelve studies conducted since the passage of the NDEA in 1958 were discussed in this section. They differed considerably in scale, populations, and methodology. Although all concerned language laboratories in some way, they did not all seek to answer the same questions other than the general one of effectiveness. For these reasons, it is difficult to draw conclusions. This body of research does not offer clear-cut confirmation of the utility of language laboratories, yet neither does it suggest that they are detrimental to language learning. Perhaps the inconclusiveness of the record is because the investigations that were conducted were not following an agreed-upon agenda. The larger educational technology community began the period with such an agenda (Allen,

1959; Meierhenry, 1962). This lack of focus was costly: Pederson (1987) claimed that it was the lack of solid research concerning courseware that led to the decline of language laboratories.

It would be hasty, however, to dismiss all language laboratory research. It can readily be determined that the use of audio resources within the foreign-language community has differed significantly from that of the larger educational technology community. Not surprisingly, this different use fostered different research. What was unique to the utilization and study of audio resources within foreign-language circles? One can first note the interest in psychophysics and the acoustic parameters of equipment. Besides Buka et al. (1962) and Freeman and Buka (1965), who were discussed previously, Hayes (1963) should be mentioned. He culled a wide range of human factors literature in order to offer standards to be used in laboratory purchase specifications. At this time, the broader educational technology community was more concerned with visual rather than auditory perception. A clear example of this pictorial bias is the fifth issue of volume 10 of the *Audio-Visual Communication Review* (1962), which was entitled "Perception Theory and AV Education." It contained no mention of the aural sense. Such a slanting of interest belies the "audio" component in the name of the flagship journal of the educational technology field at the time. More recently, Saettler's *The Evolution of American Educational Technology* (1990) shows that this inclination persists; visual media are accorded much more attention than are audio media. Related to acoustic and perceptual matters are equipment features. Some of the studies reviewed in this section of the chapter (e.g., Chomei & Houlihan, 1970; Young & Choquette, 1965) were concerned with this issue. This is also unique to the body of language laboratory research. Only the studies of compressed and expanded speech showed an interest in machine capabilities.

At the outset of this portion of the chapter, it was stated that the larger educational technology community has not fully appreciated the history of the language laboratory. The scant attention paid to them in Saettler's *The Evolution of American Educational Technology* was cited to support this point. Nor has the research that accompanied the language laboratory been acknowledged heretofore. The proof of this contention can be seen in Allen's (1971) review of past educational technology research. This essay in the *AVCR* by its longtime editor contained no mention of the many studies done in the 1960s concerning the language laboratory. This is startling when one recognized that some of the studies had attracted much attention in the

popular press. It is hoped that this chapter has filled in the glaring gap in the record.

19.3 CONCLUSION

Within the field of education, the language laboratory must be seen as a singular phenomenon. By virtue of its unique equipment and its specific pedagogy, it stands alone. There is nothing quite like it in any other discipline. At least in its golden age, the language laboratory was known and valued. The April, 1962 issue of the *Review of Educational Research* (Volume 32) was devoted to "Educational Media and Technology." It contained seven articles that summarized the literature since the publication of Volume 26 in April, 1956. Foreign language education was the only academic discipline to get its own review, namely Mathieu's (1962) piece on the language laboratory. This chapter has traced the history and summarized the research surrounding the language laboratory phenomenon with the intent of securing the lab's deserved recognition in history.

According to Last, "language teachers as a body have been more ready than most to accept and explore the pedagogical potential of new technologies as they have emerged" (1989, p. 15). No better embodiment of Last's contention can be found than the language laboratory. According to a leader of the language laboratory movement, Elton Hocking, its justification was because "Sound brings language to life, and life to language" (in Huebener, 1965, p. 140). This author was a student who used the language laboratory in the 1960s. He recalls fondly and clearly sitting in the language laboratory in 1965–66 school year as a seventh grader, listening to dialogues, repeating them, and being corrected by his teacher. A special treat was going to the lab and viewing his Spanish instructor's slides of a trip to Mexico. For him, the lab was an exotic place he enjoyed visiting. He senses that among the millions of students who passed through the language laboratory over the years, he was not alone in his appreciation. Indeed, sound brought language to many lives. Thus the huge sums expended on the language laboratory and the thousands of educators' hours devoted to its use were not in vain, even though the research did not determine the optimal lab configuration and pedagogical program. If the language laboratory as it was known during its "heyday" is now gone, it has not died. Its descendant, a computer lab equipped with foreign language software, is alive and well. The computer now fulfills all the desiderata of language educators and gives life to language for many learners.

References

Aikens, H. F., & Ross, A. J. (1977). Immediate, repetitive playback/record—a practical solution. *NAALD Journal, 11*(2), 40-46.

Allen, E. D. (1960). The effects of the language laboratory on the development of skill in a foreign language. *Modern Language Journal, 44,* 355-358.

Allen, W. H. (1959). Research on new educational media: summary and problems. *Audio-Visual Communication Review 7,* 83-96.

Allen, W. H. (1971). Instructional Media research: past, present, and future. *Audio-Visual Communication Review 19,* 5-18.

Altamura, N. C. (1970). Laboratory a liability. *French Review, 43,* 819-820.

Anderson, E. W. (1964). Review and criticism. *Modern Language Journal, 48,* 197-206.

Bagster-Collins, E. W., et al. (1930). *Studies in Modern Language teaching.* New York: Macmillan.

Barrutia, R. (1967). The past, present, and future of language laboratories. *Hispania, 50,* 888-899.

Bauer, E. W. (1964). A study of the effectiveness of two language laboratory conditions in the teaching of second year German. *International Review of Applied Linguistics, 2,* 99-112.

Benathy, B. H., & Jordan, B. (1969). A classroom laboratory instructional system (CLIS). *Foreign Language Annals, 2, 466*-473.

Bland, S. K., Noblitt, J. S., Armington, S., & Gay, G. (1990). The naive lexical hypothesis: Evidence from computer-assisted language learning. *Modern Language Journal, 74,* 440-450.

Bontempo, O. A. (1946). The language workshop. *Modern Language Journal, 30,* 319-327.

Bottke, K. G. (1944). French conversation laboratory. *French Review, 18,* 54-56.

Bräuer, G. (2001). Language learning centers: Bridging the gap between high school and college. In G. Bräuer (Ed.), *Pedagogy of language learning in higher education: An introduction* (pp. 185-192). Westport, CT: Ablex Publishing.

Brooks, N. (1960). *Language and language learning.* New York: Harcourt, Brace and Company.

Brushwood, J., & Polmantier, P. (1953). *The effectiveness of the audio-laboratory in elementary Modern Language courses.* Columbia, MO: The University of Missouri.

Buchanan, M. A., & MacPhee, E. D. (1928). *An annotated bibliography of Modern Language methodology.* Toronto, Canada: University of Toronto Press.

Buka, M., Freeman, M. K., & Locke, W. N. (1962). Language teaming and frequency response. *International Journal of American Linguistics, 28,* 62-79.

Bush, M., & Terry, R. (Eds.) (1997). *Technology-enhanced language learning.* Lincolnwood, IL: National Textbook Co.

Carroll, J. B. (1962). *A primer of programmed instruction in foreign language teaching.* Heidelberg: Julius Groos Verlag.

Carroll, J. B. (1963). Research on teaching foreign languages. In N. L. Gage (Ed.), *Handbook of research on teaching,* (pp. 1060-1100). Chicago, IL: Rand McNally.

Carroll, J. B. (1969a). Modern Languages. In R. L. Ebel (Ed.), *Encyclopaedia of educational research, 4th ed.* (pp. 866-78). New York: Macmillan.

Carroll, J. B. (1969b). What does the Pennsylvania foreign language research project tell us? *Foreign Language Annals, 3,* 214-236.

Charest, G. T. (1962). The language laboratory and the human element in language teaching. *Modern Language Journal, 46,* 268.

Charoenkul, Y. (n. d.). *The languague laboratory supplemental bibliography (1950-1977).* Lawrence, KS: Language Laboratories, University of Kansas.

Chomei, T., & Houlihan, R. (1970). Comparative effectiveness of three language lab methods using a new equipment system. *AV Communication Review, 18,* 160-168.

Clarke, C. C. (1918). The phonograph in Modern Language teaching. *Modern Language Journal, 3,* 116-22.

Claudel, C. A. (1968). The language laboratory. In J. S. Roucek, (Ed.), *The study of foreign languages* (pp. 219-36). New York: Philosophical Library.

Couch, S. (1973). Return to the language lab! *Russian Language Journal, 27,* 40-44.

Cornfield, R. R. (1966). *Foreign language instruction: Dimensions and horizons.* New York: Appelton-Century-Crofts.

Dakin, J. (1973). *The language laboratory and language teaching.* London: Longman.

Davies, N. F. (1982). Foreign/second language education and technology in the future. *NAALD Journal, 16(3/4),* 5-14.

Davison, W. F. (1973). *The language laboratory: A bibliography, 1950-1972.* Pittsburgh, PA: University Center for International Studies and The English Language Institute, University of Pittsburgh.

Delcolque, P., Annan, N., & Bramoullé, A. (2000). *The history of computer assisted language learning web exposition.* http://www.history-of-call.org/

Derthick, L. G. (1959). The purpose and legislative history of the foreign language titles in the National Defense Education Act, *1958. Publications of the Modern Language Association, 74,* 48-51.

Diekhoff, J. S. (1965). *NDEA and modern foreign languages.* New York: Modern Language Association.

Dodge, J. W. (1968). Language laboratories. In E. M. Birkmaier (Ed.), *Britannica review of foreign language education, Vol. 1,* (pp. 331-335). Chicago, IL: Encyclopaedia Britannica.

Driscoll, J. (1981). Research trends in rate-controlled speech for language learning. *NALLD Journal, 15(2),* 45-51.

Eddy, F. D. (1944). The language studio. *Modern Language Journal, 28,* 338-341.

Ek, J. D. (1974). Grant fever. *NALLD Journal, 9(1),* 17-23.

Ely, P. (1984). *Bring the lab back to life.* Oxford, England: Pergamon.

Fotos, J. T. (1955). The Purdue laboratory method in teaching beginning French classes. *Modern Language Journal, 39,* 141-143.

Freeman, M. Z., & Buka, M. (1965). Effect of frequency response on language learning. *AV Communication Review, 13,* 289-295.

Funke, E. (1949). Rebuilding a practical phonetics laboratory. *German Quarterly, 21,* 120-125.

Garrett, N. (1991). Technology in the service of language learning: Trends and issues. *Modern Language Journal, 75(1),* 74-101.

Gaudin, L. (1946). The language discothèque. *Modern Language Journal, 30,* 27-32.

Godfrey, E. P. (1967). *The state of audiovisual technology: 1961-1966.* Washington DC: Department of Audiovisual Instruction, National Education Association.

Green, J. R. (1965). Language laboratory research: a critique. *Modern Language Joumal, 49,* 367-369.

Grittner, F. (1964). The shortcomings of language laboratory findings in the IAR-Research Bulletin. *Modern Language Joumal, 48,* 207-210.

Grittner, F. (1969). *Teaching foreign languages.* New York: Harper & Row.

Gullette, C. C. (1932). Ear training in the teaching of pronunciation. *Modern Language Journal, 16,* 334-336.

Harvey, T. E. (1978). The matter with listening comprehension isn't the ear: hardware & software. *NALLD Journal, 13(1),* 8-16.

Harvigurst, R. J. (1949). Aids to language study. *School and Society, 69,* 444-445.

Hayes, A. S. (1963). *Language laboratory facilities: Technical guide for the selection, purchase, use, and maintenance.* Washington, DC: U.S. Department of Health, Education, and Welfare.

Heinich, R. (1968). The teacher in an instructional system. In F. G. Knirk & J. W. Childs (Eds.), *Instructional technology: A book of readings* (pp. 45-60). New York: Holt.

Hirsch, R. (1954). *Audio-visual aids in language teaching.* Washington, DC: Georgetown University Press.

Hocking, E. (1967). *Language laboratory and language learning, 2nd ed.* Washington, DC: Division of Audiovisual Instruction, National Education Association.

Holmes, G. (1980). The humorist in the language laboratory. *Modern Language Journal, 64,* 197-202.

Holmes, G. (1985). From the president. *NALLD Journal, 19(2),* 5-7.

Huebener, T. (1963). The New Key is now off-key! *Modern Language Journal, 47*, 375-377.

Huebener, T. (1965). *How to teach foreign languages effectively*. New York: New York University Press.

Hutchison, J. C. (1961). *Modern foreign languages in high school: The language laboratory*. Washington DC: U.S. Department of Health, Education, and Welfare.

Jarlett, F. G. (1971). The falsely accused language laboratory: 25 years of misuse. *NALLD Journal, 5*(4), 27-34.

Johnston, M. C., & Seerley, C. C. (1960). *Foreign language laboratories: In schools and colleges*. Washington, DC: U.S. Department of Health, Education, and Welfare.

Keating, L. C. (1936). Modern inventions in the language program. *School and Society, 44*, 677-79.

Keating, R. F. (1963). *A study of the effectiveness of language laboratories*. New York: Teachers College, Columbia University.

Keck, M. E. B., & Smith, W. F. (1972). *A selective, annotated bibliography for the language laboratory, 1959-1971*. New York: ERIC Clearinghouse on Languages and Linguistics.

Kelly, L. G. (1969). *25 centuries of language teaching*. Rowley, MA: Newbury.

Kennedy, A. (Ed.). (1990). *Designing the learning center of the future. Language laboratories: Today and tomorrow*. Philadelphia: International Association for Learning Laboratories.

Kenner, R. (1981). Report on the Concordia Colloquium on language laboratories. *NALLD Journal, 16*(2), 15-18.

Koekkoek, B. J. (1959). The advent of the language laboratory. *Modern Language Journal, 43*, 4-5.

Lado, R. (1964). *Language teaching: A scientific approach*. New York: McGraw-Hill.

Lange, D. L. (1968). Methods. In E. M. Birkmaier (Ed.), *Britannica Review of Foreign Language Education, Vol. 1* (pp. 281-310). Chicago, IL: Encyclopaedia Britannica.

Last, R. W. (1989). *Artificial intelligence techniques in language learning*. Chichester, England: Horwood.

Lawrason, R. (1990). The changing state of the language lab: Results of 1988 IALL member survey. *IALL Journal of Language Learning Technologies, 23*(2), 19-24.

Lawrason, R. (Ed.). (1995). *Administering the learning center: The IALL management manual*. Philadelphia: International Association for Learning Laboratories.

LeMon, R. E. (1986). Computer labs and language labs: lessons to be learned. *Educational Technology, 26*, 46-47.

Léon, P. R. (1962). *Laboratoire de langues et correction phonétique*. Paris: Didier.

Levin, L. M. (1931). More anent the phonetic laboratory method. *Modern Language Journal, 15*, 427-431.

Lorge, S. W. (1964). Language laboratory research studies in New York City high schools: A discussion of the program and the findings. *Modern Language Journal, 48*, 409-419.

Lorge, S. W. (1965). Comments on "language laboratory research: a critique." *Modern Language Journal, 49*, 369-370.

Marty, F. (1956). Language laboratory techniques. *Educational Screen, 35*, 52-53.

Marty, F. (1962). *Programing a basic foreign language course: Prospects for self-instruction*. Roanoke, VA: Audio-Visual Publications.

Marty, F. (1981). Reflections on the use of computers in second-language acquisition. *Studies in Language Learning, 3*, 25-53.

Mathieu, G. (1962). Language Laboratories. *Review of Educational Research, 32*(2), 168-178.

Mazzara, R. A. (1954). Some aural-oral devices in modern language teaching. *Modern Language Journal, 37*, 358-361.

McCoy, I. H., & Weible, D. M. (1983). Foreign languages and the new media: the videodisc and the microcomputer. In C.J. James (Ed.), *Practical applications of research in foreign language teaching*, (pp. 105-152). Lincolnwood, IL: National Textbook.

Meierhenry, W. C. (1962). Needed research in the introduction and use of audiovisual materials: A special report. *AudioVisual Communication Review, 10*, 307-316.

MLA (1956). *The language laboratory*. FL Bulletin, No. 39. New York: Modern Language Association of America.

Morin, U. (1971). Comparative study of three types of language laboratories in the learning of a second language. *Canadian Modern Language Review, 27*, 65-67.

Mueller, T., & Borglum, G. (1956). Language laboratory and target language. *French Review, 29*, 322-331.

Mullen, J. (1992). Motivation in the language laboratory. *Language Learning Journal, 5*, 53-54.

Murphy-Judy, K., & Sanders, R. (Eds.) (1997). *Nexus: The convergence of research & teaching through new information technologies*. Durham, NC: University of North Carolina.

Mustard, H., & Tudisco, A. (1959).The foreign language laboratory in colleges and universities: A partial survey of its instructional uses. *Modern Language Journal, 43*, 332-340.

Newmark, M. (1948). Teaching materials: textbooks, audiovisual aids, the language laboratory. In M. Newmark (Ed.), *Twentieth century Modern Language teaching* (pp. 456-462). New York: Philosophical Library.

Otto, S. (1989). The language laboratory in the computer age. In W. F. Smith, (Ed.), *Modern technology in foreign language education: applications and projects* (pp. 13-41). Chicago, IL: National Textbook.

Pankratz, D. (1993). LLTI highlights. *IALL Journal of Language Learning Technologies, 27*(1), 69-73.

Parker, W. R. (1960). Foreword. In F.J. Oinas (Ed.), *Language teaching today*, (pp. v-viii). Bloomington, IN: Indiana University Research Center in Anthropology, Folklore, and Linguistics.

Parker, W. R. (1961). *The national interest and foreign languages, 3d ed*. Washington, DC: U.S. Department of State.

Pederson, K. M. (1987). Research on CALL. In W. F. Smith (Ed.), *Modern media in foreign language education: Theory and implementation* (pp. 99-131). Chicago, IL: National Textbook.

Peebles, S. (1938). *The phonetics laboratory and its usefulness*. Unpublished MA thesis. Boulder, CO: University of Colorado.

Peterson, P. (1974). Origins of the language laboratory. *NALLD Journal, 8*(4), 5-17.

Porter, J. J., & Porter, S. F. (1964). A critique of the Keating report. *Modern Language Journal, 48*, 195-197.

Quinn, R. A. (1990). Our progress in integrating modern methods and computer-controlled learning for successful language study. *Hispania, 73*, 297-311.

Racle, G. L. (1976). Laboratoire de langues: problèmes et orientations. *Canadian Modern Language Review, 32*, 384-88.

Reed, J. S. (1958). Students speak about audio learning. *Educational Screen, 37*, 178-179.

Richards, J. C., & Nunan, D. (1992). Second language teaching and learning. In M. C. Aikin (Ed.), *Encyclopaedia of educational research, 6th ed*. (pp. 1200-1208). New York: Macmillan.

Saettler, P. (1990). *The evolution of American educational technology*. Englewood, CO: Libraries Unlimited.

Sanchez, J. (1959). Twenty years of modern language laboratory (an annotated bibliography). *Modern Language Journal, 43*, 228-232.

Schenk, E.H. (1930). Practical difficulties in the use of the phonetics laboratory. *Modern Language Journal, 15*, 30-32.

Scherer, G. A. C., & Wertheimer, M. (1964). *A psycholinguistic experiment in foreign-language teaching.* New York: McGraw-Hill.

Schwartz, M (1995). Computers and the language laboratory: Learning from history. *Foreign Language Annals, 28*(4), 527-535.

Science comes to languages. (1944). *Fortune, 30,* 133-135; 236; 239-240.

Scinicariello, S. (1997). Uniting teachers, learners, and machines: Language laboratories and other choices. In M. Bush & R. Terry (Eds.), *Technology-enhanced language learning* (pp. 185-213). Lincolnwood, IL: National Textbook Co.

Sisson, C. R. (1970). The effect of delayed comparison in the language laboratory on phoneme discrimination and pronunciation accuracy. *Language Learning, 20,* 69-88.

Smith, P. D. (1969a). The Pennsylvania foreign language research project: Teacher proficiency and class achievement in two Modern Languages. *Foreign Language Annals, 3,* 194-207.

Smith, P. D. (1969b). An assessment of three foreign language teaching strategies and three language laboratory systems. *The French Review, 43,* 289-304.

Smith, P. D. (1980). A study of the effect of "slowed speech" on listening comprehension of French. *NALLD Journal, 14*(3/4), 9-13.

Smith, W. F. (1970). Language learning laboratory. In D. L. Lange (Ed.), *Britannica review of foreign language education, Vol. 2* (pp. 191-237). Chicago, IL: Encyclopaedia Britannica, Inc.

Smith, W. F. (1987). *Modern media in foreign language education: Theory and implementation.* Chicago, IL: National Textbook.

Smith, W. F. (1989). *Modern technology in foreign language education: Applications and projects.* Chicago, IL: National Textbook.

Stack, E. M. (1964). The Keating report: A symposium. *Modern Language Journal, 48,* 189-210.

Stack, E. M. (1971). *The language laboratory and modern language teaching, 3rd ed.* New York: Oxford University Press.

Stiefel, W. A. (1952). Bricks with straw-the language laboratory. *Modern Language Journal, 36,* 68-73.

Stone, L. (1988). *Task-based activities: A communicative approach to language laboratory use.* Philadelphia: International Association for Learning Laboratories.

Stone, L. (Ed.). (1993). *Task-based II: More communicative activities for the language lab.* Philadelphia: International Association for Learning Laboratories.

Strei, G. (1977). Reviving the language lab. *TESOL Newsletter, 11,* 10.

Turner, E. D. (1969). *Correlation of language class and language laboratory.* New York: ERIC Focus Reports on the Teaching of Foreign Languages, No. 13.

Valette, R. M. (1969). The Pennsylvania project, its conclusions and its implications. *Modern Language Journal, 53,* 396-404.

Waltz, R. H. (1930). The laboratory as an aid to modern language teaching. *Modern Language Journal, 15,* 27-29.

Waltz, R. H. (1931). Language laboratory administration. *Modern Language Journal, 16,* 217-227.

Waltz, R. H. (1932). Some results of laboratory training. *Modern Language Journal, 16,* 299-305.

Whitehouse, R. S. (1945). The workshop: A language laboratory. *Hispania, 28,* 88-90.

Wiley, P. D. (1990). Language labs for 1990: User-friendly, expandable and affordable. *Media & Methods, 27*(1), 44-47.

Young, C. W., & Choquette, C. A. (1965). An experimental study of the effectiveness of four systems of equipment for self-monitoring in teaching French pronunciation. *International Review of Applied Linguistics, 3,* 13-49.

SOFT TECHNOLOGIES

FOUNDATIONS OF PROGRAMMED INSTRUCTION

Barbara Lockee
Virginia Tech

David (Mike) Moore
Virginia Tech

John Burton
Virginia Tech

One can gain appreciable insights to the present day status of the field of instructional technology (IT) from examining its early beginnings and the origins of current practice. Programmed Instruction (PI) was an integral factor in the evolution of the instructional design process, and serves as the foundation for the procedures in which IT professionals now engage for the development of effective learning environments. In fact, the use of the term programming was applied to the production of learning materials long before it was used to describe the design and creation of computerized outputs. Romizowski (1986) states that while PI may not have fulfilled its early promise, "the influence of the Programmed Instruction movement has gone much further and deeper than many in education care to admit" (p. 131). At the very least, PI was the first empirically determined form of instruction and played a prominent role in the convergence of science and education. Equally important is its impact on the evolution of the instructional design and development process.

This chapter addresses the historical origins of PI, its underlying psychological principals and characteristics, and the design process for the generation of programmed materials. Programmed Instruction is renowned as the most investigated form of instruction, leaving behind decades of studies that examine its effectiveness. That history of PI-related inquiry is addressed herein. Finally, the chapter closes with current applications of PI and predictions for its future use.

20.1 HISTORICAL ORIGINS OF PROGRAMMED INSTRUCTION

Probably no single movement has impacted the field of instructional design and technology than Programmed Instruction. It spawned widespread interest, research, and publication; then it was placed as a component within the larger systems movement and, finally, was largely forgotten. In many ways, the arguments and misconceptions of the "golden age" of Programmed Instruction over its conceptual and theoretical underpinnings have had a profound effect on the research and practice of our field—past, present and future. When discussing the underpinnings of Programmed Instruction it is easy to get bogged down in conflicting definitions of what the term means, which leads to disagreements as to when it first began, which leads into the arguments, efficacies and origins of particular concepts, and so forth. Since the work (and personality) of B. F. Skinner is included in the topic, the literature is further complicated by the visual array of misconceptions, misrepresentations, etc. of his work. Suffice it to say that the presentation of our view of the history of PI is just that: our view.

The term, Programmed Instruction, is probably derived from B. F. Skinner's (1954) paper "The Science of Learning and the Art of Teaching" which he presented at the University of Pittsburgh at a conference of *Current Trends in Psychology and the*

Behavioral Sciences. In that presentation, which was published later that same year, Skinner reacted to a 1953 visit to his daughter's fourth-grade arithmetic class (Vargas & Vargas, 1992). Interestingly, this paper written in part from the perspective of an irate parent, without citation or review, became the basis for his controversial (Skinner, 1958) work, "Teaching Machines," and his subsequent (1968a) work, "The Technology of Teaching." In the 1954 work, Skinner listed the problems he saw in the schools using as a specific case "for example, the teaching of arithmetic in the lower grades" (p. 90). In Skinner's view, the teaching of mathematics involves the shaping of many specific verbal behaviors under many sorts of stimulus control, and, "over and above this elaborate repertoire of numerical behavior, most of which is often dismissed as the product of rote learning, the teaching of arithmetic looks forward to those complex serial arrangements involved in original mathematical thinking" (p. 90). In Skinner's view, the schools were unable to accomplish such teaching for four reasons. First, the schools relied on aversive control in the sense that the beyond, "in some rare cases some automatic reinforcement (that) may have resulted from the sheer manipulation of the medium—from the solution of problems on the discovery of the intricacies of the number system "(p. 90) children work to avoid aversive stimulation. As Skinner says, "anyone who visits the lower grades of the average school today will observe that . . . the child . . . is behaving primarily to escape from the threat of . . . the teacher's displeasure, the criticism or ridicule of his classmates, an ignominious showing in a competition, low marks, a trip to the office 'to be talked to' by the principal" (p. 90).

Second, the school did not pay attention to the contingencies of reinforcement; for those students who *did* get answers correct, many minutes to several days may elapse before papers are corrected. He saw this as a particular problem for children in the early stages of learning who depend on the teacher for the reinforcement of being right as opposed to older learners who are able to check their own work.

The third problem that Skinner (1954) noted was "the lack of a skillful *program* which moves forward through a series of progressive approximations to the final complex behavior desired" (p. 91). Such a program would have to provide a lengthy series of contingencies to put the child in possession of the desired mathematical behavior efficiently. Since a teacher does not have time to reinforce each response, he or she must rely on grading blocks of behavior, as on a worksheet. Skinner felt that the responses within such a block should not be related in the sense that one answer depended on another. This made the task of programming education a difficult one.

Finally, Skinner's (1954) "most serious criticism of the current classroom is the relative infrequency of reinforcement" (p. 91). This was inherent in the system since the younger learner was dependent upon the teacher for being correct, and there were a lot of learners per teacher. A single teacher would be able to provide only a few thousand contingencies in the first four years of schooling. Skinner estimated that "efficient mathematical behavior at this level requires something of the order of 25,000 contingencies" (p. 91).

Interestingly, Skinner (1954) felt that the results of the schools' failure in mathematics were not just student incompetence, but anxieties, uncertainties, and apprehensions. Few students ever get to the point where "automatic reinforcements follow as the natural consequence of mathematical behavior. On the contrary, . . . the glimpse of a column of figures, not to say an algebraic symbol or an integral sign, is likely to set off—not mathematical behavior but a reaction of anxiety, guilt or fear" (Skinner, 1954, p. 92). Finally, the weaknesses in educational technologies result in a lowered expectation for skills "in favor of vague achievements—educating for democracy, educating the whole child, educating for life, and so on" (p. 92).

Important to the field of instructional design and technology, Skinner (1954) says "that education is perhaps the most important branch of scientific technology" (p. 93) and that "in the present state of our knowledge of educational practice, scheduling (of behaviors and consequences) appears to be most effectively arranged through the *design* of the material to be learned. He also discusses the potential for mechanical devices to provide more feedback and to free the teacher up from saying right or wrong (marking a set of papers in arithmetic—'Yes, nine and six are fifteen; No, nine and seven are not eighteen—is beneath the dignity of any intelligent individual,' (Skinner, 1954, p. 96) in favor of the more important functions of teaching.

In his article "Teaching Machines," published in *Science* (1958a), Skinner pushed harder for the use of technology in education that could present programming material prepared by programmers. This work also discusses the notion that whether good programming is to become a scientific technology, rather than an art, will depend on the use of student performance data to make revisions. Again, he sees the powerful rule that machines could play in collecting these data. Finally, Skinner's (1958a) work has a rather casual, almost *throw off* phrase that generated a great deal of research and controversy:

In composing material for the machine, the programmer may go directly to the point. A first step is to define the field. A second is to collect technical terms, facts, laws, principles, and cases. These must then be arranged in a plausible developmental order—*linear if possible, branching if necessary* [italics added]. (p. 974)

It may be that Skinner (1954, 1958) was the first to use the vocabulary of programmed materials and designed materials, but it was the rest of his notions which Reiser (2001) says "began what might be called a minor revolution in the field of education" (p. 59) and, according to Heinich (1970) "has been credited by some with introducing the system approach to education" (p. 123). We will briefly examine some of the key concepts.

20.1.1 Teaching Machines

Much of the research regarding Programmed Instruction was based on the use of a *teaching machine* to implement the instructional event. As Benjamin (1988) noted, "the identification of the earliest teaching machine is dependent on one's definition of such machines" (p. 703). According to Benjamin's history, H. Chard filed the first patent for a device to teach reading in 1809. Herbert Akens (a psychologist) patented a device in 1911 that presented material, required a response, and indicated whether the response was right or wrong. The contribution of this device, which was a teaching aid rather than an automatic or self-controlling device, was that it was based on psychological research. In 1914, Maria Montessori filed a patent claim for a device to train the sense of touch (Mellan, 1936, as cited in Casas, 1997). Skinner (1958a) and most others (see, for example, Hartley & Davies, 1978) credit Sidney Pressey. Beginning in the 1920s, Pressey designed machines for administering tests. Hartley and Davies (1978) correctly point out that Pressey's devices were used *after* the instruction took place, but more important to Skinner, however, was Pressey's (1926) understanding that such machines could not only test and score—they could teach. Moreover, Pressey realized that such machines could help teachers who usually know, even in a small classroom, that they are moving too fast for some students and too slow for others.

20.2 PSYCHOLOGICAL PRINCIPLES AND ISSUES

In the limited space available, we will address the primary concepts behind Programmed Instruction and their origins. For reasons of space and clarity, ancillary arguments about whether Socrates or Cicero was the first "programmer," or trying to draw distinctions between reinforcement (presumably artificial) versus feedback (automatic or natural reinforcement) will not be discussed (c.f. Merrill's, 1971, notions on cybernetics, etc.).

Similarly, the issue of overt versus covert responding has been discussed in the chapter on behaviorism in this handbook. Certainly Skinner did not distinguish between private and public behaviors except in terms of the ability of a teacher or social group to deliver consequences for the latter. It is useful to mention the notion of active responding—that is whether the learner should be required to respond at all, and if so, how often. In a behavioral sense, behaving, publicly or privately, is necessary for learning to occur. Some of the discussion may be confounded with the research/discussion on step-size that will be covered later in this chapter (see, e.g., Hartley, 1974). Others were apparently concerned that too much responding could interfere with learning.

Finally, the rather contrived distinction between programmed learning and Programmed Instruction that, for example, Hartley (1974) makes, will not be discussed beyond saying that the presumed target of the argument, Skinner (1963) stated that he was writing about a new pedagogy and the programming of materials grounded in learning theory.

20.2.1 Operational Characteristics of PI

Bullock (1978) describes PI as both a product and a process.

As a process, PI is used for developing instruction systematically, starting with behavioral objectives and using tryouts of the instruction to make sure that it works satisfactorily As a product, PI has certain key features, such as highly structured sequence of instructional units (frames) with frequent opportunities for the learner to respond via problems, questions, etc. typically accompanied by immediate feedback. (p. 3)

Lysaught and Williams (1963) suggest that Programmed Instruction maintains the following characteristics. First, it is

mediated. Beginning as print-based text, Programmed Instruction grew to leverage each new media format as technologies merged and evolved. Also, PI is replicable, as its results consistently produce the same outcomes. It is self-administrating because the learner can engage in the instructional program with little or no assistance. Its self-paced feature allows the learner to work at a rate that is most convenient or appropriate for his or her needs. Also, the learner is required to frequently respond to incrementally presented stimuli, promoting active engagement in the instructional event. PI is designed to provide immediate feedback, informing the learner of the accuracy of his or her response, as well assisting in the identification of challenges at the point of need. Additionally, PI is identified by its structured sequences of instructional units (called frames), designed to control the learner's behavior in responding to the PI.

20.2.2 Linear Versus Branching Systems

The goal of early developers of programmed instruction was to design the instructional activities to minimize the probability of an incorrect response (Beck, 1959). However, much has been made of the distinction between what some have called Crowder's (1960) multiple-choice branching versus Skinner's linear-type program (see, for example, Hartley, 1974). Crowder, like Skinner (1954, 1958a) likens his intrinsic system to a private tutor. Although Crowder himself claimed no theoretical roots, his method of intrinsic programming or "branching," was developed out of his experience as a wartime instructor for the Air Force. Crowder's method used the errors made by the recruits to send them into a different, remedial path or branch of the programming materials. Although the remediation was not in any way based on any sort of analysis of the error patterns or "procedural bugs" (see, for example Brown & VanLehn, 1980; Orey & Burton, 1992) it may well have been the first use of errors in a tutorial system. Although much has been made about the differences between Skinner and Crowder, it is clear that although the two men worked independently, Skinner was clearly aware of the use of branching and accepted it "if necessary" in 1958 (Skinner, 1958a, p. 974). Crowder began publishing his work a year later in 1959 (Crowder, 1959, 1960, 1964). In a sense they were talking about two very different things. Skinner was writing about education and Crowder was writing from his experience in the teaching complex skills to adults with widely varying backgrounds and abilities. The issue is informative, however. Neither man wanted errors per se. Skinner's goal was an error rate not to exceed 5 percent (1954). His intention was to maximize success in part in order to maximize (reinforcement) and, at least as important to minimize the aversive consequences of failure. Crowder (1964) would prefer to minimize errors also, although he accepts an 85 percent success rate (15% error rate). Recalling the context of his learner group that ran at least from college graduates to those with an 8th grade education, Crowder (1964) says:

Certainly no one would propose to write materials systematically designed to lead the student into errors and anyone would prefer programs in which no student made an error *if this could be achieved without other undesirable results.* . . . We can produce critically effort-free programs if we are careful never to assume knowledge that the most poorly prepared student does not have, never to give more information per step than the slowest can absorb, and never to require reasoning beyond the capacities of the dullest. The inevitable result of such programs is that the time of the average and better than average is wasted. (p. 149)

In short, Skinner saw errors as a necessary evil—motivational and attention getting, but essentially practicing the wrong behavior and receiving aversive consequences for it. Crowder saw errors as unavoidable given the needs of teaching complex skills to students given different backgrounds and whose ability levels varied form "dull" to "better than average." Crowder's (1960, 1964) contribution was to try to use the errors that students made to try to find the breakdown in learning or the missing prerequisite skill(s).

20.2.3   Objectives

Central to the roots of Programmed Instruction is the idea that programmers must decide what students should be to be able to do once they have completed the program. Generally, this involves some sort of activity analysis and specification of objectives. Dale (1967) traces this approach back to Franklin Bobbitt (1926, as cited in Dale) writings:

The business of education today is to teach the growing individuals, so far as their original natures will permit, to perform efficiently those activities that constitute the latest and highest level of civilization. Since the latter consists entirely of activities, the objectives of education can be nothing other than activities, and since, after being observed, an activity is mastered by performing it, the process of education must be the observing and performing of activities. (p. 33)

Charters (1924, as cited in Dale, 1967) who, like Bobbitt, was concerned with curriculum and course design contends that objectives are a primary component of the design process. Tyler (1932) used the notions of Charters in his behavioral approach to test construction. Tyler wrote that it was necessary to formulate course objectives in terms of student behavior, establish the situations or contexts in which the students are to indicate the objective, and provide the method of evaluating the student's reactions in light of each objective. Miller (1953, 1962) is generally credited with developing the first detailed task analysis methodology which working with the military (Reiser, 2001). This provided a methodology for taking a complex skill and decomposing it into objectives, sub-objectives, etc. Bloom and his colleagues (Bloom, Englehart, Furst, Hill, & Krathwohl, 1956) created a taxonomy of learner behaviors, and therefore objectives, in the cognitive domain. Robert Gagne (1956) further segmented objectives/behaviors into nine domains. His writings in the area of intellectual skills is consistent with a hierarchy of a taxonomy such that consistent with Skinner (1954, 1958b) subordinate skills need to be mastered in order to proceed to super-ordinate skills. Mager's (1962) work became the bible for writing objectives.

20.2.4   Formative Evaluation

Skinner's (1954, 1958b) early work had indicated the importance of using learner data to make revisions in instructional programs. In a sense, this technology was well established through Tyler's (1932) discussion of the use of objective-based tests to indicate an individual's performance in terms of the unit, lesson, or course objectives (Dale, 1967). Glaser (1965; Glaser & Klaus, 1962) coined the term *criterion-referenced* measurement to differentiate between measures concerned with comparing the individual against a criterion score or specific objectives and *norm-referenced* measurement which ranked the individual's performance compared to other individuals. What was needed, of course, was to change, at least in part, the use of such tests from strictly assessing student performance to evaluating program performance. Indeed, Cambre (1981) states that practitioners such as Lumsdaine, May, and Carpenter were describing methodologies for evaluating instructional materials during the Second World War and beyond. What was left was for Cronbach (1963) to discuss the need for two types of evaluation and for Scriven (1967) to label them formative and summative to distinguish between the efforts during development when the product was still relatively fluid or malleable versus the summative or judgmental testing after development is largely over and the materials are more "set." Markle's (1967) work became a key reference for the formative and summative evaluation of Programmed Instruction.

20.2.5   Learner-Controlled Instruction

Later in the chapter many variations and permutations of Programmed Instruction will be discussed, but one is briefly covered here because it was contemporary with Skinner's and Crowder's work and because it has some special echoes today. Mager's (1962) learner-controlled instruction used the teacher as a resource for answering student questions rather than for presenting material to be learned. Although largely neglected by Mager and others, perhaps in part because the approach or method did not lend itself to objectives (although the students knew them and were held accountable for them) or design, the methodology does resonate with hypermedia development and related research of the last decade. It would be interesting to see if Mager's findings that students prefer, for example, function before structure or concrete before abstract versus instructors who tend to sequence in the other direction.

20.2.6   Transfer of Stimulus Control

At the beginning of the learning sequence, the learner is asked to make responses that are already familiar to him. As the learner proceeds to perform subsequent subject matter activities that build upon but are different from these, learning takes place. In the course of performing these intermediate activities, the student transfers his original responses to new subject matter content and also attaches newly learned responses to new subject matter.

20.2.7 Priming and Prompting

Two terms that were important in the literature and are occasionally confused are priming and prompting. A prime is meant to elicit a behavior that is not likely to occur otherwise so that it may be reinforced. Skinner (1968a) uses imitation as an example of primed behavior. Movement duplication, for example, involves seeing someone do something and then behaving in the same manner. Such behaviors will only be maintained, of course, if they result in reinforcement for the person doing the imitating. Like all behaviors that a teacher reinforces, to be sustained it would have to be naturally reinforced in the environment. Skinner (1968a) also discusses product duplication (such as learning a birdcall or singing a song from the radio) and non-duplicative primes such as verbal instructions. Primes must be eliminated in order for the behavior to be learned.

Prompts are stimulus-context cues that elicit a behavior so that it can be reinforced (in the context of those stimuli). Skinner (1958a) discusses spelling as an example where letters in a word are omitted from various locations and the user required to fill in the missing letter or letters. Like a cloze task in reading, the letters around the missing element serve as prompts. Prompts are faded, or *vanished* (Skinner, 1958a) over time.

20.3 THE DESIGN OF PROGRAMMED INSTRUCTION

While no standardized approach exists for the production of Programmed Instruction (Lange, 1967), some commonalities across approaches can be identified. One author of an early PI development guide even expresses reluctance to define generalized procedures for the creation of such materials, stating that, "there is a dynamic and experimental quality about Programmed Instruction which makes it difficult and possibly undesirable to standardize the procedures except in broad terms" (Green, 1967, p. 61). In fact, the evolution of the instructional design process can be followed in the examination of PI developmental models. Early descriptions of PI procedures began with the selection of materials to be programmed (Green 1967; Lysaught & Williams 1963; Taber 1965). In 1978, long after the establishment of instructional design as a profession, Bullock, (1978) published what Tillman and Glynn (1987) suggest is "perhaps the most readable account of a PI strategy" (p. 43). In this short book, Bullock proposed his ideal approach to the creation of PI materials, the primary difference from earlier authors being the inclusion of a needs assessment phase at the beginning of the process. Additionally, upon the introduction of Crowder's (1960) notion of branching as a programming approach, future authors began to incorporate a decision phase in which programmers had to choose a particular design paradigm to follow—linear, branching, or some variation thereof—before program design could continue (Bullock, 1978; Markle, 1964).

The following description of the program development process incorporates phases and components most common across widely cited models (e.g., Bullock, 1978; Lysaught & Williams, 1963; Markle, 1964; Taber, Glaser, & Schaefer, 1965). However,

as mentioned previously, since no standardized model or approach to PI development exists, authors vary on the order and nomenclature in which these steps are presented, so the following phases are offered with the understanding that no standard sequence is intended. (For a graphical examination of the evolution of the PI process, see Hartley, 1974, p. 286.) Early in the program development process, a need for instruction is defined, along with the specification of content and the establishment of terminal performance behaviors or outcomes. Also, characteristics and needs of the target group of learners are analyzed so that the most appropriate starting point and instructional decisions can be made. Following the definition of instructional need and audience, programmers conduct a behavioral analysis to determine the incremental behaviors and tasks that will lead the student to the terminal performance. When more is known about the learners and the instructional need, the program creator selects a programming paradigm, referring to the navigation path in which the learner will engage. Typically the choice is made between linear and branching designs, as previously discussed, however, other variations of these models are described in the following section of this chapter. After the general approach to programming has been decided, the sequencing of content and the construction of programmed sequences, called frames, can begin. Although authors differ on the stage at which evaluation of the initial program should begin (Green, 1967; Lysaught & Williams, 1963; Markle, 1967), feedback is collected from students in trial runs prior to production and program revisions are based on learner feedback. The following section describes each of the aforementioned components of program development.

20.3.1 Specification of Content and Objectives

Most descriptions of the PI development process begin with a determination of what content or topic is to be taught through defining the terminal behavior and, given that, move to the delineation of the program's objectives. Several of the authors' approaches described in this section (Green, 1967; Lysaught & Williams, 1963; Mechner, 1967; Taber et al., 1965) base their discussion of defining terminal behavior and writing effective, measurable objectives on the work of Mager (1962). Once the PI developer clearly specifies the intended outcomes of the program in observable and measurable terms, then the creation of assessment items and evaluation strategies can be planned. Mager's approach to the creation of objectives, through stating what the learner will be able to do as a result of the instruction, the conditions under which the performance can occur, and the extent or level that the performance must be demonstrated, was not only the widely accepted method for PI purposes, but remains the classic approach to objective writing in current instructional design literature.

20.3.2 Learner Analysis

Authors of PI programs sought to collect relevant data about the intended learner group for which the program was to be developed. Such data was related to the learners' intelligence, ability, pre-existing knowledge of the program topic, as well as demographic and motivational information (Lysaught & Williams, 1963). Bullock (1978) describes the target audience analysis as a means to collect information regarding entry-level skills and knowledge to permit design decisions such as pre-requisite content, the program design paradigm, media requirements necessary to support instruction, and selection of representative learners for field tests and program evaluation.

20.3.3 Behavior Analysis

The process of engaging in a behavior analysis for the purpose of sequencing the instruction was commonly advocated in the literature on PI (Mechner, 1967; Taber et al., 1965). Such an analysis served as the early forerunner to the task analysis stage of current instructional design practice. Mechner suggests that most of the behaviors that are usually of interest within education and training can be analyzed in terms of discriminations, generalizations, and chains. Discriminations consist of making distinctions between stimuli. Generalizations address a student's ability to see commonalities or similarities among stimuli. When a learner can make both distinctions and generalizations regarding particular stimuli, that learner is said to have a concept. A chain is a behavioral term for procedure or process. Mechner's definition of chaining is "a sequence of responses where each response creates the stimulus for the next response" (p. 86–87). Once the discriminations, generalizations, and chains are analyzed, the programmer must determine which concepts are essential to include, considering the particular needs, abilities, strengths, and weaknesses of the target audience.

20.3.4 Selection of a Programming Paradigm

Overarching the varied approaches to sequencing PI content is the programmer's decision regarding the linearity of the program. In the early days of PI, heated debates took place over the virtues of linear versus branching programs. Linear, or extrinsic, programs were based on work of B. F. Skinner. Markle (1964) reminds the reader that while a linear design may indicate that a learner works through a program in a straight line, that linear programs also maintain three underlying design attributes—active responding, minimal errors, and knowledge of results.

Lysaught and Williams (1963) present several variations of the linear program that were developed before the notion of branching was developed. Modified linear programs allow for skipping certain sequences when responses have been accurate. Linear programs with sub-linears provide additional sequences of instruction for those who desire extra information for enrichment or supplemental explanation. Linear programs with criterion frames can be used to determine if a student needs to go through a certain sequence of material and can also be used to assign students to certain tracks of instruction.

Intrinsic programming is based on the work of Norman Crowder (1959). "The intrinsic model is designed, through interaction with the student, to present him with adaptive, tutorial instruction based on his previous responses rather than to simply inform him of the correctness or incorrectness of his replies" (Lysaught & Williams, 1963, p. 82). Taber et al. (1965) describe a variation on the intrinsic model, entitled the multitrack program. In a multitrack program, several versions of each frame are designed, each with increasing levels of prompts. If the learner cannot respond accurately to the first frame, s/he is taken to the second level with a stronger prompt. If a correct response still cannot be elicited, the learner is taken to a third level, with an even stronger prompt. This design strategy allows learners who may grasp the concept more quickly to proceed through the program without encountering an unnecessary amount of prompting.

Selection of a paradigm is based on earlier steps in programming process, such as the type of skills, knowledge, or attitudes (SKAs) to be taught, existing assumptions regarding learners, the need for adaptive work, etc. If there is a high variance in ability in a group of learners, then providing options for skipping, criterion frames, or branching would be helpful in supporting individual needs.

20.3.5 Sequencing of Content

Skinner's (1961) article on teaching machines suggested that the one of the ways that the machine helps with teaching is through the orderly presentation of the program, which in turn is required to be constructed in orderly sequences. Following the selection of an overarching programming paradigm, decisions regarding the sequencing of the content can be made. A general PI program sequence is characterized by an introduction, a diagnostic section, an organizing set/theory section (to help learner focus on primary elements of teaching/testing section), a teaching, testing section, practice section, and finally, a review or summary is presented to reinforce all of the concepts addressed in the specific program (Bullock, 1978).

Again, no standard approach exists for the sequencing of content and a variety of models are found in the literature. Lysaught and Williams (1963) describe several techniques, the first of which is the pragmatic approach, or the organization of behavioral objectives into logical sequence. "This order is examined for its internal logic and flow from beginning to end. Often an outline is developed to ensure that all necessary information/steps/components are addressed and that nothing important is omitted" (p. 92).

Another common approach to sequencing content was developed by Evans, Glaser, and Homme (1960), and is known as the RULEG system. The RULEG design is based on assumption that material to be programmed consists of rules or examples. So, the rule is presented, followed by examples and opportunities to practice. In some instances, the reverse approach, EGRUL, is used, presenting the learner with a variety of examples and guiding the behavior to comprehend the rule. Mechner (1967) suggests that the target audience should determine which approach is used. If the concept is simple or straightforward, then learners would likely benefit from the RULEG sequence. If the concept is more abstract or complex, then the EGRUL technique would be the better choice in shaping learner behavior.

In 1960, Barlow created yet another method for PI design in response to his students' dislike for the traditional stimulus-response approach, as they felt the technique was too test-like. Barlow's sequencing method was entitled *conversational chaining,* a reflection of the interconnected nature of the program's frames. The design requires the learner to complete a response to the given stimulus item, but instead of programmatic feedback about the correctness of that response within the stimulus frame; the learner checks his or her accuracy in the following frame. However, the response is not presented separately, but is integrated within the stimulus of the following frame and is typically capitalized so that it is easily identified. As such, the flow of the program is more integrated and capable of eliciting the chain of behavior targeted by the designer.

Another well known, but less widely adopted programming method was developed by Gilbert (1962). This approach, called mathetics, is a more complex implementation of reinforcement theory than other sequencing strategies. This technique is also referred to as *backwards chaining,* since the design is based on beginning with the terminal behavior and working backwards through the process or concept, in step-wise fashion.

20.3.6 Frame Composition

Taber et al. (1965) suggest that a programmed frame could contain the following items: (1) a stimulus which serves to elicit the targeted response, (2) a stimulus context to which the occurrence of a desired response is to be learned, (3) a response which leads the learner to the terminal behavior, and (4) any material necessary to make the frame more readable, understandable, or interesting (p. 90). They also contend that it may not be necessary to include each of these components in every frame. Some frames may contain only information with no opportunity for response, some may be purely directional.

One aspect of the stimulus material that is inherent in Programmed Instruction is the inclusion of a *prompt*. A prompt in Skinner's view (1957) is a supplementary stimulus, which is added to a program (in a frame or step) that makes it easier to answer correctly. The prompt is incapable of producing a "response by itself, but depends upon at least some previous learning" (Markle, 1964, p. 36). Skinner proposes two types of prompts, formal and thematic. Formal prompts are helpful in the introduction of new concepts, as learners may have little or no basis for producing their own, unsupported response. A formal prompt typically provides at least a portion of the targeted response as part of its composition, generating a low-strength response from the learner. Also, the physical arrangement of the frame may serve as a formal prompt type, suggesting to the learner cues about the intended response, such as the number of letters in the response text, underlined words for particular emphasis, the presentation of text to suggest certain patterns, etc. (Taber et al., 1965). Thematic prompts attempt to move the learner toward production and application of the frame's targeted response in more varied contexts in order to strengthen the learner's ability to produce the terminal behavior. Taber et al. describe a variety of design approaches for the creation of thematic prompts. The use of pictures, grammatical structure, synonyms, antonyms, analogies, rules, and examples are all effective

strategies that allow the programmer to create instruction that assists the learner in generating the correct response.

The strength of the prompt is another important design consideration and is defined as the likelihood that the learner will be able to produce the targeted response and is influenced by logical and psychological factors related to the design of the frame (Markle, 1964). As new content or concepts are introduced, prompts should be strong to provide enough information so that a correct response can be generated. As low-strength concepts are further developed, prompts can be decreased in strength as learners can rely on newly learned knowledge to produce accurate responses. This reduction and gradual elimination of cues is known as fading or vanishing and is another PI-related phenomenon popularized by Skinner (1958b).

Another design consideration in the programming of frames is the selection of response type. Taber et al. (1965) describe a variety of response type possibilities and factors related to the basis for selecting from constructed answer, multiple choice, true–false, and labeling, to name a few. Also, another response mode option that has been the subject of instructional research is overt versus covert responding. While Skinner (1968a) believes that active responses are necessary and contribute to acquisition of the terminal behavior, others contend that such forced production may make the learning process seem too laborious (Taber et al.). Research addressing this design issue is described in detail later in this chapter.

20.3.7 Evaluation and Revision

As stated earlier, one of the hallmarks of the Programmed Instruction process is its attention to the evaluation and revision of its products. Skinner (1958a) suggested that a specific advantage of Programmed Instruction is the feedback available to the programmer regarding the program's effectiveness; feedback available from the learner through trial runs of the product. In fact, many credit PI with the establishment of the first model of instruction that mandates accountability for learning outcomes (Hartley, 1974; Lange, 1967; Rutkaus, 1987). Reiser (2001) indicates that the PI approach is empirical in nature, as it calls for the collection of data regarding its own effectiveness, therefore allowing for the identification of weaknesses in the program's design and providing the opportunity for revision to improve the quality of the program. Markle (1967) presents perhaps the most explicit procedures for three phases of empirical product evaluation: developmental testing, validation testing, and field-testing. While other authors offer variations on these stages (Lysaught & Williams, 1963; Romiszowski, 1986; Taber et al., 1965), these phases generally represent components of formative and summative evaluation.

What factors should one consider when attempting to determine the effectiveness of a program in the production stages? Both Markle (1964) and Lysaught and Williams (1963) indicate that errors in content accuracy, appropriateness, relevance, and writing style are not likely to be uncovered by students in trial situations, and suggest the use of external reviewers such as subject matter experts to assist with initial program editing. Again, Markle (1967) provides the most intricate and rigorous accounts of formative testing, suggesting that once content has been edited and reviewed to address the aforementioned factors, then one-on-one testing with learners in controlled settings should precede field trials involving larger numbers of learners. She insists that only frame-by-frame testing can provide accurate and reliable data not only about error rates, but also information pertaining to communication problems, motivational issues, and learning variables. Some design considerations may cross these three categories, such as the "size-of-step" issue (p. 121), which is both an instructional challenge as well as a motivational factor.

Once a program has been produced, many feel that it is the program producer's obligation to collect data regarding its effectiveness in the field (Glaser, Homme, & Evans, 1959; Lumsdaine, 1965; Markle, 1967). This contention was so compelling that a joint committee was formed from members representing the American Educational Research Association, the American Psychological Association, and the Department of Audiovisual Instruction (a division of the National Education Association). The report created by this Joint Committee on Programmed Instruction and Teaching Machines (1966) offers guidance to a variety of stakeholders regarding the evaluation of program effectiveness, including programmatic effectiveness data that prospective purchasers should seek, as well as guidelines for program producers and reviewers in their production of reports for the consumer. While the committee expresses the value inherent in one-on-one and small group testing, they place stronger emphasis on the provision of data from larger groups of students and repeated testing across groups to demonstrate the program's reliability and validity in effecting its intended outcomes.

In his description of considerations for program assessment, Lumsdaine (1965) is careful to point out the need to distinguish between the validation of a specific program and the validation of Programmed Instruction as an instructional method, a distinction that has continued through present–day evaluation concerns (Lockee, Moore, & Burton, 2001). Although evaluation and research may share common data collection approaches, the intentions of each are different, the former being the generation of product-specific information and the latter being concerned with the creation of generally applicable results, or principles for instruction (Lumsdaine, 1965).

20.4 RESEARCH ON PROGRAMMED INSTRUCTION

Skinner (1968b) lamented that many devices sometimes called *teaching machines* were designed and sold without true understanding of underlying pedagogical or theoretical aspects of their use. He noted that the design and functions of teaching machines and programmed instruction had not been adequately researched. Programmed Instruction was merely a way to apply technical knowledge of behavior to that of teaching. He called for additional experimental analysis that would look at behavior and its consequences, particularly in a *programmed* or sequenced instruction (Skinner, 1968b). The study of behavior through the analysis of reinforcement suggests a "new kind of

educational research" (Skinner, 1968b, p. 414). Earlier research relied on measurement of mental abilities and comparisons of teaching methods and this led to a neglect of the processes of instruction. According to Skinner these types of comparisons and correlations are not as effective as results studied by manipulating variables and observing ensuring behavior. Moreover, in Skinner's view much of the earlier research was based upon "improvisations of skillful teachers" or theorists working "intuitively" and these types of studies had seldom "led direction to the design of improved practices (Skinner, 1968b, p. 415).

Skinner (1968b) stated that in dealing with research on Programmed Instruction, "No matter how important improvement in the students performance may be, it remains a by-product of specific changes in behavior resulting from the specific changes in the environment" (p. 415). With that said, there is a vast amount of literature on programmed instruction research that deals with student performance rather than specific changes in behavior and environment. Some proclaim a convincing array of evidence in its effectiveness; some results are provocative and unconvincing. Some research would qualify as good (in terms of methods, control, procedures) other research is no more than poor and contains repudiated techniques such as comparison studies. The 1950s and 1960s were the zenith of programmed instruction research in the literature. There are many compendiums and excellent reviews of this research. Some of these excellent sources of programmed instruction research follow. These included books by Stolurow (1961), Smith and Smith (1966), Lumsdaine and Glaser (1960), Glaser (1965), Taber et al. (1965), Ofiesh and Meirhenry (1964), Galanter (1959), and Hughes (1963) to name a few excellent research references. The research and evaluation issues and categorization of research components in program learning are many. This paper will look at general issues, research on teaching machines and devices, and variations and components of programs and programming. General issues include learning process and behavioral analysis, sole source of instruction, age level, subject matter properties and entering behavior and attitudes. Research summaries on teaching machines will review Pressey's self-instructional devices, military knowledge trainers, Skinner's teaching machines, and programmed books. Research on program variations will include programming variables response mode (such as linear and branching formats) prompts, step size, attitude, error rate, confirmation, and impact on age level.

20.4.1 A Disclaimer

The authors of this chapter, upon reviewing the research literature available found themselves in an ethical quandary. For the most part, the research conducted and published in this era of the zenith of programmed instruction use is generally poor. For example, many of the research studies conducted in the 1950s and 1960s were *comparison studies* that compared programmed materials and/or teaching machines with *conventional* or traditional methods. Despite their prevalence in this era's literature, most of these studies lack validity because the results cannot be generalized beyond the study that generated them, if at all. In addition, no program—machine-based or teacher-led, represents a whole category, nor do any two strategies differ in a single dimension. They cannot be compared because they differ in many ways (Holland, 1965). "The restrictions on interpretation of such a comparison arise from the lack of specificity of the instruction with which the instrument is compared" (Lumsdaine, 1962, p. 251). The ethical concern is that we have a large body of research that is for the most part ultimately not valid. It is also not reliable and could *not* meet the minimal standards of acceptable research. Unfortunately, much of this research was conducted by notable and experienced professionals in the field and published by the most reputable journals and organizations. Some of these problems were acknowledged early on by such researchers as Holland (1965, p. 107–109) and A. A. Lumsdaine (1962, p. 251). The authors of this chapter decided to proceed on the *buyer beware* theory. We present a limited sample of the literature addressing a variety of PI-related aspects, if for no other reason than to illustrate the breadth of the problems. For the most part, the research on programmed instruction began to die out in the early 1970s. This may have been due to editors finally realizing that the research products were poor or that the *fad* of programmed materials had slipped into history, likely the latter since it was replaced for the most part by equally flawed studies conducted on computer-assisted instruction.

Holland (1965), in recognizing the research concerns, felt that the "pseudo-experiments do not serve as a justified basis for decision" (p. 107). The answer is not to rely on this body (large) of research but to use evaluative measures, which tested against internal standards and requirements. As a result few generalizations will be made, but we will present the findings, summaries, and options of the original researchers. We will not critique the articles individually, but will allow the readers to judge for themselves.

20.4.2 Teaching Machines

20.4.2.1 Pressey's Machines. Pressey's self-instruction devices were developed to provide students with immediate feedback of results on knowledge after reading and listening to a lecture. Most of the research on Pressey's devices dealt with implementation and use of the results in order to develop a specific type of information to help the instructor change content and approach. Stolurow (1961) raised a question early on: when a programmed machine is used in conjunction with other means of instruction, which would be the cause of any effect? He felt it would be important to be able to judge how effective the programmed devices would be when used alone versus when they were used in conjunction with other types of instruction.

There was less concern about the problems of programming and sequencing in these machines (Stolurow, 1961). An example of research in this category was Peterson (1931) who evaluated Pressey's concepts with matched participants who were given objective pre- and posttests. The experimental group was given cards for self-checking their responses while the control group received no knowledge of feedback. In another version the participants were given a final test that was not the same as

the posttests. In both situations the experimental group with knowledge of results scored higher than the control group. Little (1934) compared results from groups either using a testing machine, a drill machine, or neither (control group). Both experimental groups scored significantly higher than the control group. The group using the drill machine moved further ahead than did the test machine group. Other studies during the 1940s (as cited in Smith & Smith, 1966) used the concept of Pressey's devices. These concepts included punchboard quizzes, which gave immediate feedback and were found to significantly enhance learning with citizenship and chemistry content. Angell and Troyer, (1948), Jones and Sawyer (1949), Briggs (1947), and Jensen (1949) reported that good students using self-evaluation approaches with punch cards were able to accelerate their coursework and still make acceptable scores. Cassidy (1950), (a student of Pressey) in a series of studies on the effectiveness of the punchboard, reported that the immediate knowledge of results from this device provided significant increments in the learning of content. Pressey (1950) conducted a series of studies used punchboard concepts at The Ohio State University designed to test whether punchboard teaching machines could produce better learning performance by providing immediate knowledge of results and whether these beneficial effects are limited to a particular subject (Stolurow, 1961, p. 105). This series of studies lead to the following conclusions by Pressey and his associates as reported by Stolurow.

1. The use of the punchboard device was an easy way of facilitating learning by combining feedback, test taking, and scoring.
2. Test taking programs could be transformed to self-directed instruction programs.
3. When punchboards were used systematically to provide self-instruction, content learning was improved.
4. Automatic scoring and self-instruction could be achieved by the use of the punchboard.
5. The technique of providing learners with immediate knowledge of results via the punchboard could be used successfully in a variety of subjects. (1961).

Stephens (1960) found that using a Drum Tutor (a device used with informational material and multiple-choice questions and designed that students could not progress until the correct answer was made) helped a low-ability experimental group to score higher on tests than a higher ability group. This study confirmed Pressey's earlier findings that "errors were eliminated more rapidly with meaningful material and found that students learned more efficiently when they could correct errors immediately" (Smith & Smith, 1966, p. 249). These data also suggested that immediate knowledge of results made available early within the learning situation are more effective than after or later in the process (Stolurow, 1961). Severin (1960), another student of Pressey, used a punchboard testing procedure to compare the achievement of a learners forced to make overt responses versus those who were not required to make overt responses. No differences were reported. He concluded on short or easy tasks the automated overt devices were of little value. In an electrified version of the Pressey punchboard system, Freeman (1959) analyzed learner performance in a class of students who received reinforcement for a portion of the class and no reinforcement for another portion of time. He found no significant effects related to achievement; however, he indicated that in this study there were problems in the research design, including insufficient amount of reinforced opportunity, that test items were not identical to reinforced ones, and there was little attempt to program or structure the reinforced test materials (items). Freeman also noted that rapid gains in learning might not relate to better retention.

Holland (1959), in two studies on college students studying psychology using machine instruction, required one group of students to *space* their practice versus another group of students who had to mass their practice. He reported no significant differences as a result of practice techniques.

Stolurow (1961) suggested that studies on Pressey's machines, as a way of providing learners with immediate knowledge of results indicated that these machines could produce significant increments in learning, that learning by this method was not limited to particular subject areas and that the approach could be used with various types of learners. The effectiveness of having knowledge of results made available by these machines depended a great deal upon how systematic the material was programmed, the type of test to determine retention, and the amount of reinforced practice. Smith and Smith (1966) and Stolurow (1961) indicated that, based upon reviews of Pressey's earlier experiences, that there are positive outcomes of machine-based testing of programmed material. However, they also contended that the programmed machines may be more useful when used in connection with other teaching techniques. Pressey (1960), himself, states, "certainly the subject matter for automation must be selected and organized on sound basis. But the full potentialities of machines are now only beginning to be realized" (pp. 504–505). In reference to the effectiveness of programs on machine, Stolurow (1961) concluded that they are effective in teaching verbal and symbolic skills and for teaching manipulative skills.

Please note that there is a great overlap of the research on programmed machines and materials and of other approaches and variations. Additional programmed machine research is reviewed later in this section to illustrate points, concerns, and applications of other programming variables and research.

20.4.3 Military Knowledge Trainers

A major design and development effort in the use of automated self instruction machines was conducted by the U.S. Air Force, Office of Naval Research and by the Department of Defense during and after World War II. These development projects incorporated the concepts of Pressey's punchboard device in the forms of the Subject-Matter Trainer (SMT), the Multipurpose Instructional Problem Storage Device, the Tab-Item, and Optimal Sequence Trainer (OST), and the Trainer-Tester (see Briggs, 1960 for a description of these devices). These automated self instructional devises were designed to teach and test proficiency of military personnel. The Subject Matter Trainer (SMT) was modified to include several prompting, practice, and testing modes (Briggs, 1956, 1958). The emphasis of the SMT was to teach military personnel technical skills and content (Smith & Smith, 1966). Bryan and Schuster (1959) in an experiment found the

use of the OST (which allowed immediate knowledge following a specific response) to be superior to regular instruction in a troubleshooting exam.

In an experimental evaluation of the Trainer-Tester and a military version of Pressey's punchboard, both devices were found to be superior to the use equipment mock-ups and of actual equipment for training Navy personnel in electronic troubleshooting (Cantor & Brown, 1956; Dowell, 1955). Briggs and Bernard (1956) reported that an experimental group using the SMT, study guides, and oral and written exams out performed the control group who used only the study guides and quizzes on a performance exam. However, the two groups were not significantly different on written tests. Both of these studies were related to the extent to which instruction provided by these machines was generalizeable or transferable. With respect to the effectiveness of these versions of teaching machines, these studies indicated that these programmed machines (SMT) can "be effective both for teaching verbal, symbolic skills which mediate performance and for teaching overt manipulative performance" (Stolurow, 1961, p. 115). Not all studies, however, reported superior results for the Subject Matter Trainer. He pointed out that these devices, which used military content and subjects generally, showed a consistent pattern of *rapid learning* at various ability levels and content and suggested that knowledge of results (if designed systematically) was likely to have valuable learning benefits.

20.4.4 Skinner's Teaching Machines

The research studies on Pressey's punchboard devices, and their military versions (e.g., SMT, OST, etc.), which incorporated many features of self-instruction and supported the concept that knowledge of results would likely have beneficial educational applications. However, the real impetus to self-instruction via machine and programmed instruction came from the theories and work of B.F. Skinner (e.g., 1954, 1958, 1961). Skinner's major focus was stating that self-instruction via programmed means should be in the context of reinforcement theory. He felt that Pressey's work was concerned "primarily with testing rather than learning and suggested that the important ideas about teaching machines and programmed instruction were derived from his analysis of operant conditioning" (Smith & Smith, 1966, p. 251). (See descriptions of these devices earlier in this chapter.) Skinner described his devices similar to Pressey's descriptions, including the importance of immediate knowledge of results. The major differences were that Pressey used a multiple-choice format and Skinner insisted upon *constructed* responses, because he felt they offered less chance for submitting wrong answers. Skinner's machines were designed to illicit overt responses. However, his design was modified several times over the years allowing more information to be presented and ultimately sacrificed somewhat the feature of immediate correction of errors. Skinner was most concerned about how the materials were programmed to include such concepts as overt response, size of steps, etc. As a result, much of the research was conducted on these programming components (concepts). These programming features included presenting a specific sequence of material in a linear, one-at-a-time fashion, requiring an overt response and providing immediate feedback to the response (Porter, 1958). Research on these components will be discussed later in this chapter. Much of the literature on Skinner's machines was in the form of descriptions of how these machines were used and how they worked (e.g., Holland, 1959; Meyer, 1959).

20.4.5 Crowder's Intrinsic Programming

Crowder (1959, 1960) (whose concepts were described earlier in this chapter) modified the Subject Matter Trainer to not only accommodate multiple choice questions, but to include his concept of *branching programming* in "which the sequence of items depends upon the response made by the student. Correct answers may lead to the dropping of certain items, or incorrect answers may bring on additional remedial material" (Smith & Smith, 1966, p. 273). Crowder's theories, like Skinner's were not machine specific. Much of the research was based around the various programmed aspects noted above. These programming aspects (variations) espoused by Crowder (1959, 1960) (e.g., large blocks of information, branching based upon response, etc.) will be also reviewed later in this chapter.

20.4.6 Programmed Instruction Variations and Components

As noted earlier, research on teaching machines and of programming components or program variations overlap to a great degree. Most teaching machines were designed to incorporate specific theories (e.g., Pressey—immediate knowledge of results in testing, and Skinner—overt responses with feedback in learning). Research on machines in reality became research on *program design and theory*. Because there was no general agreement on the best way to construct the machines or the programming approach much of the research deals with issues like type of programs, types of responses, size of steps, error rates, and the theoretical underpinnings of various approaches. The concept of programming refers to the way subject matter is presented, its sequence, its difficulty, and specific procedures designed into the program to enhance (theoretically) learning. It must be noted again that much of this research was conducted in the 1950s and 1960s and much of the research fell into the category of *comparison studies*. As such the reader should be weary of results and claims made by some of these researchers. The research summaries from this era and with its inherent problems provide no concrete answers or definitive results. They should, however, provide a feel for issues raised and potential insights about learning theory and their approaches.

20.4.7 Research on General Issues

20.4.7.1 Ability and Individual Differences. Glaser, Homme, and Evans (1959), suggested that individual differences of students could be important factor based upon previous research, which might affect program efficiency. Several questions arise under these assumptions: (1) Does student ability (or lack of) correlate with performance in a programmed environment,

and (2) Does performance in a programmed environment *correlate* with *conventional instructional* methods and settings? Again, there appears to be no consensus in the results or the recommendations of the research.

Porter (1959) and Ferster and Sapon (1958) reported in separate studies that there was little or no correlation between ability level and achievement on programmed materials. Detambel and Stolurow (1956) found no relationship between language ability and quantitative subtests of ACE scores (American Council on Education Psychological Examination for College) and performance on a programmed task. Keisler (1959) matched two groups on intelligence, reading ability, and pretest scores, with the experimental group using a programmed lesson; the control group received no instruction. All but one of the experimental subjects scored higher after using the programmed materials.

Two groups of Air Force pilots were matched according to duties, type of aircraft, and "other" factors, with one group having voluntary access to a programmed self-tutoring game on a Navy Automatic Rater device. After two months the experimental group with voluntary access to the programmed materials showed significant improvement on items available with the game. The control group did not show significant improvement. However, there was no difference between the groups on items not included in the programmed materials. It was concluded that a self-instructional device would promote learning even in a voluntarily used game by matched subjects (Hatch, 1959).

Dallos (1976) in a study to determine the effects of anxiety and intelligence in learning from programmed learning found an interesting interaction on difficult programs. He reported that a high state of anxiety facilitated learning from the higher intelligence students and inhibited learning for low intelligence students.

Carr (1959) hypothesized that effective self instructional devices would negate differences in achievement of students of differing aptitudes. Studies by Porter (1959), and Irion and Briggs (1957), appeared to support this hypothesis as they reported in separate studies little correlation between intelligence and retention after using programmed devices. Carr (1959) suggested that the lack of relationship between achievement and intelligence and/or aptitude is because programmed instruction renders "learners more homogeneous with respect to achievement scores" (p. 561). Studies by Homme and Glaser (1959), and Evans, Glaser, and Homme (1959) tended to also support Carr's contention, while Keisler (1959) found students using machine instruction were more variable on achievement scores than the control group not using the programmed machines. Carr (1959) called for more study to determine the relationship between achievement and *normal predictors* with the use of programmed instruction.

20.4.8 User Attitude

Knowlton and Hawes (1962) noted, "that the pull of the future has always been slowed by the drag of the past" (p. 147). But, as there is a resistance to new technology, what proves valuable is thus too accepted. This statement appears to sum up the attitude toward programmed instruction in that perception of problems is due to lack of relevant information by the programmers and researchers.

Smith and Smith (1966) reported that the general reaction of learners towards programmed instruction at all levels including adult learners was very positive. This view was borne out by a number of studies gauging attitudes of learners toward programmed self-instruction. Stolurow (1963), in a study with retarded children using programmed machines to learn mathematics, found that these students, while apprehensive at first, later became engrossed and indicated they preferred using the machines rather than having traditional instruction. However, Porter (1959), in his earlier noted study, reported that there was no relationship among the gender of the student, the level of satisfaction with the programmed method, and achievement level. Students in a high school study revealed a view that was balanced between the use of programmed programs and conventional instruction (*First Reports on Roanoke Math Materials*, 1961). Eigen (1963) also reported a significant difference between attitudes use of programmed materials and other instruction of 72 male high school students in favor of the programmed instruction. Nelson (1967) found positive attitudes in student perceptions of programmed instruction in teaching music. Likewise, several studies on attitude were conducted in college classrooms. Engleman (1963) compared attitudes of 167 students using programmed and conventional instruction (lectures, labs, etc.) and reported that 28 percent indicated programmed materials were *absolutely essential,* 36 percent felt they were useful 90 percent of the time, 21 percent considered programmed materials useful 50 percent of the time, and 14 percent indicated that programmed materials were help only occasionally or not at all. Cadets at the Air Force Academy showed moderate enthusiasm as 80 percent indicated *enjoyment* in the programmed course, however, 60 percent preferred it to conventional teaching and suggested they learned with less effort (Smith, 1962). Several opinion studies were conducted in three colleges (Harvard, State College at Genesco, and Central Washington University) comparing attitudes of students using a programmed text, *The analysis of behavior,* (Holland & Skinner, 1961) and a textbook entitled *A textbook of psychology* (Hebb, 1958). The attitudes were overwhelming positive toward the programmed text (Naumann, 1962; VanAtta, 1961). Skinner and Holland (1960) reported that 78 percent of the students "felt they learned more form the machine than from the text" (p. 169). Banta (1963) reviewed similar attitude measures at Oberlin, University of Wisconsin, and Harvard and results were somewhat less favorable than the above study, but the Harvard students' attitude scores were similarly positive. Smith and Smith (1966) speculate that because the materials were developed at Harvard, there may have been a tendency to reflect their teachers' "enthusiasm and reacted in the expected manner" (p. 302). Roth (1963) also reported results of another college graduate students' opinion of the same Holland and Skinner text. All students liked it in the beginning, but only five did at the end of the study. Several objections noted that the program was "tedious," "repetitive," "mechanized," "non-thought provoking," and "anti-insightful" (Roth, 1963, p. 279-280). In a business setting at IBM, Hughes and McNamara (1961) reported that 87 percent of trainees liked programmed materials better than *traditional* instruction. Tobias (1969a, 1969b) provided evidence that teacher and user preferences for traditional devices are negatively related to achievement in programmed instruction. There have been a variety of studies dealing with student attitude toward various aspects of the programming variables. Jones and Sawyer (1949), in a study comparing attitudes of students using a programmed machine which provided self scoring and immediate knowledge of results versus a conventional paper answer sheet found 83 percent preferred the machine program over the paper answer sheet. Two studies (Eigen, 1963; Hough & Revsin, 1963) reported conflicting results on positive attitudes toward programmed machine and programmed texts. In a study concerning anxiety and intelligence when using difficult programmed instruction, Dallos (1974) found that participants with high anxiety, but lower intelligence had unfavorable view of the programmed instruction while the high intelligent, high anxiety participants had more favorable opinions of the program. Studies on attitude and learning effectiveness of programmed instruction have indicated that positive or negative attitudes toward programmed materials have little or no predictive value in determining learning effectiveness of these programs (Eigen, 1963; Hough & Revsin, 1963; Roe, Massey, Weltman, & Leeds, 1960; Smith & Smith, 1966). Smith and Smith (1966) indicated that these findings were not surprising because of other studies on general behavior have shown similar results (e.g., Brayfield & Crockett, 1955). "The apparent fact is that *general* attitude measures predict neither learning nor performance in a particular situation" (Smith & Smith, 1966, p. 304).

20.4.9 Programmed Instruction Compared to Conventional Instruction (Comparison Studies)

Much of the research on programmed machine and programmed instruction involved comparing programs to *conventional* or *traditional* instruction (whatever that was or is). This comparison technique was flawed from the beginning, but the results using this technique were used by many as proof the program was successful or was a failure, or was it *just as good as* the other form of instruction (incorrectly interpreting the *no significant difference* result).

Anytime one method of instruction is compared with another, several issues need to be kept in mind. Sometimes the comparisons are made between small groups with limited content and for relatively short time. Secondly, the novelty may effect operates in many cases generally supporting the new technique, e.g., programmed instruction. Thirdly, there are many, many uncontrolled factors operating all at once and any of these may affect the results of the study (Smith & Smith, 1966). This noted, in a review of 15 studies comparing programmed and conventional instruction, Silberman (1962) reported that nine favored programmed instruction and six indicated no significant difference in the two approaches. All 15 studies reported that the programmed approach took less time.

Several studies reported that when specific content was taught using programmed methods, time was saved with no decrease in achievement. All reported that instruction time was saved or the program-instruction completed requirements in less time than a conventional group (Hosmer & Nolan, 1962; Smith, 1962; Uttal, 1962; Wendt & Rust, 1962). In a study to compare a traditional instruction to a programmed method of teaching spelling in the third grade, the programmed group gained significantly better grade-equivalent scores than the control group by the end of the year (Edgerton & Twombly, 1962).

Hough (1962) compared machine programs to conventional instruction in a college psychology course where time was an additional factor. When quizzes were not announced the machine-instructed group scored significantly higher, but when quizzes were announced, there was no significant difference. Hough surmised that since the conventional group could study at home, whereas the machine group could not, the additional time available to the conventional group was a factor in these results.

Hartley (1966, 1972) reviewed 112 studies that compared programmed instruction (any variety) and *conventional instruction*. He concluded that there is evidence that programmed instruction is as good, or more effective than conventional instruction. In addition, Hamilton and Heinkel (1967) concurred in Harley's findings, which found in 11 of 12 studies that compared an instructor with a programmed lesson, an instructor alone, or a program alone, that an instructor with a program was the more effective choice. Hartley (1978) states "the results. . . . allow one to make the generalizations that many programs teach as successfully as many teachers and sometimes that they do this in less time" (p. 68). Falconer (1959) believed that it is an advantage for deaf children to use teaching machines where they traditionally require a large amount of individual instruction. He suggested that his data indicated that a teaching machine might be as effective as a teacher who had to spread his/her time over many students individually. Day (1959) compared a group using a *Crowder* style programmed book with that of conventional instruction. The experimental group that used the programmed book scored 20 percent higher and made one-fourth the wrong answers than the conventional instruction group over a half semester course. Goldstein and Gotkin (1962) reviewed eight experimental studies, which compared programmed text to programmed machines. Both versions were linear in nature. Goldstein and Gotkin reported no significant differences on several factors; posttest scores, time, and attitude across both presentation modes. (Four studies indicated the programmed texts used significantly less time than the machine version, however.) Other studies have shown no significant difference between automated instruction and traditionally taught classes or were equally effective modes of instruction (Goldberg, Dawson, & Barrett, 1964; Oakes, 1960; Tsai & Pohl, 1978). Similar no significant difference results were reported in studies with learning disabled students (e.g., Blackman & Capobianco, 1965; McDermott & Watkins, 1983; Price, 1963). Porter (1959) did report results showing that second and sixth graders progressed further in spelling achievement with programmed materials in less time than in a conventional classroom setting.

Silberman (1962) reviewed eight comparative studies to determine how best to present material in a self-instruction program, e.g., small step, prompting, overt response, branching, or repetition. He reported that there was no clear pattern of success and these cases showed that some treatments favored one method or another while other treatments favored the time-on-task factor. There were no significant differences across the programmed modes.

Eighth grade students of high ability were put into three groups, one used a linear program, one used a branching program, and the third was used as a control group (conventional instruction). Time available was constant across all groups. In a result unusual for this type of study, Dessart (1962) reported that the control group did significantly better than the experimental group using the branching approach. There was no significant difference between the conventional group and the linear group or between the linear and branching groups.

Stolurow (1963) studied the effect of programs teaching learning disabled children reading, vocabulary, and comprehension. Although, the results favored the programmed version over a traditional method, Stolurow recommended altering programs with conventional instruction. His recommendation was similar to others, which suggested a variety of methods may be more effective than only using one. Klaus (1961) reported on a comparison study dealing with 15 high school physics classes. Some classes had programmed materials available but not for mandatory use. The class having access to the programs had a substantial gain in criterion scores compared to the class without these materials available. After reviewing several studies, Alter and Silverman (1962) reported there were no significant differences in learning from the use of programmed materials or conventional texts. McNeil and Keisler (1962), Giese and Stockdale (1966), Alexander (1970), and Univin (1966) in studies comparing the two versions (programmed and conventional texts) also found the similar results of no significance across methods. However, in a number of studies using primarily retarded learners, the reported results of these comparison studies found the conventional instruction to be superior (Berthold & Sachs, 1974; McKeown, 1965; Richmond, 1983; Russo, Koegel, & Lovaas, 1978; Weinstock, Shelton, & Pulley, 1973). However, the programmed devices (particularly linear ones) have the advantage over teachers in a conventional setting who, in some cases, inadvertently skip over small ideas or points, which may need to be present for understanding. Some feel these programmed devices could solve this concern (Stolurow, 1961).

When program machines were studied as the sole source of instruction, Stolurow (1961) indicated in his review that both children and adults benefited from a programmed device. He stated, "these devices not only tend to produce performance which is freer of error than conventional methods of instruction, but also reduce the amount of instruction time required" (p. 135–136).

20.4.10 Programmed Variables (Essential Components)

During the early development of programmed instruction devices and materials many ideas were expressed on how best to present information, some based in theory (e.g., Skinner's work), others based on intuition, but little on actual research. Reviews of existing literature (e.g., Silberman, 1962) yielded no clear pattern of what programming criteria was effective in improving achievement. However, as time passed more studies and analyses of programming variables were conducted.

Program or programming variables are components that are essentially general in nature and can be associated with all types of programs. For an example, these variables can deal with theoretical issues such as the effect overt versus covert responses, the impact of prompting or no-prompting, size of steps, error rate, or the confirmation of results. Other issues indirectly related to the programming variables include user attitudes toward programs the mode of presentation (e.g., linear and branching) and program effectiveness. Illustrative results are provided from representative research studies.

20.4.11 Mode of Presentation

Various studies have been conducted comparing linear to branching programs, both in terms amount of learning and time saved in instruction. Coulson and Silberman (1960), and Roe (1962) found no significant differences in test scores between the two versions, but both found significant differences in terms of time taken to learn favoring branching programs. However, Roe (1962) did find that forward branching and linear programs were significantly faster (in terms of time saved) than backward branching. Mixed results were found in other studies, for example, Silberman, Melaragno, Coulson, and Estavan (1961) found no significant difference between the versions of presentation on achievement, but in the following study, Coulson, Estavan, Melaragno, and Silberman (1962) found that the branching mode was superior to a linear presentation.

Holland (1965), Leith, (1966), and Anderson (1967) reported no significant difference in learning between linear and branching programs when compared, and indicated this was generally the case with older or intelligent learners, "younger children using linear programs were more likely to receive higher test scores, although often these still took longer to complete than did branching ones" (Hartley, 1974, p. 284).

20.4.12 Overt Versus Covert Responses

One of Skinner's principles of programmed instruction is the necessity of overt responses. It appeared to be an important research concern to determine when it is advantageous to require overt or allow covert responses that could affect learning achievement. Are covert responses as effective as overt ones? This question has been a popular research topic. Overt responses require the student to *do something* (e.g., writing or speaking an answer, while covert requires *thinking* about or reading the material). Skinner's (1958) theory requires that a response should be overt (public) because if not overt, responses often ceased (Holland, 1965). Holland (1965) suggested that covert responses are not necessarily theoretical but also practical, because all aspects (in Skinner's view) of a program necessitate getting the correct answer. "Therefore, [a] measure of a program by not answering at all circumvents the characteristics which make it a program" (p. 93). Holland (1965) continued, indicating that several conditions must be met to determine the difference between overt and covert responses, namely, (1) program design must allow the student to answer correctly, and (2) the correct answer can only be attained after the appropriate

steps in the program have been completed. Other researchers over the years have accepted this concept as important (e.g., Tiemann & Markle, 1990).

In reviews of research by Lumsdaine (1960, 1961), Feldhusen (1963), and Silberman (1962), all reported some mixed results, but the overall finding was that there was no difference in achievement between the overt or covert response groups. Results of several studies suggest that the use of overt responses was supported under some conditions (e.g., Briggs, Goldbeck, Campbell, & Nichols, 1962; Williams, 1963; Wittrock, 1963). Holland (1965) reported that when answers on a test are not contingent on important content, overt responding might not be effective. Otherwise, studies indicated a test advantage for students using overt responses. Goldbeck and Campbell (1962) found that the advantages of each type of response may vary with the difficulty of content. Additionally, several studies showed that overt responding in programmed instruction was beneficial over covert responses (Daniel & Murdock, 1968; Karis, Kent, & Gilbert, 1970; Krumboltz & Weisman, 1962; Tudor, 1995; Tudor & Bostow, 1991; Wittrock, 1963). Miller and Malott (1997) in a review of the literature on effectiveness of overt responses versus nonovert responses concluded that there was little benefit in requiring overt responses when additional learning-based incentives are present, but in situations where no incentives are present overt learning should improve learning.

A large number of other researchers found no significant difference between the effectiveness of programmed materials requiring overt responses and those using covert responses (Alter & Silberman, 1962; Csanyi, Glaser, & Reynolds, 1962; Daniel & Murdock, 1968; Goldbeck & Campbell, 1962; Goldbeck, Campbell, & Llewellyn, 1960; Hartman, Morrison, & Carlson, 1963; Kormandy & VanAtta, 1962; Lambert, Miller, & Wiley, 1962; Roe, 1960; Stolurow & Walker, 1962; Tobias, 1969a, 1969b, 1973; Tobais & Weiner, 1963). Shimamune (1992) and Vunovick (1995) found no significant difference between overt construction and discrimination responses and covert responses. However, in these studies extra credit (incentives) was given for test performance. Miller and Malott (1997) replicated Tudor's (1995) study and found that the no-incentives overt group produced greater improvement than did the covert responding group. This was also true for the incentive overt responding group as well. Their results did not support earlier studies (noted above) and concluded that overt responding was "robust enough phenomenon to occur even when an incentive is provided" (p. 500).

Evans et al. (1959) required two groups to use machine instruction except one group was required to answers overtly, the other group were required not to answer items overtly. They reported no significant difference in the approach, but the nonovert answering group took less time than the overt group. While the research reported primarily no significant difference between learners who wrote answers and thought about answers, Holland (1965), Leith (1966), and Anderson (1967) felt that there were situations in which overt answers were superior to covert answers. Hartley (1974) summarized these situations: (1) when young children were involved, (2) when materials were difficult or complex, (3) when programs were lengthy, and (4) when specific terminology was being taught. There is, however, evidence according to Glaser and Resnick (1972), and Prosser (1974) the mere questioning is important to learning, regardless of covert or overt response situations.

20.4.13 Prompting

Holland (1965) indicated that in a study of paired associates, prompting was defined as a response given prior to an opportunity to have an overt response, whereas when confirming the response item is given after the overt response. Several studies dealt with the advantages of prompting versus nonprompting in a program sequence. Cook and Spitzer (1960) and Cook (1961) reported a no significant difference between the two versions, and also indicated that overt responses were not necessary for better achievement. Angell and Lumsdaine (1961) concluded from the review several studies that programs should include both prompted and nonprompted components. Stolurow, Hasterok, and Ferrier (1960) and Stolurow, Peters, and Steinberg (1960) in preliminary results of a study reported the effectiveness of prompting and confirmation in teaching sight vocabulary to mentally retarded children. In an experiment comparing a partial degree of prompting (prompting on 3/4 of the trials) to a complete prompting (prompting on every trial) version, Angell and Lumsdaine (1961) found learning was significantly more efficient under the partial prompting condition and supported the results of Cook (1958) and Cook and Spitzer (1960).

20.4.14 Confirmation

There appears to be some controversy over the concept or interpretation of feedback, reinforcement, and confirmation. Skinner (1959) interpreted confirmation as a positive reinforcer in the operant conditioning model (Smith & Smith, 1966). Others have objected to this view suggesting that getting a student to perform a desired function for the first time is not addressed (Snygg, 1962). Lumsdaine (1962) suggested that program developers should be most interested in the manipulation of prompting cues, not manipulation of reward schedules. Smith and Smith (1966) indicated that in an operant conditioning situation the response and the reinforcement are constant while in programmed instruction the situations are continually changing.

Several studies compared programs with confirmation (after an overt answer, the correct answer is presented) to programs with no confirmation available. No significant difference was found in scores as a function of confirmation (Feldhusen & Birt, 1962; Holland, 1960; Hough & Revsin, 1963; Lewis & Whitwell, 1971; McDonald & Allen, 1962; Moore & Smith, 1961, 1962; Widlake, 1964). However, Meyer (1960), Angell (1949), and Kaess and Zeaman (1960) found significant advantages in answer confirmation. Suppes and Ginsberg (1962) found an overt correction after confirmation to be also effective. Krumboltz and Weisman (1962) in comparing continuous versus noncontinuous confirmation, reported neither had an effect on the test scores.

Repetition and review have been built into many programs. Some programs were designed to drop a question when it had been correctly answered. Because it was technically easier in the 1960s to drop out a question after only one correct response rather than after additional responses, many programs were designed this way. However, Rothkopf (1960) did try to determine if there was any advantage to dropping questions out after two correct responses or any advantage to a version where none of the questions were dropped. He reported that the two methods were equally effective.

Scharf (1961) and Krumboltz and Weisman (1962) investigated several schedules of conformation and found no significant difference. However, Holland (1965) claimed even in the absence of significant results, that there was "enough suggestion of small differences so that the importance of confirmation cannot be discounted" (p. 91). Jensen (1949), Freeman (1959), and Briggs (1949) all reported that when there is a frequent, deliberate, and systematic effort to integrate the use of knowledge-of-results, learning shows a cumulative effect in a significant manner.

Hartley (1974) in his review and summary of programmed learning research on learner knowledge of results argued that immediate knowledge affected some learners more than others. In experiments "with low-ability learners and with programs with higher error rates, immediate knowledge of results was found to be helpful" (Holland, 1965; Anderson, 1967; Annett, 1969, as cited in Hartley, 1974, p. 284).

Although reinforcement, feedback, and confirmation are central issues to programmed instruction research, this area of research is incomplete and additional information concerning variables such as amount, schedule, and delay of reinforcement was missing. There appears to be no research that explains the problem of why confirmations are not always needed or why programs exhibiting the "pall effect" (boredom induced by the program) could promote learning (Rigney & Fry, 1961, p. 22).

20.4.15 Sequence

The basic structure of programmed machines and materials is a systematic progression of behavioral steps, which takes the student through complex subject matter with the intention of knowledge acquisition. One of Skinner's major tenants was the "construction of carefully arranged sequences of contingencies leading to the terminal performance which are the object of education" (Skinner, 1953, p. 169). This sequence of information and progressions in terms of "both stimulus materials displayed to the student and the way in which he interacts with and responds to them" are a fundamental issue of programmed learning research (Taber et al., 1965, p. 167).

Gavurin and Donahue (1960) compared a sequenced order of a program with a scrambled-order version as to the number of repetitions required for an errorless trial and on the number of errors to reach criterion. For both measures the sequenced order was significantly better. Hickey and Newton (1964) also found a significant difference in favor of original sequence to another unordered one. Hartley (1974) indicated that this suggested that the "analysis of structure must be very sophisticated indeed if it is to reveal useful differences in sequencing procedures" (p. 283). Roe, Case, and Roe (1962) found no significant difference post-test scores on a scrambled ordered versus a sequenced ordered program on statistics. However, using a longer form of the same program, Roe (1962) found significant advantages for the ordered sequences, on the number of student errors on the program and amount of time needed to complete the program.

Several research studies comparing *ordered* program sequences with nonlogical or random sequences have not supported Skinner's principle of ordered sequences (Duncan, 1971; Hamilton, 1964; Hartley & Woods, 1968; Miller, 1965; Neidermeyer, Browen, & Sulzen, 1968; Wager & Broaderick, 1974). However, Wodkte, Brown, Sands, and Fredericks (1968) found some evidence that the use of logical sequences for the lower ability learner was positive. Miller's (1969) study indicated that logical sequence appears to be the best in terms of overall effectiveness and efficiency. He felt it would be of value, however, to identify which levels of sequencing would be the most effective. In a review of several studies on logical sequencing, Hartley (1974) indicated that learners could tolerate "quite considerable distortions from the original sequence . . . and that the test results obtained are not markedly different from those obtained with the original program's so-called logical sequence" (p. 282). He stressed that these studies were conducted on short programs, however.

20.4.16 Size of Step

Size of step generally refers to the level of difficulty of the content or concepts provided in a frame. In addition, step size can mean, (1) amount of materials, for example, number of words in a frame, (2) difficulty as in error rate, and (3) number of items present (Holland, 1965). Thus, research in this category varies by "increasing or decreasing the number of frames to cover a given unit of instruction" (Smith & Smith, 1966, p. 311).

Using a programmed textbook with four levels of *steps* (from 30 to 68 items), four groups of students completed the same sequence of instruction, each group with a different number of steps. Evans et al. (1959) reported in that the group using smaller steps produced significantly fewer errors on both immediate and delayed tests. Likewise, Gropper (1966) found that larger the step size, the more errors were committed during practice. This finding was significant for lower ability students.

Smith and Moore (1962) reported in a study in which step size (step difficulty) and pictorial cues were varied in a spelling program, that no significant difference was found on achievement related to step size, but the larger step program took less time. Smith and Smith (1966) opined, "very small steps and over-cueing may produce disinterest"(p. 311). Balson (1971) also suggested that programmers could "increase the amount of behavioral change required of each frame" and thus increase the error rate, but not decrease achievement levels and also have a significant saving of time in learning (p. 205). Brewer and Tomlinson (1981) reported that except for brighter students, time spent on programmed instruction is not related to either improvement in immediate or delayed performance. Shay (1961) studied the relationship of intelligence (ability level) to step size. He reported relationship and indicted that the small steps were more effective (producing higher scores) at all ability levels.

Rigney and Fry (1961) summarized various studies and indicated that programs using very small (many components to a concept) could introduce a "pall effect" (Rigney & Fry, 1961, p. 22) in which boredom was inducted by the material, particularly with brighter students. These results were later supported by Briggs et al. (1962), Feldhusen, Ramharter, and Birt (1962), and Reed and Hayman (1962).

Coulson and Silberman (1959) compared three conditions on materials taught by machine: multiple-choice versus constructed responses, small steps versus large steps and branching versus no-branching presentation. This ambitious program's results indicated (1) that small steps (more items per concept) result in higher scores, but more training time, (2) the branching versions were not significantly different, but when time and amount of learning, the differences favored the branching version, and (3) there was no significant difference in the results of the type of response.

20.4.17 Error Rate

A major tenet in programmed instruction was presenting a sequence of instruction, which has a "high probability of eliciting desired performance" (Taber et al., p. 169). This sequence can sometimes be made too easy or too difficult. Error Rate is associated closely with size of step because of the codependence of the two. Skinner's (1954) thesis is that errors have no place in an effective program. They hinder learning. Others feel it is not necessarily an easy program (with few errors) that allows more learning but the program that involves and stimulates participation.

Again the results are mixed and generally dependent upon the situation. Studies by Keisler (1959), Meyer (1960), and Holland and Porter (1961) support the concept of low error rate. While Gagne' and Dick (1962) found low correlations between error rate and learning others found the specific situation, topics, or content to be a major factor in this determination. Goldbeck and Campbell (1962) found overt responses were less effective in *easy* programs. Melaragno (1960) found that when errors occurred in close proximity in the program there was a negative outcome in achievement.

Several studies have looked at the question of the use of explanations for wrong answers. Bryan and Rigney (1956) and Bryan and Schuster (1959) found that explanations were particularly valuable with complex data. However, Coulson, Estavan, Melaragno, and Silberman (1962) found no difference in achievement between a group using linear programs with no knowledge of errors and a group using branching programs that provided explanations of errors. However, the students' level of understanding increased with explanation of errors.

20.4.18 Program Influence by Age or Level

Glaser, Reynolds, and Fullick (1963; as cited in Taber et al., 1965) conducted an extensive research study on program influence by grade level. This study was conducted within a school system using programmed materials at various grade levels, including first grade math, and fourth grade math subjects. The results were measured by program tests, teacher-made tests and by national standardized tests. One purpose of this study was to determine if very young students could work on and learn from programmed materials in a day-by-day plan. Glaser et al. reported that the students were successful in learning from the programmed materials, that students who completed the programs in the shortest time did not necessarily score the highest, that 95 percent of the students achieved 75 percent subject mastery, and 65 percent of the students at the fourth-grade level achieved 90 percent on the program and standardized test. While the researchers felt that the study was a success, they still felt that the role of the teacher *insured proficiency* by the students.

Many studies were conducted in the business and industry sector dealing with programmed instruction for training and reported significant instructional training success, a significant saving of time, or both (Hain & Holder, 1962; Hickey, 1962; Holt, 1963; Hughes & McNamara, 1961; Lysaught, 1962). A series of studies (e.g., Dodd, 1967; Evans, 1975; Mackie, 1975; Stewart & Chown, 1965) reviewed by Hartley and Davies (1978), concentrated on adults' use of programmed instruction. They concluded that there was no single *best* form (e.g., format, type) of programmed instruction, which is "appropriate for everyone at a given age doing a specific task" (p. 169). They also concluded that adults like and will work with programs longer than younger students and the more interaction built in, the more it is accepted by the adults.

20.4.19 Type of Response—Constructed vs. Multiple Choice

When errors (what some call negative knowledge) are made in a program in Skinner's (1958) view inappropriate behavior probably has occurred. Effective multiple-choice questions must contain opportunity for wrong answers and thus is out of place in the process of shaping behavior. Pressey (1960) and others claimed just the opposite, that "multiple-choice items are better *because* errors occur, permitting elimination of inappropriate behavior" (Holland, 1965, p. 86).

Several studies (Burton & Goldbeck, 1962; Coulson & Silberman, 1960; Hough, 1962; Price, 1962; Roe, 1960; Williams, 1963) compared constructed response and multiple-choice responses but found no significant differences. Fry (1960) however, found constructed responses to be the better approach.

Holland (1965) suggested a major advantage of programmed materials over other instructional methods is that they increase the probability of a correct answer. Nonprogrammed materials generally do not require an immediate answer or response, or the material is extraneous as far as the response is concerned. The more highly programmed materials have been demonstrated to be more effective in Holland's view.

20.4.20 Individual Versus Group Uses

Several studies have been conducted to assess the value of using programmed materials (various formats) in a group setting versus individual use. The results are mixed, Keisler and McNeil (1962) reported the findings of two studies using programmed materials, one showing a significant difference favoring the individual approach over the group approach. The second study found no significant difference in-group or individual approaches. Likewise, Feldhusen and Birt (1962) found no significance between individual and group approach. On the other hand, Crist (1967), reported positive results with group work with the use of programs over individual use.

20.4.21 Research Concerns

As noted earlier in the disclaimer, there has been much concern about the quality of research during the era of Programmed Instruction (Allen, 1971; Campaeu, 1974; Dick & Latta, 1970; Holland, 1965; Lockee et al., 2001; Lumsdaine, 1965; Moore, Wilson, & Armistead, 1986; Smith & Smith, 1966). There appears to be two major fundamental issues of concern, (1) poor research techniques and reporting, and (2) the preponderance of the comparison study. Smith and Smith (1966) noted several issues concerning PI research. These included:

1. Many of the comparisons used small groups, for limited subject areas and for very short study duration,
2. Because the concept of programmed instruction was relatively new in the 1950s and 1960s, the novelty effect tends to favor the new techniques, and
3. There are many uncontrolled effects apparent in many of the experiments, e.g., time.

Holland (1965) pointed out that no program or no conventional method is generic. Each program or teaching method is different in several ways (they have many, many characteristics that are uncounted for in many of these studies). The "adequacy of any *method* can be changed considerably by manipulating often subtle variables" (p. 107). Holland indicated that research on programmed learning was hampered by poor measures, test sensitivity, and experimental procedures. Campeau (1974), and Moldstad (1974) indicated rampant problems including lack of control, faulty reporting, small number of subjects, and a lack of randomization were present in many studies of this era (1950–1970). Stickell (1963) reviewed 250 comparative media studies conducted during the 1950s and 1960s and only 10 could be accurately analyzed. Most of the results were *uninterpretable*. His general assessment has great bearing on the era of programmed instruction research. The reliance on the comparison study for much of the research published during this time illustrates examples of faulty design and interpretation. Comparison studies assumed that each medium (e.g., programmed instruction) was unique and could or could not affect learning in the same way. This medium, in the researchers' views, was unique and had no other instructional attributes. These researchers give little thought to the medium's characteristics or those of the learners (Allen, 1971; Lockee et al., 2001). However, one must consider the question, "what are traditional instructional methods?" Most of these studies have used terms such as traditional or conventional instruction and have not specifically identified what these methods are. Research in which such variables are not properly identified should NOT be depended upon for valid results. Review of the many programmed instruction studies reveal incomplete, inaccurate, little or no descriptions of the treatments, methodology, and results (Moore, Wilson, & Armistead, 1986). Many of these studies, used very small samples (if they were actually samples), lacked randomization and misused and misinterpreted results. For example, a good number of this era's research studies used the statistical term, *no significant difference* to mean that variables were equally good or bad. Ask a poor question get a poor answer. Clearly any outcomes reported in these types of studies are invalid, but this fact did not stop many of the researchers, and for that matter, journal editors from misinterpreting or reporting these results (Levie & Dickie, 1973; Lockee et al., 2001).

20.4.22 Summary of Results

Stolurow (1961) felt that while research indicated that learners from learning disabled students to graduate students could effectively learn from programmed devices, additional research should continue and a systematic study of programming variables be developed.

Glaser (1960) noted early on in the era of programmed learning research that "present knowledge can scarcely fail be an improvement over anachronistic methods of teaching certain subjects by lecturing to large classes" (p. 30). Even at that time there was desire to deemphasize hardware and machines. But, that said, Glaser indicated that machines had the opportunity to offer tangibility over an existing instructional method alone and programmed machines had the opportunity to showcase the capabilities of reinforcement contingencies.

In early reviews of literature, Stolurow (1961) reported three general findings on programmed learning research: (1) a programmed machine can significantly enhance learning, (2) the advantages of programmed instruction are not limited by learning task or subject, and (3) teaching by programs are applicable to a variety of learners.

Stolurow (1961) in his summary of programmed learning literature stated that knowledge-of-results should be studied in more detail. He felt that knowledge-of-results would be more effective if given earlier in a learning situation and should be a bigger factor in programmed machine and material development.

While in Holland's (1965) view, the results of programmed variables have on paper supported the general theoretical foundations of programmed learning; the research has not "improved upon the principles because the studies have been limited to gross comparisons" (p. 92). He suggested future research, including the following aspects: (1) that the measuring and specifying of variables be more exact, and (2) that the research should be directed to improving existing procedures or developing new techniques. The *versus* statements found in many comparison study titles suggest *crude dichotomies,* without considering factors that might otherwise influence outcomes, such as other characteristics of the technology or the characteristics of the learner. "Consequently, a generalization of results is difficult since magnitudes of differences is important variables cannot be specified for either experimental materials

or programs" (Holland, 1965, p. 92). That been said, Holland goes on to state that the research that to date (1966) supported the general principles of programming and in a paradoxal statement proclaimed that "it is perhaps comforting that comparison studies almost always show large advantages for programmed instruction" (p. 107). Holland (1965) stated that a contingent relationship between answer and content was important, that low error rate had received support, sequencing content was important and public, overt responses were important.

Hoko (1986) summarized his review of literature on the effects of automated instructional and traditional approaches, by indicating that each are unique and have specific potentials. He concluded, "the two should not be compared, but investigated, each for its own truths" (p. 18).

According to Smith and Smith (1966), the most valuable aspect of the program machine and instruction literature and research as that it provided "a new objective approach to the study of meaningful learning while at the same time provides new insights into how such learning occurs" (p. 326). While much of the research on programmed learning might be described as inconclusive, contradictory or even negative, there were important contributions. These contributions included focusing attention on reinforcement learning theory and possibly its shortcomings and thus opened the possibilities of new study and experimentation. Secondly, while not necessarily the norm, there were good researchers during this time that completed solid studies that did result in significant and meaningful results. This alone should indicate a need for more variability and research control to achieve real understandings of the programming theory and methods (Smith & Smith, 1966). Some authors and researchers felt that by the middle of the 1960s changes were in order and emphasis should (was) changing from emphasizing what the learner should do to what the programmer should do (Hartley, 1974). Some educators even felt that the psychology used to justify programmed instruction was becoming restrictive (Annett, 1969). Smith and Smith (1966) and Hartley and Davies (1978) tended to believe this earlier period of programming research started to shift from looking at program variables and learner needs to dealing with interactions with entire teaching and learning systems. Smith and Smith (1966) observed that this new emphasis on "systems study will not confine its efforts to evaluating specific machines or techniques, but will broaden its interests to include all types of classroom techniques and materials" (p. 326).

Computer-assisted instruction (CAI) and computer-based instruction (CBi) can be regarded as sophisticated extensions of programmed instruction theory and concept. Although some CBI research has been conducted within the context of programmed instruction, many of these studies have been conducted outside this context. Because of the many instructional possibilities that the computer can offer, many researchers consider it to be a separate field. This chapter's literature review dealt, for the most part, only with programmed instruction regarding theory and design. It should be noted that Programmed Instruction, CBI, and CAI have similar goals—to provide instruction, effectively, efficiently, and hopefully economically. It is evident that the foundations of computer-mediated instruction are based upon Programmed Instruction theory and research.

20.5 THE FUTURE OF PROGRAMMED INSTRUCTION

While trends in educational philosophy and learning theory have shifted away from behavioral sciences to more cognitive and constructivist approaches, these authors contend that Programmed Instruction has never really ceased to exist. Its influence is apparent in the instructional design processes that have continued to serve as the standards for our field (i.e., Dick, Carey, & Carey, 2000; Gagne, Briggs, & Wager, 1992; Gustafson & Branch, 1997, 2002; Kemp, Morrison, & Ross, 1998; Smith & Ragan, 1999). Recent literature regarding current trends in instructional design and technology indicates that while the systematic instructional design process has been embraced at varying levels across different venues (Reiser & Dempsey, 2002), its behavioral origins are still evident and notions of PI are found in existing practice. From the conduct of a needs assessment, to the establishment of clearly defined and measurable objectives, to the process of task analysis, the creation of assessment instruments and approaches that reflect the specified outcomes, the provision of opportunities for practice and feedback, to evaluation of the instructional program or product—all of these aspects of instructional design developed into the formation of a cohesive process as function of the Programmed Instruction movement. Perhaps the most prominent effect of the PI tradition on education as a whole is the convergence of the science of learning with the practice of teaching, the point originating from the first discussion of PI from Skinner (1954) himself in "The Science of Learning and the Art of Teaching".

As Januszewski (1999) indicates, "politics and political overtones are likely to be an undercurrent in any historical or conceptual study of educational technology" (p. 31). In the current era of political conservatism with a strong emphasis on accountability in education (no matter the organization or institution), the pendulum may likely swing back to favor this particular learning design. Though current trends in learning theory reflect less behavioral approaches to instruction (Driscoll, 2002), factors such as high-stakes testing in K-12 environments could promote a resurgence of aspects of PI, at least in terms of identification of measurable learning outcomes, mastery learning techniques, and the evaluation of instruction.

In "Programmed Instruction Revisited," Skinner (1986) proposed that the small computer is "the ideal hardware for Programmed Instruction" (p. 110). Extending the idea of the self-paced attribute of PI is the advent of the networked learning environment, making educational opportunities available anywhere and anytime. The revolution of the desktop computer, coupled with the diffusion of the Internet on a global scale, has provided access to unlimited learning resources and programs through distance education. In fact, perhaps the most prolific and long-standing example of computer-based PI, the PLATO (Programed Logic for Automatic Teaching Operation) program, has evolved into a Web-based learning environment that offers a variety of instructional programs to learners of all ages and walks of life, including incarcerated constituents. Created as a Programmed Instruction project at the University of Illinois in 1963. PLATO has continued development and dissemination since then, following the evolution of the computer and offering a range of computer-based curriculum that is unparalleled. While the primary design philosophy behind PLATO has shifted to feature more constructivist ideals (Foshay, 1998), it still maintains some of its PI foundations. For example, it preassesses learners to determine at what point they should engage in the program and if any remediation is necessary. Also, it tracks their progress, providing immediate feedback and guiding them to make accurate responses. Its use is also heavily evaluated. These features are its hallmarks, and the aspects of the program that have perpetuated throughout the aforementioned shifts in instructional philosophy and learning theory, giving credence to the influence of PI. While CBI, CAI, and now networked computer environments have expanded to support a greater variety of instructional approaches, Programmed Instruction still remains an effective and empirically validated possibility for the design of mediated instruction.

ACKNOWLEDGMENTS

The authors would like to thank Sara M. Bishop, Krista Terry, and Forrest McFeeters for their assistance in collecting the extensive array of historical materials necessary for the production of this chapter. We sincerely appreciate their help.

References

Alexander, J. E. (1970). *Vocabulary improvement methods, college level*. Knoxville, TN: Tennessee University. (ERIC Document Reproduction Service No. ED 039095)

Allen, W. H. (1971). Instructional media research, past, present and future. *AV Communication Review, 19*(1), 5-18.

Alter, M., & Silverman, R. (1962). The response in Programmed Instruction. *Journal of Programmed Instruction, 1,* 55-78.

Anderson, R. C. (1967). Educational psychology. *Annual Review of Psychology, 18,* 129-164.

Angell, D., & Lumsdaine, A. A. (1961). Prompted and unprompted trials versus prompted trials only in paired associate learning. In A. A. Lumsdaine (Ed.), *Student response in Programmed Instruction* (pp. 389-398). Washington, DC: National Research Council.

Angell, G. W. (1949). The effect of immediate knowledge of quiz results and final examination scores in freshman chemistry. *Journal of Educational Research, 42,* 391-394.

Angell, G. W., & Troyer, M. E. (1948). A new self-scoring test device for improving instruction. *School and Society, 67,* 84-85.

Annett, J. (1969). *Feedback and human behavior.* Harmondsworth, UK: Penguin.

Balson, M. (1971). The effect of sequence presentation and operant size on rate and amount of learning. *Programmed Learning and Educational Technology, 8*(3), 202-205.

Banta, T. J. (1963). Attitudes toward a programmed text: "The analysis of behavior" with a textbook of psychology. *Audiovisual Communication Review, 11,* 227-240.

Barlow, J. (1960). *Conversational chaining in teaching machine programs.* Richmond, IN: Earlham College.

Beck, J. (1959). On some methods of programming. In E. H. Galanter (Ed.), *Automatic teaching: The state of the art* (pp. 55-62). New York: John Wiley & Sons, Inc.

Benjamin, L. (1988). A history of teaching machines. *American Psychologist, 43*(9), 703-704.

Berthold, H. C., & Sachs, R. H. (1974). Education of the minimally brain damaged child by computer and by teacher. *Programmed Learning and Educational Technology, 11,* 121-124.

Blackman, L. S., & Capobianco, R. J. (1965). An evaluation of Programmed Instruction with the mentally retarded utilizing teaching machines. *American Journal of Mental Deficiency, 70,* 262-269.

Bloom, B. S., Engelhart, M. D., Furst, E. J., Hill, W. H., & Krathwohl, D. R. (1956). *Taxonomy of educational objectives: The classification of educational goals. Handbook 1: Cognitive domain.* New York: David McKay.

Brayfield, A. H., & Crockett, W. H. (1955). Employee attitudes and employee performance. *Psychology Bulletin, 52,* 396-424.

Brewer, I. M., & Tomlinson, J. D. (1981). SIMG: The effect of time and performance with modular instruction. *Programmed Learning and Educational Technology, 18*(2), 72-86.

Briggs, L. J. (1947). Intensive classes for superior students. *Journal of Educational Psychology, 38,* 207-215.

Briggs, L. J. (1956). *A troubleshooting trainer for the E-4 fire control system.* USAF Personnel Training Research Center. Report TN 56-94.

Briggs, L. J. (1958). Two self-instructional devices. *Psychological Reports, 4,* 671-676.

Briggs, L. J. (1960). Two self-instructional devices. In A. A. Lumsdaine & R. Glaser, (Eds.), *Teaching and programmed learning* (pp. 299-304). Washington, DC: National Education Association.

Briggs, L. J., & Bernard, G. C. (1956). Experimental procedures for increasing reinforced practice in training Air Force mechanics for an electronic system. In G. Finch & F. Cameron (Eds.), *Symposium on Air Force Human Engineering Personnel and Training Research* (pp. 48-58). Washington, DC: National Academy of Science, NRC.

Briggs, L. J., Goldbeck, R. A., Campbell, V. N., & Nichols, D. G. (1962). Experimental results regarding form of response, size of step, and individual differences in automated programs. In J. E. Coulson (Ed.), *Programmed learning and computer-based instruction* (pp. 86-98). New York: Wiley.

Brown, J. S., & VanLehn, K. (1980). Repair theory: A generative theory of bugs in procedural skills. *Cognitive Science, 4,* 389-426.

Burton, B. B., & Goldbeck, R. A. (1962). *The effect of response characteristics and multiple-choice alternatives on learning during*

programed instruction (Technical report number 4). San Mateo, CA: American Institute for Research.

Bryan, G. L., & Rigney, J. W. (1956). *An evaluation of a method for shipboard training in operation knowledge USN of Naval Research* (Technical Report 18).

Bryan, G. L., & Schuster, D. H. (1959). *The effectiveness of guidance and explanation in troubleshooting training* (Technical Report No. 28). Electronics Personnel Research Group, University of Southern California.

Bullock, D. (1978). *Programmed Instruction.* Englewood Cliffs, NJ: Educational Technology Publications.

Cambre, M.A. (1981). Historical overview of formative evaluation of instructional media products. *Educational Communication and Technology Journal, 29,* 3-25.

Campeau, P. L. (1974). Selective review of the results of research on the use of audiovisual media to teach adults. *AV Communication Review, 22,* 5-40.

Cantor, J. H. & Brown, J. S. (1956). *An evaluation of the Trainer-Tester and Punch card-Tutor as electronics troubleshooting training aids* (Technical Report WAVTRADEVCEN 1257-2-1). United States Naval Training Device Center, Office of Naval Research, Port Washington, NY.

Carr, W. J. (1959). A functional analysis of self-instructional devices. In A. A. Lumsdaine & R. Glaser (Eds.), *Teaching machines and Programmed Instruction* (pp. 540-562). Washington, DC: National Education Association.

Casas, M. (1997). *The history surrounding the use of Skinnerian teaching machines and programmed instruction (1960-1970).* Unpublished master's thesis, Harvard University, Boston.

Cassidy, V. M. (1950). *The effectiveness of self-teaching devices in facilitating learning.* Unpublished dissertation. Columbus, OH: Ohio State University.

Cook, J. O. (1961). From audience participation to paired-associate learning and response analysis in paired-associate learning experiments. In A. A. Lumbsdaine (Ed.), *Student response in Programmed Instruction* (pp. 351-373). Washington, DC: National Research Council.

Cook, J. O., & Spitzer, M. E. (1960). Supplementing report: Prompting versus confirmation in paired-associate learning. *Journal of Experimental Psychology, 59,* 257-276.

Coulson, J. E., Estavan, D. P., Melaragno, R. J., & Silberman, H. F. (1962). Effects of branching in a computer controlled autoinstructional device. *Journal of Applied Psychology, 46,* 389-392.

Coulson, J. E., & Silberman, H. F. (1959). *Results of initial experiments in automated teaching* (Report number SP-73). Santa Monica, CA: Systems Development Corporation.

Coulson, J. E., & Silberman, H. F. (1960). Effects of three variables in a teaching machine. *Journal of Educational Psychology, 51,* 135-143.

Crist, R. L. (1967). Role of peer influence and aspects of group use of programmed materials. *AV Communication Review, 15,* 423-434.

Cronbach, L. J. (1963). Course improvement through evaluation. *Teachers' College Record, 64,* 672-683.

Crowder, N. A. (1959). Automatic tutoring by means of intrinsic programming. In E. Galanter (Ed.), *Automatic teaching: The state of the art* (pp. 109-116). New York: Wiley.

Crowder, N. A. (1960). Automatic tutoring by intrinsic programming. In A. A. Lumsdaine & R. Glaser, (Eds.), *Teaching machines and programmed learning* (pp. 286-298). Washington, DC: National Education Association.

Crowder, N. A. (1964). On the differences between linear and intrinsic programming. In J. P. DeCecco (Ed.), *Educational technology* (pp. 142-151). New York: Rinehart & Winston.

Csanyi, A. P., Glaser, R., & Reynolds, J. H. (1962). Programming method and response mode in a visual-oral response task. In *Investigations of learning variables in Programmed Instruction*. Pittsburgh, PA: University of Pittsburgh.

Dale, E. (1967) Historical setting of Programmed Instruction. In P. C. Lange (Ed.), *Programed Instruction: The sixty-sixth yearbook of the National Society for the Study of Education*. Chicago, National Society for the Study of Education. 28-54.

Dallos, R. (1976). The effects of anxiety and intelligence on learning from Programmed Instruction. *Programmed Learning and Educational Technology, 13*(2), 69-76.

Daniel, W. J,. & Murdock, P. (1968). Effectiveness of learning from a programmed text compared with conventional text covering the same material. *Journal of Educational Psychology, 59*, 425-431.

Day, J. H. (1959). Teaching machines. *Journal of Chemical Education, 36*, 591-595.

Dessart, D. J. (1962). A study in programmed learning. *School Science & Mathematics, 62*, 513-520.

Detambel, M. H., & Stolurow, L. M. (1956). Stimulus sequence and concept learning. *Journal of Experimental Psychology, 51*, 34-40.

Dick, W., Carey, L., & Carey, J. O. (2000). *The systematic design of instruction* (5th ed.). Reading, MA: Addison Wesley.

Dick, W., & Latta, R. (1970). Comparative effects of ability and presentation mode in computer-assisted instruction and Programmed Instruction. *AV Communication Review, 18*(1), 33-45.

Dodd, B. T. (1967). A study in adult retraining: The gas man. *Occupational Psychology, 41*, 143.

Dowell, E. C. (1955). *An evaluation of Trainer-Testers, TA and D, Air Force Technical Training* (Report No. 54-28). Keesler Air Force Base, MS.

Driscoll, M. P. (2002). Psychological foundations of instructional design. In R. A. Reiser & J. A. Dempsey (Eds.), *Trends and issues in instructional design and technology* (pp. 57-69). Upper Saddle River, NJ: Merrill/Prentice Hall.

Duncan, K. D. (1971). Fading of prompts in learning sequences. *Programmed Learning and Educational Technology, 8*(2), 111-115.

Edgerton, A. K., & Twombly, R. M. (1962). A programmed course in spelling. *Elementary School Journal. 62*, 380-386.

Eigen, L. D. (1963). High school student reactions to Programmed Instruction. *Phi Delta Kappan, 44*, 282-285.

Engelmann, M. D. (1963). Construction and evaluation of programmed materials in biology classroom use. *American Biology Teacher, 25*, 212-214.

Evans, L. F. (1975). Unconventional aspects of educational technology in an adult education program. In E. F. Evans & J. Leedham (Eds.), *Aspects of educational technology IX*, London: Kogan Page.

Evans, J. L., Glaser, R., & Homme, L. E. (1959). *A preliminary investigation of variation in properties of verbal learning sequences of the teaching machine type*. Paper presented at the meeting of the Eastern Psychological Association, Atlantic City, NJ.

Evans, J. L., Glaser, R., & Homme, L. E. (1960). A preliminary investigation of variation in properties of verbal learning sequences of the teaching machine type. In A. A. Lumsdaine & R. Glaser (Eds.), *Teaching machines and programmed learning: A sourcebook* (446-451). Washington, DC: National Education Association.

Evans, J. L., Homme, L. E., & Glaser, R. (1962). The ruleg (rule-example) system for the construction of programmed verbal learning sequences. *Journal of Educational Research, 55*, 513-518.

Falconer, G. A. (1959). *A mechanical device for teaching word recognition to young deaf children*. Unpublished doctoral dissertation, University of Illinois, Champaign, IL.

Feldhusen, J. F. (1963). Taps for teaching machines. *Phi Delta Kappan, 44*, 265-267.

Feldhusen, J. F., & Brit, A. (1962). A study of nine methods of presentation of programmed learning materials. *Journal of Educational Research, 55*, 461-465.

Feldhusen, J. F., Ramharter, H., & Birt, A. T. (1962). The teacher versus programmed learning. *Wisconsin Journal of Education, 95*(3), 8-10.

Ferster, C. D., & Sapon, S. M. (1958). An application of recent developments in psychology to the teaching of German. *Harvard Educational Review, 28*, 58-69.

First Reports on Roanoke Math Materials. (1961). *Audiovisual Instruction, 6*, 150-151.

Foshay, R. (1998). *Instructional philosophy and strategic direction of the PLATO system*. Edina, MN: PLATO, Inc. (ERIC Document Reproduction Service ED 464 603.)

Freeman, J. T. (1959). The effects of reinforced practice on conventional multiple-choice tests. *Automated Teaching Bulletin, 1*, 19-20.

Fry, E. B. (1960). A study of teaching-machine response modes. In A. A. Lumsdaine & R. Glaser (Eds.), *Teaching machines and programmed learning* (pp. 469-474). Washington, DC: National Education Association.

Fry, E. B. (1961). Programming trends. *Audiovisual Instruction, 6*, 142-143.

Gagne, R.M. (1956). *The conditions of learning*. New York: Holt, Rinehart, and Winston.

Gagne', R. M., Briggs, L. J., & Wager, W. W. (1992). *Principles of instructional design* (4th ed.). New York: Harper Collins.

Gagne', R. M., & Dick, W. (1962). Learning measures in a self-instructional program in solving equations. *Psychology Reports, 10*, 131-146.

Galanter, E. H. (1959). *Automatic teaching: The state of the art*. New York: Wiley & Sons.

Gavurin, E. I., & Donahue, V. M. (1960). *Logical sequence and random sequence teaching-machine programs*. Burlington, MA: RCA.

Giese, D. L., & Stockdale, W. A. (1966). Comparing an experimental and conventional method of teaching linguistic skills. *The General College Studies, 2*(3), 1-10.

Gilbert, T. F. (1962). Mathetics: The technology of education. *Journal of Mathetics, I*, 7-73.

Glaser. R. (1960). Christmas past, present, and future: A review and preview. In A. A. Lumsdaine & R. Glaser (Eds.), *Teaching machines and programmed learning: A sourcebook* (pp. 23-31). Washington, DC: National Education Association.

Glaser, R. (Ed.), (1965). *Teaching machines and programmed learning II*. Washington, DC. National Education Association.

Glaser, R., Homme, L. E., & Evans, J. F. (1959, February). *An evaluation of textbooks in terms of learning principles*. Paper presented at the meeting of the American Educational Research Association, Atlantic City, NJ.

Glaser, R., & Klaus, D.J. (1962). Proficiency measurement: Assessing human performance. In R. M. Gagne (Ed.), *Psychological principles in system development*. New York: Holt, Rinehart, and Winston.

Glaser, R., & Resnick, L. B. (1972). Instructional psychology. *Annual Review of Psychology, 23*, 207-276.

Glaser, R., Reynolds, J. H., & Fullick, M. G. (1963). *Programmed Instruction in the intact classroom*. Pittsburgh, PA: University of Pittsburgh.

Goldbeck, R. A., & Campbell, V. N. (1962). The effects of response mode and response difficulty on programmed learning. *Journal of Educational Psychology, 53*, 110-118.

Goldbeck, R. A., Campbell, V. N., & Llewellyn, J. E. (1960). *Further experimental evidence in response modes in automated instruction*. Santa Barbara, CA: American Institute for Research.

Goldberg, M. H., Dawson, R. I., & Barrett, R. S. (1964). Comparison of programmed and conventional instructional methods. *Journal of Applied Psychology, 48,* 110–114.

Goldstein, L. S., & Gotkin, L. G. (1962). A review of research: Teaching machines vs. programmed textbooks as presentations modes. *Journal of Programmed Instruction, 1,* 29–36.

Green, E. (1967). The process of instructional programming. In P. C. Lange (Ed.), *Programed Instruction: The sixty-sixth yearbook of the National Society for the Study of Education* (pp. 61–80). Chicago, National Society for the Study of Education.

Gropper, G. L. (1966). *Programming visual presentations for procedural learning. Studies in televised instruction.* Pittsburgh, PA: American Institute for Research in Behavioral Sciences.

Gustafson, K., & Branch, R. M. (1997). *Survey of instructional development models* (3rd Edition). Syracuse, NY. (ERIC Clearinghouse on Information & Technology.)

Gustafson, K. & Branch, R. M. (2002). What is instructional design? In R. A. Reiser & J. A. Dempsey (Eds.), *Trends and issues in instructional design and technology* (pp. 16–25). Upper Saddle River, NJ: Merrill/Prentice Hall.

Hain, K. H., & Holder, E. J. (1962). A case study in Programmed Instruction. In S. Margulies & L. D. Eigen (Eds.), *Applied Programmed Instruction* (pp. 294–297). New York: John Wiley & Sons.

Hamilton, N. R. (1964). Effect of logical versus random sequencing of items in auto-instructional program under two conditions of covert response. *Journal of Educational Psychology, 55,* 258–266.

Hamilton, R. S., & Heinkel, O. A. (1967). *An evaluation of Programmed Instruction.* San Diego, CA: San Diego City College. (ERIC Document Reproduction Service No. ED 013619.)

Hartley, J. (1966). Research report. *New Education, 2*(1), 29.

Hartley, J. (Ed.) (1972). *Strategies for Programmed Instruction.* London: Butterworths.

Hartley, J. (1974). Programmed Instruction 1954–1974: A review. *Programmed Learning and Educational Technology, 11,* 278–291.

Hartley, J. (1978). *Designing instructional text.* New York: Nichols Publishing.

Hartley, J., & Davies, I. (1978). Programmed learning and educational technology. In M. Howe (Ed.), *Adult learning: Psychological research and applications* (pp. 161–183). New York: Wiley and Sons.

Hartley, J. E., & Woods, P. M. (1968). Learning poetry backwards. *National Society for Programmed Instruction Journal, 7,* 9–15.

Hartman, T. F., Morrison, B. A., & Carlson, M. E. (1963). Active responding in programmed learning materials. *Journal of Applied Psychology, 47,* 343–347.

Hatch, R. S. (1959). *An evaluation of a self-tutoring approach applied to pilot training* (Technical Report 59-310, p. 19). USAF Wright Air Development Center.

Hebb, D. O. (1958). *A Textbook of Psychology.* New York: Saunders.

Heinich, R. (1970). *Technology and the management of instruction* (Association for Educational Communications and Technology Monograph No. 4). Washington, DC: Association for Educational Communications and Technology.

Hickey, A. E. (1962). Programmed Instruction in business and industry. In S. Margulies & L. D. Eigen (Eds.), *Applied Programmed Instruction* (pp. 282–293). New York: John Wiley & Sons.

Hickey, A. E. & Newton, J. M. (1964). *The logical basis of teaching: The effect of subconcept sequence on learning.* Newbury Port, MA: Entelek Inc.

Hoko, J. A. (1986, February). What is the scientific value of comparing automated and human instruction? *Educational Technology, 26*(2) 16–19.

Holland, J. G. (1959). A teaching machine program in psychology. In E. Galanter (Ed.), *Automatic teaching: The state of the art* (pp. 69–82). New York: John Wiley & Sons.

Holland, J. G. (1960). Design and use of a teaching machine and program. *Teacher College Record, 63,* 56–65.

Holland, J. G. (1965). Research on programming variables. In R. Glaser (Ed.), *Teaching machines and programed learning, II* (pp. 66–177). Washington, DC: National Education Association.

Holland, J. G., & Porter, D. (1961). The influence of repetition of incorrectly answered items in a teaching-machine program. *Journal of Experimental Analysis Behavior, 4,* 305–307.

Holland, J. G., & Skinner, B. F. (1961). *The analysis of behavior.* New York: McGraw-Hill.

Holt, H. O. (1963). An exploratory study of the use of a self-instructional program in basic electricity. In J. L. Hughes (Ed.), *Programmed learning: A critical evaluation* (pp. 15–39). Chicago, IL: Educational Methods.

Homme, L. E., & Glaser, R. (1959, February). *Problems in programming verbal learning sequences.* Paper presented at the meeting of the American Psychological Association, Cincinnati, OH.

Hosmer, C. L., & Nolan, J. A. (1962). Time saved by a tryout of automatic tutoring. In S. Margulies & L. D. Eigen (Eds.), *Applied Programmed Instruction* (pp. 70–72). New York: John Wiley & Sons.

Hough, J. B. (1962). An analysis of the efficiency and effectiveness of selected aspects of machine instruction. *Journal of Educational Research, 55,* 467–471.

Hough, J. B., & Revsin, B. (1963). Programmed Instruction at the college level: A study of several factors influencing learning. *Phi Delta Kappan, 44,* 286–291.

Hughes, J. E. (Ed.), (1963). *Programmed learning: A critical evaluation.* Chicago, IL: Educational Methods.

Hughes, J. L., & McNamara, W. J. (1961). A comparative study of programmed and conventional instruction in industry. *Journal of Applied Psychology, 45,* 225–231.

Irion, A. L., & Briggs, L. J. (1957). *Learning task and mode of operation and three types of learning tasks on the improved Subject Matter Trainer.* Lowry Air Force Base, Air Force Personnel and Training Research Center, CO.

Januszewski, A. (1999). Forerunners to educational technology. In R. M. Branch & M. A. Fitzgerald (Eds.), *Educational media and technology yearbook, Volume 24* (pp. 31–42). Englewood, CO: Libraries Unlimited.

Jensen, B. T. (1949). An independent-study laboratory using self-scoring tests. *Journal of Educational Research, 43,* 134–137.

Joint Committee on Programmed Instruction and Teaching Machines. (1966). Recommendations on reporting the effectiveness of Programmed Instruction materials. *AV Communication Review, 14*(1), 117–123.

Jones, H. L., & Sawyer, M. O. (1949). A new evaluation instrument. *Journal of Educational Research, 42,* 381–385.

Kaess, W., & Zeaman, D. (1960). Positive and negative knowledge of results on a Pressey-type punchboard. *Journal of Experimental Psychology, 60,* 12–17.

Karis, C., Kent, A., & Gilbert, J. E. (1970). *The interactive effect of responses per frame response mode and response confirmation on intra-frame S-R association strength. Final Report.* Boston, MA: Northwestern University. (ERIC Document Reproduction Service No. ED 040591.)

Keisler, E. R. (1959). The development of understanding in arithmetic by a teaching machine. *Journal of Educational Psychology, 50,* 247–253.

Keisler, E. R., & McNeil, J. D. (1962). Teaching science and mathematics by autoinstruction in the primary grades: An experimental strategy in curriculum development. In J. E. Coulson (Ed.), *Programmed learning and computer instruction* (pp. 99-112). New York: Wiley.

Kemp, J., Morrison, G., & Ross, S. (1998). *Designing effective instruction* (2nd ed.). New York: Merrill.

Klaus, D. J. (1961). Programming: A re-emphasis on the tutorial approach. *Audiovisual Instruction, 6,* 130-132.

Knowlton, J., & Hawes, E. (1962). Attitude: Helpful predictor of audiovisual usage. *AV Communication Review, 10*(3), 147-157.

Kormondy, E. J., & VanAtta, E. L. (1962). Experiment in self-instruction in general biology. *Ohio Journal of Science, 4,* 4-10.

Krumboltz, J. D., & Weisman, R. G. (1962). The effect of covert responding to Programmed Instruction on immediate and delayed retention. *Journal of Educational Psychology, 53,* 89-92.

Lambert, P., Miller, D. M., & Wiley, D. E. (1962). Experimental folklore and experimentation: The study of programmed learning in the Wauwatosa Public Schools. *Journal of Educational Research, 55,* 485-494.

Lange, P. C. (1967). Future developments. In P. C. Lange (Ed.), *Programed instruction: The sixty-sixth yearbook of the National Society for the Study of Education* (pp. 284-326). Chicago, National Society for the Study of Education.

Leith, G. O. M. (1966). *A handbook of programmed learning* (2nd ed.). Educational Review Occasional Publication Number 1. Birmingham, UK: University of Birmingham.

Lewis, D. G., & Whitwell, M. N. (1971). The effects of reinforcement and response upon programmed learning in mathematics. *Programmed Learning and Educational Technology, 8*(3), 186-195.

Little, J. K. (1934). Results of the use of machines for testing and for drill upon learning educational psychology. *Journal of Experimental Education, 3,* 45-49.

Lockee, B. B., Moore, D. M., & Burton, J. K. (2001). Old concerns with new distance education research. *Educause Quarterly, 24,* 60-62.

Lumsdaine, A. A. (1960). Some issues concerning devices and programs for automated learning. In A. A. Lumsdaine & R. Glaser (Eds.), *Teaching machines and programmed learning* (pp. 517-539). Washington, DC: National Education Association.

Lumsdaine, A. A. (1961). *Student response in Programmed Instruction.* Washington, DC: National Research Council.

Lumsdaine, A. A. (1962). Experimental research on instructional devices and materials. In R. Glaser (Ed.), *Training research and education* (pp. 247-294). Pittsburgh, PA: University of Pittsburgh.

Lumsdaine, A. A. (1965). Assessing the effectiveness of instructional programs. In R. Glaser (Ed.), *Teaching machines and programmed learning, II: Data and directions* (pp. 267-320). Washington, DC: National Education Association.

Lumsdaine, A. A., & Glaser, R. (Eds.) (1960). *Teaching machines and programmed learning.* Washington, DC: National Education Association.

Lysaught, J. P. (1962). Programmed learning and teaching machines in industrial training. In S. Margulies & L.D. Eigen, (Eds.), *Applied Programmed Instruction* (pp. 23-43). New York: Wiley.

Lysaught, J. P., & Williams, C. M. (1963). *A guide to programmed instruction.* New York: John Wiley and Sons.

Mackie, A. (1975). Consumer-oriented programmed learning in adult education. In L. F. Evans & J. Leedham (Eds.), *Aspects of educational technology, IX,* London: Kogan Page.

Mager, R. F. (1962). *Preparing objectives for programmed instruction.* Belmont, CA: Fearon.

Malpass, L. F., Hardy, M. M., & Gilmore, A. S. (1964). Automated instruction for retarded children. *American Journal of Mental Deficiency, 69,* 405-412.

Markle, S. M. (1964). *Good frames and bad: A grammar of frame writing.* New York: John Wiley & Sons.

Markle, S. M. (1967). Empirical testing of programs. In P. C. Lange (Ed.), *Programed Instruction: The sixty-sixth yearbook of the National Society for the Study of Education* (104-138). Chicago: National Society for the Study of Education.

McDermott, P. A., & Watkins, W. W. (1983). Computerized vs. conventional remedial instruction for learning disabled pupils. *Journal of Special Education, 17,* 81-88.

McDonald, F. J., & Allen, D. (1962). An investigation of presentation response and correction factors in Programmed Instruction. *Journal of Educational Research, 55,* 502-507.

McKeown, E. N. (1965). A comparison of the teaching of arithmetic in grade four by teaching machine, programmed booklet, and traditional methods. *Ontario Journal of Educational Research, 7,* 289-295.

McNeil, J. D., & Keisler, E. R. (1962). Questions versus statements as stimuli to children's learning. *Audiovisual Communication Review, 10,* 85-88.

Mechner, F. (1967). Behavioral analysis and instructional sequencing. In P. C. Lange (Ed.), *Programed Instruction: The sixty-sixth yearbook of the National Society for the Study of Education* (pp. 81-103). Chicago: National Society for the Study of Education.

Melaragno, R. J. (1960). Effect of negative reinforcement in an automated teaching setting. *Psychological Reports, 7,* 381-384.

Merrill, M. D. (1971). Components of a cybernetic instructional system. In M. D. Merrill (Ed.), Instructional design: Readings (pp. 48-54). Englewood Cliffs, NJ: Prentice-Hall, Inc.

Meyer, S. R. (1959). A program in elementary arithmetic: present and future. In E. Galanter (Ed.), *Automatic teaching: The state of the art* (pp. 83-84). New York: John Wiley & Sons.

Meyer, S. R. (1960). Report on the initial test of a junior high-school vocabulary program. In A.A. Lumsdaine & R. Glaser (Eds.), *Teaching machines and programmed learning* (pp. 229-246). Washington, DC: National Education Association.

Miller, H. R. (1965, April). *An investigation into sequencing and prior information variables in a programmed evaluation unit for junior high school mathematics.* Paper presented at the meeting of the Department of Audiovisual Instruction. Milwaukee, WI.

Miller, H. R. (1969). Sequencing and prior information in linear Programmed Instruction. *AV Communication Review, 17*(1), 63-76.

Miller, M. L., & Malott, R. W. (1997). The importance of overt responding in Programmed Instruction even with added incentives for learning. *Journal of Behavioral Education, 7*(4), 497-503.

Miller, R. B. (1953). *A method for man-machine task analysis* (Tech. Rep. No. 53-137). Wright-Patterson Air Force Base, Ohio: Wright Air Development Center.

Miller, R. B. (1962). Analysis and specification of behavior for training. In R. Glaser (Ed.), *Training research and education.* Pittsburgh: University of Pittsburgh.

Moldstad, J. A. (1974). Selective review of research studies showing media effectiveness: A primer for media directors. *AV Communication Review, 22*(4), 387-407.

Moore, D. M., Wilson, L., & Armistead, P. (1986). Media research: A graduate student's primer. *British Journal of Educational Technology, 3*(17), 185-193.

Moore, J. W., & Smith, W. I. (1961). Knowledge of results of self-teaching spelling. *Psychological Reports, 9,* 717-726.

Moore, J. W., & Smith, W. I. (1962). A comparison of several types of immediate reinforcement. In W. Smith & J. Moore (Eds.), *Programmed learning* (pp. 192-201). New York: VanNostrand.

Naumann, T. F. (1962). A laboratory experience in programmed learning for students in educational psychology. *Journal Programmed Instruction, 1,* 9-18.

Neidermeyer, F., Brown, J., & Sulzen, R. (1968, March). *The effects of logical, scrambled and reverse order sequences on the learning of a series of mathematical tasks at the math grade level.* Paper presented at the meeting of the California Educational Research Association, Oakland, CA.

Nelson, C. B. (1967). *The effectiveness of the use of programmed analysis of musical works on students' perception of form. Final report.* SU New York at Cortland, NY.

Oakes, W. F. (1960). The use of teaching machines as a study aid in an introductory psychology course. *Psychological Reports, 7,* 297-303.

Ofiesh, G. D., & Meirhenry (Eds.). (1964). *Trends in Programmed Instruction,* Washington, DC: National Education Association.

Orey, M. A., & Burton, J. K. (1992). The trouble with error patterns. *Journal of Research on Computers in Education, 25*(1), 1-15.

Peterson, J. C. (1931). The value of guidance in reading for information. *Trans. Kansas Academy of Science, 34,* 291-296.

Porter, D. (1958). Teaching machines. *Harvard Graduate School Education Association Bulletin, 3,* 1-5.

Porter, D. (1959). Some effects of year long teaching machine instruction. In E. Galanter (Ed.), *Automatic teaching: The state of the art* (pp. 85-90). New York: John Wiley & Sons.

Posser, G. V. P. (1974). The role of active questions in learning and retention of prose material. *Instructional Science, 2, 241-246.*

Pressey, S. L. (1926). A simple apparatus which gives tests and scores— and teaches. *School and Society, 23,* 373-376.

Pressey, S. L. (1950). Development and appraisal of devices providing immediate automatic scoring of objective tests and concomitant self-instruction. *Journal of Psychology, 29,* 417-447.

Pressey, S. L. (1959). Certain major psycho-educational issues appearing in the conference on teaching machines. In E. Galanter (Ed.), *Automatic teaching: The state of the art* (pp. 187-198). New York: John Wiley & Sons.

Pressey, S. L. (1960). Some perspectives and major problems regarding teaching machines. In A. A. Lumsdaine & R. Glaser (Eds.), *Teaching machines and Programmed Instruction* (pp. 497-506). Washington, DC: National Education Association.

Price, J. E. (1963). Automated teaching programs with mentally retarded students. *American Journal of Mental Deficiency, 68,* 69-72.

Recommendations for reporting the effectiveness of Programmed Instructional materials. (1966). Washington, DC: National Education Association.

Reed, J. E., & Hayman, J. L. (1962). An experiment involving use of English 2600, an automated instruction text. *Journal of Educational Research, 55,* 476-484.

Reiser, R. A. (2001). A history of instructional design and technology: Part II: A history of instructional design. *Educational Technology Research and Development, 49*(2), 57-67.

Reiser, R. A., & Dempsey, J. A. (2002). *Trends and issues in instructional design and technology.* Upper Saddle River, NJ: Merrill/Prentice Hall.

Richmond, G. (1983). Comparison of automated and human instruction for developmentally retarded preschool children. *TASH Journal, 8,* 79-84.

Rigney, J. W., & Fry, E. B. (1961). Current teaching-machine programs and programming techniques. *Audiovisual Communication Review, 9*(3), Supplement 3, 7-121.

Roe, A., Massey, M., Weltman, G., & Leeds, D. (1960). *Automated teaching methods using linear programs.* UCLA Department of Engineering Report, 60-105.

Roe, A. A. (1960). *Automated teaching methods using linear programs* (Project number 60-105). Los Angeles, CA: University of California.

Roe, A. A. (1962). A comparison of branching methods for Programmed Instruction. *Journal of Educational Research, 55, 407-416.*

Roe, K. V., Case, H. W., & Roe, A. (1962). Scrambled vs. ordered sequence in auto-instructional programs. *Journal of Educational Psychology, 53,* 101-104.

Romiszowski, A. J. (1986). *Developing auto-instructional materials: From programmed texts to CAL and interactive video. Instructional Development 2.* London: Kogan Page.

Roth, R. H. (1963). Student reactions to programmed learning. *Phi Delta Kappan, 44,* 278-281.

Rothkokpf, E. Z. (1960). Some research problems in the design of materials and devices for automated teaching: In A. A. Lumsdaine & R. Glaser (Eds.), *Teaching machines and programmed learning* (pp. 318-328). Washington, DC: National Education Association.

Russo, D. C., Koegel, R. L., & Lovaas, O. I. (1978). A comparison of human and automated instruction of autistic children. *Journal of Abnormal Child Psychology, 6,* 189-201.

Rutkaus, M. A. (1987). Remember programmed instruction? *Educational Technology, 27*(10), 46-48.

Scharf, E. S. (1961). A study of the effects of partial reinforcement on behavior in a programmed learning situation. In R. Glaser & J. I. Taber, (Eds.), *Investigations of the characteristics of programmed learning sequences* (Research project number 691). Pittsburgh, PA: University of Pittsburgh.

Scriven, M. (1967). The methodology of evaluation. In *Perspectives of curriculum evaluation* (American Educational Research Association Monograph Series on Curriculum Evaluation, no. 1). Chicago: Rand McNally.

Severin, D. G. (1960). Appraisal of special tests and procedures used with self-scoring instructional testing devices. In A. A. Lumsdaine & R. Glaser (Eds.), *Teaching machines and programmed learning* (pp. 678-680). Washington, DC: National Education Association.

Shay, C. B. (1961). Relationship of intelligence to step size on a teaching machine program. *Journal of Educational Psychology, 52,* 93-103.

Shimamune, S. (1992). *Experimental and theoretical analysis of instructional tasks: reading, discrimination and construction.* Unpublished dissertation, W. Michigan University, Kalamazoo, MI.

Silberman, H. F. (1962). Characteristics of some recent studies of instructional methods. In J. E. Coulson (Ed.), *Programmed learning and computer-based instruction* (pp. 13-24), New York: John Wiley & Sons.

Silberman, H. F., Melaragno, R. J., Coulson, J. E., & Estavan, D. (1961). Fixed sequence versus branching auto-instructional methods. *Journal of Educational Psychology, 52,* 166-172.

Skinner, B. F. (1953). *Science and human behavior.* New York: Macmillan.

Skinner, B. F. (1954). The science of learning and the art of teaching. *Harvard Educational Review, 24,* 86-97.

Skinner, B. F. (1957). *Verbal behavior.* New York: Appleton-Century Crofts.

Skinner, B. F. (1958a). Teaching machines. *Science, 128,* 969-977.

Skinner, B. F. (1958b). Reinforcement today. *American Psychologist, 13,* 94-99.

Skinner, B. F. (1961). Why we need teaching machines. *Harvard Educational Review, 31,* 377-398.

Skinner, B. F. (1963). Operant behavior. *American Psychologist, 18,* 503-515.

Skinner, B. F. (1968a). *The technology of teaching.* New York: Appleton-Century-Crofts Educational Division, Meredith Corporation.

Skinner, B. F. (1968b). Reflections on a decade of teaching machines. In R. A. Weisgerber (Ed.), *Instructional process and media innovation* (pp. 404-417). Chicago: Rand McNally & Co.

Skinner, B. F. (1986). Programmed instruction revisited. *Phi Delta Kappan, 68*(2),103-110.

Skinner, B. F., & Holland, J. G. (1960). The use of teaching machines in college instruction. In A. A. Lumsdaine & R. Glaser (Eds.), *Teaching machines and programmed learning* (pp. 159-172). Washington, DC: National Education Association.

Smith, K. U., & Smith, M. F. (1966). *Cybernetic principles of learning and educational design.* New York: Holt, Rinehart & Winston.

Smith, N. H. (1962). The teaching of elementary statistics by the conventional classroom method versus the method of Programmed Instruction. *Journal of Educational Research, 55,* 417-420.

Smith, P. L., & Ragan, T. J. (1999). *Instructional design (2ⁿᵈ ed.).* Upper Saddle River, NJ: Merrill Prentice Hall.

Smith, W., & Moore, J. W. (1962). Size-of-step and achievement in programmed spelling. *Psychological Reports, 10,* 287-294.

Snygg, D. (1962). The tortuous path of learning theory. *Audiovisual Instruction, 7,* 8-12.

Stephens, A. L. (1960). Certain special factors involved in the law of effect. In A. A. Lumsdaine & R. Glaser (Eds.), *Teaching machines and programmed learning* (pp. 89-93). Washington, DC: National Education Association.

Stewart, D., & Chown, S. (1965). A comparison of the effects of a continuous and a linear programmed text on adult pupils. *Occupational Psychology, 39,* 135.

Stickell, D. W. (1963). *A critical review of the methodology and results of research comparing televised and face-to-face instruction.* Unpublished doctoral dissertation, State College, PA: Pennsylvania State University.

Stolurow, L. M. (1961). *Teaching by machine.* Washington, DC: US Department of Health, Education & Welfare.

Stolurow, L. M. (1963). Programmed Instruction for the mentally retarded. *Review of Educational Research, 33,* 126-133.

Stolurow, L. M., Hasterok, S. G., & Ferrier, A. (1960). *Automation in education.* Unpublished paper presented at Allerton Park, IL Conference.

Stolurow, L. M., Peters, S., & Steinberg, M. (1960, October). *Prompting, confirmation, over learning, and retention.* Paper presented at the meeting of the Illinois Council of Exceptional Children, Chicago, IL.

Stolurow, L. M., & Walker, C. C. (1962). A comparison of overt and covert response in programmed learning. *Journal of Educational Research, 55,* 421-429.

Suppes, P., & Ginsburg, R. (1962). Experimental studies of mathematical concept formation in young children. *Science Education, 46,* 230-240.

Suppes, P., & Morningstar, M. (1969). Computer-assisted instruction. *Science, 166,* 343-350.

Taber, J. I., Glaser, R., & Schaefer, H. H. (1965). *Learning and Programmed Instruction.* Reading, MA: Addison-Wesley.

Tiemann, P. S., & Markle, S. M. (1990). *Analyzing instructional content: A guide to instruction and evaluation* (4ᵗʰ ed.) IL: Stipes Publishing Company.

Tillman, S., & Glynn, S. (1987). Writing text that teaches: Historical overview. *Educational Technology, 27*(10), 41-45.

Tobias, S. (1969a). Effect of attitudes to Programmed Instruction and other media on achievement from programmed materials. *AV Communication Review, 17*(13), 299-306.

Tobias, S. (1969b). Effect of creativity, response mode and subject matter familiarity on achievement from Programmed Instruction. *Journal of Educational Psychology, 60,* 453-460.

Tobias, S. (1973). Review of the response mode issue. *Review of Educational Research, 43,* 193-204.

Tobias, S., & Weiner, M. (1963). Effect of response made on immediate and delayed recall from programmed material. *Journal of Programed Instruction, 2,* 9-13.

Tsai, S. W., & Pohl, N. F. (1978). Student achievement in computer programming: Lecture vs. computer-aided instruction. *Journal of Experimental Education, 46,* 66-70.

Tudor, R. M. (1995). Insolating the effects of active responding in computer-based instruction. *Journal of Applied Behavior Analysis, 28,* 343-344.

Tudor, R. M. & Bostow, D. E. (1991). Computer-Programmed Instruction: The relation or required interaction to practical application. *Journal of Applied Behavior Analysis, 24,* 361-368.

Tyler, R. W. (1932). The construction of examinations in botany and zoology. *Service Studies in Higher Education* (pp. 49-50). Ohio State University Studies, Bureau of Educational Research Monographs, No. 15.

Univin, D. (1966). An organizational explanation for certain retention and correlation factors in a comparison between two teaching methods. *Programmed Learning and Educational Technology, 3,* 35-39.

Uttal, W. R. (1962). *My teacher has three arms!!* IBM Corporation, T. J. Watson Research paper, RC-788.

VanAtta, L. (1961). Behavior in small steps. *Contemporary Psychology, 6,* 378-381.

Vargas, E. A., & Vargas, J. (1992). Programmed instruction and teaching machines. In *Designs for excellence in education: The legacy of B. F. Skinner.* Longmont, CO: Sopris West, Inc.

Vunovick, P. (1995). *Discrimination training, terminal-response training and concept learning in the teaching of goal-directed-systems design.* Unpublished master's thesis, W. Michigan University, Kalamazoo, MI.

Wager, W. W., & Broaderick, W. A. (1974). Three objective rules of sequencing applied to programmed learning materials. *AV Communication Review, 22*(4), 423-438.

Weinstock, H. R., Shelton, F. W., & Pulley, J. L. (1973). Critique of criticism of CAI. *Educational Forum, 37,* 427-433.

Wendt, P. R., & Rust, G. (1962). Pictorial and performance frames in branching Programmed Instruction. *Journal of Educational Research, 55,* 430-432.

Widlake, P. (1964). English sentence construction: The effects of mode of response on learning. *Education Review, 16,* 120-129.

Williams, J. P. (1963). A comparison of several response modes in a review program. *Journal of Educational Psychology, 54,* 253-260.

Wittrock, M. C. (1963). Response mode in the programming of kinetic molecular theory concepts. *Journal of Educational Psychology, 54,* 89-93.

Wodkte, K. H., Brown, B. R., Sands, H. R., & Fredericks, P. (1968, February). *The effects of subject matter and individual difference variables on learning from scrambled versus ordered instructional programs.* Paper presented at the meeting of the American Educational Research Association, Chicago, IL.

·21·

GAMES AND SIMULATIONS AND THEIR
RELATIONSHIPS TO LEARNING

Margaret E. Gredler
University of South Carolina

21.1   INTRODUCTION

Educational games and simulations are experiential exercises that transport learners to another world. There they apply their knowledge, skills, and strategies in the execution of their assigned roles. For example, children may search for vocabulary cues to capture a wicked wizard (game), or engineers may diagnose the problems in a malfunctioning steam plant (simulation).

The use of games and simulations for educational purposes may be traced to the use of war games in the 1600s. The purpose was to improve the strategic planning of armies and navies. Since the 1800s, they have served as a component in the military planning of major world powers. In the 1950s, political–military simulations of crises, within the context of the Cold War, became a staple at the Pentagon. The first exercises involved a scenario of a local or regional event that represented a threat to international relations. Included were a Polish nationalist uprising similar to the 1956 Hungarian revolt, the emergence of a pro-Castro government in Venezuela, insurgency in India, and Chinese penetration into Burma (Allen, 1987). Each simulation began with a scenario, and the exercise unfolded as teams representing different governments acted and reacted to the situation.

Since the late 1950s, the use of simulations has become a staple of both business and medical education, and games and simulations are found in language and science education and corporate training. Further, designers have specified both the intellectual processes and the artifacts and dynamics that define games and simulations (see Gredler, 1992; Jones, 1982, 1987; McGuire, Solomon, & Bashook, 1975). Briefly, games are competitive exercises in which the objective is to win and

players must apply subject matter or other relevant knowledge in an effort to advance in the exercise and win. An example is the computer game Mineshaft, in which students apply their knowledge of fractions in competing with other players to retrieve a miner's ax.

Simulations, in contrast, are open-ended evolving situations with many interacting variables. The goal for all participants is to each take a particular role, address the issues, threats, or problems that arise in the situation, and experience the effects of their decisions. The situation can take different directions, depending on the actions and reactions of the participants. That is, a simulation is an evolving case study of a particular social or physical reality in which the participants take on bona fide roles with well-defined responsibilities and constraints.

An example in zoology is Tidepools, in which students, taking the role of researcher, predict the responses of real tidepool animals to low oxygen in a low-tide period. Another is Turbinia, in which students diagnose the problems in an oil-fired marine plant. Other examples include diagnosing and treating a comatose patient and managing the short- and long-term economic fortunes of a business or financial institution for several business quarters.

Important characteristics of simulations are as follows: (a) an adequate model of the complex real-world situation with which the student interacts (referred to as fidelity or validity), (b) a defined role for each participant, with responsibilities and constraints, (c) a data-rich environment that permits students to execute a range of strategies, from targeted to "shotgun" decision making, and (d) feedback for participant actions in the form of changes in the problem or situation. Examples of high-fidelity simulations are pilot and astronaut trainers.

In the 1980s, the increasing capabilities of computer technology contributed to the development of a variety of problem-based exercises. Some of these exercises present the student with a nonevolving straightforward problem accompanied by one or more dynamic visuals or diagrams. Such exercises are sometimes referred to as simulations or simulation models, on the basis of the graphics or the equations that express a relationship among two or three variables. However, solving a well-defined problem is not a simulation for the student. In other words, like the real world, a simulation is an ill-defined problem with several parameters and possible courses of action. Discussed in this chapter are a conceptual framework for games and simulations, current examples, and unresolved issues in design and research.

21.2 CONCEPTUAL FRAMEWORK

Two concepts are important in the analysis of games and simulations: surface structure and deep structure. Briefly, *surface structure* refers to the paraphernalia and observable mechanics of an exercise (van Ments, 1984). Examples in games are drawing cards and clicking on an icon (computer game). An essential surface structure component in a simulation, in contrast, is a scenario or set of data to be addressed by the participant.

Deep structure, in contrast, refers to the psychological mechanisms operating in the exercise (Gredler, 1990, 1992). Deep structure is reflected in the nature of the interactions (a) between the learner and the major tasks in the exercise and (b) between the students in the exercise. Examples include the extent of student control in the exercise, the learner actions that earn rewards or positive feedback, and the complexity of the decision sequence (e.g., number of variables, relationships among decisions).

Shared features of games and simulations are that they transport the student to another setting, they require maximum student involvement in learning through active responding, and the student is in control of the action. However, in addition to having different purposes, they differ in deep structure characteristics. Included are the types of roles taken by individuals, nature of the decisions, and nature of feedback.

21.2.1 Games in Education and Training

Academic games are competitive exercises in which the objective is to win. Action is governed by rules of play (including penalties for illegal action) and paraphernalia to execute the play, such as tokens, cards, and computer keys (Gredler, 1992). Examples range from simple exercises, such as matching fractions to their decimal equivalents, to more complex contests, such as classroom tournaments involving several teams. The deep structure of games includes (a) competition among the players, (b) reinforcement in the form of advancement in the game for right answers, and (c) actions governed by rules that may be imaginative. For example, the rules may specify the point values of different clues that can assist the player to find a hidden pot of gold.

21.2.1.1 Purposes. Academic games may fulfill any of four purposes: (a) to practice and/or refine already-acquired knowledge and skills, (b) to identify gaps or weaknesses in knowledge or skills, (c) to serve as a summation or review, and (d) to develop new relationships among concepts and principles. Games also may be used to reward students for working hard or as a change of pace in the classroom. Adaptations of Twenty Questions in which the goal is to identify a particular author, chemical compound, or historical event are examples.

21.2.1.2 Design Criteria. Well-designed games are challenging and interesting for the players while, at the same time, requiring the application of particular knowledge or skills. Five design criteria that are important in meeting this requirement are summarized in Table 21.1. As indicated, (1) winning should be based only on the demonstration of knowledge or skills, and (2) the game should address important concepts or content. Third, the dynamics of the game should fit the age and developmental level of the players. For older students, for example, interest may be added by assigning weights to questions according to their difficulty (1 = easy, 3 = difficult), accompanied by team choice in the level of questions to be attempted.

A problem, particularly in computer games, is that the use of sound and graphics may be distracting. Further, the learner is led to enter incorrect responses when the sound and/or graphics

TABLE 21.1. Essential Design Criteria for Educational Games

Criterion	Rationale
1. Winning should be based on knowledge or skills, not random factors.	When chance factors contribute to winning, the knowledge and, effort of other players are devalued.
2. The game should address important content, not trivia.	The game sends messages about what is important in the class.
3. The dynamics of the game should be easy to understand and interesting for the players but not obstruct or distort learning.	The goal is to provide a practical, yet challenging exercise; added "bells and whistles" should be minimal and fulfill an important purpose.
4. Students should not lose points for wrong answers.	Punishing players for errors also punishes their effort and generates frustration.
5. Games should not be zero-sum exercises.	In zero-sum games, players periodically receive rewards for game-sanctioned actions, but only one player achieves an ultimate win. The educational problem is that several students may demonstrate substantial learning but are not recognized as winners.

following a wrong answer are more interesting than the outcomes for right answers.

Finally, (4) students should not lose points for wrong answers (they simply do not advance in the game) and (5) games should not be zero-sum exercises (Gredler, 1992). In Monopoly, for example, one player wins, while others exhaust their resources. Alternatives in the educational setting include providing for several winners (e.g., team with the fewest errors, team with the best strategy) and defining success in terms of reaching a certain criterion, such as a certain number of points.

Advantages of games in the classroom are that they can increase student interest and provide opportunities to apply learning in a new context. A current problem in the field, however, is the lack of well-designed games for the classroom setting.

21.2.2 Simulations

Unlike games, simulations are evolving case studies of a particular social or physical reality. The goal, instead of winning, is to take a bona fide role, address the issues, threats, or problems arising in the simulation, and experience the effects of one's decisions. For example, corporate executives, townspeople, and government officials address the potential tourism threat of a proposed nuclear reactor near a seaside town. In another example, research teams address the health status of an ecosystem, developing and implementing models of the variables in the system, prescribing corrections for problems, and altering their hypotheses based on the effects of their decisions.

In other words, simulations can take any of several directions, depending on the actions and reactions of the participants and natural complications that arise in the exercise. They differ from role plays, which are brief, single incidents (10 to 20 min) that require participants to improvise their roles. An example of a role-playing exercise is a school principal dealing with an angry parent. In contrast, simulations address multidimensional evolving problems, run from 50 min to several days, and use role descriptions including goals, constraints, background information, and responsibilities.

21.2.2.1 Deep Structure. First, unlike games, in which the rules may be imaginative, the basis for a simulation is a dynamic set of relationships among several variables that reflect authentic causal or relational processes. That is, the relationships must be verifiable. For example, in a diagnostic simulation, in which the student is managing the treatment of a patient, the patient's symptoms, general health characteristics, and selected treatment all interact in predictable ways.

Second, simulations require participants to apply their cognitive and metacognitive capabilities in the execution of a particular role. Thus, an important advantage of simulations, from the perspective of learning, is that they provide opportunities for students to solve ill-defined problems. Specifically, ill-defined problems are those in which either the givens, the desired goal, or the allowable operators (steps) are not immediately clear (Mayer & Wittrock, 1996). Although most educational materials address discrete well-defined problems, most problems in the real world are ill-defined.

Third, feedback on participants' actions is in the form of changes in the status of the problem and/or the reactions of other participants. The medical student, for example, may make errors and inadvertently "kill" the patient and the company management team may, through poor decision making, "bankrupt" the company.

In other words, a complex scenario that can take any of several directions is a necessary, but not sufficient condition for a simulation. The related essential requirement, a key feature of the deep structure, is the experience of functioning in a bona fide role and encountering the consequences of one's actions in the execution of that role. This characteristic is referred to by Jones (1984, 1987) as "reality of function," and it includes the thoughts of participants as well as their actions or words. That is, "A chairman really is a chairman with all the power, authority, and duties to complete the task" (Jones, 1984, p. 45).

21.2.2.2 Advantages. The design and validation of simulations are time-consuming. However, simulations provide advantages not found in exercises using discrete, static problems. First, they bridge the gap between the classroom and the real world by providing experience with complex, evolving problems. Second, they can reveal student misconceptions and understandings about the content. Third, and particularly important, they can provide information about students' problem-solving strategies. For example, scoring medical students' treatment decisions in diagnostic simulations identifies strategies as constricted, shotgun, random, or thorough and discriminating (see Peterson, 2000).

The broad category of simulations includes two principal types that differ in the nature of participant roles and interface with the situation. They are experiential and symbolic simulations.

21.2.2.3 Experiential Simulations. Originally developed to provide learner interactions in situations that are too costly or hazardous to provide in a real-world setting, experiential simulations have begun to fulfill broader functions. Examples include diagnosing the learning problems of children and addressing social service needs of individuals in vocational rehabilitation.

Briefly, experiential simulations are social microcosms. Learners interact with real-world scenarios and experience the feelings, questions, and concerns associated with their particular role. That is, the learner is immersed in a complex, evolving situation in which he or she is one of the functional components. Of primary importance is the fit between the experience and the social reality it represents, referred to as fidelity or validity (Alessi, 1988). Well-known examples of high-fidelity simulations are pilot and astronaut trainers.

Three types of experiential simulations may be identified, which vary in the nature of the causal model (qualitative or quantitative) and type of professional role. They are social-process, diagnostic, and data management simulations. In the group interactions in most social-process simulations, contingencies for different actions are imbedded in the scenario description that initiates action and the various role descriptions. For example, the role cards for space crash survivors stranded on a strange planet each contain two or three unrelated bits of information

TABLE 21.2. A Comparison of Experiential Simulations

Defining characteristics	Social microcosms; individuals take different roles with particular responsibilities and constraints and interact in a complex evolving scenario.
Types	
Social process	Contingencies for different actions are imbedded in the scenario and role descriptions (a group exercise).
Diagnostic	Contingencies are based on the optimal, near-optimal, and dangerous decisions that may be made (may be an individual or a group exercise).
Data management	Contingencies are imbedded in the quantitative relationships among the variables expressed in equations (a group exercise).

important for survival (see Jones, 1982). Clear communication and careful listening by the participants are essential if they are to find food and water and stay alive.

In contrast, the model of reality in diagnostic or patient-management simulations is the patterns of optimal and near-optimal decision making expected in the real world. The sequential nature of the task links each decision to prior decisions and results. Therefore, as in real situations, errors may be compounded on top of errors as nonproductive diagnostic and solution procedures are pursued (Berven & Scofield, 1980). Diagnostic simulations typically are computer-based. The student reads a brief scenario and has several choices at each decision point, from requests for further information to solutions to the problem.

In data-management simulations, teams manage business or financial institutions. The basis for a data-management simulation is a causal model that specifies relationships among quantitative variables. Included are relationships among inputted data from participants and profitability, liquidity, solvency, business volume, inventory, and others. Each team receives a financial profile of the business or bank and makes decisions for several quarters of operation. Teams enter their decisions for each quarter into a computer, receive an updated printout from the computer on the financial condition of the institution, and make new decisions.

Table 21.2 provides a comparison of experiential simulations. Of importance in the design of experiential simulations is that the individual who is unsure of an appropriate course of action has plausible alternatives. This requirement is particularly important in diagnostic simulations in which the goal is to differentiate the problem-solution strategies of students in complex nontextbook problems.

21.2.2.4 Symbolic Simulations.
Increased computer capabilities in recent years have led to the development and implementation of symbolic simulations. Specifically, a symbolic simulation is a dynamic representation of the functioning or behavior of some universe, system, or set of processes or phenomena by another system, in this case, a computer.

A key defining characteristic of symbolic simulations is that the student functions as a researcher or investigator and tests his or her conceptual model of the relationships among the variables in the system. This feature is a major difference between symbolic and experiential simulations. That is, the role of the learner is not a functional component of the system. A second major difference is the mechanisms for reinforcing appropriate student behaviors. The student in an experiential simulation steps into a scenario in which consequences for one's actions occur in the form of other participants' actions or changes in (or effects on) the complex problem or task the student is managing. That is, the learner who is executing random strategies typically experiences powerful contingencies for such behavior, from the reactions of other participants to being exited from the simulation for inadvertently "killing" the patient.

The symbolic simulation, however, is a population of events or set of processes external to the learner. Although the learner is expected to interact with the symbolic simulation as a researcher or investigator, the exercise, by its very nature, cannot divert the learner from the use of random strategies.

One solution is to ensure, in prior instruction, that students acquire both the relevant domain knowledge and the essential research skills. That is, students should be proficient in developing mental models of complex situations, testing variables systematically, and revising their mental models where necessary. In this way, students can approach the symbolic simulation equipped to address its complexities, and the possibility of executing random strategies holds little appeal.

Two major types of symbolic simulations are laboratory-research simulations and system simulations. In the former, students function as researchers, and in the latter, they typically function as trouble shooters to analyze, diagnose, and correct operational faults in the system.

Important student skills required for interacting with symbolic simulations are relevant subject-area knowledge and particular research skills. That is, students should be proficient in developing mental models of complex situations, testing variables systematically, and revising one's mental model when necessary. For example, interacting with a model of several generations of representatives of a species requires an understanding of classical Mendelian genetics and strategies for plotting dominant and recessive genes. Table 21.3 provides a comparison of the symbolic simulations.

21.2.3 Other Technology-Based Exercises

Two technology-based experiences sometimes referred to as simulations are problem-based exercises that include simulated materials and experiences referred to as virtual reality.

TABLE 21.3. A Comparison of Symbolic Simulations

Defining characteristics	A population of events or set of processes external to the learner; individuals interact with the information in the role of researcher or investigator.
Types	
Laboratory-research simulations	Individual investigates a complex, evolving situation to make predictions or to solve problems.
System simulations	Individuals interact with indicators of system components to analyze, diagnose, and correct operational faults in the system.

21.2.3.1 Problem-Solving Exercises with Simulated Materials.

One type of exercise implements discrete problems on a particular topic for students to solve that are accompanied by dynamic visuals. Such exercises, however, are not simulations because they are discrete problems instead of student interactions with a data universe or a complex system in an open-ended exercise. That is, the task is to address well-structured finite problems that relate to a particular visual display. An example is the task of causing a space shuttle to come to a complete stop inside a circle (Rieber & Parmby, 1995). As in this example, the problems often involve only a relationship between two variables.

Other examples are the computer-based manipulatives (CMBs) in genetics developed by Horowitz and Christie (2000). The instruction combines (a) specific computer-based tasks to be solved through experimentation in two-person teams, (b) paper-and-pencil exercises, and (c) class discussions. Of interest is that a paper-and-pencil test after 6 weeks of classroom trials revealed no significant differences in the means of the computer-learning classes versus those of other classes.

Another project in science education has developed sets of physics problems on different topics accompanied by dynamic visuals. Examples include the effects of the strength of a spring on motion frequency and the influence of friction on both the frequency and the amplitude of motion (Swaak & de Jong, 2001; van Joolingen & deJong, 1996). Motion is illustrated in a small window surrounded by windows that provide instructional support to the learner in the discovery process. The learner inputs different values of a particular variable, such as the strength of a spring, in an effort to discover the relationship with an identified outcome variable (e.g., motion frequency).

The developers refer to a "simulation model" that "calculates the values of certain output variables on the basis of input variables" (van Joolingen & de Jong, 1996, p. 255). The "simulation," in other words, is the demonstrated reaction of a specified parameter that is based on the underlying relationships among the quantifiable variables. This perspective reflects the view of a simulation as "a simplified representation" (Thomas & Neilson, 1995).

The task for the learner is to infer the characteristics of the model by changing the value of an input variable or variables (de Jong & van Joolingen, 1998, p. 180). The expectation is that learners will formulate hypotheses, design experiments, interpret data, and implement these activities through systematic planning and monitoring (p. 186). The extensive problems of learners in the execution of these activities described by de Jong and van Joolingen (1998) indicate the high cognitive demands placed on the learner. That is, a lack of proficiency in

the processes of scientific discovery learning coupled with the task of discovering aspects of an unknown model overtaxes the limits of working memory and creates an excessive cognitive load that hampers learning (for a discussion see Sweller, van Merrienbaer, & Paas, 1998).

Another approach to solving problems in physics consists of (a) the portrayal, using abstract symbols, of Newton's first two laws of motion and (b) student construction of experiments on the illustrated variables (the mass, elasticity, and velocity of any object, each portrayed as a "dot") (White & Fredericksen, 2000). Students, with support from the software, carry out the process of inquiry (stating hypotheses, collecting and analyzing data, and summarizing the results) with successive modules that become increasingly complex. Also included is reflective assessment, in which students evaluate their work. Data indicated that students who completed the projects with reflective assessment outperformed students who used the software without the reflective assessment component.

These exercises differ from simulations in three ways. First, the visuals illustrate discrete relationships, not a data universe or physical or biological system. Second, in some cases, abstract symbols (e.g., dots and datacrosses) are the components of the illustrated relationships. The "simulation," in other words, is an abstract model and "models, whether on or off the computer, aren't 'almost as good as the real thing'—they are fundamentally different from the real thing" (Horowitz, 1999, p. 195).

Third, a simulation includes the actions of the participants. For example, business simulations also rely on equations to specify the relationships among such variables as balance of payments, exports, price level, imports, world prices, and exchange rate (Adams & Geczy, 1991). Also, a key component is the involvement of participants in the well-being of the financial institution as they execute their responsibilities and experience (not merely observe) the consequences of their actions. In other words, one limitation of defining a simulation as the portrayal of content is that any of a range of student activities may be permitted in the exercises. That is, an exercise as simple as the learner selecting an option in multiple-choice questions could be classified as a simulation.

21.2.3.2 Virtual Environments.

The term *virtual environment* or *virtual reality* refers to computer-generated three-dimensional environments that respond in real time to the actions of the users (Cromby, Standen, & Brown, 1996, p. 490). Examples include photographs "stitched together" to produce a computer screen that portrays a navigable 360° panorama of an urban environment (Doyle, Dodge, & Smith, 1998); total immersion systems that require headsets, earphones, and data gloves; and desktop virtual environments that implement a joystick, mouse, touch screen, or keyboard (Cromby et al., 1996). The intent is to convey a sense of presence for the participant; that is, the individual feels present in the computer-generated environment (p. 490). (For examples see Dede, Salzman, Loftin, & Ash, 2000).

Virtual environments, in other words, create particular settings and attempt to draw the participant into the setting. The question is whether virtual environments also are simulations from the perspective of learning. Again, the issue is the nature of the problem or situation the learner is addressing and the capabilities required of the learner. That is, Is it a complex, evolving reality? and What are the capabilities executed by the learner?

21.3 RESEARCH IN GAMES AND SIMULATIONS

Like other curriculum innovations, games and simulations are developed in areas where the designers perceive a particular instructional need. Examples include providing real-world decision making in the health care professions and providing opportunities for laboratory experimentation in science and psychology. Most developers, however, report only sketchy anecdotal evidence or personal impressions of the success of their particular exercise. A few documented the posttest skills of students or, in a simulation, the students' problem-solving strategies. None, however, addressed the fidelity of the experience for students for the types of simulations described in the prior section.

21.3.1 Educational Games

A key feature of educational games is the opportunity to apply subject matter knowledge in a new context. For example, the computer game Mineshaft requires the players to use fractions to retrieve a miner's ax that has fallen into the shaft (Rieber, 1996).

An innovative use of computer technology is to permit students to design their own computer games using particular content. One example, Underwater Sea Quest, involves the laws of motion. The goal is to help a diver find gold treasure while avoiding a roving shark (Rieber, 1996, p. 54).

Although educational games are accepted in elementary school, teacher and parent interest in their use declines in the later grades (Rieber, 1996). However, one use is that of providing health and human services information to adolescents, an area in which maintaining the attention of adolescents is a challenge (Bosworth, 1994). In the Boday Awareness Resource Network (BARN), AIDS information is addressed in an elaborate maze game. The object is to move through and out of a maze that is randomly generated by the computer by correctly answering questions on AIDS (p. 112). A further challenge is the capability of the computer to generate randomly a new maze for each game. Anecdotal evidence from students indicated the success of the game in enticing students to the BARN system (p. 118).

21.3.2 Experiential Simulations

Social-process simulations, one of the three categories of experiential simulations, often are developed to provide experiences in using language to communicate for various purposes. However, advances in programming have precipitated interest in developing desktop visual reality simulations in different educational settings. One suggested application is that of providing environments for learning-disabled students to develop independent living and survival skills (Cromby et al., 1996; Standen & Cromby, 1996). An example is shopping in a supermarket. The computer presented a two-aisle store with five different layouts of goods presented at random each time a student began a session. Participants used a joystick to navigate the aisles and selected items on their list with a mouse (Standen & Cromby, 1996). In the follow-up involving a trip to a real store, severely disabled students were more successful than their counterparts in a control group.

Diagnostic simulations is the second category in experiential simulations. These exercises, in which participants take professional roles that involve problem solving, may be developed for any age group. Although the majority are found in higher education, Henderson, Klemes, and Eshet (2000) describe a simulation in which second-grade students take the role of paleontologist. Entitled Message in a Fossil, the computer-based simulation allows the participants to excavate in virtual gridded dig-sites using appropriate tools (p. 107). Among the 200 fossils are dinosaur bones, fish skeletons, sea urchins, shark teeth, and fern leaves. Students predict the fossil types and then identify them through comparison with pictures in the fossil database. Posttest data indicate positive learning outcomes, internalization of scientific terminology (e.g., habitat, evidence), and personal investment in the exercise. The teacher noted that children felt like scientists by their use of statements such as "We are going to collect data" and "We are going to make observations" (p. 121).

In higher education, diagnostic simulations originally were developed for medical education. They have since expanded into related fields, such as counseling (see Frame, Flanagan, Frederick, Gold, & Harris, 1997). One related area is rehabilitation counseling, where simulations were introduced in the 1980s to enhance students' clinical problem-solving skills (see Berven, 1985; Berven & Scofield, 1980). An important characteristic of the medical model, implemented in rehabilitation counseling, is the identification of the effectiveness of students' problem-solving strategies. For example, a study by Peterson (2000) with 65 master's-degree students found four types of problem approaches. They are thorough and discriminating, constricted, shotgun (high proficiency and low efficiency scores), and random (low on both proficiency and efficiency scores). The study recommended that students with less than optimal approaches work with their mentors to develop compensatory strategies.

The largest group of experiential simulations is the data-management simulations, and their use in strategic management courses is increasing (Faria, 1998). Unlike the other experiential exercises, data-management simulations include competition among management teams as a major variable. This feature is reflected in some references to the exercises as games or gaming-simulations. Some instructors, for example, allocate as much as 25% of the course grade to student performance (Wolfe & Rogé, 1997). However, one problem associated with an emphasis on winning is that, in the real world, major quarterly decisions are not collapsed into a brief, 45-min, time period. Another is that a focus on winning can detract from meaningful strategic planning.

One analysis of the characteristics of current management simulations, a review of eight exercises, indicated that most provide some form of international competition and address, at least minimally, the elements involved in making strategic decisions (Wolf & Rogé, 1997). Identified deficiencies were that simulations did not force participants to deal with the conflicting demands of various constituencies and did not allow for the range of grand strategies currently taught in management courses (p. 436). Keys (1997) also noted that management simulations have become more robust and strategic in recent years, with more industry, realism, and technological support. Further, the simulations have included global markets, and global producing areas and finance options.

Although early research with data-management simulations compared their use to case studies or regular class instruction, the recent focus is on analyses of student behaviors in the exercises themselves. One study found, for example, that a competitive disposition in management teams is not related to performance (Neal, 1997). Further, although winning teams perceived that they had implemented the most competitive strategies, group cohesion was a major factor in performance (Neal, 1997). Another study found that students' self-efficacy (belief in one's capabilities) in using strategic management skills is not explained by the use of case studies and simulations. Predictor variables, which included teaching methods, accounted for only 14.8% of the variance in students' self-efficacy (Thompson & Dass, 2000).

Another study analyzed the factors that contributed to poor performance in a simulation that involved the management of a small garment manufacturing company (Ramnarayan, Strohschneider, & Schaub, 1997). The participants, 60 advanced students in a prestigious school of management, formed 20 teams and managed the company for 24 monthly cycles (3 hr). Factors that contributed to poor performance were (a) immediately making calculations without first developing a coherent mental model or setting goals and objectives, (b) following a "repair shop" principle (wait for problems and then respond), and (c) failing to alter plans in the face of disconfirming signals. Finally, the researchers noted that the participants were proficient in basic knowledge but lacked metaknowledge (p. 41). An important component of metacognition, metaknowledge refers to knowing what we know and what we do not know. This capability is essential to the identification of key issues in data collection to solve problems.

21.3.3 Symbolic Simulations

Symbolic simulations are referred to by some as microworlds. That is, a microworld is "a computer-based simulation of a work or decisionmaking environment" (Sauer, Wastell, & Hockey, 2000, p. 46). Of major importance for participant roles, however, is that the decision-making environment constitute a system. An example is the Cabin Air Management System (CAMS), a generic simulation of the automated life support system in a spacecraft. Developed to research the multiple effects of factors that influence human performance in complex systems, scenarios implemented with CAMS have investigated human adaptive strategies in the management of varying task demands (Sauer et al., 2000).

In science education, simulations often are viewed as a means for students to use discovery learning and usually are considered an alternative to expository instruction or hands-on laboratory exploration (Ronen & Eliahu, 2000, p. 15). In one study, one group of students received a computer disk that contained simulations of electric circuits and activities that were part of their homework. However, at the end of 6 weeks, no significant differences were found between the experimental- and the control-group classes (Ronen & Eliahu, 1998). The posttest data also indicated that both groups held key misconceptions, such as that a battery is a source of constant current. In a follow-up study 1 week later, the classes were assigned the laboratory task of building a real circuit so that the light intensity of the bulbs varied in a particular way. Experimental classes that used the simulation to test their plans outperformed the control groups, whose only opportunity to obtain feedback was in the physical trials of their circuits (Ronen & Eliahu, 2000). However, the simulation served only as a feedback device. Neither the experimental nor the control group designed their circuits using a theoretical model.

In other subject areas, the combination of hypermedia with video images can be used to create a virtual experience for students who are fulfilling roles as researchers. Examples are A Virtual Field Trip—Plant Collecting in Western New South Wales and Blue Ice: Focus on Antarctica (Peat & Fernandez, 2000). In the latter example, in addition to collecting and analyzing data, students research wild life and weather topics. Another example, used in zoology, is Tidepools, in which students (a) explore the ways in which a hypothetical tidepool animal might respond to low oxygen in the low-tide period and (b) predict the responses of four real tidepool animals (Spicer & Stratford, 2001, p. 347). To complete phase 2, students obtain relevant information on each species by searching a virtual tidepool. Students also are provided with a field notebook into which they may transfer pictures and text. Also included is a visible talking tutor who introduces the tasks and explains how to proceed and what can be done (p. 348).

Student responses to survey items were highly positive. Also of interest is that students, in unsolicited comments on their questionnaires, indicated that they learned more quickly and effectively when staff were present to discuss "emerging issues" (p. 351).

Of particular interest is that, immediately following the exercise, students perceived that Tidepools provided the same experiences as a real field trip. However, following an actual field trip, student perceptions changed significantly ($p < .0001$). That is, the majority indicated that the hypermedia experience was not a substitute. Then, following a zoology field course, students indicated that hypermedia, properly designed, can serve as preparation for field study and help them use their time more effectively. This perception is consistent with the views of Warburton and Higgitt (1997) that describe the importance of advance preparation for field trips and the role of information technology in this task.

A different type of student-researcher experience is required in general introductory psychology classes. That is, students require opportunities to conduct laboratory experiments in which they generate hypotheses, set up conditions to test the hypotheses, obtain reliable and unbiased data, and interpret the collected data.

In one software model developed for this purpose, student researchers use the clocks and counters at the bottom of the computer screen to document the extent to which an infant attends to a particular stimulus (Colle & Green, 1996). The screen portrays an infant's looking behavior, which includes both head and eye movements. In another simulation, students study the flash exchanges between fireflies during the courting behavior that precedes mating.

Other software products address the challenges involved in the operant conditioning of the bar pressing behavior of a laboratory rat. One exercise, in which the screen portrays a drawing of the side view of rat with a front paw on a bar (Shimoff & Catania, 1995), lacks the fidelity required of a simulation. Also, the exercise did not provide information to students on their skill in shaping (Graf, 1995). In contrast, Sniffy, the Virtual Rat shows Sniffy in an experimental chamber with three walls, a lever, a food dish, and a water tube. Sniffy engages in actual behavior, including wandering around, sniffing, and stretching. The program also shows the cumulative record of Sniffy's bar pressing behavior during the conditioning process (Alloway, Wilson, Graham, & Kramer, 2000).

An example of the troubleshooting role in relation to a system is the research conducted with a computer-based simulation of an oil-fired marine power plant, Turbinia (Govindaraj, Su, Vasandani, & Recker, 1996; Recker, Govindaraj, & Vasandani, 1998). Important in such simulations is that they illustrate both epistemic (structure of knowledge) fidelity and fidelity of interaction (Recker et al., 1998, p. 134). That is, the exercise should enable students to develop strategies that are consonant with the demands of real-world situations (reality of function).

The simulation models approximately 100 components of the power plant and illustrates the hierarchical representation of subsystems, components, and primitives, as well as the necessary physical and logical linkages. However, the physical fidelity is rather low.

The simulation also is accompanied by an intelligent tutoring system, Vyasa. The reason is that the purpose of the simulation is to teach diagnosing strategies and not to serve as a culminating exercise after the acquisition of basic knowledge of system faults and corrective actions. Results indicated that the less efficient students viewed more gauges and components than the efficient problem solvers. Students also seemed to implement a strategy of confirming leading hypotheses instead of choosing tests that served to disconfirm a maximum number of possible hypotheses (Recker et al., 1998, p. 150).

21.3.4 Discussion

Both experiential and symbolic simulations continue to be developed in different subject areas to meet different needs. Areas that deliver patient or client services implement simulations in which students diagnose and manage individuals' problems.

Business education, in contrast, relies on team exercises in which students manage the finances of a company or institution. Implementation of simulations in both these areas identifies students' strengths and weaknesses in planning, executing, and monitoring their approaches to solving complex problems. Similarly, research in symbolic simulations that require troubleshooting also indicates differences between effective and less effective problem solvers. One is that less effective problem solvers check a greater number of indicators (such as dials and gauges) than effective problem solvers.

Of importance for each type of simulation are the design and development of exercises with high fidelity. Required are (1) a qualitative or quantitative model of the relationships among events in the simulation, and (2) materials and required actions of participants that result in a realistic approximation of a complex reality. Hypermedia combined with video images, for example, can be used to develop virtual field trips that serve as preparatory research experiences for students (simulations). Similarly, hundreds of photographs of subtle changes in the movements or actions of laboratory-research subjects, properly programmed, can provide laboratory settings that are highly responsive to students' research designs. In contrast, photographs and video clips accompanied by explanatory information that provide a guided tour can be a useful experience, but the product is not a simulation. An example is The Digital Field Trip to the Rainforest, described by Poland (1999).

One concern for simulation design is the general conclusion that there is no clear outcome in favor of simulations (de Jong & van Joolingen, p. 181). This inference, however, does not refer to the conception of simulations that addresses the nature of the deep structure of the exercise. Instead, it refers to discrete problems with simulated materials where the student is required to engage in "scientific discovery learning" to infer the relationship between particular input variables and an outcome variable. The high cognitive load imposed on students by learning about implementing the processes of scientific discovery learning while also attempting to learn about a relationship among two variables has led to the introduction of intelligent tutoring systems to assist students. However, as indicated in the following section, instructional theory supports other alternatives that can enhance learning and contribute to the meaningfulness of the exercise for students.

21.4 DESIGN AND RESEARCH ISSUES

The early uses of simulations for military and political planning bridged the gap between the conference room and the real world. Initial expansions of simulations, particularly in business and medical education, also were designed to bridge the gap between textbook problems in the classroom and the ill-structured problems of the real world. In these exercises, participants are expected to apply their knowledge in the subject area to complex evolving problems. In other words, these simulations are culminating experiences; they are not devices to teach basic information.

In contrast, the development of interactive exercises in science education, some of which are referred to as simulations, take on the task of teaching basic content. Not surprisingly, the few comparison studies reported no differences between the classes using the computer-based exercises and control classes. These findings lend support to Clark's (1994) observation that methods, not media, are the causal factors in learning.

From the perspective of design, the key issue for developers involves two questions: Does the simulation meet the criteria for the type of exercise (symbolic or experiential)? and What is the purpose of the simulation? If the simulation is to be a culminating experience that involves the application of knowledge, then instruction must ensure that students acquire that knowledge. Research into the role of students' topic and domain knowledge indicates that it is a major factor in subsequent student learning (see, e.g., Alexander, Kulikowich, & Jetton, 1994; Dochy, Segers, & Buhl, 1999).

Interactive exercises that expect the student to infer the characteristics of a domain and to implement discovery learning face more serious difficulties. In the absence of prior instruction on conducting research in open-ended situations, the potential for failure is high. de Jong and van Joolingen (1998) note that student difficulties include inappropriate hypotheses, inadequate experimental designs, including experiments that are not intended to test a hypothesis, inaccurate encoding of data, misinterpretation of graphs, and failure to plan systematically and monitor one's performance. Hints can be provided to students during the exercise. However, this tactic of providing additional support information raises the question of what students are actually learning. Also, Butler and Winne (1995) report that students frequently do not make good use of the available information in computer exercises. Moreover, the practice of relying on hints and other information during the student's interactions with the domain runs the risk of teaching students to guess the answers the exercise expects. In that event, the exercise does not reinforce thoughtful, problem-solving behavior.

Prior to student engagement in a simulation, instruction should model and teach the expected research skills, which include planning, executing the experiment and collecting data, and evaluating (de Jong & van Joolingen, 1998, p. 180). In this way, students can acquire the capabilities needed to develop conceptual models of an aspect of a domain and test them in a systematic way. Davidson and Sternberg (1998), Gredler (2001), Holyoak (1995), and Sternberg (1998), for example, address the importance of this course of action in developing both metacognitive expertise (planning, monitoring, and evaluating one's thinking) and cognitive skills. A second reason for modeling and teaching the research skills first is to avoid the problem referred to by Sweller, van Merrienbaer, and Paas (1998, p. 262) as extraneous cognitive load. In such a situation, the limits of students' working memory are exceeded by inadequate instructional design.

Explicit teaching of these capabilities prior to engagement in a simulation is important for another reason. Specifically, it is that learners cannot develop advanced cognitive and self-regulatory capabilities unless they develop conscious awareness of their own thinking (Vygotsky, 1998a, 1998b). This theoretical principle addresses directly the concern of some researchers who note that students interacting with a simulation environment appear to be thinking metacognitively in discussions with their partners, but these skills are not evident in posttests. Students' lack of awareness of the import of a particular observation or happenstance strategy, however, may account for this phenomenon. That is, they are searching for solutions but are not focusing on their thinking.

Finally, an important issue for both design and research is to examine the assumptions that are the basis for the design of interactive exercises. One, for example, is that discovery learning environments, such as simulation environments, should lead to knowledge that is qualitatively different from knowledge acquired from more traditional instruction (Swaak & de Jong, 2001, p. 284). Important questions are, What is the nature of the knowledge? and Why should this occur? For example, if the goal is to teach scientific reasoning, as Horowitz (1999) suggests, then simulations and the associated context must be developed carefully to accomplish that purpose. In other words, addressing the prior questions is important in order to explore the potential of simulations for both cognitive and metacognitive learning.

References

Adams, F. G., & Geczy, C. C. (1991). International economic policy simulation games on the microcomputer. *Social Sciences Computer Review, 9*(2), 191–201.

Alessi, S. M. (1988). Fidelity in the design in instructional simulations. *Journal of Computer-based Instruction, 15*(2), 40–49.

Alexander, P. A., Kulikowich, J. M., & Jetton, J. (1994). The role of subject-matter knowledge and interest in the processing of linear and non-linear texts. *Review of Educational Research, 64*(2), 201–252.

Allen, T. B. (1987). *War games.* New York: McGraw–Hill.

Alloway, T., Wilson, G., Graham, J., & Kramer, L. (2000). *Sniffy, the virtual rat.* Belmont, CA: Wadsworth.

Berven, N. L. (1985). Reliability of standardized case management simulations. *Journal of Counseling Psychology, 32,* 397–409.

Berven, N. L., & Scofield, M. E. (1980). Evaluation of clinical problem-solving skills through standardized case-management simulations. *Journal of Counseling Psychology, 27,* 199–208.

Bosworth, K. (1994). Computer games and simulations as tools to reach and engage adolescents in health promotion activities. *Computers in Human Services, 11,* 109–119.

Butler, D. L., & Winne, P. H. (1995). Feedback and self-regulated learning. *Review of Educational Research, 65*(3), 245–281.

Clark, R. E. (1994). Media will never influence learning. *Educational Technology, Research, and Development, 42*(2), 21–29.

Colle, H. A., & Green, R. (1996). Introductory psychology laboratories using graphic simulations of virtual subjects. *Behavior Research Methods, Instruments, and Computers, 28*(2), 331–335.

Cromby, J. J., Standen, P. J., & Brown, D. J. (1996). The potentials of virtual environments in the education and training of people with learning disabilities. *Journal of Intellectual Disability Research, 40*(6), 489–501.

Davidson, J., & Sternberg, R. (1998). Smart problem solving: How metacognition helps. In D. J. Hacker, J. Dunlosky, & A. C. Graesser (Eds.), *Metacognition in educational theory and practice* (pp. 47–68). Mahwah, NJ: Lawrence Erlbaum Associates.

Dede, C., Salzman, M., Loftin, R. B., & Ash, K. (2000). The design of virtual learning environments: Fostering deep understandings of complex scientific language. In M. J. Jacobson & R. B. Kozma (Eds.), *Innovations in science and mathematics education: Advanced designs for technology of learning* (pp. 361–413). Mahwah, NJ: Lawrence Erlbaum Associates.

de Jong, T., & van Joolingen, W. R. (1998). Scientific discovery learning with computer simulations of conceptual domains. *Review of Educational Research, 68*(2), 179–201.

Dochy, F., Segers, M., & Buehl, M. (1999). The relation between assessment practices and outcomes of studies: The case of research on prior knowledge. *Review of Educational Research, 69*(2), 145–186.

Doyle, S., Dodge, M., & Smith, A. (1998). The potential of web-based mapping and virtual reality technologies for modeling urban environments. *Computer, Environmental, and Urban Systems, 22*(2), 137–155.

Faria, A. J. (1998). Business simulation games: Current usage levels—An update. *Simulation and Gaming, 29,* 295–309.

Frame, M. W., Flanagan, C. D., Frederick, J., Gold, R., & Harris, S. (1997). You're in the hot seat: An ethical decision-making simulation for counseling students. *Simulation and Gaming, 28*(1), 107–115.

Govindaraj, T., Su, D., Vasandani, V., & Recker, M. (1996). Training for diagnostic problem solving in complex engineered systems: Modeling, simulation, and intelligent tutors. In W. Rouse (Ed.), *Human technology interaction in complex systems,* Vol. 8 (pp. 1–66). Greenwich, CT: JAI Press.

Graf, S. A. (1995). Three nice labs, no real rats: A review of three operant laboratory simulations. *The Behavior Analyst, 18*(2), 301–306.

Gredler, M. E. (1990). Analyzing deep structure in games and simulations. *Simulations/Games for Learning, 20*(3), 329–334.

Gredler, M. E. (1992). *Designing and evaluating games and simulations.* London: Kogan Page.

Gredler, M. E. (2001). *Learning and instruction: Theory into practice* (4th ed.). Upper Saddle River, NJ: Merrill/Prentice Hall.

Henderson, L., Klemes, J., & Eshet, Y. (2000). Just playing a game? Educational simulation software and cognitive outcomes. *Journal of Educational Computing Research, 22*(1), 105–129.

Holyoak, K. J. (1995). Problem solving. In E. E. Smith & D. N. Osherman (Eds.), *Thinking.* Cambridge, MA: MIT Press.

Horowitz, P. (1999). Designing computer models that teach. In W. Feurzig & N. Roberts (Eds.), *Modeling dynamic systems.* New York: Springer-Verlag.

Horowitz, P., & Christie, M. A. (2000). Computer-based manipulatives for teaching scientific reasoning: An example. In M. A. Jacobson & R. B. Kozma (Eds.), *Innovations in science and mathematics education: Advanced designs for technologies of learning* (pp. 163–191). Mahwah, NJ: Lawrence Erlbaum.

Jones, K. (1982). *Simulations in language teaching.* Cambridge: Cambridge University Press.

Jones, K. (1984). Simulations versus professional educators. In D. Jaques & E. Tippen (Eds.), *Learning for the future with games and simulations* (pp. 45–50). Loughborough, UK: SAGSET/Loughborough, University of Technology.

Jones, K. (1987). *Simulations: A handbook for teachers and trainers.* London: Kogan Page.

Keys, J. B. (1997). Strategic management games: A review. *Simulation and Gaming, 28*(4), 395–422.

McGuire, C., Solomon, L. M., & Bashook, P. G. (1975). *Construction and use of written simulations.* Houston, TX: The Psychological Corporation.

Mayer, R., & Wittrock, M. (1996). Problem-solving transfer. In D. C. Berliner & R. C. Calfee (Eds.), *Handbook of educational psychology* (pp. 47–62). New York: Macmillan Library References.

Neal, D. J. (1997). Group competitiveness and cohesion in a business simulation. *Simulation and Gaming, 28*(4), 460–476.

Peat, M., & Fernandez, A. (2000). The role of information technology in biology education: An Australian perspective. *Journal of Biological Education, 34*(2), 69–73.

Peterson, D. B. (2000). Clinical problem solving in micro-case management: Computer-assisted instruction for information-gathering strategies in rehabilitation counseling. *Rehabilitation Counseling Bulletin, 43*(2), 84–96.

Poland, R. (1999). The digital field trip to the rainforest. *Journal of Biological Education, 34*(1), 47–48.

Ramnarayan, S., Strohschneider, S., & Schaub, H. (1997). Trappings of expertise and the pursuit of failure. *Simulation and Gaming, 28*(1), 28–43.

Recker, M. M., Govindaraj, T., & Vasandani, V. (1998). Student diagnostic strategies in a dynamic simulation environment. *Journal of Interactive Learning Research, 9*(2), 131–154.

Rieber, L. P. (1996). Seriously considering play: Designing interactive learning environments based on the blending of microworlds, simulations, and games. *Educational Technology, Research, and Development, 44*(2), 43–58.

Rieber, L. P., & Parmley, M. W. (1995). To teach or not to teach? Comparing the use of computer-based simulations in deductive versus inductive approaches to learning with adults in science. *Journal of Educational Computing Research, 13* (4), 359–374.

Ronen, M., & Eliahu, M. (1998). Simulation as a home learning environment—Students' views. *Journal of Computer Assisted Learning, 15*(4), 258–268.

Ronen, M., & Eliahu, M. (2000). Simulation—A bridge between theory and reality: The case of electric circuits. *Journal of Computer Assisted Learning, 16,* 14–26.

Sauer, J., Wastell, D. G., & Hockey, G. R. J. (2000). A conceptual framework for designing microworlds for complex work domains: A case study of the Cabin Air Management System. *Computers in Human Behavior, 16,* 45–58.

Shimoff, E., & Catania, A. C. (1995). Using computers to teach behavior analysis. *The Behavior Analyst, 18*(2), 307–316.

Spicer, J. J., & Stratford, J. (2001). Student perceptions of a virtual field trip to replace a real field trip. *Journal of Community Assisted Learning, 17,* 345–354.

Standen, P. J., & Cromby, J. J. (1996). Can students with developmental disability use virtual reality to learn skills which will transfer to the real world? In H. J. Murphy (Ed.), *Proceedings of the Third International Conference on Virtual Reality and Persons with Disabilities.* Northridge: California State University Center on Disabilities.

Sternberg, R. (1998). Abilities are forms of developing expertise. *Educational Researcher, 27*(3), 11–20.

Swaak, J., & de Jong, T. (2001). Discovery simulations and the assessment of intuitive knowledge. *Journal of Computer Assisted Learning, 17,* 284–294.

Sweller, J., van Merrienbaer, J., & Paas, F. (1998). Cognitive architecture and instructional design. *Educational Psychology Review, 10*(3), 251–296.

Thomas, R., & Neilson, I. (1995). Harnessing simulations in the service of education: The Interact simulation environment. *Computers and Education, 25*(1/2), 21-29.

Thompson, G. H., & Dass, P. (2000). Improving students' self-efficacy in strategic management: The relative impact of cases and simulations. *Simulation and Gaming, 31*(1), 22-41.

van Joolingen, W. R., & de Jong, T. (1996). Design and implementation of simulation-based discovery environments: The SMISLE solution. *Journal of Artificial Intelligence in Education, 7*(3/4), 253-276.

van Ments, M. (1984). Simulation and game structure. In D. Thatcher & J. Robinson (Eds.). *Business, health and nursing education* (pp. 51-58). Loughborough, UK: SAGSET.

Vygotsky, L. S. (1998a). Development of higher mental functions during the transitional age. In R. W. Rieber (Ed.), *Child psychology. The collected works of L. S. Vygotsky, Vol. 5* (pp. 83-149). New York: Plenum.

Vygotsky, L. S. (1998b). Development of thinking and formation of concepts in adolescence. In R. W. Rieber (Ed.), *Child psychology. The collected works of L. S. Vygotsky, Vol. 5* (pp. 29-81). New York: Plenum.

Warburton, J., & Higgitt, M. (1997). Improving the preparation for fieldwork with 'IT': Two examples from physical geography. *Journal of Geography in Higher Education, 21*(3), 333-347.

White, B. Y., & Fredericksen, J. R. (2000). Technological tools and instructional approaches for making scientific inquiry accessible to all. In M. J. Jacobson & R. B. Kozma (Eds.), *Innovations in science and mathematics education* (pp. 321-359). Mahwah, NJ: Lawrence Erlbaum.

Wolfe, J., & Rogé, J. N. (1997). Computerized management games as strategic management learning environments. *Simulations and Gaming, 28*(4), 423-441.

MICROWORLDS

Lloyd P. Rieber
The University of Georgia

22.1 MICROWORLDS

The introduction and spread of computer technology in schools since about 1980 have led to a vast assortment of educational software. Most of this software is instructional in nature, based on the paradigm of "explain, practice, and test." However, another, much smaller collection of software, known as *microworlds,* is based on very different principles, those of invention, play, and discovery. Instead of seeking to give students knowledge passed down from one generation to the next as efficiently as possible, the aim is to give students the resources to build and refine their own knowledge in personal and meaningful ways. The epistemology underlying microworlds is known as constructivism (Jonassen, 1991b). Once considered a peripheral movement in education, constructivist approaches to learning and education are now more widely endorsed and increasingly viable, due largely to advances in computer technology. While not negating the role of instruction, constructivist perspectives place central importance on a person's interaction in a domain and the relationship of this interaction with the person's prior knowledge.[1] A constructivist learning environment is characterized by students learning through active engagement, with encouragement, support, and resources to enable them to construct and communicate what they know and how they know it to others in a social context (Tinker & Thornton, 1992).

Constructivist approaches are not new to education. The progressive education ideals of John Dewey (e.g., 1916) are but one example. One of the reasons for the success of constructivist influences in education today, and perhaps the lack of success by Dewey in the first half of the twentieth century, is the widespread availability of resources that lead to rich explorations within a domain. Until only recently, it was not possible to give all students the kinds of interactive experiences in complex domains such as mathematics, physics, and biology that permit them to explore and invent in ways similar to those of mathematicians, physicists, and biologists. The technology of paper and pencil is limited to textual explanations and static drawings, thus limiting the way in which a domain can be represented and experienced. Historically, differential equations were the principal tool scientists used to study dynamic models. Such limits in representation likewise limit access to a domain's most advanced ideas to those few fortunate individuals who either have learning or metacognitive styles that are aligned with those representations or enjoy a socioeconomic status with resources and attitudes that offset such limitations to learning (Eccles & Wigfield, 1995). But the technology of computers affords a wider array of representations and experiences as well as greater availability to more people, beginning with even very young children (Resnick, 1999).

The purpose of this chapter is to review the theory and research of microworlds. The microworld literature can be confusing at times, making it difficult to distinguish microworlds from other forms of interactive software. Indeed, the term *microworld* is not used consistently even by members within the constructivist community itself. Other terms often used are *computational media* (diSessa, 1989), *interactive simulations* (White, 1992), *participatory simulations* (Wilensky & Stroup, 2002), and *computer-based manipulatives* (Horwitz & Christie, 2002). Therefore, different interpretations are reviewed, with the goal of teasing out essential characteristics of microworlds— theoretical and physical—and their relationship to other computer environments with which they are frequently compared and confused, such as computer-based simulations. Many issues remain contentious among those in the microworld community,

---

[1]Many people who ascribe to these learning principles do not necessarily characterize themselves as constructivists. See other chapters in this book for examples. Regardless, microworlds are rightly placed within a constructivist framework, if only for historical reasons.

such as model using versus model building (Feurzeig & Roberts, 1999; Penner, 2000/2001) and encouraging the use of computational media (i.e., those that require programming structures) versus tools with icon-based, or "point and click," interfaces (diSessa, Hoyles, Noss, & Edwards, 1995a).

Yet there is strong consensus on several key points within virtually all of the microworld literature. Computer-based microworlds offer the means to allow a much greater number of people, starting at a much younger age, to understand highly significant and applicable concepts and principles underlying all complex systems (e.g., White & Frederiksen, 1998). Two scientific principles deserve special mention: the vast array of rate of change problems common to all dynamic systems (Ogborn, 1999; Roschelle, Kaput, & Stroup, 2000) and decentralized systems, such as economics, ecosystems, ant colonies, and traffic jams (to name just a few), which operate on the basis of local objects or elements following relatively simple rules as they interact, rather than being based on a centralized leader or plan (Resnick, 1991, 1999). Qualitative understanding based on building and using concrete models is valued and encouraged. Indeed, many feel that the distinction between the classic concrete and the formal operations of Piaget's developmental learning theory becomes blurred and less important when students are given ready access and guidance in the use of computer-based microworlds (Ogborn, 1999). Finally, there is a reduction in the distance among learning science, doing science, and thinking like a scientist. Learning based on scientific inquiry is championed throughout the literature (again, for an example, see White & Frederiksen, 1998).

An historical context is used in this review due to the way in which advances in computer technology have directly influenced the development of microworlds. This review begins with work reported around 1980 and proceeds up to the present. The year 1980 is chosen for two reasons. First, it marks a profound juncture of education and technology—the approximate arrival and spread of the personal computer in homes and the classroom. This was the time at which the Apple computer company had begun aggressively marketing personal computers to education. The Apple II had just been introduced. The time was marked by a fascination with and enthusiasm about the potential of technology in education. Although serious work in educational computing had begun in the 1960s, the advent of the personal computer around 1980 made it possible for the first time for public-school educators to use a computer in the average classroom.

Second, the year 1980 marked the publication of a controversial book by Seymour Papert—*Mindstorms*—that offered a very different vision of education afforded by the burgeoning technology. In contrast to the emphasis on computer-assisted instruction that had dominated computer-based education up to that time (e.g., Suppes, 1980), Papert's vision focused on turning the power of the computer over to students, even those in elementary school, through computer programming. Although many computer languages were commonly used in schools around 1980, such as Pascal and BASIC, Papert and a team of talented individuals out of the Massachusetts Institute of Technology and Bolt, Baranek, and Newman began developing a radically different programming language in 1968, with

support from the National Science Foundation, based on a procedural language called Lisp (short for list processing) (Feurzeig et al., 1969; cited in Abelson, 1982). They called their new language Logo, derived from the Greek word meaning "thought" or "idea." Logo was distinguishable from other languages by how its design was influenced by a particular philosophy of education:

Logo is the name for a philosophy of education and for a continually evolving family of computer languages that aid its realization. Its learning environments articulate the principle that giving people personal control over powerful computational resources can enable them to establish intimate contact with profound ideas from science, from mathematics, and from the art of intellectual model building. Its computer languages are designed to transform computers into flexible tools to aid in learning, in playing, and in exploring. (Abelson, 1982, p. ix)

Logo was particularly distinguished from other programming languages by its use of turtle geometry. Users, as young as preschoolers, successfully learned to communicate with an object called a "turtle," commanding it to move around the screen or on the floor using commands such as FORWARD, BACK, LEFT, and RIGHT. As the turtle moved, it could leave a trail, thus combining the user's control of the computer with geometry and aesthetics. Logo was deliberately designed to map onto a child's own bodily movements in space. By encouraging children to "play turtle," thousands of children learned to control the turtle successfully in this way.

Of course, many other microworlds have become available since 1980. Besides Logo, this chapter reviews other examples in detail, including Boxer (diSessa, Abelson, & Ploger, 1991), ThinkerTools (White, 1993), SimCalc (Roschelle et al., 2000), and GenScope (Horwitz & Christie, 2000). However, because the goal of this chapter is to review research associated with microworlds in education, lengthy technical descriptions of these programs have been omitted. Other examples of microworlds not specifically examined in this chapter include Model-IT (Jackson, Stratford, Krajcik, & Soloway, 1996; Spitulnik, Krajcik, & Soloway, 1999), StarLogo (Resnick, 1991, 1999), Geometer's Sketchpad (Olive, 1998), Function Machine (Feurzeig, 1999), and Stella (Forrester, 1989; Richmond & Peterson, 1996). The work cited in this chapter represents just a fraction of the work that has been carried out in this area. Although microworld research and development is approaching 40 years of sustained effort (if you begin with Logo's emergence in the mid-1960s), it remains fresh and intriguing, advancing in step with the technology that supports it. Whether microworlds and the pedagogy that underlies them will eventually become a dominant approach in schools remains, unfortunately, a question left to speculation.

Research with microworlds has occurred during an interesting and somewhat tumultuous time in the history of educational research. Since 1980, educational research has broadened considerably to include a wide range of acceptable research methodologies. When researchers first took an interest in studying Logo, educational research was strongly dominated by quantitative, experimental research. In contrast, many of the early reports on Logo were anecdotal while, at the same time, written with enthusiasm about the technology's capabilities and potential, leading to hypish claims for their power and utility.

For example, Logo advocates suggested that it would "revolutionize" education, claims that now have the benefit of 20 years of scrutiny. These early promises, associated with data lacking scientific rigor, led to unfortunate battle lines being drawn between proponents and opponents of using microworlds and other constructivist approaches in education (an example is Tetenbaum & Mulkeen, 1984). Contemporary educational research has slowly shifted to accept alternative methods, mostly qualitative, led in part by technology-driven interpretations of the science of learning. Microworld research particularly is characterized by a history of multiple methods, of which the "design experiment" is the newest to be recognized (Barab & Kirshner, 2001; Brown, 1992; Collins, 1992; Edelson, 2002). The recent rise and formalization of design experiments are discussed later in this chapter.

22.1.1 Historical Origins of the Microworld Concept

The formal conception of a microworld, at least that afforded by computer technology, can be traced at least as far back as a chapter by Seymour Papert (1980a) in a seminal book edited by Robert Taylor entitled *The Computer in the School: Tutor, Tool, Tutee*. Papert's contribution was to the "tutee" section, that of the "computer as learner," or computer programming.[2] Papert (1980a) first defined a microworld as a

...subset of reality or a constructed reality whose structure matches that of a given cognitive mechanism so as to provide an environment where the latter can operate effectively. The concept leads to the project of inventing microworlds so structured as to allow a human learner to exercise particular powerful ideas or intellectual skills. (p. 204)

Papert clearly tried to establish the idea that a microworld is based to a large degree on the way in which an individual is able to use a technological tool for the kinds of thinking and cognitive exploration that would not be possible without the technology. In his chapter, Papert also made it clear that the concept of a microworld was not new and related the idea to the longstanding use of math manipulatives, such as Cuisenaire rods. But Papert predicted that the availability of microcomputation offered the potential for radically different learning environments to be created and adopted throughout schools. Given the benefit of more than 20 years of educational hindsight, it is tempting to be amused at Papert's naiveté. After all, the history of educational technology is filled with examples of new technologies promising similar opportunities to transform education (Saettler, 1990). Yet Papert's focus on the individual learner as contributing to the definition of a microworld distinguishes his idealism from most of the other educational innovations that had already come and gone (Cuban, 1986, 2001).

The publication of *Mindstorms* in 1980 had a large impact on educational thinking and even a modest influence on educational practice—Logo classes for teachers filled to capacity in colleges of education across the country. This was due,

again, partly to the confluence of education and technology at that time in history—there was little else available in the just-emerging educational computing curriculum. But *Mindstorms* laid out a compelling and provocative account of how computers might be used as part of the learning enterprise. It harshly criticized everything traditional in education and computing. Papert (1980b) took issue with most forms of formal instruction and imagined the computer providing a source of learning experiences that would allow a child to learn in ways that were natural and not forced:

It is not true to say that the image of a child's relationship with a computer I shall develop here goes far beyond what is common in today's schools. My image does not go beyond: It goes in the opposite direction. (p. 5)

On one hand, Papert's criticism might have helped polarize discussions about the role of technology in education, leading to factions for and against Logo, and hence for and against constructivist approaches to learning, in the schools. It could even be argued that such polarizations slowed the adoption of technology in general in schools. On the other hand, Papert's insistence that the learning environments represented by Logo offered something entirely new helped clarify differences between merely assimilating the affordances of computers into the conventional curricula and teaching approaches and changing how education happens given technology.

Despite the apparent radicalism in these early writings, Papert, unlike others writing about Logo, was not fanatical, only provocative. Though naive about education, he was not naive about learning and a learner's need for support structures. For example, he makes one other interesting point in his chapter in Taylor's book, that of how a microworld must contain design boundaries:

The use of the microworlds provides a model of a learning theory in which active learning consists of exploration by the learner of a microworld sufficiently bounded and transparent for constructive exploration and yet sufficiently rich for significant discovery. (Papert, 1980a, p. 208)

This is a telling statement because it foreshadows much of the later controversy over the role and nature of the boundaries of microworld design and whether *instructional* design could assume any place in it. While it demonstrates the importance Papert placed on exploration and discovery learning, it also shows his early acceptance of the need for a teacher or a microworld designer to identify boundaries for learning, thus contradicting the many criticisms made over the years thereafter that Papert thought that education and learning should be a "free for all" without guidance or interventions. Papert may be guilty of underestimating the difficulty of designing such boundaries, especially identifying where the boundaries lie for a particular child in a particular domain, but he certainly recognized

---

[2]Papert (1980b) later included a revised and longer version of this chapter in the provocative book *Mindstorms*. Although it is in *Mindstorms* that Papert more forcefully argued for a microworld to be a legitimate alternative learning environment to that of traditional classroom practice, I find Papert's writing in Taylor's book to be much clearer and more direct.

the need for guidance, both in the microworld itself and in the teacher's assistance to a child using it. As Papert (1980a) writes,

The construction of a network of microworlds provides a vision of education planning that is in important respects "opposite" to the concept of "curriculum." This does not mean that no teaching is necessary or that there are no "behavioral objectives." But the relationship of the teacher to learner is very different: the teacher introduces the learner to the microworld in which discoveries will be made, rather than to the discovery itself. (p. 209)

In his book *The Children's Machine,* published over a decade later, in 1993, Papert continued to explore the issue of the use and misuse of the "curriculum" and the teacher's pivotal role in the learning enterprise. Papert admitted to having little contact with teachers before *Mindstorms* and believed that teachers would be among the most difficult obstacles in transforming education given the technology. He expected very few teachers to read it. However, at the time hundreds of thousands of teachers *were* reading it, giving him a "passport into the world of teachers" (Papert, 1993), and helped change his earlier conceptions:

... My identification of "teacher" with "School" slowly dissolved into a perception of a far more complex relationship. The shift brought both a liberating sense that the balance of forces was more favorable to change than I had supposed and, at the same time, a new challenge to understand the interplay of currents in the world of teachers that favor change and that resist it. Finding ways to support the evolution of these currents may be among the most important contributions one can make to promote educational change. (p. 59)

According to Papert (1980b), the proper use of the computer for learning was in the child's total appropriation of it via learning to program:

Once programming is seen in the proper perspective, there is nothing very surprising about the fact that this should happen. Programming a computer means nothing more than communicating to it in a language that it and the human user can both "understand." And learning languages is one of the things children do best. Every normal child learns to talk. Why then should a child not learn to "talk" to a computer? (pp. 5-6)

For Papert, the difficulties in learning to program a computer stemmed not from the difficulty of the task, but from the lack of context of learning to do so, especially in the programming means available to the child. Not surprisingly, Papert, educated as a mathematician, was interested in finding ways for children to learn mathematics as naturally as they acquired language early in life. Similar to the idea that the best way to learn Spanish is to go and live in Spain, Papert conjectured that learning mathematics via Logo was similar to having students visit a computerized Mathland where the inhabitants (i.e., the turtle) speak only Logo. And because mathematics is the language of Logo, children would learn mathematics naturally by using it to communicate to the turtle. In Mathland, people do not just study mathematics, according to Papert, they "live" mathematics.

Papert's (1980a) emphasis on the learner's interaction with a microworld was rooted in Piagetian learning theory:[3]

The design of microworlds reflects a position in genetic epistemology: in particular a structuralist and constructivist position derived from Piaget that attaches great importance to the influence on the developed forms of the developmental path. (p. 208)

Interestingly, of the two principal parts of Piaget's developmental learning theory, Papert focused a great deal on one and almost ignored the second (Clements, 1989). He emphasized the stage-independent part of Piaget's theory, based on the process of equilibration, and the enabling mechanisms of assimilation and accommodation. In contrast, little attention was given to the stage-dependent part of Piaget's theory, suggesting that all people follow an invariant progression of intellectual development from birth, starting with the sensorimotor and ending with formal operations. Indeed, Papert and his colleagues felt that too much of formal education valued the formal and abstract, and too little valued the concrete.

Experience with any of the microworlds described in this chapter will lead one to see that all microworlds directly support acquiring a qualitative understanding of a problem in terms that are developmentally appropriate for a child, yet also are clearly connected to the formal, rigorous mathematics side of the domain. This value placed on the concrete and qualitative aspects of understanding permeates all of the microworld literature to the present day (see Papert's [1993, p. 148] criticism of the "supervaluation of the abstract"). This is consistent with long-standing research that indicates that novices and experts often use a qualitative approach to solve problems (Chi, Feltovich, & Glaser, 1981). Papert did not undervalue the formal and abstract side of a domain but, rather, tried to bring up to at least an equal standing the importance of an individual being able to connect to the domain through concrete, qualitative means.

Using language from Piaget's work, Papert referred to the use of the turtle as a "transitional" object, connecting what the child already knows to the domain of geometry. This is made possible by the fact that the child, like the turtle, has two attributes in common—a position and a heading. For example, a child can "play turtle" to figure out how to make the turtle draw a circle by first walking in a circle and describing the activity. The child soon learns that a circle is made by repeating a pattern of moving forward a little, followed by turning a little. Thinking of a curve in this fashion is a fundamental concept of differential calculus. Transitional objects become more sophisticated over time. A professional mathematician will construct diagrams for exactly the same purpose (which, for Papert, are also examples of microworlds). But, in all cases, such use of microworlds can be viewed as "genetic stepping stones" (Papert, 1980b, p. 206) from the learner's current understanding (without the microworld) to the internalization of powerful ideas (differential calculus) with the help of the microworld.

Mindstorms contained several fundamental ideas that continue to thrive in the vocabulary and thinking of current constructivist conceptions of learning. Among the most profound is the idea of an *object to think with,* the Logo turtle, of course, being a prime example. Thus, the turtle becomes a way for the child to grapple with mathematical ideas usually considered

[3]Papert spent 5 years studying with Piaget in Geneva, Switzerland.

too difficult or abstract. A prime role served by the turtle is the way it "concretizes" abstract ideas. A classic example is when a child learns that the number "360" has special properties in geometric space. Making a square by repeating four times the commands FORWARD 50 RIGHT 90 shows a concrete relationship between the square and 360. This idea can be expanded so that all other regular polygons can be constructed by dividing 360 by the number of sides desired.

Another important microworld idea is that of *debugging*. While obviously rooted in the process of computer programming, debugging is really concerned about learning from one's mistakes. Unlike conventional education, where errors are to be avoided at all costs, errors in problem-solving tasks such as programming are unavoidable and therefore expected. Errors actually become a rich source of information, without which a correct solution could not be found. The use of an external artifact, such as a computational microworld, as an object to think with to extend our intellectual capabilities, coupled with a learning strategy of expecting and using errors made as a route to successful problem solving, is an integral part of all contemporary learning theories (Norman, 1993; Salomon, Perkins, & Globerson, 1991).

So, as we have seen in this brief historical overview, the concept of a microworld became firmly established as a place for people of all ages to explore in personally satisfying ways complex ideas from domains usually considered intellectually inaccessible to them. These same ideas continue to be championed today, as the following contemporary definition of a microworld by Andy diSessa (2000), one of constructivism's most vocal and articulate advocates since Papert, shows:

A microworld is a genre of computational document aimed at embedding important ideas in a form that students can readily explore. The best microworlds have an easy-to-understand set of operations that students can use to engage tasks of value to them, and in doing so, they come to understanding powerful underlying principles. You might come to understand ecology, for example, by building your own little creatures that compete with and are dependent on each other. (p. 47)

Of all the possible definitions of a microworld, perhaps the most elegant comes from Clements (1989): "A microworld is a small playground of the mind" (p. 86). In the next section, we consider characteristics of microworlds that provide playful opportunities for learning.

22.2 GENERAL CHARACTERISTICS OF MICROWORLDS

So, what makes a microworld a microworld? Is it a collection of software components or characteristics, or something more? Microworlds are part of a larger set or approach to education known as *exploratory learning* (diSessa, Hoyles, Noss, & Edwards, 1995a). All exploratory learning approaches are based on the following four principles: (a) Learners can and should take control of their own learning; (b) knowledge is rich and multidimensional; (c) learners approach the learning task in very diverse ways; and (d) it is possible for learning to feel

natural and uncoaxed, that is, it does not have to be forced or contrived. These are idealistic pursuits, to say the least. These principles lead to some interesting educational outcomes or issues. For example, there is no "best approach" to teach something (at least for all but the most narrow of skill sets), nor is there a "best way" to learn. The goals of education should focus on complex learning outcomes, such as problem solving, where depth of understanding, not breadth of coverage, is valued. Furthermore, student learning should be based, at least partially, on student interests. This implies that adequate time and resources must be given to students to pursue ideas sufficiently before they are asked to move on to other educational goals. Another outcome is also very much implied: Support and resources for learning are equally diverse, coming in forms such as other people and the full range of technological innovations, including the computer, of course, but also paper and pencil. This, in turn, suggests a very social context for learning and it is expected that the personal interests of students will be tied to social situations.

There are many examples of interactive, exploratory learning environments in education. Examples include the range of hypertext and hypermedia (Jonassen, 1991a, 1992) (including the World Wide Web) and interactive multimedia (such as simulations and games). However, microworlds can be distinguished from other kinds of exploratory learning environments by their focus on immersive learning and their sensitive tuning to a person's cognitive and motivational states. It is debatable whether a software program can be rightly called a microworld based solely on the software's physical and design attributes. However, a structural view attempts to do just that by identifying a list of features, characteristics, or design attributes common to the category of software commonly labeled a microworld. Thus, if other software shares these features, one could rightly define it as a microworld. A microworld, using such a structural definition, would, according to Edwards (1995), consist of the following.

- A set of computational objects that model the mathematical or physical properties of the microworld's domain
- Links to multiple representations of the underlying properties of the model
- The ability to combine objects or operations in complex ways, similar to the idea of combining words and sentences in a language
- A set of activities or challenges that are inherent or preprogrammed in the microworld; the student is challenged to solve problems, reach a goal, etc.

While such *structural* affordances are important, the true tests of a microworld are *functional*—whether it provides a legitimate and appropriate doorway to a domain for a person in a way that captures the person's interest and curiosity (Edwards, 1995). In other words, for an interactive learning environment to be considered a microworld, a person must "get it" almost immediately—understand a simple aspect of the domain very quickly with the microworld—and then *want* to explore the domain further with the microworld (Rieber, 1996). Again, the analogy of choice for Papert was language learning because learning most math and science offers the same richness and complexity as learning a foreign language.

A functional view is based on the dynamic relationship among the software, the student, and the setting. Whether or not the software can be considered a microworld depends on this interrelationship when the software is actually used. Students are expected to be able to manipulate the objects and features of the microworld "with the purpose of inducing or discovering their properties and the functioning of the system as a whole" (Edwards, 1995, p. 144). Students are also expected to be able to interpret the feedback generated by the software based on their actions and modify the microworld to achieve their goal (i.e., debugging). And students are expected to "use the objects and operations in the microworld either to create new entities or to solve specific problems or challenges (or both)" (Edwards, 1995, p. 144).

Therefore, a microworld must be defined at the interface between an individual user in a social context and a software tool possessing the following five functional attributes:

- It is domain specific;
- it provides a doorway to the domain for the user by offering a simple example of the domain that is immediately understandable by the user;
- it leads to activity that can be intrinsically motivating to the user—the user wants to participate and persist at the task for some time;
- it leads to immersive activity best characterized by words such as play, inquiry, and invention; and
- it is situated in a constructivist philosophy of learning.

The fifth and final attribute demands that successful learning with a microworld assumes a conducive classroom environment with a very able teacher serving a dual role: teacher-as-facilitator and teacher-as-learner. The teacher's role is critical in supporting and challenging student learning while at the same time modeling the learning process with the microworld. It is important to note, perhaps surprisingly, that the principles of microworlds discussed in this section do not require that they be computer based. A child's sandbox with a collection of different-sized buckets can be considered a microworld for understanding volume. In mathematics, the use of manipulatives, such as Cuisenaire rods, can be a microworld for developing an understanding of number theory. But computational media provide unprecedented exploratory and experiential opportunities.

In summary, while both structures and functions of a microworld are important, a functional orientation is closer to the constructivist ideals of understanding interactions with technology from the learner's point of view. Of course, this means that the same software program may be a microworld for one person and not another. Microworlds can be classified as a type of cognitive tool in that they extend our limited cognitive abilities, similar to the way in which a physical tool, like a hammer or saw, extends our limited physical abilities (Jonassen, 1996; Salomon et al., 1991). However, microworlds are domain specific and carry curricular assumptions and pedagogical recommendations for how the domain, such as mathematics or physics, ought to be taught.

22.3 MICROWORLD RESEARCH WITH LOGO

To understand early research efforts involving Logo, one must understand the educational research climate at the time. Educational research around 1980 was dominated by experimental design. This, compounded with the long-standing view that media directly "affects" learning (for a summary see Clark, 1994, 2001; Kozma, 1994), led Papert to challenge the research questions being asked at the time and what methodologies were being used to generate, analyze, and interpret the data. Not surprisingly, Papert (1987) was critical of the controlled experiment in which everything except one variable is controlled and studied: "I shall argue that this is radically incompatible with the enterprise of rebuilding an education in which nothing shall be the same" (p. 22). He complained that criticism against the computer was "technocentric" in that it focused on the technology, not the student. Such a view likens computers and Logo to agents that act directly on thinking and learning and is characterized by research questions about the "effects" of computers or Logo on learning:

Consider for a moment some questions that are "obviously" absurd. Does wood produce good houses? If I built a house out of wood and it fell down, would this show that wood does not produce good houses? Do hammers and saws produce good furniture? These betray themselves as technocentric questions by ignoring people and the elements only people can introduce: skill, design, aesthetics. (Papert, 1987, p. 24)

Papert contended that these were similar to the kinds of questions being asked about the computer and Logo at the time (circa 1986). Logo, Papert (1987) said, was not like a drug being tested in a medical experiment but, instead, needed to be viewed as a cultural element: ". . . something that can be powerful when it is integrated into a culture but is simply isolated technical knowledge when it is not" (p. 24).

Papert (1987) sought to portray Logo as a "cultural building material" (p. 24). As an example, he presented the work of a teacher who had children "mess about with clocks" with the goal of trying to develop good ways to measure time. This teacher's science room was equipped with lots of everyday objects and materials—as well as computers. So the computer was just one more set of materials available to the students in their inquiry. For Papert, the way this teacher used Logo based on the students' own interests was in stark contrast to the kinds of uses of Logo that educational researchers were expecting to be studied. Papert (1987) believed that the computer must be viewed as part of the context or culture for human development: ". . . If we are interested in eliminating technocentrism from thinking about computers in education, we may find ourselves having to re-examine assumptions about education that were made long before the advent of computers" (p. 23).

Mainstream Logo research in the early 1980s was characterized by questions looking for "effects of Logo" on children's learning.[4] Probably the most careful and scholarly examples of this type of research were carried out by Douglas Clements, a mathematics educator at Kent State University. Clements conducted a series of Logo studies that investigated the effects of Logo programming on children's cognition, metacognition, and mathematical ability (examples include Clements [1984, 1986, 1987] and Clements & Gullo [1984]). He found that children working with Logo did, in fact, think differently about mathematics in deep and interesting ways. However, the results of research on whether this thinking transferred to non-Logo tasks were quite mixed. Again, the role of the teacher was central. For such transfer to occur, the teacher needed to create explicit links between the Logo activities and other mathematical activities. Clements (1987) showed that it was possible for master teachers to help students form broad mathematical understanding from their Logo activities.

In one particular study, often cited by early Logo enthusiasts, Clements studied the effects of learning Logo programming on children's cognitive style, metacognitive ability, cognitive development, and ability to describe directions. The goal was to look broadly for the types of influences that Logo programming was having on young children. He compared nine children who programmed with Logo for 12 weeks (two 40-min sessions per week) to another group of nine children who interacted with a variety of computer-assisted instruction (CAI) software packages. The rationale of such a comparison was that "...any benefits derived from computer programming can be attributed to interactive experiences with computers, rather than to the programming activity per se" (Clements & Gullo, 1984, p. 1052). It is easy to be confused today about what such a comparison would uncover, but it needs to be understood in the context of how new all of this technology was at the time. The study found very positive results favoring the Logo programming group. They outscored their CAI counterparts on virtually all measures (except cognitive development). Despite obvious methodological problems, such as the very limited sample size, Clements and Gullo concluded that the study provided evidence that programming may affect problem-solving ability and cognitive style.

Despite this positive outcome favoring Logo, Papert (1987) still felt that all such research missed the point as he critiqued the Clements and Gullo study and compared it to another done at Bank Street College (i.e., Pea & Kurland, 1984) that found negative results: "Both studies are flawed, though to very different extents, by inadequate recognition of the fact that what they are looking at, and therefore making discoveries about, is not programming but cultures that happen to have in common the presence of a computer and the Logo language" (p. 27). The work by Clements and his colleagues was carefully done

and well thought out, yet clearly at odds with the philosophical intent of Logo.[5]

Some of the most interesting microworld research also began in the early 1980s, that done by Barbara White and her colleagues. What is most noteworthy about White's work is its consistent themes, which continue to the present day. Her early research, done in collaboration with Andy diSessa, focused on middle-school students learning physics with the "dynaturtle." The dynaturtle was an extension of the familiar Logo turtle, except that in addition to position and heading, it had the attribute of velocity—it was a "dynamic" turtle. That work led to White's (1984) dissertation research, in which she developed a series of game-like physics activities for students to explore, using Logo as an authoring tool to create these activities. In the early 1990s, she was instrumental in developing ThinkerTools, a physics modeling program suitable for elementary- and middle-school students. Accompanying the tool itself was a well-crafted pedagogical approach based on scientific inquiry. The ThinkerTools software and curriculum have continually evolved. Thinker-Tools began by emphasizing how computer microworlds can facilitate learning physics and has evolved to emphasize helping students "to learn about the nature of scientific models and the process of scientific inquiry" (White & Frederiksen, 2000a, p. 321). Taken as a whole, it represents a thoughtful design and research effort. Another important aspect of White's work is the strong research program that has accompanied it. Her research results are widely cited by advocates of constructivist uses of computers.

Using the dynaturtle microworld, White conducted a series of investigations using a continually refined set of games that were designed to represent Newtonian motion phenomena clearly without unnecessary and distractive elements. Another goal was to help children focus on their own physics understanding in a reflective manner. The games she designed helped children to understand physics principles about which other research showed that they held firm misconceptions, such as the idea that objects eventually "run out of force." Interestingly, her research used a strong quantitative research methodology, comparing pretest and posttest scores of high-school students who used the computer games to those of a control group that did not. The results were very positive in favor of the dynaturtle games: Students who played the games improved their understanding of force and motion more than those who did not (White, 1984). Another interesting outcome of this line of research was the way it broadened the conception of a microworld from computer programming to interactions with "interactive simulations"[6] and modeling tools, of which ThinkerTools can be included as an example. We continue the discussion of Barbara White's work when we focus on ThinkerTools later in this chapter.

---

[4]For an additional review of early Logo research, see the chapter by Jonassen and Reeves in this volume.

[5]I had the same mindset as Clements at the time. I did a research project for my master's degree in 1983 that studied the "effects" of Logo (Rieber, 1987). It was a small study with limited exposure, yet I received over 300 requests for reprints, the most for any study I ever conducted. Such was the interest by the educational community in knowing more about what Logo was "doing to" our children.

[6]This particular study influenced my work to a great extent and led to my own research in the area of simulations and games (see Rieber, 1990, 1991; Rieber & Parmley, 1995).

22.3.1 The Emergence of a New Research Methodology: Design Experiments

The criticisms of educational research methodologies by Papert and many others in the Logo community led them to conduct field tests in cooperating schools. The formulation of partnerships between universities and schools with the desire to test a technological innovation without being restricted to the "rules" of prevalent research methods and curriculum constraints (i.e., not enough time and not enough resources) has become the preferred methodology of almost all of the microworld researchers and developers discussed in this chapter. The goal of all of these field tests is simultaneously to understand how the innovation works outside the team's rarefied development laboratories while also improving the innovation's design. This combination of a formative evaluation of the innovation (again, to improve it) and an analysis of the messy implementation process with real teachers and students has slowly led to a new research methodology called a *design experiment*. This research methodology, also referred to as design studies, design research, formative research, and development research (Richey & Nelson, 1996; van den Akker, 1999), differs from traditional educational research in which specific variables are rigidly controlled throughout an investigation. A design experiment sets a specific pedagogical goal at the beginning and then seeks to determine the necessary organization, strategies, and technological support necessary to reach the goal (Newman, 1990). Such experiments involve an iterative and self-correcting process that resolves problems as they occur. The process is documented to show what path was taken to achieve the goal, what problems were encountered, and how they were handled. Although the impact of an innovation on individual achievement is important, the unit of analysis in a design experiment is typically at the class or school level and includes social dynamics in the analysis. Vygotky's classic work on the zone of proximal development—what people can learn with and without aid—has been a clear influence on design experiments. Some of the first calls for design experiments in the early 1990s were based on the perceived need that technology would soon be adopted widely by schools, requiring a new methodology to cope with understanding what such implementation meant (Newman, 1990). Given the anticipated deluge, researchers needed to leave the laboratory and, instead, use schools themselves as their research venue.

In an early and seminal work, Collins (1992) described some of the problems and weaknesses of design experiments, at least as carried out up to that time. He cited the tendency for the researchers to be the designers of the innovation itself, hence being prone to bias due to their vested interest in seeing the innovation succeed. This also created the tendency to focus only on successful aspects of the innovation, with a temptation to exclude a wider examination of the innovation's use and implementation. The methodologies of design experiments varied widely, making it different to draw conclusions across the studies. Finally, design research is often carried out without a strong theoretical framework, thus making any results difficult to interpret. While the field has tried to solidify and elaborate on what a design experiment is and is not over the past decade, much remains to be done. It appears at present that design experiments are better viewed as explanatory frameworks for conducting research rather than clear methodologies.

In summary, the conceptual basis of design experiments and the methodology that is slowly emerging to accompany it appear to be aligned with the history and state of microworld research. Although the beginning articulation of design experiments is usually dated to the writings of Brown (1992), Collins (1992), and Newman (1990, 1992), its "unarticulated" use predates these early works by at least 10 years, as it characterizes the abundance of the field research using Logo. Much of the other research on the microworlds described in the remaining sections of this chapter also resonates with design experiments, though this work has been poorly documented, consisting of internal memos and anecdotal reports within conceptual or theoretical publications. Fortunately, the methodology of design experiments is beginning to be recognized by the educational research community at large. This acceptance, especially among research journal editors, is likely to create a small revolution in the way in which research with innovative technology and students is conducted.

22.4 GOING BEYOND LOGO: BOXER

Boxer, according to diSessa et al. (1991), "is the name for a multipurpose computational medium intended to be used by people who are not computer specialists. Boxer incorporates a broad spectrum of functions—from hypertext processing, to dynamic and interactive graphics, to databases and programming—all within a uniform and easily learned framework" (p. 3). Boxer's principal designer and advocate is Andy diSessa, of the University of California at Berkeley. Boxer's roots are closely tied to those of Logo. Boxer originated while diSessa was at MIT and part of the Logo team. Despite diSessa's admiration of Logo and what it represented, he soon became dissatisfied with Logo's limitations (Resnick's motivation to create StarLogo was based on similar dissatisfactions with Logo's limitations). For example, Logo, though an easy language to start using, is difficult to master. Children quickly learn how to use turtle geometry commands to draw simple shapes, such as squares and triangles, and even complex shapes consisting of a long series of turtle commands, but it is difficult for most children to progress to advanced features of the language, such as writing procedures, combining procedures, and using variables. Another drawback of Logo is that it is essentially just a computer programming language, a variant of LISP, though with special features, such as turtle geometry. It is difficult for students and teachers to learn Logo well enough to program it to do other meaningful things, such as journal keeping and database applications. Finally, although Logo enjoyed much success with elementary- and middle-school students, it was difficult to "grow up" using Logo for advanced computational problems. Similarly, Logo was rarely viewed by teachers as a tool that they should use for their own personal learning or professional tasks. (See diSessa [1997] for other examples of how its design transcends that of Logo.)

diSessa sought to design a new tool to overcome these difficulties by creating not just another programming language, but a "computational medium." Again, Boxer and Logo share much in common as to educational philosophy and purpose. However, Boxer was designed to take advantage of all that had been learned from observing children using Logo up to the time the Boxer research group was formed in 1981. It was meant as a successor to Logo, not just a variant.

Boxer was designed based on two major principles related to learning: concreteness and the use of a spatial metaphor. Concreteness implies that all aspects and functions of the system should be visible and directly manipulable. The use of a consistent spatial metaphor capitalizes on a person's spatial abilities for relating objects or processes. For example, the principal object is a box, hence the name Boxer. A box can contain any element or data structure, such as text, graphics, programs, or even other boxes. The use of boxes allows a person to use intuitive spatial relations such as "outside," "inside," and "next" directly in the programming. Like Logo, Boxer has gone through a slow and serious development cycle of about 15 years, with much of this work best characterized as design experiments. It has been available on typical desktop computers for only a short period of time. Although it is difficult to predict technology adoption within education, Boxer has the potential for wide-scale use within K–12 schools, especially given its ability to adapt and extend to encompass data types and teaching and learning styles. Unfortunately, the question of whether Boxer will be adopted widely in education will probably be decided by factors other than those related to learning and cognition. Other, simpler multimedia authoring tools, such as HyperStudio and PowerPoint, have been marketed very successfully, due in part to their fit to more traditional uses of technology in education. Interestingly, the latest versions of Logo, such as Microworlds Pro, have incorporated many mainstream multimedia features to compete effectively in the education market.

Boxer makes it easy for teachers and students to build small-scale microworlds in many domains. An interesting example of how children can appropriate Boxer in unexpected ways is described by Adams and diSessa (1991). In this study, they showed how a classroom of children used a motion microworld given to them. The microworld required the student to input three pieces of data, corresponding to the turtle's initial position, speed, and acceleration. For example, if the students entered the numbers 0, 4, 0, the turtle started at the 0 position on a number line at an initial speed of 4 distance units per second. Since the acceleration is 0 (the third number), the turtle moved at this uniform speed forever. If the student entered 1, 3, 2, the turtle started moving with an initial speed of 3 distance units per second from the 1 position on the number. However, the speed increased by 2 distance units each second, thus the speed of the turtle generated a list of velocities (e.g., 3, 5, 7, 9, 11, etc.) and positions (1, 4, 9, 16, 25, 36, etc.) in 1-sec increments. In many ways, such a microworld can be considered as a simple physics model that could be written with almost any programming, authoring, or modeling software. However, a difference with Boxer is that all elements of the model remain changeable or manipulable at all times. As part of their research on how students would develop in their understanding of physics and Boxer, Adams and diSessa (1991) gave these students a problem that, unknown to them, was impossible to solve. The problem was to enter the triplets of data for each

of two concurrently running turtles so that each would "pass" the other three times on the number line. There are no initial conditions that can be represented by these three numbers for each turtle that leads to such a motion. Transcripts of two students working on the problem showed their speculation that the problem could not be solved. But they soon wondered whether it was possible to alter the motion of the turtles directly by editing the velocity and position *lists* directly, thus bypassing the initial three data points. In a sense, such a direct method of manipulating the motion was cheating! However, Boxer allowed such a clever manipulation, thus also allowing the two students to reach a deeper understanding of motion. Adams and diSessa (1991) go on to describe how this technique was soon adopted by other students in the class, but through interesting negotiations with the teacher (i.e., it was permitted for difficult problems, but students were still expected to use the original method for simpler problems). Demonstrating the social dynamics of good ideas, Adams and diSessa (1991) explain: "This strategy spread in the classroom to become a communal resource for attacking the most difficult problems. The teacher and students negotiated ground rules for using these new resources productively. Although we did not plan this episode, we see it as an example of a kind of student-initiated learning that can emerge given a learning-oriented classroom and open technical designs" (pp. 88–89).

Boxer is interesting not only because of its own characteristics and affordances for learning, but also because of the history of its design within the microworld community. The roots of Boxer lie in criticisms and dissatisfactions with Logo, though diSessa and his colleagues are quick to respect all that Logo represents. Fortunately, they were willing to continue to "push the envelope" on the technology in ways that are consistent with the aims of Papert and other Logo pioneers. This is important because dissatisfaction with the state of microworld development is a powerful stimulus to improving it.

22.5 CONSTRUCTIONISM: MICROWORLD RESEARCH EVOLVES

Work with Logo in the constructivist community evolved beyond its philosophical roots in Piaget's constructivism to form a pedagogical approach called *constructionism*, a word coined by Papert (1991) to suggest another metaphor, that of "learning by building":

Constructionism—the N word as opposed to the V word—shares constructivism's connotation of learning as "building knowledge structures" irrespective of the circumstances of the learning. It then adds the idea that this happens especially felicitously in a context where the learner is engaged in constructing a public entity, whether it's a sand castle on the beach or a theory of the universe. (p. 1)

Constructionism is strongly rooted in student-generated projects. Projects offer a way critically to relate motivation and thinking and can be defined as "relatively long-term, problem-focused, and meaningful units of instruction that integrate concepts from a number of disciplines or fields of study"

(Blumenfeld et al., 1991, p. 370). Projects have two essential components: a driving question or problem and activities that result in one or more *artifacts* (Blumenfeld et al., 1991). Artifacts are "sharable and critiquable externalizations of students' cognitive work in classrooms" and "proceed through intermediate phases and are continuously subject to revision and improvement" (Blumenfeld et al., 1991, pp. 370–371).

It is important that the driving question not be overly constrained by the teacher. Instead, students need much room to create and use their own approaches to designing and developing the project. Projects, as external artifacts, are public representations of the students' solution. The artifacts, developed over time, reflect their understanding of the problem over time as well. In contrast, traditional school tasks, such as worksheets, have no driving question and, thus, no authentic purpose to motivate the student to draw or rally the difficult cognitive processes necessary for complex problem- solving.

A good example of an early constructionist research project was conducted by Harel and Papert (1990, 1991) as part of the Instructional Software Design Project (ISDP). This study is often cited among Logo and project-based learning proponents, so great attention to it is warranted here. The purpose of the ISDP was to give children the role of designer/producer of educational software rather than consumer of software. The research question of the study focused on ways in which children might use technology for their own purposes and how to facilitate children's reflection about what they are doing with technology. The study emphasized "developing new kinds of activities in which children can exercise their doing/learning/thinking" and "project activity which is self-directed by the student within a cultural/social context that offers support and help in particularly unobtrusive ways" (Harel & Papert, 1991, p. 42).

The study compared three classes: (a) 17 fourth-grade students who each worked with Logo for about 4 hr per week over a period of 15 weeks to design instructional software on fractions for use by another class (ISDP class); (b) 18 students who were also studying fractions and learning Logo, but not at the same time (control class 1); and (c) 16 students who were also studying fractions but not Logo (control class 2). Students were interviewed and tested on their understanding of fractions prior to the research. At the start of each work session, students in the ISDP group were required to spent 5–7 min writing their plans and drawing designs in their designer notebooks. The rest of the work session lasted approximately 50 min. Collaboration and sharing were encouraged. At the end of the session, students were required to write about problems and issues related to their projects confronted during the session. The projects were open-ended in the sense that students could choose whatever they wanted to design, teach, and program.

The study used both experimental and qualitative methodologies. All three classes were pretested on their knowledge of fractions and Logo. All students were then given a posttest at the end of the study. There were no significant differences among the three classes based on the pretest. During the study, observations (some videotaped) of and interviews with several students in the ISDP group were conducted, including an analysis of these students' designer notebooks and their finished

projects. All 51 students were interviewed before and after the study. Students in the ISDP group outperformed the other two groups on the fractions test: ISDP, 74%; control class 1, 66%; and control class 2, 56%. Similarly, the ISDP group also outperformed the other students on questions from a standardized mathematics test related to fractions and rational numbers. (It is important to note that the ISDP group had additional, though not formal, exposure to fractions via several focus-group sessions.)

The qualitative results focused on four issues: (a) development of concept, (b) appropriation of project, (c) rhythm of work, and (d) cognitive awareness and control. The children's early development of the concept of fractions was very rigid and spatial. Their understanding was limited to very specific prototypes, such as half of a circle. By the end of the project their understanding was much more generalized and connected to everyday objects, especially outside of school. Many children resisted the task of designing software about fractions, but they all soon appropriated the task for themselves. The openness of what could constitute a design helped with this, as well as the encouragement of socialization as part of the design work. The fact that the children had access to computers to do their work on a daily basis was very important. It allowed them to migrate between periods of intense work and periods of playful, social behavior. Students in the experimental class became very metacognitively aware of their designs and work habits. They developed "problem-finding" skills. They became aware of strategies to solve problems and also learned to activate them. They developed the ability to discard bad designs and to search for better ones. They learned to control distractions and anxiety. They learned how to practice continual evaluation of designs in a social setting. They learned to monitor their solution processes and were able to articulate their design tasks.

Harel and Papert (1991) strongly suggest that what made a difference here was not Logo or any particular group of strategies but, rather, that a "total learning environment" (p. 70) was created that permitted a culture of design work to flourish. They particularly point to the affective influences of this environment. These students developed a different "relationship with fractions" (p. 71), that is, they came to like fractions and saw the relevancy of this mathematics to their everyday lives. Many reported "seeing fractions everywhere." Harel and Papert resist any tendency to report the success as being "caused" by Logo. Instead, "learning how to program and using Logo enabled these students to become more involved in thinking about fractions knowledge" (p. 73). They point to Logo's allowing such constructions about fractions to take place. The ISDP put students in contact with the "deep structure" of rational-number knowledge, compared to the surface structure that most school curricula emphasize.

Despite the positive outcome of this early constructionist research and the enthusiastic reporting by Harel and Papert, successful project-based learning is not a panacea. Success is based on many critical assumptions or characteristics and failure in any one can thwart the experience. Examples include an appreciation of the complex interrelationship between learning and motivation, an emphasis on student-driven questions or problems, and the commitment of the teacher and his/her willingness to organize the classroom to allow the complexities of project-based learning to occur and be supported (Blumenfeld et al., 1991). Fortunately, the recent and continuing development of rich technological tools directly support both teachers and students in the creation and sharing of artifacts.

Students must be sufficiently motivated over a long period to gain the benefits of project-based learning. Among the factors that contribute to this motivation are "whether students find the project to be interesting and valuable, whether they perceive that they have the competence to engage in and complete the project, and whether they focus on learning rather than on outcomes and grades" (Blumenfeld et al. 1991, p. 375). The teacher's role is critical in all this. Teachers need to create opportunities for project-based learning, support and guide student learning through scaffolding and modeling, encourage and help students manage learning and metacognitive processes, and help students assess their own learning and provide feedback. Whether teachers will be able to meet these demands depends in large part on their own understanding of the content embedded in projects, their ability to teach and recognition of student difficulty in learning the content (i.e., pedagogical awarenesses), and their willingness to assume a constructivist culture in their classrooms. The latter point is critical, as it relates back to the holistic view of learning and motivation. Rather than perceive motivation that is done by a teacher to get a student to perform, a constructivist learning culture presupposes the need for students to take ownership of the ideas being learned and strategies for this learning. If teachers' beliefs about the nature and goals of schooling are counter to a constructivist orientation, students should not be expected to derive the benefits of project-based learning.

A good example of more recent constructionist research that has taken such project-based learning factors into account is that of Yasmin Kafai (1994, 1995; Kafai & Harel, 1991). She and her colleagues have conducted a series of studies focused on "children as designers." Their research has explored student motivation and learning while building multimedia projects, usually in the context of students building games and presentations for other, younger, students. In one example (Kafai, Ching, & Marshall, 1997), teams of fifth- and sixth-grade students were asked to build interactive multimedia resources for third graders. This research, predominantly qualitative, investigated how the students approached the task and negotiated their social roles on the team. Interestingly, the students who developed the most screens, or pages, for the team project were not necessarily those who spent the most time on the project or who exhibited the most project leadership. Upon further analysis of individual contributions, it was found that those students who spent the most time on the project focused their efforts more on developing content-related screens and animation, compared to navigational screens. Quantitative data were also included demonstrating that the students' knowledge of astronomy increased significantly as a result of their participation in the project. Research such as this demonstrates that students are able to negotiate successfully the difficult demands of designing and developing multimedia, find the projects to be motivating and relevant, and also gain content knowledge along the way.

In a similar example, in which teams of elementary-school students developed computer projects about neuroscience, Kafai and Ching (2001) found that the team-based project approach afforded many unique opportunities for discussions about science *during* the design process. Planning meetings gave students an authentic context in which to engage in systemic discussions about science. Team members who had prior experience in the team project approach often extended these discussions to consider deeper relationships.

A similar project is Project KIDDESIGNER, in which elementary- and middle-school children were asked to take roles on software design teams (Rieber, Luke, & Smith, 1998). The children's goal was to design educational computer games based on content they had just learned in school. The goal of this research was to see whether such a task would be perceived as authentic by the children and to understand how they would perform when given such design tasks in a collaborative context. Game design is both an art and a science—though games, like stories, have well-established parts, the creation of a good game demands much creativity and sensitivity to the audience that will play the games. As an interactive design artifact, it is difficult to evaluate good games just by reading their descriptions and rules. Instead, game prototypes become essential design artifacts for assessing and revising a game's design. Unlike the research by Kafai and her colleagues, the children in Project KIDDESIGNER were not expected to master a programming language, such as Logo, and then program their games. Instead, the children focused exclusively on the design activities, with the researchers acting as their programmers. The results of this study, conducted as a design experiment, showed that the children were able to handle the complexities of the design activity and were able to remain flexible in their team roles. Team members, by and large, were able to negotiate competing solutions to design problems and maintain deadlines. Of particular interest was how the resulting games provided insights into the value the children placed on the school-based content they needed to embed in the games. For example, one of the most popular games used the context of motocross racing where mathematics were embedded as a penalty for poor performance. These children saw mathematics as a punishment for not performing other tasks, which they valued, well.

22.6 MICROWORLDS MORE BROADLY CONCEIVED: GOING BEYOND PROGRAMMING LANGUAGES

Although the roots of microworlds rest in programming languages, or general computational media, such as Logo and Boxer, advances in technology have led to the development of other forms of microworlds, such as those based on direct manipulation of screen objects and attributes. The relative merits of learning text-based programming languages and those that use "point and click" methods of interaction, such as the very popular Geometer's Sketchpad, an icon-based tool for constructing geometric relationships and principles, have been hotly debated (diSessa, Hoyles, Noss, & Edwards, 1995b).

Consider the issue of "curricular fit" of these two types of systems. It is much easier to make the argument for a school to invest in a tool such as Geometer's Sketchpad as compared to Logo or Boxer because Geometer's Sketchpad more readily "maps" on to the current geometry curriculum. diSessa, Hoyles, Noss, and Edwards (1995a) suggest that systems such as Boxer and Logo are usually seen as too "subversive" by mainstream educators, hence their adoption is often resisted, whereas Geometer's Sketchpad fits easily into the curriculum, due to its alignment with traditional curriculum goals. One might argue, then, that the power and affordances of a tool such as Geometer's Sketchpad would be recognized and capitalized on less because many educators would be expected solely to integrate it into the standard way of teaching and learning, hence using it to perpetuate the "standard curriculum," though such use would also improve how the standard curriculum is taught. Another point of view is that a system like Geometer's Sketchpad could be even more subversive than Logo because, once it becomes part of the school system, its affordances may actually help to reconceptualize the boundaries of learning and teaching.

A major factor concerning the widespread adoption of these systems is the belief that each system needs to effect large-scale changes for all learners in a school population. "It is tempting—and prevalent—to attempt to design for the majority; indeed it seems many presume that an encounter with a system will produce some outcome for all. This is, of course, an underlying assumption of schooling: that it is 'good' for all. In fact, exploratory learning environments may have some claim to just the opposite, to be designed for relatively rare occurrences" (diSessa et al., 1995a, pp. 9–10).

22.6.1 ThinkerTools

ThinkerTools (http://thinkertools.soe.berkeley.edu/) is both a computer-based modeling tool for physics and a pedagogy for science education based on scientific inquiry: "...an approach to science education that enables sixth graders to learn principles underlying Newtonian mechanics, and to apply them in unfamiliar problem solving contexts. The students' learning is centered around problem solving and experimentation within a set of computer microworlds (i.e., interactive simulations)" (White & Horowitz, 1987, abstract). ThinkerTools is one of the earliest examples of how the concept of a microworld was broadened to go beyond computer programming to include interactions and model building within "interactive simulations."

In the ThinkerTools software, students explore interactive models of Newtonian mechanics. They can build their own models, or they can interact with a variety of ready-made models that accompany the software. A variety of symbolic visual representations is used. Simple objects, in the shape of balls (called "dots"), can be added to the model, each with parameters directly under the student's control. For example, each dot's initial mass, elasticity (bouncy or fragile), or velocity can be manipulated. Variables of the model's environment itself can be modified, such as the presence and strength of gravity and air friction. Other elements can be added to the model, such as barriers and targets. Forces affecting the motion of the balls can be directly controlled, if desired, by the keyboard or a joy stick, such as by giving the ball kicks in the four directions (i.e., up, down, left, right). This adds a video-game-like feature to the model.

The ThinkerTools software also includes a variety of measurement tools with which students can accurately observe distance, time, and velocity. Another symbol, called a datacross, can be used to show graphically the motion variables of the object. A datacross shows the current horizontal and vertical motion of the ball in terms of the sum of all of the forces that have acted on the ball. The motion of the object over time can also be depicted by having the object leave a trail of small, stationary dots. When the object moves slowly, the trail of dots is closely spaced, but when the object moves faster, the space between the trailing dots increases. Students can also use a "step through time" feature, in which the simulation can be frozen in time, allowing students to proceed step by step through time. This gives them a powerful means of analyzing the object's motion and also of predicting the object's future motion. The point of all of these tools is to give students the means of determining and understanding the laws of motion in an interactive, exploratory way: "In this way, such dynamic interactive simulations can provide a transition from students' intuitive ways of reasoning about the world to the more abstract, formal methods that scientists use for representing and reasoning about the behavior of a system" (White & Frederiksen, 2000b, pp. 326–327). Similar to Papert's idea of a transitional object, the ThinkerTools software acts as a bridge between concrete, qualitative reasoning of real-world examples and the highly abstract world of scientific formalism where laws are expressed mathematically in the form of equations.

The ThinkerTools software is best used, according to White, with an instructional approach to inquiry and modeling called the ThinkerTools Inquiry Curriculum. The goal of this curriculum is to develop students' metacognitive knowledge, that is, "their knowledge about the nature of scientific laws and models, their knowledge about the processes of modeling and inquiry, and their ability to monitor and reflect on these processes so they can improve them" (White & Frederiksen, 2000b, p. 327). White and her colleagues predicted that such a pedagogical approach used in the context of powerful tools such as the ThinkerTools software should make learning science possible for all students. The curriculum largely follows the scientific method, involving the following steps: (1) question—students start by constructing a research question, perhaps the hardest part of the model; (2) hypothesize—students generate hypotheses related to their question; (3) investigate—students carry out experiments, both with the ThinkerTools software and in the real world, the goal of which is to gather empirical evidence about which hypotheses (if any) are accurate; (4) analyze—after the experiments are run, students analyze the resulting data; (5) model—based on their analysis, students articulate a causal model, in the form of a scientific law, to explain the findings; and (6) evaluate—the final step is to test whether their laws and causal models work well in real-world situations, which, in turn, often leads to new research questions.

White and Frederiksen (2000b) also reported interesting insights into how teachers using ThinkerTools can affect the learning outcomes of the materials. For example, they describe teachers who contacted them to use their materials, teachers with whom they were not already associated. Eight such teachers were asked to administer the physics and inquiry tests that come with the materials and send the results back to White. Interestingly, four of the teachers reported that their focus was on using ThinkerTools as a way to teach physics. The students of these teachers showed a significant improvement on the physics test but not on the inquiry test. In contrast, the other four teachers said that their focus was on teaching scientific inquiry—their students improved significantly on both their inquiry *and* their physics expertise. Obviously, the goals of the teacher can lead to many missed opportunities for inquiry learning.

22.6.2 SimCalc

The SimCalc project (http://www.simcalc.umassd.edu/) is concerned with the mathematics of change and variation (MCV). Its mission is to give ordinary children the opportunities, experiences, and resources they need to develop an extraordinary understanding of and skill with MCV (Roschelle et al., 2000). The SimCalc project is based on three lines of innovation. The first is a deep reconstruction of the calculus curriculum, both its subject matter and the way in which it is taught. The goal is to allow all children, even those in elementary school, to access the mathematical principles of change and variation. The developers assert that this is possible through the design of visualizations and simulations for collaborative inquiry. The most notable innovation in the SimCalc curriculum is the use of piecewise linear functions as the basis of student exploration. In a velocity graph, for example, a student can build a function by putting together line segments, each of the same time duration. A series of joined horizontal segments denotes constant velocity and a set of rising or falling segments denotes increasing or decreasing speed. The second innovation is to root the learning of these mathematics principles in meaningful experiences of students. Students bring with them a wealth of mathematical understanding that is largely untapped in traditional methods of learning calculus. The SimCalc project does not require students to understand algebra before exploring calculus principles. The third innovation is the creative use of technology, namely, special software called MathWorlds.

The MathWorlds software makes extensive use of concrete visual representations, coupled with graphs that students can directly manipulate and control. The graphs can be based on data sets generated by computer-based simulations (animated clowns, ducks, and elevators), laboratory experiments, and even the students' own body movements by capturing their movements with microcomputer-based (or calculator-based) motion sensors, then importing these data into the computer.

Although mathematics educators have spent much time and effort reforming the calculus curriculum, the SimCalc project differs in two important ways from these efforts. First, unlike traditional reform, which has focused solely on the teaching of calculus in high school, the SimCalc project has reconceptualized the teaching of mathematics at all grade levels, starting with elementary school. Second, other reform efforts have focused on linking numeric, graphic, and symbolic representations, whereas the SimCalc project has put its focus on meaningful student experience based on graphs of interesting visual phenomena that students can manipulate directly. The SimCalc project places much value on students experiencing phenomena as the basis for their mathematical explorations.

The SimCalc curriculum is based on four strategies that counter traditional teaching of calculus. First, phenomena are studied and understood before delving into mathematical formalisms. Second, the mathematics are based on discrete variation before turning to continuous variation. Third, the mathematics of accumulation and integrals are taught before rates of change and derivatives. Fourth, students learn to master graphs before algebraic symbolism. So, instead of requiring algebra as a prerequisite skill for studying calculus, the SimCalc project using students' grasp of visual problem solving with graphs to enter the mathematical world of change and varying quantities.

Research with SimCalc since the project began in about 1993 has focused on two themes. The first research phase investigated the use of the MathWorlds software on student cognition, technology designs, and alternative curricular sequences. This effort resulted in a "proof of concept" curriculum largely divorced from systemic educational factors. Again, much of the research in this phase can be characterized as design experiments. The second research phase, just beginning, has focused specifically on such systemic issues as curricular integration, teacher professional development, and assessment.

Early SimCalc research was characterized as large field-test trials designed to generate formative data to improve the software and refine the SimCalc curricular approach. Although less rigorously implemented than experimental research, data from these early field trials demonstrated that the seventh-, eighth-, and ninth-grade students who participated in the SimCalc curriculum significantly improved in their understanding of rate of change problems. Interestingly, although these formative data show that middle-school students can effectively solve mathematical problems involving change and variation, the exciting possibility of introducing younger students to these principles is greatly hampered by the fact that calculus is taught only as part of the high-school curriculum. This content is considered an "add-on" to an already full middle-school mathematics curriculum. Ironically, despite the exciting potential that students could have access to such powerful mathematical ideas at a younger age, these learning opportunities are largely resisted by schools due to the curriculum constraints. Fortunately, these obstacles are exactly those that the SimCalc team hopes to study in the next phase of the project.

22.6.3 GenScope

Genscope (http://genscope.concord.org/) is an exploratory software environment "designed to help students learn to reason and solve problems in the domain of genetics" (Horwitz & Christie, 2000, p. 163). The goal of GenScope is to help students understand scientific explanations and also to gain insight into the nature of the scientific process. Horwitz and his colleagues describe GenScope as a "computer-based manipulative" and insist that it is neither a simulation nor a modeling tool. Interestingly, their intent is to have students use it to try to determine, largely through inductive reasoning, the software's underlying model (i.e., genetics). This is precisely the aim of much research on educational uses of simulations. Like other microworlds, the emphasis of GenScope is on qualitative understanding of the domain. It gives students a way to represent genetic problems and derive solutions interactively. It does not require students to master the vocabulary of genetics before effectively using genetic concepts and principles. Indeed, Horwitz and his colleagues suggest that traditional science instruction poses a significant linguistic barrier to understanding genetics—typical science textbooks often introduce more vocabulary per page than do foreign language texts. This linguistic barrier is compounded by the fact that the science terms usually do not have a direct analogue in the student's "first language" and, hence, are actually more difficult to learn than a foreign language.

Another significant barrier in understanding genetics, according to Horwitz, is the mismatch between how scientists actually study genetics and how it is taught. Understanding genetics is largely an inductive exercise, trying to determine the cause from an observed set of effects. In contrast, most science teaching is deductive, teaching the rule, followed by students having to deduce the results. Moreover, the skills that a scientist uses are rarely taught in the classroom (i.e., using the scientific method to reason inductively). Instead, most classroom practice activities are meant to let students rehearse factual information and solve similar problem sets. Of course, knowing a correct answer on a worksheet does not mean that a student actually understands the underlying concepts and principles. The GenScope curriculum was designed to have students use the GenScope tool in ways that mirror closely the methods used by actual scientists.

Genetics is the study of how an organism inherits physical characteristics from its ancestors and passes them on to its descendants, the rules of which were first postulated by Gregor Mendel in the 1800s. Learning genetics is particularly challenging because descriptions of how changes occur can be formulated at many different levels. GenScope provides students with six interdependent levels: molecules, chromosomes, cells, organisms, pedigrees, and populations. GenScope provides students with a simplified model of genetics for them to manipulate, beginning with the imaginary species of dragons. GenScope provides individual computer windows for each of the levels—students can interact with one of the levels, say via a DNA window to show the genes of an organism (i.e., genes that control whether a dragon has wings), and then see the results of their manipulation in the organism window (i.e., a dragon sprouting wings).

22.6.4 Pedagogical Approach of GenScope

Students using GenScope start by focusing on the relationships between the organism and the chromosome levels using the fictitious dragon species, progressively working up to higher levels of relationships dealing with real animals. After getting familiar with the GenScope interface for a few minutes, students are immediately given a challenge (e.g., a fire-breathing green dragon with legs, horns, and a tail but no wings). Students quickly master the ability to manipulate the genes at the chromosomal level to produce such an animal. Interestingly, the next step is to switch to a paper-and-pencil activity where students are asked to describe what a dragon would look like given printed screen shots of chromosomes. After students construct an answer, they are encouraged to use GenScope to verify, or correct, their answers. Students then progress to interrelating the DNA level to the chromosome and organism level. Students come to learn about how recessive and dominant genes can be combined to produce certain characteristics. For example, if wings are a recessive trait, a dragon would have to possess two recessive genes to be born with wings. Students then progress to the cell level and consider how two parents may pass traits to their offspring. As shown, the pedagogical approach used here is to challenge students with problems to solve in GenScope, then give them time to work alone or in pairs to solve the problems through experimentation.

A variety of research with GenScope has been conducted to test the hypothesis that students using GenScope would be better able to demonstrate genetic reasons among multiple levels than students not using GenScope. An early study compared one class of students using GenScope to another using a traditional textbook-based curriculum. Interestingly, although the GenScope students definitely showed greater qualitative reasoning as evidenced in the observations of their computer interactions, they were unable to outperform the other students on traditional paper-and-pencil tests. Horwitz and his colleagues explain these early results in several ways. First, and not surprisingly, this type of media comparison research does not lead to equal comparisons. Students were not learning the same content in similar ways or at similar rates. While, on one hand, the GenScope group was asked to solve richer and more sophisticated problems than the other group, they were doing so through the interactive and successive manipulation possible with GenScope. The textbook group was forced throughout to use genetic formalism, such as the vocabulary found on the tests (e.g., phenotype, genotype, allele, meiosis, heterozygous, homozygous, dominant/recessive).

Besides the language barrier that GenScope students faced, Horwitz and his colleagues suggest three other barriers that serve to prevent students using microworlds like GenScope to demonstrate their increased understanding on most traditional tests. The first, "shift in modality," is the barrier between shifting from computer interactions to paper-and-pencil ones. The second, "examination effect," argues that the very act of taking a test negatively affects student performance. The final barrier concerns the fact that any understanding learned in context is qualitatively different from understanding gained through abstract symbols, such as the written word. In sum, students have a very difficult time translating their GenScope-based understanding of genetics to performance on traditional paper-and-pencil tests. Horwitz and his colleagues accept this challenge given that such measures are part of the political reality of arguing for using new technologies and curricula within schools.

Other research shows that students in general biology and general science classes show much larger gains in their understanding of genetics than students in college-prep or honors biology. The larger gains were particularly evident in classrooms where teachers used curricular materials especially designed to scaffold aspects of their learning of genetics (Hickey, Kindfield, & Wolfe, 1999).

22.7 THEORETICAL BASIS FOR LEARNING IN A MICROWORLD

Based on the examples considered in this chapter, microworlds are clearly an eclectic and varied assortment of software and pedagogical approaches to learning. Is there a clear theoretical basis for suggesting that microworlds offer a more powerful representation for problem- solving with domains such as physics and mathematics? Perkins and Unger (1994) suggest that their power resides in the way microworlds represent a problem for the student. We use all sorts of representations to understand and solve problems. However, the teaching of certain domains, most notably science and mathematics, has tended to use technical representations (e.g., algebra, equations, and graphs) rather than less technical representations (e.g., analogies, metaphors, and stories).

Domains such as mathematics and physics have been represented in a variety of ways to discover the boundaries and underlying laws of the domain. The ways in which people such as Galileo, Newton, Einstein, and Feynman have chosen to represent the field of physics is a useful historical review of representation.

What role do representations play in understanding? Using the classic problem of why falling objects of different weights fall at the same rate, Perkins and Unger (1994) offer three complementary approaches using very different representations: algebraic, qualitative, and imagistic. An algebraic approach uses mathematical manipulation of the relevant formulas (e.g., Newton's second law of motion, or force equals mass times acceleration) to explain the result. In a qualitative explanation, one could reason that the greater downward force expected on a larger mass would be equally offset by the fact that a larger mass is also harder to "get moving." Finally, an imagistic explanation involves a kind of "thought experiment," such as that actually described by Galileo, to reason through the problem. For example, Galileo imagined the motion of two iron balls connected by a metal rod and how the motion would change as the balls fell if the connecting rod were made thinner and thinner, eventually being connected with just a thin thread, and then, finally, imagined the thread being cut while the balls were falling. From such reasoning through imagery, it is clear that the acceleration of the balls would not vary regardless of their mass.

Perkins and Unger (1994) suggest that microworlds offer a fourth and different kind of representation. They argue that representation facilitates explanation through active problem solving, similar to the search that a user executes in a "problem space" proposed by Newell and Simon (1972). Such a search involves an initial state, a goal state, various intermediate states, and operations that take the student from one state to another. The objective is to turn the initial state into the goal state. How to search the problem space for a path to the solution depends on a variety of factors, such as the student's knowledge of the domain in which the problem is situated (e.g., physics), the student's general abilities, and the way the problem space is represented for the student. To say that a student *understands* a problem is to mean, according to Perkins and Unger (1994), that he or she can perform the necessary explanation, justification, and prediction related to the problem topic. (They use the term *epistemic problems* to describe these sorts of problem-solving performances.)

Representations aid problem solving in three ways. First, the right representation reduces the cognitive load and allows students to use their precious working memory for higher-order tasks. For example, algebra uses symbols that are very concise and uses rules that are very generalizable to a range of problems. Of course, this is true only when the students have already mastered algebra. Qualitative representations, such as those based on analogies and metaphors, allow students to think of a problem first in terms of an example already known, such as the idea of electricity being like water in a pipe. Second, representations clarify the problem space for students, such as by organizing the problem and the search path. Again, the rules of algebra offer beginning, middle, and end states to reach and clear means of transforming equations to these different states. Qualitative representations offer the user models to use and compare. Similarly, imagistic representations help to reveal a critical factor in solving the problem, such as the absurd role played by the silk thread in Galileo's thought experiment. Third, a good representation reveals immediate implications. Regardless of how well a representation may minimize the cognitive load or clarify the problem space, if students do not see immediate applications while engaged in the problem search, then the solutions found will be devoid of meaning for, and hence understanding by, the students.

Microworlds offer the means of maximizing all three benefits of representations, when used in the context of an appropriate science teaching pedagogy, such as one based on the scientific method of hypothesis generating and hypothesis testing. For example, in the ThinkerTools microworld, students directly interact with a dynamic object while having the discrete forces they impart on the object horizontally or vertically displayed on a simple, yet effective datacross. Students can also manipulate various parameters in the microworld, such as gravity and friction. ThinkerTools ably creates a problem space in which numeric, qualitative, and visual representations consistently work together.

Not only do computer-based microworlds afford reducing the cognitive load, clarifying the problem space, and revealing immediate implications, but also, Perkins and Unger (1994) go on to suggest, microworlds afford the integration of structure-mapping frameworks based on analogies and metaphors. Similarly, a microworld can be designed so as to provide a representation that purposefully directs a student to focus on the most salient relationships of the phenomena being studied. Of course, such benefits do not come without certain costs or risks. For example, as with the use of any analogy, if the users do not correctly understand the mapping structure of the analogy, then the benefits will be lost and the students may potentially form misconceptions. The danger of a microworld's misleading students if they do not understand the structural mappings well is real. Just providing a microworld to students, without the pedagogical underpinnings, should not be expected to lead to learning. The role of the teacher and the resulting classroom practice is crucial here. Microworlds rely on a culture of learning in which students are expected to inquire, test, and justify their understanding. "Students needs to be actively engaged in the construction and assessment of their understandings by working thoughtfully in challenging and reflective problem contexts" (p. 27). (See pages 27–29 for more risks and pitfalls.)

As Perkins and Unger (1994) point out, microworld designers have a formidable task; they

have to articulate adequately the components and relationships among components of the domain to be learned. Next the designers have to construct an illustrative world exemplifying that targeted domain. Finally, the illustrative world should provide natural or familiar referents that, when placed in correspondence with one another and mapped to the target domain, yield a better understanding of the domain. (p. 30)

22.8 THE RELATIONSHIP AMONG MICROWORLDS, SIMULATIONS, AND MODELING TOOLS

There are many other examples of innovative software applications that are usually clumped in the microworld camp, the most notable being Geometer's Sketchpad (Olive, 1998). There is also the range of modeling packages to consider, such as Interactive Physics and Stella, and simulations such as SimCity. Should these be classified as microworlds? Determining the answer depends on how the user appropriates the tool using the five microworld attributes discussed earlier in this chapter. However, despite the controversy between giving users programmable media (i.e., Logo and Boxer) and giving them preprogrammed models of systems, there do seem to be benefits to including an analysis of modeling tools and simulations in a discussion of microworlds (Rieber, 1996).

There are two main ways to use simulations in education: model using and model building. Model using is when you learn from a simulation designed by someone else. This is common of *instructional* approaches where simulations are used as an interactive strategy or event, such as practice. Learning from using a simulated model of a system is different from learning from building working models in that the student does not have access to the programming of the simulation. The student is limited to manipulating only the parameters or variables that the designer of the simulation embedded into the simulation's interface. For example, in a simulation of Newtonian motion the user may have only the ability to change the mass of an object in certain increments, and not the ability to change the initial starting positions of the objects or even how many objects will interact when the simulation is run. In contrast, in model building the learner has a direct role in the construction of the simulation. This approach is closely related to work with microworlds.

The question of when a microworld is or is not a simulation often troubles people. While ThinkerTools or Interactive Physics displays trajectories of simulated falling balls, the underlying mathematical model makes the resulting representation much more "real" than a paper-and-pencil model. And although the ability to stop a ball in midflight has no analogue in the real world, features like this make understanding the real world more likely. What is important is that the mathematical models of these environments represent the phenomenon or concept in question accurately, followed by exploiting the representation for educational purposes. However, a tool like Geometer's Sketchpad is clearly *not* a simulation—its geometry is as real as it gets.

The model-using approach to simulations has had a long history in instructional technology, particularly in corporate and military settings. However, simulations have become very popular designs in the education market. There are three major design components to an educational simulation: the underlying model, the simulation's scenario, and the simulation's instructional overlay (Reigeluth & Schwartz, 1989). The underlying model refers to the mathematical relationships of the phenomenon being simulated. The scenario provides a context for the simulation, such as space travel or sports. The instructional overlay includes any features, options, or information presented before, during, or after the simulation to help the user explicitly identify and learn the relationships being modeled in the simulation. The structure and scope of the instructional overlay are of course, an interesting design question and one that has shaped my research. Mental model theory offers much guidance in the design of an effective scenario and instructional overlay, such as thinking of them as an interactive conceptual model (Gentner & Stevens, 1983; Norman, 1988). This supports the idea of using metaphors to help people interact with the simulation (Petrie & Oshlag, 1993).

de Jong and van Joolingen (1998) present one of the most thorough reviews of scientific discovery learning within computer-based simulations (of the model-using type). The goal of this type of research is to present a simulation to students and ask them to infer the underlying model on which the simulation is based. Scientific discovery learning is based on a cycle corresponding to the steps of scientific reasoning: defining a problem, stating a hypothesis about the problem, designing an experiment to test the hypothesis, collecting and analyzing data from the experiment, making predictions based on the results, and making conclusions about and possible revisions of the robustness of the original hypotheses.

The research reviewed by de Jong and van Joolingen (1998) shows that students find it difficult to learn from simulations using discovery methods and need much support to do so successfully. Research shows that students have difficulty throughout the discovery learning process. For example, students find it difficult to state or construct hypotheses that lead to good experiments. Furthermore, students do not easily adapt hypotheses on the basis of the data collected. That is, they often retain a hypothesis even when the data they collect disconfirm the hypothesis. Students do not design appropriate experiments to give them pertinent data to evaluate their hypotheses. Students are prone to *confirmation bias,* that is, they often design experiments that will lead to support their hypotheses. Students also find interpreting data in light of their hypotheses to be very challenging. In light of these difficulties de Jong and van Joolingen (1998) also review research on ways to mitigate these difficulties. One conclusion they draw is that information or instructional support needs to come *while* students are involved in the simulation, rather than prior to their working with the simulation. That is, students are likely to benefit from such instructional interventions when they are confronted with the task or challenge. This often flies in the face of conventional wisdom that students should be prepared thoroughly before being given access to the simulation. The research also shows that embedding guided activities within the simulation, such as exercises, questions, and even games, helps students to learn from the simulation. When designing experiments, students can benefit from experimentation hints, such as the recommendation to change only one variable at a time. de Jong and van Joolingen (1998) also conclude that the technique of *model progression* can be an effective design strategy. Instead of presenting the entire simulation to students from the onset, initially students are given a simplified version, then variables are added as their understanding unfolds. For example, a Newtonian simulation could be presented first with only one-dimensional motion represented, then with two-dimensional motion.

Finally, de Jong and van Joolingen (1998) also point out the importance of understanding how learning was measured in a particular study. There is a belief that learning from simulations leads to "deeper" cognitive processing than learning from expository methods (such as presentations). However, many studies did not test for application and transfer, so it is an open question whether a student who successfully learns only how to manipulate the simulation can apply this knowledge to other contexts. A student who successfully manipulates the simulation may not have acquired the general conceptual knowledge to succeed at other tasks. The review by de Jong and van Joolingen shows that there is still much researchers need to learn about the role of simulations in discovery learning and, also, about how to design supports and structure to help students use the affordances of simulations most effectively. There are also many styles and strategies beyond scientific discovery learning. For example, an experiential or inductive approach would have students explore a simulation first, followed by providing organized instruction on the concepts or principles modeled by the simulation. With this approach, the simulation provides an experiential context for anchoring later instruction.

22.9 CONCLUSION

Microworlds describe both a class of interactive exploratory software and a particular learning style. This chapter has taken a close look at the software, philosophy, and research of some of the most prominent and successful microworlds developed since about 1980—Logo, Boxer, ThinkerTools, SimCalc, and Genscope. All are incredibly creative and powerful, and all fully capture the interactive and computational affordances of computers for exploratory learning. The microworlds described in this chapter are but a few of those

developed. There are many others that deserve notice, such as Mitchell Resnick's (1991, 1994, 1996, 1999) StarLogo (http://education.mit.edu/starlogo/), a version of Logo that allows thousands of turtles to be active at the same time and all under the control of the user through a few simple commands. This powerful computational medium gives children a doorway to the world of decentralized systems, which include such complex phenomena as traffic jams, ant colonies, and even the migration of birds. Unfortunately, insufficient research is yet available on this provocative computational medium. Sadly, this reflects the fact that there is less research in the microworld literature than one would expect and hope providing evidence of their use and impact in the schools.

In the case of microworlds derived from computational media, such as Logo and Boxer, hundreds of even smaller microworlds have been developed as individual programs, though they remain open to change by the user. Probably the most successful microworld of the past 25 years has been turtle geometry, a subset of the original capabilities of the Logo language and a continuing part of many other languages (including Boxer) and programs. It is conservative to state that tens of thousands of children have successfully learned to control the turtle to make interesting geometric shapes. Most of these children, regrettably, never progressed to the higher levels of programming possible with these languages or even within the turtle geometry microworld itself. Explanations of this are speculative, the most likely being that the educational system has yet to adopt a true constructivist perspective. Although curricula in math and science supported by the respective professional associations have repeatedly called for increased attention to problem solving and scientific inquiry, most school curricula are still based on getting all students through all topics at about the same time. Until the focus turns from "covering the material" to student meaning making, it is unlikely that any microworld, no matter how powerful or persuasive, will have much influence on student learning. As David Perkins (1986) points out,

. . . Fostering transfer takes time, because it involves doing something special, something extra. With curricula crowded already and school hours a precious resource, it is hard to face the notion that topics need more time than they might otherwise get just to promote transfer. Yet that is the reality. It is actually preferable to cover somewhat less material, investing the time thereby freed to foster the transfer of that material, than to cover somewhat more and leave it context-bound. After all, who needs context-bound knowledge that shows itself only within the confines of a particular class period, a certain final essay, a term's final exam? In the long haul, there is no point to such instruction. (p. 229)

While microworld development over the past 25 years has been impressive, there is an urgent need to launch aggressive research programs so that the potential of these programs is not demonstrated in but a few special classrooms that get the chance to participate in field trials complete with able university personnel who come in to ensure that wonderful things will happen. Interestingly, most of the serious research on these systems has been completed by Ph.D. students at schools such as MIT, the University of California, Berkeley, and Harvard University for their doctoral dissertations. Some, such as the research

TABLE 22.1. Partial List of Doctoral Dissertation Research Project Microworlds

Advisor	Dissertation Title, Ph.D. Candidate, Year	Microworld
Seymour Papert	Twenty Heads Are Better Than One: Communities of children as Virtual Experts Michele Joelle Pezet Evard 1998	Logo
Seymour Papert	They Have Their Own Thoughts: Children's Learning of Computational Ideas from a Cultural Constructionist Perspective Paula K. Hooper 1998	Logo
Seymour Papert	Expressive Mathematics: Learning by Design David W. Shaffer 1998	Geometer's Sketchpad
Seymour Papert	Connected Mathematics: Building Concrete Relationships with, Mathematical Knowledge Uri J. Wilensky 1993	Logo
Seymour Papert	Beyond the Centralized Mindset: Explorations in Massively-Parallel, Microworlds Mitchel Resnick 1992	StarLogo
Seymour Papert	Learning Constellations: A Multimedia Ethnographic Research, Environment Using Video Technology for Exploring Children's Thinking (Ethnography) Ricki Goldman Segall 1990	Logo
Andy diSessa	Student Control of Whole-Class Discussions in a Community of Designers Peter Birns Atkins Kindfield 1996	Boxer
Andy diSessa	The Symbolic Basis of Physical Intuition: A Study of Two Symbol Systems in Physics Instruction Bruce L. Sherin 1996	Boxer
Andy diSessa	Students' Construction of Qualitative Physics Knowledge: Learning about Velocity and Acceleration in a Computer Microworld (Physics Education) Jeremy M. Roschelle 1991	Envisioning Machine
Andy diSessa	Learning Rational Number (Constructivism) John P. Smith, III 1990	Boxer
David Perkins	Minds in Play: Computer Game Design as a Context for Children's Learning (Vol. I and II) Yasmin B. Kafai 1993	Logo
Barbara White	Student Goal Orientation in Learning Inquiry Skills with Modifiable Software Advisors Todd A. Shimoda 1999	ThinkerTools
Barbara White	Developing Students' Understanding of Scientific Modeling Christine V. Schwarz 1998	ThinkerTools

by Barbara White, Idit Harel, and Yasmin Kafai, we have already presented. There is more, such as Jeremy Roschelle's (1991) early research on a physics microworld called the Envisioning Machine, which led to his collaborative work on MathWorlds in the SimCalc project. Table 22.1 lists a few notable examples of doctoral research carried out as part of microworld efforts.

Following in the footsteps of Papert, all of the microworld developers write persuasively about their software and pedagogical approaches. Their writings are provocative, challenging, and oftentimes inspiring. They all have interesting stories to tell about the field tests with their software. Among the lessons learned from these stories is that the potential of the software to make a difference in a child's access and understanding of complex domains, such as geometry, calculus, physics, and genetics, is great. But the challenges leading to such learning, based on constructivist orientations, are formidable. The educational system needs to change in fairly dramatic ways for the potential of these systems to be realized. Probably the most fundamental

change is allowing students adequate time, coupled with providing a master teacher who not only knows the software well, but also is a master of constructivist teaching—someone who knows how and when to challenge, provoke, suggest, scaffold, guide, direct, teach, and, most of all, leave a group of students alone to wrestle with a problem on their own terms. The word "facilitate" is often used ambiguously to denote such a teacher's actions. Such a role elevates the teacher's status and importance in the classroom, and although it can lead to a more satisfying form of teaching, it is a difficult style to master.

Without question, microworlds are among the most creative developments within educational computing and the learning sciences. Though all are defined as exploratory learning environments, all are also goal-oriented to some extent. This implies that microworlds offer a way to bridge the gap between the objectivism of instructional design methods and constructivist notions of learning. In other words, because the boundaries of a microworld are designed with certain constraints that lead and help learners to focus on a relatively narrow set of concepts and principles, microworlds complement any instructional system that requires the use of and accounting for predetermined instructional objectives (Rieber, 1992). This is not to say that conflicts do not exist. Indeed, the inability or unwillingness of schools to allow teachers and students to devote adequate time to inquiry-based activities using microworlds due to curriculum demands is a case in point. Yet, as constructivist perspectives aligned with technology innovations mature, as evidenced by the many microworld projects discussed in this chapter, there is hope that the long-rival factions within constructivist and instructivist "camps" will continue to realize more that they have in common. The current interest in and maturity of design experiments offer great promise in stimulating much more microworld research that will also be rigorously and authentically assessed.

References

Abelson, H. (1982). Logo for the Apple II. Peterborough. NH: BYTE/McGraw Hill.

Adams, S. T., & diSessa, A. (1991). Learning by "cheating": Students' inventive ways of using a boxer motion microworld. *Journal of Mathematical Behavior, 10*(1), 79-89.

Barab, S. A., & Kirshner, D. (2001). Guest editors' introduction: Rethinking methodology in the learning sciences. *Journal of the Learning Sciences, 10*, 5-15.

Blumenfeld, P. C., Soloway, E., Marx, R. W., Krajcik, J. S., Guzdial, M., & Palinscar, A. (1991). Motivating project-based learning: Sustaining the doing, supporting the learning. *Educational Psychologist, 26*(3 & 4), 369-398.

Brown, A. L. (1992). Design experiments: Theoretical and methodological challenges in creating complex interventions in classroom settings. *Journal of the Learning Sciences, 2*(2), 141-178.

Chi, M., Feltovich, P., & Glaser, R. (1981). Categorization and representation of physics problems by experts and novices. *Cognitive Science, 5*, 121-152.

Clark, R. E. (1994). Media will never influence learning. *Educational Technology Research & Development, 42*(2), 21-29.

Clark, R. E. (Ed.). (2001). *Learning from media: Arguments, analysis, and evidence*. Greenwich, CT: Information Age.

Clements, D. (1989). *Computers in elementary mathematics education*. Englewood Cliffs, NJ: Prentice Hall.

Clements, D. H. (1984). Training effects on the development and generalization of Piagetian logical operations and knowledge of number. *Journal of Educational Psychology, 76*, 766-776.

Clements, D. H. (1986). Effects of Logo and CAI environments on cognition and creativity. *Journal of Educational Psychology, 78*, 309-318.

Clements, D. H. (1987). Longitudinal study of the effects of Logo programming on cognitive abilities and achievement. *Journal of Educational Computing Research, 3*, 73-94.

Clements, D. H., & Gullo, D. F. (1984). Effects of computer programming on young children's cognition. *Journal of Educational Psychology, 76*(6), 1051-1058.

Collins, A. (1992). Toward a design science of education. In E. Scanlon & T. O'Shea (Eds.), *New directions in educational technology* (pp. 15-22). New York: Springer-Verlag.

Cuban, L. (1986). *Teachers and machines: The classroom of technology since 1920*. New York: Teachers College Press.

Cuban, L. (2001). *Oversold and underused: Computers in the classroom*. Cambridge, MA: Harvard University Press.

de Jong, T., & van Joolingen, W. R. (1998). Scientific discovery learning with computer simulations of conceptual domains. *Review of Educational Research, 68*(2), 179-201.

Dewey, J. (1916). *Democracy and education: An introduction to the philosophy of education*. New York: Macmillan.

diSessa, A. A. (1989). *Computational media as a foundation for new learning cultures*. Technical Report G5. Berkeley: University of California.

diSessa, A. A. (1997). Twenty reasons why your should use Boxer (instead of Logo). In M. Turcsányi-Szabó (Ed.), *Learning & Exploring with Logo: Proceedings of the Sixth European Logo Conference, Budapest, Hungary* (pp. 7-27).

diSessa, A. A. (2000). *Changing minds: Computers, learning, and literacy*. Cambridge, MA: MIT Press.

diSessa, A. A., Abelson, H., & Ploger, D. (1991). An overview of Boxer. *Journal of Mathematical Behavior, 10*, 3-15.

diSessa, A. A., Hoyles, C., Noss, R., & Edwards, L. D. (1995a). Computers and exploratory learning: Setting the scene. In A. A. diSessa, C. Hoyles, R. Noss, & L. D. Edwards (Eds.), *Computers and exploratory learning* (pp. 1-12). New York: Springer.

diSessa, A. A., Hoyles, C., Noss, R., & Edwards, L. D. (Eds.). (1995b). *Computers and exploratory learning*. New York: Springer.

Eccles, J. S., & Wigfield, A. (1995). In the mind of the actor: The structure of adolescents' achievement task values and expectancy-related beliefs. *Personality and Social Psychology Bulletin, 21*, 215-225.

Edelson, D. C. (2002). Design research: What we learn when we engage in design. *Journal of the Learning Sciences, 11*, 105-121.

Edwards, L. D. (1995). Microworlds as representations. In A. A. diSessa, C. Hoyles, R. Noss, & L. D. Edwards (Eds.), *Computers and exploratory learning* (pp. 127-154). New York: Springer.

Feurzeig, W. (1999). A visual modeling tool for mathematics experiment and inquiry. In W. Feurzeig & N. Roberts (Eds.), *Modeling and simulation in science and mathematics education* (pp. 95-113). New York: Springer-Verlag.

Feurzeig, W., & Roberts, N. (1999). Introduction. In W. Feurzeig & N. Roberts (Eds.), *Modeling and simulation in science and mathematics education* (pp. xv-xviii). New York: Springer-Verlag.

Forrester, J. W. (1989). The beginning of system dynamics. *International meeting of the System Dynamics Society, Stuttgart, Germany* [online]. Available: http://sysdyn.mit.edu/sdep/papers/D-4165-1.pdf.

Gentner, D., & Stevens, A. (Eds.). (1983). *Mental models*. Mahwah, NJ: Lawrence Erlbaum Associates.

Harel, I., & Papert, S. (1990). Software design as a learning environment. *Interactive Learning Environments, 1*, 1-32.

Harel, I., & Papert, S. (1991). Software design as a learning environment. In I. Harel & S. Papert (Eds.), *Constructionism* (pp. 41-84). Norwood, NJ: Ablex.

Hickey, D. T., Kindfield, A. C. H., & Wolfe, E. W. (1999, April). *Assessment-oriented scaffolding of student and teacher performance in a technology-supported genetics environment*. Paper presented at the annual meeting of the American Educational Research Association, Montreal, Quebec, Canada.

Horwitz, P., & Christie, M. A. (2000). Computer-based manipulatives for teaching scientific reasoning: An example. In M. J. Jacobson & R. B. Kozma (Eds.), *Learning the sciences of the 21st century: Research, design, and implementing advanced technology learning environments* (pp. 163-191). Mahwah, NJ: Lawrence Erlbaum Associates.

Horwitz, P., & Christie, M. A. (2002, April). *Hypermodels: Embedding curriculum and assessment in computer-based manipulatives*. Paper presented at the annual meeting of the American Educational Research Association, New Orleans, LA.

Jackson, S., Stratford, S. J., Krajcik, J. S., & Soloway, E. (1996). Making dynamic modeling accessible to pre-college science students. *Interactive Learning Environments, 4*(3), 233-257.

Jonassen, D. (1991a). Hypertext as instructional design. *Educational Technology Research & Development, 39*(1), 83-92.

Jonassen, D. (1991b). Objectivism versus constructivism: Do we need a new philosophical paradigm? *Educational Technology Research & Development, 39*(3), 5-14.

Jonassen, D. H. (1992). Designing hypertext for learning. In E. Scanlon & T. O'Shea (Eds.), *New directions in educational technology* (pp. 123-131). New York: Springer-Verlag.

Jonassen, D. H. (1996). *Computers in the classroom: Mindtools for critical thinking*. Upper Saddle River, NJ: Prentice Hall.

Kafai, Y. (1994). Electronic play worlds: Children's construction of video games. In Y. Kafai & M. Resnick (Eds.), *Constructionism in practice: Rethinking the roles of technology in learning*. Mahwah, NJ: Lawrence Erlbaum Associates.

Kafai, Y. (1995). *Minds in play: Computer game design as a context for children's learning*. Mahwah, NJ: Lawrence Erlbaum Associates.

Kafai, Y., & Harel, I. (1991). Learning through design and teaching: Exploring social and collaborative aspects of constructionism. In I. Harel & S. Papert (Eds.), *Constructionism* (pp. 85-106). Norwood, NJ: Ablex.

Kafai, Y. B., & Ching, C. C. (2001). Affordances of collaborative software design planning for elementary students' science talk. *Journal of the Learning Sciences, 10*(3), 323-363.

Kafai, Y. B., Ching, C. C., & Marshall, S. (1997). Children as designers of educational multimedia software. *Computers and Education, 29,* 117-126.

Kozma, R. B. (1994). *Will* media influence learning? Reframing the debate. *Educational Technology Research & Development, 42*(2), 7-19.

Newell, A., & Simon, H. A. (1972). *Human problem solving*. Upper Saddle River, NJ: Prentice Hall.

Newman, D. (1990). Opportunities for research on the organizational impact of school computers. *Educational Researcher, 19*(3), 8-13.

Newman, D. (1992). Formative experiments on the coevolution of technology and the educational environment. In E. Scanlon & T. O'Shea (Eds.), *New directions in educational technology* (pp. 61-70). New York: Springer-Verlag.

Norman, D. A. (1988). *The psychology of everyday things*. New York: Basic Books.

Norman, D. A. (1993). *Things that make us smart: Defending human attributes in the age of the machine*. Reading, MA: Addison-Wesley.

Ogborn, J. (1999). Modeling clay for thinking and learning. In W. Feurzeig & N. Roberts (Eds.), *Modeling and simulation in science and mathematics education* (pp. 5-37). New York: Springer-Verlag.

Olive, J. (1998). Opportunities to explore and integrate mathematics with "The Geometer's Sketchpad." In R. Lehrer & D. Chazan (Eds.), *Designing learning environments for developing understanding of geometry and space* (pp. 395-418). Mahwah, NJ: Lawrence Erlbaum Associates.

Papert, S. (1980a). Computer-based microworlds as incubators for powerful ideas. In R. Taylor (Ed.), *The computer in the school: Tutor, tool, tutee* (pp. 203-210). New York: Teacher's College Press.

Papert, S. (1980b). *Mindstorms: Children, computers, and powerful ideas*. New York: BasicBooks.

Papert, S. (1987). Computer criticism vs. technocentric thinking. *Educational Researcher, 16*(1), 22-30.

Papert, S. (1991). Situating constructionism. In I. Harel & S. Papert (Eds.), *Constructionism* (pp. 1-11). Norwood, NJ: Ablex.

Papert, S. (1993). *The children's machine: Rethinking school in the age of the computer*. New York: Basic Books.

Pea, R., & Kurland, M. (1984). On the cognitive effects of learning computer programming. *New Ideas in Psychology, 2,* 1137-1168.

Penner, D. E. (2000/2001). Cognition, computers, and synthetic science: Building knowledge and meaning through modeling. *Review of Research in Education, 25,* 1-35.

Perkins, D. N. (1986). *Knowledge as design*. Mahwah, NJ: Lawrence Erlbaum Associates.

Perkins, D. N., & Unger, C. (1994). A new look in representations for mathematics and science learning. *Instructional Science, 22,* 1-37.

Petrie, H. G., & Oshlag, R. S. (1993). Metaphor and learning. In A. Ortony (Ed.), *Metaphor and thought* (2nd ed., pp. 579-609). Cambridge: Cambridge University Press.

Reigeluth, C., & Schwartz, E. (1989). An instructional theory for the design of computer-based simulations. *Journal of Computer-Based Instruction, 16*(1), 1-10.

Resnick, M. (1991). Overcoming the centralized mindset: Towards an understanding of emergent phenomena. In I. Harel & S. Papert (Eds.), *Constructionism* (pp. 204-214). Norwood, NJ: Ablex.

Resnick, M. (1994). *Turtles, termites, and traffic jams*. Cambridge, MA: MIT Press.

Resnick, M. (1996). Beyond the centralized mindset. *Journal of the Learning Sciences, 5,* 1-22.

Resnick, M. (1999). Decentralized modeling and decentralized thinking. In W. Feurzeig & N. Roberts (Eds.), *Modeling and simulation in science and mathematics education* (pp. 114-137). New York: Springer-Verlag.

Richey, R. C., & Nelson, W. A. (1996). Developmental research. In D. Jonassen (Ed.), *Handbook of research for educational communications and technology* (pp. 1213-1245). Washington, DC: Association for Educational Communications and Technology.

Richmond, B., & Peterson, S. (1996). *STELLA: An introduction to systems thinking*. Hanover, NJ: High Performance Systems.

Rieber, L. P. (1987). LOGO and its promise: A research report. *Educational Technology, 27*(2), 12-16.

Rieber, L. P. (1990). Using computer animated graphics in science instruction with children. *Journal of Educational Psychology, 82,* 135-140.

Rieber, L. P. (1991). Animation, incidental learning, and continuing motivation. *Journal of Educational Psychology, 83,* 318-328.

Rieber, L. P. (1992). Computer-based microworlds: A bridge between constructivism and direct instruction. *Educational Technology Research & Development, 40*(1), 93-106.

Rieber, L. P. (1996). Seriously considering play: Designing interactive learning environments based on the blending of microworlds, simulations, and games. *Educational Technology Research & Development, 44*(2), 43-58.

Rieber, L. P., & Parmley, M. W. (1995). To teach or not to teach? Comparing the use of computer-based simulations in deductive versus inductive approaches to learning with adults in science. *Journal of Educational Computing Research, 13*(4), 359-374.

Rieber, L. P., Luke, N., & Smith, J. (1998). Project KID DESIGNER: Constructivism at work through play. *Meridian: Middle School*

Computer Technology Journal [online], *1*(1). http://www.ncsu. edu/meridian/archive_of_meridian/jan98/index.html.

Roschelle, J. (1991, April). *MicroAnalysis of qualitative physics: Opening the black box.* Paper presented at the annual meeting of the American Educational Research Association, Chicago. (ERIC Document ED 338 490)

Roschelle, J., Kaput, J., & Stroup, W. (2000). SimCalc: Accelerating student engagement with the mathematics of change. In M. J. Jacobson & R. B. Kozma (Eds.), *Learning the sciences of the 21st century: Research, design, and implementing advanced technology learning environments* (pp. 47–75). Mahwah, NJ: Lawrence Erlbaum Associates.

Saettler, L. P. (1990). *The evolution of American educational technology.* Englewood, CO: Libraries Unlimited.

Salomon, G., Perkins, D. N., & Globerson, T. (1991). Partners in cognition: Extending human intelligence with intelligent technologies. *Educational Researcher, 20*(3), 2–9.

Spitulnik, M. W., Krajcik, J. S., & Soloway, E. (1999). Construction of models to promote scientific understanding. In W. Feurzeig & N. Roberts (Eds.), *Modeling and simulation in science and mathematics education* (pp. 70–94). New York: Springer-Verlag.

Suppes, P. (1980). Computer-based mathematics instruction. In R. Taylor (Ed.), *The computer in the school: Tutor, tool, tutee* (pp. 215–230). New York: Teachers College Press.

Tetenbaum, T., & Mulkeen, T. (1984, November). Logo and the teaching of problem-solving: A call for a moratorium. *Educational Technology,* 16–19.

Tinker, R. F., & Thornton, R. K. (1992). Constructing student knowledge in science. In E. Scanlon & T. O'Shea (Eds.), *New directions in educational technology* (pp. 153–170). New York: Springer-Verlag.

van den Akker, J. (1999). Principles and methods of development research. In J. van den Akker, R. M. Branch, K. Gustafson, N. Nieveen, & T. Plomp (Eds.), *Design approaches and tools in education and training* (pp. 1–14). Dordrecht, The Netherlands: Kluwer Academic.

White, B. Y. (1984). Designing computer games to help physics students understand Newton's laws of motion. *Cognition and Instruction, 1*(1), 69–108.

White, B. Y. (1992). A microworld-based approach to science education. In E. Scanlon & T. O'Shea (Eds.), *New directions in educational technology* (pp. 227–242). New York: Springer-Verlag.

White, B. Y. (1993). ThinkerTools: Causal models, conceptual change, and science education. *Cognition and Instruction, 10*(1), 1–100.

White, B. Y., & Frederiksen, J. R. (1998). Inquiry, modeling, and metacognition: Making science accessible to all students. *Cognition and Instruction, 16*(1), 3–118.

White, B. Y., & Frederiksen, J. R. (2000a). Technological tools and instructional approaches for making scientific inquiry accessible to all. In M. J. Jacobson & R. B. Kozma (Eds.), *Learning the sciences of the 21st century: Research, design, and implementing advanced technology learning environments* (pp. 321–359). Mahwah, NJ: Lawrence Erlbaum Associates.

White, B. Y., & Frederiksen, J. R. (2000b). Technological tools and instructional approaches for making scientific inquiry accessible to all. In M. J. Jacobson & R. B. Kozma (Eds.), *Innovations in science and mathematics education: Advanced designs for technologies of learning* (pp. 321–359). Mahwah, NJ: Lawrence Erlbaum Associates.

White, B. Y., & Horowitz, P. (1987). *ThinkerTools: Enabling children to understand physical laws.* Cambridge, MA: Bolt, Beranek, and Newman.

Wilensky, U., & Stroup, W. (2002, April). *Participatory simulations: Envisioning the networked classroom as a way to support systems learning for all.* Paper presented at the annual meeting of the American Educational Research Association, New Orleans, LA.

· 23 ·

LEARNING FROM HYPERTEXT: RESEARCH ISSUES AND FINDINGS

Amy Shapiro
University of Massachusetts—Dartmouth

Dale Niederhauser
Iowa State University

23.1 INTRODUCTION TO THE RESEARCH ISSUES

The question of how we learn from hypertext is more complicated than that of how we learn from traditional text. Although all the same elements of character decoding, word recognition, sentence comprehension, and so forth remain the same, a number of features unique to hypertext produce added complexity. It is these features that drive the research of hypertext in education and have shaped our discussion in this chapter.

The most basic feature of hypertext, of course, is its *nonlinear structure*. How nonlinear structure alters learners' mental representations or ability to use their new knowledge has been an active area of research. This feature gives way to a number of factors related to learning. Primary among these is a *flexibility of information access*. Whereas traditional text allows the author to assume what information has already been encountered and present new information accordingly, information within a hypertext may be retrieved in a sequence specified by each user. In other words, there is a greater degree of *learner control* when engaged in hypertext-assisted learning (HAL). The shift in control of access from author to learner places a greater cognitive burden on the learner. Specifically, the learner must now monitor to a greater extent whether he or she understands what has been read, determine whether information must be sought to close information gaps, and decide where to look for that

information in the text. In short, there are greater *metacognitive demands* on the reader during HAL.

While the vast majority of research on hypertext is not specifically relevant to learning, investigation into its educational utility began to heat up in the 1980s, and many research reports and articles have been published since then. Chen and Rada (1996) conducted a metanalytic study of learning from hypertext. Of 13 studies they found comparing learning outcomes for subjects using hypertext versus nonhypertext systems, 8 revealed an advantage of hypertext. Although the combined effect size was small to medium ($r = .12$), it was highly significant ($p < .01$). In addition, they report that the effect sizes and significance levels among studies comparing learning from hypertext and linear text were heterogeneous. They interpret this result as an indication that factors such as system design, system content, and experimental design influence educational effectiveness, and a number of empirical studies have pointed to the influence of such factors on learning outcomes.

In addition to system variables, user traits such as goals, motivation, and prior knowledge are also factors in HAL. Moreover, these learner variables interact with hypertext characteristics to influence learning outcomes. We have attempted here to sort through the data to identify the variables that affect HAL most strongly and the mechanisms through which this occurs. Wherever it is appropriate, we have also tried to explain how user and system variables interact. Because of such interactions, the field is largely looking toward adaptive technology to tailor systems for the user, so we have also included a section on adaptive hypertext systems. We conclude with a discussion of problems surrounding research on HAL. First, though, we begin with a brief discussion of theories that may explain the cognitive processes underlying HAL, as these theories serve to anchor much of our discussion.

23.2 THEORETICAL VIEWS OF LEARNING FROM HYPERTEXT

Although there are no well-developed models of hypertext-based learning per se, a number of theories of reading and learning may explain the cognitive underpinnings of the process. The two models that have had the greatest impact on research and our understanding of the process are the construction-integration model (CIM; Kintsch, 1988) and cognitive flexibility theory (CFT; Spiro, Coulson, Feltovitch, & Anderson, 1988; Spiro, Feltovitch, Jacobson, & Coulson, 1992). These theories and their relationship to hypertext-based learning are presented here.

23.2.1   Construction Integration

The CIM of text processing (Kintsch, 1988) suggests a three-stage process of text comprehension. The first is character or word decoding, which is invariant across media. The second is the construction of a *textbase*. This is a mental model of the factual information presented directly in the text. The process of textbase construction is also thought to be invariant across media. The third stage in the process is the creation of the *situation model*. It is this stage that is highly relevant to our understanding of learning from hypertext. A situation model is constructed when prior knowledge is integrated with new information from a text (the textbase). According to the CIM, the integration of prior knowledge with new information is necessary to achieve a deep understanding of new material. In other words, if no situation model is formed, no meaningful learning has been achieved.

For a situation model to be developed, then, active learning is necessary. The promotion of active learning is the essence of hypertext. As Landow (1992) has noted, the act of choosing which links to follow requires that the user take an active approach. He quotes Jonassen and Grabinger (1990), who urge that "hypermedia users *must* be mentally active while interacting with the information" (cited in Landow, 1992, p. 121). Indeed, a good deal of work has shown that active use on the part of learners results in advantages of hypertext, often beyond that seen in traditional text. However, although hypertext encourages active engagement with the material, it does not require it. The fact is that hypertext may be used passively. Some of the earliest studies of hypertext identified passivity as a cause for potential educational ineffectiveness (Meyrowitz, 1986). We discuss these points in some depth later in this chapter.

As a model of learning, the CIM has had a substantial influence on the way in which researchers think about learning in general, including HAL. It is common to find references to the construction of textbases and situation models in authors' discussions of HAL. In fact, these concepts are woven so deeply into many people's understanding of HAL that they are often referred to in research articles, even when no explicit reference is made to the CIM itself. This way of thinking about mental representations has become many hypertext researchers' standard framework for understanding HAL.

23.2.2   Cognitive Flexibility

Spiro and his colleagues have proposed CFT, a constructivist theory of learning from various media (Spiro et al., 1988, 1992). Like the CIM, CFT proposes the application of prior knowledge to go beyond the information given. To account for advanced learning, however, it also stipulates that the mental representations invoked for this purpose are constructed anew, rather than retrieved as static units from memory. This model of learning is based on the supposition that real-world cases are each unique and multifaceted, thus requiring the learner to consider a variety of dimensions at once. This being the case, the prior knowledge necessary to understand new knowledge cannot be brought out from intact memories of other single cases or experiences. Rather, stored knowledge derived from aspects of a variety of prior experiences must be combined and applied to the new situation. As Spiro et al. (1988) explain, "The *re*construction of knowledge requires that it first be *de*constructed—flexibility in applying knowledge depends both on schemata (theories) and cases first being disassembled so that they may later be adaptively reassembled" (p. 186). The implication of this model is that advanced learning takes place not only as a consequence of active learning and prior knowledge use, but also as a consequence of constructing knowledge anew for each novel problem.

This perspective of learning is relevant to hypertext-based learning because hypertext offers the possibility of coming at a topic from various perspectives. Because a learner can access a single document from multiple other sites, he or she will come to that document with multiple perspectives, depending on the point of origin or learning goal. In this way, CFT predicts that the mental representations resulting from repeated, ill-structured hypertext use will be multifaceted, and one's ability to use that knowledge should theoretically be more flexible. A number of studies have supported this perspective for advanced learners (Jacobson & Spiro, 1995; Spiro, Vispoel, Schmitz, Samarapungavan, & Boerger, 1987). This evidence is discussed with relevance to the importance of system structure in a later section.

In sum, the CIM and CFT each take different approaches to the task of explaining the cognitive processes underlying HAL, but both offer enlightenment. The CIM offers a detailed description of how stable mental representations are created during learning. There is a great deal of support for the CIM in the literature and it successfully predicts some of the conditions under which HAL will succeed or fail. The CIM is informative to hypertext research because it offers an explanation of the relevance of user behavior. Specifically, it explains the research that points to user behaviors such as link choice, navigation patterns, and metacognitive practice as mediators of learning. CFT offers an explanation of meaningful learning on the part of advanced learners. It successfully explains why the exploration of identical texts can result in more flexible, transferable knowledge from a hypertext than a traditional text. It adds to our understanding of HAL because it offers a unique explanation of how mental representations are constructed, reconstructed, and altered by exposure to dynamic information structures. Each of these frameworks for understanding HAL centers on a number of learner variables. The importance of these variables to HAL is discussed throughout the remainder of this chapter.

23.3 COGNITIVE FACTORS ASSOCIATED WITH READING AND LEARNING FROM HYPERTEXT

23.3.1 Basic Reading Processes

Decades of reading research can provide valuable insights to ground our understanding of how people read and learn in hypertext learning environments. Although there are differences between reading hypertext and reading traditional text, researchers have noted similarities in the basic cognitive processes associated with reading in either context. For example, Wenger and Payne (1996) examined whether several measures of cognitive processing that have been used to assess recall and comprehension when reading traditional text (i.e., working memory span, speed of accessing word knowledge in memory, reading rate) would also hold when reading hypertext. Twenty-two university students read three hierarchically structured hypertexts and completed a battery of reading proficiency assessments. They concluded that ". . . the relationships between the information processing measures and the hypertext reading measures replicate those documented between these information processing measures and performance with normal printed (linear) text" (p. 58). This provides support for the notion that the basic reading processes that guide the design of printed text can also be applied to the design of hypertext.

As mentioned under Introduction to the Research Issues, there are also clear differences between reading traditional text and reading hypertext, because the hypertext environment provides a whole new set of issues to be addressed. Alexander, Kulikowich, and Jetton (1994) showed how subject-matter knowledge contributed to readers developing a unique self-guided text when reading hypertext. That is, readers' past experiences and prior knowledge led them to make choices about the sequence for reading information in the hypertext in ways that are not possible when reading printed text. Further, when reading hypertext, the readers' focus can be at a more global level of processing, as opposed to the microprocessing orientation typically adopted when reading printed text. When reading hypertext, readers often focus on navigating the complex system rather than deriving meaning at the word, sentence, or paragraph level (Trumbull, Gay, & Mazur, 1992).

Other differences relate to the physical attributes associated with presenting hypertext on a computer screen. The limited size of the computer screen often necessitates the use of scrolling and the presentation of text in frames (Walz, 2001).

Both of these characteristics of hypertext place an increased load on the working memory. Eye movement research has shown that during reading, the eyes move forward and backward to allow the reader to reflect on what was read, predict what is coming, and confirm meaning in the text (Nuttall, 1996; Swaffar, Arens, & Byrnes, 1991). Left-to-right scrolling features in some hypertext makes that natural reading eye movement pattern difficult, as previously read text keeps scrolling off the screen. Breaking text into frames also inhibits the reading process in that what is read in one frame must be remembered when moving to new frames if the information across multiple frames is to be integrated. Other distractions that are often found in hypertext environments include unusual color schemes; reverse contrast (light letters on a dark background); multiple fonts, type sizes, and styles; and the use of drop-down boxes that may cover portions of the text (Walz, 2001). These features tend to interrupt the normal automatic reading processes of readers and thereby change the basic reading process. However, text structures must be examined in the context of their interactions with learner variables to understand the complexity of HAL.

23.3.2 Metacognition and the Role of the Reader

Despite claims that hypertext frees the reader to create his or her own individualized text, Smith (1996) points out that there is nothing inherent in the hypertext that is "democratic or antihierarchical." Hierarchy is apparent in the maps, outlines, and menus that serve as navigation aids in the hypertext. Although the sequence of accessing information in a hypertext is not imposed, the author determines the structure and content of information and the linkages among information nodes. The reader makes choices about how to proceed, creating a linear path through the text by following the links the author has established. Actual reading of words and sentences is essentially a sequential process that is the same as reading printed text.

What differs from reading printed text is the requirement that the reader make choices about how to proceed through the text, ostensibly increasing reader interest and engaging the reader in deeper processing of the information (Patterson, 2000). According to Patterson, a fundamental shift in the reading process relates to hypertext readers having to create their own path through the text. Actively engaged readers tend to feel a greater sense of control over what they read and how they read it. Results of their choices are instantaneous and readers become part of the meaning construction as they "write" an individualized text that may differ from what the author intended. Printed text tends to formalize the role of the author, while hypertext challenges our assumptions about the roles of the author and the reader. Thus, many view educational uses of hypertext as emancipatory and empowering because it forces readers to participate actively in creating meaning from the text.

Changing the reader's role in this way places additional cognitive requirements on the reader. As in traditional reading of printed text, the learner must engage basic lower-level processes (such as letter recognition and decoding words) and higher-level processes (such as relating new information to prior knowledge). Reading hypertext requires additional metacognitive functioning like choosing what to read and deciding on the sequence for reading information. Further, less proficient computer users must use cognitive resources to operate the computer (working the mouse, pressing keys, activating on-screen buttons, etc.; Niederhauser, Reynolds, Salmen, & Skolmoski, 2000). Compounded by factors such as reading ability, subject-matter knowledge, and the cognitive load required to read and navigate, hypertext may actually *interfere* with the reader's ability to make meaning from the text (Niederhauser et al., 2000; Shapiro, 1999).

However, a number of investigations have shown that increased metacognitive activity when reading hypertext can contribute positively to HAL outcomes. For instance, Shapiro (1998a) showed that students who used a principled approach to hypertext navigation performed better on an essay posttest of conceptual understanding than their less thoughtful counterparts. In that study, a relatively ill-structured system was used to encourage thoughtful navigation. Those who were given a highly structured system were less principled in their approach, using ease of access as a major criterion for link choice. In this case, students who were forced to be more metacognitive when navigating the less structured system learned more.

In some very recent reports, investigators have attempted to encourage metacognitive skills more directly. Azevedo and colleagues (Azevedo, Guthrie, Wang, & Mulhern, 2002; Azevedo, Seibert, Guthrie, Cromley, Wang, & Tron, 2002) engaged learners with a hypertext about the human circulatory system. Subjects were either paired with a human tutor who was trained in Winne's (1995, 2001) self-regulated learning (SRL) techniques, trained on the techniques themselves, asked simply to complete a self-generated goal, or given a series of factual questions to answer. In the coregulation condition, the tutor encouraged metacognitive strategies by providing a variety of prompts. Specifically, she encouraged self-questioning, content evaluation, judgments of learning, planning, goal setting, prior knowledge activation, and other activities. In the strategy instruction condition, subjects were trained to do the same thing as the tutor but to do so as independent learners. The other two conditions provided no metacognitive prompts, tutors, or training. Analyses of posttests revealed that the sophistication of learners' mental models shifted significantly more when provided with tutors or metacognitive training than when simply given learning goals and no training. Both the tutor group and the strategy instruction group demonstrated the greatest use of effective learning strategies and the least incidence of ineffective strategies. Subjects in the simple goal conditions showed great variability in their self-regulation. This investigation shows that, given traditional learning goals with little guidance about how to work through and think about the system, users are less able to meet the challenges inherent in HAL and do not meet their full potential. Giving learners a short introduction to SRL techniques, however, can be almost as effective as providing a personal tutor.

Other investigators have experimented with using prompts or questions designed to encourage metacognition without training or tutors. Kauffman (2002) presented subjects with a hypertext designed to teach about educational measurement. Half the subjects were assigned to work with a system that presented automated self-monitoring prompts in the form of questions. The prompts appeared each time a user moved from one node to another. If students were unable to answer the question correctly, they were encouraged to go back and review the page they had just read. The other half of the subjects were able to click freely on link buttons and move to a new page without answering any questions about their understanding. Both groups performed comparably on the declarative knowledge test. Students in the metacognitive prompt condition, however, outperformed their counterparts on a posttest that assessed their ability to apply what they learned to real-world problems (a measure of situation model learning). Interestingly, the groups did not differ in their awareness of metacognition. Providing automated self-regulation prompts was an effective means of encouraging deep learning, even if subjects were unaware of how the prompts altered their thinking about their own learning. It should also be noted that, because of the small size of this hypertext, there were few link buttons and subjects received only three or four prompts during the learning period. That clear improvement in learning was observed after such a mild intervention speaks to its promise.

In sum, the nature of hypertext renders HAL a more cognitively demanding mode of learning. As such, the use of metacognitive strategies is all the more important in this context. A number of studies have shown, however, that even minimal user training or automated prompts may be used successfully to promote metacognitive strategies and augment learning outcomes.

23.3.3 Conceptual Structure

Much of the interest in using hypertext to promote learning is grounded in the notion that hypertext information structures may reflect the semantic structures of human memory (Bush, 1945; Jonassen, 1988, 1991; Jonassen & Wang, 1993; Tergan, 1997b). Researchers have asserted that developing a hypertext that provides access to an expert's semantic structures could improve the learning and comprehension of nonexperts who read it. The assumption is that "...the network-like representation of subject matter in a hypertext as well as the kind of links between information units which support associative browsing correspond to the structure of human knowledge and basic principles of the functioning of the human mind (Bush, 1945; Jonassen, 1990). Because of the suggested match, it is assumed that in learning situations information represented in hypertext may be easily assimilated by the learners' minds" (Tergan, 1997b, pp. 258–259). Thus, researchers have attempted to determine whether nonexpert users will assimilate expert conceptual structures modeled in a hypertext.

Jonassen and Wang (1993) developed a series of studies to examine whether university students' learning of the structural nature of hypertext content was enhanced by a "graphical browser" based on an expert's semantic map. The structure of the graphical browser resembled a concept map, with the concepts arranged in a weblike structure. Lines on the map indicated connections among the concepts, and descriptive phrases superimposed over the lines described the connections between the concepts. The hypertext was quite large, containing

240 informational screens and 1167 links. Seventy-five major concepts were represented in the concept nodes. Assessment measures addressed relationship proximity judgments, semantic relationships, and analogies. All were designed to assess students' structural knowledge of the content presented in the hypertext. Students read versions of the text that provided structural cues about the topic (either the graphical browser or a pop-up window explaining the connection represented by the link that was just accessed). Results showed little evidence that learners internalized the expert's semantic structures after being exposed to the structural cues in the hypertext-user interface. It should be noted that when a task was introduced that required students to construct a semantic network about the topic, their ability to represent relationships among the concepts was affected. (The importance of task variables in HAL is addressed later in the chapter.) Nonetheless, the direct measures in this study did not reveal a strong effect of system structure on learners' conceptual structures.

McDonald and Stevenson (1999) used indirect measures to examine the effects of structural cues on cognitive structures. They explored differences in learning when students used what the authors referred to as a "conceptual map" versus a "spatial map." As with Jonassen and Wang's graphical browser, the conceptual map provided a representation of the key concepts in the text and specified the relations among them. The spatial map presented a hierarchical representation of the hypertext nodes and links showing what information was available and where it could be found. In the spatial map condition the structure of the text was represented but there was no attempt to show connections among the concepts.

In their study, university students read a 4500–word hypertext (45 nodes) on human learning that used highlighted keywords to link between nodes. Assessments included a 40–question test. Twenty items tested factual knowledge and 20 items were synthesis-type questions that required a deeper understanding of the text. Students received access to a spatial map, received access to a conceptual map, or were in a control group that did not get access to any map. Results indicated that the spatial map facilitated navigation but that students in the conceptual map condition performed better on learning measures on a 1-week-delayed posttest. Thus, use of the conceptual map available in this hypertext appeared to help students gain more durable and useful knowledge.

Why the discrepancy between these results and those of Jonassen and Wang (1993)? Jonassen and Wang tried to measure semantic representations directly. They tried to demonstrate a direct relationship between expertlike structures modeled on the hypertext and the cognitive internal structures of the learners. McDonald and Stevenson inferred the nature of learners' cognitive structures based on student responses to higher-level thinking questions. Their assumption was that if users could answer synthesis-type questions, they had internalized the expertlike structures. In addition, inconsistencies may have been related to the fact that McDonald and Stevenson used a much smaller, less complex text.

There is little evidence, then, that simply working with a hypertext system designed to represent an expert's conceptual understanding of a topic can lead to a direct transfer of expertlike mental representations to the reader. Developing and changing learners' conceptualizations has long been a challenge for educational researchers (Dole & Sinatra, 1998; Posner, Strike, Hewson, & Gertzog, 1982; Strike & Posner, 1992). It seems clear that some degree of cognitive engagement is required if readers are to benefit fully from HAL. As McDonald and Stevens' (1999) work demonstrates, though, traditional assessments of learning (such as short-answer and essay tests) are clearly affected by system structure. The next section explores in detail how system structure effects HAL.

23.4 THE EFFECT OF SYSTEM STRUCTURE ON LEARNING

As the previous section showed, system structure can be communicated to users through a variety of means, including the organization of links on pages, maps, overviews, and indexes. In their metanalysis of studies on learning from hypertext, Chen and Rada (1996) searched for evidence of a learning advantage from one of these tools over another. They found no linear trend in the relationships among learning effectiveness and indexes, tables of contents, or graphical maps. They conclude that the "organizational structure of information dominates the extent that users' performance was affected and that individual components of hypertext or nonhypertext systems, such as indices, tables of contents, and graphical maps, may have a relatively weaker influence" (p. 145). Given this evidence, the present section discusses learning outcome based on the system structure in general, rather than the particular means through which the structure is communicated.

23.4.1 A Seemingly Contradictory Literature

As Chen and Rada (1996) have noted, the majority of studies have shown that system structure effects learning outcome, yet a number of studies have shown no such effect (Dee-Lucas and Larkin, 1995; Foltz, 1996; Shapiro, 1998a, 1999). This lack of effect may be due to any number of variables, including the way in which learning is assessed, users' prior knowledge, learning tasks and/or goals, navigation patterns, and actual interest in the domain. Indeed, one problem with research on HAL is that there are no standards for tests of learning outcome, user variables, or system design. (See Problems with HAL Research for more on that topic.) As such, a lack of results may often be attributable to a lack of distinction between systems or a failure to account for interacting variables. Even among studies that do demonstrate learners' sensitivity to a system's global structure, conclusions about what a "good" structure is differ greatly.

Some studies have shown advantages to using a highly organized system structure such as a hierarchy. Simpson and McKnight (1990) suggest that a well-structured system can augment learning. They presented subjects with a 2500–word hypertext on houseplants. Subjects were shown indexes listing the system content that were structured either hierarchically or alphabetically. In other words, only one system organized the information according to conceptual relationships. The differences between groups' learning outcomes were marked. The hierarchical group outperformed the alphabetical group on a posttest of content and was better able to reconstruct the organization of content on a mapping posttest.

Does this mean that highly organized, hierarchical structures are always superior? Research on learning from traditional text would suggest so. A large body of literature on the relevance to hierarchical structures to learning has shown that such well-defined structures are important to information acquisition (Bower, Clark, Lesgold, & Winzenz, 1969; Eylon & Reif, 1984; Kintsch & Keenan, 1974) and expert performance and problem solving (Chase & Simon, 1973; Chi & Koeske, 1983; De Groot, 1965; Friendly, 1977; Hughes & Michton, 1977; Johnson, 1967). This work largely influenced the design of hypertext systems from the beginning. The hypertext literature makes clear, however, that no single structure, including hierarchies, is appropriate for all learners, learning goals, or domains of study. In fact, some studies have shown no benefit of a hierarchical system structure over other nonlinear hypertexts (Dee-Lucas & Larkin, 1995; Melara, 1996). Dee-Lucas and Larkin (1995), for instance, gave subjects either a generalized or a specific learning goal while working with a hypertext on electricity. Some of the subjects received the information in a linear format, whereas others used one of two hypertext systems. One of these was hierarchical and the other was an index. Subjects were later asked to summarize what they had read. Analyses of the summaries revealed no differences between the two hypertext groups. Further, neither hypertext group outperformed the linear group when the goal was specific.

Beyond showing no advantage of hierarchies, some studies have actually found advantages of working with ill-structured hypertexts. Shapiro (1998a) presented subjects with identical systems that presented the links either within a clear, hierarchical structure or as a collection of links and nodes with no particular underlying structure. A posttest revealed that subjects in the unstructured group wrote essays that were of significantly higher quality. Their essays were also judged to reflect a significantly greater understanding of the material than did those written by the well-structured group.

To make matters even more complicated, still other studies have demonstrated the pitfalls of an ill-structured system design. Gordon, Gustavel, Moore, and Hankey (1988) were able to show that students who read a linear presentation of material actually came away with greater comprehension of the main ideas presented in the material than those who had worked with a hypertext system. In response to posttest questions about the experience of learning from these systems, those in the hypertext condition reported a feeling of disorientation; they were not sure what to expect on a document after clicking a button. Presumably, the resulting feeling of disorientation prevented subjects from creating a coherent mental representation that would allow them to store information with greater effectiveness. This study is part of a larger literature that demonstrates how a poor structure can mitigate learning by disorienting learners (Dias, Gomes, & Correia, 1999; Edwards & Hardman, 1989; Hammond, 1991).

This idea was studied in some depth by Britt, Rouet, and Perfetti (1996), who manipulated the transparency of their system's underlying structure. They presented subjects with systems designed to teach about history that presented the information either in a linear format or in a hierarchy. Each of those conditions either was scrambled or thematically organized the nodes. When the underlying structure of the material was made clear to subjects through thematic organization, subjects recalled the same amount of information on a free-recall posttest, regardless of whether they studied with a hypertext or a digitized, linear text. When the organizing information was removed and subjects were given only a "scrambled" overview of the system documents, the linear subjects actually did better than the hierarchical subjects on the recall test.

As shown here, the literature can appear to be downright contradictory but some common themes have emerged. As we see in the remainder of this section, the effectiveness of "good' structures like hierarchies tends to hinge on interactions among learners' prior knowledge, learners' goals, and the activity (or metacognitive) level of the learners' approach. In the following sections we explain two general conclusions drawn from the literature and explain the ways in which these variables interact to influence learning.

23.4.2 When a Well-Defined Structure Is Best

Learners with low prior knowledge benefit from well-formed structures like hierarchies during HAL. Several studies converge on this general conclusion. A recent study by Potelle and Rouet (2002) clearly illustrates the effect. Subjects identified as having low knowledge of social psychology were asked to use a hypertext to learn about the topic. They were assigned to use systems that presented the information as either a hierarchy, a seemingly unprincipled network, or an alphabetically structured list of topics. Subjects were given 20 min to learn about the topic and were then given posttests designed to assess the level of textbase and situation model knowledge they had gained. The results were unambiguous. On measures of textbase learning, multiple choice, and simple recall, subjects in the network condition were outperformed by those in the hierarchy or list conditions. On the posttest questions designed to assess subjects' situation models, however, subjects in the hierarchical condition outperformed those in both of the other groups.

These results strongly suggest that subjects were confused by the seemingly random (at least from their perspectives) network structure and learning was mitigated. This was so even for factual information present on individual documents (as tested by the textbase questions). When subjects were oriented by the other system structures, they were able to acquire this type of knowledge from the system. Simple orientation was not enough, however, to aid subjects in attaining a coherent, meaningful understanding of the information as a whole. Instead, subjects gained that type of knowledge best when they were shown the hierarchy. Only the hierarchical system was able to keep subjects oriented enough to create a textbase while also providing conceptual relationships that promoted deeper learning (the construction of a situation model).

System structure need not be hierarchical to benefit novices. The important characteristic for low-knowledge learners is that the conceptual relationship between documents be made clear. This was demonstrated by Shapiro (1999). In that study, subject identified as nonexperts in biology were assigned to work with either a hierarchy, an arrangement of thematic clusters, an unstructured collection of interconnected documents, or a linear (electronic) book. All system conditions presented the same documents about animal biology.

A cued-association posttest showed that subjects in all three hypertext conditions were able to recall the conceptually related topics, which were presented through system links. Subjects assigned to the electronic book condition differed significantly in this regard from those in the linked conditions. (The possibility of a repetition effect through simply seeing the link button names was ruled out with a separate control condition.) Learning across conditions was shown to be shallow, however, as all groups performed poorly on a problem-solving posttest. A closer look at the data, however, revealed that problem-solving performance was related to an interaction between the user interface and the navigation pattern. Specifically, the clustered condition presented short phrases adjacent to each link button that provided some detail about the relationship between the current document and the one represented by the link. The data revealed a significant correlation between the actual use of these buttons and performance on corresponding inferential items. Simply put, subjects were more likely to get a problem-solving question correct when they actually used the link that joined the documents relevant to the question.

In this case, not even the hierarchical structure aided subjects in creating a meaningful understanding of the material. However, the use of more explicit pointers to conceptual relationships was related to an increase in problem-solving ability. The important point about this study is that there is nothing "magical" about hierarchies for novices. Rather, any device that will explicate the conceptual relationships between topics can aid low-knowledge learners.

The importance of a clear, conceptually based system structure as it relates to meeting specific learning goals was also demonstrated by Shapiro (1998b). Specifically, she was able to show that the ability of low-prior knowledge learners to meet their goals may be mediated by a structure's compatibility with the learning goal. In the study, subjects were all pretested for knowledge of animal family resemblances and interspecies relationships within ecosystems. Subjects were included only if they had good knowledge of animal families but low knowledge of ecosystems. They were then asked to learn about a world of fictitious animals with the aid of a hypermedia program that provided an advance organizer structured around either animal families or ecosystems. They were also assigned the goal of learning about either animal families or ecosystems, with these factors fully crossed. All groups performed equivalently on posttest items that probed knowledge of animal families. These results were attributed to subjects' prior knowledge of that domain.

The posttest of ecosystem knowledge revealed how both prior knowledge and learning goals influence the effectiveness of system structure. Those who did not see the ecosystems organizer performed poorly on the ecosystems posttest items, even when they were in that goal condition. The ecosystem organizer, however, aided learners in meeting an ecosystems learning goal about which they had little or no prior knowledge. The effect was strong enough to produce incidental learning effects, as those assigned to learn about animal families also learned about ecosystems when exposed to the ecosystem organizer. In fact, subjects in the ecosystems organizer group who were *not* assigned to the ecosystems learning goal actually learned more about that topic than those in the animal families organizer condition who *were* told to learn about ecosystems. Thus, for learners with low prior knowledge of ecosystems, subjects learned about ecosystems only when they saw that structure. This result speaks to the great potential of a well-defined, goal-appropriate structure for initial learning by novices.

While most of the research examining HAL has been conducted with adult readers, work with children has been largely consistent with that with adults. Shin, Schallert, and Savenye (1994) examined the relationship between prior knowledge and learner control in learning by 110 second-grade students. A simple hypertext on food groups was presented in a free-access condition that allowed students to access every possible topic in the lesson in any order through a button-driven network structure. The same text was also presented in a limited-access form that had a hierarchical structure allowing the students to choose only topics that were related to the topic just presented. Both texts were also divided into an advisement condition, in which the program made suggestions to the reader on how to proceed, and a no-advisement condition. Students completed paper-and-pencil pre- and posttests to assess their learning of the content. According to the authors, "...High prior knowledge students seemed able to function equally well in both conditions whereas low prior knowledge students seemed to learn more from the limited-access condition than from the free access condition" (p. 43).

There have been some notable exceptions in this area of the literature. Among these is a study by Hofman and van Oostendorp (1999). Forty university students read a hierarchically structured hypertext on basic physical and biological science concepts. Half of the students had access to a graphical conceptual map that included information nodes and cause-and-effect relations between them. The remaining students read the same text, with a topic list in place of the conceptual map. Students then responded to 32 multiple-choice questions that addressed text-based recall questions and inference questions that required linking concepts from two or more screens and drawing on prior knowledge. Both types of questions addressed detailed, or micro-level, and general, or macro-level, content. Results indicated that students with low prior knowledge who had access to the conceptual map had lower scores on the inference questions than did low-prior knowledge students who did not have access to the map. The authors suggested that the conceptual map might have hindered the understanding of less knowledgeable readers because it drew students' attention away from the content of the text and focused them on macro structures. Low-prior knowledge students may have been overwhelmed by the complexity of the information system as revealed in the conceptual map.

In sum, well-structured hypertexts may offer low-knowledge learners an introduction to the ways in which topics relate to one another and an easy-to-follow introduction to a domain.

This is especially so when the structure is compatible with the learning goal. Well-defined structures also allow novices to stay oriented while exploring the information. However, some evidence has been found that contradicts this conclusion, and as Spiro et al. (1987) note, there is danger in oversimplifying a topic for learners. Providing rigid structures, especially for ill-structured domains (such as history and psychology), can impose arbitrary delineations that may impede progress as a learner advances in knowledge. For this reason, ill-structured hypertexts also offer advantages.

23.4.3 When Ill-Structured Systems Are Best

Both the CIM and CFT predict that ill-structured systems will benefit more advanced learners. From the perspective of CFT, ill-structured, multiply linked systems provide the learner with the opportunity to approach ideas from multiple perspectives, laying the groundwork for creating flexible knowledge that can be applied to new situations. The CIM also predicts gains from ill-structured systems because they promote the application of prior knowledge by encouraging the user to seek global coherence. In an article comparing and discussing three educational hypertext systems, Anderson-Inman and Tenny (1989) note that "one of the most important factors influencing whether or not studying will actually lead to knowledge acquisition is the degree to which students become actively involved in trying to make sense out of the material" (p. 27). They go on to explain how system structure can encourage this type of approach in a discussion of "exploratory" hypertexts. These are hypertexts that allow users to interact with and explore the system in ways that meet their particular goals or purposes at the moment. In other words, such systems do not impose a restricting structure on the information, allowing users to explore various aspects of relationships between ideas. Indeed, Anderson-Inman and Tenny note that exploratory hypertexts encourage learners to build their own organizational schema for the information. Since the publication of that article, empirical studies have been able to show that exploratory hypertexts can have such an effect on learning. Specifically, it has been shown that there is a relationship among system structure, active strategies, and learning.

As mentioned earlier, Shapiro (1998a) compared hierarchical and unstructured systems in a study of American history learning. Subjects in that study performed better on several measures when presented with the unstructured system. Among the measures of learning was an essay that was scored on four dimensions: (1) How well integrated was the information in the essay? (2) How clear was the author's argument? (3) How deeply does the author understand the topic about which he or she is writing? and (4) How was the overall quality of the essay? On each of these dimensions, subjects in the unstructured condition significantly outperformed those in the hierarchical condition. Further, navigation patterns differed between the system condition groups. Subjects in the hierarchical group were able to navigate more passively because the highly structured nature of the system kept them oriented in the information space. As a consequence, they used ease of access as a major criterion for link choice. Those in the unstructured system condition, however, were more principled in their movements through the information.

Taken together, the essay and navigation results suggest that the less structured system promoted more active processing and a deeper level of learning. How can these results be reconciled with Simpson and McKnight (1990) or the large literature showing the superiority of hierarchical information structures in traditional text? At least part of the answer lies in the importance of active learning as an interacting variable. Subjects who take advantage of the opportunity to work actively tend to show improved learning. Indeed, in a study of traditional text-based learning, Mannes and Kintsch (1987) note that refraining from "providing readers with a suitable schema and thereby forcing them to create their own... might make learning from texts more efficient" (p. 93). However, providing students with ill-structured hypertexts does not guarantee that active learning will occur, as not all students will thoughtfully engage with the hypertext content.

Another important point to consider when evaluating the educational value of any hypertext is the type of learning assessed. The significant difference in learning between groups in Simpson and McKnight's study was on a test of factual content (the textbase), while Shapiro (1999) examined students' answers to essay questions (the situation model). Rote learning is often aided by easily accessed structures that make fact retrieval simple. Deeper learning is aided by systems that promote a bit of "intellectual wrestling."

Jacobson and Spiro (1995) provide an excellent example of this point. In their study subjects were asked to read a number of documents about the impact of technology on society. Subjects in all conditions had been introduced to several "themes" concerning how technology influences a society. They were then randomly assigned to work with differing hypertext systems to meet a learning goal. Those in the control condition were told to explore the hypertext to identify a single theme running through the documents. Those in the experimental condition were told to identify multiple themes running through a series of "minicases." As such, they were put in a position to see multiple connections between documents, each signifying a different type of relationship. The material, then, appeared less orderly for the experimental subjects. After working with the systems for four sessions, the control group actually gained more factual knowledge than the experimental group. On the problem-solving posttest, though, the experimental group significantly outperformed the control group. Jacobson and Spiro were also able to show that those who had pretested as active, engaged learners performed better in the experimental condition than their less active counterparts in the same condition. Compared with other high-action learners, subjects performed better in the experimental than in the control condition.

The work reviewed in this section illustrates the benefits of ill-structured hypertexts for meaningful, advanced learning on the part of active, engaged learners. A cautionary note is warranted, however. Giving too little information about structure may also be detrimental. A great number of studies have examined the pitfalls of getting disoriented or "lost in hyperspace." Also, too little guidance can paralyze learners with an overwhelming cognitive load. A balance must be struck, allowing learners to reap benefits from systems that offer skill-appropriate guidance yet do not "spoon-feed" the information.

23.4.4 Conclusions

The research on organizing tools and system structure indicates that well-defined structures (such as hierarchies) are helpful if the learning goal is to achieve simple, factual knowledge (a textbase). Such structures can also be helpful (and perhaps even necessary) for beginning students. In keeping with prior research in text-based learning, however, promoting active learning is also an important consideration. By providing a structure that is highly organized or simple to follow, learners may become passive. The challenge for designers is to challenge beginning learners sufficiently while not overburdening them to the point where learning is mitigated.

Ill-structured systems are often beneficial for deep learning, especially for advanced learners. Providing less obvious organizational structures has the effect of challenging the learner to seek coherence within the system. The overall effect is to promote active strategies and improve learning. We do not claim, however, that ill-structured systems are always best for advanced learners, as learners do not always apply their prior knowledge. A passive learner will garner little from any hypertext system, beyond some facts stated explicitly in the text. The work reviewed in this section suggests that system structure and learning strategy interact to enhance advanced learning.

23.5 LEARNER VARIABLES

23.5.1 Individual Knowledge and Engagement

As discussed previously, readers come to a hypertext with differing levels of *prior knowledge,* and this variable has received considerable attention in the context of HAL. Specifically, research has yielded fairly consistent findings concerning different levels of control (Balajthy, 1990; Dillon & Gabbard, 1998; Gall & Hannafin, 1994; Large, 1996; Tergan, 1997c). That is, low-prior knowledge readers tend to benefit from more structured program-controlled hypertexts, whereas high-prior knowledge readers tend to make good use of more learner-controlled systems. Gall and Hannafin (1994) state, "Individuals with extensive prior knowledge are better able to invoke schema-driven selections, wherein knowledge needs are accurately identified *a priori* and selections made accordingly. Those with limited prior knowledge, on the other hand, are unable to establish information needs in advance, making their selections less schema-driven."

Another important individual difference that has received attention in the literature is the effect that learning style, or *cognitive style,* has on learning from hypertext under different treatment conditions. As our explanation of the interaction between active learning strategies and system structure showed, individual differences in learning style are often important to the learning outcomes. This is so largely because they interact with other factors such as system structure.

Some researchers believe that there may be a relationship between types of navigational strategies in hypertext and whether the learner is field dependent or field independent. Field-independent learners tend to be more active learners and use internal organizing structures more efficiently while learning. Thus, it would seem that degrees of structure in hypertext will be related to the learning outcomes for field-dependent or -independent learners.

Lin and Davidson-Shivers (1996) examined the effects of linking structure type and field dependence and independence on recall of verbal information from a hypertext. One hundred thirty-nine university students read one of five hypertext-based instructional programs on Chinese politics. Treatments included linking structures with varying degrees of structure from linear to random. Field dependence or independence was determined by the Group Embedded Figures Test and learning was assessed through a 30–item fact-based multiple-choice test on the content provided in the lesson. According to the authors, subjects who were more field independent had higher scores on the recall measure regardless of treatment group. That is, the authors did not find a significant interaction between linking structure type and field dependence or independence.

These measures were text-based. Thus, it is not surprising that no effect was observed, as the posttest did not assess the kind of knowledge that would be augmented by hypertext or active strategies (see Landow, 1992). However, Dillon and Gabbard (1998) have noted the frequency of such negative results and concluded that "the cognitive style distinction of field dependence/independence remains popular, but, as in most applications to new technology designs, it has failed to demonstrate much in the way of predictive or explanatory power and perhaps should be replaced with style dimensions that show greater potential for predicting behavior and performance" (p. 344). Although their sample size was small (only four studies), Chen and Rada (1996) also reported no general effect of active versus passive learning strategies in their metanalysis of HAL. As noted earlier, however, a great deal of research converges on the fact that passive engagement with a hypertext will mitigate learning outcomes when working with an unstructured hypertext. It may be that learning strategy affects learning outcomes primarily when it interacts with other factors (such as system structure). Additionally, success in meeting simplistic goals such as fact retrieval is not generally affected by learning style.

23.5.2 Reading Patterns

Researchers have attempted to identify patterns of reader navigation as they read hypertext. In an early study of navigation patterns, researchers watched subjects read hypertext and identified six distinct strategies: skimming, checking, reading, responding, studying, and reviewing (Horney & Anderson-Inman, 1994). Another effort, by Castelli, Colazzo, and Molinari (1998), examined the relationships among a battery of psychological factors and a series of navigation indexes. Based on their examinations the authors identified seven categories of hypertext users and related the kinds of cognitive characteristics associated with the various patterns. However, such studies simply addressed what readers did, not the relationship between reading patterns and learning.

Other investigations have examined how individual navigation patterns relate to learning (Lawless & Brown, 1997; Lawless & Kulikowich, 1996). For example, Lawless and Kulikowich (1996) examined navigation patterns of 41 university students who read a 150-frame hypertext on learning theories. Their purpose was to identify how students navigated and how their strategies related to learning outcomes. They identified three profiles that characterized readers' navigation of hypertext. Some students acted as knowledge seekers, systematically working through the text to extract information. Others worked as feature explorers, trying out the "bell and whistle" features to see what they did, whereas others were apathetic users who examined the hypertext at a superficial level and quit after accessing just a few screens. They found that learner interest and domain knowledge had a significant influence on readers' navigational strategies. There was also some indication that knowledge seekers tended to learn more from the text than did feature explorers.

Other research has attempted to determine underlying cognitive characteristics that are reflected in the navigation strategies employed. Balcytiene (1999) used a highly structured 19-node hypertext on Gothic art recognition. Inserted "guiding questions" were designed to focus the readers' attention. Fifteen Finnish university students read the hypertext and completed a pretest, a posttest, and an interview. The pretest and posttest involved recognizing whether artifacts were Gothic and providing a rationale for their opinions.

The authors identified two underlying characteristics for these readers. "Self-regulated readers" tended to extract systematically all of the information in the text. They were more independent and exploratory in their reading patterns. In contrast, "cue-dependent readers" focused on finding the answers to the guiding questions. They were highly task oriented, looking for the "right answer" rather than learning general concepts. The pattern of findings was interesting. Self-regulated readers went from an average of 62.5% correct on the pretest to 98% correct on the posttest, while the cue-dependent group's average scores actually declined slightly, from 91.5% to 87.5% correct. Consistent with work reported previously in this chapter, this highly structured hypertext appeared to be more beneficial to low-prior knowledge readers. Although their results were nonsignificant (probably due to the small sample size or strangely high pretest scores of the cue-dependent group), further research into the self-regulated/cue-dependent distinction may be warranted.

Hypertext navigation is not, however, always a systematic and purposeful process. An extensive area of hypertext navigation research centers on examining the effects of reader disorientation, or becoming "lost in hyperspace" on learning. According to Dede (1988; cited in Jonassen, 1988), "The richness of non-linear representation carries a risk of potential intellectual indigestion, loss of goal directedness, and cognitive entropy." Disorientation appears to stem from two factors (Dias, et al., 1999; McDonald & Stevenson, 1999). First is the complexity of the HAL task. Readers must allocate cognitive resources to navigate the text, read and understand the content, and actively integrate the new information with prior knowledge. Second is what Woods (1984; cited in McDonald & Stevenson, 1999) calls the "keyhole phenomenon." The scope of document content and the overall linking structure are not apparent when one is viewing an individual screen, causing readers to have problems locating their position in the document relative to the text as a whole.

A considerable body of research has attempted to address the keyhole phenomenon. Much of this work examines the effects of different types of user interfaces on user disorientation (e.g., Dias et al., 1999; Schroeder & Grabowski, 1995; Stanton, Taylor, & Tweedie, 1992). Unfortunately, this research has been concerned predominantly with the identification of system structures to promote ease of navigation rather than the effects of such structures on learning.

Niederhauser et al. (2000) addressed the other disorientation issue, cognitive resource allocation, by providing options to allow readers to choose their method for accessing text information and to change that method as they read. The researchers developed a hypertext describing behaviorist and constructivist learning theories that could be read in a linear fashion, moving sequentially down each branch of the hierarchy for each topic, or hypertextually, by linking between related concepts on the two topics. Reading the 83-screen hypertext was part of a regular class assignment for 39 university students who participated in the study. Students were tested on the content as part of the class. Examination of navigation patterns showed that some students adopted a purely linear approach, systematically moving through each frame for one theory, then moving through the second theory in the same manner. Other students read a screen on one theory, then used a link to compare that information with the other theory, and proceeded through the text using this compare and contrast strategy. Results indicated that students who read the text in a linear fashion had higher scores on a multiple-choice test of factual content and an essay that required students to compare and contrast the major themes in the hypertext. Increased cognitive load was hypothesized as the reason students who used the linking features did not perform as well on the posttests.

In sum, the need to navigate through a hypertext is a defining feature that differentiates reading and learning in a hypertext environment from reading and learning with traditional printed text. Initial navigation strategies may be adopted due to interest, motivation, and intrinsic or extrinsic goals of the reader. Several authors (Niederhauser et al., 2000; Shapiro, 1999; Tergan, 1997c; Yang, 1997) have discussed issues of cognitive load when engaging in HAL. (See Paas & van Merrienboer [1994], Sweller [1988], and Sweller, van Merrienboer, and Paas [1998] for more about the problem of cognitive load during instruction.) When the cognitive load associated with navigating through the text interferes with the reader's ability to make sense of the content, the reader may adopt compensatory strategies to simplify the learning task. Thus, navigation strategies may influence what the reader learns from the text and may be influenced by the conceptual difficulty associated with the content and the learning task.

23.5.3 Learning Goals

Goal-directed learning appears to have a powerful influence on HAL (Jonassen & Wang, 1993). According to Dee-Lucas and Larkin (1999), "Readers develop an internal representation of the text's propositional content and global organization, which forms their textbase. They also construct a more inclusive representation of the text topic incorporating related prior knowledge for the subject matter, which is their situation model. The nature of the representations developed by the reader reflects the requirements of the study goal . . . " (p. 283). Thus having a purpose for reading gives the learner a focus that encourages the incorporation of new information into existing knowledge structures in specific ways.

Curry et al. (1999) conducted a study to examine the effect of providing a specific learning objective to guide the reading of a hypertext. Fifty university students read a 60–frame hypertext on Lyme disease. Half of the students were given a specific task to guide their learning. They were given a scenario about a man with physical symptoms and a probable diagnosis and told to use the hypertext to determine the accuracy of the information in the scenario. The other half of the subjects were told to read the text carefully, as they would be asked a series of questions at the end. Although there were no differences found on recall measures, the concept maps that students drew did show differences. Students with a specific goal constructed more relational maps, which the authors felt demonstrated a more sophisticated internal representation of the content.

Not all specific learning goals promote deep, meaningful learning, however. In a study discussed earlier, Azevedo et al. (2002) gave some subjects a goal of answering specific questions about the human circulatory system, whereas other subjects were able to generate their own goal. Some subjects in the question-answering groups showed an increased sophistication of their mental models of circulation, but many actually showed a decrease in sophistication. None of the subjects in the learner-generated condition showed a decrease in their mental models' quality, whereas almost all showed an increase. Moreover, those in the self-generated goal condition demonstrated more effective use of metacognitive strategies.

Subjects in Curry and his colleagues' study (1999) benefited from a specific goal because it capitalized on the features offered by hypertext. The specific goal of fact-finding assigned by Azevedo et al. was not so compatible with HAL. Early in the history of hypertext in educational settings, Landow (1992) wrote about the importance of matching learning goals to the uniqueness of the technology. He points out that hypertext and printed text have different advantages and that hypertext assignments should be written that complement it. Goals like fact retrieval squander the richness of hypertext because fact-finding is not aided by multiple links. A number of studies, including that reported by Azevedo et al. (2002), exemplify this point.

What sort of learning goals do hypertext environments enhance? Landow suggests that assignments should be written to allow learners to capitalize on the connectivity. He implores educators to be explicit with learners about the goals of the course, and about the role of hypertext in meeting those goals, and to provide assignments with that in mind. In describing his own approach, Landow (1992) writes,

> . . . Since I employ a corpus of linked documents to accustom students to discovering or constructing contexts for individual blocks of text or data, my assignments require multiple answers to the same question or multiple parts to the same answer. If one wishes to accustom students to the fact that complex phenomena involve complex causation, one must arrange assignments in such a way as to make students summon different kinds of information to explain the phenomena they encounter. Since my courses have increasingly taken advantage of Intermedia's capacity to promote collaborative learning my assignments, from the beginning of the course, require students to comment upon materials and links they find, to suggest new ones, and to add materials. (p. 134)

Note how Landow's approach reflects the philosophy that grounds CFT. Indeed, Spiro, Jacobson, and colleagues have long advocated the kind of approach described by Landow (Jacobson & Spiro, 1995; Spiro & Jengh, 1990; Spiro et al., 1988).

Some work has also been reported examining the compatibility between learning goals and characteristics of hypertext structure. In a series of studies with university students, Dee-Lucas and Larkin (1995) examined the effect of segmenting hypertext into different-sized units to examine students' goal-directed searching under these conditions. Sixty-four students with limited prior knowledge of physics participated in the study. Two hypertexts on buoyant force were created. One had 22 units organized in three levels of detail, and the second had only 9 units, with each unit reading as a continuous text. Students read one version of the hypertext under two conditions, once with an information-seeking task and a second time with a problem-solving task. Readers with the more segmented hypertext tended to focus on goal-related content, resulting in detailed memory for goal units but narrower overall recall. Readers with the less-segmented hypertext tended to explore unrelated units and recalled a broader range of content. However, when the larger size of the less-segmented text blocks made information location more difficult, fewer readers completed the goal.

The authors concluded that narrow, well-defined goals that require the reader to locate and/or interrelate specific content may be more efficiently achieved with hypertext that is broken down into smaller units. Conversely, learning goals that require the reader to integrate related prior knowledge (problem solving, inferential reasoning, etc.) may benefit from reading a less-segmented hypertext. Hypertext that contains larger text blocks may promote text exploration and development of a more complex mental model. Thus, a less-segmented hypertext may be appropriate for learning goals that require readers to internalize a wide range of text content or a more thoroughly developed conceptual model of the content.

In sum, the literature shows with a fair degree of consistency that learning with hypertext is greatly enhanced when the learning goal is specific, although a clear goal is not always enough to augment learning outcomes. Tasks that do not capitalize on hypertext's unique connectivity, such as fact seeking, may be enhanced by the use of a highly segmented and indexed hypertext but can promote poor learning strategies and superficial learning. However, in most cases hypertext is designed to encourage students to seek relationships between ideas, consider multiple aspects of an issue, or otherwise promote conceptual understanding. Developers, teachers, and users who attend to these goals are most likely to reap advantages from hypertext.

23.6   ADAPTIVE EDUCATIONAL HYPERTEXT

The lion's share of work in adaptive hypertext surrounds techniques in *user modeling*. This refers to any of a number of methods used to gather information about users' knowledge, skills, motivation, or background. Such data may be gained from written surveys, test scores, hypertext navigation patterns, and so forth. Characteristics of users are then used to alter any number of system features. The most common feature adapted in hypertext systems is the links. Specifically, links can be enabled or disabled for given users, or they may be annotated. Typical types of annotations will tell users whether a document has already been viewed or if they have sufficient experience or knowledge to view a document's content. (See Brusilovsky [2001] for an extensive review of current adaptive technologies). For example, Interbook (Brusilovsky & Eklund, 1998) and ELM-ART II (Weber & Specht, 1997) both place a green ball next to links leading to documents that a learner has sufficient prior knowledge to understand. A red ball indicates that the content will be difficult because the user lacks sufficient prior knowledge. In this way, the "stoplight" indicators serve to suggest best navigation choices for each user.

Another component that may be adapted is the actual document content. Some of the best work in this area has been applied to informal learning environments, such as virtual museums (Dale et al. 1998; Milosavljevic, Dale, Green, Paris, & Williams, 1998). These systems create a user model based on which virtual exhibits a user has already visited. That information is used as an indicator of prior knowledge. The text for each exhibit is generated from a database, rather than a static text. As such, each document is tailored for each user. A visitor to an exhibit of Etruscan military helmets, for example, might read something about metal smelting during that era. If he or she had already visited a site on Etruscan jewelry, however, the system would leave out that information, because he or she would already have read it at the jewelry exhibit. The generated text is remarkably natural sounding.

Decades of work on human cognition and learning, as well as much of the hypertext work reviewed in this chapter, strongly suggest that tailoring information in these ways should benefit the learner. Whereas such technological innovation is under vigorous pursuit by engineers and computer scientists, very few empirical studies on the educational effectiveness of these technologies have been reported. A small number of studies have looked at navigation issues (e.g., Brusilovsky & Pesin, 1998), but the data do not say much about actual learning. The majority of studies that do address learning overtly are plagued by methodological problems.

One study by Weber and Specht (1997) looked at the effect of annotating nodes on student motivation, which is a predictor of learning. This was measured by how far into the material students got before quitting. They found that for novices, the annotated links had no effect on motivation. For intermediate learners, however, those who were exposed to annotated links completed much more of the lesson. While the difference was nonsignificant, the small number of participants (no more than 11 per condition) makes the study less than conclusive.

Brusilovsky and Eklund (1998) tested the same type of adaptation. This study used a larger number of subjects and also attempted to assess actual learning, rather than motivation to learn. Their initial analyses found that the annotated group did not perform better than a group working with a nonannotated system. Additional analyses showed that many of the students did not take the advice offered by the annotations, however. If the advice is not followed, it should not be expected that the annotations will have an effect. Further analysis revealed that the degree of compliance with the suggestions offered by the annotations was significantly correlated with posttest performance ($r = .67$).

In summary, we know of no studies that have investigated the educational effectiveness of adapting actual document content. The few studies reported on adaptive hypertext have concentrated on adapting links. While hardly conclusive, these studies suggest that further investigation into the educational effectiveness of adaptive systems is warranted. It is important to identify the characteristics that are most effectively used in user modeling, as well as the system characteristics that are most important to adapt. Both of these topics offer promise as fruitful areas of investigation.

23.7   PROBLEMS WITH HAL RESEARCH

As is probably clear to the reader, HAL is a complex and challenging process for educators and psychologists to address. Efforts to examine it over the past decade have met with limited success. In this section, we highlight some of the primary concerns surrounding HAL research.

23.7.1   Theoretical Issues

Tergan (1997b) has challenged several of the common theoretical assumptions underlying HAL, some of which have been explored in this chapter. The "plausibility hypothesis" holds that linked networklike subject matter representation in hypertext should be assimilatable because it matches the structure of human knowledge and the workings of the mind. The research exploring conceptual structure, which we discussed in an earlier section of this chapter, indicates that exposing students to systems structured after experts' domain knowledge is not effective in promoting expert conceptual structure. Another common misconception is that self-regulation and constructivist learning principles will be enhanced due to the active, exploratory, and metacognitive aspects of reading hypertext. Studies reviewed here also concur that hypertext use alone does not necessarily promote active learning.

Beyond these common theoretical misconceptions is the lack of a coherent theoretical framework supporting research efforts. Indeed, this is a central problem in HAL research (Gall & Hannifin, 1994; Tergan, 1997b). We have chosen to ground our review in CFT and the CIM. Others, if they addressed theoretical foundations at all, have drawn on a variety of related orientations such as schema theory (e.g., Jonassen, 1988, 1993), dual coding, and cue summation theory (e.g., Burton, Moore, & Holmes, 1995) to situate HAL. Thus, "the efforts are typically isolated in terms of their focus and foundations, obscuring their broader implications" (Gall & Hannafin, 1994).

Tergan (1997b) proposes that no current theories have the power to explain HAL because they are too rigid and broad in scope. He advocates a less reductionist and more complex and all-encompassing framework for the study of HAL. He suggests that any successful theory of learning from this media will have to encompass the many facets of technology-based instruction including learner variables, instructional methods, attributes of the learning material, the media used, and situational constraints (such as authenticity of the learning situation). Although it may be true that a more complex and inclusive set of theories is needed to capture the complexity of HAL, we must keep in mind the fact that hypertext research is in its infancy. Some degree of reductionism and variable isolation may be necessary at this stage to understand better some of the basic underpinnings of HAL. Conducting profitable hypertext research from a holistic perspective will be difficult until this is accomplished.

23.7.2 Methodological Issues

Comparing and reviewing hypertext research is difficult because of a marked lack of coherence in the field. According to Gall and Hannafin (1994), we need "... a unified, coherent framework for studying hypertext ..." (p. 207). For example, we do not share a common language. In this review we focus on Hypertext, which includes systems that are *primarily* text based but may include graphics. Others have presented hypertext as a purely textual component of hypermedia (Burton et al., 1995; Dillon & Gabbard, 1998; MacGregor, 1999), and others still view hypertext as synonymous with multimedia and hypermedia and use the terms interchangeably (Altun, 2000; Large, 1996; Unz & Hesse, 1999). This creates two problems when trying to understand the hypertext literature.

First, in this chapter we have made the case that understanding HAL should be grounded in research about learning from traditional text—that basic low-level reading processes are present regardless of the presentation medium. This allowed us to bring in a wealth of knowledge from the field of reading research and focus our attention on the set of variables unique to reading hypertext. However, the text-based reading research foundation is clearly compromised when extensive graphics and audio and video components are included in the hypertext. When these additional features are included in an experimental hypertext, the effects of learning from graphics (pictures, charts, graphs, etc.), audio, and video must be factored into the analysis. This problem is compounded in that experimental research on learning in these areas does not have the extensive history that has developed in the reading research field.

Second, there is a problem with comparing research studies when our lexicon about the field is so lacking in precision. As already mentioned, hypertext researchers do not even agree on a common definition for the most basic term—hypertext. Further, researchers may use different terms to describe similar constructs (e.g., concept map, spatial map, and semantic map; nonlinear, unstructured, and ill-structured hypertexts; and web-like and "graph of information nodes") or the same terms to describe different constructs (a conceptually easy text in one study may be equivalent to a conceptually difficult text in another). How, then, can we be confident in our claims about HAL when participants in the discussion have different meanings when using and encountering terminology in the literature? To move hypertext research forward we need a shared lexicon for the field. Gall and Hannafin (1994) proposed a framework for the study of hypertext in which they attempt to define a common language for the description and discussion of hypertext-based research. While this may be only a beginning, and not *the* definitive glossary of terms, it is certainly a step in the right direction.

In addition to the conceptual and language issues addressed above, experimental variables tend to interact and confound in the complex HAL environment. Learners with different individual characteristics (prior knowledge, field dependence or independence, activity level, goal for reading, spatial ability, etc.) are examined using different hypertext systems (level of structure, type of navigational structure, level of support, level of segmentation, etc.) and different text content (ill-structured versus well-structured domain, conceptual difficulty level, expository or narrative nature of text, etc.). This point reflects the complexity issue discussed earlier and points out the need for systematically designed programmatic research.

Finally, methodological flaws in much of the research have been widely reported in the literature. Dillon and Gabbard (1998) cite failure to control comparative variables, limited pretesting, inappropriate use of statistical tests, and a tendency to claim support for hypotheses when the data do not support them as serious concerns regarding the validity and reliability of conclusions drawn from the research base. In an extensive critique of the hypertext literature, Tergan (1997a) outlines a series of methodological problems that hamstring HAL research. In addition to confounded results due to the lack of empirical control of differential characteristics and contingencies of learners (as discussed above), he identifies lack of specificity in reporting methodology and limitations in learning criteria as major issues.

As an example of reporting specificity, Tergan points to the fact that many studies do not indicate the size of the experimental hypertext—despite the fact that there appear to be clear differences in content structure, navigability, and, therefore, learning based on the size of the text. In his critique of the limited spectrum of learning criteria, he points out that many of the measures used to examine HAL reflect traditional measures of reading—recall of factual information from the textbase and general comprehension. However, adherents claim that hypertext promotes deeper-level learning that is not addressed through these measures. Thus, "the potential of hypertext/hypermedia learning environments designed for supporting advanced learning to cope with a variety of different tasks and learning situations as well as learning criteria has not yet been explored in much detail" (Tergan, 1997a, p. 225).

23.8 GENERAL CONCLUSIONS

Despite the hype and excitement surrounding hypertext as an educational tool, there is really very little published research on the technology that is related directly to education and learning. Of the literature that does explore educational applications, there is little in the way of quality, empirical studies. As we have tried to show here, however, a number of things have been learned about HAL over the years.

Perhaps the most basic finding is that hypertext is not the panacea so many people hoped for at the time that it became widely available. Turning students loose on a hypertext will not guarantee robust learning. Indeed, doing so can actually mitigate learning outcomes in some circumstances, especially if students are novices and offered no training, guidance, or carefully planned goals. In the right circumstances, though, hypertext can enhance learning. It does so by presenting environments that offer greater opportunities for students to engage in the type of cognitive activities recognized by theorists as encouraging learning: active, metacognitive processing aimed at integrating knowledge and boosting understanding. In short, while hypertext does not offer any shortcuts for learners, it offers rich environments in which to explore, ponder, and integrate information.

Related to this point, it is clear that the effectiveness of HAL is directly related to the learning goal. Hypertext cannot help cram facts into students' heads any more effectively than most texts. It is most effective for helping students to integrate concepts, engage in problem-solving activities, and develop multifaceted mental representations and understanding. Goals and systems designed to promote such activities are most useful and productive. For this reason, learning outcome measures that explore factual knowledge alone often reveal little effect of hypertext use. Measures of deep understanding, problem-solving ability, and transfer (situation model measures) are those most likely to highlight the effectiveness of a hypertext.

Another important consideration is that, with few exceptions, there is little evidence that any single variable produces a replicable main effect on learning outcomes across diverse learners. As this review has made clear, almost every hypertext variable explored with reference to learning shows an effect primarily as an interacting variable. System structure, learning goals, prior knowledge, and learning strategies all interact. Exploration of any one of these factors without consideration of the others has tended to produce little in the way of informative results.

Finally, if future research in this area is to generate a well-grounded understanding of the processes underlying HAL, some standards for terminology and methodology will need to be developed. Only after this is done can an encompassing theory, grounded in research, emerge from the kaleidoscope of perspectives currently employed by researchers.

References

Alexander, P. A., Kulikowich, J. M., & Jetton, T. L. (1994). The role of subject-matter knowledge and interest in the processing of linear and nonlinear texts. *Review of Educational Research, 64*(2), 201–252.

Altun, A. (2000). Patterns in cognitive processes and strategies in hypertext reading: A case study of two experienced computer users. *Journal of Educational Multimedia and Hypermedia, 9*(1), 35–55.

Anderson-Inman, L., & Tenny, J. (1989). Electronic studying: Information organizers to help students to study "better" not "harder"—Part II. *The Computing Teacher, 17,* 21–53.

Azevedo, R, Guthrie, J., Wang, H.-Y., & Mulhern, J. (2001, April). *Do different instructional interventions facilitate students' ability to shift to more sophisticated mental models of complex systems?* Paper presented at the annual meeting of the American Educational Research Association, Seattle, WA.

Azevedo, R, Seibert, D, Guthrie, J., Cromley, J., Wang, H.-Y., & Tron, M. (2002, April). *How do students regulate their learning of complex systems with hypermedia?* Paper presented at the Annual Meeting of the American Educational Research Association, New Orleans, LA.

Balajthy, E. (1990). Hypertext, hypermedia, and metacognition: Research and instructional implications for disabled readers. *Journal of Reading, Writing, and Learning Disabilities International, 6*(2), 183–202.

Balcytiene, A. (1999). Exploring individual processes of knowledge construction with hypertext. *Instructional Science, 27,* 303–328.

Bower, G. H., Clark, M. C., Lesgold, A. M., & Winzenz, D. (1969). Hierarchical retrieval schemes in recall of categorized word lists. *Journal of Verbal Learning and Verbal Behavior, 8,* 323–343.

Britt, M. A., Rouet, J.-F., & Perfetti, C. A. (1996). Using hypertext to study and reason about historical evidence. In J.-F. Rouet, J. J. Levonen, A. P. Dillon, & R. J. Spiro (Eds.), *Hypertext and cognition* (pp. 43–72). Mahwah, NJ: Lawrence Erlbaum Associates.

Brusilovsky, P. (2001). Adaptive hypermedia. *User Modeling and User-Adapted Interaction, 11,* 87–110.

Brusilovsky, P., & Eklund, J. (1998). A study of user model based link annotation in educational hypermedia. *Journal of Universal Computer Science, 4*(4), 428–448.

Brusilovsky, P., & Pesin, L. (1998). Adaptive navigation support in educational hypermedia: An evaluation of the ISIS-tutor. *Journal of Computing and Information Technology, 6* (1), 27–38

Burton, J. K., Moore, D. M., & Holmes, G. A. (1995). Hypermedia concepts and research: An overview. *Computers in Human Behavior, 11*(3-4), 345–369.

Bush, V. (1945). As we may think. *Atlantic Monthly, 176,* 1, 101–103.

Castelli, C., Colazzo, L., & Molinari, A. (1998). Cognitive variables and patterns of hypertext performances: Lessons learned for educational hypermedia construction. *Journal of Educational Multimedia and Hypermedia, 7*(2-3), 177–206.

Chase, W. G., & Simon, H. A. (1973). Perception in chess. *Cognitive Psychology, 4,* 55–81.

Chen, C., & Rada, R. (1996). Interacting with hypertext: A meta-analysis of experimental studies. *Human-Computer Interaction, 11,* 125–156.

Chi, M. T. H., & Koeske, R. D. (1983). Network representation of a child's dinosaur knowledge. *Developmental Psychology, 19*(1), 29-39.

Curry, J., Haderlie, S., Ku, T., Lawless, K., Lemon, M., & Wood, R. (1999). Specified learning goals and their effect on learners' representations of a hypertext reading environment. *International Journal of Instructional Media, 26*(1), 43-51.

Dale, R., Green, S., Milosavljevic, M., Paris, C., Verspoor, C., & Williams, S. (1998, August). Using natural language generation techniques to produce virtual documents. In *Proceedings of the Third Australian Document Computing Symposium (ADCS'98)*, Sydney.

Dede, C. (1988, June). *The role of hypertext in transforming information into knowledge.* Paper presented at the annual meeting of the National Educational Computing Conference, Dallas, TX.

Dee-Lucas, D., & Larkin, J. H. (1995). Learning from electronic texts: Effects of interactive overviews for information access. *Cognition and Instruction, 13*(3), 431-468.

Dee-Lucas, D., & Larkin, J. (1999). Hypertext segmentation and goal compatibility: Effects on study strategies and learning. *Journal of Educational Multimedia and Hypermedia, 8*(3), 279-313.

De Groot, A. D. (1965). *Thought and choice in chess.* The Hague: Mouton.

Dias, P., Gomes, M., & Correia, A. (1999). Disorientation in hypermedia environments: Mechanisms to support navigation. *Journal of Educational Computing Research, 20*(2), 93-117.

Dillon, A., & Gabbard, R. (1998). Hypermedia as an educational technology: A review of the quantitative research literature on learner comprehension, control, and style. *Review of Educational Research, 68*(3), 322-349.

Dole, J. A., & Sinatra, G. M. (1998). Reconceptualizing change in the cognitive construction of knowledge. *Educational Psychologist, 33*(2/3), 109-28.

Edwards, D., & Hardman, L. (1989). 'Lost in hyperspace': Cognitive mapping and navigation in a hypertext environment. In R. McAleese (Ed.), *Hypertext: Theory into practice* (pp. 105-125). Oxford: Intellect Books.

Eylon, B., & Reif, F. (1984). Effects of knowledge organization on task performance. *Cognition and Instruction, 1,* 5-44.

Foltz, P. (1996). Comprehension, coherence, and strategies in hypertext and linear text. In Levonen, A. P. Dillon, and R.J. Spiro (Eds.), *Hypertext and Cognition* (pp. 100-136). Mahwah, NJ: Lawrence Erlbaum Associates.

Friendly, M.L. (1977). In search of the M-gram: The structure and organization of free-recall. *Cognitive Psychology, 9, 188-249.*

Gall, J., & Hannafin, M. (1994). A framework for the study of hypertext. *Instructional Science, 22*(3), 207-232.

Gordon, S., Gustavel, J., Moore, J., & Hankey, J. (1988). The effects of hypertext on reader knowledge representation. In *Proceedings of the Human Factors Society 32nd Annual Meeting* (pp. 296-300).

Hammond, N. (1991). Teaching with hypermedia: Problems and prospects. In H. Brown (Ed.), *Hypermedia, hypertext, and object-oriented databases* (pp. 107-124). London: Chapman and Hall.

Hofman, R., & van Oostendorp, H. (1999). Cognitive effects of a structural overview in a hypertext. *British Journal of Educational Technology, 30*(2), 129-140.

Horney, M. A., & Anderson-Inman, L. (1994). The electro text project: Hypertext reading patterns of middle school students. *Journal of Educational Multimedia and Hypermedia, 3*(1), 71-91.

Hughes, J. K., & Michton, J. I. (1977). *A structured approach to programming.* Englewood Cliffs, NJ: Prentice-Hall.

Jacobson, M. J., & Spiro, R. J. (1995). Hypertext learning environments, cognitive flexibility, and the transfer of complex knowledge: An empirical investigation. *Journal of Educational Computing Research, 12*(4), 301-333.

Johnson, S. C. (1967). Hierarchical clustering schemes. *Psychometrika, 32,* 241-254.

Jonassen, D. H. (1988). Designing structured hypertext and structuring access to hypertext. *Educational Technology, 28*(11), 13-16.

Jonassen, D. H. (1990). Semantic network elicitation: Tools for structuring of hypertext. In R. McAleese & C. Green (Eds.), *Hypertext: The state of the art.* London: Intellect.

Jonassen, D. H. (1991). Hypertext as instructional design. *Educational Technology Research and Development, 39*(1), 83-92.

Jonassen, D. H. (1993). Thinking technology: The trouble with learning environments. *Educational Technology, 33*(1), 35-37.

Jonassen, D. H., & Wang, S. (1993). Acquiring structural knowledge from semantically structured hypertext. *Journal of Computer-Based Instruction, 20*(1), 1-8.

Kauffman, D. (2002, April). *Self-regulated learning in web-based environments: Instructional tools designed to facilitate cognitive strategy use, metacognitive processing, and motivational beliefs.* Paper presented at the annual meeting of the American Educational Research Association, New Orleans, April 1-5.

Kintsch, W. (1988). The use of knowledge in discourse processing: A construction integration model. *Psychological Review, 95,* 163-182.

Kintsch, W., & Keenan, J. M. (1974). Recall of propositions as a function of their position in the hierarchical structure. In W. Kintsch (Ed.), *The representation of meaning in memory.* Hillsdale, NJ: Lawrence Erlbaum Associates.

Landow, G. (1992). *Hypertext: The convergence of contemporary critical theory and technology.* Baltimore, MD: The Johns Hopkins University Press.

Large, A. (1996). Hypertext instructional programs and learner control: A research review. *Education for Information, 14*(2), 95-106.

Lawless, K., & Brown, S. (1997). Multimedia learning environments: Issues of learner control and navigation. *Instructional Science, 25*(2), 117-131.

Lawless, K., & Kulikowich, J. (1996). Understanding hypertext navigation through cluster analysis. *Journal of Educational Computing Research, 14*(4), 385-399.

Lin, C., & Davidson-Shivers, G. (1996). Effects of linking structure and cognitive style on students' performance and attitude in a computer-based hypertext environment. *Journal of Educational Computing Research, 15*(4), 317-329.

MacGregor, S. K. (1999). Hypermedia navigation profiles: Cognitive characteristics and information processing strategies. *Journal of Educational Computing Research, 20*(2), 189-206.

Mannes, B., & Kintsch, W. (1987). Knowledge organization and text organization, *Cognition and Instruction, 4,* 91-115.

McDonald, S., & Stevenson, R. (1999). Spatial versus conceptual maps as learning tools in hypertext. *Journal of Educational Multimedia and Hypermedia, 8*(1), 43-64.

Melara, G. (1996). Investigating learning styles on different hypertext environments: Hierarchical-like and network-like structures. *Journal of Educational Computing Research, 14*(4), 313-328.

Meyrowitz, N. (1986). Intermedia: The architecture and construction of an object-oriented hypertext/hypermedia system and applications framework. In *Proceedings of the Conference on Object-Oriented Programming Systems, Languages, and Applications (OOPSLA '86)*, Portland, OR.

Milosavljevic, M., Dale, R., Green, S. Paris, C., & Williams, S. (1998). Virtual museums on the information superhighway: Prospects and potholes. *Proceedings of CIDOC'98, the Annual Conference of the International Committee for Documentation of the International Council of Museums,* Melbourne, Australia.

Niederhauser, D. S., Reynolds, R. E., Salmen, D. J., & Skolmoski, P. (2000). The influence of cognitive load on learning from hypertext. *Journal of Educational Computing Research, 23*(3), 237–255.

Nuttall, C. (1996). *Teaching reading skills in a foreign language.* Oxford: Heinemann.

Paas, F., and Van Merrienboer, J. (1994). Instructional control of cognitive load in the training of complex cognitive tasks. *Educational Psychology Review, 6,* 351–371.

Patterson, N. (2000). Hypertext and the changing roles of readers. *English Journal, 90*(2), 74–80.

Posner, G. J., Strike, K. A., Hewson, P. W., & Gertzog, W. A. (1982). Accommodation of a scientific concept: Toward a theory of conceptual change. *Science Education, 67*(4), 489–508.

Potelle, H., & Rouet, J.-F. (2002). Effects of content representation and readers' prior knowledge on the comprehension of hypertext. Paper presented at the EARLI-SIG "Comprehension of Verbal and Pictorial Information," Université de Poitiers, Poitieas, Agust 29–30.

Schroeder, E. E., and Grabowski, B. L. (1995). Patterns of exploration and learning with hypermedia. *Journal of Educational Computing Research, 13*(4), 313–335.

Shapiro, A. M. (1998a). Promoting active learning: The role of system structure in learning from hypertext. *Human-Computer Interaction, 13*(1), 1–35.

Shapiro, A. M. (1998b). The relationship between prior knowledge and interactive organizers during hypermedia-aided learning. *Journal of Educational Computing Research, 20*(2), 143–163.

Shapiro, A. (1999). The relevance of hierarchies to learning biology from hypertext. *Journal of the Learning Sciences, 8*(2), 215–243.

Shin, E., Schallert, D., & Savenye, W. (1994). Effects of learner control, advisement, and prior knowledge on young students' learning in a hypertext environment. *Educational Technology, Research and Development, 42*(1), 33–46.

Simpson, A., & McKnight, C. (1990). Navigation in hypertext: Structural cues and mental maps. In R. McAleese & C. Green (Eds.), *Hypertext: State of the art.* Oxford: Intellect.

Smith, J. (1996). What's all this hype about hypertext?: Teaching literature with George P. Landow's "The Dickens Web." *Computers and the Humanities, 30*(2), 121–129.

Spiro, R. J., & Jehng, J. C. (1990). Cognitive flexibility and hypertext: Theory and technology for the nonlinear and multidimensional traversal of complex subject matter. In D. Nix & R. Spiro (Eds.), *Cognition, education, and multimedia: Exploring ideas in high technology* (pp. 163–205). Hillsdale, NJ: Lawerence Erlbaum Associates.

Spiro, R., Vispoel, W., Schmitz, J., Samarapungavan, A., & Boerger, A. (1987). Knowledge acquisition for application: Cognitive flexibility and transfer in complex content domains. In B. Britton & S. Glynn (Eds.), *Executive control processes in reading* (pp. 177–199). Hillsdale, NJ: Lawrence Erlbaum Associates.

Spiro, R., Coulson, R., Feltovich, P., & Anderson, D. (1988). Cognitive flexibility theory: Advanced knowledge acquisition in ill-structured domains. In *Proceedings of the Tenth Annual Conference of the Cognitive Science Society* (pp. 375–383). Hillsdale, NJ: Lawrence Erlbaum Associates.

Spiro, R., Feltovich, P., Jacobson, M., & Coulson, R. (1992). Cognitive flexibility, constructivism, and hypertext: Random access instruction

for advanced knowledge acquisition in ill-structured domains. In T. Duffy & D. Jonassen (Eds.), *Constructivism and the technology of instruction: A conversation* (pp. 57–75). Hillsdale, NJ: Lawrence Erlbaum Associates.

Stanton, N. A., Taylor, R. G., & Tweedie, L. A. (1992). Maps as navigational aids in hypertext environments: An empirical evaluation. *Journal of Educational Multimedia and Hypermedia, 1*(4), 431–444.

Strike, K. A., & Posner, G. J. (1992) A revisionist history of conceptual change. In R. Duschl and R. Hamilton (Eds.), *Philosophy of science, cognitive psychology, and educational theory and practice* (pp. 147–176). New York: State University of New York.

Swaffar, J., Arens, K., & Byrnes, H. (1991). *Reading for meaning: An integrated approach to language learning.* Englewood Cliffs, NJ: Prentice Hall.

Sweller, J. (1988). Cognitive load during problem solving: Effects on learning. *Cognitive Science, 12,* 257–285.

Sweller, J., van Merrienboer, J. G., & Paas, F. G. (1998). Cognitive architecture and instructional design. *Educational Psychology Review, 10*(3), 251–296.

Tergan, S. (1997a). Conceptual and methodological shortcomings in hypertext/hypermedia design and research. *Journal of Educational Computing Research, 16*(3), 209–235.

Tergan, S. (1997b). Misleading theoretical assumptions in hypertext/hypermedia research. *Journal of Educational Multimedia and Hypermedia, 6*(3/4), 257–283.

Tergan, S. (1997c). Multiple views, contexts, and symbol systems in learning with hypertext/hypermedia: A critical review of research. *Educational Technology, 37*(4), 5–18.

Trumbull, D., Gay, G., & Mazur, J. (1992). Students' actual and perceived use of navigational and guidance tools in a hypermedia program. *Journal of Research on Computing in Education, 24*(3), 315–328.

Unz, D. C., & Hesse, F. W. (1999). The use of hypertext for learning. *Journal of Educational Computing Research, 20*(3), 279–295.

Walz, J. (2001). Reading hypertext: Lower level processes. *Canadian Modern Language Review, 57*(3), 475–494.

Weber, G., & Specht, M. (1997). User modeling and adaptive navigation support in WWW-based tutoring systems. In A. Jameson, C. Paris, & C. Tasso (Eds.), *Proceedings of the 6th International Conference on User Modeling* (pp. 289–300). New York: SpringerWien.

Wenger, M. J., & Payne, D. G. (1996). Human information processing correlates of reading hypertext. *Technical Communication, 43*(1), 52–60.

Winne, P. (1995). Inherent details in self-regulated learning. *Journal of Educational Psychology, 87,* 397–410.

Winne, P. (2001). Self-regulated learning viewed from models of information processing. In B. Zimmerman & D. Schunk (Eds.), *Self-regulated learning and academic achievement: Theoretical perspectives.* Mahwah, NJ: Lawrence Erlbaum Associates.

Woods, D. D. (1984). Visual momentum: A concept to improve the cognitive coupling of person and computer. *International Journal of Man-Machine Studies, 21,* 229–244.

Yang, S. (1997). Information seeking as problem-solving using a qualitative approach to uncover the novice learners' information-seeking processes in a Perseus hypertext system. *Library and Information Science Research, 19*(1), 71–92.

INSTRUCTIONAL DESIGN
APPROACHES

CONDITIONS THEORY AND MODELS
FOR DESIGNING INSTRUCTION

Tillman J. Ragan and Patricia L. Smith
University of Oklahoma

24.1 INTRODUCTION

One of the most influential and pervasive theories underlying instructional design proposes that (a) there are identifiably different types of learning outcomes and (b) the acquisition of these outcomes requires different internal and external conditions[1] of learning. In other words, this theory suggests that all learning is not qualitatively the same, that there are learning outcomes across contents, contexts, and learners that have significant and identifiable similarities in their cognitive demands on the learner. Further, each learning outcome category has significant and identifiable differences in its cognitive demands from the demands of other learning outcome categories. Finally, as this family of theories is instructional in nature, they propose that these distinctive cognitive processing demands can be supported by equally distinctive instructional methods, strategies, tactics, or conditions.

These propositions underlie what Wilson and Cole (1991) term a *conditions-of-learning* paradigm of instructional design. Models of instructional design that follow a conditions-based theory are predicated upon the seminal principles of Robert Gagné (1965b) that (a) learning can be classified into categories that require similar cognitive activities for learning (Gagné termed these *internal conditions of learning*), and therefore, (b) within these categories of learning similar instructional supports are needed to facilitate learning (Gagné termed these *external conditions of learning*).

The influence of a conditions-based perspective can be found in the task analysis, strategy development, assessment, and evaluation procedures of conditions-based instructional design. However, the point at which the conditions-based perspective has the greatest influence and most unique contribution is in the development of instructional strategies. According to conditions theory, when designing instructional strategies, instructional designers must determine the goals of instruction, categorize these goals as to outcome category, and select strategies that have been suggested as being effective for this category of learning outcome (or devise strategies consistent with the cognitive processing demands of the learning task).

Examples of conditions-based theories of design have been authored by Gagné (1985) and Gagné, Briggs, and Wager (1988), Merrill (1983), Merrill, Li and Jones (1990a), Reigeluth (1979), and Smith and Ragan (1999). Other authors, though they may not posit a complete approach to instructional design (either a model or a theory), have suggested conditions-based approaches to strategy design (e.g., Horn, 1976; Landa, 1983). Interestingly, several of these explications (Jonassen, Grabinger, & Harris, 1991; West, Farmer, & Wolf, 1991) present the instructional processes first and then suggest the learning outcomes for which these strategies might be appropriate.

The conditions theory assumption is commonplace, if not universal, in current instructional psychology and instructional design thinking, even when an author's orientation and values are not based on the cognitive science that underlies the conditions theory. For example, Nelson (1999) took care to note that

---

[1] We refer here to "conditions of learning" as described by Gagné (1985) as external conditions of learning, that is, those instructional supports that are designed to promote learning, rather than instructional conditions as described by Reigeluth et al. (1978), which are primarily learner and learning context variables.

her prescriptions for collaborative problem solving "should only be used when those types of learning are paramount" (p. 242). This care in consideration of the nature of the learning task was remarkably absent before conditions theory was developed and is remarkably consistent in its application now. Whether or not individuals formally subscribe to or have an interest in the conditions theory, it is part of the everyday work of designers and scholars of instruction and learning environments.

The purpose of this chapter is to describe the evolution of the conditions-based perspective, exemplify and compare conditions-based theories, and examine the assumptions of the conditions theory both theoretically and empirically. These assumptions are as follows:

1. Learning goals can be categorized as to learning outcome or knowledge type.
2. Learning outcomes can be represented in a predictable prerequisite relationship.
3. Acquisition of different outcome categories requires different internal processes (or, different internal processes lead to different cognitive outcomes).
4. Different internal processes are supported by identifiably different instructional processes (or, different instructional processes lead to different internal processes).

24.2 EVOLUTION OF THE CONDITIONS-BASED THEORY

The first full statement of a conditions-based theory of instruction appears to have been by R. M. Gagné in the early 1960s.[2] However, there was a considerable amount of conjecture within this paradigm by a variety of researchers prior to Gagné. In addition, Gagné and others have developed a conditions-based theory along a variety of lines of thought until the present day. In this section, we review work leading to the conditions theory, discuss Gagné's early and evolving conceptions, and review various lines of research in the conditions-based tradition that have appeared subsequent to Gagné's first work.

24.2.1 Early Work Leading to Conditions-Based Thinking

Among the earliest writing that specifically addresses the need to beware of overgeneralization of knowledge about learning, Carr (1933) cautioned that conclusions that are valid for one category of learning may not be valid for others. The categories of which Carr spoke were not within a formally defined taxonomy or system but, rather, were reflected in the different experimental tasks, research procedures, and measures employed in different studies.

Interest in devising useful categories of learning persisted over the decade, and Melton wrote, in the learning theory

chapter in the 1941 *Encyclopedia of Educational Research*, of efforts to develop a psychologically based taxonomy of learning outcomes. During this same period Tolman (1949) described six categories of learning, and Woodworth (1958) described five categories.

The behaviorist movement lent a rigor and precision to the study of learning that is perhaps difficult to appreciate today. When one looks at the work of some behaviorist learning researchers, one finds compelling (if not esoteric) evidence that there *are* different kinds of learning with different conditions for their attainment. Wickens (1962) described Spence's studies of animal learning involving both aversive conditioning and approach behaviors:

Spence (1956) has used the same approach in differentiation of the instrumental avoidance situation of the type represented by the eyelid conditioning from an approach learning represented by an animal scurrying down a runway for its daily pellet. Spence is quite specific: the antecedent of H (the intervening variable leading to the running response) in the latter case is a function only of n and not of incentive magnitude; in the former, it—the intervening variable H—is a function of n and also of magnitude of the UCS. This conclusion leads him to describe the excitatory component of behavior, E, as being a function of two intervening variables, H and D, insofar as classical aversive conditioning is concerned, while the excitatory component of runway behavior requires, for him, three intervening variables, H, D, and K. (p. 81)

Another specification of differences in learning tasks is seen in Bloom's taxonomy (Bloom, Englehart, Furst, Hill, & Krathwohl, 1956). This group's thinking about the need for a taxonomy of educational outcomes originated at an informal meeting of college examiners at the 1948 meeting of the American Psychological Association, at which "interest was expressed in a theoretical framework which could be used to facilitate communication among examiners" (Bloom et al., 1956, p. 4). The taxonomy arose not from a synthesis of research but in response to a collective need for standardization of terminology.

Applications of Bloom's taxonomy, however, have frequently assumed a stature similar to that of psychologically based approaches. For example, a study by Kunen, Cohen, and Solman (1981) investigated the cumulative hierarchical assumption of Bloom's taxonomy. The study concluded that there is "moderately strong support for the assumption that the Taxonomy represents a cumulative hierarchy of categories of cognitive operations" (p. 207). The tasks used in the study involved recall of knowledge, recall of applications, recall of words related to a synthesis task, and so forth ("the dependent variable was the number of critical words correctly free recalled" [p. 207]). As all of the tasks appear to involve recall, we have some doubt about the validity of conclusions supporting a hierarchy of cognitive operations. Furst's (1981) review of research on Bloom's taxonomy leveled a great deal of criticism of the taxonomy in terms of its lack of cumulative hierarchical structure. It seems

---

[2]A full statement of Gagné's conditions model appears in the chapter "Problem Solving," in A. W. Melton's (1964b) edited work, *Categories of Learning*. The paper on which the chapter is based was delivered at a symposium convened by Melton in January of 1962, for the purpose of exploring "the interrelationship of different categories of learning" (Melton, 1964b, p. vii).

clear that the taxonomy's uses have exceeded its original design and purpose.

24.2.1.1 Military and Industry Training Researchers.
In the 1950s and 1960s (and continuing to the present), a substantial amount of research and development related to learning and instruction was conducted by the military services and industry. Edling and associates pointed out that this group of scientists in military and industrial settings was large for its work to be so unfamiliar to many educators. Indeed, in 1963 the Army's HumRRO employed 100 "training psychologists," of whom 65 were Ph.D.'s, and the Air Force Training and Research Center at one time employed 168 psychologists, of whom 100 held Ph.D.'s (Edling et al., 1972, p. 94).

Among the contributions of these researchers were some "relatively sophisticated taxonomies of learner tasks," such as those developed by Cotterman (1959), Demaree (1961), Lumsdaine (1960), Miller (1962), Parker and Downs (1961), Stolurow (1964), and Willis and Peterson (1961). Gagné's work, also perceived as evolving within this context, was seen to be "particularly powerful" (Edling et al., 1972, p. 95).

Of these taxonomies, Miller's (1953, 1954, 1956, 1962) treatment of learning types illuminates the idea of "task analysis" as it was viewed in the 1950s and early 1960s. Miller, employed by IBM, proposed that an "equipment task analysis" description "should include analysis of perceptual, short term recall, long term recall, decision making and motor processes implied by the initial equipment task analysis" (Smode, 1962, p. 435). Miller reflected the mainstream approach by focusing on job tasks, although it is clear that consideration of cognitive processes greatly influenced much of his analysis scheme's structure and content.

Much of the progress in defining learning tasks made by the military and corporate researchers may be attributed to their employers' demands. Increasingly, technical training requirements in the military and industry were placing high demands on the skills of training designers to develop instruction in problem solving, troubleshooting, and other expertise-related tasks. Bryan (1962) discussed the pertinence of troubleshooting studies to the topics of transfer, concept formation, problem solving, decision making, thinking, and learning. To perhaps exaggerate a bit, one can envision academic colleagues running rats in the laboratories, while their counterparts who were employed by the military and large corporations were struggling with issues of human learning and skilled performance. This pressure to describe complex learning (often felt by academics as well) forced behaviorally trained psychologists to consider cognitive issues long before the mainstream and produced a unique blend of "neobehaviorism" with what we might call "precognitive" psychology. As we view Gagné's work and its evolution, this blend and transition are clearly illustrated.

24.2.1.2 Academic Learning Psychologists.
The thinking of academic psychologists about types of learning is well represented in a 1964 volume edited by A. W. Melton, *Categories of Human Learning*. In chapters by N. H. Anderson, E. J. Archer, G. E. Briggs, J. Deese, W. K. Estes, P. M. Fitts, R. M. Gagné, D. A. Grant, H. A. Kendler, T. S. Kendler, G. A. Kimble, A. W. Melton, L. Postman, B. J. Underwood, and D. D. Wickens, concerns about and progress toward understanding varieties of human learning are discussed. Two of these contributions are discussed here, for the information they contain on the state of the art and as illustrations of the categories defined during this period.

Underwood (1964b) discussed possible approaches to a taxonomy of human learning, proposing how it would be possible "to express the relationships among research findings for all forms of human learning" (p. 48). Underwood noted that a single, grand unified theory did not yet exist in which a master set of statements and relationships could lead to deductions of findings in each of the various areas of interest in learning research. A second approach that Underwood suggested in the absence of a grand unified theory was to attempt to "express the continuity for all human learning . . . in terms of phenomena produced by comparable operations. Thus, can the operations defining extinction in eyelid conditioning be duplicated in verbal learning, in motor learning, in concept formation, and so on, and, if so, do the same phenomena result from these operations?" (p. 48).

Underwood (1964b) noted that a difficulty in doing such cross-category research is that the differences among tasks make it physically impossible to manipulate them in comparable manners: "For example, it would seem difficult to manipulate meaningfulness on a pursuit rotor in the same sense that this variable is manipulated in verbal learning. Or, what operations in problem solving are comparable to variations in intensity of the conditioned stimulus in classical conditioning?" (p. 48). Underwood later described a technique for determining the similarity of learning in different situations. That technique is illustrated by work by Richardson (1958), in which "a descriptive difference between concept formation and rote verbal learning can be stated in terms of the number of identical responses to be associated with similar stimuli" (p. 49). The number of responses to a stimulus associated with a concept learning task was different from the number of responses to the same stimulus when it was part of a rote learning task, reflecting a lack of "continuity" between the two types of tasks.

In a seminal chapter in *Categories of Human Learning*, Melton (1964a) pointed out that neither the physical structures of the human organism nor its cognitive processes themselves (such as motivational, perceptual, and performance processes) provide guidance for a taxonomy of learning, as such structures would provide in classifying physical attributes. Of the need for a conditions-based approach Melton bemoans the lack of articulation between training design questions and knowledge about learning:

> When one is confronted with a decision to use massed or distributed practice, to insist on information feedback or not to insist on it, to arrange training so as to maximize or minimize requirements for contiguous stimulus differentiation, etc., and [one] discovers that the guidance received from experimental research and theory is different for rote learning, for skill learning, and for problem solving, taxonomic issues become critical and taxonomic ambiguities become frustrating, to say the least. (p. 327)

A strong element of formalism, in addition to the practical concerns noted in this quote, seems to shape Melton's thinking, and Melton's thinking is illustrative of the time in which he was writing. Melton wrote at length about a "taxonomy" of learning from the standpoint of taxonomies themselves and how they come about in science. A persistent theme is how the "primitive categories" will end up being used—to what extent they will be used and how they can conceivably be modified. The primitive categories, reflected to a large extent by chapter topics in the book, are rather long-standing areas of research and theory interest in learning psychology: conditioning, rote learning, probability learning, skills learning, concept learning, and problem solving. Apparently, Melton expected that all of these topics should, as organized in some appropriate and meaningful way, be related to one another in a taxonomic, hierarchical structure. One may notice, coincidentally perhaps, that Gagné's (1965b) first edition of *The conditions of learning* included a set of learning types that were, unlike those found in more recent editions, *in toto* a taxonomic list, in which each category in the classification scheme was prerequisite to the others (with the exception of the first category, classical conditioning). In later versions of the types of learning, Gagné included many categories that he did not propose as being in a hierarchical relationship (only the learning types within the intellectual skills category are proposed as being hierarchical in more current versions).

24.3 CONTRIBUTIONS OF R. M. GAGNÉ

As R. M. Gagné is generally identified as the primary originator of a conditions-based model of instructional design, an understanding of his evolution of thought becomes foundational to understanding the theory that extends beyond his contribution.

24.3.1 Precursors to Gagné's Conditions-Based Theory

In a review of factors that contribute to learning efficiency for a volume on programmed instruction sponsored by the Air Force Office of Scientific Research, Gagné and Bolles noted (1959) that "the learning tasks that have been most intensively studied by psychologists have been of an artificial "laboratory" variety; relatively little is known about learning in real life situations" (pp. 13–14). In 1962, as one who worked as a researcher in an academic setting, then as a researcher and research director in a military setting, and, finally, back in the academic setting, Gagné (1962b) reflected on military training research in an article entitled "Military Training and Principles of Learning."

Training research in the 1950s put Gagné in touch with a wide variety of instructional problems, representing a wide variety of learning tasks. Illustrative studies in the literature are Gagné's (1954) "An Analysis of Two Problem Solving Activities," involving troubleshooting and interpretation of aerial photographs, and Gagné, Baker, and Wylie's (1951) "Effects of an Interfering Task on the Learning of a Complex Motor Skill," involving manipulations of controls similar to aircraft controls. In a review of problem solving and thinking, Gagné (1959) pointed out the relevance of troubleshooting studies to issues in concept

formation. Wide and vigorous participation in research on learning and instruction in the military environment, along with his thorough and rigorous background as a learning psychologist, may have created the dissonance that motivated Gagné to develop the concepts of types of learning outcomes, learning hierarchies, events of instruction, and conditions of learning. A treatment of this development with personal insight into Gagné's military training involvement is provided by Spector (2000). Spector's chapter on Gagné's thinking and contributions during a long association with military training research provides illustrations of talents and quirks, in addition to achievements, which are part of his legacy.

24.3.2 Development of Types of Learning

In his chapter on problem solving for Melton's *Categories of Human Learning*, Gagné (1964) presented a table entitled "A Suggested Ordering of the Types of Human Learning" in which he proposed the following six types of learning: response learning, chaining, verbal learning (paired associates), concept learning, principle learning, and problem solving (p. 312). He did not cite a previous publication of his here, so this may be the first appearance of his types of learning scheme. This is not to say that he had not engaged in much previous thought and writing on important differences between forms of learning. However, the pulling-together of types of learning to form a totally inclusive scheme containing mutually exclusive elements appears to have taken place around the time that the Categories of Learning symposium was taking place, early in 1962.

Gagné's thinking on types of learning is illustrated by his discussion of problem solving as a form of learning. In the following, he points out how problem solving, as a form of learning, differs from other forms of learning:

...The learning situation for problem solving never includes performances which could, by simple summation, constitute the criterion performance. In conditioning and trial-and-error learning, the performance finally exhibited (blinking an eye, or tracing a path) occurs as part of the learning situation. In verbal learning, the syllables or words to be learned are included in the learning situation. In concept learning, however, this is not always so, and there is consequently a resemblance to problem solving in this respect. Although mediation experiments may present a concept during learning which is later a part of the criterion performance, many concept learning experiments do not use this procedure. Instead they require the S to respond with a performance scored in a way which was not directly given in learning (the stating of an abstraction such as "round" or "long and rectangular"). Similarly, the "solution" of the problem is not presented within the learning situation for problem solving. Concept formation and problem solving are *nonreproductive* types of learning. (Gagné, 1964, p. 311)

Perhaps the first full and complete statement of the types of learning conception appeared in the first edition of *The Conditions of Learning*, Gagné (1965b). In that work, Gagné began by reviewing learning theory and research, such as those of James, Dewey, Watson, Thorndike, Tolman, Ebbinghaus, Pavlov, and Köhler. To introduce the idea of types of learning, Gagné presented the notion of "learning prototypes":

> Throughout the period of scientific investigation of learning there has been frequent recourse to certain typical experimental situations to serve as prototypes for learning. (p.18)

The difference in kinds of learning among these prototypes is seen in the inability to "'reduce' one variety to another, although many attempts have been made" (p. 18). To clarify how these distinctive forms of learning have come to be lumped together as one form, Gagné pointed out,

> These learning prototypes all have a similar history in this respect: each of them started to be a representative of a particular variety of learning situation. Thorndike wanted to study animal association. Pavlov was studying reflexes. Ebbinghaus studied the memorization of verbal lists. Köhler was studying the solving of problems by animals. By some peculiar semantic process, these examples became prototypes of learning, and thus were considered to represent the domain of learning as a whole, or at least in large part. (pp. 18–19)

Gagné (1965b) presented eight types of learning in the first edition, in a strict hierarchical relationship. All types but the first, signal learning (classical conditioning), have prerequisite relationships with one another. The eight types of learning, with corresponding researcher links, were as follows:

1. Signal learning (Pavlov, 1927)
2. Stimulus–response learning (Kimball, 1961; Skinner, 1938; Thorndike, 1898)
3. Chaining (Gilbert, 1962; Skinner, 1938)
4. Verbal association (Underwood, 1964a)
5. Multiple discrimination (Postman, 1961)
6. Concept learning (Kendler, 1964)
7. Principle learning (Gagné, 1964)
8. Problem solving (Katona, 1940; Maier, 1930)

Regarding the distinctions among these types, Gagné (1965b, p. 59) described support for some of the distinctions. Table 24.1 summarizes that discussion.

Later editions of *The Conditions of Learning* modified the types of learning list considerably. Although the second edition (Gagné, 1970) reflected no change in the number or labeling of the eight types of learning, by the third edition (Gagné, 1977) information processing theories were added to the treatment of learning prototypes, and a large section was added on information processing along with recasting the types of learning. The information processing perspective, present in the third edition, was not part of the first or second edition, even though earlier work reflected a strong information processing background (Gagné, 1962c). Surprisingly, although Gagné's primary base

TABLE 24.1. Summary of the Etiology of Learning Types

Type 1 distinct from Type 2	Thorndike (1898)
	Skinner (1938)
	Hull (1934)
Type 3 as a distinct form	Skinner (1938)
	Hull (1943)
Type 5 distinct from Type 6	Mowrer (1960)
	Harlow (1959)

was shifting from behavioral to cognitive in the third edition, task characteristics, rather than psychological processes, began to guide the form and content of the types of learning. In Gagné's fourth edition (1985), a hierarchical, prerequisite relationship is limited to four subcategories of one major category, intellectual skills. The types of learning in the fourth edition were as follows:

1. Intellectual skills
   Discriminations
   Concepts
   Rules
   Problem solving
2. Cognitive strategies
3. Verbal information
4. Motor skills
5. Attitudes

Gagné's descriptions of the categories of problem solving and cognitive strategies have continued to evolve recent years. For example, in Gagné and Glaser (1987) combined "problem solving" into one category along with cognitive strategies. Inspection of the text reveals that, in fact, domain-specific problem solving was meant here, along with strategies for learning and strategies for remembering (see pp. 66–67). The evaluation of Gagné's problem-solving category can also be noted in his fourth edition of *The Conditions of Learning* (1985), in which problem solving was moved out of the intellectual skills category as higher-order rules and appears to have become a category separate from both the rule-based learning of intellectual skills and the domain-general category of cognitive strategy.

Gagné and Merrill (1990) described an approach to the integration of multiple learning objectives for larger, longer-term efforts that are unified through "pursuit of a comprehensive purpose in which the learner is engaged, called an enterprise" (p. 23). A learning enterprise may be defined as "a purposive activity that may depend for its execution on some combination of verbal information, intellectual skills, and cognitive strategies, all related by their involvement in the common goal" (p. 25). The storage of enterprises is discussed in terms of mental models (Gentner & Stevens, 1983), schemata (Rummelhart, 1980), and work models (Bunderson, Gibbons, Olsen, & Kearsley, 1981 and Gibbons, Bunderson, Olsen, & Robertson, 1995). Three kinds of enterprise schemata are described: denoting, manifesting, and discovering. Disappointingly, all of the examples are of individual learning, not of sets of them.

What do these categories of learning represent? Gagné (1985) described the types of learning outcomes as "learned dispositions," "capabilities," or "long term memory states" (p. 245), qualities that reside within the learner. He further described two of these categories, verbal information and intellectual skills, as having distinctly different memory storage systems. Gagné and White (1978) provided an empirical basis for the "verbal information" knowledge to be stored as propositional networks. They further described rule using (later to be called intellectual skills) as being stored in hierarchical skill structures, which at that time they called "intellectual skills."

More recently, Gagné (1985) described verbal information learning as being stored as propositional networks or schemata.

He described rules, including defining rules or concepts, as being stored as "If...then" productions. He did not suggest how problem-solving capabilities themselves are stored, although he implied that they are interconnections of schemata and productions. Nor did he explicitly conjecture regarding the storage mechanisms of attitudes, motor skills, or cognitive strategies.

As the concept of types of learning evolved from its neobehaviorist beginnings to the more cognitive orientation seen in the fourth edition of *The Conditions of Learning* (1985), the research basis for differences in conditions for their achievement appears to have been largely lost. Although the concept remains as intuitively valid as ever to many instructional technologists, direct support in the literature is shockingly absent. Kyllonen and Shute (1989) describe Gagné's types of learning as a "rational taxonomy," being developed via proposing "task categories in terms of characteristics that will foster or inhibit learned performance" (p. 120). The drawback to such an approach is that its basis does not lie in psychological processes, and therefore, such processes are unsystematically considered.

24.3.3 Development of the Learning Hierarchies Concept

A study by Gagné and Brown (1961) revealed thinking that led directly to Gagné's conceptions of learning hierarchies and types of learning. Here, in the context of programmed instruction, Gagné and Brown were concerned with the acquisition of meaningful "conceptual" learning, compared with the rote memorization or association learning that characterized the work of Holland and Skinner: "... From an examination of representative published examples of programs (e.g., Holland, 1959; Skinner, 1958) it is not immediately apparent that they are conveying 'understanding' in the sense of capability for inducing transfer to new problem situations. They appear to be concerned primarily with the usages of words in a variety of stimulus contexts" (p. 174).

The phenomenon of transfer appears to have been central to Gagné and Brown's concerns, both transfer from prerequisite learnings to higher-level outcomes (sometimes termed "vertical transfer") and transfer from the learning situation to later application (sometimes termed "lateral transfer"). Although a great deal of attention is given to the study's programmed instruction format in the report, it is clear that the authors' interests were focused on the question of vertical transfer to problem solving (the particular learning task would now be considered relational rule use).

Gagné and Brown (1961), described a study with a programmed instruction lesson teaching concepts related to number series: the terms *value* and *number*. After a common introduction to the fundamental concepts, the study employed three treatment methods to teach application of the concepts to finding the key to number series problems: rule and example (R&E), discovery (D), and guided discovery (GD). The authors considered issues such as "size of step" and others of interest in programmed instruction research of the day. However, they

concluded that "some aspect of what has been learned ... is of greater effect than how it has been learned" (p. 181). The difference in "what" is supplied by the three treatments was that the GD method required the use of previously learned concepts in a new context.

Although all three methods were effective in teaching learners to solve numerical series problems, the GD and D methods were superior to the R&E method, with the GD method being the most effective. The inferiority of the R&E method was attributed to the fact that it did not *require* learners to practice the application of concepts to a problem situation. In other conditions, learners could make the application but were believed, in general, not to have applied the concepts to the problem situation.

A postscript: It is ironic perhaps that in this early study, one that employed programmed instruction methods and reflected Gagné's thinking very much as neobehaviorist, the instructional strategies labeled *discovery* and *guided discovery* were found to provide superior instruction. It should be noted that the D method used was more structured than what many today might construct: A good amount of supplantive instruction on prerequisites preceded the D condition.

Gagné's first references to "learning hierarchies" appeared in articles published in 1962: a report of a study, "Factors in Acquiring Knowledge of a Mathematical Task"(Gagné, Mayor, Garstens, & Paradise, 1962), and another study, "The Acquisition of Knowledge" (Gagné, 1962a), which involved similar learning tasks. These reports were preceded by a study by Gagné and Paradise (1961) that formed a foundation for the latter studies. In 1961, Gagné and Paradise found support for the proposition that transfer of learning from subordinate sets of learning tasks could account for performance on a terminal learning task. In the subsequent study, Gagné et al. (1962) sought to extend and confirm the validity of the idea of the "learning hierarchy."

Gagné et al. (1962) sought to test the effects of three factors that should mediate the effectiveness of learning hierarchies: (a) identifiability, which roughly translates into "acquisition of prerequisite concepts"; (b) recallability, stimulated in the study by cueing and repetition of prerequisite concepts; and (c) integration, in this study provided by what Gagné and Briggs (1974) later termed "provision of learning guidance," which was directed toward assisting the learner in applying concepts to problem situations. Two variables, used in various combinations, served to modify a basic learning program: repetition (high and low) and guidance (high and low). The posttest supplied information about achievement of not only the terminal task (adding integers) but also the 12 prerequisite learning sets, each scored as "pass" or "fail." These data were analyzed to supply evidence of the effects of the treatments on transfer. Success in final task achievement correlated highly with the number of subordinate tasks successfully achieved for both of the two terminal learning tasks (.87 and .88). Patterns of transfer among the subordinate tasks also conformed to theoretical predictions.

In "The Acquisition of Knowledge," Gagné (1962a) began by explicating the concept of a "class of tasks," differentiating the idea from "a response" by noting that in acquiring useful knowledge, it is inadequate to consider knowledge as a set of responses because, when applied, it is impossible to identify from each specific response which skills, such as multiplication and punctuating compound sentences, the responses imply: "Any of an infinite number of distinguishable stimulus situations and an equal number of responses may be involved" (p. 229).

24.3.4 Research Confirming Learning Hierarchies

In 1973, Gagné described the idea of learning hierarchies and noted that learning hierarchies have the following characteristics: (a) They describe "successively achievable intellectual skills, each of which is stated as a performance class;" (b) they do not include "verbal information, cognitive strategies, motivational factors, or performance sets"; and (c) each step in the hierarchy describes "only those prerequisite skills that must be recalled at the moment of learning" to supply the necessary "internal" component of the total learning situation (pp. 21–22).

Gagné also described several studies on the validation of learning hierarchies. A fundamental way to accomplish this is to look at differences in transfer between groups that attain and groups that do not attain hypothesized prerequisites. The study by Gagné et al. (1962, Table 3, p. 9) was cited as an example providing positive evidence from such an approach. Other validation studies were reported, each looking in one way or another at the validity of a particular learning hierarchy: in other words, at the extent to which the hierarchy was a true description of prerequisite relationships among hypothesized subtasks. As a set, these studies can be seen to present evidence of the validity of the concept of learning hierarchies. The studies are summarized in Table 24.2.

In addition to the above, studies by Gagné and associates commonly cited to support the learning hierarchies hypothesis include the following: Gagné (1962a), Gagné and Paradise (1961), Gagné et al. (1962), Gagné and Bassler (1963), and Gagné and Staff, University of Maryland Mathematics Project (1965).

It should be noted that in "Factors in Acquiring Knowledge of a Mathematical Task" (Gagné et al., 1962) and in "The Acquisition of Knowledge" (Gagné, 1962), Gagné dealt primarily with learning hierarchies, not yet with the idea that different types of learning might require different instructional conditions. The thrust of Gagné's ideas at this point was toward the organization and sequence of instruction, not the form of encounter.

24.3.5 Development of Events of Instruction and Conditions of Learning

24.3.5.1 Events of Instruction. In "The Acquisition of Knowledge," in addition to presenting the "learning hierarchies" concept, Gagné (1962a) also introduced a precursor to the nine events of instruction. The description is of four functions for which a theory of knowledge acquisition must account.

1. Required terminal performance
2. Elements of the stimulus situation
3. High recallability of learning sets
4. Provision of "guidance of thinking"

Another foundation for the events of instruction was Gagné's thinking on the idea of internal and external conditions of learning, which is fundamental to the thesis in the first edition of *The Conditions of Learning* (1965b). Internal and external conditions were defined (p. 21) and discussion of each of the types of learning was organized essentially along lines of internal and external conditions for achievement of that type of learning. To summarize Gagné's descriptions of these two types of conditions, internal conditions were described primarily as learners' possession of prerequisite knowledge and external conditions were viewed as instruction.

The first edition of *The Conditions of Learning* (Gagné, 1965b) did not have a discussion of the *events of instruction* in the same sense in which the term later came to be used—as a listing intended to be inclusive, reflecting events that must occur, if not supplied by instruction, then generated by learners. The treatment in *The Conditions of Learning*, under the heading "External Events of Instruction," included discussion of (a) control of the stimulus situation (strategy prescriptions varied with types of learning), (b) verbally communicated "directions" (directing attention, conveying information about expected performance, inducing recall of previously learned entities, and guiding learning by discovery), and (c) feedback from learning.

The events of instruction conception may be directly attributable more to L. J. Briggs' work than to Gagné's, although the two collaborated extensively on it. For example, Briggs, Campeau, Gagné, and May's (1967) handbook for the design of multimedia instruction uses nearly all the elements of what was to become the events of instruction in its examples, but it does not present a list of the events (see Briggs, 1967,

TABLE 24.2. Results of Studies on Hierarchies

Author(s)	Date	Learning Task	Results
Wiegand	1970	Inclined plane	Transfer demonstrated
Nicholas	1970	Not stated	Replicated Wiegand (1970)
Coleman & Gagné	1970	Exports comparison	Too much mastery by control group, but better transfer to problem solving found
Eustace	1969	Concept "noun"	Hypothesized sequence better
Okey & Gagné	1970	Chemistry	Learning hierarchy revision better than original version
Resnick, Siegel, & Kresh	1971	Double classification	Successfully predicted outcomes
Caruso & Resnick	1971	Replication	Resnick et al. (1971) confirmed
Wang, Resnick, & Boozer	1972	Math curriculum	Several dependency sequences found

pp. 53–73). In another chapter in that manual, Briggs, Gagné, and May (1967, pp. 45) noted the following as "instructional functions of stimuli."

1. Set a goal in terms of performance desired
2. Direct attention
3. Present instructional content (also stimuli)
4. Elicit response
5. Provide feedback
6. Direct the next effort
7. Help the student to evaluate his or her performance

Also noted, here under "other special functions of stimuli" are (a) providing the degree of cueing or prompting desired, (b) enhancing motivation, (c) aiding the student in recall of relevant concepts, (d) promoting transfer, and (e) inducing generalizing experiences (Briggs et al., 1967, p. 45). Between the two lists, the events of instruction formulation appears to have been taking shape.

The first edition of *The Conditions of Learning* (Gagné, 1965b) contained a section called "component functions of the instructional situation" that, except for the label, was virtually identical in conception and content to the events of instruction seen in later editions of *The Conditions of Learning* as well as Gagné and Briggs' (1974) *Principles of Instructional Design*. The eight functions were (a) presenting the stimulus, (b) directing attention and other learner activities, (c) providing a model for terminal performance, (d) furnishing external prompts, (e) guiding the direction of thinking, (f) inducing transfer of knowledge, (g) assessing learning attainments, and (h) providing feedback.

24.3.5.2 Conditions of Learning.

Completing Gagné's contribution to conditions-based theory is his discussion of the internal and external conditions of learning that support each type of learning outcome. *Internal conditions* are those cognitive processes that support the acquisition of particular categories of learning outcomes. *External conditions* are those instructional conditions provided by the teacher, materials, or other learners that can facilitate the internal conditions necessary for learning. These external conditions, too, vary according to type of learning. Not surprisingly, given Gagné's transition from behavioral to cognitive theory bases, he developed the external conditions model first.

As an instructional psychologist, Gagné (1985) was particularly interested in the external conditions that might occur or could be provided to "activate and support" the internal processing necessary for learning to occur (p. 276). In fact, Gagné defined the purpose of instructional theory as "to propose a rationally based relationship between instructional events, their effects on learning processes, and the learning outcomes that are produced as a result of these processes" (p. 244). Therefore, Gagné derived the external events from the internal events of information processing.

Gagné particularized the general external events, the events of instruction, that begin to be described in his work in 1962 to specific prescriptions for external conditions for each type of learning, event by event, for each of the categories of learned

capability. Many aspects of these external conditions are logically derived from the intersection of the function of the external event (those cognitive processes that it supports) and the nature of the learning capability.

In "Domains of Learning" (1972), Gagné argued very specifically for a conditions-based theory but did not present research directly on it; rather, he presented arguments about the nature of different learning domains, buttressed often in a general fashion by research. The five domains—motor skills, verbal information, intellectual skills, cognitive strategies, and attitudes—are the level at which he argued that there is a difference in how they should be taught, particularly in terms of the kind and amount of practice required and the role of meaningful context. Additional criteria as means by which types of learning can be contrasted with regard to instructional concerns are given in Gagné's 1984 article, "Learning Outcomes and their Effects."

In Gagné and White's 1978 article, two general domains of learning outcome were discussed: knowledge stating and rule application. References used to support the distinctness of these two domains include Gagné (1972) and Olsen and Bruner (1974).

In 1987 Gagné and Glaser developed a review that included a brief survey of Gagné's early work, learning as cognition, the importance of short-term memory, learning of complex performances, knowledge organization for problem solving, mental models, and self-regulation. Table 24.3, reproduced from that

TABLE 24.3. Gagné and Glaser's Learning Categories × Conditions Summary: Effective Learning Conditions for Categories of Learned Capabilities

Type of Capability	Learning Conditions
Intellectual skill	Retrieval of subordinate (component) skills
	Guidance by verbal or other means
	Demonstration of application by student; precise feedback
	Spaced reviews
Verbal information	Retrieval of context of meaningful information
	Performance of reconstructing new knowledge; feedback
Cognitive strategy (problem solving)	Retrieval of relevant rules & concepts
	Successive presentation (usually over extended time) of novel problem situations
	Demonstration of solution by student
Attitude	Retrieval of information and intellectual skills relevant to targeted personal actions
	Establishment or recall of respect for human model
	Reinforcement for personal action either by successful direct experience or vicariously by observation of respected person
Motor skill	Retrieval of component motor chains
	Establishment or recall of executive subroutines
	Practice of total skill; precise feedback

Note. From "Foundations in Learning Research," by R. M. Gagné and R. Glaser, 1987, in R. M. Gagné (Ed.), *Instructional Technology Foundations* (p. 64), Mahwah, NJ: Lawrence Erlbaum Associates. Reproduced with permission.

review, provides an excellent summary of hypothesized differential learning conditions for types of learning.

24.3.5.3 Internal Conditions of Learning.
Gagné suggested that, for each category or subcategory of learning capability to be acquired, certain internal conditions were necessary. By 1985, Gagné described these internal conditions as being of two kinds: (a) prerequisite knowledge, which is stored in long-term memory; and (b) particular cognitive processes that bring this old knowledge and new knowledge together and store it in a retrievable form. Gagné described these cognitive processes using an information processing model: attention, selective perception, semantic encoding, retrieval, response organization, control processes, and expectancies.

It should be noted that in Gagné's detailing of the internal conditions of each type of learning, the major internal condition that he described was prerequisite knowledge. For example, Gagné specified the internal conditions for rule learning to be knowledge of (the ability to classify previously unencountered instances and noninstances of) component concepts. This may be because the research base for the identification of the specific internal conditions for each learning capability was inadequate or because, as an instructional theorist, his predominant interest was the external conditions that could support the generalized information processing mechanism and those internal conditions necessary prior to the initiation of new learning.

Gagné (1984) suggested that the internal events that may differ most across learning capabilities are "a) the substantive type of relevant prior knowledge, b) manner of encoding into long term storage, c) requirement for retrieval and transfer to new situations" (p. 514). Therefore, in his 1985 edition of *The Conditions of Learning*, he pointed out that the external events that may differ most significantly from learning category to learning category are those corresponding to the above three internal events: (a) stimulating recall of prior knowledge, (b) providing learning guidance, and (c) enhancing retention and transfer.

24.4 EXAMPLES OF CONDITIONS-BASED THEORIES

Gagné provided the intellectual leadership for a conditions-based theory of instruction. This leadership, to some extent documented in the current chapter, is well explicated in a volume dedicated to the legacy of Gagné (Richey, 2000b). Fields (2000) discusses Gagné's contributions to practice, with an emphasis on instructional design, curriculum, and transfer. Smith and Ragan (2000) discuss his contribution to instructional theory. Spector (2000) reviews Gagné's military training research and development, and Nelson (2000) concentrates on how Gagné's work relates to and has contributed to new technologies of instruction.

A number of scholars followed in Gagné's tradition by developing more detailed prescriptions of the external conditions that will support different types of learning. Three texts edited by Reigeluth, *Instructional Design Theories and Models* (1983b), *Instructional Theories in Action* (1987), and *Instructional Design Theories and Models, Volume II: A New Paradigm of Instructional Theory* (1999a), clearly delineate a number of models that we would describe as conditions-based models of design. Some of the models in these texts, such as those by Scandura, Collins, and Keller, we would not describe as full conditions-based models, as they do not describe the cognitive and instructional conditions for more than one learning type. Others, particularly in *Volume II*, employ few if any considerations of learning task and would, in any event, likely be upset by being considered as having anything to do with conditions theory and the cognitive science upon which it is built. To some, there is a conflict between "learner centered" and "content-centered" thinking, although the conflict as yet escapes us.

It is not the purpose of this chapter to replicate the thorough discussions of the conditions-based models presented by Reigeluth (1983b, 1987, 1999a). However, we briefly discuss and compare the models because it is through comparisons that many of the major issues regarding conditions-based models are revealed and exemplified. We also briefly review research and evaluation studies that have examined the effectiveness of the conditions theory as a whole or individual features of the theory. We also include in our discussion some "models" not presented in Reigeluth's texts. Some examples provided are arguably not *instructional design models* at all (such as the work of Horn [1976], Resnick [1967], and West, Farmer, & Wolf [1991], but all employ, reflect, or extend the *conditions-based theory* propositions listed in the introduction to this chapter in one important way or another.

24.4.1 Gagné and Gagné, Briggs, and Wager

We have thoroughly described Gagné's conditions-based theory of instruction elsewhere in this chapter. This theory was the basis of an instructional design model presented in *Instructional Design: Principles and Applications* (Briggs, 1977) and *Principles of Instructional Design* (Gagné & Briggs, 1974, 1979; Gagné, Briggs, & Wager, 1988, 1992).

Research examining the validity of Gagné's theory are of two types: studies that have examined the validity of Gagné's instructional theory as a cluster of treatment variables and those that have examined the individual propositions of the theory as separate variables. Research of the latter type is discussed later in this chapter. A few studies have attempted to evaluate the overall value of instruction based on Gagné's theory or portions of Gagné's theory that are not central to the conditions-based theory. We describe several examples of studies of this type. Goldberg (1987), Marshall (1986), Mengel (1986), and Stahl (1979) compared "traditional" textbook or teacher-led instruction to print-based or teacher-led instruction designed according to Gagné's principles. These studies were across age groups and subject matters. Mengal and Stahl found significant differences in learning effects for the versions developed according to Gagné's principles, and Goldberg and Marshall found no significant difference in treatments. Although we believe such gross comparison studies to be essential to the development of research in an area, they suffer from some of the same threats to the validity of conclusions as do other comparison studies. In particular, it is unclear whether the "traditional" versions did not include some features of Gagné's principles and that the "Gagnétian" versions were fully consistent with these principles. Research that has examined the principles from Gagné's instructional design models that are directly related to propositions of his theory are discussed in a later section of this chapter.

24.4.2 Merrill: Component Display Theory and Instructional Transaction Theory

Merrill's component display theory (CDT; 1983) and instructional transaction theory (ITT; 1999), extensions of Gagné's theory, are conditions-based theories of instructional design, as he prescribed instructional conditions based on the types of learning outcomes desired.

24.4.2.1 *Types of Learned Capabilities.* In CDT, Merrill classified learning objectives (or capabilities) along two dimensions: performance level (remember, use, or find) and content type (facts, concepts, principles, or procedures). So, there are conceivably 12 distinct categories of objectives that his theory addresses. Instead of having a declarative knowledge category, as Gagné does, which would include remembering facts, concept definitions, rule statements, and procedural steps, CDT makes separate categories for each of these types of declarative knowledge. Similarly, instead of having a single cognitive strategies category as Gagné does, through his intersection of the two dimensions, CDT proposes "find" operations for each of the content types: Find a fact, find a concept, find a rule, and find a procedure. In ITT, Merrill provided 13 types of learning with associated instructional strategies, which he identified as "transactions," grouped into three major categories: component transactions—identify, execute, and interpret; abstractions transactions—judge, classify, generalize, decide, and transfer; and association transactions—propagate, analogize, substitute, design, and discover (Merrill, Jones, & Li, 1992).

Merrill (1983) provided a rationale for his categorization scheme for CDT based upon "some assumptions about the nature of subject matter" (p. 298). The rationale for content type is based on five operations that he proposes can be conducted on subject matter: identity (facts), inclusion and intersection (concepts), order (procedures), and causal operations (principles). He derived his performance levels from assumptions regarding differences in four memory structures: associative, episodic, image, and algorithmic. His performance levels derived from the associative (remember: verbatim and paraphrased) and algorithmic (use and find) memory structures. Merrill did not explicitly address the internal processes that accompany the acquisition of each of these categories of learning types.

24.4.2.2 *External Conditions of Learning.* Merrill described instructional conditions as "presentation forms" in CDT and classified these forms as primary and secondary. Primary

presentation forms have two dimensions: content (generality or instance) and approach (expository or inquisitory). Secondary presentation forms are types of elaborations that may extend the primary presentations: context, prerequisite, mnemonic, mathemagenic help, representation or alternative representation, and feedback. Merrill's (1983) theory then further described for each category of capability "a unique combination of primary and secondary presentation forms that will most effectively promote acquisition of that type of objective" (p. 283).

24.4.2.3 *Research on Component Display Theory.* Researchers have examined CDT in two ways: evaluation in comparison to "traditional" approaches and examination of individual strategy variations within CDT. We briefly describe examples of both types of research.

In research across a range of content, age groups, and learning tasks, researchers have examined the effectiveness of instruction following design principles proposed by CDT to existing or "traditional" instruction. For example, Keller and Reigeluth (1982) compared more conventional mathematics instruction in both expository and discovery formats to instruction following a "modified discovery" approach suggested by CDT. They found no significant effects on acquisition of set theory concepts, concluding that it was important to learning that the generality be presented explicitly but less important whether this generality was presented prior to or following the presentation of examples. In contrast, Stein (1982) found CDT to be superior for concept learning among eighth graders, comparing four treatments: expository prose, expository prose plus adjunct questions, CDT with only primary presentation forms, and CDT with both primary and secondary presentation forms. She found that both CDT versions were significantly more effective in promoting students' ability to recognize previously presented instances of these concepts and to generalize the concept to previously unencountered instances. In addition, she found that this effect was more pronounced for the more difficult concepts. In a similar prose study, Robinson (1984) found a CDT version of a lesson on text editing to be significantly superior (on recall of the procedure; marginally superior on use of the procedure [$p = .11$]) to two other versions of prose instruction, one version with summarizing examples and one with inserted questions. Von Hurst (1984) found a similar positive effect of materials revised using CDT principles compared with the existing instructional materials in Japanese-language learning. The CDT version was found to promote significantly greater achievement and more positive affect and confidence than the original version.

Researchers have also examined individual variables in CDT. For example, Keller (1986) examined the relative benefits of generality alone, best example alone, or both generality and best example for learning graphing concepts and procedures. She found that the combined treatment was superior for remembering the steps in the procedure. None of the treatments was superior for using the procedure (only practice seemed to be critical). Further, the combined condition was superior for promoting finding a new procedural generality. Chao (1983) also examined the benefits of two expository versions of CDT (generality, example, practice, generality/generality, example, practice) and two discovery treatments (examples, practice/examples, practice, generality) for application and transfer of concepts and principles of plate tectonics. Unlike Chao and similarly to her earlier comparisons of expository and discovery sequences (Keller & Reigeluth, 1982), Keller found no statistically significant difference in the participants' performance on application or transfer measures. Although order of generality, example, and practice may not be found to affect performance, Sasayama (1985) found that for a procedure-using learning task, a rule–example–practice treatment had superior effects on learning than a rule-only, example-only, or rule–example treatment.

Many of the weaknesses of Merrill's theory are similar to those of Gagné's, such as the lack of an explicit and empirically validated tie between internal processes and external events. However, Merrill's theory conjectures even less on internal processes. It is also less complete, as his theory addresses only the cognitive domain, does not fully delineate the instructional conditions for the "find" (cognitive strategies) category, and does not have a category for complex learning reflected in what is often called "problem solving." A strength of CDT may be its evolution to fit the demands of designing intelligent CAI systems, as noted by Wilson (1987).

24.4.3 Reigeluth: Elaboration Theory

Reigeluth and his associates (Reigeluth, 1999b; Reigeluth & Darwazeh, 1982; Reigeluth & Rogers, 1980; Reigeluth & Stein, 1983; Reigeluth; Merrill, & Wilson, 1978) developed the elaboration theory as a guide for developing macrostrategies for large segments of instruction, such as courses and units. The elaboration theory is conditions based in nature, as it describes "a) three models of instruction; and b) a system for prescribing those models on the basis of the goals for a whole course of instruction" (Reigeluth & Stein, 1983, p. 340). The theory specifies a general model of selecting, sequencing, synthesizing, and summarizing content in a simple to more complex structure. The major features of the general model are an epitome at the beginning of the instruction, levels of elaboration of this epitome, learning-prerequisite sequences within the levels of elaboration, a learner-control format, and use of analogies, summarizers, and synthesizers.

The conditions-based nature of the model is obtained from Reigeluth's specification of three differing structures—conceptual, procedural, and theoretical—which are selected based on the goals of the course. Reigeluth further suggested that conceptual structures are of three types: parts, kinds, and matrices (combinations of two or more conceptual structures). He described two kinds of procedural structures: procedural order and procedural decision. Finally, he subdivided theoretical structures into two types: those that describe natural phenomena (descriptive structures) and those that affect a desired outcome (prescriptive structures).

The nature of the epitome, sequence, summarizers, prerequisites, synthesizers, and content of elaborations will vary depending on the type of knowledge structure chosen, which is based on the goals of the course. For example, if the knowledge structure is conceptual, the epitome will contain a presentation of the most fundamental concepts for the entire course. If the structure is procedural, the epitome should present the most fundamental or "shortest path" procedure. Reigeluth recommended using Merrill's CDT as the guideline for designing at the micro or lesson level within each elaboration cycle.

Increasingly Reigeluth (1992) has placed more emphasis on the importance of using a simplifying conditions method of sequencing instruction than on the sequencing and structuring of instruction based on one of the major knowledge structures. The simplifying conditions method suggests that designers "work with experts to identify a simple case that is as representative as possible of the task as a whole" (p. 81). This task should serve as the epitome of the course, with succeeding levels of elaboration "relaxing" the simplifying conditions so that the task becomes more and more complex. The theory still retains some of its conditions-based orientation, though, as Reigeluth has suggested, different simplifying conditions structures need to be developed for each of the kinds of knowledge structures he described Reigeluth & Curtis, 1987; Reigeluth & Rogers, 1980).

In recent years, Reigeluth's (1999b) discussions of elaboration theory have emphasized it as a holistic, learner-centered approach, in an effort to distance it from analytic approaches centering on learning tasks or content.

24.4.3.1 Research on Elaboration Theory. As with the previous models, some research has evaluated the effectiveness of instruction based on the principles of elaboration theory in comparison to instruction designed based on other models. Examples of this type of research are that by Beukhof (1986), who found that instructional text designed following elaboration theory prescriptions was more effective than "traditional" text for learners with low prior knowledge. In contrast, Wagner (1994) compared instruction on handling hazardous materials designed using the elaboration theory to materials designed using structural learning theory (Scandura, 1983). She found that although it took longer for learners to reach criterion performance with the structured learning materials, they performed significantly better on the delayed posttest than learners in the elaboration theory group. Wedman and Smith (1989) compared text designed according to Gagné's prescriptions and following a strictly hierarchical sequence to text designed according to the elaboration theory. They found no significant differences in either immediate or delayed principle application (photography principles). Nor did they find any interactions with a learner characteristic, field independence or dependence. In another study using the same materials, Smith and Wedman (1988) found some subtle differences between the read-think-aloud protocols of participants from the same population who were interacting with the two versions of the materials. They found that participants interacting with the elaborated version (a) required less time per page than the hierarchical version, (b) made more references to their own prior knowledge, (c) made fewer summarizing statements, (d) used mnemonics less often, and (e) made about the same types of markings and nonverbal actions as participants interacting with the hierarchical version. They concluded that although instruction designed following the two approaches may evoke subtle processing differences, these differences are not translated into differences in immediate and delayed principle application, at least within the 2 hr of instruction that this study encompassed. As Reigeluth proposed that the elaboration theory is a macrostrategy theory, effective for the design of units and courses, and recommended CDT as a micro design strategy for lessons, it is perhaps not surprising that researchers have not uniformly found positive effects of the elaboration theory designs on their shorter instruction.

Researchers have also examined design questions regarding individual variables within elaboration theory, such as synthesizers, summarizers, nonexamples in learning procedures, and sequencing. Table 24.4 summarizes the findings of several of these studies.

24.4.3.2 Evaluation of Elaboration Theory. Elaboration theory is a macrostrategy design theory that was much needed in the field of instructional design. Throughout the evolution of elaboration theory Reigeluth has proposed design principles that maintained a conditions-based orientation. Due to the strong emphasis on learning hierarchy analysis, until Reigeluth's work many designers had assumed that instruction should proceed from one enabling objective to another from the beginning to the end of a course. Reigeluth suggested a theoretically sound alternative for designing large segments of instruction. It is unfortunate that researchers in the field have not found it

pragmatically possible to evaluate the theory in comparison to alternatives with course-level instruction.

In light of advances in cognitive theory Wilson and Cole (1992) suggested a number of recommendations for revising elaboration theory. These suggestions include (a) deproceduralizing the theory, (b) removing unnecessary design constraints (including the use of primary structures, which form the basis of much of the conditions-based aspect of elaboration theory), (c) basing organization and sequencing decisions on what is known by the learners as well as the content structure, and (d) assuming a more "constructivist stance" toward content structure and sequencing (p. 76). Reigeluth (1992) responded to these recommendations in an admirable way: Regarding the deproceduralization of the elaboration theory, he pointed out that he agreed that the theory itself should not be proceduralized, but that he has always included in his discussions of elaboration theory ways to operationalize it. Reigeluth proposed that he had already removed "unnecessary design constraints" (the second Wilson and Cole recommendation) by replacing the "content structure" approach with the simplifying conditions method. This approach may more nearly reflect Reigeluth's original intentions for the elaboration theory. However, it does not eliminate the underlying conditions-based principle (which we interpret Wilson and Cole to be recommending), as the method for identifying simplified conditions seems to vary according to whether the instructional goal is conceptual, theoretical, or procedural. Reigeluth concurred with Wilson and Cole's recommendation

TABLE 24.4. Studies Examining Elaboration Theory (ET) Variables

Author(s)	Date	Variable(s)	Findings
Bentti, Golden, & Reigeluth	1983	Nonegs in teaching procedures	Greater divergence of nonegs > less diverg. Clearly labeled nonegs > nonlabeled
Carson & Reigeluth	1983	Location of synthesizers Sequencing of content: gen to detail/ detail to gen	Post > pre Gen to detail > detail to general
Chao & Reigeluth	1983	Types of synthesizers: visual,/verbal, lean or rich	NSD for visual/verbal Rich > lean for remember level
McLean	1983	Types of synthesizers: visual, verbal, both, none	Visual > verbal or none for remembering relationships Visual & verbal > none for remembering relationships
Garduno	1984	Presence/absence of nonegs in teaching procedures	NSD
Van Patten	1984	Location of synthesizers: internal, external (pre), external (post)	NSD
		Sequencing of content: gen to detail/ simple to complex	NSD
Tilden	1985	Types of summarizers	GPA × summarizer interaction (richer better for low GPA
Marcone & Reigeluth	1988	Non-egs in egs or generalities in teaching procedures	non-egs in generality > nonegs in eg form
Beissner & Reigeluth	1987	Integration of content structures	Can be effective
English & Reigeluth	1994	Formative research of ET	Suggestions for sequencing and construction of epitome

to take the learners' existing knowledge into account in the elaboration theory, although beyond some revision in the sequencing of conceptual layers (from the middle out, rather than from the top down), he did not propose that this would be formalized in his theory. Regarding the recommendation that he assume a more "constructivist stance," Reigeluth concurred that this may be important in ill-structured domains, which the elaboration theory does not currently address. However, he insightfully suggested, "People individually construct their own meanings, but the purpose of instruction—and indeed of language and communication itself—is to help people to arrive at shared meanings" (p. 81).

24.4.4 Landa

In terms of learning outcome types, Landa's (1983) algoheuristic theory of instruction, or "Landamatics," makes a distinction between knowledge and skills (ability to apply knowledge): categories that seem to be equivalent to declarative and procedural knowledge. According to Landa, learners acquire *knowledge* about objects and operations. Objects are known as a perceptive image—as a mental image or as a concept. A concept can be expressed as a proposition, but it is not necessary that this be expressed to be known. Other kinds of propositions, such as definitions, axioms, postulates, theorems, laws, and rules, can form a part of knowledge. Operations (actions on objects) are transformations of either real material objects or their mental representations (images, concepts, propositions). A skill is the ability to perform operations. Operations that transform material objects are motor operations. Operations that transform materials objects are cognitive operations. Operations can be algorithmic, "a series of relatively elementary operations that are performed in some regular and uniform way under defined conditions to solve all problems of a certain class" (p. 175) or heuristic, operations for which a series of steps can be identified but that are not as singular, regularized, and predictable as algorithms. Algorithmic operations appear to be similar to Merrill's conception of procedures, and the heuristic operations appear to be similar to Smith and Ragan's treatment of procedural rules and Gagné's problem solving (higher-order rule). A critical aspect of Landa's model is the importance that he ascribes to the verification of hypothetical description of algorithmic or heuristic process through observation, computer simulation, or error analysis. Such empirical validation is present in specifics of design models in task analysis but is generally missing in conditions-based models with regard to a generalized hypothetical cognitive task analysis for each class of outcomes that can be directly related to prescriptions for external conditions of learning.

Landa's theory suggests how to support processes that turn knowledge into skills and abilities, a transition that provides much of the substance of Anderson's (1990) ACT* theory. He suggests the following conditions for teaching individual operations.

1. Check to make sure that the learners understand the meaning of the procedure.

2. Present a problem that requires application of the procedure.
3. Have students name the operation or preview what they should do and execute the operation.
4. Present the next problem.
5. Practice until mastery.

Although he suggests a procedure for teaching students to discover procedures (algorithms), he points out that this process is difficult and time-consuming.

24.4.4.1 Research and Evaluation. Research on Landa's model is not as readily available in the literature as that on the previously reviewed models. However, Landa has reported some evaluation of his model in comparison with more "conventional" training. Landa (1993) estimated that he has saved Allstate $35 million because (a) many (up to 40) times fewer errors occur, (b) tasks are performed up to two times more rapidly, and (c) workers' confidence level is several times higher.

24.4.5 Smith and Ragan

Rather than developing a new conditions-based model, Smith and Ragan (1999) sought to exemplify and elaborate Gagné's theory. To address what they perceived to be limitations in most conditions-based models, they focused on the cognitive process necessary for the acquisition of each of the different learning capabilities.

With regard to the external conditions of learning, Smith and Ragan suggested that events of instruction as Gagné portrayed them insufficiently considered learner-generated and learner-initiated learning. Smith and Ragan restated the events so that they could be perceived as either learner supplied or instruction supported. Instruction, which predominates in learner-supplied or "generative" activities, characterizes learning environments (Jonassen & Land, 2000) and new paradigms of instruction (Reigeluth, 1999a). As instruction supplies increasing amounts of cognitive support for an instructional event, the event is seen as being increasingly "supplantive" (or mathemagenic) in character.

Smith and Ragan also proposed a model for determining the balance between generative and supplantive instructional strategies based on context, learner, and task variables. And they proposed that there is a "middle ground" between instruction-supplied, supplantive events and learner-initiated events, in which the instruction facilitates or prompts the learner to provide the cognitive processing necessary for an instructional event. Many methods associated with constructivism, including guided discovery, coaching, and cognitive apprenticeship, are examples of learner-centered events that involve external facilitation.

Although Smith and Ragan (1999) suggested that instructional strategies be as generative as possible they acknowledged that on occasion more external support may be needed "for learners to achieve learning in the time possible, with a limited and acceptable amount of frustration, anxiety, and danger" (p. 126). Smith and Ragan recommended a problem-solving approach to instructional design in which designers determine the amount of cognitive support needed for events of instruction, based on careful consideration of context, learner, and learning task.

24.4.5.1 Research and evaluation. Smith (1992) cited theoretical and empirical bases for some of the learner–task–context–strategy relationships proposed in the comparison of generative and supplantive strategies (COGSS) model, which forms the basis of the balance between instruction-supplied and learner-generated events. In this presentation she proposed an agenda for validation of the model.

24.4.6 Tennyson and Rasch

Tennyson and Rasch (1988a) described a model of how instructional prescriptions might be tied to cognitive learning theory. This work was preceded by a short paper by Tennyson (1987) that contained the key elements of the model. In this paper, part of a symposium on Clark's "media as mere vehicles" assertions, Tennyson discussed how one might "trace" the links between different treatments that media might supply and different learning processes. He described six learning processes (three storage processes—declarative knowledge, procedural knowledge, and conceptual knowledge; and three retrieval processes—differentiating, integrating, and creating), which he paired with types of learning objectives, types of knowledge bases, instructional variables, instructional strategies, and computer-based enhancements.

Tennyson and Rasch (1988a, 1988b) and Tennyson (1990) suggested that kinds of learning should refer to types of "memory systems." As with the previous conditions-based models, Tennyson and Rasch employed an information processing model as their foundation and suggested the main types of knowledge to be (a) declarative, which is stored as associative networks or schemata and relates to verbal information objectives; (b) procedural, which relates to intellectual skills objectives, and (c) contextual, which relates to problem-solving objectives and knowing when and why to employ intellectual skills. Five forms of objectives are described as requiring distinct cognitive activity (verbal information, intellectual skills, conditions information, thinking strategies, and creativity). In discussing the relationships among the types of knowledge, Tennyson and Rasch (1988a) noted that contextual knowledge is based on "standards, values, and situational appropriateness. . . . Whereas both declarative and procedural knowledge form the amount of information in a knowledge base, contextual knowledge forms its organization and accessibility" (p. 372).

In terms of instructional conditions, for declarative knowledge they recommended expository strategies, such as worked examples, which provide information in statement form on both the context and the structure of information, and question or problem repetition, which presents selected information repeatedly until the student answers or solves all items at some predetermined level of proficiency. For procedural knowledge, they recommended practice strategies in which learners apply knowledge to unencountered situations and some mon-

itoring in terms of evaluation of learner responses and advisement. To teach contextual knowledge they suggested problem-oriented simulation techniques. And for complex-problem situations, they recommended a simulation in which the consequences of decisions update the situational conditions and proceed to make the next iteration more complex.

An interesting element is a prescription of learning time for the different types of learning: 10% for verbal information, 20% for intellectual skills, 25% for conditional information, 30% for thinking strategies, and 15% for creativity. One intent of this distribution was to reflect Goodlad's (1984) prescription of a reversal of traditional classroom practice from 70% of instructional time being devoted to declarative and procedural knowledge and only 30% to conceptual knowledge and cognitive abilities. Although such general proportions may serve to illuminate general curriculum issues, specification of percentages of time to types of learning, regardless of consideration of other factors in a particular learning situation, may find limited applicability to instructional design.

24.4.6.1 Research and Evaluation. Tennyson and Rasch's model has not yet been subjected to evaluation and research. In terms of the extension of conditions-based models, some issues do emerge. Although other theorists propose this conditional knowledge, it is unclear whether the addition of a contextual type of learning will enhance the validity of the model. It is possible that such knowledge is stored as declarative knowledge that is in some way associated with procedural knowledge, such as in a mental model or problem schema. The suggestion of time that should be allocated to each type of learning is intriguing, as it attempts to point out the necessity of an emphasis on higher-order learning. However, the basis for determination of the proportion of time that should be spent on each type of outcome remains unclear.

24.4.7 Merrill, Li, and Jones: ID^2

In reaction to a number of limitations that they perceived in existing instructional design theories and models (including Merrill's own), Merrill, Li, and Jones (1990a, 1990b) have set out to construct a "second generation theory of instructional design." One of the specific goals of its developers is to expedite the design of an automated ID system, ID Expert, and thereby expedite the instructional design process itself. Ultimately, the developers hope that the system will possess both authoring and delivery environments that grow from a knowledge and rule base. Of all the models described in this chapter, ID^2 is the most ambitious in its goal to prescribe thoroughly the instructional conditions for each type of learning. The ID^2 model is being developed (a) to analyze, represent, and guide instruction to teach integrated sets of knowledge and skill, (b) to produce pedagogic prescriptions about selection and sequence, and (c) to be an open system that can respond to new theory. This model has retained its conditions-based orientation; indeed, Merrill and his associates (1990b) have elaborated on the relationships between outcomes and internal/external conditions.

a) A given learned performance results from a given organized and elaborated cognitive structure, which we will call a mental model. Different learning outcomes require different types of mental models; b) the construction of a mental model by a learner is facilitated by instruction that explicitly organizes and elaborates the knowledge being taught, during the instruction; c) there are different organizations and elaborations of knowledge required to promote different learning outcomes. (p. 8)

Within ID^2 outcomes of instruction are considered to be enterprises composed of entities, activities, or processes, which might loosely be interpreted as concepts, procedures, and principles, respectively. Merrill and his associates have spent a vast amount of effort describing the structure of knowledge relating to these types of knowledge and how these types of knowledge relate to each other.

Merrill and associates have described a number of conditions (external conditions or instructional methods) that can be placed under either system or learner control. These conditions are described as "transactions" of various classes. Evidence of Merrill's CDT can be found in the prescriptions for these transactions. To create this system based upon his ID^2, Merrill and his colleagues (Merrill, Li, & Jones, 1991; Merrill, Jones, & Li, 1992; Merrill, Li, & Jones, 1992; Merrill, Li, Jones, Chen-Troester, & Schwab, 1993) have attempted to identify the decisions that designers must make regarding the types of information to build into the system and the methods by which this information can be made available to learners. This analysis is incredibly detailed in and of itself. For example, Table 24.5 summarizes the "responsibilities" of the transactions

TABLE 24.5. Summary of ID^2 Instructional Transaction Responsibilities

Method	Parameters	Method	Parameters
Select knowledge	Selection control (learner, system)	Prioritize interactions	Strategy control (learner, system) interaction strategy type (overview, familiarity, basic, mastery, basic–remediation, mastery–remediation, learner)
Partition knowledge	Partition control (learner, system)		
	Focus (entire entity or component of entity)		
	Levels (amount of knowledge cluster below focus to include)	Expedite acquirement	Shift interaction on (learner, repetitions, criterion, response time, elapsed time)
	Coverage (all, user identifies)		Repetition
Portray knowledge	Portrayal control (learner, system)		Criterion
	View (structural, physical, functional)		Response time
	Mode (language, symbolic, literal)		Elapsed time
	Fidelity (low to high)	Enact interactions	Enactment control (learner, system)
Amplify knowledge	Ancillary information control (learner, system)	Overview knowledge	Overview control (learner, system)
			Overview view (structure, + focus, + level 1)
	Ancillary information mode (verbal, audio)		Structure format (tree, browser)
	Pronunciation availability (no, system, learner)	Present knowledge	Presentation display element control (learner, system)
	Pronunciation mode (verbal, audio)		Presentation display element availability (label, function, properties)
	Component function availability (no, learner, system)		Presentation display element timing (untimed, n seconds)
	Component function mode (verbal, audio)		Presentation display element sequence (order, simultaneous, sequential)
	Component description availability (no, learner, system)		
	Component description mode (verbal, audio)	Enable practice	Practice formats (locate, label, function, properties)
	Component aside available (no, learner, system)		Practice format sequence (sequential, simultaneous)
	Component aside mode (verbal, audio)		Response mode (recall, recognize)
Sequence knowledge	Sequence control (learner, system)		Response timing (untimed, n seconds)
Route learner	Segment sequence control (learner, system)		Practice format control (learner, system)
			Response repetition (n, contingent)
	Segment sequence type (elaboration, cumulation, accrual, learner)		Component order (learner, same, random)
	Depth (depth first, breadth first)		Feedback availability (yes, no)
	Accrual (all, isolated part, replacement)		Feedback type (intrinsic, correct answer, right–wrong, attention focusing, designer specific)
	Priority (chronological, frequency, criticality, familiarity)		Feedback control (learner, system)
Guide advancement	Shift segment on (learner, repetitions, practice, criterion, assessment criterion)		Feedback timing (immediate, schedule, delayed)
	Repetitions		Feedback schedule type (fixed interval, variable interval, fixed ratio, variable ratio)
	Criterion		
Manage interaction	Management control (learner, system)	Assess knowledge	

that may be made available in instruction, the "methods" that make up these responsibilities, and the range (or parameters) of these methods. Merrill et al. have made similar analyses of information that may be made available to learners when learning entities, activities, or processes. In addition to detailing the options of pedagogy and information that can be made available in instruction, the developers of system may also establish the "rules" by which system choices may be made about which of these options to present to learners.

24.4.7.1 Research and Evaluation.

Parts of the system have been evaluated by Spector and Muraida (1991) and by Canfield and Spector (1991). For example, one of the major evaluation questions has been, Can the target audience of novice designers use the system, and can this system expedite instructional design activities? In Spector and Muraida's study, investigating the utility of the system to expedite design, eight subjects participated in 30 hr of instruction in which they learned to use the system and developed 1 hr of instruction. The results indicated that all subjects who remained in the study were able to complete a computer-based lesson using the support of a portion of the system.

As yet there are no comparison data with more conventional design processes. In their effort to carefully explicate necessary knowledge for learning and instruction as well as the means by which these interact with each other the developers have created a model that is quite complex. One benefit of the model is that its complexity reflects and makes concrete much of the complexity of the instructional design process. Unfortunately, it seems that terminology has shifted during development. ID^2 is not without its critics. Among criticisms frequently leveled are its utility when used by novices, the lack of evidence of theory base, issues regarding sufficient agreement to generate strategies, and the likelihood of sameness of results in multiple applications.

24.4.8 Other Applications of Conditions-Based Theory

Although they have not developed complete instructional design models, a number of notable scholars within and outside the instructional design field have utilized a conditions-based theory as a basis for much of their work. We will briefly describe four of these examples, as they illustrate how pervasive and influential the conditions-based theory has been.

24.4.8.1 Jonassen, Grabinger, & Harris.

Jonassen, Grabinger, and Harris (1991) developed a decision model for selecting strategies and tactics of instruction based upon three levels of decisions: (a) scope (macro/micro), (b) instructional event (prepare learner, present information, clarify ideas, provide practice, and assess knowledge), and (c) learning outcome. Levels (b) and (c) are similar to the decisions patterns suggested by Gagné and Gagné & Briggs.

Jonassen, Grabinger, and Harris recommended making decisions regarding instructional tactics based on three major categories of learning outcomes: intellectual skills (concept or rule),

verbal information, or cognitive strategy (iconic, verbal/digital). They suggested prescriptions for instructional events based upon the learning outcome. For example, for the event of preparing the learning by supporting recall of prior knowledge of intellectual skills through presenting a verbal/oral comparative advance organizer, adapting the content of instruction to learners' prior knowledge, and reviewing prerequisite skills and knowledge.

24.4.8.2 Horn.

Horn's approach to text design has many elements of a design model and clearly employs a conditions-based set of assumptions. Horn's work, called "structured writing," presents a highly prescriptive approach to the design of instructional and informative text. In addition to format concerns, Horn proposed different treatments for different types of learning. The types of learning he identified are procedures (which explain how to do something and in what order to do it), structure (about physical things, objects that have identifiable boundaries), classification (which shows how a set of concepts is organized), process (which explains how a process or operation works, how changes take place in time), concepts (which define and give examples and nonexamples of new aspects of the subject matter), and facts (which give results of observations or measurements without supporting evidence) (Horn, 1976, p. 17). Horn described differential conditions for text presentation by identifying what elements (or "blocks") each presentation relating to a particular type of learning (or "map") must have. Horn differentiated between necessary and optional elements for each type of learning.

24.4.8.3 West, Farmer, and Wolf.

West et al. (1991) referred to three kinds of knowledge: (a) declarative, which is stored in propositional networks that may be semantic or episodic and may be structured as data or state schemata; (b) procedural knowledge, which is order specific and time dependent (p. 16); and (c) conditional knowledge, which is knowing when and why to use a procedure (similar to Tennyson and Rasch's "contextual knowledge"). They describe "cognitive strategies" that can support the acquisition of each of these learning types, which the instructional designer plans instruction to activate. In contrast to Gagné, who typically portrays cognitive strategies as instructional strategies, supplied by instruction, and in contrast to Smith and Ragan (1993a, 1999), who portray the primary load of information processing as something that should shift between learner and instruction depending on the circumstances, West et al. imply that strategies are always provided by the learner. These cognitive strategies are chunking, frames (graphic organizers), concept mapping, advance organizer, metaphor, rehearsal, imagery, and mnemonics. In terms of prescriptive or conditions-based models, West et al. prescribe the strategies as effective to support acquisition of all types of knowledge. However, they also use Gagné's five domains as types of outcomes for prescribing the appropriateness of each strategy, which is somewhat confusing, as procedural knowledge and intellectual skills, which are usually considered to refer to the same capabilities, are not given the same prescriptions for strategies. Our evaluation is that their prescriptions are for the declarative portion of higher-order knowledge types.

24.4.8.4 E. Gagné. Unlike most instructional models, E. Gagné's work (E. Gagné, Yekovich, & Yekovich, 1993) is primarily descriptive, rather than prescriptive. E. Gagné based her conditions-based propositions on Anderson's (1990) cognitive theories of learning and placed her theory base within the information processing theories. She subscribed to Anderson's types of knowledge: declarative and procedural. Gagné described the representations of declarative knowledge as propositions, images, linear orderings, and schemata (which can be composed of propositions, images, and linear orderings). Procedural knowledge is represented as a production system, which can result in domain-specific skills, domain-specific strategies, and, to a limited degree, domain-general strategies.

Although the majority of her text is more descriptive than prescriptive, E. Gagné utilized the conditions-based theory as she discussed the internal processes required in the acquisition of each of the types of knowledge and the instructional support that can promote this acquisition. She described instructional support as increasing the probability that required processes will occur, or making learning easier or faster.

A strength of E. Gagné's formulation is her description of internal processes. In addition, she provides empirical evidence of the effectiveness of the instructional support conditions.

24.5 AN EXAMINATION OF THE PROPOSITIONS OF A CONDITIONS-BASED THEORY

As noted in the introduction to this chapter, the primary propositions of conditions-based theory can be summarized as four main assertions: (a) Learning goals can be categorized as to learning outcome or knowledge type; (b) related to assertion a, different outcome categories require different internal conditions (or, one can view the proposition as "different internal conditions lead to different cognitive outcomes"); (c) outcomes can be represented in a prerequisite relationship; and (d) different learning outcomes require different external conditions for learning. In this section, issues relating to each of the primary propositions are discussed.

24.5.1 Learning Outcomes Can Be Categorized

What is meant by a learning outcome? The meaning we attribute to *outcomes* differs depending on whether we perceive these outcomes as external (as a category of task or goal) or internal (as an acquired capability, perhaps supported by a unique memory system). Gagné (1985) clearly described his classification system of outcomes as "acquired capabilities," an internal definition. Merrill (1983) has described his outcome categories as "performances," "categories of objectives," and "learned capabilities," rather a mix of internal and external connotations. Reigeluth's categorization is of "types of content," which somewhat implies the categorized of an external referent. Landa describes his kinds of knowledge as "psychological phenomena," suggesting an internal orientation. Clearly, there is no consensus even within the models described in this chapter as to what the term *learning outcomes* actually implies. Indeed, the evidence to support the validity of each category system would vary in its type and complexity, depending on whether the phenomena are viewed as entities "out there," which can be pinned down and observed, or "within," where we only see circumstantial evidence of their presence.

The statement "Learning outcomes can be categorized" is both a philosophical and a psychological assertion. Indeed, both philosophers, such as Ryle (1949), and psychologists, such as Anderson (1990), have posited ways to categorize knowledge. Interestingly, Ryle and Anderson agreed on a similar declarative or procedural classification system. Certainly, instructional theorists have suggested a variety of category systems. (However, most are compatible with the declarative or procedural classification. Gagné certainly adds additional categories to these: attitude, motor skill, and, perhaps, cognitive strategies. Tennyson and Rausch add a third class of learning—contextual knowledge.) For each group, the philosopher, the psychologist, and the instructional theorist, the evidence of the "truth" of the proposition would vary. For philosophers, this is an epistemological question, and the manner for determining its truth would depend on the philosophic school to which a particular philosopher ascribes. We do not pursue this approach for determining the validity of our assertion directly.

Reigeluth (1983b) suggested a utility criterion for determining whether a categorization system is appropriate:

When we say concepts are human-made and arbitrary, we mean phenomena can be conceptualized (i.e., grouped or categorized) in many alternative ways.... Practically all classification schemes will improve our understanding of instructional phenomena, but concepts are not the kind of knowledge for which instructional scientists are looking, except as a stepping-stone. Instructional scientists want to determine *when* different methods should be used—they want to discover principles of instruction—so that they can prescribe optimal methods. But not all classification schemes are equally useful for forming highly reliable and broadly applicable principles.... The same is true of classes of instructional phenomena: Some will have high *predictive usefulness* and some will not. The challenge to our discipline is to find out which ones are the most useful. (pp. 12–13)

The psychologist would want empirical evidence that the categories are distinct, which leads to our second proposition.

24.5.2 Different Outcome Categories Require Different Internal Conditions

Most of the models within the conditions-based theory propose that learning categories are different in terms of cognitive processing demands and activities. All of the major seven design models described in this chapter appear to make this assumption, to a greater or lesser degree. Although all models in this chapter suggest that a general information processing procedure occurs in learning, they also suggest that this processing is significantly and predictably different for each of the categories of learning that they identify. For example, R. Gagné suggested that, in particular, the cognitive processes of retrieval of prior knowledge, encoding, and retrieval and transfer of new learning would differ significantly in nature, depending upon the type of learning goal. Indeed, several of the model developers, including Gagné (1985), Merrill (1983), Smith and Ragan (1999), and Tennyson and Rasch (1988b), postulated different memory structures for different types of learning outcomes.

A slightly different statement of the proposition allows for a closer relationship to the first proposition (outcomes can be categorized): Different internal conditions lead to different cognitive outcomes. This more descriptive (and less prescriptive) assertion seems to be supported by additional educational theorists. For example, both Anderson (1990) and E. Gagné et al. (1993) proposed that different cognitive processes lead to declarative and procedural learning. They also proposed that these two types of learning have different memory systems, schemata for declarative knowledge, and productions for procedural learning. They both provided some empirical evidence that these cognitive processes and storage systems are indeed unique to the two types of learning.

We must point out that even if connectionists (Bereiter, 1991) are correct that there is only one memory system (neural networks) and only one basic cognitive process (pattern recognition), this does not necessarily preclude the possibility of different types of learning capabilities. For example, there may be generalized activation patterns that represent certain types of learning.

24.5.3 Outcomes Can Be Represented in a Prerequisite Relationship

Gagné's work on learning hierarchies would appear to be sufficient to confirm this assumption rather resoundingly, as reported previously in this chapter. In addition to work by Gagné and others working directly in his tradition, research by individuals working from entirely different frames of reference also appears solidly to confirm this assumption.

Although early learning hierarchy research appeared to be highly confirmatory, R. T. White (1973a) developed an important review of learning hierarchy research in the early 1970s. In this review, studies validating the idea of learning hierarchies were sought. Due to methodological weaknesses, White found no studies that were able to validate a complete and precise fit between a proposed learning hierarchy and optimal learning: "All of the studies suffered from one or more of the following weaknesses: small sample size, imprecise specification of component elements, use of only one question per element, and placing of tests at the end of the learning program or even the omission of instruction altogether" (p. 371).

In research following White's review, research that applied his recommendations to correct methodological weaknesses, a series of studies providing confirmation of the learning hierarchy formulation was published (White, 1974a–1974c; Linke, 1973). These results led Gagné to conclude, "The basic hypothesis of learning hierarchies is now well established, and sound practical methods for testing newly designed hierarchies exist" (White & Gagné, 1974, p. 363). Other research that may be considered within the Gagné tradition that appears to confirm

the learning hierarchy hypothesis includes that by Linke (1973), Merrill, Barton, and Wood (1970), Resnick (1967), and Resnick and Wang (1969).

Work on learning hierarchies outside the Gagné tradition, or a conditions theory perspective at all, includes studies by Winkles, Bergan and associates, and Kallison. Winkles (1986) investigated the learning of trigonometry skills with a learning hierarchy validation study identifying both lateral and vertical transfer. Two experiments with eighth- and ninth-grade students involved instructional treatments described as *achievement with understanding* and *achievement only.* Results reported that

achievement with understanding treatment is better for the development of lateral transfer for most students, and of vertical transfer for the more mathematically able students, whereas the differences between the treatment groups on tests of achievement and retention of taught skills are not significant. A small amount of additional instruction on vertical transfer items produces much better performance under both treatments. (p. 275)

Bergan, Towstopiat, Cancelli, and Karp (1982), also not working within the conditions tradition, reported a study that provided what appears to be a particularly interesting form of confirmation of the learning hierarchy concept and some insights into rule learning:

This investigation examined ordered and equivalence relations among hierarchically arranged fraction identification tasks. The study investigated whether hierarchical ordering among fraction identification problems reflects the replacement of simple rules by complex rules. A total of 456 middle-class second-, third, and fourth-grade children were asked to identify fractional parts of sets of objects. Latent class techniques reveal that children applied rules that were adequate for simple problems but had to be replaced to solve more complex problems. (p. 39)

In a follow-up study to the 1982 work, Bergan, Stone, and Feld (1984) employed a large sample of elementary-aged children in their learning of basic numerical skills. Students were presented with tasks that required rules of increasing complexity. The researchers were again studying the replacement of relatively simple rules with more complex extensions of them:

Hypotheses were generated to reflect the assumption of hierarchical ordering associated with rule replacement. In addition, restrictive knowledge and variable knowledge perspectives were evaluated. Latent-class models were used to test equivalence and ordered relations among the tasks. The results provided evidence that the development of counting skills is an evolving process in which parts of a relatively simple rule are replaced by features that enable the child to perform an increasingly broad range of counting tasks. The results also suggested that rule replacement in counting plays an important role in the development of other math skills. The results also give support for the restrictive knowledge perspective, lending credence to the stairstep learning theory. (p. 289)

An unusual and indirect, but interesting and suggestive view of the importance of hierarchies in learning intellectual skills is found in a study by Kallison (1986), who varied sequence (proper vs. manipulated, i.e., reasonable vs. modified to disrupt clarity) and explicitness of lesson organization (organization of lesson explained or organization hidden). In the disrupted sequence treatment, even though care was taken to make an unclear presentation, the hierarchical nature of content relationships was preserved. Four treatments resulted and were used with three ability levels ($2 \times 2 \times 3$). In the study, 67 college students were taught intellectual skills: numeration systems, base 10 and base 5, and how to convert from one system to the other. Although sequence modification did *not* affect achievement substantially, the explicitness of lesson organization explicit did significantly impact achievement, with the more explicit lesson structure promoting better learning. Kallison found no aptitude–treatment interactions.

Kallison was careful to point out that although the sequence was altered, nothing got in the way of learning prerequisites. He modified sequence in such a way that learning hierarchies were not interfered with, only the reasonableness or "clarity" of the lesson organization: Where care was taken *not* to violate learning hierarchy principles, the sequence could be disrupted and it did not impact learning, even with an unclear presentation. As the learning task clearly involves intellectual skills, Gagné's principle of sequencing according to learning hierarchies was not violated. Although there is already considerable evidence to validate learning hierarchies, an unusual confirmation could be obtained by replicating Kallison's study with an additional condition of sequence modified in such a way as to violate learning hierarchy principles but maintain "clarity."

In another unusual test of the validity of the idea that learning tasks can be productively cast in a prerequisite relationship, Yao (1989) sought to test Gagné's assumption that in a validated learning hierarchy, some learners should be able to skip some elements based on their individual abilities. A valid learning hierarchy represents the most probable expectation of greatest learning for an entire sample. In a carefully designed experiment, Yao confirmed that some individuals could successfully skip certain prerequisites, and she found a treatment × ability interaction regarding the pattern of skipping in which certain forms of skipping can be less detrimental for high-ability learners than for low-ability learners. However, as the theory predicts, the treatment that skipped prerequisites was less effective for both low- and high ability learners (as a group).

24.5.4 Different Learning Outcomes Require Different External Conditions

In an effort to find evidence in support of this basic tenant of the conditions theory, we engaged in a survey of research, looking across a wide scope. The following research is presented in an effort to survey the evidence. The reader may find a dizzying variety of approaches and perspectives reflected. Studies and reviews on the following topics are briefly presented to illustrate the variety of standpoints from which evidence may be found in general support of the conditions model: interaction between use of objectives and objective type, goal structure and learning task, advance organizers and learning task, presentation mode (e.g., visual presentation) and learning task,

evoked cognitive strategies and learning outcomes, expertise and learning hierarchies, teacher thinking for different types of learning, adjunct questions and type of learning, feedback for different types of learning, and provided versus evoked instructional support for different types of learning. What follows, then, is a sample of studies that lend support—in varying ways, from varying standpoints—to the theory that different instructional outcomes may best be achieved with differing types of instructional support.

24.5.4.1 Interaction of Use of Objectives and Objective Type. Hartley and Davies (1976) subjected to further examination a review by Duchastel and Merrill (1973) on the effects of providing learners with objectives. Although the original Duchastel and Merrill review found no effect, Hartley and Davies found that "behavioral objectives do not appear to be useful in terms of ultimate posttest scores, in learning tasks calling for knowledge and comprehension. On the other hand, objectives do appear to be more useful in higher level learning tasks calling for analysis, synthesis, and evaluation" (p. 250). They also noted a report by Yellon and Schmidt (1971) that pointed out a possible interference effect from informing students of objectives in problem-solving tasks by reducing the amount of reasoning required.

24.5.4.2 Goal Structure and Learning Task. Johnson and Johnson (1974) found, in a review of research on cooperative, competitive, and individualistic goal structures, that goal structure interacted with learning task. "Competition may be superior to cooperative or individualistic goal structures when a task is a simple drill activity or when sheet quantity of work is desired on a mechanical or skill-oriented task that requires little if any help from another person" (p. 220). They cite Chapman and Feder (1917), Clayton (1964), Clifford (1971), Hurlock (1927) Julian and Perry (1967), Maller (1929), Miller and Hamblin (1963), Phillips (1954), Sorokin, Tranquist, Parten, and Zimmerman (1930), and Tripplet (1897). All findings do not clearly distinguish a grouping by outcomes (declarative/procedural) condition. For example, Smith, Madden, and Sobel (1957) and Yuker (1955) found that memorization learning is also enhanced by cooperative work.

On the other hand, Johnson and Johnson pointed out, "When the instructional task is some sort of problem solving activity the research clearly indicates that a cooperative goal structure results in higher achievement than does a competitive goal structure" (p. 220). They cite Almack (1930), Deutsch (1949), Edwards, DeVries, and Snyder (1972), Gurnee (1968), Husband (1940), Jones and Vroom (1964), Laughlin and McGlynn (1967), O'Connel (1965), Shaw (1958), and Wodarski, Hamblin, Buckholdt, and Feritor (1971).

24.5.4.3 Visual Presentation Mode and Learning Task. Dwyer and Parkhurst (1982) presented a multifactor analysis (3 methods × 4 outcomes × 3 ability levels—reading comprehension). This analysis did not concentrate on different types of objectives, but apparently because different contents were used, the authors could draw this conclusion: "The results of this study indicated that (a) different methods of presenting programmed instruction are not equally effective in facilitating student achievement of all types of educational objectives" (p. 108). There were four measures, which were taken to represent four types of learning outcomes: (a) a drawing test involving generation of drawings given heart part labels such as aorta and pulmonary valve; (b) an identification test—a multiple-choice test of a matching nature covering on various heart parts; (c) a terminology test consisting of 20 multiple-choice items on knowledge of facts, terms, and definitions; and (d) a comprehension test of 20 multiple-choice items that involved looking at the position of a given heart part during a specified moment in its functioning.

Analysis of the interactions among the different outcomes was not presented in the 1982 study, however, in what appears to be a follow-on study, Dwyer and Dwyer (1987) report the analyses of interactions. The authors conclude, "All levels of depth of processing are not equally effective in facilitating student achievement of different instructional objectives" (p. 264). In Dwyer and Dwyer's studies, tasks requiring "different levels of processing" appear to these reviewers generally to reflect differing ways of eliciting declarative knowledge learning, yet meaningful differences among learning tasks were seen and reported by the authors of the studies.

24.5.4.4 Evoked Cognitive Strategies and Learning Outcomes.
Kiewra and Benton (1987) report a study that investigated relationships among note taking, review of instructor's notes, and use of higher-order questions and their effect on learning of two sorts: factual and higher order. Subjects were college students in a college class setting. Half of the class was in a condition in which they took notes themselves and reviewed them and the other half reviewed notes provided by the instructor. At the conclusion of the class, additional practice questions of a "higher-order" nature were provided to half of each group. An interaction between methodology and learning outcomes was reported. "Students who listed and reviewed the instructor's notes achieved more on factual items than did notetakers, and . . . higher-order practice questions did not differentially affect test performance" (p. 186).

A study similar to that by Kiewra and Benton (1987) was conducted by Shrager and Mayer (1989), in which some students were instructed to take notes, and others were not, as they watched videotaped information. The researchers predicted that the "note-taking would result in improved problem solving transfer and semantic recall but not verbatim recognition or verbatim fact retention for low-knowledge learners but would have essentially no effects on test performance for high-knowledge learners" (p. 263). This prediction was confirmed, supporting similar findings by Peper and Mayer (1978, 1986), who used the same design but different contents, automotive engines and statistics. This study was somewhat confounded in treatment and learner characteristics. The degree of declarative knowledge and the stage of transition from declarative to procedural (Anderson, 1990) are often the distinction between novice and expert. Instead of indicating that declarative knowledge and procedural knowledge require different instructional conditions, the study may reveal, instead, that novice learners

need more direct and explicit learning guidance in employing cognitive strategies that more knowledgeable learners will use on their own.

There is no doubt that, properly applied to the proper task, the mnemonic keyword technique is a powerful one in assisting learning: "The evidence is overwhelming that the use of the keyword method, as applied to recall of vocabulary definitions, greatly facilitates performance. . . . In short, keyword methods effects are pervasive and of impressive magnitude" (Pressley, Levin, & Delaney, 1982, pp. 70–71). The strategy, like many others, is a task-specific one: In other words, it makes no sense to apply it to other-than-appropriate tasks. Levin (1986) elaborates on this principle and brings to bear an enormous amount of research by him and his associates on particular cognitive strategies (learning strategies) that have considerable power in improving learning.

24.5.4.5 Expertise and Learning Hierarchies.
The utility and validity of learning hierarchies within authentic contexts have been studied by Dunn and Taylor (1990, 1994). In these studies, hierarchical analyses were performed on the activities of language arts teachers (1990) and medical personnel (1994). Development of expertise is encouraged to take place from "task-relevant" experience, assisted by advice strategies developed from hierarchical analysis.

24.5.4.6 Adjunct Questions.
Hamilton (1985) provided a review of research on using adjunct questions and objectives in instruction. The review contains different sections on research using of adjunct questions with different types of learning, leading to conclusions that vary with the type of learning in question.

24.5.4.7 Practice.
Some inconsistency is found in the results of studies looking at the interaction of practice and types of learning. Hannafin and Colamaio (1987) found a significant interaction between practice and type of learning. Scores on practiced items were higher than on nonpracticed items for each type of learning but the effects were proportionately greatest for factual learning and least influential for procedural learning. However, in a study by Hannafin, Phillips, and Tripp (1986), opposite results were obtained; was more helpful for factual learning than for application learning. Slee (1989), in a review of interactive video research, noted that a lack of adequacy in lesson materials may confound these studies, as they both used the National Gallery of Art Tour videodisc, which was noted to have insufficient examples and practice available.

Reiber (1989) investigated the effects of practice and animations on learning of two types: factual learning and application learning in a CBI lesson. The study looked at both immediate learning and transfer to other learning outcomes. Main effect differences were not observed for either different elaboration treatments or practice. However, a significant interaction was found between learning outcome and transfer; the lesson promoted far transfer for factual information but did not facilitate far transfer for application learning. Another interaction was observed between practice and learning outcome, in which practice improved students' application scores more than factual scores. As with Hannafin and associates' studies, unintended attributes of lesson materials may have confounded the study; in this case, as reported by the researcher, the lesson materials may have been too difficult.

24.5.4.8 *Feedback for Different Types of Learning.* Getsie, Langer, and Glass (1985) provided a meta-analysis of research on feedback (reinforcement versus punishment) and discrimination learning. They concluded that punishment is an effective form of feedback for discrimination learning: "Punishment is clearly superior to reward only, with effect sizes ranging from .10 to .31" (p. 20). The authors also concluded that reward is the least effective: "First, the most consistent finding is that compared to punishment or reward plus punishment, reward is the least efficient form of feedback during discrimination learning" (p. 20). Although discrimination learning was not compared with other forms of learning, we predict that this conclusion should not be generalized to other forms of learning (e.g., to provide punishment as feedback for practice in learning relational rules, compared with informative feedback) or to other forms of feedback, such as levels of informational feedback.

Smith and Ragan (1993b) presented a compilation of research and practice recommendations on designing instructional feedback for different learning outcomes. Using the Gagné types of learning construct as a framework, they presented feedback prescriptions for different categories of learning task. They concluded that "questions regarding the optimal content of feedback . . . really revolve around the issue of the match between the cognitive demands of the learning task; the cognitive skill, prior knowledge, and motivations of the learners; and constraints, such as time, within the learning environment" (p. 100).

An interesting insight into feedback and different types of learning was provided by a meta-analysis of research on feedback by Schimmel (1983). In attempting to explain the major inconsistencies in findings, Schimmel speculated that different characteristics of the instructional content such as "different levels of difficulty in recall" (p. 11).

24.5.4.9 *Provided Versus Evoked Instructional Support for Different Types of Learning.* Husic, Linn, and Sloane (1989) reported a study involving effects of different strategies for different types of learning. The content was learning to program in Pascal. Two college classes were studied, a beginning class in which the learning task was characterized as "learning syntax" (perhaps analogous to rule using) and an advanced class that concentrated on "learning to plan and debug complex problems" (perhaps analogous to problem solving).

The abstract of the report states,

Programming proficiency varied as a function of instructional practices and class level. Introductory students benefited from direct instruction and AP students performed better with less direct guidance and more opportunities for autonomy. Characteristics of effective programming instruction vary depending on the cognitive demands of courses. (p. 570)

24.6 CONCLUSIONS

There are some conclusions that we would draw from this review. We reflected on conclusions drawn in our chapter in the first edition of this volume (Ragan & Smith, 1996) and have modified them accordingly.

(1) It appears that conditions models have a long history of interest in psychology, educational psychology, and instructional technology. This history illustrates work that may not be widely known among instructional technologists today: work that can be instructive as to the actual base and significance of the conditions approach. Perhaps we will see fewer erroneous statements in our literature about what is known regarding types of learning, learning hierarchies, and conditions of learning.

(2) Conditions theory is characterized by a particular combination: on the one hand, its utility in helping specify instructional strategies and, on the other hand, the sizable gaps and inconsistencies that exist in current formulations. This combination creates a need for more work. We have described in this chapter many fruitful areas for further research.

(3) We have reached a conclusion about the work of R. M. Gagné that we would like to share and suggest that readers examine their own conclusions from reading. We find Gagné's work cast within so much that preceded and followed it to remain both dominating in its appeal and utility and, paradoxically, heavily flawed and in need of improvement. The utility and appeal of this work appear to derive greatly from the solid scholarship and cogent writing that Gagné brought to bear, as well as his willingness to change the formulation to keep up with changing times and new knowledge. Many of the gaps and flaws, in keeping with the paradox, appear to be a product of the very changes that he made to keep up with current interests. We believe those changes to be beneficial in the main but see a clear need for systematic and rigorous scholarship on issues raised by those changes.

(4) We continue to see utility in thinking of learning as more than one kind of thing, especially for practitioners. It is too easy, in the heat of practitioners' struggles, to slip into the assumption that all knowledge is declarative (as is so often seen in the learning outcomes statements of large-scale instructional systems) or all problem solving (as is so often assumed in the pronouncements of pundits and critics of public education) and, as a result, fail to consider either the vast arena of application of declarative knowledge or the multitude of prerequisites for problem solving. It is unhelpful to develop new systems of types of learning for the mere purpose of naming. Improvements in categorization schemes should be based on known differences in cognitive processing and required differences in external conditions.

(5) There is substantial weakness in the tie between categories of learning and external conditions of learning. What is missing is the explication of the *internal* conditions involved in the acquisition of different kinds of learning. Research on the transition from expert to novice and artificial intelligence research that attempts to describe the knowledge of experts should be particularly fruitful in helping us fill this void. Perhaps

this void is a result of the failure to place sufficient emphasis on qualitative research in our field.

(6) There is research to support the conclusion that different external events of instruction lead to different kinds of learning, especially looking at the declarative or procedural level. What appears to be lacking is any systematic body of research directly on the central tenant, not just of conditions theory but of practically anyone who would attempt to teach, much less design,

instruction: What is the relationship between *internal* learner conditions and subsequent learning from instruction. This topic seems to be a far cry from studies that would directly inform designers about procedures and techniques, yet a very great deal seems to hinge on this one question. With more insight into it, many quibbles and debates may disappear and the work of translation into design principles may begin at a new level of efficacy.

References

Anderson, J. R. (1990). *Cognitive psychology and its implications* (3rd ed). New York: W. H. Freeman.

Beissner, K., & Reigeluth, C. M. (1987). *Multiple strand sequencing using elaboration theory.* (ERIC Document Reproduction Service No. ED 314 065)

Bentti, F., Golden, A., & Reigeluth, C. M. (1983). *Teaching common errors in applying a procedure* (IDD&E Working Paper No. 17). Syracuse, NY: Syracuse University, School of Education. (ERIC Document Reproduction Service No. ED 289 464)

Bereiter, C. (1985). Toward a solution of the learning paradox. *Review of Educational Research, 55*(2), 201–226.

Bereiter, C. (1991). Implications of connectionism for thinking about rules. *Educational Researcher, 20*(3), 10–16.

Bergan, J. R., Towstopiat, O., Cancelli, A. A., & Karp, C. (1982). Replacement and component rules in hierarchically ordered mathematics rule learning tasks. *Journal of Educational Psychology, 74*(1), 39–50.

Bergan, J. R., Stone, C. A., & Feld, J. K. (1984). Rule replacement in the development of basic number skills. *Journal of Educational Psychology, 76*(2), 289–299.

Beukhof, G. (1986, April). *Designing instructional texts: Interaction between text and learner.* Paper presented at the annual meeting of the American Educational Research Association, San Francisco. (ERIC Document Reproduction Service No. ED 274 313)

Bloom, B. S., Englehart, M. D., Furst, E. J., Hill, W. H., & Krathwohl, D. R. (1956). *Taxonomy of educational objectives: The classification of educational goals, handbook 1: Cognitive domain.* New York: David McKay.

Briggs, L. J. (1967). An illustration of the analysis procedure for a group of objectives from a course in elementary science. In L. J. Briggs, P. L. Campeau, R. M. Gagné, & M. A. May (Eds.), *Instructional media: A procedure for the design of multi-media instruction, a critical review of research, and suggestions for future research* (pp. 53–73). Pittsburgh, PA: American Institutes for Research.

Briggs, L. J. (Ed.). (1977). *Instructional design: Principles and applications.* Englewood Cliffs, NJ: Educational Technology Publications.

Briggs, L. J., Campeau, P. L., Gagné, R. M., & May, M. A. (Eds.). (1967). *Instructional media: A procedure for the design of multi-media instruction; a critical review of research, and suggestions for future research.* Pittsburgh, PA: American Institutes for Research. (Final report prepared by the Instructional Methods Program of the Center for Research and Evaluation in Applications of Technology in Education, submitted to U.S. Department of Health, Education, & Welfare)

Briggs, L. J., Gagné, R. M., & May, M. A. (1967). A procedure for choosing media for instruction. In L. J. Briggs, P. L. Campeau, R. M. Gagné, & M. A. May (Eds.), *Instructional media: A procedure for the design of multi-media instruction, a critical review of research, and

suggestions for future research* (pp. 28–52). Pittsburgh, PA: American Institutes for Research.

Bryan, G. L. (1962). The training of electronics maintenance technicians. In R. Glaser (Ed.) *Training research and education,* (pp. 295–321). Pittsburgh, PA: University of Pittsburgh Press.

Bunderson, C. V., Gibbons, A. S., Olsen, J. B. & Kearsley, G. P. (1981). work models: Beyond instructional objectives. *Instructional Science 10,* 205–215.

Canfield, A. M., & Spector, J. M. (1991). A pilot study of the naming transaction shell (AL-TP-1991-0006). Brooks AFB, TX: Armstrong Laboratory, Human Resources Directorate.

Carr, H. A. (1933). The quest for constants. *Psychological Review, 40,* 514–522.

Carson, C. H., & Reigeluth, C. M. (1983). *The effects of sequence and synthesis on concept learning using a parts-conceptual structure* (IDD&E Working Paper No. 22). Syracuse, NY: Syracuse University, School of Education. (ERIC Document Reproduction Service No. ED 288 518)

Caruso, J. L., & Resnick, L. B. (1971). *Task sequence and overtraining in children's learning and transfer of double classification skills.* Paper presented at the meeting of the American Psychological Association, Miami, FL.

Chao, C. I. (1983). *Effects of four instructional sequences on application and transfer* (IDD&E Working Paper No. 12). Syracuse, NY: Syracuse University, School of Education. (ERIC Document Reproduction Service No. ED 289 461)

Chao, C. I., & Reigeluth, C. M. (1986). *The effects of format and structure of synthesizer of procedural-decision learning* (IDD&E Working Paper, No. 22). Syracuse, NY: Syracuse University, School of Education. (ERIC Document Reproduction Service No. ED 289469)

Coleman, L. T., & Gagné, R. M. (1970). Transfer of learning in a social studies task of comparing-contrasting. In R. M. Gagné (Ed.), *Basic studies of learning hierarchies in school subjects.* Berkeley: University of California. (Final report, Contract No. OEC-4-062940-3066, U.S. Office of Education)

Cotterman, T. E. (1959). *Task classification: An approach to partially ordering information on human learning* (Technical Note WADC TN 58-374). Wright Patterson Air Force Base, OH: Wright Development Center.

Demaree, R. G. (1961). *Development of training equipment planning information* (ASD TR 61-533). Wright-Patterson Air Force Base, OH: Aeronautical Systems Division (AD 267 326).

Duchastel, P. C., & Merrill, P. F. (1973). The effects of behavioral objectives on learning: A review of empirical studies. *Review of Educational Research, 75,* 250–266.

Dunn, T. G., & Taylor, C. A. (1990). Hierarchical structures in expert performance. *Educational Technology Research & Development, 38*(2), 5–18.

Dunn, T. G., & Taylor, C. A. (1994). *Learning analysis in ill-structured knowledge domains of professional practice.* Paper presented at the annual meeting of the American Educational Research Association, New Orleans, LA.

Dwyer, C. A., & Dwyer, F. M. (1987). Effect of depth of information processing on students' ability to acquire and retrieve information related to different instructional objectives. *Programmed Learning and Educational Technology, 24*(4), 264-279.

Dwyer, F. M., & Parkhurst, P. E. (1982). A multifactor analysis of the instructional effectiveness of self-paced visualized instruction on different educational objectives. *Programmed Learning and Educational Technology, 19*(2), 108-118.

Edling, J. V., Hamreus, D. G., Schalock, H. D., Beaird, J. H., Paulson, C. F., & Crawford, J. (1972). *The cognitive domain—A resource book for media specialists. Contributions of behavioral science to instructional technology, Handbook 2.* Washington, DC: Gryphon House.

English, R. E., & Reigeluth, C. M. (1994, April). *Formative research on sequencing instruction with the elaboration theory.* Paper presented at the annual meeting of the American Educational Research Association, New Orleans, LA.

Eustace, B. W. (1969). Learning a complex concept a differing hierarchical levels. *Journal of Educational Psychology, 60,* 449-452.

Fields, D. C. (2000). The impact of Gagné's theory of instructional design practice. In R. C. Richey (Ed.), *The legacy of Robert M. Gagné* (pp. 183-209). Syracuse, NY: ERIC Clearinghouse on Information and Technology.

Furst, E. J. (1981). Bloom's taxonomy of educational objectives for the cognitive domain: Philosophical and educational issues. *Review of Educational Research, 51*(5), 441-454.

Gagné, E., Yekovich, C. W., & Yekovich, F. R. (1993). *The cognitive psychology of school learning* (2nd ed.). New York: Harper Collins College.

Gagné, R. M. (1954). An analysis of two problem-solving activities *Research Bulletin 55-77.* Lockland Air Force Base, TX: USAF personnel and Training Research Center. (In Gagné, R. M. [1989], *Studies of Learning* [pp. 405-417]. Tallahassee, FL: Learning Systems Institute.)

Gagné, R. M. (1959). Problem solving and thinking. *Annual Reviews of Psychology, 10,* 147-172.

Gagné, R. M. (1962a). The acquisition of knowledge. *Psychological Review, 69,* 355-365. (In Gagné, R. M. [1989]. *Studies of learning* [pp. 229-242]. Tallahassee, FL: Learning Systems Institute.)

Gagné, R. M. (1962b). Military training and principles of learning. *American Psychologist, 17,* 83-91. (In Gagné, R. M. [1989], *Studies of learning* [pp.141-153]. Tallahassee, FL: Learning Systems Institute.)

Gagné, R. M. (1962c). Human functions in systems. In R. M. Gagné (Ed.), *Psychological principles in system development.* New York: Holt, Rinehart & Winston.

Gagné, R. M. (1964). Problem solving. In A. W. Melton (Ed.), *Categories of human learning* (pp. 293-323). New York: Academic Press.

Gagné, R. M. (1965b). *The conditions of learning.* New York: Holt, Rinehart & Winston.

Gagné, R. M. (1967). Curriculum research and the promotion of learning. In R. Stake (Ed.), *Perspectives of curriculum evaluation.* AERA monograph series on curriculum evaluation, No. 1. Chicago: Rand McNally.

Gagné, R. M. (1972). Domains of learning. *Interchange, 3,* 1-8.

Gagné, R. M. (1970). *The conditions of learning, 2nd edition.* New York: Holt, Rinehart & Winston.

Gagné, R. M. (1973). Learning and instructional sequence. In F. N. Kerlinger (Ed.), *Review of research in education* (Vol. 1, pp. 3-33). Itasca, IL: Peacock.

Gagné, R. M. (1977). *The conditions of learning, 3rd edition.* New York: Holt, Rinehart & Winston.

Gagné, R. M. (1984). Learning outcomes and their effects: Useful categories of human performance. *American Psychologist, 39,* 377-385.

Gagné, R. M. (1985). *The conditions of learning and theory of instruction* (4th ed.). New York: Holt, Rinehart & Winston.

Gagné, R. M., & Bassler, O. C. (1963, June). A study of retention of some topics of elementary nonmetric geometry. *Journal of Educational Psychology, 54,* 123-131.

Gagné, R. M., & Bolles, R. C. (1959). Review of factors in learning efficiency. In E. Galanter (Ed.), *Automatic teaching: The state of the art* (pp. 13-53). New York: Wiley.

Gagné, R. M., & Briggs, L. J. (1974). *Principles of instructional design.* New York: Holt, Rinehart & Winston.

Gagné, R. M., & Briggs, L. J. (1979). *Principles of instructional design* (2nd ed.). Fort Worth, TX: Harcourt Brace Jovanovich.

Gagné, R. M., & Brown, L. T. (1961). Some factors in the programming of conceptual learning. *Journal of Experimental Psychology, 62,* 313-321. (In Gagné, R. M. [1989]. *Studies of learning* [pp. 173-185]. Tallahassee, FL: Learning Systems Institute.)

Gagné, R. M., & Glaser, R. (1987). Foundations in learning research. In R. M. Gagné (Ed.), *Instructional technology foundations* (pp. 49-83). Mahwah, NJ: Lawrence Erlbaum, Associates.

Gagné, R. M., & Merrill, M. D. (1990). Integrative goals for instructional design. *Educational Technology Research & Development, 38*(1), 23-30.

Gagné, R. M., & Paradise, N. E. (1961). Abilities and learning sets in knowledge acquisition. *Psychological Monographs, 75*(14), Whole No. 518.

Gagné, R. M., & Staff, University of Maryland Mathematics Project. (1965). Some factors in learning non-metric geometry. *Monographs of Society for Research in Child Development, 30,* 42-49.

Gagné, R. M., & White, R. T. (1978). Memory structures and learning outcomes. *Review of Educational Research, 48*(2), 187-222.

Gagné, R. M., Baker, K. E., & Wylie, R. C. (1951). Effects of an interfering task on the learning of a complex motor skills. *Journal of Experimental Psychology, 41,* 1-9. (In Gagné, R. M. [1989]. *Studies of learning* [pp. 63-74]. Tallahassee, FL: Learning Systems Institute.)

Gagné, R. M., Mayor, J. R., Garstens, H. L., & Paradise, N. E. (1962). Factors in acquiring knowledge of a mathematical task. *Psychological Monographs, 76*(7), Whole No. 526. (In Gagné, R. M. [1989]. *Studies of learning* [pp. 197-227]. Tallahassee, FL: Learning Systems Institute.)

Gagné, R. M., Briggs, L. J., & Wager, W. W. (1988). *Principles of instructional design* (3rd ed.). Fort Worth, TX: Harcourt Brace Jovanovich.

Gagné, R. M., Briggs, L. J., & Wager, W. W. (1992). *Principles of instructional design* (4th ed.). Fort Worth, TX: Harcourt Brace Jovanovich.

Garduno, A. O. (1984). *Teaching common errors in applying a procedure* (IDD&E Working Paper No. 18). (ERIC Document Reproduction Service No. ED 289 465)

Gentner, D. & Stevens, A. L. (1983). *Mental Models.* Hillsdale, NJ: Lawrence Erlbaum Associates.

Gibbons, A. S., Bunderson, C. V., Olsen, J. B., & Robertson, J. (1995). Work models: still beyond instructional objectives. *Machine. Mediated Learning, 5,* (3 and 4), 221-236.

Getsie, R. L., Langer, P., & Glass, G. V. (1985). Meta-analysis of the effects of type and combination of feedback on children's discrimination learning. *Review of Educational Research, 55*(4), 49-22.

Gilbert, T. F. (1962). Mathetics: The technology of education. *Journal of Mathetics, 1,* 7-73.

Goldberg, N. S. (1987). An evaluation of a Gagné-Briggs based course designed for college algebra remediation. *Dissertation Abstracts International, 47*(12), 4313. (UMI No. AAC87-06313)

Goodlad, R. (1984). *Crisis in the classroom.* San Francisco: Freeman.

Hamilton, R. J. (1985). A framework for the evaluation of the effectiveness of adjunct questions and objectives. *Review of Educational Research, 55*(4), 47-85.

Hannafin, M. J., & Colamaio, M. E. (1987). The effects of locus of instructional control and practice on learning from interactive video. Paper presented at annual meeting of the Association for Educational Communications and Technology, Atlanta, GA. In M. L. Simonson & S. Zvacek (Eds.), *Proceedings of selected research paper presentations* (pp. 297-312). Ames: Iowa State University.

Hannafin, M. J., Phillips, T. L., & Tripp, S. D. (1986). The effects of orienting, processing, and practicing activities on learning from interactive video. *Journal of Computer-Based Instruction, 13*(4), 134-139.

Harlow, H. F. (1959). The development of learning in the rhesus monkey. *American Scientist, 47,* 459-479.

Hartley, J., & Davies, I. K. (1976). Preinstructional strategies: The role of pretests, behavioral objectives, overviews, and advance organizers. *Review of Educational Research, 46*(2), 239-265.

Horn, R. E. (1976). *How to write information mapping.* Lexington, MA: Information Resources.

Hull, C. L. (1934). The concept of the habit-family hierarchy and maze learning. *Psychological Review, 41,* 33-54.

Hull, C. L. (1943). *Principles of behavior.* New York: Appleton-Century-Crofts.

Husic, F. T., Linn, M. C., & Sloane, K. D. (1989). Adapting instruction to the cognitive demands of learning to program. *Journal of Educational Psychology, 81*(4), 570-583.

Johnson, D. W., & Johnson, R. T. (1974). Instructional goal structure: Cooperative, competitive, or individualistic. *Review of Educational Research, 44*(2), 213-240.

Jonassen, D. H., & Land, S. M., (Eds.). (2000). *Theoretical foundations of learning environments.* Mahwah, NJ: Lawrence Erlbaum Associates.

Jonassen, D. H., Grabinger, R. S., & Harris, N. D. C. (1991). Analyzing and selecting instructional strategies and tactics. *Performance Improvement Quarterly, 4*(2), 77-97.

Kallison, J. M. (1986). Effects of lesson organization on achievement. *American Educational Research Journal, 23*(2), 337-347.

Katona, G. (1940). *Organizing and memorizing.* New York: Columbia University Press.

Keller, B. H. (1986). The effects of selected presentation forms using conceptual and procedural content from elementary mathematics (component display theory, concept learning and development model, best example). *Dissertation Abstracts International, 47*(05), 1591. (UMI No. AAC86-17320)

Keller, B., & Reigeluth, C. H. (1982). *A comparison of three instructional presentation formats* (IDD&E Working Paper No. 6). Syracuse NY: Syracuse University, School of Education. (ERIC Document Reproduction Service No. ED 288 516)

Kendler, H. H. (1964). The concept of the concept. In A. W. Melton (Ed.), *Categories of human learning* (pp. 211-236). New York: Academic Press.

Kiewra, K. A., & Benton, S. L. (1987). Effects of notetaking, the instructor's notes, and higher-order practice questions on factual and higher order learning. *Journal of Instructional Psychology, 14*(4), 186-194.

Kunen, S., Cohen, R., & Solman, R. (1981). A levels-of-processing analysis of Bloom's taxonomy. *Journal of Educational Psychology, 73*(2), 202-211.

Kyllonen, P. C., & Shute, V. J. (1989). A taxonomy of learning skills. In P. L. Ackerman, R. J. Sternberg, & R. Glaser (Eds.), *Learning and individual differences* (pp. 117-163).

Landa, L. N. (1983). The algo-heuristic theory of instruction. In C. M. Reigeluth (Ed.), *Instructional-design theories and models* (pp. 163-211). Mahwah, NJ: Lawrence Erlbaum Associates.

Landa, L. N. (1993). Landamatics ten years later: An interview with Lev N. Landa. *Educational Technology, 32*(6), 7-18.

Levin, J. R. (1986). Four cognitive principles of learning strategy instruction. *Educational Psychologist, 2*(1 & 2), 3-17.

Linke, R. D. (1973). *The effects of certain personal and situation variables on the acquisition sequence of graphical interpretation skills.* Doctoral dissertation, Monash University.

Lumsdaine, A. A. (1960). Design of training aids and devices. In J. D. Folley (Ed.), *Human factors methods for system design.* Pittsburgh, PA: American Institutes for Research.

Maier, N. R. F. (1930). Reasoning in humans: I. On direction. *Journal of Comparative Psychology, 10,* 115-143.

Marcone, S., & Reigeluth, C. M. (1988) Teaching common errors in applying a procedure. *Educational Communications and Technology Journal, 36*(1), 23-32.

McLean, L. (1983). *The effects of format of synthesizer on conceptual learning* (IDD&E Working Paper No. 13). (ERIC Document Reproduction Service No. ED 289 462)

Melton, A. W. (1941). Learning. In W. S. Monroe (Ed.), *Encyclopedia of educational research* (pp. 667-686). New York: Macmillan.

Melton, A. W. (1964a). The taxonomy of human learning: Overview. In A. W. Melton (Ed.), *Categories of human learning* (pp. 325-339). New York: Academic Press.

Melton, A. W. (Ed.). (1964b). *Categories of human learning.* New York: Academic Press.

Mengel, N. S. (1986). The acceptability and effectiveness of textbook materials revised using instructional design criteria. *Journal of Instructional Development, 9*(2), 13-18.

Merrill, M. D. (1983). Component display theory. In C. M. Reigeluth (Ed.), *Instructional-design theories and models* (pp. 279-333). Mahwah, NJ: Lawrence Erlbaum Associates.

Merrill, M. D. (1999). Instructional transaction theory (ITT): Instructional design based on knowledge objects. In C. M Reigeluth (Ed.), *Instructional-design theories and models, Vol. II: A new paradigm of instructional theory* (pp. 397-424). Mahwah, NJ: Lawrence Erlbaum Associates.

Merrill, M. D., Barton, K., & Wood, L. E. (1970). Specific review in learning a hierarchical imaginary science. *Journal of Educational Psychology, 61,* 102-109.

Merrill, M. D., Li, Z., & Jones, M. K. (1990a). Limitations of first generation instructional design. *Educational Technology, 30*(1), 7-11.

Merrill, M. D., Li, Z., & Jones, M. K. (1990b). Second generation instructional design. *Educational Technology, 30*(2), 7-14.

Merrill, M. D., Li, Z., & Jones, M. K. (1991). Instructional transaction theory: An introduction. *Educational Technology, 31*(6), 7-12.

Merrill, M. D., Jones, M. K., & Li, Z. (1992). Instructional transaction theory: Classes of transactions. *Educational Technology, 32*(6), 12-26.

Merrill, M. D., Li, Z., & Jones, M. K. (1992). Instructional transaction shells: Responsibilities, methods, and parameters. *Educational Technology, 32*(2), 5-26.

Merrill, M. D., Li, Z., Jones, M. K., Chen-Troester, J., & Schwab, S. (1993). Instructional transaction theory: Knowledge relationships among processes, entities, and activities. *Educational Technology, 33*(4), 5-16.

Miller, R. B. (1953). *A method for man-machine task analysis* (Technical Report 53-137). Wright-Patterson Air Force Base, OH: Wright Air Development Center.

Miller, R. B. (1954). *Psychological considerations in the design of training equipment* (Technical Report 54-563). Wright-Patterson Air Force Base, OH: Wright Air Development Center.

Miller, R. B. (1956, April). *A suggested guide to position-task description* (Technical Memorandum ASPRL-TM-56-16). Lowry Air Force Base, CO: Armament Systems Personnel Research Laboratory, Air Force Personnel and Training Research Center.

Miller, R. B. (1962). Analysis and specification of behavior for training. In R. Glaser (Ed.), *Training research and education* (pp. 31-62). Pittsburgh, PA: University of Pittsburgh Press.

Mowrer, O. H. (1960). *Learning theory and the Symbolic Processes.* New York: John Wiley.

Nelson, L. M. (1999). Collaborative problem solving. In C. M Reigeluth (Ed.), *Instructional-design theories and models, Vol. II: A new paradigm of instructional theory* (pp. 241-267). Mahwah, NJ: Lawrence Erlbaum Associates.

Nelson, W. A. (2000). Gagné and the new technologies of instruction. In R. C. Richey (Ed.), *The legacy of Robert M. Gagné* (pp. 229-251). Syracuse, NY: ERIC Clearinghouse on Information and Technology.

Nicholas, J. R. (1970). *Modality of verbal instructions for problems and transfer for a science hierarchy.* Doctoral dissertation, University of California, Berkeley.

Okey, J. R., & Gagné, R. M. (1970). Revision of a science topic using evidence of performance on subordinate skills. *Journal of Research in Science Teaching, 7,* 321-325.

Olsen, D. R. & Bruner, J. S. (1974). Learning through experience and learning through media. In D. R. Olsen (Ed.), *Media and Symbols* (pp. 125-150). Chicago. IL: University of Chicago Press.

Parker, J. F., & Downs, J. E. (1961). *Selection of training media* (ASD TR 61-473). Wright-Patterson Air Force Base, OH: Aeronautical Systems Division (AD 271 483).

Pavlov, I. P. (1927). *Conditioned reflexes* (G. V. Anrep., Trans.). London: Oxford University Press.

Peper, R. J., & Mayer, R. E. (1978). Notetaking as a generative activity. *Journal of Educational Psychology, 70,* 514-522.

Peper, R. J., & Mayer, R. E. (1986). Generative effects of note-taking during science lectures. *Journal of Educational Psychology, 78,* 34-38.

Postman, L. (1961). The present status of interference theory. In C. N. Cofer (Ed.), *Verbal learning and verbal behavior.* (pp. 152-179) New York: McGraw-Hill.

Pressley, M., Levin, J. R., & Delaney, H. (1982) The mnemonic keyword method. *Review of Educational Research, 52*(1), 61-91.

Ragan, T. J., & Smith, P. L. (1996). Conditions-based models for instructional design. In D. M. Jonassen (Ed.), *Handbook of research for educational communications and technology* (pp. 541-569). New York: Macmillan.

Reiber, L. P. (1989). The effects of computer animated elaboration strategies and practice on factual and application learning in an elementary science lesson. *Journal of Educational Computing Research, 54*(4), 431-444.

Reigeluth, C. M. (1979). In search of a better way to organize instruction: The elaboration theory. *Journal of Instructional Development, 6,* 40-46.

Reigeluth, C. M. (1983b). Instructional design: What is it and why is it? In C. M. Reigeluth (Ed.), *Instructional design theories and models* (pp. 3-36). Mahwah, NJ: Lawrence Erlbaum Associates.

Reigeluth, C. M. (Ed.). (1987). *Instructional theories in action: lessons illustrating selected theories and models.* Hillsdale, NJ: Lawrence Erlbaum Associates.

Reigeluth, C. M. (1992). Elaborating the elaboration theory. *Educational Technology Research and Development, 40*(3), 80-86.

Reigeluth, C. M. (Ed.) (1999a). *Instructional-design theories and models, Vol. II: A new paradigm of instructional theory.* Mahwah, NJ: Lawrence Erlbaum Associates.

Reigeluth, C. M. (1999b). The elaboration theory: Guidance for scope and sequence decisions. In C. M. Reigeluth (Ed.), *Instructional-design theories and models Vol. II: A new paradigm of instructional theory* (pp. 425-453). Mahwah, NJ: Lawrence Erlbaum Associates.

Reigeluth, C. M., Merrill, M. D., Wilson, B. G., & Spiller, R. T. (1978). *Final report on the structural strategy diagnostic profile project.* San Diego: Navy Personnel Research and Development Center.

Reigeluth, C. M., & Curtis, R. V. (1987). Learning situations and instructional models. In R. M. Gagné (Ed.), *Instructional technology foundations* (pp. 175-206). Mahwah, NJ: Lawrence Erlbaum Associates.

Reigeluth, C. M, & Darwazeh, A. N. (1982). The elaboration theory's procedures for designing instruction: A conceptual approach. *Journal of Instructional Development, 5,* 22-32.

Reigeluth, C. M., & Rogers, C. A. (1980). The elaboration theory of instruction: Prescriptions for task analysis and design. *NSPI Journal, 19,* 16-26.

Reigeluth, C. M., & Stein, F. S. (1983). The elaboration theory of instruction. In C. M. Reigeluth, (Ed.), *Instructional design theories and models* (pp. 335-382). Mahwah, NJ: Lawrence Erlbaum Associates.

Resnick, L. B. (1967). *Design of an early learning curriculum* (Working Paper 16). Pittsburgh, PA: Learning Research and Development Center, University of Pittsburgh.

Resnick, L. B., & Wang, M. C. (1969). *Approaches to the validation of learning hierarchies.* (Preprint 50) Pittsburgh: Learning Research and Development Center, University of Pittsburgh.

Resnick, L. B., Siegel, A. W., & Kresh, E. (1971). Transfer and sequence in learning double classification skills. *Journal of Experimental Child Psychology, 11,* 139-149.

Richardson, J. (1958) The relationship of stimulus similarity and number of responses. *Journal of Experimental Psychology, 56,* 478-484.

Richey, R. C. (Ed.). (2000b). *The legacy of Robert M. Gagné.* Syracuse, NY: ERIC Clearinghouse on Information & Technology.

Robinson, E. R. N. (1984). The relationship between the effects of four instructional formats and test scores of adult civilian and military personnel when learning to use a text editor (Doctoral dissertation, University of Southern California, 1984). *Dissertation Abstracts International, 45,* 3311.

Rummelhart, D. E. (1980). Schemata: The building blocks of cognition. In Spiro, R. J., Bruce, B. C., & Brewer, W. F. (Eds.), Theoretical issues in reading comprehension (pp. 33-58). Hillsdale, NJ: Lawrence Erlbaum Associates.

Ryle, G. (1949). *The concept of Mind.* London: Hutchinson.

Sasayama, G. M. D. (1985). Effects of rules, examples and practice on learning concept-classification, principle-using, and procedure-using tasks: A cross-cultural study. *Dissertation Abstracts International, 46*(01), 65. (UMI No. AAC85-05584)

Scandura, J. M. (1983). Instructional strategies based on the structural learning theory. In C. M. Reigeluth (Ed.), *Instructional-design theories and models: An overview of their current status* (pp. 213-246). Mahwah, NJ: Lawrence Erlbaum Associates.

Schimmel, B. J. (1983, April). *A meta-analysis of feedback to learners in computerized and programmed instruction.* Paper presented at the Annual Meeting of the American Educational Research Association, Montreal. (ERIC Document Reproduction Service No. ED 233708)

Shrager, L., & Mayer, R. E. (1989). Note-taking fosters generative learning strategies in novices. *Journal of Educational Psychology, 81*(2), 263-264.

Skinner, B. F. (1938). *The behavior of organisms; An experimental analysis.* New York: Appleton-Century-Crofts.

Slee, E. J. (1989). A review of the research on interactive video. Paper presented at annual meeting of the Association for Educational Communications and Technology, Dallas, TX. In M. L. Simonson and D. Frey (Eds.), *Proceedings of selected research paper presentations* (pp. 150–166). Ames: Iowa State University.

Smith, P. L. (1992, February). *Walking, the tightrope: Selecting from Supplantive and generative instructional strategies.* paper presented at the Annual Meeting of the Association for Educational Communications and Technology, Washington, D.C.

Smith, P. L., & Ragan, T. J. (1993a). *Instructional design.* New York: Macmillan.

Smith, P. L., & Ragan, T. J. (1993b). Designing instructional feedback for different learning outcomes. In J. V. Dempsey & G. C. Sales (Eds.), *Interactive instruction and feedback* (pp. 75–103). Englewood Cliffs, NJ: Educational Technology Publications.

Smith, P. L., & Ragan, T. J. (1999). *Instructional design* (2nd ed.). Hoboken, NJ: Wiley.

Smith, P. L., & Ragan, T. J. (2000). The impact of R. M. Gagné's work on instructional theory. In R. C. Richey (Ed.), *The legacy of Robert M. Gagné* (pp.147– 181). Syracuse, NY: ERIC Clearinghouse on Information and Technology.

Smith, P. L., & Wedman, J. F. (1988, February). *The effects of organization of instruction on cognitive processing.* Paper presented at the annual convention of the Association for Educational Communications and Technology, New Orleans, LA.

Smode, A. F. (1962). Recent developments in training problems, and training and training research methodology. In R. Glaser (Ed.), *Training research and education* (pp. 429–495). Pittsburgh, PA: University Pittsburgh Press.

Spector, J. M. (2000). Gagné's influence on military training research/ development. In R. Richey (Ed.), *The legacy of Robert M. Gagné* (pp. 211–227). Syracuse, NY: ERIC Clearinghouse on Information and Technology.

Spector, J. M., & Muraida, D. J. (1991). Evaluating instructional transaction theory. *Educational Technology, 31*(10), 29–35.

Stahl, R. J. (1979, April). *Validating a modified Gagnean concept-acquisition model: The results of an experimental study using art-related content.* Paper presented at the annual meeting of the American Educational Research Association, San Francisco, CA. (ERIC Document Reproduction Service No. ED 168 942)

Stein, F. S. (1982). Beyond prose and adjunct questions: A comparison with a designed approach to instruction. *Dissertation Abstracts International, 43*(09), 2880. (UMI No. AAC82-29019)

Stolurow, L. M. (1964). *A taxonomy of learning task characteristics* (AMRL-TDR-64-2). Wright-Patterson Air Force Base, OH: Aerospace Medical Research Laboratories (AD 433 199)

Tennyson, R. D. (1987). Computer-based enhancements for the improvement of learning. Paper presented at annual meeting of the Association for Educational Communications and Technology, Atlanta, GA. In M. L. Simonson & S. Zvacek (Eds.), *Proceedings of selected research paper presentations* (pp. 25–38). Ames: Iowa State University.

Tennyson, R. D., & Rasch, M. (1988a). Linking cognitive learning theory to instructional prescriptions. *Instructional Science, 17,* 369–385.

Tennyson, R. D., & Rasch, M. (1988b). Instructional design for the improvement of learning and cognition. Paper presented at annual meeting of the Association for Educational Communications and Technology, Atlanta, GA. In M. L. Simonson & S. Zvacek (Eds.), *Proceedings of selected research paper presentations* (pp. 760–775). Ames: Iowa State University.

Thorndike, E. L. (1898). Animal intelligence: An experimental study of the associative processes in animals. *Psychology Review Monograph Supplement, 2*(4), Whole No. 8.

Tilden, D. V. (1985). The nature of review: Components of a summarizer which may increase retention (instructional design). *Dissertation Abstracts International, 45*(12), 159. (UMI No. AAC85-00771)

Tolman, E. C. (1949). There is more than one kind of learning. *Psychological Review, 56,* 144–155. (in Wickens, 1962, p. 80; also noted in Gagné, 1965).

Underwood, B. J. (1964a). The representativeness of rote verbal learning. In A. W. Melton (Ed.), *Categories of human learning* (pp. 47–78). New York: Academic Press.

Underwood, B. J. (1964b). Laboratory studies of verbal learning. In E. R. Hilgard (Ed.), *Theories of learning and instruction. Sixty-third yearbook* (pp. 133–152). Chicago: National Society for the Study of Education.

Van Patten, J. E. (1984). The effects of conceptual and procedural sequences and synthesizers on selected outcomes of instruction. *Dissertation Abstracts International, 44*(10), 2973. (UMI No. AAC84-00790)

Von Hurst, E. M. (1984). The effectiveness of component display theory in the remediation of self-instructional materials for Japanese learners (Doctoral dissertation, University of Southern California, 1984). *Dissertation Abstracts International, 45,* 794.

Wagner, K. K. (1994). A comparison of two content sequencing theories applied to hypertext-based instruction (elaboration theory, structural learning theory). *Dissertation Abstracts International, 54*(11), 101. (UMI No. AAC94-13334)

Wedman, J. F., & Smith, P. L. (1989). An examination of two approaches to organizing instruction. *International Journal of Instructional Media, 16*(4). 293–303.

West, C. K., Farmer, J. A., & Wolf, P. M. (1991). *Instructional design: Implications for cognitive science.* Upper Saddle River, NJ: Prentice Hall.

White, R. T. (1973a). Research into learning hierarchies. *Review of Educational Research, 43*(3), 361–375.

White, R. T. (1974a). A model for validation of learning hierarchies. *Journal of Research in Science Teaching, 11,* 1–3.

White, R. T. (1974b). Indexes used in testing the validity of learning hierarchies. *Journal of Research in Science Teaching, 11,* 61–66.

White, R. T. (1974c). The validation of a learning hierarchy. *American Educational Research Journal, 11,* 121–136.

White, R. T., & Gagné, R. M. (1974). Past and future research on learning hierarchies. *Educational Psychologist, 11,* 19–28. (In Gagné, R. M. [1989]. *Studies of learning* [pp. 361–373]. Tallahassee, FL: Learning Systems Institute.)

Wickens, D. D. (1962). The centrality of verbal learning: Comments on Professor Underwood's paper. In A. W. Melton (Ed.), *Categories of Human Learning* (pp. 79–87). New York: Academic Press.

Willis, M. P., & Peterson, R. O. (1961). *Deriving training device implications from learning theory principles: I. Guidelines for training device design, development, and use* (TR: NAVTRADEVCEN 784-1). Port Washington, NY: U.S. Naval Training Device Center.

Wilson, B. G. (1987). Computers and instructional design: Component display theory in transition. Paper presented at annual meeting of the Association for Educational Communications and Technology, Atlanta, GA. In M. L. Simonson & S. Zvacek (Eds.), *Proceedings of selected research paper presentations* (pp. 767–782). Ames: Iowa State University.

Wilson, B., & Cole, P. (1991). A review of Cognitive teaching, models *Educational Technology Research and Development, 39*(4), 47–64.

Winkles, J. (1986). Achievement, understanding, and transfer in a learning hierarchy. *American Educational Research Journal, 23*(2), 275–288.

Woodworth, R. S. (1958). *Dynamics of behavior*. New York: Holt, Rinehart & Winston.

Yao, K. (1989). Factors related to the skipping of subordinate skills in Gagné's learning hierarchies. Paper presented at annual meeting of the Association for Educational Communications and Technology, Dallas, TX. In M. L. Simonson & D. Frey (Eds.), *Proceedings of selected research paper presentations* (pp. 661–674). Ames: Iowa State University.

Yellon, S. L., & Schmidt, W. H. (1971). *The effect of objective sand instructions on the learning of a complex cognitive task*. Paper presented at the meeting of the American Educational Research Association, New York.

ADAPTIVE INSTRUCTIONAL SYSTEMS

Ok-choon Park[1]

Institute of Education Sciences

U.S. Department of Education

Jung Lee

Richard Stockton College of New Jersey

A central and persisting issue in educational technology is the provision of instructional environments and conditions that can comply with individually different educational goals and learning abilities. Instructional approaches and techniques that are geared to meet the needs of the individually different student are called adaptive instruction (Como & Snow, 1986). More specifically, adaptive instruction refers to educational interventions aimed at effectively accommodating individual differences in students while helping each student develop the knowledge and skills required to learn a task. Adaptive instruction is generally characterized as an educational approach that incorporates alternative procedures and strategies for instruction and resource utilization and has the built-in flexibility to permit students to take various routes to, and amounts of time for, learning (Wang & Lindvall, 1984). Glaser (1977) described three essential ingredients of adaptive instruction. First, it provides a variety of alternatives for learning and many goals from which to choose. Second, it attempts to utilize and develop the capabilities that an individual brings to the alternatives for his or her learning and to adjust to the learner's particular talents, strengths, and weaknesses. Third, it attempts to strengthen an individual's ability to meet the demands of available educational opportunities and develop the skills necessary for success in the complex world.

Adaptive instruction has been used interchangeably with individualized instruction in the literature (Reiser, 1987; Wang & Lindvall, 1984). However, they are different depending on the specific methods and procedures employed during instruction. Any type of instruction presented in a one-on-one setting can

be considered individualized instruction. However, if that instruction is not flexible enough to meet the student's specific learning needs, it cannot be considered adaptive. Similarly, even though instruction is provided in a group environment, it can be adaptive if it is sensitive to the unique needs of each student as well as the common needs of the group. Ideal individualized instruction should be adaptive, because instruction will be most powerful when it is adapted to the unique needs of each individual. It can easily be assumed that the superiority of individualized instruction over group instruction reported in many studies (e.g., Bloom, 1984; Kulik, 1982) is due to the adaptive nature of the individualized instruction.

The long history of thoughts and admonitions about adapting instruction to individual student's needs has been documented by many researchers (e.g., Como & Snow, 1986; Federico, 1980; Reiser, 1987; Tobias, 1989). Since at least the fourth century BC, adapting has been viewed as a primary factor for the success of instruction (Como & Snow, 1986), and adaptive instruction by tutoring was the common method of education until the mid-1800s (Reiser, 1987). Even after graded systems were adopted, the importance of adapting instruction to individual needs was continuously emphasized. For example, Dewey (1902/1964), in his 1902 essay, "Child and Curriculum," deplored the current emphasis on a single kind of curriculum development that produced a uniform, inflexible sequence of instruction that ignored or minimized the child's individual peculiarities, whims, and experiences. Nine years later, Thorndike (1911) argued for a specialization of instruction that acknowledged differences

---

[1] Views and opinions expressed in this chapter are solely the author's and do not represent or imply the views or opinions of the U.S. Department of Education or the Institute of Education Sciences.

among pupils within a single class as well as specialization of the curriculum for different classes. Since then, various approaches and methods have been proposed and attempted to provide adaptive instruction to individually different students (for early systems see Reiser, 1987).

Particularly since Cronbach (1957) declared that a united discipline of psychology not only will be interested in organism and treatment variables but also will be concerned with the otherwise ignored interactions between organism and treatment variables, numerous studies have been conducted to investigate what kinds of student characteristics and background variables should be considered in adapting instruction to individuals and how instructional methods and procedures should be adapted to those characteristics and variables (Cronbach, 1971; Cronbach & Snow, 1977; Federico, 1980; Snow & Swanson, 1992). It is surprising, however, how little scientific evidence has been accumulated for such adaptations and how difficult it is to provide guidelines to practitioners for making such adaptations.

This chapter has four objectives: (a) to review selectively systematic efforts to establish and implement adaptive instruction, including recently developed technology-based systems such as hypermedia and Web-based systems, (b) to discuss theoretical paradigms and research variables studied to provide theoretical bases and development guidelines of adaptive instruction, (c) to discuss problems and limitations of the current approach to adaptive instruction, and (d) to propose a response-sensitive approach to the development of adaptive instruction.

25.1 ADAPTIVE INSTRUCTION: THREE APPROACHES

The efforts to develop and implement adaptive instruction have taken different approaches based on the aspects of instruction that are intended to adapt to different students. The first approach is to adapt instruction on a macrolevel by allowing different alternatives in selecting only a few main components of instruction such as instructional goals, depth of curriculum content, and delivery systems. Most adaptive instructional systems developed as alternatives to the traditional lock-step group instruction in school environments have taken this approach. In this macroapproach, instructional alternatives are selected mostly on the basis of the student's instructional goals, general ability, and achievement levels in the curriculum structure. The second approach is to adapt specific instructional procedures and strategies to specific student characteristics. Because this approach requires the identification of the most relevant learner characteristics (or aptitudes) for the instruction and the selection of instructional strategies that best facilitate the learning process of the students who have the aptitudes, it is called aptitude–treatment interactions (ATI). The third approach is to adapt instruction on a microlevel by diagnosing the student's specific learning needs during instruction and providing instructional prescriptions for the needs. As this microapproach is designed to guide the student's ongoing learning process throughout the instruction, the diagnosis and prescription are often continuously performed from analysis of the student's performance on the task.

The degree of adaptation is determined by how sensitive the diagnostic procedure is to the specific learning needs of each student and how much the prescriptive activities are tailored to the learner's needs. Depending on the available resources and constraints in the given situation, the instruction can be designed to be adaptive using a different combination of the three approaches. However, the student in an ideal microadaptive system is supposed to achieve his or her instructional objective by following the guidance that the system provides. The rapid development of computer technology has provided a powerful tool for developing and implementing micro-adaptive instructional systems more efficiently than ever before. Thus, in this chapter micro-adaptive instructional systems and the related issues are reviewed and discussed more thoroughly than macro-adaptive systems and ATI approaches. Our review includes adaptive approaches used in recently developed technology-based learning environments such as hypermedia and Web-based instruction. However, the most powerful form of technology-based adaptive systems, intelligent tutoring systems (ITSs), is briefly reviewed on only a conceptual level here because another chapter is devoted to ITSs. Also, learner control, another form of adaptive instruction, is not discussed in depth because it is covered in another chapter.

25.2 MACRO-ADAPTIVE INSTRUCTIONAL SYSTEMS

Early attempts to adapt the instructional process to individual learners in school education were certainly macrolevel because the students were simply grouped or tracked by grades or scores from ability tests. This homogeneous grouping had a minimal effect because the groups seldom received different kinds of instructional treatments (Tennyson, 1975). In the early 1900s, however, a number of adaptive systems were developed to accommodate different student abilities better. For example, Reiser (1987) described the Burke plan, Dalton plan, and Winnetka plan that were developed in the early 1900s. The main adaptive feature in these plans was that the student was allowed to go through the instructional materials at his or her own pace. The notion of mastery learning was also fostered in the Dalton and Winnetka plans (Reiser, 1987).

Since macro-adaptive instruction is frequently used within a class to aid the differentiation of teaching operations over larger segments of instruction, it often involves a repeated sequence of "recitation" activity initiated by teachers' behaviors in classrooms (Como & Snow, 1983). For example, a typical pattern of teaching is (a) explaining or presenting specific information, (b) asking questions to monitor student learning, and (c) providing appropriate feedback for the student's responses. Several macro-adaptive instructional systems developed in the 1960s are briefly reviewed here.

25.2.1 The Keller Plan

In 1963, Keller (1968, 1974) and his associates at Columbia University developed a macroadaptive system called the Keller plan in which the instructional process was personalized for each student. The program incorporated four unique features: (a) requiring mastery of each unit before moving to the next unit, (b) allowing a self-learning pace, (c) using textbooks and workbooks as the primary instructional means, and (d) using student proctors for evaluating student performance and providing feedback. The Keller plan was used at many colleges and universities throughout the world (Reiser, 1987) during the late 1960s and early 1970s.

25.2.2 The Audio-Tutorial System

In 1961, the Audio-Tutorial System (Postlethwait, Novak, & Murray, 1972) was developed at Purdue University by applying audiovisual media, particularly audiotape. The unique feature of this audiotutorial approach was a tutorial-like instruction using audiotapes, along with other media such as texts, slides, and models. This approach was effectively used for teaching college science courses (Postlethwait, 1981).

25.2.3 PLAN

In 1967, Flanagan, Shanner, Brudner, and Marker (1975) developed a Program for Learning in Accordance with Needs (PLAN) to provide students with options for selecting different instructional objectives and learning materials. For the selected instructional objective(s), the student needed to study a specific instructional unit and demonstrate mastery before advancing to the next unit for another objective(s). In the early 1970s, more than 100 elementary schools participated in this program.

25.2.4 Mastery Learning Systems

A popular approach to individualized instruction was developed by Bloom and his associates at the University of Chicago (Block, 1980). In this mastery learning system, virtually every student achieves the given instructional objectives by having sufficient instructional time and materials for his or her learning. "Formative" examination is given to determine whether the student needs more time to master the given unit, and "summative" examination is given to determine mastery. The mastery learning approach was widely used in the United States and several foreign countries. The basic notion of mastery learning, initially proposed by Carroll (1963), is still alive at many schools and other educational institutes. However, the instructional adaptiveness of this mastery learning approach is mostly limited to the "time" variable.

25.2.5 IGE

A more comprehensive macro-adaptive instructional system, called Individually Guided Education (IGE), was developed at the University of Wisconsin in 1965 (Klausmeier, 1975, 1976). In IGE, instructional objectives are first determined for each student based on his or her academicability profile, which includes diagnostic assessments in reading and mathematics, previous achievements, and other aptitude and motivation data. Then, to accommodate different student learning abilities and styles, the teacher determines the necessary guidance for each student and selects alternative instructional materials (e.g., text, audiovisuals, and group activities) and interactions with other students. The goals and implementation methods of this program could be changed to comply with the school's educational assumptions and institutional traditions (Klausmeier, 1977). However, an evaluation study by Popkewitz, Tabachnick, and Wehlage (1982) reported that the implementation and maintenance of IGE in existing school systems were greatly constrained by the school environments.

25.2.6 IPI

The Individually Prescribed Instructional System (IPI) was developed by the Learning Research and Development Center (LRDC) at the University of Pittsburgh in 1964 to provide students with adaptive instructional environments (Glaser, 1977). In the IPI, the student was assigned to an instructional unit within a course according to the student's performance on a placement test given before the instruction. Within the unit, a pretest was given to determine which objectives the student needed to study. Learning materials required to master the instructional objectives were prescribed. After studying each unit, students took a posttest to determine their mastery of the unit. The student was required to master specific objectives for the instructional unit before advancing to the next unit.

25.2.7 ALEM

The LRDC extended the IPI with more varied types of diagnosis methods, remedial activities, and instructional prescriptions. The extended system is called the Adaptive Learning Environments Model (ALEM) (Wang, 1980). The main functions of the ALEM include (a) instructional management for providing learning guidelines on the use of instructional time and resources materials, (b) guidance for parental involvements at home in learning activities provided at school, (c) a procedure for team teaching and group activities, and (d) staff development for training teachers to implement the system (Como & Snow, 1983). An evaluation study (Wang & Walberg, 1983) reported that 96% of teachers were able to establish and maintain the ALEM in teaching economically disadvantaged children (kindergarten through grade 3) and that the degree of its implementation was associated with students' efficient use of learning time and with constructive classroom behaviors and processes.

25.2.8 CMI Systems

Well-designed computer-managed instructional (CMI) systems have functions to diagnose student learning needs and prescribe instructional activities appropriate for the needs. For example, the Plato Learning Management (PLM) System at Control Data Corporation had functions to give a test on different levels of instruction: an instructional module, a lesson, a course, and a curriculum. An instructional module was designed to teach one or more instructional objectives, a lesson consisted of one or more modules, a course consisted of one or more lessons, and a curriculum had one or more courses. A CMI system can evaluate each student's performance on the test and provide specific instructional prescriptions. For example, if a student's score has not reached the mastery criterion for a specific instructional objective on the module test, it can assign a learning activity or activities for the student. After studying the learning activities, the student may be required to take the test again. When the student demonstrates the mastery of all objectives in the module, the student will be allowed to move on to the next module. Depending on the instructor's or instructional administrator's choice, the student can complete the lesson, course, or curriculum by taking only corresponding module tests, although the student may be required to take additional summary tests on the lesson level, course level, and curriculum level. In either case, this test–evaluation–assignment process is continued until the student demonstrates the mastery of all the objectives, modules, lessons, courses, and curriculum. In addition to the test–evaluation–prescription process, a CMI system may have several other features important in adapting instruction to the student's needs and ability: (a) The instructor can be allowed to choose appropriate objectives, modules, lessons, and courses in the curriculum for each student to study; (b) the student can decide the sequence of instructional activities by choosing a specific module to study; (c) more than one learning activity can be associated with an instructional objective, and the student can have the option to choose which activity or activities to study; and (d) because most learning activities associated with a CMI system will be instructor-free, the student can choose the time to study it and progress at his or her own pace.

As described above, well-designed CMI systems provided many important macro-adaptive instructional features. Although the value of a CMI system was well understood, its actual use was limited due to the need for a central computer system that allowed the instructor to monitor and control the student's learning activities at different locations and different times. However, the dramatic increase in personal computer (PC) capability and the simple procedure to make linkages among PCs made it easy to provide a personalized CMI system.

Ross and Morrison (1988) developed a macroadaptive system combining some of the basic functions of CMI (e.g., prescription of instruction) and some of the features of microadaptive models (e.g., prediction of student learning needs). This system was designed primarily for providing adaptive instruction rather than managing the instructional process. However, the student's learning needs were diagnosed only from preinstructional data, and a new instructional prescription could not be generated until the next unit of instruction began. It consisted of three basic steps: First, variables for predicting the student's performance on the task were selected (e.g., measures of prior knowledge, reading comprehension, locus of control, and anxiety). Second, a predictive equation was developed using multiple regression analysis. Third, an instructional prescription (e.g., necessary number of examples estimated to learn the task) was selected based on the student's predicted performance. This system was developed by simplifying a microadaptive model (trajectory/multiple regression approach) described in a later section.

The macro-adaptive instructional programs just described are representative examples that have been used in existing educational systems. As mentioned at the beginning of this chapter, macro-adaptive instruction, except for CMI systems, has been a common practice in many school classrooms for a long time, although the adaptive procedures have been mostly unsystematic and primitive, with the magnitude of adaptation differing widely among teachers. Thus, several models have been proposed to examine analytically the different levels and methods of adaptive instruction and to provide guidance for developing adaptive instructional programs.

25.3 MACRO-ADAPTIVE INSTRUCTIONAL MODELS

25.3.1 A Taxonomy of Macro-Adaptive Instruction

Como and Snow (1983) developed a taxonomy of adaptive instruction to provide systematic guidance in selecting instructional mediation (i.e., activities) depending on the objectives of adaptive instruction and student aptitudes. Como and Snow distinguished two objectives of adaptive instruction: (a) aptitude development necessary for further instruction such as cognitive skills and strategies useful in later problem solving and effective decision making and (b) circumvention or compensation for existing sources of inaptitude needed to proceed with instruction. They categorized aptitudes related to learning into three types: intellectual abilities and prior achievement, cognitive and learning styles, and academic motivation and related personality characteristics. (For in-depth discussions on aptitudes in relation to adaptive instruction, see Cronbach and Snow [1977], Federico [1980], Snow [1986], Snow and Swanson, [1992], and Tobias [1987].) Como and Snow categorized instructional mediation into four types, from the least to the most intrusive: (a) activating, which mostly calls forth students' capabilities and capitalizes on learner aptitudes as in discovery learning; (b) modeling; (c) participant modeling; and (d) short-circuiting, which requires step-by-step direct instruction. This taxonomy gives a general idea of how to adapt instructional mediation for the given instructional objective and student aptitude. According to Como and Snow (1983), this taxonomy can be applied to both levels of adaptive instruction (macro and micro). For example, the activating mediation may be more beneficial for more intellectually able and motivated students, while the short-circuiting mediation may be better for intellectually low-end students. However, this level of guidance does not provide specific information about how to develop and implement an adaptive instruction. More specifically, it does not suggest how to perform ongoing learning diagnosis and instructional prescriptions during the instructional process.

25.3.2 Macro-Adaptive Instructional Models

Whereas Como and Snow's taxonomy represents possible ranges of adaptation of instructional activities for the given instructional objective and student aptitudes, Glaser's (1977) five models provide specific alternatives for the design of adaptive instruction. Glaser's first model is an instructional environment that provides limited alternatives. In this model, the instructional objective and activity to achieve the objective are fixed. Thus, if students do not have the appropriate initial competence to achieve the objective with the given activity, they are designated poor learners and are dropped out. Only students who demonstrate the appropriate initial state of competence are allowed to participate in the instructional activity. If students do not demonstrate the achievement of the objective after the activity, they are allowed to repeat the same activity or are dropped out. The second model provides an opportunity to develop the appropriate initial competence for students who do not have it. However, no alternative activities are available. Thus, students who do not achieve the objective after the activity should repeat the same activity or drop out. The third model accommodates different styles of learning. In this model, alternative instructional activities are available, and students are assessed as to whether they have the appropriate initial competence for achieving the objective through one of the alternatives. However, there are no remedial activities for the development of the appropriate initial competence. Thus, if a student does not have initial competence appropriate for any of the alternative activities, he or she is designated a poor learner. Once an instructional activity is selected based on the student's initial competence, the student should repeat the activity until achieving the objective or drop out. The fourth model provides an opportunity to develop the appropriate initial competence and accommodate different styles of learning. If the student does not have the appropriate initial competence to achieve the objective through any of the alternative instructional activities, a remedial instructional activity is provided to develop the initial competence. If the student has developed the competence, an appropriate instructional activity is selected based on the nature of the initial competence. The student should repeat the selected instructional activity until achieving the objective or drop out. The last model allows students to achieve different types of instructional objectives or different levels of the same objective depending on their individual needs or ability. The basic process is the same as the fourth model, except that the student's achievement is considered successful if any of the alternative instructional objectives (e.g., different type or different level of the same objective) are achieved.

Glaser (1977) described six conditions necessary for instantiating adaptive instructional systems: (a) The human and mental resources of the school should be flexibly employed to assist in the adaptive process; (b) curricula should be designed to provide realistic sequencing and multiple options for learning; (c) open display and access to information and instructional materials should be provided; (d) testing and monitoring procedures should be designed to provide information to teachers and students for decision making; (e) emphasis should be placed on developing abilities in children that assist them in guiding their own teaming; and (f) the role of teachers and other school personnel should be the guidance of individual students. Glaser's conditions suggest that the development and implementation of an adaptive instructional program in an existing system are

complex and difficult. This might be the primary reason why most macro-adaptive instructional systems have not been used as successfully and widely as hoped. However, computer technology provides a powerful means to overcome at least some of the problems encountered in the planning and implementing of adaptive instructional systems.

25.4 APTITUDE–TREATMENT INTERACTION MODELS

Cronbach (1957) suggested that facilitating educational development in a wide range of students would require a wide range of environments suited to the optimal learning of the individual student. For example, instructional units covering available content elements in different sequences would be adapted to differences among students. Cronbach's strategy proposed prescribing one type of sequence (and even media) for a student of certain characteristics, and an entirely different form of instruction for another learner of differing characteristics. This strategy has been termed ATI. Cronbach and Snow (1977) defined aptitude as any individual characteristic that increases or impairs the student's probability of success in a given treatment and treatment as variations in the pace or style of instruction. Potential interactions are likely to reside in two main categories of aptitudes for learning (Snow & Swanson, 1992): cognitive aptitudes and conative and affective aptitudes. Cognitive aptitudes include (a) intellectual ability constructs consisting mostly of fluid analytic reasoning ability, visual spatial abilities, crystallized verbal abilities, mathematical abilities, memory space, and mental speed; (b) cognitive and learning styles; and (c) prior knowledge. Conative and affective aptitudes include (a) motivational constructs such as anxiety, achievement motivation, and interests and (b) volitional or action-control constructs such as self-efficacy.

To provide systematic guidelines in selecting instructional strategies for individually different students, Carrier and Jonassen (1988) proposed four types of matches based on Salomon's (1972) work: (a) remedial, for providing supplementary instruction to learners who are deficient in a particular aptitude or characteristic; (b) capitalization/preferential, for providing instruction in a manner that is consistent with a learner's preferred mode of perceiving or reasoning; (c) compensatory, for supplanting some processing requirements of the task for which the learner may have a deficiency; and (d) challenge, for stimulating learners to use and develop new modes of processing.

25.4.1 Aptitude Variables and Instructional Implications

To find linkages between different aptitude variables and learning, numerous studies have been conducted (see Cronbach & Snow, 1977; Gagné, 1967; Gallangher, 1994; Snow, 1986; Snow & Swanson, 1992; Tobias, 1989, 1994). Since the detailed review of ATI research findings is beyond the scope of this chapter, a few representative aptitude variables showing relatively important implications for adaptive instruction are briefly presented here.

25.4.1.1 Intellectual Ability.

General intellectual ability consisting of various types of cognitive abilities (e.g., crystallized intelligence such as verbal ability, fluid intelligence such as deductive and logical reasoning, and visual perception such as spatial relations) (see Snow, 1986) is suggested to have interaction effects with instructional supports. For example, more structured and less complex instruction (e.g., expository method) may be more beneficial for students with low intellectual ability, while less structured and more complex instruction (e.g., discovery method) may be better for students with high intellectual ability (Snow & Lohman, 1984). More specifically, Como and Snow (1986) suggested that crystallized ability may relate to, and benefit in interaction with, familiar and similar instructional methods and content, whereas fluid ability may relate to and benefit from learning under conditions of new or unusual methods or content.

25.4.1.2 Cognitive Styles.

Cognitive styles are characteristic modes of perceiving, remembering, thinking, problem solving, and decision making. They do not reflect competence (i.e., ability) per se but, rather, the utilization (i.e., style) of competence (Messick, 1994). Among many dimensions of cognitive style (e.g., field dependence versus field independence, reflectivity versus impulsivity, haptic versus visual, leveling versus sharpening, cognitive complexity versus simplicity, constricted versus flexible control, scanning, breadth of categorization, and tolerance of unrealistic experiences), field-dependent versus field-independent and impulsive versus reflective styles have been considered to be most useful in adapting instruction. The following are instructional implications of these two cognitive styles that have been considered in ATI studies.

Field-independent persons are more likely to be self-motivated and influenced by internal reinforcement and better at analyzing features and dimensions of information and for conceptually restructuring it. In contrast, field-dependent persons are more likely to be concerned with what others think and affected by external reinforcement and accepting of given information as it stands and more attracted to salient cues within a defined learning situation. These comparisons imply some ATI research. For example, studies showing significant interactions revealed that field-independent students achieved best with deductive instruction, and field-dependent students performed best in instruction based on examples (Davis, 1991; Messick, 1994).

Reflective persons are likely to take more time to examine problem situations and make fewer errors in their performance, to exhibit more anxiety over making mistakes on intellectual tasks, and to separate patterns into different features. In contrast, impulsive persons have a tendency to show greater concern about appearing incompetent due to slow responses and take less time examining problem situations and to view the stimulus or information as a single, global unit. As some of the instructional implications described above suggest, these two cognitive styles are not completely independent of each other (Vernon, 1973).

25.4.1.3 Learning Styles.

Efforts to match instructional presentation and materials with the student's preferences and needs have produced a number of learning styles (Schmeck, 1988). For example, Pask (1976, 1988) identified two learning styles: holists, who prefer a global task approach, a wide range of attention, reliance on analogies and illustrations, and construction of an overall concept before filling in details; and serialists, who prefer a linear task approach focusing on operational details and sequential procedures. Students who are flexible employ both strategies and are called versatile learners (Messick, 1994). Marton (1988) distinguished between students who are conclusion oriented and take a deep-processing approach to learning and students who are description oriented and take a shallow-processing approach. French (1975) identified seven perception styles (print oriented, aural, oral–interactive, visual, tactile, motor, and olfactory) and five concept formation approaches (sequential, logical, intuitive, spontaneous, and open). Dunn and Dunn (1978) classified learning stimuli into four categories (environmental, emotional, sociological, and physical) and identified several learning styles within each category. The student's preference in environmental stimuli can be quiet or loud sound, bright or dim illumination, cool or warm temperature, and formal or informal design. For emotional stimuli, students may be motivated by self, peer, or adult (parent or teacher), more or less persistent, and more or less responsible. For sociological stimuli, students may prefer learning alone, with peers, with adults, or in a variety of ways. Preferences in physical stimuli can be auditory, visual, or tactile/kinesthetic. Kolb (1971, 1977) identified four learning styles and a desirable learning experience for each style: (a) Feeling or enthusiastic students may benefit more from concrete experiences, (b) watching or imaginative students prefer reflective observations, (c) thinking or logical students are strong in abstract conceptualizations, and (d) doing or practical students like active experimentation. Hagberg and Leider (1978) also developed a model for identifying learning styles, which is similar to Kolb's.

Each of the learning styles reviewed provides some practical implications for designing adaptive instruction. However, there is not yet sufficient empirical evidence to support the value of learning styles or a reliable method for measuring the different learning styles.

25.4.1.4 Prior Knowledge.

Glaser and Nitko (1971) suggested that the behaviors that need to be measured in adaptive instruction are those that are predictive of immediate learning success with a particular instructional technique. Because prior achievement measures relate directly to the instructional task, they should therefore provide a more valid and reliable basis for determining adaptations than other aptitude variables.

The value of prior knowledge in predicting the student's achievement and needs of instructional supports has been demonstrated in many studies (e.g., Ross & Morrison, 1988). Research findings have shown that the higher the level of prior achievement, the less the instructional support required to accomplish the given task (e.g., Abramson & Kagen, 1975; Salomon, 1974; Tobias, 1973; Tobias & Federico, 1984; Tobias & Ingber, 1976). Furthermore, prior knowledge has a substantial linear relationship with interest in the subject (Tobias, 1994).

25.4.1.5 Anxiety. Many studies have shown that students with high test anxiety performed poorly on tests in comparison to students with low test anxiety (see Sieber, O'Neil, & Tobias, 1977; Tobias, 1987). Since research findings suggest that high anxiety interferes with the cognitive processes that control learning, procedures for reducing the anxiety level have been investigated. For example, Deutsch and Tobias (1980) found that highly anxious students who had options to review study materials (e.g., videotaped lessons) during learning showed higher achievement than other highly anxious students who did not have the review option. Under an assumption that anxiety and study skills have complementary effects, Tobias (1987) proposed a research hypothesis in an ATI paradigm: "Test-anxious students with poor study skills would learn optimally from a program addressing both anxiety reduction and study skills training. On the other hand, test-anxious students with effective study skills would profit optimally from programs emphasizing anxiety reduction without the additional study skill training" (p. 223). However, more studies are needed to investigate specific procedures or methods for reducing anxiety before guidelines for adaptive instructional design can be made.

25.4.1.6 Achievement Motivation. Motivation is an associative network of affectively toned personality characteristics such as self-perceived competence, locus of control, and anxiety (McClelland, 1965). Thus, understanding and incorporating the interactive roles of motivation with cognitive process variables during instruction are important. However, little research evidence is available for understanding the interactions between the affective and the cognitive variables, particularly individual differences in the interactions.

Although motivation as the psychological determinant of learning achievement has been emphasized by many researchers, research evidence suggests that it has to be activated for each task (Weiner, 1990). According to Snow (1986), students achieve their optimal level of performance when they have an intermediate level of motivation to achieve success and to avoid failure. Lin and McKeachie (1999) suggested that intrinsically motivated students engage in the task more intensively and show better performance than extrinsically motivated students. However, some studies showed opposite results (e.g., Frase, Patrick, & Schumer, 1970). The contradictory findings suggest possible interaction effects of different types of motivation with different students. For example, the intrinsic motivation may be more effective for students who are strongly goal oriented, like adult learners, while extrinsic motivation may be better for students who study because they have to, like many young children.

Entwistle's (1981) classification of student-motivation orientation provides more hints for adapting instruction to the student's motivation state. He identified three types of students based on motivation orientation styles: (a) meaning-oriented students, who are internally motivated by academic interest; (b) reproducing-oriented students, who are extrinsically motivated by fear of failure; and (c) achieving-oriented students, who are motivated primarily by hope for success. Meaning-oriented students are more likely to adopt a holist learning strategy that requires deep cognitive processing, whereas reproduction-

oriented students tend to adopt a serialist strategy that requires relatively shallow cognitive processing (Schmeck, 1988). Achieving-oriented students are likely to adopt either type of learning strategy depending on the given learning content and situation. However, the specific roles of motivation in learning have not been well understood, particularly in relation to the interactions with the student's other characteristics, task, and learning conditions. Without understanding the interactions between motivation and other variables, including instructional strategies, simply adapting instruction to the student's motivation may not be useful.

Tobias (1994) examined student interest in a specific subject and its relations with prior knowledge and learning. Interest, however, is not clearly distinguishable from motivation because interest seems to originate or stimulate intrinsic motivation, and external motivators (e.g., reward) may stimulate interest. Nevertheless, Keller and his associates (Astleitner & Keller, 1995) developed a framework for adapting instruction to the learner's motivational state in computer-assisted instructional environments. They proposed a six-level motivational adaptability from fixed feedback that provides the same instruction to all students regardless of the differences in their motivational states to adaptive feedback that provides different instructional treatments based on the individual learner's motivational state represented in the computer-based instructional process.

25.4.1.7 Self-Efficacy. Self-efficacy influences people's intellectual and social behaviors, including academic achievement (Bandura, 1982). Because self-efficacy is a student's evaluation of his or her own ability to perform a given task, the student may maintain widely varying senses of self-efficacy, depending on the context (Gallangher, 1994). According to Schunk (1991), self-efficacy changes with experiences of success or failure in certain tasks. A study by Hoge, Smith, and Hanson (1990) showed that feedback from teachers and grades received in specific subjects were important factors for the student's academic self-efficacy. Although many positive aspects of high self-esteem have been discussed, few studies have been conducted to investigate the instructional effect of self-efficacy in the ATI paradigm. Zimmerman and Martinez-Pons (1990) suggested that students with high verbal and mathematical self-efficacy used more self-regulatory and metacognitive strategies in learning the subject. Although it is clear that self-regulatory and metacognitive learning strategies have a positive relationship with students' achievement, this study seems to suggest that the intellectual ability is a more primary factor than self-esteem in the selection of learning strategies. More research is needed to find factors contributing to the formation of self-esteem, relationships between self-efficacy and other motivational and cognitive variables influencing learning processes, and strategies for modifying self-efficacy. Before studying these questions, investigating specific instructional strategies for low and high self-efficacy students in an ATI paradigm may not be fruitful.

In addition to the variables just discussed, many other individual difference variables (e.g., locus of control, cognitive development stages, cerebral activities and topological localization of brain hemisphere, and personality variables) have been studied in relation to learning and instruction. Few studies, however,

TABLE 25.1. A Taxonomy of Instructional Strategies
(Park, 1983; Seidel et al., 1989)

Preinstructional Strategies

1. Instructional objective
   Terminal objectives and enabling objectives
   Cognitive objectives vs. behavioral objectives
   Performance criterion and condition specifications
2. Advance organizer
   Expository organizer vs. comparative organizer
   Verbal organizer vs. pictorial organizer
3. Overview
   Narrative overview
   Topic listing
   Orienting questions
4. Pretest
   Types of test (e.g., objective—true–false, multiple-choice,
      matching—vs. subjective—short answer, essay)
   Order of test item presentation (e.g., random, sequence,
      response sensitive)
   Item replacement (e.g., with or without replacement of presented
      items)
   Timing (e.g., limited vs. unlimited)
   Reference (e.g., criterion-reference vs. norm-reference)

Knowledge Presentation Strategies

1. Types of knowledge presentation
   Generality (e.g., definition, rules, principles)
   Instance: diversity and complexity (e.g., example and nonexample
      problems)
   Generality help (e.g., analytical explanation of generality)
   Instance help (e.g., analytical explanation of instance)
2. Formats of knowledge presentation
   Enactive, concrete physical representation
   Iconic, pictorial/graphic representation
   Symbolic, abstract verbal, or notational representation
3. Forms of knowledge presentation
   Expository, statement form
   Interrogatory, question form
4. Techniques for facilitating knowledge acquisition
   Mnemonic
   Metaphors and analogies
   Attribute isolations (e.g., coloring, underlining)
   Verbal articulation
   Observation and emulation

Interaction Strategies

1. Questions
   Level of questions (e.g., understanding/idea vs. factual
      information)
   Time of questioning (e.g., before or after instruction)
   Response mode required (e.g., selective vs. constructive; overt vs.
      covert)
2. Hints and prompts
   Formal, thematic, algorithmic, etc.
   Scaffolding (e.g., gradual withdraw of instructor supports)
   Reminder and refreshment
3. Feedback
   Amount of information (e.g., knowledge of results, analytical
      explanation, algorithmic feedback, reflective comparison)
   Time of feedback (e.g., immediate vs. delayed feedback)
   Type of feedback (e.g., cognitive/informative feedback vs.
      psychological reinforcing)

Instructional Control Strategies

1. Sequence
   Linear`
   Branching
   Response sensitive
   Response sensitive plus aptitude matched
2. Control options
   Program control
   Learner control
   Learner control with advice
   Condition-dependent mixed control

Postinstructional Strategies

1. Summary
   Narrative review
   Topic listing
   Review questions
2. Postorganizer
   Conceptual mapping
   Synthesizing
3. Posttest
   Types of test (e.g., objective—true–false, multiple choice,
      matching—vs. subjective—short answer, essay)
   Order of test item presentation (e.g., random, sequence,
      response sensitive)
   Item replacement (e.g., with or without replacement of presented
      items)
   Timing (e.g., limited vs. unlimited)
   Reference (e.g., criterion reference vs. norm reference

Note. This listing of instructional strategies is not exhaustive and the classifications are arbitrary. From *Instructional Strategies: A Hypothetical Taxonomy* (Technical Report No. 3), by O. Park, 1983, Minneapolis, MN: Control Data Corp. Adapted with permission.

have provided feasible suggestions for adapting instruction to individual differences in these variables.

25.4.2 A Taxonomy of Instructional Strategies

Although numerous teaming and instructional strategies have been studied (e.g., O'Neil, 1978; Weinstein, Goetz & Alexander, 1988), selecting a specific strategy for a given instructional situation is difficult because its effect may be different for different instructional contexts. It is particularly true for adaptive instruction. Thus, instructional strategies should be selected and designed with the consideration of many variables uniquely involved in a given context. To provide a general guideline for selecting instructional strategies, Jonassen (1988) proposed a taxonomy of instructional strategies corresponding to different processes of cognitive learning. After identifying four stages of the learning process (recall, integration, organization, and elaboration) and related learning strategies for each stage, he identified specific instructional activities for facilitating the learning process. Also, he identified different strategies for monitoring different types of cognitive operations (i.e., planning, attending, encoding, reviewing, and evaluating).

Park (1983) also proposed a taxonomy of instructional strategies (Table 25.1) for different instructional stages or activities (i.e., preinstructional strategies, knowledge presentation strategies, interaction strategies, instructional control strategies, and postinstructional strategies). However, these taxonomies are identified from the author's subjective analysis of learning and instructional processes and do not provide direct or indirect suggestions for selecting instructional strategies in ATI research or adaptive instructional development.

25.4.3 Limitations of Aptitude Treatment Interactions

In the three decades since Cronbach (1957) made his proposal, relatively few studies have found consistent results to support the paradigm or made a notable contribution to either instructional theory or practice. As several reviews of ATI research (Berliner & Cohen, 1983; Cronbach & Snow, 1977; Tobias, 1976) have pointed out, the measures of intellectual abilities and other aptitude variables were used in a large number of studies to investigate their interactions with a variety of instructional treatments. However, no convincing evidence was found to suggest that such individual differences were useful variables for differentiating alternative treatments for subjects in a homogeneous age group, although it was believed that the individual difference measures were correlated substantially with achievement in most school-related tasks (Glaser & Resnick, 1972; Tobias, 1987).

The unsatisfactory results of ATI research have prompted researchers to reexamine the paradigm and assess its effectiveness. A number of difficulties in the ATI approach are viewed by Tobias (1976, 1987, 1989) as a function of past reliance on what he terms the alternative abilities concept. Under this concept, it is assumed that instruction is divided into input, processing, and output variables. The instruction methods, which form the input of the model, are hypothesized to interact with different psychological abilities (processing variables), resulting in certain levels of performance (or outcomes) on criterion tests. According to Tobias, however, several serious limitations of the model often prevent the occurrence of the hypothesized relations, as follows.

1. The abilities assumed to be most effective for a particular treatment may not be exclusive; consequently, one ability may be used as effectively as another ability for instruction by a certain method (see Cronbach & Snow, 1977).
2. Abilities required by a treatment may shift as the task progresses so that the ability becomes more or less important for one unit (or lesson) than for another (see Burns, 1980; Federico, 1983).
3. ATIs validated for a particular task and subject area may not be generalizable to other areas. Research has suggested that ATIs may well be highly specific and vary for different kinds of content (see Peterson, 1977; Peterson & Janicki, 1979; Peterson, Janicki, & Swing, 1981).
4. ATIs validated in laboratory experiments may not be applicable to actual classroom situations.

Another criticism is that ATI research has tended to be overly concerned with exploration of simple input/output relations between measured traits and learning outcomes. According to this criticism, a thorough understanding of the psychological process in learning a specific task is a prerequisite to the development theory on the ATIs (DiVesta, 1975). Since individual difference variables are difficult to measure, the test validity can also be a problem in attempting to adapt instruction to general student characteristics.

25.4.4 Achievement–Treatment Interactions

To reduce some of the difficulties in the ATI approach, Tobias (1976) proposed an alternative model, achievement–treatment interactions. Whereas the ATI approach stresses relatively permanent dispositions for learning as assessed by measures of aptitudes (e.g., intelligence, personality, and cognitive styles), achievement–treatment interactions represent a distinctly different orientation, emphasizing task-specific variables relating to prior achievement and subject-matter familiarity. This approach stresses the need to consider interactions between prior achievement and performance on the instructional task to be learned. Prior achievement can be assessed rather easily and conveniently through administration of pretests or through analysis of students' previous performance on related tasks. Thus, it eliminates many potential sources of measurement error, which has been a problem in ATI research, since the type of abilities to be assessed would be, for the most part, clear and unambiguous.

Many studies (e.g., see Tobias 1973, 1976; Tobias & Federico, 1984) confirmed the hypothesis that the lower the level of prior achievement is, the more the instructional support is required to accomplish the given task, and vice versa. However, a major problem in the ATI approach, that learner abilities and characteristics fluctuate during instruction, is still unsolved in the achievement–treatment interaction. The treatments investigated in the studies of this approach were not generated by systematic analysis of the kind of psychological processes called on in particular instructional methods, and individual differences were not assessed in terms of these processes (Glaser, 1972). In addition to the inability to accommodate shifts in the psychological processes active during or required by a given task, the achievement–treatment interaction has another problem: In this model, some useful information may be lost by discounting possible contribution of factors such as intellectual ability, cognitive style, anxiety, and motivation.

25.4.5 Cognitive Processes and ATI Research

The limitation of aptitudes measured prior to instruction in predicting the student's learning needs suggests that the cognitive processes intrinsic to learning should be paramount considerations in adapting instructional techniques to individual differences. However, psychological testing developed to measure and classify people according to abilities and aptitudes has neglected to identify the internal processes that underlie such classifications (Federico, 1980).

According to Tobias (1982, 1987), learning involves two types of cognitive processes: (a) macroprocesses, which are relatively molar processes, such as mental tactics (Derry & Murphy, 1986), and are deployed under the student's volitional control; and (b) microprocesses, which are relatively molecular processes, such as the manipulation of information in short-term memory, and are less readily altered by students. Tobias (1989) assumed that unless the instructional methods examined in ATI research induce students with different aptitudes to use different types of macroprocesses, the expected interactions would not occur. To validate this assumption, Tobias (1987, 1989) conducted a series of experiments in rereading comprehension using computer-based instruction (CBI). In the experiments, students were given various options to employ different macroprocesses through the presentation of different instructional activities (e.g., adjunct questions, feedback, various review requirements, instructions to think of the adjunct question while reviewing, and rereading with external support). In summarizing the findings from the experiments, Tobias (1989) concluded that varying instructional methods does not lead to the use of different macrocognitive processes or to changes in the frequency with which different processes are used. Also, the findings showed little evidence that voluntary use of macrocognitive processes is meaningfully related to student characteristics such as anxiety, domain-specific knowledge, and reading ability. Although some of these findings are not consistent with previous studies that showed a high correlation between prior knowledge and the outcome of learning, they explain the reasons for the inconsistent findings in ATI research.

Based on the results of the experiments and the review of relevant studies, Tobias (1989) suggested that researchers should not assume student use of cognitive processes, no matter how clearly these appear to be required or stimulated by the instructional method. Instead, some students should be trained or at least prompted to use the cognitive processes expected to be evoked by instructional methods, whereas such intervention should be omitted for others (p. 220). This suggestion requires a new paradigm for ATI research that specifies not only student characteristics and alternative instructional methods for teaching students with different characteristics but also strategies for prompting the student to use the cognitive processes required in the instructional methods. This suggestion, however, would make ATI research more complex without being able to produce consistent findings. For example, if an experiment did not produce the expected interaction, it would be virtually impossible to find out whether the result came from the ineffectiveness of the instructional method or the failure of the prompting strategy to use the instructional method.

25.4.6 Learner Control

An alternative approach to adaptive instruction is learner control, which gives learners full or partial control over the process or style of instruction they receive (Snow, 1980). Individual students are different in their abilities for assessing the learning requirements of a given task, their own learning abilities, and instructional options available to learn the given task. Therefore, it can be considered within the ATI framework, although the decision-making authority required for the learning assessment and instructional prescription is changed to the student from the instructional agent (human teacher or media-based tutor).

Snow (1980) divided the degree of learner control into three levels depending on the imposed and elected educational goals and treatments: (a) complete independence, self-direction, and self-evaluation; (b) imposed tasks, but with learner control of sequence, scheduling, and pace of learning; and (c) fixed tasks, with learner control of pace. Numerous studies have been conducted to test the instructional effects of learner control and specific instructional strategies that can be effectively used in learner-control environments. The results have provided some important implications for developing adaptive systems: Individual differences play an important role in the success of learner control strategy, some learning activities performed during the instruction are closely related to the effectiveness of learner control, and the learning activities and effects of learner control can be predicted from the premeasured aptitude variables (Snow, 1980). For example, a study by Shin, Schallert, and Savenye (1994) showed that limited learner control and advisement during instruction were more effective for low-prior knowledge students, while high-prior knowledge students did equally well in both full and limited learner-control environments with or without advisement. These results suggest that learner control should be considered both a dimension along which instructional treatments differ and a dimension characteristic of individual differences among learners (Snow, 1980). However, research findings in learner control are not consistent, and many questions remain to be answered in terms of the learner-control activities and metacognitive processes. For example, more research is needed in terms of learner-control strategies related to assessment of knowledge about the domain content, ability to learn, selection and processing of learning strategies, etc.

25.4.7 An Eight-Step Model for Designing ATI Courseware

As just reviewed, findings in ATI research suggest that it is premature or impossible to assign students with one set of characteristics to one instructional method and those with different characteristics to another (Tobias, 1987). However, faith in adaptive instruction using the ATI model is still alive because of the theoretical and practical implications of ATI research.

Despite the inconclusive research evidence and many unresolved issues in the ATI approach, Carrier and Jonassen (1988) proposed an eight-step model to provide practical guidance for applying the ATI model to the design of CBI courseware. The eight steps are as follows: (1) Identify objectives for the courseware, (2) specify task characteristics, (3) identify an initial pool of learner characteristics, (4) select the most relevant learner characteristics, (5) analyze learners in the target population, (6) select final differences (in the learner characteristics), (7) determine how to adapt instruction, and (8) design alternative treatments. This model is basically a modified systems approach to instructional development Dick & Carey, 1985. (Gagné & Briggs, 1979). This model proposes to identify specific learner characteristics of individual students for the given task, in addition to their general characteristics. For the use of this model, Carrier and Jonassen (1988) listed important individual variables that influence learning: (a) aptitude variables, including intelligence and academic achievement; (b) prior knowledge; (c) cognitive styles; and (d) personality variables, including intrinsic and extrinsic motivation, locus of control, and anxiety (see Carrier & Jonassen, 1988, P. 205). For instructional adaptation, they recommended several types of instructional matches: remedial, capitalization/preferential, compensatory, and challenge.

This model seemingly has practical value. Without theoretically coherent and empirically traceable matrices that link the different learner variables, the different types and levels of learning requirements in different tasks, and different instructional strategies, however, the mere application of this model may not produce results much different from those with nonadaptive instructional systems. ATI research findings suggest that varying instructional methods does not necessarily invoke different types or frequencies of cognitive processing required in learning the given task, nor are individual difference measures consistently related to such processing (Tobias, 1989). Furthermore, the application of Carrier and Jonassen's (1988) model in the development and implementation of courseware would be very difficult because of the amount of work required in identifying, measuring, and analyzing the appropriate learner characteristics and in developing alternative instructional strategies.

25.5 MICRO-ADAPTIVE INSTRUCTIONAL MODELS

Although the research evidence has failed to show the advantage of the ATI approach for the development of adaptive instructional systems, research to find aptitude constructs relevant to learning, learning and instructional strategies, and their interactions continues. However, the outlook is not optimistic for the development of a comprehensive ATI model or set of principles for developing adaptive instruction that is empirically traceable and theoretically coherent in the near-future. Thus, some researchers have attempted to establish micro-adaptive instructional models using on-task measures rather than pretask measures. On-task measures of student behavior and performance, such as response errors, response latencies, and emotional states, can be valuable sources for making adaptive instructional decisions during the instructional process. Such measures taken during the course of instruction can be applied to the manipulation and optimization of instructional treatments and sequences on a much more refined scale (Federico, 1983). Thus, micro-adaptive instructional models using on-task measures are likely to be more sensitive to the student's needs.

A typical example of micro-adaptive instruction is one-on-one tutoring. The tutor selects the most appropriate information to teach based on his or her judgment of the student's learning ability, including prior knowledge, intellectual ability, and motivation. Then the tutor continuously monitors and diagnoses the student's learning process and determines the next instructional actions. The instructional actions can be questions, feedback, explanations, or others that maximize the student's learning. Although the instructional effect of one-on-one tutoring has been fully recognized for a long time and empirically

proven (Bloom, 1984; Kulik, 1982), few systematic guidelines have been developed. That is, most tutoring activities are determined by the tutor's intuitive judgments about the student's learning needs and ability for the given task. Also, one-on-one tutoring is virtually impossible for most educational situations because of the lack of both qualified tutors and resources.

As the one-on-one tutorial process suggests, the essential element of micro-adaptive instruction is the ongoing diagnosis of the student's learning needs and the prescription of instructional treatments based on the diagnosis. Holland (1977) emphasized the importance of the diagnostic and prescriptive process by defining adaptive instruction as a set of processes by which individual differences in student needs are diagnosed in an attempt to present each student with only those teaching materials necessary to reach proficiency in the terminal objectives of instruction. Landa (1976) also said that adaptive instruction is the diagnostic and prescriptive processes aimed at adjusting the basic learning environment to the unique learning characteristics and needs of each learner. According to Rothen and Tennyson (1978), the diagnostic process should assess a variety of learner indices (e.g., aptitudes and prior achievement) and characteristics of the learning task (e.g., difficulty level, content structure, and conceptual attributes). Hansen, Ross, and Rakow (1977) described the instructional prescription as a corrective process that facilitates a more appropriate interaction between the individual learner and the targeted learning task by systematically adapting the allocation of learning resources to the learner's aptitudes and recent performance.

Instructional researchers or developers have different views about the variables, indices, procedures, and actions that should be included in the diagnostic and the prescriptive processes. For example, Atkinson (1976) says that an adaptive instructional system should have the capability of varying the sequence of instructional action as a function of a given learner's performance history. According to Rothen and Tennyson (1977), a strategy for selecting the optimal amount of instruction and time necessary to achieve a given objective is the essential ingredient in an adaptive instructional system. This observation suggests that different adaptive systems have been developed to adapt different features of instruction to learners in different ways.

Micro-adaptive instructional systems have been developed through a series of different attempts beginning with programmed instruction to the recent application of artificial intelligence (AI) methodology for the development of intelligent tutoring systems (ITSs).

25.5.1 Programmed Instruction

Skinner has generally been considered the pioneer of programmed instruction. However, three decades earlier than Skinner (1954, 1958), Pressey (1926) used a mechanical device to assess a student's achievement and to provide further instruction in the teaching process. The mechanical device, which used a keyboard, presented a series of multiple-choice questions and required the student to respond by pressing the appropriate key. If the student pressed the correct key to answer the question, the device would present the next question. However, if the student pressed a wrong key, the device would ask the student to choose another answer without advancing to the next question. Using Thorndike's (1913) "Law of Effect" as the theoretical base for the teaching methodology incorporated in his mechanical device, Pressey (1927) claimed that its purpose was to ensure mastery of a given instructional objective. If the student correctly answered two questions in succession, mastery was accomplished, and no additional questions were given. The device also recorded responses to determine whether the student needed more instruction (further questions) to master the objective. According to Pressey, this made use of a modified form of Thorndike's "law of exercise." Little's (1934) study demonstrated the effectiveness of Pressey's testing–drill device against a testing-only device.

Skinner (1954) criticized Pressey's work by stating that it was not based on a thorough understanding of learning behavior. However, Pressey's work contained some noticeable instructional principles. First, he brought the mastery learning concept into his programmed instructional device, although the determination of mastery was arbitrary and did not consider measurement or testing theory. Second, he considered the difficulty level of the instructional objectives, suggesting that more difficult objectives would need additional instructional items (questions) for the student to reach mastery. Finally, his procedure exhibited a diagnostic characteristic in that, although the criterion level was based on intuition, he determined from the student's responses whether or not more instruction was needed.

Using Pressey's (1926, 1927) basic idea, Skinner (1954, 1958) designed a teaching machine to arrange contingencies of reinforcement in school learning. The instructional program format used in the teaching machine had the following characteristics: (a) It was made up of small, relatively easy-to-learn steps; (b) the student had an active role in the instructional process; and (c) positive reinforcement was given immediately following each correct response. In particular, Skinner's (1968) linear programmed instruction emphasized an individually different learning rate. However, the programmed material itself was not individualized since all students received the same instructional sequence (Cohen, 1963). In 1959, Pressey criticized this nonadaptive nature of the Skinnerian programmed instruction.

The influx of technology influenced Crowder's (1959) procedure of intrinsic programming with provisions for branching able students through the same material more rapidly than slower students, who received remedial frames whenever a question was missed. Crowder's intrinsic program was based totally on the nature of the student's response. The response to a particular frame was used both to determine whether the student learned from the preceding material and to determine the material to be presented next. The student's response was thought to reflect his or her knowledge rate, and the program was designed to adapt to that rate. Having provided only a description of his intrinsic programming, however, Crowder revealed no underlying theory or empirical evidence that could support its effectiveness against other kinds of programmed instruction. Because of the difficulty in developing tasks that required review sections for each alternative answer, Crowder's procedure was not widely used in instructional situations (Merrill, 1971).

In 1957, Pask described a perceptual motor training device in which differences in task difficulty were considered for different learners. The instructional target was made progressively more difficult until the student made an error, at which point the device would make the target somewhat easier to detect. From that point, the level of difficulty would build again. Remediation consisted of a step backward on a difficulty dimension to provide the student with further practice on the task. Pask's (1960a, 1960b) Solartron Automatic Keyboard Instructor (SAKI) was capable of electronically measuring the student's performance and storing it in a diagnostic history that included response latency, error number, and pattern. On the basis of this diagnostic history, the machine prescribed the exercises to be presented next and varied the rate and amount of material to be presented in accordance with the proficiency. Lewis and Pask (1965) demonstrated the effectiveness of Pask's device by testing the hypothesis that adjusting difficulty level and amount of practice would be more effective than adjusting difficulty level alone. Though the application of the device was limited to instruction of perceptual motor tasks, Pask (1960a) described a general framework for the device that included instruction of conceptual as well as perceptual motor tasks.

As described, most early programmed instruction methods relied primarily on intuition of the school learning process rather than on a particular model or theory of learning, instruction, or measurement. Although some of the methods were designed on a theoretical basis (for example, Skinner's teaching machine), they were primitive in terms of the adaptation of the learning environment to the individual differences of students. However, programmed instruction did provide some important implications for the development of more sophisticated instructional strategies made possible by the advance in computer technology.

25.5.2 Microadaptive Instructional Models

Using computer technology, a number of microadaptive instructional models have been developed. An adaptive instructional model differs from programmed instruction techniques in that it is based on a particular model or theory of learning, and its adaptation of the learning environment is rather sophisticated, whereas the early programmed instruction was based primarily on intuition and its adaptation was primitive. Unlike macroadaptive models, the microadaptive model uses the temporal nature of learner abilities and characteristics as a major source of diagnostic information on which an instructional treatment is prescribed. Thus, an attribute of a microadaptive model is its dynamic nature as contrasted with a macroadaptive model. A typical microadaptive model includes more variables related to instruction than a macroadaptive model or programmed instruction. It thus provides a better control process than a macroadaptive model or programmed instruction in responding to the student's performance with reference to the type of content and behavior required in a learning task (Merrill & Boutwell, 1973).

As described by Suppes, Fletcher, and Zanottie (1976), most microadaptive models use a quantitative representation and trajectory methodology. The most important feature of a microadaptive model relates to the timeliness and accuracy with which it can determine and adjust learning prescriptions during instruction. A conventional instructional method identifies how the student answers but does not identify the reasoning process that leads the student to that answer. An adaptive model, however, relies on different processes that lead to given outcomes. Discrimination between the different processes is possible when on-task information is used. The importance of the adaptive model is not that the instruction can correct each mistake but that it attempts to identify the psychological cause of mistakes and thereby lower the probability that such mistakes will occur again.

Several examples of microadaptive models are described in the following section. Although some of these models are a few decades old, an attempt was made to provide a rather detailed review because the theoretical bases and technical (nonprogramming) procedures used in these models are still relevant and valuable in identifying research issues related to adaptive instruction and in designing future adaptive systems. Particularly, having considered that some theoretical issues and ideas proposed in these models could not be fully explored because of the lack of computer power at that time, the review may provide some valuable research and development agenda.

25.5.2.1 Mathematical Model. According to Atkinson (1972), an optimal instructional strategy must be derived from a model of learning. In mathematical learning theory, two general models describe the learning process: a linear (or incremental) model and an all-or-none (or one element) model. From these two models, Atkinson and Paulson (1972) deducted three strategies for prescribing the most effective instructional sequence for a few special subjects, such as foreign-language vocabulary (Atkinson, 1968, 1974, 1976; Atkinson & Fletcher, 1972).

In the linear model, learning is defined as the gradual reduction in probability of error by repeated presentations of the given instructional items. The strategy in this model orders the instructional materials without taking into account the student's responses or abilities, since it is assumed that all students learn with the same probability. Because the probability of student error on each item is determined in advance, prediction of his or her success depends only on the number of presentations of the items.

In the all-or-none model, learning an item is not all gradual but occurs on a single trial. An item is in one of two states, a learned state or an unlearned state. If an item in the learned state is presented, the correct response is always given; however, if an item in the unlearned state is presented, an incorrect response is given unless the student makes a correct response by guessing. The optimal strategy in this model is to select for presentation the item least likely to be in the learned state, because once an item has been learned, there is no further reason to present it again. If an item in the unlearned state is presented, it changes to the learned state with a probability that remains constant throughout the procedure. Unlike the strategy in the linear model, this strategy is response sensitive. A student's response protocol for a single item provides a good index of the likelihood of that item's being in the learned state (Groen & Atkinson, 1966). This response-sensitive strategy used a dynamic programming technique (Smallwood, 1962).

On the basis of Norman's (1964) work, Atkinson and Paulson (1972) proposed the random-trial incremental model, a compromise between the linear and the all-or-none models. The instructional strategy derived for this model is parameter dependent, allowing the parameters to vary with student abilities and item difficulty. This strategy determines which item, if presented, has the best expected immediate gain, using a reasonable approximation (Calfee, 1970). Atkinson and Crothers (1964) assumed that the all-or-none model provided a better account of data than the linear model and that the random-trial increments model was better than either of them. This assumption was supported by testing the effectiveness of the strategies (Atkinson, 1976).

The all-or-none strategy was more effective than the standard linear procedure for spelling instruction, while the parameter-dependent strategy was better than the all-or-none strategy for teaching foreign vocabularies (Lorton, 1972). In the context of instruction, cost–benefit analysis is one of the key elements in a description of the learning process and determination of instructional actions (Atkinson, 1972). In the mathematical adaptive strategies, however, it is assumed that the costs of instruction are equal for all strategies, because the instructional formats and the time allocated to instruction are all the same. If both costs and benefits are significantly variable in a problem, then it is essential that both quantities be estimated accurately. Smallwood (1970, 1971) treated this problem by including a utility function into the mathematical model. Smallwood's (1971) economic teaching strategy is a special form of the all-or-none model strategy, except that it can be applied for an instructional situation in which the instructional alternatives have different costs and benefits.

Townsend (1992) and Fisher and Townsend (1993) applied a mathematical model to the development of a computer simulation and testing system for predicting the probability and duration of student responses in the acquisition of Morse code classification skills. The mathematical adaptive model, however, has never been widely used, probably because the learning process in the model is oversimplified and the applicability is limited to a relatively simple range of instructional contents.

There are criticisms of the mathematical adaptive instructional models. First, the learning process in the mathematical model is oversimplified when implemented in a practical teaching system. Yet it may not be so simple to quantify the transition probability of a learning state and the response probabilities that are uniquely associated with the student's internal states of knowledge and with the particular alternatives for presentation (Glaser, 1976). Although quantitative knowledge about how the variables in the model interact can be obtained, reducing computer decision time has little overall importance if the system can handle only a limited range of instructional materials and objectives, such as foreign-language vocabulary items (Gregg, 1970). Also, the two-state or three-state or n-state model cannot be arbitrarily chosen because the values for transitional probabilities of a learning state can change depending on how one chooses to aggregate over states. The response probabilities may not be assumed to be equally likely in a multiple-choice test question. This kind of assumption would hold only for homogeneous materials and highly sophisticated preliminary item analyses (Gregg, 1970).

Another disadvantage of the mathematical adaptive model is that its estimates for the instructional diagnosis and prescription cannot be reliable until a significant amount of student and content data is accumulated. For example, the parameter-dependent strategy supposes to predict the performance of other students or the same student on other items from the estimates computed by the logistic equation. However, the first students in an instructional program employing this strategy do not benefit from the program's sensitivity to individual differences in students or items because the initial parameter estimates must be based on data from these students. Thus, the effectiveness of this strategy is questionable unless the instructional program continues over a long period of time.

Atkinson (1972) admitted that the mathematical adaptive models are very simple, and the identification of truly effective strategies will not be possible until the learning process is better understood. However, Atkinson (1972, 1976) contended that an all-inclusive theory of learning is not a prerequisite for the development of optimal procedures. Rather, a model is needed that captures the essential features of that part of the learning process being tapped by a given instructional task.

25.5.2.2 The Trajectory Model: Multiple Regression Analysis Approach.

In a typical adaptive instructional program, the diagnostic and prescriptive decisions are frequently made based on the estimated contribution of one or two particular variables. The possible contributions of other variables are ignored. In a trajectory model, however, numerous variables can be included with the use of a multiple regression technique to yield what may be a more powerful and precise predictive base than is obtained by considering a particular variable alone.

The theoretical view in the trajectory model is that the expected course of the adaptive instructional trajectory is determined primarily by generic or trait factors that define the student group. The actual proceeding of the trajectory is dependent on the specific effects of individual learner parameters and variables derived from the task situation (Suppes et al., 1976). Using this theoretical view, Hansen et al. (1977; Ross & Morrison, 1988; Ross & Rakow, 1982) developed an adaptive model that reflects both group and individual indexes and matches them to appropriate changes for both predictions on entry and adjustments during the treatment process. The model was developed to find an optimal strategy for selecting the appropriate number of examples in a mathematical rule-learning task.

Hansen et al. (1977) assessed their trajectory adaptive model with a validation study that supported the basic tenets of the model. A desirable number of groups (four) with differential characteristics was found, and the outcomes were as predicted: superior for the adaptive group, highly positive for the cluster group, and poor for the mismatched groups. The outcome of regression analysis revealed that the pretest yielded the largest amount of explained variance within the regression coefficient. The math reading comprehension measures seemed to contribute to the assignment of the broader skill domain involved in the learning task. However, the two personality measures varied in terms of directions as well as magnitude.

This regression model is apparently helpful in estimating the relative importance of different variables for instruction. However, it does not seem to be a very useful adaptive instructional strategy. Even though many variables can be included in the analysis process, the evaluation study results indicate that only one or two are needed in the instructional prescription process because of the inconsistent or negligible contribution of other variables to the instruction. Unless the number of students to be taught is large, this approach cannot be effective since the establishment of the predictive database in advance requires a considerable number of students, and this strategy cannot be applied to those students who make up the initial database. Furthermore, a new predictive database has to be established whenever the characteristics of the learning task are changed. Transforming the student's score, as predicted from the regression equation, into the necessary number of examples is not strongly justified when a quasi-standard score procedure is used. The decision rules for adjustment of instructional treatment during on-task performance as well as for the initial instructional prescription are entirely arbitrary. Since regression analyses are based on group characteristics, shrinkage of the degrees of freedom due to reduced sample size may raise questions about the value of this approach.

To offset the shortcoming of the regression model, that is limited to the adaptation of instructional amount (e.g., selection of the number of examples in concept or rule learning), Ross and Morrison (1988) attempted to expand its functional scope by adding the capability for selecting the appropriate instructional content based on the student's interest and other background information. This contextual adaptation was based on empirical research evidence that the personalized context based on an individual student's interest and orientation facilitates the student's understanding of the problem and learning of the solution. A field study demonstrated the effectiveness of the contextual adaptation (Ross & Anand, 1986). Ross and Morrison (1988) further extended their idea of contextual adaptation by allowing the system to select different densities (or "detailedness") of textual explanation based on the student's predicted learning needs. The predicted learning needs were estimated using a multiple regression model just described. An evaluation study showed the superior effect of the adaptation of contextual density over a standard contextual density condition or learner-control condition.

Ross and Morrison's approaches for contextual adaptation alone cannot be considered microadaptive systems because they do not have capability of performing ongoing diagnosis and prescription generation during the task performance. Their diagnostic and prescriptive decisions are made on the basis of preinstructional data. The contextual adaptation approach, however, can be a significant addition to a microadaptive model like the regression analysis approach that has a limited function for adapting the quality of instruction, including the content. Although we presume that the contextual adaptation approaches were originally developed with the intent to incorporate them in the regression analysis model, this has not yet been fully accomplished.

25.5.2.3 The Bayesian Probability Model. The Bayesian
probability model employs a two-step approach for adapting instruction to individual students. After the initial assignment of
the instructional treatment is made on the basis of preinstructional measures (e.g., pretest scores), the treatment prescription
is continuously adjusted according to student on-task performance data. To operationalize this approach in CBI, a Bayesian
statistical model was used. Baye's theorem of conditional probability seems appropriate for the development of an adaptive
instructional system because it can predict the probability of
mastery of the new learning task from student preinstructional
characteristics and then continuously update the probability according to the on-task performance data (Rothen & Tennyson,
1978; Tennyson & Christensen, 1988). Accordingly, the instructional treatment is selected and adjusted.

The functional operation of this model is related to guidelines described by Novick and Lewis (1974) for determining
the minimal length of a test adequate to provide sufficient information about the learner's degree of mastery of behavior being
tested. Novick and Lewis procedure uses a pretest on a set of
objectives. From this pretest, the initial prior estimate of a student's ability per objective is combined in a Bayesian manner
with information accumulated from previous students to generate a posterior estimate of the student's probability of mastery
of each objective. This procedure generates a table of values for
different test lengths for the objectives and selects the number
of test items from this table that seems adequate to predict mastery of each objective. Rothen and Tennyson (1978) modified
Novick and Lewis (1974) model in such a way that a definite rule
or algorithm selects an instructional prescription from the table
of generated values. In addition, this prescription is updated
according to individual student's on-task learning performance.

Studies by Tennyson and his associates (see Tennyson
& Christensen, 1988) demonstrated the effectiveness of the
Bayesian probabilistic adaptive model in selecting the appropriate number of examples in concept learning. Posttest scores
showed that the adaptive group was significantly better than
the nonadaptive groups. Particularly, students in the adaptive
group required significantly less learning time than students in
the nonadaptive groups. This model was also effective in selecting the appropriate amount of instructional time for each
student based on his or her on-task performance (Tennyson &
S. Park, 1984; Tennyson, Park, & Christensen, 1985).

If the instructional system uses mastery learning as its primary goal and adjustment of the instructional treatment is critical for learning, this model may be ideal. Another advantage
of this model is that no assumption regarding the instructional
item homogeneity (in content or difficulty) is needed. A questionable aspect of the model, however, is whether or not variables other than prior achievement and on-task performance can
be effectively incorporated. Another difficulty of this model is
how to make a prior distribution from the pretest score and historical information collected from previous students. Although
Hambleton and Novick (1973) suggested the possibility of using
the student's performance level on other referral tasks for the
historical data, until enough historical data are accumulated, this
model cannot be utilized. Also, the application of this model is
limited to rather simple tasks such as concept and rule learning.

Park and Tennyson (1980, 1986) extended the function of
the Bayesian model by incorporating a sequencing strategy in
the model. Park and Tennyson (1980) developed a responsive-
sensitive strategy for selecting the presentation order of examples in concept learning from the analysis of cognitive learning requirements in concept learning (Tennyson & Park, 1982).
Studies by Park and Tennyson (1980, 1986) and Tennyson, Park,
and Christensen (1985) showed that the response-sensitive sequence not only was more effective than the non-response-
sensitive strategy but also reduced the necessary number of
examples that the Bayesian model predicted for the student.
Also, Park and Tennyson's studies found that the value of the
pretask information decreases as the instruction progresses. In
contrast, the contribution of the on-task performance data to
the model's prediction increases as the instruction progresses.

25.5.2.4 The Structural and Algorithmic Approach. The
optimization of instruction in Scandura's (1973, 1977a, 1977b,
1983) structural learning theory consists of finding optimal
trade-offs between the sum of the values of the objectives
achieved and the total time required for instruction. Optimization will involve balancing gains against costs (a form of
cost–benefit analysis). This notion is conceptually similar to
Atkinson's (1976) and Atkinson and Paulson's (1972) cost–
benefit dimension of instructional theory, Smallwood's (1971)
economic teaching strategy, and Chant and Atkinson's (1973)
optimal allocation of instructional efforts. In structural learning
theory, structural analysis of content is especially important as
a means of finding optimal trade-offs. According to Scandura
(1977a, 1977b), the competence underlying a given task domain is represented in terms of sets of processes, or rules for
problem solving. Analysis of content structure is a method for
identifying those processes.

Given a class of tasks, the structural analysis of content involves (a) sampling a wide variety of tasks, (b) identifying a set
of problem-solving rules for performing the tasks (such as an
ideal student in the target population might use), (c) identifying
parallels among the rules and devising higher-order rules that
reflect these parallels, (d) constructing more basic rule sets that
incorporate higher-order and other rules, (e) testing and refining the resulting rule set on new problems, and (f) extending
the rule set when necessary so that it accounts for both familiar
and novel tasks in the domain. This method may be reapplied
to the rule set obtained and repeated as many times as desired.
Each time the method is applied, the resulting rule set tends
to become more basic in two senses: First, the individual rules
become more simple; and second, the new rule set as a whole
has greater generating power for solving a wider variety of problems.

According to Scandura (1977a) and Wulfeck and Scandura
(1977), the instructional sequence determined by this algorithmic procedure is optimal. This algorithmically designed
sequence was superior to learner-controlled and random sequences in terms of the performance scores and the problem
solution time (Wulfeck & Scandura, 1977). Also, Scandura and
Dumin (1977) reported that a testing method based on the algorithmic sequence could assess the student's performance potential more accurately with fewer test items and less time than a

domain-reference generation procedure and a hierarchical item generation procedure. Since the algorithmic sequence is determined only by the structural characteristics of given problems and the prior knowledge of the target population (not individual students), the instructional process in structural learning theory is not adaptive to individual differences of the learner. Stressing the importance of individual differences in his structural learning theory, Scandura (1977a, 1977b, 1983) states that what is learned at each stage depends on both what is presented to the learner and what the learner knows. Based on the algorithmic sequence in the structural learning theory, Scandura and his associates (Scandura & Scandura, 1988) developed a rule-based CBI system. However, there has been no combined study of algorithmic sequence and individual differences that might show how individual differences could be used to determine the algorithmic sequences.

Landa's (1976) structural psychodiagnostic method may be well combined with Scandura's algorithmic sequence strategy to adapt the sequential procedure to individual differences that would emerge as the student learns a given task using the predetermined algorithmic sequence. According to Landa (1976), the structural psychodiagnostic method can identify the specific defects in the student's psychological mechanisms of cognitive activity by isolating the attributes of the given learning task that define the required actions and then joining these attributes with the student's logical operations.

25.5.2.5 Other Microadaptive Models.

For the last two decades, some other micro-adaptive instructional systems have been developed to optimize the effectiveness or efficiency of instruction for individual students. For example, McCombs and McDaniel (1981) developed a two-step (macro and micro) adaptive system to accommodate the multivariate nature of learning characteristics and idiosyncratic learning processes in the ATI paradigm. They identified the important learning characteristics (e.g., reading/reasoning and memory ability, anxiety, and curiosity) from the results of multiple stepwise regression analyses of existing student performance data. To compensate for the student's deficiencies in the learning characteristics, they added a number of special-treatment components to the main track of instructional materials. For example, to assist low-ability students in reading comprehension or information-processing skills, schematic visual organizers were added. However, most systems like McComb and McDaniel's are not covered in this review because they do not have true on-task adaptive capability, which is the most important criterion for qualification as a microadaptive model. In addition, these systems are task dependent, and the applicability to other tasks is very limited, although the basic principles or ideas of the systems are plausible.

25.5.3 Treatment Variables in Microadaptive Models

As reviewed in the previous section, microadaptive models are developed primarily to adapt two instructional variables: the amount of content to be presented and the presentation sequence of the content. The Bayesian probabilistic model and the multiple regression model are designed to select the amount

of instruction needed to learn the given task. Park and Tennyson (1980, 1986) incorporated sequencing strategies in the Bayesian probability model, and Ross and his associates (Ross & Anand, 1986; Ross & Morrison, 1986) investigated strategies for selecting content in the multiple regression model. Although these efforts showed that other instructional strategies could be incorporated in the model, they did not change the primary instructional variables and the operational procedure of the model. The mathematical model and the structural/algorithmic approach are designed mainly to select the optimal sequence of instruction. According to the Bayesian model and the multiple regression approach, the appropriate amount of instruction is determined by individual learning differences (aptitudes, including prior knowledge) and the individual's specific learning needs (on-task requirements). In the mathematical model, the history of the student's response pattern determines the sequence of instruction. However, an important implication of the structural/algorithmic approach is that the sequence of instruction should be decided by the content structure of the learning task as well as the student's performance history.

The Bayesian model and the multiple regression model use both pretask and on-task information to prescribe the appropriate amount of instruction. Studies by Tennyson and his associates (Park & Tennyson, 1980; Tennyson & Rothen, 1977) and Hansen et al. (1977) demonstrated the relative importance of these variables in predicting the appropriate amount of instruction. Subjects who received the amount of instruction selected based on the pretask measures (e.g., prior achievement, aptitude related to the task) needed less time to complete the task and showed a higher performance level on the posttest than subjects who received the same amount of instruction regardless of individual differences. In addition, some studies (Hansen et al., 1977; Ross & Morrison, 1988) indicated that only prior achievement among pretask measures (e.g., anxiety, locus of control) provides consistent and reliable information for prescribing the amount of instruction. However, subjects who received the amount of instruction selected based on both pretask measures and on-task measures needed less time and scored higher on tests than subjects who received the amount of instruction based on only pretask measures. The results of the response-sensitive strategies studied by Park and Tennyson (1980, 1986) suggest that the predictive power of the pretask measures, including prior knowledge, decreases, whereas that of on-task measures increases as the instruction progresses.

As reviewed above, a common characteristic of microadaptive instructional models is response sensitivity. For response-sensitive instruction, the diagnostic and prescriptive processes attempt to change the student's internal state of knowledge about the content being presented. Therefore, the optimal presentation of an instructional stimulus should be determined on the basis of the student's response pattern. Response-sensitive instruction has a long history of development, from Crowder's (1959) simple branching program to Atkinson's mathematical model of adaptive instruction. Until the late 1960s, technology was not readily available to implement the response-sensitive diagnostic and prescriptive procedures as a general practice outside the experimental laboratory (Hall, 1977). Although the development of computer technology has made the implementation of this kind of adaptive procedures possible and allowed for further investigation of their instructional effects, as seen in the descriptions of microadaptive models, they have been limited mostly to simple tasks that can be easily analyzed for quantitative applications. However, the AI methodology has provided a powerful tool for overcoming the primary limitation of microadaptive instructional models, so the response-sensitive procedures can be utilized for more broad and complex domain areas.

25.5.4 Intelligent Tutoring Systems

Intelligent tutoring systems (ITSs) are adaptive instructional systems developed with the application of AI methods and techniques. ITSs are developed to resemble what actually occurs when student and teacher sit down one-on-one and attempt to teach and learn together (Shute & Psotka, 1995). As in any other instructional systems, ITSs have components representing the content to be taught; inherent teaching or instructional strategy, and mechanisms for understanding what the student does and does not know. In ITSs, these components are referred to as the problem-solving or expertise module, student-modeling module, and tutoring module. The expertise module evaluates the student's performance and generates instructional content during the instructional process. The student-modeling module assesses the student's current knowledge state and makes hypotheses about his or her conceptions and reasoning strategies employed to achieve the current state of knowledge. The tutorial module usually consists of a set of specifications for the selection of instructional materials the system should present and how and when they should be presented. AI methods for the representation of knowledge (e.g., production rules, semantic networks, and scripts frames) make it possible for the ITS to generate the knowledge to present the student based on his or her performance on the task rather than selecting the presentation according to the predetermined branching rules. Methods and techniques for natural language dialogues allow much more flexible interactions between the system and the student. The function for making inferences about the cause of the student's misconceptions and learning needs allows the ITS to make qualitative decisions about the learning diagnosis and instructional prescription, unlike the microadaptive model, in which the decision is based entirely on quantitative data.

Furthermore, ITS techniques provide a powerful tool for effectively capturing human learning and teaching processes. It has apparently contributed to a better understanding of cognitive processes involved in learning specific skills and knowledge. Some ITSs have not only demonstrated their effects for teaching specific domain contents but also provided research environments for investigating specific instructional strategies and tools for modeling human tutors and simulating human learning and cognition (Ritter & Koedinger, 1996; Seidel & Park, 1994). Recently, ITS technology has expanded to support metacognition (Aleven, Popescu, & Koedinger, 2001; White, Shimoda, & Frederiksen, 1999). Geometry Explanation Tutor is an example of an ITS supporting metacognition processes through dialogue. This system helps students learn through self-explanation by analyzing student explanations of problem-solving steps, recognizing the type of omissions, and providing feedback. This kind of new pedagogical approach in ITSs is discussed more later.

However, there are criticisms that ITS developers have failed to incorporate many valuable learning principles and instructional strategies developed by instructional researchers and educators (Park, Perez, & Seidel, 1987). Cooperative efforts among experts in different domains, including learning/instruction and AI, are required to develop more powerful adaptive systems using ITS methods and techniques (Park & Seidel, 1989; Seidel, Park, & Perez, 1989). Theoretical issues about how to learn and teach with emerging technology, including AI, remain the most challenging problems.

25.5.5 Adaptive Hypermedia and Adaptive Web-Based Instruction

In the early 1990s, adaptive hypermedia systems inspired by ITSs were born (Beaumont, 1994; Brusilovsky, Schwarz, & Weber, 1996; Fischer, Mastaglio, Reeves, & Rieman, 1990; Gonschorek & Herzog, 1995; Kay & Kummerfeld, 1994; Pérez, Gutiérrez, & Lopistéguy, 1995). They fostered a new area of research combining adaptive instructional systems and hypermedia-based systems. Hypermedia-based systems allow learners to make their own path in learning. However, conventional hypermedia learning environments are a nonadaptive learning medium, independent from the individual user's responses or actions. They provide the same page content and the same set of links to all learners (Brusilovsky, 2000, 2001; Brusilovsky & Pesin, 1998). Also, learners choose the next task, which often leads them down a suboptimal path (Steinberg, 1991). These kinds of traditional hypermedia systems have been described as "user-neutral" because they do not consider the characteristics of the individual user (Brusilovsky & Vassileva, 1996). Duchastel (1992) criticized them as a nonpedagogical technology. Researchers tried to build adaptive and user model-based interfaces into hypermedia systems and thus developed adaptive hypermedia systems (Eklund & Sinclair, 2000). The goal of adaptive hypermedia is to improve the usability of hypermedia through the automatic adaptation of hypermedia applications to individual users (De Bra, 2000). For example, a student in an adaptive educational hypermedia system is given a presentation that is adapted specifically to his or her knowledge of the subject (De Bra & Calvi, 1998) and a suggested set of the most relevant links to pursue (Brusilovsky, Eklund, & Schwarz, 1998) rather than all users receiving the same information and same set of links. An adaptive electronic encyclopedia can trace user knowledge about different areas and provide personalized content (Milosavljevic, 1997). A virtual museum provides adaptive guided tours in the hyperspace (Oberlander, O'Donnell, Mellish, & Knott, 1998).

While most adaptive systems reviewed in the previous sections could not be developed without programming skills and were implemented in the laboratory settings, recent authoring tools allow nonprogrammers to develop adaptive hypermedia or adaptive Web-based instruction and implement it in real instructional settings. Adaptive hypermedia or adaptive Web-based systems have been employed for educational systems, e-commerce applications such as adaptive performance support systems, on-line information systems such as electronic encyclopedias and information kiosks, and on-line help systems.

Since 1996, the field of adaptive hypermedia has grown rapidly (Brusilovsky, 2001), due in large part to the advent and rapid growth of the Web. The Web had a clear demand for adaptivity due to the great variety of users and served as a strong booster for this research area (Brusilovsky, 2000). The first International Conference on Adaptive Hypermedia and Adaptive Web-Based Systems was held in Trento, Italy, in 2000 and developed into a series of regular conferences. Adaptive hypermedia and adaptive Web-based system research teams aim (a) to integrate information from heterogeneous sources into a unified interface, (b) to provide a filtering mechanism so that users see and interact with a view that is customized to their needs, (c) to deliver this information through a Web interface, and (d) to support the automatic creation and validation of links between related items to help with ongoing maintenance of the application (Gates, Lawhead, & Wilkins, 1998).

Because of its popularity and accessibility, the Web has become the choice of most adaptive educational hypermedia systems since 1996. Liberman's (1995) Letizia is one example of the earliest adaptive Web-based systems. Letizia is the system that assists users in web browsing by recommending links based on their previous browsing behaviors. Other early examples are ELM-ART (Brusilovsky, Schwarz, & Weber, 1996), InterBook (Brusilovsky, Eklund, & Schwarz, 1998), PT (Kay & Kummerfeld, 1994), and 2L670 (De Bra, 1996). These early systems have influenced more recent systems such as Medtech (Eliot, Neiman, & Lamar, 1997), AST (Specht, Weber, Heitmeyer, & Schöch, 1997), ADI (Schöch, Specht, & Weber, 1998), HysM (Kayama & Okamoto 1998), AHM (Pilar da Silva, Durm, Duval, & Olivié, 1998), MetaLinks (Murray, Condit, & Haugsjaa,1998), CHEOPS (Negro, Scarano & Simari, 1998), RATH (Hockemeyer, Held, & Albert, 1998), TANGOW (Carro, Pulido, & Rodrígues, 1999), Arthur (Gilbert & Han, 1999), CAMELEON (Laroussi & Benahmed, 1998), KBS-Hyperbook (Henze, Naceur, Nejdl, & Wolpers 1999), AHA! (De Bra & Calvi, 1998), SKILL (Neumann & Zirvas, 1998), Multibook (Steinacker, Seeberg, Rechenberger, Fischer, & Steinmetz,1998), ACE (Specht & Oppermann, 1998), and ADAPTS (Brusilovsky & Cooper, 2002).

25.5.5.1 Definition and Adaptation Methods.

In a discussion at the 1997 Adaptive Hypertext and Hypermedia Discussion forum (from Eklund & Sinclair, 2000), adaptive hypermedia systems were defined as "all hypertext and hypermedia systems which reflect some features of the user in the user model and apply this model to adapt various visible and functional aspects of the system to the user." *Functional aspects* means those components of a system that may not visibly change in an adaptive system. For example, the "next" button will not change in appearance but it will take different users to different pages (Schwarz, Brusilovsky, & Weber, 1996). An adaptive hypermedia system should (a) be based on hypertext link principles (Park, 1983), (b) have a domain model, and (c) be capable of

modifying some visible or functional part of the sytem on the basis of information contained in the user model (Eklund & Sinclair 2000).

Adaptive hypermedia methods apply mainly to two distinctive areas of adaptation: adaptation of the content of the page, which is called content-level adaptation or adaptive presentation; and the behavior of the links, which is called link-level adaptation or adaptive navigation support.

The goal of adaptive presentation is to adapt the content of a hypermedia page to the learner's goals, knowledge, and other information stored in the user model (Brusilovsky, 2000). The techniques of adaptive presentation are (a) connecting new content to the existing knowledge of the students by providing comparative explanation and (b) presenting different variants for different levels of learners (De Bra, 2000).

The goal of adaptive navigation support is to help learners find their optimal paths in hyperspace by adapting the link presentation and functionality to the goals, knowledge, and other characteristics of individual learners (Brusilovsky, 2000). It is influenced by research on curriculum sequencing, which is one of the oldest methods for adaptive instruction (Brusilovsky, 2000; Brusilovsky & Pesin, 1998). Direct guidance, adaptive sorting, adaptive annotation, and link hiding, disabling, and removal are ways to provide adaptive links to individual learners (De Bra, 2000). ELM-ART is an example of direct guidance. It generates an additional dynamic link (called "next") connected to the next most relevant node to visit. However, a problem with direct guidance is the lack of user control. An example of the hiding-link technique is HYPERTUTOR. If a page is considered irrelevant because it is not related to the user's current goal (Brusilovsky & Pesin, 1994; Vassileva & Wasson, 1996) or presents material that the user is not yet prepared to understand (Brusilovsky & Pesin, 1994; Pérez et al., 1995), the system restricts the navigation space by hiding links. The advantage of hiding links is to protect users from the complexity of the unrestricted hyperspace and reduce their cognitive load in navigation. Adaptive annotation technology adds links with a comment that provides information about the current state of the nodes (Eklund & Sinclair, 2000). The goal of the annotation is to provide orientation and guidance. Annotation links can be provided in textural form or in the form of visual cues, for example, using different icons, colors, font sizes, or fonts (Eklund & Sinclair, 2000). Also, this user-dependent adaptive hypermedia system provides different users with different annotations. The method has been shown to be especially efficient in hypermedia-based adaptive instruction. (Brusilovsky & Pesin, 1995; Eklund & Brusilovsky, 1998). InterBook, ELM-ART, and AHM are examples of adaptive hypermedia systems applying the annotation technique. To provide links, annotation systems measure the user's knowledge in three main ways: (a) according to where the user has been (history based); (b) according to where the user has been and how those places are related (prerequisite based); and (c) according to a measure of what the user has shown to have understood (knowledge based) (Eklund & Sinclair, 2000).

Brusilovsky (2000) stated that "adaptive navigation support is an interface that can integrate the power of machine and human intelligence: a user is free to make a choice while still seeing an opinion of an intelligent system" (p. 3). In other words, adaptive navigational support has the ability to decide what to present to the user, and at the same time, the user has choices to make.

25.5.5.2 User Modeling in Adaptive Hypermedia Systems.
As in all adaptive systems, the user's goals or tasks, knowledge, background, and preferences are modeled and used for making adaptation decisions by adaptive hypermedia systems. In addition, recently the user's interests and individual traits have been studied in adaptive hypermedia systems. With the developed Web information retrieval technology, it became feasible to trace the user's long-term interests as well as the user's short-term search goal. This feature is used in various on-line information systems such as kiosks (Fink, Kobsa, & Nill, 1998), encyclopedias (Hirashima, Matsuda, Nomoto, & Toyoda, 1998), and museum guides (Not et al., 1998). In these systems, the user's interests serve as a basis for recommending relevant hypernodes.

The user's individual traits include personality, cognitive factors, and learning styles. Like the user's background, individual traits are stable features of a user. However, unlike the user's background, individual traits are not easy to extract. Researchers agree on the importance of modeling and using individual traits but disagree about which user characteristics can and should be used (Brusilovsky, 2001). Several systems have been developed for using learning styles in educational hypermedia (Carver, Howard, & Lavelle 1996; Gilbert & Han, 1999; Specht & Oppermann, 1998).

Adaptation to the user's environment is a new kind of adaptation fostered by Web-based systems (Brusilovsky, 2001). Since Web users are virtually everywhere and use different hardware, software, and platforms, adaptation to the user's environment has become an important issue.

25.5.5.3 Limitations of Adaptive Hypermedia Systems.
The introduction of hypermedia and the Web has had a great impact on adaptive instructional systems. Recently, a number of authoring tools for developing Web-based adaptive courses have even been created. SmexWeb is one of these Web-based adaptive hypermedia training authoring tools (Albrecht, Koch, & Tiller, 2000). However, there are some limitations of adaptive hypermedia systems: They are not usually theoretically or empirically well founded. There was little empirical evidence for the effectiveness of adaptive hypermedia systems. Specht and Oppermann's study (1998) showed that neither link annotations nor incremental linkages in adaptive hypermedia system have significant separate effects. However, the composite of adaptive link annotations and incremental linking was found to produce superior student performance compared with to that of students receiving no annotations and static linking. The study also found that students with a good working knowledge of the domain to be learned performed best in the annotation group, whereas those with less knowledge appeared to prefer more direct guidance. Brusilovsky and Eklund (1998) found that adaptive link annotation was useful to the acquisition of knowledge for users who chose to follow the navigational advice. However, in a subsequent study (Eklund & Sinclair, 2000), link annotation was not found to influence user performance on the subject. The authors

concluded that the adaptive component was a very small part of the interface and insignificant in a practical sense. Also, De Bra pointed out that if prerequisite relationships in adaptive hypermedia systems are omitted by the user or just wrong, the user may be guided to pages that are not relevant or that the user cannot understand. Bad guidance is worse than no guidance (De Bra, 2000). Evaluating the learner's state of knowledge is the most critical factor for the successful implementation of the system.

25.6 APTITUDES, ON-TASK PERFORMANCE, AND RESPONSE-SENSITIVE ADAPTATION

As reviewed, microadaptive systems, including ITSs, demonstrate the power of on-task measures in adapting instruction to students' learning needs that are individually different and constantly changing, while ATI research has shown few consistent findings. Because of the theoretical implications, however, efforts to apply aptitude variables selectively in adaptive instruction continue. Integrating some aptitude variables in microadaptive systems has been suggested. For example, Park and Seidel (1989) recommended including several aptitude variables in the ITS student model and using them in the diagnostic and tutoring processes.

25.6.1 A Two-Level Model of Adaptive Instruction

To integrate the ATI approach in a microadaptive model, Tennyson and Christensen (1988; also see Tennyson & Park, 1987) have proposed a two-level model of adaptive instruction. This two-level model is based partially on the findings of their own research on adaptive instruction over two decades. First, this computer-based model allows the computer tutor to establish conditions of instruction based on learner aptitude variables (cognitive, affective, and memory structure) and context (information) structure. Second, the computer tutor provides moment-to-moment adjustment of instructional conditions by adapting the amount of information, example formats, display time, sequence of instruction, instructional advisement, and embedded refreshment and remediation. The microlevel adaptation takes place based on the student's on-task performance, and the procedure is response sensitive (Park & Tennyson, 1980). The amount of information to be presented and the time to display the information on the computer screen are determined through the continuous decision-making process of the Bayesian adaptive model based on on-task performance data. The selection and presentation of other instructional strategies (sequence of examples, advisement, embedded refreshment, and remediation) are determined based on the evaluation of the on-task performance. However, the response-sensitive procedure used in this microlevel adaptation has two major limitations, as discussed for the Bayesian adaptive instructional model: (a) problems associated with the quantification process in transforming the learning needs into the Bayesian probabilities and (b) the capability to handle only simple types of learning tasks (e.g., concept and rule learning). For variables to be considered in the macroadaptive process, Tennyson and Christensen (1988) identified the types of learning objectives, instructional variables, and enhancement strategies for different types of memory structures (i.e., declarative knowledge, conceptual knowledge, and procedural knowledge) and cognitive processes (storage and retrieval). However, the procedure for integrating components of learning and instruction are not clearly demonstrated in their Minnesota Adaptive Instructional System.

25.6.2 On-Task Performance and Response-Sensitive Strategies

Studies reviewed for microadaptive models demonstrated the superior diagnostic power of on-task performance measures compared to pretask measures and the stronger effect of response-sensitive adaptation over ATI or nonadaptive instruction. These results indicate the relative importance of the response-sensitive strategy compared to ATI methods. The student's on-task performance or response to a given problem is the reflection of the integrated effect of all the variables, identifiable or unidentifiable, involved in the student's learning and response-generation process. As discussed earlier, a shortcoming of the ATI method is adapting instructional processes to one or two selected aptitude variables despite the fact that learning results from the integrated effects of many identifiable or unidentifiable aptitude variables and their interactions with the complex learning requirements of the given task. Some of the aptitude variables involved in the learning process may be stable in nature, whereas others are temporal. Identifying all of the aptitude variables and their interactions with the task-learning requirements is practically impossible.

Research evidence shows that some aptitude variables (e.g., prior knowledge, interest, intellectual ability) (Tobias, 1994; Whitener, 1989) are important predictors in selecting instructional treatments for individual students. However, some studies (Park & Tennyson, 1980, 1986) suggest that the predictive value of aptitude variables decreases as the learning process continues, because the involvement of other aptitude variables and their interactions may increase as learning occurs. For example, knowledge the student has acquired in the immediately preceding unit becomes the most important factor in learning the next unit, and the motivational level for learning the next unit may not be the same as that for learning the last unit. Thus, the general intellectual ability measured prior to instruction may not be as important in predicting the student's performance and learning requirements for the later stage or unit of the instruction as it was for the initial stage or unit.

In a summary of factor analytic studies of human abilities for learning, Fleishman and Bartlett (1969) provided evidence that the particular combinations of abilities contributing to performance change as the individual works on the task. Dunham, Guilford, and Hoepner (1968) also found that definite trends in ability factor loading can be seen as a function of stage of practice on the task. According to Fredrickson (1969), changes in the factorial composition of a task might be a function of the

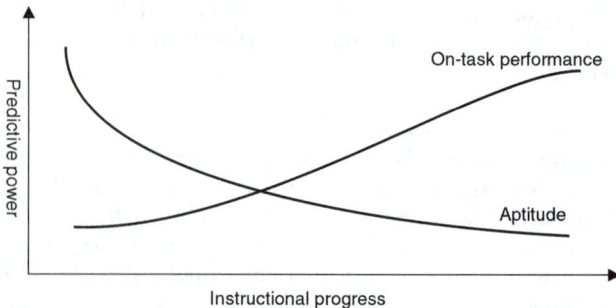

FIGURE 25.1. Predictive power of aptitudes and on-task performance.

student's employing cognitive strategies early in the learning task and changing the strategies later in the task. Because the behavior of the learner changes during the course of learning, including the learner's strategies, abilities that transfer and produce effects at one stage of learning may differ from those that are effective at other stages.

25.6.3 Diagnostic Power of Aptitudes and On-Task Performance

As discussed in the previous section, the change of aptitudes during the learning process suggests that the diagnostic power of premeasured aptitude variables for assessing the user's learning needs, including instructional treatments, decreases as learning continues. In contrast, the diagnostic power of on-task performance increases because it reflects the most up-to-date and integrated reflection of aptitude and other variables involved in the learning. Also, students' on-task performance in the initial stage of learning may not be as powerful as in the later stage of learning because, in the initial stage, they may not have sufficient understanding of the nature of the task or specific learning requirements in the task and their own ability related to the learning of the task. Therefore, during the initial stage of instruction, specific aptitude variables such as prior knowledge and general intellectual ability may be most useful in prescribing the best instructional treatment for the student. The decrease in the predictive power of premeasured aptitude variables and the increase in that of on-task performance are represented in Fig. 25.1.

25.6.4 Response-Sensitive Adaptation

Figure 25.1 suggests that an adaptive instructional system should be a two-stage approach: adaptation to the selected aptitude variable and response-sensitive adaptation. In the two-stage approach, the student will initially be assigned to the best instructional alternative for the aptitude measured prior to instruction, and then response-sensitive procedures will be applied as the student's response patterns emerge to reflect his or her knowledge or skills on the given task. A representative example of this two-stage approach is the Bayesian adaptive instructional model. In this model, the student's initial learning needs are estimated from the student's performance on a pretest, and the estimate is continuously adjusted by reflecting the student's on-task performance (i.e., correct or incorrect response to the given question). As the process for estimating student learning needs continues in this Bayesian model, the pretest performance data become less important, and the most recent performance data become more important.

The response-sensitive procedure is particularly important because it can determine and use learning prescriptions with timeliness and accuracy during instruction. The focus of a response-sensitive approach is that the instruction should attempt to identify the psychological cause of the student's response and thereby lower the probability that similar mistakes will occur again rather than merely correcting each mistake. The effectiveness of a response-sensitive approach (e.g., Atkinson, 1968; Park & Tennyson, 1980, 1986) has been empirically supported. Also, some of the successful ITSs (e.g., SHERLOCK) diagnose the student's learning needs and generate instructional treatments based entirely on a student's response to the given specific problem, without an extensive student-modeling function.

Development of a response-sensitive system requires procedures for obtaining instant assessment of student knowledge or abilities and alternative methods for using those assessments to make instructional decisions. Also, the learning requirements of the given task, including the structural characteristics and difficulty level, should be assessed continuously by on-task analysis. Without considering the content structure, the student's response, reflecting his or her knowledge about the task, cannot be appropriately analyzed, and a reasonable instructional treatment cannot be prescribed. The importance of the content structure of the learning task was well illustrated by Scandura's (1973, 1977a, 1977b) structural analysis and Landa's (1970, 1976) algo-heuristics approaches.

To implement a response-sensitive strategy in determining the presentation sequence of examples in concept learning, Tennyson and Park (1980) recommended analyzing on-task error patterns from the student's response history and content and structural characteristics of the task. Many ITSs have incorporated functions to make inferences about the cause of a student misconception from the analysis of the student's response errors and the content structure and instantly to generate instructional treatment (i.e., knowledge) appropriate for the misconception.

25.6.5 On-Task Performance and Adaptive Learner Control

A curve similar to that for the instructional diagnostic power of aptitudes (Fig. 25.1) can be applied in predicting the effect of the learner-control approach. In the beginning stage of learning, the student's familiarity with the subject knowledge and its learning requirements will be relatively low, and the student will not be able to choose the best strategies for learning. However, as the process of instruction and learning continues and external or self-assessment of the student's own ability is repeated, his or her familiarity with the subject and ability to learn it will increase. Thus, as the instruction progresses, the student will be able to make better decisions in selecting strategies for learning the subject. This argument is supported by research evidence that a strong effect of learner-control strategies is found mostly in relatively long-term studies (Seidel, Wagner, Rosenblatt, Hillelsohn, & Stelzer, 1978; Snow, 1980), whereas scattered effects are usually found in short-term experiments (Carrier, 1984; Ross & Rakow, 1981).

The speed, degree, and quality of obtaining self-regulatory ability in the learning process, however, will differ between students (Gallangher, 1994), because learning is an idiosyncratic process influenced by many identifiable and unidentifiable individual difference variables. Thus, an on-task adaptive learner control, which gradually gives learners the options for controlling the instructional process based on the progress of their on-task performance, should be better than non- or predetermined adaptive learner control, which gives the options without considering individual differences or is based on aptitudes measured prior to instruction. An on-task adaptive learner control will decide not only when is the best time to give the learner-control option but also which control options (e.g., selection of contents and learning activities) should be given based on the student's on-task performance. When the learner-control options are given adaptively, the concern that learner control may guide the student to put in less effort (Clark, 1984) would not be a serious matter.

25.7 INTERACTIVE COMMUNICATION IN ADAPTIVE INSTRUCTION

The response-sensitive strategies in CBI have been applied mostly to simple student–computer interactions such as multiple-choice, true–false, and short-answer types of questioning and responding processes. However, AI techniques for natural language dialogues have provided an opportunity to apply the response-sensitive strategy in a manner requiring much more in-depth communications between the student and the computer. For example, many ITSs have a function to understand and generate natural dialogues during the tutoring process. Although the AI method of handling natural languages is still limited and its development has been relatively slow, it is certain that future adaptive instructional systems, including ITSs, will have a more powerful function for handling response-sensitive strategies.

The development of a powerful response-sensitive instructional system using emerging technology, including AI, requires a communication model that depicts the process of interactions between the student and tutor. According to Wenger (1987), the development of an adaptive instructional system is the process of software engineering for constructing a knowledge communication system that causes and/or supports the acquisition of one's knowledge by someone else, via a restricted set of communication operations.

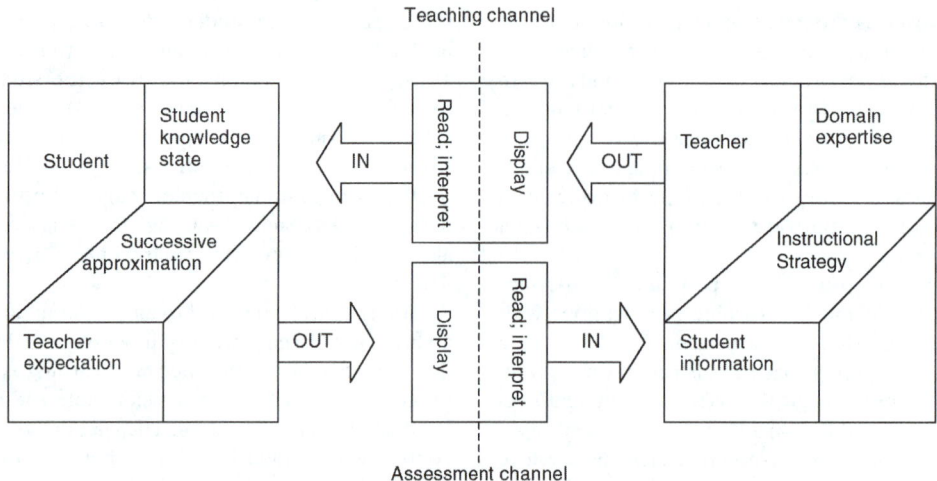

FIGURE 25.2. Process of instructional communication. From *Project IMPACT, Description of Learning and Prescription for Instruction* (Professional Paper 22–69), by R. J. Seidel, J. G. Compton, F. F. Kopstein, R. D. Rosenblatt, and S. See, 1969, Alexandria, VA: Human Resources Research Organization.

25.7.1 The Process of Instructional Communication

To develop a communication model for instruction, the process of instructional communication should first be understood. Seidel, Compton, Kopstein, Rosenblatt, and See (1969) divided instructional communication into teaching and assessment channels existing between the teacher and the student (Fig. 25.2 is adopted from Seidel et al. with modifications). Through the teaching channel, the teacher presents the student communication materials via the interface medium (e.g., computer display). The communication materials are generated from the selective integration of the teacher's domain knowledge expertise and teaching strategies based on information he or she has about the student. The student reads and interprets the communication materials based on the student's own current knowledge and the perceived teacher's expectation. The student's understanding and learning of the materials are communicated through his or her response or questions. The questions and responses by the student through the interface medium are read and interpreted by the teacher. Seidel et al. (1969; Seidel, 1971) called the communication process from the student to the teacher the assessment channel. Through this process, the teacher updates or modifies his or her information about the student and generates new communication materials based on the most up-to-date information. The student's knowledge successively approximates the state that the teacher plans to accomplish or expects.

The model of Seidel and his associates (1969) describes the general process of instruction. However, it does not explain how to assess the student's questions or responses and generate specific communication materials. Because specific combinations of questions and responses between the student and the teacher occurring in the teaching and assessment process are mostly task specific, it is difficult to develop a general model for describing and guiding the process.

25.7.2 Diagnostic Questions and Instructional Explanations

Most student–system interactions in adaptive instruction consist of questions that the system asks to diagnose the student's learning needs and explanations that the system provides based on the student's learning needs. Many studies have been conducted to investigate classroom discourse patterns (see Cazden, 1986) and the effect of questioning (Farrar, 1986; Hamaker, 1986; Redfield & Rouseau, 1981). However, few principles or procedures for asking diagnostic questions in CBI or ITSs have been developed. Most diagnostic processes in CBI and ITSs take place from the analysis of the student's on-task performance. For assessing the student's knowledge state and diagnosing his or her misconceptions, two basic methods have been used in ITSs: (a) the overlay method for comparing student's current knowledge structure with the expert's and (b) the buggy method for identifying specific misconceptions from a precompiled list of possible misconceptions. In both methods, the primary source for identifying the student's knowledge structure or misconceptions is the student's on-task performance data.

From the analysis of interactions between graduate students and undergraduates they are tutoring in research methods, Graesser (1993) identified a five-step dialogue pattern to implement in an ITS: (a) tutor asks question; (b) student answers question; (c) tutor gives short feedback on answer quality; (d) tutor and student collaboratively improve on answer quality; and (e) tutor assesses student's understanding of the answer. According to Graesser's observation, tutor questions were motivated primarily by curriculum scripts and the process of coaching students' idiosyncratic knowledge deficits. This five-step dialogue pattern suggests only a general nature of tutoring interactions rather than specific procedures for generating interactive questions and answers.

Collins and Stevens (1982, 1983) generated a set of inquiry techniques from analyses of teachers' interactive behaviors in a variety of domain areas. Nine of their most important strategies are (a) selecting positive and negative examples, (b) varying cases systematically, (c) selecting counterexamples, (d) forming hypotheses, (e) testing hypotheses, (f) considering alternative predictions, (g) entrapping students, (h) tracing consequences to a contradiction, and (i) questioning authority. Although these techniques are derived from the observation of classroom teachers' behaviors rather than experienced tutors', they provide valuable implications for producing diagnostic questions.

Brown and Palincsar (1982, 1989) emphasize expert scaffolding and Socratic dialogue techniques in their reciprocal teaching. Whereas expert scaffolding provides guidance for the tutor's involvement or provision of aids in the learning process, Socratic dialogue techniques suggest what kinds of questions should be asked to diagnose the student's learning needs. Five ploys are important in the diagnostic questions: (a) Systematic varied cases are presented to help the student focus on relevant facts, (b) counter examples and hypothetical cases are presented to question the legitimacy of the student's conclusions, (c) entrapment strategies are presented in questions to lure the student into making incorrect predictions or premature formulations of general rules based on faulty reasoning, (d) hypothesis identifications are forced by asking the student to specify his or her work hypotheses, and (e) hypothesis evaluations are forced by asking the student's prediction (Brown & Palincsar, 1989).

Leinhardt's (1989) work provides important implications for generating explanations for the student's misconceptions identified from the analysis of on-task performance or response. She identified two primary features in expert teachers' explanations: explicating the goal and objectives of the lessons and using parallel representations and their linkages. A model of explanation that she developed from the analysis of an expert tutor's explanations in teaching algebra subtraction problems shows that explanations are generated from various relations (e.g., pre-, co-, and postrequisite) between the instructional goal and content elements and the constraints for the use of the learned content.

As the preceding review suggests, efforts for generating principles of tutoring strategies (diagnosis and explanation) have continued, from observation of human tutoring activities (e.g., Berliner, 1991; Borko & Livingston, 1989; Leinhardt, 1989; Putnam, 1987) and from simulation and testing of tutoring processes in ITS environments (Ohlsson & Rees, 1991). However, specific principles and practical guidelines for generating questions and explanations in an on-task adaptive system have yet to be developed.

25.7.3 Generation of Tutoring Dialogues

Once the principles and patterns of tutoring interactions are defined, they should be implemented through interactions (particularly dialogues) between the student and the system. However, the generation of specific rules for tutoring dialogues is an extremely difficult task. After having extensively studied human tutorial dialogues, Fox (1993) concluded that tutoring languages and communication are indeterminate, because a given linguistic item (including silence, face and body movement, and voice tones) is in principle open to an indefinite number of interpretations and reinterpretations. She argues that indeterminacy is a fundamental principle of interaction and that tutoring interactions should not be rule governed. Also, she says that tutoring dialogues should be contextualized, and the contextualization should be tailored to fit exactly the needs of the student at the moment. The difficulty of developing tutoring dialogues in an adaptive system suggests that the development of future adaptive systems should focus on the application of the advantageous features of computer technology for the improvement of the tutoring functions of the adaptive system rather than simulating human tutoring behaviors and activities. As discussed earlier, however, AI methods and techniques have provided a much more powerful tool for developing and implementing flexible interactions required in adaptive instruction than traditional programming methods used in developing ordinary CBI programs. Also, the development of computer technology, including AI, continuously provides opportunities to enrich our environment for instructional research, development, and implementation.

25.8 NEW PEDAGOGICAL APPROACHES IN ADAPTIVE INSTRUCTIONAL SYSTEMS

During the eighties and early nineties, adaptive CBI focused mainly on the acquisition of conceptual knowledge and procedural skills (see microadaptive models), the detection of predominant errors and misconceptions in specific domains, and the nature of dialogues between program (or tutor) and student (Andriessen and Sandberg, 1999). Ohlsson (1987, 1993) and others criticized ITSs and other computer-based interactive learning systems for their limited range and adaptability of teaching actions compared to rich tactics and strategies employed by human expert teachers. In the late nineties, researchers began to incorporate more complex pedagogical approaches such as metacognitive strategies, collaborative learning, constructivist learning, and motivational competence in adaptive instructional systems.

25.8.1 The Constructivist Approach

Constructivist learning theories emphasize active roles for learners in constructing their own knowledge through experiences in a learning context in which the target domain is integrated. The focus is on the learning process. The learners experience the learning context through the process rather than the acquisition of previously defined knowledge and construct their own knowledge based on their understanding. Meanwhile, most adaptive instructional systems have emphasized representation of knowledge, inference of the learner's state of knowledge, and planning of instructional steps (Akhras & Self, 2000). Akhas and Self argued, "Alternative views of learning, such as constructivism, may similarly benefit from a system intelligence in which the mechanisms of knowledge representation, reasoning, and decision making originate from a formal interpretation of the values of that view of learning" (p. 345). Therefore, it is important to develop a different kind of system intelligence to support the alternative views and processes of learning. The constructivist intelligent system shifts the focus from a model of *what* is learned to a model of *how* knowledge is learned. Akhras and Self presented four main components of a constructivist intelligence system: context, activity, cognitive structure, and time extension. In the constructivist system, the context should be flexible enough to allow and accommodate different levels of learning experience within the context. Learning activities should be designed for learners to interact with the context and facilitate the process of knowledge construction through the interactions. The cognitive structure should be carefully designed so that learners' previously constructed knowledge influences the way they interpret new experiences. Also, learners should have chances to practice their previously developed knowledge to connect new knowledge over time (Akhras & Self, 2000).

Akhras and Self's approach was implemented in INCENSE (INtelligent Constructivist ENvironment for Software Engineering learning). INCENSE is capable of analyzing a time-extended process of interaction between a learner and a set of software-engineered situations and providing a learning situation based on the learner's needs. The goal of this system is to support further processes of learning experiences rather than the acquisition of target knowledge.

25.8.2 Vygotsky's Zone of Proximal Development and Contingent Teaching

According to Vygotsky (1978), "The zone of proximal development is those functions that have not yet matured, but would be possible to do under adult guidance or in collaboration with more capable peers" (p. 86). Based on Vygotsky's theory, providing immediate and appropriately challenging activities and contingent teaching based on learners' behavior is necessary for them to progress to the next level. He believed that minimal levels of guidance are best for learners. Recently, this theory has been deployed in several ways in CBI.

Compared to traditional adaptive instruction, one of the distinctions of this contingent teaching system is that there is no model of the learner. The learner's performance is local and situation constrained by contingencies in the learner's current activity. Since the tutor's actions and reactions occur in response to the learner's input, the theory promotes an "active" view of the learner and an account of learning as a collaborative and constructive process (D. Wood & H. Wood, 1996). The assessment of learners' prior knowledge with the task is critical to applying contingent teaching strategy to computer-based adaptive instruction. Thus, the contingent tutoring system generally provides two assessment methods: model tracing and knowledge tracing (du Boulay & Luckin, 2001). The purpose of model tracing is to keep track of all the student's actions as the problem

is solved and flag errors as they occur. It also adapts the help feedback according to the specific problem-solving context. The purpose of knowledge tracing is to choose the next appropriate problem so as to move the student though the curriculum in a timely but effective manner.

David Wood (2001) provided examples of tutoring systems based on Vygotsky's zone of proximal development (ZPD). ECOLAB is one. ECOLAB, which helps children aged 10–11 years learn about food chains and webs, provides appropriately challenging activities and the right quantity and quality of assistance. The learner model tracks both learners' capability and their potential to maintain the appropriate degree of collaborative assistance. ECOLAB ensures stretching learners beyond what they can achieve alone and then providing sufficient assistance to ensure that they do not fail.

Other examples are SHERLOCK (Karz & Lesgold, 1991; Karz, Lesgold, Eggan, & Gordin, 1992), QUADRARIC (H. Wood & D. Wood, 1999), DATA (H. Wood, Wood, & Marston, 1998), and EXPLAIN (D. Wood, Shadbolt, Reichgelt, Wood, & Paskiewitcz, 1992). In SHERLOCK, there is adjustment both to the nature of the activities undertaken by the user and to the language in which these activities are expressed. The working assumption is that more abstract language is harder and it moves from the concrete toward the abstract. QUADRARIC provides contingent, on-line help at the learner's request. The tutor continually monitors and logs learner activity and, in response to requests for help, exploits principles of instructional contingency to determine what help to provide. DATA was designed to undertake on-line assessment prior to tutoring. Based on on-line assessment, all learners are offered tutoring in the classes of problems with which they have shown evidence of error during the assessment. EXPLAIN (Experiments in Planning and Instruction) challenges learners to master tasks with presentation of manageable problems. This involves tutorial decisions about what challenges to set for the learner, if and when to intervene to support them as they attempt given tasks, and how much help to provide if they appear to need support.

However, these contingent-based learning systems have limitations. Hobsbaum, Peters, and Syla (1996) argue that the specific goals for tutorial action often arise out of the process of tutorial interactions and the system does not appear to follow a prearranged program. Learners often develop their own problem-solving strategies that differ from those taught. A competent tutor should be able to provide help or guidance contingent on any learner's conceptions and inputs. However, these systems cannot reliably diagnose such complex idiosyncratic conceptions and hence have limitation to provide useful guidance contingent on such conceptions.

25.8.3 Adaptation to Motivational State

Some new adaptive instructional systems take account of students' motivational factors. Their notion suggests that a comprehensive instructional plan should consist of a "traditional" instructional plan combined with a "motivational" plan. Wasson (1990) proposed the division of instructional planning into two streams: (a) content planning for selecting the topic to teach next and (b) delivery planning for determining how to teach the selected topic. Motivational components should be considered while designing delivery planning.

For example, in new systems, researchers try to incorporate gaze, gesture, nonverbal feedback, and conversational signals to detect and increase students' motivation. COSMO and MORE are examples of adaptive systems that focus on motivational components. COSMO supports a pedagogical agent that can adapt its facial expression, its tone of voice, its gestures, and the structure of its utterances to indicate its own affective state and to add affective force during its interactions with learners (du Boulay & Luckin, 2001). MORE detects the student's motivational state and reacts to motivate the distracted, less confident, or discontented student or to help sustain the disposition of the already motivated student (du Boulay & Luckin, 2001).

25.8.4 Teaching Metacognitive Ability

Metacognitive skill is students' understanding of their own cognitive processes. Educational psychologists including Dewey, Piaget, and Vygotsky argued that understanding and control of one's own cognitive processes play a key role in learning. Carroll and McKendree (1987) criticized the fact that most tutoring systems do not promote students' metacognitive thinking skills. White et al. (1999) considered that metacognitive processes are easily understood and observed in a multiagent social system, which integrates cognitive and social aspects of cognition within a social framework. Based on this conceptual framework, they developed the SCI-WISE program. It houses a community of software agents, such as an Inventor, an Analyzer, and a Collaborator. The agents provide strategic advice and guidance to learners as they undertake research projects and as they reflect on and revise their inquiry. Therefore, students express their metacognitive ideas as they undertake complex sociocognitive practices. Through this exercise, students will develop explicit theories of the social and cognitive processes required for collaborative inquiry and reflective learning (White et al., 1999).

Another example focusing on improving metacognitive skills is the Geometry Explanation Tutor program, developed by Aleven et al. (2001). They argue that self-explanation is an effective metacognitive strategy. Explaining examples or problem-solving steps helps students learn with greater understanding (Chi, Bassok, Lewis, Reimann, & Glaser, 1989). Originally, Geometry Explanation Tutor was created by adding dialogue capabilities to the PACT Geometry tutor. The current Geometry Explanation Tutor engages students in a restricted form of dialogue to help them state general explanations that justify problem-solving steps. The tutor is able to respond to the types of incomplete statements in the student's explanations. Although its range of dialogue strategies is currently very limited, it promotes students' greater understanding of geometry.

25.8.5 Collaborative Learning

Adaptive CBI systems including ITSs are no longer viewed as stand-alone but as embedded in a larger environment in which students are offered additional support in the learning process (Andriessen & Sandberg, 1999). One new pedagogical approach

of adaptive instructional systems is to support collaborative learning activities. Effective collaboration with peers is a powerful learning experience and studies have proved its value (Piaget, 1977; Brown & Palinscar, 1989; Doise, Mugny, & Perret-Clermont, 1975). However, placing students in a group and assigning a group task does not guarantee that they will have a valuable learning experience (Soller, 2001). It is necessary for teachers (tutors) to provide effective strategies with students to optimize collaborative learning. Through his Intelligent Collaborative system, Soller (2001) identified five characteristics of effective collaborative learning behaviors: participation, social grounding, performance analysis, group processing and application of active learning conversation skills, and promotive interaction. Based on these five characteristics, he listed components of an intelligent assistance module in a collaborative learning system, which include a collaborative learning skill coach, an instructional planner, a student or group model, a learning companion, and a personal learning assistant.

Erkens (1997) identified four uses of adaptive systems for collaborate learning: computer-based collaborative tasks (CBCT), cooperative tools (CT), intelligent cooperative systems (ICS), and computer-supported collaborative learning (CSCL).

1. CBCT: Group learning or group activity is the basic method to organize collaborative learning. The system presents a task environment in which students work with a team, and sometimes, the system supports the collaboration via intelligent coaching. SHERLOCK (Karz & Lesgold, 1993) and Envisioning Machines (Roschell & Teasley, 1995) are examples.
2. CT: The system is a partner that may take over some of the burden of lower-order tasks while students work with higher-order activities. Writing Partner (Salomon, 1993), CSILE, and Case-based Reasoning Tool are examples.
3. ICS: The system functions as an intelligent cooperative partner (e.g., DSA), a colearner (e.g., People Power), or a learning companion (e.g., Integration-Kid).
4. CSCL: The system serves as the communication interface such as a chat tool or discussion forum, which allows students to involve collaboration. The systems in this category provide the least adaptability to learners. Owing to the development of Internet-based technology (Web), however, this kind of system has been improving rapidly with the strong adaptive capability.

Although these systems are still in the early developmental stage, their contribution to the adaptive instructional system field cannot be ignored; they not only facilitate group activities, but also help educators and researchers gain further understanding of group interaction and determine how to support collaborative learning better.

25.9 A MODEL OF ADAPTIVE INSTRUCTIONAL SYSTEMS

In the preceding section, we emphasized the importance of on-task performance or a response-sensitive approach in the development of adaptive instructional systems. However, a complete adaptive system should have the capability to update

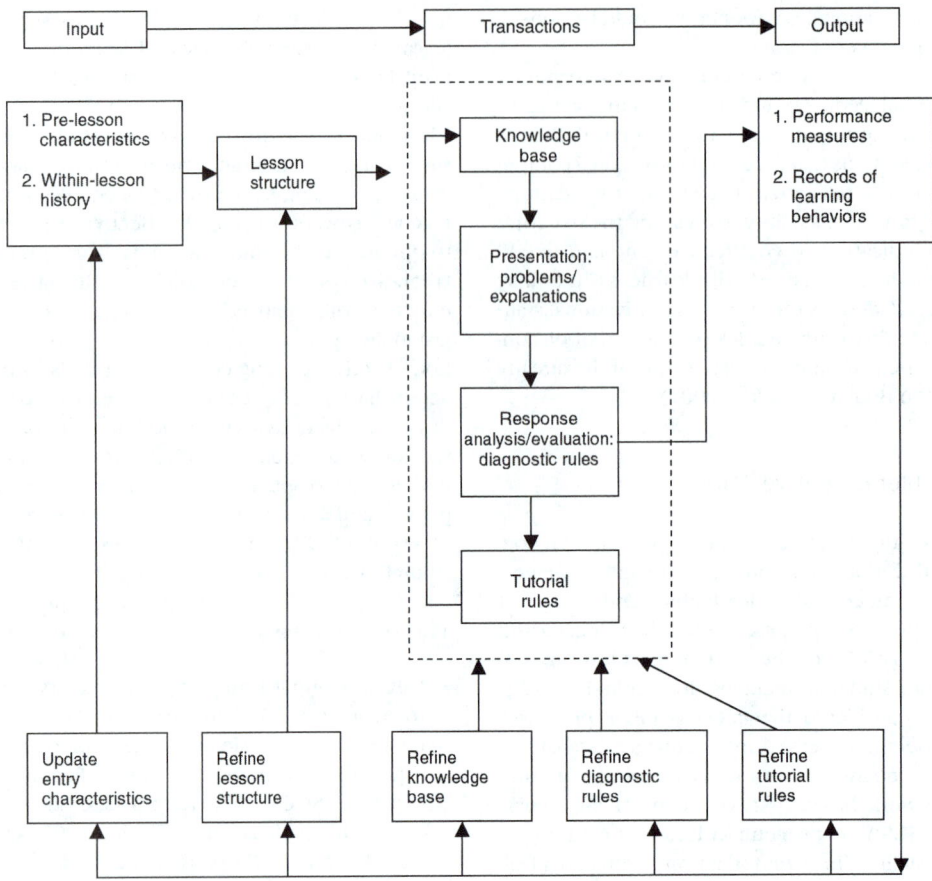

FIGURE 25.3. A model of adaptive instruction (Park et al., 1987). Originally from *Theories and Strategies Related to Measurement in Individualized Instruction* (Professional Paper 2–72), by R. J. Seidel, 1971, Alexandria, VA: Human Resources Research Organization.

continuously every component in the instructional system based on the student's on-task performance and the interactions between the student and the system. However, almost all adaptive instructional systems, including ITSs, have been developed with an emphasis on a few specific aspects or functions of instruction. Therefore, we present a conceptual model for developing a complete adaptive instructional system (Fig. 25.3). This model is adopted from the work of Seidel and his associates (Seidel, 1971), with consideration of recent developments in learning and instructional psychology and computer technology (Park et al., 1987).

This model does not provide specific procedures or technical guidelines for developing an adaptive system. However, we think that the cybernetic metasystem approach used in the model is generalizable as a guide for developing the more effective and efficient control process required in adaptive instructional systems. The model illustrates what components an adaptive system should have and how those components should be interrelated in an instructional process. Also, the model shows what specific self-improving or updating capabilities the system may need to have.

As Fig. 25.3 shows, this model divides the instructional process into three stages: input, transactions, and output. The input stage basically consists of the analysis of the student's entry characteristics. The student's entry characteristics include not only his or her within-lesson history (e.g., response history) but also prelesson characteristics. The prelesson characteristics may include information about the student's aptitudes and other variables influencing his or her learning. As discussed earlier, the aptitude variables measured prior to instruction will be useful for the beginning stage of instruction but will become less important as the student's on-task performance history is accumulated. Thus, the within-lesson history should be continuously updated using information from the evaluation of the performance (i.e., output measures).

The transaction stage consists of the interactions between the student and the system. In the beginning stage of the instruction, the system will select problems and explanations to present based on the student's entry characteristics, mainly the premeasured aptitudes. Then the system will evaluate the student's responses (or any other student input such as questions or comments) to the given problem or task. The response evaluation provides information for diagnosing the student's specific learning needs and for assessing overall performance level on the task. The learning needs will be inferred according to diagnostic rules in the system. Finally, the system will select new display presentations and questions for the student according to the tutorial rules. The tutorial rules should be developed in consideration of different learning and instructional theories (e.g., see Snelbecker, 1974; Reigeluth, 1983), research findings (e.g., see Gallangher, 1994; Weinstein & Mayer, 1986), expert heuristics (Jonassen, 1988), and response-sensitive strategies discussed earlier in this chapter.

The output stage consists mainly of performance evaluation. The performance evaluation may include not only the student's overall achievement level on a given task and specific performance on the subtasks but also the analysis of complete learning behaviors related to the task and subtasks. According to the performance evaluation and analysis, the instructional components will be modified or updated. The instructional components to be updated may include contents in the knowledge base (including questions and explanations), instructional strategies, diagnostic and tutorial rules, the lesson structure, and entry characteristics. If the system does not have the capability to modify or update some of the instructional components automatically, a human monitor may be required to perform that task.

25.10 CONCLUSION

Adaptive instruction has a long history (Reiser, 1987). However, systematic efforts aimed at developing adaptive instructional systems were not made until the early 1900s. Efforts to develop adaptive instructional systems have taken different approaches: macroadaptive, ATI, and microadaptive. Macroadaptive systems have been developed to provide more individualized instruction on the basis of the student's basic learning needs and abilities determined prior to instruction. The ATI approach is to adapt instructional methods, procedures, or strategies to the student's specific aptitude information. Microadaptive systems have been developed to diagnose the student's learning needs and provide optimal instructional treatments during the instructional transaction process.

Some macro-adaptive instructional systems seemed to be positioned as alternative educational systems because of their demonstrated effectiveness. However, most macrosystems were discontinued without much success because of the difficulty associated with their development and implementation, including curriculum development, teacher training, resource limitation, and organizational resistance. Numerous studies have been conducted to investigate ATI methods and strategies because of ATI's theoretically appealing and practical application possibilities. However, the results are not consistent and have provided little impetus for developing adaptive instructional systems.

Using computer technology, a number of micro-adaptive instructional systems have been developed. However, their applications had been mostly in laboratory environments because of the limitation of their functional capability to handle the complex transaction processes involved in the learning of various types of tasks by many different students. In the last decade, with the advent of the Web and adaptive hypermedia systems, their applications have moved out of the laboratory and into classrooms and workplaces. However, empirical evidence of the effectiveness of the new systems is very limited.

Another reason for the limited success of adaptive instructional systems is that unverified theoretical assumptions were used for their development. Particularly, ATI, including achievement and treatment interactions, has been used as the theoretical basis for many studies. However, the variability of ATI research findings suggests that the theoretical assumptions used may not be valid, and the development of a complete taxonomy of all likely aptitudes and instructional variables may not be possible. Even if it is possible to develop such a taxonomy, its instructional value will be limited because learning will be influenced by many variables, including aptitudes. Also, the instructional value of aptitude variables measured prior to instruction decreases as the instruction progresses. In the meantime, students' on-task performance (i.e., response to the given problem or task) becomes more important for diagnosing their learning needs (see Fig. 25.1) because on-task performance is the integrated reflection of many verifiable and unverifiable variables involved in learning.

Therefore, we propose an on-task performance and treatment interaction approach. In this approach, response-sensitive methods will be used as the primary strategy. Many studies (e.g., Atkinson, 1974; Park & Tennyson, 1980, 1986) have demonstrated the effects of response-sensitive strategies. However, application of the response-sensitive strategy has been limited to simple tasks such as vocabulary acquisition and concept learning because of the technical limitations in handling the complex interactions involved in the learning and teaching of more sophisticated tasks such as problem solving. However, ITSs created in the last two decades have demonstrated that technical methods and tools are now available for the development of more sophisticated response-sensitive systems. Unfortunately, this technical development has not contributed significantly to an intellectual breakthrough in the field of learning and instruction. Thus, no principles or systematic guidelines for developing questions and explanations necessary in the response-sensitive strategy have been developed. In this chapter, we have reviewed several studies that provide some valuable suggestions for the development of response-sensitive strategies, including asking diagnostic questions and providing explanations (Collins & Stevens, 1983; Brown & Palincsar, 1989; Leinhardt, 1983). Further research on asking diagnostic questions and providing explanations is needed for the development of response-sensitive adaptive systems.

Since response-sensitive diagnostic and prescriptive processes should be developed on the basis of many types of information available in the system, we propose to use a complete model of adaptive instructional systems described by Park et al. (1987). This model consists of input, transactions, and output stages, and components directly required to implement the response-sensitive strategy are in the transaction stage of instruction. To develop an adaptive instructional system using this model will require a multidisciplinary approach because it will require expertise from different domain areas such as learning psychology, cognitive science or knowledge engineering, and instructional technology (Park & Seidel, 1989). However, with the current technology and our knowledge of learning and instruction, the development of a complete adaptive instructional system like the one shown in Fig. 25.3 may not be possible in the immediate future. It is expected that cognitive scientists will further improve the capabilities of current AI technology such as natural language dialogues and inferencing processes for capturing the human reasoning and cognitive process. In the meantime, the continuous accumulation of research findings in learning and instruction will make a significant contribution to instructional researchers' and developers' efforts to create more powerful adaptive instructional systems.

References

Abramson, T., & Kagen, E. (1975). Familiarization of content and different response modes in programmed instruction. *Journal of Educational Psychology, 67,* 83-88.

Akhras, F. N., & Self, J. A. (2000). System intelligence in constructivist learning. *International Journal of Artificial Intelligence in Education, 11,* 344-376

Albrecht, F., Koch, N., & Tiller, T. (2000). SmexWeb: An adaptive Web-based hypermedia teaching system. *Journal of Interactive Learning Research, Special Issue on Intelligent Systems/Tools in Training and Life-Long Learning, 11*(3/4).

Aleven, V., & Koedinger, K. R. (2000). Limitations of student control: Do students know when they need help? *In* G. Gauthier, C. Frasson, & K. VanLehn (Eds.), *Intelligent tutoring systems. Lecture notes in computer science* (Vol. 1839, pp. 292-303). Berlin: Springer Verlag.

Aleven, V., Popescu, O., & Koedinger, K. R. (2001). Towards tutorial dialog to support self-explanation: Adding natural language understanding to a cognitive tutor. *In* J. D. Moore, C. L. Redfield, & W. L. Johnson (Eds.), *Artificial intelligence in education: AI-ED in the wired and wireless future, proceedings of AI-ED 2001,* 246-255.

Andriessen, J., & Sandberg, J. (1999). Where is education heading and how about AI? *International Journal of Artificial Intelligence in Education, 10,* 130-150.

Astleitner, Hermann; Keller, & John M. (1995). A Model for Motivationally Adaptive Computer-Assisted Instruction. *Jouranl of Research on Computing in Education, 27*(3) 270-80.

Atkinson, R. C. (1968). Computerized instruction and the learning process. *American Psychologist, 23,* 225-239.

Atkinson, R. C. (1972). Ingredients for a theory of instruction. *American Psychologist, 27,* 921-931.

Atkinson, R. C. (1974). Teaching children to read using computer. *American Psychologist, 29,* 169-178.

Atkinson, R. C. (1976). Adaptive instructional systems: some attempts to optimize the learning process. *In* D. Klahr (Ed.), *Cognition and instruction.* New York: Wiley.

Atkinson, R. C., & Crothers, E. J. (1964). A comparison of paired-associate learning models having different acquisition and retention axioms. *Journal of Mathematical Psychology, 2,* 285-315.

Atkinson, R. C., & Fletcher, J. D. (1972). Teaching children to read with computer. *The Reading Teacher, 25,* 319-327.

Atkinson, R. C., & Paulson, J. A. (1972). An approach to the psychology of instruction. *Psychological Bulletin, 78,* 49-61.

Bandura, A. (1982). Self-efficacy mechanism in human agency. *American Psychologist, 37,* 122-148.

Beaumont, I. (1994). User modeling in the interactive anatomy tutoring system ANATOM-TUTOR. *User Modeling and User-Adapted Interaction, 4,* 121-145.

Berliner, D. C. (1991). Educational psychology and pedagogical expertise: new findings and new opportunities for thinking about training. *Educational Psychologist, 26,* 145-155.

Berliner, D. C., & Cohen, L. S. (1973). Trait-treatment interaction and learning. *Review of Research in Education, 1,* 58-94.

Block, J. H. (1980). Promising excellence through mastery learning. *Theory and Practice, 19,* 66-74.

Bloom, B. S. (1984). The 2 sigma problem: The search for methods of group instruction as effective as one-to-one tutoring. *Educational Researcher, 13,* 4-16.

Borko, H., & Livingston, C. (1989). Cognition and improvisation: Differences in mathematics instruction by expert and novice teachers. *American Educational Research Journal, 26,* 474-498.

Brown, A. L., & Palincsar, A. S. (1982). Reciprocal teaching of comprehension strategies: A natural history of one program for enhancing learning. *In* J. D. Day & J. Borkowski (Eds.), *Intelligence and exceptionality. New directions for theory, assessment and instructional practice.* Norwood, NJ: Ablex.

Brown, A. L., & Palincsar, A. S. (1989). Guided, cooperative learning and individual knowledge acquisition. *In* L. Resnick, (Ed.), *Knowledge, learning, and instruction: Essays in honor of Robert Glaser* (pp. 307-336). Mahwah, NJ: Lawrence Erlbaum Associates.

Brusilovsky, P., & Pesin, L. (1994). An intelligent learning environment for CDS/ISIS users. *In* J. J., Levonen, & M. T. Tukianinen, (Eds.), *Proceedings of the Interdisciplinary Workshop on Complex Learning in Computer Environments* (CLCE94), Joensuu, Finland, 29-33.

Brusilovsky, P., Schwarz, E., & Weber, G. (1996). ELM-ART: An intelligent tutoring system on World Wide Web. In: Frasson, C., Gauthier, G., & Lesgold, A. (Eds.), *Intelligent tutoring systems. Lecture notes in computer science* (Vol. 1086, pp. 261-269). Berlin: Springer-Verlag.

Brusilovsky, P., & Vassileva, J. (1996). Preface. *User Modeling and User-Adapted Interaction, 6*(2-3), v-vi.

Brusilovsky, P., & Pesin, L. (1998). Adaptive navigation support in educational hypermedia: An evaluation of the ISIS-Tutor. *Journal of Computing and Information Technology, 6*(1), 27-38.

Brusilovsky, P., & Eklund, J. (1998). A Study of User Model Based Link Annotation in Educational Hypermedia. *Journal of Universal Computer Science, 4*(4), 429-448. Springer Science Online.

Brusilovsky, P., Eklund, J., & Schwarz, E. (1998). Web-based education for all: A tool for developing adaptive courseware. *Computer Networks and ISDN Systems, 30*(1-7), 291-300.

Brusilovsky, P. (2000). Adaptive hypermedia: From intelligent tutoring systems to Web-based education. *In* G. Gauthier, C. Frasson, & K. VanLehn (Eds.), *Intelligent tutoring systems. Lecture notes in computer science* (Vol. 1839, pp. 1-7). Berlin: Springer Verlag.

Brusilovsky, P. (2001, June). Adaptive educational hypermedia. In *Proceedings of Tenth International PEG Conference,* Tampere, Finland, 8-12.

Brusilovsky, P., & Cooper, D. W. (2002). Domain, task, and user models for an adaptive hypermedia performance support system. *In* Gil, Y., & Leake, D. B. (Eds.), *Proceedings of 2002*

International Conference on Intelligent User Interfaces (pp. 23–30). San Francisco, CA: ACM Press.

Burns, R. B. (1980). Relation of aptitude learning at different points in time during instruction. *Journal of Educational Psychology, 72,* 785–797.

Calfee, R. C. (1970). The role of mathematical model in optimizing instruction. *Scientia: Revue Internationale de Sythese Scientifique, 105,* 1–25.

Carrier, C. (1984). Do learners make good choices? *Instructional Innovator, 29,* 15–17, 48.

Carrier, C., & Jonassen, D. H. (1988). Adapting courseware to accommodate individual differences. *In* D. Jonassen (Ed.), *Instructional designs for microcomputer courseware.* Mahwah, NJ: Lawrence Erlbaum Associates.

Carro, R. M., Pulido, E., & Rodrígues, P. (1999). TANGOW: Task-based Adaptive learNer Guidance on the WWW. In *Computer sciences reports* (pp. 49–57). Eindhoven: Eindhoven University of Technology.

Carroll, J. B. (1963). A model of school learning. *Teachers College Record, 64,* 723–733.

Carroll, J., & McKendree, J. (1987). Interface design issues for advice-giving expert systems. *Communications of the ACM, 30*(1), 14–31.

Carver, C., Howard, R., & Lavelle, E. (1996). Enhancing student learning by incorporating learning styles into adaptive hypermedia. In *Proceedings of the AACE Worldwide Conference on Educational Hypermedia and Multimedia.*

Cazden, C. B. (1986). Classroom discourse. *In* M. C. Wittrock (Ed.), *Handbook of research on teaching* (3rd ed.). New York: Macmillan.

Chant, V. G., & Atkinson, R. C. (1973). Optimal allocation of instructional effort to interrelated learning strands. *Journal of Mathematical Psychology, 10,* 1–25.

Chi, M., Bassok, M., Lewis, M., Reimann, P., & Glaser, R. (1989). Self-explanations: How students study and use examples in learning to solve problems. *Cognitive Science, 13,* 145–182.

Clark, R. (1984). Research on student thought processes during computer-based instruction. *Journal of Instructional Development, 7,* 2–5.

Cohen, I. S. (1963). Programmed learning and the Socratic dialogue. *American Psychologist, 17,* 772–775.

Collins, A., & Stevens, A. (1982). Goals and strategies of effective teachers. *In* R. Glaser (Ed.), *Advances in instructional psychology 2.* Mahwah, NJ: Lawrence Erlbaum Associates.

Collins, A., & Stevens, A. (1983). A cognitive theory of inquiry teaching. *In* C. M. Reigeluth (Ed.), *Instructional-design theories and models: An overview of their current status.* Mahwah, NJ: Lawrence Erlbaum Associates.

Como, L., & Snow, E. R. (1986). Adapting teaching to individual differences among learners. *In* M. C. Wittrock (Ed.), *Handbook of research on teaching* (3rd ed.). New York: Macmillan.

Cronbach, L. J. (1957). The two disciplines of scientific psychology. *American Psychologist, 12,* 671–684.

Cronbach, L. J. (1971). How can instruction be adapted to individual differences? *In* R. A. Weisgerber (Ed.), *Perspective in individualized learning.* Itasca, IL: Peacock.

Cronbach, L. J., & Snow, R. E. (1977). *Aptitudes and instructional methods. A handbook for research on interactions.* New York: Irvingston.

Crowder, N. W. (1959). *Automatic tutoring: The state of art.* New York: Wiley.

Davis, J. K. (1991). Educational implications of field dependence-independence. *In* S. Wapner & J. Demick (Eds.), *Field dependence-independence: Cognitive style across the life span* (pp. 149–76). Mahwah, NJ: Lawrence Erlbaum Associates.

De Bra, P. (1996). Teaching hypertext and hypermedia through the Web. *Journal of Universal Computer Science, 2,* 12, 797–804.

De Bra, P. (2000). Pros and cons of adaptive hypermedia in Web-based education. *Journal on CyberPsychology and Behavior, 3*(1), 71–77.

De Bra, P., & Calvi, L. (1998). AHA! An open adaptive hypermedia architecture. *New Review of Hypermedia and Multimedia, 4,* 115–139.

Dear, R. E., Silberman, H. F., Estavan, D. P., & Atkinson, R. C. (1967). An optimal strategy for the presentation of paired-associate items. *Behavioral Science, 12,* 1–13.

Derry, S. J., & Murphy, D. A. (1986). Designing systems that train learning ability: From theory to practice. *Review of Educational Research, 56,* 1–39.

Deutsch, T., & Tobias, S. (1980). *Prior achievement, anxiety, and instructional method.* Paper presented at the annual meeting of the American Psychological Association, Montreal, Canada.

Dewey, J. (1902/1964). The child and the curriculum. *In* R. D. Archambault (Ed.), *John Dewey on education: Selected writings.* New York: Modern Library.

Dick, W., & Carey, L. (1985). *The systematic design of instruction* (2nd ed.). Glenview, IL: Scott, Foresman.

DiVesta, F. J. (1975). Trait-treatment interactions, cognitive processes, and research on communication media. *AV Communication Review, 23,* 185–196.

Doise, W., Mugny, G., & Perret-Clermont, A. (1975). Social interaction and the development of cognitive operations. *European Journal of Social Psychology, 5*(3), 367–383.

du Boulay, B., & Luckin R. (2001). Modelling human teaching tactics and strategies for tutoring systems. *International Journal of Artificial Intelligence in Education, 12,* 235–256.

Duchastel, P. (1992). Towards methodologies for building knowledge-based instructional systems. *Instructional Science, 20*(5–6), 349–358.

Dunham, J. L., Guilford, J. P., & Hoepner, R. (1968). Multivariate approach to discovering the intellectual components of concept learning. *Psychological Review, 75,* 206–221.

Dunn, R., & Dunn, K. (1978). *Teaching students through their individual learning styles: A practical approach.* Reston, VA: Reston.

Eklund, J., & Sinclair, K. (2000). An empirical appraisal of adaptive interfaces for instructional systems. *Educational Technology and Society Journal, 3*(4), 165–177.

Eliot, C., Neiman, D., & Lamar, M. (1997). Medtec: A Web-based intelligent tutor for basic anatomy. *In* S. Lobodzinski & I. Tomek (Eds.), *Proceedings of WebNet'97, World Conference of the WWW, Internet and Intranet,* Toronto, Canada, AACE, 161–165.

Entwistle, N. (1981). *Styles of learning and teaching.* New York: Wiley.

Erkens, G. (1997). *Cooperatief probleemoplossen met computers in het onderwijs: Het modelleren van cooperatieve dialogen voor de ontwikkeling van intelligente onderwijssystemen [Cooperative problem solving with computers in education: Modelling of cooperative dialogues for the design of intelligent educational systems].* Ph.D. thesis, Utrecht University, Utrecht, The Netherlands.

Farrar, M. T. (1986). Teacher questions: The complexity of the cognitive simple. *Instructional Science, 15,* 89–107.

Federico, P. (1980). Adaptive instruction: Trends and issues. *In* R. E. Snow, P. Federico, & W. E. Montague (Eds.), *Aptitude, learning and instruction, Vol. 1: Cognitive process analyses of aptitude.* Mahwah, NJ: Lawrence, Erlbaum Associates.

Federico, Pat-Anthony. (1983). Changes in The Congnitive Components of Achievement as Students Proceed through Computer-Managed Instruction. *Journal of Computer-Based Instruction, 9*(4) 156–68.

Fink, J., Kobsa, A., & Nill, A. (1998). Adaptable and adaptive information provision for all users, including disabled and elderly people. *New Review of Hypermedia and Multimedia, 4,* 163–188. http://www.ics.uci.edu/~kobsa/papers/1998-NRMH-kobsa.ps.

Fischer, G., Mastaglio, T., Reeves, B., & Rieman, J. (1990). Minimalist explanations in knowledge-based systems. In *Proceedings of 23rd Annual Hawaii International Conference on System Sciences,* Kailua-Kona, HI, IEEE, 309–317.

Fisher, D. F., & Townsend, J. T. (1993). *Models of Morse code skill acquisition: Simulation and analysis* (Research Product 93-04). Alexandria, VA: US. Army Research Institute.

Flanagan, J. C., Shanner, W. M., Brudner, H. J., & Marker, R. W. (1975). An individualized instructional system: PLAN. *In* H. Talmage (Ed.), *Systems of individualized education.* Berkeley, CA: McCutchan.

Fleishman, E. A., & Bartlett, C. J. (1969). Human abilities. *Annual Review of Psychology, 20,* 349–380.

Fox, B. A. (1993). *The human tutoring dialogue project: Issues in the design of instructional systems.* Mahwah, NJ: Lawrence Erlbaum Associates.

Frase, L. X., Patrick, E., & Schumer, H. (1970). Effect of question position and frequency upon learning from text under different levels of incentives. *Journal of Educational Psychology, 61,* 52–56.

Fredrickson, C. H. (1969). Abilities, transfer and information retrieval in verbal learning. *Multivariate Behavioral Research Monographs, 2.*

French, R. L. (1975). Teaching strategies and learning processes. *Educational Considerations, 3,* 27–28.

Gagné, R. M., (1967). *Learning and individual differences.* Columbus, OH: Merrill.

Gagné, R. M., & Briggs, L. J. (1979). *Principles of instructional design,* (2nd ed.). New York: Holt.

Gallangher, J. J. (1994). Teaching and learning: New models. *Annual Review of Psychology, 45,* 171–195.

Gates, K. F., Lawhead, P. B., & Wilkins, D. E. (1998). Towards an adaptive WWW: A case study in customized hypermedia. *New Review of Hypermedia and Multimedia, 4,* 89–113.

Gilbert, J. E., & Han, C. Y. (1999). Arthur: Adapting instruction to accommodate learning style. *In* P., De Bra, & J. Leggett, (Eds.), *Proceedings of WebNet'99, World Conference of the WWW and Internet,* Honolulu, HI, 433–438.

Glaser, R. (1972). Individual and learning: The new aptitudes. *Educational Researcher, 6,* 5–13.

Glaser, R. (1976). Cognitive psychology and instructional design. *In* D. Klahr (Ed.), *Cognition and instruction.* New York: Wiley.

Glaser, R. (1977). *Adaptive education: Individual, diversity and learning.* New York: Holt.

Glaser, R., & Nitko, A. J. (1971). Measurement in learning and instruction. *In* R. L. Thorudike (Ed.), *Educational Measurement,* (2nd ed.). Washington, DC: American Council of Education.

Glaser, R., & Resnick, L. B. (1972). Instructional psychology. *Annual Review of Psychology, 23,* 207–276.

Gonschorek, M., & Herzog, C. (1995). Using hypertext for an adaptive helpsystem in an intelligent tutoring system. *In* Greer, J. (Ed.), *Proceedings of AI-ED'95, 7th World Conference on Artificial Intelligence in Education,* Washington, DC, 274–281.

Graesser, A. C. (1993). *Questioning mechanisms during tutoring, conversation, and human-computer interaction* (Office of Naval Research Technical Report 93-1). Memphis, TN: Memphis State University.

Gregg, L. W. (1970). Optimal policies of wise choice? A critique of Smallwood's optimization procedure. *In* W. H. Holtzman, (Ed.), *Computer-assisted instruction, testing and guidance.* New York: Harper & Row.

Groen, G. J., & Atkinson, R. C. (1966). Models for optimizing the learning process. *Psychological Bulletin, 66,* 309–320.

Hagberg, J. O., & Leider, R. J. (1978). *The inventures: Excursions in life and career renewal.* Reading, MA: Addison–Wesley.

Hall, K. A. (1977). A research model for applying computer technology to the interactive instructional process. *Journal of Computer-Based Instruction, 3,* 68–75.

Hamaker, C. (1986). The effects of adjunct questions on prose learning. *Review of Educational Research, 56,* 212–242.

Hambleton, R. K., & Novick, M. R. (1973). Toward an integration of theory and method for criterion-referenced tests. *Journal of Educational Measurement, 10,* 159–170.

Hansen, D. N., Ross, S. M., & Rakow, E. (1977). *Adaptive models for computer-based training systems* (Annual Report to Navy Personnel Research and Development Center). Memphis, TN: Memphis State University.

Henze, N., Naceur, K., Nejdl, W., & Wolpers, M. (1999). *Adaptive hyperbooks for constructivist teaching. Künstliche Intelligenz, 4,* 26–31.

Hirashima, T., Matsuda, N., Nomoto, T., & Toyoda, J. (1998). Toward context-sensitive filtering on WWW. *WebNet 98.*

Hobsbaum, A., Peters, S., & Sylva, K. (1996). Scaffolding in reading recovery. *Oxford Review of Education, 22*(1), 17–35.

Hockemeyer, C., Held, T., & Albert, D. (1998). RATH—A relational adaptive tutoring hypertext WWW-environment based on knowledge space theory. *In* C. Alvegård, (Ed.), *Proceedings of CALISCE'98, 4th International Conference on Computer Aided Learning and Instruction in Science and Engineering,* Göteborg, Sweden, 417–423.

Hoge, D., Smith, E., & Hanson, S. (1990). School experiences predicting changes in self-esteem of sixth- and seventh-grade students. *Journal of Educational Psychology, 82,* 117–127.

Holland, J. G. (1977). Variables in adaptive decisions in indi-vidualized instruction. *Educational Psychologist, 12,* 146–161.

Jonassen, D. H. (1988). Integrating learning strategies into courseware to facilitate deeper processing. *In* D. H. Jonassen (Ed.), *Instructional designs for microcomputer courseware.* Mahwah, NJ: Lawrence Erlbaum Associates.

Katz, S., & Lesgold, A. (1991). Modeling the student in Sherlock II. *In* J. Kay, & A. Quilici (Eds.), *Proceedings of the IJCAI-91 Workshop W.4: Agent modelling for intelligent inteaction,* 93–127. Sydney, Australia.

Katz, S., Lesgold, A., Eggan, G., & Gordin, M. (1992). Self-adjusting Curriculum Planning in Sherlock II. *Lecture Notes in Computer Science: Proceedings of the Fourth Internationsl Conference on Computers in Learning (ICCAL '92).* Berlin: Springer Verlag.

Kay, J., & Kummerfeld, R. J. (1994). An individualised course for the C programming language. In *Proceedings of Second International WWW Conference,* Chicago, IL.

Kayama, M., & Okamoto, T. (1998). A mechanism for knowledge-navigation in hyperspace with neural networks to support exploring activities. *In* G. Ayala (Ed.), *Proceedings of Workshop "Current Trends and Applications of Artificial Intelligence in Education" at the 4th World Congress on Expert Systems,* Mexico City, ITESM, 41–48.

Keller, F. S. (1968). Goodbye Teacher.... *Journal of Applied Behavior Analysis, 1,* 79–89.

Keller, F. S. (1974). Ten years of personalized instruction. *Teaching of Psychology, 1,* 4–9.

Klausmeier, H. J. (1975). IGE: An alternative form of schooling. *In* H. Talmage (Ed.), *Systems of individualized education.* Berkeley, CA: McCutchan.

Klausmeier, H. J. (1976). Individually guided education: 1966–1980. *Journal of Teacher Education, 27,* 199–205.

Klausmeier, H. J. (1977). Origin and overview of IGE. *In* H. J. Klausmeier, R. A. Rossmiller, & M. Saily (Eds.), *Individually guided elementary education: Concepts and practice.* New York: Academic Press.

Kolb, D. A. (1971). *Individual learning styles and the learning process.* Cambridge, MA: MIT Press.

Kolb, D. A. (1977). *Learning style inventory: A self-description of preferred learning modes.* Boston, MA: McBer.

Kulik, J. A. (1982). Individualized systems of instruction. *In* H. E. Mitzel, (Ed.), *Encyclopedia of educational research* (5th ed.). New York: Macmillan.

Landa, L. N. (1970). *Algorithmization in learning and instruction.* Englewood Cliffs, NJ: Educational Technology.

Landa, L. N. (1976). *Instructional regulation and control.* Englewood Cliffs, NJ: Educational Technology.

Laroussi, M., & Benahmed, M. (1998). Providing an adaptive learning through the Web case of CAMELEON: Computer Aided MEdium for LEarning on Networks. In Alvegård, C. (Ed.), *Proceedings of CALISCE'98, 4th International Conference on Computer Aided Learning and Instruction in Science and Engineering,* 411–416.

Leinhardt, G. (1989). Development of expert explanation: An analysis of a sequence of subtraction lessons. *In* L. Resnick (Ed.), *Knowledge, learning, and instruction: Essays in honor of Robert Glaser* (pp. 67–124). Mahwah, NJ: Lawrence Erlbaum Associates.

Lewis, B. N., & Pask, G. (1965). The theory and practice of adaptive teaching systems. *In* R. Glaser (Ed.), *Teaching machines and programmed learning II.* Washington, DC: National Educational Association.

Liberman, H. (1995). Letizia: An agent that assists web browsing. *Proceedings of the Fourteenth International Joint Conference on Artificial Intelligence,* 924–929.

Lin, Yi-Guang; McKeachie, & Wilbert J. (1999). College Student Intrinsic and/or Extrinsic Motivation and Learning. Paper presented at the Annul Conference of the American Psychological Association, Boston, MA, August (1999).

Little, K. L. (1934). Results of use of machines for testing and for drill, upon learning in educational psychology. *Journal of Experimental Education, 3,* 45–49.

Lorton, P. (1972). *Computer-based instruction in spelling: An investigation of optimal strategies for presenting instructional material.* Unpublished doctoral dissertation, Stanford University.

Marton, F. (1988). Describing and improving learning. *In* R. R. Schmeck (Ed.), *Learning strategies and learning styles.* New York: Plenum.

McClelland, D. C. (1965). Toward a theory of motive acquisition. *American Psychologist, 33,* 201–211.

McCombs, B. L., & McDaniel, M. A. (1981). On the design of adaptive treatments for individualized instructional systems. *Educational Psychologist, 16,* 11–22.

Merrill, M. D. (1971). *Instructional design: Reading.* Upper Saddle River, NJ: Prentice Hall.

Merrill, M. D., & Boutwell, R. C. (1973). Instructional development: Methodology and research. *In* F. Kerlinger (ed.), *Review of research in education.* Itasca, IL: Peacock.

Messick, S. (1994). The matter of style: Manifestations of personality in cognition, learning and teaching. *Educational Psychologist, 29,* 121–136.

Milosavljevic, M. (1997). Augmenting the user's knowledge via comparison. In *Proceedings of the 6th International Conference on User Modelling,* Sardinia, 119–130.

Murray, T., Condit, C., & Haugsjaa, E. (1998). MetaLinks. A preliminary framework for concept-based adaptive hypermedia. In *Proceedings of Workshop "WWW-Based Tutoring" at 4th International Conference on Intelligent Tutoring Systems,* San Antonio, TX

Negro, A., Scarano, V., & Simari, R. (1998). User adaptivity on WWW through CHEOPS. In *Computing science reports,* (pp. 57–62). Eindhoven: Eindhoven University of Technology.

Neumann, G., & Zirvas, J. (1998). SKILL—A scallable internet-based teaching and learning system. *In* H., Maurer, & R. G. Olson, (Eds.), *Proceedings of WebNet'98, World Conference of the WWW, Internet, and Intranet,* Orlando, FL, 688–693.

Norman, M. F. (1964). Incremental learning on random trials. *Journal of Mathematical Psychology, 2,* 336–350.

Not E., Petrelli, D., Sarini M., Stock, O., Strapparava C., & Zancanaro M. (1998). Hypernavigation in the physical space: Adapting presentations to the user and to the situational context [Technical note]. *New Review of Hypermedia and Multimedia, 4,* 33–46.

Novick, M. R., & Jackson, P. H. (1974). *Statistical methods* for *educational and psychological research.* New York: McGraw-Hill.

Novick, M. R., & Lewis, C. (1974). *Prescribing test length for criterion-referenced measurement. 1. Posttests* (ACT Technical Bulletin No. 18). Iowa City, IA: American College Testing Program.

Oberlander, J., O'Donnell, M., Mellish, C., & Knott, A. (1998). Conversation in the museum: Experiments in dynamic hypermedia with the intelligent labelling explorer. *New Review of Hypermedia and Multimedia, 4,* 11–32.

Ohlsson, S. (1987). Some principles of intelligent tutoring. *In* R. W. Lawler & M. Yazdani (Eds.), *Artificial intelligence and education* (pp. 203–237). Norwood, NJ: Ablex.

Ohlsson, S. (1993). Learning to do and learning to understand: A lesson and a challenge for cognitive modeling. *In* P. Reimann & H. Spada (Eds.), *Learning in humans and machines* (pp. 37–62). Oxford: Pergamon Press.

Ohlsson, S., & Rees, E. (1991). The function of conceptual understanding in the learning of arithmetic procedures. *Cognition and Instruction, 8,* 103–179.

O'Neil, H. F., Jr. (1978). *Learning strategies.* New York: Academic Press.

Park, O. (1983). *Instructional strategies: A hypothetical taxonomy* (Technical Report No. 3). Minneapolis, MN: Control Data Corp.

Park, O., & Seidel, R. J. (1989). A multidisciplinary model for development of intelligent computer-assisted instruction. *Educational Technology Research and Development, 37,* 72–80.

Park, O., & Tennyson, R. D. (1980). Adaptive design strategies for selecting number and presentation order of examples in coordinate concept acquisition. *Journal of Educational Psychology, 72,* 362–370.

Park, O., & Tennyson, R. D. (1986). Computer-based response-sensitive design strategies for selecting presentation form and sequence of examples in learning of coordinate concepts. *Journal of Educational Psychology, 78,* 23–28.

Park, O., Pérez, R. S., & Seidel, R. J. (1987). Intelligent CAI: Old wine in new bottles or a new vintage? *In* G. Kearsley (Ed.), *Artificial intelligence and instruction: Applications and methods.* Boston, MA: Addison–Wesley.

Pask, G. (1957). Automatic teaching techniques. *British Communication and Electronics, 4,* 210–211.

Pask, G. (1960a). Electronic keyboard teaching machines. *In* A. A. Lumsdaine & R. Glaser (Eds.), *Teaching machines and programmed learning I.* Washington, DC: National Educational Association.

Pask, G. (1960b). Adaptive teaching with adaptive machines. *In* A. A. Lumsdaine & R. Glaser (Eds.), *Teaching machines and programmed learning I.* Washington, DC: National Educational Association.

Pask, G. (1976). Styles and strategies of learning. *British Journal of Educational Psychology, 46,* 128–148.

Pask, G. (1988). Learning strategies, teaching strategies, and conceptual or learning style. *In* R. R. Schmeck (Ed.), *Learning strategies and learning styles,* (pp. 83–100). New York: Plenum.

Pérez, T., Gutiérrez, J., & Lopistéguy, P. (1995). An adaptive hypermedia system. *In* J. Greer (Ed.), *Proceedings of AI-ED'95, 7th World Conference on Artificial Intelligence in Education,* Washington, DC, 351-358.

Peterson, P. L. (1977). Review of human characteristics and school learning. *American Educational Research Journal, 14,* 73-79.

Peterson, P. L., & Janicki, T. C. (1979). Individual characteristics and children's learning in large-group and small-group approaches. *Journal of Educational Psychology, 71,* 677-687.

Peterson, P. L., Janicki, T. C., & Swing, S. (1981). Ability X treatment interaction effects on children's learning in large-group and small-group approaches. *American Educational Research Journal, 18,* 453-473.

Piaget, J. (1977). *The development of thought: Equilibration of cognitive structures.* New York: Viking Penguin.

Pilar da Silva, D., Durm, R. V., Duval, E., & Olivié, H. (1998). Concepts and documents for adaptive educational hypermedia: A model and a prototype. In *Computing science reports* (pp. 35-43). Eindhoven: Eindhoven University of Technology.

Popkewitz, T. S., Tabachnick, B. R., & Wehlage, G. (1982). *The myth of educational reform: A study of school response to a program of change.* Madison: University of Wisconsin Press.

Posdethwait, S. N. (1981). A basis for instructional alternatives. *Journal of College Science Teaching, 21,* 446.

Posdethwait, S. N., Novak, J., & Murray, H. T. (1972). *The audio-tutorial approach to learning* (3rd ed.). Minneapolis, MN: Burgess.

Pressey, S. L. (1926). A simple apparatus which gives tests and scores and teaches. *School and Society, 23,* 373-376.

Pressey, S. L. (1927). A machine for automatic teaching of drill material. *School and Society, 25,* 1-14.

Pressey, S. L. (1959). Certain major educational issues appearing in the conference on teaching machines. *In* E. H. Galanter (Ed.), *Automatic teaching: The state of art.* New York: Wiley.

Putnam, R. T. (1987). Structuring and adjusting content for students: A study of live and simulated tutoring addition. *American Educational Research Journal, 24,* 13-48.

Redfield, D. L., & Rousseau, E. W. (1981). A meta-analysis of experimental research on teacher questioning behavior. *Review of Educational Research, 51,* 237-245.

Reigeluth, C. M. (1983). *Instructional-design theories and models: An overview of their current status.* Mahwah, NJ: Lawrence Erlbaum Associates.

Reiser, R. A. (1987). Instructional technology: A history. *In* R. Gagné (Ed.), *Instructional technology. Foundations.* Mahwah, NJ: Lawrence Erlbaum Associates.

Ritter, Steven, Koedinger, & Kenneth, R. (1996). An Architecture for Plug-In Tutor Agents. *Journal of Artificial Intelligence in Education, 7*(3-4), 315-47.

Roschelle, J., & Teasley, S. D. (1995). Construction of shared knowledge in collaborative problem solving. *In* C. O'Malley (Ed.), *Computer-supported collaborative learning.* New York: Springer-Verlag.

Ross, S. M. (1983). Increasing the meaningfulness of quantitative materials by adapting context to student background. *Journal of Educational Psychology, 75,* 519-529.

Ross, S. M., & Anand, F. (1986). *Using computer-based instruction to personalize math learning materials for elementary school children.* Paper presented at the annual meeting of the American Educational Research Association, San Francisco, CA.

Ross, S. M., & Morrison, G. R. (1986). Adaptive instructional strategies for teaching rules in mathematics. *Educational Communication and Technology Journal, 30,* 67-74.

Ross, S. M., & Morrison, G. R. (1988). Adapting instruction to learner performance and background variables. *In* D. Jonassen (Ed.), *Instructional designs for microcomputer courseware* (pp. 227-243). Mahwah, NJ: Lawrence Erlbaum Associates.

Ross, S. M., & Rakow, E. A. (1981). Learner control versus program control as adaptive strategies for selection of instructional support on math rules. *Journal of Educational Psychology, 73,* 745-753.

Rothen, W., & Tennyson, R. D. (1978). Application of Bayes' theory in designing computer-based adaptive instructional strategies. *Educational Psychologist, 12,* 317-323.

Salomon, G. (1972). Heuristic models for the generation of aptitude treatment interaction hypotheses. *Review of Educational Research, 42,* 327-343.

Salomon, G. (1974). Internalization of filmic schematic operations in interaction with learner's aptitudes. *Journal of Educational Psychology, 66,* 499-511.

Salomon, G. (1995) On the nature of pedagogical computer tools: The case of the Writing Partner. *In* S. Lajoie, & S. Derry, (Eds.), Computers as Cognitive Tools. Hillsdale, New Jersey: Lawrence Erlbaum.

Scandura, J. M. (1973). *Structural learning L theory and research.* New York: Gordon & Breach Science.

Scandura, J. M. (1977a). *Problem solving: A structural/processes approach with instructional implications.* New York: Academic.

Scandura, J. M. (1977b). Structural approach to instructional problems. *American Psychologist, 32,* 33-53.

Scandura, J. M. (1983). Instructional strategies based on the structural learning theory. *In* C. M. Reigeluth (Ed.), *Instructional-design theories and models: An overview of their current status* (pp. 213-249). Mahwah, NJ: Lawrence Erlbaum Associates.

Scandura, J. M., & Dumin, J. H. (1977). Assessing behavior potential: Test of basic theoretical assumptions. *In* J. M. Scandura (Ed.), *Problem solving: A struciural/proeesses approach with instructional implications.* New York: Academic.

Scandura, J. M., & Scandura, A. B. (1988). A structured approach to intelligent tutoring. *In* D. H. Jonassen (Ed.), *Instructional designs for microcomputer courseware.* Mahwah, NJ: Lawrence Erlbaum Associates.

Schöch, V., Specht, M., & Weber, G. (1998). "ADI"—An empirical evaluation of a tutorial agent. *In* T. Ottmann & I. Tomek (Eds.), *Proceedings of ED-MEDIA/ED-TELECOM'98, 10th World Conference on Educational Multimedia and Hypermedia and World Conference on Educational Telecommunications,* Freiburg, Germany, AACE, 1242-1247.

Schmeck, R. R. (1988). Strategies and styles of learning: An integration of varied perspectives. *In* R. R. Schmeck (Ed.), *Learning strategies and learning styles.* New York: Plenum.

Schunk, D. H. (1991). Self-efficacy and academic motivation. *Educational Psychologist, 26,* 207-231.

Schwarz, E., Brusilovsky, P., & Weber, G. (1996, June). *World wide intelligent textbooks.* Paper presented at the World Conference on Educational Telecommunications, Boston, MA.

Seidel, R. J. (1971). *Theories and strategies related to measurement in individualized instruction* (Professional paper 2-72). Alexandria, VA: Human Resources Research Organization.

Seidel, R. J., & Park, O. (1994). An historical perspective and a model for evaluation of intelligent tutoring systems. *Journal of Educational Computing Research, 10,* 103-128.

Seidel, R. J., Compton, J. G., Kopstein, F. F., Rosenblatt, R. D., & See, S. (1969). *Project IMPACT. description of learning and prescription for instruction* (Professional paper 22-69). Alexandria, VA: Human Resources Research Organization.

Seidel, R. J., Wagner, H., Rosenblatt, R. D., Hillelsohn, M. J., & Stelzer, J. (1978). Learner control of instructional sequencing with-in an adaptive tutorial CAI environment. *Instructional Science 7,* 37-80.

Seidel, R. J., Park, O., & Perez, R. (1989). Expertise of CAI: Development requirements. *Computers in Human Behaviors, 4*, 235-256.

Shin, E. C., Schallert, D. L., & Savenye, W. C. (1994). Effects of learner control, advisement, and prior knowledge on young students' learning in a hypertext environment. *Educational Technology Research and Development, 42*, 33-46.

Shute, V. J., & Psotka, J. (1995). Intelligent tutoring systems: Past, present and future. *In* D. Jonassen (Ed.), *Handbook of research on educational communications and technology.* New York: Scholastic.

Sieber, J. R., O'Neil, H. E., Jr., & Tobias, S. (1977). *Anxiety, learning and instruction.* Mahwah, NJ: Lawrence Erlbaum Associates.

Skinner, B. F. (1954). The science of learning and the art of teaching. *Harvard Educational Review, 24*, 86-97.

Skinner, B. F. (1958). The teaching machines. *Science, 128*, 969-977.

Skinner, B. F. (1968). *The technology of teaching.* New York: Appleton-Century-Crofts.

Smallwood, R. D. (1962). A *decision structure for teaching machines.* Cambridge, MA: MIT Press.

Smallwood, R. D. (1970). Optimal policy regions for computer-directed teaching systems. *In* W. H. Holtzman (Ed.), *Computer-assisted instruction, testing and guidance.* New York: Harper & Row.

Smallwood, R. D. (1971). The analysis of economic teaching strategies for a simple learning model. *Journal of Mathematical Psychology, 8*, 285-301.

Snelbbecker, G. E. (1974). *Learning theory, instructional theory, and psychoeducational design.* New York: McGraw-Hill.

Snow, E. R. (1980). Aptitude, learner control, and adaptive instruction. *Educational Psychologist, 15*, 151-158.

Snow, E. R. (1986). Individual differences and the design of educational program. *American Psychologist, 41*, 1029-1039.

Snow, E. R., & Lohman, D. F. (1984). Toward a theory of cognitive aptitude for learning from instruction. *Journal of Educational Psychology, 76*, 347-376.

Snow, E. R., & Swanson, J. (1992). Instructional psychology: Aptitude, adaptation, and assessment. *Annual Review of Psychology, 43*, 583-626.

Soller, A. L. (2001). Supporting social interaction in an intelligent collaborative learning system. *International Journal of Artificial Intelligence in Education, 12*, 40-62.

Specht, M., & Oppermann, R. (1998). ACE—Adaptive courseware environment. *New Review of Hypermedia and Multimedia, 4*, 141-161.

Specht, M., Weber, G., Heitmeyer, S., & Schöch, V. (1997). AST: Adaptive WWW-courseware for statistics. *In* P., Brusilovsky, J., Fink, & J. Kay, (Eds.), *Proceedings of Workshop "Adaptive Systems and User Modeling on the World Wide Web" at 6th International Conference on User Modeling*, UM97, Chia Laguna, Sardinia, Italy, 91-95.

Steinacker, A., Seeberg, C., Rechenberger, K., Fischer, S., & Steinmetz, R. (1998). Dynamically generated tables of contents as guided tours in adaptive hypermedia systems. In *Proceedings of ED-MEDIA/ED-TELECOM'99, 11th World Conference on Educational Multimedia and Hypermedia and World Conference on Educational Telecommunications*, Seattle, WA.

Steinberg, E. R. (1991). *Computer-assisted instruction: A synthesis of theory, practice, and technology.* Mahwah, NJ: Lawrence Erlbaum Associates.

Suppes, P., Fletcher, J. D., & Zanottie, M. (1976). Models of individual trajectories in computer-assisted instruction for deaf students. *Journal of Educational Psychology, 68*, 117-127.

Tennyson, R. D. (1975). *Adaptive Instructional Models for Concept Acquisition Education Technology, 15*(4) 7-15.

Tennyson, R. D., & Christensen, Dean L. (1985). Educational Research and Theory Perspectives on Intelligent Computer-Assisted Instruction. 1989.

Tennyson, R. D. (1981). Use of adaptive information for advisement in learning concepts and rules using computer-assisted instruction. *American Educational Research Journal, 73*, 326-334.

Tennyson, R. D., & Christensen, D. L. (1988). MAIS: An intelligent learning system. *In* D. Jonassen, (Ed.), *Instructional designs for micro-computer courseware* (pp. 247-274). Mahwah, NJ: Lawrence Erlbaum Associates.

Tennyson, R. D., & Park, O. (1987). Artificial intelligence and computer-based learning. *In* R. Gagné (Ed.), *Instructional technology: Foundations.* Mahwah, NJ: Lawrence Erlbaum Associates.

Tennyson, R. D., & Park, S. (1984). Process learning time as an adaptive design variable in concept learning using computer-based instruction. *Journal of Educational Psychology, 76*, 452-465.

Tennyson, R. D., & Rothen, W. (1977). Pre-task and on-task adaptive design strategies for selecting number of instances in concept acquisition. *Journal of Educational Psychology, 69*, 586-592.

Tennyson, R. D. Park, O., & Christensen, D. L. (1985). Adaptive control of learning time and content sequence in concept learning using computer-based instruction. *Journal of Educational Psychology, 77*, 481-491.

Thorndike, E. L. (1911). *Individuality.* Boston, MA: Houghton Mifflin.

Thorndike, E. L. (1913). *The psychology of learning: Educational psychology II.* New York: Teachers College Press.

Tobias, S. (1973). Review of the response mode issues. *Review of Educational Research, 43*, 193-204.

Tobias, S. (1976). Achievement-treatment interactions. *Review of Educational Research, 46*, 61-74.

Tobias, S. (1982). When do instructional methods make a difference? *Educational Researcher, 11*, 4-9.

Tobias, S. (1987). Learner characteristics. *In* R. Gagné, (Ed.), *Instructional technology: Foundations.* Mahwah, NJ: Lawrence Erlbaum Associates.

Tobias, S. (1989). Another look at research on the adaptation of instruction to student characteristics. *Educational Psychologist, 24*, 213-227.

Tobias, S. (1994). Interest, prior knowledge, and learning. *Review of Educational Research, 64*, 37-54.

Tobias, S., & Federico, P. A. (1984). Changing aptitude-achievement relationships in instruction: A comment. *Journal of Computer-Based Instruction, 11*, 111-112.

Tobias, S., & Ingber, T (1976). Achievement-treatment interactions in programmed instruction. *Journal of Educational Psychology, 68*, 43-47.

Townsend, J. T. (1992).*Initial mathematical models of early Morse code performance* (Research Product 93-04). Alexandria, VA: US. Army Research Institute.

Vassilveva, J., & Wasson, B. (1996). Instructional planning approaches: From tutoring towards free learning. *Proceedings of Euro-AIED'96, Lisbon, Portugal*, 1-8.

Vernon, P. E. (1973). Multivariate approaches to the study of cognitive styles. *In* J. R. Royce (Ed.), *Multivariate analysis and psychological theory* (pp. 125-141). New York: Academic Press.

Vygotsky, L. (1978). *Mind in society: The development of higher psychological processes.* Cambridge, MA: Harvard University Press.

Wang, M. (1980). Adaptive instruction: building on diversity. *Theory into Practice, 19*, 122-128.

Wang, M., & Lindvall, C. M. (1984). Individual differences and school learning environments. *Review of Research in Education, 11*, 161-225.

Wang, M., & Walberg, H.J. (1983). Adaptive instruction and classroom time. *American Educational Research Journal, 20*, 601-626.

Wasson, B. B. (1990). *Determining the focus of instruction: Content planning for intelligent tutoring systems.* Ph.D. thesis, Department of Computational Science, University of Saskatchewan.

Weiner, B. (1990). History of motivational researcher in education. *Journal of Educational Psychology, 82,* 616–622.

Weinstein, C. F., & Mayer, R. (1986). The teaching of learning strategies. *In* M. C. Wittrock (Ed.), *Handbook of research on teaching* (3rd ed.). New York: Macmillan.

Weinstein, C. F., Goetz, E. X., & Alexander, P. A. (1988).*Learning and study strategies.* San Diego, CA: Academic Press.

Wenger, E. (1987). *Artificial intelligence and tutoring systems: Computational and cognitive approaches to the communication of knowledge.* Los Altos, CA: Kaufmann.

White, B. Y., Shimoda, T. A., & Frederiksen, J. R. (1999). *Enabling students to construct theories of collaborative inquiry and reflective learning: Computer support for metacognitive development.*

Whitener, E. M. (1989). A meta-analytic review of the effect on learning of the interaction between prior achievement and instructional support. *Review of Educational Research, 59,* 65–86.

Wood, D. (2001). Scaffolding, contingent tutoring and computer-supported learning. *International Journal of Artificial Intelligence in Education, 12,* 280–292.

Wood, D., & Wood, H. (1996). Contingency in tutoring and learning. *Learning and Instruction, 6*(4), 391–398.

Wood, D., Shadbolt, N., Reichgelt, H., Wood, H., & Paskiewicz, T. (1992). EXPLAIN: Experiments in planning and instruction. *AISB Quarterly, 81,* 13–16.

Wood, H. A., & Wood, D. J. (1999). Help seeking, learning and contingent tutoring. *Computers and Education, 33*(2/3), 153–170.

Wood, H., Wood, D., & Marston, L. (1998). *A computer-based assessment approach to whole number addition and subtraction.* (Technical Report No. 56). Nottingham, UK: Centre for Research in Development, Instruction & Training, University of Nottingham.

Wulfeck, W. H., II, & Scandura, J. M. (1977). Theory of adaptive instruction with application to sequencing in teaching problem solving. *In* J. M. Scandura (Ed.), *Problem solving: A structural processes approach with instructional implications.* New York: Academic.

Zimmerman, B. J., & Martinez-Pons, M. (1990). Student differences in self-regulated learning: Relating grade, sex, and giftedness to self-efficacy and strategy use. *Journal of Educational Psychology, 82,* 51–59.

AUTOMATING INSTRUCTIONAL DESIGN: APPROACHES AND LIMITATIONS

J. Michael Spector and Celestia Ohrazda
Syracuse University

26.1 INTRODUCTION

In the last half of the previous century, many tasks that had been regarded as best accomplished by skilled workers have been shifted partially or entirely to computers. Examples can be found in nearly every domain, including assembly line operations, quality control, and financial planning. As technologies and knowledge have advanced, the tasks of scientists, engineers, and managers have become considerably more complex. Not surprisingly, there has been a tendency to apply computer technologies to the more complex and challenging tasks encountered by the user. Instructional design (ID)[1] represents a collection of complex and challenging tasks.

This discussion reviews the history of automation in the domain of ID. An overview of automation in the domain of software engineering is provided, which introduces key distinctions and types of systems to consider. This historical context sets the stage for a review of some of the more remarkable efforts to automate ID. Systems reviewed herein illustrate important lessons learned along the way. Consequently, the historical review of systems is not intended to be comprehensive or complete. Rather, it is designed to introduce key distinctions and to highlight what the instructional design community has learned through these attempts. The main theme of this chapter is that regardless of success or failure (in the sense of continued funding or market success), attempts to automate a complex process nearly always provide a deeper understanding of the complexities of that process.

26.2 HISTORICAL OVERVIEW

One way to approach the history of ID automation would be to trace the history of automation in teaching and learning. However, this would take the discussion into areas outside the focus of this discussion, requiring a discussion of teaching machines (Glaser, 1968; Silverman, 1960; Taylor, 1972) among other forms of automation in teaching and learning. Rather than extend the discussion that far back into the twentieth century, the focus will remain on the latter half of the twentieth century and on automation intended to support ID activities.

Several researchers have pointed out that developments in instructional computing generally follow developments in software engineering with about a generation delay (Spector, Polson & Muraida, 1993; Spector, Arnold, & Wilson, 1996; Tennyson, 1994). Some may argue that this is because ID and training development are typically perceived as less important than developments in other areas. A different account for this delay, however, is that educational applications are typically more complex and challenging than applications in many business and industry settings. Evidence in support of both accounts exists. The point to be pursued here is twofold: (a) to acknowledge that automation techniques and approaches in instructional settings generally follow automation in other areas, and (b) then to look at developments in other areas as a precursor to automation in ID.

Merrill (1993, 2001) and others (e.g., Glaser, 1968; Goodyear, 1994) have argued persuasively that ID is an engineering

---

[1]See Appendix 1 for abbreviations used and Appendix 2 for glossary of key terms.

discipline and that the development of instructional systems and support tools for instructional designers is somewhat similar to the development of software engineering systems and support tools for software engineers. Consequently, automation in software engineering serves as the basis for a discussion of automation in instructional design. What have been the trends and developments in computer automation in the field of software engineering?

To answer this question, it is useful to introduce the phases typically associated with a systems approach to engineering design and development. These phases include (a) analysis of the situation, requirements, and problem; (b) planning and specification of solutions and alternatives; (c) development of solutions or prototypes, with testing, redesign, and redevelopment; (d) implementation of the solutions; and (e) evaluation, maintenance, and management of the solutions. Clearly these phases overlap; they are interrelated in complex ways; they are less discrete than typically presented in textbooks, and they are often accomplished in a nonlinear and iterative manner (Tennyson, 1993). Although these software engineering phases become somewhat transparent in rapid prototyping settings, they are useful for organizing tasks that might be automated or supported with technology.

It is relevant to note that these software engineering phases may be regarded as collections of related tasks and that they correspond roughly with the generic ID model called ADDIE—analysis, design, development, implementation, and evaluation. Additionally, these phases can be clustered into related sets of processes: (a) *front-end* processes such as analysis and planning; (b) *middle-phase* processes including design, development, refinement, and delivery; and (c) *follow-through* processes, including summative and confirmative evaluation, life-cycle management, and maintenance. These clusters are useful in categorizing various approaches to automation. Goodyear (1994) clusters these phases into *upstream* and *downstream* phases, with the upstream phase including analysis and planning activities and the downstream phase including the remaining activities.

Reviewing automation in software engineering, it is possible to identify a number of support tools for computer engineers and programmers. Syntax-directed, context-sensitive editors for coding were developed in response to a recognized need to create more readable and more easily modified programming code. Such editors improved the productivity of programmers in middle-phase activities (development and implementation) and had an impact on overall program maintenance in the life cycle of a software product (follow-through activities). In short, downstream activities in both the second and the third clusters were and still are supported with such tools.

More aggressive support for front-end and early middle-phase activities developed soon thereafter. IBM developed a flowchart-based language (FL-I and FL-II) that allowed a software engineer to specify the logic of a program in terms of a rigorously defined flowchart, which then automatically generated Fortran code to implement the flowchart specification. This was clearly a form of automation aimed at the intersection of the front-end and middle phases of software engineering, which suggests that the clustering of phases is somewhat arbitrary and that the phases, however clustered, are interrelated.

In the 1980s computer-assisted software engineering (CASE) systems were developed that attempted to integrate such tools with automated support for additional analysis and management tools so as to broaden the range of activities supported. These CASE systems have evolved and are now widely used in software development. CASE systems and tools provide support throughout all phases and address both upstream and downstream activities.

About the same time that code generators and syntax-directed editors were being integrated into CASE performance support systems, object-oriented systems developed. This resulted in the reconceptualization of software engineering in terms of situated problems rather than in terms of programming or logical operations, which had been the focus in earlier software development systems. This shift emphasized how people think about problems rather than how machines process solutions to problems. Moreover, in an object-oriented system, there is strong emphasis on a long-term enterprise perspective that explicitly addresses reuse of developed resources.

Whereas code generators actually replaced the human activity of coding with an automatic process, syntax-directed editors aimed to make human coders more efficient in terms of creating syntactically correct and easily readable code. The first kind of automation has been referred to as strong support, and the second type of system is called weak support (Goodyear, 1994, 1995; Halff, 1993; Spector, 1999). Strong systems are aimed at replacing what a human can do with something to be accomplished by a computer. Weak systems are aimed at extending what humans can do, often to make less experienced practitioners perform more like experts. Weak systems have generally met with more success than strong systems, although those strong systems that are narrowly focused on a limited set of well-defined actions and activities have met with success as well (Spector, 1999).

Automated support for the middle phases occurred first and was given primary consideration and emphasis. Automated support for front-end and for follow-through activities and processes have been less aggressively pursued and developed late in the evolution of the automation of software engineering processes. Integrated systems are now the hallmark of automation within software engineering and can be characterized as primarily providing weak support across a variety of phases and activities for a wide variety of users. The integrated and powerful performance support found in many CASE systems adopted tools and capabilities found in computer-supported collaborative work systems and in information management systems. These tools have now evolved into still more powerful knowledge management systems. Capabilities supported by a knowledge management system typically include (a) communications support for a variety of users; (b) coordination of various user activities; (c) collaboration among user groups on various project tasks and activities involving the creation of products and artifacts; and (d) control processes to ensure the integrity of collaborative activities and to track the progress of projects (Spector & Edmonds, 2002). Knowledge management systems can be found in a number of domains outside software engineering and represent a full spectrum of support across a variety of tasks and users.

This short review of automation in software engineering suggests several questions to consider in examining the automation of ID and development processes.

1. Which phases are targeted for support or automation?
2. Is the type of automation intended to replace a human activity or to extend the capability of humans performing that activity?
3. Is how designers think and work being appropriately recognized and supported?
4. Are a long-term enterprise and organizational perspective explicitly supported?

Of course other questions are possible. We have chosen these questions to organize our discussion of exemplary automated ID systems because we believe that these questions and the systems that illustrate attempted answers serve to highlight the lessons learned and the issues likely to emerge as critical in the future. These four questions form the basis for the selection of systems that are examined in more detail. Before looking at specific systems, however, we discuss relevant distinctions, definitions, and types of systems.

26.3 DISTINCTIONS AND DEFINITIONS

To provide a background for our review of automated ID systems, we briefly discuss what we include in the concept of ID and what we consider automation to involve. We then identify the various characteristics that distinguish one system from another. These characteristics are used in subsequent sections to categorize various types of ID automation and also to provide a foundation for concluding remarks about the future of automated ID.

26.3.1 ID

ID, for the purpose of this discussion, is interpreted broadly and includes a collection of activities to plan, implement, evaluate, and manage events and environments that are intended to facilitate learning and performance. ID encompasses a set of interdependent and complex activities including situation assessment and problem identification, analysis and design, development and production, evaluation, and management and maintenance of learning process and the ID effort (Gagné, Briggs, & Wager, 1992).

The terms *instructional design, instructional development, instructional systems development* (ISD), and *instructional systems design* are used somewhat ambiguously within the discipline (Gustafson & Branch, 1997; Spector, 1994). Some authors and programs take pains to distinguish ID from instructional development, using one term for a more narrow set of activities and the other for a larger set of activities. Most often, however, ISD is used to refer to the entire set of processes and activities associated with ID and development. ISD has also been associated with a narrow and outdated behavioral model that evokes much negative reaction. It is not our intention here to resolve any terminological bias, indeterminism, or ambiguity. Rather, it is our aim to consider ID broadly and to look at various

approaches, techniques, and tools that have been developed to support ID.

The examination of automated support systems for ID largely ignores the area of instructional delivery, although authoring systems are mentioned in the section on types of support. There are two reasons for this. First, there are simply too many systems directed at instructional delivery to consider in this rather brief discussion. Second, the most notable aspect of automation in instructional delivery concerns intelligent tutoring systems and these systems have a significant and rich body of research and development literature of their own, which interested readers can explore. Our focus is primarily on upstream systems and systems aimed specifically at planning and prototyping, because these areas probably involve the most complex and ill-defined aspects to be found in ID.

It is worth adding that the military research and development community has contributed significantly to the exploration of automation within the domain of ID (Spector et al., 1993). Baker and O'Neil (2003) note that military training research contributed advances such as adaptive testing, simulation-based training, embedded training systems, and several authoring systems in the period from the 1970s through the 1990s. A question worth investigating is why the military training research and development community made such progress in the area of ID automation compared with the rest of the educational technology research and development community in that period.

26.3.2 Automation and Performance Support

For the purposes of our discussion, a process involves a purposeful sequence and collection of actions and activities. Some of these actions might be performed by humans and some by machines. Automation of a process may involve replacing human actions and activities with those performed by a computer (nonhuman intelligent agent). As noted earlier, this kind of automation is referred to as a strong form of support. When automation is aimed at extending the capability of a human rather than replacing the human, the support is categorized as weak and the associated system is called a weak system. Weak systems in general constitute a form of performance support.

Job aids provide the most common example of performance support. A calculator is one such form of job aid to support humans required to make rapid and accurate calculations. Performance support may also involve paper-based items such as checklists or much more sophisticated computer-based support such as a tool that automatically aligns or centers items.

Performance support systems that keep hidden the rationale or process behind the decision or solution are referred to as black box systems. Systems that make much of the system's reasoning evident and provide explanations to those using the system are called glass box or transparent systems. If users are not expected to acquire expertise, then a black box system may be more desirable and efficient. However, if users desire to acquire expertise or if they are expected to acquire higher-order capabilities, then a glass box may be preferable.

When a computer-based support system is embedded within a larger system it is generally called an electronic performance support system (EPSS). An example of such a system is an aircraft maintenance system that includes an electronic troubleshooting guide that is integrated with the specific device status and history of the aircraft. Some EPSSs provide intelligent support in the sense that they make at least preliminary decisions based on their assessment and diagnosis of the situation.

26.3.3 Intelligent Support Systems

Our definition of an intelligent system is derived from Rich and Knight (1991): Intelligent systems are those systems in which computers provide humanlike expert knowledge or performance. Early intelligent systems included those aimed at providing a medical diagnosis based on a preliminary review of a patient's condition and a sequence of follow-up examinations aimed at isolating the underlying problem. Expert system technology of the kind used in diagnostic systems is only one form of artificial intelligence. Artificial neural networks represent another important category of intelligent systems; they have been used to recognize complex patterns and to make judgments based on the pattern recognized. Applications can be found in a number of areas including quality control and security systems. Intelligent systems may be either weak or strong.

Expert advisory systems are generally weak systems that extend or enhance the capability of a human decision maker. Intelligent tutoring systems are strong systems in that the burden for deciding what to present next to a learner is shifted entirely from a human (either the teacher or the student) to the instructional delivery system.

26.3.4 Collaborative Learning and Knowledge Management Systems

Additional characteristics that serve to distinguish systems are the number of users and the number of various uses. In software engineering, systems have evolved to support multiple users and multiple uses. A parallel development is beginning to occur with regard to automated support for ID. Given the growing interest in collaborative learning and distributed decision making, it is not surprising to find increasing interest in the use of multiple-user applications in various design and development environments (Ganesan, Edmonds, & Spector, 2001). This development is further evidence of the pattern reported earlier; advances in instructional computing are about a generation behind similar developments in software engineering.

26.3.5 Instructional Perspective

A final characteristic to consider is the issue of the underlying perspective or paradigm. This issue is more complex in the area of ID than in software engineering, where we have already noted the trend to adopt an object-oriented perspective. With regard to automated support for ID, there are additional

perspectives to consider. Some of the prevailing instructional paradigms include constructionism (Jonassen, Hernandez-Serrano, & Choi, 2000), cognitive apprenticeship (Collins, Brown, & Newman, 1989), transaction theory (Merrill, 1993), and socially shared cognition (Resnick, 1989). The assumptions underlying these perspectives include the nature of knowledge, the learning environment, the role of the learner, and the role of the learner and instructional support. Does the system or support tool provide active and relevant support for a single versus a multiple learning paradigm or perspective? If software engineering continues to provide important clues about the future of ID technology, then the inclination will be toward flexible use and reuse, allowing for support of more than a single learning perspective or paradigm.

26.4 TYPES OF AUTOMATED ID SYSTEMS

Kasowitz (1998) identified the following types of automated ID tools and systems: (a) advisory/critiquing systems, (b) expert systems, (c) information management systems, (d) electronic performance support systems, and (e) authoring tools. Although these categories do overlap somewhat, they provide a reasonable organizational framework for considering automated ID systems developed in the latter half of the twentieth century.

26.4.1 Advisory/Critiquing ID Systems

The notion of an advisory critiquing system was introduced by Duchastel (1990). Duchastel proposed an advisory system that would be used to provide an ID team with a critique of a prototype or instructional solution given a set of desired outcomes and system goals. The system envisioned by Duchastel was never constructed, although an advisory system called PLANalyst created by Dodge (1994) did provide limited advisory feedback in addition to assisting in other planning activities. The lack of an advisory critiquing system reflects the complexity of such an enterprise. Such an advisory critiquing system would require sophisticated pattern recognition capabilities as well as a great deal of expert knowledge. Moreover, the prototypes and sample solutions provided would require some form of instructional tagging that has yet to be developed as well as access to extensive libraries of reusable learning objects (Wiley, 2001) and system evaluations and assessments (Baker & O'Neil, in press). Such an advisory/critiquing system remains a desirable long-term goal.

26.4.2 Expert ID Systems

In the latter part of the twentieth century, expert systems met with interest and success in various domains, including the domain of ID (Jonassen & Wilson, 1990; Spector, 1999; Welsh & Wilson, 1987). Some of these expert ID systems focused on specific tasks, such as generating partially complete programming problems in an intelligent tutoring system (van Merriëboer &

Paas, 1990) or automating the production of technical documentation for instructional and other systems (Emmott, 1998). Many such expert systems for focused tasks in ID can be found (Locatis and Park, 1992). Focused applications of expert system technology in general have met with more success than more general applications, although there were several notable developments of more ambitious expert ID systems in this period, including

1. Instructional Design Environment (IDE; Pirolli & Russel, 1990)—a hypermedia system for designing and developing instructional materials;
2. ID Expert (Merrill, 1998)—an expert system for generating instruction based on second-generation instructional transaction theory (which evolved into a commercial system called Electronic Trainer and influenced the development of XAIDA, which is described in more detail); and
3. IDioM (Gustafson & Reeves, 1990)—a rule-based, hypermedia system for instructional design and course development (which evolved into a system called ID Bookshelf for the Macintosh).

Among the applications of expert systems in ID are those that support the development of intelligent tutoring systems. van Merriënboer & Paas (1990) developed an intelligent tutoring system for teaching programming that included several rule-based systems to accomplish specific tasks, including the generation of partially solved programming problems. A wide variety of applications of expert systems within the context of intelligent tutoring systems is given by Regian and Shute (1992). Most of these are focused on the delivery aspects of instruction—creating a dynamic model of a learner's understanding within a domain to generate a new problem to the learner. A remarkable exception to this use of expert systems within the context of intelligent tutoring was the Generic Tutoring Environment (GTE), which used an expert rule base and a robust instructional model to generate intelligent tutoring systems (Elen, 1998). GTE is elaborated in more detail in the next section.

26.4.3 Information Management and ID Systems

Information and knowledge management within the domain of ID have been largely based on other ID systems and developments as components and capabilities have been integrated and made interoperable (Spector & Edmonds, 2002). For example, although the expert, hypermedia system IDE is no longer in existence, the idea was to create an entire environment for instructional development (Pirolli & Russell, 1990). Significant developments in this area have emerged from the cognitive informatics research group (LICEF) at Télé-université, the distance-learning university of the University of Québec. The LICEF research group consists of nearly a hundred individuals working in the fields of cognitive informatics, telecommunications, computational linguistics, cognitive psychology, education, and communication who have contributed to the development of methods, design and development tools, and systems to support distance learning (Paquette, 1992). This group has

developed a range of tools that support the creation of a knowledge model for a subject domain, the development of a method of instruction for that domain, and the environment for the delivery of instruction in that domain (Paquette, Aubin, & Crevier, 1994). MOT, one of the knowledge modeling tools created by this group, is described in more detail in the next section.

26.4.4 EPSSs for ID

EPSSs are typically embedded within a larger application (e.g., an airplane) and provide targeted support to humans performing tasks on those larger systems (e.g., aircraft maintenance technicians). Within the context of ID, there have been commercial EPSSs (e.g., Designer's Edge and Instructional Design-Ware) as well as R&D EPSSs (e.g., IDioM). NCR Corporation commissioned the development of an EPSS for ID based on a development methodology called quality information products process (Jury & Reeves, 1999). Another example of an EPSS in ID is CASCADE, a support tool aimed at facilitating rapid prototyping within ID (Nieveen, 1999). An example of an EPSS for ID that is not tightly coupled with an authoring tool is the Guided Approach to Instructional Design Advising, which is described in more detail in the following section.

26.4.5 ID Authoring Tools

There has been a plethora of authoring tools to enable instructors and instructional developers to create computer- and Web-based learning environments (Kearsley, 1984). Early authoring systems were text based and ran on mainframes (e.g., IBM's Instructional Interaction System and Control Data Corporation's Plato System). Widely used course authoring systems include Macromedia's Authorware and Click2Learn's ToolBook. Many other course authoring systems have been developed and are still in use, including IconAuthor, Quest, and TenCore, which, along with other authoring languages, was developed from Tutor, the authoring language underlying the Plato System.

Specific languages have been developed to make the creation of interactive simulations possible. The creation of meaningful simulations has proven to be a difficult task for subject experts who lack specific training in the creation of simulations. The system that comes closest to making simulation authoring possible for those with minimal special training in simulation development is SimQuest (de Jong, Limbach, & Gellevij, 1999). SimQuest includes a building blocks metaphor and draws on a library of existing simulation objects, making it also an information and knowledge management tool for ID.

The Internet often plays a role in instructional delivery and many authoring environments have been built specifically to host or support lessons and courses on the World Wide Web. Among the better-known of the commercial Web-based course management systems are BlackBoard, Learning Space, TopClass, and WebCT. Although there have been many publications about courses and implementations in such environments, there has been very little research with regard to effects of the systems on instruction. TeleTop, a system developed at the University of Twente, is a notable exception that documents the particular time burdens for instructors leading Web-based courses (Gervedink Nijhuis & Collis, 2003).

26.5 A CLOSER LOOK AT FOUR SYSTEMS

In this section we briefly describe a variety of automated instructional design systems, including the following:

- GAIDA (Guided Approach to ID Advising—later called GUIDE)
- GTE (Generic Tutoring Environment)
- MOT (Modélisation par Objets Typés)
- XAIDA (Experimental Advanced Instructional Design Associate—called an advisor in early publications)

26.5.1 GAIDA—Guided Approach to ID Advising

An advisory system to support lesson design was developed as part of the Advanced Instructional Design Advisor project at Armstrong Laboratory (Spector et al., 1993). This advisory system is called GAIDA. The system uses completely developed sample cases as the basis for helping less experienced instructional designers construct their lesson plans. GAIDA is designed explicitly around the nine events of instruction (Gagné, 1985). Gagné participated in the design of the system and scripted the first several cases that were included in the system while at

Armstrong Laboratory as a Senior National Research Council Fellow (Spector, 2000). GAIDA allows users to view a completely worked example, shown from the learner's point of view (see Fig. 26.1). The user can shift from this learner view to a designer view that provides an elaboration of why specific learner activities were designed as they were. The designer view allows the user to take notes and to cut and paste items that may be relevant to a lesson plan under construction.

GAIDA was also designed so that additional cases and examples could easily be added. Moreover, the design advice in GAIDA could be easily modified and customized to local practices. Initial cases included lessons about identifying and classifying electronic components, performing a checklist procedure to test a piece of equipment, checking a patient's breathing capacity, handcuffing a criminal suspect, performing a formation flying maneuver, and integrating multiple media into lessons. GAIDA was adopted for use in the Air Education and Training Command's training for technical trainers. As part of the U.S. government's technology transfer effort in the 1990s, GAIDA became a commercial product called GUIDE—Guided Understanding of Instructional Design Expertise—made available through the International Consortium for Courseware Engineering with three additional cases.

As a commercial product, GUIDE was only marginally successful, although GAIDA continues to be used by the Air Force in the technical training sequence. The utility of this advising system is that it provides a concrete context for the elaboration of ID principles without imposing rigidity or stifling creativity. The user can select examples that appear to be relevant to a current project and borrow as much or as little as desired. Gagné's basic assumption was that targeted users were bright (all were subject

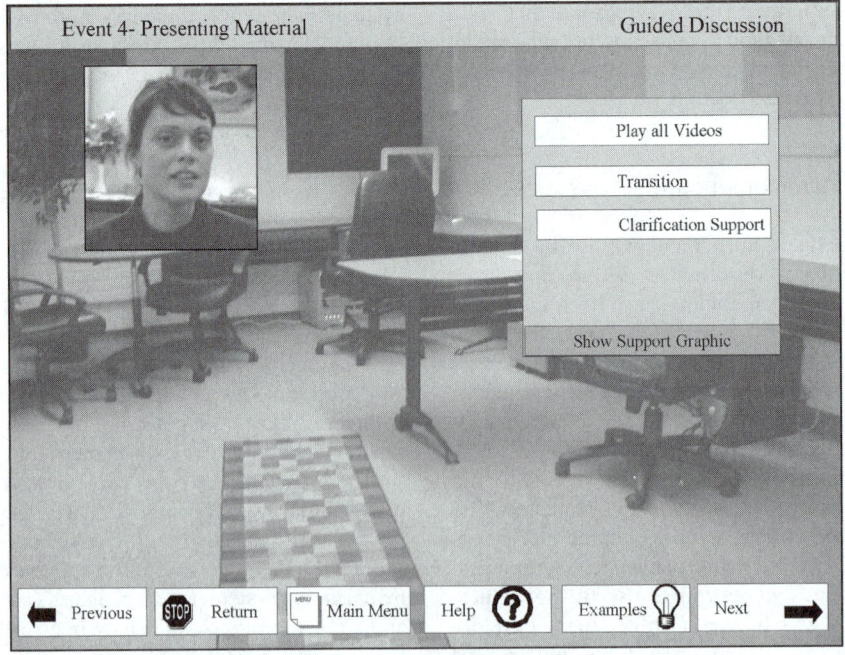

FIGURE 26.1. Adapted from screen from GAIDA/GUIDE.

matter experts who had advanced to a recognized level of expertise in their fields) and motivated. All that was required to enable such users to produce meaningful lesson plans were relevant examples elaborated in a straightforward manner. GAIDA/GUIDE achieved these goals. Users quickly advanced from a beginning level to more advanced levels of ID competence based on the advice and elaborated examples found in GAIDA.

26.5.2 GTE—Generic Tutoring Environment

GTE grew out of an international collaboration involving academic and industrial communities in several countries and was focused on providing support for intelligent tutoring systems. GTE proceeds from a particular educational philosophy and explicitly adopts a particular psychological perspective involving the nature of expertise (Ericsson and Smith, 1991; Resnick, 1989). A cognitive processing perspective informs the design of GTE (van Marcke's, 1992a, 1992b, 1998). van Marcke (1998), the designer of GTE, argues that teaching is primarily a knowledge-based task. Experienced teachers are able to draw on specific teaching knowledge in addition to extensive domain knowledge. A primary task for an intelligent tutoring system is to integrate that instructional knowledge in the system in a way that allows the system to adapt to learners just as expert teachers do.

van Marcke took an intentionally narrow view of the instructional context, confined instructional decision making to teachers, and did not explore the decisions that might be made by instructional designers, textbook authors, test experts, and so on.

GTE combines a reductionist perspective with a pragmatic approach. The tutor-generation task is reduced to two tasks: (a) determining all of the relevant components and relationships (an instructional semantic network), and (b) determining how and when to provide and combine these components to learners so as to promote learning (Fig. 26.2). The domain perspective in GTE consists of a static semantic network. According to van Marcke (1998), this network is used for sequencing material within a topic area, for indexing instructional objects, and for stating learning objectives. GTE makes use of an object-oriented network so that components can be meaningfully combined and reused.

Although a reductionist approach lends itself to automation in the strong sense, there are limitations. As van Marcke (1998) claims, (a) teaching is an inherently complex activity, (b) there are only incomplete theories about how people learn, and (c) strong generative systems should include and exploit expertlike instructional decision making.

However, it is not completely clear how expert human designers work. Evidence suggests that experts typically use a case-based approach initially to structure complex instructional

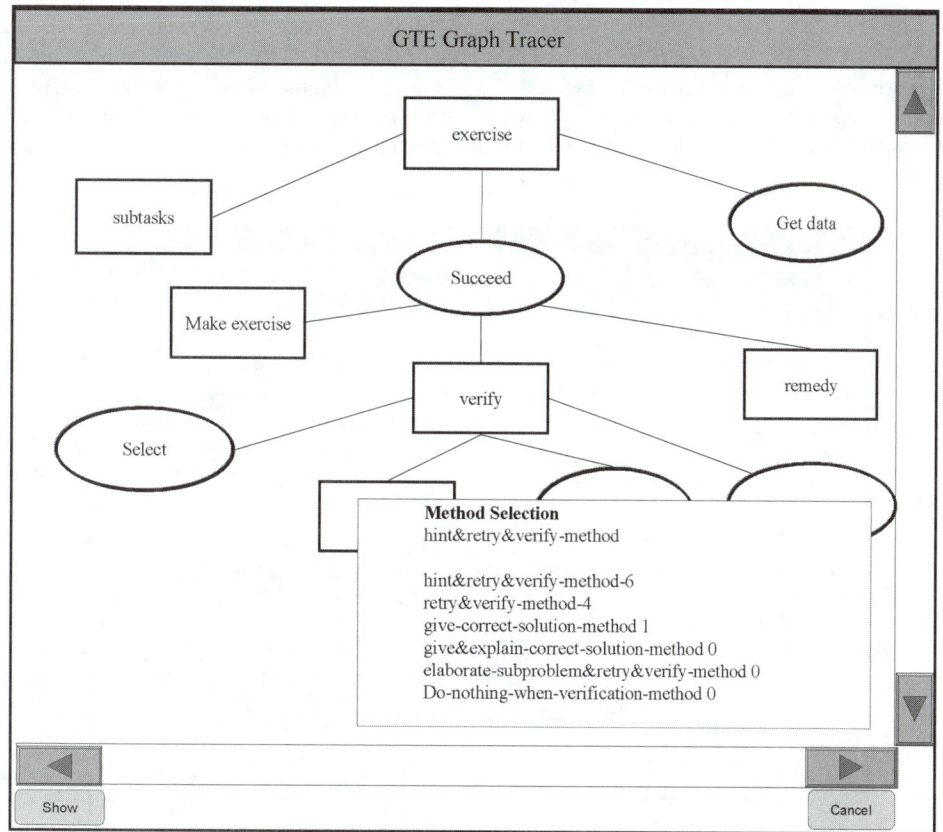

FIGURE 26.2. Sample GTE method selection screen (adapted from van Marcke, 1992b).

planning tasks (Perez & Neiderman, 1992; Rowland, 1992). The rationale in case-based tools is that inexperienced instructional planners lack case expertise and that this can be provided by embedding design rationale with lesson and course exemplars. This rationale informed the development of GAIDA.

However, cases lack the granularity of the very detailed objects described by van Marcke (1998). A significant contribution of GTE is in the area of object-oriented instructional design. GTE aimed to generate computer-based lessons and replace a human developer in that process. GTE does not directly support student modeling in the sense that this term has been used in the intelligent tutoring literature, although van Marcke (1998) indicates that GTE's knowledge base can be linked to student modeling techniques. GTE contains a number of instructional methods with detailed elaborations and basic rules for their applicability within a dynamic generative environment. When these instructional rules break down, it is possible to resort to human instructional intervention or attempt the computationally complex and challenging task of maintaining a detailed and dynamic student model. By not directly supporting student modeling, GTE remains a generic tool, which is both a strength and a weakness.

One might argue that it is only when a case-based approach fails or breaks down that humans revert to overtly reductionistic approaches. What has been successfully modeled and implemented in GTE is not human instructional expertise. Rather, what has been modeled is knowledge about instruction that is likely to work when human expertise is not available, as might be the case in many computer-based tutoring environments.

Because teaching is a complex collection of activities, we ought to have limited expectations with regard to the extent that computer tutors are able to replace human tutors. Moreover, it seems reasonable to plan for both human and computer tutoring, coaching, and facilitation in many situations. Unfortu-

nately, the notion of combining strong generative systems (such as GTE) with weak advising systems (such as GAIDA) has not yet established a place in the automation of instructional design. We return to this point in our concluding remarks.

26.5.3 MOT—Modélisation par Objets Typés

MOT is a knowledge-based modeling tool aimed at assisting instructional designers and developers in determining what kind of content knowledge and skills are involved, how these items are related, and how they might then be sequenced for learning and instruction. MOT grew out of an earlier effort at Télé-université LICEF, a research laboratory for cognitive informatics and training environments at the University of Québec, to develop a didactic engineering workbench (Paquette, 1992; Paquette et al., 1994).

MOT allows a subject matter expert or designer to create a semantic network of a subject domain at a level of detail appropriate for instructional purposes (Fig. 26.3). The semantic network has two interesting features: (a) It is designed specifically for instructional purposes (e.g., there are links to indicate relationships that have instructional significance), and (b) the objects in the network are part of an object-oriented network (e.g., they can be instantiated at various points in a curriculum/course and retain relevant aspects).

MOT can be used as a stand-alone tool or in concert with other tools developed at Télé-université, including a design methodology tool (ADISA) and a Web-based delivery environment tool (Explor@). The suite of tools available provides the kind of integration and broad enterprise support found in other domains. This entire suite of tools can be regarded as a knowledge management system for ID (Spector & Edmonds,

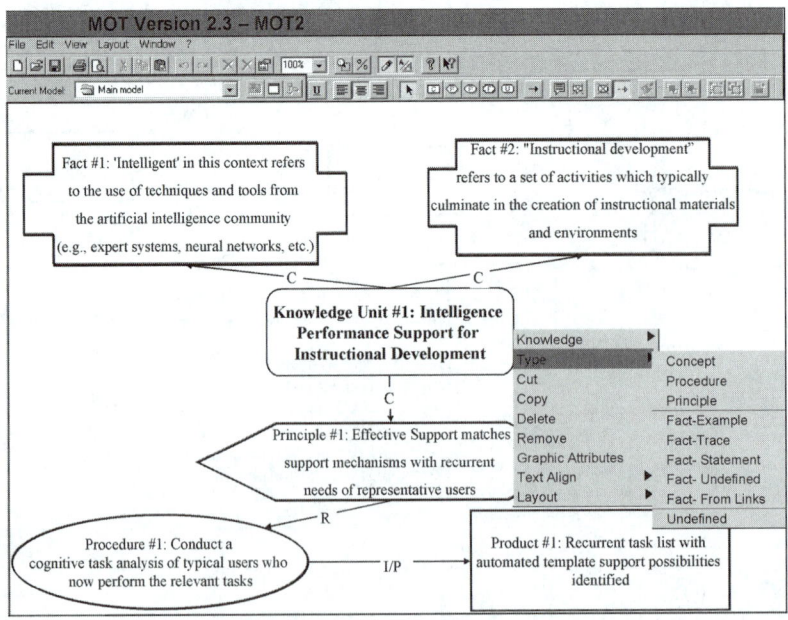

FIGURE 26.3. Sample MOT knowledge modeling screen.

2002). ADISA embraces an instructional perspective that is similar to cognitive apprenticeship (Collins et al., 1989) and is actively supportive of situated learning (Paquette, 1996; Paquette et al., 1994).

MOT is a weak system in that it extends the ability of designers to plan instruction based on the knowledge and skills involved. The rationale in MOT is not as transparent as the rationale offered in GAIDA, which provides elaborations of specific cases. However, whereas GAIDA left the user to do whatever seemed appropriate, MOT imposes logical constraints on instructional networks (e.g., a user cannot create an instance that governs a process). Moreover, the object-oriented approach of MOT and its place in the context of a larger knowledge management system for ID has great potential for future developments.

26.5.4   XAIDA—Experimental Advanced Instructional Design Associate

Like GAIDA, XAIDA was developed as part of the Advanced Instructional Design Advisor project at Armstrong Laboratory (Spector et al., 1993). Whereas GAIDA explicitly adopted a weak approach to automated support, XAIDA aggressively adopted a strong approach with the goal of generating prototype computer-based instruction based on content information and a description of the learning situation provided by a subject matter expert or technical trainer. The underlying instructional model was based on ID^2 (second-generation instructional design) and ID Expert (Merrill, 1993, 1998). A commercial version of ID Expert known as Electronic Trainer met with substantial success and the underlying structure is part of other systems being offered by Leading Way Technologies in California.

XAIDA was aimed at entry-level and refresher aircraft maintenance training (Fig. 26.4). In short, the domain of application was appropriately constrained and targeted users were

reasonably well defined. As with the other strong system described here in GTE, such constraints appear to be necessary when attempting to automate a complex process completely. Whereas expert human designers can make adjustments to the many variations in domains, learners, and learning situations, a strong generative system cannot benefit from such expertise in ill-defined domains. Setting proper constraints is a practical way to address this limitation.

One of the more remarkable achievements of XAIDA was its linkage to the Integrated Maintenance Information System (IMIS), which consisted of two databases: One contained technical descriptions and drawings of the avionic components of a military aircraft, and the other contained troubleshooting procedures for those components (Spector et al., 1996). The basic notion of this innovation was to address a scenario such as the following: A technical supervisor has determined that an apprentice technician requires some refresher training on how to remove, troubleshoot, repair, and replace the radar in a particular aircraft. The supervisor goes to XAIDA-IMIS, selects the component about which *just-in-need* instruction is desired, and selects the type of training desired. XAIDA-IMIS then generates a module based on the current version of the equipment installed in the aircraft. IMIS has current information on installed equipment. Cases in technical training schools usually involve earlier versions of equipment. The XAIDA-IMIS module is specific to the need and to the equipment actually installed. The entire process of generating a *just-in-need* lesson required about 5 min—from the identification of the need to the delivered lesson.

Despite this remarkable demonstration of efficiency and effectiveness, the Air Force has since abandoned this effort. Nevertheless, the linkage to databases represents another extension of automated support into the domain of knowledge management for ID. Additionally, the requirement to constrain strong systems again demonstrates the limitations of automation within a complex domain.

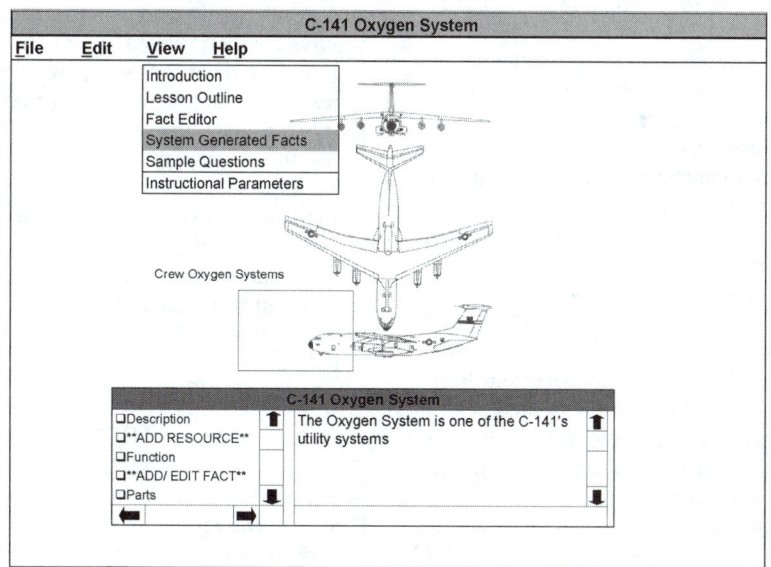

FIGURE 26.4. Example of an XAIDA-generated lesson and interaction screen.

TABLE 26.1. Automated Support for Instructional Design and Development

Type of Automation or Support	GAIDA	MOT	GTE	XAIDA
Strong or weak	Weak	Weak	Strong	Strong
Black box or glass box	Glass	Glass	Black	Opaque
Upstream or downstream	Up	Up	Down	Down
Single-user or multiple-user	Single	Group	Single	Group
Learning paradigm(s) supported	Multiple	Single	Single	Single

These four unique systems are summarized in Table 26.1. The intention of this section was to illustrate a representative variety of ID automated systems so as to motivate a discussion of current trends and issues and to provide a foundation for speculation about the future of automation in the domain of ID.

26.6 RESEARCH FINDINGS

There has been considerable research conducted on these four systems as well as others mentioned earlier. What can be learned from the research on automated ID systems? First, evaluating automated ID systems is a complex problem (Gros & Spector, 1994). There are numerous factors to consider, including the type of system, the goals of the instruction developed, the ID team, and the instructors and learners for whom systems are created. Jonassen and Wilson (1990) propose a number of evaluation criteria similar to those developed for the evaluation of CASE tools. Montague and Wulfeck (1982) propose an instructional quality inventory to be used in evaluating instructional systems. Halff (1993) distinguishes three levels of evaluation for ID systems: quality review, formative evaluation, and summative evaluation. Halff also emphasizes the requirement to assure quality prior to conducting formative and summative evaluations. Gayeski (1991) argues that an evaluation of automated ID systems requires consideration of uses by novice as well as expert designers and organizational considerations. In short, it is difficult to evaluate automated ID systems.

Most of the published research presents formative evaluations of systems or evaluations of learning environments created using particular systems. These research findings do not address the deeper issues associated with the four questions raised earlier, as it is difficult to link features of an ID system to improved learning and instruction or to longer-term trends in the development of learning environments. Two kinds of evaluation findings are worth noting. First, productivity improvements have occurred due to systems that provide performance support or automate portions of ID (Bartoli & Golas, 1997; Merrill, 1998; Spector et al., 1993). While results vary, using support tools can achieve an order of magnitude improvement in the productivity of a design team. Second, learning outcomes can result from systems that enable designers to adapt systems to particular learning needs. The promise of intelligent tutoring systems was to raise learning outcomes by two standard deviations, similar to that noted for one-to-one human tutoring situations (Farr & Psotka, 1992). While such significant outcomes did not occur, there are many instances of significant improvement (as much as a standard deviation) in learning outcomes with

regard to well-structured learning goals (e.g., beginning programming and simple troubleshooting) (Farr & Psotka, 1992; Regian & Shute, 1992). In addition to such findings, some evaluation findings with regard to the four systems described earlier are mentioned next.

GAIDA has been evaluated in numerous settings with both novice and expert designers (Gettman, McNelly, & Muraida, 1999). Findings suggest that expert designers found little use for GAIDA, whereas novice designers made extensive use of GAIDA for about 6 months and then no longer felt a need to use it. GTE proved to be useful in generating intelligent tutors across a variety of subject domains, as long as the subject domains were sufficiently well structured (Elen, 1998). MOT has been used by novice and experienced designers for a variety of domains ranging from well-structured to ill-structured knowledge domains (e.g., organizational management). Paguette and colleagues (1994) found consistent improvements in both productivity (about an order of magnitude; similar to the productivity improvements of other systems) and quality (consistency of products and client satisfaction were the primary measures). XAIDA was evaluated during every phase of its development (Muraida, Spector, O'Neil, & Marlino, 1993). Perhaps unique to the XAIDA project was a serious evaluation of the design plan, along with subsequent evaluations of XAIDA as it was developed. The final evaluation of XAIDA focused on productivity and the results are again remarkable. As noted earlier, XAIDA was linked by software to electronic databases that described aircraft subsystems and provided standard troubleshooting procedures for each subsystem. When XAIDA was linked to these databases, a technical supervisor could generate a lesson for refresher training for an apprentice technician on a selected subsystem in less than 10 minutes (Spector et al., 1996).

We found no published research findings on the organizational impact of these systems, although anecdotal reports on nearly every system mentioned are easily found. Rather than review additional evaluation studies or present anecdotal evidence of the effects of these systems, we move next to a discussion of trends and issues likely to follow given what has already been accomplished with and learned from these systems.

26.7 TRENDS AND ISSUES

Although the attempts to automate ID are not by any means limited to the four systems outlined in the preceding section, we have used these systems for illustrative purposes. We believe that they serve as a representation of the major trends, issues, and possibilities that have been encountered in the process.

Two very reachable possibilities pertaining to efficiency and effectiveness of intelligent performance support for courseware engineering come to mind. The first concerns connecting object-oriented approaches with case-based advising, and the second concerns the creation of easily accessible, reusable electronic databases. The key to achieving both of these possibilities revolves around the key notions of object orientation, knowledge modeling, instructional tagging, learning objects, and instructional standards. These key ideas have been demonstrated in the systems here and exist in other systems as well.

First, let us consider connecting object-oriented approaches with case-based advising. Case-based advising has been demonstrated in GUIDE. Case-based advising could be made much more flexible if it were constructed within an object-oriented framework. This would mean that cases could be constructed as needed to suit specific and dynamic requirements rather than relying on prescribed cases, as found in GAIDA/GUIDE.

The notion of knowledge objects has emerged from object orientation in software engineering and the development of object-oriented programming languages such as SIMULA (Dahl & Nygaard, 1966). Basically the notion of object orientation is to think in terms of (a) classes of things with more or less well-defined characteristics or attributes, (b) objects that inherit most or all of the characteristics of a class and have additional built-in functionality that allows them to act and react to specific situations and data, and (c) methods that specify the actions associated with an object. A knowledge object might be considered as an instance within an information processing class that has the purpose of representing information or promoting internal representation and understanding. A knowledge object that is explicitly intended to facilitate learning is called a learning object (Wiley, 2001). Knowledge objects might be considered the building blocks of a knowledge construction set within an instructional system, although this metaphor should not be taken literally or casually.

The general notion of object orientation is twofold: to promote analysis and problem solving in terms that closely parallel human experience rather than in terms that are tightly linked to machine processing features, and (2) to promote reuse. Object orientation was initially conceptualized in terms of improved productivity, although there has been a clear shift toward viewing object orientation in education as being aimed primarily at improving understanding. The value of knowledge objects in promoting organizational learning is recognized in many knowledge management systems.

Second, dramatic improvements in development time and cost are now a reasonable goal. An object-oriented approach allows instructional objects to be constructed dynamically and flexibly, as ably illustrated by GTE (van Marke 1992a, 1998).

The temptation will most likely be to base strong automated support for ID on knowledge objects and metatagging (Table 26.2). Identifying a sufficient set of instructional tags and then devising a facile way to support tagging of existing and new electronic databases are a significant and challenging undertaking but would be eminently worthwhile.

There is an active effort to create a standardized extensible markup language called XML (Connolly, 1997). This language is similar to HTML but it is intended to provide a syntax for defining

TABLE 26.2. Instructional Tags

Notional Instructional Tag	Instructional Purpose
key_definition	Identify a key definition; automatically generate of glossary entries
good_example_of	Highlight an exemplifying item; generate an introductory example or reminder item
non_example_of	Emphasize a boundary case or exception or contrasting example; generate an elaboration sequence
bad_example_of	Highlight an important distinction; generate an elaboration sequence.
moral_of_story	Summarize a main point; generate a synthetic sequence
theme_of_article	Provide a very short abstract sentence; generate an introductory sequence
main_point_of_paragraph	Summarize a short module or sequence; generate a remedial or refresher sequence

a specialized or customized markup language, returning to the original notion behind SGML (Standard Generalized Markup Language) with the advantage of a decade of experience. Basically, XML is a low-level syntax for creating new declarative representations for specific domains. Several such instantiations have been developed including MathML for mathematical expressions and SMIL for scheduling multimedia presentations on the Internet. A quite natural research and development project that could be associated with the XML effort would be to create, implement, and evaluate an instructional markup language using XML as the underlying mechanism.

Clearly, the use of object-oriented approaches makes it possible in principle to reuse previous courses, lessons, databases, and so on. Two long-range goals come to mind. One has to do with connecting object-oriented design with case-based advising and guidance (for learners, instructors, and designers). Case-based advising could be made much more flexible if it were constructed within an object-oriented framework. Cases could be constructed from collections of smaller objects and could be activated according to a variety of parameters. Thus, cases could be constructed as needed to suit specific and dynamic requirements rather than relying on prescribed cases or a case base.

Both object orientation and case libraries are making their way into commercial authoring products as well. For example, PowerSim, an environment for creating system dynamics-based systems, has tested the ability to provide model builders with partially complete, preconstructed generic structures with all the relevant properties of reusable objects (Gonzalez, 1998). Such reusable, generic structures (adaptive templates) will most likely appear in other commercial systems as well. Creating reusable objects and case libraries makes more poignant the need for advising those who must select relevant items from these new ID riches.

Knowledge management systems developed somewhat independently of object orientation in software engineering. They have evolved from early information management systems that were an evolution from earlier database management systems. Databases were initially collections of records that contained individual fields representing information about some collection of things. Early databases typically had only one type of user, who had a specific use for the database. As information processing enjoyed more and more success in enterprise-wide situations, multiple users became the norm, and each user often had different requirements for finding, relating, and using information from a number of different sources. Relational databases and sophisticated query and user access systems were developed to meet these needs in the form of information management systems. As the number and variety of users and uses grew, and as the overall value of these systems in promoting organizational flexibility, productivity, responsiveness, and adaptability became more widely recognized, still more powerful knowledge management systems were developed. Knowledge management systems add powerful support for communication, coordination, collaboration, and control of information management systems and generally make use of some kind of fundamental object orientation system.

26.8   CONCLUDING REMARKS

Attempts to automate aspects of ID have led to deep insights into the more general processes of ID and development. Indeed, the theme of this chapter is that we have only begun to witness the many ways in which intelligent support can be provided to instructional designers and developers; however, we would be wrong to expect computers to replace human expertise in crucial areas of ID and development.

In the process of attempting to automate ID, key lessons include the following:

1. Strong systems work only in narrow and well-defined domains; there will continue to be opportunities to develop intelligent agents in support of learning, more so in the delivery domain (downstream activities) and less so in the planning and analysis phases (upstream activities).
2. Knowledge management systems are by nature weak systems and have a definite place in ID, which is by nature complex and often involves teams and enterprise-level learning and performance issues; some components of a knowledge management system for ID may involve strong and intelligent support, as in an intelligent agent to perform a particular task.
3. The value of knowledge objects and reuse is likely to be realized only when humans are kept involved and systems kept open.
4. We learn a lot about a process by trying to automate it; we find out how much human involvement is required and when and why such involvement is advisable. We should not discourage or denigrate attempts to automate more ID processes—we always learn something in the process.
5. The temptation will be to base strong automated support for ID on knowledge objects and metatagging.
6. Human involvement in the ID process will still be necessary and the real value of reusability and knowledge management in support of ID will be realized only if humans are involved in the process (Ganesan et al., 2001).

In conclusion, it seems safe to say that the future of intelligent performance support for courseware engineering will be filled with interesting opportunities and challenges. The most interesting opportunities may arise in inter- and multidisciplinary settings, which appear to be essential to making significant advances. The big challenge will be to remain humble with regard to how little we really know about human learning and intelligence.

As we develop newer and more sophisticated techniques for creating learning environments, we should remember that learning cultures are dynamic. When only mainframe, text-based systems were available, users and learners came to expect certain types of screens and interactions. Today's learners are more accustomed to highly interactive, multimedia environments, often attached to the World Wide Web. Learning environments that do not take these expectations into account may fall short of their intended effectiveness. Moreover, humility should remind us that machines are not likely to replace all aspects of human intelligence and expertise in the area of ID and development.

APPENDIX 1.   ABBREVIATIONS AND ACRONYMS

AIDA	Advanced Instructional Design Advisor
CASE	Computer-assisted software engineering
EPSS	Electronic performance support system
GAIDA	Guided Approach to Instructional Design Advising
GTE	Generic Tutoring Environment
GUIDE	Guidance for Understanding Instructional Design Expertise
HTML	Hypertext Markup Language
ID	Instructional design (broadly conceived; sometimes also called instructional development)
ID^2	Second-generation instructional design
IDE	Instructional Design Environment
IMIS	Integrated Maintenance Information System
ISD	Instructional systems development
IPSS	Intelligent performance support system
KQML	Knowledge Query Markup Language
MOT	Modélisation par Objets Typés (a knowledge modeling tool)
SCORM	Sharable Content Object Reference Model
SGML	Standard Generalized Markup Language
XAIDA	Experimental Advanced Instructional Design Associate
XML	Extensible Markup Language

APPENDIX 2.   GLOSSARY OF KEY TERMS

Advisory system: In instructional design (ID) a computer system that implements principles and rules (analyze, design, develop, implement, evaluate) in guiding the developer through the instructional design process.

Black box system: Performance support systems that keep hidden from the user the rationale behind the decisions being made and the processes performed.

Courseware engineering: An emerging set of practices, tools, and methodologies that result from an engineering approach to instructional computing systems. An engineering approach is in contrast to a craft or artisan approach and emphasizes the use of principled methods rather than intuition; an engineering approach values the replicability of processes and results rather than idiosyncratic creativity.

Downstream support: Support for implementation-intensive activities, such as the production of graphics, during the courseware development process.

Electronic performance support system: An interactive computer-based environment or infrastructure, embedded within a larger system, that provides support to facilitate performance. This includes capturing, storing, and distributing knowledge, information, advice, and learning experiences with minimum support from other people.

Expert system: A computer-based representation of the domain-specific knowledge of an expert in a form that can accessed by others for problem solving and decision making. An expert system typically contains a set of rules, a way to represent various situations, and an inference engine to determine which rule to activate given a particular situation.

Generative approach: Systems that take over the more routine aspects of ID and accelerate the process of the production of instruction, leaving the more conceptual aspects of ID to the designer.

Intelligent systems: Those systems in which computers provide humanlike expert knowledge or performance. Expert system technology represent one type of intelligent systems; artificial neural networks represent another category of intelligent systems.

Knowledge management systems: An evolution from earlier information management systems in which support for a variety of users is included. This leads to power support for communication, coordination, collaboration, and control on top of information management systems.

Knowledge objects: Provide a way to organize a knowledge base so that different instructional algorithms can use the same knowledge objects to teach the same subject matter content.

Learning object: Any entity, digital or nondigital, that can be used or referenced in technology-supported learning.

Metadata: Data about data that describe something about the data intended to promote reuse and usability in general. In the past, metadata have largely been of concern to programmers and specialists; however, as the number of learning objects continues to increase, creators of learning objects should also create metadata categories and values.

Multiple-paradigm support: The ability to support more than one instructional perspective in accordance with an analysis of features of the situation at hand.

Multiple-user support or groupware: Various techniques that allow users to share documents, media, and other items in a database, exchange remarks, and create alternative versions of these items.

Object orientation: A way to think in terms of (a) classes of things with more or less defined characteristics, (b) objects that inherit characteristics of classes and have a built-in functionality that allows them to react to specific situations and data, and (c) methods that specify the actions associated with the objects.

Process automation: Automation of a process involves replacing human actions with those performed by a computer or nonintelligent agent.

Strong support: A performance support system that intends to replace part of an activity or process previously performed by a human with an automatic process is characterized as a strong system.

Transparent systems or glass box systems: Performance support systems that provide an explanation and make much of the systems' reasoning evident to the user.

Upstream support: Support for analysis and design-intensive activities, such as definition of the target audience, information to be learned, learning goals, and objectives.

Weak support: A performance support systems that intends to extend the capability of one or more humans performing various actions and activities is characterized as a weak form of automation or a weak system.

References

Baker, E. L., & O'Neil, H. F., Jr. (2003). Evaluation and research for technology: Not just playing around. *Evaluation and Program Planning, 26*(2), 169–176.

Bartoli, C. S., & Golas, K. C. (1997, December). *An approach to automating development of interactive courseware.* Paper presented at the annual meeting of the Interservice/Industry Training, Simulation and Education Conference, Orlando, FL.

Collins, A., Brown, J. S., & Newman, S. E. (1989). Cognitive apprenticeship: Teaching the crafts of reading, writing, and mathematics. In L. B. Resnick (Ed.), *Knowing, learning, and instruction: Essays in honor of Robert Glaser* (pp. 453–494). Mahwah, NJ: Lawrence Erlbaum Associates.

Connolly, D. (Ed.). (1997). XML: Principles, tools, and techniques. *World Wide Web Journal, 2*(4), 1–266.

Dahl, O. J., & Nygaard, K. (1966). SIMULA—An algol based simulation language. *Communications of the ACM, 9*(9), 671–678.

de Jong, T., Limbach, R., & Gellevij, M. (1999). Cognitive tools to support the instructional design of simulation-based discovery learning environments: The SimQuest authoring system. In J. V. D. Akker, R. M. Branch, K. Gustafson, N. Nieveen, & T. Plomp (Eds.), *Design approaches and tools in education and training* (pp. 215–224). Dordrecht: Kluwer.

Dodge, B. J. (1994, February). *Design and formative evaluation of PLANalyst: A lesson design tool.* Paper presented at the annual meeting of the Association for Educational Communications and Technology, Nashville, TN.

Duchastel, P. C. (1990). Cognitive design for instructional design. *Instructional Science, 19*(6), 437–444.

Elen, J. (1998). Automating I.D.: The impact of theoretical knowledge bases and referent systems. *Instructional Science, 26*(3/4), 281-297.

Emmott, L. C. (1998). Automating the production of interactive technical documentation and EPSS. *Journal of Interactive Instruction Development, 11*(1), 25-34.

Ericsson, K. A., & Smith, J. (Eds.). (1991). *Toward a general theory of expertise: Prospects and limits.* New York: Cambridge University Press.

Farr, M. J., & Psotka, J. (Eds.). (1992). *Intelligent instruction by computer: Theory and practice.* Bristol, PA: Taylor & Francis.

Gagné, R. M. (1985). *Conditions of learning* (4th ed.). New York: Holt, Rinehart and Winston.

Gagné, R. M., Briggs, L. J., & Wager, W. W. (1992). *Principles of instructional design* (4th ed.) Fort Worth, TX: Harcourt Brace Jovanovich.

Ganesan, R., Edmonds, G. S., & Spector, J. M. (2001). The changing nature of instructional design for networked learning. In C. Jones & C. Steeples (Eds.), *Networked learning in higher education* (pp. 93-109). Berlin: Springer-Verlag.

Gayeski, D. (1991). Software tools for empowering instructional developers. *Performance Improvement Quarterly, 4*(4), 21-36.

Gervedink Nijhuis, G., & Collis, B. (2003). Using a web-based course-management system: An evaluation of management tasks and time implications for the instructor. *Evaluation and Program Planning, 26*(2), 193-201.

Gettman, D., McNelly, T., & Muraida, D. (1999). The guided approach to instructional design advising (GAIDA): A case-based approach to developing instructional design expertise. In J. V. D. Akker, R. M. Branch, K. Gustafson, N. Nieveen, & T. Plomp (Eds.), *Design approaches and tools in education and training* (pp. 175-181). Dordrecht: Kluwer.

Glaser, R. (1968). *The design and programming of instruction* (Technical paper). Pittsburgh, PA: Learning Research & Development Center, University of Pittsburgh.

Gonzalez, J. J. (1998, April). *Internet simulators (WebSims) and learning environments.* Presented at the Annual Meeting of the American Educational Research Association, San Diego, CA.

Goodyear, P. (1994). Foundations for courseware engineering. In R. D. Tennyson (Ed.), *Automating instructional design, development, and delivery* (pp. 7-28). Berlin: Springer-Verlag.

Goodyear P. (1995). Infrastructure for courseware engineering. In R. D. Tennyson & A. E. Barron (Eds.), *Automating instructional design: Computer based development and delivery tools.* Berlin: Springer-Verlag.

Gros, B., & Spector, J. M. (1994). Evaluating automated instructional design systems: A complex problem. *Educational Technology, 34*(5), 37-46.

Gustafson, K. L., & Branch, R. M. (1997). *Survey of instructional development models* (3rd ed.). Syracuse, NY: ERIC Clearinghouse on Information and Technology.

Gustafson, K. L., & Reeves, T. C. (1990, March). A platform for a course development expert system. *Educational Technology,* 19-25.

Halff, H. M. (1993). Prospects for automating instructional design. In J. M. Spector, M. C. Polson, & D. J. Muraida (Eds.), *Automating instructional design: Concepts and issues* (pp. 67-132). Englewood Cliffs, NJ: Educational Technology.

Jonassen, D. H., & Wilson, B. G. (1990, April). *Analyzing automated instructional systems: Metaphors from related design professions.* Paper presentation at the convention of the Association for Educational Communications and Technology.

Jonassen, D. H., Hernandez-Serrano, J., & Choi, I. (2000). Integrating constructivism and learning technologies. In J. M. Spector & T. M. Anderson (Eds.), *Integrated and holistic perspectives on learning, instruction and technology* (pp. 103-128). Dordrecht: Kluwer.

Jury, T., & Reeves, T. (1999). An EPSS for instructional design: NCR's quality information products process. In J. V. D. Akker, R. M. Branch, K. Gustafson, N. Nieveen, & T. Plomp (Eds.), *Design approaches and tools in education and training* (pp. 183-194). Dordrecht: Kluwer.

Kasowitz, A. (1998, August). Tools for automating instructional design. *ERIC Digest* [On-line], EDO-IR-1998-1. Available: http://www.ericit.org/digests/EDO-IR-1998-01.shtml.

Kearsley, G. (1984). Instructional design and authoring software. *Journal of Instructional Development, 7*(3) 11-16.

Locatis, C., & Park, O. (1992). Some uneasy inquiries into ID expert systems. *Educational Technology Research & Development, 40*(3), 87-94.

Merrill, M. D. (1993). An integrated model for automating instructional design and delivery. In J. M. Spector, M. C. Polson, and D. J. Muraida (Eds.), *Automating instructional design: Concepts and issues* (pp. 147-190). Englewood Cliffs, NJ: Educational Technology.

Merrill, M. D. (1998). ID Expert: A second generation instructional development system. *Instructional Science, 26*, 243-262.

Merrill, M. D. (2001). First principles of instruction. *Journal of Structural Learning and Intelligent Systems, 14*(4), 459-466.

Montague, W. E., & Wulfeck, W. H. (1982). *Improving the quality of Navy training: The role of R&D in support of instructional systems design* (Technical Report NPRDC-SR-82-19). San Diego, CA: Navy Personnel Research and Development Center.

Muraida, D. J., Spector, J. M., O'Neil, H. F., Jr., & Marlino, M. R. (1993). Evaluation. In J. M. Spector, M. C. Polson, & D. J. Muraida, *Automating instructional design: Concepts and issues* (pp. 293-324). Englewood Cliffs, NJ: Educational Technology.

Nieveen, N. (1999). Prototyping to reach product quality. In J. V. D. Akker, R. M. Branch, K. Gustafson, N. Nieveen, & T. Plomp (Eds.), *Design approaches and tools in education and training* (pp. 125-135). Dordrecht: Kluwer.

Paquette, G. (1992). An architecture for knowledge-based learning environments. In *Proceedings of EXPERSYS-92,* Ottawa, Canada, (pp. 31-36).

Paquette, G., Aubin, C., & Crevier, F. (1994). An intelligent support system for course design. *Educational Technology, 34*(9), 50-57.

Perez, R. S., & Neiderman, E. C. (1992). Modeling the expert training developer. In R. J. Seidel and P. Chatelier (Eds.), *Advanced training technologies applied to training design.* New York: Plenum Press.

Pirolli, P., & Russell, D. M. (1990). The instructional design environment: Technology to support design problem solving. *Instructional Science, 19*(2), 121-144.

Regian, J. W., Jr., & Shute, V. (Eds.). (1992). *Cognitive approaches to automated instruction.* Mahwah, NJ: Lawrence Erlbaum Associates.

Resnick, L. B. (Ed.). (1989). *Knowing, learning, and instruction.* Mahwah, NJ: Lawrence Erlbaum Associates.

Rich, E., & Knight, K. K. (1991). *Artificial intelligence* (2nd ed.). New York: McGraw-Hill.

Romiszowski, A. J. (1987). Expert systems in education and training: Automated job aids or sophisticated instructional media. *Educational Technology, 27*(10), 22-30.

Rowland, G. (1992). What do instructional designers actually do? An initial investigation of expert practice. *Performance Improvement Quarterly, 5*(2), 65-86.

Silverman, R. E. (1960). *Automated teaching: A review of theory and research* (Technical Report for the U.S. Navy). San Diego, CA: Navy Personnel Research and Development Center.

Spector, J. M. (1994). Integrating instructional science, learning theory and technology. In R. D. Tennyson (Ed.), *Automating instructional design, development, and delivery* (pp. 243-260). Berlin: Springer-Verlag.

Spector, J. M. (1999). Intelligent support for instructional development: Approaches and limits. In J. V. D. Akker, R. B. Branch, K. Gustafson, N. Nieveen, & T. Plomp (Eds.), *Design approaches and tools in education and training* (pp. 279–290). Dordrecht: Kluwer.

Spector, J. M. (2000). Gagné's influence on military training research and development. In R. Richey (Ed.), *The legacy of Robert M. Gagné* (pp. 211–228). New York: ERIC-IT Clearing House and the International Board of Standards for Training, Performance and Instruction.

Spector, J. M., & Edmonds, G. S. (2002, September). Knowledge management in instructional design. *ERIC Digest* [On-line], EDO-IR-2002-02. Available at http://www.ericit.org/digests/EDO-IR-2002-02.shtml.

Spector, J. M., Polson, M. C., & Muraida, D. J. (Eds.). (1993). *Automating instructional design: Concepts and issues*. Englewood Cliffs, NJ: Educational Technology.

Spector, J. M., Arnold, E. M., & Wilson A. S. (1996). A Turing test for automatically generated instruction. *Journal of Structural Learning, 12*(4), 301–313.

Tennyson, R. D. (1993). The instructional design models and authoring activities. In J. M. Spector, M. C. Polson, & D. J. Muraida (Eds.), *Automating instructional design: Concepts and issues*. Englewood Cliffs, NJ: Educational Technology.

Tennyson, R. D. (Ed.). (1994). *Automating instructional design, development, and delivery*. Berlin: Springer-Verlag.

van Marcke, K. (1992a). A generic task model for instruction. In S. Dijkstra (Ed.), *Instructional models in computer-based learning environments* (NATO ASI Series, Vol. F104). Berlin: Springer-Verlag.

van Marcke, K. (1992b). Instructional expertise. In G. Frasson, G. Gauthier, & G. I. McCalla (Eds.), *Intelligent tutoring systems* (pp. 234–243). Berlin: Springer-Verlag.

van Marcke, K. (1998). GTE: An epistemological approach to instructional modelling. *Instructional Science, 26*(3/4), 147–191.

van Merriënboer, J. J. G., & Paas, F. G. W. C. (1990). Automation and schema acquisition in learning elementary computer programming: Implications for the design of practice. *Computers in Human Behavior, 6*(3), 273–289.

Welsh, J. R., & Wilson, B. G. (1987). Expert system shells: Tools to aid human performance. *Journal of Instructional Development, 10*(2), 15–19.

Wiley, D. A. (Ed.). (2001). *The instructional use of learning objects*. Agency for Instructional Technology and Association for Educational and Communications Technology. Bloomington, IN.

USER-DESIGN RESEARCH

Alison Carr-Chellman and Michael Savoy
Penn State University

> Knowledge and human power are synonymous.
> —Sir Francis Bacon

27.1 INTRODUCTION

The purpose of this chapter is to describe the state of research and theory in the area of user design in instructional and informational sciences. In recent decades the importance of the learner and user has increased considerably. However, a comprehensive consideration of the underlying theories that contribute to user design as a construct, as well as a careful explication of the research that contributes to our understanding of engaging users, is currently lacking in the literature. This is particularly the case in the educational technology literature.

Traditionally, the quest for and attainment of knowledge have been restricted, for various reasons, to those select few in the upper echelons of society. And this is surely the case within instructional design thoroughly steeped in jargon and special techniques for taking best advantage of the findings of instructional science. Academics conduct research to gain deeper knowledge and understanding of the powerless majority of society to compel that majority to utilize the results of the research through products that are *unveiled* to the users. However, the users of this expert-conducted and designed research have had little say about the products with which they were presented. This has led to many innovations being less than acceptable or usable and rarely effectively implemented. The instructional sciences have not been exempt from this type of one-sided, often-unsuccessful *diffusion* of innovation. The experts' and practitioners' frustrations with the lack of relevant useful results have led to more collaborative efforts to design, develop, implement, and benefit from research, processes, and products.

We begin this chapter with a definition of user design and delineation between user design and other progressive archetypes such as learner-centered, user-centered, and emancipatory design models. This is followed by a discussion of the foundations of user-design research including the Scandinavian design literature and stakeholder participation. Within these related disciplines, we consider what the empirical research tells us and what gaps remain to be filled to build a robust research agenda for the user-design discipline. We then turn our attention to a brief discussion of obstacles to user design and conclude the chapter with a description of a potential research agenda and associated methods for advancing user design. Each section of this chapter begins with an explication of the specfics of the concepts and theories of the various related areas and user design. This is followed by a careful discussion of empirical evidence that helps to frame the relationship to user design and the need for further and specific research as well as a brief discussion of the methods needed to further user-design inquiry.

27.2 DEFINING USER DESIGN AND USER-DESIGN RESEARCH

The engagement of end users in the creation of new artifacts is not an entirely new concept. For example, the architect works closely within the boundaries of what the end users want, need, and hope for their new home while lending his or her expertise to the project (Hooper, 1986). In contrast, the instructional designer who closely follows instructional science methods for the creation of learning materials has not traditionally consulted with the end users. In a traditional instructional design model, a needs assessment is conducted in which the instructional designer finds the problem and begins to create a solution to it. This solution is then negotiated with *administrators* and eventually imposed on the end users or learners. Typically, the learners are considered as part of a learner analysis, and usually they engage in the formative evaluation stage. However, in most cases these processes are limited engagements and tend toward something being done *to* rather than *with* the learner.

User design, in contrast, empowers the users to engage authentically in the decision-making process that *is* design. In this case, the end users are empowered to play a central role in the creation of their own systems. Schuler and Namioka (1993) set out the Scandinavian roots of user design as they apply to the creation of information technology interfaces. Scandinavian participatory design research focuses not only on improved product development as a result of user participation, but also on the political structure between management and labor. However, the Scandinavian work force is characterized by high education levels, strong unions, and prolabor policies and legislation regulating management/union relations. This context represents an almost-ideal situation for user participation compared to typical instructional design situations in the United States or most other Western cultures.

User design, when applied to instructional design, represents a dramatic shift in power dynamics from traditional instructional design approaches (Carr, 1997; Reigeluth, 1996). In traditional instructional design the designer analyzes, creates, and negotiates, and the leaders initiate, approve and decide. Unfortunately, the users are left to accept or reject the innovation and much literature has focused on better and better ways to encourage adoption, or compliance from the end users (Evans, 1996; Rogers, 1995; Valente & Davis, 1999). This approach, however, ignores savvy users who realize that they are being, in large part, controlled by the negotiated agenda of the designer and the administrator. Typically, those products or processes that are truly designed by users tend to build ownership among users and create a significantly different adoption process than is typical of more manipulative (Rogers, 1995) models of innovation adoption. Rogers' approach, or the "colonial" approach, to design and diffusion has been critiqued because of the disempowerment of users and the lack of respect afforded indigenous knowledge (Carmen, 1990; Yapa, 1996a, 1996b). This traditional approach is deficient in terms of the robustness necessary given the variability of many current contexts (Larsen & McGuire, 1998). Thus, in user design, actions such as initiation, approval, rejection, design, and decision making are negotiated among the users, designers, and leaders.

Though user design has empowering potential, many users still need a little convincing. Ehn (1993) interprets Ackoff (1974) as concluding that three conditions are necessary for users to be motivated to participate in design efforts. "(1) it makes a difference for the participants, (2) implementation of the results is likely, and (3) it is fun" (p. 74). Ehn (1993) further states that user design not only means users being involved in the design, but also designers participating in its use. Designers must be more than outside researchers, consultants, or even facilitators. They must be users as well, thereby increasing their stake in the effectiveness of the design process and eventual product. In addition, where designers are users, power differentials are increasingly mitigated.

One important distinction to make with regard to defining user design is what it is *not*. It is not the practice of increasing "user involvement in acquiring, maintaining and manipulating essential institutional data" for the purpose of "incorporating user input into systems design and development (Hurley & Lipp, 1980)." It is also not user-based (Abels, 1997) design in which focus groups and questionnaires are used to gather user perspectives for application to the design of systems. Although these approaches are good strategies for soliciting input and garnering user support, they rarely significantly change what designers do. User-design empirical research on instructional systems is almost nonexistent. The field of instructional design has not yet taken many of the lessons from Scandinavian user-design models and applied them to the creation of learning environments. The notable exception here is the study of home nursing agents (Carr-Chellman, Cuyar, & Breman,1998) that found that user design, while possible, was very time-consuming and resource hungry. In this case study a group of full-time nurses was engaged in the creation of a computer interface system that they were to use within home settings. A series of meetings was held and observed, participants were interviewed, and one of the authors was within the organization, lending to the complete telling of the story. It was found that the process of user design, truly engaging the nurses in the creation of their own interface, was extremely time-consuming. It led to fundamental considerations about power relations within the organization at a macro level, uncomfortable discussions between nurses and leaders about the future job prospects for home nurses, and careful and, at times, contentious discussion about what nurses do in any particular home visit at a micro level. This was not a surprising finding, and the length of time that was required clearly pointed to resource expenditures that made the leadership, in particular, quite uncomfortable. Resources in terms of time and people were required for this user-design attempt, and the second (M.S.), author who was the Chief Information Officer for the agency conducting the study, insisted that the organization would not attempt this level of user engagement, much less true user design, again soon. This study, however, was both naive in its attempt to apply user-design principles to an organizational setting and unskilled at the actualizing of appropriate research methods. Thus, user design in instructional systems is almost a blank slate. This is not particularly surprising to us. To pursue user-design research is to begin to deny the power and expertise of instructional design as a field (Carr-Chellman, in press). It is to devote precious time and research resources to an issue that is essentially out of alignment with our expert-based capitalistic society. There are, however, a number of empirical studies in related areas such as user-centered design, human–computer interface design, and others, which may help to build an appropriate research agenda by identifying gaps in those literatures.

User design embraces the conflict inherent in power dynamics present in most organizations and social systems and brings this conflict into clear relief by engaging users in empowered decision making through design. User design is, however, perhaps not quite as clear as this definition suggests. We have found that there is a variety of levels of user engagement that encompass several levels of user design and empowerment. The next section addresses these levels and sublevels of user design and related user engagement and each level's associated research findings.

27.3   LEVELS OF USER PARTICIPATION

Noyes and Baber (1999) define *user* as the "human component" of design. However, this definition gives no detail as to who actually uses and/or benefits from the designed product or process. It also does not define the level of knowledge these users possess. In operational settings, users range from trainees to masters, governance structures range from frontline workers to top executives, HCI/technology users range from novice to expert or laggards to early adopters, and users in society range from the disenfranchised to the empowered.

User participation occurs in various ways depending on the context, participants, resources, and intentionality with which user engagement is proscribed. There is much confusion about the differences among *levels* of user participation, i.e., user centered, learner centered, student centered, and user design. Whereas some researchers make no distinction among sublevels of user-centered design (Sugar, 2001), others distinguish between user centered and user participation (Salvo, 2001), and some clearly define various levels of user design (Schulze, 2001).

Regardless of the sublevel of user design, the designer and/or leader typically determines the extent to which users are engaged in the creation of their own systems. Thus, grassroots movements (T. Jackson, 1993; Merrifield, 1993; Olson, 1990) are infrequently possible. Because the leader typically maintains power in most organizational contexts, and is usually uncomfortable giving it up, true user participation requires a different perspective on organizational structure and radically different communication systems.

Power is an issue that may not be completely understood by those not familiar with the ways in which power can be employed for and against users. In essence, power can be invested—not given to (which implies a certain patronization of users), but invested in users. This would be understood as empowerment of users. The idea of power is pretty transparent, actually. Persons in power are usually able to get persons with less power to carry out their wishes. Often persons in power, leaders, for example, believe that they have the best intentions for the organization or the users or workers themselves. Persons in power often have a global view of the organization and may employ that advantage to set direction, plan initiatives, and make changes as they see fit. Persons in power are able to manipulate systems and organizations to their own or others' benefits. Typically, though, for persons in power, the power itself may not be recognized. They may feel that they are overwhelmed leaders (Oshry, 1995) rather than powerful participants in the shaping of the organization's future. Power is, for them, a natural consequence and they often do not recognize their own power. In addition, the powerful rarely recognize that the power they wield will tend to benefit some and not others, and they even more rarely will carefully examine the intended and unintended consequences of their powerful actions on a variety of stakeholders at lower levels.

Perhaps the best way to understand the types or sublevels of user design is to array these levels of user participation on a continuum of empowerment (see Fig. 27.1). A few of the associated researchers and theorists are listed under each design model. Further explication of each of these design models (excluding the traditional instructional systems design [ISD] model, which is well discussed elsewhere [Dick, Carey, & Carey, 2001; Reigeluth, 1999; Romiszowski, 1981; Schiffman, 1995]) follows.

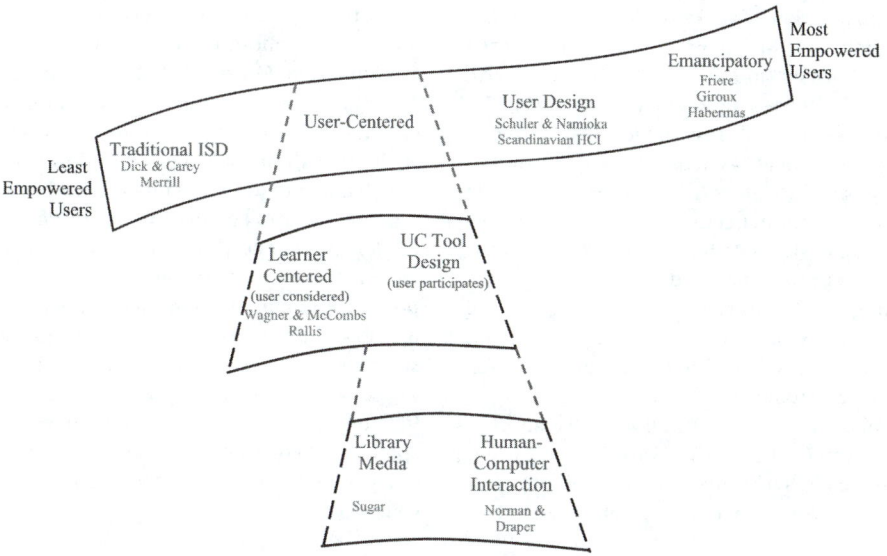

FIGURE 27.1. Continuum of empowerment in user-participation levels. ISD, instructional systems design; UC, user-centered.

27.3.1 User-Centered Design

In earlier work, we distinguished broadly between user-*centered* design and user design (Carr, 1997). In that earlier work, user-centered design and learner-centered design are used synonymously. However, for the purposes of clarity, we can divide user-centered design into two broad groups of models and corresponding literature. The first is concerned primarily with learners, whereas the second is more concerned with end users. In general, learners are engaged primarily in structured or semistructured learning experiences, whereas end users are engaged in tool use. We explore learner-centered design first and user-centered tool design second and distinguish between user-centered tool design for human–computer interfaces and library media tools.

27.3.1.1 Learner-Centered Design. In traditional instructional situations the teacher defines what the learner will learn based on external mandates from, for example, curriculum and assessment standards. Consideration of the learner is given through pretests, learner analyses, and sensitivity to individual learner differences, however, the learner does not actually have a say in what, when, how, and to what extent he or she learns. Learner-centered design differs from other types of user design in that the focus is on learning and pedagogy rather than tool use as is the case in human–computer interface design. Learner-centered design emanates from learner-centered psychological principles (American Psychological Association [APA], 1993), particularly those associated with metacognition, cognition, and affective, developmental, and social psychology. Perhaps the most well-known theorist to extend learner-centered principles from situated cognition (Brown & Duguid, 1994), constructivism (Duffy, Lowyck, & Jonassen, 1993; Jonassen, 1999) and systems theories (Banathy, 1973, 1996; Senge, 1990) was Barbara McCombs (2001; McCombs & Whistler, 1997), and most of the design models that have passed into the instructional design field come from this foundation (Wagner & McCombs, 1995).

According to Wagner and McCombs the learner-centered model for instructional design (in this case for distance learning) strongly considers the needs of different learners during the design process. Learner-centered design encourages active collaboration and engaging learners "as active participants in the generation of learning plans." (Wagner & McCombs, 1995, P. 33) However, the principles of learner-centered psychology (APA) and their implications for design practice (Wagner & McCombs) maintain and reify the standard role for designers. The principles are primarily phrased, "The learner...," indicating that the audience for the work is a designer who should know and understand these psychological principles *about* learners to design better learner-centered environments.

There is little discussion of the shifts in power that are necessary to engage learners in substantive ways in the current literature. Future research literature needs to highlight the shift from imposing education *on* learners to designing education

with learners (Norman & Spohrer, 1996). One notable exception is Hannafin and Land's work (1997) in technology-enhanced student learning[1] environments where we encounter "students-as-designers" (p. 168). Thus, although the learners are not precisely *engaged* in the process of designing their own instruction or information systems in the majority of learner-centered design literature, they are considered to be the center of what the designer is doing. All things should focus on successful outcomes for the learner rather than other extraneous concerns such as administrator desires, contextual cues, or resource limitations. This position argues that learners ought to be afforded a serious opportunity to influence their own learning (Wagner & McCombs, 1995) and to allow learners to take a more active role. This represents a significant departure from traditional instructional design models (Wagner & McCombs, 1995).

In terms of empirical studies in the area of student-centered or learner-centered environments, there are a number of strands of research. The seminal author in this area is McCombs. She has three studies in particular that indicate positive findings for learner-centered classrooms. Weinberger and McCombs (2001) examined students in grades 4 through 8 using the Assessment of Learner Centered Practices (ALCP) survey and found that as students feel or perceive that their teachers are more learner centered in their approach, students' academic performance, attendance, and motivation increase, whereas disciplinary problems tend to decrease. These findings are of particular interest, in Wienberger and McCombs' view, to those students who are at risk of failure in more traditional teacher-centered classroom structures. Two additional survey studies by McCombs (2001; McCombs & Quiat, 2000) found strong links between a positive predilection toward learner-centeredness and positive motivation, performance, climate for learning, and student–teacher relationships. Daniels, Kalkman, and McCombs (2001) looked at learner-centered and non-learner-centered primary classrooms and surveyed these young learners about what they valued in a teacher. They found that primary students valued similar things in all teachers and that those in learner-centered classrooms tended to be more interested in schoolwork and learning. In McCombs and Quait (2000) the Community for Learning (CFL) program, a K–12 reform effort, was evaluated to determine the extent to which it was meeting its learner-centered goals. Here again, the ALCP was administered to students and teachers of fourth and fifth grades in inner-city schools that were all in various stages of implementation of the CFL program. Naturally, high implementers and those open to learner-centered approaches were more adept at and more willing to implement the CFL approach. Students of these high-implementing teachers tended to show higher test scores and higher motivation levels than students who were in classrooms taught by low implementers. These survey results may not be completely reliable because high-implementer teachers likely have other qualities that inspire excellence and motivation in their learners and that is likely to be separate from the learner-centered approach of the CFL program.

---

[1]Because sorting out the language associated with various design models (user centered, learner centered, etc.) is the main purpose of this portion of the chapter, it is important to note that we consider *learner centered* and *student centered* to be synonymous.

The remainder of empirical studies on learner-centered approaches can be loosely broken down into two categories: studies that examine teacher philosophies, perceptions, and abilities toward learner-centered classrooms and studies that examine specific learning outcomes as a result of learner-centered classrooms. Paris and Combs (2000) studied teachers from elementary, secondary, and postsecondary contexts who were involved in the Foxfire curriculum innovation. In interviews they found that teachers' understandings of learner-centered classrooms included five specific characteristics; the teacher focuses on learners, guides and facilitates learning, promotes active learner engagement, promotes learning through interactive decision making, and participates as a reflective, ongoing learner. However, simple understanding is not sufficient for effective implementation. As Williams (1996) found in a survey of 435 teachers' philosophies and attitudes about learner-centered instruction, teachers are, in fact, faced with a variety of conflicts. In this study of 10 public high schools in an urban school system, she administered both the Kerlinger's Education Attitude Scale and the McREL School Practices survey and found that whereas teachers prefer to see themselves as progressive, they are ambivalent about both progressive and traditional philosophies. Williams explains this ambivalence as either moderation between two extreme positionalities or, possibly, the realities of classroom life forcing a more moderate stand.

Learner-centered studies, which focus more on learning outcomes, are by and large positive. Smrekar (1997), in her study of learner-centered second-language classrooms, found that students with limited English skills, in learner-centered classrooms, enjoyed more language growth than those in more teacher-centered classrooms. This study utililzed the Preschool Teacher Verbal Behavior Index (PTVBI) to determine the extent of learner centeredness in four second-language classrooms. This was combined with observations over a 16-week period. While the group examined is very small, and it may not be surprising to find that one teacher was learner centered, one was not, and two were slightly more learner centered, the final conclusion is that the use of the PTVBI is helpful in understanding classroom communication and studying it further. Jackson, Stratford, Krajcik, and Soloway (1996) utilized computer modeling as a case study of learner-centered software design and found that their modeling tools allowed even novice learners to construct computer models easily. This study was a case study that described the application of the ScienceWare Model-It software to high-school science learning. In this case, novice high-school learners were able to create simulations and test hypotheses using the software. Ruiter (1971) utilized learner-centered techniques at the university level in basic electricity instruction. He found that learner-centered instruction was superior to conventional methods in terms of both achievement of learning goals and efficiency as measured by number of experiments on electricity completed. Nelson (1999) examined learner-centered telecourses, by examining the application of four media—cable TV, face-to-face, print, and Web page—to health education at the undergraduate level. A battery of surveys and questionnaires was administered in this study including a Telecourse Readiness Questionnaire, additional questions on learner style and learner independence, the Canfield Learning Styles Inventory, the

Rotter Internal–External Locus of Control Scale, Kolb's Learning Style Inventory, and an end-of-course evaluation survey. Additional data sources included midterm and final examiniations and student projects and portfolios. The treatments all utilized competency-based strategies, and in the end, the study found that this approach (competency-based telecourse) resulted in overall higher retention rates despite higher early withdrawals. In addition, students had increased satisfaction rates with instructor preparedness, quality of interaction, feedback, GPAs and self-regulation. Soloway et al. (1996) offer two case studies implementing computer-based learner-centered environments. The first is based on the earlier work by Jackson et al. (1996) with Model-It high-school science learning. The second case study involves NoRIS, a problem-solving environment designed for nuclear engineering learning. In both cases, based on think-aloud learner interviews, the authors found that these learners used their tools effectively and that their reflection and engagement in learning tasks increased with the use of learner-centered environments. In addition, they found that these tools offered helpful structure to the students and assisted with enculturation into professional fields of study.

Salisbusy-Glennon, Gorrell, Sanders, Boyd & Kamen (1999) examined an entire school that was implementing learner-centered philosophies. Their large-scale, multimethod study looked at the effects of learner centeredness on an urban middle-class school among sixth and seventh graders. The study found that certain self-regulation strategies such as seeking, organizing, and transforming information were used more often than memorizing, self-evaluation, and record-keeping for those in the learner-centered school. The students in the study tended to be more oriented toward the development of new skills, self-improvement, and intrinsic rewards of learning itself. This finding is consonant with Brush and Saye's (2000) case study of a single U.S. history class (one teacher and 21 students) in which learner-centered approaches were attempted. Their evaluative case study used classroom observations, interviews, teacher debriefings, and analysis of student products. The study found that learner-centered strategies hinge on specific classroom and learner characteristics. For example, Brush and Saye found that learners, to be successful in learner-centered environments, need high levels of self-monitoring and other metacognitive skills. In addition, Brush and Saye advocate for sufficient structure to support learners in learner-centered environments to avoid high levels of learner disorientation and frustration.

Methodologically, these studies truly run the gamut from surveys, to pre–post test experiments, to interviews and observations. The findings are not completely holistic; they do not always build on one another but, rather, examine bits and pieces of the largest issues associated with learner-centered learning environment design. However, these studies do not approach learner-centered learning from a truly learner-empowered position, nor should we expect that they would. Taken together, the studies on learner-centered learning are hopeful, encouraging, and overall positive with regard to using learner-centered approaches. They tend to use a variety of methods and find that teachers and learners, in the proper mindset and the proper contexts, can make learner-centered approaches work well. Turning learning entirely or primarily over to the learner is still not a part of this dialogue.

27.3.1.2 User-Centered Design for Tool Usage.

The application of user-design principles to the creation of artifacts and tools for human productivity (Sugar & Boling, 1995) has been utilized primarily in two areas, human–computer interface design (Norman & Draper, 1986) and library media use (Fidel, 1994; Morris, 1994; Wilson, 1995)

27.3.1.2.1 User-Centered Design for Human–Computer Interfaces.

User design for the creation of computer-based software tools and online resources has focused more on the "how to" (work with users) than on learner-centered models (Muller & Czerwinski, 1999; Soloway & Pryor, 1996). Although it is most often true that the designer is not the primary user of the tool he or she designs, it still has become very good business practice to be customer centered (Smart & Whiting, 2001). The customer-centered orientation typically takes the same perspective on power dynamics that other forms of user-centered design take. Specifically, the user is considered, not empowered; research has centered on better understanding the user and the context in which the user works so as to manipulate their adoption rates (Karat, 1997; Vredenburg, 1999).

Thus, the fact remains that most user-centered design literature maintains power in the hands of the designers and only touches on user considerations in actual design. For example, engaging frontline users in the process of usability testing or formative evaluation (Corry, Frick, & Hansen, 1997) still puts the designer in the most powerful position of creation followed by approval, suggestion, or implementation by the user. Sugar and Boling (1995) advocate for early user engagement and iterative processes to represent user desires most effectively in final products. In general, Sugar's (1999, 2001) work in user-centered design advocates for stronger roles for users, while recognizing that it rarely occurs. Sugar (2001) would like to see users in a powerful position regardless of what the process is called but recognizes that the novice designer has misconceptions about true user-centered principles and their implementation.

Norman and Draper's (1986) edited text, on *User-Centered System Design,* seems to focus primarily on how best to engage users in the creation of their own systems. For example, the chapter by Riley (1986) focuses on what fundamental understandings users need to have to engage effectively with designers.

The empirical research on user-centered design for human–computer interfaces consists of approximately six studies, primarily cases and observations that tell us that user feedback on the creation of computer interfaces is useful instrumentally. Vredenburg (1999) conducted a case study indicating that user *testing* increases user ease of adoption. In this case, user-centered design was implemented at IBM prior to the release of DB2, a universal database program. Vredenburg concurs with most research that user-centered design is still very labor-intensive and offers a number of possible strategies for minimizing the resources necessary for user-centered design such as groupware. Smart and Whiting (2001) present a 2-year case study of a technical documentation design team. In their study, the

authors utilized contextual inquiry methods where members of design teams worked directly with users in the context of their work environment. Researchers engaged with users in conversation about their work and what that work meant for the future design of technical documents. Smart and Whiting found that working with user feedback is good business, particularly when it concerns technology. This, they assert, is because it is all too common in our society today that the end user is not the same person as the designer. Corry et al. (1997) conducted a case study with World Wide Web design for higher-education administrators and found that user-centered design is particularly useful from an instrumental perspective. In their study of the University Computing Services (UCS) at Indiana University (Bloomington), Corry et al. conducted interviews, tabulated questions asked by patrons of various UCS offices and categorized them, and conducted think-aloud protocols with users. The new system that resulted from the user engagement was adopted in 1995. Sugar and Boling (1995) conducted a case study of the Virtual Textbook project at Indiana University. In their study, five groups of three or four students each were videotaped as they created a time line for the history of rock and roll. The authors do not specify precisely how these 2.5-hr videotaped sessions were analyzed other than "viewing" them. Sugar and Boling found that user-centered design should be considered as part of instructional systems design because it (a) condenses the ISD process, (b) refines the prescriptive methods, (c) encourages cyclical (iterative) processes, and (d) focuses on the human element. Both the Cory et al. and the Sugar and Boling studies would essentially be considered usability testing. On the other hand, sometimes usability testing is not terribly effectives, such as in Sugar's (2001) study of hypermedia design teams' use of iterative feedback. Sugar examined 11 part-time graduate students(6 males and 5 females) as they developed a prototype hypermedia system. Data included interviews, student demonstrations, and class materials. These data sources were examined both before and after usability sessions and a control group was utilized. As noted above, Sugar found that user-centered design is sometimes superficial, particularly with novice designers, who made very few changes as a result of user input. Karat, Atwood, Dray, Rantzer, and Wixon (1996) conducted an "informal survey" that certainly highlights the problems of common language associated with this area. They found that there is no agreed-on definition of user centered design (much less user design in instructional systems). They also found that consideration of context and understanding of the user are lacking among user-centered designers. It should be noted, however, that this particular study, as it was an informal survey, is not really a strong source of empirical evidence.

All of these studies illustrate a lack of robust user design and, rather, focus on user-*centered* design. They illustrate the difficulties with a common language and agreed-on standards for calling an approach true user design or user-centered design. The studies draw conflicting conclusions in terms of whether user-centered design, and usability testing, is instrumentally valuable. None of these studies are interested in loftier issues of empowerment, moral value, or power issues. In addition, all of these studies employ case inquiry methodology, leaving many gaps in the literature when we consider a variety of other research methods.

27.3.1.2.2 *User-Centered Design for Media Usage.* In the case of library media usage, user-centered design has primarily meant conducting user surveys to design better the library resources and systems for patrons' use (DeCandido, 1997; Rockman, 1980; Wilson, 1995). Starting in the mid 1980s information retrieval methods were increasingly influenced by advancements in technology (McCandless et al., 1985). These advancements coincided with library/media center users wanting information systems that were characterized by easy, adaptive, user-friendly interfaces and navigation tools (Payette & Rieger, 1998). These systems needed to be suitable for novice technology users and handicapped individuals as well as the typical library patron.

The design and creation of the user-centered library/media facility sparked a number of empirical research reports. Most of this research describes results of surveys of library patron usage patterns and preferences. The expectation here is that other library/media center staff or designers will learn valuable lessons from the results of surveys of particular library patron populations. This generalization assumption may not be altogether valid, however, the studies are of interest here in terms of what they generally say about the evolution of library/media centers and the place of user design in that evolution. In Dowlin's (1980) study of library user preferences between the card catalog and the computer terminal, he found that users actually preferred the terminals (as long as they were readily available) to the card catalog. Reasons for this included speed, efficiency, and increased availability of additional information such as location, number, and availability of resources. Miller (1980), in her case study of the use of automated library systems at Ohio State University, employed a number of inquiry methods but relied most heavily on staff interviews and surveys and found that library patrons were quite willingly accepting new technologies, particularly when they increased information access. She also found that more men than women utilized the electronic terminals rather than the card catalogs. Kaske and Sanders' (1980) report on more than 200 group and individual interviews focused on user methods of accessing library information. They found that users have strong preferences for design of subject databases to include a "knowledge tree, transparent translation from term entered to index term, more access points, summary of author credentials, book status, and various delimiters." (P. 58). However, Kaske and Sanders also called for more research to determine which of these user requests is really feasible and cost-effective. It seems in their report as if they discount user preferences as "pie in the sky" requests that are too expensive to implement.

In a more recent survey of library patrons, Wilson (1995) looked at preferences among library users at the University of Washington. She reported on a number of changes they made as a result of user feedback on their systems. One of the more interesting shifts evident was the importance of responsiveness, in direct opposition to Kaske and Sanders' views of a decade earlier. "When we work to connect with users, and tell them we care about their input, we are obliged to do something with

what they tell us, unlike the suggestion box in Hell" (p. 300). The remainder of the study described specific changes made as a result of user input including a number of policy changes. Payette and Rieger (1998) continued this strand of inquiry by examining scholarly library usage through surveys, focus groups, and semistructured interviewing at the Mann library at Cornell University. They found that "scholars will benefit from adaptive, flexible user interfaces that enable easy navigation of a complex information landscape" (p. 121). Specific changes included different application of metaphors, more user-centric opening screens, easier access, shortcuts, and multi-navigational pathways.

Taken as a group, these studies are of interest in terms of opening of practitioners' minds to the importance and validity of the indigenous knowledge present in library patrons' minds. Although the research is, in our view, overly reliant on survey techniques, the basic idea of implementing user designs for library systems does seem to have progressed substantially in the past two decades. This stream of research is, however, only tangentially related to what user-centered design for instructional purposes has meant. User-centered design for instructional systems has been more closely aligned with Donald Norman's (1983, 1989) understanding of design for human–computer interfaces.

27.3.2 Emancipatory Design

Emancipatory design models take the mission of empowerment beyond user design. The emancipatory design team hopes to inspire transformation, to alter some significant, and often historically intractable, aspect of society. The goal of emancipatory design is more to create change and to vest the users and front-line workers in organizational outcomes than it is actually to create a working instructional system.

Emancipation as it is applied to action in the form of research, education, or design emanates from Paolo Freire's (1970) work with Chilean illiteracy. It was Freire's contention that knowledge collaboratively constructed is the key to changes in practice. He asserted that research itself is a project of social change and his understandings were extended to the popular education movement (Morrow & Torres, 2002) in South America during the 1960s and 1970s (Carr, 1990; Gerhardt, 1986; Melo and Benavente, 1978). Emancipatory ideas, then, have been used in education and research but more rarely in design activities. Designers have been more interested in the creation of appropriate, implementable, cost-effective artifacts than in how those artifacts may serve to free oppressed populations.

In the case of both user design and emancipatory design, the payoffs for the corporation or educational institution are tertiary rather than primary or even secondary. That is, the rewards are usually more to the users than to the management. There exists little in the way of literature on what we are calling emancipatory design. This is quite possibly because it brings into sharp focus the conflict between users and designers or between labor and management, as the case may be (Bjerknes & Bratteteig, 1995). It may be seen as completely impractical or impossible to implement, particularly in capitalistic societies where return on investment is primary. In the case of emancipatory design, users are in charge; their power, their indigenous knowledge are *more* powerful and respected than those of the expert designer. Even more than fully empowered users, emancipatory design asks users to find ways to create systems for themselves that serve themselves primarily. Thus, the extent to which the organization flourishes and succeeds is the extent to which *users* flourish and succeed. Because of this positionality, emancipatory design draws heavily on critical theories, which have as their central focus who benefits and who is disempowered by any innovation, policy, or product (Horkheimer & Adorno, 2002).

There is a good series of Scandinavian case studies from corporate applications of user design. Included among these is a series of trade union projects from three Scandinavian countries. The first involved the introduction of new technology through the Norwegian Iron and Metal Workers' Union (Nygaard & Bergo, 1974). The second looked at the introduction of technology among Swedish skilled workers with the basic assumption that the technology was meant to deskill work (Ehn & Sandberg, 1979). The third was an examination of the unions' influence on the introduction of computer systems among Danish workers (Kyng & Mathiassen, 1979). All of these projects took the position of emancipation of workers. They diametrically opposed labor and management and considered the researcher's moral obligations to reside with the disempowered population being studied (typically labor). Generally, these studies found that "working life democracy can be reached through trade unions as institutions representing a workers' collective." (Bjerknes & Bratteteig, 1995). These studies are considered case studies, though they generally do not follow recent trends in qualitative research or the typical case study research methods.

Perhaps one of the most underresearched areas we report on in this chapter, other than strict definitions of user-design inquiry, is emancipatory design. Rossman and Rallis (1998) described emancipatory research thus: "The research—process and results—becomes a source of empowerment both to the individual's immediate daily life and to change structures that dominate and oppress. The participants are not generating knowledge simply to inform or enlighten an academic or social science community. They are collaboratively producing knowledge to improve their work and their lives" (p. 15).

Carmen (1990) approached emancipatory diffusion of change and innovation with particular attention to the differentiation between Rogers and Friere. In this text, three case studies are presented: Kenyan educational development, West African and Zimbabwean rural progress through indigenous nongovernmental organizations, and Kenyan democratic participation in theater and cultural space/event design. Carmen examined these cases from an emancipatory perspective. Generally, Carmen found these cases to be empowering and presents several criteria, that these cases by and large meet, including horizontal participatory communication, investigation–education praxis, and impact/effectiveness as measured largely by popularity. These cases are very helpful in illuminating emancipatory design, however, all of the research that we currently have on the topic is case based and there is a clear need for further definitional and (primarily) qualitative research to further this vein of inquiry.

27.4 FOUNDATIONS OF USER-DESIGN MODELS

The foundations of user-design research and theory are drawn from a wide variety of philosophical stances, research traditions, and theoretical perspectives. Considerable work has already been done to explicate many of these foundations, though their relationship and contribution to the aims of user design have not been drawn. The purpose of this section is to describe briefly the foundations of user-design models and to indicate their relationships and contributions to the discipline of user design broadly defined.

27.4.1 Scandinavian User Design

Scandinavian researchers have a long history of user-centered, user-design, and emancipatory design literatures. Their active involvement of users in systems development traces back two decades or more .(Bansler, 1989; Bødker, 1996). Certainly Schuler and Namioka's (1993) text *Participatory Design: Principles and Practices* is one of the seminal texts in the field. While their primary emphasis is on HCI tool use, many of the ideas are useful for instructional design (Carr, 1997). Perhaps one of the best reviews of research in Scandinavian user design was offered by Bjerknes and Bratteteig (1995), who focused primarily on the relationship between users and administrators and the inherent contextual issues that are defined by user design. They traced the roots of user design back to a series of research projects involving trade unions and defined two strategic perspectives—conflict or harmony. In this case, Bjerknes and Bratteteig suggested that the conflict perspective recognizes the inherent contextual conflict between users/labor and administration/employers and called on the researcher to work on behalf of the less powerful (that is the users, labor, or employees) to empower them. The harmony perspective suggests that all are working for the betterment of the organization and so all interests are aligned rather than being oppositional. Growing out of this review is a careful explication of the relationship of critical theory, democracy, and social change.

The vast majority of Scandinavian empirical user-design research has focused on human–computer interface and tool design. There has been some theoretical work looking specifically at work contexts and the design of jobs for democracy (Elden, 1979). In fact, the Scandinavian cultures take the user-design process so seriously that in some cases, such as Denmark employment law and the Norwegian Worker Protection and Working Environment Act, it has been legislated (AML, 1977; Norrbom, 2001; Otten, 1991). The relationship between Scandinavian user-design research and the application of user design to instructional design is still quite limited. Very few instructional design and technology scholars are utilizing (we suspect they may be unaware of) the Scandinavian human–computer interface research on engaging users. Thus user design, as a relatively new model for the instructional design community, embraces the somewhat unknown Scandinavian models for user design of interface tools. Conceptually, the Scandinavian research on user design typically creates more diametrically opposed forces between users and administrators than the application of user-design principles for instructional design. Although Carr (1997; Carr-Chellman, in press) recognizes the inherent power shifts necessary for effective user design, Scandinavian researchers tend more toward a deconstruction of the social context of work in an effort to uncover the inherent conflicts as obstacles to user engagement.

The empirical work in Scandinavian user participation and systems development was well reviewed by Bjerknes and Bratteteig (1987). Some of this work has already been reviewed in this chapter (the union projects discussed in the emancipatory design section above), but there are several additional strands of research worthy of review. There have been three studies of design for the skilled worker in several Scandinavian countries including the UTOPIA Project, which involved several Scandinavian research organizations and the Nordic Graphical Union (UTOPIA Project Group, 1981). In this case, the workers were deeply involved in the creation of a pilot–computer interface for a text and image processing system. The various tools for this system were indeed developed in cooperative ways. And although there was a strong sense that trade unions and labor's voice were strengthened through the project overall, it was not found that it ultimately contributed to universal stakeholder involvements in particular, women and unskilled men were largely removed from the process. The Florence project focused on the creation of a computer system for nurses in their daily work. It was interested not only in individuals, but also in organizational change (Bjerknes & Bratteteig, 1987). The case report of the Florence project found that working at the organizational level requires certain compromises between and among the interests of a variety of stakeholder groups. The FIRE project also examined the design of computer systems for whole organizations and found that there is a problem with attempting to meet all the needs of many workers within an organization. This stakeholder-based process can lead to serious and practical compromises that may be acceptable to all but end up being manipulative (Ehn & Kyng, 1987). However, value was found in the *redesign* process, as it can serve to facilitate user participation if properly organized. Bjerknes and Bratteteig (1995) make the final synopsis of all of these studies clear in one of their concluding comments: "The challenge for future research is to contribute to democracy in a changing working life and workplaces. To achieve this, it is not obvious that user participation in system development activities is a means or the only means." Thus, the final analysis of the Scandinavian empirical literature is, as has been the case with most of our review, mixed in terms of the impacts of user participation.

Ultimately, these reviews of the findings of Scandinavian user research expose certain gaps in the literature including the over-reliance on the case study method and the somewhat narrow definitions associated with user participation in the Scandinavian tradition. Although this foundational area has much to offer those involved in user-design research, there are also important changes that could be made to create a more robust research product to speak to the critics of user design.

27.4.2 Stakeholder Participation

User design extends stakeholder involvement beyond mere input to create empowered users who have design and decision-making powers. However, linkage to stakeholder participation literature and research is an important foundation for user design. Stakeholder approaches from the performance technology arena include organizational design (Jewell & Jewell, 1992) and cultural change (Lineberry & Carleton, 1992). As both of these enterprises attest, enacting substantive change requires more than a simple open invitation to stakeholders to participate. Each unique situation determines who the users are, and each user has a different experience and knowledge level.

Understanding the ways in which leaders can enable stakeholders to take a decision-making role in the design of their own systems of human learning is the next step toward effective implementation of technology and educational practices. In the most effective cases of both user design and stakeholder participation, control percolates from the bottom up. Grassroots movements, although rare, are perhaps our strongest cases of true user design built on the foundation of effective stakeholder participation. Kevin Kelly (1994) describes the problem of control over distributed systems (such as most social systems) by equating this problem to the example of bees in a hive. He asserts that within social systems where everything is connected to everything else (a lesson we are rapidly learning firsthand in the global economy of today), things happen quickly and "simply route around any central authority"(p. 469). Stakeholder researchers have, for some time, realized that stakeholder participation is one way to stem ineffective implementation of innovations due to this "routing around" authority.

User participation, as with stakeholder participation, becomes more complex as the size of the system involved increases. For example, stakeholder research informs us that successful participation requires multilevel and multistake participation (Daresh, 1992; Stevenson & Pellicer, 1992). This means that for something as complex as a school system, for example, stakeholders from teachers to administrators, from community members to parents, must engage in the design or participation processes at many levels including policymaking at the classroom, school building, district, and even state levels. Stakeholder participation theory and research offer the user-designer a number of similar lessons about effective implementation of empowering methods (Berube, 1970; Cooper, 1992; Davies, 1981; Epstein, 1997; Fantini, Gittell, & Magat, 1970; Sarason, 1995).

The empirical research in stakeholder participation represents a large and well-defined body of literature. For our purposes we have divided the literature into two broad areas, public-school participation and social systems participation. Within public-school participation, there are studies focused on site-based management and a series of studies that consider a number of other stakeholder participation or involvement approaches from planning to evaluation.

Although there are a number of articles on site-based management, very few of them seriously consider the question from an empirical standpoint. Two exceptions are worthy of note here as exemplars of what the literature says generally. Holcomb's (1993) study of school-based instructional leadership essentially described the progress of a large site-based instructional leadership (SBIL) program. One of the larger efforts, this study described the sessions in which 909 educators and stakeholders were involved in SBIL and data sources included anecdotal reports, evaluation forms and surveys, and a follow-up study. Holcomb found that stakeholders felt positively about their participation and were highly satisfied with the outcomes as well as their training for their changed roles. Carr's (1996) examination of stakeholder site-based management in four public middle schools found that leadership philosophies are critical to stakeholder satisfaction—that more transformative leaders tend to encourage stakeholder participation and sustain stakeholder satisfaction. In that study, data sources included leader interviews, staff and parental interviews, observations, and analysis of school-based documents when available. Based on the same study, Carr (1994) found that for stakeholder participation to be truly effective, it must be apparent to the stakeholders that the effort involved is worth their while. Specifically, phone interviews, personal interviews, observations, and document analysis led to a clear indication that community member participation is logistically difficult, and therefore, stakeholders will participate only if they feel strongly that their voice will not only be heard, but be heeded. In addition to these two studies, there are a number of cases that are detailed in an edited book focused on site-based management (Lane & Epps, 1992). Daresh's (1992) case study of Cincinnati's schools and Stevenson & Pellicer's (1992) case study of South Carolina's schools were both loosely empirical. Although they were based on real cases, the work tends to be reflective and theoretical, but both chapters found that site-based management was a useful tool and an important aspect of larger reform efforts.

In terms of the more general set of empirical studies associated with stakeholder participation in the public schools, there are six studies of note, which look at a variety of approaches. Wang, Haertel, and Walberg (1995) examined six urban school sites selected for their diversity of certain variables. Fully two-thirds of the programs in these schools specifically identified stakeholder participation as a key to successful planning. Likewise, Hafner (1992), in her review of promising practices in public-school district information systems design, found that obtaining stakeholder participation was one of the keys to success. Hafner examined three schools in California and Maryland and created profiles of each school to describe their information systems. Whereas she found that most administrators do not utilize available sources of information, such as student information, for the purposes of decision making, she did find that these districts shared "obtaining stakeholder participation" as one of the most promising practices. Henry, Dickey, and Areson (1991) reported on a case study of Virginia's creation of an educational-performance monitoring system. In this case, a stakeholder approach to development was utilized and stakeholders felt that their impact and input were significant to the final product. The study found that teachers, in particular, were

positive about their efficacy. In contrast to that study is one that considered *student* participation in the creation of program attributes (Brandon, Lindberg, & Wang, 1993). In this case study, students were involved by offering input, and although faculty retained the final decision-making power, the end product was seen by all as better than it would have been without student involvement. Similarly, Brandon (1999) found that although males participated more than females in stakeholder participation opportunities, the resulting product was stronger because of everyone's input. However, there are certainly studies that are more cautious in their advocacy of stakeholder participation. Keith, Abrams, and McLaughlin (1993), for example, balanced their enthusiastic use of stakeholders in the creation of special-education services with realistic understandings of the costs and resource demands of truly effective participation. In their study, part of a larger 18-month research project aimed at evaluating the influences of class size and inclusion of disabled learners, stakeholders were surveyed about their expectations, perspectives, and opinions. Among other findings, Keith et al. advocated for researchers to serve as teachers of research to the participating stakeholder groups.

Empirical research on social systems' stakeholder participation ranges in context from homeless children and youth programs through agricultural development. Here, again, in general, stakeholder participation is seen as a positive force for improved planning, evaluation, and social change, however, some studies are more mixed. Brandon, Newton, and Harmon (1993) conducted a study that would be considered similar to needs assessment to look at homeless children's problem issues and found that the scope of problems identified by stakeholder groups was significantly broader than that found in previous similar efforts that did not involve collaboration among stakeholder groups. Saegert (1996) also found positive effects of stakeholder participation in her case study of New York City urban housing. She found that a cooperative neighborhood program called Homebuilders was more successful than other similar tenant programs with less stakeholder participation. Jennifer Greene conducted a series of four empirical studies on stakeholder participation, which also found positive associations. Greene's (1988b) examination of troubled youth programs (such as Big Brother and Big Sister) found support for the positive effects of stakeholder involvement in terms of the utilization of evaluation findings for positive programmatic change. In her 1987 case study of two social service agencies, Greene found that stakeholder participation is worth the time and resources needed to do it well, however, only in certain circumstances—that stakeholders are truly interested, motivated, and knowledgeable and hold legitimacy as stakeholders (Greene, 1987). She also found that participation's success is contextually bound. Finally, conditional to the success of stakeholder involvement is that the process (and, we feel, the leaders) must take participant decision making seriously. In two related papers based on these same two cases, Greene found that "key elements of a participatory evaluation process can be linked to meaningful and multiple forms of results utilization through cognitive and political uses of the evaluation process" (1988a, p. 341) and that, when social action is the desired final goal, less diversity among stakeholders may be more desirable than more diversity (Mathie & Greene, 1997).

Similarly, some concerns were raised by Grudens-Schuck (2001) in her study of Canadian agricultural education programs. This qualitative single-case study focused on the Ontario Environmental Farm Plan program. The method involved 36 2-hr interviews, observations of farm workshop sessions, document analysis, and observation of other events such as farm shows. Although Grudens-Schuck found that stakeholder participation is useful, she tempered this finding with specific challenges such as conflicts among stakeholders. In addition, she asserted that there are actually few data that show the specific positive effects of stakeholder involvement.

In general, the findings of these studies point to positive, effective uses of stakeholders as sources of information, but this is more in the user-input vein than the user-design vein of change. That is, few cases of real decision-making power accorded to stakeholders are present in this set of studies. In addition, it is difficult to know whether or not this body of research represents reliable, objective data for positive effects of stakeholder participation. Although we generally reject the positivistic notion of truth, these studies are putting forward attempts at generalized findings; however, there is no deep engagement with researcher identity, and so it is impossible to be sure whether these findings are colored by researcher bias or researcher role in the context studied.

Methodologically, the studies of stakeholder participation in all of these contexts (site based, public schools, and social systems) represent a number of approaches, techniques, and strategies. Most of these studies, however, lack significant methodological attention and rigor. Only one study, that by Hafner (1992), based out of the Far West Lab, truly seems to consider qualitative research from within a carefully and appropriately triangulated framework of observations, document analysis, and interviews. Most of the above studies use strategies and techniques that mix and match in somewhat less intentional ways and rarely display the rigor associated with excellent qualitative or quantitative inquiry.

27.5   OBSTACLES TO USER DESIGN

Engaging users in the creation of their own systems does indeed carry with it certain inalienable obstacles. The primary obstacle is the problem of power and the reticence of the powerful to truly engage users (less powerful factions) in decision making (Carr, 1997). In other cases, a design team may decide to plunge into user design too late in the process, potentially at the prototype stage rather than at the analysis stage. In this case, a product is already completed and the user is left with adoption or rejection as the only option. Instead, user design optimally engages users from analysis through evaluation.

Another very important obstacle is the tendency to categorize most or all users into a single monolithic group possessing a single set of characteristics, desires, and stakes in the design. In fact, users are typically such a diverse group that there is almost no way to suggest that what one user wants is *necessarily* what others will want as well. This makes the user-design enterprise significantly more complex than one might initially imagine. For example, as a society Americans have not managed to

negotiate effectively among community members locally or nationally what the purpose of schooling is. This lack of consensus has wide-ranging impacts on our ability to reform or improve education. Other obstacles to user design are dealt with primarily in the human–computer interface literature and include user motivation and apathy, user identification, communication, value conflicts, user access, acquisition of user feedback, and effective implementation user feedback (Grudin, 1993). One final obstacle is the tendency to ignore context in expert-driven design efforts. For example, software designers often engage users in ensuring software usability, but these tasks are often accomplished outside the context in which the software is to be *used,* making effective adoption in context particularly elusive.

In any the situation, user design may be affected by the knowledge level of the users. In addition, the benefit enjoyed by users varies. Doing the work of design is difficult, requiring extensive conversation (Bohm, 1996; Jenlink & Carr, 1996). No part of this process is easy. However, in the traditional constructivist notion of learning by doing (Dewey, 1916, 1938), it is clear that the process of design offers great hope not only for increased adoption rates and ethical design practice, but *also* for human learning (Wiggins, 1998). Just as students who have been enculturated into the learning processes of traditional classrooms complain about the work of active learning of any sort, users who are asked to engage in the design of their own systems can be expected to react similarly.

27.6   RESEARCH METHODS AND AGENDA

27.6.1   Agenda for Further Research on User Design

This review has revealed several important issues associated with research in user design. First, there is almost no research that is specific to the field of user design within instructional systems. Second, there are significant gaps and problems with the majority of the related research literature on user design, such as user-centered, learner-centered, tool use, human–computer interface, media, and emancipatory design. This leads us to propose a specific research agenda for the further development of user design as a discipline. Most of this research agenda will be useful for user design in many contexts and not solely purposed for instructional systems.

The first step in establishing user-design research is to create a clear, shared language around user-design concepts. We hope that this chapter has, in fact, helped take that step by distinguishing among many similar (though not precisely the same) concepts such as learner centered, user centered, and other terms that may cause confusion between user design and other, potentially less robust forms of participant engagement. However, this first step needs substantially more theoretical thought and articulation. Defining user design clearly and ensuring a common language, which is also *used* in a common fashion, are imperative for a truly significant research agenda. One of the important projects associated with these definitional studies is a litmus test for what constitutes user design and what should be relegated to other categories. As has been the case with many similar movements (e.g., total quality management, alternative

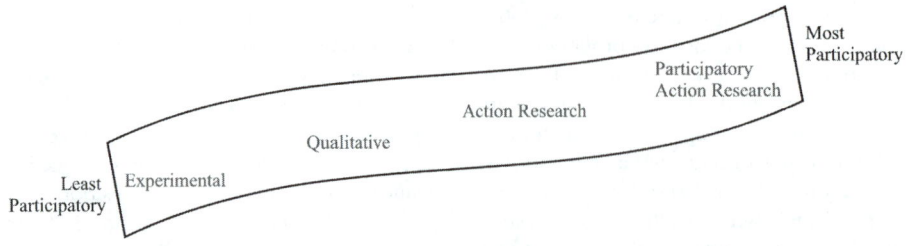

FIGURE 27.2. Continuum of empowerment in research approaches.

assessment, and site-based management) where power is usurped, there is a tendency to compromise the fundamentals of the theory to make it potentially more palatable to management, leaders, and those in power. This would completely undermine the goals of user design, and therefore, it is imperative that some level of oversight and standards be available for those who wish to call their efforts true user design.

The second step for the research agenda, in our view, is a series of studies examining user-design implementation by a number of specific variables such as individual differences (including individual motivation, metacognitive abilities, race, class, gender, and learning style), subject area (including levels of cognitive process), and mode and/or medium of delivery. For example, one might consider how user design at a micro level, in the classroom, works for rote learning, compared to higher-order thinking skills; in what ways user design works—or does not work—with learners of high or low motivation levels; and whether there are any differences among various classes, races, or genders in terms of users' abilities to engage in user design and overcome some of the theoretical obstacles that have already been discussed in the literature. Although this series of empirical studies may appear, on the face of it, to require traditional quantitative controlled experiments, nothing could be further from the truth. In fact, these studies should be primarily exploratory at this point and should engage a variety of research methods, primarily qualitative and participatory action research. Methods of research are detailed below.

The third step in this agenda building process is a series of studies examining what might be considered more traditional measures of effectiveness. Whereas we do feel that these goals may be out of alignment with the fundamental values of user design, we also see their value in terms of policymakers and the traditional inquiry community. There is value in gaining credibility through research and using it further to empower users and alternative modes of inquiry. That said, the fairly reasonable third step would be a series of studies examining user design's return on investment, efficiency in terms of time and money spent to actualize user-design goals, implementation sustainability, cost and feasibility, effects on student learning, and, finally, user empowerment from a moral standpoint.

27.6.2 Methods for User-Design Inquiry

To examine and build this research agenda effectively, the user-design inquirer should seriously consider the extent to which the research model chosen is in alliance with the basic values

and philosophies associated with user design. Based on this review, we feel that it would be extremely difficult to attain, particularly, the moral level of inquiry that user design demands utilizing traditional experimental research models. However, we do recognize the need for a variety of research modalities to bring the above research agenda to full fruition. Based on this need, in Fig. 27.2 we have constructed a continuum matched with Fig. 27.1. Perhaps the clearest statement of research methods that the user-designer might engage includes ethnographic field methods, cooperative design, and action research-based user design, which are more fully discussed by Carr (1997) and Schuler and Namioka (1993).

Traditional research models have attempted to remain value neutral (Denzin & Lincoln, 1994). The ethics of research and researcher were not in question and research was not linked to some sort of social action in these more traditional conceptions of inquiry. The user-designer is not necessarily informed by all types of research; rather the user-designer is best informed by certain types of inquiry that tend to engage participants in more powerful ways. Participatory action research (PAR) is one such model. PAR is research with a purpose, in context, to improve an organization with practical applications (Whyte, 1991). It is collaborative research where the "community" is in control (Stoecker, 1999). PAR makes research more accessible to those being studied and distributes knowledge to the academic researcher as well as the participants. Knowledge becomes a tool for fighting oppression. PAR empowers those who have traditionally had research done *to* them instead of actually participating in the design, implementation, and subsequent application of the results of research. The oppressed transform their own environment, with the traditional researcher playing a supporting role (Rahman, 1993).

PAR is full of surprise problems and outcomes. Unlike traditional research, participatory action researchers do not define problems ahead of time but determine, in collaboration with the participants, the problems throughout the research process. It therefore engages all of the potential problems also associated with user design such as apathy, lack of knowledge, communication, and value conflicts. Validity and practicality of research are of paramount importance in PAR. The results of the research must be clear to all involved and delivered in a timely manner for the action objective to be met. All users should have access to this information for them to be an integral part of the design process. Thus, communication and dissemination of information are an ongoing process.

PAR is the research model that is most closely aligned with user design, although user design, to this point, has had very little specific research conducted on either process or product (Carr-Chellman, Cuyar, & Breman, 1998). Therefore, we cannot say with any certainty that PAR is the best *match* to measure the results or processes of user design but, rather, that ideologically PAR is the most closely *aligned* research model. It seems to us, on the face of it, wrong-headed to attempt to measure the results of user design with those of more traditional, particularly quantitative or experimental, research methods. This is primarily because it seems difficult, if not impossible, to measure the true worth of user design using models that are strikingly oppositional in their value systems. PAR offers the user-design community a number of important lessons regarding engaging participants in the social action of research. For example, the North Bonneville, USA, Experience (Comstock & Fox, 1993) gives the user-designer insights into the purposes of engaging users, the positionality of knowledge, empowered knowledge creation, power issues, the democratic method, and the validity of results.

A number of other examples are illuminating to those engaged in user design, including Hansen, Ramstead, Richer, Smith, and Stratton's (2001) work with school community research, Davies and Johnson's (1996) family/school relationship research, Walker's (1993) rehabilitation research, Kaplan and Alsup's (1995) AIDS prevention research, Petras and Porpora's (1993) PAR models, and McTaggart's (1997) collection of PAR around the world. Taken together, these examples form a strong corollary for user-designers to draw on in their continued practice of user-design inquiry.

We recognize the realities of empirical research as it is tied to policymaking. This leads us to suggest that whereas the methods that are most appropriate for user-design inquiry are qualitative, particularly PAR, more traditional empirical studies such as controlled experiments may be useful for public meetings and policy decisionmaking. However, in general, we feel that these studies, for example, comparing pre- and posttest scores are not really getting at the critical issues associated with user-design implementation.

27.7 CONCLUSION

This chapter has reviewed the basic definition of user design and distinguished it from a number of related user-oriented progressive design models such as learner-centered, user-centered, and emancipatory design. The primary distinction, as laid out here, is the elevation of user to true partnership in the design process. Empirical research in related areas of user design such as user-centered, learner-centered, and emancipatory design for the most part showed positive findings for involvement of users in the creation of their own systems part. However, these studies were overly reliant on certain forms of research methods, such as case studies and surveys, and were not holistic in terms of understanding complete disciplines. Foundations of user design were drawn from Scandinavian user design and the large research base in stakeholder participation. The brief review of obstacles to user design recognized the inherent difficulties that rest in the actual practice of user design. We concluded the chapter with a brief review of a research agenda and corresponding recommendations for appropriate research approaches. True user design, as messy, inefficient, overwhelming, difficult, contentious, and perturbing as it may be to the system, goes beyond mere consultation to elevate the user to the role of a designer. It is our belief that user design offers us the clearest, most hopeful way to approach design with faithful inclusion and, consequently, more consistent and facile adoption and implementation. This elevation is a difficult, but entirely worthwhile enterprise, which we hope future instructional designers will integrate into their practices.

References

Abels, E. G. (1997). *The Development and implementation of user-based design process in web site design*. Report to Disclosure, Inc.

Ackoff, R. L. (1974). *Redesigning the future: A systems approach to societal problems*. New York: Wiley.

American Psychological Association. (1993). *Learner-centered psychological principles: Guidelines for school redesign and reform* (ERIC Document Reproduction Service No. ED371994). Washington, DC: Presidential Task Force on Psychology in Education.

AML. (1977). *Law of workers' protection and working environment*. Oslo, Norway: AML.

Banathy, B. H. (1973). *Developing a systems view of education: The systems-model approach*. Belmont, CA: Siegler/Fearon.

Banathy, B. H. (1996). *Designing social systems in a changing world*. New York: Plenum Press.

Bansler, J. (1989). Systems development research in scandinavia: Three theoretical schools. *Scandinavian Journal of Information Systems, 1,* 3–20.

Berube, M. (1970). Community control: Key to educational achievement. *Social Policy, 1*(2), 42.

Bjerknes, G., & Bratteteig, T. (1987). Florence in wonderland: System development with nurses. In G. Bjerknes, P. Ehn, & M. M. Kyng (Eds.), *Computers and democracy: A Scandinavian challenge* (pp. 279–295). Aldershot, UK:Gower.

Bjerknes, G., & Bratteteig, T. (1995). User participation and democracy: A discussion of Scandinavian research on system development. *Scandinavian Journal of Information Systems, 7*(1), 73–98.

Bødker, S. (1996). Creating conditions for participation: Conflicts and resources in systems development. *Human-Computer Interaction, 11*(3), 215–236.

Bohm, D. (1996). *On dialogue*. New York: Routledge.

Brandon, P. R. (1999). Involving program stakeholders in reviews of evaluators' recommendations for program revisions. *Evaluation and Program Planning, 22,* 363–372.

Brandon, P. R., Lindberg, M. A., & Wang, Z. (1993). Involving program beneficiaries in the early stages of evaluation: Issues of consequential validity and influence. *Educational Evaluation and Policy Analysis, 15*(4), 420–428.

Brandon, P. R., Newton, B. J., & Harman, J. W. (1993). Enhancing validity through beneficiaries' equitable involvement in identifying and prioritizing homeless children's educational problems. *Evaluation and Program Planning, 16,* 287-293.

Brown, J. S., & Duguid, P. (1994). Borderline issues: Social and material aspects of design. *Human-Computer Interaction, 9,* 3-36.

Brush, T., & Saye, J. (2000). Implementation and evaluation of a student-centered learning unit: A case study. *Educational Technology Research and Development, 48*(3), 79-100.

Carmen, R. (1990). *Communication, education and empowerment* (ERIC Document Reproduction Service No. ED362649). Manchester, UK: Centre for Adult and Higher Education, Manchester University.

Carr, A. A. (1994). Community participation in systemic educational change. *Educational Technology, 34*(1), 43-50.

Carr, A. A. (1996). Leadership and community participation: Four case studies. *Journal of Curriculum and Supervision, 12*(2), 152-168.

Carr, A. A. (1997). User-design in the creation of human learning systems. *Educational Technology Research and Development, 45*(3), 5-22.

Carr, I. C. (1990). The politics of literacy in Latin America. *Convergence, 23*(2), 50-68.

Carr-Chellman, A. A. (in press). Power, expertism, and the practice of instructional design: Empowering the users. In G. J. Anglin (Ed.), *Instructional technology: Past, present and future.* Englewood, CO: Libraries Unlimited.

Carr-Chellman, A. A., Cuyar, C., & Breman, J. (1998). User-design: A case application in health care training. *Educational Technology Research and Development, 46*(4), 97-114.

Comstock, D. E., & Fox, R. (1993). Participatory research as critical theory: The North Bonneville, USA, Experience. In P. Park, M. Brydon-Miller, B. Hall, & T. Jackson (Eds.), *Voices of change.* Westport, CT: Bergin & Garvey.

Cooper, B. S. (1992). A tale of two cities: Radical school reform in chicago and london. In J. J. Lane & E. G. Epps (Eds.), *Restructuring the schools: Problems and prospects.* Berkeley, CA: McCutchan.

Corry, M. D., Frick, T. W., & Hansen, L. (1997). User-centered design and usability testing of a web site: An illustrative case study. *Educational Technology Research and Development, 45*(4), 65-76.

Daniels, D. H., Kalkman, D. L., & McCombs, B. L. (2001). Young children's perspectives on learning and teacher practices in different classroom contexts: Implications for motivation. *Early Education and Development, 12*(2), 253-273.

Daresh, J. C. (1992). Impressions of school-based management: The cincinnati story. In J. J. Lane & E. G. Epps (Eds.), *Restructuring the schools: Problems and prospects.* Berkeley: CA: McCutchan.

Davies, D. (1981). Citizen participation in decision making in the schools. In D. Davies (Ed.), *Communities and Their Schools* (pp. 83-119). New York: McGraw-Hill.

Davies, D., & Johnson, V. (1996). *Crossing boundaries: Multi-national action research on family-school collaboration.* (ERIC Document Reproduction Service No. ED394718)

DeCandido, G. A. (1997). *After the user survey, what then? Issues and innovations in transforming libraries.* Washington, DC: Systems and Procedures Exchange Center.

Denzin, N. K., & Lincoln, Y. S. (1994). Introduction: Entering the field of qualitative research. In N. K. Denzin & Y. S. Lincoln (Eds.), *Handbook of qualitative research.* Thousand Oaks, CA: Sage.

Dewey, J. (1916). *Democracy and education.* New York: Macmillan.

Dewey, J. (1938). *Experience and education.* New York: Macmillan.

Dick, W., Carey, L. M., & Carey, J. O. (2001). *The systematic design of instruction* (5th ed.). New York: Addison–Wesley Educational.

Dowlin, K. (1980). On-line catalog user acceptance survey. *RQ, 20*(1), 44-47.

Duffy, T. M., Lowyck, J., & Jonassen, D. H. (1993). *Designing environments for constructive learning.* Berlin: Springer-Verlag.

Ehn, P. (1993). Scandinavian design: On participatioin and skill. In D. Schuler & A. Namioka (Eds.), *Participatory design: Principles and practices.* Hillsdale, NJ: Lawrence Erlbaum Associates.

Ehn, P., & Kyng, M. (1987). The collective resource approach to systems design. In G. Bjerknes, P. Ehn, & M. M. Kyng (Eds.), *Computers and democracy: A Scandinavian challenge* (pp. 279-295). Aldershot, UK:Gower.

Ehn, P., & Sandberg, Å. (1979). *Management control and wage earners' power.* Falköping: Prisma.

Elden, M. (1979). Three generations of worker democracy research in Norway. In C. L. Cooper & E. Mumford (Eds.), *The quality of work life in Europe.* London: Associate Business Press.

Epstein, J. L. (1997). *School, family, and community partnerships: Your handbook for action.* Thousand Oaks, CA: Corwin Press.

Evans, R. (1996). *The human side of change: Reform, resistance, and the real-life problems of innovation.* San Francisco: Jossey–Bass.

Fantini, M., Gittell, M., & Magat, R. (1970). *Community control and the urban school.* New York: Praeger.

Fidel, R. (1994). User-centered indexing. *Journal of the American Society for Information Science, 45*(8), 572-576.

Freire, P. (1970). *Pedagogy of the oppressed* (M. B. Ramos, Trans.). New York: Seabury Press.

Gerhardt, H. P. (1986). *Brazil's popular education in the eighties: Essentials, fundamentals and realpolitik.* (ERIC Document Reproduction Service No. ED291877)

Greene, J. C. (1987). Stakeholder participation in evaluation design: Is it worth the effort? *Evaluation and Program Planning, 10,* 379-394.

Greene, J. C. (1988a). Communication of results and utilization in participatory program evaluation. *Evaluation and Program Planning, 11,* 341-351.

Greene, J. C. (1988b). Stakeholder participation and utilization in program evaluation. *Evaluation Review, 12*(2), 91-116.

Grudens-Schuck, N. (2001). Stakeholder effect: A qualitative study of the influence of farm leaders' ideas on a sustainable agriculture education program for adults. *Journal of Agricultural Education, 42*(4), 1-11.

Grudin, J. (1993). Obstacles to participatory design in large product development organizations. In D. Schuler & A. Namioka (Eds.), *Participatory design: Principles and practices.* Hillsdale, NJ: Lawrence Erlbaum Associates.

Hafner, A. L. (1992). *Developing model student information systems: Promising practices* (ERIC Document Reproduction Service No. ED358516). San Francisco, CA: Far West Laboratory for the Educational Research and Development.

Hannafin, M. J., & Land, S. M. (1997). The foundations and assumptions of technology-enhanced student-centered learning environments. *Instructional Science, 25,* 167-202.

Hansen, H. P., Ramstead, J., Richer, S., Smith, S., & Stratton, M. (2001). Unpacking participatory research in education. *Interchange, 32*(3), 295-322.

Henry, G. T., Dickey, K. C., & Areson, J. C. (1991). Stakeholder participation in educational performance monitoring systems. *Educational Evaluation and Policy Analysis, 13*(2), 177-188.

Holcomb, E. L. (1993). *School-based instructional leadership: A staff development program for school effectiveness and improvement.* Paper presented at the Annual Meeting of the International Congress for School Effectiveness and Improvement, Norrkoping, Sweden.

Hooper, K. (1986). Architectural design: An analogy. In D. A. Norman & S. W. Draper (Eds.), *User centered system design: New perspectives on human-computer interaction.* Hillsdale, NJ: Lawrence Erlbaum Associates.

Horkheimer, M., & Adorno, T. W. (2002). *Dialectic of enlightenment: Philosophical fragments* (E. Jephcott, Trans.). Stanford, CA: Stanford University Press.

Hurley, D. E., & Lipp, M. E. (1980). A method for gathering user input to achieve a successful design system. *Cause/Effect, 3*(3), 22–27.

Jackson, S. L., Stratford, S. J., Krajcik, J. S., & Soloway, E. (1996). *Model-it: A case study of learner-centered software design for supporting model building* (ERIC Document Reproduction Service No. ED446903). Arlington, VA: National Science Foundation.

Jackson, T. (1993). A way of working: Participatory research and the aboriginal movement in Canada. In P. Park, M. Brydon-Miller, B. Hall, & T. Jackson (Eds.), *Voices of change*. Westport, CT: Bergin & Garvey.

Jenlink, P., & Carr, A. A. (1996). Conversation as a medium for change in education. *Educational Technology, 36*(1), 31–38.

Jewell, S. F., & Jewell, D. O. (1992). Organization design. In H. D. Stolovitch & E. J. Keeps (Eds.), *Handbook of human performance technology*. San Francisco, CA: Jossey–Bass.

Jonassen, D. H. (1999). Designing constructivist Learning environments. In C. M. Reigeluth (Ed.), *Instructional-design theories and models: A new paradigm of instructional theory* (Vol. 2). Mahwah, NJ: Lawrence Erlbaum Associates.

Kaplan, S. J., & Alsup, R. (1995). Participatory action research: A creative response to AIDS prevention in diverse communities. *Convergence, 28*(1), 38–56.

Karat, J. (1997). Evolving the scope of user-centered design. *Communications of the ACM, 40*(7), 33–38.

Karat, J., Atwood, M. E., Dray, S. M., Rantzer, M., & Wixon, D. R. (1996, April). *User centered design: Quality or quakery.* Paper presented at the CHI 96.

Kaske, N. K., & Sanders, N. P. (1980). On-line subject access: The human side of the problem. *RQ, 20*(1), 52–58.

Keith, P. B., Abrams, P., & McLaughlin, J. (1993). *Using stakeholders in special education research: How does it influence the research process?* Paper presented at the Annual Meeting of the American Educational Research Association, Atlanta, GA.

Kelly, K. (1994). *Out of control: The rise of neo-biological civilization.* Reading, MA: Addison–Wesley.

Kyng, M., & Mathiassen, L. (1979). A "new systems development": Trade union and research activities. In Å. Sandberg (Ed.), *Computers dividing man and work* (pp. 54–74). Malmö: Swedish Center for Working Life.

Lane, J. J., & Epps, E. G. (Eds.). (1992). *Restructuring the schools: Problems and prospects.* Berkley, CA: McCutchan.

Larsen, T. J., & McGuire, E. (1998). *Information systems innovation and diffusion: Issues and directions.* Hershey, PA: Idea Group.

Lineberry, C., & Carleton, J. R. (1992). Culture change. In H. D. Stolovitch & E. J. Keeps (Eds.), *Handbook of human performance technology*. San Francisco, CA: Jossey–Bass.

Mathie, A., & Greene, J. C. (1997). Stakeholder participation in evaluation: How important is diversity? *Evaluation and Program Planning, 20*(3), 279–285.

McCandless, P., et al. (1985). *University of Illinois Library. The invisible user: User needs assessment for library public services.* Washington, DC: Association of Research Libraries.

McCombs, B. L. (2001). What do we know about learners and learning? The learner-centered framework: Bringing the educational system into balance. *Educational Horizons, 79*(4), 182–193.

McCombs, B. L., & Quiat, M. (2000). *Results of pilot study to evaluate the community for learning (CFL) program.* Philadelphia, PA: Mid-Atlantic Lab for Student Success.

McCombs, B. L., & Whisler, J. S. (1997). *The learner-centered classroom and school: Strategies for increasing student motivation and achievement.* San Francisco, CA: Jossey–Bass.

McTaggart, R. (1997). *Participatory action research: International contexts and consequences.* (ERIC Document Reproduction Service No. ED420669)

Melo, A., & Benavente, A. (1978). *Experiments in popular education in Portugal.* (ERIC Document Reproduction Service No. ED182086)

Merrifield, J. (1993). Putting scientists in their place: Participatory research in environmental and occupational health. In P. Park, M. Brydon-Miller, B. Hall, & T. Jackson (Eds.), *Voices of change*. Westport, CT: Bergin & Garvey.

Miller, S. L. (1980). The changing role of a circulation system: The OSU experience. *RQ, 20*(1), 47–52.

Morris, R. C. T. (1994). Toward a user-centered information service. *Journal of the American Society for Information Science, 45*(1), 20–30.

Morrow, R. A., & Torres, C. A. (2002). *Reading Freire and Habermas: Critical pedagogy and transformative social change.* New York: Teachers College Press.

Muller, M. J., & Czerwinski, M. (1999). Organizing usability work to fit the full product range. *Communications of the ACM, 42*(5), 87–90.

Nelson, L. M. (1999). *Increasing retention of adult learners in telecourses through the incorporation of learning-centered instructional strategies and the use of multiple modalities for content delivery and interaction.* Unpublished Praticum, Nova Southeastern University.

Norman, D. A. (1983). *Design principles for human-computer interfaces.* Paper presented at the Conference on Human Factors and Computing Systems, Boston, MA.

Norman, D. A. (1989). The electronic library: How will the user cope. *Bulletin of the American Society of Information Science, 15*(5), 8–9.

Norman, D. A., & Draper, S. W. (1986). *User centered system design: New perspectives on human-computer interaction.* Mahwah, NJ: Lawrence Erlbaum Associates.

Norman, D. A., & Spohrer, J. C. (1996). Learner-centered education. *Communications of the ACM, 39*(4), 24–27.

Norrbom, M. (2001). Employment law in Denmark. *International Financial Law Review,* 23–25.

Noyes, J. M., & Baber, C. (1999). *User-centred design of systems.* New York: Springer.

Nygaard, K., & Bergo, O. T. (1974). *Planning, control, and computing. Basic book for the trade unions.* Oslo: Tiden Norsk Forlag.

Olson, L. (1990). "Jury still out" on re:learning's grassroots reform experiments. *Education Week, 10*(5), 1, 18–19.

Oshry, B. (1995). *Seeing systems.* San Francisco: Berrett–Koeher.

Otten, M. (1991). Changing the workplace to fit human needs: The norwegian work environment act. *Economic and Industrial Democracy, 12*(4) 487–500.

Paris, C., & Combs, B. (2000). *Teachers' perspectives on what it means to be learner-centered.* Paper presented at the Annual Meeting of the American Educational Research Association, New Orleans, LA.

Payette, S. D., & Rieger, O. Y. (1998). Supporting scholarly inquiry: Incorporating users in the design of the digital library. *Journal of Academic Librarianship, 24*(2), 121–129.

Petras, E. M., & Porpora, D. V. (1993). Participatory research: Three models and an analysis. *American Sociologist, 24,* 107–125.

Rahman, A. (1993). *People's self-development: Perspectives on participatory action research.* London: University Press.

Reigeluth, C. M. (1996). A new paradigm of ISD? *Educational Technology, 36*(3), 13–20.

Reigeluth, C. M. (1999). *Instructional-design theories and models: A new paradigm of instructional theory* (Vol. 2). Mahwah, NJ: Lawrence Erlbaum Associates.

Riley, M. S. (1986). User understanding. In D. A. Norman & S. W. Draper (Eds.), *User centered system design*. Mahwah, NJ: Lawrence Erlbaum Associates.

Rockman, I. F. (1980). The potential of on-line circulation systems as public catalogs: An introduction. *RQ, 20*(1), 39-58.

Rogers, E. M. (1995). *Diffusion of innovations*. New York: Free Press.

Romiszowski, A. J. (1981). *Designing instructional systems: Decision making in course planning and curriculum design*. London: Kogan Page.

Rossman, G. B., & Rallis, S. F. (1998). *Learning in the field*. Thousand Oaks, CA: Sage.

Ruiter, W. W. (1971). *An analysis of the effectiveness of a learner-centered teaching system compared to that of a conventional teaching of basic electricity to university students*. Unpublished Dissertation, Oregon State University.

Saegert, S. (1996). *Growing the seeds of strength in high risk urban neighborhoods*. Paper presented at the Annual Meeting of the American Psychological Association, Toronto, Ontario, Canada.

Salisbury-Glennon, J. D., Gorrell, J., Sanders, S., Boyd, P., & Kamen, M. (1999). *Self-regulated learning strategies used by the learners in a learner-centered school*. Paper presented at the Annual Meeting of the American Educational Research Association, Montreal, Quebec, Canada.

Salvo, M. J. (2001). Ethics of engagement: User-centered design and rhetorical methodology. *Technical Communication Quarterly, 10*(3), 273-290.

Sarason, S. (1995). *Parental involvement and the political principle*. San Francisco, CA: Jossey-Bass.

Schiffman, S. S. (1995). Instructional systems design: Five views of the field. In G. J. Anglin (Ed.), *Instructional technology: Past, present and future*. Englewood, CO: Libraries Unlimited.

Schuler, D., & Namioka, A. (1993). *Participatory design: Principles and practices*. Mahwah, NJ: Lawrence Erlbaum Associates.

Schulze, A. N. (2001). User-centered design for information professionals. *Journal of Education for Library and Information Science, 42*(2), 116-122.

Senge, P. (1990). *The fifth discipline: The art & practice of the learning organization*. New York: DoubleDay.

Smart, K. L., & Whiting, M. E. (2001). Designing systems that support learning and use: A customer-centered approach. *Information and Management, 39,* 177-190.

Smrekar, J. L. (1997). *The impact of learner-centered classrooms on second language learning: Communicating with educators*. Paper presented at the Annual Meeting of the American Educational Research Association, Chicago, IL.

Soloway, E., & Pryor, A. (1996). The next generation in human-computer interaction. *Communications of the ACM, 39*(4), 16-18.

Soloway, E., Jackson, S. L., Klein, J., et al. (1996). *Learning theory in practice: Case studies of learner-centered design*. Paper presented at the Conference on Human Factors and Computing Systems, Vancouver, British Columbia, Canada.

Stevenson, K. R., & Pellicer, L. O. (1992). School-based management in South Carolina: Balancing state-directed reform with local decision making. In J. J. Lane & E. G. Epps (Eds.), *Restructuring the schools: Problems and prospects*. Berkeley: CA: McCutchan.

Stoecker, R. (1999). Are academics irrelevant? Roles for scholars in participatory research. *American Behavioral Scientist, 42*(5) 840-854.

Sugar, W. A. (1999). Novice designers' myths about usability sessions: Guidelines to implementing user-centered design principles. *Educational Technology,* 40-44.

Sugar, W. A. (2001). What is so good about user-centered design? Documenting the effect of usability sessions on novice software designers. *Journal of Research on Computing in Education, 33*(3), 235-250.

Sugar, W. A., & Boling, E. (1995). *User-centered innovation: A model for "early usability testing."* Paper presented at the Annual National Convention of the Association for Educational Communications and Technology, Anaheim, CA.

UTOPIA Project Group. (1981). *Training, technology, and product from the quality of work perspective* (Utopia report no. 1). Stockholm: Swedish Center for Working Life.

Valente, T. W., & Davis, R. L. (1999). Accelerating the diffusion of innovations using opinion leaders. *Annals of the American Academy of the Political and Social Sciences, 566,* 55-67.

Vredenburg, K. (1999). Increasing ease of use. *Communications of the ACM, 42*(5), 67-71.

Wagner, E. D., & McCombs, B. L. (1995). Learner centered psychological principles in practice: Designs for distance education. *Educational Technology, 35*(2), 32-35.

Walker, M. L. (1993). Participatory action research. *Rehabilitation Counseling Bulletin, 37*(1), 2-5.

Wang, M. C., Haertel, G. D., & Walberg, H. J. (1995). *Effective features of collaborative school-linked services for children in elementary school: What do we know from research and practice?* (ERIC Document Reproduction Service No. ED399309). Nairobi, Kenya/Philadelphia, PA: Coordinating Centre for Regional Information Training.

Weinberger, E., & McCombs, B. L. (2001). *The impact of learner-centered practices on the academic and non-academic outcomes of upper elementary and middle school students*. Paper presented at the Annual Meeting of the American Educational Research Association, Seattle, WA.

Whyte, W. F. (Ed.). (1991). *Participatory action research*. Newbury Park, CA: Sage.

Wiggins, G. P. (1998). *Understanding by design*. Alexandria, VA: Association for Supervision and Curriculum Developmen.

Williams, P. A. (1996). *Relationships between educational philosophies and attitudes toward learner-centered instruction*. Paper presented at the Georgia Educational Research Association, Atlanta, GA.

Wilson, L. A. (1995). Building a user-centered library. *RQ, 34*(3), 297-301.

Yapa, L. (1996a). Innovation diffusion and paradigms of development. In C. Earle, K. Mathewson, & M. Kenzer (Eds.), *Concepts in human geography* (pp. 231-270). Lanham, MD: Rowman & Littlefield.

Yapa, L. (1996b). What causes poverty? A postmodern view. *Annals of the Association of American Geographers, 86*(4), 707-728.

Part

·V·

INSTRUCTIONAL STRATEGIES

·28·

GENERATIVE LEARNING CONTRIBUTIONS TO THE DESIGN OF INSTRUCTION AND LEARNING

Barbara L. Grabowski
Penn State University

28.1 INTRODUCTION

28.1.1 Learning or Instruction

Over the past 30 years, attention has gradually shifted from investigating the effects of the external, physical form *of instruction* to examining the internal processes of *learning* that are stimulated or induced by external stimuli. As a result, models and prescriptions for learning are founded on theoretical and empirical evidence about cognitive functioning, processes, and structure of memory. Using a learning foundation, designers develop a conception of the thinking that occurs within the learner and use this conception to guide the design of environments for learning. Instructional and learning environments both contain information; the key difference is who does what with that information. In a learning environment, the learners and their learning processes, styles, and goals take on prime importance. In an instructional environment, the roles of the learner and the instructor or designer are reversed. A learning environment is not devoid of instruction or an instructor, but rather the external stimuli simply take on a secondary role. In an instructional environment, the materials provided for the learners take on prime importance, with the assumption that learner characteristics have been taken into account and the belief that material design and presentation can affect learning.

The designers' beliefs about learning, that is, their epistemology, control their perception of their identity, roles, and responsibilities, which thereby affect whether a learning, an instructional, or a combination approach to design is taken (Grabowski et al., 2002; Jonassen, Marra, & Palmer, 2003). The locus for controlling learning (instruction or learner) has been debated throughout the history of the field, fueled by

researchers' ability to gather evidence for their positions. The evolution of this understanding has been greatly influenced by the development of more refined research methodologies and advances in technology. Armed with new methods, designers, who hold the belief that both the learner and learning environments are of equal importance, that intentionality on the part of the designer *and* the learner is critical, are most likely to design promising instruction and learning environments that blend the extreme beliefs held by behaviorists and constructivists (Grabowski, 2002; Grabowski et al., 2002).

Generative learning theory, with its companion model, generative teaching, is one such area of blending whose theoretical foundation lies in neural research, research regarding the structure of knowledge and cognitive development, with a focus on selecting appropriate, learner centric instructional activities for the learner. This theory is one that combines the importance of learner and instructional intentionality. Bonn and Grabowski (2001) call generative learning theory the "practical cousin of constructivism." Perhaps it also provides a more complete perspective on learning, making it a "second cousin" to behaviorism. The theory blends our understanding of learners and design of external stimuli or instruction.

This chapter defines generative learning and its foundation, reviews relevant research that tests the theory, describes the generative model of teaching and implications for instructional design, and concludes with a discussion of applications of generative learning theory in face-to-face and e-learning environments.

28.1.2 Generative Learning Foundations

Wittrock (1974a, 1974b) was the founder of generative learning theory. His beliefs about learning were influenced by research in several areas of cognitive psychology, including cognitive development, human learning, human abilities, information processing, and aptitude–treatment interactions. His work explains and prescribes teaching strategies to maximize reading comprehension. Whereas most of the original research deals specifically with reading comprehension, in theory there is much transferability to learning for understanding in general, regardless of the medium or form of the external stimuli. This chapter embraces the broader interpretation of this theory and model of learning and teaching.

In his theory, Wittrock emphasized one very significant and basic assumption: The learner is not a passive recipient of information; rather he or she is an active participant in the learning process, working to construct meaningful understanding of information found in the environment. Wittrock (1974b) states, "Although a student may not understand sentences spoken to him by his teacher, it is highly likely that a student understands sentences that he generates himself" (p. 182). It is, as Harlen and Osborne (1985) call it, "learning through the person" (p. 137). This assumption is evident in each process of Wittrock's four-part model.

Wittrock (1990, 1991, 1992) felt that the process of generation distinguished his from other theories and models of learning. He emphasized the importance of and difference between two types of learner-generated relationships: first, among the different parts of the external stimuli (information being perceived) and, second, between that information and the learner's prior knowledge. Comprehension occurs from formulating connections, rather than solely by the function of "placing" information or "transferring" information in memory. The subtle difference lies in the *creation of new* understanding of the information by the learner, rather than *changing* of the presented information. Comprehension, therefore, is not the result of a Brunerian discovery learning approach, but rather it is attributed to the process of generating relationships. A learner-self, learner–teacher, learner–learner, or learner–instruction dialogue or interaction becomes key to learning. The teacher or designer's role is "knowing how and when to facilitate the learner's construction of relations[hips]" (Wittrock, 1990, p. 352), making the learner and teacher or instruction partners in the learning process (Kourilsky, Esfandiari, & Wittrock, 1996; Mayer & Wittrock, 1996). (An analogy characterizing these important and subtle differences is presented in the next section in which generative learning is compared with other theories.)

Wittrock's three other component processes that explain learning are motivational processes, learning processes, and knowledge creation processes. Metacognitive processes also play a key role in his model, although in most cases he folds this idea into the knowledge creation process component. The concept maps in Figs. 28.1 and 28.2 are illustrative of generative learning in action. These figures represent my comprehension of the ideas presented in Wittrock's (1974a, 1974b, 1985, 1990, 1991, 1992) writings regarding the progression of generative learning from neural brain processes research to models of thinking and teaching. The lines depict personally generated relationships between different concepts and ideas presented in his writings.

As shown in Fig. 28.1, Wittrock conceptualized this model of generative learning based on a neural model of brain functioning and cognitive research on the process of knowing. From this foundation, the four components of the model are presented in shaded, rounded-off rectangles, with examples of each process presented as ovals below. For example, attribution is one example of motivational processes, and preconceptions is one example of knowledge creation processes. The process of generation is divided into two types of possible relationship creations—*coding* among different parts of the information in the text and *integration* of the information in the text with prior learning and experience. Figure 28.1 also implies a flow between the processes of the model, with motivational processes activating learning processes, which in turn affect whether the process of generation will occur. Knowledge creation processes also affect the process of generation, but in a different way: Beliefs, preconception, prior concepts, and metacognition influence the quality and type of links that learners create. Depending on the type of relationship generated, the four components converge for the purpose of learner-constructed organization, reorganization, elaboration, or reconceptualization of the information, resulting ultimately in comprehension, as shown by the hexagons. Each of these four processes is discussed in detail in later.

Figure 28.2 depicts the research by Luria (1973), as described by Wittrock (1992), on which generative learning was founded. As depicted here, Luria identified three functional units of the brain that are activated through the ascending and descending reticular activating systems and the frontal lobes of the cortex. Cognitive functioning originates in each of these units, which then activates or manages one of the processes of knowing, which then influences one of the four components of Wittrock's generative learning model—again depicted by shaded, rounded-off rectangles.

The first unit, arousal and intention, influences an individual's learning processes and motivation. External stimuli arouse attention through the ascending reticular activating system; however, without active, dynamic, and selective attending of environmental stimuli, it follows that meaning generation cannot occur regarding those stimuli. The influence of arousal on attention flows from the environment outside of the learner but interacts internally, another indication of the partnership between the learner and the instruction or teacher. Intention is activated by the descending reticular activating system, which stimulates attribution and interest. Attribution and interest influence the motivation of the learner. Attribution of effort, or the process of giving credit for success or failure to one's own effort, can influence whether or not the learner will exert the effort to be "attentive to the underlying structure of the information to be learned" (Wittrock, 1985, p. 123) and thereby become actively involved in generating understanding. If learners attribute success to themselves, it follows that motivation to exert effort will be greater than if they attribute success to external forces (Weiner, 1979). The influence of intention on motivation for meaning generation flows from within the learner.

The second functional unit is the unit for receiving, analyzing, and storing information. The coding of information is managed by the frontal lobes of the cortex. The functions of the brain in this unit influence the knowledge creation processes.

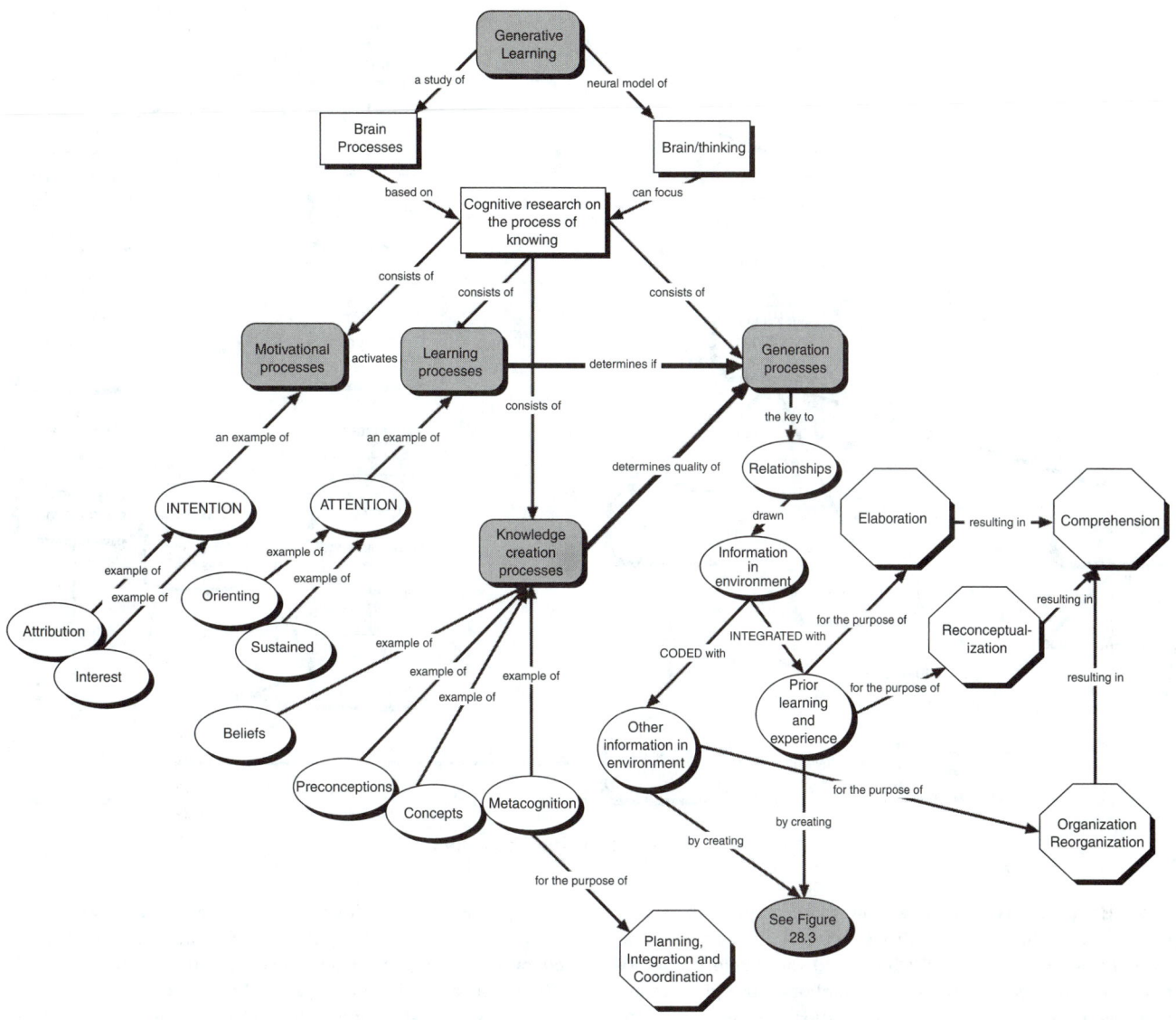

FIGURE 28.1. Generative learning concept map.

Wittrock identifies many parts to the knowledge creation processes in several of his writings. Primarily, he includes beliefs, concepts, preconceptions, metacognitions, and experiences (see Fig. 28.1). In other words, these are the components of memory. It is between these existing beliefs, concepts, preconceptions, etc., and environmental stimuli that relationships are formed, and thereby, understanding and comprehension are generated. According to Wittrock (1974a), "Cognitive theory implies that learning can be predicted and understood in terms of what the learners bring to the learning situation, how they relate the stimuli to their memories, and what they generate from their previous experiences" (p. 93).

The third functional unit is the unit for planning, organizing, and regulating cognition and behavior. This unit also operates through the frontal lobes of the cortex to coordinate learning and integrate information. These are the processes of metacognitive monitoring and generative processes—the heart and soul of generative learning theory. By generating relationships between parts of what the learners see and hear, and by integrating that information with what exists in memory, learners reorganize, elaborate, and/or reconceptualize information, not simply "stuff in more information." It is a process for which meaningful understanding and comprehension are predicted outcomes (see Fig. 28.1).

Wittrock (1990) claimed that there are two types of learning activities that can be judged as generative. Activities that generate organizational and reorganizational relationships among different components of the environment include "titles,

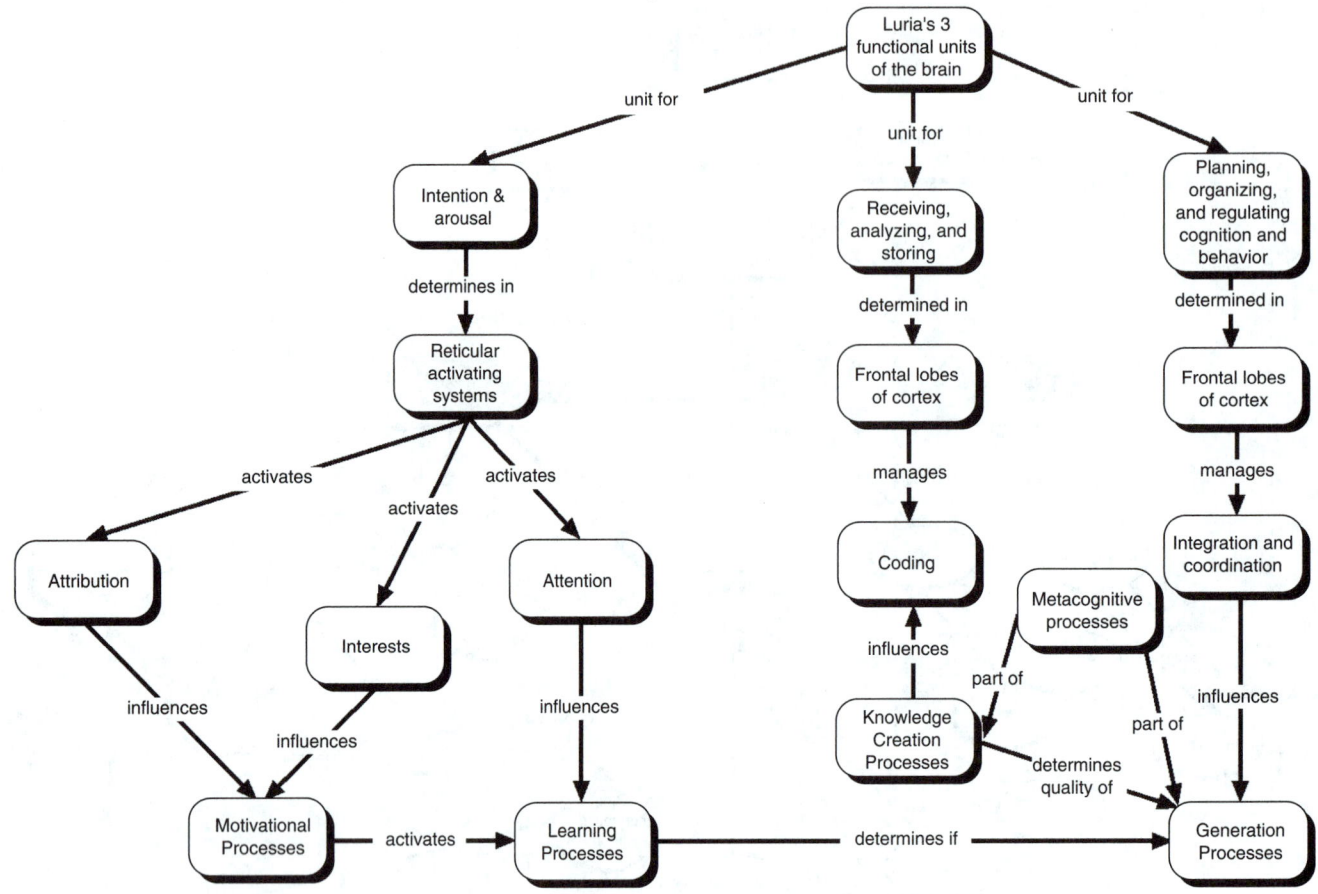

FIGURE 28.2. Neural functions concept map.

headings, questions, objectives, summaries, graphs, tables, and main ideas," whereas those that generate integrated relationships between the external stimuli and the memory components include "demonstrations, metaphors, analogies, examples, pictures, applications, interpretations, paraphrases, and inferences" (p. 354). In Fig. 28.3, these examples are shown in the ovals connected to one of the two types of relationships. From other activities proposed by DiVesta (1989), Goetz (1983), and Jonassen (1986), concept maps, diagrams, outlines, and identifying scripts within narratives seem to be appropriate additions to the organizational relationship list. Mnemonics, clarifying, and predicting seem appropriate for his second list, the integrated relationships, linking external stimuli to internal components of memory. Notetaking, diagrams, and concept maps could be appropriate for both lists, depending on which cognitive processes were used to create which type of link—organizational or integrative. That is, if learners were only relating different ideas extracted directly from a text passage, their list would be classified as organizational, whereas if they related the information to prior knowledge, it would qualify as integrative. Based on Wittrock's definition of organization and integration, Figs. 28.1 to 28.3 represent my organizational maps. Table 28.1, on the other hand, portrays generation as integration through reconceptualization and elaboration.

Only those activities that involve the actual *creation* of relationships and meaning would be classified as examples of generative learning strategies. Restructuring of environmental information by definition requires the learner to generate either organizational or integrated relationships and construct personal meaning, thereby qualifying as generative. If this activity were simply tracing, with no generation of relationships or meaning, the activity would not qualify as generative. Other controversial activities such as highlighting and underlining can be argued not to be generative, because they involve examining only single components, even though the learner may be selecting author-written main ideas. Even if learners are integrating the sentences with prior knowledge, there is no covert evidence of that integration, as the focus of the activity is a task in which they are simply selecting from among many parts. An activity must involve *meaning making* to qualify as generative. An activity in which the learner simply selects sentences that someone else has already composed cannot be considered generative. The generated main idea must relate all the ideas presented in the passage. If learners are relating the textual information to their own prior experience, knowledge, or preconception, however, it could be argued that highlighting or underlining is generative (Grabowski, 1995). As discussed later, under Applied Research, Rickards (1979) would support this notion.

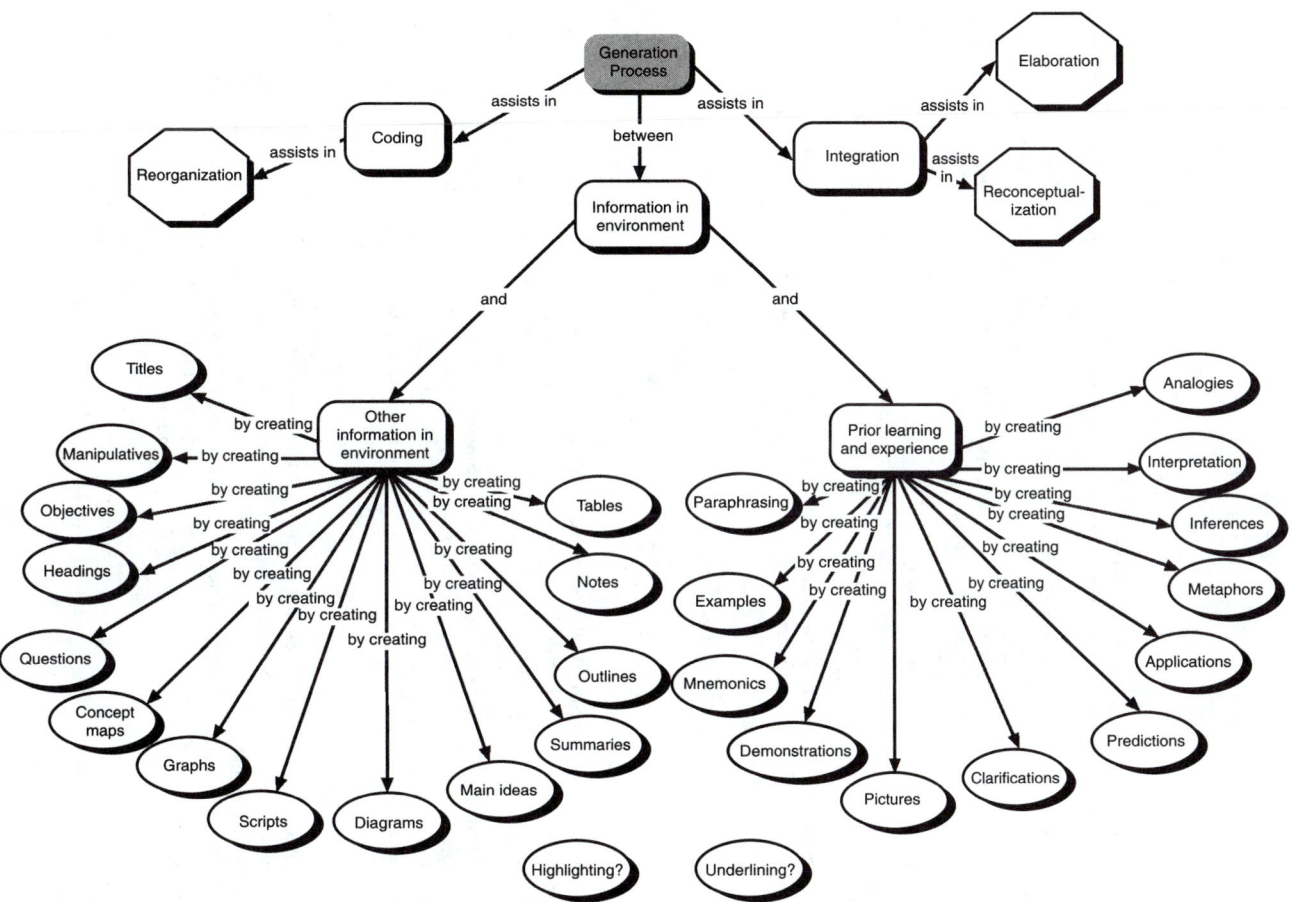

FIGURE 28.3. Generative activities concept map.

28.1.3 Relationship of Generative Learning to Other Schools of Thought

Wittrock (1991, 1992) often compares his own theory with others. These comparisons are quite useful for understanding the nuances of his teaching recommendations. In Table 28.1, generative learning theory is compared with other contemporary schools of thought: behaviorism, connectionism, schema theory, information processing, and constructivism with an integrative restructured elaboration.

These schools of thought differ in many ways, the most significant being what unit of analysis is examined and explained and how thinking and learning are defined and exemplified. These basic differences are often subtle, yet they contribute directly to the type of model that has been constructed and the implications that are drawn for instruction. The purpose of this section is not to describe each of these theories in detail (see other chapters for further description); rather, it is to discuss overall salient differences between the various models and generative learning theory and what these differences imply for instruction. The last two rows in Table 28.1 depict those differences, one directly and the other in an analogical reconceptualization.

Of all the theories, behaviorism (Skinner, 1990) presents the most extreme difference from generative learning. That difference lies in how the role of the learner is perceived and what this perception implies for learning. For generative learning, the learner is the key–the controller of whether or not information is learned. Understanding all of the neural processes that affect learning, from intention to components in memory to attribution, will aid the designer in selecting or creating appropriate activities that take these factors into account. The learner must also be actively and consciously relating ideas. For behaviorism, the learner plays no role, except as a passive recipient of information. The behavioral design of instruction must center on creating a stimulating message that reinforces by positive or negative feedback. Higher-level coding or integration is irrelevant in the prescription. An important contribution to generative learning, however, comes from extensive research on message design—this is how the external message can gain attention and be driven by designer or teacher intentionality. This contribution provides an incomplete notion of learning comprehension, thereby making it an indirect "second cousin."

Connectionisin (Wittrock, 1992) is similar to behaviorism, in that its intent is in strengthening associations. However,

TABLE 28.1. Comparison of Related Schools of Thought

Comparison	Generative Learning Theory (Wittrock, 1992)	Behaviorism (Skinner, 1990)	Connectionism (Wittrock, 1992)	Schema Theory (Rummelhart, 1981)	Information Processing (Bell-Gredler, 1986)	Constructivism (Jonassen, 1991)
A study of	Brain as controller	Neural connections	Memory associations	Knowledge representation in memory	Stages and levels of processing	Philosophy of constructed meaning
Learning defined by	Learner-generated relationships	Behavioral change	Associations	Creation of, addition to, restructuring of, or fine-tuning of schema	Process of encoding information for retrieval	Individually constructed understanding
Type of thinking	Brain as model builder by controlling the 4 processes	Automatic paired response in stimulus–response chain	Neurally induced	Schemata construction and reconstruction	Transference of external stimulus to memory so that it may be retrieved	Building understanding from experiences
Levels of thinking	Comprehension/ understanding— coding, elaboration, reorganization, reconceptualization	Unnecessary unit of analysis	Conceptual	Comprehension	Rehearsal, coding, organization, conceptualization, integration, and translation	Unspecified
Type of model	Neurally controlled learning	Stimulus–response chains	Subconceptual network model of memory	Structural (networked) knowledge representation of memory	Representation of the sequence of mental operation and form of stored knowledge	n/a
Components of theory	Four processes: motivation, learning, knowledge creation, and generation	Operant conditioning, response formation, shaping, reinforcement schedules	Networks of patterns and weights of nodes and connections	Schema, schemata, scripts, and plans	Stages—sensory receptors, short-term storage, working memory, long-term memory; levels—deep and surface processing	Source of reality, learner as builder
Implications for instruction	Activities that guide (induce) mental processes relating information	Careful construction of the physical form of messages with repeated, rewarded practice	Activities that strengthen connections through repetition	Activities that relate new to existing knowledge so that it is retrievable	Activities that activate attention, facilitate processing in working memory, and facilitate transfer into long-term memory	Creation of contextualized learning environment

724

Comparison with generative learning theory	n/a	Claims a very different role for the learner, as passive recipient rather than active generator	Explains learning as external neural induction instead of being neurally controlled internally; externally imposed, not necessarily personally relevant	Explains the basic knowledge unit used in generative learning theory	Explains learning as a transformation of information rather than generation	Provides a philosophical basis rather than a neurological explanation of learning
Comparative analogy: task—purchasing clothing for an outing	Approach: Active and conscious selection of items	Approach: Passive and reinforced by salesperson	Approach: Passive, externally driven	Approach: Not specified, but rather the units of clothing that can be chosen are more representative here	Approach: Active but not necessarily internally controlled; represents the process one goes through from attending to those items in the store, trying various combinations, and then taking them home to store in the closet using a variety of grouping strategies	Approach: Active—represents a philosophy that what is fashionable is constructed by individual tastes and individually defined needs rather than predefined combinations proffered in society or by salespersons
	Item purchased: The intent is creating a new fashion statement	Item purchased: Outfit created and selected by another	Item purchased: Selection of combination of items for outfit determined by those most commonly worn by peers or in magazines	Item purchased: Something to add to an existing outfit, tailoring of an old item, or creation of a new combination of items	Item purchased: Something to add to an existing outfit, tailoring of an old item, or creation of a new combination of items	Item purchased: That which has been created by the individual rather than the salesperson

the network of individual memory is important, as in generative learning theory. Connectionists, however, establish networks by strengthening associations by externally driven, repeated practice rather than creating personally drawn relationships between and among ideas. Understanding is internally created in generative learning theory, making repetitions unnecessary.

Schema theory (Rummelhart, 1981; Rummelhart & Ortony, 1977) is similar to connectionism in that it deals with patterns of data points or schemata. Basically, these data points form the knowledge units that are manipulated in generative learning theory. Because of the way knowledge is stored, instructional and learning activities must connect new to existing knowledge so that it is easily retrievable. This connection is made by adding information to a schema, restructuring it, or fine-tuning it. Although connections are made by links, those linkages are not defined or labeled, as in creating a pattern note without labeling the lines. Generative learning theory, on the other hand, is similar in concept to creating a pattern note with all the links labeled. Activities designed by schema theorists include those that remind learners of prior knowledge and relate the information to what learners already know. Who selects those connection points is less relevant than the fact that they are made.

Information processing theory (Bell-Gredler, 1986) explains the process of thinking and memory storage, in other words, the stages and levels of processing. What we take from information processing theory is an emphasis on how we think, rather than on what we think or *that* we think. Its focus is on that process of transforming external stimuli into some recallable form to be stored in memory. The emphasis of generative learning theory is on the generation of *new* conceptual understandings, not just on transforming information.

Finally, constructivism. (Jonassen, 1991) is a philosophy that underlies learning. It parallels generative theory in considering the learner to be an active processor of information; however, it is extreme in its position about the nonexistence of an objective reality. Wittrock has not addressed this approach in any of his writings, but because of its foundation, Bonn and Grabowski (2001) call generative learning theory its "practical cousin."

To explain some of these subtle differences, a comparative analogy of an individual tasked with purchasing clothing for an outing was generated showing how the approach to the task (the purchase process) and the ultimate outcome (what item would ultimately be purchased) differ between these schools of thought. The approach in generative buying would be exemplified as a buyer-controlled activity, with intention, motivation, and prior conceptions and beliefs about the outing and the people invited. These factors would drive what types and styles of clothing are perceived as needed. The generative buyer would purchase cloth and create a *new* style based on those internally stimulated factors. The salesperson, also an active participant in the purchase process, will query the buyer on how each article fits with those other influences and how the articles would go with other items the buyer had at home. Intentionality is shared, however, the buyer seeks a totally new fashion statement, rather than one already prepared.

A behavioristic example is simple: In a salesperson-driven environment, the approach is very passive, with an outfit having been preselected and the salesperson giving much praise

for purchasing the item. In a connectionism scenario, the approach is also passive. Choices are driven by society-defined fashion that has been repeatedly seen (connected) in fashion magazines, on television, and on peers. A buyer purchases an outfit based on the frequency of seeing the outfit. Intention or personal conception would already have been programmed.

Following schema theory, the buyer and seller play equal roles. Though the approach is not specified by this theory, the articles of available clothing in the store and at home will play the key role. How these articles are combined is the important aspect of this theory. Accessories could be added, items rearranged, the outfit tailored to reach different desired effects. The coordination factors, however, would remain undefined. Intention, personal conceptions, or the generation of some new fashion item are irrelevant.

For information processing, both the buyer and the sales environment are essential players, meaning that the approach by the buyer is active but not necessarily internally controlled. The information processing buyer would attend to featured items that catch his or her attention, select a few, try on various combinations, and purchase a standard outfit, embellish it with accessories, or ask for it to be tailored. The key difference here is that what is purchased is transformed from a rack in a store into an appropriate outfit following established rules of fashion, rather than generating totally new fashion statements or a totally new garment from different pieces of cloth.

A constructivistic buyer would hold a philosophy that what is fashionable is constructed by individual tastes and needs rather than predefined combinations proffered by society. The approach would be very active, independent, and individually driven. The ultimate item or combination of items would make an individual statement.

In each case, the notable difference is in the role of the buyer (learner) as he or she is related to the salesperson (instructor) or store items (instruction). This is exemplified through the approach (learning process) taken to the task and the final selection of the item (learning).

28.2 APPLIED RESEARCH

Studies investigating the viability of the generative model of learning have tested the effects of simple coding strategies such as underlining, note taking, and adjunct or inserted questions; more complex coding organizational strategies such as creation of hierarchies, headings, summaries, and concept maps or manipulation of objects; elaborative integration strategies such as imaging and creation of examples, interpretations, or analogies; and, finally, metacognitive generative learning training. Table 28.2 organizes and summarizes some of the most significant work testing Wittrock's theory. The table divides the types of research into those that represent a coding generative activity and those that represent an integrative generative activity. Those that exemplify coding interrelate concepts from the instruction together to create one level of understanding through various levels and types of organizational activities. Those exemplifying integration interrelate the concepts from the instruction with prior knowledge to create a higher level of understanding by

TABLE 28.2. Summary of Selected Applied Generative Research Studies

Generative Activity	Author/Year	Dependent Variable	Content	Age Level	Results
			Coding		
Underlining					
Underlining	Rickards & August (1975)	Reading comprehension	Educational psychology	College students	Increased achievement on posttest when learner underlined most relevant information.
Note taking					
Note taking	Peper & Mayer (1986)	Recall, problem solving	Auto engines	High-school & college students	Note taking increased achievement for far-transfer problem solving but not near-transfer fact retention.
Note taking	Shrager & Mayer (1989)	Recall, problem solving	How to use a camera	College students	Confirmed above findings; also significant differences for students with low prior knowledge.
Note taking, elaborated and simple review; instructor-provided and learner-generated notes	Barnett, DiVesta, & Rogozenski (1981)	Immediate and delayed recall	History	College students	Note taking produced better results than no note taking, but no significant difference between elaborated review and simple review of notes. Review of instructor-prepared notes resulted in greater learning than review of learner-generated notes. Delayed retention scores higher for questions from learner notes.
Writing summaries during note taking	Davis & Hult (1997)	Domain-specific immediate and delayed recall and free recall	Introductory psychology	College students	Summary group scored significantly higher on free recall and delayed retention test.
Précising vs. rereading underlining, or signaling	McGuire (1999)	Comprehension	Reading	ESL learners	Précising results in higher comprehension over rereading, underlining, or signaling.
Adjunct questions					
Adjunct questions: frequency, nature of, need for feedback, overt/covert responses	Anderson & Biddle (1975)	Facts, motivation, and higher-order thinking	Across content areas	Across age levels	Better learning with more frequent questions. No difference if feedback is given. Overt response needed depending on if questions were embedded.

Continues

727

TABLE 28.2. *continued*

Generative Activity	Author/Year	Dependent Variable	Content	Age Level	Results
Adjunct postquestions with no overt responses	Sutliff (1986)	Facts, inference	Electrical engineering	Low- and upper-ability college students	No significant differences between groups.
Adjunct questions: super-subordinate postquestions	Burton, Niles Lalik, & Reed (1986)	Recall of main ideas and details	Description of a mythical country	Undergraduates	More main ideas were recalled. General questions were more engaging than detailed ones.
Adjunct postquestions	Woods & Bernard (1987)	Recall of intentional and incidental ideas	Weather forecasting	Adults aged 60 or older	Adjunct questions aided recall of intentional ideas only.
Adjunct pictures	Brody & Legenza (1980)	Reading comprehension	History	Undergraduates	Postpictures were more beneficial than prepictures.
Organizational strategies Organization hierarchies	Wittrock & Carter (1975)	Free recall	Mineral tables	Undergraduates	Learner-generated hierarchies for disorganized lists significantly better than simply reproducing them. Reproducing organized hierarchies significantly better than learner-generated ones.
Organization headings, sentence meaning	Doctorow, Wittrock, & Marks (1978)	Reading comprehension	SRA literature	Elementary-school students	Learner-generated sentences combined with experimenter-provided headings produced increased comprehension, followed by generative only.
Concept vs. semantic maps	Beissner, Jonassen, & Grabowski (1993)	Drawing, identification, terminology, comprehension, and problem solving	Heart content	Undergraduates	Learner-generated concept maps better strategy for holists. Learner-generated semantic maps better for serialists for problem-solving learning only.
Concept maps	Smith & Dwyer (1995)	Drawing, identification, terminology, and comprehension	Heart content	Undergraduates	Learners using instructor-provided concept maps performed better on identification tests only. No other differences found.
Graphic organizers	Kenny (1995)	Immediate and delayed (retention) nursing assessments and interventions	Nursing elderly patients	University nursing students and faculty	Significantly poorer performance on the immediate learning and retention tests for those generative graphic organizers than those given a graphic organizer.

Strategy	Study	Task/Test	Content	Population	Findings
Concept maps—partial and total learner-generated by feedback	Taricani (2002)	Identification, terminology, comprehension tests	Heart content	Undergraduate students	Providing feedback resulted in higher terminology scores on partially generated map.
Manipulation of objects Physical manipulation of objects	Sayeki, Ueno, & Nagasaka (1991)	Calculating an area	Math	Elementary-school children	Posttest showed physical manipulation facilitated problem solving.
Mouse-manipulated graphics	Haag & Grabowski (1994)	Terminology, identification, comprehension, and problem solving	Heart content	Undergraduates	Learner-manipulated graphics increased problem solving over static or computer-manipulated graphics.
Individual and group concept mapping and object manipulation; sequence of activities	Ritchie & Volkl (2000)	Immediate, intermediate, and delayed recall	Science	Sixth-grade children	No difference between concept mapping and manipulatives on immediate recall, and those who worked in teams versus those who worked individually. Significantly better performance for those who created concept maps first and then used the manipulatives on the delayed posttest. Interaction found between strategy and individual/team on immediate and delayed recall—those who created concept maps in teams performed significantly better than those who used the manipulatives in teams. The opposite effect was found for intermediate recall.

Integration

Strategy	Study	Task/Test	Content	Population	Findings
Imaging Imaging	Anderson & Kulhavey (1972)	Prose learning	Fictitious description of a tribe of people	High-school seniors	Significant differences in favor of those who actually used an imaging strategy.
Imaging—experimenter provided/learner generated	Bull & Wittrock (1973)	Recall of verbal definitions	Definitions of nouns	Elementary-school children	Recall was significantly higher for imaging than verbal/copying strategy.
Verbal and image elaborations: *sequence*	Kourilsky & Wittrock (1987)	Economic understanding	Economics	High-school students	Verbal-to-image elaborations significantly better than image to verbal or either used singularly.

Continues

TABLE 28.2. *continued*

Generative Activity	Author/Year	Dependent Variable	Content	Age Level	Results
Verbal only, image only, and combined elaborations	Laney (1990)	Reasoning in decision making	Economics	Third-grade children	Verbal-only and verbal-to-image integrated strategies facilitated reasoning better than imagery only.
Elaborations					
Elaborations elaborated sentences	Stein & Bransford (1979)	Retention	Language arts	Undergraduates	Performance facilitated only when elaborations clarified precise objectives prompting encouraged subjects to ask more relevant questions.
Elaboration examples	DiVesta & Peverley (1984)	Concept attainment near and far transfer	Fictitious concepts	Undergraduates	Students who generated their own examples did significantly better on far-transfer tasks than those given instructor-provided examples.
Elaboration interpretation	Johnsey, Morrison, & Ross (1992)	Recall, recognition, application, type of elaborations	Professional development	Adults	Results favored the use of embedded vs. detached elaboration strategies. Elaborations better than no elaborations. No difference between learner-generated and experimenter-provided.
Combination of Coding and Integration					
Images, verbalization of the image and summaries, structural adjunct questions,	Carnine & Kinder (1985)	Reading comprehension	Social studies and science	Low-performing elementary-school children	Comprehension increased significantly but not more than when inserted questions on passage structure were used.
Summaries, and analogies	Wittrock & Alesandrini (1990)	Text	Marine life	Undergraduates	Summaries facilitated reading comprehension better than analogies, and both did better than reading alone.
Summaries and analogies: alone and in pairs	Hooper, Sales, & Rysavy (1994)	Achievement, efficiency, and generations	Marine life	Undergraduates	Those who generated summaries performed better than those who generated analogies. Students working alone did better than those working in pairs.
Combination of generative strategies—images summary sentences, and analogies/metaphors	Linden & Wittrock (1981)	Factual retention and comprehension	Reading	Elementary-school children	All generations increased and correlated with comprehension. More generations were produced when images were produced before verbal elaborations. *No* difference by generation sequence. Results were mixed for factual recall.

Strategy	Citation	Measure	Context	Population	Results
Self-questioning, summarizing, and note taking	King (1992)	Immediate and delayed recall	Generic lecture	Underprepared undergraduate students	Immediate: Summarizers performed better than self-questioners, who performed better than note takers. Delayed: Self-questioners performed better than summarizers, who performed better than note takers.
Summaries, analogies, and question answering in different sequences	Boulaoude & Tamin (1998)	Comprehension and preference	Science	Seventh-grade students	No differences for strategy or sequence. Preferred summaries the most, and questions because they were easy, analogies for fun, and summaries for their helpfulness.
Strategy orientation (underlining, headings, and analogies) by guided vs. active activity	McKeague & DiVesta (1996)	Memory, organization, and application	Radar	Undergraduates	No effect by strategy. Students performed better in the guided activities than the active learner groups.

Metacognitive Strategies

Strategy	Citation	Measure	Context	Population	Results
Generative learning processes training	Kourilsky & Wittrock (1992)	Comprehension, confidence, misunderstanding	Economics	High-school seniors	Generative learning procedures significantly increased confidence and decreased level of misunderstanding.
Generative teaching training	Kourilsky (1993)	Comprehension, misunderstanding	Economics	Professional teachers	Pre- to posttest gains on both exams were significant when misconceptions were clarified and learning covered again.
Instruction on summary writing versus reflection training	Friend (1999)	Judging importance of content/construction of a thesis statement	Reading comprehension	Unskilled undergraduate writers	Instruction on how to write effective summaries was more effective.

reconceptualization and elaboration. A discussion and summary of the results from each of these areas are provided. This discussion begins with the most controversial—underlining—so that it neither gets lost among the other significant, noncontroversial studies nor is given the same importance as many of the other studies reported here.

28.2.1 Simple Coding

28.2.1.1 Underlining. As discussed previously, an argument can be made for activating generative processes by having the learner consciously and interactively relate information in the passage with prior beliefs and conceptions. This is, in essence, what Rickards and August (1975) did in their study. They investigated subject-generated versus experimenter-provided underlining strategies under six treatment conditions. Their results indicated that when college students had an opportunity to underline text that they considered most relevant, they performed better on the posttests on both objective-specific and incidental learning (total recall). In fact, a very interesting result was that in the learner-generated condition, in which the subjects were asked to underline the least important items, they did poorest of all. Rickards (1979) explained that because learners were asked to underline those sentences that were more relevant to them, a mental interaction between sentences and between what they read and their own preconceptions had to occur, thereby establishing plausible evidence that learner-constructed generative learning occurred.

28.2.1.2 Note Taking. Note taking is also considered an organizational coding strategy by some. Others would argue that no generation of understanding occurs when a learner simply copies sentences from a page. As with the Rickards' argument, however, a learner that rewords sentences to combine ideas from the passage or relate them to prior knowledge is engaging in generative activity. This is an important distinction for teachers as they teach learners how to take notes and provide feedback in the process. To illustrate, five studies have been selected that include high-school and college students in vocational education, liberal arts, and English as a second language (ESL).

Peper and Mayer (1986) found from two experiments, one with high-school and one with college-level students, that note takers performed better than non-note takers on far-transfer tasks of problem solving but worse on near-transfer tasks of fact retention and verbatim recognition (p. 34). Shrager and Mayer's (1989) study of college students instructed to take notes or not to take notes of a videotaped lesson confirmed these findings and found that the effect on recall and transfer was highest for learners with low prior knowledge. Peper and Mayer also tested the effects of other generative strategies, such as taking summary notes and answering conceptual questions during breaks in lectures, and produced similar results. This study points out the importance of examining the effects of generative strategies on the type of learning that results.

Davis and Hult (1997) added another dimension to note taking—that of writing summaries as specified periods during note taking in introductory psychology classes. Their results support the findings of Barnett, DiVesta, and Rogozenski (1981) that writing summaries during pauses in the lecture note-taking activity significantly improved free recall and delayed retention. The summaries added an important generative dimension to the note-taking activity. McGuire (1999) compared précis writing (summaring) to rereading, underlining, or signaling for ESL learning. Her contribution to this body of work is the positive effect of summarizing for ESL.

Note taking in two studies by Barnett et al. (1981) was hypothesized to aid college students' processing of information. Note taking produced better results in learning from text than no note taking, but elaboration of the notes during a review period, a generative activity, produced similar results in terms of amount of learning as those who simply reviewed their notes. An interesting dimension to this study was the inclusion of instructor-prepared notes vs. learner-generated notes. For immediate recall tests during which learners had an opportunity to review or elaborate on instructor-prepared notes, they performed better than the learner-generated notes group. The second study tested whether the effects were the same for different types of questions: those common to the group, those from their own notes, those from others' notes, and those from others' elaborations. Scores for the delayed test using questions written from student's own notes were dramatically higher than for the other groups. This provides a strong case for note taking causing generative effects. In other words, these results showed that learners remembered what they originally perceived and encoded versus what others had intended them to remember.

To summarize these studies, note taking has shown positive effects, but there were mixed findings compared with type of learning. Note taking may be a highly generative activity; however, quality of notes, type of elaborations, and opportunity for review can affect what, how much, and for how long information is learned. Another important implication is that for a learning partnership to occur between the instruction or instructor and the learner, an interaction is required—a dialogue between the learner and the instructor about the match between instructor intention and learner generation.

28.2.1.3 Adjunct or Inserted Questions. Wittrock (1990) classified adjunct questions as a generative activity. They function as a scaffold for coding and organizing external stimuli. Whereas learners can generate questions, Wittrock believes that providing questions intentionally induces generative thinking by stimulating attention and intention of the learner to relate ideas from a passage together, thereby creating personally meaningful understanding.

Over the past 35 years, the effects of inserted or adjunct questions have been studied extensively across content areas and age levels. Two important reviews of this research have summarized those findings. Anderson and Biddle (1975) and Rickards (1979) have concluded that inserted postquestions have been shown to increase recall of incidental learning (where criterion questions are unrelated to the inserted questions) as well as increasing recall on intentional learning (i.e., where criterion questions are the same as the inserted questions). Prequestions have been shown to increase intentional learning only.

According to Anderson and Biddle (1975), adjunct questions have been examined in terms of frequency, need for feedback, nature of the question, need for overt responding, and motivation. They summarized the findings as follows: The more frequent the questions, the better; feedback increased learning, but so did inserted questions without feedback; whereas most of the research focused on fact-level questions, there was also a positive effect for higher-level questions; free recall was generally better than multiple choice; a need for overt responding was dependent on how the questions were embedded; and the questions did motivate learners in some cases. They also found that these effects held across age level, content, length of text, and medium used.

Sutliff (1986) investigated the effect of inserted questions on reducing passivity in a self-instructional slide–tape presentation as evidenced by increased learning of facts (direct learning) and inference (indirect learning). His findings were opposite those of Anderson and Biddle in that there were no significant differences between groups. He interpreted the nonsignificance to be a result of not requiring overt responses to the questions, again contrary to previous research. Because of this "veto power over learning," described by Rothkopf (1976, p. 94), results such as this need to be examined further to determine just where overt manifestations may be necessary to ensure that processing occurs.

Burton, Niles, Lalik, and Reed (1986) investigated the effect of superordinate and subordinate questions on the amount of mental effort (level of cognitive capacity engagement) by using a secondary task probe technique and a passage about a mythical country. They found that superordinate questions have a greater learning effect and that the effect carries over into subsequent text. The overall results indicated that more main ideas were recalled than details. The explanation of the effect was that superordinate information is pulled into short-term memory more frequently, so it gets more practice. In other words, they found that general questions are more mentally engaging than detailed ones.

Woods and Bernard (1987) also found effects contrary to those of the reviews by Anderson and Biddle and by Rickards. They investigated the effects of adjunct conceptual postquestions for encouraging greater depth of processing of verbal information of adults 60 and older. From results on intentional and incidental free-recall tests, they found that adjunct questions helped older learners process only intentional text at a greater depth.

In an interesting twist on the research question, Brody and Legenza (1980) studied the effect on learning of inserted pictures as opposed to inserted questions and hypothesized that the effect would be the same as the results on adjunct questions. Their findings supported their hypothesis that postpictures were more beneficial to reading comprehension than prepictures.

To summarize the numerous studies: Postquestions and postpictures have been shown to be most effective for increasing both intentional and incidental learning, superordinate questions have been more effective than subordinate detail questions, and overt responses have been more effective than allowing covert responses.

28.2.2 Complex Coding

28.2.2.1 Organizational Strategies.

This topic deals with a variety of coding and organizational activities including creating hierarchies, headings, and sentence meanings and mapping techniques across all age levels, from elementary-school children to professionals, in a variety of topics, from science to language arts. These organizational tasks require learners to relate ideas from a passage together by using a variety of symbolic representations. Each addresses at least one of three key questions regarding the generative model of learning: the effect of learner-generated learning vs. the effect of learner-reproductive learning; the effect of learner-generated vs. instructor-provided constructions of meaning, including organization as a variable; or the general effects of generated elaborations.

Wittrock and Carter (1975) studied free-recall responses of undergraduates in generative vs. reproductive treatments using hierarchies with varying degrees of order. The generative group was directed to organize the hierarchies, whereas the reproductive group was directed to simply copy them. The results showed better performance for the generative treatment groups than for the reproductive groups for the disorganized and randomly organized hierarchies. However, the organized reproductive group performed better than the unrelated generative group. This means that organization within the stimuli can compensate somewhat for a lack of learner-generated strategies, but providing organization in the instruction *and* opportunities for generative activity will be the best.

In two experiments with elementary-school children, Doctorow, Wittrock, and Marks (1978) studied the effect of learner-generated vs. experimenter-provided paragraph headings and sentence meanings on comprehension. Again, the combination of text organized through the use of headings plus learner-generated sentences about the paragraphs produced dramatic gains in comprehension and recall. Generative instructions without experimenter-provided headings followed as the next most effective, and paragraph headings alone were more effective than the control group. This strategy also increased comprehension more for high-ability students than for low-ability students, perhaps because high-ability students have better organizational cognitive abilities to make sense out of disorganized information.

Beissner, Jonassen, and Grabowski (1993) tested the effects of two organizational strategies against learner differences at four levels of learning. Their findings showed an interaction between learner-generated concept vs. semantic maps and serialist or holist learners on the problem-solving questions only, with serialists performing better with semantic maps and holists performing better with concept maps. Although this study did not compare their results with instructor-provided maps, it does contribute evidence to the importance of individual cognitive strengths and patterns of thinking when selecting organizational learning activities.

Also studying the effects of concept maps, Smith and Dwyer (1995) found a significant difference only on lower-level terminology tasks in favor of instructor-provided maps. This result is consistent with that found by Wittrock and Carter (1975). For lower-level tasks, organization helps, especially when a learner is tested with questions that show similarity to the organization that an instructor may have possessed when creating the test.

Two other studies (Kenny, 1995; Taricani, 2002) found no effects of learner generated graphic organizers or concept maps. In the Kenny (1995) study, it appeared that the computer-based interactive instruction lacked an organization that the instructor provided graphic organizer provided. Subsequent subject interviews supported this notion. In the Taricani (2002) study, feedback was also tested against generativity, testing the notion that learner generation can create misconceptions that are corrected before testing. Her results support this hypothesis for the terminology test in the partially generated treatment group.

To summarize the findings of these studies, the results are mixed when comparing learner generativity. Some studies show that learner-generated activities are more effective in improving achievement than instruction-provided organizational schemes and that performance is increased even more when the text is organized. However, other studies found that instructor-provided activites produced better results when the instruction is disorganized and when feedback is provided. Finally, the selection of activities should be tempered by cognitive ability. Given these results, it is clear that more research is needed to understand these results more fully, especially in the area of concept map generation.

28.2.2.2 *Manipulation of Objects.*

The next organizational activity is manipulating objects. Although this activity extends beyond the printed page as designated by Wittrock's work, it qualifies as a generative activity because a relationship is being drawn and extended between parts of the environment.

Sayeki, Ueno, and Nagasaka (1991), in a very interesting study, investigated the effects of transforming mediation objects in the learning of mathematical principles. Their results supported the hypothesis that manipulatives increase comprehension. Although they do not specifically call this a generative activity, the act of creating understanding by generating both mental and physical relationships from different shapes of a manipulable rectangle manifests the same required attributes defined by Wittrock. Their results from mathematics should be tested for conceptual learning and problem solving in other content areas.

Haag and Grabowski (1994) extended this work to computer-manipulated graphics. Most applications of moving or manipulated graphics are done through generated animation. In this study, they found that learners who manipulated the graphics on the screen using a preorganized framework increased problem solving over those using no organizational framework or having the computer create the graphic statically. These results are consistent with those of other organizational strategies reported in the previous section.

Ritchie and Volkl (2002) found no difference between concept mapping and object manipulation—perhaps due to the generative nature of both activities. However, they did find a difference between these two strategies when sequence was added to the mix. Those students who *first* created concept maps and then used the manipulatives performed better on a delayed posttest. They also tested the team vs. individual generation

effect and found an interaction between strategy and individual or team interaction.

These studies lend support to the use of manipulatives for generating understanding for children and undergraduates in math and science. Compared with concept mapping, however, sequence played a part in its effectiveness.

28.2.3 Integration Strategies

The next series of studies examines the effects of activities that require a student to relate information to prior knowledge. In these activities, learners are integrating information through imaging, elaborations, and analogies.

28.2.3.1 *Imaging.*

The effects of imaging have been investigated extensively in four of those studies summarized here. They include fictitious descriptions, language arts, and economics topics studied by elementary- or high-school students.

Anderson and Kulhavey (1972) studied prose learning of high-school seniors to determine the effect of imaging. In this study, half of the subjects were told to image, and the other half were not. Results indicated no difference in prose learning between the groups. On further probing, the researchers discovered that not all of the students in the imaging group actually created images (only 50% did), and many in the control group created images (about one-third)! Comparing subjects from both groups who actually used imaging with those who did not showed significant differences in favor of the imaging strategy. These results illustrate the fact that mental activity cannot be strictly controlled by instruction and, again, raises the issue that requiring an overt response may be more effective in encouraging the desired result than just simply providing direction to image, as Sutliff (1986) found with adjunct questions.

Bull and Wittrock (1973) compared the effect of experimenter-provided vs. learner-generated imagery with elementary-school children. Groups were directed to draw, trace, or copy definitions. As predicted, results showed that the group that generated images performed significantly better than those who copied definitions; however, there was no significant difference between the imagery provided (tracing) and the copied definitions groups.

Kourilsky and Wittrock (1987) investigated what effect the sequence of the use of verbal or imaging generative activities would have on economic understanding by high-school students. They found that using verbal elaborations first, followed by imaging, significantly increased economic understanding. They also found significantly greater gains using both generative activities (verbal and imaged) than using just verbal elaboration only.

Laney (1990) found a slightly different result. Examining economic reasoning of third-graders, he found that the verbal-only and integrated strategies were more effective than the imaging-only strategy. Whereas using both symbol systems increased learning in both studies, the verbal-only elaboration was more effective than both the imaging-only strategy and the use of dual-symbol systems. He felt that his results were consistent with Wittrock's notion that the effective use of imaging is developmental. Laney's third-grade subjects had not yet developed this ability and were more familiar with verbal instruction. These are important results given the confusion that could result from the use of a generative imaging strategy too early in a learner's developmental cycle.

In summary, these studies have shown that overt imaging is more effective than covert; learner-generated imaging is more effective than instruction-provided imaging; and visual images may be more effective than verbal ones, only in cases in which students have progressed developmentally to the point where they can understand images. The sequence of generative activity also played a part in the results found for imaging.

28.2.3.2 Elaborations.
Stein and Bransford (1979) conducted two studies to determine the effects of learner-generated or experimenter-provided sentence elaborations by type. They hypothesized that congruence of the elaboration with the topic would be the determining variable and, in fact, did find differences in two experiments with undergraduates. In those cases in which elaborations were incongruent, students did worse than those in the treatments with no elaborations at all. Two important findings indicated that "elaborations facilitated performance only when they clarify the precise significance of target concepts ... and that prompting subjects to ask relevant questions facilitated both the precision of elaboration and subsequent retention" (p. 769).

DiVesta and Peverley (1984), in a very complex study, tested learner-organized vs. preorganized examples on near and far transfer in a concept attainment lesson. Additional variables included variability of examples and sequence. Their results on the active vs. passive element of their study indicated that students who generated their own examples did significantly better on both transfer tests than the preorganized group.

Johnsey, Morrison, and Ross (1992) investigated the effects of embedded vs. detached and learner-generated vs. experimenter-provided elaboration on recall, recognition, and application learning. The type of elaborations tested in this study in the area of adult professional development included two types of statements relating the content of the lesson to their job and stating implications of the information presented to their job environment. When these elaborations were embedded in the CAI training, significant gains were found; however, there were no differences between the learner-generated and the experimenter-provided elaborations. Teaching students how to generate elaborations at the time they will need them appears to be consistent with "just-in-time" training, especially when the technique may be new or more mentally difficult to implement.

To summarize these findings, elaborations that are congruent with intentional targets, student-generated question elaborations, student-generated examples, and student-generated relevant questions seem to improve retention and transfer, but not always more than instructor-provided elaborations.

28.2.4 Combination and Comparison of Coding and Integration Strategies

Carnine and Kinder (1985) expanded on the Anderson and Kulhavey (1972) study on imaging. In their investigation,

elementary-school subjects were asked to form an image and verbalize it and were then given corrective feedback. They were also asked to create a summary at the end. This strategy was compared to a "schema-based strategy" in which learners were asked structurally related questions about the passage composition. They found significant gains in reading comprehension from pre- to posttests for both narrative and expository text for both treatments. One cannot be sure whether the positive results were due to the additional instructional effects or the feedback. Nevertheless, the question of the need for feedback on learner-generated activities is an important one because significant differences favoring adjunct questioning over the imaging strategy were observed for learning of expository materials.

Linden and Wittrock (1981) conducted a study with elementary-school children that found that students who were asked to generate text-related summaries, analogies, metaphors, and pictures had better comprehension than those who were not. When instructed to generate images before verbal explanations, students produced more generations.

Wittrock and Alesandrini (1990) also investigated the effects of learner-generated summaries and analogies by analytic and holist undergraduates. The results followed the predicted rank ordering, with the most positive effects found for generating summaries, followed by generating analogies, both of which were significantly better than the control group containing no generative activities. They also found that individual differences in analytic and holist ability correlated with learning differently in the three treatments: analytic ability with learning in the generate analogies group, holist ability with the text-only control group, and both analytic and holist abilities in the generate summaries treatment.

Hooper, Sales, and Rysavy (1994) tested individual and paired undergraduates on achievement efficiency and generations when given summaries and analogies. They found that those who generated summaries performed better than those who generated analogies. Contrary to expected predictions, students working alone did better than those working in pairs.

BouJaoude and Tamin (1998) and McKeague and DiVesta (1996) also studied the effects of summaries and analogies. BouJaode and Tamin (1998) added question answering to the mix. They found no differences for stategy or sequence of the strategy. What was important in their study was the finding about preferences. Overall, their seventh-grade students preferred summaries the most often, but reasons stated for preferences noted ease for the questions, fun for analogies, and helpfulness for summaries. McKeague and DiVesta (1996) also found no strategy difference among underlining, headings, and analogies, but they did find that those who were guided performed better than those in the active learner group.

Finally, King (1992) examined the effect of self-questioning, summarizing, and note taking on immediate and delayed recall of underprepared college students. On the immediate recall, summarizers performed better than self-questioners, who were better than note takers, indicating a progressive generative effect. Self-questioners performed best on the delayed tests, indicating that deeper processing may occur in more generative tasks like self-questioning.

To summarize, earlier research suggests that when using a combination of strategies, the difficulty of the task must be taken into consideration, and, where possible, the effects of cognitive strengths factored in. Imaging is a more difficult task than adjunct questions, and analogies are more difficult than summaries. Also, self-questioning may be more difficult than writing summaries. If learners are not developmentally ready for such a task, it may cause more frustration than positive effects. Sequencing the tasks may also contribute to preparing the learner for more complex cognitive processing. However, more recent research found no results for strategy for undergraduates or middle-school children. More research is needed to tease out the variables causing this effect in the later, more complex studies.

28.2.5 Metacognitive Processes

Kourilsky and Wittrock (1992), in a very powerful study, investigated the effect of teaching the overall generative model of teaching, including its four processes and activities, to senior high-school students. The seniors were taught economics in cooperative learning groups. Those students who were taught this way of thinking were found to be more confident, had significantly fewer misconceptions, and had greater comprehension than those without this training. A fascinating result consistent with the Hooper et al. (1994) study was that using cooperative learning groups alone did not produce as great an effect.

Kourilsky (1993) taught professional teachers generative teaching strategies and economic misconceptions. She found that pre- to posttest gains on exams of comprehension and misunderstanding were significant when misconceptions were clarified. This result also provides support for the notion of partnership among the learner, instructor, and instruction. Without a dialogue, misconceptions can be generated and sustained.

Finally, Friend (2001) tested the effect of providing training on judging the importance of content and construction of a thesis statement over providing reflective thinking training. Their results showed a positive effect of the training on noting argument repetition and generalization. These findings are important in that they indicate that cognitive skill may play a large role in generative activity selection.

These studies lend support for teaching generative thinking to students, making them independent learners. One caution is noted, however. In their generation or understanding, students may actually create misconceptions about the content.

28.2.6 Summary

A variety of studies reporting on results of generative strategies has been summarized here. This section was not intended to be exhaustive; rather the studies were selected as representative of the kind of research that has been conducted across content areas, learning types, and age levels. However, all articles that could be found that specify generative learning as the theory being tested were included. In general, results have shown

increased gains in learning when the learner is an active partner versus a passive participant in the learning process and when instruction includes activities that relate new information together and new information to prior knowledge. These studies on generative learning have shown that, in most cases, active learner involvement produced increased learning, i.e., learner-generated activities have resulted in significant gains in learning, although issues of misconception, provision of feedback, and developmental appropriateness require investigation regarding differences in effect.

28.3 THE GENERATIVE MODEL OF TEACHING AND IMPLICATIONS FOR INSTRUCTIONAL DESIGN

Instructional designers engage in the systematic process of analyzing, designing, developing, evaluating, and implementing instruction. Although "effective instruction [in the generative model of learning] causes the learner to generate a relationship between new information and previous experience" (Wittrock, 1974a, p. 182), it is brought about by considering the four processes defined by generative learning theory. Ignoring any one of these processes could result in the learner's taking a "passive," mentally disengaged approach to learning. Generative learning theory is most applicable to the design and development phases, although there are implications for analysis and evaluation. Four of the five phases of the instructional design process, therefore, can be matched to the four generative processes that work in tandem to create learning: motivation, learning, knowledge creation, and generation. See Table 28.3.

The goal of the analysis phase is to understand the task and the learner. The goal of the design phase is to select appropriate strategies and tactics that match needs defined in the analysis phase. The goal of the development phase is to create effective instruction through effective message design that is organized and causes some level of mental activity on the part of the learner (Grabowski, 1991). The goal of the evaluation phase is to determine if the instruction that was created was effective. Specific implications of each of the four processes are noted in Table 28.3. These were selected from the many practical guidelines and suggestions offered by the generative model of teaching and generative learning theory that extend beyond simply suggesting those learning activities that induce relationship building. Creating a teaching model to provide practical prescriptions for teachers was Wittrock's original intent in pursing this area of research. As such, he provides some important recommendations that affect the four processes of his model.

28.3.1 Motivation Processes

Wittrock (1991) specifies interest and attribution as the two essential and linked components of motivation processes (see Figs. 28.1 and 28.2) that are activated by arousal and intention through the descending reticular activation system. Research from other areas suggests that attribution of effort, or the process of giving credit for success or failure to one's own effort,

TABLE 28.3. Instructional Development Process Matched with Generative Learning Theory

Instructional Development Process	Processes of Generative Learning Theory	Implications
Analysis	Motivation	Understanding learner's concept of self as learner
	Learning	Understanding current interests
	Knowledge creation	Understanding learner's beliefs, concepts, metacognitive ability, and prior experiences
	Generation	Understanding cognitive processes required of the task
Design	Motivation and knowledge creation	Strategies selected to help learners attribute learning to their own effort; create satisfaction; control for one's own learning.
	Knowledge creation	Select activities that match cognitive strengths *or* include instruction on how to engage in the generative activity.
	Generation	Select strategies that engage learners in the process of relating information or relating information to themselves.
Development	Learning	Use effective message design strategies to gain and maintain attention.
Evaluation	Generation	Evaluate whether the learner engaged in the generative activity.
		Evaluate the products generated by the learner to note misconceptions.

can influence whether or not the learner will exert the effort to learn actively. If learners attribute success to themselves, it follows that motivation to exert effort will be greater than if they attribute success to external forces (Weiner, 1979). The influence of intention on motivation for meaning generation flows from within the learner. Wittrock (1990, 1991) suggests that addressing this component means providing opportunities for the learner to "take control and responsibility for being active in learning" (p. 175). Teaching and design strategies that deal with attribution should result in enduring interest, persistence, and motivation. He suggests those activities or teaching strategies that

- attribute learning to learners' own effort,
- improve learners' self-concept,
- create satisfaction from the process of learning,
- modify learners' perception of themselves as learners,
- create control and increase responsibility and accountability for learning, and
- use rewards and praise that can be directly attributable to learners' own effort.

28.3.2 Learning Processes

Arousal and intention in the brain also influence an individual's learning processes. External stimuli arouse attention through the ascending reticular activating system. Without active, dynamic, and selective attending of an environmental stimulus, it follows that meaning generation cannot occur regarding that environmental stimulus. The influence of arousal on attention flows from the environment outside of the learner but interacts internally. The learning process that is key to this model is

attention. Without attention, learning cannot occur. Teaching and design activities that can assist in gaining and maintaining attention include those that

- provide attention training by self-control, planning, and organizing;
- provide behavioral objectives and adjunct questions;
- provide interpretation of the importance of the topic selected;
- use problems, mysteries, inconsistencies, suspense, and enigmas; and
- direct students' voluntary attention to meaning.

28.3.3 Knowledge Creation Processes

Knowledge creation processes are those components of memory—including preconceptions, beliefs, concepts, metacognitions, and experiences—activated through the frontal lobes of the cortex, which manage the receipt, coding, and storage of information. It is between these existing beliefs, concepts, preconceptions, etc., and environmental stimuli that relationships are formed, and, thereby, understanding and comprehension are generated (Wittrock, 1990, 1991). Much of Wittrock's writing and research with colleagues addresses the notion of preconceptions as they influence learning misconceptions (Kourilsky & Wittrock, 1987; Benson, Wittrock, & Bauer, 1993). Some would assert that creating dissonance in the learner is one way to "unteach" misconceptions. Wittrock (1990) would argue that those dissonant situations must be carefully selected experiences that are real to the learner so that the learner cannot easily dismiss the situation as untrue. He also suggests teaching scientific conceptions early—before preconceptions are formed.

TABLE 28.4. Match of Generative Activity with Level of Processing

Level of Cognitive Processing	Recommended Generative Activity
Coding	Creating titles and labels
Organization	Outlining
	Summarizing
	Diagramming
Conceptualization	Paraphrasing
	Explaining/clarifying
	Creating concept maps
	Identifying important information
Integration	Creating relevant examples
	Relating to prior knowledge
	Creating analogies
	Creating metaphors
	Synthesizing
Translation	Evaluating
	Questioning
	Analyzing
	Predicting
	Inferring

Preconceptions about learning and the learning process also function as a primary influence on learning. It may be necessary to change one's beliefs about learning and the learner's role to understand the value of participating in generative activities.

Other strategy recommendations offered by Wittrock (1990, 1991) include the following.

- relating instruction to background knowledge and interest;
- teaching metacognitive processes to monitor learning actively;
- demonstrating tangible results from active learning.

28.3.4 Generation Processes

"The art of generative teaching is knowing how and when to facilitate the learner's construction of relations among the parts of the text and their knowledge" (Wittrock, 1990, p. 353). Stimulated by the frontal lobes of the cortex, learners generate relationships between parts of what they see and hear. By integrating that information with what exists in memory, learners reorganize, elaborate, and/or reconceptualize information.

Two types of activities can be judged as generative. Those that generate organizational relationships among different components of the environment include "titles, headings, questions, objectives, summaries, graphs tables, and main ideas." Those that generate integrated relationships between the external stimuli and the memory components include "demonstrations, metaphors, analogies, examples, pictures, applications, interpretations, paraphrases, inferences" (Wittrock, 1990, p. 354).

Both of these types of activities can be used in an instructor-provided or a learner-generated format. In other words, the teacher can create titles and headings as organizers or ask the learner to create a title or heading. When the instructor provides the actual relationship, it should be done in a manner that will direct attention. One way to do that is to relate those

connections to ideas that are highly relevant to the learner. They should capture attention *and* motivate learners to think actively about the information. Wittrock advises that even though the instructor makes connections for the learners, learners must make those connections actively themselves to learn them. Passive observation will not suffice.

Given that there are many types of relationship-building activities that can be selected, a guide for selecting from among those activities is appropriate. Although Wittrock claims that levels of thinking are not represented in his theory and designates only two types of relationship building, it is evident that, by examining the level of mental effort required for each of these activities, the two categories can be broken down even further. Those activities that relate parts of the information in the environment together include coding, organization, and conceptualization levels of thinking, whereas those that relate parts of the information to prior knowledge include integration and translation tasks. Those activities that relate to the various levels are listed in Table 28.4 (Grabowski, 1995).

28.4 SUMMARY

The recommendations that follow from Wittrock's writings provide straightforward ideas to be implemented by teachers and designers for any instructional medium. Whether we are designing for the computer, print, television, or instructor-led training, face-to-face, or e-learning environments, these principles hold. Engaging the learner in active processing of the information should be our primary goal.

The computer can be exploited as a powerful means to engage learners by tapping its capability as a mental construction tool, rather than as an automated page-turner (Jonassen, 2000). Following Wittrock's principles, one should put the control of learning in the hands of the learner by creating an advisory environment in which learners manipulate information by moving text, graphics, and media segments around mentally or physically, testing their own ideas. This does not mean placing the learner in a total learner-controlled *information* environment but, rather, in one in which success can be guided, rewarded, and reinforced.

Creating a transactive environment (between the learner and the materials) is a greater challenge when designing for more static media, but it can be done cleverly by giving conscious attention to the design of the message to induce thinking—such as "stop and think activities" (Arnone & Grabowski, 1992), incomplete messages, and rhetorical adjunct questions to direct and engage thought.

The second important message from Wittrock is that more time and effort be spent on identifying important factors about the learner than is traditionally spent in the instructional design process. Identifying the learner has always been an important step in the instructional design process; however, how to do this, or what kind of key information to gather, is rarely specified. Wittrock's writings show some clear elements: Gather learners' conceptual preconceptions, preconceptions about their learning the topic, preconceptions about their role as learners, prior knowledge relating to the topic, general prior knowledge, and metacognitive abilities. This information is input into the design phase during which strategies are selected to help learners attribute learning to their own effort and create satisfaction in and control over learning. It also aids in the selection of activities appropriate for learners that engage them in personally generated understandings of the topic. The information also feeds into the actual development following effective message design that gains and maintains attention. During the evaluation phase, designers need to know if the learner actually engaged in the generative activity to be able to interpret effectiveness data. This knowledge, combined with a good understanding of appropriate activities that draw relationships, should result in very effective instruction.

28.5 IMPLICATIONS FOR FURTHER RESEARCH

Past research validates Wittrock's basic premise of active learner engagement; however, further research could help designers select from among the various types and modes of activity and understand the implication of the types of activities on levels of information processing. In other words, we need to ask which generative activities are more appropriate than others, whether they should be used in an instructor-provided format or a learner-generated one, and on what basis designers can make activity selection.

28.5.1 Selection of the Type of Generative Activity

Table 28.4 matches generative activities to desired levels of cognitive processing. This matching must be empirically tested. Questions such as the following take this into account.

1. What are the effects of each generative activity on higher-level learning? Much of the previous research has emphasized fact and concept-level learning and has not dealt with

higher-level learning such as application, synthesis, or problem solving.
2. Are there clusters of generative activities that are best used for specific learning tasks or levels of learning? What types of learning tasks are more appropriately coded versus integrated?
3. Are the activities classified appropriately by type of information processing—coding or integration—or can another level of processing be added to the theory to make it more prescriptive?

28.5.2 Use of Generative Activities

Previous research has also indicated mixed results from activities requiring overt/covert responses. Because of the "veto power over learning," described by Rothkopf (1976, p. 94), further research should explore the conditions that may require overt manifestations to ensure that processing occurs.

4. Is there a differential effect from requiring or not requiring overt manifestations of generative activity? What are the best strategies (instructional and mechanical) for ensuring that information is manipulated in the mind?

28.5.3 Motivation, Learner, and Knowledge Creation Processes

Another very significant area of research is identifying strategies that will enhance the perception of learner responsibility. This indicates a need to merge the learner control research with that on generative learning. From Wittrock's writing, it seems apparent that learner control with advisement would be recommended, but it needs to be empirically tested with questions such as the following.

5. What are the best methods for providing advisory feedback on learner-generated conceptions of the instruction content? and What are their effects?
6. What is the effect on learning of directive, embedded, or inductive control when the motivation level varies?

Various researchers have proposed several strategies. Directive control, as defined by Rothkopf (1976), takes the form of directions that are given to a learner to perform a particular task. Embedded strategies are similar to Rothkopf's inductive control in that they may not be obvious to the learner. Inductive control does not force a response, however, whereas an embedded strategy expects the learner to perform the behavior before going on (Rigney, 1980).

28.5.4 Instructor Provided or Learner Generated?

Some of the research results reported earlier indicate that both developmental and cognitive strengths may play a part in selecting appropriate and successful activities. Besides learner-generated activities in which the learner actively makes connections, Bovy (1981) suggests that instructor-provided activities

TABLE 28.5. Theoretical Match of Generative Activity with Cognitive Strengths

Cognitive Style Type	Cognitive Strength	Learner-Generated Activity	Instructor-Provided Activity
		Brendth of Categorization—Organizational Thinking	
	Broad	Create summaries	Provide outlines
		Create main ideas	
	Narrow	Outline	Provide summaries
			Provide main ideas
		Organizational Patterns—Organizational Thinking	
	Global	Create summaries	Provide outline
		Create diagrams	
	Analytic	Create outline	Provide summaries
			Provide diagrams
		Variation in Memory—Organizational Thinking	
	Leveling	Create summaries	Provide outlines
	Sharpening	Create outlines	Provide summaries
		Conceptual Styles—Conceptualization	
	Relational	Create concept maps	Explain/clarify
			Identify important information
			Provide paraphrases
	Analytic/descriptive	Explain/clarify	Provide concept maps
		Identify important information	Provide paraphrases
	Categorical/inferential	Paraphrase	Provide concept maps
			Explain/clarify
			Identify important information
		Cognitive Dimension—Integration	
	Complexity (abstract)	Create analogies	Provide relevant examples
		Create metaphors	Relate to prior knowledge
	Simplicity (concrete)	Create relevant examples	Provide analogies
		Relate to prior knowledge	Provide metaphors
		Thinking Patterns—Organization, Conceptualization, Integration, Translation	
Organizational	Convergent	Creating outlines	Provide summaries
		Creating diagrams	
Conceptualization		Explaining/clarifying	Provide concept maps
		Identifying important information	Paraphrase
Integration		Relate to prior knowledge	Provide analogies
		Create relevant examples	Provide metaphor
Translation		Evaluation	Question
		Analysis	Provide predictions
		Inference	
Organizational	Divergent	Create summaries	Provide outlines
			Provide diagrams
Conceptualization		Create concept maps	explain/clarify
		Paraphrase	Identify important information
Integration		Create analogies	Relate to prior knowledge
		Create metaphors	Provide relevant examples
Translation		Question	Evaluation
		Make predictions	Analysis
			Inference

supplant cognitive connections that are provided for the learner by the instruction itself (instructor generated, not learner generated, but personally relevant). There is also another category of instruction in which no control is provided: offering no suggestions, no forced responses, and no supplanted cognitive strategies. Table 28.5 proposes a matching of cognitive strengths with levels of thinking and recommended generative activities. If the activity is one that matches the cognitive strengths of individuals, then perhaps it should be presented in a learner-generated format. If it is an activity that would frustrate the learner, i.e., it is not a cognitive strength, then it should be presented in an instructor-provided format, so that the mental effort can be concentrated on the meaning of the message, rather than on a frustrated attempt at using a technique that does not match one's cognitive style. Providing no guidance may best be saved for learners with well-developed metacognitive abilities (see Table 28.5).

Research designs should then test the effect of these three presentational strategies (learner generated, supplanted, or no control) for each generative learning strategy matched by cognitive style or other individual difference factors against desired levels of learning or the cognitive processing requirements of the specific task. Cognitive developmental issues should also be considered. The following research questions should yield very important prescriptions.

7. Is there an appropriate use for supplanted vs. generated learning? Does this vary by task or learner?
8. Which activities match with developmental levels of learners?

28.6 CONCLUSION

The principles behind generative learning offer the instructional designer much guidance for developing environments that emphasize the learner as an active partner in the instructional process. Generative activities can be selected based on the type and level of cognitive processing desired. Generative learning theory is not discovery learning but student-centric learning with specified activities for actively constructing meaning. Generative learning activities require internal processing of external stimuli. A generative learning environment is not limited to open-ended resources, although it can engender those, and

includes carefully crafted external stimuli that are ready for individual processing. Generative activities are what exist between external stimuli and the learner. Generative learning theory does not assume dominance of the role of the learner or the instructor or instruction, but partnership in the process. As a "practical cousin" to constructivism and a more complete "second cousin" to behaviorism, generative learning theory is easily applied to any learning or instructional setting. The subtle differences between this theory and other theories account for differences in the "where the sage belongs" debate. For behaviorism, the sage is on the stage. For constructivism, the sage is viewed as a guide. For generative learning theory, the *sage, guide,* and *learner* are in the center. Content, instructional expertise, and instructional intention are expected of the sage and guide. Active engagement, attention, and learning intention are also expected of the learner. There is much research that has been done to support this position, and there is much research left to do to establish specific guidelines that help the designer create a learning environment that stimulates attention and intention and promotes active mental processing at all stages and levels of learning. The evidence indicates, in my view, that generative learning theory is very applicable to instructional design and that research defining types of processing should continue.

References

Anderson, R. C., & Biddle, W. B. (1975). On asking people questions about what they are reading. *In* G. Bower (Ed.), *Psychology of learning and motivation* (Vol. 9). New York: Academic Press.

Anderson, R. C., & Kulhavey, R. W. (1972). Imagery and prose learning. *Journal of Educational Psychology, 63*(3), 242-243.

Arnone, M., & Grabowski, B. L. (1992). Effects of variation in learner control over an interactive video lesson children's achievement and curiosity. *Educational Technology: Research and Development, 40*(1), 15-27.

Barnett, J. E., DiVesta, F. J., & Rogozenski, L. T. (1981). What is learned in notetaking? *Journal of Educational Psychology, 73*(2), 181-192.

Barry, R. J. (1974). The concept of mathemagenic behaviors: An analysis of its heuristic value. *Perceptual and Motor Skills, 38,* 311-321.

Beissner, K., Jonassen, D., & Grabowski, B. L. (1993). Using and selecting graphic techniques to convey structural knowledge. *In* M. R. Simonson (Ed.), *Proceedings of selected research paper presentations* (pp. 79-114). Ames: Iowa State University.

Bell-Gredler, M. E. (1986). *Learning and instruction: Theory into practice.* New York: Macmillan.

Benson, D. L., Wittrock, M. C., & Baur, M. E. (1993). Student's preconceptions of the nature of gases. *Journal of Research in Science Teaching, 30*(6), 587-597.

Blanchard, J., Chang, F., Logan, L., & Smith, K. (1985). An investigation of computer based mathemagenic activities. *Texas Tech Journal of Education, 12*(3), 159-174.

Bonn, K. L., & Grabowski, B. L. (2001, January). *Generative learning theory: A practical cousin to constructivism.* Paper presented at the Joint Meeting of Mathematics, New Orleans, LA.

BouJaoude, S., & Tamin, R. (1998, April). *Analogies, summaries, and question answering in middle school life science: Effect on achievement and perceptions of instructional value.* Paper presented at

the annual meeting of the National Association for Research in Science Teaching, San Diego, CA. (ERIC Document 420 503).

Bovy, R. C. (1981). Successful instructional methods: A cognitive information processing approach. *Educational Communications and Technology Journal, 29*(4), 203-217.

Brody, P., & Legenza, A. (1980). Can pictorial attributes serve Mathemagenic functions? *Educational Communications and Technology Journal, 28*(1), 25-29.

Bull, B. L., & Wittrock, M. C. (1973). Imagery in the learning of verbal definitions. *British Journal of Educational Psychology, 43*(3), 289-293.

Burton, J. K., Niles, J. A., Lalik, R. M., & Reed, M. W. (1986). Cognitive capacity engagement during and following interspersed mathemagenic questions. *Journal of Educational Psychology, 78*(2), 147-152.

Carnine, D., & Kinder, C. (1985). Teaching low-performing students to apply generative and schema strategies to narrative and expository materials. *Remedial and Special Education, 6*(1), 20-30.

Davis, M., & Hult, R. E. (1997). Effects of writing summaries as a generative learning activity during note taking. *Teaching of Psychology, 24*(1), 47-49.

DiVesta, F. T. (1989). Applications of cognitive psychology to education. *In* M. C. Wittrock & F. Farley (Eds.), *The future of educational psychology.* Mahwah, NJ: Lawrence Erlbaum Associates.

DiVesta, F. T., & Peverley, S. (1984). The effects of encoding variability, processing activity, and rule-examples sequence on the transfer of conceptual rules. *Journal of Educational Psychology, 76*(1), 108-119.

Doctorow, M., Wittrock, M. C., & Marks, C. B. (1978). Generative processes in reading comprehension. *Journal of Educational Psychology, 70*(2), 109-118.

Friend, R. (1999). Effects of strategy instruction on summary writing of college students. *Contemporary Educational Psychology, 26*, 3-24.

Goetz, E. (1983). *Elaborative strategies: Promises and dilemmas for instruction in large classes.* (ERIC Document 24307)

Grabowski, B. (1991). Message design. In G. Anglin (Ed.), *Instructional technology: Past, present and future.* Denver: Libraries Unlimited, pp. 202-212.

Grabowski, B. L. (1995). Mathemagenic and generative learning: A comparison and implications for designers. *In* A. J. Romiszowski & C. Dills (Eds.), *Instructional developments: State of the art, Vol 3: The paradigms.* Englewood Cliffs, NJ: Educational Technology.

Grabowski. B. L.(2002, November). *Applying theory to the design of instruction: An e-learning perspective.* Paper presented to the 2002 Singapore Educational Research Association, Singapore.

Grabowski, B. L., Hsieh, M., Hsieh, W., Wei, S., Liu, Y., & Dudley, V. (2002). *IT identity: Who we perceive ourselves to be.* Paper presented to the Association for Educational Communications and Technology, Dallas, TX.

Haag, B. B., & Grabowski, B. L. (1994). The effects of varied visual organizational strategies within computer-based instruction on factual, conceptual and problem solving learning. *In* M. R. Simonson, N. Maushak, & K. Abu-Omar (Eds.), *16th annual proceedings of selected research and development presentations,* (pp. 235-246B). Ames: Iowa State University.

Harlen, W., & Osborne, R. (1985). A model for learning and teaching applied to primary science. *Journal of Curriculum Studies, 17*(2), 133-146.

Hooper, S., Sales, G., & Rysavy, S. (1994). Generating summaries and analogies alone and in pairs. *Contemporary Educational Psychology, 19*, 53-62.

Johnsey, A., Morrison, G. R., & Ross, S. M. (1992). Using elaboration strategies training in computer-based instruction to promote generative learning. *Contemporary Educational Psychology, 17*, 125-135.

Jonassen, D. H. (1986). *Technology of text (Vol. 2).* Englewood Cliffs, NJ: Educational Technology.

Jonassen, D. H. (1991). Objectivism versus constructivism: Do we need a new philosophical paradigm? *Educational Technology: Research and Development, 39*(3), 15-26.

Jonassen, D. H. (2000). *Computers as mindtools for schools: Engaging critical thinking.* (2nd ed.). Upper Saddle River, NJ: Merrill.

Jonassen, D. H., Marra, R. M., & Palmer, E. (2003). Epistemological development: An implicit entailment of constructivist learning environments. In Seel, N. M., & Dijkstra, S. (Eds.), *Curriculum, plans and processes of instructional design: International perspectives.* Mahwah, NJ: Lawrence Erlbaum Associates.

Kenny, R. (1995). The generative effects of instructional organizers with computer-based interactive video. *Journal of Educational Computing Research, 12*(3), 275-296.

King, A. (1992). Comparison of self-questioning, summarizing, and note taking review as strategies for learning from lectures. *American Educational Research Journal, 29*, 303-323.

Kourilsky, M. (1993). Economic education and a generative model of mis-learning and recovery. *Journal of Economic Education, 25*(Winter), 23-33.

Kourilsky, M., & Wittrock, M. C. (1987). Verbal and graphical strategies in teaching economics. *Teaching and Teacher Education, 3*(1), 1-12.

Kourilsky, M., & Wittrock, M. C. (1992). Generative teaching: An enhancement strategy for the learning of economics in cooperative groups. *American Educational Research Journal, 29*(4), 861-876.

Kourilsky, M., Esfandiari, M., & Wittrock, M. C. (1996). Generative teaching and personality characteristics of student teachers. *Teaching & Teacher Education, 12*(4), 355-363.

Laney, J. D. (1990). Generative teaching and learning of costbenefit analysis: An empirical investigation. *Journal of Research and Development in Education, 23*(3), 136-144.

Linden, M., & Wittrock, M. C. (1981). The teaching of reading comprehension according to the model of generative learning. *Reading Research Quarterly, 17*(1),44-57.

Luria, A. (1973). *The working brain: An introduction to neuropsychology* (B. Haigh, Trans.). New York: Basic Books.

Mayer, R. E., & Wittrock, M. (1996). Problem-solving transfer. In D. Berliner, & R. C. Calfee (Eds.), *Handbook of educational psychology.* (pp. 47-62). New York: Macmillan.

McGuire, K. M. (1999). *Generative précising as a reading comprehension strategy for adult ESL learners.* Digital Dissertation, University of California, Los Angeles. (AAT 9940540)

McKeague, C. A., & DiVesta, F. J. (1996). Strategy outcomes, learner activity, and learning outcomes: Implications for instructional support of learning. *Educational Technology Research and Development, 44*(2), 29-42.

Peper, R. J., & Mayer, R. E. (1986). Generative effects of note taking during science lectures. *Journal of Educational Psychology, 78*(1), 34-38.

Rickards, J. P. (1979). Adjunct post-questions in text: A critical review of methods and processes. *Review of Educational Research, 49*(2), 181-196.

Rickards, J. P., & August, G. J. (1975). Generative underlining strategies in prose recall. *Journal of Educational Psychology, 67*(6),860-865.

Rigney, J. W. (1980). Cognitive learning strategies and dualities in information processing. *In* R. E. Snow, P. Frederico, & W. E. Montague, (Eds.), *Aptitude, learning and instruction* (Vol. 1). Mahwah, NJ: Lawrence Erlbaum Associates.

Ritchie, D., & Volkl, C. (2000). Effectiveness of two generative learning strategies in the science classroom. *School Science and Mathematics, 100*(2), 83-89.

Rothkopf, E. Z. (1976). Writing to teach and reading to learn: A perspective on the psychology of written instruction. *In* N. L. Gagné (Ed.), *The psychology of teaching methods.* Chicago: University of Chicago Press.

Rummelhart, D. E. (1981). *Understanding understanding* (Technical Report). Washington, DC: National Science Foundation. (ERIC Document 198-497).

Rummelhart, D. E., & Ortony, A. (1977). The representation of knowledge in memory. *In* R. C. Anderson, R. J. Spiro, & W. E. Montague (Eds.), *Schooling and the acquisition of knowledge.* Mahwah, NJ: Lawrence Erlbaum Associates.

Sayeki, Y., Ueno, N., & Nagasaka, T. (1991). Mediation as a generative model for obtaining an area. *Learning and Instruction, 1,* 229-242.

Shrager, L., & Mayer, R. E. (1989). Note-taking fosters generative learning strategies in novices. *Journal of Educational Psychology, 81*(2), 263-264.

Skinner, B. F. (1990). Can psychology be a science of mind? *American Psychologist, 45*(11), 1206-1210.

Smith, K., & Dwyer, F. M. (1995). The effect of concept mapping strategies in facilitating student achievement. *International Journal of Instructional Media, 22*(1), 25-31.

Stein, B. S., & Bransford, J. P. (1979). Constraints on effective elaboration: Effects of precision and subject generation. *Journal of Verbal Learning and Verbal Behavior, 18*(6), 769-777.

Sutliff, R. (1986). Effect of adjunct postquestions on achievement. *Journal of Industrial Teacher Education, 23*(3), 45-54.

Taricani, E. (2002). Effect of the level of generativity in concept mapping with knowledge of correct response feed back on learning. Unpublished dissertation, Pennsylvania State University.

Weiner, B. (1979). A theory of motivation for some classroom experiences. *Journal of Educational Psychology, 71*(1), 3-25.

Wittrock, M. C. (1974a). Learning as a generative process. *Educational Psychologist, 19*(2), 87-95.

Wittrock, M. C. (1974b). A generative model of mathematics education. *Journal for Research in Mathematics Education, 5*(4), 181-196.

Wittrock, M. C. (1985). Teaching learners generative strategies for enhancing reading comprehension. *Theory into Practice, 24*(2), 123-126.

Wittrock, M. C. (1990). Generative processes of comprehension. *Educational Psychologist, 24,* 345-376.

Wittrock, M. C. (1991). Generative teaching of comprehension. *Elementary School Journal, 92,* 167-182.

Wittrock, M. C. (1992). Generative learning processes of the brain. *Educational Psychologist, 27*(4), 531-541.

Wittrock, M. C., & Alesandrini, K. (1990). Generation of summaries and analogies and analytic and holistic abilities. *American Educational Research Journal, 27,* 489-502.

Woods, J. H., & Bernard, R. M. (1987). Improving older adults retention of text: A test of an instructional activity. *Educational Gerontology, 13*(2), 107-120.

Wittrock, M. C., & Carter, J. (1975). Generative processing of hierarchically organized words. *American Journal of Psychology, 88*(3),489-501.

·29·

FEEDBACK RESEARCH REVISITED

Edna Holland Mory
University of North Carolina at Wilmington

29.1 INTRODUCTION

In a previous examination of feedback research (Mory, 1996), the use of feedback in the facilitation of learning was examined extensively according to various historical and paradigmatic views of the past feedback literature. Most of the research presented in that volume in the area of feedback was completed with specific assumptions as to what purpose feedback serves. This still holds true, and even more so, because our theories and paradigms have expanded, and the field of instructional design has undergone and will continue to undergo rapid changes in technologies that will afford new advances to take place in both the delivery and the context of using feedback in instruction. It is not surprising that feedback may have various functions according to the particular learning environment in which it is examined and the particular learning paradigm under which it is viewed. In fact, feedback is incorporated in many paradigms of learning, from the early views of behaviorism (Skinner, 1958), to cognitivism (Gagné, 1985; Kulhavy & Wager 1993) through more recent models of constructivism (Jonassen, 1991, 1999; Mayer, 1999; Willis, 2000), settings such as open learning environments (Hannafin, Land, & Oliver, 1999), and views that support multiple approaches to understanding (Gardner, 1999), to name just a few. While feedback has been an essential element of theories of learning and instruction in the past (Bangert-Drowns, Kulik, Kulik, & Morgan, 1991), it still pervades the literature and instructional models as an important aspect of instruction (Collis, De Boer, & Slotman, 2001; Dick, Carey, & Carey, 2001).

29.2 DEFINITION OF FEEDBACK

The basic meaning of feedback has remained the same in *Webster's New World Dictionary* from the 1984 edition to the current one. *Webster's* (2001) continues to define feedback as

"a process in which the factors that produce a result are themselves modified, corrected, strengthened, etc. by that result" and "a response, as one that sets such a process in motion" (p. 520). Whereas this definition could fit a host of situations or systems, most educational researchers consider the term "feedback" in the context of instruction. Feedback has been widely perceived as an important component of general systems operations and may be viewed under a variety of settings (Kowitz & Smith, 1985, 1987). In the purely instructional sense, feedback can be said to describe any communication or procedure given to inform a learner of the accuracy of a response, usually to an instructional question (Carter, 1984; Cohen, 1985; Kulhavy, 1977; Sales, 1993). This type of feedback acts as one of the events of instruction described by Gagné (1985) and usually follows some type of practice task. More broadly, feedback allows the comparison of actual performance with some set standard of performance (Johnson & Johnson, 1993). In technology-assisted instruction, it is information presented to the learner after any input with the purpose of shaping the perceptions of the learner (Sales, 1993). Information presented via feedback in instruction might include not only answer correctness, but other information such as precision, timeliness, learning guidance, motivational messages, lesson sequence advisement, critical comparisons, and learning focus (Hoska, 1993; Sales, 1993). In fact, Wager and Wager (1985) refer to feedback in computer-based instruction as being *any* message or display that the computer presents to the learner after a response.

Most studies that have examined feedback use contrived experimental learning situations where feedback is given from an external source after a learner responds to a question during instruction. The main purpose of this feedback is to confirm or change a student's knowledge as represented by answers to practice or test questions. However, some researchers (Butler & Winne, 1995) have suggested that viewing feedback in such a unilateral context fails to take into account variances in behavior that might be the result of self-regulation and student engagement. Further, feedback can also be viewed in even less traditional settings, such as its role in program evaluation. When used in situations that are not necessarily instructional, the best definition of feedback is information presented that allows comparison between an actual outcome and a desired outcome. Tucker (1993) points out that feedback is particularly important when evaluating dynamic instructional programs because its presence or absence can "dramatically affect the accuracy required of human judgment and decision making" (p. 303).

New learning environments have erupted into a wide range of potential uses of feedback that were not utilized or considered before, as the ability to provide rapid information from and to learners is facilitated through a myriad of new technologies and simulations. There is quite a difference between Skinner's programmed instruction of the 1960s, which presented a linear series of steps, to that of interactive microworlds, gaming environments, open learning environments, and rapid transfer of information through advanced technologies such as the World Wide Web.

To illustrate some of the purposes of feedback, the next section presents the evolution of feedback research in instruction from its early beginnings through the present. The principal feedback variables that have interested researchers are then discussed.

29.3   A HISTORY OF FEEDBACK RESEARCH

Many of us may assume that the most recent studies of feedback are the result of several current trends and accepted paradigms—for example, the information processing model and newer theories of motivation. However, three definitions of feedback dating back to the early 1900s are surprisingly similar to the ones we use today. Kulhavy and Wager (1993) refer to these as the "feedback triad" (p. 5) and point out that these definitions still prevail in the views of feedback we currently hold. First, feedback served as a motivator or incentive for increasing response rate and/or accuracy. Second, feedback acted to provide a reinforcing message that would automatically connect responses to prior stimuli—the focus being on correct responses. Finally, feedback provided information that learners could use to validate or change a previous response—the focus falling on error responses.

29.3.1   The Law of Effect

The earliest studies of feedback date back to E. L. Thorndike's Law of Effect, which postulated that feedback would act as a "connector" between responses and preceding stimuli (see Kulhavy & Wager, 1993). Researchers such as Thorndike were examining the use of postresponse information as early as 1911 (cited in Kulhavy & Wager, 1993). Thorndike's work showed that a response followed by a "satisfying state of affairs" is likely to be repeated and increases the likelihood of learning. The view of feedback as information emphasized the role that the learner

had in learning, with the ability to adapt his or her response according to information in the feedback and thus correct his or her errors. The first researcher to emphasize error correction was Sidney Pressey (1926). However, a later study using his "teaching machine" emphasized both the error-correcting function of feedback and its acting as a punishment for errors—a Thorndike viewpoint that supports the notion of feedback as a reinforcer (Pressey, 1927). Thus we see that the confusion in the feedback research began quite early and that, given the early "feedback triad," the research has not evolved as much as one might expect.

29.3.2   Programmed Instruction

Thorndike's pioneering work paved the way for the next avenue of research on feedback, B. F. Skinner's (1958) study of programmed instruction. Using principles from the Law of Effect and the application of reinforcement on learners, Skinner proposed that a solution to instructional problems lied in the use of strategically designed classroom materials that would take learners through information in a step-by-step fashion, shaping behavior and strengthening desired responses. By the year 1960, the programmed instruction movement was well under way, purporting that feedback in programmed instruction served as both a reinforcer and a motivator, perpetuating a confusion between learning and incentive. During this period, instructional errors were either ignored or considered "aversive consequences" to be avoided (Skinner, 1968). The fact that errors were deemed as aversive implies an emotional element from which the early motivational view of feedback was derived. The viewpoint that incorrect responses cause distress and influence self-concept is used even today (Fischer & Mandl, 1988). Kulhavy and Wager (1993) suggest that such motivational variables should be separated from the feedback message, keeping them extrinsic to the lesson content itself. Certainly this would help remove the confusion between the instructional content of feedback and other factors that might affect performance.

29.3.3   Feedback as Reinforcement

Programmed instruction emphasized an operant approach to learning—one that had the concept of reinforcement at its heart. Programs were designed to shape a student's responses using a small lock-step approach with a high level of redundancy. Operant psychologists of the time argued that learning tasks should be analyzed and broken down into small enough steps that the probability of a successful response was ensured (Cohen, 1985). By telling a student that an answer is correct, the student is "reinforced" to answer correctly again on a later test (Kulhavy, 1977).

Around 1970, most researchers began to doubt the feedback-as-reinforcement view. In fact, 10 years of research under this paradigm showed no systematic effects for feedback (see Kulhavy & Wager, 1993). Studies provided little evidence that feedback following positive responses acts in a reinforcing manner (Anderson, Kulhavy, & Andre, 1972; Bardwell, 1981; Barringer & Gholson, 1979; Kulhavy, 1977; Roper, 1977). Researchers then had to look at the basic functions of feedback to discover what was actually occurring. A series of studies by R. C. Anderson and his colleagues found that students will not use feedback as the researcher intends unless this use is controlled (Anderson, Kulhavy, & Andre, 1971, 1972). For instance, students will simply copy answers from feedback if allowed to do so, with little or no processing or learning of information. Kulhavy (1977) coined the term *presearch availability* to describe the ease with which learners can find a correct answer without reading the lesson material. If presearch availability is high, then students will usually copy the answer itself, bypassing the instruction and yielding little learning (Anderson & Faust, 1967). In programmed material, feedback significantly facilitates learning only if students must respond *before* seeing the feedback.

29.3.4 Feedback as Information

The data collected by Anderson and his colleagues (1971, 1972) not only provided insight into the importance of the learner's processing of the lesson material before his or her response to a question, but also, and perhaps more importantly, provided indication that feedback functions primarily to correct errors, not merely to "reinforce" correct answers. Numerous studies during this time supported feedback's ability to correct inaccurate information (Anderson et al., 1971, 1972; Bardwell, 1981; Barringer & Gholson, 1979; Kulhavy, 1977; Kulhavy & Anderson, 1972; Roper, 1977; Tait, Hartley, & Anderson, 1973). Concurrent shifts toward cognitive psychology led researchers to focus on how feedback influenced primary cognitive and metacognitive processes within a learner (Briggs & Hamilton, 1964; Kulhavy, 1977).

Examining feedback from an information-processing perspective, the learner participates in the system to correct his or her errors. Kulhavy and Stock (1989) use the concept of servocontrol theory, contrasting the two feedback systems (feedback as reinforcement vs. feedback as information) as open-loop versus closed-loop. Feedback acting as reinforcement is an example of an open-loop system, in which errors are ignored because the system is not affected by input information. The operant approach does not provide error-correcting mechanisms. In contrast, the feedback-as-information position acts as a closed-loop system. Because this type of system has ways of correcting errors, errors are of primary importance. Studies indeed emerged that made the correction and analysis of errors a major goal (Anderson et al., 1971; Birenbaum & Tasuoka, 1987; Elley, 1966; Gilman, 1969; Kulhavy & Parsons, 1972), with a predominant focus on all the metacognitive processes involved in this type of error correction.

It is from the information processing perspective that most research of the past 20 years has been conducted. In a later section of this chapter, the prevailing concerns of researchers from that period to the present are discussed in detail. But first,

it is helpful to present two current models of feedback as a framework for what follows.

29.4 MAJOR MODELS OF FEEDBACK

29.4.1 A Connectionist Model of Feedback Effects

Perhaps the most recent reference to any type of feedback model, per se, lies in the work of Clariana (1999, 2000) in the area of using a connectionist model to explain feedback effects. "Connectionist models apply various mathematical rules within neural network computer simulations in an effort, among other things, to mimic and describe human memory associations and learning" (Clariana, 2000, p. 83). He describes the theory of connectionism as comprising several families of models, which include "simple feedforward networks, pattern associators, multilayer networks with backpropagation, competitive networks, and recurrent networks" (p. 83). These apparently differ little in how the nodes of the network are interconnected but are vastly different in terms of the type of processing that they are able to accomplish (McLeod, Plunkett, & Rolls, 1998). Neural networks have been used to determine pattern matching, pattern completion, and retrieval by content, recognition, prototype extraction, and classification (Haberlandt, 1997; as cited in Clariana, 2000).

The crux of the model lies in a view of learning as involving the interaction of information given by instruction with existing information that is already in the learner's memory (Ausubel, 1968; Bruner, 1990). When a learner "commits" to a lesson response, that response reflects the learner's immediate understanding of a particular instructional instance. Clariana terms this the initial lesson response (ILR) and uses it to provide a measure of a learner's existing information. He then relates this to what happens to the learner's memory traces of ILRs that are error responses, to determine if these initial errors interfere with attaining correct responses. He views this as one key to our understanding of how feedback works and has researched this approach using the *delta rule* to predict posttest memory activation levels of ILR errors and of correct responses for immediate and delayed feedback (Clariana, 1999).

The delta rule apparently is one of the simplest and most common of connectionist rules that implies the effect of feedback on learning (Shanks, 1995; Widrow & Hoff, 1960). It describes the change in association weight between an input unit and an output unit at each learning trial. Application of the delta rule in this setting assumes that lesson average item difficulty values are reasonable estimates of the association weights of correct responses.

Use of the delta rule involves the use of delta equations and assigned values for learner responses, so that the association weight increases with correct responses and decreases with incorrect responses. Or in simpler terms, when feedback is provided as part of the responding instance, correct responses are strengthened and incorrect responses weakened. The amount of this increase or decrease can be determined by the delta rule

(Clariana, 2000). When given the lesson item difficulty (the initial response), the delta rule should be able to predict posttest item difficulties after feedback has been presented.

Clariana postulates that this has implications for the effectiveness of immediate versus delayed feedback. He suggests several ways in which this would occur. For correct lesson responses, memory of ILRs and of correct responses would be strengthened in general for both immediate and delayed feedback, as the application of the delta equation result would be positive. For lesson errors, the ILR association with the item stem would be weakened for immediate feedback, as the equation produces a negative result, but would not be for delayed feedback.

For delayed feedback, the connectionist model predicts that ILR errors would actually be strengthened. Typically in associated learning within living systems, there is a small portion of time during the specific input pattern activation when associations can be strengthened or weakened. Clariana suggests that immediate feedback provides the necessary feedback information within this time frame, whereas delayed feedback does not.

Based on a previous study (Clariana, 1999), three hypotheses were postulated in the Clariana (2000) study:

1. Retention test memory of ILRs will be considerably greater for delayed feedback than for immediate feedback at all item difficulty levels.
2. Both types of feedback will obtain the across the range of possible lesson to posttest gain with difficult lesson items.
3. Retention test memory of correct responses will vary across the range of possible lesson item difficulty values for the delayed and immediate forms, with immediate feedback slightly better than delayed feedback with more difficult lesson items and delayed feedback slightly better than immediate feedback with easier lesson items. (p. 85)

Clariana (2000) also tried to separate any effects observed from immediacy versus multiple exposures by including multiple-try feedback. The study utilized two levels of questions, verbatim versus inferential, depending on their relationship either directly to one or to multiple propositions in the text. The three alternate feedback treatments were delayed feedback, single-try immediate feedback, and multiple-try immediate feedback.

Results confirmed that retention of initial lesson responses is greater for delayed feedback compared to immediate feedback across all item difficulties, but particularly with difficult lesson items. The essential value in this result is that it can help instructional designers use initial question responses to broaden understanding, particularly when answers are not absolutely "right" or "wrong" but function as learning transitions to broaden students' understanding. Feedback was also suggested to have its greatest effect with difficult lesson items, thus suggesting that future feedback studies should consider and control lesson item difficulty so as not to confound results. However, feedback timing did not interact with lesson item difficulty as predicted. Clariana suspects that the lesson items were not difficult enough in the study to produce the hypothesized interaction.

In terms of feedback effects, multiple-try feedback was much more like single-try feedback in retention test memory of ILRs,

suggesting that feedback's immediacy does indeed serve to reduce memory of ILR errors—what Clariana (2000) terms a "retroactive interference effect" (p. 89). The multiple-try feedback group fell midway between the single-try feedback (immediate) and the delayed feedback (multiple-item exposure) groups. He suggests that this indicates that both feedback timing and number of exposures combine or interact to impact retention test memory, particularly for memory of correct responses. A similar study (Clariana, Wagner, & Murphy, 2000) also supports the use of a connectionist model for explaining instructional feedback effects

29.4.2 A Certitude Model of Feedback

Kulhavy and Stock (1989) have proposed a model of feedback in written instruction that attempts to clarify and explain previous findings in the literature. Their model also goes beyond these basic explanations to make testable predictions under girded by theoretical rationales. The model has been scrutinized (Bangert-Drowns et al., 1991; Dempsey, Driscoll, & Swindell, 1993; Mory, 1991, 1992, 1994) and tested by current researchers (Kulhavy & Stock, 1989; Kulhavy, Stock, Hancock, Swindell, & Hammrich, 1990; Kulhavy, Stock, Thornton, Winston, & Behrens, 1990; Mory, 1991, 1994; Swindell, 1991, 1992; Swindell, Peterson, & Greenway, 1992). It is cited as the most comprehensive treatment of feedback in facilitating learning from written instruction (Dempsey, Driscoll, & Swindell, 1993), as it integrates the factors of learner confidence, feedback complexity, and error correction and has been investigated under different modes of presentation and timing. (Note that each of these components is discussed individually and in depth later.)

Kulhavy and Stock (1989) assert that much of the prior research on feedback is conceptually flawed. For one thing, researchers always treated responses as being absolutely right or wrong—a dichotomy that virtually ignored the complexity of learning behavior. Consider that a correct answer may be just a lucky guess or that a wrong answer may be anything from a careless mistake to a total miscomprehension of the material. Even more puzzling were studies that resulted in initial correct answers being *changed* to *wrong* responses on a posttest and instances in which initial errors were never corrected, despite what was included in the feedback (Lhyle & Kulhavy, 1987; Peeck, van den Bosch, & Kreupeling, 1985).

The model proposes that the feedback process is made of three cycles that constitute each instructional episode. In Cycle I, the learner is presented with a task to which he or she needs to respond. In Cycle II, feedback is presented based upon the input from the learner in Cycle I. In Cycle III, the original task is presented again as a test item to which the learner responds. Within each cycle, a common series of steps ensues. Put succinctly, each cycle involves an input from the task at hand to the learner, a comparison of the input to some sort of reference standard that then results in an output. The degree of mismatch between the perceived stimulus and the reference standard results in a measure of error. The discrepancy between these two entities causes the system to exert effort to reduce the discrepancy. Dempsey, Driscoll, and Swindell (1993) have

INPUT ⟶ LEARNER ⟶ OUTPUT

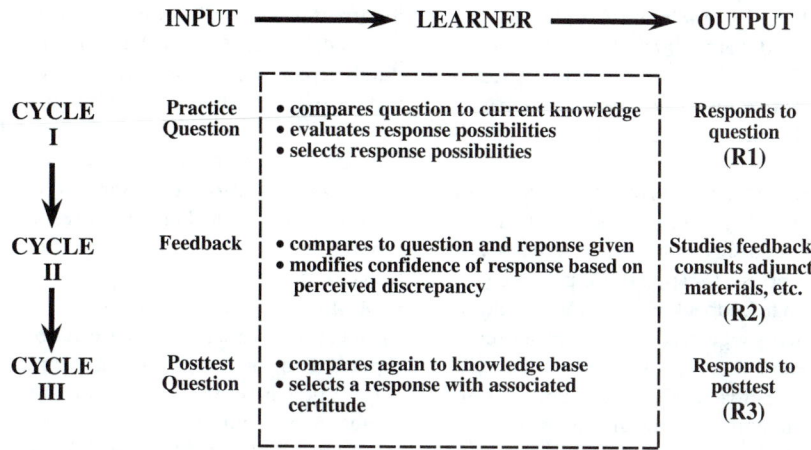

FIGURE 29.1. Representation of Kulhavy and Stock's (1989) certitude model of text-based feedback (from Dempsey, Driscoll, & Swindell, 1993). From *Interactive Instruction and Feedback* (p. 42), by J. V. Dempsey and G. C. Sales (Eds.), 1993, Englewood Cliffs, NJ: Educational Technology. Copyright 1993 by Educational Technology Publications. Reprinted with permission.

graphically represented the Kulhavy and Stock model as shown in Fig. 29.1.

During each cycle, the learner engages in mental activity aimed at processing the input and preparing an appropriate response. The model emphasizes the learner's level of certainty (termed *response certitude*) between the demands of the instructional task in Cycle I and his or her prior knowledge and current understanding of that task. If this perceived match is good, the learner will select a response with a high level of certainty or confidence. The worse the match, the lower the learner's confidence level will be. In Cycle II, when the learner receives feedback on his or her response, the feedback acts as verification to allow the learner to compare the response to the information contained in the feedback. When this verification is combined with the learner's initial response confidence level, a discrepancy value results. If learners receive verification of a correct answer when they are certain they were correct, there is no discrepancy. Conversely, learners who are informed that their answer was wrong when they were confident that their answer was correct will produce a high level of discrepancy.

Kulhavy has represented this discrepancy value in the equation

$$f_v \cdot c = d,$$

where f_v is the verification component, c is the initial certitude level, and d is the discrepancy. The verification component f_v is set to equal $(-1)^m$, where $m = 0$ for initial error responses and $m = 1$ for initial corrects. This is explained as having the effect of assigning an algebraic sign to d, where $[(-1)^0 = +1]$ for errors and $[(-1)^{-1} = -1]$ for correct responses. The response certitude variable, c, usually employing a 5-point Likert-type scale, results in a discrepancy (d) from (-5) to $(+5)$ (Kulhavy & Stock, 1989; Kulhavy, Stock, Hancock et al., 1990).

In this model, it is predicted that the level of discrepancy is a major factor influencing how much time and effort a student will naturally expend in error correction. In the case of a high-certitude correct answer (low discrepancy), students have little need for extensive or elaborated feedback. But when students think an answer is correct that is in reality an incorrect response (high discrepancy), they will exert much effort to find out what was remiss in their thinking. In the case of low-certitude responses, regardless of whether students' answer is correct or wrong, they likely do not understand the information and would benefit from feedback that acts as new instruction. Even in Kulhavy's (1977) prior research we see that high-confidence correct answers yield the shortest feedback study times, high-confidence errors yield the longest time, and low-confidence responses fall somewhere in between (Kulhavy, White, Topp, Chan, & Adams, 1985; Kulhavy, Yekovich, & Dyer, 1976, 1979). Obviously, discrepancy must mediate effects of different types of feedback in terms of their complexity or elaboration. Further, according to the model, prescriptions can be made as to how much and what type of information to include in feedback for the varying levels of discrepancy.

Kulhavy and Stock's (1989) predictions have been shown to prevail in a number of conditions, thus suggesting its robustness. In testing the model, they performed three studies relating to discrepancy and feedback times and the durability of correct answers under low discrepancy. As predicted by the model, learners who thought they answered correctly when in fact they were in error (high discrepancy) spent more time studying feedback. To test this finding further, students in a second study (Kulhavy & Stock, 1989) were told that an answer was wrong when it was in fact correct, and vice versa. Because the students *thought* their answer was wrong when they had assumed they were correct (even though in actuality the answer *was* correct), they indeed spent more time studying the feedback. Again, these results support the model. And in their third study, Kulhavy and Stock (1989) demonstrated that the probability of a correct posttest response increased with the initial response certainty level, particularly when practice responses were also correct. In this way, feedback served to increase the durability of initially correct responses.

Several other studies have also supported the model. Kulhavy and his associates (Kulhavy, Stock, Hancock et al., 1990) found that in the absence of feedback, response confidence and the probability of a correct posttest response are positively related. The model suggests that feedback elaboration should be useful in correcting particularly high-certitude errors, a prediction that a study by Swindell (1991) supports. One problem in the Swindell study, however, is that feedback elaboration consisted of presenting the stem and all of the alternatives listed, with the correct alternative designated by an asterisk. As discussed later, feedback elaborations usually provide more information than was operationalized in the Swindell (1991) study, usually informing the learner of why an answer is incorrect or re-presenting a portion of the original instruction.

The prediction that there is a direct relationship between increases in discrepancy and increased study effort is supported by another study by Swindell (1992). In that study, she also constrained the time that students were allowed to study feedback, expecting that as the feedback reading time became increasingly constrained, the probability of a correct posttest response would decrease. This was generally true, but for groups receiving feedback at both slow and average presentations speeds, high certitudes resulted in lower probabilities of correct responses and lower certitudes resulted in higher probabilities. Swindell explained this through interference theory, suggesting that in the case of errors, certitude may reflect response competition that results in an inaccurate perception of comprehension. Her study was not able to support the durability hypothesis that high-certitude response alternatives would be better remembered and carry over to a posttest and that low-certitude judgments are more likely to be forgotten over time and are less likely to be chosen again on a posttest. No systematic relationship could be determined from her study.

Swindell, Peterson, and Greenway (1992) have also attempted to extend the model to younger learners, as the original model was developed from a research base of adult learners. Certainly the developmental stage of children will determine whether or not they are able to assess their own learning confidence accurately. The results of the study suggest that fifth graders demonstrated the pattern that high-confidence errors (maximum discrepancy) were more likely to be corrected on a posttest than were low-confidence errors. However, third graders in the study demonstrated the opposite pattern: High-confidence errors were less likely to be corrected than those of low confidence. Further, fifth graders were more likely to correct high-confidence errors than were third graders.

Dempsey, Driscoll, and Swindell (1993) point out that the Kulhavy and Stock (1989) model also provides a useful framework for past research results. The durability hypothesis explaining why initially correct responses are better remembered than errors, assuming that learners are more likely to make higher-confidence judgments for correct responses than for incorrect responses, is supported by Peeck and Tilleman (1979) and Peeck et al. (1985). Measures of response certitude and durability should be positively related because high confidence should represent better comprehension and will therefore be better remembered. Further, the model supports the finding that learners not only were more likely to recall initially correct responses, but also were more likely to correct initial errors if they could recall their initial response. And a recent study (Swindell, Kulhavy, & Stock, 1992) found similar response patterns for durability as well.

Although the Kulhavy and Stock (1989) model of feedback is the most comprehensive to date, it does have some problematic aspects. For one thing, response certitude is a self-report measure. Whereas response certitude judgments do provide some useful information about the cognitive status of the learner (Kulhavy et al., 1976; Metcalfe, 1986; Nelson, Leonesio, Landwehr, & Narens, 1986), the nature of determining certitude has some underlying problems. The idea behind response certainty lies in the learner's metacognitive process of predicting his or her criterion performance on a task. This process can be related to "feeling of knowing" research (Butterfield, Nelson, & Peck, 1988; Metcalfe, 1986; Nelson, 1988; Nelson et al., 1986). Feeling of knowing has been shown to be accurately predicted for memory recognition tasks and has been found to exist over all age groups, and the reliability of feeling of knowing has been found to be generally excellent. However, the stability of an individual's feeling of knowing accuracy has been found to fluctuate significantly (Nelson, 1988). In Nelson's (1988) findings, when a subject gives a higher feeling-of-knowing rating to one item over another, there is perfect retest reliability in that the same outcome occurs if the person subsequently makes feeling-of-knowing responses on those same items (Nelson et al., 1986). Conversely, individuals having a relatively high level of feeling-of-knowing accuracy at one time do not also have a relatively high level of feeling-of-knowing accuracy at another time (see Nelson, 1988). Since individual differences of feeling-of-knowing accuracy may be inconsistent, it raises the question of whether or not a response certitude estimate is valid for prescribing feedback, if certitude statements may not be a stable measure of an individual's true knowledge. Perhaps if a variable or variables could be identified that influence these changes, researchers would have more insight into the process. For example, learners' general level of self-esteem or motivation might be influencing their perceptions of certainty.

Further inconsistency predominates when comparing the levels of tasks involved in feeling-of-knowing research. Learners were able to predict their feeling of knowing in memory tasks accurately but overestimated their likelihood of success on problem-solving tasks or problems requiring insight (Metcalfe, 1986). Other researchers (Driscoll, 1990) have found a contrary finding, that students learning concepts tended to underestimate their feelings of answer correctness. These cases of over- and underestimation show that students generally possess an inaccurate perception of their own knowledge. Of further concern, most feedback studies using response certitude have employed verbal information tasks only; in fact, the model itself was built upon a vast well of studies that involved rote memorization of verbal information. As researchers are discovering (Dempsey & Driscoll, 1994; Mory, 1991, 1994), tasks of learning intellectual skills may produce different results, especially in light of the prior findings suggesting that subjects tend to estimate their feeling of knowing incorrectly during studies using higher-level tasks. Indeed, this was the case in a recent study (Mory, 1994) that used response certitude estimates as part of the feedback cycle for both verbal information and concept learning tasks. Students tended to have a high level of certitude for concept questions, regardless of actual answer correctness. Thus, low-certitude feedback designed to give the most information was not encountered when it was truly needed. Learners simply were not able to give accurate assessments of their own abilities to classify a particular concept.

Another issue that regards the application of response certitude estimates within an instructional situation is that of efficiency. Corrective efficiency results from taking the total number of correct answers on a posttest and dividing it by the amount of time spent during an instructional task. Kulhavy and his associates (1985) examined efficiency using two separate measures. One measure isolated the amount of time spent reading the instruction, thus accounting for the efficiency of only the instruction or "text" portion of the lesson. When this measure was tested across varying feedback groups, there were no significant differences found. The second measure used was the amount of time spent just in studying the feedback, as less complex forms of feedback are usually more time efficient in terms of what Kulhavy and his colleagues (1985) call "posttest yield per unit of study time invested" (p. 289). The amount of time a learner spends on feedback is affected by two things: (a) the amount of information included in the feedback message (load) and (b) the response certitude levels. Results from the study confirmed that the less complex forms of feedback were more time efficient and, also, that efficiency rose as a function of increases in confidence values. Considering that high-confidence responses should reflect an understanding of subject matter and content, the learner would be more likely to make efficient use of the feedback presented (Kulhavy et al., 1985).

One should note that the Kulhavy study (Kulhavy et al., 1985) examined efficiency in terms of the feedback portion of a lesson only. But the process of giving a response confidence rating for each question could possibly add considerable time and interference to the overall lesson for the student. Mory (1991, 1994) investigated adaptive feedback that was based on levels of discrepancy and prescriptions of the model. The study supported that feedback efficiency can be increased by varying the amount of feedback information according to levels of discrepancy, however, the added time for response certitude evaluations resulted in lower overall lesson efficiency. Further, when a typical nonadaptive feedback sequence was compared with an adaptive one that employed response certitude as part of the cycle, adaptive feedback was significantly less efficient than traditional feedback in terms of overall lesson efficiency (Mory, 1994).

And finally, one might question the generality of a model that was built around experimental testing environments and usually limited to the use of multiple-choice questions (see Kulik & Kulik, 1988). Many of the studies present brief paragraphs of

text information, followed by multiple-choice questions based on the preceding paragraph (Chanond, 1988; Kulhavy et al., 1976, 1979; Lhyle & Kulhavy, 1987). Many of these studies used generic topics with limited relevance to current topics being studies by learners within the experimental groups. And to confound matters further, in several studies students were not given instruction at all, but questions and feedback alone served as "instruction" (Anderson et al., 1971, 1972; Kulhavy & Anderson, 1972; Kulhavy & Stock, 1989; Swindell, 1991). In fact, recent findings (Clariana, Ross, & Morrison, 1991) support the notion that feedback effects tend to be stronger in conditions where materials involve no text but use questions and feedback only than in conditions in which text was used before questions and feedback. This leads to the question of whether or not the model will be supported in "real world" instructional environments. Researchers (Chanond, 1988; Dempsey, Driscoll, & Litchfield, 1993; Mory, 1991, 1992, 1994; Peterson & Swindell, 1991) are beginning to recommend that the model be examined under more typical classroom learning situations.

Researchers interested in exploring the Kulhavy and Stock (1989) model further should consider some of the aforementioned issues, both supportive and problematic. Dempsey, Driscoll, and Swindell (1993) point out that the model has made more precise predictions for high-confidence responses than for low-confidence responses and that midrange levels of confidence have no such predictions. This means that the entire range of metacognitive judgments should be examined. Further, if response confidence could be linked to a variable other than self-report, the adaptation of feedback might more readily fit the needs of the learner. For example, Dempsey and others (Dempsey, 1988; Dempsey, Driscoll, & Litchfield, 1993) used levels of fine and gross discrimination error during a concept learning task to adapt feedback to the needs of learners.

29.4.3 A Five-Stage Model of Mindfulness

Bangert-Drowns and his associates (1991) organize the findings of previous researchers' investigations of text-based feedback into a five-stage model, describing the state of the learner as he or she is going through a feedback cycle. The model emphasizes the construct of mindfulness (Salomon & Globerson, 1987), described as "a reflective process in which the learner explores situational cues and underlying meanings relevant to the task involved" (Dempsey, Driscoll, & Swindell, 1993, p. 38). They describe both behavioral and cognitive operations that occur in learning. To direct behavior, a learner needs to be able to monitor physical changes brought about by the behavior. Learners change cognitive operations and, consequently, activity by adapting it to new information and matching it with their own expectations about performance (Bangert-Drowns et al., 1991). These researchers emphasize that

any theory that depicts learning as a process of mutual influence between learners and their environments must involve feedback implicitly or explicitly because, without feedback, mutual influence is by definition impossible. Hence, the feedback construct appears often as an essential element of theories of learning and instruction. (p. 214)

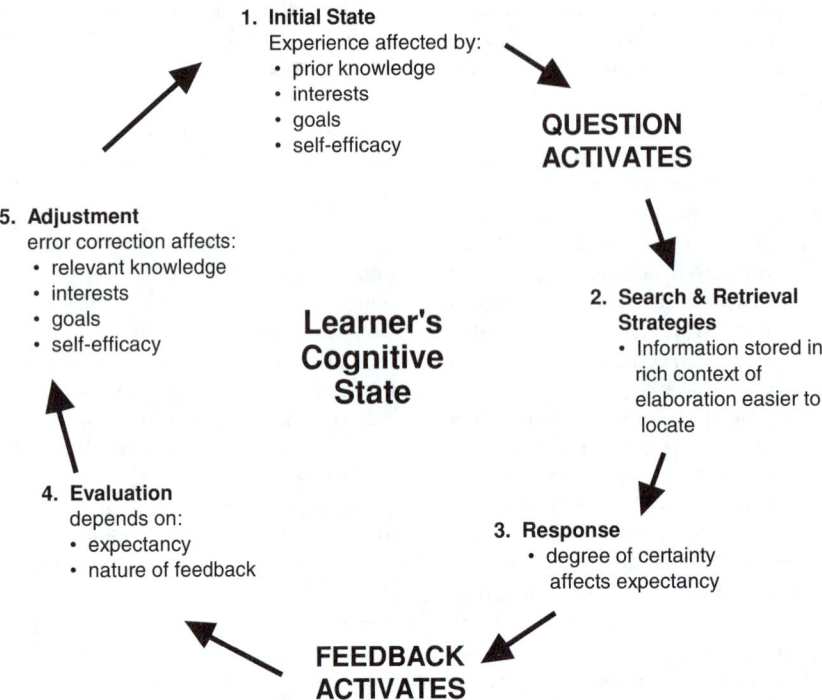

FIGURE 29.2. The state of the learner receiving feedback based on Bangert-Drowns et al. (1991; from Dempsey, Driscoll, & Swindell, 1993). From *Interactive Instruction and Feedback* (p. 40), by J. V. Dempsey and G. C. Sales (Eds.), 1993, Englewood Cliffs, NJ: Educational Technology. Copyright 1993 by Educational Technology Publications. Reprinted with permission.

The five stages are (1) the learner's initial state, (2) what search and retrieval strategies are activated, (3) the learner's response, (4) the learner's evaluation of the response, and (5) adjustments the learner makes. A graphic representation of the model by Dempsey, Driscoll, and Swindell (1993) is shown in Fig. 29.2.

This model emphasizes the construct of mindfulness, in which activities are exactly the opposite of automatic, over-learned responses. Feedback can promote learning if it is received mindfully. However, it also can inhibit learning if it encourages mindlessness, as when the feedback message is made available before learners begin their memory search or if the instruction is too easy or redundant. The inhibition of learning effect relates to research conducted on processes that "kill" learning (Clark, Aster, & Hession, 1987) and presearch availability (Anderson et al., 1971, 1972; Kulhavy, 1977).

Bangert-Drowns et al. (1991) examined 40 studies using metanalytic procedures looking at such variables as type of feedback, timing of feedback, and error rates in terms of their various effect sizes. They reported generally weak effects of feedback on achievement. Also, feedback indicating only whether an answer was correct or wrong resulted in lower effect sizes than feedback containing the correct answer. Further, using a pretest within a study significantly lowered effect sizes, as did uncontrolled presearch availability of answers.

Dempsey, Driscoll, and Swindell (1993) pointed out that the emphasis on mindfulness is an important framework for future research involving text-based feedback. Whereas the studies examined by the Bangert-Drowns et al. (1991) metanalysis "may be too simple or specific" (p. 234), it leads us to believe that future studies should examine feedback in more complex environments that involve higher-learning outcomes.

29.5 FEEDBACK RESEARCH VARIABLES OF INTEREST

Several common areas have prevailed in the research literature on feedback. These include type of information content, amount of information (load), complexity of feedback, timing of feedback (immediate versus delayed), type and analysis of errors, type of learning outcomes being studied, and various motivational functions that feedback might provide.

29.5.1 Information Content and Load

29.5.1.1 Complexity. Feedback complexity refers to how much and what information should be included in the feedback messages. There is an abundance of literature concerning feedback complexity. Dempsey, Driscoll, and Swindell (1993) have organized the major variables of interest in most corrective feedback studies as follows.

1. *No feedback* means the learner is presented a question and is required to respond, but no indication is provided as to the correctness of the learner's response.
2. *Simple verification feedback or knowledge of results (KR)* informs the learner of a correct or incorrect response.
3. *Correct response feedback or knowledge or correct response (KCR)* informs the learner what the correct response should be.
4. *Elaborated feedback* provides an explanation for why the learner's response is correct or incorrect or allows the learner to review part of the instruction.
5. *Try-again feedback* informs the learner when an incorrect response and allows the learner to one or more additional attempts to try again. (p. 25)

If feedback is to serve a corrective function, even in its most simple form feedback should verify whether the student's answer is right or wrong. This verification is usually combined with an elaboration component to provide more information to the learner. Studies that have examined the type and amount of information in feedback have not yielded very consistent results (Kulhavy, 1977; Schimmel, 1988).

What types of elaborative information have been used along with the verification component in the feedback message? In a review of the feedback literature, Kulhavy and Stock (1989) suggest that there are basically three possible elaboration types to employ during feedback. They categorize them as (a) *task specific,* which is drawn from the initial task demand or initial question (e.g., restatement of the correct answer), (b) *instruction based,* which contains information derived from the specific lesson material but not directly from the actual question completed before the feedback (e.g., explanation of why an answer is correct, based on the original instruction, or a display of the original instructional text that contains the correct answer), and (c) *extrainstructional,* which is the addition of information from outside the immediate lesson environment (e.g., new information to clarify meaning). The majority of elaboration studies fall within the task-specific and instruction-based types.

First, consider task-specific types of feedback, where the feedback is a restatement of the correct answer. Usually studies that contain this type of feedback have examined changes in the amount of information, sometimes referred to as *load.* A study by Phye (1979) examined three types of feedback for multiple-choice questions. One contained the question stem and only the correct alternative; another contained the stem and designated correct answer, with incorrect alternatives from the question; and a third contained the stem and designated correct answer, with the two incorrect alternatives from the question plus two previously unseen incorrect alternatives. No differential effect was produced by type of feedback on the posttest. However, in the second experiment in the study, immediate feedback in the form of only the correct answer plus an answer sheet from the practice was superior to other forms of feedback. Thus, the type of feedback thought to provide the least information produced the greatest improvement on the posttest. Phye suggests

a threshold hypothesis to account for this unexpected finding, positing that when more than sufficient information needed to correct or confirm an answer is provided to students, it does not have a facilitative effect on their ability to use the feedback.

Some studies that have added increases of task information to feedback have actually produced lower scores on a posttest. Phye, Gugliamella, and Sola (1976) used feedback very similar to that used in the Phye (1979) study, adding either the correct answer only, the initial item plus all original distracters, or the correct alternative and three extralist distracters. Feedback in the form of correct answer only was superior to the other types that contained more information. This would imply that the feedback with more load contained considerable distracting information in the form of incorrect alternatives.

Another similar finding was provided by Sassenrath and Yonge (1969) in providing two types of feedback cues: with or without the stem of the question and with or without correct plus wrong alternative answers. Students who received information feedback without the stem of the question performed better than those who received information feedback with the question stem. This goes against the results of a previous study they completed (Sassenrath & Yonge, 1968) in which students receiving the stem of the question and the alternatives performed better on a retention test than those receiving only the alternatives. The researchers explain this discrepancy by the fact that the earlier (1968) study gave feedback after the students had responded to the entire list of questions, so that the question stem conveyed valuable information in addition to the alternatives. But in the second study (1969), feedback was presented after each item response, and it is suggested that the stem was distracting when used in feedback given within such a short time lapse after a response.

Wentling (1973) compared the effects of (a) partial feedback that contained knowledge of results to (b) total feedback that contained knowledge of correct answer and required a re-response or (c) no feedback at all. The partial feedback treatment exceeded the other two treatments on immediate achievement scores, and surprisingly, the total feedback treatment was least effective in terms of immediate achievement.

Another study (Hanna, 1976) comparing partial feedback, total feedback, and no feedback found that partial feedback produced highest scores for high-ability students, and total feedback produced the highest scores for lower-ability students. There were no differential effects between partial and total feedback for middle-ability students, but both of these types of feedback were superior to no feedback.

Three studies do show positive results for task-specific item elaborations. Roper (1977) provided students with either no feedback, yes–no verification, or an opportunity to restudy the correct answer. Scores on the posttest increased as more information was added to the feedback. There was also evidence that the correction of errors and not just reinforcement of responses was the major effect of feedback. Also, Winston and Kulhavy (cited in Kulhavy & Stock, 1989) found that using feedback consisting of a multiple-choice item stem plus the correct response and all of the original distracter alternatives was more effective at correcting errors than using feedback containing the stem plus only the correct alternative. And finally, an early study (Travers, van Wagenen, Haygood, & McCormick, 1964) gave an interesting variation of task-specific feedback for corrects and wrongs. One group received verification for both corrects and wrongs, a second group received verification only for wrongs and nothing for corrects, a third group received verification only for corrects and verification plus the correct answer for wrongs, and a fourth group received nothing for corrects and verification plus the correct answer for wrongs. A relationship between information content of the feedback condition and extent of learning was found to exist. Highest criterion test performance occurred under the latter two feedback conditions—the ones that were the most information laden. The second feedback condition, merely saying "That's wrong," was significantly inferior to all the other conditions studied.

An even more inconsistent pattern of results is found in studies that have used instruction-based elaborations, in which information in the feedback is taken from the instruction itself. The information used in this type of feedback has been quite diverse, including explaining of the correct answer (Gilman, 1969), supplying solution rules (Birenbaum & Tatsuoka, 1987; Lee, 1985; J. Merrill, 1987), and re-presenting original instruction (Peeck, 1979).

Gilman (1969) employed "additive" feedback, comparing (1) no feedback to (2) feedback of "correct" or "wrong," (3) feedback of correct response choice, (4) feedback appropriate to the student's response, or (5) a combination of 2, 3, and 4. The means of the groups that had guidance toward the correct answer (groups 3–5) performed better than the groups that had to search for the correct answer. Gilman points out that providing learners with a statement of which response was correct or with a statement of why the correct response is correct may be of more value than merely telling the learner "correct" or "wrong." In terms of error correction, knowledge-of-results feedback resulted in the lowest number of corrected errors. In terms of retention rates, Gilman suggests that extensive information in feedback messages show advantages in retention rates.

Merrill employed both corrective feedback and attribute isolation feedback in his 1987 study of feedback to aid concept acquisition. Corrective feedback informed the learners of the correctness or incorrectness of their answers and also provided the full text of the correct answer when a student's answer was wrong. The full text consisted of a single word, phrase, or short paragraph. Attribution isolation feedback also informed the learners of the correctness of their responses, but then included the attributes of the concepts being studied. Attribution isolation is used to help focus attention on the variable attributes of a concept (M. Merrill & Tennyson, 1977). No main effects for feedback form were found, possibly due to the attribute isolation feedback being presented after two incorrect responses and, consequently, not being encountered enough times in the lesson to make a difference.

Another study (Lee, 1985) that provided solution rules in its feedback used either (1) "right/wrong" feedback only, (2) "right/wrong" plus the correct answer after an error, or (3) "right/wrong" plus the rule restated and the correct answer after an error. No significant main effects were found in the feedback treatments.

One unique approach using feedback solution rules was devised by Tatsuoka and her colleagues (cited in Kulhavy & Stock, 1989). The seriousness of instructional errors was analyzed from a pretest to assess the effect of additive feedback elaborations on a later criterion measure. Students received feedback as either (1) "OK/NO" verification, (2) the correct answer to the problem, or (3) a statement of correct and incorrect rules for solving the problem. They found that for nonserious errors, more feedback elaborations result in a greater probability of these errors being corrected. But for serious errors, correction was relatively unaffected by the amount of elaboration. This finding suggests that more complex errors or misunderstandings are not as likely to be corrected by typical feedback treatments.

Schloss, Sindelar, Cartwright, and Schloss (1987) presented either instructions to try again or a re-presentation of the instruction after student errors in computer-assisted instructional modules to test if error correction procedures would interact with question type such that higher cognitive questions with feedback loops and factual questions with re-presentation of questions would yield maximum results. They concluded that when factual questions are used in CAI modules, allowing a student to attempt a second answer after an error results in more learning than re-presenting the part of the instruction in which the answer appears.

Sassenrath and Garverick (1965) compared more traditional classroom types of feedback: looking up wrong answers in the textbook to having answers discussed by the instructor or checking over answers from correct ones written on the board. These three feedback groups did perform significantly better on a retention test than a no feedback control group. The discussion group also performed better than the groups that looked up answers in the textbook.

Students in a different study (Peeck, 1979) were either given feedback sheets identical to immediate test sheets, with the correct alternatives circled, or were given both the original text and the feedback sheets with correct alternatives circled. Also, to test if the effectiveness of different forms of feedback was influenced by the kind of test question presented, both fact and inference multiple-choice questions were used. There was little difference in scores between the two feedback conditions. More inference questions were answered correctly when subjects could refer to the original text during the feedback. But for fact questions, subjects were more successful on a delayed test when the text was absent during the feedback.

Similarly, two types of questions (factual and application) and two types of feedback (correct answer feedback, self-correction feedback, and no feedback control) were employed in a study by Andre and Thieman (1988). Both types of feedback facilitated performance on the same concept questions but did not facilitate the application to new examples. This suggests that such feedback may be helpful in tasks where the students memorize an answer, but be ineffective for tasks which require application to new cases.

Even large-scale additions to the feedback have failed to influence posttest performance, as was the case for Kulhavy and his colleagues (1985). Four types of feedback were developed additively. Four components could be used in the feedback:

(1) the test item stem and the correct alternative, (2) incorrect response alternatives, (3) four sentences, each explaining why one of the error choices was incorrect, and (4) the relevant section of the passage in which the correct answer was identified. One group received only component 1; a second group, components 1 and 2; a third group, components 1, 2, and 3; and a fourth group, all four components. The principle was that increases in the feedback complexity are closely tied to corresponding increases in the amount of information available to the learner. Results showed that more complex versions of feedback had a small effect on error correction, with the least complex feedback correcting a significantly greater portion of errors than the more complex third feedback group.

In a computer-assisted instruction (CAI) drill and practice program using a concept learning task, it was indicated that immediate extended feedback following both correct and incorrect responses is superior to minimal feedback (Waldrop, Justen, & Adams, 1986). In the first of three treatment conditions, subjects received only minimal feedback of "correct" or "incorrect." In a second treatment condition, subjects received minimal feedback ("that's correct") if a response was correct but received minimal feedback ("that's incorrect") for three trials if a response was wrong. After the third trial, if a response was still incorrect, students were provided extended feedback relating the example given to the definition of the type of consequence involved in that example. The third treatment condition provided a detailed explanation of the correct answer following both correct and incorrect responses. The results of this study agree with a suggestion made by Gilman (1969) that providing the student with a statement of which response was correct after errors and reasons for correctness of a correct response is essential.

Noonan (1984) examined the presence or position of knowledge of results, knowledge of correct response, elaborated, and try-again feedback. In this study, knowledge of results with an explanation and a second attempt was no less effective than giving knowledge of correct response and moving on or giving knowledge of correct response and another second attempt. In support of error analysis, Noonan suggests that explanations should depend more on the type of error made by the learner, and not merely on the correct answer.

Varying types and amounts of information in feedback given after specific combinations of answer correctness and response certitude in a CAI lesson were used by Chanond (1988). If a subject's answer was correct, and he or she was confident of the answer, the subject received knowledge of result feedback. If a subject's answer was correct, but he or she was not confident of the answer, the subject received knowledge of result feedback and a statement of why the response was correct. If a subject's answer was incorrect, but he or she was confident of the answer, the subject received knowledge of result, a statement of why the response was incorrect, knowledge of correct response, and a statement of why the correct answer was correct. If a subject's answer was incorrect, and he or she was not confident of the answer, the subject received knowledge of result, knowledge of correct response, and a statement of why the correct answer was correct.

Subjects were given both an immediate and a delayed posttest at the end of the lesson. Results indicated that for immediate retention of verbal information in terms of overall correct responses, the feedback had a significant effect. No significant effect was found for delayed retention, however. Further analyses indicated that, regardless of the level of confidence for the response, feedback following incorrect responses had a significant effect on both immediate and delayed retention.

The use of extrainstructional feedback types has been studied very little (Kulhavy & Stock, 1989). However, adaptive feedback that additively used all three feedback types, task specific, instruction based, and extrainstructional, was implemented by Mory (1991) and involved two levels of learning tasks: verbal information and concepts. Varying combinations of task-specific, instruction-based, and extrainstructional feedback were prescribed according to a combined assessment of answer correctness and response certitude level for an adaptive feedback group. Compared to nonadaptive feedback that utilized task-specific and instruction-based elaborations only, there were no significant differences in posttest performance for either verbal information or concept tasks.

To summarize the feedback elaboration literature, only half of the studies utilizing task-specific feedback produced any significant improvements in learning. An even greater inconsistency is found in studies using information-based feedback, perhaps due partially to the diverse types of information manipulations tried. Such variance has made it difficult to prescribe any set rule for the use of either type of elaboration (Kulhavy & Stock, 1989). Extrainstructional feedback types have not been researched enough to draw conclusions as to their effectiveness on learning.

29.5.2 Timing of Feedback

Recall from the early reports of feedback research that the idea of feedback as reinforcement—a Skinnerian view—would suggest that feedback should follow a response as closely in time as possible in order to be most effective. Skinner himself is quoted as saying, "... The lapse of only a few seconds between response and reinforcement destroys most of the effect" (cited in Kulhavy & Wager, 1993, p. 13). But when researchers began comparing the effects of immediate versus delayed feedback, discrepancies from such an operant approach were soon discovered. Kulhavy (1977) reported that studies showed repeatedly that delaying the presentation of feedback for a day or more results in significant increases in student retention on posttest scores (Sassenrath & Yonge, 1968, 1969; Sturges, 1969, 1972). This phenomenon was termed the delay-retention effect (DRE) (Brackbill, Bravos, & Starr, 1962; Brackbill & Kappy, 1962) and was found to occur predominantly in studies concerned with multiple-choice testing. The explanation for the DRE is thought to lie in the proactive interference from initial error responses on the acquisition of correct answers given via immediate feedback. That is, when a learner is presented immediate feedback showing the correct response after an error, his or her error response interferes with the correction of the response due to the immediacy of the feedback. Thus delayed feedback eliminates this type of interference, and the learner is better able to remember the correct response. Several studies support this hypothesis, e.g., the interference-perseveration hypothesis, explains the DRE through the assumption that initial errors tend to be forgotten over time (Bardwell, 1981; Kulhavy & Anderson, 1972; Kulik & Kulik, 1988; Sassenrath, 1975; Surber & Anderson, 1975). But others have found either that the delay did not make a difference (Peeck et al., 1985; Phye et al., 1976), that initial responses were not forgotten (Peeck & Tillema, 1979), or that the DRE was not present when subjects were required to re-respond (Phye & Andre, 1989).

In a 1988 metanalysis conducted by Kulik and Kulik, the issue of immediate versus delayed feedback was examined more thoroughly. In analyzing the available research on the timing of feedback, they found that studies using actual classroom quizzes and materials usually found that immediate feedback was more effective than delayed feedback. Apparently the studies that supported the effects of delayed feedback over immediate feedback for improving retention of material were conducted using contrived, experimental learning situations, such as list learning. These findings challenge both the use of delayed feedback in more practical learning environments and the explanations afforded by the interference-perseveration hypothesis in "real-world" learning situations.

Dempsey, Driscoll, and Swindell (1993) suggest that delaying feedback in many instructional contexts "is tantamount to withholding information from the learner that the learner can use" (p. 24). And a pragmatic suggestion postulated by Tosti (1978) and Keller (1983) is to present feedback containing pertinent information from the learner's prior performance right before the next learning trial, when the learner would be able to use the information to improve his or her subsequent learning. As Dempsey Driscoll, and Swindell (1993) point out, this amounts to providing feedback at what is commonly referred to as "the teachable moment" (p. 24). An interesting variation involving a delay of feedback was designed by Richards (1989) using a declarative knowledge task involving labels and facts. In this case, feedback was more effective when delayed temporarily and the learner was required to respond covertly a second time to the question—that is, a covert second try, *prior* to feedback.

In a 1989 study conducted to examine the timing of feedback with respect to the acquisition of motor skills, shorter feedback times improved acquisition and performance while feedback was present, but delayed feedback resulted in improved subsequent performance once feedback had been withdrawn (Schmidt, Young, Swinnen, and Shapiro, 1989). They explain these findings in terms of what is termed the guidance hypothesis. The guidance hypothesis suggests that during the initial stages of skill acquisition, immediate feedback guides the learner and results in superior initial performance. But this guidance can lead to dependence on the feedback and obscure the need to learn the secondary skills (such as detection and self-correction) necessary to perform the task without feedback (Schmidt et al., 1989).

The guidance hypothesis is supported by a previous study that examined the effects of immediate versus delayed feedback within the context of an adventure game on subsequent

performance (Lewis & Anderson, 1985). Subjects that received immediate feedback were more likely to select appropriate operators, but those that received delayed feedback were better able to detect errors. But a differing trend was found by Anderson, Conrad, and Corbett (1989) when assessing the effects of immediate and delayed feedback within the context of the GRAPES LISP Tutor. Subjects receiving immediate feedback moved through the material more quickly than did those subjects receiving delayed feedback, but there was no significant difference in test performance. A more recent study by Schooler and Anderson (1990) found that when students were acquiring LISP skills, subjects receiving immediate feedback went through the training material in 40% less time than those receiving delayed feedback, yet with no detrimental effects on learning. In a second experiment during the same study, subjects used an improved LISP editor and less supportive testing conditions. During this trial, subjects in the immediate feedback group completed the problems 18% faster than those in the delayed feedback group, but they were slower on the test problems and made twice as many errors. The final experiment, a partial replication of the first two experiments, indicated that delayed feedback was an advantage in terms of errors, time on task, and percentage of errors that subjects self-corrected. They suggest that immediate feedback competes for working memory resources, forcing out necessary information for operator compilation—a finding that would support the interference-perseveration hypothesis mentioned above. In contrast, delayed feedback in the study fostered the development of secondary skills such as error detection and self-correction (Schooler & Anderson, 1990).

Regarding which to recommend, immediate or delayed feedback, several researchers concur (Dempsey, Driscoll, & Swindell, 1993; Kulhavy, 1977; Kulik & Kulik, 1988) that in most learning situations delayed feedback appears to function to hinder the acquisition of needed information. Only in under very special experimental situations has the use of delayed feedback helped learning. As Kulik and Kulik (1988) point out,

The experimental paradigms that show superiority of delayed feedback are very similar to paradigms used for testing effects of massed versus distributed practice. When experiments deviate from this paradigm, they show results similar to those in applied studies. In such experiments, immediate feedback produces a better effect than delayed feedback does. (p. 94)

One only has to look at the myriad of definitions that past researchers have used in the areas of both immediate and delayed feedback to understand why this field of study has always been muddied. Dempsey and Wager (1988) have summarized the types of immediate and delayed feedback as reported in Table 29.1.

Some researchers suggest that as newer technologies offer more instructional delivery options and a wider variety of modalities through which to deliver feedback, these issues will become even more complex (Dempsey, Driscoll, & Swindell, 1993). Perhaps as delivery options increase, researchers will be better able to determine when delayed feedback might aid learners.

TABLE 29.1. Immediate and Delayed Feedback with Computer-Based Instruction: Definitions and Categories (from Dempsey & Wager, 1988)

Immediate feedback is informative corrective feedback given to a learner or examinee as quickly as the computer's hardware and software will allow during instruction or testing.

Types of immediate feedback

1. Item by item
2. Learner controlled
3. Logical content break
4. End of module (end of session)
5. Break by learner
6. Time controlled (end of session)

Delayed feedback is informative, corrective feedback given to a learner or examinee after a specified programming delay interval during instruction or testing.

Types of delayed feedback

1. Item by item
2. Logical content break
3. Less than 1 hr (end of session)
4. 1–24 hr (end of session)
5. 1–7 days (end of session)
6. Extended delay (end of session)
7. Before next session

29.5.3 Error Analyses

In the early 1930s, Thorndike demonstrated that errors made in rote learning tasks tend to persist. By the year 1958, Skinner argued that errors made within programmed instruction will tend to persist as well. Elley (1966) tested the hypothesis that errors play different roles in rote and meaningful learning tasks. Results supported the hypothesis, showing that fewer errors were associated with better retention in rote tasks but not in meaningful types of learning. Both experiments supported the hypothesis that errors are undesirable in rote learning and tend to be repeated even with immediate feedback. however, when learners were given meaningful problems, incidence of errors was unrelated to ultimate performance.

The current view considers an error to be a valuable opportunity to clarify misunderstanding in the learner. Thus errors play an important role in feedback studies today. The belief that feedback's main function lies in correcting errors makes error analyses more critical for gaining insight into the corrective process.

Kulhavy and Parsons (1972) examined errors that are never corrected, or that "perseverate" to a posttest. They suggest that error perseveration is a function of at least three factors: (a) the rated meaningfulness of the items used, (b) the amount of incorrect material available during learning, and (c) the response mode required of the learner. In their study, students were forced to respond incorrectly to see if these errors would be repeated on a posttest. But their analyses revealed that forcing a student to make an error does not automatically result in the transference of that error to the posttest.

Patterns of pretest-posttest responses were introduced in a limited way by Phye and his colleagues (1976). This work was later extended to include three error types (Peeck & Tillema, 1979; Phye, 1979). An error analysis model was developed independently by Peeck and Tillema (1979) and Phye (1979), and this model has been used by several researchers (Peeck, 1979; Phye & Andre, 1989; Phye & Bender, 1989). Their research has served to help understand further how feedback is being used by learners in most experimental settings.

Whenever informative feedback is used in a pretest-feedback-posttest design, five possible outcomes for pretest-posttest response sequences exist. First, when feedback has a *confirmatory* function, the feedback serves to confirm a correct answer at pretest (a combination sequence of correct-correct). Second, when feedback has a *corrective* function, it serves to correct an error made on the pretest (a sequence combination of wrong-correct). And finally, feedback can have *no* function, as in cases when errors result on the posttest (Phye & Bender, 1989).

The three error types where feedback is considered nonfunctional are described as follows. One type is a *same* error and is perseverative in nature. A same error occurs when an initial incorrect response reoccurs on the posttest, regardless of any correct answer feedback that was provided. The second type of error is a *different* error, in which an item is missed on both the pretest and the posttest but was not the same error across trials. That is, the posttest error was a different error than the pretest error. Perhaps insufficient information was encoded during feedback so that on the posttest the learner remembers that his or her initial response was wrong but does not remember information well enough to respond correctly. The final type of error is a *new* error, in which an item was initially correct on the pretest or practice but for some reason was changed to a wrong answer, or new error, on the posttest. Perhaps in this instance, the initial response was a lucky guess, feedback was basically ignored, and a new error resulted on the test.

Thus, the five possible combinations of pretest-posttest responses are (1) correct-correct, (2) wrong-correct, (3) wrong-same wrong, (4) wrong-different wrong, and (5) correct-new wrong (see Fig. 29.3).

When put into a response pattern profile in terms of percentage of occurrence, a more exhaustive account of test performance is facilitated (Peeck et al., 1985). Response pattern profiles have been used for multiple-choice formats (Peeck, 1979; Phye, 1979). Some researchers (Peeck et al., 1985) argue that to interpret the cognitive processes involved in such sequences, it is important to determine to what extent learners remember their initial responses after the pretest. Peeck et al. (1985) included "guess questions" that could not be answered from the text and "factual questions" that could be answered from the text. The most important finding was that learners remembered their initial responses in the wrong-changed-to-correct category. This indicates that retention of initial responses did not prevent subjects from learning the correct answer from feedback, casting serious doubt, incidentally, on the assumption that subjects tend to forget their responses on the initial task after a delay and that error tendencies interfere with learning the correct answers from feedback—an assumption that was a major component of the interference-perseveration interpretation of the delayed-retention effect studies (Kulhavy & Anderson, 1972).

Error Analysis

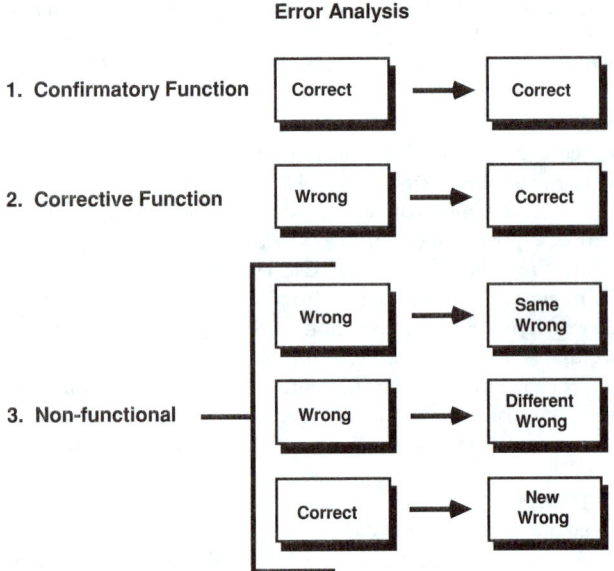

1. **Confirmatory Function** Correct → Correct

2. **Corrective Function** Wrong → Correct

3. **Non-functional**
   Wrong → Same Wrong
   Wrong → Different Wrong
   Correct → New Wrong

FIGURE 29.3. Five response pattern combinations based on Phye and Bender's (1989) response pattern analysis.

Data also indicated that when subjects changed their initial response after feedback (correct to a new wrong, wrong to correct, and wrong to a different wrong), the highest identification scores were obtained in the category of corrected errors (wrong to correct).

The construct validity of error analysis was addressed by Phye and Bender (1989) and demonstrated when Peeck et al. (1985) examined pooled data from four previous experiments. Proportional frequencies for the three error types when averaged across the four studies were 0.10 for same errors, 0.06 for different errors, and 0.05 for new errors. These averages were quite similar compared to results of Phye and Bender (1989) in which same errors equaled 0.08, different errors equaled 0.05, and new errors equaled 0.04. These data contribute to the construct validity of the error analysis model and suggest its value when combined with correct response and conditional probability data to assess feedback effectiveness.

Further research from an information processing perspective should address feedback effectiveness and efficiency by considering not only correct responses but also an analysis of processing errors (Phye & Bender, 1989). Error data, when used with correct response data and conditional probability data, "provides a multivariate account of feedback utilization by the learner in a learning situation involving practice" (p. 109).

Another way of analyzing errors is to classify them in some way that is related to the specific learning outcome involved. In rule using tasks, an example would be the classification of errors as "serious" or "nonserious" as was done in an analysis developed by Tatsuoka (see Birenbaum & Tatsuoka, 1987). The measure of seriousness of error types indicated to what extent a wrong rule deviates from the right rule. Using an "error vector" system to analyze signed-number problems, error codes were developed based on the absolute number operation and the

sign operation involved in solving problems. Students' response patterns to test items were then classified into three categories: serious errors, nonserious errors, and correct answers.

In concept learning, errors are categorized according to three kinds of concept classification errors: overgeneralization, undergeneralization, and misconception (cited in Tennyson & Cocchiarella, 1986). When students are learning to classify a member of a concept class, they must make discriminations between examples and nonexamples of the concept. Certain nonexamples may be quite difficult to discriminate from a given concept example (termed a "close-in" nonexample), and others may be easy to discriminate from an example (termed a "far-out" nonexample) (Dempsey, 1988). When a learner is consistently making a particular overgeneralization error of accepting nonexamples, it is likely that he or she is having a problem with fine discrimination of the concept. Fine discrimination errors occur when close-in nonexamples are classified by the learner as an example of a concept. But if the student is regularly classifying a far-out nonexample as a true example, he or she may be undergeneralizing by rejecting the examples, resulting in an error of gross discrimination. In general, fine discrimination errors result from classification problems on close-in nonexamples, whereas gross discrimination errors result from a student's having classification problems on far-out nonexamples. Because close-in nonexamples are more difficult to discriminate from examples than are far-out nonexamples, more close-in errors (or fine discrimination errors) should be expected to occur. This indeed was the case in a study by Dempsey (1988). In the same study, it was found that learners who made fewer fine discrimination errors during instruction scored significantly higher on a retention test. In fact, 4 of 10 errors made during the instruction were those that were predetermined as fine discrimination errors. These findings encourage the analysis of close-in and far-out nonexamples associated with fine and gross discrimination errors when employing concepts learning tasks.

Finally, Meyer (1986) identified four errors reflected in a review of research on teachers' correction of students: (a) lack-of-information errors, (b) motor errors, (c) confusions, and (d) rule application errors. Lack-of-information errors result when a student's mistakes are caused by missing knowledge. Motor errors result when a student knows the information but cannot express it. Confusions occur when students fail to discriminate correctly between concepts and ideas. And rule application errors result when students apply rules incorrectly in problem-solving situations. Meyer asserts that feedback should be designed to fit each type of misunderstanding.

Because the correction of errors appears to be where feedback has its most promising effects, researchers should continue to examine ways in which to manipulate feedback to maximize this outcome. As Noonan (1984) pointed out, more sophisticated procedures that involve analysis of common errors or error patterns might be more useful than traditional correct answer feedback. Adaptive feedback information can easily be facilitated within a computer-based instruction environment, where the computer can record and analyze the types of errors being made and give appropriate feedback based upon error types.

29.5.4 Learning Outcomes

A detailed overview of suggested feedback for various learning outcomes has been offered by Smith and Ragan (1993). These researchers discuss their views of what information to include for each type of learning outcome according to Gagné's taxonomy. Instructional design theorists have proposed that different types of learning tasks require different strategies and instructional methods (Gagné, 1985; Merrill, 1983; Reigeluth & Stein, 1983). Very few researchers have attempted to investigate the differences in feedback needs for differing types of learning. Schimmel (1983) found differences in informative feedback given for declarative knowledge versus procedural knowledge. The studies that have been conducted are summarized below. In terms of testing current views of feedback, recall that results from the Mory (1991) study indicated that predictions from the Kulhavy and Stock (1989) model held for verbal information learning but not for concept acquisition. Swindell (1991) also reported a study attempting to examine the same model (Kulhavy & Stock, 1989) under the conditions of higher-level learning. Although results of the study claim to suggest the generalizability of the model to higher learning, questions required recall of verbal information only, with no guarantee that intellectual skill learning had occurred.

The vast majority of feedback studies have dealt with verbal information tasks (Schimmel, 1988). Consequently, it is not known if certain patterns or inconsistencies that have emerged from these studies would necessarily result when involving other types of learning. This question has been acknowledged by a few researchers, an example of which is clear in Andre and Thieman's (1988) statement, "Whether feedback on questions facilitates concept learning as well as factual learning is not known from available research" (p. 297). Indeed, Schimmel discovered differences in the value of informative feedback for declarative knowledge versus procedural learning in the results of a 1983 metaanalysis.

Smith and Ragan (1993) estimate feedback requirements for different learning outcomes based on the theoretical cognitive processing requirements of each outcome. Thus their suggestions are predominantly theory based, and the reader should note that each area is a source of much needed research to test these conjectures. The following sections address the feedback requirements suggested by either research, theory, or both.

29.5.4.1 Learning Outcome Comparisons.

In an effort to bridge the gap between learning outcome differences, some researchers have compared declarative information tasks with higher cognitive tasks. Lee (1985) compared verbal information with rule using, hypothesizing that feedback for rule using tasks should be more complex than feedback for learning verbal information. Three levels of feedback were compared. Correct answer feedback was the same for all three levels (i.e., "right"). Differences in feedback occurred only if the student missed the question. For an error, students in the first level of feedback simply received the statement, "Wrong." Students in the second level were told, "Wrong. The answer is. . . ." for errors made. Errors for the students in the third level of feedback were presented with, "Wrong. The rule is. . . . The correct answer is. . . . " There were no significant differences between feedback levels, suggesting that more complex feedback did not prove more effective in either task. An additional finding was that there were no differences between feedback that was given immediately or feedback that was delayed.

Another study comparing verbal information with rule using was completed by Char (1978). Char refers to his intellectual skill task as "higher-order learning," which he describes as both identifying concepts and applying rules. The purpose was to examine the effects of both informative feedback versus no feedback and delayed versus immediate feedback on retention of verbal information and higher-order learning. As one might predict, informative feedback did significantly enhance retention of both verbal information and higher-order learning. There were no differences between immediate and delayed feedback. It is regrettable that Char did not categorize each higher-order question separately as being either a concept or a rule application, so as to delineate more clearly the specific kinds of learning being applied.

S. U. Wager (1983) also compared verbal information learning with a type of intellectual skill—specifically, defined concepts. She examined the effects of timing and type of feedback on retention of an instructional task involving verbal information and defined concepts learning. Both immediate and delayed feedback timing were used, and feedback was either simple or elaborated. Simple feedback presented a knowledge of results only, and elaborated feedback presented a combination of knowledge of results, knowledge of correct response, and response contingent feedback, which explained why a particular response choice was or was not correct. Results indicated that neither timing of feedback nor type of feedback made any significant differences between groups. These results were attributed partially to the fact the feedback may have assumed a lesser role when students were given tutorial instruction.

Gaynor (1981) also compared across verbal tasks and higher-level tasks. Rather than using Gagné's categorizations of "verbal information" and "intellectual skill," Gaynor classified her materials according to Bloom's taxonomy. She compared test items that fell into three levels of intellectual ability: knowledge, comprehension, and application. She concluded that when degree of original learning is equated, immediate feedback, end of session feedback, or even no feedback has little effect on short- or long-term retention of materials at Bloom's first three taxonomy levels.

Mory (1991, 1994) attempted to test the Kulhavy and Stock (1989) model of response certitude using two types of learning outcomes for her subjects to try to determine if the model would generalize to a concept learning task. The model was derived from studies that used predominantly verbal information and rote memorization of facts. In the Mory (1991, 1994) study, feedback was adaptive based on a combined assessment of answer correctness and level of certitude. The rationale was that by varying the type and amount of information contained in the feedback to fit the prescriptive state of learners under high- and low-certitude conditions and correct and error responses, learners would be given only the most "economic" form of feedback. Further, this type of adaptive feedback treatment was compared with a traditional form of nonadaptive feedback that essentially contained a verification component combined with knowledge of correct response. Whereas there were no significant differences in posttest performance between the adaptive and the nonadaptive groups, there was a significant increase in feedback efficiency for the adaptive group. Mory postulates that one reason that adaptive feedback did not seem to improve scores in the higher-level learning task of concept learning was that students did not accurately predict their answer correctness and thus were not able to receive the appropriate feedback for that condition. Data in the study revealed that certitude levels tended to be high throughout the adaptive program, regardless of actual answer correctness. This means that students did not receive low-certitude feedback when it was needed most. Learners simply could not give accurate assessments of their own abilities to classify a particular concept. As stated earlier, these findings are supported by previous studies involving "feeling of knowing" judgments (which are similar to response-certitude estimates) that proposed that when learning involved higher-level tasks, judgments tended to be overestimated by learners (Metcalfe, 1986). In contrast to this, some researchers have found that students learning concepts tended to underestimate their belief about their answer correctness (M. P. Driscoll, personal communication, August 30, 1990). Despite the opposing nature of these two separate results, it would appear that learners do not accurately predict their knowledge in higher cognitive tasks.

29.5.4.2 Declarative Knowledge.
This type of knowledge is what is referred to as verbal information in Gagné's (1985) taxonomy and specifically by Smith and Ragan (1993) as including labels, facts, lists, and organized discourse. For labels and facts, feedback should give some evaluation of whether the learner's response is complete and whether the learner's associations are complete. Lists will possibly involve the elements of both completeness and sequence to be evaluated. They suggested that feedback might point out errors in incorrect combinations of associations and that simple correct or incorrect feedback may be sufficient. In Schimmel's work (1983), confirmation feedback was found to be more potent than correct answer feedback in verbal information tasks. Simpler feedback was more effective than complex feedback in a study by Siegel and Misselt (1984). Further, Kulhavy and his colleagues (1985) found that knowledge of correct response was more beneficial than more complex feedback.

In terms of organized discourse, Smith and Ragan (1993) asserted that feedback must act as an intelligent evaluator or provide model responses. This "intelligent" evaluation may be provided by a knowledgeable human being or by computerized intelligent tutors. In terms of a model response, feedback should be constructed with attention to modeling organization, links of information, and elaborations that would be considered essential for an appropriate answer.

29.5.4.3 Concept Learning.
Four feedback studies were found that dealt specifically with concept learning tasks. Although already described with the feedback elaboration research, they are discussed in this section for their importance

as involving concepts. But before discussing these studies, an overview of concepts is presented from the major tenets of concepts learning research.

Concepts are types of classifying rules (Gagné & Driscoll, 1988; Gagné et al., 1992) that are used to facilitate the classification of instances through acquiring definitions, attributes, and examples (Tessmer, Wilson, & Driscoll, 1990). The two categories of concepts are concrete concepts and defined concepts (Gagné & Driscoll, 1988). Concrete concepts represent categories determined on the basis of perceptual features, whereas defined concepts represent semantic categories that may or may not have a perceptual basis (Tessmer et al., 1990). Defined concepts must be identified through the use of a definition, rather than by actual sight.

Concepts have both declarative and procedural components that require instruction designed to convey both of these learning outcomes. Declarative strategies help make information about the concept meaningful to the learner, and procedural strategies produce accuracy and ease in performance of concept classification skills (Tessmer et al., 1990). Conceptual knowledge is more than just the storage of declarative (or verbal information) knowledge, embodying also an understanding of a concept's operational structure within itself and of structure between associated concepts (Park & Tennyson, 1986; Tennyson & Cocchiarella, 1986). Because conceptual knowledge is the storage and integration of information, and procedural knowledge is the retrieval of knowledge in the service of solving problems, instruction could typically include portions that focus on verbal information outcomes (the declarative component) and intellectual skill (concept) outcomes (the procedural component). Although testing how well a student has stored information in the form of verbal information outcomes is not a guarantee that the student also understands and can integrate the information, it still is an indicator of how much he or she can remember in order to apply it.

The primary method of teaching concepts usually involves presenting a definition or classification rule, followed by sets of examples and nonexamples. Examples and nonexamples are in the form of both (a) statement presentations to the student (expository instances) and (b) question presentations to the student (interrogatory instances) (Tennyson & Cocchiarella, 1986). Additionally, critical attributes of a concept may be presented. Critical attributes are what define a concept and must be present in any given case to be an example of the concept. The presence of these critical attributes constitutes both "necessary and sufficient conditions for judging the presence of the concept" (Wilson, 1986, p. 16). The test of whether a concept has been learned is to present the student with new instances of the concept not previously encountered to see if he or she can classify the instance correctly.

Further, a concept is a set of specific objects, symbols, or events that share common characteristics (critical attributes) and can be categorized by a particular name or symbol (Tennyson & Park, 1980). Most concepts do not exist in isolation but as part of a set of related concepts. The placement of a given concept in relation to other concepts having similar attributes implies that certain concepts would be subordinate, whereas others would be superordinate. Those concepts that are placed in the same general location in the content structure and are neither subordinate nor superordinate may be defined as coordinate concepts (M. Merrill & Tennyson, 1977; Tennyson & Park, 1980). Coordinate concepts fall at the same level of specificity, and the members of any coordinate class are not members of any other coordinate class (Klausmeier, 1976). For coordinate concept learning, the nonexamples of one concept are examples of other coordinate concepts. Usually a set of concepts is presented simultaneously, making it easy for the learner to confuse specific attributes of one concept with another one and resulting in an error of misclassification. But simultaneous presentation is helpful in enabling learners to compare and contrast similarities and differences between concepts and thus aid in clarification of individual concepts (Litchfield, 1987).

The first study to involve both feedback and concepts was by Waldrop, Justen, and Adams (1986). They approach feedback with an emphasis on feedback being effective only under *certain conditions,* relating the importance of this when using feedback in CAI. They compared three types of feedback during a drill- and- practice CAI program. The program presented a series of 20 examples of four types of consequences for behavior (positive reinforcement, negative reinforcement, punishment, and extinction). Although the classification of concepts was used in the practice, they did not test the learning of the concepts by giving them new instances on the posttest. Instead, the criterion measure consisted of the same 20 items used in the CAI modules, only presented in a random order and within a test booklet. At least in terms of retention of the original examples, immediate extended feedback following both correct and incorrect responses was superior to minimal feedback. It would have been of value if the researchers had tested the concepts in the manner typically in line with what theorists would say constitutes successful learning of the concept—that is, being able to classify previously unencountered examples—and not merely by a repetition of the same examples.

The second feedback study to employ the use of concepts was by J. Merrill (1987). High- and low-level questions were used in combination with corrective feedback and attribute isolation feedback to form four versions of a computer-based science lesson that taught Xenograde terminology concepts. J. Merrill chose attribute isolation feedback based on M. Merrill and Tennyson's (1977) proposition that the correct classification of newly encountered examples of a concept is more likely if attribution isolation is presented both in the instructional presentation of examples and in the feedback given after practice examples. The primary hypothesis of the study was that students who received high-level questions and attribute isolation feedback would perform better than the other groups. Although there was a question-level main effect of students in the high-level question treatments performing significantly better than those in low-level question treatments, there was an absence of a feedback form main effect. J. Merrill suggests that this absence may be due to the fact that potential benefits of either feedback form were not fully available to the students. The attribute isolation feedback was presented only after two wrong responses and, consequently, was not encountered very often. This is unfortunate considering results from previous studies

(cited in J. Merrill, 1987) that yielded significant posttest results from the addition of attribute isolation to the concept learning task.

Andre and Thieman (1988) approached the concept issue by directly addressing the problem that feedback research has used tests that measure only factual learning and thus has stood "mute on the issue of concept/principle acquisition" (p. 297). Unlike the Waldrop et al. (1986) study, these researchers measured both retention of the presented examples and performance on new instances of the concept. They broke student scores into performance on four types of questions: (a) repeated factual, (b) repeated application, (c) new factual, and (d) new application. Performance on the new application questions was cited as the main variable of interest, as the major purpose of the study was to determine the effects of type of question and type of feedback on concept learning. Subjects were given either factual, application, or both types of adjunct questions immediately after reading an instructional passage. A day later, subjects were given either no feedback, correct answer feedback, or self-correction feedback, in which the students received a list of incorrect items without the correct answer, the instructional passage, and instructions to find the correct answers to the incorrect items.

One major finding of the study was that adjunct application questions significantly improved student performance on later use of concepts and that this improvement occurred without any loss of incidental factual learning. This beneficial effect was obtained only when application questions were used in isolation. When both factual and application adjunct questions were used in the practice, poor performance occurred on new application items. This suggests some sort of interference when the two types of questions are presented together.

A second major finding was that feedback did not influence concept learning (i.e., performance on new instances) but did influence performance on repeated examples of concepts. Thus, feedback did not facilitate the acquisition of a concept that could be applied to new examples. They suggested that more than one trial of feedback may have been insufficient to induce concept acquisition and cited Park and Tennyson's (1980) finding that students required approximately four examples to learn a particular concept.

Dempsey and his associates (Dempsey, 1988; Dempsey, Driscoll, & Litchfield, 1993) examined concepts in terms of achievement on a retention test, feedback study time, and type and numbers of discrimination errors. These studies examined the effects of four methods of immediate corrective feedback on retention, discrimination error, and feedback study time in computer-based instruction. Also, the studies explored the relationship between types of corrective feedback and types of errors made by learners. The four feedback conditions were (a) feedback that gave knowledge of correct response only, (b) feedback that informed students of the correct response and then required that they make that response, (c) feedback that gave knowledge of the correct response and also presented anticipated wrong answer feedback, and (d) feedback that gave knowledge of correct response and allowed a second try to answer the question. No significant differences in retention rates resulted for any feedback group, but the group receiving knowledge of correct response only used significantly less feedback study time and was more efficient than the other conditions. Type of feedback made no difference in the number of errors during instruction. Students making fewer fine discrimination errors during the instruction performed better on a retention test. More fine than gross discrimination errors were made on the retention test. Regarding feedback study times and discrimination error, almost twice as much feedback study time was consumed for fine discrimination errors. This finding may suggest a link between fine discrimination errors and high-certitude errors from Kulhavy's work, as in both cases, the longest feedback study times resulted.

29.5.4.4 Rule Learning.
According to Smith and Ragan (1993), rules may be one of two types: relational rules and procedural rules. Relational rules involve relationships between two or more concepts, often being described in terms of "if–then" or "cause–effect" (p. 84). Relational rules have also been referred to as propositions, principles, laws, axioms, theorems, and postulates. These researchers (Smith & Ragan, 1993) describe suggested feedback for rule learning in terms of various practice stages for using the rule. When practicing verbalizing or visualizing the rule, feedback should provide information concerning the key concepts of the rule and their relationships. Note that this would basically qualify as verbal information, and not rule utilization itself.

When practice involves the recognition of situations in which the rule is applicable, feedback should identify (a) whether the rule is applicable and (b) what features of the situation make the rule applicable or not. Smith and Ragan (1993) suggest that the explanatory portion of the feedback be placed under learner control, as explanatory feedback has been shown to confuse some learners (Phye, 1979).

When learners begin actually applying the rule, feedback should provide the outcome of the application of the rule. Explanatory feedback might include a step-by-step solution of the problem, highlighting critical features that influence the application of the rule or illustrating in graphic form how a solution can be drawn. Such explanatory feedback was found to be significantly superior to simple correct/incorrect feedback on college students' ability to apply rules in computer programming (Lee, Smith, & Savenye, 1991).

When learners determine whether a rule has been correctly applied, feedback should include simple correct answer feedback. For situations in which the rule has been applied incorrectly, feedback should point out the specific error in application and give the correct way that rule should have been applied. Feedback might also serve to provide hints for modification of the learner's use of a rule or be adapted to correct specific misconceptions or error patterns that a learner is making (Smith & Ragan, 1993).

The second type of rules, procedural, involves learning a series of steps to reach a specific goal. Procedural rules may be simple, with only one set of steps to complete linearly, or they may be complex, with many decision points leading to different baths or branches. The first step in learning procedural rules involves determining if the procedure is required. Smith and Ragan (1993) recommend feedback that is confirmatory, informing the learner whether he or she has appropriately identified the situations that require the application of the procedure. Learners should also be given feedback as to the accuracy of their completion of each step in the procedure. During initial practice stages, feedback should be detailed and given during the practice of each step of the procedure. Then as the learner is able to perform the entire procedure, feedback would both determine whether each step was correctly completed and provide qualitative information concerning selection, criterion, and precision and efficiency. Smith and Ragan (1993) also recommend that feedback be given as to the remembrance of steps in the procedure and their correct sequence of completion. And, finally, feedback should be provided as to the appropriateness of a completed procedure in the form of correct answer feedback.

Departing from the usual fare of verbal learning studies in the feedback elaboration research, only a few experimenters have chosen to look at rule using alone. Birenbaum and Tatsuoka (1987) examined the seriousness of errors committed by eighth graders using rules to add signed numbers in a CAI task. For serious errors, it did not matter how much elaboration was in the feedback, correction was relatively unaffected by feedback. Feedback elaborations for nonserious errors did have an increasing probability of being corrected as more information was added to the feedback.

A second group of researchers (Tait et al., 1973) examined rule using in a CAI environment designed to help children multiply two- and three-digit numbers by one-digit numbers. Treatment conditions included (a) no feedback, (b) passive feedback, and (c) active feedback. The active feedback procedure required an overt response to be given for each step in the procedure for computing the answer. The passive procedure merely printed a message to the student and required no overt response. The active feedback was designed to alleviate the problem of children not attending to feedback messages that explained the procedure. Children seemed to be copying the answer presented at the end of the feedback and ignoring other information in the feedback. Active feedback required the student's active engagement with the feedback at each step in solving the problem. Additionally, active feedback contained more information than did passive feedback.

Even when using both active and passive feedback, there was still little improvement from pretest to posttest. The researchers concluded that with the active feedback, children were still able to copy answers without understanding the procedure behind them. Consequently, a second experiment was designed that required the pupils to repeat the question until it had been answered correctly. The correct answer was required in both passive and active feedback groups before the child was allowed to continue on to a new problem. Even under these conditions, active feedback was no more beneficial than passive feedback. However, pupils who had scored low on the pretest did perform much better on the posttest when given active feedback than similar pupils in the passive feedback group.

29.5.4.5 Problem Solving.
In the domain of problem solving, a learner must select and combine multiple rules to reach a solution. This may require that learners use declarative knowledge and cognitive strategies within a content domain

and combine previously learned relational and procedural rules to solve a previously unencountered problem (Gagné, 1985). According to Smith and Ragan (1993), the following stages often occur during a problem-solving task, and not necessarily in the same sequence:

1. Clarify the given state, including any obstacles or constraints.
2. Clarify the goal state, including criteria for knowing when the goal is reached.
3. Search for relevant prior knowledge of declarative, rule, or cognitive strategies that will aid in solution.
4. Decompose problem into subproblems with subgoals.
5. Determine a sequence for attacking subproblems.
6. Consider possible solution paths to each subproblem using related prior knowledge.
7. Select solution path and apply production knowledge (rules) in appropriate order.
8. Evaluate to determine if goal is achieved. If not revise by returning to (1) above. (p. 92)

Because this type of learning involves the use of several other types of learning, feedback during a problem-solving task must work to help the learner see where his or her strategies or information gaps are occurring. According to Smith and Ragan's (1993) suggestions, initial feedback may be in the form of hints or guiding questions. It may include data on which information has been used or misused, the appropriateness of selected solutions, whether individual phases of the solution have been correctly performed, and the efficiency of the solution process. As learners transition from novice to expert, their approaches to a problem should become more automatic. At this expert level, learners will need feedback on the efficiency or speed of their problem solving. The extent of this type of feedback will depend on the extent that genuine expertise is an expected part of the learning goal.

In simulations, feedback is often provided in terms of presenting learners with the consequences of their decisions. Open-ended response questions may be followed by feedback presenting a model of the solution process. And during the initial stages of practice, immediate feedback will be most helpful for intermediate stages, when responses can keep the learner from an eventual successful solution (cited in Smith & Ragan, 1993).

It should be noted that more recent views of problem solving are found in the literature on constructivism, presented later in this chapter. In particular, recent research in the areas of anchored instruction, situated cognition, situated learning, and generative learning have examined what might be thought to be "problem solving," but with very different philosophical assumptions about the way in which learning takes place (Cognition and Technology Group at Vanderbilt [CTGV], 1990, 1991a, 1991b, 1992a, 1992b, Young, 1993). It is from this broadened perspective that researchers will find the most need for research on types of feedback that can aid learners as they construct solutions to authentic problems.

29.5.4.6 Cognitive Strategies. Cognitive strategies are techniques that learners use to help them attend to, organize, elaborate, manipulate, and retrieve knowledge, thus controlling their own cognitive processes (see Gagné, 1985). Smith and Ragan (1993) relate the use of cognitive strategies with problem solving, as the selection, application, and evaluation of a cognitive strategy are similar to problem-solving techniques. Given that similarity, feedback will have some of the same functions as stated for problem solving—that of modeling appropriate decisions and stating explicitly whether the decisions and performance of the learner were adequate. Feedback should also contain explanations as to why the model is appropriate. Characteristics such as the learners' capabilities, requirements of the task, learner efficacy, and applications of various strategies should be considered as well. They (Smith & Ragan, 1993) suggest that for open-ended trials toward a solution, feedback should involve reviewing appropriateness of a particular strategy and the critical details of the strategy for a given problem or solution.

In a study by Ahmad (1988), college-age learners participating in a guided discovery lesson were taught strategies that were either compatible or incongruent with their prior cognitive strategies. When feedback on the effective or ineffective use of a particular strategy was provided, better performance resulted when the strategy was compatible with previously employed strategies. But when the strategy used by learners was incompatible with their prior strategy use, feedback containing only whether a solution was correct or incorrect proved to be more effective.

Because cognitive strategies can be very subject domain oriented, it would probably be fruitful to explore the uses of various cognitive strategies within specified subject areas and contexts. Also, as stated above, researchers should consider examining cognitive strategies in terms of their applications to a learner's construction of solutions of more authentic learning tasks. In fact, one of the important goals underlying the development of the Jasper series (CTGV, 1990, 1991a, 1992a, 1992b) was helping students learn to become independent thinkers, to identify and define issues and problems on their own (CTGV, 1992a). Cognitive strategies should begin to be viewed as "generative learning" (CTGV, 1990, 1992a), as the learners themselves generate the relevant subproblems and data necessary to satisfy subgoals that they have generated on their own.

29.5.4.7 Psychomotor Skills. Psychomotor learning involves skills that are physical in nature, often with coordinated muscular movements. Psychomotor skills require a cognitive component, particularly in the early stages of learning the skill. As the skill becomes more automatic, the cognitive awareness becomes an unconscious part of performing the skill. Two components of psychomotor skill are (a) executive subroutines to control decisions and supply subordinate hierarchical skills and (b) temporal patterning of skills to integrate the sequence of performance over time, involving pacing and anticipation (cited in Smith & Ragan, 1993). Further, psychomotor skills are sometimes classified on a continuum from "closed" to "open." Closed skills are predictable and do not require much adaptation to the environment, thus they are referred to as being "internally paced" (Singer, as cited in Smith & Ragan, 1993). Open skills, on the other hand, must be adapted to unpredictable aspects of a changing environment.

The function of feedback in the learning of psychomotor skills is to provide a surrogate for the learners' self-evaluation, at least until learners reach a skill level at which they can provide this role for themselves. However, as Smith and Ragan (1993) point out, this transfer is more pronounced than in other types of learning tasks. Learners are able, through their own seeing and hearing, to determine when a skill has been performed correctly, thus providing themselves a type of internal feedback.

Feedback may be given about (a) the product (the quality of the response outcome) or (b) the process (what causes the response outcome). During the beginning practice stages of motor skill, feedback serves the critical function of providing information about the process of executing the motor skill. Then, as learners advance in their ability to execute the skill, feedback can focus on the response outcome (product) itself. Ho and Shea (cited in Smith & Ragan, 1993) found that learners appeared to learn simple motor skills better when feedback was withdrawn or at least not given after every single response. Also, quantitative feedback (using a measurable criterion) appears to be superior to qualitative feedback (e.g., "too fast," "too low") (Smoll, as cited in Smith & Ragan, 1993). However, there is an optimal precision point to include in feedback, past which point the feedback can result in detrimental learning (Rogers, as cited in Smith & Ragan, 1993).

Graphic representations can be very beneficial to learners when included in feedback about the quality of a psychomotor response. Sometimes referred to as "kinematic" feedback, it can increase both the efficiency and the effectiveness of the learner during the acquisition of a psychomotor skill. Further, feedback that is interspersed throughout the learning of a motor task is more effective than massed feedback at the end of practice (cited in Smith & Ragan, 1993).

29.5.4.8   Attitude Learning.

The final type of learning capability discussed in this section is attitude learning. The desired outcome of attitude learning is that a learner will choose to behave in a particular way. A person's attitude about something is reflected in the decisions or choices he or she makes. The goal of instruction for attitude learning would be to influence what a learner chooses to do after the instruction is completed (Gagné, 1985; Gagné et al., 1992). Obviously before a person can "choose" to do something, there are cognitive and behavioral components that have to be learned beforehand. The person has to cognitively "know how" to practice the attitude. Also, a person has to see the need to apply the attitude, behaviorally responding to opportunities to make decisions and make the particular choice. This can be accomplished through his or her own experience or vicariously through others' experiences. The affective side of attitude learning merely involves "knowing why."

Feedback for the cognitive and behavioral components can simply include information concerning whether learners have successfully employed the knowledge or skill that the attitude will require. Feedback can also include information about the congruency of their responses with the desired attitude. In terms of mediating attitudes through feedback, learners can be presented with information concerning the anticipated consequences of their choices, incorporating the affective component of why the behavior that reflects the attitude is important (Smith & Ragan, 1993).

29.5.5   Motivation

When one begins to speak of motivation in feedback, it is easy to bring to mind the reinforcement view of feedback, and indeed, theories of motivation have tended to focus on behavioral reinforcement and performance rather than on increasing motivation through instructional means (Jacobs & Dempsey, 1993). To understand ways in which feedback can be used to help the motivational level of students, whether from a behavioral or a cognitive view, it will be useful to examine briefly some of the basic theories of motivation that psychologists have constructed to explain motivation in the learning process.

29.5.5.1   Goals and Goal Discrepancy Feedback.

Past research in the area of motivation (cited in Covington & Omelich, 1984) has shown that for a learner to remain motivated and involved depends on a close match between a learner's aspirations or goals and his or her expectations that these goals can be met. If these aspirations are set so high that they are unattainable, the learner will likely experience failure and discouragement. Conversely, when goals are set so low that their attainment is certain, success loses its potency in promoting further effort (Birney, Burdick, & Teevan, 1969). Covington and Omelich (1984) have suggested that setting performance goals beyond present capabilities, particularly in the case of low self-perception of success, can become a main source of gratification. Apparently the statement of a worthy goal is enough to boost self-regard irrespective of goal attainment. One might say that feedback is a means to allow a learner to study and "retest" information, actions that, according to some researchers, would encourage greater performance aspirations coupled with increased confidence to achieve these elevated goals. Findings suggest that motivation is a key mediating factor in the performance of learners (Covington & Omelich, 1984).

Feedback can be a powerful motivator when it is given in response to goal-driven efforts Some researchers suggest that the learner's goal orientation should be considered when designing instruction, particularly when feedback can encourage or discourage a learner's effort, thus regulating sustained effort and future goal orientations (Dempsey, Driscoll, & Swindell, 1993). Other researchers claim that feedback enters into the actual goal-setting process, as a basis for evaluating assigned goals and in guiding the formation of a learner's personal goals (Erez & Zidon, 1984; Locke, Shaw, Saari, & Latham, 1981). Malone (1981) asserts that there are certain attributes that a goal must have to challenge the learner to attain them. First, they should be personally meaningful and easily generated by the learner. This is supported by Locke et al. (1981), who contend that goals may enhance performance only when the learner conscientiously accepts them. Indeed, Erez and Zidon (1984) found a linear decrease in performance after assigned goals were rejected.

Malone (1981) also suggests that learners need some type of performance feedback as to whether or not they are achieving their goals. This notion was explored in a study by Vance and Coella (1990) in which goal discrepancy feedback (GDF) and past-performance discrepancy feedback (PDF) were used to examine acceptance of assigned goals and personal goal levels of learners. GDF conveyed to what level learners were performing above or below the assigned goals. PDF indicated the learner's performance level from one trial to the next. Interestingly, assigned goals were designed to become increasingly difficult over given trials. This meant that, concurrently, the GDF became increasingly negative, and consequently, the learner's acceptance of the goals because less likely. Learners were found to switch over to PDF for evaluating assigned goals and for selecting new goals, what one would expect given the uncomfortable nature of the GDF over time.

Hoska (1993) refers to goals in terms of whether they help in acquiring something desirable or in avoiding something undesirable. These *acquisition* and *avoidance goals* can be external (in which the learner's focus is performing for others) or internal (in which the learner's focus is on learning for him- or herself). Several researchers (Dweck, 1986; Dweck & Legget, 1988; Nolen-Hoeksema, Seligman, & Girgus, 1986) have found that an individual's general goal orientation falls on a continuum from an ego-involved performing goal orientation to a task-involved learning goal orientation. Hoska further explains that learners who have performing goals want to demonstrate high ability and to avoid poor performance. They tend to view their success as a display of their abilities, which they measure in terms of the perceived abilities of others. To ego-involved learners, ability is their key to success, and effort is merely a means to achieve such external goals. In contrast, individuals who have learning goals pursue learning and extend effort to gain skills. They view their competence as improved mastery, attained through effort. To a task-involved learner, effort is perceived as being beneficial, as it helps the learner attain mastery.

When learners are successful, individual goal orientation is not a critical issue because success breeds the desire to extend effort, regardless of the goal. But when looking at instances of performance failure, the two goal orientations can produce very different results. If an individual with a learning goal orientation perceives an impending failure, it results in his or her exerting more effort on the task. To this task-focused individual, obstacles are a challenge to be overcome through effort. Task-involved learners believe that effort, not ability, is the key to success, and consequently, they will look for ways to overcome any difficulties that arise. Their satisfaction lies in effort, which has been shown to result in higher mastery scores and produces 50% more work than by other learners (Dweck, 1986).

In contrast, learners with a performance goal orientation will react quite differently to an impending failure. Obstacles become a threat to success and, therefore a threat to their self-worth. Even high ability learners in this group will set up defenses to protect themselves against the emotional threat. These self-defense reactions include such tactics as discounting (Kelley, 1973); avoiding the task, feigning boredom, or engaging in task-irrelevant actions to bolster their self-image (Dweck & Legget, 1988); and using inefficient strategies, resulting in learned helplessness (Seligman, Maier, & Geer, 1968).

According to Hoska (1993), if learners begin a task without a predisposition toward one of these two goal orientations, they will probably approach the task with the goals of both learning and performing. If learners do not receive cues favoring one type of goal over another, they will act according to their predisposition. But if a learning situation is structured to foster a particular type of goal, learners will respond. Thus a learner's goal orientations can be temporarily and, over time, permanently altered by intervention. This is where feedback can have a great effect on this aspect of motivation.

Providing lesson feedback can be used to influence learners' goal orientation by increasing their incentives to learn and minimize their incentives to perform. Hoska (1993) classifies these modifications into three approaches: (a) changing the learner's view of intelligence, (b) modifying the goal structure of the learning task, and (c) controlling the delivery of learning rewards. In terms of modifying a learner's view of intelligence, feedback can help learners view intelligence in a way that helps them see that ability and skill can be developed through practice, that effort is critical to increasing this skill, and that mistakes are part of the skill-developing process.

In terms of altering a learner's goal structure, one should consider the type of learning environment in which the lesson is taking place. Often goal structures are set within competitive, cooperative, and individualistic learning environments. Competitive goal structures emphasize performance success and failure and causes learners to become ego-involved. Cooperative goal structures teach a learner that the task is important, thus helping to foster learning goals (Johnson & Johnson, 1993). In individualized goal structures, although noncompetitive, learners will not necessarily be task-focused, but their orientation will be determined by the reward system of the learning experience.

Finally, the control of the delivery of learning awards usually involves providing external awards, offering praise and blame feedback, and offering unrequested help that can increase the learner's chance for success and comparison of the learner's performance to that of others.

Unfortunately, providing external rewards to learners can easily undermine any personal learning goals that they have. Researchers have found that learners will often select less difficult tasks to increase their probability of success (Deci, 1972; McCullers et al., 1987), and this effect increases under competitive conditions (Covington & Omelich, 1979). Further, learners often think that only difficult or boring tasks require reward (McCullers et al., 1987). Hoska (1993) offers the suggestion that feedback on the development of skills at various stages of a learning task can help redirect the learner to a focus on internal rewards.

Praise and blame feedback, once thought to provide positive and negative reinforcement, has been shown to be interpreted by learners as an estimate of their ability (Deci, 1972). While most learners associate praise and blame in terms of how much effort they expended, ego-involved learners and learners in competitive tasks often interpret praise and blame feedback as an indicator of both ability and success levels, sometimes even producing learned helplessness (Koestner, Zuckerman, & Koestner, 1987). Hoska (1993) summarizes the effects of praise and blame feedback in terms of whether or not the learner felt the comments were warranted, the difficulty of the task involved, and the goal structure of the learning environment. She points out that praise has the most potential for being misinterpreted by learners. When high praise occurs after successful completion of an easy task, it is interpreted to mean that the evaluator thinks the learner must have low ability. When minimal praise occurs after the successful completion of a difficult task, learners may believe that the evaluator thinks they have high ability, with success occurring due to this high ability rather than effort. And when praise or no feedback occurs after a failure, learners will tend to believe that this indicates low ability.

Blame feedback for incorrect responses can have more positive effects than praise feedback does for successes. Learners will tend to perceive blame as a result of their withheld effort. Hoska (1993) cautions that blame feedback must be used carefully because it also can be harmful in instances when a learner has invested a high degree of effort and has achieved at least some level of success. In such cases, the feedback can teach learners that small sustained improvements do not help them reach mastery—an undesirable outcome. In general, praise and blame feedback should focus on individual learner responses rather than overall success levels so as to associate the feedback with effort and not with ability.

It should be noted that having the option of being retested, in which a learner is given feedback and allowed to improve, also increases the number of failures experienced by a learner (Covington & Omelich, 1982). These failures have been shown to lead to decreases in self-estimates of ability, which in turn trigger hopelessness, shame, and anxiety (Covington, 1983; Covington & Omelich, 1981). But under a mastery format, positive perceptions of ability have been shown to be maintained even in the event of failure, as long as learners eventually reached their grade goals or showed improvement (Covington & Omelich, 1984). In the same study (Covington & Omelich, 1984), although isolated failures were temporarily demoralizing, they were shown to play little part in determining overall motivational reactions. When students do not have the opportunity to make good their failures, the result is greater demoralization even though they experience fewer failures. The study makes the point that task-oriented learning may be especially beneficial for slow learners, who may require several tries before mastering the subject matter.

Although the mastery learning approach is not new, nor is the idea of mastery being a desirable approach for slow learners, it is important to note here that the motivational element at work in such approaches should not be ignored. This line of motivation research suggests that students who are given the chance to improve through practice and feedback of some sort will have a positive perception of ability and will retain a high level of motivation overall. Thus the "retesting" effects of feedback have implications for improving and sustaining motivation, irrespective of the numbers of errors made.

29.5.5.2 Self-Efficacy and Expectancy.
Self-efficacy and task expectancy have been said to be equally important in determining how a learner will respond to a learning task (Hoska, 1993). Self-efficacy is the learner's perception of how well he or she can perform the learning tasks to achieve his or her goals.

It helps the learner select attainable goals and determine the amount of effort that will be involved for reaching success. Self-efficacy affects learning because it influences how much effort a learner will invest in a task. For example, low self-efficacy can cause learners to dwell on their deficiencies, resulting in inaccurate personal assessments of task difficulty and excessive attention devoted to the possibility of failure, resulting in a learning detriment (Bandura; cited in Hoska, 1993). On the other hand, high self-efficacy does not always result in maximum effort because the amount of effort extended by learners is said to depend on not only self-efficacy, but also goal incentives and the perceived demand or load of a task. Hoska (1993) points out that when learners are aware that a task is demanding, high self-efficacy will usually result in the effort needed for optimal performance. But when learners perceive tasks as being easy, high self-efficacy may cause them to feel that minimal effort is needed.

Bandura (1977) cites three information sources from which learners derive their general sense of self-efficacy. One is through vicarious experiences, in which self-efficacy is increased through viewing others' successes or decreased by viewing others' failures. Self-efficacy is also developed through the learner's own personal performance. The impact of a success or failure affects self-efficacy by how the learner interprets the outcome. Any success that is achieved through a minimal amount of effort is viewed to indicate high ability and can result in increased self-efficacy. Some learners view success that requires high effort to mean low ability, thus reducing their self-efficacy. The third area from which learners build their self-efficacy is verbal persuasion. Verbal persuasion comes in the form of opinions from parents, teachers, and peers concerning the learners' ability to perform various tasks and tend to affect learners' own perceptions about their abilities. Even learners with an initially high level of self-efficacy are said to have their own opinions of their ability affected by continual exposure to negative criticism (Hoska, 1993). Self-efficacy levels can also be temporarily affected by the learner's physiological state (Bandura, 1977), role assignment, familiarity with a task, or the presence of a highly confident person (Bandura, 1982).

Expectancy is determined by the amount of effort a learner deems as appropriate for a task, based on the learner's goal incentives. Hoska (1993) describes several elements of expectancy as follows:

- Belief that an outcome, or goal, is possible given the current situation. (Learner must feel that he or she has some control over goal attainment; this goal may or may not be task completion.)
- Belief that an outcome, which can be achieving either an acquisition or an avoidance goal, will have desired consequences. (The consequences of goal achievement must have some value to the learner.)
- Determination of the amount of effort appropriate for goal attainment. (The greater the goal incentive, the more effort the learner is willing to invest to achieve the goal.)
- Determination of whether or not the selected amount of effort will lead to goal attainment. (p. 119)

Keller and Suzuki (1986) assert that learners tend to evaluate outcomes against their own expectations. Recall that Kulhavy's

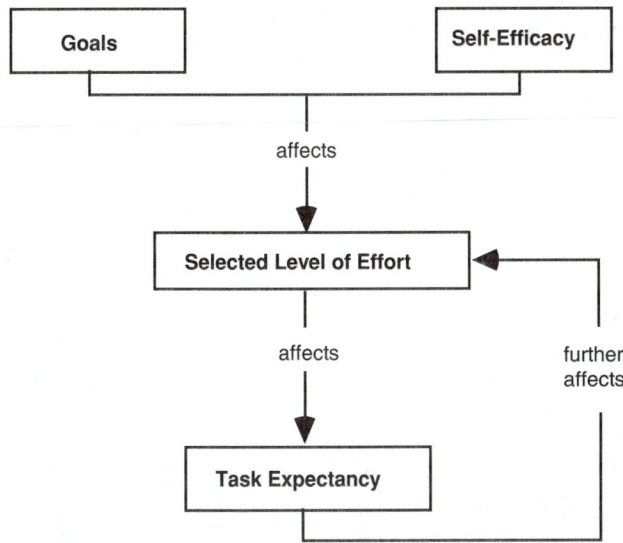

FIGURE 29.4. Relationship among a learner's goals, self-efficacy, selected level of effort, and task expectancy (from Hoska, 1993, p. 121). From *Interactive Instruction and Feedback* (p. 121), by J. V. Dempsey and G. C. Sales (Eds.), 1993, Englewood Cliffs, NJ: Educational Technology. Copyright 1993 by Educational Technology Publications. Reprinted with permission.

research in the area of response certitude supports the importance of the learner's expectancy level. Dempsey, Driscoll, and Swindell (1993) note that Kulhavy's work supports the hypothesis that "corrective feedback should be personally relevant to the learner and tailored to the learner's expectancy for success" (p. 28) and that this link has major implications for both motivational and instructional designs.

Hoska (1993) asserts that self-efficacy and expectancy levels can be modified. Figure 29.4 depicts the relationship between learners' goals and self-efficacy and their selected with level of effort and task expectancy.

As shown in the figure, a learner's self-efficacy and strength of task goals influence the level of effort that the learner will decide to invest in the task. This selected level of effort will then affect the learner's task expectancy, which will in turn influence further effort decisions. Learners' level of effort can be increased by providing them with experiences that are positive and internally satisfying, such as experiencing continually increasing levels of competence. Another method of increasing self-efficacy is by modifying the learner's attributes of success and failures (see the following section).

29.5.5.3 Attribution Theory.
One classic approach to motivation emphasizes the importance of causal attributions in explaining the consequences of academic failure and success (Weiner, 1972, 1979, 1980). According to attribution theory, a learner's achievement, affective reactions, and expectations concerning future outcomes are determined in part by the learner's attributional conclusions. Following performance on a

learning task, students will react in a generally positive or negative manner, formulate causes to explain their performance (causal attributions), and then experience affect and expectancy changes dependent on the nature of these attributions. Note how closely this last description matches what Kulhavy and his associates (Kulhavy, 1977; Kulhavy & Stock, 1989) described for a learner's processing of feedback and the comparison of his or her response to the feedback information. Recall that Kulhavy explained how a learner's level of response confidence combined with the actual correctness of response determined how feedback was used.

Forsyth and McMillan (1981) describe Weiner's proposed model of educational attributions and attempt to assess the relationship among the attributions, affect, and expectations of college students following a course exam. They cite previous research that suggests that when students attribute their success to factors such as ability or the nature of the task, their expectations for success increase, whereas students who attribute their success to luck or effort report less positive expectancies. Further, according to self-worth theory, "failure is more likely to lead to shame, depressed expectations, and lowered self-worth when it is ability linked rather than effort linked" (p. 394). Effort is something that is within the learner's control and has been found to have a strong relationship to affect. In the Forsyth and McMillan (1981) study, the affective reactions of students who felt that their performance was caused by factors they could control were more positive than the reactions of students who believed that they did not control the cause of their outcome. This supports studies of learned helplessness in that even students who did well on the test yet believed that they could not control their outcomes reported less positive affect.

Learned helplessness has been described by Seligman (1990) as "the giving-up reaction, the quitting response that follows from the belief that whatever you do doesn't matter" (p. 15). In his 25 years of research in this area, Seligman has isolated what he believes to be "the great modulator of learned helplessness," *explanatory style*. When events, whether good or bad, happen to a person, he or she has an habitual manner of explaining those events. These explanatory styles can either prevent helplessness or spread helplessness, depending on the person's explanations of events. Seligman further divides these explanations into the areas of *permanence, pervasiveness,* and *personalization*. He has found that if you can alter the way in which pessimistic people explain a success or failure—that is, alter the levels of permanence, pervasiveness, and personalization with which they surround their self-talk—you can change their outlook to one of optimism. Optimism, in turn, prevents people from remaining in a state of helplessness so that they can be more productive individuals.

Because students' "perceived noncontingency" (Forsyth & McMillan, 1981, p. 400) is associated with loss of achievement motivation, it seems reasonable to suggest that feedback could help students see a direct link between their level of effort and success and provide information concerning various factors that the learners have under control. This is elaborated on in the next section, in which strategies for modifying learners' motivational perspectives are examined.

TABLE 29.2. Motivating Learners Through Feedback (modified from Hoska, 1993, pp. 126–129)

Type of Feedback	Function of the Feedback	Technique	Cautions
Feedback to strengthen the incentive of learning goals	Help learner view his or her abilities as improvable. Present a task-focused, noncompetitive learning environment.	In intro. To lesson or as feedback when learner has difficulty: • Suggest that abilities are skills that can be developed. • Identify the skills that the lesson is aimed at developing. • Indicate that effort is the main tool for increasing skills. • Treat mistakes as an important part of skill development. When presenting feedback for both correct and incorrect responses: • Keep comments task focused. • Have the learner set goals related to completion of small-task stages. • Do not tie goals to accuracy rate or the time required for mastery. • Avoid comparisons. Do not rate the learner's progress against the progress of previous lesson users. • Do not offer rewards such as bonus points.	Help learner view his or her abilities as improvable. If learners are working in pairs or small groups, set up a cooperative environment.
Feedback to minimize the effect of difficulty level	In the case of CBI feedback, counteract learners tendency to view the computer as solely an entertainment source. Convince learner that difficulties and challenges are positive and do not reflect ability level.	As an introduction to the lesson and intermittently within feedback, reinforce the idea that the lesson is designed to help the learner develop skills. During feedback, occasionally stress the importance of paying close attention to presented information. Introduce the idea that the learner may easily complete some parts of the lesson, while having difficulty with others. Present the need for increasing levels of difficulty as a necessary part of skill development.	Do not suggest that the learner needs to work hard before he or she is presented with a learning task. This may cause him or her to overestimate task difficulty.
Feedback to increase a learner's self-efficacy	Steadily increase the self-efficacy of learners.	To develop a sense of self-efficacy, use the following strategy throughout the lesson: 1. Use feedback that provides support during the early stages of learning a task. Either give the learner some type of advised control over help sequences or attempt to put some aspect of forced support under learner control. 2. As the learner progresses, slowly reduce the amount of available help, letting the learner know that he or she is starting to do well on his or her own. 3. As the learner gains skill, begin to give him or her increasing control over the lesson. Let learners know that they have earned the ability to direct their study. If trackable factors are present, such as the speed at which the learner selects answers to questions, indicate that poor performance may be due to guessing; suggest to the learner that guessing is a waste of time, and lesson mastery is possible if he or she takes time and concentrates.	Do not offer high verbal praise for successes; a learner can easily misinterpret praise as a sign of low ability. Simple verification of a success is usually enough. Do not admonish learners every time they do poorly. If a learner with low self-efficacy is trying, blame may cause him or her to give up. Do not always force help on a learner. Provide help only when the learner really needs it.
Learner gains a sense of control over his or her learning	Help learner to attribute his or her success and failures to effort.	Provide feedback related to effort levels for both successes and failures. Track the learner's performance and: • If a learner responds incorrectly to several problems in a row, suggest that the difficulty does not mean failure. Encourage effort and suggest that if the learner tries hard, he or she will achieve success. Follow this advice with a slightly less-different problem. • If a learner has had difficulty and is now improving, point out the success and suggest that the cause is effort. Encourage continued effort. Follow this advice with a problem the learner has a fairly good chance of answering correctly. • If the learner is having difficulty, guide the learner to select a different, more-effective strategy. Relate the search for and use of strategies to effort.	Make certain that the learning environment is task focused and noncompetitive. Present the effort feedback after the learner responds to a problem. Offer effort-directed feedback only when the learner is working on problems of medium difficulty.

29.5.5.4 Modifying Learner's Perspectives Through Feedback. Hoska (1993) cites several steps that learners go through when they select and perform tasks, based on Weiner (1979).

Step 1. Learner selects a goal.

Step 2. Learner evaluates task difficulty.

Step 3. Learner evaluates his or her abilities and develops a level of self-efficacy.

Step 4. Learner selects an effort level and decides if that level will yield task success.

Step 5. Learner invests effort to complete the task and evaluates progress toward task completion.

Step 6. Learner determines and dimensions the cause of the success or failure.

Step 7. Learner modifies his or her learner perspective.

As learners go through these steps, Hoska suggests feedback according to its motivational function. This is summarized in Table 29.2.

29.5.5.5 ARCS Model of Motivation. Some researchers (Keller, 1983, 1987a, 1987b, 1987c; Keller & Kopp, 1987; Keller & Suzuki, 1987) have developed a model for increasing student motivation through instructional design, emphasizing instructional components that serve to motivate learners. The model grew from a macro theory, which motivation and instruction developed by Keller (1983). It is grounded in expectancy-value theory, which assumes that "people engage in an activity if it is perceived to be linked to the satisfaction of personal needs (the value aspect), and if there is a positive expectancy for success (the expectancy aspect)" (Keller, 1987a, pp. 2–3). The model came about by dividing the value components into the categories of *interest* and *relevance*. *Interest* refers to attentional factors in the environment, and *relevance* refers more to goal directed activities (p. 3). The expectancy component remained as a category, and a fourth category was added which was originally called *outcomes*. *Expectancy* refers to one's own expectation for being successful, and *outcomes* refers to the reinforcing value of instruction. Outcomes include reinforcement as described in operant conditioning theory but also include any environmental outcomes that help maintain intrinsic motivation (see Deci, 1972).

The ARCS model was created by generating a large list of motivational strategy statements, derived from research findings and from practices that have resulted in motivated learners. The four original categories of *interest, relevance, expectancy,* and *outcomes* were renamed to strengthen the central feature of each component and to generate a useful acronym (Keller, 1987a). The model now focuses on the four categories, attention, relevance, confidence, and satisfaction, and is hence referred to as the ARCS model. By using each of these four categories as a framework, instructional designers are able to incorporate strategies that relate to each.

When Keller (1987a) refers to *attention,* he is referring to the interest level of the learner—whether or not the learner's curiosity is aroused and is sustained over an appropriate period of time. Whether the learner perceives the instruction to satisfy

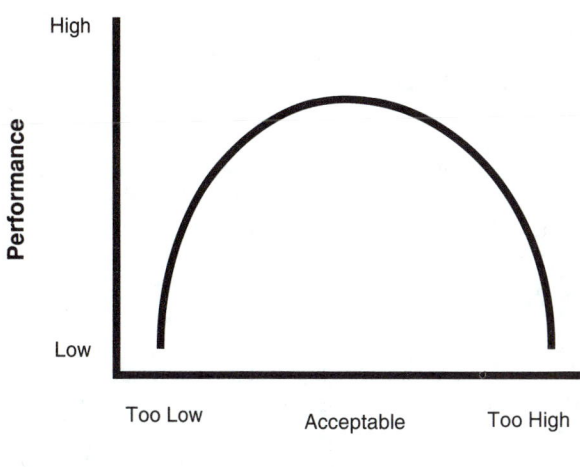

FIGURE 29.5. Inverted-U curve depiction of the relationship between motivation and performance (based on Keller, 1987).

personal needs or to help achieve personal goals is referred to by the *relevance* component of the model. *Confidence* refers to the learner's perceived likelihood of success (expectancy) and whether the learner perceives success as being under his or her control. Intrinsic and extrinsic motivation are referred to under the *satisfaction* component and focuses on the learner's intrinsic motivation and response to extrinsic awards.

Keller (1987c) notes that one of the challenges of motivation is that it is just as detrimental to learning and performance for learners to be overmotivated as it is for them to be undermotivated. Undermotivation results in low productivity levels, whereas overmotivation results in high error rates and poor efficiency due to stress and overconfidence (pp. 2–3). The typical graphical representation of this is the inverted-U curve, illustrating this result (see Fig. 29.5).

Keller (1987c) uses this inverted-U depiction when he completes audience analyses, plotting the levels of attention, relevance, confidence, and satisfaction on the curve. The rise and fall in performance in relationship to levels of motivation have implications for instruction. It appears that enhancing motivation for learning is an area that should be of concern to researchers: and, as we shall see momentarily, an area that feedback potentially may influence.

In Keller's (1983) original description of the motivational design of instruction, he lists several strategies to enhance motivation, some of which recommend the use of feedback to the learner. For our purposes of considering areas for future feedback research, these deserve closer inspection. They are as follows.

"Increase expectancy for success," which is now included in the model as *confidence,* "by using *attributional feedback* and other devices that help students *connect success* to personal effort and ability" (Keller, 1983, p. 420).

Attributional feedback is important when a student does not perceive a connection between his or her effort and its consequences. This is what was referred to earlier as *learned helplessness.* A person who has developed learned help-lessness toward a task does not perceive any causal link between behavior (effort) and its consequences. This type of learner cannot see the connection between ability and persistence as the key to success. When working with this type of learner, a sequence of problems or assignments should be developed that is initially easy but becomes challenging. After each success, feedback should be given as encouragement to keep trying, and after success on more difficult problems, attributional feedback should be presented. Basically attributional feedback tells learners that their success occurred because they kept trying. Keller (1993) refers to this feedback as being given verbally by a teacher in a classroom situation, but it is easily conceivable that adaptive feedback in other forms that contains the same type of messages would be appropriate.

Enhancing the learner's perception of outcome, now referred to as *satisfaction,* involves both intrinsic and extrinsic motivation. Keller (1983) recommends the following.

1. To maintain intrinsic satisfaction with instruction, use *verbal praise* and *informative feedback* rather than threats, surveillance, or external performance evaluation.
2. To maintain quantity of performance, use *motivating feedback* following the response.
3. To improve the quality of performance, provide *formative* corrective) feedback when it will be immediately useful, usually just *before* the next opportunity to practice. (pp. 426–427)

The first strategy is concerned with the types of consequences that will enhance or suppress intrinsic motivation. Keller (1983) points out that intrinsic motivation is more likely to flourish in a context of positive but noncontrolling consequences than when excessive evaluation and aversive forms of control are used (p. 426). In terms of motivating feedback in the second strategy, the behavioral view of operant conditioning using positive reinforcement again surfaces. As Keller emphasizes, we are more likely to repeat behaviors that have pleasurable consequences than those that do not. When a learner receives positive reinforcement following a desired response, it affects the quantity of performance. One might contest this view of feedback in light of the evolution of feedback research from this type of behavioral view to that of cognition only. But it does make sense in terms of increasing and maintaining motivation or morale.

The third strategy refers to formative feedback, used to affect the quality of performance. It signals a gap between the given performance of the student and the desired performance, and it indicates the actions to take to close the gap. Again, it is easy to see that this is feedback with the purpose of correcting errors, as seen in the latest feedback studies that view feedback from a cognitive standpoint with a predominantly corrective function.

A prototype of motivationally adaptive CAI has been developed using the ARCS model (Song & Keller, 1999, 2001). One study (1999) focused on how three versions of motivationally adaptive CAI affected student achievement, perceived motivation, efficiency, and continuing motivation. The three types of adaptive motivational feedback were (a) motivationally adaptive, (b) motivationally saturated, and (c) motivationally minimized. The motivationally adaptive group showed higher levels of effectiveness, overall motivation, and attention than the other two groups.

In the ARCS model area of relevance, the motivationally adaptive group ranked higher than the motivationally saturated group, but not any higher than the motivationally-minimized group. In the areas of confidence and satisfaction, the motivationally adaptive CAI group did not prove to be more effective than the other two groups. In the case of efficiency, both the motivationally adaptive and the motivationally minimized groups were more efficient than the motivationally saturated CAI group; however, the efficiency of the motivationally adaptive group was identified as the area that offers practical importance to future design. In terms of continuing motivation, the groups were not significantly different, however, a significant correlation was found between students' overall motivation and their continuing motivation across the three groups. This study does support the notion that motivationally adaptive CAI can be an effective, efficient, and motivating form of instruction and that it also may enhance students' continuing motivation (Song & Keller, 1999).

Song and Keller (2001) also examined the prototype of motivationally adaptive CAI on the dynamic aspects of motivation—that is, changes in learner motivation that might occur over time through a lesson. Their results suggest that CAI can respond to changes in motivation levels of learners across time. They also support the use of the ARCS model areas of attention, relevance, confidence, and satisfaction as a useful and effective tool in the design of such dynamic aspects of motivation.

29.6 FEEDBACK FROM A CONSTRUCTIVIST VIEW

29.6.1 Paradigm Shifts

The majority of feedback studies in the literature have examined feedback under the traditional learning theory paradigms of behaviorism and information processing. Both of these theories can be classified as viewing learning from an *objectivist* perspective. The philosophy of objectivism basically holds that "reliable knowledge about the world" exists (Jonassen, 1991, p. 8) and that instruction serves to present this real world knowledge to the student, who will in turn be tested and "give back" this knowledge to demonstrate effective learning. Feedback would then serve to correct misinformation about this external, objective reality. This is, indeed, how most feedback studies are conceived.

The latest philosophy of learning, however, postulates that there is no external knowledge the student merely "takes in"; rather, the student must *construct* his or her own reality or knowledge, and this construction will be based on the learner's prior experiences, mental structures, and beliefs (Brown, Collins, & Duguid, 1988; Cooper, 1993; Duffy & Jonassen, 1991; Jonassen, 1991). Put succinctly, "Knowledge is constructed in the mind of the learner" (Bodner, 1986, p. 873). Thus espouses the philosophy called "constructivism,"

TABLE 29.3. Assumptions of Objectivism (from Jonassen, 1991b) and Suggested Use of Feedback

Objectivism	
Assumption	Feedback
• Reality is external to knower	• Feedback is based upon response match to external reality
• Mind acts as processor of symbols	• Feedback contains symbols for learner to process
• Thought is independent of human experience; reflects external reality	• Feedback not related to human experience; reflects external reality
• Meaning corresponds to categories in the world	• Meaning within feedback information corresponds to categories in the world
• Symbols represent external reality	• Feedback contains symbols that represent external reality

in which each learner constructs his or her own reality through interpretation of experiences of the external world. And given this new view of learning, feedback will likely function differently than from an objectivist view of learning (Mory, 1995).

Recall how early studies of feedback evolved from a behavioral view of feedback as reinforcement to more recent research that advocates an information processing perspective with an emphasis on error correction. Feedback's main function is providing corrective information. Recall also the recently developed models of feedback (Bangert-Drowns et al., 1991; Kozma & Bangert-Drowns, 1987; Kulhavy, 1977; Kulhavy & Stock, 1989) that attempt to explain what happens within the feedback process. These models also contribute to an organization of the many variables that have been examined or even overlooked in past research. All of these studies were conceived under a philosophy of learning that embraces certain assumptions about learning from an objectivist viewpoint. These assumptions and the resulting use of feedback are listed in Table 29.3.

Although there has been progress in determining ways in which feedback can best be used under certain conditions, there are still many areas in which the feedback literature is not consistent and yet other areas that have been left unexplored. One must critically examine feedback in light of the philosophical assumptions underlying these studies to highlight how feedback functions within such contrived experimental settings. The basic assumptions of the objectivist philosophy are presented (Table 29.3) to contrast them with those of a constructivist view. Suggestions for the use and function of feedback within the constructivist philosophy are presented in light of these basic

assumptions in an effort to identify areas in need of further research (see Table 29.4).

Given such an array of inconsistencies in the feedback literature, it is essential to question whether or not researchers are focusing on feedback variables that have real value in the world of the classroom. Many feedback studies are computer-based training (CBT) studies and are not intended to be generalized to a large group setting such as a "typical classroom." In most instructional settings, feedback is presented within some sort of interactional environment, not necessarily one of computer-based or programmed instruction. Perhaps some of the most potent feedback is received within a setting in which the student interacts with some problem he or she is trying to solve, with feedback resulting as a natural phenomenon of the context of instruction. For example, students who are trying to learn to play a musical instrument receive constant feedback from their mistakes just by hearing the sounds that are being produced, regardless of whether or not there is any other external mechanism in place to correct these sounds. Feedback occurs as a natural result of interactions between the learner and his or her own constructions of knowledge. Further, the topics usually being presented in traditional feedback studies are usually a far cry from being anything the learner would be motivated to learn, this being purposefully the case in order to maximize feedback differences. The context in which learning takes place in most of these studies is often artificial and distanced from what a typical learner's interactions with a problem would be. Certainly the inconsistencies in the feedback literature warrant some fresh ideas and perspectives. This researcher proposes that feedback be critically examined within a paradigm that embraces the philosophy of constructivism, in which the learner

TABLE 29.4. Assumptions of Constructivism (from Jonassen, 1991b) and Suggested Use of Feedback

Constructivism	
Assumption	Feedback
• Reality is determined by knower	• Feedback is to guide learner toward internal reality; facilitates knowledge construction
• Mind acts as builder of symbols	• Feedback aids learner in building symbols
• Thought grows out of human experience	• Feedback in context of human experience
• Meaning does not rely on correspondence to world; determined by understander	• Meaning within feedback information determined by internal understanding
• Symbols are tools for constructing an internal reality	• Feedback provides generative, mental construction "tool kits"

must construct his or her own knowledge based on interactions within authentic learning environments.

29.6.2 Applications of Feedback in Constructivism

The philosophy of constructivism opens a new avenue for feedback research. Feedback in a constructivist context would provide intellectual tools and serve as an aid to help the learner construct his or her internal reality. Because learners would be solving complex problems through social negotiation between equal peers and in contextual settings, feedback might also occur in the form of discussion among learners and through comparisons of internally structured knowledge.

Perhaps to understand better what feedback would represent in a constructivist paradigm, consider the earlier transition of research foci from a behavioral view (reinforcement) to a cognitive view (information). As Cooper (1993) suggests,

The move from behaviorism through cognitivism to constructivism represents shifts in emphasis away from an external view to an internal view. To the behaviorist, the internal processing is of no interest; to the cognitivist, the internal processing is only of importance to the extent to which it explains how external reality is understood. In contrast, the constructivist views the mind as a builder of symbols—the tools used to represent the knower's reality. External phenomena are meaningless except as the mind perceives them. (p. 16)

One constructivist principle is that instruction should occur in relevant contexts (Brown et al., 1989; Jonassen, 1991a). Referred to as *situated cognition,* the notion is that learning occurs most effectively in context and that the context becomes part of the actual knowledge base for that learning (Jonassen, 1991b). One approach to this is called *cognitive apprenticeship* (Brown et al., 1989; Collins, Brown, & Newman, 1987), in which learners engage in activity and make deliberate use of both social and physical context, just as an apprentice would do. Feedback in this view would occur in the form of the interactions between the learner and the activity of solving real-world problems. Rather than providing predetermined instructional sequences, feedback could be used as a coaching mechanism that analyzes strategies used to solve these problems (Jonassen, 1991b).

Another constructivist strategy has been termed *cognitive flexibility theory* and involves the presentation of multiple perspectives to learners (Jonassen, 1991b; Spiro, Feltovich, Jacobson, & Coulson, 1991a, 1991b). By stressing conceptual interrelatedness, providing multiple representations of content, and emphasizing "case-based instruction" that includes inherent multiple themes (Jonassen, 1991b), feedback can help learners acquire advanced knowledge in ill-structured domains. Spiro and associates (1991a, 1991b) propose the use of multidimensional and nonlinear hypertext systems to convey ill-structured aspects of knowledge domains and thus promote cognitive flexibility. When a learner approaches a problem from a certain perspective, feedback can serve to guide the learner to revisit the same material in a rearranged context, for a different purpose, from a different conceptual perspective (Spiro et al., 1991a),

or any combination of these. Although implementing cognitive flexibility theory is not just a matter of, using a computer to "connect everything with everything else," as Spiro et al. (1991a, p. 30) state, feedback can be designed into a hypertext system to lead the learner to approach concepts from new perspectives and to provide locator information when a learner feels lost in a "labyrinth of incidental or *ad hoc* connnections" (p. 30). Feedback traditionally has been used to allow the learner to evaluate preset goals through reinforcement of matching responses or through control of instruction. But in the constructivist view, evaluation provided by feedback would become more of a tool for self-analysis (Jonassen, 1991a).

Another constructivist invention is that of the *microworld*—"a small but complete subset of reality in which one can go to learn about a specific domain through personal discovery and exploration" (cited in Rieber, 1992, p. 94). Instructional applications of microworlds conform to Vygotsky's idea of the "zone of proximal development," in which learners who are on the threshold of learning are often unable to attain understanding without some external intervention or assistance (Rieber, 1992). Rieber contends that learning environments such as microworlds should be designed with a "self-oriented feedback loop" (p. 100) that provides a rich and continual stream of information to help students establish and maintain goal setting and goal monitoring. Further, because many complex problems contain so many individual variables that can inundate a novice to the point of frustration, microworlds offer a way to structure the learning environment to a finite set of variables, something Piaget termed *variable stepping* (Rieber, 1992). Feedback received can be judged against a learner's individually defined goals. Rieber (1992) also suggests using a variety of feedback features to complement one another, such as presenting verbal feedback at the same time as visual feedback.

A report by Edwards (1991) focused on how children used feedback from a computer microworld for transformational geometry to discover and correct instances of overgeneralizations that emerged as they solved problems with the microworld. Although there was a tendency toward symbolic overgeneralization in some activities, the children were able to use visual feedback from the microworld and discussions with their partners to correct their own errors.

A summary of the functions of feedback under a constructivist philosophy is presented in Table 29.5. Researchers

TABLE 29.5. Suggested Constructivist Functions
of Feedback (Mory, 1995)

- Aids learner in constructing an internal reality by providing intellectual tools
- Helps learner solve complex problems within contextual, relevant settings
- Occurs as social negotiation between equal peers
- Provides guidance for multiple modes of representation
- Guides learner through ill-structured domains, reminding learner of goals
- Challenges learner toward potential development

are encouraged to pursue the study of feedback under this paradigm.

29.7 BRIDGING THE GAP: A SYNTHESIS MODEL OF FEEDBACK WITH SELF-REGULATED LEARNING

The most recent synthesis of contemporary feedback models views feedback in the context of self-regulated learning (SRL; Butler & Winne, 1995). Butler and Winne (1995) propose a more elaborated examination of feedback that takes into account how feedback affects cognitive engagement with tasks and how engagement relates to achievement. Self-regulated students are aware of aspects of their own knowledge, beliefs, motivations, and cognitive processing, and the most effective learners are self-regulating. The model couples elements from traditional feedback research with processes involved in self-regulation. My view is that the Butler and Winne (1995) model quite possibly may supply the "missing link" between the findings presented in recent reviews (Bangert-Drowns et al., 1991; Kulhavy & Stock, 1989; Mory, 1992) and elements of motivation theory and constructivistic philosophies. Butler and Winne (1995) point out that many studies of SRL have looked at global or aggregate results of multiple SRL activities, rather than at individual instances of self-regulation. They suggest a more "fine-grained analysis of feedback's roles in dynamic cognitive activities that unfold during SRL" (p. 247).

Whereas most studies of feedback have focused on externally provided information, Butler and Winne (1995) postulate that internal feedback is also inherent, as self-regulated learners monitor their own engagement in tasks. The most effective learners develop their own distinct cognitive routines for creating this internal feedback, which in turn affects how they will use information presented within feedback externally. Thus, the feedback serves a multidimensional role in aiding knowledge construction that fits into a model of self-regulation.

Although not usually found in feedback or SRL research, Butler and Winne (1995) cite several areas of research and integrate these areas to aid in understanding the process of self-regulation as it relates to feedback. These include (a) how affect relates to persistence during self-regulation, (b) the role that learner-generated feedback plays in decision making, (c) how students' beliefs affect learning, and (d) what beliefs learners have in the process of conceptual change or restructuring when faced with misconceptions.

Self-regulation is the recursive process of interpreting information based on beliefs and knowledge, goal setting, and strategy applications to generate both mental and behavioral products (see Fig. 29.6). Mental products can include both cognitive and affective domains. Learners monitor their own process of engagement and updated products through internal feedback. They then reinterpret the task and their own engagement, which affects subsequent engagement. Modifications can include altering goals or setting new ones, reviewing and adapting their strategies of learning, and developing new skills. At this point, if external feedback is provided, additional information can be added to help the learner in this process (see Fig. 29.6).

29.7.1 Self-Regulated Engagement

Four lines of research are featured in Butler and Winne's (1995) review of self-regulation. One is a model of self-regulation in

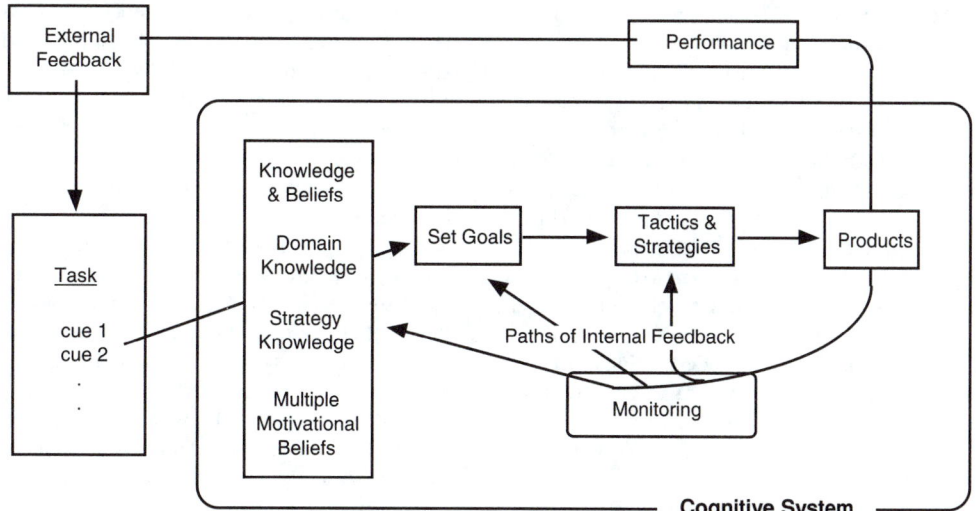

FIGURE 29.6. A model of self-regulated learning). From "Feedback and Self-Regulated Learning," by D. L. Butler and P. H. Winne, 1995, *Review of Educational Research, 65,* 248. Copyright 1995 by the American Educational Research Association. Reprinted with permission.

terms of engagement and affect. Several researchers (Bandura, 1993; Carver & Scheier, 1990; Kuhl & Goschke, 1994; Mithaug, 1993; Zimmerman, 1989) have found that "students' goals couple with motivational beliefs and affective reactions to shape self-regulation" (Butler & Winne, 1995, p. 249). Positive affect results when progress is achieved faster than predicted, and negative affect results when the learner's rate of progress is slower than predicted. According to this model of SRL (Carver & Scheier, 1990), it is predicted that when learners make progress exactly as planned, the affect level that results is neutral rather than positive and that, under some conditions, achievement actually results in a negative affect. These affect levels influence future engagement in the task by shaping confidence judgments during the learner's internal monitoring process (Carver & Scheier, 1990; Eisenberger, 1992; Kuhl & Goschke, 1994).

29.7.2 A Lens Model

The second line of SRL research is from the viewpoint of what is termed a lens model, in which both task characteristics and students' progress on tasks are used to predict final performance. Traditional feedback studies focus on *outcome feedback,* often referred to as knowledge of results. Whereas several studies do focus on adding elaborations to outcome information, most have ignored the role of giving learners guidance that can aid in their own self-regulation. Butler and Winne (1995) propose that data on students' perceptions of cues and their value, along with expectations of success and perceptions of actual achievement, can help researchers know what to provide in elaborated feedback to support self-regulated engagement and to enhance self-calibration. Such feedback has been termed *cognitive feedback* (Balzer, Doherty, & O'Connor, 1989) and can provide learners information that links cues and achievement. Cognitive feedback includes (a) task validity feedback, (b) cognitive validity feedback, and (c) functional validity feedback. *Task validity feedback* includes information provided from an external source that describes that source's perceived relationship between a task's cues and achievement (Butler & Winne, 1995; Elawar & Corno, 1985; Winne, 1989, 1992; Zellermayer, Salomon, Globerson, & Givon, 1991). *Cognitive validity feedback* includes information describing the learner's own perceptions about the cue and achievement relationship (Butler & Winne, 1995). And *functional validity feedback* describes the relationship between the learner's own achievement estimation and the actual end performance. In a review by Balzer and associates (1989), feedback that provided various forms of validity-related information was found to be more effective than outcome feedback, and task validity feedback was somewhat more effective in supporting learning and problem solving than cognitive validity feedback information alone.

Several implications of examining feedback from a lens model viewpoint become evident. When providing outcome feedback, researchers should realize that the effectiveness of the feedback depends on several learner characteristics and behaviors. Students must be attentive to many cues, have accurate memories of cue features when receiving outcome feedback, and be strategic enough to generate effective internal feedback

to themselves. Outcome feedback provides little guidance to the learner on how to self-regulate. However, when applying cognitive feedback, researchers should use information that helps students identify cues and monitor their own task engagement. This monitoring is an essential part of self-regulation.

29.7.3 Learners' Beliefs.

The third line of SRL research examines the relationships among the learner's beliefs about learning, use of strategies, and resulting performance (Schommer, 1990, 1993; Schommer, Crouse, & Rhodes, 1992). Beliefs about learning can affect a student's persistent effort on a given task and goal orientation (Boekaerts, 1994; Carver & Scheier, 1990). These beliefs thus influence subsequent engagement on a task.

29.7.4 Misperceptions in Content

A learner's prior misconceptions about content area can hinder his or her subsequent revisions of that incorrect knowledge (Chinn & Brewer, 1993; Perkins & Simmons, 1988). Whereas students can be receptive and correct misunderstandings through feedback, Chinn and Brewer (1993) identify six negative responses to feedback under such conditions. Students can (a) ignore the feedback, (b) reject the feedback, (c) judge the feedback to be irrelevant, (d) consider the feedback to be unrelated to the belief, (e) reinterpret the feedback to fit the misconceived belief, or (f) make superficial as opposed to fundamental changes in the erroneous belief. In this way, feedback is "filtered" through a learner's existing beliefs about the content.

Butler and Winne (1995) conclude that SRL is inherent in students' construction of knowledge. They assert that differentiating functions of feedback using a broadly framed model of self-regulation synthesizes the diversity of students on feedback and instruction. They identify the potential roles of feedback in remedying both strategy implementation failure and ineffective monitoring.

Students' knowledge and beliefs are linked with their self-regulated engagement in tasks. In addition to their epistemological beliefs, research on self-regulation also points to four other types of knowledge that learners bring to a task: domain knowledge, task knowledge, strategy knowledge, and motivational beliefs. In terms of domain knowledge, students' strong incorrect knowledge structures within a domain result in erratic application of productive learning strategies (Burbules & Linn, 1988). As domain knowledge increases, students tend to acquire, use, and transfer cognitive strategies that support SRL (Salomon & Perkins, 1989). Task knowledge influences self-regulation as well, and learners' beliefs or interpretations of tasks can influence the goals they establish, as well as the cues attended to and acted on as they work on a task (Schommer, 1990).

Strategy knowledge results as students complete tasks. Winne and Butler (1994) identify three types of strategy knowledge. The first, declarative knowledge, involves stating what the strategy is. The second, procedural knowledge, involves how to use a particular strategy. And the third, conditional knowledge, addresses the utility of a strategy, such as when and where to use a strategy and how much effort will be required.

Finally, motivational knowledge involves learners' "beliefs about their capabilities to exercise control over their own level of functioning and over events that affect their lives" (Bandura, 1993, p. 118), referred to as *self-efficacy*. Self-efficacy affects the goals learners will set and their commitment to those goals, decision making while striving to reach those goals, and persistence (Bandura, 1993).

As mentioned in the research on motivation, students can adopt two types of task-related goals—learning goals and performance goals. Butler and Winne (1995) hypothesize that cognitive feedback containing information about task cues will be most effective when given to students that adopt learning goals. Further, the effects of feedback depend on both students' overall goal and the item-to-item change in their total knowledge as they review their wrong answers. The goals that students adopt may be different from the goals intended by the instructor, designer, or researcher. When that is the case, feedback will probably have less stable or predictable effects. Because goals are central in the process of SRL, feedback must address the types of goals students adopt and support their processes for prioritization, selection, and maintenance of these goals (cited in Butler & Winne, 1995).

In terms of students selecting and generating strategies to reach their goals, Winne (1982) notes four particular problems that students encounter. First, learners may fail to recognize the conditions under which to employ the strategy. Second, learners may not understand the task or perceive the task goals and mismatch strategies to goals. Third, students may select good strategies but not know how to apply them. And, finally, students may lack the motivation to expend effort in applying a strategy.

Monitoring is another important aspect of SRL. Monitoring generates internal feedback in the learner that links his or her past performance to the next successive task. The points of linkage are the prime times at which feedback should be given to be most useful (Butler & Winne, 1995).

The ideas put forth by Butler and Winne (1995) may well be the key to linking the two areas of motivation and constructivist philosophy presented earlier in this chapter. Through the blending of SRL research with research on feedback, both the motivational elements involved in learning and the philosophy of constructivism can be addressed. Their model (Butler & Winne, 1995) suggests that feedback is contextualized according to the learner's prior knowledge and beliefs and, consequently, provides insufficient information to affect knowledge construction. They further suggest that for learning in authentic complex tasks, feedback should provide information about cognitive activities that promote learning and the relationships between cues and successive states of achievement.

Note also that the Kulhavy and Stock (1989) model emphasizing response certitude judgments adds credence to the notion that learners both set goals and monitor themselves. But Butler and Winne (1995) fine-tune the issue by hypothesizing that students actually monitor their own *calibration*. Calibration is the extent to which monitoring creates accurate certitude judgments. Butler and Winne (1995) suggest that high-confidence errors result in longer and more intense study of feedback because it is at this point that calibration is at its worst.

Traditional feedback research has been directed narrowly to the effects of feedback on achievement. The Butler and Winne (1995) model is a bridge allowing us to combine diverse studies on feedback, self-regulation, and instruction in such a way that future researchers have a schema for integrating instruction, self-regulation, feedback, and knowledge construction.

Recent research has included the study of the interaction of cognitive styles with varying levels of feedback in multimedia (Khine, 1996), the use of student-to-teacher feedback in Web-based courses (Hazari & Schnorr, 1999), the examination of varying types and uses of tutor feedback (Anderson, Benson, & Lynch, 2001), and the use of global and local feedback in relationship to motivation and anxiety in students (Wiltse, 2001).

In specialized areas of feedback research, metacognitive feedback in SRL resulted in improved performance in mathematical reasoning and explanations. Metacognitive feedback was based on SRL using metacognitive questions that served as cues for understanding math problems (Kramarski & Zeichner, 2001). In self-directed learning in a Web course, elaborative feedback was found to be more valuable to students than just knowledge of a score (Cennamo & Ross, 2000). And in a distance learning course designed for the development of higher-level cognitive skills, evaluation is described as feedback, and not a performance measurement, and, as such, must be diagnostic and prescriptive, be formative and iterative, and involve peers and group assessment (Notar, Wilson, & Ross, 2002).

29.8 ADVANCES IN TECHNOLOGY

The development of the microcomputer and its use for instruction has been perhaps the most important technology for allowing for adaptive feedback. Unlike many technologies of the past decades, the computer opened a door to interactivity, the precise recording of student response information, and the ability to adapt feedback and instruction to the changing needs of the learner within the interactive environment almost instantaneously.

Further, developments in the use of multimedia and hypermedia open a vast set of questions for researchers to consider. For example, how does feedback function when presented via different modes of sensory input? Multimedia PCs common today involve the use of both auditory and visual stimuli to aid learning. What was once possible only through the integration of specialized media such as the interactive laser disc now becomes more commonplace as newer technologies such as CD-ROM and DVD become increasingly common and available. Hypertext and hypermedia designs await the learner using today's interactive CD software, with icons and "hotwords" linking vast amounts of information in the form of text, pictures, animations, and sounds.

A common problem with such open hypermedia environments is that learners often get lost along their exploratory way, unaware of how they were taken to the point at which they now rest. Navigation is just one of many variables to consider when examining such complex environments. Search (1994) suggests that if the communication potential of hypermedia is to be realized designers must develop interfaces with orientation cues that help users navigate through large, multimedia databases. As she phrases it, "Hypermedia computing is a temporal medium in which spatial relationships change dynamically, leaving the user with few references for orientation" (p. 369).

To understand adequately how the nature of computer-based learning has evolved, it is helpful to consider how differently it was utilized in the 1960s compared with how it is used now for interactive computer-based instruction, hypermedia environments, simulations and microworlds, and Web-based instruction (WBI). Jonassen (1993) notes that even early CAI was merely programmed instruction delivered on a computer. The evolutionary path unfolded from programmed instruction, computer-based drills and tutorials, adaptive tutorials, and simulations. An important conceptual framework for hypertext and hypermedia environments is presented by Jonassen (1993). The growth of hypertext, hypermedia, and multimedia since the 1980s has provided designers with the capabilities necessary to develop complex, content-oriented learning environments. To make such large quantities of information more accessible, a variety of conceptual models is being "mapped" onto these environments. The subsequent rapid expansion of information connectivity of the Internet during the 1990s has provided designers with the capabilities necessary to develop complex, content-oriented learning environments.

As Jonassen (1993) so aptly described it,

Recent advances in learning theory have fueled a more rapid and extensive revolution in computer-supported learning systems. Rather than using the computer as a delivery vehicle for displaying and purvey information, generative learning systems and knowledge construction environments are designed to form partnerships with learners/users, to distribute the cognitive load and responsibility to the part of the learning systems that performs the best. Learners are engaged by these environments because their intellectual involvement in the learning process is essential. They are no longer passive recipients of information . . . they are actively involved in knowledge construction and meaning making. The computer's computational functionality is being used to support those processes rather than to present information. (p. 332)

The open architecture of hypermedia and multimedia has made them the platform of choice for implementing such knowledge construction environments. The computers of the future will function as "intellectual toolkits for enhancing the intellectual and perceptual capacities of humans" (p. 333).

A useful framework for designing feedback by incorporating the powers of emerging instructional technologies to present, manipulate, control, and manage educational activities has been proposed by Hannafin et al. (1993). They point out that emerging technologies provide the potential for a dramatic range of varied feedback not possible or practical before.

Feedback design helps in the ability to present information and support encoding. The range of presentation dimensions includes visual, verbal, sensory, and multiple modalities. To optimize both individual processing capabilities and technological potential requires an expansion of our notion of both feedback and technology.

According to Hannafin et al. (1993), emerging technologies have provided six major areas of improvement for instruction: adaptability, realism, hypermedia, open-endedness, manipulability, and flexibility. To design feedback effectively requires the psychological, technological, and pedagogical foundations of lesson design (Hannafin, 1989). The use of the World Wide Web as a delivery system and information database for on-line instruction has enhanced the computer's capabilities and connectivity dramatically.

29.8.1 Web-Based Instruction

The advances and growth in Web-based instruction have certainly changed the types of feedback mechanisms that are being actively used by students. WBI lends itself to a student-centered or constructivist approach that involves learner-to-learner interaction options and provides meaningful peer and instructor feedback (Dabbagh, 2002). The role of feedback in on-line teaching is critical for students' success in the on-line environment. Students have stressed that "they needed regular feedback to know how their performance was judged, how they could improve, and how their final grade was calculated" (Bischoff, 2000, p. 62). Effective elements of on-line teaching are known to include frequent and consistent on-line feedback, timely on-line feedback, diplomatic on-line feedback, and evaluative on-line feedback (Bischoff, 2000).

Schwartz and White (2000) emphasize the distinction between *formative* feedback, which modifies a student's thinking or behavior for the purpose of learning, and *summative* feedback, which assesses how well a student accomplishes a task or achieves a result for the purpose of grading. These researchers emphasize the importance of the need for on-line feedback to be (a) multidimensional, (b) nonevaluative, (c) supportive, (d) student controlled, (e) timely, and (f) specific. These equate to the following qualities that students expect from feedback in the on-line environment.

- Prompt, timely, and thorough on-line feedback
- Ongoing formative feedback about on-line group discussions
- Ongoing summative feedback about grades
- Constructive, supportive, and substantive on-line feedback
- Specific, objective, and individual on-line feedback
- Consistent on-line feedback

Others (Ritchie & Hoffman, 1997) suggest that there should be a relationship between descriptors and the links they represent by the use of a meaningful system. "A more meaningful system would be to use words such as 'definition,' 'example,' or 'nonexample' when teaching concepts or principles; 'definition' or 'mnemonic' when teaching facts; and 'shortest path' or 'alternative path' when teaching a procedure" (p. 137). They also recommend requiring students to make an informed choice among alternatives after engaging a segment of instruction. Another, more complex method of providing feedback uses CGI (Common Gateway Interface) codes to provide learners with detailed information and alternative choices. With such CGI scripts, information that students place in text fields, buttons, or check boxes can be compared to preset answers in a database or text file. This allows for feedback to provide students with a deeper explanation of the consequences of their choices, along with active links to guide them to additional information. The use of feedback in Web-based assignments is also discussed in detail in terms of pedagogical aspects of feedback, the frequent lack of feedback in on-line courses in higher education, and instructor support for feedback in a Web system by other researchers (Collis et al., 2001).

The use of dynamic Web databases opens up an extremely fertile area for both gathering student information that can be used to give individual feedback based on background variables, as well as providing specific feedback about various misconceptions or insights during on-line learning. Dynamic databases are currently being studied and implemented to facilitate collaboration, knowledge construction, and communication in on-line courses (McNeil & Robin, 2000a, 2000b).

Other emphases in on-line learning environments include the need for building on-line communities (Ravitz, 1997) and interactions in both synchronous and asynchronous modes (Vrasidas & McIsaac, 2000). Feedback can be used to help foster on-line learning communities and a feeling of "connectedness" through peer-to-peer interactions as well as student-to-instructor interactions. The type and the timing of such interactions in terms of synchronous and asynchronous are a ripe area for researchers to begin to study the effects of these communications in terms of feedback in the learning environment. Web-based learning opens the door for more of a constructivist view of learning and its implications for new ways of utilizing feedback (see also Mory, 1996).

Psychological foundations emphasize the role of the learner in processing inputs, organizing and restructuring knowledge, and generating responses. Particularly relevant are processing requirements, the role of prior knowledge, the role of active processing, and strength encoding (Hannafin et al., 1993, p. 272).

Technological foundations concern the capabilities of the actual hardware and devices for providing output, receiving input, and processing data. Emphasis is on input–output capability, symbol manipulation, and management. In many instances, technological capabilities far exceed human processing capacity. Therefore, what is most important is not what the outer limits of technology are but, rather, how to utilize those technological capacities (Hannafin et al., 1993).

Pedagogical foundations of design are rooted in beliefs about how to organize lesson knowledge, how to sequence activities in the lesson, and how to support the learner as he or she acquires knowledge. Many times pedagogical factors are identified during a needs assessment or front-end analysis and include the resources and constraints of learner, task, and setting characteristics (Hannafin et al., 1993).

As one might expect, even with emerging, high-profile technologies, distinctions of "good instruction, bad instruction" hold true (Hannafin et al., 1993). This includes the design of "good and bad" feedback within instruction as well. Research issues in the area of motivating students within the WBI environment have been examined by Song (2000), looking individually at the motivation to initiate, motivation to persist, and motivation to continue within such an environment. Song (2000) has identified motivational issues related to each area, and Song and Keller (1999, 2001) have suggested motivational adaptations in the area of CAI (detailed under *Motivation*). One can easily understand how results from the CAI studies (Song & Keller, 1999, 2001) could easily be transferred to the WBI environment.

29.9 RECOMMENDATIONS TO FUTURE RESEARCHERS

To summarize areas in feedback research that need further attention, this author offers the following suggestions.

1. Examine how feedback functions within a wider variety of learning domains. Higher-order learning such as concept acquisition, rule use, problem solving, and the use of cognitive strategies offers a rich source for researchers to explore.
2. Analyze individual learner motivations and attitudes and prescribe feedback based on factors such as tenacity, self-efficacy, attributions, expectancy, and goal structure.
3. Identify measurable variables that can reflect internal cognitive and affective processes of learners that might potentially affect how feedback is perceived and utilized.
4. Examine how feedback functions within constructivist learning environments and test new feedback strategies within these environments.
5. Examine the role of monitoring and how both external and internal feedback generation affects the learning from a viewpoint of self-regulation.
6. As technologies continue to advance, design feedback that utilizes the improved capabilities for instruction.
7. Continue to identify and test interactive patterns among the learner, the environment, individual internal knowledge construction, and varying types of feedback.

One could venture to say that no learning would occur unless some type of feedback mechanism was at work. What we do know is that feedback serves a critical function in knowledge acquisition, regardless of the particular learning paradigm through which we choose to examine it.

Although the study of feedback in instruction has a vast history and an ever-evolving set of variables of interest, researchers are challenged to go back and study further the complexities of feedback under the variety of models and conditions described here and in past reviews (Mory, 1992, 1996). There are many questions that have been left unresolved from older paradigms and theoretical views. And yet there is an ever-increasing need to consider how new technologies and views of learning change and impact the functions of feedback, its forms, and its dynamic potential for use in instructional settings. Future researchers are encouraged to consider past research variables, carefully, in combination with new pedagogical views of learning and changes in learning environments as technology continues to develop, as they seek to tease out how feedback is used by learners in various learning environments. Particularly as learning environments become more disparate in terms of time and space, feedback is going to be an increasingly complex and critical aspect of successful learning.

References

Ahmad, M. (1988). The effect of computer-based feedback on using cognitive strategies of problem solving. *Proceedings of selected research papers, Association for Educational Communications and Technology, Research and Theory Division* (pp. 1-22). New Orleans, LA: AECT.

Anderson, K., Beson, C., & Lynch, T. (2001). Feedback on writing: Attitudes and uptake. *Edinburgh Working Papers in Applied Linguistics, 11,* 1-20.

Anderson, J. R., Conrad, C. G., & Corbett, A. T. (1989). Skill acquisition and the LISP Tutor. *Cognitive Science, 13,* 467-505.

Anderson, R. C., & Faust, G. W. (1967). The effects of strong formal prompts in programmed instruction. *American Educational Research Journal, 4,* 345-352.

Anderson, R. C., Kulhavy, R. W., & Andre, T. (1971). Feedback procedures in programmed instruction. *Journal of Educational Psychology, 62,* 148-156.

Anderson, R. C., Kulhavy, R. W., & Andre, T. (1972). Conditions under which feedback facilitates learning from programmed lessons. *Journal of Educational Psychology, 63,* 186-188.

Andre, T., & Thieman, A. (1988). Level of adjunct question, type of feedback, and learning concepts by reading. *Contemporary Educational Psychology, 13,* 296-307.

Ausubel, D. P. (1968). *Educational psychology: A cognitive view.* New York: Holt, Rinehart and Winston.

Balzer, W. K., Doherty, M. E., & O'Connor, R. (1989). Effects of cognitive feedback on performance. *Psychological Bulletin, 106,* 410-433.

Bandura, A. (1977). Self-efficacy: Toward a unifying theory of behavior change. *Psychological Review, 84*(2), 191-215.

Bandura, A. (1982). Self-efficacy mechanism in human aging. *American Psychologist, 37*(2), 122-147.

Bandura, A. (1993). Perceived self-efficacy in cognitive development and functioning. *Educational Psychologist, 28,* 117-148.

Bangert-Drowns, R. L., Kulik, C. C., Kulik, J. A., & Morgan, M. T. (1991). The instructional effect of feedback in test-like events. *Review of Educational Research, 61*(2), 218-238.

Bardwell, R. (1981). Feedback: How does it function? *Journal of Experimental Education, 50,* 4-9.

Barringer, C., & Gholson, B. (1979). Effects of type and combination of feedback upon conceptual learning by children: Implications for research in academic learning. *Review of Educational Research, 49*(3), 459-478.

Birenbaum, M., & Tatsuoka, K. K. (1987). Effects of "on-line" test feedback on the seriousness of subsequent errors. *Journal of Educational Measurement, 24*(2), 145-155.

Birney, R. C., Burdick, H., & Teevan, R. C. (1969). *Fear of failure.* New York: Van Nostrand.

Bischoff, A. (2000). The elements of effective online teaching: Overcoming the barriers to success. In K. W. White & B. H. Weight (Eds.), *The online teaching guide: A handbook of attitudes, strategies, and techniques for the virtual classroom* (pp. 57-72). Boston: Allyn and Bacon.

Bodner, G. M. (1986). Constructivism: A theory of knowledge. *Journal of Chemical Education, 63,* 873-878.

Boekaerts, M. (1994). Action control: How relevant is it for classroom learning? In J. Kuhl & J. Beckmann (Eds.), *Volition and personality: Action versus state orientation* (pp. 427-435). Seattle, WA: Hogrefe & Huber.

Brackbill, Y., & Kappy, M. S. (1962). Delay of reinforcement and retention. *Journal of Comparative and Physiological Psychology, 55,* 14-18.

Brackbill, Y., Bravos, A., & Starr, R. H. (1962). Delay improved retention of a difficult task. *Journal of Comparative Psychology, 55,* 947-952.

Briggs, L. J., & Hamilton, N. R. (1964). Meaningful learning and retention: Practice and feedback variables. *Review of Educational Research, 34,* 545-558.

Brown, J. S., Collins, A., & Duguid, P. (1989). Situated cognition and the culture of learning. *Educational Researcher, 18*(1), 32-42.

Bruner, J. (1990). *Acts of meaning.* Cambridge, MA: Harvard University Press.

Burbules, N. C., & Linn, M. C. (1988). Response to contradiction: Scientific reasoning during adolescence. *Journal of Educational Psychology, 80,* 67-75.

Butler, D. L., & Winne, P. H. (1995). Feedback and self-regulated learning: A theoretical synthesis. *Review of Educational Research, 65*(3), 245-281.

Butterfield, E. C., Nelson, T. O., & Peck, V. (1988). Developmental aspects of the feeling of knowing. *Developmental Psychology, 24*(5), 654-663.

Carter, J. (1984). Instructional learner feedback: A literature review with implications for software development. *The Computing Teacher, 12*(2), 53-55.

Carver, C. S., & Scheier, M. F. (1990). Origins and functions of positive and negative affect: A control-process view. *Psychological Review, 97,* 19-35.

Cennamo, K. S., & Ross, J. D. (2000, April). *Strategies to support self-directed learning in a web-based course.* Paper presented at the Annual Meeting of the American Educational Research Association, New Orleans, LA.

Chanond, K. (1988). The effects of feedback, correctness of response and response confidence on learners' retention in computer-assisted instruction. (Doctoral dissertation, University of Texas at Austin, 1988). *Dissertation Abstracts International, 49,* 1358A.

Char, R. O. (1978). The effect of delay of informative feedback on the retention of verbal information and higher-order learning, for college students. (Doctoral dissertation, Florida State University, 1978). *Dissertation Abstracts International, 40,* 748A.

Chinn, C. A., & Brewer, W. F. (1993). The role of anomalous data in knowledge acquisition: A theoretical framework and implications for science instruction. *Review of Educational Research, 63,* 1-49.

Clariana, R. B. (1999, February). *Differential memory effects for immediate and delayed feedback: A delta rule explanation of feedback timing effects.* Paper presented at the Association for Educational Communications and Technology annual convention, Houston, TX.

Clariana, R. B. (2000, October). *A connectionist model of instructional feedback effects.* Annual Proceedings of Selected Research and

Development Papers presented at the National Convention of the Association for Educational Communications and Technology, Denver, CO.

Clariana, R. B., Ross, S. M., & Morrison, G. R. (1991). The effects of different feedback strategies using computer-administered multiple-choice questions as instruction. *Educational Technology Research & Development, 39*(2), 5-17.

Clariana, R. B., Wagner, D., & Murphy, L. C. (2000). Applying a connectionist description of feedback timing. *Educational Technology Research and Development, 43*(3), 5-21.

Clark, R. E., Aster, D., & Hession, M. A. (1987, April). *When teaching kills learning: Types of mathemathantic effects.* Paper presented at the annual meeting of the American Educational Research Association, Washington, DC.

Cognition and Technology Group at Vanderbilt. (1990). Anchored instruction and its relationship to situated cognition. *Educational Researcher, 19*(6), 2-10.

Cognition and Technology Group at Vanderbilt. (1991a). Technology and the design of generative learning environments. *Educational Technology, 31*(5), 34-40.

Cognition and Technology Group at Vanderbilt. (1991b). Some thoughts about constructivism and instructional design. *Educational Technology, 31*(9), 16-18.

Cognition and Technology Group at Vanderbilt. (1992a). The Jasper experiment: An exploration of issues in learning and instructional design. *Educational Technology Research & Development, 40*(1), 65-80.

Cognition and Technology Group at Vanderbilt. (1992b). The Jasper Series as an example of anchored instruction: Theory, program description, and assessment data. *Educational Psychologist, 27*(3), 291-315.

Cohen, V. B. (1985). A reexamination of feedback in computer-based instruction: Implications for instructional design. *Educational Technology, 25*(1), 33-37.

Collins, A., Brown, J. S., & Newman, S. E. (1987). Cognitive apprenticeship: Teaching the craft of reading, writing, and mathematics. In L. Resnick (Ed.), *Learning, knowing, and instruction: Essays in honor of Robert Glaser* (pp. 453-494). Hillsdale, NJ: Lawrence Erlbaum.

Collis, B., De Boer, W., & Slotman, K. (2001). Feedback for web-based assignments. *Journal of Computer Assisted Learning, 17,* 306-313.

Cooper, P. A. (1993, May). Paradigm shifts in designed instruction: From behaviorism to cognitivism to constructivism. *Educational Technology,* 12-19.

Covington, M. V. (1983). Motivated cognitions. In S. G. Paris, G. M. Olson, & H. W. Stevenson (Eds.), *Learning and motivation in the classroom.* Hillsdale, NJ: Lawrence Erlbaum.

Covington, M. V., & Omelich, C. L. (1979). Are causal attributions causal? A path analysis of the cognitive model of achievement motivation. *Journal of Personality and Social Psychology, 37,* 1487-1504.

Covington, M. V., & Omelich, C. L. (1981). As failures mount: Affective and cognitive consequences of ability demotion in the classroom. *Journal of Educational Psychology, 73,* 796-808.

Covington, M. V., & Omelich, C. L. (1982). Achievement anxiety, performance and behavioral instruction: A cost/benefits analysis. In R. Schwarzer, H. van der Ploeg, & C. Speilberger (Eds.), *Test anxiety research* (Vol. 1). Amsterdam: Swets & Zeitlinger.

Covington, M. V., & Omelich, C. L. (1984). Task-oriented versus competitive learning structures: Motivational and performance consequences. *Journal of Educational Psychology, 76*(6), 1038-1050.

Cunningham, D. J. (1991). Assessing constructions and constructing assessments. *Educational Technology,* 13-17.

Dabbagh, N. (2002). The evolution of authoring tools and hypermedia learning systems: Current and future implications. *Educational Technology, 42*(4), 24-31.

Deci, E. L. (1972). Intrinsic motivation, extrinsic reinforcement, and inequity. *Journal of Personality and Social Psychology, 22*(1), 113-120.

Dempsey, J. V. (1988). The effects of four methods of immediate corrective feedback on retention, discrimination error, and feedback study time in computer-based instruction. (Doctoral dissertation, Florida State University, 1988). *Dissertation Abstracts International, 49,* 1434A.

Dempsey, J. V., & Driscoll, M. P. (1994). *Conceptual error and feedback: The relationship between content analysis and confidence of response.* Manuscript submitted for publication.

Dempsey, J. V., & Wager, S. U. (1988). A taxonomy for the timing of feedback in computer-based instruction. *Educational Technology, 28*(10), 20-25.

Dempsey, J. V., Driscoll, M. P., & Litchfield, B. C. (1993). Feedback, retention, discrimination error, and feedback study time. *Journal of Research on Computing in Education, 25*(3), 303-326.

Dempsey, J. V., Driscoll, M. P., & Swindell, L. K. (1993). Text-based feedback. In J. V. Dempsey and G. C. Sales (Eds.), *Interactive instruction and feedback* (pp. 21-54). Englewood Cliffs, NJ: Educational Technology Publications.

Dick, W., Carey, L,.& Carey, J. O. (2001). *The systematic design of instruction* (5th ed.). New York: Addison, Wesley, Longman.

Duffy, T. M., & Jonassen, D. (1991, May). Constructivism: New implications for instructional technology? *Educational Technology,* 7-12.

Dweck, C. S. (1986). Motivational processes affecting learning. *American Psychologist, 41*(10), 1040-1048.

Dweck, C. S., & Legget, E. L. (1988). A social-cognitive approach to motivation and personality. *Psychology Review, 95*(2), 256-273.

Edwards, L. D. (1991). Children's learning in a computer microworld for transformation geometry. *Journal for Research in Mathematics Education, 22*(2), 122-137.

Elawar, M. C., & Corno, L. (1985). A factorial experiment in teachers' written feedback on student homework: Changing teacher behavior a little rather than a lot. *Journal of Educational Psychology, 77,* 162-173.

Eisenberger, R. (1992). Learned industriousness. *Psychological Review, 99,* 248-267.

Elley, W. B. (1966). The role of errors in learning with feedback. *British Journal of Educational Psychology, 35-36,* 296-300.

Erez, M., & Zidon, I. (1984). Effect of goal acceptance on the relationship of goal difficulty to performance. *Journal of Applied Psychology, 69,* 69-78.

Ferguson, G. A. (1981). *Statistical analysis in psychology and education* (5th ed.). New York: McGraw-Hill.

Fischer, P. M., & Mandl, H. (1988). Knowledge acquisition by computerized audio-visual feedback. *European Journal of Psychology of Education, 111,* 217-233.

Forsyth, D. R., & McMillan, J. H.(1981). Attributions, affect, and expectations: A test of Weiner's three-dimensional model. *Journal of Educational Psychology, 73*(3), 393-403.

Gagné, R. M. (1985). *The conditions of learning* (4th ed.). New York: CBS College.

Gagné, R. M., & Driscoll, M. P. (1988). *Essentials of learning for instruction* (2nd ed.). Upper Saddle River, NJ: Prentice Hall.

Gagné, R. M., Briggs, L. J., & Wager, W. W. (1992). *Principles of instructional design* (4th ed.). New York: Holt, Rinehart and Winston.

Gardner, H. (1999). Multiple approaches to understanding. In C. M. Reigeluth (Ed.), *Instructional-design theories and models: A new paradigm of instructional theory Vol. II* (pp. 69-89). Mahwah, NJ: Lawrence Earlbaum Associates.

Gaynor, P. (1981). The effect of feedback delay on retention of computer-based mathematical material. *Journal of Computer-Based Instruction, 8*(2), 28–34.

Gilman, D. A. (1969). Comparison of several feedback methods for correcting errors by computer-assisted instruction. *Journal of Educational Psychology, 60*(6), 503–508.

Hanna, G. S. (1976). Effects of total and partial feedback in multiple-choice testing upon learning. *Journal of Educational Research, 69,* 202–205.

Hannafin, M. J. (1989). Interactive strategies and emerging instructional technologies: Psychological perspectives. *Canadian Journal of Educational Communication, 18*(3), 167–180.

Hannafin, M. F., Hannafin, K. M., & Dalton, D. W. (1993). Feedback and emerging instructional technologies. In J. V. Dempsey and G. C. Sales (Eds.), *Interactive instruction and feedback* (pp. 263–286). Englewood Cliffs, NJ: Educational Technology.

Hannafin, M., Land, S., & Oliver, K. (1999). Open learning environments: Foundations, methods, and models. In C. M. Reigeluth (ed.), *Instructional-design theories and models: A new paradigm of instructional theory Vol. II* (pp. 115–140). Mahwah, NJ: Lawrence Earlbaum Associates.

Hazari, S., & Schnorr, D. (1999). Leveraging student feedback to improve teaching in Web-based courses. *T.H.E. Journal, 26*(11), 30–37.

Hoska, D. M. (1993). Motivating learners through CBI feedback: Developing a positive learner perspective. In J. V. Dempsey & G. C. Sales (Eds.), *Interactive instruction and feedback* (pp. 105–132). Englewood Cliffs, NJ: Educational Technology.

Jacobs, J. W., & Dempsey, J. V. (1993). Simulation and gaming: Fidelity, feedback, and motivation. In J. V. Dempsey & G. C. Sales (Eds.), *Interactive instruction and feedback* (pp. 197–227). Englewood Cliffs, NJ: Educational Technology.

Johnson, D. W., & Johnson, R. T. (1993). Cooperative learning and feedback in technology-based instruction. In J. V. Dempsey & G. C. Sales (Eds.), *Interactive instruction and feedback* (pp. 133–157). Englewood Cliffs, NJ: Educational Technology.

Jonassen, D. H. (1988). Interactive designs for courseware. In D. H. Jonassen (Ed.), *Instructional designs for microcomputer courseware* (pp. 97–102). Hillsdale, NJ: Lawrence Erlbaum.

Jonassen, D. H. (1990, May). Thinking technology: Toward a constructivist view of instructional design. *Educational Technology,* 32–34.

Jonassen, D. H. (1991a). Context is everything. *Educational Technology, 31*(6), 33–34.

Jonassen, D. H. (1991b). Objectivism versus constructivism: Do we need a new philosophical paradigm? *Educational Technology Research and Development, 39*(3), 5–14.

Jonassen, D. H. (1993). Conceptual frontiers in hypermedia environments for learning. *Journal of Educational Multimedia and Hypermedia, 2*(4), 331–335.

Jonassen, D. H. (1999). Designing constructivist learning environments. In C. M. Reigeluth (Ed.), *Instructional-design theories and models: A new paradigm of instructional theory Vol. II* (pp. 215–239). Mahwah, NJ: Lawrence Earlbaum Associates.

Keller, J. M. (1983). Motivational design of instruction. In C. M. Reigeluth (Ed.), *Instructional-design theories and models: An overview of their current status* (pp. 383–434). Hillsdale, NJ: Lawrence Erlbaum.

Keller, J. M. (1987a). Development and use of the ARCS model of instructional design. *Journal of Instructional Development, 10*(3), 2–10.

Keller, J. M. (1987b). Strategies for stimulating the motivation to learn. *Performance & Instruction, 26*(8), 1–7.

Keller, J. M. (1987c). The systematic process of motivational design. *Performance and Instruction, 26*(9), 1–8.

Keller, J. M., & Kopp, T. (1987). An application of the ARCS model of motivational design. In C. M. Reigeluth (Ed.), *Instructional theories in action: Lessons illustrating selected theories and models* (pp. 289–320). Hillsdale, NJ: Lawrence Erlbaum Associates.

Keller, J. M., & Suzuki, K. (1987). Use of ARCS motivation model in courseware design. In D. H. Jonassen (Ed.), *Instructional designs for microcomputer courseware* (pp. 409–434). Hillsdale, NJ: Lawrence Erlbaum Associates.

Kelley, H. H. (1973). The processes of causal attribution. *American Psychologist, 28,* 107–128.

Khine, M. S. (1996). The interaction of cognitive styles with varying levels of feedback in multimedia presentation. *International Journal of Instructional Media, 23*(3), 229–236.

Klausmeier, H. J. (1976). Instructional design and the teaching of concepts. In J. R. Levin & V. L. Allen (Eds.), *Cognitive learning in children* (pp. 191–217). New York: Academic Press.

Koestner, R., Zuckerman, M., & Koestner, J. (1987). Praise involvement and intrinsic motivation. *Journal of Personality and Social Psychology, 53*(2), 383–390.

Kowitz, G. T., & Smith, J. C. (1985, October). The dynamics of successful feedback. *Performance & Instruction Journal,* 4–6.

Kowitz, G. T., & Smith, J. C. (1987, October). The four faces of feedback. *Performance & Instruction,* 33–36.

Kozma, R., & Bangert-Drowns, R. L. (1987). *Design in context: A conceptual framework for the study of computer software in higher education.* Ann Arbor: University of Michigan, National Center for Research to Improve Postsecondary Teaching and Learning. (ERIC Document Reproduction Service No. 287 436)

Kramarski, B., & Zeichner, O. (2001). Using technology to enhance mathematical reasoning: Effects of feedback and self-regulation learning. *Education Media International.* http://www.tandf.co.uk/journals.

Kuhl, J., & Goschke, T. (1994). A theory of action control: Mental subsystems, modes of control, and volitional conflict-resolution strategies. In J. Kuhl & J. Beckmann (Eds.), *Volition and personality: Action versus state orientation* (pp. 93–124). Seattle, WA: Hogrefe & Huber.

Kulhavy, R. W. (1977). Feedback in written instruction. *Review of Educational Research, 47*(1), 211–232.

Kulhavy, R. W., & Anderson, R. C. (1972). Delay-retention effect with multiple-choice tests. *Journal of Educational Psychology, 63*(5), 505–512.

Kulhavy, R. W., & Parsons, J. A. (1972). Learning-criterion error perseveration in text materials. *Journal of Educational Psychology, 63*(1), 81–86.

Kulhavy, R. W., & Stock, W. A. (1989). Feedback in written instruction: The place of response certitude. *Educational Psychology Review, 1*(4), 279–308.

Kulhavy, R. W., & Wager, W. (1993). Feedback in programmed instruction: Historical context and implications for practice. In J. V. Dempsey & G. C. Sales (Eds.), *Interactive instruction and feedback* (pp. 3–20). Englewood Cliffs, NJ: Educational Technology.

Kulhavy, R. W., Yekovich, F. R., & Dyer, J. W. (1976). Feedback and response confidence. *Journal of Educational Psychology, 68*(5), 522–528.

Kulhavy, R. W., Yekovich, F. R., & Dyer, J. W. (1979). Feedback and content review in programmed instruction. *Contemporary Educational Psychology, 4,* 91–98.

Kulhavy, R. W., White, M. T., Topp, B. W., Chan, A. L., & Adams, J. (1985). Feedback complexity and corrective efficiency. *Contemporary Educational Psychology, 10,* 285–291.

Kulhavy, R. W., Stock, W. A., Hancock, T. E., Swindell, L. K., & Hammrich, P. (1990). Written feedback: Response certitude and durability. *Contemporary Educational Psychology, 15,* 319-332.

Kulhavy, R. W., Stock, W. A., Thornton, N. E., Winston, K. S., & Behrens, J. T. (1990). Response feedback, certitude and learning from text. British *Journal of Educational Psychology, 60,* 161-170.

Kulik, J. A., & Kulik, C.-L. C. (1988). Timing of feedback and verbal learning. *Review of Educational Research, 58*(1), 79-97.

Lebow, D. (1993). Constructivist values for instructional systems design: Five principles toward a new mindset. *Educational Technology Research & Development, 41*(3), 4-16.

Lee, O. M. (1985). The effect of type of feedback on rule learning in computer based instruction (Doctoral dissertation, Florida State University, 1985). *Dissertation Abstracts International, 46,* 955A.

Lee, D., Smith, P. L., & Savenye, W. (1991). The effects of feedback and second try in computer-assisted instruction for rule-learning task. *Proceedings of selected research papers, Association for Educational Communications and Technology, Research and Theory Division* (pp. 441-432). Orlando, FL: AECT.

Lewis, M. W., & Anderson, J. R. (1985). Discrimination of operator schemata in problem solving: Learning from examples. *Cognitive Psychology, 17,* 26-65.

Lhyle, K. G., & Kulhavy, R. W. (1987). Feedback processing and error correction. *Journal of Educational Psychology, 79*(3), 320-322.

Litchfield, B. C. (1987). The effect of presentation sequence and generalization formulae on retention of coordinate and successive concepts and rules in computer-based instruction (Doctoral dissertation, Florida State University, 1987). *Dissertation Abstracts International, 49,* 486A.

Locke, E. A., Shaw, K. N., Saari, L. M., & Latham, G. P. (1981). Goal setting and task performance: 1969-1980. *Psychological Bulletin, 90,* 125-152.

Malone, T. W. (1981). Toward a theory of intrinsically motivating instruction. *Cognitive Science, 4,* 333-369.

Mayer, R. H. (1999). Designing instruction for constructivist learning. In C. M. Reigeluth (ed.), *Instructional-design theories and models: A new paradigm of instructional theory Vol. II* (pp. 141-159). Mahwah, NJ: Lawrence Earlbaum Associates.

McCullers, J. C., Fabes, R. A., & Moran, J. D., III (1987). Does intrinsic motivation theory explain the adverse effects of rewards on immediate task performance? *Journal of Personality and Social Psychology, 52*(5), 1027-1033.

McLeod, P., Plunkett, K., & Rolls, E. T. (1998). *Introduction to connectionist modeling of cognitive processes.* Oxford, UK: Oxford University Press.

McNeil, S. G., & Robin, B. R. (2000a, February). *Using web database tools to facilitate the construction of knowledge in online courses.* Proceedings of the Society for Information Technology and Teacher Education International Conference, San Diego, CA.

McNeil, S. G., & Robin, B. R. (2000b, November). *Using web database tools to facilitate the construction of knowledge in online courses.* WebNet 2000 World Conference on the WWW and Internet Proceedings, San Antonio, TX.

Merrill, J. (1987). Levels of questioning and forms of feedback: Instructional factors in courseware design. *Journal of Computer-Based Instruction, 14*(1), 18-22.

Merrill, M. D. (1983). Component display theory. In C. M. Reigeluth (Ed.), *Instructional design theories and models* (pp. 279-333). Hillsdale, NJ: Lawrence Erlbaum Associates.

Merrill, M., & Tennyson, R. (1977). *Teaching concepts: An instructional design guide.* Englewood Cliffs, NJ: Educational Technology.

Metcalfe, J. (1986). Feeling of knowing in memory and problem solving.

Journal of Experimental Psychology: Learning, Memory, and Cognition, 12(2), 288-294.

Meyer, L. (1986). Strategies for correcting students' wrong responses. *Elementary School Journal, 87,* 227-241.

Mithaug, D. E. (1993). *Self-regulation theory: How optimal adjustment maximizes growth.* Westport, CT: Praeger.

Mory, E. H. (1991). *The effects of adaptive feedback on student performance, feedback study time, and lesson efficiency within computer-based instruction.* Unpublished doctoral dissertation, Florida State University, Tallahassee.

Mory, E. H. (1992). The use of informational feedback in instruction: Implications for future research. *Educational Technology Research and Development, 40*(3), 5-20.

Mory, E. H. (1994). The use of response certitude in adaptive feedback: Effects on student performance, feedback study time, and efficiency. *Journal of Educational Computing Research, 11*(3), 263-290.

Mory, E. H. (1995, February). *A new perspective on instructional feedback: From objectivism to constructivism.* Paper presented at the annual meeting of the Association for Educational Communications and Technology, Anaheim, CA.

Mory, E. H. (1996). Feedback research. In D. H. Jonassen (Ed.), *Handbook of research for educational communications and technology.* New York: Simon & Schuster Macmillan.

Nelson, T. O. (1988). Predictive accuracy of the feeling of knowing across different criterion tasks and across different subject populations and individuals. In M. M. Gruneberg, P. E. Morris, & R. N. Sykes (Eds.), *Practical aspects of memory* (Vol. 1, pp. 190-196). New York: John Wiley & Sons.

Nelson, T. O., Leonesio, R. J., Landwehr, R. S., & Narens, L. (1986). A comparison of three predictors of an individual's memory performance: The individual's feeling of knowing versus the normative feeling of knowing versus base-rate item difficulty. *Journal of Experimental Psychology: Learning, Memory, and Cognition, 12*(2), 279-287.

Nolen-Hoeksema, S., Seligman, M. E., & Girgus, J. S. (1986). Learned helplessness in children: A longitudinal study of depression, achievement, and explanatory style. *Journal of Personality and Social Psychology, 51*(2), 435-442.

Noonan, J. V. (1984). *Feedback procedures in computer-assisted instruction: Knowledge-of-results, knowledge-of-correct-response, process explanations, and second attempts after errors.* Unpublished doctoral dissertation, University of Illinois, Urbana-Champaign.

Notar, C. E., Wilson, J. D., & Ross, K. G. (2002). Distant learning for the development of higher-level cognitive skills. *Education, 122*(4), 642-650.

Park, O. C., & Tennyson, R. D. (1986). Computer-based response-sensitive design strategies for selecting presentation form and sequence of examples in learning of coordinate concepts. *Journal of Educational Psychology, 78*(2), 153-158.

Peeck, J. (1979). Effects of differential feedback on the answering of two types of questions by fifth- and sixth-graders. *British Journal of Educational Psychology, 49,* 87-92.

Peeck, J., & Tillema, H. H. (1979). Delay of feedback and retention of correct and incorrect responses. *Journal of Experimental Education, 47,* 171-178.

Peeck, J., van den Bosch, A. B., & Kreupeling, W. J. (1985). Effects of informative feedback in relation to retention of initial responses. *Contemporary Educational Psychology, 10,* 303-313.

Perkins, D. N., & Simmons, R. (1988). Patterns of misunderstanding: An integrative model for science, math, and programming. *Review of Educational Research, 58,* 303-326.

Peterson, S. K., & Swindell, L. K. (1991, April). *The role of feedback in written instruction: Recent theoretical advance.* Paper presented at the annual meeting of the American Educational Research Association, Chicago, IL.

Phye, G. D. (1979). The processing of informative feedback about multiple-choice test performance. *Contemporary Educational Psychology, 4,* 381-394.

Phye, G. D., & Andre, T. (1989). Delayed retention effect: Attention, perseveration, or both? *Contemporary Educational Psychology, 14,* 173-185.

Phye, G. D., & Bender, T. (1989). Feedback complexity and practice: Response pattern analysis in retention and transfer. *Contemporary Educational Psychology, 14,* 97-110.

Phye, G. D., Gugliamella, J., & Sola, J. (1976). Effects of delayed retention on multiple-choice test performance. *Contemporary Educational Psychology, 1,* 26-36.

Pressey, S. L. (1926). A simple device which gives tests and scores—and teaches. *School and Society, 23,* 373-376.

Pressey, S. L. (1927). A machine for the automatic teaching of drill material. *School and Society, 25,* 549-552.

Ravitz, J. (1997, February). *An ISD model for building online communities: Furthering the dialogue.* Proceedings of Selected Research and Development Presentations at the national convention of the Association for Educational Communications and Technology, Albuquerque, NM.

Reigeluth, C. M., & Stein, F. S. (1983). The elaboration theory of instruction. In C. M. Reigeluth (Ed.), *Instructional design theories and models* (pp. 335-381). Hillsdale, NJ: Lawrence Erlbaum Associates.

Richards, D. R. (1989). A comparison of three computer-generated feedback strategies. *Proceedings of selected research papers, Association for Educational Communications and Technology, Research and Theory Division* (pp. 357-368). Dallas, TX: AECT.

Rieber, L. P. (1992). Computer-based microworlds: A bridge between constructivism and direct instruction. *Educational Technology Research & Development, 41*(1), 93-106.

Ritchie, D. C., & Hoffman, B. (1997). Incorporating instructional design principles with the World Wide Web. In B. H. Khan (Ed.), *Web-based instruction.* Englewood Cliffs, NJ: Educational Technology.

Roper, W. J. (1977). Feedback in computer-assisted instruction. *Programmed Learning and Educational Technology, 14,* 43-49.

Sales, G. C. (1993). Adapted and adaptive feedback in technology-based instruction. In J. V. Dempsey & G. C. Sales (Eds.), *Interactive instruction and feedback* (pp. 159-175). Englewood Cliffs, NJ: Educational Technology.

Salomon, G., & Globerson, T. (1987). Skill may not be enough: The role of mindfulness in learning and transfer. *International Journal of Educational Research, 11,* 623-637.

Sassenrath, J. M. (1975). Theory and results on feedback and retention. *Journal of Educational Psychology, 67*(6), 894-899.

Sassenrath, J. M., & Garverick, C. M. (1965). Effects of differential feedback from examinations on retention and transfer. *Journal of Educational Psychology, 56*(5), 259-263.

Sassenrath, J. M., & Yonge, G. D. (1968). Delayed information feedback, feedback cues, retention set, and delayed retention. *Journal of Educational Psychology, 59*(2), 69-73.

Sassenrath, J. M., & Yonge, G. D. (1969). Effects of delayed information feedback and feedback cues in learning on delayed retention. *Journal of Educational Psychology, 60*(3), 174-177.

Schimmel, B. J. (1983, April). *A meta-analysis of feedback to learners in computerized and programmed instruction.* Paper presented at the annual meeting of the American Educational Research Association, Montreal. (ERIC Document Reproduction Service No. ED 233 708)

Schimmel, B. J. (1988). Providing meaningful feedback in courseware. In D. H. Jonassen (Ed.), *Instructional designs for microcomputer courseware* (pp. 183-195). Hillsdale, NJ: Lawrence Erlbaum Associates.

Schloss, P. J., Sindelar, P. T., Cartwright, P. G., & Schloss, C. N. (1987-1988). The influence of error correction procedures and question type on student achievement in computer assisted instruction. *Journal of Educational Technology Systems, 16*(1), 17-27.

Schmidt, R. A., Young, D. E., Sinnen, S., & Shapiro, D. C. (1989). Summary knowledge of results for skill acquisition: Support for the guidance hypothesis. *Journal of Experimental Psychology: Learning, Memory, and Cognition, 15*(2), 352-359.

Schommer, M. (1990). Effects of beliefs about the nature of knowledge on comprehension. *Journal of Educational Psychology, 82,* 498-504.

Schommer, M. (1993). Epistemological development and academic performance among secondary students. *Journal of Educational Psychology, 85,* 406-411.

Schommer, M., Crouse, A., & Rhodes, N. (1992). Epistemological beliefs and mathematical text comprehension: Believing it is simple does not make it so. *Journal of Educational Psychology, 84,* 435-443.

Schooler, L. J., & Anderson, J. R. (1990). The disruptive potential of immediate feedback. *Proceedings of the Twelfth Annual Conference of the Cognitive Science Society* (pp. 702-708). Cambridge, MA.

Schwartz, F., & White, K. (2000). Making sense of it all: Giving and getting online course feedback. In K. W. White & B. H. Weight (Eds.), *The online teaching guide: A handbook of attitudes, strategies, and techniques for the virtual classroom* (pp. 57-72). Boston: Allyn and Bacon.

Search, P. (1993). HyperGlyphs: Using design and language to define hypermedia navigation. *Journal of Educational Multimedia and Hypermedia, 2*(4), 369-380.

Seligman, M. E. (1990). *Learned optimism.* New York: Alfred A. Knopf.

Seligman, M. E., Maier, S. F., & Geer, J. H. (1968). Alleviation of learned helplessness in the dog. *Journal of Abnormal Psychology, 73,* 256-262.

Shanks, D. R. (1995). *The psychology of associative learning.* Cambridge, UK: Cambridge University Press.

Siegel, M. A., & Misselt, A. L. (1984). Adaptive feedback and review paradigm for computer-based drills. *Journal of Educational Psychology, 76,* 310-317.

Skinner, B. F. (1958). Teaching machines. *Science, 128,* 969-977.

Skinner, B. F. (1968). *The technology of teaching.* New York: Appleton-Century-Crofts.

Smith, P. L., & Ragan, T. J. (1993). Designing instructional feedback for different learning outcomes. In J. V. Dempsey & G. C. Sales (Eds.), *Interactive instruction and feedback* (pp. 75-103). Englewood Cliffs, NJ: Educational Technology.

Song, S. H. (2000). Research issues of motivation in web-based instruction. *Quarterly Review of Distance Education, 1*(3), 225-229.

Song, S. H., & Keller, J. M. (1999, February). The ARCS Model for developing motivationally-adaptive computer-assisted instruction. In *Proceedings of selected research and development papers presented at the national Convention of the Association for Educational Communications and Technology,* Houston, TX.

Song, S. H., & Keller, J. M. (2001). Effectiveness of motivationally adaptive computer-assisted instruction on the dynamic aspects of motivation. *Educational Technology Research and Development, 49*(2), 5-22.

Spiro, R. J., Feltovich, P. J., Jacobson, M. J., & Coulson, R. L. (1991a, May). Cognitive flexibility, constructivism, and hypertext: Random access instruction for advanced knowledge acquisition in ill-structured domains. *Educational Technology, 24*-33.

Spiro, R. J., Feltovich, P. J., Jacobson, M. J., & Coulson, R. L. (1991b, September). Knowledge representation, content specification, and the development of skill in situation-specific knowledge assembly: Some constructivist issues as they relate to cognitive flexibility theory and hypertext. *Educational Technology*, 22-25.

Sturges, P. T. (1969). Verbal retention as a function of the informativeness and delay of information feedback. *Journal of Educational Psychology, 60*, 11-14.

Sturges, P. T. (1972). Information delay and retention: Effect of information in feedback and tests. *Journal of Educational Psychology, 63*, 32-43.

Surber, J. R., & Anderson, R. C. (1975). Delay-retention effect in natural classroom settings. *Journal of Educational Psychology, 67*(2), 170-173.

Swindell, L. (1991, April). *Testing a model of feedback in written instruction.* Paper presented at the annual meeting of the American Educational Research Association, Chicago, IL.

Swindell, L. K. (1992). Certitude and the constrained processing of feedback. *Contemporary Educational Psychology, 17*, 30-37.

Swindell, L. K., Kulhavy, R. W., & Stock, W. A. (1992). *The role of response confidence in comprehension and memory for written instruction.* Manuscript submitted for publication.

Swindell, L. K., Peterson, S. E., & Greenway, R. (1992). Children's use of response confidence in the processing of instructional feedback. *Contemporary Educational Psychology, 17*, 379-385.

Tait, K., Hartley, J. R., & Anderson, R. C. (1973). Feedback procedures in computer-assisted arithmetic instruction. *British Journal of Educational Psychology, 43*, 161-171.

Tennyson, R. D., & Cocchiarella, M. J. (1986). An empirically based instructional design theory for teaching concepts. *Review of Educational Research, 56*(1), 40-71.

Tennyson, R. D., & Park, O. C. (1980). The teaching of concepts: A review of instructional design research literature. *Review of Educational Research, 50*(1), 55-70.

Tessmer, M., Wilson, B., & Driscoll, M. (1990). A new model of concept teaching and learning. *Educational Technology Research and Development, 38*(1), 45-53.

Tosti, D. T. (1978). Formative feedback. *NSPI Journal, 13*, 19-21.

Travers, R. M., van Wagenen, R. K., Haygood, D. H., & McCormick, M. (1964). Learning as a consequence of the learner's task involvement under different conditions of feedback. *Journal of Educational Psychology, 55*(3), 167-173.

Tucker, S. A. (1993). Evaluation as feedback in instructional technology: The role of feedback in program evaluation. In J. V. Dempsey & G. C. Sales (Eds.), *Interactive instruction and feedback* (pp. 301-342). Englewood Cliffs, NJ: Educational Technology.

Vance, R. J., & Coella, A. (1990). Effects of two types of feedback on goal acceptance and personal goals. *Journal of Applied Psychology, 75*(1), 68-76.

Vrasidas, C., & McIsaac, M.S. (2000). Principles of pedagogy and evaluation for web-based learning. *Education Media International.* http://www.tandf.co.uk/journals.

Wager, S. U. (1983). The effect of immediacy and type of informative feedback on retention in a computer-assisted task. (Doctoral dissertation, Florida State University, 1983). *Dissertation Abstracts International, 44*, 2100A.

Wager, W., & Wager, S. (1985). Presenting questions, processing responses, and providing feedback in CAI. *Journal of Instructional Development, 8*(4), 2-8.

Waldrop, P. B., Justen, J. E., & Adams, T. M. (1986). A comparison of three types of feedback in a computer-assisted instruction task. *Educational Technology, 26*, 43-45.

Webster's new world dictionary of the American language, 4th ed., (2001). Foster City, CA: IDG Books Worldwide.

Weiner, B. (1972). *Theories of motivation: From mechanism to cognition.* Chicago: Rand McNally.

Weiner, B. (1979). A theory of motivation for some classroom experiences. *Journal of Educational Psychology, 71*, 3-25.

Weiner, B. (1980). *Human motivation.* New York: Holt, Rinehart & Winston.

Wentling, T. L. (1973). Mastery versus nonmastery instruction with varying test item feedback treatments. *Journal of Educational Psychology, 65*(1), 50-58.

Widrow, B., & Hoff, M.E. (1960). Adaptive switching circuits. *1960 IRE WESCON Convention Record* (Pt. 4), 96-104.

Willis, J. (2000). The maturing of constructivist instructional design: Some basic principles that can guide practice. *Educational Technology, 40*(1), 5-16.

Wilson, B. (1986). What is a concept? Cognitive teaching and cognitive psychology. *Performance and Instruction, 25*(10), 16-18.

Wiltse, E. M. (2001, August). *The effects of motivation and anxiety on students' use of instructor comments.* Paper presented at the Annual Meeting of the Association for Education in Journalism and Mass Communication

Winne, P. H. (1989). Theories of instruction and intelligence for designing artificially intelligent tutoring systems. *Educational Psychologist, 24*, 229-259.

Winne, P. H. (1992). State-of-the-art instructional computing systems that afford instruction and bootstrap research. In M. Jones & P. H. Winne (Eds.), *Foundations and frontiers of adaptive learning environments* (pp. 349-380). Berlin: Springer-Verlag.

Young, M. F. (1993). Instructional design for situated learning. *Educational Technology Research & Development, 41*(1), 43-58.

Zellermayer, M., Salomon, G., Globerson, T., & Givon, H. (1991). Enhancing writing-related metacognitions through a computerized writing partner. *American Educational Research Journal, 28*, 373-339.

Zimmerman, B. J. (Ed.). (1990). Self-regulated learning and academic achievement [Special issue]. *Educational Psychologist, 25*(1).

Zimmerman, B. J., & Martinez-Pons, M. (1992). Perceptions of efficacy and strategy use in the self-regulation of learning. In D. H. Schunk & J. L. Meece (Eds.), *Student perceptions in the classroom* (pp. 185-207). Hillsdale, NJ: Lawrence Erlbaum.

·30·

COOPERATION AND THE USE OF TECHNOLOGY

David W. Johnson and Roger T. Johnson
University of Minnesota

30.1 TECHNOLOGY IN THE CLASSROOM

We live in an historical period in which knowledge is the most critical resource for social and economic development and people need to be able to participate in a networked, information-based society. Whereas previously people engaged in manufacturing-based work where they generally competed with or worked independently of each other, now people engage in information- and technological-rich work where they work in teams. People need to be able to work collaboratively in designing, using, and maintaining the tools of technology. Technology and teamwork will continuously play a larger role in most people's lives. Children, adolescents, and young adults have no choice but to develop and increase their technological and teamwork literacy. There is no better place for them to begin than in school. Learning in cooperative groups while utilizing the tools of technology should occur at all grade levels and in all subject areas.

Because the nature of technology used by a society influences what the society is and becomes, individuals who do not become technologically literate will be left behind. Influences of a technology include the nature of the medium, the way the medium extends human senses, and the type of cognitive processing required by the medium. Harold Adam Innis (1964, 1972) proposed that media biased toward lasting a long time, such as stone hieroglyphics, lead to small, stable societies because stone was difficult to edit and rewrite and was too heavy to distribute over great distances. In contrast, media biased toward traveling easily across distances, such as papyrus, enabled the Romans to build and run a large empire. Marshall McLuhan (1964) believed that the way the media technology balances the senses creates its own form of thinking and communicating and eventually alters the balance of human senses. He believed that oral communication makes hearing dominant and thought simultaneous and circular. Written communication makes sight

dominant and thought may be linear (one thing follows another), rational (cause and effect), and abstract. Electronic technology tends to recreate the village on a global scale through instantaneous and simultaneous communication in which physical distance between people becomes irrelevant. On a more negative note, Neil Postman (1985) expressed fears that our ability to reason with rigor and self-discipline is being eroded as fewer people read systematically and more people watch and listen to electronic media. Their thinking may become more reactive and impressionistic.

Given the pervasive and powerful effects media that technologies can have on the nature of society and the thinking and communicating of its members, there can be little doubt that technology will increasingly be utilized in instructional situations. In the past, however, teachers and schools have been very slow in adopting new technologies and very quick in discontinuing their use (Cuban, 1986). There tends to be a cycle in which (a) the potential of a technology leads to fervent claims and promises by advocates, (b) its utility is demonstrated by academic research in a small set of classrooms rich with human and technical support, (c) teachers who have little or no resources adopt the technology and are frustrated by their failure to make it work, and (d) the use of the new technology gradually declines. With the invention of motion pictures, for example, Thomas Edison predicted that films of great teachers would replace live classroom teachers. When radio was invented the prediction was made that teachers would soon be obsolete because all over the country students could sit and listen to great minds lecture via the radio. Similar predictions were made when television and computers were first invented.

The failure of schools to adopt available instructional technologies and to maintain (let alone continuously improve) their use may be due at least in part to two barriers: (a) the individual assumption underlying most hardware and software development and (b) the failure to utilize cooperation learning as an inherent part of using instructional technologies. The purpose of this chapter is to clarify the interdependence between instructional technologies and cooperation among students in using the technologies. To understand how cooperative learning may be used with technologies, the nature of cooperative learning needs to be defined, the theoretical foundations on which it is based need to be clarified, the research validating its use needs to be reviewed, distinctions between cooperative learning and other types of instructional groups need to be make, and the basic elements that make cooperation work must be defined. At that point, the interrelationships between cooperative learning and technology-supported instruction can be noted and their complementary strengths delineated. The future of technology-assisted cooperative learning can then be discussed.

30.2 THE INDIVIDUAL ASSUMPTION

Before the 1990s, most of the research on computer-supported learning was based on the single-learner assumption. The *individual assumption* is that instruction should be tailored to each student's personal aptitude, learning style, personality characteristics, motivation, and needs. Computers were viewed as an important tool for individualizing learning experiences, especially for computer-assisted instruction programs based on programmed learning, but also for learning experiences derived from constructivist principles (Crook, 1994). Many hardware and software designers (as well as teachers) assumed that all technology-supported instruction should be structured individualistically (one student to a computer) and computer programs were written accordingly.

The ability of designers to adapt instruction sequences to the cognitive and affective needs of each learner, however, is limited by three factors.

1. Substantial variation exists in types of learning styles and personality traits, and although many of them are sometimes correlated with achievement, few have been shown to predict achievement consistently.
2. Little agreement exists on how to translate differences in learning styles and personal traits into instructional prescriptions. The only design rule that is widely accepted is that students should control the flow of information.
3. Creating algorithms to adapt instruction to individual needs and designing and producing multiple versions of lessons are both time-consuming and expensive.

Thus, the potential for individualized instruction may be limited due to the difficulties associated with identifying individual differences and translating them into instructional prescriptions. In addition, individualized instruction has several shortcomings:

1. Individual work isolates students and working alone for long periods may lower personal motivation by increasing boredom, frustration, anxiety, and the perception that learning is impersonal.
2. Individual instruction limits the resources available to themselves and the technology. The support and encouragement

of peers and the cognitive benefits associated with explaining to peers and developing shared mental models are lost.
3. Individualized instruction greatly increases development and hardware costs. A workstation is required for each learner, which entails considerable hardware expense. Considerable development and software expenses are required, as the lessons have to be designed to personalize instruction and to adapt the instructional sequenced to individual processing requirements.

The difficulties associated with identifying and accommodating individual needs severely limit designers' ability to individualize instruction. The shortcomings of individualized instruction call into question the wisdom of designing individualized programs. Despite these problems, however, much of the instructional software has been and is designed, developed, and marketed for individual use.

This omission of social interaction in computer-based learning experiences worried many educators in the 1980s (Baker, 1985; Cuban, 1986; Hawkins, Sheingold, Gearhart, & Berger, 1982; Isenberg, 1992). Given the limitations of the individual assumption, and its shortcomings, technology may be more productively used when it is used in combination with cooperation learning. The spontaneous cooperation often reported around technology, in addition, both casts doubt on the individual assumption made by hardware and software designers and points toward the use of cooperative learning in technology-supported instruction (Dyer, 1994). To use cooperative learning, however, educators must understand its nature.

30.3 THE NATURE OF COOPERATIVE LEARNING

There are advantages to embedding technology-supported instruction in cooperative learning. Cooperative learning may be distinguished from traditional "direct transfer" models of instruction in which the instructor is assumed to be the distributor of knowledge and skills. To understand technology-supported cooperative learning, you must understand the nature of cooperative learning, the theoretical foundations on which it is based, the research validating its use, the distinctions between cooperative learning and other types of instructional groups, and the basic elements that make cooperation work (Fig. 30.1).

30.3.1 Cooperative Learning

Cooperation is working together to accomplish shared goals. Within cooperative activities individuals seek outcomes that are beneficial to themselves and beneficial to all other group members. *Cooperative learning* is the instructional use of small groups so that students work together to maximize their own and each other's learning. In cooperative learning situations there is a positive interdependence among students' goal attainments; students perceive that they can reach their learning goals if and only if the other students in the learning group also

Social Interdependence		
Cooperative	Competitive	Individualistic
Research: Why Use Cooperative Learning		
Effort To Achieve	Positive Relationships	Psychological Health
Five Basic Elements				
Positive Inter-dependence	Individual Accountability	Promotive Interaction	Social Skills	Group Processing
Cooperative Learning		
Formal Coop Learning	Informal Coop Learning	Coop Base Groups
Make Preinstructional Decisions	Conduct Introductory Focused Discussion	Opening Class Meeting To Check Homework, Ensure Members Understand Academic Material, Complete Routine Tasks Such As Attendance
Explain Task And Cooperative Structure	Conduct Intermittent Pair Discussions Every Ten Or Fifteen Minutes	Ending Class Meeting To Ensure Members Understand Academic Material, Homework Assignment
Monitor Learning Groups And Intervene To Improve Taskwork & Teamwork	Conduct Closure Focused Discussion	Members Help And Assist Each Other Learn In-Between Classes
Assess Student Learning And Process Group Effectiveness		Conduct Semester Or Year Long School Or Class Service Projects
Cooperative School		
Teaching Teams	Site-Based Decision Making	Faculty Meetings
Constructive Conflict			
Students		Faculty	
Academic Controversy	Negotiating, Mediating	Decision-Making Controversy	Negotiating, Mediating
Civic Values				
Work For Mutual Benefit, Common Good	Equality Of All Members	Trusting, Caring Relationships	View Situations From All Perspectives	Unconditional Worth Of Self, Diverse Others

FIGURE 30.1. Cooperative learning.

reach their goals (Deutsch, 1962; D. W. Johnson & R. Johnson, 1989).

Technology-supported cooperative learning exists when the instructional use of technology is combined with the use of cooperative learning groups. Cooperative learning is usually contrasted with **competitive learning** (students working to achieve goals that only a few can attain; students can succeed if and only if the other students in the class fail to obtain their goals) and **individualistic learning** (students working alone on goals independent from the goals of others) (Deutsch, 1962; D. W. Johnson & R. Johnson, 1989).

30.3.2 Collaborative Learning

Cooperative learning is sometimes differentiated from **collaborative learning**, which has its roots in the world of Sir James Britton (1990) and others in England in the 1970s. Quoting Vygotsky (1978), Britton notes that just as the individual mind is derived from society, a student's learning is derived from the community of learners. Britton is quite critical of educators who wish to provide specific definitions of the teacher's role. He recommends placing students in groups and letting them generate their own culture, community, and procedures for learning.

Britton believed in ***natural learning*** (learning something by making intuitive responses to whatever our efforts throw up) rather than ***training*** (the application of explanations, instructions, or recipes for action). The source of learning is interpersonal; learning is derived from dialogues and interactions with other students and sometimes the teacher. He viewed structure provided by teachers as manipulation that creates training, not learning, and therefore teachers should assign students to groups, provide no guidelines or instructions, and stay out of their way until the class is over. As an educational procedure, therefore, collaborative learning has historically been much less structured and more student directed than cooperative learning, with only vague directions given to teachers about its use. The vagueness in the role of the teacher and students results in a vagueness of definition of the nature of collaborative learning. Although there is a clear definition of cooperative learning, there is considerable ambiguity about the meaning of collaborative learning. The two terms (cooperative learning and collaborative learning) are, therefore, usually used as interchangeable and synonymous.

30.3.3 Types of Cooperative Learning

There are four types of cooperative learning that may be used in combination with instructional technology: formal cooperative learning, informal cooperative learning, cooperative base groups, and academic controversy.

Formal cooperative learning is students working together, for one class period to several weeks, to achieve shared learning goals and complete jointly specific tasks and assignments (such as decision making or problem solving, completing a curriculum unit, writing a report, conducting a survey or experiment, reading a chapter or reference book, learning vocabulary, or answering questions at the end of a chapter; D. W. Johnson, Johnson, & Holubec, 1998a, 1998b). Any course requirement or assignment may be reformulated to be cooperative. In formal cooperative learning groups, teachers:

1. **Make a number of preinstructional decisions.** A teacher has to decide on the objectives of the lesson (both academic and social skills objectives), the size of groups, the method of assigning students to groups, the roles students will be assigned, the materials needed to conduct the lesson, and the way the room will be arranged.
2. **Explain the task and the positive interdependence.** A teacher clearly defines the assignment, teaches the required concepts and strategies, specifies the positive interdependence and individual accountability, gives the criteria for success, and explains the expected social skills to be engaged.
3. **Monitor students' learning and intervene within the groups to provide task assistance or to increase students' interpersonal and group skills.** A teacher systematically observes and collects data on each group as it works. When it is needed, the teacher intervenes to assist students in completing the task accurately and in working together effectively.
4. **Evaluate students' learning and help students process how well their groups functioned.** Students' learning is carefully assessed and their performances are evaluated. Members of the learning groups then process how effectively they have been working together.

Informal cooperative learning consists of having students work together to achieve a joint learning goal in temporary, ad-hoc groups that last from a few minutes to one class period (D. W. Johnson et al., 1998b; D. W. Johnson, Johnson, & Smith, 1998). During a lecture, demonstration, or film they can be used to focus student attention on the material to be learned, set a mood conducive to learning, help set expectations as to what will be covered in a class session, ensure that students cognitively process the material being taught, and provide closure to an instructional session. Informal cooperative learning groups are often organized so that students engage in 3- to 5-min ***focused discussions*** before and after a lecture and 2- to 3-min ***turn-to-your-partner*** discussions interspersed every 15 min or so throughout a lecture.

Cooperative base groups are long-term, heterogeneous cooperative learning groups with stable membership (D. W. Johnson et al., 1998b; D. W. Johnson, Johnson, & Smith, 1998). The purposes of the base group are to give the support, help, encouragement, and assistance each member needs to make academic progress (attend class, complete all assignments, learn) and develop cognitively and socially in healthy ways. Base groups meet daily in elementary school and twice a week in secondary school (or whenever the class meets).

The fourth type of cooperative learning is ***academic controversy,*** which exists when one student's ideas, information, conclusions, theories, and opinions are incompatible with those of another, and the two seek to reach an agreement (D. W. Johnson & R. Johnson, 1979, 1995). Teachers structure academic controversies by choosing an important intellectual issue, assigning students to groups of four, dividing the group into two pairs, and assigning one pair the pro position and the other pair a con position. Students then follow the five-step controversy procedure of (a) preparing the best case possible for their assigned position, (b) persuasively presenting the best case possible for their position to the opposing pair, (c) having an open discussion in which the two sides argue forcefully and persuasively for their position while subjecting the opposing position to critical analysis, (d) reversing perspectives, and (e) dropping all advocacy coming to a consensus as to their best reasoned judgment about the issue.

In all four types of cooperative learning, repetitive lessons can be scripted so they become classroom routines. ***Cooperative learning scripts*** are standard cooperative procedures for conducting generic, repetitive lessons and managing classroom routines (D. W. Johnson et al., 1998a, 1998b). They are used to organize course routines and generic lessons that occur repeatedly. Some examples are checking homework, preparing for and reviewing a test, drill-reviewing facts and events, reading textbooks and reference materials, writing reports and essays, giving presentations, learning vocabulary, learning concepts, doing projects such as surveys, and problem solving. All of these instructional activities may be done cooperatively and, once planned and conducted several times, will become automatic activities in the classroom. They may also be used in combination to form an overall lesson.

Cooperative learning is being used throughout preschools, elementary and secondary schools, colleges, and adult education programs because of its blend of theory, research, and practice. It is being used throughout the world, that is, throughout North America and Europe and in Central and South America, Africa, the Middle East, Asia, and the Pacific Rim. Cooperative learning's popularity is based on its theoretical basis, which has been validated by hundreds of research studies.

30.4 THEORETICAL FOUNDATIONS OF COOPERATIVE LEARNING

Whereas computers have been used as educational tools since the 1970s, integrating the design and deployment of computers with educational theory has been difficult and largely absent. Technology-supported instruction, for example, needs to be integrated into the theories underlying the use of cooperative learning. There are at least three general theoretical perspectives that have guided research on cooperative learning—cognitive-developmental, behavioral, and social interdependence. The *cognitive developmental or constructivist perspective* is based largely on the theories of Piaget and Vygotsky. The work of Piaget and related theorists is based on the premise that when individuals cooperate on the environment, sociocognitive conflict occurs that creates cognitive disequilibrium, which in turn stimulates perspective-taking ability and cognitive development. The work of Vygotsky and related theorists is based on the premise that knowledge is social, constructed from cooperative efforts to learn, understand, and solve problems. The *behavioral learning theory perspective* focuses on the impact of group reinforcers and rewards on learning. Skinner focused on group contingencies, Bandura focused on imitation, and Homans as well as Thibaut and Kelley focused on the balance of rewards and costs in social exchange among interdependent individuals. While the cognitive-developmental and behavioral theoretical orientations have their followings, the theory dealing with cooperation that has generated by far the most research is the *social interdependence theory*.

Social interdependence exists when individuals share common goals and each person's success is affected by the actions of the others (Deutsch, 1962; D. W. Johnson & R. Johnson, 1989). It may be differentiated from *social dependence* (i.e., the outcomes of one person, are affected by the actions of a second person, but not vice versa) and *social independence* (i.e., individuals' outcomes are unaffected by each other's actions). There are two types of social interdependence: cooperative and competitive. The absence of social interdependence and dependence results in individualistic efforts.

Theorizing on *social interdependence* began in the early 1900s, when one of the founders of the Gestalt School of Psychology, Kurt Koffka, proposed that groups were dynamic wholes in which the interdependence among members could vary. One of his colleagues, Kurt Lewin, refined Koffka's notions in the 1920s and 1930s while stating that (a) the essence of a group is the interdependence among members (created by common goals), which results in the group being a "dynamic whole," so that a change in the state of any member or subgroup changes the state of any other member or subgroup, and (b) an intrinsic state of tension within group members motivates movement toward the accomplishment of the desired common goals. In the late 1940s, one of Lewin's graduate students, Morton Deutsch (1949, 1962), extended Lewin's reasoning about social interdependence and formulated a theory of cooperation and competition. Deutsch conceptualized three types of social interdependence—positive, negative, and none. Deutsch's basic premise was that the type of interdependence structured in a situation determines how individuals interact with each other, which in turn largely determines outcomes. Positive interdependence tends to result in promotive interaction, negative interdependence tends to result in oppositional or contrient interaction, and no interdependence results in an absence of interaction. Depending on whether individuals promote or obstruct each other's goal accomplishments, there is substitutability, cathexis, and inducibility. The relationship between the type of social interdependence and the interaction pattern it elicits is assumed to be bidirectional. Each may cause the other. Deutsch's theory has served as a major conceptual structure for the study of social interdependence since the late 1940s.

30.5 RESEARCH ON SOCIAL INTERDEPENDENCE

The research on social interdependence is notable for the sheer amount of work done, the long history of the work, the wide variety of dependent variables examined, the generalizability and external validity of the work, and the sophistication of the research reviews.

A great deal of research on social interdependence has been conducted. In North America, the first study was published in 1898. Between that time and 1989, over 550 experimental and 100 correlational studies were conducted on social interdependence (see D. W. Johnson & R. Johnson, 1989, for a complete listing of these studies). Hundreds of other studies have used social interdependence as the dependent rather than the independent variable. In our own research program at the Cooperative Learning Center at the University of Minnesota since the late 1960s we have conducted over 90 studies to refine our understanding of how cooperation works. In terms of sheer quantity of research, social interdependence theory is one of the most examined aspects of human nature.

The research on social interdependence has been conducted in 11 historical decades. Research subjects have varied as to age, sex, economic class, ethnicity, nationality, and cultural background. A wide variety of research tasks, ways of structuring social interdependence, and measures of the dependent variables has been used. Many researchers with markedly different theoretical and practical orientations working in different

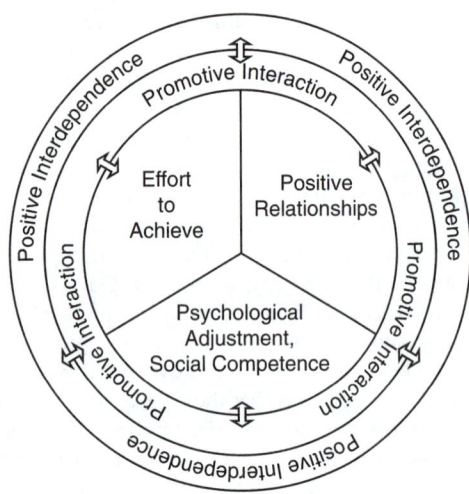

FIGURE 30.2. Outcomes of cooperation. From *Coopration and Competition: Theory and Research*, by D. W. Johnson and R. Johnson, 1989 Edina, MN: Interaction Book Company. Reprinted by permission.

settings and even in different countries have conducted the research. The diversity of subjects, settings, age levels, and operationalizations of social interdependence and the dependent variables give this work an external validity and a generalizability rarely found in the social sciences.

A wide variety of dependent variables has been examined in the research on social interdependence. These numerous dependent variable may be subsumed within the broad categories of (D. W. Johnson & R. Johnson, 1989) interaction pattern, effort to achieve, positive interpersonal relationships, and psychological health (Fig. 30.2).

30.5.1 Interaction Patterns

Two heads are better than one.
—Heywood

Positive interdependence creates promotive interaction. ***Promotive interaction*** occurs as individuals encourage and facilitate each other's efforts to reach the group's goals (such as maximizing each member's learning). Group members promote each other's success by (D. W. Johnson & R. Johnson, 1989):

1. Giving and receiving help and assistance. In cooperative groups, members both give and receive work related and personal help and support. Hooper (1992a) found a positive and significant correlation between achievement and helping behaviors.
2. Exchanging resources and information. Group members seek information and other resources from each other, comprehend information accurately and without bias, and make optimal use of the information provided (e.g., Cosden &

English, 1987; Hawkins et al., 1982; Webb, Ender, & Lewis, 1986). There are a number of beneficial results from (a) orally explaining, elaborating, and summarizing information and (b) teaching one's knowledge to others. Yueh and Alessi (1988) found that a combination of group and individual rewards resulted in increased peer teaching. Explaining and teaching increase the degree to which group members cognitively process and organize information, engage in higher-level reasoning, attain insights, and become personally committed to achieving. Listening critically to the explanations of groupmates provides the opportunity to utilize other's resources.

3. Giving and receiving feedback on taskwork and teamwork behaviors. In cooperative groups, members monitor each other's efforts, give immediate feedback on performance, and, when needed, give each other help and assistance. Carrier and Sales (1987) found that students working in pairs chose elaborative feedback more frequently than did those working alone.
4. Challenging each other's reasoning. Intellectual controversy promotes curiosity, motivation to learn, reconceptualization of what one's knows, higher-quality decision making, greater insight into the problem being considered, higher-level reasoning, and cognitive development (D. W. Johnson & R. Johnson, 1995). LOGO environments may especially engender conflicts among ideas and subsequent negotiation and resolution of that conflict (Clements & Nastasi, 1985, 1988; Lehrer & Smith, 1986).
5. Advocating increased efforts to achieve. Encouraging others to achieve increases one's own commitment to do so.
6. Mutually influencing each other's reasoning and behavior. Group members actively seek to influence and be influenced by each other. If a member has a better way to complete the task, groupmates usually quickly adopt it.
7. Engaging in the interpersonal and small group skills needed for effective teamwork.
8. Processing how effectively group members are working together and how the group's effectiveness can be continuously improved.

Negative interdependence typically results in oppositional interaction. ***Oppositional interaction*** occurs as individuals discourage and obstruct each other's efforts to achieve. Individuals focus both on increasing their own success and on preventing any one else from being more successful than they are. ***No interaction*** exists when individuals work independently without any interaction or interchange with each other. Individuals focus only on increasing their own success and ignore as irrelevant the efforts of others.

Each of these interaction patterns affects outcomes differently. The outcomes of social interdependence may be organized into three major areas.

30.5.1.1 Effort to Achieve. Between 1898 and 1989, researchers conducted over 375 experimental studies on social interdependence and achievement (D. W. Johnson & R. Johnson,

TABLE 30.1. Mean Effect Sizes for Impact of Social Interdependence on Dependent Variables

Condition	Achievement	Interpersonal attraction	Social Support	Self-Esteem
Total studies				
Coop vs. comp	0.67	0.67	0.62	0.58
Coop vs. ind	0.64	0.60	0.70	0.44
Comp vs. ind	0.30	0.08	−0.13	−0.23
High-quality studies				
Coop vs. comp	0.88	0.82	0.83	0.67
Coop vs. ind	0.61	0.62	0.72	0.45
Comp vs. ind	0.07	0.27	−0.13	−0.25
Mixed operationalizations				
Coop vs. comp	0.40	0.46	0.45	0.33
Coop vs. ind	0.42	0.36	0.02	0.22
Pure operationalizations				
Coop vs. comp	0.71	0.79	0.73	0.74
Coop vs. ind	0.65	0.66	0.77	0.51

Note: Coop, cooperation; comp, competition; ind, Individualistic. Form *Cooperation and Competition: Theory and Research*, by D. W. Johnson and R. Johnson, 1989, Edina, MN: Interaction Book Company. Reprinted by permission.

1989). A metaanalysis of all studies indicates that cooperative learning results in significantly higher achievement and retention than do competitive and individualistic learning (see Table 30.1). The more conceptual and complex the task, the more problem solving required, and the more creative the answers need to be, the greater the superiority of cooperative over competitive and individualistic learning. When we examined only the methodological high-quality studies, the superiority of cooperative over competitive or individualistic efforts was still pronounced.

Some cooperative procedures contained a mixture of cooperative, competitive, and individualistic efforts, whereas others contained pure cooperation. The original jigsaw procedure (Aronson, 1978), for example, is a combination of resource interdependence and an individualistic reward structure. Teams-games–tournaments (DeVries & Edwards, 1974) and student-teams–achievement–divisions (Slavin, 1986) are mixtures of cooperation and intergroup competition. Team-assisted instruction (Slavin, Leavey, & Madden, 1982) is a mixture of individualistic and cooperative learning. When the results of "pure" and "mixed" operationalizations of cooperative learning were compared, the pure operationalizations produced higher achievement.

Besides higher achievement and greater retention, cooperation, compared with competitive or individualistic efforts, tends to result in more (D. W. Johnson & R. Johnson, 1989):

1. Willingness to take on difficult tasks and persist, despite difficulties, in working toward goal accomplishment.
2. Long-term retention of what is learned.
3. Higher-level reasoning (critical thinking) and metacognitive thought. Cooperative efforts promote a greater use of higher-level reasoning strategies and critical thinking than do competitive or individualistic efforts (effect sizes = 0.93 and 0.97, respectively). Even on writing assignments, students working cooperatively show more higher-level thought.

4. Creative thinking (process gain). In cooperative groups, members more frequently generate new ideas, strategies, and solutions that they would think of on their own.
5. Transfer of learning from one situation to another (group to individual transfer). What individuals learn in a group today, they are able to do alone tomorrow.
6. Positive attitudes toward the tasks being completed (job satisfaction). Cooperative efforts result in more positive attitudes toward the tasks being completed and greater continuing motivation to complete them. The positive attitudes extend to the work experience and the organization as a whole.
7. Time on task. Cooperators spend more time on task than do competitors (effect size = 0.76) or students working individualistically (effect size = 1.17).

Kurt Lewin often stated, *"I always found myself unable to think as a single person."* Most efforts to achieve are a personal but social process that requires individuals to cooperate and to construct shared understandings and knowledge. Both competitive and individualistic structures, by isolating individuals from each other, tend to depress achievement.

30.5.2 Positive Interpersonal Relationships

Heartpower is the strength of your corporation.
  —Vince Lombardi (famous coach of the Green Bay Packers)

Since 1940, over 180 studies have compared the impact of cooperative, competitive, and individualistic efforts on interpersonal attraction (D. W. Johnson & R. Johnson, 1989). Cooperative efforts, compared with competitive and individualistic experiences, promoted considerably more liking among individuals (see Table 30.1). The effect sizes were higher for (a) high-quality studies and (b) studies using pure operationalizations of cooperative learning than for studies using mixed operationalizations. These positive feelings were found to extend to superiors in the organizational structure. Thus, individuals tend to care more about each other and to be more committed to each other's success and well-being when they work together cooperatively than when they compete to see who is best or work independently from each other.

A major extension of social interdependence theory, is social judgment theory, which focuses on relationships among diverse individuals (D. W. Johnson & R. Johnson, 1989). Cooperators tend to like each other not only when they are homogeneous, but also when they differ in intellectual ability, handicapping conditions, ethnic membership, social class, culture, and gender. Individuals working cooperatively tend to value heterogeneity and diversity more than do individuals working competitively or individualistically. The positive impact of heterogeneity results from a process of acceptance that includes frequent and accurate communication, accurate perspective taking, mutual inducibility (openness to influence), multidimensional views of each other, feelings of psychological acceptance and self-esteem, psychological success, and expectations of rewarding and productive future interaction.

Besides liking each other, cooperators give and receive considerable social support, both personally and academically (D. W. Johnson & R. Johnson). Since the 1940s, over 106 studies comparing the relative impact of cooperative, competitive, and individualistic efforts on social support have been conducted. Social support may be aimed at enhancing another person's success (task-related social support) or at providing support on a more personal level (personal social support). Cooperative experience promoted greater task-oriented and personal social support than did competitive (effect size = 0.62) or individualistic (effect size = 0.70) experiences. Social support tends to promote achievement and productivity, physical health, psychological health, and successful coping with stress and adversity.

30.5.2.1 Psychological Health.

Ashley Montagu was fond of saying, "With few exceptions, the solitary animal is, in any species, an abnormal creature." Karen Horney said, "The neurotic individual is someone who is inappropriately competitive and, therefore, unable to cooperate with others." Montagu and Horney recognized that the essence of psychological health is the ability to develop and maintain cooperative relationships. Psychological health may be defined, therefore, as the ability to develop, maintain, and appropriately modify interdependent relationships with others to succeed in achieving goals (D. W. Johnson & R. Johnson, 1989). To manage social interdependence, individuals must correctly perceive whether interdependence exists and whether it is positive or negative, be motivated accordingly, and act in ways consistent with normative expectations for appropriate behavior within the situation. The major variables related to psychological health studied by researchers interested in social interdependence are psychological adjustment, self-esteem, perspective-taking ability, social skills, and a variety of related attitudes and values.

A number of studies have been conducted on the relationship between social interdependence and psychological health (D. W. Johnson & R. Johnson, 1989). Working cooperatively with peers and valuing cooperation results in greater psychological health than does competing with peers or working independently. **Cooperativeness** is positively related to a number of indexes of psychological health, such as emotional maturity, well-adjusted social relations, strong personal identity, ability to cope with adversity, social competencies, and basic trust in and optimism about people. Personal ego-strength, self-confidence, independence, and autonomy are all promoted by being involved in cooperative efforts. **Individualistic attitudes** tend to be related to a number of indices of psychological pathology such as emotional immaturity, social maladjustment, delinquency, self-alienation, and self-rejection. **Competitiveness** is related to a mixture of healthy and unhealthy characteristics. Cooperative experiences are not a luxury; they are an absolute necessity for healthy psychological development.

Interested researchers have examined the relationship between social interdependence and self-esteem. Since the 1950s there have been over 80 studies comparing the relative impact of cooperative, competitive, and individualistic experiences on self-esteem (D. W. Johnson & R. Johnson, 1989). Cooperative experiences promoted higher self-esteem than did competitive (effect size = 0.58) or individualistic (effect size = 0.44) experiences. Our research demonstrated that cooperative experiences tend to be related to beliefs that one is intrinsically worthwhile, others see one in positive ways, one's attributes compare favorably with those of one's peers, and one is a capable, competent, and successful person. In cooperative efforts, students (a) realize that they are accurately known, accepted, and liked by one's peers, (b) know that they have contributed to own, others, and group success, and (c) perceive themselves and others in a differentiated and realistic way that allows for multidimensional comparisons based on complementarity of own and others' abilities. Competitive experiences tend to be related to conditional self-esteem based on whether one wins or loses. Individualistic experiences tend to be related to basic self-rejection.

Cooperative experiences tend to increase perspective-taking ability (the ability to understand how a situation appears to other people) while competitive and individualistic experiences tend to promote egocentrism (being unaware of other perspectives other than your own [effect sizes of 0.61 and 0.44, respectively] D. W. Johnson & R. Johnson, 1989). Individuals who are part of a cooperative effort learn more social skills and become more socially competent than do persons competing or working individualistically. Finally, it is through cooperative efforts that many of the attitudes and values essential to psychological health (such as self-efficacy) and learned and adopted.

30.5.2.2 Everything Affects Everything Else.

Deutsch's (1985) crude law of social relations states that the characteristic processes and effects elicited by a given type of social interdependence also tends to elicit that type of social interdependence. Thus, positive interdependence elicits promotive interaction and promotive interaction tends to elicit positive interdependence. Deutsch's law may also be applied to the three types of outcomes resulting from cooperative experiences. The more individuals work together to achieve, the more caring and committed their relationships tend to be; the more individuals care about each other the harder they will work to achieve mutual goals. The more individuals work together to achieve, the greater their psychological adjustment, self-esteem, and social competence; the healthier psychologically individuals are, the better able to they are to work with others to achieve mutual goals. The better individuals' psychological health, the more caring and committed their relationships tend to be; the more caring and committed their relationships, the more healthy psychologically they tend to be. Because each outcome can induce the others, you are likely to find them together. They are a package, with each outcome a door into all three. Together they induce positive interdependence and promotive interaction.

The research outcomes noted occur only when the efforts are truly cooperative. Not all groups are cooperative groups. To be cooperative, five basic elements must be present in a group.

30.6 THE BASIC ELEMENTS OF COOPERATION

30.6.1 Potential Group Performance

Not all groups are cooperative (D. W. Johnson & F. Johnson, 2003). Placing people in the same room, seating them together, telling them they are a group, does not mean they will cooperate effectively. Project groups, lab groups, committees, task forces, departments, and councils are groups, but they are not necessarily cooperative. Many groups are ineffective and some are even destructive. Almost everyone has been part of a group that has wasted time and produced poor work. Ineffective and destructive groups are characterized by a number of dynamics (D. W. Johnson & F. Johnson) such as social loafing, free riding, group immaturity, uncritical and quick acceptance of members' dominant response, and group-think. Such hindering factors are eliminated by carefully structuring the five essential elements of cooperation. Those elements are positive interdependence, individual and group accountability, promotive interaction, appropriate use of social skills, and group processing.

30.6.2 Positive Interdependence: We Instead of Me

All for one and one for all.
—Alexander Dumas

The heart of cooperation is positive interdependence (see D. W. Johnson & R. Johnson, 1989, 1992a, 1992b). *Positive interdependence* exists when one perceives that one is linked with others in a way so that one cannot succeed unless they do (and vice versa) and/or that one must coordinate one's efforts with the efforts of others to complete a task (Deutsch, 1962; D. W. Johnson & R. Johnson, 1989). There are two major categories of interdependence: outcome interdependence and means interdependence (D. W. Johnson & R. Johnson). When persons are in a cooperative or competitive situation, they are oriented toward a desired outcome, end state, goal, or reward. If there is no outcome interdependence (goal and reward interdependence), there is no cooperation or competition. In addition, the means through which the mutual goals or rewards are to be accomplished specify the actions required on the part of group members. Means interdependence includes resource, role, and

task interdependence (which are overlapping and not independent from each other).

The authors have conducted a series of studies investigating the nature of positive interdependence and the relative power of the different types of positive interdependence (Frank, 1984; Hwong, Caswell, Johnson, & Johnson, 1993; D. W. Johnson, Johnson, Stanne, & Garibaldi, 1990; Johnson, Johnson, Ortiz, & Stanne, 1991; Lew, Mesch, Johnson, & Johnson, 1986a, 1986b; Mesch, Lew, Johnson, & Johnson, 1986; Mesch, Johnson, & Johnson, 1988). Our research indicates that positive interdependence provides the context within which promotive interaction takes place, group membership and interpersonal interaction among students do not produce higher achievement unless positive interdependence is clearly structured, the combination of goal and reward interdependence increases achievement over goal interdependence alone, and resource interdependence does not increase achievement unless goal interdependence is present also.

30.6.3 Individual Accountability/Personal Responsibility

What children can do together today, they can do alone tomorrow.
—Vygotsky (1978)

Using cooperative groups requires structuring group and individual accountability. *Group accountability* exists when the overall performance of the group is assessed and the results are given back to all group members to compare against a standard of performance. *Individual accountability* exists when the performance of each individual member is assessed, the results given back to the individual and the group to compare against a standard of performance, and the member is held responsible by groupmates for contributing his or her fair share to the group's success. On the basis of the feedback received, (a) efforts to learn and contribute to groupmates' learning can be recognized and celebrated, (b) immediate remediation can take place by providing any needed assistance or encouragement, and (c) groups can reassign responsibilities to avoid any redundant efforts by members.

The purpose of cooperative groups is to make each member a stronger individual in his or her own right. Individual accountability is the key to ensuring that learning cooperatively in fact strengthens all group members. There is a pattern to classroom learning. **First,** students learn knowledge, skills, strategies, or procedures in a cooperative group. **Second,** students apply the knowledge or perform the skill, strategy, or procedure alone to demonstrate their personal mastery of the material. Students learn it together and then perform it alone. Archer-Kath, Johnson, and Johnson (1994) found that individual feedback resulted in greater achievement and perceptions of cooperation, goal interdependence, and resource interdependence than did group feedback. Hooper, Ward, Hannafin and Clark (1989) found that cooperative technology-supported instruction resulted in higher achievement when individual accountability was structured than when it was not.

30.6.4 Promotive Interaction

In an industrial organization it's the group effort that counts. There's really no room for stars in an industrial organization. You need talented people, but they can't do it alone. They have to have help.

—John F. Donnelly (President, Donnelly Mirrors)

Promotive interaction exists when individuals encourage and facilitate each other's efforts to complete tasks in order to reach the group's goals. Through promoting each other's success, group members build both an academic and a personal support system for each member. Promotive interaction is characterized by individuals providing each other with efficient and effective help and assistance, exchanging needed resources such as information and materials and processing information more efficiently and effectively, providing each other with feedback in order to improve subsequent performance, challenging each other's conclusions and reasoning in order to promote higher-quality decision making and greater insight into the problems being considered, advocating the exertion of effort to achieve mutual goals, influencing each other's efforts to achieve the group's goals, acting in trusting and trustworthy ways, being motivated to strive for mutual benefit, and having a moderate level of arousal characterized by low anxiety and stress.

Traditionally, promotive interaction was viewed as being face-to-face. Technology, through the use of local and wide area networks and mediating tools such as e-mail, electronic bulletin boards, conferencing systems that can include live video, and specialized groupware, enables individuals to promote each other success all across the world, in ways that were never possible before. Such electronic communication is growing exponentially, but it does not always substitute for face-to-face interaction. Face-to-face communication has a richness that electronic communication may never match (Prusak & Cohen, 2001). There is evidence that up to 93% of people's intent is conveyed by facial expression and tone of voice, with the most important channel being facial expression (Druckman, Rozelle, & Baxter, 1982; Meherabian, 1971). Harold Geneen, the former head of ITT, believed that his response to requests was different face-to-face than through electronic means. *"In New York, I might read a request and say no. But in Europe, I could see that an answer to the same question might be yes...it became our policy to deal with problems on the spot, face-to-face"* (cited in Trevino, Lengel, & Draft, 1987). A number of businesses are building office facilities that maximize human interaction. The biggest complaint of students in a virtual high school was that interactions with on-line students just did not measure up to face-to-face context (Allen, 2001). On the other hand, Bonk and King (1998) suggest that promotive interaction in electronic environments has some advantages over live discussion in terms of engagement in learning, depth of discussion, time on task, and the promotion of higher-order thinking skills. Instructional programs, therefore, may be most effective when they include multiple ways for students to promote each other's success, both electronically and face to face whenever possible.

30.6.5 Interpersonal and Small Group Skills

I will pay more for the ability to deal with people than any other ability under the sun.

—John D. Rockefeller

Using cooperative learning requires group members to master the small group and interpersonal skills they need to work effectively with each other and function as part of a group. The greater the members' teamwork skills, the higher will be the quality and quantity of their learning. Cooperative learning is inherently more complex than competitive or individualistic learning because students have to engage simultaneously in taskwork and teamwork. To coordinate efforts to achieve mutual goals, students must (a) get to know and trust each other, (b) communicate accurately and unambiguously, (c) accept and support each other, and (c) resolve conflicts constructively (D. W. Johnson, 1991, 2003; D. W. Johnson & F. Johnson, 2003).

The more socially skillful students are, and the more attention teachers pay to teaching and rewarding the use of social skills, the higher the achievement that can be expected within cooperative learning groups. In their studies on the long-term implementation of cooperative learning, Marvin Lew and Debra Mesch (Lew et al., 1986a, 1986b; Mesch et al., 1986, 1988) investigated the impact of a reward contingency for using social skills as well as positive interdependence and a contingency for academic achievement on performance within cooperative learning groups. In the cooperative skills conditions students were trained weekly in four social skills and each member of a cooperative group was given two bonus points toward the quiz grade if all group members were observed by the teacher to demonstrate three of four cooperative skills. The results indicated that the combination of positive interdependence, an academic contingency for high performance by all group members, and a social skills contingency promoted the highest achievement. Archer-Kath et al. (1994) found that individual feedback was more effective in teaching students social skills than was group feedback. Putnam, Rynders, Johnson, and Johnson (1989) demonstrated that, when individuals were taught social skills, were observed by their superior, and were given individual feedback as to how frequently they engaged in the skills, their relationships became more positive.

30.6.6 Group Processing

Take care of each other. Share your energies with the group. No one must feel alone, cut off, for that is when you do not make it.

—Willi Unsoeld (renowned mountain climber)

Group processing occurs when members discuss how well they are achieving their goals and maintaining effective working relationships among members. Cooperative groups need to describe what member actions are helpful and unhelpful and make decisions about what behaviors to continue or change. The purposes of group processing are to clarify and improve the effectiveness of members in contributing to the cooperative efforts to achieve the group's goals by (a) enabling groups to improve continuously the quality of member's work, (b) facilitating the learning of teamwork skills, (c) ensuring that members receive feedback on their participation, and (d) enabling groups to focus on group maintenance (D. W. Johnson, 2003; D. W. Johnson et al., 1998a). Groups that process how effectively members are working together tend to achieve higher than do groups that do not process or individuals working alone, the combination of teacher and student processing resulted in greater problem-solving success than did the other cooperative conditions, and the combination of group and individual feedback resulted in higher achievement (Archer-Kath et al., 1994; D. W. Johnson et al., 1990; Yager, Johnson, & Johnson, 1985).

Group processing leads to self-monitoring and self-efficacy. Discussing the observations of members' actions results in (a) a heightened self-awareness of the effective and ineffective actions taken during the group meetings, (b) public commitment to increase the frequency of effective actions and decrease the frequency of ineffective actions, and (c) an increased sense of having the ability to be more effective if appropriate effort is exerted (i.e., self-efficacy). Sarason and Potter (1983) examined the impact of individual self-monitoring of thoughts on self-efficacy and successful performance and found that having individuals focus their attention on self-efficacious thoughts is related to greater task persistence and less cognitive interference. They concluded that the more that people are aware of what they are experiencing, the more aware they will be of their own role in determining their success. The greater the sense of self- and joint efficacy promoted by group processing, the more productive and effective group members and the group as a whole become.

Effective processing focuses group members on positive rather than negative behaviors. Sarason and Potter (1983) found that when individuals monitored their stressful experiences they were more likely to perceive a program as having been more stressful than did those who did not, but when individuals monitored their positive experiences they were more likely to perceive the group experience as involving less psychological demands, were more attracted to the group and had greater motivation to remain members, and felt less strained during the experience and more prepared for future group experiences. When individuals are anxious about being successful and are then told that they have failed, their performance tends to decrease significantly, but when individuals anxious about being successful are told that they have succeeded, their performance tends to increase significantly (Turk & Sarason, 1983).

30.7 THE COOPERATIVE SCHOOL

The new electronic tools are radically changing the way people access and use information and, therefore, have profound implications for the educational process. Education, on the other hand, is stuck with organizational patterns and professional traditions that negate many of the advantages of the new technologies. For technology to be fully utilized in schools, the organizational structure of the school has to change, as well as the organizational structure of the classroom. To utilize the new technologies most effectively, schools need to change from a mass-manufacturing organizational structure to a team-based, high-performance organizational structure. This new organizational structure is created when cooperative learning is used the majority of the time in the classroom and cooperation is used to structure faculty and staff work in (a) colleagial teaching teams, (b) school-based decision making, and (c) faculty meetings (D. W. Johnson & R. Johnson, 1994).

Just as the heart of the classroom is cooperative learning, the heart of the school is *colleagial teaching teams.* **Colleagial teaching teams** are small cooperative groups in which members work to improve continuously each other's (a) instructional expertise and success in general and (b) expertise in using cooperative learning in specific. Administrators may also be organized into colleagial support groups to increase their administrative expertise and success.

School-based decision making may be structured through the use of two types of cooperative teams. A *task force* considers a school problem and proposes a solution to the faculty as a whole. The faculty is then divided into *ad hoc decision-making groups* and considers whether to accept or modify the proposal. The decisions made by the ad hoc groups are summarized, and the entire faculty then decides on the action to be taken to solve the problem.

Faculty meetings represent a microcosm of what administrators think the school should be. The clearest modeling of cooperative procedures in the school may be in faculty meetings and other meetings structured by the school administration. All four types of cooperative learning (formal, informal, base groups, and controversy) may be used in faculty meetings to increase their productivity, build faculty cohesion, and improve the faculty's social competence.

Technological innovation lags in schools. A key obstacle to the use of technology in schools is the limited support teachers have for integrating unfamiliar technologies into instruction. Just as students group together to learn cooperatively how to use new software or hardware, teachers need to group together to learn how to use the new technologies and then how to integrate them into the instruction. As long as each teacher works in isolation from his or her peers, the implementation of technology represents a personal decision on the part of each teacher, rather than an organizational change at the school and district levels. Many teachers are unfamiliar with the new technologies and feel unable to master them. To implement technology fully, the organizational structure of the school has to change from the old mass-manufacturing organizational structure to a team-based, high-performance organizational structure where teams of teachers can explore the new technologies, learn how to use them, and implement them together.

30.8 COOPERATIVE LEARNING AND TECHNOLOGY-SUPPORTED INSTRUCTION

To enhance learning, technology must promote cooperation among students and create a shared experience. Crook (1996) has widely analyzed how computers can facilitate collaborative learning in schools. He makes a distinction between:

1. Interacting around computers. The first perspective stresses the use of computers as tools to facilitate face-to-face communication between student pairs or in a small group. Crook (1996, pp. 189–193) states that technology may serve to support cooperation by providing students with points of shared reference. He states that the traditional classroom does not have enough available anchor points at which action and attention can be coordinated. The capabilities of computers can be used as mediating tools that help students to focus their attention on mutually shared objects.

2. Interacting through computers. This refers to the use of networks. Local area networks (LAN) and wide area networks (WAN) and the global version of the latter (Internet) provide education with a variety of mediating tools for cooperation (email, electronic bulletin boards, conferencing systems, and specialized groupware).

30.8.1 Interacting Around Computers

30.8.1.1 Single-User Programs Reapplied to Cooperative Learning. Many computer programs were developed to tailor learning situations to individual students. Field experiments, however, indicate several advantages of the importance of cooperation among students in using these programs (Crook, 1994; Hawkins et al., 1982). The technical extension of the tradition LOGO (Papert, 1980) to legoLOGO, where Lego bricks robots can be controlled by LOGO programs has been an especially promising tool for creating cooperation among students (e.g., Eraut, 1995; Jarvela, 1996). Cooperative learning has been promoted by many different program types, such as databases, spreadsheets, math programs, programming languages, simulations, multimedia authoring tools, and so forth (Amigues & Agostinelli, 1992; Brush, 1997; Eraut, 1995; Lehtinen & Repo. 1996).

30.8.1.2 Programs Developed To Promote Cooperation. For cooperation to take place, students must have a joint workspace. One of the promises of the computer is to allow students to create shared spaces. Instead of sharing a blackboard or a worktable, students can share a computer screen. Such groupware (aimed at supporting group rather than individual work) has expanded dramatically the past ten years. Numerous programs in a variety of subject areas have been developed to externalize the problem-solving process by displaying the student's solution or learning paths on the screen, and they generally tend to be helpful for both individual reflection and cooperative problem solving (Lehtinen, Hamalainen, & Malkonen, 1998). The ways in which technology and cooperative learning have been integrated are so numerous that even a small fraction cannot be mentioned. Some of the more widely used methods of computer-supported cooperative learning (CSCL) are CSILE, the Belvedere System, and CoVis.

CSILE (Computer-Supported Intentional Learning Environment) was originally developed in the late 1980s (Scardamalia, Bereiter, McLearn, Swallow, & Woodruff, 1989) and uses a network to help students build, articulate, explore, and structure knowledge. The system contains tools for text and chart processing and a communal database for producing, searching, classifying, and linking knowledge. The Belvedere system was developed by Lesgold, Weiner, and Suthers (1995) and it focuses and prompts students' cognitive activity by giving them a graphical language to express the steps of hypothesizing, data gathering, and weighing of information. CoVis (Learning Through Collaborative Visualization Project) focuses on cooperative project work in high-school science (Pea, Edelson, & Gomez, 1994), with advanced networking technologies, collaborative software, and visualization tools to enable students and others to work together in classrooms and across the country at the same time (synchronously) or at different times (asynchronously). These and many other groupware systems are providing new and powerful opportunities for cooperative learning.

30.8.2 Cooperation Through Computers

There has been a rapid expansion of computer network technology that allows students all over the world to create powerful shared spaces on the computer screen. The future of technology-supported cooperative learning may depend on the software and hardware that creates workspaces that network group members and groups throughout the world. Networking has had a strong influence on the tools and methods of technology-supported cooperative learning. In a network-based environment, students and teachers can interact through the computer free of the limitations of time and place. The speed at which asynchronous and distance communication may be completed opens new opportunities for cooperative learning. It makes more intensive cooperative possible with the out-of-school experts, brings students from different schools into contact with each other, and creates powerful tools for joint writing and knowledge sharing. There are, however, different levels at which the network environment supports cooperation. From a series of studies, Bonk and King (1995) concluded that networks can (a) change the way students and instructors interact, (b) enhance cooperative learning opportunities, (c) facilitate class discussion, and (d) move writing from solitary to more active, social learning. The network tools include the following.

1. Local Area Network-Based Client-Server Systems. There are many software programs based on local area networks and client–server architecture, such as CSILE, the Belvedere System, and CoVis.

2. E-Mail for Cooperative Learning. E-mail is used to deliver information to students, supervise students, and support national and international communication between cooperative learning groups and schools located far away from each other. With the help of mailing lists, groups of students can use e-mail to share joint documents and comment on each other's work.

3. The Internet and World Wide Web and Cooperative Learning. Internet-based conferencing systems and e-mail systems are very similar. Computer conferencing has existed since the first computer networks but has only recently been

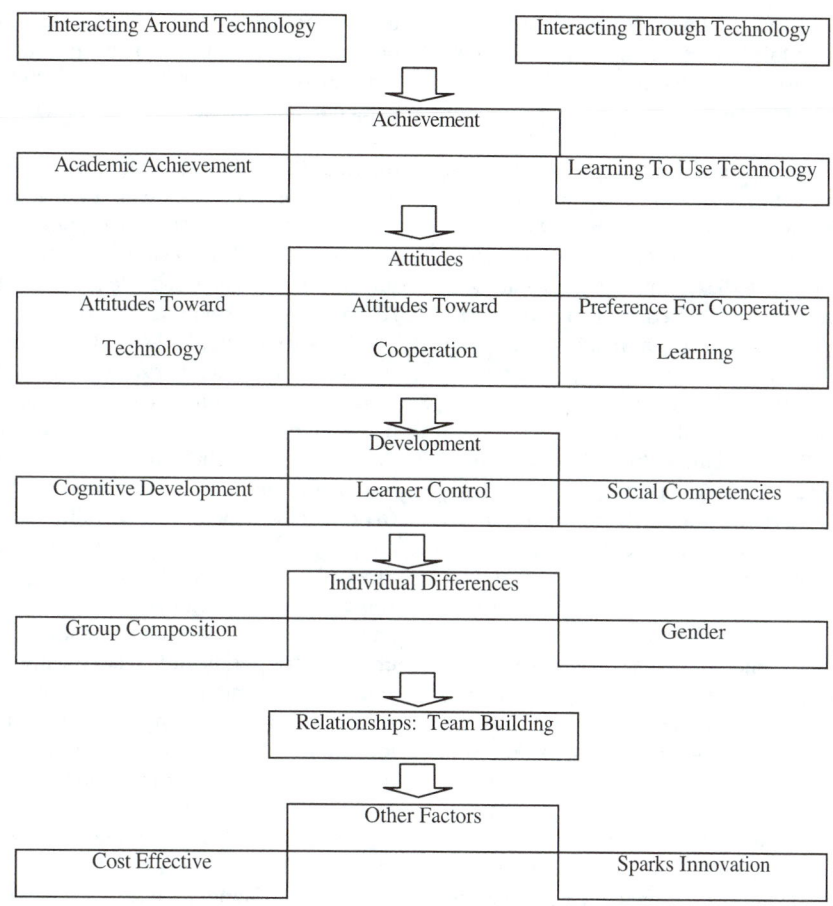

FIGURE 30.3. Outcomes of technology-supported cooperative learning.

implemented as part of cooperative learning. Web-based cooperative learning is time independent and location independent, thus allowing a combination of synchronous and asynchronous discussions. It is similar to e-mail lists but, in addition, has user-control, document structures, shared databases, and interaction styles that make it especially effective for cooperative work (Bates, 1995; Harasim et al., 1995; Malikowski, 1998). Creating and using shared databases is especially helpful for network-based cooperative-learning systems. On the World Wide Web, conferencing may require "threading" (the ability to sequentially read the messages that make up one discussion). Woolley (1995) listed about 150 internet conferencing systems. It is now possible to have live video of individuals and groups conferencing with each other.

Adding technology to a lesson inherently increases the lesson's complexity. When students participate in technology-supported instruction, they have the dual tasks of (a) learning how to use the technology (i.e., the hardware and software required by the lesson) and (b) mastering the information, skills, procedures, and processes being presented within the technology. When cooperative learning groups are used, students have the additional task of learning teamwork procedures and skills. Consequently, the initial use of technology-supported cooperative learning may take more time, but once students and teachers master the new systems, the results will be worth the effort. Technology-supported cooperative learning tends to be cost effective way of teaching students how to use technology. In addition, increasing academic achievement, giving learners control over their learning, creating positive attitudes toward technology-based instruction and cooperative learning, promoting cognitive development, and increasing social skills. Computers themselves promote cooperative interaction among learners. The composition of the group and the gender of the learners are factors that have been hypothesized to affect the success of technology-supported cooperative learning (see Fig. 30.3).

30.8.3 Achievement

30.8.3.1 Academic Achievement. Two large metaanalysis on the effectiveness of computer-assisted instruction concluded that the use of technology markedly improved learning outcomes (e.g., Fletcher-Finn & Gravatt, 1995; Khalili & Shashaani, 1994). These metaanalysis, however, did not differentiate among teaching practices and the ways technology was implemented in classrooms. It is not possible, therefore, to draw any conclusions about the effectiveness of technology-supported cooperative learning from these metaanalysis.

We conducted several studies examining the use of cooperative, competitive, and individualistic learning activities at the computer (D. W. Johnson, Johnson, & Stanne, 1989; D. W. Johnson et al., 1990; R. Johnson, Johnson, & Stanne, 1985, 1986; R. Johnson, Johnson, Stanne, Smizak, & Avon, 1987; Johnson, Johnson, Richards, 1986). The studies included eighth-grade students through college freshmen and lasted from 3 to 30 instructional hr. The tasks were a computerized navigational and map reading problem-solving task and word processing assignments. Computer-assisted cooperative learning, compared with competitive and individualistic efforts at the computer, promoted (a) a higher quantity of daily achievement, (b) a higher quality of daily achievement, (c) greater mastery of factual information, (d) greater ability to apply one's factual knowledge in test questions requiring application of facts, (e) greater ability to use factual information to answer problem-solving questions, and (f) greater success in problem solving. Cooperation at the computer promoted greater motivation to persist on problem-solving tasks. Students in the cooperative condition were more successful in operating computer programs. In terms of oral participation, students in the cooperative condition, compared with students in the competitive and individualistic conditions, made fewer statements to the teacher and more to each other, made more task-oriented statements and fewer social statements, and generally engaged in more positive, task-oriented interaction with each other (especially when the social skill responsibilities were specified and group processing was conducted). Finally, the studies provided evidence that females were perceived to be of higher status in the cooperative than in the competitive or individualistic conditions.

In addition to our work, there are a number of studies that have found that students using a combination of cooperative learning and computer-based instruction learn better than do students using computer-based instruction while working individualistically (Anderson, Mayes, & Kibby, 1995; Cockayne, 1991; Cox & Berger, 1985; Dalton, 1990a, 1990b; Dalton, Hannafin, & Hooper, 1987; Dees, 1991; Hooper, 1992b; Hooper, Temiyakarn, & Williams, 1993; Hythecker et al., 1985; Inkpen, Booth, Klawe, & Upitis, 1995; Lin, Wu, & Liu, 1999; Love, 1969; McInerney, McInerney, & Marsh, 1997; Mevarech, 1993; 1987; Mevarech, Silber, & Fine, 1991; Mevarech, Stern, & Levita, Okey & Majer, 1976; Postthast, 1995; Reglin, 1990; Repman, 1993; Rocklin et al., 1985; Shlecter, 1990; Stephenson, 1992; Underwood, McCaffrey, 1990; Webb, 1984; Whitelock, Scanlon, Taylor, & O'Shea, 1995; Yeuh & Alessi, 1988). There are also a number of studies that found no statistically significant differences in achievement between subjects who worked in groups and subjects who worked alone (Carrier & Sales, 1987; Cosden & English, 1987; Hooper & Hannafin, 1988; Trowbridge & Durnin, 1984). No study has reported significantly greater learning when students work alone. Many of these studies, however, are short-term experiments focused on a small number of students. Several experiments provide evidence that well-known CSCL programs like CSIKE and Belvedere have proved to be

helpful for higher-order social interaction and, subsequently, for better learning in terms of deep understanding (Scardamalia, Bereiter, & Lamon, 1994; Suthers, 1998). What is still lacking is evidence that the same results could be found in normal classrooms. There are CSCL projects like CoVis that are widely implemented (Pea, Edelson, & Gopmez, 1994), but there have been few well-controlled follow-up evaluations published.

Simon Hooper and his colleagues have conducted a series of studies on technology-supported cooperative learning involving fifth through eighth-grade and college students (Dyer, 1993; Hooper, 1991; Hooper & Hannafin, 1988, 1991; Hooper et al., 1989; Huang, 1993; McDonald, 1993). They found that (a) cooperative group members achieved significantly higher than did students working under individualistic conditions, (b) cooperative learning groups in which individual accountability was carefully structured achieved higher than did cooperative learning groups in which no individual accountability was structured, (b) the achievement of low-ability students in heterogeneous cooperative groups was consistently higher than the achievement of low-ability students in homogeneous groups, (c) there was a positive and significant correlation between achievement and helping behaviors, and increases in achievement and cooperation were significantly related within heterogeneous groups, and (d) cooperative (compared with individualistic) learning resulted in greater willingness to learn the material, options selection, time on task, perceived interdependence, and supportiveness for partners. Carlson and Falk (1989) and Noell and Carnine (1989) found that students in cooperative groups perform higher than students working alone on learning tasks involving interactive videodiscs. Adams, Carson, and Hamm (1990) suggest that cooperative learning can influence attention, motivation, and achievement when students use the medium of television.

Fletcher (1985), on the other hand, investigating cognitive facilitation, found on a computer task calling for solving equations in an earth spaceship game that individuals who were told to verbalize their decisions did as well in problem-solving performance on the game as groups told to come to consensus (both of which had results superior to those of individuals working silently). King (1989) asked groups of fourth graders to reproduce a stimulus design using LOGO computer graphics after they had watched a videotape modeling of "think aloud problem solving." The groups were instructed to think aloud as they performed their task. More successful groups asked more task-related questions, spent more time on strategy, and reached higher levels of strategy elaboration than did groups who were less successful on the task.

30.8.3.2 Learning How to Use Technology. Cooperative learning may reduce hardware and software problems that interfere with achievement when students work alone (Hativa, 1988). Students naturally form groups when learning how to use a new technology or software program (Becker, 1984). In his description of the implementation of the Apple Classrooms of Tomorrow, Dwyer (1994) notes that the cooperative, task-related interaction among students was spontaneous and more extensive than in traditional classrooms, with students interacting with one another while working at computers, spontaneously helping each other, showing curiosity about each other's activities, wanting to share what they had just learned to do, working together to build multimedia presentations about diverse topics, and combining their group's work into whole class, interdisciplinary projects.

When technology-supported lessons require new, complex procedures (such as learner-controlled lessons), cooperative learning tends to promote quicker and more thorough mastery of the procedures than competitive or individualistic learning. Trowbridge and Durnin (1984) found that students working in groups of two or three seemed more likely to interpret program questions as the authors of the materials intended. Discussions of multiple interpretations tended to converge on the correct interpretation. Hooper (1992a) reported that students were frustrated and could not master the computer-assisted, learner-controlled lesson when they worked alone. Keeler and Anson (1995) used cooperative learning in a software application lab course and found that both students' performance and their retention were significantly improved. Dyer (1993) compared structured cooperative pairs, unstructured cooperative pairs, and individuals working alone to solve computer-assisted math problem solving lessons. Structured cooperative pairs communicated more frequently and used the computer more efficiently and skillfully than did the unstructured cooperative pairs or the students in the individualistic condition. McDonald (1993) found that students in the learner-controlled/cooperative learning condition selected more options during the lesson and spent more time interacting with the tutorial than did the learner-controlled/individual learning condition. Hooper et al. (1993) found that cooperative learning established a mutually supportive learning environment among group members in which both cognitive difficulties and navigational disorientation were overcome in using the computer to complete a symbolic-reasoning task. Students studying alone had greater difficulty reading and understanding lesson directions, used the help option more often, and required more attempts to master embedded quizzes than did students in cooperative learning groups. In learning how to use computers, Webb (1984) and Webb et al. (1986) found that in cooperative groups, explaining how to do computer programming was not related to skill in doing so and receiving explanations influenced only the learning of basic commands (not the interpretation of programs or the ability to generate programs). Generally, this evidence indicates that students will learn how to use hardware and software more quickly and effectively when they learn in cooperative groups rather than alone. When teachers wish to introduce new technology and new software programs of some complexity, they will be well advised to use cooperative learning.

30.8.4 Cognitive and Social Development

30.8.4.1 Cognitive Development: Cooperation and Controversy. Social-cognitive theory posits that cognitive development is facilitated by (Bearison, 1982; D. W. Johnson & R. Johnson, 1979, 1995; Perret-Clermont, 1980) (a) individuals working cooperatively with peers on tasks that require coordination of actions or thoughts, (b) cooperators contradicting and challenging each other's intuitively derived concepts and points of view (i.e., engaging in academic controversy), thereby creating cognitive conflict within and among group members, and (c) the successful and equitable (members contributing approximately equally) resolution of those conflicts (learners have to go beyond mere disagreement to benefit from cognitive conflict; [Bearison, Magzament, & Filardi, 1986; Damon & Killen, 1982). To create the conditions under which cognitive development takes place, students must work cooperatively, challenge each other's points of view, and resolve the resulting cognitive conflicts. Clements and Nastasi conducted a series of studies on the occurrence of cooperation and controversy in technology-supported instruction (Battista & Clements, 1986; Clements & Nastasi, 1985, 1988; Nastasi & Clements, 1992; Nastasi, Clements, & Battista, 1990). They have found that both LOGO and CAI/CBI-W computer environments promoted considerable cooperative work and conflict (both social and cognitive). The LOGO environment (compared to CAI/CBI-W computer and traditional classroom tasks environments) promoted (a) more peer interaction focused on learning and problem solving, (b) self-directed problem solving (i.e., learners solve problems they themselves have posed) in which there is mutual "ownership" of the problem, (c) more frequent occurrence and resolution of cognitive conflicts, (d) greater development of executive-level problem-solving skills (planning, monitoring, decision making), higher-level reasoning, and cognitive development. The development of higher-level cognitive processes seemed to be facilitated by the resolution of cognitive conflict that arises out of cooperating. They also found that the LOGO (compared with the CAI) computer environment resulted in more learner satisfaction and expressions of pleasure at the discovery of new information and their work, variables reflective of intrinsic and competence motivation.

More recently, Bell (2001) has developed a software program to create arguments to be used in discussions with other students (the SenseMaker argumentation tool). It is designed to support a rhetorical construction of arguments by individuals by connecting evidence dots with claim frames. The intent is to teach students the nature of scientific inquiry by coordinating emerging evidence with an existing set of theories. The use of SenseMaker to develop arguments to be used in an academic controversy could significantly advance students' level of reasoning and learing.

30.8.4.2 Learner Control. Combining cooperative learning and technology-supported instruction results in students having more control over their learning. Hooper and his associates (Hooper, 1992a; Hooper et al., 1993) note that three forms of lesson control are used in the design of technology-based instruction: learner, program, and adaptive control. Learner control involves delegating instructional decisions to learners so that they can determine what help they need, what difficulty level or content density of material they wish to study, in what sequence they wish to learn the material, and how much they want to learn. Learner-controlled environments include simulations, hypermedia, and online databases. Program or linear control prescribes an identical instructional sequence for all students regardless of interest or need. Adaptive control modifies lesson features according to student aptitude (e.g., Snow, 1980), prior performance (e.g., Tobias, 1987), or ongoing lesson needs (e.g., Tennyson, Christensen, & Park, 1984). Linear or program control may impose an inappropriate lesson sequence on learners and thereby lower their motivation, and adaptive instruction may foster learner dependence (Hannafin & Rieber, 1989). As learner control increases so does (a) instructional effectiveness and efficiency (Reigeluth & Stein, 1983) and (b) learner independence, efficiency, mental effort, and motivation (Federico, 1980; Salomon, 1983, 1985; Steinberg, 1984).

Technology-supported cooperative learning tends to increase the effectiveness of learner control. When students work alone, in isolation from their peers, they tend not to control the learning situation productively, making ineffective instructional decisions and leaving instruction prematurely (Carrier, 1984; Hannafin, 1984; Milheim & Martin, 1991; Steinberg, 1977, 1989). Students working cooperatively tend to motivate each other to seek elaborative feedback to their responses to practice items during learning control and to seek a greater variety of feedback types more frequently than did those working alone (Carrier & Sales, 1987). Cooperative pairs spent longer times inspecting information on the computer screen as they discussed which level of feedback they needed and the answers to practice items. Students in the learner-controlled/cooperative learning condition selected more options during the lesson, and spent more time interacting with the tutorial, than did students in the learner-controlled/individual learning condition (McDonald, 1993). Hooper et al. (1993) found that students in the program-control conditions attempted more than four times as many examples and nearly twice as many practice questions as did the students in the learner-control conditions. The LOGO computer environment tends to promote more actual learner control over the task structure and the making of rules to govern it than does the CAI computer environment (Battista & Clements, 1986; Clements & Nastasi, 1985, 1988; Nastasi et al., 1990). Learner control seems to be most effective when prior knowledge is high or when students possess well-developed metacognitive abilities (Garhart & Hannafin, 1986). What these studies imply is that cooperative learning is an important variable in improving the effectiveness of learner controlled environments.

30.8.4.3 Increasing Social Competencies.
If students are to work effectively in cooperative groups they must have the teamwork skills to do so. To examine the importance of social skills training on the productiveness of cooperative groups, it is possible to compare studies that have included cooperative skills training and those that have not. Numerous studies on technology-supported cooperative learning have demonstrated positive effects on the amount and quality of social interaction (e.g., Amigues & Agostinelli, 1992; Crook, 1994; Davis & Huttenlocher, 1995; Fishman & Gomez, 1997; McConnell, 1994; Rysavy & Sales, 1991). A number of studies have found that when teamwork procedures and skills are present, cooperative learning results in higher achievement in technology-supported instructional lessons than individualistic learning (Hooper & Hannafin, 1991; Hooper & Hannafin, 1988, 1991; R. Johnson et al., 1985, 1986; Susman, 1998). In studies where teamwork

procedures and skills were not emphasized, reliable differences in achievement in cooperative and individualistic technology-assisted instruction tend not to be found (Mevarech et al., 1987; Hooper et al., 1989; Susman, 1998; Underwood & McCaffrey, 1990).

Software designers may be able to facilitate the development use of the interpersonal and small group skills required for teamwork in several ways.

1. Before students engage in the actual instruction, they might first be required to complete a tutorial activity designed to introduce or refresh their understanding of cooperative skills. This could include a discussion of each member's role and its value in determining the overall group success.
2. Teachers' guides could suggest roles to assign to each group member to perform in the group (keyboarder, recorder, checker for understanding, encourager of participation).
3. Time for group processing to analyze and discuss how effectively they are working together and how they might work together more effectively in the future could be provided. Software could be designed to include pauses during which group members are directed to focus on their progress, discuss the records they are keeping, or reflect on improvements or changes they might make to increase performance.
4. The software could periodically remind students to monitor their own performance and to assist in optimizing group performance.
5. Yeuh and Alessi (1988) suggest that group reward is crucial to provide a group goal motivating everyone to work well together and individual accountability is needed to create a feelings of fairness among group members. Tangible prizes are recognition for individual successes and for group achievement offers motivation to succeed on both levels. One computer-generated reward would be a printout of collective characters, coupons, or certificates that are assigned points or a relative value or are valued based on the number accumulated. These items could be displayed by students where they would be acknowledged by the teacher and other classmates.

30.8.5 Attitudes

30.8.5.1 Attitudes Toward Technology-Based Instruction.
Students are more likely to learn from and to use technology-based instruction in the future when their self-efficacy toward technology and attitudes about technology-based instruction are positive. Sutton (1991) found that students developed more positive attitudes toward the computer-based instructional lesson and learning with a computer when they worked in cooperative learning groups than when they worked individually (Hooper et al., 1993; Huang, 1993; McDonald, 1993). Students tend to enjoy using the computer to engage in cooperative activities.

30.8.5.2 Attitudes Toward Cooperative Learning.
Mevarech et al. (1985) found that students who learned in pairs were more positive in their attitudes toward cooperative

learning than were students who worked individually with the computer. Evaluations obtained by Rocklin et al. (1985) from students involved in computer-based cooperative learning were more positive toward cooperative learning and how it affected them personally than were subjects who worked individually. Hooper et al. (1993) found that students working in cooperative pairs developed more positive attitudes toward cooperative learning than did students working alone, that is, students rated cooperative learning in a computer-assisted lesson almost a point higher on a 5-point scale than did students who worked alone. A number of studies found that students in the structured cooperative learning conditions developed more positive attitudes toward working cooperatively than did students in the unstructured cooperative learning or the individualistic learning condition (Dyer, 1993; Hooper et al., 1993; Huang, 1993; McDonald, 1993).

30.8.5.3 Preference for Using Technology Cooperatively.
There is a natural partnership between technology and cooperation. The introduction of computers into classrooms tends to increase cooperative behavior and task-oriented verbal interaction (Chernick & White, 1981, 1983; Hawkins et al., 1982; Levin & Kareev, 1980; Rubin, 1983; Webb, 1984). Individuals prefer to work cooperatively at the computer (Hawkins et al., 1982; Levin & Kareev, 1980; Muller & Perlmutter, 1985). Students are more likely to seek each other out at the computer than they normally would for other schoolwork. Even when students play electronic games they prefer to have partners and associates. Working at a computer cooperatively with classmates seems to be more fun and enjoyable as well as more effective for most students.

30.8.6 Individual Differences

30.8.6.1 Group Composition.
A factor hypothesized to affect the success of technology-supported cooperative learning is whether members of cooperative groups are homogeneous or heterogeneous. There is considerable disagreement as to which is the most effective composition. Advocates of heterogeneous grouping point out that (a) students are more likely to gain sophistication and preparation for life in a heterogeneous society by working cooperatively with classmates from diverse cultures, attitudes, and perspectives, (b) high-achieving students benefit from the cognitive restructuring that occurs when providing in-depth explanations to peers, and (c) less academically successful students benefit from the extra attention, alternative knowledge representations, and modeling that more academically successful students provide (D. W. Johnson & R. Johnson, 1989; Webb, 1989). Students in heterogeneous ability groups tend to learn more than students in homogeneous ability groups (Yager, Johnson, & Johnson, 1985; Yager, Johnson, Johnson, & Snider, 1986). Beane & Lemke (1971) found that high ability students benefited more from heterogeneous than homogeneous grouping. The academic discussion and peer interaction in heterogeneous (compared with homogeneous) groups promote the discovery of more effective reasoning strategies (Johnson & Johnson, 1979; Berndt, Perry, & Miller, 1988).

Proponents of homogeneous ability grouping, however, state that heterogeneous ability grouping may fail to challenge high-ability students (Willis, 1990) and that less academically successful students benefit at the expense of their more successful partners (Mills & Durden, 1992; Robinson, 1990). Many of the most carefully conducted studies aimed are resolving this controversy have been focused on ability grouping in technologically-assisted instruction. In a week-long study on the learning of LOGO, Webb (1984) investigated whether the higher-ability students in cooperative groups of three would try to monopolize the computer. She found that (a) student ability did not relate to contact time with the computer and (b) student success in programming was predicted by different profiles of abilities and by group process variables such as verbal interaction. Yeuh and Alessi (1988) used group ability composition as one of their treatments for students utilizing the computer to learn three topics in algebra. They formed groups of medium-ability students and groups of mixed-ability students and found that group composition had no significant effect on achievement. Hooper and Hannafin (1988), in a study with 40 eighth-grade students, found that on a computer task low ability students working with high-ability partners achieved higher than did low ability students studying in homogeneous groups or alone, without lowering the achievement of high-ability students. In a subsequent study involving 125 sixth- and seventh-grade students, Hooper and Hannafin (1991) randomly assigned students to homogeneous or heterogeneous pairs, and pairs to cooperative or individualistic conditions. High-ability students interacted equally across treatments, but low-ability students interacted 30% more when placed in heterogeneous pairs. Students in the heterogeneous groups achieved and cooperated significantly more than did students in the homogeneous pairs (or the individualistic condition).

Simsek and Hooper (1992) compared the effects of cooperative and individual learning on student performance and attitudes during interactive videodisc instruction. Thirty fifth- and sixth-grade students were classified as high or low ability and randomly assigned to cooperative or individual treatments. Students completed a level II interactive video disc science lesson. The achievement, attitudes, and time on task of high- and low-ability students working alone or in cooperative groups were compared. Results indicated that both high- and low-ability students performed better on the posttest when they learned in cooperative groups than did their counterparts who learned alone. Students who worked individually spent less time on task. Members of cooperative groups developed more positive attitudes toward instruction, teamwork, and peers than did students studying alone.

Simsek and Tsai (1992) compared the effects of homogeneous versus heterogeneous ability grouping on performance and attitudes of students working cooperatively during interactive videodisc instruction. After two cooperative training sessions, 80 fourth- through sixth-grade students, classified as high and low ability, were randomly assigned to treatments. Students completed a level II interactive video disc science lesson. The amount of instructional time for each group was also recorded. Homogeneous low-ability groups scored significantly lower than the other three groups, while the difference in achievement of high-ability students in homogeneous versus heterogeneous groups was not statistically significant. Homogeneous low-ability groups consistently used the least amount of time. Low-ability students in heterogeneous groups had significantly more positive attitudes than did their high-ability groupmates.

Hooper (1992b) compared individual and cooperative learning in an investigation of the effects of ability grouping on achievement, instructional efficacy, and discourse during computer-based mathematics instruction. A total of 115 fifth- and sixth-grade students were classified as having high or average ability and were randomly assigned to group or individual treatments. Students in the cooperative condition were assigned to either heterogeneous or homogeneous dyads, according to ability. Results indicated that students completed the instruction more effectively in groups than alone. In groups, achievement and efficiency were highest for high-ability homogeneously grouped students and lowest for average-ability homogeneously grouped students. Generating and receiving help were significant predictors of achievement, and average-ability students generated and received significantly more help in heterogeneous groups than in homogeneous ones.

Hooper et al. (1993) compared cooperative and individualistic learning on academically high- and average/low-performing students. They classified 175 fourth-grade students as high or average/low performing academically and randomly assigned them to pairs or individualistic conditions strategies by performance level. Performance level was determined by scores on the mathematics subscale of the California Achievement Test. All cooperative pairs consisted of one high- and one average/low-performing student. They found that the students in the cooperative conditions performed higher on a computer-assisted symbolic reasoning task than did the students in the individualistic conditions. The greatest benefactors from the group learning experience appeared to be the highest-performing students. Overall achievement increased by almost 20% for high-academic ability students but only 4% for average-ability students. High-ability students may have benefited from generating explanations of their less able partners and less able partners might have adopted more passive roles. Mulryan (1992) found that the highest-achieving students adopted the more active roles in cooperative learning groups and the least able students demonstrated high levels of passive behavior, a pattern that, according to Webb (1989), further decreases the achievement of the passive students.

The results of these studies indicate that cooperative learning may be used effectively with both homogeneous and heterogeneous groups but that the greatest educational benefits may be derived when heterogeneous groups work with technology-supported instruction. In heterogeneous cooperative learning groups, low-ability students increased their achievement considerably and high-ability students generally either increased their achievement or achieved at the same level as did their counterparts in homogeneously high groups.

30.8.6.2 Gender. The gender of group members has been hypothesized to be an important factor in determining the success of technology-supported cooperative learning. D. W. Johnson,

Johnson, Richards, and Buckman (1986) found that computer-assisted cooperative learning, compared with competitive and individualistic computer-assisted learning, increased the positiveness of female students' attitudes toward computers, equalized the status and respect among group members regardless of gender, and resulted in a more equal participation pattern between male and female members. Whereas females in cooperative groups liked working with the computer more than males did, there was no significant difference in oral interactions between males and females. Dalton et al. (1987) examined interactions between instructional method and gender and found that cooperative learning was rated more favorably by low-ability females than by low-ability males. Other studies noted no significant differences in performance between males and females in computer-based instruction cooperative learning settings (Mevarech et al., 1987; Webb, 1984). Carrier and Sales (1987) compared female pairs, male pairs, and mixed pairs among college juniors and noted that female pairs verbalized the most, whereas male pairs verbalized the least, and that male–female pairs demonstrated the most off-task behavior. Lee (1993) found that males tended to become more verbally active and females tended to become less verbally active in equal-ratio, mixed-gender groups.

A study that looked at mixed-gender groups versus single-gender groups was done by Underwood and McCaffrey (1990) in England. Two classes of students between 10.5 and 11.4 years of age from a single school participated in the study. The 40 females and 40 males were randomly assigned to male/male, female/female, or male/female pairs. The study was divided into three sessions. The first session had the subjects working individually. In the second session subjects worked in pairs. The third session also involved pairs, but subjects who were in mixed pairs were shifted to single-gender pairs and single-gender pairs were assigned to mixed pairs. The subjects worked with a computer program in language tasks that required them to place missing letters into text. The results showed that single-gender pairs completed more stories and had more correct responses than did mixed-gender pairs. When subjects were shifted from single-gender pairs to mixed-gender pairs, their level of activity decreased but there was no change in their overall performance. The study found no overall differences for gender on any of the measures. No cooperative training was given and mixed pairs rarely discussed their answers. Rather, one subject operated the keyboard and the other gave directions.

Overall, there is mixed evidence concerning the impact of technology-supported instruction on males and females. A conservative interpretation of the existing research is that there will be no performance differences between males and females on technology-supported cooperative learning, but females will have more positive attitudes toward using technology when they learn in cooperative groups.

30.8.7 Relationships: Networking into Teams

Technology such as electronic mail, bulletin boards, and conferences can be used to create teams of individuals who are widely separated geographically. In an electronically networked team, interaction no longer has to be face-to-face, team members can be anywhere in the world. Meetings require only that members be at their terminals. Communication between meetings can be asynchronous and extremely fast in comparison with telephone conversations and interoffice mail. Participation may be more equalized and less affected by prestige and status (McGuire, Kiesler, & Siegel, 1987; Siegel, Dubrovsky, Kiesler, & McGuire, 1986). The egalitarian "network" structures may coexist with substantial hierarchy and centralization in patters of communication.

Electronic communications influence interaction style and work flow. The use of electronic mail compared to telephones, for example, enables workers to control the pace of their response and thus facilitates multitasking. Digital conferencing may make employees less risk averse and render group decision making less predictable, more time-consuming, and more egalitarian (Sproull & Kiesler, 1991; Wellman et al. 1996). Whether these effects on decision making enhance organizational performance or will continue as the technologies develop and change is uncertain in part because they depend on the specific ways in which the technological systems are designed and implemented (O'Mahony & Barley, 1999; Sproull & Kiesler, 1991).

Electronic communication, however, relies almost entirely on plain text for conveying messages, text that is often ephemeral, appearing on and disappearing from a screen without any necessary tangible artifacts. It becomes easy for a sender to be out of touch with his or her audience. And it is easy for the sender to be less constrained by conventional norms and rules for behavior in composing messages. Communicators can feel a greater sense of anonymity, detect less individuality in others, feel less empathy, feel less guilt, be less concerned over how they compare with others, and be less influenced by social conventions (Kiesler, Siegel, & McGuire, 1984; Short, Williams, & Christie, 1976). Such influences can lead both to more honesty and more "flaming" (name calling and epithets).

Hara, Bonk, and Angeli and his associates (2000) conducted a content analysis of on-line discussions. They examined participation rates, interaction patterns, social cues within student messages, cognitive and metacognitive components, and depth of processing. They concluded that messages became more lengthy and cognitively deeper over time. The messages were also embedded with peer references, became more interactive over time, and were thus indicative of a student-oriented environment.

30.8.8 Other Factors

30.8.8.1 Cost Effectiveness. The use of cooperative learning increases the cost effectiveness of technology. Although the range of technology that could be used in schools is increasing yearly (Hancock & Betts, 1994), the cost of adopting new technologies is an inhibiting factor to its use. Ensuring that every student is provided with the latest technology is beyond the financial resources of most school districts. Giving each cooperative learning group access to the latest technology is much more cost effective. An historical example is the adoption of computers by schools. By having groups work at computers (instead of

individuals) schools were able to reduce significantly the cost of obtaining and maintaining computers (Johnson & Johnson, 1985; Wizer, 1987).

30.8.8.2 Innovation in Groupware and Hardware. In creating joint workspaces for team members to work together, and in creating hardware and communication networks that facilitates teamwork, considerable innovation has taken, is taking, and will take place. The promise of the current technology is that in the future, more effective, efficient, and productive ways of teaming will be created through technology.

Of special interest for technology-supported cooperative learning is the use of self-powered, palm-sized computers and low-cost, high-bandwidth wireless communications. Just as computers made communication asynchronous, these mobile innovations make communication independent of place. The ability to communicate with anyone at anytime and anywhere geometrically increases the possibilities of technology-supported cooperative learning. And the widespread use of such technologies will undoubtedly inspire even more effective ways to use hardware and software to enhance human cooperation. Both students and teachers, furthermore, benefit from high-bandwidth, as it allows various technologies (i.e., high-quality video, sophisticated teleconferencing, and Internet-based communication and assessment tools) to converge and be delivered together, thereby providing richer content and stimulating cooperative interaction.

30.9 QUESTIONS ABOUT TECHNOLOGY-SUPPORTED COOPERATIVE LEARNING

Given the powerful effects of cooperation on achievement, relationships, and psychological health, and given the numerous advantages of using technology-supported cooperative learning, there are a number of questions about the use of technology that may tentatively be answered. First, *Does technology effect achievement or is it merely a means of delivering instruction?* In a review of research, Clark (1983) concluded that technology is merely a means of delivering instruction. There are cognitive consequences of discussing what one is learning with classmates that technology may not be able to duplicate. The extent to which social interaction is essential for effective learning, the transformation of the mind, and the development of expertise is unclear.

Second, *Is a "dialogue" with a computer as effective in promoting achievement, higher-level reasoning, and ability to apply learning as a dialogue with a peer?* The answer is probably no. It takes more than the presentation of information to have a dialogue. There needs to be an exchange of knowledge that leads to epistemic conflict and intellectual challenge and curiosity. Such an exchange is personal as well as informational. It involves respect for and belief in each other's abilities and commitment to each other's learning. Our results and the results of other researchers indicate that a dialogue with a peer is far more powerful than one with a computer.

Third, *Can a computer pass as a person?* The answer, again, is probably no. A person interacts quite differently with a computer than he or she does with another person. Machines and people are not equally interesting or persuasive. With other people there is a commitment to their learning and well-being. It is rare to feel the same emotions toward a machine.

Fourth, *Is the effectiveness of a message separate from the medium?* Generally, the research on cognitive development indicates that the same information, presented in other formats (especially nonsocial formats) is only marginally effective in promoting genuine cognitive development (Murray, 1983; D. W. Johnson & R. Johnson, 1989).

Fifth *Is technology an amplifier or a transformer of the mind?* An **amplifier** serves a tool function like note taking or measuring. A **transformer** leads to the discovery and invention of principles. If technological learning devices are transformers, the habitual technology users eventually will be in a new stage of mental functioning. Postman (1985) believes that the introduction into a culture of a technique such as writing or a clock is not merely an extension of humans' power to record information or bind time but a transformation of their way of thinking and the content of human culture. Generally, therefore, it may be concluded that technology such as the computer is a tool to amplify the minds of students. As a tool, the computer (as well as the calculator) can free students from the rote memorization of methods of mathematical formulation and formula-driven science, allowing more time for underlying concepts to be integrated with physical examples. A danger of the computer is that student will know what button to push to get the right answer without understanding the underlying process or developing the ability to solve the problem on his or her own without the computer. There is far more to expertise than knowing how to run hardware and software.

Finally, *Can technology such as computers prepare a student for the "real world"?* Technological expertise is helpful in finding and holding a job. Working in a modern organization, however, requires team skills such as leadership and conflict management and the ability to engage in interpersonal problem solving. Although it is clear that cooperative learning is an analogue to modern organizational life, experience in using technology in and of itself may only marginally improve employability and job success. A person has to have interpersonal competence as well as technical competence.

30.10 THE FUTURE OF TECHNOLOGY-SUPPORTED COOPERATIVE LEARNING

The interdependence between the use of technology-supported instruction and cooperative learning is relatively unexplored. Technologies can either facilitate or obstruct cooperation. The ways in which technology may enhance or interfere with cooperative efforts have not been conceptualized, placed in a theoretical framework, researched, and applied in classrooms. Cooperative learning has a well-formulated theory validated by hundreds of research studies, translated into a set of practical procedures that teachers and administrators may use, and actually implemented in tens of thousands of classrooms throughout the world. Technology is transforming the way in which work and communication are conducted. Despite the success of cooperative learning and technology, there are a number of shortcomings of the work on technology-supported cooperative learning.

First, there is a lack of theorizing. If technology-supported cooperative learning is to continue to develop, it needs to become more articulate about the theories that underlie its use. Currently, social interdependence theory is the most clearly spelled out theoretical base for cooperative learning, but the way in which technology provides unique opportunities for cooperation have not been tied to social interdependence theory. John Dewey has been widely quoted, but his work does not provide a precise theory on which to base either cooperative learning or technology-supported instruction. The same may be said for Vygotsky. Conceptual models of how technology and teamwork may be productively integrated are practically nonexistent. The variables unique to the combination of technology and cooperation have not been identified and defined. Two theoretical perspectives are needed that can be contrasted and compared in research studies. The field needs such rivalry to develop.

Second, relatively little research has been done. Overall, the quality of the existing research is quite high. Only a few of the potential outcomes, however, have been studied. There are many gaps in the research on technology-supported cooperative learning. The unique strengths of technology-supported cooperative learning have not been assessed and documented. The impact of technology-based cooperative learning on relationships among students (especially in face-to-face and non-face-to-face situations and among diverse individuals) has not been studied. The specific ways that use of technology affects various aspects of psychological health (such as social adjustment, personal happiness, self-esteem, anxiety levels, social competencies, and ability to cope with stress and diversity) is largely unknown. Almost all of the research that has been conducted has focused on the effectiveness of technology-based computer instruction or specific software programs without testing theory. In the future, theoretically oriented research needs to be conducted.

Third, the lack of conceptual models and the scarcity of research have created a corresponding lack of operational procedures for practice. Operational procedures are needed for designing and implementing instructional procedures that optimize the impact of technology-supported cooperative learning. Equivalent procedures need to be designed for work environments where technology and teamwork are used together. Once the operational procedures are clarified, decisions about training teachers and students can be made. Teachers can be trained to implement cooperative learning, but training in the specific procedures for implementing technology-supported cooperative learning is underdeveloped. The nature and amount of training students need to work together cooperatively while utilizing technology are largely unknown. Whereas the social skills required to cooperate have been clear for some time (D. W. Johnson, 1991, 2003; D. W. Johnson & F. Johnson, 2003), the social skills required to utilize technology cooperatively have generally been ignored. More needs to be known about the skills students need to maximize the constructiveness of technology-supported cooperative learning.

In addition to using validated theory to operationalize teacher and student procedures, new software development should be more closely tied to validated theory. Effective cooperation depends on the existence of five basic elements (positive interdependence, individual accountability, promotive interaction, appropriate use of social skills, and group processing) in operational procedures (D. W. Johnson & Johnson, 1989). Whereas there are many groupware programs, the extent to which groupware incorporates the five basic elements of cooperation has not been discussed or researched, and whether there are other elements essential to technology-supported cooperative learning programs has not been determined by research. Attention to ensuring that the groupware developed is based on social interdependence theory as well as on technology hardware and software potentialities is needed.

In summary, what is needed is a theory to stimulate research that, in turn, will validate and modify the theory. The results need to be used to design specific procedures for operationalizing technology-supported cooperative learning at every grade level and in every subject area. Groupware needs to be tied more closely to theory. Without this combination of theory, research, and operational procedures and software, proponents of technology-supported cooperative learning cannot present a persuasive case for adoption or an effective training program for teachers. On the positive side, there has been so little research on technology-supported cooperative learning that the future is wide open to interested social scientists.

There are, however, several areas on which researchers can focus. First, there is a need for long-term studies that track the use of technology-supported cooperative learning across at least 1 school year and, ideally, several years. Short-term studies of initial use are not enough. The real question is whether the use of technology-supported cooperative learning will be maintained over several years.

Second, the critical factors that result in technology and cooperative learning enhancing each other need to be identified and researched. One important factor may be epistemic conflict, that is, the collision of adverse opinion. Cognitive growth and the development of problem-solving skills depend on epistemic conflict (D. W. Johnson & R. Johnson, 1979, 1995; Piaget, 1950). Students need the opportunity to experience and resolve academic controversies. Technology rarely engages students in intellectual conflict the same way other students can. The role of technology in promoting and facilitating intellectual conflicts among students has not been thoroughly investigated.

Third, there is a question whether technology-supported instruction will increase inequality in educational outcomes (Becker & Sterling, 1987). Students who have access to the new technologies in their homes will be more skilled and sophisticated in their uses than will students who do not. Equality in the classroom may require heterogeneous grouping where students who are skilled in the use of instructional technologies work with students who are not. Cooperative learning is an essential aspect of such equalization. New studies need to be conducted

on group composition focusing on the ability of students to use instructional technologies.

Fourth, the implementation process by which technology-supported cooperative learning is institutionalized within schools needs to be documented and studied. Whereas advocates of technology see a revolution coming in instruction, historians point to the virtual absence of lasting or profound changes in classroom practice over the past 100 years. Despite brief periods of popularity, new instructional technologies such as educational television, language laboratories, and programmed learning were tried and dropped. Life in classrooms remains largely unchanged. Lepper and Gurtner (1989) argue that the last "technology" to have had a major impact on the way schools are run is the blackboard. Most often new technologies are used in ways that do not disrupt regular classroom practices, which means that they can be dropped with no disruption to ongoing classroom life. Similarly, software selection is often conducted with the intention of supporting existing classroom practices rather than transforming them. Considerably more research is needed on the implementation process by which the combination of cooperative learning and learning technologies becomes integrated and institutionalized in classroom and schools.

Fifth, studies need to focus on the role of teachers and administrators in the implementation process. No matter how good technology is, unless teachers decide to use it and gain some expertise in how to implement it, the technology will not be adopted by schools.

Sixth, studies need to examine the support services required for technology to be used in the classroom. Who repairs the technology and how often repairs are needed are important questions. Teachers, for example, cannot be expected to be computer technicians. As the quantity of research on technology-supported cooperative learning has grown, so has the networking among interested social scientists and educators. In 1996 an international conference on computer-supported cooperative learning took place, followed by similar conferences in Toronto in 1997, at Stanford University in 1999, in The Netherlands in 2001, and in Boulder, Colorado, in 2002. Conferences such as these are helpful in advancing the development of relevant theory, research, and operational procedures and software.

30.11 SUMMARY

We live in a networked, information-based society in which teams and technology are needed to manage the complexity of learning, work, and living. Schools have become a strategic place. For education to develop the technological and teamwork competencies of children, adolescents, and young adults, if must overcome the individualistic assumption historically connected with technology-supported instruction and utilize cooperative learning as an inherent part of instruction. The **individual assumption** is that instruction should be tailored to each student's personal aptitude, learning style, personality characteristics, motivation, and needs. Computers were originally viewed as an important tool for providing individualized learning experiences. The difficulties and shortcomings of individualizing instruction call into question the wisdom of focusing technology on delivering individualized instruction. Technology may be more productively used when it is used in combination with cooperation learning.

Cooperative learning is the instructional use of small groups so that students work together to maximize their own and each other's learning. There are four types of cooperative learning—formal cooperative learning, informal cooperative learning, base groups, and academic controversies. **Technology-supported cooperative learning** exists when the instructional use of technology is combined with the use of cooperative learning groups. What underlies cooperative learning's worldwide use is that it is based on a well-formulated theory that has been validated by numerous research studies and operationalized into practical procedures that can be used at any level of education. The three theoretical perspectives that have contributed to cooperative learning are cognitive-developmental theory, behavioral learning theory, and social interdependence theory. The latter has had the most profound influence on the development of cooperative learning. Between 1898 and 1989, over 550 experimental and 100 correlational studies were conducted comparing the relative effectiveness of cooperative, competitive, and individualistic efforts. Generally, cooperative efforts result in higher achievement, more positive relationships, and greater psychological health than do competitive or individualistic efforts. Not all groups, however, are cooperative groups. To be a cooperative group, five basic elements must be structured within the learning situation—positive interdependence, promotive interaction, individual accountability, social skills, and group processing. For schools to adopt technology and maintain its use over time, the school organizational structure must change from a mass-manufacturing structure to a team-based, high-performance structure (which is known as the cooperative school).

There is a growing body of research on technology-supported cooperative learning. The results indicate that compared with technology-supported instruction, cooperative learning tends to increase achievement (both academic achievement and learning how to use technology), promote positive attitudes (toward technology and cooperation), promote development (cognitive development, learning control, social competencies), promote positive relationships with team members, promote positive effects on both high- and low-performing students and both male and female students, be cost effective, and promote innovation in groupware and hardware. What this research illuminates is that cooperative learning and technology-supported instruction have complementary strengths. The more technology is used to teach, the more necessary cooperative learning is. The computer, for example, can control the flow of work, monitor accuracy, give electronic feedback, and do calculations. Cooperative learning provides a sense of belonging, the opportunity to explain and summarize what is being learned, social models, respect and approval for efforts to achieve, encouragement of divergent thinking, and interpersonal feedback on academic learning and the use of the technology.

A number of questions must be asked about technology-supported instruction. Does technology affect achievement, or is it only a means for delivering instruction? Current evidence indicates that computers deliver instruction but they do not effect achievement in and of themselves. Is a dialogue with the computer as effective as a dialogue with another person in promoting achievement and higher-level reasoning? The answer seems to be no. Can the computer pass as a person? The answer seems to be no. Cooperators are people, not machines. Is the effectiveness of a message separate from the medium? The answer seems to be yes, messages from other people are more powerful and influential than are messages from machines. Is technology an amplifier or a transformer of the mind? The answer seems to be an amplifier. Technology amplifies communication, but it takes other people to transform each other's minds.

The future of technology-supported cooperative learning depends largely on the cycle of theory–research–practice. The unique opportunities of technology-supported cooperative learning need to be tied to social interdependence theory (or another theory underlying cooperative learning), research needs to be conducted to validate or disconfirm the theoretical predictions, and operational procedures and groupware need to be developed directly based on the validated theory.

Finally, technologies can either facilitate or obstruct cooperation. The ways in which technology may enhance or interfere with cooperative efforts have not been conceptualized, placed in a theoretical framework, researched, and applied in classrooms. Despite the success of cooperative learning and technology, there are a number of shortcomings of the work on technology-supported cooperative learning. Among other issues, long-term studies of the use of technology-supported cooperative learning are needed, the role of factors that enhance or interfere with cooperation (such as epistemic conflict) need to be studied, the impact of implementation on equality of opportunity needs to be researched, and the role of the teacher and support services needed to be investigated.

Few educational innovations hold the promise that technology-supported cooperative learning does. The combination of cooperation and technology has a potential that is changing the way courses are being delivered and instruction is taking place. More theorizing, research, and refinement of practice is needed to help the field actualize its possibilities.

References

Adams, D., Carson, H., & Hamm, M. (1990). *Cooperative learning and educational media.* Englewood Cliffs, NJ: Educational Technology.

Allen, R. (2001, Fall). Technology and learning. *Curriculum Update,* 1–3, 6–8. Association for Supervision and Curriculum Development.

Ames, R., & Lau, S. (1982). An attributional analysis of student help-seeking in academic settings. *Journal of Educational Psychology,* 74, 414-423.

Amigues, R., & Agostinelli, S. (1992). Collaborative problem-solving with computer: How can an interactive learning environment be designed? *European Journal of Psychology of Education,* 7(4), 325-337.

Anderson, A., Mayes, T., & Kibby, M. (1995). Small group collaborative discovery learning from hypertext. In C. O'Malley (Ed.), *Computer supported collaborative learning, NATO ASI Series F: Computer and systems sciences* (Vol. 129, pp. 23-28). Heidelberg, Berlin: Springer-Verlag.

Archer-Kath, J., Johnson, D. W., & Johnson, R. (1994). Individual versus group feedback in cooperative groups. *Journal of Social Psychology,*

Aronson, E. (1978). *The jigsaw classroom.* Beverly Hills, CA: Sage.

Baker, C. (1985). The microcomputer and the curriculum. A critique. *Journal of Curriculum Studies,* 17, 449-451.

Bandura, A. (1977). *Social learning theory.* Englewood Cliffs, NJ: Prentice Hall.

Bates, A. (1995). *Tecnology, open learning and distance education.* London: Routledge.

Battista, M., & Clements, D. (1986). The effects of Logo and CAI problem-solving environments on problem-solving abilities and mathematics achievement. *Computers in Human Behavior, 2,* 183-193.

Beane, W., & Lemke, E. (1971). Group variables influencing the transfer of conceptual behavior. *Journal of Educational Psychology,* 62(3), 215-218.

Bearison, D. (1982). New directions in studies of social interaction and cognitive growth. In F. Serafica (Ed.), *Social-cognitive development in context* (pp. 199-221). New York: Guildford Press.

Bearison, D., Magzamen, S., & Filardo, E. (1986). Socio-cognitive conflict and cognitive growth in young children. *Merrill-Palmer Quarterly,* 32, 51-72.

Becker, H. (1984). *School uses of microcomputers: Reports from a national survey* (Issue No. 6). Baltimore, MD: Johns Hopkins University, Center for Social Organization of Schools.

Becker, H. (1985). *The second national U.S. school users of microcomputers survey.* Paper presented at the Second World Conference on Computers in Education, Norfolk, VA.

Becker, H., & Sterling, C. (1987). Equity in schools computer use: National data and neglected considerations. *Journal of Educational Computing Research, 3,* 289-311.

Bell, P. (2001). Using argument map representations to make thinking visible in the classroom. In T. Koschmann, R. Hall, & N. Miyake (Eds.), *CSCL2: Carrying forward the conversation* (pp. 449-485). Mahwah, NJ: Lawrence Erlbaum Associates.

Berndt, T., Perry, T., & Miller, K. (1988). Friends' and classmates' interactions on academic tasks. *Journal of Educational Psychology, 80,* 506-513.

Bonk, C., & King, K. (Eds.). (1998). *Electronic collaborators: Learner-centered technologies for literacy, apprenticeship, and discourse.* Mahwah, NJ: Lawrence Erlbaum.

Bonk, C., Medury, P., & Reynolds, T. (in press). Cooperative hypermedia: The marriage of collaborative writing and mediated environments. *Computers in the Schools,*

Britton, J. (1990). Research currents: Second thoughts on learning. In Brubacher, M., Payne, R., & Richett, K. (Eds.), *Perspectives on small group learning: Theory and practice* (pp. 3-11). Oakville, Ontario: Rubicon.

Brush, T. (1997). The effects on student achievement and attitudes when using integrated learning systems with cooperative pairs. *Educational Technology Research and Development,* 45(1), 51-64.

Carlson, H., & Falk, D. (1989). Effective use of interactive videodisc instruction in understanding and implementing cooperative group learning with elementary pupils in social studies. *Theory and Research in Social Education,* 17(3), 241-158.

Carrier, C. (1984). Do learners make good choices? A review of research on learner control in instruction. *Instructional Innovator,* 29(2), 15-17.

Carrier, C., & Sales, G. (1987). Pair versus individual work on the acquisition concepts in a computer-based instructional lesson. *Journal of Computer-Based Instruction,* 14(1), 11-17.

Chernick, R., & White, M. (1981). *Pupils' interaction with microcomputers vs. interaction in classroom settings.* New York: Teachers College, Columbia University, Electronic Learning Laboratory.

Chernick, R., & White, M. (1983, May). *Pupil cooperation in computer learning vs. learning with classroom materials.* Paper presented at the New York State Psychological Association, Liberty, NY.

Clark, R. (1983). Reconsidering research on learning from media. *Review of Educational Research,* 53, 445-459.

Clements, D. (1986). Research on Logo and social development. *Logo Exchange,* 5(3), 22-24.

Clements, D., & Nastasi, B. (1985). Effects of computer environments on social-emotional development: Logo and computer-assisted instruction. *Computers in the Schools,* 2(2/3), 11-31.

Clements, D., & Nastasi, B. (1988). Social and cognitive interaction in educational computer environments. *American Educational Research Journal,* 25, 87-106.

Cockayne, S. (1991, February). Effects of small group sizes on learning with interactive videodisc. *Educational Technology,* 43-45.

Cohen, E. (1986). *Designing groupwork: Strategies for heterogeneous classrooms.* New York: Teachers College Press.

Cosden, M., & English, J. (1987). The effects of grouping, self-esteem, and locus of control on microcomputer performance and help seeking by mildly handicapped students. *Journal of Educational Computing Research, 3,* 443-460.

Cox, D., & Berger, C. (1985). The importance of group size in the use of problem-solving skills on a microcomputer. *Journal of Educational Computing Research, 1,* 459-468.

Crook, C. (1994). *Computers and the collaborative experience of learning.* London: Routledge.

Cuban, L. (1986). *Teachers and machines: The classroom use of technology since 1920.* New York: Teachers College Press.

Dalton, D. (1990a). The effects of cooperative learning strategies on achievement and attitudes during interactive video. *Journal of Computer-Based Instruction,* 17, 8-16.

Dalton, D. (1990b, April). *The effects of prior learning on learner interaction and achievement during cooperative computer-based instruction.* Paper presented at the annual meeting of the American Educational Research Association, Boston, MA.

Dalton, D., Hannafin, M., & Hooper, S. (1987). Effects of individual and cooperative computer-assisted instruction on student performance and attitudes. *Educational Technology Research and Development,* 37(2), 15-24.

Damon, W., & Killen, M. (1982). Peer interaction and the process of change in children's moral reasoning. *Merrill-Palmer Quarterly, 28,* 347-367.

Davis, J., & Huttenlocher, D. (1995). Shared annotation for cooperative learning. *Proceedings of CSCL95: First International Conference on Computer Support for Collaborative Learning.* Mahwah, NJ: Lawrence Erlbaum.

Dees, R. (1991). The role of cooperative learning in increasing problem-solving ability in a college remedial course. *Journal for Research in Mathematics Education,* 22(5), 409-421.

Deutsch, M. (1949). A theory of cooperation and competition. *Human Relations, 2,* 129-152.

Deutsch, M. (1962). Cooperation and trust: Some theoretical notes. In M. R. Jones (Ed.), *Nebraska symposium on motivation* (pp. 275–319). Lincoln: University of Nebraska Press.

DeVries, D., & Edwards, K. (1974). Student teams and learning games: Their effects on cross-race and cross-sex interaction. *Journal of Educational Psychology, 66*(5), 741–749.

Dickson, W., & Vereen M. (1985). Two students at one microcomputer. *Theory into Practice, 22*(4), 296–300.

Druckman, D., Rozelle, R., & Baxter, J. (1982). *Nonverbal communication: Survey, theory, and research.* Beverly Hills, CA: Sage.

Dwyer, D. (1994). Apple classrooms of tomorrow: What we've learned. *Educational Leadership, 51*(7), 4–10.

Dyer, L. (1993). *An investigation of the effects of cooperative learning on computer monitored problem solving.* Ph.D. Dissertation, University of Minnesota.

Eraut, M. (1995). Groupwork with computers in British primary schools. *Journal of Educational Computing Research, 13*(1), 61–87.

Federico, P. (1980). Adaptive instruction: Trends and issues. In R. Snow, P. Federico, & W. Montague (Eds.), *Aptitude, learning, and instruction: Vol. 1. Cognitive process analysis of aptitude* (pp. 1–26). Hillsdale, NJ: Lawrence Erlbaum.

Fishman, B., & Gomez, L. (1997, December). How activities foster CMC tool use in classrooms. In R. Hall, N. Miyake, & N. Enyedy (Eds.), *Computer support for cooperative learning 1997. Proceedings of the Second International Conference on Computer Support for Collaborative Learning* (pp. 37–44). Toronto, Ontario, Canada.

Fletcher, B. (1985). Group and individual learning of junior high school children on a micro-computer-based task. *Educational Review, 37,* 252–261.

Fetcher-Flinn, C., & Gravatt, B. (1995). The efficacy of computer assisted instruction (CAI): A meta-analysis. *Journal of Educational Computing Research, 12*(3), 219–241.

Frank, M. (1984). A comparison between an individual and group goal structure contingency that differed in the behavioral contingency and performance-outcome components (Doctoral dissertation, University of Minnesota). *Dissertation Abstracts International, 45*(05), 1341-A.

Garhart, C., Hannafin, M. (1986). The accuracy of cognitive monitoring during computer-based instruction. *Journal of Computer-Based Instruction, 13,* 88–93.

Hancock, V., & Betts, F. (1994). From the lagging to the leading edge. *Educational Leadership, 51*(7), 24–29.

Hannafin, M. (1984). Guidelines for using locus of instructional control in the design of computer-assisted instruction. *Journal of Instructional Development, 7*(3), 6–10.

Hannafin, M., & Rieber, L. (1989). Psychological foundations of instructional design for emerging computer-based interactive technologies: Part II. *Educational Technology Research and Development, 37*(2), 102–114.

Hara, N., Bonk, C., & Angeli, C. (2000). Content analysis of online discussion in an applied educational psychology course. *Instructional Science, 28,* 115–152.

Harasim, L., Hiltz, R., Teles, L., & Turoff, M. (1995). *Learning networks: A field guide to teaching and learning online.* Cambridge, MA: MIT press.

Hawkins, S., Sheingold, K., Gearhart, M., & Berger, C. (1982). Microcomputers in schools: Impact on the social life of elementary classrooms. *Journal of Applied Developmental Psychology, 3,* 361–373.

Hill, G. (1982). Group versus individual performance: Are N + 1 heads better than one? *Psychological Bulletin, 91,* 517–539.

Hooper, S. (1992a). Effects of peer interaction during computer-based mathematics instruction. *Journal of Educational Research, 85*(3), 180–189.

Hooper, S. (1992b). Cooperation learning and computer-based instruction. *Educational Technology Research and Development, 40*(3), 21–38.

Hooper, S., & Hannafin, M. (1988). Cooperative CBI: The effects of heterogeneous versus homogeneous groups on the learning of progressively complex concepts. *Journal of Educational Computing Research, 4*(4), 413–424.

Hooper, S., & Hannafin, M. (1991). The effects of group composition on achievement, interaction, and learning efficiency during computer-based cooperative instruction. *Educational Technology Research and Development, 39*(3), 27–40.

Hooper, S., Ward, T., Hannafin, M., & Clark, H. (1989). The effects of aptitude composition on achievement during small group learning. *Journal of Computer-Based Instruction, 16,* 102–109.

Hooper, S., Temiyakarn, C., & Williams, M. (1993). The effects of cooperative learning and learner control on high- and average-ability students. *Educational Technology Research and Development, 41*(2), 5–18.

Hwong, N., Caswell, A., Johnson, D. W., & Johnson, R. (1993). Effects of cooperative and individualistic learning on prospective elementary teachers' music achievement and attitudes. *Journal of Social Psychology, 133*(1), 53–64.

Huang, C. (1993). *The effects of feedback on performance and attitude in cooperative and individualized computer-based instruction.* Doctoral Dissertation, University of Minnesota.

Hythecker, V., Rocklin, T., Dansereau, D., Lambiotte, J., Larson, C., & O'Donnell, A. (1985). A computer-based learning strategy training module: Development and evaluation. *Journal of Educational Computer Research, 1*(3), 275–283.

Inkpen, K., Booth, K., Klawe, M., & Upitis, R. (1995). Playing together beats playing apart, especially for girls. In J. Schnase & E. Cunnius (Eds.), *Proceedings of CSCL 1995: The First International Conference on Computer Support for Collaborative Learning* (pp. 177–181). Hillsdale, NJ: Erlbaum.

Innis, H. (1964). *The bias of communication.* Toronto: University of Toronto Press.

Innis, H. (1972). *Empire and communication.* Toronto: University of Toronto Press.

Isenberg, R. (1992). Social skills at the computer. *The Cooperative Link, 2*(6), 1–2.

Jarvela, S. (1996). New models of teacher-student interaction: A critical review. *European Journal of Psychology of Education, 6*(3), 246–268.

Johnson, D. W. (1991). *Human relations and your career.* Englewood Cliffs, NJ: Prentice Hall.

Johnson, D. W. (2003). *Reaching out: Interpersonal effectiveness and self-actualization.* Boston: Allyn & Bacon.

Johnson, D. W., & Johnson, F. (2003). *Joining together: Group theory and group skills* (7th ed.). Boston: Allyn & Bacon.

Johnson, D. W., & Johnson, R. (1979). Conflict in the classroom: Controversy and learning. *Review of Educational Research, 49,* 51–70.

Johnson, D. W., & Johnson, R. (1986). Computer-assisted cooperative learning. *Educational Technology, 26*(1), 12–18.

Johnson, D. W., & Johnson, R. (1989). *Cooperation and competition: Theory and research.* Edina, MN: Interaction Book.

Johnson, D. W., & Johnson, R. (1992a). Positive interdependence: Key to effective cooperation. In R. Hertz-Lazarowitz & N. Miller (Ed.), *Interaction in cooperative groups: The theoretical anatomy of group learning* (pp. 174–199). Cambridge, UK: Cambridge University Press.

Johnson, D. W., & Johnson, R. (1992b). *Positive interdependence: The heart of cooperative Learning.* Edina, MN: Interaction Book.

Johnson, D. W., & Johnson, R. (1994). *Leading the cooperative school* (2nd ed.). Edina, MN: Interaction Book.

Johnson, D. W., & Johnson, R. (1995). *Creative controversy: Intellectual challenge in the classroom* (3rd ed.). Edina, MN: Interaction Book.

Johnson, D. W., Johnson, R., & Holubec, E. (1998a). *Cooperation in the classroom* (6th ed.). Edina, MN: Interaction Book.

Johnson, D. W., Johnson, R., & Holubec, E. (1998b). *Advanced cooperative learning* (2nd ed.). Edina, MN: Interaction Book.

Johnson, D. W., Johnson, R., & Richards, P. (1986). A scale for assessing student attitudes toward computers: Preliminary findings. *Computers in the Schools, 3*(2), 31–38.

Johnson, D. W., Johnson, R., & Smith, K. (1998). *Active learning: Cooperation in the college classroom* (2nd ed.). Edina, MN: Interaction Book.

Johnson, D. W., Johnson, R., & Stanne, M. (1989). Impact of goal and resource interdependence on problem-solving success. *Journal of Social Psychology, 129*(5), 621–629.

Johnson, D. W., Johnson, R., Stanne, M., & Garibaldi, A. (1990). The impact of group processing on achievement in cooperative groups. *Journal of Social Psychology, 130,* 507–516.

Johnson, D. W., Johnson, R., Richards, S., & Buckman, L. (1986). The effect of prolonged implementation of cooperative learning on social support within the classroom. *Journal of Psychology, 119,* 405–411.

Johnson, R., & Johnson, D. W. (1979). Type of task and student achievement and attitudes in interpersonal cooperation, competition, and individualization. *Journal of Social Psychology, 116,* 211–219.

Johnson, D. W., Johnson, R., Ortiz, A., & Stanne, M. (1991). Impact of positive goal and resouce interdependence on achievement, interaction, and attitudes. *Journal of General Psychology, 118*(4), 341–347.

Johnson, R., Johnson, D. W., & Stanne, M. (1985). Effects of cooperative, competitive, and individualistic goal structures on computer-assisted instruction. *Journal of Educational Psychology, 77,* 668–677.

Johnson, R., Johnson, D. W., & Stanne, M. (1986). A comparison of computer-assisted cooperative, competitive, and individualistic learning. *American Educational Research Journal, 23,* 382–392.

Johnson, R., Johnson, D. W., Stanne, M., Smizak, B., & Avon, J. (1987). *Effect of composition pairs at the word processor on quality of writing and ability to use the word processor.* Minneapolis: Cooperative Learning Center, University of Minnesota.

Keeler, C., & Anson, R. (1995). An assessment of cooperative learning used for basic computer skills instruction in the college classroom. *Journal of Educational Computing Research, 19*(4), 379–393.

Khalili, A., & Shashaani, L. (1994). The effectiveness of computer applications: A meta-analysis. *Journal of Research on Computing in Education, 27*(1), 48–62.

Kiesler, S., Siegel, J., & McGuire, T. (1984, October). Social psychological aspects of computer-mediated communication. *American Psychologist, 39*(10), 1123–1134.

King, A. (1989). Verbal interaction and problem solving within computer-assisted cooperative learning groups. *Journal of Educational Computing Research, 5*(1), 1–15.

Lee, M. (1993). Gender, group composition, and peer interaction in computer-based cooperative learning. *Journal of Educational Computing Research, 9*(4), 549–577.

Lehrer, R., & Smith, P. (1986, April). *Logo learning: Are two heads better than one?* Paper presented at the annual meeting of the American Educational Research Association, San Francisco.

Lehtinen, E., & Repo, S. (1996). Activity, social interaction and reflective abstraction: Learning advanced mathematics in a computer environment. In S. Vosniadou, E. DeCorte, R. Glaser, & H. Mandl (Eds.), *International perspectives on the design of technology supported learning environments* (pp. 105–128). Mahwah, NJ: Lawrence Erlbaum.

Lehtinen, E., Hamalainen, S., & Malkonen, E. (1998, April). *Learning experimental research methodology and statistical inference in a computer environement.* Paper presented at the American Educational Research Association Annual Meeting, San Diego.

Lepper, M., & Gurtner J. (1989). Children and computers: Approaching the twenty-first century. *American Psychologist, 44*(2), 170–178.

Lesgold, A., Weiner, A., & Suthers, D. (1995, August). *Tools for thinking about complex issues.* Paper presented at the 6th European Conference for Research on Learning and Instruction, Nijmegen, The Netherlands.

Levin, J., & Kareev, Y. (1980). Problem-solving in everyday situations. *Quarterly Newsletter of the Laboratory of Comparative Human Cognition, 2,* 47–51.

Lew, M., Mesch, D., Johnson, D. W., & Johnson, R. (1986a). Positive interdependence, academic and collaborative-skills group contingencies and isolated students. *American Educational Research Journal, 23,* 476–488.

Lew, M., Mesch, D., Johnson, D. W., & Johnson, R. (1986b). Components of cooperative learning: Effects of collaborative skills and academic group contingencies on achievement and mainstreaming. *Contemporary Educational Psychology, 11,* 229–239.

Lin, J., Wu, C., & Liu, H. (1999). Using SimCPU in cooperative learning laboratories. *Journal of Educational Computing Research, 20*(3), 259–277.

Love, W. (1969). *Individual versus paired learning of an abstract algebra presented by computer assisted instruction.* Ph.D. Dissertation, Florida State University. (ERIC Document Reproduction Service No. ED 034 403).

Malikowski, S. (1998). *WEB-based conferencing for education.* The Center for Excellence in Education.

McConnell, D. (1994). Managing open learning in computer supported collaborative learning environments. *Studies in Higher Education, 19*(3), 175–191.

McDonald, C. (1993). *Learner-controlled lesson in cooperative learning groups during computer-based instruction.* Ph.D. Dissertation, University of Minnesota.

McGuire, T., Kiesler, S., & Siegel, J. (1987). Group and computer-mediated discussion effects in risk decision making. *Journal of Personality and Social Psychology, 52,* 917–930.

McInerey, V., McInerney, D., & Marsh, H. (1997). Effects of metacognitive strategy training within a cooperative group learning context on computer achievement and anxiety: An aptitude-treatment interaction study. *Journal of Educational Psychology, 89*(4), 686–695.

McLuhan, M. (1964). *Understanding media: The extensions of man.* New York: New American Library.

Mehrabian, A. (1971). *Silent messages.* Belmont, CA: Wadsworth.

Mesch, D., Lew, M., Johnson, D. W., & Johnson, R. (1986). Isolated teenagers, cooperative learning and the training of social skills. *Journal of Psychology, 120,* 323–334.

Mesch, D., Johnson, D. W., & Johnson, R. (1988). Impact of positive interdependence and academic group contingencies on achievement. *Journal of Social Psychology, 128,* 345–352.

Mevarech, Z. (1993). Who benefits from cooperative computer-assisted instruction? *Journal of Educational Computing Research, 9*(4), 451–464.

Mevarech, Z., Stern, D., & Levita, I. (1987). To cooperate or not to cooperate in CAI: That is the question. *Journal of Educational Research, 80*(3), 164–167.

Mevarech, Z., Silber, O., & Fine, D. (1991). Learning with computers in small groups: Cognitive and affective outcomes. *Journal of Educational Computing Research, 7*(2), 233–243.

Milheim, W., & Martin, B. (1991). Theoretical bases for the use of learner control: Three different perspectives. *Journal of Computer-Based Instruction, 18*(3), 99-105.

Mills, C., & Durden, W. (1992). Cooperative learning and ability groups: An issue of choice. *Gifted Child Quarterly, 36*(1), 11-16.

Muller, A., & Perlmutter, M. (1985). Preschool children's problem-solving interactions at computers and jigsaw puzzles. *Journal of Applied Developmental Psychology, 6,* 173-186.

Mulryan, C. (1992). Student passivity during cooperative small groups in mathematics. *Journal of Educational Research, 85,* 261-273.

Murray, F. (1983). *Cognitive benefits of teaching on the teacher.* Paper presented at American Educational Research Association Annual Meeting, Montreal, Quebec.

Nastasi, B., & Clements, D. (1992). Social-cognitive behaviors and higher-order thinking in educational computer environments. *Learning and Instruction, 2,* 215-238.

Nastasi, B., Clements, D., & Battista, M. (1990). Social-cognitive interactions, motivation, and cognitive growth in logo programming and CAI problem-solving environments. *Journal of Educational Psychology, 82,* 150-158.

Noell, J., & Carnine, D. (1989). Group and individual computer-based video instruction. *Educational Technology, 29*(1), 36-37.

Okey, J., & Majer, K. (1976). Individual and small-group learning with computer-assisted instruction. *AV Communication Review, 24*(1), 79-86.

O'Mahony, S., & Barley, S. (1999). Do digital telecommunications affect work and organization? The state of our knowledge. *Research on Organizational Behavior, 21,* 125-161.

Pea, R., Edelson, E., & Gomez, L. (1994, April). *The CoVis Collaboratory: High school science learning supported by a broadband educational network with scientific visualization, videoconferencing, and collaborative computing.* Paper presented at the Annual Meeting of the American Educational Research Association, New Orleans, LA.

Perret-Clermont, A. (1980). *Social interaction and cognitive development in children.* New York: Academic Press.

Piaget, J. (1950). *The psychology of intelligence.* New York: Harcourt.

Postman, N. (1985). *Ourselves to death: Public discourse in the age of show business.* New York: Viking Penguin.

Postthast, M. (1995, April). *Cooperative learning experiences in introductory statistics.* Paper presented at the annual meeting of the American Educational Research Association, San Francisco.

Putnam, J., Rynders, J., Johnson, R., & Johnson, D. W. (1989). Collaborative skills instruction for promoting positive interactions between mentally handicapped and nonhandicapped children. *Exceptional Children, 55,* 550-557.

Reglin, G. (1990). The effects of individualized and cooperative computer assisted instruction on mathematics achievement and mathematics anxiety for prospective teachers. *Journal of Research on Computing in Education, 22,* 404-412.

Reigeluth, C., & Stein, F. (1983). The elaborative theory of instruction. In C. Reigeluth (Ed.), *Instructional design theories and models* (pp. 335-382). Hillsdale, NJ: Lawrence Erlbaum.

Repman, J. (1993). Collaborative, computer-based learning: Cognitive and affective outcomes. *Journal of Educational Computing Research, 9*(2), 149-163.

Riel, M. (1990). Cooperative learning across classrooms in electronic learning circles. *Instructional Science, 19,* 445-466.

Robinson, A. (1990) Cooperation or exploitation? The argument against cooperative learning for talented students. *Journal of Education of the Gifted, 14*(3), 9-27.

Rocklin, T., O'Donnell, A., Dansereau, D., Lambiotte, J., Hythecker, Va., &

Larson, C. (1985). Training learning strategies with computer-aided cooperative learning. *Computers in Education, 9*(1), 67-71.

Rubin, A. (1983). The computer confronts language arts: Cans and shoulds for education. In A. Wilkinson (Ed.), *Classroom computers and cognitive science* (pp. 201-218). San Diego, CA: Academic Press.

Rysavy, D., & Sales, G. (1991). Cooperative learning in computer-based instruction. *Educational Technology Research and Development, 39*(2), 70-79.

Salomon, G. (1983). The differential investment of mental effort in learning from different sources. *Educational Psychologist, 18*(1), 42-50.

Salomon, G. (1985). Information technologies: What you see is not (always) what you get. *Educational Psychologist, 20*(4), 207-216.

Sarason, I., & Potter, E. (1983*). Self-monitoring: Cognitive processes, and performance.* Seattle: University of Washington, Research Report.

Scardamalia, M., Bereiter, C., McLearn, R., Swallow, J., & Woodruff, D. (1989). Computer supported intentional learning environments. *Journal of Educational Computing Research, 5*(1), 51-68.

Scardamalia, M., Bereiter, K., & Lamon, M. (1994). The CSILE project: Trying to bring the classroom into world 3. In K. McGilly (Ed.), *Classroom lessons: Integrating cognitive theory and classroom practice* (pp. 201-228). Cambridge, MA: Bradford Books/MIT Press.

Sherman, L. (2000). Cooperative learning and computer-supported intentional learning experiences. In C. Wolfe (Ed.), *Learning and teaching on the world wide web* (pp. 113-130). New York: Academic Press.

Shlechter, T. (1990). The relative instructional efficiency of small group computer-based training. *Journal of Educational Computing Research, 6,* 329-341.

Short, J., Williams, E., & Christie, B. (1976). *The social psychology of telecommunications.* London: Wiley.

Showers, C., & Cantor, N. (1985). Social cognition: A look at motivated strategies. In M. Rosenzweig & L. Porter (Eds.), **Annual review of psychology,** (Vol. 36, pp. 275-306). Palo Alto, CA: Annual Reviews.

Siann, G., & MacLeod, G. (1986). Computers and children of primary school age: Issues and questions. *British Journal of Educational Technology, 17,* 133-144.

Siegel, J., Dubrovsky, V., Kiesler, S., & McGuire, T. (1986). Group processes in computer-mediated communication. *Organizational Behavior and Human Decision Processes, 37,* 157-187.

Simpson, J. (1986). Computers and collaborative work among students. *Educational Technology, 26*(10), 37-44.

Simsek, A., & Hooper, S. (1992). The effects of cooperative versus individual videodisc learning on student performance and attitudes. *International Journal of Instructional Media, 19*(3), 209-218.

Simsek, A., & Tsai, B. (1992). The impact of cooperative group composition on student performance and attitudes during interactive videodisc instruction. *Journal of Computer-Based Instruction, 19*(3), 86-91.

Slavin, R. (1986). *Using student team learning.* Baltimore, MD: Center for Social Organization of Schools, Johns Hopkins University.

Slavin, R., Leavey, M., & Madden, N. (1982). *Team-assisted individualization: Mathematics teacher's manual.* Baltimore: Center for Social Organization of Schools, Johns Hopkins University.

Snow, R. (1980). Aptitude, learner control, and adaptive instruction. *Educational Psychologist, 15,* 151-158.

Sproull, L., & Kiesler, S. (1991). Computers, networks and work. *Scientific American, 65,* 116-123.

Steinberg, E. (1977). Review of student control in computer-assisted instruction. *Journal of Computer-Based Instruction, 3*(3), 84-90.

Steinberg, E. (1984). *Teaching computers to teach.* Hillsdale, NJ: Lawrence Erlbaum.

Steinberg, E. (1989). Cognition and learner control: A literature review, 1977-1988. *Journal of Computer-Based Instruction, 16*(4), 117-124.

Stephenson, S. (1992). Effects of student-instructor interaction and paired/individual study on achievement in computer-based training (CBT). *Journal of Computer-Based Instruction, 19*(1), 22-26.

Susman, E. (1998). Cooperative learning: A review of factors that increase the effectiveness of cooperative computer-based instruction. *Journal of Educational Computing Research, 18*(4), 303-332.

Suthers, D. (1998, January). *Computer aided education and training initiative*. Technical Report 12.

Swing, S., & Peterson, P. (1982). The relationship of student ability and small group interaction to student achievement. *American Educational Research Journal, 19*, 259-274.

Tennyson, R., Christensen, D., & Park, O. (1984). The Minnesota Adaptive Instructional System: A review of its theory and research. *Journal of Computer-Based Instruction, 11*(1), 2-13.

Trevino. L., Lengel, R., & Daft, R. (1987). Media symbolism, media richness, and media choice in organizations: A symbolic interactionist perspective. *Communication Research, 14*, 553-574.

Tobias, S. (1987). Mandatory text review and interaction with student characteristics. *Journal of Educational Psychology, 79*, 154-161.

Trowbridge, D., & Durnin, R. (1984). *Results from an investigation of groups working at the computer*. Washington, DC: National Science Foundation.

Turk, S., & Sarason, I. (1983). *Test anxiety and causal attributions*. Seattle: University of Washington, Department of Psychology.

Underwood, G., & McCaffrey, M. (1990). Gender differences in a cooperative computer-based language task. *Educational Research, 32*, 44-49.

Vygotsky, L. (1978). *Mind in society*. Cambridge, MA: Harvard University Press.

Webb, N. (1982). Group composition, group interaction, and achievement in cooperative small groups. *Journal of Educational Psychology, 74*(4), 475-484.

Webb, N. (1984). Microcomputer learning in small groups: Cognitive requirements and group processes. *Journal of Educational Psychology, 76*, 1076-1088.

Webb, N. (1987). Peer interaction and learning with computers in small groups. *Computers in Human Behavior, 3*, 193-209.

Webb, N. (1989). Peer interaction and learning in small groups. *International Journal of Educational Research, 13*, 21-39.

Webb, N., Ender, P., & Lewis, S. (1986). Problem solving strategies and group processes in small group learning computer programming. *American Educational Research Journal, 23*(2), 243-261.

Wellman, B., Salaff, J., Dimitrova, D., Garton, L., Gulia, M., & Haythornwaite, C. (1996). Computer networks as social networks: collaborative work, telework, and virtual community. *Annual Review of Sociology, 22*, 213-238.

Whitelock, D., Scanlon, E., Taylor, J., & O'Shea, T. (1995). Computer support for pupils collaborating: A case study on collisions. In J. Schnase & E. Cunnius (Eds.), *Proceedings of CSCL 1995: The First International Conference on Computer Support for Collaborative Learning* (pp. 380-384). Hillsdale, NJ: Erlbaum.

Willis, S. (1990). Cooperative learning fallout. *ASCD Update, 32*(8), 6, 8.

Woolley, J. (1995). Children's understanding of fictional versus epistemic mental representation: Imagination and belief. *Child Development, 66*(4), 1011-1021.

Yager, S., Johnson, D. W., & Johnson, R. (1985). Oral discussion, group-to-individual transfer, and achievement in cooperative learning groups. *Journal of Educational Psychology, 77*(1), 60-66.

Yager, S., Johnson, R., Johnson, D. W., & Snider, B. (1986). The impact of group processing on achievement in cooperative learning groups. *Journal of Social Psynology, 126*, 389-397.

Yeuh, J., & Alessi, S. (1988). The effects of reward structure and group ability composition on cooperative computer-assisted instruction. *Journal of Computer-Based Instruction, 15*, 18-22.

Zimmerman, B. (1986). Becoming a self-regulated learner: Which are the key subprocesses? *Contemporary Educational Psychology, 11*, 303-313.

·31·

COGNITIVE APPRENTICESHIP IN EDUCATIONAL PRACTICE: RESEARCH ON SCAFFOLDING, MODELING, MENTORING, AND COACHING AS INSTRUCTIONAL STRATEGIES

Vanessa Paz Dennen
Florida State University

31.1   INTRODUCTION

Apprenticeship is an inherently social learning method with a long history of helping novices become experts in fields as diverse as midwifery, construction, and law. At the center of apprenticeship is the concept of more experienced people assisting less experienced ones, providing structure and examples to support the attainment of goals. Traditionally apprenticeship has been associated with learning in the context of becoming skilled in a trade or craft—a task that typically requires both the acquisition of knowledge, concepts, and perhaps psychomotor skills and the development of the ability to apply the knowledge and skills in a context-appropriate manner—and far predates formal schooling as it is known today. In many nonindustrialized nations apprenticeship remains the predominant method of teaching and learning. However, the overall concept of learning from experts through social interactions is not one that should be relegated to vocational and trade-based training while K–12 and higher educational institutions seek to prepare students for operating in an information-based society. Apprenticeship as a method of teaching and learning is just as relevant within the cognitive and metacognitive domain as it is in the psychomotor domain.

In the last 20 years, the recognition and popularity of facilitating learning of all types through social methods have grown tremendously. Educators and educational researchers have looked to informal learning settings, where such methods have been in continuous use, as a basis for creating more formal instructional methods and activities that take advantage of these social constructivist methods. Cognitive apprenticeship—essentially, the use of an apprentice model to support learning in the cognitive domain—is one such method that has gained respect and popularity throughout the 1990s and into the 2000s.

Scaffolding, modeling, mentoring, and coaching are all methods of teaching and learning that draw on social constructivist learning theory. As such, they promote learning that occurs through social interactions involving negotiation of content, understanding, and learner needs, and all three generally are considered forms of cognitive apprenticeship (although certainly they are not the only methods). This chapter first explores prevailing definitions and underlying theories of these teaching and learning strategies and then reviews the state of research in these area.

31.2   TERMINOLOGY AND KEY CONCEPTS RELATED TO COGNITIVE APPRENTICESHIP

One of the challenges when researching or discussing cognitive apprenticeship in general, and the techniques of scaffolding, mentoring, and coaching in particular, is getting a clear sense of how the terminology is being used. There is no standard taxonomy or classification of these social constructivist methods; for example, some refer to mentoring and/or coaching as a form of scaffolding (e.g., McLoughlin, 2002), some refer to scaffolding as an aspect of coaching (e.g., Collins, Brown, & Newman, 1989), and others maintain that they are separate strategies falling under the larger classification of cognitive apprenticeship (e.g., Enkenberg, 2001; Jarvela, 1995). Additionally, the terms *coach* and *mentor* are commonly used in everyday practice to identify people who play particular roles regardless of whether the learning support that they foster and provide truly falls within the pedagogical definitions of the terms. Whereas the work being done in this overall area appropriately tends to focus more on improving teaching and learning than on developing consistency in terminology, the terms nevertheless are important to our ability to discuss, share, and further knowledge in cognitive apprenticeship. This section presents the dominant thought and definitions related to cognitive apprenticeship, scaffolding, modeling, mentoring, and coaching.

31.2.1 Cognitive Apprenticeship

A cognitive apprenticeship is much like a trade apprenticeship, with learning that occurs as experts and novices interact socially while focused on completing a task; the focus, as implied in the name, is on developing cognitive skills through participating in authentic learning experiences. Collins et al. (1989, p. 456) succinctly define it as "learning-through-guided-experience on cognitive and metacognitive, rather than physical, skills and processes." Core to cognitive apprenticeship as a method of learning are the concepts of situatedness and legitimate peripheral participation, both described by Lave and Wenger (1991). Situated learning occurs through active participation in an authentic setting, founded on the belief that this engagement fosters relevant, transferable learning much more than traditional information-dissemination methods of learning. However, it is more than just learning by doing; situated learning requires a deeper embedding within an authentic context. Human actions of any nature are socially situated, affected by cultural, historical, and institutional factors (Wertsch, 1998). This situatedness is a key component of the learning environment and thus needs to be considered in a cognitive apprenticeship.

Learning in a cognitive apprenticeship occurs through legitimate peripheral participation, a process in which newcomers enter on the periphery and gradually move toward full participation. It is not a technique or strategy, as it tends to happen quite naturally on its own. Legitimate peripheral participation is perhaps easiest to understand through a workplace example of traditional apprenticeship. Lave and Wenger (1991) present the example of legitimate peripheral participation as apprentices learn the trade of becoming a tailor:

Consider, for instance, the tailors' apprentices, whose involvement starts with both initial preparations for the tailors' daily labor and finishing details on completed garments. The apprentices progressively move backward through the production process to cutting jobs. (This kind of progression is quite common across cultures and historical periods.) Under these circumstances, the initial "circumferential"

perspective—running errands, delivering messages, or accompanying others—takes on new significance: It provides a first approximation to an armature of the structure of the community of practice. (p. 96)

Essentially, the apprentices are learning about both the overall process of the larger task and profession and criteria for evaluating performance through the completion of small tasks. As they gain experience, they are offered larger, more central tasks to complete. Their understanding of how these tasks affect the end product in a holistic manner supports their performance, as does their knowledge of the criteria that will be used to assess the end product.

What does this mean for school-based education? According to J. S. Brown (1998), "The central issue in learning is becoming a practitioner, not learning about practice" (p. 230). In an argument for adopting cognitive apprenticeship in formal educational settings, Enkenberg (2001) criticizes university education because the learning tends to occur separately from expert practice. This separation is problematic because expert practice is critical to real-world performance and is difficult to simply teach by lecture or explanation. For many of today's students, skills and knowledge are being taught in an abstract manner, which makes it difficult for them to apply them in concrete, real-world situations (Collins et al., 1989). The implications of this problem, taken to the extreme, are that our schools could rely solely on information transmission methods of instruction and universities could rely solely on faculty and graduate students who know many facts but are ill prepared to apply them in a practical context to provide educational experiences. Although the reality is not this extreme, many students still fail to see the relationship between traditional school-based learning and real-world applications, and many educators who are competent practitioners fail to provide learning experiences that adequately connect theory to practice. During the last two decades, educational researchers have been addressing this problem by looking for ways to integrate cognitive apprenticeship in the classroom. This research is discussed later in this chapter.

Teaching and learning through cognitive apprenticeship requires making tacit processes visible to learners so they can observe and then practice them (Collins et al., 1989). The following methods support the goals of cognitive apprenticeship.

1. Modeling: meaning the demonstration of the temporal process of thinking.
2. Explanation: explaining why activities take place as they do.
3. Coaching: meaning the monitoring of students' activities and assisting and supporting them where necessary.
4. Scaffolding: meaning support of students so that they can cope with the task situation. The strategy also entails the gradual withdrawal of teacher from the process, when the students can manage on their own.
5. Reflection: the student assesses and analyses his performance.
6. Articulation: the results of reflection are put into verbal form.
7. Explorations: the students are encouraged to form hypotheses, to test them, and to find new ideas and viewpoints. (Enkenberg, 2001, p. 503)

Enkenberg's list is not considered the definitive one, but it nevertheless presents various strategies that may be used in a cognitive apprenticeship. Collins et al. (1989) refer to modeling, coaching, and fading as the predominant methods of cognitive apprenticeship, with scaffolding mentioned as part of the coaching process. Note that these strategies refer to the teacher's or expert's actions; the learners in a cognitive apprenticeship are engaged in acts of observation, practice, and reflection.

31.2.2 Scaffolding Defined

The concept of scaffolding draws on the work of Vygotsky (1978), although the term first came into use in an article written by Wood, Bruner, and Ross (1976). In education, scaffolding is a metaphor for a structure that is put in place to help learners reach their goals and is removed bit by bit as it is no longer needed, much like a physical scaffold is placed around a building that is under construction and removed as the building nears completion. Whereas some believe this is an appropriate metaphor for providing support during instruction that can be removed as the learner no longer needs it (J. S. Brown, Collins, & Duguid, 1989), Duffy and Cunningham (1996, p. 183) find this metaphor "unfortunate" because "it suggests a guiding and teaching of the learner toward some well-defined (structural) end" and is teacher centered. In practice, however, scaffolding is a learner-centered strategy whose success is dependent on its adaptability to the learner's needs. Additionally, scaffolding is much more than a physical support in a learning context, addressing student learning of concepts, procedures, strategies, and metacognitive skills (McLoughlin, 2002).

Scaffolding has been described as either directive or supportive, depending on where the impetus for the support originates (Lenski & Niersheimer, 2002). Directive scaffolding is part of a more teacher-centered approach, in which the instructor devises skills and strategies to teach specified content. Supportive scaffolding, in contrast, is learner centered and occurs as the learner coconstructs knowledge with others. In practice, the former may be manifest as a teacher providing learners with strategies of successful students, whereas the latter would involve instruction tailored to specific learner needs based on current ability and interest.

Rogoff (1990) discusses scaffolding in terms of adult structure of child's learning activities. Adults provide children with metacognitive support by breaking down tasks from those that are beyond the child (learner's) abilities into smaller, more manageable ones that are within the child's grasp. Within this method it is important to ensure that the learners' participation is still meaningful and clearly contributes to the overall goal; tasks should not be broken down and segmented to the extent that learners no longer feel like participants in the overall process or cannot see how their work contributes to the end result. There are many ways in which one may scaffold instruction, but there are a few central concepts that are common and critical to scaffolding in any form: the zone of proximal development (ZPD), intersubjectivity, and fading.

31.2.2.1 *Zone of Proximal Development.* The ZPD is a concept put forth by Vygotsky (1978), who suggested that learning activities should provide adequate challenges to the learner based on his or her current knowledge state but at the same time not be so challenging as to be unattainable. The ZPD is a dynamic region that is just beyond the learner's present ability level; as learners gain new skills and understanding, their ZPD moves with their development. This space between actual and potential performance is assessed through social interaction between the learner and someone who is more experienced—potentially a teacher, parent, or even an advanced peer. Rogoff (1990) adds that cultural learning and development, in addition to individual cognitive development, occur a result of teaching and learning in the ZPD: "Interactions in the zone of proximal development are the crucible of development *and* of culture, in that they allow children to participate in activities that would be impossible for them alone, using cultural tools that themselves must be adapted to the specific practical activities at hand" (p. 16). This observation again stresses the situated nature and social interconnectedness of learning through cognitive apprenticeship.

The ZPD is a critical concept to consider when providing scaffolding. Scaffolding affects learners both cognitively and emotionally, impacting not just learner skill and knowledge, but also learner motivation and confidence when approaching a task. Cognitively, it supports the selection of activities and the use of a variety of assists to ensure that learning takes place, such as hints, models, analogies and demonstrations. Emotionally, it helps students keep from getting mired in feelings of failure through the various supports that are focused on learner success (Bean & Patel Stevens, 2002). Both cognitively and emotionally, these successes rely on scaffolding that is directed appropriately at the learner's current ability level. In other words, it must occur within the learner's ZPD.

The learner may write off some tasks as too easy and lose interest quickly, whereas other tasks may seem so daunting at the onset—even if the learner does possess the technical capability to succeed—that the learner may essentially declare defeat before even trying. Optimal instruction and learning tasks occur in the middle zone, which is neither too simple nor too difficult and is open for learning. I liken this situation of finding the appropriate middle zone to a parent teaching a child to swim, a learning situation that often relies on scaffolding. Initially, the task may be broken into smaller pieces by the parent; the child may practice kicking with the assistance of a kickboard, breathing while holding onto the side of the pool, and arm strokes while being supported afloat by the parent. To do all three parts together initially would be too difficult for the child, but once they are individually mastered the child may try them together as a coordinated whole with the assistance of inflatable water wings, which ensure that he or she will not sink. When the parent determines that the child has the necessary skills to swim on his or her own, the child may still be nervous and uncertain of the ability both to stay afloat and to move forward—yet without trying, the child will never know if he or she can succeed. Additionally, the parent must observe the child in motion to diagnose any difficulties. Thus, the adult provides the child with small challenges that are constantly being adjusted to match the child's ability and confidence. Initially the parent may stand 2 ft from the child and challenge him or her to swim; this distance provides a small challenge but keeps the parent close enough for the child to feel safe. On success, the parent may challenge the child again, this time continuously moving backward as the child moves forward, maintaining or perhaps increasing the distance between them. The child is not only learning the mechanics of swimming, but also learning that he or she can succeed at swimming alone. Gradually the child realizes that he or she does not need the parent's assistance any more and sets new, independent learning goals, such as swimming from one side of the pool to another. Throughout this example the parent's role is to determine an appropriate challenge for the child and the necessary support for learning and achievement.

Tharp and Gallimore (1988) discuss learning as a four-stage model that involves progress through the learner's ZPD and returns recursively to the first stage with each new concept learned. Stage I occurs firmly within the learner's ZPD, with assistance being provided by more experienced others, often through directions and modeling. In Stage II, learners begin to help themselves and the expert scaffolding recedes. At the end of Stage II learners have succeeded in the task at hand and thus have passed through the ZPD; learners then engage in a process of internalization (Stage III) and, finally, deautomatization of performance (Stage IV), which leads back recursively to Stage I. This model demonstrates the dynamic nature of learning and the ZPD.

Assisting students within their ZPD is a personalized process. The ZPD is not determined by age or grade level, which is how schools normally approach instruction; learners will have different individual needs. A task that is too difficult and requires scaffolding for one third-grade student may be completed without any assistance by a peer. Individual learners have been found to have different scaffolding needs as well (Roehler & Cantlon, 1997); for example, students with a narrower ZPD may need more frequent and detailed assistance (Day & Cordon, 1993). This reliance on individualization can prove challenging for teachers who have many children in a class, each with different needs.

31.2.2.2 Intersubjectivity.
Scaffolding requires shared understanding among participants in the learning situation. Vygotsky (1977) stated that the processes of knowing and understanding are connected to one's sociohistorical experience; knowledge is shaped by the individual's culture and background. Teachers and learners come to the learning situation with their own understandings and must find a shared meaning to succeed in the learning activity. This shared understanding, called intersubjectivity, is constantly negotiated in our everyday lives, helping in the process of "bridging between the known and the new in communication" (Rogoff, 1990, p. 72). In Tharp and Gallimore's (1988) four-stage model of progression through the ZPD, intersubjectivity is focused in Stage I. The learner and the assister may not similarly conceive the learning goal and the negotiation will take place at the beginning of this stage.

Matusov (2001), in a review of research on intersubjectivity, notes that having a shared goal is a critical component of the teaching–learning situation. When intersubjectivity is lacking, it can be evident in the form of learning conflict, nonparticipation, or unexpected outcomes. An example of conflict is a situation in which the learner does not know how to complete a desired task and perceives the scaffolding assistance as irrelevant to his or her goal. At this point a negotiation of meaning may take place. Failing that, it is likely that the learner will not complete the task as expected or will follow the assistance that is given but fail to learn because he or she does not understand the purpose of the scaffolded activity.

31.2.2.3 Fading.
Fading of scaffolding occurs as the learner gains independence and no longer needs support to complete the desired task. Returning to the construction metaphor, Greenfield (1999) points out that scaffolding would not be used when workers are just a few feet from the ground. To move the learner toward self-sufficiency there must initially be an external (adult) regulation of the learning activity, followed by the learner's (child's) redefinition of the activity, followed by a shifting of responsibility (Diaz, Neal, & Amaya-Williams, 1990). When this shift occurs—in the transition from Stage I to Stage II (per Tharp & Gallimore, 1988)—the assister's lessening of assistance is referred to as fading. Fading is not an abrupt process; it is evidenced by hints and feedback that gradually become less frequent and less detailed (Collins et al., 1989).

How does fading work? Reciprocal teaching (A. L. Brown & Palincsar, 1989; Palincsar & Brown, 1984; Palincsar, Brown, & Campione, 1993; Rosenshine & Meister, 1994) is a method of scaffolding for teaching reading comprehension that provides a clear example of how fading would occur. There are four sequential guided learning strategies that are part of reciprocal teaching; after reading a text, a cooperative learning group gathers with an adult leader and engages in

1. questioning, in which a content-oriented question is asked, opening the dialogue;
2. summarizing, in which the gist of the test is summarized and the group can work toward consensus;
3. clarifying, in which any misunderstandings or disagreements in meaning are addressed; and
4. predicting, in which likely future text content is discussed.

Throughout this process the teacher scaffolds their learning by rephrasing or elaborating on statements and asking questions (Rosenshine & Meister, 1994). As scaffolding is removed, students take greater responsibility over facilitating the reciprocal teaching process, which requires them to be primary instigators in the construction of knowledge; as the teacher ceases to scaffold and hands over responsibility to the learners, fading is taking place.

31.2.3 Modeling Defined

Modeling, a form of demonstration followed by imitation, frequently is used as a way of helping the learner progress through the ZPD (Tharp & Gallimore, 1988). The work of Bandura (1977) showed that modeling is a more efficient way of learning than trial and error. Jonassen (1999) discusses two types of modeling, behavioral and cognitive modeling. The former is one most people are familiar with, as it is arguably the easiest way to teach a psychomotor skill and involves imitation of the demonstrated act. Cognitive modeling, however, is more complex (Tharp & Gallimore, 1988). For example, a teacher might model a decision-making process by talking aloud about the considerations taken and explaining the rationale for the end result. The learner in this case would not be engaged in direct imitation but, rather, use of similar strategies in a related context. Per Tharp and Gallimore (1988), the concept of imitation as mimicry is too simple to be considered modeling. During the learning process, modeled activities are coded through the use of labels or imagery. Using a psychomotor example, dancers often use their hands to mark the presence of particular moves in a choreographed piece as they watch it being demonstrated; these smaller motions help them remember the modeled moves when it is their turn to practice.

Learners may observe the target action (behavioral modeling) or reasoning (cognitive modeling) as presented by an expert or more experienced peer. In fact, peer modeling is an activity in which learners tend to engage even without instructor design or direction, manifest through learners observing and following the strategies used by others who are working on similar tasks nearby (King, 1999). This form of modeling, unintentionally offered, has a major impact on socialization and enculturation of children and adults in new environments (Gallimore & Tharp, 1990). The impact of modeling is strongest when it is an explicit process. Individuals who engage in a process of expert observation, reflection, and practice being more likely to be able to apply the learned knowledge in a different setting than those who receive a passive model (Cooper, 1999).

31.2.4 Mentoring and Coaching Defined

A mentor, by its most basic definition, is one who mediates expert knowledge for novices, helping that which is tacit become more explicit. The two most common uses of the word *mentoring* are to describe (a) a professional development relationship in which a more experienced participant assists a less experienced one in developing a career and (b) a guiding relationship between an adult and a youth focused on helping the youth realize his or her potential and perhaps overcome some barriers or challenges. In both cases it is the mentor who provides advice and support and may serve as a role model. Whereas these examples generally imply long-term relationships, mentoring can be used as an instructional strategy on a smaller scale.

In a phenomenological review of the mentoring literature, Roberts (2000, p. 151) notes that there are eight "attributes" of mentoring that commonly appear.

1. A process form
2. An active relationship
3. A helping process
4. A teaching-learning process
5. Reflective practice
6. A career and personal development process
7. A formalized process
8. A role constructed by or for a mentor

Certainly notions of helping, teaching and learning, and reflection all seem central to mentoring, which is a process that involves relationships. Not mentioned directly, but implied, is the concept of expertise. Mentors are expected to provide expert knowledge to protégés, which involves that they both have said expertise and know how to effectively share it with others (Little, 1990). Mentors may use strategies such as verbal descriptions and diagrams to help concretize or reveal expert knowledge such as why things are done in a certain way and the relationship between parts. However, mentors should not take an overly directive role with mentees; instead they should use strategies like questioning to help mentees articulate their understanding, a process that supports the development of intersubjectivity as well as assessment of progress (Billet, 1994).

Enerson (2001) points out that teacher-centered terms like *sage, actor,* and *pedagogue* have long been used as metaphors for the teacher's role and suggests that *mentor* more appropriately puts the focus on the learner. Essentially, the teaching-learning situation changes from being about teacher performance to being about learner needs. One may act without an audience, but it is not possible to mentor without a mentee. One might evaluate an actor's performance without regard for the audience's reaction, but a mentor cannot effectively be evaluated without consideration of the mentee.

For most people, the term *coach* initially brings to mind sports. Coaching also is commonly heard in reference to technology (people who provide just-in-time, task-based assistance) and business settings (people who are hired to provide guidance on a particular task at the individual or organizational level). Collins et al. (1989) quite simply describe coaching as assistance from a master. In many ways a coach and a mentor do the same thing, and in practice the terms often are used interchangeably, so how do we differentiate them? Parsloe and Wray (2000), who discuss practical applications of coaching and mentoring in the learning process, distinguish coaching from mentoring by suggesting that a mentor is one who provides support of a more general nature in an ongoing capacity and a coach is typically focused on assistance for meeting a particular goal. By this definition, within the context of career development a mentor would help guide the career choices and workplace skills of the mentee, while a coach would be involved in more concrete, goal-oriented tasks such as getting a new job or promotion.

Burton, Brown, and Fischer (1999, p. 149) state that there are four goals for a coach to accomplish:

1. ensure that appropriate subskills are acquired,
2. design appropriate exercises and supply the required technology,
3. demonstrate the student's performance in the interest of highlighting problems, and
4. provide clear explanation and instruction.

Additionally, a coach maintains focus on the goal, determining when learner exploration is fruitless and when a learner is ready to move onward.

Still others rely on a more modest definition of *coach*, considering it a scaffold and believing that coaching is the process of helping a student work through an activity (Guzdial, 1995; Jarvela, 1995). The difference here seems to be in designating coaching as technique—one of many strategies an expert might use to assist someone who is more novice—from coaching as career.

31.3 TYPES OF COGNITIVE APPRENTICESHIP RESEARCH

A constant across research in cognitive apprenticeship is consideration of learning environment and context; in other words, it is an awareness of the situated nature of learning. Roth (2001) suggests that in any instance of educational research an observation must be considered as a result of the interaction of three factors: the activity, the individual, and the community. These elements are interrelated and continuously changing and affecting each other and, thus, the learning that results.

Research interests in cognitive apprenticeship grew throughout the late 1980s and early 1990s, with studies largely focused on children's learning processes (e.g., Palincsar & Brown, 1984; Palincsar et al., 1993; Rogoff, 1990; Rogoff, Mosier, Mistry, & Goncu, 1993). This growth pattern is no surprise, as the roots of the field grew out of renewed interest in Vygotsky's (1977, 1978) work on the social nature of cognitive development in children that came about as part of the constructivist movement. Bonk and Kim (1998), in a review of research, found little research looking at sociocultural theory as it relates to adult learning in formal settings; instead the focus tends to be on K–12 environments. They suggest that more research is needed to determine if adult learners benefit from the same forms of scaffolding as children; if there are differences in needs among young, middle, and adult learners; and how to determine the ZPD in adult learners. Such research conducted in higher education and adult learning settings has grown with advances in technology; educational researches have seized the challenge of determining how technology can help offer learning experiences that use cognitive apprenticeship strategies that are simultaneously more effective than traditional instruction and more efficient than non-computer-based methods.

Research on cognitive apprenticeship has taken various approaches. For organizational purposes, I have divided them into three groups that are representative of the kinds of research that has been done in the last 20 years.

1. **In situ** *research.* This type of research seeks to capture elements of cognitive apprenticeship for the purpose of documenting a learning experience and guiding further work, both in theory and in practice. These studies do not have designed interventions or experimental groups and favor a case study methodology. Also included in this category are evaluations—both formative and summative—of mentoring programs.
2. *Designed interventions and experimental studies.* This group includes experimental studies and studies of prescriptive instructional designs. In addition, to determine whether particular interventions are effective, some studies

have sought to find out how cognitive apprenticeship-based classroom experiences compare to more traditional ones.
3. *Research on technology* and how it might support cognitive apprenticeship. This category of research includes studies of technology used as a teaching enhancement, with participants collocated in a live setting; as a teaching medium, with participants potentially located in different settings and communicating through the computer; and as a teacher, in which learners receive support from the computer.

Each category of cognitive apprenticeship research is discussed separately, although the technology studies certainly do overlap with the other two categories.

31.4 IN SITU STUDIES

In situ studies of cognitive apprenticeship can be important to our understanding of how students best learn. Lave and Wenger (1991) suggest that the analysis of legitimate peripheral participation may uncover aspects of the learning experience that have previously been overlooked. The research done in this area is responsible for the initial theories of cognitive apprenticeship. It has served to develop knowledge bases of expert performance and preliminary recommendations of what methods are likely to work under particular conditions and in particular settings.

31.4.1 Cognitive Apprenticeship in Everyday Practice

In a study of a community of writers at an urban nonprofit organization, Beaufort (2000) explored the roles the writers played and how new writers were integrated into the community following an apprenticeship model. Fifteen roles were observed in this example, ranging from observer, reader/researcher, and clerical assistant on the novice end up to author, inventor, and coach on the expert end. New or less experienced writers learned the process through taking on roles such as the clerical assistant (a role reserved for new members), which allowed for extended observation of the expert writers at work. New employees gained both experience and responsibility as time passed through this model, which exhibited Lave and Wenger's (1991) legitimate peripheral participation. Although the act of learning was not formalized or labeled by participants, and much learning occurred through observation, more experienced employees would serve as mentors and illuminate the tacit components of the writing process as needed. This model of learning worked for most participants, but one employee did not succeed and was let go. The results suggest that learning writing through a social process with authentic tasks is effective, and the researcher states that a similar model may be useful in school settings, where writing has traditionally been an individual, general skills learning activity.

Similar to analysis of legitimate peripheral participation, analysis of expert performance can be used to help determine ways in which novice performance may be supported. For example, the process of *in situ* knowledge construction by a competitive table tennis player was documented through the player's reflective commentary on watching a videotape of a recent match (Sève, Saury, Thereau, & Durand, 2002). The player was able to articulate the underlying thought behind his actions during the game, demonstrating points at which he was learning about his opponent's game and strategies and integrating that knowledge with his knowledge about the game in general as well as his past experiences competing against this opponent. The knowledge generated by this study—and in-depth exploration of situated actions—can be used to build a model of expert actions within table tennis. Such models are useful for teachers and coaches to draw on and use to support their students.

31.4.2 *In Situ* Studies of Scaffolding

Focusing more directly on techniques used in a formal learning situation, Roehler and Cantlon (1997) examined the use of scaffolds in two social constructivist classrooms, exploring the types and characteristics of scaffolding in learning conversations taking place during elementary-school language instruction. Two constructivist classrooms were observed in this study, including an English as a second language (ESL) class. An analysis of lesson transcripts from the ESL classroom resulted in five types of scaffolding that were commonly used.

1. Offering explanation
2. Inviting student participation
3. Verifying and clarifying student understanding
4. Modeling desired behaviors
5. Inviting students to contribute clues

Over time, students took more responsibility for learning in this environment and the amount of scaffolding used by the instructor lessened.

Savery (1998) noted that instructors in a business writing course made use of all six of Gallimore and Tharp's (1990) forms of scaffolded assistance (instructing, questioning, modeling, feeding back, cognitive structuring, and contingency management), although each occurred in different amounts based on student need. Instructing, questioning, modeling, and cognitive structuring were part of the teachers' interaction with the students. Feedback occurred through grades and comments on assignments. Finally, contingency management was largely unspoken, although it had been designed into the course itself that students would face repercussions for unproductive behavior. Also using Gallimore and Tharp's framework, Sugar and Bonk (1998) found, in their analysis of electronic mentoring in an adventure learning program for middle- and high-school students, that 75% of the mentors' time was spent engaged in questioning, feedback, and cognitive structuring. Contingency management and task structuring (as per Tharp, 1993) were minimally used and modeling did not occur at all. Sugar and Bonk hypothesized that had the mentors engaged in modeling there might have been more student interactions. This hypothesis is consistent with the findings of Dennen (2001), in

which modeling was the most effective way to generate desired student performance across classes in an on-line forum.

31.4.3 Scaffolding, Modeling, and Reflection in the Classroom

Scaffolded learning and modeling followed by learner reflection have been suggested as a way to help learners achieve what they would not be able to do on their own and then to make sense of and to internalize the experience. As mentioned earlier, a learner working within her ZPD initially requires assistance but then takes responsibility for the task and internalizes it (Tharp & Gallimore, 1988); reflection would occur as the learner comes to understand her activities. Reflection as a learning activity has become in vogue during recent years, but best practices in scaffolding reflection still remain to be determined.

Bean and Patel Stevens (2002) looked at how scaffolding affected the reflection process for teacher education students enrolled in university-level courses. A group of preservice teachers was divided into five groups of five students each and asked to participate in a bulletin board discussion base on instructor prompts. Their instructor provided scaffolding in the form of modeling and suggesting response types. A group of inservice teachers was also studied. They were asked to keep weekly journals relating concepts from their assigned readings to their own classroom experiences. Analyzed using constant comparative and critical discourse methods, a purposive sample of work completed by each group yielded similar results. The students' written work followed the models given as a scaffold but did not extend in any substantial way beyond the scaffold. The students stated their personal beliefs related to teaching and learning and integrated reading concepts, as they had been asked and supported to do, but they did not reach the point of addressing issues related teaching and learning in the larger arena of critical discourse. Interestingly, preservice teachers avoided mention of local contexts, keeping their comments focused on their personal belief systems, whereas inservice teachers tended to discuss their localized situations at length without really commenting on institutional and societal levels. The authors conclude that whereas scaffolding had a clear effect, it did not help achieve all of the instructional goals, but they are not sure whether this is inherent in scaffolding or indicative of a scaffold that did not fully meet the learners' needs.

Parker and Hess (2001) used modeling followed by reflection to prepare student teachers for leading discussions in their classroom. They hypothesized that by experiencing a well-designed class discussion and engaging in reflection on the activity, learners would be able to adapt and use the same methods with another group of learners. Whereas the scaffolding in this instance resulted in productive in-class discussion for the learners (student teachers), it did not in turn teach them how to lead discussion themselves. Thus, modeling and reflection were effective methods of addressing course content, but simply engaging in and using the methods was not enough to prepare the learners in turn to serve as instructors using those same methods. One suggested reason for the ineffectiveness was that the class discussions that the learners engaged in were exemplars in terms of process, resulting in a seamless focus on the content being discussed, with little to no emphasis on the method itself. In other words, learners saw and succeeded in using the model of how to participate in discussion—which was what they were asked to do—but because their attention had not been called to it and they were not asked to engage in the practice of it, they did not pick up on the instructor's modeling of how to lead discussion.

Another way in which students may need scaffolding assistance is task structuring (Tharp, 1993), which may include activities such as "chunking, sequencing, detailing, reviewing, or any other means to structure the task and its components so as to fit it into the learner's zone of proximal development" (Sugar & Bonk, 1998, p. 142). Dennen (2000), in a qualitative study of students engaged in month-long computer-mediated collaborative problem-based learning scenarios, found that scaffolds in the form of chunking and sequencing helped motivate students and enabled them to focus more on the content-based learning goals than on project management elements of the assignment.

Critical to success in scaffolding is shared understanding. In a descriptive study of learner interactions in a "model culture" environment called Fifth Dimension, Kaptelinin and Cole (2001) found three phases of intersubjectivity that affect the ability to communicate productively in this social learning context. The first phase precedes intersubjectivity and involves the coordination of individuals' goals. The premise here is that the participants need to have a sense of their own goals before anything else can take place. This individually focused phase is followed by a phase in which a group identity emerges (intersubjectivity), which in turn is followed by a third and final phase in which the group experience is translated back to the individual (postintersubjectivity). As a result of this analysis, the researchers suggest that consideration be given to fostering these phases when designing instruction. Savery (1998), in the above-mentioned study of collaborative computer-based writing in a business course, also argues that the successful teams were developing intersubjectivity. In this instance it took the form of learning about each others' interests and preferences through the process of working together, which in turn helped them work more productively.

31.4.4 Scaffolding in One-on-One Learning Situations

In a qualitative study examining the effects of electronic peer mentoring in a university physical therapy class, it was found that both mentors and mentees learned through the process of reflection and articulation (Hayward et al., 2001). Protégés benefited from the mentors' stories and experiences, which made the learning more concrete and authentic, whereas mentors reinforced concepts already learned by connecting theory to practice and perhaps doing a bit of new research in order to address mentees' questions effectively. The technology, although initially considered a barrier to students who chose the field of physical therapy in part out of a desire for face-to-face interactions, did not inhibit the usefulness of the mentoring activity and

these peers did engage in computer-mediated social exchanges much as one would anticipate in a face-to-face meeting.

Mentor teaching strategies were studied as well, with integrative teaching being the most popular. In this strategy, the mentor combines theory and practice in their explanation to the mentee. Hayward et al. (2001) found that most mentors provided far more information than the mentees had requested. About one-third of the mentors used a strategy called *expert push,* in which a mentor did not directly answer the mentee's question but instead returned questions that would hopefully help him find the right answer.

Peers also may serve as mentors to each other, with learners in some instances identifying on their own both their knowledge gap (given their learning goals) and peers who can help them attain their learning goals. Engaging in study groups and asking for peer assistance is a common practice in many educational settings, as students realize that their peers can often supply the learning assistance that they need. Loong (1998) studied the peer apprenticeship that developed between two students engaged in a computer-mediated mathematical task. Initially the students had different approaches and worked rather independently, with one student focused on mathematical rules and the other focused more on concepts. Over time, however, the rule-focused student noticed that the concept-focused student's expertise was needed, and he assigned himself to this peer in an apprentice role.

In a case study of teacher educators (university faculty) who received technology coaching from preservice teachers, coaching was found to be a mutually beneficial activity (Matthew, Callaway, Letendre, Kimbell-Lopez, & Stephens, 2002). The faculty learned new technology skills while the student coaches gained teaching experience. Coaching was found to be a particularly appropriate teaching and learning method for this audience because they tend to have just-in-time technology learning needs and are unlikely to engage in formal learning opportunities to learn new technology skills. Additionally, it was deemed more relevant for the teacher-educators to learn under authentic, situated conditions.

Expert tutors both teach and motivate well, as evidenced by the effects on their tutees and high scores on independent measures (Lepper, Drake, & O'Donnell-Johnson, 1997). Some of the scaffolding methods used by the expert tutors, as observed in 30- to 60-min math sessions with students who have a history of academic difficulties, included their selection of the problem to work through, problem presentation (which includes motivational elements), and encouragement of the learner to solve the problem independently, although subtle intervention or debugging strategies may be used as needed.

31.4.5 In Situ Practices and Effects of Mentoring Programs

Traditional programs pair up mentors and mentees, often considering personal preferences and interests in the process. Programs may have guidelines for the pairs to follow, training for the mentors, and/or points at which their progress is reported or evaluated. It is these programs that tend to be researched, as we seek to find out what types of interactions occur, which ones are effective, and how the participants perceive the usefulness of the relationship. Evaluations also tend to be conducted on funded mentoring programs to determine whether or not the funding is well spent or the program is meeting its goals. Not all mentoring occurs within a program, but studies on informal mentoring practices are less common. Many mentor–protégé pairs develop informally; not only would locating such pairs and determining how representative they are be difficult, but also identifying the participants of informal mentoring would affect the very nature of their interaction by making them consider labels and roles for their intuitive relationship. A third area of potential study is technology-mediated mentoring, which is discussed later.

The results of a review of 10 evaluations of youth mentoring programs (Jekielek, Moore, Hair, & Scarupa, 2002) found that their impacts fell into multiple areas, including academic achievement (in terms of attendance, attitudes, and continuing education, although not necessarily grades), health and safety (in terms of preventing and reducing negative behaviors), and social and emotional development. Productive mentoring practices were found to be structure, regular meetings, mentor training and preparation, and a focus on the mentees' needs rather than the mentors' expectations.

Lucas .(2001) studied an after-school mentoring program for sixth-grade students. Mentors were college undergraduates who were enrolled in a for-credit course. This mentoring program, called Project Mentor, was voluntary and extracurricular for the mentee participants but promised them support for academic achievement. Lucas suggests based on her research that there is true interdependence between the role of mentor and that of mentee. She found that the relationship between mentor and mentee is heavily based on individual factors including personal preferences, prior experiences, and goals and expectations; essentially, the nature of the experience transcends any traditional definition or training that may take place and is heavily shaped by the individuals who are involved in it. Lucas also found a much greater desire to engage in mentor–mentee interaction when it was focused around an activity that the mentee could not successfully complete alone. She also found that successfully collaborating on such activities generally created a closer relationship between the mentoring pair.

Langer (2001), in his study of the nature of mandatory mentoring at SUNY Empire State College (ESC), found a gap between his results and the predominant views in the theoretical literature about mentoring. Whereas the literature base tends to place a heavy emphasis on the close interpersonal relationships developed between mentors and mentees, Langer observed a process that was focused almost exclusively on goal attainment. This is not to say that faculty mentors and their students at ESC never develop close relationships but that the task focus and school-year time frame relegate the development of a social bond to a secondary status. What Langer and ESC are referring to as mentoring might better fit the definition of coaching, which is more task-focused than relationship-focused.

Billet (2000) studied the learning process of mentees in a formal workplace mentoring program over a 6-month period. This prolonged engagement allowed him to identify learning sources and strategies that were influential on the mentees' development. Mentors were trained in workshops that introduced guided learning strategies such as questioning, modeling, and coaching and helped them to identify ways that these strategies might be used in their workplace. Engagement in everyday work was found to have the greatest influence on mentee development, supporting the concept of situated cognition, and Billet suggests that the guided learning strategies were used to enhance this engagement. A specific analysis of guided learning strategies showed that the ones that were used most frequently, such as questioning, modeling, and coaching, were perceived as the most useful. Less-used strategies, such as diagrams and analogies, were less valued by the mentees; mentors reported greater challenges finding ways to draw upon and use these strategies spontaneously with their mentees.

Young and Perrewé (2000) looked at career and social support factors and their effects on participant perceptions of the success of a mentoring relationship, finding that mentors' expectations generally were met when a protégé was involved in career support behavior. Conversely, protégés tended to measure the success of their mentoring relationship in terms of the amount of social support they received. Young and Perrewé hypothesize that this difference in perception may be due to the mentors' established status, which may have them focused on successes directly related to the mentoring goal (career enhancement), whereas their more novice protégés may not yet be able to predict the impact of particular career-related behaviors but will look for encouragement and friendship as indicators that they are performing as expected.

Although none of the results presented in this section are generalizable, given the methodologies used, they are nonetheless quite valuable to the field. They confirm theoretical principles and strategies and represent what is possible in everyday educational settings with regular teachers and students.

31.5 DESIGNED INTERVENTIONS AND EXPERIMENTAL STUDIES

An organized program of experimental studies is much needed at this point in the development of cognitive apprenticeship theory and practice. The various theories of how cognitive apprenticeship works and the results from *in situ* research both need to be studied with rigor in the interest of attaining generalizability. Small pockets of experimental studies have been conducted to date, but many of these studies occur in isolation rather than in a related series.

31.5.1 Effectiveness of Cognitive Apprenticeship

To gain support for a paradigm shift regarding methods of learning and instruction, it is necessary to demonstrate the effectiveness of cognitive apprenticeship. Hendricks (2001) conducted an experimental study to determine whether situated instruction was more likely to result in transferable knowledge than traditional instruction. The content area was causality, with a learning goal focused on students being able to determine whether or not a cause–effect relationship was present in particular research studies. The control group received "abstract instruction" in the form of a lecture and practice activity, whereas the treatment group's "situated instruction" followed the instructional model set forth by J. S. Brown et al. (1989), beginning with discussion, then modeling, and, finally, coaching and scaffolding to assist the learners in applying the knowledge. Scaffolding was faded and control ceded to individual students as they demonstrated the ability to identify causality, and, finally, students were asked to reflect aloud, articulating what they had learned. The results demonstrated that students in the treatment group outperformed the control group on a posttest administered at the end of the instruction, but there was no significant difference in performance on a far-transfer task 2 weeks later. However, the results still show that the differences in instruction had some effect. Whereas only two students successfully completed the transfer task, both had been in the treatment group and both indicated that they had already applied the learned information at home. Additionally, students in the situated group had a more favorable reaction to the instruction than those who received the lecture and practice intervention. Hendricks suggests that although these results counter claims that situated learning is more likely to result in knowledge that is transferable to real life, they may simply be indicative of how challenging it is to produce far transfer given any kind of instruction and may be affected by the use of a fabricated situation to measure transfer.

The use of expert concept map structures as a form of scaffolding has been demonstrated to be effective. Chang, Sung, and Chen (2001) studied the impact of three variations of a concept mapping activity on student learning in a biology class. In one treatment, called "construct by self," students had access to a computer-based concept mapping tool that had hints built into the system; the hints compared the learner's concept map with that of an expert. In the other treatment, called "construct on scaffold," students were given a blank outline of an expert's concept map to fill in using the same computer-based tool. The control group was asked to create a pencil-and-paper concept map with no form of assistance. Results of a posttest showed that there was no significant difference in terms of performance of the students in the control group and the construct-by-self treatment group. The construct-on-scaffold treatment group, however, had a higher level of mastery. A postsurvey of student impressions of concept mapping showed that students using the computer-based tool in either treatment group preferred concept mapping as a learning activity much more than those using pencil and paper in the control group. The researchers theorize that the students in the construct-on-scaffold group learned more because the expert's outline helped reduce their cognitive load while keeping them focused on the material that was relevant to learning biology.

Coltman, Petyaeva, and Anghileri (2002) conducted a study of the impact of adult support in a discovery learning process for young children. In the study, children were given building blocks and were asked to complete abstract tasks related to three-dimensional shapes, such as recognizing size and shape equivalence in different formations of building blocks. All subjects were pretested to ensure novice status in this area. Learners in the control group were to complete the tasks unaided; those

in the treatment group were offered graded levels of support. There were four support levels, starting with contextualization of the task, followed by guided reflection, modeling, and, finally, direct demonstration. In practice, the second level (reflection) was sufficient scaffolding for 28% of the students in the study, and the remaining 72% performed the task correctly when modeling was offered; the fourth available support, demonstration, was not used with any subject. A posttest 3 days after the task intervention was used to measure learning gains. Children in the treatment group outperformed those in the control group, with respective posttest task completion rates of 90.7% and 33.3%, respectively. This study suggests that discovery alone is not sufficient to ensure that learning will take place and demonstrates the value of scaffolding—particularly in the form of modeling—in the learning process of children.

In a study of mathematics learning in peer groups, Webb, Troper, and Fall (1995) found that the level of help students received (ranging from none to receiving just the right answer to various levels of explanation of the concepts) is a predictor of student engagement in constructive activity, which in turn is a predictor of student achievement. Students who received no help or who were told the right answer tended to avoid engagement with the learning exercise, whereas those who received explanations engaged in activities like reworking a problem. Essentially, these results support using level-appropriate explanations to scaffold mathematics instruction, as they foster a learning climate that may lead to greater student achievement. Similarly, King (1994) found that when students are guided by both lesson-based questions and questions that cue and connect prior knowledge with the present lesson, they perform better than students who have only the lesson-based questions. These results suggest that providing students with help oriented toward making connections with material and conceptual support rather than answers is a useful form of scaffolding.

31.5.1.1 Research on Intersubjectivity. Mutual understanding is a key part of being able to communicate clearly and to ensure that learning goals have been met, but exactly how this understanding is developed remains somewhat of a puzzle. Illustrating this challenge is a study conducted by Hallam and Hazel (1998) in which postgraduate students with similar backgrounds were paired. Each person individually read a text and then discussed it with his or her partner. The results showed that the individuals were likely to have differences in understanding and interpretation of the passages read, particularly in parts that were connected to areas in which they had prior knowledge or experience, although the participants generally expected their partners to have a common understanding. Given the frequency with which students are asked to read passages and then participate in class discussions, the lack of mutually agreed-on interpretations of readings is particularly problematic.

Jarvela (1995) studied the relevance of social interactions between students and teachers based on a cognitive apprenticeship model used in a technologically rich environment. Jarvela was interested in the key parts of shared cognition in learning interactions and in how much the expert should be controlling the interaction. Specifically, Jarvela studied the work of seventh-grade boys using a Legologo environment to determine if modeling, scaffolding, and reflection fostered appropriate task involvement; whether cognitive apprenticeship fostered worthwhile social interactions for teachers and learners; and how the technology affected the learning interactions. Findings indicated that a reciprocal understanding of the task at hand was important; if teacher and student did not conceive of the task similarly, scaffolding and modeling might fail. Learners who did not share their teachers' understanding tended to be frustrated when modeling occurred and when reflection was required; indeed, it was found that teacher modeling did not create reciprocal understanding. In this study, the technology was found to be of assistance to the learning process because it fostered reflection activities and thus made students' thought processes more visible to the teacher.

As shown through the studies by Jarvela (1995) and Hallam and Hazel (1998), much remains to be known about how intersubjectivity can be efficiently developed in a classroom environment with multiple participants. Although the consequences of our failure to do so seem to highlight its importance very effectively, and we have been able to document when it does and does not occur, we do not yet know how to develop and support intersubjectivity efficiently among participants in a learning situation.

31.5.2   Studies of Reciprocal Teaching

Reciprocal teaching, described earlier, is one of the first-studied methods of scaffolded instruction, and research has looked at the method itself as well as a variation that involves direct instruction on the method followed by a reciprocal teaching episode. Studies of reciprocal teaching have proven it to be a successful technique for improving reading comprehension (A. L. Brown & Palincsar, 1989; Palincsar & Brown, 1984; Palincsar et al., 1993; Rosenshine & Meister, 1994). For example, results from Greenway's (2002) quasi-experimental study, albeit limited by the lack of a control group, indicated that students' reading comprehension scores and self-confidence both improved due to the reciprocal teaching intervention. Another study of reciprocal teaching (Brand-Gruwel, Aarnoutse, & Van Den Bos, 1998) looked at its effects on students with both reading comprehension and decoding problems (as opposed to students with only comprehension problems, as studied by Palincsar and Brown, 1984). Participants came from both regular and special schools. The study provided instruction and practice on the four reciprocal teaching strategies—questioning, summarizing, clarifying, and predicting—in alternating reading and listening activities. Student skills were measured using a pretest, a posttest, and a retention test. Results indicated a clear effect on student performance shortly following the intervention, but long-term performance differences between the control and the treatment group were not statistically significant. Also, there were no significant differences in performance related to school type (regular or special).

Related to reciprocal teaching, particularly the concept of shifting responsibility for process from teacher to learner, Chou, Lin, and Chan (2002) created a computer-based reciprocal tutoring system (RTS) that contains a virtual tutor and tutee. This tutor is programmed to trace a human tutee's actions and to scaffold his or her learning process through timely guidance. When the roles are reversed, with the human playing tutor and the RTS playing tutee, the human learner will observe the computer attempt to solve a problem (programmed to have difficulties) and will be required to diagnose any problems that arise. The human tutor's actions are monitored by the system and feedback is provided in the instance of an incorrect diagnosis.

31.6   TECHNOLOGY STUDIES

Up to this point, cognitive apprenticeship has been discussed as an activity engaged in by human participants, which is appropriate given the dynamic nature of the ZPD. However, computer use in conjunction with scaffolding, mentoring, and coaching of various kinds is being explored. In some instances the computer is being used as a medium through which scaffolding is provided; I refer to this as *computer-mediated* cognitive apprenticeship. Finally, there are researchers and developers who believe in the promise of what is called "software-realized scaffolding" (Guzdial, 1995; Shabo, Guzdial, & Stasko, 1997), in which the ability to scaffold is built into a software program and enacted by the computer in response to a user's actions; I refer to this as *computer-based* cognitive apprenticeship.

31.6.1   Computer-Mediated Cognitive Apprenticeship

Interest in computer-mediated cognitive apprenticeship has grown with the Web-based education trend of the last decade. As learning experiences move to an on-line environment, educators and researchers have sought to determine what constitutes worthwhile computer-mediated interactions between teachers and learners. Learner-centered strategies, including mentoring and scaffolding collaboration, have been hailed as the solution (Bonk & Dennen, 1999), moving away from information transmission models of learning, which tend to result in static content and flat interactions in an on-line environment. Oliver and Herrington (2000) state that coaching and scaffolding are essential to achieve deep levels of asynchronous discussion. McLouglin (2002) theorizes about how scaffolding might be used in distance learning situations, noting that in such settings "the metaphor of scaffolding is appealing in principle, yet elusive and problematic." Why is scaffolding in an on-line environment so challenging? In part because it brings into question whether or not traditional roles of teacher and learner will be relied on.

McLouglin suggests a variety of technology interventions that rely on scaffolding, including computer-supported intentional learning environments (CSILEs), which are collaborative learning spaces in which the teacher is a facilitator and the student is tasked with communicating and creating knowledge objects (e.g., Scardamalia & Bereiter, 1994); intelligent tutoring systems (ITSs), which help break down and manage specific tasks; and goal-based scenarios (GBSs), which engage students in authentic tasks and provide computer-based resources and scaffolding in the form of task assistance and hints as needed (e.g., Schank, Berman, & McPherson, 1999). Whereas the latter two fall under the category of computer-based learning experiences, CSILE would be considered a computer-mediated form of cognitive apprenticeship.

31.6.1.1 Computer-Mediated Scaffolding. Oshima and Oshima (2001) studied ways to improve learning for novices through the use of discourse scaffolding. Two groups of learners were studied in successive years, the first with a comprehension-oriented learning objective and the second with a synthesis-oriented one. The learners used the WebCSILE (Computer-Supported Intentional Learning Environment) tool to support their interactions. The second group had the addition of learning supports in the form of a schedule discussion and a page providing tips for writing ideas. These scaffolds were developed based on the feedback from the first group. Statistically, these two groups used the tool in similar ways, generating and reading about the same number of messages. A comparative analysis of the resulting discourse shows that whereas students in the first group discussed contents at the metacognitive level, those in the second group did not, and the quality of writing did not improve in the second group. This was surprising to the researchers, who surmised that this may have been because the scaffolding alone was not sufficient to promote greater knowledge advancement and, in fact, may in some ways have limited the interactions that took place. Learners in the second group used the provided scaffolding as a directive for what to do and followed its suggestions quite literally, like a task list. More extensive and tailored instructor intervention is planned for future studies.

Pear and Crone-Todd (2002) examined ways of using computers to provide feedback to students in a manner consistent with the tenets of social constructivism. The setting for this study is a college-level course, which used a teaching system called a computer-aided personalized system of instruction (CAPSI). Drawing on the concept of scaffolding, course material was arranged in manageable units. A peer-tutor model was developed in which more advanced learners provided feedback to their classmates in an open-ended question practice test environment. Although the findings of this study show that the method works to help ensure that students receive a high amount of feedback while keeping the process manageable for instructors, it neglects to comment on the impact of this intervention on the learning process for either the students who received the feedback or the peer tutors who provided it.

Guzdial and Turns (2000) recommend the use of anchors, or topics that students wish to discuss to stimulate interest and motivation. Using the Collaborative and Multimedia Interactive Learning Environment (CaMILE), a discussion tool, students identify a note type they wish to use, which essentially labels the nature of their contribution and gives them a sentence prompt. For example, if students choose a New Idea note, they may be given the prompt "I propose...." In CaMILE, Web pages are linked from notes and used as anchors to begin particular discussion threads. Guzdial and Turns compared the use of CaMILE to support anchored discussion with the use of a newsgroup tool lacking its management, facilitation, and anchoring features, hypothesizing that the anchored threads would be more effective (defined as having broad participation and being on-topic) than the unanchored ones. In an initial study, which looked at participation across multiple classes, findings indicated that discussion threads in CaMILE were longer than those in the newsgroup, with low variability of length in the newsgroups but high variability in CaMILE. There was no significant difference between the two tools in terms of the number of active participants. A second study focused on discussion within a single class. Findings in this study indicated that the students who used CaMILE participated more extensively than their newsgroup counterparts and that teacher participation was greater in number of messages but far less in percentage of messages.

31.6.1.2 Computer-Mediated Mentoring. The advent of the Internet has encouraged the exploration of mentoring in environments where mentors and learners are not collocated. Bonk and his colleagues at Indiana University investigated the effects of on-line mentoring of pre-service teachers in a project called Conference on the Web (COW), which spanned multiple years and involved collaborations from faculty and preservice teachers at other schools and universities internationally (Bonk, Angeli, Malikowski, & Supplee, 2001; Bonk, Daytner, Daytner, Dennen, & Malikowski, 2001; Bonk, Hara, Dennen, Malikowski, & Supplee, 2000). Students in the COW environment were asked to post case-based reflections based on observations in their early teaching experiences and connect these observations to theory learned in their teacher preparation classes. Mentors, in the form of peers, graduate students, university faculty, and in-service teachers, provided case posters with feedback on their ideas. Postclass surveys and interviews indicated that the students valued the mentoring they received and felt that the computer-mediated forum was an appropriate outlet. Indeed, this forum allowed communication among parties who would otherwise not meet. The quality of student reflection was not as high as it might be, and further work is needed to develop better scaffolding and mentoring strategies for use in online environments.

Russell and Cohen (1997) shared their experiences and reflections as participants in a reflective colleague relationship over e-mail. This relationship was similar to what others would call mentoring or coaching, although the authors chose a different term to help indicate the peer nature of their interaction, using Schon's (1983) description of reflective practitioners as those who articulate their thoughts and experiences, reflect on them, and then discuss these reflections with critical friends. In particular, Russell and Cohen explored the impact that e-mail had as a medium, finding that the asynchronous technology provided two important advantages to this mentorlike relationship: (a) It allowed them to complete the articulation and reflection process without any interjections or distractions, and (b) it resulted in a written archive of the reflection that could be used later for further reflection. They also commented on how the process of being reflective colleagues helped them both grow, whether they were playing the role of the reflector or the role of the critical friend.

31.6.2 Computer-Based Cognitive Apprenticeship

Davis and Linn (2000) and Davis (2003) studied the use of prompts to scaffold the reflection process for middle-school science students working within a computer-based system called Knowledge Integration Environment (KIE) developed by Bell, Davis, and Linn (1995). This system supports the scientific process by prompting students through related activities, such as identifying the needed evidence to support claims and determining whether presented evidence is adequate.

Davis and Linn found in two related studies that reflective prompts in KIE promoted knowledge integration in students working on science projects. Students in Study 1 were assigned to two conditions, those receiving activity prompts and those receiving both activity prompts and reflective self-monitoring prompts. In Study 2, three conditions were used: (a) belief prompts, which were unlikely to impact work on the project (control group); (b) activity prompts; and (c) self-monitoring prompts. They found that the self-monitoring prompts, which encouraged and scaffolded reflective behavior, had the greatest impact on knowledge integration as evidenced by performance on student projects. Davis and Linn suggest that the reflective articulation that is involved in responding to self-monitoring prompts helps students better self-assess their understanding and thus engages them in knowledge integration.

In Davis' 2003 study, students working in pairs received either generic prompts, basically asking students to share their thoughts at that point in the activity, or directed prompts. Directed prompts took one of three forms: Thinking Ahead prompts, which pushed learners to think about task structuring and information needs; Checking Our Understanding prompts, which asked learners to identify current knowledge gaps; and Thinking Back prompts, which asked learners to think about what they might do differently next time. She found that the learners who receive the generic prompts were more likely to develop a coherent understanding of the overall project in which they were participating than those who received the more heavily scaffolded or controlled direct prompts. Learner autonomy was also a factor, with autonomous learners demonstrating the greatest comprehension benefits from the generic prompts. It is possible that the directed prompts, which were programmed into the KIE, were too limiting or narrow for these learners or did not challenge them enough. It is also possible that the learners' understanding of the material was different from that expected and thus the prompts were not fully relevant to their thought processes.

This study demonstrates one of the challenges of providing computer-based scaffolding; it is difficult to meet learners' needs with respect to providing instruction within the learner's ZPD that is relevant to the learner's current understanding without human diagnosis and intervention. Whereas computers can be programmed to understand and react to different input patterns, they lack the ability to make the subtle judgments that human teachers do and to identify accurately and consistently each learner's ZPD (Ainsworth, Wood, & O'Malley, 1998).

Can computers actually respond to learner input at an appropriate level to provide cognitive support? Hague and Benest (1996) suggest that computers can provide "over-the-shoulder"

guidance to students, essentially playing the role of a coach. Based on the premise that information and problems should be presented to learners in a scaffolded manner, graded by difficulty, and within the ZPD, they discuss the challenge of programming a computer-aided learning system to diagnose correctly the student's learning difficulty based on an incorrect response. Their solution is to build hot spots or hyperlinks into the material so students can access clues as needed. These clues will assist the students but will not supply them with the correct answer. Their system has not yet been tested in classrooms for practical *in situ* effectiveness but, nonetheless, is indicative of directions being explored.

Shabo et al. (1997) designed scaffolding into *Graphica*, a computer-based environment focused on graphics learning. Graphica provides scaffolds that are built into learning exercises in the form of resources (hints, descriptions of expert processes), coaching (computer-based critiques of student work that are available on demand), and articulation (a newsgroup; the one form of human–human interaction built into the program). In a formative evaluation of Graphica, they found that many students were unsure how to use its various components to support their learning processes. The practice exercises and visualization components were popular, but scaffolds such as the expert analyses and hints were not heavily used. The challenge for users of Graphica and similar programs is that they must have sufficient metacognitive development to identify their own learning needs, and their learning goals must be in-line with the goals designed into the system.

31.7 LOOKING TO THE FUTURE: RESEARCH AND PRACTICE

The most essential statement that can be made with reference to research in cognitive apprenticeship is, quite simply, "We need more." The present body of research, with exceptions in a few key areas such as reciprocal teaching, is largely scattered across personal interest areas rather than focused on a program of research that will lead to greater generalizability of results and the development of prescriptive knowledge to guide practitioners. *In situ* and experimental research studies should be designed to work together, complementing each other in the knowledge production process. Although individual studies of unique or proprietary programs and software are interesting and have some value, there is a greater need for results that clearly demonstrate (a) whether or not (and under what conditions) cognitive apprenticeship is preferable to traditional instruction and (b) how to implement and support a cognitive apprenticeship model of learning through scaffolding, mentoring, and coaching activities. All of this work needs to be done within the context of what is reasonably operational within today's standard educational contexts. Research on cognitive apprenticeship has already demonstrated its great potential as a method of facilitating learning; now we need to determine whether it is suitable, practical, and efficient as well.

There are some definite challenges to implementing cognitive apprenticeship methods on a grand scale in K–12 education given the reality of today's classrooms. Large class size limits the teacher's ability to interact with and assess individual student's needs. Diverse cultural and communication styles can further inhibit teacher ability to meet many students' needs in a cognitive apprenticeship. Curricular and time pressures tend to favor the use of other, seemingly more efficient teaching methods. Dominant and required methods of assessment do not always align with and measure the learning outcomes. State-mandated learning goals may leave little room for development and negotiation of students' personal learning goals. Teachers need methods, templates, and tools to help simplify and support the process as well as the backing of other stakeholders such as administrators and parents.

Hogan and Pressley (1997) suggest that whole-class scaffolding is possible though reaction to and elaboration on student comments in a class discussion. The teacher can use discussion as a way of prompting student thinking, focusing the direction of the discussion. Such strategies involve requesting explanation, elaboration, clarification, and extension of student contributions. A range of instructional goals and philosophies can be addressed through this method, which balances student-centeredness with subject-centeredness. Conceptually, this idea sounds good. However, what remains is to prove the practical soundness of this idea and generate empirical-based prescriptions for putting it into practice.

In higher education, the focus of cognitive apprenticeships likely will continue in the same vein as for the last 5 years, with mentoring programs (both live and on-line), scaffolded on-line discussion and reflection activities, and computer-based tools to support self-study. Research in on-line learning in general has been robust, including the study of closely related learning methods such as problem-based learning. Technology seems to hold great promise and interest as both a mediator of and a provider of scaffolding, modeling, mentoring, and coaching. Whereas proprietary programs are essential to furthering knowledge and capabilities in this area, the next steps in research should focus on developing and researching techniques that will work with the commercial programs that educational institutions have already invested in rather heavily, in terms of both adoption and training.

In closing, although the historical roots of cognitive apprenticeship in education are clear, the future is not. It seems likely that corporate and continuing education will continue to use methods of cognitive apprenticeship, which are appropriately focused on moving one's ability from novice-level to expert-level skills. It is also probable that distance learning initiatives will continue to embrace methods such as mentoring and components of scaffolding such as modeling and task structuring that have already proven to be useful in managing the learning process. However, whether cognitive apprenticeship will be widely adopted in K–12 education and on face-to-face college campuses in the current climate of high-stakes standardized testing—performance on which is likely better supported through other instructional methods—remains unknown.

References

Ainsworth, S., Wood, D., & O'Malley, C. (1998). There is more than one way to solve a problem: Evaluating a learning environment that supports the development of children's multiplication skills. *Learning and Instruction, 8*(2), 141-157.

Bandura, A. (1977). *Social learning theory*. Englewood Cliffs, NJ: Prentice-Hall.

Bean, T. W., & Patel Stevens, L. (2002). Scaffolding reflection for preservice and inservice teachers. *Reflective Practice, 3*(2), 205-218.

Beaufort, A. (2000). Learning the trade: A social apprenticeship model for gaining writing expertise. *Written Communication, 17*(2), 185-223.

Bell, P., Davis, E. A., & Linn, M. C. (1995). *The knowledge integration environment: Theory and design*. Paper presented at the Computer Supported Collaborative Learning Conference (CSCL '95), Bloomington, IN.

Billet, S. (1994). Situated learning in the workplace: Having another look at apprenticeships. *Industrial and Commercial Training, 26*(11), 9-16.

Billet, S. (2000). Guided learning at work. *Journal of Workplace Learning, 12*(7), 272-285.

Bonk, C. J., & Dennen, V. P. (1999). Getting by with a little help from my pedagogical friends. *Journal of Computing in Higher Education, 11*(1), 3-28.

Bonk, C. J., & Kim, K. A. (1998). Extending sociocultural theory to adult learning. In M. C. Smith & T. Pourchot (Eds.), *Adult learning and development: Perspectives from educational psychology* (pp. 67-88). Mahwah, NJ: Lawrence Erlbaum.

Bonk, C. J., Hara, N., Dennen, V. P., Malikowski, S., & Supplee, L. (2000). We're in TITLE to dream: Envisioning a community of practice, "The Intraplanetary Teacher Learning Exchange." *CyberPsychology and Behavior, 3*(1), 25-39.

Bonk, C. J., Angeli, C., Malikowski, S., & Supplee, L. (2001, August). *Holy COW: Scaffolding case-based "Conferencing on the Web" with preservice teachers*. Retrieved October 22, 2002, from http://www.usdla.org/html/journal/AUG01_Issue/article01.html

Bonk, C. J., Daytner, K., Daytner, G., Dennen, V. P., & Malikowski, S. (2001). Using Web-based cases to enhance, extend, and transform preservice teacher training: Two years in review. *Computers in the Schools, 18*(1), 189-211.

Brand-Gruwel, S., Aarnoutse, C. A. J., & Van Den Bos, K. P. (1998). Improving text comprehension strategies in reading and listening settings. *Learning and Instruction, 8*(1), 63-81.

Brown, A. L., & Palincsar, A. S. (1989). Guided, cooperative learning and individual knowledge acquisition. In L. B. Resnick (Ed.), *Knowing, learning, and instruction: Essays in honor of Robert Glaser* (pp. 393-451). Hillsdale, NJ: Lawrence Erlbaum Associates.

Brown, J. S. (1998). Internet technology in support of the concept of "communities-of-practice": The case of Xerox. *Accounting, Management and Information Technology, 8*, 227-236.

Brown, J. S., Collins, A., & Duguid, P. (1989). Situated cognition and the culture of learning. *Educational Researcher, 18*(1), 32-42.

Burton, R., Brown, J. S., & Fischer, G. (1999). Skiing as a model of instruction. In B. Rogoff & J. Lave (Eds.), *Everyday cognition: Development in social context* (pp. 139-150). Cambridge, MA: Harvard University Press.

Chang, K. E., Sung, Y. T., & Chen, S. F. (2001). Learning through computer-based concept mapping with scaffolding aid. *Journal of Computer Assisted Learning, 17,* 21-33.

Chou, C.-Y., Lin, C.-J., & Chan, T.-W. (2002). An approach to developing computational supports for reciprocal tutoring. *Knowledge-Based Systems, 15,* 407-412.

Collins, A., Brown, J. S., & Newman, S. E. (1989). Cognitive apprenticeship: Teaching the craft of reading, writing, and mathematics. In L. B. Resnick (Ed.), *Knowing, learning, and instruction: Essays in honor of Robert Glaser* (pp. 453-494). Hillsdale, NJ: Lawrence Erlbaum Associates.

Coltman, P., Petyaeva, D., & Anghileri, J. (2002). Scaffolding learning through meaningful tasks and adult interaction. *Early Years, 22*(1), 39-49.

Cooper, M. A. (1999). Classroom choices from a cognitive perspective on peer learning. In A. M. O'Donnell & A. King (Eds.), *Cognitive perspectives on peer learning* (pp. 215-233). Mahwah, NJ: Lawrence Erlbaum.

Davis, E. A. (2003). Prompting middle school science students for productive reflection: Generic and directed prompts. *Journal of the Learning Sciences, 12*(1), 91-142.

Davis, E. A., & Linn, M. C. (2000). Scaffolding students' knowledge integration: Prompts for reflection in KIE. *International Journal of Science Education, 22*(8), 819-837.

Day, J. D., & Cordon, L. A. (1993). Static and dynamic measures of ability: An experimental comparison. *Journal of Educational Psychology, 85,* 75-82.

Dennen, V. P. (2000). Task structuring for online problem-based learning. *Educational Technology and Society, 3*(3), 330-336.

Dennen, V. P. (2001). *The design and facilitation of asynchronous discussion activities in Web-based courses.* Unpublished Doctoral Dissertation. Indiana University.

Diaz, R. M., Neal, C. J., & Amaya-Williams, M. (1990). The social origins of self-regulation. In L. C. Moll (Ed.), *Vygotsky and education: Instructional implications and applications of socio-historical psychology* (pp. 127-154). Cambridge: Cambridge University Press.

Duffy, T. M., & Cunningham, D. J. (1996). Constructivism: Implications for the design and delivery of instruction. In D. H. Jonassen (Ed.), *Handbook of research for educational communications and technology* (pp. 170-198). New York: Macmillan.

Enerson, D. M. (2001). Mentoring as metaphor: An opportunity for innovation and renewal. In A. G. Reinarz & E. R. White (Eds.), *Beyond teaching to mentoring* (Vol. 85, pp. 7-13). San Francisco: Jossey-Bass.

Enkenberg, J. (2001). Instructional design and emerging models in higher education. *Computers in Human Behavior, 17,* 495-506.

Gallimore, R., & Tharp, R. (1990). Teaching mind in society: Teaching, schooling, and literate discourse. In L. C. Moll (Ed.), *Vygotsky and education: Instructional implications and applications of socio-historical psychology*. New York: Cambridge.

Greenfield, P. M. (1999). A theory of the teacher in the learning activities of everyday life. In B. Rogoff & J. Lave (Eds.), *Everyday cognition: Development in social context* (pp. 116-138). Cambridge, MA: Harvard University Press.

Greenway, C. (2002). The process, pitfalls and benefits of implementing a reciprocal teaching intervention to improve the reading comprehension of a group of Year 6 pupils. *Educational Psychology in Practice, 18*(2), 113-137.

Guzdial, M. (1995). Software-realized scaffolding to facilitate programming for science learning. *Interactive Learning Environments, 4*(1), 1-44.

Guzdial, M., & Turns, J. (2000). Effective discussion through a computer-mediated anchored forum. *Journal of the Learning Sciences, 9*(4), 437-469.

Hague, A. C., & Benest, I. D. (1996). Towards over-the-shoulder guidance following a traditional learning metaphor. *Computers & Education, 26*(1), 61-70.

Hallam, S., & Hazel, F. (1998). Is my understanding yours? A study of higher education students' reading for understanding and the effects of different texts. *Learning and Instruction, 8*(1), 83-95.

Hayward, L. M., DiMarco, R., Blackmer, B., Canali, A., Wong, K., & O'Brien, M. (2001). Curriculum-based electronic peer mentoring: An instructional strategy for integrative learning. *Journal of Physical Therapy Education, 15*(4), 14-25.

Hendricks, C. C. (2001). Teaching causal reasoning through cognitive apprenticeship: What are the results from situated learning. *Journal of Educational Research, 94*(5), 302-311.

Hogan, K., & Pressley, M. (1997). Scaffolding scientific competencies within classroom communities of inquire. In K. Hogan & M. Pressley (Eds.), *Scaffolding student learning: Instructional approaches and issues* (pp. 74-107). Cambridge, MA: Brookline.

Jarvela, S. (1995). The cognitive apprenticeship model in a technologically rich learning environment: Interpreting the learning interaction. *Learning and Instruction, 5,* 237-259.

Jekielek, S. M., Moore, K. A., Hair, E. C., & Scarupa, H. J. (2002). *Mentoring: A promising strategy for youth development* [Research Brief]. Washington, DC: Child Trends.

Jonassen, D. H. (1999). Designing constructivist learning environments. In C. M. Reigeluth (Ed.), *Instructional-design theories and models: A new paradigm of instructional theory* (pp. 215-239). Mahwah, NJ: Lawrence Erlbaum.

Kaptelinin, V., & Cole, M. (2001). Individual and collective activities in educational computer game playing. In T. Koschmann, R. Nelson, & N. Miyake (Eds.), *CSCL 2: Carrying forward the conversation* (pp. 303-315). Mahwah, NJ: Lawrence Erlbaum.

King, A. (1994). Guiding knowledge construction in the classroom: Effects of teaching children how to question and how to explain. *American Educational Research Journal, 31*(2), 338-368.

King, A. (1999). Discourse patterns for mediating peer learning. In A. M. O'Donnell & A. King (Eds.), *Cognitive perspectives on peer learning* (pp. 87-115). Mahwah, NJ: Lawrence Erlbaum.

Langer, A. M. (2001). Confronting theory: The practice of mentoring non-traditional students at Empire State College. *Mentoring & Tutoring, 9*(1), 49-62.

Lave, J., & Wenger, E. (1991). *Situated learning: Legitimate peripheral participation*. Cambridge: Cambridge University Press.

Lenski, S. D., & Nierstheimer, S. L. (2002). Strategy instruction from a sociocognitive perspective. *Reading Psychology, 23*(2), 127-143.

Lepper, M. R., Drake, M. F., & O'Donnell-Johnson, T. (1997). Scaffolding techniques of expert human tutors. In K. Hogan & M. Pressley (Eds.), *Scaffolding student learning: Instructional approaches and issues* (pp. 108-144). Cambridge, MA: Brookline.

Little, J. W. (1990). The mentor phenomenon and the social organisation of teaching. *Review of Research in Education, 16,* 297-351.

Loong, D. H. W. (1998). Epistemological change through peer apprenticeship learning: From rule-based to idea-based social constructivism. *International Journal of Computers for Mathematical Learning, 3*(1), 45-80.

Lucas, K. F. (2001). The social construction of mentoring roles. *Mentoring & Tutoring, 9*(1), 23-47.

Matthew, K., Callaway, R., Letendre, C., Kimbell-Lopez, K., & Stephens, E. (2002). Adoption of information communication technology by teacher educators: One-on-one coaching. *Journal of Information Technology for Teacher Education, 11*(1), 45-62.

Matusov, E. (2001). Intersubjectivity as a way of informing teaching design for a community of learners classroom. *Teaching and Teacher Education, 17,* 383-402.

McLoughlin, C. (2002). Learning support in distance and networked learning environments: Ten dimensions for successful design. *Distance Education, 23*(2), 149-162.

Oliver, R., & Herrington, J. (2000). Using situated learning as a design strategy for Web-based learning. In B. Abbey (Ed.), *Instructional and cognitive aspects of Web-based education* (pp. 178-191). Hershey, PA: Idea.

Oshima, J., & Oshima, R. (2001). Next step in design experiments with networked collaborative learning environments: Instructional interventions in the curriculum. In T. Koschmann, R. Hall, & N. Miyake (Eds.), *CSCL 2: Carrying forward the conversation* (pp. 99-109). Mahwah, NJ: Lawrence Erlbaum.

Palincsar, A. S., & Brown, A. L. (1984). Reciprocal teaching of comprehension-fostering and monitoring activities. *Cognition and Instruction, 1,* 117-175.

Palincsar, A. S., Brown, A. L., & Campione, J. C. (1993). First-grade dialogue for knowledge acquisition and use. In E. A. Forman, N. Minick, & C. A. Stone (Eds.), *Contexts for learning* (pp. 43-57). New York: Oxford University Press.

Parker, W. C., & Hess, D. (2001). Teaching with and for discussion. *Teaching and Teacher Education, 17,* 273-289.

Parsloe, E., & Wray, M. (2000). *Coaching and mentoring: Practical methods to improve learning.* London: Kogan Page.

Pear, J. J., & Crone-Todd, D. E. (2002). A social constructivist approach to computer-mediated instruction. *Computers & Education, 38*(1-3), 221-231.

Roberts, A. (2000). Mentoring revisited: A phenomenological reading of the literature. *Mentoring & Tutoring, 8*(2), 145-170.

Roehler, L. R., & Cantlon, D. J. (1997). Scaffolding: A powerful tool in social constructivist classrooms. In K. Hogan & M. Pressley (Eds.), *Scaffolding student learning: Instructional approaches and issues* (pp. 6-42). Cambridge, MA: Brookline.

Rogoff, B. (1990). *Apprenticeship in thinking: Cognitive development in social context.* New York: Oxford University Press.

Rogoff, B., Mosier, C., Mistry, J., & Goncu, A. (1993). Toddlers' guided participation with their caregivers in cultural activity. In E. A. Forman, N. Minick, & C. A. Stone (Eds.), *Contexts for learning* (pp. 230-253). New York: Oxford University Press.

Rosenshine, B., & Meister, C. (1994). Reciprocal teaching: A review of the research. *Review of Educational Research, 64*(4), 479-487.

Roth, W.-M. (2001). Situating cognition. *Journal of the Learning Sciences, 10*(1, 2), 27-61.

Russell, A. L., & Cohen, L. M. (1997). The reflective colleague in e-mail cyberspace: A means for improving university instruction. *Computers & Education, 29*(4), 137-145.

Savery, J. R. (1998). Fostering ownership for learning with computer-supported collaborative writing in an undergraduate business communication course. In C. J. Bonk & K. S. King (Eds.), *Electronic collaborators: Learner-centered technologies for literacy, apprenticeship, and discourse* (pp. 103-127). Mahwah, NJ: Lawrence Erlbaum Associates.

Scardamalia, M., & Bereiter, C. (1994). Computer support for knowledge-building communities. *Journal of the Learning Sciences, 3*(3), 265-283.

Schank, R. C., Berman, T., & McPherson, J. (1999). Learning by doing. In C. M. Reigeluth (Ed.), *Instructional design theories and models: A new paradigm of instructional theory* (pp. 161-181). Mahwah, NJ: Lawrence Erlbaum.

Schon, D. A. (1983). *The reflective practitioner.* New York: Basic Books.

Sève, C., Saury, J., Thereau, J., & Durand, M. (2002). Activity organization and knowledge construction during competitive interaction in table tennis. *Cognitive Systems Research, 3,* 501-522.

Shabo, A., Guzdial, M., & Stasko, J. (1997). An apprenticeship-based multimedia courseware for computer graphics studies provided on the World Wide Web. *Computers & Education, 29*(2/3), 103-116.

Sugar, W. A., & Bonk, C. J. (1998). Student role play in the World Forum: Analyses of an Arctic Adventure learning apprenticeship. In C. J. Bonk & K. S. King (Eds.), *Electronic collaborators: Learner-centered technologies for literacy, apprenticeship, and discourse* (pp. 131-155). Mahwah, NJ: Lawrence Erlbaum Associates.

Tharp, R. (1993). Institutional and social context of educational reform: Practice and reform. In E. A. Forman, N. Minnick, & C. A. Stone (Eds.), *Contexts for learning: Sociocultural dynamics in children's development* (pp. 269-282). New York: Cambridge University Press.

Tharp, R., & Gallimore, R. (1988). *Rousing minds to life: Teaching, learning and schooling in social context.* Cambridge: Cambridge University Press.

Vygotsky, L. S. (1977). The development of higher psychological functions. *Soviet Psychology, 16,* 60-73.

Vygotsky, L. S. (1978). *Mind in society: The development of higher psychological processes.* Cambridge, MA: Harvard University Press.

Webb, N. M., Troper, J. D., & Fall, R. (1995). Constructive activity and learning in collaborative small groups. *Journal of Educational Psychology, 87*(3), 406-423.

Wertsch, J. V. (1998). *Mind as action.* Oxford: Oxford University Press.

Wood, D. J., Bruner, J. S., & Ross, G. (1976). The role of tutoring in problem solving. *Journal of Child Psychology and Psychiatry, 17,* 89-100.

Young, A. M., & Perrewé, P. L. (2000). What did you expect? An examination of career-related support and social support among mentors and protégés. *Journal of Management, 26*(4), 611-632.

·32·

CASE-BASED LEARNING AIDS

Janet L. Kolodner, Jakita N. Owensby, and Mark Guzdial
Georgia Institute of Technology

32.1   WHAT IS A CASE-BASED LEARNING AID?

A case-based learning aid is a support that helps learners interpret, reflect on, and apply experiences—their own or those of someone else—in such a way that valuable learning takes place. Case-based learning aids have cases at their core. The creation and importance of case-based learning aids arose out of work done in two disciplines—work in computer science on case-based reasoning (CBR) and work in education on constructivist approaches to education.

CBR, inspired by people, was developed as a model for creating intelligent systems—systems that could reason by reference to their previous experiences. Such systems, it was conjectured, had the potential to behave more like real experts than could traditional expert systems. Reasoning based on experience would allow them to be more flexible and less brittle than rule-based systems, and with learning from experience built into their architectures, they would become more capable over time (Hammond, 1989; Kolodner & Simpson, 1989; Schank, 1982). Many experimental automated case-based reasoners have been created (see the lists, e.g., in Kolodner, 1993), and indeed, CBR has proven to be quite a useful technology. More interesting to education, however, are the implications CBR holds as a model of cognition—implications about what it means to be a learner and implications about learning and education.

CBR is a special kind of analogical reasoning. A previous experience might suggest a solution to a new problem or a way of interpreting a situation, may warn of a problem that will arise, or may allow the potential effects of a proposed solution to be predicted. CBR has as its core (a) analogy in the context of solving real-world problems and understanding real-world situations and (b) research methodology of computational modeling, aimed at deriving hypotheses about cognition. Whereas analogical reasoning focuses on analogy as a single reasoning method, put into play when a rule-based approach is failing, CBR sees analogical reasoning as the centerpiece of our ability to function as human beings. It posits that our most natural and powerful learning strategies are the automatic ones that situate learning in real-world experience. According to CBR's model, we naturally bring our previous experience and knowledge to bear in interpreting new situations we encounter; we naturally try to explain when things are not as expected (based on the predictions made by our previous experiences and knowledge); we naturally draw conclusions based on explanations and on similarities between situations; and once we draw conclusions, we naturally anticipate, at least a little bit, when this new thing we learned might be applicable. To be able to do all these things so automatically, we must also have some internal processes and representations that allow a new experience to call up similar ones from memory.

CBR also helps us understand how we might develop expertise and how an expert uses his or her own experiences and those of others to reason and learn. Consider, for example, an architect designing an office building. She calls on her experiences and those of others who have designed buildings that address similar needs to make decisions about how to proceed. She knows that many modern office buildings have atriums. Should this new building have an atrium? To answer that, she first looks at the reasons for including atriums in those buildings. In some, it was to provide light to inside offices; in others, to provide a friendly informal space to meet. Are those goals in the new design? They are, but she wonders whether the noise of a central meeting space might be problematic. She examines those buildings again, looking at the effects of the atriums on use of its offices. Indeed, some did cause too much noise, but others were quite successful. Why did some succeed and some fail? The architect looks to see the reasons for failures. Will they be present in the new building? If so, is there a way to avoid the failure by doing it another way (perhaps suggested by one of the successful atria), or should an atrium not be used?

CBR suggests the kinds of content we should extract from our experiences to be able to reuse effectively what we can learn from them, and the kinds of reflection that are effective for doing this, suggesting several critical processes that promote good transfer (Kolodner, 1993, 1997). In particular, CBR suggests five important facilitators for learning effectively from hands-on activities and vicarious experiences: (a) having the kinds of experiences that afford learning what needs to be learned; (b) interpreting those experiences so as to recognize what can be learned from them, to draw connections between their parts so as to transform them into useful cases, and to extract lessons that might be applied elsewhere; (c) anticipating their usefulness so as to be able to develop indexes for these cases that will allow their applicability to be recognized in the future; (d) experiencing failure of one's conceptions to work as expected, explaining those failures, and trying again (iteration); and (e) learning to use cases effectively to reason.

With respect to what the right kinds of experiences are, CBR suggests (a) that they be experiences that afford concrete, authentic, and timely feedback, so that learners have the opportunity to confront their conceptions and identify what they still need to learn; (b) that learners have the opportunity to move iteratively toward better and better development of the skills and concepts they are learning so as to experience them in a range of situations and under a variety of conditions; and (c) that they be experiences that allow cases to be compared and contrasted.

CBR's suggestions about promoting learning have informed three contributions to educational practice and the use of software tools for education.

- **Supports for reflection**: Prompts and other guidance for learners aimed at promoting productive reflection.
- **Case libraries as a resource**: Collections of cases and experiences that can act as external memory for a reasoner.
- **Engineering of the learning environment:** Effective sequencing of activities and facilitation of discussions so as to increase the frequency and impact of having the right kinds of experiences.

CBR's implications for supporting learning are in-line with those made by constructivist approaches to learning and the constructionist approach to education. All focus on promoting the kinds of thinking that will allow learners to construct productive mental models from concrete experiences. Constructionism goes on to say that experiences of actively constructing an artifact are particularly good for promoting such construction. Similarly, CBR begins by suggesting that we create environments that promote the kinds of hands-on experiences and active construction that will lead to good learning. But CBR goes farther. It provides a model of cognition (including processes and knowledge structures) that can be turned to for advice and predictions and that can be simulated on a computer as a test of ideas. This model, in turn, makes suggestions about how to orchestrate and facilitate students' experiences so that they can draw productive lessons from their experiences and makes suggestions about how to encourage transferable learning—so that

lessons learned may be applied in new situations. CBR's cognitive model provides explanations of how learning happens and, from there, makes suggestions about how to ensure that active construction activities produce the results they afford.

32.2 CBR AS A MODEL OF COGNITION

CBR has been explored for many years in artificial intelligence as a way of creating more intelligent computer software. Several experimental case-based reasoners serve as the basis for CBR's cognitive model. The earliest case-based reasoner was CYRUS (Kolodner, 1983a, 1983b), a case library that knew about the life of statesman Cyrus Vance. When CYRUS was asked a question, it answered it by constructing a model of what the answer was likely to look like and then searching its memory for a matching case (a process of *reconstructing* the stories it held in its memory). Sometimes it did not find a case but, rather, answered questions by using this construction process to construct plausible stories. It was the first attempt to deal with retrieval and management of a case library. Early CBR systems, such as MEDIATOR (Kolodner & Simpson, 1989), CHEF (Hammond, 1989), and JULIA (Kolodner, 1993), showed us many of the processes involved in reasoning with cases. CHEF, which created recipes (plans for cooking), taught us much about the role of failure in learning and the role experience can play in helping us anticipate pitfalls as we are reasoning. A later system, called CELIA (Redmond, 1992), modeled the troubleshooting and learning of an apprentice mechanic. From CELIA we learned about the powerful role one's experiences can play before one has a full understanding of a domain and how important it is for a reasoner to have a variety of similar experiences so as to be able to extract the subtleties and nuances of the lessons it is learning and when each one applies. Still later reasoners, such as Creative-JULIA (Kolodner & Penberthy, 1990), IMPROVISOR (Kolodner & Wills, 1993), and ALEC (Simina & Kolodner, 1997; Simina, Kolodner, Ram, & Gorman, 1998) show us the role of CBR in creativity. The lesson from those models is that the quality of one's explorations before giving up on an idea, anticipation of the circumstances in which one might go back to it, immersion of oneself in an environment where one is likely to come upon such circumstances, and willingness to try, fail, and explain are all essential to reasoning that goes beyond the obvious.

CBR, as a cognitive model, values the concrete over the abstract (Kolodner, 1993). Whereas most traditional theories of cognition emphasize how general-purpose abstract operators are formed and applied, CBR makes concrete cases, representing experience, primary. CBR suggests that we think in terms of cases—interpretations of our experiences that we apply to new situations. To find the milk in a supermarket I've never been in, for example, I walk around the perimeter of the store until I reach the dairy section. Why? Because the dairy section of the supermarket I usually shop in is around its perimeter. When I throw a ball in the air, I expect it to come down because that's what I've always seen before. When I do strategic planning for my organization, I call on previous situations to suggest strategies and tactics and to warn of pitfalls. When I plan a dinner party, I consult menus I've served before as part of my planning; I may even serve the same meal I served another time if it worked well and different guests are invited this time.

Those schooled in traditional models of cognition will notice that CBR puts little explicit emphasis on abstract operators in the mind. There is no hierarchy of production rules, nor do we discuss networks of neuronlike components. Rather, we emphasize concrete experience in the form of stories that can be manipulated directly. CBR in many ways corresponds to our own introspection on how we think—in terms of stories and experiences. However, CBR does not exclude abstractions altogether. Rather, it places abstraction in roles that promote productive use of concrete experience: (a) for organizing similar cases in the case library so that one can choose one or a small number from the category from which to reason; (b) for creating indexing vocabulary; and (c) for managing partial matching—to allow the reasoner to recognize that two things that are similar but not identical are a close enough match. According to CBR's model, abstractions are extracted from concrete experience and formed as needed.

CBR explicitly integrates memory, learning, and reasoning. A reasoner, it says, is a being in the world that has goals. It seeks to navigate its world in such a way that its goals are successfully achieved. It has experiences, some of them successful and some not as successful, some pleasant and some not so pleasant, that allow it to learn about its environment and ways of using that environment to achieve its goals. As it has experiences, it seeks to learn the skills and concepts that will allow it to achieve its goals more productively in the future. It is engaged, therefore, in recording its experiences, interpreting its experiences to derive lessons useful to its future, anticipating when those lessons might be useful, and labeling its experiences appropriately so that it will be able to recognize the applicability of an experience in a later situation. A case-based reasoner is also engaged in noticing the similarities and differences between similar situations and experiences so that it can draw conclusions about its world and notice the subtle differences that suggest when each of the lessons it has learned is most appropriately applicable. Essential to its learning is failure—it needs to attempt to apply what it thinks is applicable and fail at that in order to know to focus its attentions on subtleties of which it had not previously been aware.

CBR suggests three components of cognition that we need to focus on: cases, case indexes, and the case processor.

Cases: Cases are interpretations of experiences. Cases have several subcomponents, just as stories do: their setting, the actors and their goals, a sequence of events, results, and explanations linking results to goals, and the means of achieving them. The better the interpretations of each of these pieces, and the better the explanations linking them to each other, the more useful a case will be when it is remembered later. For example, if we know that a plan carried out in a case failed, we can wonder whether it might fail again in a new similar situation, but we cannot make predictions. If, on the other hand, we know what caused the failure, we can check to see if the conditions that led to failure are present in the new situation. If they are, we can predict failure; if not, we might reuse the old plan.

The explanations that tie pieces of a case together allow us to derive lessons that can be learned from the case—its *lessons*

learned. For example, if I unknowingly served fish to vegetarians, and they didn't eat, I might explain the failure as being due to my not having inquired about whether any of my guests were vegetarians or had special eating requirements. The lesson learned is that I should make those inquiries whenever I invite guests for dinner. On recall of a case, the lessons one has derived from it are available for application to the new situation, as are the explanations from which those lessons were derived. Lessons in a case can identify why things went wrong and why things worked and can help learners make predictions about the results of an experience given certain criteria and constraints. For maximum usefulness, cases should be interpreted with the goal of deriving lessons learned.

Cases can reside in one's memory, and the set of cases in one's memory is referred to as one's *case library* or *library of cases.* Cases in one's case library may be derived from one's own experiences or from the experiences of others. For example, one might read about someone else's experience and remember its lessons to apply in the future. In general, one's own cases will be more embellished, but the cases of others play a very important role in learning and reasoning, filling in where one's own experience is deficient.

Case indexes: A library is as good as the indexes and indexing scheme available for locating something on its shelves. So too with one's case library. We can find the right cases in our memories if we "indexed" them well when we entered them into the library and if the indexing scheme is defined well enough that we can recreate an index for an appropriate case when we are trying to locate something in memory. If reasoners cannot recognize a past experience as being applicable in a new situation, they will have no case to apply.

A good indexing scheme for case-based reasoners allows them to see a past situation as being relevant to the one now facing them. Thus, a case's *indexes* should allow us to find it at times when it might be productive to apply it. Good indexes are critical for *transfer,* the ability to apply knowledge or skills derived in one kind of situation in a situation that might be quite different.

The best indexing results from anticipating the circumstances when a lesson learned from a case might be useful and marking the case so that it will be recalled in such circumstances. For example, if I index the case where vegetarians didn't eat the fish I served under "serving fish as the main course at a dinner party," I will be reminded of that case each time I plan to serve fish at a dinner party. Remembering the case would remind me to apply the lesson it teaches: Ask guests if they have any special eating requirements. Or I might index the case more specifically under "having a dinner party," allowing me to be reminded that I ought to ask guests for their eating requirements even before I begin planning dinner.

It is important to keep in mind, though, that it is almost always impossible to identify every lesson an experience might teach and every situation in which it might be applicable. It is common to have an experience that one does not completely understand or appreciate until much later—sometimes because one is lacking the knowledge necessary to interpret it, sometimes because one is lacking the experience to know whether a result is positive or negative, sometimes for other reasons. We may recognize that our understanding is incomplete at the time of an experience, or we may come to realize that our understanding was incomplete only when attempting to use the case later and finding that its application led to poor results. Either way, indexing will be incomplete.

But incomplete indexing does not have to mean that cases are inaccessible IF the reasoner engages in *situation assessment* at the time that he, she, or it is trying to address a new situation. Situation assessment is a process of analyzing a new situation so as to understand it better. One attempts to infer unknown details of a new situation or to look at the situation from several perspectives. This interpretation process allows the reasoner to construct a better description of the new situation than he or she has available. Though the description is hypothetical, it plays a critical role in reasoning: The hypothetical interpretation of the new situation serves as an index that allows old cases to be recalled. One way to look at situation assessment is as a process of imagining, "If I'd encountered a situation like this in the past, what would it have looked like, and how would it have been described?"

Nor does a poor index at the time one encounters or experiences a situation mean that the situation can never be described well as a case or indexed well. Situation assessment allows a reasoner to remember a case that was not well indexed. If, after a case is recalled and used, the reasoner is better able to interpret it, he, she, or it might extract new lessons from the case or identify something critical about it and reinterpret the case and update the indexes associated with it at that time.

The case processor: A reasoner's case processor has a variety of responsibilities. This component needs to carry out the processing that results in understanding and indexing one's experiences, finding appropriate cases in memory, applying them in a new situation, and learning:

- interpreting a new situation in such a way that relevant cases can be located in the case library;
- deciding which of the old cases that is remembered is most applicable;
- applying the lessons learned from an old case to the new situation, for example, decomposing and recomposing pieces of old cases to create a new solution, adapting an old solution to fit a new situation, or choosing a strategy for moving forward;
- noticing results and explaining the reasons why some scheme did or did not work;
- structuring an experience as a case and choosing ways of indexing it; and
- when necessary, reinterpreting and reindexing an old case in light of new findings (e.g., derived by applying its lessons learned and finding that they did not work as expected).

Each of these components is important to productive use of cases for reasoning and learning. Together, they promote learning from cases, productive use of cases, reflection upon experiences so that they are indexed with future use in mind, and application of a lesson learned in one situation in another where it applies. One can find more detail about CBR and early case-based reasoners in Kolodner (1993), more detail about CBR as a cognitive model in Kolodner (1993, Chap. 4, 1997), and more detail about CBR's implications for learning and education in Kolodner (1997), Kolodner, Crismond, Gray, Holbrook, and Puntambekar (1998), Kolodner et al. (2003, in press), and Schank (1999).

32.3 IMPLICATIONS FOR EDUCATION

We can derive a variety of specific suggestions about promoting effective learning from the discussions of case libraries and CBR's cognitive model.

- CBR's focus on the role of failure in promoting learning suggests the importance of acquiring feedback on decisions made, in order to be able to identify holes in one's knowledge and to generate goals for additional learning. CBR's approach emphasizes the need for students actually to carry out and test their ideas, not just think about them.

- CBR's focus on explanation suggests that the learners should be pushed both to predict and to explain and that they should be helped to do both successfully. One cannot recognize a need to explain without first seeing a difference between what was expected and what happened. Thus prediction is important so that students can recognize holes in what they know.

- CBR's focus on indexing as the key to reuse of what is learned from experience suggests that, in addition to having experiences, students should reflect on and assess those experiences to extract both what might be learned from them and the circumstances in which those lessons might be appropriately applied, in order to index their experiences well for reuse.

- CBR's focus on iterative refinement suggests that learners should have the opportunity to try out their ideas in a variety of situations and to cycle through application of what they are learning, interpretation of feedback, and explanation and revision of conceptions several times—that we should not expect one application to promote accurate learning.

- CBR's focus on the role previous experience plays in reasoning suggests that learners should be encouraged to reuse their own previous experiences as they solve "school" problems. It also suggests that they might be helped along to solve more complex problems than they could by themselves by having access to the cases (experiences of others).

These suggestions have informed the creation of two approaches to sequencing activities for learning—Goal-based scenarios (Schank, Fano, Bell, & Jona, 1994) and Learning by Design (Kolodner et al., 1998, 2003, in press). They also suggest two roles for computers:

- Software might support student reflection, especially that involved in explaining their experiences, interpreting them to make them accessible and easily applicable, and anticipating the applicability of lessons that can be learned from them.

- Case libraries might serve as a resource to provide suggestions to learners as they are engaging in problem solving, explanation, or other reasoning.

That is, software can help students process their experiences to make them into cases that can be stored in their memories and later accessed and applied, and software can supply students with cases as resources that they can use to reason. A range of case-based learning aids has been designed with each of these functionalities in mind. Table 32.1 characterizes each of the case-based learning aids that will be described later in the chapter by the responsibilities that they take on. These case-based learning aids support the student as a case processor in taking on these responsibilities with the hope that, as the student interacts with the learning aid more and more, he or she will be able to begin taking on these responsibilities without the support of the case-based learning aid. Based on the needs of a particular learning environment, appropriate tools can be chosen or created that fulfill the needs of a learner.

We provide introductions to each of these kinds of case-based learning aids in this section, along with short examples, and in later sections, we provide detail on the two approaches to sequencing activities that CBR has informed and the design and use of the case-based learning aids introduced here.

32.3.1 CBR-Informed Supports for Reflection

It has been over 10 years since Alan Collins and John Seeley Brown (1988) first suggested that the computer could be used to support reflection. In that first conceptualization, the emphasis was on skills and process learning. Collins and Brown talked about capturing an expert's process, then allowing the student to compare his or her process to that of the expert. The computer's role was to record the expert's reasoning, making it available whenever it could be useful and to whoever needed it. In this way, the computer was supporting a kind of reflection that was difficult to do without a computer.

More recent supports for reflection have emphasized the use of design journals as a way of getting students to reflect on their plans and past experiences. In Idit Harel's (1991) Instructional Software Design Project, the only daily requirement for students was that they had to write down what they had done each day and what they planned to do the next. The hope was that they would articulate how they did things and what they were learning.

Collins and Brown's work has also been used as the basis for supporting reflection during reasoning or during project activity. KIE (Bell, Davis, & Linn, 1995) prompts students to think about evidence and its uses as they are creating a scientific argument. Reciprocal teaching (Palincsar & Brown, 1984) helps students to recognize the questions they need to ask themselves as they are trying to understand something they are reading. CSILE (Scardamalia, Bereiter, & Lamon, 1994) prompts students to think about their actions and their discussion as they are having knowledge-building conversations.

We know that reflection is an important component of learning, and each of these approaches helps students reflect in a way that that will help them learn a difficult-to-learn skill by suggesting important times for reflection and/or providing helpful prompts for reflection.

TABLE 32.1. Case-Based Learning Aids and the Responsibilities They Support

	Interpreting a New Situation	Deciding Which Old Case Is Most Applicable	Applying Lessons Learned from an Old Case to a New Situation	Noticing Results & Explaining Reasons Why Some Scheme Did or Did Not Work	Structuring an Experience as a Case & Choosing Ways of Indexing It	Reinterpreting & Reindexing an Old Case in Light of New Findings
Reflective Learner	X			X	X	
Archie-2 (as a resource)		X		X	X	
Archie-2 (as an authoring tool)	X		X	X	X	X
STABLE (as a resource)	X	X		X		X
Design Discussion Area	X			X	X	
Case Authoring Tool		X	X	X		
Case Application Suite	X	X	X	X		
JavaCAP/Storyboard Author	X			X	X	
Smile	X	X	X	X	X	

CBR allows us to go the next steps. Because it makes explicit the role of reflection in learning, it allows us to understand the kinds of reflection that are productive at different times and to understand what the results of those reflections ought to be. In particular, CBR tells us that reflection is critical for (a) interpreting an experience to connect its pieces together and extract what might be learned from it, (b) creating indexes, and (c) creating and evaluating solutions. In other words, CBR tells us that we should help learners understand their experiences in ways that will help them describe and index them well so as to be able to use them well later (Kolodner, Hmelo, & Narayanan, 1996) and that we should help them reuse their experiences productively and in ways that help them gain better understanding of the experiences they are using.

CBR-inspired support for reflection encourages students to think about (a) the kinds of problems they have faced in solving a problem or developing a skill or achieving a design challenge, (b) the kinds of solutions they constructed, and (c) the future situations in which the solutions might be used again, focusing particularly on how the lessons learned from an experience might be utilized in new ways. For example, Turns' Reflective Learner (Turns, Newstetter, Allen, & Mistree, 1997) helps students write "learning essays" about their design experiences. Puntambekar has described good results with paper-based, CBR-informed *design diaries* (Puntambekar, Nagel, Hubscher, Guzdial, & Kolodner, 1997; Puntambekar & Kolodner, 1998, submitted) in which students keep records of their project experiences.

Motivating students to reflect is a critical issue in learning, and the computer provides a motivation that children find compelling. For example, Shabo's JavaCAP (Shabo, Nagel, Guzdial, & Kolodner, 1997) and its successors, Kolodner and Nagel's (1999) Storyboard Author and Voida and Kolodner's (2002) Lessons Learned, help students summarize their project experiences and write them up as stories for publication in a permanently accessible case library for use by other students. The networked computer creates motivation for the students' reflection: Students enhance their own learning as they are trying to write summaries that can act as guides and supports to future students.

Kolodner and Nagel's (1999) Design Discussion Area uses the computer similarly to encourage reflection during hands-on activities. It provides a forum for students to share their ideas with others, to get advice and criticism of their own ideas from others, and to provide advice and criticism to others. Students write up the results of experiments they have done, ideas about achieving design challenges or solving problems they are working on, or what happened when they constructed and tested a design idea. They publish it for others to see. The computer prompts students to include relevant information in their write-ups. Publishing their materials makes the materials available to others to incorporate into their solutions. Reading the ideas of others gives them ideas. Commenting on others' ideas requires consideration of how the ideas of others work. Comments from others encourage deeper thought about the implications of their own ideas.

Owensby and Kolodner's (2002) Case Application Suite uses the computer to encourage interpretation, application, and assessment of old experiences and expert cases. Recognizing that an old experience or an expert case may be applicable,

identifying which case to apply, and applying that case are skills that must be developed. The Case Application Suite scaffolds the examination and application of expert cases to the challenge the learners are trying to solve through the use of prompting, hints, examples, and chunking. Students can glean lessons learned (rules of thumb) from the experiences of the experts, and once their attempt at applying the lessons learned has been published, those experiences can serve as cases to be used by their peers.

There are several challenges to creating good CBR-informed supports for reflection.

- ***Motivating reflection:*** Reflection is hard to do and offers few extrinsic rewards. Motivating good reflection is a real challenge.
- ***Generating feedback:*** Computer-based supports for reflection can rarely respond intelligently about a students' reflection. In several of the tools listed, collaborative discussion areas are used to generate feedback on the students' reflections, but this kind of feedback will necessarily occur after the reflection is complete and is dependent on the quality of the discussants.
- ***Encouraging quality reflection:*** Reflection is hard to do but easy to "fake," that is, generating text that sounds reflective but really is not (Ng & Bereiter, 1995). Encouraging students to reflect about things that can lead to better learning is hard to prompt and structure.
- ***Not overdoing it:*** Periodic reflection while attempting to solve a problem or understand a situation is productive, as is summative reflection when one is finished. It is easy to identify times when reflection would be productive, but it is also easy to overdo it—to try to force reflection at times when it interferes with other reasoning or so often that it becomes a hated activity. We need to find that happy medium—a way of promoting reflection at productive times and without damaging a train of thought.

Computer tools can aid reflection, but the wanting to reflect, helping learners reflect better, and managing when to reflect have to be handled from elsewhere. Both sequencing approaches suggested by CBR (goal-based scenarios and Learning by Design) suggest pragmatic approaches to these issues. Other approaches (e.g., problem-based learning [Barrows, 1986], Project-Based Inquiry [Blumenfeld et. al, 1991]) also provide suggestions about managing these hard problems, and the kinds of reflective tools CBR suggests could, in principle, be easily inserted into any of those frameworks.

32.3.2 Supporting Learning with Case Libraries

The most common place where CBR has influenced the design of software tools to support learning is in the creation of case libraries. A case library offers two opportunities: the opportunity to learn from *others'* experiences and the opportunity to learn by sharing one's own experiences with others. Case libraries can offer a variety of kinds of information of value to learners.

- *Advice in the form of stories*: When we first think about case libraries, we normally think of stories—from experts, from peers, from people in unusual situations. Stories about success are valuable for the advice they give about how to proceed or what strategies to use. Stories about failure provide advice about what to avoid or issues on which to focus. Stories can also provide the basis for predicting what might happen if one tries out one's solution. Valuable stories are those that help a student understand a situation, the solution that was derived and why it was derived that way, and what happened as a result, as well as the explanations that tie those pieces together. Stories may be presented in a variety of media; the important thing is to present them in ways that make their points, or lessons that can be learned from them, most clear. Also important is that stories be indexed in ways that anticipate their use. That is, the indexer needs to think about the ways the case library will be used and the questions with which a user might come to the case library. He or she indexes stories so that it will be easy to find stories that address those questions (Kolodner, 1993).

- *Vicarious experience using a concept or skill:* We know that it takes several encounters with a concept or skill to learn it well (Redmond, 1992)—encounters that cover the range of applicability of the concept or skill allow the learner to see its varied uses and the other concepts or skills to which it is related, and to debug its applicability and refine its definition. But there usually is not time in school for students to experience actively the full range of applicability of a concept. Sharing experiences with other students or looking at the ways experts have applied concepts and skills can fill those gaps. In Learning by Design (Kolodner et al., 1998), such sharing is built into the system of activities students do in class in three ways—students engage in "gallery walks," sharing their design experiences with each other several times in the course of every design challenge in which they engage; students use DDA (Kolodner & Nagel, 1999) to write up their design experiences after in-class gallery walks to share across classes; and students write up what they have learned at the end of a unit (using StoryBoard Author), and the best are put it in an archive (Peer Publications) for students in following years. In all of these instances, students have the opportunity both to present their work and to engage in discussion with other students about it—they clarify for others, answer questions about why they did things a certain way, and then entertain suggestions about how to improve their designs.

- *The lay of the domain and guidance on focus*: An on-line case library's indexing system, if it is available for examination, can serve as an advanced organizer for students or even scaffolding for how students might think about their own cases (Spiro, Feltovich, Jacobson, & Coulson, 1991). For example, the system of indexes in Archie-2, which helped architectural students design public libraries, helped students develop an understanding of the issues that need to be addressed in designing libraries, the kinds of spaces libraries have, and the perspectives different kinds of library users might take on how well it functions. In this role, the case library's indexing system provides a view of the domain's major concepts and their relationships and guidance on what to focus on when designing or solving problems.

- *Strategies and procedures*: Sometimes what is most valuable about a story is not the solution itself, but the strategies employed or even just the starting point. For novices in a domain, the biggest problem is sometimes how to start (Guzdial, 1991)—What is the first thing to do or to try or to explore? In many models of design, simply defining the problem is the most challenging aspect (Schon, 1982). Cases that describe somebody's problem-solving or design process can show how others have defined problems and proceeded through to a solution.

- *How to use cases*: Learning about others' experiences in such a way that learners can reuse the lessons learned in novel situations is a complex metacognitive activity (Silver, Branca, & Adams, 1980). Cases that are about applying someone else's case can help students understand how experts reuse cases. Case libraries that prompt for the kind of analysis that is necessary in deciding whether a case is relevant and how to adapt it for reuse can help learners develop CBR skills.

The context in which case libraries are used is critical to their effectiveness. Case libraries have proven most useful as a resource that provides information as needed as students are engaged in constructive learning activities. In a project-based learning situation (Blumenfeld et al., 1991) a case library may provide guidance for getting started, for moving forward, and so on—if its cases answer the project-related issues that arise as students are working on a project. In a problem-based learning (Barrows, 1986) or learning-from-doing (Schank & Cleary, 1994) situation or in a learning-from-design situation (Kolodner, 1997), cases can provide those same benefits. But in a more traditional, lecture-based or fact-based classroom, cases may not be useful or may even be ignored by the students.

Common sense suggests that for cases to be a useful resource to students, the students must be engaged in an activity in which their impasses might be answered by cases in the case library. If the students are simply memorizing facts, then the challenges that the students will face (e.g., learning to memorize a particularly complicated fact) will not lead them to need or want to use a case library. However, if students are facing challenges that arise naturally in problem solving (e.g., "How do I model a situation like this?" or "What is a good starting point for this kind of problem?"), then a case library of relevant situations and problems can help them address those impasses.

Building case libraries can be as valuable educationally as using case libraries, as suggested above, sometimes even more valuable than simple use. Students building a case library explicitly have to deal with issues of identifying appropriate indexes, identifying strategies and process elements, and decomposing the case for others to use. By making these activities explicit, the intention is to induce learning goals in the student that are appropriate to generating transferable knowledge (Ram & Leake, 1995). The activity of building a case library is frequently motivating for students, as it is creating a public artifact whose purpose is to help future students. This is the same kind of motivating activity on which Harel and other constructionists have been building (Harel & Papert, 1990; Papert, 1991). Cognitively, the need to explain to others in a way that will allow them to understand requires reflecting on a situation, sorting out its complexities, making connections between its parts, and organizing what one has to say into coherent and memorable chunks. Storytelling can aid making sense and remembering (Schank, 1982, 1999).

Case libraries can be a particularly rich source for educational content and process. As a content resource, case libraries offer resources for students to study and to use in actual problem-solving activity. As a process resource, case libraries offer opportunities for students to articulate knowledge and reflect on their experiences in a way that other hands-on activities do not usually provide.

32.4 CBR'S SUGGESTIONS ABOUT ENGINEERING THE LEARNING ENVIRONMENT

CBR's suggestions have also been used to inform the design of learning environments that employ cases as a way to help students learn. Following is a discussion of two such learning environments—goal-based scenarios and Learning by Design.

32.4.1 Goal-Based Scenarios

One of the originators of CBR is Roger Schank. In his work on learning supports, he has been applying the lessons of CBR to creating a new kind of learning environment called a *goal-based scenario* (Schank et al., 1994).

Key to Schank's vision of learning is that motivation is a critical aspect of learning. Basing his claims on the cognitive model implied by CBR, he claims that unless students have a *reason* for wanting to learn or do something, nothing that anybody wants them to learn will make sense to them. Further, until a student fails (reaches an impasse) at something, Schank (1982) believes that they have no reason to question what they are doing and therefore no reason to want to learn anything new. For example, case libraries play a significant role in a goal-based scenerio, but setting up their *context* of use so that students will have a reason to want to use the case library and a context for understanding what it is offering is as important as creating the content of the case library itself.

A goal-based scenario is a learning environment that places students in a situation where they have to achieve some interesting goal that requires them to learn whatever is in the curriculum goals. In one goal-based scenario, for example, students play the role of advisors to the President in dealing with a hostage situation in a foreign land (Bareiss & Beckwith, 1993), in the process learning about several hostage-taking events that have happened in history and also learning some foreign policy. In another, students advise couples about their risk of having children with sickle-cell anemia (Schank et al., 1994), in the process learning about genetics in the context of sickle-cell disease. Using Broadcast News, students put together a news story, in the process learning both history and writing skills. Students learn about history or genetics or writing because they need

to learn those things to achieve successfully the challenge set for them. The trick, of course, is to design challenges that both engage the students and focus them on the content and skills we want them to be learning.

Students engaged in a goal-based scenario are provided with a case library of videos of experts telling their stories, strategies, and perspectives that might help them with their task. When they reach an impasse in achieving their goal, they ask a question of the case library, and an appropriate video is retrieved and shown. Sometimes a story will suggest a topic they should learn more about or a skill they need to learn; other times it will tell how that expert dealt with some difficult issue the student is addressing. Students are in a situation where the case library is relevant for their impasses. Students engaged in a well-designed goal-based scenario take on goals that lead them to want to know and apply the recorded experiences of others.

Based on suggestions made by the case library, students move forward with their task—choosing a policy to recommend to the President, choosing a blood test, making a recommendation to a couple about whether or not they should have children, or deciding how to refer to a leader. In all goal-based scenarios that have been implemented on the computer, there are clear *right* answers to each small task they are working on, and the software can detect when the students have selected the *wrong* answer. The software informs students when they have failed at their task, and through use of cases in the case library, it helps them explain and recover from their failures and move forward successfully.

This second context for a case use—recognizing, explaining, and recovering from failure—suggests that case libraries used as part of a GBS need to index their cases in two ways—by content and also by their applicability helping a learner explain why his or her action failed and how to recover. A story told to the student after a failure can successfully lead to learning when the student is in a context where he or she needs that particular story to move forward.

Case libraries used in a goal-based scenario focus their indexing very tightly on the context in which a retrieved case will be used: On what task is the student working? What is his or her solution in progress? What difficulty is the student having? and On what poor answer has the student settled? When building a case library to be used as part of a goal-based scenario, case indexes are chosen by anticipating the situations in which a student will want to hear a story. By focusing indexing on the learner's goals, these case libraries can act as very powerful supports for learning.

Research papers by Schank and his students report more details of how the cases in a goal-based scenario should be organized and accessed (Bareiss & Osgood, 1993; Ferguson, Bareiss, Birnbaum, & Osgood, 1992; Schank, Berman, & Macpherson, 1999). Most critical to keep in mind is that the design of a goal-based scenario requires anticipating learner's goals when working on a challenge. This, in turn, requires anticipating the tasks students will carry out, the avenues of thought and strategies they will pursue, and the kinds of choices they will make. By using a students' tasks to promote goals students will pursue, the designer of a goal-based scenario can anticipate the kinds of impasses students will encounter and therefore the kinds of stories the case library needs to include and the ways those stories ought to be indexed for easy access.

32.4.2 Learning by Design

Like goal-based scenarios, Learning by Design (LBD) (Kolodner, 1997, Kolodner et al., 1998, 2003, in press) takes CBR's cognitive model seriously in the design of learning environments. But whereas the goal-based scenario approach focuses on designing computer programs that help a learner achieve an exciting challenge, LBD focuses on using CBR's model to suggest how to orchestrate a classroom environment. In addition to suggesting ways of integrating the computer into the classroom, LBD is explicit about teacher roles and about the sequencing of individual, small-group, and whole-class activities.

LBD curriculum units ask middle-school students (ages 12–14, grades 6–8) to achieve design challenges as compelling contexts for learning science concepts and skills. Design challenges provide opportunities for engaging in and learning complex cognitive, social, practical, and communication skills. For example, students design parachutes made from coffee filters to learn about air resistance and gravity and their relationship; miniature vehicles and their propulsion systems to learn about forces, motion, and Newton's laws; and ways of managing the erosion on barrier islands to learn about erosion, water currents, and the relationship between people and the environment. Construction and trial of real devices give students the motivation to want to learn, the opportunity to discover what they need to learn, the opportunity to experience uses of science, and the opportunity to test their conceptions and discover the bugs and holes in their knowledge. The teacher helps students reflect on their experiences in ways that help them extract and articulate and keep track of both the content and the skills they are learning.

CBR tells us that learning requires impasses and expectation failures—to show us what we do not know, to focus us on what we need to learn, and to motivate us to want to learn. This suggests an iterative approach to learning from experience—try to solve a problem or achieve a challenge, use the impasses and failures of expectation to show what needs to be learned, investigate in some way to learn more, and try again. But how can failures of expectation be engineered into students' activities? CBR suggests that the best learning experiences will be those that afford real feedback in a timely way. Designing, building, and testing working devices provide that kind of feedback. Based on these suggestions from CBR, LBD's curriculum units are centered on the design and construction of working devices or working models that illustrate physical phenomena or that measure phenomena (e.g., to get feedback about biological function).

CBR tells us that learning from experience requires reflecting on experiences in ways that will allow learners to derive well-articulated cases from their experiences and insert them well into their own memories. We also know that learning is most effective when learners have been able to identify what they need to learn—when they have had a chance to think about what they do know and how to apply that and then identified where the gaps are. LBD includes in its activities a system of classroom rituals that promotes such derivations. "Messing about" is guided play done in small groups that promotes making connections between a design challenge and what students already know. Playing with toy cars, for example, seeing which ones can go over hills and which ones cannot, gets students thinking about what it takes to get a vehicle over a hill and the different ways they have made things move. "Whiteboarding," borrowed from problem-based learning (Barrows, 1985), follows messing about and is a whole-class activity in which learners articulate together what they discovered during messing about and generate ideas about how to proceed and learning issues to pursue. "Poster sessions" are presentation venues where students present their investigation procedures and results to each other. "Pinup sessions," borrowed from the architecture design studio, give small groups the opportunity to share their plans with the whole class and hear other students' ideas. "Gallery walks," adapted from pinups, provide a venue for presenting one's designs in progress to the rest of the class. All three types of presentations require students to articulate what they are doing well enough for others to understand; they also provide students with ideas to build on in moving forward, a venue for getting feedback on their articulations (Are they communicating well?), for asking for advice and getting suggestions, and for vicarious experience applying the concepts and skills they are learning.

Using guidelines from case-based reasoning, LBD provides (a) libraries of cases for students to use as resources; (b) paper-and-pencil and software tools that allow students to keep track of their design experiences so that they can remember what they did and draw lessons from their experiences; (c) a system of classroom activities that help students make contact with their own previous experience and bring it to bear (messing about), help them anticipate what they need to learn more about (whiteboarding), and help them share their ideas with each other (poster sessions, gallery walks, and pinup sessions); (d) software tools that prompt students to explain their design decisions and design experiences to each other and get feedback from their peers; (e) software tools that prompt students to extract and articulate the content and skills they are learning from their experiences and write them up as stories to share with other students; (f) software tools that help students read the cases written by experts and extract from them the science and advice that can help them with their design challenge; and (g) teacher guidelines for facilitating reflective discussions and other activities in ways that help students to turn their experiences into cases—stored in their memories in ways that allow them to remember and apply them in later situations (e.g., helping them identify what they learned, how they learned it, under what conditions it might be applicable, and when such conditions might come up in the future). The tools LBD provides act as resources, help students create cases for others to use, help students keep track of what they have been doing; and help students reflect on their experiences and turn them into cases in their own memories. Each tool is used in the context of other classroom activities and discussions that support their use and is designed to enhance LBD activities. Some LBD teachers have integrated the use of software tools into their classrooms; some have not. More detail on LBD's software tools is provided in the next section.

32.5 EXAMPLES OF CBR-INFORMED LEARNING AIDS

CBR and case libraries have a rich research history, but educational applications of CBR are relatively new and still relatively few. We select a few projects and describe them below to provide concrete examples of how CBR can inform the creation of learning supports. They fit three categories: supports for reflection on and interpretation of one's own experience, support for use of case libraries, and hybrids that support both.

32.5.1 Supports for Reflection and Interpretation of One's Experiences

32.5.1.1 Reflective Learner. Students in undergraduate project-based design courses face a huge number of challenges as part of their learning. They have to do design at the same time that they are learning about design, using theory and engineering principles that they may have just learned a term before (Turns, Guzdial, Mistree, Allen, & Rosen, 1995a). Often, they are working in groups, so they have to deal with issues of collaborative work at the same time (Turns et al., 1995b).

What Turns discovered in her ethnographic studies of students in engineering design courses was that students often did not even know what they were supposed to be learning, why they were engaging in the activities they were being asked to engage in, and, worse yet, how to reflect on their activities in order to learn from them (Turns et al., 1997). She decided to build a support for learning that directly addressed the issue of reflection.

Her tool, Reflective Learner, supports students in producing "learning essays" about their experiences. The requirement for the students to write learning essays already existed in the engineering design class that she chose to study. However, the unsupported learning essays were not particularly satisfying to the teacher or students. Students still seemed confused about why they were doing what they were being asked to do.

Reflective Learner provides scaffolding in the form of prompts to help students write learning essays in a more effective manner. Its prompts are directly informed by CBR's suggestions about the reflection needed to be able to learn from and reuse one's experiences. It asks students

- to identify and describe a problem that they had encountered when undertaking the current phase of their design project,
- to describe their solution to the problem,
- to say what they had learned from the experience, and
- to anticipate the kinds of situations in which a similar solution might be useful.

Turns' interviews and discussions with students suggest that they found this activity useful and that it helped them to understand why they were doing what they were doing.

32.5.1.2 The Design Discussion Area (DDA) and Its Successor Tools in Smile. An important lesson learned from exploration of apprenticeship and case-based learning (Redmond, 1992) was that it takes several encounters with a concept or skill to learn it well. The first encounter allows the learner to build an impoverished picture of the concept or skill. Later encounters, in which that impoverished picture is applied and fails to work as expected, let learners know that their knowledge base is incomplete or incorrect, prompting engaged learners to want to revise their knowledge, cases, or indexing so that it works better. But school does not provide the time for students to have the full range of experiences that would allow them to build up a complete understanding. LBD's poster sessions, gallery walks, and pinup sessions, and their electronic extension, the DDA (Kolodner & Nagel, 1999), are designed to help students share their experiences with each other so that they can learn vicariously from each other's experiences.

For such learning to happen, students need to be able to present their design ideas coherently, and for students to learn science from their own experiences and those of others, they need to talk the talk of science as they are presenting their ideas and conversing with others. The DDA is designed with two learning goals in mind: (a) to help small groups of students present their design ideas and results to others coherently and using the right kinds of vocabulary and (b) to guide students in other work groups through conversations about those design ideas.

Figure 32.1 shows a design idea and short discussion about it along with the simple prompts the DDA provides to aid discussion. The DDA helps students articulate their design ideas by providing three kinds of scaffolding—a structuring of the writing area into well-organized chunks ("our solution idea," "functions it satisfies," and "how it will work" can be seen in Figure 32.1), hints for what belongs in each of those structured paragraphs, and examples to examine. The intention is that for each design idea or design experience they report on, students will report the design decisions they made, why they made those decisions, the evidence they used to come to that decision, and, if they have applied it, what happened, their explanation of why, and anything new they feel they need to learn. After small groups of students complete their reports and "publish" them in the case library, the DDA provides another set of prompts to help peers comment on published material. These prompts, shown on the right side of Fig. 32.2 similar to those in CSILE (Scardamalia & Bereiter, 1991), invite students to identify the kind of contribution they are making to a design discussion. We invited them to "praise," "wonder," and "suggest"; they can also make other kinds of comments if they specify the type.

When we used the DDA in the classroom of a very masterful teacher (Kolodner & Nagel, 1999), we found that when students used it before making presentations to the class, their presentations were of a higher caliber. But we also discovered that he was providing a great deal of scaffolding to students in addition to what we provided in the tool. In particular, for each of the kinds of presentations students made in the classroom (of experimental results, design ideas, and solutions in progress), the teacher was giving them different kinds of instructions about how to use

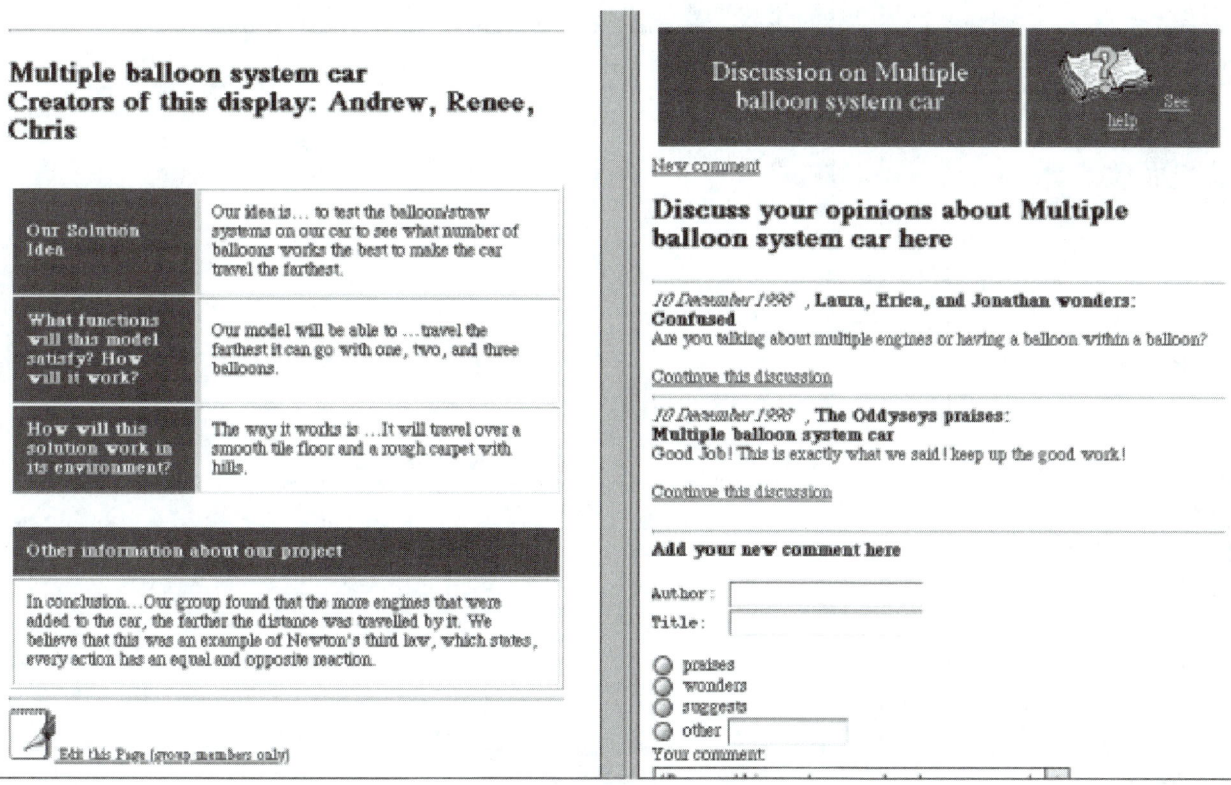

FIGURE 32.1. Design discussion area prompts.

Multiple balloon system car
Creators of this display: Andrew, Renee, Chris

Our Solution Idea	Our idea is... to test the balloon/straw systems on our car to see what number of balloons works the best to make the car travel the farthest.
What functions will this model satisfy? How will it work?	Our model will be able to ...travel the farthest it can go with one, two, and three balloons.
How will this solution work in its environment?	The way it works is ...It will travel over a smooth tile floor and a rough carpet with hills.

Other information about our project

In conclusion...Our group found that the more engines that were added to the car, the farther the distance was travelled by it. We believe that this was an example of Newton's third law, which states, every action has an equal and opposite reaction.

Edit this Page (group members only)

Discussion on Multiple balloon system car
help   See

New comment

Discuss your opinions about Multiple balloon system car here

18 December 1998, **Laura, Erica, and Jonathan wonders:**
Confused
Are you talking about multiple engines or having a balloon within a balloon?

Continue this discussion

18 December 1998, **The Oddyseys praises:**
Multiple balloon system car
Good Job! This is exactly what we said! keep up the good work!

Continue this discussion

Add your new comment here

Author:
Title:

○ praises
○ wonders
○ suggests
○ other
Your comment:

FIGURE 32.2. Design idea with discussion.

the tool. Our analysis of the situation led us to predict that if we rewrote the software, maintaining the same types of scaffolding but creating tools for each of the kinds of planning activities and presentations students engaged in, the software would be easier to use and provide better guidance. In response to these predictions, the DDA has grown to encompass several tools in Smile, each providing prompting specific to the kind of experience being reflected on and the kind of presentation that needs to be made. Figures 32.3–32.5 show a selection of those tools. In these screen shots, the left-hand side of the screen provides organizing structure to whatever task students are working on, and the right side holds hints, examples, and templates to help with completing the task.

An example of one of these tools is the Experiment Result Tool (Fig. 32.3). After students have conducted experiments and gathered data, this tool helps them analyze their results, with the aim of reflecting on their experimental methodology and understanding what lessons their results suggest. The Experiment Result Tool prompts them to do that—students record their data, compare their results to the predictions they made when planning their experiment, and create a rule of thumb based on their analysis. After using the tool to help them make sense of their results, they present their results to the class in a poster session. After discussion with their peers, they might edit their on-line write-up and publish it for others to see, comment on, and use.

The Pin-Up Tool helps students use the results of investigations to come up with their best solution to their project challenge. Students are asked to formulate design decisions and justify them with evidence—from experiments just performed, rules of thumb extracted, and science laws read about. We provide a template to help them line up their design decisions with their justifications. Students are asked to list their design decision, justify why they have chosen that

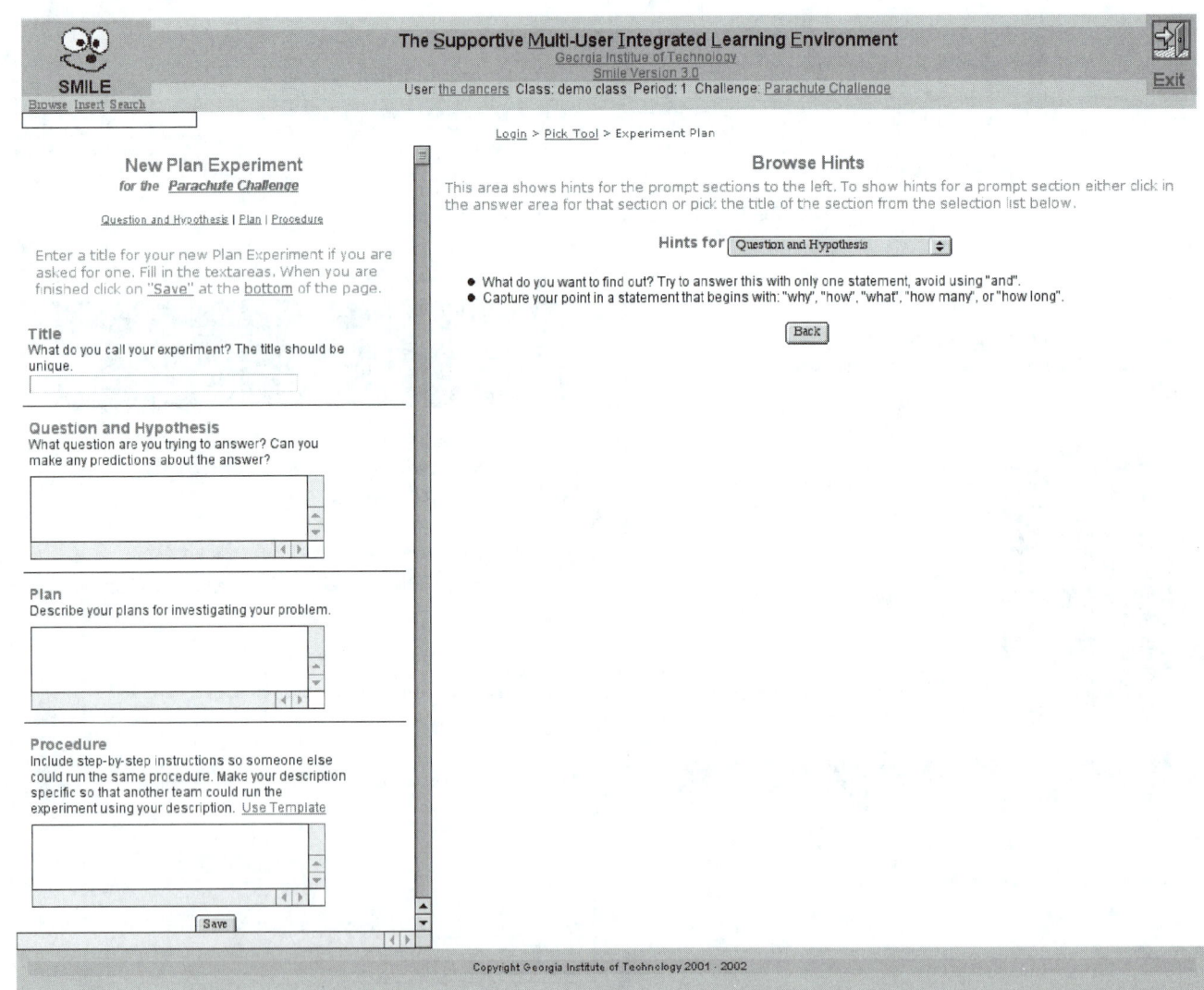

FIGURE 32.3. Reporting on an experimental result.

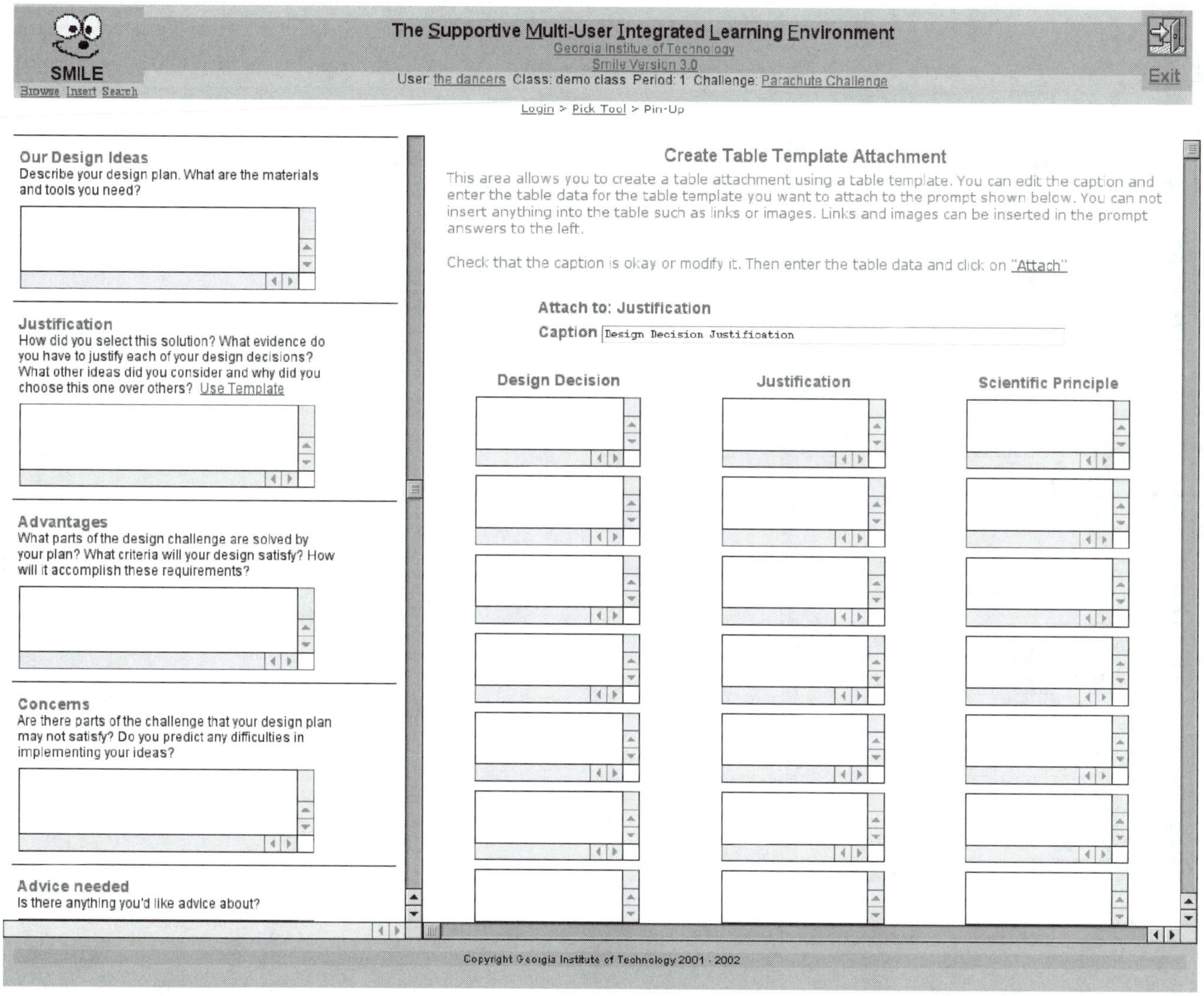

FIGURE 32.4. Coming up with design plans using the Pin-Up Tool.

decision, and provide a scientific principle that supports the decision.

The Gallery Walk Tool scaffolds students as they reflect on their design experiences and plan presentations of their solutions in progress for their peers. Their first time through, students have constructed a solution based on design decisions reported in their pinup presentation. But those solutions do not work exactly as they had thought. After trying out those ideas, this tool helps them look back on the decisions they made and articulate what happened differently than they had imagined. It then prompts them to explain, if they can, why their solution behaved differently than they had predicted. To facilitate this, the Gallery Walk Tool is linked to the Pin-Up Tool so that students can see their decisions and justifications as they are analyzing their results. Students can also edit their old decision and justification chart to show changes they will make in their next iteration. If students use the Gallery Walk Tool after each

of their iterations, then at the end of their design challenge, they will have a full documentation that chronicles the decisions that were made at each iteration and why those decisions were made. This set can serve not only as a means of reflecting over the iterations of a design, but also as cases to be used by other students as they are engaging in the same challenge in the future.

After a team publishes its investigations, design ideas, and/or design experiences, their published artifact is available to other teams by clicking on its hyperlinked title in Smile's library. Looking at another team's idea will open two side-by-side windows: the presentation on the left and a comment window on the right. This anchored collaboration (Guzdial et al., 1997), similar to that in the original DDA, ties each student presentation to its own threaded discussion space. Other students may add a new comment or question for the team (a new thread) or insert a comment into an existing discussion. Scaffolding is quite

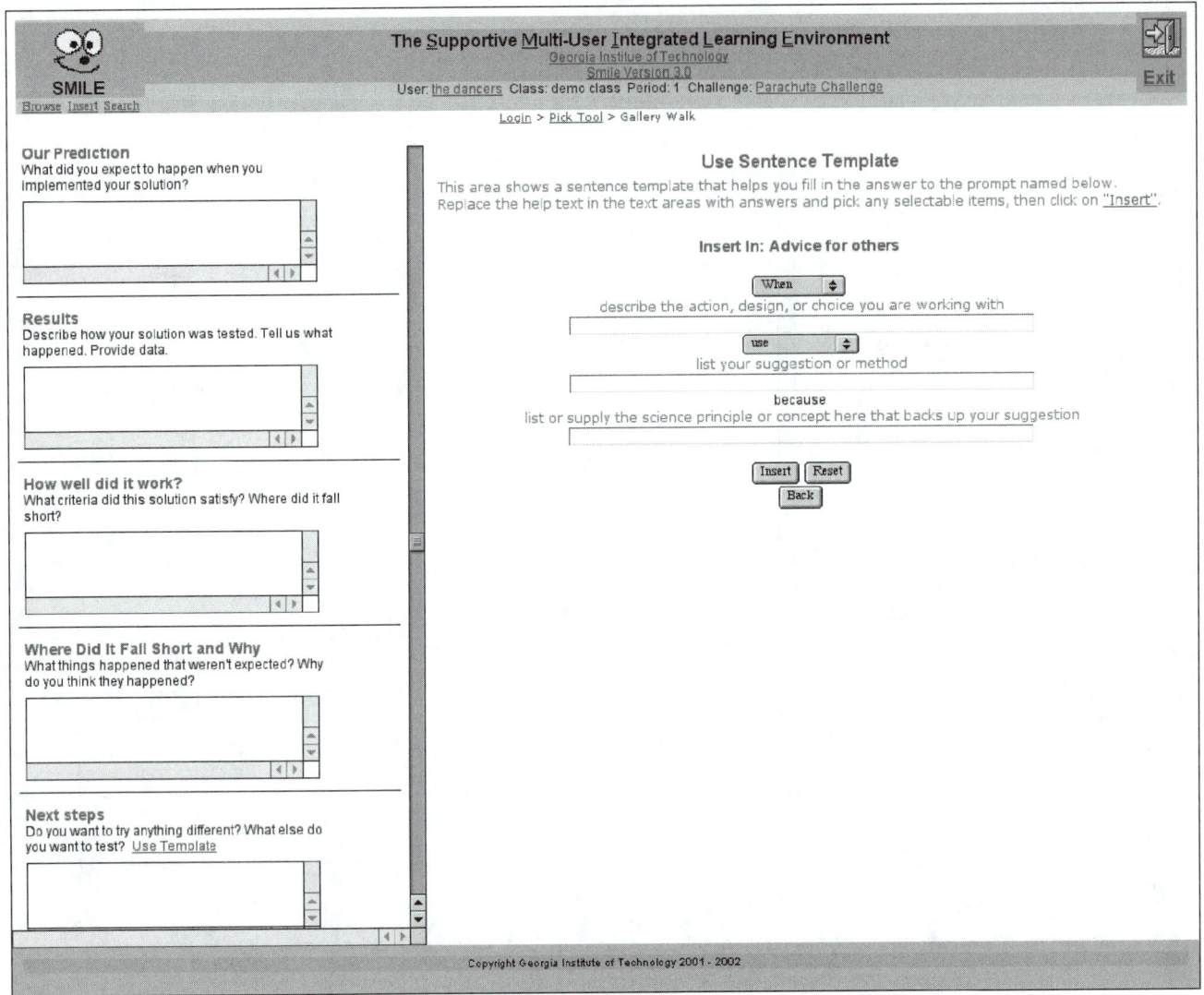

FIGURE 32.5. The Gallery Walk Tool.

minimal, so as not to get in the way, but serves two essential purposes: (a) It helps students differentiate between continuing an old discussion and beginning a new one; and (b) it makes suggestions to students about the kinds of comments they might want to make—"praises," "wonders," and "suggests" for new threads and "replies," "wonders," and "suggests" for continuing threads. As in the DDA, students can also add their own new types.

32.5.1.3 Case-Authoring Tool (CAT).
Some design challenges do not lend themselves to exploration with real materials. It is hard, for example, to mess about with managing erosion in any way that gets across the complexities of managing erosion when winds and currents and tides are all interacting. For these kinds of situations, LBD has a different way for students to gain perspective on the challenge they are addressing—by looking at real-world cases that address those same sets of issues. For

example, students working on the erosion problem read about the ravages of erosion on islands up and down the East Coast of American and around the world and the ways engineers have tried to control erosion and the problems that come with it. Those working on a tunneling problem read about cases where interesting tunnels have been built and what went into building them—e.g., the Chunnel, railroad tunnels through the Rockies, and the sewer system in New York. But reading expert cases is difficult, and knowing what might be learned from such a case can be difficult as well. CAT (Nagel & Kolodner, 1999) was designed to provide that guidance. It helps students divide their challenging task into manageable chunks and provides hints and examples for each. Figure 32.6. shows some of the help CAT gives students in articulating the solution the experts came up with. Three kinds of help are provided (as in the DDA): structuring of what they need to articulate into manageable chunks, hints for each of those chunks, and examples. CAT provides

CAT

The Solution: The St. Gotthard Tunnel
Alternatives and Justification
Team members: David

Hints for Solution   Example of Solution   Exit to Contents

The Solution
What did they decide to do?

> They blasted through the huge tunnel in 6 diffrent sections upper
> left, up, upper right, lower, lower
> left, and lower right.

Science and Technology Used ...
What science was used? What technologies were used? How were these applied?

> Pyrotechnics were the newest
> technology to carve through rock.
> They used it to blast through the
> rock.
> ,little cost as possible
> little manpower as possible
> little or no casualties

Alternative Implementations
What other ways of accomplishing this were considered?
Why were they not chosen?

> Drilling, they didn't choose it
>   because it would have taken a life
> time.

The Criteria
What criteria were used to select a solution?

> Use as little money as possible
> while maintaining a safe and
> efficent mode of transportation.

Favorable Outcomes
What parts of the challenge were solved?
What are the good results of this solution?

> Easier and faster transportation of
> people and goods through the Alps

Unfavorable Outcomes
What parts of the challenge were not solved?
Were there any bad results from this solution?

> Bad result: men who worked did not
> live past a year. To supply food,

FIGURE 32.6. Case Authoring Tool's help with articulating expert solutions.

similar prompting to help students record the challenges the experts were up against and the issues they had to address and to record the results and how they affected the people and environment.

Our intention in designing CAT was that students would use it in small groups to read an article, extract what it says, and write that up for the rest of the class. We suggested that they first use CAT's prompts to skim the article they are reading and extract some of its important parts, then use the prompts to see where they should pay special attention in reading the article, and read those parts of it and write down what they have read. We suggested that they then do another iteration of rewriting their notes to compose a presentation of the case that others could use as a reference. As with the DDA, we wanted them to use CAT to help them read and interpret the expert case, present their case to the class, and then, after making small clarification changes in their on-line presentation, publish it as a resource. We did not, however, provide in this tool the kind of help students would need in applying a case to their new situation. We have designed CAT's successor, the Case Application Suite (Owensby & Kolodner, 2002), to provide both kinds of help and discuss it later as a case library tool.

32.5.1.4 JavaCAP and Its Descendants: StoryBoard Author and Lessons Learned. In LBD, students are asked to achieve a challenge, and along the way, they must investigate, analyze, and interpret component experiences. Although tools like the DDA and its successors help students interpret component experiences that are part of their full design project, they do not provide help with connecting those component experiences by pulling together the lessons learned from a full project experience. JavaCAP (Shabo et al., 1997), StoryBoard Author (Nagel & Kolodner, 1999), and Lessons Learned were designed to help students reflect on an entire project experience, summarize it and put it into perspective, extract from it what they have learned, and write that up in ways from which other students can learn. Our intention has been to provide guidelines in the software tool that will encourage students to look back over a long-term project experience to extract what they learned in productive ways.

JavaCAP (Fig. 32.7) was our first attempt at helping students reflect on their experiences and extract from them what they have learned. In JavaCAP, students began by describing their design problem and went on to describe the alternative solutions they came up with, why they chose the particular solution they

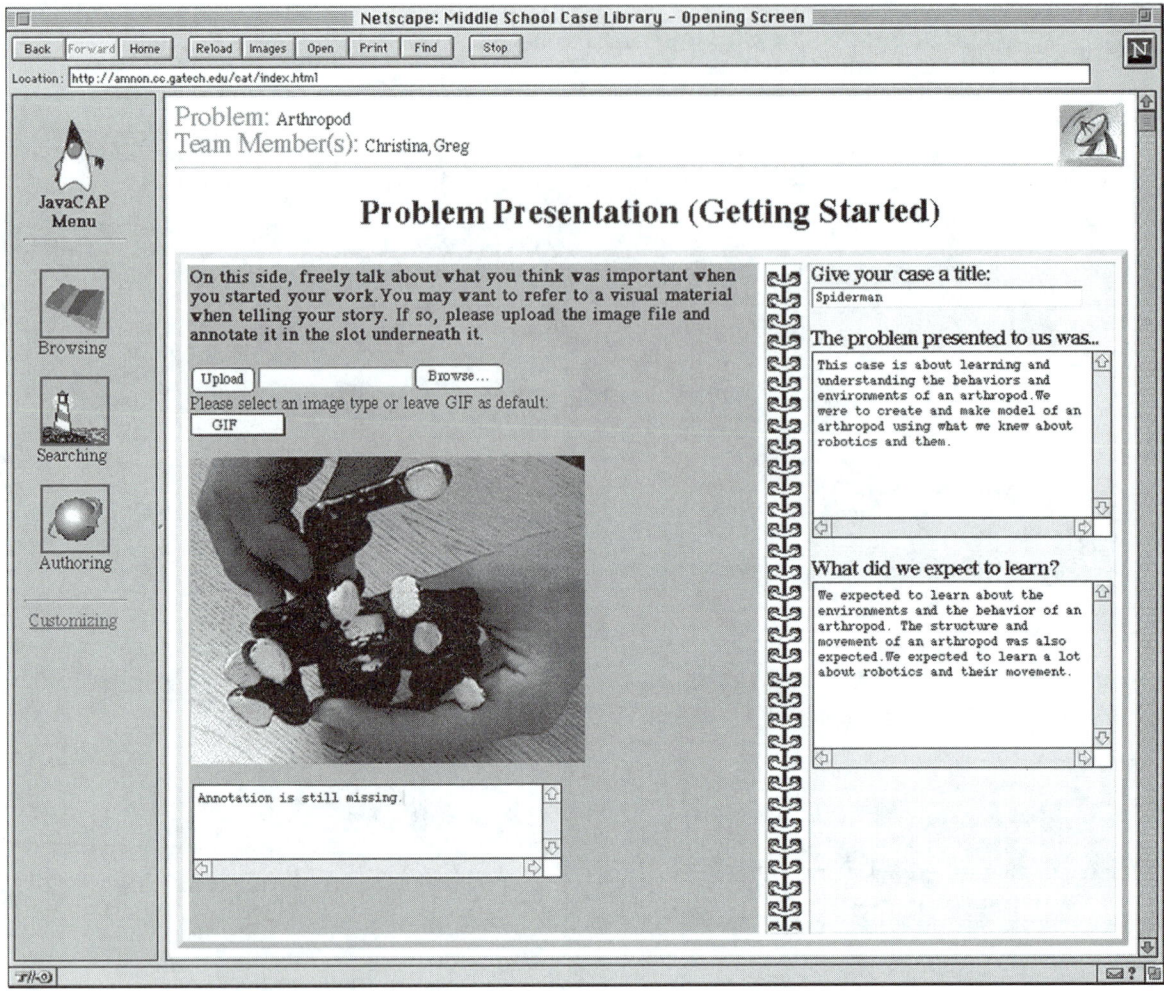

FIGURE 32.7. JavaCAP's scaffolding for presenting the problem.

did, and what they learned overall. Although students were able to articulate their design problem and describe their solutions, the scaffolding we provided for having them discuss what they had learned was quite limited. The open-ended prompting we provided led most students to write about the importance of research and the importance of the collaborative process, but our scaffolding was far too generic to support students in thinking deeply about the science they had used and its implications. As with the DDA, it has taken several iterations to get to scaffolding with the appropriate specificity.

StoryBoard Author (Fig. 32.8) was our next attempt to provide such scaffolding. More structured and specifically tailored prompting was added to help students put their experiences into perspective. Indeed, we took our cues from CAT, designed to help students read the cases of others, and in StoryBoard Author, we used the same kinds of prompts that we found they needed to understand the stories of others as guidance as they thought about and reported on their own experiences. Students were specifically prompted for reconstruction of their project experience in ways that would get at the details, and affect was

used to help them remember the most interesting parts of their experience (e.g., What were you proud of?). In StoryBoard Author, students are asked to articulate the challenge they have been addressing, their solution to it and how they came to that solution, the science they applied in getting to the solution, and how well their solution works. Figure 32.8 shows prompts provided to students in StoryBoard Author to help them articulate a description of their project challenge.

To help students identify what they have learned, StoryBoard Author asks them to think back on the things that used to confuse them but do not anymore, the things that still confuse them, surprises they encountered, things that made them angry, and things that made them happy. It asks them to jot down short notes to themselves on the computer about these things, and it helps them sort each of those into one of three categories: science or technology concepts (e.g., gravity, inertia), science or technology skills (e.g., choosing variables, measuring), and project skills (e.g., collaboration, communication, planning). For each category, StoryBoard Author provides prompts and examples to help them tell the story of what they learned and how

Challenge Presentation
Who, What, When and Where?
Team members: Kim, Jamie, Blair

Hints for Presenting the Challenge   Example of a Challenge   Exit to Contents

Give your case a title:

The Headline Story Is...

The Challenge ...
What was the challenge?

Issues...
What issues were important? Were there
sub-problems to the challenge?

When and where did this challenge take place?
What is the setting for this challenge?

Who or what was affected by the challenge?
How were they affected?

Actions: Save Challenge   Back to Opening

Navigation: The Solution   Things We Learned

FIGURE 32.8. StoryBoard Author.

they learned it. Figure 32.9 shows our first attempts at helping students write stories about what they learned about science concepts.

The intention was that students would use StoryBoard Author to prepare presentations about their projects for their classmates. As with the DDA, the tool prompts for the kinds of things they should include in their presentations. After presentation to the class and discussion that helps them better articulate what they meant, they go back to software, revise their presentations, and publish them for others to learn from.

Experience with the different tools in Smile has allowed us to learn how to structure this tool better, and a new iteration, called Lessons Learned, will become part of Smile's tool suite. In addition to the functions initially included in StoryBoard Author, this tool will focus more on helping students write more technically—to be more specific about what they learned and to help them use scientific terminology and phraseology in their summaries.

32.5.1.5 Lessons Learned About Designing Case Based-Inspired Tools for Reflection.
Earlier tools in each of the foregoing categories were less sophisticated in a variety of ways than later ones. Indeed, we have been able to extract several lessons about the design of these tools from experiences designing across the whole set.

All of our earlier versions of tools were far too general in the support they gave—either the full range of uses of the tool was not supported (as in the DDA and CAT) or the specific details of articulation students would have trouble with were not anticipated (as in JavaCAP and the DDA). Later versions of each tool that addressed these issues help students write more complete and more specific reports of their work, require less help from the teacher in getting to detailed reports, and raise the level of discussion in the classroom. We learned an important lesson about the design of scaffolding from this set of experiences:

Scaffolding the remembering and articulation of an experience. *Particular reasoning tasks students will engage in during case understanding and application should be identified and each scaffolded specifically according to its needs. Creating a suite of tools, each specific to a task, make both the pieces of that task and the task as a whole easier to grasp and manage.*

Two kinds of collaboration are needed in project-based classrooms for students to have the full range of productive discussions that allow them to connect their projects to the content they are learning (Puntambekar et al., 1997)—collaboration within groups and collaboration across groups. In our earlier versions of tools, we focused on providing anchored collaboration areas where discussions across groups could happen.

Things We Learned
Science, Technology and Project concepts and skills
My Year in Science
CUL8R Team members: Kim, Jamie, Blair

Storyboard

Hints for Things We Learned   Examples of Things We Learned   Exit to Contents

Things We Learned About

Use this area to list any ideas!

Save Your Ideas

Hints for Jogging Your Memory

- List as many items as come to your mind!
- What are you proud of?
- What have you gotten better at?
- Are there concepts you understand better?
- What skills are you better at now?
- Do you have stories to tell about your group's work on the project?
- Did anything surprise you? Make you angry? Make you happy? Make you sad?
- Were any of your failures educational?
- Did you learn about technology concepts?
- Compare your ideas to the categories listed below.

Science and Technology Concepts and Skills		Project Skills
Edit Your Concepts:	**Edit Your Skills:**	**Edit Your Project Skills:**
Gravity		Justifying Design Decisions
Select Science or Technology Concept:	**Select Science or Technology Skill:**	**Select Project Skills:**
Newtons Third Law / Vectors / Newtons First Law / Mass / Velocity and Speed	Measuring / Data Presentation / Optimizing / Designing Experiments / Controlling Variables	Presenting to an Audience / Communication / Good Arguments / Making Decisions / Learning from Experience / Justifying Design Decisions

FIGURE 32.9. Encouraging students to write stories about science concepts.

We designed procedural facilitation as in CSILE (Scardamalia & Bereiter, 1991) to help students respond well to their peers. But the discussions they were able to have with their peers on line were limited (Kolodner & Nagel, 1999) because small groups had not been given the support they needed to be able to write coherent reports of their activities. From this, we learned a lesson about designing tools for collaboration.

Supporting collaborative discussions about experiences across groups. *Good collaboration across groups depends on small groups being able to articulate their ideas to others well. It is important in building collaboration tools for classrooms to support the articulation of things that will be shared across groups in order for good cross-group discussion to happen. It is often difficult for young students to articulate the stories of their experiences. When we revised the DDA to provide the specifics students needed to articulate their experiences (supporting their within-group collaboration better), the level of discussion between groups increased both in the software and in the classroom (Kolodner & Nagel, 1999).*

In our earliest tool (JavaCAP), based on advice about software-realized scaffolding (in EMILE; Guzdial, 1993, 1995), we provided the equivalent of "worksheets" for users to help them with their reflection and interpretation—pages that structured the entries they would make. But students had trouble sometimes knowing how detailed their entries should be. In later versions of our tools, we therefore added to the structuring two other kinds of scaffolding—hints to help them know our intentions of what they should be writing about in their entries, and examples to show the detail expected and to provide a template that we hoped would model what we expected. Later, when we found that some items we wanted students to think about and write about could be best expressed as lists or charts or other templates, we created specialized templates to help them frame their thinking (e.g., design decisions in the Pin-Up Tool, rules of thumb in the Experimental Results Tool). No one way of scaffolding would have worked by itself; it is the system of different scaffolds supporting each other that we think has provided success. Whereas we cannot predict the full range of systems of scaffolding that might be useful, we have learned a lesson about a system of scaffolds that seems appropriate for promoting good planning and good articulation of experiences.

The pragmatics of designing scaffolding systems. *To help learners report on their experiences and pull out what they have learned, four kinds of scaffolding working together in a system seems to work: structuring of the task they are carrying out in pieces of a manageable size, hints about what is expected for each, examples as models of the way to address each, and templates for those responses that themselves have a regular structure.*

32.5.2   Case Libraries as Resources

Case libraries are very important resources, providing models of case application to be reused as well as providing examples of successful and unsuccessful attempts at problem solving. However, applying cases to new situations is not always easy. Many times, students have difficulty recognizing that a case can be applied to a new situation; other times, students have difficulty figuring out how to adapt the case to meet their needs. Early case libraries like Archie-2 and Stable supplied cases and focused on structuring them so that learners could easily understand them. More recent case library tools, such as our own Case Application Suite, also try to help students with case application.

32.5.2.1   *Archie-2 and Its Descendants.*   Archie-2 (Zimring, Do, Domeshek, & Kolodner, 1995) was created as a case-based design aid for professional architects. Its cases describe public buildings, focusing on libraries and courthouses. The intent was that as a designer was working on the design of a public building, he or she would consult Archie-2 periodically for advice. To get started, the architect would use Archie-2 much as architects use file cabinets, architectural journals, and the library—to find projects similar in intent to the new one and to see how others had handled the issues. The authors' intent was that an architect would browse Archie-2's library, looking briefly to see what issues other architects had addressed and how they had addressed them. An architect designing courthouses would browse the courthouses; one designing libraries would browse the libraries. Later, while addressing a particular issue (e.g., placement of the children's section in a library, lighting reading areas, access to management), the architect, they thought, would go back to Archie-2 again, this time focusing on that particular issue.

To ensure that such access could happen easily, they needed to structure cases for easy usability and accessibility. Usability was an issue because architectural cases are very large (whole public buildings). They cannot simply be presented to users in all of their complexity. Rather, users needed to be able to examine each case in parts. The big issues, then, became (a) how to divide a large complex case into easily usable parts, (b) how to provide a map of a case that would provide a big picture of the case and a map to its parts, and (c) how to provide access to a case's parts. They divided cases into parts, called *snippets* or *stories,* based on a physical and functional breakdown of the physical artifact coupled with an issue that was addressed with respect to that component and for which there was an interesting solution. The case library of public library cases, for example, had stories associated with it about placement of the children's space, lighting in the checkout area, way-finding, placement of bathrooms, and so on. Cases had tens of stories associated with them, each indexed by a relevant component of the artifact and the issue it addressed. To make it easy for users to navigate around these tens of stories a single case included, Archie-2's designers found that they had to provide several different maps of each case, as there were many ways of thinking about each.

Easy accessibility had several parts to it. (a) They wanted users to be able to ask for and then browse all cases of a kind (e.g., library, courthouse). (b) They wanted users to be able to ask for and then browse all snippets of cases that addressed the same issues (e.g., way-finding, placement of children's area). (c) From a case, they wanted users to be able to examine all stories that were about how a particular physical area or functional system was being handled. Figure 32.10 shows how that structuring looked to users. At the bottom is a spatial view of the Buckhead Library in Atlanta, with blue dots representing the spaces that had stories associated with them. The user has clicked on one dot, and a short summary of the story associated with that space in the library shows on the left. A complete version of that story shows in the top middle pane, with a general description of the problem that needed to be addressed to its left and a general description of the strategy it used to address that problem to its right. Users could see other instances of stories from other cases that addressed a similar problem by clicking in the Problem pane; they could see stories from other cases that enacted a similar kind of solution by clicking in the Response pane, and they could look at other stories about the Buckhead Library by clicking on another dot in the bottom Design frame. They also had other views of the Buckhead Library available to them that showed different ways of grouping the many Buckhead Library stories (e.g., according to functional subsystem in the building).

Though Archie-2 was designed for practicing architects, architecture faculty told its designers that they thought its cases would be useful to students working on design projects. Archie-2 was used by students in an architectural design studio who had the assignment of designing public libraries. Once they learned how to navigate Archie-2's case library, they found it quite useful. It suggested issues to focus on as well as suggestions. But, Archie's case library, as we had created it, was really useful only for assignments of library design or courthouse design (later prison design), and it was quite time-consuming to collect and format all the data necessary to build additional case libraries.

Luckily, another faculty member of the College of Architecture had an idea about how to build case libraries easily. A teacher of industrial design, he wanted to create a case library for learning about the design of simple mechanical appliances.

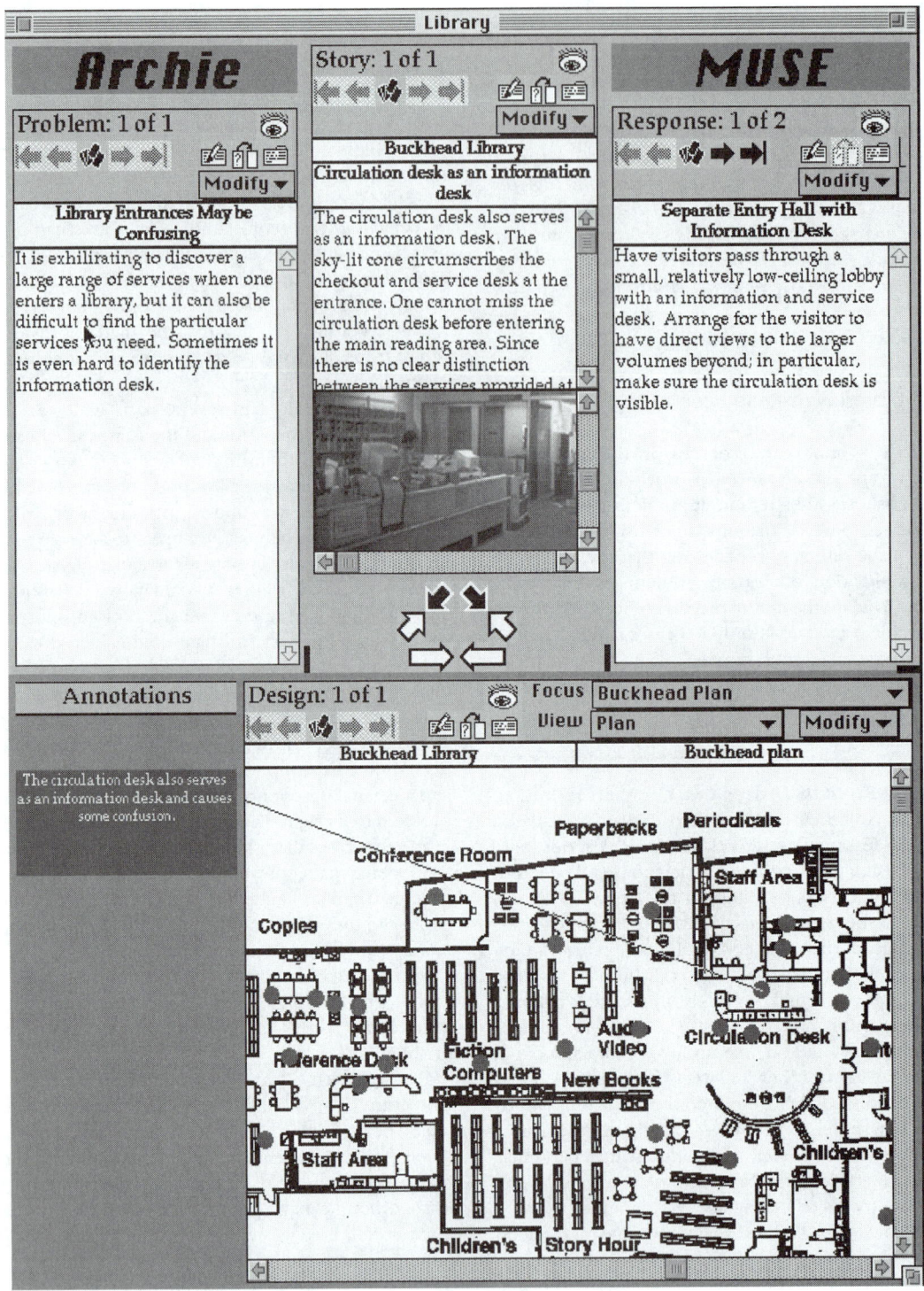

FIGURE 32.10. Archie-2.

He was teaching two classes—a lower-level (freshman) class where students were examining and evaluating such devices and a higher-level (junior) class where students were doing design. He had the students in the lower-level class record their descriptions and evaluations in a case library, using Archie-2's case-authoring tool, called DesignMuse (Domeshek & Kolodner, 1993). He was quite happy with the depth of what students in the lower-level course learned and also quite happy with the way students in the design course used the case library.

Since then, DesignMuse has been used to create libraries of skyscrapers and of airplane's hydrolic systems, and Archie-2 has been rewritten to be simpler to use. It has been used extensively in architecture studios at Georgia Tech (Zimring et al., 1995).

32.5.2.2 Stable.

Complete goal-based scenarios are difficult to design in software if the learning goal for the student is a design challenge. There is no single correct solution to a design challenge, and even defining a space of correct solutions is very difficult in most design fields. The goal-based scenario approach of presenting a story at the point of failure becomes nearly impossible, because it is impossible to anticipate all failures and because failure is often nearly impossible to determine for sure.

One way around this is to build case library frameworks that are indexed by the general kinds of issues that arise in design tasks of some kind and by the kinds of failures and judgment errors that are known to come up frequently. This is essentially what was done in Archie-2—the case libraries about courthouses and public libraries were indexed by the kinds of architectural issues that arise in designing public buildings and the kinds of failures experts in the field have encountered. The case library cannot anticipate all errors that students might make, but it can provide reasonable guidance for design.

Stable (SmallTalk Apprenticeship-Based Learning Environment) is a descendant of Archie-2 designed to help students learn the skills involved in doing object-oriented design and programming. Whereas Archie-2 focused on helping students make design decisions, Stable goes the next steps in helping students learn design and programming skills. Stable uses a Web-based (hypermedia) collection of cases made from previous students' work. Students using Stable were learning object-oriented design and programming in a required computer science course. The problems that the students were asked to solve were related to the cases in Stable, at varying levels of relation. For example, students were asked to create a spreadsheet that accepted functions for cell entries, where a spreadsheet that did not accept generic functions was already in Stable. Students were asked to create a discrete event simulation of a subway system with multiple possible routes, where Stable contained several solutions to a simulation problem involving a bus system on a single basic route.

Since Stable's intent was to support skill learning, its was based on theories of apprenticeship learning (Collins, Brown, & Newman, 1989). In apprenticeship learning, a student attempts problems under the supervision and coaching of a master in the domain. The master uses a variety of methods to help the student learn. These methods are often referred to as *scaffolding*. For example, the master might model the process for the student but would be cautious about telling the student too much. Later, the master might ask leading questions to help the student focus. In successful apprenticeship learning, the master would answer questions but would not explicitly volunteer the rationale for his or her actions, to encourage students to generate the rationale themselves (Redmond, 1992). In this way, the master scaffolds or structures students' learning, encouraging them to think for themselves and solve problems on their own.

Stable was designed to provide a large amount of information but scaffolded in such a way that students were encouraged to think for themselves and request only the information they needed (Fig. 32.11).

- Each step of a design process was provided at three or more levels of detail, where the initial visit to a step was at the lowest level of detail (Fig. 32.12).

- Strategy information ("Why was this step done now or in this way?") was available, but not initially presented.

- Potential problems and solutions were presented, but mostly as links to previous steps. For example, a given step might say "A problem like this might occur" and "If it does, the cause probably occurred during this step," with a hyperlink provided to the previous step.

- Each step was linked to expert's observations on the case (e.g., "This is an example of a part–whole object relationship"), and the observations were also linked to other steps, to provide more concrete examples of an abstract observation.

it was successful in improving student performance and learning.

- Students were able to solve more complicated problems earlier in the term. We gave students a more complicated version of a problem that had been attempted in a previous term. Students did solve the problem (explicitly using Stable), and a coding of the STABLE-using students' problems showed that they were of a higher quality than the earlier problems.

- Students were able to solve design problems on a final exam better than students in previous years. STABLE-using students were asked to repair a faulty design. STABLE-using students did better on the repair task than previous students. We believe that STABLE-using students demonstrated this improved design repair skill due to their seeing more and more varied designs (e.g., multiple design solutions for the same problem) than previous students had.

Surprisingly, though, students expressed several complaints about Stable. Students were identifying cases that they wanted to compare and contrast with each other that were not already connected with each other by hyperlinks, and such comparisons were hard to do. For example, someone might become interested in how objects are created and want to look at several examples where objects were created. Or a student might be interested in how a user interface is created in an object-oriented program and, thus, want to compare how multiple cases implemented user interfaces. STABLE was designed to offer various levels of details *about a case.* It was not designed to offer much in the way of support for *comparing cases,* except through experts' observations.

The lesson learned from Stable was that a case library to support students engaged in design activities can facilitate student learning, be successful in supporting design, and be placed in a curricular setting that creates the relevant context that Schank has identified as being critical for successful learning from cases. However, Stable also showed that what students see as "relevant" is important to determine, and it may not always be evident. Several iterations of a tool are needed to ensure that all the

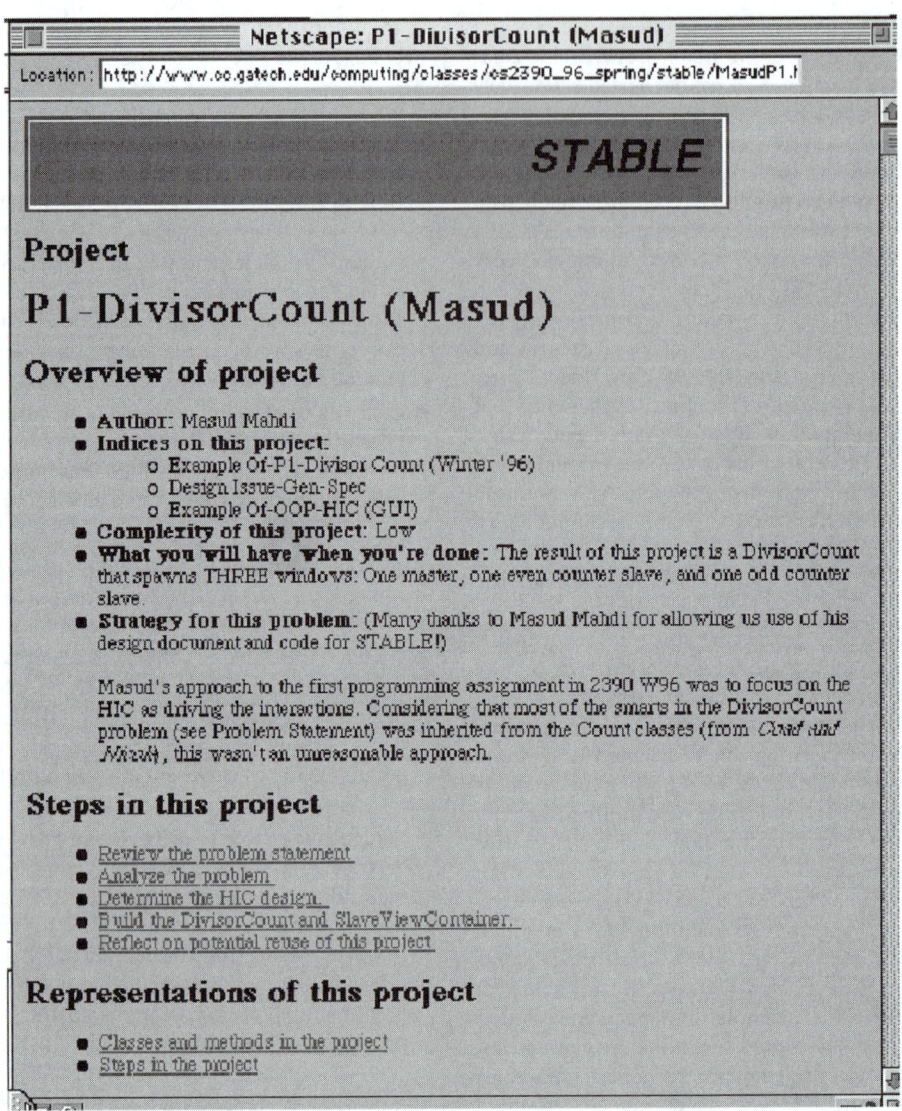

FIGURE 32.11. A STABLE project page, with steps and representation links visible.

capabilities that need to be in it for productive use are indeed included. There are open and interesting research questions on what relevance means in a case library context and how best to support it.

32.5.2.3 *The Case Application Suite.* The literature tells us that case application is difficult for novices. For example, given a standard physics problem, a novice problem solver will use the superficial characteristics of the problem (i.e., known and unknown variables) to search for a problem that has similar known and unknown variables and then attempt to apply the equation used to solve the previous problem to this current problem (Chi, Feltovich, & Glaser, 1981). A novice problem solver will most likely overlook the fact that there are categories of problems based on the structural characteristics they share. However, an expert in physics will recognize that the problem is of a certain category of problems (i.e., conservation of energy), drawing a

diagram that represents the problem pictorially or by analyzing a diagram given. From there, the expert will recall a previous problem in that category that was successfully solved in the past, notice the strategy used to solve that problem, and either use that strategy as is or modify the strategy to accommodate the context of the problem. Important features of the problem, the relationship between those important features, and using that information to identify the type of problem they are trying to solve helps the expert problem solver identify which cases to recall from memory and which aspects of the case to apply. Without that understanding, application is impossible. Good case application requires several things (Owensby & Kolodner, 2002):

• an understanding of both the new situation and old ones thorough enough to recognize similarities between cases that might be applicable and the situation students have been presented with to which they wish to apply the case,

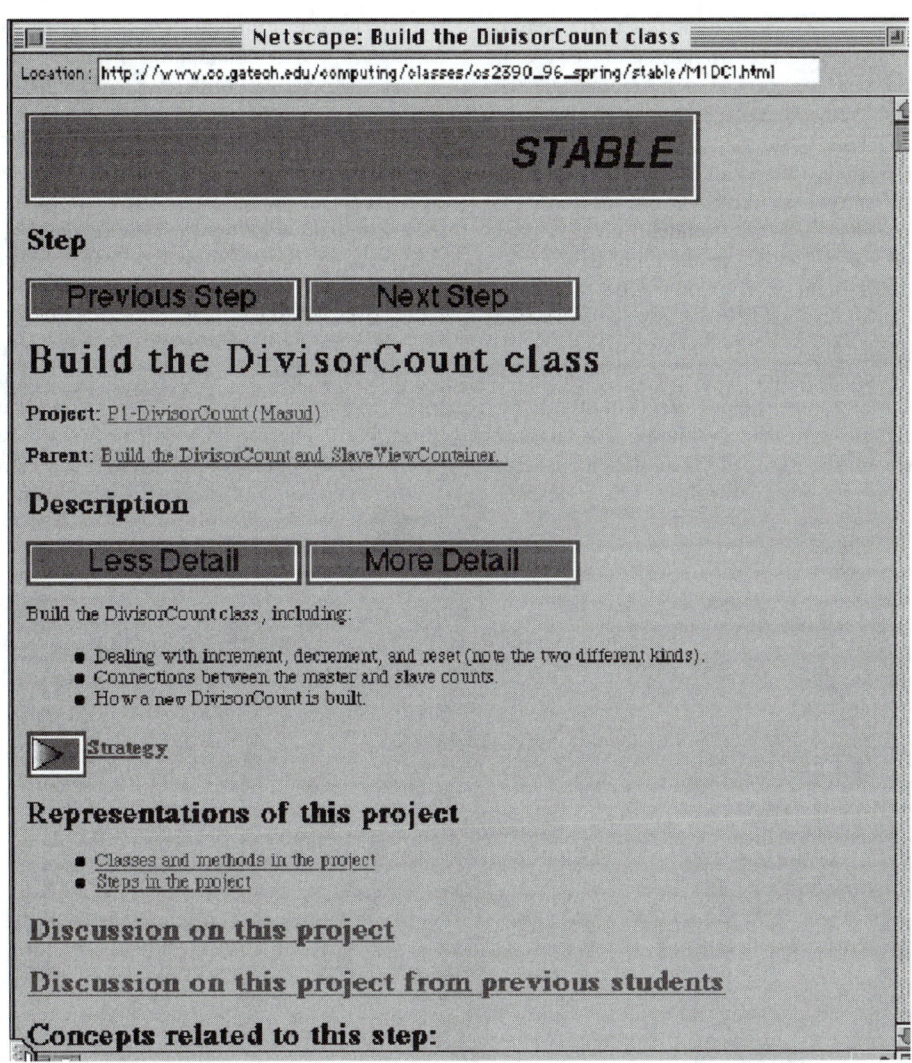

FIGURE 32.12. A Stable step page. Note the ability to increase or decrease the amount of detail on the step, as well as the link to strategy information.

- the ability to recognize what is known that might be applicable, and
- an available library of applicable cases that makes the job of remembering the right cases at the right times easier.

Keeping both the difficulties of students and the lessons learned from the earlier tool design in mind, we have turned CAT, (discussed earlier) into a suite of tools that supports three stages of case application: one for gaining an initial understanding of the case (Case Interpretation), one for thinking about how that understanding might apply in the new situation (Case Application), and one for predicting the success of the derived (Solution Assessment). Together, these tools make up the Case Application Suite. Its scaffolding aims to provide support to small groups as they engage in case interpretation and application, especially helping them to articulate and record

their interpretations and the reasoning behind their case application suggestions. Hints, examples, and templates are designed to help students articulate appropriate content.

A big issue we had to address was how to help students apply an old situation to a new one. The first approach was to look to the analogical reasoning literature for advice on mapping between cases, but whereas there are several model constraints on such mapping (e.g., Gentner, 1983; Holyoak & Thagard, 1995), there was little in the way of articulation of step-by-step procedures for getting to such mapping, and such mappings seemed too hard for middle-schoolers.

Instead, a successful methodology for application that was derived for our physical science LBD units from CBR was used—the "design rule of thumb" as a representation of a lesson learned (Ryan, Camp, & Crismond, 2001). Rules of thumb in LBD's physical science classes are used to help students connect their design experiences and the process of designing to the science they are learning (e.g., To make a car go farther, make sure the wheels don't rub on the chassis because such rubbing adds friction [a negative force] to the system). Having students derive rules of thumb has resulted in students using scientific terminology and illustrating an understanding of scientific principles (Ryan et al., 2001). The Case Application Suite uses rules of thumb similarly as a vehicle for helping students make connections between expert cases they are reading and design challenges they are trying to achieve. The application process revolves around pulling out lessons learned from cases as rules of thumb, analyzing their applicability and applying them to a challenge, and then predicting the effects of the solution and assessing how well it meets the challenge. A rule-of-thumb template helps student articulate their rules of thumb. The intention is to scaffold students so that they can create detailed rules of thumb and use scientific principles to justify the lessons learned.

The Case Interpretation Tool (Fig. 32.13) scaffolds the examination and understanding of an expert case, focusing on sequencing, general understanding, highlighting of alternative solutions, the science used, and the rules of thumb that can be derived. It plays the same role as the previous Cat, but it is somewhat more streamlined. Figure 32.13 shows its structuring—with the case being interpreted on the left, the structuring prompts in the middle pane (and modeled after CAT), and hints and examples in the right-hand pane. Figure 32.14 shows the rule-of-thumb template.

Based on the rules of thumb that are created, the Case Application Tool (Fig. 32.15) helps students analyze those rules of thumb in light of their challenge and determine if those rules of thumb can be applied to their solution. Students are prompted to analyze a rule of thumb's applicability with respect to their design goals, issues and subissues, and criteria and constraints. Figure 32.15 shows this tool's general setup (with the

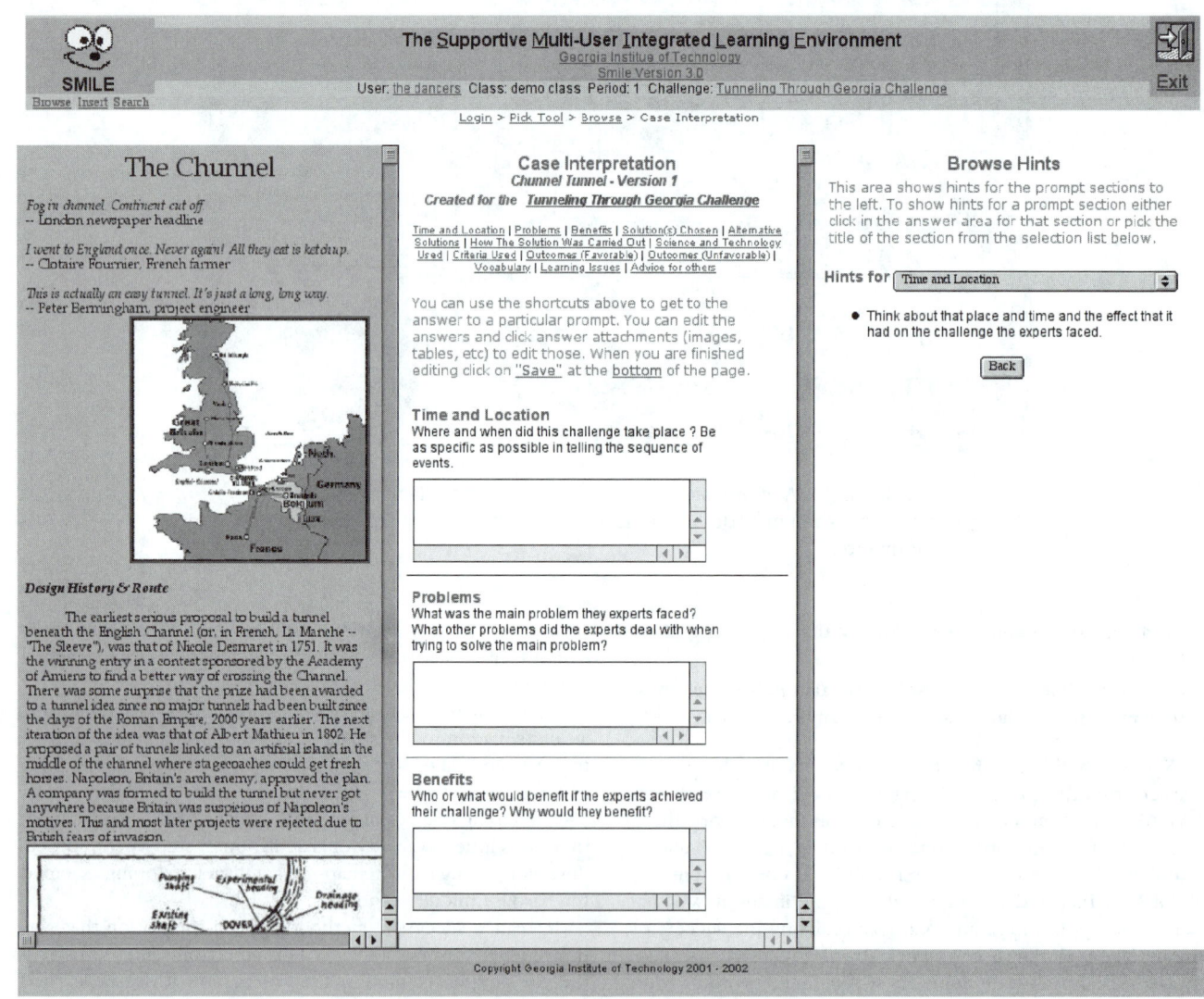

FIGURE 32.13. The Case Interpretation Tool.

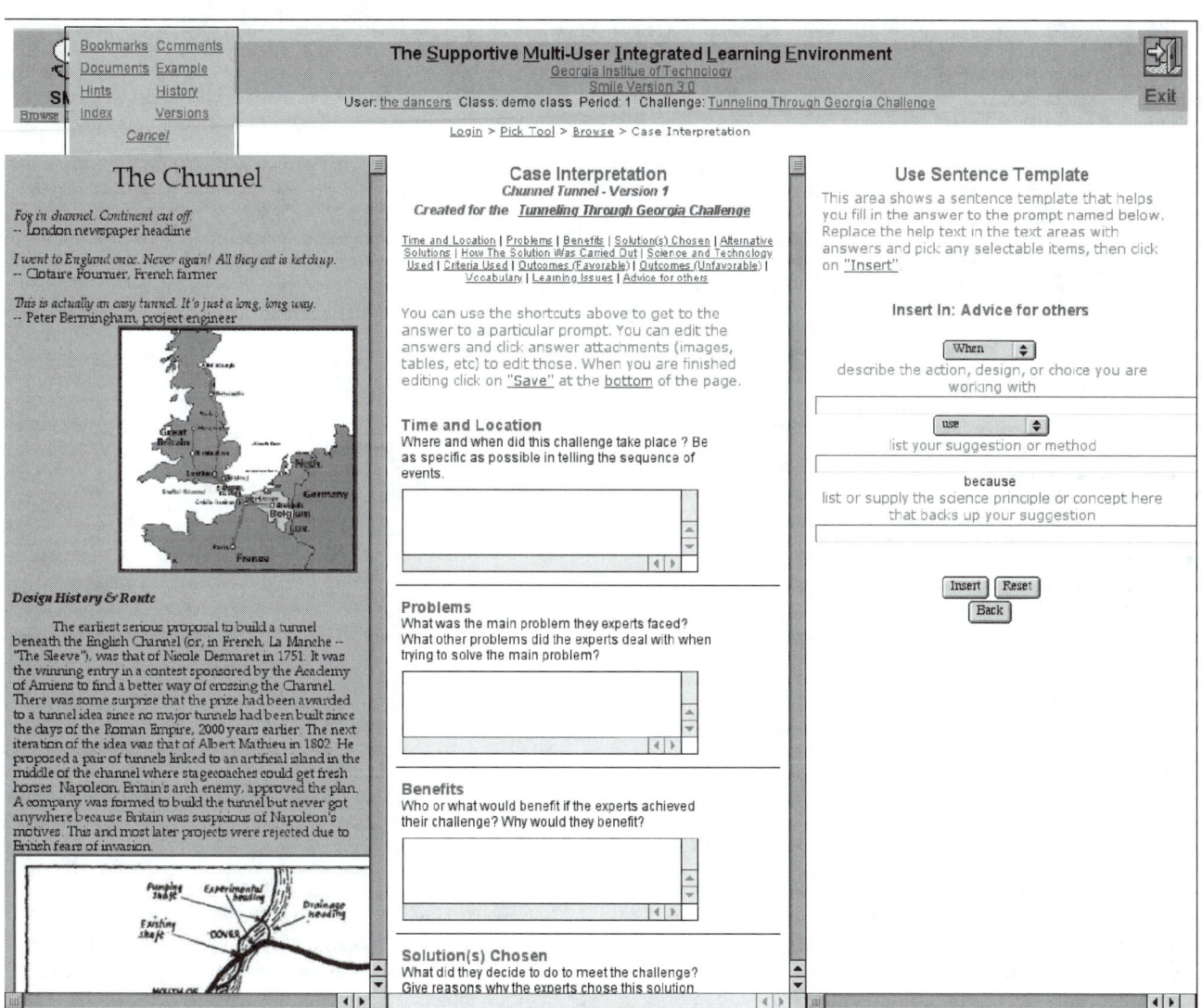

FIGURE 32.14. The Rule-of-thumb template (right frame).

case interpretation on the left, the structuring scaffolding in the middle, and hints and examples on the right). Figure 32.16 shows some of the scaffolding to help with application of a rule of thumb. Table 32.2 shows the full set of structuring prompts (middle para of each tool) across CAS' three tools.

When using the Case Application Tool, the students think about whether their solution can be improved using this rule of thumb and decide whether they should apply it. Once a solution or partial solution is derived, the results of applying a case or rule of thumb must be assessed, which is the goal of the Solution Assessment Tool (Fig. 32.17).

32.5.3 Hybrids

As part of the LBD project, researchers have created a variety of tools for helping students reason about their own experiences

and reason about and apply the lessons learned from expert cases. As alluded to previously, development of early tools in that suite (e.g., the DDA) influenced the design of later tools in the suite (e.g., the tools in the Case Application Suite). Not only did researchers find that the kinds of scaffolding needed for each were similar (structuring, hints, examples, templates), but also they found that the use of the tools and their integration into classroom project-based activities seemed to be similar. Each provided tools that were good for small groups to work with to interpret their own or some expert experience, but students were not able to do a real quality job of those interpretations without also getting help from their peers and their teacher—usually as a result of a presentation and then a full-class discussion. Smile (Guzdial et. al., 1997; Nagel & Kolodner, 1999) was designed to pull together all of these functionalities across the variety of scaffolding tools. It includes in it refined versions of each of the original tools described previously, and as

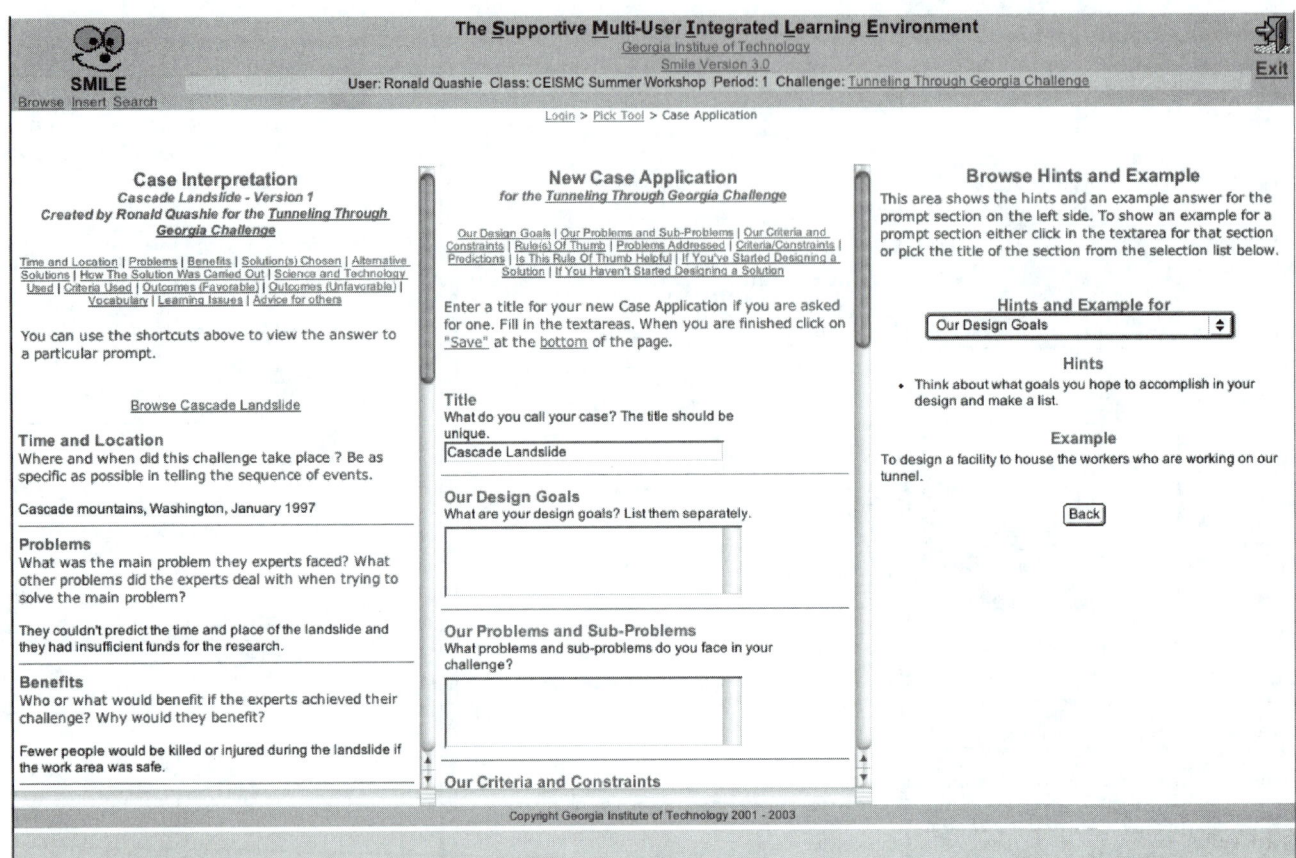

FIGURE 32.15. The Case Application Tool.

a whole, its tools promote the many kinds of reflection that CBR suggests are needed to learn from experience. Its suite of tools supports the full range of design discussions suggested earlier, helping students plan investigations and designs and interpret investigative results and behaviors of solutions in progress. Students use its tools while planning and to prepare for poster sessions, pinup sessions, and gallery walks. SMILE also includes the Case Application Suite (for guiding interpretation of expert cases), and it will include the redesigned StoryBoard Authoring tool, Lessons Learned (for summarizing over an extended project experience and extracting lessons that can be learned from it).

Each of Smile's tools helps students organize their thoughts and provides prompting in the form of hints and examples to help them make their presentations technical and complete. As discussed earlier, CBR informs on the content of that scaffolding—the structuring and prompts we provide are those needed to make connections among their goals, their plans, and what happened, to connect the disparate parts of their entire design experience, and to analyze their experiences so as to be able to index them as cases for future use. Students collaborate in groups as they use SMILE. Once they write up a presentation, they publish it in SMILE's library for public access and comment, facilitating collaboration across groups and access by students

to their peers' experiences as well as their own. Although SMILE was designed for LBD classrooms, it provides facilities appropriate for any project-based inquiry classroom, whether in science or in other subjects. In any inquiry environment, students design, run, and report on investigations, plan solutions to project challenges, make their solutions work, and extract out what they have learned. Smile's tools are designed to help students get more from those experiences by reflecting on them better.

32.6   RESULTS

We have already discussed many lessons learned about the design of tools for collaborative reflection. This section discusses some of the evaluation results collected from pilots and field tests of CBR approaches and the use of case-based learning aids and other lessons we can glean from them. Many of the findings discussed are preliminary, consisting of mostly formative assessment around issues of usability and general student performance; the most research has been done with respect to LBD. Nonetheless, the findings for these systems, with respect to the usefulness of and support provided by case-based learning aids, are promising.

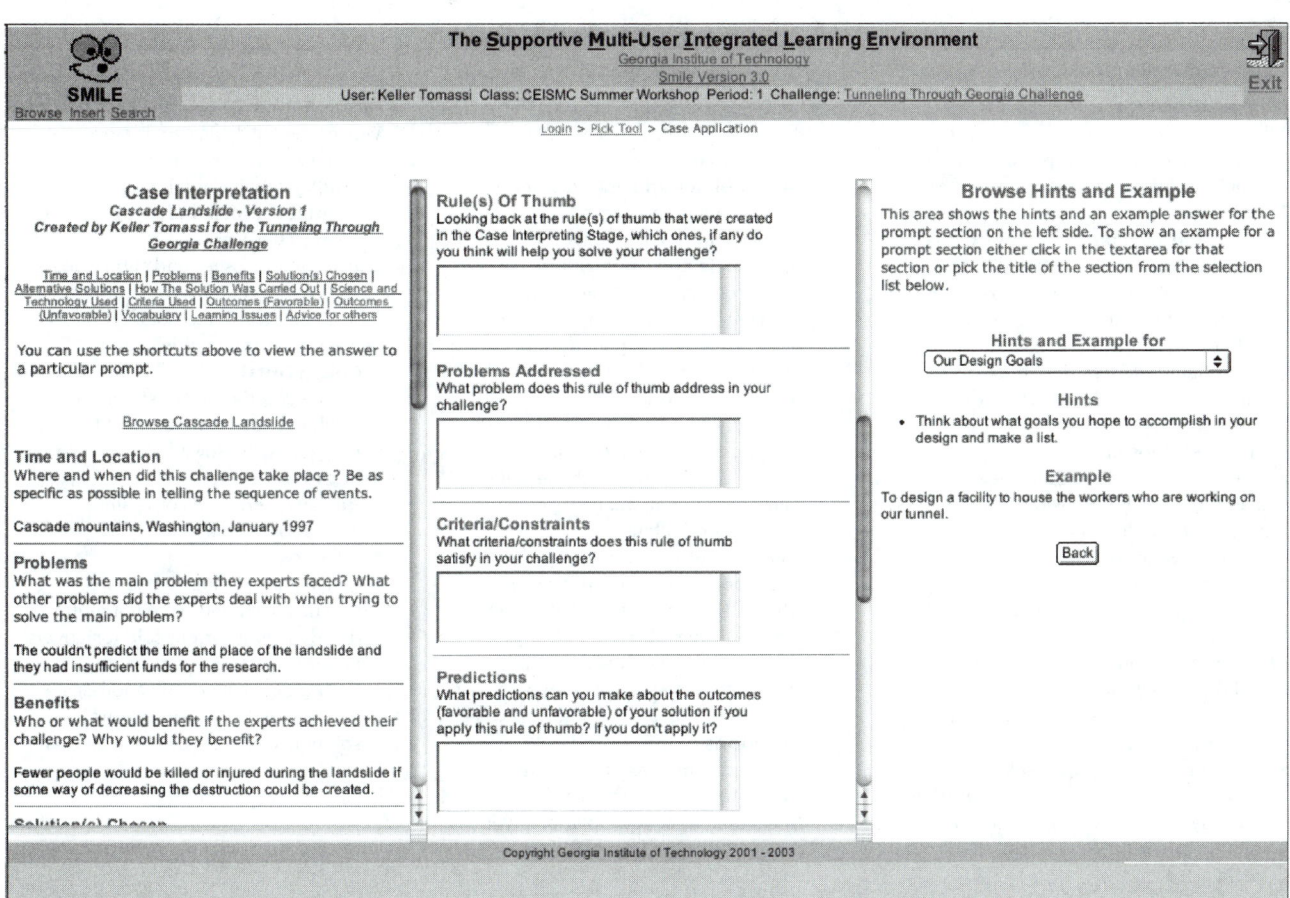

FIGURE 32.16. Scaffolding to help with application of a rule of thumb.

32.6.1 Environments That Make Use of Case-Based Learning Aids

Whereas goal-based scenarios and LBD use cases to promote learning in somewhat different ways, results from both approaches suggest that students who engage in these approaches have a better understanding of the domain and are more capable of applying that knowledge in useful ways than comparison groups.

32.6.1.1 *Goal-Based Scenarios.* Goal-based scenarios are designed around the idea that the best and most connected learning takes place when appropriately contextualized knowledge is learned in the context of actively pursuing a meaningful problem-solving goal that employs that contextualized knowledge. Because goal-based scenarios are designed around the task learners are working on and anticipating the learners' goals when working on the challenge, the case libraries used in goal-based scenarios are indexed based on where learners are within the task and what support they may need at that point. In particular, designers of goal-based scenarios want to know whether the indexing used is appropriate and helpful and, in a more

general sense, whether the goal-based scenario has enabled the user to learn the information or skill presented and whether the user has learned the conditions that are necessary to apply that knowledge or skill. The evaluation of goal-based scenarios, like Sickle Cell Couselor (Bell, 1996; Bell, Bareiss, & Beckwith, 1993; Bell, 1996), suggests that goal-based scenarios are effective for teaching contextualized skills and knowledge. Data suggest that the counseling/role-playing aspect of goal-based scenarios effectively promotes understanding and learning the circumstances in which new knowledge is useful, compared with presenting comparable material without the counseling/role-playing aspect. The principal result is that embedding the target knowledge within the cover story promotes recall of relevant information (Bell et al., 1994).

32.6.1.2 *Learning by Design.* Our hypothesis is that learning environments that encourage the natural use of CBR to achieve challenges of real-world complexity and that are orchestrated in ways that promote repeated practice, promote articulation of the skills and practices being used, and explicitly encourage reuse of lessons learned from old experiences will promote transferable learning, of both content and skills. LBD was designed with this hypothesis in mind, and

TABLE 32.2. Case Application Suite Prompts

Case Interpretation Tool	Case Application Tool	Solution Assessment Tool
Time and Location Where and when did this challege take place? Be as specific as possible in telling the sequence of events. **Problems** What was the main problem they experts faced? What other problems did the experts deal with when trying to solve the main problem? **Benefits** Who or what would benefit if the experts achieved their challenge? Why would they benefit? **Solution(s) Chosen** What did they decide to do to meet the challenge? Give reasons why the experts chose this solution. **Alternative Solutions** Were other ways of meeting the challenge that were considered? Why were they not chosen? **How The Solution Was Carried Out** How did they put the solution into practice? What steps did they take to carry the solution out? **Science and Technology Used** What science and technology were used in choosing the solution? In putting the solution into practice? **Criteria Used** What criteria were used to select a solution? To select hoe the solution would be put into practice? **Outcomes (Favorable)** Were any of the outcomes favorable? What short-term effects did these outcomes have? Long-term? **Outcomes (Unfavorable)** Were any of the outcomes unfavorable? What short-term effects did these outcomes have? Long-term? **Learning Issues** Do you know everything you need to know about this case to move on? Do you have any questions about whether this case can help you solve your challenge? **Advice For Others** Do you have any 'rules of thumb' for others?	**Our Design Goals** What are your design goals? List them separately. **Our Problems and Sub-Problems** What problems and sub-problems do you face in your challenge? **Our Criteria and Constraints** What criteria and constraints are present in your challenge? How do they affect each of your design goals? Issues and sub-issues? **Rule(s) Of Thumb** Looking back at the rule(s) of thumb that were created in the Case Interpreting Stage, which ones, if any do you think will help you solve your challenge? **Problem Addressed** What problem does this rule of thumb address in your challenge? **Criteria/Constraints** What criteria/constraints does this rule of thumb satisfy in your challenge?… **Predictions** What predictions can you make about the outcomes (favorable and unfavorable) of your solution if you apply this rule of thumb? If you don't apply it? **Is This Rule Of Thumb Helpful** Is this rule of thumb helpful to use to design a solution for your challenge? Justify.	**Assess Solution (Design Goals)** Which specific design goals are successfully met by your new solution? Which are not? **Potential Problems That Were Seen Along The Way** Which specific issues and sub-issues are successfully met by your new solution? Which are not? **Assess Solution (Criteria and Constraints)** Were the criteria and constrains in your challenge taken into account by your new solution? How? **Things Overlooked** Were any criteria and constraints overlooked? How? **Next Steps** If design goals, issues/sub-issues, or criteria/constraints were not met, decide if your current solution covers enough to stand alone, whether it should be meshed with another solution to make a more complete solution, or if it should be abandoned.

analyses of LBD's effectiveness allow us both to evaluate that hypothesis and to gain an understanding of LBD's strengths and weaknesses.

Our design of LBD predicts three aspects of learning that stand to gain from the approach: (a) content knowledge in the target domain, (b) specific science process skills such as those involved in designing experiments, and (c) more general learning practices such as collaborative skills. Because LBD puts

major focus on learning of science and collaboration practices, we have expected that LBD students would perform science and collaboration practices significantly better than non-LBD students. We have also expected LBD students to learn science content more deeply than their counterparts, but as it is notoriously difficult to show that based on multiple-choice tests, we did not know whether or not would find evidence for that.

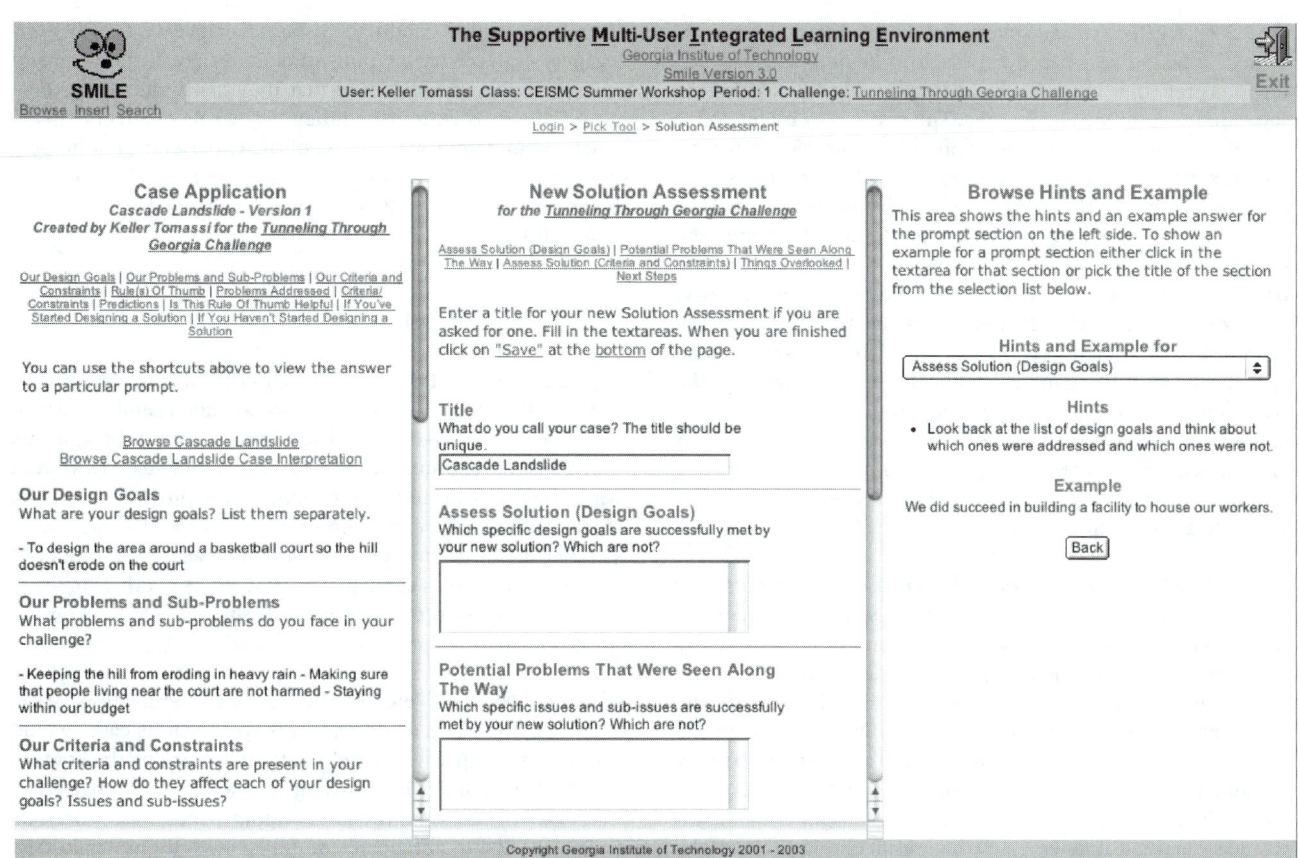

FIGURE 32.17. The Solution Assessment Tool.

We have carried out field tests in over a dozen classrooms and compared the knowledge and capabilities of students participating in LBD environments to those of students in matched comparison classes (with matched teachers). We have used two major strategies of formal assessment: (a) assessing content learning by comparing change from pre- to postcurriculum on written, mostly multiple-choice, exams, and (b) assessing students' application of science practices as they occur during data-gathering and analysis activities and during experimental design activities. Our results show that LBD students consistently learn science content as well as or better than comparison students, judged by standard-format multiple-choice tests. We are working on a deeper analysis of their learning, and preliminary results show greater understanding among LBD students (Kolodner et al., 2003), but it is early to make that claim. On the other hand, analysis of our performance data shows large, consistent differences between all LBD classes and their comparisons. While they are engaging in science activities, LBD students recall more of what they have learned than do comparison students, and they greatly outperform comparison students in their abilities to design experiments, plan for data gathering, and collaborate. Indeed, some of our mixed-achievement LBD classes outperform comparison honors students on these measures. We have found, too, through observation, that the skills acquired by LBD students often transfer to areas outside of their LBD experience and that LBD students connect with its activity structures, understand what each affords, and use them outside the LBD classroom to help them understand and investigate similar problems (Kolodner, Gray, & Fasse, 2003). See Holbrook, Gray, and Kolodner (2001), Kolodner et al., (2001), and Gray, Camp, Holbrook, and Kolodner (2001) for more detail.

32.6.2 Supports for Reflection and Interpretation of One's Experiences

In general, results for tools that support student reflection and interpretation of experiences show that although students can be scaffolded to reflect, interpret, and articulate their experiences better, designing scaffolding for middle schoolers (grades 6–8) that succeeds in having them carry out those tasks in a way that makes their reflections useful to others is tricky. We have presented the lessons we learned about how to do this in a preceding section; in this section we report on results of use of several of the tools.

32.6.2.1 Reflective Learner.

Reflective Learner was designed to take a case-based approach to helping learners better interpret their experiences as they engaged in writing essays about what they had learned. The scaffolding in Reflective Learner represents CBR's suggestions at their simplest and most direct. Reflective Learner simply prompts college students to articulate their goals, how they went about achieving them, what was difficult, and what could be learned from that. Despite the simplicity of its prompts, analysis showed that students who used Reflective Learner wrote longer, more structured essays and received significantly higher grades than those who did not (Turns, 1997). Students report that the system was useful and easy to use, and although their initial use was motivated by the scaffolding provided for essay writing, their use continued because of the ability of the system to handle and manage their electronically submitted essays. Students were able to retain more of what they learned, and students became more responsible and active in their learning (Turns, 1997).

32.6.2.2 The Design Discussion Area and Its Successor Tools in Smile.

The designers of the DDA and its successors have been trying to understand how to support teams of students as they engage in writing about their design efforts and discussing those efforts with each other and with the class. The first version of the DDA was trialed with 200 students in the classrooms of two masterful teachers, and although it was easy for students to use, integration of the tool into the classroom activities did not happen exactly the way the designers thought it would (Nagel & Kolodner, 1999). As a result of this, the scaffolding provided was not always the kind of support the students needed, and, thus, was not as useful as the designers had originally thought. After revising the DDA so that it specifically supported all three of LBD's presentation forums (poster sessions, pinup sessions, gallery walks), it was trialed again the following year, in the classrooms of one of those teachers. This time write-ups created with the system were far more complete and articulate, and the level of classroom discussion was far higher.

32.6.2.3 JavaCAP and Its Descendants: Storyboard Author and Lessons Learned.

The designers of JavaCAP were interested in understanding how well the tool's use of narrative structure helped students reflect on and write about their experiences and whether those reflections were written in such a way that they could be used by others. Two studies of JavaCAP showed that it is usable and well understood by students and teachers, having the potential to be an excellent reflective tool, but that the authoring process needed to be scaffolded more specifically (Shabo et al., 1997). StoryBoard Author (Nagel & Kolodner, 1999) was an attempt to use what had been learned in designing other tools to provide such scaffolding. Unfortunately, teachers had students use only the "lessons learned" part of it, not taking the time to have students reconstruct their project experience before trying to remember what they had learned. Results were therefore disappointing; students were often unable to express what they had learned. On the other hand, this experience confirmed an original hypothesis in building this tool, that one cannot expect learners to remember what they have learned without asking them to reconstruct the experience as a whole. Studies conducted using several versions of Lessons Learned showed that helping students to recall the details of an experience in such a way that they can write about them in useful ways is extremely difficult. The role of affect helps to situate them within the context of the experience, but helping them to explain the lessons they learned in a way that connects the experience to the science remains a challenge (Kolodner & Voida, 2002).

32.6.3 Case Libraries

In general, results for tools that support student use of case libraries show that case libraries can be quite useful resources. They also show two somewhat surprising results. First, students were able to get as much as or more from building cases as from using them if a useful case structure was provided to them. Second, comparing and contrasting two cases to each other seems to be an important part of using cases. The model of applying one case to solve a new problem is overly simplistic, and our results show that case libraries should provide an option of looking at two cases at the same time.

32.6.3.1 Archie-2 and Its Descendants.

Predictions in designing Archie-2 and its descendants were that its cases would offer resources that would help both with learning the content of the domain and with learning the how-to's of what architects do—in particular, the issues about which they worry. Its designers tried to anticipate the trajectories users would take in making their way through the system's cases and stories and tried to design navigation aids that would promote productive navigation. Its designers wondered, too, if student creation of cases would lead to deeper learning. Archie-2 and its authoring tool, Design Muse, were used in four classes—a junior-level architecture class where students were designing public libraries, a graduate level architecture class, a freshman-level industrial design class, and a junior-level industrial design class (Zimring et al., 1995). Although some users found the interface overly complex, in all three classes, users were happy with the navigation it allowed them to do and found its cases and case structures understandable. Students in the architecture class found that Archie's indexing scheme indeed helped them figure out what issues they needed to pay attention to in designing, and students in that class seemed to be able to design well using its cases. In the industrial design classes, freshman students used Design Muse to create cases, and students in the junior-level class used those cases to inform about designing. The teacher reported that he was pleased with the learning of both sets of students, but no formal evaluations were done. Most interesting, perhaps, was the graduate level architecture course. In this class, students who enaged in *building* cases seemed to be learning as much as or more than the students who were *using* the case library in their design work.

32.6.3.2 STABLE.

The designers of STABLE were interested in whether use of STABLE's case library would help students learn design and programming skills better. The evaluation of STABLE was conducted to find out whether STABLE could improve student performance and learning. This evaluation focused on ease of use, student performance while using STABLE, and ability of students to use the knowledge and skills they acquired in the absence of STABLE. The evaluation showed that students using STABLE performed better while using STABLE, and they were able to employ what they learned in the absence of STABLE. Although students found STABLE sometimes difficult to use, overall they found the information in STABLE useful (Guzdial & Kehoe, 1998). This evaluation of STABLE also led to the finding that it is quite important to allow those using a case library to be able to compare and contrast cases side by side as they are working.

32.6.3.3 The Case Application Suite.

The designers of the Case Application Suite are trying to understand how much and what kinds of scaffolding are needed to help students not only understand a second-hand expert experience, but also identify and use the lessons the experts learned in such a way that their solution to the challenge is the best it can be. During Fall 2003, the Case Application Suite was used in three LBD classrooms, one where the teacher had students interpret cases without much introduction and two where the teacher modeled case interpretation before students read their cases. In each classroom, some students used the tool, and some did not. Early analysis shows that, in general, the tools were easily usable, that students using the Case Interpretation Tool were able to extract rules of thumb far better than those who did not use the tool; that when the teacher had not modeled case interpretation well for students before using the tool, they were able to interpret a case well, and that even when the teacher did model case interpretation well, those students using the tool wrote more cogent summaries of their cases than those who did not use the tool. Analysis has not yet been done of the other tools in the suite, and statistics have not yet been run on analyses that have been completed.

32.7 CONCLUDING THOUGHTS

CBR makes a variety of suggestions about how to promote better learning. CBR suggests ways of making learning from hands-on activities more effective: (a) by making sure that students have the opportunity to apply iteratively what they are learning—getting real feedback about what they have done so far, being helped to explain what happened if it was not what was expected, and having an opportunity to try again and again until they are successful and come to a full understanding of what they are learning; (b) by making sure to include in the classroom rituals the kinds of discussions and activities that ask students to reflect on their experiences, extract what they are doing and learning, and articulate it for themselves or others; and (c) by making sure that students anticipate the kinds of future situations in which they will be able to apply what they are learning.

- CBR suggests resources that might be useful during learning—well-indexed libraries of expert cases and well-indexed libraries that hold the ideas and lessons learned by their peers.
- CBR suggests activities that can enhance learning in any setting—writing cases to share with others, reading the cases of experts, and preparing them for other students to learn from.
- CBR suggests ways of managing a student-centered problem-based, project-based, or design-based classroom so that students help each other move forward at about the same pace—gallery walks for sharing ideas keep everyone at about the same pace and archives of on-line cases allow those who can move forward at a faster pace to gain from the experiences of those who came before.
- CBR suggests ways of creating useful case libraries without an undue amount of up-front work by the teacher—seed a case library with several cases that model what is expected, and then have students add to that case library each year for students in the years to come.

This is a simple list. But we do not want readers to walk away thinking that CBR has all the answers, and if one simply does these things, learning will be enhanced. We hope that the discussions of the different systems and what makes them effective will help readers to understand that a great deal of planning and thought is needed to integrate these kinds of activities into a classroom in ways that work. We hope too that the discussions will provide some guidelines on how to get started.

ACKNOWLEDGMENTS

Writing of this chapter was supported in part by the National Science Foundation and the National Physical Science Consortium. Any opinions, findings, and conclusions or recommendations expressed in this material are those of the authors and do not necessarily reflect the views of the funding organizations.

References

Barrows, H. S. (1985). *How to design a problem-based curriculum for the preclinical years*. New York: Springer.

Bareiss, R., & Beckwith, R. (1993). *Advise the President: A hypermedia system for teaching contemporary American history*. Paper presented at the annual meeting of the American Educational Research Association.

Bareiss, R., & Osgood, R. (1993). Applying AI models to the design of exploratory hypermedia systems. *Proceedings of the ACM Conference on Hypertext*, pp. 94–105.

Barrows, H. S. (1986). A taxonomy of problem-based learning methods. *Medical Education, 20*, 481–486.

Bell, B. (1996). *A special-purpose architecture for the design of educational software* (Technical report 70). Institute for the Learning Sciences, Northwestern University.

Bell, B., Bareiss, R., and Beckwith, R. (1993). Sickle Cell Counselor: A prototype goal-based scenario for instruction in a museum environment. *Journal of the Learning Sciences, 3*(4), 347-386.

Bell, P., Davis, E., & Linn, M. C. (1995). The knowledge integration environment: Theory and design. In T. Koschmann (Ed.), *Proceedings of the Computer Support for Collaborative Learning 1995 Conference (CSCL'95)*. Bloomington, IN.

Blumenfeld, P. C., Soloway, E., Marx, R. W., Krajcik, J. S., Guzdial, M., & Palincsar, A. (1991). Motivating project-based learning: Sustaining the doing, supporting the learning. *Educational Psychologist, 26*(3, 4), 369-398.

Chi, M. T. H., Feltovich, P. J., & Glaser, R. (1981). Categorization and representation of physics problems by experts and novices. *Cognitive Science, 5*, 121-152.

Collins, A., & Brown, J. S. (1988). The computer as a tool for learning through reflection. In H. Mandl & A. Lesgold (Eds.), *Learning issues for intelligent tutoring systems* (pp. 1-18). New York: Springer.

Collins, A., Brown, J. S., & Newman, S. E. (1989). Cognitive apprenticeship: Teaching the craft of reading, writing, and mathematics. In L. B. Resnick (Ed.), *Knowing, learning, and instruction: Essays in honor of Robert Glaser* (pp. 453-494). Hillsdale, NJ: Lawrence Erlbaum and Associates.

Domeshek, E., & Kolodner, J. L. (1993). Using the points of large cases. *Artificial Intelligence for Engineering Design, Analysis and Manufacturing (AIEDAM), 7*(2), 87-96.

Ferguson, W., Bareiss, R., Birnbaum, L., & Osgood, R. (1992). ASK systems: An approach to the realization of story-based teachers. *Journal of the Learning Sciences, 2*(1), 95-134.

Gentner, D. (1983). Structure-mapping: A theoretical framework for analogy. *Cognitive Science, 7*, 155-170. (Reprinted in A. Collins & E. E. Smith (Eds.), *Readings in cognitive science: A perspective from psychology and artificial intelligence*. Palo Alto, CA: Kaufman).

Gray, J., Camp, P. J., Holbrook, J. K., Fasse, B. B., & Kolodner, J. L. (2001). Science talk as a way to assess student transfer and learning: Implications for formative assessment. Paper presented at the Meeting of the American Educational Researchers Association, Seattle, WA, April 2001. http://www.cc.gatech. edu/projects/lbd/pubtopic.html#assess.

Guzdial, M. J. (1991). The need for education and technology: Examples from the GPCeditor. *Proceedings of the National Educational Computing Conference*, pp. 16-23. Phoenix, AZ.

Guzdial, M. J. (1993). *Emile: Software-realized scaffolding for science learners programming in mixed media*. Unpublished Ph.D. dissertation, University of Michigan.

Guzdial, M. (1995). "Software-realized scaffolding to facilitate programming for science learning." *Interactive Learning Environments, 4*(1). 1-44.

Guzdial, M., & Kehoe, C. (1998). Apprenticeship-based learning environments: A principled approach to providing software-realized scaffolding through hypermedia. *Journal of Interactive Learning Research, 9*(3/4).

Guzdial, M., Hmelo, C., Hubscher, R., Nagel, K., Newstetter, W., Puntambakar, S., Shabo, A., Turns, J., & Kolodner, J. L. (1997). Integrating and guiding collaboration: Lessons learned in computer-supported collaboration learning research at Georgia Tech. In R. Hall, N. Miyake, & N. Enyedy (Eds.), *Proceedings of Computer-Supported Collaborative Learning '97* (pp. 91-100). Toronto, Ontario.

Hammond, K. J. (1989). *Case-based planning: Viewing planning as a memory task*. Boston: Academic Press.

Harel, I. (1991). *Children designers: Interdisciplinary constructions for learning and knowing mathematics in a computer-rich school.* Norwood, NJ: Ablex.

Harel, I., & Papert, S. (1990). Software design as a learning environment. *Interactive Learning Environments, 1*(1), 1-32.

Holyoak, K. J. and Thagard, P. (1995). *Mental Leaps*. Cambridge: The MIT Press.

Holbrook, J. K., Gray, J., Fasse, B. B., Camp, P. J., and Kolodner, J. L. (2001). *Assessment and Evaluation of the Learning by Design Physical Science Unit, 1999-2000: A Document in Progress.* http://www.cc.gatech.edu/projects/lbd/pubtopic.html#assess.

Kolodner, J. L. (1983a). Maintaining organization in a dynamic long-term memory. *Cognitive Science, 7*(4).

Kolodner, J. L. (1983b). Reconstructive memory: A computer model. *Cognitive Science, 7*(4).

Kolodner, J. (1993). *Case based reasoning*. San Mateo, CA: Morgan Kaufmann.

Kolodner, J. L. (1997). Educational implications of analogy: A view from case-based reasoning. *American Psychologist, 52*, 57-66.

Kolodner, J. L., & Nagel, K. (1999). The Design Discussion Area: A collaborative learning from problem-solving and design activities. *Proceedings of CSCL '99. Palo Alto, CA*, 300-307.

Kolodner, J. L., & Penberthy, L. (1990). *A case-based approach to creativity in problem-solving*. In Proceedings of the Twelfth Annual Conference of the Cognitive Science Society (pp. 978-985). Mahwah, NJ: Lawrence Erlbaum Associates.

Kolodner, J. L., & Simpson, R. L. (1989). *The MEDIATOR: Analysis of an early case-based problem solver. Cognitive Science, 13*(4), 507-549.

Kolodner, J. L., & Wills, L. (1993, July). *Paying attention to the right thing: Issues of focus in case-based creative design*. Proceedings of the Ninth Annual Conference of the Cognitive Science Society.

Kolodner, J. L., Hmelo, C. E., & Narayanan, N. H. (1996). Problem-based learning meets case-based reasoning. In D. C. Edelson & E. A. Domeshek (Eds.), *Proceedings of the International Journal of the Learning Sciences (ICLS '96)*, Charlottesville, VA: AACE, pp. 188-195.

Kolodner, J. L., Crismond, D., Gray, J., Holbrook, J., & Puntambekar, S. (1998). Learning by design from theory to practice. In A. Bruckman, M. Guzdial, J. Kolodner, & A. Ram (Eds.), *Proceedings of International Conference of the Learning Sciences 1998* (pp. 16-22). Atlanta, GA.

Kolodner, J. L., Camp, P. J., Crismond, D., Fasse, B., Gray, J., Holbrook, J., Puntembakar (2003). Problem-Based Learning Meets Case-Based Reasoning in the Middle-School Science Classroom: Putting Learning-by-Design™ into Practice. *Journal of the Learning Sciences*, Vol.12, No.4, pp. 495-548.

Koloder, J. L., & Voida, A (2002). Articulating Lessons Learned: Scaffolding and Collaboration for Summative Reflection. *http://www.cc.gatech.edu/projects/lbd/pubtopic.html#software*.

Kolodner, J. L., Camp, P. J., Crismond, D., Fasse, B. B., Gray, J., Holbrook, J., & Ryan, M. (in press). Promoting deep science learning through case-based reasoning: Rituals and practices in Learning by Design™ classrooms. In Seel, N. M. (Ed.), *Instructional Design: International Perspectives*. Mahwah, NJ: Lawrence Erlbaum Associates.

Nagel, K., & Kolodner, J. L. (1999). *SMILE: Supportive Multi-User Interactive Learning Environment*. (Poster presented at CSCL '99. Palo Alto, CA.) *http://www.cc.gatech.edu/projects/lbd/pubtopic.html#software*.

Ng, E., & Bereiter, C. (1995). Three levels of goal orientation in learning. In A. Ram & D. B. Leake (Eds.), *Goal-driven learning* (pp. 354-370). Cambridge, MA: MIT Press.

Owensby, J., & Kolodner, J. L. (2002, January). Case application suite: Promoting collaborative case application in Learning by

Design™classrooms. In *Proceedings of the International Conference on Computer Support for Collaborative Learning, CSCL-2002,* pp. 505-506.

Palinscar, A., & Brown, A. (1984). Reciprocal teaching of comprehension-fostering and comprehension monitoring activities. *Cognition and Instruction, I*(2), 117-175.

Papert, S. (1991). Situating constructionism. In I. Harel & S. Papert (Eds.), *Constructionism* (pp. 1-11). Norwood, NJ: Ablex.

Puntambekar, S., & Kolodner, J. L. (1998). The Design Diary: Development of a Tool to Support Students Learning Science by Design. *Proceedings International Conference of the Learning Sciences '98,* pp. 280-236.

Puntambekar, S., & Kolodner, J. L. (submitted). Distributed Scaffolding: Helping Students Learn from Design.

Puntambekar, S., Nagel, K., Hubscher, R., Guzdial, M., & Kolodner, J. L. (1997). Intragroup and intergroup: An exploration of learning with complementary collaboration tools. In R. Hall, N. Miyake, & N. Enyedy (Eds.), *Proceedings of Computer-Supported Collaborative Learning '97* (pp. 207-214). Toronto, Ontario.

Ram, A., & Leake, D. B. (1995). Learning, goals, and learning goals. In A. Ram & D. B. Leake (Eds.), *Goal-driven learning* (pp. 1-37). Cambridge, MA: MIT Press.

Redmond, M. (1992). *Learning by observing and understanding expert problem solving.* Unpublished Ph.D. Thesis, College of Computing, Georgia Institute of Technology.

Ryan, M., Camp, P., & Crismond, D. (2001). Design rules of thumb—Connecting science and design. Paper presented at AERA 2001, Seattle, WA.

Scardamalia, M., & Bereiter, C. (1991). Literate expertise. In K. A. Ericsson, & J. Smith (Eds.), *Toward a general theory of expertise: Prospects and limits* (pp. 172-194). Cambridge: Cambridge University Press.

Scardamalia, M., Bereiter, C., & Lamon, M. (1994). The CSILE Project: Trying to bring the classroom into World 3. In K. McGilly (Ed.), *Classroom lessons: Integrating cognitive theory and classroom practice* (pp. 201-228). Cambridge, MA: MIT Press.

Schank, R. C. (1982). *Dynamic memory* . Cambridge: Cambridge University Press.

Schank, R. C. (1999). *Dynamic memory revisited.* New York: Cambridge University Press.

Schank, R. C., & Cleary, C. (1994). *Engines for education.* Mahwah, NJ: Lawrence Erlbaum Associates. *http://www.ils.nwu.edu/~e_for_e.*

Schank, R. C., Fano, A., Bell, B., & Jona, M. (1994). The design of goal-based scenarios. *Journal of the Learning Sciences, 3*(4), 305-346.

Schank, R. C., Berman, T. R., & Macpherson, K. A. (1999). Learning by doing. In C. Reigeluth (Ed.), *Instructional design theories and models* (pp. 161-181) Mahwah, NJ: Lawrence Erlbaum Associates.

Schon, D. A. (1982). *The reflective practitioner: How professionals think in action.* New York: Basic Books.

Shabo, A., Nagel, K., Guzdial, M., & Kolodner, J. (1997). JavaCAP: A collaborative case authoring program on the WWW. In R. Hall, N. Miyake, & N. Enyedy (Eds.), *Proceedings of Computer-Supported Collaborative Learning '97* (pp. 241-249). Toronto, Ontario.

Silver, E. A., Branca, N. A., & Adams, V. M. (1980). Metacognition: The missing link in problem solving? In R. Karplus (Ed.), *Proceedings of the Fourth International Conference for the Psychology of Mathematics Education* (pp. 213-222). Berkeley: University of California.

Simina, M., & Kolodner, J. (1997). *Creative design: Reasoning and understanding. Proceedings of the International Conference on Case-Based Reasoning* (ICCBR97), Providence, RI.

Simina, M., Kolodner, J. L., Ram A., & Gorman, M. (1998, August). *Opportunistic enterprises in invention. Proceedings of the Twentieth Annual Conference of the Cognitive Science Society,* Madison, WI.

Spiro, R. J., Feltovich, P. J., Jacobson, M. J., & Coulson, R. L. (1991). Cognitive flexibility, constructivism, and hypertext: Random access instruction for advanced knowledge acquisition in ill-structured domains. *Educational Technology, 31*(5), 24-33.

Turns, J. (1997). *learning essays and the reflective learner: Supporting assessment in engineering design education.* Unpublished Doctoral Dissertation. School of Industrial and Systems Engineering. Georgia Institute of Technology. Atlanta, GA.

Turns, J., Guzdial, M., Mistree, F., Allen, J. K., & Rosen, D. (1995a). *I wish I had understood this at the beginning: Dilemmas in research, teaching, and the introduction of technology in engineering design courses. Proceedings of the Frontiers in Education Conference,* Atlanta, GA.

Turns, J., Mistree, F., Rosen, D., Allen, J., Guzdial, M., & Carlson, D. (1995b, June). *A collaborative multimedia design learning simulator.* Paper presented at the ED-Media 95: World Conference on Educational Multimedia and HyperMedia, Graz, Austria.

Turns, J. A., Newstetter, W., Allen, J. K., & Mistree, F. (1997). *The reflective learner: supporting the writing of learning essays that support the learning of engineering design through experience. Proceedings of the 1997 American Society of Engineering Educators Conference.* Milwaukee, WI.

Zimring, C. M., Do. E., Domeshek, E., & Kolodner, J. (1995). Supporting case-study use in design education: A computational case-based design aid for architecture. In J. P. Mohsen (Ed.), *Computing in Engineering: Proceedings of the Second Congress.* New York: American Society of Civil Engineers.

Part

·VI·

INSTRUCTIONAL MESSAGE DESIGN

·33·

VISUAL REPRESENTATIONS AND LEARNING:
THE ROLE OF STATIC AND ANIMATED GRAPHICS

Gary J. Anglin
University of Kentucky

Hossein Vaez
Eastern Kentucky University

Kathryn L. Cunningham
University of Kentucky

With the proliferation of illustrations in instructional materials, it becomes increasingly important to investigate their effects on student learning. The use of illustrations in instructional materials has been pervasive for a considerable amount of time (Feaver, 1977; Slythe, 1970). A substantial research literature has already accumulated concerning the role of illustrations in instructional materials. The purpose of this chapter is to introduce researchers in instructional technology and others to the primary theories of picture perception and to provide a survey and critique of the visual representation research that incorporates static animated illustrations.

33.1 SCOPE

The effective use of illustrations (pictures, charts, graphs, and diagrams) in instructional materials is an important facet of instructional message design. Fleming (1993) defines a message as "a pattern of signs (words, pictures, gestures) produced for the purpose of modifying the psychomotor, cognitive, or affective behavior of one or more persons" (p. x). We define pictures as illustrations that have some resemblance to the entity that they stand for, whereas nonrepresentational graphics including charts, graphs, and diagrams are more abstract but do use spatial layout in a consequential way (Knowlton, 1966; Levie & Dickie, 1973; Rieber, 1994; Winn, 1987). Levie (1987) has suggested that there are at least four lines of research on illustrations: (a) picture perception, (b) memory for pictures, (c) learning and cognition, and (d) affective responses to pictures. In this chapter we first present several theories of picture perception. We then present a brief discussion of selected memory models that have been used to describe how words and pictures are encoded and two related topics, cognitive load theory and multiple representations in multimedia. Next, knowledge acquisition studies incorporating static and animated pictures are reviewed. Finally, we critically analyze the literature and offer suggestions for future research and practice based on results of primary research and all literature reviews discussed in the chapter. Given the magnitude of the literature, our own expertise, and the economics of publishing, we reviewed only comparative experimental research studies. Visual message design studies completed using other research methods are certainly reasonable and appropriate. There are many variables to consider when designing visual instructional messages. Our system of classification represents only one perspective on the literature. We reviewed a wide range of studies but we do not claim that the review is exhaustive.

33.2   PICTURE PERCEPTION

33.2.1   Theories of Picture Perception

When is a surface with marks on it a "picture"? How do pictures carry meaning? What kinds of meaning can pictures carry? Is there a grammar of picturing? Is picture perception essentially innate, or is it a skill that must be learned?

Questions such as these have provoked conjecture from philosophers, psychologists, art historians, semioticians, and computer scientists. It is a fascinating, disputatious literature: one with implications for researchers in educational communication and technology—although widely neglected.

This section provides a concise introduction to the major scientific theories of picture perception. To set the discussion of modern theories in historical context, we begin with a description of the theory of linear perspective developed during the Italian Renaissance. Then two major conflicting theories are introduced: James J. Gibson's resemblance theory, in which meaning is based on the picture's resemblance to the visual environment, and E. H. Gombrich's constructivist theory, in which meaning is based upon pictorial conventions. Next a compromise position by Margaret Hagen is described. Then a third major theory is presented: Rudolph Arnheim's Gestalt approach, followed by the views of Julian Hochberg, who is in opposition to Arnheim, and John M. Kennedy, who supports Arnheim.

Next the discussion shifts to two approaches from the field of semiotics: James Knowlton's analysis of the iconic sign and Nelson Goodman's theory of symbol systems. Finally, some emerging approaches from cognitive science are noted, exemplified by David Marr's computational theory of vision.

Only the gist of each approach is presented, but suggestions for further reading are provided. Overviews to the area can be found in several edited books containing chapters on a wide range of issues: Crozier and Chapman (1984), Hagen (1980b, 1980c), Mitchell (1980), Nodine and Fisher (1979), Olson (1974), and Perkins and Leondar (1977).

33.2.1.1   Renaissance Perspective Theory: Brunelleschi.
The technique of linear perspective by which three-dimensional scenes are represented on two-dimensional surfaces has its origins in ancient Greek architecture and scene design. It was not until 1420, however, that a theoretical basis for the technique was elucidated by Filippo Brunelleschi of Florence. The technique involves using the pattern of light rays emanating from a natural scene. The artist draws the composition that is projected onto a picture plane—a cross section of the straight lines connecting the artist's viewpoint with the objects in the scene. Accordingly, our ability to understand pictures is due to the optical equivalence between pictures and their real-world referents. Because the picture is an optical surrogate for the scene, picture perception is thought to be straightforward and essentially automatic.

But there are problems with this theory. According to the theory a picture will be perceived accurately only when the person viewing the picture assumes the point of observation taken by the artist. Viewing the picture from a different position should result in distorted perception—an outcome that does not occur in practice. For example, when we look at a portrait from an oblique angle we do not conclude that the person portrayed actually has an elongated head; we take notice of our orientation to the picture surface and judge shapes as though our viewpoint were perpendicular to the picture (although modest distortion due to oblique viewing may occur; Goldstein, 1987).

Another problem is that successful pictures often violate perspective theory. For example, artists rarely obey the rules of perspective in the vertical dimension. When a tall building is seen from ground level, the rules of three-point perspective stipulate that the sides of the building should be drawn as converging lines. Such drawings are usually judged to look unnatural. On the other hand, when artists violate perspective in the third dimension the "error" is visually noticed only by those few who are attuned to watch for it. Another violation is that artists often use more than one station point. Often each major figure in a picture is drawn from a different station point, a fact that goes unnoticed by most viewers. On the other hand, pictures drawn from a single station point can look distorted if the station point is very close to the subject. Yet another problem—and there are several more—is that the shapes on the picture plane are ambiguous, as they can be the result of the projections of more than one three-dimensional object.

Thus the techniques of pictorial composition used in post-Renaissance Western culture often disobey the geometric rules of perspective. In practice, pictures are very rarely the optical equivalence of the sense they represent, and Renaissance perspective theory cannot serve as an adequate explanation of picture perception.

Detailed treatments of the geometry of perspective are provided by Hagen (1986) and Kubovy (1986). Other commentary on this topic is given by Greene (1983), Haber (1979), Penrice (1980), and Pirenne (1970).

33.2.1.2   Resemblance Theory: James J. Gibson.
The laws of linear perspective were the starting point for Gibson's resemblance theory of picture perception (sometimes called "projective theory" or the "direct perception" approach). Although modified somewhat by his final position on the status of pictures (Gibson, 1979), Gibson's (1971) best-known definition of "picture" is, "A picture is a surface so treated that a delimited optic array to a point of observation is made available that contains the same kind of information that is found in the ambient optic arrays of an ordinary environment" (p. 31).

But what is this "kind of information" that is found in both the picture and the environment? According to Gibson it is something beyond the static lines and shapes in the picture; it is a higher-order kind of information consisting of formless, timeless invariants. The concept of an invariant is described by Gibson (1979):

When a young child sees the family cat at play, the front view, side view, rear view, top view, and so on are not seen, and what gets perceived is the *invariant* cat. Hence, when the child first sees a picture of a cat he is prepared to pick up the invariants, and he pays no attention to the frozen cartoon. It is not that he sees an abstract cat, or a conceptual cat, or the common features of the class of cats; ... what he gets is the information for the persistence of that peculiar, furry, mobile layout of surfaces. (p. 271)

These stable, enduring structures that are picked up from the environment are also present in the optic array provided by a picture and are used to interpret the picture. An example of an invariant is the texture of surfaces such as sand or fur. Such textures are represented in photographs and act as optical gradients that guide judgments of distances (Gibson & Bridgeman, 1987). Although it is not equally clear how we are able to perceive the invariant shapes of the objects in a picture (e.g., What does an "invariant cat" look like?), Gibson uses the concept to avoid some of the problems of perspective theory (e.g., How can we identify an object in a picture if it is depicted from a point of view we have never seen?). Nevertheless, Gibson's theory of pictorial representation is based primarily on the optical correspondence of the picture and the environment, and it is the structure of the stimulus that is the driving force in picture perception.

For recent discussion of Gibson's work see Cutting (1982, 1987), Fodor and Pylyshyn (1981), Natsoulas (1983), Reed and Jones (1982), Rogers and Costall (1983), and Wilcox and Edwards (1982).

33.2.1.3 Constructivism: E. H. Gombrich. Perception, as Neisser (1976) puts it, is where reality and cognition meet. Whereas Gibson assigns the major role in this meeting to reality, constructivists such as Gombrich emphasize the role of cognition. Pictures do not "tell their own story," Gombrich argues, the viewer must *construct* a meaning.

Pictures will be interpreted differently depending on the attitude taken by the eye of the beholder. What we see, or think we see, is filtered through a variety of mental sets and expectations. For example, briefly shown playing cards in which hearts are colored black are sometime seen as purple (Bruner & Postman, 1949).

One special class of expectations consists of the artistic conventions in common use. Gombrich (1969) traces the history of Western art showing how cultural and technological changes have altered the criteria for pictorial realism. What is judged to be a "good likeness" is a function of the conventions and drawing techniques that now look "wrong" and amateurish to our modern eye.

A more pervasive example of a system of pictorial convention in use today is the outline drawing. The use of lines to represent the edges of objects is a substantial departure from nature. The objects in the world are not bounded by lines, and it is due to convention that we perceive outline drawings as depicting shapes rather than arrangements of wires. Whereas the convention that shapes can be represented by outlines is a rapidly acquired understanding, the ability to interpret some conventions such as implied motion cues may require extensive experience or even direct instruction (Levie, 1978).

Such conventions are not arbitrary. Artists are not free to adopt any technique they choose. In fact, the history of naturalistic art can be thought of as a series of innovations in the technique of approximating what is seen by viewing the

environment. But Gombrich argues that realism in art is more than just an effort to record the optical data present in nature. The artists must produce an "illusion of reality" that matches the viewer's concept (schema) of what a picture of a given kind *should* look like. And how are these schemata acquired? By repeated exposure to the art of the day. These schemata then function as the standards for judging reality in subsequent picture viewing.

Such schemata can also affect our perceptions of nature. "We not only believe what we see: to some extent we see what we believe" (Gregory, 1970, p. 86). Our experience with art may lead us to look at the natural environment in new ways. For example, the sensitive museum visitor may note that the pastel patches of impressionist paintings can be observed in nature as well. So the ways of representing nature can become ways of seeing nature. Similarly, artists vacillate between painting what they see in nature and seeing in nature what they paint on canvas.

One controversial claim by Gombrich (1972) is that pictures lack the "statement function" of words. For example, he argues that the statement "The cat sits on the mat" cannot be directly pictured. A picture of a cat on a mat depicts a particular cat in a particular environment as seen from a particular viewpoint. An equivalent verbal message would be something like "There is a cat seen from behind." Gombrich would not, however, propose that pictures are a poor source of ideas. Indeed, the conceptual richness of pictorial representation is a central theme of his work.

For further comment on this approach see Blinder (1983), Carrier (1983), Gregory (1973, 1981), Heffernan (1985), and Katz (1983).

33.2.1.4 A Generative Theory: Margaret Hagen. Is picture perception primarily a bottom-up process, as Gibson claims, or a top-down process, as Gombrich claims? Hagen (1978, 1980a) provides a generative theory of representation that suggests a reconciliation: "Meaning is not given by the head to the unstructured stimulus, nor is it given by the stimulus to the unstructured head. The "relation between the two is reciprocal and symmetrical" (1980a, p. 45).

In developing her thesis, Hagen describes differences between how we perceive the natural world and how we perceive "the world within the picture." For example, compared to natural perception, picture perception compresses the perceived third dimension and increases the awareness of the angle among objects (the spread). Thus picture perception has a special character that is based partly on ecological geometry (the natural perspective of the visual environment) and partly on the creativity or generativity of the perceiver.

Recently Hagen (1986) has provided a category system for describing the geometrical foundations of many styles of representational art—early Egyptian art, Roman murals, Northwest Coast Indian art, Japanese art, Mayan art, and Ice Age cave art, to name just a few. For example, there are several options for the location of the artist's station point. It can be close to the subject of the picture, at a moderate distance, or at optical infinity—in which case vanishing points and the convergence of parallel lines (e.g., railroad tracks meeting at the horizon) are obviated. Also, the system can involve the use of a single station point or multiple station points. Hagen observes that each system of depiction is "correct" when judged according to its assumptions. Thus in evaluating the art of other times and cultures we must reject the premise that the prevailing post-Renaissance system of Western art is the only valid system for representing reality—a position also taken by Arnheim.

33.2.1.5 A Gestalt Approach: Rudolf Arnheim.
According to Arnheim, picture perception is not primarily an act of direct perception as Gibson claims, nor is it a response to changing conventions as Gombrich claims. Picture perception is primarily a matter of organizing the lines and other elements of a picture into shapes and patterns according to innate laws of structure. Arnheim (1954) applies the principles of Gestalt psychology to the study of art. He shows how the laws of organization (e.g., the rules of grouping, the laws of simplicity and good continuation) can be found in the art of many periods. Meaning, he argues, has always been embodied in the Gestalt, the whole that is greater than the sum of its parts. Picture-making is also derived from Gestalt principles:

The urge to create simple shapes . . . cannot be explained as an urge to copy nature; it can be understood only when one realizes that perceiving is not passive recording but understanding, that understanding can take place only through the conception of definable shapes. For this reason art begins not with attempts to duplicate nature, but with highly abstract general principles that take the form of elementary shapes. (Arnheim, 1986, pp. 161–162)

Arnheim observes that our judgment of the art of other times and cultures suffers from "a prejudice generated by the particular conventions of Western art since the Renaissance" (p. 159). Furthermore, current technique is so pervasive that we assume that it is the only correct way to make pictures. But the techniques of unfamiliar art styles are not, as sometimes supposed, due to lack of skill or accidentally acquired convention; nor are they deliberate distortions devised for some artistic purpose. Each style is based on an internally consistent system of solutions to visual problems, solutions that are no more in need of justification than contemporary technique.

Arnheim (1969) is also known for his advocacy of "visual thinking." He rejects the belief that reasoning occurs only through the use of language. In fact he argues that thinking occurs primarily through abstract imagery. Arnheim champions the role of art in education and stresses the importance of teaching students to become fluent in thinking with shapes.

Another recurrent theme in Arnheim's work is the nature of abstraction. Representational art involves one kind of abstraction. Portraits, for example, are more abstract than their real-world referents. In such cases, "abstractness is a means by which a picture interprets what it portrays" (Arnheim, 1969, p. 137). On the other hand, pictures may be less abstract than the concepts they symbolize. For example, the silhouette of a cow on a roadside sign, although quite abstract, is still less abstract than the concept "cattle crossing." Arnheim (1974) discusses some of the problems faced by educators in determining the most effective kind and level of abstraction to use in instructional illustrations.

Although Gestalt ideas have been eschewed by cognitive psychologists, recent discoveries in visual anatomy and physiology and the study of perceptual organization have attracted some renewed interest in the area (Hoffman & Dodwell, 1985; Kubovy, 1981).

33.2.1.6 Picture Perception as Purposive Behavior: Julian Hochberg.
Hochberg opposes the Gestalt approach, arguing that "the whole stimulus configuration cannot in general be taken as the effective determinant for perception" (Peterson & Hochberg, 1983, p. 192). Here is why: All aspects of a picture cannot be perceived in a single glance. Vision is sharp only in a small central area of the visual field—an area about the size of your thumbnail when held at arm's length. On the retina of the eye, acuity falls off rapidly from this area (the fovea). Because detailed discriminations are possible only on the fovea, it is necessary to scan pictures to take in all the details. Scanning does not occur in smooth sweeps but, rather, as a series of very rapid jumps called "saccades" and brief stops called "fixations"—normally about 0.33 s each. The information obtained from these separate fixations must be integrated into a mental map. Thus "at any given time most of the picture as we perceive it is not only the retina of the eye, nor on the plane of the picture—it is in the mind's eye" (Hochberg, 1972). So the whole is not perceived directly, as Arnheim claims; it is the result of synthesis based on the analysis of parts. These interactions among the picture, eye movements, and cognitions are "highly skilled sequential purposive behaviors" that are, according to Hochberg, the keys to understanding picture perception.

Hochberg (1979, 1980) describes how certain techniques used in painting can be thought to mimic the workings of the visual system. For example, in some of Rembrandt's paintings most of the canvas is blurred; only a few areas are rendered in sharp detail, simulating what is registered by the eye in a series of fixations. Similarly, techniques used in impressionistic paintings (which Hochberg calls "painting for parafoveal viewing"), pointillist paintings, and Op Art (Vitz & Glimcher, 1984) mirror processes of the human perceptual system.

Another issue discussed by Hochberg concerns the question of which picture of an object is the "best" picture. Hochberg (1980) uses the term "canonical form" to refer to "the most readily recognized and remembered view or 'clean up' version of some form or object" (p. 76). Canonical form preserves the most distinctive features of an object and eliminates noninformative features. Another factor in determining canonical form is the point of view from which an object is depicted.

33.2.1.7 A Mentalistic Approach: John M. Kennedy.
Kennedy is supportive of Arnheim's approach and opposed to Gibson and Gombrich. He argues that we will learn very little about how pictures are perceived by studying the optical geometry of naturalistic art. Understanding picture perception should begin with the realization that pictures are made by people trying to communicate to receivers who are themselves intelligent perceivers striving to grasp the sender's intent. Pictures are made to communicate ideas, not just show scenes. To

exemplify his approach, Kennedy (1985) discusses the pictorial metaphor:

Imagine a picture of a businessman with as many arms as an octopus, each hand holding a telephone. Or imagine a picture of a bride looking into a mirror and seeing a harried housewife. These pictures violate the laws of physics; they break the rules that Gibson called on. . . . And they do so precisely because the artist wants to put across *ideas:* that business men are overworked; that present bliss gives rise to future stress. (p. 38)

Metaphoric pictures present two meanings: one false, the other intended. Understanding the perception of such pictures requires a "mentalistic analysis" in which assumptions are made about the experience and mental processes of the sender and the receiver. "The person who makes the metaphor expects the recipient to notice both meanings, and expects the recipient to know which was intended, and expects the recipient to know which was intended, and expects the recipient to know the maker expected all this from the recipient" (Kennedy, 1984b, p. 901). Kennedy also argues that pictorial cues such as implied motion cues can be conceived of as metaphor rather than as pictorial convention.

As a historical footnote, Kennedy was Gibson's student at Cornell and, at one time, followed in his footsteps, writing a survey of the field that was based largely on Gibsonian ideas (1974). But a decade later Kennedy (1984a) would write, "Regrettably scientific psychology as found in our universities can never be anything more than a trivial pursuit. By its very nature it is incapable of profound insights into humankind" (p. 30). Although this represents a dramatic change in philosophy on Kennedy's part, the attack on a competing approach is by no means unusual. The picture perception literature is an intellectual battlefield delightfully seasoned with charge and counter charge. Theorists are robustly combative in attacking opposing views while defending their own.

33.2.1.8 A Semiotic Approach: James Knowlton.
The theories discussed so far approach the topic from points of view related to visual perception, either by way of perceptual psychology or through the analysis of visual art. The next two theories have a different starting point; they derive from a concern with symbol using in general, thus placing the discussion of picture perception in a broader context.

The boundaries of semiotics—the science of signs—are wide and indistinct. The domain includes questions of the meaning of as well as the communication of meaning. Among the central figures in this field are Cassirer (1944), Morris (1946), Pierce (1960), and Sebeok (1976). For further commentary on the contribution of semiotics to picture perception see Cassidy (1982), Eco (1976), Holowka (1981), Langer (1976), Sless (1986), and Veltrusky (1976).

Here, however, we focus on the theorist in this tradition who speaks most directly to our present concerns with visual message design research: James Knowlton. Knowlton (1964, 1966) develops a metalanguage for talking about pictures beginning with the term *sign*. A sign is a stimulus intentionally produced for the purpose of making reference to some other object or concept. A key distinction is that between digital signs and iconic signs. Digital signs bear no resemblance to their referents. For example, the physical appearance of the signs "man" and "hombre" do not in any way look like their referent. Examples of digital signs are words, numbers, Morse code, Braille, and semaphore. Iconic signs, on the other hand, are not arbitrary in their appearance. In some way, iconic signs include drawings, photographs, maps, and blueprints.

Usually pictures are thought to resemble their referents in terms of visual appearance. Resemblance can, however, take other forms. Knowlton broadens the concept of *picture* to include *logical pictures* and *analogical pictures*. Logical pictures resemble their referents in terms of the relationships between elements. An electrical writing schematic, for example, bears no visual resemblance to the piece of apparatus it represents; it is a picture of the pattern of connections between elements. Flowcharts and diagrams are other examples of logical pictures. In analogical pictures, the intent is to portray a resemblance in function. For example, a pictorial analogy could be made between a suit of armor and an insect's exoskeleton. Thus Knowlton's definition of "resemblance" goes far beyond Gibson's concept, in which resemblance is based on the optical equivalence of pictures and their referents. And even when resemblance is based on physical appearance, the resemblance of a picture to its referent can, according to Knowlton, be slight. Sometimes a simple silhouette will do the job. Additionally, the ways in which resemblance functions in pictorial communication often depend on factors that are extrinsic to the picture itself:

Resemblance does not designate a single relation between pictures and their subjects; it designates the members of a fairly comprehensive class of relations—a class whose boundaries are not clear. And relations of resemblance are not always immediately evident to the uneducated eye. Knowing how to look at a picture is required to discern the ways it resembles its subject. Knowledge of other matters may be required as well—pictorial conventions, referential connections, historical, scientific, or mythical lore that sets the context of the work. Such matters are not taken in at a glance. (Elgin, 1984, p. 919)

The most extreme and controversial position on the role of resemblance is taken by Goodman (1978). He asserts that resemblance between picture and nature is not necessary and that "a picture is realistic to the extent that it is correct under the accustomed system of representation" (p. 130).

33.2.1.9 Symbol Systems Theory: Nelson Goodman.
Goodman (1976) has devised a detailed theory of symbol systems. A symbol system consists of a set of inscriptions (e.g., phonemes, numbers) organized into a scheme that correlates with a field of reference. For example, musical staff notation consists of five horizontal lines on which notes and other marks are placed that correlate with a musical performance. As another example, maps consist of lines, shapes, and symbols that correlate with a musical performance. Also, maps consist of lines, shapes, and symbols that correlate with roads, boundaries, and landmarks. Thus the analysis of a symbol system involves an examination of (a) the scheme of representation, (b) the field of reference, and (c) the rules of correspondence between the two.

Goodman provides several conceptual tools that can be used for analyzing symbol systems. One key concept is notationality.

Notationality is the degree to which the elements of a symbol system are distinct and are combined according to precise rules. Music is high in notationality. The notes on the scale are distinct in terms of pitch and duration, and the rules for combining them are clear. Mathematics systems are also high in notationality; each number is distinct and the rules for "making statements" are precise. Pictures, on the other hand, are nonnotational. The "elements" of picturing are overlapping, confusable, and lacking in syntax. The lines and shadings that pictures are built from are without limit, and the ways they are combined to produce a symbol are undefined.

Notationality is an aspect of symbol using that may have implications for human information processing. Gardner (1982) speculates that "a case can be made that the left hemisphere of the human brain is relatively more effective than the right at dealing with notational symbol systems, . . . while the right hemisphere is more at ease in dealing with . . . non-notational systems" (p. 59).

Another key concept in Goodman's theory is repleteness. Some symbol schemes, such as most pictures, are replete (or dense), whereas other schemes, such as printed words, are lacking in repleteness. The degree of repleteness is an index of how many aspects of a scheme are significant. In printed text, changes in the typeface, boldness, ink color, and other physical parameters do not necessarily alter meaning in any significant way. Drawings, on the other hand, are relatively replete, as several aspects of the marks in a drawing are often critical. Paintings are very high in repleteness. "Everything about a painting is part of it—design, coloration, brush stroke, texture and so on. A painting is "unrepeatable in the strict sense of the term" (Kolers, 1983, p. 146).

Goodman distinguishes three primary functions of symbol systems. Symbols can *represent* concepts by denoting or depicting them. Symbols can *exemplify* ideas or qualities by providing a sample of the concept. And symbols can *express* affective meaning (emotions).

Symbol systems differ with respect to the ease with which they can perform the functions of representation, exemplification, and expression. For example, music, although richly expressive, has no literal denotation. Music in the absence of a title or lyrics is not "about" anything. Number systems are limited in a different way. Numbers represent (quantities), but they normally have no expressive function. Most pictorial systems are versatile. Line drawings, photographs, and representational paintings can depict, exemplify, and express forcefully.

Pictures exemplify qualities such as color and shape through the possession and presentation of them. The qualities exemplified are properties of the picture. Pictures express through "metaphorical exemplification"—the figurative possession and presentation of emotion. For example, when a picture expresses sorrow, the feeling can be said to be "in the picture." We must, however, learn how to decode the expressive features of pictorial systems. "Emotions are everywhere the same; but the artistic expression of them varies from age to age and from one country to another" (Goodman, 1976, p. 90).

For other comments on Goodman's theory see Coldron (1982), Gardner, Howard, and Perkins (1974), Roupas (1977), Salomon (1979a, 1979b), and Scruton (1974).

33.2.1.10 Cognitive Science: David Marr. Artificial intelligence research on computer vision is a rapidly developing area that may contribute to understanding picture perception by humans. One focus of this work involves determining the computations that are required to program a computer to see. To do this, it is necessary to specify the nature of the visual input, to describe how this input is transformed into data that can be handled by a computer, and to enumerate the computations that are carried out on-line to produce solutions to visual problems. Such problems include the detection of shape contours and surface textures.

A central figure in this area is David Marr. Marr's (1982) theory of vision involves the analysis of visual input through a series of stages that culminates the meaningful interpretation of an image. In Marr's theory an initial analysis involves the detection of features such as boundaries. These determinations are used to construct a "primal sketch" that distinguishes the sections of the display. From these sections, surface data such as shading are used to define the simple three-dimensional shapes in the scene. Finally, "generalized cones" form the basis for the representation and recognition of complex shapes such as animals.

Marr (1982) asserts that since the early days of the Gestalt school "students of the psychology of perception have made no serious attempts at an overall understanding of what perception is" (p. 9). Some psychologists are equally skeptical of the reciprocal value of Marr's work. Kolers (1983), for example, comments that "although the study of human perceiving may continue to inform the study of machine vision, it remains to be seen whether students of computer vision will teach us much about human perceiving" (p. 160). For comments on Marr's work and other recent approaches to computer vision see Connell and Brady (1987), Fischler and Firschein (1987), Gregory (1981), Jackendoff (1987), Kitcher (1988), Kolers and Smythe (1984), Lowe (1987), and Rosenfeld (1986).

A theory that is closely related to Marr's approach has been proposed by Biederman (1985, 1987). Biederman describes a process by which an object in a two-dimensional image can be recognized. The process uses a set of primitive elements: 36 generalized-cone components called *geons*. These geons are derived from the combination of only five aspects of the edges of objects (e.g., curvature and symmetry). The process of interpreting a picture involves detecting the edge elements in an image, generating the resulting geons, combining these geons to produce meaningful forms, and matching them to known forms in the visual environment. Only 36 geons are needed for the perception of all possible images, a situation that is analogous to speech perception in which only 44 phonemes are needed to encode all the words in the English language. Biederman invokes evidence showing that the recognition of objects is robust across a wide range of viewing conditions (e.g., occluded views) and viewpoints (e.g., rotations in depth). Biederman's theory would appear to be in opposition to most other theorists, who contend that it makes little sense to talk of a "vocabulary" and "grammar" of picturing.

Another area that should be mentioned is neurophysiology. Kosslyn (1986, 1987) suggests how neurophysiology might be combined with artificial intelligence computational theory to yield a more complete understanding of vision. After all, Kosslyn observes, perception and cognition are something the brain does. The extreme belief regarding the potential importance of neurophysiology is expressed by Kitcher (1988): "Ultimately, all phenomena currently regarded as psychological will either be explained by neurophysiology or not at all" (p. 10).

33.2.2 Implications for Media Researchers: An Example

Picture perception theorists have challenged many of our orthodox beliefs about pictures. For example, consider the question of what constitutes "realism" in pictures. In the media research literature, realism is generally defined as matter of faithfully copying nature. A picture is said to be "realistic" to the degree that it mirrors the visual information provided by the real-world referent, and researchers studying the effects of pictorial realism have manipulated "realism cues" such as amount of detail, color, and motion. The outcomes of this research have been frequently disappointing.

Picture perception theorists have offered alternatives to the simple "copy theory" of realism. Although Gibson's approach stresses the fidelity of picture to referent, he adds the qualification that a successful picture copies the *invariant* visual information in nature—the optical data about reality that remains constant across time and across different views of an object. Goodman (1976) contends that realism is ". . . not a matter of copying but of conveying. It is more a matter of 'catching a likeness' than of duplicating—in the sense that a likeness lost in a photograph may be caught in a caricature" (p. 14). For Gombrich, the criteria for realism are not in nature, but in the perceiver's head in the form of expectations for what pictures of a given type "should" look like. These expectations are built up during extensive experience with the prevailing pictorial system and function as the standards for judging realism. Arnheim argues that perceptions of realism are relative to pictorial style and are particularly influenced by how a style represents what we know about an object (conceptual reality) compared to what the object looks like (perceptual reality). Marr and Biederman propose bottom-up theories that focus on the match between abstract elementary forms in pictures and their referents.

Thus contrasting the copy theory of pictorial realism with those of picture perception theorists, the copy theory emphasizes the exact visual match between pictures and referents, whereas theorists emphasize the nature of departures of picture from reality—surface level vs. deeper semantic, psychological stimulus only vs. contribution of perceiver also.

33.3 MEMORY MODELS, COGNITIVE LOAD THEORY, AND MULTIPLE REPRESENTATIONS

33.3.1 Memory Models

There is significant evidence that generally memory for pictures is better than memory for words. This consistent finding is referred to as the *picture superiority effect*. At least three significant theoretical perspectives have been used to explain the picture superiority effect, including (a) the dual-code model, (b) the single-code model, and (c) the sensory-semantic model.

Proponents of the dual-code theory argue that there are two interdependent types of memory codes, verbal and nonverbal, for processing and storing information (Paivio, 1971, 1978, 1990, 1991). The verbal code is a specialized system for processing and storing verbal information such as words and sentences. The nonverbal system "includes memory for all nonverbal phenomenon, including such things as emotional reactions, this system is most easily thought of as a code for images and other 'picture-like' representations (although it would be inaccurate to think of this as pictures stored in the head)" (Rieber, 1994, p. 111). If it is assumed, as Paivio does, that the dual coding of pictures in verbal and nonverbal memory is more likely to occur for pictures than words, then the "picture superiority effect" could be explained using dual-coding theory.

Proponents of a single-code model argue that visual information is transformed into abstract propositions stored in semantic memory (Anderson, 1978; Kieras, 1978; Kosslyn, 1980, 1981; Pylyshyn, 1981; Rieber, 1994; Shepard, 1978). Advocates for a single-code model argue that pictures activate a single semantic memory system differently than do words. Individuals "provided with pictures just naturally spend more time and effort processing pictures" (Rieber, 1994, p. 114).

Picture superiority can also be explained using a sensory-semantic model (Nelson, 1979). There may be a more distinctive sensory code for pictures or the probability that pictures will be processed semantically is greater than that for words (Levie, 1987; Nelson, Reed, & Walling, 1976; Smith & Magee, 1980). In many cases researchers in educational communications and technology have neglected the work that has been done concerning memory models.

33.3.1.1 Cognitive Load Theory. We believe that it is critical for instructional design researchers to be aware of the knowledge and breakthroughs that have been made by researchers in cognitive science concerning human cognitive architecture and a particular instructional theory based on current cognitive science research. In this section we provide a brief summary of a particular information processing view (IPV) of human cognitive architecture similar to the one presented in the learning and memory section. We then describe an instructional theory based on this IPV.

In our discussion of memory models we presented an IPV of human cognitive architecture. An IPV assumes that humans have a limited working (conscious) memory and a long-term memory (Miller, 1956). There is evidence that only seven elements can be stored in working memory at a given time (Miller). Individuals are not conscious of the information stored in long-term memory. On the other hand, there is evidence that humans have the ability to store almost unlimited amounts of information in long-term memory (Sweller, Van Merrienboer, & Pass, 1998). Sweller et al. suggest that individuals real intellectual power lies in their knowledge stored in long-term memory. The implications for instructional design are that we should not emphasize general reasoning strategies that use working memory but, rather, promote the acquisition of knowledge in specific domains.

An additional component of human cognitive architecture is that of schema. A schema is a network of information or classification of elements according to the way that they will be used. Schemas are stored in long-term memory. Consider the following example. If one asks an educational researcher to write a research paper using APA style, an experienced writer will already know what APA style is and will have knowledge of the following elements: order of presentation, heading structure, in-text citation format, and reference list. A schema has been developed and stored for "APA" style. Most researchers that are true experts at writing research papers using APA style will automatically be able to recall and use their schema for an APA-style paper without performing any means–ends analysis including the elements of APA style.

In summary, humans have limited working memory and almost-unlimited long-term memory, and they develop schemas that may become automated and used to solve particular problems. The result of schema development is a reduction in the load on working memoy. The goal of instruction should be to help learners develop and automate schemas.

Cognitive load refers to the resources used by working memory at a given point in time. Two types of cognitive load have been identified in particular: instrinsic cognitive load and extraneous cognitive load (Sweller et al., 1998). Intrinsic cognitive load refers to the load placed on working memory by "difficult-to-learn" content. Extraneous cognitive load is the working memory load resulting from poorly designed instructional message materials and poor instructional designs. In any case, if working memory is cognitively overloaded, the desired learning will not be accomplished. We believe that researchers investigating how pictures and animated graphics can help or hinder learning should consider the implications of cognitive load theory.

33.3.1.2 Multiple Representations.
It is now common for multiple representations to be used in instructional programs and situations. For example, students can now learn how to solve quadratic equations algebraically, or they can learn to draw the "right" picture. Concepts and content can be represented using pictures, animations, spreadsheets, graphs, and a number of other external representations. Research on using multiple representations in instruction has yielded conflicting results (Ainsworth, 1999). Ainsworth suggests that one finding that is consistent across a number of studies investigating multiple representations in multimedia. It is difficult for students to see the relationship between the multiple representations used. The translation process may place a heavy demand on short-term memory and cognitive overload occurs. Ainsworth suggests that if we are to develop principles for incorporating effective multiple external representations (MERs) in learning situations, we must consider the functions of MERs.

Anisworth (1999) identifies three primary functions of MERs in learning environments, "to complement, constrain, and construct" (p. 134). The complimentary function involves using "representations that contain complementary information or support complementary cognitive processes"; when using the constrain function of MERs, "one representation is used to constrain possible (mis)interpretations in the use of another"; the construct function involves using MERs to "'construct deeper' understanding of a situation" (p. 134). For each of the functions of MERs Ainsworth has identified, she has also identified a number of subfunctions and discussed using MERs to support more than one function. We attempt to present only the gist of her perspective her. A detailed discussion can be found in Ainsworth (1999).

Ainsworth also suggests that the selection of particular MERs has implications for how learning will be measured when incorporating MERs in instructional situations. For example, when MREs are used to complement information or processes or to constrain interpretation, it is not critical for the learner to understand the relationship between the representations, so that measurement of performance on MERs in isolation is appropriate. In contrast, for MERs designed to facilitate deeper understanding, it is important to assess the relationship between MERs. As with cognitive load theory, the authors believe that Ainsworth's discussion of the functions of multiple representations can be very useful to researchers interested in the effect of static pictures and animated graphics on learning.

33.4 PICTURES AND KNOWLEDGE ACQUISITION

33.4.1 Literature Search and Reviews

Through various on-line and manual literature searches, 2,235 primary research studies, reviews, books, conceptual papers, and magazine articles were identified, collected, and catalogued. The literature search was limited to the categories of static and animated graphics and knowledge acquisition. Many of the documents collected were not appropriate for the current review. For example, numerous papers reported the results of memory recognition studies including pictures. In addition, several studies were not included because of methodological flaws such as failing to include a control group or appropriate statistics. Many of the papers identified were not primary research studies or theoretical in nature. A total of 168 primary research studies was included across the two categories (static illustrations and animated graphics) used for the review. We first report the results of earlier literature reviews. Then an abridged guide to the literature is presented.

33.4.1.1 Static Pictures and Knowledge Acquisition.
In this section we first present a summary of earlier reviews of the literature concerning the role of static pictures in the acquisition of knowledge. We then discuss the results of our literature search and summary. A similar approach is used for animated pictures and knowledge acquisition.

33.4.1.2 Static Pictures and Knowledge Acquisition: Literature Reviews.
Spaulding (1955) reviewed 16 research studies using pictorial illustrations conducted between 1930 and 1953. Based on the findings of the 16 studies, Spaulding concluded that illustrations (a) are effective interest-getting devices, (b) help the learner interpret and remember the

content of the illustrated text, (c) are more effective in realistic color than black and white, but the amount of effectiveness might not always be significant, (d) will draw more attention if they are large, and (e) should conform to eye movement tendencies.

Samuels (1970) reviewed a series of 23 studies that investigated the effects of pictures on learning to read words, on reading comprehension, and on reader attitudes. Samuels's review covered the time span from 1938 to 1969. The studies reviewed included such treatments as (a) learning to read words in isolation with and without pictures, (b) acquiring a sight vocabulary with and without pictures, (c) using pictures as a response alternative in a reading program, and (d) using pictures as prompts. Samuels concluded that (a) most studies show that, for acquisition of a sight vocabulary, pictures interfere with learning to read, (b) the majority of studies indicate that pictures used as adjuncts to printed text do not facilitate comprehension, and (c) pictures can influence attitudes. Many of the studies reviewed by Samuels were narrowly focused on the use of illustrations to learn to decode words in isolation. Illustrations used in the context of learning to read have generally not proved to facilitate learning.

An analysis of the pictorial research in science instruction has also been conducted (Holliday, 1973). The general conclusions reached by Holliday concerning the effect of pictures on science education were that (a) pictures used in conjunction with related verbal material can aid recall of a combination of verbal and pictorial information; (b) pictures will facilitate learning if they relate to relevant criterion test items; (c) pictorial variables such as embellishment, size, and preference are complex issues, and there are almost-infinite interrelationships among picture types, presentation formats, subject content, and individual learner characteristics.

Concannon (1975) reviewed a number of studies on the effects of illustrations in children's texts (mainly basal readers). Concannon summarized the results of her review with the single conclusion that when pictures are used as motivating factors, they do not contribute significantly to helping a young reader decode the textual information.

Levin and Lesgold (1978) reviewed studies of prose learning with pictures and concluded that pictures do facilitate prose learning when five ground rules are adhered to.

1. Prose passages are presented orally;
2. The subjects are children;
3. The passages are fictional narratives;
4. The pictures overlap the story content; and
5. Learning is demonstrated by factual recall. (pp. 234–235)

Although Levin and Lesgold (1978) focused on oral prose, they also suggest that pictures may benefit individuals reading for comprehension.

Schallert (1980) reviewed a number of research studies and presented the case for and against pictures in instructional materials. In the case against pictures Shallert reviewed the work of Samuels (1967, 1970) and others. Shallert states that "the most convincing evidence against the use of illustrations in children's text has been marshaled by Samuels" (p. 505). Shallert noted

that many of the early reviews completed by Samuels, Concannon, and others reported that the use of pictures serving as motivating factors do not facilitate a child's ability to decode text information. Shallert indicated that some of the reasons the pre-1970 studies did not identify picture effects were that (a) the primary emphasis in the word acquisition treatments were speed and efficiency—with the words being spoken aloud, pictures used in that context are of little value; (b) the illustrations used in many studies were not meant to convey new information and were used only as adjuncts to the text; (c) many illustrations used in basal readers vaguely relate to the contextual information in the text; and (d) the effects of illustrations on long-term memory were not measured in these earlier studies.

In the case supporting positive picture effects Shallert (1980) reviewed a series of studies that covered the time period from 1972 to 1977. The general conclusions reached by Schallert were that pictures can help subjects learn and comprehend text (a) when the pictures illustrate information central to the text, (b) when they represent new content important to the overall message being presented, (c) when they help depict the structural relationships covered by the text, and (d) if the illustrated information contributes more than a simple second rehearsal of the text.

Readence and Moore (1981) conducted a metanalytic review of the literature on the effect of experimenter-provided adjunct pictures on reading comprehension. The 16 studies reviewed included 2,227 subjects and incorporated a total of 122 measures of association between the use of adjunct pictures and reading comprehension. The overall results across all studies revealed only minimal positive effects on reading text and subsequent reading comprehension when using adjunct pictures. The magnitude of picture effects was more substantial for university subjects who read text containing adjunct pictures.

One of the most comprehensive reviews of the effects of illustrated text on learning was done by Levie and Lentz (1982). The Levie and Lentz (1982) review compared three separate areas concerning the role of illustration in learning: (a) learning illustrated text information, (b) learning nonillustrated text information, and (c) learning using a combination of illustrated and nonillustrated text information. Studies included in the Levie and Lentz review cover the time period from 1938 to 1981. Levie and Lentz also present a functional perspective, which could be used to explain how illustrations might function to facilitate learning. Functional frameworks are covered in detail in a later section.

Summarizing the results across all studies included in their review, Levie and Lentz (1982) drew three primary conclusions: (a) Learning will be facilitated when the information in the written text is depicted in the illustrations; (b) learning of text material will not be helped or necessarily hindered with illustrations that are not related to the text; and (c) when the criterion measure of learning includes both illustrated and nonillustrated text information, a modest improvement may often result from the addition of pictures.

Using Levin's (1981) framework to classify pictures according to the function they serve in prose learning, Levin, Anglin, and Carney (1987) conducted a metanalysis of the pictures in prose studies. The reviewers concluded that for pictures (not

TABLE 33.1. Summary of Primary Research Studies Included in the Literature Survey

Studies	Total Number	Audience by Experiment			Results by Study	
		Y	H	A	SD	NSD
Static pictures	90	75	16	29	81	33
Animation	78	15	5	72	43	27

Note. Subject classifications: Y—young children, elementary school, and middle school; H—high school; A—adult. SD, significant differences; NSD, nonsignificant differences. Mixed effects were identified in selected studies. Some studies included more than one experiment.

mental images), serving a representation, organization, interpretation, or transformation function yielded at least moderate degrees of facilitation. A substantial effect size was identified for the transformation function.

One of the most significant programs of research on visual learning has been conducted by Dwyer and his associates (Dwyer, 1972, 1978, 1987; Levie & Lentz, 1982; Rieber, 1994). The research program is unique in several ways. The studies in the Dwyer series used similar stimulus materials. In particular, the stimulus materials included a 2,000-word prose passage describing the parts, locations, and functions of the human heart along with various types of visual materials including line drawings, shaded drawings, and photographs in black and white and in color. The materials were delivered in a number of formats and combinations including written prose with illustrations, a slide tape program with audio, television, and computer-based. In addition, a rationale was provided for the inclusion of visual illustrations in the treatments. If the information tested in a particular section of the text material was not difficult for the student (did not require external visualization), visual information would not be included and tested for this section of the text. Several types of criterion measures were developed by Dwyer and his associates including a drawing test, an identification test, a terminology test, and a comprehension test. The research has been conducted with over 48,000 students (Dwyer, 1972, 1978, 1987).

Levie and Lentz (1982) conducted a metanalysis using the treatments developed by Dwyer and presented in a text format or programmed booklet. All studies included in the metanalysis included a text-only condition. Based on 41 comparisons of treatments with text plus prose vs. with text only using four criterion measures (drawing test, identification test, terminology test, comprehension test), Levie and Lentz (1982) reported that 36 comparisons favored illustrated text and 4 favored text alone (see Appendix 33.1). As with other reviews of literature discussed, one conclusion that can be drawn from the work of Dwyer and his colleagues is that visuals are "effective some of the time under some conditions" (Rieber, 1994, p. 132). Space limitations do not permit a more detailed discussion of the Dwyer (1972, 1978, 1987) series.

33.4.1.3 Guide to the Literature: Static Illustrations.
Based on our literature search, 90 studies investigating the role of static pictures in knowledge acquisition were identified. The 90 studies were conducted with more than 13,528 subjects ranging from elementary-school children to adults. (See Table 33.1.) All of the studies included at least one comparison of learning with prose and static visual illustrations of various types vs. with a prose-only treatment. A number of the studies included written

prose materials, whereas others included prose presented orally. It should be noted that many of the studies summarized included other comparisons irrelevant to this review, and they are not discussed. In the 118 experiments included in the 90 studies, 102 significant effects for treatments including text and visual illustrations vs. text only were identified. The results of the "box score" summary indicate that static visuals can have a positive effect on the acquisition of knowledge by students. The treatments used were varied and many of the studies were not based on a particular theoretical perspective. In many of the studies it was not possible to identify the role or function of the visual illustrations in the instructional treatments. Examples of visuals and criterion measure items should be included more regularly in published studies. It was also difficult to determine what type of information was tested using the criterion measures in many of the studies. The reliability coefficients of the criterion measures were infrequently reported in the studies reviewed. In addition, few of the studies have been replicated. Notable exceptions are the research programs of Dwyer and Levin. A more detailed summary of each study is reported in Appendix 33.2. The studies by Dwyer and his associates that are reported in Appendix 33.1 are not duplicated in Appendix 33.2.

Based on our review of reviews of the literature and our own literature summary concerning the role of visual illustrations and knowledge acquisition, we still agree with a conclusion stated by Levie (1987):

It is clear that "research on pictures" is not a coherent field of inquiry. An aerial view of the picture research literature would look like a group of small topical islands with only a few connecting bridges in between. Most researchers refer to a narrow range of this literature in devising their hypotheses and in discussing their results. Similarly, authors of picture memory models, for example, take little notice of theories of picture perception. (p. 26)

One of the primary reasons much of the research on the role of visual illustrations in knowledge acquisition is not easily integrated is that the role or function of the pictures and illustrations in the instructional treatments is not identified. We feel that it is critically important to determine, in advance of conducting research, the particular functions of the visual illustrations.

33.4.1.4 The Use of Functional Frameworks in Static Visual Research.
Despite the considerable amount of research concerning how static visuals facilitate learning, many empirical research studies reflect an unclear perception on the part of researchers of the manner in which illustrations function in facilitating learning. A number of researchers have provided a variety of functional frameworks that may provide assistance

in classifying static visuals into meaningful functional categories (Alesandrini, 1984; Brody, 1984; Duchastel & Waller, 1979; Levie & Lentz, 1982; Levin, 1981; Levin et al., 1987). We provide a brief summary of several functional frameworks.

Two taxonomies have been proposed that take a morphological approach (what an illustration physically looks like) to picture classification (Fleming, 1967; Twyman, 1985). But classifying the role of pictures on the basis of "form" rather than "function" has not proven to be very useful (Duchastel & Waller, 1979). According to Duchastel and Waller, what is needed is not a taxonomy of illustrations but a grammar of illustrations that provides a functional set of principles that relate illustrations to the potential effects they may have on the learner.

Duchastel (1978) identified three general functional roles of illustrations in text: (a) an attentional role, (b) a retentional role, and (c) an explicative role. The attentional role relies on the fact that pictures naturally attract attention. The retentional role aids the learner in recalling information seen in an illustration, and the explicative role explains, in visual terms, information that would be hard to convey in verbal or written terms (Duchastel & Waller, 1979). Duchastel and Waller concluded that the explicative role of illustrations provides the most direct means with which to classify the role of illustrations in text. Seven subfunctions of explicative illustrations were identified by Duchastel and Waller.

1. Descriptive. The role of the descriptive function is to show what an object looks like physically.
2. Expressive. The expressive role is to make an impact on the reader beyond a simple description.
3. Constructional. The intent of the constructional role is to show how the parts of a system form the whole.
4. Functional. The functional role allows a learner to visually follow the unfolding of a process or the organization of a system.
5. Logico-Mathematical. The purpose of this role is to show mathematical concepts through curves, graphs, etc.
6. Algorithmic. The algorithmic role is used to show action possibilities.
7. Data-Display. The functional role of data-display is to allow quick visual comparison and easy access to data such as pie charts, histograms, dot maps, or bar graphs. (pp. 21–24)

An alternative functional framework, offered by Levie and Lentz (1982), suggests that a functional framework include classifying illustrations in text based on how they impact a learner in attending, feeling, or thinking about the information being presented. Their framework contains four major functions: (a) attentional, (b) affective, (c) cognitive, and (d) compensatory. The attentional function attracts or directs attention to the material. The affective function enhances enjoyment or, in some other way, affects emotions and attitude. Illustrations serving a cognitive function facilitate learning text content through improving comprehension, improving retention, or providing additional information. The last functional role identified by Levie and Lentz is the compensatory role, which is used to accommodate poor readers. Levie and Lentz, after reviewing a large number of studies containing 155 experimental comparisons of learning, have found much empirical support for the utility of their functional framework. Such a framework can help researchers sort out the functions that illustrations perform and

can be used to identify the ways illustrations should be designed and used for specific cases (Levie & Lentz).

A functional framework that has proved to be useful in explaining differences in research studies concerning pictures and prose is provided by Levin (1981). Levin contended that different types of text-embedded pictures serve five prose learning functions: (a) decoration, (b) representation, (c) organization, (d) interpretive, and (e) transformation. The decoration function is associated with text-irrelevant pictures (e.g., pictures used to make a written text more attractive) and does not represent the actors, objects, and activities happening in the text. Representational pictures are associated with text-relevant pictures and do represent the actors, objects, and activities happening in the text. The role of organizational pictures is to provide an organizational structure giving the text more coherence. Interpretational pictures serve to clarify passages and abstract concepts or ideas that are hard to understand. Transformational pictures are unconventional and not often found in traditional textbooks. Transformational pictures are designed to have a direct impact on a learner's memory (e.g., pictures used as a mnemonical aid serves a transformation function).

After reviewing the frameworks offered by Duchastel, Levin, Levie and Lentz, and others, Brody (1984) suggests that many of the specific functions identified within these frameworks do not clarify how pictures function in instructional settings. First, some functions are too broad or general in nature and add little to gaining an understanding of the instructional roles served by visuals. As an example, Brody contends that a single picture can increase comprehension in multiple ways such as gaining attention, repeating information, offering new information, and providing additional examples. A broad functional role such as increasing prose comprehension does not provide an adequate explanation of how a picture is to be used to affect prose comprehension (Brody). Brody also suggests that many previously defined functional roles of pictures are often too narrow in their view. In an effort to ameliorate the limitations of previously identified functional roles of pictures, Brody offers his own set of representative instructional functions served by illustrations. Brody's approach to creating a potentially more useful functional framework was to identify functions in terms of what occurs during the instructional process. Another prime objective was to make the functional framework as general as possible in scope; that is, to make the functions independent of the specific form of instruction, content area, or types of learning skills being taught. Brody identified 20 representative instructional functions served by pictures. A potential problem with Brody's classification system for determining the role of illustrations in instructional materials is that it already contains a large number of categories. To extend his classification scheme further would make it less practical for identifying the role of pictures in either research or instructional design practice.

Alesandrini (1984) states that some of the previous functional frameworks dealt only with representational pictures, that is, pictures that represent the actors, objects, and activities taking place in the text. Alesandrini notes that other frameworks also include arbitrary or nonrepresentational roles of pictures such as graphs and flowcharts in the functional mix. Alesandrini offers a functional framework based on how instructional pictures convey meaning. Based on previous work by Grooper and Knowlton, Alesandrini classifies the role of instructional pictures into three functions: (a) representational, (b) analogical, and (c) arbitrary. Representational pictures can convey information in a direct way through tangible objects or concepts or indirectly by the portrayal of intangible concepts that have no physical existence. Photos and drawings, or models and manipulatives, are examples of representational illustrations. Analogical pictures convey meaning by acting as a substitute and then implying a similarity for the concept or topic being presented. Arbitrary pictures (sometimes referred to as logical pictures) are highly schematized visuals that do not look like the things they represent but are related in some conceptual or logical way. Arbitrary illustrations include schematized charts and diagrams, flowcharts, tree diagrams, maps, and networks.

33.4.1.5 Static Visuals and Knowledge Acquisition: Conclusions.
Based on the conclusions of our review of earlier literature reviews and the studies we summarize in Appendixes 33.3 and 33.4, we conclude that static visual illustrations can facilitate the acquisition of knowledge when they are presented with text materials. However, the facilitative effects of illustrations are not present across all learning situations. It is very difficult to integrate the results across all studies due to the lack of connections (theoretical or functional) among many of them. We do offer the following broad conclusions regarding the effects of illustrated visuals on learning: (a) Illustrated visuals used in the context of learning to read are not very helpful; (b) illustrated visuals that contain text-redundant information can facilitate learning; (c) illustrated visuals that are not text-redundant neither help nor hinder learning; (d) illustration variables (cueing) such as size, page position, style, color, and degree of realism may direct attention but may not act as a significant aid in learning; and (e) there is a curvilinear relationship between the degree of realism in illustrations and the subsequent learning that takes place.

There has been substantial progress in understanding how static illustrations affect the learning process. However, much remains to be done. Validations for many of the functional frameworks summarized in this chapter need to be completed. Theory-based studies that are informed by both memory research and theories of picture perception are lacking. Specific studies incorporating a particular theory of picture perception and a particular memory model need to be conducted. Theory-based research will provide us with a deeper understanding of the mechanisms that contribute to the effectiveness or ineffectiveness of static illustrations in instructional materials. It is also not clear how students use illustrations in instructional materials or that they even know how to use them. A number of methods including eye movement measurements, student surveys, and simply questioning students while they are using visual illustrations will provide useful data on how students use or do not use illustrations. These data will be complementary to the results of the recall and comprehension studies already completed. In addition, studies are needed that attempt to identify effective strategies for using illustrations included in instructional materials. Assuming that strategies for effectively using illustrations are identified, studies will then be needed that consider effective ways to train students to use these strategies. The issue

of what constitutes "realism" in illustrations also needs to be reconsidered in light of the theories of picture perception discussed in this chapter. Many of the criterion measures (recall or comprehension tests) are administered immediately after the presentation of the instructional treatments. It is also important to determine if the illustration effects identified in many of the studies reviewed in this chapter are durable over time. Finally, few of the studies reviewed systematically controlled for the type of text or picture included. Perhaps the effects of illustrations on learning will vary according to the type of prose passage or picture used.

33.4.2 Animated Pictures and Knowledge Acquisition

In this section we first review the early research on the effect of animated visuals on learning. We then summarize more recent reviews of the literature concerning the role of animated visual displays and knowledge acquisition. Finally, we present the results of our literature search and analysis.

33.4.2.1 Animated Pictures and Knowledge Acquisition: Literature Reviews.
Early studies examining the effects of animated visuals on learning can be found in instructional film research. Freeman (1924) summarized 13 research studies that compared the effectiveness of various forms of visual instruction. The treatment formats used in the 13 studies included film, slides, lectures, still pictures, prints, live demonstrations, and stereographs. The motion treatments in these studies included the use of action pictures, animated drawings, and maps or cartoons. Based on the results of the 13 studies, it was concluded that motion or animated sequences in film are effective when (a) motion is a critical attribute of the concept being presented, and (b) motion is used to cue or drew the viewer's attention to the material being presented. It should be noted that the methodologies used in the 13 studies do not meet current standards for conducting comparative experimental research. A number of other investigators have conducted instructional film research that examined the effect of animated visuals on learning (Lumsdaine, Sultzer, & Kopstein, 1961; May & Lumsdaine, 1958; Weber, 1926). Several conclusions can be drawn based on the early research on the role of animated visuals in instructional materials, including that (a) animation (motion) can lead to positive learning effects if it is a critical attribute of the concept(s) being presented, (b) animation (motion) can increase learning of a complex procedural task, and (c) motion or action used primarily to enhance the realism of the presentation does not appear to have a significant effect on learning. It should be noted that the conclusions drawn are based on a limited number of studies where the motion variables were not usually tightly controlled.

Rieber (1990) summarized the results of 13 empirical studies investigating the role of animated graphics in computer-based instruction. Significant effects for animated treatments were found in five of the primary research studies reviewed. Based on the results of the 13 studies reviewed, Rieber presented three design recommendations for the use of animated visuals in instructional materials, including that (a) "animation should be incorporated only when its attributes are congruent to the learning task" (p. 79), (b) "evidence suggests that when learners are novices in the content area, they may not know how to attend to relevant cues or details provided by animation" (p. 82), and (c) "animation's greatest contributions to CBI may lie in interactive graphic applications (e.g., interactive dynamics)" (p. 82).

As discussed in the review of static visuals, a number of frameworks have been provided to classify static visual material. A similar functional approach would be appropriate for animated visual research. Rieber (1990) suggests that "generally, animation has been used in instruction to fulfill or assist one of three functions: attention-gaining, presentation, and practice" (p. 77).

More recently, Park and Hopkins (1993) identified five important instructional roles of animated visuals.

1. As an attention Guide—the animated visual can serve to guide and direct the subject's attention.
2. As an aid for illustration—dynamic visuals can be used as an effective aid to represent the structural and functional relations among components in a domain of knowledge.
3. As a representation of domain knowledge—movement and action can be used to effectively represent certain domain knowledge.
4. As a device model for forming a mental image—graphical animation can be used to represent system structures and functions which are not directly observable (e.g. blood flowing through the heart).
5. As a visual analogy or reasoning anchor for understanding abstract and symbolic concepts or processes—animation can make abstract and symbolic concepts (e.g. velocity) become more concrete and directly observable. (p. 19)

When both the characteristics of the domain knowledge and the characteristics of the subjects require one or more of these five instructional roles to be used, then animated visuals will most likely be effective (Park & Hopkins).

Using their functional framework, Park and Hopkins (1993) produced a research summary of 25 studies investigating the effects of animated versus static visual displays. The delivery medium for 17 of the studies was computer-based instruction, whereas the delivery medium for the remaining 8 studies was film or television. Fourteen of the studies yielded significant effects for animated visual displays. However, "the research findings do not consistently support the superior effect of animated visual displays. The conflicting findings seem to be related to the different theoretical rationales and methodological approaches used in various studies..." (p. 427).

One of the most interesting and rigorous programs of research on the effect of animation on learning has been conducted by Rieber (1989, 1994). The animation research conducted by Rieber included students across age groups, with realistic instructional content (Newton's laws of motion) and higher-level learning outcomes. As with the static visual research of Dwyer and his associates, the Rieber series of studies used animated graphics only when there was a need for external visualization. Results from the Rieber series are mixed and do not support the use of animated graphics across the board.

In summary, conclusions drawn from early reviews of the animation research literature are mixed. Rieber (1990) states that the few serious attempts to study the instructional attributes of animation have reported inconsistent results. "... CBI

designers... must resist incorporating special effects, like animation, when no rationale exists..." (p. 84).

33.4.2.2 Guide to the Literature.

Forty-two studies were located that included at least one animation treatment. Information concerning the authors, treatments, subjects, and results is reported in Appendix 33.5 (see also Appendix 33.6). Initially, we attempted to classify the animated treatments according to the function they performed (Park & Hopkins, 1993). However, we later abandoned the approach due to lack of specific information concerning the treatments. It was also difficult to classify many of the animated treatments as performing a single role using the classification system.

From the group of 42 studies a total of 45 comparisons was identified that included at least one animation treatment. Significant animation effects were identified in 21 of these comparisons. Animated treatments used by investigators have included various visual content such as animated illustrations, diagrams and visuals, real-time motion graphics, animated spatial visualization graphics, and animated interactive maps with blinking dots. General content areas covered by these studies include general science, physics, geometry, mathematics, statistics, and electronics. Subjects for these experiments ranged from mature adults to primary-school children in the first, second, and third grade. A variety of tests was used to measure learning outcomes including (a) learning of facts, concepts, and procedures, (b) problem solving and visual thinking, and (c) acquisition of cognitive skills that are primarily spatial or perceptual in nature.

How can the mixed results of the animation research be interpreted? Based on these "box score" results only, one could conclude that the use of animated graphics does not facilitate learning. However, methodological issues need to be considered. For example, in many of the studies it was not indicated if it was determined that there was a need for external visuals, static or animated. Perhaps reading text alone is adequate. In addition, many of the investigators did not provide a rationale for why motion is needed to indicate either changes over time or changes in direction. Text or text plus static graphics may be the optimal treatment if motion is not required. Many of the research reports reviewed did not specifically indicate that the animated sequences were text relevant or at least congruent with the text information presented. Also, both the information tested and the test type are critical considerations when investigating the learning effects for both static and animated graphic displays. It was not always possible to determine if the information tested was presented only in the animation, only in the animated sequence, or in both. It was also difficult to determine the function of the animated sequences. Using the lessons learned from static graphic research, more attention needs to be given to the functional role of animated sequences in research studies.

Such methodological problems call into question the results of these studies reporting insignificant animation effects. We believe that the comments of Rieber and of Park and Hopkins are still timely and appropriate. Rieber (1990) stated that "while speculative explanations for these studies which did not produce effects have been offered, many rival hypotheses linger rooted in general procedural flaws such as poor conceptualization of the research problem or inappropriate implementation of methods" (p. 84).

In a later review of the literature Park and Hopkins (1993) suggested that

> probably the most profound discrepancy separating the research is theoretical in nature. One important difference between studies which found significant effects of DVDs [animated visuals] and studies which found no such effects is that the former were guided by theoretical rationales which derived the appropriate uses for animated and static features of visual displays and their presumed effect. Accordingly, learner variables, the learning requirements in the task, and/or the medium characteristics were appropriately coordinated in most of the studies that found significant effects. (p. 439)

As is the case for static graphics, it is clear that facilitative effects are not present for animated treatments across all learning situations.

33.4.2.3 Animated Visuals and Knowledge Acquisition: Conclusions.

Unlike research pertaining to static visuals, which encompass many additional studies and dozens of treatment conditions, research on the effects of animated visuals is very limited. The early research lacked appropriate controls so that the specific effects of animation on learning cannot be determined. Results from the limited number of completed studies of the effect of animated visuals on learning are mixed. As discussed earlier, a number of the studies are methodologically flawed. Thus, the verdict is still out on the effect of animated treatments on student learning.

More research needs to be completed concerning the functions of animated visuals in learning materials. Rieber's and Park and Hopkins' contributions have provided a starting point for further work. Refinement and validation of the functional frameworks suggested by Rieber and by Park and Hopkins are needed. In addition, it has not been demonstrated if or how learners use an animated sequence in the learning process. The effect of experience, prior knowledge, and aptitude patterns on the effective use of animated visual displays needs to be considered. Also, will students who are naive to specific instructional content be able to determine that an animated sequence indicates changes over time or changes in direction and relate these changes to the specific content they are learning.? Perhaps students need specific training on how to use animated sequences for learning. In almost all of the animation studies we reviewed, students in an animated treatment condition received visualized instruction (an animated sequence) and were then tested verbally. It is an open question whether a verbal test covering content displayed in a visual animated sequence measures the learning that has occurred. Also, many animated sequences particularly in simulations include a significant amount of information incidental to the particular purpose of the instructional package. Studies investigating the effect of such animated treatments on incidental learning are needed. Few of the animation studies we reviewed considered the effects of developmental level on learning. Animated treatments may differentially affect older vs. younger students. Finally, as discussed earlier, Rieber has suggested that animation may be most effective in computer-based instruction when used in interactive graphic applications. Much work needs to be done in this promising area of inquiry. In any case, future research investigating the effect of animated visual displays on learning should (a) be based on a functional framework (i.e., Rieber or Park and Hopkins), (b) include content for which external visual information is needed and that requires the illustration of motion or the trajectory of an object, and (c) control for the effect of static graphics.

Whereas some progress had been made since the review by Anglin, Towers, and Levie (1996), it is apparent that we still know very little about the effect of animated visual displays on student learning. Given the proliferation of visual information in instructional material, it is imperative that the most effective strategies for using animated visuals be determined. Relative to the production of static visuals and text materials, the cost of producing animated sequences is high. Caraballo-Rios (1985) stated that "insisting on the used of computer animation in cases where it is not absolutely necessary should be considered an extravagance" (p. 4). Many additional theory-based studies including a range of content areas, audiences, treatment conditions, and learner characteristics are needed.

33.4.3 The Role of Static and Animated Visuals: Conclusions

We have emphasized the need for future research on the effect of static and animated graphics on learning. Some of the studies we reviewed are theory based, whereas others are not. It is difficult to draw general conclusions across all studies given the wide variety of topics and perspectives represented in the studies. This is true particularly for the studies incorporating animated graphics. It was also pointed out that functional frameworks have been helpful when attempting to explain conflicting results identified across various studies. The functional frameworks developed for static graphics have been particularly useful. However, we think it is now time for researchers to revaluate the functional frameworks that they are using in light of what we know about human learning and cognition. Consideration of cognitive load theory in conjunction with Ainsworth's (1991) taxonomy of multiple representations could provide a perspective that incorporates recent breakthroughs in human cognitive science with a functional framework that could be used for various external representations of concepts and content in instructional materials, including static animated and graphics (Sweller et al., 1998). Consideration of cognitive load theory and taxonomy of multiple representations would lead to a new set of research questions related to the effectiveness of static and animated graphics. Do the static pictures or animated graphics we include in instructional materials overload working memory, or do such pictures help reduce cognitive load and help the learner develop automated schemas? When should pictures and animated graphics be used as external representations? How should pictures and animated graphics function when used with other forms or external representation or with each other? Should they complement information and processes, constrain interpretation, or promote deeper understanding (Ainsworth, 1999)? What strategies will be effective is helping the learner understand the relationships among multiple representations when appropriate? In addition to new research questions, the use of cognitive load theory and a taxonomy of multiple representations also has implications for the assessment method researchers would use. In some cases it would be appropriate to assess the effectiveness of a single external representation on learning; in other cases it would be necessary to assess weather learners understand the relationships between multiple representations. In conclusion, we think that it is critical that new research concerning the effectiveness of visual representations on learning be well grounded in theory and that the functions of external representations, including static pictures and animated graphics, be identified.

33.5 CONCLUSIONS

We have briefly reviewed theories of picture perception, memory models, and cognitive load theory and presented a taxonomy of multiple external representations in instructional materials. Then a survey of existing studies and reviews concerning the effect of static and animated visuals on learning was presented. Significant progress has been made concerning our understanding of the effect of static and animated visuals on learning. Several problems are evident in the research reviewed.

For both static and animated graphics, the research is fragmented and sporadic. Notable exceptions are the research programs of Dwyer, Levin, and Rieber. Over the last 6 years, the scope of animation research has broadened. In addition, many of the researchers in instructional communication and technology have neglected the work on human cognitive architecture, memory models, perspectives on multiple external representations, and theories of pictures perception. Future research related to visual learning should derive from theories of picture perception and incorporate memory models. We believe that consideration of cognitive load theory and Ainsworth's (1999) taxonomy of multiple external representations would be very useful to researchers interested in examining the effect of static and animated graphics on student learning. There is much that we do not know about how to design effective visual representations. Future research strategies should be selected carefully to assure that we continue to make significant progress.

APPENDIX 33.1

TABLE 33.A1. Summary Matrix of Studies by Dwyer and His Associates

Study	Learners (N)	Drawing Test			Identification Test			Terminology Test			Comprehension Test		
		Better Version	Effect Size	Mean IT/ Mean TA	Better Version	Effect Size	Mean IT/ Mean TA	Better Version	Effect Size	Mean IT/ Mean TA	Better Version	Effect Size	Mean IT/ Mean TA
Dwyer (1967)	College (86)	IT	0.35	1.14	IT	0.34	1.09	IT	0.23	1.06	IT	0.02	1.00
Dwyer (1968)	9th grade (141)	IT	0.82	1.28	IT	0.57	1.24	TA	−0.10	0.96	TA	−0.17	0.94
Delayed retest	9th grade (129)	IT	0.36	1.09	IT	0.42	1.14	IT	0.27	1.06	IT	0.50	1.18
Dwyer (1969)	College (175)	IT	1.23	1.37	IT	0.67	1.17	IT	0.80	1.16	NSD	—	—
Dwyer (1972)	College (266)	IT	0.43	1.12	IT	0.26	1.07	IT	0.16	1.04	IT	0.11	1.03
Dwyer (1975)	College (587)	IT	0.82	1.16	IT	0.47	1.13	IT	0.52	1.11	TA	−0.04	0.99
Arnold & Dwyer (1975)	10th Grade (185)	—	—	—	—	—	—	IT	0.77	1.27	IT	0.90	1.22
Joseph (1978)	10th Grade (414)	IT	0.41	1.07	IT	0.14	1.02	TA	−0.12	0.98	IT	0.01	1.00
Delayed retest	10th Grade	IT	0.24	1.03	IT	0.13	1.02	IT	0.47	1.10	IT	0.23	1.04
de Melo (1980)	High school (48)	—	—	—	IT	0.23	1.11	IT	0.34	1.18	IT	0.36	1.15
Pictorial test	High school (48)	—	—	—	IT	1.42	1.72	IT	1.11	1.50	IT	0.52	1.23

Note. IT, illustrated text; TA, text alone; NSD, no significant difference. Dashes indicate that the value was not provided in the published report. From "Effects of Text Illustrations: A Review of Research," by W. H. Levie and R. Lentz, 1982, *Educational Communication and Technology Journal, 30*,30(4) p. 212, pp. 195–232. Copyright 1982 by the Association for Educational Communications and Technology. Reprinted by permission of the AECT.

APPENDIX 33.2   REFERENCE LIST OF DWYER SERIES REVIEWED BY W. HOWARD LEVIE (SEE APPENDIX 33.1)

Arnold, T. C., & Dwyer, F. M. (1975). Realism in visualized instruction. *Perceptual and Motor Skills, 40,* 369–370.

de Melo, H. T. (1981). Visual self-paced instruction and visual testing in biological science at the secondary level (Doctoral dissertation, Pennsylvania State University, 1980). *Dissertation Abstracts International, 41,* 4954A.

Dwyer, F. M., Jr (1967). The relative effectiveness of varied visual illustrations in complementing programed instruction. *Journal of Experimental Education, 36,* 34–42.

Dwyer, F. M. (1968). The effectiveness of visual illustrations used to complement programed instruction. *Journal of Psychology, 70,* 157–162.

Dwyer, F. M. (1969). The effect of varying the amount of realistic detail in visual illustrations designed to complement programmed instruction. *Programmed Learning and Educational Technology, 6,* 147–153.

Dwyer, F. M. (1972). The effect of overt responses in improving visually programmed science instruction. *Journal of Research in Science Teaching, 9,* 47–55.

Dwyer, F. M. (1975). On visualized instruction effect of students' entering behavior. *Journal of Experimental Education, 43,* 78–83.

Joseph, J. H. (1979). The instructional effectiveness of integrating abstract and realistic visualization (Doctoral dissertation, Pennsylvania State University, 1978). *Dissertation Abstracts International, 39,* 5907A.

APPENDIX 33.3 (pp. 880–893)

TABLE 33.A3. Summary Matrix of Research Results for Static Visuals

Study	Treatment	Contents	Subjects (N)	Depedent Variable(s)	Prose Type	Result(s)
Alesandrini & Rigney (1981) Experiment 1	1. Verbal + interactive graphics expansion 2. Verbal + computer game 3. Verbal + verbal expansion 4. Verbal + game	Science (battery cell)	Undergraduate (98)	1. A 37-item verbal test 2. A 27-item picture recognition test	Written	SD
Experiment 2	1. Verbal + pictorial review 2. Verbal + verbal review	Same	Undergraduate (50)	1. A 60-item verbal test 2. A 27-item picture recognition test	Same	NSD (verbal) SD (picture)
Alesandrini (1981)	1. Pictorial + learning strategy (3) 2. Verbal + learning strategy (3) 3. Verbal (read twice)	Science (battery cell)	College (383)	A 60-item test of (a) Knowledge (b) Comprehension (c) Application	Written	SD (holistic learning strategy)
Anglin & Stevens (1986)	1. Prose + pictures 2. Prose only	Science (water clock)	Undergraduate (42)	A 12-item multiple-choice test Immediate and 28 day delayed	Written	SD (immediate) NSD (delayed)
Anglin (1986) Experiment 1	1. Prose + picture 2. Prose only	Three human interest stories	Graduate (52)	15 short-answer paraphrase questions; immediate and 14 day delayed	Written	SD (immediate & delayed)
Experiment 2	Same	Same	Graduate (47)	Same, except delay increased to 28 days	Same	SD (immediate and delayed)
Anglin (1987)	1. Prose + picture 2. Prose	Three human interest stories	Graduate (30)	Recall test had 15 paraphrase questions on text-redundant information, 5 short-answer questions on text-only information (immediate and 55- day-delayed recall)	Written	SD for text-redundant information on immediate & delayed NSD for text only information
Arnold & Brooks (1976)	1. Verbal + pictorial integrated organizer 2. Verbal + pictorial nonintegrated organizer 3. Verbal + verbal integrated organizer 4. Verbal + verbal nonintegrated organizer	Eight organizationally complex paragraphs about unusual situations	Elementary school (32)	1. Total responses 2. Inferential responses 3. Recall responses 4. Correct responses	Oral	SD dependent on age and organizer type
Beck (1984)	1. Prose + pictorial cues 2. Prose + textual cues 3. Prose + combinational cues 4. Prose + noncues	12 passages and pictures based on carnivorous plants	Elementary school (256)	Recall 1-day-delayed multiple-choice test	Written	SD for combin-rational cueing only
Bender & Levin (1978)	1. Story + illustrations 2. Story + generate visual images 3. Story (listen twice) 4. Story (listen once)	20 sentence fictitious story	Mentally retarded children (96)	Recall scores 10 verbatim + 10 paraphrased questions	Oral	SD (illustrations) NSD (other 3 conditions)

880

Study	Conditions	Materials	Participants (N)	Dependent measures	Mode	Results
Bernard, Petterson, & Ally (1981)	1. Verbal organizer 2. Contextual image (picture) 3. No-organizer control 4. Placebo control	An 800-word passage about function of the brain	Undergraduate (104)	Recognition 18 paraphrase and nonparaphrase questions Immediate & delayed testing (2 weeks)	Written	SD for both verbal and image organizers NSD between them
Bieger & Glock (1984)	1. Ten combinations of text + pictures by information type 2. Nothing control Information types: nonoperational, operational, contextual, spatial, operational + contextual, operational + spatial	Two assembly tasks (hand truck & wall hanging)	Undergraduate (120)	1. Mean assembly times 2. Mean number of assembly errors	Written	SD depending on information type
Bluth (1973)	1. Prose + illustrations 2. Prose only	Two different cloze passages of 126 words each	Elementary school (80)	Cloze test measure of comprehension	Written	SD (good readers)
Borges & Robins (1980)	1. Story + appropriate context picture 2. Story + partial context picture 3. Story + no picture	Character motivation story	Undergraduate (120)	1. Recall based on 14 idea units 2. Mean comprehension rating	Oral	SD, appropriate > partial > no picture Bransford & Johnson (1972)
Bransford & Johnson (1972) Experiment 1	1. No context 1 (heard prose passage) 2. No context 2 (heard prose passage twice) 3. Context after (picture after passage) 4. Partial context (partial picture before passage) 5. Context before (picture before passage)	Fictitious prose passage	High school (50)	1. Mean comprehension 2. Mean recall score	Oral	SD, context picture before passage
Covey & Carroll (1985)	1. Text + line drawings 2. Text only	Three expository science passages of approximately 300 words each	Elementary school (132)	Recognition using 36-item multiple-choice test	Written	SD
Dean & Enemoh (1983)	1. Pictures before reading text 2. Pictures after reading text 3. Text only	Difficult geology passage containing 262 words	Undergraduate (90)	Total number of "idea units" recalled	Written	SD, picture before passage
DeRose (1976)	1. Prose + experimenter-provided illustration 2. Prose + instructions to summarize 3. Prose + experimenter-provided summary 4. Prose + instructions to image 5. Prose-only control	A 490-word passage from a social studies textbook	Middle school (192)	14 short-answer questions	Written	SD for experimenter-provided illustrations
Digdon, Pressley, & Levin (1985)	1. Object picture + no imagery instruction 2. Partial picture + no imagery instruction 3. Object picture + imagery instruction 4. Partial picture + imagery instruction	Two 10-sentence prose stories	Young children (160)	Set of cued recall questions	Oral	SD for object + partial pictures with and without imagery instruction

Continues

TABLE 33.A3. (Continued)

Study	Treatment	Contents	Subjects (N)	Depedent Variable(s)	Prose Type	Result(s)
	5. Object picture + partial picture + imagery instruction 6. Object picture + partial picture + no imagery instruction 7. Prose + imagery instruction 8. Prose + no imagery instruction					
Duchastel (1980)	1. Prose only 2. Prose + illustrations (illustrations conveyed the topical ideas)	A 750-word prose passage on energy	High school (77)	Retention by 1. Summary 2. Free recall 3. 30 short answers	Written	NSD
Duchastel (1981)	1. Prose + illustrations 2. Prose only	A 1,700-word history passage	High school (77)	1. Topical recall 2. Cued recall (36 questions) Immediate & 2 week delayed	Written	SD on 2-week-delayed only (recall test)
Durso & Johnson (1980) Experiment 1	1. Words (verbal orienting task) 2. Pictures (verbal orienting task) 3. Words (imaging orienting task) 4. Pictures (imaging orienting task) 5. Words (referential orienting task) 6. Pictures (referential orienting task) (pictures were line drawings of each of the 140 word concepts)	Contained 140 words, each a concept, chosen from Kucera & Francis word norms	Undergraduate (120)	A response of either a picture or a word was taken as an indication that the item was remembered as having been present during acquisition	Oral	SD for verbal orienting tasks only
Experiment 2	Same	Same	Undergraduate (60)	Free recall of the items presented	Same	Same
Gibbons et al. (1986)	1. Prose + visuals 2. Prose only	Dolls as actors performing in several settings	Young children (96)	1. Free recall 2. Reconstruction of story content	Oral	SD, audiovisual condition
Goldberg (1974)	1. Prose (incidental information) + Illustrations 2. Prose (incidental information)	Spelling and grammar exercise	Elementary school (216)	Incidental information: 12 recognition and 12 recall questions	Written	SD
Goldston & Richman (1985)	1. Prose + partial pictures during study 2. Prose + partial sentence repetition during study 3. Prose only	10-sentence narrative story	Elementary school (288)	Cued-recall measures	Oral	SD for partial pictorial cues
Guttmann, Levin, & Pressley (1977), Experiment 1	1. Imagery + prose 2. Partial pictures + prose 3. Complete pictures + prose 4. Prose only	Two short stories, each with a person, object, and thing	Young children & elementary school (240)	Cued recall, 20 questions	Oral	SD, kindergarten, for complete pictures only SD, third graders, for imagery = partial = complete SD, second graders, for complete > partial > imagery > control

882

Study	Materials	Conditions	Grade level (n)	Dependent measure	Mode	Results
Hannafin (1988)	Fictitious children's story	1. Pictures + oral 2. Pictures 3. Prose only	Elementary school (168)	Recall test-containing 24-item short answer of abstract and concrete items Immediate and delayed	Oral	SD, oral + pictures, immediate & delayed
Haring & Fry (1979)	A 360-word version of "Mercury and the Woodcutter"	1. Top-level + lower-level pictures + Prose 2. Top-level pictures + prose 3. Prose only (text-redundant line drawings)	Elementary school & middle school (150)	Free recall of both levels of idea units Immediate and 5 day delayed	Written	SD for top-level idea units for both immediate & delayed
Hayes & Readence (1983)	Four 400-word prose passages from illustrated educational texts	1. Two line drawings + prose + no instructions 2. Two line drawings + prose + instructions to pay careful attention to pictures 3. Prose + instruction to form images 4. Prose + no instructions	Middle school (108)	1. Mean score on information recalled 2. Mean proportion of inferences per information unit recalled	Written	SD of both illustrated conditions NSD between illustrated conditions
Hayes & Readence (1982)	Four 300-word science texts about simple machines	1. Two line drawings + prose + no instructions 2. Two line drawings + prose + instructions to pay careful attention to pictures 3. Prose + instruction to form images 4. Prose + no instructions	Middle school (82)	Student success at working study problems with text available	Written	SD, illustrated text with or without instructions
Hayes & Henk (1986)	How to tie a "bowline" knot	1. Pictures only 2. Pictures + prose 3. Prose only (five simple line drawings)	High school (102)	Nonverbal applied performance Immediate and 2 week delayed	Written	SD, pictures + prose & pictures, immediate testing only NSD between them
Holliday (1975)	Verbal prose (23 pages) about plant growth hormones	1. Textbook-like illustrations + verbal 2. Verbal	High school (80)	Verbal comprehension, 30-item multiple choice, administered orally	Oral	SD
Holliday & Harvey (1976)	Biology lesson on density, pressure, and Archimedes' principle	1. Adjunct labeled line drawings + prose 2. Prose only	High school (61)	Verbal quantitative (non-pictorial), multiple-choice test	Written	SD
Holmes (1987)	Fifteen passages of 150–200 words each; material from popular magazines	1. Prose + picture 2. Pictures 3. Prose only	Elementary school & middle school (116)	25 inferential questions	Written	SD, pictures + text > pictures > prose NSD, pictures vs. prose

Continues

883

TABLE 33.A3. (Continued)

Study	Treatment	Contents	Subjects (N)	Depedent Variable(s)	Prose Type	Result(s)
Jagodzinska (1976)	1. Prose + schematic correspondent illustration 2. Prose + realistic correspondent illustration 3. Prose + schematic supplement illustration 4. Prose + realistic supplement illustration 5. Prose Note: Above instructional conditions crossed with 2 text types (essential & nonessential), giving 10 total conditions	Two versions of a biology lesson	Middle school (200)	1. Reproduction (amount of material reproduced) 2. Text organization Both immediate and 2-week-delayed testing	Written	SD depending on picture type and its relationship to the text type
Jahoda et al. (1976) Experiment 1	1. Pictures + prose 2. Pictures 3. Prose only 4. Control	Expository text designed to be culturally free	Middle school & High school (938), Scotland, India, Ghana, Kenya	Recall scores, 10 pictorial or verbal questions of picture and text-redundant information	Written	SD for pictures + text NSD, pictures alone vs. text alone
Jonassen (1979)	1. Prose + single-screen presentation 2. Prose + three-screen presentation 3. Prose + four-screen presentation 4. Prose only	Biology lesson on four plant types	Middle school (363)	Criterion test of a verbal and visual classification exercise Immediate and 2 week delayed	Oral	SD, Four-screen condition on visual classification, immediate & delayed
Koenke & Otto (1969)	1. Prose + illustrations (both specifically relevant and generally relevant to passage) 2. Prose only	Three 198-word passages from Readers Digest	Elementary school & middle school (60)	Comprehension of main ideas	Written	SD (both picture types), sixth graders only
Koran & Koran (1980)	1. Picture before text 2. Picture after text 3. Text only	Science lesson on hydrologic cycle	Middle school (84)	23-item completion consisting of transformed and paraphrase questions	Written	SD for seventh graders regardless of picture placement NSD for eighth graders
Lesgold & DeGood & Levin (1977)	1. Prose + subject-illustrated story using cutouts on a background 2. Prose + coloring simple figures in a booklet	Sixteen prose stories, four of each type (50 vs. 100 words; one vs. two locations)	Elementary school (32)	Free and cued-recall scores	Oral	SD
Lesgold et al. (1975) Experiment 1	1. Prose + subjects made up illustrations from cutouts (some potentially interfering) 2. Prose + subjects copied or colored geometric forms during illustration phase	Five single-episode stories of 30–50 words each	Elementary school (24)	Oral recall	Oral	NSD

Experiment	Conditions	Materials	Subjects	Test		Results
Experiment 2a	1. Prose + subjects made up illustrations from fewer cutouts than experiment 1 2. Prose + subjects copied or colored geometric forms during illustration phase	Three stories of 5 sentences each	Elementary school (48)	Oral recall, both free and cued	Same	SD
Experiment 2b	1. Prose + experimenter-provided pictures 2. Prose + subjects copied or colored geometric forms during illustration phase	Same as 2a	Elementary school (24)	Same as 2a	Same	SD for both picture conditions NSD between the two picture conditions
Experiment 3	1. Prose + experimenter-provided pictures 2. Prose + subjects made up illustrations from fewer cutouts than experiment 1 2. Prose + subjects copied or colored geometric forms during illustration phase	Same as 2a	Elementary school (36)	Same as 2a	Same	SD for experimenter-provided pictures only
Levin & Berry (1980)						
Experiment 1	1. Prose + one colored, main-idea line drawing per passage 2. Prose only	Five human interest and novelty stories, from local newspapers, approximately 100 words each	Elementary school (50)	Six short-answer paraphrase questions per passage (30 total); half the questions about information in the pictures, the other half about information not in pictures	Oral	SD for pictured information
Experiment 2	Same (change was in time of testing only)	A sixth passage added	Elementary school (37)	Same but testing took place on 3-day-delayed basis	Same	SD
Experiment 3a	1. Single main idea picture + prose 2. Prose + prompt (verbal analogue of main idea for each passage)	Same	Elementary school (36)	16 main-idea questions	Same	SD
Experiment 3b	1. One main-idea picture/passage + prose 2. Prose + no prompting	Same as 3a	Elementary school (36)	16 main-idea questions plus 24 non-main-idea questions	Same	SD (both question types)
Levin (1976)						
Experiment 2	1. Prose + experimenter-provided culminating pictures 2. Prose + Experimenter-provided nonculminating pictures 3. Repetition condition (passage repeated once) 4. Activity control (passage + nonrelevant coloring activity) 5. Nonactivity control (passage only)	Three single-episode stories of 30 to 75 words each	Elementary school (61)	Cued-recall, 5 short-answer questions	Oral	SD
Experiment 3	Same (minus the activity control condition)	Two 10-sentence passages	Elementary school (64)	Cued recall, 10 questions/story	Same	SD

Continues

TABLE 33.A3. (Continued)

Study	Treatment	Contents	Subjects (N)	Dependent Variable(s)	Prose Type	Result(s)
Levin et al. (1983) Experiment 1	1. Prose + colored mnemonic illustrations 2. Prose only	Learn numerical order of 10 U.S. presidents	Middle school (46)	1. Total recall 2. Serial-position profile 3. Response latencies	Oral	NSD on total recall
Experiment 2 Experiment 3	Same + additional study trials added Same + 3 study trials added	Same Same	Middle school (40) High school (32)	Same + name recall added Total recall scores only	Same Same	NSD on total recall SD
Levin et al. (1982) Experiment 1	1. Key word context (word list + contextually explicit colored "key word" illustration) 2. Control condition (word list + experimenter read aloud + use own strategy)	Learn meanings of 12 challenging vocabulary words	Elementary school (30)	Total number of words defined correctly	Oral	SD
Experiment 2	1. Key word context (word list + contextually explicit colored "key word" illustration) 2. Picture context (colored illustration of words definition + read definition aloud) 3. Experiential context (read 3 sentences with definition + application question with word) 4. Control condition (word list + experimenter read aloud + use own strategy)	14 words to learn	Elementary school (64)	Same	Same	SD, Key word context best Picture better than experiential
Levin et al. (1983) Experiments 1a & 1b	1. Prose + organized mnemonic "key word" picture 2. Prose + organized single picture 3. Prose + separate pictures 4. Prose + subjects use own learning strategy	Short prose passages about distinguishing attributes of fictitious towns	Middle school (178)	1. Total number of attributes remembered via matching questions 2. Clustering score	Oral	SD, organized mnemonic "key word" NSD, separate picture
Experiments 2a & 2b	Same without organized separate picture condition (No. 2 above)	Same	Middle school (113)	Subject responses of (a) Verbatim correct (b) Essence correct	Same	SD, organized mnemonic "key word" NSD, separate picture
Levin et al. (1986) Experiment 1	1. Text + mnemonic pictures 2. Text + summary using fact mapping 3. Text + free study instructions	A 540-word text about minerals organized around "names"	Middle school (53)	Name and attribute recall testing	Written	SD for mnemonic pictures
Experiment 2	Same	Same except text organized around "attributes"	Middle school (115)	Same	Same	SD for mnemonic pictures

Study	Conditions	Materials	Population (n)	Dependent measure	Test format	Results
Mange & Parknas (1962)						
Experiment 1	1. Picture information slide + picture test slide 2. Picture information slide + word test slide 3. Word slide + picture test slide 4. Word slide + word test slide	Biology lesson on plant types	Middle school (228)	Retention of pictorial or verbal information	Written	SD when retention measured by pictorial testing
Experiment 2	Same	Same	College (81)	Same	Same	SD (same condition)
Experiment 3	1. Prose + filmstrip 2. Prose	Lesson on Greenland	Middle school (192)	Retention using both verbal and pictorial questions	Same	SD (same condition)
Main & Griffiths (1977)	1. Printed text + printed and pictorial supplement 2. Printed text + audio and pictorial supplement 3. Printed text + printed supplement 4. Printed text (control)	12 passages from a chapter on weather	Adult (120)	1. Vocabulary test 2. A 100-item sentence completion part 3. A 55-item multiple-choice section	Written Oral	SD, all experimental groups vs. control NSD between experimental groups
Mayer (1989)						
Experiment 1	1. Text + illustrations including labels 2. Text only	Vehicle braking systems	College (34)	95 idea units of both explanatory and nonexplanatory information	Written	SD on recall of explanatory information
Experiment 2	1. Text + labeled illustrations 2. Text + nonlabeled illustrations 3. Text only	Same	College (44)	Same	Same	SD on recall of explanatory information for labeled illustrations
McCormick et al. (1984)	1. Related text + separate mnemonic illustrations 2. Related text + integrated mnemonic illustration 3. Noninterference control (read 3 unrelated passages) 4. Interference control (read 3 related but potentially interfering passages)	Three fictitious biographical stories	College (160)	11 short-answer recall questions	Written	SD for integrated mnemonic illustrations
McCormick & Levin (1984)						
Experiment 1	1. Text + mnemonic pictures (key word-paired) 2. Text + mnemonic pictures (key word-chained) 3. Text + mnemonic pictures (key word-integrated) 4. Simple control (text + additional study each sentence) 5. Cumulative control (text + cumulative study of all sentences)	Four fictitious biographies	Middle school (220)	20 cued-recall questions	Written	SD for all three mnemonic conditions NSD between them
Experiment 2	Same except delete condition 2 above	Same	Middle school (82)	Name–attribute recognition test, both immediate and 2 day delayed	Same	SD for key word conditions, both immediate and delayed

Continues

887

TABLE 33.A3. (Continued)

Study	Treatment	Contents	Subjects (N)	Dependent Variable(s)	Prose Type	Result(s)
Miller (1938)	1. Prose + illustrations 2. Prose only	Three stories from basal readers	Elementary school (600)	Comprehension	Written	NSD
Moore (1975)	1. Illustrations + prose together 2. Illustrations before prose 3. Illustrations after prose 4. Prose only	Text on learning time from a sundial	Elementary school (63)	Comprehension, 20-item multiple-choice	Written	NSD
Nugent (1982) Experiment 1	1. Visuals + print + audio. 5. Visuals 2. Visuals + print. 6. Print. 3. Visuals + audio. 7. Audio. 4. Print + audio. 8. Control	Film about factual life of a cheetah	Elementary school & middle school (201)	23 multiple-choice comprehension test	Oral	NSD, single medium SD, dual media SD, three media
O'Keefe & Solman (1987) Experiments 1 & 2	1. Complex pictures before prose 2. Complex pictures after prose 3. Normal pictures before prose 4. Normal pictures after prose	Stories about 470 words in length	Elementary school (118)	Recall of semantic and logical network of story information	Written	NSD
Peeck (1974)	1. Prose + pictures 2. Pictures 3. Prose only	Passage from "Rupert Bear" story	Elementary school (71)	40 item retention test Immediate, 1-day- and 1-week-delayed testing	Written	SD, immediate and delayed testing
Peng & Levin (1979)	1. Prose + colored line drawings 2. Prose only	Two 10-sentence narrative stories	Elementary school (64)	Cued recall using paraphrase verbatim questions, both immediate and 3 day delayed	Oral	SD, immediate and delayed testing
Popham (1969)	1. Cartoon-embellished tape/slide version 2. Unembellished tape/slide version 3. Programmed text version	Program developed for public-school administrators	College (175)	1. Cognitive achievement (58 items) 2. Anonymous response (4 items)	Written Oral	NSD
Pressley, Pigott, & Bryant (1982) Experiment 1	1. Prose + completely matched picture 2. Prose + actor action picture 3. Prose + actor static picture 4. Prose + mismatched picture/object incorrect 5. Prose + incorrect object picture 6. Prose only.	Two lists of concrete sentences	Young children (126)	Correct recall responses	Oral	SD, matched pictures > prose only, prose only > mismatched pictures
Experiment 2	1. Prose + completely matched picture 2. Prose + actor action/object correct picture 3. Prose + actor static/object object picture 4. Prose only	Same	Young children (52)	Same	Same	SD, Matched pictures > action object > static object > prose only NSD, action object and static object

Study	Conditions	Materials	Population (N)	Test	Written/Oral	Result
Pressley et al. (1983) Collapsed experiments 1, 2, 2A, 3, & 3A	1. Prose + matched pictures 2. Prose + mismatched pictures 3. Prose only Note: Above basic conditions were combined with explicit or nonexplicit instructions regarding picture–text relationships	33 concrete sentences or 6 moderately difficult stories	Elementary school (414)	1. Cued-recall questions 2. Picture recognition in some instances	Written Oral	SD in all cases for matched pictures NSD for mismatched pictures vs. prose only
Rankin & Culhane (1970)	1. Typed format text with no illustrations 2. Printed format text with illustrations	A passage from "Pioneer Life in America"	Middle school (57) High school (22)	50 item cloze comprehension test	Written	NSD
Rasco et al. (1975) Experiment 1	1. Prose + drawings + Instructional strategy 2. Prose + drawings 3. Prose + instructional strategy 4. Prose only	A 2,511-word prose passage	Undergraduate (91)	35-item test with 28 true/false, 1 constructed response, and 6 multiple-choice questions on the verbal information in the text	Written	NSD
Experiment 2	Same	Same	High school (80)	Same	Same	NSD
Experiment 3	Same	Two shorter passages (429 words and 633 words)	Elementary school (93)	20 multiple-choice questions on verbal information	Same	SD, prose + strategy + pictures
Reid, Briggs, & Beveridge (1983)	1. Prose + colored illustrations 2. Prose + black-&-white illustrations 3. Prose only	Specifically written science topic, "structure and function of the mammalian heart"	Middle school (338)	1. Cloze test immediately 2. Objective test items, delayed 15 min	Written	SD for pictures on objective test NSD for pictures on cloze testing
Rice, Doan, & Brown (1981)	1. Prose + pictures 2. Prose only	Prose story, "Little Bear"	Elementary school (60)	Reading comprehension with an 11-item test	Written	SD
Riding & Shore (1974)	1. Prose + visuals 2. Prose only	Prose passage from "A Story of Rhodpis" containing 185 words	High school (100)	Recall test with 43 questions	Oral	SD
Rohwer & Matz (1975)	1. Prose + pictures 2. Prose only	Prose containing three passages	Elementary school (128)	Total number of assertions correctly verified	Oral	SD
Rohwer & Harris (1975)	1. Oral prose + written prose + pictures 2. Written prose + pictures 3. Oral prose + pictures 4. Oral prose + written prose 5. Pictures only 6. Oral prose only 7. Written prose only	Passages about two types of monkeys	Elementary school (186)	1. Short answers 2. Free recall 3. Verification of statements in text	Oral Written	SD, oral + pictures was superior
Royer & Cable (1976)	1. Abstract passage + illustrations 2. Unembellished abstract passage 3. Abstract passage with analogues 4. Concrete passage 5. Unrelated prose (control)	Science lesson on heat flow and electrical conductivity	College (80)	Recall of "idea units"	Written	SD

Continues

TABLE 33.A3. (Continued)

Study	Treatment	Contents	Subjects (N)	Depedent Variable(s)	Prose Type	Result(s)
Ruch & Levin (1977)	1. Partial test (partial pictures with each question) 2. Partial study (look at partial pictures during narrative) 3. Repetition (each sentence twice in succession) 4. Control (listened to text once).	Two 10-sentence narrative passages	Elementary school (112)	Cued recall 10 verbatim 10 paraphrase	Oral	SD (relative to other 3 conditions) for partial pictures during study on paraphrase questions only
Ruch & Levin (1979) Experiment 1	1. Reinstated picture condition (prose + partial picture at onset of passage and at question time) 2. Partial picture condition (prose + partial picture at onset of each passage) 3. Prose only	Two-sentence narrative passage making reference to an object	Elementary school (48)	Set of 10 "Wh—" questions containing both paraphrase and verbatim information	Oral	SD for reinstated picture condition only
Experiment 2	1. Reinstated descriptions (prose + partial picture at onset of passage & two-sentence verbal description prior to each question) 2. Reinstated pictures (prose + partial pictures both during story and questions) 3. Partial pictures only during story presentation 4. Prose only	Same plus two-sentence verbal description developed for each picture added	Elementary school (42)	Same	Same	SD, reinstated pictures > reinstated descriptions
Rusted & Coltheart (1979b)	1. Prose + simple line drawings 2. Prose only	Two sets of concrete nouns plus a short prose passage	Elementary school (32)	Mean recall, recognition and pronunciation scores	Written	SD
Rusted & Coltheart (1979a) Experiment 1	1. Prose + line drawings 2. Prose only	Six short factual passages of highly unusual plant or creatures	Elementary school (72)	Free recall, both immediate and 5–7 min delayed	Written	SD, both immediate and delayed testing
Experiment 2	1–3. Prose + three picture types 4–6. Three picture types alone 7. Prose Picture types: (a) line drawing, (b) colored drawing, (c) color and background	Same	Elementary school (100)	Number of features recalled, both immediate and delayed testing	Same	SD independent of picture type, both immediate and delayed testing
Rusted & Hodgson (1985)	1. Text + text-relevant and text-nonrelevant pictures 2. Text only	One factual and one fictitious passage	Middle school (40)	Oral recall scores	Written	SD for factual/expository text
Scruggs et al. (1985)	1. Mnemonic instruction (10 interactive illustrations) 2. Direct study (realistic colored illustration) 3. Free study (text only)	Passage describing 8 North American minerals	High school + LD (56)	Recall of mineral attributes	Written	SD, mnemonic condition

890

Study	Conditions	Materials	Subjects (N)	Measure	Presentation	Results
Sewell & Moore (1980)	1. Cartoon text (text + 43 cartoon embellishments) 2. Visual only (cartoon embellishment) 3. Audio/visual (audio + slides of cartoons) 4. Audio only 5. Printed text only	Cartoon strip used as passage	College (150)	Comprehension using 25-item multiple-choice test	Written Oral	SD, audio/visual
Sherman (1976)	1. Graphic partial before passage 2. Graphic partial after passage 3. Graphic complete before passage 4. Graphic complete after passage 5. Verbal partial before passage 6. Verbal partial after passage 7. Verbal complete before passage 8. Verbal complete after passage	Eight 70-word paragraphs (both concrete and abstract versions)	High school (144)	Free recall Total words, idea units, and thematic intrusions recalled	Written	SD for all graphics vs. all verbal conditions
Shriberg et al. (1892) Experiment 1	1. Prose + pictures plus (colored "key word" line drawings + 2 additional pieces of incidental information) 2. Prose + pictures (colored "key word" line drawings) 3. Prose (12 passages)	12 three-sentence passages about famous people	Middle school (48)	12 sets of test questions relating to passages	Written	SD for pictures NSD between picture conditions
Experiment 2	1. Prose + pictures plus (colored "key word" line drawings + 4 additional pieces of incidental information) 2. Imagery + name & key word pages	Same	Middle school (48)	Same	Same	SD
Silvern (1980)	1. Picture (listen + picture) 2. Play (listen + pretend in story) 3. Repetition (listen twice) 4. Control (listen once)	Two stories, each 10 sentences long	Young children (40)	Comprehension using 10 "Wh—" questions	Oral	NSD
Snowman & Cunningham (1975)	1. Pictures before relevant text 2. Pictures after relevant text 3. Pictures & questions before relevant text 4. Pictures & questions after relevant text 5. Questions before relevant text 6. Questions after relevant text 7. Text with no adjunct aids	A 2,189-word fictitious passage	Undergraduate (63)	Recall of specific factual information for both practiced and nonpracticed items	Written	NSD (with respect to type of adjunct aid)
Stone & Glock (1981)	1. Prose + text-redundant line drawings 2. Text-redundant line drawings 3. Text only	Directs for assembly of a "hand truck" toy	Undergraduate (90)	1. Number of assembly errors 2. Comprehension of reading the instructions	Written	SD (drawing + text)
Strommes & Nyman (1974)	1. Prose + mnemonic illustrations preceding each sentence 2. Prose only	Two 30-sentence stories of connected discourse	High school (30)	Immediate paced recall with pictures or empty frames; paced and free recall 1 year delayed	Written	SD for immediate but NSD for delayed testing

891

Continues

TABLE 33.A3. (Continued)

Study	Treatment	Contents	Subjects (N)	Depedent Variable(s)	Prose Type	Result(s)
Talley (1989)	1. Basal text + basal pictures 2. Story grammar + story grammar pictures 3. Literature + pictures 4. Basal text 5. Story grammar 6. Literature	Four stories from basal readers	Elementary school (72)	1. Comprehension questions 2. Recall measures	Written	SD for picture conditions
Thomas (1978)	1. Color photographs + text 2. Simplified line drawings + text 3. Text only	Prose from a science textbook	Elementary school (108)	1. Literal comprehension 2. Inferential comprehension	Written	NSD
Towers (1994) Experiment 1	1. Prose only 2. Prose + static visuals	Weather patterns	College (69)	10 short-answer paraphrase questions	Written	SD
Experiment 2	Note: These two experiments also contained an animated treatment that is not included in this summary	Same	College (64)	13 short-answer paraphrase questions + 4 comprehension questions	Same	NSD
Vernon (1953) Series 1 & 2	1. Prose + photographs 2. Prose + graphs (series 1 only) 3. Prose only	Expository short stories of 700–800 words each	High school (62)	Oral recall of verbal information (major points)	Written	NSD
Vernon (1954) Experiment 1	1. Prose + pictures 2. Prose only	Text from two small books 755 and 940 words in length	Elementary school & middle school (24)	Six fairly general questions related to text on recall measures	Written	NSD
Experiment 2	1. Prose + pictures cutout from book 2. Prose + four simple line drawings 3. Text + photographs	Text taken from book, *The Shape of Things*	Elementary School (60)	1. Number of items remembered 2. Question to test understanding	Oral	NSD
Vye et al. (1986)	1. Sentence + picture 2. Picture 3. Sentence Note: Above instructional conditions crossed with elaboration type (precise, imprecise), crossed with retrieval cue (verbal, pictorial), yielding 12 total instructional conditions	20 precise sentences and 20 imprecise sentences	Undergraduate (168)	Cued recall	Oral	SD for sentence + picture condition superior

892

Study	Conditions	Materials	Population (n)	Measures	Presentation	Results
Waddill, McDaniel, & Einstein (1988)						
Experiment 1	1. Prose + detailed pictures 2. Prose + relational pictures 3. Prose only	Two text types, a narrative fairy tale and an expository text	College (172)	1. Comprehension 2. Free recall 3. Cued recall	Written	SD dependent on text type and picture type
Experiment 2	Same + subjects instructed to attend to the type of information, not normally encoded from each text type	Same	College (72)	Same	Same	SD dependent on text type and picture type
Weintraub (1960)	1. Prose + pictures 2. Pictures only 3. Prose only	Three stories from selected basal readers	Elementary school (104)	Questions dealing with comprehension	Written	NSD
Weisberg (1970)	1. Prose + advanced organizer (graph) 2. Prose + advanced organizer (map) 3. Prose + advanced organizer (verbal) 4. Prose + no advanced organizer	Earth science concepts	Middle school (96)	40 questions, verbal multiple choice of knowledge content	Written	SD, map > graph > verbal > prose
Woolridge et al. (1982)	1. Partial pictures during prose & question phases 2. Partial pictures during question phase 3. Partial pictures during prose phase 4. Prose only	Two 10-sentence narrative paragraphs	Elementary school (80)	Two 10-sentence narrative paragraphs	Oral	SD

Note. NSD, nonsignificant difference; SD, significant static graphic effect.

APPENDIX 33.4. STUDIES LISTED IN THE MATRIX FOR STATIC VISUALS (SEE APPENDIX 33.3)

Alesandrini, K. L. (1981). Pictorial-verbal and analytic-holistic learning strategies in science learning. *Journal of Educational Psychology, 73*, 358-368.

Alesandrini, K. L., & Rigney, J. W. (1981). Pictorial presentation and review strategies in science learning. *Journal of Research in Science Teaching, 18*(5), 465-474.

Anglin, G. J. (1986). Prose-relevant pictures and older learners' recall of written prose. *Educational Communication and Technology Journal, 34*(3), 131-136.

Anglin, G. J. (1987). Effect of pictures on recall of written prose: How durable are picture effects? *Educational Communication and Technology Journal, 35*(1), 25-30.

Anglin, G. J., & Stevens, J. T. (1986). Prose-relevant pictures and recall from science text. *Perceptual and Motor Skills, 63*(3), 1143-1148.

Arnold, D. J., & Brooks, P. H. (1976). Influence of contextual organizing material on children's listening comprehension. *Journal of Educational Psychology, 68*, 711-716.

Beck, C. R. (1984). Visual cueing strategies: Pictorial, textual, and combinational effects. *Educational Communication and Technology Journal, 32*, 207-216.

Bender, B. G., & Levin, J. R. (1978). Pictures, imagery, and retarded children's prose learning. *Journal of Educational Psychology, 70*, 583-588.

Bernard, R. M., Petersen, C. H., & Ally, M. (1981). Can images provide contextual support for prose? *Educational Communication and Technology Journal, 29*, 101-108.

Bieger, G. R., & Glock, M. D. (1984). Comprehending spatial and contextual information in picture-text instructions. *Journal of Experimental Education*, 181-188.

Bluth, L. F. (1973). A comparison of the reading comprehension of good and poor readers in the second grade with and without illustration (Doctoral dissertation, University of Illinois at Urbana-Champaign, 1972). *Dissertations Abstracts International, 34*, 637A.

Borges, M. A., & Robins, S. L. (1980). Contextual and motivational cue effects on the comprehension and recall of prose. *Psychological Reports, 47*, 263-268.

Bransford, J. D., & Johnson, M. K. (1972). Contextual prerequisites for understanding: Some investigations of comprehension and recall. *Journal of Verbal Learning and Verbal Behavior, 11*, 717-726.

Covey, R. E., & Carroll, J. L. (1985, October). *Effects of adjunct pictures on comprehension of grade six science texts under three levels of text organization*. Paper presented at the annual meeting of the Evaluation Network/Evaluation Research Society, San Francisco, CA. (ERIC Document Reproduction Service No. 259-946)

Dean, R. S., & Enemoh, P. A. (1983). Pictorial organization in prose learning. *Contemporary Educational Psychology, 8*, 20-27.

DeRose, T. (1976). *The effects of verbally and pictorially induced and imposed strategies on children's memory for text*. Madison: Wisconsin Research and Development Center for Cognitive Learning, University of Wisconsin. (ERIC Document Reproduction Service No. 133-709).

Digdon, N., Pressley, M., & Levin, J. R. (1985). Preschoolers' learning when pictures do not tell the whole story. *Educational Communication and Technology Journal, 33*, 139-145.

Duchastel, P. C. (1980). Test of the role in retention of illustrations in text. *Psychological Reports, 47*, 204-206.

Duchastel, P. C. (1981). Illustrations in text: A retentional role. *Programmed Learning and Educational Technology, 18*, 11-15.

Durso, F. T., & Johnson, M. K. (1980). The effects of orienting tasks on recognition, recall, and modality confusion of pictures and words. *Journal of Verbal Learning and Verbal Behavior, 19*, 416-429.

Gibbons, J., et al. (1986). Young children's recall and reconstruction of audio and audiovisual narratives. *Child Development, 57*(4), 1014-1023.

Goldberg, F. (1974). Effects of imagery on learning incidental material in the classroom. *Journal of Educational Psychology, 66*, 233-237.

Goldston, D. B., & Richman, C. L. (1985). Imagery, encoding, specificity, and prose recall in 6-year-old children. *Journal of Experimental Child Psychology, 40*, 395-405.

Guttmann, J., Levin, J. R., & Pressley, M. (1977). Pictures, partial pictures, and young children's oral prose learning. *Journal of Educational Psychology, 69*, 473-480.

Hannafin, M. J. (1988). The effects of instructional explicitness on learning and error persistence. *Contemporary Educational Psychology, 13*, 126-132.

Haring, M. J., & Fry, M. A. (1979). Effect of pictures on children's comprehension of written text. *Educational Communication and Technology Journal, 27*, 185-190.

Hayes, D. A., & Henk, W. A. (1986). Understanding and remembering complex prose augmented by analogic and pictorial illustration. *Journal of Reading Behavior, 18*(1), 63-77.

Hayes, D. A., & Readance, J. E. (1983). Transfer of learning from illustration-dependent text. *Journal of Educational Research, 76*, 245-248.

Hayes, D. A., & Readence, J. E. (1982). Effects of cued attention to illustrations in text. In G. A. Niles & L. A. Harris (Eds.), *New inquiries in reading research and instruction* (pp. 60-63). *Thirty-first year book of the National Reading Conference*. Rochester NY: National Reading Conference.

Holliday, W. G. (1975). The effects of verbal and adjunct pictorial-verbal information in science instruction. *Journal of Research in Science Teaching, 12*, 77-83.

Holliday, W. G., & Harvey, D. A. (1976). Adjunct labeled drawings in teaching physics to junior high school students. *Journal of Research in Science Teaching, 13*, 37-43.

Holmes, B. C. (1987). Children's inferences with print and pictures. *Journal of Educational Psychology, 79*(1), 14-18.

Jagodzinska, M. (1976). The role of illustrations in verbal learning. *Polish Psychological Bulletin, 7*, 95-104.

Jahoda, G., Cheyne, W. M., Deregowski, J. B., Sinha, D., & Collingsbourne, R. (1976). Utilization of pictorial information in classroom learning: A cross cultural study. *AV Communication Review, 24*, 295-315.

Jonassen, D. H. (1979). Implications of multi-image for concept acquisition. *Educational Communication and Technology Journal, 27*(4), 291-302.

Koenke, K., & Otto, W. (1969). Contribution of pictures to children's comprehension of the main idea in reading. *Psychology in the Schools, 6*, 298-302.

Koran, M. L., & Koran, J. J. J. (1980). Interaction of learner characteristics with pictorial adjuncts in learning from science text. *Journal of Research in Science Teaching, 17*(5), 477-483.

Lesgold, A. M., DeGood, & Levin, J. R. (1977). Pictures and young children's prose learning: A supplementary report. *Journal of Reading Behavior, 9*, 353-360.

Lesgold, A. M., Levin, J. R., Shimron, J., & Guttmann, J. (1975). Pictures and young children's learning from oral prose. *Journal of Educational Psychology, 67*, 636-642.

Levin, J. R. (1976). What have we learned about maximizing what children learn? In J. R. L. & & V. L. Allen (Eds.), *Cognitive learning in children: Theories and strategies.* (pp. 105-134). New York: Academic Press.

Levin, J. R., & Berry, J. K. (1980). Children's learning of all the news that's fit to picture. *Educational Communication and Technology Journal, 28,* 177-185.

Levin, J. R., McCormick, C. B., Miller, G. E., Berry, J. K., & Pressley, M. (1982). Mnemonic versus nonmnemonic vocabulary-learning strategies for children. *American Educational Research Journal, 19,* 121-136.

Levin, J. R., Morrison, C. R., McGivern, J. E., Mastropieri, M. S., & Scruggs, T. E. (1986). Mnemonic facilitation of text-embedded science facts. *American Educational Research Journal, 23,* 489-506.

Levin, J. R., et al. (1983). Learning via mnemonic pictures: Analysis of presidential process. *Educational Communication and Technology Journal, 31*(3), 161-173.

Levin, J. R., Shriberg, L. K., & Berry, J. K. (1983). A concrete strategy for remembering abstract prose. *American Educational Research Journal, 20*(2), 277-290.

Magne, O., & Parknas, L. (1962). The learning effects of pictures. *British Journal of Educational Psychology, 33,* 265-275.

Main, R. E., & Griffiths, B. (1977). Evaluation of audio and pictorial instructional supplements. *AV Communication Review, 25*(2), 167-179.

Mayer, R. E. (1989). Systematic thinking fostered by illustrations in scientific text. *Journal of Educational Psychology, 81*(2), 240-246.

McCormick, C. B., & Levin, J. R. (1984). A comparison of different prose-learning variations of the mnemoic keyword method. *American Education Research Journal, 21,* 379-398.

McCormick, C. B., Levin, J. R., Cykowski, F., & Danilovics, P. (1984). Mnemonic-strategy reduction of prose-learning interference. *Educational Communication and Technology Journal, 32,* 154-152.

Miller, W. A. (1938). Reading with and without pictures. *Elementary School Journal, 38,* 676-682.

Moore, A. M. (1975). Investigation of the effect of patterns of illustrations on third graders' comprehension of information (Doctoral dissertation, Kent State University, 1974). *Dissertation Abstracts International, 36,* 1275A.

Nugent, G. C. (1982). Pictures, audio, and print: Symbolic representation and effect on learning. *Educational Communications and Technology Journal, 30*(3), 163-174.

O'Keefe, E. J., & Solman, R. T. (1987). The influence of illustrations on children's comprehension of written stories. *Journal of Reading Behavior, 19*(4), 353-377.

Peeck, J. (1974). Retention of pictorial and verbal content of a text with illustrations. *Journal of Educational Psychology, 66,* 880-888.

Peng, C. Y., & Levin, J. R. (1979). Pictures and children's story recall: Some questions of durability. *Educational Communication and Technology Journal, 27,* 179-192.

Popham, W. J. (1969). Pictorial embellishments in a tape-slide instructional program. *AV Communication Review, 17*(1), 28-35.

Pressley, M., Levin, J. R., Pigott, S., LeComte, M., & Hope, D. J. (1983). Mismatched pictures and children's prose learning. *Educational Communication and Technology Journal, 31,* 131-143.

Pressley, M., Pigott, S., & Bryant, S. L. (1982). Picture content and preschoolers' learning from sentences. *Educational Communication and Technology Journal, 30,* 151-161.

Rankin, E. F., & Culhane, J. W. (1970). One picture equals 1,000 words? *Reading Improvement, 7,* 37-40.

Rasco, R. W., Tennyson, R. D., & Boutwell, R. C. (1975). Imagery instructions and drawings in learning prose. *Journal of Educational Psychology, 67,* 188-192.

Reid, D. J., Briggs, N., & Beveridge, M. (1983). The effect of pictures upon the readability of a school science topic. *British Journal of Educational Psychology, 53,* 327-335.

Rice, D. R., Doan, R. L., & Brown, S. J. (1981). The effects of pictures on reading comprehension, speed and interest of second grade students. *Reading Improvement, 18,* 308-312.

Riding, R. J., & Shore, J. M. (1974). A comparison of two methods of improving prose comprehension in educationally subnormal children. *British Journal of Educational Psychology, 44,* 300-303.

Rohwer, W. D., & Matz, R. D. (1975). Improving aural comprehension in white and in black children. *Journal of Experimental Child Psychology, 19,* 23-36.

Rohwer, W. D. J., & Harris, W. J. (1975). Media effects of prose learning in two populations of children. *Journal of Educational Psychology, 67,* 651-657.

Royer, J. M., & Cable, G. W. (1976). Illustrations, analogies, and facilitative transfer in prose learning. *Journal of Educational Psychology, 68,* 205-209.

Ruch, M. D., & Levin, J. R. (1977). Pictorial organization versus verbal repetition of children's prose: Evidence for processing differences. *AV Communication Review, 25,* 269-280.

Ruch, M. D., & Levin, J. R. (1979). Partial pictures as imagery-retrieval cues in young children's prose recall. *Journal of Experimental Child Psychology, 28,* 268-279.

Rusted, J., & Coltheart, M. (1979a). Facilitation of children's prose recall by the presence of pictures. *Memory and Cognition, 7*(5), 354-359.

Rusted, J., & Coltheart, V. (1979b). The effect of pictures on the retention of novel words and prose passages. *Journal of Experimental Child Psychology, 28,* 516-524.

Rusted, J., & Hodgson, S. (1985). Evaluating the picture facilitation effect in children's recall of written texts. *British Journal of Educational Psychology, 55*(3), 288-294.

Scruggs, T. E., Mastropieri, M. A., Levin, J. R., & Gaffney, J. S. (1985). Facilitating the acquisition of science facts in learning disabled students. *American Educational Research Journal, 22,* 575-586.

Sewell, E. H., & Moore, R. L. (1980). Cartoon embellishments in informative presentations. *Educational Communication and Technology Journal, 28,* 39-46.

Sherman, J. L. (1976). Contextual information and prose comprehension. *Journal of Reading Behavior, 8,* 369-379.

Shriberg, L. K., Levin, J. R., McCormick, C. B., & Pressley, M. (1982). Learning about "famous" people via the keyword method. *Journal of Educational Pscyhology, 74,* 238-247.

Silvern, S. B. (1980). Play, pictures, and repetition: Mediators in aural prose learning. *Educational Communication and Technology Journal, 28,* 134-139.

Snowman, J., & Cunningham, D. J. (1975). A comparison of pictorial and written adjunct aids in learning from text. *Journal of Educational Psychology, 67,* 307-311.

Stone, D. E., & Glock, M. D. (1981). How do young adults read directions with and without pictures? *Journal of Educational Psychology, 73,* 419-426.

Stromnes, F. J., & Nyman, J. (1974). Immediate and long-term retention of connected concrete discourse as a function of mnemonic picture-type sequence and context. *Scandinavian Journal of Psychology, 15,* 197-202.

Talley, J. E. (1989). The effect of pictures and story text structure on recall and comprehension. (Doctoral dissertation, Auburn University, 1988). *Dissertation Abstracts International, 49,* 2604A.

Thomas, J. L. (1978). The influence of pictorial illustrations with written text and previous achievement on the reading comprehension of fourth grade science students. *Journal of Research in Science Teaching, 15,* 401-405.

Towers, R. L. (1994). *The effects of animated graphics and static graphics on student learning in a computer-based instructional format.* Doctoral dissertation, University of Kentucky.

Vernon, M. D. (1953). The value of pictorial illustration. *British Journal of Educational Psychology, 23,* 180–187.

Vernon, M. D. (1954). The instruction of children by pictorial illustration. *British Journal of Educational Psychology, 24,* 171–179.

Vye, N. J., Bransford, J. D., Symons, S. E., & Acton, H. (1986, April). *Constraints on elaborations in visual domains.* Paper presented at the meeting of the American Educational Research Association, San Francisco.

Waddill, M. A., & McDaniel, M. A. (1988). Illustrations as adjuncts to prose: A text-appropriate processing approach. *Journal of Educational Psychology, 80*(4), 457–464.

Weintraub, S. (1960). The effect of pictures on the comprehension of a second grade basal reader (Doctoral dissertation, University of Illinois, 1960). *Dissertation Abstracts International, 21,* 1428.

Weisberg, J. S. (1970). The use of visual advance organizers for learning earth science concepts. *Journal of Research in Science Teaching, 7,* 161–165.

Woolridge, P., Nall, L., Hughes, L., Rauch, T., Stewart, G., & Richman, C. L. (1982). Prose recall in first-grade children using imagery, pictures, and questions. *Bulletin of the Psychonomic Society, 20,* 249–252.

APPENDIX 33.5 (pp. 898–912)

APPENDIX 33.6. STUDIES LISTED IN THE MATRIX FOR DYNAMIC VISUALS (SEE APPENDIX 33.5)

Al-Mulla, A. (1995). The influence of computer animation on learning (Doctoral dissertation, University of Kansas, 1995). *Dissertation Abstracts International, 57,* 0993A.

Alesandrini, K. L., & Rigney, J. (1981). Pictorial representation and review strategies in science learning. *Journal of Research in Science Teaching 1*(5), 465–474.

Atlas, R., Cornett, L., Lane, D. M., & Napier, A. (1977). The use of animation in software training: Pitfalls and benefits. In M. A. Quinones & A. Ehrenstein (Eds.), *Training for a Rapidly Changing Workplace* (pp. 281–302). Washington DC: American Psychological Association.

Avons, S. E., Beveridge, M. C., Hickman, A. T., & Hitch, G. J. (1983). Teaching journey graph with microcomputer animation. *Human Learning, 2,* 93–105.

Baek, Y. K., & Layne, B. H. (1988). Color, graphics, and animation in a computer-assisted learning tutorial lesson. *Journal of Computer-Based Instruction, 15*(4), 131–135.

Beichner, R. (1990). The effects of simultaneous motion presentation and graph generation in a kinematics lab. *Journal of Research in Science Teaching, 27*(8), 803–815.

Blake, T. (1977). Motion in instructional media: Some subject-display mode interactions. *Perceptual and Motor Skills, 44,* 975–985.

Brasell, H. (1987). The effects of real-time laboratory graphing on learning graphic representations of distance and velocity. *Journal of Research in Science Teaching, 24*(4), 385–395.

Caputo, D. J. (1982). An analysis of relative effectiveness of a graphic-enhanced microcomputer-based remedial system in a university basic mathematical skills deficiency removal plan. (Doctoral dissertation, University of Pittsburgh, 1981.) *Dissertation Abstracts International, 42,* 3482A.

Caraballo, J. N. (1985). The effect of various visual display modes in computer-based instruction and language background upon achievement of selected educational objectives (Doctoral dissertation, Pennsylvania State University, 1985). *Dissertation Abstracts International, 46*(6), 1494A.

Caraballo-Rios, A. (1985). An experimental study to investigate the effects of computer animation on the understanding and retention of selected levels of learning outcomes (Doctoral dissertation, Pennsylvania State University, 1985). *Dissertation Abstracts International, 46,* 1494A.

ChanLin, L. (1996). Enhancing computer graphics through metaphorical elaboration. *Journal of Instructional Psychology, 23*(3), 196.

ChanLin, L. (1998). Animation to teach students of different knowledge levels. *Journal of Instructional Psychology, 25*(3), 166.

ChanLin, L. (1999). Visual treatment for different prior knowledge. *International Journal of Instructional Media, 26*(2), 213–220.

ChanLin, L. (2000). Attributes of animation for learning scientific knowledge. *Journal of Instructional Psychology, 24*(4), 228–238.

Chien, S. C. (1986). The effectiveness of animated and interactive microcomputer graphics on children's development of spatial visualization ability/mental rotation skills (Doctoral dissertation, Ohio State University, 1986). *Dissertation Abstracts International, 46,* 1494A.

Collins, A., Adams, M. J., & Pew, R. W. (1978). Effectiveness of an interactive map display in tutoring geography. *Journal of Educational Psychology, 70*(1), 1–7.

Dwyer, F. (1969). The instructional effect of motion in varied visual illustrations. *Journal of Psychology, 73,* 167–172.

Dyck, J., L. (1995). Problem solving by Macintosh users: The effects of animated, self-paced written, and no instruction. *Educational Computing Research, 12*(1), 29–49.

Hativa, N., & Reingold, A. (1987). Effects of audiovisual stimuli on learning through microcomputer-based class presentation. *Instructional Science, 16,* 287–306.

Hays, T. A. (1996). Spatial abilities and the effects of computer animation on short-term and long-term comprehension. *Educational Computing Research, 14*(2), 139–155.

Houston, J. M., Joiner, C. L., Uddo, F., Harper, C., & Stroll, A. (1995). Computer animation in mock juries' decision making. *Psychological Reports, 76,* 987–993.

Johnson, N. C. (1985). Using a microcomputer to teach a statistical concept (Doctoral dissertation, University of Minnesota, 1986). *Dissertation Abstracts International, 47,* 455A.

Kann, C., Lindeman, R. W., & Heller, R. (1977). Integrating algorithm animation into a learning environment. *Computers Education, 28*(4), 223–228.

King, W. A. (1975). *A comparison of three combinations of text and graphics for concept learning.* Navy Personnel Research and Development Center, Report No. NPRDC-TR-76-16, San Diego, CA. (ERIC Document Reproduction Service No. ED 112936)

Kini, A. S. (1994). *Effects of cognitive style and verbal and visual presentation mode on concept learning in CBI.* Paper presented at the meeting of the American Educational Research Association, New Orleans, LA.

Kinzer, C. K., Sherwood, R. D., & Loofbourrow, M. C. (1989). Simulation software vs expository text: A comparison of retention across two instructional tools. *Reading Research and Instruction, 28*(2), 41–49.

Klein, D. (1986). Conditions influencing the effectiveness of animated and non-animated displays in computer assisted instruction (Doctoral dissertation, University of Illinois at Urbana–Champaign, 1985). *Dissertation Abstracts International, 46,* 1878A.

Lai, S. (1998). The effects of visual display on analogies using computer-based learning. *International Journal of Instructional Media, 25*(2), 151-161.

Lai, S. (2000). Influence of audio-visual presentations on learning of abstract concepts. *International Journal of Instructional Media, 27*(2), 199-207.

Laner, S. (1954). The impact of visual aid displays showing a manipulative task. *Quarterly Journal of Experimental Psychology, 6,* 95-106.

Laner, S. (1955). Some factors influencing the effectiveness of an instructional film. *British Journal of Psychology, 46,* 280-294.

Large, A., Beheshti, J., Breuleux, A., & Reneud, A. (1995). Multimedia and comprehension: The relationship among text, animation, and captions. *Journal of the American Society for Information Science, 46*(5), 340-347.

Lumsdaine, A. A., Sultzer, R. L. & Kopstein, F. F. (1961). The effect of animation cues and repetition of examples on learning from an instructional film. In A. A. Lumsdaine (Ed.), *Student response in programmed instruction* (pp. 241-269). Washington, DC: National Research Council.

Mayer, R. E., & Anderson, R. B. (1991). Animation needs narration: an experimental test of a dual-coding hypothesis. *Journal of Educational Psychology, 83*(4), 484-90.

Mayer, R. E., & Anderson, R. B. (1992). The instructive animation: Helping students build connections between words and pictures in multimedia learning. *Journal of Educational Psychology, 84*(4), 444-452.

Mayer, R. E., Moreno, R., Boire, M., & Vagge, S. (1999). Maximizing constructivist learning from multimedia communications by minimizing cognitive load. *Journal of Educational Psychology, 81*(4), 638-643.

Mayer, R. E., & Moreno, R. (1998). A split-attention effect in multimedia learning: Evidence for dual processing systems in working memory. *Journal of Educational Psychology, 90*(2), 312-320.

Mayer, R. E., & Sims, V. K. (1994). For whom is a picture worth a thousand words? Extensions of dual-coding theory of multimedia learning. *Journal of Educational Psychology, 86*(3), 389-401.

Mayton, G. B. (1990). The effects of the animation of visuals on the learning of dynamic progresses through microcomputer-based instruction (Doctoral dissertation, Ohio State University, 1990). *Dissertation Abstracts International, 51,* 4097A.

McCloskey, M., & Kohl, D. (1983). Naive physics: The curvilinear impetus principle and its role in interactions with moving objects. *Journal of Experimental Psychology: Learning Memory and Cognition, 9*(1), 146-156.

Mccuiston, P. J. (1990). Static vs dynamic visuals in computer-assisted instruction. (Doctoral dissertation, Texas A&M University, 1989). *Dissertation Abstracts International, 42,* 4409A.

Moore, M. V., Nawrocki, L. H., & Simutis, Z. M. (1979). The instructional effectiveness of three levels of graphic displays for computer-assisted instruction. *Army Research Center, ARI-TP-359,* 2-14. (ERIC, ED No. 178 057)

Myers, K. N. (1990). An exploratory study of the effectiveness of computer graphics and simulations in a computer-student interactive environment in illustrating random sampling and the central limit theorem (Doctoral dissertation, Florida State University, 1990). *Dissertation Abstracts International, 51,* 441A.

Nicholls, C., & Merkel, S. (1996). The effect of computer animation on students' understanding of microbiology. *Journal of Research on Computing in Education, 28*(3), 359-372.

Palmiter, S., Elkerton, J., & Baggett, P. (1991). Animated demonstrations vs written instructions for learning procedural tasks: A preliminary investigation. *Instructional Journal of Man-Machine Studies, 34,* 687-701.

Palmiter, S., & Elkerton, J. (1993). Animated demonstrations for learning procedural computer-based tasks. *Human-Computer Interaction, 8,* 193-216.

Park, O. (1998). Visual displays and contextual presentations in computer-based instruction. *Educational Technology Research and Development, 46*(3), 37-50.

Park, O., & Gittelman, S. (1992). Selective use of animation and feedback in computer-based instruction. *Educational Technology Research and Development, 40*(4), 27-38.

Payne, S. J., Chesworth, L., & Hill, E. (1992). Animated demonstrations for exploratory learners. *Interacting with Computers, 4*(1), 3-22.

Peters, H. J., & Daiker, K. C. (1982). Graphics and animations as instructional tools: A case study. *Pipeline, 7*(1), 11-13.

Ponick, D. A. (1986). Animation used as a logical organizer in visualization for concept learning (Doctoral dissertation, University of Minnesota, 1986). *Dissertation Abstracts International, 47,* 3300A.

Ram, S. P., & Phua, K. K. (1997). The effectiveness of a computer-aided instruction courseware developed using interactive multimedia concepts for teaching phase III MD students. *Medical Teacher, 19*(1), 51-53.

Reed, S. K. (1985). Effects of computer graphics on improving estimates to algebra word problems. *Journal of Educational Psychology, 77*(3), 285-298.

Rieber, L. P., & Hannafin, M. J. (1988). Effects of textual and animated orienting activities and practice on learning from computer-based instruction. *Computers in Schools, 5*(1/2), 77-89.

Rieber, L. P. (1989). The effects of computer animated elaboration strategies and practice on factual and application learning in an elementary science lesson. *Journal of Educational Computing Research, 5*(4), 431-444.

Rieber, L. P. (1990). Using computer animated graphics in science instruction with children. *Journal of Educational Psychology, 82*(1), 135-140.

Rieber, L. P., Boyce, M. J., & Assad, C. (1990). The effects of computer animation on adult learning and retrieval tasks. *Journal of Computer-Based Instruction, 17*(2), 46-52.

Rieber, L. P. (1991a). Animation, incidental learning, and continuing motivation. *Journal of Educational Psychology, 83*(3), 318-328.

Rieber, L. P. (1991b). Effects of visual grouping strategies of computer-animated presentations on selective attention in science. *Educational Technology Research and Development, 39*(4), 5-15.

Rieber, L. P. (1996a). Animation as feedback in a computer-based simulation: Representation matters. *Educational Technology Research and Development, 44*(1), 5-22.

Rieber, L. P. (1996b). Animation as a distractor to learning. *International Journal of Instructional Media, 23*(1), 53-57.

Rieber, L. P., Smith, M., Al-gharry, S., Strickland, B., Chu, G., & Spahi, F. (1996). The role of meaning in interpreting graphical and textual feedback during a computer-based simulation. *Computers & Education, 27*(1), 45-58.

Rigney, J. W., & Lutz, K. A. (1976). Effects of graphic analogies of concepts in chemistry on learning and attitude. *Journal of Educational Psychology, 68*(3), 305-311.

Roshal, S. M. (1961). Film mediated learning with varying representations of the task: Viewing angle, portrayal of demonstration, motion, and student participation. In A. A. Lumsdaine (Ed.), *Student response in programmed instruction* (pp. 155-175). Washington, DC: National Research Council.

Sanger, M. J., & Greenbowe, T. J. (2000). Addressing student misconceptions concerning electron flow in aqueous solutions with instruction including computer animations and conceptual change strategies. *International Journal of Science Education, 22*(5), 521-537.

(Continues on p. 913)

TABLE 33.A5. Summary Matrix of Research Results for Dynamic Visuals

Study	Treatment	Content	Subjects	Dependent Variable (s)	Results
Al-Mulla (1995)	1. Static visuals 2. Animated visuals	Aerodynamic, air-conditioner, & joystick	50 adults	Immediate and delayed posttests	SD for animation on aerodynamic intellectual skills delayed posttest, overall intellectual skills delayed posttest, and immediate and delayed joystick intellectual skills
Alesandrini & Rigney (1981)					
Expt 1	1. Pictorial lesson & pictorial review 2. Pictorial lesson & no review 3. Verbal lesson & pictorial review 4. Verbal lesson & no review	Function of a battery	96 adults	Pictorial test & verbal test	SD for animation on picture recognition NSD among groups for verbal test
Expt 2	1. Verbal lesson & pictorial review 2. Verbal lesson & verbal review		50 adults		
Atlas, Cornett, Lane, & Napier (1997)					
Expt 1	1. Text 2. Animation 3. Animation plus verbal information	Training in HyperCard authoring tasks	39 adults	Immediate test & 7 day delayed test	Mixed results: Animated group performed better on immediate test but worse on delayed test
Expt 2	1. Text 2. Animation plus verbal information	22 adults			Training in animation plus verbal information led to greater improvement on delayed test
Avons, Beveridge, Hickman, & Hitch (1983)					
Expt 1	1. Active vertical 2. Active horizontal 3. Passive vertical 4. Passive horizontal 5. Optimal condition	Relationship between speed and corresponding slopes of the graph in an animated simulation of a moving car	60 children, 9 to 11 years old 48 children, 10 to 11 years old	Posttest measuring comprehension, production, and conceptual understanding	In both experiments, NSD were found among the groups for conceptual, comprehension, and production tests. However, children performed better on comprehension and production tests
Expt 2	1. Vertical label (VL) 2. Vertical (V) 3. Horizontal (H) 4. Label only (L)				

898

Study	Treatment conditions	Content	Sample	Dependent measure	Results
Baek & Layne (1988)	1. Animated group (color) 2. Graphics group (color) 3. Text group (color) 4. Animated group (B/W) 5. Graphics group (B/W) 6. Text group (B/W)	Tutorial lessons about the mathematical rules for calculating speed	119 high-school children	Score on performance test and time to finish computer module	SD among the groups for both performance test and completion time. Animated groups performed better than graphics and text groups, and graphics groups performed better than text groups on performance test. For completion time, animated groups had the slowest time. Color had no effects on learning
Beichner (1990)	1. Videograph technique, viewed the real motion 2. Videograph technique, did not view the real motion 3. Traditional technique, viewed the real motion 4. Traditional technique, did not view the real motion	MBL experiments showing the physical events along with their graphical representations	237 mixed subjects (165 high-school students and 72 adults)	Score on pretest and posttest (understanding graphs)	NSD among groups
Blake (1977)	1. Still condition (only slides) 2. Arrow condition (slides plus cueing arrows) 3. Motion condition showing standard motion video	Learning the movement of chess pieces	84 adults	Score on test consisting of 32 diagrams of chessboard	Mixed result. SD found among groups for low-spatial ability students. The still condition performed worse than either one of the motion conditions, which did not differ from each other. NSD found among groups for high-spatial ability students
Brasell (1987)	1. Standard (real-time graphing) 2. Delayed (delayed-graphing) 3. Test only 4. Control (paper only)	Experiments for learning graphing skills	93 high-school students	Score on pretest and posttest (understanding graphs)	SD found among groups in favor of animation (real-time graphing).
Caputo (1982)	1. Dynamic graphic CAI 2. Verbal CAI 3. Checklist CAI	Upgrading certain basic mathematical skills	109 adults	Score on basic mathematical skills retake test. Also, course grade average for computer science	SD among groups
Caraballo (1985)	1. No instruction 2. Text only 3. Text plus still graphics 4. Text plus still graphics plus animated graphics	Learner's achievement and language background	80 adults	Four criterion tests (terminology, identification, drawing, and comprehension) and total scores	NSD
Caraballo-Rios (1985)	1. Text 2. Text plus still pictures 3. Text plus still pictures plus animation	Concepts and rules in geometry	72 adults	Immediate and delayed posttests on performance	NSD among groups

Continues

899

33.A5. (Continued)

Study	Treatment	Content	Subjects	Dependent Variable (s)	Results
ChanLin (1996)	1. Nongraphic w/ metaphors 2. Static graphics w/ metaphors 3. Animated graphics w/ metaphors 4. Animated graphics w/o metaphors 5. Static graphics w/o metaphors 6. Nongraphics w/o metaphors	CAI explaining concepts of biotechnology	120 college students	Criterion referenced test, Keller's IMMS (Instructional Materials Motivational Survey)	SD for student performance metaphorical elaboration w/ animation treatment. NSD for no metaphors w/graphic representation. SD for student motivational scores w/ metaphors & animated graphics
ChanLin (1998)	1. No graphics 2. Still graphics 3. Animated graphics	Biotechnology	135 adults	Tests of procedural and descriptive facts	Mixed results
ChanLin (1999)	1. Text (control group) 2. Still graphics 3. Animated graphics	Biotechnology	135 adults	Criterion referenced test	SD among groups for animation
ChanLin (2000)	1. Text 2. Graphics with text 3. Animation with text	Physics lesson	357 children	Descriptive test and procedural knowledge test	Mixed results
Chien (1986)	1. Hands-on simulations 2. Animated interactive graphics	Spatial visualization	72 children, 1st, 2nd, and 3rd graders	Posttest on performance	NSD among groups
Collins, Adams, & Pew (1978)	1. SCHOLAR map system (interactive) condition 2. A labeled map condition 3. An unlabeled map condition	Learning geography	9 high-school students and 9 adults	Score on pretest and posttest (number of correct responses)	SD among groups in favor of animation. Scores on posttest showed that the SCHOLAR condition performed significantly better than the labeled map condition, which in turn scored significantly better than the unlabeled map condition
Dwyer (1969)	1. Control group (G1), text-only group 2. Simple line representations (G2) 3. Detailed shaded drawings (G3) 4. Photographs of the heart model (G4) 5. Realistic heart photographs (G5)	Function of human heart	139 adults	A pretest, a drawing test, an identification test, a terminology test, and a total criterion test	SD among groups for drawing tests. G2 performed better than G1. SD among groups for terminology test. G2 performed significantly better than G1 SD among groups for total criterion test. G2 & G5 performed significantly better than G1. NSD among groups for identification and comprehension tests
Dyck (1995)	1. No instruction 2. Mouse/icon manual 3. File manipulation manual 4. Animated instruction (Mac tour)	Macintosh operating system	48 adults	Posttest measuring the task completion time and proportion of tasks completed with familiar and unfamiliar tasks	NSD among groups for either completion time or proportion of tasks completed

Study	Groups/Conditions	Topic	Sample	Measures	Results
Hativa & Reingold (1987)	1. Stimulus group with sound, animation, and color 2. Nonstimulus without sound, animation, or color	Learning Euclidean geometry	92 9th graders	Immediate and delayed posttests measuring the aptitude for learning and understanding of geometry	SD found for both understanding and aptitude on both immediate and delayed posttests. The stimulus group performed better. Animation was helpful in gaining attention, creating positive attitude, and helping students understand the subjects
Hays (1996)	1. Text alone 2. Text and static visuals 3. Text plus animation	Concepts involving time and motion (diffusion)	131 6th, 7th, and 8th graders	Two tests: 1. Sentence verification technique (SVT) to measure short-term comprehension for spatial ability, and presentation mode 2. Concept evaluation statement (CES) to measure long-term comprehension for spatial ability and presentation mode	Short-term comprehension: SD among groups for SVT test. Animation helped low-spatial ability students. NSD among groups for mode of presentation. Long-term comprehension: SD for CES test. Animation helped both low- and high-spatial ability students to gain higher score on conceptual understanding. However, low-spatial ability students benefited the most
Houston, Joiner, Uddo, Harper, & Stroll (1995)	1. Reading out loud group, listening to the transcript of the voice recorder 2. Voice recorder's written transcript & audiotape group 3. Animated group listening to the cockpit's voice and flight recorder	Plane crash investigation	72 adults	A questionnaire for rating the blame on the crew for the crash A questionnaire to measure the subject s recall of information about the crash	SD among groups. Subjects in the animated group put less of the blame on the flight crew NSD found among groups for recall of information and retention
Kann, Lindeman, & Heller (1977)	1. N group (no animation) 2. V group (viewed animation of the algorithm) 3. C group (control group, wrote programs without any instruction) 4. VC group (subjects wrote programs after viewing the animation)	Knapsack algorithm	28 adults	Posttest measuring students' ability to recognize the type of program (declarative, procedural, analytical, and recursion) Quality of the written codes	SD among groups for recognizing the recursive-type programs. The animated group performed better on the posttest. The animated group also performed better on the posttest than the others for the procedural- and declarative-type problem SD among groups for writing programs. The animated group performed much better than the other groups.
King (1975)	1. Text and animation 2. Text & still graphics 3. Text only	Sine-ratio concepts	45 adults	Posttest measuring students' understanding of the sine-ratio concepts	NSD among groups. However, the mean score of the animated group was the highest on the posttest

901

Continues

33.A5. (Continued)

Study	Treatment	Content	Subjects	Dependent Variable (s)	Results
Kini (1994)	1. Text only 2. Text plus animated graphics 3. Field independence–field dependence 4. Preferred perceptual mode (verbal–visual)	Concepts of velocity and acceleration in one-dimensional space	192 adults	Concept test	NSD among groups
Kinzer, Sherwood, & Loofbourrow (1989)	1. Computer animation 2. Text	Understanding the food chain	52 children, 5th graders	Posttest measuring students' understanding of the food chain	SD among groups in favor of the text group
Klein (1986)	1. Temporal animated, easy 2. Temporal animated, difficult 3. Temporal nonanimated, easy 4. Temporal nonanimated, difficult 5. Spatial animated, easy 6. Spatial animated, difficult 7. Spatial nonanimated, easy 8. Spatial nonanimated, difficult	Problem solving	38 adults	Time between presenting the problem and receiving answers from students	Mixed results
Lai (1998)	1. Text only 2. Text with static graphics 3. Animation	Learning computer-based programming language through analogies	78 children and adults	A multiple-choice test measuring the understanding of programming concepts and functions	SD among groups in favor of text with static graphics
Lai (2000)	1. Text with audio instruction 2. Treatment 1 plus static graphics 3. Treatment 1 plus animated graphics	Computer programming languages	169 adults	A multiple-choice test measuring concepts; an attitude questionnaire (Likert type)	SD among groups for animation NSD among groups for attitude
Laner (1954)	1. Students' film group 2. RAF film group 3. RAF film strip	Moving film showing the repair of a sash-cord window	75 adults	Individual tests of performance	NSD among groups. However, students who viewed the film performed better than both RAF groups
Laner (1955)	1. Film 2. Text and two static pictures	Moving films about the Bren-Gun trigger mechanism	50 adults	Individual performance test for drawing the mechanism, naming parts, and performing the assembly	SD among groups for performance. This means that moving film did not have any effects on performance
Large, Beheshti, Breuleux, & Reneud (1995)	1. Text-only group 2. Text plus animation 3. Text plus animation plus captions 4. Captions plus animation	Multimedia learning. The procedural task of "how to find south"	71 6th graders	Individual test for recall of information and performance of the procedure	NSD among groups for recall of information SD among groups for performance The animated group and the caption groups performed better than the text-only group

Study	Treatment	Content	Sample	Measure	Results
Lumsdaine et al. (1961)	1. Animated group given the prefilm test 2. Animated group given film with 6 examples 1. Animated group given film with 3 examples 2. Animated group with supplemental sound 3. Nonanimated group with prefilm test 4. Nonanimated group given film with 6 examples 5. Nonanimated group given film with 3 examples 6. Nonanimated group with supplemental sound	Instrument reading skills	1,300 Air Force basic trainees	Ability to read the value of the micrometer settings	SD among groups. The animated prefilm test group performed significantly better than the animated group not given the prefilm test. Animated group also performed better in the replication trials
Mayer & Anderson (1991) Expt 1	1. Words with pictures 2. Words before pictures	Operation of a bicycle pump	30 adults	A problem-solving test (four essay questions)	SD among groups in favor of words with picture group
Expt 2b	1. Control 2. Words only 3. Pictures only 4. Words with pictures	Same as above	48 adults	A problem-solving test and a verbal recall test	SD among groups for problem solving NSD among groups for recall
Mayer & Anderson (1992) Expt 1	1. Concurrent group, 3 (A+N) 2. Successive group, 3 (AN, NA, A, N, N, A) 3. Animation-alone group 4. Narration-alone group 5. No instruction group (control group)	Operation of a bicycle pump	136 adults	A posttest measuring recall of information and number of solutions generated to fix the given problems	SD among groups for retention and problem solving in favor of the experimental groups. The concurrent group performed better than any other group on problem solving. All experimental groups performed better than the control group, but their performance did not differ from each other.
Expt 2	Same treatment as Expt 1	Operation of an automobile braking system	144 adults	Same as Expt 1	SD among the experimental groups and the control group for problem solving. All experimental groups, except AAA group performed significantly better than the control group.

Continues

903

33.A5. (Continued)

Study	Treatment	Content	Subjects	Dependent Variable (s)	Results
Mayer, Moreno, Boire, & Vagge (1999) Expt 1	1. Concurrent presentation 2. Small bites of narration before animation 3. Small bites of animation before narration 4. Large bites of narration before animation 5. Large bites of animation before narration	How lightening forms, and how automobile braking system operates	60 adults	Retention test, matching test, and transfer test (open response and open-ended questions)	SD among groups for both experiments, except NSD found for the matching test in Expt 2.
Expt 2, replication of Expt 1					
Mayer & Moreno (1998) Expt 1	1. Concurrent animation plus narration (AN group) 2. Concurrent animation plus text (AT group)	Process of lighting formation	78 adults	A matching test, to measure students' ability to match each animation frame to a particular sentence that describes it, a retention test, and a transfer test, to assess students' ability to apply the learned knowledge to a new situation	SD among groups. In both experiments; the AN group outperformed the AT group in all tests.
Expt 2	1. Concurrent animation plus narration (AN group) 2. Concurrent animation plus text (AT group)	Operation of an automobile braking system	68 adults		
Mayer & Sims (1994) Expt 1	1. Concurrent group, 3(A+N), consisted of 10 HSA & 12 LSA 2. Successive group, 3 (AN,NA), consisted of 21 HAS and 22 LSA 3. Control group (no instruction), consisted of 7 HAS and 14 LSA	Operation of an automobile breaking system	86 adults	A posttest measuring the number of solutions generated for the given problem by high- and low-spatial ability students	SD among groups for the number of solutions generated for each problem. The performance of the concurrent group was significantly better than that of the successive or no instruction groups, which did not differ from each other. SD among the spatial ability groups for problem solving. The high-spatial ability students who viewed concurrent animation generated twice as many solutions as the high-spatial ability students who received successive animation.

904

Study	Groups	Topic	N	Tests/Measures	Results
Expt 2	1. Concurrent group, 3 (A+N) 2. Successive group, 3 (N,A) 3. Control group (no instruction)	Operation of human respiratory system	97 adults	Posttest measuring the number of solutions generated by the high- and low-spatial ability students	The results were almost similar to experiment #1. SD was found for problem solving. The presentation of animation and narration generated 50% more solutions to the given problems.
Mayton (1990)	1. Static graphics 2. Static graphics with some imagery cues 3 Animated graphics & imagery cues	Functions of the human heart	72 adults	Five tests. T1 & T2 to identify the heart parts in both free and cued recall. T3 to identify parts of the human heart. T4 & T5 to measure the understanding of the heart's functions, with cued and free recall.	SD found among groups. Animated group outperformed the other groups
McCloskey & Kohl (1983) Expt 1	1. Computer animation 2. Computer animation showing the possible trajectories 3 Visual graphics with no motion	Perceiving trajectories in the ball-and-string problem	90 adults	Finding the correct trajectory for the ball	NSD found among the groups in each experiment
Expt 2	1. The no-motion group (chose the correct path without viewing animation 2. The trajectory group (Viewed an animation, then picked the correct path from the given six alternatives)		72 adults		
Expt 3	1. Same instructions for all on the task		50 adults		
Mccuistion (1990)	1. Static visual 2. Dynamic visual	Spatial abilities	137 adults	A performance test and a mental rotation test	NSD among groups
Moore, Nawrocki, & Simutis (1979)	1. Low-level graphic group, consisted of alphanumerics and schematics 2. Medium-level graphic group, consisted of line drawing 3. High-level graphic group, consisted of line drawing and animation	How the inner ear works	90 adults	Five tests were used: one test to measure the completion time of the lesson; other content tests used to measure terminology, facts, identification, and principles	NSD among groups for completion time NSD among groups for the other four tests
Myers (1990)	1. Traditional lecture 2. Interactive method	Learning statistical concepts	52 adults	A concept test and an application test	SD among groups for concept test NSD among the groups for application test

Continues

Study	Treatment	Content	Subjects	Dependent Variable (s)	Results
Nicholls & Merkel (1996)	1. Animated tutorial 2. Text with still diagram	Nitrogen cycle	44 adults	10 multiple-choice questions and six short-answer questions	NSD among groups
Palmiter, Elkerton, and Baggett (1991)	1. Animated demonstration group 2. Written-text group	Performing authoring tasks in HyperCard on the Macintosh	28 adults	Immediate and delayed posttests on different, identical, and similar tasks measuring initial acquisition, retention, and transfer	NSD among groups. There was a trade-off between training performance and later speed and transfer. The animated group was 50% faster in the training session than the text group, but their performance was worse on both immediate and delayed posttest.
Palmiter & Elkerton (1993)	1. Text-only group 2. Animated demo-only group 3. Text plus animated demo group	Performing HyperCard tasks	48 adults	Immediate and delayed tests (7 days) measuring acquisition, retention, and transfer of HyperCard tasks	NSD among groups. The demo groups were faster and more accurate than the text group during the training session but became slower during the test sessions. There were NSD between the demo group and the demo plus text group.
Park (1998)	1. Animation 2. Static graphics w/ motion cues. 3. Static graphic w/o motion cues	Electronic circuits and troubleshooting procedures	96 adults	Test of performance and test of transfer (troubleshooting)	SD among groups for animated groups
Park & Gittelman (1992)	1. Animation with natural feedback 2. Animation with knowledge of results feedback 3. Animation with explanatory feedback 4. Static visuals with natural feedback 5. Static visuals with knowledge of results feedback 6. Static visuals with explanatory feedback	Problem solving, teaching electronics troubleshooting	90 adults	A test measuring number of trials attempted to fix the faulty circuits and time spent on the faulty circuit during practice and test sessions	SD among groups for number of trials and in favor of animation NSD among groups for time spent on circuit and feedback type
Payne, Chesworth, & Hill (1992) Expt 1	1. No instruction group 2. Cards-only instructions 3. Video-only instructions 4. Card and video instructions	Performing tasks on the MacDraw software package Understanding and performing different tasks in MacDraw	32 adults	Amount of time spent to complete all six tasks	SD among groups in favor of animation. The animated groups performed all tasks in 38 min less than the text group SD among groups in favor of animation for understanding and performance. The animated group finished all four tasks 15 min faster than the control group

Study	Treatments/Groups	Content	Sample	Measure	Results
Expt 2	1. Video (animated) group 2. Control (no instruction) group		16 adults	Amount of time spent to perform all four tasks	NSD among groups
Peters & Daiker (1982)	1. Animation-only group 2. Interaction-only group 3. Animation plus interaction group 4. Control group: played an unrelated game	Understanding organic chemistry	35 adults	Score on the posttest	SD among the animated group and static visual groups. Subjects assigned to animated treatment (No. 4) performed significantly better on learning concepts related to mathematical functions than subjects assigned to static graphics treatments
Ponick (1986)	1. Random selection with sequential presentation 2. Random selection with simultaneous presentation 3. Guided selection with sequential presentations 4. Guided selection with simultaneous presentation)	Concept learning in mathematical curve sketching	71 adults	Identifying the function that represented the given graph, from the set of six alternatives	
Ram & Phua (1997)	1. Conventional lecture 2. Animation courseware	Review of congenital heart disease.	64 adults	10 multiple-choice questions	SD among groups in favor of animation
Reed (1985)	1. Experimental group, viewing simulations with regard to speed estimation, filling tank estimation, and mixture estimation 2. Control group, receiving unrelated information	Teaching algebra word problems related to: 1. Speed simulation 2. Tank filling 3. Mixing of different concentrations	180 adults	Net gain in students estimate of the problem from the prequestionnaire to the posttest questionnaire	Mixed results were reported. Watching simulation (animation) was useful when feedback was provided (learning by doing). However, in most cases viewing alone (learning by seeing) was not enough. This means that graphics displays alone did not produce an increase in instructional effectiveness.
Rieber & Hannafin (1988)	1. Text group with practice 2. Text group without practice 3. Animation group with practice 4. Animation group without practice 5. Text plus animation group with practice 6. Text plus animation group without practice 7. No-activity group with practice 8. No-activity group without practice	Rule using and problem solving, Newton's laws of motion	111 4th, 5th, and 6th graders	A 24-item posttest measuring rule using and problem solving	NSD among groups for orienting activities. No main effect was found for practice. A significant interaction was found between practice and learning outcomes. These results suggests that "orienting activities whether text-based or animated do not exert influence on learning" (p. 85)

907

Continues

Study	Treatment	Content	Subjects	Dependent Variable (s)	Results
Rieber (1989)	1. Static graphics 2. Static graphics without relevant practice 3. Static graphics without text 4. Static graphics 5. Animated graphics with relevant practice 6. Animated graphics without relevant practice 7. Animated graphics without text 8. Animated graphics with text 9. No graphics with relevant practice 10. No graphics 11. No graphics without text 12. No graphics	Newton's laws of motion	192 4th, 5th and 6th graders	A posttest measuring learning outcomes and transfer	NSD among groups for learning outcomes. This means no animation effects.
Rieber (1990)	1. Static graphics with behavioral practice 2. Static graphics with cognitive practice 3. Static graphics with no practice 4. Animated graphics with behavioral practice 5. Animated graphics with cognitive practice 6. Animated graphics with no practice	Newton's laws of motion	119 4th and 5th graders	A posttest measuring six learning objectives (p. 137)	SD among groups for visual elaboration. Significant interaction between visual elaboration and practice. Students in the cognitive group scored higher than the other groups on the posttest. SD among groups for learning objectives in favor of animation
Rieber, Boyce, & Assad (1990)	This is the replication of the 1990b study using adult subjects.	Newton's laws of motion	141 adults	A posttest measuring six learning objectives (p. 48)	NSD among groups for visual elaboration Significant interaction between visual elaboration and practice. The practice had more effects on learning than the strategy. The animated group outperformed the other groups when there was no feedback. SD among groups for learning objectives and response latency in favor of animation
Rieber (1991a)	1. Animation with questions/simulations. 2. Animation with simulation/questions 3. Static graphics with questions/simulations	Newton's laws of motion	70 children, 4th graders	A 24-item posttest (immediate and 2 days delayed) measuring both types of rule learning: intentional and incidental	SD among groups for incidental learning in both immediate and delayed posttest in favor of animation SD among groups for intentional learning in favor of animation

Study	Conditions	Topic	Subjects	Measure	Findings
	4. Static graphics with simulations/questions				SD among groups for time latency. The animated groups took significantly less time to answer the incidental questions. This was not the case for intentional learning.
Rieber (1991b)	1. Grouped animation (chunked) 2. Ungrouped animation (no chunking) 3. Grouped static graphics (chunked) 4. Ungrouped static graphics (no chunking)	Newton's laws of motion	39 children, 4th graders	A 24-item posttest measuring incidental and intentional learning	SD among groups in favor of animation. The chunked group scored significantly better on the posttest than the static groups. NSD between the ungrouped animated condition and any of the other three groups. SD among groups on incidental learning in favor of animation NSD among groups for intentional learning
Rieber (1996a) Expt 1	1. Animated feedback group 2. Textual feedback group 3. Textual plus animated feedback	Learning the relationship between speed & velocity of a ball	40 adults	A 12-item pretest and posttest to measure score (time/s), interactivity (No. of hits on keys), and frustration level	NSD among simulation versions for the performance test. SD for the game score. The animated feedback group had a lower score SD among simulation versions for interactivity. The animated feedback version had a lower interactivity level (understood the relationship between speed and velocity). NSD found among the simulation versions for the level of frustrations.
Expt 2	This is the replication of Expt 1. The only changes are the amount of practice and the number of subjects.		49 adults		SD among simulation versions. The animated feedback and animated feedback plus text groups performed significantly better than the textual group. SD among the simulation groups for score and interactivity. The animated feedback version had the lowest time and number of hits. SD found for frustration level in favor of the animated groups.
Rieber (1996b)	1. High-distraction condition (spaceship moved from L to R) 2. Medium-distraction condition (spaceship moved at top of page) 3. No-distraction condition (no spaceship)	Newton's laws of motion	364 5th graders	A posttest measuring performance and processing time (time needed by each student to process each instructional frame)	NSD among groups for performance test. The distracter did not affect students' performance on the posttest. SD among groups for processing time. The high- and medium-distraction groups paid attention to the distracters and took less time to view the instructional frames.

Continues

Study	Content	Subjects	Treatment	Dependent Variable (s)	Results
Rieber et al. (1996)	Understanding Newton's laws of motion through simulated games (miniature golf)	41 adults	1. Meaningful context group 2. Arbitrary context group	A pretest and posttest measured students' performance; game score, interactivity, and frustration level also measured	NSD among groups for performance. NSD among groups for interactivity. However, subjects did better with animated feedback. NSD among groups for frustration level. SD among groups for score in favor of animation.
Rigney & Lutz (1976)	Learning the concept of a simple battery	40 adults	1. Verbal treatment group (verbal only) 2. Imagery group (verbal information plus animation)	One recognition (memory) test and three recall tests (knowledge, comprehension, and application)	SD among groups for recall and attitude in favor of animated group. NSD among groups for recognition test. However, the animated group performed better on the recognition test.
Roshal (1949)	Tying three types of knots	3314 adults (Navy recruit trainees)	1. Group 1 2. Group 2 3. Group 3 4. Group 4 5. Group 5 6. Group 6 7. Group 7 8. Group 8	Performing the task correctly (tying the knots)	SD among groups in favor of motion. Portraying continuous changes through movement was an effective learning strategy.
Sanger & Greenbowe (2000)	Chemical processes	135 adults	1. Animation 2. Conceptual change instruction	Eight multiple-choice questions and one essay	NSD among groups
Spangenberg (1973) Expt 1	Learning the disassembly procedure for an M-85 machine gun	40 adults (Army soldiers)	1. Animated video group 2. Still-Sequence group	Individual performance test	SD among groups. The percentage of subjects who correctly disassembled the procedure was 59% for the video group and 25% for the still-sequence group.
Expt 2		80 adults (enlisted soldiers)	1. Animated video group 2. Animated video group plus cueing arrows 3. Still-sequence group 4. Still-sequence group plus cueing arrows		SD among groups. The percentage of subjects who correctly disassembled the procedure was 43% for the video groups and 15% for the still-sequence groups.
Spangler (1994)	Depicting 2D and 3D objects	57 adults	1. Traditional instruction 2. Animation with color 3. Animation without color 4. Static pictures with color 5. Static pictures without color	A 2D & 3D test; mental rotation test	NSD among groups
Spotts & Dwyer (1996)	Learning parts and functions of human heart	63 adults	1. Text plus static graphics 2. Text plus animation 3. Text plus animation plus simulation	Four criterion tests: drawing, identification, terminology, and comprehension tests	SD among groups for drawing test in favor of the animation plus text group. SD among groups for total criterion test (combination of the four criterion tests). The animation plus text group outperformed the simulation group. The addition of simulated blood flow did not affect learning.

Study	Conditions	Task	Sample	Test	Results
Swezey, Prez, & Allen (1991)	1. Procedural group: (a) video presentation, (b) slide presentation; 2. Generic system structure and function group: (a) video presentation, (b) slide presentation; 3. Integrated group: combination of the above	Troubleshooting electromechanical systems in a diesel engine	120 adults	Four tests: a criterion-based reference task, a hands-on transfer task, an abstract transfer task, and a conceptual knowledge task	NSD among subjects who received static versus dynamic presentations of the training materials, regardless of the instructional strategy conditions employed
Szabo & Poohkay (1996)	1. Text only; 2. Text plus static graphics; 3. Text plus animated graphics	Construction of a triangle using a compass	173 adults	Construction problem test and Likert-type attitude test	NSD among groups
Thompson & Riding (1990)	1. No computerized illustration group; 2. Pythagorean program with illustrations; 3. Pythagorean program with computerized animation (experimental group)	Learning Pythogoras' theorem through mathematical demonstrations	108 children, 11 to 14 years old	Two tests given to measure students' understanding of the rotations and shears	SD among groups in favor of animation. The mean score of the animated group was significantly higher than the mean scores of the other two groups.
Todorov, Shadmehr, & Bizzi (1997) Expt 1	1. Viewed real performance plus verbal coaching; 2. Viewed simulated performance and animated paddle (pilot group); 3. Viewed simulated performance showing animated paddle and ball (training group)	Learning difficult motor skills (hitting a ping-pong ball)	42 adults	Number of times to hit the target for two sets of 50-ball trials	Significant interaction reported. The performance of the pilot group was similar to that of the control group for the first 50 trials and worse for the second 50 trials. SD among groups in the second trial. The simulated training group performed significantly better than the other groups. SD for performance. The training group that practiced in the simulator performed better than the control group that practiced on the task in the real environment.
Expt 2	1. Control group (real practice); 2. Training group (simulating practice)		21 adults		
Towers (1994) Expt 1	1. Text only; 2. Text plus static visuals; 3. Text plus animated visuals	Prediction of weather pattern	49 adults	A 10-item recall test	SD among groups in favor of text

Continues

Study	Treatment	Content	Subjects	Dependent Variable (s)	Results
Expt 2	1. Text only 2. Text plus static visuals 3. Text plus animated visuals		64 adults	An immediate test and a 14-day-delayed test on recall and comprehension of information	NSD among groups
Vaez (2000)	1. Pure animation 2. Animation plus textual narration 3. Animation plus verbal narration	Operation of an internal combustion engine	60 adults	Immediate and delayed tests consisting of a 33-item retention test, an 11-item matching test, and a 7-item transfer test	SD among groups for treatment NSD among groups for exposure time to animation. NSD among groups for sequence of viewing
Westendorp (1996)	1. Text plus spatial information 2. Text only 3. Picture w/ spatial information only 4. Picture only 5. Animation with / spatial information 6. Animation only	Setting up a telephone system	Not given	Time spent reading instructions; time spent performing 13 tasks immediately after instruction and 1 week later	SD among groups for immediate test. In the delayed test NSD among groups for performance
Williams & Abraham (1995) Unit 5	1. Static visuals (control group) 2. Animation in lectures 3. Animation in lectures and laboratories	Understanding the molecular behavior of matters (PNM)	124 adults	For both units: Test of conceptual understanding (PNMET), course achievement test, reasoning ability test (TOLT), and attitude test (BAR)	For Units 5 and 7: SD among groups for conceptual understanding. Both animated groups performed 50% better than the control group (effect size of 0.5). However, they did not differ from each other.
Unit 7	1. Static visuals (control group) 2. Animation in lectures 3. Animation in lectures and laboratories		124 adults		NSD among groups for reasoning abilities, attitude toward instruction, and course achievement
Zavotka (1987)	1. No animation (control group) 2. Animation order 1 3. Animation order 2 4. Animation order 3	Understanding 3D orthographic drawings	101 adults	A mental rotation pretest, an immediate mental rotation test, and a final identification test	Mixed results: NSD among groups for mental rotation test. Animation did not have any effect on the mental rotation test. SD among groups for identification test. One experimental order (natural 3D to natural 2D to a 3D wire frame to a 2D flat line drawing form) scored higher than the control group.

Note. Adult subjects are undergraduate and graduate students. Others are specified.

Spangenberg, R. W. (1973). The motion variable in procedural learning. *AV Communication Review, 21*(4), 419–436.

Spangler, R. D. (1994). *The effects of computer-based animated and static graphics on learning to visualize three-dimensional objects.* Unpublished doctoral dissertation, University of Kentucky.

Spotts, J., & Dwyer, F. (1996). The effects of computer-generated animation on student achievement of different types of educational objectives. *International Journal of Instructional Media, 23*(4), 365–375.

Swezey, R. W. (1991). Effects of instructional strategy and motion presentation conditions on the acquisition and transfer of electromechanical troubleshooting skill. *Human Factors, 33*(3), 309–323.

Szabo, M., & Poohkay, B. (1996). An experimental study of animation, mathematics achievement, and attitude toward computer-assisted instruction. *Journal of Research on Computing in Education, 28*(3), 390–403.

Thompson, S. V., & Riding, R. J. (1990). The effect of animated diagrams on the understanding of a mathematical demonstration in 11- to 14-year-old pupils. *British Journal of Educational Psychology, 60*, 93–98.

Todorov, E., Shadmehr, R., & Bizzi, E. (1997). Augmented feedback presented in virtual environment accelerates learning of a difficult motor task. *Journal of Motor Behavior, 29*(2), 147–158.

Towers, R. (1994). The effects of animated graphics and static graphics on student learning in a computer-based instructional format (Doctoral dissertation, University of Kentucky, 1994). *Dissertation Abstracts International, 55*, 1184A.

Vaez, H. (2000). Effects of narrated computer animation versus pure computer animation on understanding of the operation of an internal combustion engine (Doctoral dissertation, University of Kentucky, 2000). *Dissertation Abstracts International 61*, 4280A.

Westendorp, P. (1996). Learning efficiency with text, pictures, and animation in on-line help. *Journal of Technical Writing and Communication, 26*(4), 401–417.

Williamson, V. M., & Abraham, M. R. (1995). The effects of computer animation on the particulate mental models of college chemistry students. *Journal of Research in Science Teaching, 32*(5), 521–534.

Zavotka, S. L. (1987). Three-dimensional computer animated graphics: A tool for spatial skill instruction. *Educational Communication Technology Journal, 35*(3), 133–144.

References

Ainsworth, S. (1999). The functions of multiple representations. *Computers and Education, 33*, 131–152.

Alesandrini, K. L. (1984). Pictures and adult learning. *Instructional Science, 13*, 63–77.

Anderson, J. R. (1978). Arguments concerning representations for mental imagery. *Psychological Review, 85*, 249–277.

Anglin, G. J., Towers, R. L., & Levie, W. H. (1996). Visual message design and learning: The role of static and animated illustrations. In D. H. Jonassen (Ed.), *Handbook of research for educational communications and technology* (pp. 755–794). New York: Simon & Schuster Macmillan.

Arnheim, R. (1954). *Art and visual perception: A psychology of the creative eye.* Berkeley: University of California Press.

Arnheim, R. (1969). *Visual thinking.* Berkeley: University of California Press.

Arnheim, R. (1974). Virtues and vices of the visual media. In D. R. Olsen (Ed.), *Media and symbols: The forms of expression, communication, and education. The 73 yearbook of the National Society for the Study of Education* (pp. 180–210). Chicago: University of Chicago Press.

Arnheim, R. (1986). *New essays on the psychology of art.* Berkeley: University of California Press.

Biederman, I. (1985). Human image understanding: Recent research and a theory. *Computer Vision, Graphics, and Image Processing, 32*, 29–73.

Biederman, I. (1987). Recognition-by components: A theory of human image understanding. *Psychological Review, 94*, 115–147.

Blinder, D. (1983). The controversy over conventionalism. *Journal of Aesthetics and Art Criticism, 41*, 253–264.

Brody, P. J. (1984). In search of instructional utility: A function-based approach to pictorial research. *Instructional Science, 13*, 47–61.

Bruner, J. S., & Postman, L. (1949). On the perception of incongruity: A paradigm. *Journal of Personality, 18*, 206–223.

Caraballo-Rios, A. L. (1985). An experimental study to investigate the effects of computer animation on the understanding and retention of selected levels of learning outcomes (Doctoral dissertation, Pennsylvania State University, 1985). *Dissertation Abstracts International, 46*, 1494A.

Carrier, D. (1983). Gombrich on art historical explanations. *Leonardo, 16*, 91–96.

Cassidy, M. F. (1982). Toward integration: Education, instructional technology, and semiotics. *Educational Communication and Technology Journal, 30*, 75–89.

Cassirer, E. (1944). *An essay on man.* New Haven, CT: Yale University Press.

Coldron, J. (1982). Peltz on Goodman on exemplification. *Journal of Aesthetic Education, 16*, 88–93.

Concannon, S. J. (1975). Illustrations in books for children: Review of research. *The Reading Teacher, 29*, 254–256.

Connell, J. H., & Brady, M. (1987). Generating and generalizing models of visual objects. *Artificial Intelligence, 31*, 159–183.

Crozier, W. R., & Chapman, A. J. (Eds.). (1984). *Cognitive processes in the perception of art.* Amsterdam: Elsevier Science.

Cutting, J. E. (1982). Two ecological perspectives: Gibson vs. Shaw and Turvey. *American Journal of Psychology, 95*(2), 199–222.

Cutting, J. E. (1987). Perception and information. *Annual Review of Psychology, 38*, 61–90.

Duchastel, P. C. (1978). Illustrating instructional texts. *Educational Technology, 11*, 36–39.

Duchastel, P., & Waller, R. (1979, November). Pictorial illustration in instructional texts. *Educational Technology, 20*–25.

Dwyer, F. M. (1972). *A guide for improving visualized instruction.* State College, PA: Learning Services.

Dwyer, F. M. (1978). *Strategies for improving visual learning.* State College, PA: Learning Services.

Dwyer, F. M. (Ed.). (1987). *Enhancing visualized instruction—Recommendations for practitioners.* State College, PA: Learning Services.

Eco, U. (1976). *A theory of semiotics.* Bloomington: Indiana University.

Elgin, C. Z. (1984). Representation, comprehension, and competence. *Social Research, 51*(4), 905-925.

Feaver, W. (1977). *When we were young: Two centuries of children's book illustration*. London: Thames & Hudson.

Fischler, M., & Firschein, O. (Eds.). (1987). *Readings in computer vision: Issues, problems, principles, and paradigms*. Palo Alto, CA: Morgan Kaufmann.

Fleming, M. (1967). Classification and analysis of instructional illustrations. *AV Communication Review, 15*(3), 246-258.

Fleming, M. (1993). Introduction. In M. Fleming & W. H. Levie (Eds.), *Instructional message design: Principles from the behavioral and cognitive sciences* (p. x). Englewood Cliffs, NJ: Educational Technology.

Fodor, J. H., & Pylyshyn, Z. W. (1981). How direct is visual perception? Some reflections on Gibson's "ecological approach." *Cognition, 9,* 139-196.

Freeman, F. N. (Ed.). (1924). *Visual education: A comparative study of motion pictures and other methods of instruction*. Chicago: University of Chicago Press.

Gardner, H. (1982). *Art, mind, and brain: A cognitive approach to creativity*. New York: Basic Books.

Gardner, H., Howard, V. A., & Perkins, D. (1974). Symbol systems: A philosophical, psychological, and educational investigation. In D. R. Olson (Ed.), *Media and symbols: the forms of expression, communication, and education. The 73 yearbook of the National Society for the Study of Education* (pp. 27-55). Chicago: University of Chicago Press.

Gibson, J. J. (1971). The information available in pictures. *Leonardo, 4,* 27-35.

Gibson, J. J. (1979). *The ecological approach to visual perception*. Boston, MA: Houghton Mifflin.

Gibson, J. J., & Bridgeman, B. (1987). The visual perception of surface texture in photographs. *Psychological Review, 49,* 1-5.

Goldstein, E. B. (1987). Spatial layout, orientation relative to the observer, and perceived projection in pictures viewed at an angle. *Journal of Experimental Psychology: Human Perception and Performance, 13*(2), 256-266.

Gombrich, E. H. (1969). *Art and illusion: A study in the psychology of pictorial representation*. Princeton, NJ: Princeton University Press.

Gombrich, E. H. (1972). The visual image. *Scientific American, 227*(3), 82-96.

Goodman, N. (Ed.). (1976). *Languages of art: An approach to a theory of symbols* (2nd ed.). Indianapolis, IN: Hackett.

Goodman, N. (1978). *Ways of worldmaking*. Indianapolis, IN: Hacket.

Greene, R. (1983). Determining the preferred viewpoint in linear perspective. *Leonardo, 16,* 97-102.

Gregory, R. L. (1970). *The intelligent eye*. New York: McGraw-Hill.

Gregory, R. L. (1973). *Eye and brain*. New York: McGraw-Hill.

Gregory, R. L. (1981). Questions of pattern and object perception by man and computer. In J. Long & A. Baddeley (Eds.), *Attention and performance IX* (pp. 97-116). Hillsdale, NJ: Lawrence Erlbaum.

Haber, R. N. (1979). Perceiving the layout of space in pictures: A perspective theory based upon Leonardo da Vinci. In C. F. Nodine & D. F. Fisher (Eds.), *Perception and pictorial representation* (pp. 84-99). New York: Praeger.

Hagen, M. A. (1978). An outline of an investigation into the special character of pictures. In H. L. J. Pick & E. Saltzman (Eds.), *Modes of perceiving and processing information* (pp. 23-38). New York: John Wiley.

Hagen, M. A. (1980a). Generative theory: A perceptual theory of pictorial representation. In M. A. Hagen (Ed.), *The perception of pictures, Vol. 2* (pp. 3-46). New York: Academic Press.

Hagen, M. A. (Ed.). (1980b). *The perception of pictures, Vol. 1. Alberti's window: The projective model of pictorial information*. New York: Academic Press.

Hagen, M. A. (Ed.). (1980c). *The perception of pictures, Vol. 2. Durer's devices: Beyond the projective model of pictures*. New York: Academic Press.

Hagen, M. A. (1986). *Varieties of realism: Geometries of representational art*. New York: Cambridge University Press.

Heffernan, J. A. (1985). Resemblance, signification, and metaphor in the visual arts. *Journal of Aesthetics and Arts Criticism, 44*(2), 167-180.

Hochberg, J. (1972). The representation of things and people. In E. H. Gombrich, J. Hochberg, & M. Black (Eds.), *Art, perception, and reality* (pp. 47-94). Baltimore: Johns Hopkins Press.

Hochberg, J. (1979). Some of the things that paintings are. In C. F. Nodine & D. F. Fisher (Eds.), *Perception and pictorial representation* (pp. 17-41). New York: Praeger.

Hochberg, J. (1980). Pictorial functions and perceptual structures. In M. A. Hagen (Ed.), *The perception of pictures, Vol. 2* (pp. 47-93). New York: Academic Press.

Hoffman, W. C., & Dodwell, P. C. (1985). Geometric psychology generates the visual Gestalt. *Canadian Journal of Psychology, 39,* 491-528.

Holliday, W. G. (1973). Critical analysis of pictorial research related to science education. *Science Education, 57*(2), 201-214.

Holowka, T. (1981). On conventionality of signs. *Semiotica, 33,* 79-86.

Jackendoff, R. (1987). On beyond zebra: The relation of linguistic and visual information. *Cognition, 26,* 89-114.

Katz, S. (1983). R. L. Gregory and others: The wrong picture of the picture theory of perception. *Perception, 12,* 269-279.

Kennedy, J. M. (1974). *A psychology of picture perception*. San Francisco: Jossey-Bass.

Kennedy, J. M. (1984a). Gombrich and Winner: Schema theories of perception in aesthetics. *Visual Arts Research, 10*(2), 30-36.

Kennedy, J. M. (1984b). How minds use pictures. *Social Research, 51*(4), 885-904.

Kennedy, J. M. (1985). Arnheim, Gestalt theory and pictures. *Visual Arts Research, 11,* 23-44.

Kieras, D. (1978). Beyond pictures and words: Alternative information processing models for imagery effects in verbal memory. *Psychological Bulletin, 85,* 532-554.

Kitcher, P. (1988). Marrs's computational theory of vision. *Philosophy of Science, 55,* 1-24.

Knowlton, J. Q. (1964). *A socio- and psycho-linguistic theory of pictorial communication*. Bloomington: Indiana University.

Knowlton, J. Q. (1966). On the definition of "picture." *AV Communication Review, 14,* 157-183.

Kolers, P. A. (1983). Perception and representation. *Annual Review of Psychology, 34,* 129-166.

Kolers, P. A., & Smythe, W. E. (1984). Symbol manipulation: Alternatives to the computational view of mind. *Journal of Verbal Learning and Verbal Behavior, 23,* 289-314.

Kosslyn, S. M. (1980). *Image and mind*. Cambridge, MA: Harvard University Press.

Kosslyn, S. M. (1981). The medium and the message in mental imagery: A theory. *Psychological Review, 88,* 46-66.

Kosslyn, S. M. (1986). Toward a computational neuropsychology of high-level vision. In T. J. Knapp & L. C. Robertson (Eds.), *Approaches to cognition: Contrasts and controversies* (pp. 223-242). Hillsdale, NJ: Lawrence Erlbaum.

Kosslyn, S. M. (1987). Seeing and imagining in the cerebral hemispheres: A computational approach. *Psychological Review, 94*(2), 148-175.

Kubovy, M. (1986). *The psychology of perspective and Renaissance art*. New York: Cambridge University Press.

Langer, S. (1976). *Philosophy in a new key* (3rd ed.). Cambridge, MA: Harvard University Press.

Levie, W. H. (1978). A prospectus for instructional research on visual literacy. *Educational Communication and Technology Journal, 26*, 25-36.

Levie, W. H. (1987). Research on pictures: A guide to the literature. In D. M. Willows & H. A. Houghton (Eds.), *The psychology of illustration: Volume 1 Basic research* (pp. 1-50). New York: Springer-Verlag.

Levie, W. H., & Dickie, K. E. (1973). The analysis and application of media. In R. M. W. Travers (Ed.), *Second handbook of research on teaching* (pp. 858-882). Chicago: Rand McNally.

Levie, W. H., & Lentz, R. (1982). Effects of text illustrations: A review of research. *Educational Communication and Technology Journal, 30*(4), 195-232.

Levin, J. R. (1981). On the functions of pictures in prose. In F. J. Pirozzolo & M. C. Wittrock (Eds.), *Neuropsychological and cognitive processes in reading* (pp. 203-228). New York: Academic Press.

Levin, J. R., & Lesgold, A. M. (1978). On pictures in prose. *Educational Communication and Technology Journal, 26*, 233-243.

Levin, J. R., Anglin, G. J., & Carney, R. N. (1987). On empirically validating functions of pictures in prose. In D. M. Willows & H. A. Houghton (Eds.), *The psychology of illustration* (pp. 51-80). New York: Springer-Verlag.

Lowe, D. G. (1987). Three-dimensional object recognition from single two-dimensional images. *Artificial Intelligence, 31*, 355-395.

Lumsdaine, A. A., Sultzer, R. L., & Kopstein, F. F. (1961). The effect of animation cues and repetition of examples on learning from an instructional film. In A. A. Lumsdaine (Ed.), *Student Response in Programmed Instruction* (pp. 241-269). Washington, DC: National Research Council.

Marr, D. (1982). *Vision: A computational investigation into the human representation and processing of visual information*. San Francisco: W. H. Freeman.

May, M. A., & Lumsdaine, A. A. (1958). *Learning from films*. New Haven, CT: Yale University Press.

Miller, G. A. (1956). The magical number seven plus or minus two: Some limits on our capacity for processing information. *Psychological Review, 63*, 81-97.

Mitchell, W. J. T. (Ed.). (1980). *The languages of images*. Chicago: University of Chicago Press.

Morris, C. W. (1946). *Signs, language and behavior*. Englewood Cliffs, NJ: Prentice Hall.

Natsoulas, T. (1983). What are the objects of perceptual consciousness? *American Journal of Psychology, 96*(4), 435-467.

Neisser, U. (1976). *Cognition and reality*. San Francisco: W. H. Freeman.

Nelson, D. L. (1979). Remembering pictures and words: Appearance, significance, and name. In L. S. Cermak & F. I. M. Craik (Ed.), *Levels of processing in human memory* (pp. 45-76). Hillsdale, NJ: Erlbaum.

Nelson, D. L., Reed, V. S., & Walling, J. R. (1976). The pictorial superiority effect. *Journal of Experimental Psychology: Human Learning and Memory, 2*, 523-528.

Nodine, C. F., & Fisher, D. F. (Eds.). (1979). *Perception and pictorial representation*. New York: Praeger.

Olson, D. R. (Ed.). (1974). *Media and symbols: The forms of expression, communication, and education. The 73 yearbook of the National Society for the Study of Education*. Chicago: University of Chicago Press.

Paivio, A. (1971). *Imagery and verbal processes*. New York: Holt, Rinehart & Winston.

Paivio, A. (1978). A dual coding approach to perception and cognition. In J. & H. L. Pick, Jr. & E. Saltzman (Eds.), *Modes of perceiving and processing information* (pp. 39-51). Hillsdale, NJ: Erlbaum.

Paivio, A. (1990). *Mental representations: A dual coding approach* (2nd ed.). New York: Oxford University Press.

Paivio, A. (1991). Dual coding theory: Retrospect and current status. *Canadian Journal of Psychology, 45*, 255-287.

Park, O., & Hopkins, R. (1993). Instructional conditions for using animated visual displays: A review. *Instructional Science, 22*, 1-24.

Penrice, L. (1980). The background to perspective. *Information Design Journal, 1*, 190-203.

Perkins, D. N., & Leondar, B. (Eds.). (1977). *The arts and cognition*. Baltimore, MD: Johns Hopkins University Press.

Peterson, M. A., & Hochberg, J. (1983). Opposed-set measurement procedure: A quantitative analysis of the role of local cues and intention in form perception. *Journal of Experimental Psychology: Human Perception and Performance, 9*, 183-193.

Pierce, C. S. (1960). *The icon, index, andd symbol (1902): Collected papers*. Cambridge, MA: Harvard University Press.

Pirenne, M. H. (1970). *Optics, painting, and photography*. Cambridge: Cambridge University Press.

Pylyshyn, Z. W. (1981). The imagery debate: Analogue media versus tacit knowledge. *Psychological Review, 88*, 16-45.

Readence, J. E., & Moore, D. W. (1981). A meta-analytic review of the effect of adjunct pictures on reading comprehension. *Psychology in the Schools, 18*, 218-224.

Reed, E., & Jones, R. (Eds.). (1982). *Reasons for realism: Selected essays of James J. Gibson*. Hillsdale, NJ: Erlbaum.

Rieber, L. P. (1989, February). *A review of animation research in computer-based instruction*. Proceedings of selected research papers presented at the annual meeting of the Association for Educational Communications and Technology, Dallas, TX. (ERIC Document Reproduction Service No. 308-832)

Rieber, L. P. (1990). Animation in computer-based instruction. *Educational Technology Research and Development, 38*(1), 77-86.

Rieber, L. P. (1994). *Computers, graphics, and learning*. Madison, WI: WCB Brown & Benchmark.

Rogers, S., & Costall, A. (1983). On the horizon: Picture perception and Gibson's concept of information. *Leonardo, 16*, 180-182.

Rosenfeld, A. (1986). *Human and machine vision II*. New York: Academic Press.

Roupas, T. G. (1977). Information and pictorial representation. In D. Perkins & B. Leondar (Eds.), *The arts and cognition* (pp. 48-79). Baltimore: Johns Hopkins Press.

Salomon, G. (1979a). *Interaction of media, cognition, and learning: An exploration of how symbolic forms cultivate mental skills and affect knowledge acquisition*. San Francisco: Jossey-Bass.

Salomon, G. (1979b). Media and symbol systems as related to cognition and learning. *Journal of Educational Psychology, 71*, 131-148.

Samuels, S. J. (1967). Attentional process in reading: The effect of pictures on the acquisition of reading responses. *Journal of Educational Psychology, 58*(6), 337-342.

Samuels, S. J. (1970). Effects of pictures on learning to read, comprehension and attitudes. *Review of Educational Research, 40*, 397-407.

Schallert, D. L. (1980). The role of illustrations in reading comprehension. In B. Spiro & W. F. Brewer (Eds.), *Theoretical Issues in Reading Comprehension* (pp. 503-523). Hillsdale, NJ: Lawrence Erlbaum.

Scruton, R. (1974). *Art and imagination*. New York: Harper & Row.

Sebeok, T. A. (1976). *Contributions to the doctrine of signs: Studies in semiotics, Vol. 5*. Bloomington: Indiana University Press.

Shepard, R. N. (1978). The mental image. *American Psychologist, 33*, 125-137.

Sless, D. (1986). Reading semiotics. *Information Design Journal, 4,* 179-189.

Slythe, R. M. (1970). *The art of illustration 1750-1900.* London: The Library Association.

Smith, M. C., & Magee, L. E. (1980). Tracing the time course of picture-word processing. *Journal of Experimental Psychology: General, 109,* 373-392.

Spaulding, S. (1955). Research on pictorial illustration. *AV Communication Review, 3,* 35-45.

Sweller, J. (1988). Cognitive load during problem solving: Effects on learning. *Cognitive Science, 12,* 257-285.

Sweller, J., Van Merrienboer, J. J. G., & Pass, F. G. W. C. (1998). Cognitive architecture and instructional design. *Educational Psychology Review, 10*(3), 251-296.

Twyman, M. (1985). Using pictorial language: A discussion of the dimensions of the problem. In T. M. D. & R. Waller (Eds.), *Designing usable texts* (pp. 245-312). New York: Academic Press.

Veltrusky, J. (1976). Some aspects of the pictorial sign. In L. Matejka & I. R. Titunik (Eds.), *Semiotics of art* (pp. 245-264). Cambridge, MA: MIT Press.

Vitz, P. C., & Glimcher, A. B. (1984). *Modern art and modern science.* New York: Praeger.

Weber, J. J. (1926). Three important studies on the use of educational films. In A. P. Hollis (Ed.), *Motion pictures for instruction* (pp. 162-196). New York: Century.

Wilcox, S., & Edwards, D. A. (1982). Some Gibsonian perspectives on the ways that psychologists use physics. *Acta Psychologica, 52,* 147-163.

Winn, B. (1987). Charts, graphs, and diagrams in educational materials. In D. M. Willows & H. A. Houghton (Eds.), *The psychology of illustration* (pp. 152-193). New York: Springer-Verlag.

·34·

DESIGNING INSTRUCTIONAL AND INFORMATIONAL TEXT

James Hartley
University of Keele

34.1 INTRODUCTION

This chapter is divided into eight sections as follows.

1. Introduction
2. Typographical Considerations in the Design of Text
3. Navigating Text: Structure and Access
4. Making Text Easier to Understand
5. Measuring the Difficulty of Text
6. Designing Text for Readers with Special Needs
7. Using Textbooks
8. Future Directions

My aim in each section is to present a particular argument, supported by references to empirical research. In addition, I hope that these references will allow interested readers to follow up the issues raised more widely, should they wish. Regrettably I have decided that there is no one clear theoretical perspective that I could take in writing this chapter so, accordingly, none is offered. However, references to particular paradigms in text design are made where it seems appropriate. One important aspect of instructional and informational text design omitted in this chapter is that of the design and positioning of elements such as tables, diagrams, graphs, and figures. These issues are discussed in other chapters.

34.2 TYPOGRAPHICAL CONSIDERATIONS IN THE DESIGN OF TEXT

34.2.1 Page Sizes

Printed materials come in many shapes and sizes. There are no specific rules or guidelines that might suggest to writers, designers, or printers why they should choose one particular page size in preference to any other. The research literature on legibility, textbook, and informational design offers little help, for page size is not an issue that features in many books on this topic. Why, then, do I choose to start this chapter by discussing page sizes?

Many people expect a chapter such as this to begin with issues such as type sizes, typefaces, and line lengths. However, it is important to realize that the choices for these variables are already constrained by earlier decisions. Clearly we do not expect to find large type sizes in a pocket dictionary or a single column of print in a daily newspaper. These examples are extreme, but they illustrate the point. The choice of page size comes first, and this affects the choices that are available for subsequent decisions.

The size of the page (and these days, the electronic screen) determines the size of the overall visual display. The reader needs to be able to scan, read, and focus on both the gross and the fine details of this display. The size of the page (or screen) constrains the decisions that writers and designers make about these details.

The choice of an appropriate page size for printed text is not always easy. A number of factors contribute to decisions about which size to employ. Perhaps the most important one is knowledge of how the information is going to be used. Others are reader preferences, the costs of production and marketing, basic paper sheet sizes, and, more generally, the need to conserve resources and avoid waste (Hartley, 1994a; Spencer, 1969).

34.2.2 Standard Page Sizes

The page sizes that we commonly see for printed text are cut from much larger basic sheets that have been folded several

TABLE 34.1. The ISO A Series of Trimmed Paper Sizes

Designation	Size (mm)
A0	841 × 1,189
A1	594 × 841
A2	420 × 594
A3	297 × 420
A4	210 × 297
A5	148 × 210
A6	105 × 148
A7	74 × 105
A8	52 × 74
A9	37 × 52
A10	26 × 37

times. The present-day variety in page sizes results from the manufacturers using different sizes for their basic printing sheets and folding them in different ways. If the basic printing sheets were all one standard size, however, and if the method of folding them allowed for little if any wastage at the cutting stage, then great economies could be achieved.

The need to rationalize paper sizes has long been discussed in the history of information printing. In 1798, for example, the French government prescribed a standard for official documents based on the proportion of width:height 1:1.41, with a basic printing sheet 1m^2 in area. In 1911, Wilhelm Oswald proposed the ratio 1:1.414 (that is, 1: $\sqrt{2}$) as the "world format." In 1922 the German standard, DIN 476, was published. For this standard the ratio of width:height 1: $\sqrt{2}$ was retained, with a basic printing sheet size of 1m^2. This German standard, together with the A, B, and C series of sizes, was adopted in 1958 by the International Standards Organization (ISO). Today the ISO series is recommended by the 50 or more national standards bodies that together make up the ISO.

The dimensions of the sizes in the ISO A series are set out in Table 34.1. In the United Kingdom the A series is used widely, especially the A4 and A5 sizes. The unifying principle of the ISO-recommended range of sizes is that a rectangle with sides at a 1:$\sqrt{2}$ can be halved or doubled to produce a series of rectangles, each of which retains the proportions of the original. A rectangle of any other proportion will generate geometrically similar rectangles only at every other point in the process of halving or doubling (see Fig. 34.1).

As the pages of a book are made by folding the larger basic printing sheet in half—once, twice, three times, or more—all the pages made from a standard-size basic sheet will be at the ratio 1:$\sqrt{2}$. Basic sheets that do not conform to this standard do not exhibit this property of geometric similarity when folded, and this creates waste.

We may note at this point, of course, that a page can be bound in a vertical (*portrait*) or a horizontal (*landscape*) style. Pages can be also bound at the top (as in a notebook) as well as on the left. These variations allow for a variety of page layouts (see Fig. 34.2). Curiously enough, there is almost no research comparing the effects of setting the same texts in portrait or landscape style (Hartley & Johnson, 2000).

It is considerations such as these that come first when designing instructional and informational text. Once these decisions have been made (but not necessarily finalized) the designer can begin to think more about the details of the typography. The next step is to consider the number of columns of print required, their widths, and that of the margins.

34.2.3 Margins

In many books, the margins appear to be planned like a picture frame around a rectangle of print. Tinker (1965) reported that the space devoted to margins in this way could sometimes occupy as much as 50% of the page. However, if we take a functional approach rather than an aesthetic one, it seems to be fairly well agreed that a margin of about 10 mm is necessary at the top and the bottom of the page. But the inner, or binding-edge, margin is a special case. Here thought needs to be given to factors that suggest the need for a wider margin. For example, the printed page may be copied at some time, and the copies punched or clipped for filing with other material. The binding system itself may involve the punching of pages, or it may be of the kind that causes some part of the edge of the page to be hidden from view. Indeed, the binding system may be such that text or diagrams printed too close to the binding edge may curve inward and be difficult to read (or to copy). So, because text appears on both the front and the back of the page, a margin of about 25 mm is usually necessary for both the left- and the right-hand margins.

34.2.4 Column Widths

The choice of column widths also depends on the size of the page, the widths of the margins, and the nature of the text. For printed text it is normal to consider one, two, or even three columns of print (depending on the page size and its orientation). A decision to use three columns of print may be appropriate for text that is not very complex (typographically speaking), especially in a landscape format. Other variations, such as one wide column and one narrow one, are possible with larger (portrait) page sizes, and it is useful to consider this when planning the size and positioning of illustrative materials (see Hartley, 1994a, and Misanchuk, 1992, for a fuller discussion).

34.2.5 Type Sizes

Several researchers have made suggestions concerning the appropriate type sizes for reading matter and have given advice on related issues such as line length and line spacing. Tinker (1963, 1965) and Watts and Nisbet (1974) provide good summaries of the earlier literature in this respect, and Black (1990) and Schriver (1997) provide more up to date accounts.

Unfortunately much of the early research on type sizes was not very helpful to designers of instructional or informational text. This was principally because the variables such as type size, line length, and interline space were not studied in the "real-life"

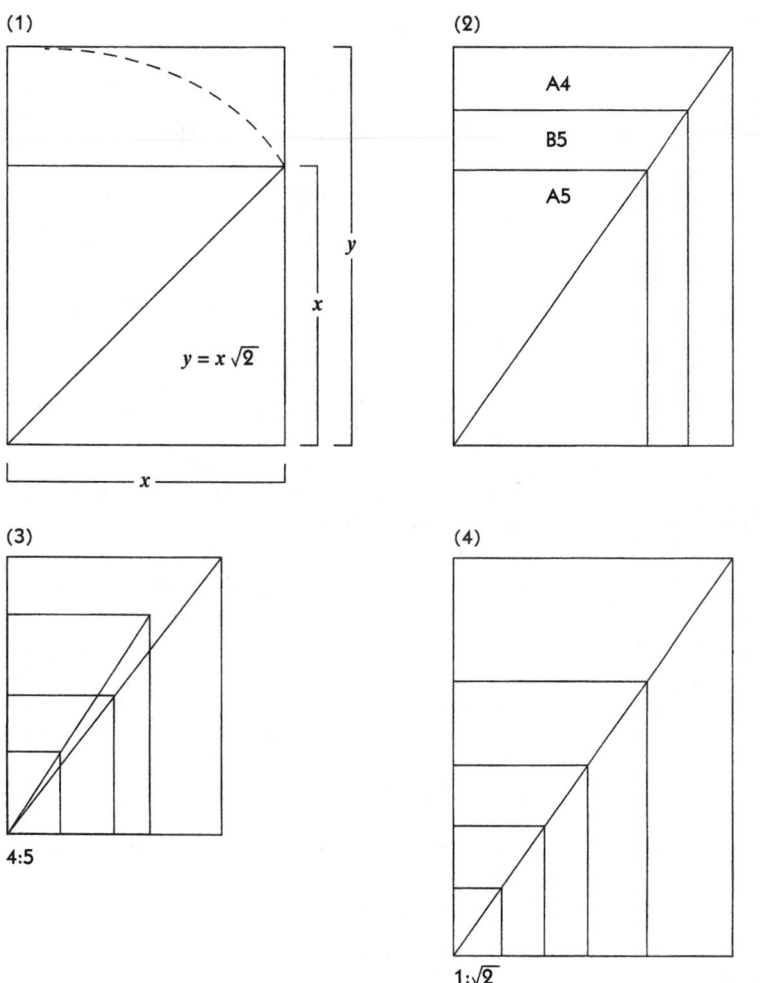

1. This diagram illustrates the principle of construction and shows that the ratio of the sides of the rectangle is the same as that of the side of a square to its diagonal.

2. This illustrates the fit between the A and the B series of sizes. For example, B5 falls between A5 and A4 and is geometrically similar.

3. A rectangle of nonstandard proportions. Note that the process of halving generates two geometrically dissimilar series of rectangles.

4. A rectangle of standard proportions. This case is unique in that halving generates geometrically similar rectangles at each point in the series.

FIGURE 34.1. The principles underlying the recommended page sizes of the International Standards Organization.

context of instructional materials. Most early researchers, for example, considered issues of type size with short, simple settings of continuous prose (e.g., see Paterson & Tinker, 1929). Furthermore, the generalizations that emerged from this research did not take into account the difficulties that arose from the fact that different typefaces with the same designated type sizes do not, in fact, look the same.

There are many different measurement systems used in the printing industry but, with the advent of computer-aided printing, these will undoubtedly be rationalized. One measure that still seems to remain for some reason, however, is the *point*. (A point measures 0.0138 inc.) Typical type sizes in textbooks are 10, 11, and 12 point. The "small print" (in legal documents, for example) may be 6 or 8 point, but this is too small for most people to read with ease. Larger sizes (such as 14, 18, and 24 point) are used for headings and display purposes. The typographic setting of a text is often described, for example, as "10-on-12" point. This indicates that there is an extra space of 2 points between the lines of print to facilitate reading.

However, as noted above, a confusing aspect of past research in this field has been the tendency to recommend the use of specific type sizes without proper regard for the fact that the specified size of a particular typeface (say 12 point) does not actually refer to the size of the image of the printed characters as seen by the reader. The specified size refers instead to the original depth of space that was required by a line of metal type when it was set with minimum line-to-line spacing. Letters were originally carved on the top of the metal shanks that took up this space. Consequently, the size and style of the letters on the top of the shank could vary, although the measure of the particular shank remained the same.

Figure 34.3, for instance, shows the same sentence printed in one size of type but in five different typefaces. As can be seen, at best, type size is but a first approximation to image size. The effect is more dramatic when

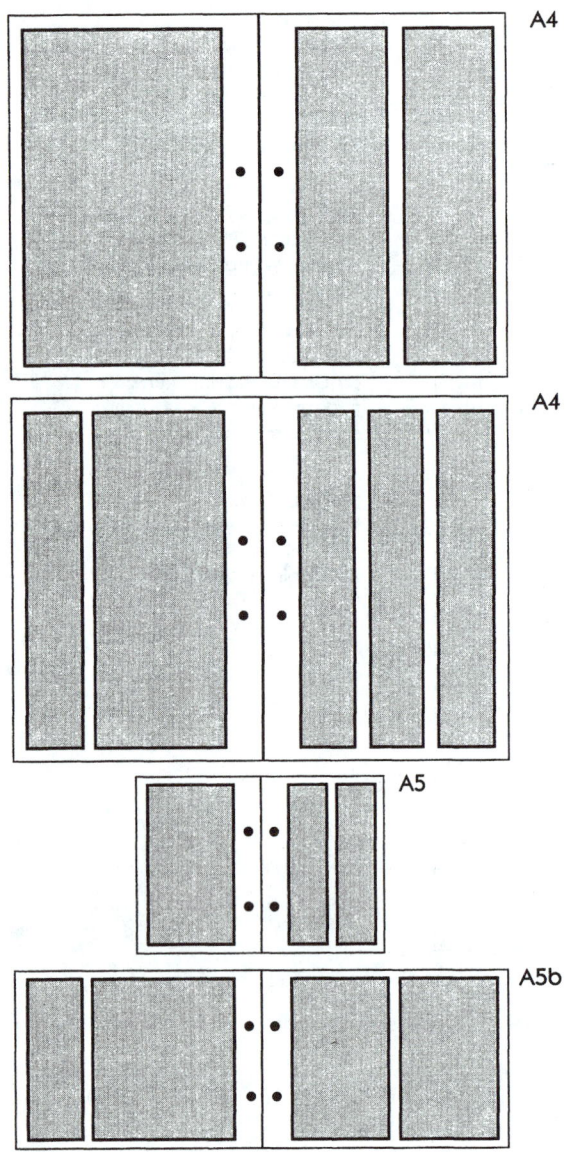

FIGURE 34.2. How a standard-size sheet can be arranged to provide a variety of page layouts.

whole paragraphs, rather than single sentences, are considered. This particular paragraph is printed in 12-point Arial. The following paragraph is printed in 12-point Bookman to illustrate the point.

So it is not my intention here to recommend specific type sizes for use in printing instructional materials. However, I would like to outline one approach to the problem of choosing a type size for a text. At root, this concerns choosing the

This is 12-point Times Roman

This is 12-point Palatino

This is 12-point Helvetica

This is 12-point Century Schoolbook

This is 12-point Bookman

FIGURE 34.3. How different typefaces with the same designated type size actually differ in size.

maximum permissible line length that, when related to the type size, will not obstruct the proper and sensible phrasing of the information.

Designers need to examine their text carefully to look for problems that can arise if they choose too large a typeface. For example, in children's reading books, the maximum permissible line length is often limited by the use of large type sizes to being only three or four words long. In this case, it is often difficult to group syntactically the words in the lines. Indeed, some children think that sentences are completed at the end of each line (Raban, 1982). Thus, as shown in the preceding Bookman paragraph, one of the primary dimensions to be considered when thinking about type sizes is the width of the character groups and syntactically structured word strings, and not just the vertical dimension of the characters.

34.2.6 Typefaces

One particular source of confusion for novice designers is how to choose an appropriate typeface from the bewildering range of typefaces currently available. For example, one encyclopedia of typefaces published in 1930 listed over 2,350 entries. Today there must be several thousands of typefaces available, and designers are frequently encouraged to create their own. So how does one decide?

In practice, as Black (1990) points out, choosing a typeface really means

1. considering the purpose of the text,
2. making sure that the chosen sizes and weights required for the text (e.g., light, medium, bold) are available,
3. making sure that the character set contains not only the commonly used signs but also any additional special characters called for by the text (e.g., mathematical symbols), and
4. considering how well particular typefaces will withstand repeated copying.

Certain typefaces seem more appropriate in some situations than others. Neither Gothic nor Balloon, for example, would seem very helpful for instructional text, although they may be appropriate for party invitations. Typefaces thus have emotional connotations (see Lewis & Walker, 1989; Tannenbaum,

Jacobson, & Norris, 1964). Spencer (1969) provides a review of earlier studies in this respect. Furthermore, some readers have personal preferences (see Misanchuk, 1992). These individual differences suggest that it may be wiser to stick to conventional and familiar typefaces than it is to employ idiosyncratic ones. Black (1990) and Schriver (1997) provide useful full-length treatments of these issues.

One way of classifying familiar typefaces is in terms of those that have serifs (finishing strokes at the ends of letters) and those that do not (sans serifs). For example, this paragraph is printed in a serif typeface. The following paragraph is printed in a sans serif face, to illustrate the effects.

The available research gives no clear guidance on which typefaces are best. Some designers recommend that faces with serifs be used for the body of the text and that faces without serifs be used for headings or for other purposes (such as to differentiate examples from the body of the text). Others consider that typefaces without serifs are more legible in the smaller sizes (e.g., 6 and 8 point) and go on to argue that such sans serif typefaces are better for text that is not intended for continuous reading (e.g., reference works, tables, catalogs). Others indeed suggest that sans serif faces are more appropriate for older readers (see below).

Berger (1991), Misanchuk (1992), and Schriver (1997) review the relevant literature in this field. They conclude that one has to make decisions here that are based on good practice and common sense. I would add, too, that there are so many typefaces within each group (serif or sans serif) that it makes little sense to generalize in terms of comparing faces with serifs with those without them. It is better to consider how different typefaces compare and to specify which ones are being discussed.

34.2.7 Capital Letters

Words printed in capital letters contain less distinctive information per unit of space than do words set in lowercase characters of the same type size (Tinker, 1965; Tinker & Paterson, 1928).

THUS IT IS GENERALLY BELIEVED THAT WHOLE PARAGRAPHS OF TEXT SET IN CAPITAL LETTERS ARE MORE DIFFICULT TO READ THAN ARE PARAGRAPHS SET IN NORMAL UPPER- AND LOWERCASE LETTERS. THE USE OF STRINGS OF WORDS IN CAPITALS FOR MAIN HEADINGS (OR SMALL CAPITALS FOR SECONDARY HEADINGS) MAY BE SATISFACTORY BECAUSE SUCH HEADINGS ARE NORMALLY SURROUNDED BY SPACE, WHICH AIDS THEIR PERCEPTION. ON THE WHOLE, THOUGH, THE USE OF CAPITAL LETTERS SHOULD BE KEPT TO A MINIMUM. APART FROM SPECIALIZED USE IN MATHEMATICAL WORK, CAPITAL LETTERS ARE BEST RESERVED FOR THE FIRST LETTER OF A SENTENCE (INCLUDING HEADINGS) AND FOR THE FIRST LETTER OF PROPER NOUNS.

34.2.8 Italicized Letters

Sloping or italic characters were originally introduced into printed books in the sixteenth century. With italics you could have more characters to the line, the style of letters being more compressed than the vertically drawn and rounded forms of the normal lowercase character set. Again, it is commonly believed that continuous italic text is harder to read than the more conventional typographic settings. (See Misanchuk, 1992, and Schriver, 1997, for further discussion.) Today, italicized characters are often used in instructional text for emphasizing words, for book titles when these appear in the text or in bibliographic references, and sometimes for setting summaries or abstracts.

34.2.9 Color

Color can be used in textbooks in many ways. Sometimes, for example, colored headings are used simply to make the text more appealing. In other situations subtexts may be set in a different color to differentiate them from the main content.

There is a considerable amount of research on the effectiveness of color in printed instructional text (see Dwyer, 1978; Keys, 1993; Tinker, 1965) and this is an issue that is also prominent in current work with multimedia. As it happens there appear to be few clear generalizations that one can make but it does seem that

- readers have color preferences;
- readers like additional color; and
- color can help learning (see Dwyer, 1978); but
- extra colors have to be used sparingly and consistently if they are not to confuse the readers;
- some colors stand out more than others, so it is unhelpful to use a range of colors on the same page;
- certain combinations of colored inks on colored papers are more legible than others—thus, for example, black ink on white or yellow paper is generally preferable to red ink on these colors, and black ink on dark red or purple paper is generally to be avoided (see Dwyer, 1978, and Keys, 1993, for further details); and
- certain colors and combinations of colors do not copy well in black and white (so details may get lost when black and white copies are made). (This consideration also applies to screens when some readers only have black-and-white visual display units.)

It must be remembered, of course, that young readers cannot be expected to know automatically why any change from the traditional norm has taken place. This particularly applies to the printing of individual words in bold, capitals, italics, or color. Early readers need to be taught these conventions. And, in addition, we need to remember that all of these devices need to be used sparingly—as they can lose their significance when they are used in combination or to excess (see, e.g., Foster, 1979; Hershberger & Terry, 1965; Murphy, Duffy, & Goodrum, Welsh, 1993).

Finally, we should also note in this section that it is not wise to present readers with text that continually changes its size, its spacing, and its typefaces. A brief rule of thumb might be that there is no need to use three or more additional cues when one or two will do.

34.2.10   Spacing the Text

One of the main arguments in this chapter is that the way in which the designer uses the space on the page greatly affects how easily the reader can understand and retrieve the information from it. Although the text is important—one cannot do without it—I argue that the clarity of the text can be enhanced by a rational and consistent use of the "white space" (Hartley, 1994a).

But first a bit more history. Most people today know what a textbook looks like and how it is arranged. But, as Small (1997) points out, books began originally as vertical rolls. The concept of a page did not exist, and there were no page breaks or page numbers. Furthermore, in Classical Greek times, there were no breaks between words, sentences, or even paragraphs. (The paragraph as a unit of text on the page did not appear until the sixteenth century.) Cross-references were very vague, like "see above" and "see below." The letters forming the words were of the same height and, often, of the same width. Line lengths were equal, and words were split at the ends of lines without hyphenation. Figure 34.4 simulates what such text used to look like. It is clear to our modern eyes that punctuation and spacing, together with upper- and-lowercase letters, make text easier to read.

Space thus plays an important role in clarifying text. It is space that separates letters from each other. It is space that separates words from each other. It is space (with punctuation) that separates phrases, clauses, and paragraphs from each other; and it is space (with headings and subheadings) that separates subsections and chapters from one another.

There is some evidence from eye-movement research that shows that these spatial cues are important aids to understanding text (Rayner, Kambe, & Duffy, 2000). It is argued, for instance, that with increasing maturity and experience, readers come to rely more heavily on such spatial cues to enhance their reading and search efficiency (e.g., see Fisher, 1976). It has

BOOKXXXIVCONTENTSCOPPERMETALKINDSOFCOPPERC
ORINTHIANDELIANAEGINETANONBRONZEDININGCOUC
HESONCANDELABRAONTEMPLEDECORATIONSOFBRON
ZEFIRSTBRONZEIMAGEOFAGODMADEATROMEONTHEO
RIGINALSTATUTESA

Book XXXIV. Contents: Copper metal. Kinds of copper:
Corinthian, Delian, Aeginetan. On bronze dining
couches; on candelabra; on temple decorations of
bronze; first bronze. . . .

FIGURE 34.4. The top illustration shows schematically the original way of presenting Classical Greek text. The bottom illustration shows the conventional way of presenting text today. Note that the original text would also have been in handwriting, which would have made it even more difficult to read. (Figure based on illustrations from Small, 1998, and reproduced with permission.)

been found that the beginning of a line—and not its end—has a more marked effect on eye-movement fixations and that text that starts in an irregular manner, such as poetry, produces more regressive fixations (look backs) than does regularly spaced text (Carpenter & Just, 1977).

In this chapter I maintain that consistent spacing helps readers to

1. see redundancies in the text and thus to read faster,
2. see more easily which bits of the text are personally relevant for them,
3. see the structure of the document as a whole, and
4. grasp its organization.

34.2.10.1   Vertical Spacing. The spacing of a page can be considered from both a vertical and a horizontal point of view. Let us consider vertical spacing first. The argument here is that the underlying structure of complex text can be made more apparent to the reader by the consistent and planned use of vertical spacing. In practice this means that predetermined increments of line space can be used consistently to separate out the components of the text—such as sentences, paragraphs, and sub- and major headings.

One simple way of using line space in this way is to use it in a proportional system. One can, for example, separate paragraphs by one line space, separate subheadings from paragraphs by two extra lines above and one below them, and separate main headings from text by four extra lines above and two below them. With more complex text one can even start each sentence on a new line within each paragraph.

What is the effect of such an approach? Figure 34.5a shows a traditionally spaced piece of text, and Figure 34.5b shows a revised version using the system described above. Such a proportional system is an effective way of determining that the amount of space between the component parts of a piece of text is consistent throughout the work. Other systems (not proportional but equally consistent) can be used. Indeed, for even more complex text one might wish to introduce indentation into the text to convey further substructure.

Research has shown that readers usually prefer lengthy paragraphs to be set in a more open manner (e.g., see Hartley, Trueman, & Burnhill, 1980). Readers thus generally prefer text set in the style of Fig. 34.5b to that of Fig. 34.5a. Finally, in this section on vertical spacing, we should note that if the vertical spacing between the components of the text is to be consistent throughout the text, this leads to the idea that the text will have a "floating baseline." This means that, in contrast to most textbooks, the text does not stop at the same place on every page, irrespective of its content. With a floating baseline the stopping point for each page is determined by the content and the structure of the text rather than by the need to fill the page.

As a rule of thumb we can say that each page of a printed text should have a specified number of lines plus or minus two. This flexibility allows the designer to avoid *widows* or *orphans*—where a page starts with the last line of a previous paragraph or ends with a heading or the first line of a new paragraph—without changing the underlying spacing of the

General

This section describes the care, maintenance, and inspection of insulating rubber blankets. This section is reissued to delete reference to the KS-13602 cleaner; this has been superseded by the B cleaning fluid (AT-8236).

Description

An insulating rubber blanket is made of flat, flexible sheets of black rubber. These sheets do not contain either beaded edges or eyelets. The blankets are approximately 36 inches square, $^1/_{10}$ inch thick, and weigh approximately 7 pounds. The electrical, weather, and chemical resistance properties of the blanket are very good.

Rubber-stamped on each blanket is a "return for test" date. Blankets must be returned for testing by that date to the Western Electric Company or other authorized agent. The blankets should be returned in rolls (3½ inches in diameter) and wrapped properly so as to avoid damage. A replacement blanket will be made available when a blanket is returned for testing.

FIGURE 34.5(a). A traditionally spaced piece of text.

General

This section describes the care, maintenance, and inspection of insulating rubber blankets.
This section is reissued to delete reference to the KS-13602 cleaner; this has been superseded by the B cleaning fluid (AT-8236).

Description

An insulating rubber blanket is made of flat, flexible sheets of black rubber.
These sheets do not contain either beaded edges or eyelets.
The blankets are approximately 36 inches square, $^1/_{10}$ inch thick, and weigh approximately 7 pounds.
The electrical, weather, and chemical resistance properties of the blanket are very good.

Rubber-stamped on each blanket is a "return for test" date.
Blankets must be returned for testing by that date to the Western Electric Company or other authorized agent.
The blankets should be returned in rolls (3½ inches in diameter) and wrapped properly so as to avoid damage.
A replacement blanket will be made available when a blanket is returned for testing.

FIGURE 34.5(b). A revised version of Fig. 34.5a with a proportionally based spacing system.

text. In traditional settings the internal spacing is sometimes stretched or squeezed to force the text to finish at the same point on each page. Normally this has little effect in pages of continuous prose, but Hartley (1991a) provides an illustration of where such a policy can mislead the reader.

34.2.10.2 *Horizontal Spacing.* One can consider the horizontal spacing of text in much the same way that we have considered the vertical spacing. That is, we can also look to see how we can use the horizontal spacing to separate and to group components of the text and how we can vary the stopping point of horizontal text in accord with its content, rather than using arbitrary rules about line lengths.

In the printed edition of this book all the lines of text are set *justified*. This means that all of the lines within the columns were of equal width and that the columns have straight left- and right-hand edges. Such a procedure is quite typical in printed texts. The straight edges are achieved by varying the spacing between the words on each line and, occasionally, by hyphenating or breaking words at the ends of lines. Indeed, in text that has very narrow columns (e.g., in newspapers or advertising copy), the spaces between the letters forming the words are also often varied to force the text to fit a given length of line.

A different approach to setting the text is to provide a consistent space between each word. Such a procedure produces what is called *unjustified* text. Here there is the same amount of space between each word, and usually there are no word breaks (or hyphenation) at the ends of lines. Consequently the text has a ragged right-hand edge. This kind of text is more common in screen-based presentations.

There has been much debate over the relative merits of justified and unjustified text in printed text. Misanchuk (1992) and Muncer, Gorman, Gorman, and Bibel (1986) provide representative reviews, and Kinross (1994) provides an interesting

historical footnote. It would appear that it does not matter much which setting is used as far as understanding conventional text is concerned: the decision concerning which format to use is largely a matter of choice. There is some evidence, however, that unjustified text might be more helpful for less able readers, be they younger children or older adults (see Hartley, 1999; Schriver, 1997).

Nonetheless, it is doubtful whether the studies reviewed by Misanchuk and by Muncer et al. fully considered all of the possible advantages of unjustified text. One clear advantage is that one does not have to fill up each line with text: we can consider (as with vertical spacing) where best to end each line. With unjustified text, for instance, it is possible to specify that no line should end with the first word of a new sentence or that, if the last word on a line is preceded by a punctuation mark, then this last word should be carried over to the next line. And, of course, it is possible to consider the starting points of each line too. Figure 34.6a shows a piece of justified text. Figure 34.6b shows what happens to this text when space is used to show its underlying structure. Research has shown that readers often recall more from text set in the manner shown in Fig. 34.6b than they do from text set in the manner of Fig. 34.6a (see Jandreau & Bever, 1992). And, curiously enough, when asked to write out their recalls of short texts set in these different formats, readers usually write them out in the formats in which they are presented (Hartley, 1993).

Now the sons of Jacob were twelve. The sons of Leah; Reuben, Jacob's firstborn, and Simeon, and Levi, and Judah, and Issachar, and Zebulun. The sons of Rachel; Joseph, and Benjamin: And the sons of Bilhah, Rachel's handmaid; Dan, and Naphtali. And the sons of Zilpah, Leah's handmaid; Gad, and Asher. These are the sons of Jacob, which were born to him in Padan-aram.

FIGURE 34.6(a). A piece of text with a traditional justified setting.

Now the sons of Jacob were twelve:
   The sons of Leah;
      Reuben, Jacob's firstborn,
      and Simeon, and Levi, and Judah,
      and Issachar, and Zebulun:
   The sons of Rachel;
      Joseph, and Benjamin:
  And the sons of Bilhar, Rachel's handmaid;
      Dan, and Naphtali:
  And the sons of Zilpah, Leah's handmaid;
      Gad, and Asher:
These are the sons of Jacob, which were born
to him in Padan-aram.

FIGURE 34.6(b). The same text with an unjustified setting. Note here that in this case the settings of both the beginnings and the endings of the lines are determined by syntactic considerations. Normally, of course, only the endings of the lines are unjustified.

34.2.10.3 *Combining Vertical and Horizontal Spacing.*

So far we have discussed vertical and horizontal spacing as though they are separate issues—which, of course, they are not. For all texts interrelated decisions need to be taken that depend on the nature of the text. If the text consists of nothing but continuous prose, then (on a smallish page) a single-column structure with normal paragraph indentation may be perfectly acceptable. If, however, the text consists of numerous small elements, many of which start on new lines, then using traditional indentation to denote new paragraphs can be misleading. It is for reasons such as these that I generally advocate the use of line spacing rather than indentation to denote the start of new paragraphs in instructional and informational text (Hartley, 1994a; Hartley, Burnhill, & Davies, 1972).

34.2.10.4 *Common Mistakes.* If the text contains a mixture of text, diagrams, instructions, and other typical instructional material, then one has to think much harder about the appropriate way of presenting it. The key point here, of course, is that instructional text should not be designed, as often happens, on a "let's put this here" basis for every page, and text should certainly not be wrapped around a figure or printed over it (Hartley, 1998a). Decisions concerning the vertical and the horizontal spacing of the full text need to be made in advance of keyboarding it, and these decisions have to be adhered to throughout. To help with this many designers advocate using

what is called a *typographical reference grid* (e.g., see Hartley, 1994a; Schriver, 1997; Swann, 1989). This tool—where layout decisions are mapped out in terms of grid modules—allows the designer to plan for standard units of space to separate out the components within the text. Thus, for example, one can specify in advance how many units of line space to allow between the text and a table or figure caption.

A good example of the difficulties that can arise when the spacing of the text is not properly considered occurred in the U.S. presidential election in 2000. Here many voters in Florida found themselves voting inadvertently for the wrong candidate because the punch holes for voting for each candidate were not systematically aligned with the candidates' names (Clay, 2001). If the text had been properly aligned and a punch hole placed systematically to the right of each candidate's name, then this mistake would not have occurred.

34.3 NAVIGATING TEXT: STRUCTURE AND ACCESS

So far I have discussed matters of typography that I believe help readers to find their way around a text and to grasp its underlying structure. I now turn to discuss those devices that are specifically used by writers and designers to help readers further in this respect. I have labeled this section "structure and access" because these devices—perhaps unwittingly— both clarify the structure of the text and help the readers gain access to it. Readers do not simply read instructional and informational text from beginning to end: They skim, search, re-read, etc. Devices that help them to do this include titles, contents pages, summaries, outlines, headings and subheadings, and numbering systems. In addition, authors use linguistic devices—such as "signals"—to help readers follow the organization of their arguments (Meyer, 1985; Waller, 1979).

34.3.1 Titles

Titles aim to describe the content of a text in the fewest words possible— but these are often supplemented with a subtitle (Michelson, 1994). Such succinct descriptions help to focus attention and expectations. Niegemann (1982) showed that titles aided the recall of what the text was about and, more recently, Sadoski, Goetz, and Rodriguez (2000) showed that concrete titles rather than abstract ones improved undergraduate students' recall, comprehension, and interest. Other studies have shown that titles can affect the readers' perception and interpretation of ambiguous text (e.g., Bransford, 1979). However, it is to be hoped that the titles for instructional and informational text will not be ambiguous!

Unfortunately, I know of no research on typographic variables connected with the setting of titles (e.g., type sizes, typefaces, weights) and little, apart from the references cited by Michelson (1994) and Zeller and Farmer (1999), on the more interesting problems of using different title formats (e.g., statements, questions, quotations).

34.3.2 Summaries

Summaries in text can have different positions and roles. Beginning summaries tell the readers what the text is about, they help the readers to decide whether or not they want to read it, and they help the readers who do read it to organize their subsequent reading. Interim summaries summarize the argument so far and indicate what is to come. End summaries list or review the main points made and, thus, aid the recall of important points in the text. End summaries can use the more technical vocabulary introduced in the text: Beginning summaries might not. There is considerable research on the effectiveness of *author-provided* summaries (e.g., see Hartley & Trueman, 1982; Lorch & Lorch, 1995; Sherrard, 1988) and on the effectiveness of *reader-generated* summaries (e.g., see Coleman, Brown, & Rivkin, 1997; Kirby & Pedwell, 1991; Thiede & Anderson, 2000). Other research has shown that findings concerning summaries might be less clear-cut, especially when summaries are combined with other variables (Mayer et al., 1996).

Summaries can be typeset in many different ways: in medium, bold, or italic, in large or small type, boxed in, etc. To my knowledge, there is no research on the effect of such typographic variables in this context, although there is some indication that readers dislike journal abstracts set in a smaller type size than the main body of the text (Hartley, 1994b, 2000).

34.3.3 Outlines

Outlines can have much the same function as a summary, although it is likely that outlines depict the structure of the text more clearly. Often outlines are provided in a graphic form, sometimes in the form of a tree diagram or flowchart (Guri-Rozenblit, 1989). Such displays facilitate understanding and recall in at least two ways. First, readers can see the organizing structure of the text all at once. Second, readers can follow different routes within this structure. This allows them to compare and contrast different parts in the order of their choice. The argument, as in hypermedia, is no longer linear, and it is not obscured by lengthy paragraphs of text. Research reviewing the effectiveness of outlines has been reported on and summarized by, among others, Foos, Mora, and Tkacz (1994), Hall, Hall, and Saling (1999), and Hofman and van Oostendorp (1999).

34.3.4 The Role of Boxed Asides

Authors frequently seek to extend the reader's comprehension of the main ideas by including supporting material, such as examples, anecdotes, and bibliographies. Often, one way of handling such material is to treat the information as a figure, to box it off from the main body of the text, and to use a different typeface and/or typographic setting. Presumably the idea here is that, by being separated from the main text, the information in the box is seen as separate and adjunct. It is less likely to interfere with either the author's presentation or the reader's comprehension of the main ideas.

Some authors have provided interesting comments on the problems of dealing with ancillary material (e.g., Armbruster & Anderson, 1985; Schumacher, 1885), but there is little research on the effectiveness of boxed asides. Three studies that did examine the effects of boxes in texts for schoolchildren all failed to have control groups that read the texts without them (Boscolo, Cisotto, & Lucca, 1992; Lucca, Boscolo, & Cisotto, 1991, 1994). Nonetheless, even if there is no evidence for or against boxed asides, some people have firm opinions. Consider, for example, this extract from James Thomas' (1984) review of an introductory psychology textbook:

On the negative side the text includes many boxed inserts presenting "Critical Issues" and "Applications". I object to this common approach for two reasons. First, these inserts disrupt the logical flow of the running text. If the application or issue is important enough for it to be boxed, why not include it in the running text and avoid breaking the reader's train of thought? Second, the boxed inserts exaggerate the importance of single, nonreplicated research findings. In many cases, these boxes report unusual, unexpected, or sensational research or applications that have not been adequately evaluated. Their appearance in an introductory textbook, especially in a highlighted position, seems to legitimize these findings and applications, whereas they should still be regarded as tentative. These concerns apply to three of the texts under review.

34.3.5 Headings

Headings in text may be written in the form of questions or statements or (as here) with one- or two-word labels. Headings may be placed in the margin or in the body of the text.

In a series of experiments with 12- to 14-year-old schoolchildren Mark Trueman and I investigated the role of different kinds of heading (questions versus statements) and their position (marginal versus embedded). We concluded that headings significantly aided search, recall, and retrieval but that the position and the kinds of heading that we used had no significant effects with the texts that we employed (Hartley & Trueman, 1985). More studies still need to be carried out on factors such as

- the nature of the text (technical versus semi-literary),
- the frequency of headings, and
- the typographic denotation of headings of different levels (primary, secondary, tertiary: see Spyridakis & Williams, 1992).

Additional research indicating the effectiveness of headings has been provided (see, e.g., Lorch & Lorch, 1995; Spyridakis, 1989a, 1989b; Townsend, Moore, Tuck, & Wilton, 1990). Wilhite (1989) showed, intriguingly, that headings were particularly effective with students who had high prior knowledge of the topic in question.

34.3.6 Questions

Questions may be interspersed in the text itself—or presented in a list at the end of a chapter to provide material for exercises. There is some indication that readers tend to ignore questions given at the ends of chapters (see the following), so it might be more appropriate to consider how they can best be embedded in the text. It appears that factual questions, placed in a passage before paragraphs of relevant material, often lead to specific learning, whereas similar questions placed in the passage after the relevant content will sometimes lead to more general learning as well (see Allington & Weber, 1993; Hamaker, 1986; Hamilton, 1985). The level of difficulty of these questions, too, may be important (see Allington & Weber, 1993; Armbruster & Ostertag, 1993; Lee & Hutchison, 1998). Lockwood (1995) and Martens and Valcke (1995) emphasize the value of such embedded study support devices in materials produced for distance learning.

Some early research suggested that headings written in the form of questions were particularly suitable for less able readers, but later (better designed) studies failed to confirm this (see Hartley & Trueman, 1985). Nonetheless, it might be important to consider headings in this form for certain kinds of text. Cataldo and Cornoldi (1998) for instance found that headings in the form of questions helped the self-monitoring of both poor and good readers.

34.3.7 Sequencing Information

Information in printed texts is—normally—presented in a linear sequence. But the sequencing of the items within a text can be considered at different levels. For example, we might move from considering the order of the chapters in a book, to the subdivisions within the chapters, to the paragraphs within the subdivisions, to the sentences within the paragraphs, and, finally, to the sequence of the actual words themselves within the sentences. Research has taken place at different levels in this sequencing. Some people have been interested in how a sequence within sections might be interrupted by the positioning of other components, such as tables and pictures (Hartley, 1991b). Another set of researchers has been interested in the sequencing of information within paragraphs, with the aim of putting higher-order or more important information before lower-order information (e.g., Isakson & Spyridakis, 1999; Meyer, 1997; Meyer, Young, & Bartlett, 1989). Others have examined the sequencing of individual sentences: These people suggest that sentences that are coherently ordered are better understood than sentences that are not (e.g., Bransford & Johnson, 1972; Carroll & Korukina, 1999). However, these effects might be greater in narrative than they are in expository text.

Another body of early work, in the context of programmed instruction, suggested that violations in natural sequences provided little difficulty for most readers. But what is a "natural" sequence? Posner and Strike (1978) contrasted 17 ways of sequencing text to show that sequencing is not a simple matter, and Van Patten, Chao, and Reigeluth (1986) developed their arguments further.

One thing, however, that does seem to be generally agreed is that readers find it easier to follow a sequence in which the events in the sequence match the temporal order in which they occur. Compare "Before the machine is switched on, the lid must be closed and the powder placed within its compartment" with "The powder must be placed within its compartment, and the lid closed, before the machine is switched on." And consider this odd sequence of instructions that I once found for using an electric razor.

1. To gain access to the heads for cleaning, press the button on the side of the appliance (see Fig. 4).
2. To remove the razor from its packaging . . .

Finally, in this section it is worth noting that the ordering of information in instructional and informational text can have considerable practical significance. Morrow and Leirer (1999), for example, showed how important it was for the order of information presented in patient information leaflets to match the order expected by the reader. Prentice-Dunn, Floyd, and Flournoy (2001) found that it was better—in leaflets about breast cancer—to present more threatening information before information on how to cope.

34.3.8 Itemizing Lists

It is fairly common in instructional writing to find sentences containing embedded lists of items such as this:

Five devices that aid the reader are (i) skeleton outlines for each chapter, (ii) headings in the text, (iii) an end summary, (iv) a glossary for new technical terms, and (v) a comprehensive subject and author index.

However, research suggests that readers prefer text that has such lists or numbered items spaced out and separated, rather than run-on in continuous prose. The above example would be better thus:

Five devices that aid the reader are:

- skeleton outlines for each chapter;
- headings in the text;
- an end summary;
- a glossary for new technical terms; and
- a comprehensive subject and author index.

34.3.9 Numbers in Text

Numbers are often used to clarify the structure of a piece of text. Lorch and Chen (1986) showed that when making a series of points within paragraphs, it was helpful to list and enumerate them. Other commentators have suggested that it is best to use Arabic numbers when there is an order or sequence to the points being made—and that *bullets,* as used in the preceding list, are more appropriate when each point is of equal value (Seki, 2000).

The structure and the organization of a piece of text can often be made clearer for the reader by the use of numbered paragraphs (as in this text). Such numbering systems can be used to organize information in many ways, e.g., Section 1, 2, 3 or 1.01, 1.02, 1.03, etc. However, there has been little research on the effectiveness of such systems. Many people undoubtedly feel that they are useful—particularly for cross-reference purposes. But such systems can be abused if they are overdone and they can lead to extraordinary confusion (see Smith & Aucella, 1983; and Waller, 1980).

34.3.10 Signaling

A rather different way of making text organization more explicit is to use verbal *signals*. Signals have been defined by Meyer et al. (1989) as "non-content words that serve to emphasize the conceptual structure or organization of the passage." Words and phrases such as *however, but,* or *on the other hand* signal to the reader that some form of comparison is to be made. Similarly, words and phrases such as *first, second, three reasons for this are . . .* , and *a better example, however, might be . . .* signal the structure of the argument (and comparisons with subsections). Likewise, words and phrases such as *therefore, as a result, so that, in order to,* and *because* signal causal relationships. Studies have shown that such signals help readers to grasp the underlying structure of the author's argument (e.g., see Meyer et al., 1989; Rice, Meyer, & Miller, 1989; Spyridakis & Standal, 1987). However, there may be some confusion over the use of the term *signal.* Ii is now common to find it being used to cover a range of devices such as headings, overviews, previews, and summaries, as well as "noncontent" words and logical connectives (Glover et al., 1988; Lorch, Lorch, & Inman, 1993; Spyridakis, 1989a, 1989b).

34.3.11 Conclusions

This section on navigating text has shown that there is a good deal of research available on the variety of methods that have been used to help readers to grasp the structure of a text and to gain access to it. However, most of this research is uncoordinated and atheoretical. Most researchers focus on one device or another in a single study, and few consider systematically the myriad factors affecting the effectiveness of one or other particular device. Even fewer consider effects of several such devices in combination. Exceptions to these general criticisms are Dwyer's work on illustrations, Dansereau's work on outlines, Meyer's work on signals, Spyridakis' work on headings, previews, and logical connectives, and possibly my own on headings. Such theories as there are are thus buried below a welter of specific instances rather than being subjected to any rigorous analysis that might, in the long term, lead to deeper understanding.

34.4 MAKING TEXT EASIER TO UNDERSTAND

A separate area of research relevant to the design of instructional and informational text concerns itself with assessing how difficult or easy a text might be for its intended readers and, indeed, whether or not difficulty per se is a bad thing. The title of a book by Chall and Conard (1991) puts the question succinctly: *Should Textbooks Challenge Students? The Case for Easier or Harder Books.* Making text easier to understand has been examined from numerous points of view (e.g., see Chall & Conard, 1991; Davison & Green, 1988; Schriver, 1997). Here I want simply to report on some of the issues and findings.

Again, if we start with an historical perspective, it is probably true to say that the instructional and informational materials available today are more spaciously arrayed. Furthermore, they also contain shorter paragraphs, sentences, and words than did similar texts published some 50 years ago. What can research tell us about these features of text difficulty?

34.4.1 Paragraph Length and Denotation

Few researchers have commented on the effects of long chapters and long paragraphs on readability. It would seem, other things being equal, that short chapters, and short paragraphs within them, make a text easier to read. In addition, the ways in which new paragraphs are denoted may be important. One problem is knowing how best to format paragraphs without unduly breaking the readers' flow. In an early study, Hartley et al. (1978) suggested that different methods of paragraph denotation can affect the speed and accuracy of location and access, as well as the recall of information. Four methods were compared in both single- and double-column texts on an A4 page:

1. indent,
2. indent plus line space,
3. line space without indent, and
4. no line space and no indent.

The results showed that readers did best (at finding information) with the two-column text in condition 1, that is, with indentation to display the start of new paragraphs. However, the authors commented that their prose materials were not typographically complex and that they did not contain any large tables, diagrams, or figures—which can cause problems for two-column settings.

34.4.2 Sentence Length

It is generally considered that long sentences—such as the one you are now reading—are difficult to understand because they often contain a number of subordinate clauses that, because of their parenthetical nature, make it difficult for you to bear all of their points in mind and, in addition, because there are often so many of them, make it harder for you to remember the first part of the sentence when you are reading the last part. Long sentences overload the memory system. Short sentences do not. I once wrote,

As a rule of thumb, sentences less than 20 words long are probably fine. Sentences 20 to 30 words long are probably satisfactory. Sentences 30 to 40 words long are suspect, and sentences containing over 40 words will almost certainly benefit from rewriting.

Perceptive readers will notice that many of my sentences contain more than 30 words—but at least they have been scrutinized! I am now inclined to the view that the length of sentences is also a function of the topic being written about and the level at which it is pitched. Furthermore, my advice ignores the advice given by many other commentators (e.g., Berger, 1993; Williams, 1997), that sentences (and paragraphs) should vary in length if they are to entertain the reader. Nonetheless, long sentences today are often flagged in computer aided writing systems and it seems unwise to ignore this information.

34.4.3 Word Length

Long words—like long sentences—can also cause difficulty. It is easier to understand short, familiar words than technical terms that mean the same thing. If, for example, you wanted to sell thixotropic paint, you would probably do better to call it nondrip! One author on style quoted a letter writer in *The Times* who had asked a government department how to obtain a book. He was "authorized to acquire the work in question by purchasing it through the ordinary trade channels"—in other words, "to buy it." Concrete words and phrases are shorter and clearer than abstract ones. Fowler and Fowler (1906)—almost 100 years ago—put the matter well when they said, "Anyone who wishes to become a good writer should endeavor, before he allows himself to be tempted by the more showy qualities, to be direct, simple, brief, vigorous and lucid."

34.4.4 Difficult Short Sentences

It does not necessarily follow, of course, that passages written in short sentences and short words will always be better understood. Alphonse Chapanis (1965, 1988) provides many examples of short pieces of text that are difficult to understand. The one I like best is the notice that reads

PLEASE
WALK UP ONE FLOOR
WALK DOWN TWO FLOORS
FOR IMPROVED ELEVATOR SERVICE

People interpret the notice as meaning "To get on the elevator I must either walk up one floor or go down two floors" or even "To get on the elevator I must first walk up one floor and then down two floors." When they have done this they find the same notice confronting them! What this notice means, in effect, is "Please, don't use the elevator if you are only going a short distance." Chapanis' articles are well worth studying. They are abundantly illustrated with short sentences that are hard to understand and (in some cases) potentially lethal. Later research using this particular warning notice showed how the principles of text design advocated in this chapter led to significant improvements (Wogalter, Begley, Scancorelli, & Brelsford, 1997).

34.4.5 Reducing Ambiguities

Many short (and indeed many long) sentences can turn out to be ambiguous. Consider "Then roll up the three additional blankets and place them inside the first blanket in the canister." Does this sentence mean that each blanket should be rolled inside the other or that the three rolled blankets should be placed side by side and a fourth one wrapped around them? (An illustration would clarify this ambiguity.)

Ambiguities, or at least difficulties, often result from the use of abbreviations or acronyms (strings of capital letters that form real or pseudo-words, e.g., NATO). I once counted over 20 such acronyms in a two-page text distributed by my university computer center. Chapanis (1988) provides additional examples, also from the field of computing. The meanings of acronyms may be familiar to the writer but they need to be explained to the reader. Furthermore, readers easily forget what an author's abbreviations stand for when they are not familiar with the material and when they come from another country.

34.4.6 Verbal Quantifiers

Numerical data in text are often difficult to understand and prose descriptions of them seem more helpful. Everyday words that act as rough quantifiers, e.g., "nearly half the group," seem adequate for most purposes and are handled with reasonable consistency (Moxey & Sanford, 1993; Windschitl & Wells, 1996). Young children, of course, may have greater difficulty with some of these terms (Badzinski, Cantor, & Hoffner, 1989).

Issues such as these are important because verbal quantifiers are widely used in a variety of situations, including surveys, questionnaires, and educational materials. Furthermore, people forget that the interpretation and use of these verbal quantifiers are affected by the context in which they appear. For example, how we respond to one quantifier in a questionnaire may well be affected by the other choices in the set (Haddock, 1998; Hartley, Trueman, & Rodgers, 1984) as well as by what is being discussed. Thus we might reply "often" to situations that vary widely in their frequency (e.g., compare "We often go abroad for our summer holidays" with "We often eat out during the week"), and what is "often" for some might be "rarely" for others.

Nonetheless, research by Hartley et al. (1984) suggested that the following phrases could be used with reasonable confidence with adults.

Numerical value to be conveyed	Suitable phrase
Above 85%	Almost all of . . .
60%–75%	Rather more than half of . . .
40%–50%	Nearly half of . . .
15%–35%	A part of . . .
Under 10%	A very small part of . . .

However, it may be better (or at least clearer for the reader) if more exact verbal equivalents of numbers are given, as follows.

Numerical value to be conveyed	Suitable phrase
100%	All of …
75%	Three-quarters of …
50%	Half of …
25%	A quarter of …
0%	None of …

Verbal descriptions of probabilities are also more comfortable for most people than are actual probability statements. People are less consistent, however, in their interpretations of verbal descriptions of probability than they are in their interpretations of verbal descriptions of quantity (Moxey & Sanford, 1993). Some people, for example, say "fifty-fifty" when they mean that the chances are equal, and others say "fifty-fifty" when they mean that they have no idea of what the probability might be (Bruine de Bruin, Fischoff, Millstein, & Halpern-Felsher, 2000). If precision is required, actual quantities can be given with a verbal quantifier. For example, one can say, "Nearly half the group—43%—said…" or "There was a distinct chance ($p < 0.06$) that…."

34.4.7 Clarifying Text

Generally speaking, text is usually easier to understand when:

1. Writers produce few sentences containing more than two subordinate clauses. The more subordinate clauses or modifying statements there are, the more difficult it is to understand a sentence. Consider, for example, the problems posed for an anxious student by this examination rubric: "Alternative C: Answer four questions including at least one from at least two sections (1–5)."
2. Writers use the active rather than the passive voice. Compare the active form, "We found that the engineers had a significantly higher interocular transfer index than the chemists" with the passive form, "For the engineers, as compared with the chemists, a significantly higher interocular transfer index was found." (Riggle, 1998, provides qualifications to this general view.)
3. Writers use positive terms (e.g., more than, heavier than, thicker than) rather than negative ones (e.g., less than, lighter than, thinner than). Compare "The rain is heavier today" with "The rain was lighter yesterday."
4. Writers avoid negatives, especially double or triple ones. Negatives can often be confusing. I once saw, for example, a label fixed to a machine in a school workshop that read, "This machine is dangerous: it is not to be used only by the teacher." Harold Evans (1972) provides another example. Compare "The figures provide no indication that costs would have not been lower if competition had not been restricted" with "The figures provide no indication that competition would have produced higher costs." Negative qualifications can be used, however, for particular emphasis and for correcting misconceptions. Double negatives in imperatives (e.g., "Do not … unless…") are sometimes easier to understand than single ones. Jordan (1998) offers an interesting discussion of these points.

5. Writers use concrete phrases and terminology rather than abstract expressions (Sadoski et al. 2000; Hartley, 1998a). Compare "Tell people quickly if there is a fire" with "It is of the utmost importance that persons in a building which is on fire should be given immediate warning."
6. Writers avoid nominalizations. Nouns derived from verbs are called nominalizations. Williams (1997) wittily points out that the word "nominalization" itself is a nominalization from the verb to nominalize. Other, simpler examples, are nouns typically ending in *-tion, -ment, -ence,* and so on. So, it would be easier to read "The agency investigated the matter" than "the agency conducted an investigation into the matter." Spyridakis and Isakson (1998) reviewed the early research on nominalizations and conducted their own experiment with nominalizations in technical text. They concluded that denominalized text was more helpful for native speakers of English but that nominalized text worked well with nonnative speakers.
7. Writers include examples. Students often rely heavily on examples to learn materials. The research suggests that examples can be made clearer by including greater detail, by increasing their frequency, and by making them more familiar. Students also learn more if they have to answer questions about the examples (Atkinson, Derry, Renkl, & Wortham, 2000; Lee & Hutchison, 1998; Robertson & Kahney, 1996). It is also helpful to place examples close to where they are referred to in the text.
8. Writers make text more interesting. Lively examples and anecdotes make the text more memorable—or do they? Research has indicated that vivid anecdotes and the like can indeed make text more interesting (e.g., see Hidi & Harackiewicz, 2000; McDaniel, Waddill, Finstad, & Bourg, 2000) but this is often at a cost. Apparently many readers tend to recall such "seductive details" at the expense of the main information in the passage (Harp & Mayer, 1998; Schraw, 1998). Boostrom (2001) provides another—interesting—perspective on this discussion.
9. Writers personalize texts. In one unpublished study Cathryn Brown and I compared two medical audiotapes. The first tape began

Welcome to the Health Department's Medical Directory. This tape is about multiple sclerosis: what causes it, and what you can do about it.

The second tape began

Welcome to the Health Department's Medical Directory. My name is Nick and I want to tell you about multiple sclerosis. I am able to do this because I am suffering from the disease. In this tape I will tell you about what causes multiple sclerosis and what you can do about it.

Both tapes contained the same information but, while the first tape was formal, the second tape conveyed the information in a more personal way. Students listening to this tape recalled more information from it than they did from the first one. Czuchry and Dansereau (1998), Moreno and Meyer (2000), and Rook (1987) provide similar results.

Personalizing instruction, of course, can take many forms. It is possible to insert the appropriate names of people and places in computer-generated texts (Jones et al, 1999; Lucke, 1998) and problems can be tailored to students' backgrounds. For example, the same mathematical problems can be presented in different contexts for nursing, teaching, and psychology students (e.g., see Davis-Dorsey, Ross & Morrison, 1991). Again, age and ability differences are important considerations in this field. Bracken (1982), for example, found that personalizing stories helped less able fourth graders but had no effect with those of average ability.

34.5 MEASURING TEXT DIFFICULTY

Much of the text that we see around us—on screen as well as on paper—can be written and presented more effectively. And, in order to help us achieve these goals, psychologists (and others) have devised numerous tools and methods for measuring the difficulty text. Schriver (1989, 1997) has grouped these methods under three headings: expert-based, reader-based, and text-based methods, respectively.

- *Expert-based* methods are ones that use experts to make assessments of the effectiveness of a piece of text. Subject-matter experts might be asked to use checklists to evaluate the quality of an instructional textbook. Referees might complete rating scales to judge the quality of an article submitted for publication in a scientific journal.

- *Reader-based* methods are ones that involve actual readers in making assessments of the text. Readers might be asked to complete questionnaires, to comment on sections of text that they find difficult to follow, or to carry out instructions or be tested on how much they can remember.

- *Text-based* measures are ones that can be used without recourse to experts or to readers. They examine the text on its own. Such measures include computer-based readability formulas and computer-based measures of style and grammar.

34.5.1 Expert-Based Measures

Experts in this context are people who have a high level of knowledge about (a) a particular subject matter, (b) the potential readership of a text, and (c) the skills of writing. Such people typically use their judgment to assess texts. Teachers, for example, may want to decide if a textbook is suitable for their students. In examining a particular textbook they will be concerned about whether it meets their teaching objectives and if it is written at an appropriate level. They will also be concerned with whether or not there are any outdated materials, important omissions, or biases of any kind— academic, national, racial, and sexual. They will consider the depth and breadth of the contents and how much the text may need to be supplemented by other materials.

Making such judgments is a subjective activity. However, there are ways of making them more objective. One way to do this is to increase the number of judges. Another is to provide some sort of checklist to ensure that all the judges evaluate the same concerns. Figure 34.7 provides an example of part of such a checklist. This kind of approach is commonly used in evaluating school textbooks in countries with state-controlled school systems such as the United States. Although such checklists are useful in making the judges' ratings more systematic and consistent, there are no *standard* tools that everyone can use. Different people with different interests tend to create their own measures. In one early study, for instance, Farr and Tulley

Please rate the book in the spaces provided on each of the items given, using a scale of 0 (very poor) to 5 (very good).

____	General appearance	____	Relevance of content
____	Practicality of size	____	Ease of reading
____	Durability of binding	____	Use of chapter subheadings
____	Quality of paper	____	Use of illustrative materials (tables, figures, and graphs)
____	Appeal of page layout	____	Degree of challenge for able students
____	Legibility of typefaces	____	Suitability for less able students
____	Usability of index		

FIGURE 34.7. An excerpt from a typical checklist for judging the quality of a textbook.

TABLE 34.2. Some Examples of Concurrent and Retrospective Reader-Based Text Evaluation Measures

Concurrent	Retrospective
Eye-movement patterns	Comprehension tests (including cloze)
Verbal commentaries	Readers' judgments of difficulty
Oral reading errors	Readers' preferences
Search tasks	Readers' feedback sheets
Reading times	
Cloze tests	

(1985) reported that the number of items on the checklists that they studied for evaluating school textbooks ranged from 42 to 180, with an average number of 73.

Such checklists are usually completed *before* recommending a particular textbook for use. However, this kind of information can also be collected *after* textbooks have been used by teachers and students. Information gained in this way is helpful in deciding whether or not to use a book again and in informing authors who are planning subsequent editions. Indeed, information can also be collected from colleagues and readers concerning chapters as they are being written. The information collected in this way can be used by authors in finalizing their chapters.

34.5.2 Reader-Based Measures

Reader-based tools for evaluating text require the readers to carry out some activities. Such activities can be many and varied. Schriver (1989, 1997) distinguishes between those that are *concurrent* with the reading activities and those that are *retrospective*, or come after them. Table 34.2 lists examples of different reader-based measures under these two headings. Here I consider two of them in more detail.

34.5.2.1 Cloze Tests. The cloze test was originally developed by Taylor (1953) to measure people's understanding of text. Here samples of a passage are presented to readers with, say, every sixth word missing. The readers are then required to fill in the missing words.

Technically speaking, if every sixth word is deleted, then six versions should be prepared with the gaps each starting from a different point. However, it is more common _____ prepare one version and, perhaps _____ to focus the gaps on _____ words. Whatever the procedure, the _____ are scored either (a) by _____ accepting as correct those responses _____ directly match what the original _____ actually said, or (b) by _____ these together with acceptable synonyms. Because the two scoring methods, a and b, correlate highly, it is more objective to use the tougher measure of matching exact words (in this case, "to," "even," "important," "passages," "only," "which," "author," and "accepting").

The scores obtained can be improved by

- having the gaps more widely dispersed (say every tenth word),
- varying the lengths of the gaps to match the lengths of the missing words,
- providing dashes to indicate the number of letters missing in each word,
- providing the first of the missing letters,
- providing multiple-choice alternative solutions, and
- having readers work in pairs or small groups.

These minor variations, however, do not affect the main purpose of the cloze procedure, which is to assess readers' comprehension of the text and, by inference, its difficulty.

The cloze test can be used by readers both concurrently and retrospectively. It can be presented concurrently (as above) as a test of comprehension, and readers required to complete it. It can be presented retrospectively and readers asked to complete it after they have read the original text. In the latter case the test can serve as a measure of recall as well as comprehension. The cloze test can also be used to assess the effects of different textual organization, readers' prior knowledge, and other textual features, such as illustrations, tables, and graphs (e.g., see Couloubaritsis, Moss, & Abouserie, 1994; Reid, Briggs, & Beveridge, 1983).

34.5.2.2 Readers' Judgments and Preferences. A rather different but useful measure of text difficulty is to ask readers to judge the difficulty for themselves. One simple procedure here is to ask readers to circle in the text those areas, sentences, or words that they think *readers less able than themselves* will find difficult. In my experience, if you ask readers to point out difficulties *for others* they will be much more forthcoming than if you ask them to point out their own difficulties.

An elaboration of this technique is to ask readers to give a running commentary on the difficulties that they experience as they are using or reading a text. This technique has proved extremely valuable in evaluating complex text such as that provided in instructional manuals, where there can be a rich interplay between text and diagrams (see Shriver, 1997). Some critics of this approach suggest that talking about a task while trying to do it can cause difficulties, and this does seem to be a reasonable objection. However, such problems can be partly overcome by videotaping readers using the text to complete a particular task and then asking them to talk through the resulting tape—which can be stopped at any point to allow them to make an extended commentary.

Readers can also be asked to state their preferences for different kinds of texts and for different layouts of a specific text. Some experts dismiss such preference judgments by readers because they think that their preferences might be based on inappropriate considerations (such as a lavish use of different colors rather than the clarity of the wording). However, most people have clear views about what they like in texts and how they expect texts to perform.

A common method of measuring preferences is to ask people to rate (on a scale of 1–10) original and revised texts. The results can tell you whether a revised text is preferred to the original, whether people see no difference, or whether people prefer the original version. However, one has to be careful here. For some reason or other, when people rate two things on a scale of 1–10, they often rate one of them 5 or 6 and the other one 8 (Hartley and Ganier, 2000). So it is useful to have a baseline text for comparison. The same text might be rated 5 or 8, depending on what it is being compared with.

Another useful tool to use here, if you want preference judgments for a number of texts that vary in different ways, is the method of *paired comparisons*. Suppose, for example, that you have 15 designs for a poster. You could ask potential readers to judge them (overall or on some specific aspect) and to make paired comparisons. Essentially this involves each judge comparing design 1 with design 2 and recording the preference, then design 1 with design 3, 1 with 4, 1 with 5, and so on, until 1 with 15 is reached. Then the judge starts again, this time comparing 2 with 3, 2 with 4, 2 with 5, and so on, until 2 with 15. This procedure is repeated again, starting with 3 with 4, 3 with 5, 3 with 6, etc., 4 with 5, 4 with 6, 4 with 7, etc., until all the designs have been systematically compared. Finally, you total the number of preferences recorded for each design to see which one has been preferred the most.

34.5.3 Text-Based Measures

Text-based tools for evaluating text can be used without recourse to readers. These measures, too, can be applied concurrently—while one is writing the text and, retrospectively, once it has been written—either by the author(s) or by others who might be thinking of using it. Here I describe two computer-based tools for evaluating written text.

34.5.3.1 Computer-Based Measures of Readability.
Readability formulas were originally developed to predict the age at which children, on average, would have the necessary reading skills and abilities to understand a particular text. And this is still their main aim today, although the scope of application has widened.

Most readability formulas are in fact not as accurate at predicting this age as one might wish (and different formulas produce slightly different results), but the figures they provide do give a rough guide. Furthermore, if the same formula is used to compare two different texts, or to compare an original with a revised version, then you do get a good idea of the relative difficulty of the texts.

Readability formulas typically combine two main measures to predict the difficulty of text. These are (a) the average sentence length of samples of the text, and (b) the average word length in these samples. One simple formula—the Gunning Fog Index—is as follows.

- Take a sample of 100 words.
- Calculate the average number of words per sentence in the sample.
- Count the number of words with three or more syllables in the sample.
- Add the average number of words per sentence to the total number of words with three or more syllables.
- Multiply the result by 0.4.

TABLE 34.3. The Relationship Among the Flesch Reading Ease (RE) Score, Difficulty, and Suggested Reading Ages

RE Value	Description of Style	Required Reading Skill
90–100	Very easy	5th grade
80–90	Easy	6th grade
70–80	Fairly easy	7th grade
60–70	Standard	8th–9th grade
50–60	Fairly difficult	10th–12th grade
30–50	Difficult	13th–16th grade
0–30	Very difficult	College graduate

The result is the "reading grade level" as used in U.S. schools (Grade 1, 6 years old; Grade 2, 7 years old; etc.). Most readability formulas, however, are much more complex to calculate than the Gunning Fog Index—hence the interest in computer-based methods. One better-known formula, but one that is harder to calculate by hand, is the Flesch Reading Ease (RE) formula:

$$RE = 206.835 - 0.846w - 1.015s,$$

where w is the number of syllables per 100 words and s is the average number of words per sentence.

In this case, the higher the RE score, the easier the text. Table 34.3 shows the relationship among RE, difficulty, and suggested reading ages. One computer program—Microsoft's *Office 97*—gives the results from the Flesch RE formula. (Other programs sometimes give the measures from several formulas.) When I tried *Office 97* on an earlier section in this chapter the outcome was 41.1, suggesting that that section was relatively easy to read for the audience of this text—but that it might be difficult for thirteen to sixteen graders. Different formulas will produce slightly different results. Furthermore, an additional difficulty has arisen with computer-based readability formulas because different programmers have worked out different ways of computerizing what are ostensibly the same formulas. Thus you might find that, for example, if you use the *Word for Windows* version of the Flesch RE measure, you will get an RE result slightly different from that provided by, say, *Grammatik 5* or *Office 97*. This problem is not too serious with simple texts, but it can become more of an issue when working with complex ones (Sydes & Hartley, 1997). So the moral is always use the same computer program when evaluating different texts.

To summarize, the basic idea underlying readability formulas is that the longer the sentences and the more complex the vocabulary in these sentences, the more difficult the text will be. Clearly such a notion, although generally sensible, has its limitations. For example:

- Some technical abbreviations are short (e.g., "DNA") but difficult for people who have not heard of them.
- Some words are long but, because of their frequent use, become quite familiar (e.g., "readability" in this context).
- Clearly there is more to text than just sentence and word lengths—otherwise it would be easy to make text simple

Scientists divide the different forms of life into two main groups. There are animals called *vertebrates* that have backbones, and there are animals called *invertebrates* that do not. *Vertebrates* can be divided into several subgroups. There are *reptiles* such as snakes and crocodiles; *amphibians*, such as frogs and toads; *fish*, such as salmon and sharks; *birds*, such as sparrows and eagles; and *mammals*, such as dogs, horses, and people.

Scientists divide the different forms of life into two main groups. There are animals called *vertebrates* that have backbones. There are animals called *invertebrates* that do not. *Vertebrates* can be divided into several subgroups. There are *reptiles*—such as snakes and crocodiles. There are *amphibians*—such as frogs and toads. There are *fish*—such as salmon and sharks. There are *birds*—such as sparrows and eagles. And there are *mammals*—such as dogs, horses, and people.

FIGURE 34.8. The effects on readability measures achieved simply by shortening sentences. The top passage has a Flesch reading age of 15–17 years. The bottom passage has one of 13–14 years. But the top passage flows more easily than the bottom one.

by just shortening the words and the sentences (Davison & Green, 1988). However, studies by Beck and her colleagues have shown that in some circumstances more readable texts can score less well on readability formulas than less readable ones (Beck, McKeown, & Worthy, 1995; Loxterman, Beck, & McKeown, 1994).

- Text that has short, choppy sentences can be difficult to read (see Fig. 34.8).
- Readability formulas do not take into account the order of the words and the sentences, nor do they assess the effects of other devices used to aid comprehension (e.g., typographical layout, tables, graphs, and illustrations).
- Most importantly (unlike reader-based tools), readability formulas ignore the readers' motivation, abilities, and prior knowledge.

34.5.3.2 Computer-Based Style and Grammar Checkers.
Most readers who use word processors will be familiar with spelling checkers, tools that enable you to check the spelling in your documents. Style and grammar checkers, as their names suggest, are but an extension of this idea—they aim to help with style and grammar. Essentially the procedure is to run these checkers over the text once you have completed it (but it can be done concurrently). The checker stops at every point where the program detects a possible stylistic or grammatical error. Figure 34.9 indicates the kinds of errors picked up by the program *Grammatik 5*.

Early investigations of style and grammar checkers focused on assessing how useful they were to writers. This research suggested that many people found them rather tedious to use but that they did find them helpful (Hartley, 1994a). More recent research has focused on making comparison studies between different programs to see which is the most effective. Typically what one does here is to assemble a set of ungrammatical or poorly written sentences or passages and then try out different grammar checkers on them to see which errors are detected and what sort of advice is given (e.g., see Kohut & Gorman, 1995; Pedler, 2001). Other, more theoretical research in this

Programs that indicate grammatical errors:

- Adjective errors
- Adverb errors
- Article errors
- Clause errors
- Comparative/superlative use
- Double negatives
- Incomplete sentences
- Noun phrase errors
- Object of verb errors
- Possessive misuse
- Preposition errors
- Pronoun errors
- Sequence of tense errors
- Subject-verb errors
- Tense changes
- etc.

Programs that indicate mechanical errors:

- Spelling errors
- Capitalization errors
- Double word
- Ellipsis misuse
- End-of-sentence punctuation errors
- Incorrect punctuation
- Number style errors
- Question mark errors
- Quotation mark misuse
- Similar words
- Split words
- etc.

Programs that indicate stylistic errors:

- Long sentences
- Wordy sentences
- Passive tenses
- End-of-sentence prepositions
- Split infinitives
- Cliched words/phrases
- Colloquial language
- Americanisms
- Archaic language
- Gender-specific words
- Jargon
- Abbreviation errors
- Paragraph problems
- Questionable word usage
- etc.

FIGURE 34.9. Examples of different errors detected by *Grammatik 5*.

area concerns itself with developing more sophisticated programs than the ones currently available (e.g., see Harrison &
Bakker, 1998; Pennebaker & King, 1999; Woolls & Coulthard,
1998).

Grammar checkers are good at spotting the minutiae of errors in punctuation and grammar, but naturally, they cannot
help with matters of content. In my experience it is best to use
both computer-based and human editors (experts and readers)
to evaluate the effectiveness of style.

34.5.4 Combining Different Measures

Experiments have been carried out to see whether or not the
information provided from these different kinds of measure is
equally effective in improving texts. de Jong and Lentz (1996),
for instance, compared the usefulness of expert versus reader
feedback in assessing the effectiveness of a public information
brochure about rent subsidies. Here the criticisms of 15 expert
technical writers were compared with those of 15 members
of the public. The main conclusions of this study were that
criticisms of the two groups were very different. The readers
pointed out significantly more problems associated with the typographic design of the brochure and with their understanding
of it. The technical writers pointed out significantly more problems with the use of appropriate expressions and conventions
and with matters of writing style.

In another study, Weston, Le Maistre, McAlpine, and Bordonaro (1997) gave suggestions from experts, readers, and instructional designers for rewriting a six-page instructional unit
on diet and cancer to a new set of instructional designers. These
new designers most frequently used the suggestions from the
readers and the previous instructional designers in making their
revisions. However, subsequent comprehension tests showed
that the most important information for improving the comprehension of the passage came from the readers' earlier comments.

In a third study, Wilson et al. (1998) reported, among
other things, the responses of medical practitioners and patients to questions concerning the content and usefulness of
patient information leaflets. Both the practitioners and the
patients thought that the leaflets were useful, but they had
widely disparate views about the content. Thus, for example,
80% of the practitioners responded "No" and 75% of the patients responded "Yes" to the question, "Is there anything you
feel is essential to include but is omitted?" Similarly, 86% of
the practitioners responded "No" and 46% of the patients responded "Yes" to the question, "Is there anything you feel
should be left out that is included?" Finally, 86% of the practitioners responded "No" and 50% of the patients "Yes" to
the question, "Is there anywhere where you feel the style of
the language is not appropriate (e.g., patronising/confusing)?"
Berry, Michas, Gillie, and Forster (1997) reported similar
results.

A different kind of study (Hartley & Benjamin, 1998) showed
how using multiple measures could be more informative than
using single ones. Here comparisons were made between traditional abstracts (summaries) of journal articles and what are
called *structured* abstracts. (These contain subheadings, such
as Background to the Study, Aims, Methods, Results, and Conclusions.) In this investigation the effects of these changes were
assessed in five ways. The results showed the following.

- In terms of *length* the structured abstracts were significantly
  longer.
- In terms of *information content* the structured abstracts were significantly more informative—as assessed by
  readers.
- In terms of *readability* the structured abstracts were significantly more readable—as assessed by computer-based readability formulas.
- In terms of *searchability* the readers were able to find information more quickly with the structured abstracts.
- In terms of *preferences* the authors of the abstracts were almost unanimous in their preferences for the structured versions.

The results from combining these measures suggested that
the structured abstracts were more effective than the traditional
ones—but that they took up more journal space to achieve this.
This use of several evaluation methods—rather than just one—
strengthened this conclusion.

34.6 DESIGNING TEXT FOR READERS WITH SPECIAL NEEDS

In this section I turn to issues of text design for two sets of readers with special needs—the elderly and the visually impaired.
These two groups of people can, of course, overlap.

34.6.1 Text Design for Older Readers

The proportion of elderly people in society has been gradually increasing over the years. Life expectancy at birth in the
United Kingdom increased by over 50% in the last century, and
4 in every 10 British people are now over 50. In the United
States currently 12% of the population is 65 years of age or
older, and the number of Americans 65 years of age or older is
expected to double to 65 million by the year 2030 (Qualls &
Abeles, 2000). Thus people are living longer and the number of
elderly people in the community is getting larger. Consequently
there are more older people reading traditional and screen-
based texts and more materials being produced especially for
them.

Research on the effects of aging can be described in terms
of three overlapping areas, physiological, cognitive, and social.
Physiological research looks at the biology of aging and its physiological correlates. Most people, for example, experience a decline with age in eyesight and other senses. *Cognitive* research
on aging focuses on changes in memory, learning, and judgment. Such cognitive changes have implications for text design,
as we shall see. *Social* research on aging examines, for example,

how societies expect their older members to perform. Studies of "agism," for example, focus on how commonly held attitudes and beliefs about what elderly people should do (and should *not* do) determine to a considerable extent what, in fact, they do do.

It is difficult to summarize in a few lines the main findings of studies on aging and their implications for text design. (Fuller expositions are given by Hartley, 1999, Morrell, 2001, and Wright, 2000). Here, for the sake of argument, I would like to suggest two points that I think it helpful to bear in mind when thinking about these issues.

1. Working memory capacity (i.e., information held in memory and used in ongoing tasks) declines as people get older.
2. The more difficult the task and the older the person, the more disproportionally difficult that task becomes.

Thus, for example, older people may recall narrative texts relatively well but find expository texts more difficult. But summarizing these expository texts will be much more difficult the older the readers are (Byrd, 1985).

Meyer et al. (1989) and Meyer (1997) suggest that it is important to consider three overlapping variables when considering designing instructional and informational texts for older learners.

- Reader variables—such as verbal ability and prior knowledge
- Text variables—such as text structure, genre, and difficulty
- Task variables—such as remembering and following instructions

Thus one might not expect differences between older and younger readers when the verbal ability of the readers is high, when they have good prior knowledge, when the texts are clearly presented, and when the tasks are relatively straightforward. Differences, however, might be expected to emerge with less able readers, less familiar materials, poorly designed text, and more complex tasks.

34.6.1.1 Improving Typographically Simple Layouts.
Generally speaking, studies on the effects of aging suggest that texts will be easier for older people when their perceptual and memory-processing loads are reduced. One would imagine, therefore. that this might be achieved by, for example,

- using larger type sizes;
- using clearer layouts;
- using more readable text; and
- clarifying the structure of the text by using, for example, summaries, headings, systematic spacing, and signals.

In another review I summarized the results from some 15 studies that examined these various aspects of text design with older readers (Hartley, 1999). These studies used what I call relatively simple typographic layouts, that is, mainly continuous run-on text. Table 34.4 shows that, unfortunately, there were

TABLE 34.4. The Number of Studies with Older People for Each Aspect of Text Design Listed in the Text

Number of Studies	Text Design Feature
5	Type size
3	Unjustified text
2	Underlining
2	Advance organizers
1	Signals
1	Questions in text
1	Text structure and organization

Note. From "What Does It Say? Text Design, Medical Information and Older Readers," by J. Hartley, 1999, in D. C. Park, R. W. Morrell, and K. Shifrin (Eds.), *Processing of Medical Information in Aging Patients* (pp. 233–247), Mahwah, NJ: Lawrence Erlbaum Associates. Reproduced by permission.

insufficient studies to make any clear generalizations from their findings, except for the area of type size.

All five studies on type size indicated that larger type sizes were suitable for older readers. It appears—ignoring my earlier caveats about measuring type sizes—that 12- or 14-point type is more appropriate for older readers.

The three studies with unjustified text suggested that there were advantages for unjustified text with *less able* older readers when the line lengths were short (seven or eight words).

The two studies on underlining and the two on advanced organizers had mixed results: one positive and one neutral in each case. The two studies on making texts more readable showed that, in these studies, this had no effect with age. However, there were age effects for the studies with questions, signals, and variations in text structure. Older readers did less well than younger ones, but high-ability older readers were helped by the textual variable being considered.

My review highlighted three issues in this research.

1. There were ability effects rather than age effects in about half of these studies. The more able participants did better than the less able ones, irrespective of age.
2. Six of the studies showed interactions between conditions and ability. Three of them showed that the text device in question helped the more able participants, and three of them showed that it helped the less able ones.
3. Very few of the investigators reported working with text that was appropriately designed to take into account the visual problems of their older readers. Only one or two checked that their participants could in fact read the texts. None reported on increasing the type size when looking at other variables, and none appeared to consider the value of improving the lighting. Thus, one might argue, the older readers in many of these studies were probably working under additional handicaps.

34.6.1.2 Improving Typographically Complex Texts.
So far I have discussed research with texts that had a relatively simple typographic structure. I now turn to studies of older people using materials that are more complex—both typographically and literally. Such materials include, for example, bus and train schedules, labels on medicine bottles, food packaging, and government forms. In my earlier review (Hartley, 1999)

I examined the results from 10 studies in this more complex area. These covered work on medical insurance policies, informed consent forms, medicine bottle labels, prescription information, food labels, inland revenue forms in the United Kingdom, diagrams, models, flowcharts, and procedural instructions for assembly tasks.

Eight of the ten studies with these more complex materials found that their older participants fared worse than their younger ones when using this kind of text (but not always significantly so). And the two of them that reported ability data reported that high-ability participants did better than low-ability ones, irrespective of age. What was of more interest, however, was that the changes made ostensibly to help older people with these materials *actually appeared to make the texts more difficult for them*. Further work is need with elderly people on the use of diagrams, charts, and tables, for example, to see if this really is the case.

In the light of these findings it is likely—although this has not been studied—that presentation methods that hinder legibility for the young (e.g., printing text over photographs, using poor color contrast, using three-dimensional bar charts instead of two-dimensional ones) might cause even more difficulty for elderly readers.

Clearly, more work needs to be done in this area of instructional and informational design. Indeed, it would be wise to ensure that older people are included in the evaluation studies of any textual materials. Text designed for older readers is unlikely to confuse younger ones. However, text designed for younger readers may well confuse older ones.

34.6.2 Designing Text for the Visually Impaired

During 1986 and 1987 the Royal National Institute for the Blind (RNIB) conducted a survey of the needs of blind and partially sighted adults in Britain, and a final report was published in 1991 (Bruce, McKennell, & Walker, 1991). A similar report on the needs of blind and partially sighted children was published in 1992 (Walker, Tobin, & McKennell, 1992). And, although these reports describe the situation in the United Kingdom, we can anticipate that the problems are similar in other developed countries and worse in developing ones.

The 1991 U.K. report indicated that the number of blind and partially sighted adults in Great Britain, was approaching 1 million (960,000), many more than were actually registered (239,000). The prevalence rates (for those registered) were as follows:

- 3 per 1,000 among 16- to 59-year-olds,
- 23 per 1,000 among 60- to 74-year-olds, and
- 152 per 1,000 among those over 75 years of age.

Thus one person in seven aged 75 or over was blind or partially sighted, and this prevalence rate was almost certainly higher among those over 80 and those over 85.

It is, of course, important to realize that the great majority of these people are not completely blind but are, in fact, partially sighted. The RNIB 1991 report estimated that only 20% of "blind" people are completely blind (and this number includes people who can perceive light but nothing more). Thus 80% of the blind have varying degrees of visual impairment and, as we shall see, many can read large print.

Similar findings were presented in the 1992 report on blind and partially sighted children. It was estimated that there were at least 10,000 children in Great Britain with significant visual impairments, and possibly as many as 25,000. As many as 80% of the children in the sample were reported to have had their sight problems from birth.

For some children (and adults for that matter) spectacles, contact lenses, and other magnifying devices mean that they can in fact read and write using print and new technological devices rather than Braille. In this children's sample,

- over 80% used tape recordings for learning and/or entertainment,
- 40% could read normal-size print,
- 63% were using microcomputers in school,
- 36% were using microcomputers at home, and
- 90% liked listening to the radio and listening to and watching television.

Today, of course, new technology allows print to be turned into Braille or speech, and speech to be turned into print or Braille. These developments, of course, are beyond the scope of this chapter, but Nisbet, Spooner, Arthur, and Whittaker (1999) provide a useful summary.

The RNIB reports point out that the needs of blind and partially sighted are complex. Many of them have additional disabilities, and many cannot use Braille or computers because of additional learning or physical difficulties.

34.6.2.1 Large Print. The RNIB considers that 10-point type (as used in many textbooks) is too small for many readers, not just the blind and partially sighted. They recommend 12-point type for most documents and 14 point as the minimum type size for material intended for the blind and partially sighted. Other recommendations are given in Fig. 34.10. Similar guidelines have been produced in the United States by the American Association of Retired Persons (AARP, 1986), by the Civil Rights Division of the U.S. Department of Justice (1988), and by the Society for Environmental Graphic Design (1993). These guidelines share some common characteristics: They make good sense but occasionally imply too strongly that they are based on known research findings. It is important to remember, as noted earlier, that with large print the width of the text expands as well as the depth. This may make it difficult to perceive the syntactical groupings of words if the page size stays the same. So, simply enlarging a text may not always be a sensible solution to the problem: One might take the opportunity to reconsider its design (see Hartley, 1994a).

There have been few actual studies of designing printed instructional and informational texts for the partially sighted. Mansfield, Legge, and Bane (1996) compared the legibility of two typefaces—Courier and Times. They found that there were

- *Contrast.* There needs to be good contrast between the type and the paper on which it is printed or photocopied. Contrast is affected by paper color, print color, type size, and weight. Black type on white or yellow paper gives a very good contrast. Pale-colored papers provide better contrast than dark ones. Black or very dark-colored print can be used if the paper is very pale. The print should not run across photographs or illustrations.

- *Type sizes.* 14 or 16 point is acceptable when printing for the partially sighted (see the text).

- *Type weights.* Avoid light typefaces, especially in small sizes. Medium and bold type weights are more appropriate in this context.

- *Typefaces.* Most typefaces in common use are suitable. Avoid bizarre or indistinct typefaces. Numbers need to be printed clearly: Blind and partially sighted people can easily misread 3, 5, and 8 in some faces, and even 0 and 6.

- *Capital letters.* Avoid long strings of text in capital letters, as they are harder to read than lower-case ones.

- *Line lengths.* These, ideally, should be in the range of 50–65 characters. Blind and partially sighted people may prefer shorter lines than this. Avoid hyphenation at the ends of lines.

- *Spacing.* Keep to regular word spacing: Do not stretch or condense lines of type, that is, avoid justified typesettings. Allow the line spacing to be equivalent to the type size plus the word spacing. Use a line space between paragraphs, and use space to show the underlying structure of the text. Additional lines or "rules" may help keep separate unrelated sections. Do not rotate text or wrap it around illustrations. (It is also worth noting that blind and partially sighted people often need more generous space on forms for handwritten responses, as their handwriting tends to be larger than average.)

- *Paper.* Print on glossy paper can be difficult to read. Very thin papers also cause problems because text can show through from the reverse.

FIGURE 34.10. Recommendations for designing text for the visually impaired. Guidelines adapted from the RNIB's *See It Right: Clear Print Guidelines, Fact Sheet 2*. Reproduced with permission of the RNIB.

small but significant advantages for Courier for low-vision participants but that the two typefaces were more or less equivalent for participants with normal vision. DeMarco and Massof (1997) assessed the distribution of print sizes used in American newspapers and noted that the print size for front-page articles had increased by 20% over the past 50 years. Nonetheless, they concluded, much text in newspapers was printed in a type size too small for elderly and visually impaired readers. Other investigators have commented on how keyboards, smart cards, and screen-based text presents particular problems for readers with special needs (e.g., see Gill, 1997, 2001).

Shaw (1969) provides a good review of the earlier literature and reports on a detailed study with adults. Shaw asked her participants to read aloud short passages that varied in typeface (Gill and Plantin), type size (from 10 to 24 point), weight (bold and medium), and spatial settings (see Fig. 34.11).

Shaw reported that an increase in type size achieved a 16% improvement in reading performance; an increase in weight, 9%; and a change from Plantin (a serif face) to Gill Sans (a sans serif face), a 4% improvement. (This typeface change was particularly helpful for readers over 50 years of age.)

These results must, of course, be considered with caution in view of the fact that the participants were asked to read the texts out loud and that the texts themselves, as shown in Fig. 34.11, were very odd.

34.6.3 Presenting Text in Braille

The Braille system—where each character is conveyed by one of six embossed dots in a 2 × 3 matrix—is well known to many and is illustrated in Fig. 34.12. Braille text was originally produced on thick card, but today it is more likely to be produced by a thermoform system with heated, paper-thin plastic sheets. This system also allows one to produce tactile maps and line drawings. To the sighted reader a page of Braille may look like a large and cumbersome equivalent of a piece of conventionally printed text. But this would be naive. Completely blind readers cannot see the top and the bottom of the page simultaneously—they have to work out which is which. They cannot see headings and subheadings at a glance. They cannot see at a glance how many paragraphs there are on the page and, thus, how dense the text is. They cannot tell until they start whether the language of the text is going to be easy or difficult. To discover what is there blind readers must start at the beginning and work through to the end without knowing (for the most part) when the end is coming.

Face: GILL
Weight: ROMAN
Size: 12 POINT

Main floors escape special loads. Foreign glories arrange careful
bills. Returning fathers concern large merchants. Valuable
shadows know frequent corn. Lower money beats straight
diseases. Last oils enjoy

Spacing: "normal"

Wild life claims perfect witnesses. Loud beauties
move demanding chairs. Sad wages attract silent
populations. Exact spaces please ideal dinners.
Appointed plates see lost farms. Deep newspapers
expect square

Spacing: extra space between
letters and words

Next season allows set companions. Modern banks paint
vain trade. Brave adventures marry extreme churches.
Ancient machinery shoots future currents. Important
stories take late posts. Black clubs seize twenty

Spacing: extra space between
words only

Noble ways sing other bread. Long stores perform second
teeth. Religious fashions compose wide factories. Excellent
officials appear usual towns. Sorry coals walk five defences.
Numerous flowers speak wrong

Spacing: extra space between
lines only

FIGURE 34.11. An example of the materials used in Alison Shaw's experiments. Note that the experimental design meant that each participant read 4 texts of a possible 32. (Figure reproduced with permission
of the U.K. Library Association.)

In this chapter I have described how instructional text can
be improved by paying attention to the typographic layout, to
the wording or language of the text, and to the use of headings,
summaries, numbering systems, and other such devices. Much
of the research that I have described seems to be applicable
to the setting of Braille text. Despite the fact that many Braille
texts seem to be devoid of clear spatial cues—perhaps because
of the assumption that there is no need to include space because
blind people cannot see it—it seems to me that the structure of
Braille texts could be clarified by the methods discussed above.
My observations of skilled Braille readers indicate that they can
indeed "look ahead" by quickly scanning (with both forefin-
gers) and that they welcome devices such as headings (Hartley,
1989).

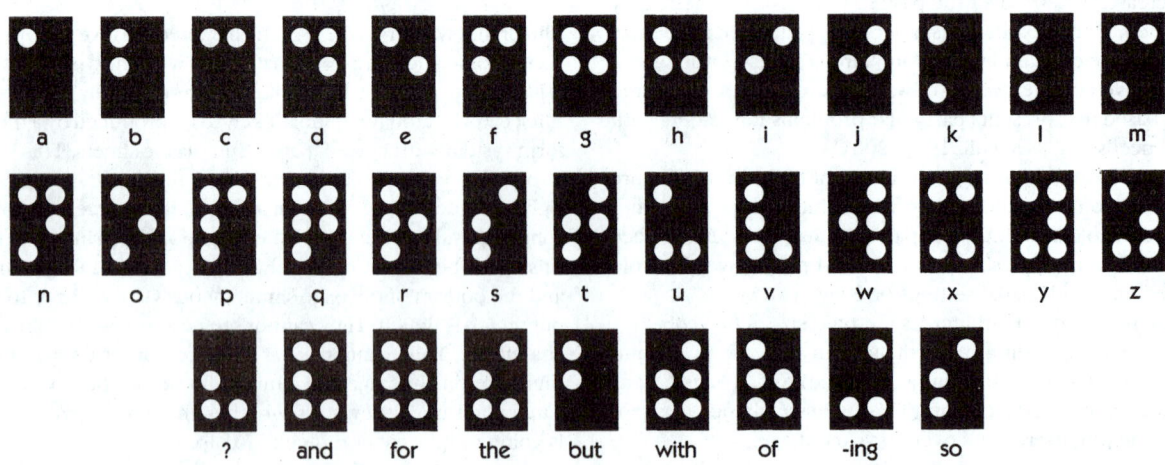

FIGURE 34.12. The Braille code.

Version A

Kanski, J. J. and Packard, R. B. S., **Cataract and Lens Implant Surgery**, Churchill Livingstone, 1985, 60pp, £26.00, ISBN 0 443 03205.

Gilbert, P., **Mental Handicap: a practical guide for social workers**, Community Care, 1985, 130pp, pbk £3.95, ISBN 0617 00447 1.

Dechesne, B. H. H, Pons, C. and Schellen, A. M. C. M. (eds.), **Sexuality and Handicap: problems of motor handicapped people**, Woodhead-Faulkner, 1985, 234pp, pbk £19.95, ISBN 0 85941 231 8.

Holloway, C. and Otto, S., **Getting Organised**, Bedford Square Press, 1985, 70pp, pbk £4.95, ISBN 0 7199 1162 1.

Version B

Cataract and Lens Implant Surgery,
Kanski, J. J. and Packard, R. B. S.
Churchill Livingstone, 1985,
60pp, £26.00, ISBN 0 443 03205.

Mental Handicap: a practical guide for social workers,
Gilbert, P.
Community Care, 1985,
130pp, pbk £3.95, ISBN 0617 00447 1.

Sexuality and Handicap: problems of motor handicapped people,
Dechesne, B. H. H, Pons, C. and Schellen, A. M. C. M. (eds.),
Woodhead-Faulkner, 1985,
234pp, pbk £19.95, ISBN 0 85941 231 8.

Getting Organised,
Holloway, C. and Otto, S.,
Bedford Square Press, 1985,
70pp, pbk £4.95, ISBN 0 7199 1162 1.

FIGURE 34.13. Version A shows an excerpt from a list of references as typically presented in the *British Journal of Visual Impairment.* Version B shows the same text using space rather than typographic cueing to show the structure of the entries in the list. The argument is that Version B would be more helpful in Braille than Version A.

Blind readers require practical information (e.g., telling them how long an article is going to be) and contextual information (e.g., the use of overview summaries). If headings are numbered and phrased in the form of questions (e.g., who, what, when, where, why, how), then blind and visually impaired readers can read with such questions in mind and they will know when they have reached the end of particular sections. Overview summaries and headings enable readers to look ahead more easily and, thus, to reduce their memory load while reading.

In addition, it might also be profitable to think of how one can convey information differently without the array of typographical devices available in printed text. In Fig. 34.13, for instance, I contrast the traditional sequence used in presenting references in a scientific journal with what might be appropriate in a Braille version. In Version A—the traditional setting—the text is continuous and different sections of the references are denoted by different typographic cues. In Braille versions of this material it is conventional to follow this continuous sequence of the printed version. In Version B, however, I have shown that resequencing the elements, and placing the key elements on different lines, makes the text easier to search even though it has no typographic cues. Clearly making changes such as these may be costly in terms of the additional space required but such changes may be more cost-effective if readers find the resulting text easier to read.

At present, of course, we do not know whether respacing traditional Braille settings would be of value to blind readers: it may make little difference to those blind from birth. However, it is likely that those who become blind in later life and who wish to learn to read Braille do carry with them a repertoire of expectations about text layout that is currently not realized in Braille.

34.7 USING TEXTBOOKS

In this penultimate section of this chapter I want to turn from discussing textbook design, where design is taken to be the equivalent of typography, to considering the situation where design is taken to be synonymous with control. In short, I am interested in how one might use the knowledge we have gained to manipulate the text so that learners can read and use it more effectively.

One aspect of this research that is of interest here is to find out what readers actually value in different text features, both separately and in combination. For example, Thompson and Maniam (two of my undergraduates) asked a group of university students to indicate their preferences for four various designs for tabular layouts presented by Ehrenberg (1977) and illustrated in Hartley (1994a). Strong support was found for Ehrenberg's personal judgments. In another study, Kim Little (another undergraduate) asked 87 adolescents aged between 12 and 16 for their preferences for various features of the design of textbooks. Access structures were clearly appreciated, but devices that required work (tables, graphs, questions, and suggestions for further reading) were not as popular.

Several authors have examined the features of text design present in various introductory textbooks in psychology, and some have collected student ratings of their value and their probable use (e.g., Griggs & Koenig, 2001; Schallert, Anderson, & Goetz, 1988). Table 34.5 shows the percentage of features found in introductory psychology textbooks by Marek, Griggs, and Christopher (1999) and the rank orderings of students' estimates of their probability of use in both this study and one (of several) by Weiten, Deguara, Rehmke, and Sewell (1999).

TABLE 34.5. The Rank Ordering of Pedagogical Features in Introductory Psychology Textbooks and Students' Estimates of Their Probability of Using Them

Feature (%)	Rank Probability of Estimated Use	
	Study 1	Study 2
Chapter outlines (100)	15	10
Boldface terms (100)	1	1
Italicized terms (97)	7	4
Chapter summaries (84)	4	2
Discussion questions (70)	14	3
Running glossaries (54)	2	6
Learning checks (46)	8	11
Section summaries (35)	6	13
Glossaries with pronunciations (22)	11	11
Questions as organizers (19)	8	15
Chapter glossaries (16)	3	7
Demonstrations (14)	12	14
Learning objectives (14)	13	9
Review exercises (11)	10	7
Self-tests (8)	4	4

Note. From "Pedagogical Aids in Textbooks: Do College Students' Perceptions Justify Their Prevalence?" by P. Marek, R. A. Griggs, and N. Christopher, 1999, *Teaching of Psychology*, 26(1), pp. 11–18. Also from "University, Community College, and High-School Students' Evaluations of Textbook Pedagogical Aids," by W. Weiten, D. Deguara, E. Rehmke, and L. Sewell, 1999, *Teaching of Psychology*, 26(1), pp. 19–21. Adapted by permission.

It is clear that different groups of students make different estimates but that some features are clearly judged more useful than others in both studies. Marek et al. also noted that the number of pedagogical aids increased in inverse proportion to the instructors' perceived difficulty level of the text.

There have also been detailed reports—with case-histories—of how students use distance-learning materials (e.g., see Marland, Patching, Putt, & Store, 1984; Marland, Patching, Putt, & Putt, 1990; Marland, Patching, & Putt, 1992). These studies have tended to focus on how such students allocate their time, what sections they read (or do not read), and in what order they carry out the assignments requested of them. Marland et al. (1990) drew attention to the fact that different groups of students paid attention to different features. Some focused on the course objectives, but others never looked at these. Few paid much attention to the headings, but tables were inspected closely. Some students were bemused by author-provided underlining. Overall there was little indication that any of the students sought to develop a broad, integrated understanding of the text.

Newton (1984) described some early British studies with university students and with teacher training college students reading science textbooks. In the 1984 report he outlined the results he obtained from examining how twelfth-grade pupils used textbooks in physics, chemistry, and biology. Basically Newton found—in these British studies—that it was rare for students to be asked to read the complete texts. It appeared that on average just over one-third of the physics text was read, slightly less than half of the chemistry text, and just over one-half of the biology text. In all cases it was common for the texts to be read after the appropriate lessons rather then before them, and there were great variations in the amounts read by individual students. The main uses that the students made of the texts were to help them answer specific questions, to help them revise, and to provide supplementary reading. Newton concluded that the main role of the textbook in this study was to act as "a surrogate teacher" and a provider of supplementary reading.

In fact there has been surprisingly little research on how teachers, as opposed to students, actually use textbooks and on which features they appreciate. Three early American studies (Alverman, 1989; Hinchman, 1987; Zahorik, 1991) suggested that teachers, overall, appeared to have three ways of using textbooks in class:

- to provide authoritative content,
- to provide basic material that they could embellish, and/or
- to provide material for discussion.

Zahorik found that over 80% of the teachers in his sample said that they would use a textbook when teaching a particular lesson but that over 40% said that they would not have their pupils read it from cover to cover. Other investigators have provided accounts—with case histories—of how teachers use textbooks in class (e.g., see DiGisi & Willett 1995; Garner & Alexander, 1994; Roth & Anderson, 1988).

Newton (1984) suggested that the ways that textbooks were used in class restricted the ways in which textbooks were written and designed. Authors, he wrote, "can assume nothing," and "the expositional style adopted has tended to give the reader a passive role." There is, indeed, some evidence to support these notions as is apparent from the listing of the percentage of pedagogical aids in Table 34.5. Features that require students to do something (such as review exercises and self-test questions) have low ranks in the hierarchy. Similar findings were reported by Schallert et al. (1988). These authors examined the strategies designed to encourage text processing in five popular introductory psychology and biology texts. Table 34.6 shows the strategies that they found, together with estimates of their approximate frequency. Schallert et al. concluded that, despite the presence of these cues, these authors generally required little effort and activity from their readers. They wrote,

Pictures and graphs were provided. Directed imagery where an author might ask readers to imagine or construct a mental representation, was never used in our sample. Summaries were provided, but readers were not asked to summarize for themselves. . . . The most effort demanding cues that were used with any substantial frequency were questions to be answered by the reader. These were usually found at the ends of chapters and may have been easily overlooked during studying.

Armbruster and Ostertag (1993) and Turner (1989) point out that the quality of these questions may leave something to be desired.

It appears, then, that such a passive view of studying is fairly common among textbook authors. This view neglects the fact that readers vary enormously in their reasons for studying, in their ability and motivation, and in their methods of approach.

One particular distinction currently receiving much attention in Europe is that between "surface" and "deep" approaches

TABLE 34.6. The Strategies Used by Authors of Five Psychology and Five Biology Introductory Textbooks to Help Their Readers

Proportion of Use:		Strategies Used by Authors
Psychology Textbooks	Biology Textbooks	
45%	29%	Cues that direct the reader's attention (e.g., objectives, questions, boldfaces, italics)
25%	31%	Cues to signal content and organization (e.g., headings, summaries, overviews, outlines, intertextual references, text to graphic references)
10%	22%	Cues that help the reader to elaborate (e.g., examples, paraphrases, applications, marginal comments)
5%	11%	Cues to support the communication (e.g., tables, graphs, referenced drawings, photographs)
3%	5%	Cues that relate text material to familiar information (e.g., familiar quotes, allusions to common experiences and comparisons)
6%	2%	Cues that arouse and motivate the reader (e.g., humor, unreferenced illustration, photographs)

Note. Data based on Schallert et al. (1988).

to studying and reading (Hartley, 1998b; Richardson, 2000). Readers with a surface approach skim the text, retain isolated facts, and are not much concerned with the overall structure or argument of the text. Readers with a deep approach, however, search for the underlying structure of the text, question it, relate ideas in the text to their own prior knowledge and experience, and so on. Table 34.7 suggests how these different study strategies may manifest themselves. This distinction between deep and surface learning, of course, is only one of many similar ones. Whatever the terminology used, the question I am asking here is, How can one design instructional text to encourage readers to take a deeper and a more active approach to reading? One answer, I think, is to identify successful learning strategies for reading and to write the text in such a way that it encourages readers to practice them.

TABLE 34.7. The Effects of the Two Study Orientations on Reading

Characteristics	Study Orientations	
	X	Y
Motivation	Intrinsic, professional • Improve teaching • Improve self-knowledge • Develop understanding of teaching • Get more out of course • Put more effort into course (not concerned about grades)	Extrinsic • Obtain graduate qualifications • Achieve higher status • Get salary increment • Enhance employment prospects
Study strategies	Optimizing • Read beyond course materials • Process material three times • Generate own questions • Use textual material to evaluate own teaching whenever appropriate or interested	Satisficing • Select textual material for study that is relevant to assessment • Process material once • Complete minimal requirements • Use textual material to evaluate own teaching when required • Evaluate ideas in text when required
Student role	• Diverge from assigned or implied student role when necessary, appropriate	
General characteristics	Information processing is generally deep Student is: • More professionally oriented • Not text bound • An optimizer (that is, tries to get the most out of study)	Information processing is generally surface unless otherwise required Student is: • Assessment oriented • Text bound • A satisficer (that is, is satisfied with getting by on what is required by assessment)

If, as Newton (1984) suggested, we consider a book as a device to think with, and if we consider that active participation is more likely to foster understanding than is a passive role, then we must consider how, as textbook designers, we might achieve this. Newton suggested, for example, that we can use self-test questions ("not necessarily difficult ones"), outlines, and advance organizers to help pupils enter into a dialogue with the author. Also, he suggested, pupils can be encouraged to use the materials provided in an active way (for example, by constructing tables and drawing diagrams). Marland et al. (1990), in their study of distance-learning materials, similarly suggested that their findings had implications for text design. They wrote,

It may be helpful if writers were to: reduce the scope of the content to allow for more in-depth study of the text; be explicit about the expectations as to study strategies to be employed, level or quality of student response and types of cognitive processes to be used when completing the in-text activity; structure the text in such a way that emphasises a cumulative, interactive organic view of learning rather than a view of learning as the acquisition of isolated bits of knowledge; design assessment activities which require re-interpretation and integration of substantial chunks of content; use outcomes of in-text activities as prerequisite knowledge for further study and make completion of some in-text activities compulsory.

Just how this might be achieved can be seen in a study by Portier and van Buuren (1995). These authors described a computer-aided text prepared for a distance-learning course that allowed students to access the course materials in a flexible way. Students using this text were able to choose whether or not they wished to read any of the text support devices such as examples, exercises, illustrations, and simulations. The authors found that students with high prior knowledge made *greater* use of the support devices in the electronic text than did students with low prior knowledge. Students with low prior knowledge preferred to stick to the basics; students with high prior knowledge were able to accommodate the extra information more easily.

In a chapter that I wrote in 1987 I listed 13 such strategies that writers, teachers, and students might use that would encourage deeper text processing. Jones (1988) similarly described a curriculum with such learning strategies embedded within it. Thus Newton, Marland, Jones, and I were arguing, along with others (e.g., Armbruster & Anderson, 1985; Rowntree, 1992), for what we called more *coherent* texts. Such texts

- are written for specific groups of readers;
- use language with which the readers are familiar;
- include experiences that readers share;
- provide meaningful examples;
- ask readers questions as they go along—not just in the headings or at the; end;
- provide examples and problems that readers actually have to work through in order to follow the exposition; and
- can be supplemented by other kinds of reading materials (see Lapp, Flood, & Ranck-Buhr, 1995).

I have written elsewhere chapters that illustrate how writers can use questions that readers have to answer in order to understand the following exposition (Hartley, 1985, 1986). More recent examples of coherent texts include Collins and Kneale's (2001) *Study Skills for Psychology Students,* Girden's (2001) *Evaluating Research Articles,* and books in the American Psychological Association's series, *Psychology in the Classroom.* Given the preponderance of textbooks in our schools, changing the ways in which we write them can make a major improvement to instructional practice.

34.8 FUTURE DIRECTIONS

In the sections above I have described a good deal of research on designing instructional and informational text. Much of this research, however, as I noted previously, is uncoordinated and atheoretical. Most researchers focus on one particular feature of text design, few consider the effects of several features in combination, few focus on what readers do with particular features and thus concentrate solely on the outcomes, and few carry out carefully developed programmatic studies.

In addition, most researchers work within a particular framework. Researchers with a leaning toward a cognitive approach, for instance, might look, for example, at how prior knowledge affects the usefulness of headings or other support devices (e.g., Portier & van Buuren, 1996; Wilhite, 1989). In contrast, researchers following a constructivist approach might focus on how getting readers to generate their own outlines, headings, or questions might be more advantageous than simply reading author-provided ones (e.g., see Foos et al., 1994; Speigel & Barufaldi, 1994). This distinction between author-provided and reader-provided devices occurs in research on summaries, outlines, headings, questions, and underlining. Presumably, too, it also affects how one writes instructional text.

Furthermore, we need to remember that textbooks are constantly evolving. Weiten and Wight (1992) provided a good example of this in their historical analysis of introductory textbooks in psychology. Currently British textbooks lag behind American ones in this evolutionary process. British textbooks use far less color and far fewer graphics, although things are changing. In 5 to 10 years, no doubt, our schoolchildren and our university students will be familiar with multimedia interactive text that they will read on colorful screens. Textbooks, *as we currently know them,* may become a thing of the past. Some people (e.g., Jonassen, 1992; Schlosser, 1994) have already predicted the demise of the textbook and described current textbooks as obsolescent. Although I think these people go too far, I do agree that the physical nature of instructional and informational text may change. New technology already allows visually handicapped students to print out text in the type sizes and typefaces that they prefer. Readers are already able to download or read on screen materials in their preferred fonts, type sizes, line lengths, margins, etc. Thus, with the help of new technology, students can customize their own materials (Lucke, 1998; MacArthur & Haynes, 1995). They can choose, for example,

- different typefaces,
- different type sizes,
- the presence or absence of inserted questions,
- summaries listed before or after the text prose,
- concept maps or outlines,
- embedded or marginal headings,
- headings written as statements or questions, and
- specific chapters from the ones available.

In other words, the future directions of instructional and informational design may be more under the control of the readers than the authors. Research in instructional design may never answer the question "Which typeface/type size/line length/etc. is best?" for every individual occasion, but it may allow us to present readers of the future with appropriate menus from which to choose.

ACKNOWLEDGMENTS

I am grateful to my reviewers, Thomas Anderson, Gary Morrison, and David Jonassen for helpful comments on earlier versions of this chapter and to anonymous editors for designing the screen-based presentation.

References

AARP (1986). *Truth about aging: Guidelines for accurate communications*. Washington, DC: American Association of Retired Persons.

Allington, R. L., & Weber, R. (1993). Questioning questions in teaching and learning from text. In B. K. Britton, A. Woodward, & M. Binkley (Eds.), *Learning from textbooks: Theory and practice* (pp. 47–68). Hillsdale, NJ: Erlbaum.

Alverman, D. (1989). Teacher-student mediation of content area texts. *Theory into Practice, 27,* 142–147.

Armbruster, B. B., & Anderson, T. H. (1995). Producing "considerate" expository text: Or easy reading is damned hard writing. *Journal of Curriculum Studies, 17,* 247–274.

Armbruster, B. B., & Ostertag, J. (1993). Questions in elementary science and social studies textbooks. In B. K. Britton, A. Woodward, & M. Binkley (Eds.), *Learning from textbooks: Theory and practice* (pp. 69–94). Hillsdale, NJ: Erlbaum.

Atkinson, R. A., Derry, S. J., Renkl, A., & Wortham, D. (2000). Learning from examples: Instructional principles from worked examples research. *Review of Educational Research, 70, 2,* 181–214.

Badzinski, D. M., Cantor, J., & Hoffner, C. (1989). Children's understanding of quantifiers. *Child Study Journal, 19*(4), 241–258.

Beck, I. L., McKeown, M. G., & Worthy, J. (1995). Giving a text voice can improve students' understanding. *Reading Research Quarterly, 30*(2), 220–238.

Berger, A. A. (1993). *Improving writing skills: Memos, letters, reports and proposals.* Newbury Park, CA: Sage.

Berger, S. (1991). *The design of bibliographies: Observations, references and examples.* London: Mansell.

Berry, D. C., Michas, I. C., Gillie, T., & Forster, M. (1997). What do patients want to know about their medicines, and what do doctors want to tell them? A comparative study. *Psychology and Health, 12*(4), 467–480.

Black, A. (1990). *Typefaces for desktop publishing: A user guide.* London: Architecture Design and Technology Press.

Boostrom, R. (2001). Wither textbooks? *Journal of Curriculum Studies, 33*(2), 229–245.

Boscolo, P., Cisotto, L., & Lucca, A. (1992). Text comprehension and typographical features of elementary school textbooks. In B. van Hout-Wolters & W. Schnotz (Eds.), *Text comprehension and learning from text* (pp. 72–83). Amsterdam: Swets & Zeitlinger.

Bracken, B. A. (1982). Effect of personalized basal stories on the reading comprehension of fourth-grade poor and average readers. *Contemporary Educational Psychology, 7,* 320–324.

Bransford, J. D. (1979). *Human cognition.* Belmont, CA: Wadsworth.

Bransford, J. D., & Johnson, M. K. (1972). Contextual prerequisites for understanding: Some investigations of comprehension and recall. *Journal of Verbal Learning and Verbal Behavior, 11* 716–726.

Bruce, I., McKennell, A., & Walker, E. (1991*). Blind and partially sighted adults in Britain: The RNIB Survey, Vol. 1.* London: HMSO.

Bruine de Bruin, W. B., Fischhoff, B., Millstein, S. G., & Halpern-Felsher, B. L. (2000). Verbal and numerical expressions of probability: "It's a fifty-fifty chance." *Organizational Behavior and Human Decision Processes, 81*(1), 115–131.

Byrd, M. (1985). Age differences in the ability to recall and summarize textual information. *Experimental Aging Research, 16*(3), 151–154.

Carpenter, P. A., & Just, M. A. (1977). Reading comprehension as the eyes see it. In M. A. Just & P. A. Carpenter (Eds.), *Cognitive processes in comprehension* (pp. 109–139). Hillsdale, NJ: Erlbaum.

Carroll, M., & Korukina, S. (1999). The effect of text coherence and modality on metamemory judgements. *Memory, 7*(3), 309–322.

Cataldo, M. G., & Cornoldi C. (1998). Self-monitoring in poor and good reading comprehenders and their use of strategy. *British Journal of Developmental Psychology, 16* 155–165.

Chall, J. S., & Conard, S. S. (1991). *Should textbooks challenge students? The case for easier or harder books.* New York: Teachers College Press.

Chapanis, A. (1965). Words, words, words. *Human Factors, 7*(1), 1–17.

Chapanis, A. (1988). "Words, Words, Words" revisited. *International Review of Ergonomics, 2* 1–30.

Clay, R. A. (2001). It was bad design, not dumb voters. *Monitor on Psychology, 32*(3), 30–31.

Coleman, E. B., Brown, A. L., & Rivkin, I. D. (1997). The effect of instructional explanations on learning from scientific texts. *Journal of the Learning Sciences, 6*(4), 347–365.

Collins, S. Y., & Kneale, P. E. (2001). *Study skills for psychology students.* London: Arnold.

Couloubaritsis, A., Moss, G. D., & Abouserie, R. (1994). Evaluating curriculum materials: Do Greek children understand their history textbook? *Education Training and Technology International, 31*(4), 268–275.

Czuchry, M., & Dansereau, D. F. (1998). The generation and recall of personally relevant information. *Journal of Experimental Information, 66*(4), 293–315.

Davis-Dorsey, J. D., Ross, S. M., & Morrison, G. R. (1991). The role of rewording and context personalization in the solving of mathematical word problems. *Journal of Educational Psychology, 83,* 61–68.

Davison, A., & Green, G. (Eds.). (1988). *Linguistic complexity and text comprehension: Readability issues re-considered.* Hillsdale, NJ: Erlbaum.

de Jong, M. D. T., & Lentz, L. R. (1996). Expert judgements versus reader feedback: A comparison of text evaluation techniques. *Journal of Technical Writing, 26*(4), 507-519.

DeMarco, L. M., & Massof, R. W., (1997, January-February). Distributions of print sizes in U.S. newspapers. *Journal of Visual Impairment and Blindness,* 9-13.

DiGisi, L. L., & Willett, J. B. (1995). What high school biology teachers say about their textbook use: A descriptive study. *Journal of Research in Science Teaching, 32*(2), 123-142.

Dwyer, F. M. (1978). *Strategies for improving visual learning.* State College, PA: Learning Services.

Ehrenberg, A.S.C. (1977). Rudiments of numeracy. *Journal of the Royal Statistical Society, A, 140,* 227-297.

Evans, H. (1972). *Editing and design, Vol. 1.* London: Heinemann.

Farr, R., & Tulley, M. A. (1985). Do adoption committees perpetuate mediocre textbooks? *Phi Delta Kappan, 66*(7), 467-471.

Fisher, D. (1976). Spatial factors in reading and research: the case for space. In R. A. Monty & J. W. Senders (Eds.), *Eye-movements and psychological processes* (pp. 417-428). Hillsdale, NJ: Erlbaum.

Foos, P. W., Mora, J. J., & Tkacz, S. (1994). Student study techniques and the generation effect. *Journal of Educational Psychology, 86*(4), 567-576.

Foster, J. J. (1979). The use of visual cues in text. In P. A. Kolers, M. E. Wrolstad, & H. Bouma (Eds.), *Processing of visible language, Vol. 1* (pp.189-203). New York: Plenum.

Fowler, H. W., & Fowler, F. G. (1906). *The King's English* (1st ed.). Oxford: Clarendon Press.

Garner, R., & Alexander, P. A. (Eds.). (1994). *Beliefs about text and instruction with text.* Hillsdale, NJ: Erlbaum.

Gill, J. (1997). *Access prohibited? Information for designers of public access terminals.* London: RNIB.

Gill, J. (2001). *Keeping step? Scientific and technological research for visually impaired people.* London: RNIB.

Girden, E. R. (2001). *Evaluating research articles* (2nd ed.). Thousand Oaks, CA: Sage.

Glover, J. A., Dinnel, D. L., Halpain, D. R., McKee, R. K., Corkhill, A. J., & Wise, S. L. (1988). Effects of across-chapter signals on recall of text. *Journal of Educational Psychology, 80*(1), 3-15.

Griggs, R. A., & Koenig, C. S. (2001). Brief introductory textbooks: A current analysis. *Teaching of Psychology, 28*(1), 36-40.

Guri-Rozenblit, S. (1989). Effects of a tree diagram on students' comprehension of main ideas in an expository text with multiple themes. *Reading Research Quarterly, 14*(2), 226-247.

Haddock, G. (1998). The influence of response scale alternatives on judgements of future academic expectations. *British Journal of Educational Psychology, 68,* 113-119.

Hall, R. M., Hall, M. A., & Saling, C. B. (1999). The effects of graphical postorganization strategies on learning from knowledge maps. *Journal of Experimental Education, 67*(2), 101-112.

Hamaker, C. (1986). The effects of adjunct questions on prose learning. *Review of Educational Research, 56*(2), 212-242.

Hamilton, R. J. (1985). A framework for the evaluation of the effectiveness of adjunct questions and objectives. *Review of Educational Research, 55*(1), 47-85.

Harp, S. F., & Mayer, R. E. (1998). How seductive details do their damage: A theory of cognitive interest in science learning. *Journal of Educational Psychology, 90*(3), 414-434.

Harrison, S., & Bakker, P. (1998). Two new readability predictors for the professional writer. *Journal of Research in Reading, 21*(2), 121-138.

Hartley, J. (1985). Developing skills of learning. In A. Branthwaite & D. Rogers (Eds.), *Children growing up* (pp. 112-121). Milton Keynes, UK: Open University Press.

Hartley, J. (1986). Learning skills and their improvement. In A. Gellatly (Ed.), *The skillful mind* (pp. 143-155). Milton Keynes, UK: Open University Press.

Hartley, J. (1989). Text design and the setting of Braille (with a footnote on Moon). *Information Design Journal, 5*(3), 183-190.

Hartley, J. (1991a). Thomas Jefferson, page design and desktop publishing. *Educational Technology, XXXI*(1), 54-57.

Hartley, J. (1991b). Tabling information. *American Psychologist, 46*(6), 655-656.

Hartley, J. (1993). Recalling structured text: Does what goes in determine what comes out? *British Journal of Educational Technology, 24*(3), 85-91.

Hartley, J. (1994a). *Designing instructional text* (3rd ed.). East Brunswick, NJ: Nichols.

Hartley, J. (1994b). Three ways to improve the clarity of journal abstracts. *British Journal of Educational Psychology, 64*(2), 331-343.

Hartley, J. (1998a). Return to sender. Why written communications fail. *The Psychologist, 11*(10), 477-480.

Hartley, J. (1998b). *Learning and studying: A research perspective.* London: Routledge.

Hartley, J. (1999). What does it say? Text design, medical information and older readers. In DC. Park, R. W. Morrell, & K. Shifrin (Eds.), *Processing of medical information in aging patients* (pp. 233-247). Mahwah, NJ: Erlbaum.

Hartley, J. (2000). Typographic settings for structured abstracts. *Journal of Technical Writing and Communication, 30*(4), 355-365.

Hartley, J., & Benjamin, M. (1998). An evaluation of structured abstracts in journals published by the British Psychological Society. *British Journal of Educational Psychology, 68*(3), 443-456.

Hartley, J., Burnhill, P., & Davies, L. (1978). The effects of line-length and paragraph denotation on the retrieval of information from prose text. *Visible Language, 12*(2), 183-194.

Hartley, J., & Ganier, F. (2000). Which do you prefer? Some observations on preference measures in studies of structured abstracts. *European Science Editing, 26*(1), 4-7.

Hartley, J., & Johnson, M. (2000). Portrait or landscape? Typographical layouts for patient information leaflets. *Visible Language, 34*(3), 296-309.

Hartley, J., & Trueman, M. (1982). The effects of summaries on the recall of information from prose text. *Human Learning, 1,* 63-82.

Hartley, J., & Trueman, M. (1985). A research strategy for text designers: The role of headings. *Instructional Science, 14*(2), 99-155.

Hartley, J., Trueman, M., & Burnhill, P. (1980). Some observations on producing and measuring readable writing. *Programmed Learning and Educational Technology, 17*(3), 164-174.

Hartley, J., Trueman, M., & Rodgers, A. (1984). The effects of verbal and numerical quantifiers on questionnaire responses. *Applied Ergonomics, 11,* 149-155.

Hershberger, W. A., & Terry, D. F. (1965). Typographic cueing in conventional and programmed texts. *Journal of Applied Psychology, 49*(1), 55-60.

Hidi, S., & Harackiewicz, J. M. (2000). Motivating the academically unmotivated: A critical issue for the 21st century. *Review of Educational Research, 70*(2), 151-179.

Hinchman, K. (1987). The textbook and those content-area teachers. *Reading Research and Instruction, 26,* 247-263.

Hofman, R., & van Oostendorp, H. (1999). Cognitive effects of a structural overview in a hypertext. *British Journal of Educational Technology, 30*(2), 129-140.

Isakson, C. S., & Spyridakis, J. H. (1999). The influence of semantics and syntax on what readers remember. *Technical Communication, 3rd Quarter,* 366–381.

Jandreau, S., & Bever, T. G. (1992). Phrase-spaced formats improve comprehension in average readers. *Journal of Applied Psychology, 77,* 143–146.

Jonassen, D. H. (1982). Introduction to Section III: Electronic text. In D. H. Jonassen (Ed.), *The technology of text: Principles for structuring, designing and displaying text* (pp. 379–381). Englewood Cliffs, NJ: Educational Technology.

Jones, B. F. (1988). Text learning strategy instruction: guidelines from theory and practice. In C. E. Weinstein, E. Goetz, & P. A. Alexander (Eds.), *Learning and study strategies* (pp. 233–260). San Diego, CA: Academic Press.

Jones, R., Pearson, J., McGregor, S., Cawsey, A. J., Barrett, A, Craig, N., Atkinson, J. M., Gilmour, W. H., & McEwen, J. (1999). Computers that personalise: Randomised trials of personalised computer-based information for cancer patients. *British Medical Journal, 319,* 1241–1247.

Jordan, M. P. (1998). The power of negation in English: Text, context and relevance. *Journal of Pragmatics, 29,* 705–702.

Keys, E. (1993). Typography, color and information structure. *Technical Communication, 40*(4), 638–654.

Kinross, R. (1994). Unjustified text and the zero hour. *Information Design Journal, 7*(3), 243–252.

Kirby, J. R., & Pedwell D. (1991). Students' approaches to summarisation. *Educational Psychology, 11,* 297– 307.

Kohut, G. F., & Gorman, K. J. (1995). The effectiveness of leading grammar/style software packages in analysing business students' writing. *Journal of Business and Technical Communication, 9*(3), 341–361.

Lapp, D., Flood, J., & Ranck-Buhr, W. (1995). Using multiple text formats to explore scientific phenomena in middle school classrooms. *Reading and Writing Quarterly: Overcoming Learning Difficulties, 11,* 173–186.

Lee, A. Y., & Hutchison, L. (1998). Improving learning from examples through reflection. *Journal of Experimental Psychology: Applied, 4*(3), 187–210.

Lewis, C., & Walker, P. (1989). Typographic influences on reading. *British Journal of Psychology, 80*(2), 241–258.

Lockwood, F. (1995). A cost benefit analysis model to describe the perception and use of activities in self-instructional texts. *European Journal of the Psychology of Education, 10*(2), 145–152.

Lorch, R. F., & Chen, A. H. (1986). Effects of number signals on reading and recall. *Journal of Educational Psychology, 78*(4), 263–270.

Lorch, R. F., & Lorch, E. P. (1995). Effects of organizational signals on test-processing strategies. *Journal of Educational Psychology, 87*(4), 537–544.

Lorch, R. F., Lorch, E. P., & Inman, W. I. (1993). Effects of signalling topic structure on text recall. *Journal of Educational Psychology, 85*(2), 281–290.

Loxterman, J. A., Beck, I. L., & McKeown, M. G. (1994). The effects of thinking aloud during reading on students' comprehension of more or less coherent text. *Reading Research Quarterly, 29*(4), 353–368.

Lucca, A., Boscolo, P., & Cisotto, L. (1991). Unpublished paper. (Cited in Lucca, Boscolo, & Cisotto, 1994.)

Lucca, A., Boscolo, P., & Cisotto, L. (1994). Typographical cueing and text comprehension: The effect of written signalling and text structure. In F. P. C. M. de Jong & B. van Hout-Walters (Eds.), *Process oriented instruction and learning from text* (pp. 205–214). Amsterdom: V. U. University Press.

Lucke, K. (1998). Customized digital books on demand: Issues in the creation of a flexible document format. *Visible Language, 32*(2), 128–149.

MacArthur, C. A., & Haynes, J. B. (1995). Student assistant for learning from text (SALT): A hypermedia reading aid. *Journal of Learning Disabilities, 28*(3), 150–159.

Mansfield, J. S., Legge, G., & Bane, M. C. (1996). Psychophysics of reading XV: Font effects in normal and low vision. *Investigative Ophthalmology & Visual Science, 37*(8), 1492–1591.

Marek, P., Griggs, R. A., & Christopher, N. (1999). Pedagogical aids in textbooks: Do college students' perceptions justify their prevalence? *Teaching of Psychology, 26*(1), 11–18.

Marland, P., Patching, W., Putt, I., & Store, R. (1984). Learning from distance-teaching materials: A study of students' mediating responses. *Distance Education, 5*(2), 215–236.

Marland, P., Patching, W., Putt, I., & Putt, R. (1990). Distance learners' interactions with text while studying. *Distance Education,11*(1), 71–91.

Marland, P., Patching, W., & Putt, I. (1992). *Learning from text: Glimpses inside the minds of distance learners.* Townsville, Australia: James Cook University of North Queensland.

Martens, R., & Valcke, M. (1995). Validation of a theory about functions and effects of embedded support devices in distance learning materials. *European Journal of the Psychology of Education, 10*(2), 181–196.

Mayer, R. E., Bove, W., Bryman, A., Mars, R., & Tapangeo, L. (1996). When less is more: Meaningful learning from visual and verbal summaries of science textbook lessons. *Journal of Educational Psychology, 88*(1), 64–73.

McDaniel, M. A., Waddill, P. J., Finstad, K., & Bourg, T. (2000). The effects of text-based interest on attention and recall. *Journal of Educational Psychology, 92*(3), 492–502.

Meyer, B. J. F. (1985). *The organisation of prose and its effects upon memory.* New York: Elsevier.

Meyer, B. J. F. (1997). Contextualization—Text structure. In A. Ram (Ed.), *Computational models of reading and understanding.* Cambridge, MA: MIT Press.

Meyer, B. J. F., Young, C. J., & Bartlett, B. J. (1989). *Memory improved: Reading and memory enhancement across the life-span through strategic text structures.* Hillsdale, NJ: Erlbaum.

Michelson, G. (1994). Use of colons in titles and journal status in industrial relations journals. *Psychological Reports, 74,* 657–578.

Miles, J. (1987). *Design for desktop publishing.* San Francisco: Chronicle Books.

Misanchuk, E. R. (1992). *Preparing instructional text: Document design using desktop publishing.* Englewood Cliffs, NJ: Educational Technology.

Moreno, R., & Mayer, R. E. (2000). Engaging students in active learning: The case for personalized multi-media messages. *Journal of Educational Psychology, 92*(4), 724–733.

Morrell, R. W. (2001). *Older adults, health information, and the World Wide Web.* Mahwah, NJ: Erlbaum.

Morrow, D., & Lierer, V. (1999). Designing medical instructions for older adults. In D. C. Park, R. W. Morrell & K. Shifren (Eds.), *Processing of medical information for aging patients* (pp. 249–265). Mahwah, NJ: Erlbaum.

Moxey, L. M., & Sanford, A. J. (1993). *Communicating quantities: A psychological perspective.* London: Erlbaum.

Muncer, S. J., Gorman, B. S., Gorman, S., & Bibel, D. (1986). Right is wrong: An examination of the effect of right justification on reading. *British Journal of Educational Technology, 17*(1), 5–10.

Newton, D. P. (1994). Textbooks in science teaching. *School Science Review, 66,* 235, 388–391.

Niegemann, H. M. (1982). Influences of titles on the recall of instructional texts. In A. Flammer & W. Kintsch (Eds.), *Discourse processing.* Amsterdam: North-Holland.

Nisbet, P., Spooner, R., Arthur, E., & Whittaker (1999). *Supportive writing technology*. Edinburgh: CALL Centre, University of Edinburgh.

Paterson, D. G., & Tinker, M. (1929). Studies of typographical factors influencing speed of reading. II. Size of type. *Journal of Applied Psychology, 13,* 120-130.

Pedler, J. (2001). Computer spellcheckers and dyslexics—A performance survey. *British Journal of Educational Technology, 32*(1), 23-37.

Pennebaker, J. W., & King, L. A. (1999). Linguistic styles: Language use as an individual difference. *Journal of Personality and Social Psychology, 77*(6), 1296-1312.

Portier, S. J., & van Buuren, H. A. (1995). An interactive learning environment (ILE) to study statistics: effects of prior knowledge on the use of embedded support devices. *European Journal of Psychology of Education, X*(2), 197-207.

Posner, G. J., & Strike, K. A. (1976). A categorisation scheme for principles of sequencing content. *Review of Educational Research, 46,* 685-690.

Prentice-Dunn, S., Floyd, D. L., & Flournoy, J. M. (2001). Effects of persuasive message order on coping with breast cancer information. *Health Education Research, 16*(1), 81-84.

Qualls, S. H., & Abeles, N. (Eds.). (2000). *Psychology and the aging revolution: How we adapt to longer life.* Washington, DC: American Psychological Association.

Raban, B. (1982). Text display effects on the fluency of young readers. *Journal of Research in Reading, 5*(1), 7-28.

Rayner, K., Kambe, G., & Duffy, S. A. (2000). The effect of clause wrap-up on eye-movements during reading. *Quarterly Journal of Experimental Psychology, 53A*(4), 1061-1080.

Reid, D. J., Briggs, N., & Beveridge, M. (1983). The effects of pictures upon the readability of a school science topic. *British Journal of Educational Psychology, 53,* 327-335.

Rice, G. E., Meyer, B. J. F., & Miller, D. C. (1989). Using text structure to improve older adults' recall of important medical information. *Educational Gerontology, 15,* 527-542.

Richardson, J. T. E. (2000). *Researching student learning.* Buckingham, UK: Open University Press.

Riggle, K. B. (1998). Using the active and passive voice appropriately in on-the-job writing. *Journal of Technical Writing and Communication, 28*(1), 85-117.

Robertson, I., & Kahney, H. (1996). The use of examples in expository texts: Outline of an interpretation theory for text analysis. *Instructional Science, 24,* 93-123.

Rook, K. (1987). Effects of case-history versus abstract information on health attitudes and behaviors. *Journal of Applied Social Psychology, 17*(6), 533-553.

Roth, K., & Anderson, C. (1988). Promoting conceptual change learning from science textbooks. In Ramsden, P. (Ed.), *Improving learning: New perspectives* (pp. 109-141). London: Kogan Page.

Rowntree, D. (1992). *Exploring open and distance learning.* London: Kogan Page.

Sadoski, M., Goetz, E. T., & Rodriguez, M. (2000). Engaging texts: Effects of concreteness on comprehensibility, interest, and recall in four text types. *Journal of Educational Psychology, 92*(1), 85-95.

Schallert, D. L., Alexander, P. A., & Goetz, E. (1988). Implicit instruction of strategies for learning from text. In C. E. Weinstein, E. Goetz, & P. A. Alexander (Eds.), *Learning and study strategies* (pp. 193-214). San Diego, CA: Academic Press.

Schlosser, B. (1994, August). Books have already entered the stage of obsolescence. *APA Monitor 25*(8).

Schraw, G. (1998). Processing and recall differences among seductive details. *Journal of Educational Psychology, 90*(1), 3-12.

Schriver, K. A. (1989). Evaluating text quality: The continuum from text-focused to reader-focused methods. *IEEE Transactions on Professional Communication, 32*(4), 238-255.

Schriver, K. A. (1997). *Dynamics of document design.* New York: Wiley.

Schumacher, G. M. (1985). Reaction to "Americans Develop Plans for Government." *Journal of Curriculum Studies, 17*(3), 263-267.

Seki, Y. (2000). Using lists to improve text access: The role of layout in reading. *Visible Language, 34*(3), 280-295.

Shaw, A. (1969). *Print for partial sight.* London: Library Association.

Sherrard, C. (1988). What is a summary? *Educational Technology, 28*(9), 47-50.

Small, J. P. (1997). *Wax tablets of the mind: Cognitive studies of classical antiquity.* New York: Routledge.

Smith, S. L., & Aucella, A. F. (1983). Numbering formats for hierarchic lists. *Human Factors, 25*(3), 343-348.

Society for Environmental Graphic Design. (1993). The Americans with Disabilities Act white paper: *SEGD's clarification and interpretation of the ADA signage requirements.* Cambridge, MA: Society for Environmental Graphic Design.

Spencer, H. (1969). *The visible word.* London: Lund Humphries.

Spiegel, G., & Barufaldi, J. P. (1994). The effects of a combination of text structure awareness and graphic postorganizers on recall and retention of scientific knowledge. *Journal of Research in Science Teaching, 31*(9), 913-932.

Spyridakis, J. H. (1989a). Signaling effects: A review of the research—Part 1. *Journal of Technical Writing and Communication, 19*(3), 227-240.

Spyridakis, J. H. (1989b). Signaling effects: increased content retention and new answers—Part 2. *Journal of Technical Writing and Communication, 19*(4), 395-415.

Spyridakis, J. H., & Isakson, C. S. (1998). Nominalizations vs. denominalizations: Do they influence what readers recall? *Journal of Technical Writing and Communication, 28*(2), 163-188.

Spyridakis, J. H., & Standal, T. C. (1987). Signals in expository prose: Effects on reading. *Reading Research Quarterly, 12*(3), 285-298.

Spyridakis, J. H., & Williams, T. R. (1992). Text headings: Do readers perceive what we think they do? In *Proceedings of the 39th Conference of the Society for Technical Communication, Atlanta, May* (pp. 433-435).

Swann, A. (1989). *How to design grids.* London: Phaedon.

Sydes, M., & Hartley, J. (1997). A thorn in the Flesch: Observations on the unreliability of computer-based readability formulae. *British Journal of Educational Technology, 28*(2), 143-45.

Tannenbaum, P., Jacobson, H., & Norris, E. (1964). An experimental investigation of typeface connotations. *Journalism Quarterly, 41*(1), 65-73.

Taylor, W. L. (1953). Cloze procedure: A new tool for measuring readability. *Journalism Quarterly, 30,* 415-433.

Thiede, K. W., & Anderson, M. C. M. (2001). *Summarizing can improve metacomprehension accuracy.* Paper presented at the Annual Convention of the American Educational Research Association.

Thomas, J. M. (1984). Four introductions to psychology. *Contemporary Psychology, 29*(8), 629-632.

Tinker, M. A. (1963). *Legibility of print.* Ames: Iowa State University Press.

Tinker, M. A. (1965). *Bases for effective reading.* Ames: Iowa State University Press.

Tinker, M. A., & Paterson, D. G. (1928). Influence of type form on speed of reading. *Journal of Applied Psychology, 12*(4), 359-368.

Townsend, M. A. R., Moore, D. W., Tuck, B. F., & Wilton, K. M. (1990). Headings within multiple-choice tests as facilitators of test performance. *British Journal of Educational Psychology, 60,* 153-160.

Turner, T. N. (1989). Using textbook questions intelligently. *Social Education, 53,* 58-60.

U.S. Department of Justice. (1988). *Access to printed information by visually-impaired persons.* Technical Assistance Guide: Civil Rights Division.

Van Patten, B., Chao, C. I., & Reigeluth, C. M. (1986). A review of strategies for sequencing and synthesising information. *Review of Educational Research, 56,* 437-472.

Walker, E., Tobin, M., & McKennell, A. (1992). *Blind and partially sighted children in Britain: The RNIB survey, Vol. 2.* London: HMSO.

Waller, R. (1979). Typographic access structures for educational texts. In P. A. Kolers, M. E. Wrolstad, & H. Bouma (Eds.), *Processing of visible language, Vol. 1* (pp. 175-188). New York: Plenum.

Waller, R. (1980). Notes on transforming No. 4: Numbering systems in text. In J. Hartley (Ed.), *The psychology of written communication* (pp. 145-153). London: Kogan Page.

Watts, L., & Nisbet, J. (1974). *Legibility in children's books.* London: National Foundation for Educational Research.

Weiten, W., & Wight, R. D. (1992). Portraits of a discipline: An examination of introductory textbooks in America. In A. E. Puente, J. R. Matthews, & C. L. Brewer (Eds.), *Teaching psychology in America: A history.* Washington, DC: American Psychological Association.

Weiten, W., Deguara, D., Rehmke, E., & Sewell, L. (1999). University, community college, and high-school students' evaluations of textbook pedagogical aids. *Teaching of Psychology, 26*(1), 19-21.

Welsh, T., Murphy, K., Duffy, T. M., & Goodrum, D. A. (1993). Accessing elaborations on core information in a hypermedia environment. *Educational Technology Research and Development, 41*(2), 19-34.

Weston, C., Le Maistre, C., McAlpine, L., & Bordonaro, T. (1997). The influence of participants in formative evaluation on the learning from written instructional materials. *Instructional Science, 25,* 368-386.

Wilhite, S. C. (1989). Headings as memory facilitators: The importance of prior knowledge. *Journal of Educational Psychology, 81,* 115-117.

Williams. J. M. (1997). *Style: Ten lessons in clarity and grace* (5th ed.). New York: Longman.

Wilson, R., Kenny, T., Clark, J., Moseley, D., Newton, L., Newton, D., & Purves, I. (1998). Ensuring the readability and understandability and efficacy of patient information leaflets. *Prodigy Publication, No. 30.* Newcastle, UK: Sowerby Centre for Health Informatics, Newcastle University.

Windschitl, P. D., & Wells, G. L. (1996). Measuring psychological uncertainty: Verbal versus numeric methods. *Journal of Experimental Psychology: Applied, 2*(4), 343-364.

Wogalther, M. S., Begley, P., Scancorelli, L. F., & Brelsford, J. W. (1997). Effectiveness of elevator signs: Measurement of perceived understanding, willingness to comply and behaviour. *Applied Ergonomics, 28*(3), 181-187.

Woolls, D., & Coulthard, R. M. (1998). Tools for the trade. *Forensic Linguistics: The International Journal of Speech, Language and Law, 5*(1), 33-57.

Wright, P. (2000). Supportive documentation for older people. In P. Westendorp, C. Jansen, & R. Punselie (Eds.), *Interface Design and Document Design* (pp. 81-100). Amsterdam: Rodopi.

Zahorik, J. A. (1991). Teaching styles and textbooks. *Teaching and Teacher Education, 7*(2), 185-196.

Zeller, N., & Farmer, F. M. (1999). Catchy, clever titles are not acceptable: Style, APA, and qualitative reporting. *International Journal of Qualitative Studies in Education, 12*(1), 3-21.

·35·

AUDITORY INSTRUCTION

Ann E. Barron
University of South Florida

35.1 INTRODUCTION

As noted by Winn (1993), "Human speech is the most powerful and expressive medium the designer has available for use in instructional messages" (p. 117). Speech is naturally expressive, and by varying the qualities of loudness, pitch, pace, and tone, designers can use audio to motivate and inform students. Three primary audio elements are used in educational technology—music, speech, and sound effects (Beccue, 2001; Kerr, 1999). Through these elements, audio can deliver information, direct attention, convey emotions, and provide feedback. In fact, "Audio is so integral a part of multimedia that most users would recognize its importance only by its absence" (Lehrman & Tully, 1991).

Although audio in an important instructional tool, it has not been studied as much as other media (Bishop & Cates, 2001; Jaspers, 1995; Thompson, Simonson, & Hargrave, 1996; Wilkinson, 1980). This chapter focuses on published research studies related to audio. Beginning with evaluation research and media comparison studies, the focus is then shifted to auditory memory and multichannel communication. A multimedia section focuses on design guidelines for incorporating audio in multimedia instruction. Finally, an overview of time-compressed speech and a summary are provided.

The chapter is presented in seven parts.

1. Introduction
2. History of Audio Technologies and Research
3. Auditory Memory
4. Multichannel Research Related to Audio
5. Audio in Interactive Multimedia
6. Time-Compressed Speech
7. Recommendations

35.2 SCOPE OF THE AUDITORY INSTRUCTION REVIEW

Because of the enormous amount of information related to sound and audio, this literature review is limited in its scope. The focus is on the use of verbal audio (speech); it does not address the instructional applications of sound effects or music, nor does it include the applications of audio that are specifically designed for students with disabilities.

35.3 HISTORY OF AUDIO TECHNOLOGIES AND RESEARCH

35.3.1 Introduction

Sound, as a physical form, can be described as "vibrations that set into motion longitudinal waves of compression and rarefaction propagated through molecular structures such as gas, liquids, and solids" (Alten, 2002, p. 14). For example, if you hit a drum or a tuning fork, it will vibrate, causing variations in the air pressure around it to reach your ears (Barron, Orwig, Ivers, & Lilavois, 2002). From a physiological aspect, sound is generally described as a phenomenon that is capable of being detected by the organs of hearing—generally between 20 and 20,000 Hz (American Heritage Dictionary, 1982).

Communication and instruction through sound (in the form of speech) have been used throughout time. Especially in the days prior to the printing press, oral instruction was a primary means of education and communication. After the printing press was invented in 1455, it became possible to reach a large audience by disseminating books. From then until the present, university-level instruction has relied primarily on text (Ives, 1992).

Leon Scott is credited with devising the first method of "recording" sound waves, in 1857 (Purcell & Hemphill, 1997). His device, called a phonoautograph, used a large horn, bristle, membrane, and lever to etch a pattern of a sound's frequency. This provided a "picture" of the sound, but it could not be played back. Then, in the late 1800s, the first of many technologies was invented that would allow the storage, duplication, and delivery of audio waves (the phonograph). Audio, in the forms of language, music, nature, and environmental sounds, is now an integral part of our lives and our education—it is perhaps second only to the written word as the distribution medium for instruction (Unwin & McAleese, 1988).

35.3.2 Timeline of Audio Technologies

With technological developments in the late nineteenth century and throughout the twentieth century, additional tools were added to teachers' arsenals of instructional devices. These audio technologies enabled educators to communicate verbally with students located in remote places, bring the voices and music of experts into the classroom, and record and distribute students' audio projects. A time line of approximate dates related to the major technologies is presented in Fig. 35.1 (Access Science, 2003, Fang & Ross, 1966; Motion-Picture Technology, 2003).

35.3.3 Audio in Instruction

As indicated in Fig. 35.1, a variety of audio technologies has been developed and has transitioned from analog to digital formats. Although the adoption time frame and degree of penetration for each technology varied (depending on the price of the hardware, the availability of educational software and other factors), they all had an impact on education. Through these technologies, educators have been able to use audio in both synchronous and asynchronous modes.

One of the oldest synchronous technologies (telephone) is still extremely valuable in educational settings. Whether talking to a parent or interacting with distant students, synchronous communications are essential. With the advent of digital technologies, synchronous communications have evolved to include audio conferencing via the Internet, satellite, leased data lines, and wireless connections.

Asynchronous audio technologies began with the phonograph and radio and evolved into audiotape and television. After digital audio formats emerged, audio disc, computers, DVD, HDTV, and other technologies replaced the analog formats.

As the synchronous and asynchronous audio technologies were developed, evaluation studies took place to ascertain their ability to deliver effective instruction. This section provides a review of some of the major studies associated with the various technologies, as well as a synopsis of the media comparison debate.

35.3.4 Telephone

The initial applications of teaching via telephone began in the 1930s and 1940s. Since the 1970s, the trend toward distance education has resulted in expanded use of the telephone in teaching (Olgren, 1977; Olgren & Parker, 1983). "Teaching by telephone may be one of the original distance education media, but it still has an important place in the array of media available for distance learning" (Olgren, 1997, p. 59).

In 1958, Cutler, McKeachie, and McNeil conducted a study concerning the relative effectiveness of teaching via the telephone. Two matched groups of 10 participants were selected. One group was taught elementary psychology in the traditional manner; the other, by telephone alone. No text was used, but a list of suggested readings was furnished. The telephone group was connected to a system in which all participants could speak to each other. Gains in knowledge were found in both groups, and there was no significant difference in the gain between

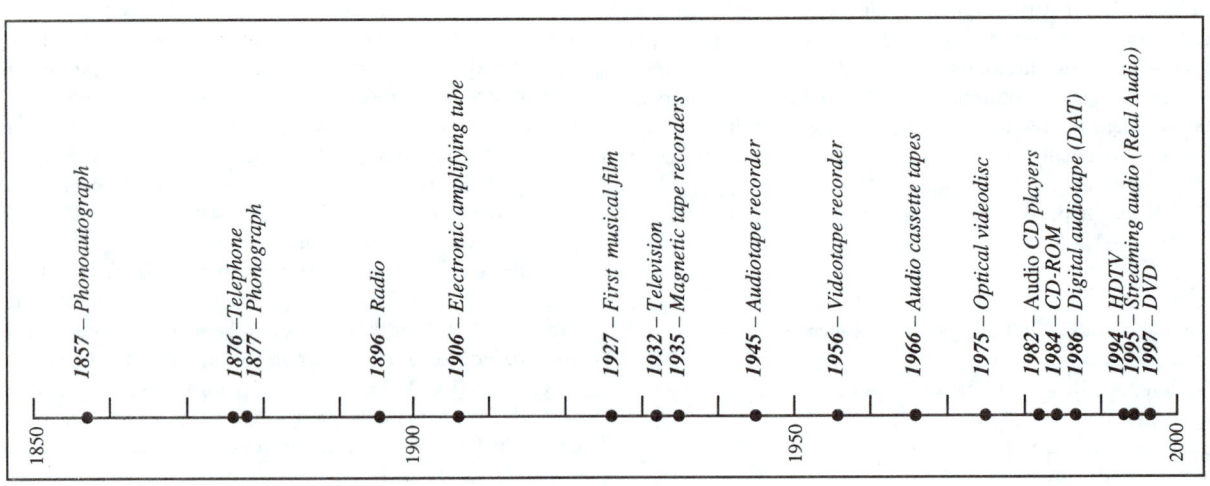

FIGURE 35.1. Approximate dates associated with audio technologies.

the two classes. Although there was evidence of a novelty effect, the method appeared practical. Rao (1977) summarized the limited research on telephone teaching and concluded, "... The research done on the effectiveness of teleteaching indicates that teleteaching is an economical and effective tool" (p. 483).

35.3.5 Phonographic Recordings

Rulon (1943a), using phonographic recordings, conducted an experiment to compare the amount of information gained by students who listened and those who studied the same material in printed form. Time was equalized. A total of 418 students listened to the recordings; 426 students studied the printed material. All students involved took a pretest, a posttest, and a test 1 week after the experiment was completed. Separate t tests were used to compare means of the pretest and posttest and also the delayed test. According to Rulon, the study of the printed material was superior to the method employing the recordings. However, a comparison in tests taken after a week showed little difference in methods employed. From this result, he concluded that recordings make more of a lasting impression than printed materials.

Rulon (1943b) later conducted a similar experiment to compare the amount of information gained by students using phonographic recordings with the amount gained by students who studied a unit incorporating the same material presented in a textbook. This experiment probably was closer to an actual classroom situation, although in this case, the textbook was prepared using the recordings as a primary source. Instructional methods using the textbook were not controlled. Testing procedures were similar to the previous study. The results, also using the t test, showed that phonographic recordings failed to show any superior effectiveness in teaching the "informational" aspects of the lesson.

In a third study on the effects of phonographic recordings, Rulon (1943c) investigated the motivational values of recordings. Using the same recordings and textbooks prepared for the earlier experiment, two groups of students were given access to supplementary reading materials after one group had heard the recordings and the other had read the material. Motivation was measured by which group used more supplementary reading materials. A total of 193 students used the recording, and 187 used the textbook presentation. Rulon's study showed no difference between the groups in terms of motivation to use supplementary reading material.

35.3.6 Loudspeakers

Educational use of the loudspeaker also attracted the attention of researchers. In 1937, Loder compared the retention of factual materials presented over a loudspeaker system with those presented directly by a speaker. Two groups totaling 449 students were rotated in the experiment. A pretest, a test immediately after the lesson, a test 1 day later, and another test 20 days later were given. One group saw the speaker, and the other group heard him from another room. The direct group performed better, but the means were not significantly different.

Kramer and Lewis (1951) investigated whether there was a difference in memory and comprehension between two groups of students in which one group sees and hears the speaker and another group only hears him. There were 128 students in the visual group and 120 in the audio group. Both groups were located in the same lecture room, separated by a large, heavy curtain. Loudspeakers were used, and the lecture was given simultaneously to both groups. After the lecture, both groups took the same test. Both groups had been told that grades would not be counted. Kramer and Lewis reported that the mean of the visual group was higher than that of the audio group and that the visual group had a wider range. They concluded that the speaker's visible action somehow contributed to the ability to understand and remember the ideas in the lecture.

35.3.7 Radio

Educational radio began at the University of Iowa in 1911 (Wolcott, 1993). The University of Wisconsin followed in 1919, and the Ohio School of the Air was established in 1929. Other "schools of the air" were established at many institutions, but the Wisconsin effort appears to have been the most successful. Various attempts were made to evaluate the effectiveness of radio broadcasts, and Saettler (1990) reports on two important ones. The first, the Ohio Evaluation of School Broadcasts Project, began in 1937 and ended in 1943. The project's goals were to analyze the educational values of radio and to study the social and psychological effects of radio on children. "Without question, the evaluation of school broadcasts project made a significant contribution to educational broadcasting and educational technology. It provided valuable factual evidence and produced helpful aids to the educational broadcaster in the planning and effective use of educational broadcasts" (Saettler, 1990, p. 242).

The second evaluation study, the Wisconsin Research Project, compared radio instruction with conventional instruction in six subject areas (grades 5-12) from 1937 to 1939. The differences were not significant. "The comparisons consistently favored the radio groups only in the field of music, and even there the differences were not large enough to be statistically significant" (Saettler, 1990, p. 242). Although there are not many other studies, those that exist (e.g., Constantine, 1964; Cook, 1964; NHK, 1956) typically showed that radio students performed at least as well as live audiences.

Bates (1983) reported that the British Open University's experience with radio instruction showed that the broadcasts tended to help the weaker students more than the successful ones. It must be remembered that Open University courses were taught primarily through correspondence texts and that the radio broadcasts were intended to supplement the texts. It is not surprising that students who found the texts difficult would welcome the added help afforded by the radio.

Radio is no longer widely used in education in the wealthier countries, but Wolcott (1993) reports that interactive radio is still used where long distances are involved, as in Alaska and Australia. In the poorer nations, radio is used widely because it is cost effective compared to other more sophisticated technologies. Radio is not expensive to produce or receive and can cover long distances using the AM band. The Agency for International Development (no date) reports that from 1974 to 1990 radio instruction programs existed in Nicaragua, Thailand, Kenya, Nepal, the Dominican Republic, Papua New Guinea, Honduras, Bolivia, Lesotho, Costa Rica, Ecuador, Belize, Swaziland, and Guatemala. Reported results were encouraging. For example, in Bolivia effect sizes as large as 0.91 were reported for radio math compared to traditional math. By dividing effect size by cost per pupil, a measure of cost effectiveness was obtained. According to data from the Agency for International Development, interactive radio was generally much more cost effective than textbooks or teacher training. In a related case study of radio-assisted community basic education (Eshgh, Hoxeng, Provenzano, & Casals, 1988) in the Dominican Republic, gains in both math and reading as a result of radio instruction were reported.

Although the history of the use of radio in education is long, there is not a plethora of empirical data concerning its effectiveness. Saettler (1990) gave an institutional history of early educational radio in the United States but did not mention more than a few empirical studies. After World War II, interest in instructional radio declined, so the situation did not improve. As with other media, radio instruction has been found to be at least as effective as conventional instruction. In certain circumstances, such as when conventional instruction is inadequate, the radio can be a cause of improved learning. Given the cost and reach of radio, it appears to be a viable medium in places where other media are too expensive or unavailable. A 1999 ERIC Digest provides information on applications and activities for using radios in the classroom (Ninno, 1999).

35.3.8 Film and Television

The first "talking picture," *The Jazz Singer*, by Warner Brothers, was produced in 1927 (Motion-Picture Technology, 2003). Since then, audio has been an important component of film and television production. When sound films reached academia in the early 1930s, a series of research studies examined their effectiveness. Hoban and Van Ormer (1970) summarized the research from 1918 through 1950 and concluded that films can be equivalent to good instructors and that using films in the classroom can reduce instructional time. In 1966, Campeau published a review of the literature that reported no significant differences between traditional instruction and motion pictures.

Television cameras were invented in 1923, and the first TV broadcast in the United States took place in 1930. By the 1950s, televisions were appearing in schools and instructional settings. In separate literature reviews, both Stickell (1963) and Chu and Schramm (1968) found no significant differences in the majority of the studies that compared face-to-face instruction and television.

35.3.9 Audiotape/Disc

The ability to record audio or to purchase professionally developed audio instruction has had a substantial impact on education and entertainment. Over the years, storage options have evolved from reel-to-reel, cartridges, and cassette to compact disc. These formats have been used to deliver instruction and to provide audio feedback. Because playback units are inexpensive and are readily available in homes and cars, these media offer tremendous versatility for classroom and remote instruction.

Gibson (1958, 1959, 1960) reported a 3-year experimental comparison of a tape-teaching program with conventional instruction at an Omaha, Nebraska, junior high school. Two areas were chosen to study the effectiveness of tape recording: spelling and conversational Spanish. Oral and written tests were used. Results included the assertion that tape instruction was superior to conventional instruction when the criterion was the number of words correctly spelled. Both methods were equally effective for recognition of words misspelled. Spanish classes taught by a non-Spanish teacher using Spanish tapes and classes taught by a Spanish teacher were similar in achievement scores. The following conclusions were made: (a) Tape recording is an effective method for teaching conversational Spanish to seventh graders; (b) regular classroom teachers can effectively teach conversational Spanish by means of tape prepared by Spanish specialists; (c) students can learn to spell as effectively with a tape as with conventional classroom procedures; (d) with proper orientation, large groups can be taught spelling effectively; and (e) teaching with tapes produced no adverse effect on attitudes toward the subject.

Popham (1962) studied the effectiveness of tape-recorded lectures in teaching a college-level education class. Thirty-six students were divided into 18 matched pairs. Chi-square analyses revealed no significant difference among variables. One group was a conventional lecture discussion; the other group was taught by tape-recorded lectures with student-led discussions. This experiment continued over one semester. Pretests in achievement and a test to measure student opinion were given. Both tests were repeated at the completion of the course. Popham reported that both groups had increased performance on the achievement tests; there was no significant difference between them. There was no significant difference on reactions to the courses; however, the opinions of the tape-lecture sections were generally favorable toward the technique.

In a similar study, Menne, Klingenschmidt, and Nord (1969) provided taped lectures, tape recorders, and printed notes to 209 college students. Another 408 students attended regular lectures. Overall, there was no significant difference, but students in the lowest quartile showed an advantage in the tape condition. Also, the dropout rate was lower for the students using tape.

There are few cases of the large-scale, systematic application of audio technology to instruction. One interesting and extensive implementation of audio for instructional purposes is Postlethwaite's "audiotutorial instruction" (ATI). This approach, which has been widely reported (Button, 1991; Postlethwaite, 1970, 1972, 1978, 1980; Svoboda, 1978), is more a complete instructional system than just an application of audio; however, its long history and wide application make it an important source of information.

ATI began almost by accident in 1961 at Purdue University (Postlethwaite, Novak, & Murray, 1972), when Postlethwaite was attempting to provide supplementary materials for weaker students in freshman botany. Simple lecture material was made available on a self-study basis through the audiovisual department. During the semester, these tapes evolved into programmed experiences that directed the students' attention to sections of the textbook, pictures, and diagrams, as well as live plants. Eventually experiments were added, and the entire week's study could be covered without attending any formal sessions. Student reaction was favorable, so in 1961–1962, an experimental section of 36 students was taught entirely by the audiotutorial method. Results on the conventional exam showed that the experimental group performed as well as the regular students. Interviews with the students led to the creation of a completely restructured course.

In designing the new course, Postlethwaite studiously avoided using words like lecture, recitation, and laboratory, which he felt connoted formality and passivity. The new course consisted of independent study sessions (with an audiotape as a tutor and guide to activities), general assembly sessions (for exams and group lectures), and small assembly sessions (which included integrated oral and written quiz sessions). Additional activities were sometimes included.

It appears that Postlethwaite was acutely aware that an audiotape-mediated course might take on the appearance of impersonality. To avoid this, several measures were taken. The tapes were made with an informal, conversational quality. The instructors in the learning center were apparently told to maintain a pleasant personal manner. The senior instructor spent 3 hours per week in the small quiz sessions, meeting with about 48 students. Another 3 hours were spent informally visiting the learning center. He also held a weekly coffee hour to which all students were invited. Finally, he held an open house (for 600 students!) at his home once a semester. Postlethwaite considered this emphasis on personal contact and a well-structured sequence of learning events to be the essential ingredients of ATI.

Joseph Novak (of the previous Postlethwaite group) developed elementary science lessons using ATI. In an extensive longitudinal investigation of the effects of ATI, Novak and Musunda (1991) reported a 12-year study of science concept learning. Twenty-eight of their best science concept ATI lessons were provided to 191 first- and second-grade children. Each lesson required 15 to 25 min to complete. As with the Postlethwaite materials, students were directed by the tape to interact with materials and pictures. Data collection evolved into Piagetian clinical interviews that were then translated into concept maps. Concept maps were then graded for valid and invalid notions. Instructed subjects showed significantly more valid concept understandings and fewer misconceptions. A significant interaction showed that instructed subjects, over the 12 years, had a greater tendency to increase their number of correct concepts and decrease the number of incorrect concepts. This study strongly supports the validity of ATI even under conditions where the instructors are not well trained. Valid concepts were learned from ATI and evidently "scaffolded" more learning throughout the children's 12 years of schooling.

The most comprehensive review of ATI is by Kulik, Kulik, and Cohen (1979). This metanalysis of 48 reports of ATI found a small but significant achievement effect for ATI over conventional instruction. However, ATI had little effect on course evaluations or withdrawal rates. Also, aptitude and achievement correlated highly, indicating that ATI did not have a leveling effect as might have been expected with such a self-directed, self-paced approach.

Several recent studies focus on the efficiency and effectiveness of providing audiotaped feedback for students, as opposed to written feedback. Pearce and Ackley (1995) conducted a review of the literature and summarized the following points (p. 32).

- All studies that reported on the measure found that audiotaping provided more and better feedback than written comments.
- Audiotaping typically required either less or the same amount of time and improved the context, leading to a better understanding of the feedback provided.
- Students liked or were motivated better by taped feedback, although the results on grades and quality were mixed.

In summary, ATI is the most complete and most well-documented method of auditory presentation. It has a general record of success, and although it is not noticeably superior to conventional approaches, it has many valuable applications.

35.3.10 Audioconferencing and Audiographics

In distance education, audio-based technologies are proliferating. Audioconferencing (both audio only and audioconferencing with images or data) is now possible through existing public telephone lines and other connections. Audiographic technologies such as the fax machine, streaming audio, and electronic whiteboards are becoming common. Freeman, Grimes, and Holliday (2000) conducted an experiment in which a 14-week course in statistics was delivered via four treatments: (a) audio-data collaboration,(b) satellite-delivered instructional television, (c) face-to-face instruction in the television studio, and (d) face-to-face instruction in a traditional classroom. Results suggest that "there is no difference in student learning performance between the hybrid audio-data collaboration and instructional television or face-to-face modes" (p. 112). Students in the audiographic group were more satisfied with the technical aspects of the medium than those in the instructional television group. For additional studies related to audioconferencing and other technologies, see *The No Significant Difference Phenomenon as Reported in 355 Research Reports, Summaries, and Papers* (Russell, 1999).

35.3.11 Computer and Web-Based Audio

At its inception, audio on computers was primarily a monotonous feature (such as a beep or a buzz) for inappropriate input by the computer user. As hardware and software improved, digital audio became a viable means of computer-based instruction (Barron & Kysilka, 1993). Several large-scale research studies that focused on computer-based education (with and without audio) have been conducted. In a general sense, these studies have found computer-based, interactive programs to be at least as effective as traditional instruction (Kulik, 1994; Mann, Shakeshaft, Becker, & Kottkamp, 1999; Schacter, 1999; Sivin-Kachala, 1998; Sivin-Kachala & Bialo, 2000). Research related specifically to digital audio in interactive formats is presented under *Audio in Interactive Multimedia* later in this chapter.

Although limited initially by storage space, audio in computer-based education flourished after CD-ROMs were developed. Currently, audio is a very common component of educational software programs. In the initial phases of the Internet and the Web, audio was again a limited commodity because of bandwidth constraints—although audio files could be downloaded and played, the transfer time was excessive. However, in the mid 1990s, technologies that allowed audio to be streamed over the Internet (rather than downloaded and played) were developed. Thanks to streaming technologies and advancements in compression algorithms, audio is becoming a common element in interactive, Web-based training.

Streaming audio is also used to deliver linear "lectures" via the Internet. A 1998 study by Ingebritsen and Flickinger found that achievement grades for an Internet section of a biology course were slightly higher (though not statistically significant) than the scores for a traditional section. Student attitudes toward the course were also very good. A similar study was conducted by Hurlburt (2001) with an introductory statistics course. Although a significant difference was not noted between course grades (of the traditional classroom and the "lectlet" group), the researcher noted that streaming audio effectively presented the course content and allowed a great deal more flexibility for students (who could record them and replay them at any time).

35.3.12 Reading vs. Listening; Print vs. Audio

In addition to the technology-focused studies, there are historical studies that focused on reading vs. listening, without involving a specific technology. Erickson and King (1917) performed one of the earliest studies of the effectiveness of the auditory medium. Four groups of students from third to ninth grade were chosen, and each group was divided in half. One-half received the lesson from silent reading; the other half was given similar material orally by the teacher. The following day, the order was reversed as to which half read and which listened. This procedure was followed two more times, for a total of four lessons. At the third- and fourth-grade level, the median score for the oral group was much higher than the median for the group that read. At the fifth- and sixth-grade levels, the results were inconclusive. At the seventh-, eighth-, and ninth-grade levels, the medians for the oral groups were much higher than for the groups that read the lesson. Needless to say, in these early studies experimental design was not what might be desired. Specific variables, such as teachers' skill and interest, were not taken into account, nor was the subject matter. Also, the only datum that was examined was the median score of the group.

Young (1936) tested comprehension via hearing and reading with 2,000 intermediate students from Iowa and Texas. Four modes were used to present the material: (a) The teacher read aloud to students, (b) the teacher read aloud and students read the selection silently, (c) students read the selection once; and (d) students read for the time allotted the teacher to read orally. At the end of each presentation, a comprehension test was given; a delayed test was given 1 month later. Young reported that the oral presentation was more effective than either of the silent readings, both immediately and after a month. Nevertheless, gains by all groups were poor. He also found that the children who did poorly in comprehending through reading also did poorly in comprehending through hearing.

Larsen and Feder (1940) asked whether psychological abilities differentiate between the processes involved in reading and those involved in listening comprehension. After hearing and reading selected materials that varied in difficulty, 151 students were given both reading and listening comprehension tests. On these tests, there was a superiority of performance on reading comprehension over listening comprehension. However, this superiority depended on the aptitude of the student. Students with lower aptitudes tended to show equal results in listening and reading. The higher-ability groups showed a superiority in the reading comprehension tests.

Taylor (1964) concurred that less competent students retained more from listening than from reading—possibly due to the additional cues provided by the speaker's expressions, gestures, and phrasing. He also noted that younger students prefer listening over reading, and older students prefer reading. "Above grade 7, there is a distinct preference for reading over listening in most learning situations, and better retention results from reading" (p. 17).

Reading and listening seem to demand the same underlying linguistic competence (Mosenthal, 1976–1977). However, comparisons of learning from audio and print have been contradictory. Nugent (1982) and Rohwer and Harris (1975) found no differences for children, and Nasser and McEwen (1976) found no differences for college students. However, in a series of studies involving children and adults, Furnham, Gunter, and others consistently found superiority of print over audio (Furnham & Gunter, 1989; Furnham, Gunter, & Green, 1990; Furnham, Proctor, & Gunter, 1988; Gunter & Furnham, 1986; Gunter, Furnham, & Leese, 1986).

Tripp (1994) tested the differences between audio and print in a direct comparison that attempted to hold other factors constant, including reviewability and novelty, by presenting the same text by computer through either the audio or the video (printed text) medium. As found by Furnham and Gunter, the students who read the text remembered significantly more correct semantic units than the students who heard the passage. Perhaps, as Travers (1970) remarked, "One cannot reasonably ask the general question whether the eye or the ear is more efficient for the transmission of information, since clearly some information is better transmitted by one sensory channel than by another" (p. 85).

35.3.13 Media Comparison Studies: The Great Debate

Over the years, numerous researchers have criticized comparison studies and called for a change in research focus. In 1961, Kumata concluded that, despite numerous research studies that focused on the effect of television (as compared to face-to-face instruction), it did not seem to matter whether or not television was present. He urged that new areas of research, beyond the "comparability" studies, be conceived and "that the emphasis should be shifted to the totality of the teaching-learning process" (Saettler, 1968, p. 340).

In 1969, Gordon noted that the results of measuring technologies (not media) by their impact on academic grades did not help to assess any differences between the media themselves. He stated, "These experiments have shown that the same kind of teaching operates more or less the same way with and without technological aids" (p. 118). A similar sentiment was expressed by Clark (1983, 1994) in his statement, "The best current evidence is that media are mere vehicles that deliver instruction but do not influence student achievement any more than the truck that delivers our groceries causes changes in our nutrition" (1983, p. 445). He defended his position by arguing that even where apparent differences are detected, they are rendered dubious by various forms of confounding factors. Some of the forms of confounding variables that Clark cited are the novelty effect, the "John Henry effect" (where participants in a control group exert extra effort because of the sense of competition), unequal instructional strategies, unequal opportunity to learn, and unequal quality of instructional design.

Kozma (1994) responded to Clark, noting that different media possess different attributes and capabilities. He suggested that instead of asking, "Do media influence learning?" we ask "In what ways can we use the capabilities of media to influence learning for particular students, tasks, and situations?" (p. 18). Jonassen, Campbell, and Davidson (1994) then entered the debate, suggesting that we shift from an instruction and media-centered focus to a learner-centered conception of learning. Others, such as Morrison (1994), Reiser (1994), Ross (1994), and Shrock (1994), have voiced opinions about the debate and the pertinent questions related to media.

Salomon (1994) emphasizes that media are not discrete, invariant entities and that "the examination of media, when made from a cognitive-psychological and educational point of view, should not adopt a holistic approach but rather focus on specific critical qualities of media" (p. 26). Salomon defines these critical qualities as the symbol systems—media's ways of structuring and presenting information. Koumi (1994) agreed, urging that we "try to develop and refine the criteria for deploying of media to best effect" (p. 47).

It should be noted, however, that even Clark and Salomon (1986) do not think that all studies that compare or evaluate media are pointless. "The shortcomings of overall media comparisons do not render such studies useless for all purposes. The evaluation of particular products, the weighting of a medium's overall cost effectiveness, and the close monitoring of a medium's employment in practice can all benefit from one or another kind of media comparison"(p. 466).

35.3.14 Summary

Numerous technologies, designed to store and deliver audio, have emerged in the last century. From the ability to speak to someone over a primitive telephone to streaming audio on the Web, education has been enhanced through audio communication. As new technologies appeared in educational settings, there was a natural interest in ascertaining their value to instruction. To that end, a number of studies were conducted, usually comparing instruction delivered through the new technology to instruction delivered in a classroom by a teacher. Most found no significant differences. For instructional designers and teachers, this was good news—their repertoire of instructional classroom tools increased, and they could effectively teach remote students via radio, audiotapes/discs, and computers.

However, it should be noted that many of the predictions of technology-delivered instruction did not bear fruit. As Cuban (1986) points out, radio, film, television, and computers met with only marginal success in schools, and instructional practices in classrooms have changed very little since 1900. The prophesies that films would revolutionize the educational system, that radio would bring the world to the classroom, and that television would relieve crowded classrooms were all doomed to fail (Cuban, 2001; Oppenheimer, 1997; Saettler, 1990). There are many reasons for these failures, few of which have to do with the capabilities of the technology. Technology can be used to "make us smart," but we need to focus on the learner and cognition (Norman, 1993). Hence, we now turn the focus of this chapter to the research related to the perception, attention, and memory of auditory information.

35.4 AUDITORY MEMORY

35.4.1 Introduction

A great deal of research has centered on the question of how we process, store, and retrieve auditory information. Although the quantity and depth of literature related to physiology and psychoacoustics are far beyond the scope of this chapter, an overview of the research that focuses on how verbal information presented via the audio modality is perceived, processed, and remembered is presented. For a more in-depth investigation, see *Thinking in Sound: The Cognitive Psychology of Human Audition* (McAdams & Bigand, 1993) and other publications.

35.4.2 Auditory Processing

Prior to the 1960s, most psychologists did not differentiate between short-term memory (STM) and long-term memory (LTM); instead, they proposed models with a unitary memory structure (Baddeley, 1998). Since then, numerous researchers have postulated two-part or three-part memory systems, and they have investigated potential differences in the processing of visual information and auditory information.

In 1967, Neisser wrote about early-stage, sensory memory systems and labeled them iconic (visual) and echoic (auditory). In 1968, Atkinson and Shiffrin proposed a model that has been nicknamed the "modal model." This model postulates three kinds of memory—sensory memory, STM, and LTM. The model depicts information from the environment initially entering through parallel sensory stores (visual, auditory, and haptic). Most of the information in the sensory store is lost; however, some may enter the limited capacity of the short-term store and may be placed in permanent, long-term store.

Baddeley (1998) also postulates a three-part memory structure, for both visual and auditory information. In particular, he states," Evidence suggests that auditory sensory memory can be split into at least three types, echoic memory extending over a matter of milliseconds, auditory short term memory extending up to perhaps 5 or 10 seconds, and auditory long-term memory" (p. 20).

35.4.3   Echoic Sensory Store

Echoic storage (also referred to as echoic memory) is similar to an echo that lingers after a sound has been heard (similar to the persistence of vision in iconic memory). As a part of the perceptual process, information in the sensory store either fades rapidly or is displaced by subsequent information (Penney, 1975).

Research focusing on echoic memory has investigated its duration and capacity. The duration of echoic memory is generally predicted to be about 200–350 ms (Baddeley, 1998; Cowan, 1984; Efron, 1970; Guttman & Julesz 1963; & Massaro & Loftus, 1996). A few studies, involving pure tones, have resulted in longer durations (Elliott, 1970; Erickson and Johnson 1964; Massaro, 1975).

As far as the capacity, Hawkins and Presson (1986) state that it is "impossible to assign a specific value to the amount of information the echoic memory system can hold" (pp. 26–36). They note that factors that can impact the capacity include the physical similarity of items, the difficulty of discrimination, temporal relations, and the subject's prior knowledge related to the stimuli.

35.4.4   Short-Term Auditory Memory

Whereas echoic sensory memory is passive, STM is active. In STM (which is equated with working memory by some researchers), some of the information in the sensory store is attended to and processed. Selective attention and divided attention are two phenomena that can affect the processing of auditory information.

Selective attention is the ability to focus on or attend to one particular sound or voice. For example, in a crowded cafeteria, the noise level is high, yet it is possible to attend to one conversation while mentally blocking the others. Early research conceptualized a filter, which selected information for further processing (Broadbent, 1958; Cherry, 1953). However, through laboratory experiments, it became clear that even the information that was not directly attended to could sometimes be recalled (Hawkins & Presson, 1986). Many researchers propose a process of resource allocation, wherein the limited resources of working memory can be allocated to various senses or streams of information, based on the task, the stimulus, or its relevance (Kahneman, 1973).

A similar concept is referred to as *divided attention* or *split attention*. In selective attention, the listener seeks to attend to one message or channel among several; in divided attention, "the task is to attend to several simultaneously active input channels or messages, responding to each as needed" (Hawkins & Presson, 1986). A classic example, attributed to Boring (1950), recounts nineteenth-century astronomers who were counting clock beats to measure the time required for a star to traverse a given distance. Unable to obtain agreement among several observers, they concluded that it was impossible to attend to both the clock beats and the star movements simultaneously (Hawkins & Presson, 1986). Although early researchers supported the "law of prior entry"—that attention is indivisible—many now believe that multiple sources of information can be processed in parallel to a certain point and then serially beyond that point (Hawkins & Presson, 1986). Olson (1989) noted that processing multiple streams of information simultaneously can degrade performance, depending on the processing loads and other factors. He concludes: "Concurrent streams of information are processed incompletely, although attention can be switched to sample from one stream to another, often quite rapidly, and inferential processes can attempt to fill in missing information" (p. 57). Experiments involving split attention and its impact on cognitive load and instructional design have recently been conducted by Kalyuga, Chandler, and Sweller (1999) and Mayer and Moreno (1998).

The debate continues over whether the audio and visual modalities share a common resource pool/processor or are allocated different resources/processors (Basil, 1992). Support for the theory of different processing systems derives from findings that audio information is almost always recalled at a higher rate than visual information (Penney, 1975). This short-term "modality effect" has been the focus of numerous research studies and theories. For example, a study by Gelder and Vroomen (1997) tested the immediate, serial recall of spoken words, sounds, written words, and pictures. They found that the recency (being able to remember the last few items in the list of eight terms) was highest for spoken words, intermediate for sounds, and negligible for printed words and pictures. Likewise, Rummer and Engelkamp (2001) found a clear modality effect for audio in tests that involved short-term recall of sentences presented in auditory and visual modes.

There are several theories that seek to explain this recency effect and the advantage of auditory information over visual information in STM (for tasks related to immediate, serial recall). When Murdock and Walker (1969) found evidence of a modality effect, beyond that which could be explained by echoic memory, they promoted the theory of separate STM stores for visual and audio information.

Penney (1989a) hypothesized that auditory and visual information are processed in separate streams, each with different properties and capabilities. She defines three properties of the auditory stream (p. 415):

1. There is a large capacity for storing sensory information. The sensory information persists for periods of up to a minute in the absence of subsequent auditory information.
2. The echo does not decay; rather, it is highly susceptible to interference from subsequent auditory input.

3. There is an automatic generation and maintenance of the acoustic code (referred to as A code).

Whereas speech is encoded in an acoustic and a phonological code, sounds might be encoded in only auditory code, and visual items are encoded in visual and phonological code. The acoustic code is hypothesized to be "rich and very durable relative to a visual sensory code" (p. 399).

Other researchers also suggest the presence of separate channels for processing visual and auditory information. Baddeley (1998) promotes a sensory–based process, which consists of a visual–spatial sketch pad (for visually presented material) and a phonological loop (for verbal material presented in auditory form and for information converted to auditory form through subvocalization). These two processors (referred to as slave systems) operate independently but are governed by a central executive, which regulates retrieving, processing, and storing the information. In this model, verbal input in auditory form (speech) has an advantage in STM because it automatically enters the phonological loop, whereas visual input requires recoding (which takes time and resources) to enter the phonological loop (Gelder & Vroomen, 1997).

Paivio's (1986) dual-coding theory is based primarily on presentation modes—the verbal channel processes spoken or written text, and the visual (i.e., nonverbal) channel processes pictorial materials and nonverbal sounds. In a 1994 study, Thompson and Paivio conducted an experiment with three stimulus lists—pictures, sounds, and picture–sound pairs. The "additive recall of dual-modality stimuli was found to be reliable and robust" (p. 390). They concluded that memory traces could be encoded in separate, modality-specific verbal and nonverbal components.

Mayer (2001) has proposed a sensory-modalities combination approach that recognizes both sensory input (audio vs. visual) and presentation mode (verbal vs. nonverbal). This model is illustrated in Fig. 35.2. Note that spoken words would enter sensory memory through the ears. If some or all of the words are attended to, they will then enter working memory as sounds and be coded as verbal information before being integrated with other information in short-term memory and with prior knowledge (visual and verbal) that was retrieved from

long-term memory. In both Paivio's and Mayer's models, there is a semantic cross-connection between verbal and nonverbal memory where one code is accessible by the other.

Estimates of the duration and capacity of STM are generally 2–20 seconds for duration (Baddeley, 1998) and 5–9 chunks for capacity (Miller, 1956). There seems to be considerable disagreement, however, on the distinction between the echoic store and STM, the duration of STM, and the systems involved in processing auditory and visual information (Baddeley, 1998; Engle, 1996; Morra, 2000; Palmer, 2000; Penney, 1989a; Robinson & Molina, 2002). As noted by Crowder (1993), "Issues of perception, coding and immediate memory are notoriously difficult to disentangle" (in Gelder & Vroomen, 1997, p. 100).

35.4.5 Long-Term Auditory Memory

Experimental psychologists define LTM as "information that is stored sufficiently durably to be accessible over a period of anything more than a few seconds" (Baddeley, 1999, p. 16). The capacity and duration of LTM are difficult to assess; most assume that it is extremely large (perhaps unlimited) and has a very long duration (perhaps infinite). Exactly how the information is coded and stored in LTM is not completely understood. Psychologists have yet to agree if LTM is a unitary, dual, or multiple system and whether or not there are distinct audio and visual channels or stores (Baddeley, 1999).

According to Baddeley (1998), a lot of the information that is presented in the audio mode (such as speech) is probably stored in LTM in terms of its meaning, rather than its sound. However, some auditory information, such as music, voices, and sound effects, are assumed to be stored in a strictly audio form. Although there is general agreement about the modality effect in STM, results related to modalities in LTM memory have been more complex and contradictory. To test the possible modality effects in LTM, the subjects are generally presented with a series of words or numbers in either visual or audio format. An interference task is then introduced (to ensure that the memory being tested is long-term rather than short-term). Finally, the subjects are asked to recall as many of the items as possible.

Modality effects in LTM were found by Engle and Mobley (1976) and Glenberg, Eberhardt, and Belden (1987), giving rise

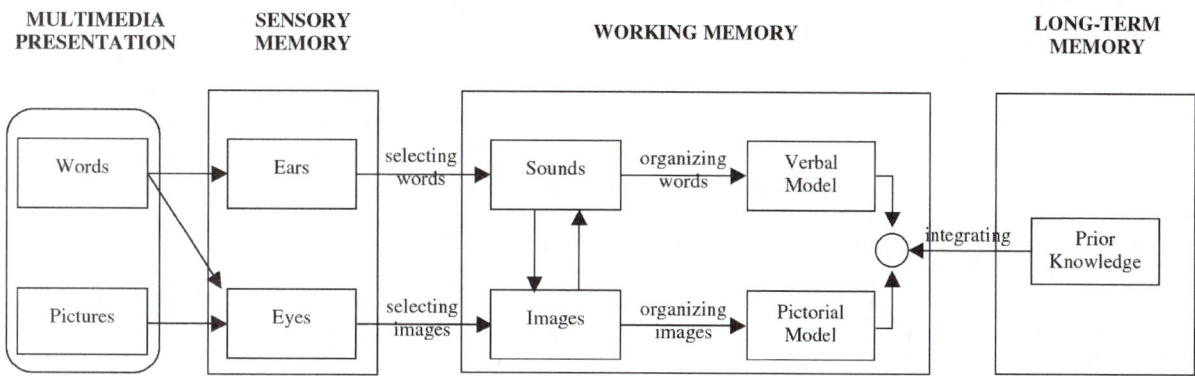

FIGURE 35.2. Mayer's cognition model.

to hypotheses such as auditory items being more distinctive than visual items and temporal information being encoded more precisely. However, in a 1989 study, Penney found a visual superiority for recall and recognition. She concluded that "where modality effects are found in long-term memory, the general effect will not consistently be an auditory superiority, but, rather, as interaction between task requirements and presentation modality" (1989b, pp. 468–469).

In 1994, Duis, Dean, and Derks also investigated the modality effects in STM and LTM. They found an auditory superiority in STM; however, they did not find evidence of a modality effect in LTM. They concluded that previous research designs may have favored audio and stated, "It seems possible that auditory and visual information are processed differently and that an understanding of these differences may lead to the conclusion that auditory superiority may, in fact, be due to the sequential presentation of stimuli that is common to so many experiments investigating the modality effect" (p. 6).

35.4.6 Summary

By examining the differences in people's ability to recall auditory vs. visual information, researchers have sought to learn more about how the human brain processes, stores, and retrieves information. Thus far, the majority of the studies have found a modality effect for STM. That is, audio information (generally a sequence of several words or numbers) is recalled better than the same information presented visually. This finding supports the theory that audio information is processed differently from (and perhaps independently of) visual data in STM. Similar studies investigating modality effects in LTM have produced conflicting results.

As experimental psychologists wrestle with models and theories that focus on differences in modalities, they may help to unravel issues that relate to the design and effectiveness of auditory instruction. As Estes (1989) noted, "Whether information is presented via films, lectures, readings, or other kinds of experiences, the process of adding the information to the stock of knowledge and skill in the mind of the student in usable form is complex and subject to many uncertainties" (p. 3).

35.5   MULTICHANNEL RESEARCH RELATED TO AUDIO

35.5.1   Introduction

Audio instruction is very rarely presented in isolation (Jaspers, 1995)—even with telephone and radio instruction, guidelines dictate having complementary visual materials. This dual approach derives from the fact that many educators believe that more learning will occur if instruction is presented through two sensory channels as opposed to one. This belief was responsible, in part, for the rush to use instructional television and film in the early and middle twentieth century. However, Travers (1970) stated that the assumption was based on

"the most flimsy evidence" (p. 104). He disputed many of the early multichannel research studies based on the fact that they were conducted without solid research designs or statistical tests of significance.

Studies investigating channels of transmission have been ongoing for decades and continue in the present. The research typically centers on an auditory or visual channel and compares it with a combined audiovisual presentation. In some cases, the visual channel is further subdivided into a pictorial channel (nonverbal) and a print channel (visual–verbal). Although there are many theories related to multichannel communications, this section concentrates on five that are often cited in research related to auditory instruction.

1. Single-channel processing theory: There is only one channel to higher centers of the brain; therefore, dual-channel transmission can be equal to, but not greater than, the single-channel processing. In fact, if both stimuli arrive at the same time, information jamming may occur and cause the dual-channel effectiveness to be less than that of either of the single channels.
2. Cue summation theory: Dual-channel presentations result in more learning than single-channel presentations because the number of stimuli or cues is increased. "This theory suggests that when pictures are added to the message, the number of cues relevant to the message increases" (Lang, 1995, p. 88).
3. Limited-capacity information processing: If the combined amount of information of two single channels exceeds the upper limit of the central nervous system capacity, then interference may occur, causing equal or less gain to take place. If combined stimuli are less than the capacity, however, then the dual-channel presentation is more efficient and effective.
4. Dual-coding theory: Information is processed in either a verbal or a nonverbal form. By coding semantically connected information in both formats, recall and recognition can be enhanced because information from one code acts as a retrieval cue for information in the other mental store.
5. Cognitive load theory: Working memory is limited; therefore, designers should seek to structure the learning materials to minimize the requirements on STM (by using two modalities, reducing the complexity, organizing the material, etc.).

35.5.2   Single-Channel Processing Theory

Broadbent's (1958) theory of perception was constructed on the assumption that there is only a single channel to the brain's higher centers. By conducting various experiments, Broadbent found that when the limit of the central nervous system has been met, some information is stored in a holding area. Because his system generally handles only one message at a time, it is referred to as the *single-processing theory* or *single-channel theory*. According to this theory, if information (from one or more sources) reaches the brain at a very slow rate, all of the information can be processed. However, when the limit is reached, only one source will be able to enter the system; the others will be excluded.

In 1964, Van Mondfrans and Travers conducted a study that assigned 72 male and female undergraduate students to three modes of presentation. Modes consisted of a series of learning trials with stimulus materials of differing degrees of meaningfulness and redundancy presented in an auditory, a visual, or an audiovisual format. One-fourth of each group received stimuli at the rate of one stimulus every 4 seconds, one-fourth at the rate of one stimulus every 2 seconds, one-fourth at a 1-second rate, and one-fourth at the rate of one stimulus every 0.6 seconds. Results revealed no significant differences between the visual and the audiovisual modes of presentation across all types of stimulus material. Travers (1967) noted, "The use of a single channel for transmitting information seems to be a safe rule except where the information transmission requires the use of more than one sense modality" (p. 145).

Based on a series of research studies and Broadbent's (1958) theoretical model of the perceptual system as a single-channel system, Travers (1970) arrived at the following conclusions regarding multichannel transmission of information.

- The transmission of redundant information through two perceptual systems will not lead to more effective information transmission than the use of a single modality except when the rate of information transmission is very slow (p. 105).
- When non-redundant information is transmitted through two different perceptual systems . . . the two channels together do not result in the retention of greater quantities of information than when one channel is used alone (p. 106).
- The main factor limiting the rate at which information is received and at least temporarily stored depends on events at the highest levels of the nervous system and not on the number of perceptual systems through which information is transmitted (p. 106).
- The bottleneck in the information processing occurs "upstairs," in the brain, and both auditory and visual information seem to encounter either the same bottleneck or bottlenecks of equal size (p. 92).

35.5.3 Cue Summation Theory

Results demonstrating increased learner achievement utilizing two channels of instruction (audiovisual) rather than one channel were realized by several studies. In 1950, the Office of Naval Research sponsored two studies at the Pennsylvania State University with 430 ROTC trainees. Experiments (utilizing film) yielded the following conclusions (Nelson & Moll, 1950, p. 1).

- Significant learning accrues from the presentation of film as a whole than from the presentation of either the audio or the video channel alone.
- Neither channel is consistently better than the other.
- Both channels together are consistently better than either one alone.

An eminent study that compared a single presentation of audio or print with the combined presentation was conducted by Hartman (1961a). This study included 1,184 freshmen at the Pennsylvania State University. The design of the experiment provided subjects with a 5-second exposure to a photograph on motion picture film. For the audio treatment, a professional announcer spoke the person's name in the photograph, paused 1 second and then repeated it; for the print treatment, the name was printed on the lower portion of the frame and appeared simultaneously with the picture throughout the exposure. Hartman's (1961a) conclusion was that "redundant information simultaneously presented by the audio and print channels [was] more effective in producing learning than [was] the same information in either channel alone" (p. 42).

Hartman (1961b) further investigated the relationship to redundant audio/print stimuli in a review of literature and published the following results:

Of nine studies comparing simultaneous audio-print presentations with audio presentations of the information, four indicated superiority for the combined channels, two favored audio, and three indicated no differences. With regard to the comparisons of simultaneous audio-print with print, seven studies supported the simultaneous presentation, and two found the presentations equivalent.

Hartman concluded, "It is apparent that a simultaneous audio-print presentation is more effective than either audio or print alone when the information simultaneously presented is redundant" (p. 244). He supported his findings with the cue summation theory. This theory predicts that learning of discriminations is increased as the number of available cues or stimuli is increased. Some researchers add the caveat that cues must also be available in a situation wherein discrimination is tested.

In another study, Severin (1968) designed a series of treatment conditions: audio with relevant pictures (cue summation condition), audio only, visual only, audio and print (redundant condition), and audio and unrelated pictures. The sample population consisted of 246 seventh-grade students, and the task was recognition. Results demonstrated that the cue summation combination was significantly superior to the redundant condition, and the visual-only treatment was superior to the audio-only treatment. Although Severin's findings agreed with Hartman's and others, he stressed the distinction between redundant, relevant, and related information. His general conclusions were as follows.

1. Multichannel communications that combine words with closely related and relevant illustrations can provide significant gains because of the summation of cues between channels.
2. Multichannel communications that combine redundant words in two channels (speech and print) do not result in significantly greater gain than single-channel communications because the added channel does not provide additional cues.
3. Multichannel communications with unrelated cues in two channels causes interference between channels and can result in less information gain than if one channel were presented alone.

Severin emphasizes the importance of relevant cues in his interpretation of the cue summation theory. He states that "these results suggest that multi-modality stimulus materials may be capable of producing increments in learning under certain conditions; they also suggest what one of these conditions might be: use of the second channel to carry additional related cues rather than simply redundant cues" (p. 9).

35.5.4 Limited-Capacity Information Processing

A study that was not completely consistent with Broadbent's model was conducted by Hsia (1968b). In this study, 912 students in the seventh grade were randomly assigned to test conditions. The content of treatments was verses of English poetry. Six conditions were set up in differing combinations of channel treatments (audio, visual, and audiovisual) and noise factors (noise and no-noise conditions). The noise factor was either auditory noise (white noise at 25% intensity) or visual noise (random black dots scattered over visual stimuli). After the presentation of each verse, subjects were given just enough time to recall what they had seen on the screen or heard from the tape recorder or both and to write down those recollections. Scoring was based on the aggregate number of words recalled, erred, lost, and presented. Data results for the total amount of recalled information revealed that neither audio nor visual was significantly better. An audiovisual treatment, however, was significantly superior to both the audio and the visual treatments. Hsia concluded that "data showed that both communication efficiency and dependability were higher in the AV channel than in the A and V channels alone" (p. 342).

In the discussion of his experiment and in a follow-up review of research, Hsia (1968b) remarked that Broadbent's single information processing channel was "demonstrably insufficient" (p. 326). He criticized Broadbent's "mechanical model," which expounds that the information system can process only audio or visual information, thereby limiting the amount of information gain in an audiovisual presentation to that of a single channel (Hsia, 1971, p. 52). Hsia based his finding on the capacity limit theorem (Shannon & Weaver, 1949) of the central nervous system. Simply stated, he asserted that

if the combined amount of information of audio and visual stimuli exceeds the upper limit of the central nervous system capacity, then both selection processes and interference take place; yet so long as neither audio nor visual stimuli reach the limit of the central nervous system, an audio-visual presentation is generally a more efficient method of presenting communication materials. (Hsia, 1968a, p. 253)

Hsia (1971) also pointed out that with the use of between-channel redundancy, the amount of information received from an audiovisual presentation is less than the amount received from the sum of the audio and visual components. In other words, "the total information provided by a stimulus or a message with a number of dimensions cannot be equal to but is always less than the sum of the information in each dimension" (p. 63). In addition, one channel can provide cues and clues for the other, thereby eliminating probable interference or information jamming.

In an attempt to reconcile findings of the cue summation theory and Broadbent's theory, Hsia (1971) hypothesized that man is a multiple-channel organism when input is optimal. In other words, he is capable of processing information through multiple channels, "so long as the inflow is within the limit of his information processing capacity. When input is far beyond this information processing capacity, it is possible that man may act as 'a single communication channel'" (p. 65).

35.5.5 Dual-Coding Theory

The dual-coding theory evolved over a 30-year period from a series of experiments and hypotheses related to imagery (Paivio, 1991). At the core of the theory is the relationship between symbolic systems and specific sensorimotor systems. Verbal systems refer to properties of language and include both text (visual) and speech (audio). Nonverbal systems refer to nonlinguistic items, such as graphics (visual), sound effects (audio), and objects (visual).

Imagery, concreteness, and verbal associative processes are important tenets of dual-coding theory. For example, "lessons containing concrete information and evoking vivid images will be easier to comprehend and remember than lessons that are abstract and not image-arousing" (Clark and Paivio, 1991, p. 173). Although the dual-coding theory has wide-ranging implications for memory, language, and cognition, it is the combination of verbal and nonverbal aspect that is most often cited in multichannel literature. For example, the *Theory Into Practice* website lists the following principle for dual coding: "Recall/recognition is enhanced by presenting information in both visual and verbal form" (Kearsley, 2001, p. 1). A key feature of dual coding is the cross-connection between information in the linguistic and that in the visual–spatial store. Hence, the viability of dual coding depends, to a large degree, on the semantic overlap between both types of information during initial encoding. As noted by Hannafin and Hooper (1993) in *Instructional Message Design*, "Information depicted in each modality must be congruent. Dual coding of text and graphics, for example, is affected by the degree to which the graphics and text reflect redundant information. Nonredundant information increases the processing requirements of the task and may hinder encoding" (p. 196). Based on this principle, many research studies and development projects combine visual (nonverbal) and verbal information, such as graphics with text or speech with graphics. "Dual coding is ineffective when both sources of information employ identical coding mechanisms. Identical presentation of words in sound and text, for example, should be avoided" (p. 196).

Not all theorists agree with the dual-coding theory, and it is often applied in a very broad sense. In the 1996 edition of this handbook, Braden noted that there had not been a direct conflict between the dual-coding and the cue summation theories. Nor had there been any attempts to reconcile or combine them.

35.5.6 Cognitive Load

The cognitive load theory can also provide important theoretical guidance to multichannel instruction. Basically, cognitive load refers to the limitations of working memory. As there is general agreement that STM is severely limited in capacity and duration (see *Auditory Memory*), designers should seek to reduce working memory load. In contrast, LTM is theoretically unlimited and consists of hierarchically organized schemas. "Schemas allow us not only to store learned information in long-term memory but, because multiple elements of information are treated as a single element in working memory, schemas also reduce the burden on working memory" (Kalyuga et al., 1999, p. 351).

Sweller and others differentiate between intrinsic and extraneous cognitive load (Sweller, 1999; Sweller & Chandler, 1994). Intrinsic cognitive load relates to the difficulty of the material as defined by the magnitude of the body of knowledge to be learned and the degree of interrelatedness among its elements. If the information is complex or complicated, the intrinsic cognitive load will be high. For example, the cognitive load involved in learning human anatomy is intrinsically high because of the large number of terms that must be learned. Extraneous cognitive load refers to the way the instruction is designed and organized—if the instruction contains irrelevant information or other material that causes inefficient cognitive processing, the extraneous cognitive load will be high.

With the assumption that there are two separate systems for modalities in STM (audio and visual), "the effective size of working memory may be increased by presenting information in a mixed (auditory and visual mode) rather than in a single mode" (Mousavi, Low, & Sweller, 1995, p. 320). In this manner, there would be an increase in the capacity of working memory, thereby allowing an increase in the amount of information that could be processed (Andres & Petersen, 2001/2002; Goolkasian, 2000; Kalyuga et al., 1999).

Several research studies have tested this theory. In a series of experiments involving high-school students and geometry lessons, Moursavi, et al. (1995) provided instruction in visual/visual (text/graphic) or audio/visual (speech/graphic) formats. The results indicated that the mixed audio/visual format was more effective than the visual/visual format, and they concluded that "when students must split their attention between multiple sources of information that require mental integration, cognitive resources available for learning can be increased by presenting some of the verbal materials in auditory rather than written form" (p. 333).

In a study involving adults, electrical content, and a computer-based instructional program, Kalyuga et al. (1999) employed variations of modality mixes and color coding to reduce cognitive load. Using the cognitive load theory, they provide the following guidance for instructional designers (when dealing with split-source diagrams and text).

1. Textual materials should be presented in auditory rather than written form.
2. Textual materials should not be presented in both auditory and written form.
3. If textual materials must be presented in written form, search for diagrammatic referents should be reduced by using appropriate markers or guides such as colour-coding. (p. 369)

In similar research, Tindall-Ford, Chandler, and Sweller (1997) conducted three experiments where audio text with visual diagrams or tables was presented to some participants and visual text with visual diagrams was presented to other participants. The results (obtained only for instructions with a high intellectual content) showed that the audio/visual treatment resulted in increased performance over the visual/visual treatment. Basing their results on the cognitive load theory, the researchers stated the following.

1. When students are faced with intellectually difficult materials requiring mental integration between multiple sources of information, results suggest that mental integration may be easier if written information is transferred into an auditory form (p. 285).
2. Audio-visual presentations are unlikely to be beneficial if the auditory component is structured in such a way that it overloads working memory—for example, if it is too long in length (p. 283).
3. If the audio component makes excessive memory demands because of its inherent complexity (even if it is short in length), it may overload working memory and render audio-visual instruction ineffective (p. 284)
4. Audio-visual instruction also may not be ideal in situations when the audio component is unnecessary or redundant for understanding (p. 284)

35.5.7 Review of the Literature

In an investigation into some of the apparent contradictions in the multichannel research, Lang (1995) conducted an extensive review of the literature. She analyzed 22 research studies (from the 1960s through the early 1990s) that were related to audio/video redundancy (primarily television). Based on the review, she identified four factors that were contributing to the conflicting results (p. 87).

1. **Overall theoretical perspective guiding the research.** Lang notes that although several theories "have been used to attempt to explain why pictures might (or might not) improve memory, they have not been used consistently to guide the conceptualization and operationalization of audio/video redundancy or memory" (p. 88).
2. **Conceptual definition of audio/video redundancy.** Variations in definitions may have accounted for a great deal of the conflicting results. In particular, three definitions of redundancy were noted in the studies (p. 90):
   a. the presence of two channels rather than a single channel,
   b. an exact match in content between the audio and the video channels, and
   c. a relationship in semantic meaning between the audio and the video channels.
3. **Operational definition of audio/video redundancy.** Lang identified 24 different operational comparisons for testing redundancy, including single words spoken aloud, single words flashed on screens, simultaneous audio/video single words, audio words with visually redundant or conflicting stills, narration with redundant text on screen, narration with redundant video, and narration with conflicting video. For her analysis, Lang grouped all of the operational comparisons into four categories—single-channel presentations, multiple-channel redundant presentations, audio/video conflicting, and talking heads.

4. *Operational definitions of memory.* There were multiple definitions of memory, including recognition, cued recall, and free recall.

Using the limited-capacity information processing model, Lang hypothesized that multiple-channel redundant information and talking head video were unlikely to overload the processing system and would thus result in increased processing and memory (over single-channel and multiple-channel conflicting information). By stratifying the studies based on consistent definitions of redundancy and memory measure, Lang concluded that her analysis showed the following effects of audio–video redundancy on memory (pp. 111–112).

- Her research suggests quite strongly that multiple-channel redundant presentations are better than single-channel presentations at every level of processing (e.g., encoding, storage, and retrieval).
- Memory for visual information is not much affected by audio/video redundancy at any stage of processing. But information for audio information is sadly compromised when redundancy between the two channels falls. This appears to be due primarily to a superiority of visual information both at recognition and recall.
- Having pictures—even conflicting pictures—appears to have the largest impact at retrieval.

She also noted, "This review reveals abundant evidence already reported in the literature that visual processing may require less capacity than audio processing and that a lack of audio/video redundancy has a much greater detrimental effect on memory for audio information than it does on memory for video information" (p. 111).

35.5.8 Summary

When examining the research studies and theories presented in this section, one can see many similarities and differences. As noted by Lang (1995), the variations in research results can often be attributed to different definitions of terms (such as redundancy, channel, cue), different philosophical perspectives, and variations in research designs. It seems evident that there are many variables that influence optimal combinations of audio and visual information, including the type and complexity of the information, the attributes of the target audience, and the level of redundancy.

The theories presented in this section serve as examples of theoretical foundations that have been used to analyze the implementation of audio. Other theories, such as interference, schema, and generative learning, are also valuable components in the quest to understand modality-based instruction. Although the controversy over multichannel processing of information is not over, guidelines are beginning to emerge; those that relate to multimedia instruction are presented in the next section, *Audio in Interactive Multimedia.*

35.6 AUDIO IN INTERACTIVE MULTIMEDIA

35.6.1 Introduction

Multimedia instruction can be loosely defined as educational programs integrating media elements (text, graphics, animation, sound, and video) in an interactive environment controlled by a computer or similar processor (Barron et al., 2002). This definition encompasses many other terms from education, commercial, and military environments, such as the following.

- Computer-based education
- Computer-assisted instruction
- Computer-based training
- Computer-assisted learning
- Computer-assisted instruction
- Technology-based training
- Interactive courseware
- Interactive videodisc
- Interactive multimedia instruction
- Multimedia learning
- Web-based training
- Internet-based learning
- e-Learning

Educational materials delivered via a computer date back to the 1960s when PLATO and TICCIT used mainframe computers and "dumb" terminals to disseminate instruction. At that time, audio was not a part of the instruction, other than perhaps a beep for an incorrect answer. When interactive videotape and interactive videodisc appeared, audio, in analog form, became a component of some programs and the related research (for example, the report by Fletcher, 1990, included programs with audio).

Although it was possible to digitize audio and incorporate it into computer programs in the 1980s, it was not practical. The primary limitation was the storage requirements. One minute of digitized audio can consume several megabytes of storage if it is stored in high-quality (44.1-kHz), 16-bit, stereo format (Barron et al., 2002). Finally, in the early 1990s, the advent of large hard drives and compact discs, along with improved, standardized compression techniques and formats, created an environment wherein incorporating audio into multimedia was feasible, easy, and relatively inexpensive (Barron and Varnadoe, 1992).

35.6.2 Applications of Audio in Multimedia Instruction

There are numerous ways to employ digital audio in interactive multimedia, including the following.

- Gaining attention. Audio (in multimedia instruction) can be used to draw attention to a program or direct attention to the most important parts of the screen (Aarntzen, 1993). "In fact, research by Kohlfeld (1971) and Posner, Nissen, and Klein (1976) has confirmed that sounds generally are more effective than images for gaining attention" (Bishop & Cates, 2001, p. 13).

- Temporal sounds. Temporal sounds can be defined as "spoken information provided about future and past events that present highlights and details about static or moving visuals" (Mann, 1995, p. 402). Mann advocates using sound as epitomes (similar to an advanced organizer, except that the key ideas are presented) or verbal summaries to help in the interpretation of the message.

- Assessments. There are several advantages to incorporating sound into computerized assessments, including meeting the needs of nonreaders and visually impaired examinees. In addition, audio can be incorporated into the user interface (spoken directions and interactions) or it can be used to test listening skills (Parshall, 1999).

- Interface. Sounds are commonly used to provide human–computer interactions through interfaces (Gaver, 1997). Operating systems provide audio feedback when a computer boots up or when a dialog box must be closed (Helander, Landauer, & Prabhu, 1997). Multimedia courseware can also be programmed to provide audio cues for navigation, such as menus.

- Instruction. Recorded voice is often used to provide the mainstream of instruction (Aarntzen, 1993). A narrator speaks to the student as text, graphics, and/or animations appear on the screens. Sound effects may also be provided, such as heartbeats for medical programs and sonar signals for the military. "Sounds can communicate information when visual attention is focused elsewhere, when tasks do not require constant visual monitoring, or when the visual channel is overburdened" (Bishop & Cates, 2001, p. 14).

- Prompts and feedback. Some instructional multimedia programs use audio to provide prompts or feedback for the students (Anderson-Inman, 1990; Jongekrijg & Russell, 1999). One approach is to have one voice or character used for instruction and another for hints or feedback.

35.6.3 Research Focusing on Audio in Multimedia

When digital audio became feasible and designers began incorporating it into multimedia courseware, there were few guidelines to follow. Consequently, very little of the design or development was based on instructional theory or research (Barron & Atkins, 1994; Daniels, 1995; Kozma, 1991; Moore, Myers, & Burton, 1996; Moreno & Mayer, 1999). In recent years, several research studies have emerged that focus on specific design options for audio in multimedia courseware. This section presents research related to textual and audio redundancy, temporal contiguity, coherence, audio feedback, aptitudes of learners, and cost/time issues.

35.6.3.1 Textual and Audio Redundancy. Speech is ephemeral, and Winn (1993) noted that "the most serious drawback to using speech (or any sounds for that matter) in

instructional messages is that they lack the permanence of text or illustration" (p. 116). There are many ways to counter this drawback, such as repeating the information (as a paraphrase) or providing a button that the student can click to repeat the audio segment (Barron & Kysilka, 1993). Another approach is to provide redundancy of the information through other channels, such as text or images.

There are several options for presenting verbal information through audio/visual combinations in multimedia programs. Assuming that all of the programs contain static or animated graphics, the following combinations of text and audio can be used.

1. Full text mirrored by verbatim audio
2. Full text combined with audio highlights
3. Full text used without spoken audio
4. Partial text combined with full audio
5. No text combined with full audio

The optimal combination of text/audio is a perplexing issue for multimedia developers, and numerous research studies have investigated this matter. Several theories related to the multiple modality of working memory (Baddeley, 1992) and dual coding (Paivio, 1986) promote the premise that combinations of verbal and nonverbal information, using both visual and audio modalities, can increase working memory. Tindall-Ford et al. (1997) explored this hypothesis with three experiments involving adults. Their results, based on the cognitive load theory, were, "When students are faced with intellectually difficult material requiring mental integration between multiple sources of information, results suggest that mental integration may be easier if written information is transferred into an auditory form. Alternatively, when information is not intellectually challenging, the mode of presentation may be of less importance" (p. 285). Their results appear to support option 5 no text combined with full audio in the preceding list. However, the researchers note that many variables must be considered. For example, if the audio segment is long or extremely complex, it may exceed working memory, and a modality effect is not likely to be observed.

Whereas the research by Tindall-Ford et al. contained static graphics and tables, Mayer and Moreno (1998) and Moreno and Mayor (1999) conducted research investigating the combination of animations and audio. They found that in four of four studies, the combination of verbal audio with animations was better than the combination of text and animations. They provided a similar rationale for the findings "When pictures and words are both presented visually (i.e., as animation and text), the visual/pictorial channel can become overloaded but the auditory/verbal channel is unused. When words are presented auditory, they can be processed in the auditory/verbal channel, thereby leaving the visual/pictorial channel to process only the pictures" (Mayer, 2001, p. 134).

A study by Koroghlanian and Klein (2000) is similar to Mayer's research in that it employed both static illustrations and animations, with and without audio. A biology lesson with 109 high-school students was used to determine the effects of instructional mode (audio vs. text), illustration mode (static illustration vs. animation), and spatial ability (high vs. low) on achievement. Contrary to the findings by Mayer and

Tindall-Ford, this research yielded no significant differences, except that the high-spatial ability students achieved more than the low-spatial ability participants. Although the text vs. audio versions did not differ in completion time, the animation treatment took significantly more time than the static illustration treatment.

Kalyuga et al. (1999) have conducted numerous experiments investigating split attention, cognitive load, and redundancy. Some of these experiments included an audio variable.

According to the cognitive load theory, learning might be inhibited when learners must split their attention between and mentally integrate text and graphics because the integration process might overburden limited working memory capacity. However, when textual information is presented in auditory form, mental integration with a diagram may not overload working memory because working memory may be enhanced by the use of both visual and auditory channels. Such a dual mode of presentation might be used to circumvent cognitive load problems caused by split-attention This phenomenon will be referred to as the instructional modality effect. (p. 353)

One experiment that tested this modality effect involved 34 adults and a training module focused on soldering. The audio-only version was superior to both the text-only and the redundant audio/text versions (Kalyuga et al., 1999). Similar results were reported in 2000—the auditory presentation of text was better than the visual-only presentation and the combined visual and auditory forms. However, in this study, the research team also noted that the results differed, based on the experience level of the learners (Kalyga, Chandler, & Sweller, 2000).

There are other recent studies that did not demonstrate instructional modality effects. For example, Shih and Alessi (1996) compared three treatments (text, voice, text and voice) for 141 college undergraduates. They included two types of information (spatial vs. temporal). The results did not show any significant differences between groups or any significant interactions among treatment groups and type of learning. However, 82% of the students reported that they preferred the combination of text and voice to the other methods of delivery.

Quealy and Langan-Fox (1998) conducted a study that involved 60 adults in three treatments: (a) stills (graphic/text screens), (b) audio (graphic/text screens with verbatim audio), and (c) video (video/text screens with verbatim audio). The results showed no significant group effect for recall.

Rehaag and Szabo (1995) assigned 82 high-school students (low ability and high ability) to either a text-based or a text plus full-audio version of a mathematics program. The program was originally designed as a text-based program, and audio was added to 3 of the 110 lessons. They did not find any significant differences in achievement or attitudes between the two main treatment groups.

Three studies used the amount of text as a variable, using treatments of (a) full text, (b) full text and full audio, and (c) partial text and full audio (Barron & Atkins, 1994; Barron & Kysilka, 1993; Koroghlanian & Sullivan, 2000). All three of the studies found no significant differences, prompting the researchers to conclude that the partial-text/full-audio approach (which is common in industrial and military multimedia programs) is at least as effective as full text/full audio. The partial-text approach is often used to conserve screen real estate in multimedia instruction and allow space for complex simulations or images. The question has been raised as to whether this decrease in visual text would adversely affect learning. As indicated in these studies, the impact was not significant.

A study that investigated audio in a hypertext dictionary environment was conducted by adding sound to the textual definitions. It was hypothesized that the encoding of two modalities would result in better retrieval of vocabulary. The results, however, indicated that the audio resources did not have a significant effect on retention (Tripp & Roby, 1994).

Based on these studies, it seems clear that verbatim audio, along with text does not generally increase achievement over a text-only approach. Some of the studies also indicate that full-audio/partial-text and full-audio/full-text delivery can achieve the same results. However, it is not clear when eliminating the text entirely (and using full audio) will increase achievement. There are obviously additional variables that could be studied. For example, Jeung, Chandler, and Sweller (1997) suggested that dual-mode instruction would be beneficial when mental resources were not required for extensive visual searching. Other variables that could be investigated include the content, duration, and pacing of multimedia instruction. For example, some researchers have noted that many of the studies conducted by Mayer and associates (that favored spoken audio over text) consisted of short segments (less than 3 minutes), focused on technical content, and did not include learner-pacing. In experiments that included different content, length, and pacing, Tabbers, Martens, and van Merrienboer (2001) found, "In the two groups in which the students set the pace of the instruction, no modality effect is found at all. Not only do the students in the visual-user group perform almost equally well on the transfer test, on the retention test they even outperform the students in the audio-user group" (p. 1029). Tabbers (2002) recommends, "Only in situations in which time-on-task is a crucial variable and the instructions are system-paced based on the pace of the narration, should spoken text be first choice in multimedia instruction" (p. 79).

35.6.3.2 Temporal Contiguity. In 1992, Mayer and Anderson proposed a contiguity principle, which recommended that words and pictures should be presented concurrently, rather than sequentially. In a 1999 article, Moreno and Mayer divided the contiguity principle into a temporal-contiguity effect (visual and spoken materials) and a spatial-contiguity effect (printed text and pictures). The rationale behind these effects is that if two stimuli are presented simultaneously, it will be easier for the learner to integrate them in STM. Likewise, if there is only a short time lapse between stimuli (as opposed to a longer one), the learners may be able to build the connections required to integrate the information. Mayer and others tested the principle on a series of experiments that involved low-ability students with high spatial ability. The results in three of five tests measuring retention and eight of eight tests measuring transfer supported the temporal contiguity principle (Mayer, 2001; Mayer

& Anderson, 1991; 1992; Mayer & Sims, 1994; Mayer, Moreno, Boire, & Vagge, 1999; Moreno & Mayer, 1999).

35.6.3.3 Coherence.

The term *seductive details* refers to the addition of interesting, entertaining, yet perhaps distracting, information in a lesson or text (Garner, Gillingham, & White, 1989). For example, a textual passage might provide interesting, but irrelevant, information in addition to the main idea (Wade, Schraw, Buxton, & Hayes, 1993). If the learners then recall the extraneous details, to the detriment of the main idea, it is referred to as the seductive detail effect. Centering on research in reading of informative text, a controversy ensued in the early 1990s. Wade (1992) concluded that "the practice of adding anecdotes and seductive details does not facilitate and may even interfere with the learning of important information "(p. 264). Other researchers agreed (Garner, Brown, Sanders, & Menke, 1992; Hidi, 1990).

However, in a review of the seductive detail literature related to reading, Goetz and Sadoski (1995a) concluded that there was insufficient evidence to confirm or deny the construct. Citing methodological problems, they remarked that "it is impossible to determine whether readers were being bewitched by distracting details, bothered by incoherent text, or bewildered by incomprehensible abstraction" (1995b, p. 509).

Recently, several research studies have investigated a similar construct, referred to as the coherence effect, in multimedia. In 11 of 11 experiments, students who received a concise presentation of a multimedia program performed significantly better (in both retention and transfer measures) than those who received a lesson with extraneous material (Harp & Mayer, 1997, 1998; Mayer, Bove, Bryman, Mars, & Tapagco, 1996; Mayer, Heiser, & Lonn, 2001; Moreno & Mayer, 2000). For example, one experiment included four different treatments of an animated lesson that focused on the phenomenon of lightning: concurrent narration (N); narration with sound effects (NS); narration, along with background music (NM); and narration, sound effects, and background music (NSM). The results supported the coherence effect in that the NSM group recalled significantly less information than all of the other groups, the NM group recalled significantly less than the N and NS groups, and groups N and NS did not differ from each other (Moreno & Mayer, 2000). A related study using a different animation and sound effects (which were not as closely related to the content) noted a detrimental impact of the sound effects as well as the music, prompting the researchers to suggest that "in multimedia lessons, the more relevant and integrated sounds are, the more they will help students' understanding of the materials" (p. 124). Based on the compiled evidence of several research studies, Mayer (2001) provides the following coherence principles (p. 133).

- Student learning is hurt when interesting but irrelevant words and pictures are added to a multimedia presentation.

- Student learning is hurt when interesting but irrelevant sounds and music are added to a multimedia presentation

- Student learning is improved when unneeded words are eliminated from a multimedia presentation.

35.6.3.4 Audio Feedback.

Sales and Johnston (1993) conducted a research study focused on the use of digitized speech as feedback in multimedia instruction. The subjects were 145 sixth-grade students who received feedback in one of three ways: spoken audio, printed and spoken, or spoken by an animated character. Although the results were not significant, the researchers provided the following recommendations that related to audio.

1. The gender of the speaker may result in differing levels of performance. When a female agent was used, female students outperformed male students.
2. Digitized speech can help overcome reading limitations of students.
3. Students were more on-task when they wore headphones.
4. Clients expect speech enhancements to software, much as they expect color to be used in the lesson.
5. Important symbol systems related to audio include gender of the speaker, tone, mode, pacing, cultural cues, and message. These have different degrees of importance to individual learners.

In another study that focused on feedback, Huang (1995) provided audio only; audio with text; or audio with text and animation feedback for a computer-based lesson about tennis. Sixty-eight adults were categorized as having high or low prior knowledge and randomly assigned to a feedback treatment. Results indicate that there was no interaction between ability and feedback type. However, the elaborate (audio with text and animation) feedback was significantly more effective.

35.6.3.5 Learner Characteristics.

It seems obvious that the aptitudes and interests of the learners can and do interact with other variables related to multimedia instruction. Although too numerous to detail, almost every study mentioned in this section provides some information about the learners' characteristics and possible interactions with the treatment. This information is invaluable when findings are generalized to additional audiences. For example, Mayer noted a difference in the effects of various design strategies between low-knowledge and high-knowledge learners and between learners with low spatial and high spatial ability. Observing that design effects were stronger for low-knowledge and high-spatial learners, he concluded that the high-knowledge learners were better able to compensate for less-than-optimal design approaches. Likewise, the low-spatial learners did not benefit as much, possibly because they had less capacity to integrate images and text in working memory (Mayer, 2001). Many of Mayer's studies included only low-knowledge and high-spatial ability students.

In their article, "*Levels of Expertise and Instructional Design*," Kalyuga, Chandler, and Sweller (1998) emphasize the importance of "knowing one's students" (p. 12). Once individual differences are determined, multimedia designers can adapt the instruction to "accommodate differences in ability, style, or preferences among individuals" (Jonassen & Grabowski, 1993, p. 19). For example, in the article, "*When Using Sound with a*

Text or Picture Is Not Beneficial for Learning," Kalyuga (2000) noted that if a diagram is self-explanatory, experienced learners performed better with the diagram alone—without verbal audio. The researcher offered the following principle: "When presented in auditory form, textual explanations should be easily turned off or otherwise ignored by more experienced learners" (p. 171). One option is to present the instruction in various methods, allowing the learners to select the most appropriate strategy or modality (Mayer, 2001).

35.6.3.6 Impact on Time and Cost. Cost is an important issue that must be considered prior to incorporating audio into multimedia instruction. It could easily cost several thousand dollars per courseware hour to hire a professional narrator, record and edit the audio files, and integrate them with an authoring program. Additional development costs would be incurred for digitizing equipment, editing software, and streaming servers. Given these financial considerations, some researchers have concluded that audio is not worth the price. Based on a study involving 120 adults, Main and Griffiths (1977) concluded that the additional cost and effort involved with the addition of audio "are not warranted until it can be demonstrated that audio and pictorial supplements provide instructional advantages that cannot be duplicated in other ways that are less expensive and easier to implement" (p. 178).

In industrial settings, time often equates to money; therefore, an investigation of audio's impact on time was the focus of several studies. Since audio is time-based, and text is not, it seems likely that programs with full audio could require more time for students to complete. This was, in fact, the case in experiments conducted by Barron and Kysilka (1993). They found that multimedia instruction with full audio required significantly more time to complete than the same program without audio (1993). Likewise Koroghlanian and Sullivan (2000) noted that the full-audio groups required more time. Rehaag and Szabo (1995) conducted a study using two treatments—full audio and full text. They found that the higher-ability students required more time in the full-audio treatment than in the text treatment. However, lower-ability students required equal time for both treatments. They surmised that the higher-ability students were able to scan the text version quickly and thus spend less time. The high-ability, full-audio group also expressed significantly more negative responses to the statement "I felt I could work at my own pace."

35.6.4 Summary

Audio is a major component of many multimedia programs, and instructional designers have many choices to make dealing with when, where, and how the audio elements should be implemented. The design decisions are extremely complex because other media elements, the content, and learners' characteristics must be considered. As Quealy and Langan-Fox (1998) remarked, "The real world (even, when only 'modeled') is awash with uncontrolled variables in a shifting dynamic equilibrium" (p. 275). The good news is that research studies are targeting the use of audio in multimedia design; the bad news is that we

have a long road to travel before all of the variables are identified and concise guidelines are available.

35.7 TIME-COMPRESSED SPEECH

35.7.1 Introduction

Unlike text, speech is inherently time-based—it cannot easily or effectively be skimmed. Several research studies have noted that a multimedia program with full narration will take significantly longer for a student to complete than a multimedia program with on-screen text (Barron & Kysilka, 1993; Koroghlanian & Sullivan, 2000). As the use of audio proliferates in multimedia learning and other venues, techniques to minimize students' time commitments are being investigated (He & Gupta, 2001).

An interesting paradox is that people can understand speech faster than narrators can speak—even the fastest talkers reach a physiological barrier at about 215 wpm (words per minute; Beasley & Maki, 1976). Conversation typically takes place at approximately 150 wpm (Benz, 1971; Nichols & Stevens, 1957). Since, in conversation, one is simultaneously listening and composing speech, it was assumed that perhaps another 125 to 150 wpm of unused processing capacity might be available in simple listening. Because the rate for speed reading is 250 to 300 wpm (Taylor, 1965) and the rate for silent reading is 275–300 wpm (Junor, 1992), it was assumed that a similar capacity might be available for listening. In fact, Fairbanks, Guttman, and Miron (1957) found that good intelligibility is possible when speech is compressed up to 50% of its original time length—up to 300 wpm.

35.7.2 Compression Technology

In early studies, time-compressed speech was produced by playing back a recording at a speed faster than the original recording. Although this method is simple to produce, the vocal pitch and intelligibility are affected (the "chipmunk effect"). The limitations of this technique generally rendered research findings questionable.

Miller and Lichlinder (1950) first demonstrated the tape-sampling method accomplished by deleting small segments of the speech signal. A switching device was used that turned off the signal periodically. Garvey (1953) performed further experimentation in compressed speech by editing out segments of the audiotape and splicing the ends of the retained tape together. Although Garvey's technique was successful, it was deemed too tedious except for research purposes. Fairbanks, Everitt, and Jaeger (1954) produced the first electromechanical apparatus that allowed both the expansion and the compression of recorded tape.

A relatively simple technique is the sampling, or Fairbanks method, which consists of removing small portions of the signal at regular time intervals (Arons, 1994). A cross-fade can then be performed between segments to improve the perceived quality. Currently, a common, linear time-compression technique is the synchronized overlap-and-add (SOLA) technique (Roucos & Wilgus, 1985). The SOLA compression method can be completed in real time (on a desktop computer). It improves the quality of speech (over the Fairbanks method) by computing the cross-correlation and locating the optimal match between segments before applying the cross fades (Arons, 1992). Both the Fairbanks and the SOLA techniques are referred to as linear time compression because the algorithms are applied consistently, and all segments are reduced by equal proportions.

Nonlinear time compression (in which the compression rates may vary from point to point) can also be applied. Nonlinear compression techniques are used to reduce redundancies, such as pauses and long vowel sounds. Combinations of linear and nonlinear are common (Arons, 1992). For example, some of the silent segments may be reduced prior to applying the SOLA technique, or the SOLA technique may be applied prior to compressing the vowel sounds.

Advanced algorithms, involving dichotic presentations for the ears or complex, adaptive compression methods, have also been developed (Arons, 1994; Covell, Withgott, & Slaney, 1998; He & Gupta, 2001). These sophisticated algorithms have been able to demonstrate increased compression rates, and at very high compression ratios, users prefer them. However, most advanced algorithms have failed to show a significant advantage in intelligibility or comprehension at the speech rates that are comfortable for listeners because intelligibility reaches a ceiling at about twice the normal speaking rate; this "ceiling" rate can be attained very easily by the linear techniques (Janse, Nooteboom, & Quene, 2001). For example, He and Gupta (2001) tested various linear and nonlinear compression techniques. They found that, regardless of the sophistication of the algorithm, the participants reached a ceiling level. Because the linear techniques, such as SOLA, are easier to implement and are equally effective below the ceiling level, they continue to be the most common (He & Gupta, 2001).

35.7.3 Comprehension

Intelligibility and comprehension are discrete, yet related constructs. Intelligibility refers to being able to identify isolated words, and it has been achieved with compression rates up to 10 times normal speech (Arons, 1997). Comprehension refers to understanding the content of a passage (measured by answering questions related to the content).

Numerous researchers have varied the rate of compression and measured the resulting effect on comprehension. Fairbanks et al. (1957) found little difference in intelligibility of selections compressed to 141, 201, and 282 wpm. Diehl, White, and Burke (1959) determined that listening comprehension was unaffected by changes between 126 and 175 wpm. Foulke and Sticht (1967) tested the intelligibility and comprehension of different rates of speech with 100 college students. Using rates of 225, 275, 325, 375, and 425 wpm, they found intelligibility scores of 93, 91, 89, 85, and 84%, respectively. The comprehension scores were 73, 66, 67, 56, and 53%, respectively. These results demonstrate a 6% loss in comprehension between 225 and 325 wpm and a loss of 14% between 325 and 425 wpm. These and other studies (Boyle, 1969; Carver, 1973; Foulke, 1968; Foulke & Sticht, 1969; Rossiter, 1970; Sticht, 1968; Wasserman & Tedford, 1973; Williams, Moore, & Sewell, 1983–1984) indicated that as word rate is increased beyond about 250 to 300 wpm, there is a decline in comprehension.

However, numerous intervening variables must be considered before a determination of the optimum degree of compression can be made (Duker, 1974). Researchers believe that the ability of subjects to comprehend compressed speech may be dependent on the difficulty of the material. Foulke (1962) determined that the comprehension of a scientific selection was less than the comprehension of a literary work at normal speed. However, at various levels of compression, the comprehension scores of the scientific selection declined less than those for the literary selection. This phenomenon may be because the comprehension scores for the scientific selection were lower at the normal rate; therefore the range in which they could vary was relatively small (Duker, 1974). His data showed that for college students, listening to compressed materials written at the eighth-grade level produced the greatest efficiency. Raising the difficulty level of the materials caused comprehension to drop off abruptly.

Length of presentation may also be a factor in comprehension and memory. Adelson (1975) examined comprehension by a group of college students listening to a 1-hr lecture at 175 wpm, as compared to the same group of college students listening to an equated 1-hr lecture compressed at 275 wpm for 40 min. Compressed materials produced less comprehension than did the normal rate materials. The author concluded that with compressed materials, the length of presentation appeared to be a critical factor, perhaps because of attentional fatigue or other factors.

Learner characteristics may influence the comprehension of compressed speech. Some of these variables include the subject's sex, age, intelligence, and reading ability. Duker (1974) determined that the comprehension scores of male and female subjects revealed no sex-related differences for word rates varying from 174 to 475 wpm. This conclusion is supported by other research studies conducted by Bell (1969), Foulke and Sticht (1967), Klavon (1975), Ludrick (1974), Orr and Friedman (1964), and Ross (1964).

Fergen (1954) and Wood (1966) found that ability to comprehend compressed speech increases with age and grade level of school children. However, beyond age 12, little difference was noted until age 60 or so. Wingfield, Poon, Lombardi, and Lowe (1985) proposed that the decline in comprehension for older people may be the result of a decline in information processing resources and that it becomes more apparent with more complex stimuli. Letowski and Poch (1996) noted a 20% decline in comprehension of time-compressed speech between middle-aged (fifth-decade) and older (seventh-decade) adults. Gordon-Salant and Fitzgibbons (2001) also investigated the relationship among age, content, and comprehension of time-compressed speech. Their research included four compression techniques (linear or selective compression of pauses, vowels, or consonants) and three stimulus forms (sentences, syntactic sets, or

random-order words). They reported three major findings related to older listeners.

1. Reduced linguistic cues resulted in reduced comprehension.
2. Acoustic alteration of consonants affected comprehension
   more than alteration of vowels or pauses.
3. A combination of time compression with reduced contextual
   cues resulted in a reduction of comprehension.

Aptitude or intelligence may also interact with comprehension. Eckhardt (1970) used a 1-hr multimedia presentation at
various rates of compression with Air Force recruits of varying
aptitudes. Eckhardt concluded that test differences between the
groups were due to aptitude and an aptitude–rate interaction.
There was a comprehension loss for lower aptitude subjects
at the higher compression levels. Sticht and Glasnap (1972) determined that low-aptitude men learned easier material better
than more difficult material as a function of decreased words
per minute. High-aptitude men tended to learn material best
at 175 wpm, independent of difficulty level. However, other researchers (Sticht, 1968; Watts, 1971; Williams et al., 1983–1984)
found that subjects with lower aptitudes or lower reading ability
performed as well at higher rates of compression as at normal
rates.

Reading ability may also influence comprehension of compressed speech. Breed (1977) tested adult vocational technical school students to determine the differences in listening
comprehension when subjects were categorized according to
reading ability. The subjects in Breed's study listened to tapes
that were time expanded and time compressed, varying in rate
from 60 to 240 wpm. Breed indicated that listening comprehension and reading ability appear to be related to verbal skills.
The poorest readers exhibited the poorest listening comprehension, and better readers were better listeners as measured
by scores on tests of listening comprehension. Goldstein (1940)
and Orr, Friedman, and Williams (1965) found a positive correlation between reading rate and ability to comprehend compressed speech. Conversely, both studies further determined
that practice in listening to compressed speech resulted in
an improved reading rate. Robertson (1977) determined that
the comprehension of subjects is not affected when they are
presented recorded materials within two reading levels below
or three reading levels above their particular grade level. In
general, it appears that a relationship between better reading ability and the comprehension of compressed speech can
be established, although this may reflect an underlying verbal
ability.

Although most of the studies reported in this section are
based on limits measured in words per minute, some researchers
feel that the limiting factor is compression ratios (and resulting
quality) rather than words per minute (Omoigui, He, Gupta,
Grudin, & Sanoeki, 1999). Heiman, Leo, Leighbody,& Bowler,
(1986) suggest that if a passage is compressed at 50%, all of the
redundant information has been removed. Because the original
passage may vary in the number of words per minute, they
conclude that the compression ratio (50%) is the limiting factor,
not the number of words per minute.

35.7.4 Preference

Several studies have been conducted to determine which level
of time compression listeners would select if they were presented with several options. Foulke (1969), found that college
students preferred a rate of about 207 wpm (approximately 1.38
the normal rate). This rate was less than the 275 wpm speed preferred by blind college students (Foulke, 1965). The researcher
surmised that if sighted students had more practice listening to
compressed speech, they might prefer the higher rates also.

In a 1995 study, Harrigan offered time-compressed lectures
to students at three distinct speeds (1.0, 1.18, and 1.36 the speed
of the original lecture). Results showed that 75% of the time,
the students preferred the 1.36-rate lecture. Similarly, Omoigui
et al. (1999) and Li, Gupta, Senoeki, He, and Yong, (1999)
conducted a study that found comfortable speedup rates at
approximately 1.4 the rate of normal speech. He and Gupta
(2001) concluded that when people were instructed to assume
they were in a hurry, rates of 1.6–1.7 the original speed were
acceptable.

Wingfield and Ducharme (1999) conducted a study to investigate possible effects of age and passage difficulty on listening-
rate preferences. They found that older adults preferred significantly slower rates than did younger adults. Both groups
preferred slower rates for difficult passages (as measured by
cloze predictability) than for easy passages. The researchers
concluded that both age groups were equally effective in their
ability to monitor the difficulty and adjust the rate.

There are some interesting affective factors to consider
when using compressed speech. Listener attitudes toward the
speaker are improved significantly (Maclachlan, 1982). Maclachlan notes that people associate fast, fluent speech with confidence, knowledge, and enthusiasm. Because attitude learning is
influenced strongly by feelings toward the speaker, compressed
speech may be appropriate in such situations. Also, Boyle (1969)
found a preference for listening over reading in young students
(under about 14 years old), presumably because of their slow
reading rates. Likewise, college students prefer listening to compressed speech over normal recording (Short, 1977) apparently
because of the time savings.

35.7.5 Training

It has often been speculated that practice might influence comprehension of compressed speech. Voor and Miller (1965) exposed subjects to five listening sessions at 380 wpm. Test scores
indicated that comprehension increased as a function of exposure up to 7 min, and remained constant thereafter. Orr et al.
(1965) exposed blind subjects to listening material presented
initially at 325 wpm and increased at 25-wpm intervals to a
rate of 475 wpm. Subjects were tested for comprehension at
475 wpm and compared to equivalent pretraining test scores.
An improvement of 29.3% was noted. Friedman, Orr, Freedle,
and Norris (1966) compared the comprehension scores of subjects given 35 hours of massed practice with the test scores
of subjects given 14 to 21 hours of distributed practice in listening to compressed speech. The authors concluded that the

comprehension of the distributed-practice group was as good as or better than the comprehension demonstrated by the mass-practiced group. Duker (1974) suggested that gradually increasing the words per minute rate might have some benefit on comprehension of compressed speech. Klavon (1975) tested this idea, without effect, in an attempt to provide a controlled transition period. In general, studies have found that although no particular method of training or practice appears to be any more effective than another, even small exposure to compressed speech can improve comprehension (Foulke, Amster, Bixler, & Nolan, 1962; Friedman, Orr, & Norris, 1966).

35.7.6 Applications

Time-compressed speech has application in voice mail systems, training materials for business and industry, and instruction for populations with special needs. Speech compressor/expanders are also used to speed up or slow down foreign languages in language labs and to normalize speech from a voice recognition program. Given the research on the stability of the comprehension levels when speech is presented at an increased pace, the ease with which speech can be compressed, and the amount of speech used in communication and instruction, one might assume that time compression is a common practice. In contrast, Arons (1992) states, "While the utility of time compressing recordings is generally recognized, surprisingly, its use has not become pervasive" (p. 169). Most audio used in education is available at one speed—normal.

One factor that may increase the use of time-compressed audio is the ability to select a playback speed for streaming audio on the web. For example, IBM's Web lecture interface has a slider that allows the user to adjust the speed of the narration. Similar approaches are being implemented for streaming media by Microsoft and Real Networks (He & Gupta, 2001). For example the 2xAV plug-in from Real allows the user to play audio (by moving a slider) at from 0.33 to 2.5 the normal speed (Enounce, 2002); the Microsoft encoder allows users to adjust pause removal and other parameters, which reduces the playback time (Microsoft Corporation, 2002).

The ability to skim or scan audio is another application for time-compressed speech. As more and more companies and universities are making audio-enhanced lectures, webcasts, and digital videos available, there needs to be a way to scan the contents and obtain the pertinent information. When skimming audio, 100% comprehension is not essential; therefore, higher compression rates can be used (Arons, 1997; Harrigan, 2000; He & Gupta, 2001).

35.7.7 Efficiency

The original impetus for speech compression was potential efficiency. However, the instructional implications of using compressed speech for efficiency are somewhat contradictory. When the time saved in compression was used to elaborate certain parts of the text, comprehension for that part of the text increased (Fairbanks et al., 1957). However, as Sticht (1971)

pointed out, the time saved in compression was lost in elaboration, and overall comprehension was not improved. Schramm (1972) reported similar results. However, in a recent research study conducted by Omoigui et al. (1999), a task-time savings of 22% was reported when users were allowed to select the most comfortable compression rate; however, comprehension was not measured.

35.7.8 Summary

Research studies have confirmed the hypothesis that listeners can process information at a much higher rate than normal conversational speech. Usually, any short exposure to compressed speech will result in improved comprehension. In general, few differences were detected for ages between about 12 and 50. However, some differences in the ability to comprehend compressed speech may be due to aptitude or verbal ability. Compressed speech may be preferred to normal speech because of the time efficiency. However, the early hopes that time-compressed speech would be fully utilized appear to be unjustified. As interfaces with increased user control are implemented, it is anticipated that time-compression will become more prevalent. For additional information on time-compressed speech (prior to 1972), see the three-volume series, *Time-Compressed Speech: An Anthology and Bibliography,* by Duker (1974).

35.8 RECOMMENDATIONS

35.8.1 Introduction

Sound and speech have existed for thousands of years. However, the technologies that can record, store, and distribute audio have only been available in the last century. Research related to auditory instruction has varied over the years. When audio technologies were first introduced into schools, a series of evaluation studies was conducted to determine whether or not students could learn from a particular technology (Kerr, 1999). Media comparison studies were also quite common—comparing the effectiveness of audio vs. visual presentations in various subject areas and age levels. Another thread of research has focused on the theories that serve as foundations for auditory memory and multichannel communications. More recently, a number of studies have been conducted to determine optimal techniques and strategies for incorporating an audio component in multimedia instruction. This chapter has presented many studies that were conducted in a variety of settings, using different metrics and research designs.

Throughout the literature, several researchers have remarked on the lack of substantiated research related to audio instruction (Barron & Atkins, 1994; Beccue, Vila, & Whitley, 2001; Bishop & Cates, 2001; Thompson et al., 1996). Aarntzen (1993) notes that although multimedia designers and developers are "inclined to use audio (and speech in particular)... hardly anything is known about the use of audio in instruction with respect to the processing of visual and auditive information, learner characteristics, events of instruction, and audio characteristics" (p. 354).

Now that audio components are a feasible, and often expected, component of instruction, researchers in educational technology should continue to provide guidelines for designers that are based on empirical research and cognitive theory.

35.8.2 Recommendations for Future Research

Throughout this chapter, information has been provided about research findings and implications. This section serves as a finale to the chapter by presenting a synopsis of a few "calls" for future research.

35.8.2.1 Auditory Processing and Memory. There are many unanswered questions about how auditory information is perceived, processed, stored, and retrieved (Baddeley, 1998). More definitive answers to issues such as modality effects may lead to better understanding of appropriate applications and designs for audio in instruction. "Future research is needed, concentrating on the exact cognitive mechanisms underlying modality effects in memory performance and in which the findings are extended to more natural stimuli, such as prose passages" (Haan, Appels, & Aleman, 2000, p. 582). Other aspects of modality effects that bear investigation include the differential effects of sequential and simultaneous processing of audio and visual information (Duis et al., 1994) and effects on memory for items generated by the subject instead of the researcher (Penney, 1989b).

McAdams and Bigand (1993) point out that

one of the areas that has not received much attention, with the exception of some studies in young children, is the understanding of the role of auditory cognitive processes and their integration with those of other sensory and more general cognitive systems in everyday activity.... Research programmes addressing some of these issues are sure to demonstrate a more important role for audition in everyday activity than has been granted to this perceptual system to date". (p. 5)

According to Grace-Martin (2001), "Designing instructional materials with multimedia is a bit like walking a tight rope: the designer tries to provide a rich, informational learning experience for the learner while at the same time not exceeding his or her ability to process and assimilate the information" (p. 407). Additional research into factors that impact cognitive load and appropriate multimodal strategies would be very beneficial (Mayer, 2001; Sweller, 1988; Sweller, Merrienboer, & Paas, 1998).

35.8.2.2 Media Selection. With the popularity of blended solutions in e-learning, emphasis is being placed on determining the optimal combinations of media, technologies, and instructional approaches. Audio, in the form of audio conferencing, multimedia, and streaming audio, is an important component of e-learning. As noted by Koumi (1994), the most common current practice is to design instruction without using a media selection model, "in which case, it is no wonder that allocation of media has been controlled more by practical, economic, and human/political factors than by pedagogic considerations" (p. 56).

Mann (1995) agrees and points out, "Forty-five years of intuitive combinations of audio-visual information have produced only mixed results" (p. 16). Structural and functional attributes such as those in Mann's structured sound function (SSF) model may be one approach to producing more consistent, effective implementations of audio. Distinctive attributes and symbols related to audio (as mentioned by Salomon, 1994) need to be defined further so that instructional designers and developers can develop and refine the criteria for the deployment of media to best effect (Koumi, 1994).

The literature does not offer much assistance in media selection. Results related to multichannel communication are complex and contradictory. Based on a review of literature related to learning abstract concepts through audiovisual redundancy, Lai (2000) concluded, "It is clear that the results are inconsistent and there are only few instructional design guidelines available for the optimal relationship between audiovisual redundancy and ability level" (p. 278). Lang (1995) had a similar conclusion about redundancy research when she stated, "Forty years of research has yielded a hodgepodge of contradictory conclusions" (p. 86). Still unanswered are questions such as when, where, and how audio should be integrated with other media.

There are obviously numerous variables that must be considered when deciding whether or not to use audio, with or without additional media (Sutcliffe, 1999). In some cases, the selection of audio as an instructional medium is self-evident. For example, audio is essential to learn a foreign language, study music, or discriminate sound effects such as heartbeats or sonar signals. Audio may also be the optimal (and, in most cases, the only) solution for interacting with distant students, especially in geographically remote or economically disadvantaged areas. In addition, children who have not learned to read and adults who are unable to read at a functioning level can benefit from audio instruction (Beccue, Vila, & Whitley, 2001).

The issue of where and how to use audio in multimedia programs is considerably more complicated. In literature and textbooks that focus on the design and development of multimedia, there is a great deal more attention given to visuals than to audio (Jaspers, 1991). In fact, it is almost impossible to find more than a cursory reference (if any) to design guidelines for incorporating audio into interactive programs in many current books (see, for example, Lee & Owens, 2000; Horton, 2000; Kruse & Keil, 2000; Allen, 2003).

The situation is exacerbated when the few guidelines that exist are often contradictory. For example, Gibbons and Fairweather (1998) advised designers to "avoid echoing text with audio" (p. 375); Clark and Mayer (2003) agree, recommending that designers "avoid e-learning courses that contain redundant on-screen text presented at the same time as on-screen graphics" (p. 100). However, Aarntzen (1991) stated that "when speech is used as the mainstream provider of information it should be accompanied by that same text on the computer's screen" (p. 363). Alessi and Trollip (2001) acknowledge that although including both speech and text helps to meet the needs of students with visual or auditory impairment, the best approach may be to "provide controls that encourage learners to use *either* the text or audio presentation, not both at the same time" (p. 75).

Although the addition of audio in computer-based training has not consistently shown a significant increase in achievement, there are other advantages to audio-enhanced courseware, such as realism and motivation. Some results, such as Mayer's (2001) research on the effectiveness of using audio with animations, offer a good beginning to the types of research-based guidelines that are needed by instructional designers. Mayer, cautions, however, that design principles based on research "must be qualified with respect to different kinds of learners. Additional research is needed to pinpoint the role of individual differences in multimedia learning" (p. 189).

Shih and Alessi (1996) seem to agree with Mayer about the need for qualifications in media research. They stated, "Media is a tool or a learning environment; we educators or researchers must have a better understanding of it before we can wisely use and design it. Therefore, further and multiple dimensions of research on using audio (sound or voice) in education and multimedia are suggested" (p. 217).

35.8.3 Conclusion

A wide range of research is relevant for auditory instruction. As new technologies mature, such as voice recognition, interactive agents, wearable computers, virtual reality, and PDAs, even more tools that can deliver auditory instruction will be available. In his article "Multimedia Learning: Are We Asking the Right Questions?" Mayer (1997) noted, "At this time, the technology for multimedia education is developing at a faster pace than a corresponding science of how people learn in multimedia environments" (p. 4). From the experimental psychologists who are investigating the way in which auditory information is processed and stored to the instructional designers who are seeking to structure optimal environments and strategies for learners, pertinent research areas abound.

Audio technologies offer powerful tools for educators; tools that can entice, motivate, persuade, inform, reinforce, and reward. Sound is a natural part of our lives and environment; it should also be a natural part of our education.

References

Aarntzen, D. (1993). Audio in courseware: Design knowledge issues. *Educational and Training Technology International, 30*(4), 354–356.

Access Science (2003). *McGraw-Hill encyclopedia of science and technology*. Retrieved April 29, 2003, from http://www.accessscience.com

Adelson, L. (1975). Comprehension by college students of time compressed lectures. *Journal of Experimental Education, 44*, 53–59.

Allen, M. (2003). *Guide to e-learning: Building interactive, fun, and effective learning programs for any company*. Hoboken, NJ: John Wiley & Sons, Inc.

Alten, S. R. (2002). *Audio in media*. 6th edition. Belmont, CA: Wadsworth/Thomson Learning.

American Heritage Dictionary. (1982). Boston: Houghton Mifflin Company.

Anderson-Inman, L. (1990). Enhancing the reading-writing connection: Classroom applications. *Writing Notebook, 7*(3), 12–15.

Andres, H. P., & Petersen, C. (2001/2002). Presentation media, information complexity, and learning outcomes. *Journal of Educational Technology Systems, 30*(3), 225–246.

Arons, B. (1992). *Techniques, perception, and applications of time-compressed speech*. Proceedings of 1992 Conference, American Voice I/O Society, Sept., (pp. 169–277). Available from http://xenia.media.mit.edu/~barons/avios92.html

Arons, B. (1994). *Efficient listening with two ears: Dichotic time compression and spatialization*. Proceedings of the Second International Conference on Auditory Display, Santa Fe, NM, (pp. 171–177). Available from http://lucy.media.mit.edu/~barons/icad94.html

Arons, B. (1997). SpeechSkimmer: A system for interactively skimming recorded speech. *ACM Transactions on Computer-Human Interaction, 4*(1), 3–38.

Atkinson, R. C., & Shiffrin, R. M. (1968). Human memory: A proposed system and its control processes. In K. W. Spence (Ed.), *The psychology of learning and motivation: Advances in research and theory* Vol. 2 (pp. 89–195). New York: Academic Press.

Baddeley, A. D. (1992). Working memory. *Science, 255*, 556–559.

Baddeley, A. D. (1998). *Human memory: Theory and practice*. Boston: Allyn and Bacon.

Baddeley, A. D. (1999). *Essentials of human memory*. East Sussex, UK: Psychology Press Ltd.

Barron, A., & Varnadoe, S. (1992). Digital audio: A sound design element. *Instruction Delivery Systems, 6*(1), 6–9.

Barron, A. E., & Atkins, D. (1994). Audio instruction in multimedia education: Is textual redundancy important? *Journal of Educational Multimedia and Hypermedia, 3*(3–4), 295–306.

Barron, A. E., & Kysilka, M. L. (1993). The effectiveness of digital audio in computer-based training. *Journal of Research on Computing in Education, 25*, 277–289.

Barron, A. E., Orwig, G. W., Ivers, K. S., & Lilavois, N. (2002). *Technologies for education: A practical guide*. Englewood, CO: Libraries Unlimited.

Basil, M. D. (1992). *Attention to and memory for audio and video information in television scenes*. Paper presented at the Annual Meeting of the International Communication Association, Miami, FL, (pp. 1–52). (ERIC Document ED 347 592)

Bates, A. W. (1983). Adult teaming from educational television: The open university experience. In M. J. A. Howe (Ed.), *Learning from television: psychological and educational research* (213–27). Washington, DC: American Psychological Association.

Beasley, D. S., & Maki, J. E. (1976). Time- and frequency-altered speech. In N. J. Lass Ed.), *Contemporary issues in experimental phonetics* (Ch. 12, pp. 419–458). New York: Academic Press.

Beccue, B., Vila, J., & Whitley, L. K. (2001). The effects of adding audio instructions to a multimedia computer based training environment. *Journal of Educational Multimedia and Hypermedia, 10*(1), 47–67.

Bell, R. (1969). *An analysis of certain elements of an audio-tape approach to instruction*. Unpublished doctoral dissertation, University of Washington.

Benz, C. R. (1971). *Effects of time compressed speech upon the comprehension of a visual oriented television lecture.* Unpublished doctoral dissertation, Wayne State University.

Bishop, M. J., & Cates, W. M. (2001). Theoretical foundations for sound's use in multimedia instruction to enhance learning. *Educational Technology Research and Development, 49*(3), 5-22.

Boring, E. G. (1950). *A history of experimental psychology* (2nd ed.). New York: Appleton-Century-Crofts.

Boyle, V. A. (1969). Visual stimulation and comprehension of compressed speech. *Dissertation Abstracts International, 30,* 5221B.

Braden, R. A. (1996). Visual literacy. In D. Jonassen (Ed.), *The handbook of research for educational communications and technology.* Washington, DC: AECT.

Breed, P. A. (1977). *The relative effect of the controlled reader and the speech compressor on reading rate and comprehension.* Unpublished doctoral dissertation, Northern Illinois University.

Broadbent, D. (1958). *Perception and communication.* New York: Pergamon Press.

Button, G. E. (1991). Audio-tutorial biology, andragogy, and self-esteem: Relationships among independent and dependent variables. *Dissertation Abstracts International, 53*/02, 457. (University Microfilms No. AAC).

Campeau, P. L. (1966). Selective review of the results of research on the use of audio visual media to teach adults. In L. J. Briggs, P. L. Campeau, R. M. Gagne, & M. A. May (Eds.), *Instructional media: A procedure for the design of multi media instruction and suggestions for future research,* Monograph 2 (pp. 99-176). Pittsburgh, PA: American Institutes for Research.

Carver, R. P. (1973). Understanding, information processing, and teaming from prose materials. *Journal of Educational Psychology, 64,* 76-84.

Cherry, C. (1953). Some experiments on the recognition of speech with one and two ears. *Journal of the Acoustical Society of America, 23,* 915-919.

Chu, G. D., & Schramm, W. (1968). *Learning from television: What the research says.* Palo Alto, CA: Institute for Communication Research, Stanford University.

Clark, J. M., & Paivio, A. (1991). Dual coding theory and education. *Educational Psychology Review, 3*(3), 149-210.

Clark, R. C., & Mayer, R. E. (2003). *E-Learning and the science of instruction: Proven guidelines for consumers and designers of multimedia learning.* San Francisco, CA: Jossey-Bass Publishers.

Clark, R. E. (1983). Reconsidering research on learning from media. *Review of Educational Research, 53*(4), 445-459.

Clark, R. E. (1994). Media will never influence learning. *Educational Training Research and Development, 42*(2), 21-29.

Clark, R. E., & Salomon, G. (1986). Media in teaching. In M. Wittrock (Ed.), *Handbook of research on teaching* (3rd ed.). New York: Macmillan.

Constantine, M. (1964). Radio in the elementary school. *Science Education, 48,* 121-32.

Cook, H. R. (1964). *The effects of learning of structural drills in Spanish broadcast via high frequency AM radio* (NDEA Title VII Project No. 1018). Bloomington, IN. Indiana University.

Covell, M., Withgott, M., & Slaney, M. (1998, May). *Mach1: Nonuniform time-scale modification of speech.* Proceedings of the IEEE International Conference on Acoustics, Speech, and Signal Processing, Seattle WA. Available from http://www.slaney.org/covell/interval/1997-061/writeup.html

Cowan, N. (1984). On short and long auditory stores. *Psychological Bulletin, 96,* 341-370.

Crowder, R. G. (1993). Short-term memory: Where do we stand? *Memory and Cognition, 21,* 142-145.

Cuban, L. (1986). *Teachers and machines: The classroom use of technology since 1920.* New York: Teachers College Press.

Cuban, L. (2001). *Oversold and underused: Computers in the classroom.* Cambridge, MA: Harvard University Press.

Cutler, R. L., McKeachie, W. J. & McNeil, E. B. (1958). Teaching psychology by telephone. *The American Psychologist, 13*(9), 551-52.

Dahlem, W. E. (1985). The effects of supplemental auditory information on the reading comprehension performance of learning disabled, high school students. *Dissertation Abstracts International, 46,* 2396A.

Daniels, L. (1995). *Audio-vision: Audio-visual interaction in desktop multimedia.* Annual Conference of the International Visual Literacy Association. Tempe, AZ, October 12-16.

Diehl, C. F., White, R. D., & Burke, K. (1959). Rate and comprehension. *Speech Monographs, 26,* 229-232.

Duis, S. S., Dean, R. S., & Derks, P. (1994). The modality effect: A result of methodology? *International Journal of Neuroscience, 78,* 1-7.

Duker, S. (1974). *Time compressed speech.* Metuchen, NJ: Scarecrow.

Eckhardt, W. X. (1970). *Learning in multi-media programmed instruction as a function of aptitude and instruction rate controlled by compressed speech.* Unpublished doctoral dissertation, University of Southern California.

Efron, R. (1970). The relationship between the duration of a stimulus and the duration of a perception. *Neuropsychologia, 8,* 37-55.

Elliott, L. L. (1970). Pitch memory for short tones. *Perception and Psychophysics, 8,* 379-384.

Engle, R. (1996). Working memory and retrieval: An inhibition-resource approach. In J. Richards (Ed.), *Working memory and human cognition* (pp. 89-119). New York: Oxford University Press.

Engle, R. W., & Mobley, L. A. (1976). The modality effect: What happens in long-term memory. *Journal of Verbal Learning and Verbal Behavior, 15,* 519-528.

Enounce Inc. (2002). *2xAV Plug-in for RealPlayer.* Available from http://www.enounce.com/products/real/2xav/index.shtml

Erickson, C. I., & King, I. (1917). A comparison of visual and oral presentations of lessons in the case of pupils from third to ninth grade. *School and Society, 6*(136), 146-48.

Erickson, C. W., & Johnson, H. J. (1964). Storage and decay characteristics of nonattended auditory stimuli. *Journal of Experimental Psychology, 8,* 28-36.

Eshgh, R., Hoxeng, J., Provenzano, J. & Casals, B., eds. (1988). *Radio-assisted community basic education (RADECO).* Pittsburgh, PA: Duquesne University Press.

Estes, W. K. (1989). Learning theory. In A. Lesgold & R. Glaser (Eds.), *Foundations for a Psychology of Education.* Hillsdale, NJ: Lawrence A. Erlbaum Associates.

Fairbanks, G., Everitt, W. L., & Jaeger, R. P. (1954). Method for time or frequency compression-expansion of speech. *Transactions of the Institute of Radio Engineers, Professional Groups on Audio, AU 2,* 7-12.

Fairbanks, G., Guttman, N., & Miron, M. S. (1957). Auditory comprehension of repeated high speech messages. *Journal of Speech and Hearing Disorders, 22,* 23-32,

Fang, I., & Ross, K. (1996). *Media history project: Timeline by chronology.* Minneapolis, MN: School of Journalism and Mass Communication. Retrieved April 29, 2003, from http://www.mediahistory.umn.edu/index2.html.

Fergen, G. K. (1954). *Listening comprehension at controlled rates for children in grades iv, v, and vi.* Unpublished doctoral dissertation, University of Missouri.

Fletcher, J. D. (1990). *The effectiveness of interactive videodisc instruction in defense training and education* (IDA paper P-2372).

Arlington, VA: Institute for Defense Analyses, Science and Technology Division.

Foulke, E. (1965). *A survey of the acceptability of rapid speech* (Tech. Rep. Project No. 2430). Cooperative Research Branch, Dept. of HEW, Office of Education. Louisville, KY: Performance Research Laboratory, U. Louisville.

Foulke, E. (1968). Listening comprehension as a function of word rate. *Journal of Communication, 18,* 198–206.

Foulke, E. (1969). *Comprehension of rapid speech by the blind: Part III. Final progress report on cooperative research project no. 2430 covering the period from March 1, 1964 to June 30, 1968.* Louisville, KY: U. Louisville.

Foulke, E., Amster, C. H., Bixler, R. H., & Nolan, C. X. (1962). The comprehension of rapid speech by the blind. *Exceptional Children, 11,* 134–141.

Foulke, E. A. (1962, Mar.). *A comparison of two methods of compressing speech.* Symposium at the Southeastern Psychological Association, Louisville, KY.

Foulke, E. A., & Sticht, T. G. (1967). *The intelligibility and comprehension of accelerated speech.* Proceedings of the Louisville Conference on Time Compressed Speech, Louisville, KY, (pp. 21–28).

Foulke, E. A., & Sticht, T. G. (1969). In *Proceedings of the second Louisville conference on rate and/or frequency controlled speech.* Louisville, KY. University of Louisville. (ERIC Document Reproduction Service No. Ed 61682)

Foulke, E. A. & Sticht, T. G. (1969). Review of research on the intelligibility and comprehension of accelerated speech. *Psychological Bulletin, 72,* 50–62.

Freeman, M. W., Grimes, L. W., & Holliday, J. R. (2000). Increasing access to learning with hybrid audio-data collaboration. *Educational Technology & Society, 3*(3), 112–121.

Friedman, H. L., Orr, D. B., Freedle, R. O., & Norris, C. M. (1966). *Further research on speeded speech as an educational medium* (Report No. AIR-E-50-7-66-TR-3). Silver Spring, MD: American Institute for Research in the Behavioral Sciences. (ED 044 903)

Friedman, H. L., Orr, D., & Norris, C. (1966). *Further research on speeded speech as an educational medium-the use of listening aids* (Report No. 3.). Silver Spring, MD: American Institute for Research in Behavioral Sciences. (ED 044 903)

Furnham, A., & Gunter, B. (1989). The primacy of print: Immediate cued recall of news as a function of the channel of communication. *Journal of General Psychology, 116*(3), 305–310.

Furnham, A., Gunter, B., & Green, A. (1990). Remembering science: The recall of factual information as a function of the presentation mode. *Applied Cognitive Psychology, 4*(3), 203–212.

Furnham, A., Proctor, E., & Gunter, B. (1988). Memory for material presented in the media: The superiority of written communication. *Psychological Reports, 63*(3), 935–938.

Garner, R., Brown, R., Sanders, S., & Menke, D. (1992). "Seductive details" and learning from text. In K. A. Renninger, S. Hidi, & A. Krapp (Eds.), *The role of interest in learning and development* (pp. 239–254). Hillsdale, NJ: Lawrence A. Erlbaum Associates.

Garner, R., Gillingham, M., & White, C. (1989). Effects of "seductive details" on macroprocessing and microprocessing in adults and children. *Cognition and Instruction, 6,* 41–57.

Garvey, W. D. (1953). The intelligibility of speeded speech. *Journal of Experimental Psychology, 45,* 102–108.

Gaver, W. W. (1997). Auditory interfaces. In M. G., Landauer, T. K., and Prabhu, P. V. (Eds.), *Handbook of Human-Computer Interaction.* Helander, NY: Elsevier.

Gelder, B., & Vroomen, J. (1997). Modality effects in immediate recall of verbal and non-verbal information. *Psychology Press, 9*(1), 97–110.

Gibson, R. (1958). Tape recordings are used to teach seventh grade students in Westside Junior-Senior High School, Omaha, NE. *Bulletin of the National Association of Secondary Principals, 42,* 81–93.

Gibson, R. (1959). The tape recordings experiment is expanded in Westside Junior-Senior High School, Omaha, NE. *Bulletin of the National Association of Secondary Principals, 43,* 49–72.

Gibson, R. (1960). Final report on the Westside High School teaching by-tape project. *Bulletin of the National Association of Secondary Principals, 44,* 56–62.

Glenberg, A. M., Eberhardt, K. A., & Belden, T. M. (1987). The role of visual interference in producing the long-term modality effect. *Memory and Cognition, 15*(6), 504–510.

Goetz, E. T., & Sadoski, M. (1995a). The perils of seduction revisited: A reply to Wade, Alexander, Schraw, and Kulikowich. *Reading Research Quarterly, 30*(3), 518–519.

Goetz, E. T., & Sadoski, M. (1995b). Commentary: The perils of seduction: Distracting details or incomprehensible abstractions? *Reading Research Quarterly, 30*(3), 500–511.

Goldstein, H. (1940). Reading and listening comprehension at various controlled rates. *Teacher College Contributions to Education,* No. 821.

Goolkasian, P. (2000). Pictures, words, and sounds: From which format are we best able to reason? *Journal of General Psychology, 127*(4), 439–459.

Gordon, G. N. (1969). *The languages of communication.* New York: Hastings House.

Gordon-Salant, S., & Fitzgibbons, P. J. (2001, August). Sources of age-related recognition difficulty for time-compressed speech. *Journal of Speech, Language, and Hearing Research, 44*(4), 709–719.

Grace-Martin, M. (2001). How to design educational multimedia: A "loaded" question. *Journal of Educational Multimedia and Hypermedia, 4,*(10) 397–409.

Gunter, B., Furnham, A., & Leese, J. (1986). Memory for information from a party political broadcast as a function of channel of communication. *Social Behaviour, 1,* 135–142.

Gunter, G., & Furnham, A. (1986). Sex and personality differences in recall of violent and non-violent news from three presentational modalities. *Personality and Individual Differences, 7,* 829–837.

Guttman, N., & Julesz, B. (1963). Lower limits of auditory periodicity analysis. *Journal of the Acoustical Society of America, 35,* 610.

Haan, E. H. F., Appels, G., & Aleman, A. (2000). Inter- and intramodal encoding of auditory and visual presentation of material: Effects on memory performance. *The Psychological Record, 50*(3), 577–586.

Hannafin, M. & Hooper, S. (1993). Learning principles. In Fleming M., & Levie, H. (Eds.). *Instructional message design: Principles from the behavioral and cognitive sciences.* Englewood Cliffs, NJ: Educational Technology Publications.

Harp, S. F., & Mayer, R. E. (1997). The role of interest in learning from scientific text and illustrations: On the distinction between emotional interest and cognitive interest. *Journal of Educational Psychology, 89,* 92–102.

Harp, S. F., & Mayer, R. E. (1998). How seductive details do their damage: A theory of cognitive interest in science learning. *Journal of Educational Psychology, 90,* 414–434.

Harrigan, K. (1995, Spring). THE SPECIAL System: Self-paced education with compressed interactive audio listening. *Journal of Research on Computing in Education, 27*(3), 361–370.

Harrigan, K. (2000). The SPECIAL system: Searching time-compressed digital video lectures. *Journal of Research on computing in Education, 33*(1), 77–86.

Hartman, F. R. (1961a, January/February). Recognition learning under multiple channel presentation and testing conditions. *AV Communication Review, 9*(1), 24–43.

Hartman, F. R. (1961b, November/December). Single and multiple channel communications: A review of research and a proposed model. *AV Communication Review, 9*(6), 235–262.

Hawkins, H. and Presson, J. (1986). Auditory information processing. In K. R. Boff, L. Kaufman, & J.P. Thomas (Eds.), *Handbook of perception and human performance.* New York: Wiley.

He, L., & Gupta, A. (2001). *Exploring benefits of non-linear time compression.* Proceedings of ACM International Conference on Multimedia, Ottawa, Canada, (pp. 382–391).

Heiman, G. W., Leo, R. J., Leighbody, G., & Bowler, K. (1986). Word intelligibility decrements and the comprehension of time-compressed speech. *Perception and Psychophysics, 40*(6). 407–411.

Helander, M. G., Landauer, T. K., & Prabhu, P. F. (1997). *Handbook of human-computer interaction.* Amsterdam: Elsevier.

Hidi, S. (1990). Interest and its contribution as a mental resource for Learning. *Review of Educational Research, 60*(4), 549–571.

Hoban, C. F., & Van Ormer, E. B. (1970). *Instructional film research 1918–1950.* New York: Arno Press.

Horton, W. (2000). *Designing web-based training: How to teach anyone anything anywhere anytime.* New York: John Wiley & Sons, Inc.

Hsia, H. J. (1968a). On channel effectiveness. *AV Communication Review, 16,* 245–267.

Hsia, H. J. (1968b, December). Output, error, equivocation and recalled information in auditory, visual and audiovisual information processing. *Journal of Communication, 18,* 325–353.

Hsia. H. J. (1971, Spring). The information processing capacity of modality and channel performance. *AV Communication Review, 19*(1), 51–75.

Huang, J. C. (1995). *Digitized speech as feedback on cognitive aspects of psychomotor performance during computer-based instruction.* Proceedings of the 1995 Annual National Convention of the Association for Educational Communications and Technology. Anaheim, CA.

Hurlburt, R. T. (2001). "Lectlets" deliver content at a distance; Introductory statistics as a case study. *Teaching of Psychology, 28*(1), 15–20.

Ingebritsen, T. S., & Flickinger, K. A. (1998). *Development and assessment of web courses that use streaming audio and video technologies. Distance Learning '98.* Proceedings of the Annual conference on Distance Teaching & Learning, Madison, WI, August 5–7.

Ives, W. (1992). Evaluating new multimedia technologies for self-paced instruction. *Evaluation and Program Planning, 15,* 287–295.

Janse, E., Nooteboom, S., & Quene, H. (2001, August). *Word-level intelligibility of time-compressed speech: Prosodic and segmental factors.* The Netherlands: Utrecht Institute of Linguistics. Available from http://www.let.uu.nl/~Sieb.Nooteboom/personal/timecompressed.pdf

Jasper, F. (1991). The relationship sound-image. *International Journal of Instructional Media, 18*(2), 161–174.

Jaspers, A. (1995). Focus on audio in communication and instruction: An overview. *Educational Media International, 32,* 176–181.

Jeung, H., Chandler, P., & Sweller, J. (1997). The role of visual indicators in dual sensory mode instruction. *Educational Psychology, 17,* 329–348.

Jonassen, D. H., Campbell, J. P., & Davidson, M. E. (1994). Learning with media: Restructuring the debate. *Educational Training Research and Development, 42*(2), 45–48.

Jonassen, D. H., & Grabowski, B. L. (1993). *Handbook of individual differences, learning, and instruction.* Hillsdale, NJ: Lawrence A. Erlbaum Associates.

Jongekrijg, T. & Russell, J. D. (1999). Alternative techniques for providing feedback to students and trainees: A literature review with guidelines. *Educational Technology, 39*(6), 54–58.

Junor, L. (1992). Teaching by tape: Some benefits, problems, and solutions. *Distance Education, 13*(1), 93–107.

Kahneman, D. (1973).*Attention and effort.* Englewood Cliffs, NJ: Prentice-Hall.

Kalyuga, S. (2000). When using sound with a text or picture is not beneficial to learning. *Australian Journal of Educational Technology, 16*(2), 161–172. Available from http://www.ascilite.org/ajet/ajet16/kalyuga.html

Kalyuga, S., Chandler, P., & Sweller, J. (1998). Levels of expertise and instructional design. *Human Factors, 40*(1), 1–17.

Kalyuga, S., Chandler, P., & Sweller, J. (1999). Managing split-attention and redundancy in multimedia instruction. *Applied Cognitive Psychology, 13,* 351–372.

Kalyuga, S., Chandler, P., & Sweller, J. (2000). Incorporating learner experience into the design of multimedia instruction. *Journal of Educational Psychology, 92*(1), 126–136.

Kearsley, G. (2001). *Dual coding theory (A. Paivio). Theory into practice.* Retrieved July 28, 2002, from http://tip.psychology.org/paivio.html

Kerr, B. (1999). *Effective use of audio media in multimedia presentation.* Proceedings of the Mid-South Instructional Technology Conference, Murfreesboro, TN, March 28–30, (pp. 1–10).

Klavon, A. J. (1975). *Time-compressed lecture: an alternative for increased teacher learner interaction.* Unpublished doctoral dissertation, University of Maryland.

Kohlfeld, D. L. (1971). Simple reaction time as a function of stimulus intensity in decibels of light and sound. *Journal of Experimental Psychology, 88,* 251–257.

Koroghlanian, C. M., & Klein, J. D. (2000). *The use of audio and animation in computer-based instruction.* Paper presented at the National Convention of the Association for Educational Communications and Technology. Denver CO, October 25–28.

Koroghlanian, C. M., & Sullivan, H. J. (2000). Audio and text density in computer-based instruction. *Journal of Educational Computing Research, 22*(2), 217–230.

Koumi, J. (1994). Media comparison and deployment: A practitioner's view. *British Journal of Educational Technology, 25*(1), 41–57.

Kozma, R. B. (1991). Learning with media. *Review of Educational Research, 61*(2), 179–211.

Kozma, R. B. (1994). Will media influence learning? Reframing the debate. *Educational Training Research and Development, 42*(2), 7–19.

Kramer, E. J., & Lewis, T. R. (1951). Comparison of visual and non-visual listening. *Journal of Communication, 1*(2), 16–20.

Kruse, K., & Keil, J. (2000). *Technology-based training: The art and science of design, development, and delivery.* San Francisco: Jossey-Bass/Pfeiffer.

Kulik, J. A. (1994). Meta-analytic studies of findings on computer-based instruction. In E. L. Baker & H. F. O'Neil, Jr. (Eds.), *Technology assessment in education and training.* Hillsdale, NJ: Lawrence Erlbaum Associates.

Kulik, J. A., Kulik, C.-L. C., & Cohen, P.A. (1979). Research on audio-tutorial instruction: a meta-analysis of comparative studies. *Review of Educational Research, 11,* 321–341.

Kumata, H. (1961). *History and progress of instructional television research in the United States.* Report presented at the International Seminar on Instructional Television, Oct. 8–18, Purdue University, Lafayette, IN.

Lai, S. (2000). Increasing associative learning of abstract concepts through audiovisual redundancy. *Journal of Educational Computing Research, 23*(3), 275–289.

Lang, A. (1995). Defining audio/video redundancy from a limited-capacity informaitn processing perspective. *Communications Research, 22*(1) 86-115.

Larsen, R. P., & Feder, D. D. (1940). Common and differential factors in reading and hearing comprehension. *Journal of Educational Psychology, 31,* 241-251.

Lee, D. (1994). *Audio-vision: Audio-visual interaction in desktop multimedia.* Selected Readings from the Annual Conference of the International Visual Literacy Association. Tempe AZ, October 12-16, (pp. 1-8).

Lee, W. W., & Owens, D. L. (2000). *Multimedia-based instructional design.* San Francisco: Jossey-Bass/Pfeiffer.

Lehrman, P. D., & Tully, J. (1991, October). Catch a wave: Digital audio. *MacUser,* 94-103.

Letowski, T., & Poch, N. (1996). Comprehension of time-compressed speech: Effects of age and speech complexity. *Journal of American Academy of Audiology, 7,* 447-457.

Li, F., Gupta, A., Sanocki, E., He, L., & Yong, R. (1999, September). *Browsing digital video.* Proceedings of ACM Conference Computer Human Interaction 2000, pp. 169-176. Available from ftp://ftp.research.microsoft.com/pub/tr/tr-99-67.doc

Loder, L. E. (1937). A study of aural learning with and without the speaker present. *Journal of Experimental Education, 6,* 46-60.

Ludrick, L. A. (1974). *A study of the effects of controlled delivery instruction upon the achievement of college students using compressed speech audio and television pictorials.* Unpublished doctoral dissertation, the University of Oklahoma.

Maclachlan, J. (1982). Listener perception of time-compressed spokespersons for radio commercials. *Journal of Advertising, 22,* 47-51.

Main, R. E., & Griffiths, B. (1977). Evaluation of audio and pictorial instructional supplements. *Educational Communication & Technology, 25*(2), 167-179.

Mann, B. L. (1995, Summer). Focusing attention with temporal sound. *Journal of Research on Computing in Education, 27*(4), 402-424.

Mann, D., Shakeshaft, C., Becker, J., & Kottkamp, R. (1999). *West Virginia's basic skills/computer education program: An analysis of student achievement.* Santa Monica, CA: Milken Family Foundation.

Massaro, D. (1975). Backward recognition masking. *Journal of the Acoustical Society of America, 58,* 1059-1064.

Massaro, D. W., & Loftus, G. R. (1996).*Sensory and perceptual storage.* In E. L. Bjork & R. A. Bjork (Eds.), *Memory,* San Diego, CA: Academic Press.

Mayer, R. E. (1997). Multimedia learning: Are we asking the right questions? *Educational Psychologist, 32*(1), 1-19.

Mayer, R. E. (2001). *Multimedia learning.* New York: Cambridge University Press.

Mayer, R. E., & Anderson, R. B. (1991). Animations need narrations: An experimental test of a dual-coding hypothesis. *Journal of Educational Psychology, 83,* 484-490.

Mayer, R. E., & Anderson, R. B. (1992). The instructive animation: Helping students build connections between words and pictures in multimedia learning. *Journal of Educational Psychology, 84,* 444-452.

Mayer, R. E., Bove, W., Bryman, A., Mars, R., & Tapangco, L. (1996). When less is more: Meaningful learning from visual and verbal summaries of science textbook lessons. *Journal of Educational Psychology, 88,* 64-73.

Mayer, R. E., Heiser, J., & Lonn, S. (2001). Cognitive constraints on multimedia learning: When presenting more material results in less understanding. *Journal of Educational Psychology, 93*(1), 187-198.

Mayer, R. E., & Moreno, R. (1998). A split-attention effect in multimedia learning: Evidence for dual processing systems in working memory. *Journal of Educational Psychology, 90,* 312-320.

Mayer, R. E., Moreno, R., Boire, M., & Vagge, S. (1999). Maximizing constructivist learning from multimedia communications by minimizing cognitive load. *Journal of Educational Psychology, 91,* 638-643.

Mayer, R. E., & Sims, V. K. (1994). For whom is a picture worth a thousand words? Extensions of a dual-coding theory of multimedia learning. *Journal of Educational Psychology, 84,* 389-401.

McAdams, S., & Bigand, E. (Eds.) (1993). *Thinking in sound: The cognitive psychology of human audition.* Oxford: Clarendon Press.

Menne, J. W., Klingenschmidt, L. E., & Nord, D. L. (1969, Mar.). *The feasibility of using taped lectures to replace class attendance.* Paper presented at the annual meeting of American Educational Research Association, Los Angeles.

Microsoft Corporation. (2002). *Windows media technologies: Encoder 7.0.* Available from http://www.microsoft.com/windows/windowsmedia/wm7/encoder.asp

Miller, G. A. (1956). The magical number seven, plus or minus two: Some limits on our capacity for processing information. *Psychological Review, 63,* 81-97.

Miller, G. A., & Lichlinder, J. C. (1950). The intelligibility of interrupted speech. *Journal of the Acoustical Society of America, 22,* 167-173.

Moore, D. M., Myers, R. J., & Burton, J. K. (1996). Multiple-channel communication: The theoretical and research foundations of multimedia. In Jonassen, D. (Ed.), *Handbook of research on communication and educational technology.* Washington, DC: Association for Educational Communications and Technology.

Moreno, R., & Mayer, R. E. (1999). Cognitive principles of multimedia learning: The role of modality and contiguity. *Journal of Educational Psychology, 91,* 358-368.

Moreno, R., & Mayer, R. E. (2000). A coherence effect in multimedia learning: The case for minimizing irrelevant sounds in the design of multimedia messages. *Journal of Educational Psychology, 92,* 117-125.

Morra, S. (2000). A new model of verbal short-term memory. *Journal of Experimental Child Psychology, 75,* 191-227.

Morrison, G. R. (1994). The media effects questions: "Unresolvable" or asking the right question. *Educational Training Research and Development, 42*(2), 41-44.

Mosenthal, P. (1976-77). Psycholinguistic properties of aural and visual comprehension as determined by children's abilities to comprehend syllogisms. *Reading Research Quarterly, 12,* 55-92.

Motion-Picture Technology. (2003). *Encyclopedia Britannica.* Retrieved April 29, 2003, from http://search.eb.com/eb/article?eu=119928

Mousivi, S., Low, R., & Sweller, J. (1995). Reducing cognitive load by mixing auditory and visual presentation modes. *Journal of Educational Psychology, 87,* 319-334.

Murdock, B. B., Jr., & Walker, K. (1969). Modality effects in free recall. *Journal of Verbal Learning and Verbal Behavior, 8,* 665-676.

Nasser, D. L., & McEwen, W. J. (1976). The impact of alternate media channels: recall and involvement with messages. *AV Communication Review, 24,* 263-272.

Neisser, U. (1967). *Cognitive psychology.* New York: Appleton-Century-Crofts.

Nelson, H. E. and Moll, K. R. (1950) Comparison of audio and video elements of instructional films. Technical Report No. SDC 269-17-18. Instructional Film Program. Naval Training Devices Centre-Office of Naval Research: Port Washington.

NHK Radio-Television Cultural Research Institute. (1956). *The listening effect of radio English classroom.* Tokyo: NHK.

Nichols, R. G., & Stevens, L. A. (1957). *Are you listening?* New York: McGraw-Hill.

Ninno, A. (1999). Radios in the classroom: Curriculum integration and communication skills. *ERIC Digest.* Syracuse, NY: ERIC Clearinghouse on Information and Technology.

Norman, D. A. (1993). *Things that make us smart.* Reading, MA: Addison-Wmesley.

Novak, J. D. & Musunda, D. (1991). A twelve-year longitudinal study of science concept learning. *American Educational Research Journal 28,* 117-53.

Nugent, G. C. (1982). Pictures, audio, and print: symbolic representation and effect on learning. *Educational Communication and Technology Journal, 30,* 163-174.

Olgren, C. H. (1997). Teaching by telephone. *New Directions for Teaching and Learning, 71,* 59-66.

Olgren, C. H., & Parker, L. A. (1983). *Teleconferencing technology and applications.* Dedham, MA: Artech House.

Olson, G. M. (1989). Intellectual development. In A. Lesgold & R. Glaser (Eds.), *Foundations for a Psychology of Education.* Hillsdale, NJ: Lawrence Erlbaum Associates.

Omiogui, N., He, L., Gupta, A., Grudin, J., & Sanocki, E. (1999). *Time-compression: Systems concerns, usage, and benefits.* Available from http://www.research.microsoft.com/research/coet/Compression/MM2001/paper.doc

Oppenheimer, T. (July 1997). The computer delusion. *The Atlantic Monthly.* Available from http://www.theatlantic.com/atlantic/issues/97jul/computer.htm

Orr, D. B., & Friedman, H. L. (1964). *Research on speeded speech as an educational medium.* (Progress Report, Grant No. 7-48-7670-203.) Washington, DC: U.S. Department of Health, Education, and Welfare, Office of Education.

Orr, D. B., Friedman, H. L., & Williams, J. D. (1965). Trainability of listening comprehension of speeded discourse. *Journal of Educational Psychology, 56,* 148-156.

Paivio, A. (1986). *Mental representations: A dual coding approach.* Oxford, England: Oxford University Press.

Paivio, A. (1991). Dual coding theory: Retrospect and current status. *Canadian Journal of Psychology, 45*(3), 255-287.

Palmer, S. (2000). Working memory: A developmental study of phonological recoding. *Memory, 8*(3), 179-193.

Parshall, C. G. (1999). *Audio CBTs: Measuring more through the use of speech and non-speech sound.* Paper presented at the Annual Meeting of the American Educational Research Association, Montreal, Canada, April 19-23.

Pearce, C. G., & Ackley, R. J. (1995). Audiotaped feedback in business writing: An exploratory study. *Business Communication Quarterly, 58*(3), 31-34.

Penney, C. G. (1975). Modality effects in short-term verbal memory. *Psychological Bulletin, 82,* 68-84.

Penney, C. G. (1989a). Modality effects and the structure of short-term verbal memory. *Memory and Cognition, 17*(4), 398-422.

Penney, C. G. (1989b). Modality effects in delayed free recall and recognition: Visual is better than auditory. *The Quarterly Journal of Experimental Psychology, 17*(4), 398-422.

Popham, W. J. (1962). Tape recorded lectures in the college classroom 11. *AV Communication Review, 10,* 94-101.

Posner, M. I., Nissen, M. J., & Klein, R. M. (1976). Visual dominance: An information-processing account of its origins and significance. *Psychological Review, 83,* 157-171.

Postlethwaite, S. N. (1970). The audio-tutorial system. *American Biology Teacher, 32,* 31-33.

Postlethwaite, S. N. (1972). The audio-tutorial system: incorporating mini course and mastery. *Educational Technology, 12*(9), 35-37.

Postlethwaite, S. N., Novak, L & Murray, H. T., Jr. (1972). *The audio-tutorial approach to learning,* 3d ed. Minneapolis, MN: Burgess.

Postlethwaite, S. N. (1975). Students are a lot like people! *American Biology Teacher, 37,* 205.

Postlethwaite, S. N. (1978). Principles behind the audio-tutorial system. *NSPI Journal, 17,* 3-4,18.

Postlethwaite, S. N. (1980). Improvement of science teaching. *Bio-Science, 30,* 601-604.

Purcell, L., & Hemphill, J. (1997). *Interactive audio.* New York: Wiley.

Quealy, J., & Langan-Fox, J. (1998). Attributes of delivery media in computer-assisted instruction. *Ergonomics, 41*(3), 257-279.

Quereshi, S. U. H. (1974). Speech compression by computer. In S. Duker (Ed.), *Time-compressed speech* (pp. 618-623). Metuchen, NJ: Scarecrow.

Rao, P. X. (1977). Telephone and instructional communication. In I. D. S. Pool (Ed.), *The social impact of the telephone* (pp. 473-486). Cambridge, MA: MIT Press.

Rehaag, D., & Szabo, M. (1995). *An experiment on effects of redundant audio in computer based instruction on achievement, attitude, and learning time in 10th grade math.* (ERIC Document ED380123)

Reiser, R. A. (1994). Clark's invitation to the dance: An instructional designer's response. *Educational Training Research and Development, 42*(2), 45-48.

Robertson, E. M. (1977). *The effects of different rates of recorded speech on the listening comprehension of adult remedial readers.* Unpublished doctoral dissertation, University of Georgia.

Robinson, D. H., & Molina, E. (2002). The relative involvement of visual and auditory working memory when studying adjunct displays. *Contemporary Educational Psychology, 27,* 118-131.

Rohwer, W. D., & Harris, W. J. (1975). Media effect on prose learning in two populations of children. *Journal of Educational Psychology, 67,* 651-657.

Ross, R. A. (1964). Look at listeners. *Elementary School Journal, 64*(7), 369-372.

Ross, S. M. (1994). Delivery trucks or groceries? More food for thought on whether media (will, may, can't) influence learning. *Educational Training Research and Development, 42*(2), 5-6.

Rossiter, C. M., Jr. (1970). *The effects of rate of presentation on listening test scores for recall of facts, recall of ideas, and generation of inferences.* Unpublished doctoral dissertation, Ohio University.

Roucos, S., & Wilgus, A. M. (1985). *High quality time-scale modification for speech.* Proceedings of the International Conference on Acoustics, Speech, and Signal Processing, IEEE, (pp. 493-496).

Rulon, P. X. (1943a) A comparison of phonographic recordings with printed material in terms of knowledge. *The Harvard Educational Review, 8,* 63-76.

Rulon, P. X. (1943b). A comparison of phonographic recordings with printed material in terms of knowledge gained through their use in a teaching unit. *The Harvard Educational Review, 8,* 163-175.

Rulon, P. X. (1943c). A comparison of phonographic recordings with printed motivation to further study. *The Harvard Educational Review, 8,* 246-255.

Rummer, R., & Engelkamp, J. (2001). Phonological information contributes to short-term recall of auditorily presented sentences. *Journal of Memory and Language, 45,* 451-467.

Russell, T. L. (1999). *The No Significant Difference Phenomenon: As reported in 355 Research Reports, Summaries and Papers* (5th ed.). Raleigh, NC: North Carolina State University.

Saettler, P. (1968). *A history of instructional technology.* NY: McGraw-Hill, Inc.

Saettler, P. (1990). *The evolution of American educational technology.* Englewood, CO: Libraries Unlimited.

Sales, G. C., & Johnston, M. D. (1993). *Digitized speech as feedback in computer-based instruction*. Proceedings of Selected Research and Development Presentations at the Convention of the Association for Educational Communications and Technology. New Orleans, LA, January 13-17.

Salomon, G. (1994). *Interaction of media, cognition, and learning*. Hillsdale, NJ: Lawrence Erlbaum Associates.

Schacter, J. (1999). *The impact of educational technology on student achievement: What the most current research has to say. Milken Exchange on Educational Technology*. Retrieved July 28, 2002, from http://web.mff.org/publications/publications.taf?page=161

Schramm, W. (1972). What the research says. In W. Schramm (Ed.), *Quality instructional television* (pp. 44-79). Honolulu, HI: University Press of Hawaii.

Schramm, W. (1973). *Big media, little media: A report to the Agency for International Development*. Stanford, CA: Institute for Communication Research, Stanford University.

Schrock, S. A. (1994). The media influence debate: Read the fine print, but don't lose sight of the big picture. *Educational Training Research and Development, 42*(2), 49-53.

Severin, W. (1967, Fall). Another look at cue summation. *AV Communication Review, 15*(3), 233-245.

Severin, W. (1968). *Cue summation in multiple-channel communication. Report from the Media and Concept Learning Project* (Tech. Rep. No. 37). Washington DC: Bureau of Research.

Shannon, C. E., & Weaver, W. (1949). *The mathematical theory of communication*. Urbana, IL: University of Illinois Press.

Shih, Y., & Alessi, S. M. (1996). Effects of text versus voice on learning in multimedia courseware. *Journal of Educational Multimedia and Hypermedia, 5*(2), 203-218.

Short, H. S. (1977). A comparison of variable time-compressed speech and normal rate speech based on time spent and performance in a course taught by self-instructional methods. *British Journal of Educational Technology, 8*, 146-157.

Sivin-Kachala, J. (1998). *Report of the effectiveness of technology in schools, 1990-1997*. Software Publisher's Association.

Sivin-Kachala, J., & Bialo, E. R. (2000). *Report on the effectiveness of technology in schools* (7th ed.). Washington, DC: Software and Information Industry Association.

Sticht, T. G. (1968). Some relationships of mental aptitude, reading ability, and listening ability using normal and time-compressed speech. *Journal of Communication, 18*, 243-258.

Sticht, T. G. (1969, Summer). Comprehension of repeated time-compressed recordings. *The Journal of Experimental Education, 37*(4), 60-62.

Sticht, T. G. (1971). Failure to increase learning using the time saved by the time compression of speech. *Journal of Educational Psychology, 62*, 55-59.

Sticht, T. G., & Glasnap, D. R. (1972). Effects of speech rate, selection difficulty, association strength, and mental aptitude on learning by listening. *Journal of Communication, 22*, 174-188.

Stickell, D. W. (1963). A critical review of the methodology and results of research comparing televised and face-to-face instruction. *Dissertation Abstracts International, 24*(08), 3239.

Sutcliffe, A. G. (1999). A design method for effective information delivery in multimedia presentations. *The New Review of Hypermedia and Multimedia, 5*, 29-58.

Svoboda, R. G. (1978). *Audio-tutorial courses for college algebra and trigonometry: a progress report*. Fort Wayne, IN: Indiana University. (ED 167125)

Sweller, J. (1988). Cognitive load during problem solving: Effects on learning, *Cognitive Science, 12*, 257-285.

Sweller, J. (1999). *Instructional design in technical areas*. Camberwell, Australia: ACER Press.

Sweller, J., & Chandler, P. (1994). Why some material is difficult to learn. *Cognition and Instruction, 12*, 185-233.

Sweller, J., Merrienboer, J. J. B. van, Paas F. G. W. C. (1998). Cognitive architecture and instructional design. *Educational Psychology Review, 10*(3), 251-296.

Tabbers, H. K., Martens, R. L., & Van Merriënboer, J. J. G. (2001). The modality effect in multimedia instructions. In J. D. Moore & K. Stenning (Eds.), *Proceedings of the 23rd annual conference of the Cognitive Science Society* (pp. 1024-1029). Mahwah, NJ: Lawrence Erlbaum Associates.

Tabbers, H. K. (2002). *The modality of text in multimedia instructions: Refining the design guidelines*. Unpublished doctoral dissertation, Open University of the Netherlands, Heerlen.

Taylor, S. E. (1964). *Listening: What research says to the teacher*. Washington, DC: National Education Association of the United States.

Taylor, S. E. (1965). Eye movements in reading: facts and fallacies. *American Educational Research Journal, 2*, 187-202.

Thompson, A. D., Simonson, M. R., & Hargrave, C. P. (1996). *Educational Technology: A review of the research*. Washington DC: Association of Educational Communications and Technology.

Thompson, V. A., & Paivio, A. (1994). Memory for pictures and sounds: Independence of auditory and visual codes. *Canadian Journal of Experimental Psychology, 48*(3), 380-396.

Tindall-Ford, S., Chandler, P., & Sweller, J. (1997). When two sensory modes are better than one. *Journal of Experimental Psychology, 3*(4), 257-287.

Travers, R. M. W. (1967). *Research and theory related to audiovisual information transmission* (rev. ed.). U.S. Department of Health, Education and Welfare. Kalamazoo, MI: Western Michigan University.

Travers, R. M. W. (1970). *Man's information system: A primer for media specialists and educational technologists*. Scranton, PA: Chandler Publishing Company.

Tripp, S., & Roby, W. (1994). The effects of various information resources on learning from a hypertext bilingual lexicon. *Journal of Research on Computing in Education, 27*(1), 92-102.

Tripp, S. D. (1994, Aug. 5). *Do media affect memory?* Paper presented at the 3d Practical Aspects of Memory Conference, College Park, MD.

Unwin, D., & McAleese, R. (Eds.). (1988). *The Encyclopedia of Educational Media Communications and Technology*. New York: Greenwood Press.

Van Mondfrans, A., & Travers, R. M. W. (1964). Learning of redundant materials presented through two sensory modalities. *Perceptual and Motor Skills, 19*, 743-751.

Voor, J. B., & Miller, J. M. (1965). The effect of practice on the comprehension of time compressed speech. *Speech Monographs, 32*, 452-454.

Wade, W. (1992). How interest affects learning from text. In K.A. Renninger, S. Hidi, & A. Krapp (Eds.), *The role of interest in learning and development* (pp. 255-277). Hillsdale, NJ: Erlbaum.

Wade, S. E., Schraw, G., Buxton, W. M., & Hayes, M. T. (1993). Seduction of the strategic reader: Effects of interest on strategies and recall. *Reading Research Quarterly, 28*, 92-114.

Wasserman, H. M., & Tedford, W. H. (1973). Recall of temporally compressed auditory and visual information. *Psychological Reports, 32*, 499-502.

Watts, M. W., Jr. (1971). Differences in educational level and subject matter difficulty in the use of compressed speech with adult military students. *Adult Educational Journal, 21*, 27-36.

Wilkinson, G. L. (1980). *Media in instruction: 60 years of research*.

Washington DC: Association of Educational Communications and Technology.

Williams, D. L., Moore, D. M., & Sewell, E. H., Jr. (1983-84). Effects of compressed speech on comprehension of community college students. *Journal of Educational Technology Systems, 12,* 273-284.

Wingfield, A., & Ducharme, J. L. (1999, May). Effects of age and passage difficulty on listening-rate preferences for time-altered speech. *Journals of Gerontology, Series B: Psychological Sciences and Social Sciences, 54B*(3), 199-202.

Wingfield, A., Poon, L. W., Lombardi, L., & Lowe, D. (1985). Speed of processing in normal aging: Effects of speech rate, linguistic structure, and processing time. *Journal of Gerontology, 40,* 579-585.

Winn, W. (1993). Perception principles. In Fleming M., & Levie, H. (Eds.). *Instructional message design: Principles from the behavioral and cognitive sciences*. Englewood Cliffs, NJ: Educational Technology Publications.

Wolcott, L. L. (1993). Audio tools for distance education. In B. Willis (Ed.), *Distance education: strategies and tools* (pp. 135-164). Washington, DC: American Psychological Association.

Wood, C. D. (1966). *Comprehension of compressed speech by elementary school children*. Indiana University, Bloomington, IN. (ED 003 216)

Young, W. E. (1936). The relation of reading comprehension and retention to hearing comprehension and retention. *Journal of Experimental Education, 5*(1), 30-39.

MULTIPLE-CHANNEL COMMUNICATION: THE THEORETICAL AND RESEARCH FOUNDATIONS OF MULTIMEDIA

David M. (Mike) Moore, John K. Burton, and Robert J. Myers
Virginia Polytechnic Institute and State University

36.1 INTRODUCTION

The ability of technology to make information available quickly and provide an individualized learning opportunity has long been discussed and dreamed of. These desires go back to Pressey's teaching machines of the 1920s and Bush's theoretical *Memex* information retrieval system of the 1940s. Since the beginning of the microcomputer computer revolution in the late 1970s, however, the dream has become a reality. Proponents have extolled the virtues of instruction supported, assisted, or conducted by the computer (e.g., Papert, 1977; Suppes, 1980). Others have exercised less enthusiasm about the effects of any media per se. Clark (1983), for example, said that mediated environments are merely sufficient, not necessary for the learning process. Teachers, as practitioners, will ultimately decide whether incorporation of new technologies into the classroom is worth the time and effort (Moore, Myers, & Burton, 1994).

This chapter focuses on the theories and effects related to multiple-channel communication, which undergirds notions of multimedia instruction. Because cognitive notions of learning currently have widespread acceptance, we use it as the perspective for the review. Specifically, we use the information processing view of the cognitive system because it, like current views of multimedia itself, relies so heavily on the computer. The information processing approach focuses on how the human memory system acquires, encodes retrieves, and uses information. This approach applies information theory and

computer analogies to human learning. Within the information processing model, topics and research reviewed include multiple-channel communication—including modalities of instruction, cue summation and stimulus generalization, channel interference, and capacity. We resisted, however, the temptation to include, and thus report on, cueing strategies and other remotely related theories. Related research literature in the areas of multiimage and subliminal perception are also investigated and summarized.

The term *multimedia* has been used for a long time by educators as well as those in the technology industry, yet there is little consensus as to what, exactly, the concept includes (Strommen & Ravelle, 1990). Until recently, the term has meant the use of several media devices in a coordinated fashion (e.g., synchronized slides with audiotape). Advances in technology, however, have combined these media so that information previously delivered by several devices is now integrated into one device (Kozma, 1987, 1991). Obviously the computer plays a central organizing role in this environment, and just as obviously the computer allows interactivity and, constrained only by the size of the lesson, unlimited branching. Because of this history, many authors (see, e.g., Matchett & Elliot, 1991) argue that multimedia should encompass interactive systems. This allows the notion of multimedia not only to accommodate interactive video, for example, but also to absorb the historically older concept of hypermedia (Moore et al., 1994). In part because we do not agree (we tend to see multimedia as a special case of hypermedia with one, linear path specified) and in part because of the more practical reason that such things as interactive video are covered elsewhere in this handbook, we limit our definition, and hence our coverage, to systems that include two or more of the following: motion, voice, data, text, graphics, and still images.

Multimedia research is evaluated with the intent of answering the question: Does multimedia really work? Speculation on multimedia message design based on past and current research concludes this chapter.

36.2 INFORMATION PROCESSING APPROACH TO HUMAN COGNITION

36.2.1 Historical Perspectives

Notions such as seeing with our *mind's eye* and *listening to our inner voices* portray an ancient metaphor of a mind with sense organs much like the body. The mind feels pain (e.g., "It hurts me when I think about..."), has a sense of taste (e.g., "I want this so bad I can taste it") and smell (e.g., "The more I think about this the more it smells"), etc. Moreover, our language reflects specific, organ-based memories as in "I'll never forget the look on his face or the sound of his voice" or "I can still feel (or smell) it after all these years." Yet the nature of sensory image processing, storage, interpretation, and generation is not nearly as clear (or as noncontroversial) as our conversational descriptions would imply.

Images are mentioned in Greek scrolls that date back as early as 500 B.C. A few hundred years later, a building collapsed during an earthquake; Simonodes, a survivor, related his use of mental images to recreate the seating arrangement at the feast he had been attending in the building. The power of the mind to *see* is exemplified, for example, by authors such as St. Augustine (who refers to inner sight or insight) and De Cartes (who believed that during dream states the mind could both see and hear during its *travels*).

To understand the current views of these historical concepts, however, it is necessary to take a position on how the human memory system works. For simplicity, and to make discussions about modalities, channels, etc., easier, we have selected the model that began the current rise of cognitive psychology: information processing.

36.2.2 Cognitive Overview

The information processing approach to human cognition relies on the computer as a metaphor. Gardner (1985) states that cognitive science was *officially* recognized at the Symposium on Information Theory held at MIT in 1956. Although Broadbent (1958) published the first model, it was Neisser, in his 1967 book, *Cognitive Psychology,* who synthesized earlier attempts to apply information theory and computer analogies to human learning (see, e.g., Bartlett, 1958; Broadbent, 1958; Miller, 1953; Posner, 1964).

The information processing approach focuses on how the human memory system acquires, transforms, compacts, elaborates, encodes, retrieves, and uses information. The memory system is divided into three main storage structures: sensory registers, short-term memory (STM), and long-term memory (LTM). Each structure is synonymous with a type of processing.

The first stage of processing is registering stimuli in the memory system. The sensory registers (one for each sense) briefly hold raw information until the stimulus pattern is recognized or lost. Pattern recognition is the matching of stimulus information with previously acquired knowledge. Klatzky (1980) referred to this complex recognition process as assigning meaning to a stimulus. Unlike the sensory registers, STM does not hold information in its raw sensory form, (e.g., visual—*icon,* auditory—*echo*) but in its recognized form. For example, the letter *A* is recognized as a letter rather than as just a group of lines. STM can maintain information longer than the sensory registers through a holding process known as maintenance rehearsal, which recycles material over and over as the system works on it. Without rehearsal, the information would decay and be lost from STM.

Another characteristic of STM is its limited capacity for information. Miller (1956) determined that STM has room for about seven items (chunks) of information. Moreover, STM has a *limited pool of effort* or cognition capacity (see, e.g., Britton, Meyer, Simpson, Holdredge, & Curry, 1979; Kahneman, 1973; Kerr, 1973). This limited pool is assumed to effect everything from decision making to the sizes of visual images that can be processed (e.g., Kosslyn, 1975). Klatzky (1980) defined STM as a *work space* in which information may be rehearsed, elaborated, used for decision making, lost, or stored in the third memory structure: LTM.

LTM is a complex and permanent storehouse for individuals' knowledge about the world and their experiences in it. LTM processes information to the two other memory structures and in turn receives information from the sensory registers and STM. First, the stimulus is recognized in the sensory registers through comparison with information in LTM. Second, information manipulated in STM can be permanently stored in LTM.

Perception is an interpretive process involving a great deal of unconscious inference (Helmholtz, 1866, as cited in Malone, 1990). An important characteristic of STM, for our purposes, is that, despite the fact that it *can* apparently manipulate visual information (e.g., Cooper & Shepard, 1973), phonemic coding is the preferred modality (Baddeley, 1966; Conrad, 1964; Sperling, 1960). Related to this phenomena is that STM apparently treats printed text and spoken words the same: acoustically (e.g., Pellegrino, Siegel, & Dhawan, 1974, 1976a, 1976b). Basic research studies not only tend to confirm this treatment, but suggest that whereas people can remember information as being presented by picture or spoken word, printed text is identified as printed (versus spoken) at about a chance level (Burton, 1982; Burton & Bruning, 1982).

To understand how an individual is able to interpret information, the researcher must first focus on decisions made at each memory storage structure. Within the information processing model, attention and pattern recognition determine the environmental factors that are processed. A large amount of information impinges on the sensory registers but is quickly lost if not attended to. Attention, therefore, plays an important role in selecting sensory information.

Early information processing models viewed attention as a filter or bottleneck (e.g., Broadbent, 1958). For example, an individual could follow an auditory message across many *ears* (headphones) but could attend to only one message; the rest were filtered out. Work by Cherry (1953, 1957), Moray (1959), and Treisman (1960) indicated, however, that information in an unattended channel (same modality) *could* penetrate this proposed bottleneck. Current models (e.g., Shiffrin & Geisler, 1973) view attention as attenuation (much like a volume control on a TV or radio) with unlimited capacity for recognition of stimuli coming from different channels at the same time. Recognizing a stimulus in one channel does not disturb the process of recognizing a second stimulus in another channel (Bourne, Dominowski, Loftus, & Healy, 1986). Attention is conceived of as being a very limited mental resource (Anderson, 1985). It is difficult to perform two demanding tasks at the same time. Although the sensory registers register all information, only information attended to and processed to a more permanent form is retained. Bruner, Goodnow, and Auston (1967) stated that a person tends to focus attention on cues that have seemed useful in the past. Pattern recognition enables the individual to organize perceptual features (cues) so that relevant knowledge from LTM is activated. In other words, recognition *is* attention (Norman, 1969). Pattern recognition integrates information from a complex interaction that uses both bottom-up and top-down processing (Anderson, 1985). Bottom-up processing is the use of sensory information in pattern recognition. Top-down processing is the use of pattern context and general knowledge. Attention is assumed to use both processes, that is, it is interactive (Neisser, 1967). Once relevant information is activated from LTM, the individual focuses attention on the relevant stimulus and brings it into the working memory (STM).

LTM contains large quantities of information that have to be organized efficiently so they can be effectively encoded, stored, and retrieved. These three processes are interdependent. For example, the method of presentation determines how information is stored and retrieved (Klatzky, 1980). Encoding is related to the amount of elaboration and rehearsal conducted in STM. Elaboration uses information received from LTM after the stimulus is recognized. As new information is compared to the old and manipulated information, it is either added or subsumed into the existing schema, then encoded in LTM (Anderson, Greeno, Kline, & Neves, 1981). This schema or *set of past experiences* is the cognitive structure that, when related to new information, causes meaning (Mayer, 1983, p. 68). As information is restructured and added, new structures are formed that result in new conceptualizations (Magliaro, 1988). These knowledge structures combine information in an organized manner. Evidence for memory storage indicates that representations can be both meaning-based and perception-based. Retrieval of information is also an active process. Information is accessed by a search of the memory structures. The speed and accuracy of retrieval are directly dependent on how the information was encoded and the attention being given to the stimulus. To be recalled from LTM, information must be activated. The level of activation seems to depend on the associative strength of the path. The strength of the activation increases with practice and with the associative properties (Anderson, 1985).

36.2.3 Dual Coding

Imagery theorists obviously make a distinction between the codes used for images and those used for verbal information. Paivio (1971, 1986) developed the dual-code model, which stated that the two types of information (verbal and imaginal) are encoded by separate subsystems, one specialized for sensory images and the other specialized for verbal language. The two systems are assumed to be structurally and functionally distinct. Paivio (1986) defined structure as the difference in the nature of representational units and the way in which these units are organized into higher-order systems. Structure, therefore, refers to LTM operations that correlate with perceptually identifiable verbal or visual objects and activities.

It is important to note that Paivio defines his two systems very broadly. An image can be a picture or a sound or even perhaps a taste, whereas the verbal store, on the other hand, is construed broadly to mean a language store (Burton & Bruning, 1982). In Paivio's (1971) words, image refers

...to concrete imagery, that is, *nonverbal* memory representations of concrete objects and events, or nonverbal modes of thought (e.g.., imagination) in which such representations are actively generated and manipulated by the individual. This will usually be taken to mean *visual* imagery, although it is clear that other modalities (e.g., auditory) could be involved and when they are, this must be specified. Imagery, so defined, will be distinguished from verbal symbolic processes, which will be assumed to involve implicit activity in an auditory-motor speech system. (p. 12)

Functionally, Paivio's two hypothesized subsystems are independent, meaning that either can operate without the other or both can work parallel to each other. Even though independent of one another, these two subsystems are interconnected so that a concept represented as an image can also be converted to a verbal label in the other system, or vice versa (Klatzky, 1980). Paivio is very explicit, however, about the power of images: Whereas words that can be imaged *may* be, images (and presumably all concrete sensory input) that can be translated *will* be, automatically. Paivio argues that this is why pictures are often remembered better than verbal information (Pressley & Miller, 1987).

Dual-code theorists accept that mental images are not exact copies of pictures but, instead, contain information that was encoded from a sensory event after perceptual analysis and pattern recognition (Klatzky, 1980). It is thought that the images are organized into subunits at the time of perception (Anderson, 1978). Paivio (1986) further explained that mental representations have their developmental beginnings in perceptual, motor, and affective experience and are able to retain these characteristics when being encoded so that the structures and the processes are modality specific. For example, a concrete object such as the ocean would be recognized by more than one modality—by its appearance, sound, smell, and taste. Therefore, a continuity between perception and memory as well as between behavioral skills and cognitive skills is implied (Paivio).

There are, however, the same limits on imaginal processing that we see throughout the information processing model. The concept of limited space was demonstrated by Kosslyn (1975), who asked students to visualize two named objects and then to answer questions about one of the objects. Students were slower to find parts that were next to an elephant than to find those next to a fly. STM for visuals appeared to have a processing limitation. Large objects like elephants (or even *very large* flies) *fill up* the system and slow it down. Retrieval of visually coded material also differs from other forms of internal representation. As previously stated, information is available simultaneously rather than by a sequential search and can be located by template or by an unlimited-capacity parallel search (Anderson, 1978).

Dual-coding theory can account for our personal impression of having images. The theory is often supported by research studies that conclude that individuals have a continuous and analogue ability to judge space from images, in at least some cases (Kosslyn, 1975), and, finally, by studies that indicate strong visual memory abilities. Paivio's theory is also able effectively to support the recurrent finding that memory for pictures is better than memory for words (Shepard, 1967), otherwise known as the *pictorial superiority effect* (Levie, 1987). Imagery theories have been used by researchers to construct and test hypotheses on learning from graphics (Winn, 1987) and seem a fruitful heuristic source for multimodality research in the future.

36.2.4 Detail and Experience

In terms of simple recognition, text modality detail does not seem to be important. Nelson, Metzler, and Reed (1974), for example, varied visual representations of the same scene from nondetailed drawings to photographs and compared recognition for the visuals versus text descriptions. As we would expect, pictures were superior in recognition tests, but there were no differences among the detail levels used. For recall, however, detail is important in at least two ways. Mandler and Parker (1976) showed that the locations of detail elements are best recalled if they are organized in a meaningful way. Thus, for example, graphic elements of classroom items that are placed in their *usual* locations are superior to the same elements when they are not organized in a meaningful manner. Obviously, *meaningful* reflects prior knowledge, including culture. In a related way, specific expertise impacts memory for visuals. Egan and Schwartz (1979) demonstrated that skilled electronics technicians showed superior recall for circuit diagrams relative to novices *as long as* the diagrams made sense, that is, were organized in a meaningful manner.

Images can also be used to organize incoming information. The classic demonstration of this use of visuals to make sense of subsequent textual information is Bransford and Johnson's (1972) *Balloons* passage. In their study, people found text without the visuals (or the visual following the text) to be difficult to comprehend and remember relative to the same text following an organizing visual. A related effect, *priming* (see, e.g., Neely, 1977; Posner & Snyder, 1975), has been demonstrated with text. Basically, a categorical prime, such a bird, facilitates access to a specific bird, such as a robin. Conversely, an incorrect categorical prime inhibits access. A representative of the category in whatever modality should produce a similar effect (Miller & Burton, 1994).

Theory, basic research, and applied research predict and support the efficacy of images (and instructions to image) in learning and memory. Yet images are prone to the same processes (and problems) that affect all aspects of the human system: distortions of *reality*. We assume that human sensation is about the same for all of us. When confronted with a visual stimulus, we assume that our rods, cones, optic nerves, and so forth, react about the same. Perceptually, however, we do not *see* the same things. We extract (and create) meaning from visual stimuli just as we do from text. Therefore, our prior experience, inferences, expectations, beliefs, physical state, and other factors determine what we see as surely as the stimulus before us. A similar process operates when we recall an image from memory: We reconstruct from our constructed images. Naturally, as in memory for text, we forget details (Miller & Burton, 1994).

Finally, where there are gaps, we unconsciously fill them. As you will see in other chapters, images are effective for connecting items to be remembered and, if the level of detail is correct, for learning new facts and relationships. However, these tasks are rather low level and rote. In general, unless images are entrained to the point of pattern recognition, we can assume that the human memory system deals with images as it deals with text: generally or prototypically. The system is great at *gist* or meaning and poor at specifics. Thus, images may work *better* than text in many applications, but they probably do not work differently (Miller & Burton, 1994).

36.3 MULTIPLE-CHANNEL COMMUNICATION

Of major interest to communication theorists and instructional designers is whether humans can accommodate simultaneous audio and visual stimuli and, if so, the amount and types of information that can be so processed. Multiple-channel communication involves simultaneous presentations of stimuli "... through different sensory channels (i.e., sight, sound, touch, etc.) which will provide additional stimuli reinforcement" (Dwyer, 1978, p. 22).

Broadbent (1958) and later Feigenbaum and Simon (1963) espoused the single-channel theory, in which, if information arrives simultaneously in separate channels, information jamming will occur. Broadbent (1958, 1965) suggests that one reason for reduced learning in multiple-channel presentations is a result of the filtering process (bottleneck) occurring in an individual's information processing system, which reduces superfluous elements and permits only essential or basic information to be received; the nervous system acts as a single channel. Similarly, research conducted by Hernandez-Peon (1961) has led to a hypothesis known as the *Hernandez-Peon* effect, which contends that when information is being processed via one sense, this act may cause an impediment to the processing of a stimuli through other senses. Likewise, Jacobson (1950, 1951) contended that the brain is able to process only small proportions of the large amounts of stimuli received. Thus, regardless of the amount of information presented in which sensory modality, learners are able to accept only limited amounts in the information processing center (Attneave, 1954; Brown, 1959; Dwyer, 1972; Livingstone, 1962). Broadbent (1958) asserts that the human information processing can receive information from only one source at a time—the additional information is temporarily stored (in the sensory register). However, Hartman (1961b) also points out that Broadbent's thesis regarding the filtering of information in the central nervous system is based on data obtained from presenting unrelated information to learners through two or more modalities simultaneously. If, after this momentary storage, the information is not used, it is not retained. Thus, people viewing multiple-channel presentations are presented with the problem of switching from one channel to another (Broadbent, 1956, 1965). Other researchers including Cherry (1953), Shannon and Weaver (1949), and Spaulding (1956) support this theory. Corballis and Reaburn (1970), Clark (1969), Herman (1965), and Welford (1968) have documented the reduction (impairment) of the processing of information in multiple-channel communication situations. Travers (1968) concurs in his review of multiple-channel communication. He suggests that there is no convincing evidence that *multiple-channel communications* were any more effective in producing learning than single-channel inputs. There appear to be major concerns, however, involved in determining the amount of information a human can process at any one time. Travers (1968) indicates unequivocally that the human processing system is one of limited capacity (see also Miller, 1956). To recognize information simultaneously, the various receptors (eyes, ears) would have to analyze a great variety of different cues. At this initial stage, the system *does* function as a multiple-channel system. But once recognition has occurred (and hence attention; see also Norman, 1969), the remainder of operations on the incoming information is undertaken by a system with a limited capacity, STM. The system from this point on operates as a single-channel system. Travers states, ". . . Unless the rate at which the incoming information being received is less than the capacity of the system for handling information. Only under the latter condition can two separate and distinct sequences of messages be received at the same time" (p. 10). Humans are able to deal with the vast complexities of various types of data from the environment. These data are then simplified to be handled by the perceptual system. Much of the simplification of this huge amount of complex data involves the discarding of redundant information. This process is referred to as *information compression* (Travers, 1968, p. 11).

Given the complexity of multimedia and its close relationship to cognitive and information processing theories, it is helpful to review a perspective known as cognitive load theory to understand the possible implications of multichannel processing on cognitive structures (K. Smith, 2001). Mayer's (2001) discussion of limited capacity assumptions suggests that humans are limited in the amount of information that can be processed in each channel at one time. Mayer distinguishes between two types of cognitive load. Intrinsic cognitive load "depends on the inherent difficulty of the material—how many elements there are and how they interact with each other" (p. 50). Extraneous cognitive load, on the other hand, depends on the way the instructional message is designed, organized, and presented (p. 50). Mayer also cites metacognitive strategies as techniques for allocating, monitoring coordinating, and adjusting limited cognitive resources (K. Smith).

Sweller and Chandler (1994) provide empirical evidence related to the analysis of both intrinsic and extraneous cognitive load and conclude that such analysis can lead to instructional design that will generate gains in learning efficiency. Sweller and Chandler base their conclusions on the following assumptions.

- Schema acquisition and automation are major learning mechanisms.
- Limited working memory makes it difficult to assimilate multiple elements of information simultaneously.
- Multiple elements must be assimilated when the elements interact.
- Heavy cognitive load is caused by material with a high level of interactivity.
- High levels of interactivity may be caused by the nature of the material being learned and by the method of presentation.
- If intrinsic element interactivity and consequent cognitive load are low, extraneous load may not be important (K. Smith, 2001).

Sweller and Chandler (1994) also suggest that schema acquisition and automatic processing become important mechanisms that could be fostered to prevent issues with cognitive load. They define schemata as "cognitive constructs that organize information according to the manner in which it will be dealt" (p. 186). Automation, on the other hand, occurs with time and practice and allows cognitive process to occur with out conscious control. Sweller and Chandler additionally caution against such design issues as split-attention and redundancy effects. The split-attention effect occurs when instructional material requires students to split their attention among multiple sources of information and then integrate that information (K. Smith, 2001). The redundancy effect is a phenomenon that deals with segments of information that can be understood in isolation. Chandler and Sweller (1991) found that by adding redundant elements such as text, students may associate those elements with a diagram, which may increase the element interactivity and lead to cognitive overload.

Cognitive load is also related to the information processing system's strength: gist. Travers' perceptual model thus includes a high-capacity information system up to the point of recognition and a very limited system beyond. Lack of retention and lack of understanding of many multiple-channel presentations are examples of this model in action. Travers' (1964a, 1964b, 1966) studies support this contention that humans cannot receive more information if exposed to two or more sources simultaneously than if exposed to just one source or if the information is transmitted by two different modalities. Van Mondfrans (1963), in a study using nonsense syllables and words, showed no advantage of an audiovisual presentation over presentations via audio and visual modalities alone. Cherry (1953) concluded that the utilization of information by the brain could be represented by single-channel input. Travers (1968) continues and states that since the perceptual channel is very limited, we must assume that the receiver (learner) cannot process multiple-channel inputs as efficiently as "designers of audiovisual materials have commonly assumed" (p. 10).

Other researchers have supported the efficacy of single-channel presentations. These include Fleming (1970), who reviewed research studies dealing with single- and multiple-channel presentations and noted the possibility that many instructional programs are already "perceptually overloaded." He suggests that additional "jamming" of the perceivers' senses through multiple media (channels) may have negative results. Fleming suggests that the only possible instructional situation where "stepped up sensory environments" are useful is when the desire is to "overwhelm, impress or to exhilarate" (pp. 69–100). Hartman (1961a) concludes that multiple-channel presentations do not produce increases in learning (however defined) over single-channel communication unless the situation in which the learning takes place also contains the necessary additional cues. Hartman (1961b) has also expressed concern about the act of increasing the number of cues and/or the number of channels used with the expectation that more learning will occur. He states,

A common practice among multiple-channel communicators has been to fill the channels, especially the pictorial, with as much information as possible. The obvious expectation is for additional communication to result from the additional information. However, the probability of interference resulting from the additional cues is very high. The hoped-for enhanced communication resulting from a summation of cues occurs only under special conditions. Most of the added cues in the mass media possess a large number of extraneous cognitive associations. The possibility that these associations will interfere with one another is probably greater than that they will facilitate learning. (p. 255)

Hsia (1971) drew several conclusions from an extensive review of literature comparing multiple and single-channel presentations. These include the following: (a) Human information processing functions as a multiple-channel system until the capacity of the system is overloaded; (b) when the input becomes greater than the system's capacity, the system reverts to a single-channel system; and (c) an increase in the amount of information presented does not necessarily increase the rate of information transmission. Hsia (1971) asserts that, because all incoming information needs to be coded prior to being processed by the human processing system, it would seem reasonable that all extraneous, irrelevant, and superfluous information be eliminated or reduced at that time. Hsia (1971) contends that by reducing this *extra* information, the learner is spared from having to discriminate the relevant from the irrelevant. In addition to filtering information, a large portion of redundancy and noise is eliminated. Hsia (1971) and Carpenter (1953) feel that the physiological aspects of the individual limit the processing capability of an individual. A person can receive far more stimuli than they can effectively process. Clark (1969), Corballis and Reaburn (1970), Herman (1965), and Welford (1968) indicate that there are a substantial number of research results that support the position that single-channel communication can be as effective as multiple-channel orientations. Dwyer (1978) cites approximately 50 studies in which the contention that additional cues—"provided by the use of two or more information channels simultaneously—or excessive realistic cues within a single-channel may be distracting or even evoke responses in opposition to the desired types of learning" (pp. 29–30).

There is also much criticism of the research that supports the single-channel view. For example, Norberg (1966) takes Travers to task for basing his assumption concerning single-channel communication on experiments using verbal material in both auditory and visual channels (i.e., no pictures presented). Norberg explains that Travers' studies

. . . deal exclusively with verbal symbols, whereas most two-channel presentations actually used in instructional situations typically combine nonverbal signs in the visual channel with verbal auditory stimuli. . . . But it is still necessary to distinguish carefully between the actual experimental findings and theoretical statements regarding nonverbal "realistic" stimuli which have not entered into the experimental work cited. . . . it is one thing to say that the "density" of information in stimulus materials presented to the leaner may become a factor impeding efficient transmission; i.e., some presentations may be too realistic. (p. 307)

Other criticisms of single-channel research are that many of the data collected were from studies where unrelated and/or contradictory stimuli were presented to the learners simultaneously. It would seem reasonable in these circumstances that a person would attend to one stimulus (message) and not the other. The following section looks at multiple-channel communication and the influences of the cue summation theories.

36.4 CUE SUMMATION AND MULTIPLE-CHANNEL COMMUNICATION

It is relatively easy to find current literature extolling the virtues of multimedia or hypermedia environments. Among the commonly mentioned advantages are

- the ability to place learners in a context-rich environment;
- an increase in learning due to the combination of text, graphics, full-motion video, and signs;
- the ability to navigate complex nonlinear *hyperspace*; and
- an increase in motivation due to intrinsic aspects of the media.

Desktop hardware and software have become more powerful, flexible, and sophisticated in the types of presentations that they can author and deliver. Moreover, such systems are within the budgets of many, if not most, K–12 classrooms. There has been a proliferation of authoring packages and CD-ROM-based programs that can deliver high-fidelity sound, realistic color images in stills, graphics, and full-motion video. The central issue in this chapter, however, is whether multiple-channel presentations provided by multimedia environments contribute to an increase in the amount of learning.

The terms *multiple-channel communication* and *cue summation* are routinely used interchangeably in the literature. Is there a difference? The cue summation principle of learning theory predicts that learning is increased as the number of available cues or stimuli is increased (Severin, 1967a). Does this mean the addition of cues within a single-channel (such as adding color to a picture)? or Does it mean adding cues across channels (such as adding audio to visual a presentation)? For the purposes of this review cue summation includes the addition of cues both within and across channels. Therefore the multiple-channel communication research in this review may be subsumed under the cue summation theories. Supporting this approach is Miller's (1957) view concerning cue summation, which is frequently cited:

When cues from different modalities (or different cues within the same modality) are used simultaneously, they may either facilitate or interfere with each other. When cues elicit the same responses simultaneously, or different responses in the proper succession, they should summate to yield increased effectiveness. When the cues elicit incompatible responses, they should produce conflict and interference. (p. 78)

Hoban (1949), in a summary of the instructional value of increasing the number of cues and/or realistic detail (which some call *single-channel realism theory*) in a visual presentation, concluded that the power of a medium of communication is determined by "the richness of the symbols employed" (p. 9) within that medium. These cues lead to greater understanding of the message by the audience.

Miller (1957) cites his views on the need to increase the number of cues in a presentation. He states that if one stimulus complex is to be identified versus another, the individual may use any number (even one) of available cues to make this discrimination. Increasing the number of available cues will increase the likelihood of an individual making the correct discrimination over time and the likelihood of a number of individuals making the correct discrimination simultaneously.

Dwyer (1978) suggests that the above views can be classified under the theoretical orientation collectively referred to as *realism theories*. The assumption is that "learning will be more complete as the number of cues in the learning situation increases. They suggest that an increase in realism in the existing cues in a learning situation increases the probability learning will be facilitated" (p. 6). (It should be noted that making a learning situation more complex does not necessarily make it more realistic).

Allen and Cooney (1963) suggest that age and maturity have effects on recall of information from multiple- or single-channel presentations. The mode of presentation has less effect on learning than maturity. Hsia (1969) studied the relationships between modalities and learner intelligence; he concluded that less intelligent learners would be assisted positively if input, noise, and redundancy were controlled. Audiovisual (multiple-channel) presentations rather than single-channel presentations were suggested to optimize the information processing rate of less intelligent subjects. Further, Hsia recommended keeping cross-channel redundancy high in audiovisual (multiple-channel) presentations. Hsia (1968) similarly states that

... in dual or multi-channel information processing, dimensionality of information generally increases, and one channel provides cues and clues for the other, provided that the amount of information to be presented has not reached the capacity limit, thereby eliminating probable interference or information jamming. Increase in dimensionality usually results in the increase of information processing. (p. 326)

Severin (1967b) suggests that "multiple-channel communications appear to be superior to single-channel communications when relevant cues are summated across channels, neither is

superior when redundant between channels, and are inferior when irrelevant cues are combined (presumably because irrelevant cues cause interference between them)" (p. 397). Severin's theory of cue summation differs slightly from others in that he stresses the addition of *relevant* cues. This is somewhat of a caveat to the general theory of cue summation, which states that any increase in cues will summate in more learning. Severin (1967c) also places emphasis on the use of pictorial presentations as the vehicle to add cues.

Van Mondfrans and Travers (1964) found that redundant information presented over two-sense modalities (auditory plus visual) resulted in no better learning than from either sense modality used alone. Severin (1967a) points out that the work of Van Mondfrans and Travers did not deal with nonredundant information presented over two channels. Their work looked at verbal material in both channels—omitting the use of pictorial information.

Baggett and Ehrenfeucht (1983) reported that when college students are watching a film presentation, and related information is presented simultaneously across two mediums—visual and auditory—there is no competition for resources. When encoding visual and auditory information sequentially the extraction of information is not increased. They concluded that synchronous visual and auditory input is an efficient way to present information. Baggett (1984) reported superiority of a simultaneous presentation of narrative and visuals over a presentation of the narration prior to the corresponding visual sequence, but speech given slightly after a visual sequence resulted in recall just as good as that of a simultaneous presentation. Nugent (1982) studied redundancy of content across three channels and found that when the content was the same, subjects learned equally well from all modes and, by combining modes, generally maximized learning.

It is not surprising that much of the multiple-channel (audiovisual) research has been conducted in the television venue, particularly with studies dealing with questions of redundancy. Findahl (1971), Reese (1983), and Drew and Grimes (1987) reported the superiority of redundant audio and video presentations in recall, retention of verbal information, and understanding of content. Likewise, Pezdek and Stevens (1984) found that with kindergarten students audio and video channels with *matched* information were better for memory than *mismatched* channels. They concluded that a high degree of redundancy helps learning in the audio channel and hinders it in the visual channel. With nonredundant material the students relied primarily on the video for meaning, however. Calvert, Huston, Watkins, and Wright (1982) reported that children learned more when verbal content was supported by understandable video than when abstract audio was accompanied by recognizable video.

Rolandelli (1989) reports that, in television presentations, the visual mode is more important than the auditory mode when the visual component competes with an incongruent audio tract, but when visual superiority is confounded with complexity and comprehensibility, comprehensibility appears to be a more critical factor in viewer behavior. Audio can enhance comprehensibility by signaling what is worthy of attention and conveys information, which can be understood independently of the visual mode (being present). Studies exploring irrelevant visual distractions (Bither, 1972; Festinger & Maccoby, 1964; Ostehouse & Brock, 1970) found that irrelevant visual distractions have an adverse effect on audio recall.

Lumsdaine and Gladstone (1958), Kale, Grosslight, and McIntyre (1955), and Kopstein and Roshal (1954) found the use of pictorial information or picture–word combinations to be more effective than words alone. Setting out to develop a hypothesis for these findings, Severin (1967a) suggested that the principles of cue summation and stimulus generalization accounted for the improvement in learning. Stimulus generalization implies that learning improves as testing situations become more similar to the presentation situation.

Additional studies have shown the superiority of the multiple-channel presentations of information. Severin (1967b, 1967c) reported that participants receiving information with audio and related pictures received the highest scores of four treatments (sound only, picture only, sound and pictures, sound and unrelated pictures). He also reported finding that individual intelligence scores were less important in predicting learning than types of treatments. Hartman (1961a), in summarizing his study on multiple-channel effectiveness, indicated that "redundant information simultaneously presented by the audio and print channels is more effective in producing learning than the same information in either channel alone" (p. 42). Likewise, reviews of literature by Day and Beach (1950), which focused on the comparisons of audio and print channels, and the Hoban and Van Ormer studies (1950a), which concentrated on pictorial comparisons, made similar conclusions. However, Hartman (1961a) distinguished four relationships between multiple-channel messages in those studies: redundant, related, unrelated, and contradictory. If multiple-channel messages are unrelated or contradictory, they compete with each other, and information interference is the result. That is why multiple-channel presentations were less effective in some studies. But if audio and visual messages were identical or closely related, they complement the other to form one thought and improve learning (Hanson, 1989; Ketcham & Heath, 1962). In educational practices, we seldom deliver unrelated or contradictory messages through multiple-channels. Therefore, an improvement of learning is expected by adopting the multiple-channel approach (Yang, 1993).

The implications of this work for development of multimedia products are considerable. It suggests that the addition of *bells and whistles* may contribute unrelated cues. As Severin (1967b) says, "If interference is accidentally introduced between channels, then much effort, time, and money is wasted, for one channel could then communicate more effectively" (p. 399). This work could provide advice for those engaged in the development of multimedia products for *at-risk* audiences. For these groups, less emphasis on print material combined with the summation of cues using relevant material in the other channels may be more appropriate.

K. U. Smith and Smith (1966) critiqued earlier multiple-channel research (sometimes called *audiovisual research*). The Smiths state,

Implicit in many of the older research designs which tried to make direct comparisons between different techniques was the assumptions that different types of instruction promoted the same type of learning—presumably the learning of verbal knowledge. These experimental comparisons usually were based on verbal criterion tests, for it was not realized that specialized audiovisual procedures might teach specialized non-verbal knowledge. (p. 142)

Dwyer (1978) identified 19 factors that complicate interpretation and cause contradictory results of the single- and multiple-channel communication research studies. Some criticisms include weakness in experimental design, studies lacking hypotheses, research conducted in nonrealistic situations, and lack of relationship content used in one channel versus another.

Hartman (1961b), commenting on a review of 30 studies of channel comparisons, suggested that for presenting related information through either one or two channels, there is a strong indication of an advantage of combining channels. Severin (1967a) points out, however, that most of these studies were completed prior to 1940 and many contained poor research designs, lacked controls, and had test-channel bias. Interference between channels due to unrelated or opposing information was not recognized in many of the studies. Severin (1967a) continues that a common practice among many communication researchers was to fill all channels in a multiple-channel situation with as much information (cues) as possible, with the expectation that this additional information would increase communication. The probability is quite high, however, that the additional information will only "evoke irreverent cues" (p. 234). Also see a strikingly similar statement by Hartman (1961b, p. 255).

Severin (1967a) attempts to explain the contradictory research findings of those who have studied multiple-channel and single-channel communication. Severin asks why some studies show an increase in learning in cross (multiple)-channel redundancy and others do not. Severin (1967a) suggests that educators sometime use multiple channels without understanding the possibilities of interference between them, and information may be presented via two channels and testing mode presented via only one channel. If, as Broadbent (1957) suggests, the central nervous system is a single system, separate presentations across two channels may not exceed its capacity but, together, could overload and jam it. Gulo and Baron (1965) and Williams and Ogilvie, (1957) suggest that presentations do not always use the second channel to convey information and, thus, add nothing, even redundancy, and might cause interference.

Hsia (1968) also questions the inconsistent findings. He feels that a major cause is the failure to take into account the capacity limit theorem and redundancy. First, redundancy causes information processing to fluctuate. Second, overloading the capacity limit causes equivocation (loss of information). Hsia suggests that decreasing input information in accordance with the information processing capacity will eliminate or reduce equivocation. Adjusting redundancy to an optimum level so that maximum transfer may take place, he submits, will eliminate error.

Conway (1968), however, suggests that "the distinction between redundant and related information must now be regarded as an artifact of faulty conceptualization" (p. 409). He opines that equivalence in referential function is the criterion for redundancy. That is, "two items are redundant in that as sign vehicles they are interpreted to make reference in an equivalent fashion" (p. 409). Two important issues are implied in this discussion. First, Conway questions Severin's hypotheses concerning cue summation and stimulus generalization and the criteria on which they are based. Second, Conway goes to some length discussing whether relationships involving two signs or two modalities are redundant or related. If, as Conway proposes, most of the above relationships are redundant, as opposed to related, then there is no advantage in combining signs or sensory modalities. In refuting the hypothesis that presentations combining two sensory modalities are more efficient than either one of the modalities used alone, Conway cites findings of Van Mondfrans and Travers (1964) and Severin (1967a, 1967c). Severin's (1967a) position states that there is no advantage in using *redundant* information over two modalities versus either one used alone. An example is a presentation of the spoken word *moose* and the written word *moose*. Severin (1967a) hypothesizes that *related or relevant* presentations using two signs offer the greatest gain in communications. An example of the latter would be a picture of a *moose* and the written word *moose* or a picture of a *moose* along with the spoken word *moose*.

Conway (1968), in an attempt to analyze the cue summation and stimulus generalization theories, tested word plus picture presentations against other conditions. He found that the present-picture/test-picture condition to be superior to those of presentword/testword plus picture or present word/test word. He failed to find significance in the present-word/test-picture and present-picture/test-word conditions. Conway suggests that the dual-coding theory (Paivio, 1971) may account for the failure to support the stimulus generalization theory. For example, "...Simple pictorial (line drawing) sign vehicles, although presented as single units, are, it is suggested, most likely to be coded and stored in two internal forms and therefore more likely than either word or word plus picture presentations to be readily assessed by the sign-vehicle presentations used to test memory" (p. 412). Using somewhat analogous reasoning to explain Van Mondfrans and Travers' (1964) failure to support an advantage to combined spoken and printed-word presentations, Conway suggests that these messages are functionally equivalent and are already stored in word form. Therefore, using either spoken- or printed-word presentations would be equal in learning to a combined presentation. It would follow that recall would also be equal under either stimulus because the material is stored as a verbal string under both modes of presentation.

Much kinder to cue summation theory and Severin's (1967a, 1967b) views is Hsia (1968, 1971). He submits, "... Tangible evidence suggests the possibility that when the amount of information to be processed is optimal, the audiovisual channels may be a more effective means of communication than either single channel" (1968, p. 246). Hsia (1971) makes a very thorough literature review of the discrete ranges of audio, visual, and audiovisual information processing rates and capacities. One of his conclusions is that combined audiovisual presentations produce more dimensionality than audio or visual alone. This dimensionality, he says, brings about an increase in information transfer within the information processing capacity.

Hsia (1968) cautions, however, that multimodal information processing seems to reach the overloading point faster than using single channels alone, especially when the between-channel redundancy is low. In essence, Hsia is proposing that designers remain cognizant of the principle that audiovisual communications will provide dimensionality and address individual learner differences when used within the capacity of the nervous system. He also addresses individual learner traits. For example, he cites research that supports use of the audio channel for young children, poor readers, and those of limited ability. In dealing with literate subjects, however, he provides evidence for using visual presentations. We could easily deduce that this information supports a need for multiple-channel presentations, especially when resources do not permit developing for specific learner types. Severin (1967a) makes the following predictions based on research comparing single-channel communication and multiple-channel communication. Multiple-channel presentations, which combine words and relevant visuals across channels, will be the most effective and superior to single-channels alone. This is due to cue summation across the channels. Multiple-channel communication with unrelated cues across both channels will cause interference and thus single channel presentations will be superior. Single-channel communication will be as effective as multiple-channel presentations when words (aurally and visually) are combined across channels.

Whether one subscribes to Severin's (1967) theory of using related multiple-channel communications or the more generally held notion of using redundant information (Hsia, 1968), there is a considerable body of research supporting combined presentations (Levie & Lentz, 1982). From a review of over 155 experiments, Levie and Lentz suggest that using attention-getting pictorials increases the possibility that material will be looked at, using text-redundant illustrations will facilitate learning of the textual material, illustrations will help learners understand and remember readings, learners often need prompting to pay attention to critical information found in illustrations, learners' enjoyment and affective reactions may be evoked by illustrations, poor readers may benefit from illustrations, and learner-generated imaginal pictures are generally less useful than supplied illustrations.

Supporting both cue summation and stimulus generalization were two studies by Beck (1987). His findings indicated that labeled pictures used during instruction provided more effective encoding cues than arrowed or noncued pictures. During evaluation, the repetition of identical cues appeared to assist learners in retrieving critical information. Mayer (1989) also found evidence that the use of labeled illustrations helped students with limited prior knowledge of mechanical systems recall more explanative information and perform better on problem-solving transfer. He suggested that a meaningful learning model using illustrations helps focus attention on explanative textual information and assimilate the information into useful mental models. Similarly, Rigney and Lutz (1976) found that the addition of images significantly improved learning of complex concepts. Students also found the graphics versions to be more enjoyable. The enjoyment, it appears, increases involvement so those students may acquire concepts from verbal instructional materials. Their research also supports Levie and Lentz's (1982) findings that supplied illustrations are better than user-generated imaginal pictures.

Mayer and Gallini (1990) tested two major features of illustrations that would assist learners in building mental models: system topology and component behavior. The former portrays each major system component; the latter portrays state changes in major components and the relationships of the components as the system functions. An example is the major components of a braking system and the changes each component undergoes in relation to the others as the system is employed. Findings supported their hypothesis that these illustrations would assist explanative recall and improve creative problem solving for low prior knowledge learners.

Mayer and Anderson (1991) extended previous research (Mayer, 1989; Mayer & Gallini, 1990) by using voice narration and animation. Although inconclusive, the results supported the theory that coordinated presentation of narrative and visuals (animation) results in better performance on tests of creative problem solving than presentation of the word before pictures. This research on integrated dual coding was adapted from Paivio's (1971) dual-code hypothesis. This extended theory posits that learners can build both visual and verbal representations as well as connections between them. Significant for designers was the finding that animation without narration had about the same effect as no instruction. Further, presenting unconnected words and pictures is not as useful as presenting coordinated verbal narration simultaneously with animation.

Reynolds and Baker (1987) were interested in the notion of selective attention and its influence on using text and graphical representations. They found that texts with graphs and texts without graphs did not differ in amounts of learning. Presenting materials on a computer, however, did increase attention and learning. Further, that interactive, graphical representation increased attention. The amount learned, although not significant, did show an increase. Their research suggested that when attention was increased, so was the amount of learning.

As noted earlier, questions over the superiority of individual channels have intrigued researchers for years. Conflicting results can be found that favor either channel. Katz and Deutsch (1963) and Travers (1964), for example, reported results that supported the visual channel over the auditory channel. However, Carterette and Jones (1967), Hartman (1961a, 1961b), Henneman (1952), and Mowbray (1952) determined that auditory presentations were superior for young children and had more resistance to interference. Other researchers (Beagles-Roos & Gat, 1983; Meringoff, 1980) found that recall by children is comparable for visual and auditory modalities. However, Hayes, Kelly, and Mandel (1986) disagree and feel verbal information recalled was incidental to the central plot of a televised program. Mudd and McCormick (1960) reported that provided that the information is related, auditory cues of various dimensions appreciably decrease the time involved in a visual search task. Warshaw (1978) reported on a series of experiments where subjects were shown commercials with various juxtapositioning of different levels of audio and video information. He reported that when auditory information was presented without background video (a blank screen), more content was recalled than when audio appeared simultaneously with relevant video, regardless of the level of information content in the second channel. Warshaw continued and stated that multiple-channel presentations do attract more attention than either channel alone, but perceptual interference across multiplechannels will hamper assimilation of the content.

Other studies (supporting the single-channel, nervous system theory; Broadbent, 1958) found no difference between modalities (Baker & Alluisi 1962; Hill & Hecher, 1966). Lorch, Bellock, and Augsback (1987) also noted, in televised presentations, that children's recall of "central" content was comparable to audio only, visual only, or simultaneous across both modes. Grimes (1991) continued, that in studies conducted with television where two channels—audio and visual—are highly redundant, people view the two channels as components of a single message. In a medium-redundancy situation, attention was shifted away from the visual channel and more attention was applied to the auditory channel. He reported contradictory results for a nonredundant presentation; in one study the group attended to the video, and in another study they did not. However, in the two experiments with nonredundant presentations, viewers' memory dropped for auditory messages and suggested low visual attention but high visual memory.

Another area very closely akin to the theoretical base of multiple-channel research is multiple external representations (MERs). Students are given more than one representation (usually visual and words) for the same concept or idea. Moving from one representation of a concept to another is neither automatic nor intuitive. Students do have the opportunity to *see* a concept from a different visual perspective or a different organizational pattern. Ainsworth (1999) suggests a speculative taxonomy for the study and design of multiple external representations.

Ainsworth (1999) asserts that the concept of multimedia and multirepresentational learning environments are essentially the same. The reasons for using MERs are to increase learner's interest and to promote effective learning. The use of such multirepresentational learning environments appear to becoming more widespread but research ". . . has produced mixed results and implies a degree of caution in their use" (p. 132). Research finds that learners have difficulty in translating information from one representation to another and making links across multiple representations is not automatic (Schoenfeld, Smith, & Arcavi, 1993; Yerushalmy, 1991). Ainsworth (1999) argues that MERs must be used for specific purposes, and the failure to take this into account explains some of the conflicting research studies. The specific functions for MERs need to be categorized. Ainsworth (1999) proposes a taxonomy consisting of three separate functions: (a) to support complementary processes and information, (b) to constrain interpretations, and (c) to provide for deeper understandings. Identifying these functions that MERs play should allow the opportunity for learning goals to be supported. Function a means providing alternative representations, which present a different view and different strategies for solving or presenting a problem. This function is supportive and explains the same solutions in a different ways. Constraining interpretations (function b) can be seen as "the more that the format and operators of two representations differ, the harder it will be for the learner the appreciate the relations between them" (p. 147). Function c is when the purpose is to develop a deeper understanding of the situation. These can be done through abstracting, generalizing, or teaching the relationship between the two representations (see also Trepanier-Street, 2000). Ainsworth (1999) suggests that if MERs are designed to support concepts or information, then the relationships should be evident; if they are designed to constrain interpretations, then the relationships should be automatic; if they are to develop deeper understanding, then the relationships should be scaffolded or addative.

36.5 MULTI-IMAGE PRESENTATIONS

The concept of multi-image is closely akin to properties of cue summation research, which suggests increased learning from more cues within a single channel or using more cues across (multiple) channels. Multi-image research was very popular in the 1960s and 1970s. The multi-image format in these earlier studies generally referred to the use of more than one image, with or without audio synchronization, on single- or multiple-projection screens. Millard (1964) stated that simultaneous images can be used advantageously in instructional situations that require comparisons, the development of interrelated concepts, illustrations, of relationships, or the presentation of dimensional and spatial characteristics of objects. Perrin's (1969) theory of using multi-images is based on the simultaneous presentation of images in which images interact; this may be of significance in making comparisons and establishing relationships. Film, slides, television, etc. (not current interactive multimedia formats), presented content and images in a sequential, linear format; the meaning was based on the context (content that preceded) of the image. However, multi-image, as Perrin states, allows ". . . the viewer to process larger amounts of information in a very short time. Thus information density is effectively increased, and certain kinds of information are more efficiently learned" (p. 369). However, questions raised earlier by Hartman (1961), Hsia (1971), and others concerning the efficacy of simultaneously presenting information across (and within) channels also apply to the concept of multi-image presentations.

Burke and Leps (1989) indicated that there might have been a *failure* by multiple image enthusiasts to prove its effectiveness. Multi-image, like other specific technologies, has always had to use traditional media comparison studies, with their inherent problems. Fradkin (1974, 1976) noted that although there was wide use of multi-image in education, there was little empirical evidence in support of increased learning. Moreover, Burke and Leps (1989) note that little research on multi-image presentations has investigated the validity of aspects of Perrin's theory and that many studies of multiple-image presentations have been limited to self-serving individuals involved in the hardware and production processes.

All of these instructional situations require association, which, according to Gagné (1965), is one of the basic mechanisms of learning. According to Perrin (1969), the number of instances available to the viewer to make associations by visual comparison is greater with simultaneously presented

images than with sequentially presented images. Low (1968) pointed out that in single-image presentations one image follows another, thus determining the interrelationships between images. In multiple-image presentations, several images appear simultaneously and "interact upon each other *at the same time,* and this is of significant value in making comparisons and relationships" (Perrin, 1969, p. 90).

Perrin (1969) stressed that images are especially rich in information and in the range of associations they stimulate. Without careful control by the communicator, there is the possibility that some associations can conflict with the intended message, causing interference. Relevance, realism, and simplicity have been found to be important in learning from book illustrations (Spaulding, 1956) and in learning from films (May & Lumsdaine, 1958). These factors are equally important in presentations utilizing multiple-imagery (Perrin, 1969). A viewer's ability to determine relationships between images has an effect on memory and recall (Berger, 1973; Low, 1968). Low stated that no single image can establish certain memory combinations, but a group of images perceived simultaneously often recalls long forgotten memories. Berger (1973) found that multi-image techniques are effective in expediting the recall of events and thought-feeling associations in analytic psychology. The recall of memories and of events attributed to simultaneous images may be a function of viewers' freedom to select their own sequence (Bruner, 1967; Gagné & Briggs, 1974). Therefore, as Perrin (1969) pointed out, presenting images simultaneously and allowing viewers to select their own sequential order may have an effect on the learning taking place. Roshka (1960), Malandin (cited in Perrin, 1969), and Allen and Cooney (1963) found simultaneous presentation of images effective in instruction with younger children. Roshka (1960) found that simultaneous images had less effect with older children, and Allen and Cooney (1963) stated that simultaneous images had a significant effect on learning of sixth graders but not eighth graders. Malandin (cited in Perrin, 1969) found that primary classes had difficulty with recall from sequential images but that grouping the images permitted an increase in the number of recollections and organization of the recollections. These studies support Perrin's (1969) view that image simultaneity is a significant factor in some learning situations. Beck (1983), in a study, that supported Perrin's views, found that subjects exposed to simultaneous picture formats achieved significantly higher scores than subjects exposed to successive (linear) formats. Goldstein (1975) stated that the simultaneous presentation of multiple images is in many respects "like the environment, it contains meaningful material, it surrounds us, and it is constantly changing" (p. 63).

A caution that emerges from the literature concerning the simultaneity of multiple images is that the theory of cue summation may not be valid in some contexts. (Recall that cue summation, as noted earlier, is the general theory positing that the more cues that are given through various communications channels, the more learning occurs [Whitley, 1977].) Perrin (1969) notes that the use of simultaneous multiple images places a burden on the visual channel and that, in the multiplication of visual stimuli, irrelevant as well as relevant detail is increased. Therefore, care must be taken to assure that the visual stimuli are clear and simple and that detail included is relevant.

Otherwise the result is not cue summation, but confusion. A study by Fradkin and Meyrowitz (1975) supports this hypothesis that cue summation and the avoidance of conflicting cues are important in the design of multiple-image presentations produced for cognitive learning situations.

36.5.1 Screen Size

The use of a large screen coupled with the simultaneous projection of two or more images has been cited as one of the major, inherent advantages of multiple-imagery. A large screen provides better approximations of *real* environments by supplying the physical and psychological factors necessary for realism and involvement (Perrin, 1969).

Blackwell (1968) indicated that tasks requiring high visual acuity, such as detecting differences in texture or patterns, might benefit from the use of large screen presentations. Schlanger (1966) identified two factors affecting usefulness of large screens: visual impact and visual task. Visual impact is the amount and forcefulness of information available to the sense of sight. The visual impact is proportional to the amount of the viewer's field of view that the screen occupies. According to Blackwell, visual impact on the viewer is greater in large screen presentations because more of the viewer's field of vision is occupied by the projected image—therefore limiting the chance of distraction from the surrounding environment. Schlanger stated that large screens can produce information rich in detail for the visual channel and simulate real environments, but Blackwell warned that any channel of communication loaded with information details might be distracting if the details are irrelevant to the learning situation. Travers (1966), in attempting to deal with excess details, hypothesized that line drawings would be advantageous because they eliminated superfluous detail. His experiments with oversimplified drawings, however, indicate poor transfer of learning to real situations. Blackwell stated that the advantage of a large screen to reduce the visual task factor is conditional. Presented images, for example, must contain enough irrelevant detail to convey the proper message (which may not have been the situation in Travers' experiments) but not so much detail as to distract learners. Barr (1963) stated that a large screen opens up the frame and gives a greater sense of continuous space. The more open the frame, the greater the impression of depth; the image is more vivid. This suggests simultaneous images produce an increase in information density during presentations.

36.5.2 Information Density

A higher density of information is possible with multiple than with linear imagery. There are several dimensions to information density in multiple-image presentations (Whitley, 1977). Perrin (1969) believes that it is important to distinguish between the method of presentation and the mechanism of perception. He states that the theory of multiple images suggests that for making contrasts and comparisons, and for learning relationships, "simultaneous images reduce the task of memory (a dimension of visual task) and enable the viewer to make immediate comparisons" (p. 376).

Langer (1957) utilizes the terms *linear* and *nonlinear* to distinguish between verbal and iconic signs. She stresses the sequential ordering, the *strung-out* arrangement of linear (verbal) signs in time and contrasts this with the *all-at-once* (parallel) character inherent in pictorial signs (p. 83). Her position is that even single pictures shown in sequential order are essentially nonlinear (Whitley, 1977).

Nonlinearity and simultaneity go hand in hand. The use of visual images, inherently nonlinear, allows the presentation of a great deal of information simultaneously rather than sequentially, as with words arranged in sentences and thus bound to grammatical ordering and syntax. Perrin (1969) expands this line of analysis and hypothesizes that when visual images are combined in multi-image presentations, the result is an increase in the amount of information that is presented simultaneously or in the information density of the presentation.

Information density can be increased further if the information is organized properly (Whitley, 1977). McFee (1969) believes that visual organization is more important than the actual amount of information present. Much of our responding occurs so quickly that we are unaware of our own processing. Selecting and organizing visuals in advance make the information easier to assimilate for the user (p. 85).

Investigative confirmation of the importance of organization is illustrated by the introduction of a carefully organized and automated televised instructional system called TeleMation at the University of Wisconsin. Hubbard found (1961) that information density could be increased significantly through proper organization without loss of material or loss of learning by students. A similar finding resulted when the Army Ordinance Guided Missile School conducted a series of evaluative studies in 1958 (U.S. Army, 1959). Instruction time was reduced 19.5% to 41% for a similar level of achievement, and an increase in learning was reported for the experimental groups 9 weeks later. Allen and Cooney (1963), however, suggested that time saved in instruction was as much a function of care in preparation as it was a function of the multi-imaged delivery of the subject matter.

Commercial producers claim that information density created through multiple-imagery results in motivation and arousal. A serious question is whether or not this arousal is beneficial (Whitley, 1977). Research on motivation indicates that an increase in motivation improves performance (R. L. Smith, 1966) but that there is an optimum level. Eysenck (1963) found that for complex tasks, optimum performance is achieved when the drive is relatively low; only for simple tasks is the optimum achieved with a relatively high drive. Kleinsmith and Kaplan (1963, 1964) and Kleinsmith, Kaplan, and Tarte (1963) found that there is some confusion between learning and performance, with individuals sometimes performing very poorly in highly arousing situations, yet tending to remember most vividly those incidents in their lives that were most traumatic or arousing. These researchers measured skin conductivity, and their findings indicated that high-arousal associates showed stronger permanent memory and weaker immediate memory than low-arousal associates did. Low arousal was accompanied by the normal forgetting curve. High-arousal subjects showed poor immediate recall. This may explain some inconsistencies in research with regard to long-term retention. For example, Vander-Meer (1951) found that color films did not increase immediate learning but produced greater long-term retention. The findings of Kleinsmith suggest that the cause may have been the arousal produced by the color films.

Fleisher (1969) stated that the mind and eye have proven to be capable of tremendous speed and versatility in accepting multiple impressions and that during a multi-image presentation the viewer's eyes explore the entire screen and keep the viewer very conscious of what is happening. In contrast, Goldstein (1975) indicated that multi-image presentation might cause information overload by presenting more information than the viewer can process and thus create arousal through frustration. This arousal may cause multi-image presentations to be highly motivating but not very informative (Kreszock, 1981). Goldstein stated that when presenting specific concepts or highly technical information, multi-image presentations should be used with restraint. Perrin (1969) concluded that it is clear that high densities of information can be *perceived* during a multi-image presentation, but he went on to question whether great amounts of information were *learned* from these perceptions.

Several studies have compared different aspects of single-image and multi-image presentations. Lombard (1969) used both a single-image and a multi-image format to teach synthesis skills in history to eleventh-grade students. He found no significant differences in males between the single-image and the multi-image presentations at any achievement level, and the only female group to demonstrate any significant difference were the low achievers. These low-achieving females who received the multi-image presentations surpassed both the males and the females in the average and high-achieving groups that received the single-image format. Some of the procedures used in Lombard's study, however, make his findings dubious.

Conducting a study to explore the affective impact of multi-image presentations, Bollman (1970) experimented to see if there was any difference in the amount of shift in evaluative meaning of audiences viewing multi-image presentations versus audiences viewing single-image presentations and to ascertain if the person's relationship to the screen had any effect on shifts in evaluative meaning. In his conclusions, Bollman stated that this experiment did not produce significant statistical evidence or conclusive answers.

Atherton (1971) conducted a study to determine if a multi-image slide presentation would result in greater affective and cognitive learning than similar content presented by a 16-mm film. No significant differences were found between groups in the amount of attitudinal change elicited as a result of the presentation or between treatment of groups relative to the cognitive learning resulting from viewing the presentations. These analyses indicated that one treatment was not more effective (or even affective) than the other in producing positive increases in affective or cognitive learning (Atherton, 1971). Didcoct (1958) conducted a study of the cognitive and affective responses of college students to single-image and multi-image presentations. He found no difference in attitude or cognitive retention between a group viewing a single-image presentation and a group viewing a multi-image presentation.

Westwater (1972), in conducting a descriptive study to gather information about the field use of a multi-image presentation, found that about 80% of the teachers who participated in the study would like to use such presentations to a greater degree. Westwater, however, pointed out two major limitations to the development of multi-image presentations: Few teachers were familiar with the characteristics and capabilities of large multi-image presentations, and there was a lack of knowledge concerning their utility.

Jonassen (1979) states that it is generally believed that research on multi-image presentation revolves around linear vs. simultaneous presentation factors. Using Perrin's (1969) theory, most researchers predict that learning will increase (however that is measured) when "the viewer makes his own montage of different image elements, increasing the probability of learning comparative information" (p. 369). Jonassen indicates that the mere presentation of simultaneous images do not necessarily lead to simultaneous mental processing. The viewer still must provide a cognitive strategy for processing and making sense of the presentation order. Just as linear sequenced material must be processed based on content and syntactic associations, so must multi-image presentations. Jonassen finds that the literature on multi-image (simultaneous) presentations has yielded contradictory results. He feels that incomplete questions were asked in the research hypothesis instead of just asking about linearity vs. simultaneity. Researchers should consider "how simultaneous images can best be structured to facilitate specific types of learning behavior" (p. 292). Jonassen continues by indicating that proponents have assumed that multi-image presentations are a unique form of communication. Multi-imagery is *not a medium;* it is a presentation mode that can manipulate visual perception. Therefore, study of multi-image presentations should be based on established principles of concept learning. To date, little research in this area has been conducted with concept teaching in mind. An exception would be the study conducted by Whitley and Moore (1979), which found a significant interaction between a student perceptual type (visual vs. haptics) and presentation mode (linear vs. simultaneous). Haptics scored higher with multi-image presentations. Another exception was completed by Ausburn (1975), who found that both haptics and visuals benefited from multi-image presentations.

Burke and Leps (1989), gleaning information from the limited (and possibility flawed) research on multi-image presentations, feel that multi-imagery as a concept offers little to learners to improve cognitive potential or *affective impact.* This is due to conceptually weak studies. The limited number of reviews concerning multiple-image research (Allen & Cooney, 1964; Burke, 1987; Burke & Leps, 1989) has revealed few usable results. There is, of course, the seemingly ever-present problem of research design and implications. These basic problems included retention studies comparing single-images and multiple-image presentations, which were flawed by the presence of unnecessary recall data in both sound tracks. In addition, " the comparisons were usually of single and multiple-screen versions of the same material, thereby canceling out Perrin's theoretical call for multi-image to enhance a basic message" (Burke & Leps, 1989, p. 185). Burke and Leps, however, feel that multi-image presentations were given little opportunity to prove themselves due to cost and technical execution of the presentations.

36.6 SUBLIMINAL PERCEPTION AND INSTRUCTION

Subliminal perception refers to visual and auditory information presented at a speed and or intensity that is below the conscious threshold of perception through one or more channels and thus not readily apparent to the person (Moore, 1982). Subliminal perception, like multi-image presentations, is closely related to the theoretical bases of cue summation and multiple-channel research. All are interested in providing the learner with the maximum amount of usable cues, with the idea that these cues will support and reinforce each other. This is similar to multiple-channel theory, which suggests that additional simultaneous cues within and across sensory channels provide greater reinforcement in organizing and structuring information.

Experiments using subliminal exposure to visual and audio stimuli have been reported in psychological journals since 1863 (*Application of Subliminal Perception in Advertising*, 1958). Reviews of experimentation in subliminal perception have contributed summaries of various points of view. Three excellent sources on the subject were published by Miller (1942), Adams (1957), and McConnell, Cutler, and McNeil (1958). All three sources indicate that research results have differed widely (DeChenne, 1975).

In reviewing three summaries of research on subliminal perception (Bevan, 1964; Dixon, 1971; McConnell et al., 1958), several generalizations become apparent. Susceptibility to subliminal stimulation varies among people and is dependent on factors such as anxiety, attentiveness, and need state. Sensitivity to subliminal effects tends to be cumulative, as repeated viewing of subliminal materials tend to make a person more aware of the technique. Differences in awareness thresholds also determine whether subliminal messages are perceived. Perception thresholds can be lowered if the duration of the subliminal exposure increases or if the message is of a different brightness than the surrounding visual field. In other words, the closer the material is to being consciously visible, the more likely it is to be perceived (Moore, 1982).

Early experiments were designed to provide evidence that the psychological phenomenon of subliminal perception was a reality. Hollingworth (1919) reported one of the earliest of these experiments. Others include experiments by Maker (1937), Coyne, King, Zubin, and Landis (1943), McGinnus (1949), Lazarus and McClearey (1951), and Wilcot (1953). All except Wilcot reported results that there had been definite unconscious recognition or influence by stimuli below the conscious threshold. These studies gained attention for the concept of subliminal perception but brought about additional research that was often inconclusive and contradictory (Moore, 1982). More recent experiments have focused on determining relationships between subliminal perception and behavior. Studies of this type include those by Klein, Spence, Holt, and Gourevtich (1958) and G. J. W.

Smith, Spence, and Klein (1959), both of which reported tendencies of a positive nature concerning the effectiveness of subliminal perception.

Several studies have been conducted to determine whether subliminal shapes or words could be detected when superimposed on a still or moving picture. One method of operationalizing subliminal stimulation is to superimpose a message at a very low relative brightness for a long period of time. DeFleur and Petranoff (1959) used this method in one of the first studies of subliminal perception using television as a carrier medium. The subliminal material in this experiment was superimposed as an extremely faint image relative to the main program. Analysis of the results indicated that significantly more correct guesses had occurred than would have been expected by chance. It was not reported if the participants were asked whether they had consciously seen any of the shapes during the film. Nevertheless, the results seemed to indicate that TV images of extremely low brightness influenced their responses.

Moore (1982) commented that the low-intensity, constant-image technique that used by DeFleur and Petranoff could result in the subliminal image being consciously visible. Because the visual field of the motion picture was dynamic (the images moved and changed), the faint subliminal words or shapes that were on the screen may have become partially unmasked at times as the foreground images changed. For example, if the constantly superimposed, subliminal images were white and the foreground images (the motion picture) in the same area of the screen were momentarily dark, then the resulting contrast differences may have been sufficient to unmask and reveal the subliminal word or shape or an identifiable segment of it. If the superimposed words or shapes were flashed quickly rather than exposed constantly, then the visual threshold of viewers would remain higher and the images would more likely remain subliminal (Moore).

Several other researchers have reported similar experiments. In these experiments, the subliminal shapes or words were non-moving images on a neutral background, compared to the moving foreground images used by DeFleur and Petranoff (1959). Schiff (1961) and King, Landis, and Zubin (1944) reported positive results, whereas Calvin and Dollenmayer (1959) and Champion and Turner (1959) concluded that there was no definitive evidence that behavior was altered by subliminal presentations. The relationship between subliminal stimulation and cognitive functions has been studied in a number of experiments. Kolars (1957) (two studies) and Gerard (1960) used a problem-solving task in which rows of geometric figures were presented simultaneously by a tachistoscope. Kolars concluded that the presentations of subliminal stimuli did influence the frequency of correct answers in both studies. Gerard tested participants' ability to mentally reconstruct a composite, geometric figure into alternative assemblies. One group saw the correct solution, another group saw an incorrect solution, and the control group saw no subliminal solution.

The results indicated that the control group did better than either of the subliminal treatment groups. However, the group shown the correct answers did better than the group shown the incorrect answers, as hypothesized. Gerard's results partially confirmed Kolers' findings, however, that subliminal presentations could affect performance on problem solving tests (DeChenne, 1975; Moore, 1982; Moore & Moore, 1984).

The research described above (Calvin & Dollenmayer, 1959; DeFleur & Petranoff, 1959; Gerald, 1960; Kolers, 1957) indicates that subliminal perception can occur among certain people in laboratory settings. In contrast to Murch (1965) and Sharp (1959), who demonstrated that choice behavior could be altered in a test-taking situation, the experiments of DeChenne (1975), Skinner (1969), and Taris (1970) failed to demonstrate that direct teaching by subliminal perception can occur. Although various laboratory experiments have produced evidence that subliminal perception can occur, field experiments conducted to test direct teaching by subliminal perception have not yielded collaborative results.

Moore (1982) contends that when teaching by a subliminal means under conditions when the subject matter to be taught is transmitted with films that are unrelated and/or irrelevant to the subject matter, the possibility for content interference is great and the lack of conductive and focused learning setting would seem to hinder learning further. "Expecting subliminally produced learning to occur now seems less realistic than expecting a classroom teacher to teach while students are watching an Abbott and Costello comedy" (pp. 19–20).

A number of studies investigated the possibilities that motivation might be influenced by subliminal perception. Among these were studies by Byrne (1959) and Goldstein and Davis (1961), whose results indicated no influence on the subjects. Goldstein and Barthal (1968) and Zuckerman (1960) conducted studies to determine whether subliminal stimulation could influence elaborative thinking. In both studies positive and negative words were subliminally flashed with pictures from the Thematic-Apperception Test. Both studies reported contradictory results when participants were asked to create and elaborate on stories and the amount written as directed in the subliminal constructions. Shevrin and Luborsky (1958) and Johnson and Erikson (1961) reported similar results to support their theory that there was a tendency for tachiscopically presented material to appear in daydreams and dreams.

In addition to content reinforcement, Moore (1982) asked what effect individual cognitive style differences may have on learning from subliminal media treatments. Most early subliminal perception research limited consideration of individual participant differences to sex, race, and IQ. Other (undetected) differences in sample populations might explain why many replication attempts have failed to confirm original findings and why many findings are contradictory. In a review of subliminal research, McConnell et al. (1958) stated that individual differences "must be taken into account by anyone who wishes to deal with individuals. It is quite likely that many differences in the perception of subliminal stimuli do exist between individuals of differing classes, ages, and sexes" (p. 236). Allison (1963), Murch (1965), and Sackeim, Packer, and Gur (1977) have shown that individual differences such as thought strategies, cognitive set, and hemisphericity were related to susceptibility to subliminal stimulation. DeChenne (1975) and Skinner (1969) did not collect data on individual differences in learning styles or abilities within their samples. This would have made detecting the effect of the treatment more difficult if aptitude–treatment

interaction effects were occurring, as the slight increase in treatment effectiveness in these two studies may indicate. The term *individual differences* is also associated with the concept of cognitive styles.

Past studies questioned whether subliminal perception could be a useful tool for producers of educational television and explored the feasibility of teaching one topic while students were watching a program unrelated in content (DeChenne, 1975; Skinner, 1969; Taris, 1970). The results indicated that subliminal messages were generally not powerful enough to cause learning when students were concentrating on an unrelated topic. In other words, it is unrealistic for educational producers to expect that students could be taught two topics simultaneously, one through normal channels and the other through subliminal perception (Moore, 1982; Moore & Moore, 1984). However, there was some evidence (DeChenne, 1975) that some students seeing subliminal cues performed better on a criterion task. This suggested that individual differences such as intelligence or perceptual abilities may be related to the ability to profit from subliminal messages implanted in a television program. This is generally consistent with Calvin and Dollenmayer (1959), Gerard (1960), Murch (1965), and Sharp (1959).

The properties of visual subliminal messages include being faintly and quickly embedded within a surrounding visual field. A student's ability to profit from subliminal messages could be related to the ability to dissembe the message from the surrounding television picture. Therefore, it was thought that the cognitive style of field dependence might have some relationship to the potential usefulness of subliminal perception. People have different ways of perceiving their environment, and these differences may have been associated with the differences in subliminal learning seen in various studies (Calvin & Dollenmayer, 1959; DeChenne, 1975; Gerard, 1960; Kolers, 1957). Based on the literature, it also could be expected that field-independent individuals, because they have highly developed skills at dissembedding one object or image from a surrounding array of objects or images, should likewise be able to distinguish the embedded subliminal messages in a television picture (Greco & McClung, 1979; Hessler, 1972). The real benefit in learning, however, could occur for those students who are field dependent, as they typically benefit from more salient content organization cues (Witkin, Moore, Goodenough, & Cox, 1977). Thus, the use of subliminal reinforcement cues (captions) could be of most value to field-dependent students, because the captions would supplant students' reduced ability to distinguish between relevant and nonrelevant cues and would make the relevant cues more salient.

In Moore's (1982) experiment, these differences in cognitive style were studied as a possible intervening factor for consideration in the production and utilization of subliminal materials. In the analysis of data, it was found that students having prior experience with the subject matter, such as in a previous course, averaged highest on the recall test, as one would execute. These students were eliminated from subsequent analysis, as their prior knowledge may have reflected outside influence.

The available experiments and observations on subliminal perception seem to indicate that in certain instances human subjects are capable of responding to audio and visual stimuli that are so weak in duration, intensity, or clarity that they are not consciously aware of them. Researchers have varying opinions as to the effectiveness of subliminal stimulation and there is no conclusive evidence as to its ineffectiveness or effectiveness. However, the body of evidence does indicate that, effective or not, there is perception below the threshold of awareness (DeChenne, 1975). There appear to be major concerns, however, involved in determining the amount of information a human can process at any one time. To recognize information simultaneously, the various receptors (eyes, ears) would have to analyze a great variety of different cues. All the findings noted in the previous sections, e.g., multiple-channel, communication, multi-imagery, and subliminal perception, have import to the design of multimedia presentations. Basic decisions have to be made to determine concerning how the presentation is to be developed, the number of cues to be available, and the number of channels to be used.

36.7 MULTIMEDIA RESEARCH

Technology does not stand still. As the debate as to the efficacy of technology's impact on learning continues, microcomputers become more powerful and flexible. Compared to the first microcomputers, today's classroom machines can have easily thousands of times the amount of internal memory. Audio and visual capabilities will soon exceed those of today's television, and auxiliary storage will soon be practically unlimited (Moore et al., 1994). Because of these (and related technological advances in software), everyday users, and most particularly educators, have access to systems called multimedia and hypermedia. Yet the development of the interactive technologies that we now call multimedia has not been without controversy or unfulfilled promises (Gleason, 1991).

Although the concept of multimedia has been present for a long time, educators and the technology industry cannot decide exactly what the concept of multimedia includes (Strommen & Revelle, 1990). Until recently, the term has meant the use of several media devices, sometimes in a coordinated fashion (e.g., synchronized slides with audio tape) Advances in technology, however, have combined these media so that information previously delivered by several devices is now integrated into one device (Kozma, 1991, p. 199). The computer now plays a central organizing role in this environment. Questions remain. For example, does multimedia include, interactive video, CDI, and DVI as well as traditional slide shows supplemented by sound and many other media formats?

The most commonly accepted definition of multimedia appears to support the concept of computer-driven interactivity with the learner's ability to determine and control the sequence and content selection. Matchett and Elliott (1991) argue that interactive multimedia should include motion, voice plus data, text, and graphic and still images. This definition permits multimedia to *absorb* the historically older and somewhat broader notion of hypermedia—which is discussed in more detail later. As such, interactive video is a *high-bandwidth* source in the sense that a great deal of information, in many modes, or channels, is available at once (i.e., parallel fashion). DeBloois (1982)

indicates that "it is important to realize that interactive video (multimedia) is not merely a merging of video and computer mediums; it is an entirely new media with characteristics quite unlike each of the composites" (p. 33). The attraction of interactive multimedia is that it includes two of the more powerful educational technologies: the computer and video. Unlike some of the earlier linear technologies that allowed the user to remain passive, the new interactive programs not only allow viewers to become involved but demand it (Gleason, 1991). By doing so, these technologies have closed the gap between learner control and learning styles in some of the earlier theories. Interactive multimedia allows the user to see, hear, and do.

Others attempt more elaborate definitions of multimedia, especially as it pertains to its role in learning (K. Smith, 2001). Mayer (2001) defines three ways in which multimedia can be viewed: based on the delivery media, the presentation modes, and the sensory modalities involved in the process of receiving instructional messages. The delivery media view focuses on the physical system used to deliver the information. The combinations of two or more delivery devices comprise a multimedia system. Mayer (2001) rejects this view because the focus is on technology rather than on the learner. The presentation mode view focuses the combination of technologies, e.g., sound and image. This view became more learner centered based on a cognitive theory that assumes that learners have separate information processing channels (Paivio, 1971). The third view, the sensory modality view, focuses on the sensory receptor that the learner uses to perceive the material. Examples of this type of view include the use of animation, which can be perceived visually along with narration. This view became more learner centered because it takes into account the learner's information processing activity (Mayer, 2001). Through this mix of presentation techniques, interactive multimedia can appeal to learners who prefer to receive information by reading, those who learn best through hearing and those who prefer hands-on environments (Moore et al., 1994).

36.7.1 Multimedia

Research concerning the learning impact of this medium is still sketchy. Its potential is important because it can combine all the symbol systems discussed above. An important distinction in this medium, however, is that the computer controls the use of the various system states. Distinct potential advantages accrue when using this media-rich environment. The learner can develop pattern recognition skills from the video and access information (in all modes) in a random manner. The latter capability takes the learner out of the traditional sequential environment and into one in which he or she can explore the domain from multiple perspectives (Cognition and Technology Group at Vanderbilt, 1990). Using interactive videodisc, the learner can be placed into contexts that simulate the *real world*. This type of learning has been referred to as *situated cognition* (Brown, Collins, & Duguid, 1989) because the information learned is tied to retrieval cues in the environments it will be needed.

An excellent example of situated cognition is the *anchored instruction work* done by the Cognition and Technology Group at Vanderbilt (1990). They believed that young students learn better in meaningful, socially organized contexts. Their research indicated that problem-oriented approaches are more effective than fact-oriented approaches in overcoming inert knowledge (knowledge people know but often fail to use in problem-solving situations). The methodology is designed to help students develop rich mental models as the basis for future learning, create environments that permit sustained exploration by students and teachers, help students explore the domain from multiple perspectives, and develop integrated knowledge structures that help students transfer knowledge to more complex tasks. (It should be noted that the preceding comments are speculative and are not confirmed by direct research.).

36.7.2 Hypermedia

This technology parallels mental models by permitting associations or links among various ideas to be formed, then constructing meaning among these relationships (Kozma, 1991). Research suggests that a number of concepts can be explored by using hypermedia's cognitive flexibility. For example, users might be interested in pursuing information about land navigation. Searching in this area might turn up information about magnetic principles, topography, uses of the compass, terrain orientation, the coordinate system, and celestial navigation. The learner could follow one or all of these links—all of which would provide further links. There might also be an opportunity to watch a video of participants engaged in the sport of orienteering or simulations using triangulation to determine location. Although research on hypermedia is in its infancy, the learner will have access to a multitude of information. This information will allow the formation (and tracking) of mental models or schemata on unlimited types of domains.

Kozma (1991) suggested that " various aspects of the learning process are influenced by cognitively relevant characteristics of media: their technologies, symbol systems, and processing capabilities" (p. 205). He also submits that learning is influenced by taking "... advantage of the medium's cognitively relevant capabilities to complement the learner's cognitive abilities and prior knowledge and cognitive skills" (p. 205). The discussion has considered basic cognitive learning theory and the dual-code theory, which links learning to the symbol systems inherent in multimedia. Also important is the strategy used by the instructional designer or teacher to take advantage of cognitive psychology in employing media. The discussion now turns to two approaches in which multimedia applications demonstrate the use of cognitive theory.

Liao (1999) conducted a metanalysis on 46 studies conducted from 1996 to 1998, which compared the effects of hypermedia versus nonhypermedia instruction. These studies came from computer searches of ERIC, Comprehensive Dissertation Abstracts, and bibliographies from review and computer searches. Liao noted that his findings acknowledge the concerns noted by Clark (1983) about the problems of comparison studies and suggested that Clark "might overlook the fact that certain media attributes make certain methods possible, particularly

when new technology such as hypermedia, is used as the delivery system" (p. 256).

Liao (1999) reported that in the 46 studies included in his metanalysis, 61% (28) favored hypermedia instruction (including interactive videos, computer simulations, and interactive multimedia) compared to nonhypermedia instruction (e.g., traditional instruction, computer-assisted instruction or videotapes). Thirty-seven percent of these comparison studies favored the nonhypermedia instruction groups and 2% found no differences in the two. Likewise, regarding the effect size of 143 comparisons within the 46 studies reviewed, 60% (86) were positive and favored the hypermedia instruction group, whereas 37% (53) were negative and favored the nonhypermedia instruction groups. Liao suggested that these results clearly indicated the positive effects of hypermedia instruction over nonhypermedia instruction and "should not be confused with the uncontrolled effects of instructional method noted by Clark" (p. 270). (Note: The authors of this chapter are still quite concerned about the reliability and validity of these *comparison studies,* Liao's earlier comments not withstanding. Moreover, Liao's type of interpretation is a good example of what Orey, Garrison, and Burton [1989] have described as accepting the null hypothesis but not embracing it as true. This situation creates some interesting assumptions between so-called *hard* and so-called *soft* sciences. For example, Meehl [1967] articulated that a major concern about social science research was the tendency to 'treat disconfirming instances with equal methodological respect as if one could, so to speak, 'count noses,' so that if a theory has somewhat more confirming instances it is in pretty good shape evidentially' [p.112].)

Tergan (1997) reviewed several empirical studies, conducted a theoretical analysis, and suggested that the literature made the following assumptions concerning hypertext and/or hypermedia research.

1. Structural and functional features of hypertext/hypermedia mimic the structure and function of the human mind (p. 258).
2. Hypermedia/hypertext match instructional principles for self-regulation and constructivist learning (p. 262).
3. Hypermedia/hypertext match cognitive principles of multiple modes for the mental representation of knowledge (p. 271).

Tergan's (1997) review indicated that research on multimedia has been based on technology rather than on new instructional concepts that use technology but are not driven by it. He continued that most multimedia research is not theoretically sound. Many cognitive theories do not cope with complex self-regulated hypermedia-based learning, because these theories have been misinterpreted, e.g., "like the constructivist principle which has conceptually been put on the same level with exploratory cognitive processing itself-regulated interactive learning" (p. 276). Knowledge acquisition and transfer to complex hypermedia environments have been overgeneralized. For instance, Tergan suggested that in the apparent match of the technical features of multimedia, neither theory nor empirical evidence matches the functions of the human mind (p. 262). His second review dealt with the assumption that hypermedia technical functions match the instructional function of self-regulation and constructivist learning. He concluded that hypermedia did not "induce incidentally efficient autonomous constructive cognitive processes," (p. 269). When positive results are reported, it is based on the learners themselves, independent of the hypermedia itself (see Dee-Lukas & Larkin, 1992; Jonassen & Wang, 1992; Jonassen, 1993). Only under conditions of "self-regulating competencies, well defined roles, and explicit scaffolding" are learners' cognitive processing functions supported by hypermedia structures (p. 269). (See also Rouet, 1992; Jonassen, 1993; and Jacobson, Maouri, Mishra, & Kolar, 1995.) Tergan's summary of the third assumption (that hypermedia functions match the multiple modes of mental representation of knowledge) concluded that these "theories based upon assumptions concerning possible additive and integrative effects of multimedia are underdetermined, because of possible interactions of psychologically relevant media with learner prerequisites, cognitive requirements of the task to be accomplished, and (the) constraints of instructional design are not taken into account" (p. 275). Also see Clark (1983).

36.7.3 Using the Evidence to Evaluate Multimedia Programs

Does multimedia really work? To answer this question, it is necessary to note some of the earlier-mentioned learning theories but also to note earlier media-related research. It may also be useful to differentiate between evaluation studies and research. Evaluation is practical and is concerned with how to improve a product or whether to buy/use a product. Studies that compare one program or media against another (or a control for that matter) are primarily evaluations. Evaluation seeks to find programs that *work* more cheaply, efficiently, quickly, and effectively. Research, on the other hand, tends to be more concerned with testing theoretical concepts and constructs or attempting to isolate variables to observe their contributions to a process or outcome. Having said this, we should point out that the two terms evaluation and research are often used interchangeably in the fields of education and media (Moore et al., 1994).

Multimedia is a combination of many technologies, most notably the computer, which allows for true interaction. Strommen and Revelle (1990) stress the importance of existing research literature on computer usage for understanding the pragmatic requirements of developing interactive tasks in the multimedia programs that were developed at the Children's Television Workshop. This literature helped "take children's special needs into account and . . . [delineate] what the content of our interactive tasks should be and how those tasks should be structured" (pp. 77–78).

E. E. Smith (1987) indicated that there are three major sectors in our society that use, and conduct research on the effects of interactive multimedia: the military, the industry, and education. Educational use of multimedia programs is still limited and, in most cases, still experimental. Two multimedia formats (videodisc and videotape) predominate in education. As you would expect, multimedia researchers are still debating their relative values and virtues (Smith, 1987). However, the

marketplace may decide the winner and DVI technologies such as CD-ROM and Quicktime may well settle the debate in a practical sense. Despite the short duration of multimedia's availability, Smith reports evidence for both the effectiveness and the efficiency of the interactive media in learning. Other researchers argue that there is little to support the contentions of the effectiveness of interactive media. They contend that little progress has been made since Clark (1983) argued that media in general have little substantial impact on learning (Hannafin, 1985; Slee, 1989). Hannafin (1985) asserts that although the interactive technology, as noted earlier, offers interesting potential, interactive video differs little from the allied technology from either *learning or cognitive perspectives*.

Ragan, Boyce, Redwine, Savenye, and McMichael (1993) summarized the findings of seven major reviews of research on multimedia. The 139 reviews were from a variety of settings, but the majority concerned adults. Among their (obviously not independent) findings were the following:

(1) multimedia is at least as effective as conventional forms and has substantial cost and efficiency, benefits
(2) frequently, multimedia instruction is more effective than conventional instruction, and
(3) multimedia is more efficient in terms of learning time than conventional instruction (30% savings).

Ragan et al. (1993) stated that they were unable to determine why multimedia was appreciably more effective than conventional instruction and cautioned that it would be inappropriate to say that multimedia is always the most effective delivery system. They suggested that certain instructional design features appear to enhance the quality of multimedia instruction. Among them are higher levels of interactivity, program or advised learner control, integration of multimedia with other delivery forms, and structured rather than totally exploratory learning.

P. L. Smith, Hsu, Azzarello, and McMichael (1993) reviewed 28 group-based multimedia studies. They indicate that group-based multimedia can be as effective as individualized multimedia, and it can be as effective as, or more so than, traditional forms of instruction. They also found that learners prefer group-based multimedia to individualized multimedia and traditional instruction. Again, Smith et al. stated that they were unable to predict what situations are appropriate for group-based multimedia and that it would be erroneous to that state group-based multimedia is always superior to traditional instruction or individualized multimedia.

Through hypermedia is relatively new, there are hundreds of reports and studies about its implementation. However, most of them deal with the excitement of adopting this new technology or envision its potentials in education (Yang, 1993). Only a few of these reports are experimental studies. In these limited studies, some positive results of using hypermedia have been reported. Abrams and Streit (1986) as well as Jones and Smith (1989) reported significant gains in learning achievement. Janda (1992) found a positive attitude toward the use of hypermedia systems. Higgins and Boone (1992) reported a decreased demand on teaching time. Hardiman and Williams (1990) noted that the completion rate of courses was increased with the use of hypermedia. Liu (1992) found that hypermedia was very effective in the teaching of English as a second language. In a review, E. E. Smith (1987) summarized the findings thus: "The effective evidence seems to indicate that the medium is both effective and efficient. . . " (p. 2). Thompson, Simonson, and Hargrave (1992) also suggested that hypermedia was promising in a learning context (Yang, 1993).

One of the more unique and interesting inquiries into the effects of multimedia was conducted by Gerlic and Jausovec (1999), who investigated the cognitive processes involved in multimedia (sound and video), text, and image-oriented presentations using electroencephalographic (EEG) measures. The results indicate that the multimedia (sound and video) and image presentations induced visualization strategies, whereas the text presentations generated mental processes related to verbal processing. This study has shown promise in employing methods developed in brain research and relating them to cognitive psychology.

From a review of research literature dealing with simulations, Reigeluth and Schwartz (1989) suggest 3-D simulation and video and graphics representation forms for physical movement procedures. Rieber (1990) cautions that special effects including animation and 3-D graphic displays should be used only if the learning tasks require them. Likewise Harrington and Oliver (1999) conducted a qualitative study describing students' use of higher-order thinking in an interactive multimedia program based on a situated learning framework. They concluded that this environment could provide the setting that would support and maintain high levels of higher-order thinking.

Park (1998) investigated the instructional effects of three types of visual presentations including animation and static graphics without motion cues. Parks concluded that the dynamic aspects of static graphics with motion cues were as effective as those of the animation presentation. The results suggest that if static graphics contain "appropriate cues," they can facilitate understanding of the dynamic functions and formation of appropriate mental models (p. 38). Others like Bagui (1998) reviewed the research literature and touted the "success of multimedia" (p. 15) for increasing learning. He suggests that this success is due to dual coding (Paivio, 1986) and cites Shih and Alessi (1996) and Najjar (1996) in his contention that verbal and visual codes interact with each other and blend and support each other without a "clear division." Bagui restates oft-stated advantages of multimedia including that multimedia allows students to control pace and direction and develop more of a constructivist approach to learning (as cited in Jurden, 1995), allows interactivity (Najjar, 1996), and is flexible.

What does the research say about multimedia and its interactive technologies? Unfortunately, not much. The terms *multimedia* and *interactivity* are defined universally by neither the developers nor the researchers. Many of the current guidelines for the development of multimedia programs can be traced to just a few sources. One source is the behaviorist learning theory tradition of Thorndike and Skinner; the second is existing research investigating computer-assisted instruction. The most prevalent sources however, are assumption, intuition, and (apparently) common sense. Another source for much of the *supposed* support for the use of multimedia instruction lies in the many *comparison studies,* which essentially compare multimedia instruction with traditional or conventional classroom instruction. These studies are legion (e.g., Fletcher, 1990; Erwin & Rieppi, 1999; Mayer, 1997; Stoloff, 1995). Whereas these studies generally show support for multimedia use or *no significant difference* in presentations, one thing in common is the fundamental methodological flaws (Clark, 1983; Lookatch, 1995; Lockee, Moore, & Burton, 2001). Najjan (1996) contends that much of the support for multimedia appears to be from personal opinion or thoughts other than research studies. After reflection on an extensive review of the literature, there appears to be little useful research on multimedia (Moore et al., 1994). Quite frankly, with few exceptions there is *NOT* a body of research on the design, use, and value of multimedia systems. The few exceptions include the metanalysis of some 60 studies by McNeil and Nelson (1991), the work at the Children's Television Workshop (Strommen & Revelle, 1990), and the reviews by Ragan et al. (1993) and Mayer (1997, 2001).

Mayer (1997) and Reiber (1990) contend that the technological advancements in the area of multimedia environments have outstripped the research on how people learn from pictures and words. Mayer (1977, 2001) has conducted extensive research on learning from multimedia based on a generative theory of learning (based on earlier work by Wittrock, 1989; Paivio 1986, and Mayer, 1992). Mayer's (1997) hypothesis says that meaningful learning occurs when learners

1. select relevant information from what is presented,
2. organize information into a mental representation,
3. integrate the new information, and
4. separate the information into two information processing systems (visual and verbal) as suggested by Paivio (1986).

"(T)he learner is viewed as a knowledge constructor who actively selects and connects pieces of visual and verbal knowledge" (p. 4).

Reiterating Clark's view (1994) that studying the effectiveness of a particular media is no longer productive but focusing on how "instructional treatments affect the cognitive processing within the learner" (p. 7), Mayer and his associates have conducted an extensive program of research to test his generative theory of multimedia learning in which learners select, organize, and integrate visual and verbal information. Mayer and associates, in eight studies, compared problem-solving transfer performance of students who viewed coordinated multiple representations (words and pictures) with that of students receiving only verbal expansions. Overall, Mayer found that students who received the coordinated word and image presentations produced 75% more creative solutions than did students receiving only information in a verbal form (Mayer, 1997). Mayer then compared students receiving visual and verbal information in a linear fashion. Although acknowledging some methodological concerns Mayer reported that the coordinated presentations created more creative solutions than the linear presentations (p. 12). Looking then at the interactions between high- and low-prior knowledge learners and coordinated multimedia presentations, the results indicated that multimedia presentations were effective for students with low prior knowledge and relatively ineffective for students with high prior knowledge (Mayer & Gallini, 1990; Mayer, Steinhoff, Bower, & Mars, 1995). An additional study by Mayer and Sims (1994) reviewed the interaction between high- and low-spatial ability students and coordinated multiple presentations and linear presentations. They found strong effects for high-spatial ability students on coordinated presentations, but not for low-spatial ability students. Mayer (1997) concluded that the theoretical aspects of the generative theory are supported by his research in that coordinated presentations of words and images guide and select relevant information, help serve as organizers to build cause-and-effect relationships, and make connections between actions in the visual and verbal representations (pp. 27–28).

The lack of research concentrating on the interactive features that maximize learning effectiveness has been noted by both practitioners and researchers alike. Specific programs of research have been suggested to fill these gaps, e.g., Hannafin (1985) and Kozma (1991). Until these calls are taken seriously multimedia development will have a less than adequate research base (Moore et al., 1994).

36.8 DISCUSSION AND SUMMARY

"Design decisions are not made based solely on a given foundation, but upon presumed processing requirements, the strategies and methods deemed reasonable in supporting those processes, and the manner in which technology options support or hinder combinations of learning strategies and cognitive processes" (Park & Hannafin, 1993, p. 67). Among the important variables are teacher–student interactions, methods, learner traits, and motivation. Based on our review of the literature, a multiple-channel research article that addressed more than one of these variables is an exception. At the beginning of this chapter, we highlighted the information processing model, its impact on research, and the implications research results have for instructional design.

To recap, briefly the information processing model hypothesizes several information storage areas governed by processes that convert stimuli to information. The goal for instructional designers is to take advantage of suggestions from multiple-channel research to facilitate cognitive processes, particularly in the development of multimedia presentations.

Our review has focused on the effectiveness of multiple-channel communications, cue summation, and related areas such as multi-image and subliminal perception research in learning situations. Unfortunately, most literature addressing these issues is conflicting and/or dated. Not once did we encounter research that thoroughly investigated these theories in the context of hypermedia or multimedia. In addition, much of the research reported is based on the well-documented limitations of media comparison studies. We also feel that the literature dealing with multiple-channel communications and cue summation should provide a portion of the foundation from which to design learning environments in the multimedia arena. Based on the review of pertinent research on the antecedents of the concept of multimedia, e.g., multiple-channel, presentations, cue

summation, multi-imagery, and subliminal perception, what did we find? We feel that instructional designers, looking for simple rationale, methods, or guidelines for effective multimedia (multiple-channel) presentation will be disappointed in the relevant research. Although much of the evidence from the research studies appears to support multiple-channel design, the overall evidence on the effectiveness of single-channel versus multiple-channel presentations is confusing at best. The human information processing system appears to function as a multiple-channel system until the system capacity overloads. When the system capacity is reached, the processing system seems to revert to a single-channel system. In other words, a fixed cognitive capacity limits the absolute amount of information that the individual can *handle*. Adding information channels does not enlarge the system; rather it distributes the system capacity across the additional input channels. Conflicting research results are also present concerning the use of redundant information presented across two or more channels. People apparently view highly redundant information presented over two or more channels as components of a single message. Research on the cue summation and stimulus generalization theories has produced opposing results (no surprise). However, there appears to be some evidence to suggest that multiple-channel presentations are superior to single-channel presentations when cues are summated across channels but neither channel is superior when content is redundant or irrelevant across channels. Redundancy may cause information processing to fluctuate and become less efficient. There also may be failure to take into account the human processing capacity theory. It is suggested that designers sometimes do not understand the possibility that, in multiple-channel communication, irrelevant cues in either channel can cause interference. Research on multi-image presentations suggests that the mere presentation of simultaneous images does not necessarily lead to simultaneous mental processing. Like the other research in this area, multi-image research has revealed few usable results. The familiar problem of how much information an individual processes at any one time is also raised by multi-image presentations and studies on subliminal perception. Inconclusive results leave us with no definite evidence as to subliminal perception's effectiveness or ineffectiveness. However, there appears to be evidence that there is human perception below the threshold of awareness. Where does this leave us in relationship to multimedia? First, educators appear to be unable to determine a universal definition for the concept of multimedia. Second, there is little research concerning the design and value of multimedia systems. Certainly, use of the research and theoretical antecedents of multimedia reviewed in this paper (e.g., multiple-channel communication and cue summation theory) has not, for the most part, made it into the research literature on multimedia. Most of the literature appears to deal with their adoption, their implementation, or visions for their potential use. Some of the evaluative studies available, however, tend to support the use of such presentations.

There is a rather obvious lesson to be learned in reviewing the literature in this area and, we suspect, many of the areas that this handbook is meant to deal with: theory-based research such as that grounded in dual-coding theory, cue summation theory, etc., adds up over time: research comparing media against media, which we have characterized as evaluations, does not. As Clark (1983) readily acknowledges, such studies were criticized long before he put forth his delivery truck metaphor. This metaphor does not seem counterintuitive or, for that matter, controversial. We invite you to look up the term *media* in a dictionary. It will say *vehicle, as in television or radio,* or words to that effect. The concept, though blindingly simple, is still misunderstood. Evaluating media against media in terms of learning outcomes (as in film versus television, etc.) has not helped us. Even testing media attributes per se (e.g., text and audio) against each other has not helped us much. Neither approach is grounded in a theory that explains what happens from a human learning or memory point of view. Clark and others suggest that there are *deeper processes* at work in learning and that the various media attributes employed are surrogates for those processes that can be cued or accessed in many ways. Simply put,

learning may be unaffected by a particular media and learning of any type can be achieved through a variety of paths (media) if the methods of providing information are well designed, have a theoretical base, and are well executed (Hergert, 1994). If work in multimedia does not move quickly from evaluation to theory-based research, not only will we repeat the mistakes of the past, but we, as a discipline, will be made redundant by the workers in human–computer interface and industrial systems engineering, who *are* grounding their work in theory.

ACKNOWLEDGMENTS

The authors appreciate the research assistance of James A. DeChenne, Helen B. Miller, John F. Moore, Krista P. Smith, and Joanne B. Whitley.

References

Adams, J. K. (1957). Laboratory studies of behavior without awareness. *Psychological Bulletin, 54,* 383–405.

Abrams, A., & Streit, L. (1986). Effectiveness of interactive video in teaching basic photography. *T.H.E. Journal, 14*(2), 92–96.

Ainsworth, S. (1999). The functions of multiple representations. *Computers & Education, 33,* 131–152.

Allen, W. H., & Cooney, S. M. (1963). *A study of the non-linearity variable in filmic presentation.* NDEA Title VII, Project No. 422. Los Angeles: University of Southern California.

Allen, W. H., & Cooney, S. M. (1964). Non-linearity in filmic presentation. *AV Communication Review, 12*(2), 164–176.

Allison, J. (1963). Cognitive structure and receptivity to low-intensity stimulation. *Journal of Abnormal and Social Psychology, 67,* 132–138.

Anderson, J. R. (1985a). *Cognitive psychology and its implications.* New York: Freeman.

Anderson, J. R. (1985b). *Theories of learning* (5th ed.). Englewood Cliffs, NJ: Prentice Hall.

Anderson, J. R. (1978). Arguments concerning representations for mental imagery. *Psychological Review, 85,* 249–277.

Anderson, R. C., Greeno, J. G., Kline, P. J., & Neves, D. M. (1981). Acquisition of problem solving skill. In J. R. Anderson (Ed.), *Cognitive skills and their acquisition.* Hillsdale, NJ: Erlbaum.

Anglin, G. J., & Morrison, G. R. (2001, November). *Cognitive load theory: Implications for instructional design research and practice.* Paper presented at the annual conference of the Association for Educational Communications and Technology. Atlanta, GA.

Application of subliminal perception in advertising. (1958). New York: Advertising Research Foundation.

Atherton, L. L.(1971). A comparison of movie and multi-image presentation techniques on affective and cognitive learning. (Doctoral dissertation, Michigan State University). *Dissertation Abstracts International, 32*(6-A), 5924. (University Microfilms, No. 71-31,154)

Attneave, F. (1954). Some informational aspects of visual perception. *Psychological Review, 61,* 183–193.

Ausburn, F. B. (1975). *Multiple versus linear imagery in the presentation of a comparative visual location task to visual and haptic college students.* Unpublished doctoral dissertation, University of Oklahoma.

Baddeley, A. D. (1966). Short term memory for word sequences as a function of acoustic, semantic, and formal similarity. *Quarterly Journal of Experimental Psychology, 18,* 362–365.

Baggett, P. (1984). Role of temporal overlap of visual and auditory material in forming dual media associations. *Journal of Educational Psychology, 76,* 408–417.

Baggett, P., & Ehrenfecucht, A. (1983). Encoding and retaining information in the visuals and verbals of an educational movie. *Educational Communication and Technology, 31*(1), 23–32.

Bagui, S. (1998). Reasons for increased learning from multimedia. *Journal of Educational Multimedia and Hypermedia, 7*(1), 3–18.

Baker, E. J., & Alluisi, E. A. (1962). Information handling aspect of visual and auditory form perception. *Journal of Engineering Psychology, 1,* 159–179.

Bartlett, F. C. (1958). *Thinking.* New York: Basic Books.

Beagles-Roos, J., & Gat, I. (1983). Specific impact of radio and television on children's story comprehension. *Journal of Educational Psychology, 75,* 128–137.

Beck, C. R. (1983). Successive and simultaneous picture and passage formats: Visual, tactual, and topical effects. *Educational Communications and Technology, 31*(3), 145–152.

Beck, C. R. (1987). Pictorial cueing strategies for encoding and retrieving information. *International Journal of Instructional Media, 14*(4), 332–346.

Berger, M. M. (1973). A preliminary report on the multi-image immediate impact on video self-confrontation. *American Journal of Psychiatry, 130,* 304–306.

Bevan, W. (1964). Subliminal stimulation: A pervasive problem for psychology. *Psychological Bulletin, 61,* 81–99.

Bither, S. W. (1972). Effects of distraction and commitment on the persuasiveness of television advertising. *Journal of Marketing Research, 9,* 1–5.

Blackwell, H. R. (1968). Lighting in the learning module. *American Annals of the Deaf, 113*(5), 1063–1074.

Bollman, C. G. (1970). The effect of large screen multi-image display of evaluative meaning. (Doctoral dissertation, Michigan State University). *Dissertation Abstracts International, 31*(11-A), 5924. (University Microfilms, No. 71-11,789)

Bourne, C. E., Dominowski, R. L., Loftus, E. F., & Healy, A. F. (1986). *Cognitive processes* (2nd ed.). Englewood Cliffs, NJ: Prentice Hall.

Bransford, J. D., & Johnson, M. K. (1972). Contextual prerequisites for understanding: Some investigations of comprehension and recall. *Journal of Verbal Learning and Verbal Behavior, 11,* 717-726.

Bransford, J. D., Sherwood, R., Vye, N. J., & Rieser, J. (1986). Teaching thinking and problem solving: Research foundations. *American Psychologist, 41*(10), 1078-1079.

Britton, B. K., Meyer, B. J. F., Simpson, R., Holdredge, T., & Curry, C. (1979). Effects of organization of text on memory: Test of two implications of selective attention. *Journal of Experimental Psychology: Human Learning and Memory, 5,* 496-506.

Broadbent, D. E. (1956). Successive responses to simultaneous stimuli. *Quarterly Journal of Experimental Psychology, 8,* 145-152.

Broadbent, D. E. (1957). Immediate memory and simultaneous stimuli. *Quarterly Journal of Experimental Psychology, 9,* 1-11.

Broadbent, D. E. (1958). *Perception and communication.* New York: Pergamon Press.

Broadbent, D. E. (1965). Information processing in the nervous system. *Science, 150,* 457-462.

Brown, J. (1959). Information, redundancy, and decay of the memory trace. In *Mechanization of the thought,* Vol. 2. National Physical Laboratory, Symposium No. 10. London: Her Majesty's Stationery Office.

Brown, J. S., Collins, A., & Duguid, P. (1989). Situated cognition and the culture of learning. *Educational Researcher, 18*(1), 32-41.

Bruner, J. S. (1967). *Towards a theory of instruction.* Cambridge, MA: Harvard University Press.

Bruner, J. S., Goodnow, J. J., & Auston, G. A. (1967). *A study of thinking.* New York: John Wiley & Sons.

Burke, K. (1987). *AMI research bibliography.* AMI Archives and Clearinghouse No. CAb1.

Burke, K., & Leps, A. A. (1989). Multi-Image research: A thirty-year retrospective. *International Journal of Instructional Media, 16*(3), 181-195.

Burton, J. K. (1982). Dual coding of pictorial stimuli by children. *Journal of Mental Imagery, 6*(1), 159-168.

Burton, J. K., & Bruning, R. H. (1982). Interference effects on the recall of pictures, printed words, spoken words. *Contemporary Educational Psychology, 7,* 61-69.

Byrne, D. (1959). The effect of a subliminal food stimulus on verbal responses. *Journal of Applied Psychology, 43,* 249-252.

Calvert, S. L., Huston, A. C., Watkins, B. A., & Wright, J. C. (1982). The relation between selective attention to television forms and children's comprehension of content. *Child Development, 53,* 601-610.

Calvin, A. D., & Dollenmayer, K. S. (1959). Subliminal perception: Some negative findings. *Journal of Applied Psychology, 43,* 187-188.

Carpenter, C. R. (1953). A theoretical orientation for instructional film research. *AV Communication Review, 1,* 38-52.

Carterette, E. C., & Jones, M. H. (1965). Visual and auditory information processing in children and adults. *Science, 156,* 986-988.

Champion, J. M., & Turner, W. W. (1959). An experimental investigation of subliminal perception. *Journal of Applied Psychology, 43,* 382-384.

Chandler, P., & Sweller, J. (1991). Cognitive load theory and jthe format of instruction. *Cognition and Instruction, 8,* 293-332.

Cherry, C. E. (1953). Some experiments on the recognition of speech with one and two ears. *Journal of the Acoustical Society of America, 25,* 965-974.

Cherry, C. E. (1957). *On human communication: A review, a survey, and a criticism.* New York: John Wiley.

Clark, R. E. (1983). Reconsidering research on learning from media. *Review of Educational Research, 53,* 445-459.

Clark, R. E. (1994). Media will never influence learning. *Educational Technology Research and Development, 42*(2), 21-30.

Clark, S. E. (1969). Retrieval of color information from preperceptual memory. *Journal of Experimental Psychology, 82,* 263-266.

Cognition and Technology Group at Vanderbilt (1990). Anchored instruction and its relationship to situated cognition. *Educational Researcher, 19*(5), 2-10.

Conrad, R. (1964). Acoustic confusions in immediate memory. *British Journal of Psychology, 55,* 75-84.

Conway, J. K. (1967). Multiple-sensory modality communication and the problem of sign types. *AV Communication Review, 15*(4), 371-383.

Conway, J. K. (1968). Information presentation, information processing, and the sing vehicle. *AV Communication Review, 16*(4), 403-414.

Cooper, L. A., & Shepard, R. N. (1973). Chronometric studies of the rotation of mental images. In W. G. Chase (Ed.), *Visual information processing.* New York: Academic Press.

Corballis, M. C., & Raeburn, B. J. (1970). Recall strategies in three-channel immediate memory. *Canadian Journal of Psychology, 24,* 109-116.

Coyne, J. W., King, H. E., Zubin, J., & Landis, C. (1943). Accuracy of recognition of subliminal auditory stimuli. *Journal of Experimental Psychology, 33,* 508-513.

Day, W. F., & Beach, B. R. (1950). *A survey of the research literature comparing the visual and auditory presentation of information.* Charlottesville: University of Virginia (Contract No. W33-039-ac-21269, E.O. No. 694-37).

DeBlois, M. L. (1982). *Videodisc/microcomputer courseware design.* Englewood Cliffs, NJ: Educational Technology.

DeChenne, J. A. (1975). An experimental study to determine if a task involving psychomotor and problem solving skills can be taught subliminally (Doctoral dissertation, Virginia Polytechnic Institute and State University). *Dissertation Abstracts International, 37,* 1947a. (University Microfilms No. 76-23213)

Dee-Lukas, D., & Larkin, J. H. (1992). *Text representation with traditional text and hypertext* (Technical Report H.P.21). Carnegie Mellon University, Department of Psychology.

DeFleur, M. L., & Petranoff, R. M. (1959). A televised test of subliminal persuasion. *Public Opinion Quarterly, 23,* 168-180.

Didcoct, D. H. (1958). *Comparison of the cognitive and affective responses of college students to single-image and multi-image audiovisual presentations.* Unpublished doctoral dissertation, Cornell University.

Dixon, N. F. (1971). *Subliminal perception: The nature of a controversy.* New York: McGraw-Hill.

Drew, D. G., & Grimes, T. (1987). Audio-visual redundancy and TV news recall. *Communication Research, 14,* 452-461.

Dwyer, F. M. (1972). *A guide for improving visualized instruction.* State College, PA: Learning Services.

Dwyer, F. M. (1978). *Strategies for improving visual learning.* State College, PA: Learning Services.

Egan, D. E., & Schwartz, B. J. (1979). Chunking in recall of symbolic drawings. *Memory & Cognition, 7,* 149-158.

Eggen, P. D., & Kauchak, D. (1992). *Educational psychology: Classroom connections* New York: Merrill.

Emmer, E. T. (1981). *Effective management in junior high mathematics classrooms* (R&D Report No. 6111). Austin, TX: University of Texas.

Erwin, T. D. (1999). Comparing multimedia and traditional approaches in undergraduate psychology classes. *Computers in Teaching, 26*(1), 58-61.

Evertson, C. M., Anderson, L. M., & Brophy, J. E. (1978). *Process-outcome relationships in the Texas junior high school study: Compendium.*

Washington, DC: National Institute of Education. (ERIC No. ED 166 192)

Eysenck, N. J. (1963). *The measurement of motivation.* Reprinted from *Scientific American* (May). Print No. 477. New York: W. H. Freeman.

Feigenbaum, E. A., & Simon, H. A. (1963). Brief notes on the EPAM theory of verbal learning. In C. N. Confer & B. S. Musgrave (Eds.), *Verbal behavior and learning.* New York: McGraw–Hill.

Festinger, L., & Maccoby, N. (1964). On resistance to persuasive communications. *Journal of Abnormal and Social Psychology, 68,* 359–366.

Findahl, O. (19781). *The effect of visual illustrations upon perception and retention of news programmes.* (ERIC Document Reproduction Service No. ED 054 631)

Fleisher, R. (1969). Multiple-image technique for "The Boston Strangler." *American Cinematographer,* 202–205 *et passim.*

Fletcher, J. (1990). *Effectiveness and cost of interactive videodisc instruction in defense training and education* (IDA Paper P-2372). Washington, DC: Institute for Defense Analysis.

Fleming, M. L. (1970). Perceptual principles for the design of instructional material. *Viewpoints, Bulletin of the School of Education,* 69–200. Bloomington: Indiana University.

Fortune, J. C. (1967). *A study of the generality of presenting behavior in teaching.* Memphis, TN: Memphis State University. ERIC No. ED 016 285)

Fradkin, B. M. (1974). Effectiveness of multi-image presentations. *Journal of Educational Technology Systems, 2,* 231–326.

Fradkin, B. (1976). *A review of multiple image presentation research* (Contract No. WIE-C-74-0027). Washington, DC. National Institute of Education. (ERIC No. ED130 680)

Fradkin, B. M., & Meyowitz, J. (1975). *Design of multi-image instructional presentations.* Paper presented at the national convention of the Association for Educational Communications and Technology, Dallas, TX.

Gardner, H. (1985). *The mind's new science: A history of the cognitive revolution.* New York: Basic Books.

Gerard, E. O. (1960). Subliminal stimulation in problem solving. *American Journal of Psychology, 73,* 121–126.

Gerlic, I., & Jausovec, N. (1999). Multimedia: Differences in cognitive processes observed with EEG. *Educational Technology Research and Development, 47,*(3), 5–14.

Gersten, R. M., Carine, D. W., & Williams, P. B. (1982). Measuring implementation of a structural educational model in a urban school district: An observational approach. *Educational Evaluation and Policy Analysis, 4,* 67–79.

Gleason, J. (1991). *Development of an interactive multimedia presentation for use in a public delivery setting.* Unpublished doctoral dissertation, Virginia Tech University.

Goldstein, B. (1975). The perception of multiple images. *AV Communication Review, 23*(1), 34–68.

Goldstein, M. J., & Barthol, R. P. (1960). Fantasy responses to subliminal stimuli. *Journal of Abnormal and Social Psychology, 60,* 22–26.

Goldstein, M. J., & Davis, D. (1961). The impact of stimuli registering outside of awareness. *Journal of Personality, 29,* 247–257.

Greco, A., & McClung, C. (1979). Interaction between attention directing and cognitive style. *Educational Communications and Technology Journal, 27,* 97–102.

Grimes, T. (1991). Mild auditory-visual dissonance in television news may exceed viewer attentional capacity. *Human Communication Research, 18*(2), 268–298.

Gulo, E., & Baron, A, (1965). Classroom learning of meaningful prose by college students as a function of sensory mode of stimulus presentation. *Perceptual and Motor Skills, 21,* 183–186.

Hannafin, M. J. (1985). Empirical issues in the study of computer assisted

interactive video. *Educational Communication and Technology, Journal, 33*(4), 235–247.

Hanson, L. (1989). Multichannel learning research applied to principles of television production: A review and synthesis of the literature. *Educational Technology, 29*(10), 15–19.

Hardiman, B., & Williams, R. (1990). Teaching developmental mathematics: The interactive video approach. *T.H.E. Journal, 17,* 63–65.

Harrington, J., & Oliver, R. (1999). Using situated learning and multimedia to investigate higher-order thinking. *Journal of Educational Multimedia and Hypermedia, 8,*(4), 401–421.

Hartman, F. R. (1961a). Investigation of recognition learning under multiple-channel presentation and testing conditions. *AV Communication Review, 9,* 24–43.

Hartman, F. R. (1961b). Single and multi channel communication: A review of research and a proposed model. *AV Communication Review, 9,* 235–262.

Hayes, D. S., Kelly, S. B., & Mandel, M. (1986). Media differences in children's story synopses: Radio and television contrasted. *Journal of Educational Psychology, 78,* 341–346.

Henneman, R. H. (1952). Vision and audition as sensory channels for communication. *Journal of Speech, 38,* 161–166.

Hergert, T. (1994). *Research on instructional technology.* Unpublished paper. Virginia Polytechnic Institute and State University.

Herman, L. M. (1965). Study of the single channel hypothesis and input regulation within a continuous, simultaneous task situation. *Quarterly Journal of Experimental Psychology, 17,* 37–46.

Hernandez-Peon, R. (1961). Reticular mechanisms of sensory control. In W. A. Rosenblith (Ed.), *Sensory communication.* (pp. 497–517). New York: John Wiley & Sons.

Hessler, D. W. (1972). Interaction of 'visual compression' and field-dependence in relation to self-instruction and transfer (Doctoral dissertation, Michigan State University, 1972). *Dissertation Abstracts International, 33,* 6235a. (University Microfilms No. 73-12735)

Higgins, K., & Boone, R. (1992). Hypermedia computer study guides: Adapting a Canadian history text. *Social Education, 56*(3), 154–159.

Hill, S. D., & Hecker, E. E. (1966). Auditory and visual learning of paired associate tasks by second grade children. *Perceptual & Motor Skills, 23,* 814.

Hoban, C. F. (1949). *Some aspects of learning from films.* Incidental Report No. 2. State College: Pennsylvania State College, Instructional Film Research Program.

Hoban, C. F., & VanOrmer, E. B. (1950). *Instructional film research.* University Park: Pennsylvania State University (SDC 269-7-19).

Hollingworth, H. L. (1919). *Advertising and selling.* New York: D. Appleton.

Hooper, S., & Hannafin, M. J. (1991). Psychological perspectives on emerging instructional technologies: A critical analysis. *Educational Psychologist, 26*(1), 69–95.

Hsia, H. J. (1968). On channel effectiveness. *AV Communication Review, 16,* 245–267.

Hsia, H. J. (1969). Intelligence in auditory, visual, and audiovisual information processing. *AV Communication Review, 17,* 272–282.

Hsia, H. J. (1971). The information processing capacity of modality and channel performance. *AV Communication Review, 19*(1), 51–75.

Hubbard, R. D. (1961). Telemation: AV automatically controlled. *Audio-Visual Instruction, 6,* 437–439.

Jacobson, H. (1950). The informational capacity of the human ear. *Science, 112,* 143–144.

Jacobson, H. (1951). The informational capacity of the human eye. *Science, 113,* 292–293.

Jacobson, M. J., Maouri, C., Mishra, P., & Kolar, C. (1995). Learning with hypertext learning environments: Theory, design and research.

Journal of Educational Multimedia and Hypermedia, 4(4), 321–364.

Janda, K. (1992). Multimedia in political science: Sobering lessons from a teaching experiment. *Journal of Educational Multimedia and Hypermedia, 1,* 341–354.

Johnson, H., & Eriksen, C. W. (1961). Preconscious perception: A re-examination of the Poetzl phenomenon. *Journal of Abnormal and Social Psychology, 62,* 497–503.

Jonassen, D. (1979). Implications of multi-image for concept acquisition. *Educational Technology Communication Journal, 27*(4), 291–302.

Jonassen, D. H. (1993). Effects of semantically structured hypertext knowledge bases on usuer's knowledge structures. In C. Mcknight, A. Dillon, & J. Richardson (Eds.), *Hypertext. A psychological perspective* (pp. 153–168). Chichester, UK: Horwood.

Jonassen, D. H., & Wang, S. (1992, July). *Acquiring structural knowledge from semantically structured hypertext.* Paper presented at the European Conference on Educational Research, Twente, The Netherlands.

Jones, L. L., & Smith, S. G. (1989). Lights, camera, reactions! The interactive videodisc: A tool for teaching chemistry. *T.H.E. Journal, 16,* 78–85.

Jurden, F. H. (1995). Individual differences in working memory and complex cognition. *Journal of Educational Psychology, 87*(1), 93–102.

Kahneman, D. (1973). *Attention and effort.* Englewood Cliffs, NJ: Prentice Hall.

Kale, S. U., Grosslight, J. H., & McIntyre, D. J. (1955). *Exploratory studies in the use of pictures and sound for teaching foreign language vocabulary* (Technical Report SDC 269-7-53). Port Washington, NY: Special Devices Center.

Katz, P. A., & Deutsch, M. (1963). *Visual and auditory efficiency and its relationship to reading in children.* Final Report, Project 1009, Washington, DC: Office of Education.

Kerr, B. (1973). Processing demands during mental operations. *Memory and Cognitions, 1,* 401–412.

Ketcham, C. H., & Heath, R. W. (1962). Teaching effectiveness of sound with pictures that do not embody the material being taught. *AV Communication Review, 10,* 89–93.

King, H. E., Landis, C., & Zubin, J. (1944). Visual subliminal perception where a figure is obscured by the influences upon conscious thought. *Journal of Experimental Psychology, 34,* 60–69.

Klatzky, R. L. (1980). *Human memory: Structures and processes.* New York: Freeman.

Klein, G. S., Spence, D. P., Holt, R. R., & Gourevitch, S. (1958). Cognition without awareness: Subliminal influences upon conscious thought. *Journal of Abnormal and Social Psychology, 57,* 255–266.

Kleinsmith, L. J., & Kaplan, S. (1963). Paired-associate learning as a function of arousal and interpolated interval. *Journal of Experimental Psychology, 65,* 190–193.

Kleinsmith, L. J., & Kaplan, S. (1964). Interaction of arousal and recall interval in nonsense syllable paired-associate learning. *Journal of Experimental Psychology, 67,* 124–126.

Kleinsmith, L. J., Kaplan, S., & Tarte, R. D. (1963). The relationship of arousal to short- and long-term verbal recall. *Canadian Journal of Psychology, 17,* 393–397.

Kolers, P. A. (1957). Subliminal stimulation in problem solving. *American Journal of Psychology, 70,* 437–441.

Kopstein, F. F., & Roshal, S. M. (1954). Learning foreign vocabulary from pictures versus words. *American Psychologist, 9,* 407–408.

Kosslyn, S. M. (1975). Information representation in visual images. *Cognitive Psychology, 7,* 341–370.

Kozma, R. B. (1987, November). The implications of cognitive psychology for computer-based learning tools. *Educational Technology,* 20–25.

Kozma, R. B. (1991). Learning with media. *Review of Educational Research, 61*(2), 179–211.

Kreszock, C. M. (1981). *An experimental study to compare the affective and cognitive responses of female and male college students to single-image, multi-image, and time compressed single-image presentations.* Unpublished doctoral dissertation, Virginia Tech University.

Langer, S. D. (1957). *Philosophy in a new key: A study of the symbolism of reason, rite, and art.* Cambridge, MA: Harvard University Press.

Lazarus, R. S., & McCleary, R. A. (1951). Automatic discrimination without awareness: A study of subception. *Psychological Review, 58,* 113–122.

Levie, W. L. (1987). Research on pictures: A guide to the literature. In D. M. Willows & H. A. Houghton (Eds.), *The psychology of illustration.* New York: Springer-Verlag.

Levie, W. H., & Lentz, R. (1982). Effects of text illustrations: A review of research. *Educational Communications and Technology Journal, 30*(4), 195–232.

Liao, Y. C. (1999). Effects of hypermedia on students' achievement: A meta-analysis. *Journal of Educational Multimedia and Hypermedia, 8*(3), 255–277.

Lillie, D. L., Hannum, W. H., & Stuck, G. B. (1989). *Computers and effective instruction.* White Plains, NY: Longman.

Liu, M. (1992). *The application of research-based instructional design principles in developing a hypermedia assisted instruction courseware for second language learning.* Paper presented at the 34th ADCIS meting.

Livingstone, R. B. (1962). An adventure shared psychology and neurophysiology. In S. Koch (Ed.), *Psychology: A study of science.* New York: McGraw-Hill.

Lockee, B. B., Moore, D. M., & Burton, J. K. (2001). Old concerns with new distance education research. *Educause Quarterly, 24*(2), 60–62.

Lombard, E. S. (1969). *Multi-channel, multi-image teaching of synthesis skills in 11th grade U.S. history.* Unpublished doctoral dissertation, University of Southern California.

Lorch, E. P., Bellack, D. R., & Augsbach, L. H. (1987). Young children's memory for televised stories: Effects of importance. *Child Development, 58,* 453–462.

Low, C. (1968). Multi-screen and Expo 67. *Journal of the Society of Motion Picture and Television Engineers, 77,* 185–186.

Lumsdaine, A. A., & Gladstone, A. (1958). Overt practice and audiovisual embellishments. In M. A. May and A. A. Lumsdaine (Eds.), *Learning from films.* New Haven, CT: Yale University Press.

Magliaro, S. (1988). *Expertise in problem identification: A descriptive analysis of the cue selection and hypothesis generation of reading diagnosticians.* Unpublished doctoral dissertation, Virginia Polytechnic Institute and State University.

Malandin, C. (n.d.). *Research on the understanding of filmstrips.* Mimeo. Ministere de l'Education Nationale, Ecole Normale Superieur de Saint-Cloud, France.

Mandler, J. M., & Parker, R. E. (1976). Memory for descriptive and spatial information of complex pictures. *Journal of Experimental Psychology: Human and Learning Memory, 2,* 38–48.

Matchett, J. R., & Elliott, S. A. (1991). Multimedia: The potential is startling, but.... *Inform, 6*(4), 48–50.

May, M. A., & Lumsdaine, A. A. (Eds.), (1958). *Learning from films.* New Haven, CT: Yale University Press.

Mayer, R. E. (1983). *Thinking, problem solving, cognition.* New York: W. H. Freeman.

Mayer, R. E. (1984). Aids to text comprehension. *Educational Psychologist, 19,* 30–42.

Mayer, R. E., & Anderson, R. B. (1991). Animations need narrations: An experimental test of a dual-coding hypothesis. *Journal of Educational Psychology, 83*(4), 484–490.

Mayer, R. E. (1989). Systematic thinking fostered by illustrations in scientific text. *Journal of Educational Psychology, 81*(2), 240–246.

Mayer, R. E. (1992). Knowledge and thought: Mental models that support scientific **reasoning**. In R. A. Duschl & R. J. Hamilton (Eds.), *Philosophy of science, cognitive psychology, and educational theory and practice* (pp. 226–243). Albany, NY: SUNY Press.

Mayer, R. E. (1997). Multimedia learning: Are we asking the right questions? *Educational Psychologist, 32*(1), 1–19.

Mayer, R. E. (2001). *Multi-media learning.* New York: Cambridge University Press.

Mayer, R. E., & Gallini, J. K. (1990). When is an illustration worth ten thousand words? *Journal of Educational Psychology, 82*(4), 715–726.

Mayer, R. E., & Sims, V. K. (1994). For whom is a picture worth a thousand words? Extensions of a dual-coding theory of multimedia learning. *Journal of Educational Psychology, 86,* 389–401.

Mayer, R. E., Steinhoff, K., Bower, G., & Mars, R. (1995). A generative theory of textbook design: Using annotated illustrations to foster meaningful learning of science text. *Educational Technology Research and Development, 43*(1), 31–44.

McConnell, J. W., Cutler, R. L., & McNeil, E. B. (1958). Subliminal stimulation: An overview. *American Psychologist, 13,* 229–242.

McFee, J. K. (1969). Visual communication. In R. V. Wiman & M. C. Meierhenry (Eds.), *Educational media: Theory into practice.* Columbus, OH: Charles E. Merrill.

McGinnus, E. (1949). Emotionality and perceptual defense. *Psychological Review, 56,* 244–251.

McNeil, B. J., & Nelson, K. R. (1991). Meta-analysis of interactive video instruction: A 10 year review of achievement effects. *Journal of Computer-Based Instruction, 18*(1), (1–6).

Meekl, P. E. (1967). Theory-testing in psychology and physics: A methodological paradox. *Philosophy of Science, 34,* 103–115.

Meringoff, L. K. (1980). Influence of the medium on children's story apprehension. *Journal of Educational Psychology, 72,* 240–249.

Millard, W. L. (1964). Visual teaching aids: Production and use. *In The Encyclopedia of Photography.* New York: Greystone Press.

Miller, G. A. (1953). What is information measurement? *American Psychologist, 17,* 748–762.

Miller, G. A. (1956). The magical number seven, plus or minus two: Some limits on our capacity for processing information. *Psychological Review, 63,* 81–97.

Miller, H. B., & Burton, J. K. (1994). Images and imagery theory. In D. M. Moore & F. M. Dwyer (Eds.), *Visual literacy: A spectrum of visual learning* (pp. 65–85). Englewood Cliffs, NJ: Educational Technology.

Miller, J. G. (1942). *Unconsciousness.* New York: Wiley & Sons.

Miller, N. E. (Ed.). (1957). Graphic communication and the crisis in education. In collaboration with W. A. Allen, et al. *AV Communication Review, 5,* 1–120.

Moore, D. M., Myers, R. J., & Burton, J. K.(1994). What multimedia might do and. . . What we know about what it does. In A. Ward (Ed.), *Multimedia and learning: A school's leaders guide.* Alexandria, VA: National School Boards Association.

Moore, J. F. (1982). *An exploratory study of subliminal perception and field dependence in a concept learning task taught by television.* Unpublished doctoral dissertation, Virginia Polytechnic Institute and State University.

Moore, J. F., & Moore, D. M. (1984). Subliminal perception and cognitive style in a concept learning task taught via television. *British Journal of Educational Technology, 3*(15), 22–31.

Moray, N. (1959). Attention in dichotic listening: Affective cues and the influence of instructions. *Quarterly Journal of Experimental Psychology, 11,* 59–60.

Mowbray, G. H. (1952). Simultaneous vision and audition: The detection of elements from over learned sequences. *Journal of Experimental Psychology, 44,* 292–300.

Mudd, S. A., & McCormick, E. J. (1960). A The use of auditory cues in a visual search task. *Journal of Applied Psychology, 44,* 184–188.

Murch, G. M. (1965). A set of conditions for a consistent recovery of subliminal stimulus. *Journal of Applied Psychology, 49,* 257–260.

Myers, R. (1993). *Problem-based learning: A case study in integrating teachers, students, methods, and hypermedia databases.* Unpublished doctoral dissertation, Virginia Polytechnic Institute and State University.

Najjar, L. J. (1996) Multimedia information and learning. *Journal of Educational Multimedia and Hypermedia, 5*(2), 129–150.

Neely, J. H. (1977). Semantic priming and retrieval from lexical memory: Roles of inhibitionless spreading activation and limited-capacity attention. *Journal of Experimental Psychology: General, 106,* 226–254.

Neisser, U. (1967). *Cognitive psychology.* New York: Appleton-Century–Crofts.

Nelson, T. O., Metzler, J., & Reed, D. A. (1974). Role of details in the long-term recognition of pictures and verbal descriptions. *Journal of Experimental Psychology, 102,* 184–186.

Norberg, K. (1966). Visual perception theory and instructional communication. *AV Communication Review, 14,* 301–316.

Norman, D. A. (1969). *Memory and attention.* New York: Wiley.

Nugent, G. C. (1982). Pictures, audio, and print: Symbolic representation and effect on learning. *Educational Communication and Technology, 30*(3), 163–174.

Nuthall, G., & Alton-Lee, A. (1990). Research on teaching and learning: Thirty years of change. *Elementary School Journal, 90*(5), 547–570.

Orey, M. A., Garrison, J. W., & Burton, J. K. (1989). A philosophical critique of null hypothesis testing. *Journal of Research and Development in Education, 22*(3), 12–21.

Osterhouse, R. A., & Brock, T. C. (1970). Distraction increases yielding to propaganda by inhibiting counterarguing. *Journal of Personality and Social Psychology, 15,* 344–358.

Paivio, A. (1971). *Imagery and verbal processes.* New York: Holt, Rinehart & Winston.

Paivio, A. (1986). *Mental representations: A dual coding approach.* New York: Oxford Press.

Papert, S. (1977). A learning environment of children. In R. J. Seidel & M. Rubin (Eds.), *Computers and communications: Implications for education* (pp. 271–278). New York: Academic Press.

Park, I., & Hannifin, M. J. (1993). Empirically-Based guidelines for the design of interactive multimedia. *Educational Technology Research and Development, 41*(3), 63–85.

Park, O. (1998). Visual displays and contextual presentations in computer-based instruction. *Educational Technology Research and Development, 46*(3), 37–50.

Pellegrino, J. W., Siegel, A. W., & Dhawan, M. (1974). Short-term retention of pictures and words: Evidence for dual coding systems. *Journal of Experimental Psychology: Human Learning and Memory, 1,* 95–102.

Pellegrino, J. W., Siegel, A. W., & Dhawan, M. (1976a). Short-term retention of pictures and words as a function of type of distraction and length of delay interval. *Memory & Cognition, 4,* 11–15.

Pellegrino, J. W., Siegel, A. W., & Dhawan, M. (1976b). Differential distraction effects in short-term and long-term retention of pictures and words. *Journal of Experimental Psychology: Human Learning and Memory, 2,* 541-547.

Perrin, D. G. (1969). A theory of multiple-image communication. *AV Communication Review, 17*(4), 368-382.

Pezdek, K., & Stevens, E. (1984). Children's memory for auditory and visual infomration on television. *Developmental Psychology, 210,* 212-218.

Posner, M. I. (1964). Information reduction in the analysis of sequential tasks. *Psychology Review, 71,* 491-504.

Posner, M. I., & Snyder, C. R. R. (1975). Facilitation and inhibition in the processing of signals. In P. M. A. Rabbitt & S. Dornic (Eds.), *Attention and Performance, Vol. 5.* New York: Academic Press.

Pressley, M., & Miller, G. (1987). Effects of illustrations on children's listening comprehension and oral prose memory. In D. M. Willows & H. A. Houghton (Eds.), *The psychology of illustration.* New York: Springer-Verlag.

Ragan, T., Boyce, M., Redwine, D., Savenye, W. C., & McMichael J. (1993). *Is multimedia worth it? A review of the effectiveness of individualized multimedia instruction.* A paper presented at the Association for Educational Communications and Technology Convention, New Orleans, LA.

Reed, S. K. (1985). Effect of computer graphics on improving estimates to algebra word problems. *Journal of Educational Psychology, 77*(3), 285-298.

Reese, S. D. (1983). *Improving Audience Learning from Television News Through Between-Channel Redundancy.* (ERIC Document Reproduction Service No. ED 229 777).

Reigeluth, C. M., & Schwartz, E. (1989). An instructional theory for the design of computer-based simulations. *Journal of Computer-Based Instruction, 16,* 1-10.

Reynolds, R. E., & Baker, D. R. (1987). The utility of graphical representations in text: Some theoretical and empirical issues. *Journal of Research in Science Teaching, 24*(2), 161-173.

Rieber, L. P. (1990). Animation in computer-based instruction. *Educational Technology Research and Development, 38,* 77-86.

Rigney, J. W., & Lutz, K. A. (1976). Effect of graphic analogies of concepts in chemistry on learning and attitude. *Journal of Educational Psychology, 68,* 305-311.

Rolandelli, D. R. (1989). Children and television: The visual superiority effect reconsidered. *Journal of Broadcasting & Electronic Media, 33*(1), 69-81.

Roshka, A. U. (1960). Conditions facilitating abstraction and generalization., *Voprosy Psikhologii, 4*(6), 89-96. (Reported by I. D. London, *Psychological Abstracts, 34,* 85.)

Rouet, R. F. (1992). Cognitine processing of hyperdocuments: When does non-linearity help? In D. Lucarella, J. Nanard, M. Narard, & P. Palolina (Eds.), *Proceedings of the 4th ACM Conference on Hypertext* (pp. 1331-140). New York: Academic Press.

Sackeim, H. A., Packer, I. K., & Gur, R. C. (1977). Hemisphericity, cognitive set, and susceptibility to subliminal perception. *Journal of Abnormal Psychology, 86,* 624-630.

Samuels, S. J. (1970). Effects of pictures on learning to read, comprehension and attitudes. *Review of Educational Research, 40*(3), 397-407.

Schiff, W. (1961). The effect of subliminal stimuli on guessing accuracy. *American Journal of Psychology, 74,* 54-60.

Schoenfeld, A. H., Smith, J. P., & Arcavi, A. (1993). Learning: The microgenetic analysis of one students evolving understanding of a complex subject matter domain. In R. Glaser (Ed.), *Advances in instructional psychology, Vol. 4,* (pp. 55-175). Hillsdale, NJ: Erlbaum.

Severin, W. J. (1967a). *Cue summation in multiple-channel communication.* Unpublished doctoral dissertation, University of Wisconsin.

Severin, W. J. (1967b). Another look at cue summation. *AV Communication Review, 15*(4), 233-245.

Severin, W. J. (1967c). The effectiveness of relevant pictures in multiple-channel communication. *AV Communication Review, 15*(4), 386-401.

Shannon, C. E., & Weaver, W. (1949). *The mathematical theory of communication.* Urbana: University of Illinois Press.

Sharp, H. C. (1959). Effect of subliminal cues on test results. *Journal of Applied Psychology, 43,* 369-371.

Sheehan, J. (1992). Multimedia down under. *Multimedia and Videodisc Monitor, 10*(6), 20.

Shepard, R. N. (1967). Recognition memory for words, sentences, and pictures. *Journal of Verbal Learning and Verbal Behavior, 6,* 156-163.

Shevrin, H., & Luborsky, L. (1958). The measurement of preconscious perception in dreams and images: An investigation of the Poetzl phenomenon. *Journal of Abnormal and Social Psychology, 56,* 285-294.

Shiffrin, R. M., & Geisler, W. S. (1973). Visual recognition in a theory of information processing. In R. L. Solso (Ed.), *Contemporary issues in cognitive psychology: The Loyola symposium.* Washington, DC: V. H. Winston.

Shih, Y. F., & Alessi, S. M. (1996). Effects of text verus voice on learning in multimedia courseware. *Journal of Educational Multimedia and Hypermedia, 5*(2), 203-218.

Skinner, W. S. (1969). *The effect of subliminal and supraliminal words presented via video taped motion pictures on vocabulary development of ninth grade students* (Doctoral dissertation, Arizona State University, 1969). University Microfilms No. 69-20802.

Slee, E. J. (1989). *A review of the research on interactive video.* Paper presented at the Educational Communications and Technology Annual Meeting, Dallas, TX.

Smith, E. E. (1987). Interactive video: An examination of use and effectiveness. *Journal of Instructional Development, 10*(2), 2-10.

Smith, R. L. (1966). *Monotony and motivation: A theory of vigilance.* Santa Monica, CA: Dunlap and Associates.

Smith, G. J. W., Spence, D. P., & Klein, G. S. (1959). Subliminal effects of verbal stimuli. *Journal of Abnormal and Social Psychology, 59,* 167-176.

Smith, K. (2001). *New designs for multimedia learning.* Unpublished paper, Virginia Tech University.

Smith, K. U., & Smith, M. F. (1966). *Cybernetic principles of learning and educational design.* New York: Holt, Rinehart and Winston.

Smith, P. L., Hsu, S, Azzarello, J., & McMichael, J. (1993). *Group based multimedia: Research conclusions and future question.* Paper presented at the Association for Educational Communications and Technology Convention, New Orleans, LA.

Smith, S. M., Glenbert, A., & Bjork, R. A. (1978). Environmental context and human memory. *Memory and Cognition, 6,* 342-353.

Spaulding, S. (1956). Communication potential of pictorial illustration. *AV Communication Review, 4,* 31-46.

Sperling, G. (1960). The information available in brief visual presentations. *Psychological Monographs, 74,* 1-29.

Strommen, E. F., & Revelle, G. L. (1990). Research in interactive technologies at the Children's Television Workshop. *Educational Technology Research and Development, 38*(4), 65-80.

Suppes, P. (1980). The teacher and computer-assisted instruction. In R. P. Taylor (Ed.), *The computer in the school: Tutor, tool, tutee* (pp. 231-235). New York: Teachers College Press.

Sweller, J., & Chandler, P. (1991). Evidence for cognitive load. *Cognition and Instruction, 8*(4), 351-362.

Sweller, J., & Chandler, P. (1994). Why some material is difficult to learn*. *Cognition and Instruction, 12,* 185-233.

Taris, L. J. (1970). *Subliminal perception: An experimental study to determine whether a science concept can be taught subliminally to fourth grade pupils.* (Doctoral dissertation, Boston University, 1970). University Microfilms No. 70-22527.

Tergan, S. (1997). Misleading theoretical assumptions in hypertext/hypermedia research. *Journal of Educational Multimedia and Hypermedia, 6*(3/4), 257-283.

Thompson, A. D., Simonson, M. R., & Hargrave, C. P. (1992). *Educational technology: A review of the research.* Washington, DC: Association for Educational Communications and Technology.

Travers, R. M. W. (1964a). The transmission of information to human receivers. *AV Communication Review, 12,* 373-385.

Travers, R. M. W. (Ed.). (1964b). *Research and theory related to audiovisual information transmission.* Salt Lake City: Bureau of Educational Research, University of Utah.

Travers, R. M. W. (1967). *Research and theory related to audiovisual information transmission* (rev. ed.; Contract No. 3-20-003), Washington, DC: U.S. Department of Health, Education and Welfare.

Travers, R. M. W. (1968, April). *Theory of perception and the design of audiovisual materials.* Paper presented at the Faculty on Educational Media, Bucknell University.

Travers, R. M. W. et al. (1966). *Studies related to the design of audiovisual teaching materials* (Final Report Contract No. 3-20-003). Washington, DC: U.S. Department of Education.

Treisman, A. M. (1960). Contextual cues in selective listening. *Quarterly Journal of Experimental Psychology, 12,* 242-248.

Trepanier-Street, M. (2000, April). *Multiple forms of representation in long-term projects.* Paper presented at the annual conference of the Association for Childhood Education International, Toronto, Canada.

U. S. Army (1959). *Training by television and television prompting equipment.* New York: Redstone Arsenal, Ordnance Guided Missile School.

VanderMeer, A. W. (1951). *Relative effectiveness of color and black and white in instructional films.* (Technical Report No. SDC-269-7-28). Port Washington, NY: Office of Naval Research, Human Engineering Division, Special Devices Center.

Van Mondfrans, A. P. (1963). *An investigation of the interaction between the level of meaningfulness and redundancy in the content of the stimulus material, and the mode of presentation of the stimulus material.* Unpublished master's thesis, University of Utah.

Van Mondfrans, A. P., & Travers, R. M. W. (1964). Learning of redundant materials presented through two sensory modalities. *Perceptual and Motor Skills, 19,* 743-51.

Warshaw, P. R. (1978. Application of selective attention theory to television advertising displays. *Journal of Applied Psychology, 63*(3), 366-372.

Webb, N. M. (1982). Group composition, group interaction and achievement in cooperative small groups. *Journal of Educational Psychology, 74,* 475-484.

Westwater, J. N. (1973). A wide-screen multi-image presentation used as a multidimensional resource for experimental education: A study of teacher-user perceptions (Doctoral dissertation, Ohio State University). *Dissertation Abstracts International, 33*(8-a), 3976. (University Microfilms No. 73-02, 159)

Whitley, J. B. (1977). *The effects of perceptual type and presentation mode in a visual location task.* Unpublished doctoral dissertation, Virginia Polytechnic Institute and State University.

Whitley, J. B., & Moore, D. M. (1979). The effects of perceptual type and presentation mode in a visual location task. *Educational Communication and Technology Journal, 27*(4), 281-290.

Wilcot, R. C. (1953). A search for subthreshold conditioning at four different auditory frequencies. *Journal of Experimental Psychology, 46,* 271-277.

Williams, D., & Ogilvie, J. (1957). Mass media, learning, and retention. *Canadian Journal of Psychology, 11,* 157-163.

Winn, B. (1987). Charts, graphs, and diagrams in educational materials. In D. M. Willows & H. A. Houghton (Eds.), *The psychology of illustration.* New York: Springer-Verlag.

Witkin, H. A., Moore, C. A., Goodenough, D. R., & Cox, P. W. (1977). Field-dependent and field-independent cognitive styles and their educational implications. *Review of Educational Research, 47,* 1-64.

Wittrock, M. C. (1989). Generative process of comprehension. *Educational Psychologist, 24,* 345-376.

Welford, A. T. (1968). *Fundamentals of skills.* London: Methuen.

Yang, C. S. (1993). *Theoretical foundations of hypermedia.* Unpublished paper, Virginia Polytechnic Institute and State University.

Yerushalmy, M. (1991). Student perceptions of aspects of algebraic function using multiple representation software. *Journal of Computer Assisted Instruction, 7,* 42-57.

Zuckerman, M. (1960). The effects of subliminal and supraliminal suggestion on verbal productivity. *Journal of Abnormal and Social Psychology, 60,* 404-411.

Part

·VII·

RESEARCH METHODOLOGIES

PHILOSOPHY, RESEARCH, AND EDUCATION

J. Randall Koetting, and Mark Malisa
University of Nevada, Reno

Research always conveys a commitment to philosophical beliefs even if this is unintended and even though it remains implicit and unacknowledged....[Researchers] cannot evade the responsibility for critically examining and justifying the philosophical ideas that their enquiries incorporate. It follows that philosophical reflection and argumentation are central features of the methods and procedures of educational research.

—W. Carr, 1995 (as quoted in Bridges, 1997, p. 179)

Indeed...adapting from Plato on a different but not unrelated matter, one might say that there may be no good educational practice until all professional teachers become—rather than school effectiveness, action researchers or other empirical researchers—educational philosophers.

—D. Carr, (2001, p. 475)

The problems we face are not really technical—they are moral, they are ethical. A reliance on technical solutions leaves us still gasping, still empty.

—M. Greene (as quoted in Ayers & Miller, 1998, p. 6)

37.1 INTRODUCTION: PHILOSOPHY AND PERSONAL STRUGGLE

The purpose of this chapter in the First Edition of this handbook was to engage the reader in a discussion of concepts/issues in philosophy and to suggest how philosophical inquiry is a form of critical inquiry, philosophy as a way of doing research. The concepts/issues were (are) presented (re-presented) as follows.

1. Education is a moral undertaking and therefore our practice within education must be open to inquiry.
2. To engage in philosophical inquiry is to theorize, to analyze, to critique, to raise questions about, and/or to pose as problematic that which we are investigating.
3. Theory can be derived from other systems of thought; derived from social, political, and/or economic situations; and constructed from practice.
4. Philosophical inquiry is concerned with (i.e., "inquires into") the nature of reality, knowledge, and value.
5. Philosophical inquiry can be descriptive, normative, and/or analytic. It can be interpretive and/or critical.
6. Modes of philosophical inquiry have interests: Interpretive inquiry has an interest in understanding, critical inquiry has an interest in emancipation.
7. Critical inquiry is a mode of philosophical inquiry that questions reality, looking for contradictions. Critical inquiry is change/action-oriented.

8. The major task of philosophy is the posing of questions. It is the foundation of research. Without good questions there is no inquiry.
9. Philosophical inquiry is doing philosophy.
10. Philosophical inquiry is philosophical research.

The struggle for the first author in writing the first-edition chapter was twofold: to establish that philosophy is more than an "academic distraction" and to present to the reader a philosophical discussion of the relationship/connectedness of philosophy and research. Eisner (1991) provided insight into understanding my struggle, stating that some researchers within the social sciences viewed philosophy as an "academic distraction" because

Philosophy is nagging. It conjoles students into asking questions about basic assumptions, it generates doubts and uncertainties, and, it is said, it keeps people from getting their work done. Many appear to believe that it is better to leave the unanswerable questions and unsolvable problems alone and get down to brass tacks. I regard such attitudes as short-sighted. Core concepts in the social sciences are philosophical in nature: Objectivity, Validity, Truth, Fact, Theory, Structure. Why neglect to examine them, even if their examination will never yield a single unassailable meaning? (pp. 4–5)

Trying to deal with the "big picture" in education gets complicated. There is a greater sense of urgency felt today to come up with answers to educational "problems." Philosophy takes too much time. There is the sense of "Lets get down to brass tacks." Like Eisner, I experience philosophy as a study that does nag at my thinking because, at its best, it has me question and doubt. Because I question and doubt, sometimes it keeps me from getting my work done. Also, I agree with Eisner that core concepts in the social sciences are philosophical in nature. And this is my struggle, also taken up by my coauthor.

Our perspective in this chapter is that of teacher–student. We find value in the study of philosophy, which has helped us to understand issues in education better. Our purpose in this chapter is to convey to the reader the importance of philosophy for research into education. We discuss and analyze, in a philosophical way, philosophy, education, and research. We do this by situating our discussion of philosophy, inquiry, and education within a general discussion of educational research. We then examine education as a moral undertaking, and that inquiry is foundational (theoretical), diverse, and critical. We argue that the study of philosophy/philosophy of education will provide a framework needed for inquiry into schooling that is foundational (theoretical), diverse, and critical. We briefly look at the notion of theory and the importance of having or taking a theoretical (foundational) perspective. Modes of philosophical inquiry are discussed throughout the chapter.

Greene (1978) provides insight into what is implicit in the writing of this chapter and suggests the philosophical issues imbedded in the work of teachers, hence the importance of and need for philosophical inquiry:

The concern of teacher educators must remain normative, critical, and even political. Neither the teachers' colleges nor the schools can change the social order. Neither colleges nor schools can legislate democracy.

But something can be done to empower teachers to reflect upon their own life situations, to speak out in their own ways about the lacks that must be repaired, the possibilities to be acted upon in the name of what they deem decent, humane, and just. (p. 71)

The study of philosophy/philosophy of education can provide the possibility for the empowering possibilities and practices that Greene identifies: reflection on one's own life situation, one's own voice with which to speak, and the possibility for action based on decency, humaneness, and justice.

37.2 EDUCATION AND RESEARCH

We begin with a brief definition and discussion of what we consider a mainstream position on what constitutes educational research (Anderson, 1990). We do this to situate our discussion of philosophy, research, and education:

Research in education is a disciplined attempt to address questions or solve problems through the collection and analysis of primary data for the purpose of description, explanation, generalization and prediction. (Anderson, 1990, p. 4)

Anderson's discussion in his first chapter, entitled "The Nature of Educational Research," expands this definition. He views educational research as primarily problem solving as opposed to testing of hypotheses. This research is based on "systematic and objective observation, recording and analysis"; it seeks to find "general principles and theories which can lead to the prediction of behaviors and events in the future"; its goals are "understanding, prediction and ultimately control"; controlled, accurate observation and recording information allow for prediction to be "accurately measured and assessed"; the researcher should be "unbiased" and strive for "objectivity" (p. 5). Furthermore, "research is a scientific process which assumes that events in the world are lawful and orderly" and that the laws are "discoverable." This lawfulness provides the meaning of determinism and the

... researcher acts in the belief that the laws of nature can be understood and ultimately controlled to at least some degree. In a nutshell, educational research is the systematic process of discovering how and why people in educational settings behave as they do. (pp. 4–5)

As stated above, we believe that this is a mainstream position on educational research.

Anderson (1990) also identifies "four different levels at which educational research takes place: descriptive, explanatory, generalization and basic or theoretical" (p. 7). It is within the basic/theoretical level that Anderson places philosophy as an associated discipline:

While philosophy does not typically incorporate primary source data, empirical evidence, or observation, it is included as an associated discipline since it relies on similar approaches to other forms of theoretical research. (p. 7)

At the same time, in a previous passage, philosophy is not considered research within the definition quoted earlier:

There is another domain of investigation which some scholars consider research. It includes philosophical analysis, especially conceptual analysis, the situation of educational issues within a philosophical tradition, the examination of epistemological and axiological assumptions, criticism and so forth. I view such activities as scholarship, but not as research in the sense in which it is used in this text. The principal difference is the lack of primary data in those approaches which rely entirely on critical thinking and analysis of existing literature and theory. (p. 5)

The above discussion places philosophy outside legitimate educational research and identifies it as "scholarship." In this framework, scholarship does not qualify as research because it is not "empirical."

Whereas the impression is that in the sciences there is a detached empiricism, researchers in the sciences also have a commitment to philosophical beliefs, although at times the philosophical beliefs might not be explicit. They, too (researchers in the sciences), have a responsibility to society, and that responsibility is usually justified in philosophical terms. Thus, there is no neutral research even in the natural/hard sciences. For example, researchers in medicine and in civil engineering (e.g., building highways, large buildings, bridges) have to consider ethical implications of their work. They are concerned with finding cures for human maladies, safer transportation and buildings, etc. There is no veiled claim to neutrality. Hence, philosophy is implicit in research. Bridges (1997) observes that scientific research usually operates in such a way that the researcher is "artificially invisible" (p. 179). With philosophical research, however, although there are particular methodologies in use (e.g., "Socratic questioning, Cartesian doubting, or linguistic analysis"), oftentimes the research process itself is less visible, whereas the researcher is highly visible. "One curious consequence is that of course we have relatively little public evidence of the way in which philosophers go about their business: we have rather the fruits of that business" (p. 179). We do not believe that this makes an associated discipline of one and genuine research of the other.[1]

37.3   EDUCATION UNDERSTOOD AS A MORAL UNDERTAKING

The study of philosophy/philosophy of education can provide greater insight and understanding into the complexities of schooling. By complexities of schooling we mean that educational practice does not "just happen," does not take place as an isolated activity. Wingo (1974) identifies the complexities of the school setting:

Behind every approach to teaching method, behind every plan for administrative organization of the schools, behind the structure of every school curriculum stands a body of accepted doctrine—assumptions, concepts, generalizations, and values. In short, every practical approach to the art of teaching is shored up by some constellation of accepted ideas. Very often, however, the very presence of this body of ideas goes unnoticed. Its acceptance is largely unconscious and based on tradition. (p. 6)

To be more explicit about this, as educators, we are concerned with philosophical issues and perspectives in our daily work within classrooms. As we debate curricular issues, as we decide educational policy, as we work with students and their "behavior," as we "test" students' "knowledge," etc., we are concerned with philosophy. However, as Wingo stated, the underlying ideas behind our practice may go unnoticed, may be unconscious, may be unquestioned. The importance of philosophical inquiry in education is exactly at this point: It can illuminate, inform, call into question, etc., the taken-for-granted notions that we have. Philosophical inquiry and analysis can help conceptual clarification, as well as inform our praxis, and vice versa.

37.3.1   Traditional Philosophical Questions

The Western tradition in philosophy has wrestled with the following questions: What is real? (metaphysics/ontology), How do we know? (epistemology), and What is of value? (axiology). Understanding and identifying the nature of reality, what counts for knowledge, and what is of value, are all philosophical positions. We use the term *philosophical inquiry* to mean a form of questioning (inquiring into) the nature of reality, knowledge, and value. This notion of inquiry is the beginning of doing philosophy, of inquiring into the nature of things (Greene, 1974).

The three questions/positions regarding the nature of reality, knowledge, and value also identify the nature of the concerns of schooling as well as forming the basis for philosophical inquiry. If this is so, the lives of educators/researchers are rooted in philosophical and moral struggles and questions, and consequently they cannot view their work as a neutral enterprise. Their lives are rooted in philosophical, moral, and nonneutral (political) realities because educators, schools, communities, interest groups, legislators, religious organizations, private and corporate enterprise, etc., presuppose some conception of reality that they wish to transmit, or pass on to the young. As Childs (1950) stated,

... Deliberate education is never morally neutral. A definite expression of preference for certain human ends, or values, is inherent in all efforts to guide the experience of the young. No human group would ever bother to found and maintain a system of schools were it not concerned to make of its children something other than they would become if left to themselves and their surroundings. (p. 19)

School practice reflects the interests of divergent groups. The metaphysical/ontological, epistemological, and axiological

---

[1]As we stated in the Introduction, modes of philosophical inquiry are discussed throughout the chapter. Also, see Kincheloe (1991), especially Chapter 3, on "Exploring Assumptions Behind Educational Research: The Nature of Positivism," pp. 48–66.

questions of philosophy are educational questions as well. Research in education reflects this. The differing groups mentioned have interests, and those interests identify the political nature of education.

School curricula reflect multiple worldviews. Curricula reflect the possibilities of humankind. Curricula can raise critical questions about the nature of the social world and how we know that world, or it can dogmatically repress such exploration. To choose a specific curriculum is to choose from among many possibilities. Curricular decision making is hence a political decision. To say that "... education is a moral undertaking involves choices that make a difference in the individual and social lives of human beings" (Morris & Pai, 1976, p. 18).

The concept of moral as used here is from Child's work (1950), *Education and Morals*. He uses the term quite specifically regarding educators' intervention in the lives of their students. Moral refers to

... the more elemental fact that choices among genuine life-alternatives are inescapably involved in the construction and the actual conduct of each and every educational program. These choices necessarily have consequences in the lives of the young, and through them in the life of the society. Viewed from this perspective, education undoubtedly ranks as one of the outstanding moral undertakings of the human race. (p. 20)

Furthermore, education is rooted in philosophical and political realities. The philosophical and political roots come in when we are required to make choices from among many possible worldviews.[2]

Boyd (1997) echoes this notion of education as a moral undertaking. He states that to be involved in education "is to be engaged, ultimately, with the question of what it means to be fully human" (p. 4). He goes on to state,

... Education is one of the main ways we have as humans to define our humanity, to practice our humanity, to maintain our humanity, and to change our humanity. It is how we seek to connect ourselves today with ourselves of the past and it is how we project ourselves into the future. Although it is tempting to view much of what goes on in contemporary schools in much less grandiose terms, to do so risks losing sight of what schools are there for in the end. (p. 5)

If education is a moral undertaking as Childs rightly suggests, and a way for us to define our humanity, as Boyd suggests, it is incumbent on educators to "inquire into their work," to question their theory and practice. Philosophical inquiry provides various ways of doing that.

37.4 PHILOSOPHY AND INQUIRY

Although we were critical of Anderson's (1990) discussion of philosophy and research, we do think he accurately represented

the processes of philosophical inquiry: conceptual analysis, situating educational issues within a philosophical tradition, and examination of epistemological and axiological assumptions, criticism, etc. He also emphasized critical thinking and analysis of existing literature and theory as part of philosophical inquiry. These processes are modes of philosophical inquiry, ways of doing philosophy.

Our criticism of Anderson's position centered on his viewing philosophy as an "associated discipline" for research, whereas we believe it to be a foundation (theory) for educational research. Philosophical conclusions are the fruit of research, not simple speculation. To begin to address philosophy as foundation, we return to the three questions that have concerned philosophers within the Western traditions from the beginning.

What is the nature of reality? What is the nature of knowledge? and What is of value? (metaphysics, epistemology, and axiology, respectively). These questions provide a *conceptual framework* that gives coherence to the study of philosophy. These questions also identify the major concerns of education and provide the possibility for coherence in educational practice. By coherence we mean that they provide educators with a possible framework for posing questions from multiple perspectives that allow us to reflect on our work. For example, they allow us to pose multiple questions regarding the nature of curricula. They allow us to examine whose knowledge we are promoting and, even prior to that, what knowledge is of most worth. Questions of value ask us why we choose this particular knowledge and leave all of the rest out, etc. (see Apple, 1979, 1996). Engaging in this questioning is philosophical inquiry, is doing philosophy.

Another framework we can use in looking at the relationship among philosophy, research, and education, is an examination of the differing approaches to the study of philosophy. Wingo (1974) states that we can approach the study of philosophy in three ways (these ways may also be looked at as the main functions of philosophy): the descriptive, the normative, and the analytic (pp. 15–16).

To engage in descriptive philosophical inquiry, a student would be involved in the study of the history of philosophy. He or she would be studying "... what is (and has been) the field of philosophy. Working comprehensively, he is trying to picture the general development of philosophical thought" (Wingo, 1974, p. 15). This is more than studying "intellectual history." As Wingo points out, it is possible to study about what philosophers have said and, at the same time, be doing philosophy in that students are "analyzing and clarifying concepts and the language in which ideas are expressed" (p. 15). This is the area that Anderson (1990) identified as situating educational issues within a philosophical tradition. For example, educational issues looked at from the viewpoint of different philosophies, and what writers within those philosophical traditions said about the issues, how they would go about making sense of those issues, establish a worldview (metaphysics/ontology), a way of knowing (epistemology), and a way to make decisions regarding

---

[2]Recent educational critics suggest that we have lost this sense of education as a moral undertaking. Representative essays of a philosophical nature are those by Aronowitz and Giroux (1985), Beyer (1998), Giroux (1988), and Purpel (1993).

action (axiology). Philosophy of education textbooks are good examples of the descriptive perspective.[3]

To engage in normative philosophical inquiry a student would be involved with values (axiology). Interests could focus on

ethics or aesthetics. He will be involved with advocating some ends or objectives (values) that he believes to be desirable and with explaining the reasons for their desirability. He may also be involved in suggesting means for advocating these values. His main concern is not what is, but what ought to be. (Wingo, 1974, p. 15)

Normative philosophical inquiry explores and critiques philosophical positions, as well as making decisions as to the "rightness and wrongness" of those positions (see Webb, Metha, & Jordan, 1992). The normative perspective reflects Anderson's (1990) earlier position regarding examination of epistemological and axiological assumptions, as well as critical thinking and analysis of existing literature and theory as part of inquiry.[4]

To engage in analytic philosophical inquiry is to engage in the "analysis of language, concepts, theories, and so on" (Wingo, 1974, p. 15). This is the practice that analytic philosophers consider "doing philosophy." According to Webb et al. (1992), analytic philosophy has as its goal

... to improve our understanding of education by clarifying our educational concepts, beliefs, arguments, assumptions. For example, an analytic philosophy of education would attempt to understand such questions as: What is experience? What is understanding? What is readiness? (pp.174–175)

Anderson (1990) referred to the analytic perspective as conceptual analysis.[5]

The framework of the "functions" of philosophy suggests the foundations position mentioned earlier. Each of these three functions can provide multiple possibilities for educational research and, more specifically, philosophical inquiry. The descriptive, normative, and analytic forms of philosophical inquiry suggest in-depth study of the philosophy of education. Looking at different philosophical traditions with regard to metaphysics/ontology, epistemology, and axiology requires study in philosophy. Movements in education, e.g., reconstructionism, perrenialism, Marxism and education, and more recent movements rooted in critical theory, postmodern analyses, and renewed emphasis on democratic schooling and forms of emancipatory practice, represent major areas of study for researchers. These areas of study have their own world-views and concerns. Writers within these positions offer differing conceptual frameworks, differing questions posed, and hence challenges to status quo practice. And they all engage the student in philosophical inquiry.

The study of the philosophy of education from the normative, descriptive, and analytic perspectives offers critical means of inquiry into educational realities for researchers. Writing within these frameworks is doing philosophy. Doing philosophy is doing research. The descriptive perspective works out of systems of philosophical thought, schools of thought, offering foundational positions from which to work; the normative perspective offers a "process of inquiry into ideas and basic beliefs that will enable us to form reasoned attitudes about the important issues of our time" (Wingo, 1974, p. 22). The analytic perspective allows us to inquire into the use of language, the meaning, and clarification of language used to talk about education. This is philosophical inquiry/philosophical research.

Education is a complex social undertaking, having myriad important dimensions that can be examined from psychological, sociological, and political perspectives, yet there is one question that is uniquely philosophical: "the question of determining the ends of education" (Wingo, 1974, p. 22). The means and ends of education are inseparably united. Wingo quotes Max Black:

All serious discussion of educational problems, no matter how specific, soon leads to consideration of educational aims, and becomes a conversation about the good life, the nature of man, the varieties of experience. But these are the perennial themes of philosophical investigation. It might be a hard thing to expect educators to be philosophical, but can they be anything else? (p. 22)

Conceptualizations about "the good life," the nature of humankind, etc., are problematic in the sense that there are no final, all-inclusive, agreed-on positions on these concepts. Inquiry into these issues can take place through the descriptive, normative, and analytic perspectives. Each of these perspectives, again, will demand different questions be posed. This process is doing philosophy, doing philosophical inquiry.

To understand how the three perspectives can be used in the study of education, Wingo (1974) suggests that there are three assumptions that underlie the nature of philosophical inquiry in education. These three assumptions are critical to an understanding of the importance, scope, and possibility the study of philosophy has for the study of education. As obvious as it may seem, the first assumption is, "The primary subject matter of philosophy of education is education itself" (p. 24). Thus the phenomena of education, in all its myriad forms, are the "subject matter" for study. From a research point of view this can mean looking at curricula, the outcomes of learning, testing, organizational matters, place of schools within the social setting, the means–ends of education, etc.

The second, and perhaps the most insightful and critical assumption, states that "education always takes place within a certain constellation of cultural conditions and therefore it cannot be studied as a set of universal and independent phenomena" (Wingo, 1974, p. 24). This assumption means that there is no "one best system" to model schools after and no single answer to complex educational situations. This assumption suggests that we need to view education relationally, in context (cf. Apple, 1979; Beyer, 1986; Purpel, 1993), and clearly identifies the

---

[3]Examples of descriptive philosophical inquiry can be found in the following philosophy of education texts: Gutek (1997), Ozmon and Craver (1995), and Wingo (1974).
[4]See Dewey, 1904/1964 and Kaufman (1966) for examples of normative philosophical inquiry.
[5]Examples of analytic inquiry are Tom (1984) and Wilson (1963).

complex nature of understanding education. At the same time this assumption suggests the myriad possibilities for inquiry into the process of schooling. By this we mean that the nature of the inquiry is dependent on the researcher. It is not standardized, it is not given (cf. Eisner, 1991).

The third assumption states that the "basic purpose of philosophy of education applies to the ends and means of education and their interrelationships" (Wingo, 1974, p. 24). The assumption suggests the complexity of educational experience and the many variables/factors that influence the process. These assumptions clearly call for the descriptive, normative, and analytic perspectives of viewing educational realities but also point toward the need for expanding our decision to accommodate other perspectives such as interpretive and critical forms of inquiry, as well as the empirical.

A way to expand our discussion to accommodate other perspectives that can be used in looking at the relationship among philosophy, inquiry, and education can be found in examining research paradigms. This framework (research paradigms) extends the more traditional descriptive, normative, and analytic perspectives by looking at methodological/epistemological viewpoints. This framework allows the researcher to identify human interests within modes of inquiry.[6]

Bredo and Feinberg (1982) discuss differing paradigms according to the research methodologies utilized. These methodologies have inherent interests in the kind of research findings sought and generated. The paradigms identified are the positivistic, the interpretive, and the critical approaches to social and educational research. These paradigms have fundamental differences that separate the positivistic from the interpretive and critical approaches. These differences are of a philosophical nature concerning metaphysics, subject–object dualism, generalization, causality, and axiology (Koetting, 1985).

If we pose the question "Why do we do research?" our response will allow us to explore the framework (research paradigms) as follows. We do research to gain a clear/clearer perception of reality and our relationship to that reality. This clearer perception can be of benefit to us and others depending on our interests: What are we searching for? (Truth? Knowledge? Information? Understanding? Explanation? Emancipation?). This notion of interest also bears on why we ask certain research questions, as well as what the nature of the research question/problem/situation under investigation might be. Positivist science has an interest in technical control, interpretive science has an interest in understanding, and critical science has an interest in emancipation. For example, I may try to control reality better to make predictions, develop lawlike theories or explanations, establish causal relationships, etc. This would correspond to the positivist, empirical approach to research. I may want to understand reality better and, hence, understand myself and others within a particular context. I may want to understand the meanings attached to social customs, the diversity of meaning in multiple interpretations of singular events, etc. This would

correspond to the interpretive approach to research. I may want to understand reality better and, hence, understand myself and others within a particular context in order to act within that context, to effect change. This corresponds to the critical approach to social and educational research.

There are fundamental differences that separate forms of inquiry, and the differences are of a philosophical nature. The differences are concerned with the three questions of philosophy stated earlier: metaphysics/ontology, epistemology, and axiology (also, cf. Koetting, 1985, 1993). These concerns keep us rooted in doing philosophy.

Although we have used the term "foundations" frequently in this section, We are not talking about the establishment of a "metanarrative" (Hlynka and Yeaman, 1992; Lyotard, 1984). We are not talking about "doing philosophy in the grand manner" of building systems of thought (Wingo, 1974). We do not believe that there is only one complete explanation or understanding of our social world and that, given the time and effort, we will be able to "figure things out." What we are saying about foundations is the way in which philosophy is carried out, within philosophical inquiry, the problem posing, the questioning, the search for clarification, the quest for seeing things relationally, provides multiple ways of inquiring into the world of social and educational realities.

Martusewicz and Reynolds (1994) state a similar position regarding foundations. They see the "job" of foundations as being

... to raise questions and offer points of view that ask us to see what we do as teachers or as students in new or at least unfamiliar ways, from another side, perhaps from the inside, or perhaps from both inside and outside. It is an invitation to look at education both socially and historically as well as practically, that is, from the inside (the complex processes, methods, and relations that affect individuals in schools, for example) within the context of the outside (the larger social, economic, and political forces that have affected those processes over time). (p. 2)

This notion of inside/outside (school/world) suggests the "flux of boundaries" and allows the researcher/participant to see the relationships of seemingly separate realities, as well as questioning the idea of foundations as a "stable set of knowledges, concepts, or principles to be discovered, defined, and then presented in a unilinear way" (p. 3; also see Greene, 1974). Again, there is no one best way to explain what happens in the world or in education. Possibilities for understanding, however, can take place when we pay "particular attention to perspectives that maintain a critical stance, a willingness to put existing assumptions and interpretations into question" (Mantusewicz and Reynolds, 1994, p. 3).

As we become engaged in this form of critical inquiry, we become involved in theory (foundations). There are multiple theoretical perspectives on the world, knowledge, value.[7] However, there is no metanarrative. There is no grand philosophy (Greene, 1974, 1994; Martusewicz & Reynolds, 1994). Returning to an assumption made earlier in this chapter from Wingo (1974),

---

[6]The foundational (theoretical) text that influenced my (first author) study was that by Jurgen Habermas (1971): also, as secondary texts, those by Bernstein (1978), who offers an historical perspective and overview of mainstream social science and moves through theoretical positions of language, analysis, phenomenology, and critical theory, and Schroyer (1973).

[7]Note the chapters in this volume on postmodernism and poststructural theory and on critical theory.

education always takes place within a certain constellation of cultural conditions and therefore it cannot be studied as a set of universal and independent phenomena. Some set of relations among education, politics, and social institutions is inevitable and cannot be ignored in any useful analysis. (p. 24)

There are multiple explanations/understandings of schooling, and of the "world," and multiple ways of knowing. In the next section we turn to a discussion of theory. Understanding the notion of theory can provide insight into the multiple interpretations of the world and experience. Theorizing is a mode of philosophical inquiry that suggests the complexities and possibilities for creating/constructing knowledge.

37.4.1 Theory and Philosophical Inquiry

Theorizing is a mode of philosophical inquiry. It is an important mode of inquiry in that, as educators/researchers, we take a theoretical stance with regard to our work (Koetting, 1993). Stated another way, as educators/researchers, we work out of a theoretical framework that is very closely related to our orientation to the world. This happens whether we are conscious of it or not. Furthermore, it is important that we reflect on that stance, we try to understand how that stance affects our practice and, vice versa, how the practice influences our theoretical stance. This is directly related to the earlier discussion of the moral nature of our work (we intervene in the lives of people).

How do we define/talk about theory that helps shape our practice, and practice that helps to shape theory? Stated simply, theory is a "worldview, a way of looking at and explaining a set of phenomena" (Martusewicz and Reynolds, 1994, p. 5). In relation to philosophy and education, Gutek (1997) refers to theory as a "grouping or clustering of general ideas or propositions that explain the operations of an institution, such as school, or a situation, such as teaching or learning" and says that these ideas are "sufficiently abstract or general that they can be transferred and applied to situations other than those in which they are directly developed" (p. 259). Theory can also refer to an "opinion that originates from trying to establish generalizable patterns from facts, information, or practices" (p. 259).

Where do educational theories come from? How do educators arrive at theoretical positions? Gutek (1997) discusses three sources of educational theory. Educational theory can be derived from philosophies or ideologies; educational theory can be constructed from reactions to certain "social, political, and economic situations"; and theories can be constructed from educational practice. We discuss each of these sources.

First, theories are derived from philosophies and ideologies. This is the study of philosophy of education. Education is examined within the broader context of individual philosophical systems. Although these systems may not have dealt specifically with education, educators, writers, and scholars derive educational positions from these philosophies and apply principles from their study to schooling. For example, progressivism, as a theory of education, is derived from elements of pragmatism and naturalism. Similarly, we can derive a theory of education from ideological positions. For example, a view of the Ameri-

can democratic ideology can be found in public-school settings. Theories of education can be derived from a Marxist ideology. And, finally, educational theories can be derived from blending philosophy and ideology, as in social reconstructionism, a blending of philosophical elements found in Pragmatism and ideological elements found in Utopianism (cf. Gutek, 1997, pp. 259–262). This theorizing is philosophical inquiry.

Second, educational theory can be developed from reactions to certain "social, political, and economic situations." Gutek (1997) suggests studying the history of American education to understand the reactive nature of educational theories. For example, in the late nineteenth and early twentieth century, educational critics said that

... schools had become too formal, devitalized, and geared to rote learning. In some of the big cities school systems were mired in political patronage and corruption. Progressivism as an educational movement and the various experimental schools that it simulated, including John Dewey's at the University of Chicago, were reactions designed to bring about the reform of American society and education. (p. 252)

This examination and critique of existing literature (cf. Anderson, 1990) are philosophical inquiry, are doing philosophy.

Finally, educational theories can be constructed from educational practice. The effective schools movement provides an example of theory derived from practice (Gutek, 1997). Schools, teachers, administrators are singled out for their effectiveness in bringing about higher levels of student achievement. Research is conducted, findings are analyzed, generalizations and principles are offered. A research report is published by the Department of Education entitled *What Works: Research About Teaching and Learning* (1986, quoted in Gutek). The report

... is based on a research investigation and analysis of school practices. Information about these practices is organized as findings. These findings have sufficient generality about them that they can be applied in various school settings. In other words, they represent an emerging theory of education. (pp. 261–262)

Examples of theoretical generalizations and principles from the report are

Parents are their children's first and most influential teachers. What parents do to help their children learn is more important to academic success than how well-off the family is.

and

Children learn science best when they are able to do experiments, so they can witness "science in action."

and, finally,

Belief in the value of hard work, the importance of personal responsibility, and the importance of education itself contribute to greater success in school. (pp. 261–262)

These three sources allow us to engage in philosophical inquiry, theorizing possible understandings of realities/schooling. This theorizing is a mode of doing research, a way of doing philosophy. As stated at the beginning of this section, theorizing, inquiry happens whether we are aware of it or not and suggests the importance of "thinking about what we are doing" (Arendt, cited in Greene, 1974, p. 6). This theorizing, this doing philosophy, is what Greene refers to as "wide-awakeness," thinking about commitment and action wherever we "work and make" our lives. "In other words, we shall attempt to do philosophy with respect to teaching, learning, the aims and policies of education, the choices to be made in classrooms, the goods to be pursued" (p. 6).

Another way of talking about theory, to identify the nature of differing theoretical positions, is to view theory in relation to method and interest (Koetting and Januszewski, 1991). From this viewpoint, knowledge of the world is constructed through a dialectical relationship with that world, i.e., we are shaped by our world, and we help to shape that world. Thus

. . . theorizing about that world is part of a social process, and therefore, theory itself can be considered a social construction. Theorizing, as a social construction/social process, arises out of humankind's desire to explain and/or understand and/or to change the world. (Koetting and Januszweski, 1991, p. 97)

This analysis is based on the work of Habermas (1971) and thus has a philosophical position within critical theory. Habermas' theory of knowledge and interests has three forms/processes of inquiry: empirical-analytic, historical-hermeneutic, and critical. Drawing on a previous work (Koetting and Januszweski, 1991), we briefly present these processes.[8]

Theory can serve to explain both the conscious and the unconscious. Theory can be seen as a "hypothetical position which can be proven/disproven through empirical testing." It suggests causal relationships.

This notion of explaining things is the basis for rational thought. Nomological knowledge is the result of such endeavours. Nomological suggests law-like propositions based on the results of the testing of hypotheses. This form of theory (empirical/analytic theory) has an interest in prediction and control. (Koetting and Januszweski, 1991, p. 97)

Theory can serve to help us better understand/make sense of the world as well as ourselves and others within that world. When we are engaged in this form of investigation, our interest is not explanation, but understanding. Thus we are involved in an

. . . interpretive mode of understanding/theorizing and this theoretical stance to the world sees reality as a social construction. This form of theory (historical/hermeneutic theory) has an interest in better understanding that social construction through consensual agreement. (Koetting and Januszweski, 1991, pp. 97–98)

The third use of theory can help us gain insight into seemingly "given" realities. Through a process of reflective critique we can

. . . examine the social construction of reality and seek ways to analyze the contradictions found in reality (the 'is' and the 'ought'). Through a shared vision we can begin to set about the enormous difficulty of changing (our) individual and group context. (Koetting and Januszewski, 1991, p. 98)

To effect change within that context a different understanding of reality is needed. This form of theorizing (critical theory) has an interest in emancipation. In this context emancipation means

. . . the possibility of individuals freeing themselves from "law-like rules and patterns of action in 'nature' and history so that they can reflect and act on the dialectical process of creating and recreating themselves and their institutions" (Apple, 1975, p.126). In this sense, emancipation is a continual process of "critique of everyday life." (Koetting and Januszweski, 1991, p. 98)

This discussion of theory/theorizing returns us to the main focus of this chapter: philosophy, research, and education. There are fundamental differences within the empirical, hermeneutical, and critical modes of knowing and theorizing, and these differences are of a philosophical nature. Each form of inquiry has its own understanding of the nature of reality, the nature of knowledge, and the nature of value (metaphysics, epistemology, axiology). Hence theory and theorizing raise questions of a philosophical nature. To become engaged in raising these questions is philosophical inquiry, is doing philosophy. This is the sense in which Eisner (1991) referred to philosophy as being nagging, "conjoling us" into asking more questions about the nature of things, generating "doubt and uncertainties," and perhaps, hindering us in getting our work done.

Theory and theorizing do lead us to ask philosophical questions. Giarelli and Chambliss (1984) state that it is the philosopher's "task to ask the unasked questions" (p. 36). They state that "without a formulated question, there can be no inquiry" (p. 36). They identify the special task of philosophy as

. . . the formulation of questions for reflective thought. The philosopher, as a qualitative thinker, tries to cultivate a sensitivity to the situation as a whole and to the qualities that regulate it. . . . For the philosopher, the issue always is, "What is the problem?" which in turn depends on a prior question, "What is this all about?" (p. 37)

The philosopher as "qualitative thinker" does not seek certain knowledge or truth but, rather, is concerned with meaning. In this sense,

philosophy does not aim at making the world, for its concern is not action, but qualities. Rather, philosophy serves an educational role. It mediates between immediate experience and experiment and promotes the intelligent development of value. (p. 38)

The educational role of philosophy can be seen within public philosophy of education. Public philosophers of education "see the context of educational problems to be social and cultural

---

[8]This discussion of theorizing relates to our earlier discussion of research paradigms and interest.

life" (p. 40). The social and historical processes of education include the interactions of differing institutions and participants whose intent is to conserve, create, and criticize culture. Public philosophy focuses on creating a context for understanding the process of education as a whole.

Their methods are synthetic rather that analytic and aim to integrate and give synoptic meaning to knowledge from all perspectives (e.g., history, sociology, economics, anthropology, psychology, etc.), about all educative institutions (e.g., family, school, work-place, church, community, media, etc.), in order to construct a context or a vision of education in its widest cultural sense. Without such a context, efforts to resolve educational problems will be short-sighted and short-lived. (p. 40)

This position of the public philosophers of education relates to Wingo's (1974) second assumption that underlies the nature of inquiry in the study of philosophy and education, namely, that "education always takes place within a certain constellation of cultural conditions and therefore it cannot be studied as a set of universal and independent phenomena" (p. 24). Giarelli and Chambliss (1984) build on Wingo's assumption and show the broader context of the discussion.[9] They discuss the nature of questioning:

All questions arise from within a perceptual field, a whole, a context, or a situation. Inquiry is the exploration of questions (or queries) that arise and take particular shape in a situation. The same may be said for "research," which word comes from the Latin re-circere, "to go around again." Research is going around, exploring, looking within a situation, context, or field. Inquiry, then, is not simply questioning or searching. It is questioning and searching with an intent, with some limits, or with an object in mind. (p. 36)

This questioning is a mode of philosophical inquiry and will help to identify the fundamental problems in education, which depend on an aesthetic judgment (axiology) of "where the difficulty is and on qualitative thinking to bring these difficulties into the form of questions and problems that can be researched" (p. 45). In other words, these "questions and problems that can be researched" are not arbitrary, they do not just "appear." They are contextual, purposive, and limited in scope, necessitating further questioning, and have a particular "object" in mind that changes as we question, search, requestion, re-search.

Our discussion in this section has gone from theory and theorizing as philosophical inquiry to the nature of questioning within the context of a public philosophy of education. The nature of questioning, our engagement in the process of questioning, is philosophical inquiry, is doing philosophy.

The present status of "doing philosophy," particularly philosophy of education, has broadened into multiple discourses. Ozmon and Craver (1999) suggest that the "current mood" in philosophy of education is moving away from "overriding systems of thought" and is concerned with problems and issues in particular contexts, becoming the new arena for philosophy of education At the same time, the philosophical task remains one of "constant probing and inquiry" (p. xxv). This suggests to us the

notion of public philosophy of education mentioned previously in the work by Giarelli and Chambliss (1984). This "new arena of philosophy" is what was meant by the construction of a "context or vision of education in its widest cultural sense" (p. 40).

Quantitative research also relies on philosophical inquiry. Sherman, Webb, and Andrews (1984) argue that even a study (e.g., a dissertation) that has a "quantitative formulation" has a

. . . qualitative context out of which it grows and to which its conclusions must be put. The "statement of the problem" in such a study, to be made clearly, calls on philosophy, and the chapter in which conclusions are suggested to be important (for further research or for practice) is philosophical in its axiological import. And one may see a "review of the literature" in any study as an historical account of what has been tried in reference to the problem at hand. (p. 33)

Sherman and co-workers' position captures the sense in which we believe philosophy and its modes of inquiry are the foundation for educational research.

37.5 CONCLUDING DISCUSSION: DOING PHILOSOPHY

We want to revisit some concepts/terms used during the course of this chapter, similar to how we began:

- To engage in philosophical inquiry is to theorize, to analyze, to critique, to raise questions about, and/or to pose as problematic that which we are investigating.
- Philosophical inquiry is concerned with the nature of reality, knowledge, and value.
- Philosophical inquiry can be descriptive, normative, and/or analytic. It can be interpretive and/or critical.
- Modes of philosophical inquiry have interests: Interpretive inquiry has an interest in understanding; critical inquiry has an interest in emancipation.
- Critical inquiry is a mode of philosophical inquiry that questions reality, looking for contradictions. Critical inquiry is change/action-oriented.
- The major task of philosophy is the posing of questions. It is the foundation of research. Without good questions there is no inquiry.
- Philosophical inquiry is philosophical research.

As we have stressed throughout this chapter, philosophical inquiry is doing philosophy. Maxine Greene (1974) has captured in a very insightful and existential way what it means to do philosophy. We have used her work in the course of this chapter and would like to present more of her insights on what it means to do philosophy (also see Ayers & Miller, 1998).

Greene (1974) regards philosophy as a way to approach (a way to look at, or to take a stance with respect to) knowledge gained through study of the sciences and the arts, as well as the

---

[9]Giarelli and Chambliss (1984) identify Dewey's *Democracy and Education* (1944) as a "classic example" of public philosophy of education. Also, cf. Aronowitz and Giroux (1985).

personal understandings and insights that each of us acquires through daily life. Philosophy allows us a way to ask questions that have to do with

...what is presupposed, perceived, intuited, believed, and known. It is a way of contemplating, examining, or thinking about what is taken to be significant, valuable, beautiful, worthy of commitment. It is a way of becoming self-aware, of constituting meanings in one's life-world. Critical thinking is demanded, as are deliberate attempts to make things clear. (p. 7)

There is the exploration of "background consciousness" and boundaries; there is the creation of "unifying perspectives"; there is normative thinking; there is the "probing of what might be, what should be" and the "forging of ideals." Doing philosophy is becoming conscious of the world as it presents itself to our consciousness. "To do philosophy, as Jean-Paul Sartre says, is to develop a fundamental project, to go beyond the situations one confronts and refuse reality as given in the name of a reality to be produced" (p. 7).

To do educational philosophy we must become critically aware of the complexities of the teaching and learning context. We must clarify the meanings of education and the language of schooling. We must become clear about preferences for the "good" and the "right" that motivate pressure groups as they place demands on schools (Greene, 1974, p.7). This calls for critical, analytic, and normative philosophical inquiry.

We do philosophy (theorize) when, for whatever reason, we are

...aroused to wonder about how events and experiences are interpreted and should be interpreted. We philosophize when we can no longer tolerate the splits and fragmentations in our pictures of the world, when we desire some kind of wholeness and integration, some coherence which is our own. (Greene, 1974, pp. 10–11)

This requires that we be "wide awake" within our world, with others, within our communities. To be closed off because of

...snobbery, ignorance, or fear is to be deprived of the content that makes concepts meaningful. It is, as well, to be deprived of the very ground of questioning. For this reason, the teacher who dares to do philosophy must be open to such a multiplicity of realities. He cannot do so if he cannot perceive himself, in both his freedom and his limitations, as someone who must constitute his own meanings with the aid of what his culture provides. Nor can he do so if he is incapable of 'bracketing,' or setting aside, on occasion the presuppositions that fix his vision of the world. (p. 11)

We sense this feeling of a fractured, fragmented world is part of the human condition, our sense of not being at home in the world. To remain open to multiple perspectives of the world, to create our own meanings and yet have to bracket them to understand another, etc., leaves one with a sense of unquietness

(cf. Koetting, 1994). And yet not to be able to do this leaves us (teachers), like our students, to live in a world that is primarily prefabricated by others for what they consider to be "the public." Thus,

on occasion, he must be critically attentive; he must consciously choose what to appropriate and what to discard. Reliance on the natural attitude—a commonsense taking for granted of the everyday—will not suffice. In some fashion, the everyday must be rendered problematic so that questions may be posed. (Greene, 1974, p. 11)

Greene is speaking of the difficult task of maintaining a philosophical attitude, a person/teacher who sees philosophically and can communicate that attitude to students, that sense of empowerment to transform their situations. Thus students

...need to be enabled- through habituation and stimulation- to initiate inquiries. To be equipped for inquiry is to be equipped to engage in a process through which objects and events can be seen in connection with other objects and events in the experienced world. (p. 158)

This is working with students to do philosophy, to develop the philosophical attitude/orientation; this is seeing realities relationally and not in isolation. We need to show, as well as believe, that students are capable of doing philosophy.

Maxine Greene identifies what it means to do philosophy, to engage in philosophical inquiry. We have presented in this chapter many of the theoretical positions that she demonstrates. We have referred to this as the philosophical attitude/orientation. There are many texts that will convey this attitude that would be helpful for initiating or continuing study in educational research.

There are texts on inquiry that are of a philosophical nature, that present in great depth the theoretical positions, the modes of inquiry, and examples of critical research.[10] There are texts within the field of educational technology that convey the theoretical positions for engaging in multiple forms of research.[11] We believe that it is important for those in technology/educational technology to engage in educational philosophy/research. Educational technology is founded on philosophical assumptions, and the designers of educational technology (and of technology in general) work under certain interpretive and normative processes that are essentially philosophical. The dichotomy between technology and philosophy is somewhat superficial, as both impact each other. Although our focus in this chapter has been on education, the connection among educational technology, philosophy of education, and educational research suggests the opportunity for a mutually critical and enriching dialogue. And there are texts of critical essays that are examples of the forms of philosophical inquiry discussed in this chapter.[12] They are examples of doing philosophy.

---

[10]For example, Bredo and Feinberg (1982), Carr and Kemmis (1986), Cherryholmes (1988), Eisner (1991, 1994), Kincheloe (1991) and Popkewitz (1984).

[11]For example, Hlynka and Belland (1991), Muffoletto and Knupfer (1993), and Yeaman, Ketting, and Nichols (1994).

[12]For example, Apple (1999), Beyer and Apple (1998), Greene (1978), Martusewicz and Reynolds (1994), McLaren and Leonard (1993), Pinar (1988), and Short (1991).

37.5.1 A Final Word

Six years have passed since the First Edition of *Handbook of Research on Educational Communications and Technology* was published. In a review of the *Handbook* in *Educational Technology, Research, and Development* (Braden, 1997), specific reference was made to this chapter on "Philosophy, Research, and Education." The chapter was identified as a "surprise." The reviewer stated that the chapter was a "philosophical statement that warrants intellectual consideration. But it is no more than that" (p. 100). As the author of the chapter for the First Edition, I (Koetting) was pleased that the chapter was received as a "philosophical statement that warrants intellectual consideration" because I did struggle with how to discuss and analyze,

in a "philosophical way," philosophy, research, and education. The reviewer went on to say,

... This controversial chapter is one about which each reader will have to make her or his own judgment. Certainly, when we talk about research we should enter into both the discussion and the process with open minds. (Braden, 1997)

We re-present this chapter in the hope that readers will find a viable understanding of educational research that goes beyond the common notions of what it means to do research. It is our belief that philosophy, and philosophy of education, opens the discussion for examining educational issues within a framework of philosophical inquiry (philosophical research).

References

Anderson, G. (1990). *Fundamentals of educational research*. New York: Falmer Press.

Apple, M. W. (1979). *Ideology and curriculum*. London: Routledge.

Apple, M. W. (1996). *Cultural politics and education*. New York: Teachers College Press.

Apple, M. W. (1999). *Power, meaning, and identity: Essays in critical educational studies*. New York: Peter Lang.

Aronowitz, S., & Giroux, H. A. (1985). Education and the crisis of public philosophy. In S. Aronowitz & H. A. Giroux (Eds.), *Education under siege: The conservative, liberal and radical debate over schooling*. South Hadley, MA: Bergin & Garvey.

Aronowitz, S., & Giroux, H. A. (1991). *Postmodern education: Politics, culture, and social criticism*. Minneapolis: University of Minnesota Press.

Ayers, W. C. (1998). Doing philosophy: Maxine Greene and the pedagogy of possibility. In W. C. Ayers & J. L. Miller (Eds.), *A light in dark times: Maxine Greene and the unfinished conversation*. New York: Teachers College Press.

Ayers, W. C., & Miller, J. L. (Eds.). (1998). *A light in dark times: Maxine Greene and the unfinished conversation*. New York: Teachers College Press.

Bernstein, R. J. (1978). *The restructuring of social and political theory*. Philadelphia: University of Pennsylvania Press.

Beyer, L. E. (1986). Beyond elitism and technicism: Teacher education as practical philosophy. *Journal of Teacher Education, 37*(2), 33–41.

Beyer, L. E. (1998). Schooling for democracy: What kind? In L. E. Beyer & M. W. Apple (Eds.), *The curriculum: Problems, politics, & possibilities* (2nd ed.). Albany: State University of New York Press.

Beyer, L. E. & Apple, M. W. (Eds.). (1998). *The curriculum: Problems, politics, & possibilities* (2nd ed.). Albany: State University of New York Press.

Boyd, D. (1997). The place of locating oneself(ves)/myself(ves) in doing philosophy of education. *Philosophy of Education 1997*. Retrieved September 25, 2001, from *http://www.ed.uicu.edu/EPS/PES-yearbook/97_docs/boyd.html*.

Braden, R. A. (1997). Review of *Handbook of Research on Educational Communications and Technology*. *Educational Technology, Research & Development, 45*(1), 98–101.

Bredo, E., & Feinberg, W. (1982). *Knowledge and values in social and educational research*. Philadelphia, PA: Temple University Press.

Bridges, D. (1997). Philosophy and educational research: A reconsideration of epistemological boundaries. *Cambridge Journal of Education, 27*(2), 177–190.

Carr, D. (2001). Educational philosophy, theory and research: A psychiatric autobiography. *Journal of the Philosophy of Education Society of Great Britain, 35*(3), 461–476.

Carr, W., & Kemmis, S. (1986). *Becoming critical: Education, knowledge, and action research*. Philadelphia, PA: Falmer Press.

Carspecken, P. F. (1996). *Critical ethnography in educational research: A theoretical and practical guide*. New York: Routledge.

Cherryholmes, C. (1988). *Power and criticism: Poststructural investigations in education*. New York: Teachers College Press.

Childs, J. L. (1950). *Education and morals*. New York: John Wiley & Sons.

Dewey, J. (1944). *Democracy and education: An introduction to the philosophy of education*. New York: Free Press.

Dewey, J. (1904/1964). *The relation of theory to practice in education*. New York: Modern Library.

Eisner, E. W. (1991). *The enlightened eye: Qualitative inquiry and the enhancement of educational practice*. New York: Macmillan.

Eisner, E. W. (1994). *The educational imagination: On the design and evaluation of school programs* (3rd ed.). New York: Macmillan.

Giarelli, J. M., & Chambliss, J. J. (1984). Philosophy of education as qualitative inquiry. *Journal of Thought, 19*(2), 34–46.

Giroux, H. A. (1988). *Teachers as intellectuals: Toward a critical pedagogy of learning*. Boston, MA: Bergin & Garvey.

Greene, M. (1974). *Teacher as stranger: Educational philosophy for the modern age*. Belmont, CA: Wadsworth.

Greene, M. (1978). *Landscapes of meaning*. New York: Teachers College Press.

Greene, M. (1994). Epistemology and educational research: The influence of recent approaches to knowledge. In L. Darling-Hammond (Ed.), *Review of research in education*. Washington, DC: AERA.

Gutek, G. L. (1997). *Philosophical and ideological perspectives on education* (3rd ed.). Boston, MA: Allyn and Bacon.

Habermas, J. (1971). *Knowledge and human interests*. Boston, MA: Beacon Press.

Hlynka, D., & Belland, J. C. (Eds.). (1991). *Paradigms regained: The uses of illuminative, semiotic, and post-modern criticism as modes of inquiry in educational technology*. Englewood Cliffs, NJ: Educational Technology.

Hlynka, D., & Yeaman, A. R. J. (1992). Postmodern educational technology. *ERIC Digest*, EDO-IR-92-5.

Kaufmann, W. (1966). Educational development from the point of view of a normative philosophy. In G. Barnett (Ed.), *Philosophy and educational development*. Boston, MA: Houghton Mifflin.

Kincheloe, J. L. (1991). *Teachers as researchers: Qualitative inquiry as a path to empowerment*. New York: Falmer Press.

Koetting, J. R. (1979). *Towards a synthesis of a theory of knowledge and human interests, educational technology and emancipatory education: A preliminary theoretical investigation and critique*. Unpublished doctoral dissertation, University of Wisconsin-Madison.

Koetting, J. R. (1983). *Philosophical foundations of instructional technology. Proceedings, Selected Research Papers*, RTD-AECT, Dallas.

Koetting, J. R. (1985). Foundations of naturalistic inquiry: Developing a theory base for understanding individual interpretations of reality. *Media and Adult Learning, 6*(2), 8–18.

Koetting, J. R. (1993). Educational technology, curriculum theory, and social foundations: Toward a new language of possibility. In R. Muffoletto & N. N. Knupfer (Eds.), *Computers in education: Social, political, and historical perspectives*. Cresskill, NJ: Hampton Press.

Koetting, J. R. (1994). Postmodern thinking in a modernist cultural climate: The need for an unquiet pedagogy. *Educational Technology, 34*(2), 55–56.

Koetting, J. R., & Januszweski, A. (1991). The notion of theory and educational technology: Foundation for understanding. *Educational and training technology international, 28*(2), 96–101.

Lyotard, J.-F. (1984). *The postmodern condition: A report on knowledge*. Minneapolis: University of Minnesota Press.

Martusewicz, R. A., & Reynolds, W. M. (Eds.). (1994). *Inside/out: Contemporary critical perspectives in education*. New York: St. Martin's Press.

McLaren, P., & Leonard, P. (Eds.). (1993). *Paulo Freire: A critical encounter*. New York: Routledge.

Morris, V. C., & Pai, Y. (1976). *Philosophy and the American school: An introduction to the philosophy of education*, (2nd ed.). Boston, MA: Houghton Mifflin.

Muffoletto, R., & Knupfer, N. N. (Eds.). (1993). *Computers in education: Social, political, and historical perspectives*. Cresskill, NJ: Hampton Press.

Nichols, R. (1995). Critical theory and educational technology. In D. H. Jonassen (Ed.), *Handbook of research on educational technology*. New York, Macmillan.

Ozmon, H., & Craver, S. (1995). *Philosophical foundations of education*. (5th ed.). Englewood Cliffs, NJ: Merrill.

Ozmon, H., & Craver, S. (1999). *Philosophical foundations of education* (6th ed.). Upper Sasdle River, NJ: Merrill/Prentice Hall.

Pinar, W. F. (Ed.). (1988). *Contemporary curriculum discourses*. Scottsdale, AZ: Gorsuch Scarisbrick.

Popkewitz, T. S. (1984). *Paradigm and ideology in educational research: The social functions of the intellectual*. New York: Falmer Press.

Purpel, D. E. (1993). Educational discourse and global crisis: What's a teacher to do? In H. Shapiro & D. E. Purpel, (Eds.), *Critical social issues in American education: Toward the 21st century*. New York: Longman.

Robinson, R. S. (Ed.). (1990). *Journal of Thought, 25*(1&2).

Schroyer, T. (1973). *The critique of domination*. Boston, MA: Beacon Press.

Schubert, W. H. (1991). Philosophical inquiry: The speculative essay. In E. C. Short (Ed.), *Forms of curriculum inquiry*. Albany: State University of New York Press.

Sherman, R. R., Webb, R. B., & Andrews, S. D. (Gues Eds.). (1984). Qualitative inquiry: An introduction. *Journal of Thought, 19*(2).

Short, E. C. (Ed.). (1991). *Forms of curriculum inquiry*. Albany: State University of New York Press.

Simon, R. I. (1992). *Teaching against the grain: Texts for a pedagogy of possibility*. Boston, MA: Bergin & Garvey.

Tom, A. R. (1984). Teaching as a moral craft. United Kingdom: Longman group.

Webb, L. D., Metha, A., & Jordan, K. F. (2003). *Foundations of American education* (4th ed.). Upper Saddle River, NJ: Merrill/Prentice Hall.

Wilson, J. (1969). *Thinking with concepts*. Cambridge: University Press.

Winch, P. (1958). *The idea of a social science and its relation to philosophy*. London: Routledge.

Wingo, M. (1974). *Philosophies of education: An introduction*. Lexington, MA: D. C. Heath.

Yeaman, A. R. J., Koetting, J. R., & Nichols, R. G. (1994). Critical theory, cultural analysis, and the ethics of educational technology as social responsibility. *Educational Technology, 34*(2), 5–13.

Yeaman, A. R. J., Hlynka, D., Anderson, J. H., Damarin, S. K., & Muffoletto, R. (1995). Postmodern and poststructural theory. *In Handbook of research for educational communications and technology*. New York: Macmillan.

·38·

EXPERIMENTAL RESEARCH METHODS

Steven M. Ross
The University of Memphis

Gary R. Morrison
Wayne State University

38.1 EVOLUTION OF EXPERIMENTAL RESEARCH METHODS

Experimental research has had a long tradition in psychology and education. When psychology emerged as an infant science during the 1900s, it modeled its research methods on the established paradigms of the physical sciences, which for centuries relied on experimentation to derive principals and laws. Subsequent reliance on experimental approaches was strengthened by behavioral approaches to psychology and education that predominated during the first half of this century. Thus, usage of experimentation in educational technology over the past 40 years has been influenced by developments in theory and research practices within its parent disciplines.

In this chapter, we examine practices, issues, and trends related to the application of experimental research methods in educational technology. The purpose is to provide readers with sufficient background to understand and evaluate experimental designs encountered in the literature and to identify designs that will effectively address questions of interest in their own research. In an introductory section, we define experimental research, differentiate it from alternative approaches, and identify important concepts in its use (e.g., internal vs. external validity). We also suggest procedures for conducting experimental studies and publishing them in educational technology research journals. Next, we analyze uses of experimental methods by instructional researchers, extending the analyses of three decades ago by Clark and Snow (1975). In the concluding section, we turn to issues in using experimental research in educational technology, to include balancing internal and external validity, using multiple outcome measures to assess learning processes and products, using item responses vs. aggregate scores as dependent variables, reporting effect size as a complement to statistical significance, and media replications vs. media comparisons.

38.2 WHAT IS EXPERIMENTAL RESEARCH?

The experimental method formally surfaced in educational psychology around the turn of the century, with the classic studies by Thorndike and Woodworth on transfer (Cronbach, 1957). The experimenter's interest in the effect of environmental change, referred to as "treatments," demanded designs using standardized procedures to hold all conditions constant except the independent (experimental) variable. This standardization ensured high internal validity (experimental control) in comparing the experimental group to the control group on the dependent or "outcome" variable. That is, when internal validity was high, differences between groups could be confidently attributed to the treatment, thus ruling out rival hypotheses attributing effects to extraneous factors. Traditionally, experimenters have given less emphasis to external validity, which concerns the generalizability of findings to other settings, particularly realistic ones. One theme of this chapter is that current orientations in instructional theory and research practices necessitate achieving a better balance between internal and external validity levels.

During the past century, the experimental method has remained immune to paradigm shifts in the psychology of learning, including behaviorism to cognitivism, objectivism to cognitivism, and instructivism to constructivism (see Jonassen, 1991; Jonassen, Campbell, & Davidson, 1994). Clearly, the logical positivism of behavioristic theory created a fertile, inviting framework for attempts to establish causal relationships between variables, using experimental methods. The emergence of cognitive learning theory in the 1970s and 1980s initially did little to change this view, as researchers changed the locus of inquiry from behavior to mental processing but maintained the experimental method as the basic way they searched for scientific truths. Today, the increasing influences of constructivist theories are making the fit between traditional scientific methods and current perspectives on learning more difficult. As Jonassen et al. (1994) state, it is now viewed as much more difficult "...to isolate which components of the learning system, the medium, the attributes, the learner, or the environment affect learning and in what ways" (p. 6). Accordingly, without knowing the ultimate impact or longevity of the constructivist view, we acknowledge its contribution in conveying instruction and learning as less orderly than preceding paradigms had depicted and the learner rather than the "treatment" as deserving more importance in the study of learning processes. Our perspective in this chapter, therefore, is to present experimental methods as continuing to provide valuable "tools" for research but ones whose uses may need to be altered or expanded relative to their traditional functions to accommodate the changing complexion of theory and scientific inquiry in instructional technology.

38.2.1 Types of Experimental Designs

Complete descriptions of alternative experimental designs are provided in Campbell and Stanley (1963) and conventional research textbooks (e.g., Borg, Gall, & Gall, 1993; Creswell, 2002; Gliner & Morgan, 2000). For purposes of providing common background for the present chapter, we have selected four major design approaches to review. These particular designs appeared to be the ones instructional technology researchers would be most likely to use for experimental studies or find in the literature. They are also "core" designs in the sense of including basic components of the more complex or related designs not covered.

38.2.1.1 True Experiments.
The ideal design for maximizing internal validity is the true experiment, as diagrammed below. The R means that subjects were randomly assigned, X represents the treatment (in this case, alternative treatments 1 and 2), and O means observation (or outcome), for example, a dependent measure of learning or attitude. What distinguishes the true experiment from less powerful designs is the random assignment of subjects to treatments, thereby eliminating any systematic error that might be associated with using intact groups. The two (or more) groups are then subjected to identical environmental conditions, while being exposed to different treatments. In educational technology research, such

treatments frequently consist of different instructional methods (discussed later).

$$X_1 O$$
$$R \quad X_2 O$$

Example. An example of a true experiment involving an educational technology application is the study by Clariana and Lee (2001) on the use of different types of feedback in computer-delivered instruction. Graduate students were randomly assigned to one of five feedback treatments, approximately 25 subjects per group, comprised of (a) a constructed-response (fill-in-the-blank) study task with feedback and recognition (multiple-choice) tasks with (b) single-try feedback, (c) multiple-response feedback, (d) single-try feedback with overt responding, and (e) multiple-try feedback with overt responding. All subjects were treated identically, with the exception of the manipulation of the assigned feedback treatment. The major outcome variable (observation) was a constructed-response achievement test on the lesson material. Findings favored the recognition-study treatments with feedback followed by overt responding. Given the true experimental design employed, the authors could infer that the learning advantages obtained were due to properties of the overt responding (namely, in their opinion, that it best matched the posttest measure of learning) rather than extraneous factors relating to the lesson, environment, or instructional delivery. In research parlance, "causal" inferences can be made regarding the effects of the independent (manipulated) variable (in this case, type of feedback strategy) on the dependent (outcome) variable (in this case, degree of learning).

38.2.1.2 Repeated Measures.
A variation of the above experimental design is the situation where all treatments (X_1, X_2, etc.) are administered to all subjects. Thus, each individual (S1, S2, etc.), in essence, serves as his or her own control and is tested or "observed" (O), as diagrammed below for an experiment using n subjects and k treatments. Note that the diagram shows each subject receiving the same sequence of treatments; a stronger design, where feasible, would involve randomly ordering the treatments to eliminate a sequence effect.

$$S1: \quad X_1 0 - X_2 0 \ldots X_k O.$$
$$S2: \quad X_1 0 - X_2 0 \ldots X_k O.$$
$$Sn: \quad X_1 0 - X_2 0 \ldots X_k O.$$

Suppose that an experimenter is interested in whether learners are more likely to remember words that are italicized or words that are underlined in a computer text presentation. Twenty subjects read a paragraph containing five words in each form. They are then asked to list as many italicized words and as many underlined words as they can remember. (To reduce bias, the forms in which the 10 words are represented are randomly varied for different subjects.) Note that this design has the advantage of using only one group, thereby effectively doubling the number of subjects per treatment relative to a two-group (italics only vs. underline only) design. It also ensures that the ability level of subjects receiving the two treatments will be the same. But there is a possible disadvantage that may distort results. The observations are not independent. Recalling an italicized word may help or hinder the recall of an underlined word, or vice versa.

Example. An example of a repeated-measures design is the recent study by Gerlic and Jausovec (1999) on the mental effort induced by information present in multimedia and text formats. Three presentation formats (text only, text/sound/video, text/sound/picture) were presented in randomly determined orders to 38 subjects. Brain wave activity while learning the material was recorded as electroencephalographic (EEG) data. Findings supported the assumption that the video and picture presentations induced visualization strategies, whereas the text presentation generated mainly processes related to verbal processing. Again, by using the repeated-measures design, the researchers were able to reduce the number of subjects needed while controlling for individual differences across the alternative presentation modes. That is, every presentation mode was administered to the identical samples. But the disadvantage was the possible "diffusion" of treatment effects caused by earlier experiences with other modes. We will return to diffusion effects, along with other internal validity threats, in a later section.

38.2.1.3 Quasi-experimental Designs.
Oftentimes in educational studies, it is neither practical nor feasible to assign subjects randomly to treatments. Such is especially likely to occur in school-based research, where classes are formed at the start of the year. These circumstances preclude true-experimental designs, while allowing the quasi-experiment as an option. A common application in educational technology would be to expose two similar classes of students to alternative instructional strategies and compare them on designated dependent measures (e.g., learning, attitude, classroom behavior) during the year.

An important component of the quasi-experimental study is the use of pretesting or analysis of prior achievement to establish group equivalence. Whereas in the true experiment, randomization makes it improbable that one group will be significantly superior in ability to another, in the quasi-experiment, systematic bias can easily (but often unnoticeably) be introduced. For example, although the first- and third-period algebra classes may have the same teacher and identical lessons, it may be the case that honors English is offered third period only, thus restricting those honors students to taking first-period algebra. The quasi-experiment is represented diagrammatically as follows. Note its similarity to the true experiment, with the omission of the randomization component. That is, the Xs and Os show treatments and outcomes, respectively, but there are no Rs to indicate random assignment.

$$X_1 O$$

$$X_2 O$$

Example. Use of a quasi-experimental design is reflected in a recent study by the present authors on the long-term effects of computer experiences by elementary students (Ross, Smith, & Morrison, 1991). During their fifth- and sixth-grade years, one class of students at an inner-city school received classroom and home computers as part of a computer-intensive learning program sponsored by Apple Classrooms of Tomorrow (ACOT). A class of similar students, who were exposed to the same curriculum but without computer support, was designated to serve as the control group. To ensure comparability of groups, scores on all subtests of the California Achievement Test (CAT), administered before the ACOT program was initiated, were analyzed as pretests; no class differences were indicated. The Ross et al. (1991) study was designed to find members of the two cohorts and evaluate their adjustment and progress in the seventh-grade year, when, as junior-high students, they were no longer participating in ACOT.

Although many more similarities than differences were found, the ACOT group was significantly superior to the control group on CAT mathematics. Can this advantage be attributed to their ACOT experiences? Perhaps, but in view of the quasi-experimental design employed, this interpretation would need to be made cautiously. Not only was "differential selection" of subjects a validity threat, so was the "history effect" of having each class taught in a separate room by a different teacher during each program year. Quasi-experimental designs have the advantage of convenience and practicality but the disadvantage of reduced internal validity.

38.2.1.4 Time Series Design.
Another type of quasi-experimental approach is time series designs. This family of designs involves repeated measurement of a group, with the experimental treatment induced between two of the measures. Why is this a quasi-experiment as opposed to a true experiment? The absence of randomly composed, separate experimental and control groups makes it impossible to attribute changes in the dependent measure directly to the effects of the experimental treatment. That is, the individual group participating in the time series design may improve its performances from pretesting to posttesting, but is it the treatment or some other event that produced the change? There is a variety of time series designs, some of which provide a higher internal validity than others.

A single-group time series design can be diagrammed as shown below. As depicted, one group (G) is observed (O) several times prior to receiving the treatment (X) and following the treatment.

$$G \quad O_1 \quad O_2 \quad O_3 \quad X \quad O_4 \quad O_5$$

To illustrate, suppose that we assess on 3 successive days the percentage of students in a class who successfully complete individualized computer-based instructional units. Prior to the fourth day, teams are formed and students are given additional team rewards for completing the units. Performance is then monitored on days 4 and 5. If performance increases relative to the pretreatment phase (days 1 to 3), we may infer that the CBI units contributed to that effect. Lacking a true-experimental design, we make that interpretation with some element of caution.

A variation of the time series design is the single-subject study, in which one individual is examined before and after the introduction of the experimental treatment. The simplest form is the A–B design, where A is the baseline (no treatment) period and B is the treatment. A potentially stronger variation is the A–B–A design, which adds a withdrawal phase following the treatment. Each new phase (A or B) added to the design provides further data to strengthen conclusions about the treatment's impact. On the other hand, each phase may inherit cumulative contaminating effects from prior phases. That is, once B is experienced, subsequent reactions to A and B may be directly altered as a consequence.

Example. An example of a time series design is the study by Alper, Thoresen, and Wright (1972), as described by Clark and Snow (1975). The focus was the effects of a videotape on increasing a teacher's positive attention to appropriate student behavior and decreasing negative responses to inappropriate behavior. Baseline data were collected from a teacher at two times: (a) prior to the presentation of the video and feedback on ignoring inappropriate behavior and (b) prior to the video and feedback on attending to positive behavior. Teacher attention was then assessed at different points following the video modeling and feedback. Interestingly, the analysis revealed that, although the teacher's behavior changed in the predicted directions following the video–feedback interventions, undesirable behavior tended to reappear over time. The time series design, therefore, was especially apt for detecting the unstable behavior pattern. We see relatively few time series designs in the current research literature. Perhaps one reason is that "human subjects" criteria would generally discourage subjecting individuals to prolonged involvement in a study and to repeated assessments.

38.2.1.5 Deceptive Appearances: The Ex Post Facto Design.
Suppose that in reviewing a manuscript for a journal, you come across the following study that the author describes as quasi-experimental (or experimental). The basic design involves giving a class of 100 college educational psychology students the option of using a word processor or paper and pencil to take notes during three full-period lectures on the topic of cognitive theory. Of those who opt for the two media (say, 55 for the word processor and 45 for paper and pencil), 40 from each group are randomly selected for the study. Over the 3 days, their notes are collected, and daily quizzes on the material are evaluated. Results show that the word processor group writes a greater quantity of notes and scores higher on the quizzes.

Despite the appearances of a treatment comparison and random assignment, this research is not an experiment but rather an ex post facto study. No variables are manipulated. Existing groups that are essentially self-selected are being compared: those who chose the word processor vs. those who chose paper and pencil. The random selection merely reduced the number of possible participants to more manageable numbers; it did not assign students to particular treatments. Given these properties, the ex post facto study may look sometimes like an experiment but is closer in design to a correlational study. In our example, the results imply that using a word processor is related to better performance. But a causal interpretation cannot be made, be-

cause other factors could just as easily have accounted for the outcomes (e.g., brighter or more motivated students may have been more likely to select the word-processing option).

38.2.2 Validity Threats

As has been described, internal validity is the degree to which the design of an experiment controls extraneous variables (Borg et al., 1993). For example, suppose that a researcher compares the achievement scores of students who are asked to write elaborations on a computer-based instruction (CBI) lesson vs. those who do not write elaborations on the same lesson. If findings indicate that the elaborations group scored significantly higher on a mastery test than the control group, the implication would be that the elaborations strategy was effective. But what if students in the elaborations group were given more information about how to study the material than were control students? This extraneous variable (i.e., additional information) would weaken the internal validity and the ability to infer causality.

When conducting experiments, instructional technology researchers need to be aware of potential internal validity threats. In 1963, Campbell and Stanley identified different classes of such threats. We briefly describe each below, using an illustration relevant to educational technology interests.

38.2.2.1 History.
This validity threat is present when events, other than the treatments, occurring during the experimental period can influence results.

Example. A researcher investigates the effect of using cooperative learning (treatment) vs. individual learning (control) in CBI. Students from a given class are randomly assigned to different laboratory rooms where they learn either cooperatively or individually. During the period of the study, however, the regular teacher begins to use cooperative learning with all students. Consequently, the control group feels frustrated that, during the CBI activity, they have to work alone. Due to their "history," with cooperative learning, the control group's perceptions were altered.

38.2.2.2 Maturation.
During the experimental period, physical or psychological changes take place within the subjects.

Example. First-grade students receive two types of instruction in learning to use a mouse in operating a computer. One group is given active practice, and the other group observes a skilled model followed by limited practice. At the beginning of the year, neither group performs well. At the end of the year, however, both substantially improve to a comparable level. The researcher (ignoring the fact that students became more dexterous, as well as benefiting from the training) concluded that both treatments were equally effective.

38.2.2.3 Testing.
Exposure to a pretest or intervening assessment influences performance on a posttest.

Example. A researcher who is interested in determining the effects of using animation vs. static graphics in a CBI lesson pretests two randomly composed groups of high-school students on the content of the lesson. Both groups average close to 55% correct. One of the groups then receives animation, and the other the static graphics on their respective lessons. At the conclusion of the lesson, all students complete a posttest that is nearly identical to the pretest. No treatment differences, however, are found, with both groups averaging close to 90% correct. Students report that the pretest gave them valuable cues about what to study.

38.2.2.4 Instrumentation.

Inconsistent use is made of testing instruments or testing conditions, or the pretest and posttest are uneven in difficulty, suggesting a gain or decline in performance that is not real.

Example. An experiment is designed to test two procedures for teaching students to write nonlinear stories (i.e., stories with branches) using hypermedia. Randomly composed groups of eighth graders learn from a modeling method or a direct instruction method and are then judged by raters on the basis of the complexity and quality of a writing sample they produce. The "modeling" group completes the criterion task in their regular writing laboratory, whereas the "direct instruction" group completes it on similar computers, at the same day and time, but in the journalism room at the local university. Results show significantly superior ratings for the modeling group. In fact, both groups were fairly comparable in skills, but the modeling group had the advantage of performing the criterion task in familiar surroundings.

38.2.2.5 Statistical Regression.

Subjects who score very high or very low on a dependent measure naturally tend to score closer (i.e., regress) to the mean during retesting.

Example. A researcher is interested in the effects of learning programming on the problem-solving skills of high-ability children. A group of 400 sixth graders is pretested on a problem-solving test. The 50 highest scorers are selected and randomly assigned to two groups of 25 each. One group learns programming during the semester, whereas the other learns a spreadsheet application. At the end of the year, the students are posttested on the same problem-solving measure. There are no differences between them; in fact, the means for both groups are actually slightly lower than they were on the pretest. These very high scorers on the pretest had regressed to the mean (due, perhaps, to not having as "good of a day" on the second testing).

38.2.2.6 Selection.

There is a systematic difference in subjects' abilities or characteristics between the treatment groups being compared.

Example. Students in the fourth-period American history class use an electronic encyclopedia during the year as a reference for historical events, whereas those in the sixth-period class use a conventional encyclopedia. The two classes have nearly identical grade point averages and are taught by the same teacher using the exact same materials and curriculum. Comparisons are made between the classes on the frequency with which they use their respective encyclopedias and the quality of the information they select for their reports. The control group is determined to be superior on both of these variables. Further examination of student demographics, however, shows that a much greater percentage of the control students are in

advanced placement (AP) courses in English, mathematics, and science. In fact, the reason many were scheduled to take history sixth period was to avoid conflicts with AP offerings. Differential selection therefore resulted in higher-achieving students being members of the control group.

38.2.2.7 Experimental Mortality.

The loss of subjects from one or more treatments during the period of the study may bias the results.

Example. An instructional designer is interested in evaluating a college-level CBI algebra course that uses two learning orientations. One orientation allows the learner to select menu and instructional support options (learner-control treatment); the other prescribes particular options based on what is considered best for "typical" learners (program-control treatment). At the beginning of the semester, 40 students are assigned to each treatment and begin work with the corresponding CBI programs. At the end of the semester, only 50 students remain in the course, 35 in the learner-control group and 15 in the program-control group. Achievement results favor the program-control group. The greater "mortality" in the program-control group probably left a higher proportion of more motivated or more capable learners than in the learner-control group.

38.2.2.8 Diffusion of Treatments.

The implementation of a particular treatment influences subjects in the comparison treatment.

Example. A researcher is interested in examining the influences on attitudes and achievement of fifth graders' writing to pen pals via electronic mail. Half the students are assigned pen pals; the other half complete the identical assignments on the same electronic mail system but send the letters to "fictitious" friends. The students in the latter group, however, become aware that the other group has real pen pals and feel resentful. On the attitude measure, their reactions toward the writing activities are very negative as a consequence. By learning about the experimental group's "treatment," the perceptions and attitudes of the control group were negatively influenced.

38.2.3 Dealing With Validity Threats

In many instances, validity threats cannot be avoided. The presence of a validity threat should not be taken to mean that experimental findings are inaccurate or misleading. By validity "threat," we mean only that a factor has the potential to bias results. Knowing about validity threats gives the experimenter a framework for evaluating the particular situation and making a judgment about its severity. Such knowledge may also permit actions to be taken to limit the influences of the validity threat in question. Examples are as follows:

- Concern that a pretest may bias posttest results leads to the decision not to use a pretest.
- Concern that the two intact groups to be used for treatment comparisons (quasi-experimental design) may not be equal in

ability leads to the decision to pretest subjects on ability and employ a statistical adjustment (analysis of covariance) if the groups significantly differ.

- Concern that subjects may mature or drop out during the period of the experiment leads to the decision to shorten the length of the treatment period, use different types of subjects, and/or introduce noncontaminating conditions (e.g., incentives) to reduce attrition.

- Concern that the posttest may differ in difficulty from the pretest in an experiment design to assess learning gain leads to the decision to use each test form as the pretest for half the students and the posttest for the other half.

- Concern about the artificiality of using abstract symbols such as Xs and Os as the stimulus material for assessing computer screen designs leads to the addition of "realistic" nonsense words and actual words as supplementary treatments.

- Concern that subjects might not be motivated to perform on an experimental task leads to the development of an actual unit of instruction that becomes an alternative form of instruction for the students in a class.

Even after all reasonable actions have been taken to eliminate the operation of one or more validity threats, the experimenter must still make a judgment about the internal validity of the experiment overall. In certain cases, the combined effects of multiple validity threats may be considered inconsequential, whereas in others, the effects of a single threat (e.g., differential sample selection) may be severe enough to preclude meaningful results. When the latter occurs, the experiment needs to be redone. In cases less severe, experimenters have the obligation to note the validity threats and qualify their interpretations of results accordingly.

38.3 THE PRACTICE OF EXPERIMENTATION IN EDUCATIONAL TECHNOLOGY

38.3.1 How to Conduct Experimental Studies: A Brief Course

For the novice researcher, it is often difficult to get started in designing and conducting experimental studies. Seemingly, a common problem is putting the cart before the horse, which in typical cases translates into selecting methodology or a research design before deciding what questions to investigate. Research questions, along with practical constraints (time and resources), should normally dictate what type of study to do, rather than the reverse. To help readers avoid such problems, we have devised the following seven-step model, which presents a sequence of logical steps for planning and conducting research (Ross & Morrison, 1992, 1993, 2001). The model begins at a level where the individual is interested in conducting research (such as for a dissertation or scholarly activity) but has not even identified a topic. More advanced researchers would naturally start at the level appropriate to their needs. To illustrate the various steps, we discuss our recent experiences in designing a

research study on applications of an interactive computer-based chemistry unit.

38.3.1.1 Step 1. Select a Topic. This step is self-explanatory and usually not a problem, except for those who are "required" to do research (e.g., as part of an academic degree program) as opposed to initiating it on their own. The step simply involves identifying a general area that is of personal interest (e.g., learner control, picture perception, mathematics learning) and then narrowing the focus to a researchable problem (step 2).

Chemistry CBI Example. In our situation, Gary Morrison received a grant from FIPSE to develop and evaluate interactive chemistry units. We thus had the interest in as well as the formal responsibility of investigating how the completed units operated.

38.3.1.2 Step 2. Identify the Research Problem. Given the general topic area, what specific problems are of interest? In many cases, the researcher already knows the problems. In others, a trip to the library to read background literature and examine previous studies is probably needed. A key concern is the importance of the problem to the field. Conducting research requires too much time and effort to be examining trivial questions that do not expand existing knowledge. Experienced researchers will usually be attuned to important topics, based on their knowledge of the literature and current research activities. Novices, however, need to be more careful about establishing support for their idea from recent research and issues-oriented publications (see step 3). For experts and novices alike, it is always a good practice to use other researchers as a sounding board for a research focus before getting too far into the study design (steps 4 and 5).

Chemistry CBI Example. The topic and the research problem were presented to us through the objectives of the FIPSE grant and our interest in assessing the "effectiveness" of the completed CBI chemistry units. The research topic was "CBI usage in teaching college chemistry courses"; the research problem was "how effectively interactive CBI units on different chemistry concepts would teach those concepts." Later, this "problem" was narrowed to an examination of the influences on student learning and attitudes of selected features of a specific CBI unit, Gas Laws.

38.3.1.3 Step 3. Conduct a Literature Search. With the research topic and problem identified, it is now time to conduct a more intensive literature search. Of importance is determining what relevant studies have been performed; the designs, instruments, and procedures employed in those studies; and, most critically, the findings. Based on the review, direction will be provided for (a) how to extend or compliment the existing literature base, (b) possible research orientations to use, and (c) specific research questions to address. Helpful information about how to conduct effective literature reviews is provided in other sources (e.g., Borg et al., 1993; Creswell, 2002; Ross & Morrison, 2001).

Chemistry CBI Example. For the chemistry study, the literature proved important in two ways. First, it provided general background information on related studies in the content area (chemistry) and in CBI applications in general. Second, in considering the many specific features of the chemistry unit that interested us (e.g., usage of color, animation, prediction, elaboration, self-pacing, learner control, active problem solving), the literature review helped to narrow our focus to a restricted, more manageable number of variables and gave us ideas for how the selected set might be simultaneously examined in a study.

38.3.1.4 Step 4. State the Research Questions (or Hypotheses).
This step is probably the most critical part of the planning process. Once stated, the research questions or hypotheses provide the basis for planning all other parts of the study: design, materials, and data analysis. In particular, this step will guide the researcher's decision as to whether an experimental design or some other orientation is the best choice.

For example, in investigating uses of learner control in a math lesson, the researcher must ask what questions he or she really wants to answer. Consider a question such as, How well do learners like using learner control with math lessons? To answer it, an experiment is hardly needed or even appropriate. A much better choice would be a descriptive study in which learners are interviewed, surveyed, and/or observed relative to the activities of concern. In general, if a research question involves determining the "effects" or "influences" of one variable (independent) on another (dependent), use of an experimental design is implied.

Chemistry CB1 Example. The questions of greatest interest to us concerned the effects on learning of (a) animated vs. static graphics, (b) learners predicting outcomes of experiments vs. not making predictions, and (c) learner control vs. program control. The variables concerned were expected to operate in certain ways based on theoretical assumptions and prior empirical support. Accordingly, *hypotheses* such as the following were suggested: "Students who receive animated graphics will perform better on problem-solving tasks than do students who receive static graphics," and "Low achievers will learn less effectively under learner control than program control." Where we felt less confident about predictions or where the interest was descriptive findings, research *questions* were implied: "Would students receiving animated graphics react more positively to the unit than those receiving static graphics?" and "To what extent would learner-control students make use of opportunities for experimenting in the 'lab'?"

38.3.1.5 Step 5. Determine the Research Design.
The next consideration is whether an experimental design is feasible. If not, the researcher will need to consider alternative approaches, recognizing that the original research question may not be answerable as a result. For example, suppose that the research question is to determine the effects of students watching CNN on their knowledge of current events. In planning the experiment, the researcher becomes aware that no control group will be available, as all classrooms to which she has access receive the CNN broadcasts. Whereas an experimental study is implied by the original "cause–effect" question, a descriptive study examining current events scores (perhaps from pretest to posttest) will probably be the most reasonable option. This design may provide some interesting food for thought on the

possible effects of CNN on current events learning, but it cannot validly answer the original question.

Chemistry CBI Example. Our hypotheses and research questions implied both experimental and descriptive designs. Specifically, hypotheses concerning the effects of animated vs. static graphics and between prediction vs. no prediction implied controlled experimental comparisons between appropriate treatment conditions. Decisions needed to be made about which treatments to manipulate and how to combine them (e.g., a factorial or balanced design vs. selected treatments). We decided on selected treatments representing targeted conditions of interest. For example, we excluded static graphics with no prediction, as that treatment would have appeared awkward given the way the CBI program was designed, and we had little interest in it for applied evaluation purposes. Because subjects could be randomly assigned to treatments, we decided to use a true-experimental design.

Other research questions, however, implied additional designs. Specifically, comparisons between high and low achievers (in usage of CBI options and relative success in different treatments) required an ex post facto design, because members of these groups would be identified on the basis of existing characteristics. Research questions regarding usage of learner control options would further be examined via a descriptive approach.

38.3.1.6 Step 6. Determine Methods.
Methods of the study include (a) subjects, (b) materials and data collection instruments, and (c) procedures. In determining these components, the researcher must continually use the research questions and/or hypotheses as reference points. A good place to start is with subjects or participants. What kind and how many participants does the research design require? (See, e.g., Glass & Hopkins, 1984, p. 213, for a discussion of sample size and power.) Next consider materials and instrumentation. When the needed resources are not obvious, a good strategy is to construct a listing of data collection instruments needed to answer each question (e.g., attitude survey, achievement test, observation form).

An experiment does not require having access to instruments that are already developed. Particularly in research with new technologies, the creation of novel measures of affect or performance may be implied. From an efficiency standpoint, however, the researcher's first step should be to conduct a thorough search of existing instruments to determine if any can be used in their original form or adapted to present needs. If none is found, it would usually be far more advisable to construct a new instrument rather than "force fit" an existing one. New instruments will need to be pilot tested and validated. Standard test and measurement texts provide useful guidance for this requirement (e.g., Gronlund & Linn, 1990; Popham, 1990). The experimental procedure, then, will be dictated by the research questions and the available resources. Piloting the methodology is essential to ensure that materials and methods work as planned.

Chemistry CB1 Example. Our instructional material consisted of the CBI unit itself. Hypotheses and research questions implied developing alternative forms of instruction (e.g., animation–prediction, animation–no prediction, static–prediction) to compare, as well as original (new) data collection instruments because the instructional content was unit-specific. These instruments included an achievement test, attitude survey, and on-line assessments for recording of lesson option usage (e.g., number of lab experiments selected), learning time, and predictions.

38.3.1.7 Step 7. Determine Data Analysis Techniques.
Whereas statistical analysis procedures vary widely in complexity, the appropriate options for a particular experiment will be defined by two factors: the research questions and the type of data. For example, a *t* test for independent samples would be implied for comparing one experimental group (e.g., CBI with animation) to one control group (CBI with static graphics) on an interval-dependent measure (e.g., performance on a problem-solving test). Add a third treatment group (CBI without graphics), and a one-way analysis of variance (ANOVA) would be implied for the same interval data, but now comparing more than two means. If an additional outcome measure were a categorical response on, say, an attitude survey ("liked the lesson" or "didn't like it"), a chi-square analysis would be implied for determining the relationship between treatment and response on the resultant *nominal* data obtained.

Educational technology experimenters do not have to be statisticians. Nor do they have to set analytical procedures in stone prior to completing the research. Clearly formulated research questions and design specifications will provide a solid foundation for working with a statistician (if needed) to select and run appropriate analyses. To provide a convenient guide for considering alternative analysis, Table 38.1 lists common statistical analysis procedures and the main conditions under which they are used. Note that in assessing causal relationships, experiments depend on analysis approaches that compare outcomes associated with treatments (nominal or categorical variables) such as *t* tests, ANOVA, analysis of covariance, and chi-square, rather than correlational-type approaches.

38.3.2 Reporting and Publishing Experimental Studies

Obviously, for experimental studies to have impact on theory and practice in educational technology, their findings need to be disseminated to the field. Thus, part of the experimenter's role is publishing research in professional journals and presenting it at professional meetings. Discussing these activities in any detail is beyond the scope of the present chapter; also, articles devoted to these subjects can be found elsewhere (e.g., Ross & Morrison, 1991, 1993, 2001; Thyer, 1994). However, given the special features and style conventions of experimental reports compared to other types of educational technology literature, we consider it relevant to review the former, with a specific concentration on journal publications. It is through referred journals—such as *Performance Improvement Quarterly*, and *Educational Technology Research and Development*—that experimental studies are most likely to be disseminated to members of the educational technology field. The following is a brief description of each major section of the paper.

38.3.2.1 Introduction.
The introduction to reports of experimental studies accomplishes several functions: (a) identifying the general area of the problem (e.g., CBI or cooperative learning), (b) creating a rationale to learn more about the problem (otherwise, why do more research in this area?), (c) reviewing relevant literature, and (d) stating the specific purposes of the study. Hypotheses and/or research questions should directly follow from the preceding discussion and generally be stated explicitly, even though they may be obvious from the literature review. In basic research experiments, usage of hypotheses is usually expected, as a theory or principle is typically being tested. In applied research experiments, hypotheses would be used where there is a logical or empirical basis for expecting a certain result (e.g., "The feedback group will perform better than the no-feedback group"); otherwise, research questions might be preferable (e.g., "Are worked examples more effective than incomplete examples on the CBI math unit developed?").

38.3.2.2 Method.
The *Method* section of an experiment describes the participants or subjects, materials, and procedures. The usual convention is to start with *subjects* (or participants) by clearly describing the population concerned (e.g., age or grade level, background) and the sampling procedure. In reading about an experiment, it is extremely important to know if subjects were randomly assigned to treatments or if intact groups were employed. It is also important to know if participation was voluntary or required and whether the level of performance on the experimental task was consequential to the subjects.

Learner motivation and task investment are critical in educational technology research, because such variables are likely to impact directly on subjects' usage of media attributes and instructional strategies (see Morrison, Ross, Gopalakrishnan, & Casey, 1995; Song & Keller, 2001). For example, when learning from a CBI lesson is perceived as part of an experiment rather than actual course, a volunteer subject may be concerned primarily with completing the material as quickly as possible and, therefore, not select any optional instructional support features. In contrast, subjects who were completing the lesson for a grade would probably be motivated to take advantage of those options. A given treatment variable (e.g., learner control or elaborated feedback) could therefore take very different forms and have different effects in the two experiments.

Once subjects are described, the type of design employed (e.g., quasi-experiment, true experiment) should be indicated. Both the independent and the dependent variables also need to be identified.

Materials and *instrumentation* are covered next. A frequent limitation of descriptions of educational technology experiments is lack of information on the learning task and the context in which it was delivered. Since media attributes can impact learning and performance in unique ways (see Clark, 1983, 2001; 1994; Kozma, 1991, 1994; Ullmer, 1994), their full

TABLE 38.1. Common Statistical Analysis Procedures Used in Educational Technology Research

Analysis	Types of Data	Features	Example	Test of Causal Effects?
t test Independent samples	Independent variable = nominal; dependent = one interval-ratio measure	Tests the differences between 2 treatment groups	Does the problem-based treatment group surpass the traditional instruction treatment group?	Yes
t test Dependent samples	Independent variable = nominal (repeated measure); dependent = one interval-ratio measure	Tests the difference between 2 treatment means for a *given group*	Will participants change their attitudes toward drugs, from pretest to posttest, following a videotape on drug effects?	Yes
Analysis of variance (ANOVA)	Independent variable = nominal; dependent = one interval-ratio measure	Tests the differences between 3 or more treatment means. If ANOVA is significant, follow-up comparisons of means are performed.	Will there be differences in learning among three groups that paraphrase, summarize, or neither?	Yes
Multivariate analysis of variance (MANOVA)	Independent variable = nominal; dependent = two or more interval-ratio measures	Tests the difference between 2 or more treatment group means on 2 or more learning measures. Controls Type I error rate across the measure. If MANOVA is significant, an ANOVA on each individual measure is performed.	Will there be differences among 3 feedback strategies on problem solving and knowledge learning?	Yes
Analysis of covariance (ANCOVA) or multivariate analysis of covariance (MANCOVA)	Independent variable = nominal; dependent = one or more interval-ratio measures; covariate = one or more measures	Replicates ANOVA or MANOVA but employs an additional variable to control for treatment group differences in aptitude and/or to reduce error variance in the dependent variable(s)	Will there be differences in concept learning among learner-control, program-control, and advisement strategies, with differences in prior knowledge controlled?	Yes
Pearson *r*	Two ordinal or interval-ratio measures	Tests relationship between two variables	Is anxiety related to test performance?	No
Multiple linear regression	Independent variable = two or more ordinal or interval-ratio measures; dependent = one ordinal or interval-ratio measure	Tests relationship between set of predictor (independent) variables and outcome variable. Shows the relative contribution of each predictor in accounting for variability in the outcome variable.	How well do experience, age, gender, and grade point average predict time spent on completing a task?	No
Discriminant analysis	Nominal variable (groups) and 2 or more ordinal or interval-ratio variables	Tests relationship between a set of predictor variables and subjects' membership in particular groups	Do students who favor learning from print materials vs. computers vs. television differ with regard to ability, age, and motivation?	No
Chi-square test of independence	Two nominal variables	Tests relationship between two nominal variables	Is there a relationship between gender (male vs. females) and attitudes toward the instruction (liked, no opinion, disliked)?	

description is particularly important to the educational technologist. Knowing only that a "CBI" presentation was compared to a "textbook" presentation suggests the type of senseless media comparison experiment criticized by Clark (1983, 2001) and others (Hagler & Knowlton, 1987; Knowlton, 1964; Morrison, 2001; Ross & Morrison, 1989). In contrast, knowing the specific attributes of the CBI (e.g., animation, immediate feedback, prompting) and textbook presentations permits more meaningful interpretation of results relative to the influences of these attributes on the learning process.

Aside from describing the instructional task, the overall method section should also detail the instruments used for data collection. For illustrative purposes, consider the following excerpts from a highly thorough description of the instructional materials used by Schnackenberg and Sullivan (2000).

The program was developed in four versions that represented the four different treatment conditions. Each of the 13 objectives was taught through a number of screens that present the instruction, practice and feedback, summaries, and reviews. Of the objectives, 9 required selected responses in a multiple-choice format and 4 required constructed responses. The program tracked each participant's response choice on a screen-by-screen basis. (p. 22)

The next main methodology section is the *procedure*. It provides a reasonably detailed description of the steps employed in carrying out the study (e.g., implementing different treatments, distributing materials, observing behaviors, testing). Here, the rule of thumb is to provide sufficient information on what was done to perform the experiment so that another researcher could replicate the study. This section should also provide a time line that describes sequence of the treatments and data collection. For example, the reader should understand that the attitude survey was administered *after* the subjects completed the treatment and *before* they completed the posttest.

38.3.2.3 Results.
This major section describes the analyses and the findings. Typically, it should be organized such that the most important dependent measures are reported first. Tables and/or figures should be used judiciously to supplement (not repeat) the text.

Statistical significance vs. practical importance. Traditionally, researchers followed the convention of determining the "importance" of findings based on statistical significance. Simply put, if the experimental group's mean of 85% on the posttest was found to be significantly higher (say, at $p < .01$) than the control group's mean of 80%, then the "effect" was regarded as having theoretical or practical value. If the result was not significant (i.e., the null hypothesis could not be rejected), the effect was dismissed as not reliable or important.

In recent years, however, considerable attention has been given to the benefits of distinguishing between "statistical significance" and "practical importance" (Thompson, 1998). Statistical significance indicates whether an effect can be considered attributable to factors other than chance. But a significant effect does not necessary mean a "large" effect. Consider this example:

Suppose that 342 students who were randomly selected to participate in a Web-based writing skills course averaged 3.3 (out of 5.0) on the state assessment of writing skills. The 355 students in the control group, however, averaged 3.1, which, due to the large sample sizes, was significantly lower than the experimental group mean, at $p = .032$. Would you advocate the Web-based course as a means of increasing writing skill? Perhaps, but the findings basically indicate a "reliable but small" effect. If improving writing skill is a priority goal, the Web-based course might not be the most effective and useful intervention.

To supplement statistical significance, the reporting of effect sizes is recommended. In fact, in the most recent (fifth) edition of the *APA Publication Manual (2001)*, effect sizes are recommended as "almost always necessary" to include in the results section (pp. 25–26). Effect size indicates the number of standard deviations by which the experimental treatment mean differs from the control treatment mean. Thus an effect size of +1.00 indicates a full standard deviation advantage, a large and educationally important effect (Cohen, 1988). Effect sizes of +0.20 and +0.50 would indicate small and medium effects, respectively. Calculation of effect sizes is relatively straightforward. Helpful guidance and formulas are provided in the recent article by Bruce Thompson (2002), who has served over the past decade as one of the strongest advocates of reporting effect sizes in research papers. Many journals, including *Educational Technology Research and Development (ETR&D)*, presently require effect sizes to be reported.

38.3.2.4 Discussion.
To conclude the report, the *discussion* section explains and interprets the findings relative to the hypotheses or research questions, previous studies, and relevant theory and practice. Where appropriate, weaknesses in procedures that may have impacted results should be identified. Other conventional features of a discussion may include suggestions for further research and conclusions regarding the research hypotheses/questions. For educational technology experiments, drawing implications for practice in the area concerned is highly desirable.

38.3.3 Why Experimental Studies Are Rejected for Publication

After considering the above discussion, readers may question what makes an experimental study "publishable or perishable" in professional research journals. Given that we have not done a formal investigation of this topic, we make only a brief subjective analysis based on our experiences with *ETR&D*. We strongly believe, however, that all of the following factors would apply to every educational technology research journal, although the relative importance they are assigned may vary. Our "top 10" listing is as follows.

Low internal validity of conditions: Treatment and comparison groups are not uniformly implemented. One or more groups have an advantage on a particular condition (time, materials, encouragement) other than the independent (treatment) variable. Example: The treatment group that receives illustrations and text takes 1 hr to study the electricity unit, whereas the text-only group takes only 0.5 hr.

Low internal validity of subject selection/assignment:
Groups assigned to treatment and comparison conditions are
not comparable (e.g., a more experienced group receives the
treatment strategy). Example: In comparing learner control vs.
program control, the researcher allows students to select the
orientation they want. The higher-aptitude students tend to select program control, which, not surprisingly, yields the better
results!

Invalid testing: Outcomes are not measured in a controlled
and scientific way (e.g., observations are done by the author
without validation of the system or reliability checks of the
data). Example: In a qualitative study of teachers' adaptations to
technology, only one researcher (the author) observes each of
the 10 teachers in a school in which she works part-time as an
aide.

Low external validity: Application or importance of topic
or findings is weak. Example: The findings show that nonsense
syllables take more time to be identified if embedded in a border
than if they are isolated. We should note, however, that there are
journals that do publish basic research that has a low external
validity but a high internal validity.

Poor writing: Writing style is unclear, weak in quality (syntax, construction), and/or does not use appropriate (APA) style.
Example: The *method* section contains no subheadings and in-
termixes descriptions of participants and materials, then discusses the procedures, and ends with introducing the design of
the study. Note that the design would be much more useful as
an organizer if presented first.

Trivial/inappropriate outcome measures: Outcomes are
assessed using irrelevant, trivial, or insubstantial measures.
Example: A 10-item multiple-choice test is the only achievement outcome in a study of cooperative learning effects.

Inadequate description of methodology: Instruments, materials, or procedures are not described sufficiently to evaluate
the quality of the study. Example: The author describes dependent measures using only the following: "A 10-item posttest was
used to assess learning of the unit. It was followed by a 20-item
attitude scale regarding reactions to the unit. Other materials
used. . . . "

Inappropriate analyses: Quantitative or qualitative analyses
needed to address research objectives are not properly used or
sufficiently described. Example: In a qualitative study, the author
presents the "analysis" of 30 classroom observations exclusively
as "holistic impressions," without reference to any application
of systematic methods of documenting, transcribing, synthesizing, and verifying what was observed. *Inappropriate discussion
of results*: Results are not interpreted accurately or meaningfully to convey appropriate implications of the study. Example:
After finding that motivation and performance correlated significantly but very weakly at $r = +.15$, the author discusses for
several paragraphs the importance of motivation to learning, "as
supported by this study." (Note that although "reliable" in this
study, the .15 correlation indicates that motivation accounted
for only about 2.25% of the variable in performance: $.15 \times .15 =
.0225$).

Insufficient theoretical base or rationale: The basis for
the study is conveyed as manipulating some combination of
variables essentially "to see what happens." Example: After

reviewing the literature on the use of highlighting text, the
author establishes the rationale for his study by stating, "No
one, however, has examined these effects using color vs. no-
color with males vs. females." The author subsequently fails to
provide any theoretical rationales or hypotheses relating to the
color or gender variable. A similar fault is providing an adequate
literature review, but the hypotheses and/or problem statement
are not related or supported by the review.

38.4 THE STATUS OF EXPERIMENTATION IN EDUCATIONAL TECHNOLOGY

38.4.1 Uses and Abuses of Experiments

The behavioral roots of educational technology and its parent disciplines have fostered usage of experimentation as the
predominant mode of research. As we show in a later section,
experiments comprise the overwhelming proportion of studies
published in the research section of *Educational Technology
Research and Development (ETR&D)*. The representation of
alternative paradigms, however, is gradually increasing.

***38.4.1.1 The Historical Predominance of Experimenta-
tion.*** Why is the experimental paradigm so dominant? According to Hannafin (1986), aside from the impetus provided from
behavioral psychology, there are three reasons. First, experimentation has been traditionally viewed as the definition of
"acceptable" research in the field. Researchers have developed
the mentality that a study is of higher quality if it is experimental
in design. Positivistic views have reinforced beliefs about the importance of scientific rigor, control, statistical verification, and
hypothesis testing as the "correct" approaches to research in the
field. Qualitative researchers have challenged this way of thinking, but until recently, acceptance of alternative paradigms has
been reluctant and of minimal consequence (Creswell, 2002,
pp. 47–48).

Second, Hannafin (1986) proposes that promotion and
tenure criteria at colleges and universities have been strongly
biased toward experimental studies. If this bias occurs, it is probably attributable mainly to the more respected journals having
been more likely to publish experimental designs (see next paragraph). In any case, such practices are perpetuated by creating
standards that are naturally favored by faculty and passed down
to their graduate students.

Third, the research journals have published proportionately
more experimental studies than alternative types. This factor
also creates a self-perpetuating situation in which increased exposure to experimental studies increases the likelihood that beginning researchers will also favor the experimental method in
their research.

As discussed in later sections, in the 17 years since Hannafin
presented these arguments, practices have changed considerably in the direction of greater acceptance of alternative methodologies, such as qualitative methods. The pendulum may have
even swung far enough to make the highly controlled experiment with a low external validity less valued than eclectic

orientations that use a variety of strategies to balance internal and external validity (Kozma, 2000).

38.4.1.2 When to Experiment.

The purpose of this chapter is neither to promote nor to criticize the experimental method but, rather, to provide direction for its effective usage in educational technology research. On the one hand, it is fair to say that, probably for the reasons just described, experimentation has been overused by educational technology researchers. The result has frequently been "force-fitting" the experiment in situations where research questions could have been much more meaningfully answered using an alternative design or a combination of several designs.

For example, we recall a study on learner control that was submitted to *ETR&D* for review several years ago. The major research question concerned the benefits of allowing learners to select practice items and review questions as they proceeded through a self-paced lesson. The results showed no effects for the learner-control strategy compared to conventional instruction on either an achievement test or an attitude survey. Despite the study's being well designed, competently conducted, and well described, the decision was *not* to accept the manuscript for publication. In the manner of pure scientists, the authors had carefully measured outcomes but totally omitted any observation or recording of how the subjects used learner-control. Nor did they bother to question the learners on their usage and reactions toward the learner-control options. The experiment thus showed that learner control did not "work" but failed to provide any insights into why.

On the other hand, we disagree with the sentiments expressed by some writers that experimental research conflicts with the goal of improving instruction (Guba, 1969; Heinich, 1984). The fact that carpentry tools, if used improperly, can potentially damage a bookcase does not detract from the value of such tools to skilled carpenters who know how to use them appropriately to build bookcases. Unfortunately, the experimental method has frequently been applied in a very strict, formal way that has blinded the experimenter from looking past the testing of the null hypothesis to inquire why a particular outcome occurs. In this chapter, we take the view that the experiment is simply another valuable way, no more or less sacrosanct than any other, of increasing understanding about methods and applications of educational technology. We also emphasize sensitivity to the much greater concern today than there was 20 or 30 years ago with applying experimental methods to "ecologically valid" (realistic) settings. This orientation implies assigning relatively greater focus on external validity and increased tolerance for minor violations (due to uncontrollable real-world factors) of internal validity. A concomitant need is for contextually sensitive interpretations of findings coupled with replicability studies in similar and diverse contexts.

38.4.1.3 Experiments in Evaluation Research.

In applied instructional design contexts, experiments could potentially offer practitioners much useful information about their products but will typically be impractical to perform. Consider, for example, an instructional designer who develops an innovative way of using an interactive medium to teach principles of chemistry. Systematic evaluation of this instructional method (and of the unit in particular) would comprise an important component of the design process (Dick, Carey, & Carey, 2001; Morrison, Ross, & Kemp, 2001). Of major interest in the evaluation would certainly be how effectively the new method supports instructional objectives compared to conventional teaching procedures. Under normal conditions, it would be difficult logistically to address this question via a true experiment. But if conditions permitted random assignment of students to "treatments?" without compromising the integrity (external validity) of the instruction, a true experimental design would likely provide the most meaningful test. If random assignment were not viable, but two comparable groups of learners were available to experience the instructional alternatives, a quasi-experimental design might well be the next-best choice. The results of either category of experiment would provide useful information for the evaluator, particularly when combined with outcomes from other measures, for either judging the method's effectiveness (summative evaluation) or making recommendations to improve it (formative evaluation). Only a very narrow, shortsighted approach would use the experimental results as isolated evidence for "proving" or "disapproving" program effects.

In the concluding sections of this chapter, we further examine applications and potentialities of "applied research" experiments as sources of information for understanding and improving instruction. First, to provide a better sense of historical practices in the field, we will turn to an analysis of how often and in what ways experiments have been employed in educational technology research.

38.4.2 Experimental Methods in Educational Technology Research

To determine practices and trends in experimental research on educational technology, we decided to examine comprehensively the studies published in a single journal. The journal, *Educational Technology Research and Development* (*ETR&D*), is published quarterly by the Association for Educational Communications and Technology (AECT). *ETR&D* is AECT's only research journal, is distributed internationally, and is generally considered a leading research publication in educational technology. The journal started in 1953 as *AV Communication Review* (*AVCR*) and was renamed *Educational Communication and Technology Journal* (*ECTJ*) in 1978. *ETR&D* was established in 1989 to combine *ECTJ* (AECT's research journal) with the *Journal of Instructional Development* (AECT's design/development journal) by including a research section and a development section. The research section, which is of present interest, solicits manuscripts dealing with "research in educational technology and related topics." Nearly all published articles are blind refereed, with the exception of infrequent solicited manuscripts as part of special issues.

38.4.2.1 Analysis Procedure.

The present analysis began with the Volume I issue of *AVCR* (1953) and ended with Volume

49 (2001) of *ETR&D*. All research studies in these issues were examined and classified in terms of the following categories.

Experimental Studies. This category included (a) true experimental, (b) quasi-experimental, (c) single-subject time series, and (d) repeated-measures time series studies.

Nonexperimental (Descriptive) Studies. The nonexperimental or descriptive studies included correlational, ex post facto, survey, and observational/ethnographic approaches, but these were not used as separate categories—only the experimental studies were classified. A total of 424 articles was classified into one of the four experimental categories or into the overall nonexperimental category. Experimental studies were then classified according to the two additional criteria described below.

Stimulus Materials: *Actual content.* Stimulus materials classified in this category were based on actual content taught in a course from which the subjects were drawn. For example, Tennyson, Welsh, Christensen, and Hajovy (1985) worked with a high-school English teacher to develop stimulus materials that were based on content covered in the English class.

Realistic content. Studies classified in this category used stimulus materials that were factually correct and potentially usable in an actual teaching situation. For example, in examining Taiwanese students' leaning of mathematics, Ku and Sullivan (2000) developed word problems that were taken directly from the fifth-grade textbook used by the students.

Contrived content. This stimulus material category included both nonsense words (Morrison, 1986) and fictional material. For example, Feliciano, Powers, and Kearl (1963) constructed fictitious agricultural data to test different formats for presenting statistical data. Studies in this category generally used stimulus materials with little if any relevance to subjects' knowledge base or interests.

Experimental setting: *Actual setting.* Studies in this category were conducted in either the regular classroom, the computer lab, or an other room used by the subjects for real-life instruction. For example, Nath and Ross (2001) examined student activities in cooperative learning groups on real lessons in their actual classrooms.

Realistic setting. This category consisted of new environments designed to simulate a realistic situation. For example, in the study by Koolstra and Beentjes (1999), elementary students participated in different television-based treatments in vacant school rooms similar to their actual classrooms.

Contrived setting. Studies requiring special equipment or environments were classified in this study. For example, Niekamp's (1981) eye movement study required special equipment that was in-lab designed especially for the data collection.

The final analysis yielded 311 articles classified as experimental (81%) and 71 classified as descriptive (19%). In instances where more than one approach was used, a decision was made by the authors as to which individual approach was predominant. The study was then classified into the latter category. The authors were able to classify all studies into individual design categories. Articles that appeared as literature reviews or studies that clearly lacked the rigor of other articles in the volume were not included in the list of 388 studies. The results of the analysis are described below.

38.4.2.2 Utilization of Varied Experimental Designs. Of the 311 articles classified as experimental, 223 (72%) were classified as true experiments using random assignment of subjects, 77 (25%) of the studies were classified as using quasi-experimental designs, and 11 (35%) were classified as employing time series designs. Thus, following the traditions of the physical sciences and behavioral psychology, use of true-experimental designs has predominated in educational technology research.

An analysis of the publications by decade (e.g., 1953–1962, 1963–1972, 1973–1982) revealed the increased use of true-experimental designs and decreased use of quasi-experimental designs since 1953 (see Fig. 38.1). In the first 10 years of the journal (1953–1962), there was a total of only six experimental studies and three descriptive studies. The experimental studies included two true-experimental and four quasi-experimental designs. During the next 30 years, there was an increase in the number of true-experimental articles. However, in the most recent (abbreviated) decade, from 1993–2001, the percentage of true experiments decreased from the prior decade from 77% to 53% of the total studies, whereas descriptive studies increased from 13% to 45%. This pattern reflects the growing influence of

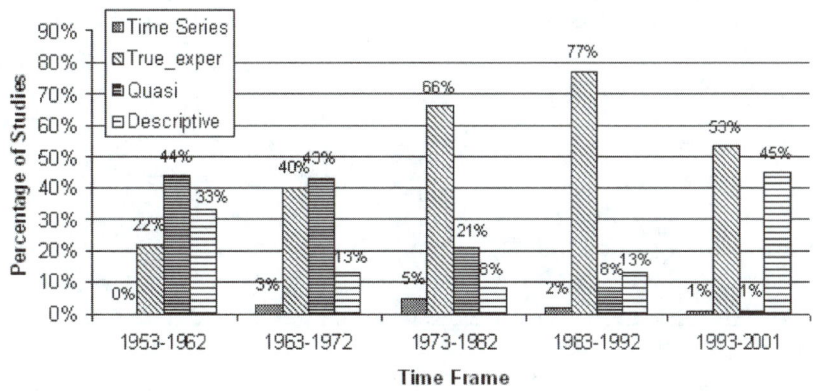

FIGURE 38.1. Experimental design trends.

TABLE 38.2. Designs × Time Frame

Design	1953–1962	1963–1972	1973–1982	1983–1992	1993–2001
Time series	0	3	5	2	1
True experimental	2	40	70	70	41
Quasi-experimental	4	43	22	7	1
Descriptive	3	13	9	12	34

qualitative designs such as case studies. Table 38.2 presents the number of articles published with each design in each of the five decades. It is interesting to note that quasi-experimental designs reached a peak during the 1963-1972 period, with 43 articles, and then decreased to only 1 article in the 1993–2001 time period.

38.4.2.3 Utilization of Stimulus Materials.

An additional focus of our analysis was the types of stimulus materials used in the studies. For example, did researchers use actual materials that were either part of the curriculum or derived from the curriculum? Such materials would have a high external validity and provide additional incentive for the subjects to engage in learning process. Figure 38.2 illustrates the three classifications of materials used by the various studies published during the past 40 years. In the period 1963 to 1972, actual materials were clearly used more often than realistic or contrived. Then, starting in 1972, the use of actual materials began a rapid decline, whereas the use of realistic materials tended to increase. There are two possible explanations for this shift from actual to realistic materials. First is the increasing availability of technology and improved media production techniques. During the 1963-1972 time frame, the primary subject of study was film instruction (actual materials). The increased utilization of realistic materials during the 1973-1982 period may have been the result of the availability of other media, increased media production capabilities, and a growing interest in instructional design as opposed to message design. Similarly, in the 1983-1992 time frame, the high utilization of realistic materials may have been due to the increase in experimenter-designed CBI materials using topics appropriate for the subjects but not necessarily based on curriculum objectives. Interestingly, in 1993-2001, relative to the prior decade, the percentage of studies using realistic content almost doubled, from 18% to 31%. This trend seems

attributable to increased interest in external validity in contemporary education technology research.

38.4.2.4 Utilization of Settings.

The third question concerns the settings used to conduct the studies. As shown in Fig. 38.3, actual classrooms have remained the most preferred locations for researchers, with a strong resurgence in the past 9 years. Again, it appears that increased concern about the applicability (external validity) of findings has an created impetus for moving from the controlled laboratory setting into real-world contexts, such as classrooms and training centers.

38.4.2.5 Interaction Between Usage Variables.

Extending the preceding analyses is the question of which types of stimulus materials are more or less likely to be used in different designs. As shown in Fig. 38.4, realistic materials were more likely to be used in true-experimental designs (48%), whereas actual materials were used most frequently in quasi-experimental designs. Further, as shown in Fig. 38.5, classroom settings were more likely to be chosen for studies using quasi-experimental (82%) than for those using true-experimental (44%) designs. These relationships are predictable, since naturalistic contexts would generally favor quasi-experimental designs over true-experimental designs given the difficulty of making the random assignments needed for the latter. The nature of educational technology research seems to create preferences for realistic as opposed to contrived applications. Yet the trend over time has been to emphasize true-experimental designs and a growing number of classroom applications. Better balances between internal and external validity are therefore being achieved than in the past. Changes in publishing conventions and standards in favor of high experimental control have certainly been influential. Affecting present patterns is the substantive and still growing usage and acceptance of qualitative methods in educational

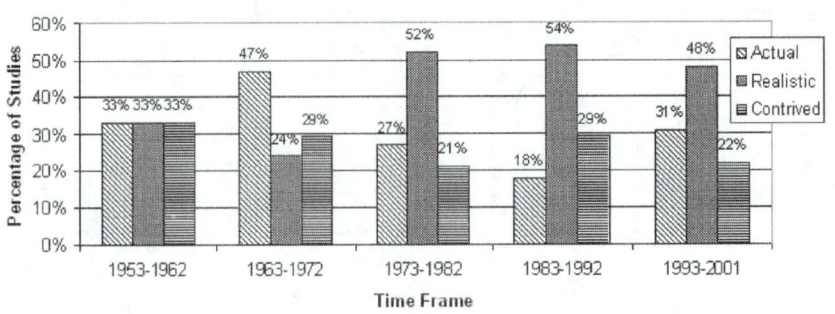

FIGURE 38.2. Trends in stimulus material.

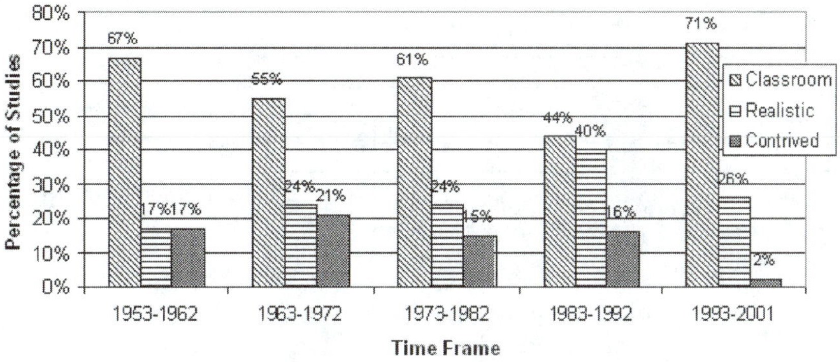

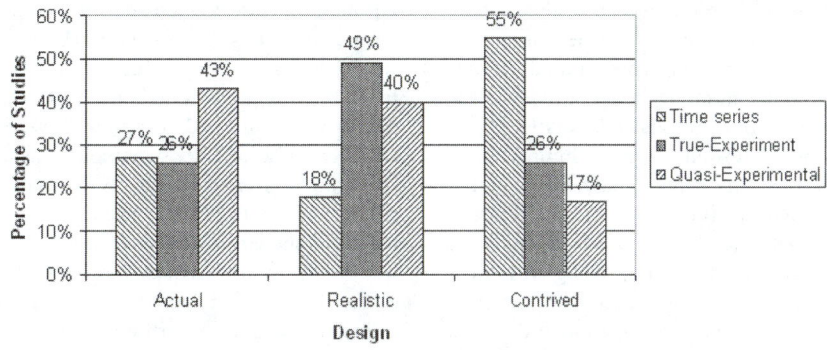

FIGURE 38.3. Trends in settings.

technology research. In our trends analysis, that pattern first became noticeable in the reviewed studies published in 1992 or later.

38.5 CONTEMPORARY ISSUES IN EDUCATIONAL TECHNOLOGY EXPERIMENTATION

38.5.1 Balancing Internal and External Validity

Frequently in this chapter, we have discussed the traditional importance to experimenters of establishing a high internal validity by eliminating sources of extraneous variance in testing treatment effects. Consequently, any differences favoring one treatment over another can be attributed confidently to the intrinsic properties of those treatments rather than to confounding variables, such as one group having a better teacher or more comfortable conditions for learning (see, e.g., reviews by Ross & Morrison, 1989; Slavin, 1993).

The quest for high internal validity orients researchers to design experiments in which treatment manipulations can be tightly controlled. In the process, using naturalistic conditions (e.g., real classrooms) is discouraged, given the many extraneous sources of variance that are likely to operate in those contexts. For example, the extensive research conducted on "verbal

learning" in the 1960s and 1970s largely involved associative learning tasks using simple words and nonsense syllables (e.g., see Underwood, 1966). With simplicity and artificiality comes greater opportunity for control.

This orientation directly supports the objectives of the basic learning or educational psychology researcher whose interests lie in testing the generalized theory associated with treatment strategies, independent of the specific methods used in their administration. Educational technology researchers, however, are directly interested in the interaction of medium and method (Kozma, 1991, 1994; Ullmer, 1994). To learn about this interaction, realistic media applications rather than artificial ones need to be established. In other words, external validity becomes as important a concern as internal validity.

Discussing these issues brings to mind a manuscript that one of us was asked to review a number of years ago for publication in an educational research journal. The author's intent was to compare, using an experimental design, the effects on learning of programmed instruction and CBI. To avoid Clark's (1983) criticism of performing a media comparison, i.e., confounding media with instructional strategies, the author decided to make the two "treatments" as similar as possible in all characteristics except delivery mode. This essentially involved replicating the exact programmed instruction design in the CBI condition. Not surprisingly, the findings showed no difference between treatments, a direct justification of Clark's (1983) position. But, unfortunately, this result (or one showing an actual treatment

FIGURE 38.4. Experimental designs × materials.

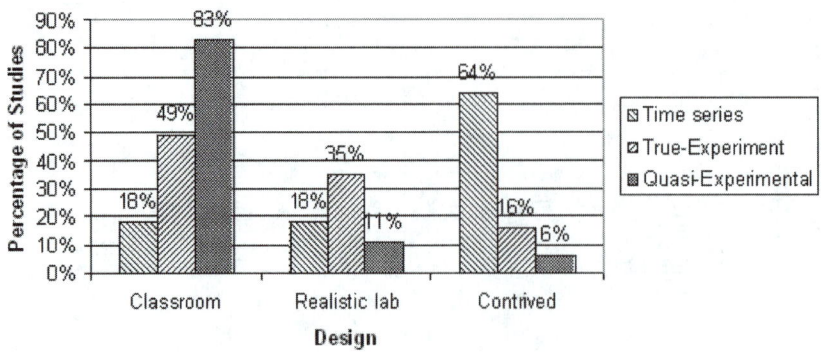

FIGURE 38.5. Experimental design × setting.

effect as well) would be meaningless for advancing theory or practice in educational technology. By stripping away the special attributes of a normal CBI lesson (e.g., interaction, sound, adaptive feedback, animation), all that remained were alternative forms of programmed instruction and the unexciting finding, to use Clark's (1983) metaphor, that groceries delivered in different, but fundamentally similar, ways still have the same nutritional value. Needless to say, this study, with its high internal validity but very low external validity, was evaluated as unsuitable for publication. Two more appropriate orientations for educational technology experiments are proposed in the following sections.

38.5.1.1 Randomized Field Experiments.
Given the importance of balancing external validity (application) and internal validity (control) in educational technology research, an especially appropriate design is the randomized field experiment (Slavin, 1997), in which instructional programs are evaluated over relatively long periods of time under realistic conditions. In contrast to descriptive or quasi-experimental designs, the randomized field experiment requires random assignment of subjects to treatment groups, thus eliminating differential selection as a validity threat.

For example, Nath and Ross (2001) randomly assigned elementary students working in cooperative learning dyads to two groups. The treatment group received training in cooperative learning over seven sessions during the school year, while the control group participated in unrelated ("placebo") group activities. At eight different times, the cooperative dyads were observed using a standardized instrument to determine the level and types of cooperative activities demonstrated. Results indicated that in general the treatment group surpassed the control group in both communication and cooperative skills. Students in grades 2–3 showed substantially more improvement than students in grades 4–6. The obvious advantage of the randomized field experiment is the high external validity. Had Nath and Ross (2001) tried to establish cooperative groupings outside the regular classroom, using volunteer students, the actual conditions of peer interactions would have been substantially altered and likely to have yielded different results. On the other hand, the randomized field experiment concomitantly sacrifices internal validity, because its length

and complexity permit interactions to occur with confounding variables. Nath and Ross' (2001) results, for example, might have been influenced by students' discussing the study and its different conditions with one another after class (e.g., diffusion of treatments). It was definitely influenced, as the authors describe in detail, by the teachers' level of expertise in cooperative learning pedagogy, the cooperative learning tasks assigned, and the ways in which learning conditions were established in the particular class. The experimental results from such studies, therefore, reflect "what really happens" from combined effects of treatment and environmental variables rather than the pure effects of an isolated instructional strategy.

38.5.1.2 Basic–Applied Design Replications.
Basic research designs demand a high degree of control to provide valid tests of principles of instruction and learning. Once a principle has been thoroughly tested with consistent results, the natural progression is to evaluate its use in a real-world application. For educational technologists interested in how learners are affected by new technologies, the question of which route to take, basic vs. applied, may pose a real dilemma. Typically, existing theory and prior research on related interventions will be sufficient to raise the possibility that further basic research may not be necessary. Making the leap to a real-life application, however, runs the risk of clouding the underlying causes of obtained treatment effects due to their confounding with extraneous variables.

To avoid the limitations of addressing one perspective only, a potentially advantageous approach is to look at both using a replication design. "Experiment 1," the basic research part, would examine the variables of interest by establishing a relatively high degree of control and high internal validity. "Experiment 2," the applied component, would then reexamine the same learning variables by establishing more realistic conditions and a high external validity. Consistency of findings across experiments would provide strong convergent evidence supporting the obtained effects and underlying theoretical principles. Inconsistency of findings, however, would suggest influences of intervening variables that alter the effects of the variables of interest when converted from their "pure" form to realistic applications. Such contamination may often represent "media effects," as might occur, for example, when feedback strategies used with print material are naturally made more adaptive (i.e., powerful and effectual) via interactive CBI (see Kozma, 1991). (For example, a learner who confuses discovery learning with inquiry learning in response to an inserted lesson question may be branched immediately to a remedial CBI frame that differentiates between the two approaches, whereas his or her counterpart in a parallel print lesson might experience the same type of feedback by having to reference the response selected on an answer page and manually locate the appropriate response-sensitive feedback in another section of the lesson.) The next implied step of a replication design would be further experimentation on the nature and locus of the altered effects in the applied situation. Several examples from the literature of the basic–applied replication orientation follow.

Example 1. In a repeated-measures experiment that we conducted several years ago, we asked adult subjects to indicate their preferences for screen designs representing differing degrees of text density (Morrison, Ross, Schultz, & O'Dell, 1989). In one experiment, high internal validity was established by having learners judge only the initial screen of a given text presentation, thus keeping the number of displays across higher- and lower-density variations constant. In realistic lessons, however, using lower-density displays requires the use of additional screens (or more scrolling) to view the content fully. Accordingly, a parallel experiment, having a higher external validity but a lower internal validity, was conducted in which the number of screens was allowed to vary naturally in accord with the selected density level.

Both experiments produced similar results, supporting higher- over lower-density displays, regardless of the quantity of screens that conveyed a particular density condition. Consequently, we were able to make a stronger case both for the theoretical assumption that higher density would provide greater contextual support for comprehending expository text and for the practical recommendation that such density levels be considered for the design of actual CBI lessons.

Example 2. In a design used by Winn and Solomon (1993), nonsense syllables served as verbal stimuli in experiment 1. Findings indicated that the interpretation of diagrams containing verbal labels (e.g., "Yutcur" in box A and "Nipden" in box B) was determined mainly by syntactic rules of English. For example, if box B were embedded in box A, subjects were more likely to select, as an interpretation, "Yutcur are Nipden" than the converse description. However, when English words were substituted for the nonsense syllables (e.g., "sugar" in box A and "spice" in box B) in experiment 2, this effect was overridden by common semantic meanings. For example, "Sugar is spice" would be a more probable response than the converse, regardless of the diagram arrangement. Taken together, the two experiments supported theoretical assumptions about the influences of diagram arrangement on the interpreted meaning of concepts, while suggesting for designers that appropriate diagram arrangements become increasing critical as the meaningfulness of the material decreases.

Example 3. Although using a descriptive rather than experimental design, Grabinger (1993) asked subjects to judge the readability of "model" screens that presented symbolic notation as opposed to real content in different formats (e.g., using

or not using illustrations, status bars, headings). Using multidimensional scaling analysis, he found that evaluations were made along two dimensions: organization and structure. In a second study, he replicated the procedure using real content screens. Results yielded only one evaluative dimension that emphasized organization and visual interest. In this case, somewhat conflicting results from the basic and applied designs required the researcher to evaluate the implications of each relative to the research objectives. The basic conclusion reached was that although the results of study I were free from content bias, the results of study 2 more meaningfully reflected the types of decisions that learners make in viewing CBI information screens.

Example 4. Morrison et al. (1995) examined uses of different feedback strategies in learning from CBI. Built into the experimental design was a factor representing the conditions under which college student subjects participated in the experiment: simulated or realistic. Specifically, in the simulated condition, the students from selected education courses completed the CBI lesson to earn extra credit toward their course grade. The advantage of using this sample was increased internal validity, given that students were not expected to be familiar with the lesson content (writing instructional objectives) or to be studying it during the period of their participation. In the realistic condition, subjects were students in an instructional technology course for which performance on the CBI unit (posttest score) would be computed in their final average.

Interestingly, the results showed similar relative effects of the different feedback conditions; for example, knowledge of correct response (KCR) and delayed feedback tended to surpass no-feedback and answer-until-correct (AUC) feedback. Examination of learning process variables, however, further revealed that students in the realistic conditions performed better, while making greater and more appropriate use of instructional support options provided in association with the feedback. Whereas the simulated condition was valuable as a more basic and purer test of theoretical assumptions, the realistic condition provided more valid insights into how the different forms of feedback would likely be used in combination with other learning resources on an actual learning task.

38.5.2 Assessing Multiple Outcomes in Educational Technology Experiments

The classic conception of an experiment might be to imagine two groups of white rats, one trained in a Skinner Box under a continuous schedule of reinforcement and the other under an intermittent schedule. After a designated period of training, reinforcement (food) is discontinued, and the two groups of rats are compared on the number of trials to extinction. That is, how long will they continue to press the bar even though food is withheld?

In this type of experiment, it is probable that the single dependent measure of "trials" would be sufficient to answer the research question of interest. In educational technology research, however, research questions are not likely to be resolved in so straightforward a manner. Merely knowing that one instructional strategy produced better achievement than another provides little insight into how those effects occurred or about other possible effects of the strategies. Earlier educational technology experiments, influenced by behavioristic approaches to learning, were often subject to this limitation.

For example, Shettel, Faison, Roshal, and Lumsdaine (1956) compared live lectures and identical film lectures on subjects (Air Force technicians) learning fuel and rudder systems. The dependent measure was immediate and delayed multiple-choice tests on three content areas. Two outcomes were significant, both favoring the live-lecture condition on the immediate test. Although the authors concluded that the films taught the material less well than the "live" lectures, they were unable to provide any interpretation as to why. Observation of students might have revealed greater attentiveness to the live lecture, student interviews might have indicated that the film audio was hard to hear, or a problem-solving test might have shown that application skills were low (or high) under both presentations.

Released from the rigidity of behavioristic approaches, contemporary educational technology experimenters are likely to employ more and richer outcome measures than did their predecessors. Two factors have been influential in promoting this development. One is the predominance of cognitive learning perspectives in the past two decades (Bransford, Brown, & Cocking, 1999; Snow & Lohman, 1989; Tennyson, 1992); the other has been the growing influence of qualitative research methods.

38.5.2.1 Cognitive Applications.
In their comprehensive review paper, Snow and Lohman (1989) discuss influences of cognitive theory on contemporary educational measurement practices. One key contribution has been the expansion of conventional assessment instruments so as to describe more fully the "cognitive character" of the target. Among the newer, cognitively derived measurement applications that are receiving greater usage in research are tests of declarative and procedural knowledge, componential analysis, computer simulations, faceted tests, and coaching methods, to name only a few.

Whereas behavioral theory stressed learning products, such as accuracy and rate, cognitive approaches also emphasize learning processes (Brownell, 1992). The underlying assumption is that learners may appear to reach similar destinations in terms of observable outcomes but take qualitatively different routes to arrive at those points. Importantly, the routes or "processes" used determine the durability and transferability of what is learned (Mayer, 1989). Process measures may include such variables as the problem-solving approach employed, level of task interest, resources selected, learning strategies used, and responses made on the task. At the same time, the cognitive approach expands the measurement of products to include varied, multiple learning outcomes such as declarative knowledge, procedural knowledge, long-term retention, and transfer (Tennyson & Rasch, 1988).

This expanded approach to assessment is exemplified in a recent experiment by Cavalier and Klein (1998). The focus of the study was comparing the effects of implementing cooperative versus individual learning and orienting activities during CBI. Students working in cooperative dyads or individually completed a CBI earth science program that contained advance organizers, instructional objectives, or no orienting activities. Results indicated that students who received the instructional objectives performed highest on the posttest. This information alone, however, would have provided little insight into how learning objectives might be used by students and, in the case of dyads, how they might influence the dynamics of learner interactions. Accordingly, Cavalier and Klein also examined interaction behaviors while students were learning under the different orienting activities. Findings revealed, for example, that cooperative dyads receiving objectives exhibited more helping behaviors and on-task behaviors than those not receiving orienting activities. Qualitative data from attitude surveys provided further insight into how students approached the instructional task and learning structure. Using these multiple outcome measures, the researchers acquired a clearer perspective on how processes induced by the different strategies culminated in the learning products obtained.

Use of special assessments that directly relate to the treatment is illustrated in a study by Shin, Schallert, and Savenye (1994). Both quantitative and qualitative data were collected to determine the effectiveness of leaner control with elementary students who varied in prior knowledge. An advisement condition that provided the subject with specific directions as to what action to take next was also employed. Quantitative data collected consisted of both immediate and delayed posttest scores, preferences for the method, self-ratings of difficulty, and lesson completion time. The qualitative data included an analysis of the path each learner took through the materials. This analysis revealed that nonadvisement students became lost in the hypertext "maze" and often went back and forth between two sections of the lessons as though searching for a way to complete the lesson. In contrast, students who received advisement used the information to make the proper decisions regarding navigation more than 70% of the time. Based on the qualitative analysis, they concluded that advisement (e.g., orientation information, what to do next) was necessary when learners cauld freely access (e.g., learner control) different parts of the instruction at will. They also concluded that advisement was not necessary when the program controlled access to the instruction.

Another example of multiple and treatment-oriented assessments is found in Neuman's (1994) study on the applicability of databases for instruction. Neuman used observations of the students using the database, informal interviews, and document analysis (e.g., review of assignment, search plans, and search results). This triangulation of data provided information on the design and interface of the database. If the data collection were limited to the number of citations found or used in the students' assignment, the results might have shown that the database was quite effective. Using a variety of sources allowed the researcher to make specific recommendations for improving the database rather than simply concluding that it was beneficial or was not.

38.5.2.2 Qualitative Research.
In recent years, educational researchers have shown increasing interest in qualitative research approaches. Such research involves naturalistic inquiries using techniques such as in-depth interviews, direct

observation, and document analysis (Patton, 1990). Our position, in congruence with the philosophy expressed throughout this chapter is that quantitative and qualitative research are more useful when used together than when either is used alone (see, e.g., Gliner & Morgan, 2000, pp. 16–28). Both provide unique perspectives, which, when combined, are likely to yield a richer and more valid understanding.

Presently, in educational technology research, experimentalists have been slow to incorporate qualitative measures as part of their overall research methodology. To illustrate how such an integration could be useful, we recall conducting an editorial review of a manuscript submitted by Klein and Pridemore (1992) for publication in *ETR&D*. The focus of their study was the effects of cooperative learning and need for affiliation on performance and satisfaction in learning from instructional television. Findings showed benefits for cooperative learning over individual learning, particularly when students were high in affiliation needs. Although we and the reviewers evaluated the manuscript positively, a shared criticism was the lack of data reflecting the nature of the cooperative interactions. It was felt that such qualitative information would have increased understanding of why the treatment effects obtained occurred. Seemingly, the same recommendation could be made for nearly any applied experiment on educational technology uses. The following excerpt from the *published* version of the Klien and Pridemore paper illustrates the potential value of this approach:

... Observations of subjects who worked cooperatively suggested that they did, in fact, implement these directions [to work together, discuss feedback, etc.]. After each segment of the tape was stopped, one member of the dyad usually read the practice question aloud. If the question was unclear to either member, the other would spend time explaining it ... [in contrast to individuals who worked alone] read each question quietly and would either immediately write their answer in the workbook or would check the feedback for the correct answer. These informal observations tend to suggest that subjects who worked cooperatively were more engaged than those who worked alone. (p. 45)

Qualitative and quantitative measures can thus be used collectively in experiments to provide complementary perspectives on research outcomes.

38.5.3 Item Responses vs. Aggregate Scores as Dependent Variables

Consistent with the "expanded assessment" trend, educational technology experiments are likely to include dependent variables consisting of one or more achievement (learning) measures, attitude measures, or a combination of both types. In the typical case, the achievement or attitude measure will be a test comprised of multiple items. By summing item scores across items, a total or "aggregate" score is derived. To support the validity of this score, the experimenter may report the test's internal-consistency reliability (computed using Cronbach's alpha or the KR-20 formula) or some other reliability index. Internal consistency represents "equivalence reliability"— the extent to which parts of a test are equivalent (Wiersma & Jurs, 1985). Depending on the situation, these procedures could

prove limiting or even misleading with regard to answering the experimental research questions.

A fundamental question to consider is whether the test is designed to measure a unitary construct (e.g., ability to reduce fractions or level of test anxiety) or multiple constructs (e.g., how much students liked the lesson and how much they liked using a computer). In the latter cases, internal consistency reliability might well be low, because students vary in how they perform or how they feel across the separate measures. Specifically, there may be no logical reason why good performances on, say, the "math facts" portion of the test should be highly correlated with those on the problem-solving portion (or why reactions to the lesson should strongly correlate with reactions to the computer). It may even be the case that the treatments being investigated are geared to affect one type of performance or attitude more than another. Accordingly, one caution is that, where multiple constructs are being assessed by *design*, internal-consistency reliability may be a poor indicator of construct validity. More appropriate indexes would assess the degree to which (a) items within the separate subscales intercorrelate (subscale internal consistency), (b) the makeup of the instruments conforms with measurement objectives (content validity), (c) students answer particular questions in the same way on repeated administrations (test–retest reliability), and (d) subscale scores correlate with measures of similar constructs or identified criteria (construct or predictive validity).

Separate from the test validation issue is the concern that aggregate scores may mask revealing patterns that occur across different subscales and items. We explore this issue further by examining some negative and positive examples from actual studies.

38.5.3.1 Aggregating Achievement Results. We recall evaluating a manuscript for publication that described an experimental study on graphic aids. The main hypothesis was that such aids would primarily promote better understanding of the science concepts being taught. The dependent measure was an achievement test consisting of factual (fill-in-the-blank), application (multiple-choice and short answer), and problem-solving questions. The analysis, however, examined total score only in comparing treatments. Because the authors had not recorded subtest scores and were unable to rerun the analysis to provide such breakdowns (and, thereby, directly address the main research question), the manuscript was rejected.

38.5.3.2 Aggregating Attitude Results. More commonly, educational technology experimenters commit comparable oversights in analyzing attitude data. When attitude questions concern different properties of the learning experience or instructional context, it may make little sense to compute a total score, unless there is an interest in an overall attitude score. For example, in a study using elaborative feedback as a treatment strategy, students may respond that they liked the learning material but did not use the feedback. The overall attitude score would mask the latter, important finding.

For a brief illustration, we recall a manuscript submitted to *ETR&D* in which the author reported only aggregate results on a postlesson attitude survey. When the need for individual item information was requested, the author replied, "The KR-20 reliability of the scale was .84; therefore, all items are measuring the same thing." Although a high internal consistency reliability implies that the items are "pulling in the same direction," it does not also mean necessarily that all yielded equally positive responses. For example, as a group, learners might have rated the lesson material very high, but the instructional delivery very low. Such specific information might have been useful in furthering understanding of why certain achievement results occurred.

Effective reporting of item results was done by Ku and Sullivan (2000) in a study assessing the effects of personalizing mathematics word problems on Taiwanese students' learning. One of the dependent measures was a six-item attitude measure used to determine student reactions to different aspects of the learning experience. Rather than combining the items to form a global attitude measure, the authors performed a MANOVA comparing the personalized and control treatments on the various items. The MANOVA was significant, thereby justifying follow-up univariate treatment comparisons on each item. Findings revealed that although the personalized group tended to have more favorable reactions toward the lesson, the differences were concentrated (and statistically significant) on only three of the items—ones concerning the students' interest, their familiarity with the referents (people and events) in the problems, and their motivation to do more of that type of math problem. More insight into learner experiences was thus obtained relative to examining the aggregate score only. It is important to keep in mind, however, that the multiple statistical tests resulting from individual item analyses can drastically inflate the chances of making a Type I error (falsely concluding that treatment effects exists). As exemplified in the Ku and Sullivan (2000) study, use of appropriate statistical controls, such as MANOVA (see Table 38.1) or a reduced alpha (significance) level, is required.

38.5.4 Media Studies vs. Media Comparisons

As confirmed by our analysis of trends in educational technology experimentation, a popular focus of the past was comparing different types of media-based instruction to one another or to teacher-based instruction to determine which approach was "best." The fallacy or, at least, unreasonableness of this orientation, now known as "media comparison studies," was forcibly explicated by Clark (1983) in his now classic article (see also Hagler & Knowlton, 1987; Petkovich & Tennyson, 1984; Ross & Morrison, 1989; Salomon & Clark, 1977). As previously discussed, in that paper, Clark argued that media were analogous to grocery trucks that carry food but do not in themselves provide nourishment (i.e., instruction). It, therefore, makes little sense to compare delivery methods when instructional strategies are the variables that impact learning.

For present purposes, these considerations present a strong case against experimentation that simply compares media. Specifically, two types of experimental designs seem particularly unproductive in this regard. One of these represents treatments as amorphous or "generic" media applications, such as

CBI, interactive video, and Web-based instruction. The focus of the experiment then becomes which medium "produces" the highest achievement. The obvious problem with such research is the confounding of results with numerous media attributes. For example, because CBI may offer immediate feedback, animation, and sound, whereas a print lesson does not, differences in outcomes from the two types of presentations would be expected to the extent that differentiating attributes impact criterion performance. More recently, this type of study has been used to "prove" the effectiveness of distance education courses. A better approach is an evaluation study that determines if the students were able to achieve the objectives for the course (Morrison, 2001). Little can be gained by comparing two delivery systems in comparison to determining if a course and the strategies are effective in helping the students achieve the stated objectives. A second type of inappropriate media comparison experiment is to create artificially comparable alternative media presentations, such that both variations contain identical attributes but use different modes of delivery. In an earlier section, we described a study in which CBI and a print manual were used to deliver the identical programmed instruction lesson. The results, which predictably showed no treatment differences, revealed little about CBI's capabilities as a medium compared to those of print lessons. Similarly, to learn about television's "effects" as a medium, it seems to make more sense to use an actual television program, as in Koolstra and Beentjes' (1999) study of subtitle effects, than a simulation done with a home videocamera. So where does this leave us with regard to experimentation on media differences? We propose that researchers consider two related orientations for "media studies." Both orientations involve conveying media applications realistically, whether "conventional" or "ideal" (cutting edge) in form. Both also directly compare educational outcomes from the alternative media presentations. However, as explained below, one orientation is deductive in nature and the other is inductive.

38.5.4.1 Deductive Approach: Testing Hypotheses About Media Differences. In this first approach, the purpose of the experiment is to test a priori hypotheses of differences between the two media presentations based directly on analyses of their different attributes (see Kozma, 1991, 1994). For example, it might be hypothesized that for teaching an instructional unit on a cardiac surgery procedure, a conventional lecture presentation would be superior to an interactive video presentation for facilitating retention of factual information, whereas the converse would be true for facilitating meaningful understanding of the procedure. The rationale for these hypotheses would be based directly on analyses of the special capabilities (embedded attributes or instructional strategies) of each medium in relation to the type of material taught. Findings would be used to support or refute these assumptions.

An example of this a priori search for media differences is the study by Aust, Kelley, and Roby (1993) on "hyperreference" (on line) and conventional paper dictionary use in foreign-language learning. Because hyperreferences offer immediate access to supportive information, it was hypothesized and confirmed that learners would consult such dictionaries more frequently and with greater efficiency than they would conventional dictionaries.

38.5.4.2 Inductive Approach: Replicating Findings Across Media.

The second type of study, which we have called *media replications* (Ross & Morrison, 1989), examines the consistency of effects of given instructional strategies delivered by alternative media. Consistent findings, if obtained, are treated as corroborative evidence to strengthen the theoretical understanding of the instructional variables in question as well as claims concerning the associated strategy's effectiveness for learning. If inconsistent outcomes are obtained, methods and theoretical assumptions are reexamined and the target strategy subjected to further empirical tests using diverse learners and conditions. Key interests are why results were better or worse with a particular medium and how the strategy might be more powerfully represented by the alternative media. Subsequent developmental research might then explore ways of incorporating the suggested refinements in actual systems and evaluating those applications. In this manner, media replication experiments use an inductive, post hoc procedure to identify media attributes that differentially impact learning. At the same time, they provide valuable generalizability tests of the effects of particular instructional strategies.

The classic debate on media effects (Clark, 1983, 1994, 2001; Kozma, 1994) is important for sharpening conceptualization of the role of media in enhancing instruction. However, Clark's focal argument that media do not affect learning should not be used as a basis for discouraging experimentation that compares educational outcomes using different media. In the first orientation reviewed above, the focus of the experiment is hypothesized effects on learning of instructional strategies embedded in media. In the second orientation, the focus is the identified effects of media in altering how those strategies are conveyed. In neither case is the medium itself conceptualized as the direct cause of learning. In both cases, the common goal is increasing theoretical and practical understanding of how to use media more effectively to deliver instruction.

38.6 SUMMARY

In this chapter, we have examined the historical roots and current practices of experimentation in educational technology. Initial usage of experimental methods received impetus from behavioral psychology and the physical sciences. The basic interest was to employ standardized procedures to investigate the effects of treatments. Such standardization ensured a high internal validity or the ability to attribute findings to treatment variations as opposed to extraneous factors.

Common forms of experimentation consist of true experiments, repeated-measures designs, quasi-experiments, and time series designs. Internal validity is generally highest with true experiments due to the random assignment of subjects to different treatments. Typical threats to internal validity consist of history, maturation, testing, instrumentation, statistical regression, selection, experimental mortality, and diffusion of treatments.

Conducting experiments is facilitated by following a systematic planning and application process. A seven-step model suggested consists of (1) selecting a topic, (2) identifying the research problem, (3) conducting a literature search, (4) stating research questions or hypotheses, (5) identifying the research design, (6) determining methods, and (7) identifying data analysis approaches.

For experimental studies to have an impact on theory and practice in educational technology, their findings need to be disseminated to other researchers and practitioners. Getting a research article published in a good journal requires careful attention to writing quality and style conventions. Typical write-ups of experiments include as major sections an introduction (problem area, literature review, rationale, and hypotheses), method (subjects, design, materials, instruments, and procedure), results (analyses and findings), and discussion. Today, there is increasing emphasis by the research community and professional journals on reporting effects sizes (showing the magnitude or "importance" of experimental effects) in addition to statistical significance.

Given their long tradition and prevalence in educational research, experiments are sometimes criticized as being overemphasized and conflicting with the improvement of instruction. However, experiments are not intrinsically problematic as a research approach but have sometimes been used in very strict, formal ways that have blinded educational researchers from looking past results to gain understanding about learning processes. To increase their utility to the field, experiments should be used in conjunction with other research approaches and with nontraditional, supplementary ways of collecting and analyzing results.

Analysis of trends in using experiments in educational technology, as reflected by publications in *ETR&D* (and its predecessors) over the last five decades, show consistent trends as well as some changing ones. True experiments have been much more frequently conducted over the years relative to quasi-experiments, time series designs, and descriptive studies. However, greater balancing of internal and external validity has been evidenced over time by increasing usage in experiments of realistic but simulated materials and contexts as opposed to either contrived or completely naturalistic materials and contexts.

Several issues seem important to current uses of experimentation as a research methodology in educational technology. One is balancing internal validity and external validity, so that experiments are adequately controlled while yielding meaningful and applicable findings. Two orientations suggested for achieving such balance are the randomized field experiment and the "basic–applied" design replication. Influenced and aided by advancements in cognitive learning approaches and qualitative research methodologies, today's experimenters are also more likely than their predecessors to use multiple data sources to obtain corroborative and supplementary evidence regarding the learning processes and products associated with the strategies evaluated. Looking at individual item results as opposed to only aggregate scores from cognitive and attitude measures is consistent with the orientation.

Finally, the continuing debate regarding "media effects" notwithstanding, media comparison experiments remain interesting and viable in our field. The goal is not to compare media generically to determine which are "best" but, rather, to further understanding of (a) how media differ in their capabilities for conveying instructional strategies and (b) how the influences of instructional strategies are maintained or altered via different media presentations.

References

Alper, T., Thoresen, C. E., & Wright, J. (1972). *The use of film mediated modeling and feedback to change a classroom teacher's classroom responses.* Palo Alto, CA: Stanford University, School of Education, R&D Memorandum 91.

Aust, R., Kelley, M. J. & Roby, W. (1993). The use of hypereference and conventional dictionaries. *Educational Technology Research & Development, 41*(4), 63-71.

Borg, W. R., Gall, J. P., & Gall, M. D. (1993). *Applying educational research* (3rd ed.). New York: Longman.

Bransford, J. D., Brown, A. L., & Cocking, R. R. (1999). *How people learn: Brain, mind, experience, and school.* Washington, DC: National Academy Press.

Brownell, W. A. (1992). Reprint of criteria of learning in educational research. *Journal of Educational Psychology, 84,* 400-404.

Campbell, D. T., & Stanley, J. C. (1963). Experimental and quasi-experimental designs for research on teaching. In N. L. Gage (Ed.), *Handbook of research on teaching* (pp. 171-246). Chicago, IL: Rand McNally.

Cavalier, J. C., & Klein, J. D. (1998). Effects of cooperative versus individual learning and orienting activities during computer-based instruction. *Educational Technology Research and Development, 46*(1), 5-18.

Clariana. R. B., & Lee, D. (2001). The effects of recognition and recall study tasks with feedback in a computer-based vocabulary lesson. *Educational Technology Research and Development, 49*(3), 23-36.

Clark, R. E. (1983). Reconsidering research on learning from media. *Review of Educational Research, 53,* 445-459.

Clark, R. E. (1994). Media will never influence learning. *Educational Technology Research and Development, 42*(2), 21-29.

Clark, R. E. (Ed.). (2001). *Learning from media: Arguments, analysis, and evidence.* Greenwich, CT: Information Age.

Clark, R. E., & Snow, R. E. (1975). Alternative designs for instructional technology research. *AV Communication Review, 23,* 373-394.

Cohen, J. (1988). *Statistical power analysis for the behavioral sciences* (2nd ed.). Hillsdale, NJ: Erlbaum.

Creswell, J. W. (2002). *Educational research.* Upper Saddle River, NJ: Pearson Education.

Cronbach, L. J. (1957). The two disciplines of scientific psychology. *American Psychologist, 12,* 671-684.

Dick, W., Carey, L., & Carey, J. (2001). *The systematic design of instruction* 4th ed.). New York: HarperCollins College.

Feliciano, G. D., Powers, R. D., & Kearl, B. E. (1963). The presentation of statistical information. *AV Communication Review, 11,* 32-39.

Gerlic, I., & Jausovec, N. (1999). Multimedia differences in cognitive processes observed with EEG. *Educational Technology Research and Development, 47*(3), 5-14.

Glass, G. V., & Hopkins, K. D. (1984). *Statistical methods in education and psychology.* Englewood Cliffs, NJ: Prentice Hall.

Gliner, J. A., & Morgan, G. A. (2000). *Research methods in applied settings: An integrated approach to design and analysis.* Mahwah, NJ: Lawrence Erlbaum Associates.

Grabinger, R. S. (1993). Computer screen designs: Viewer judgments. *Educational Technology Research & Development, 41*(2), 35-73.

Gronlund, N. E., & Linn, R. L. (1990). *Measurement and evaluation in teaching* (6th ed.). New York: Macmillan.

Guba, E. G. (1969). The failure of educational evaluation. *Educational Technology, 9*(5), 29-38.

Hagler, P., & Knowlton, J. (1987). Invalid implicit assumption in CBI comparison research. *Journal of Computer-Based Instruction, 14,* 84-88.

Hannafin, M. J. (1986). Ile status and future of research in instructional design and technology. *Journal of Instructional Development, 8,* 24-30.

Heinich, R. (1984). The proper study of educational technology. *Educational Communication and Technology Journal, 32,* 67-87.

Jonassen, D. H. (1991). Chaos in instructional design. *Educational Technology, 30,* 32-34.

Jonassen, D. H., Campbell, J. P., & Davidson, M. E. (1994). Learning with media: Restructuring the debate. *Educational Technology Research & Development, 42*(2), 31-39.

Klein, J. D., & Pridemore, D. R. (1992). Effects of cooperative learning and the need for affiliation on performance, time on task, and satisfaction. *Educational Technology Research & Development, 40*(4), 39-48.

Knowlton, J. Q. (1964). A conceptual scheme for the audiovisual field. *Bulletin of the School of Education: Indiana University, 40*(3), 1-44.

Koolstra, C. M., & Beentjes, J. W. J. (1999). Children's vocabulary acquisition in a foreign language through watching subtitled television programs at home. *Educational Technology Research & Development, 47*(1), 51-50.

Kozma, R. B. (1991). Learning with media. *Review of Educational Research, 61,* 179-212.

Kozma, R. B. (1994). Will media influence learning? Refraining the debate. *Educational Technology Research and Development, 42*(2) 7-19.

Kozma, R. B. (2000). Reflections on the state of educational technology research and development: A reply to Richey. *Educational Technology Research and Development, 48*(1), 7-19.

Ku, H-Y., & Sullivan, H. (2000). Learner control over full and lean computer-based instruction under personalization of mathematics word problems in Taiwan. *Educational Technology Research and Development, 48*(3), 49-60.

Mayer, R. E. (1989). Models for understanding. *Review of Educational Research, 59,* 43-64.

Morrison, G. R. (1986). Communicability of the emotional connotation of type. *Educational Communication and Technology Journal, 43*(1), 235-244.

Morrison, G. R. (2001). New directions: Equivalent evaluation of instructional media: The next round of media comparison studies. In R. E. Clark (Ed.), *Learning from media: Arguments, analysis, and evidence* (pp. 319-326). Greenwich, CT: Information Age.

Morrison, G. R., Ross, S. M., Schultz, C. X., & O'Dell, J. K. (1989). Learner preferences for varying screen densities using realistic stimulus materials with single and multiple designs. *Educational Technology Research & Development, 37*(3), 53-62.

Morrison, G. R., Ross, S. M., Gopalakrishnan, M., & Casey, J. (1995). The effects of incentives and feedback on achievement in computer-based instruction. *Contemporary Educational Psychology, 20,* 32-50.

Morrison, G. R., Ross, S. M., & Kemp, J. E. (2001). *Designing effective instruction: Applications of instructional design.* New York: John Wiley & Sons.

Nath, L. R., & Ross, S. M. (2001). The influences of a peer-tutoring training model for implementing cooperative groupings with elementary students. *Educational Technology Research & Development, 49*(2), 41-56.

Neuman, D. (1994). Designing databases as tools for higherlevel learning: Insights from instructional systems design. *Educational Technology Research & Development, 41*(4), 25-46.

Niekamp, W. (1981). An exploratory investigation into factors affecting visual balance. *Educational Communication and Technology Journal, 29,* 37-48.

Patton, M. G. (1990). *Qualitative evaluation and research methods,* (2nd ed.). Newbury Park, CA: Sage.

Petkovich, M. D., & Tennyson, R. D. (1984). Clark's "Learning from media": A critique. *Educational Communication and Technology Journal, 32*(4), 233-241.

Popham, J. X. (1990). *Modern educational measurement: A practitioner's perspective* (2nd ed.). Englewood Cliffs, NJ: Prentice Hall.

Ross, S. M., & Morrison, G. R. (1989). In search of a happy medium in instructional technology research: Issues concerning external validity, media replications, and learner control. *Educational Technology Research and Development, 37*(1), 19-34.

Ross, S. M., & Morrison, G. R. (1991). Delivering your convention presentations at AECT. *Tech Trends, 36,* 66-68.

Ross, S. M., & Morrison, G. R. (1992). Getting started as a researcher: Designing and conducting research studies in instructional technology. *Tech Trends, 37,* 19-22.

Ross, S. M., & Morrison, G. R. (1993). How to get research articles published in professional journals. *Tech Trends, 38,* 29-33.

Ross, S. M., & Morrison, G. R. (2001). *Getting started in instructional technology research* (3rd ed.). Bloomington, IN: Association for Educational Communication and Technology. https://www.aect.org/intranet/Publications/Research/index.html.

Ross, S. M., Smith, L. S., & Morrison, G. R. (1991). The longitudinal influences of computer-intensive learning experiences on at risk elementary students. *Educational Technology Research & Development, 39*(4), 33-46.

Salomon, G., & Clark, R. W. (1977). Reexamining the methodology of research on media and technology in education. *Review of Educational Research, 47,* 99-120.

Schnackenberg, H. L., & Sullivan, H. J. (2000). Learner control over full and lean computer-based instruction. *Educational Technology Research and Development, 48*(2), 19-36.

Shettel, H. H., Faison, E. J., Roshal, S. M., & Lumsdaine, A. A. (1956). An experimental comparison of "live" and filmed lectures employing mobile training devices. *AV Communication Review, 4,* 216-222.

Shin, E. C., Schallert, D. L., & Savenye, W. (1994). Effects of learner control, advisement, and prior knowledge on students' learning in a hypertext environment. *Educational Technology Research and Development, 42*(1), 33-46.

Slavin, R. E. (1993). *Educational psychology.* Englewood Cliffs, NJ: Prentice Hall.

Slavin, R. E. (1997). *Educational psychology* (5th ed.). Needham Heights, MA: Allyn & Bacon.

Snow, R. E., & Lohman, D. F. (1989). Implications of cognitive psychology for educational measurement. *In* R. L. Linn (ed.). *Educational measurement* (3rd ed., pp. 263-331). New York: Macmillan.

Song, H. S., & Keller, J. M. (2001). Effectiveness of motivationally-adaptive computer-assisted instruction on the dynamic aspects of motivation. *Educational Technology Research and Development, 49*(2), 5-22.

Tennyson, R. D., (1992). An educational learning theory for instructional design. *Educational Technology, 32,* 36-41.

Tennyson, R. D., & Rasch, M. (1988). Linking cognitive learning theory to instructional prescriptions. *Instructional Science, 17,* 369-385.

Tennyson, R. D., Welsh, J. C., Christensen, D. L., & Hajovy, H. (1985). Interactive effect of information structure sequence of information and process learning time on rule learning using computer-based instruction. *Educational Communication and Technology Journal, 33,* 212-223.

Thompson, B. (1998). Review of *What if there were no significance tests? Educational and Psychological Measurement, 58,* 332-344.

Thompson, B. (2002). "Statistical," "practical," and "clinical": How many kinds of significance do counselors need to consider? *Journal of Counseling & Development, 80,* 64-70.

Thyer, B. A. (1994). *Successful publishing in scholarly journals.* Thousand Oaks, CA: Sage.

Ullmer, E. J. (1994). Media and learning: Are there two kinds of truth? *Educational Technology Research & Development, 42*(1), 21-32.

Underwood, B. J. (1966). *Experimental psychology.* New York: Appleton-Ceatury-Crofts.

Wiersma, W., & Jurs, S. G. (1985). *Educational measurement and testing.* Newton, MA: Allyn & Bacon.

Winn, W., & Solomon, C. (1993). The effect of spatial arrangement of simple diagrams on the interpretation of English and nonsense sentences. *Educational Technology Research & Development, 41,* 29-41.

QUALITATIVE RESEARCH ISSUES AND METHODS: AN INTRODUCTION FOR EDUCATIONAL TECHNOLOGISTS

Wilhelmina C. Savenye
Arizona State University

Rhonda S. Robinson
Northern Illinois University

Educational technology research methods are changing as new questions and concerns arise. Assumptions, questions, methods, and paradigms that formerly dominated research in the field are changing. Research questions and methods that might once have been deemed unacceptable are gaining acceptability; studies using a variety of qualitative methods and based on alternate paradigms may now be published. Are these "new methods" really so new? Are they based on the same perceptions of quality as the well-established quantitative methods? Are we losing the big picture in research? Are researchers really calling for the end of quantitative research, the positivistic research paradigm, all that has gone before?

It is the goal of this chapter to introduce educational technology researchers, both new and experienced, to the conceptual basis and methods of qualitative research. The goal is a modest one, due to the need for brevity in a single chapter in a large handbook. Controversy is not sidestepped but does not dominate our discussions or cause us to deviate from our goals. Readers are introduced, for example, to the "paradigm debate" currently swirling in the field and to the assumptions of various researchers who adhere to one view or another. Just as one cannot learn to conduct research by reading one book, a researcher who determines to conduct research to be labeled qualitative will need to study sources beyond this chapter to determine his or her own assumptions on which to base the work. The researcher must thus enter the debate, and will be responsible for describing the foundational ideas of the study. He or she will want to conduct the study with the utmost attention to quality, and, therefore, will want to turn to more detailed texts to learn more deeply how to apply qualitative methods. This chapter points the researcher to such references and resources; we do not intend the chapter to be a definitive self-study text in conducting qualitative research. We intend to make the chapter a useful tool, a simple guide to assist educational technologists in learning and making decisions about qualitative research. It is thus intended as a beginning point, a brief tour of qualitative methods that may serve an educational technology researcher well in preparing to answer chosen questions and serve the field in allowing new questions to be explored.

Objectives

The objectives of this chapter are listed below. It is hoped that after reading this chapter, educational technology researchers will be able to do the following.

1. Define the term qualitative research and compare it with other terms, including naturalistic inquiry and ethnography.

2. Describe some of the assumptions underlying qualitative research and compare these assumptions with those underlying quantitative research.
3. Describe and select from various qualitative research methods.
4. Begin to be able to use qualitative research methods at a basic level in research studies.
5. Describe common problems in conducting—and evaluate the quality of—qualitative research studies.
6. Describe a few of the ethical issues involved in conducting qualitative research.
7. Describe issues related to analyzing and reporting qualitative findings.

39.1 INTRODUCTION TO QUALITATIVE RESEARCH

39.1.1 What Is Qualitative Research?

Qualitative research is a term with varying meanings in educational research. Borg and Gall (1989), for example, suggest that the term is often used interchangeably with terms such as *naturalistic, ethnographic, subjective, and postpositivistic.* Goetz and LeCompte (1984) choose to use the term ethnographic as an overall rubric for research using qualitative methods and for ethnographies. In this chapter, *qualitative research* is defined as research devoted to developing an understanding of human systems, be they small, such as a technology-using teacher and his or her students and classroom, or large, such as a cultural system. Qualitative research studies typically include ethnographies, case studies, and generally descriptive studies. They often are called *ethnographies,* but these are somewhat more specific. For instance Goetz and LeCompte (1984), define ethnographies as "analytic descriptions or reconstructions of intact cultural scenes and groups" (p. 2). A case study may indeed be viewed as an ethnography; however, the investigator may have set out to answer a particular question rather than to describe a group or scene as a whole.

Qualitative research methods typically include interviews and observations but may also include case studies, surveys, and historical and document analyses. Case study and survey research are also often considered methods on their own. Survey research and historical and document analysis are covered in other chapters in this book; therefore they are not extensively discussed in this chapter.

Qualitative research has several hallmarks. It is conducted in a natural setting, without intentionally manipulating the environment. It typically involves highly detailed rich descriptions of human behaviors and opinions. The perspective is that humans construct their own reality, and an understanding of what they do may be based on why they believe they do it. There is allowance for the "multiple realities" individuals thus might construct in an environment. The research questions often evolve as the study does, because the researcher wants to know "what is happening" and may not want to bias the study by focusing the investigation too narrowly. The researcher becomes a part of the study by interacting closely with the subjects of the study. The researcher attempts to be open to the subjects' perceptions of "what is"; that is, researchers are bound by the values and worldviews of the subjects. In qualitative research, it is not necessarily assumed that the findings of one study may be generalized easily to other settings. There is a concern for the uniqueness of a particular setting and participants.

In the following section, we present some of the many points of debate about the definition and use of qualitative methods.

39.1.2 Comparisons Between Qualitative and Quantitative Methods

Some authors have chosen to posit qualitative and quantitative research as diametrically opposed constructs. This may confuse a beginning researcher in that it simplistically implies that qualitative research might never use numbers, whereas quantitative research might never use subjects' perceptions. (Discussion of quantifying qualitative data will follow, but for an example the reader need only look at the title of Johnson's, 1978, introduction to qualitative research design, *Quantification in Cultural Anthropology.*)

More useful, perhaps, is the comparison by Borg and Gall (1989), who name the two approaches *positivistic* and *naturalistic* and compare them on the dimensions of the vision of the nature of reality, the relationship of the researcher to the research subject, issues of generalizability, discussion of causality, and the role of values.

Lincoln and Guba (1985) and Denzin and Lincoln (1994) define the term *paradigm* as a systematic set of beliefs, and their accompanying methods, that provide a view of the nature of reality. They contend that the history of inquiry can be divided into eras based on people's view of the world and how to study it. They argue that scientific inquiry is defined by the positivist paradigm, which has prevailed until recently. They call the earliest era the *prepositivist era,* which included human scientific endeavor at about the time of Aristotle to the middle of the 1700s. This was the precursor to a more modern perspective. Lincoln and Guba say that research during this era consisted of passive observation and description. They consider the modern scientific method to have emerged in the positivist era, from about the middle 1700s to the present. Positivism, they note, can be identified by scientific research that involves hypotheses, manipulation, active observation of occurrences, and, thus, testing of hypotheses. These authors argue that the positivist paradigm is limited and is challenged currently by the emerging postpositivist paradigm, which they also call the *naturalistic paradigm.* (Readers unfamiliar with the evolution of paradigms in research may refer to Kuhn's, 1970, seminal work, *The Structure of Scientific Revolutions,* although Lincoln and Guba, 1985, appear to consider Kuhn's views part of the positivist paradigm.)

This conception of the naturalistic paradigm is echoed by Erlandson, Harris, Skipper, and Allen (1993), who note in their book, *Doing Naturalistic Inquiry,* that naturalistic inquiry is a new paradigm as opposed to the older prevailing positivist one. They say that although naturalistic research may use qualitative research methods, it cannot be equated with these methods.

They mention the "paradigm wars" raging in research in general. They note that constructivism and naturalistic inquiry have evolved together. (Readers may refer to Guba's, 1990, book, *The Paradigm Dialog,* in the first few chapters of which these points of view are explored further, for newer views of educational technology research.)

The paradigm debate as it has evolved in educational technology is more recent. The introduction of critical theory issues, the presentation of qualitative workshops at AECT national conferences, and the discussion of alternative research techniques are all indicators of change (see Driscoll, 1995; Robinson, 1995; Robinson & Driscoll, 1993; Yeaman, Koetting, & Nichols, 1994). One aspect of the paradigm debate is the issue of how one's perspective directs the type of research questions studied and how methods are chosen. Some believe that researchers must declare a paradigm from which they work and that the paradigm naturally dictates methods and questions. This point of view comes from strong convictions but may cause limitations in the variety of questions posed for research. It is a different approach from that taken in this chapter, namely, that methods may be chosen based on questions to be studied.

Other authors, such as Goetz and LeCompte (1984), contend that it is perhaps not useful to build simplistic dichotomies of research models. They argue that dichotomies such as generative–verificative, inductive–deductive, subjective–objective, and constructive–enumerative to describe research models must be examined carefully and that "all factors must be balanced in composing a research design" (p. 48).

Although many of the authors above use the term *naturalistic inquiry,* it is perhaps more useful for that term to be applied to the paradigm as Lincoln and Guba (1985) and Erlandson et al. (1993) apply it. Goetz and LeCompte use the term *ethnographic* for research using qualitative methods, but ethnography is just one form that qualitative research may take. In this chapter, we use the term *qualitative research.* This seems to be a less value-laden term and one that has come to the fore recently. (As evidence, one major publisher of textbooks for social science research, Sage Publications, California, publishes an extensive series of references for all aspects of conducting this type of research under the title "qualitative methods.") It remains to be seen whether this is the term that in decades hence will continue to be used.

In sum, in this chapter we agree that forcing a choice between using qualitative and using quantitative methods limits and inhibits the quality of research. Our argument is that the questions a researcher strives to answer should drive the choice of methods. Although it may be true that those approaching research from a postpositivistic perspective consider very different questions to have value, we acknowledge that both perspectives can create interesting and valid research questions. Our assumption is that there is no reason data-gathering methods cannot be combined in a study, that a researcher can investigate carefully and creatively any questions he or she chooses. Rather than limiting our endeavors in this time of tremendous strides in technology development, this approach should enable researchers to take chances, to make leaps, to enhance development in the field by yielding both "answers" and "understanding." As will be seen in the next section, this approach has a solid tradition in educational communications and technology.

That said, given the tremendous ferment in educational research today, it behooves any researcher using qualitative methods to be aware of the varying viewpoints in discussions. A researcher may choose to follow his or her beliefs regarding the postmodern perspective or may construct a study based on emerging questions for research. Either way, a research project could be structured to use quantitative, qualitative, or mixed methods. One could build a study using qualitative methods to answer certain questions, in a study that blends these methods with experimental or quasi-experimental methods. The researcher may design an entirely qualitative study to come to a deep understanding about what is happening in a setting or how the participants perceive of their world. This study may stand on its own or be used as a sort of pilot study to generate questions and hypotheses prior to conducting further research. In any case, the researcher should be specific about how he or she defines the assumptions of the study and why what was done was done—in short, to be able to enter into the current and upcoming discussions as a thoughtful, critical, and creative researcher.

39.1.3 How Has Qualitative Research Historically Been Defined in Educational Technology?

In educational communications and technology research, and in educational research in general, there is similar debate about the definition and purpose of qualitative methods. This can be viewed as a natural consequence of discussion in education about the utility of constructivist as opposed to positivist views of education. This discussion can be enjoyed at national and regional conferences in the field and in the journals. It can be said that the larger debate regarding naturalistic versus positivistic research is creating a more open arena in which studies can be presented and published. Indeed, the editors of the leading journals in the field have indicated that they welcome the submission of well-crafted qualitative studies. Although fewer such reports have been published, it is hoped that this chapter may positively influence the future. It may come as a surprise to some that the use of qualitative perspectives and data collection methods has a long tradition in educational technology research. Early research efforts often used qualitative methods to evaluate and describe the use of media in the classroom. Classroom uses of film, for instance, were investigated through observing teachers and students and by reviewing student work. On the other hand, experimental researchers have often used qualitative methods to collect attitude data, for instance, to yield possible explanations of students' behavior. These data are typically collected using surveys but may be collected using interviews. It is not unusual for an experimental researcher to inform the study further by conducting observations of the subjects. Researchers often conduct a case study to learn more unobtrusively about students, teachers, and trainers who use a new technology. Case studies present detailed data that create a picture of perceptions, use, attitudes, reactions, and learner/teacher environments. Case study data cannot be generalized, however, they may be used to derive questions later to be investigated in an experiment. Evaluation researchers have long used qualitative methods, in particular, surveys, interviews, observations, and historical and document analyses.

Although not researchers per se, instructional systems designers have always used the qualitative methods of surveys, interviews, and observations during the front-end analysis and evaluation phases of development. Markle (1989), for example, contends that even in the early, more "behaviorist" days of instructional design, developers listened to their learners, watched them carefully, and humbly incorporated what learners taught them into their drafts of instructional materials. Similarly, what recent authors, especially computer scientists, are calling testing in "software engineering" (Chen & Shen, 1989), "prototype evaluation" (P. L. Smith & Wedman, 1988), "prototype testing," "quality assurance" (McLean, 1989), or "quality control" (Darabi & Dempsey, 1989–1990) is clearly formative evaluation, usually incorporating some qualitative methods. Beyond these basic uses of qualitative methods, however, there have been calls in the field to use these methods to address new research questions.

With the increasing use of computer-based interactive technologies and distance-learning technologies in education and industry, opportunities, and at times the responsibility, to explore new questions about the processes of learning and instruction have evolved. Educational technologists have issued the call for the use of more qualitative research methods to explore training and school processes (Bosco, 1986; Clark, 1983). Driscoll (1995) suggests that educational technologists select research paradigms based on what they perceive as the most critical questions. Noting the debate regarding paradigms, she adds that educational technology is a relatively young field in which "numerous paradigms may vie for acceptability and dominance" (p. 322). Robinson (1995) and Reigeluth (1989) concur, noting the considerable debate within the field regarding suitable research questions and methods. Winn (1989) also calls for more descriptive studies yielding information about learning and instruction. Clark agrees with Winn, calling for reconsideration of how media are studied (1983) and stating that researchers should conduct planned series of studies, selecting methods based on extensive literature reviews (1989). He recommends that prescriptive studies be conducted to determine why instructional development methods work. Qualitative methods can serve these purposes admirably.

The approach taken in this chapter, that choosing qualitative or quantitative methods need not be an either/or proposition, is similar to the approach of Hannafin and his associates (Hannafin & Rieber, 1989; Hooper & Hannafin, 1988) in their development of the ROPES guidelines for designing instruction. Their guidelines blend behaviorist with cognitive principles in what they call applied cognitivism.

In our field, new educational technologies are continually being developed. Recent developments have been interactive multimedia, new distance-learning systems, information technologies such as hypertext databases and the Internet, interactive learning environments, microworlds, and virtual-reality systems. Many teachers, trainers, administrators, managers, community members, and institutional leaders contend that the evolution of new technologies will continue to change the nature of teaching, training, instruction, and learning (Ambron & Hooper, 1990, 1988; Lambert & Sallis, 1987; Schwartz, 1987; Schwier, 1987; U.S. Congress, OTA, 1988).

It is not only new technologies that require new research methods. The more recent developments in critical theory, postmodernism, and philosophical thought presented in this handbook and elsewhere (see Yeaman et al., 1994) also suggest distinctive changes and additions to our research endeavors and to the questions and problems in education with which technology is involved.

A recent study that investigated new technologies and combined qualitative and quantitative data collection methods is that by Abraham (2000). In his dissertation, he combined techniques to examine the viability and use of media distribution technology in a high school. His examination included quantitative data collected by the system on use, length of time, number of classrooms, number of students, types of materials, and so on. He surveyed all teachers regarding their use of and reaction to the distribution system installed in the building and analyzed the data for frequencies of use and for opinion data. He also interviewed a percentage of the teachers to discover how and why they were using the system and how it changed their teaching. The overall research question was "How does the implementation of a media distribution system change the teaching in a high school?" New technologies also enable researchers to study learners and learning processes in new ways. Computers allow sophisticated tracking of the paths that learners take through a lesson. We can view each decision a learner makes and analyze the relationship among the patterns of those decisions and their performance and attitudes (Dwyer & Leader, 1995).

New technologies may also require that we ask new questions in new ways. We may need to expand our views of what we should investigate and how. For instance, a qualitative view of how teachers and their students use a new technology may yield a view of "what is really happening" when the technology is used. Developers are well aware that instruction is not always delivered as designed, and this holds true for technology-based instruction. The history of educational technology includes records of the failures of a technological approach, often for reasons stemming from poorly planned implementation. We need to know what is really occurring when technologies or new approaches are used. Newman (1989) holds that learning environments can affect instructional technologies. He writes, "How a new piece of educational technology gets used in a particular environment cannot always be anticipated ahead of time. It can be argued that what the environment does with the technology provides critical information to guide design process" (p. 1). He adds, "It is seldom the case that the technology can be inserted into a classroom without changing other aspects of the environment" (p. 3).

A lucid discussion of the issues related to using qualitative techniques in investigating aspects of the technology of computer-based instruction is presented by Neuman (1989). She presents, for example, her findings on teacher perceptions and behaviors for integrating this type of interactive technological innovation into their classrooms. In another qualitative study of an instructional innovation, Jost (1994) investigated aspects of effective use of calculators in teaching calculus for discussions of the impact of new technologies and research in educational technology.

The use of qualitative methods for research has been increasing, especially among doctoral students conducting their dissertation research. A review of the University of Northern Colorado's Web directory of educational technology dissertations reveals that since 1990, over 15 dissertations have used "qualitative" in the title. The subject matter varies in these studies from examinations of instructional design processes, to distance-eductation environments, to hypermedia and multimedia platforms. No doubt a closer look at the abstracts from this period would reveal more dissertations that have used qualitative methods.

39.1.4 Assumptions of this Chapter

Well-designed research is never easy to conduct. Qualitative research studies typically require considerably more time to design, collect, and analyze data and to report the results than do quantitative studies. Yet professors in the field often hear students stating that they plan to do a qualitative study because it will be easier or require less knowledge of statistics. Unfortunately, all too often poorly conceived and conducted studies are called "qualitative" in an effort to avoid defining and describing methods used to collect data, to avoid assumptions of the study, and even to describe results clearly. At conferences, one often hears editors of the leading journals exhorted to publish more qualitative research. Editors reply that they will publish such studies, provided that reviewers and editors can determine that the studies are sound and relevant. (See, for example, M. L. Smith's [1987] paper signifying that the *American Educational Research Journal* [*AERJ*] welcomes the submission of qualitative reports.)

It should be noted that there is still some concern regarding the acceptance of qualitative research by journals. Many editors and reviewers have not become expert in recognizing well-developed research reports of qualitative studies. Questions of sample size and validity may be inappropriately raised about qualitative studies, indicating that reviewers may need more experience with qualitative methods or that reviewers with more experience with qualitative methods could be selected.

The concerns with regard to quality of research are not confined to educational technology. Lincoln and Guba (1985) note that "the naturalistic inquirer soon becomes accustomed to hearing charges that naturalistic studies are undisciplined; that he or she is guilty of 'sloppy' research, engaging in 'merely subjective' observations, responding indiscriminately to the 'loudest bangs or brightest lights'" (p. 289).

Methods for evaluating the soundness of a qualitative study, and for conducting a study ethically, are presented in a later section. However, before discussing the methods qualitative researchers use, it is critical to illustrate the characteristics of good qualitative research. Not all will be present in any one study, as each study is designed differently to investigate different issues. However, it is worth considering what makes a study "qualitative."

In addition to the characteristics described in the earlier definition of qualitative research, in this chapter many of Lincoln and Guba's (1985) characteristics of naturalistic research are assumed to apply to qualitative research. Qualitative research is done in a natural setting. The main data-gathering instrument is the human researcher. The researcher uses tacit, that is, intuitive or felt, knowledge, as well as propositional knowledge. Qualitative methods are used generally, but not to the exclusion of quantitative methods. Sampling is often purposive or theoretical rather than random or representative. Data analysis is typically inductive rather than deductive, but again, not exclusively. In naturalistic studies, theory is grounded in the data rather than determined a priori, although in qualitative studies theories often do drive the processes used in the investigation.

In contrast to experimental studies, in qualitative studies the design often emerges as the research progresses, with the researcher continually refining the methods and questions. Similarly, the focus of the study determines what data are collected, and the boundaries of what is studied may change during the research as new issues and questions emerge. In qualitative research, the "reality" or the meaning of a situation and setting is negotiated among the researcher and those studied, with the understanding that multiple realities are always present. Many qualitative studies use a case study approach in the report, rather than a scientific report; some, in fact, describe the results by building a narrative or sort of story. A qualitative researcher tends to interpret results of a study or draw conclusions based on the particulars of that study, rather than in terms of generalizability to other situations and settings. Similarly, such a researcher is likely to be hesitant about advocating broad application of the findings of one study to other settings (Lincoln & Guba, 1985).

A final assumption of this chapter is that qualitative studies can be evaluated for quality, and rigor is not tossed out because a study is not quantitative in nature. Although some of the criteria may be different from those used in quantitative research, many criteria for evaluating what Lincoln and Guba call the "trustworthiness" of a qualitative study are discussed in this chapter, many related to the particular methods used in qualitative research. For some practical questions to pose and perspectives to consider as research ideas are being debated, see the chapter on qualitative research in Leedy, Newby, and Ertmer (1996). Their guide provides some simple continua to help a new researcher understand the qualitative perspective. As qualitative research courses have increased in number, professors are beginning to discuss the differences between qualitative and quantitative studies. For instance, we could describe these differences along the continuum of social/human research paradigms. On one end of this continuum are quanitative data in which numbers have been assigned to values of a variable and used to describe mathematical, statistical relationships among variables, thereby to generalize from a sample to a population. On the other end of the continuum are qualitative data, gathered through interviews with individuals or groups, or through observing human activities using a variety of methods, in an attempt to describe human meanings and experiences.

In summary, we concur with the call of Salomon (1991) that it is time to transcend the debate about qualitative versus quantitative research. In a stronger message, Robinson (1995) suggests that "the paradigm debate should be declared a draw.... [We should] accept the dual perspectives of our paradigm debate, if we are to meet the challenges of the future and be at all helpful in shaping the educational success of the next century" (pp. 332–333). Robinson continues, "All ways of knowing and all social constructs should be equally accepted and represented in our literature... individuals should be encouraged to question and consider how they approach the world, how they understand learning, and how they believe knowledge is achieved" (p. 332).

The range of methods we may use to conduct qualitative research is explored in the next section. Examples of educational technology studies that use these methods are woven into the discussion. As this chapter is an introduction, issues of analysis and reporting are briefly introduced, but not in great detail.

39.2 QUALITATIVE RESEARCH METHODS

Designing qualitative studies is quite different from designing experimental studies. In fact, designs and methods are continually refined while the researcher conducts a qualitative study. As suggested by Jacobs (1987), the researcher initially chooses methods based on the questions to be addressed; however, the questions, issues, and topics of the study themselves may change as the researcher's conception of the reality of the "world" being studied changes. This may be uncomfortable for those experienced with more quantitative, experimental, or quasi-experimental research. However, most qualitative researchers recommend this process of continual refinement. Goetz and LeCompte (1984), for example, note that methods are "adjusted, expanded, modified, or restricted on the basis of information acquired during the mapping phase of field-work.... Only after final withdrawal from the field can researchers specify the strategies they actually used for a particular study" (p. 108).

Lincoln and Guba (1985) address the contradictory idea of "designing" a naturalistic study completely prior to beginning the study, calling this a "paradox" in that most funding agencies require specificity regarding methods, whereas methods in a good qualitative study may be expected to change as the study progresses. Erlandson et al. (1993) take the middle road. They say that the answer to whether a naturalistic study should be designed in advance is "Yes—to some extent" (p. 66). They recommend beginning the study by specifying a research problem, selecting a research site, developing working hypotheses, and using interactive processes to refine the research questions. They further suggest that the researcher plan for the stages of conducting the study. These may include negotiating entry to the site, planning for purposive (rather than random) sampling and for data collection, planning for data analysis, determining how quality will be ensured in the study, deciding how the findings of the study will be disseminated, and developing a logistical plan. (For further information regarding the logistical operations of field research, the reader may refer to Fiedler's, 1978, book, *Field Research: A Manual for Logistics and Management of Scientific Studies in Natural Settings.*) Erlandson et al. (1993) also recommend reviewing the design of the study regularly.

In determining what the research problem is, Bernard (1988, p. 11) suggests that researchers ask themselves five questions:

1. Does this topic (i.e., setting, school, organization, institution—and data collection method) really interest me?
2. Is this a problem that is amenable to scientific inquiry?
3. Are adequate resources available to investigate this topic? (To study this population? To use this particular method?)
4. Will my research question, or the methods I want to use, lead to unresolvable ethical problems? (Ethical issues are addressed later in this chapter.)
5. Is the topic (community, method) of theoretical interest?

Once a question or issue has been selected, the choice of qualitative methods falls roughly into the categories of observations, interviews, and document and artifact analyses. Qualitative methods, however, form continua on various dimensions, and researchers espouse many views of how methods may be categorized and conceptualized.

Pelto and Pelto (1978), in their frequently cited text on anthropological research methods, remind us that the human investigator is the primary research instrument. These authors categorize methods as either verbal or nonverbal techniques. Verbal techniques include participant observation, questionnaires, and various forms of structured and unstructured interviews. Nonverbal techniques include observations and measures of interactions; proxemics, kinesics, and research involving videotaped observations; use of various types of technical equipment for collecting data; content analysis; and analysis of artifacts and records. Pelto and Pelto add that methods may be described as having an "emic" or insider's view, as in participant observation, versus an "etic" or outsider's view, as in nonparticipant stream-of-behavior analyses.

Other researchers use variations of these taxonomies. Goetz and LeCompte (1984) divide methods into interactive (participant observation and several types of interviews) versus noninteractive methods (forms of nonparticipant observation, as well as artifact collection and analysis). Lincoln and Guba (1985) classify methods as those that collect data from human sources (observations and interviews) as opposed to those that collect data from nonhuman sources (documents and records).

Other authors, however, note that methods can rarely be classified as simple dichotomies, such as interactive or not, in large part because the researcher is a human being, and thus involved, and plays a role even in nonparticipant observation (see Atkinson & Hammersley, 1994). Bogdan and Biklen (1992) provide the example of the "participant/observer continuum" (p. 88), describing the ways in which observers who refrain from being overt participants may still interact to varying degrees with those subjects. Researchers who work using an ethnographic perspective consider all methods "doing fieldwork" (cf. Bogdan & Biklen, 1992). Similarly, Bernard (1982) calls participant observation the "foundation of anthropological research" (p. 148); some would say that this deep, involved method of interacting with subjects defines qualitative research.

It is assumed that educational technologists will use methods ethically and with a view to doing quality research but may not always be bound by anthropological tradition. We are in another field with questions to answer other than those in which anthropologists or sociologists may be interested. For instance, it is now possible to design instruction using a multitude of techniques, using many delivery systems. As noted by McNeil and Nelson (1991) and Reeves (1986), many design factors contribute to the success of instruction using new technologies, such as distance education, interactive multimedia, and Internet-based delivery systems. Educational technologists may successfully use and adapt qualitative methods to investigate new and challenging questions.

In this chapter, we discuss specific methods that may be called observations, interviews, and document and artifact analyses. As in all qualitative research, it is also assumed that educational technology researchers will use and refine methods with the view that these methods vary in their degree of interactiveness with subjects. Each of these methods, in their various forms, along with several research perspectives, is examined in detail below.

39.2.1 Grounded Theory

Grounded theory is considered a type of qualitative methodology. Strauss and Corbin (1994), however, in their overview of grounded theory, note that it is "a general methodology for developing theory that is grounded in data systematically gathered and analyzed" (p. 273), adding that it is sometimes called the constant comparative method and that it is applicable as well to quantitative research. In grounded theory, the data may come from observations, interviews, and videotape or document analyses, and, as in other qualitative research, these data may be considered strictly qualitative or may be quantitative. The purpose of the methodology is to develop theory, through an iterative process of data analysis and theoretical analysis, with verification of hypotheses ongoing throughout the study. A grounded theory perspective leads the researcher to begin a study without completely preconceived notions about what the research questions should be, assuming that the theory on which the study is based will be tested and refined as the research is conducted.

The researcher collects extensive data with an open mind. As the study progresses, he or she continually examines the data for patterns, and the patterns lead the researcher to build the theory. Further data collection leads to further refinement of the questions. The researcher continues collecting and examining data until the patterns continue to repeat and few relatively, or no clearly, new patterns emerge. The researcher builds the theory from the phenomena, from the data, and the theory is thus built on, or "grounded" in, the phenomena. As Borg and Gall (1989) note, even quantitative researchers see the value of grounded theory and might use qualitative techniques in a pilot study without completely a priori notions of theory to develop a more grounded theory on which to base later experiments.

A recent example of a grounded-theory approach in an educational technology study is that of McNabb (1996). This study investigated the teaching of writing in a college computer laboratory. Asking instructors to describe orally critical incidents in their teaching, and using the files created as accompanying data, McNabb investigated the role of the computer-assisted learning environment on instructors and students in assessing and guiding the development of writing skills. In analyzing and explaining the data, McNabb discovered that Vygotsky's theory of the Zone of Proximal Development was a contributing theoretical construct through which to understand her findings.

An earlier grounded theory study looked at two-way television teaching (Oliver, 1992). This research investigated and described the activities used in a university televised distance-education system, analyzing the use of camera techniques as they related to interaction in class. Oliver videotaped hours of two-way video instruction and analyzed the amount and kind of classroom interactions that occurred. She also examined and described the various television shots and transitions used. Outside observers also coded the videotapes. Using grounded-theory techniques, Oliver used the data she transcribed and the emerging categories of data to create a theory of televised instruction. The theory involved the use of close-up camera techniques and the "clean-cut" transition to enhance interaction.

39.2.2 Participant Observation

Participant observation is a qualitative method frequently used in social science research. It is based on a long tradition of ethnographic study in anthropology. In participant observation, the observer becomes "part" of the environment, or the cultural context. The method usually involves the researcher's spending considerable time "in the field," as anthropologists do. Anthropologists typically spend a year or more in a cultural setting in order really to understand the culture in depth, even when they begin the study with a broad overall research question. The hallmark of participant observation is interaction among the researcher and the participants. The main subjects take part in the study to varying degrees, but the researcher interacts with them continually. For instance, the study may involve periodic interviews interspersed with observations so that the researcher can question the subjects and verify perceptions and patterns. These interviews may themselves take many forms, as noted in an upcoming section. For example, a researcher may begin by conducting open-ended unstructured interviews with several teachers to begin to formulate the research questions. This may be followed by a set of structured interviews with a few other teachers, based on results of the first series, forming a sort of oral questionnaire. Results of these interviews may then determine what will initially be recorded during observations. Later, after patterns begin to appear in the observational data, the researcher may conduct interviews asking the teachers about these patterns and why they think they are occurring or if, indeed, these are categories of information. Similarly, a researcher might conduct videotaped observations of a set of teachers, analyze the tapes to begin to make taxonomies of behaviors, and then conduct interviews with the teachers, perhaps while they view the tapes together, to determine how the teachers themselves categorize these behaviors. Thus, the researcher becomes a long-term participant in the research setting.

Educational researchers have come under some criticism, at times legitimately so, for observing in educational settings for very brief periods of time, such as once for a few hours, and then making sweeping generalizations about teachers, schools, and students from these brief "slices of time." Yet educational researchers typically do not have the resources to "live" in the observed settings for such extended periods of time as anthropologists do. There are several exceptions, including, but not limited to, Harry Wolcott's studies of a Kwakiutl village and school (1967) and of one year in the life of a school principal (1973); John Ogbu's (1974) ethnography of urban education; and Hugh Mehan's (1979) collaborative study of social interactions in a classroom, done with Courtney Cazden and her cooperating teacher, LaDonna Coles.

It is reasonable that fine educational technology research can be conducted using participant observation techniques, with somewhat limited research questions. Not every phenomenon can possibly be recorded. Most qualitative observational studies rely on the researcher's writing down what occurs in the form of extensive field notes. The researcher then analyzes these notes soon after observations are carried out, noting patterns of behaviors and events and phenomena to investigate in further observations. Still, the researcher is the instrument in most participant observations and, being human, cannot observe and record everything. Therefore, in most educational research studies, the investigator determines ahead of time what will be observed and recorded, guided but not limited by the research questions.

In an example of a limited participant observation case study, Robinson (1994) observed classes using "Channel One" in a midwestern middle school. Although Robinson was not there for more than one semester, she did observe and participate in the class discussions for many hours of classroom instruction, as well as interview about 10% of the students. She did not focus on all school activities, or on all the categories of interaction within the classrooms, but focused her observations and field notes on the use of the televised news show and the reaction to it from students, teachers, administrators, and parents.

A more involved and longer participant observation study was conducted in a case study by Turner (2000). She participated as the instructor in a two-way televised classroom and gathered data through surveys, observations, analyzing videotapes, and examining class assignments and assessment instruments given in class, as well as by interviewing all participants. The massive amounts of data collected were recorded in a more fluid, narrative style for her report, which details the experiences and perceptions of the students in a distance education setting.

It should be noted that novice observers initially think they can avoid the observational limitations by simply videotaping everything that goes on in the setting, such as the classroom. The use of videotape and audiotape in data collection is useful, particularly in nonparticipant observational studies of particular behaviors and phenomena. However, it can be readily seen that videotaping everything is usually not a way to avoid defining or focusing research questions. For instance, without an exceptionally wide-angle lens, no videocamera can record all that goes on in one classroom. If such a lens is used, then the wide view will preclude being able to see enough detail to understand much of what is going on. For example, computer screens will not be clearly visible, nor will specific nonverbal

behaviors. In addition, if conversations are of interest in order to understand the types of behaviors students are engaged in, no one camera at the back of the room will be able to record all the conversations. Finally, those who have conducted microanalysis of videotaped classroom observations find that it is not unusual to require 10 hr to analyze the behaviors and language recorded in 1 hr of videotape. It can easily be seen that the decision to videotape dozens of hours of classroom behaviors with one camera in the room might result in few useful data being collected, even after hundreds of hours of analysis. Videotape can successfully be used in data collection when the researcher knows what he or she wants to analyze. The preceding note of caution is just a reminder to the qualitative researcher that "shotgun" data collection is no substitute for determining ahead of time what the study is all about.

What can happen with videotape can also happen with written field notes. Trying to glean meaning by sifting through notebook after notebook of descriptions of classroom happenings, especially long after observations were made, is nearly impossible. What is needed is for observations to be at least loosely guided by purposes and questions. Even in studies using a grounded theory approach, observers generally analyze for patterns in observations throughout the entire data collection phase.

Spradley's (1980) book details how to conduct participant observations. He discusses the variety of roles the observer might take, noting that the observer becomes to varying degrees an "insider," in line with what Pelto and Pelto (1978) call the emic view. Spradley suggests that the research site and setting, of course, be selected best to answer the research questions, but with an eye toward simplicity, accessibility, the possibility of remaining relatively unobtrusive, permissibleness, assurance that the activities of interest will occur frequently, and the degree to which the researcher can truly become a participant.

Spradley (1980) provides specific techniques for conducting observations, for conducting iterative interviews with subjects, and for analyzing behaviors, especially language used by informants in interviews. In particular, he notes that cultural domains, or categories of cultural meaning, can be derived from interviews and observations with participants. Finally, he provides advice regarding how to analyze data and write the ethnography.

The stages of participant observation, from an anthropological perspective, have been delineated by Bernard (1988). He describes the excitement, and sometimes fear, of the initial contact period; the next stage, which is often a type of shock as one gets to know the culture in more detail; a period of intense data collection he identifies with discovering the obvious, followed by the need for a real break; a stage in which the study becomes more focused; followed by exhaustion, a break, and frantic activity; and, finally, carefully taking leave of the field setting.

Spradley (1980) advises that ethical issues be addressed throughout the study. These issues are common to most types of qualitative research methods. For instance, Spradley advises that the researcher consider the welfare and interests of the informants, that is, the collaborating subjects first. He says that informants' rights, interests, and sensibilities must be safeguarded; informants should not be exploited. Subjects should be made aware of the purposes of the research study. Their privacy should be protected. Many of these issues are common to all types of research. However, Spradley adds that reports should be made available to informants, so that they too are participants in the study. In some of the interview techniques described later, in fact, verifying analyses and preliminary reports with subjects is one way to ensure the authenticity of the results and to delve more deeply into the research questions. Ethical issues in qualitative research, as well as criteria for evaluating the rigor and quality of such research, are discussed in further detail later in this chapter.

Borg and Gall (1979) discuss the types of questions one might address using participant observation techniques. These include such questions as who the participants are; their typical and atypical patterns of behavior; and where, when, how, and why the phenomena occur. In short, participant observation is often successfully used to describe what is happening in a context and why it happens. These are questions that cannot be answered in the standard experiment.

Another example of participant observation is described by Reilly (1994). His use of videotaping and video production instruction as a project in a California high school involved defining a new type of literacy, combining print, video, and computer technologies. Students produced videotapes that were then transferred to disc and made available for others' use. The research involved many hours of in-school data collection and analysis and was very action oriented, with a product from the students as well as a written report from the researcher.

The work of Higgins and Rice (1991) is another excellent example of a qualitative study with an educational technology focus. These researchers investigated teachers' perceptions of testing. They used triangulation, by using a variety of methods to collect data; however, a key feature of the study was participant observation. Researchers observed six teachers for a sample of 10 hr each. Trained observers recorded instances of classroom behaviors that could be classified as assessment.

Another exemplary study that used multiple methods to triangulate data but that relied primarily on participant observation is that by Moallem (1994). This researcher investigated an experienced teacher's model of teaching and thinking by conducting a series of observations and interviews over a 7-month period. Using a constant comparative style, she analyzed the data, which allowed categories of the teacher's frames of reference, knowledge and beliefs, planning and teaching techniques, and reflective thinking to emerge. She then built a model of the teacher's conceptions. This study may also be called a form of case study.

The study and the triangulation of data and refinement of patterns using progressively more structured interviews and multidimensional scaling are described in more detail later in this chapter.

39.2.3 Nonparticipant Observation

Nonparticipant observation is one of several methods for collecting data considered to be relatively unobtrusive. Many recent authors cite the early work of E. J. Webb, Campbell, Schwartz, and Sechrest (1966) as laying the groundwork for use of all types of unobtrusive measures.

Several types of nonparticipant observation have been identified by Goetz and LeCompte (1984). These include stream-of-behavior chronicles, recorded in written narratives or using videotape or audiotape; proxemics and kinesics, that is, the study of uses of social space and movement; and interaction analysis protocols, typically in the form of observations of particular types of behaviors, categorized and coded for analysis of patterns. Bernard (1988) describes two types of nonparticipant observation, which he calls disguised field observation and naturalistic field experiments. He cautions in the first case for care to be taken that subjects are not harmfully deceived. Reflecting recent postmodern and constructivist (as well as deconstructionist) trends, Adler and Adler (1994) extend paradigms of observational research to include dramaturgical constructions of reality, and auto-observation, as well as more typical ethnomethodology.

In nonparticipant observation, the observer does not interact to a great degree with those he or she is observing (as opposed to what Bernard, 1988, calls direct, reactive observation). The researcher primarily observes and records and has no specific role as a participant. Usually, of course, the observer is "in" the scene and, thus, affects it in some way; this must be taken into account. For instance, observers often work with teachers or instructors to have them explain to students briefly why the observer is there. Care should be taken once more not to bias the study. It is often desirable to explain the observations in general terms rather than to describe the exact behaviors being observed, so that participants do not naturally increase those behaviors. Some increase may occur; if the researcher suspects this, it is appropriate to note it in the analyses and report.

As with participant observation, nonparticipant observers may or may not use structured observation forms but are often more likely to do so. In this type of study, often several trained observers make brief sampled observations over periods of time, and observation forms help to ensure consistency of the data being recorded.

Nonparticipant observation is often used to study focused aspects of a setting, to answer specific questions within a study. This method can yield extensive detailed data, over many subjects and settings, if desired, to search for patterns or to test hypotheses developed as a result of using other methods, such as interviews. It can thus be a powerful tool in triangulation. Observational data may be coded into categories, frequencies tabulated, and relationships analyzed, yielding quantitative reports of results.

Guidelines for conducting nonparticipant observation are provided by Goetz and LeCompte (1984), among others. They recommend that researchers strive to be as unobtrusive and unbiased as possible. They suggest verification of data by using multiple observers. Before the study is begun in earnest, the units of analysis, and thus the data to be recorded, should be specified; recording methods should be developed; strategies for selection and sampling of units should be determined; and, finally, all processes should be tested and refined.

Examples of studies in which observations were conducted that could be considered relatively nonparticipant observation are Savenye and Strand's (1989) in the initial pilot test and Savenye's (1989) in the subsequent larger field test of a science videodisc- and computer-based curriculum. Of most concern during implementation was how teachers used the curriculum. Among other questions researchers were interested in are: how much teachers followed the teachers' guide, the types of questions they asked students when the system paused for class discussion, and what teachers added to or did not use from the curriculum. In the field test (Savenye, 1989), a careful sample of classroom lessons was videotaped and the data were coded. For example, teacher questions were coded according to a taxonomy based on Bloom's (1984), and results indicated that teachers typically used the system pauses to ask recall-level rather than higher-level questions.

Analysis of the coded behaviors for what teachers added indicated that most of the teachers in the sample added examples to the lessons that would provide relevance for their own learners and that almost all of the teachers added reviews of the previous lessons to the beginning of the new lesson. Some teachers seemed to feel that they needed to continue to lecture their classes; therefore they duplicated the content presented in the interactive lessons.

Developers used the results of the studies to make changes in the curriculum and in the teacher training that accompanied it. Of interest in this study was a comparison of these varied teacher behaviors with the student achievement results. Borich (1989) found that learning achievement among students who used the interactive videodisc curriculum was significantly higher than among control students. Therefore, teachers had a great degree of freedom in using the curriculum, and the students still learned well.

If how students use interactive lessons is the major concern, researchers might videotape samples of students using an interactive lesson in cooperative groups and code student statements and behaviors, as did Schmidt (1992). In a study conducted in a museum setting, Hirumi, Savenye, and Allen (1994) used qualitative methods to measure what visitors learned from an interactive videodisc-based natural history exhibit.

Nonparticipant observations may be used in studies that are primarily quantitative experimental studies in order to answer focused research questions about what learners do while participating in studies. For instance, a researcher may be interested in what types of choices learners make while they proceed through a lesson. This use of observations to answer a few research questions within experimental studies is exemplified in a series of studies of cooperative learning and learner control in television- or computer-delivered instruction by Klein, Sullivan, Savenye, and their colleagues.

Jones, Crooks, and Klein (1995) describe the development of the observational instrument used in several of these studies. Klein and Pridemore (1994), in a study of cooperative learning in a television lesson, observed four sets of behaviors. These were coded as helping behaviors, on-task group behaviors, on-task individual behaviors, and off-task behaviors. In a subsequent experimental study using a computer-based lesson, Crooks, Klein, Jones, and Dwyer (1995) observed students in cooperative dyads and recorded, coded, and analyzed helping, discussion, or off-task behaviors.

In another study of cooperative use of computer-based instruction (Wolf, 1994), only one behavior was determined to be most related to increased performance, and that was giving elaborated explanations, as defined by Webb (1991, 1983). Instances of this behavior, then, were recorded and analyzed.

An example of using technology to assist in recording and analyzing behaviors is given in Dalton, Hannafin, and Hooper's (1989) study on the achievement effects of individual and cooperative use of computer-based instruction. These researchers audiotaped the conversations of each set of students as they proceeded through the instruction.

A variation on nonparticipant observations represents a blend with trace behavior, artifact, or document analysis. This technique, called read-think-aloud protocols, takes the form of asking learners to describe what they do and why they do it, that is, their thoughts about their processes, as they proceed through an activity, such as a lesson. P. L. Smith and Wedman (1988) describe using this technique to analyze learner tracking and choices. Researchers may observe and listen as subjects participate, or researchers can use audiotape or videotape to analyze observations later. In either case, the resulting verbal data must be coded and summarized to address the research questions. Techniques for coding are described by Spradley (1980). However, protocol analysis (cf. Ericsson & Simon, 1984) techniques could be used on the resulting verbal data. These techniques also relate to analysis of documentary data, such as journals, discourse, recalled learning measures, and even forms of stories, such as life or career histories.

Many qualitative studies using observational techniques are case studies, and many in educational technology have involved the use of computers in schools. One such study was conducted by Dana (1994), who investigated how the pedagogical beliefs of one first-grade teacher related to her classroom curriculum and teaching practices. The teacher was an experienced and creative computer user who modeled the use of computers for her peers. Many hours of interviews and observations of the classes were made. Classroom videotapes were coded by outside reviewers who were trained to identify examples of the teacher's beliefs, exemplified in classroom practice. This study provided insights into the pedagogy, methodology, and teaching and learning in a computer-rich environment. She suggested changes that schools could make to encourage teachers to become better able to incorporate technology into their classrooms in ways congruent with their teaching beliefs.

Another qualitative case study was conducted by Pitts (1993). She investigated students' organization and activities when they were involved in locating, organizing, and using information in the context of a research project in a biology class. Pitts relied on cognitive theory and information models in developing her theoretical construct. She described how students conducted their research leading to their preparation and use of video to present the results of their research.

39.2.3.1 Scope.
A study using observational techniques may investigate a broad set of research questions, such as how a reorganization has affected an entire institution, or it may be much more narrowly focused. The outcome of the study may take the form of a type of "rich story" that describes an institution or a

classroom or another type of cultural setting. A more narrowly focused participant observation study, however, may investigate particular aspects of a setting, such as the use of an educational innovation or its effects on particular classroom behaviors.

Whereas some qualitative researchers might believe that only studies rich in "thick description," as described by Lincoln and Guba (1985; cf. Geertz, 1973), are legitimate, other researchers might choose to use qualitative techniques to yield quantitative data. This blend of qualitative and quantitative data collection is also being used in anthropological studies. An example of a more narrowly focused relatively nonparticipant observation study is the Savenye and Strand (1989) study described earlier, in which the researchers chose to focus primarily on what types of interactive exchanges occurred between students and teachers while they used an electronic curriculum.

39.2.3.2 Biases.
Educational researchers who choose to do observational studies would do well to remember that although they do not spend years observing the particular instructional community, they may quickly become participants in that community. Their presence may influence results. Similarly, their prior experiences or upbringing may bias them initially toward observing or recording certain phenomena and, later, in how they "see" the patterns in the data. In subsequent reports, therefore, this subjectivity should be honestly acknowledged, as is recommended in ethnographic research.

39.2.3.3 The Observer's Role.
In participant observation studies, the researcher is a legitimate member in some way in the community. For instance, in the videodisc science curriculum study mentioned above, Strand was the senior instructional designer of the materials, Savenye had been an instructional design consultant on the project, and both researchers were known to the teachers through their roles in periodic teacher-training sessions. Observers have limited roles to play in the setting, but they must be careful not to influence the results of the study, that is, to make things happen that they want to happen. This may not seem so difficult, but it may be—for example, if the researcher finds himself or herself drawn to tutoring individuals in a classroom, which may bias the results of the study. Schmidt (1992) describes an example in which she had difficulty not responding to a student in class who turned to her for help in solving a problem; in fact, in that instance, she did assist. More difficult would be a researcher observing illegal behaviors by students who trust the researcher and have asked him or her to keep their activities secret. Potential bias may be handled by simply describing the researcher's role in the research report, but the investigator will want to examine periodically what his or her role is and what type of influence may result from it.

39.2.3.4 What Should Be Recorded.
What data are recorded should be based on the research questions. For example, in a study of classroom behaviors, every behavior that instructors and students engage in could potentially be recorded and analyzed, but this can be costly in money and time and is often not possible. A researcher using a completely "grounded-theory" approach would spend considerable time in the field recording as much as possible. However, another researcher

might legitimately choose to investigate more narrowly defined research questions and collect primarily data related to those questions. Again, what is excluded may be as important as what is included.

Therefore, even in a more focused study, the researcher should be observant of other phenomena occurring and be willing to refine data collection procedures to collect emerging important information, or to change the research questions as the data dictate, even if this necessitates added time collecting data.

39.2.3.5 Sampling.
In observational research, sampling becomes not random but purposive (Borg & Gall, 1989). For the study to be valid, the reader should be able to believe that a representative sample of involved individuals was observed. The "multiple realities" of any cultural context should be represented. The researcher, for instance, who is studying the impact of an educational innovation would never be satisfied with observing only the principals in the schools. Teachers and students using the innovation would obviously need to be observed. What is not so obvious is that it is important in this example to observe novice teachers, more experienced teachers, those who are comfortable with the innovation and those who are not, along with those who are downright hostile to the innovation. Parents might also be observed working with their youngsters or interacting with the teachers. How these various individuals use the innovation becomes the "reality of what is," rather than how only the most enthusiastic teachers or experienced technologists use it.

39.2.3.6 Multiple Observers.
If several observers are used to collect the data, and their data are compared or aggregated, problems with reliability of data may occur. Remember that human beings are the recording instruments, and they tend to see and subsequently interpret the same phenomena in many different ways. It becomes necessary to train the observers and to ensure that observers are recording the same phenomena in the same ways. This is not as easy as it may sound, although it can be accomplished with some effort. A brief description of these efforts should be described in the final research report, as this description will illustrate why the data may be considered consistent.

One successful example of a method to train observers has been used by Klein and his colleagues in several of the studies described earlier (cf. Klein & Pridemore, 1994; Klein, Erchul, & Pridemore, 1994). In the study investigating effects of cooperative learning versus individual learning structures, Crooks et al. (1995) determined to observe instances of cooperative behaviors while students worked together in a computer-based lesson. Several observers were trained using a videotape made of a typical cooperative-learning group, with a good-quality audio track and with close views of the computer screens. Observers were told what types of cooperative behaviors to record, such as instances of asking for help, giving help, and providing explanations. These behaviors were then defined in the context of a computer-based lesson and the observation record form reviewed. Then observers all watched the same videotape and recorded instances of the various cooperative behaviors in the appropriate categories. The trainer and observers next discussed their records, and observers were given feedback regarding any errors. The following segment of videotape was viewed, and the observers again recorded the behaviors. The training was repeated until observers were recording at a reliability of about 95%. Similarly, in her study Wolf (1994) trained observers to record instances of just one behavior, providing elaborated explanations.

It should be noted that in studies in which multiple observers are used and behaviors counted or categorized and tallied, it is desirable to calculate and report interrater reliability. This can easily be done by having a number of observers record data in several of the same classroom sessions or in the same segments of tape and then computing the degree of their agreement in the data.

Other references are also available for more information about conducting observational studies in education, for example, Croll's (1986) book on systematic classroom observation.

39.2.4 Interviews

In contrast with the relatively noninteractive, nonparticipant observation methods described earlier, interviews represent a classic qualitative research method that is directly interactive. Interview techniques, too, vary in how they may be classified, and again, most vary in certain dimensions along continua, rather than being clearly dichotomous. For instance, Bernard (1988) describes interview techniques as being structured or unstructured to various degrees. He describes the most informal type of interviewing, followed by unstructured interviewing that has some focus. Next, Bernard mentions semistructured interviewing and, finally, structured interviews, typically involving what he calls an interview schedule, which others call interview protocols, that is, sets of questions, or scripts. Fontana and Frey (1994) expand this classification scheme by noting that interviews may be conducted individually or in groups. Again, exemplifying modern trends in qualitative research, these authors add that unstructured interviews now may include oral histories and creative and postmodern interviewing, the latter of which may include use of visual media and polyphonic interviewing, that is, almost-verbatim reporting of respondents' words, as well as gendered interviewing in response to feminist concerns.

Goetz and LeCompte (1984) note that other classification schemes may include scheduled versus nonscheduled or standardized versus nonstandardized. However, their division of interview techniques into key-informant interviews, career histories, and surveys represents a useful introduction to the range of interviewing techniques.

An interview is a form of conversation in which the purpose is for the researcher to gather data that address the study's goals and questions. A researcher, particularly one who will be in the setting for a considerable period of time or one doing participant observations, may choose to conduct a series of relatively unstructured interviews that seem more like conversations with the respondents. Topics will be discussed and explored in a somewhat loose but probing manner. The researcher may return periodically to continue to interview the respondents in more depth, for instance, to focus on questions further or to triangulate with other data.

In contrast, structured interviews may be conducted in which the researcher follows a sort of script of questions, asking the same questions, and in the same order, of all respondents. Goetz and LeCompte (1984) consider these to be surveys, whereas other authors do not make this distinction, and some consider surveys and questionnaires to be instruments respondents complete on their own without an interview.

Interviews or a series of interviews may focus on aspects of a respondent's life and represent a standard technique in anthropology for understanding aspects of culture from an insider's view. Fontana and Frey (1994) call these oral histories. Goetz and LeCompte (1984) note that for educators such interviews, which focus on career histories, may be useful for exploring how and why subjects respond to events, situations, or, of interest to educational technologists, particular innovations.

Guidelines for conducting interviews are relatively straightforward if one considers that both the researcher, as data-gathering instrument, and the respondents are human beings, with their various strengths and foibles in communicating. The cornerstone is to be sure that one truly listens to respondents and records what they say, rather than to the researcher's perceptions or interpretations. This is a good rule of thumb in qualitative research in general. It is best to maintain the integrity of raw data, using respondents' words, including quotes, liberally. Most researchers, as a study progresses, also maintain field notes that contain interpretations of patterns, to be refined and investigated on an ongoing basis. Bogdan and Biklen (1992) summarize these ideas: "Good interviews are those in which the subjects are at ease and talk freely about their points of view.... Good interviews produce rich data filled with words that reveal the respondents' perspectives" (p. 97).

Bernard (1988) suggests letting the informant lead the conversation in unstructured interviews and asking probing questions that serve to focus the interview at natural points in the conversation. Whereas some advocate only taking notes during interviews, Bernard stresses that memory should not be relied on, and tape recorders should be used to record exact words. This may be crucial later in identifying subjects' points of view and still later in writing reports.

Ensuring the quality of a study by maintaining detailed field journals is also emphasized by Lincoln and Guba (1985). They suggest keeping a daily log of activities, a personal log, and a methodological log. They add that safeguards should be implemented to avoid distortions that result from the researcher's presence and bias that arises from the researcher, respondents, or data-gathering techniques. They add that participants should be debriefed after the study.

Stages in conducting an interview are described by Lincoln and Guba (1985). They describe how to decide whom to interview, how to prepare for the interview, what to say to the respondent as one begins the interview (Bogdan and Biklen, 1992, mention that most interviews begin with small talk), how to pace the interview and keep it productive, and, finally, how to terminate the interview and gain closure.

One example of the use of interviews is described by Pitlik (1995). As an instructional designer, she used a case study approach to describe the "real world" of instructional design and development. Her primary data source was a series of interviews with individuals involved in instructional design. She conducted group interviews with members of the International Board of Standards for Performance and Instruction and conducted individual interviews with about 15 others. From the data she collected, she approached questions about the profession, professional practices, and the meaning of the term instructional designer. Her data included interview transcripts and literature on the profession. She coded her data and found that themes that emerged described four distinct types of practitioners. Her results led to recommendations for programs that train instructional designers, as well as for practitioners.

Many old, adapted, new, and exciting techniques for structured interviewing are evolving. For example, Goetz and LeCompte (1984) describe confirmation instruments, participant-construct instruments, and projective devices. Confirmation instruments verify the applicability of data gathered from key-informant interviews or observations across segments of the population being studied. (It may be added that this type of structured interview could be adapted as a questionnaire or survey for administering to larger subject groups). Participant-construct instruments may be used to measure degrees of feelings that individuals have about phenomena or in having them classify events, situations, techniques, or concepts from their perspective. Goetz and LeCompte say that this technique is particularly useful in gathering information about lists of things, which respondents can then be asked to classify.

One example of such a use of interviews occurred in the Higgins and Rice (1991) study mentioned earlier. At several points during the study teachers were asked to name all the ways they test their students. In informal interviews, they were asked about types of assessment observers recorded in their classrooms. The researchers later composed lists of the types of tests teachers mentioned and asked them to sort the assessment types into those most alike. Subsequently, multidimensional scaling was used to analyze these data, yielding a picture of how these teachers' viewed testing.

A third type of structured interview mentioned by Goetz and LeCompte is the interview using projective techniques. Photographs, drawings, other visuals, or objects may be used to elicit individuals' opinions or feelings. These things may also be used to help the researcher clarify what is going on in the situation. Pelto and Pelto (1978) describe traditional projective techniques in psychology, such as the Rorschack inkblot test and the Thematic Apperception Test. Spindler (1974), for example, used drawings to elicit parents', teachers', and students' conceptions of the school's role in a German village. McIssac, Ozkalp, and Harper-Marinick (1992) effectively used projective techniques with subjects viewing photographs.

Types of questions to be asked in interviews are also categorized in a multitude of ways. Goetz and LeCompte (1984) describe these as "experience, opinion, feeling questions, hypothetical questions, and propositional questions" (p. 141). Spradley (1980) provides one of the more extensive discussions of questions, indicating that they may be descriptive, structural, or contrast questions. He further explains ways to conduct

analyses of data collected through interviews and observations. In an earlier work, Spradley (1972) explicates how cultural knowledge is formed through symbols and rules and describes how language can be analyzed to begin to form conceptions of such knowledge.

Of particular use to educational technologists may be the forms of structured interviews that Bernard (1988) says are used in the field of cognitive anthropology. Educational technologists and psychological researchers are interested in how learners learn and how they conceive of the world, including technological innovations. Some of the techniques that Bernard suggests trying out include having respondents do free listing of taxonomies, as done in the Higgins and Rice (1991) study of teachers' conceptions of testing. The items listed can later be ranked or sorted by respondents in various ways. Another technique is the frame technique or true/false test. After lists of topics, phenomena, or things are developed through free listing, subjects can be asked probing questions, such as, "Is this _ an example of _?" Triad tests are used to ask subjects to sort and categorize things that go together or do not. Similarly, respondents can be asked to do pile sorting, to generate categories of terms and how they relate to each other, forming a type of concept map. Bernard adds that other types of rankings and ratings can also be done.

To learn further techniques and the skills needed to use them, the reader may refer to Weller and Romney's (1988) book, *Systematic Data Collection*. Also, for a more in-depth perspective on analyzing verbal protocols and interview data for insight into cognitive processes, one may look to several chapters in the Spradley (1972) work mentioned earlier. For instance, Bruner, Goodnow, and Austin (1972) discuss categories and cognition, and Frake (1972) presents uses of ethnographic methods to study cognitive systems. More recent works include work in semiotics (Manning & Cullum-Swan, 1994).

The earlier-mentioned study by Moallem (1994) relied heavily on use of interviews along with participant observation to build the model of an experienced teacher's teaching and thinking. Both of the earlier mentioned studies, Turner (2000) and Donaldson (2000), used extensive interviews, and their reports featured in-depth quotations as part of the data. Another good study in educational technology that used interview techniques as one of several methods to gather data is that of Reiser and Mory (1991). These researchers investigated the systematic planning techniques of two experienced teachers. The teachers were administered a survey at the beginning of the year and were interviewed early in the year about how they planned and designed lessons. They were subsequently observed once a week while they taught the first science unit of the year.

Before and after each observation, the teachers were interviewed in depth. In addition, copies of their written plans were collected (a form of document analysis; discussed later in this chapter). Thus a deep case study approach was used to determine the ways in which experienced teachers plan their instruction. In this study, the teacher who had received instructional design training appeared to use more systematic planning techniques, whereas the other planned instructional activities focused on objectives.

As with observations, interviews may be conducted as part of an experimental, quantitative study in educational technology. For instance, Nielsen (1989) conducted an experimental study to determine the effects of informational feedback and second attempt at practice on learning in a computer-assisted instructional program. He incorporated interviews with a sample of the learners to explain his findings further. He found that some of his learners who received no feedback realized that their performance depended more on their own hard work, so they took longer to study the material than did those who determined that they would receive detailed informational feedback, including the answers.

Other detailed examples of how interview techniques may be used are illustrated in Erickson and Shultz's (1982) work, *The Counselor as Gatekeeper*.

39.2.5 Document and Artifact Analysis

Beyond nonparticipant observation, many unobtrusive methods exist for collecting information about human behaviors. These fall roughly into the categories of document and artifact analyses but overlap with other methods. For instance, the verbal or non-verbal behavior streams produced during videotaped observations may be subjected to intense microanalysis to answer an almost-unlimited number of research questions. Content analysis, as one example, may be done on these narratives. In the Moallem (1993), Higgins and Rice (1991), and Reiser and Mory (1991) studies of teachers' planning, thinking, behaviors, and conceptions of testing, documents developed by the teachers, such as instructional plans and actual tests, were collected and analyzed.

This section presents an overview of unobtrusive measures. (Readers interested in more detailed discussion of analysis issues may refer to DeWalt and Pelto's, 1985, work, *Micro and Macro Levels of Analysis in Anthropology*, as well as other resources cited in this chapter.)

Goetz and LeCompte (1984) define artifacts of interest to researchers as things that people make and do. The artifacts of interest to educational technologists are often written, but computer trails of behavior are becoming the objects of analysis as well. Examples of artifacts that may help to illuminate research questions include textbooks and other instructional materials, such as media materials; memos, letters, and, now, e-mail records, as well as logs of meetings and activities; demographic information, such as enrollment, attendance, and detailed information about subjects; and personal logs kept by subjects. E. J. Webb et al. (1966) add that archival data may be running records, such as those in legal records or the media, or they may be episodic and private, such as records of sales and other business activities and written documents.

Physical traces of behaviors may be recorded and analyzed. E. J. Webb et al. (1966) describe these as including types of wear and tear that may appear on objects or in settings naturally, as in police tracing of fingerprints or blood remains.

In recent studies in educational technology, researchers are beginning to analyze the patterns of learner pathways and decisions they make as they proceed through computer-based lessons. Based on the earlier work of Hicken, Sullivan, and Klein (1992), Dwyer and Leader (1995) describe the development of a Hypercard-based researcher's tool for collecting data from counts of keypresses to analyze categories of choices made within computer-based instruction, such as the mean numbers of practice or example screens chosen. In their study, Savenye et al. (1996) used this tool to collect information about the types of choices learners made in a fully student-controlled, computer-based learning environment. In a similar use of computers to record data, Shin, Schallert, and Savenye (1994) analyzed the paths that young learners took when using a computer-based lesson to determine the effects of advisement in a free-access, learner-controlled condition.

As noted earlier, the records made using videotape or audiotape to collect information in nonparticipant observation may be considered documentary data and may be subjected to microanalysis.

Guidelines for artifact collection are provided by Goetz and LeCompte (1984). They identify four activities involved in this type of method: "locating artifacts, identifying the material, analyzing it, and evaluating it" (p. 155). They recommend that the more informed the researcher is about the subjects and setting, the more useful artifacts may be identified and the more easily access may be gained to those artifacts.

Hodder (1984) suggests that from artifacts, a theory of material culture may be built. He describes types of objects and working with respondents to determine how they might be used. (Anyone who has accompanied older friends to an antique store, especially one that includes household tools or farm implements from bygone eras, may have experienced a type of interactive description and analysis of systems and culture of the past based on physical artifacts.) Hodder continues with discussion of the ways in which material items in a cultural setting change over time and reflect changes in a culture.

Anthropologists have often based investigations about the past on artifacts such as art pieces, analyzing these alone or using them in concert with informant and projective interviews. As noted in some of the current debate in anthropology or regarding museum installations that interpret artifacts, the meaning of artifacts is often intensely personal and subjective, so that verification of findings through triangulation is recommended. (The reader intrigued with these ideas may wish to refer to some of the classic anthropological references cited here, or to current issues of anthropology and museum journals. Two interesting examples appear in the January 1995 issue of *Smithsonian* magazine. I. Michael Heyman discusses the many points of view represented in the public's perceptions of the initial form of the installation of the Enola Gay exhibit. In a different vein, Haida Indian artist Robert Davidson describes how he used art and dance and song to help elders in his tribe remember the old ways and old tales [Kowinski, 1995.])

Content analysis of prose in any form may also be considered to fall into this artifact-and-document category of qualitative methodology. Pelto and Pelto (1978) refer to analysis of such cultural materials as folktales, myths, and other literature, although educational technologists would more likely analyze, for example, content presented in learning materials. For more information about content analysis see, for instance, Manning and Cullum-Swan (1994).

This concludes our introduction to general methods in conducting qualitative research. We can look forward to other methods being continually added to the repertoire.

39.3   ANALYZING QUALITATIVE DATA

Qualitative data are considered to be the "rough materials researchers collect from the world they are studying; they are the particulars that form the basis of analysis" (Bogdan & Biklen, 1992, p. 106). As described earlier, qualitative data can take many forms, such as photos, objects, patterns of choices in computer materials, and videotapes of behaviors. However, words often are the raw materials that qualitative researchers analyze, and much advice from researchers discusses analyzing these words.

The need for brevity in this chapter precludes an extensive discussion of analyzing qualitative data. However, we introduce the researcher to the issues underlying decisions to be made and provide several views of how to analyze data. As noted by Miles and Huberman (1994) in their in-depth sourcebook, beginning researchers may quake in the face of the "deep, dark question" regarding how to have confidence that their approach to analysis is the right one (p. 2). Yet we concur with the thoughtful but practical approach of these authors, that one must just begin and that more energy is often spent discussing analysis, and research for that matter, than "doing it." Miles and Huberman note, in a decidedly unnaive approach, that "...any method that works, that will produce clear, verifiable, credible meanings from a set of qualitative data," is "grist for their mill." They add, "...The creation, testing, and revision of simple, practical, and effective analysis methods remain the highest priority of qualitative researchers," adding that, "We remain convinced that concrete, shareable methods do indeed belong to 'all of us'" (p. 3). It is in this spirit that we present approaches to analyzing qualitative data.

One of the major hallmarks of conducting qualitative research is that data are analyzed continually, throughout the study, from conceptualization through the entire data collection phase, and into the interpretation and writing phases. In fact, Goetz and LeCompte (1984) describe the processes of analyzing and writing together in what they call analysis and interpretation. How these activities may be done is explored here.

39.3.1   Overall Approaches to Analyzing Qualitative Data

Qualitative researchers choose their analysis methods not only by the research questions and types of data collected but also based on the philosophical approach underlying the study. For example, Miles and Huberman (1994) outline three overall approaches to analyzing qualitative data. An "interpretive" approach would be phenoniological in nature or based on social interactionism. Researchers using this approach would seek to present a holistic view of data rather than a condensed view. They might seek to describe a picture of "what is." They would

generally not choose to categorize data to reduce it. Miles and Huberman note that the interpretive approach might be used by qualitative researchers in semiotics, deconstructivism, aesthetic criticism, ethnomethodology, and hermeneutics.

The second approach described by these researchers is "collaborative social research," often used by action researchers in partnerships composed of members of many, and sometimes opposing, organizations.

The final approach to analyzing data described by Miles and Huberman is that of "social anthropology," which relies primarily on ethnography. Researchers using this approach seek to provide detailed, or rich, descriptions across multiple data sources. They seek regular patterns of human behavior in data, usually sifting, coding, and sorting data as they are collected, and following up analyses with ongoing observations and interviews to explore and refine these patterns, in what Goetz and LeCompte call a recursive approach (1994). Researchers using a social anthropology approach also tend to be concerned with developing and testing theory. Researchers who develop life histories, work in grounded theory and ecological psychology, and develop narrative studies, applied studies, and case studies often base their analyses on this social anthropology approach. Many of the methods for, and views about, analyzing qualitative data can be seen to be based on this social anthropology approach.

39.3.2   Methods for Analyzing Qualitative Data

Depending on the basic philosophical approach of the qualitative researcher, many methods exist for analyzing data. Miles and Huberman state that qualitative data analysis consists of "three concurrent flows of activity: data reduction, data display, and conclusion drawing/verification" (1994, p. 10). Most researchers advocate that reducing and condensing data, and thereby beginning to seek meaning, should begin as the study begins and continue throughout data collection.

39.3.2.1   Data Reduction. Goetz and LeCompte (1994) describe the conceptual basis for reducing and condensing data in this ongoing style as the study progresses. The researcher theorizes as the study begins and builds and tests theories based on observed patterns in data continually. Researchers compare, aggregate, contrast, sort, and order data. These authors note that although large amounts of raw data are collected, the researcher may examine in detail selected cases or negative cases to test theory. They describe analytic procedures researchers use to determine what the data mean. These procedures involve looking for patterns, links, and relationships. In contrast to experimental research, the qualitative researcher engages in speculation while looking for meaning in data; this speculation will lead the researcher to make new observations, conduct new interviews, and look more deeply for new patterns in this "recursive" process.

Researchers may derive patterns in many ways. They may, for example, engage in what Goetz and LeCompte call "analytic induction" (p. 179), reviewing data for categories of phenomena, defining sets of relationships, developing hypotheses, collecting more data, and refining hypotheses accordingly. As noted earlier, interpretivists would be unlikely to use this method. They would not tend to categorize but would scan for patterns to build a picture or tell a story to describe what is occurring.

Another method, constant comparison, would be relied on by those using a grounded-theory approach. This method involves categorizing, or coding, data as they are collected and continually examining data for examples of similar cases and patterns. Data collection can cease when few or no new categories of data are being encountered. Goetz and LeCompte contend that researchers using constant-comparison code data look for patterns as do those using analytic induction, but the categories are thus processed differently.

Bogdan and Biklen (1992) describe in detail practical approaches to writing up field notes, one of the main forms the "words" that make up qualitative data take. They recommend writing field notes with large margins in which to write later notes as data are later analyzed, as well as in which to write codes for these data. They also advise that text be written in blocks with room left for headings, notes, and codes.

It should be noted that virtually all researchers who use an ethnographic approach advocate writing up field notes immediately after leaving the research site each day. Observations not recorded will quickly be forgotten. Researchers may not realize the importance of some small phenomenon early on, so these details should be recorded each day. Most authors further recommend that researchers scan these data daily, analyzing thoughtfully for patterns and relationships and, perhaps, adding to or modifying data collection procedures accordingly.

Field notes consist of observations and the researcher's interpretations. Bogdan and Biklen (1984) call these two types of field notes contents the descriptive part (p. 108) and the reflective part (p. 121). They state that the descriptive part consists of detailed descriptions of the subjects and settings, the actual dialogue of participants, and descriptions of events and activities, as well as descriptions of the observer's behavior, to enable determining how this may have influenced participants' behaviors. The reflective part of field notes, they add, consists of the observer/researcher's analysis. The researcher records speculations about patterns and how data can be analyzed, thoughts about methods and ethical concerns, and even ideas about his or her own state of mind at the time. Bogdan and Biklen provide many pages of actual field notes from studies done in elementary and secondary education classrooms, which the beginning researcher will find helpful.

If researchers collect data using audiotape or videotape, written transcripts of language recorded are often prepared. Later analysis can be done, but notes should still be recorded immediately after being in the field. Such notes, for instance, will include observations about participants' nonverbal behaviors, what was occurring in the immediate surroundings, or activities in which participants were engaging. Even in the case of interviews, notes might include these descriptions, as well as what participants were doing just prior to interviews. As noted in the discussion of data collection methods, audiotapes and videotapes may be subjected to detailed microanalysis. Usually data are coded and counted, but due to the labor-intensive nature of this type of analysis, segments of these "streams of behavior" are often systematically selected for analysis.

It is advisable to collect data in its raw, detailed form and then record patterns. This enables the researcher later to analyze the original data in different ways, perhaps to answer deeper questions than originally conceived. The researcher many weeks into data collection may realize, for example, that some phenomena previously considered unimportant hold the keys to explaining participants' views and actions. In addition, preserving the raw data allows other researchers to explore and verify the data and the interpretations.

If researchers have collected documents from subjects, such as logs, journals, diaries, memos, and letters, these can also be analyzed as raw data. Similarly, official documents of an organization can be subjected to analysis.

Collecting data in the form of photographs, films, and videotapes, those produced either by participants or by the researcher, has a long tradition in anthropology and education. These data, too, can be analyzed for meaning. (See, for instance, Bellman & Jules-Rosette, 1977; Bogaart & Ketelaar, 1983; Bogdan & Biklen, 1992; Collier, 1967; Collier & Collier, 1986; Heider, 1976; and Hockings, 1975.)

39.3.2.2 Coding Data.
Early in the study, the researcher will begin to scan recorded data and to develop categories of phenomena. These categories are usually called codes. They enable the researcher to manage data by labeling, storing, and retrieving it according to the codes. Of course, the codes created depend on the study, setting, participants, and research questions, because the codes are the researchers' way of beginning to get at the meaning of the data. There are therefore as many coding schemes as researchers. Still, examples of coding schemes are provided here in an attempt to guide the reader.

Miles and Huberman (1994) suggest that data can be coded descriptively or interpretively. Unlike some authors, they suggest creating an initial "start list" (p. 58) of codes and refining these in the field. Researchers using a strictly inductive approach might choose not to create any codes until some observations and informal interviews were conducted from which codes could be induced.

Bogdan and Biklen (1992) recommend reading data over at least several times to begin to develop a coding scheme. They describe coding data according to categories and details of settings; types of situation observed; perspectives and views of subjects of all manner of phenomena and objects; processes, activities, events, strategies, and methods observed; and social relationships. Goetz and LeCompte (1984) describe coding to form a taxonomic analysis, a sort of outline of what is related to what, and in what ways.

In one of many examples he provides, Spradley (1979) describes in extensive detail how to code and analyze interview data, which are semantic data, as are most qualitative data. He describes how to construct domain, structural, taxonomic, and componential analyses. We discuss, as one example, domain analysis. Domains are names of things. Spradley proposes "universal semantic relationships," which include such categories as "strict inclusion" (that is, "X is a kind of Y"), "spatial" ("X is a place in Y, X is a part of Y"), "cause–effect," "rationale," "location of action," "function," "means–end," "sequence," and "attribution" (p. 111). Spradley provides an example from his own research. In a study on tramps, he found from interviews that the cover term *flop,* as a place to sleep, included such things as box cars, laundromats, hotel lobbies, and alleys.

An example of the types of codes that might be developed to investigate patterns of teacher use of an educational technology innovation is presented in the Savenye and Strand (1989) observational study described earlier. The researchers videotaped teachers and students using the multimedia science course in 13 physical science classrooms in four states. Samples of videotapes from three teachers were selected for approximate equivalence; in the samples, the teachers were teaching approximately the same content using the same types of lesson components. The researchers were interested not in all the behaviors occurring in the classrooms but in the types of language expressed as teachers taught the lessons.

After reviewing the videotaped data several times, the researchers developed codes for categorizing teacher language. Most of these codes were created specifically for this study. For example, the most frequent types of teacher language observed were instances of "teacher statements," which included data coded as "increasing clarity or coherence of information presented." Examples of codes in this category included PR, for providing preview or organizers of lessons; RP, reminding students to remember prior knowledge; EL, elaborating by providing new information about a scientific concept in the lesson; and R, providing a review of lesson content. Another example of a code created for teacher statements was REL, for instances of when a teacher relates content to students' own experience with everyday examples.

Savenye and Strand were also interested in the types of questions teachers added to the curriculum to encourage their students to participate actively during the whole-class presentations of content. Along with a few created codes, the researchers developed codes based on Bloom's (1984) taxonomy of cognitive objectives. Such codes included REC, for questions that asked students to recall information just presented by the multimedia system; APP, for questions that required students to apply or extend lesson content to new content or situations; and ANAL/SYN, for questions that require a student to analyze a situation to come up with solutions or to synthesize a solution. In a result similar to those of many studies of teacher-questioning strategies, but that may disappoint multimedia developers, the majority of the teachers' questions simply asked students to recall information just presented, rather than to apply or analyze or synthesize knowledge learned.

In this study, as in most qualitative studies, coding schemes were continually added to, collapsed, and refined as the study progressed. However, in some studies, only preassigned codes are used to collect and/or analyze data. As in the use of Bloom's categories by Savenye and Strand (1989), usually these codes have been derived from studies and theories of other researchers or from pilot studies conducted by the researchers themselves. These studies may use observational coding forms or protocols on which data are recorded in the coding categories.

Another example of using preassigned codes is a study conducted to investigate how visitors to a botanical garden use interactive signs (Savenye, Socolofsky, Greenhouse, & Cutler, 1995). Among other types of data collected in this study, these researchers trained observers to record behaviors visitors engaged in while they used signs. Observers recorded whether visitors stopped to read a sign at all; if so, for how long; and the level of interactivity visitors exhibited. Based on the work of Bitgood (1990), interactivity was coded as stopping briefly and glancing only; obviously reading the sign and looking at the plant exhibit near it; and, finally, engaging in highly active behaviors, such as reading the sign aloud, pointing to the plants displayed, discussing information being learned, and pulling friends and family over to the sign to read it. In a blend of coding methods typical in many studies, observers also wrote ethnographic-style notes to describe what if any content on the signs was being discussed, what misconceptions appeared, what excited visitors most, etc. In this study, visitor surveys and interviews were also used.

In any qualitative study, codes can be used to count frequencies or, as Goetz and LeCompte call it, conduct enumeration (1984) to develop quantitative data, as done in the studies just described. Similarly, quantitative data, such as attendance or production figures, from other sources, may be analyzed. Most researchers suggest caution that the "big picture" is not lost when counting, and, also, note that quantitative data from other sources can also be biased. Even what is collected in a school district, for instance, may be determined by financial, administrative, and political concerns.

For more examples of coding schemes and strategies, see Strauss (1987).

39.3.2.3 Data Management.

39.3.2.3.1 Physically Organizing Data. Analysis of data requires examining, sorting, and reexamining data continually. Qualitative researchers use many means to organize, retrieve, and analyze their data. Many researchers simply use notebooks and boxes of paper. Bogdan and Biklen (1992) describe what they call two mechanical means to organize and begin to review data. One way they describe is to write initial codes in margins of field notes, photocopy the notes, and store the originals, then cut up and sort the text segments into piles according to codes. These coded data can be stored in boxes and resorted and analyzed on an ongoing basis. The second method they describe is to record field notes on pages on which each line is numbered, code the field notes, and then write the page number, line numbers, and a brief description of each piece of data on a small index card. These cards can then be sorted and analyzed. The authors note that this second method is better suited for small sets of data, as it often requires returning to the original field notes to analyze the actual data.

39.3.2.3.2 Organizing Data Using Computers. Computers are increasingly the tool of choice for managing and analyzing qualitative data. It is interesting to note that computers have long been used in anthropological analysis. (See, e.g., Hymes, 1965.) Computers may be used simply for word processing in developing field notes. However, there is now considerable software specifically developed for qualitative research, and it can be expected that many new programs will be developed in the upcoming decade. Some software uses text entered with a word processor to retrieve words and phrases or to manage text in databases. Software is also available to code and retrieve data, and some programs also allow for building theories and conceptual networks. Programs are available for IBM (e.g., QUAL-PRO, The Ethnograph) or for Macintosh microcomputers (e.g., HyperQual, SemNet) or multiple systems (QSR NUD-IST) (Miles & Weitzman, 1994). For much more on using computers for analysis, the reader may refer to the following books: Tesch's (1990), *Qualitative Research: Analysis Types and Software Tools* and Wietzman and Miles' (1995), *A Software Sourcebook: Computer Programs for Qualitative Data Analysis*.

39.3.2.3.3 Data Display. Seeking the meaning in data is made easier by displaying data visually. Research data are displayed using charts, graphs, diagrams, tables, matrices, and any other devices, such as drawings, that researchers devise. Frequency tables are typically developed for categories of coded behaviors. In the Reiser and Mory (1991) study, for example, teachers' planning behaviors were coded and tables of behaviors presented.

Miles and Huberman (1994) hold that data display is a critical and often underutilized means of analysis. They describe many forms of data display, illustrated with examples of actual data. They recommend that researchers initially create categories of data, code data, and revise codes, as do other authors. They note that increasingly qualitative research involves analyzing what they call within-case data, for instance, from one classroom or one school, as well as "cross-case" data, from many participants and many sites. Whereas in one case study, it may not be necessary to present visual displays—narrative descriptions may suffice—studies involving data from many cases can greatly benefit from visual displays. Miles and Huberman present many options. For example, for within-case data they show context charts and checklist matrices, but they also discuss using a transcript as a poem. They also illustrate time-ordered displays, role-ordered displays, and conceptually ordered displays. For cross-case studies, these researchers mention some of the earlier displays for reviewing and presenting data, along with case-ordered displays. They illustrate other displays for examining cross-case data and provide extensive advice for creating matrix displays.

An example of the use of matrix displays is the Higgins and Rice (1991) participant observation study described earlier. The researchers analyzed teachers' conceptions of all the activities that represent "assessment." These data were derived from a series of structured interviews with the teachers, conducted in conjunction with observations of the teachers and their students. The researchers analyzed these data using multidimensional scaling and displayed the data using a matrix to show the relationships among types of assessments teachers used and how different teachers conceived of them differently.

That data analysis is woven into interpreting results and writing up the study is indicated by the fact that Miles and Hubetinan describe the third type of data analysis activity as drawing and verifying conclusions. Similarly, Goetz and LeCompte (1984) include writing up the study in their chapter on analysis and interpretation of data, describing the writing phase as developing an ethnographic analysis and integrating and interpreting

the study. While recognizing that analysis continues as the research report is written, and that writing should begin during analysis, in this chapter, we present ideas and issues for writing up a study.

39.4 WRITING QUALITATIVE RESEARCH REPORTS

The report of a qualitative study may take many forms, both those common to more quantitative research and forms likely to be unfamiliar to those who conduct only experimental research. The best advice for the beginning researcher is to recognize that it is not unusual for even experienced researchers to feel overwhelmed by the amount of data to be analyzed and described, as well as to feel a lack of confidence that the interpretations and conclusions the researcher has drawn represent "the truth." Most authors simply advise writers to "do it," or to "begin" to write and refine and write and refine. A later section discusses ethical issues and criteria for evaluating the quality of a study. As with analysis, there exist many entire books of guidelines and advice for writing qualitative research. In this section we briefly discuss a few of the issues.

In writing up a qualitative study, researchers have many choices of presentation styles. Bogdan and Biklen (1984) consider qualitiative researchers fortunate in that there is not one accepted convention for writing qualitative reports. For example, the qualitative report may take the form of a case study, as in the Reiser and Mory (1991) study. If a case study, the report may include considerable quantification and tables of enumerated data, or it may take a strictly narrative form. Recent studies have been reported in more nontraditional forms, such as stories, plays, and poems showing what is happening for these participants in that setting.

A few examples of less traditional approaches to reporting results are the presentations by Barone and Lather at the 1995 conference of the American Educational Research Association (AERA). Barone (1995) presented an arts-based phenomological inquiry in a narrative format. Lather, in an AERA Qualitative Research SIG interactive symposium on reframing the narrative voice, discussed her study, in which she divided pages in her report into three sections in which she presented her interpretation, the participants' interpretation, and then her response to the participants (Tierney et al., 1995.)

Richardson (1995) describes other components and styles of less traditional writing, including ways to reference historical contexts, using metaphors, using documentary styles, and various experimental representations, including "narrative of the self," "ethnographic fictional representations," "poetic representations," "ethnographic dramas," and "mixed genres" (pp. 521–522). Richardson additionally provides advice to the researcher who wishes to explore these experimental formats.

Fetterman (1989) explicates the nature of qualitative writing. As do many others, he stresses the use of "thick description" and liberal use of verbatim quotations, that is, the participants' own words, to illustrate the reality of the setting and subjects. (This serves as another reminder to the researcher to record and preserve raw data in the participants' language with quotes.)

Fetterman adds that ethnographies are usually written in what he calls the "ethnographic present" (p. 116), as if the reality is still ongoing, however, in educational technology research, in which innovations are often described, the researcher may or may not choose to use this approach. Qualitative reports typically will be woven around a theme or central message and will include an introduction, core material, and a conclusion (Bogdan & Biklen, 1984). However, what constitutes the core of the report will vary, of course, depending on the style of the writing.

A cogent and enjoyable manual for writing up qualitative research is that by Wolcott (1990). (For additional information about writing reports of qualitative studies, see Meloy, 1994, and Van Maanen, 1988.)

39.5 ETHICAL ISSUES IN CONDUCTING QUALITATIVE RESEARCH

In addition to the ethical issues raised by authors cited earlier in discussions of specific methodologies, there continues to be great concern that qualitative researchers conduct and report their studies in an ethical manner. Punch, 1994, however, suggests that qualitative researchers not be daunted or deterred by ethical issues. In fact, under the heading, "Just do it!" he advises that "fieldwork is fun; it is easy; anyone can do it; it is salutary for young academics to flee the nest; and they should be able to take any moral or political dilemmas encountered in their stride" (p. 83). He describes the ethical issues that are common with most scientific research, such as biomedical research, in this country at this time. For instance, all researchers must be concerned with preventing subjects from being harmed, protecting their anonymity and privacy, not deceiving them, and securing their informed consent. In discussing recent debate about qualitative methods, however, Punch adds other issues that arise. Such questions may include, "Does the pursuit of scientific knowledge justify the means? What is public and what is private? When can research be said to be 'harming' people? [and] Does the researcher enjoy any immunity from the law when he or she refuses to disclose information?" (p. 89). Punch discusses the concepts of codes, consent, privacy, confidentiality, and trust and betrayal in detail. He further describes three developments that have stirred up the debate. These include the women's movement and its attendant concern that women have been studied as subjects/objects, the trend toward conducting action research in which participants are partners or stakeholders to be empowered and therefore not to be duped, and, finally, the concern of funding agencies for ethics that has led to requirements for the inclusion of statements of ethics in proposals and reports. Croll (1986) addresses similar issues and recommends that researchers conduct their studies in good faith and that the research should be not only not harmful to subjects, but worthwhile.

Erlandson et al. (1993), in their discussion of ethical issues, echo the previously mentioned concerns with regard to privacy, confidentiality, harm, deception, and informed consent. They add that in contracted research, situations may arise that could compromise the research by restricting freedom or encouraging suppression of negative results. From a more "action research" type of perspective, these authors add to Croll's idea that studies should be of value to subjects, that they should educate subjects. Educational technology researchers must determine for themselves their answers to ethical questions, realizing that their work may or may not fall into the category of action research.

For a broader and more in-depth discussion of ethical issues, the reader may wish to refer to *Ethics and Anthropology: Dilemmas in Fieldwork,* by Rynkiewich and Spradley (1976); the Beauchamp, Faden, Wallace, and Walters (1982) book, *Ethical Issues in Social Science Research;* or the Bower and de Gasparis (1978) book, *Ethics in Social Research: Protecting the Interest of Human Subjects.*

Many authors blend concerns for ethics with criteria for evaluating the quality of qualitative studies, in that an unethically conducted study would not be of high quality. The criteria to use in determining whether a qualitative study is sound and strong are illustrated in the following section.

39.6 CRITERIA FOR EVALUATING QUALITATIVE STUDIES

Criteria for evaluating the quality and rigor of qualitative studies vary somewhat, based on methods used. Most concerns, however, apply to most studies. Adler and Adler (1994) say that one of the primary criticisms of observational studies, whether participant or nonparticipant methods are used, is the question of their validity, due to the subjectivity and biases of the researcher. These authors contend that this concern is one of the reasons studies based solely on observations are rarely published. They suggest that validity can be increased in three ways. Multiple observers in teams can cross-check data and patterns continually. The researcher can refine and test propositions and hypotheses throughout the study, in a grounded theory approach. Finally, the researcher can write using "verisimilitude" or "vraisemblance" (p. 383), or writing that makes the world of the subjects real to the reader; the reader recognizes the authenticity of the results. Adler and Adler also address the issue of reliability in observational studies. They suggest systematically conducting observations repeatedly under varying conditions, particularly varying time and place. Reliability would be verified by emergence of similar results.

Borg and Gall (1989) listed several criteria for evaluating the quality of participant observation studies, including the following.

1. Using involved participant observers is less likely to result in erroneous reported data from individuals or organizations.
2. The researcher should have relatively free access to a broad range of activities.
3. The observations should be intense, that is, conducted over a long period of time.
4. In more recent studies, both qualitative and quantitative data are collected.

5. Using a "triangulation of methodology" (p. 393), researchers can be assured that the picture they present of the reality of a setting or situation is clear and true. Multiple methods may be used to address research questions, but also, in line with Adler and Adler's (1994) recommendations for enhancing reliability, the same data may be collected from other samples at other times and in other places.

6. Researchers should strive to gain an overall view of the issues and context and then sample purposely to collect data that represent the range of realities of participants in those settings. Borg and Gall, as do others, caution that researchers be sensitive to both what is excluded and what is included.

7. Finally, in all observational studies they recommend that researchers should be ready to observe, record, and analyze not just verbal exchanges but subtle cues by using unobtrusive measures.

Ethical issues also relate to the quality of a study. Issues specific to conducting interviews are delineated by Fontana and Frey (1994). They add to the general concerns already mentioned the issues of informed consent, right to privacy, and protection. They mention that there is some debate regarding whether covert methods for gathering data are ethical, although they may reflect real life. They describe the dilemma a researcher may face in deciding how involved to become with respondents and suggest some degree of situational ethics, cautioning that a researcher's participation may enable or inhibit certain behaviors or responses. Finally, they raise the issue of interviewing itself being manipulative, still treating humans as objects.

Hammersley (1990) provides additional criteria for assessing ethnographic research, many of which will apply to most qualitative studies. He puts forward two main criteria for judging ethnographic studies, namely, validity and relevance. He discusses the validity of a study as meaning the "truth" of the study. He suggests three steps for assessing the validity of ethnographic finds or conclusions. He recommends asking, first, if the findings or claim are reasonable and, second, "whether it seems likely that the ethnographer's judgement of matters relating to the claim would be accurate given the nature of the phenomena concerned, the circumstances of the research, the characteristics of the researcher, etc." (p. 61); finally, in cases in which the claim does not appear to be plausible or credible, evidence of validity is required to be examined. Clearly in reports of qualitative research studies, the reader must be provided enough information about the perspective, sampling and choice of subjects, and data collected to determine with some confidence the validity or "truth" represented in a study.

With regard to the second criterion, relevance, Hammersley (1990) advises that studies have broadly conceived public relevance or value. On a practical level, Nathan (1979), in Abt's book on the costs and benefits of applied social research, provides what he calls rules for relevant research. A selection follows.

1. Be as evenhanded as you can.
2. Focus on the most policy-relevant effects.
3. When faced with a choice between the direct and the more elaborate expression of statistics and concepts, choose the former.

4. Get your hands dirty.
5. Be interdisciplinary.
6. Sort out carefully description, analysis, and your opinions. (pp. 113–115).

Lincoln and Guba (1985) describe criteria that are frequently cited for evaluating qualitative studies. They address the criticisms leveled at naturalistic research and determine that quality rests in trustworthiness of the study and its findings. They agree with others that conventional criteria are inappropriate for qualitative studies and that alternate criteria do exist. These criteria are (a) credibility, (b) transferability, (c) dependability, and (d) confirmability. These authors go on to recommend activities the researcher may undertake to ensure that these criteria will be inherent in the study. In particular, to make credible findings more likely, they recommend that prolonged engagement, persistent observation, and triangulation be done. Further, they recommend peer debriefing about the study and its methods, opening the researcher and the methods up for review. They also recommend analyzing negative cases to revise hypotheses; testing for referential adequacy, by building in the critical examination of findings and their accompanying raw data; and conducting checks of data, categories used in analysis, interpretations and findings, with members of the subject audience.

Lincoln and Guba (1985) provide a similar level of helpful suggestions in the area of ensuring confirmability. They recommend triangulation with multimethods and various sources of data, keeping a reflexive journal, and, most powerfully, conducting a confirmability audit. In their book they include detailed descriptions of the steps in conducting an audit and recommend the following categories of data that can be used in the audit, including raw data, products of data analysis, products of the synthesis of data such as findings and conclusions, process notes, personal notes about intentions, and information about how instruments were developed.

In the tradition of Lincoln and Guba, Erlandson et al. (1993) describe the following techniques for ensuring the quality of a study.

- Prolonged engagement
- Persistent observation
- Triangulation
- Referential adequacy
- Peer debriefing
- Member checking
- Reflexive journal
- Thick description
- Purposive sampling
- Audit trail.

The Association for Educational Communications and Technology (AECT) has shown strong support for qualitative research in the field. For several years the ECT Foundation and the Research and Theory Division supported the Special Research Award. The ECT Foundation has also supported a Qualitative Research Award. Ann DeVaney (2000), formerly the chair of this award committee, provided the following criteria, developed by numerous AECT members, that are used to evaluate the quality of papers submitted for this award:

1. Is the problem clearly stated; does it have theoretical value and currency; does it have practical value?
2. Is the problem or topic situated in a theoretical framework; is the framework clear and accessible; does the document contain competing epistemologies or other basic assumptions that might invalidate claims?
3. Is the literature review a critique or simply a recapitulation; is it relevant; does it appear accurate and sufficiently comprehensive?
4. Are the theses stated in a clear and coherent fashion; are they sufficiently demonstrated in an accessible manner; are there credible warrants to claims made about the theses? (If applicable)
5. Does the method fit the problem and is it an appropriate one given the theoretical framework? (If applicable)
6. Do the data collected adequately address the problem; do they make explicit the researcher's role and perspective; do the data collection techniques have a "good fit" with the method and theory? (If applicable)
7. Are the data aggregates and analysis clearly reported; do they make explicit the interpretive and reasoning process of the researcher? (If applicable)
8. Does the discussion provide meaningful and warranted interpretations and conclusions?

Lest it appear that there is universal agreement about the quality criteria, it may be noted that the postmodern trend toward questioning and deconstruction have led to continued debate in this area. Wolcott (1994), in his book about transforming qualitative data, argues for rejecting validity in qualitative research and then describes activities he undertakes to address the challenge of validity. These include "talk a little, listen a lot... begin writing early... let readers 'see' for themselves... report fully... be candid... seek feedback... try to achieve balance... write accurately" (pp. 348–356).

39.7 TRENDS IN QUALITATIVE RESEARCH IN EDUCATIONAL TECHNOLOGY

This handbook represents the Second Edition of the version published in 1996. Since that earlier publication we set out to determine whether the use of qualitative methods in educational technology research has increased and what topics are generally being investigated using qualitative methods.

39.7.1 Beyond the "Alternate Research" Paradigm Debate

We began with a review of recent articles describing the types of research being conducted in educational technology. DeVaney (2000), for instance, has suggested broadening our

lines of inquiry, addressing social/cultural issues, and addressing poststructural/analytical questions. The work of Driscoll and Dick (1999), Kozma (2000a, 2000b), and Richey (1998) was featured in a series of special issues of *Educational Technology Research and Development* (*ETR&D*). Driscoll and Dick, using an earlier article by Briggs (1984), discuss the need to conduct studies that represent "culture four" research, that is, investigations involving actual curriculum materials, accurate classification of learning outcomes, and systematically designed and evaluated materials, along with assessment instruments that match learning outcomes. Driscoll and Dick reviewed 5 years of *ETR&D* articles (1992–1996) and concluded that disappointingly few culture four research studies are being conducted.

Luetkehans and Robinson (2000) have argued that the field of educational technology, as defined by Richey (2000), goes beyond instructional design and so our research, too, should go beyond even culture four research. Echoing the views of Kozma (2000a), these authors contend that educational technology research has been limited by the focus on instructional design and even more so by the adaptation of simply psychology-oriented views of research. For instance, Kozma (2000a) reviewed, and has advocated, research that more broadly encompasses design in combination with advanced technologies, new collaborations, and large-scale implementation. Luetkehans and Robinson note that almost two decades have passed since leaders in the field have encouraged research using other paradigms. They have called for an end to the paradigm debate, ceasing the use of the term *alternative research* to describe nonexperimental designs based on more qualitative modes of thinking.

One example of a study that goes beyond instructional design or even culture four research is that of Luetkehans (1998, 1999). This researcher developed a case study of a distance-learning course delivered via multiple media, a study that represents a deep view of design and technology that is situated in an authentic context. Case study methodology was selected for this research in order to understand the uniqueness and complexity of an authentic context, the participants, their experience in the course, and interactions among them. Data were captured through surveys, observations, semistructured interviews, computer transcripts, participant debriefings, and focus group interviews. The researcher was a "participant observer," in that she collaborated with the instructional team, as well as the student participants. Rigor and validation were achieved through member checking and triangulation.

Another example of a study using qualitative methods to illuminate perspectives on the field is that by Julian (2001). This researcher conducted a series of deep, reflective interviews to develop views of instructional designers' perspectives on their work and their professional preparation.

Research conducted using action research methods and approaches is another trend in the field. Duffield and Robinson (1999), for instance, report the results of a study that focused on teachers' concerns and solutions. Projects reported by Luetkehans and Robinson (2000) include those investigating questions regarding Internet use in the classroom, staff development initiatives, engaged learning in science, e-pals and motivation, and research skills and information sequencing, among others. These authors describe issues that have emerged in these efforts, such as the amount of time involved in conducting an action research project and the level of self-assessment involved. They conclude that action research studies not only aid us in gaining an understanding of teachers' involvement with technology, but enable researchers to build productive partnerships that support teachers, too, to conduct research that informs both their and our practice.

Part of the discussion regarding the value of qualitative research must include the more emancipatory possibilities of action research based upon postmodern perspectives. Social research in a postmodern age, as Apple (1991) has pointed out, must turn away from the hope of constructing an "ultimate truth" (p. ix.) Action research may provide ways of empowering educators to investigate and resolve instructional technology issues for themselves, in their own contexts. Postmodern and critical literature in education would point to the need for research done thoughtfully by the participants themselves and would recommend the critical reflection and action of participants that embody action research. (See Lather, 1991.)

Lather (1991) uses postpositivist theories to construct a chart defining the categories of knowledge claims to include prediction, understanding, emancipation, and deconstruction. Educational technology could benefit from research conducted not just to predict and to understand phenomena, but to emancipate participants in educational arenas. Action research has that potential. The results of action research projects, although individual and reflective, could also be collected into new and distinctly different views of the utility, possibility, and power of educators and technology.

39.7.2 Dissertations in Educational Technology

One indication of an increase in the amount of research using qualitative methods has been described by Caffarella (1999). This researcher conducted a content analysis on the titles of the 2,689 dissertation studies in educational technology listed in the *Doctoral Research in Educational Technology: A Directory of Dissertations, 1977–2001* (Caffarella, 2002) database. Caffarella categorized methods used in empirical studies as either delphi, qualitative, ethnographic, naturalistic, experimental, or comparative. He then combined studies that were described as using qualitative, naturalistic, or ethnographic methods as all using "qualitative" designs. It should be noted that the number of dissertation studies that clearly represent empirical research appears to be small. For instance, of 73 studies in 1998 and another 73 in 1997, only 3 each year appear to be empirical. Disapointingly, the number of empirical dissertations may be decreasing, as in the previous 20 years from 101 to 150 dissertations per year are listed. Nevertheless, Caffarella reports that in 8 of the 10 most recent years, from 1980 to 1998, the number of studies that used qualitative designs exceeded the number that used experimental designs. In contrast, for the 10 years before that, 1979 to 1988, in only 3 years did the number of studies that used qualitative designs exceed the number that used experimental designs. Again, caution must be used in interpreting these findings, as the total number of empirical studies is small,

ranging from 3 to 16 of 73 to 150 total dissertations reported per year.

39.7.3 Content of Recent Issues of ETR&D and *Performance Improvement Quarterly*

The recent editors of *ETR&D* have indicated an openness to receiving more submissions of articles that describe qualitative studies (J. D. Klein, personal communication, March 20, 2002; S. M. Ross, personal communication, March 20, 2002.) These editors have also indicated that the numbers of qualitative reports submitted may be increasing. As he became editor of the development section of *ETR&D,* Klein (1997) reported the results of a study he conducted to aid in determining the direction of the journal. Klein reviewed the content of 100 articles published in the development section of *ETR&D* from 1989 to 1997. He reported that the largest percentage of these articles represented descriptions of projects (49%), followed by 21% representing literature reviews, 18% case studies, and just 12% representing empirical research. He added that when he surveyed the consulting editors of this section of the journal, the majority called for an increase in articles that use data to draw conclusions, that is, data drawn from many types of studies, including applied research, case studies, evaluations, and qualitative, as well as quantitative, studies.

With regard to the research section, Reeves (1995) concluded that the main type of study published in the research section of the *ETR&D* journal in the 5 years from 1989 to 1994 was empirical research using quantitative methods and theoretical literature reviews.

For an admittedly brief look at how the journal may be changing, we examined six recent issues of *ETR&D,* that is, the four issues in Volume 50, 2001, and the first two issues in Volume 51, 2002. We adapted the categories used by Klein (1997) to classify articles in both the research and the development sections, as representing literature reviews, theoretical papers, descriptions of one project, or empirical research, using either experimental designs, qualitative designs, case study, or a combination of these methods. Several articles, in fact, represented not only mixed methods, but also empirical tests of theoretical models.

With the qualifier that the number of articles discussed here is small, it still appears that the percentage of articles in *ETR&D* that represent data-based reports of any type is increasing and that the use of qualitative methods, whether alone or in combination with other methods, is also increasing. In the research section, in 2001, for instance, the journal published 12 articles. Of these, three-quarters (nine) represented empirical research, whereas two were literature reviews and one was a theoretical article. Of the nine empirical studies, two-thirds used some qualitative methods, including fully qualitative designs, a mix of qualitative and experimental methods, and a mix of case study with qualitative methods, whereas only three were described as using mainly experimental designs. In the first two issues published in 2002, five articles were published in the research section, with three representing empirical research and two being theoretical articles. Of the three empirical articles, two were experimental and one represented an exploratory study that used some qualitative methods.

In reviewing the development section of the journal, we found that in 2001, of the 10 articles published, only 3 represented literature reviews. In contrast, seven articles represented empirical studies, most of which included qualitative methods. For instance, three articles described cases that included qualitative results, two described studies that involved both quantitative and qualitative data, one described a theoretical model that was tested using a mix of case study and qualitative approaches, and one was primarily a case study. In 2002 four articles were published in the development section in the first two issues of the journal. Of these two were theoretical papers, one was a literature review, and only one represented an empirical study, however, that study did use a combination of a case study and a qualitative approach.

More recently, in 2002, Klein also conducted a content analysis of 138 articles published from 1997 to 2002 in another leading journal in our field, *Performance Improvement Quarterly*. Klein concluded that only 36% of the articles published in these recent years represented empirical research studies. He called for more data-based studies of training interventions and recommended such qualitative methods as direct observation of on-the-job performance, cost-consequence analysis, and investigations of the value a performance intervention adds to organizations and society.

39.7.4 Literature Review of 20 Years of Educational Technology and Qualitative Research

Finally, in the spirit of triangulation, we offer the reader one more view of trends in qualitative research. We conducted a literature review using the ERIC database of publications and papers from the 20 years from 1980 to 2000. There is no doubt that publications in our field and those using qualitative methods are increasing. Entering just the search term *educational technology* yielded 20,785 publications. Entering the term *research* yielded 327,408 publications, whereas entering the term *qualitative* yielded 8,645. Combining the terms *educational technology* and *qualitative research* yielded a final set of 100 publications, which we analyzed. Of these 100 publications, 90% were published in the 10 years from 1990 to 2000, with two-thirds of these (58) published in the 5 years from 1996 to 2000 and almost half (46) published in just the more recent 3 years.

We also reviewed the content described in the titles of the 100 publications. The majority of the publications involved aspects of technology (42), including 15 publications about specific technologies, such as hypermedia, games, interactive video, the Internet, CDI/CDTV, electronic databases, and electronic performance support systems. In this category, we also included 11 publications about classroom technology such as computers and classroom media along with technology integration, 6 about technology planning, 4 about subject-specific applications of technology, 2 about assistive/adaptive technology, 2 related to gender issues, and 1 each about equity of technology access and educational technology service at one university.

Reflecting trends in our field, the next most common category of qualitative research areas of investigation included studies of distance education and Web-based education (13), combined with computer-mediated communications and telecommunications (4).

The third most common topic of the educational technology and qualitative research publications was research itself (14), with articles about methodologies and approaches, as well as themes in research, and calls to action. Four additional articles discussed specifically the use of qualitative methods in educational technology. Other topics included in these 100 publications were student perceptions (four), instructor perceptions (two), project-based learning (three), collaborative practices (three), and other individual topics (seven); there were five collections of conference proceedings.

39.7.5 A "Call to Action"

Luetkehans and Robinson (2000) have argued that qualitative research represents not simply a methodology, but a worldview, paradigm, or perspective. They contend that researchers should approach educational technology questions not just from an instructional design perspective, as recommended by Richey (1998) and Driscoll and Dick (1999), but from a broader perspective. That broader perspective would enable researchers to study, for instance, aspects of instructional settings, interactions and views of participants, and the politics or economics of the reality of a complex learning situation.

For the past two decades, educational technology researchers have explored qualitative research issues. We support and congratulate those researchers and encourage them and the next generation of researchers to expand the questions and types of inquiry being conducted in our field. Qualitative research will continue to illuminate our practice of educational technology.

39.8 LEARNING MORE ABOUT DOING QUALITATIVE RESEARCH

The preceding discussions of evaluating qualitative studies and trends in qualitative research, rather than being conclusive, form a fitting beginning point from which you, the researcher, can go onward and conduct your studies. It is hoped that this chapter has served as an introduction, pointing you toward more useful resources and references.

Below is a subjective list of the authors' "top" books, listed in alphabetical, not ranked order, for learning about qualitative research in education (full citations are given in the References).

Bogdan and Biklen (1992). *Qualitative research for education* (2nd ed.).
Denzin and Lincoln (Eds.) (1994). *Handbook of qualitative research*.
Eisner (1991). *The enlightened eye: Qualitative inquiry and the enhancement of educational practice*.

Erlandson, Harris, Skipper, and Allen (1993). *Doing naturalistic inquiry: A guide to methods.*

Fetterman (1989). *Ethnography: Step by step.*

Goetz and LeCompte (1984). *Ethnography and qualitative design in educational research.*

Lincoln and Guba (1985). *Naturalistic inquiry.*

Marshall and Rossman (1999). *Designing qualitative research.*

Meloy (1994). *Writing the qualitative dissertation: Understanding by doing.*

Miles and Huberman (1994). *Qualitative data analysis: An expanded sourcebook* (2nd ed.)

Spradley (1980). *Participant observation.*

Strauss (1987). *Qualitative analysis for social scientists.*

Van Maanen (1988). *Tales of the Field: On writing ethnography.*

Wolcott (1990). *Writing up qualitative research.*

Wolcott (1994). *Transforming qualitative data: Description, analysis, and interpretation.*

Yin (1989). *Case study research.*

Additional references appear in Robinson and Driscoll's (1993) handout for their AECT workshop on qualitative methods.

The researcher is also wise to keep up with new publications in methodology, including new editions of these books and others. Several journals specialize in publishing qualititive research, including *International Journal of Qualitative Studies in Education, Journal of Contemporary Ethnography, Journal of Visual Literacy,* and the research section of *Educational Technology.* In addition, researchers may wish to join the Qualitative Research Listserv for the Human Sciences (QUALS-L), which can be reached via Judith Preissle at the University of Georgia listserv@uga.cc.uga.edu

We wish you well in your explorations!

ACKNOWLEDGMENTS

The authors would like to thank Marcy Driscoll, David Jonassen, and Susan Tucker for their comments.

References

Abraham, R. P. (2000). *Examining the impact a media distribution system has on a high school classroom environment: A case study.* Unpublished doctoral dissertation, Northern Illinois University.

Adler, P. A., & Adler, P. (1994). Observational techniques. In N. K., Denzin, & Y. S. Lincoln (Eds.), *Handbook of qualitative research* (pp. 377-392). Thousand Oaks, CA: Sage.

Altheide, D. L., & Johnson, J. M. (1994) Criteria for assessing interpretive validity in qualitative research. In N. K., Denzin, & Y. S. Lincoln (Eds.), *Handbook of qualitative research* (pp. 485-499). Thousand Oaks, CA: Sage.

Ambron, S., & Hooper, K. (Eds.). (1988). *Interactive multimedia: visions of multimedia for developers, educators, & information providers.* Redmond, WA: Microsoft Press.

Ambron, S., & Hooper, K. (Eds.). (1990). *Learning with interactive multimedia: developing and using multimedia tools in education.* Redmond, WA: Microsoft Press.

Anderson, W. (2001). *Children's television: A content analysis of communication intent in* Arthur *and* Rugrats. Unpublished doctoral dissertation, Northern Illinois University.

Apple, M. W. (1991). Series editor introduction. In P. Lather (Ed.), *Getting smart.* New York: Routledge.

Atkinson, P., & Hammersley, M. (1994) Ethnography and participant observation. In N. K. Denzin & Y. S. Lincoln, (Eds.) *Handbook of qualitative research* (pp. 248-261). Thousand Oaks, CA: Sage.

Barone, T. (1995, April). *An example of an arts-based phenomenological inquiry.* Paper presented at the annual conference of the American Educational Research Association, San Francisco, CA.

Beauchamp, T. L., Faden, R. R., Wallace, R. J., Jr., & Walters, L. (1982). *Ethical issues in social science research.* Baltimore: The Johns Hopkins University Press.

Bellman, B. L., & Jules-Rosette, B. (1977). *A paradigm for looking: cross-cultural research with visual media.* Norwood, NJ: Ablex.

Bernard, H. R. (1988). *Research methods in cultural anthropology.* Newbury Park, CA: Sage.

Bitgood, S. (1990, November). *The role of simulated immersion in exhibition.* Jacksonville, AL: Center of Social Design.

Bloom, B. S. (1984). *Taxonomy of educational objectives. Handbook 1: Cognitive domain.* New York: Longman.

Bogaart, N. C. R., & Ketelaar, H. W. E. R. (Eds.). (1983). *Methodology in anthropological filmmaking: Papers of the IUAES—Intercongress, Amsterdam, 1981.* Gottingen: Edition Herodot.

Bogdan, R. C., & Biklen, S. K. (1992). *Qualitative research for education: An introduction to theory and methods* (2nd ed.). Boston, MA: Allyn and Bacon.

Borg, W. R., & Gall, M. D. (1989). *Educational research: An introduction* (5th ed.). New York: Longman.

Borich, G. D. (1989). *Outcome evaluation report of the TLTG Physical Science Curriculum, 1988-89.* Austin: Texas Learning Technology Group of the Texas Association of School Boards.

Bosco, J. (1986). An analysis of evaluationsof interactive video. *Educational Technology, 16*(5), 7-17.

Bower, R. T., & de Gasparis, P. (1978). *Ethics in social research: Protecting the interests of human subjects.* New York: Praeger.

Briggs, L. J. (1984). Trying to straddle four research cultures. *Educational Technology, 22*(8), 33-34.

Bruner, J. S., Goodnow, J. J., & Austin, G. A. (1972). Categories and cognition. In J. P. Spradley (Ed.), *Culture and cognition: Rules, maps, and plans* (pp. 168-190). San Francisco, CA: Chandler.

Caffarella, E. P. (1999, February). The major themes and trends in doctoral dissertation research in educational technology from 1977 through 1998. In *Proceedings of selected research and development papers presented at the national convention of the Association for Educational Communications and Technology* (AECT), Houston, TX, pp. 483-490.

Caffarella, E. P. (2002). *Doctoral research in educational technology: A directory of dissertations. 1977-2001.* Greeley, CO: University of Northern Colorado. Retrieved December 15, 2002, from http://www.edtech.unco.edu/disswww/dissdir.htm.

Chen, J. W., & Shen, C. W. (1989, September). Software engineering: A new component for instructional software development. *Educational Technology, 9*, 9-15.

Clark, R. E. (1983). Reconsidering research on learning from media. *Review of Educational Research, 53*(4), 445-459.

Clark, R. E. (1989). Current progress and future directions for research in instructional technology. *Educational Technology Research and Development, 37*(1), 57-66.

Collier, J. (1967). *Visual anthropology: Photography as a research method*. New York: Holt, Rinehart and Winston.

Collier, J., & Collier, M. (1986). *Visual anthropology: Photography as a research method*. Albuquerque: University of New Mexico Press.

Croll, P. (1986). *Systematic classroom observation*. London: Falmer Press.

Crooks, S. M., Klein, J. D., Jones, E. K., & Dwyer, H. (1995, February). *Effects of cooperative learning and learner control modes in computer-based instruction*. Paper presented at the annual meeting of the Association for Communications and Technology, Anaheim, CA.

Dalton, D. W., Hannafin, M. J., & Hooper, S. (1989). Effects of individual and cooperative computer-assisted instruction on student performance and attitude. *Educational Technology Research and Development, 37*(2), 15-24.

Dana, A. S. (1993). *Integrating technology into the classroom: Description of a successful first-grade teacher*. Unpublished manuscript. DeKalb, IL: Northern Illinois University.

Darabi, G. A., & Dempsey, J. V. (1989-1990). A quality control system for curriculum-based CBI projects. *Journal of Educational Technology Systems, 18*(1), 15-31.

Denzin, N. K., & Lincoln, Y. S. (Eds.). (1994). *Handbook of qualitative research*. Thousand Oaks, CA: Sage.

DeVaney, A. (2000, February). *What positions should educational technology researchers take in this brave new world of cyberspace? What should we address?* Presented at the annual meeting of the Association for Educational Communications and Technology, Long Beach, CA.

DeWalt, B. R., & Pelto, P. J. (Ed.). (1985). *Micro and macro levels of analysis in anthropology*. Boulder, CO: Westview Press.

Donaldson, J. A. (2000). *Promises unfulfilled: A university/school district partnership study*. Unpublished doctoral dissertation, Northern Illinois University.

Driscoll, M. P. (1995). Paradigms for research in instructional systems. In G. J. Anglin (Ed.), *Instructional technology: Past, present and future* (2nd ed., pp. 322-329). Englewood, CO: Libraries Unlimited.

Driscoll, M., & Dick, W. (1999). New research paradigms in instructional technology: An inquiry. *Educational Technology Research and Development, 47*(2), 7-18.

Duffield, J., & Robinson, R. (1999, April). *Collaborative models for technology integration in schools through school-university partnerships*. Paper presented at the annual meeting of the American Educational Research Association, Montreal, Quebec, Canada.

Dwyer, H., & Leader, L. (1995, February). *The researcher's HyperCard Toolkit II*. Paper presented at the annual meeting of the Association for Educational Communications and Technology, Anaheim, CA.

ECT Foundation. (1995). *Suggested criteria for qualitative research*. Association for Educational Communications and Technology.

Eisner, E. (1991). *The enlightened eye: Qualitative inquiry and the enhancement of educational practice*. New York: Macmillan.

Erickson, F., & Shultz, J. (1982). *The counselor as gatekeeper: Social interaction in interviews*. New York: Academic Press.

Ericsson, K. A., & Simon, H. A. (1984). *Protocol analysis—Verbal reports as data*. Cambridge, MA: MIT Press.

Erlandson, D. A., Harris, E. L., Skipper, B. L., & Allen, S. D. (1993). *Doing naturalistic inquiry: A guide to methods*. Newbury Park, CA: Sage.

Fetterman, D. M. (1989). *Ethnography: Step by step*. Applied Social Research Methods Series, Vol. 17. Newbury Park, CA: Sage.

Fiedler, J. (1978). *Field research: A manual for logistics and management of scientific studies in natural settings*. San Fransisco, CA: Jossey-Bass.

Fontana, A., & Frey, J. H. (1994). Interviewing: The art of science. In N. K., Denzin, & Y. S. Lincoln, (Eds.), *Handbook of qualitative research* (pp. 361-377). Thousand Oaks, CA: Sage.

Frake, C. O. (1972). The ethnographic study of cognitive systems. In J. P. Spradley (Ed.), *Culture and cognition: Rules, maps, and plans*. (pp. 191-205). San Francisco, CA: Chandler.

Geertz, C. (1973). Thick description. In C. Geertz (Ed.), *The interpretation of cultures* (pp. 3-30). New York: Basic Books.

Goetz, J. P., & LeCompte, M. D. (1984). *Ethnography and qualitative design in educational research*. Orlando, FL: Academic Press.

Guba, E. G. (Ed.). (1990). *The paradigm dialog*. Newbury Park, CA: Sage.

Hammersley, M. (1990). *Reading ethnographic research: A critical guide*. London: Longman.

Hammersley, M., & Atkinson, P. (1983). *Ethnography: Principles in practice*. London: Tavistock.

Hannafin, M. J., & Rieber, L. P. (1989). Psychological foundations of instructional design for emerging computer-based instructional technologies: Part 1. *Educational Technology Research and Development, 37*(2), 91-101.

Heider, K. G. (1976). *Ethnographic film*. Austin: University of Texas Press.

Heyman, I. M. (1995, January). Smithsonian perspectives. *Smithsonian*, p. 8.

Hicken, S., Sullivan, H., & Klein, J. (1992). Learner control modes and incentive variations in computer delivered instruction. *Educational Technology Research and Development, 40*(4), 15-26.

Higgins, N., & Rice, E. (1991). Teachers' perspectives on competency-based testing. *Educational Technology Research and Development, 39*(3), 59-69.

Hirumi, A., Savenye, W., & Allen, B. (1994). Designing interactive videodisc-based museum exhibits: A case study. *Educational Technology Research and Development, 42*(1), 47-55.

Hockings, P. (Ed.), (1975). *Principles of visual anthropology*. The Hague, Netherlands: Mouton.

Hodder, I. (1994) The interpretation of documents and material culture. In N. K., Denzin, & Y. S., Lincoln (Eds.), *Handbook of qualitative research* (pp. 393-402). Thousand Oaks, CA: Sage.

Hooper, S., & Hannafin, M. J. (1988). Learning the ROPES of instructional design: Guidelines for emerging interactive technologies. *Educational Technology, 28*, 14-18.

Hymes, D. (Ed.). (1965). *The use of computers in anthropology*. London: Mouton.

Jacobs, E. (1987). Qualitative research traditions: A review. *Review of Educational Research, 57*(1), 1-50.

Johnson, A. W. (1978). *Quantification in cultural anthropology*. Stanford, CA: Stanford University Press.

Jones, E. K., Crooks, S., & Klein, J. (1995, February). *Development of a cooperative learning observational instrument*. Paper presented at the annual meeting of the Association for Communications and Technology, Anaheim, CA.

Jost, K. L. (1994, February). *Educational change: The implementation of technology and curriculum change*. Paper presented at the annual meeting of the Association for Communications and Technology, Nashville, TN.

Julian, M. F. (2001, October). *Learning in action: The professional preparation of instructional designers*. Paper presented at the annual meeting of the Association for Communications and Technology, Atlanta, GA.

Klein, J. D. (1997). ETR&D-development: An analysis of content and survey of future direction. *Educational Technology Research and Development, 45*(3), 57-62.

Klein, J. D. (2002). Empirical research on performance improvement. *Performance Improvement Quarterly, 15*(1), 99-110.

Klein, J. D., & Pridemore, D. R. (1994). Effects of orienting activities and practice on achievement, continuing motivation, and student behaviors in a cooperative learning environment. *Educational Technology Research and Development, 41*(4), 41-54.

Klein, J. D., Erchul, J. A., & Pridemore, D. R. (1994). Effects of individual versus cooperative learning and type of reward on performance and continuing motivation. *Contemporary Educational Psychology, 19,* 24-32.

Kowinski, W. S. (1995, January). Giving new life to Haida art and the culture it expresses. *Smithsonian,* pp. 38-46.

Kozma, R. (2000a). Reflections on the state of educational technology research and development. *Educational Technology Research and Development, 48*(1), 5-18.

Kozma, R. (2000b). The relationship between technology and design in educational technology research and development: A reply to Richey. *Educational Technology Research and Development, 48*(1), 19-21.

Kuhn, T. S. (1970). *The structure of scientific revolutions* (2nd ed.). Chicago: University of Chicago Press.

Lambert, S., & Sallis, J. (Eds.). (1987). *CD-I and interactive videodisc technology.* Indianapolis, IN: Howard W. Sams.

Lather, P. (1991). *Getting smart.* New York: Routledge.

Lather, P. (1995, April). *At play in the field of theory: From social scientism to paradigm proliferation.* Paper presented at the annual conference of the American Educational Research Association, San Francisco, CA.

Leedy, P., D., Newby, T. J., & Ertmer, P. A. (1996). *Practical research: Planning and design* (5th ed.). New York: Prentice Hall.

Lincoln, Y. S., & Guba, E. G. (1985). *Naturalistic inquiry.* Beverly Hills, CA: Sage.

Luetkehans, L. M. (1998). *A case study of using a computer supported collaborative learning tool to supplement a distance learning course in educational telecommunications.* Unpublished doctoral dissertation, University of Georgia.

Luetkehans, L. (1999, February). A case study of using groupware to support collaborative activities in a distance learning course. In *Proceedings of selected research and development papers presented at the national convention of the Association for Educational Communications and Technology* (AECT), Houston, TX, pp. 491-502.

Luetkehans, L., & Robinson, R. (2000, April). *Qualitative methods in educational technology research: An examination of recent studies.* Paper presented at the annual meeting of the American Educational Research Association, New Orleans, LA.

Manning, P. K., & Cullum-Swan, B. (1994). Narrative, content, and semiotic analysis. In N. K., Denzin, & Y. S. Lincoln (Eds.), *Handbook of qualitative research* (pp. 463-477). Thousand Oaks, CA: Sage.

Markle, S. M. (1989, August). The ancient history of formative evaluation. *Performance & Instruction,* 27-29.

Marshall, C., & Rossman, G. (1999). *Designing qualitative research* (3rd ed.). Newbury Park, CA: Sage.

McIsaac, M. S., Ozkalp, E., & Harper-Marinick, M. (1992). Crossgenerational perspectives on gender differences and perceptions of professional competence in photographs. *International Journal of Instructional Media, 19*(4), 349-365.

McLean, R. S. (1989). Megatrends in computing and educational software development. *Education & Computing, 5,* 55-60.

McNabb, M. L. (1996). *Toward a theory of proximal instruction: Pedagogical practices for college composition within a computerized*

learning environment. Unpublished doctoral dissertation, Northern Illinois University.

McNeil, B. J., & Nelson, K. R. (1991). Meta-analysis of interactive video instruction: A 10 year review of achievement effects. *Journal of Computer-Based Instruction, 18*(1), 1-6.

Mehan, H. (1979). *Learning lessons: Social organization in the classroom.* Cambridge, MA: Harvard University Press.

Meloy, J. M. (1994). *Writing the qualitative dissertation: Understanding by doing.* Hillsdale, NJ: Lawrence Erlbaum Associates.

Miles, M. B., & Huberman, A. M. (1994). *Qualitative data analysis: An expanded sourcebook* (2nd ed.). Thousand Oaks, CA: Sage.

Miles, M. B., & Weitzman, E. A. (1994). Appendix: Choosing computer programs for qualitative data analysis. In M. B., Miles, & A. M. Huberman (Eds.), *Qualitative data analysis: An expanded sourcebook* (2nd ed., pp. 311-317). Thousand Oaks, CA: Sage.

Moallem, M. (1994, February). *An experienced teacher's model of thinking and teaching: an ethnographic study on teacher cognition.* Paper presented at the annual meeting of the Association for Communications and Technology, Nashville, TN.

Nathan, R. (1979). Ten rigorous rules for relevant research. In C. C. Abt (Ed.), *Perspectives on the costs and benefits of applied social research.* Cambridge, MA: Abt Books.

Neuman, D. (1989). Naturalistic inquiry and computer-based instruction: Rationale, procedures, and potential. *Educational Technology Research and Development, 37*(3), 39-51.

Newman, D. (1989, March). *Formative experiments on technologies that change the organization of instruction.* Paper presented at the annual conference of the American Educational Research Association, San Francisco, CA.

Nielsen, M. C. (1989). *The effects of varying levels of informational feedback on concept learning in CAI programs.* Unpublished doctoral dissertation, University of Texas at Austin.

Ogbu, J. U. (1974). *The next generation: An ethnography of education in an urban neighborhood.* New York: Academic Press.

Oliver, E. L. (1992). *Interaction at a distance: Mediated communication in televised courses.* Unpublished doctoral dissertation, Northern Illinois University.

Pelto, P. J., & Pelto, G. H. (1978). *Anthropological research: The structure of inquiry* (2nd Ed.). Cambridge: Cambridge University Press.

Pitlik, D. (1995). *A description of the real profession of instructional design.* Unpublished doctoral dissertation, Northern Illinois University.

Pitts, J. M. (1993). *Personal understandings and mental models of information: A qualitative study of factors associated with the information seeking and use of adolescents.* Unpublished doctoral dissertation, Florida State University.

Punch, M. (1994). Politics and ethics in qualitative research. In N. K., Denzin, & Y. S. Lincoln (Eds.), *Handbook of qualitative research* (pp. 83-97). Thousand Oaks, CA: Sage.

Reeves, T. C. (1985). *Questioning the questions of instructional technology research.* Retrieved December 15, 2002, from http://www.gsu.edu/~wwwitr/docs/dean/index.html.

Reeves, T. C. (1986). Research and evaluation models for the study of interactive video. *Journal of Computer-Based Instruction, 13*(4), 102-106.

Reigeluth, C. M. (1989). Educational technology at the crossroads: New mindsets and new directions. *Educational Technology Research and Development, 37*(1), 67-80.

Reilly, B. (1994). Composing with images: A study of high school video producers. *Proceedings of ED-MEDIA 94, Educational multimedia and hypermedia.* Charlottesville, VA: Association for the Advancement of Computing in Education.

Reiser, R. A., & Mory, E. H. (1991). An examination of the systematic planning techniques of two experienced teachers. *Educational Technology Research and Development, 39*(3), 71- 82.

Richardson, L. (1994) Writing: A method of inquiry. In N. K., Denzin, & Y. S. Lincoln (Eds.), *Handbook of qualitative research* (pp. 516–529). Thousand Oaks, CA: Sage.

Richey, R. C. (1998). The pursuit of usable knowledge. *Educational Technology Research and Development, 46*(4), 7–22.

Richey, R C. (2000). Reflections on the state of educational technology research and development: A response to Kozma. *Educational Technology Research and Development, 48*(1), 16–18.

Robinson, R. S. (1994). Investigating Channel One: A case study report. In DeVaney, A. (Ed.), *Watching Channel One*. Albany, NY: SUNY Press.

Robinson, R. S. (1995). Qualitative research—A case for case studies. In G. J. Anglin (Ed.), *Instructional technology: Past, present and future* (2nd ed., pp. 330–339). Englewood, CO: Libraries Unlimited.

Robinson, R. S., & Driscoll, M. (1993). Qualitative research methods: an introduction. In M. R. Simonson, & K. Abu-Omar, (Eds.), *15th annual proceedings of selected research and development presentations at the 1993 national convention of the Association for Educational Communications and Technology, New Orleans, LA.* (pp. 833–844). Ames: Iowa State University.

Rynkiewich, M. A., & Spradley, J. P. (Eds.). (1976). *Ethics and anthropology: Dilemmas in fieldwork*. New York: John Wiley.

Salomon, G. (1991). Transcending the qualitative–quantitative debate: The analytic and systemic approaches to educational research. *Educational Researcher, 20*(6), 10–18.

Savenye, W. C. (1989) *Field test year evaluation of the TLTG interactive videodisc science curriculum: effects on student and teacher attitude and classroom implementation*. Austin: Texas Learning Technology Group of the Texas Association of School Boards.

Savenye, W. C., & Strand, E. (1989, February). Teaching science using interactive videodisc: Results of the pilot year evaluation of the Texas Learning Technology Group Project. In M. R. Simonson, & D. Frey (Eds.), *Eleventh annual proceedings of selected research paper presentations at the 1989 Annual Convention of the Association for Educational Communications and Technology in Dallas, Texas*. Ames: Iowa State University.

Savenye, W., Socolofsky, K., Greenhouse, R., & Cutler, N. (1995, February). *Evaluation under Sonoran sun: Formative evaluation of a desert education exhibit*. Paper presented at the annual conference of the Association for Educational Communications and Technology, Anaheim, CA.

Savenye, W., Leader, L., Dwyer, H., Jones, E., Schnackenberg, H., & Jiang, B. (1996, February). *Relationship among patterns of choices, achievement, incentive, and attitude in a learner-controlled computer-based lesson for college students*. Paper presented the annual conference of the Association for Educational Communications and Technology, Indianapolis, IN.

Schmidt, K. J. (1992). *At-risk eighth grade student feelings, perceptions, and insights of computer-assisted interactive video*. Unpublished doctoral dissertation, University of Texas at Austin.

Shin, E. J., Schallert, D., & Savenye, W. C. (1994). Effects of learner control, advisement, and prior knowledge on young students' learning in a hypertext environment. *Educational Technology Research and Development, 42*(1), 33–46.

Smith, M. L. (1987). Publishing qualitative research. *American Educational Research Journal, 24*(2), 173–183.

Smith, P. L., & Wedman, J. F. (1988). Read-think-aloud protocols: A new data-source for formative evaluation. *Performance Improvement Quarterly, 1*(2), 13–22.

Spindler, G. D. (1974). Schooling in Schonhausen: A study in cultural transmission and instrumental adaptation in an urbanizing German village. In G. D. Spindler (Ed.), *Education an cultural process: Toward an anthropology of education*. New York: Holt, Rinehart and Winston.

Spradley, J. P. (1972). *Culture and cognition: rules, maps, and plans*. San Francisco, CA: Chandler.

Spradley, J. P. (1979). *The ethnographic interview*. New York: Holt, Rinehart and Winston.

Spradley, J. P. (1980). *Participant observation*. New York: Holt, Rinehart and Winston.

Straus, A. L. (1987). *Qualitative analysis for social scientists*. Cambridge: Cambridge University Press.

Strauss, A. L., & Corbin, J. M. (1994). Grounded theory methodology: An overview. In N. K., Denzin, & Y. S. Lincoln (Eds.), *Handbook of qualitative research* (pp. 273–285). Thousand Oaks, CA: Sage.

Tesch, R. (1990). *Qualitative research: Analysis types and software tools*. New York: Falmer Press.

Tierney, W., Polkinghorne, D. E., Lincoln, Y. S., Denzin, N. K., Kincheloe, J., Lather, P., & Pinar, W. (1995, April). *Representation and text: Reframing the narrative voice*. Interactive symposium presented at the annual conference of the American Educational Research Association, San Francisco, CA.

Turner, A. M. (2000). *Voices of the people: Experiences with two-way interactive television in the City Colleges of Chicago*. Unpublished doctoral dissertation, Northern Illinois University.

U.S. Congress, Office of Technology Assessment. (1988, September). *Power On! New Tools for Teaching and Learning* (OTA-SET-379). Washington, DC: U.S. Government Printing Office.

Van Maanen, J. (1988). *Tales of the field: On writing ethnography*. Chicago: University of Chicago Press.

Webb, E. J., Campbell, D. T., Schwartz, R. D., & Sechrest, L. (1966). *Unobtrusive measures: Nonreactive research in the social sciences*. Chicago: Rand McNally.

Webb, N. M. (1983). Predicting learning from student interaction: defining the interaction variable. *Educational Psychologist, 18*(1), 33–41.

Webb, N. M. (1991). Task-related verbal interaction and mathematics learning in small groups. *Journal of Research in Mathematics Education, 22*(5), 366–389.

Weitzman, E. A., & Miles, M. B. (1995). *A software sourcebook: Computer programs for qualitative data analysis*. Thousand Oaks, CA: Sage.

Weller, S. C., & Romney, A. K. (1988). *Systematic data collection*. Newbury Park, CA: Sage.

Winn, W. (1989). Toward a rationale and theoretical basis for educational technology. *Educational Technology Research and Development, 37*(1), 35–46.

Wolcott, H. F. (1967). *A Kwakiutl village and school*. New York: Holt, Rinehart & Winston.

Wolcott, H. F. (1973). *The man in the principal's office*. New York: Holt, Rinehart & Winston.

Wolcott, H. F. (1990). *Writing up qualitative research*. Newbury Park, CA: Sage.

Wolcott, H. F. (1994). *Transforming qualitative data*. Thousand Oaks, CA: Sage.

Wolf, B. A. (1994). *Effects of cooperative learning and learner control in computer-based instruction*. Unpublished doctoral dissertation, Arizona State University.

Yeaman, A., Koetting, J., & Nichols, R. (1994). Special issue: The ethical position of educational technology in society. *Educational Technology, 34*(2), 5–72.

Yin, R. K. (1989). *Case study research* (2nd ed.). Beverly Hills, CA: Sage.

·40·

CONVERSATION ANALYSIS FOR EDUCATIONAL TECHNOLOGISTS: THEORETICAL AND METHODOLOGICAL ISSUES FOR RESEARCHING THE STRUCTURES, PROCESSES, AND MEANING OF ON-LINE TALK

Joan M. Mazur
University of Kentucky

40.1   INTRODUCTION

Research in education technology encompasses a wide range of quantitative and qualitative methods (Savenye & Robinson 1996). Methods and approaches formerly applied in the broader realm of qualitative educational research have become important to researchers in educational technology. Conversation analysis (CA) is one such qualitative approach that has recently become highly relevant for examining educational phenonmena related to discourse supported by the plethora of tools and resources for computer-mediated communication. In this chapter, which focuses on CA situated within the tradition of discourse analysis, I make several assumptions. I assume that the reader is acquainted with qualitative inquiry and such terms as grounded theory, intersubjectivity, participant and nonparticipant observation, sampling, and recursion in the analytic phases of inquiry are familiar.

Concurrent with the remarkable growth of networked, interactive communication technologies during the last decade, educational technologists are beginning to see the need to scrutinize people's on-line conversations as evidence of educational processes and outcomes. As ever-increasing numbers of people use on-line chats, listservs, threaded discussions, and video and audio conferencing for educational purposes, questions about these on-line conversations arise:

- What are characteristics of on-line conversations, and how does virtual talk-in-interaction relate to instruction, learning, and communication?
- What relationships exist between conversation and cognition or the social, distributed construction of knowledge?
- To what extent does the type of technology limit or support the discourse required for various modes of instruction?
- What are these discourses of on-line instruction?
- How can structures and processes inherent in conversation assist in the development of instructional contexts that support interactions that result in meaningful learning?
- To what extent can we take the robust body of previous research on classroom talk, which has yielded valuable information on instruction and learning, and apply it to investigations of on-line conversation?

- What are the social or ideological dimensions of on-line conversations and how do they affect learning and instruction. Are roles changing? How and why? Who has (and who does not have) access to the virtual "floor?"

What participants in on-line conferencing say—talk—is the evidence used to examine these questions related to conversation. CA techniques are not new, but the application and modification of CA to computer-mediated systems and on-line social networks by educational technologists are relatively unexplored.

There are three goals of this chapter. The first is to articulate the theoretical and methodological issues related to CA, the basic foundational principles and concepts related to a CA, and the kinds of questions that can be addressed using this approach. The second is to provide the educational technologist with practical guidelines and specific examples for conducting a CA. The third goal is to provide a research synthesis reviewing the literature related to CA focused on computer-mediated "virtual" and "actual" conversations and to discuss directions for further research on the structure, processes, and meaning of on-line talk.

40.2   OBJECTIVES

The objectives of this chapter are detailed below. After reading this chapter education technology researchers will be able to:

1. define the term *conversation analysis* and situate the method within the larger contexts of discourse analysis and ethnomethodology from which it is drawn;
2. demonstrate awareness of previous research investigating talk in educational, work, and other social settings;
3. describe the underlying epistemological, theoretical, and methodological assumptions for CA associated with two prevalent approaches: the process–product and the sociocultural traditions (paradigms);
4. define salient aspects of investigating talk and interaction and how they relate to understanding aspects of learning, cognition, instruction, and design in on-line social computing environments;
5. describe the currently available technologies that support on-line conversation;
6. discuss the methods and mechanics of conducting CA and select among them to address research questions related to interaction appropriately;
7. understand the various computer tools (hardware and software) that are available to collect, prepare, and analyze on-line conversational data;
8. conduct a conversation analysis to examine content, interaction patterns, social networking, or other dimensions of social interaction, evidenced by talk in on-line contexts; and
9. discuss areas for future research for CA of on-line talk.

40.3   SITUATING CA IN TRADITIONS OF DISCOURSE ANALYSIS

The focus of this chapter is CA. CA is embedded in the broader field of discourse analysis. In this section an overview of this broader field of discourse analysis is presented and CA is situated within that framework. Two criteria for defining conversation are discussed and two kinds of CA are articulated.

The ubiquity of words in human communication can easily lead one to take its significance and complexities for granted. In fact, the use of language is so common that the study of its structures and processes as they relate to education and communication was minimal until the 1960s, when researchers in many fields began to see its importance. There were efforts to explore theory and methods to understand its structural, cultural, and cognitive dimensions. That is the starting point for this chapter: What is discourse, and how is it studied?

Discourse in its most everyday sense is comprised of *forms of language use,* usually spoken language or ways of speaking, whether public or private speech (van Dijk, 1997, p. 2). Another common use of the term discourse refers not only to the language used but to the ideas and philosophies extended through their use. Thus we speak of a neoconservative discourse and mean both the words and the political or social rhetoric inherent in using language to disseminate the ideas. A discourse analysis moves beyond this ordinary sense of language use and includes additional elements of interest—who uses the language, how, why, and when.

The study of discourse is considered multidisciplinary drawing from the diverse fields of linguistics, social psychology, communication, educational psychology and education, sociology of communication, and, more recently, human–computer interaction (van Dijk, 1997). Discourse studies focus on theory and analysis of text and talk in virtually all disciplines. Discourse analysis includes a broad range of areas and topics including linguistic forms and functions, style and rhetoric, psychological studies, and sociocultural research. The data for discourse analyses are drawn from informal and formal dialogue in both individual and institutional contexts documented in language, in its many forms, from spoken talk to written texts. Analyses of these types of data can be conducted at many levels: abstract analyses of linguistic function and structures of discourse, the organization of talk by language users, structures of coconstructed dialogic meaning, breakdowns in communicative patterns, and examinations of the multilayered cultural and social implications of discourse.

Language use, the communication of beliefs (cognition), and interaction are three main dimensions of discourse. Language is not simply *used*: It is used *for something;* it is functional. Primarily, language functions as a *communicative event* (Coulthard, 1993). Regardless of function, when people use language they are, in fact, doing something—they are interacting (verbally interacting). Within each of these dimensions there are levels of analyses. For instance, a focus on language use would include more obvious observable levels of the utterance or expression and move into more complex, even covert aspects such as form, meaning, and action (Joshi, Webber, & Sag, 1981). Discourse analyses tend to focus on several topics: discourse as verbal structure, discourse as cognition, discourse and society, and discourse as action and interaction. Descriptions of these topics are outlined in the sections that follow.

40.3.1   Discourse as Verbal Structure

Words, gestures, sounds, and body language are the observable aspects or expression of discourse. Expression is symbiotic with language use, and attention to the phonological (sound) or haptic (gesture) features of spoken language, for example, can be key to understanding the structure of the discourse. Intonation may denote a question, signal a change of speaker, or close a segment of dialogue. Written discourse is multimodal and an analysis of a written text provides opportunities to examine a range of communications and representations within one text, what Kress, Leite-Garcia, and van Leeuen (1997) term the *semiotic landscape.* The language of chat rooms, threaded discussions, and instant messaging on the Internet contains a new hybrid language of "written speech" with its own evolving semiotics (emoticons, for example) and verbal structure. Nonverbal activity such as gestures, body position, laughter, and the like occur with talk and must be analyzed as part of the communicative event.

The primary modes of discourse are talk and text. Spoken discourses such as conversations, debates, meetings, and lawyer–client, teacher–student, designer–client interactions are among the kinds of discourse to be studied. Texts, such as newpaper articles, fiction, poetry, textbooks, and advertising are written modes of discourse. van Dijk (1997), extending the work of Sinclair, Hoey, and Fox (1993) and Coulthard (1985), has noted that the analysis of the verbal structure of discourse routinely includes attention to order and form, meaning, style, rhetoric, and schema.

40.3.1.1   *Order and Form.* The order and form of discourse are examined through the decomposition of word order, phrases or clauses, or other aspects related to syntax. Discourse analysts explore form beyond the boundary of the sentence, the traditional unit of linguists, to determine the influences of surrounding texts or talk. Thus in discourse analysis the "completeness" of a grammatical utterance is relative. For example, a single noun may be incomprehensible grammatically but, in relation to a previous or following sentence, may be a significant part of an exchange. Word order in sentences in any language is of course not arbitrary and required for comprehension (for example, the noun–verb structure of most English sentences). But word order can also signal emphasis or contrast. Syntactical study of discourse in the type of strict linguistic sense described above is increasingly being integrated with other levels and dimensions of discourse such as how the information contained in previous sentences affects the discourse (Cumming and Ono, 1997). This brings us to another aspect of the analysis of verbal structure of discourse—meaning.

40.3.1.2   *Meaning.* Semantics is the study of meaning. Semantic representations in discourse in a linguistic sense usually refer to the abstract or conceptual meaning of words. Psychologists and sociologists, however, are more pragmatic in their approach. The participants ascribe meaning to a discourse. It is the language user who understands the meaning in terms of his or her prior knowledge, understanding, and experience. A proposition is the term for the meaning of a clause or sentence. Understanding the meaning of clauses or sentences is subject to a discursive relativity principle described by van Dijk (1997, p. 9). According to this principle, any proposition is influenced by what comes before or after it in the discourse. Another key semantic concept is that of coherence (Tannen, 1986). The notion of coherence, like so many terms in discourse (and, as the reader will note later, in CA as well) has both a common-sense meaning and a more technical, theoretical one. On its face, coherence is obvious—the connectedness of the discourse. A text or conversation that loses focus and seems to have many topics or tangents lacks coherence. From a more technical perspective coherence is achieved through several linguistic devices and coherence conditions must be met. Although a full explication of these kinds of linguistic devices and conditions is beyond the scope of this review, I include the example of prosody (Gumperz, Kaltman, & O'Connor, 1984) as an exemplum. Prosody includes intonation, stress, tone, and other paralinguistic signals and speakers' mutual understandings of these signals establish coherence conditions. Thus, a semantic analysis can include topics, themes, how focus is achieved/maintained/eroded, or discourse referents (who or what the talk is about). Semantic chunks such as headlines in a newspaper often signal boundaries for the discourse (between news stories, for example). At the global or macro level of discourse semantics the analyst will emphasize discernment of topics or themes over the linguistics and grammar that one might expect to encounter at a microlevel of syntactical or grammatical semantic analysis.

40.3.1.3   *Style.* Style is the component of the verbal structure of a discourse related to variation and most often evinced in word choice. Are students in conversation between teachers referred to as "members," "collaborators," or "participants"? Such distinctions are usually a product of the context (who is speaking, their role, the medium, etc.). As van Dijk (1997, p. 12) notes "a stylistic analysis may also define a collection of typical discursive characteristics of a genre (story vs. report), a speaker (calm vs. emotional), a group (women vs. men), a social situation (formal vs. informal) or even a whole culture (Anglo vs. Latino)."

40.3.1.4   *Rhetoric.* The rhetoric of a discourse is evinced in the use of figures of speech within the talk or text. Persuasive-type speech structures such as metaphor, irony, or hyperbole are among the types of rhetorical devices. Again, invoking the discourse relativity principle (van Dijk, 1997, p. 20) the function of such rhetorical structures are often dependent on coherence or meaning.

40.3.2   Cognition as Discourse

Talk and text as expression of language use are also expressions of the knowledge of the speaker or writer. Knowledge as represented in mind is both a mental and a cultural phenomenon. Psychological dimensions of knowledge and skills are processes and representations stored in memory and play out in talk about thoughts and beliefs. Cultural and social dimensions of knowledge play out as shared meanings, judgments, and understandings of those expressed thoughts and beliefs. Amann and Knorr-Cetina (1989) note that it is plausible to "assume that [humans] will evolve cultural 'vehicles of thinking' other than thought that routinely supplement and replace their central [mental] operations" (p. 6). They referred to spoken discourse as one such "machinery" and that "when embedded in talk, thinking is *interactively accomplished* [their emphasis] . . . what we get instead of mentally–induced problem solutions are conversationally-induced utterances which . . . trigger certain non-obvious interpretations or performance recommendations" (p. 6). Thus, investigations of discourse also yield insight into the structure and process of cognition. The early cognitive theories of discourse were based in other fields such as text linguistics (Halliday and Hasan, 1976; van Dijk, 1972;), artificial intelligence (Shank and Abelson, 1977), and pragmatics (Grice, 1975; Searles, 1969). Early work in the cognitive context of discourse analysis focused on determining the extent to which the structure and function of texts could account for experimental psychological findings. As the theory base and methods evolved, discourse analysis shifted to investigation of text comprehension and production and away from studies of spoken conversation (Grasser, Gernsbacher, & Goldman, 1997).

40.3.2.1 Symbolic and Connectionist Models of Discourse. Cognitive models of discourse have been highly influenced by two cognitive theories: symbolic and connectionist theories. Using symbolic theories, psychologists generated descriptions of discourse production rules in the form of "IF, THEN" forms—when the condition exists the production "fires" and results in an action. Production rules can encompass physical and mental actions: IF [a beeper goes off and a person has a cell phone in her pocket], THEN [the person searches for her cell phone and runs out of a classroom] or IF [a letter sequence P-I-Z-Z-A is perceived], THEN [activate the concept of "pizza" in working memory]. Using connectionist theories, psychologies generated descriptions of discourse as representations and processes distributed among distinct units. This neural net metaphor is used to describe patterns of activation. For example, determining the meaning of a representation at a point of comprehension requires activation values for all the units and thus is distributed throughout the network. The two most influential cognitive models of discourse are Kintch's (1988) construction-integration (CI) model and the collaborative activiation-based production system (CAPS) model (Just & Carpenter, 1992). The CI model simulates dynamic changes in the activation values for units in a network. The values change as comprehension proceeds, words build on words, sentences on sentences, and so forth. In the construction phase a person creates units associated with particular text and external knowledge. In the integration phase stable patterns of activation values are established and maintained in working memory. Working memory is a factor in the CI model because capacity is

fixed, though information not in working memory continues to be resourced in long-term memory. The CAPS model uses the symbolic-connectionist foundations but brings in semantic representation and deals with capacity limits in working memory differently than the CI model. Partial pattern recognition can occur as portions of words (PIZZ, to use the previous letter sequence example) that activate the networked units without having to put all in working memory, thus freeing up space for other textual components. A combined CI/CAPS model was developed by Goldman and Varma (1995). Their model replaced the fixed buffer memory of the CI model with the CAPS method of allocating activation in working memory. The Goldman–Varma model also integrated the goals and strategies of the reader into the comprehension mechanism. Cognitive discourse analysis focused on detecting structure-building frameworks and how language structures reflect mental comprehension processes, how information is mapped in text comprehension and production, and how inference is constructed through text and situation models that include the people, setting, states, events, and actions of the mental microworld of the text description.

40.3.3 Discourse and Society

Social context is a crucial element of discourse analysis regardless of whether the focus of the analysis is verbal structure or cognition. Context is the sum of the dimensions and properties of the social situation that relate to the evolution, production or reception of discourse. Context and discourse are mutually constitutive. Discourse is affected by context, and in turn discourse can shape or modify context. Cazden (1986) noted two definitions of context as they apply to discourse analysis from the perspective of the speaker. "There are two types of context. The one the speaker brings to the situation and the one that evolves in the course of a conversation" (p. 436). van Dijk (1997) has articulated several contextual elements to consider in discourse analysis: gender, ethnicity, culture, social discourse analysis, and critical discourse analysis.

40.3.3.1 Gender, Ethnicity, and Discourse Analysis. The work of Tannen (cf. 1996, 2001) provides many excellent examples of how gender affects discourse. In fact, Tannen argues that the influences of the sociocultural constructions of gender are so strong as to render the discourse of one gender virtually incomprehensible to the other. Whether you agree with her theses on this matter, Tannen has used discourse analysis to examine how talk affects relationship, both personal and social. The communicative disparities in gender can be extended to issues of ethnicity. Inter- and intracultural discourses evolve as speech patterns develop among and within ethnic groups. Historically, talk has been a rich source of understanding how discourse is a source of social reproduction through prejudiced talk about ethnic or racial minorities and other types of hate speech.

40.3.3.2 The Explanatory Elements of Cultural Context: The Critical Turn. Discourse occurs in a cultural context, encompassed by social institutions, roles, and practices. Misunderstandings occur as participants misread or mishear the semantics and pragmatics of discourse with which they are unfamiliar. Rules for politeness, topic changes, and giving commands change across cultures. Acceptance of difference or intolerance and even exclusion and oppression of less powerful voices can be examined through analysis of discourse. The move to situating the discourse in a larger sociocultural context adds a key element to discourse analysis. Insight into the culture through an examination of talk becomes the point of discourse analysis. Analyses at the microlevels of internal language structures, cognitive function or pragmatic purpose, and meaning have limited explanatory power. To understand how talk and text function as mirrors of mind and action, the analysis must be contextualized within the larger cultural milieu. Critical discourse analysis involves explicit articulation of the political or social posture of discourse analyst as he or she engages in the process of understanding talk or text. If the goal of the analysis is change, in addition to science or scholarship, it is critical. The critical discourse analyst argues for a moral-social dimension in research and works to make public findings regarding how discourse can oppress, silence, dominate, or prejudice.

40.3.4 Discourse as Action and Interaction: Speech Act Theory and Conversation Analysis

Discourse analysis necessarily includes the notion of discourse as interaction and action. The concept of language as action—the move from linguistic form to linguistic action—was first defined by John Austen (1962), a philosopher of language who articulated speech act theory. The central tenet of speech act theory is that speech is action. Talk implies motivation and thus talk both IS and RESULTS in action. Prior to Austen's assertions, speech was virtually unconsidered as part of communication because it was considered a passive and "fixed" phenomenon that was analyzed as "texts" and "discourses" [in the static not the dynamic sense that has come to be a more common parlance today]. Speech act theory defines specific *speech acts* as its basic units of analysis. For example, *locutionary acts* are those that produce utterances in some language. *Semantic* or *prepositional* acts are used to convey meaning in language use. When people *use* language, they are *doing* something—they are acting through words. Utterances are produced, these utterances have meaning, and utterances have a sociocultural dimension. Pragmatics is the field of study focused on the study of language use as action in social context. Speech acts do not occur as individual utterance in isolation. People talk to each other, they write texts for readers, they interact. Interaction takes many forms: turn-taking in conversation, agreeing and disagreeing, questioning and answering, opening and closing conversation, preparing to engage in and enter conversation, developing persona in conversation, saving face, attacking or defending, and persuading or explaining. These interactions in their social context are the subject of conversation analysis, a subset of discourse studies of interaction.

40.3.5 Definitions of Conversation and Conversation Analysis

Conversation—people talking with each other—is one of the most commonplace of all human activities. Despite its prevalence in human interaction, the study of conversation as a serious disciplinary endeavor only began in the 1960s based on the concepts and principles of speech act theory. Prior to that time, the discourse on conversation was primarily written texts that described how one should speak rather than how they actually *did* speak. Conversation occurs when any people talk with each other and can be used to indicate any activity of interactive talk, regardless of its purpose (ten Have, 1999, p. 4). The term *conversation analysis* can be construed in a broad sense to mean any study of people talking together in oral communication or language use. However, as a subdiscipline of discourse analysis, CA refers to a tradition of analysis founded by Harvey Sacks and his colleagues, including Emanuel Schegloff and Gail Jefferson. It is in this particular tradition that the term conversation analysis is used throughout most of this chapter. However, in concluding this chapter, I offer a discussion of the necessity to broaden this stricter sense of CA through theory building and new methodologies based on how conversation and interaction continue to be redefined and reshaped by computer-mediated communication technologies. Such revisions will enable researchers interested in the ever-proliferating worlds of on-line conversation to translate the traditions of CA to investigations of computer-mediated conversations.

40.4 ELEMENTS OF TALK-IN-INTERACTION

In this section, key elements of talk-in-interaction, the phenomena of interest for CA, are presented. The central purpose of CA is to investigate the norms and conventions that speakers use *in interaction* to establish communicative understandings. Traditional CA was concerned only with the speech of the conversants as an observable, external event. The seminal CA work by Sacks, Schegloff, and Jefferson (1974) articulated three basic facts about conversation: (a) turn-taking occurs, (b) one speaker tends to speak at a time, and (c) turns are taken with as little overlap between them as possible (the speakers coordinate their interactions as much as possible to avoid overlap). These basic tenets presume a continuity of time and space in face-to-face conversations and is called into question later in the examination of virtual conversations. However, for purposes of describing foundational elements of CA, they will stand, as will the presumption of shared time and space. Although the following descriptions are highly detailed, it is important to remember that the conversation analyst is not working from an abstract prescriptive definition of what constitutes a turn construction, for example, in the manner in which a linguist may define a sentence. Rather, what the turn construction consists of in an situated segment of conversation is a concern for the speakers themselves. This tension between the technical methods of analyzing conversation and its socially constituted nature is a continual challenge to researchers working with CA to maintain perspective on this problematic.

40.4.1 Turn-Taking

The principle of turn-taking has been established as one of the central interests of CA, as it is the basic component of all conversation. The *turn form*, *the turn content*, and the *turn length* are all of interest when examining turn-taking in conversation. Turn form, turn content, and turn length are affected by the formality or informality of a situation. Turns between teachers and students, clients and lawyers, have more boundaries defined by the formal context, whereas telephone conversations among friends are freely variable and determined by elements within the interaction. Turns have two components: a turn-construction component and a turn distribution component.

Turn constructions have turn construction units that often correspond to linguistic elements such as sentences, phrases, or single words (e.g., "Yo!" or "What?"). Turn construction units have two prominent properties. One is called *projectability*. It is possible for a speaker to project, as the turn construction unit proceeds, what kind of a unit it is and when it is likely to end. This leads to the second property, *transition-relevant places*. These occur at the boundaries of the turn construction unit and make it possible for transition between speakers. These two properties are shown in the following transcript excerpt.

1. *Art:* Why don't you drop by and we'll work on the assign[ment]
2. *Ann:* [that would
3.   really help me understand
4. *Art:* I'm happy to help

Ann recognizes Art's utterance "Why don't you drop by and we'll work on the assignment?" as a form of invitation and responds with an acceptance prior to Art's finishing the statement. Ann's projection on the transition-relevance place is correct, as it turns out. This is shown by Art's response. Ann projects the end of the turn construction unit *and* shows her understanding of what kind of unit that invitation represents.

However, if Ann's projection about the transition-relevance place was incorrect, the exchange might have been very different. If Art was going to say "... work on the assignment next Tuesday," making the invitation much more specific, Ann's response may have been very different. Such a situation would exemplify the second component of turn-taking, turn distribution.

40.4.1.1 Turn-Taking Rules. Turn distribution has some "simple rules" as articulated by Sacks et al. (1974) that occur at the initial transition-relevant place in a turn. I paraphrase these as follows.

Rule 1: (a) If the current speaker designates the next speaker, that speaker should take the turn at that place. (b) If no such selection occurs, then any speaker can self-select, with the first volunteer having the right to speak first. (c) If no speaker is selected, the first speaker may (or may not) continue speaking with another turn construction unit, unless or until another speaker self-selects, at which point that speaker has the floor.

Rule 2: However the participants work out the turn distribution, then rules 1a–1c are reiterated at the point of the next transition-relevant place.

If Ann's response at her projected transition-relevant place had been incorrect—if Art's invitation was for next Tuesday, he could have redistributed the turn by means of rule 1b and repaired the exchange. Even if Ann's projected transition-relevant place were incorrect, it probably would not have mattered in the context of achieving understanding. Schegloff (1992) notes that speakers project to possible not actual transition points because in natural spoken conversation the optimum condition is for as little time as possible to occur between turns. This is practical, as waiting for any speaker to finish completely would result in gaps that would erode the natural flow and meaning as well as lessen the opportunity for any speaker to enter the conversation because either someone else does or the current speaker continues.

According the Sacks et al. (1974) such rules of turn distribution are intended as descriptors of practices that speakers exhibit in the actual occasion of turn-taking in conversation; again, they are not meant to be prescriptive but, rather, are *practices* that are in evidence in transcriptions of talk.

The point of these detailed descriptions of conversational practice or use is to provide empirically grounded descriptions of how speakers interactively manage and organize communication in myriad social contexts and for an array of everyday social actions. Traditional CA has used the focus on turns to develop insightful accounts of the structural organization of topic shifts (Jefferson, 1986), agreement and disagreement (Pomerantz, 1984), laughter (Jefferson, Sacks, & Schegloff, 1987), repair and correction (Schegloff, 1986), invitations (Drew, 1984), and overlapping talk (Jefferson, 1986).

40.4.1.2 Sequential Organization and Intersubjectivity. In CA, participants' understandings are displayed in interaction and displayed for the conversationalists chiefly through the sequential organization of turn-taking. The fact that talk-in-interaction is organized by turns leads to an important distinction for CA. Turns occur one after the other, in a serial order. However, the relationship between turns is not serial but sequential. This distinction is crucial because the talk does not just occur in a series of responses; rather the talk is organized in sequences of two or more in which conversants show their understanding of the kind of turn the prior turn was intended to be (their understanding of the turn construction). This concept is known as the adjacency pair sequence. Clear case examples are invitations that make acceptance or deferral relevant as the next move or questions that make an answer relevant as the next move. The insight here is not just that answers follow questions but that responses are conditionally relevant to utterances in prior turns. The second pair part is conditional on the first—it is normative. The normative constraints on adjacency pairs are important to CA because the researcher can draw inferences in the cases where typical responses do not occur. For example, a lack of an answer to a question may imply evasion. Moreover, the resolution of the meaning of the break in normative constraint is confirmed in subsequent turns through what in CA is called the next-turn proof procedure. Consider the following example of a discussion between a teacher and student regarding an upcoming open house at school.

1. *Teacher:*   Do you know who will be at the open house?

The question is ambiguous. It may be a legitimate request for information or it may be a preannouncement, a foundation for an announcement the speaker wishes to convey regarding who will be at the open house. In CA, the problem here is not whether the student can technically decode the utterance but, rather, how the conversants show their understanding or interpretation of the utterance. Comprehension is worked out in the next few turns.

1. *Teacher:*   Do you know who will be at the open house?
2. *Student:*   No, who?
3. *Teacher:*   I'm asking you, I can't know who's coming
4. *Student:*   Uh, oh, my mom, my dad is working

Here we see that the students' projections were not on target; the teacher was actually seeking information, not making an announcement. Based on that misunderstanding the student's response to the preannouncement was to encourage the first speaker to continue with the announcement. This example points up that the general conceptual orientation of CA is not cognitive but social. Regardless of whether the student or teacher knew (cognitively) the potential answer(s) to the question, the participants in this exchange relied on the social organization of the interaction (its context) to shape their contributions to the conversation. This process is constitutive of publicly achieved understanding and intersubjectivity.

40.4.1.3 *Strategies and Goals.* Despite strong ties to pragmatics and social psychology, CA takes an opposing view of the nature and relevance of goals and strategies in common everyday conversation. CA uses the many nuances and details of talk-in-interaction to observe through the empirical evidence of the exchanges in the transcript the subtleties of how communication and shared understanding is achieved. Consider this exchange between two sisters discussing an aunt's recent trip to the doctor (Mazur, 1989).

1. *Mary:*   Hi: mmm:::uh:::Aunt Bessie called, have you talked to her↑ she (.)
2.   was very↓ weak sounding and (0.7) ((sniffling sound)) well it's [not↓
3. *Claire:*   [this doesn't sound good
4. *Mary:*   [I waited 'til after the kids were in bed to call (.) With her history::
5. *Claire:*   = [Oma had breast cancer
6. *Mary:*   It's malignant. She has about six months. OH GOD ((sobbing))↑

On its face, this is a conversation about a cancer diagnosis. Note how the first speaker does not actually announce the bad news, but rather as the turns play out the recipient infers and announces an exchange that would have been impossible without the shared knowledge of the aunt's medical history. The communication was accomplished through interactive negotiation of

the information through conversational turn-taking. This is not the same as noting that Mary's strategy was to be evasive and get Claire to say the bad news. As sisters there may be other socially constrained frames on the production of this exchange; perhaps one speaker (Claire) is aware that the other (Mary) may not be able to continue with the announcement (by hearing her sniffling) even though Mary initiated the conversation and wishes to convey the information. Of course, conversants have goals and strategies and the CA perspective does not deny that they play a key part in communication. However, the interest of CA in goals and strategies is how conversants show their understandings and orientations to each other using their talk as evidence.

40.5   SOCIAL, EPISTEMOLOGICAL, AND MORAL ASSUMPTIONS OF THE CA PARADIGM

The purpose of this section is to examine the historical and theoretical roots of CA and to lay out the social, epistemological, and moral assumptions inherent in the classic CA paradigm. The section ends with some reflections on the goodness of fit of the classic CA model for conversations that occur in a computer-mediated context toward the purpose of raising issues that may arise as the CA paradigm and methods are applied to talk-in-interaction in on-line settings.

40.5.1   Sociolinguistics, Pragmatics, and Ethnomethodology

CA evolved at the nexus of paradigm shifts in linguistics toward sociolinguistics and pragmatics (Grice, 1975; Hymes, 1977) and ethnomethodology in sociology (Garfinkel, 1967; Goffman, 1963; Sacks, 1972; Schegloff & Sacks, 1973). Ethnomethodology, as first described by Garfinkel (1967), was a study of practical theorizing in everyday practices and focused on legitimizing common sense reasoning and examining procedures in common-sense activities. Schegloff and Sacks, two of the pioneering practitioners of CA, were sociology students of Goffman's (1963) at Berkeley. They followed in his interests in researching face-to-face interactions in the real-world contexts of talk and interaction. It is Sacks who is generally credited with formulating procedures that came be known as CA through his analysis of a collection of tape-recorded calls to a Los Angeles Suicide Prevention Center.

Heritage (1997, p. 162) notes that there are currently two prevalent branches of analytic conversation research. One kind examines the institution of interaction as an entity with its own structural, social, and moral characteristics. The other prevalent type of analysis focuses on the management of social institutions IN interaction. ten Have refers to the first kind as *pure CA* and to the second kind as *applied CA* (ten Have, 1999, p. 8). Within the applied CA framework the organization of interaction (such as turn-taking, the distribution of speakers' rights, and openings and closings of conversation) can be examined. Additionally, the specfic interaction situation, the local, unique interaction requirements, and how the conversants understand

and demonstrate their orientations toward these "rules" can be examined. Sacks (1974) and others were careful to articulate that these are *not* prescriptive rules but, rather, rules that develop within and *through* the interaction. Thus, within the applied CA framework, CA is a systematic method to observe the production of intention or the achievement of understandings in the turns of talk between human speakers.

40.5.1.1 Social Assumptions of CA.
It is important to note that historically the CA paradigm is a decidedly *local* and *specific* endeavor. Based in the sociological perspective of ethnomethodology (described below), CA focused on the *interactions* of ordinary people talking in ordinary and naturally occurring circumstances—situations that have come to be known as talk-in-interaction. The phenomenon of interest was defined as talk in natural settings rather than formal, laboratory, or experimentally contrived situations and discourse. Based on this foundational tenet, of the local, the *in situ,* and the particular, CA is clearly a qualitative research effort. However, partially because of its relationship to linguistics and partially because of its focus on interaction (and the complexities of such activities), CA researchers realized from the first that a new methodology would be required. Until the proliferation of on-line exchanges in the form of typed "virtual" conversations, data in CA studies consisted primarily of audio recordings of talk in naturally occurring settings. The development of procedures and protocols for transcribing these data and development of frameworks for analyses of these data were crucial for achieving the systematic rigor required of any disciplined field of inquiry. Despite these efforts toward rigor that necessarily resulted in rules (practices) from inductive analysis of conversational patterns, the notion of the socially constituted, mutually understood character of conversations is paramount to implementing the CA approach. However, to reiterate a key point, the notion that conversation is normative does not mean that its structures and "rules" are prescriptive. This is certainly the case because all conversation is contextualized by the social circumstances in which it occurs and thus prescription is precluded.

40.5.1.2 Epistemological Assumptions of CA.
The epistemological perspective of the CA paradigm appears to be somewhat ambiguous. However, I would assert that this ambiguity is both ironic and semantic, directly related to the very focus of CA—words. As I have alluded to in previous sections, the use of such terms as rules for turn distribution gives the CA a prescriptive, frame that not evident in the actual conduct of CA research. As Sacks conceded, the use of these terms is unfortunate and he could have just as easily described such rules as practices, thereby countering the algorithmic, predictive connotation. CA is interpretative, with an emphasis as on the local and the particular. Although (as the reader will see) CA methods are circumscribed by very specific procedures, the practice of CA analysis is largely inductive. The CA researcher, working within the classical CA tradition, confines the basis for analysis to the transcribed text in naturally occurring settings. Based on the evidence of the transcript of the actual recorded conversation, the CA researcher discerns patterns in talk, using primarily the strategies related to case analysis—clear case, discrepant case,

and the like from the transcription. Meaning is inferred in the context of the social interaction of the coconstructed conversation. Clearly the relationship of the knower to the known in the CA analytic process is a mutually constitutive one. The CA analyst is "reading" the transcript, which has distinct features related to turn-taking and structure, and bringing her own interpretative frames and lenses to this task. The analytic task is recursive and folds back on itself. This recursion occurs not only in the context of the actual dialogic expressions that are interdependent (the discursive relativity principle defined by van Dijk), but also in the procedure of the researcher in moving back and forth within the data, confirming or denying clear and discrepant cases.

40.5.1.3 Moral Assumptions of CA.
The moral perspectives inherent in CA are impulses toward equity and multivocal participation, in the privileging of the actual voices of participants in everyday settings. In particular, in the case of critical social analysis, the expressed purpose of the analytic effort is toward understanding deep-seated or hidden power relations evidenced within the talk-in-interaction. Morally, findings from these types of CA have great potential to raise issues of status, empowerment, silencing, and other forms of oppression. Taking Austen at his word, that speech is action, critical feminist philosophers have examined the power of hate speech as an insidious means to shape attitudes and prompt action (Callahan, 2001). Critical social analysis in CA can provide powerful evidence from everyday talk for the necessity for change.

40.6 TECHNOLOGY AND CONVERSATION

40.6.1 Technology-Involved Conversation

Defining the parameters and participants in technology-involved conversations has been greatly complicated over the past three decades by advances in computer science that have appropriated intricate psycholinguistic and psychomotor models and applied them to the design of interactive computing technologies, in both desktop and networked environments. Thus, it is important to distinguish in a general sense between two terms, often used interchangeably, and to settle on the use of one for the purpose of this review. These terms are *computer-mediated communication* (CMC; cf. the chapter on CMC in this handbook) and *human–computer interaction* (HCI; cf. Suchman, 1990). Computer-mediated contexts include e-mail, digital videoconferencing, asynchronous threaded discussions, and real-time chats. (HCIs can relate to the technologies described above with reference to CMC) but use a distinctly different metaphor to describe the relationship between human and machine. Rather than mediational descriptors (computer-supported, for example), the emphasis is on interactional descriptors. Thus, in HCI, humans' interactions with machine can be characterized as "conversations" by denoting the sequencing of "give and take" involved in the use of expert systems as "turns." The computer anticipates and responds to users' actions. For example, in the HCI paradigm, machines "interact" with humans by beeping announcements of the arrival of new e-mail. Remarkably, in an extension of the HCI framework, machines can also "talk" to other machines as in the case of enforcing constraints on automated "computerized" stock market trading. The information in this chapter is confined to the tools of CMC as defined by Romiszowki and Mason (1986). However, although an analysis of useful overlaps in the HCI literature (cf. Jacko & Sears, 2002) and CMC is beyond the scope of this discussion, there are unquestionably concepts from that discipline that can relate directly to the conduct of a conversation analysis focused on talk that occurs in on-line settings. One such concept is the notion of an "affordance" as advanced by Gibson (1979).

40.6.1.1 *Affordances and On-Line Talk.*
Technologies are not neutral (Ellul, 1964). Communication technologies affect the quality and conduct of conversation and interaction. There is a complex relationship between the normative structures of conversational interaction and the communicative affordances of various forms of technology (Hutchby, 2001). The notion of an affordance is drawn from the perceptual psychology work of Gibson (1979). Affordances are possibilities for action that are suggested by the physical features and inherent properties of objects. For example, door knobs afford grasping and pulling, telephones *afford* grasping and talking and listening, and wireless headsets make it possible to eliminate the action of holding the phone. Gibson emphasized that affordances can enable or constrain based on their physical properties. These properties are not interpreted by human actors but, rather, are real, material dimensions of objects. Humans perceive affordances based on these physical properties and these properties do not change regardless of how the object is used. Specifically, in one of Gibson's classic examples, the "grasp-ability" of the door knob does not depend on someone's opening or closing a door. An examination of the material aspects of objects is important for conversations in CMC, particularly in reference to the potential to enable or constrain the ways in which a conversation is carried out. For example, speech is simply not possible in a threaded discussion or bulletin board conversation where typed text is the method by which exchanges occur. The chat window and the distance between client and server machines affect turn-taking and the sequential organization of the on-line "typed" talk. These characteristics of the talk-in-interaction relate to the affordances of the technologies used and these affordances need to be considered as part of the context of the conversation.

Interestingly, it was distinct affordances of the new audiovisual medium of the tape recorder that proved critical to the initial development of CA methodology. The audio tape recorder made it possible to access actual speech as raw data and to support systematic and rigorous research in ethnomethodology (ten Have, 1999, p. 8). After Schegloff and Sacks broke away from the examination of formal discourses and planned interaction to focus on everyday conventions and social interaction, the actual documentation of these conversations remained a problem to be addressed. By using more portable audiotape recorders just being commercially mass-produced at that time, documentation of field conversations was possible. Currently we have similar "revolutionary" means for the documentation of on-line conversations. Computer tracking utilities (Gay &

Mazur, 1993; Misanchuk & Schwier, 1992), network proxy log aggregation (Watt, 1999), text archives of on-line chats, and bulletin boards, and e-mail as well as other kinds of internal computing devices for recording screen actions and sound (Gay and Bennington, 1999) are among the tools available. The use of these new tools is discussed later, under The Researcher's Toolkit.

40.6.2 Virtual Conversation: The Special Case of Text-Based On-Line Conversation

In text-based CMC such as synchronous chats, asynchronous bulletin boards, or threaded discussions, the participants affect "talk" by typing in their "speech," and the Internet Relay Chat (IRC) or threaded discussion software archives the interactions via a text-based, time-coded transaction log. Thus, conversation analysts are challenged to consider these virtual conversations as potentially rich sources of data about how on-line learning, instruction, or work may occur. Theoretical discussions of the status of virtual conversations have just recently begun to surface in the CA literature (Hutchby, 2001). Issues such as interpersonal relations, social identities, and frameworks for participation have been researched (Jones, 1995). Garcia and Jacobs (1999) conducted a comparative analysis of turn-taking in a synchronous chat with the two-party turn-taking structures identified by Sacks et al. (1974) that revealed that these virtual conversations indeed (a) have normative characteristics, (b) exhibit unique forms of expression, and (c) contain procedures by which newcomers to the conversational environment are initiated in the use of both a and b. For example, the chat environment differs from dyadic face-to-face conversation norms in that simultaneous, multiple-party turn-taking is possible. Nonetheless, conventions for turn-taking exist and it is possible to achieve coherence through the turns in talk. The on-line talk is influenced by the affordances of the chat technology and interface (such as the window to enter talk on the speaker's screen and the public display of all entries on a shared scrolling collection window). Figure 40.1 shows the affordances of a typical chat interface from Blackboard, a widely used Internet course management software package.

Hutchby (2001, pp. 183–184) found four ways (paraphrased below) in which virtual conversations on an IRC differ from face-to-face conversations.

1. Participants can take a turn only by entering text in the text line box and pressing the enter key.
2. There is a temporal lag. The "turn" reaches others only when the sent message is accepted and distributed by the remote server.
3. The lag described in 2 results in disjointed sequential relationships between when talk is produced and when it is "enunciated" or displayed on the public talk space.
4. While all of the above is happening, the conversation is conducted in a scrolling window on the shared public space. Depending on the volume of traffic to the server, prior contributions tied to a specific response or turn may scroll off the screen by the time it reaches the public display.

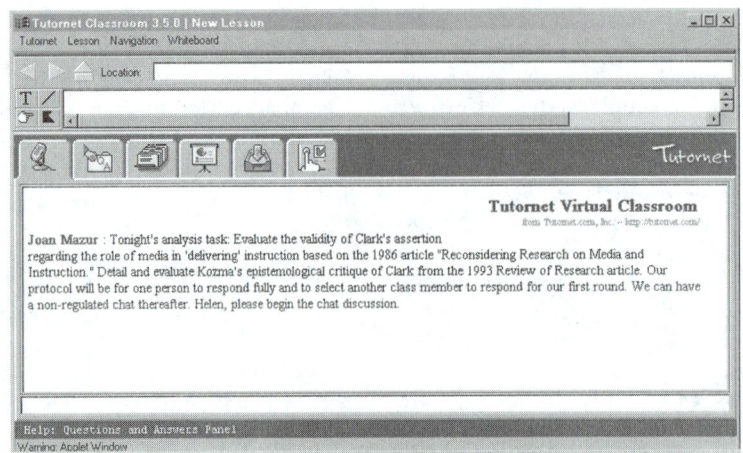

FIGURE 40.1. The Chat tool from the BlackBoard Virtual Classroom feature.

This leads to multichannel conversation that develops coherence through specific word-based strategies such as "naming" (directing a comment to a specific speaker's previous comment) or through the use of another sensory resource: sight. By looking at the text, speakers (as reader/listeners) can maintain turn-taking and develop coherence, even in light of the disappearing scrolling text. These distinct features of virtual conversation imply the need for specific transcription techniques when using the archive of an on-line chat as a data source. These conventions are necessarily still evolving, but some specific strategies that have been employed (Egbert, 1997; Garcia & Jacobs, 1999; Herring, 1999; Hutchby, 2001; Mazur and Jones, 2002) are discussed in the sections on data preparation and transcription that follow.

Unique forms of expression, emoticons, have evolved that approximate sociolinguistic components of speech in text-based talk. Emoticons are iconic representations of emotions that are interspersed with the text-talk to indicate a range of affective responses such as displeasure, :(, or surprise, >:-o. In fact, the use of some emoticons has become so routine in text-based communication that many word processors default to an automatic insertion of a graphic happy face ☺ when one types a :).

As regards initiation into the conventions of on-line talk, any search engine query for Netiquette reveals standardized norms for communicating in text-based communication environments and neophytes to an on-line forum are warned about participation rules, usually including sanctions for "spamming" or other inappropriate behaviors.

40.7 CONDUCTING CA RESEARCH: RESEARCH QUESTIONS AND DATA COLLECTION AND ANALYSIS

The purpose of this section is to lay out in practical terms some of the procedures for conducting a CA for talk that occurs in computer-mediated contexts. These procedures are meant as guidelines rather than formulas or recipes because, as must be clear to the reader by this point, there is much to be explored in both the theoretical and the methodological arenas concerned with the analysis of on-line conversation in its many situated occurrences. Issues related to developing central questions, sampling, data collection, and preparation and data analysis are the topics discussed.

40.7.1 Develop Focus Questions for Research Related to Naturally Occurring Talk

The design of a CA study is similar in approach to any qualitative research design and includes these characteristic features: formulating initial focus questions related to talk-in-interaction, making a plan for obtaining or making recordings of *naturally occurring* interactions, transcribing or obtaining a transcript (in the case of the text archive of an on-line chat), developing inductive, analytic strategies, and elaborating the analysis in conclusions and implications. Questions such as those raised in the Introduction are among those that could be addressed through a rigorous analysis of on-line conversation as it applies to how learning and instruction proceed in these contexts. In the sections that follow specific issues related to CA data collection and analysis are discussed: sampling, collecting, and producing records of conversation, transcription, and other preparation of conversation records.

40.7.2 Sampling Using a "Specimen" Approach

In an insightful discussion of sampling Alasuutari (1995) elaborates on an important methodological point related to the distinctive sampling procedures used in CA. Sampling, in the quantitative sense, represents what he calls a *factist* perspective. This factist perspective is contrasted to what he terms a *specimen* perspective. In the factist approach, sampling is required because the reality under study is not observable and thus indicators of parameters of a population are specified to determine the sample. A researcher cannot directly observe opinions and thus uses a survey to ascertain them from a subject pool. Consequently, to make the results generalizable to the entire population, the sample must be representative.

Using a specimen approach, drawn from techniques in naturalist observation and biology, the reality under study is directly observable in the particular individual. For example, a biologist examining a species of tadpoles would simply choose individuals from that species. Perhaps, by observing the species in some natural setting, the biologist would not choose one that seemed highly unusual, but there would be no need for a statistical sample of tadpoles, as it is the category of species, the specimen, that is of interest. Similarly, a CA study might focus on any *category* of talk-in-interaction such as repairs and then simply select any specimen of conversation generated in a naturalistic setting. As Hutchby (2001, p. 51) has claimed, "The logic of CA, however, in terms of data selection suggests that *any* [his emphasis] specimen is a 'good' one, that is, worthy of intense and detailed examination." From a common-sense perspective as well as from the key disciplinary tenet of CA that conversation has normative dimensions, one can imagine that in any specimen of a data log from an on-line chat one might expect to find exchanges to examine such as greetings, announcements, repairs, and the like. How these types of exhanges are accomplished by conversants using typed, synchronous, or asynchronous postings of text would be an insight that a conversation analysis might illuminate.

40.7.3 Collecting/Producing Records of Conversation

The most important caveat for collecting and producing data for CA is rooted in the concept of *naturally occurring* conversation. Regardless of how it is produced or recorded, the data for CA are always in a sense "primary sources" of talk-in-interaction. Although the more general field of discourse analysis might potentially consider descriptions of witnessed talk-in-interaction as data, those types of accounts would not be considered appropriate for CA. Following is a list of sources of CA information that are typically used to analyze talk-in-interaction. For a discussion of the potentially intrusive effects of recording equipment and how such devices affect the behavior of participants and the natural setting of data collection, the reader is referred to Chapter 39, on qualitative research.

40.7.3.1 Audio Recordings (Analog and Digital). As previously mentioned audio recording, whether analog or digital, was for many years the essential and required source data for CA. Audio recording captured actual speech and recorded the natural sequencing, intonation, and content of conversation. Digital recording has improved on the original method in two key ways. Digital recording maintains its high quality despite repeated playback. Specimens can be more easily selected from the complete conservation because of both random access and the capacities of some tools (such as Imovie software for the Macintosh) easily to provide time-stamped recordings. In computer-mediated contexts such as distributed audio or video

conferencing, analog or digital audio recordings of actual speech continue to be a viable means for documenting interaction.

40.7.3.2 Video Recordings (Analog and Digital). Perhaps simply because of the tradition of using audio recordings, video recordings of talk-in-interaction are not the preferred device of CA researchers, though some recent researchers have been working with video transcripts and have done much to advance the use of video transcripts (Goodwin, 1995; Heath, 1997). In addition to visual aspects of interaction (such as noting gaze, which has been related to turn distribution), video is particularly appropriate when aspects of the physical setting of the conversations are intrinsic to the conversation such as engineers discussing design models. Gestures and other body language are often highly relevant in the context of social activity. In computer-mediated contexts such as distributed digital videoconferencing and compressed video, analog or digital video recordings are a viable (and relatively untapped) means of documenting interaction.

40.7.3.3 Text Logs from On-Line Forums (Synchronous or Asynchronous). Transcriptions of audio or video recordings were for decades the primary source of CA data, and the process of transcription is a time-consuming and arduous task. In today's worlds of CMC, perhaps from some impulse to make the virtual more real and, more practically, because the conversations often occur via the use of typed text that is exchanged between and among on-line conversants, massive text logs of synchronous and asynchronous chats and bulletin boards are available for CA. To prepare a text log "transcription" many modifications to the traditional CA conventions are required. However, the text logs themselves contain "naturally occurring" conversant-generated indications of some of the sociolinguistic dimensions evinced in recordings of speech. The use of emoticons—typed graphics such as ;) to indicate a textual "wink," are an example of this phenomenon quite prevalent in text-based on-line conversations. A discussion of issues regarding transcription for on-line talk is contained in a section that follows.

40.7.3.4 Digital Screen Recordings of On-Line Interactions (Screen Playback). Some kinds of on-line conversations take place within the virtual space of the desktop such as point-to-point videoconferencing. MSN Messenger and Yahoo are two Internet Service Providers who offer on-screen services of this type. Using an inexpensive, small eyeball camera, conversants can engage in computer-mediated face-to-face talks. Using a screen recorder such as HyperCam that captures screen images and stores them as digital movies, a researcher could conduct CA on these types of conversations. Using these types of tools, however, will also require transcription and modifications to the more traditional conventions. For example, transcription conventions such as the use of the symbol (.) to indicate a microsecond pause or the use of parentheses with the numeric symbol (0.7) to denote time delay in talk have to be amended to denote when pauses" are related to technical affordances such as network bandwidth constraints or are actually "pauses" in the conversation. Of course, these technological constraints become part of the social context of the talk and become part of how participants "project" turn constructions, which are participants' determinations of transition relevant places and turn distributions.

40.7.4 Transcription and Other Preparation of Records of Conversation

40.7.4.1 Classic Transcription of Audio and Video Recording. Any discussion of classic CA transcription convention credits Gail Jefferson (1972) with developing the canon of transcription conventions that continues to have utility in the preparation of transcribed verbal interactions to the current day. Table 40.1 contains a modified listing of these standardized conventions. The purpose of this table is illustrative, not exhaustive. Jefferson developed many indicators of nuance and was always alert to opportunities to add to conventions as they played out

TABLE 40.1. Excerpts from Gail Jefferson's Transcription Conventions

Sequencing	
[	A single left bracket indicates the point of the beginning of the overlap.
]	A single right bracket indicates that the point of the utterance or utterance part stops with reference to another utterance.
=	Equal signs, one at the end of a line and one at the beginning of the next, indicate no gap between the lines, often referred to as "latching."
Timed intervals	
(0.0)	The number in parentheses is the elapsed time in silence by tenths of a second. For example, (2.5) is a 2.5-s pause.
(.)	This indicates a miniscule gap pause in or between utterances.
Speech production	
Word	Underscored words indicate a form of stress in pitch or loudness; sometimes an alternative is used, printing the stressed part of the word in *italics*.
::	Colons are used to indicate elongation of the immediately preceding sound. Multiple colons are used to indicated a more prolonged sound.
.,??	Punctuation marks are used to show characteristics of speech production. For example, question marks are used to show rising intonation; a period to show falling intonation; and so on.
↑↓	Arrows up or down show rising tone, pitch, amplitude in words.
WORD	Uppercase letters are used to show especially loud sounds compared to words preceding or following.
Transcriber doubts	
( )	Empty parentheses show that the transcriber could not hear words.
(( ))	Double parentheses show the transcriber's additions or descriptions, not actual transcription.

in specific social contexts, such as joking, directing, evaluating, and other social or cognitive functions of talk. As the reader will note, the inclusion of sociolinguistic elements such as raised tone of voice presumes either an audio or a video record of the conversation. In the case of CA for computer-mediated contexts such as audio and video conferencing, these same kinds of conventions would certainly be applicable, with modifications for affordances of the technologies as discussed in a previous section.

These transcription conventions show the arduous task of transcribing talk from speech in naturally occurring situations. The goal of the transcription is to capture descriptively as many dimensions of the talk as is observable in the specimen. By articulating these minute dimensions, the conversation analyst aspires to understand how these dimensions work in concert to create a normative, meaningful interchange.

40.7.4.2 "Transcription" of Real-Time Log Data for Text-Based On-Line Conversation. The task of working from the "transcription" of an on-line, text-based talk-in-interaction differs from the task of transcribing actual natural speech that may be conducted using CMC, although both instances are legitimate subjects for CA. The on-line record of the synchronous chat archive is already in a text form, obviating the process of transcribing speech. However, the logs may still be in need of processing that approximates the conceptual task of transcription, which is to provide descriptive detail to the words to assist in analysis of the normative characteristics of the talk-in-interaction. Do examples of such processing of on-line archived texts exist in the literature? Hutchby (2001, p. 178) uses an arrow to focus on a speaker and threads in a multiparty conversation from on-line chat. In the example in Table 40.2 of a chat from my own data, turn-taking is indicated by an arrow (pseudonym initials replace users' actual names). In addition to indicating turn-taking in a thread of conversation, one can also note the use of capital letters by DT when she types the word TYPO! indicating emphasis. Actually, DT is conducting nearly simultaneous threads with RD and LN. One of the most important methodological issues when preparing a chat archive transcript is to indicate clearly, through the use of a Key, the emoticons or typographical "inflections" of participants and those such as the arrows used to indicate the turn-taking thread between LN and DT inserted by the researcher for purposes of analysis.

Clearly the conventions developed by Jefferson and elaborated on by countless researchers in the CA tradition need to be modified and extended for documenting the range of social action accomplished through talk in these on-line contexts where multithread, multiple-participant conversation is possible. For example, in a recent analysis, the use of a *conversation map*, a technique that built on the work of Levin, Kim, and Riel (1990) using message maps and Herring's (1999) multiple-thread schematics, was helpful to orient spatially the various topic threads occurring over time in a synchronous chat (Mazur & Jones, 2002).

40.7.4.3 Documentation of the Affordances and Conventions of the CMC Forum Environment. In preparing the data for analysis it is obviously crucial to describe thoroughly the

TABLE 40.2. Excerpt from an On-Line Chat Used for Teacher Professional Development (Mazur & Jones, 2002)

	RCMC:120300
1	RD: What are you currently doing in class?
2	DT: Just finished the Connected Math unit "Prime
3	Time"—dealt with factors, multiples, LCM & GCF. Will be beginning the unit
4	"Bits & Pieces" this
5	week—decimals, fractions & percents. Also, we are very heavily using Accelerated Math
6	RD: I don't know whether you looked at Pizza Pirate,
7	but that activity was chosen for doing decimals, fractions, and percents.
8	RD: welcome back LN
9	RD: When you come back like that, do you see the
10	comment by DT about she has just been doing in class?
11	LN: I accidentally hit refresh.
12 →	LN: Yes, I'm not familiar with this material, but I'd
13	like to learn more.
14 →	DT: Yes! I have used it in the past and emailed class
15	members trying to find it again. I cannot locate mine. PR and I were
16	wanting to use it with
17	a class we are teaching as part of our 21st CCLCI
18	RD: OK, I had no idea who are requested it because I
19	didn't recognize the username.
20 →	DT: RD, Would you possibly be able to find a
21	hard copy of Pizza Pirate?
22 →	LN: What is the 21st CCLCl?
23	RD: Of the problem statement?
24 →	DT: TYPO! 21st Century Community Learning
25	Center

affordances and known conventions or normative behaviors of the computer-mediated conversational environment. This means articulating the communication channels such as audio, visual, or textual and, in the case of most on-line newsgroups, chats or bulletin boards, articulating the posted or known "rules" for engagement (so to speak). Also, it is important to ascertain the possible roles that participants may have in the computer-mediated context. For example, participants may be ordinary speakers, moderators, sysops (system operators), chanops (channel operators), or other roles within the formal computer-mediated system.

The necessary linear presentation in the preceding sections on data preparation belie the interactive, inductive nature of conversation analysis. Although it is useful to use a word processor to number lines and to search and replace names with pseudonyms, for example, the process of grounding theory in the data and the particular circumstances of the observed phenomena is an iterative one. Once data are produced, collected, and transcribed, how exactly might one proceed with the analysis?

40.7.5 Steps for Conducting an Analysis of Conversation

In CA, the analysis proceeds from the perspective of what Psathias (1995) has referred to as "unmotivated looking (p. 45)."

The purpose of this posture toward the data is to affect openness toward induction. The stance is neither atheoretical nor naïve with respect to acknowledging the frames or biases the researcher brings to the qualitative task. Rather, this stance of unmotivated looking is simply a way to achieve an "examination not prompted by pre-specified goals" (Schegloff, 1996).' Given this general frame on the analytic task for conversation analysis, how might one proceed?

Several researchers in many contexts have offered suggestions for the task of systematically analyzing conversation (Pomerantze & Fehr, 1997; Schegloff, 1989; ten Have, 1999). I have summarized and synthesized the work of these three researchers, whose works offer the most concrete suggestions for doing a CA that I have read.

40.7.5.1 Select a Sequence. Select either a purposive or an arbitrarily selected segment of a transcript and carefully read and reread the segments, focusing on how the talk is organized. Sequences can be difficult to define, especially in multithreaded on-line conversation. A good tip is that a sequence has usually ended when speakers are no longer responding to a prior action (initiation, repair) or topic. Stay open to the possibility that discrepant cases involving unusual initiations or cues or unusual closures that spur other sequences may be in evidence.

40.7.5.2 Characterize the Sequence. Answer the question, "What is the speaker doing in this turn?" What is the topic of the conversation? Is the person trying to initiate, repair (clarify, elaborate), or close an interaction? Keeping in mind that the interpretations of the action may change as the analysis proceeds, try to understand what is accomplished in the turns (Does the speaker try to get the floor? Is the attempt successful? What reference terms are used? How does the talk set up options for recipients?). What is the meaning of the interaction? How is meaning conveyed, received, coconstructred through interaction? What do participants talk about, and how do they signal topic changes or the need to stay on a certain point? Understanding the purpose of the turn can be a complicated task, and inference is necessarily ambiguous.

40.7.5.3 Consider the Rights, Obligations, and Expectations Constituted in the Talk. In the course of establishing conventions within talk-in-interaction, inferences can be drawn about the identities, roles, and relationships among and between the participants. These conventions are often obvious in who initiates topics, who closes sequences, and the ways in which these closures or initiations are understood by participants. Aspects of how talk can be used to mount a social critique within the context and issues related to social status as it plays out in talk often emerge within this dimension of analysis. Keep in mind that silence has a powerful voice in conversation and that, as is often the case in qualitative analysis, what is not present can be as telling as what is.

By reading and rereading and focusing in on particular dimensions of conversation such as the sequences of turn-taking or repairs that support topic shifts, the conversation analysis proceeds. Observing and documenting unique patterns that become conventional modes of interacting to inquire, confirm, contradict, or elaborate discussed topics is at the core of the analysis of conversation.

40.7.6 Ethical Considerations When Collecting Conversational Data

40.7.6.1 *The Notion of a "Public" On-Line Forum.* Even though an on-line chat or forum may indeed be "public," that is, the chat logs are archived and available for group inspection, it is important for the researcher to maintain an ethical posture toward informing participants that their work will be the subject of an analysis either by a "participant-observer" or by an external researcher. Additionally, even if access to an on-line conversation is "password" protected, it is still possible to be in virtual attendance without the specific knowledge of the participants. This can occur most easily if the researcher obtains a password or permission to join the on-line conversation from the facilitator but not the participants. Unless there is a specific, conceptually justifiable rationale to deceive participants, I recommend obtaining permission to participate or view retrospectively conversational data in on-line chats or discussion forums. On-line information is highly accessible and it is (perhaps) too easy simply to print it off and import it into your word processor as electronic text overlooking a critical tenet of ethical research, informed consent.

40.7.6.2 *Requirements for Informed Consent from Participants.* In checking with the Institutional Research Boards (IRB) at several Carnegie Research Institutions, I was told that publicly available data, that is, public chat forums or discussion boards that *do not* use passwords, *do not* require informed consent of participants or any contact with the IRB. However, when a password is required to participate, some expectation of privacy is inferred and thus a researcher should take steps to obtain informed verbal or written consent as deemed appropriate by the governing IRB. Regardless of whether the research is conducted as part of university work or for independent consulting firms, ethical issues need to be considered. As an example, to conduct a CA of an on-line chat (which required a password) used for professional development by middle-school mathematics teachers, I first contacted the university faculty moderator by e-mail, then via a phone interview (Mazur & Jones, 2002). After explaining the purpose of the research, supported by an independent, nonacademic business leadership group interested in educational change, I asked the moderator if he would introduce me to the chat group and elicit their consent for me to "lurk"—my intention was to observe, not participate in the chat. Finally, I requested that the moderator ask chat group members to e-mail their verbal consent to me "off-chat" to deter any implication of pressure to comply by requiring that participants publicly accept my participation and monitoring of the group's on-line chatting. In this case all of the participants consented. Had a participant refused consent, I had decided that that person's talk would not be included in any analysis. However, I did not have to deal with that issue. The extent to which excluding

segments of conversation based on a participant's failure to consent affects the overall CA remains an open methodological question.

40.7.7 A Case Example: Conducting a CA of an On-Line Chat

The conduct of a CA is a time-consuming and detailed task. The analysis of 9 months of a once-weekly 2-hr chat took this author and a graduate assistant 6 months (and there remains an additional year of chats to analyze!). To give a concrete example of CA in a computer-mediated context, I outline below the steps we took to conduct the CA of this particular on-line chat. The chat forum was used for ongoing professional development and follow-up to a middle-school mathematics teacher academy (Mazur & Jones, 2002). A cautionary note: The step-by-step approach detailed here is intended to be succinct and informative and is *not* intended to be formulaic or prescriptive. Although I believe that these procedures are essential elements of a CA, they are by no means all inclusive or mandatory. The character of the particular forum and the context in which it is situated should be overarching frames for deciding on the procedures that will yield the richest analysis.

Of course, any inquiry begins with *a question*. For this study our question was "How does the teachers' talk (within the chat environment) support/hinder the development of a community of practice as defined by Wenger (1999)?" our procedures in this case are outlined below.

Step 1: Obtain Required Permissions to Observe or Participate in the On-Line Forum

For this case, research done external to a university environment, formal IRB approval was not required. However, permissions to observe the forum were obtained from participants nonetheless through an appeal for introductions and permission to the forum moderator.

Step 2: Compile the Entire Record of the On-Line Talk

The chat archives were accessed, and with the use of a word processor for cutting and pasting, we compiled the entire 10 months' of weekly chat interactions into a single text record (the transcript) of the chat.

Step 3: Prepare the Transcript for Analysis

The complete chat record was "scrubbed" of identifying data and electronic text "noise" such as symbols like <email address> that made reading the text difficult. Be careful *not* to delete emoticons, etc., that are cogent to the meaning of the text-based conversation. Decisions were also made about changing actual names or "handles" to initials to ensure anonymity further. The lines for the complete record were numbered and dates were converted to numerics (e.g., January 3, 2001, was 010301) to denote sections of chat "sessions." See Table 40.2 above for an example of the cleaned data.

Step 4: Read the Transcript

We read the entire transcript to familiarize ourselves with the participants, content, and other elements of the chat. During this initial read one can begin to be cognizant of turn-taking, who is talking, what topics are being discussed, the length of sessions, and the like. This particular chat had from 7 to 15 regular participants. Summaries of the chat logs were developed. The following summary of data was compiled from the entire 10-month chat log. This summary reports the following information: the dates participants went on-line to chat (or attempt to chat), the number of participants in the chat room at one time, and, finally, the number of minutes the chat was active.

Dates of conversations (or attempts):

a. 9/24 (attempt/2 participants)
b. 9/25 (attempt-time to meet suggested/2 participants)
c. 9/26 (attempt-time to meet established/1 participant)
d. 9/27 (full conversation/1 participant w/facilitator; 55 min)
   9/28 (attempt, full conversation w/facilitator and 1 participant, 16 min)
f. 10/02 (full conversation w/facilitator and 1 participant, 20 min; 1 participant attempted afterward,16 min)
g. 10/05 (4 participants w/facilitator, 76 min)
h. 10/12 ((4 participants w/facilitator, 64 min)
i. 10/13 (attempt/facilitator waited 12 minutes after check in)
j. 10/19 (5 participants w/facilitator, 141 min)

There are, of course, much larger chat forums that would require the researcher to observe or participate for a specified period of time (a week, a month, etc.). Then data-based decisions to focus on several specific participants or on one topic or day, etc., might be in order.

Step 5: Define the Sample "Specimen"
Related to Step 4 is the decision regarding the "specimen" sample. In the case of the middle-school math teachers' chat, a content specimen (that involved two, 2-hr consecutive weekly chats) was selected that focused on the discussion of the classroom implementation of an activity related to proportional reasoning using a pizza pie as a "manipulative." Because the purpose of the on-line chat was for professional development and to build an on-line community of practice (1999), we were interested in their use of conversation to learn, use, or discuss content.

Step 6: Analyze the Specimen: Examine the CA Elements
With content in the defined specimen as the frame, we examined the specimen for exchanges (greetings, repairs, etc.), turn-taking and sequencing, and related conversational elements (expressions of emotion). We also used Burnett's (2002) typology of exchanges to characterize the participation in the online conversation.

Step 7: Contextualize the CA Theoretically
Because the analysis in this case study was focused on how participants *used* talk to share or learn content and build a community of practice (Wenger, 1999), elements of CA such as turn-taking and sequencing were related to how they supported development of a community of practice along each of four dimensions: identity, community, practice, and meaning. Thus, the highly consistent rules and interactions regarding patterns in greetings when participants entered the chat were related conceptually to the development of community (learning as belonging according to Wenger). The normative characteristics of participants' conversations comprised the specific evidence of the development of a community of practice through their talk.

This case illustrates one approach to the use of a specific on-line chat for teacher professional development. A subsequent section, Research Synthesis, further explores additional possibilities for using on-line conversations as a basis for understanding the experiences of participants in a variety of on-line communication forums.

40.8 THE RESEARCHER'S TOOLKIT: HARDWARE, NETWORK TOOLS, AND SOFTWARE FOR CA

When Renata Tesch wrote *Qualitative Research: Analysis Types and Software Tools* in 1990, she legitimized the use of computer software for the qualitative analysis of complex, richly layered narrative, interview, and/or observational data. These tools have continued to improve and today educational technologists who embark on CA have many options for their toolkit. Moreover, very recent advances in digitizing audio and video have addressed some mundane, but critical, issues in data manipulation. For example, the erosion of quality inherent in analog magnetic audiotape data reproduction through multiple replays and the difficulties in precisely locating information inherent in the use of analog recording technology are obviated by digital audio records. In the following sections I discuss several (but by no means do I claim all) tools that may be useful for CA.

40.8.1 Word Processors

The remarkable functions of the word processor to process text-based data of all kinds clearly make it a key tool for CA. Features typical in all current versions of word processors include line numbering, search and replace, and symbol and character maps, and myriad options for formatting and displaying text representations through the use of tables, inserted graphics, and other text enhancements are invaluable for processing data for transcriptions used in CA.

40.8.2 Qualitative Text Analysis Programs

Qualitative text analysis software such as ATLASti (Scolari, 2002) and NVIVO (QSR, Inc., 2002) may also prove useful for CA. These types of programs provide tools for coding and restructuring the data along categorical dimensions defined by the researcher. Using this kind of software, which typically utilizes multiple windows to categorize, link, and sort data, it is possible to develop graphical "tree" displays of related text data chunks and to group data in "families" to support complex analyses. ATLASti (Fig. 40.2) can accommodate audio and visual data.

Although this author has used these programs for various projects, CA has not been among them. Certainly grouping exchanges, turn-taking, multiple threads, or message content graphically might prove to be very illuminating examples of how these tools can be used for documenting and categorizing conversations. Candidly, I would note that some users report that these kinds of programs do have a rather steep learning

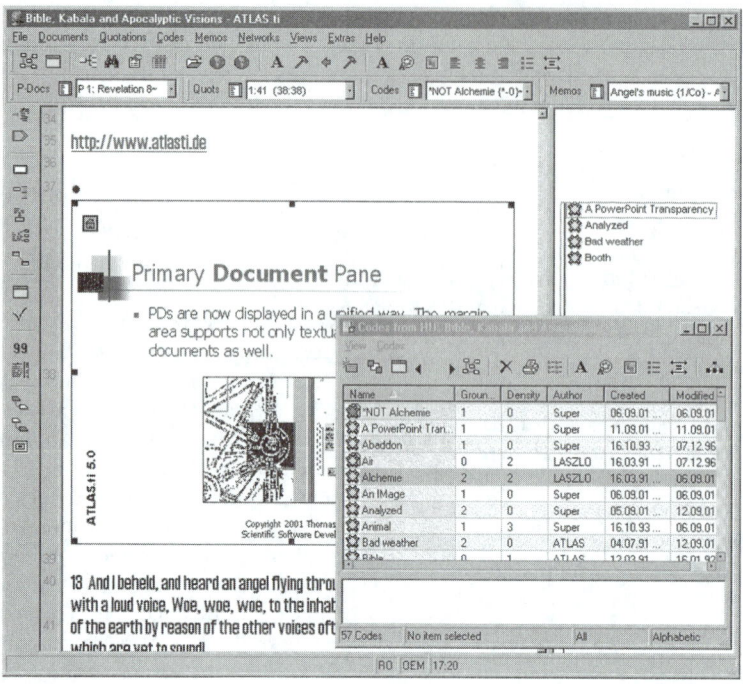

FIGURE 40.2. The ATLASti interface displaying numerous features and tools for categorizing and relating qualitative data.

curve; the CA neophyte may find word processors just as useful for many kinds of analysis tasks.

40.8.3 Graphical Cluster Displays of "Neural Net" Text Data

CATPAC is software described by the program's creators as

a neural network program that has been designed to read and understand text of any kind. CATPAC, available at *http://www. thegalileocompany.com*, works by learning the interrelationships among words and phrases in the text, and can identify the underlying concepts in a text after only a single reading.

CATPAC works by sliding a window through the text, typically seven words at a time, so that the window will first contain words 1 through 7, then words 2 through 8, and so on. Each word that CATPAC "sees" is associated with an artificial neuron in the program's simulated brain. Whenever two or more neurons are "active"—that is, present in the window—the connection between them is strengthened by a small amount. Connections are also weakened through a simulation of forgetting. The program has the capacity to generate a "dendogram," a graphical display of the density of the text as shown in Fig. 40.3.

I have included this tool because I suspect that it has untapped potential to assist in the analysis of conversation transcriptions. For example, a recent study of the content of an on-line community of practice used this tool to examine the density of the discourse on various topics (deLaat, 2001).

To use text excerpts in CATPAC an ASCII text is required and thus the possibility of stripping out key transcription tags is

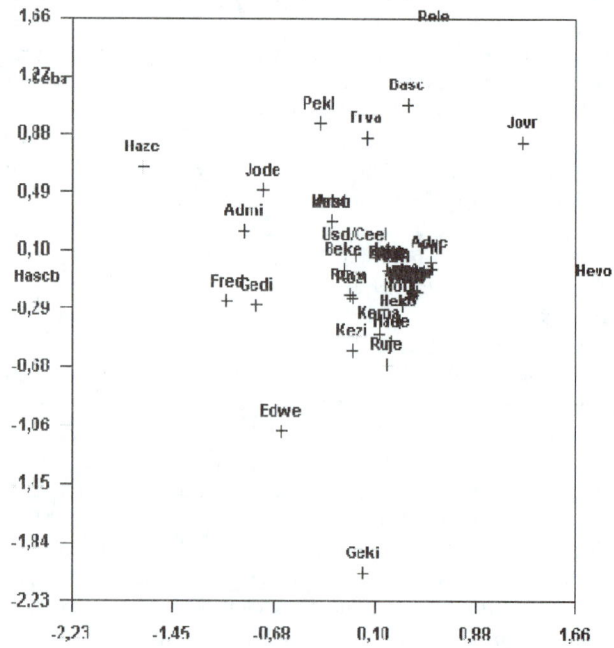

FIGURE 40.3. Graphical CATPAC display shows the density of word occurrences arrayed on an arbitrary scale that denotes relationships of themes or codes (adapted from deLaat, 2001).

possible. Certainly, clusters of certain text representations such as emoticons might prove useful as part of a CA.

40.8.4 Transcription of Video Data

Transana, software developed by Fastnach and maintained by D. Woods and at the University of Wisconsin Center for Education Research, is available as a free download at http://www.transana.org. According to the Web site description, Transana

facilitates the transcription and analysis of video data. It provides a way to view video, create a transcript, and link places in the transcript to frames in the video. It provides tools for identifying and organizing analytically interesting portions of videos, as well as for attaching keywords to those video clips. It also features database and file manipulation tools that facilitate the organization and storage of large collections of digitized video.

Be cautioned that the download contains digital video examples and is in excess of 80 Mb. The Transana screen is shown in Fig. 40.4.

40.8.5 Computer Tracking Logs

The internal archiving features of any text-based on-line chat, bulletin board, newsgroup, or threaded discussion are essentially time-and date-stamped text logs of the typed-in talk. The software for these on-line forums typically keeps track of general use statistics such as how many users participate (often astonishingly high numbers, in the thousands in any 24-hr period), the type of conversation tool used (a synchronous chat or asynchronous threaded discussion), and the amount of time spent in the forum. Without the specific text of the conversation, such "statistics" are of little interest to those interested in discourse analysis or CA.

There are also internal tracking tools that operate on the network servers that support these on-line forums. These tools are available as inexpensive Internet downloads, which may have as yet untapped potential for documenting on-line talk-in-interaction. The AXS tracking utility is available at http://www.xav.com/scripts/axs. The installation of this utility on a server may require some technical assistance to accommodate the Perl programming language. This AXS utility provides graphical and real-time log data analysis. Another free, open-source Internet data-gathering option that uses Active Server Page (ASP) programming and Access for the database function is available at http://www.2enetworx.com/dev/projects/statcountex.asp. Specifically, one can envision the need to document a student's "hits" in a Web-based instructional unit that might be cross-referenced with on-line synchronous mentoring of a student who was exploring the information on that site. Again, although these kinds of on-line talk-in-interaction are not commonly used or researched, the potential for this type of conversation clearly exists. In fact, the entire area of on-line facilitation and

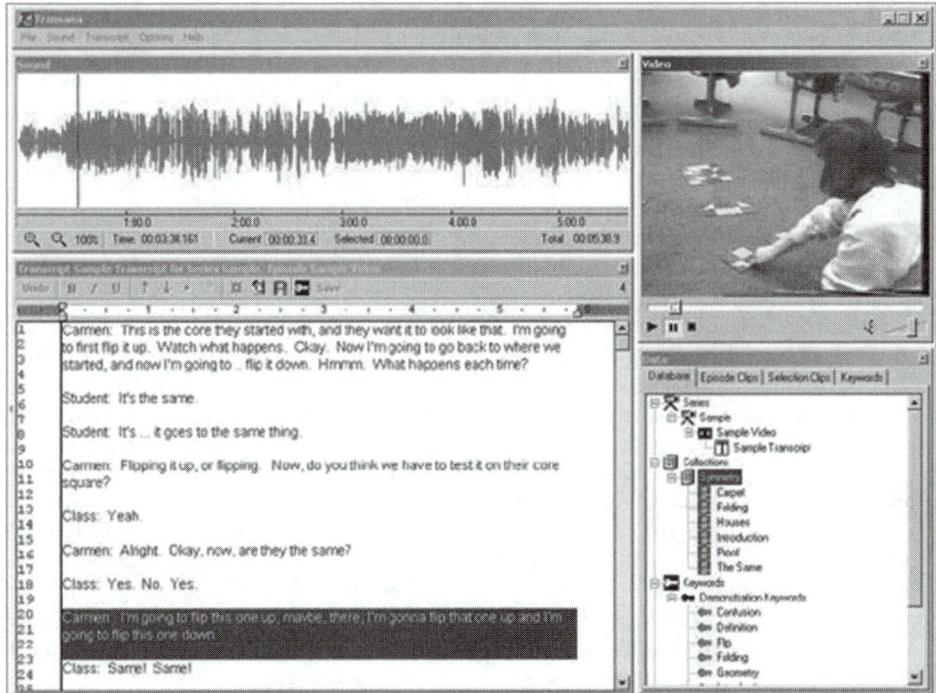

FIGURE 40.4. The main Transana screen showing multiple windows for displaying video, transcription, and database options.

so-called e-moderating has only recently received serious attention (Collison, Elbaum, Haavind, & Tinker, 2000; Salmon, 2000).

40.8.6 Screen Recorders of On-Screen Interactions

In complex, multimedia on-line environments it may be fruitful to consider the use of a "playback" screen recorder. In some ways this type of tool may be better suited to research that focuses on HCIs, but clearly the data produced—real-time visual archives of each click or mouse movement—may be required in multiple-mode conversational environments such as the use of Instant Messaging (which is not archived in the typical chat sense) in conjunction with digital video record of a desktop videoconference conversation. Hypercam is an excellent screen recorder tool for the PC that is available for about $30 at http://www.hyperionics.com.

40.8.7 Additional Tools for Visualizing Conversation

Donath, Karahalios, and Viegas (1999) have noted insightfully that whereas archival text data of on-line conversations is searchable and highly useful in many respects, the text display is not particularly useful for depicting the inherent social patterns and relationships. These representational problems are exacerbated in graphical "microworld"-type environments available on the World Wide Web for chatting that use avatars to represent conversants. Two tools, Chat Circles, a graphical interface for synchronous conversation, and Loom, a visualization of threaded discussions (p. 2), have been developed for the purposes of investigating these underlying social patterns in these kinds of highly visual, graphically represented on-line conversation forums. The Chat Circle tool displays a "Conversation Landscape," which is a two dimensional model that shows conversations as lines that become wider with the length of the message. Periods of silence are brought into sharp focus with this kind of conversation representation. Loom uses connected lines on a two-dimensional display to illustrate connections between postings. Various types of conversation groups (focused on narrow topics or free-for-all forums, for example) yield very different visual "gestalts" in their Loom display patterns, more intricate threading from user to user in the more open-ended forum.

By using Internet search engines many tools of these kinds can be found. Some are associated with quality control and performance improvement consulting companies, and the tools accompany those services. Others are available as freeware or shareware for purposes of documenting on-line interactions. The tools for researching conversation in on-line environments noted in this section mirror the many-faceted dimensions of on-line talk and interaction and reflect the diversity of the possibilities for inquiry into how, what, and why on-line talk has become such a part of daily life.

40.9 RESEARCH SYNTHESIS: HISTORICAL PERSPECTIVE AND FRAMES FOR THE ANALYSIS OF ON-LINE CONVERSATION FOR EDUCATIONAL TECHNOLOGISTS

In this section, I provide an historical overview and synthesis of salient research findings related to the foundational work on classroom talk and to research trends in CA as it is being applied to research on new modes of technology-involved conversation. This synthesis is intended to be illustrative of the research traditions in CA as they might be most applicable to the work of educational technologists interested in examining computer-mediated conversation. As a part of that task, I include several frameworks that have a research base and for which there seems to be much promise for developing a multifacet research agenda for investigating on-line talk-in-interaction. Several topics are presented in this section.

1. a brief historical overview that begins with salient work in classroom talk;
2. the interaction analysis model developed by an in-depth qualitative investigation of a global on-line debate, a pioneering effort to investigate such a networked conversation in light of social knowledge construction;
3. social network analysis, a framework borrowed from communication theory that has many potential applications to CMC conversation and interaction;
4. a typology of exchanges within a virtual community, a framework that addresses the conversational and communal aspects of on-line interaction; and, finally,
5. The social, linguistic, and interactional frames contained in the area of researching so-called *persistent conversation*—work that has integrated strategically interests from linguistics, social communication and learning, and CA—to investigate specifically how and why on-line conversations "persist" in the face of the many challenges that communicating in on-line environments poses.

40.9.1 A Brief Historical Overview

40.9.1.1 *Building on Previous Work Investigating Classroom Talk.* Although CA is clearly embedded in sociology and its elaboration in ethnomethodology, it is its application to educational contexts that concerns the efforts in this chapter. The appropriation of discourse analysis and CA techniques from sociology and linguistics in educational research began in the late 1960s and seemed to reach a zenith in the mid-1980s. Although it is my hope that research on on-line interaction will avoid the pitfall of superficial, inappropriate comparisons with "face-to-face" conversations (as often occurs, for example, between distance education and face-to-face learning), there is unquestionably a valuable history of examining classroom talk (Edwards & Westgate, 1987) that can inform our investigations of current

on-line conversation. In fact, some of the strongest evidence for the "teacher-centeredness" of classroom instruction was provided by the analysis of classroom interactions. In 1978 Mehan reported findings on a persistent, widely evidenced interaction pattern in classroom talk. The initiation–response–evaluation (I-R-E) model he induced through the use of a constant comparison technique is so prevalent that it can be identified in virtually all classrooms to this day. Constant comparison involves defining a typology based on evidence and discarding it only when a discrepant case is found. According to Mehan's model, the instructor asks a question or poses a problem, the student responds, and the instructor then "evaluates" (often by repeating and intoning finality and correctness) the student's response. Once aware of the I-R-E pattern one can easily see how the authority of the teacher's talk (and ideas) is achieved as speech in action. If the "evaluation" response by the teacher is absent, students get the idea the response is faulty in some way. Carlsen (1990) provided a comprehensive review of questioning in classrooms in which he reviews research in terms of two prevalent paradigms focused on teacher–student interaction: the "process–product" paradigm and the "sociolinguistic" paradigm (p. 157). Within the process–product paradigm research findings focus on the relationship between discrete observable teacher practices and student outcomes. Using taxonomies of teacher behaviors, such as those developed by Flanders (1970), the effects of teacher action and talk on student outcomes are deduced. These actions can be experimentally manipulated and researchers in the process–product tradition seek to modify student outcomes by changing teacher behaviors. Within the sociolinguistic paradigm, the central beliefs are that classroom talk is context dependent and that contexts are constituted and modified by speakers in the course of conversation. Research in the sociolinguistic tradition of research has yielded insight into the context of questions, the content of questions and the responses, and participants' reactions to questions. The epistemological differences in these two paradigms are apparent, and although each tradition has offered insight into classroom practices related to teacher action and talk, the sociolinguistic tradition of research on classroom talk is clearly more consonant with the perspectives on discourse analysis and CA described in this chapter.

40.9.1.2 Research on e-Mail and On-Line Networked Conferencing: Mid 1980s–Early 1990s. From the mid-1980s into the early 1990s there was a bubble of research activity in fields traditionally unrelated to education technology that sought to understand the emerging discourse patterns within the contexts of new communication technologies. The fields of sociology and linguistics continued to pursue CA in the context of the then-emerging on-line technology of choice, electronic mail. Journals such as *Discourse Processes*, *Written Communication*, *Human Society*, *Research on Language and Social Interaction*, *The American Journal of Sociology*, and *Studies in Social Interaction* were among the publications in which discourse analysis of e-mail appeared. Evidence began to accumulate that on-line forums might encourage broader and deeper participation in group activities (Kiesler, Siefel, & McGuire,

1984; Pullinger, 1986; Spitzer, 1989). CMC was seen to enable participation of handicapped students (Batson, 1988) and to encourage the participation of students often marginalized in face-to-face classroom settings such as women and minorities (Hiltz, 1986; Meeks, 1985). In 1991, Selfe and Meyer challenged some of those rosier assumptions in an exploratory study of the gender and power relationships that tested the claims of the so-called equalizing effects of anonymity in on-line forums used for student-centered collaborative writing. This work followed on the 1990 work by Cooper and Selfe related to evolving power relations in on-line contexts. These researchers found evidence that mutually constructed conversations formed normative discourse patterns of resistance related to authority roles in computer conferences. The October 1991 issue of *Written Communication* included research on the use of e-mail as a vehicle for peer response (Mabrito, 1991) that found that there were differences in conversation strategies of high- and low-apprehensive college writers in giving and accepting feedback about their writing. Sproul and Kessler (1988) reported on the problem of reduced social context cues as impediments to clear communication. Rice and Love (1987) examined socioemotional content in a computer mediated network. These researchers found that such content was essential to the engagement of participants and helped to establish "elationships" that played out in the both the content of the talk and the turn-taking conventions. Other researchers were focusing on how the affordances of on-line conferencing technologies were disrupting the usual temporal and spatial situations of face-to-face conversation (Black, Levin, Mehan, & Quinn, 1983).

Daly et al. (1987) developed a protocol analysis technique using accomplished typists as subjects. They used a think-aloud protocol to elicit subjects' cognitions while the subjects used the text channel on a computer conferencing tool to converse. Using this admittedly flawed though inventive technique, these researchers were able to provide corroborating evidence for three general cognitive processes in conversation: inferencing, planning, and coping with maxim violations (p. 229). Maxims, as defined by Grice (1975), have to do with expectations between conversants related to contributions to conversation. The "quantity" maxim asserts that one should say enough but not too much, whereas the quality maxim relates to truthfulness. Research in this vein relates to cognitive models of discourse and conversation.

40.9.1.3 Revived Interest in Features of Electronic Discourse: The Late 1990s. For reasons that are unclear, after some years of waning interest, research activity in on-line or electronic discourse picked up in the late 1990s. Quite possibly the surge of participation in on-line communities that use both synchronous and asynchronous forums for purposes as diverse as Internet dating, professional development, and primary training for business and industry spurred researchers to focus again on these CMC contexts. Abdullah (1998) asserts that despite the fact that on-line conversation is written, it has nonetheless evolved to have a distinctly informal and conversational tone through the use of incomplete sentences, the use of lowercase letters to begin sentences, and uncorrected spelling.

These indiscretions, totally unacceptable in formal written communications, affect the casual immediacy of spoken interaction. Moreover, "readers" as listeners in these on-line conversations overlook the grammatical transgressions and focus on the emoticons and other cues, including the umms and errrs embedded in the text as clues to the tone and import of various phrases (Davis & Brewer, 1997). A manual called *Wired Style: Principles of English Usage in the Digital Age* also signals the standardization of on-line text-talk conventions (Hale, 1996). A more serious question for education researchers is how to evaluate the extent to which postings to on-line discussions and chats represent evidence of students' knowledge, reasoning, and understanding. The situational rhetoric on on-line conversation differs markedly from the erudite discourse of academia.

Issues of power, identity, and critical theoretical analysis have also resurfaced. Kolko (1998, 1999, 2000) has examined the use of linguistic patterns to represent identity discursively in on-line conversations. As more participants become entrenched in on-line forums and communities of discourse and rhetoric evolve, examinations of the extent to which on-line forums are sites for various aspects of social reproduction will become critical to our understanding of how conversation might be used mitigate those effects. Privacy and the balance of public and private space are also a concern as the tension between the containment of the individual and the coconstructed nature of self in community evolves.

40.9.2 Social Interaction and On-Line Community: New Frames for Conversation Analysis for the Twenty-first Century

As often occurs in educational research, some paradigms seem to recycle in somewhat modified forms as investigations of new contexts for learning are conducted. The context of the online community has begun to surface as a central notion in examinations of conversation and interaction in on-line forums. Of course language is central to a learning community to support negotiation and collaboration among peers. Information sharing through conversation and dialogic interaction is endemic to the functions of a learning community (John-Steiner & Mahn, 1996). Interestingly, research in the traditions of both the process–product paradigm and the sociolinguistic paradigms articulated by Carlsen (1991) seem to be in evidence as this current body of research accumulates. However, in the process–product vein, rather than focusing on how teacher behaviors might change outcomes within classroom interactions, the focus is on how self-directed behavior or group behavior might change learning outcomes or perceptions of outcomes. In their article "Socio-cognitive Constructs and Characteristics of Classroom Communities: An Exploration of Relationships," Gallini and Zhang (1997) conclude that factors such as "preferences to work independently" and "preferences to work in groups" constituted a "task structure" variable. Presumably manipulation of this variable would affect outcomes for these students. These variables are predetermined and can be experimentally manipulated using quasi-experimental methods. Although the authors

conclude that "through e-mail, students become immersed in the discourse structures of inquiry, conjecture, evidence and proof (p. 336)", their methods include no conversation analysis to support this claim. A sociolinguistic approach would have utilized more inferential methods and CA to examine how the e-mail transcriptions of talk-in-interaction achieved these constructivist learning outcomes.

More consonant with the sociolinguistic paradigm, several frameworks have been used recently to analyze on-line interaction and talk in on-line networked environments.

40.9.2.1 An Interaction Analysis Model for the Examination of Social Knowledge Construction. Gunawardena, Lowe, and Anderson (1997) developed their pioneering *interaction analysis model* to address lacunae in the research on participant interaction in on-line forums. Despite the technical capacity to log and tabulate more superficial aspects of participation, such as who participates or the duration and pattern of on-line activity, such research does not address the quality of the interaction. Information about how or if learning or knowledge constructions (or coconstructions in the case of on-line talk) occurred or insights into how such learning or knowledge construction may be supported or hampered was unavailable. Such analyses can be achieved only through careful attention to the content of the particular on-line interactions. By asserting this problem, Gunawardena and her colleagues encountered another lack: the paucity of analytic frameworks through which to examine the quality of on-line interaction.

An analysis of the content of messages exchanged during a week-long, global on-line "debate" with 554 list subscribers was conducted as part of preconference activities for the 1995 XVI World Conference of the International Council on Distance Education. The researchers developed an interaction analysis model based on the content of the on-line talk in this debate forum for the specific purpose of understanding the processes of negotiating meaning and coconstruction of knowledge in a collaborative learning environment. Prior to elaborating their interaction analysis model, they are careful to articulate the local circumstances and context of the data source. First, the participants were participants in a distance-education conference, and the topic was a controversial one, proposed as a purposely reduced statement, "No Interaction, No Debate," to fuel partisan participation. Second, although participants were free to chose whether to participate on the affirmative or negative side of the question, the debate had rules that circumscribed the general content of postings during the week-long event. For example, on day 1 the first affirmative was posted by the team leader and arguments in favor of the proposition had to be posted within that 24-hr period. The "team leader" was tasked with summarizing the day's postings on the affirmative side. This organizational scheme was applied throughout the week, alternating elements typical of general debate formats, first negative, affirmative rebuttal, and so forth. Consequent to the formalizing functions of this debate format, many of the social dimensions that might be evident in a more loosely structured forum were not in evidence in the on-line talk of these participants.

Using the naturally occurring talk of the debaters, the researchers used the transcripts of the debate and developed the framework in several stages. First, they critically reviewed currently available interaction models and definitions of interaction and interaction analysis. Next, these models were tested on the debate transcript and a new model was developed based on deficiencies seen as part of that exercise. Finally, a new interaction analysis model was developed and then applied to an inductive analysis of themes, patterns, and phases evident in the debate transcript.

The interaction analysis model has five phases related to social knowledge construction in computer conferencing. Each phase is comprised of several operations that can be used to analyze the content of talk-in-interaction. For each phase listed, illustrative operations, rather than complete lists, are noted

Phase I: Sharing/comparison of information. Within this phase operations include (a) a statement of observation or opinion and (b) a statement of agreement from one or more other participants.

Phase II: Discovery and exploration of dissonance or inconsistency among ideas, concepts, or statements. Within this phase operations include (a) identifying and stating areas of disagreement and (b) asking and answering questions to clarify the source and extent of disagreement.

Phase III: Negotiation of meaning/coconstruction of knowledge. Within this phase operations include (a) negotiation or clarification of the meaning of terms and (b) negotiation of the relative weight to be assigned to types of argument.

Phase IV: Testing and modification of proposed synthesis or coconstruction. Within this phase operations include (a) testing the proposed synthesis against "received fact" as shared by participants and/or their culture and (b) testing against existing cognitive schema.

Phase V: Agreement statement(s)/application of newly constructed meaning. Within this phase operations include (a) summarization of agreement and (b) applications of new knowledge.

Gunawardena and her colleagues have added to the discourse on the analysis of on-line talk by adopting the more inclusive definition of interaction as

the totality of interconnected and mutually-responsive messages which make up the conference, and perhaps more: 'interaction' is the entire gestalt formed by the on-line communication among the participants... the process observed in the debate is akin to Salomon's (1993) thinking on "distributed cognitions" where he states individual and "distributed cognitions" interact over time, affecting each other and developing from each other. (p. 407)

These researchers caution against using more fine-grained and detailed analyses of "threaded" language forms and turn-taking (such as the methods described in the preceding sections), which have the potential of losing site of the big picture—losing the forest in the trees, so to speak. They believe that their approach is more useful for understanding the ongoing processes of talk-in-interaction as an ongoing process of knowledge construction rather than threads of conversation that may open or close, knowledge of which does not particularly lead to rich understandings of the interactional activity.

Of course, this position can be countered with attention to the sociological roots of conversation analysis and the hopes that, by understanding naturally occurring talk, we can understand the larger processes, social and cognitive, that are in evidence in on-line talk. Gunawardena and her colleagues point to the phenomenon of a conference that has run its course or "threads" that seem to "dry up" (p. 428). From the perspective of CA, the possibilities to examine the power relationships inherent in the talk, for example, may give clues to the function (or lack thereof) of the forum for the participants. Perhaps threads dry up because participants are cued not to explore "offensive" topics further. Or perhaps, in a more positive vein, they simply have no more to say and closure in turns indicates satisfaction, not dissatisfaction, with the interaction. Quite possibly a combination of CA methods and the interaction analysis model approach might provide triangulation data for research assertions.

40.9.2.2 Social Network Analysis.
Incorporating the levels of interaction from the Gunawardena et al. (1997) model and social network analysis (SNA; Scott, 1991; Wasserman and Faust, 1997), deLaat (2001) analyzed the interaction patterns of an online community of practice within a Dutch police organization. The purpose of the analysis was to ascertain how active the participants were and in the discourse, who the central participants were, and how dense the participation was within the network and to examine the quality of the discourse. SNA was conducted by aggregating the total number of messages sent (as taken from server logs) and detailing the various recipients as "nodes" in the network. When closely examined the researcher discovered that many messages were initiations to which no replies were posted. However, in rechecking the data, deLaat found that some messages that were apparently new messages were in fact "latched" to previous threads. This research indicates how conversation analysis provides the fine-grained tools to examine closely the actual discursive interactions, rather than relying on grosser indicators such as "messages sent." However, the use of the SNA did empirically identify and display the range of interaction within the community. To assess the quality of the discourse, the 233 messages in deLaat's study were coded using the Gunawardena et al. scheme.

40.9.2.3 A Typology of Exchanges Within a Virtual Community.
Another approach to the examination of interaction has been developed by Burnett (2002). At first glance this approach appears to draw on the tradition of discourse as cognition and takes a view of interaction as "information seeking," and Burnett denotes information exchange as the phenomenon of interest in a virtual community. However, the typology developed is based conceptually on Savolainen's (1995) research of nonwork, everyday life information seeking as "a natural component of everyday practices (p. 261; quoted in Burnett, 2002, p. 3). The typology focuses on the *behaviors* of participants as they interact, often within the dislocations of time and space inherent in on-line talk and interaction. The typology with summary explanations is reported here.

40.9.2.3.1 Noninteractive Behaviors.
The noninteractive behavior category is interesting because it provides a framework

for examining participation that seemingly does not exist. Specifically this category refers to the activities of participants who do not type in talk but are actively following along as reader/listeners in the discussion. This activity, often termed *lurking* in on-line forums, might be elaborated to include a more positive term with less voyeuristic connotations, *listeners,* for example. Still, these nonparticipants have been shown to be a large portion of on-line users. Smith (1992) reported that 50% of all messages were written by only 1% of those logged on. By including this category in his typology, Burnett focuses our attention on a significant, though hard to examine, constituency in on-line interaction.

40.9.2.3.2 Interactive Behaviors. The interactive behavior category encompasses the range of posting or active message writing that constitutes the talk-in-interaction of on-line CMC. Interactive behaviors are further broken down into hostile and collaborative/positive behaviors.

A. Hostile Behaviors: Hostile behaviors are comprised of online behaviors that are impolite, uncivil, or outright antisocial in character. Flaming is on-line argumentation usually characterized by large amounts of CAPITALIZED TEXT and emoticons as well as inappropriate or disrespectful language such as the use of racial slurs or profanity. Trolling, the term for deliberate postings of inflammatory or provacative messages, is often used as a form of "initiation" right within the on-line community. Newcomers (termed *newbies*) may be prompted to post corrective, though naïve responses and thus draw the disdainful comments of more seasoned community members. Spamming, the on-line equivalent of junk mail or excessive verbiage, is usually unsolicited and therefore distracting and annoying to participants. Cyber-rape, explicit sexual verbal assaults directed personally at specific participants, is a particularly vicious form of hostile behavior. Among the most well-known cases is perhaps the incident that occurred on LambdaMOO, where a participant was verbally gang-raped by a group of anonymous assailants (Dibbell, 1998). Some argue that the instances of name-calling, hate speech, and other hostile behaviors mirror those in face-to-face interactions, and such behaviors are rooted in personal orientation, rather than communication media. On the other hand, it is plausible to make the case that the anonymity afforded participants is surely related to some users' temerity in expressing hostile behavior through on-line talk.

B. Collaborative Interactive Behaviors: Clearly, the overarching purposes of message exchange are generally positive ones. Collaborative interactive behaviors are further divided into (1) behaviors not specifically oriented toward information and (2) behaviors directly related to either information seeking or providing information to other community members.

(1) Behaviors not specifically oriented toward information include neutral behaviors such as pleasantries and gossip, humorous behaviors, and empathic behaviors that offer emotional or moral support.

(2) Behaviors directly related to either information seeking or providing information to other community members include announcements, queries or specific requests for information (made by community members or participants outside the community or queries presented directly to the community), and group-directed projects.

Taxonomic approaches such as the one taken by Burnett can seem to impose an overly restrictive structure on naturally occurring on-line talk. However, the possibilities to use the techniques and analysis frames from CA as it can be applied within this typology are rich areas for further research. A key element in this typology is the emphasis on the on-line message content and exchange as "behavior" harkening back to the speech act theory roots of CA.

40.9.3 Persistent Conversation

Given that humans are social creatures bent on communicating regardless of the barriers, it should not be surprising that despite the difficulties in achieving contact, coherence, and interaction, conversation using digital, on-line technologies has persisted (Erickson, 1999). No one disputes that CMC differs from the face-to-face experience (Walther, 1996). However, as "persistent conversations" continue in a variety of on-line environments, researchers investigating the ubiquitous phenomenon of on-line talk have begun to integrate the linguistic, social, and moral traditions from which conversation analysis evolved.

Susan Herring (1996) has been a pioneer in investigations of how, despite the purported incoherence of on-line conversation, participants in either asynchronous or synchronous forums have established conventions that reclaim the coherence and personality of conversational interaction. To counter the lacks in simultaneous feedback and disruptions in turn adjacencies, this linguist and others (Cherney, 1999; Condon and Cech, 1996) assert that conversants have adapted to affordances in the medium and normative elements of on-line conversation in evidence. Herring's (1999) research shows consistent evidence for several normative elements: (a) backchannels are minimal postturn responses such as "nods," "giggles," and (?) questioning looks (Cherny, 1999, p. 186); (b) turn change signals are agreed-on cues that denote that one is (or is not) ready to cede the floor; (c) cross-turn references are used especially in multiuser synchronous environments that begin the posting with the user name or the intended recipient, a convention Werry (1996) terms *addressivity*; and (d) topical organization, particularly in asynchronous environments, is achieved through the familiar practice of threading discussions using topical outline formatting to promote coherence in on-line talk. The success of this strategy is a straightforward demonstration of the need to employ elements of the technology of text (Jonassen, 1982) in designing conversational environments. The archiving functions of text-based chat and discussion forums also contribute to the quite literal persistence of conversation in the legacy of an archive of the on-line talk. The archive is a vehicle for so-called lurkers and nonconversants to participate as "readers" of the conversation. This kind of involvement is not trivial and nonconversants can actually feel a part of a conversation in which they have not spoken a word (Mazur, David, Kanappel, & Coe, 2002).

Language is inherent in community and several researchers have refocused efforts along the sociolinguistic dimension (Paolillo, 1999). The effects of how users in CMC environments adapt, reshape, and use new linguistic conventions to retain elements of social interaction are the focus of this work. Through the use of language, "tie strength" and "connections" among participants are in evidence. Although language is clearly a factor in social connection, Paolillo's work has shown that there exists a "more complex arrangement of linguistic variables" that support shared discourse and tie strength in evolving virtual speech communities. How these kinds of ties relate to the capacities for on-line conversation to be used for instruction, learning, and knowledge is as yet uncharted water.

The notion of community has proved to be an enduring one in understanding persistent conversation in cyberspace (Rheingold, 1993). Work has begun to appear examining virtual discourse and networking in the formulation of professional communities (Davis, 1998; Mavis & Brocato, 1998) and communities organized around mutual interest (Carroll & Rosson, 1996) and for a myriad of formal and informal purposes (Isaacs, Tang, & Morris, 1996; Rosson, 1999; Whittaker, 1996). One certainty exists. As computer-mediated conversation persists, so too must research efforts in order to understand the complex interactions among technological affordances, linguistic and sociolinguistic communication, and social learning efforts.

40.10 DIRECTIONS FOR FUTURE RESEARCH: PROMISES AND PROBLEMS OF THE CA APPROACH

Increasingly, the use of CMC for training, instruction, continuing education, and professional development involves conversation and on-line discourse in varying degrees of formal and informal interaction. As on-line talk in its many forms proliferates, the use of CA techniques may be useful to inform the design and evaluation of instruction. For CA to be useful in these tasks, much work needs to be done regarding our understanding of the contexts, content, participant response and reaction, and the social relationships inherent in all this on-line talk-in-interaction. Echoing Mason (1991), I challenge researchers interested in on-line learning and the social dimensions of knowledge, cognition, and instruction to take on the task of in-depth examinations of the content, structures, processes, and meaning of on-line conversation and talk-in-interaction, arduous and time-consuming though it might be. Such investigations can only enhance our understanding of how best to use and design educational experiences for this seemingly ubiquitous communication context.

There are new technology tools for accumulating data for CA. However, new transcription conventions and how best to use these tools to support sophisticated and thoughtful analyses are as yet untapped.

Perhaps the most productive avenue to further research on talk in the naturally occurring settings of these burgeoning on-line communities would be to propose a larger frame of discourse analysis and, within that frame, examine the many aspects of interaction, conversation, and behavior, as they might further inform us on the experiences of participants as they use talk-in-interaction as the primary vehicle for information sharing, knowledge construction, and the development of social relationships that are inherent in all educational endeavors.

ACKNOWLEDGMENTS

I wish to thank David Jonassen and Barb Bischelmeyer for feedback, questions, and comments that improved the content of this chapter and helped clarify my thinking.

References

Abdullah, M. H. (1998). Electronic discourse: Evolving conventions in on-line academic environments. *ERIC Digest*. Available at http://www.ed.gov/databases/ERIC-Digests/ed422593.html.

Alasuutari, P. (1995). *Researching culture: Qualitative method and cultural studies*. Thousand Oaks, CA: Sage.

Amann, K., & Knorr-Cetina, K. (1989). Thinking through talk: An ethnographic study of a molecular biology laboratory. *Knowledge and Society: Studies in the Sociology of Science Past and Present, 8*, 2–26.

Auer, P., Couper-Kuhlen, E., & Muller, F. (1999). *Language in time: The rhythm and tempo of spoken interaction*. New York: Oxford University Press.

Austen, J. (1962). *How to do things with words*. Oxford: Oxford University Press.

Batson, T. (1988, February/March). The ENFI project: A networked classroom approach to writing instruction. *Academic Computing, 32–33*, 55–56.

Black, S. D., Levin, J. A., Mehan, H., & Quinn, N. C. (1983). Real and non-real time interaction: Unraveling multiple threads of discourse. *Discourse Processes, 6*, 59–75.

Brown, G., & Yule, G. (1983). *Discourse analysis*. New York: Cambridge University Press.

Burnett, G. (2002). *Information exchange in virtual communities: A typology*. [On-line]. Available at http://informationr.net/ir/5-4/paper82.html.

Carlsen, W. (1991). Questioning in classroom: A sociolinguistic perspective. *Review of Educational Research, 61*(2), 157–178.

Carroll, J. M., & Rosson, M. B. (1992). Developing the Blacksburg electronic village. *Communications of the ACM, 39*(12), 181–212.

Cazden, C. (1986). Classroom discourse. In M. Wittrock (Ed.), *The handbook of research on teaching* (pp. 432–463). New York: Macmillan.

Cherny, L. (1999). *Conversation and community: Chat in a virtual world*. Stanford, CA: CSLI.

Collison, G., Elbaum, B., Haavind, S., & Tinker, R. (2000). *Facilitating on-line learning*. Madison, WI: Atwood Press.

Cooper, M. M., & Selfe, C. L. (1990). Computer conferences and learning: Authority, resistance, and internally persuasive discourse. *College English, 52*, 847–869.

Condon, S. L., & Cech, C. G. (1996). Functional comparisons of face-to-face and computer-mediated decision making interactions. In S. Herring (Ed.), *Computer-mediated communication: Linguistic, social and cross-cultural perpectives* (pp. 65–80). Amsterdam: John Benjamins.

Coulthard, M. (1985). *Introduction to discourse analysis* (2nd ed.) Harlow: Longman.

Coulthard, M. (1994). *Advances in written and text analysis*. London, New York: Routledge.

Cumming, S., & Ono, T. (1997). Discourse and grammar. In T. Van Dijk (Ed.), *Discourse as structure and process* (pp. 257–291). Thousand Oaks, CA: Sage.

Daly, J. A., Vangelisti, A. L., & Daughton, S. M. (1987). The nature and correlates of communication sensitivity. *Human Communication Research, 14,* 167–202.

Davis, B. H., & Brewer, J. P. (1997). *Electronic discourse: linguistic individuals in virtual space*. Albany: State University of New York. (Available as an on-line e-book.)

Davis, M. (1997). Fragmented by technologies: A community in cyberspace. *Interpersonal Computing and Technology, 5*(1–2), 7–19.

deLaat, M. (2001). *Network and content analysis in an online community discourse*. Paper presented at the Computer-Supported Collaborative Learning Conference. Boulder CO. Available at http://newmedia.colorado.edu/cscl/62.pdf.

Dibbell, J. (1998). *My tiny life: Crime and passion in a virtual world*. New York: Henry Holt.

Donath, J., Karahalios, K., & Vieges, F. (1999). Visualizing conversation. *Journal of Computer-Mediated Communication, 4*(4). www.ascusc.org/jcmc/vol4/issue4/herring.html.

Drew, P. (1984). Speakers' reportings in invitation sequences. In J. M. Atkinson & J. Heritage (Eds.), *Structures of social actions: Studies in conversation analysis* (pp. 57–101). Cambridge: Cambridge University Press.

Edwards, A. D., & Westgate, D. P. G. (1987). *Investigating classroom talk*. Phildelphia, PA: Falmer Press.

Egbert, M. (1997). Schisming: The collaborative transformation from a single conversation to multiple conversations. *Research on Language and Social Interaction, 31,* 1–51.

Ellul, J. (1964). *The technological society*. New York: Vintage Books.

Erickson, T. (1999). Persistent conversation: An introduction. *Journal of Computer-Mediated Communication, 4*(4). www.ascusc.org/jcmc/vol4/issue4/herring.html.

Ericsson, K. A., & Simon, H. A. (1984). *Protocol analysis: Verbal reports as data*. Cambridge, MA: MIT Press.

Flanders, N. (1970). *Analysing teacher behaviour*. Reading, MA: Addison–Wesley.

Gallini, J. K., & Zhang, Y. (1997). Socio-cognitive constructs and characteristics of classroom communities: An exploration of relationships. *Journal of Educational Computing Research, 17*(4), 321–339.

Garcia, A. C., & Jacobs, J. B. (1999). The eyes of the beholder: Understanding the turn-taking system in quasi-synchronous computer-mediated communication. *Research on Language and Social Interaction, 32,* 337–367.

Garfinkel, H. (1967). *Studies in ethnomethodology*. New York: Prentice Hall.

Gay, G., & Bennington, T. (1999). *Information technologies in evaluation: Social, moral, epistemological and practical implications*. San Francisco: Jossey–Bass.

Gay, G., & Mazur, J. (1993, April). The utility of computer tracking tools for user centered design. *Educational Technology*.

Gibson, J. J. (1979). *The ecological approach to perception*. London: Houghton Mifflin.

Gilbert, N., Wooffitt, R., & Fraser, N. (1990). Organizing computer talk. In P. Luff, N. Gilbert, & D. Frohlich (Eds.), *Computers and conversation* (pp. 235–258). London: Academic Press.

Goldman, S. R., & Varma, S. (1995). CAPin the construction-integration model of discourse comprehension. In C. Weaver, S. Mannes, & C. Fletcher (Eds.), *Discourse comprehension: Models of processing revisited*. Hillsdale, NJ: Erlbaum.

Goodwin, M. H. (1995). Assembling a response: Setting and collaboratively constructed work talk. In P. ten Have & G. Psathas (Eds.), *Situated order: Studies in the social organization of talk and embodied activities* (pp. 173–186). Washington, DC: University Press of America.

Goffman, E. (1963). *Behavior in public places: Notes of the social organization of gatherings*. New York: Free Press.

Gresser, A., Gernsberger, M., & Goldman, S. (1997). Cognition. In T. Van Dijk (Ed.), *Discourse as structure and process* (pp. 257–291). Thousand Oaks, CA: Sage.

Grice, H. P. (1975). Logic and conversation. In P. Cole & J. L. Morgan (Eds.), *Syntax and semantics. Vol. 3. Speech acts* (pp. 41–58). New York: Academic Press.

Gumperz, J., Kaltman, H., & O'Connor, M. (1984). Cohesion in spoken and written discourse: Ethnic style and the transition to literacy. In D. Tannen (Ed.), *Coherence in spoken and written discourse* (pp. 3–20). Norwood, NJ: Ablex.

Gunawardena, C., Lowe, C., & Anderson, T. (1997). Analysis of a global online debate and the development of an interaction analysis model for examining social construction of knowledge in computer conferencing. *Journal of Educational Computing Research, 17*(4), 397–431.

Hale, C. (1996). *Wired style: Principles of English usage in the digital age*. San Francisco: HardWired.

Halliday, M. A. K. (1985). *An introduction to functional grammar*. London: Edward Arnold.

Halliday, M. A. K. & Hasan (1976). *Cohesion in english*. London: Longman.

Heath, C. (1997). The analysis of activities in face to face interaction using video. In D. Silverman (Ed.), *Qualitative research: Theory, method and practice* (pp. 183–200). London: Sage.

Heritage, J. (1984). *Garfinkel and ethnomethodology*. Cambridge: Polity Press.

Heritage, J. (1997). Conversational analysis and institutional talk: Analyzing data. In D. Silverman (Ed.), *Qualitative research: Theory, method and practice* (pp. 161–182). London: Sage.

Herring, S. (1996). *Computer-mediated communication: Linguistic, social and cross-cultural perspectives*, Pragmatics and Beyond Series. Amsterdam: John Benjamin.

Herrring, S. (1999). Interactional coherence in CMC. *Journal of Computer-Mediated Communication, 4*(4). www.ascusc.org/jcmc/vol4/issue4/herring.html.

Hiltz, S. R. (1986). The 'virtual classroom': Using computer-mediated communication for university teaching. *Journal of Communication, 36,* 94–105.

Hopper, R. (1992). *Telephone conversation*. Bloomington: Indiana University Press.

Hutchby, I. (2001). *Conversation and technology: From the telephone to the internet*. Malden, MA: Polity Press/Blackwell.

Hutchby, I., & Wooffitt, R. (1998). *Conversation analysis*. Cambridge: Polity Press.

Hymes, D. (1977). *Foundations in sociolinguistics: An ethnographic approach*. London: Tavistock.

Isaacs, E., Tang, J. C., & Morris, T. (1996). Piazza: A desktop environment supporting impromptu and planned interactions. In M. Ackerman (Ed.), *CSCW '96, Proceedings of the Conference on Computer-Supported Cooperative Work* (pp. 315–324). New York: ACM.

Jacko, J., & Sears, A. (2002). *The human-computer interaction handbook: Fundamentals, evolving technologies and emerging applications.* Upper Saddle River, NJ: Lawrence Erlbaum Associates.

Jefferson, G. (1972). Side sequences. In D. Sudnow (Ed.), *Studies in social interaction* (pp. 294–338). New York: Free Press.

Jefferson, G. (1985). An exercise in the transcription and analysis of laughter. In T. A. van Dijk (Ed.), *Handbook of discourse analysis, Vol. III* (pp. 25–34). London: Academic Press.

Jefferson, G. (1986). Notes on latency in overlap onset. *Human Studies, 9*, 153–183.

Jefferson, G., Sacks, H., & Schegloff, E. A. (1987). Notes on laughter in pursuit of intimacy. In G. Button & J. R. E. Lee (Eds.), *Talks and social organization* (pp. 152–205). Cleveland: Multilinguial Matters.

John-Steiner, V., & Mahn, H. (1996). Sociocultural approaches to learning and development: A Vygotskian framework. *Educational Psychologist, 31*(3/4), 191–200.

Jonassen, D. H. (1982). *The technology of text: Principles for structuring, designing, and displaying text.* Englewood Cliffs, NJ: Educational Technology.

Joshi, A., Webber, B., & Sag, I. (1981). *Elements of discourse understanding.* New York: Cambridge University Press.

Kiesler, S., Siefel, J., & McGuire, T. (1984). Social psychological aspects of computer-mediated communication. *American Psychologist, 39*, 1123–1134.

Kolko, B. (1998). We are not just words: Learning the literacies of culture, body and politics. In I. Ward & T. Taylor (Eds.), *Literacy theory in the age of the Internet.* New York: Columbia University Press.

Kolko, B. (1999). Discursive citizenship: The body politic in cyberspace. *International Journal of Virtual Reality.*

Kolko, B. (2000*). Eracing @race: Going white in the (inter)face.* In B. Kolko, L. Nakamura, & G. Rodman (Eds.). London: Routledge.

Kress, G., Leite-Garcia, R., & van Leeuwen, T. (1997). Discourse semiotics. In T. Van Dijk (Eds.), *Discourse as structure and process* (pp. 257–291). Thousand Oaks, CA: Sage.

Levin, J., Kim, H., & Riel, M. (1990). Analyzing instructional interactions on electronic message networks. In L. Harasim (Ed.), *Online education.* New York: Praeger.

Luff, P., Gilbert N., & Frohlich, D. (Eds.) (1990). *Computers and conversation.* London: Academic Press.

Mabrito, M. (1991). Electronic mail as a vehicle for peer response. *Written Communication, 8*(4), 509–532.

Malone, M. (1997). *Worlds of talk: The presentation of self in everyday conversation.* Malden, MA: Polity Press/Blackwell.

Mason, R. (1991). Methodologies for evaluating applications of computer conferencing. In A. R. Kaye (Ed.), *Collaborative learning through computer conferencing.* Heidelberg: Springer-Verlag.

Mavis, B., & Brocato, M. P. A. (1998). Virtual discourse: Evaluating DR-ED as a computer mediated communications network for medical education. *Journal of Educational Computing Research, 19*(1), 53–65.

Mazur, J. (1989). *Using concept maps in therapy with substance abusers.* Unpublished master's thesis, Cornell University.

Mazur, J., & Jones, P. (2002). *Talking and working in an on-line context: A conversation analysis of a Web-based synchronous chat used for teacher professional development.* Paper presented at the Annual Conference of the Association for Educational Communications Technology (AECT), Dallas, TX.

Mazur, J., David, J., Kanappel, P., & Coe, P. (2002). *Missing in action: The use of technology in Kentucky's teacher content academies.* Technical report to the Partnership for Kentucky Schools. Lexington: Partnership for Kentucky Schools.

Mehan, H. (1978). Structuring school structure. *Harvard Educational Review, 48*(1), 32–64.

Mehan, H. (1979). "What time is it, denise?" Asking known questions in classroom practice. *Theory into Practice, 18*(4), 285–294.

Misanchuk, E., & Schwier, R. (1992). Representing interactive multimedia and hypermedia audit trails. *Journal of Educational Multimedia and Hypermedia, 1*(3), 55–72.

Paolillo, J. (1999). The virtual speech community: Social network and language variation on IRC. *Journal of Computer-Mediated Communication, 4*(4). www.ascusc.org/jcmc/vol4/issue4/herring.html.

Pomeranz, A. (1984). Agreeing and disagreeing with assessments: Some features of preferred/dispreferred turn shapes. In J. M. Atkinson & J. Heritage (Eds.), *Structures of social actions: Studies in conversation analysis* (pp. 57–101). Cambridge: Cambridge University Press.

Postman, N. (1988). *Conscientious objections: Stirring up trouble about language, technology and education.* New York: Vintage Books.

Pomeranz, A., & Fehr, B. J. (1997). Conversation analysis: An approach to the study of social action as sense making practices. In T. A. van Dijk (Ed.), *Discourse studies: A multidisciplinary introduction* (pp. 64–91). London: Sage.

Psathias, G. (1995). *Conversation analysis: The study of talk-in-interaction.* Thousand Oaks, CA: Sage.

Pullinger, D. J. (1986). Chit-chat to electronic journals. Computer conferencing supports scientific communication. In V. Arms (Ed.), *IEEE Transactions of Professional Communications, PC29*, 30–33.

QSR, Inc. (2002). *Nvivo* (N6) qualitative analysis software. Available at www.qsr.com/au/home/home.html.

Rheingold, H. (1993). *The virtual community: Homesteading on the electronic frontier.* Reading, MA: Addison–Wesley.

Rice, R. E., & Love, G. (1987). Electronic emotion: Socio-emotional content in a computer-mediated communication network. *Communication Research, 14*, 85–105.

Romiszowski, A., & Mason, R. (1986). Computer-mediated communication. In D. Jonassen (Ed.), *Handbook of research for educational communications and technology* (pp. 438–456). New York: Simon and Schuster Macmillan.

Rosson, M. B. (1999). I get by with a little help from my cyber-friends: Sharing stories of good and bad times on the web. *Journal of Computer-Mediated Communication, 4*(4). www.ascusc.org/jcmc/vol4/issue4/herring.html.

Sacks, H. (1972). On the analyzability of stories by children. In J. J. Gumperz & D. Hymes (Eds.), *Directions in sociolinguistics: The ethnography of communication* (pp. 329–345). New York: Holt, Rinehart and Winston.

Sacks H. (1984). Notes on methodology. In J. M. Atkinson & J. Heritage (Eds.), *Structures of social action: Studies in conversation analysis* (pp. 21–27). Cambridge: Cambridge University Press.

Sacks, H., Schegloff, E. A., & Jefferson, G. (1974). A simplest systematic for the organization of turn-taking for conversation. *Language, 50*, 696–735.

Salomon, G. (1993). No distribution without individuals' cognitions: A dynamic interactional view. In G. Saloman (Ed.), *Distributed cognitions* (pp. 111–138). Cambridge: Cambridge University Press.

Salmon, G. (2000). *E-moderating: The key to teaching and learning online.* London: Kogan Page.

Schegloff, E. A. (1986). Routine as achievement. *Human Studies, 9*, 111–152.

Schegloff, E. A. (1991). Reflections on talk and social structure. In D. Boden & D. Zimmerman (Eds.), *Talk and social structure* (pp. 44–70). Cambridge, MA: Polity Press.

Schegloff, E. A. (1992). Repair after next turn: The last structurally provided defense of intersubjectivity in conversation. *American Journal of Sociology, 97*, 1295–1345.

Schegloff, E. A. (1996). Confirming allusions: Towards an empirical account of action. *American Journal of Sociology, 104*, 161-217.

Schegloff, E. A., & Sacks, H. (1973). Opening up closings. *Semiotica*, 7, 289-326.

Scolari Company. (2002). ATLAS.ti Qualitative Analysis Software. Available at www.scolari.co.uk/atlasti/atlasti.html.

Scott, J. (1991). *Social network analysis. A handbook*. London: Sage.

Selfe, C. L., & Meyer, P. R. (1991). Testing claims for on-line conferences. *Written Communication, 8*(4), 163-193.

Shank, R. C., & Abelson, R. P. (1977). *Scripts, plans, goals, and understanding: An inquiry into human knowledge structures*. Hillsdale, N J: Erlbaum.

Sinclair, J., & Coulthard, R. M. (1975). *Towards an analysis of discourse*. Oxford: Oxford University Press.

Sinclair, J. M., Hoey, M., & Fox, G. (1993). *Techniques of description: Spoken and written discou*rse. London: Routledge.

Smith, M. A. (1992). *Voices from the WELL: The logic of the virtual commons* [On-line]. http://www.usyd.edu.au/su/social/papers/virtcomm.htm.

Spitzer, M. (1989). Computer conferencing: An emerging technology. In G. Hawisher & S. Selfe (Eds.), *Critical perspectives on computers and composition instruction* (pp. 187-199). New York: Teachers College Press.

Sproull, L., & Kiesler, S. (1988). Reducing social context cues: Electronic mail in organizational communication. In I. Grief (Ed.), *Computer-supported cooperative work: A book of readings*. San Mateo, CA: Morgan Kaufman.

Suchman, L. (1990). What is human-machine communication? In S. P. Robertson, W. Zachary, & J. B. Black (Eds.), *Cognition, computing and cooperation* (pp. 24-55). Norwood, NJ: Ablex.

Tannen, D. (1986). *Coherence in spoken and written discourse*. Norwood, NJ: Ablex.

Tannen, D. (1996). *Gender and discourse*. Oxford: Oxford University Press.

Tannen, D. (2001). *You just don't understand: Women and men in conversation*. New York: Quill.

ten Have, P. (1999). *Doing conversation analysis*. Thousand Oaks, CA: Sage.

Tesch, R. (1992). *Qualitative research: Analysis types and software tools*. New York: Falmer Press.

Tolbert, C. A., & Bittner, A. C., Jr. (1991). Applications of verbal protocol analysis during the system development cycle. In W. Karwowski & J. W. Yates (Eds.), *Advances in industrial ergonomics and safety III* (pp. 855-862). Bristol, PA: Taylor & Francis.

van, T. Dijk. (Ed.). (1985). *Handbook of discourse analysis*. London: Academic Press.

van Dijk, T. (1997).*Discourse as structure and process*. Thousand Oaks, CA: Sage.

Walther, J. B. (1996). Computer-mediated communication: Impersonal, interpersonal, and hyperpersonal interaction. *Communication Research, 23*(1), 3-43.

Wasserman, S., & Faust, K. (1997). *Social network analysis. Methods and applications*. Cambridge: Cambridge University Press.

Watt, J. (1999). Researching large web-based data sets. In G. Gay & T. Bennington (Eds). *New directions in evaluation* (pp. 23-44). Jossey-Bass, San Francisco, CA.

Welch, K. (1999). *Electric rhetoric*. Cambridge, MA: The MIT Press.

Wenger, E. (1999). *Communities of practice*. New York: Cambridge University Press.

Werry, C. C. (1996). Linguistic and interactional features of internet relay chat. In S. Herring (Ed.) *Computer-mediated communication: Linguistic, social and cross-cultural perpectives* (pp. 65-80). Amsterdam: John Benjamins.

Whalen, J. (1995). Expert systems for experts: Computer-aided dispatch as a support system in real-world environments. In P. Thomas (Ed.), *The social and interactional dimensions of human-computer interfaces* (pp. 161-184). Cambridge: Cambridge University Press.

Whittaker, S. (1996). Talking to strangers: An evaluation of the factors affecting electronic collaboration. In M. Ackerman (Ed.), *CSCW '96, proceedings of the conference on computer-supported cooperative work* (pp. 315-324). New York: ACM.

Wooten, A. (1975). *Dilemmas of discourse*. New York: Holmes & Meier.

·41·

DEVELOPMENTAL RESEARCH: STUDIES OF INSTRUCTIONAL DESIGN AND DEVELOPMENT

Rita C. Richey
Wayne State University

James D. Klein
Arizona State University

Wayne A. Nelson
Southern Illinois University at Edwardsville

41.1 INTRODUCTION

The field of instructional technology has traditionally involved a unique blend of theory and practice. This blend is most obvious in developmental research, those studies that involve the production of knowledge with the ultimate aim of improving the processes of instructional design, development, and evaluation. Such research is based on either situation-specific problem solving or generalized inquiry procedures. Developmental *research*, as opposed to simple instructional development, has been defined as "the systematic study of designing, developing and evaluating instructional programs, processes and products that must meet the criteria of internal consistency and effectiveness" (Seels & Richey, 1994, p. 127). In its simplest form, developmental research can be either

- the study of the process and impact of specific instructional design and development efforts; **or**
- a situation in which someone is *performing* instructional design, development, or evaluation activities and *studying* the process at the same time; **or**
- the study of the instructional design, development, and evaluation process as a whole or of particular process components.

In each case the distinction is made between performing a process and studying that process. Reports of developmental research may take the form of a case study with retrospective analysis, an evaluation report, or even a typical experimental research report.

The purposes of this chapter are to

- explore the nature and background of developmental research;
- describe the major types of developmental research by examining a range of representative projects;
- analyze the methodological approaches used in the various types of developmental research;
- describe the issues, findings, and trends in recent developmental research; and
- discuss the future of this type of research in our field.

41.2 THE NATURE OF DEVELOPMENTAL RESEARCH

Today, even amid the calls for increased use of alternative research methodologies, the notion of developmental research is often unclear, not only to the broader community of educational researchers, but to many instructional technology researchers as well. An understanding of this topic is rooted in the nature of development and research in general, as well as a more specific understanding of the purpose, focus, and techniques of developmental research itself.

41.2.1 The Character of Development

Development, in its most generic sense, implies gradual growth, evolution, and change. This concept has been applied to diverse areas of study and practice. For example, organization development is a strategy for changing "the beliefs, attitudes, values, and structure of organizations so that they can better adapt to new ... challenges" (Bennis, 1969, p. 2). Educators are familiar with the notion of professional or staff development. Lieberman and Miller (1992) define this as "the knowledge, skills, abilities, and the necessary conditions for teacher learning on the job" (p. 1045). This same concept is often applied to other professional areas. In the corporate arena, the term "executive development" also refers to learning processes, and in this setting learning, as a developmental activity, often integrates both classroom instruction and work experience (Smith, 1993). The most common use of the term "development," however, is in relation to human growth and the field of developmental psychology. The term *developmental research* is most often confused with research in this field that concentrates on particular age groups, such as in the areas of adolescent development or life-span development.

In the field of instructional technology, development has a particular, somewhat unique, connotation. The most current definition views development as "the process of translating the design specifications into physical form" (Seels & Richey, 1994, p. 35). In other words, it refers to the process of *producing* instructional materials. Development is viewed as one of the five major domains of theory and practice in the field.[1] Even though this varies from many other uses of the term *development,* it is consistent with the fundamental attribute of being a process of growth, and in our field development is a very creative process.

Historically *development* has been an ambiguous term to many instructional technologists and has generated considerable discussion regarding its proper interpretation. This debate has focused typically on the distinctions between instructional *design* and instructional *development.* Heinich, Molenda, Russell, and Smaldino (2002) define instructional development as "the process of analyzing needs, determining what content must be mastered, establishing educational goals, designing materials to reach the objectives, and trying out and revising the program in terms of learner achievement" (p. 445). They have been consistent in this orientation since the early editions of their influential book. Yet to many, this is a definition of the instructional systems design (ISD) process.

The confusion has been further exacerbated. In 1977, Briggs defined *instructional design* as "the entire process of analysis of

learning needs and goals and the development of a delivery system to meet the needs; includes development of instructional materials and activities; and tryout and revision of all instruction and learner assessment activities" (p. xx). In this interpretation design is the more generic term, encompassing *both* planning and production. The 1994 definition of the field attempts to clarify these issues by viewing design as the planning phase in which specifications are constructed, and development as the production phase in which the design specifications are actualized (Seels & Richey, 1994). This is not a new distinction (Cronbach & Suppes, 1969; National Center for Educational Research and Development, 1970), even though the past use of the term *instructional developer* (see Baker, 1973) typically referred to a person who was doing what today we would call both design and development. All would agree, however, that design and development are *related* processes, and Connop-Scollard (1991) has graphically demonstrated these relationships in a complex chart which identified hundreds of interrelated concepts.

However, the word *development* has a broader definition when it is used within the research context than it has when used within the context of creating instructional products. The focus is no longer only on production, or even on both planning and production. It also includes comprehensive evaluation. As such, developmental research may well address not only formative, but also summative and confirmative evaluation. It may address not only needs assessment, but also broad issues of front-end analysis, such as contextual analysis issues as conceived by Tessmer and Richey (1997). When evaluation is approached in a comprehensive manner, the scope of the research effort is often correspondingly expanded to encompass product utilization and management, as well as product creation. Table 41.1 displays the scope of development as discussed in this chapter.

The next step beyond "Utilization & Maintenance" in the Table 41.1 schemata would be "Impact," the follow-up analysis of the effects of an instructional product or program on the organization or the learner. This type of research typically falls within the scope of traditional evaluation research.

41.2.2 The Character of Research

Although research methodologies vary, there are key attributes that transcend the various research orientations and goals. An understanding of these characteristics can shed light on the process of developmental research.

41.2.2.1 The Dimensions of Research.
Research is typically viewed as a type of systematic investigation, and in education it typically is an empirical process that employs the systematic method (Crowl, 1996). One result of such efforts is the creation of knowledge. Even though research is typically rooted in societal problems, all knowledge produced by research is not necessarily in a form conducive to quick resolution of society's problems. Some knowledge (which is usually generated by *basic* research) must be specifically transformed to enable its application to a given problem. Other knowledge (which is usually

---

[1]In addition to development, the domains also include design, management, utilization, and evaluation.

TABLE 41.1. The Scope of Development in a Research Context

Design	Development	Utilization & Maintenance
Analysis and Planning for Development, Evaluation, Utilization, & Maintenance	Production & Formative Evaluation	Usage, Management, Summative & Confirmative Evaluation

generated by *applied* research) lends itself to the immediate solution of practical problems. Developmental research clearly falls in the latter category. In this respect, it is similar to other methodologies such as action research.

Although the objective of research is to produce knowledge, these products may take a variety of forms. Diesing (1991) has noted that

... the philosophers suggest that social science produces at least three kinds of knowledge: (1) systems of laws which describe interconnected regularities in society; (2) descriptions, from the inside, of a way of life, community, person, belief system, or scientific community's beliefs; (3) structural models, mathematical or verbal, of dynamic processes exemplified in particular cases. (p. 325)

Research orientations tend to conform to the pursuit of a particular type of knowledge. Experimental research tends to contribute to the construction of a system of laws. Characteristic of this method is a series of routine checks to ensure self-correction throughout the research, and in the logical positivist tradition, such checks are considered to be rooted in objectivity (Kerlinger, 1964). Qualitative research primarily contributes to the development of "mirrors for man" so that we can see ourselves better (Kluckhohn, as noted in Diesing, 1991). In the various forms of qualitative research, context and contextual influences become an integral part of the investigation (Driscoll, 1991; Mishler, 1979).

Diesing's third type of knowledge is process knowledge presented in model form. This is usually of great interest to instructional designers and developers, given our history of working with many kinds of process models, such as the graphic models of systematic design procedures and the models of media selection. When inquiry procedures result in this type of knowledge, these endeavors can legitimately be placed in the research realm.

Another traditional characterization of research is as a facilitator of understanding and prediction. In this regard "understanding results from a knowledge of the process or dynamics of a theory. Prediction results from investigation of the outcomes of a theory" (Schwen, 1977, p. 8). These goals can be achieved by either (a) providing a logical explanation of reality, (b) anticipating the values of one variable based on those of other variables, or (c) determining the states of a model (Dubin, as cited by Schwen, 1977). While these ends, especially the first two, can be achieved through traditional research methodologies, the third is uniquely matched to the goals of developmental research. This was emphasized by Schwen (1977):

Inquiry in educational technology may be associated with the planning, implementing, and/or evaluation of the management-of-learning process, where that process employs systematic technological analysis and

synthesis ... current definitions of technological process may be found in development models ... (having) the common attributes of 1) disciplined analysis of problem, context, constraints, learners, and task, and 2) disciplined synthesis involving the design of replicable forms of instruction and formative and summative evaluation. (p. 9)

41.2.2.2 The Relationships Between Research and Development.

The traditional view of research is as the discovery of new knowledge and that of development is as the translation of that knowledge into a useful form (Pelz, 1967). This conceptual framework not only has been commonly subscribed to, but was subsequently extended into the research, development, and diffusion model (Brickell, Clark & Guba, as cited in Havelock, 1971). Early research methods texts addressed development as the "research and development" process (Borg & Gall, 1971). The processes were separate, though related, dependent, and sequential. In some situations this orientation still prevails. This view emphasizes development's function of linking practice to research and theory and recognizes the likelihood that instructional development can highlight researchable problems and, thus, serve as a vehicle for stimulating new research (Baker, 1973).

Stowe (1973) has shown the parallels between scientific research and the general methodology of instructional systems design (ISD). He notes that both

- are objective, empirical problem-solving approaches;
- employ procedural models "couched in the language of mathematics" (p. 167);
- have a predictive power dependent on the degree to which they represent the most critical aspects of reality; and
- can generate new problems and hypotheses.

Nonetheless, Stowe rejected the proposition that systematic design procedures can be viewed as research to a great extent because of the inability of ISD to discover generalizable principles and its intent to produce context-specific solutions. In addition, Stowe cited the distinctions between ISD's orientation toward explanations of "how" as opposed to research's orientation toward explanations of "why."

In the contemporary orientation toward research, Stowe's arguments can be interpreted as an overly rigid expression of positivist philosophy. The contextual richness of the typical design and development task increases the likelihood that research on such topics be especially ripe for a qualitative orientation. The ability to provide process explanations exemplifies a type of knowledge production using the Diesing framework, and an avenue to understanding and prediction using Schwen's paradigm. Stowe's arguments, drafted 30 years ago, could lead to diametrically opposite conclusions today, providing one accepts the premise that research can have a broader function than the creation of generalizable statements of law. We are taking the position that research can also result in context-specific knowledge and can serve a problem-solving function. This is true of developmental research, as it has commonly thought to be true of evaluation research.

While instructional development typically *builds* on previous research, developmental research attempts to produce the models and principles that guide the design, development, and evaluation processes. As such, *doing* development and *studying* development are two different enterprises.

41.2.3 The Background of Developmental Research

The field of instructional technology as it exists today emerged primarily from a convergence of the fields of audiovisual education and instructional psychology. In audiovisual education the emphasis was on the role of media as an enhancement of the teaching/learning process and an aid in the communication process, and there was much interest in materials production. On the other hand, in instructional psychology the nature of the learner and the learning process took precedence over the nature of the delivery methodology, and there was much interest in instructional design. Complementing the instructional psychology roots was the application of systems theory to instruction that resulted in the instructional systems design movement (Seels & Richey, 1994). This conceptual and professional merger came to fruition in the 1960s and 1970s. During this period instructional design and development came to assume the role of the "linking science" that John Dewey had called for at the turn of the century (Reigeluth, 1983).

Not surprisingly, it was during this same period that the term *developmental research* emerged. This new orientation was exemplified by the shift in topics between the first and the second *Handbook of Research on Teaching* (Gage, 1963; Travers, 1973). In the 1963 handbook, media was addressed as an area of research with a major emphasis on media comparison research, and all research methodologies considered were quantitative. In the 1973 handbook, media continued to be included as a research area, but the research methodologies were varied, including Eva Baker's chapter on "The Technology of Instructional Development."[2] This chapter describes in detail the process of systematic product design, development, and evaluation. Of significance is the fact that the entire methodology section was titled "Methods and Techniques of Research *and Development*".

This was a period in which federal support of educational research mushroomed. Regional research and development laboratories were established and the ERIC system was devised for dissemination. Clifford (1973) estimated that appropriations for educational "research and development for 1966 through 1968 alone equaled three-fourths of all funds ever made available" (p. 1). Research-based product and program development had

become firmly established as part of the scientific movement in education. At this time, Wittrock (1967) hailed the use of empirical measurement and experimentation to explain product effectiveness. Such activities "could change the development of products into research with empirical results and theory generalizable to new problems" (p. 148).

Hilgard (1964) characterized research as a continuum from basic research on topics not directly relevant to learning through the advocacy and adoption stages of technological development. Saettler (1990) maintained that the last three of Hilgard's research categories were directly within the domain of instructional technology. These included laboratory, classroom, and special teacher research; tryout in "normal" classrooms; and advocacy and adoption. Note that these are portrayed as types of research, rather than applications of research, and they are all encompassed within the framework of developmental research.

Although instructional technology is not the only field concerned with learning in applied settings, few would dispute the critical role played by these three types of research in our field. Moreover, our uniqueness among educational fields is not only our concern with technology, but rather our emphasis on the design, development, and use of processes and resources for learning (Seels & Richey, 1994). Given this definition of the field, developmental research is critically important to the evolution of our theory base.

41.2.4 The Character of Developmental Research

The distinctions between "doing" and "studying" design and development provide further clarification of developmental research activities. These distinctions can be described in terms of examining the focus, techniques, and tools of developmental research.

41.2.4.1 The Focus of Developmental Research. The general purposes of research have been described as knowledge production, understanding, and prediction. Within this framework, developmental research has particular emphases that vary in terms of the extent to which the conclusions are generalizable or contextually specific. Table 41.2 portrays the relationships between the two general types of developmental research.

The most straightforward developmental research projects fall into the first category in Table 41.2. This category typically involves situations in which the product development process used in a particular situation is described and analyzed and the final product is evaluated, such as McKenney's (2002) documentation of the use of CASCADE-SEA, a computer-based support tool for curriculum development. Driscoll (1991) has used the term *systems-based evaluation* to describe a similar research paradigm. van den Akker (1999), on the other hand, prefers to label Type I research *formative research*. He further defines this type of research as "activities performed during the entire development process of a specific intervention,

---

[2]A history of instructional development is given by Baker (1973), who primarily summarizes the work in research-based product development from the turn of the century to 1970. Baker, however, does not address developmental research as it is presented in this chapter.

TABLE 41.2. A Summary of the Two Types
of Developmental Research

	Type 1	Type 2
Emphasis	Study of specific product or program design, development, &/or evaluation projects	Study of design, development, or evaluation processes, tools, or models
Product	Lessons learned from developing specific products and analyzing the conditions that facilitate their use	New design, development, and evaluation procedures &/or models, and conditions that facilitate their use
	Context-specific Conclusions ⇒ ⇒ ⇒	**⇒ Conclusions** Generalized

from exploratory studies through (formative and summative) evaluation studies" (p. 6).

Some Type 1 developmental studies reflect traditional evaluation orientations in which the development process is not addressed, and only the product or program evaluation is described. An example of this type of study is O'Quin, Kinsey, and Beery's (1987) report on the evaluation of a microcomputer training workshop for college personnel. Regardless of the nature of the Type 1 study, the results are typically context and product specific, even though the implications for similar situations may be discussed.

The second type of developmental study is oriented toward a general analysis of design, development, or evaluation processes, addressed either as a whole or in terms of a particular component. They are similar to those studies Driscoll (1991) calls "model development and technique development research." van den Akker (1999) calls them "reconstructive studies." His term emphasizes the common (but not exclusive) situation in which this research takes place after the actual design and development process is completed.

Tracey's (2002) study is an example of Type 2 developmental research that has a global design orientation. She constructed and validated an instructional systems design model that incorporated Gardner's notion of multiple intelligences. Taylor and Ellis' (1991) study had a similar orientation, although their orientation was far different. They evaluated the use of instructional systems design in the Navy. Other studies in this category focus on only one phase of the design/development/evaluation process, such as Jonassen's (1988) case study of using needs assessment data in the development of a university program. Type 2 research may draw its population either from one target project such as King and Dille's (1993) study of the application of quality concepts in the systematic design of instruction at the Motorola Training and Education Center or from a variety of design and development environments. Examples of the latter approach include Riplinger's (1987) survey of current task analysis procedures and Hallamon's similar study conducted in 2001. Typically, conclusions from Type 2 developmental research are generalized, even though there are instances of context-specific conclusions in the literature.

41.2.4.2 Nondevelopmental Research in the Field. A critical aspect of any concept definition is the identification of

nonexamples as well as examples. This is especially important with respect to developmental research, as it often seems to overlap with other key methodologies used in the field. Even so, developmental research does *not* encompass studies such as the following:

- instructional psychology studies,
- media or delivery system comparison or impact studies,
- message design and communication studies,
- policy analysis or formation studies, and
- research on the profession.

While results from research in these areas impact the development process, the study of variables embedded in such topics does not constitute developmental research. For example, design and development is dependent on what we know about the learning process. We have learned from the research literature that transfer of training is impacted by motivation, organizational climate, and previous educational experiences. Therefore, one may expand a front-end analysis to address such issues, or even construct design models that reflect this information, but the foundational research would not be considered developmental. If the new models were tested, or programs designed using such models were evaluated, this research would qualify as developmental.

A fundamental distinction should be made between reports that analyze actual development projects and *descriptions* of recommended design and development procedural models. Although these models may represent a synthesis of the research, they do not constitute research in themselves. A good example of the latter situation is Park and Hannafin's (1993) guidelines for designing interactive multimedia. These guidelines are generalized principles that speak to the development process, and they are based on a large body of research. Nonetheless, the identification and explanation of the guidelines is not in itself an example of developmental research. The instructional technology literature includes many examples of such work. They often provide the stimulus for a line of new research, even though these articles themselves are not considered to be research reports themselves. There are many examples today of such work, including explorations of topics such as cognitive task analysis (Ryder & Redding, 1993) and the nature of design and designer decision making (Rowland, 1993).

41.2.4.3 The Techniques and Tools of Developmental Research. Developmental researchers employ a variety of research methodologies, applying any tool that meets their requirements. Summative evaluation studies often employ classical experimental designs. Needs assessments may incorporate qualitative approaches. Process studies may adopt descriptive survey methods. Even historical research methods may be used in developmental projects.

Traditional research tools and traditional design tools facilitate the developmental endeavor. Expertise is often required in statistical analysis, measurement theory, and methods of establishing internal and external validity. Likewise, the developmental researcher (even those studying previously designed instruction) requires a command of design techniques and theory. Additional design proficiency is frequently required when using electronic design systems and aids, conducting environmental analyses, and defining ways to decrease design cycle time.

A developmental research project may include several distinct stages, each of which involves reporting and analyzing a data set. Merely conducting a comprehensive design and development project does not constitute conducting a developmental research project even using its most narrow Type 1 definition. One must also include the analysis and reporting stage to warrant being classified as developmental research.

Developmental research projects may include a number of component parts. Substudies may be conducted to analyze and define the instructional problem, to specify the content, or to determine instrument reliability and validity. Substudies may be conducted to provide a formative evaluation, a summative evaluation, or a follow-up of postinstruction performance. Consequently, reports of developmental research are frequently quite long, often prohibiting publication of the full study.

Reports of developmental projects can often be found in

- professional journals,
- doctoral dissertations,
- Educational Resource Information Center (ERIC) collections of unpublished project reports, and
- conference proceedings.

The nature of these reports varies depending on the dissemination vehicle. Sometimes, full developmental projects are split into more easily publishable units (or even summarized) to facilitate publication in the traditional research journals. Developmental research reports are also published in practitioner-oriented journals and magazines, and the methodology and theoretical base of the studies are omitted to conform to the traditions of those periodicals. The next section further defines the nature of developmental research by summarizing studies that are representative of the wide range of research in this category.

41.3 A REVIEW OF REPRESENTATIVE DEVELOPMENTAL RESEARCH

We have identified representative developmental research studies in the literature so that we might

- further describe the character of this type of research,
- identify the range of settings and foci of developmental research,
- summarize developmental tools and techniques commonly used,
- identify the range of research methodologies used, and
- describe the nature of the conclusions in such research.

The literature is described in terms of the two types of developmental research. This review covers research from the past 20 years, with a concentration on the most recent work.

41.3.1 Type 1 Developmental Research

Type 1 research is the most context-specific inquiry. These studies are essentially all forms of case studies and emanate from a wide range of educational needs. Table 41.3 presents an analysis of 56 studies representative of this category of research. These studies are described in terms of their focus, their methodology, and the nature of their conclusions. Focus is examined in terms of the

- type of program or product developed;
- particular design, development, or evaluation process emphasized in the study;
- particular tools and techniques emphasized; and
- organizational context for which the product is intended.

The most common characteristics among the studies are found in relation to their process foci, the research methodologies employed, and the nature of their conclusions. The product and technique focus and the user context seem to reflect individual researcher interests or participant availability more than they reflect the inherent nature of this type of research.

41.3.1.1 Process Foci of Type 1 Developmental Research. Type 1 research studies originate with the design and development of an instructional product or program. This is the crux of Type 1 research. Frequently, the entire design, development, and evaluation process is documented. Consistent with predominant practice in the field, the procedures employed usually follow the tenets of ISD, encompassing front-end analysis through formative or summative evaluation. One-third of the studies cited in Table 41.3 describe in detail the entire design, development, and evaluation process as it occurred in a particular environment. (See Table 41.3 for studies classified in terms of an "A" process focus.)

Two studies provide an example of this kind of research. Petry and Edwards's (1984) description of the systematic design, development, and evaluation of a university applied phonetics course is a classic Type 1 study with a course focus. They describe the application of a particular ISD model as well as the use of elaboration theory in content sequencing. The study also addresses the production of course materials, as well as the results of an evaluation of student performance and attitudes in the revised course. Hirumi, Savenye, and Allen's (1994) report of the analysis, design, development, implementation, and evaluation of an interactive videodisc museum exhibit is an example of a Type 1 study with a program focus. This study provides evidence that an ISD model can be adapted to informal educational settings.

Studies that did not document the entire design, development, and evaluation process tended to emphasize a particular phase of ISD such as needs assessment or formative evaluation.

For example, Link and Cherow-O'Leary (1990) document the needs assessment procedures followed by the Children's Television Workshop (CTW) to determine the needs and interests of elementary school teachers. They also describe formative evaluation techniques for testing the effectiveness of children's and parent's magazines. Klein et al. (2000) describe a needs assessment conducted to determine the optimal instructional content and delivery method for an introductory course in educational technology. The results of the needs assessment were used to revise an existing course. Fischer, Savenye, and Sullivan (2002) report on the formative evaluation of a computer-based training course for an on-line financial and purchasing system. The purpose of the study was to evaluate the effectiveness of the training and to identify appropriate revisions to incorporate into the program.

Type 1 developmental research studies often concentrate on the production aspect of the ISD approach. (See Table 41.3 for studies classified in terms of an "E" process focus.) Often these studies concerned the development of technology-based instruction, such as Bowers and Tsai's (1990), Crane and Mylonas' (1988), and Harris and Cady's (1988) research on the use of hypertext as a vehicle for creating computer-based instructional materials. The reports describe authoring procedures so specifically that one could replicate the innovative development processes. These same tactics were employed with respect to developing instructional television by Albero-Andes (1983), and they were used in interactive videodisc projects by Alessi (1988) and C. M. Russell (1990). Similar studies can be found in the research of our field as each new technological advancement emerges.[3]

Type 1 developmental studies demonstrate the range of design and development procedures currently available to practitioners. In addition, these studies commonly encompassed an evaluation of the products and programs that were created, including an examination of the changes in learners who had interacted with the newly developed products.

41.3.1.2 Research Methodologies Employed in Type 1 Developmental Research.
A basic premise of this chapter is that the design–development–evaluation process itself can be viewed as a form of inquiry. This is accomplished in a developmental research project by embedding traditional research methodologies into the development projects. The type of research method used in a particular project tends to vary with the type of developmental research, and Type 1 studies frequently employ case study techniques. (See Table 41.3 for studies classified in terms of an A methodology use.)

The manner in which case study techniques are used varies widely in developmental research. Most commonly, the case study is seen as a way in which one can explore or describe complex situations, which consist of a myriad of critical contextual

variables as well as process complexities. For example, Dick (1991) described a corporate design project in Singapore aimed at training instructional designers. The report of his Type 1 study focuses upon the needs assessment and actual design phases rather than the entire design–development–evaluation process. In another Type 1 study, Carr-Chellman, Cuyar, and Breman (1998) document how user design was implemented to create an information technology system in the context of home health care. This case study explored the complexities of systemic change as the organization used an educational systems design process. Both of these projects were approached from a research point of view in a qualitative manner.

Less often do studies heed the admonition of Yin (1992), who indicates that case studies are more appropriate when one is attempting to establish causal relationships rather than simply provide detailed descriptions. This approach requires a more quantitative orientation to the development case study as one seeks to explain (as well as describe) the nature of the development process. More often quantitative aspects of a Type 1 developmental research project concern efforts to determine the effectiveness or impact of the resulting instruction. In these cases the studies have experimental designs, with or without the case study component. (See Table 41.3 for studies classified in terms of an E methodology use.) An example of this methodological approach is the study by Plummer, Gillis, Legree, and Sanders (1992), which used two research methodologies—case study and experimental—in conjunction with the design and development task. This project involved the development of a job aid used by the military when operating a complicated piece of communications equipment. The experimental phase of the evaluation of the job aid was a study to evaluate the effectiveness of the job aid. Three instructional situations were compared— using the job aid alone, using it in combination with a demonstration, and using the technical manual in combination with a demonstration. Consequently, not only was impact information secured, but also information relating to the superior conditions for using the newly developed product was obtained.

Evaluation methods are frequently used in Type 1 developmental research studies (see Table 41.3 for studies classified as a "D" methodology use). Evaluation instruments such as learner surveys, achievement tests, and performance measures are often used to collect data. For example, Martin and Bramble (1996) conducted an in-depth evaluation of five video teletraining courses for military personnel by collecting survey data from students and instructors who participated in the courses. Achievement and proficiency tests were also used. Quinn (1994) evaluated a curriculum project in which graduate students served as instructional developers in a corporate environment. He used learner, instructor, and client evaluations to determine the impact of the project. Sullivan, Ice, and Niedermeyer (2000) field-tested a K–12 energy education curriculum

---

[3]Although this is not the emphasis of this chapter, one could construct a type of history of the field of instructional technology by tracing the Type 1 developmental research. The audiovisual emphasis could be documented through a series of studies such as Greenhill's (1955) description of producing low-cost motion pictures with sound for instructional purposes. Procedural changes could be traced through studies such as those by Rouch (1969) and Gordon (1969), who describe early applications of the systems approach to designing education and training programs. Programmatic trends could be seen in studies of the design and development of competency-based teacher education programs, such as Cook and Richey (1975). Today the development of new technologies is documented in a variety of studies, many of which are discussed here.

TABLE 41.3. An Analysis of Representative Type 1 Developmental Research Literature

Reference	Product or Program Focus	Process Focus	Use Context	Tools and Techniques Emphasized	Research Method(s) Used	Nature of Conclusions
Albero-Andes (1983)	C, F, I	A, E, F	A	B	A	B
Alessi (1988)	J	A, H	B	H, K	A	C
Aukerman (1987)		G, J	D	H	D, G, I	A
Bednar (1988)	B	B	B	A, B	A	B
Blackstone (1990)	H	E, F, I, J	F		A, E, D, J	A
Borras (1993)	B, J, L	D, F	B	K	E	B
Bowers & Tsai (1990)	J	E, G	G	K	A, E	D
Buch (1989)	C	A, J	C	B, F	A, D, E	B
Cantor (1988)		E	E	K	A, D	B
Capell & Dannenberg (1993)	J	C, D	A, B	F, G, L	A, D	B
Carr-Chellman, Cuyar, & Breman (1998)	J	D, F, G	D	L	A	B
Chou & Sun (1996)	J	A	B,H	L	D	A
Corry, Frick, & Hansen (1997)	L	B, F	B	B, L	A	A
Coscarelli & White (1982)	A	A, G, H	B	E	A, D	B
Coyle (1986)	B, J	G, J	B		A, G	B
Coyle (1992)	B	E, G	B		D	A
Crane & Mylonas (1988)	J	E	B	K	A	A
Cregger Metzler (1992)	A	A, G, H	B	G	A, D, J	B
Dabbagh et al. (2000)	A	A	B		A	B
Dick (1991)	B	B, D	C, H	B, F,	A	A
Fischer, Savenye, & Sullivan (2002)	J	F	G	J	D	B
Fox & Klein (2002)	A	B	B	B	J	B
Gay & Mazur (1993)	J	E, H	G	K	A, F	C
Gettman, McNelly, & Muraida (1999)	M	D	E		D	A
Gustafson & Reeves (1990)	K	A	G	B, C, D, E, H	D	C
Harris and Cady (1988)	J	E	A	K	A	A
Herrington & Oliver (2000)	J, L	D, E, G	B	K	I	B
Hirumi, Savenye, & Allen (1994)	B	A	F		A	B
Jonassen (1988)	B	B, D	B	B	J	A
Jones (1986)	C	J	B		A, C, E, J	A
Kanyarusoke (1985)	A, F	A, B, C, J	B		A, B, J	A
Kearsley (1985)	J	G	I	K	D	B
Klein et al. (2000)	A	B, C	B	B	J	A
Lewis, Stern, & Linn (1993)	H, J	E	A		A, B	A
Li & Merrill (1991)	J	C, D	I		A, D	C

Link & Cherow-O'Leary (1990)	D	B, F	A, F, G	J	B, G, J	B
Martin & Bramble (1996)	A	A	E		D	B
McKenney (2001)	J, M	A	A, H	B, C, L	G, I, J	B
Medsker (1992)	A, B	A, H, J	B, C, G	A	A, B	B
Mendes & Mendes (1996)	J	D, E, F	A, H		D	D
Mielke (1990)	I	A	A, F		A	A
Munro & Towne (1992)	I	D, E	A, B, E, G	K	A, D	A
Nieveen & van den Akker (1999)	J, M	F	I	L	A, G, J	B
Noel (1991)	B	A, B	A, H	C	A	C
O'Quin, Kinsey, & Beery (1987)	C, J	I, J	B, G		D, E	A
Petry & Edwards (1984)	A	A	B	G	A	A
Pirolli (1991)	J	C, D	I	F, G, K	A, D	B
Pizzuto (1983)	C, H	A, C, E, F, I, J	C		A, D, G, J	A
Plummer, Gillis, Legree, & Sanders (1992)	G	E, I	C		A, E, J	A
Quinn (1994)	A	A	B, C, G	J	D	D
Ross (1998)	A	G	B, C		I	A
Russell (1990)	J	A, E, F, G, J	B	D, E	D, E	B
Russell (1988)	J	C, D	I	F, G, K	A, D	B
Sullivan (1984)	B	D, F, G	A		A	C
Sullivan, Ice, & Niedermeyer (2000)	B	D, F, G	A	J	D	D
Watson & Belland (1985)	E					

Legend 1
A. Full course
B. Full program
C. Workshop
D. Gen. print mat.
E. Instruct. module
F. Study guide
G. Job aid
H. Games/simulation
I. Instruct. television
J. Computer-based
K. Any project
L. Multimedia/Web-based
M. Performance support system

Legend 2
A. Gen. des/devel./evaluation proc.
B. Needs assessment
C. Content selection
D. Design/development
E. Production
F. Form. evaluation/usability
G. Implementation/utilization/delivery
H. Management
I. Summative evaluation
J. Learner outcomes
K. No dev. involved

Legend 3
A. K-12 schools
B. Postsecondary
C. Business and industry
D. Health care
E. Military and govt.
F. Continuing and community educ.
G. Employee trng.—other
H. International
I. Context-free

Legend 4
A. Problem analysis
B. Needs assessment
C. Environm'tal anal.
D. Job analysis
E. Task analysis
F. Learning hierarchy
G. Sequencing
H. Cost analysis
I. Dissemination
J. Learner verification
K. Specific technique
L. Prototype/usability testing

Legend 5
A. Case study
B. Descriptive
C. Ethnography
D. Evaluation
E. Experimental
F. Historical
G. Observational
H. Philosophical
I. Qualitative
J. Survey
K. Other

Legend 6
A. Context/product specific
B. Context/product specific with some generalization
C. Generalizations with some context/product specific
D. Generalizations

by implementing student and teacher attitude surveys and student achievement tests. In most cases, Type 1 developmental studies using evaluation research methods employ several techniques for collecting data.

41.3.1.3 The Nature of Conclusions from Type 1 Developmental Research.
Type 1 studies are characterized by their reliance on contextually specific projects and contextually specific conclusions that emerge from such research. This is consistent with the more qualitative orientation of the research, with the applied nature of the research, and with the field's history of using practitioner experience as a source of knowledge.

Over three-quarters of the Type 1 representative developmental studies identified in Table 41.3 have conclusions that are either exclusively directed toward the target product and situation in which the project occurred or have predominantly context-specific conclusions, even though they did generalize to some extent to other situations. (See Table 41.3 for studies classified in terms of A and B types of conclusions.) These context-specific conclusions address issues such as the following:

- *Suggested improvements in the product or program* (Albero-Andres, 1983; Coyle, 1986; Corry, Frick, & Hansen, 1997; Crane & Mylonas, 1988; Cregger & Metzler, 1992; Fischer, Savenye, & Sullivan, 2002; Kanyarusoke, 1985; Klein et al., 2000; Link & Cherow-O'Leary, 1990; Martin & Bramble, 1996; McKenney, 2002; Mendes & Mendes, 1996; Munro & Towne, 1992; C. M. Russell, 1990)

- *The conditions that promote successful use of the product or program* (Borras, 1993; Dabbagh et al., 2000; Hirumi et al., 1994; McKenney, 2002; Munro & Towne, 1992; Pizzuto, 1983; Quinn, 1994; Ross, 1998)

- *The impact of the particular product or program* (Aukerman, 1987; Blackstone, 1990; Cantor, 1988; Fischer et al., 2002; Jones, 1986; Kearsley, 1985; Martin & Bramble, 1996; Petry & Edwards, 1984; Pirolli, 1991; Plummer et al., 1992; D. M. Russell, 1988)

- *The conditions that are conducive to efficient design, development, and/or evaluation of the instructional product or program* (Albero-Andres, 1983; Bednar, 1988; Blackstone, 1990; Buch, 1989; Capell & Dannenberg, 1993; Chou & Sun, 1996; Coyle, 1992; Dick, 1991; Harris & Cady, 1988; Herrington & Oliver, 2000; Jonassen, 1988; Jones, 1986; Kearsley, 1985; Link & Cherow-O'Leary, 1990; Martin & Bramble, 1996; McKenney, 2002; Mielke, 1990; Munro & Towne, 1992; Petry & Edwards, 1984; Pirolli, 1991; Quinn, 1994; C. M. Russell, 1990; D. M. Russell, 1988; Sullivan et al., 2000; Watson & Bellend, 1985)

Even though these conclusions are directed toward a particular product or program, it is clear that the foundational design and development procedures are as important as the product. However, it is possible for these conclusions, even though they are context specific, to provide direction to others who are confronting similar design and development projects.

Some Type 1 studies did present conclusions that were directed toward applications of a more general nature. It should be noted that these studies (see C and D classifications, Table 41.3) were published in journals with a national audience. This may have influenced the manner in which the report was written, or it may have been recommended by a reviewer or even a condition of publication. In any case, many journal articles tend to be less focused on context-specific conclusions than dissertation research reports. The conclusions of these studies, especially those with a less formal quantitative design or with a more descriptive qualitative design, tend to be presented as "lessons learned" rather than as hypothesized relationships or predictions. These generalized lessons are often supported by and discussed in the context of current related literature as well as the design, development, and evaluation project that prompted them. The content of the conclusions in the studies identified in Table 41.3 with more generalized conclusions relate to the conditions that are conducive to efficient design, development, and/or evaluation of instructional products or programs (Alessi, 1988; Bowers & Tsai, 1990; Gay & Mazur, 1993; Medsker, 1992; Noel, 1991; Quinn, 1994; Sullivan, 1984; Sullivan et al., 2000).

41.3.1.4 Typical Type 1 Developmental Studies.
This section has described the nature of Type 1 developmental research in terms of their focus, specifically examining the design, development, and evaluation processes addressed, the research methodologies employed, and the nature of their conclusions. While recent studies have been used to exemplify the range of Type 1 research, thus far particular studies have not been described in detail. Here, we summarize the research by McKenney (2002) and Sullivan et al. (2000) as studies that are representative of the group. These studies reflect the two key Type 1 research formats; McKenney's work was a doctoral dissertation and Sullivan and his co-researchers' was a long-term ID project published in a research journal.

The McKenney (2002) study examined the development of a computer program to support curriculum materials development in the context of secondary science and mathematics education in southern Africa. As with any traditional research project, the study was guided by predetermined questions and was embedded into a conceptual framework supported by current literature on curriculum development, teacher professional development, and computer-based performance support. The project was a careful and extensive documentation of the phases of ISD—needs and context analysis, design, development, and formative evaluation of several prototypes, and summative evaluation. Each phase included different expert and novice participant groups; a total of 510 participants from 15 countries was involved. Like many developmental research projects, the researcher used several different types of instruments for data collection including interviews, questionnaires, observations, logbooks, and document analysis. However, this study included more data collection than most; a total of 108 instruments was employed. Also typical of many Type 1 studies, the conclusions were focused on context-specific variables. McKenney (2002) discusses the validity, practicality, and potential impact of the computer-based performance support program. In addition, she discusses the design principles followed and provides suggestions for conducting developmental research.

McKenney's work (2002) is a detailed report of an extensive study that includes both context-specific and some generalized conclusions, although the clear focus of the study is on the design, development, and evaluation of a computer program to support curriculum development in Africa. As it is a study completed as part of the requirements of a doctoral degree, length is not an issue and the format was undoubtedly dictated by the degree requirements. On the other hand, the Sullivan et al. (2000) study was reported in a research journal. Consequently, it takes on a different form, even though it too is representative of Type 1 developmental research.

Sullivan et al. (2000) describe the development and implementation of a comprehensive K-12 energy education curriculum. When the article was published, the program had been implemented over a 20-year period and used by more than 12 million students in the United States. The report describes the components of the program itself including instructional objectives and test items covering a variety of learning outcomes such as facts, concepts, problem solving, and behavior change. A description of the instructional materials is also provided. Field test data such as posttest scores and student and teacher attitudes are reported and the implementation phase of the project is discussed in detail. Based on two decades of experience with the program, the authors provide 10 guidelines for long-term instructional development projects. The conclusions and recommendations are written in a more general tone; they are lessons learned from a specific practical situation.

The McKenney (2002) dissertation and Sullivan et al. (2000) article exemplify Type 1 developmental research. They are studies that

- describe and document a particular design, development, and evaluation project;
- employ standard design and development procedures;
- utilize a range of research methodologies and data collection instruments;
- draw conclusions from their research which are context specific; and
- tend to serve as dissemination vehicles for exemplary design, development, and/or evaluation strategies.

41.3.2 Type 2 Developmental Research

Type 2 developmental research is the most generalized of the various orientations and typically addresses the design, development, and evaluation processes themselves rather than a demonstration of such processes. The ultimate objective of this research is the production of knowledge, often in the form of a new (or an enhanced) design or development model. This research tends to emphasize

- the use of a particular design technique or process, such as formative evaluation; or
- the use of a comprehensive design, development, or evaluation model; or
- a general examination of design and development as it is commonly practiced in the workplace.

Fifty-eight examples of Type 2 research have been analyzed using the same framework previously employed in the analysis of Type 1, and the results are presented in Table 41.4.

41.3.2.1 Process Foci of Type 2 Developmental Research. We have previously distinguished between *doing* development and *studying* development. In Type 1 research there is a pattern of combining the doing and the studying in the process of discovering superior procedures. However, Type 2 research often does *not* begin with the actual development of an instructional product or program. These studies are more likely to focus on the more generic use of development processes, offering implications for *any* design or development project.

Type 2 studies are more likely to concentrate upon a particular ISD process, rather than the more comprehensive view of development. (See those studies in the Table 41.4 Process Focus column that are labeled B through J as opposed to those labeled A.) For example, Abdelraheem (1990) and Twitchell, Holton, and Trott (2000) both studied evaluation processes, one with respect to instructional module design and the other in reference to the practices of technical trainers in the United States. But while Abdelraheem was involved in a specific design and development project, Twitchell et al. were not. They studied the extent to which technical trainers employ accepted evaluation methods and techniques. The key difference between Type 1 and Type 2 studies that focus on a particular aspect of the total process is that goals of Type 2 studies tend to be more generalized, striving to enhance the ultimate models employed in these procedures. Type 1 research, on the other hand, is more confined to the analysis of a given project.

Type 2 developmental research projects span the entire range of design and development process components from needs assessment and performance analysis (Cowell, 2000; Kunneman & Sleezer, 2000; Tessmer, McCann, & Ludvigsen, 1999) to evaluation (Le Maistre, 1998; Phillips, 2000; Twitchell et al., 2000). In addition, there are studies that address design processes in a more generic fashion. Sample studies of this nature include those by Adamski (1998), Nelson (1990), Rowland (1992), Rowland and Adams (1999), Tracey (2002), Visscher-Voerman (1999), Klimczak and Wedman (1997), and Wedman and Tessmer (1993). This research is part of the growing body of literature contributing to an understanding of the nature of designer decision making. It provides another topical orientation in addition to those studies that examine the various components of traditional instructional systems design models.

Although the majority of the studies cited in Table 41.4 do not tackle the entire design and development process in a comprehensive fashion, some do. For example, Spector, Muraida, and Marlino (1992) proposed an enhanced ISD model for use in courseware authoring, which is grounded in cognitive theory. This use of this model was then described and evaluated in a military training environment. This is a good example of a Type 2 study. Likewise, Richey (1992) proposed a modified ISD procedural model that was based on an empirical examination of those factors that influence employee training effectiveness. This is another example of a comprehensive Type 2 study.

Recently, a few Type 2 studies have examined how ISD models can be applied in settings outside of traditional education

TABLE 41.4. An Analysis of Representative Type 2 Developmental Research Literature

Reference	Product or Program Focus	Process Focus	Use Context	Tools and Techniques Emphasized	Research Method(s) Used	Nature of Conclusions
Abdelraheem (1990)	E	F, J	A, H	J, K	E	C
Adamski (1998)	G	A	C	A, J, K	E, I, K, L	C
Beauchamp (1991)	K	A	A	B	J	D
Burkholder (1981–82)	E, A	F	B	K	E	D
Capell (1990)	J	A	B		B, I	D
Carliner (1998)		D	F		I	C
Cowell (2000)	K	B	C	B	J	D
Cummings (1985)	K	B	C		I	D
Driscoll & Tessmer (1985)	E, K	D, J	A	G, J	E	D
English & Reigeluth (1996)	D	D	B	G	D, I	D
Ford & Wood (1992)	K	D	I	E, F, G	D	C
Forsyth (1997)	B	A	F		I, D, K	C
Fuchs & Fuchs (1986)	A, K	F	A	J	K	D
Gauger (1987)	B	I	B, D		D	C
Goel & Pirolli (1988)	K	A, K	C		G, I	D
Hallamon (2001)	K	C	I	E	J	D
Harrison et al. (1991)	B	A, G, H	B		I, J	C
Higgins & Reiser (1985)	K	D	C		E	D
Jones & Richey (2000)	E	A	C	A, J	Q	D
Julian (2001)	K	A	I		I	C
Keller (1987)	A, K	D	A, I	J	E, J, K	C
Kerr (1983)	A, E	A	A, B		J	C
Kim (1984)	K	A	H			C
King & Dille (1993)	K	A	C		A	B
Klimczak & Wedman (1997)	K	A	G	H	I, J	C
Kress (1990)	A	A	C		E, J	D
Kunneman & Sleezer (2000)	K	K	C		A	B
Le Maistre (1998)	K	F	I		I	B
Le Maistre & Weston (1996)	D	F	C		E	B
Luiz (1983)	K	A	I		H	D
McAleese (1988)	K	D	I	E, F, G	D	C
Means, Jonassen, & Dwyer (1997)	D, E	J	B		E	B
Nadolski, Kirschner, van Merrienboer, & Hummel (2001)	J	D	B	E, G	A, D, I	C
Nelson (1990)	K	A, K	G	A, D, E	G, I	D
Nicolson (1988)	K	D, E	B	E, F, G	D	C
Phillips (2000)	K	I	C	K	I	D
Piper (1991)	K	H	C	J	A	D
Pirolli (1991)	K	D, E	I	E, F, G	D	D
Plass & Salisbury (2002)	L	A	C, E	L	D	C

Reference	Type of product	Design/development phase	Context	Technique	Research method	Generalizability
Richey (1992)	C, K	A, J	C	B, C	I, J	D
Riplinger (1987)	K	B, C	J	E	B, J	D
Rojas (1988)	C	I	C		D	D
Rowland (1992)	K	A, K	B, C, E		G, I	D
Rowland & Adams (1999)	K	A	B, C		J	D
Roytek (1999)	K	D	C	L	A, I, K	B
Shambaugh & Magliaro (2001)	A	A	B	J	A	C
Shellnut (1999)	K	A	A, B, C, D, E	K	J	D
Spector, Muraida, & Marlino (1992)	J	A, E	E	K	G	B
Taylor & Ellis (1991)	A	A	E		D	B
Tessmer, McCann, & Ludvigsen (1999)	B	B	C, D	B	A	D
Tracey (2002)	K	A	I		E, I, K	
Twitchell, Holton, & Trott (2000)	K	F, I	C, G		J	D
Visscher-Voerman (1999)	K	A	I		A, I	D
Wagner (1984)	A, K	I	B	J, K	E	D
Wedman & Tessmer (1993)	K	A, K	C		J	D
Weston, McAlpine, & Bordonaro (1995)	K	F	I		B	D
Wreathall & Connelly (1992)	K	I, J	E	J, K	A, J	C
Zemke (1985)	K	A, K	C		J	B

Type of product
A. Full course
B. Full program
C. Workshop
D. Gen. print mat.
E. Instruct. module
F. Study guide
G. Job aid
H. Games/simulation
I. Instruct. television
J. Computer-based
K. Any project
L. Multimedia/Web-based
M. Performance support system

Design/development phase
A. Gen. des/devel./evaluation proc.
B. Needs assessment
C. Content selection
D. Design/development
E. Production
F. Form. evaluation/usability
G. Implementation/utilization/delivery
H. Management
I. Summative evaluation
J. Learner outcomes
K. No dev. involved

Context
A. K–12 schools
B. Postsecondary
C. Business and industry
D. Health care
E. Military and govt.
F. Continuing and community educ.
G. Employee trng.—other
H. International
I. Context-free

Technique
A. Problem analysis
B. Needs assessment
C. Environmental anal.
D. Job analysis
E. Task analysis
F. Learning hierarchy
G. Sequencing
H. Cost analysis
I. Dissemination
J. Learner verification
K. Specific tech.
L. Prototype/usability testing

Research method
A. Case study
B. Descriptive
C. Ethnography
D. Evaluation
E. Experimental
F. Historical
G. Observational
H. Philosophical
I. Qualitative
J. Survey
K. Other

Generalizability
A. Context/product specific
B. Context/product specific with some generalization
C. Generalizations with some context/product specific
D. Generalizations

and training. For example, Plass and Salisbury (2002) described and evaluated a design model for a Web-based knowledge management system. Carliner (1998) conducted a naturalistic study of design practices in a museum setting and proposed an enhanced model of instructional design for informal learning in museums. Both of these studies included empirical data to support the use of the ISD approach to nontraditional products and settings.

41.3.2.2 Research Methodologies Employed in Type 2 Developmental Research.
While the case study served as the dominant methodological orientation of Type 1 developmental research, it is far less prominent in Type 2 studies. This is not surprising given the fact that Type 2 research typically does not involve a specific design and development project. There is a much greater diversity of research methods employed in the representative Type 2 studies identified in Table 41.4. Not only are experimental and quasi-experimental studies common, but this table even shows a study using philosophical techniques, as well as a variety of qualitative methodologies. (See Table 41.4's Research Methods Used column.)

Even though case studies are not the overwhelming norm in Type 2 research, they are nonetheless found. (See Table 41.4 for studies classified in terms of an A-type research methodology.) As with other developmental studies, case study techniques are sometimes employed in Type 2 research, which includes a description of the actual design and development processes followed in the creation of a particular product or in the demonstration of a particular process. Wreathall and Connelly (1992) document the development of a method of using performance indicators as a technique for determining training effectiveness. In true Type 1 fashion they describe the technique and the manner in which they applied it in a given context. This facet utilizes case study methods. However, they extend their study to verify the relevance of their technique through the use of a structured survey interview of other professionals in the field. (The latter phase of the research warrants its classification as a Type 2 study.) The Wreathall and Connelly study is typical of the Type 2 research, which uses case study methods in that the methods are used in combination with other research techniques.

Experimental and quasi-experimental techniques can serve a variety of functions in Type 2 developmental research. (See Table 41.4 for studies classified in terms of an E-type research methodology.) They are often used as a way of verifying the procedure in terms of learner outcomes. Means, Jonassen, and Dwyer (1997) examined the impact of embedding relevance strategies into instruction following the ARCS model by using experimental design to determine their influence on achievement and motivation. Keller (1987) used quasi-experimental methods to test the impact of the ARCS model as it was applied to the development of teacher in-service training workshops. Le Maistre and Weston (1996) used a counterbalanced design to examine the revision practices of instructional designers when they are provided with various types of data sources. In these studies, the experimentation is critical to the verification and evaluation of a particular design and development technique. This is not unlike the use of experimental and quasi-experimental techniques in other types of research.

Surveys are frequently used in Type 2 developmental studies. In Type 1 studies surveys were typically another means of determining product impact or effectiveness with learners and/or instructors in a given education or training situation. This technique is also used in Type 2 research as in the studies by Keller (1987) and Richey (1992). However, in Type 2 studies the survey is frequently used as a means of gathering data from designers in a variety of settings. Beauchamp (1991), Hallamon (2002), Klimczak and Wedman (1997), Rowland and Adams (1999), Twitchell et al. (2000), and Wedman and Tessmer (1993) all conducted surveys across a range of typical design environments—Beauchamp to validate the use a wide range of affective variables in the instructional design process, Hallamon to investigate the factors that influence the use of task analysis, Klimczak and Wedman to examine success factors in instructional design projects, Rowland and Adams to explore designers' perspectives toward systems thinking, Twitchell et al. to determine evaluation practices in technical training settings, and Wedman and Tessmer to analyze the nature of designer decisions.

Qualitative research methods are often employed in Type 2 developmental research studies. (See Table 41.4 for studies classified in terms of an I-type research methodology.) These studies frequently employ a structured interview to gather data from participants. For example, Nadolski, Kirschner, van Merrienboer, and Hummel (2001) used structured interviews to determine how different types of practitioners approached cognitive task analysis. Jones and Richey (2000) interviewed instructional designers and customers to investigate the use of rapid prototyping. Interviews are sometimes used in combination with other data collection methods. Visscher-Voerman (1999) conducted interviews of professional designers and analyzed project documents to determine the design strategies used in various training and education contexts. Richey (1992) conducted structured personal interviews with trainees to verify and/or expand the more quantitative data collected in her study. Similarly, Rowland (1992) used a systematic posttask interview in addition to other data collection techniques designed to document one's decision-making processes.

In addition to interviews, other qualitative methods are used in Type 2 studies. English and Reigeluth (1996) used qualitative data analysis techniques to examine the use of elaboration theory for sequencing instruction. Harrison et al. (1991) used qualitative data in the development of a distance education assessment instrument. Nelson's (1990) Le Maistre's (1998), Nelson's (1990), and Rowland's (1992) use of "think-aloud protocols" reflects not only a cognitive orientation, but also a qualitative one.

41.3.2.3 The Nature of Conclusions from Type 2 Developmental Research.
Type 2 studies are unique among developmental research in that they are ultimately directed toward general principles, which are applicable in a wide range of design and development projects. Those studies described in Table 41.4 are typical. Most of these studies present generalized conclusions (see the studies in Table 41.4 that are classified in terms of C and D types of conclusions), and the majority of these studies have *all* generalized conclusions.

The nature of the conclusions in Type 2 research also varies somewhat from that in Type 1. The most noticeable difference is that the Type 2 conclusions pertain to a technique or model, as opposed to a product or program. The issues that are addressed in these conclusions can be summarized in the following manner.

- *Evidence of the validity and/or effectiveness of a particular technique or model* (Adamski, 1998; Beauchamp, 1991; Burkholder, 1981–1982; Driscoll & Tessmer, 1985; English & Reigeluth, 1996; Forsyth, 1998; Fuchs & Fuchs, 1986; Gauger, 1987; Harrison et al., 1991; Keller, 1987; Kim, 1984; Kress, 1990; Kunneman & Sleezer; 2000; Means et al., 1997; Nadolski et al., 2001; Plass & Salisbury, 2002: Richey, 1992; Shambaugh & Magliaro, 2001; Shellnut, 1999; Tessmer et al., 1999; Twitchell et al., 2000; Tracey, 2002; Wagner, 1984; Weston, McAlpine, & Bordonaro, 1995; Wreathall & Connelly, 1992)
- *Conditions and procedures that facilitate the successful use of a particular technique or model* (Abdelraheem, 1990; Adamski, 1998; Beauchamp, 1991; Burkholder, 1981–1982; Cowall, 2001; Cummings, 1985; English & Reigeluth, 1996; Ford & Wood, 1992; Forsyth, 1998; Fuchs & Fuchs, 1986; Gauger, 1987; Goel & Pirolli, 1988; Hallamon, 2002; Jones & Richey, 2000; Keller, 1987; Kim, 1984; King & Dille, 1993; Kress, 1990; Le Maistre & Weston, 1996; Nelson, 1990; Nicholson, 1988; Phillips, 2000; Piper, 1991; Rowland, 1992; Rowland & Adams, 1999; Roytek, 2000; Shambaugh & Magliaro, 2001; Shellnut, 1999; Spector et al., 1992; Tracey, 2002; Twitchell et al., 2000; Visscher-Voerman, 1999)
- *Explanations of the successes or failures encountered in using a particular technique or model* (Cowall, 2001; Higgins & Reiser, 1985; Jones & Richey, 2000; Kerr, 1983; King & Dille, 1993; Klimczak & Wedman, 1997; Kress, 1990; Le Maistre & Weston, 1996; McAleese, 1988; Means et al., 1997; Nicolson, 1988; Pirolli, 1991; Roytek, 2000; Taylor & Ellis, 1991; Tracey, 2002; Wedman & Tessmer, 1993; Zemke, 1985)
- *A synthesis of events and/or opinions related to the use of a particular technique or model* (Carliner, 1998; Cowall, 2001; Jones & Richey, 2000; Julian, 2001; Le Maistre; 1998; Luiz, 1983; Nadolski et al., 2001; Phillips, 2000; Pirolli, 1991; Riplinger, 1987; Rojas, 1988; Roytek, 2000; Visscher-Voerman, 1999; Weston et al., 1995)
- *A new or enhanced design, development, and/or evaluation model* (Adamski, 1998; Beauchamp, 1991; Carliner, 1998; Forsyth, 1998; Jones & Richey, 2000; King & Dille, 1993; McAleese, 1988; Nadolski et al., 2001; Plass & Salisbury, 2002: Richey, 1992; Spector et al., 1992; Tessmer et al., 1999; Tracey, 2002; Wedman & Tessmer, 1993)

It is not uncommon for a given Type 2 study to generate more than one type of conclusion. This was less likely to be the case with respect to Type 1 developmental research.

41.3.2.4 Typical Type 2 Developmental Studies.
We now illustrate two typical Type 2 research studies in more detail. Tessmer et al. (1999)[4] described a theoretical and procedural model for conducting a type of needs assessment, called *Needs reassessment*. According to the authors, "Needs reassessment is a hybrid process, one that has the purposes of needs assessment and the timing of summative evaluation" (p. 86). The model is used to reassess existing training programs to determine if training excesses and deficiencies exist. Like many other authors in the field who propose a new ISD model, Tessmer et al. (1999) use an acronym for their model—CODE—which stands for the four foci of the needs reassessment process (criticality, opportunity, difficulty, and emphasis). However, unlike many recent ISD models, the validity of the CODE model was empirically tested. Tessmer et al. (1999) report on two studies—a needs reassessment of corporate training program and a medical training program reassessment. Both employed the case study method to examine the application of the CODE model. A variety of data sources was used including surveys, interviews, and extant data analysis. The authors provide generalized conclusions but wisely caution that their model requires further validation in other instructional settings.

Another example of Type 2 developmental research is a study by Jones and Richey (2000). These authors conducted an in-depth examination of the use of rapid prototyping methods in two instructional design projects in natural work settings. The study used qualitative methods; data were collected from structured personal interviews, activity logs, and a review of extant data. Participants included two experienced instructional designers who employed rapid prototyping to the design and development of two projects—a 1-day instructor led course with a matching on-line tutorial for the automotive industry and a 1-day instructor led training program in the health-care industry. In addition, one client was interviewed to obtain perceptions of product quality and usability, cycle time reduction, and customer satisfaction. After discussing how rapid prototyping was successfully used in the context of the study, Jones and Richey (2000) provide generalized conclusions and suggest a revised model of ISD that includes rapid prototyping.

Each of these studies represents Type 2 developmental research. They are typical of Type 2 studies because of the following characteristics:

- an orientation toward studying the design and development process, rather than demonstrating particular strategies;
- a tendency toward the use of multiple sources of data;
- a tendency to develop generalized principles and conclusions with respect to the design and development process, or a part of the process; and
- an effort to identify, describe, explain, or validate those conditions that facilitate successful design and development.

41.4 THE METHODOLOGY OF DEVELOPMENTAL RESEARCH

The aim of this section is to provide some methodological direction to those entertaining a developmental research project. In

---

[4]The article by Tessmer et al. won the 1999 ETR&D Award for Outstanding Research on Instructional Development. The award is given by the development section of *Educational Technology Research and Development (ETR&D)* for the best paper describing research findings that can be used to improve the process of instructional design, development, and evaluation.

essence, it is a discussion of establishing the credibility of a given developmental study by assuring authenticity and methodological rigor. Because many topics can be addressed in a number of ways, this section may also help one recognize the potential of a given problem to be addressed as a developmental topic. This section describes developmental methodologies in terms of the traditional stages of planning and reporting research projects:

- problem definition,
- literature reviews, and
- research procedures.

41.4.1 Defining the Research Problem

The perceived authenticity of a particular developmental research project often depends on the problem selected. Is the problem one that is common to many designers and developers? Is it one that is currently critical to the profession? Does the problem reflect realistic constraints and conditions typically faced by designers? Does the problem pertain to cutting-edge technologies and processes? Answers to these questions predict not only interest in the project, but also whether the research is viewed as relevant. "Explorations of research relevance are typically examinations of shared perceptions, the extent to which researchers' notions of relevance are congruent with the perceptions and needs of practitioners" (Richey, 1998, p. 8). This is particularly true with developmental research, where the object of such research is clearly not simply knowledge, but knowledge that practitioners consider usable.

41.4.1.1 Focusing the Problem. Given a relevant topic, the research project must first be given a "developmental twist." This begins in the problem definition stage. It is done by focusing the research problem on a particular aspect of the design, development, or evaluation *process,* as opposed to focusing on a particular variable that impacts learning or, perhaps, the impact of a type of media (to name two alternative approaches). Type 1 developmental studies focus upon a given instructional product, program, process, or tool. They reflect an interest in identifying either general development principles or situation-specific recommendations. These studies may ultimately validate a particular design or development technique or tool. Type 2 studies, on the other hand, focus on a given design, development or evaluation model or process. They may involve constructing and validating unique design models and processes, as well as identifying those conditions that facilitate their successful use.

The problem definition stage must also establish the research parameters. At the minimum, this involves determining whether the research will be conducted as the design and development is occurring or whether retrospective data will be collected on a *previously* developed program or set of materials. Then the scope of the study must be established. How much of the design and development process will be addressed? Will the research address

- all parts of the *design* of the instruction?
- the *development* (or part of the development) of the instruction?

- the *evaluation* of the instruction? If so, will formative, and summative, and confirmative evaluation be addressed?
- the *revision* and *retesting* of the instruction?

Developmental studies often are structured in phases. For example, comprehensive Type 1 studies may have an analysis phase, design phase, a development phase, and a try-out and evaluation phase. Another organization of a Type 1 study would include phases directed toward first analysis, then prototype development and testing, and, finally, prototype revision and retesting. McKinney (2001) is an example of this type of study. Type 2 studies may have a model construction phase, a model implementation phase, and a model validation phase. Forsyth (1998), Adamski (1998), and Tracey (2002) followed this pattern. In these studies the model construction phase was further divided to include comprehensive literature reviews, model construction, and model revision phases.

41.4.1.2 Framing the Problem. Seels (1994) describes typical processes one uses to explain the goals of a developmental research project. For example, *research questions,* rather than hypotheses, commonly serve as the organizing framework for developmental studies. This tactic is appropriate if there is not a firm base in the literature that one can use as a basis for formulating a hypothesis. This is often the case with such research, especially if the problem focuses on emerging technologies. However, research questions are also more appropriate for qualitative research, a common developmental methodology.

41.4.1.3 Identifying Limitations. Because developmental research is often context specific, one must be particularly concerned with the limitations or unique conditions that may be operating in a particular study. Such limitations will effect the extent to which one may generalize the conclusions of the study. The results may be applicable only in the situation studied or to others with similar characteristics, rather than being generalizable to a wider range of instructional environments.

41.4.2 Review of Related Literature

Typically, literature reviews concentrate on the specific variables being studied, usually the independent and dependent variables. This orientation may not prove useful in many developmental studies. The goal of the literature review, however, remains the same as with other types of research projects. It is to establish the conceptual foundations of the study.

The literature review in Type 1 developmental studies, for example, may address topics, such as

- procedural models that might be appropriate for the task at hand;
- characteristics of similar effective instructional products, programs, or delivery systems;
- factors that have impacted the use of the target development processes in other situations; and

- factors impacting the implementation and management of the target instructional product, program, or delivery system in other situations.

Literature reviews in Type 2 studies may address topics such as

- a description of models (either formally published or currently in use) similar to the one being studied, including their strengths and weaknesses;
- research on the targeted process (for example, task analysis or evaluation of organizational impact); and
- research on factors impacting the use of a given model or process (for example, factors that facilitate the use of rapid prototyping models).

Both types of studies often address the methodology of developmental research itself in the literature review.

In developmental studies directed toward innovative instructional environments or innovative design and development processes, it would not be unusual to find little research in the literature that is *directly* relevant. In such cases the researcher must still identify literature that is relevant to the foundational theory of the project, even though the link may be indirect. For example, there *is* literature on factors that affect the use of computers and other media in instruction, but there may be little on factors related to the specific use of virtual reality as a delivery system. In developmental research the conceptual framework for the study may be found in literature from actual practice environments (such as an evaluation report) as well as from traditional research literature directed toward theory construction.

41.4.3 Research Procedures

Often developmental research occurs in natural work environments. This tends to enhance the credibility of the research, as well as create methodological dilemmas for the researcher. Nonetheless, whether the research is conducted during the design and development process or retrospectively, the best research pertains to actual projects, rather than simulated or idealized projects. Perhaps it is the "real-life" aspect of developmental research that results in studies that frequently take even more time to complete than other types of research. There are often more changes in one's research plans and procedures as a result of unanticipated events than is typical in other types of research. Consequently, detailed research procedures and time lines are most important.

41.4.3.1 Participants. There are often multiple types of participants in a given developmental research project, and if the study is conducted in phases, the participants may vary among phases. The nature of the participating populations tends to vary with the type of developmental research being conducted. Typical populations include

- designers, developers, and evaluators;
- clients;
- instructors and/or program facilitators;

TABLE 41.5. Common Participants in Developmental Research Studies

Developmental Research	Function/Phase	Type of Participant
Type 1	Product design & development	Designers, Developers, Clients
Type 1	Product evaluation	Evaluators, Clients, Learners, Instructors, Organizations
Type 1	Validation of tool or technique	Designers, Developers, Evaluators, Users
Type 2	Model development	Designers, Developers, Evaluators, Researchers, Theorists
Type 2	Model use	Designers, Developers, Evaluators, Clients
Type 2	Model validation	Designers, Developers, Evaluators, Clients, Learners, Instructors, Organizations

- organizations;
- design and development researchers and theorists; and
- learners and other types of users.

Table 41.5 shows the array of persons that most commonly participate in these projects and the various phases of the project in which they tend to contribute data.

For example, participants in the Tracey (2002) study included researchers and theorists in model development, designers in model use, and learners and instructors in model validation. This was a comprehensive Type 2 study. The participants in Jones and Richey's (2000) Type 2 study were designers, developers, and clients. This study primarily addressed model use. McKenney's research (2002) was a Type 1 study. Here, in the phase addressing the construction and prototyping of an electronic design tool, the participants were developers, users, evaluators, and a variety of ID experts. Then, in the phase evaluating and validating the tool, participants were users (preservice and in-service teachers and curriculum developers, i.e., designers) and experts.

41.4.3.2 Research Design. It is not uncommon for a developmental research project to also utilize multiple research methodologies and designs, with different designs again being used for different phases of the project. Table 41.6 presents a summary of those research methods that are most frequently used in the various types and phases of developmental research. This table reflects those studies presented in Tables 41.3 and 41.4.

Table 41.6 highlights some typical methodology patterns used in developmental studies. In Type 1 studies critical design and development processes are often explicated using case study methods. Interviews, observations, and document analysis are techniques used to gather the case study data and to document the processes used and the conditions under which they are employed as well. Pizzuto's (1983) development of a simulation game is a classic example of this type of methodology.

TABLE 41.6. Common Research Methods Employed in Developmental Research Studies

Developmental Research Type	Function/Phase	Research Methodologies Employed
Type 1	Product design & development	Case study, In-depth interview, Field observation, Document analysis
Type 1	Product evaluation	Evaluation, Case study, Survey, In-depth interview, Document analysis
Type 1	Validation of tool or technique	Evaluation, Experimental, Expert review, In-depth interview, Survey
Type 2	Model development	Literature review, Case study, Survey, Delphi, Think-aloud protocols
Type 2	Model use	Survey, In-depth interview, Case study, Field observation, Document analysis
Type 2	Model validation	Experimental, In-depth interview, Expert review, Replication

Evaluation research techniques are often employed in Type 1 studies to determine the effectiveness of the resulting product or the particular techniques used during the design and development project. As with all evaluation research, a variety of data collection techniques is possible. Sullivan and co-Researchers' (2000) examination of the development and use of a K-12 energy education program employed a formal evaluation design, in addition to a case study. Smith (1993) used in-depth interviews and document analysis techniques in her evaluation of an executive development program. Sometimes, a full experiment is constructed to test the product or technique.

In Type 2 research models of the full design and development process, or of a particular part of the process, are constructed in a variety of ways, including the following.

- By conducting surveys of designers and developers with regard to projects in which they have been involved, such as Shellnut's (1999) study of motivation design or Phillip's (2000) study of organizational impact evaluation techniques
- By synthesizing models from the literature, such as Adamski's (1998) reviews of instructional technology, human factors, and aviation literature in his efforts to devise an initial model for designing job performance aids for use in high-risk settings
- By arriving at a consensus of opinion of respects experts in the field using Delphi techniques, such as Tracey's (2002) methods of finalizing her multiple intelligence design model
- By conducting experiments to validate particular design and development models, such as Tracey's (2002) and Adamski's (1998) projects

Developmental researchers are commonly confronted by methodological dilemmas. One is the need to account for contextual variables, especially in those studies taking place in a natural work setting. For example, to what extent do the client's design experience and sophistication, or designer expertise, or time pressures impact the success of a particular project? Because it is typically not possible to control such factors in the research design, the researcher is then obligated to describe

(and measure, if possible) these variables carefully in an effort to account for their impact.

Another common situation that is potentially problematic is when the researcher is also a participant in the study, such as when the researcher is also the designer or developer. Although this situation is not preferable, it is not unusual. Care must be taken to ensure objectivity through consistent, systematic data collection techniques and the collection of corroborating data, if possible. Often structured logs and diaries completed by several project participants according to a regularly established schedule create a structure that facilitates the generation of reliable and comparable data.

Another frequent problem is maintaining the integrity of recall data. Many studies rely on self-reports of past projects. Others use structured interviews of participants. Using previously prepared documents or data from others involved in the same project facilitates a triangulation process to validate the data collected.

41.4.3.3 Collecting, Analyzing, and Reporting Data.
Data collection in a developmental study takes a variety of forms depending on the focus of the research. The validity of the conclusions is often dependent on the richness of the data set as well as the quality of the research design. Typical types of data collected in developmental research relate to

- documentation of the design, development, and evaluation tasks, including profiling the design and development context and collecting data such as work time and expenses, problems encountered and decisions made, adjustments made in the original plans, designer reactions and attitudes, or records of concurrent work patterns;
- documentation of the conditions under which the development and implementation took place, including factors such as equipment and resources available, participant expertise and background, or time and client constraints; and
- identification of the results of predesign needs assessments, formative, summative, and confirmative evaluations,

including documentation of the target populations and the implementation context and measures of learning, transfer, and the impact of the intervention on the organization.

As with all research projects, participants must be fully informed of the nature of the research, not be coerced to be involved, and be assured that the data will be both anonymous and confidential. Not only must the participants be informed and give their consent, but often written consent from their organizations is required as well. Data may be sensitive and proprietary in nature, and researchers must be attuned to these issues and their ramifications.

Data analysis and synthesis in a developmental study are not unlike those in other research projects. There are likely to be descriptive data presentations and qualitative data analyses using data from documentation, interviews, and observations. Traditional quantitative data analyses techniques are used as well.

The best techniques for reporting developmental data, however, have not been firmly established. There can be a massive amount of data, especially with Type 1 studies. Journals do not provide for a detailed documentation of such data. Often, the raw data sets are too massive even to include in a dissertation appendix.

In response to this dilemma, some researchers are using Web sites as data repositories. For example, full results of a needs assessment may be included in a Web site, or complete copies of electronic tools can be provided, or full transcripts of designer interviews can be presented. Assuming that these Web sites are stable and accurate, this solution allows for full disclosure of data that should prove valuable to practitioners and researchers alike. With full data sets, practitioners should be to apply general lessons to their own work environments. With full data sets, researchers should have opportunities for secondary analysis of data (an option seldom available to researchers in this field), as well as opportunities to replicate fully the research in other settings.

41.5 RECENT INNOVATIVE DEVELOPMENTAL RESEARCH

Recently, innovative lines of developmental research have extended the boundaries of the more traditional orientation to developmental research previously discussed in this chapter. This work concerns mainly the development of instruction using newer models and procedures of instructional design that reflect the influence of cognitive science, especially with respect to higher-level cognitive skills (van Merrienboer, Jelsma, & Paas, 1992). Moreover, constructivist influences are evident in the emphasis on the role of context in design (Richey & Tessmer, 1995), in examination of the social and collaborative nature of learning (Duffy & Jonassen, 1992), and in the development of new approaches to instruction such as anchored instruction (Bransford, Sherwood, Hasselbring, Kinzer, & Williams, 1990), or case-based instruction (Schank, Berman, & Macpherson, 1999). The more recent research to be considered here addresses areas such as designer decision making, knowledge acquisition tools, and the use of automated development tools.

By its very nature, the research on designer decision making is Type 2 research aimed at understanding and improving the design process. The other research tends to focus on improving the design process through the development of new tools and techniques. Sometimes this is Type 1 research involving a particular product or context, but more frequently it is Type 2 research oriented toward the development of generic tools. The following section summarizes important findings and issues emerging from these research activities.

41.5.1 Trends in Research on Design and Designer Decision Making

Design has been described as decision making, simulation, a creative activity, a scientific process or "a very complicated act of faith" (Freeman, 1983, p. 3). Research on how people design, regardless of what is being designed, has shown that designers select certain elements from a large number of possibilities and combine these elements to develop a functional and aesthetically pleasing solution to a problem (Zaff, 1987). Although a definitive, unified description of how people design is yet to be fully developed (Shedroff, 1994), most researchers agree that design combines both rational and intuitive thought processes that are derived from the knowledge and creativity of the designer (Nadin & Novak, 1987).

To understand the design process, it is necessary to distinguish design activities from other forms of thinking. The theoretical basis for most studies of design comes from the literature on human problem solving, where Simon (1981) suggests an all-encompassing view of design that incorporates nearly any kind of planning activity. In fact, he considers design as a fundamental characteristic of human thought: Everyone designs who devises courses of action aimed at changing existing situations into preferred ones. Simon's conception of design as problem solving leads to the characterization of design as a process of optimization among various solution alternatives.

An alternative theoretical orientation views design as an experiential, constructive process where an individual designer shapes the problem and solution through cycles of situated action and reflection (Suchman, 1987). In this sense, design problems are constructed by the designer through a process of "dialogue" with the situation in which the designer engages in metaphorical processes that relate the current design state to the repertoire of objects/solutions known by the designer. Design typically flows through four major stages: *naming* (where designers identify the main issues in the problem), *framing* (establishing the parameters of the problem), *moving* (taking an experimental design action), and *reflecting* (evaluating and criticizing the move and the frame). Schon (1983, 1985, 1987) has noted that designers reflect on moves in three ways: by judging the desirability and consequences of the move, by examining the implications of a move in terms of conformity or violation of earlier moves, and by understanding new problems or potentials the move has created. In part, this involves "seeing" the current situation in a new way (Rowland, 1993). As a designer moves through the design process, the situation "talks back" to the designer and causes a reframing of the problem. This reframing is often accomplished by relating the current situation to previous experiences. Obstacles or difficulties in the design situation provide opportunities for new insights into the problem. Because of its cyclical nature, design thinking naturally benefits from reflection in action, and designers often maintain sketchbooks and diaries to support reflection (Cheng, 2000; Webster, 2001). These and other aspects of reflection assume that a designer possesses a willingness to be thoughtful and reflective, is able to understand the context in which assumptions and actions are formed, and is willing to explore alternatives and be exposed to interpretive considerations through dialogue with others (Moallem, 1998). In some sense, a designer is engaged in learning as well as design, because the designer's personal knowledge structures are altered by the information present in the design environment (McAleese, 1988).

From a social view, design is a collaborative activity where conversation, argumentation, and persuasion are used to achieve consensus about perspectives and actions that might be taken to solve the design problem (Bucciarelli, 2001; Lave & Wenger, 1991; Stumpf & McDonnell, 1999). The design process, therefore, includes both shared and distributed cognition (Lanzara, 1983; Roth, 2001), with the design team developing a shared understanding of the problem through conversations and representations (Hedberg & Sims, 2001; Rowland, 1996), and a solution to the problem through individual and collaborative design efforts (Hutchins, 1991; Walz, Elam, & Curtis, 1993). Often, collaborative design processes generate questions and requests for information and opinions among group members. Conflicting viewpoints are debated and differences of opinion are negotiated. Mutually agreeable solutions result from rethinking, restructuring, and synthesizing alternate points of view. In this way, dialogue transforms individual thinking, creating collective thought and socially constructed knowledge within the team (Sherry & Myers, 1998).

41.5.1.1 The Instructional Design Task Environment.
What makes design a special form of problem solving, in part, is the nature of design problems. Reitman (1964) has identified a category of problems that he calls "ill defined," where starting states, goal states, and allowable transformations of the problem are not specified. Simon (1973) proposes a similar classification but notes that problems can fall along a continuum between well defined and ill defined. The point at which a problem becomes ill defined is largely a function of the problem solver, in that the goals, attitudes, and knowledge of the problem solver determine the degree to which a problem may be ill defined. Goel and Pirolli (1988) take issue with Simon's broad characterization of design. They identify several features that distinguish design from other forms of problem solving, including the initial "fuzziness" of the problem statement, limited or delayed feedback from the world during problem-solving activities, an artifact that must function independently from the designer, and "no right or wrong answers, only better and worse ones" (Goel & Pirolli, 1988, p. 7). Chandrasekaran (1987) concurs, noting that at one extreme are those rare design problems that require innovative behavior where neither the knowledge sources nor the problem-solving strategies are known in advance. Such activity might be more properly termed creating or inventing,

and results in a completely new product. Other design problems are closer to routine but may require some innovation because of the introduction of new requirements for a product that has already been designed.

Certainly, how a designer functions in the design environment is related to what is being designed (the design task environment). Initially, design goals are often poorly specified and can involve the performance goals for the object or system, constraints on the development process (such as cost), or constraints on the design process (such as time required for completion). Part of the designer's task is to formulate more specific goals based on the constraints of the problem. The designer then identifies criteria for selecting and eliminating various elements and, finally, makes decisions based on these criteria (Kerr, 1983). Pirolli and Greeno (1988) noted that the instructional design task environment consists of "the alternatives that a problem solver has available and the various states that can be produced during problem solving by the decisions that the problem solver makes in choosing among alternatives" (p. 182). They suggest that instructional design has three levels of generality: global, intermediate, and local. At each level, designers are concerned with three types of issues: goals and constraints, technological resources, and theoretical resources. Global-level design decisions are concerned mainly with the content and goals of instruction. At the intermediate level, lessons and activities are identified and sequenced. At the local level, instructional designers make decisions about how information is to be presented to learners and how specific learning tasks are to be organized. This description of the instructional design task environment is similar in many respects to the "variables" of instruction identified by Reigeluth (1983a). Hwoever, Pirolli and Greeno (1988) also noted an interesting gap in instructional design research: nearly all of the descriptive and prescriptive theories of instructional design focus on instructional products, while there is little research dedicated to describing the instructional design process. A few researchers have subsequently addressed issues surrounding the instructional design task environment (Dijkstra, 2001; Murphy, 1992), attempting to draw parallels to other design domains. Rathbun (1999) has provided a comprehensive activity-oriented analysis of the work of instructional design that confirms many of the theoretical predictions of design studies in other areas. Other researchers have established that the way the process is portrayed visually impacts a designer's impression of the process (Branch, 1997; Branch & Bloom, 1995; Rezabek & Cochenour, 1996). New approaches to instructional design have emerged as designers explore procedural techniques from other fields, such as rapid prototyping (Rathbun, 1997) and situated instructional design (Rowland, 1993; Wilson, 1995). Research has also focused on collaborative aspects of the instructional design and development process, to understand and improve design team interactions (Hedberg & Sims, 2001), content production procedures (Keppel, 2001), and project management strategies (McDaniel & Liu, 1996; Phillips, 2001)

41.5.1.2 Design Thinking and Instructional Design.
Studies of the cognitive processes of designers in domains other than instructional design indicate that the design process is iterative and cyclical, with two distinct categories of

designer behavior: problem structuring and problem solving (Akin, Chen, Dave, & Pithavadian, 1986). Problem structuring transforms the information obtained through functional analysis into scenarios that partition the design space into a hierarchical organization of design units along with the parameters of the units and relationships between units. The design units are then arranged in various ways until a solution is found that meets the requirements and constraints established earlier. Furthermore, the structure of the problem can affect the designer's performance. When the information of a design problem is provided in a more hierarchical structure, solutions tend to be faster, more clustered, stable, and more successful in satisfying design requirements (Carroll, Thomas, Miller, & Friedman, 1980). While problem structuring establishes the problem space, problem solving completes the design task by producing solutions that satisfy the requirements and constraints for each design unit. Solution proceeds under a control structure that is established through problem structuring and consists of successive generate/test actions that progress toward the final solution. Problem solving in design also contains a feedback component that communicates results of the solution to higher levels, where restructuring of the problem space can be undertaken if the partial solution demands such an action (Akin et al., 1986).

In their studies of the design process, Goel and Pirolli (1988) noted a number of additional characteristics of design problem solving. Observations of three experienced designers (an architect, a mechanical engineer, and an instructional designer) using think-aloud protocols revealed that during the design task these designers engaged in extensive problem structuring (decomposing the problem into modules) and performance modeling of the artifact at various stages of its design. Each designer also employed evaluation functions and "stopping rules" that controlled the decomposition of the problem. Designers tended to evaluate their decisions at several levels continuously through the process, employing cognitive strategies to decompose problems into "leaky modules" (Goel & Pirolli, 1988, p. 20). Although extensive restructuring of the design problem into several modules was observed, the designers did not encapsulate each module, but rather they monitored the design process to assure that decisions made in one module did not adversely affect other modules. The designers handled "leaks" between modules by "plugging" the leaks, that is, ignoring the effects of low-level decisions in one module after making high-level assumptions about the other modules.

Several other studies have provided valuable insights into the design process. Kerr (1983) studied the thought processes of 26 novice instructional designers using interviews and planning documents produced by the designers during a graduate course in instructional design. He found that the processes employed by the designers were not systematic, that their solutions were generated based largely on their personal experiences in various instructional settings, and that problem constraints greatly influenced their solutions. Using a think-aloud task and protocol analysis, Nelson (1990) studied the initial phase of problem structuring in four experienced instructional designers. Although the experimental task only approximated a "first pass" at the problem, the designers tended to focus on information related to available resources, the learners, and the skills to

be trained. Specific information regarding content and learning tasks was not examined in detail. It was also apparent that specific pieces of information constrained the possible solutions that the designers considered. In other words, a "stopping rule" was evoked that led the designers to a particular solution without considering additional alternatives (Goel & Pirolli, 1988). A more comprehensive study of instructional designers was reported by Rowland (1992), where four expert and four novice designers were given a task to design instruction for an industrial setting involving training employees to operate two hypothetical machines. Verbal reports of the designers' thoughts while completing the task were coded and analyzed, and the results of this study suggest that the design process alternates between two phases that Rowland terms *problem understanding* and *solution generation* (p. 71). Experts tended to take much more time in the problem understanding phase, constructing a rich representation of the problem that was guided by a template, or mental model, of the process (Rowland, 1992). Novices did not develop a rich representation of the problem, relying on the materials given rather than making inferences about the constraints of the problem or the structure of the content. They also quickly began to generate possible solutions after briefly examining the problem materials and frequently returned to the problem materials as the process unfolded. Consequently, their problem representation grew as they progressed through the solution generation phase.

Observations of designer behavior using a case study methodology (Spector et al., 1992) have revealed that many variables affect the ability of designers to author computer-based instruction effectively, especially prior experience (both as a designer and with computer-based authoring systems). In another context, a naturalistic study of instructional design for informal learning settings noted the effects of constraints on the design process (Carliner, 1998). Other studies of instructional design practice have employed self-report methods using surveys to elicit designers' opinions about how they actually practice instructional design. Zemke's (1985) survey indicated that instructional designers in business and industry are selective in terms of the design activities in which they engage, often ignoring needs assessment, task analysis, and follow-up evaluations. Similar results were found by Mann (1996). Wedman and Tessmer (1993) extended this work by examining the factors that might contribute to the selective use of instructional design activities. Surveys of more than 70 instructional design professionals indicated that activities such as writing learning objectives, developing test items, and selecting media and instructional strategies are nearly always completed. On the other hand, these designers reported that needs assessment, task analysis, assessing entry-level skills, and pilot testing instruction are performed selectively, if ever. Reasons for not performing some activities included lack of time and that the decisions had already been made by others. Interestingly, lack of money or expertise in performing the activity was rarely cited as a reason the activities were not performed.

41.5.1.3 The Role of Knowledge in the Design Process.
The success of the designer's problem-solving processes is directly related to the designer's experience and knowledge

in the design task environment. Researchers have speculated about general cognitive structures for design that contain both the elements of a designed product and the processes necessary for generating the design (Akin, 1979; Jeffries, Turner, Polson, & Atwood, 1981). Goel and Pirolli (1988) also discuss the role of knowledge in the design process, noting that the personal knowledge of expert designers is organized in rich and intricate memory structures that contain both general knowledge (extracted from the totality of an individual's life experiences) and domain-specific knowledge derived from their professional training. This knowledge is used in many cases as a template for understanding the characteristics of the design task, as well as generating solutions.

So it seems that a well-organized knowledge base for instructional design is crucial to the process. The knowledge available to instructional designers, either individual knowledge stored in memory or other forms of knowledge embodied in the models and tools used for design, will influence the kinds of instruction they create (Nelson & Orey, 1991). An instructional designer's knowledge base should include not only conceptual and procedural structures for controlling the design process, but also cases or scenarios of exemplary instructional products and solutions that can be recalled and applied to particular situations (Nelson, Magliaro, & Sherman, 1988; Rowland, 1993). It is also necessary for an instructional designer to be familiar with concepts and procedures derived from general systems theory, psychological theory, instructional theory, and message design (Richey, 1993). In fact, it has been argued that successful implementation of instructional design procedures ultimately depends on whether designers have "adequate understanding and training in higher-order problem-solving principles and skills such that the necessary expertise can be applied in the process" (McCombs, 1986, p. 78). More recent studies suggest that complex case studies grounded in real-world, ill-defined problems are effective in developing the kind of knowledge and expertise necessary to be an effective instructional designer.

41.5.1.4 Overview of Designer Decision-Making Studies as Developmental Research.
Designer decision-making research is typically Type 2 research and has the ultimate goal of understanding the design process and, at times, producing design models that more closely match actual design activity. The populations of the studies are naturally designers—not learners—and frequently designers are classified as either novice or expert. The effort to identify the impact of various design environments is a common secondary objective. Consequently, the project itself is often a second unit of analysis and data are collected on the nature of the content, work resources, and constraints. Methodologically the studies tend to be more qualitative in nature, although survey methods are not uncommon.

41.5.2 Trends in Research on Automated Instructional Design and Development

The systematic instructional design and development procedures common to our field have been developed as a means to organize and control what is essentially a very complicated engineering process. Even with systematic methods, however, the instructional design process can become very time-consuming and costly (O'Neil, Faust, & O'Neil, 1979). As computer technology has proliferated in society, and as more training has become computer based, it is not surprising that efforts in the instructional design field have concentrated on the development of computer-based tools intended to streamline the design and development of instruction, for both novice designers and expert designers.

41.5.2.1 Tools for Content Acquisition.
One of the major tasks to be completed by the instructional designer is to identify and structure the content of instruction. Both instructional designers and instructional developers consult with subject matter experts to determine the content that must be acquired by the learners, and the forms in which this content might best be communicated to the learners. In this respect, instructional design activities are similar to the knowledge engineering process that is utilized in the development of expert systems and intelligent tutoring systems (McGraw, 1989; Nelson, 1989; Rushby, 1986). Knowledge engineers typically work with subject matter experts to identify and organize the knowledge that is necessary for solving problems in a domain. Although the ultimate goals of content acquisition for instructional design and knowledge engineering differ, the processes and tools used by instructional designers and knowledge engineers are complementary. In fact, many of the techniques and tools used in knowledge engineering are becoming common in instructional design.

Until recently, the procedures utilized for content acquisition in instructional design and development relied largely on task analysis (e.g., Merrill, 1973) and information processing analysis (Gagné, Briggs, & Wager, 1988). A large number of task analysis procedures have been employed for instructional design and development, as summarized by Jonassen, Hannum, and Tessmer (1989). In general, these analysis techniques are used by designers to describe the nature of the learning tasks and to identify and sequence the content of the instruction. Information processing analysis further delineates the decision-making processes that may underlie a task, allowing the designer to identify any concepts or rules that may be necessary to complete the task. The process of content acquisition generally follows several stages, including (a) a descriptive phase, where basic domain concepts and relations are identified; (b) a structural phase, where the information is organized into integrated structures; (c) a procedural phase, where the reasoning and problem-solving strategies are identified; and (d) a refinement phase, where the information structures procedures, and strategies are tested with a wider range of problems and modified as needed (Ford & Wood, 1992; McGraw, 1989). Using structured interviews and a variety of documentation activities, concepts and relations can be identified during the descriptive phase of content acquisition. McGraw (1989) recommends the use of concept dictionaries or cognitive maps to represent the major domain concepts graphically. Many of the automated tools for instructional design discussed later feature some kind of graphical representation tool to help define domain concepts and relations (e.g., McAleese, 1988; Nicolson,

1988; Pirolli, 1991). During the structural phase, the concepts and relations identified earlier are organized into larger units. This phase has been described as "a precondition to effective instructional design" (Jones, Li, & Merrill, 1990, p. 7) and is critical to the specification of content. Interviewing is the most widely employed technique, however, at this stage it is important to begin prompting the expert to clarify distinctions between concepts in order to structure the knowledge (Ford & Wood, 1992). Besides interviews, various statistical procedures such as multidimensional scaling (e.g., Cooke & McDonald, 1986), path analysis (Schvaneveldt, 1990), ordered trees (Naveh-Benjamin, McKeachie, Lin, & Tucker, 1986), and repertory grid techniques (Boose, 1986; Kelly, 1955) can be used to help structure the knowledge.

Content does not consist solely of concepts and relations. Experts also possess highly proceduralized knowledge in the form of rules and heuristics that help them solve problems. A variety of methods can be used to identify and describe these procedures. Task analysis methods yield a description of the tasks that constitute performance, along with the skills necessary to perform each task (Jonassen et al., 1989). Additional methods that provide useful descriptions of domain expertise include time-line analysis for sequencing tasks, information processing analysis for describing decision making, and process tracing to determine the thinking strategies used by the expert during task performance (McGraw, 1989). Protocol analysis (Ericsson & Simon, 1984) is a particularly effective process tracing technique, although it is time-consuming because of the extensive data analysis that is required. Observations, constrained tasks (Hoffman, 1987), and simulations can also be useful at this stage of knowledge acquisition, especially when two or more experts collaborate to solve or "debug" a problem (Tenney & Kurland, 1988). It is also advisable to perform similar analyses of novices in order to identify specific difficulties that learners are likely to encounter (Means & Gott, 1988; Orey & Nelson, 1993).

Advances in database technologies and Web-based delivery systems have created new opportunities for research in content acquisition, management, and delivery. The focus in recent research has been on the feasibility of creating and maintaining reusable, scalable, and distributed content. Much research has been devoted to the definition and organization of "learning objects" or "knowledge objects" (Wiley, 2000; Zielinski, 2000). Systems to store and deliver content modules that are "tagged" with descriptors related to various learning or instructional characteristics of the content modules, as well as the characteristics of the content itself, are being developed and tested. The modules can be retrieved and dynamically assembled by the system based on learner actions or requests.

Standards for structuring and tagging content objects have been developed and evaluated (Cuddy, 2000). Several models for automating the delivery process have been proposed and tested, including Merrill's (1999) instructional transaction theory, interactive remote instruction (Maly, Overstreet, Gonzalez, Denbar, Cutaran, & Karunaratne, 1998), and learning engines (Fritz & Ip, 1998). Other research has focused on assembling content and demonstrating the effectiveness of learning object technologies (Anderson & Merrill, 2000; Merrill, 2001). The impact of these approaches is evident in the rapid adoption of open architectures for learning objects (Open Courseware, 2002) and the proliferation of shared content databases (Labeuf & Spalter, 2001).

41.5.2.2 Knowledge-Based Design Tools.
Knowledge-based design systems are becoming common in many design professions as researchers strive to acquire and represent in computer systems the kinds of knowledge and reasoning necessary to interpret design problems, control design actions, and produce design specifications (Coyne, Rosenman, Radford, Balachandran, & Gero, 1990). Some computer-based design environments have been developed as extensions of the tools used by designers, such as the computer-aided design (CAD) systems used in professions where sketches or blueprints are used as a part of the design specifications (architecture, electronics, automobiles, etc.). Other systems have been developed around "libraries" or "templates" of primitive design elements or as critiquing environments that monitor the designer's activities and suggest alternatives when an action that may be inappropriate is taken (Fischer, 1991). These types of knowledge-based design systems require an extensive database of rules that functions in the background as the designer works with the system.

Although a wide variety of approaches to knowledge-based instructional design has been attempted, all are characterized by the need to formalize the knowledge and decision-making processes necessary for effective instructional design. These efforts began with attempts to provide "job aids" for novice instructional designers, especially those in military settings (Schulz & Wagner, 1981). Early efforts using computers to automate various instructional development tasks focused on the production of print-based materials for programmed instruction (Braby & Kincaid, 1981; Brecke & Blaiwes, 1981), adaptive testing systems (Weiss, 1979), and, more recently, paper-based training materials (Cantor, 1988). A more ambitious project was undertaken in conjunction with the PLATO system. Beginning with libraries of code to produce various types of test items, Schulz (1979) completed extensive research to produce and test a number of on-line authoring aids designed to be integrated with the military's IPISD model. Various activities specified by the model were identified and the associated tasks analyzed. Flowcharts of the design activities were then converted to interactive instructional segments that could be accessed by users as on-line aids during authoring activities. Findings indicated that the aids were accepted by the authors and that development time was significantly decreased.

41.5.2.3 Design Productivity Tools.
Numerous tools based on expert system technology have been developed to aid instructional designers in making decisions about various aspects of instructional design. These tools function as intelligent "job aids" where the designer enters information about the present situation in response to system queries, and the system then provides a solution based on domain-specific rules and reasoning strategies. Such tools do not provide a complete working environment for the design task but, rather, can serve as an expert consultant when the designer is not sure how to proceed in a particular situation (Jonassen & Wilson, 1990). A number of expert system tools for instructional design have been

developed by Kearsley (1985) to provide guidance for classification of learning objectives, needs assessment, cost benefit analysis, and decisions about the appropriateness of computers for delivery of instruction. Other expert system tools have been developed to aid in media selection (Gayeski, 1987; Harmon & King, 1985) and job/task analysis (Hermanns, 1990), while researchers in artificial intelligence are developing tools to analyze a curriculum for an intelligent tutoring system based on prerequisites and lesson objectives (Capell & Dannenberg, 1993).

Expert system technology has also been employed in the development of integrated instructional design systems that provide guidance and support for the complete design process. Merrill (1987) was an early advocate for the development of authoring systems for computer-based instruction that provide guidance for the user throughout the design process. His work has focused on a comprehensive instructional design environment that queries the user about the nature of the problem, guides in the specification and structuring of content, and recommends strategies and instructional transactions (Li & Merrill, 1991; Merrill & Li, 1989; Merrill & Thompson, 1999). Nicolson (1988) has described a similar system named SCALD (Scriptal CAL Designer) that was developed to produce automatically computer code for computer-assisted instruction systems. Using a script representation, SCALD users enter descriptions of the instructional components of the system by filling out forms to specify the script for each component. The system then creates an appropriately organized and sequenced "shell" from the scripts, and content (specific questions, information, graphics, etc.) can then be added to the shell by the developer.

Alternative approaches to rule-based expert system technologies for knowledge-based instructional design have been examined by other researchers. Some of these systems serve as working environments for the instructional designer but without the system-controlled advisory sessions common to expert system approaches. Instead, these systems provide structured environments and tools to facilitate the instructional design process, sometimes in very specific domains such as the tools described by Munro and Towne (1992) for the design and development of computer-based simulations and sometimes comprehensive systems to support all aspects of the instructional design process, including tutorials and support for novice designers (Gayeski, 1987; Seyfer & Russell, 1986; Spector & Song, 1995; Whitehead & Spector, 1994). IDioM (Gustafson & Reeves, 1990) is an instructional design environment used by Apple Computer employees to aid in their training design activities. Consisting of several modules related to analysis, design, development, evaluation, implementation, and management activities, IDioM helps to impose structure on the design process while maintaining flexibility for the designer to engage in various design and development activities. The Instructional Design Environment (IDE), developed at Xerox, is a similar system that allows designers to enter and manipulate the information necessary for analysis and specification activities (Pirolli, 1991). The environment is completely open, allowing the designer to represent the problem in a way that is comfortable and appropriate for the situation. Tools are provided to assist the designer in activities related to

task and content analysis, sequencing, delivery, and evaluation. Another set of tools, the IDE-Interpreter, has been developed to generate automatically instructional plans based on the specifications previously stored in the IDE knowledge base by the designer (D. M. Russell, 1988). Research in this area has expanded in recent years to include new commercial products such as Designer's Edge (Chapman, 1995) and Design Station 2000 (Gayeski, 1995), as well as tools for Web-based learning environments (Wild, 2000)

41.5.2.4 *The Practicality of Automated Instructional Design.* The question that remains unanswered with respect to research in the area of knowledge-based instructional design systems is whether such systems will be used by practicing instructional designers. Gayeski (1988, 1990) has pointed out several problems with automating instructional design processes, especially the difficulty of representing instructional design expertise as decision algorithms that can be executed by a computer. She also speculates that using an automated instructional design system may stifle creativity and that systems may need to be customized and tailored to the design procedures and practices of a particular organization. On the other hand, there has been growth in the development of these tools (Kasowitz, 1998) and increased interest in design and utilization issues (Tennyson & Baron, 1995) The open-ended workbench approach to knowledge-based instructional design can pose problems for some users, even though it may be a more appropriate architecture given the nature of the instructional design task (Duchastel, 1990). Because of the high degree of user control, an instructional design workbench can be useful for experienced instructional designers, helping them to streamline their work and providing assistance in documenting and managing the design process. But a system such as Designer's Edge is not designed to provide guidance to novice instructional designers and, therefore, may not be useful in many situations where trained instructional designers are in short supply.

The most appropriate architecture for knowledge-based instructional design systems may be a hybrid system that incorporates open-ended tools for experts along with an advisory system and solution library for novices. Fischer (1991) has developed such a system for architectural design that includes several modules: a construction kit, a simulation generator, a hypertext database of design principles, and a design catalog. As the designer works, an on-line design critic monitors activities, interrupting the user when a design principle has been violated. At such times, the design critic module presents an argument for modification of the design, supporting the argument with a design principle retrieved from a hypertext database along with examples of correct designs in the design catalog. The user can then browse both modules to obtain more information about the principle that was violated and other related principles and examples. The user can also access the simulation generator to test the current design using "what if" scenarios that simulate usage in various situations.

Even if we never use a knowledge-based instructional design system on a daily basis, research in this area has not been futile. In part, the interest in developing automated instructional design systems has precipitated research into the nature of the instructional design process (Pirolli, personal communication). Work in this area may also help to identify those instructional design tasks that can be successfully automated, leaving the tasks that require creativity and "fuzzy" reasoning to human designers. And finally, attempts to acquire and represent instructional design expertise will result in a better understanding of the nature of that expertise, suggesting alternative approaches to teaching instructional design (Rowland, 1992).

41.5.2.5 Overview of Studies of Automated Instructional Design and Development.
These studies are Type 2 research directed toward the production and testing of tools that would change design procedures, although some studies focus on only one phase of the design process—predesign content identification and analysis. The research on content is directed primarily toward producing new content analysis tools and procedures and then determining the conditions under which they can be best used. There are often multiple units of analysis in these studies, including designers, subject-matter experts, and the design tasks themselves. Much of this research is based on "artificial" design tasks, or projects that have been devised solely for the purposes of the research. Again, it is common for researchers to use qualitative techniques in these studies.

Research on automated design tools and systems is also primarily Type 2 research, however, Type 1 studies that would describe and analyze design projects using these new automated tools and evaluate the impact on learners of the materials produced using these tools are not precluded. The focus of analysis in the Type 2 studies of automated design tools tends to be the tools themselves, and in some instances the designers who use such tools are also studied. The studies are typically descriptive and observational in nature and typically seek to identify those conditions that facilitate successful use.

41.6 CONCLUSIONS

Developmental research methodologies facilitate the study of new models, tools, and procedures so that we can reliably anticipate their effectiveness and efficiency and, at the same, time address the pressing problems of this field. Such research can identify context-specific findings and determine their relevance for other teaching and learning environments. It can also identify new principles of design, development, and evaluation. Developmental research techniques not only expand the empirical methodologies of the field, but also expand the *substance* of instructional technology research. As such, it can be an important vehicle in our field's efforts to enhance the learning and performance of individuals and organizations alike.

The history of developmental research parallels the history and growth of instructional technology. Findings from past research provide a record of the technological development of the field, as well as a record of the development of the instructional design movement. The impetus for developmental research lies in the concerns of the field at any point in time. For example, the field is currently preoccupied with the idiosyncrasies of e-learning, while it continues to grapple with ways of reducing design and development cycle time while maintaining quality standards. It is concerned with the implications of globalization and diversity for instructional design. Issues such as these should give rise to new research, and developmental projects are well suited to address many of these problems.

References

Abdelraheem, A. Y. (1990). Formative evaluation in instructional development: A multiple comparison study (Doctoral dissertation, Indiana University, 1989). *Dissertation Abstracts International—A, 50*(10), 3381.

Adamski, A. J. (1998). The development of a systems design model for job performance aids: A qualitative developmental study (Doctoral dissertation, Wayne State University, 1998). *Dissertation Abstracts International—A, 59*(03), 789.

Akin, O. (1979). Exploration of the design process. *Design Methods and Theories, 13*(3/4), 115–119.

Akin, O., Chen, C. C., Dave, B., & Pithavadian, S. (1986). A schematic representation of the designer's logic. *Proceedings of the Joint International Conference on CAD and Robotics in Architecture and Construction* (pp. 31–40). London: Kogan-Page.

Albero-Andres, M. (1983). The use of the Agency for Instructional Television instructional development model in the design, production, and evaluation of the series of Give and Take (Doctoral dissertation, Indiana University, 1982). *Dissertation Abstracts International—A, 43*(11), 3489.

Alessi, S. M. (1988). Learning interactive videodisc development: A case study. *Journal of Instructional Development, 11*(2), 2–7.

Anderson, J. R., Boyle, C. F., Corbett, A. T., & Lewis, M. W. (1990). Cognitive modeling and intelligent tutoring. *Artificial Intelligence, 42*(1), 7–49.

Anderson, T. A., & Merrill, M. D. (2000). A design for standards-based knowledge components. *Journal of Computing in Higher Education, 11*(2), 3–29.

Andrews, D. H., & Goodson, L. A. (1980). A comparative analysis of models of instructional design. *Journal of Instructional Development, 3*(4), 2–16.

Aukerman, M. E. (1987). Effectiveness of an interactive video approach for CPR recertification of registered nurses (Doctoral dissertation, University of Pittsburgh, 1986). *Dissertation Abstracts International—A, 47*(06), 1979.

Baghdadi, A. A. (1981). A comparison between two formative evaluation methods (Doctoral dissertation, Indiana University, 1980). *Dissertation Abstracts International, 41*(08), 3387.

Baker, E. L. (1973). The technology of instructional development. In R. M. W. Travers (Ed.), *Second handbook of research on teaching* (pp. 245–285). Chicago: Rand McNally.

Beauchamp, M. (1991). The validation of an integrative model of student affect variables and instructional systems design (Doctoral dissertation, Wayne State University, 1990). *Dissertation Abstracts International—A, 51*(6), 1885.

Bednar, A. K. (1988). Needs assessment as a change strategy: A case study. *Performance Improvement Quarterly, 1*(2), 31-39.

Bennis, W. G. (1969). *Organizational development: Its nature, origins, and prospects.* Reading, MA: Addison-Wesley.

Blackstone, B. B. (1990). The development and evaluation of a simulation game about being a believer in the Soviet Union (Doctoral dissertation, University of Pittsburgh, 1989). *Dissertation Abstracts International—A, 50*(7), 2024.

Boose, J. H. (1986). *Expertise transfer for expert system design.* New York: Elsevier.

Borg, W. R., & Gall, M. D. (1971). *Educational research: An introduction* (2nd ed.). New York: David McKay.

Borras, I. (1993). Developing and assessing practicing spoken French: A multimedia program for improving speaking skills. *Educational Technology Research and Development, 41*(4), 91-103.

Bowers, D., & Tsai, C. (1990). Hypercard in educational research: An introduction and case study. *Educational Technology, 30*(2), 19-24.

Braby, R., & Kincaid, J. P. (1981). Computer aided authoring and editing. *Journal of Educational Technology Systems, 10*(2), 109-124.

Branch, R. M. (1997, October). *Perceptions of instructional design process models.* Paper presented at the annual meeting of the International Visual Literacy Association, Cheyenne, WY.

Branch, R. M., & Bloom, J. R. (1995, October). *The role of graphic elements in the accurate portrayal of instructional design.* Paper presented at the annual meeting of the International Visual Literacy Association, Tempe, AZ.

Bransford, J. D., Sherwood, R. D., Hasselbring, T. S., Kinzer, C. K., & Williams, S. M. (1990). Anchored instruction: Why we need it and how technology can help. In D. Nix & R. Spiro (Eds.), *Cognition, education, and multimedia* (pp. 115-142). Hillsdale, NJ: Lawrence Erlbaum.

Brecke, F., & Blaiwes, A. (1981). CASDAT: An innovative approach to more efficient ISD. *Journal of Educational Technology Systems, 10*(3), 271-283.

Briggs, L. J. (Ed.). (1977). *Instructional design: Principles and applications.* Englewood Cliffs, NJ: Educational Technology.

Bucciarelli, L. (2001). Design knowing and learning: A socially mediated activity. In C. M. Eastman, W. M. McCracken, & W. C. Newstetter (Eds.), *Design knowing and learning: Cognition in design education* (pp. 297-314). Amsterdam, NY: Elsevier Science.

Buch, E. E. (1989). A systematically developed training program for microcomputer users in an industrial setting (Doctoral dissertation, University of Pittsburgh, 1988). *Dissertation Abstracts International—A, 49*(4), 750.

Burkholder, B. L. (1981-1982). The effectiveness of using the instructional strategy diagnostic profile to prescribe improvements in self-instructional materials. *Journal of Instructional Development, 5*(2), 2-9.

Cantor, J. A. (1988). An automated curriculum development process for Navy Technical Training. *Journal of Instructional Development, 11*(4), 3-12.

Capell, P. (1990). A content analysis approach used in the study of the characteristics of instructional design in three intelligent tutoring systems: The LISP tutor, Bridge, and Piano Tutor (Doctoral dissertation, University of Pittsburgh, 1989). *Dissertation Abstracts International—A, 50*(7), 2024.

Capell, P., & Dannenberg, R. B. (1993). Instructional design and intelligent tutoring: Theory and the precision of design. *Journal of Artificial Intelligence in Education, 4*(1), 95-121.

Carl, D. (1978). A front-end analysis of instructional development in instructional television (Doctoral dissertation, Indiana University, 1977). *Dissertation Abstracts International—A, 38*(9), 5198.

Carliner, S. (1998). How designers make decisions: A descriptive model of instructional design for informal learning in museums. *Performance Improvement Quarterly, 11*(2), 72-92.

Carr-Chellman, A., Cuyar, C., & Breman, J. (1998). User-design: A case application in health care training. *Educational Technology Research and Development, 46*(4), 97-114.

Carroll, J. M., Thomas, J. C., Miller, L. A., & Friedman, H. P. (1980). Aspects of solution structure in design problem solving. *American Journal of Psychology, 95*(2), 269-284.

Chandrasekaran, B. (1987). Design as knowledge-based problem solving activity. In B. Zaff (Ed.), *Proceedings of a Symposium on the Cognitive Condition of Design* (pp. 117-147). Columbus: Ohio State University.

Chapman, B. L. (1995). Accelerating the design process: A tool for instructional designers. *Journal of Interactive Instructional Development, 8*(2), 8-15.

Cheng, N. (2000, September). *Web-based teamwork in design education.* Paper presented at SiGraDi 2000: 4th Iberoamerican Congress of Digital Graphics, Rio de Janiero.

Chou, C., & Sun C. (1996). Constructing a cooperative distance learning system: The CORAL experience. *Educational Technology Research and Development, 44*(4), 71-84.

Clifford, G. J. (1973). A history of the impact of research on teaching. In R. M. W. Travers (Ed.), *Second handbook of research on teaching* (pp. 1-46). Chicago: Rand McNally.

Connop-Scollard, C. (1991). The ID/D chart: A representation of instructional design and development. *Educational Technology, 31*(12), 47-50.

Cook, F. S., & Richey, R. C. (1975). A competency-based program for preparing vocational teachers. *Journal for Industrial Teacher Education, 12*(4), 29-38.

Cooke, N. M., & McDonald, J. E. (1986). A formal methodology for acquiring and representing expert knowledge. *Proceedings of the IEEE, 74*(1), 1422-1430.

Corry, M. D., Frick, T. W., & Hansen, L. (1997). User-centered design and usability testing of a web site: An illustrative case study. *Educational Technology Research and Development, 45*(4), 65-76.

Coscarelli, W. C., & White, G. P. (1982). Applying the ID process to the guided design teaching strategy: A case study. *Journal of Instructional Development, 5*(4), 2-6.

Cowell, D. M. (2001). Needs assessment activities and techniques of instructional designers: A qualitative study (Doctoral dissertation, Wayne State University, 2000). *Dissertation Abstracts International—A, 61*(10), 3873.

Coyle, K. (1986). The development and evaluation of an experimental computer simulation for animal science students (Doctoral dissertation, Iowa State University, 1985). *Dissertation Abstracts International—A, 46*(12), 3581.

Coyle, L. (1992). Distance education project: Extending extension programming via telecommunications technology. *Educational Technology, 32*(8), 57-58.

Coyne, R. D., Rosenman, M. A., Radford, A. D., Balachandran, M., & Gero, J. S. (1990). *Knowledge-based design systems.* Reading, MA: Addison-Wesley.

Crane, G., & Mylonas, E. (1988). The Perseus project: An interactive curriculum on classical Greek civilization. *Educational Technology, 28*(11), 25-32.

Cregger, R., & Metzler, M. (1992). PSI for a college physical education basic instructional program. *Educational Technology, 32*(8), 51-56.

Cronbach, L. J., & Suppes, P. (Eds.). (1969). *Research for tomorrow's schools—Disciplined inquiry for education.* Report of the Committee on Educational Research of the National Academy of Education. London: Macmillan, Callien Macmillan.

Crowl, T. K. (1996). *Fundamentals of educational research* (2nd ed.). Madison, WI: Brown & Benchmark.

Cuddy, C. (2000). Metadata evaluation: The road toward meeting our objectives. *Proceedings of the ASIS Annual Meeting, 37,* 67.

Cummings, O. W. (1985). Comparison of three algorithms for analyzing questionnaire-type needs assessment data to establish need priorities. *Journal of Instructional Development, 8*(2), 11–16.

Dabbagh, N. H., Jonassen, D. H., Yueh, H., & Samouilova, M. (2000). Assessing a problem-based learning approach to an introductory instructional design course: A case study. *Performance Improvement Quarterly, 13*(2), 61–83.

Dick, W. (1991). The Singapore project: A case study in instructional design. *Performance Improvement Quarterly, 4*(1), 14–22.

Diesing, P. (1991). *How does social science work? Reflections on practice.* Pittsburgh, PA: University of Pittsburgh Press.

Dijkstra, S. (2001). The design space for solving instructional design problems. *Instructional Science, 29*(4–5), 275–290.

Driscoll, M. P. (1991). Paradigms for research in instructional systems. In G. Anglin (Ed.), *Instructional technology: Past, present, and future* (pp. 310–317). Englewood, CO: Libraries Unlimited.

Driscoll, M. P., & Tessmer, M. (1985). The rational set generator: A method for creating concept examples for teaching and testing. *Educational Technology, 25*(2), 29–32.

Duchastel, P. C. (1990). Cognitive design for instructional design. *Instructional Science, 19,* 437–444.

Duffy, T. M., & Jonassen, D. H. (1992). *Constructivism and the technology of instruction.* Mahwah, NJ: Lawrence Erlbaum Associates.

English, R. E., & Reigeluth, C. M. (1996). Formative research on sequencing instruction with the elaboration theory. *Educational Technology Research and Development, 44*(1), 23–42.

Ericsson, K. A., & Simon, H. A. (1984). *Protocol analysis.* Cambridge, MA: MIT Press.

Fischer, G. (1991). Supporting learning on demand with design environments. In L. Birnbaum (Ed.), *The International Conference on the Learning Sciences: Proceedings of the 1991 Conference.* Charlottesville, VA: Association for the Advancement of Computing in Education.

Fischer, K. M., Savenye, W. C., & Sullivan, H. J. (2002). Formative evaluation of computer-based training for a university financial system. *Performance Improvement Quarterly, 15*(1), 11–24.

Ford, J. M., & Wood, L. E. (1992). Structuring and documenting interactions with subject-matter experts. *Performance Improvement Quarterly, 5*(1), 2–24.

Forsyth, J. E. (1998). The construction and validation of a model for the design of community-based train-the-trainer instruction (Doctoral dissertation, Wayne State University, 1997). *Dissertation Abstracts International—A, 58*(11), 4242.

Fox, E. J., & Klein, J. D. (2002). *What should instructional designers know about human performance technology?* Paper presented at the annual meeting of the Association for Educational Communication and Technology, Dallas, TX.

Freeman, P. (1983). Fundamentals of design. In P. Freeman (Ed.), *Software design tutorial* (pp. 2–22). New York: IEEE Computer Society Press.

Fritz, P., & Ip, A. (1998, June). *Learning engines—A functional object model for developing learning resources for the WWW.* Paper presented at the World Conference on Educational Multimedia and Hypermedia, Freiburg, Germany.

Fuchs, L. S., & Fuchs, D. (1986). Effects of systematic formative evaluation: A meta-analysis. *Exceptional Children, 53*(3), 199–208.

Gage, N. L. (Ed.). (1963). *Handbook of research on teaching.* Chicago: Rand McNally.

Gagné, R. M. (1985). *The conditions of learning and theory of instruction* (4th ed.). New York: Holt, Rinehart and Winston.

Gagné, R. M., Briggs, L. J., & Wager, W. W. (1988). *Principles of instructional design* (3rd ed.). New York: Holt, Rinehart and Winston.

Gauger, E. P. (1987). The design, development, and field test of a prototype program evaluation approach for medical residency rotations (Doctoral dissertation, Michigan State University, 1985). *Dissertation Abstracts International—A, 47*(1), 69.

Gay, G., & Mazur, J. (1993). The utility of computer tracking tools for user-centered design. *Educational Technology, 33*(4), 45–59.

Gayeski, D. M. (1987). *Interactive toolkit.* Ithaca, NY: OmniCom Associates.

Gayeski, D. M. (1988). Can (and should) instructional design be automated? *Performance and Instruction, 27*(10), 1–5.

Gayeski, D. M. (1990). Are you ready for automated design? *Training and Development Journal, 44*(1), 61–62.

Gayeski, D. M. (1995). Design Station 2000: Imagining future realities in learning systems design. *Educational Technology, 35*(3), 43–47.

Gettman, D., McNelly, T., & Muraida, D. (1999). The guided approach to instructional design advising (GAIDA): A case-based approach to developing instructional design expertise. In J. van den Akker, R. M. Branch, K. Gustafson, N. Nieveen, & T. Plomp (Eds.), *Design approaches and tools in education and training* (pp. 175–181). Dordrecht: Kluwer.

Goel, V., & Pirolli, P. (1988). *Motivating the notion of generic design within information processing theory: The design problem space* (Report No. DPS-1). Washington, DC: Office of Naval Research. (ERIC Document Reproduction Service No. ED 315 041)

Gordon, J. J. (1969). A system model for civil defense training and education. *Educational Technology, 9*(6), 39–45.

Greenhill, L. P. (1955). *A study of the feasibility of local production of minimum cost sound motion pictures* (Pennsylvania State University Instructional Film Research Program). Port Washington, NY: U.S. Naval Training Device Center, Office of Naval Research, Technical Report No. SDC 269-7-48.

Gustafson, K. L., & Reeves, T. C. (1990). IDioM: A platform for a course development expert system. *Educational Technology, 30*(3), 19–25.

Gustafson, K. L., & Reeves, T. C. (1991). Introduction. In L. J. Briggs, K. L. Gustafson, & M. H. Tillman (Eds.), *Instructional design: Principles and applications* (2nd ed., pp. 3–16). Englewood Cliffs, NJ: Educational Technology.

Hallamon, T. C. (2002). A study of factors affecting the use of task analysis in the design of instruction (Doctoral dissertation, Wayne State University, 2001). *Dissertation Abstracts International—A, 62*(12), 4131.

Harmon, P., & King, D. (1985). *Expert systems: Artificial intelligence in business.* New York: Wiley.

Harris, M., & Cady, M. (1988). The dynamic process of creating hypertext literature. *Educational Technology, 28*(11), 33–40.

Harrison, P. J., Seeman, B. J., Behm, R., Saba, F., Molise, G., & Williams, M. D. (1991). Development of a distance education assessment instrument. *Educational Technology Research and Development, 39*(4), 65–77.

Havelock, R. G. (1971). The utilisation of educational research and development. *British Journal of Educational Technology, 2*(2), 84–98.

Hedberg, J., & Sims, R. (2001). Speculations on design team interactions. *Journal of Interactive Learning Research, 12*(2–3), 193–208.

Heinich, R., Molenda, M., Russell, J. D., & Smaldino, S. E. (2002). *Instructional media and the new technologies of instruction* (7th ed.). Englewood Cliff, NJ: Prentice Hall.

Hermanns, J. (1990). Computer-aided instructional systems development. *Educational Technology, 30*(3), 42–45.

Herrington, J., & Oliver, R. (2000). An instructional design framework for authentic learning environments. *Educational Technology Research and Development, 48*(3), 23-48.

Higgins, N., & Reiser, R. (1985). Selecting media for instruction: An exploratory study. *Journal of Instructional Development, 8*(2), 6-10.

Hilgard, E. R. (Ed.). (1964). *Theories of learning and instruction.* 63rd National Society for the Study of Education Yearbook. Chicago: University of Chicago Press.

Hirumi, A., Savenye, W., & Allen, B. (1994). Designing interactive videodisc-based museum exhibits: A case study. *Educational Technology Research and Development, 42*(1), 47-55.

Hoffman, R. R. (1987). The problem of extracting the knowledge of experts from the perspective of experimental psychology. *AI Magazine, 8*(2), 53-67.

Hutchins, E. (1991). The technology of team navigation. In L. B. Resnick, J. M. Levine, & S. D. Teasley (Eds.), *Perspectives on socially shared cognition* (pp. 283-307).Washington, DC: American Psychological Association.

Jeffries, R., Turner, A. A., Polson, P. G., & Atwood, M. E. (1981). The processes involved in designing software. In J. R. Anderson (Ed.), *Cognitive skills and their acquisition* (pp. 255-283). Hillsdale, NJ: Lawrence Erlbaum.

Jonassen, D. H. (1988). Using needs assessment data to design a graduate instructional development program. *Journal of Instructional Development, 11*(2), 14-23.

Jonassen, D. H., Grabinger, R. S., & Harris, N. D. C. (1991). Analyzing and selecting instructional strategies and tactics. *Performance Improvement Quarterly, 4*(2), 77-97.

Jonassen, D. H., Hannum, W. H., & Tessmer, M. (1989). *Handbook of task analysis procedures.* New York: Praeger.

Jonassen, D. H., & Wilson, B.G. (1990). Analyzing automated instructional design systems: Metaphors from related design professions. In M. R. Simonson (Ed.). *Proceedings of Selected Research Paper Presentations at the 1990 Annual Convention of the Association of Educational Communications and Technology* (pp. 309-328). Washington, DC: Association of Educational Communications and Technology. (ERIC Document Reproduction Service No. ED 323 912)

Jones, M. K., Li, Z., & Merrill, M. D. (1990). Domain knowledge representation for instructional analysis. *Educational Technology, 30*(10), 7-32.

Jones, R. H. (1986). The development and analysis of an interactive video program for paralegal students in a university setting (Doctoral dissertation, University of Pittsburgh, 1985). *Dissertation Abstracts International—A, 46*(6), 1604.

Jones, T., & Richey, R. C. (2000). Rapid prototyping methodology in action: A developmental study. *Educational Technology Research & Development, 48*(2), 63-80.

Julian, M. F. (2001). Learning in action: The professional preparation of instructional designers (Doctoral dissertation, University of Virginia). *Dissertation Abstracts International—A, 62*(01), 136.

Kanyarusoke, C. M. S. (1985). The development and evaluation of an external studies form of the introductory course in educational communications and technology (Doctoral dissertation, University of Pittsburgh, 1983). *Dissertation Abstracts International—A, 45*(2), 387.

Kasowitz, A. (1998). *Tools for Automating Instructional Design.* ERIC Digest Report No. EDO-IR-98-01.

Kearsley, G. (1985). An expert system program for making decisions about CBT. *Performance and Instruction, 24*(5), 15-17.

Kearsley, G. (1986). Automated instructional development using personal computers: Research issues. *Journal of Instructional Development, 9*(1), 9-15.

Kelly, G. A. (1955). *The psychology of personal constructs.* New York: W. W. Norton.

Keppel, M. (2001). Optimizing instructional designer-subject matter expert communication in the design and development of multimedia projects. *Journal of Interactive Learning Research, 12*(2/3), 209-227.

Kerlinger, F. N. (1964). *Foundations of behavioral research: Educational and psychological inquiry.* New York: Holt, Rinehart and Winston.

Kerr, S. T. (1983). Inside the black box: Making design decisions for instruction. *British Journal of Educational Technology, 14*(1), 45-58.

Kim, S. O. (1984). Design of an instructional systems development process for Korean education in harmony with Korean culture (Doctoral dissertation, Ohio State University, 1983). *Dissertation Abstract International—A, 44*(4), 974.

King, D., & Dille, A. (1993). An early endeavor to apply quality concepts to the systematic design of instruction: Successes and lessons learned. *Performance Improvement Quarterly, 6*(3), 48-63.

Klein, J. D., Brinkerhoff, J., Koroghlanian, C., Brewer, S., Ku, H., & MacPherson-Coy, A. (2000). The foundations of educational technology: A needs assessment. *Tech Trends, 44*(6), 32-36.

Klimczak, A. K., & Wedman, J. F. (1997). Instructional design project success factors: An empirical basis. *Educational Technology Research & Development, 45*(2), 75-83.

Kress, C. (1990). The effects of instructional systems design techniques on varying levels of adult achievement in technical training (Doctoral dissertation, Wayne State University, 1989). *Dissertation Abstracts International—A, 50*(11), 3447.

Kunneman, D. E., & Sleezer, C. M. (2000). Using performance analysis for training in an organization implementing ISO-9000 manufacturing practices: A case study. *Performance Improvement Quarterly, 13*(4), 47-66.

Labeuf, J. R., & Spalter, A. M. (2001, June). *A component repository for learning objects: A progress report.* Paper presented at the Joint Conference on Digital Libraries, Roanoke, VA.

Lanzara, G. F. (1983). The design process: Frames, metaphors and games. In U. Briefs, C. Ciborra, & L. Schneider (Eds.), *Systems design for, with and by the users.* Amsterdam: North-Holland.

Lave, J., & Wenger, E. (1991). *Situated learning: Legitimate peripheral participation.* Cambridge, MA: Cambridge University Press.

Le Maistre, C. (1998). What is an expert instructional designer? Evidence of expert instructional designer? Evidence of expert performance during formative evaluation. *Educational Technology Research & Development, 46*(3), 21-36.

Le Maistre, K., & Weston, C. (1996). The priorities established among data sources when instructional designers revise written materials. *Educational Technology Research and Development, 44*(1), 61-70.

Lewis, E. L., Stern, J. L., & Linn, M. C. (1993). The effect of computer simulations on introductory thermodynamics understanding. *Educational Technology, 33*(1), 45-58.

Li, Z., & Merrill, M. D. (1991). ID Expert 2.0: Design theory and process. *Educational Technology Research and Development, 39*(2), 53-69.

Lieberman, A., & Miller, L. (1992). Professional development of teachers. In M.C. Alkin (Ed.), *Encyclopedia of educational research* (6th ed., pp. 1045-1051). New York: Macmillan.

Link, N., & Cherow-O'Leary, R. (1990). Research and development of print materials at the Children's Television Workshop. *Educational Technology Research & Development, 38*(4), 34-44.

Luiz, T. (1983). A comparative study of humanism and pragmatism as they relate to decision making in instructional development processes (Doctoral dissertation, Michigan State University, 1982). *Dissertation Abstracts International—A, 43*(12), 3839.

Maly, K. Overstreet, C. M., Gonzalez, A., Denbar, M. L., Cutaran, R., & Karunaratne, N. (1998, June). *Automated content synthesis for interactive remote instruction.* Paper presented at the World Conference on Educational Multimedia and Hypermedia, Freiburg, Germany.

Mann, E. (1996). A case study of instructional design practices: Implications for instructional designers. In M. R. Simonson, M. Hays, & S. Hall (Eds.), *Proceedings of selected research papers presented at the 1996 Annual Convention of the Association of Educational Communications and Technology* (pp. 455-463). Washington, DC: Association of Educational Communications and Technology.

Martin, B., & Bramble, W. (1996). Designing effective video teletraining instruction: The Florida teletraining project. *Educational Technology Research and Development, 44*(1), 85-99.

McAleese, R. (1988). Design and authoring: A model of cognitive processes. In H. Mathias, N. Rushby, & R. Budgett (Eds.), *Designing new systems for learning* (pp. 118-126). New York: Nichols.

McCombs, B. L. (1986). The instructional systems development model: A review of those factors critical to its implementation. *Educational Technology and Communications Journal, 34*(2), 67-81.

McDaniel, K., & Liu, M. (1996). A study of project management techniques for developing interactive multimedia programs: A practitioner's perspective. *Journal of Research on Computing in Education, 29*(1), 29-48.

McGraw, K. L. (1989). Knowledge acquisition for intelligent instructional systems. *Journal of Artificial Intelligence in Education, 1*(1), 11-26.

McKenney, S. (2002). Computer-based support for science education materials development in Africa: Exploring potentials (Doctoral dissertation, Universiteit Twente, The Netherlands, 2001). *Dissertation Abstracts International—C, 63*(03), 355.

Means, B., & Gott, S. (1988). Cognitive task analysis as a basis for tutor development: Articulating abstract knowledge representations. In J. Psotka, L. D. Massey, & S. A. Mutter (Eds.), *Intelligent tutoring systems: Lessons learned* (pp. 35-57). Hillsdale, NJ: Erlbaum.

Means, T. B., Jonassen, D. H., & Dwyer, F. M. (1997). Enhancing relevance: Embedded ARCS strategies vs. purpose. *Educational Technology Research & Development, 45*(1), 5-17.

Medsker, K. L. (1992). NETwork for excellent teaching: A case study in university instructional development. *Performance Improvement Quarterly, 5*(1), 35-48.

Mendes, A. J., & Mendes, T. (1996). AIDA: An integrated authoring environment for educational software. *Educational Technology Research and Development, 44*(4), 57-70.

Merrill, M. D. (1973). Cognitive and instructional analysis for cognitive transfer tasks. *Audio Visual Communications Review, 21*(1), 109-125.

Merrill, M. D. (1987). Prescriptions for an authoring system. *Journal of Computer-Based Instruction, 14*(1), 1-10.

Merrill, M. D. (1999). Instructional transaction theory: Instructional design based on knowledge objects. In C. M. Reigeluth (Ed.), *Instructional design theories and models* (Vol. 2). Mahwah, NJ: Lawrence Erlbaum Associates.

Merrill, M. D. (2001). A knowledge object and mental model approach to a physics lesson. *Educational Technology, 41*(1), 36-47.

Merrill, M. D., & Li, Z. (1989). An instructional design expert system. *Journal of Computer-Based Instruction, 16*(3), 95-101.

Merrill, M. D., Li, Z., & Jones, M. K. (1990a). Limitations of first generation instructional design. *Educational Technology, 30*(1), 7-11.

Merrill, M. D., Li, Z., & Jones, M. K. (1990b). Second generation instructional design. *Educational Technology, 30*(2), 7-14.

Merrill, M. D., Li, Z., & Jones, M. K. (1991). Instructional transaction theory: An introduction. *Educational Technology, 31*(6), 7-12.

Merrill, M. D., & Thompson, B. M. (1999). The IDXelerator: Learning-centered instructional design. In J. Vd Akker, R. M. Branch, K. Gustafson, N. Nieveen, & T. Plomp (Eds.), *Design approaches and tools in education and training* (pp. 265-277). Dordrecht: Kluwer Academic.

Mielke, K. W. (1990). Research and development at the Children's Television Workshop. *Educational Technology Research & Development, 38*(4), 7-16.

Milazzo, C. (1981). Formative evaluation process in the development of a simulation game for the socialization of senior nursing students (Doctoral dissertation, Columbia University Teachers College). *Dissertation Abstracts International—A, 42*(5), 1935.

Mishler, E. G. (1979). Meaning in context: Is there any other kind? *Harvard Educational Review, 49*(1), 1-19.

Moallem, M. (1998). Reflection as a means of developing expertise in problem solving, decision making, and complex thinking of designers. In N. J. Maushak, C. Schlosser, T. N. Lloyd, & M. Simonson (Eds.), *Proceedings of Selected Research and Development Presentations at the National Convention of the Association for Educational Communications and Technology* (pp. 281-289). Washington, DC: Association for Educational Communications and Technology.

Munro, A., & Towne, D. M. (1992). Productivity tools for simulation-centered training development. *Educational Technology Research and Development, 40*(4), 65-80.

Murphy, D. (1992). Is instructional design truly a design activity? *Educational and Training Technology International, 29*(4), 279-282.

Nadin, M., & Novak, M. (1987). MIND: A design machine. In P. J. W. ten Hagen & T. Tomiyama (Eds.), *Intelligent CAD Systems I* (pp. 146-171). New York: Springer-Verlag.

Nadolski, R., Kirschner, P., van Merrienboer, J., & Hummel, H. (2001). A model for optimizing step size of learning tasks in competency-based multimedia practicals. *Educational Technology Research & Development, 49*(3), 87-103.

National Center for Educational Research and Development. (1970). *Educational research and development in the United States.* Washington, DC: United States Government Printing Office.

Naveh-Benjamin, J., McKeachie, W. J., Lin, Y., & Tucker, D. G. (1986). Inferring students' cognitive structures and their development using the "ordered tree technique." *Journal of Educational Psychology, 78,* 130-140.

Nelson, W. A. (1989). Artificial intelligence knowledge acquisition techniques for instructional development. *Educational Technology Research and Development, 37*(3), 81-94.

Nelson, W. A. (1990). Selection and utilization of problem information by instructional designers (Doctoral dissertation, Virginia Polytechnic Institute and State University, 1988). *Dissertation Abstract International—A, 50*(4), 866.

Nelson, W. A., Magliaro, S. G., & Sherman, T. M. (1988). The intellectual content of instructional design. *Journal of Instructional Development, 11*(1), 29-35.

Nelson, W. A., & Orey, M. A. (1991). *Reconceptualizing the instructional design process: Lessons learned from cognitive science.* Paper presented at the annual meeting of the American Educational Research Association, Chicago, IL. (ERIC Document Reproduction Service No. ED 334 268)

Nicolson, R. (1988). SCALD—Towards an intelligent authoring system. In J. Self (Ed.), *Artificial intelligence and human learning* (pp. 236-254). London: Chapman and Hall.

Nieveen, N., & van den Akker, J. (1999). Exploring the potential of a computer tool for instructional developers. *Educational Technology Research & Development, 47*(3), 77-98.

Noel, K. (1991). Instructional systems development in a large-scale education project. *Educational Technology Research & Development, 39*(4), 91-108.

O'Neil, H. L., Faust, G. W., & O'Neil, A. F. (1979). An author training course. In H. L. O'Neil (Ed.), *Procedures for instructional systems development* (pp. 1-38). New York: Academic Press.

O'Quin, K., Kinsey, T. G., & Beery, D. (1987). Effectiveness of a microcomputer-training workshop for college professionals. *Computers in Human Behavior, 3*(2), 85-94.

Open Courseware. (2002). Open Courseware: Simple idea, profound implications. *Syllabus, 15*(6), 12-14.

Orey, M. A., & Nelson, W. A. (1993). Development principles for intelligent tutoring systems: Integrating cognitive theory into the development of computer-based instruction. *Educational Technology Research and Development, 41*(1), 59-72.

Parer, M. (1978). A case study in the use of an instructional development model to produce and evaluate an instructional television program (Doctoral dissertation, Indiana University, 1977). *Dissertation Abstracts International—A, 38*(6), 3229.

Park, I., & Hannafin, M. J. (1993). Empirically-based guidelines for the design of interactive multimedia. *Educational Technology Research and Development, 41*(3), 63-85.

Pelz, D. C. (1967, July). Creative tensions in the research and development climate. *Science,* 160-165.

Petry, B. A., and Edwards, M. L. (1984). Systematic development of an applied phonetics course. *Journal of Instructional Development, 7*(4), 6-11.

Phillips, J. H. (2000). Evaluating training programs for organizational impact (Doctoral dissertation, Wayne State University, 2000). *Dissertation Abstracts International—A 61*(03), 840.

Phillips, R. (2001). A case study of the development and project management of a web/CD hybrid application. *Journal of Interactive Learning Research, 12*(2/3), 229-247.

Piper, A. J. (1991). An analysis and comparison of selected project management techniques and their implications for the instructional development process (Doctoral dissertation, Michigan State University, 1990). *Dissertation Abstracts International—A, 51*(12), 4010.

Pirolli, P. (1991). Computer-aided instructional design systems. In H. Burns, J. W. Parlett, & C. L. Redfield (Eds.), *Intelligent tutoring systems: Evolutions in design* (pp.105-125). Hillsdale, NJ: Lawrence Erlbaum Associates.

Pirolli, P. L., & Greeno, J. G. (1988). The problem space of instructional design. In J. Psotka, L. D. Massey, & S. A. Mutter (Eds.), *Intelligent tutoring systems: Lessons learned* (pp. 181-201). Hillsdale, NJ: Lawrence Erlbaum.

Pizzuto, A. E. (1983). The development and evaluation of a simulation game demonstrating diffusion communications in a corporate organization (Doctoral dissertation, University of Pittsburgh, 1982). *Dissertation Abstracts International—A, 43*(4), 1273.

Plass, J. L., & Salisbury, M. W. (2002). A living-systems design model for web-based knowledge management systems. *Educational Technology Research & Development, 50*(1), 35-57.

Plummer, K. H., Gillis, P. D., Legree, P. J., & Sanders, M. G. (1992). The development and evaluation of a job aid to support mobile subscriber radio-telephone terminal (MSRT). *Performance Improvement Quarterly, 5*(1), 90-105.

Quinn, J. (1994). Connecting education and practice in an instructional design graduate program. *Educational Technology Research and Development, 42*(3), 71-82.

Rathbun, G. A. (1999). Portraying the work of instructional design: An activity-oriented analysis. In K. E. Sparks & M. R. Simonson (Eds.), *Proceedings of Selected Research and Development Papers Presented at the 1999 Annual Convention of the Association of Educational Communications and Technology* (pp. 391-402). Washington, DC: Association of Educational Communications and Technology.

Rathbun, G., Saito, R., & Goodrum, D. A. (1997). Reconceiving ISD: Three perspectives on rapid prototyping as a paradigm shift. In O. Abel, N. J. Maushak, K. E. Wright, & M. R. Simonson (Eds.), *Proceedings of Selected Research and Development Presentations at the 1997 Annual Convention of the Association of Educational Communications and Technology* (pp. 291-296). Washington, DC: Association of Educational Communications and Technology.

Reigeluth, C. M. (1983). Instructional design: What is it and why is it? In C. M. Reigeluth (Ed.), *Instructional design theories and models: An overview of their current status* (pp. 3-36). Hillsdale, NJ: Lawrence Erlbaum Associates, Publishers.

Reigeluth, C. M., & Curtis, R. V. (1987). Learning situations and instructional models. In R. M. Gagné (Ed.), *Instructional technology: Foundations* (pp. 175-206). Hillsdale, NJ: Lawrence Erlbaum.

Reitman, W. (1964). *Cognition and thought.* New York: John Wiley.

Rezabek, L. L., & Cochenour, J. J. (1996). Perceptions of the ID process: The influence of visual display. In M. R. Simonson, M. Hays & S. Hall (Eds.), *Proceedings of Selected Research and Development Presentations at the 1996 Annual Convention of the Association of Educational Communications and Technology* (pp. 582-593). Washington, DC: Association of Educational Communications and Technology.

Richey, R. C. (1992). *Designing instruction for the adult learner: Systemic training theory and practice.* London/Bristol, PA: Kogan Page/Taylor and Francis.

Richey, R. C. (1993). *The knowledge base of instructional design.* Paper presented at the 1993 Annual Meeting of the Association for Educational Communications and Technology in New Orleans, LA.

Richey, R. C. (1998). The pursuit of useable knowledge in instructional technology. *Educational Technology Research and Development, 46*(4), 7-22.

Richey, R. C., & Tessmer, M. (1995). Enhancing instructional systems design through contextual analysis. In B. Seels (Ed.), *Instructional design fundamentals: A reconsideration* (pp. 189-199). Englewood Cliffs, NJ: Educational Technology.

Riplinger, J. A. (1987). A survey of task analysis activities used by instructional designers (Doctoral dissertation, University of Iowa, 1985). *Dissertation Abstracts International—A, 47*(3), 778.

Rojas, A. M. (1988). Evaluation of sales training impact: A case study using the organizational elements model. *Performance Improvement Quarterly, 1*(2), 71-84.

Ross, K. R. (1998). Blending authentic work projects and instructional assignments: An adaptation process. *Educational Technology Research and Development, 46*(3), 67-79.

Roth, W. M. (2001). Modeling design as a situated and distributed process. *Learning and Instruction, 11*(3), 211-239.

Rouch, M. A. (1969). A system model for continuing education for the ministry. *Educational Technology, 9*(6), 32-38.

Rowland, G. (1992). What do instructional designers actually do? An initial investigation of expert practice. *Performance Improvement Quarterly, 5*(2), 65-86.

Rowland, G. (1993). Designing and instructional design. *Educational Technology Research and Development, 41*(1), 79-91.

Rowland, G. (1996). "Lighting the fire" of design conversations. *Educational Technology, 36*(1), 42-45.

Rowland, G., & Adams, A. (1999). Systems thinking in instructional design. In J. van den Akker, R. M. Branch, K. Gustafson, N. Nieveen, & T. Plomp (Eds.), *Design approaches and tools in education and training* (pp. 29-44). Dordrecht: Kluwer.

Rowland, G., Parra, M. L., & Basnet, K. (1994). Educating instructional designers: Different methods for different outcomes. *Educational Technology, 34*(6), 5-11.

Roytek, M. A. (2000). Contextual factors affecting the use of rapid prototyping within the design and development of instruction (Doctoral dissertation, Wayne State University, 1999). *Dissertation Abstracts International—A, 61*(01), 76.

Rushby, N. (1986). A knowledge-engineering approach to instructional design. *Computer Journal, 29*(5), 385-389.

Russell, C. M. (1990). The development and evaluation of an interactive videodisc system to train radiation therapy technology students on the use of the linear accelerator (Doctoral dissertation, University of Pittsburgh, 1988). *Dissertation Abstracts International—B, 50*(3), 919.

Russell, D. M. (1988). IDE: The interpreter. In J. Psotka, L. D. Massey, & S. A. Mutter (Eds.), *Intelligent tutoring systems: Lessons learned* (pp. 323-349). Hillsdale, NJ: Lawrence Erlbaum.

Saettler, P. (1990). *The evolution of American educational technology.* Englewood, CO: Libraries Unlimited.

Schank, R. C., Berman, T. R., & Macpherson, K. A. (1999). Learning by doing. In C. M. Reigeluth (Ed.), *Instructional design theories and models*: *Vol. II.* Mahwah, NJ: Lawrence Erlbaum Associates.

Schon, D. A. (1983). *The reflective practitioner: How professionals think and act.* New York: Basic Books.

Schon, D. (1985). *The design studio: An exploration of its traditions and potentials.* Portland, OR: RIBA Publications for RIBA Building Industry Trust.

Schon, D. A. (1987). *Educating the reflective practitioner: Toward a new design for teaching and learning in the professions.* San Francisco: Jossey-Bass.

Schulz, R. E. (1979). Computer aids for developing tests and instruction. In H. L. O'Neil (Ed.) *Procedures for instructional systems development* (pp. 39-66). New York: Academic Press.

Schulz, R. E., & Wagner, H. (1981). *Development of job aids for instructional systems development* (ARI Technical Report No. ARI-TR-527). Alexandria, VA: U.S. Army Research Institute. (ERIC Document Reproduction Service No. 205 202)

Schvaneveldt, R. W. (1990). *Pathfinder associative networks: Studies in knowledge organization.* Norwood, NJ: Ablex.

Schwen, T. M. (1977). Professional scholarship in educational technology: Criteria for judging inquiry. *Audio Visual Communication Review, 25*(1), 5-24.

Seels, B. (1994). *An advisor's view: Lessons learned from developmental research dissertations.* Paper presented at the 1994 Annual Meeting of the Association for Educational Communications and Technology, Nashville, TN.

Seels, B. B., & Richey, R. C. (1994). *Instructional technology: The definition and domains of the field.* Washington, DC: Association for Educational Communications and Technology.

Seyfer, C., & Russell, J. D. (1986). Success story: Computer managed instruction development. *Performance and Instruction, 25*(9), 5-8.

Shambaugh, N., & Magliaro, S. (2001). A reflexive model for teaching instructional design. *Educational Technology Research & Development, 49*(2), 69-92.

Shedroff, N. (1994). *Information interaction design: A unified field theory of design* [On-line]. Available at: http://www.nathan.com/thoughts/unified/.

Shellnut, B. J. (1999). The influence of designer and contextual variables on the incorporation of motivational components to instructional design and the perceived success of a project (Doctoral dissertation, Wayne State University, 1999). *Dissertation Abstracts International—A, 60*(06), 1993.

Sherry, L., & Myers, K. M. (1998). The dynamics of collaborative design. *IEEE Transactions on Professional Communication, 41*(2), 123-139.

Simon, H. A. (1973). The structure of ill-structured problems. *Artificial Intelligence, 4,* 181-201.

Simon, H. A. (1981). *The sciences of the artificial* (2nd ed.). Cambridge, MA: MIT Press.

Smith, M. (1993). Evaluation of executive development: A case study. *Performance Improvement Quarterly, 6*(1), 26-42.

Spector, J. M., Muraida, D. J., & Marlino, M. R. (1992). Cognitively based models of courseware development. *Educational Technology Research and Development, 40*(2), 45-54.

Spector, J. M., & Song, D. (1995). Automated instructional design advising. In R. D. Tennyson & A. E. Baron (Eds.), *Automating instructional design: Computer-based development and delivery tools.* New York: Springer-Verlag.

Stowe, R. A. (1973). Research and the systems approach as methodologies for education. *Audio-Visual Communications Review, 21*(2), 165-175.

Stumpf, S. C., & McDonnell, J. T. (1999). Relating argument to design problem framing. *Proceedings of the 4th Design Thinking Research Symposium,* Cambridge, MA.

Suchman, L. (1987). *Plans and situated actions: The problem of human/machine communication.* New York: Cambridge University Press.

Sullivan, H. J. (1984). Instructional development through a national industry-education partnership. *Journal of Instructional Development, 7*(4), 17-22.

Sullivan, H., Ice, K., & Niedermeyer, F. (2000). Long-term instructional development: A 20-year ID and implementation project. *Educational Technology Research and Development, 48*(4), 87-99.

Taylor, B., & Ellis, J. (1991). An evaluation of instructional systems development in the Navy. *Educational Technology Research and Development, 39*(1), 93-103.

Taylor, R. L. M. (1987). An analysis of development and design models for microcomputer-based instruction (Doctoral dissertation, Syracuse University, 1986). *Dissertation Abstracts International—A, 47*(8), 3011.

Tenney, Y. J., & Kurland, L. J. (1988). The development of troubleshooting expertise in radar mechanics. In J. Psotka, L. D. Massey, & S. A. Mutter (Eds.), *Intelligent tutoring systems: Lessons learned* (pp. 59-83). Hillsdale, NJ: Erlbaum.

Tennyson, R. D., & Baron, A. E. (1995). *Automating instructional design: Computer-based development and delivery tools.* New York: Springer-Verlag.

Tessmer, M., McCann, D., & Ludvigsen, M. (1999). Reassessing training programs: A model for identifying training excesses and deficiencies. *Educational Technology Research and Development, 47*(2), 86-99.

Tessmer, M., & Richey, R. C. (1997) The role of context in learning and instructional design. *Educational Technology Research and Development, 45*(2), 85-115.

Tracey, M. W. (2002). The construction and validation of an instructional design model for incorporating multiple intelligences (Doctoral dissertation, Wayne State University, 2001). *Dissertation Abstracts International—A, 62*(12), 4135.

Travers, R. M. W. (Ed.). (1973). *Second handbook of research on teaching.* Chicago: Rand McNally.

Twitchell, S., Holton, E. F., & Trott, J. W. (2000). Technical training evaluation practices in the United States. *Performance Improvement Quarterly, 13*(3), 84-110.

van den Akker, J. (1999). Principles and methods of development research. In J. van den Akker, R. M. Branch, K. Gustafson, N. Nieveen,

& T. Plomp (Eds.), *Design approaches and tools in education and training* (pp. 1–14). Dordrecht: Kluwer Academic.

van Merrienboer, J. J. G. V., Jelsma, O., & Paas, R. G. W. C. (1992). Training for reflective expertise: A four-component instructional design model for complex cognitive skills. *Educational Technology Research and Development, 40*(2), 23–43.

Visscher-Voerman, J. I. A. (1999). *Design approaches in training and education: A reconstructive study.* Doctoral dissertation, Universiteit Twente, The Netherlands.

Wagner, N. (1984). Instructional product evaluation using the staged innovation design. *Journal of Instructional Development, 7*(2), 24–27.

Walz, D., Elam, J., & Curtis, B. (1993). Inside a design team: Knowledge acquisition, sharing and integration. *Communications of the ACM, 36*(10), 63–77.

Watson, J. E., & Belland, J. C. (1985). Use of learner data in selecting instructional content for continuing education. *Journal of Instructional Development, 8*(4), 29–33.

Webster, H. (2001, September). *The design diary: Promoting reflective practice in the design studio.* Paper presented at the Architectural Education Exchange, Cardiff, UK.

Wedman, J., & Tessmer, M. (1993). Instructional designers' decisions and priorities: A survey of design practice. *Performance Improvement Quarterly, 6*(2), 43–57.

Weiss, D. J. (1979). Computerized adaptive achievement testing. In H. L. O'Neil (Ed.), *Procedures for instructional systems development* (pp. 129–164). New York: Academic Press.

Wenger, E. (1987). *Artificial intelligence and tutoring systems.* Los Altos, CA: Morgan Kaufmann.

Weston, C., McAlpine, L., & Bordonaro, T. (1995). A model for understanding formative evaluation in instructional design. *Educational Technology Research and Development, 43*(3), 29–48.

Whitehead, L. K., & Spector, M. J. (1994, February). *A guided approach to instructional design advising.* Paper presented at the International Conference of the Association for the Development of Computer-Based Instructional Systems, Nashville, TN.

Wild, M. (2000). Designing and evaluating an educational performance support system. *British Journal of Educational Technology 31*(1), 5–20.

Wiley, D. A. (Ed.). (2000). *Instructional use of learning objects.* Indianapolis, IN: Association for Educational Communications and Technology.

Wilson, B. G. (1995, April). *Situated instructional design.* Paper presented at the annual meeting of the American Educational Research Association, San Francisco, CA.

Wittrock, M. C. (1967). Product-oriented research. *Educational Forum, 31*(1), 145–150.

Wreathall, J., & Connelly, E. (1992). Using performance indicators to evaluate training effectiveness: Lessons learned. *Performance Improvement Quarterly, 5*(3), 35–43.

Yin, R. K. (1992). Case study design. In M. C. Alkin (Ed.), *Encyclopedia of educational research* (pp. 134–137). New York: Macmillan.

Zaff, B. S. (Ed.). (1987). The cognitive condition of design. *Proceedings of a Symposium on the Cognitive Condition of Design.* Columbus: Ohio State University.

Zemke, R. (1985, October). The systems approach: A nice theory but . . . . *Training,* 103–108.

Zielinski, D. (2000). Objects of desire. *Training, 37*(9), 126–134.

AUTHOR INDEX

Green, G., 927, 933, *944*
Green, J. R., 534, *539*
Green, P., 226, *239*
Green, P. S., 469, *492*
Green, R., 578, *579*
Green, S., 616, *619*
Greenbaum, T., 422, *427*
Greenberg, B. S., 281, 282, 288, 309, 319, *321, 325*
Greenberg, M. G., 282, *324*
Greene, B., 380, *391*
Greene, J. C., 710, *714, 715*
Greene, K., 295, *327*
Greene, M., 1010, 1011, 1014, 1016, 1017, 1018, *1019*
Greene, R., 866, *914*
Greenfield, P., 66, 67, *75*
Greenfield, P. M., 66, 67, *75*, 816, *827*
Greenhill, L. P., 15, 16, *28*, 254, 255, 256, 259, *322, 325*, 1105, *1125*
Greenhouse, R., 1061, *1071*
Greenleaf, W., 472, 489, *492*
Greeno, J. G., 12, 13, *30*, 98, 103, *107, 144, 166*, 169, *176*, 199, *212*, 218, 223, *240*, 447, *457*, 981, *999*, 1118, *1128*
Greenspun, D., 260, *324*
Greenstein, J., 268, *325*
Greenway, C., 823, *827*
Greenway, R., 748, 750, *783*
Greer, D., 66, *75*, 270, *325, 326*
Greer, J. E., 194, *196*
Gregg, L. W., 663, 664, *680*
Gregor, P., 26, *34*
Gregory, E., 385, *392*
Gregory, R. L., 227, *240*, 867, 870, *914*
Greschler, D., 473, 486, *492*
Gresser, A., 1076, *1096*
Greve, H. R., 122, *138*
Grice, H. P., 1076, 1079, 1091, *1096*
Gridina, N., 295, 296, *333*
Griffiths, B., 966, *975*
Griggs, R. A., 939, 940, *944, 945*
Grimes, L. W., *973*
Grimes, T., 985, 988, *1000*
Grimes, W., 467, *492*
Grinberg, J., 413, *430*
Grinter, R. E., 408, *428*
Grittner, F., 526, 533, *539*
Groan, G. J., 663, *680*
Groebel, J., 295, *325*
Groen, G. J., 94, *109*
Gronlund, N. E., 1027, *1042*
Grooms, D., 304, *324*
Gropper, G. L., 15, 16, 18, *30*, 102, *107*, 255, *325*, 560, *566*
Gros, B., 694, *698*
Gross, L. E., 64, 65, *75*, 269, 271, 285, *325, 328*
Grossen, B., 25, *28*
Grosslight, J. H., 986, *1002*
Group, M. S. M. T. A. P., 144, *166*
Grover, R., 516, *520*
Grudens-Schuck, N., 711, *714*
Grudin, J., 711, *714*, 968, 969, *976*

Guan, Y., 173, *177*
Guba, E. G., 1032, *1042*, 1046, 1047, 1049, 1050, 1055, 1056, 1064, 1068, *1069, 1070*
Guedj, R. A., 461, 471, 474, *491*
Gugliamella, J., 753, 756, 757, *782*
Guha, R. V., 90, *107, 108*
Guilford, J. P., 670, *679*
Gulia, M., 407, *431*, 803, *811*
Gullette, C. C., 524, 530, *539*
Gullo, D. F., 589, *601*
Gulo, E., 986, *1001*
Gumperz, J., 1075, *1096*
Gunawardena, C. N., 25, *32*, 362, 363, 365, 371, 372, 374, 375, 379, 380, 381, 382, 383, 384, 385, *390, 391, 392, 393, 394*, 434, 435, *457, 458, 393*, 1092, 1093, *1096*
Gunstone, R. F., 103, *106*
Gunter, B., 64, *75*, 266, 285, 286, 287, 289, 302, 303, 304, 316, 317, 319, *323, 325*, 954, *973*
Gupta, A., 966, 967, 968, 969, *974, 975, 976*
Gur, R. C., 993, *1004*
Guri-Rozenblit, S., 925, *944*
Gurtner J., 805, *809*
Guskey, T. R., 23, 26, *30*
Gustafson, K., L., 18, *30*, 342, *352*, 499, 515, 519, *520*, 563, *566*, 687, 689, *698*, 1106, 1122, *1125*
Gustavel, J., 610, *619*
Gutek, G. L., 1012, *1019*
Guthrie, J., 608, 615, *618*
Gutiérrez, J., 667, 668, *682*
Guttman, N., 956, 966, 967, 969, *972, 973*
Guzdial, M. J., 592, 593, *601*, 817, 823, 824, 825, *827, 828*, 834, 835, 838, 841, 843, 845, 846, 853, 858, 859, *860, 861*

H

Haag, B. B., *213*, 398, *428*, 729, 734, *742*
Haan, E. H. F., 970, *973*
Haavind, S., 1090, *1095*
Haber, R. N., 866, *914*
Habermas, J., 187, *195, 196*, 1014, 1016, *1019*
Habermas, Jürgen, 43, *55*
Hackman, M. Z., 363, 383, *392*
Haddad, W., 388, *392*
Haddock, G., 928, *944*
Haderlie, S., 615, *619*
Hadley, M., 123, 129, 135, *138, 141*
Haefner, M. J., 280, 281, *325*
Haertel, G., 269, 271, 272, *333*
Haertel, G. D., 710, *716*
Haertle, E., 269, 271, 272, *333*
Haferkamp, C. J., 283, *325*
Haffer, A., 447, *458*
Hafner, A. L., 710, 711, *714*
Hafner, K., 470, 480, *492*
Hagan, N., 363, *390*

Hagberg, J. O., 656, *680*
Hagen, M. A., 866, 867, *914*
Hagerstown: The Board of Education, 255, *325*
Hagler, P., 1030, 1040, *1042*
Hague, A. C., 825, *827*
Hahn, 454, *459*
Hain, K. H., 561, *566*
Haines, V. A., 407, *427*
Hair, E. C., 821, *827*
Hajovy, H., 1033, *1043*
Hakkarainen, K., 338, 343, 344, *352, 353*
Hale, C., 1092, *1096*
Hale, J., *492*
Halff, H. M., 26, *30*, 686, 694, *698*
Hall, A., 407, *431*
Hall, Arthur, 41, *55*
Hall, E. R., 301, *324*
Hall, E. T., 144, *166*, 385, *392*
Hall, G., 122, *138*
Hall, J., 64, *76*
Hall, K. A., 666, *680*
Hall, M. A., 925, *944*
Hall, R., 125, *142*
Hall, R. M., 925, *944*
Hall, S., 69, *75*
Hall, T., 461, *492*
Hallam, S., 822, 823, *827*
Hallamon, T. C., 1110, 1112, 1113, *1125*
Hallaway, D., 465, *492*
Halliday, M. A. K., 1076, *1096*
Halloran, M. E., 440, *457*
Halpain, D. R., 927, *944*
Halpern, D. F., 65, *75*
Halpern, W., 260, 269, *325*
Halpern-Felsher, B. L., 929, *943*
Hamaker, C., 672, *680*, 926, *944*
Hamalainen, S., 796, *809*
Hambleton, R. K., 665, *680*
Hamilton, J., 466, 472, *492*
Hamilton, N. R., 560, *566*, 747, *778*
Hamilton, R. J., 642, *646*, 926, *944*
Hamilton, R. S., 17, *30*, 557, *566*
Hamilton-Pennell, C., 512, *520, 521*
Hamit, F., 461, 462, 467, 469, 474, *492*
Hamlin, W. C., 378, *390*
Hamm, M., 798, *806*
Hammer, Michael, 46, *55*
Hammersley, M., 1050, 1064, *1068, 1069*
Hammond, K. J., 829, 830, *860*
Hammond, L., 208, 211, *214*
Hammond, N., 610, *619*
Hammrich, P., 748, 749, 750, *780*
Hamreus, D. G., 625, *645*
Han, C. Y., 668, 669, *680*
Han, S., 435, 451, 453, *457*
Hancock, D. R., 133, *138*
Hancock, T. E., 748, 749, 750, *780*
Hancock, V., 803, *808*
Hankey, J., 610, *619*
Hanks, W., 145, *166*
Hanks, W. F., 144, 145, 147, 155, 158, 159, *166*

SUBJECT INDEX